# THE Billboard. BOOK OF

# NUMBER

# HITS

## UPDATED AND EXPANDED 5TH EDITION

**THE INSIDE STORY BEHIND EVERY NUMBER ONE SINGLE
ON BILLBOARD'S HOT 100 FROM 1955 TO THE PRESENT**

## FRED BRONSON

BILLBOARD BOOKS
An imprint of Watson-Guptill / New York

Senior Acquisitions Editor: Bob Nirkind
Editor: Anne McNamara
Cover Design: Spencer Drate
Graphic Design: Michelle Gengaro, Bob Fillie
Production Manager: Hector Campbell
Text set in 8-point Century Expanded BT Roman.

First published by Billboard Books,
an imprint of Watson-Guptill Publications,
a division of VNU Business Media, Inc.,
770 Broadway, New York, NY  10003-9595

ISBN 0-8230-7677-6


**Library of Congress Cataloging-in-Publication Data**
Bronson, Fred.
      The Billboard book of number one hits / Fred Bronson.— Rev. and
updated 5th ed.
        p.   cm.
   ISBN 0-8230-7677-6 (paperback : alk. paper)
   1.  Popular music—United States—Discography.
  2.  Rock music—United States—Discography.
  3.  Musicians—United States—Biography.
  I. Title: Book of number one hits. II. Title: Number one hits. III. Title.
    ML156.4.P6B76 2004
    016.78164'0973'0266—dc22          2003016910


Manufactured in the United States of America

First printing, 2003

1 2 3 4 5 6 7 8 / 09 08 07 06 05 04 03

*To my parents,*
*Irving and Mildred Bronson,*
*for their love and support*
*and for letting me spend all*
*of my allowance on records.*

# Contents

# CONTENTS

# CONTENTS

# CONTENTS

# CONTENTS

# CONTENTS

# CONTENTS

# Introduction

Buried in a box of my childhood souvenirs is a cardboard disc, recorded in a booth at the Thrifty drugstore on Sunset Boulevard and Vermont Avenue in Los Angeles when I was six years old. Although I could no more carry a tune at that age than I can now, this recording of "Love and Marriage" is the best evidence I have that I was interested in music at an early age.

Well, there are some vague memories of staying up late to see Dorothy Collins and Gisele MacKenzie on "Your Hit Parade," to find out if "Shrimp Boats" was still number one. That would have been my earliest awareness that not only were there such things as songs, but there were ways to keep track of which ones were the most popular.

That concept didn't hold any further meaning for me until 1960, when Roger Beck, Records Editor of the *Los Angeles Mirror-News,* ran his annual Music Poll contest. The idea was to vote for your favorites in several categories, including best record, male singer, female singer, vocal group, band and instrumental group. The entries were tallied, and whoever voted for the most category winners was the ultimate winner of the contest. I had just turned 11 and was not all that familiar with the music and artists of 1959, but it seemed to me that "Mack the Knife" was the record of the year. So I decided to enter.

After voting for Bobby Darin and Connie Francis, I had to guess at the others. I didn't really know who Duane Eddy was, but he had won the previous year in the instrumental category, so I figured he'd win again. Lawrence Welk and the Kingston Trio seemed like good guesses too. Beck ran the results on February 29, 1960. The winners were "Mack," Darin, Francis, Welk, the Kingston Trio and Eddy. And me. My prize was lunch with "Hawaiian Eye" star Connie Stevens at the Warner Brothers commissary in Burbank, a drive around the lot in her little red sports car, a peek at the set of "77 Sunset Strip" and a handful of promotional LPs. Thanks to Roger and Connie, I realized that keeping track of records and artists wasn't such a bad idea.

It wasn't until January, 1963, that I took a dedicated interest in the weekly countdown of top 30 records on radio station KRLA. It dawned on me that if I wrote down the titles of the songs as they were counted down from 30 to number one, I would have a copy of the station's survey that I could refer back to days—or months or years—later. Then, one day during the week of March 15, I made an important discovery.

I was sitting behind Allan Levin in geometry class when I learned possibly the most important fact of my junior high school education. Allan was well-connected with the music industry; he was the cousin of Larry Levine, the engineer on Phil Spector's records. This was even *before* the Ronettes had recorded "Be My Baby" and I was still very impressed. I remember Allan turning around and showing me a green piece of 8 x 14-inch paper, folded over once. On the first page it said KRLA Tune-Dex. It was a printed list of the station's top 50 records (20 more than they revealed on the air!). I couldn't believe they would take the trouble to print this— and that I would no longer have to write the titles down as I heard them every Friday afternoon.

The number one song on KRLA that week was "He's So Fine" by the Chiffons, and every week for the next several years, I faithfully picked up a copy of the KRLA Tune-Dex. But there was more information yet to be revealed. The next step in my musical education took place two months after Allan gave me that copy of the KRLA survey. While shopping in downtown Los Angeles with my mother, I wandered into a record store. Sitting on the counter was a magazine, and as it related to records, I glanced through it. Inside was a list of the nation's 100 best-selling singles. *This thing was bigger than I thought.* The gentleman behind the counter graciously offered to tear the chart out of the magazine so I could take it home and study it.

Soon after, I was a regular weekly reader of *Billboard.* I didn't know it when I started reading the magazine, but *Billboard* began publishing on November 1, 1894, "devoted to the interests of advertisers, poster printers, billposters, advertising agents and secretaries at fairs." Over more than 100 years, *Billboard* has evolved from a trade paper covering those 19th century issues to the 21st century "international newsweekly of music, video and home entertainment" that it is today.

One of the most significant developments in the history of *Billboard* was the introduction of the first "Music Popularity Chart" on July 20, 1940. "I'll Never Smile Again" by Tommy Dorsey (vocals by Frank Sinatra) was the very first number one record. From that date on, *Billboard* has reported every week what the most popular records in the U.S. are. During the first 15 years after that initial chart was published, artists like Bing Crosby, Perry Como, Patti Page, the Andrews Sisters, Rosemary Clooney and the Ink Spots shared the same achievement—they all had number one singles in *Billboard.*

Everything was going smoothly right up to and including the week that "Cherry Pink and Apple Blossom White" by Perez Prado went to number one. The record that succeeded it was "(We're Gonna) Rock Around the Clock" by Bill Haley and His Comets, the first rock and roll record to top the

*Billboard* chart. Nothing would ever be the same again.

*The Billboard Book of Number One Hits* begins at this point, the intangible, chronological boundary line that divides all prehistory and the first 48 years of what we call the "rock era." "Rock Around the Clock" wasn't just another number one record—it was a brilliant signal flare, warning that all that followed would be different from all that came before. It was the musical harbinger that foreshadowed Elvis Presley, the Supremes and the Beatles. It was rock and roll.

Until 1958, *Billboard* published more than one pop chart each week. These included Best Sellers in Stores, Most Played in Juke Boxes, Most Played by Jockeys and the Honor Roll of Hits. Although a Top 100 was published as early as November 12, 1955, the true test of a record's popularity was the Best Sellers in Stores list, later known as Best Selling Pop Singles in Stores. Based on retail sales, this survey is the source for the first 39 number one singles in this book.

On August 4, 1958, *Billboard* introduced the Hot 100, the pop singles survey that remains the definitive industry chart to this day. The first number one on the Hot 100 was "Poor Little Fool" by Ricky Nelson, and beginning with this record, the Hot 100 is the source for all number one songs.

Before January 13, 1962, *Billboard*'s issue date differed from the chart date listed in the magazine. To avoid unnecessary confusion, the dates listed in this book are for the *Billboard* issue date. As of January 13, 1962, both the issue and chart dates are the *week ending* dates. Thus, an event taking place on October 4, 1965, would fall under the reign of the Beatles' "Yesterday," which was number one for the week ending October 9, 1965.

One of the joys of writing *The Billboard Book of Number One Hits* was talking to many of the people responsible for creating the greatest songs of the rock era. Over the past 19 years, almost 450 artists, writers, producers and label executives have taken the time to talk to me and a group of researchers about their achievements. I want to thank all of them for sharing their memories, shattering myths and—in some cases—revealing information that may surprise, delight, and/or anger you.

There are many people who deserve thanks for contributing to the ongoing editions of this book. First, there is Brian Carroll, who single-handedly did all of the research for the fourth and fifth editions. I appreciate his journalistic skills, his devotion to detail and his friendship. I also am indebted to the small army of people who contributed to the research of this book's earliest editions: Marj Baker, Drea Besch, Linda Merinoff, Barbara Pepe, Jim Richliano, Michael Ross, Marcia Rovins and Donna Schwartz.

Thanks also to others who have made contributions over the past 19 years, including Ken Barnes, Brady L. Benton, Bill Buster, Keith Caulfield, Dennis Clark, Larry Cohen, Sherman Cohen, Ted Cordes, Bill Derby, Robert Dilley, Su and Joe DiLuzio, Louie Dorado, Steve Drummond, Jim Durkin, Michael Ellis, Todd Etelson, Beatrice Goldman, Joan Gosewisch, Ron Hamill, Johnny Hayes, Ronnie Hertzman, Jimmy Hillman, Louis Iacueo, Jeff James, Alan Jones, Mark Katz, Barry Lazell, Danny Lemos, Michael Linah, Lois Linden, Geoff Mayfield, Mark Milett, Gail Mitchell, Melinda Newman, Jose Promis, Dafydd Rees, Steve Resnick, Linda Rouse, Susan Sackett, Ken Schlager,

Gene Sculatti, Lou Simon, Horst Stipp, Phil Swern, Chuck Taylor, Wayne Volat, Merrick Wolfe, Stephen Wunderlich, Mark Young and Guy Zapoleon.

It's difficult to recognize pivotal moments at the instant they are happening to you. I've been fortunate enough to have several pivotal moments when I encountered people who deeply influenced my life. I want to acknowledge Donald E. Mack and May Carpenter for helping me to realize my creative potential; Jerry Lishon, Hank Rieger, and Joel Tator for trusting me with new levels of responsibility; Rob Eichberg, for reminding me that we are radiant energy, dancing playfully through life, and all we have to give and receive is love; Adam White for believing I should write this book and telling the right people; Gene Roddenberry for being not just a visionary but a real human being who offered friendship and support during his lifetime; and Larry Klein for asking me to jump into the deep end by writing ABC's three-hour live coverage of Live-Aid, thus earning my membership in the Writers Guild of America.

I'm grateful to Dick and Kari Clark for reasons too numerous to list here (but including the opportunity to write "The American Music Awards" and collaborate with Dick on the book *Dick Clark's American Bandstand*), as well as past and present employees of dick clark productions, also too numerous to mention here.

A few months after the third edition of this book was published, I became a contributor to *Billboard*, writing the weekly Chart Beat column. Four years later, my duties expanded to writing a weekly section of Billboard.com, and after another two years, I was asked to write the weekly show "The Billboard Radio Countdown," heard at www.billboardradio.com. This work has connected me to the entire world in ways I couldn't have imagined. Thanks to all the readers of Chart Beat, both in print and online, for their kind words—and for keeping me on my toes. I also appreciate the many *Billboard* employees, past and present, who have extended their friendship and support. I can't imagine a better group of people to work with, and I miss the ones who have moved on to other endeavors.

To the editorial staff of Watson-Guptill, thanks for being there from start to finish. Bob Nirkind, thank you for your guidance, expertise and understanding, and for bringing Billboard Books to new heights. Anne McNamara, it was a special pleasure to work with you as my editor for two books in a row because you make everything seem so effortless, even when we're both actually working very hard. I've been privileged to work with only the best editors over the multiple versions of this book, including Amy Handy, Paul Lukas, Joy Aquilino, Fred Weiler, Tad Lathrop and Marisa Bulzone. A special thanks to Bob Fillie, whose art direction has always made this book look spectacular. David Lewis, thanks for getting this off the ground. Hector Campbell, LaMarre Dyson and Lee Wiggins, thanks for your hard work as well.

Finally, there would be no book without the men and women who have written, produced and recorded the 933 number one singles of the rock era. Thank you for the music.

FRED BRONSON
www.billboard.com
fbronson@billboard.com
*September 2003*

DECCA 29124 **(We're Gonna) Rock Around the Clock**
BILL HALEY AND HIS COMETS

**1**

*Writers: Max Freedman*
*Jimmy DeKnight*

*Producer: Milt Gabler*

*July 9, 1955*
*8 weeks*

THE typical record industry executive picking up the July 9, 1955 issue of *Billboard* might have taken notice that the new number one single on the Best Sellers in Stores chart was "(We're Gonna) Rock Around the Clock" by Bill Haley and His Comets, and then moved on to the more pressing news stories of the day. It would have been impossible to know that Haley's number one single created a dividing line between all that came before and all that followed. It's only from our perspective several decades later that we can see the impact this song had on our culture. It was the beginning of the rock era.

"Rock Around the Clock" was not the first rock and roll song. Historians disagree on what exactly was, but many suggest it was "Rocket 88," recorded by Jackie Brenston in Memphis and released on the Chess label in 1951 (actually, the record was by the Ike Turner Band, and vocalist Brenston was Turner's saxophonist). "Rocket 88" was recorded by Haley that same year, making it the first rock and roll recording by a white artist.

Haley didn't invent the term "rock and roll," either. Credit for that goes to disc jockey Alan Freed, who coined the term from the 1947 R&B hit "We're Gonna Rock, We're Gonna Roll" by Wild Bill Moore.

What Haley did was bring rock and roll to the consciousness of America—and the world. His career did not reach the stratospheric heights of Elvis Presley, but he will always be known as the "father of rock and roll."

He was born William John Clifton Haley Jr. in Highland Park, Michigan on July 6, 1925. His father, a textile worker, played the banjo and his mother was a piano teacher who sometimes played organ in a neighborhood Baptist Church. When Bill was seven, the family moved to Wilmington, Delaware, and soon after he was playing his own homemade cardboard guitar.

Answering an ad in *Billboard*, Haley was hired as a singing yodeller for the Downhomers. He left the group to become a disc jockey at WSNJ in Bridgeport, New Jersey. In 1948, he moved to WPWA in Chester, Pennsylvania, where he formed a singing group, the Four Aces of Western Swing. He disbanded them in 1949 and started the Saddlemen, who signed with Dave Miller's Holiday Records a year later. In 1952 they recorded "Rock This Joint," a song which blended a country sound with rhythm and blues.

The Saddlemen became the Comets in 1953, and their first chart hit, "Crazy Man, Crazy," went to number 15 on *Billboard* and is the first rock and roll record to ever make the chart.

That same year, songwriters Max Freedman and Jimmy DeKnight (Jimmy Myers, a New York music publisher) wrote a song with Haley in mind. But Dave Miller disliked Myers and refused to let Haley record the song. When his contract with Miller expired, Haley and Myers went to see Milt Gabler at Decca Records. Gabler signed Bill Haley and the Comets immediately, and on April 12, 1954, they went into the studio to record two tracks: "Thirteen Women" and the song Miller refused to record: "(We're Gonna) Rock Around the Clock."

The song was only mildly successful. It was Haley's next single, a cover version of Joe Turner's "Shake, Rattle and Roll" that hit the top ten and made Haley a national star. Two more Top 20 Records followed, "Dim, Dim the Lights" and "Mambo Rock."

Myers had not given up on "Rock Around the Clock." To promote the song, he sent copies to everyone he could think of in Hollywood. In the spring of 1955, MGM released *The Blackboard Jungle*, starring Glenn Ford as a high school teacher confronted by violent students. The song heard under the opening credits was "Rock Around the Clock."

It created a sensation. There were riots in theaters. Clare Booth Luce denounced the film as degenerate, causing it to be pulled from the Venice Film Festival. And Haley's song was re-released and shot to number one—the rock era had begun.

In 1956, movie producer Sam Katzman signed Haley and the Comets to star in a film titled *Rock Around the Clock*. It established a new trend in marrying rock and roll with the silver screen. Haley never matched the record success of his number one single, but he did concert tours all over the world. He was very popular in Europe in the last half of the 60s, and enjoyed renewed success in the U.S. after appearing at a Richard Nader rock and roll revival show.

But in the 70s, Haley fell victim to alcoholism and increasing paranoia. He died on February 9, 1981, in his home in Harlingen, Texas. Cause of death was listed as "natural causes, most likely heart attack."

## THE TOP FIVE
*Week of July 9, 1955*

1 **Rock Around the Clock**
Bill Haley and His Comets

2 **Cherry Pink and Apple Blossom White**
Perez Prado

3 **Blossom Fell/If I May**
Nat (King) Cole

4 **Unchained Melody**
Les Baxter

5 **Learnin' the Blues**
Frank Sinatra

# 2 The Yellow Rose of Texas COLUMBIA 40540
## MITCH MILLER

*Writer: Don George*

*Producer: Mitch Miller*

*September 3, 1955*
*6 weeks*

It's no small irony that Mitch Miller's "The Yellow Rose of Texas" became the second number one single of the rock era, for Miller was a frequent critic of rock and roll at the same time he was one of the chief architects of pop music. While he would never claim to have the same kind of influence as a Bill Haley or an Elvis Presley, in his position as head of artists and repertoires for Columbia Records he was responsible for the successful careers of Frankie Laine, Rosemary Clooney, Johnnie Ray, Patti Page, Tony Bennett, Doris Day, Johnny Mathis, Guy Mitchell and the Four Lads.

Mitch remained one of the most important behind-the-scenes figures

## THE TOP FIVE
*Week of September 3, 1955*

1  **Yellow Rose of Texas**
   Mitch Miller

2  **Ain't That a Shame?**
   Pat Boone

3  **Rock Around the Clock**
   Bill Haley

4  **Learnin' the Blues**
   Frank Sinatra

5  **Seventeen**
   Boyd Bennett

in the music industry until he was thrust into the public spotlight by the success of "The Yellow Rose of Texas," an 1853 marching song written for travelling minstrel shows by an anonymous author, known only as "J.K." It became popular during the Civil War in both the North and South, and there were several different permutations, including "The Gallant Hood of Texas" and "The Song of the Texas Rangers."

In 1955, a Cleveland disc jockey, Bill Randle, suggested to Don George that the song had potential as a pop hit. George adapted it, giving it a marching beat. The song appeared in an album of Civil War songs, where Miller discovered it. He gave it a new arrangement, adding snare drums (one of the first times they had been featured in a pop record). Miller liked the finished product so much, he ordered 100,000 singles to be pressed. A shocked Columbia Records executive protested the large order, so Mitch offered to buy back all the unsold copies at cost—15 cents apiece.

Mitch never had to lay out a penny. The record sold over a million copies.

Mitchell William Miller was born July 4, 1911, in Rochester, New York. He learned to play piano at age six, and took up the oboe when he was 11. He studied at the Eastman School of Music, and after graduation joined the Rochester Philharmonic Orchestra as an oboist. He played with the CBS Symphony and the Budapest String Quartet. In the 1940s, he joined Mercury Records as head of pop music, and worked with Eddy Howard, Patti Page and Frankie Laine (whom he convinced to record "Mule Train").

When Mannie Sacks left Columbia Records to go to RCA Victor, Mitch

was brought in to head up A&R. The label had not been doing well, but after Mitch joined the company in 1951, their artist roster and chart fortunes improved quickly.

*Sing Along with Mitch*, his first album of standards performed by a vocal chorus, was released in August, 1958. It was accompanied by lyrics so people could sing with the tunes and was an immediate success that led to a series of albums, and an NBC special, telecast May 24, 1960 on "Startime." The concept proved popular enough to prompt NBC to give Mitch his own series, which ran from January 27, 1961, to September 2, 1966. Viewers could sing along with lyrics flashed on the screen, and soon Mitch Miller's beard (fashioned after a portrait of King Feisal) was seen in homes coast-to-coast.

"The Yellow Rose of Texas" went to number one on September 3, 1955. Its six week run was interrupted on October 8 by the Four Aces' "Love Is a Many Splendored Thing."

DECCA 29625 **Love Is a Many Splendored Thing** **3**
THE FOUR ACES

*Writers: Sammy Fain*
*Paul Francis Webster*

*Producer: Milt Gabler*

*October 8, 1955*
*2 weeks*

"LOVE IS A MANY SPLENDORED THING" is the first song specifically written for a motion picture to be number one in the rock era. It's true that "(We're Gonna) Rock Around the Clock" was heard in *The Blackboard Jungle*, but even though it became an integral part of the film, it had been composed two years earlier. Sammy Fain and Paul Francis Webster, Oscar winners for writing Doris Day's "Secret Love" from *Calamity Jane*, were asked to write a title song for *Love is a Many Splendored Thing* starring William Holden and Jennifer Jones. Their efforts won them a second Oscar.

Although the Four Aces eventually recorded "Love Is a Many Splendored Thing" and took it to number one, they weren't the first artists approached to sing the tune— and the song itself was not the first choice for the title song.

Fain and Webster were asked by producer Buddy Allen to write a title song for his new film, "A Many Splendored Thing." The two collaborators wrote an intricate song with that title. Confident he had fulfilled his obligation, Fain flew to New York. "I received a phone call from Buddy Allen," Fain recalls. "He said he loved the song and it should be a

big hit, but they decided to change the title of the film to *Love Is a Many Splendored Thing* because it said more on a theater marquee."

Fain rushed back to Los Angeles and quickly wrote a new melody. Webster came over to his house and wrote words for the new tune, and they took it to Allen. He sent them over to see Al Newman who was scoring the picture, and told Fain to sing it for him. Newman loved it, and the song's place in the picture was assured.

The original title tune was abandoned, although Webster later tried to write new lyrics for it. Nothing ever came of it. Meanwhile, Fain was taking his demo of "Love Is a Many Splendored Thing" to well-known artists to find someone to sing it in the film. He played it for Eddie Fisher, Tony Martin, Doris Day and Nat "King" Cole. They all turned him down.

Finally, the song went to the Four Aces, a vocal group on the verge of breaking up. They had been recording since 1951, when their first single of "Sin" made the top five. Before the rock era began, they placed 16 songs on the *Billboard* chart, including the Oscar-winning "Three Coins in the Fountain" in 1954.

The Four Aces were from Chester, Pennsylvania. Al Alberts was the lead vocalist; Dave Mahoney sang tenor, Sol Vaccaro sang baritone and Lou Silvestri sang bass. After they financed the recording of "Sin" for the Victoria label, Decca Records signed them to a contract. When

Alberts eventually left for a solo career, the group faded from the scene.

After the Four Aces recorded "Love Is a Many Splendored Thing" and it went to number one, all of the artists who had turned it down recorded their own versions. And William Holden and Jennifer Jones aren't the only screen lovers who fanned the flames of love to the song; 23 years later, John Travolta and Olivia Newton-John gazed into each others' eyes on a deserted beach in the opening scene of *Grease*, as strains of "Love Is a Many Splendored Thing" were heard in the background.

"Love Is a Many Splendored Thing" went to number one on October 8, 1955 for one week, and returned to the top spot on October 22 for one more week.

### THE TOP FIVE
*Week of October 8, 1955*

1 **Love is a Many-Splendored Thing**
Four Aces

2 **Yellow Rose of Texas**
Mitch Miller

3 **Autumn Leaves**
Roger Williams

4 **Ain't That a Shame?**
Pat Boone

5 **Moments to Remember**
Four Lads

# 4 | Autumn Leaves KAPP 116
## ROGER WILLIAMS

Writers: *Joseph Kosma*
*Jacques Prevert*
*Johnny Mercer*

Producer: *Dave Kapp*

*October 29, 1955*
*4 weeks*

THE first instrumental number one song of the rock era was "Autumn Leaves" by Roger Williams. It was Williams' first chart hit ever, and the most successful of his career.

"Autumn Leaves" was originally a popular French melody written by Joseph Kosma as "Les Feuilles Mortes." Poet Jacques Prevert added French lyrics, and Juliette Greco sang it in the French motion picture *Les Portes de la Nuit*. Capitol Records asked Johnny Mercer to write English lyrics. More than a dozen artists recorded it, including Bing Crosby and Jo Stafford, but no one came close to having a hit with it until Williams cut his piano version.

A year after Williams took it to number one, Nat "King" Cole sang it over the opening and closing credits of the film *Autumn Leaves*, starring Joan Crawford.

Surprisingly, only two seasons of the year have ever been mentioned in the titles of number one songs. "Summer" is the leader, appearing in two songs, by Percy Faith and the Lovin' Spoonful. This song is autumn's only mention.

Born in Omaha, Nebraska as Lou Weertz, Roger Williams was a child prodigy. He learned to play the piano before he was three years old, and had written his first song by the time he was four. When he was eight, he had mastered a dozen other instruments. At high school, in Des Moines, Iowa, he conducted the school's orchestra and choir. His father, a Lutheran minister, taught his son to box—some would consider that hazardous for a piano player—and Williams won a boxing title while serving in the Navy during World War II (in 1959 Williams sparred with Swedish champion Ingemar Johansson at his training camp in the Catskills).

After the war, Williams enrolled at Idaho State College. He received his M.A. degree in music from Drake University and later earned a Doctorate in music. In 1952, Williams enrolled at Juilliard and while in New York, won on "Arthur Godfrey's Talent Scouts" television show. A year later, he was playing piano at the Madison Hotel lounge, where Dave Kapp, president of Kapp Records, heard him. Kapp signed the pianist to his label, but insisted on a name change. "He had to have a name that would stand up anywhere," Kapp told *Newsweek*. So Kapp named him after the founder of Rhode Island, Roger Williams.

DJs named Williams their favorite solo instrumentalist in 1960. He was an early proponent of stereo recordings, and in 1957 he invented a miniature electronic piano that played songs automatically and simulated speech.

His second biggest recording was an instrumental version of the "Born Free" movie theme, which peaked at number seven in 1966.

## THE TOP FIVE
*Week of October 29, 1955*

1 **Autumn Leaves**
Roger Williams

2 **Love is a Many Splendored Thing**
Four Aces

3 **Yellow Rose of Texas**
Mitch Miller

4 **Moments to Remember**
Four Lads

5 **Shifting, Whispering Sands (Parts I & II)**
Billy Vaughn

Writer: *Merle Travis*

Producer: *Lee Gillette*

*November 26, 1955*
*7 weeks*

CAPITOL Records' first number one single of the rock era was recorded by that little ole pea-picker, "Tennessee" Ernie Ford. When "Sixteen Tons" was released, Ford was already a popular television personality, appearing every weekday on NBC's daytime schedule. That may be one of the reasons "Sixteen Tons" became the fastest-selling single in the history of the record business to date, moving more than one million copies in three weeks and rising to the top of the chart in the same amount of time, beating the previous record held by "The Yellow Rose of Texas."

"Sixteen Tons" was written in 1947 by country singer Merle Travis. He was recording a 78 rpm album for Capitol entitled *Folk Songs of the Hills*, and was asked by the label to include several mining songs. When he couldn't find any, he wrote some himself, like "Nine-Pound Hammer" and "Sixteen Tons." Travis' father was a coal miner in Kentucky and was fond of saying he was "another day older and deeper in debt," a quotation that became part of the

chorus of "Sixteen Tons."

Ford was so busy with his five-times-a-week TV show, he was behind in his recording schedule for Capitol. After several phone calls from label executives telling him he needed to release new material, Ford picked two songs he had sung on television and headed for Capitol's recording studios. The songs were "You Don't Have to Be a Baby to Cry" and "Sixteen Tons."

While rehearsing the latter song, Ford was snapping his fingers to set the tempo. Producer Lee Gillette was in the control booth and told Ford to leave the snapping in when he recorded the song.

Ernest Jennings Ford was born February 13, 1919, in Bristol, Tennessee. By the age of four, he was singing "The Old Rugged Cross" at family gatherings. After high school graduation, Ernie was hired as an announcer for a local radio station at the salary of $10 a week. He studied voice at the Cincinnati Conservatory of Music, and went to work for a station in Atlanta at twice his previous wage. In 1941, he was paid $25 a week to work for a Knoxville station, a job he kept until joining the Air Force in December.

During World War II he was a bombardier and a bombing instructor, and after his discharge in 1945 he moved to California with his wife

Betty. Ford worked at radio stations in San Bernadino, California and Reno, Nevada. He got his first big break by being hired as a hillbilly DJ on KXLA, Pasadena, the station that evolved into top 40 KRLA in the late 1950s.

"Just for the heck of it, I used to run into the studio where my buddy Cliffie Stone was doing his country-western program, swap a few jokes, sing a hymn with the group and leave. It was all for fun and didn't pay a thing," Ford remembers. But there was a pay-off: Stone asked Ernie to be a regular on his Saturday night show.

Gillette, an A&R man at Capitol Records before he became Ford's producer, heard Ernie singing along with a record on KXLA one morning while driving to work. As soon as he got to the office he called Stone and told him to bring Ford in at once. On January 21, 1949, Capitol Records signed "Tennessee" Ernie Ford to a contract. He hit the charts with "Mule Train," "The Cry of the Wild Goose" and a song he wrote himself, "Shotgun Boogie." His biggest hit prior to "Sixteen Tons" was a duet with Kay Starr (see 7—"Rock and Roll Waltz"), "I'll Never Be Free," which went to number three in the summer of 1950.

Ford starred in his own NBC-TV variety series, seen on Thursday nights from October, 1956 to June, 1961. In September of 1991, he was in Washington, D.C. to attend a White House state dinner when he was stricken at Dulles International Airport and hospitalized with a liver ailment. He died on October 17.

---

## THE TOP FIVE
*Week of November 26, 1955*

1  **Sixteen Tons**
   Tennessee Ernie Ford

2  **Autumn Leaves**
   Roger Williams

3  **Love is a Many-Splendored Thing**
   Four Aces

4  **Moments to Remember**
   Four Lads

5  **I Hear You Knockin'**
   Gale Storm

## 6 Memories Are Made of This CAPITOL 3295
### DEAN MARTIN

*Writers: Terry Gilkyson*
*Richard Dehr*
*Frank Miller*

*Producer: Lee Gillette*

*January 14, 1956*
*5 weeks*

**D**EAN MARTIN says he became a singer because he was tired of cleaning windshields and getting punched in the mouth. He was 27 by the time he decided to sing professionally, and before that he held a wide variety of jobs, including gas station attendant, boxer, steel worker, coal miner, drugstore clerk, mill hand and blackjack dealer.

He was born Dino Crocetti on June 7, 1917 in Steubenville, Ohio. He dropped out of school in the ninth grade, and when his father, a barber, gave him five dollars to go to barber school, Dino became a boxer ("Kid Crochet") instead, until someone punched him in the nose too hard. He started singing with Sammy Watkins' band in Cleveland, then struck out on his own, changing his name and getting a nose job. He was earning $750 a week by 1946, the year he played the 500 Club in Atlantic City. On the same bill was a 20-year-old comedian who lip synched to records, and the owner of the club suggested that Dean team up with the talented newcomer, Jerry Lewis. Their scripted opening night show was a disaster, so the following evening they tried ad-libbing, and brought the house down. Soon, they were earning $25,000 as the hottest comedy team in America.

Dean and Jerry were headlined at the Copa in New York, Ciro's on Sunset Strip and Chez Paree in Chicago. They made 16 films together, starting with *My Friend Irma* in 1949. Kinescopes of their early TV appearances are collectors' items today.

Dean signed with Capitol Records in 1948. His pre-rock era hits include "I'll Always Love You," "If," "You Belong to Me," "That's Amore" and "Sway." In 1955 he recorded "Memories Are Made of This," written by Terry Gilkyson, who had belonged to the folksinging group, the Weavers. Gilkyson and co-writers Richard Dehr and Frank Miller formed a group, the Easyriders, and sang backing vocals for Martin on "Memories Are Made of This." In the spring of 1957, they went to number four with their own single, "Marianne."

"Memories Are Made of This" started 1956 off in a good fashion for Dean. It was the first number one single of the year, and Dean's most successful single ever. But later in the year, Martin and Lewis made headlines all over the country when they went their separate ways. The press predicted that Dean would have a difficult time as a solo performer, and at first, it seemed they might be right. His first film without Jerry, *10,000 Bedrooms*, was a flop. So Martin decided to go after good parts in important films and ask for less money. He was cast in *The Young Lions*, *Some Came Running* and *Rio Bravo*, and earned praise from the critics.

Dean Martin had been suffering with failing health for a length of time when he died of acute respiratory failure at his home in Beverly Hills on December 25, 1995. Martin was 78.

### THE TOP FIVE
*Week of January 14, 1956*

1 **Memories Are Made of This**
Dean Martin

2 **Sixteen Tons**
Tennessee Ernie Ford

3 **Great Pretender**
Platters

4 **I Hear You Knockin'**
Gale Storm

5 **Band of Gold**
Don Cherry

RCA 6359 **Rock and Roll Waltz** 7
KAY STARR

*Writers: Dick Ware*
*Shorty Allen*

*Producer: Joe Carlton*

*February 18, 1956*
*1 week*

"ROCK AND ROLL WALTZ" was the first number one single by a female singer in the rock era, the first to have "rock and roll" in the title and the first number one single for RCA Records. Kay Starr had been with Capitol Records since 1948, where she became well-known for hits like "Side by Side" and the number one single "Wheel of Fortune." "Rock and Roll Waltz" was her first recording for RCA.

Kay remembers the recording session. "It was in a huge studio, nothing cozy about it. It was completely foreign to any kind of recording I had done before. I had never sung with strings before. I was in awe of the whole thing. I was never comfortable recording for RCA, with such high ceilinged studios. I wanted the ceilings down, I wanted to feel like part of the band."

Kay also remembers her reaction when RCA's A&R staff asked her to record "Rock and Roll Waltz." "I was so used to singing gutbucket songs

that were loud and boisterous or un-requited love songs. When they handed me this, I thought they were playing a joke on me. I looked at it and said, 'What is this?' It was so simple, it was almost like they were insulting my intelligence. I thought, what are they doing to me? I made the switch from Capitol to RCA, and they're gonna give me this stuff to sing? Well, I found out they were certainly serious about it. It was pleasant, but I didn't feel my heart was in it, I couldn't relate to this nursery rhyme kind of thing."

Despite the song's chart success and its million-plus sales, no one ever requested Kay to sing the song at a personal appearance. "It will always be a puzzlement to me, when it sold a million, no one asked me to sing it on TV or anywhere. People still asked me to do 'Wheel of Fortune.'" Still, Kay loves the song today, and people do ask her to sing it now. "I see the response. When I see people reaching over and touching—if you can get people to touch and communicate, I believe you've done your job."

Kay was born Katherine La Verne Starks in Dougherty, Oklahoma. Her father worked for the Automatic Sprinkler Company, and her mother raised chickens. When she was a little girl, Kay would take

an apple box into the chicken coop, stand on it and sing to the chickens. "I don't know if you know how chickens roost, but they roost in levels. It really looks like an amphitheatre." Her Aunt Nora heard her singing for the chickens and entered her in a yo-yo contest. She sang while she "yo-yoed" and won third prize. She won a local radio station talent contest so many times, the station manager asked if she'd like her own 15-minute show three times a week.

The family moved to Memphis, and at age 15 Kay got a job singing for jazz violinist Joe Venuti's dance orchestra. When Marion Hutton, Glenn Miller's vocalist, was hospitalized briefly, Kay filled in for her, and recorded two songs with Miller, "Baby Me" and "Love With a Capital U." She sang with Bob Crosby and Charlie Barnet's bands, then went to California and stayed with Venuti and his wife.

During World War II, Kay sang in different army camps. She traveled on uncomfortable army transport planes and caught a terrible cold. She developed pneumonia and spent time in an army hospital. Eventually, she developed nodes on her vocal chords and required surgery. She lost the use of her voice completely—no talking, no whispering and *no* singing. She communicated by writing notes, and after six months was able to regain some use of her voice. It was a year-and-a-half before she was able to sing with a full band again. When her voice came back, it was "huskier and tighter," and she used it well, recording "I'm the Lonesomest Gal in Town," "You Were Only Foolin'" and "Bonaparte's Retreat" for Capitol.

## THE TOP FIVE
*Week of February 18, 1956*

1 **Rock and Roll Waltz**
Kay Starr

2 **Lisbon Antigua**
Nelson Riddle

3 **Great Pretender**
Platters

4 **Memories Are Made of This**
Dean Martin

5 **No, Not Much**
Four Lads

## 8 Lisbon Antigua CAPITOL 3287
### NELSON RIDDLE

*Writers: Raul Portela*
*Jose Galhardo*
*Amadeu do Vale*
*Harry Dupree*

*Producer: Lee Gillette*

*February 25, 1956*
*4 weeks*

Twenty-seven years before he arranged Linda Ronstadt's *What's New* album, Nelson Riddle topped the chart with "Lisbon Antigua." The song was written in 1937 by three Portugese writers as "Lisboa Antigua," which translates "In Old Lisbon."

Riddle learned of the song through Nat "King" Cole's manager's sister, who lived near Mexico City. A band known as Los Churambalis were having a local hit with it, and she thought Riddle would be interested. Executives at Riddle's label, Capitol, told him to copy the version exactly.

Later in 1956, Riddle was hired to score a motion picture starring Ray Milland and Maureen O'Hara, titled *Lisbon*, and he used "Lisbon Antigua" as the film's theme.

Riddle was born June 1, 1921, in Oradell, New Jersey. His father was a sign painter and commercial artist who also had an amateur band, which rehearsed once a week in Nelson's living room. Riddle became interested in music through his father, and started taking piano lessons at age eight. At 14 he took up the trombone. After graduating high school, he played in Charlie Spivak and Bob Crosby's orchestras. In 1944, he

spent a year travelling with Tommy Dorsey.

After his Army service, he joined NBC Radio as a staff arranger in April, 1947. Three years later, with the advent of television, his boss was fired and he lost his job. Then Les Baxter asked Riddle to come up with some arrangements for a Nat "King" Cole album.

"I wrote two arrangements for Nat that he liked very much," Riddle recalls. "One was 'Mona Lisa' and one was 'Too Young.' They both came out under the heading 'Les Baxter and His Orchestra'...the mistake that Mr. Baxter made was that he also took credit for the arrangements. That was a little much for me."

Cole discovered that Riddle did the arrangements, and after that they worked together for about 10 years. After a couple of years with Cole, Riddle asked Capitol for his own artists' contract.

While at Capitol, Riddle worked

closely with Frank Sinatra. In 1958 Riddle arranged *Frank Sinatra Sings for Only the Lonely*, which included three songs that would end up on Ronstadt's *What's New*. One afternoon in 1982, producer Peter Asher [see 150—"A World Without Love"] called Riddle and asked if he would arrange one song for a new Ronstadt album. Riddle said he didn't do single arrangements, he did albums. Linda had already recorded the songs for *What's New* with a different arranger and was unhappy with them. Asher gladly hired Riddle to arrange the entire album, a definite factor in its huge success.

Riddle is also acclaimed for his film and television scoring. His TV credits include the theme song for the "Route 66" series (he talked the producer out of using the Bobby Troup song) as well as "The Untouchables" and "Newhart."

On October 6, 1985, Riddle died of cardiac and kidney failure. He was 64.

### THE TOP FIVE
*Week of February 25, 1956*

1 **Lisbon Antigua**
   Nelson Riddle

2 **Rock and Roll Waltz**
   Kay Starr

3 **Great Pretender**
   Platters

4 **Memories Are Made of This**
   Dean Martin

5 **No, Not Much**
   Four Lads

*Writers: Marguerite Mannot*
*Jack Lawrence*
*Rene Rouzaud*

*Producer: Lee Gillette*

*March 24, 1956*
*4 weeks*

LES BAXTER'S "Poor People of Paris" (his only number one single) followed Nelson Riddle's "Lisbon Antigua" into the number one position, the only time in the history of the rock era that two instrumentals have reached number one back to back. Both songs also featured the names of international cities in their titles—quite a remarkable coincidence considering that only five out of more than 850 number one songs have non-American cities in their titles (the other three honored locales are Calcutta, Winchester and Glasgow).

Actually, "Poor People of Paris" was only so titled by mistake. The song, popularized in France by Edith Piaf, was called "La Goulante du Pauvre Jean," which should have translated as "The Ballad of Poor John." Capitol Records' representative in the Paris office cabled the wrong title to Hollywood, writing *gens* for Jean. *Gens* translates as people, and the error was never corrected.

The song had been written in France by lyricist Rene Rouzaud and composer Marguerite Mannot, who wrote the score for *Irma la Douce*. "Poor John" was the kind of guy who kept meeting the "bad girls" of Paris. Jack Lawrence wrote English lyrics for the song.

Baxter was born on March 14,

## THE TOP FIVE
*Week of March 24, 1956*

1 **Poor People of Paris**
Les Baxter

2 **Lisbon Antigua**
Nelson Riddle

3 **Rock and Roll Waltz**
Kay Starr

4 **No, Not Much**
Four Lads

5 **Great Pretender**
Platters

1922 in Mexia, Texas. He has been a musician ever since he was five years old, when he learned to play the piano. As a child, he studied at the Detroit Conservatory of Music, and was composing songs before he entered high school. He skipped his senior year to attend Pepperdine College in Los Angeles on a scholarship.

In the 1930s he became a well-known conductor for many Hollywood-based radio shows, for celebrities like Bob Hope and Abbott and Costello. He also conducted the orchestra for the world-famous Cocoanut Grove at the Ambassador Hotel, and sang with Mel Torme's Meltones.

In 1950, he signed a contract with Capitol Records. His album *Music Out of the Moon* was considered somewhat exotic, and over the next

few years, he recorded a number of songs for Capitol, including "Blue Tango," "April in Portugal," "Ruby," "The High and the Mighty," "Unchained Melody" and "Wake the Town and Tell the People."

"Poor People of Paris" rode the crest of a wave of European melodies imported and adapted for American audiences. In addition to predecessors like Roger Williams' "Autumn Leaves" and Nelson Riddle's "Lisbon Antigua," the charts were full of records such as Percy Faith's "Valley Valparaiso," Ray Anthony's "Madeira," Jackie Gleason's "Capri in May" and Sophia Loren's "Woman of the River."

Baxter, who also wrote Martin Denny's hit "Quiet Village," was 73 when he died of a heart attack on January 15, 1966, in Newport Beach, California.

## 10 Heartbreak Hotel RCA 6420
### ELVIS PRESLEY

Writers: *Mae Boren Axton*
*Tommy Durden*
*Elvis Presley*

Producer: *Steve Sholes*

*April 21, 1956*
*8 weeks*

"HEARTBREAK HOTEL" was Elvis Presley's first recording for RCA Victor and his first number one single. It marked Elvis' transition from a local southern sensation to a national phenomenon, and it built on the foundation begun by Bill Haley's "(We're Gonna) Rock Around the Clock" to establish rock and roll as a musical force that was simply not going to go away. The king of rock and roll had just ascended to his throne.

Elvis Aaron Presley was born on January 8, 1935 in Tupelo, Mississippi to Gladys Love Smith Presley and Vernon Presley. A twin brother, Jesse Garon, was stillborn and was buried the next day in Priceville Cemetery. The Presley family was not far above the poverty line, but nothing prevented them from attending the First Assembly of God Church, and singing gospel music at revival meetings. When he was in the fifth grade, Elvis sang Red Foley's "Old Shep" in school, and his teacher and principal were so impressed, they entered Elvis in a talent show at the Mississippi-Alabama State Fair. He won second place, and four months later received his first guitar from his mother as a birthday present. It cost $12.98.

In September, 1948, the family moved suddenly to Memphis, where Elvis enrolled at L.C. Humes High School. After graduation, he worked briefly for the Precision Tool Company before getting a job as a truck driver for Crown Electric. One Saturday in the closing days of summer, 1953, Elvis stopped during a lunch break at the Memphis Recording Service to record two songs for his mother, which eventually led to a recording contract with Sun Records [see 12—"I Want You, I Need You, I Love You"].

On November 22, 1955, RCA announced the purchase of Elvis' contract and his singles and unreleased masters from Sam Phillips of Sun

Records for an unprecedented sum of $40,000 ($35,000 to Sun and a $5,000 bonus to Elvis). Elvis' first recording session for RCA took place in Nashville on January 10 and 11, 1956. Producer Steve Sholes intended to capture the "Sun sound" and brought in musicians Elvis had already worked with: guitarist Scotty Moore, bassist Bill Black and drummer D.J. Fontana. They were joined by Chet Atkins on guitar, Floyd Cramer on piano and three members of the Jordanaires on backing vocals.

Among the five songs recorded during those two days were "Heartbreak Hotel" and its flip side, "I Was the One." Elvis had been told a few months before that he would be

recording "Heartbreak Hotel"—by co-writer Mae Axton. She handled public relations for Col. Tom Parker in Florida, and when he became Elvis' manager, Mae told Elvis he needed one more thing: "I said, 'you need a million seller, and I'm going to write it for you,'" she recounts.

Soon after, Tommy Durden brought Mae a front page newspaper story about a suicide victim who had left a one-line note: "I walk a lonely street." It was Mae who suggested to co-writer Tommy Durden they put a heartbreak hotel at the end of the lonely street, and 22 minutes later they had written and recorded on tape "Heartbreak Hotel." Mae called Elvis in Memphis and told him to meet her in Nashville to hear his first million seller. She flew there while he drove in, and when she played it for him, he asked to hear it again—and again—until he had listened to it 10 times.

"Heartbreak Hotel" was released on January 27, 1956. The next day, Elvis made his network television debut on Tommy and Jimmy Dorsey's "Stage Show" on CBS. Over the next two months, he was a guest on the live show five more times, singing "Heartbreak Hotel" on his third, fifth and sixth appearances.

On April 3, Elvis sang "Heartbreak Hotel" on NBC's "Milton Berle Show," with an audience estimated at one-quarter of the American population. Eighteen days later, "Heartbreak Hotel" became the 10th number one single of the rock era. At the end of 1956, *Billboard* rated it as the year's number one single.

---

### THE TOP FIVE
*Week of April 21, 1956*

1 **Heartbreak Hotel**
   Elvis Presley

2 **Hot Diggity/Jukebox Baby**
   Perry Como

3 **Poor People of Paris**
   Les Baxter

4 **Blue Suede Shoes**
   Carl Perkins

5 **Lisbon Antigua**
   Nelson Riddle
   & His Orchestra

*Writers: Stan Lebousky*
*Herb Newman*

*Producer: Buddy Bregman*

*June 16, 1956*
*6 weeks*

**D**ID singer Gogi Grant's name come from a dream or from the name of a New York restaurant? Only Dave Kapp, who headed A&R for RCA Records before he founded Kapp Records, knows for sure. Audrey Arinsberg was using her married name, Audrey Brown, when she signed with RCA. Her manager changed her name to Audrey Grant, and she used that for two months while performing in the Borscht Belt. Then Dave Kapp came up with the name "Gogi." "He told me, and you can believe it or not believe it, it came to him in a dream," she reveals. "But Dave used to go to lunch every day in New York at Gogi's La Rue. Some of Dave's friends suspected that's where he got the name."

Audrey was born September 20, 1924 in Philadelphia, the eldest of six children. The family moved to Los Angeles when she was 12. She always sang as a child, but never considered it as a career. Her high school classes included typing and shorthand, and she was thinking of teaching or becoming a commercial artist.

That changed after friends insisted she enter a weekly talent contest at the Macambo nightclub on the Sunset Strip. Through an orchestra leader there, she met a vocal coach and worked with her for three months. Then she went to Gold Star recording studios to make a demo record. Studio owner Stan Ross set up an interview with an agent at MCA's talent agency, but he and Gogi agreed she wasn't ready.

Three days later, Ross called her with the news that MCA was in an uproar. Audrey had inadvertently left her demo record on the turntable, which was in the office of the head of the music department. He had returned from a vacation in Tahiti and played the disc, a recording of "I'm Yours." His orders: find that voice!

Through MCA, she auditioned for RCA Records and signed a contract the same day. Her first RCA release, "Where There's Smoke, There's Fire," failed to chart, as did subsequent recordings. Kapp left RCA to start his own label and through Buddy Bregman, Gogi signed with Era Records, a Los Angeles label run by Herb Newman.

A song was selected for her, and when she met the writers, they played some other things they had written. One of them was "Suddenly There's a Valley." "I said I'd like to try that song. They all looked at each other strangely and said 'fine, but we thought we should have a male singer sing this song.' They had it in reserve for the first big male voice they found." Gogi recorded it instead of the song chosen for her, and went on a 28-city promotional tour. By the time she arrived in the first city, there were five cover versions. "If I hadn't gone on that publicity trip, I would have lost that record."

"Suddenly There's a Valley" went to number nine, and Gogi recorded a follow-up, "Who Are We," which took most of a three-hour recording session. While going over the arrangements, label owner Newman asked Gogi to come into his office. "Herb pulled out this manuscript; it was brown with age," Gogi remembers. It was a song Newman had written with Stan Lebousky when they were students at UCLA. It was also written for a man to sing, but Gogi felt something in the song. She changed some lyrics to sing the song from a woman's point of view, and, with 15 minutes of studio time remaining in the "Who Are We" session, recorded "The Wayward Wind."

"Who Are We" peaked at 62, so "The Wayward Wind" was released. Five weeks after entering the chart, it knocked "Heartbreak Hotel" out of the number one position.

## THE TOP FIVE
*Week of June 16, 1956*

1 **Wayward Wind**
Gogi Grant

2 **Moonglow and Theme from "Picnic"**
Morris Stoloff

3 **Heartbreak Hotel**
Elvis Presley

4 **Standing on The Corner**
Four Lads

5 **I'm in Love Again**
Fats Domino

## 12 I Want You, I Need You, I Love You RCA 6540

### ELVIS PRESLEY

*Writers: Maurice Mysels*
*Ira Kosloff*

*Producer: Steve Sholes*

*July 28, 1956*
*1 week*

ALTHOUGH he preferred not to fly, Elvis arrived for his third RCA recording session in Nashville by airplane. The flight did not build his confidence in air travel: one of the twin engines cut out and the charter craft was forced to make an emergency landing on a small, deserted runway.

That may be why Elvis only recorded one song during a recording session scheduled for April 11, 1956—"I Want You, I Need You, I Love You." The final track is an edit of the 14th and 17th takes; in 1976, an alternative recording was issued in which Elvis mistakenly sang "I Need You, I Want You, I Love You."

The single was released in May, and on June 5 Elvis made his second appearance on Milton Berle's show. He sang "I Want You, I Need You, I Love You" as well as his next single, "Hound Dog" [see 14]. While Ed Sullivan said he would never have Elvis on his show, time period rival Steve Allen had no qualms, and Elvis earned $7,500 for singing the same two songs on Allen's Sunday night show on July 1.

The first record Elvis ever made was an acetate of two songs he wanted to give his mother as a present. On a Saturday afternoon in late summer, 1953, Elvis parked his truck in front of Sam Phillips' Memphis Recording Service at 706 Union Avenue. It was also the office of Phillips' label, Sun Records. Phillips wasn't there, but his assistant, Marion Keisker, collected

Elvis' four dollars and helped him record "My Happiness" (an Ink Spots song) and "That's When Your Heartaches Begin" (a country song recorded by Bob Lamb). Sam had always told Marion, "If I could find a white boy who could sing like a Negro, I could make a million dollars." Halfway through "My Happiness," Marion thought she had found that white boy, and she quickly turned on a tape recorder.

Phillips listened to the tape and disagreed with Marion—he didn't think Elvis had anything. Presley returned to the studio on January 4, 1954 to cut two more songs: "Casual Love Affair" and "I'll Never Stand in Your Way." Still, Phillips was not taken with Elvis' voice. A few months later, Phillips received a demo of a song called "Without You." When he couldn't locate the original singer, Marion suggested they bring in Presley to record it.

Legend has it that Presley arrived at the studio before Phillips could hang up the phone. He recorded "Without You"—and it was terrible. Then Phillips asked him to record "Rag Mop," with similiar results. Finally, Sam asked Elvis what he could sing, and Elvis did his repertoire of rhythm and blues, country and western, gospel and Dean Martin hits. Phillips was impressed at last; he asked guitarist Scotty Moore to work with Elvis. Later that night, neighbor Bill Black came over to

Scotty's house to join them, and the following Monday they had their first Sun recording session.

The date was July 5, 1954. Elvis recorded "I Love You Because" and "Blue Moon of Kentucky." During a break, Elvis picked up his guitar and started playing Arthur Crudup's "That's All Right, Mama." Scotty and Bill joined in, and Phillips rushed out of the control booth and asked what they were doing. They stopped, but he told them to keep going—he wanted to capture the song on tape. It was the combination of white singer and black song that he had been looking for.

Two days later, WHBQ's Dewey Martin played an acetate of "That's All Right, Mama" on his "Red, Hot and Blue" show. The station was inundated with calls from people who wanted to hear the song again. Elvis shied away from hearing the broadcast, and went to watch *High Noon* at the local movie house. His parents raced there and brought him to the station for an interview on Martin's show. The DJ made a point to ask Elvis what high school he attended. It was only when he answered "Humes High" that the audience realized Presley was white.

Between July, 1954 and November, 1955, Sun Records would issue five singles by Elvis. Although none made the pop charts, the final two ("Baby Let's Play House" backed with "I'm Left, You're Right, She's Gone" and "Mystery Train" backed with "I Forgot to Remember to Forget") made number 10 and number one, respectively, on *Billboard's* country and western chart.

### THE TOP FIVE
*Week of July 28, 1956*

1 **I Want You, I Need You, I Love You**
Elvis Presley

2 **Wayward Wind**
Gogi Grant

3 **I Almost Lost my Mind**
Pat Boone

4 **My Prayer**
Platters

5 **More**
Perry Como

*Writers: Jimmy Kennedy*
  *Georges Boulanger*

*Producer: Buck Ram*

*August 4, 1956*
*2 weeks*

THE Platters were the first black artists to have a number one single on the pop charts. Their style was in the tradition of the Mills Brothers and the Ink Spots, and under the guidance of producer/manager Buck Ram, they were the most popular vocal group during the first five years of the rock era.

The Platters were already a quartet when Buck Ram met them in late 1953. Tony Williams, Herbert Reed, David Lynch and Alex Hodge signed a management contract with Buck on February 15, 1954. In May, Buck decided to add a female to the Platters. He recruited 15-year-old Zola Taylor from the girl group, Shirley Gunter and the Queens. Two months later, Hodge had trouble with the law, and was replaced by Paul Robi.

The group was signed to Federal Records, where they first released "Only You (And You Alone)," which didn't do very well. But they worked consistently, often earning $150 a night. When the Penguins, a Los Angeles doo-wop group that had a national hit with "Earth Angel," found out the Platters were earning three times as much money without having any hit records, they signed a management deal with Buck as well.

Mercury Records wanted to sign the Penguins away from the Dootone label, and Ram agreed on one condition: they sign the Platters, too. Buck credits west coast label executive John Sippel, later a *Billboard* reporter, with urging the Chicago-based label to take both groups.

The Platters' first release on Mercury was a new recording of "Only You." It was issued on a purple label, indicating the record was R&B. Ram successfully argued that the Platters sang pop music, and the record was reissued on Mercury's standard black label.

"Only You" did not do well at first, as the Penguins were a much higher priority for Mercury. Platter Tony Williams' wife was a secretary to Hunter Hancock, an influential white R&B disc jockey in Los Angeles. He played the record on his show, where it was heard by visiting Seattle DJ Bob Salter. Salter went back home and played the record, creating a demand that turned "Only You" into a national hit.

Mercury Records was anxious for a follow-up. "I file away ideas in my head," Buck explains. "The A&R man from Mercury said, 'you've had a big hit, we need another tune.' I said, 'I've got just the tune.' I thought

quickly and said, 'The Great Pretender.' I hadn't even written it yet. I went back to my hotel, went to the washroom and in 30 minutes wrote 'The Great Pretender.' Tony Williams didn't want to sing it because it was a 'hillbilly' song."

Lead singer Williams and producer Ram often had differences of opinion, but Ram was the group's manager and had the final word. As usual, he was correct and "The Great Pretender" was a smash.

English songwriter Jimmy Kennedy stopped Buck on the street one day and said he was very impressed with the sound of the Platters. He offered several of his songs to the group, and the one Buck liked best was "My Prayer," a French song originally written by Georges Boulanger as "Avant de Mourir." Kennedy had written English lyrics in 1939.

"It was the first song ever written that had a slow introduction and verse, then the chorus," Buck claims. "Mercury would not release 'My Prayer.' Then an A&R man heard the Four Aces were recording it. The minute they heard that, they rushed it out."

## THE TOP FIVE
*Week of August 4, 1956*

1  **My Prayer**
  Platters

2  **I Want You, I Need You,**
  **I Love You**
  Elvis Presley

3  **I Almost Lost my Mind**
  Pat Boone

4  **Wayward Wind**
  Gogi Grant

5  **Whatever Will Be, Will Be**
  Doris Day

<table>
<tr><td>14</td></tr>
</table>

# Don't Be Cruel / Hound Dog RCA 6604
## ELVIS PRESLEY

*Writers: Otis Blackwell*
*Elvis Presley*
*Jerry Leiber*
*Mike Stoller*

*Producer: Steve Sholes*

*August 18, 1956*
*11 weeks*

At 11 WEEKS, "Don't Be Cruel" / "Hound Dog" had the longest run at number one until "End of the Road" by Boyz II Men in 1992. "Don't Be Cruel" was composed by Otis Blackwell, a Brooklyn songwriter whose credits include "Fever," "Great Balls of Fire," "Breathless" and many later Elvis hits, including "Return to Sender," "One Broken Heart for Sale," "(Such an) Easy Question" and the number one single "All Shook Up." Elvis no more wrote "Don't Be Cruel" than he wrote "Heartbreak Hotel"—it was simply a demand by Colonel Tom Parker that Elvis should be listed as a songwriter so that he would receive a share of the writing royalties.

"Hound Dog" was written in 1952 by Jerry Leiber and Mike Stoller, two East Coast songwriters who met in Los Angeles through a drummer who was a mutual friend. Leiber and Stoller were as responsible as any performer for laying the foundation of rock and roll, writing and producing for the Coasters, the Drifters and the Clovers. They began writing R&B songs in the summer of 1950, and two years later were asked by Johnny Otis to write for the singers in his band, including Little Esther and Big Mama Thornton.

After watching Thornton perform at a rehearsal, Leiber and Stoller went home and wrote "Hound Dog" as a country blues tune. They helped Otis produce the session, and "Hound Dog" went to number one on the R&B chart.

On April 23, 1956, Elvis made his debut in Las Vegas at the Frontier Hotel. The middle-aged audience watched in unappreciative silence,

and the two-week run was cancelled after the first week. But Elvis made a fateful visit to the lounge and listened to Freddie Bell and the Bellboys, who did a comedic version of "Hound Dog" in their act, adding lyrics like "You ain't never caught a rabbit, and you ain't no friend of mine." Elvis liked their treatment of the song enough to add it to his repertoire.

Elvis introduced "Hound Dog" to a national audience on June 5, during his second appearance on Milton Berle's TV show. His pelvic undulations caused an uproar and the press lambasted him. Ed Sullivan announced he would never have Presley on his Sunday night show, but that didn't stop Steve Allen, whose NBC variety series aired opposite Sullivan, from booking Elvis. On July 1, Elvis sang "Hound Dog" on Allen's show, only this time, dressed in a tuxedo and blue suede shoes, with explicit instructions to stand still. Elvis simply sang "Hound Dog" to a sad-eyed basset hound.

Steve Allen received a 55 share, and Sullivan quickly changed his mind about booking Elvis, who was paid $50,000 for three appearances. He sang "Don't Be Cruel" and "Hound Dog" on September 9 and October 28 of 1956 and January 6, 1957.

The day after appearing on Steve Allen's show, Elvis recorded "Don't Be Cruel" and "Hound Dog" at RCA Studios in New York City. Despite the latter song's success in his stage act, he was reluctant to record it, but producer Steve Sholes insisted. It was the last time Elvis ever recorded in New York.

In the early summer of 1956, Mr. and Mrs. Mike Stoller vacationed in Europe. They returned home to New York on the Italian liner Andrea Doria, which, on the night of July 25, was rammed by the Swedish-American liner Stockholm. Fifty people were killed or missing, but the Stollers were among the 1,652 survivors. They escaped in a lifeboat and were rescued at sea. A frantic Jerry Leiber rushed to the docks to greet the freighter that brought the Stollers home. Grateful to be alive, the Stollers disembarked and were greeted by an excited Leiber, who exclaimed, "Elvis Presley recorded Hound Dog!'"

### THE TOP FIVE
*Week of August 18, 1956*

1  **Don't Be Cruel/Hound Dog**
   Elvis Presley

2  **My Prayer**
   Platters

3  **Whatever Will Be, Will Be**
   Doris Day

4  **Flying Saucer (Parts I & II)**
   Buchanan & Goodman

5  **I Want You, I Need You,
   I Love You**
   Elvis Presley

use Elvis' coterie of musicians (Scotty Moore, Bill Black and D.J. Fontana), believing they couldn't do justice to his music. The musicians playing on the soundtrack are the Ken Darby Trio.

David Weisbart, the man who produced James Dean's *Rebel Without a Cause*, was an appropriate choice to produce *Love Me Tender*. On the first day of filming, Presley talked to Weisbart about starring in a film biography of the late James Dean that the producer was considering.

Richard Egan, Debra Paget and Neville Brand were Elvis' co-stars in *Love Me Tender*, a Civil War story about Confederate soldiers who are unaware the war has ended. Elvis plays Cliff Reno, a young man who marries his dead brother's fiancee. One small problem: the brother wasn't killed in the war after all, and comes home to a romantic triangle. Before Cliff is killed by Brand, Elvis gets to sing all four songs.

*Love Me Tender* opened in New York City on November 16, and 20th Century Fox released 550 prints to theaters, more than any other film had ever issued. RCA had been forced to release the title song in the first week of October, due to the demand created after Elvis sang it on his first Ed Sullivan appearance on September 9.

In 1978, WCBM disc jockey Ray Quinn edited Elvis' recording of "Love Me Tender" with a then-new version by Linda Ronstadt, creating an ersatz duet which received much radio airplay, but for obvious contractual reasons was never released.

*Writers: Elvis Presley*
*Vera Watson*

*Producer: Steve Sholes*

*November 3, 1956*
*5 weeks*

WHEN "LOVE ME TENDER" succeeded "Don't Be Cruel" and "Hound Dog" as the nation's number one song, it was the first of only three occasions in the rock era when an artist had consecutive number one hits. The only other acts to accomplish this were the Beatles [see 144—"She Loves You"] and Boyz II Men [see 811—"End of the Road"].

On October 20, 1956, "Love Me Tender" was number two while "Don't Be Cruel" and "Hound Dog" were number one, and the following week they reversed positions, marking the first time the same artist occupied the top two positions on *Billboard*'s pop chart.

Even before his first RCA original release, "Heartbreak Hotel," went to number one, Elvis flew to Hollywood for a screen test with Hal Wallis at Paramount Pictures. Presley wasn't asked to sing; they already knew he

could do that. He performed a scene with character actor Frank Faylen, and on April 1, 1956, Wallis made a three-picture deal with Col. Tom Parker.

Elvis was to make his film debut in *The Rainmaker* with Burt Lancaster and Katharine Hepburn, and if he had, it would have been the most serious dramatic role of his career. But that was not the direction Col. Parker wanted him to follow, and the first of his 33 films set the pattern of simple, uncomplicated plots with beautiful female guest stars and a few songs thrown in for good measure.

Elvis' first film was originally titled *The Reno Brothers*, but by the time production started on August 22, it was called *Love Me Tender*. Before filming began at 20th Century Fox, four songs were recorded, including the title track. Based on an 1861 folk ballad called "Aura Lee," the song was credited to Elvis and a songwriter named Vera Watson, but was actually written by Vera's husband, Ken Darby, musical director of the film. Darby wrote the entire score for the movie, and refused to

---

## THE TOP FIVE
### *Week of November 3, 1956*

1  **Love Me Tender**
   Elvis Presley

2  **Don't Be Cruel/**
   **Hound Dog**
   Elvis Presley

3  **Green Door**
   Jim Lowe

4  **Just Walkin' in the Rain**
   Johnnie Ray

5  **Honky Tonk (Parts I & II)**
   Bill Doggett

## 16 Singing the Blues  COLUMBIA 40769
### GUY MITCHELL

*Writer: Melvin Endsley*

*Producer: Mitch Miller*

*December 8, 1956*
*9 weeks*

"SINGING THE BLUES" by Guy Mitchell is the first of six singles in the rock era to have a nine-week run at number one. The others are "Mack the Knife" by Bobby Darin in 1959, "Theme From 'A Summer Place'" by Percy Faith in 1960, "Hey Jude" by the Beatles in 1968, "Bette Davis Eyes" by Kim Carnes in 1981 and "Endless Love" by Diana Ross and Lionel Richie, also in 1981.

Melvin Endsley, a 20-year-old songwriter from Arkansas, wrote "Singing the Blues" in 1954. A victim of polio when he was three years old, Endsley was confined to a wheelchair. This song was his first successful composition.

Marty Robbins recorded the song first, also for Columbia Records, but the label was more interested in making him a country star. Mitchell heard Robbins' version and asked Mitch Miller if he could record it, too. Both versions entered the Best Sellers in Stores chart on November 3, 1956. Robbins peaked at 17.

Guy Mitchell was born Al Cernick on February 27, 1927 in Detroit, Michigan. His parents were of Yugoslavian descent. They decided to move to Los Angeles when Guy was 11 years old, and on the fateful train journey west, a passenger approached Guy's mother and handed her a business card. He said her son had a beautiful voice and she should contact him after she was settled in Los Angeles. True to his word, he arranged an audition with Warner Brothers, who signed Al to a contract for grooming as a child star.

Al took acting, dancing, voice and diction lessons, and sang on the studio's radio station, KFWB, but his parents moved to San Francisco, ending his early chances for stardom. He continued to sing while attending Mission High in the Bay Area, and during the summers he worked on a ranch in the San Joaquin Valley. There, country singer Dude Martin heard him and invited Al to appear regularly on his KYA and KGO radio shows, a job interrupted by a 16-month stint in the Navy.

In 1947, Cernick joined Carmen Cavallaro's orchestra as a vocalist and made his first recordings, on December 17. "I Go in When the Moon Comes Out" and "Ah But It Happens" were released on Decca. Al was supposed to appear with Cavallaro at the Astor Room in New York, but a throat infection prevented him from singing. He decided to stay in New York anyway to make the rounds of the record companies.

Al recorded for King Records in 1949, the same year he was a winner on "Arthur Godfrey's Talent Scouts." His biggest break came a year later when Frank Sinatra refused to record two songs for Mitch Miller at Columbia Records. The studio was booked, the band was waiting and an angry Mitch wanted to find a replacement vocalist immediately. He remembered hearing the voice of Al Cernick on demo records and called all over town to find him. Two hours later, Al was in the studio recording "My Heart Cries for You" and its flip side, "The Roving Kind." Both songs made the top five in early 1951.

Mitch thought Al Cernick was not an appropriate name for a performer, so he took his own first name and added it to the fact that Al was "a nice guy" to come up with Guy Mitchell.

### THE TOP FIVE
*Week of December 8, 1956*

1 **Singing the Blues**
  Guy Mitchell

2 **Love Me Tender**
  Elvis Presley

3 **Green Door**
  Jim Lowe

4 **Blueberry Hill**
  Fats Domino

5 **Just Walking in the Rain**
  Johnnie Ray

*Writers: Lee Rosenberg*
*Bernard Weinman*

*Producer: Steve Sholes*

*February 9, 1957*
*3 weeks*

Gᴜʏ Mɪᴛᴄʜᴇʟʟ's "Singing the Blues" finally relinquished the top spot after nine weeks, and Elvis Presley had his first number one single of 1957, "Too Much." The previous year had been good for Presley. In 1956, he topped the chart four times and occupied the number one position for 25 weeks, a total unmatched by any other artist in any other year. He would not let up the pace in '57—in fact, he would tie his own record by being number one for 25 weeks this year, again with four singles.

Elvis premiered "Too Much" on his third Ed Sullivan appearance, on January 6, 1957. Guest starring on Sullivan's show gave Presley national credibility, especially after Ed had given Elvis his personal endorsement during his second appearance on October 28. Sullivan had been ill when Presley made his first guest appearance on September 9, 1956— Charles Laughton was the substitute emcee that night. TV Guide, selecting what they felt was the most noteworthy event on television that week, ran a cover story: "The Plain Truth About Elvis Presley."

Despite this growing public acceptance of Presley by the adult population of America, on the January 6 Sullivan show, Elvis was seen only from the waist up; the cameramen ordered not to pan their lenses down to the verboten pelvic region. Elvis sang seven songs that night· "Hound Dog," "Love Me Tender," "Heartbreak Hotel," "Peace in the Valley," "When My Blue Moon Turns to Gold Again" as well as "Don't Be Cruel" and "Too Much." It was the last time Presley ever appeared on Sullivan's show.

Elvis recorded "Too Much" and its flip side, "Playing for Keeps," at a three-day session in Hollywood, beginning September 1, 1956. "Too Much" had been recorded in 1954 by Bernard Hardison, and songwriter Lee Rosenberg handed the song to Elvis as he was boarding a train for Los Angeles.

Although Ken Darby refused to employ Scotty Moore, Bill Black and D.J. Fontana for the *Love Me Tender* sessions, these three musicians were flown to Hollywood for the recording of "Too Much" and the songs that would comprise Elvis' second RCA album. That LP, titled simply *Elvis*, was released in October, 1956, and "Too Much" was held for release in January, 1957.

A month before "Too Much" was issued, Elvis took part in a recording session that has taken on legendary proportions. He was home in Memphis to visit his family, when he stopped by the Sun Recording Studio on December 4, 1956. Label owner Sam Phillips was producing a session for Carl Perkins ("Matchbox") that day. Two other Sun artists were in the studio: Jerry Lee Lewis (who had just recorded his first Sun single, "Crazy Arms") had been hired to play the piano for Perkins' and Johnny Cash (in the national top 20 with "I Walk the Line") was a guest.

With that much talent in the room, it was inevitable that music would be made. Elvis replaced Jerry Lee at the piano, and while Sam Phillips discreetly turned on a tape recorder, the sounds of "Blueberry Hill" filled the studio, along with gospel numbers like "Just a Little Talk With Jesus" and "Walk That Lonesome Valley." For 25 years, the only evidence of this almost-mythical session was a newspaper photo of the four participants and a report by Memphis Press-Scimitar columnist Robert Johnson.

It wasn't until April 1, 1981, when Sun Records in Great Britain released the album *Million Dollar Quartet*, that anyone actually heard what was recorded that day. As it turned out, only Presley, Lewis and Perkins are on the album, lending credence to the story that after having his picture taken, Cash went shopping.

Just after "Too Much" descended from number one, Elvis purchased a new home in the Whitehaven suburb of Memphis. He paid $100,000 for the two-story mansion, built of Tennessee limestone, and the 13 3/4 acres of land the house sat on. Elvis bought the house from Mrs. Ruth Brown Moore. It had been built by her husband, Dr. Thomas Moore, and named after her aunt, Grace Toof. Elvis kept the name: Graceland.

## THE TOP FIVE
*Week of February 9, 1957*

1 **Too Much**
Elvis Presley

2 **Young Love**
Sonny James

3 **Don't Forbid Me**
Pat Boone

4 **Young Love**
Tab Hunter

5 **Singing the Blues**
Guy Mitchell

# Young Love DOT 15533
## TAB HUNTER

Writers: *Carole Joyner*
*Ric Cartey*

Producer: *Billy Vaughn*

*March 2, 1957*
*4 weeks*

When the rock era was young, it was common for several singers to record the same song simultaneously and fight each other for airplay and sales. Publishers wanted as many artists as possible to cover their songs and provide more revenue for them; sometimes more than one version became popular and increased their income even more. The most hotly contested cover battle of the rock era was over the song "Young Love," recorded first by the song's co-writer, Ric Cartey, on RCA. When his version failed, he played it for country singer Sonny James, who liked it enough to record it.

Randy Wood, president of Dot Records in Gallatin, Texas, thought Sonny's version would do well on the country charts, and wanted a pop singer to cover it. He contacted actor Tab Hunter, who remembers the conversation: "Randy called me up and said, 'I've got a record I want you to hear. If you can carry a tune at all, we'd like you to record it.'"

Tab's vocal experience had been confined to the school choir, but he liked the song and agreed to record it. Ten days later it was available in record stores. Sonny's country version bounded up the pop charts, but Tab was right behind him until March 2, 1957, when Hunter went to number one. Sonny peaked at number two.

Tab's recording career was short-lived. Warner Brothers had him under contract for films, and objected strongly to his recording for Dot. The studio sent him on a national promotion tour for the film *The Spirit of St. Louis*. "Everybody knew the plane landed safely...so they kept saying, 'tell us about your new record.' Warners was furious," Tab laughs.

When Warner Brothers started their own label in 1958, Tab was among the first artists signed. He feels he was one of the reasons the film company decided to have their own label, so their talent wouldn't be earning money for other companies.

Tab was born Arthur Andrew Kelm on July 11, 1931, in New York City. Later, he used his mother's maiden name, Gelien. He joined the Coast Guard at 15, and after a two-year stint became a competitive ice skater. He loved horses, and was working at a stable when he was spotted by talent agent Dick Clayton. He introduced Arthur to Henry Willson, Hollywood agent for Rock Hudson. "Harry always gave strange names to people," says Hunter. "Rory Calhoun, Guy Madison, Rock Hudson, Rhonda Fleming. And he said, 'We've got to tab you something'...I used to show horses, hunters and jumpers. It could have been Tab Jumper instead of Tab Hunter."

Willson got Tab into his first film, *Island of Desire*, with Linda Darnell in 1952. He made many films in the 1950s, but perhaps the best was the musical *Damn Yankees*, in which he was the only leading actor who hadn't been in the Broadway cast. He asked for and secured his release from Warner Brothers, then continued to make films in Europe.

He starred for one season in a half-hour situation comedy, "The Tab Hunter Show," which premiered on NBC September 18, 1960. He played a bachelor cartoonist and was up against the last 30 minutes of "The Ed Sullivan Show."

In 1977, when Mary Hartman's father, George Shumway, fell into a vat of rustoleum, he came out looking like Tab Hunter in "Forever Fernwood," the series that succeeded "Mary Hartman, Mary Hartman" after Louise Lasser departed. For 19 episodes, Tab Hunter took Philip Bruns' place in the role of George Shumway.

Tab's recent film work includes *Polyester*, a 1981 film which also starred Divine. Tab sang the title song, written by Debbie Harry and Chris Stein of Blondie. In 1982, Tab had a role in *Grease 2*. He has since formed his own production company and teamed up with Divine again for a western film, *Lust in the Dust*.

## THE TOP FIVE
*Week of March 2, 1957*

1 **Young Love**
Tab Hunter

2 **Too Much**
Elvis Presley

3 **Don't Forbid Me**
Pat Boone

4 **Young Love**
Sonny James

5 **Banana Boat (Day-O)**
Harry Belafonte

*Writers: Buddy Knox*
*Jimmy Bowen*

*Producer: Norman Petty*

*March 30, 1957*
*1 week*

**B**UDDY WAYNE KNOX, born July 20, 1933 in Happy, Texas, was the first artist of the rock era to write his own number one song (Elvis Presley was listed as songwriter on two of his number one hits before "Party Doll," but didn't actually participate in writing either one [see 14—"Don't Be Cruel" / "Hound Dog"]). He was also one of the innovators of the southwestern style of rockabilly that became known as "Tex-Mex" music, as exemplified by many singers who recorded at Norman Petty's studios in Clovis, New Mexico, just 10 steps from the Texas border.

Buddy went to West Texas State University on a sports scholarship and met two other students who were on partial sports scholarships, Jimmy Bowen and Don Lanier. They formed a group called the Serenaders, named for their habit of serenading the women's dorms at two in the morning. Buddy Holly and Roy Orbison performed on campus. and when Knox became friendly with them, both suggested he take his songs over to producer Petty's studio and record them.

One of those songs was "Party Doll," which Buddy had written in 1948. "I really don't remember writing 'Party Doll,'" he confesses, "but I did, out on the farm, behind a haystack." Around the same time, he also wrote another future hit, "Hula Love." The original idea came from an Edison wax cylinder recording made on February 14, 1910, by the Metropolitan Opera Quartet, "My Hula Hula Love," and from the motion picture *Bird of Paradise* starring Deborah Paget and Louis Jordan.

"When I got into college, those were really about the only songs I knew outside of a few Fats Domino things. Then we started hearing about Elvis Presley and Jerry Lee Lewis and Chuck Berry, and found out we were doing the same kind of music they were doing."

Buddy, Jimmy and Don arrived at Clovis Studios with $60 in their pockets. "We didn't know if that was the right price or not for a session," Buddy says. Petty laughed and spent three days recording "Party Doll" and two other songs. "We suddenly discovered Jimmy Bowen couldn't play bass. There was a black fellow in town who played pretty good bass, so we hired him for 'Party Doll.'"

Dave Alldred, drummer with the Norman Petty Trio, played drums—sort of. He didn't have a complete set of drums, so a cardboard box was filled with cotton and a microphone was stuffed inside. A girl from the Clovis High School marching band played cymbals, and Buddy's sister and her two girlfriends sang backing vocals.

When the three days were over, Norman gave each member of the group a couple of acetates of their recordings. "We just went back home with the darn things. We knew nothing about the business at all...the only thing that we really went to record for was just to have a couple of copies of the record."

Chester Oliver, a farmer from Plainview, Texas, asked if he could press 1,500 copies of "Party Doll" to sell in local stores. They formed a small label, Triple-D, named after Dumas, Texas radio station KDDD where Bowen had worked. A DJ in Amarillo, Dean Kelly, played the record and it became a local hit.

Don Lanier's sister called Morris Levy at Roulette Records in New York, and he was interested enough to send the group plane tickets and sign them to contracts. "We called ourselves the Orchids originally, because we all had orchid-colored shirts. When we got to New York, the people at Roulette decided it wasn't such a jazzy name, so they changed it to the Rhythm Orchids," says Buddy.

As soon as Roulette released "Party Doll," there were three other versions. Wingy Manone and Roy Brown had R&B versions which charted in the bottom half of the Hot 100, but Steve Lawrence's pop version went to number five.

With four months to go before getting his masters degree in accounting, Buddy quit school to be a full-time performer. Today he tours 11 months out of the year, and lives with his wife on a farm about 50 miles out of Winnipeg, Manitoba, Canada, near the American border.

## THE TOP FIVE
*Week of March 30, 1957*

1  **Party Doll**
   Buddy Knox

2  **Round and Round**
   Perry Como

3  **Butterfly**
   Charlie Gracie

4  **Butterfly**
   Andy Williams

5  **Teen-Age Crush**
   Tommy Sands

# Round and Round
RCA 6815

## PERRY COMO

*Writers: Joe Shapiro*
*Lou Stallman*

*Producer: Joe Reisman*

*April 6, 1957*
*1 week*

PERRY COMO was signed to the same record label longer than any one else who has had a number one record. In fact, he was an RCA recording artist longer than many other singers have been alive. He signed with the label on June 17, 1943, and released an RCA album as recently as 1987. On June 21, 1983, RCA's chairman and chief executive officer Thornton F. Bradshaw and RCA Records president Robert D. Summer hosted a dinner for Como at the Rainbow Grill in New York's Rockefeller Center, to honor his 40th year with RCA Records and his 50th year in show business.

"Round and Round" is his only number one single of the rock era, but he had eight number ones between 1945-1954. He first sang "Round and Round" on his weekly NBC variety show, and the audience response was so great, RCA decided to release it as a single.

He was born Pierino Roland Como on May 18, 1912 in Canonsburg, Pennsylvania. He was the seventh son of a seventh son, the first of Pietro and Lucia Como's 13 children to be born in the United States. Canonsburg was a mining town, but Perry avoided working in the coal pits by becoming an apprentice barber at age 11. By the time he was 14, he had opened his own shop, where his customers received a shave and a

## THE TOP FIVE
*Week of April 6, 1957*

1 **Round and Round**
Perry Como

2 **Little Darlin'**
Diamonds

3 **Party Doll**
Buddy Knox

4 **Butterfly**
Charlie Gracie

5 **I'm Walkin'**
Fats Domino

haircut *and* a song. Perry was a full-time barber for seven years, until, while on vacation in Cleveland in 1933, he auditioned for Freddy Carlone's band. He was offered $28 a week, and said yes—giving up the security of $125 a week as a barber.

Perry married his childhood sweetheart, Roselle Belline, on July 31, 1933, and four days later started touring with Carlone's band. One night, three years later, Perry was singing with the the group at a gambling casino in Warren, Ohio, when bandleader Ted Weems came in to play roulette. He won at the table, then went downstairs to hear Perry sing. He offered him a job on the spot as lead vocalist with his band. Perry accepted the $50-a-week job.

In 1942, Weems disbanded because of the war, and Perry returned to Canonsburg, intending to be a barber once more. He was negotiating a lease for a new shop when General Artists Corporation offered him a network radio show, nightclub bookings and a chance to sign to RCA Victor as a solo artist. He was reluctant, but Roselle said he could always go back to barbering if it didn't work out. Perry said yes.

During the next three years, Perry became a national celebrity. His first single for RCA, "Goodbye, Sue" was released. His NBC radio show. "The Chesterfield Supper

Club" was a hit. He received rave reviews for his shows at the Copacabana and the Paramount Theater in New York. He signed a seven-year movie contract with 20th Century Fox and made his film debut in *Something for the Boys* with Vivian Blaine, Phil Silvers and Carmen Miranda.

His first number one single was "Till the End of Time" in the fall of 1945, followed by hits like "Prisoner of Love," "Don't Let the Stars Get in Your Eyes" and "Hot Diggity (Dog Ziggity Boom)."

Perry's first television series, "The Chesterfield Supper Club," premiered on NBC on December 24, 1948 in the 7:00-7:15 p.m. time period on Friday nights. He went to CBS in 1950, and returned to NBC in September, 1955 with a weekly one-hour show on Saturday nights. In the fall of 1959 he moved to Wednesday nights at 9 p.m., a time period he secured until his last program on June 12, 1963.

Unlike many of his contemporaries who criticized rock and roll, Como was never one to put down the new music and in fact welcomed many new artists as guests on his television series.

On May 12, 2001, Perry Como died in his sleep at his home in Jupiter Beach Inlet Colony, Florida, after a long illness. He was 88.

Writers: *Otis Blackwell*
*Elvis Presley*

Producer: *Steve Sholes*

April 13, 1957
8 weeks

"ALL SHOOK UP" was Elvis Presley's first number one single in Britain. "Heartbreak Hotel" and "Hound Dog" had both peaked at two in the United Kingdom, but it took this song written by Otis Blackwell (but credited to Blackwell and Presley) to put him on top. "All Shook Up" was the first of 17 British number ones for Elvis, an odd coincidence considering that he also had 17 American number ones. Only six titles reached the top in both countries; in Britain, his charttoppers included such non-American number ones as "One Night," "A Fool Such As I," "Can't Help Falling in Love" and "The Wonder of You."

Elvis' British total of 17 number one hits ties him with the Beatles for the greatest amount of number one singles; in America, that same total is only good enough for second place behind the Beatles.

Despite Elvis' incredible success in Britain, he never toured there. British fans always held hope the king of rock and roll would come to their country, but in fact, Elvis never toured outside of North America. Many reasons and excuses were given over the years, but it was only in the biography *Elvis* by Albert Goldman, published in 1981, that the truth became apparent. Elvis' manager, Col. Tom Parker, was not born in West Virginia, as his biographies had always stated. His real name was Andreas Cornelis van Kuijk and he was born in Breda, Holland on June 26, 1909. At 18, he came to America, lived briefly with a Dutch family, then rode freight trains all over the country. After one year, he returned to Holland with gifts for his family. But he longed to return to the States, and returned in 1929, entering the U.S. Army a year later.

He wrote to his family and sent money, but by January, 1932, there was no further word from van Kuijk, who had been signing his letters "Tom Parker." His family did not know of his fate until 1961, when they saw a magazine photo of Elvis and the Colonel. The resemblance to one of his brothers was so strong, the family recognized him immediately.

Col. Parker couldn't obtain a U.S. passport because he wasn't a U.S. citizen, and he couldn't leave the United States because there was no assurance he would be allowed back in. He made certain he wouldn't have to leave the country by keeping Elvis on the American continent.

"All Shook Up" was recorded at Radio Recorders in Hollywood on January 12, 1957. The two-day session was divided between secular material and gospel songs. "That's When Your Heartaches Begin" was recorded on January 13, and was the flip side of "All Shook Up." The single was released in March, followed in April by the "Just for You" EP with songs that were recorded on January 19 and February 23. The same month, RCA released the "Peace in the Valley" EP with four songs recorded at the "All Shook Up" session. Two more songs from that session found their way to the *Loving You* soundtrack, released in July.

"All Shook Up" was the number one single of 1957, according to *Billboard*. It was the second year in a row that Elvis had the top single of the year [see 10—"Heartbreak Hotel."] No other artist has ever topped the year-end charts for two consecutive years.

## THE TOP FIVE
*Week of April 13, 1957*

1 **All Shook Up**
Elvis Presley

2 **Little Darlin'**
Diamonds

3 **Party Doll**
Buddy Knox

4 **Round and Round**
Perry Como

5 **Butterfly**
Andy Williams

# Love Letters in the Sand DOT 15570
### PAT BOONE

**22**

*Writers: Nick Kenny*
*Charles Kenny*
*J. Fred Coots*

*Producer: Randy Wood*

*June 3, 1957*
*5 weeks*

Even after he had a couple of hit records, Pat Boone wasn't sure he would pursue a singing career. "I thought I was going to be a schoolteacher," he recalls. As for recording, "I thought it was a hobby for me. Growing up in Tennessee in a church background, I thought I had too many strikes against me in self-imposed limitations brought about by my faith and conscience....It was only after several million selling records and I had a couple of million dollar contracts that the thought occurred I might make a career out of it."

It was a wise career choice. Pat Boone is the second most successful artist of the rock era's first half-decade, behind Elvis Presley. His first single for Dot Records was a cover of an R&B song, "Two Hearts, Two Kisses" by Otis Williams and the Charms. It established a pattern that saw Pat record pop versions of Fats Domino's "Ain't That a Shame" and Little Richard's "Long Tall Sally," among others. That practice elicited harsh criticism from people like DJ Alan Freed, who refused to play Boone's releases on the grounds he was denying black artists a chance to have hits with their own material. Pat sees it differently.

"Ninety per cent of radio stations in America wouldn't play R&B hits no matter how big they were. To get them on radio, other artists had to do them. I talked to Fats and Little Richard. There was a definite ceiling on how far they could go. When a white artist came along and sang their songs, they were introduced to audiences they couldn't get to themselves."

With his handsome, youthful looks, it was inevitable that Hollywood would be interested in Pat Boone. He did a screen test for 20th Century Fox, which signed him to a seven-year contract and cast him in the lead of *Bernadine*, opposite Terry Moore.

Originally, there were no songs included in the film, but the producers realized it would be silly to have Pat Boone in a movie without music. Two numbers were added: Johnny Mercer's title tune and a song that Pat had already recorded, "Love Letters in the Sand."

Rudy Vallee and Bing Crosby recorded it before Pat, and Randy Wood, owner of Dot Records, knew it was a hot item. "Randy had a little store called Randy's Record Shop in Gallatin, Tennessee, and he merchandised records on the radio. He kept getting requests for 'Love Letters in the Sand' over a ten-year period," Boone explains.

Pat's version sat on a shelf while other songs he recorded at the same time went on to be hits. When the producers of *Bernadine* agreed to include it in the film, Randy had Pat record a version for the soundtrack. For single release, Pat recorded it for a third time, but after listening to all three versions, Randy decided to release the very first one as the 45.

"It's always been a mystery to me why it had universal appeal," Pat admits. "There's nothing exciting about the arrangement or the way I sang it." Still, it's Boone's most successful single, with five weeks at number one and 23 weeks on the Best Sellers chart.

## THE TOP FIVE
*Week of June 3, 1957*

1 **Love Letters in the Sand**
  Pat Boone

2 **White Sport Coat**
  Marty Robbins

3 **All Shook Up**
  Elvis Presley

4 **I'm Walkin'**
  Ricky Nelson

5 **So Rare**
  Jimmy Dorsey

*Writers: Kal Mann*
*Bernie Lowe*

*Producer: Steve Sholes*

*July 8, 1957*
*7 weeks*

THE teddy bear was created by Morris Michton, president of the Ideal Toy Company, in 1902. The name "Teddy" came from President Theodore Roosevelt, and the original teddy bear is on display at the Smithsonian Institute in Washington, D.C.

Somehow, a rumor started that Elvis collected teddy bears. He didn't, but fans the world over sent him teddy bears for his collection, and suddenly, he had one. Kal Mann and Bernie Lowe, the founders of Cameo-Parkway Records in Phila-delphia, were inspired by Elvis' "affinity" for the cuddly toys to write this song for the film *Loving You*.

Elvis recorded "(Let Me Be Your) Teddy Bear" and its flip side, the title track from *Loving You*, at Radio Recorders Studio in Hollywood dur-ing sessions that took place in February and March of 1957. It was at these sessions that Elvis recorded the other tracks for the soundtrack of *Loving You*, his second motion pic-ture.

*Loving You* went into production in February. Originally titled *Lone-some Cowboy*, it was produced by Hal B. Wallis and directed by Hal Kanter for Paramount Pictures. Elvis starred as Deke Rivers, a character not unlike Elvis himself. Deke is a truck driver who becomes a famous rock singer and is besieged by young

## THE TOP FIVE
*Week of July 8, 1957*

1  **(Let Me be Your) Teddy Bear**
   Elvis Presley

2  **Bye Bye Love**
   Everly Brothers

3  **Love Letters in The Sand**
   Pat Boone

4  **So Rare**
   Jimmy Dorsey

5  **Searchin'**
   Coasters

girls who want to tear his clothes off, their boyfriends who want to tear his head off and business managers who just want to rip him off. Deke falls for a girl singer with his band, but she's fired to help pay for expensive publicity stunts. Somehow, Deke ends up with the girl anyway and there's a happy ending, unlike Elvis' first film, *Love Me Tender*.

*Loving You* was Elvis' first color film, and the other actors were Liz-abeth Scott, Wendell Corey, Dolores Hart and James Gleason. "(Let Me Be Your) Teddy Bear" went to number one on July 8, and the motion picture opened the next day.

The film featured plenty of footage of Elvis singing on stage, and in the last concert scene, two extras enjoying Elvis' music are very recog-nizable: Vernon and Gladys Presley. After his mother's death in August, 1958, Elvis was never able to watch this scene again.

It was during the reign of "(Let Me Be Your) Teddy Bear" that a development significant to the future of rock and roll was taking place in Philadelphia. On August 5, Dick Clark's "American Bandstand" made its network debut on ABC-TV. The program had been a local Philadelphia institution for four years, and Clark became the host in 1956. The first guests on the network premiere were the Chordettes. Ironically, only two major artists have never appeared on the show: Elvis Presley and Rick Nelson. The series is the longest-running variety show in the history of TV. It moved into syndication in Sep-tember, 1987.

As for Elvis' teddy bear collec-tion—on the day after Christmas of 1957, Elvis donated thousands of teddy bears to the National Founda-tion for Infantile Paralysis.

### 24 Tammy CORAL 61851
### DEBBIE REYNOLDS

*Writers: Jay Livingston*
*Ray Evans*

*Producer: Not Known*

*August 26, 1957*
*3 weeks*

"TAMMY" by Debbie Reynolds was the only single by a female vocalist to go to number one between July 28, 1956 and December 1, 1958. It is one of the longest periods of male domination of the number one position in the entire rock era.

The only song to break through during this bloc of time was from a film about a teenager who nurses an injured pilot back to health—*Tammy and the Bachelor*. Debbie Reynolds and Leslie Nielsen starred in the 1957 release, which was produced by Ross Hunter and directed by Joseph Pevney. Debbie sang the title tune in the film, and when it was nominated

for an Oscar, she was invited to sing it at the Academy Awards on March 26, 1958.

Debbie recorded the song accompanied only by a piano. More instruments and a Henry Mancini arrangement were added to the track before it went into the movie. Bob Thiele, head of Coral Records, didn't expect it to sell and released the song without any further embellishments. The song went to number one and boosted the sagging box office of the film.

Debbie was born Mary Frances Reynolds on April Fool's Day of 1932 in El Paso, Texas. When she was eight, her father was transferred by Southern Pacific Railroad to California, and the family moved to Burbank. At 16, she entered the Miss Burbank contest, winning with an imitation of Betty Hutton singing "My Rockin' Horse Ran Away." Talent scouts from Warner Brothers and

MGM were there, and they flipped a coin to see which studio would interview Debbie. The man from Warners won. Jack Warner changed Mary Frances' name to Debbie, but two films and one year later the studio dropped her.

MGM was still interested, and Debbie's first film for the studio was *Three Little Words* in 1950. Her next film, *Two Weeks in Love*, produced Debbie's first million-selling single, "Aba Dabba Honeymoon." Next came the classic *Singin' in the Rain* with Gene Kelly.

On September 26, 1955, Debbie married Eddie Fisher. They teamed up in *Bundle of Joy* (1956) and gave birth to their first child, Carrie Frances (whose own acting career would begin 21 years later when she starred as Princess Leia in the *Star Wars* trilogy), on October 21, 1956. It was soon after Carrie's birth that MGM loaned Debbie to Universal to star in *Tammy and the Bachelor*.

In March, 1958, Debbie and Eddie's close friend, Mike Todd, was killed in an airplane crash. Eddie comforted the grieving widow, Elizabeth Taylor, and married her on May 12, 1959, after Debbie agreed to a divorce. As the wronged woman, Debbie's box office value soared.

In 1966 she became the only number one artist to play the life story of *another* number one artist. She accomplished this by starring in the title role of MGM's *The Singing Nun* [see 141—"Dominique"].

"Tammy" held on to the number one position for two weeks, then gave way to Paul Anka for a week. "Tammy" returned to the top on Sept. 16, 1957 for an additional week.

### THE TOP FIVE
*Week of August 26, 1957*

1 **Tammy**
   Debbie Reynolds

2 **(Let Me be Your) Teddy Bear**
   Elvis Presley

3 **Diana**
   Paul Anka

4 **Searchin'**
   Coasters

5 **Love Letters in The Sand**
   Pat Boone

ABC-PARAMOUNT 9831 **Diana**
PAUL ANKA

**25**

and Frankie Laine.

When Paul was 13, he spent the summer in Los Angeles, working at the Civic Playhouse, where he parked cars and sold candy. His summer project was to write a book report for school on *Prestor John* by John Buchan. Paul wrote a song based on an African town in the novel, *Blau Wildebeeste Fontaine*.

He spent his free time at Wallich's Music City, the huge record store at the corner of Sunset and Vine, listening to the latest records in customer booths. One of the songs he heard at Wallich's was "Stranded in the Jungle" by the Cadets, and noticing the label's offices were based in nearby Culver City, he went to see A&R director Ernie Freeman. Paul played him "Blau Wildebeeste Fontaine" and Freeman loved it. He recorded it two weeks later, with the Cadets singing background. The record didn't do well, and Paul returned home to Ottawa, a failure at 14.

The following summer Paul went to New York, courtesy of Campbell's Soup. Paul entered a supermarket contest to collect soup wrappers, and was so determined to win he scoured garbage cans and took a job in the market to be close to the soup cans. He won a train trip to Manhattan. He was so taken by the city, he borrowed $100 from his father and returned later that summer with four songs he had written. The first person he went to see was Don Costa at ABC-Paramount Records, and Costa was so impressed with "Diana," he told Paul to have his parents come to New York immediately so they could sign contracts.

*Writer: Paul Anka*

*Producer: Don Costa*

*September 9, 1957*
*1 week*

"Diana" by Paul Anka topped the chart for only one week in America, but it was one of four songs to spend nine weeks at number one in Britain during the rock era. It shares that honor with "Mull of Kintyre" by Wings, "You're the One That I Want" by John Travolta and Olivia Newton-John and "Two Tribes" by Frankie Goes to Hollywood.

"Diana" is tied for the sixth-longest-running number one hit of the rock era in the U.K. The top three are Bryan Adams' "(Everything I Do) I Do It for You" (16 weeks), Wet Wet Wet's "Love Is All Around" (15 weeks) and Queen's "Bohemian Rhapsody" (14 weeks).

Paul was 15 years old when he wrote "Diana," a love song for his younger brother and sister's babysitter. She was three years older than Paul, and despite his mad crush on her, wanted nothing to do with him. He found her rejection traumatic, so he wrote a poem and sent it to her. Later he set it to music and it became an international hit. When Paul returned home from touring the world, she wanted to talk things over with him, but by then it was too late. He had lost interest in Diana.

Six years later Paul recorded a "sequel," called "Remember Diana," but it didn't duplicate the success of the original.

Paul was born on July 30, 1941, in Ottawa, Ontario, Canada. His parents owned restaurants and were supportive of Paul's interest in music. By the age of 12, he thought he would become a journalist or a lawyer, but he dropped out of a shorthand class to study music. He entered amateur talent contests and did impersonations of Johnnie Ray

## THE TOP FIVE
*Week of September 9, 1957*

1 **Diana**
Paul Anka

2 **Tammy**
Debbie Reynolds

3 **Whole Lotta Shakin' Goin' On**
Jerry Lee Lewis

4 **(Let Me be Your) Teddy Bear**
Elvis Presley

5 **That'll Be The Day**
Crickets

# That'll Be the Day BRUNSWICK 55009
## THE CRICKETS

*Writers: Jerry Allison*
*Buddy Holly*
*Norman Petty*

*Producer: Norman Petty*

*September 23, 1957*
*1 week*

*"I can't remember if I cried,*
*When I read about his widowed bride,*
*But something touched me deep inside,*
*The day the music died."*

I N the short span of three years, Buddy Holly created a timeless body of work that influenced almost every major artist of the rock era, especially the Beatles, the Rolling Stones, Bob Dylan, Elton John, Linda Ronstadt, John Denver, Bobby Vee, Tommy Roe, Elvis Costello and a list too long to complete here. No one knows what more Buddy would have contributed if he had lived beyond his 22 years.

On Monday, February 2, 1959, the "Winter Dance Party" tour played to over a thousand people at the Surf Ballroom in Clear Lake, Iowa. Top of the bill were Buddy Holly and the Crickets, the "Big Bopper" (J.P. Richardson), Ritchie Valens and Dion and the Belmonts. Tired of travelling on a broken-down tour bus that didn't have proper heating, Holly chartered a private plane to take him and his band (Waylon Jennings and Tommy Allsup) to their next stop in Fargo, North Dakota, so they could get their laundry done and have a good night's sleep. Valens and Richardson wanted to travel by plane as well, so Valens tossed a coin with Allsup for his seat. Valens won the toss. Richardson had a cold and talked Jennings into trading places with him on the bus.

The Beechcraft Bonanza took off just after 1 a.m. in a heavy snowstorm. A few minutes later, the plane crashed into a frozen cornfield on the farm of Albert Juhl in Ames, Iowa. The three singers and the 21-year-old pilot were all killed. The date was February 3, 1959. It was the day the music died.

Charles Hardin Holley was born September 7, 1936 in Lubbock, Texas. His mother suggested he be called Buddy. She had him take piano lessons when he was 11, but a year later he was hooked on the guitar. In junior high he met Bob Montgomery and they formed a duo. A Lubbock

DJ, Hi-pockets Duncan, became their manager and added bass player Larry Welbourn to make them a trio. An agent from Nashville, Eddie Crandall, heard them support Bill Haley and the Comets and helped Buddy sign a record deal with Decca.

On July 22, 1956, Buddy recorded a song inspired by a John Wayne quote from the film *The Searchers*: "That'll Be the Day." Decca executives didn't like it, and they didn't release it. In January, 1957, Buddy's contract with Decca expired. Impressed with Norman Petty's production on Buddy Knox's "Party Doll," Holly went to Petty's studio in Clovis, New Mexico. Buddy wanted to sign with Knox' label, Roulette, so on February 25, 1957, they cut a demo of "That'll Be the Day." Roulette passed on the tape, and so did Columbia, RCA and Atlantic. Finally, Bob Thiele at Coral/Brunswick Records (a Decca subsidiary, ironically) heard the demo and signed Holly.

Because Decca owned "That'll Be the Day" by Buddy Holly, Thiele released it under the group name of the Crickets. Over the next two years, songs were released by the Crickets on Brunswick and by Holly on Coral, but the distinction was arti-

ficial. All songs were recorded by Buddy Holly and the Crickets.

Holly and Petty had a parting of the ways after a U.S. tour in October, 1958. The Crickets (Jerry Allison, Joe B. Mauldin and Niki Sullivan) remained with Petty, so Holly recruited Jennings and Allsup as new Crickets. Holly moved to New York with his bride, Maria Elena. There, he recorded his last studio track, "It Doesn't Matter Anymore," which became a posthumous hit. His final recordings were made in his Greenwich Village apartment before setting out on the winter tour.

Buddy Holly was not acknowledged as a legend until years after his death. Songs like "Everyday," "Peggy Sue," "Oh Boy," "Words of Love" and "Raining in My Heart" continue to be recorded by contemporary artists, and the "Tex-Mex" sound of Buddy Holly lives on.

Gary Busey was nominated for an Oscar for his portrayal of Holly in the 1978 motion picture *The Buddy Holly Story*. Paul McCartney bought the publishing rights to most of Holly's songs, and is instrumental in making sure that "Buddy Holly Week" is celebrated every year in England during the first week in September, the anniversary of Buddy's birth.

## THE TOP FIVE
### Week of September 23, 1957

1  **That'll Be The Day**
   Crickets

2  **Tammy**
   Debbie Reynolds

3  **Diana**
   Paul Anka

4  **Honeycomb**
   Jimmie Rodgers

5  **Whole Lotta Shakin' Goin' On**
   Jerry Lee Lewis

*Writer: Bob Merrill*

*Producers: Hugo Peretti*
*Luigi Creatori*

*September 30, 1957*
*2 weeks*

JAMES FREDERICK RODGERS was born September 18, 1933, in Camas, Washington, about 30 miles from the Oregon border. His mother was a piano teacher, and while Jimmie was very young she gave him lessons and instilled a love of music in him. He majored in music at Vancouver Clark College in Washington, but with the idea of becoming a teacher, not a performer.

He left college before graduation to enlist in the United States Air Force. He volunteered for Korean War duty and was transferred to Seoul, where he made the fateful purchase of a beat-up guitar from another airman. Jimmie learned how to play the instrument and, with some of his Air Force buddies, formed a group, the Rhythm Kings. They played military installations in Korea for a year, until Jimmie was transferred to Stewart Air Force Base in Nashville. Here he began winning Air Force talent shows, and was hired to perform at Nashville's Unique Club.

Another performer at the club sang "Honeycomb" one night, and Jimmie liked it so much he rearranged it to suit his own style. Jimmie's Air Force stint ended and he returned home to Washington state, where he was booked into Vancouver's Fort Cafe. He was so popular, the club kept him on for 17 weeks.

Across the street in the Frontier Room, singer Chuck Miller was appearing. He dropped in to see Jimmie's show one night and was so impressed, he insisted that Jimmie go to New York to audition for "Arthur Godfrey's Talent Scouts" television program and for Hugo Peretti and Luigi Creatore at Roulette Records. Miller even lent Jimmie the cost of the airfare so he could go.

Jimmie won on Godfrey's show, and sang "Honeycomb" for Hugo and Luigi. He returned to Camas and renewed his wedding vows with his first wife, Colleen. As the ceremony ended, a telegram arrived from Morris Levy, president of Roulette, asking Jimmie to return to New York and sign with the label. He recorded "Honeycomb" as his first release.

Jimmie had a run of hits during the next 12 months, including "Kisses Sweeter Than Wine," "Oh-Oh, I'm Falling in Love Again" and "Secretly." He was signed to star in his own weekly variety series on NBC, which premiered on March 31, 1959. A year later, he starred in a film, *The Little Shepherd of Kingdom Come.*

In 1967 Jimmie signed with A&M Records and was cast in a motion picture scheduled to shoot in Europe. He released one album on A&M but never started the movie. In the early morning hours of December 1, 1967, he was returning home from a party when he was pulled over by an off-duty police officer for suspected traffic violations. Two policemen in uniform were called for assistance. A few hours later, Rodgers was found unconscious in his car by his musical conductor, Ed Samuels. Rodgers had a fractured skull and a broken wrist. The Los Angeles District Attorney's report said the injuries were the result of a fall. Rodgers filed an $11 million lawsuit against the city, claiming the officers had assaulted him.

Rodgers underwent three brain operations and has a 23″ steel plate in his skull. After a long period of recuperation, he returned to show business with a concert at L.A.'s Cocoanut Grove on January 28, 1969.

A year later, he told Digby Diehl in *TV Guide*: "It's great to be alive. I guess when you've been as close to death as I have, you begin to appreciate how beautiful life is. When I go into a room now, I notice everything—even the color of the wallpaper. Things that didn't seem important before become very important."

## THE TOP FIVE
*Week of September 30, 1957*

1 **Honeycomb**
Jimmie Rodgers

2 **Tammy**
Debbie Reynolds

3 **That'll Be The Day**
Crickets

4 **Diana**
Paul Anka

5 **Whole Lotta Shakin' Goin' On**
Jerry Lee Lewis

## 28 Wake Up Little Susie CADENCE 1337
### EVERLY BROTHERS

*Writers: Felice Bryant*
*Boudleaux Bryant*

*Producer: Archie Bleyer*

*October 14, 1957*
*1 week*

THE harmonies of Simon and Garfunkel, the Beach Boys, the Mamas and the Papas and even the Beatles can all be traced back to one source: Don and Phil Everly, two brothers from Brownie, Kentucky who influenced a generation of country and rock singers with their pure pop harmony.

There was a set of Everly Brothers that performed before Don and Phil were born. Their father, Ike, was a coal miner until he grew tired of the perils underground and went to Chicago with his two brothers to sing.

The family was living in Shenadoah, Iowa, when the boys' mother, Margaret, asked if they'd like to sing on the radio. The Everly family had a half-hour show on KMA every morning at 6 a.m., before Don and Phil would go to school. When he was seven years old, Don had his own 15-minute show on Saturday mornings, "The Little Donnie Show." After six years in Shenadoah and a brief spell at a radio station in Knoxville, Tennessee, there was no more live radio work, so the family act broke up.

Ike went into the construction business and Margaret became a beautician. Don had already sold "Thou Shalt Not Steal" to Kitty Wells, so he and Phil went to Nashville, hung around the Grand Ole Opry and tried to sell more songs. They recorded an audition tape for Archie Bleyer, but they were broke and told the studio owner after the tape was finished that they couldn't pay for it. When they left the studio, they discovered their car had been towed away, so they returned to the studio and borrowed some money to get their vehicle out of the impound lot.

Bleyer turned the tape down, and so did most other companies in Nashville. Columbia Records took a chance and signed the brothers to record four sides for the label in November, 1955, including their first single, "The Sun Keeps Shining."

Ike asked his friend Chet Atkins to introduce Don and Phil to publisher Wesley Rose, who signed the brothers. When their CBS option was not picked up, Rose persuaded Bleyer to listen to their tape again. Looking for a country act to sign to his New York record label, Cadence, this time he agreed to take the Everly Brothers.

Archie had a song published by Acuff-Rose he wanted Don and Phil to record. It had been turned down by 30 other artists, including Cadence's other signing, Gordon Terry. Don and Phil didn't care, because they knew they would make at least $64 each just for recording the song, which was Felice and Boudleaux Bryant's "Bye Bye Love."

Don and Phil went on a "tent-show" tour of Mississippi, Alabama and Florida. By the time they returned home, "Bye Bye Love" was climbing up the national charts, where it eventually peaked at number two.

Rose became their manager and worked with Bleyer on their career. It took four recording sessions to cut their next single, "Wake Up Little Susie." Bleyer didn't like the song because of the lyrics; it sounded like Susie and her boyfriend had been sleeping together at the drive-in. Released despite his objection, the record was banned by some radio stations for its "suggestive" lyrics. But that didn't stop it from becoming the Everly Brothers' first number one single.

### THE TOP FIVE
*Week of October 14, 1957*

1 **Wake Up Little Susie**
Everly Brothers

2 **Honeycomb**
Jimmie Rodgers

3 **Tammy**
Debbie Reynolds

4 **Jailhouse Rock/Treat Me Nice**
Elvis Presley

5 **Diana**
Paul Anka

RCA 7035 **Jailhouse Rock / Treat Me Nice**
ELVIS PRESLEY 29

*Writers: Jerry Leiber*
*Mike Stoller*

*Producer: Steve Sholes*

*October 21, 1957*
*7 weeks*

"JAILHOUSE ROCK" was the first record to enter the British singles chart at number one. It's happened five times in America, but in the United Kingdom, where BBC Radio is heard nationally, it is easier for a record to capture the attention of the entire country in the short time period of one week. Since the day when Elvis accomplished this amazing feat, more than 65 singles have debuted at number one in Great Britain. Still, until "Jailhouse Rock" did it on January 24, 1958, it was considered impossible.

"Jailhouse Rock" and "Treat Me Nice" were both written by Jerry Leiber and Mike Stoller, who had penned tunes for Elvis' second film, *Loving You*. In the book *Baby, That Was Rock & Roll*, author Robert Palmer quotes Leiber: "We would get a script marked off where they

wanted some type of song, like Scene II, Elvis is with so-and-so and needs a love song. The love songs were a great problem, because I really can't write love songs. But that was the least of it. I certainly would never have written a song like 'Jailhouse Rock,' for example, if somebody hadn't said, Look, there's going to be a big production number in a jail.'"

That big production number in a jail was the highlight of *Jailhouse Rock*, Elvis' third film. Elvis choreographed the number himself, and the resulting sequence is one of the best-remembered scenes from any Elvis motion picture.

Despite writing "Hound Dog" and songs for *Loving You*, Leiber and Stoller didn't meet Presley until the recording session for "Jailhouse Rock" on May 2, 1957, at MGM Studios in Culver City, California. Stoller, who had a cameo role in the movie as a piano player in Elvis' band, tells Palmer about Elvis: "We were very impressed with him. We were impressed with how good he was. He would do a great take and then insist on another and another

and still another. When he was in the mood he could do 50 takes of a number and go on to the next tune without taking a break. To unwind, he'd sit down at the piano and sing a hymn. He never looked at the clock."

Although "Treat Me Nice" was recorded at the same session as "Jailhouse Rock," the track laid down that day was not used. Instead, Elvis recorded it again on September 5 at Radio Recorders in Hollywood, at the session for his first Christmas album. With the exception of "Treat Me Nice," the "A" side of Elvis' next single and "My Wish Came True," all the other songs recorded at that session appeared on *Elvis' Christmas Album*, released in November, 1957.

*Jailhouse Rock* opened in theaters on October 21, 1957, the same day the title track became Elvis' eighth number one single. The film's cast includes Judy Tyler, Mickey Shaughnessy, Jennifer Holden and Dean Jones. Elvis stars as convict Vince Everett, who is encouraged to pursue a singing career by his cellmate after appearing on a televised prison talent show. Released from jail, Vince forms a small record company and releases a single, which is played by an influential disc jockey. Vince becomes a big star, but when his cellmate gets out of prison, they fight over a contract and Vince receives a blow to the throat, silencing his singing voice. There's another happy ending: Vince gets his voice back and he gets the girl.

Elvis got something, too. Three weeks after "Jailhouse Rock" fell from the top of the chart, his draft notice from the United States Army arrived.

## THE TOP FIVE
*Week of October 21, 1957*

1 **Jailhouse Rock/Treat Me Nice**
Elvis Presley

2 **Wake Up Little Susie**
Everly Brothers

3 **Honeycomb**
Jimmie Rodgers

4 **Tammy**
Debbie Reynolds

5 **Chances Are**
Johnny Mathis

## 30  You Send Me   KEEN 34013
### SAM COOKE

*Writer: Sam Cooke*

*Producer: Richard 'Bumps' Blackwell*

*December 2, 1957*
*2 weeks*

SAM COOKE broke away from his early gospel musical training to join the secular world of pop singers, and in his short life established a body of work that influenced many of his successors, black and white.

He was born January 22, 1935 in Chicago, son of the Rev. Charles S. Cooke. With two of his sisters and one brother, he performed at age nine in a church group known as The Singing Children. At Wendell Phillips High School, he and his brother sang in a gospel group called The Highway Q.C.'s, but he became a star on the gospel circuit when he replaced R. H. Harris as lead singer of the popular Soul Stirrers.

In 1956, "Bumps" Blackwell, an A&R man with Specialty Records, approached Cooke about recording some pop sides. Cooke was interested, but gospel singers did not cross over into secular music. Blackwell released a single, "Lovable," under the pseudonym Dale Cooke. The smooth, creamy voice was too obvious to disguise and the Soul Stirrers fired Cooke. Art Rupe, owner of Specialty Records, refused to release any more of Cooke's singles, so Blackwell bought his contract and took him to Keen Records. His third single for the label, "You Send Me," became his first chart record and his only number one single. In January, 1960, RCA Records paid Cooke $100,000 to join the label.

Cooke's influence can be heard in singers as disparate as Otis Redding, Rod Stewart, Marvin Gaye and Mick Jagger. His catalog of songs has been covered by artists spanning all the decades of rock. A partial list would include: "Cupid" (Johnny Rivers, Johnny Nash and the Spinners), "Only Sixteen" (Dr. Hook), "Little Red Rooster" (Rolling Stones), "Bring It on Home to Me" (Animals, Eddie Floyd), "Wonderful World" (Herman's Hermits, Art Garfunkel and Bryan Ferry), "Another Saturday Night" (Cat Stevens), "Twistin' the Night Away" (Stewart) and "Shake" (Redding) [see 238—"(Sittin' on) The Dock of the Bay"].

Cooke's life was not untouched by tragedy. On November 10, 1958, he and Lou Rawls were injured in an automobile accident in Marion, Arkansas, that put Rawls in critical condition. A year later, Cooke's first wife was killed in an automobile accident in Fresno, California. In the summer of 1963, Cooke's youngest child, Vincent, drowned in the family swimming pool.

On the evening of December 10, 1964, Cooke met a woman named Elisa Boyer at a Hollywood restaurant. He took her, allegedly against her wishes, to the Hacienda Motel in South Los Angeles. When she fled his room with his clothes, Cooke chased after her and, apparently thinking she had sought refuge in the office of the manager, Mrs. Bertha Franklin, knocked forcefully on her door. A scuffle ensued and Mrs. Franklin shot Cooke three times at close range, and when he came at her, clubbed him with a stick. He died on her office floor.

The coroner's jury returned a verdict of justifiable homicide. Funeral services were held in Los Angeles and Chicago with almost 200,000 grieving fans paying their last respects.

### THE TOP FIVE
*Week of December 2, 1957*

1  **You Send Me**
   Sam Cooke

2  **Jailhouse Rock/Treat Me Nice**
   Elvis Presley

3  **Wake Up Little Susie**
   Everly Brothers

4  **Silhouettes**
   The Rays

5  **Raunchy**
   Bill Justis

DOT 15660 **April Love**
PAT BOONE
**31**

*Writers: Sammy Fain*
*Paul Francis Webster*

*Producer: Randy Wood*

*December 23, 1957*
*2 weeks*

COMPETING against Elvis Presley, the Everly Brothers and Buddy Holly for the top spot on the charts, Pat Boone didn't think the pretty but slow-moving arrangement of "April Love" was commercial enough to be a hit.

The title song to his film *April Love* was written for Boone by Sammy Fain and Paul Francis Webster, Academy Award winners for "Love Is a Many Splendored Thing" [see 3] and "Secret Love." "I was honored," says Pat, "but at the same time it didn't sound commercial. In the heyday of rock and roll, what chance did a sweet, simple little song have?

"In the recording session, I said to Billy Vaughn, who arranged it, we need something to goose this song up a little bit. I said we need something to make it sound important." Pat thought the proper intro would say that something was about to happen, so he sat down in the corner and wrote the ten notes that open the song.

Years later, Pat would have another use for those notes. "I bought a Ferrari in Italy and shipped it home. The air horn played 'April Love.' It took two air horns to convey that melody. I liked the horn better than I liked the car. Eventually I sold it to Tommy Smothers."

Pat was born Charles Eugene Boone on June 1, 1934, in Jacksonville, Florida, the great-great-great-great grandson of frontiersman Daniel Boone. Later, the family moved to Nashville, and his mother taught him and his younger brother, Nick (who would later record for Dot as Nick Todd), how to sing harmony on songs like "Sentimental Journey." The brothers sang at family gatherings, and then at church and school.

Pat won the semi-final round of Ted Mack's "The Original Amateur Hour," but before the finals he appeared on "Arthur Godfrey's Talent Scouts" and won. "You can't win an amateur show after you've won on a professional show, so winning on Arthur Godfrey disqualified me from winning on Ted Mack. I blew a $6,000 college scholarship for a $600 fee for appearing on Godfrey."

After appearing on those shows in New York, Pat was returning home to his wife, Shirley, in Denton, Texas, when he decided to stop in Nashville and visit his parents. While there, his friend Hugh Cherry, a DJ at WMAK, introduced him to Randy Wood, owner of Dot Records. Wood had seen Boone's performances on the Ted Mack and Arthur Godfrey shows, and told him he should be making records.

Six months later, Wood asked Boone to come to Chicago and record "Two Hearts, Two Kisses."

While concentrating on his recording and acting careers, Pat also signed with ABC-TV to star in "The Pat Boone-Chevy Showroom," a weekly prime-time variety series that premiered one month before "April Love" entered the chart on November 4, 1957. The half-hour series ran for three years, at 9 p.m. on Thursday nights.

With all his success, Pat never stopped attending college. In June, 1958, he graduated *magna cum laude*, with a degree in speech and English, from Columbia University. His wife and four daughters attended his graduation.

## THE TOP FIVE
*Week of December 23, 1957*

1 **April Love**
   Pat Boone

2 **At The Hop**
   Danny and the Juniors

3 **Jailhouse Rock/Treat Me Nice**
   Elvis Presley

4 **Raunchy**
   Bill Justis

5 **You Send Me**
   Sam Cooke

## 32 At the Hop ABC-Paramount 9871
### DANNY AND THE JUNIORS

*Writers: Arthur Singer*
*John Medora*
*David White*

*Producer: Arthur Singer*

*January 6, 1958*
*5 weeks*

THE first number one single of 1958 was "At the Hop" by Danny and the Juniors, a group that had its origins on the street corners of Philadelphia. The four members all grew up in the city of brotherly love and started singing together in high school as the Juvenairs.

The quartet consisted of Danny Rapp, lead singer; Dave White, first tenor; Frank Maffei, second tenor; and Joe Terranova, baritone. They performed at school dances, private parties and in local clubs, where they were discovered by Artie Singer, who owned a small, independent record label, Singular Records. Singer became their vocal coach and suggested they change their name to Danny and the Juniors.

Philadelphia was also home to Dick Clark's "American Bandstand," and the most popular dance on the show in the summer of 1957 was the Bop. Singer, White and songwriter John Medora teamed up to write a

song about this dance craze, "Do the Bop." The group recorded it as a demo, and Singer brought it to Clark to see what he thought of it.

Clark gave him some excellent advice: the Bop was on the way out, and the song would be coming out too late to take advantage of its popularity. Clark thought it was a good song that needed new lyrics, and suggested they try "At the Hop." The group went back into the studio and re-cut it, and Singer brought it to Clark again. This time, Clark told him, he had a hit. He was right.

It was the only song ever to make the top 10 for the group. Their next single, "Rock and Roll Is Here to Stay," was written in response to attacks against rock music that included a display of smashing records, sponsored by KWK, a St. Louis radio station. It made it to number 19, and the group continued to place records on the Hot 100 until early 1963.

White released a solo album, *Pastel, Paint, Pencil and Ink* in 1971 under his real name, David White Tricker. Terranova and Maffei and a new first tenor, Bill Carlucci, reformed the group in the 1970s and have toured America for as many as 50 weeks a year. Danny Rapp committed suicide in an Arizona

hotel room in April, 1983.

In a 1982 interview with Dick Clark, Terranova expressed one regret, common to many young groups popular in the early days of rock and roll: "I think when we had our shot in the beginning, if we had been a little more serious about it, we could have done much more with it, but being so young...we couldn't wait to get home and hang out on the corner. I guess we were just regular street kids. I think if we'd just had a little better guidance we'd have been in better shape."

### THE TOP FIVE
*Week of January 6, 1958*

1 **At The Hop**
Danny and the Juniors

2 **Great Balls of Fire**
Jerry Lee Lewis

3 **April Love**
Pat Boone

4 **Stood Up**
Ricky Nelson

5 **Peggy Sue**
Buddy Holly

Writers: *Jerry Leiber*
*Mike Stoller*
*Rose Marie McCoy*
*Kelly Owens*

Producer: *Steve Sholes*

*February 10, 1958*
*5 weeks*

ELVIS PRESLEY started 1958 with his ninth number one single, "Don't" (his first "A" side to feature a ballad since "Love Me Tender") and "I Beg of You." He ended 1957 with his draft notice from the United States Army, received December 20. The next day, Paramount Pictures requested a two-month delay in the January 20 induction date, so Elvis could complete the filming of his fourth movie, *King Creole.*

"I Beg of You" was recorded first—originally, at the January 12-13, 1957 session that produced "All Shook Up." But the take that resulted that day was not released. Elvis re-recorded the song on Feb. 23 at Radio Recorders Studio in Hollywood, and the final track was his 34th take.

"Don't" was recorded on September 6, on the second day of a three-day session where Elvis recorded the songs for his first Christmas album. It was written by Jerry Leiber and Mike Stoller, who had already written two of Elvis' number one singles: "Hound Dog" and "Jailhouse Rock," both rockers that sharply contrasted with the slow pace of "Don't."

Elvis began filming *King Creole* on January 13, 1958. The movie was

originally titled *A Stone for Danny Fisher*, after the Harold Robbins novel on which it's based. Danny Fisher was a boxer in Robbins' book; in the film, he's a singer. The setting was New York in the book; in the movie it's New Orleans. *King Creole* was the first Elvis film shot on location, and it's the movie Elvis always said was his favorite. The strong supporting cast includes Walter Matthau, Dean Jagger, Carolyn Jones and Vic Morrow.

Elvis recorded the songs for the movie during the month of January at Radio Recorders. On February 1, he had his final recording session before joining the U.S. Army. It also took place at Radio Recorders, and only four tracks were completed, including

his next single, "Wear My Ring Around Your Neck."

Elvis was inducted into the Army on March 24, 1958. It was a rainy Monday morning when he arrived at Local Draft Board 86 in Memphis. Elvis was accompanied by his parents and a friend, Lamar Fike. The media turned out in full force, and Col. Tom Parker passed out balloons promoting *King Creole.* Elvis became Private Presley, US 53310761, and boarded the bus for Fort Chaffee, Arkansas.

Elvis' monthly salary dropped from $100,000 to $78. The fans and Col. Parker were concerned, but for different reasons. Elvis' fans besieged the Memphis Draft Board, protesting their idol's induction. Parker was more worried that two years out of public sight would permanently derail Elvis' career.

## THE TOP FIVE
*Week of February 10, 1958*

1 **Don't/I Beg of You**
Elvis Presley

2 **At The Hop**
Danny and the Juniors

3 **Get a Job**
Silhouettes

4 **Stood Up**
Ricky Nelson

5 **Sail Along Silvery Moon**
Billy Vaughn

## 34 **Tequila** CHALLENGE 1016
### THE CHAMPS

*Writer: Chuck Rio*

*Producer: Joe Johnson*

*March 17, 1958*
*5 weeks*

THE CHAMPS are more famous for who was *not* in the group when they recorded "Tequila." It was only after they had a number one song that Glen Campbell, Jim Seals and Dash Crofts joined the band. Campbell went on to have two number one singles [see 415—"Rhinestone Cowboy" and 461—"Southern Nights"], and Seals and Crofts formed a group called The Dawnbreakers before recording as a duo and scoring with hits like "Summer Breeze" and "Diamond Girl."

The original Champs formed more by happenstance than design. Lead guitarist Dave Burgess was head of A&R and the first artist signed to Gene Autry's Challenge label. He released three singles as "Dave Dupre" and a fourth under his own name, but all failed to chart. Then he recorded an instrumental, "Train to Nowhere," with session musician Danny Flores on saxophone and piano.

While recording instrumental tracks for a Jerry Wallace album, Burgess had some studio time left and decided to record a "B" side for "Train to Nowhere." The musicians present included Flores, drummer Gene Alden, guitarist Buddy Bruce and bass guitarist Cliff Hils.

Flores came up with a song he had written while visiting Tijuana. Burgess liked it, and suggested Danny shout "tequila" in his low voice at the appropriate breaks. The track was considered a throwaway, and none of the musicians hung around the studio long enough to hear a playback.

A group name was needed to release the single, and someone suggested they name themselves after Gene Autry's horse, Champion. The Champs were born. At the same time, Flores changed his name— using his middle name, Carlos, and his father's middle name, Del Rio, he came up with Chuck Rio.

"Train to Nowhere" was released on December 26, 1957, and that's exactly where it went, until DJs started to play the flip side. The February 3, 1958 issue of *Billboard* reviewed "Tequila"—by the Champs and by Eddie Platt on ABC-Paramount Records. A cover battle was on.

Both versions entered the chart on March 3. Platt made it to number 20, but the Champs were unstoppa-

ble. They made it to number one in three weeks, establishing several firsts:

—They were the first instrumental group to go to number one with their first release.

—"Tequila" was the first song to move into the number one position from outside of the top 10, moving from 12 to 1.

—"Tequila" was number one on the R&B chart for four weeks, and won the first Grammy ever awarded for "Best R&B Performance."

The personnel of the Champs changed continually over the years, a process that began as soon as "Tequila" was recorded. Buddy Bruce and Cliff Hils had no desire to tour, and were replaced by Dave Norris and Joe Burnas. Burnas left soon after, replaced by Van Norman. A few months later, Flores and Alden left, and Flores recorded on his own as Chuck Rio. Three people were brought in as replacements: Dean Beard and two members of his group, Seals and Crofts. Norman was killed in an automobile accident and was replaced by Bobby Morris. Then Beard left and the group was a quintet again. Campbell joined the Champs when Burgess decided to only work in the studio and not go on the road.

Although there were more changes, the Champs were never able to match the success of "Tequila." Two songs made it to number 30: "El Rancho Rock" and "Too Much Tequila," and in 1965 Burgess decided to call an end to the Champs.

---

### THE TOP FIVE
*Week of March 17, 1958*

1 **Tequila**
   The Champs

2 **Sweet Little Sixteen**
   Chuck Berry

3 **Don't/I Beg of You**
   Elvis Presley

4 **A Wonderful Time Up There**
   Pat Boone

5 **Twenty-Six Miles**
   Four Preps

*Writers: Buck Ram*
*Al Nevins*
*Morton Nevins*
*Artie Dunn*

*Producer: Buck Ram*

*April 21, 1958*
*1 week*

Long before he worked with the Platters, Samuel Buck Ram was arranging songs for several swing bands. After working on popular tunes of the day, he turned to his wife and said, "I can write as good as that!" So he quit arranging and started songwriting. His first composition was "Afterglow."

In college, Buck liked to write poems, and composed one called "Twilight Time." In 1944, he set his poem to music with the help of the Three Suns, a trio made up of Al Nevins on guitar, his brother Morty on accordion and their cousin Artie Dunn on organ and lead vocals. It was recorded by the Three Suns in 1946 and sold over a million copies, a feat duplicated by the Platters when they recorded it in 1958.

But Mercury Records' A&R department didn't believe the song would be a hit, and relegated it to the "B" side. While Buck was in Australia, the Platters were booked for "The Dick Clark Saturday Night Beechnut Show." The producer informed Buck's assistant, Jean Ben-

nett, that the group was to sing either "Only You" or "The Great Pretender," plus "Out of My Mind," the designated "A" side of their new single.

"I grabbed a cab and went right over to their office," recalls Bennett. "I told them Buck was gonna kill me if he came back from Australia and found out they hadn't sung 'Twilight Time.'" She suggested they only mention their earlier hits, and allow the group to sing both sides of their new single. The producer was adamant, so Jean insisted he get Dick Clark on the phone in Philadelphia. "We played 'Twilight Time' over the phone, and he said, 'That's the hit! Of course we'll play both sides.' Monday morning Mercury's switchboard lit up with orders for 'Twilight Time.'"

It didn't seem to bother anyone who knew the Three Suns' version that Tony Williams had sung the wrong melody—not even Buck, who liked it enough to keep it in.

The sales reports of "Twilight Time" sounded the death knell for an endangered species: the 78 rpm disc. With one-and-a-half million copies sold, Irwin Steinberg, vice president of Mercury, announced that 98.2 per cent of the record's sales were on 45 rpm, and only 1.8 per cent were on 78 rpm. So it was no surprise that in the June 9, 1958 issue of *Billboard*, Mercury Records became the first major label to announce it was abolishing the production of 78s, effective immediately.

A month later, Mercury made another important announcement involving a Platters single. From the July 14 issue of *Billboard*: "Mercury Records is quietly working on a major new technique for getting plugs via the mushrooming media of TV platter shows....The label has produced two three-minute films, one of the Platters and one of the Diamonds, performing their current plug tunes, which they will rush to make available to a list of almost 200 TV deejays....Ed Sullivan had offered to buy the Platters' film for several thousand dollars...(Mercury) decided not to sell but to reap its value by giving it away to the afternoon teenage programs."

And so was born the music video.

---

**THE TOP FIVE**

*Week of April 21, 1958*

1 **Twilight Time**
Platters

2 **He's Got The Whole World in His Hands**
Laurie London

3 **Tequila**
The Champs

4 **Believe What You Say**
Ricky Nelson

5 **Witch Doctor**
David Seville

# Witch Doctor LIBERTY 55132
## DAVID SEVILLE

*Writer: Ross Bagdasarian*

*Producer: Ross Bagdasarian*

*April 28, 1958*
*2 weeks*

IF every now and then you find yourself dusting the house and you suddenly burst into song with "Oo-ee, oo-ah-ah, ting-tang, walla walla bing-bang," you can blame Ross Bagdasarian, who in his alter ego of David Seville recorded 1958's novelty hit, "Witch Doctor."

He got the idea from a book title in his library, "Duel with the Witch Doctor," and with his trusty tape recorder, came up with the idea of playing back music and vocals at different speeds. The voice of the witch doctor was recorded at halfspeed and played back at normal speed, a device that would eventually lead Bagdasarian to create a multi-million dollar empire centered around three friendly rodents [see 47—"The Chipmunk Song"].

Bagdasarian was born January 27, 1919 in Fresno, California. His father was a grape grower, and expected his son to follow in his footsteps. But by age 19, Ross knew he wanted to be an actor, and went to New York to work with his cousin, author William Saroyan.

After working in the theater in New York, Ross served four years in the Air Force and spent time in England, France and Spain. When World War II ended, he returned to Fresno and married a woman named Armen. They tried, unsuccessfully, to be

## THE TOP FIVE
*Week of April 28, 1958*

1 **Witch Doctor**
   David Seville

2 **Wear My Ring**
   **Around Your Neck**
   Elvis Presley

3 **Twilight Time**
   Platters

4 **He's Got The Whole World**
   **in His Hands**
   Laurie London

5 **Tequila**
   The Champs

grape farmers again.

The family moved to Los Angeles with only $200 in their pockets. Bagdasarian had collaborated on a song with his cousin Saroyan, but it had been rejected by everyone for being "too ethnic." Mitch Miller at Columbia Records liked it and persuaded Rosemary Clooney to record it. "Come on-a My House" went to number one in the summer of 1951. Three years later, Ross wrote another hit, Dean Martin's "Hey, Brother, Pour the Wine."

In 1956 he composed an instrumental song named for his wife, "Armen's Theme." Executives at Liberty Records told him Bagdasarian was difficult to pronounce and suggested he come up with a different name. He had been stationed near Seville, Spain, and always liked the city, so he created the alter-ego of David Seville.

The music for "Witch Doctor" was recorded two months before the vocals. It took Seville that much time to figure out how to record the voice. Si Waronker, one of the owners of Liberty, loved the final product and released it immediately.

"Witch Doctor" sold enough copies to prevent Elvis Presley's "Wear My Ring Around Your Neck" from going to number one. Significantly, it was the first new Elvis single since he signed to RCA Victor that missed going all the way to the top of the chart.

"Witch Doctor" was the first of three novelty songs to go to number one in 1958, making it the most successful year ever for this genre. Sheb Wooley and some friends of David Seville helped set this benchmark for the novelty song.

*Writers: Felice Bryant*
*Boudleaux Bryant*

*Producer: Archie Bleyer*

*May 12, 1958*
*4 weeks*

THE second Everly Brothers number one single was also a triumph for the songwriting team of Felice and Boudleaux Bryant, the Nashville couple who provided many of the Everly's early hits.

Boudleaux and Felice were both interested in music before they met. His ambition was to become a concert violinist, and he played for radio station WSB and the Atlanta Philharmonic Orchestra; she was a singer who performed at USO shows and won several amateur talent contests.

Felice grew up in Milwaukee. She was employed as an elevator operator at the Sherwood Hotel when Boudleaux played a date there with a jazz band. She recognized his face immediately—she had seen him in a dream when she was eight years old! They were married in September, 1945, and started collaborating on songs; he wrote music and she wrote lyrics. Their first hit was "Country Boy" by Little Jimmy Dickens in 1949, and a year later they moved to Nashville. They wrote hits for Eddy Arnold and Joe Smith before the Everly Brothers recorded their "Bye Bye Love," and Buddy Holly recorded their "Raining in My Heart," which became a posthumous hit in 1959.

## THE TOP FIVE
*Week of May 12, 1958*

1 **All I Have to do is Dream**
Everly Brothers

2 **Witch Doctor**
David Seville

3 **Twilight Time**
Platters

4 **Wear My Ring**
**Around Your Neck**
Elvis Presley

5 **He's Got The Whole World**
**in His Hands**
Laurie London

"All I Have to Do Is Dream" was written in about 15 minutes, but Phil Everly considers it one of the most important songs the brothers ever recorded. The song has charted in every decade of the rock era. Richard Chamberlain took it to number 14 in 1963; Glen Campbell and Bobbie Gentry peaked at number 27 in 1970; and Andy Gibb and Victoria Principal attempted a version in 1981 that made it to number 51.

The flip side of the Everly Brothers' recording also received a lot of airplay. "Claudette" was written by Roy Orbison [see 91—"Running Scared" and 157—"Oh, Pretty Woman"] about his wife.

After "All I Have to Do is Dream," the Everly Brothers had five more top 10 songs on Cadence before parting company with Archie Bleyer over royalty disputes. After "Bird Dog," "Devoted to You" and "Problems" came two notable departures: "('Til) I Kissed You" was recorded with the Crickets [see 26—"That'll Be the Day"] backing up the Everlys, and "Let It Be Me" was recorded in New York, the first time the Everlys ventured out of Nashville

to cut a record, and the first time they used strings instead of guitars. A full-page ad run by Archie Bleyer in *Billboard* proclaiming "Everlys Record in New York" was followed by a denial the next week from publisher Wesley Rose that the boys were changing their style: "They are not going uptown."

Two events significant to the future of the record industry took place while "All I Have to Do Is Dream" was number one. RCA Records released 55 stereo albums, the first stereo recordings by a major record company. Some record executives at other labels were quick to proclaim that stereo was a passing fad and that the monaural disc would always be around, but it was the beginning of the end of mono.

On May 28, the National Association of Recording Arts and Sciences held their first meeting at the Park Sheraton Hotel. One of the NARAS founders, George Avakian, said at the meeting the organization planned to give annual awards for various "bests" in the recording field. Later, those awards would be called Grammys.

## 38 | The Purple People Eater MGM 12651
### SHEB WOOLEY

*Writer: Sheb Wooley*

*Producer: Neely Plumb*

*June 9, 1958*
*6 weeks*

A SONGWRITING friend of Sheb Wooley's repeated a joke that his kids had heard in school: "What has one eye, flies, has a horn and eats people?" The answer was, of course, "A one-eyed, one-horned, flying people eater." Sheb thought that had the makings of a song.

Shortly after he wrote it, he had a meeting with the president of his record label, MGM, at the Beverly Hills Hotel. After singing all his ballads, Sheb was asked what else he had. He said he had a song that was the "bottom of the barrel" and proceeded to sing "The Purple People Eater." Within three weeks of release, it was the number one song in America.

Using a recording technique similar to David Seville [see 36—"Witch Doctor"], Wooley recorded the voice of the people eater and his saxophone at a reduced speed and played it back at high speed.

The success of the song led to merchandising of hats (with horns attached), T-shirts and even ice cream. Other record companies rushed out answer records, such as Joe South's "The Purple People Eater Meets the Witch Doctor."

Shelby Wooley was born April 10, 1921, in Erick, Oklahoma. With his three brothers, he roped steers for neighboring ranchers. But music was more important to him than cattle, and by the time he was 11, he talked his father into trading a shotgun for a

### THE TOP FIVE
*Week of June 9, 1958*

1 **Purple People Eater**
   Sheb Wooley

2 **All I Have to do is Dream**
   Everly Brothers

3 **Witch Doctor**
   David Seville

4 **Return to Me**
   Dean Martin

5 **Secretly**
   Jimmie Rodgers

friend's beat-up old guitar.

He formed a band in high school, the Melody Boys. By 19, he was married and working as a welder in Long Beach, California. After World War II, he took the songs he had been writing to Nashville, where he also worked at radio station WLAC.

He returned to California in 1950, seeking work as an actor. He made his film debut in *Rocky Mountain* with Errol Flynn and was later cast in *Giant* with Rock Hudson, Elizabeth Taylor and James Dean. In early 1958 he started working with Clint Eastwood in the new

"Rawhide" series. For four-and-a-half years, he played cattle drive scout Pete Nolan.

His "Rawhide" production schedule left little time for him to promote "The Purple People Eater," but as it turned out, he didn't have to.

Wooley only had two more chart entries after "The Purple People Eater," but he continued to have success as his alter ego, Ben Colder. Between 1962-1968 he had five chart entries that all were parodies of well-known songs such as "Harper Valley P.T.A.," "Still" and "Almost Persuaded."

*Writer: Claude De Metrius*

*Producer: Steve Sholes*

*July 21, 1958*
*2 weeks*

"**H**ARD HEADED WOMAN" and the film it came from, *King Creole*, were both released in June, 1958. The movie opened on June 4 and the record entered *Billboard's* chart on June 30. Three weeks later, it became Elvis' tenth number one hit.

"Hard Headed Woman" was recorded during the January, 1958 sessions where Elvis recorded all of the songs for the *Kid Creole* soundtrack. When it went to number one, Elvis was in Fort Hood, Texas, doing basic training. Many thought that Elvis would be sent to Special Services, where he could entertain the troops, but despite being one of the most famous soldiers ever to be in the United States Army, he was treated like any other G.I.—and sometimes less.

Elvis rented a home for his parents in Texas while he was at Fort Hood. But as "Hard Headed Woman" was moving up the chart, his mother Gladys fell ill. She was taken home to Memphis by train and admitted to Methodist Hospital, where her condition was diagnosed as acute severe hepatitis. Her condition worsened, and Elvis requested leave. The Army had a dilemma: they believed if Elvis was granted permission to go home, they would be accused of showing him special preference. His request was refused. Gladys continued to worsen, and Elvis was determined to go home no matter what the Army said. In truth, any ordinary soldier would have been granted leave, and finally, the powers-that-were consented to a seven-day emergency leave. Elvis went home to Memphis to visit his mother.

Elvis went to the hospital on August 12 and stayed day and night. He finally went home to get some rest, and at 3:15 in the morning on August 14, his mother died of a heart attack. His father telephoned home to give him the news.

Funeral services were held on August 15 at the National Funeral Home. Elvis collapsed more than once during the ceremonies, and over 700 fans attended. After a few days at home, Elvis returned to Fort Hood and prepared for transfer to Germany. The Army bent their rules and allowed a press conference to be held on September 22 at the Brooklyn Army Terminal.

Elvis answered the press' questions. He told them he had made a lot of new friends in the Army, and his buddies treated him like any other G.I., especially when he pulled K.P. duty. He told them he liked the song "Volare" [see 41]. And he answered questions about his late mother.

"She was very close, more than a mother," Elvis said. "She was a friend who would let me talk to her any hour of the day or night if I had a problem. I would get mad sometimes when she wouldn't let me do something. But I found out she was right about almost everything. She would always try to slow me up if I ever thought I wanted to get married. She was right."

## THE TOP FIVE
*Week of July 21, 1958*

1   **Hard Headed Woman**
    Elvis Presley

2   **Yakety Yak**
    Coasters

3   **Purple People Eater**
    Sheb Wooley

4   **Splish Splash**
    Bobby Darin

5   **Poor Little Fool**
    Ricky Nelson

## 40 Poor Little Fool IMPERIAL 5528
### RICKY NELSON

*Writer: Sharon Sheeley*
*Producer: Ricky Nelson*

*August 4, 1958*
*2 weeks*

On August 4, 1958, *Billboard* introduced the Hot 100, the weekly singles chart that would become the industry standard to determine the best-selling, most-played records in America. The very first song to top the Hot 100 was "Poor Little Fool" by Ricky Nelson, his sixth hit single.

After Ricky's first hit, a cover of Fats Domino's "I'm Walking" on Verve Records, no one would ever underestimate the power of television again. "The Adventures of Ozzie and Harriet" had premiered on radio in 1944, with former band leader Ozzie Nelson and his wife, vocalist Harriet Hilliard Nelson, playing themselves. Two child actors portrayed their sons, David and Ricky, until their real-life counterparts suggested they play their own characters. David (born October 24, 1936) and Ricky (born Eric Hilliard Nelson on May 8, 1940 in Teaneck, New Jersey) joined the show in 1949, and when it debuted on ABC-TV on October 3, 1952, the entire family continued in their roles.

Ricky was a student at Hollywood High School, dating a girl named Arline. As he drove her home one evening, an Elvis Presley song came on the radio. She raved about Presley and his singing, and a defensive Ricky announced he would be making a record, too. Arline just laughed, not believing him for a second. At that moment, Ricky became determined to make a record, even if it meant only pressing one disc and handing it to her personally.

Ricky asked his father if he could use the TV series' orchestra to record a demo. He chose "I'm Walking" because it contained the two chords he knew how to play. The series had already established in a previous episode that Ricky was putting together his own band, so it was a natural next step for him to sing "I'm Walking" on the episode telecast April 10, 1957.

On May 6, the single entered the chart. The flip side, "A Teenager's Romance," proved to be even bigger,

peaking at number two. Imperial Records, which had released the Fats Domino version, became interested in Ricky, and when label owner Lou Chudd discovered a contract with Verve had never been signed, he pacted Ricky immediately.

His first single for Imperial, "Be-Bop Baby," went to number three. The next two 45s, "Stood Up" and "Believe What You Say," charted at number two and four, respectively.

"Poor Little Fool" was written by Sharon Sheeley, a prolific songwriter who became the girlfriend of singer Eddie Cochran ("Summertime Blues," "C'mon Everybody"). She travelled with Cochran to Britain for a 1960 tour that included singer Gene Vincent. When the first half of the tour concluded, Eddie and Sharon decided to take a break and return briefly to America to get married. After appearing at the Hippodrome in Bristol, they hired a taxi to take them to the airport in London. In the early

morning hours of April 17, while travelling on the A4 near Chippenham, one of the tires burst and the taxi smashed into a lamppost. Sheeley and Vincent were badly injured, but recovered. Several hours later, Cochran died of severe head injuries.

### THE TOP FIVE
*Week of August 4, 1958*

1 **Poor Little Fool**
Ricky Nelson

2 **Patricia**
Perez Prado

3 **Splish Splash**
Bobby Darin

4 **Hard Headed Woman**
Elvis Presley

5 **When**
Kalin Twins

DECCA 30677 **Volare (Nel Blu Dipinto di Blu)**
DOMENICO MODUGNO  **41**

*Writers: Franco Migliacci*
*Domenico Modugno*
*Mitchell Parish*

*Producer: Not Known*

*August 18, 1958*
*6 weeks*

**T**HE only record to originate in Italy and top the American chart was Domenico Modugno's "Volare (*Nel Blu Dipinto di Blu*)." Hailed as "the music genius of Italy," Modugno was a four-time winner in that country's San Remo Festival of Music, an annual event to select the best new song of the year.

The first time he won was in 1958 with "*Nel Blu Dipinto di Blu*," a song that captured the fancy of the jury, the press and the public, who bought almost a million copies in Italy alone.

Franco Migliacci, a friend of Domenico's, was inspired by the back of a pack of cigarettes. He brought the idea to Domenico, who wrote the music and together they wrote the lyrics. The song describes a dream—a man painting his hands in blue and singing, and flying through the "blue painted in blue." English lyrics were added later by Mitchell Parish, and a flood of releases hit the American market to compete with Domenico's original version. The July 21, 1958 issue of *Billboard* reviews seven versions of the song by different artists (including Dean Martin, Nelson Riddle, Jesse Belvin, Umberto Marcato, Alan Dale and Linda Ross) and indicates that three more were to be released.

## THE TOP FIVE
*Week of August 18, 1958*

1  **Volare**
   **(Nel Blu Dipinto Di Blu)**
   Domenico Modugno

2  **Little Star**
   Elegants

3  **My True Love**
   Jack Scott

4  **Poor Little Fool**
   Ricky Nelson

5  **Patricia**
   Perez Prado

Dean Martin was the only real competitor; his recording peaked at number 12 while Domenico's version was *Billboard's* number one single of 1958. It also won three Grammys for Best Male Vocal Performance, Song of the Year and Record of the Year. In 1960, Bobby Rydell took the song to number four, and Al Martino charted with it in 1975.

Modugno was born on January 9, 1928, in Polignano a Mare, Italy. He dropped out of school and, with less than five dollars in his pocket, took off for Rome to seek fame and fortune. He wrote his first song when he was 14, a lullaby titled "*Ninna Nanna*."

He worked as a waiter and factory worker in Rome, and wanted to enroll in a school for screen actors when he was drafted. After completing military service, he did enter the school, where one of his "fellow" students was Sophia Loren. In the next two years, Domenico won some small film roles, but his big break came when he played a balladeer in *Il Mantello Rosso* (The Red Cloak). That led to a contract to appear on a radio series hosted by an Italian comedian, Walter Chiari.

Domenico toured America in 1955 and a year later played Athos in a TV series based on "The Three Musketeers." In 1957 he won second place in the Neapolitan Song Festival with "*Lazzarella*."

Domenico's other San Remo wins were for "*Piove*" in 1959, "*Addio, Addio*" in 1962 and "*Dio Come Ti Amo*" in 1966. In 1960, he had a couple of brushes with the Italian law over his songs: a judge absolved him of plagiarism charges brought against "Volare" by an opera composer and copies of his recording of "Libero" were seized by police because the flip side, "*Nuda*," contained the lyric "I would like to hold you nude in my arms." Banned by RAI radio and television and criticized by the church, "*Nuda*" was replaced by another "B" side and "*Libero*" was re-released. Public demand for "*Nuda*" did not abate, and after the courts ruled it was not an immoral song, it was released again as an "A" side.

Domenico Modugno was 66 years old when he died of a heart attack on August 6, 1994, while vacationing at his summer villa on the island of Lampedusa near Sicily.

## 42 Little Star APT 25005
## THE ELEGANTS

*Writers: Arnold Venosa*
*Vito Picone*

*Producer: Not Known*

*August 25, 1958*
*1 week*

SHERMAN COHEN is the program director of radio station KHYT in Tucson, Arizona. By compiling a list of songs that were number one on your birthday through the years, Sherman will give you a reading, much as an astrologer or numerologist might with their own criteria. The song that was number one on the day you were born will have the most influence on your life, according to Sherman. Those of you who are scoffing at this new art may want to reconsider when you learn that on August 29, 1958, while the Elegants' *Little Star* was number one, a baby named Michael Jackson was born in Gary, Indiana.

If Sherman's theory is correct, Michael may have benefitted more from "Little Star" than the Elegants, who are the first of four ultimate one-hit-wonders of the rock era. To qualify for this distinction, one must have a solitary number one single and then no other records on the chart—ever.

The nucleus of the Elegants was made up of two young singers from Staten Island, New York. Lead singer Vito Picone and baritone Carmen Romano joined a group called the Crescents in 1956. When that group disbanded a year later, Vito and Carmen looked for local singers to form a new group. They recruited a mutual friend, Artie Venosa, to sing first tenor. Frankie Fardogno, a friend of Vito's from school, became second tenor. The fifth member of the quintet was a friend of Artie's, bass singer Jimmy Moschella.

A billboard advertising Schenley's Whiskey said it was the "liquor of elegance," and that inspired the new group's name of the Elegants. For their first song, Vito and Artie took Mozart's "Twinkle, Twinkle, Little Star" and adapted it into a rock and roll song, "Little Star."

The Elegants took their song to a New York label, Hull Records. They leased the song to a larger company, ABC-Paramount Records, which was just starting a new label. The May 19, 1958 issue of *Billboard* announced that Apt Records was readying its first release of four singles, including the track by the Elegants.

One of the group's problems was constant touring, which started as "Little Star" entered the chart on July 28. A month later, it was number one, and the Elegants were appearing all over the United States and in the possession of Hawaii. Being on the road meant not being in the studio, and the results hurt: the Elegants never returned to the Hot 100 again.

The records they did release all sounded like "Little Star" anyway, and despite recording for several different labels, the group never regained their momentum. Two members of the group were drafted into the army, one was married and Vito was laid up for six months after an accident. By 1962, the Elegants had broken up for good.

## THE TOP FIVE
*Week of August 25, 1958*

1 **Little Star**
Elegants

2 **Volare**
**(Nel Blu Dipinto Di Blu)**
Domenico Modugno

3 **Bird Dog**
Everly Brothers

4 **Just a Dream**
Jimmy Clanton

5 **My True Love**
Jack Scott

Tommy was born on February 17, 1922 in Richmond, Virginia. He had his own radio show in Richmond during the 40s, singing and playing the piano. His ambition was to write songs, and in 1946, he wrote "That Chick's Too Young to Fry," later recorded by R&B singer Louis Jordan.

Tommy moved to New York in 1950. He recorded demos of his songs and took them to record companies and music publishers. MGM signed him, but more for his voice than his material. He recorded four tracks, including his own "All Over Again."

The success of the revitalized "It's All in the Game" in 1958 encouraged other artists to re-cut their pre-rock era hits in a modern style. MGM released three updated singles: Fran Warren's "Sunday Kind of Love," Bill Farrell's "Circus" and Johnny Desmond's *"C'est Si Bon Cha Cha."* Columbia and Mercury did the same with Guy Mitchell and Billy Eckstine, respectively.

Edwards had eight more chart records in the next two years, including a new version of "Morning Side of the Mountain" in 1959. His last chart entry was "It's Not the End of Everything" in 1960. But in chart terms, it was.

Although Tommy found it difficult to have more hit records, "It's All in the Game" fared quite well. It is one of a handful of number one singles to make the top 30 three times. Cliff Richard took it to number 25 in 1964, and the Four Tops went to number 24 with it in 1970, just six months after Tommy Edwards died at the age of 47 in Henrico County, Virginia.

*Writers: Charles Gates Dawes
        Carl Sigman*

*Producer: Harry Myerson*

*September 29, 1958
6 weeks*

In 1912, a Chicago banker by the name of Charles Gates Dawes wrote the music for a tune he called "Melody in A Major." Dawes, who was an amateur flutist, is perhaps better known (well, maybe not that much better known) for being the vice president of the United States during the second administration of President Calvin Coolidge (1925-29). Unless Al Gore suddenly writes a hit for Madonna, Dawes will remain the only American vice president to ever write a number one song.

In 1951, songwriter Carl Sigman added lyrics to Dawes' music, and the result was "It's All in the Game," a song recorded that year by Sammy

Kaye, Carmen Cavallaro, Dinah Shore and Tommy Edwards. The latter was the biggest hit version, entering the *Billboard* chart on October 5 and climbing to number 18.

Edwards had already had a hit with "Morning Side of the Mountain," but after "It's All in the Game" he found it difficult to maintain momentum. By 1958, MGM Records was ready to drop him from the artist roster. But stereo recording was just coming into vogue, and this new technology helped save Tommy's career.

With one session left to record under his MGM contract, Edwards was asked by label executive Morty Craft to re-cut "It's All in the Game" in stereo. Instead of using the 1951 arrangement, he updated it to a rock and roll ballad. MGM liked the new version well enough to release it as a single, and six weeks after it entered the Hot 100, it topped the chart. In November, it also went to number one in Britain.

## THE TOP FIVE
*Week of September 29, 1958*

1 **It's All in the Game**
  Tommy Edwards

2 **Volare
  (Nel Blu Dipinto Di Blu)**
  Domenico Modugno

3 **Bird Dog**
  Everly Brothers

4 **Rock-In' Robin**
  Bobby Day

5 **Little Star**
  Elegants

## 44 It's Only Make Believe MGM 12677
### CONWAY TWITTY

*Writers: Conway Twitty*
*Jack Nance*

*Producer: Jim Vinneau*

*November 10, 1958*
*2 weeks*

HAROLD LLOYD JENKINS could have been a major league baseball player or a Bible-thumping preacher. Instead he renamed himself after two towns on a map of the southern United States (Conway, Arkansas and Twitty, Texas) and became a rock and roller and a country superstar.

Named after silent screen actor Harold Lloyd, he was born September 1, 1933, in Friars Point, Mississippi, the son of a ferry boat pilot on the Mississippi River. His grandfather bought him his first guitar, and in his spare time he'd sit in the pilot house of his father's boat and practice strumming and singing. When he was ten years old, he formed a band, the Phillips County Ramblers, and they had their own show on Helena, Arkansas radio station KFFA.

During his teens he preached at church revivals and considered becoming a minister, but by age 17 was disillusioned with his church deacons and gave up the idea. When he graduated from high school, he had a .450 batting average and was offered a contract with the Philadelphia Phillies. His desire to own his own car was so strong, he decided to work in Chicago for International Harvester for a few months before accepting the Phillies' offer. By the time he had

enough money to buy a 1948 Buick, he returned home and found his draft notice.

Serving in the Far East, he formed a band called the Cimmarrons and played clubs in Japan. When he returned home, the Phillies renewed their offer, but Jenkins had heard Elvis Presley sing "Mystery Train," and was inspired to follow a new direction.

One of the Cimmarons had told him to contact manager Don Seat, who decided Harold Jenkins was not a name with star quality. After the name change, Seat signed Twitty to Mercury Records. Three unremarkable singles later, Twitty and his new band were booked into the Flamingo Lounge in Toronto. One night during intermission, Twitty and band member Jack Nance wrote "It's Only Make Believe."

Twitty was signed to a five-year contract with MGM and recorded the song in Nashville with the Jordanaires. After a long wait, Twitty was convinced the song would not be a hit, until he received a call from a Columbus, Ohio DJ who said the record was a smash in his city.

Twitty was so strongly identified as a rock and roll singer that he became the model for Conrad Birdie in the Broadway musical *Bye Bye Birdie*. In his heart he wanted to sing country music, and he toyed with the idea of recording country songs as Harold Jenkins and keeping his Conway Twitty identity for rock and roll. In the summer of 1965 he walked off stage in the middle of a song in a New Jersey club and never looked back at rock.

Since then, he has recorded for Decca, MCA, Elektra and Warner Brothers Records. He has had 35 number one singles as a solo artist (and five with Loretta Lynn) on the country chart, more than any other artist.

For years he lived on a nine-acre complex called Twitty Ciy, a tourist attraction that also housed a museum, a gift shop, his offices and his children's homes.

On June 4, 1993, Twitty performed in Branson, Missouri. He was returning to Nashville on his tour bus when he was stricken with an abdominal aneurism. He died the next day at age 59.

### THE TOP FIVE
*Week of November 10, 1958*

1 **It's Only Make Believe**
   Conway Twitty

2 **Tom Dooley**
   Kingston Trio

3 **It's All in the Game**
   Tommy Edwards

4 **Topsy II**
   Cozy Cole

5 **To Know Him is to Love Him**
   Teddy Bears

album, released June 1, 1958. Two DJs at KLUB in Salt Lake City liked "Tom Dooley" a lot and started giving it heavy airplay. Slowly, the song started to spread to other cities, and Capitol Records was forced to release the track as a single.

Dave, Bob and Nick stayed together until 1961. Unhappy with the trio's choice of material and disappointed with their manager and music publisher, Guard left and formed a new folk group, The Whiskey Hill Singers. They recorded one album and contributed to the soundtrack of *How the West Was Won* before breaking up.

Guard's replacement in the Kingston Trio was John Stewart, who had been writing their arrangements and composing some of their songs. This second line-up remained together until 1967. Since then, Bob has carried on the Kingston Trio name with a couple of different group rosters. Stewart has had a successful solo career and has written hit songs for other artists [see 233—"Daydream Believer"].

In November, 1981, Tom Smothers hosted "The Kingston Trio and Friends Reunion," taped for PBS. Bob Shane, Roger Gambill and George Grove appeared with Dave, Nick and John. It was the first time Dave had performed with Bob and Nick since 1961, and "The Kingston Trio and Friends" show proved to be an emotional reunion.

In March, 1991, Guard died of lymphoma at age 56. Two months earlier, Reynolds had visited him and found him in remission. "We were talking about doing a reunion," Nick said.

*Writer: Dave Guard*

*Producer: Voyle Gilmore*

*November 17, 1958*
*1 week*

---

**T**HE KINGSTON TRIO was the forerunner of the modern folk movement in the rock era. Their popularity in the late fifties and early sixties paved the way for Peter, Paul and Mary; Bob Dylan; Joan Baez; Judy Collins; John Denver and Gordon Lightfoot.

Their number one single, "Tom Dooley," was a century-old Blue Ridge Mountains folk tune, originally titled "Tom Dula." Dula was a mountaineer hanged for murder in 1868, and after The Kingston Trio's record went to number one, his forgotten grave in North Carolina was restored and steps were taken to give him an official pardon.

The Trio formed in San Francisco, where Dave Guard was attending nearby Stanford University, and Bob Shane and Nick Reynolds were students at Menlo College. Dave, Nick and two other people were playing at a club called the Cracked Pot as Dave

Guard and the Calypsonians. Frank Werber, a San Francisco publicist who had worked at the Purple Onion nightclub, saw Guard's group and suggested they could do without their bass player. Soon after, when the bass player and his female vocalist girlfriend left, Shane joined the group, and Werber offered to manage them. He sent them to a vocal coach, Judy Davis; put them through extensive rehearsals; and helped pick a new name that sounded collegiate yet retained a calypso flavor: The Kingston Trio. He booked them at the Hungry i in San Francisco, and when Phyllis Diller cancelled an appearance at the Purple Onion, the trio filled in for her and went on to work seven straight weeks.

Jimmy Saphier, Bob Hope's television agent, saw the group and told Voyle Gilmore at Capitol Records about them. Gilmore flew up north and signed them to a contract.

One night at the Purple Onion, they heard a singer named Tom audition for the club with "Tom Dooley." Although they never did learn Tom's last name, they liked the song, and included it on their first Capitol

---

## THE TOP FIVE
*Week of November 17, 1958*

1 **Tom Dooley**
Kingston Trio

2 **It's Only Make Believe**
Conway Twitty

3 **Topsy II**
Cozy Cole

4 **It's All in the Game**
Tommy Edwards

5 **To Know Him is to Love Him**
Teddy Bears

## 46    To Know Him Is to Love Him   DORE 503
### THE TEDDY BEARS

*Writer: Phil Spector*

*Producer: Phil Spector*

*December 1, 1958*
*3 weeks*

PHIL SPECTOR graduated from Fairfax High School in June, 1958, and a month later organized a group called the Teddy Bears with two friends, Marshall Leib and Harvey Goldstein. At the same time, Phil was dating a girl named Donna, and her best friend, 15-year-old Annette Kleinbard, loved to sing. Phil fell in love with her voice and asked her to join the group. Before they could record anything, Harvey departed, leaving the Teddy Bears a trio.

First they recorded a song Phil wrote, "Don't You Worry, My Little Pet." Then Phil told Annette he was going to write a song especially for her voice. Phil was inspired by a photograph of his father's tombstone in Beth David Cemetery in New York. The inscription read: "To Know Him Was to Love Him."

Annette Kleinbard, who later changed her name to Carol Connors ("I had to grow up under Annette Funicello's ears...I hated the name because of her") and gained fame as a songwriter ("Hey Little Cobra, "Gonna Fly Now (Theme from

'Rocky')," "With You I'm Born Again"), says Phil called her and sang "To Know Him Is to Love Him" over the telephone. She told him she didn't think much of the song, but agreed to sing it. They rehearsed in Marshall's garage, and it took 20 minutes to record the song in two takes at Gold Star Studios in Hollywood, with Sandy Nelson on drums.

"To Know Him Is to Love Him" was released in August on a new Southern California label, Dore, and broke out in Los Angeles and Minneapolis. It debuted on the Hot 100 on September 22, and took 10 weeks to rise to number one. It was the first hit for writer/producer Phil Spector, born in the Bronx on December 26, 1940. His father died when he was nine, and he moved to Hollywood with his mother Bertha, and his sister Shirley. Phil's first public flirtation with music was a Fairfax Junior High talent show, where he performed Lonnie Donegan's "Rock Island Line." Phil's first group was called the Sleepwalkers, who disbanded before he formed the Teddy Bears.

He went on to produce hits like "Corrine, Corrrina" for Ray Peterson, "I Love How You Love Me" for the Paris Sisters, "Pretty Little Angel Eyes" and "Under the Moon of Love" for Curtis Lee and "Every

Breath I Take" for Gene Pitney. In 1961, Spector started his own label, Philles, which flourished with the "wall of sound" production for artists such as the Crystals [see 119—"He's a Rebel"], the Ronettes, Bob B. Soxx and the Blue Jeans, Darlene Love and the Righteous Brothers [see 166—"You've Lost That Lovin' Feelin'"].

The Teddy Bears disbanded for several reasons, including Phil's reluctance to be a performer and Annette's car accident, in which she drove off a cliff and required several operations for plastic surgery.

Recovering from the terrible accident, Annette finally changed her name to Carol and enrolled at UCLA to study anthropology. "One day I woke up and said, 'what do you really want to do with your life,'" Carol explains. "I wanted to write songs." She quit school and recorded a song she wrote herself, "My Diary." In 1963, she formed a group with her younger sister Cheryl and a friend, Steve Barri [see 183—"Eve of Destruction"]. Called the Storytellers, they had a local Los Angeles hit with "When Two People." At the same time, Carol and her brother wrote "Hey Little Cobra," a song they brought to Terry Melcher. Melcher and his partner Bruce Johnston (a future Beach Boy) were producing and singing lead vocals for the Rip Chords, and they took "Hey Little Cobra" to number four.

"I was the only girl to ever write a hot rod song," Carol laughs. "Brian Wilson said it had to be written by a girl, because you can't take your Cobra out of gear and let it coast to the line!"

### THE TOP FIVE
*Week of December 1, 1958*

1 **To Know Him is to Love Him**
Teddy Bears

2 **Tom Dooley**
Kingston Trio

3 **It's Only Make Believe**
Conway Twitty

4 **Beep Beep**
Playmates

5 **One Night**
Elvis Presley

SIMON ALVIN THEODORE

*Writer: Ross Bagdasarian*

*Producer: Ross Bagdasarian*

*December 22, 1958*
*4 weeks*

CAN you name a musical trio from the 1950s who were still popular enough in the 1980s to have their own weekly Saturday morning TV show? Right: The Chipmunks, whose NBC-TV series was a consistent time period winner, knocking off the competition left and right.

The Chipmunks were created by Ross Bagdasarian, who as David Seville had a number one song earlier in 1958 [see 36—"Witch Doctor"]. The speeded-up voices in "Witch Doctor" had no name or identity; it was only after that song was a hit that Bagdasarian came up with the Chipmunks. He was driving through Yosemite, California, when a chipmunk in the road refused to budge for his automobile. Inspiration struck.

The chipmunk survived.

Ross named his three characters after executives at Liberty Records. Alvin was named for Al Bennett, president of the company; Simon was named after Bennett's partner, Si Waronker; and Theodore was named for Ted Keep, recording engineer.

The role model for the mischievious Alvin was Ross' youngest son, Adam, who had a penchant for asking in September if it was Christmas yet. Bagdasarian figured if his son was asking about the holiday so early, other children were probably doing the same thing.

The song went through three versions before the Bagdasarian family approved of Ross' efforts. Version one was an instrumental; two was called "In a Village Park" and number three was the charm. Within three weeks of release, the song had sold more than 2,500,000 copies and was the fastest selling record of 1958.

At the first annual Grammy Awards, Bagdasarian walked away with three awards: Best Recording

for Children, Best Comedy Performance and Best Engineered Record.

The Chipmunks' popularity did not abate after "The Chipmunk Song." A follow-up, "Alvin's Harmonica," peaked at number three in the spring of 1959. A prime-time animated series, "The Alvin Show," premiered on CBS on October 4, 1961 and ran for a full season. The series was repeated on CBS' Saturday morning schedule for three years, beginning in June of 1962.

Early in 1964, Liberty released an album called *The Chipmunks Sing the Beatles*, which resulted from Bagdasarian seeing the fab four on Ed Sullivan's show. But by 1967, Ross decided to let the Chipmunks retire. He wanted to be thought of as a serious songwriter again and not be known just for his novelty material.

On January 16, 1972, Ross died of a heart attack. The return of the Chipmunks in 1980 began with a radio station playing Blondie's "Call Me" at a faster speed and announcing, in jest, that it was by the Chipmunks. So many requests came in for the "new" Chipmunks song, that Ross Bagdasarian Jr. and his wife, Janice Karman, recorded an album called *Chipmunk Punk*.

With Ross providing the voices of Alvin, Simon and David Seville, and Janice giving a new dimension to Theodore, the Chipmunks recorded a sequel album, *Urban Chipmunk*. Ross and Janice created a "live" touring Chipmunks show and sold a new series of Chipmunk adventures to NBC for their Saturday morning schedule. The program premiered in September, 1983.

## 48 | Smoke Gets in Your Eyes MERCURY 71383
### THE PLATTERS

*Writers: Otto Harbach*
*Jerome Kern*

*Producer: Buck Ram*

*January 19, 1959*
*3 weeks*

JEROME KERN'S widow wasn't exactly thrilled to learn that the Platters had recorded her late husband's "Smoke Gets in Your Eyes," a song he had written with Otto Harbach for the 1933 stage musical *Roberta.* In fact, she had her lawyer get in touch with the song's publisher, Max Dreyfus, about seeking an injunction against the Platters to prevent their recording from being distributed.

What Mrs. Kern didn't know was that Dreyfus had pushed for the Platters to record the song in the first place. After all, songs don't make money unless someone keeps recording them, and publishers are *supposed* to keep their inventory active.

Two things helped change Mrs. Kern's mind. Oscar Hammerstein publicly thanked Buck Ram and the Platters for reviving a dead song. And Dreyfus mentioned to Mrs. Kern's lawyer that the new recording of "Smoke Gets in Your Eyes" could sell over a million copies. The idea of an injunction was dropped.

By the autumn of 1958, the Platters were an international success, touring Europe and receiving rave reviews, especially in Paris and Athens. In October, the Platters recorded "Smoke Gets in Your Eyes" in Paris, to the dismay of Mercury executive Art Talmadge, who told Buck the group should be recording more modern material, like "Short Shorts," instead of tired old standards.

The Platters' reign as the world's most popular vocal group was suddenly interrupted on August 10, 1959, when the four male members of the group were arrested in a Cincinnati hotel room on morals charges. They were accused of using drugs and soliciting prostitutes. The fall-out from the incident did irreparable damage to their career. Their records were dropped from radio playlists and some venues refused to book them. Ren Grevatt, writing in the August 17 issue of *Billboard*, put the incident in perspective:

"The story...is a good illustration of the kind of pressure any performer...is constantly under to avoid those human failings in which many people—stars and the common man—become involved....It has already been noted that had the four Platters been four itinerant businessmen and had an issue of race not been involved, the matter would not have become a subject of scrutiny....Is it fair to let this grievous incident become the source of permanent damage to the career of the Platters?"

At their trial, the Platters were told by the judge that they had a duty to their fans to keep their record clean. The case was dismissed.

What really ended the five-year reign of the Platters was the departure of lead singer Tony Williams in 1960. The Platters continued with a new lead singer, Sonny Turner, but Mercury sued the group and Williams for breach of contract. Ram, who had passed the bar but had not become a lawyer, knew the members of the Platters were not signed as individuals to Mercury. He won, and from that point on, record companies rewrote their contracts so members of a group were also signed as individuals.

Zola Taylor and Paul Robi eventually left the Platters, and were replaced by Sandra Dawn and Nate Nelson. After a four-year absence from the Hot 100, the Platters had a brief resurgence in 1966-1967 with five records on Musicor, including "I Love You 1000 Times" and "With This Ring."

The Platters name was copyrighted all over the world, but that didn't stop a great number of ersatz groups from appearing as the Platters. Ram had been involved in almost 50 lawsuits against imitation Platters until there was only one set, managed by Jean Bennett. Ram (who produced an album for them in 1984) died January 1, 1991, of natural causes, in Las Vegas. He was 83.

### THE TOP FIVE
*Week of January 19, 1959*

1 **Smoke Gets in Your Eyes**
Platters

2 **My Happiness**
Connie Francis

3 **The Chipmunk Song**
David Seville & the Chipmunks

4 **Donna**
Ritchie Valens

5 **16 Candles**
Crests

*Writers: Lloyd Price*
*Harold Logan*

*Producer: Don Costa*

*February 9, 1959*
*4 weeks*

**A**LONG with Fats Domino, Lloyd Price is one of the major rock and roll artists to come out of New Orleans. His biggest hit was "Stagger Lee," but he earned the nickname "Mr. Personality" from his second biggest hit, "Personality" ("Cause o-o-over and over, I'll be a fool for you...").

Price was born in New Orleans on March 9, 1933. There were a lot of musicians in the family, and his mother, a gospel singer, encouraged him to sing in the church choir. He played trumpet in high school and formed a five-piece band to play for school dances. As a sophomore, he got his group a regular job playing music on radio station WBOK.

Price wrote station-break jingles, and one of them was so popular, listeners phoned the station to request it. Price recorded a full-length version and took it to Specialty Records. The song, "Lawdy Miss Clawdy," became a number one R&B song in 1952. Price's idol, Domino, played piano on the session.

Price had a few more R&B hits, until he was drafted in 1954. He formed a military band and toured bases in Korea and Japan. He was discharged in 1956, and returned to live in Washington, D.C. There he met up with an old friend, Harold Logan, who became his business partner. They formed KRC, the Kent Record Company, and leased their masters to ABC-Paramount. The first one, "Just Because," was Price's first national pop hit, peaking at number 29 in the spring of 1957.

A year later, Price and Logan took an old folk song, "Stack-O-Lee," about the tragic fate of two gamblers, and rewrote it as an R&B song, "Stagger Lee." It went to number one on the Hot 100, and was a top 30 hit again for Wilson Pickett in 1967 and Tommy Roe in 1971.

Price's most successful year was 1959, with four big hits: "Where Were You (On Our Wedding Day)," "Personality," "I'm Gonna Get Married" and "Come into My Heart." Four years later, he formed his own label, Double-L. He had a couple of minor hits on the label, which is best remembered for launching Pickett's career.

Price is also indirectly responsible for the career of another artist. When Price left Specialty Records, they hired his valet—Larry Williams. His hits include "Bony Moronie," "Short Fat Fannie" and two songs later recorded by the Beatles—"Dizzy Miss Lizzy" (a parody of Price's "Lawdy Miss Clawdy") and "Slow Down."

After Price's career slowed down, he toured the country with a nine-piece band and established a fund to provide scholarships for black students to attend college. In the early 70s, he opened a night club in New York City, "Lloyd Price's Turntable."

## THE TOP FIVE
*Week of February 9, 1959*

1 **Stagger Lee**
Lloyd Price

2 **16 Candles**
Crests

3 **Donna**
Ritchie Valens

4 **Smoke Gets in Your Eyes**
Platters

5 **All American Boy**
Bill Parsons

## 50 **Venus** CHANCELOR 1031
### FRANKIE AVALON

*Writer: Ed Marshall*

*Producers: Peter De Angelis*
         *Bob Marcucci*

*March 9, 1959*
*5 weeks*

Frankie Avalon grew up in Philadelphia, the same city that nurtured Bobby Rydell, James Darren, Chubby Checker, Fabian, Dick Clark's "American Bandstand" and Kenny Gamble and Leon Huff's sound of Philadelphia International.

Born Francis Thomas Avallone on September 18, 1939, his first interest was boxing. That was preempted after seeing Kirk Douglas in the film *Young Man With a Horn*. Avalon recalls: "It inspired me so much, I asked my father if I could get a trumpet. He was elated, being a frustrated musician himself. So not having money to buy me a horn, he borrowed the money and went to a pawn shop, where he bought my first trumpet for $15."

Avalon became a child prodigy on the trumpet, recording for RCA Victor's subsidiary, X Records, and appearing on television shows like "TV Teen Club" hosted by Paul Whiteman, the man who suggested the new name of Frankie Avalon.

During summer vacation, Frankie played the horn for Bobby Boyd and the Jazz Bums. He was too young to travel with the band while school was in session, so he joined a local group, Rocco and the Saints. There were already two vocalists with the band, but Frankie had Rocco's support to also sing a song in each set.

One day Frankie received a phone call from a neighborhood friend he had known since childhood. "Bob Marcucci was starting a new record label. He asked me if I knew of singers for the label. I told him there were two singers in our band. He and his partner came to Mary's Inn and listened to the band. The two singers did their numbers and I did mine. I asked him, 'What do you think?' He said, 'I want to record you.'"

Despite Avalon's protests that he was a trumpet player and not a vocalist, Marcucci insisted. He signed the whole band to Chancellor Records and recorded "Cupid" backed with "Jivin' with the Saints." Marcucci had the band audition for a film, *Disc*

*Jockey Jamboree.* They won a small role and Avalon's first solo vocal single, "Teacher's Pet," came from the film. Like "Cupid," it failed to chart.

Marcucci was certain Avalon would be a star, but Frankie wanted to stay with the band. Convinced he should record one more song before giving up, Frankie cut a song written by Peter De Angelis and Marcucci. "I walked into the studio and they were rehearsing it. The rhythm sounded very stacatto to me, so I started singing along with it, holding my nose. Bob came out and said, 'What are you doing?' I said I was having a good time. They said, 'Let's make a couple of takes like that.'" The result, a nasal "Dede Dinah," was Avalon's first hit, peaking at number seven. One of the follow-ups, "Ginger Bread," was another "nose job," and it went to number nine.

A ballad, "I'll Wait for You," followed, and established a more romantic image for Frankie. His next song was brought to him by writer Ed Marshall. "He came to my house and asked if I would listen to a song....He sat down at the piano and started playing 'Venus.' I listened to it and the first time it just caught me immediately. I said play it again and he played it again, and I asked him, 'Has anybody heard this song?' He said, 'Al Martino...likes it very much

but thinks it's a good album cut.'"

Frankie called Marcucci and asked him to come over immediately. Three days later Frankie was in a New York studio, where he recorded it in nine takes. He waited until 4 a.m. to get the acetate and returned to Philadelphia, where he stayed awake all day playing the song. A couple of days later, while doing a live telephone interview with Clark on "American Bandstand," Frankie said he had just recorded a smash hit single. A week later it was released on Chancellor, and four weeks after it entered the Hot 100 at number 99 it had gone all the way to number one.

---

### THE TOP FIVE
*Week of March 9, 1959*

1  **Venus**
   Frankie Avalon

2  **Charlie Brown**
   Coasters

3  **Stagger Lee**
   Lloyd Price

4  **Donna**
   Ritchie Valens

5  **Alvin's Harmonica**
   David Seville & the Chipmunks

DOLPHIN 1 **Come Softly to Me**
THE FLEETWOODS **51**

*Writers: Gary Troxel
         Gretchen Christopher
         Barbara Ellis*

*Producer: Bob Reisdorff*

*April 13, 1959
4 weeks*

Barbara Ellis was born in Olympia, Washington on February 20, 1940. Nine days later, Gretchen Christopher was born in the same hospital and for a few days both babies were in the maternity ward together. It was the beginning of a perfect harmony.

When they were five years old, they lived in the same neighborhood and played together. Both girls attended Lincoln Elementary School, until Gretchen's father bought a waterfront farm and the Christophers moved to the country. Barbara and Gretchen were reunited at Washington Junior High School, where they were both cheerleaders and did some singing together. But they went to different high schools until their senior year, when they were both at Olympia High. Then Gretchen suggested they sing together again, and they auditioned several girls to complete a trio. None were suitable, so they remained a duo and called themselves the Saturns, to complement a local rock group called the Blue Comets.

"We worked up an arrangement of 'Stormy Weather,' Gretchen remembers, "and we wanted a blues trumpet behind us, so we asked the Blue Comets if they knew anybody. They brought in this young man that we'd never seen before, and he was pretty arresting looking, with smouldering dark eyes. That was Gary Troxel. He tried to play a blues trumpet behind us, but he couldn't play in our key and we couldn't sing in his, so that was the beginning and end of that.

"He walked me downtown after school that day, and we were standing on the corner waiting for my mother to pick us up and he began humming this, 'Dum dum, dum-bee-doo-wah,'...and I could tell it was based on the same chord progression as a song I had been writing, 'Come Softly.' I said, 'Let's do it for Barbara, and if she likes it we'll incorporate the song and you into the group.'"

Gary made the group a trio and they performed "Come Softly" at the senior class talent assembly. The students loved it. "For weeks after, they came up to me in the halls and said, 'How does it go, it's driving me crazy.' We sang it a second time after a football game at a school dance." This time their friends said they should record the song. Gretchen was singing and dancing at a local club, The Colony, where Pat Suzuki was starring. The club owner introduced Gretchen to Pat's record promoter, Bob Reisdorff, who told her to make a tape.

Barbara and Gary met Gretchen at her parents' farmhouse and recorded the song a cappella. Gretchen boarded a Greyhound Bus by herself and took the tape to Reisdorff in Seattle, who loved it enough to start his own label, Dolphin Records.

Recording started right after high school graduation in June, and took six tedious months to complete. Reisdorff thought the title too suggestive and extended it to "Come Softly to Me," although those words are never heard in the lyrics. He also didn't care for the group's name, Two Girls and a Guy. In the days before all-digit dialing, the three members had the same telephone exchange, FLeetwood, and during a long-distance phone conversation with Gretchen, Bob suggested they call themselves the Fleetwoods.

The single was released and started doing well in the Pacific Northwest. Gretchen was attending Whitman College, and Barbara called one day to tell her she'd have to leave school to go on tour. "I called Bob and begged him to let me stay in school. He said he would on one condition, that I would leave with no argument if the song hit nationally." As the record climbed higher and higher, Gretchen's hopes for college sunk lower and lower.

The Fleetwoods flew to New York to appear on the April 11, 1959 edition of "The Dick Clark Saturday Night Beechwood Show." Gretchen recalls, "It was morning when we arrived, and the theater was dark. Out of the shadows stepped Frankie Avalon. He stuck out his hand and said, 'Congratulations. "Come Softly to Me" has just knocked "Venus" out of the number one spot.'"

## THE TOP FIVE
*Week of April 13, 1959*

1 **Come Softly to Me**
   Fleetwoods

2 **Venus**
   Frankie Avalon

3 **Pink Shoelaces**
   Dodie Stevens

4 **It's Just a Matter of Time**
   Brook Benton

5 **Tragedy**
   Thomas Wayne

## 52 The Happy Organ CLOCK 1009
### DAVE "BABY" CORTEZ

*Writers: Dave "Baby" Cortez*
*Ken Wood*

*Producer: Dave "Baby" Cortez*

*May 11, 1959*
*1 week*

"THE HAPPY ORGAN" was a happy accident for Dave "Baby" Cortez, who wrote the song under the title "The Dog and the Cat." It was meant to be a vocal accompanied by piano, but fate stepped in. "The vocal didn't come off, I didn't like it," Dave explains. In the studio, he needed to add a melody. "I saw an organ in the corner, and said, Hey, let me try the organ.' People thought of the organ as a church instrument. I was the first to use the organ commercially."

It was unusual to hear an organ in a rock or R&B song, and Cortez helped popularize the electric organ beyond the jazz field, where people

like Jimmy Smith were using it. Dave still plays the organ today, but the original Hammond organ which he used to record "The Happy Organ" is resting in his father's home in Detroit, "gathering dust."

Before he signed with Clock Records and recorded "The Happy Organ," Cortez was a studio musician, playing keyboards for many artists, including Gladys Knight and the Pips, the Isley Brothers and the Chantels. He was touring with Little Anthony and the Imperials, earning $200 a week, when "The Happy Organ" was released. "We had the radio on all night long, a little transistor radio, and I heard 'The Happy Organ,'" says Dave. "The disc jockey said it was fast becoming a number one record." Sure enough, Dave's agent called him in Washington, D.C., to tell him that the song had gone to number one on *Billboard's* Hot 100. He told Anthony that he

was leaving the tour.

*Billboard's* review of the single called it a "snappy reading of a tune based on 'Shortnin' Bread.'" Asked about this, Dave replied, "I don't know. People have been telling me for years it's got to be 'Shortnin' Bread:' I really don't know!"

Born David Cortez Clowney on August 13, 1938 in Detroit, Michigan, he became interested in the piano because his father enjoyed playing. As a child, Dave was taken to a Duke Ellington show and remembers being impressed. An older brother played drums, a younger brother played trumpet, and soon Dave was taking piano lessons. It was too early for Detroit to be an important musical center—Berry Gordy's Motown was a few years away—so Dave headed for New York with a singing group, the Pearls. He preferred to just play piano, but he was told he had to sing second tenor as well. The group signed with Aladdin Records, then Atco, and had some R&B hits.

The follow-up to "The Happy Organ" was called "The Whistling Organ," but it didn't duplicate the success of the original, peaking at number 61. After Clock records folded, Dave recorded an organ instrumental, "Rinky Dink" on his own label. Al Silver, owner of Herald Records, advanced him $400 for it, but decided not to release it. Leonard Chess bought it for Chess Records, and it soared to number 10. Silver sued Chess Records, and the label made a token payment to Silver for the single.

### THE TOP FIVE
*Week of May 11, 1959*

1 **The Happy Organ**
Dave (Baby) Cortez

2 **Sorry, I Ran All the Way Home**
Impalas

3 **Come Softly to Me**
Fleetwoods

4 **Kookie, Kookie (Lend Me Your Comb)**
Edward Byrnes with Connie Stevens

5 **A Fool Such as I**
Elvis Presley

Writers: *Jerry Leiber*
*Mike Stoller*

Producer: *Bobby Robinson*

*May 18, 1959*
*2 weeks*

**O**NE of the earliest songs written by Jerry Leiber and Mike Stoller was "Kansas City," a 1952 composition that they recorded with Texas bluesman Little Willie Littlefield on Federal Records. Pioneer R&B producer Ralph Bass thought the initials "K.C." were hipper, and changed the title to "K.C. Lovin'," to Leiber and Stoller's disappointment.

Seven years later, while producing the Coasters, Leiber and Stoller were told by King Curtis that he had just been at a recording session where someone's friend did a hot version of "Kansas City." The friend was Wilbert Harrison.

Harrison was born January 6, 1929, in Charlotte, North Carolina. He won first prize in a Miami amateur talent contest in 1953 singing "Mule Train." Four years later, he moved to Newark, New Jersey, where he told Herman Lubinsky of Savoy Records that he wanted to record "K.C. Lovin'." Lubinsky sent Harrison to Bobby Robinson at Fury Records, and Wilbert recorded the song under its original title of "Kansas City" in March, 1959.

On March 27, Leiber and Stoller called Teddy Reig, producer of Joe Williams at Roulette Records, to see if he'd be interested in recording "Kansas City." They couldn't get hold of Reig, and on Monday, *Billboard* gave a spotlight pick to five different versions of the song. The review said: "The song is a finger-snappin' blues with a highly contagious sound."

Contagious was a good word. Wilbert Harrison's record was the top pick, followed by versions from Hank Ballard and the Midnighters, a re-issue of Little Willie Littlefield, Rocky Olson and Rockin' Ronald and the Rebels. The following week, a sixth version by Little Richard was reviewed.

Olson, Ballard and Little Richard all managed to chart on the Hot 100, but Harrison bested them all. It didn't look that way at first—Harrison's version is the first song ever to enter the chart in the anchor position—number 100—and still go all the way to number one.

Harrison became a virtual one-man band, playing guitar, drums, harmonica and piano. After "Kansas City," he didn't have another chart record for 10 years. His "Let's Work Together" went to number 32 in early 1970, and was covered later by Canned Heat and Bryan Ferry (as "Let's Stick Together").

"Kansas City" has achieved a degree of immortality, thanks to the Beatles, who recorded it for the British *Beatles for Sale* album. They had been performing the song in a medley with Little Richard's "Hey, Hey, Hey Hey" since their days in Hamburg, Germany. But the recording of the song only identified Leiber and Stoller as the writers and did not include the title of Little Richard's song.

The mistake was noticed by Dorothy Rupe, vice president of Venice Music, when she was reading the book *All Together Now*, which indicated the song had really been a medley. Venice Music, the publisher of "Hey, Hey, Hey, Hey" had not received any royalties from the Beatles' recording.

Rupe quickly contacted Capitol Records in the United States and EMI in Britain. "There was never any question of disputing the validity of the claim," Laurie Hall, EMI business manager said in *Rolling Stone*. "It was just an oversight. It never came to a question of court proceedings. It's just a matter of figuring out a realistic figure."

It's estimated that Little Richard eventually received over $30,000 in royalties for the Beatles' recording of "Kansas City/Hey, Hey, Hey, Hey."

## THE TOP FIVE
*Week of May 18, 1959*

1 **Kansas City**
Wilbert Harrison

2 **Sorry, I Ran All the Way Home**
Impalas

3 **The Happy Organ**
Dave (Baby) Cortez

4 **Kookie, Kookie (Lend Me Your Comb)**
Edward Byrnes with Connie Stevens

5 **A Teenager in Love**
Dion and the Belmonts

## 54 The Battle of New Orleans COLUMBIA 41339
### JOHNNY HORTON

*Writer: Jimmy Driftwood*

*Producer: Don Law*

*June 1, 1959*
*6 weeks*

ON the eighth of January in the year 1815, Andrew Jackson and his men defeated the British forces of Commander Pakenham at New Orleans. It was the final battle of the War of 1812, which had officially ended two weeks earlier. Celebrating the victory was a folk song soon played by fiddlers all over the United States: "The Eighth of January."

It wasn't until the year 1955 that Jimmy Driftwood, a teacher from Snowball, Arkansas, wrote lyrics for that song and retitled it "The Battle of New Orleans."

Four years later, country singer Johnny Horton recorded it and took it to number one, making New Orleans the second American city to be immortalized in the title of a number one single during the rock era (the first had been "Kansas City,"

only a week before).

The popularity of "The Battle of New Orleans" helped keep the "saga song" alive, a trend that began with the Kingston Trio's "Tom Dooley." Demands for Driftwood's songwriting grew so strong that he had to resign his teaching job and devote all his time to the music business.

The song was also the first pop hit for Horton, who had been recording country songs since he signed with Cormac Records in 1951. He signed with Columbia Records in 1956, after working for the Mercury and Abbott labels.

The date and place of his birth vary in different sources, but a majority agree that John Gale Horton was born in Los Angeles on November 30, 1929. His family moved to Tyler, Texas, when he was a child. His parents did migrant farm work, and Johnny's mother taught him to play the guitar. He excelled at basketball and received an athletic scholarship for Baylor University. He was attending the University of Seattle when he decided to drop out and

move to Alaska, where he worked in the fishing industry. He became a proficient fisherman and designed his own equipment, a talent that would earn him the nickname "the singing fisherman."

In 1950, Johnny moved back to Los Angeles and, at the urging of friends, entered a talent contest at the Harmony Park Corral. He won, leading to a guest spot on Cliffie Stone's "Hometown Jamboree" on KLAC and his own radio show on KXLA in Pasadena. A year later, he was signed to a regular spot on the "Louisiana Hayride Radio Show" on KWKH in Shreveport.

"The Battle of New Orleans" won two Grammys: one for Song of the Year and one for Best Country and Western Recording. *Billboard* ranked it as the number one single of 1959. Horton followed it with other saga songs, including "Sink the Bismarck" and "North to Alaska," the title song for the John Wayne movie.

Horton was invited to the premiere of the film in Alaska, but was having premonitions of his own death, and cancelled plans to go. He refused to fly on airplanes and rescheduled appearances.

On the fifth of November in 1960, he was performing at the Skyline club in Austin, Texas—the same club where Hank Williams made his final appearance before his death. Driving home to Shreveport on foggy U.S. Highway 79, Horton was killed in a head-on collision that also took the life of his guitarist, Gerald Tomlinson. In a sad coincidence, Horton's widow, Billie Jean, had once been married to Hank Williams.

### THE TOP FIVE
*Week of June 1, 1959*

1  **The Battle of New Orleans**
   Johnny Horton

2  **Kansas City**
   Wilbert Harrison

3  **Dream Lover**
   Bobby Darin

4  **Quiet Village**
   Martin Denny

5  **Personality**
   Lloyd Price

ABC-PARAMOUNT 10022 **Lonely Boy**
PAUL ANKA
**55**

*Writer: Paul Anka*

*Producer: Don Costa*

*July 13, 1959*
*4 weeks*

**B**Y 1959, Paul Anka was one of the youngest, most successful singer/songwriters in the business. He followed his number one single "Diana" [see 25] with several hits, including "You Are My Destiny." He was internationally famous, travelling all over the world. But success was not everything. When he was 17, a tragedy made him realize that in some ways, he truly was a "Lonely Boy."

Paul had always been particularly close to his mother. She was the one who lent him her car to drive to another province to enter a talent contest. She was the one who listened to his songs in the basement of their home before he would play them for others. And Paul, a loving son, bought her a new house, a new car and did anything he could for her. He was in Pittsburgh when he was informed via telephone that she had died of a liver ailment. She was only 39.

Paul sang "Lonely Boy" in the film *Girls Town*, in which he starred with Mamie Van Doren and Mel Torme. Directed by Charles Haas, it was the story of a "bad girl" sent to prison for a crime she didn't commit. It was Paul's second movie, following *Let's Rock* in 1958. "Lonely Boy" also became the title of an award-winning documentary about Anka.

After "Lonely Boy" went to number one, Paul had two number two hits: "Put Your Head on My Shoulder" and "Puppy Love." The latter was written about a crush he had on Annette Funicello. They worked on an album and toured together, but Paul's feelings for her were frowned upon by Disney officials, who couldn't see their prime female attraction falling in love with a young pop star. Paul was told he was just experiencing puppy love, which inspired the song.

On November 13, 1961, ABC-Paramount Records announced they had agreed to early termination of Anka's contract. A week later, RCA Victor signed Paul to a worldwide deal. Anka stayed with RCA through the end of the sixties and returned for a brief association in 1978.

Although he never had his own top ten single while signed to RCA, he did write some very big hits for other people. His success as a songwriter for others was foreshadowed in 1958 when he wrote "It Doesn't Matter Anymore" for his friend, Buddy Holly [see 26—"That'll Be the Day"]. The song charted less than three weeks after Holly was killed in an airplane crash on February 3, 1959.

In 1971 Anka wrote Tom Jones' biggest hit, "She's a Lady." The song he will always be remembered for writing was adapted from a French ballad he heard in 1968, *"Comme d'Habitude."* Paul bought the rights to the melody, wrote new words to it and gave it to Frank Sinatra to record under its new English title: "My Way."

Paul also wrote the music for the film "The Longest Day." He had a small role in the movie, and asked producer Daryl Zanuck if he could write the score. Zanuck said there would be no music in the film, but when he heard Anka's proposed compositions, he relented.

Another Paul Anka theme that was heard five times a week, to the tune of $30,000 a year in royalties, was the theme for NBC-TV's "The Tonight Show Starring Johnny Carson."

## THE TOP FIVE
*Week of July 13, 1959*

1 **Lonely Boy**
Paul Anka

2 **The Battle of New Orleans**
Johnny Horton

3 **Personality**
Lloyd Price

4 **Waterloo**
Stonewall Jackson

5 **Lipstick on Your Collar**
Connie Francis

# 56 A Big Hunk O' Love RCA 7600
## ELVIS PRESLEY

*Writers: Aaron Schroeder*
*Sid Jaxon*

*Producers: Steve Sholes*
*Chet Atkins*

*August 10, 1959*
*2 weeks*

WHEN Elvis Presley was inducted into the United States Army, RCA was desperate for him to record enough material to provide them with songs to release during his military stay. But Col. Tom Parker had other plans—he purposefully kept Elvis away from the studio to let the surplus of material dry up. Col. Parker wanted the public to be hungry for a new Elvis release when he got out of the Army in 1960; it's possible he also wanted leverage in contract negotiations due that year as well.

Elvis only had one recording session during his two-year Army hitch. He returned home to Nashville on his first furlough in June, 1958. He was in good physical condition from his basic training, and the vocal chords weren't in bad shape, either. It was June 10 when he went into RCA's Nashville studios for a two-day recording session.

Most of Elvis' regular musicians were there, except for Scotty Moore and Bill Black. Scotty was working for Fernwood Records in Memphis, but would work with Elvis again. Bill would not. He formed The Bill Black Combo and signed with Hi Records, scoring 17 chart entries on the Hot 100 between 1959-1965. He was 39 years old when he died on Oct. 21, 1965, four months after surgery for removal of a brain tumor.

Elvis recorded five songs during the two days: "(Now and Then There's) A Fool Such As I," "Ain't That Lovin' You Baby," "I Got Stung," "I Need Your Love Tonight" and "A Big Hunk O' Love."

On Sept. 19, Elvis set sail for Germany. The press conference he gave before leaving was recorded and released as an EP in March, 1959, "Elvis Sails." The USS General Randall arrived at Bremerhaven on October 1 and Elvis was taken to the Army base at Friedburg, just north of Frankfurt, where he would become a jeep driver.

"A Fool Such As I" was released in March, 1959, and only went to number two. "A Big Hunk O' Love" was the only other single released until Elvis' discharge. It came out in June and entered the Hot 100 on July 6. Five weeks later it was number one.

While "A Big Hunk O' Love" settled in for a two-week run at the top, a more important turn of events was affecting Elvis in Germany. He was introduced to Priscilla Beaulieu, 14-year-old stepdaughter of Capt. Joseph P. Bealieu. They saw each other often and fell in love; when Elvis left Germany, Priscilla was one of thousands of fans waving goodbye at the airport. He invited her to come to America and spend Christmas at Graceland in 1960. The next year, Elvis called Capt. Beaulieu in Germany and asked if Priscilla could complete her schooling in Memphis and live at Graceland under the supervision of Vernon Presley. She arrived in May, 1962, and attended Immaculate Conception High School until she graduated in June, 1963. Elvis and Priscilla were married on May 1, 1967 in Las Vegas. Their daughter, Lisa Marie, was born nine months to the day later, on February 1, 1968. Elvis and Priscilla were divorced on October 11, 1973.

## THE TOP FIVE
*Week of August 10, 1959*

1 **A Big Hunk O'Love**
Elvis Presley

2 **Lonely Boy**
Paul Anka

3 **My Heart is an Open Book**
Carl Dobkins, Jr.

4 **There Goes My Baby**
Drifters

5 **Lavender Blue**
Sammy Turner

*Writers: Jean Villard*
*Bert Reisfield*
*Dick Manning*

*Producer: Chet Atkins*

*August 24, 1959*
*4 weeks*

"THE THREE BELLS" was originally a French song, *"Les Trois Cloches,"* written by Jean Villard in 1945 and popularized around the world by Edith Piaf. *Les Compagnons de la Chanson*, also from France, recorded it as well, and when Bert Reisfield added English lyrics in 1948, they recorded that version, too. They performed it in England in 1951 and in America a year later, on Ed Sullivan's show.

Watching at home that Sunday night in Pine Bluff, Arkansas, was high school senior Jim Ed Brown. He loved the song, and not just because the hero was named Jimmy Brown. His high school choir added the song to their repertoire.

After graduation, Jim Ed entered a talent show on a dare from his sister, Maxine. He won first prize and called her up to the stage to sing a duet. That night, Little Rock radio station KLRA signed them to perform on the "Barnyard Frolics" show. They were signed as regulars for the "Louisiana Hayride" show in Shreveport, and younger sister Bonnie joined them to make the Browns a trio.

They signed with RCA Victor in 1956 and recorded a top ten country song, "I Take the Chance." The family's youngest sister, Norma, was called to fill in for Jim Ed Brown while he served in the Army. Continued success proved difficult, and in 1959 the family travelled to RCA's offices in Nashville to announce the break-up of the act.

They recorded what they thought would be their final song—"The Three Bells," which they had wanted to cut since their high school days. The song was six minutes long, so with the help of Chet Atkins and Anita Kerr, they edited it down to three minutes for single release.

"The Three Bells" entered the Hot 100 at number 63 on July 27, 1959, and was number one four weeks later, putting an end to any plans for breaking up the trio.

Instead, the group had two more top 20 hits—"Scarlet Ribbons (For Her Hair)" and "The Old Lamplighter"—and they continued to record together until 1967. On October 10 of that year, they made their final appearance, at the 42nd anniversary of the Grand Ole Opry. Maxine and Bonnie both retired and Jim Ed began a very successful solo career. By 1981 he had amassed more than 50 country chart entries.

## THE TOP FIVE
*Week of August 24, 1959*

1 **The Three Bells**
   Browns

2 **Sea of Love**
   Phil Phillips

3 **Lavender Blue**
   Sammy Turner

4 **A Big Hunk O'Love**
   Elvis Presley

5 **My Heart is an Open Book**
   Carl Dobkins, Jr.

# 58 Sleep Walk CANADIAN-AMERICAN 103
## SANTO AND JOHNNY

*Writers: Santo Farina*
*Johnny Farina*
*Ann Farina*

*Producer: Not Known*

*September 21, 1959*
*2 weeks*

Twenty-five instrumental songs have made it to number one in the rock era. More than half of them occurred between 1955-1962, followed by a five-year gap in which *no* instrumentals made it to the top of the pop chart. And only two instrumentals topped the Hot 100 in the '80s.

The final instrumental number one of the fifties was "Sleep Walk," a guitar duet by two brothers from Brooklyn who recorded for Canadian-American, a label that made its debut earlier in 1959.

Santo Farina was born on October 24, 1937, and his younger brother Johnny was born on April 30, 1941. Santo learned to play the steel guitar when he was nine years old, and he taught Johnny how to play. Johnny mastered the rhythm guitar when he was 12, and the two brothers were popular in school, where they played for dances and parties.

Santo and Johnny wrote "Sleep Walk" with their sister Ann and recorded it at Trinity Music in Manhattan. In February of 1959, Gene Orndorf of Minot, North Dakota, started a new label with offices in New York and Winnipeg, Manitoba, Canada. The label was appropriately named Canadian-American Records, and they leased the Santo and Johnny track. It entered the Hot 100 on July 27, and eight weeks later it was number one.

For the next three years, Santo and Johnny toured North America extensively, travelling over 100,000 miles. They continued to have chart records on Canadian-American through the beginning of 1964.

"Sleep Walk" was released in Europe, but there were more than 20 cover versions on the continent as well, including *"Grido"* by Niki Davis in Italy, *"Loa"* by Wim Van De Velde in Belgium and Holland, and *"Shada"* and *"Nuit Bleu,"* both by Caterina Valente, in Germany and France, respectively. Despite British cover versions by the Sleepwalkers, the Johnny Boys and Ken Kakintosh, Santo and Johnny's version went to number 22 in the United Kingdom.

"Sleep Walk" was the sixth number one instrumental of the rock era. Although 1959 was a good year for instrumentals, the best year was 1962, when three instrumentals went to number one [see 110—"Stranger on the Shore," 112—"The Stripper" and 121—"Telstar"]. But then no instrumentals went to the top of the chart in the years 1963-1967. The drought was broken in 1968 by Paul Mauriat [see 237—"Love Is Blue"]. In another five-year period, 1980-1984, the only number one instrumental was Vangelis' "Chariots of Fire," the main title theme from the Oscar-winning Best Picture.

## THE TOP FIVE
*Week of September 21, 1959*

1 **Sleep Walk**
  Santo and Johnny

2 **The Three Bells**
  Browns

3 **I'm Gonna Get Married**
  Lloyd Price

4 **('Til) I Kissed You**
  Everly Brothers

5 **Sea of Love**
  Phil Phillips

ATCO 6147 **Mack the Knife** **59**
BOBBY DARIN

*Writers: Kurt Weill*
*Berthold Brecht*
*Marc Blitzstein*

*Producer: Ahmet Ertegun*

*October 5, 1959*
*9 weeks*

"I'D like to be a legend by the time I'm 25 years old," Bobby Darin told Shana Alexander in *Life* magazine. It was a quote used against him to prove his arrogance and conceit. Few understood that Bobby felt he *had* to achieve greatness by the time he was 25; he didn't believe he would still be alive at 30.

Darin was well on his way to legendary status in the fall of 1959 when "Mack the Knife" topped the Hot 100 for nine weeks. But he knew his time was limited. As a child, he suffered from rheumatic fever attacks, and as an adult, he had a history of heart trouble. On December 10, 1973, he called for an ambulance to take him to Cedars-Sinai Medical Center in Los Angeles. Suffering from congestive heart failure, he slipped into a coma on December 18 and died two days later.

Darin was born Walden Robert Cassoto on May 14, 1936. His mother, Nina, was 17 years old. When she returned home from the Foundling Hospital for unwed mothers, she assumed the role of her child's "sister," and her mother, Polly, raised the boy as her own son. It wasn't until February, 1968 that Nina revealed their true relationship.

As a teenager, Darin graduated from the Bronx School of Science. After dropping out of Hunter College, he wrote some songs with another Bronx Science student, Don Kirshner. They brought one of their tunes to Connie Francis' manager, George Scheck, who arranged for Bobby to sign with Decca Records. The label released four singles that failed and dropped Darin, but Kirshner told his friend Ahmet Ertegun at Atlantic Records about this new singer, and Bobby was signed to the company's Atco subsidiary.

Three more failures followed, and Darin recorded what looked like his final single for Atco, a song with a title suggested by the mother of DJ Murray the K. The first single recorded on Atlantic's new eight-track machine, "Splish Splash" went to number three.

Unfortunately, Bobby had calculated it would not be a hit, and assuming his contract with Atco would not be renewed, recorded "Early in the Morning" for Brunswick Records as "the Rinky Dinks." When "Splish Splash" became a hit, Brunswick released their single. Atco retaliated and demanded Brunswick recall the record. Brunswick complied, but had Buddy Holly record the song to compete with Darin's version.

In a September 1, 1958 interview in *Billboard*, Darin stressed his desire to not be known just for singing rock and roll: "It's the only way to build a future in this business. In night clubs I lean to other things...I even do 'Mack the Knife' from *The Threepenny Opera.*"

Inspired by Louis Armstrong's recording of that Kurt Weill-Berthold Brecht song, Darin included it in his album "That's All." Darin didn't want it released as a 45, but Atco issued it anyway, resulting in Darin's biggest hit ever and two Grammy Awards, for Best New Artist of 1959 and Best Vocal Performance by a Male.

Darin left Atco for Capitol Records in 1962, but returned to Atlantic in 1966, when he scored with Tim Hardin's "If I Were a Carpenter." Robert Kennedy's death deeply affected him, causing him to drop out of show business for a year and retire to Big Sur. He came back in 1969 with a thoughtful album of self-written songs on his own label. His final label affiliation was with Motown in 1972-1973.

In his lifetime, Darin excelled not only in records, but in motion pictures (receiving an Oscar nomination for Best Supporting Actor for his role in *Captain Newman, M.D.* in 1963), television (starring in his own NBC prime time variety series in the summer of 1972 and the winter of 1973) and personal appearances (headlining in Las Vegas at age 23).

Numerologists may want to take note: "Mack the Knife" is the 59th number one single of the rock era; it entered the Hot 100 at number 59, and it was *Billboard's* number two single of the year 1959.

"Mack the Knife's" nine-week run at number one was interrupted on November 16, 1959 by the Fleetwoods.

## THE TOP FIVE
*Week of October 5, 1959*

1 **Mack the Knife**
Bobby Darin

2 **Put Your Head on my Shoulder**
Paul Anka

3 **Sleep Walk**
Santo and Johnny

4 **('Til) I Kissed You**
Everly Brothers

5 **The Three Bells**
Browns

## 60 Mr. Blue DOLTON 5
## THE FLEETWOODS

*Writer: Dewayne Blackwell*

*Producer: Bob Reisdorff*

*November 16, 1959*
*1 week*

"**M**R. BLUE" was the Fleetwoods' second number one single, but lead singer Gary Troxel didn't think it would be a big hit. Producer Bob Reisdorff, who had assured the group it would be very difficult to find a song that would do as well as "Come Softly to Me" [see 51], was convinced "Mr. Blue" would sell a million. He was willing to let Gary drive his Corvette for two weeks if the song went to number one. When it did, Gary borrowed Bob's Corvette and then bought one for himself.

He didn't get to drive it around his native Olympia, Washington, for very long. Before the Fleetwoods recorded "Come Softly to Me," Gary had signed up for the Naval Reserves in high school. After the success of their two number one singles, the group had offers to tour Europe and Australia, but had to turn them down. "Gary was always 30 days away from the gallows," Gretchen Christopher notes.

Finally, he had to serve. He was stationed in San Diego, and Gretchen and Barbara Ellis would meet him in Los Angeles when he was on leave to record new singles and albums. Touring was out, but they made an appearance at the Hollywood Bowl.

"Mr. Blue" was written for the Platters by Dewayne Blackwell, but he didn't know how to get the song to them. Blackwell, a songwriter who performed with his brother and sis-

ter, met a record promoter in Washington state who knew Reisdorff. Accompanied by his family, Dewayne met the Fleetwoods in a hotel room to play his songs for them.

He sang "Mr. Blue," and Gretchen recalls: "We said, 'it's a great song, why don't you record it yourselves?' and he said, 'if we ever record it, it'll never be heard of. If the Fleetwoods record it, every DJ in the country will play it automatically.'" A few days later, Blackwell received a telegram from the group, telling him they were recording "Mr. Blue" as the "A" side of their new single.

It was the biggest hit of Blackwell's songwriting career, although he had several more chart records, including the Everly Brothers' "The Ferris Wheel" (written with his brother), Bobby Vee's "Hickory, Dick and Doc" and Sam the Sham and the Pharaohs' "Oh That's Good, No That's Bad."

The Fleetwoods continued to chart on Dolton Records (the original label name, Dolphin, was changed because of a conflict with a publishing

company using that name) until 1963. Their final hit, a cover version of "Goodnight My Love," featured Barbara as lead singer. Gary had been lead singer on most of their tracks, a source of irritation for the two women in the Fleetwoods, and "Goodnight My Love" was only meant to be an album track, until radio airplay forced its release as a single.

The Fleetwoods parted ways in 1966, but reunited in 1971 for four sold-out shows at the New York Academy of Music. They continued to perform through 1973. They came back together to appear at the Bumbershoot Festival in Seattle with Dolton labelmates the Ventures. Liberty Records, which distributed and eventually bought Dolton, unearthed a cache of unreleased masters, and Gretchen helped edit them into a new album, *Buried Treasure*, released in 1983. While Barbara chose to spend time at home with her family in Southern California, Gary and Gretchen continued to tour as the Fleetwoods with the addition of partner Cheryl Huggins.

### THE TOP FIVE

*Week of November 16, 1959*

1 **Mr. Blue**
  Fleetwoods

2 **Mack the Knife**
  Bobby Darin

3 **Don't You Know**
  Della Reese

4 **Put Your Head on my Shoulder**
  Paul Anka

5 **Heartaches by the Number**
  Guy Mitchell

COLUMBIA 41476 **Heartaches by the Number** **61**
GUY MITCHELL

*Writer: Harlan Howard*

*Producer: Mitch Miller*

*December 14, 1959*
*2 weeks*

Guy Mitchell's biggest hit, "Singing the Blues" [see 16], was originally recorded by Marty Robbins for the country market; lightning struck twice when Guy recorded Ray Price's country hit "Heartaches by the Number" and turned that into a number one pop hit, too.

Mitchell's follow-ups to "Singing the Blues" were not big hits. "Knee Deep in the Blues" did go as high as 16, and "Rock-a-Billy" even went to 10—but it was "Heartaches by the Number" that put him back on top.

Mitchell pursued dual careers during the fifties and sixties. All the time he was having hits on the charts, he was also working full time as an actor. His first film role was in Paramount's *Those Redheads from Seattle*, starring Rhonda Fleming, Gene Barry and Teresa Brewer. Guy had a hit song from the film, "Chicka Boom."

A year later, he starred in *Red Garters* with Jack Carson, Rosemary Clooney and Barry again. From this movie came another hit song for Guy, "A Dime and a Dollar."

Guy became a television star, too. "The Guy Mitchell Show," a half-hour variety series, premiered on ABC on October 7, 1957 and ran for three months at 8 p.m. on Monday nights. He was also cast as Detective George Romack in "Whispering Smith," an NBC series starring Audie Murphy that was supposed to debut in the fall of 1959. After seven episodes were filmed, Guy broke his shoulder and the series' premiere was postponed until May 15, 1961. It ran for only four months.

Guy also became a big star in Britain, where his version of "Singing the Blues" battled a cover version by English actor Tommy Steele. At one point, both versions held the top two positions on the British chart, with Mitchell at number one.

He made three whirlwind tours of England. In 1952, he filled in for an ailing Jack Benny at the London Palladium and sold out every seat of his two-week stand. Two years later, he was invited, along with Frankie Laine, to sing for Queen Elizabeth II at the Royal Command Performance. He was a guest star in the first showing of ITV's "Sunday Night at the London Palladium," and had his own one-hour British TV special.

Mitchell's last appearance on the Hot 100 was in 1960. Two years later, Columbia Records dropped him from the label. He released some singles on the Joy label and then recorded briefly for Reprise before signing with Starday Records in Nashville. When that label folded, he released a couple of singles on his own GMI label.

Mitchell died in Las Vegas on July 1, 1999, of complications following surgery. He was survived by his widow, two sons and five grandchildren.

## THE TOP FIVE
*Week of December 14, 1959*

1 **Heartaches by the Number**
Guy Mitchell

2 **Mr. Blue**
Fleetwoods

3 **Mack the Knife**
Bobby Darin

4 **In the Mood**
Ernie Fields

5 **Why**
Frankie Avalon

## 62 Why CHANCELLOR 1045
### FRANKIE AVALON

Writers: Bob Marcucci
   Peter DeAngelis

Producers: Bob Marcucci
    Peter DeAngelis

December 28, 1959
1 week

THE final number one song of the fifties was "Why," the shortest title yet of any chart-topping song. It was the second number one for Frankie Avalon, the South Philadelphian singer discovered by Bob Marcucci.

Marcucci's life story was fictionalized in the 1980 motion picture *The Idolmaker*, starring Ray Sharkey. Marcucci was technical advisor to the film, which told of a frustrated performer who discovers two teen idols. In reality, Marcucci discovered and managed Avalon, who then told his manager about a 15-year-old student who looked like a cross between Elvis Presley and Ricky Nelson—Fabiano Forte, better known as Fabian.

Marcucci and his partner Peter DeAngelis wrote "Why" for Avalon. "I was always a firm believer in the team of Marcucci-DeAngelis because I think they had a real good feel for writing songs," Frankie says. "I thought 'Why' was a nice song—not a number one song, but they thought it was."

As "Why" climbed to the chart summit, Frankie was embarking on an acting career. Marcucci told him to diversify, so he took acting and voice lessons. He won a part in *Guns of the Timberland* with Alan Ladd and followed that with a role in *The Alamo*

starring John Wayne. Avalon says he couldn't take full advantage of the success of "Why": "While it was riding the chart, I was on location for four months in the middle of Racketville, Texas, riding a horse."

Avalon's concentration on movie work detracted from his recording career. "Why" was his seventh and final top 10 song, and none of his subsequent singles were able to break through to the top 20. His final chart single was a disco version of his first number one record, "Venus," recorded for De-Lite Records in late 1975.

Frankie's motion picture credits include *Voyage to the Bottom of the Sea*, *The Carpetbaggers*, and *Panic in the Year Zero* with Ray Milland. The latter film was a turning point in Avalon's film career because he developed a good relationship with

the production company, American International Pictures. With his manager, his agent and the screenwriter of *Panic in the Year Zero*, Avalon developed the idea for AIP's beach party movies. They all thought Frankie's one-time girlfriend, Annette Funicello, would be the perfect female lead, and Disney Studios agreed to loan her out. The films are still popular on television, and Frankie and Annette starred in a 1987 update: *Back to the Beach*.

In 1978, Frankie had a cameo role in the highest-grossing movie musical of all time, *Grease*. Appearing in a fantasy sequence, he sang "Beauty School Dropout."

Avalon has given up Philadelphia for the suburbs of Los Angeles. He lives in the San Fernando Valley with his wife and eight children—four sons and four daughters.

### THE TOP FIVE
*Week of December 28, 1959*

1 **Why**
 Frankie Avalon

2 **El Paso**
 Marty Robbins

3 **The Big Hurt**
 Toni Fisher

4 **It's Time to Cry**
 Paul Anka

5 **Way Down Yonder in New Orleans**
 Freddy Cannon

*Writer: Marty Robbins*

*Producer: Don Law*

*January 4, 1960*
*2 weeks*

*I always wanted to write a song about El Paso, because traditionally that is where the West begins....Had I been born a little sooner, the cowboy life is the kind of life I'd have liked to have lived.*
—MARTY ROBBINS

"**E**L PASO" is a landmark song in many ways. It was the first number one single of the sixties, the first country song to win a Grammy and the longest single to go to number one to date. At 4:40, it was so long that Columbia Records rejected Robbins' request to release "El Paso" as a single. Instead, he and the label mutually agreed to put it on an album titled *Gunfighter Ballads and Trail Songs.* The album was in release for four weeks when the requests for a single of "El Paso" became so strong, company executives relented and decided to release a 45 despite its unusual length.

The cowboy/hero who sings "El Paso" dies at the end, but a resurrection was attempted in 1977 in a sequel, "El Paso City." That song may not be on the tip of your tongue, but "El Paso" is and probably always will be the definitive song about the Texas city. Despite that, the song has never been considered for the city's official song. According to the *Los Angeles Times,* on October 14, 1980, the city council of El Paso adopted a song written by resident Leona Washington. The city clerk did not know the name of the song, nor could he find it in the municipal records.

Marty Robbins said he had been fascinated with the city and its name ever since he was a child, growing up in a state that borders El Paso: Arizona. Born September 26, 1925 as Martin D. Robinson, he was raised in Glendale, Arizona. His family moved to Phoenix when he was 12.

Robbins learned to play the guitar during his three-year hitch in the Navy. After his discharge he returned to Phoenix and worked as a ditch digger, a truck driver and labored in the oil fields. He hated all

of it, and one night filled in when a guitarist failed to show up for a friend's band. When the lead singer became sick, Marty took over those duties, too.

Robbins and his band were working for radio station KPHO when Columbia Records artist Little Jimmy Dickens guest starred on the "Caravan" show with Marty. Dickens was so impressed, he told his label to sign Robbins. After his first single, "Love Me or Leave Me Alone," Marty guest starred on Nashville's "Grand Ole Opry" and became a regular in February, 1953. On March 1, 1958, after an argument with WSM station manager Robert Cooper, Robbins was fired from the Opry, but five days later, after apologies on both sides, he was hired back. Robbins remained with the Opry through four decades, and was both the last person to perform in Ryman Auditorium and the first person to appear on stage at the Opry's new home, Opryland.

He had several pop hits between 1956-1962, including "A White Sport Coat (And a Pink Carnation)," "Don't

Worry" and "Devil Woman." He continued to have hits on the country charts until his death on December 8, 1982. He had suffered a heart attack in 1969 and underwent arterial heart surgery, but recovered and returned to recording and performing. He was having a quadruple bypass operation at St. Thomas Hospital in Nashville when he died of a heart attack.

---

## THE TOP FIVE
*Week of January 4, 1960*

1  **El Paso**
   Marty Robbins

2  **Why**
   Frankie Avalon

3  **The Big Hurt**
   Toni Fisher

4  **Running Bear**
   Johnny Preston

5  **Way Down Yonder in New Orleans**
   Freddy Cannon

## 64 Running Bear Mercury 71474
### JOHNNY PRESTON

*Writer: J.P. Richardson*

*Producer: J.P. Richardson*

*January 18, 1960*
*3 weeks*

WHEN Buddy Holly was killed in a plane crash [see 26—"That'll Be the Day"], he left behind a collection of songs that has made him a legendary figure in rock music. Two other artists died in the fateful accident, Ritchie Valens and J.P. Richardson, better known as "The Big Bopper." While they have not been as influential as Holly, their careers were too short for us to know what heights they may have reached. All that's left is speculation, based on the brief amount of time they spent with us.

Jape Richardson was a singer, a songwriter and a disc jockey. He was born October 24, 1930, in Sabine Pass, Texas. Not fond of his given name, he used J.P. Richardson on the air at KTRM in Beaumont, Texas,

and recorded rockabilly songs as "The Big Bopper." When Mercury Records executive Shelby Singleton came to Texas looking for new talent, he signed Richardson and his protege, Johnny Preston.

The Big Bopper's big hit was "Chantilly Lace," which peaked at number three on November 3, 1958. He had only one more chart record before he was killed on February 3, 1959, and he did not live long enough to see his song "Running Bear" by Johnny Preston go to number one on January 18, 1960.

John Preston Courville was born August 18, 1939 in Port Arthur, Texas. He sang in the high school choir and organized a band, the Shades, which became popular in southern Texas. The Shades were playing at a club in Beaumont when Richardson and a friend, record producer Bill Hall, spotted Preston and liked his singing enough to approach him about recording.

Preston's first session did not go

well at all. The teenager was too nervous to sing well, and the results were too poor to even be considered for release. Richardson still believed in the young singer, and wrote a song for him that was inspired by a commercial for Dove soap. He asked him to record again, but wouldn't tell him anything about the new song. Accompanied by singer George Jones, Preston drove to Houston where J.P. played "Running Bear" for him.

Johnny was not impressed. But Richardson insisted, and Preston agreed to record the song. Richardson, Jones and Bill Hall sang the "oom-pah-pah" Indian chant in the background while Johnny sang about the Indian brave Running Bear and his love for little White Dove.

Mercury was ready to release the single when Richardson was killed. After his death, label execs decided to postpone issuing the song. It finally came out in the autumn of 1959, debuting on the Hot 100 on October 12. Amazingly, it faltered and actually fell off the chart. It re-entered the survey on November 23, becoming the first song to exit the chart, then re-enter and go all the way to number one.

Preston had two more hits, "Cradle of Love" and a cover version of Shirley and Lee's "Feel So Good," retitled "Feel So Fine." He had two more chart entries, including a version of Little Willie John's "Leave My Kitten Alone" (a song also recorded by the Beatles). But without his mentor, Preston couldn't sustain his career and had his last chart record in 1961.

### THE TOP FIVE
*Week of January 18, 1960*

1 **Running Bear**
Johnny Preston

2 **Why**
Frankie Avalon

3 **El Paso**
Marty Robbins

4 **The Big Hurt**
Toni Fisher

5 **Way Down Yonder
in New Orleans**
Freddy Cannon

*Writer: Jean Surrey*
*Red Surrey*

*Producer: Jim Vinneau*

*February 8, 1960*
*2 weeks*

IF rock and roll records were filed by the Dewey Decimal System, there would be a separate classification set aside for tragedy songs. There have been some classics over the years, like Ray Peterson's "Tell Laura I Love Her," the Everly Brothers' "Ebony Eyes" and J. Frank Wilson's "Last Kiss," but preceding all of them was Mark Dinning's "Teen Angel."

Mark was surrounded by music while growing up in Grant County, Oklahoma, although his future seemed set when he won first prize in his local 4H club for raising turkeys. His father was an evangelist minister, his baby sitter was Clara Ann Fowler (later to be known as Patti Page) and three of his sisters formed a vocal group in the 1940s, the Dinning Sisters (they had a top 10 single in 1948 with the Oscar-winning "Buttons and Bows").

At 17, Mark took up the electric guitar and appeared in local clubs with his brother Ace. It was goodbye turkey farming, hello rock and roll. He was drafted after graduating from high school, and made a decision while serving in the army that he would sign a recording contract when he was discharged.

Back in civilian life in 1957, Mark auditioned for publisher Wesley Rose in Nashville. Rose liked what he heard and telephoned his friend Mitch Miller at Columbia Records in New York. Miller had signed a new recording artist that very day—his name was Johnny Mathis—and wasn't looking for any other new male singers. Within six weeks, Rose had signed Mark to MGM Records.

Mark's sister Jean, one of the three performing Dinning sisters, was reading a magazine article in 1959 about juvenile delinquency. The author suggested that good kids needed a name, and offered "teen angels." "Being a songwriter, I said that's a title, what can I do with it?" Jean explains. She wrote half of the song, then woke up in the middle of the night and, as if someone had handed her a lyric, suddenly knew what the rest of the words would be.

At a family dinner at her parents' farm in Tennessee, Jean played several demos, including "Teen Angel" for Mark while he was eating. He asked to hear "Teen Angel" again, and before the dinner dishes could be cleared a microphone and tape recorder were set up on the table so he could record it. "We had some 45s made," says Jean. "We mailed one to Mark, and waited a month to hear from him. We finally called and he said he hadn't opened the package yet because he didn't have a record player."

Jean told him to take it to the nearest record store and play it immediately. A crowd gathered around the listening booth and asked where they could buy the record, and Mark excitedly took the demo to Rose. Wesley became hooked on it, and Felice Bryant suggested changing "are you flying up above" to "are you somewhere up above." Wesley called Jean in Chicago and invited her to the recording session to sing backing vocals, but she had just given birth to her daughter and couldn't make the trip.

Many radio stations were reluctant to play the song, but Howard Miller in Chicago was a Dinning Sisters fan, and was the first to play it. Jean was listening at home when Miller asked his audience to phone in their reaction to the tragic storyline, and the approval was overwhelming. On February 8, 1960, Jean received a phone call from her sister Lou in California, telling her to grab a copy of *Billboard*, because "Teen Angel" had gone to number one.

Despite its success, some radio stations still refused to play the song. Jean still remembers a headline in a British trade paper, "Blood Runs in the Grooves."

A footnote about the writing credits on "Teen Angel": Jean made an agreement with her husband at the time, Red Surrey, that both their names would go on any songs either one of them wrote. "When we were divorced, 'Teen Angel' was turned back over to me as part of the settlement. It didn't seem like a hot property at the time and was past its peak. Not long after, a friend called and said 'Teen Angel' was in a movie...*American Grafitti*."

## THE TOP FIVE

*Week of February 8, 1960*

1 **Teen Angel**
  Mark Dinning

2 **Running Bear**
  Johnny Preston

3 **Where or When**
  Dion & the Belmonts

4 **El Paso**
  Marty Robbins

5 **Handy Man**
  Jimmy Jones

## 66 Theme from 'A Summer Place' COLUMBIA 41490
### PERCY FAITH

*Writer: Max Steiner*

*Producer: Percy Faith*

*February 22, 1960*
*9 weeks*

THE most successful instrumental single of the rock era is "Theme from 'A Summer Place'" by Percy Faith. It was number one on the Hot 100 for nine weeks, ranking it well above the other 24 instrumental songs that have topped the chart since July, 1955. It was also *Billboard's* number one single of 1960.

Max Steiner composed the score for the 1959 film *A Summer Place*, which starred Dorothy McGuire,

Richard Egan, Sandra Dee, Troy Donahue and Arthur Kennedy. Critics likened it to a steamier *Peyton Place*, released the year before.

Faith had already experienced success with recording film themes; in 1953, his "Song from Moulin Rouge" was the best-selling single of the year. He duplicated that feat with "Theme from 'A Summer Place,'" the number one single of 1960.

Faith was born April 7, 1908, in Toronto, Canada. He learned to play the violin when he was seven. At 11, he was already working, playing piano at a silent film theater. He gave his first concert recital at 15, at the Toronto Conservatory of Music.

A tragic accident occured when he was 18. His sister's clothing caught fire, and Faith stamped out the flames with his hands. His burns were so severe that doctors told him he could not play the piano for five years.

He turned to composing and conducting, and seven years later was hired by the Canadian Broadcasting Company to be staff arranger and conductor. His radio show, "Music by Faith," became popular all over Canada, and after two years, the Mutual Broadcasting System picked it up for America.

Faith moved to the United States in 1940 to conduct "The Carnation Contented Hour," and by the end of the decade he had become an American citizen. Mitch Miller hired him to be director of popular music for Columbia Records in 1950, where he arranged other artists' material and recorded his own songs.

Aside from "Song from Moulin Rouge," his biggest pre-rock era hits were "Delicado" (also number one), "I Cross My Fingers," "All of My Love" and "On Top of Old Smokey," with Burl Ives. In 1955, Faith was nominated for an Oscar for scoring *Love Me or Leave Me*.

"Theme from 'A Summer Place'" was not an immediate hit. It was reviewed in the September 28, 1959 issue of *Billboard*, but didn't enter the Hot 100 until January 11, 1960. Six weeks later it began its nine-week run at number one.

Percy recorded a disco version of the song in 1976. On February 9 of that year, he died, a victim of cancer.

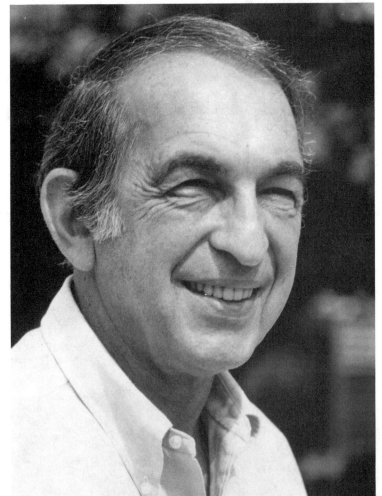

### THE TOP FIVE
*Week of February 22, 1960*

1 **Theme from 'A Summer Place'**
Percy Faith

2 **Teen Angel**
Mark Dinning

3 **Handy Man**
Jimmy Jones

4 **He'll Have to Go**
Jim Reeves

5 **What in the World's Come Over You**
Jack Scott

Writers: *Aaron Schroeder*
*J. Leslie McFarland*

Producer: *Steve Sholes*

*April 25, 1960*
*4 weeks*

**O**N March 1, 1960, Elvis Presley's Army unit threw a farewell party for the world's most famous G.I. By an odd coincidence, the party was organized by Capt. Marion Keisker—the woman who was Sam Phillips' assistant when Elvis wandered into the Memphis Recording Company in 1953 to record two songs for his mother.

She had left Sun to join the military, and was working with the Armed Forces Television Network in Germany.

Elvis arrived at Fort Dix, New Jersey in the middle of a blizzard. He was discharged on March 5 and RCA couldn't wait to get him into a recording studio. Anticipation of a new Elvis single was so great that, without knowing what the song title would be, RCA had racked up advance orders of 1,275,077—the highest advance sale of any single to date.

The catalog number 7740 was already assigned to this greatly-awaited single when Elvis went into RCA's Nashville studios on March 20. The two-day session produced six songs: "A Mess of Blues," "Soldier Boy," "It Feels So Right," "Make Me Know It," "Fame and Fortune" and "Stuck on You." The last two became Elvis' first post-Army single, and his first to be released in stereo.

On March 26, Elvis was a guest star on "The Frank Sinatra-Timex Show," taped in the Grand Ballroom of the Hotel Fontainebleu in Miami Beach. Col. Parker negotiated a salary of $125,000 for the appearance, Elvis' last on television for eight years. Elvis sang both "Stuck on You" and "Fame and Fortune," and performed Sinatra's "Witchcraft" while Sinatra sang "Love Me Tender." The *Billboard* review preferred Frank's other guest stars: "The impression lingers...that Presley has much to learn before he can work in the same league with pros like Sinatra, Joey Bishop and especially Sammy Davis Jr."

"Stuck on You" entered the Hot 100 on April 4, and was number one three weeks later, where it remained on May 12, the date the Sinatra special was telecast.

In addition to resuming his recording career, it was time for Elvis to go back to work in Hollywood. He reported to Paramount Studios to star in his fifth movie, *G.I. Blues*, directed by Hal Wallis. Background footage had already been shot while Elvis was in Germany, and the plot paralleled his army career. He portrays Tulsa McLean, a soldier based in West Germany who starts a musical group with some Army buddies. The cast includes Juliet Prowse, James Douglas and Robert Ivers.

The critics, the fans and even Elvis were disappointed with *G.I. Blues*. The thin characters, see-through plot and innocuous songs didn't prevent the film from grossing over four million dollars, but Elvis told the Colonel to find a better role for his next movie.

## THE TOP FIVE
*Week of April 25, 1960*

1 **Stuck on You**
Elvis Presley

2 **Greenfields**
Brothers Four

3 **Sink the Bismarck**
Johnny Horton

4 **Theme from 'A Summer Place'**
Percy Faith

5 **He'll Have to Go**
Jim Reeves

## 68 Cathy's Clown Warner Brothers 5151
### EVERLY BROTHERS

Writers: *Don Everly*
*Phil Everly*

Producer: *Wesley Rose*

*May 23, 1960*
*5 weeks*

**A**FTER nine consecutive hits on Archie Bleyer's Cadence Records, the Everly Brothers signed a 10-year, $1,000,000 contract with a brand-new label based in Burbank, California: Warner Brothers. Their very first single for their new company, "Cathy's Clown," became their biggest U.S. hit ever. It was also their most successful British single—of their five number ones there, it was on top the longest (seven weeks). It was also the first single to be number one simultaneously in America and Great Britain.

The break with Archie was a result of disagreements about royalty payments and the direction their music would take. The Warner Brothers offer meant financial security for a decade—not to be taken lightly when no one knew if rock and roll would survive longer than the five years it had dominated the music business.

"Cathy's Clown" was written just after a tour. Home in Nashville, Don and Phil were under pressure from Warner Brothers to come up with a first single. They had recorded eight songs already, but didn't feel that any of them were right. Phil was living with his parents, and one day he got a call from Don to come over to his house and finish a song. Phil helped Don write the verses, and two days later they recorded "Cathy's Clown."

The Everlys had six more top ten songs on Warner Brothers, including "When Will I Be Loved," "Ebony Eyes" and "Crying in the Rain." But after "That's Old Fashioned (That's the Way Love Should Be)" in 1962, they never made the top 30 again. They joined the Marine Corps

Reserves that year and were on active duty for six months. When they returned to civilian life, they were never able to regain their momentum.

They continued to record and perform together, and in 1970 they hosted a summer replacement show for Johnny Cash, a weekly one-hour TV series called "Johnny Cash Presents the Everly Brothers Show."

One of the saddest days in their career was Friday, the 13th of July in 1973. They were performing together on stage at the John Wayne Theater in Knott's Berry Farm in Buena Park, California, when Phil threw his guitar down and stormed off stage, leaving Don to tell the stunned audience that the Everly Brothers were through, forever.

During the next ten years, they did not perform together, and the press reported that they did not even speak to each other. Both recorded solo material, and Phil had a top ten single in England—a duet with Cliff Richard called "She Means Nothing to Me."

Their emotional reunion concerts took place September 22 and 23, 1983 at the Royal Albert Hall in London. Singing together in perfect harmony again, it was as if no time had passed at all. A live double album of the concert was released, and Home Box Office broadcast a two-hour video of the show. Don and Phil connected with Dave Edmunds, who produced their first new studio album in a decade. And Paul McCartney, who with John Lennon once referred to themselves as the "Foreverly Brothers," wrote their comeback single, "On the Wings of a Nightingale."

### THE TOP FIVE
*Week of May 23, 1960*

1 **Cathy's Clown**
Everly Brothers

2 **Stuck on You**
Elvis Presley

3 **Good Timin'**
Jimmy Jones

4 **Greenfields**
Brothers Four

5 **Night**
Jackie Wilson

MGM 12899 **Everybody's Somebody's Fool**
CONNIE FRANCIS

Writers: *Jack Keller*
*Howard Greenfield*

Producers: *Joe Sherman  Arnold Maxin*

*June 27, 1960*
*2 weeks*

IF someone asked you to name a Connie Francis song, you'd be more likely to think of "Who's Sorry Now," "Stupid Cupid" or "Where the Boys Are" before you would name any of her three number one songs. The first was the country-flavored "Everybody's Somebody's Fool," and it was an international hit, thanks to Connie's decision to record it in many other languages, starting with German.

Howard Greeenfield had already written hits for Connie with his regular partner, Neil Sedaka [see 114—"Breaking Up is Hard to Do"] when Connie telephoned him to write a special type of song. "I called Howie and asked him to write me a country song," explains Connie. "A couple of months later, when I came back from Europe, I was looking specifically for a country song to put foreign lyrics to."

Connie asked Greenfield if the song was ready. "He said, 'Well, it's not country—we wrote a kind of LaVern Baker-type blues ballad.' I said forget about that—just take your ballad and play it uptempo like 'Heartaches by the Number.' "

"Everybody's Somebody's Fool" was completed in two takes and became Connie's first number one song. But it was a long road to the top, and Connie almost quit before she got there.

She was born Concetta Rosa Maria Franconero on December 12, 1938 in Newark, New Jersey. Her father, George, was a roofing contractor who played the concertina for a hobby. When his daughter was three, he gave her a 12-bass accordion and soon she was singing at church benefits, family gatherings, hospitals and clubs. She appeared on "Arthur Godfrey's Talent Scouts" and Godfrey suggested the name change to the more Americanized Connie Francis.

At age 11, she and her father went into Manhattan to get Connie on a children's television show, "Startime." Connie remembers: "We flagged down the producer of the show, George Scheck, who was hailing a taxi cab, and my father said to

**THE TOP FIVE**
*Week of June 27, 1960*

1  **Everybody's Somebody's Fool**
   Connie Francis

2  **Cathy's Clown**
   Everly Brothers

3  **Alley-Oop**
   Hollywood Argyles

4  **Burning Bridges**
   Jack Scott

5  **Because They're Young**
   Duane Eddy

him, 'Would you listen to my daughter Connie sing.' He said, 'I'm up to here with singers, I can't use singers,' and that's when the accordion saved my life." Connie's father said his daughter played the accordion and Scheck handed them his card and said he would give the young girl an audition. Connie was on "Startime" for four years.

But she got rid of the accordion right away. Ted Mack told her to drop it; Godfrey said she should lose it and even Scheck, who became her manager, agreed. "So I said 150 Americans can't be wrong, this thing's got to be a loser...in 1967 there was a big flood in my basement and the accordion died. I threw a real big party."

Her recording career started by singing demos for music publishers. She would have to sound like Patti Page, or Kay Starr, or Jo Stafford—anyone but Connie Francis. "When I was 16 years old, a music publisher by the name of Lou Levy put up about $5,000 necessary for me to record my first very own session. They brought it around to every recording company in the business and everywhere they heard the same story—they were turned down. I remember Mitch Miller at Columbia said, 'Save your money, this girl's got nothing.' Thanks, Mitch. And finally over at MGM Harry Myerson signed me to my first recording contract."

Connie's first single for MGM was "Freddy." "That dippy song proved to be a stroke of good luck for me...the reason I got signed to the contract in the first place by Myerson was not because he thought I would be the hottest thing on wax, but because he had a son by the name of Freddy, and he thought it would be a cute birthday present...talk about luck!"

Yes, talk about luck...Connie didn't have any for her first *ten* singles. Not a one made the chart. She was selecting songs for her final MGM recording session—the label had lost interest in her and she decided to accept a scholarship to New York University and give up the record business—when her father came up with a suggestion Connie considered much too square: a 1923 song, "Who's Sorry Now."

# 70 Alley-Oop LUTE 5905
## THE HOLLYWOOD ARGYLES

*Writer: Dallas Frazier*

*Producers: Kim Fowley*
*Gary S. Paxton*

*July 11, 1960*
*1 week*

THE HOLLYWOOD ARGYLES have the reputation of being one of the rock era's one-hit-wonders. They had one number one single, "Alley-Oop," then never made the chart again. Actually, when "Alley-Oop" was recorded, there were no Hollywood Argyles. Gary Paxton, who had scored two hits ("It was I," "Cherry Pie") as the latter half of Skip and Flip, had been advised that he was still under contract to his former record label, Brent Records, when he came to Hollywood and recorded "Alley-Oop." To avoid any legal hassles, he made up a fictitious group named after the street in Hollywood that intersected Sunset Boulevard where the studio was located: Argyle.

It was only later that Paxton found out he was no longer under contract to Brent. Had he known that at the time, he explains, he would have recorded "Alley-Oop" under his real name of Gary Paxton instead of dreaming up the Hollywood Argyles.

Gary was attending the University of Arizona in Tucson when he formed his first group, the Pledges, with fellow student Clyde Battin. Battin was working as a disc jockey at local radio station KMOP, and later became Skip to Gary's Flip. Personal differences broke up the duo, and Gary moved to Washington and Oregon before deciding to try his luck in Hollywood.

### THE TOP FIVE
*Week of July 11, 1960*

1  **Alley-Oop**
   Hollywood Argyles

2  **I'm Sorry**
   Brenda Lee

3  **Everybody's Somebody's Fool**
   Connie Francis

4  **Because They're Young**
   Duane Eddy

5  **Mule Skinner Blues**
   Fendermen

"I'm coming down the freeway and I didn't know where Hollywood was," Paxton explains. "I pulled off at Universal (studios) and drove into a filling station at two in the morning. There were two guys sitting on top of a desk at this all-night station. I asked,'You know where Hollywood is?'"

One of the two men was songwriter Dallas Frazier. He recognized Gary from his Skip and Flip days. "They said, 'We'll lead you to Hollywood when we get off work at six in the morning.'"

In Hollywood at last, Gary found an apartment for $7.50 a week at the corner of Selma and El Centro. There he met record producer Kim Fowley, and they started hanging out at a Chevron Station at the fateful corner of Sunset and Argyle. They formed a music publishing company, Maverick Music, and used the pay phone at the station for their business number. Through Fowley's friend Terry Melcher [see 178—"Mr. Tambourine Man"], Gary met the owner of Lute Records, Al Kavlin.

Gary recorded Frazier's song "Alley-Oop" for Lute. Because there were problems with finding a distributor in New York, Larry Uttal, President of Manhattan-based, Madison Records, released a cover version of the song by Dante and the Evergreens. They gave Paxton some competition, especially in the New York area, but they only reached number 15 on the Hot 100 while the Hollywood Argyles went to number one. After the song was a hit, Gary put together a Hollywood Argyles band to make personal appearances, but after one album he felt he hadn't been paid what he was due and left the label.

Paxton started his own label, Garpax, and produced a number one single for Bobby 'Boris' Pickett [see 118—"Monster Mash"]. In the '80s Paxton and his wife had a daily Christian radio talk show in Nashville. He has recorded gospel albums, and spent several months working on a brand-new Christian Youth Center for Nashville.

Writers: Ronnie Self
 Dub Albritton

Producer: Owen Bradley

July 18, 1960
3 weeks

"SHE liked music even when she was a baby," said Brenda Lee's mother, Grace Tarpley, in a 1966 *Billboard* interview. "When she was eight months old, she loved to listen to music on the radio." By the time she was three, Brenda could hear a song twice and sing part of it back. "She was a very smart child. Before she was five she could sing a song all the way through. I'm sure it was a God-given talent."

Brenda Mae Tarpley, born December 11, 1944, in Atlanta, Georgia, put that talent to use early. She was just five when she sang "Take Me Out to the Ball Game" at a talent and beauty contest for her school district. She was the first student from Conyers Elementary School to ever win a prize; she placed first in talent and second in beauty. As a result, Brenda was invited to sing every Saturday on "Starmakers Revue," a weekly Atlanta radio show. A year later, while watching a local television program called "TV Ranch," Brenda told her mother she'd like to be on the show.

The producer, who had never hired a child singer, reluctantly granted an audition. An hour-and-a-half after singing Hank Williams' "Hey, Good Lookin'" for him, she appeared on the show.

Brenda continued to appear on "TV Ranch" with the full support of her mother and her father, carpenter Ruben Tarpley. Brenda was just nine when her father was fatally injured in a tragic on-the-job accident.

A year later, Peanut Faircloth, an Augusta DJ, signed Brenda to appear on his television series. It was a fateful move. In early 1956, country singer Red Foley and his manager, Dub Albritton, came to Augusta. Faircloth cornered them and insisted they listen to Brenda sing. They consented to let Brenda open for Foley and were so impressed, they signed her to appear on Foley's ABC-TV show, "Ozark Jubilee." Hearst columnist Jack O'Brien caught her on the show, and a column praising her

resulted in a booking on Perry Como's television program. Before making her first record, she had also appeared with Ed Sullivan and Steve Allen.

Brenda's recording career began later in 1956, when Albritton signed her to Foley's long-time label, Decca Records. At her first session, held July 30 in Nashville, Brenda recorded "Jambalaya" and "BIgelow 6-200." *Billboard* reviewed the single in the September 22 issue, saying she "has the projection, voice and sincerity that can skyrocket her to great heights, not only in the country field but in the pop field as well."

Brenda's first chart entry was "One Step at a Time" in 1957, but by 1959 she was still without a hit record. Albritton decided a trip to Paris might increase her popularity at home. She was set to open at the Olympia Music Hall in Paris on March 18, 1959, until the promoter suddenly realized she wasn't the adult he thought she was. Albritton saved the day by planting a story in the French newspapers that Brenda Lee was a 32-year-old midget. He

then denied the stories, and the resulting controversy made her so newsworthy, the promoter had no choice but to go on with the show. Brenda was a smash and *Le Figaro* said, "Never before since Judy Garland has anyone caused as much clapping of hands and stamping of feet."

Brenda was held over for five weeks at the Olympia and then toured Germany, Italy and England, returning home an international star. Before 1959 was over, she toured South America and received a similar reception. The worldwide acclaim finally paid off with a hit record at home: "Sweet Nothin's" went to number four in early 1960.

"I'm Sorry" was cut at the tail end of a session, with just five minutes of recording time left. Producer Bradley said in a *Billboard* interview: " 'I'm Sorry' was one of the first sessions in Nashville to use strings. We used four strings—now we use 10—and you might sum it up by saying that everybody faked it but the fiddle players....We decided to let the fiddles answer—when Brenda sang 'I'm Sorry,' the fiddles would answer 'I'm Sorry.' "

Brenda loved the recording, but Decca executives were concerned that a 15-year-old teenager was too young to be singing about unrequited love. It was several months before the label decided to release the ballad, and when they did, it was considered to be the flip side of the more uptempo "That's All You Gotta Do." Both sides made *Billboard's* top 10, but "I'm Sorry" was the clear winner, climbing to number one on July 18, 1960.

## THE TOP FIVE
*Week of July 18, 1960*

1 **I'm Sorry**
 Brenda Lee

2 **Alley-Oop**
 Hollywood Argyles

3 **Everybody's Somebody's Fool**
 Connie Francis

4 **Only the Lonely**
 Roy Orbison

5 **Because They're Young**
 Duane Eddy

# 72 Itsy Bitsy Teenie Weenie Yellow Polka Dot Bikini LEADER 805
## BRIAN HYLAND

*Writers: Paul Vance*
*Lee Pockriss*

*Producer: Richard Wolfe*

*August 8, 1960*
*1 week*

ITSY BITSY TEENIE Weenie Yellow Polka Dot Bikini is a true story. Paula Vance, two-year-old daughter of songwriter Paul Vance, was cavorting on the beach in her yellow polka dot bikini and inspired her father to write a song about her antics. Vance asked a songwriting friend of his, Jack Siegal, to co-write the tune, but Siegal said it wasn't his kind of song. So Paul turned to collaborator Lee Pockriss, and together they wrote the song and recorded a demo.

"I usually sang on our demos, but I thought it would sound cuter with a female vocal," Vance recalls. A session singer named Sandy recorded it, and publisher Geroge Pincus dropped by the studio when the demo was being recorded. He liked the song and insisted on publishing it. Vance and Pockriss were planning on publishing it themselves, but they figured the song was a novelty and would not be the hottest copyright in their catalogues. Based on his enthusiasm, they agreed to let Pincus have 100 percent of the publishing.

Pincus took it to Dave Kapp [see 11—"The Wayward Wind"], founder of Kapp Records. The label was known for its middle-of-the road artists like Jane Morgan and Roger Williams [see 4—"Autumn Leaves"]. Jay Lasker, later the president of Motown Records, was vice president in charge of sales for Kapp at the time. Lasker remembers that Dave "didn't like rock and roll, nor did he want to be associated with it." Lasker did convince Kapp to set up a budget of $10,000 to make some rock and roll records. "We couldn't let them be (released) on Kapp Records. He didn't want to lower the image of the label."

A subsidiary was invented, Leader Records. "My father had a cousin from Brooklyn named Leader," explains Mickey Kapp, now working in special projects at Warner Brothers Records.

The song was to be recorded by a new, 16-year old singer who had just signed with Kapp. Brian Hyland was a student at Franklin K. Lane High School in Brooklyn when he showed up to record "Itsy Bitsy Teenie Weenie Yellow Polka Dot Bikini." Worried that record producer Richard Wolfe would not handle his novelty song properly, Vance went to the recording session.

After hearing what Wolfe had done to his song, Vance protested. It didn't sound close enough to the demo, and he insisted it be recorded over. Wolfe objected. Although there were a couple of mistakes in the recording—an incorrect note on bass guitar and a wrong word sung by one of the singers—the producer thought the take felt right.

Before the record was a hit, Vance received a call from Dave Kapp. He was concerned about the song being too risqué. Vance explained that the girl wearing the yellow polka dot bikini was two years old, and the lyrics were perfectly innocent. Kapp not only released the single, he moved it over to the Kapp label when it became a huge hit.

Brian recorded one more single for the company, a Vance-Pockriss tune called "(The Clickity Clack Song) Four Little Heels." It ambled up to number 73, and then Brian, still a minor, disavowed his contract. He signed with ABC-Paramount Records and had a couple of medium-sized hits with "Let Me Belong to You" and "Ginny Come Lately." In the summer of 1962, he had a top three song, "Sealed With a Kiss."

He subsequently recorded for Philips and Dot, but his next top three hit didn't come until he signed with Uni Records in 1970 and released a cover version of the Impressions' "Gypsy Woman," produced by Del Shannon [see 88—"Runaway"].

## THE TOP FIVE
### *Week of August 8, 1960*

1  **Itsy Bitsy Teenie Weenie Yellow Polka Dot Bikini**
   Brian Hyland

2  **I'm Sorry**
   Brenda Lee

3  **It's Now or Never**
   Elvis Presley

4  **Only the Lonely**
   Roy Orbison

5  **Alley-Oop**
   Hollywood Argyles

*Writers: Aaron Schroeder*
*Wally Gold*

*Producers: Steve Sholes*
*Chet Atkins*

*August 15, 1960*
*5 weeks*

"**I**T'S NOW OR NEVER" is Elvis Presley's biggest-selling single, with total international sales topping 20 million, according to *The Guinness Book of Recorded Sound*. It was number one for eight weeks in Britain, a longer run than any of his U.K. charttoppers, and it replaced "Don't Be Cruel" as Elvis' personal favorite of all his songs.

It also marked a distinct change in style for Elvis. He had sung ballads before, but "It's Now or Never" had a more adult, operatic sound than anything he had ever recorded. That may be because the song was based on "*O Sole Mio*," an Italian song written in 1901 by G. Capurro (words) and Eduardo di Capua (music) and made popular by Mario Lanza. Tony Martin sang an English adaptation in 1949, "There's No Tomorrow," and Aaron Schroeder and Wally Gold wrote new English lyrics for Elvis.

Elvis recorded "It's Now or Never" at a productive, marathon two-day session at RCA's Nashville studios that began April 3, 1960. Many of the songs recorded during this session were for the first post-G.I. album, *Elvis Is Back*, released later in April. "It's Now or Never" and the flip side, "A Mess of Blues," were held for release until July. The

## THE TOP FIVE
*Week of August 15, 1960*

1  **It's Now or Never**
   Elvis Presley

2  **Itsy Bitsy Teenie Weenie**
   **Yellow Polka Dot Bikini**
   Brian Hyland

3  **I'm Sorry**
   Brenda Lee

4  **Only the Lonely**
   Roy Orbison

5  **Walk, Don't Run**
   Ventures

record, Elvis' second post-Army single, debuted on the Hot 100 on July 18, 1960 at number 44, and took four more weeks to climb to number one.

"It's Now or Never" was released much later in Britain, due to copyright disputes over the original "*O Sole Mio*." RCA needed to release a follow-up to "Stuck on You" in England, so they put "A Mess of Blues" on the "A" side and backed it with "The Girl of My Best Friend," a 1961 American hit for Ral Donner. It went to number two in Britain, and kept British fans happy until "It's Now or Never" could be released in November. By the time it finally came out, the anticipation was so high that it became Elvis' second single to enter the British chart at number one, and, according to *Billboard*, the fastest-selling single in the country's history. Reports from London said that dealers were having trouble coping with the demand for the single, and one shop closed for two hours on a Saturday to all customers except those wanting to buy the Presley record.

"It's Now or Never" opened new

doors for Elvis in America, where many easy listening stations found they could play a Presley single for the first time. This helped create a wider adult audience for the King, as did two other factors. His Army stint gave him more respectability—he was no longer just a rock and roll singer who swivelled his hips; he was an American who had served his country instead of choosing an easy way out just because he was famous. And many of the teenagers who were screaming for Elvis in 1956 were now becoming adults themselves.

Just before "It's Now or Never" debuted on the American chart, Elvis' father Vernon remarried. He had met Davada "Dee" Stanley in Germany during Elvis' army stint, when she was married to a Master Sergeant who had been Gen. Patton's bodyguard during World War II. After her divorce, she and Vernon visited Elvis in the hospital in June of 1959 to discuss their marriage (Elvis was having his tonsils out). Vernon and Dee were married on July 3, 1960. Elvis, who was in Hollywood filming *G.I. Blues*, did not attend.

## 74 The Twist Parkway 811
### CHUBBY CHECKER

*Writer: Hank Ballard*

*Producer: Kal Mann*

*September 19, 1960*
*1 week*

*January 13, 1962*
*2 weeks*

"THE TWIST" BY CHUBBY CHECKER is the only single in the history of the Hot 100 to go to number one twice in separate chart runs—first in September, 1960, for one week, and then again in January, 1962, when it remained in pole position for two weeks. The song, issued on Cameo's Parkway label, had a cumulative chart run of 39 weeks, longer than any other number one single until UB40's "Red Red Wine" [see 710]. Not bad for a former chicken plucker from Philadelphia.

The phenomenon of "The Twist" started in 1958 with a Detroit group, Hank Ballard and the Midnighters. Best known for a big R&B hit that was banned by many radio stations in the early 50s ("Work With Me Annie"), the group's first pop hit was "Teardrops on Your Letter." The flip side of that single was a song Ballard had written after seeing some teenagers do a new dance in Tampa, Florida: "The Twist."

But DJs played the "A" side and "The Twist" went mostly unnoticed, until the dance spread across the country. When it became the hottest dance on Dick Clark's "American Bandstand," Clark suggested that Danny and the Juniors record a cover version. When they didn't come up with anything, Clark called some friends at Philadelphia's most successful record company, Cameo-Parkway, and made a suggestion of who should record the song.

It had been December of 1958 when Clark and his then-wife Bobbie went to Cameo Records to find someone to record an audio "Christmas card" they could send to their friends. Cameo had a new artist, Ernest Evans, who impressed Dick with his ability to impersonate other singers, especially Fats Domino. Evans recorded a song called "The Class," which Dick used for his Christmas card. Evans had been nicknamed "Chubby" by a friend who

came into the produce market where he used to work, and Bobbie Clark added the last name "Checker" as a take-off of "Fats *Domino*."

"The Class" was such a hit with Clark's friends, that Cameo-Parkway released it as a commercial single in the spring of 1959. The novelty recording was Chubby's first Hot 100 entry, peaking at number 38.

So Chubby Checker was recruited to record a new version of "The Twist." It took him 35 minutes to do three takes, backed by a vocal group known as the Dreamlovers. He made several appearances on "American Bandstand," giving "Twist" lessons and promoting his single. On August 1, 1960, "The Twist" entered the Hot 100 at number 49.

Hank Ballard was floating in a swimming pool in Miami, Florida the first time he heard Chubby's song on the radio. It was so carefully copied note for note from the original version that Hank thought he was listening to himself on the radio. While many people thought Ballard was cheated out of a hit record by the cover version, he has since expressed his gratitude to Chubby and Dick Clark—as the writer of the song, Ballard's royalties over the years have amounted to a nice sum.

As the twist faded from the dance scene and was replaced by the slop, the mashed potato, the fly and the popeye, Chubby went on to record other dance songs. But while the twist was passe for teenagers, it was just catching on with adults. Society columnist "Cholly Knickerbocker" mentioned that Prince Serge Obolensky was seen dancing the twist at Manhattan's Peppermint Lounge, and suddenly it was a worldwide sensation, drawing the elite to discotheques to twist the night away.

Because of the dance's new found acceptance, Chubby was invited to sing "The Twist" on Ed Sullivan's show on October 22, 1961, prompting a re-release of the single. A full-page ad in *Billboard* said it all: "'The Twist' dance rage explodes into the adult world!" This time around it was the grown-ups buying Chubby's single, and they bought enough copies to return it to the Hot 100 on November 13, and send it all the way to number one again just after the new year.

### THE TOP FIVE
*Week of September 19, 1960*

1  **Twist**
   Chubby Checker

2  **My Heart Has
   a Mind of Its Own**
   Connie Francis

3  **It's Now or Never**
   Elvis Presley

4  **Mr. Custer**
   Larry Verne

5  **Chain Gang**
   Sam Cooke

MGM 12923 ## My Heart Has a Mind of Its Own
### CONNIE FRANCIS

*Writers: Howard Greenfield  Jack Keller*

*Producers: Joe Sherman*
*Arnold Maxin  Jesse Kaye*

*September 26, 1960*
*2 weeks*

WHEN "My Heart Has a Mind of Its Own" displaced Chubby Checker's "The Twist" from the top of the chart, Connie Francis became the first female singer to have two consecutive singles go to number one.

It was a dramatic turnaround from her first ten singles, all of which failed to make *Billboard's* chart [see 69—"Everybody's Somebody's Fool"]. When Connie chose material to record at what was going to be her final MGM session, she played the songs for her father. "He said, 'They stink. Here's your hit, dummy.'" And he handed her "Who's Sorry Now."

"I reluctantly did that song and squeezed it in as the last song on a four-hour recording session, and we did it in about 15 minutes." Released by MGM, the song lingered for three-and-a-half months without any signs of becoming a hit.

"It was going nowhere," Connie recalls. "And then it was January 1st of 1958, and about four o'clock in the afternoon we were all seated down to one of those monstrous Italian meals with all the family there. I got up, and like 8.5 million other American teenagers, I tuned my black-and-white TV set to 'American Bandstand.' And I heard Dick Clark mention something about a new girl singer and that she was going right

to the top and I said, 'well, good luck to her'—sour grapes—and then all of a sudden he played 'Who's Sorry Now.' It was an incredible feeling because it was such a surprise. I screamed...and I said, 'Dad, Dick Clark is playing 'Who's Sorry Now.' (And dad said) 'Naw, it can't be, the thing's dead' with his usual optimism."

It wasn't dead, it was finally showing signs of life. It became Connie's first chart record, peaking at number four in America and going all the way to number one in Britain.

Her first American number one, "Everybody's Somebody's Fool," was written by Howard Greenfield and Jerry Keller, and for the follow-up, Connie asked them for another song in the same country vein. "Howie used to call me up in the middle of the night and throw titles out at me...if I love the title, I almost

always record the song. And when he called me up and said, 'My Heart Has a Mind of Its Own,' I said, 'That's a smash! Great title!' 'You haven't heard the song yet,' he said. 'Doesn't matter, it's a great title!'"

A few months after "My Heart Has a Mind Of Its Own" was number one, Connie made her film debut in MGM's *Where the Boys Are*. She found it difficult to convince Hollywood film executives that two New York songwriters, Neil Sedaka and Howard Greenfield, should write the title song. Connie called Greenfield anyway, and told them they had four days to come up with a suitable tune. He said it was impossible, but four days later he and Neil had written *two* songs called "Where the Boys Are." One they loved and one they hated. Producer Joe Pasternak picked the latter and it went to number four on the Hot 100.

## THE TOP FIVE
*Week of September 26, 1960*

1  **My Heart Has a Mind of Its Own**
   Connie Francis

2  **Twist**
   Chubby Checker

3  **Chain Gang**
   Sam Cooke

4  **Mr. Custer**
   Larry Verne

5  **A Million to One**
   Jimmy Charles

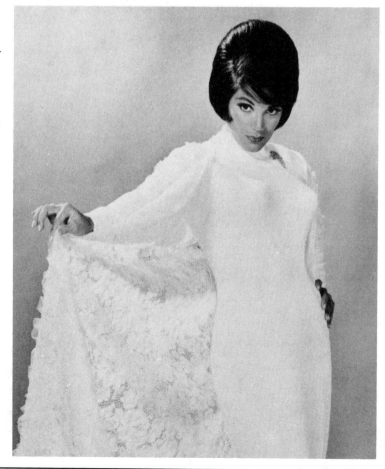

## 76 Mr. Custer ERA 3024
### LARRY VERNE

*Writers: Fred Darian*
*Al DeLory*
*Joe Van Winkle*

*Producers: Fred Darian*
*Al DeLory*
*Joe Van Winkle*

*October 10, 1960*
*1 week*

On Sunday, June 25, 1876, thirty years of warfare between the white man and the red man came to an end. The climactic battle was fought at Little Big Horn, where 700 U.S. Cavalry troops under the command of General George Custer fought 3,000 Sioux Indians loyal to Chief Sitting Bull. Within a half-hour of Custer's attack, he and all of his troops lay dead.

Eighty-four years, three months and 15 days later, Larry Verne's novelty song, about a soldier's comical plea to Mr. Custer that he didn't want to fight, was the number one song in America.

The song was developed by three friends who worked in the music industry in Hollywood. Fred Darian, Al de Lory and Joe Van Winkle were dubbing a song at Gold Star studios one night when de Lory came up with, "Mr. Custer, I don't want to go" and "Forward, ho!" and someone else made the sound effect of an arrow piercing the air. "'Mr. Custer' was not a song you just sat down and wrote," explains Darian. "It was a succession of incidents that brought it about. It just developed as we were going along. We came up with a phrase we thought was funny, we rolled over and slapped each other on the back, and as time went on the thought provoked us to try and do something with the idea."

The three writers first met at Coffee Dan's, a Hollywood hang-out that was close to Wallich's Music City at Sunset and Vine. They formed a vocal group, the Balladeers, and had a small office on Sunset, for which they paid $40 a month rent. Down the hall was a photographer's studio, where a young man named Larry Verne worked in the darkroom developing pictures. He spoke with a drawl, and Van Winkle asked him to sing lead vocal on a demo of "Mr. Custer." Did he know Verne could

sing? No, but they required an actor, not a singer.

The song was only in outline form until they took Verne into the studio, where a two-hour session with guitar, bass, drums, background vocals and noises by the three writer/producers resulted in a four-and-a-half minute track.

"Everybody turned it down," Van Winkle reveals. "I mean everybody. I don't think we missed any of the majors. Then we hit the independents. The crowning disappointment came when we went into a storefront that someone had taken over to make a record company. We went in the back and there was an old woman and a thirty-ish guy. They had a little record player sitting on a table. They put 'Mr. Custer' on and listened. They never smiled, never said a word. When it was over they gave the record back and she said, 'That's the most horrible thing I ever heard in my life.'"

Finally, Bob Keene of Del-Fi Records gave them a $300 advance so he could release the record. After waiting an interminable amount of time, Darian called and asked when it would be coming out. "He said, 'You know, I don't think it's so funny anymore.'"

The original dub was wearing out from airplay, so they went back to Gold Star to cut a new one. Herb Newman, owner of Era Records, listened in the hallway and asked if they wanted him to put it out. Ten months after it was recorded, a shortened version of "Mr. Custer" was released. Darian credits the late Bob Crane, a Los Angeles DJ at the time, with being the first to play the song on the radio.

### THE TOP FIVE
*Week of October 10, 1960*

1  **Mr. Custer**
   Larry Verne

2  **Chain Gang**
   Sam Cooke

3  **My Heart Has
   a Mind of Its Own**
   Connie Francis

4  **Save the Last Dance For Me**
   Drifters

5  **Twist**
   Chubby Checker

ATLANTIC 2071 **Save the Last Dance for Me** 77
THE DRIFTERS

*Writers: Doc Pomus*
*        Mort Shuman*

*Producers: Jerry Leiber*
*          Mike Stoller*

*October 17, 1960*
*3 weeks*

THERE have been 30 different singers who, at one time or another, were members of the group known as the Drifters, and there have been two completely different sets of Drifters—the original group, which formed in 1953, and a new group which came together in 1959 to record "There Goes My Baby."

The original Drifters formed around Clyde McPhatter, lead tenor of Billy Ward's group the Dominoes, who had an early R&B hit in 1951 with "Sixty Minute Man." When Clyde left the Dominoes in 1953 (to be replaced by Jackie Wilson), he was signed to Atlantic Records by Ahmet Ertegun. McPhatter recruited members of a gospel singing group, the Civitones, to form a new outfit, and because they had all drifted in and out of different groups, they called themselves the Drifters.

Hits like "Money Honey" and "Honey Love" did well on the R&B charts, but in 1954 McPhatter was drafted into the armed forces. He recorded with the Drifters when he was on leave, but he also did some solo sessions, and when he was dis-

charged in 1956, he decided to leave the group and pursue a solo career. He only had two big hits on his own ("A Lover's Question" and "Lover Please"), and he died on June 13, 1972, at the age of 38.

There were six different lead singers after McPhatter, and the group continued recording until 1958, when disagreements with manager George Treadwell led to the entire group being fired. Treadwell owned the Drifters' name, but he had one small problem: in 1954, he signed a contract with Harlem's Apollo Theater stipulating that the Drifters would appear there twice a year for ten years. Now, there were no Drifters.

Treadwell was at the Apollo one night when he saw a group called the Five Crowns. They were low on the bill, but he was impressed with their lead singer, Benjamin Nelson. With help from Atlantic's Jerry Wexler, Treadwell persuaded the group to change their name to the Drifters.

Nelson changed his name, too, to Ben E. King. Atlantic Records put producers Jerry Leiber and Mike Stoller in charge of the Drifters' recording sessions, and their first single, "There Goes My Baby," is considered to be the first rock and roll single to have a full orchestral backing.

After writing a couple of hits for the Drifters, Leiber and Stoller turned to other songwriters for material, including Doc Pomus and Mort

Shuman. Pomus and Shuman had already written songs for the Five Crowns and knew King's voice: they fashioned "This Magic Moment" for him, and then "Save the Last Dance for Me." Many Phil Spector fans believe he assisted Leiber and Stoller with "Save the Last Dance for Me." The truth may never be known, but Phil was apprenticed to them at the time, and the production sounds enough like early Spector to lend credence to this legend.

Spector did work closely with Ben E. King when he left the Drifters right after "Save the Last Dance for Me," co-writing and co-producing "Spanish Harlem."

Rudy Lewis replaced King as lead singer of the Drifters, beginning with "Some Kind of Wonderful." He's also the lead voice on "Up on the Roof" and "On Broadway," but he suffered a fatal heart attack in 1964. Johnny Moore, who had been in the earlier incarnation of the Drifters (from 1955-1957), assumed lead vocal duties beginning with "Under the Boardwalk."

After Treadwell died in 1965, his widow, Faye, took over management of the group. She signed them with Bell Records in the United Kingdom in 1972, and they had a succession of British-only hits over a four-year period, including "Like Sister and Brother," "Kissin' in the Back Row of the Movies" and "There Goes My First Love."

"Save the Last Dance for Me" went to number one on October 17, 1960 for one week, and returned to the top for two more weeks on October 31.

## THE TOP FIVE
*Week of October 17, 1960*

1   **Save the Last Dance For Me**
    Drifters

2   **My Heart Has
    a Mind of Its Own**
    Connie Francis

3   **Chain Gang**
    Sam Cooke

4   **I Want to be Wanted**
    Brenda Lee

5   **Twist**
    Chubby Checker

**78**

# I Want to Be Wanted DECCA 31149
## BRENDA LEE

*Writers: Kim Gannon*
*Pino Spotti*
*A. Testa*

*Producer: Owen Bradley*

*October 24, 1960*
*1 week*

"I WANT TO BE WANTED" was far away from Brenda Lee's country-gospel roots. About five thousand miles away. The song came from Italy, where it was included in the original production of *Never on Sunday*. When Brenda first heard it, there was only a melody, and she had to contact the writers in Italy to have the lyrics sent to her.

"I Want to Be Wanted" was Brenda's second number one single [see 71—"I'm Sorry"]. She followed it with a succession of top 10 songs, including "Emotions," "Dum Dum" and "Fool #1," a song Loretta Lynn wanted to record as her first single for Decca. Brenda's producer, A&R man Owen Bradley, wanted to sign Loretta to Decca but didn't think that song was right for her. Brenda got the song, Loretta got a contract and everyone was happy.

The top 10 hits kept coming: "Break It to Me Gently," "All Alone Am I" and "Losing You," a song that was moving up the Hot 100 when Brenda married Charles Ronald Shacklett, son of a Nashville city councilman, on April 24, 1963. After an eight-day honeymoon, she flew to New York to open at the Copacabana. *Billboard* gave her a rave review: "Brenda has the fire,

the drive, the movement and the vocalistics that led one ringsider to characterize her as a teen-aged Sophie Tucker."

In July, 1963, Decca announced that Brenda had signed a 20-year pact, guaranteeing her $35,000 a year. The new contract included a two-picture deal with Universal. Although she didn't reach the top 10 again after "Losing You," she held her own during the British invasion with top 20 hits like "The Grass Is Greener" and "As Usual." She recorded in London with producer Mickie Most and came up with another top 20 hit, "Is It True?" Her last major hit was "Coming On Strong," which peaked at number 11 in 1966. It was a song that inspired Dutch rockers Golden Earring to mention Brenda in the lyrics of their 1974 hit "Radar Love" ("Brenda Lee

is coming on strong...").

Brenda's final Hot 100 entry was "Nobody Wins," a Kris Kristofferson song that went to number one on the country charts. In 1977, Brenda asked to be released from her contract, six years before its expiration date. Loretta Lynn's manager, David Skepner, arranged for her to sign with Elektra Records. She recorded one single for Elektra, then returned to MCA (which had absorbed its subsidiary, Decca Records) in 1979. That year, she said in a *Billboard* interview:

"I want to let people know I'm still very much alive and active. A lot of people think that just because they've seen me and heard my records for so many years, I must be a 60-year-old invalid by now. They forget that I started my singing career when I was only 10."

## THE TOP FIVE
*Week of October 24, 1960*

1  **I Want to be Wanted**
   Brenda Lee

2  **Save the Last Dance For Me**
   Drifters

3  **Twist**
   Chubby Checker

4  **My Heart Has
   a Mind of Its Own**
   Connie Francis

5  **Chain Gang**
   Sam Cooke

ABC-PARAMOUNT 10135 **Georgia on My Mind** 79
RAY CHARLES

*Writers: Hoagy Carmichael*
*Stewart Gorrell*

*Producer: Sid Feller*

*November 14, 1960*
*1 week*

**Q**UINCY JONES said of Ray Charles: "Ray doesn't follow others. He's an innovator." *Time* magazine confirmed, "There is no modern singer who has not learned something from him."

When the people whose business it is to make music are asked who had the most influence on them, no individual singer is mentioned more often than Ray Charles. Through his career, he blended jazz, blues, soul, country and pop until the divisions that normally separate these categories of music dissolved. All that was left was the music.

His first number one single was the 1930 standard, "Georgia on My Mind." His driver, Tommy Brown, suggested he record it because he was always singing it on the road anyway. Ray thought that was a good idea and asked Ralph Burns, Woody Herman's pianist, to handle the arrangement. The song was recorded in New York in four takes,

less than the usual 10-12 takes Ray was used to.

He was born Ray Charles Robinson on September 23, 1930 in Albany, Georgia, but he grew up in Greenville, Florida. His father, Bailey, was a handyman who did odd jobs, and his mother, Aretha, took in washing. His early life was beset by tragedies. When Ray was four years old, his younger brother George fell into a wash basin in the front yard and drowned before Ray could summon his mother for help.

At age five, Ray began to have problems with his eyes. His vision slipped away in increments, and the family was too poor to afford an eye specialist. By the time he was seven, Ray was completely blind. Years later, doctors analyzed the problem as glaucoma, but Ray is not sure. He remembers being fascinated with the sun and staring into its red-hot mass.

Ray also remembers his mother's words: "You're blind, not stupid. You lost your sight, not your mind." He was 10 when his father died. Ray went to St. Augustine's School for the Deaf and Blind in Orlando, Florida, and when he was 15 he received the news that his mother had passed away.

His teachers at St. Augustine's taught him classical music, but he loved to play boogie woogie like the music he heard as a three-year-old from his neighbor, Wylie Pittman, who had an old beat up piano on his front porch that he used to let Ray play.

Shortly after he was orphaned, Ray left school to go to Jacksonville, Florida, where he played in a hillbilly band and a group called the Honeydippers. Three years later, he was ready to leave the south behind. He asked a friend to take a map and find the furthest point away from Florida that would still be in the United States. New York was five inches away, but too intimidating. Los Angeles was seven inches away, but Ray wasn't ready for L.A. Seattle was eight inches away, and Ray arrived there with $600 in his pocket.

He was hired to play at a club, the Rockin' Chair, where he impressed audiences with his vocal similarity to Nat "King" Cole and Charles Brown. People kept telling Ray how much he sounded like them until he tired of the "compliments" and decided to sing in his own voice. That landed him a deal with a Los Angeles label, Swingtime, and he recorded "Confession Blues." But there was a musicians' strike, and Ray violated it by recording the song. He was fined his entire $600 and left penniless.

Other musicians violated the strike, but claimed they recorded their tracks before the strike began. "I only made one mistake," he said, years later. "I was so stupid I didn't know I was supposed to lie."

## THE TOP FIVE
*Week of November 14, 1960*

1 **Georgia on my Mind**
Ray Charles

2 **Poetry in Motion**
Johnny Tillotson

3 **You Talk Too Much**
Joe Jones

4 **I Want to be Wanted**
Brenda Lee

5 **Save the Last Dance For Me**
Drifters

# 80 Stay HERALD 552
## MAURICE WILLIAMS AND THE ZODIACS

*Writer: Maurice Williams*

*Producers: Phil Gernhard*
*Johnny McCullough*

*November 21, 1960*
*1 week*

**O**NE of the early classics of rock and roll was "Little Darlin'" by the Diamonds, a quartet of four white males who kept the song at number two for an amazing eight weeks. Most people who can still sing the distinctive "Yi-yi-yi-yi" don't realize that the song was written and originally recorded by Maurice Williams, with his group the Gladiolas. It was not unusual for white artists to cover black records to make them acceptable to pop radio in the 1950s, and the Diamonds' copied Williams' record note-for-note.

Unhappy at having his record "stolen" from him, Williams got financial backing in Columbia, South Carolina, to record new songs. "Stay" was recorded in a defunct television studio. Producers Phil Gernhard and Johnny McCullough took the song to New York and started knocking on record company doors. They were turned down everywhere. Jerry Wexler at Atlantic said the song didn't have a plot line and warned them it was a tough business.

Finally, they walked into the offices of Al Silver at Herald Records. Silver was on the telephone and sent his A&R man, Bill Darnell, to meet with them. After listening to several songs, Darnell picked out "Stay" for Silver to listen to. He wanted it, but there were two problems.

First, the song wasn't recorded at a level high enough for quality reproduction. "None of us knew what the hell we were doing," Gernhard admits. "He drew a VU meter for us

and said, 'go back and rerecord it, and keep the needle up in this area.' We took the piece of paper with us."

Second, "It had a line in it that was objectionable," Phil says. "It said, 'Let's have another smoke.' He said radio wouldn't play anything that encouraged young people to smoke cigarettes."

The group returned to Columbia and recorded the song again, keeping the VU needle where the drawing indicated and changing the offensive line. When the single was released, southern stations favored the flip side, "Do You Believe." "Stay" finally broke north of the Mason-Dixon line, in Detroit. It entered the Hot 100 at number 86 on October 3, 1960. When it topped the chart seven weeks later, it became the shortest number one single of the rock era, clocking in at one minute and 37 seconds.

"Stay" has proven to be an ever-

green, hitting the top 20 two more times. The Four Seasons took it to number 16 in 1964, and Jackson Browne's version peaked at number 20 in 1978. In Britain, the Hollies recorded it in 1963.

Maurice Williams was born April 26, 1938 in Lancaster, South Carolina. He sang in church, and organized his first group, The Royal Charmers, while in high school. They raised money from their parents and local business owners to finance a trip to Nashville so they could audition for Excello Records. At the last moment, the lead singer's mother said he couldn't go—which upset Williams, as he had written "Little Darlin'" especially for his voice. When they auditioned for the head of the label, Ernie Young, Williams had to sing "Little Darlin'," and that was the song Young picked for their first release. He also gave them their new name, the Gladiolas. When they left the label, Young insisted on retaining the name, forcing the group to choose a new one. The bass player saw an automobile at a repair shop called a Zodiac and suggested they use that.

## THE TOP FIVE
*Week of November 21, 1960*

1  **Stay**
   Maurice Williams & the Zodiacs

2  **Are You Lonesome Tonight?**
   Elvis Presley

3  **Poetry in Motion**
   Johnny Tillotson

4  **Last Date**
   Floyd Cramer

5  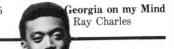 **Georgia on my Mind**
   Ray Charles

was released. At the same time, Elvis was already filming his sixth motion picture, *Flaming Star*, which was released December 20—in time for Christmas vacation. It was Elvis' first western, and his first dramatic, non-singing role. There was no soundtrack album, just an EP with the title song and three other non-movie songs, including "Are You Lonesome Tonight" and "It's Now or Never."

Elvis starred as half-breed Pacer Burton, a role that had been turned down by Marlon Brando. Don Siegal, who directed the original *Invasion of the Body Snatchers* and would one day direct Clint Eastwood in the *Dirty Harry* series, was the film's director. The cast included Barbara Eden, Dolores Del Rio, Richard Jaeckel, John McIntyre and Steve Forrest.

Col. Tom Parker did not consider the film a success. The box office was lower than most Elvis films, and the idea of an Elvis film without songs appealed to the Colonel as much as it appealed to most Elvis fans—not at all. *Flaming Star* would be the last non-singing role until the 1969 attempt at a spaghetti western, *Charro*.

His next film, *Wild in the Country*, was already in production, however. Like *Flaming Star*, it was meant to show off Elvis the actor, not Elvis the singer. Hope Lange, Tuesday Weld, Gary Lockwood, Rafer Johnson, Millie Perkins and John Ireland were also in the cast. It was Elvis' final film for 20th Century Fox, and he recorded five songs for the soundtrack on the studio lot in October, 1960.

*Writers: Roy Turk*
*Lou Handman*

*Producers: Steve Sholes*
*Chet Atkins*

*November 28, 1960*
*6 weeks*

"**A**RE You Lonesome Tonight," a song written in 1926 that was first recorded by Al Jolson, and made popular again in 1959 by Jaye P. Morgan, became Elvis Presley's 14th number one single in America. It was recorded April 4, 1960, at the same two-day marathon session that produced "It's Now or Never." Like that more adult-oriented song, "Are You Lonesome Tonight" received airplay on easy listening stations that were unaccustomed to playing Elvis Presley songs.

"Are You Lonesome Tonight" entered the chart at number 35, higher than any other Elvis Hot 100 record to date. Two weeks later, it was number one. It topped the British chart on January 26, 1961 for four weeks, his sixth number one in the United Kingdom.

No doubt the song's popularity was boosted by a long, spoken narration by Elvis in the middle of the song, which paraphrased Shakespeare's sentiments on all the world being a stage. The song inspired a flood of answer records, including four female versions of "Yes I'm Lonesome Tonight" by Dodie Stevens, Linda Lee, Ricky Page and Thelma Carpenter. Jeanne Black released another answer, "Oh How I Miss You Tonight."

Just a little over three weeks before "Are You Lonesome Tonight" made the American chart, *G.I. Blues*

## THE TOP FIVE

*Week of November 28, 1960*

1 **Are You Lonesome Tonight?**
Elvis Presley

2 **Last Date**
Floyd Cramer

3 **Stay**
Maurice Williams & the Zodiacs

4 **Poetry in Motion**
Johnny Tillotson

5 **A Thousand Stars**
Kathy Young and the Innocents

## 82 Wonderland by Night DECCA 31141
### BERT KAEMPFERT

*Writers: Klauss-Gunter Neuman*
*Lincoln Chase*

*Producer: Bert Kaempfert*

*January 9, 1961*
*3 weeks*

BERT KAEMPFERT is the only number one artist who was involved with the careers of the Beatles, Elvis Presley and Frank Sinatra. Presley and Sinatra both recorded songs written by Kaempfert: Presley sang "Wooden Heart" [see 95] in *G.I. Blues*, and Sinatra recorded an English translation of "Strangers in the Night" [see 202].

Kaempfert played a more crucial role in the Beatles' history. He produced the first session they ever recorded, which resulted in "My Bonnie Lies Over the Ocean" and "When the Saints Go Marching In" for singer/guitarist Tony Sheridan as well as the Beatles' own "Ain't She Sweet" and "Cry for a Shadow."

Kaempfert was born in Hamburg, Germany, on October 16, 1923. He studied at the Hamburg School of Music, and became proficient on the piano, accordion, clarinet and saxophone. After World War II he formed his own band, which became a popular attraction in West Germany. He was hired by Polydor Records as a producer, and had two big hits in 1959, "Morgen" by Ivo Robic and *"Die Gitarre und Das Meer"* by Freddy Quinn.

*"Wunderland bei Nacht"* was the instrumental title theme for a film that told of the dark side of Germany's "economic miracle." Kaempfert arrived in New York in

### THE TOP FIVE
*Week of January 9, 1961*

1 **Wonderland by Night**
Bert Kaempfert

2 **Are You Lonesome Tonight**
Elvis Presley

3 **Exodus**
Ferrante & Teicher

4 **Last Date**
Floyd Cramer

5 **Will You Love Me Tomorrow**
Shirelles

October, 1959, to place the song with an American publisher. After several rejections, Hal Fein at Roosevelt Music bought the tune. The song was a hit in Germany as well as Japan before it met with success in the United States. By the end of September, 1960, Fein telephoned Kaempfert in Hamburg to predict the song would be a million-seller.

Under its English title, the song entered the Hot 100 on November 14, 1960—the same month that a club called the Top Ten opened in Hamburg, featuring British vocalist Tony Sheridan. On January 9, 1961, "Wonderland by Night" was the number one song in America. Three months later, the Beatles were booked to play at the Top Ten, alternating sets with Sheridan's band. One night, Kaempfert came to the club to check out Sheridan's act, and signed him to Polydor. The British singer suggested his friends the Beatles be hired as his backing band, and Kaempfert agreed.

At the recording session, John Lennon and Paul McCartney asked

Bert to listen to some songs they had written, but he didn't think they were ready to record their own material yet. As a favor, he consented to let them record two songs after Sheridan completed his tracks. John sang lead on a song they performed at the Top Ten, "Ain't She Sweet." George had an instrumental that was meant to be a parody of Britain's most popular instrumental group, the Shadows. It was recorded under the title "Cry for a Shadow."

Kaempfert didn't think the name Beatles would mean much in Germany, so he renamed them the Beat Brothers and paid them a flat fee for their work—300 marks each, worth about $125 in 1961.

Kaempfert had 10 more chart entries after "Wonderland by Night," all instrumentals. Among them were two of his own compositions, "Red Roses for a Blue Lady" and "Spanish Eyes," released under the title "Moon Over Naples."

Kaempfert was 56 when he died on June 21, 1980, in Zug, Switzerland.

SCEPTER 1211 **Will You Love Me Tomorrow** 83

THE SHIRELLES

*Writers: Gerry Goffin*
*Carole King*

*Producer: Luther Dixon*

*January 30, 1961*
*2 weeks*

THE SHIRELLES were the very first girl group to have a number one single. Other girl groups had made the top 30, like The Chantels ("Maybe," "He's Gone") and the Chordettes ("Born to Be With You," "Lollipop"), and others would follow into the number one spot, like The Marvelettes, The Crystals, The Supremes and The Shangri-Las. But the Shirelles got there first.

Shirley Owens and Addie "Micki" Harris were grammar school friends in Passaic, New Jersey. They met Doris Kenner and Beverly Lee in junior high and while Shirley and Bev were baby-sitting, they decided to start a singing group. They asked Micki to join them, and after hearing Doris sing in the school choir, they asked her to complete the quartet. Their classmate Mary Jane Greenberg wanted them to audition for her mother Florence, who had a small record company called Tiara Records.

The girls were not interested, but Mary Jane pursued them for two years. She was so insistent, that eventually the girls would hide when they saw her coming. After winning a school talent contest with a tune they composed, "I Met Him on a Sunday,"

they finally agreed to meet Mary Jane's mother. Florence loved them and signed them up immediately—with their parents' permission.

Unhappy with the group name the *Poquellos* (Spanish for little birds), Florence suggested the Honeytones. The girls thought it was corny and said no. Florence told them they had to have a name by the following day for label copy on their first release. In the taxi cab on the way home from the office, they mused over names that would be similar to their favorite group, the Chantels. They considered the Chanels, but it was too close. Shirley says no one can remember who first came up with the Shirelles, and the other girls deny they named themselves after Shirley (who was not lead singer at this point—Doris was), but it was the name they unanimously chose.

"I Met Him on a Sunday" was released on Tiara, but Florence felt she couldn't promote the song like a major label could, so she leased it to Decca. The song went to number 49 in the spring of 1958.

Two follow-ups on Decca did not chart, so Florence took the girls back for her own label, now renamed Scepter Records. She signed Luther Dixon, a former member of the Four Buddies, to write and produce the Shirelles. For their first single, the girls brought Florence a song they said they had written. When it came time to sign the songwriters' contract, they had to admit they did not

write "Dedicated to the One I Love." It was written by two members of the group they heard performing it at the Howard Theater in Washington, D.C., The Five Royales.

"Dedicated" faltered at number 83. Their next single, "Tonight's the Night," was written by Shirley and Luther, and it fought off a cover version by the Chiffons to peak at number 39.

For their next single, Dixon told the girls he owed songwriters Gerry Goffin and Carole King a favor, and had promised to record one of their tunes. Shirley heard Carole's demo of "Will You Love Me Tomorrow" and hated it. She thought it sounded like a country and western song and disliked it all through rehearsals.

But during the recording session she changed her mind. Dixon's production had changed it into a pop song, and Carole, unhappy with one of the musicians, played kettle drums herself. The result was not only the first girl group number one, but the first chart-topper for the songwriting team of Goffin and King.

"Will You Love Me Tomorrow" has proven to be a timeless song, recorded by artists like the Four Seasons, Melanie, Laura Branigan, Carole herself on 1971's legendary *Tapestry* album and most recently, Dionne Warwick.

Dionne rose to fame in the early 60s on the Scepter label, and she begins her version, produced by Luther Vandross, with a spoken intro: "Some things I'll never let go of, like friends. My friends like Doris, Beverly and Shirley..." And then Shirley sings the first few lines of "Will You Love Me Tomorrow."

## THE TOP FIVE

*Week of January 30, 1961*

1 **Will You Love Me Tomorrow**
Shirelles

2 **Calcutta**
Lawrence Welk

3 **Exodus**
Ferrante & Teicher

4 **Wonderland by Night**
Bert Kaempfert

5 **Shop Around**
Miracles

## 84 | Calcutta DOT 16161
### LAWRENCE WELK

*Writers:* Heino Gaze
Paul Vance
Lee Pockriss

*Producers:* Randy Wood
George Cates
Lawrence Welk

*February 13, 1961*
*2 weeks*

THREE weeks after Bert Kaempfert's "Wonderland by Night" was number one, another German instrumental topped the American chart. Written in 1958 by composer Heino Gaze as "Tivoli Melody," it was retitled "Take Me Dreaming," then "Nicolette" and in 1960 the Werner Muller Orchestra recorded it in Germany as *"Kalkutta Liegt am Ganges."* When Randy Wood, the president of Dot Records, brought the song to Lawrence Welk to record, it received its fifth title: "Calcutta."

The Welk version added a harpsichord, which complicated recording in the studio. A microphone was placed inside the instrument while harpsichordist Frank Scott wore earphones to hear what he was playing. The rest of Welk's orchestra couldn't hear the harpsichord, but it was recorded in one take. The song was intended to be the flip side of "My Grandfather's Clock," until radio stations started playing "Calcutta."

Welk was born on March 11, 1903, in Strasburg, North Dakota, where his parents (Ludwig and Christina) fled after escaping Bismarck's Prussian invasion of Alsace-Lorraine in 1878. They left with the clothes they were wearing and one family possession, handed down from father-to-son

for three generations: an antique accordion.

In America, Ludwig and Christina had eight children. One son, Lawrence, showed interest in the accordion, and by the time he was 13 was playing well enough to entertain at community dances and church socials. His parents bought him a "mail-order" accordion, but Welk was strong from farm work, and the fragile instrument could not stand up to his hours of practice. Lawrence promised he would remain on his parents' farm until he was 21 if they would loan him $400 to buy a new, professional accordion.

When he turned 21, Lawrence paid his parents back and left home—against their better judgment, but with their blessing. At first he was a soloist, but in Aberdeen, South Dakota, he formed his first orchestra. They were invited to appear on a

daily radio show on WNAX, a pioneer midwest station. By 1927, Welk's orchestra was well-known on the east coast, where a friend in Pittsburgh said their music had a "bubbly, frothy quality." "Champagne Music" was born.

Welk headed west and in 1951 began a six-week engagement at the Aragon Ballroom in Pacific Ocean Park, California. He stayed 10 years. In 1961, he moved to the Hollywood Palladium. Welk made his local TV debut in 1952 on KTLA and on July 2, 1955, his series was picked up by the ABC network.

Welk's first chart single was "Don't Sweetheart Me" on Decca in 1944. He recorded for Coral from 1953–1959 and then signed with Dot just as the Coral contract was about to expire.

On May 17, 1992, he died in Santa Monica, California, of pneumonia. He was 89.

### THE TOP FIVE
*Week of February 13, 1961*

1 **Calcutta**
Lawrence Welk

2 **Will You Love Me Tomorrow**
Shirelles

3 **Shop Around**
Miracles

4 **Calendar Girl**
Neil Sedaka

5 **Exodus**
Ferrante & Teicher

*Writers: Don Covay*
*John Berry*

*Producer: Kal Mann*

*February 27, 1961*
*3 weeks*

THE man who immortalized "The Twist" had his biggest hits with songs about dances. The limbo, the popeye, the fly, the hucklebuck were all subjects of Chubby Checker songs, and so was the pony, in his second number one single, "Pony Time."

And like his first number one [see 74—"The Twist"], "Pony Time" was a cover of the original version. Don Covay, who wrote the song with John Berry, recorded it as a member of the Goodtimers in late 1960. The song was adapted from "Boogie Woogie," a 1928 composition by Clarence "Pinetop" Smith. Chubby's version debuted on the Hot 100 the same week as the Goodtimers, but he took it all the way to number one, while they stalled at number 60.

Chubby was born Ernest Evans on October 3, 1941, in South Carolina. With his parents and two brothers (Spencer and Tracy), he moved to Philadelphia, where he decided, by age five, that someday he would be a big singing star. His mother, a strongly religious woman, discouraged that notion, but Ernest formed his own singing group when he was eight years old.

In high school, Ernest played the piano and drums, and learned to do vocal impressions of famous singers.

Before and after classes, he worked in a local poultry market, where he was a chicken plucker. He often sang for the customers, and the market owner, Henry Colt, was impressed enough to take his young employee to meet Kal Mann and Dave Appell, producers at Philadelphia's Cameo-Parkway Records.

"Pony Time" went to number one five months after "The Twist" topped the chart for the first time. But Chubby wasn't finished with the twist. In the summer of 1961, he had a top 10 hit with "Let's Twist Again." During the second chart run of "The Twist," the flip side, "Twistin' U.S.A," also received airplay. In the spring of 1962, Chubby recorded a duet with labelmate Dee Dee Sharp called "Slow Twistin'," which went to number three. And finally, in the summer of 1963, he made the top 30

with "Twist It Up."

Chubby charted with two more dance records, although neither was a big hit. "She Wants T'Swim" was released in the summer of 1964, but Bobby Freeman made the dance his own with "C'mon and Swim." The following year, Chubby sang "Let's Do the Freddie," but he couldn't beat Freddie and the Dreamers at their own game.

Chubby Checker had a chart entry with a cover version of the Beatles' "Back in the U.S.S.R.," a song they never released as a single. In 1981 he signed with MCA Records, and had a hit on the dance chart with "Running."

In 1964, Chubby married Catharina Lodders, a Dutch beauty queen who was Miss World in 1962. They have three children and are still happily married today.

### THE TOP FIVE
*Week of February 27, 1961*

1 **Pony Time**
Chubby Checker

2 **Calcutta**
Lawrence Welk

3 **There's a Moon Out Tonight**
Capris

4 **Surrender**
Elvis Presley

5 **Don't Worry**
Marty Robbins

## 86 Surrender RCA 7850
### ELVIS PRESLEY

*Writers: Doc Pomus*
*Mort Shuman*

*Producer: Steve Sholes*

*March 20, 1961*
*2 weeks*

"I'T'S NOW OR NEVER" was Elvis Presley's biggest-selling single, so it was no surprise that he turned to another beginning-of-the-century Italian song for his 15th number one single. "Surrender" was based on *"Torna a Sorrento"* ("Come Back to Sorrento"), written in 1911 by Ernesto and B.G. de Curtis. Doc Pomus and Mort Shuman wrote English lyrics, and the song entered the Hot 100 at number 24 on February 20, 1961. It became the highest new entry on the Hot 100 of any Elvis song to date, beating the record set by "Are You Lonesome Tonight."

Elvis returned to RCA's Nashville studios on October 30 and 31, after recording in Hollywood for six months. "Surrender" was the only secular song recorded during these two days; the rest of the time was devoted to cutting 13 gospel songs. Twelve of these were released on the religious album *His Hand in Mine* in December, 1960. "Crying in the Chapel" was held back until 1965, when it broke a dry spell and went to number three.

While "Surrender" was number one, Elvis appeared live in concert in Hawaii—his final live performance for the next seven years. It was Col. Tom Parker's plan to have Elvis release three films a year with accompanying soundtrack albums and

### THE TOP FIVE
*Week of March 20, 1961*

1 **Surrender**
   Elvis Presley

2 **Pony Time**
   Chubby Checker

3 **Don't Worry**
   Marty Robbins

4 **Where the Boys Are**
   Connie Francis

5 **Dedicated to the One I Love**
   Shirelles

singles, but to stay off the live circuit, so as to keep the public hungry for Elvis.

On February 25, Elvis did a benefit concert in his hometown, and raised $51,000 for the Memphis Charities. Exactly one month later, he did another charity show, this time at Bloch Arena in Pearl Harbor to raise money for the USS Arizona Memorial Fund. Jimmy Stewart and Minnie Pearl also appeared, and they raised $53,000. Elvis sang 17 songs, concluding with "Hound Dog." He wouldn't sing another live note on stage until 1968.

While in Hawaii, Elvis shot some footage for his next movie, originally titled *Hawaii Beach Boy*. By the time it was released on November 14,

1961, the title had been changed to *Blue Hawaii*. Angela Lansbury played Elvis' domineering mother, who wants him to go into the family pineapple business instead of marrying his girlfriend, played by Joan Blackman.

It was Elvis' eighth movie, and set the pattern for most of the films that would follow. The plot was lightweight and the songs were plentiful: 14 in all, including "Can't Help Falling in Love." Like its predecessor, "(Marie's the Name) His Latest Flame" backed with "Little Sister," it failed to go to number one, but made the top five. When Elvis finally returned to performing, "Can't Help Falling in Love" replaced "Hound Dog" as his finale.

*Writers: Richard Rodgers*
*Lorenz Hart*

*Producer: Stu Phillips*

*April 3, 1961*
*3 weeks*

**W**HEN Rodgers and Hart wrote "Blue Moon" in 1934, their wildest dreams couldn't have produced the 1961 version by the Marcels. It's doubtful that lyricist Hart would have added "Dang-a-dang-dang, ding-a-dong-ding" to any of his songs.

"Blue Moon" was the only song by Rodgers and Hart to become a hit without originating in a stage or screen musical. Actually, "Blue Moon" was the third revision of a song that was intended to be in a show. After writing successful Broadway shows like *The Garrick Gaieties* (1925), *A Connecticut Yankee* (1927) and *Present Arms* (1928), Richard Rodgers and Lorenz Hart moved to Hollywood in 1931 to write a score for Paramount. They stayed for three years. In 1933, they wrote several songs for a movie starring Jean Harlow, including "Make Me a Star." Harlow and the song were dropped from the film. Hart wrote new lyrics for Rodgers' melody, and the song became "The Bad in Every Man." The song was given to MGM for *Manhattan Melodrama*, but was rejected. But MGM had their own publishing company, Robbins Music, and Jack Robbins liked the melody, too. He asked for new lyrics, and within one day he had "Blue Moon" on his desk.

The song was a hit, and appeared in several motion pictures, including *Words and Music* in 1948, *Malaya* in 1949, *East Side, West Side* in 1950 and *With a Song in My Heart* in 1952. Elvis Presley recorded a standard version of it in 1954, seven years before the Marcels released their version on Colpix.

The Marcels were a quintet from Pittsburgh. The group, named after a popular hair style, consisted of lead singer Cornelius Harp, first tenor Ronald Mundy, second tenor Gene Bricker, baritone Dick Knauss and bass singer Fred Johnson.

Their repertoire consisted of 1950s R&B songs when they met Colpix staff producer Stu Phillips. Stu had orders to devote all his time to another new artist on the label, but he believed in the Marcels enough to defy his boss and bring them into the studio at 8 p.m., after everyone else had gone home.

The Marcels had three songs to record and needed one more. Phillips didn't like any of the other songs the group chose, except for one excerpt from a song that had the same chord changes as "Heart and Soul" and "Blue Moon." Stu asked them if they knew "Heart and Soul," and they didn't, but one of the Marcels knew "Blue Moon." "So I gave him an hour to teach it to the others," Stu says.

The group learned the middle section of the melody wrong, but they recorded it anyway. The excerpt Stu liked became the intro to "Blue Moon." There were eight minutes of studio time left when the group recorded it. It was completed in two takes, both without stopping.

A new Colpix promotion man heard the tape and asked for a copy. Stu obliged, not realizing it would be given to Murray the K at WINS radio in New York. He loved it and played it 26 times on one show. The next day Stu was called in to his boss' office to explain how Murray the K had an "exclusive" on the Marcels.

"Blue Moon" went to number one in America and Britain. In 1980, producer/director Jon Landis used all "moon" songs in the soundtrack of *An American Werewolf in London*. Bobby Vinton's "Blue Moon" was heard over the opening credits, and the Marcels' version over the closing credits.

**THE TOP FIVE**
*Week of April 3, 1961*

1 **Blue Moon**
   Marcels

2 **Apache**
   Jorgen Ingmann

3 **Surrender**
   Elvis Presley

4 **Pony Time**
   Chubby Checker

5 **Dedicated to the One I Love**
   Shirelles

## 88  Runaway  BIG TOP 3067
### DEL SHANNON

*Writers: Charles Westover*
*Max Crook*

*Producers: Harry Balk*
*Irving Micahnik*

*April 24, 1961*
*4 weeks*

DEL SHANNON was the first person to take a John Lennon-Paul McCartney song into the Hot 100. Shannon was appearing at London's Royal Albert Hall with the Beatles in 1963, while "From Me to You" was the number one single in Britain. Shannon told Lennon he was going to record "From Me to You" for America, and John responded, "That'll be fine." But just as John went on stage, he turned to Del and said, "Don't do that!" Del thinks John must have realized the consequences of other artists competing against the Beatles with their own songs.

Despite John's last-minute command, Del recorded "From Me to You" before he left London. Del's version was released in America just as Vee Jay issued the Beatles' original. Shannon bested the Beatles, debuting on the Hot 100 on June 29. The Beatles would not enter the American chart until January, 1964 [see 143—"I Want to Hold Your Hand"].

Del Shannon was born Charles Westover in Coopersville, Michigan on December 30, 1939. The first instrument he played was a kazoo, providing melody for a neighbor accordionist. His mother taught him to play "Doodlee-Doo" on the ukulele, and he soon graduated to guitar. "I wanted to play so bad, my fingers used to bleed," he confesses.

There weren't too many people in Coopersville who could teach him to play the guitar, so young Charles would go to clubs on Saturday nights and observe guitarists in country bands, transposing what he saw from the point of view of the audience. "If they knew you were watching, they'd turn their backs."

He started singing in school. "My first introduction to echo was in the men's shower room." A sympathetic school principal would let him practice his guitar in the gym a couple of hours a day, and he'd sing Ink Spots songs at pep rallies ("that's where I got the falsetto").

Drafted after high school, he entertained troops for five months until a general changed the law about how long a soldier could be in special services. After his discharge, he returned to Battle Creek, Michigan. He played guitar in a club for a singer who drank too much, and ended up taking his place. When one of his band members quit, drummer Dick Parker suggested Max Crook as a replacement. Crook's specialty was playing the "musitron," an electronic organ that was a forerunner of the synthesizer.

They played the Hi-Lo club as Charlie Johnson and the Big Little Show Band, but Westover wasn't happy with that name. A Hi-Lo patron who dreamed of becoming a professional wrestler wanted to call himself Mark Shannon, and Charles liked that last name. During the day, he sold carpets, and the store owner owned a Cadillac Coupe de Ville, which inspired the first name of Del.

Ollie McLaughlin, a black DJ from WGRV in Ann Arbor, heard Del play and took him to Detroit, where he introduced him to Harry Balk and Irving Micahnik. They signed Del to Big Top Records, and sent him to New York to record a couple of songs. Ollie thought they were too slow to be singles, and suggested Del

find an uptempo tune. Back at the Hi-Lo, Crook hit an unusual chord change on the organ one night, going from A-minor to G, and Del stopped the show and told him to play it again. The next day, Del telephoned Max from the carpet shop and told him to bring a tape recorder to the Hi-Lo that night to record a new song he had written using those chord changes, "Runaway."

They performed it for the next three months, then drove back to New York in 10°F weather with a broken heater so they could record "Runaway." "I just said to myself, if this record isn't a hit, I'm going to go into the carpet business."

By the time the single was selling 80,000 copies a day, Balk told Del to quit selling carpets and come to Brooklyn for a gig at the Paramount Theater, where he would earn more than he made in a year at the carpet shop.

Del's next hit, "Hats Off to Larry," was a title he always thought would make a good Everly Brothers song. He signed with Amy Records in 1964, and recorded hits such as "Keep Searchin' (We'll Follow the Sun") and "Stranger in Town." In the late sixties, he discovered the group Smith with Gayle McCormick and arranged their version of the Shirelles' "Baby It's You." He also produced Brian Hyland's version of "Gypsy Woman."

On February 8, 1990, Del Shannon was found dead in his home in Santa Clarita, California, the victim of a self-inflicted gunshot wound. He had already recorded an album with producer Jeff Lynne. It was posthumously released in 1991.

---

### THE TOP FIVE
*Week of April 24, 1961*

1  **Runaway**
   Del Shannon

2  **Blue Moon**
   Marcels

3  **Mother-In-Law**
   Ernie K-Doe

4  **But I Do**
   Clarence "Frogman" Henry

5  **On the Rebound**
   Floyd Kramer

*Writer: Allen Toussaint*

*Producer: Allen Toussaint*

*May 22, 1961*
*1 week*

*"The word is poison, I know."\**

LET the record show that the Mothers-in-Law of America never expressed their appreciation to singer Ernie K-Doe or writer/producer Allen Toussaint for making "Mother-in-Law" the number one song in the land. Little wonder, considering it was the ultimate mother-in-law joke, suggesting she was "sent from down below."

Nevertheless, the song earned a place in rock history by spreading the gospel piano of the New Orleans sound, as championed by Toussaint. He was the head of A&R for Minit, a label formed in 1960. In March of that year, Minit scored with Jessie Hill's "Ooh Poo Pah Doo," which peaked at number 28.

Before "Mother-in-Law," Ernie K-Doe was Ernest Kador Jr. Born in New Orleans on February 22, 1936, he was the ninth of 11 children. His father was the Reverend Ernest Kador, Sr., a Baptist minister, and young Ernest began singing in his father's New Home Baptist church choir at age seven.

His mother lived in Chicago, so Ernie was raised by his aunt in New Orleans. By the time he was 15, he was entering local talent shows and singing in nightclubs while finding time to letter in football, basketball and track at Booker T. Washington High School.

Ernie visited his mother in Chicago, where she signed permission slips for him to sing in clubs. After two years in the Windy City, he returned to New Orleans and joined the Blue Diamonds. They released one single on Savoy Records and performed at the city's famed night spot, the Club Tijuana. It was the same club where artists like Johnny Ace, Chuck Willis and Little Richard had performed.

Talent scouts from record companies often checked out the performers at the Tijuana, and one of them signed Ernie to Specialty, the same label that had Little Richard under contract. Ernie recorded his first solo single, "Do Baby Do," the same day Little Richard recorded "Tutti Frutti." After another single on Ember, Ernie signed with Minit, a label owned by Joe Banashak. It was Banashak who suggested Kador was too difficult to pronounce, and the phonetic K-Doe would be a better stage name. Later, Ernie would legally change his name to K-Doe and copyright it as well.

Ernie found "Mother-in-Law" in Toussaint's trash—it was a song he had written and thrown away. Ernie was having marital problems at the time and thought his mother-in-law was responsible for some of them, so he told Toussaint he wanted to record the discarded song.

The irresistable hook in the song is Benny Spellman's deep bass voice intoning "mother-in-law" after K-Doe pauses at the appropriate places. Ernie returned the favor the following year by singing on Spellman's "Lipstick Traces (On a Cigarette)."

"Mother-in-Law" was K-Doe's only top 50 hit. His final chart entry was "Popeye Joe" in February, 1962. He continued to record for Minit until it was sold to Liberty in 1965, and then signed with Duke Records. After three years, he returned to producer Toussaint, but without productive results. K-Doe died of liver failure at University Hospital in New Orleans on July 5, 2001. He was 65.

## THE TOP FIVE
*Week of May 22, 1961*

1 **Mother-In-Law**
Ernie K-Doe

2 **Runaway**
Del Shannon

3 **Daddy's Home**
Shep and the Limelites

4 **One Hundred Pounds of Clay**
Gene McDaniels

5 **Travelin' Man**
Ricky Nelson

## Travelin' Man IMPERIAL 5741
### RICKY NELSON

*Writer: Jerry Fuller*

*Producer: Ricky Nelson*

*May 29, 1961*
*2 weeks*

"Travelin' Man" was a comeback record of sorts for Ricky Nelson, who had eight consecutive top 10 singles between 1957-1959, including his first number one [see 40—"Poor Little Fool"]. After "Just a Little Too Much" in the summer of '59, Ricky failed to make the top 10 with his next four releases. In 1961, the two-sided smash "Travelin' Man" and "Hello Mary Lou" broke the spell.

"Travelin' Man" was written by Jerry Fuller while he was waiting for his wife in a park. He had a world atlas with him, and picked out different locales around the world to write about. He wrote the song for Sam Cooke, and recorded a demo with Glen Campbell and Dave Burgess of the Champs [see 34—"Tequila"] backing him. Fuller took the completed demo to Cooke's manager, J.W. Alexander, whose office was adjacent to Lou Chudd's, head of Ricky's label, Imperial Records.

Alexander played the demo, thanked Fuller, and threw the tape away as soon as he had gone. But Nelson's bass player, Joe Osbourne, was in Chudd's office and heard the song. He went in and asked Alexander if he could hear that song again. Cooke's manager pulled it out of the garbage and gave it to him. Fuller heard the song on "The Adventures of Ozzie and Harriet" one night, as Ricky continued his tradition of sing-ing a song at the end of every episode.

The flip side of "Travelin' Man" was written by Gene Pitney, who had already recorded it himself with no success. "Hello Mary Lou" peaked at number nine.

After "Travelin' Man," Ricky had several more big hits on Imperial, including "Young World," "Teenage Idol" and "It's Up to You." His contract with Imperial was set to expire at the end of 1962, and a major bidding war erupted. The ultimate winner was Decca Records, owned by MCA, which offered Ricky one million dollars over a 20-year-period.

There were only two major hits on Decca, "Fools Rush In" and "For You." America had seen Ricky grow from a precocious eight-year-old boy to a happily married adult (his real-life wife, Kris Nelson, played his wife on the series) on television, and when the series ended in 1966, Ricky—now known as Rick—found his recording career in a slump.

In 1969, a more mature Rick Nelson returned to the charts with a version of Bob Dylan's "She Belongs to Me," backed by the Stone Canyon Band. Three years later, he headlined one of Richard Nader's rock and roll revival shows at Madison Square Garden. After playing some of his biggest hits, Rick turned to his newer material. The audience turned too, against him. Their ungrateful reaction resulted in the song "Garden Party," in which Rick vented his frustration at his fans who wanted him to remain in an early sixties time warp. The song went to number six on the Hot 100.

After his 20-year pact with MCA ended, Rick recorded an album for Epic in 1977 and one for Capitol in 1981. He continued his acting career, starring as the principal in an NBC-TV movie, "High School, U.S.A.," in 1983. His secretary was played by his mother, Harriet. Rick also performed in concert frequently, sometimes doing up to 200 dates in one year. On December 30, 1985, Nelson and his band played at PJ's Lounge in Guntersville, Alabama. The next day they were en route to Dallas for a New Year's Eve show at the Park Suite Hotel. Their chartered twin-engine DC-3 crashed at 5:15 p.m. CST in a hayfield near De Kalb, 135 miles east of Dallas. Rick Nelson was killed along with his fiancée, Helen Blair, four members of his band and one of his road crew.

---

## THE TOP FIVE
### *Week of May 29, 1961*

1 **Travelin' Man**
  Ricky Nelson

2 **Daddy's Home**
  Shep and the Limelites

3 **Runing Scared**
  Roy Orbison

4 **Mama Said**
  Shirelles

5 **Mother-In-Law**
  Ernie K-Doe

*Writers: Roy Orbison*
*Joe Melson*

*Producer: Fred Foster*

*June 5, 1961*
*1 week*

**A**LONG with Elvis Presley, Carl Perkins and Jerry Lee Lewis, Roy Orbison recorded for Sam Phillips' Sun Records in Memphis. Like his label-mates, he is one of the most influential figures of the rock era. Devotees of Orbison's music include the Beatles, Bob Dylan and Bruce Springsteen.

Many of Orbison's songs are based on personal experience. A self-confessed introvert, Orbison and his writing partner, Joe Melson, wrote "Running Scared" in five minutes, just slightly longer than it takes to sing the song. But they had spent several non-productive writing sessions working on it.

Orbison almost gave his first national hit, "Only the Lonely," to Elvis and the Everly Brothers before recording it himself. After writing the song with Melson, the two collaborators took "Only the Lonely" to Memphis to play it for Presley. But they arrived from Texas at 6:00 a.m. and found people at Graceland still sleeping.

Elvis suggested they meet later that day in Nashville. Orbison and Melson drove there, but instead of waiting for Elvis, they played it for Phil Everly (the Everly Brothers had recorded Orbison's "Claudette," a song he had written about his wife). Too shy to tell Phil he wanted him to record "Only the Lonely," Orbison

patiently listened while Phil responded by playing one of his new songs. Finally, Orbison just decided to record the song himself. It went to number two in America and number one in Britain.

Roy Kelton Orbison was born on April 23, 1936, in Vernon, Texas and raised in the town of Wink. His father, Orbie, worked in the oil fields and his mother, Nadine, was a nurse. His father gave him a guitar when he was six years old, and by the time he was eight he was playing on a Sunday morning country show on KVWC, a radio station in Kermit, Texas. At 13, he formed his own group, the Wink Westerners, with members of his high school band. In the next two years, he came to realize he was a better singer than a guitarist and started writing songs for himself.

At North Texas University, he was inspired by the success of fellow student Pat Boone. Roy liked a song written by two college fraternity brothers, "Ooby Dooby," and took his new group, the Teen Kings, to Norman Petty's studios in Clovis, New Mexico, to record it. It was released on Petty's Je-Wel label, but it didn't fare well. Meanwhile, Orbison hosted a local television show and met Johnny Cash, who suggested Roy contact Sam Phillips at Sun Records in Memphis.

Roy was signed to Sun and recorded a stronger version of "Ooby Dooby," which was his first chart entry. Phillips wanted Roy to record rock and roll like the rest of the Sun artists, and Roy preferred to sing ballads. Through the Everly Brothers, Orbison came under the management guidance of Wesley Rose, who secured a recording contract with RCA. After a brief association with the label and producer Chet Atkins, Rose took Orbison to a brand-new label: Fred Foster's Monument Records. Although his first two recording sessions for Monument weren't very successful, it was at the third session that he cut "Only the Lonely," the first of nine top 10 songs he would record for Monument.

## THE TOP FIVE
*Week of June 5, 1961*

1 **Running Scared**
Roy Orbison

2 **Travelin' Man**
Ricky Nelson

3 **Daddy's Home**
Shep and the Limelites

4 **Mama Said**
Shirelles

5 **I Feel So Bad**
Elvis Presley

## 92 Moody River DOT 16209
### PAT BOONE

*Writer: Gary Bruce*

*Producer: Randy Wood*

*June 19, 1961*
*1 week*

"MOODY RIVER" may hold the record for the number one single that made it from the recording studio to the airwaves in the shortest amount of time.

Randy Wood, Pat Boone's producer and the owner of Dot Records, remembered the country version of "Moody River" by Chase Webster and thought it could be a pop hit for Pat. While Boone's movie and television careers were going great guns, his luck on the record charts had diminished considerably. After two number one singles and many top ten hits, Pat was finding it difficult in 1959-1960 to match his earlier success. In fact, of his last 13 chart records, only two had cracked the lower regions of the top 20.

Pat reminisces about the recording session for "Moody River": "We'd done it in a very high key, cause Randy wanted me to sound really in pain, and I was, trying to sing that high. I went from the studio to a friend's house to pick up my wife—she had been visiting for a little while. We were about to go home. They had their radio tuned to a top 40 station, and we were about to walk out the door when I heard...the intro to either my record or Chase Webster's. I turned it up just in time to hear the disc jockey say over the intro, 'And now our brand new pick

hit of the week, Pat Boone's "Moody River.'"

"I'm not home from the studio from recording the song yet, and it's already pick hit of the week on a major top 40 radio station!

"What had happened was Randy believed in it so much, he had an acetate made from the master tape, went right over to the radio studio, met the program director, said 'here's the song Pat just recorded, what do you think?' and the guy said, 'you know, it's time for a new pick hit of the week, let's just put it right on the air.'"

Pat was with Dot Records for 13 years. By the time he left, Randy Wood had sold the label to Paramount, which in turn was sold to Gulf + Western. Boone went to Capitol, and then to Tetragrammaton Records, a label owned by comedian

Bill Cosby and Roy Silver. When they closed their doors, Boone went with Mike Curb at MGM and through him later signed with Motown's country label, Melodyland. His daughters, recording as the Boones, also signed with Motown.

Then Pat and his daughters signed with Warner/Curb Records. Cherry, Lindy, Debby and Laury released some more singles until Debby tried one on her own [see 475—"You Light Up My Life"].

Pat also became an author. He recorded a song named after his first book, *Twixt Twelve and Twenty*, a guide for teenagers. All royalties were donated to the Northeastern Institute of Christian Education.

Pat limited his recording activities, but he remained an active television personality. For some time, he hosted a nationally syndicated weekly show.

### THE TOP FIVE
*Week of June 19, 1961*

1. **Moody River**
   Pat Boone

2. **Travelin' Man**
   Ricky Nelson

3. **Quarter to Three**
   Gary U. S. Bonds

4. **Stand by Me**
   Ben E. King

5. **Raindrops**
   Dee Clark

*Writers: Gene Barge*
*Frank Guida*
*Gary Anderson*
*Joe Royster*

*Producer: Frank Guida*

*June 26, 1961*
*2 weeks*

Gary U.S. Bonds was playing a New Jersey club called the Red Baron in 1978, when he thought he'd give a local kid who seemed fairly popular a break by bringing him up on stage. Although he didn't know who the guy was, the audience liked the idea, so Gary introduced Bruce Springsteen. The reaction overwhelmed Bonds, as he sang a duet on "Quarter to Three" with this "new kid." It was only later that Gary found out just who Bruce Springsteen was, and that "the Boss" usually sang "Quarter to Three" as an encore number in his own act.

After that incredible evening, Springsteen asked Gary if they could work on an album together. It took two years for Bruce to complete his own album, *The River*, but when it was done he and Miami Steve Van Zandt produced the *Dedication* album that gave Gary his first hit in 19 years, "This Little Girl."

The Gary U.S. Bonds story starts on June 6, 1939, when Gary Anderson was born in Jacksonville, Florida. His family moved to Norfolk, Virginia, where Gary formed a group, the Turks, and sang doo-wop on street corners. He was discovered by Frank Guida, owner of the Norfolk Recording Studios. Guida and a shoe salesman named Joe Royster had written a country and western sounding song, "New Orleans," and asked 19-year-old Gary to record it. Gary changed the arrangement by adding a chorus and a drum beat. When the record was released, Gary was surprised to find out his name wasn't listed as the artist—the label read "U.S. Bonds."

There was a logical explanation. A delicatessen was located next door to the studio, and the owner was a strong believer in Uncle Sam. He had posters in the deli that reminded customers to buy savings bonds, and Gary speculates that Guida was inspired one day while eating a pastrami sandwich.

It was too late to go back to Gary Anderson, so future releases listed his name as Gary U.S. Bonds, confusing fans who thought U.S. Bonds was a group name.

Celebrating the success of "New Orleans," which went to number six, Gary was in the studio with the members of another Legrand recording act, the Church Street Five. Their instrumental single, "A Night with Daddy G," wasn't doing very well, and after everyone had more than enough to drink, Daddy G (Barge) asked Bonds to write lyrics for it. Ten minutes later Gary had come up with some words and the band started jamming on the arrangement.

Although many rock historians claim the resulting song, "Quarter to Three," was recorded accidentally, Bonds has said in interviews that he turned on the tape recorder.

Over the next 15 months Gary had a few more hits, including "School Is In," "School Is Out," "Dear Lady Twist" and "Twist, Twist Senora." After reaching the lower rungs of the chart with "Copy Cat" in the summer of 1962, Bonds was out of the picture until "This Little Girl" hit in the spring of 1981.

Bonds recorded two albums with Springsteen and Van Zandt for EMI-America Records, then left the label and his two "mentors" to produce his own album, *Standing in the Line of Fire* for the independent Phoenix label.

## THE TOP FIVE
*Week of June 26, 1961*

1  **Quarter to Three**
   Gary U. S. Bonds

2  **Raindrops**
   Dee Clark

3  **Moody River**
   Pat Boone

4  **Tossin' and Turnin'**
   Bobby Lewis

5  **Travelin' Man**
   Ricky Nelson

## 94 Tossin' and Turnin' BELTONE 1002
### BOBBY LEWIS

*Writers: Ritchie Adams*
*Joe Rene*

*Producer: Joe Rene*

*July 10, 1961*
*7 weeks*

"TOSSIN' AND TURNIN'" by Bobby Lewis is one of the longest-running number one hits by a solo male artist in the rock era. The only solo male singers who have bested the seven-week run are Elvis Presley, Eminem, Guy Mitchell, Bobby Darin and 50 Cent. Those who tied are Tennessee Ernie Ford, Marvin Gaye, Michael Jackson, Andy Gibb, Bryan Adams, Snow, Montell Jordan and Nelly.

Bobby Lewis was born February 17, 1933 in Indianapolis, Indiana. He grew up in an orphanage, where his musical talent was recognized early.

At five years old, Bobby was given piano lessons and during school he sang with the glee club and in class productions. He was adopted at age 12 and went to live with his new family in Detroit. Before he was 16, he worked as a janitor, an ice man, a truck driver and a hotel clerk, none of which satisifed him as much as playing music.

He sang in a downtown nightclub and became friendly with Jackie Wilson, whose manager introduced him to the head of Parrot Records, a Chicago-based label. In 1956, Bobby recorded "My Love Is Solid as a Rock," for Parrot, his first single release. Returning to Detroit, Bobby appeared on Soupy Sales' local late-night variety show and was asked back on a regular basis. In 1958, Bobby recorded "Mumbles Blues" on the Spotlight label, but it suffered

the same fate as his Parrot release.

Jackie Wilson was having great success, and urged Bobby to go to New York. Bobby declined, but his wife suggested he would never be more successful if he remained in Detroit. When Wilson wired money for a train ticket to Manhattan, Lewis accepted.

Jackie and his manager tried to help Bobby, but he was turned down by many record companies. Bobby continued to knock on doors and sing in clubs. He played a week at the Apollo Theater, where he gave encouragement to a nervous group of white singers, the Fireflies, who had a hit in 1959 with "You Were Mine."

Three weeks later, Bobby was making more rounds of labels when he found Beltone Records. He liked the name immediately, because he had sung in a gospel group called the Belltones. He asked for an audition, and sat down at the piano when he recognized a familiar face—the lead singer of the Fireflies, Ritchie Adams. Surprised to see him, Bobby learned that Adams was signed to Beltone. He and label owner Joe Rene listened to some of Bobby's songs, and then Ritchie pulled out a song he had written and asked Bobby to try it. When Bobby sang, "I couldn't sleep at all last night," Ritchie knew he had found the right person to record "Tossin' and Turnin'."

Bobby had one more top 10 single, "One Track Mind." Two more singles, including "I'm Tossin' and Turnin' Again," made the lower region of the Hot 100 before Lewis disappeared from the chart forever.

### THE TOP FIVE
*Week of July 10, 1961*

1  **Tossin' and Turnin'**
   Bobby Lewis

2  **Boll Weevil Song**
   Brook Benton

3  **Quarter to Three**
   Gary U. S. Bonds

4  **Raindrops**
   Dee Clark

5  **The Writing on the Wall**
   Adam Wade

Writers: *Bert Kaempfert*
*Kay Twomey*
*Fred Wise*
*Ben Weisman*

Producer: *Shelby Singleton, Jr.*

*August 28, 1961*
*1 week*

**O**N THE DAY before Joe Dowell was to record his first four songs in Nashville for Mercury Records' Smash label, producer Shelby Singleton, Jr., went to see a screening of Elvis Presley's fifth movie, *G. I. Blues* [see 67—"Stuck On You"]. One of the songs Shelby heard in the movie was "Wooden Heart *(Muss I Denn)*," a part-English, part-German adaptation of a German folk song, "*Muss I Denn zum Staedele Hinaus.*" Singleton was already familiar with the song because he had been watching a version by Gus Bacchus move up the German pop chart. Elvis Presley had another single climbing the Hot 100 ("I Feel So Bad"), so it seemed unlikely that RCA would release "Wooden Heart" by Elvis. Shelby decided to record a cover version of the song with Dowell.

Joe arrived for the session at 11 AM and was given three hours to learn the song. "A man named Eddie Wilson came in to the office to teach me to sing '*Muss I Denn, Muss I Denn.*' I didn't have any idea what I was singing; I learned the song phonetically," Joe recalls.

Elvis' version of the song featured tuba and organ. Joe remembers how Singleton came up with a more commercial sound: "Jerry Kennedy mimicked the tuba with a bass guitar, and Ray Stevens [see 274—"Everything is Beautiful"] played an organ, mimicking an accordion." Dowell's version of "Wooden Heart" was rushed out in three days and he was sent on a one-month "barnstorming tour." There were four other cover versions of "Wooden Heart" plus the Elvis original competing with his recording, but Joe's promotional tour helped win airplay for his own version. Joe's "Wooden Heart" entered the Hot 100 at number 98 on June 26, 1961, and moved to number one nine weeks later.

In Britain and throughout Europe, Elvis' "Wooden Heart" was already a single. In the United Kingdom, it was number one for six weeks. "It's Now or Never" and "Are You Lonesome Tonight," Elvis' previous two singles, had also gone to number one, making Presley the first artist to score three chart-toppers with consecutive British releases.

"Wooden Heart" was adapted by Bert Kaempfert [see 82—"Wonderland by Night"], Kay Twomey, Fred Wise, and Ben Weisman. The German folk song is sung in the dialect of the Hessian state, and a translation of the German line that Dowell sang would read something like, "I have to leave our little town and you, my darling, have to stay behind."

Joe Dowell was born on January 23, 1940, in Bloomington, Indiana. The family moved a year later when Joe's father, an executive with the Boy Scouts of America, was offered a better job in Bloomington, Illinois. When he was 13, Joe bought a ten-dollar guitar and wrote his first song, "Tell Me."

He was in the ninth grade when he made his first public performance, singing "Unchained Melody" at an amateur talent show. He competed in country fair talent contests while majoring in radio and television at the University of Illinois. "I listened to WLS radio after and during homework," Joe says. "I tried to envision that I would be on the radio. I could

actually hear my own voice on WLS." With that dream in mind, he went to Nashville on a semester break, three weeks before his twenty-first birthday, to find a record company that would sign him.

He borrowed a friend's VW and drove to Nashville, where he rented a room for three dollars a night at the YMCA. A week of knocking on doors proved fruitless. On his last day in Nashville, he went to the office of Teddy and Doyle Wilburn, regular singers on the Grand Ole Opry show. They liked his voice and introduced him to a gentleman in an adjoining office. That was Shelby Singleton, Jr., of Mercury Records, who was impressed with Dowell's voice and his "all-American Jack Armstrong look."

Joe resumed his studies, then returned to Nashville by train the following May for his first recording session. He followed "Wooden Heart" with two more singles on Smash, "The Bridge of Love" (number 50) and "Little Red Rented Rowboat" (number 23), then was dropped from the label at age 23. He had completed his degree in radio-television, and found a new career writing commercials. At first he had his own radio show in Illinois and wrote jingles for his sponsors, then moved on to being a spokesperson for financial institutions.

He gave up the world of advertising in 1980 to devote time to writing a book, which he completed in 1985. He has also written a new song, "Homeward on the Wind," and plans to record it with producer Al DeLory.

## THE TOP FIVE
*Week of August 28, 1961*

1 **Wooden Heart (Muss I Denn)**
Joe Dowell

2 **Tossin' and Turnin'**
Bobby Lewis

3 **Michael**
Highwaymen

4 **Last Night**
Mar-Keys

5 **You Don't Know What You've Got (Until You Lose It)**
Ral Donner

## 96 Michael UNITED ARTISTS 258
### THE HIGHWAYMEN

Writer: (Traditional) Dave Fisher

Producer: Dave Fisher

September 4, 1961
2 weeks

THE five members of the Highwaymen were all freshmen from the same fraternity at Wesleyan University in Middletown, Connecticut. They got together to perform at a campus party in 1959, and were so well-received, they decided to keep the act going. The result was international success, giving them a number one single in America (the first for the United Artists label) and, one month later, in Britain as well.

The song was a traditional folk song, sung in the 19th century by slaves who lived on the islands off the coast of Georgia and travelled to work on the mainland each day by boat.

Dave Fisher, who adapted "Michael," organized the group. He played the banjo and was first tenor, as well as arranging their songs. The other four members were: Bob Burnett, the college's pole vault champion, who sang tenor and played bongos and maracas; Steve Trott, the fraternity's president, who played guitar and sang third tenor; Steve Butts, a polio victim as a child who was the sportscaster for the campus radio station and sang bass; and Chan Daniels, a baritone who played a South American instrument called a charango, made from the shell of an armadillo.

The group performed folk songs from many different countries, often singing in French, Spanish, Hebrew and other languages as well as English. They rehearsed in the basement of their frat house and were very suc-

cessful on a local basis, when someone suggested they get in touch with talent agents in New York. They met Ken Greengrass in November of 1960. He became their manager and set up an audition with United Artists Records.

One of the songs they recorded for their first album was "Michael." It was released as a single in January, 1961, but nothing happened for six months. Finally, Dick Smith, a DJ at WORC in Worcester, Massachussetts, started playing the record, and it entered Billboard's chart at number 100 on July 10, 1961.

The quintet had many offers to tour, but turned a majority of them down to pay attention to studying. They had one more top 20 hit, "Cottonfields," in early 1962. But when Burnett and Trott graduated that year, they left the group and the record business. The group added Gil Robbins and became a quartet, until Burnett returned in 1963. A year later, the Highwaymen disbanded. ABC Records bought the name, and put together an entirely new group to become "the Highwaymen."

The original members reunited in the latter half of the 1970s to record an updated version of "Michael," but it wasn't a hit. Fisher has concentrated on his songwriting. Robbins went into acting, while Butts became an administrator at a college. Burnett became an attorney and Trott joined the Los Angeles District Attorney's staff. Daniels earned a graduate degree from Harvard and worked at MGM Records until he died of pneumonia on August 2, 1975.

---

### THE TOP FIVE
*Week of September 4, 1961*

1  **Michael**
   Highwaymen

2  **Wooden Heart (Muss I Denn)**
   Joe Dowell

3  **Tossin' and Turnin'**
   Bobby Lewis

4  **You Don't Know What You've Got (Until You Lose It)**
   Ral Donner

5  **School Is Out**
   Gary U.S. Bonds

LIBERTY 55354 **Take Good Care of My Baby**
BOBBY VEE

**97**

*Writers: Gerry Goffin*
*Carole King*

*Producer: Snuff Garrett*

*September 18, 1961*
*3 weeks*

THE year was 1959, and 15-year-old Robert Velline was excitedly looking forward to the first-ever rock and roll concert to come to his home town of Fargo, North Dakota. Velline was a guitarist himself, and just two weeks before the big concert, he formed a band with one of his older brothers on drums and a friend on bass. That didn't seem important on the morning of February 3. All that mattered was that night, he would see the greatest rock stars in the world: Dion and the Belmonts, the Big Bopper, Ritchie Valens and Velline's idol, Buddy Holly.

Velline came home from school for lunch and heard the terrible news. A plane had crashed in a cornfield in Iowa. All the passengers had been killed. Buddy Holly, Ritchie Valens and J.P. Richardson, the Big Bopper, were dead.

Fargo's top 40 station, KFGO, put out a call for help. Was there a local group that could play that night? Bobby's group volunteered.

They bought matching ties and sweaters, came up with the name the Shadows and rehearsed the Buddy Holly songs they knew. With nervous anticipation, they showed up at the auditorium. They were second on the bill and they were a hit. A local promoter, Bing Bingstrom, was

impressed enough to start booking them.

Velline, now Bobby Vee, wrote a Holly-inspired song called "Suzy Baby" and recorded it on June 1. It was a local hit in Minneapolis and San Diego. The Shadows thought about hiring a piano player, and interviewed an 18-year-old kid who had played with Conway Twitty. He called himself Elston Gunn, but his real name was Robert Zimmerman. He didn't work out for the Shadows, but did nicely on his own later, as Bob Dylan.

Bobby Vee and the Shadows were signed to Liberty Records under the guidance of producer Snuff Garrett.

After a few flops, Garrett took Vee to Norman Petty's studio in Clovis, New Mexico, where Buddy Holly recorded his hits. One of the songs he recorded was an old R&B tune by the Clovers, "Devil or Angel," and it became Vee's first national hit, peaking at number six. Vee's next hit, "Rubber Ball," was written by Aaron Schroeder and Gene Pitney (under his mother's name) and it also peaked at six.

In 1961, Garrett made one of his many trips to New York to find material for Bobby to record. Meet-

ing with publisher Don Kirshner at Aldon Music, Garrett heard a demo of Carole King singing "Take Good Care of My Baby," a song she had written with her husband, Gerry Goffin. Garrett told Kirshner he wanted it, but the publisher knew that Garrett didn't want material that had already been recorded by someone else. Kirshner told him someone else had already recorded it.

Garrett asked who, and was informed that Dion had cut it, but wasn't going to release it. Garrett wanted it anyway, but he felt the song needed an introductory verse and sat down with Carole to work out, "My tears are falling, cause you've taken her away..."

The song became Vee's only number one record, and the second for the Goffin-King team [see 83—"Will You Love Me Tomorrow"]. Dion's original version, without the introduction, was eventually released as an album track on *Runaround Sue*. In 1972, Bobby re-recorded "Take Good Care of My Baby" as a ballad. It appeared on the album "Nothin' Like a Sunny Day" by Robert Thomas Velline, with no mention of "Bobby Vee" anywhere to be found.

## THE TOP FIVE

*Week of September 18, 1961*

1 **Take Good Care of My Baby**
Bobby Vee

2 **Michael**
Highwaymen

3 **My True Story**
Jive Five

4 **(Marie's the Name)**
**His Latest Flame**
Elvis Presley

5 **Crying**
Roy Orbison

## 98 Hit the Road Jack ABC-PARAMOUNT 10244
### RAY CHARLES

Writer: *Percy Mayfield*

Producer: *Sid Feller*

*October 9, 1961*
*2 weeks*

*Ray Charles is the only genius in our business.*
—FRANK SINATRA
*I believe genius is a higher category. And I don't believe Ray Charles is even near it.*
—RAY CHARLES

Ray CHARLES recorded "Hit the Road Jack," his second number one single, after his good friend, the late songwriter Percy Mayfield, brought it to him. Mayfield said the song would work on two levels. Some people would think it was funny, and for others, it would be real. Ray thought it was cute and liked the "call-and-response" that featured so strongly in his first big hit, "What'd I Say." That song was released on Atlantic Records, a New York label that was the leader in the R&B field in the fifties. They bought Ray's contract

from Swingtime Records in 1954, and a year later Ray called Atlantic executive Jerry Wexler and said he was ready to record a song called "I Got a Woman." Wexler met Charles in Atlanta and the song was recorded at a radio station so small that while they were recording, an announcer was doing a news broadcast from the control room, preventing them from playing anything back.

"I Got a Woman" introduced the genius of Ray Charles to white audiences, but it was "What'd I Say" that gave him his first top 10 single. The song originated at a dance one night when Ray had played everything he knew and the audience wanted more. He told his seven-piece band to follow him, and his quartet of back-up singers, the Raelets, to repeat what he said when he paused. The result was so popular he had to repeat the spontaenous song the next night.

On June 26, 1959, Ray recorded a country song, "I'm Movin' On." The title proved prophetic, for ABC-Paramount Records offered him a contract that was so rewarding he found it impossible to reject. In fairness to his friends at Atlantic, he approached them and told them if they would match ABC, he would stay with them. Unable to meet ABC's generous offer, Atlantic gave Ray blessings to leave. It was an amiable but sad parting, and even when he was signed to ABC, Ray was always able to call on Atlantic for support. The label even allowed then-engineer Tom Dowd to come to California and help build Ray's recording studio.

ABC assigned Sid Feller to produce Ray, and their first collaboration took place in Hollywood on December 29, 1959. The label's faith in Ray was well-rewarded. His second release, "Georgia on My Mind," shot to number one. He recorded jazz for ABC's subsidiary label, Impulse, and had a top 10 song with the instrumental "One Mint Julep" in 1961. But Ray's most successful recording project was still a year away.

### THE TOP FIVE
*Week of October 9, 1961*

1 **Hit the Road Jack**
  Ray Charles

2 **Crying**
  Roy Orbison

3 **Take Good Care of My Baby**
  Bobby Vee

4 **Runaround Sue**
  Dion

5 **Bristol Stomp**
  Dovells

Writers: *Dion DiMucci*
*Ernie Maresca*

Producer: *Gene Schwartz*

*October 23, 1961*
*2 weeks*

**H**EARING a Dion song from the early 1960s summons up an image of tough, cool doo-wop singers on a Bronx street corner. They really weren't that tough and cool, but Dion didn't admit until years later that his real feelings and emotions had been bottled up inside while he projected the right image for his neighborhood.

He sure didn't tell his friends that he enjoyed listening to his father's Al Jolson records, or that he accidentally found a country music station on the radio, and had fallen in love with the songs of Hank Williams, which he played on the Gibson guitar his parents bought him when he was eight years old.

Dion was in a neighborhood gang, the Fordham Baldies, when he recorded four songs (including Fats Domino's "Rosalie" and Carl Perkins' "Boppin' the Blues") as a Valentine's Day gift for his mother. She played them for all her friends, including one who knew someone at a small label, Mohawk Records. As a result, Dion went into the recording studio to cut "The Chosen Few" with a backing track by a vocal group he never met, the Timberlanes. Dion describes them as sounding "counterfeit." "I told

them, if you really want to hear some singing, I'll bring some guys down here." Dion searched the pool halls, candy stores and streets of several Bronx neighborhoods and found Angelo D'Aleo, Freddie Milano and Carlo Mastrangelo, who named themselves after Belmont Avenue in the Bronx.

Dion and the Belmonts recorded two more singles for Mohawk, including "Tag Along," written by Gene Schwartz. "There was one guy in the company who thought we sang flat, and we got into a disagreement," Dion recalls. "That's how Laurie Records got started." Schwartz started the Laurie label and signed the group. Their first release, "I Wonder Why," peaked at 19, and they had seven more hit records (including the top three "Where or When") before Dion decided to go solo.

Dion's biggest hit was "Runaround Sue," a song he wrote with Ernie Maresca, who went on to have his own hit, "Shout! Shout! (Knock Yourself Out)." Although Dion married a woman named Sue, he remembers the song being written about a girl named Roberta. "The song was put together in a schoolyard. We used to hang out and just bang on cardboard boxes and get these riffs going that you could sing to. That was one of those things that worked and I put some words to it."

The Del Satins were the un-credited backing vocal group on

"Runaround Sue" and Dion's next hit, "The Wanderer." After four more hits on Laurie, including "Lovers Who Wander" and "Little Diane," Dion signed with Columbia Records, where he was influenced by A&R man John Hammond, Sr., to record more country, folk and blues songs like "Ruby Baby," "Be Careful of Stones That You Throw" and "Drip Drop."

Dion was living in Miami in 1968 when Gene Schwartz at Laurie asked producer Phil Gernhard to bring him Dick Holler's "Abraham, Martin and John." Reluctant at first to record a song about assassinations, Dion changed his mind when he saw the positive message in the song. It went to number four, but the reunion with Laurie was brief. They released an edited version of Dion singing Joni Mitchell's "Clouds," and he felt they had destroyed the meaning of the song. He signed with Warner Brothers and recorded the critically acclaimed "Your Own Back Yard," which dealt honestly with the drug addiction he had suffered since being a teenager, and his kicking the habit.

For years, Dion had been turning down invitations to appear on oldies shows, but in 1972 he had a one-night-only triumphant reunion with the Belmonts on stage at Madison Square Garden. In 1975, a Dion album produced by Phil Spector was released in Britain only. Dion's next few albums reflected his turn toward Christianity. But in 1989 he returned to the world of secular music with the album *Yo, Frankie*, produced by Dave Edmunds and Bryan Adams. It was released by Arista.

## THE TOP FIVE
*Week of October 23, 1961*

1  **Runaround Sue**
   Dion

2  **Bristol Stomp**
   Dovells

3  **Big Bad John**
   Jimmy Dean

4  **Hit the Road Jack**
   Ray Charles

5  **Sad Movies (Make Me Cry)**
   Sue Thompson

## 100 Big Bad John COLUMBIA 42175
### JIMMY DEAN

*Writer: Jimmy Dean*

*Producer: Don Law*

*November 6, 1961*
*5 weeks*

THE 100th number one single of the rock era was written in an hour-and-a-half on a plane ride to Nashville by a man who introduced many future country stars to the nation on his weekly television series.

Jimmy Dean was born Seth Ward on August 10, 1928, in Plainview, Texas. His mother taught him to play the piano, and he soon took up the harmonica and accordion. When he was 18, he left home to join the Air Force and was stationed at Bolling Air Base near Washington, D.C.

Some of the men at the base worked after hours playing music at a local nightclub. When the fiddle player took ill, they asked Dean to sit in with them and play the accordion in exchange for a fourth of the tips. When the fiddle player tried to return, the band said they wanted to keep Dean instead.

Once out of the Air Force, Dean got a job on WARL radio in Arlington, Virginia playing country music. That led to work with the ABC-TV affiliate in Washington and, in 1958, a job with the CBS radio network in New York.

Jimmy was also pursuing a recording career. He released his first single, "Bumming Around," in 1953 on the Four Star label. He signed with Columbia Records in 1957.

In 1961, Jimmy was flying to a recording session in Nashville with only three songs to record. "At that time, you recorded four sides a session," he recalls. "I had to do something. I had worked with a guy in summer stock named John Mentoe. He was six-foot-five and skinny as a rail, but he was the only guy in the troupe taller than me, and I used to call him Big John. It had a powerful ring to it. So I put him in a mine and killed him on a plane going to Nashville. It took me an hour-and-a-half to write."

Dean thought the "A" side of his new single would be "I Won't Go Huntin' With You Jake, But I'll Go Chasin' Women." He was wrong. Disc jockeys went for the "B" side, "Big Bad John." The song became an immediate hit, but there was one slight problem with Columbia Records.

"Their legal department had not renewed my contract because I wasn't selling records," Jimmy explains. "A&R didn't know so they released this sucker. Well, I didn't know it either, but I found out in a hurry...by the time we got around to signing another contract with Columbia, it was one of the better ones they had ever issued."

Dean had several more hits with Columbia, including "Cajun Queen," which resurrected Big John against Dean's better judgment. "I hated that when I recorded it," Jimmy admits. The million-selling "I.O.U." in 1976 was a sentimental ode to his mother, which Jimmy doesn't sing since she passed away.

Dean's major contribution to country music was his prime time variety series, which ran for three seasons on ABC (1963-1966). He introduced acts like Roger Miller and Roy Clark, and gave network exposure to Jim Henson's Muppet hound, Rowlf. Today Jimmy still performs occasionally, and has many business interests, including The Jimmy Dean Meat Company, which produces pork sausage, and a chain of family-style restaurants.

### THE TOP FIVE
*Week of November 6, 1961*

1 **Big Bad John**
   Jimmy Dean

2 **Runaround Sue**
   Dion

3 **Bristol Stomp**
   Dovells

4 **Hit the Road Jack**
   Ray Charles

5 **Fool #1**
   Brenda Lee

TAMLA 54046 **Please Mr. Postman**
THE MARVELETTES

**101**

Writers: *Brian Holland*
*Robert Bateman*
*William Garrett*
*Georgia Dobbins*

Producers: *Brian Holland*
*Robert Bateman*

*December 11, 1961*
*1 week*

"**P**LEASE MR. POSTMAN" took longer to reach the number one position than any record that had come before—but it didn't matter to Berry Gordy, Jr., the founder of the Motown Record Corporation. It was the first number one single for the Detroit label and a sure sign to the world that Motown was here to stay.

In the early 1950s, Gordy was running a record shop in Detroit that specialized in jazz. When his business went bankrupt, he turned to writing and producing records.

He was going to name his first label after Debbie Reynolds' hit song "Tammy," but because of copyright changed it to Tamla. His first act to chart was The Miracles, and their "Shop Around" went all the way to number two.

It was a female quintet from the Detroit suburb of Inkster that gave Gordy his first number one single. They formed a group while attending Inkster High School, and called themselves the Casinyets, a contraction of "can't-sing-yet." In 1961 they entered the school talent contest, knowing the winners would get an audition with Motown. They came in fourth.

But their teacher, Mrs. Sharpley, thought they sounded too good to lose. She asked the principal if the girls could go with the top three acts to the auditions at Motown, and he agreed. Strongly influenced by The Chantels and the Shirelles, the Casinyets sang "He's Gone" and "I Met Him on a Sunday" at the audition. Motown was impressed, but told the girls to come up with some original material.

Group member Georgia Dobbins asked a songwriter friend, William Garrett, if he had anything for them. He offered a blues song called "Please Mr. Postman." Georgia asked if she could take the song and work on it, and overnight wrote completely new lyrics, saving only the title. She told the group's organizer, Gladys Horton, to learn how to sing it, because Georgia was dropping out of the group to take care of her ill mother.

Gladys' search for a replacement led her to Wanda Young, a nursing student who had already graduated from Inkster High. She agreed to join the group, and with Gladys and Katherine Anderson, Georgeanna Tillman and Juanita Cowart went back to Motown to play their new song for producers Brian Holland and Robert Bateman.

Holland and Bateman loved it. They rehearsed for two weeks and then recorded it (with 22-year-old Marvin Gaye playing drums). Berry re-named the girls The Marvelettes, and the song began its climb up the Hot 100. It inched up to 79 and fell to

81. It surged again. It reached 30 and fell to 33. Then it jumped to 19 and began its climb to number one, reaching the apex on Dec. 11, 1961, 15 weeks after it entered the chart.

The Beatles recorded "Please Mr. Postman" and so did the Carpenters, [see 390], who took the song to number one again in January, 1975. It is one of only seven songs to be number one by different artists.

The Marvelettes had hits with "Playboy" and "Beechwood 4-5789" in 1962, and enjoyed a resurgence of popularity when Smokey Robinson wrote and produced "Don't Mess With Bill" and "The Hunter Gets Captured by the Game" in 1966-67. Gladys and Wanda had always shared lead singing duties, with Gladys singing most of the early hits and Wanda singing Smokey's songs.

Juanita quit the group in the early 60s, and Georgeanna left to marry Billy Gordon of the Contours. On Jan. 6, 1980, she died after a long illness. Wanda married Bobby Rogers of the Miracles and took a brief leave of absence to give birth to the first of their three children. Katherine married Joe Schaffner, road manager for the Temptations. In 1968, Gladys departed after the birth of her first son, Sammy. She was replaced by Anne Bogan.

Gladys made some attempts to re-unite the group, but Katherine was busy being a Girl Scout Leader and Wanda didn't want to leave Detroit. Finally, when Ian Levine formed his Motorcity label in the U.K., Gladys and Wanda re-formed the Marvelettes with two new female singers. *The Marvelettes . . . Now!* was released in 1990.

## THE TOP FIVE
*Week of December 11, 1961*

1 **Please Mr. Postman**
 Marvelettes

2 **Big Bad John**
 Jimmy Dean

3 **Goodbye Cruel World**
 James Darren

4 **The Twist**
 Chubby Checker

5 **Walk On By**
 Leroy Van Dyke

# 102 The Lion Sleeps Tonight RCA 7954
## THE TOKENS

Writers: Hugo Peretti    Albert Stanton
    Luigi Creatore  Paul Campbell
    George Weiss    Roy Ilene

Producers: Hugo Peretti
    Luigi Creatore

December 18, 1961
3 weeks

In the summer of 1959, Phil Margo worked as a piano player at a club in the Catskills. When he returned home to Brighton Beach, Brooklyn, in the fall, he got together with Hank Medress and Jay Siegal, two friends who were in a group called Daryl and the Oxfords, and recorded an instrumental track. Though nothing came of it, they decide to write some songs together. Working at the Margo home, Hank learned that Phil's 12-year-old brother Mitch was a mean harmony singer. The first time Hank, Phil and Mitch sang together was December 7, 1959, the date the Tokens came into being.

In July, 1960, Phil and Hank took a day off from work and stayed home with Mitch to write "Tonight I Fell

in Love." They asked Jay to join the group and sing lead on the track, and when it was finished, signed with Morty Kraft's Warwick label. When Kraft wavered on releasing it, the group confronted him. He said he would put it out, but he needed a group name. "We wanted to call ourselves 'Those Guys,' but that was unheard of in 1960. It had to be 'the somethings,'" says Phil. Hank had been in a high school group called the Tokens with Neil Sedaka [see 114—"Breaking Up Is Hard to Do"], so he chose to use that name again.

"Tonight I Fell in Love" went to number 15 on the Hot 100, and the Tokens went to producers Hugo Peretti and Luigi Creatore to get a deal with RCA Records. They auditioned with a South African folk song called "Wimoweh," which had been sung by Miriam Makeba in Zulu a decade earlier. The Weavers, an American folk group, sang the song in their act as well.

Hugo and Luigi decided to add new lyrics to the song, and had the Tokens record it under the title "The Lion Sleeps Tonight" at their second RCA recording session in May, 1961. "We were embarassed by it," recalls

Phil, "and tried to convince Hugo and Luigi not to release it. They said it would be a big record and it was going out. They released it October 17, 1961."

While listening to Murray the K one day soon after, Phil was surprised to hear him play "Tina," a Portugese folk song they had recorded for the flip side. Someone at RCA had decided to push "Tina." It was Dick Smith, a DJ at WORC in Worcester, Massachussets, who played "The Lion Sleeps Tonight" and started the record on its climb to number one.

While roaring up the charts on RCA, the Tokens signed a production deal with Capitol Records. Over the next 12 years, members of the Tokens were responsible for producing the Chiffons [see 127—"He's So Fine"], the Happenings, Tony Orlando and Dawn [see 287—"Knock Three Times"] and Robert John, who went to number three with a new version of "The Lion Sleeps Tonight" in 1972.

In the summer of 1973, Phil, Mitch and Jay recorded as Cross Country. They made one album for Atco and had a top 30 single with an adult contemporary version of Wilson Pickett's "In the Midnight Hour." They had little taste left for touring and performing, and disbanded after a year.

The Tokens had gone out with a whimper, gradually dissolving because of ego problems. The bang didn't come until October 3, 1981, when Phil, Mitch, Jay and Hank were reunited on stage at Radio City Music Hall for a final performance as the Tokens. "It was just the nicest way to go out," says Phil, who has spent the last few years acting and writing screenplays. "We never had a proper curtain. Now I can bury that part of my life."

After "The Lion Sleeps Tonight" had a three week run at the top, a unique event in the rock era took place. For the first and only time, a song that had been number one 17 months earlier returned to the number one position. Thanks to renewed interest in the popular dance, Chubby Checker's "The Twist," which had topped the Hot 100 on September 19, 1960 [see 74], went back to number one for two more weeks.

## THE TOP FIVE
### Week of December 18, 1961

1  **The Lion Sleeps Tonight**
   Tokens

2  **Please Mr. Postman**
   Marvelettes

3  **Run to Him**
   Bobby Vee

4  **The Twist**
   Chubby Checker

5  **Walk On By**
   Leroy Van Dyke

ROULETTE 4401 **Peppermint Twist - Part 1**
JOEY DEE AND THE STARLITERS
**103**

*Writers: Joey Dee
Henry Glover*

*Producer: Henry Glover*

*January 27, 1962
3 weeks*

**F**IFTEEN years before Studio 54 attracted the trendy set, *the* place to dance in New York was the Peppermint Lounge on West 45th Street. The house band was a New Jersey outfit known as Joey Dee and the Starliters, and in 1961 they recorded their own twist song, the "Peppermint Twist."

Dee was born Joseph DiNicola on June 11, 1940 in Passaic, New Jersey. At Passaic High, he studied the clarinet and played in the school band. His classmates included the Shirelles, and like them, Dee signed with Florence Greenberg's Scepter Records, for which he recorded four songs (the Shirelles sang background on one).

Joey put together The Starliters, who were Carlton Latimor, Willie Davis, Larry Vernieri and David Brigati. They played weddings, Bar Mitzvahs, proms and high school dances all over northern New Jersey. One night at a club called Oliveri's, an agent from New York offered

them a job at the Peppermint Lounge. The club gained worldwide publicity when some socialites came in to dance the Twist. The next day, the newspapers were full of stories and pictures about the Peppermint Lounge.

Thanks to the media coverage, four record labels offered Dee a recording contract. He chose Roulette Records, because they promised to speed the release, and Dee knew timing was crucial before the Twist craze faded.

Dee starred in two films. First was *Hey, Let's Twist* with Gary Crosby and Teddy Randazzo, and second was *Two Tickets to Paris* with Charles Nelson Reilly and Kay Medford. A song from the film's soundtrack, "What Kind of Love Is This," written by Johnny Nash [see 322—"I Can See Clearly Now"], was a top 20 hit for Dee in 1962.

Joey worked with several soon-to-be famous acts. A female trio that was part of his revue at the Peppermint Lounge became the Ronettes. In 1964, after Dee opened his own New York club, The Starliter, his band consisted of Felix Cavaliere, Gene Cornish and Eddie, the younger brother of original Starliter David Brigati. They later became The Young Rascals [see 197—"Good Lovin'"]. A year later, when Dee sold the night club and began touring, his guitar player was named Jimi Hendrix.

Today Joey lives in the Bronx, and with his keyboard player, Joey Dee, Jr., often appears in "Dick Clark's Good Ol' Rock 'n' Roll" shows.

## THE TOP FIVE
*Week of January 27, 1962*

1 **Peppermint Twist-Part I**
Joey Dee & the Starliters

2 **The Twist**
Chubby Checker

3 **I Know**
Barbara George

4 **Can't Help Falling in Love**
Elvis Presley

5 **Norman**
Sue Thompson

**Duke of Earl** VEE JAY 416
GENE CHANDLER

---

*Writers: Bernice Williams*
*Eugene Dixon*
*Earl Edwards*

*Producer: Carl Davis*

*February 17, 1962*
*3 weeks*

---

Eugene Dixon was born July 6, 1937 on the south side of Chicago, where he grew up listening to doo-wop groups like the Spaniels and the El Dorados. In high school, he performed with a group called the Gaytones, and they won a talent contest at Chicago's Trianon Ballroom which resulted in a singing job on a local radio program. Another neighborhood group, the Dukays, asked Dixon to be their lead singer and he appeared with them at local night clubs.

He left the Dukays to join the armed forces in 1957, and returned to the group after a three-year stint. One night, a woman named Bernice Williams came to see them perform, and approached the group about managing them. She took the group to Bill "Bunky" Sheppard, who signed them to Nat Records. Williams wrote "The Girl's a Devil" and "Night Owl" for them, and both songs made the Hot 100.

Dixon had written a song that began with "doo doo doo," going up the scale. It turned into "duke, duke, duke" and he added the name of one of the Dukays, Earl, to come up with "Duke of Earl," which was recorded at the same session as "Night Owl." Dixon had been reluctant to record it, because he wanted strings on the track and the budget didn't permit that extravagance. But the group and producer Carl Davis liked the song so much, they insisted on recording it.

Nat Records didn't like the song, according to Gene, and released "Night Owl" instead. Another prominent Chicago label, Vee Jay, owned the publishing for "Night Owl," and their A&R man, Calvin Carter, was so excited about "Duke of Earl" that he telephoned label president Ewart Abner in Paris to get the okay to purchase the recording from Nat. Abner didn't want to hear the song—he told Carter that if it was important enough to call him in France, it had to be great.

Small problem. Eugene Dixon was signed to Nat Records as a member of the Dukays. But as a solo artist, he could record for another label, so Dixon decided to go out on his own. Davis shortened his first name to Gene and borrowed a new last name from his favorite actor, Jeff Chandler.

"Duke of Earl" became the first million-seller for Vee Jay Records, and Chandler took on the identity of the Duke, dressing up in cape, top hat and monocle for public appearances and a role in the movie *Don't Knock the Twist*. His follow-up single, "Walk on With the Duke," and *The Duke of Earl* album were released under the name Duke of Earl instead of Gene Chandler. In the album's liner notes, Chandler is only thanked in fine print for "his talent and cooperation in behalf of this album."

Chandler reverted to his "real" name for his late 1962 double-sided hit, "You Threw a Lucky Punch" (an answer record to Mary Wells' "You Beat Me to the Punch") and "Rainbow" (written by Curtis Mayfield).

When Abner left Vee Jay in 1963 and formed Constellation Records, Chandler went with him and had nine chart singles. He then recorded for Brunswick Records and in 1970 moved to Mercury, where he had the second-biggest hit of his career, "Groovy Situation." He also recorded

an album with label-mate Jerry Butler for Mercury.

Chandler became a label executive himself by running Bamboo Records and forming the Mr. Chand label. For the former, he produced a top 10 single, "Backfield in Motion" by Mel and Tim. In the late 70s, he became executive vice president of Carl Davis' Chi-Sound Records, and recorded a few songs for the label.

Chandler had several hits in Britain, but "Duke of Earl" was not one of them. He first charted in the United Kingdom in 1968 with "Nothing Can Stop Me." "Duke of Earl" was a British hit by the Darts, who took it to number six in the summer of 1979.

---

## THE TOP FIVE
*Week of February 17, 1962*

1 **Duke of Earl**
  Gene (Duke of Earl) Chandler

.2 **Peppermint Twist-Part I**
  Joey Dee & the Starliters

3 **The Twist**
  Chubby Checker

4 **Norman**
  Sue Thompson

5 **The Wanderer**
  Dion

Writers: *Margaret Cobb*
*Bruce Channel*

Producers: *Major Bill Smith*
*Marvin Montgomery*

*March 10, 1962*
*3 weeks*

WITH "Hey! Baby" at the top of the American charts and in second place in Britain, Bruce Channel toured England in 1962. One of the stops on the tour was the Castle in New Brighton, near Liverpool. While Bruce was busy talking to the press before the show, his harmonica player, Delbert McClinton, wandered over to the dressing room of one of the acts that was lower on the bill—the Beatles. McClinton spent about 15 minutes with them, and John Lennon was particularly impressed with his distinctive harmonica introduction to "Hey! Baby." John asked Delbert to show him how to play it, and a year later the Beatles released "Love Me Do," with a harmonica solo that was "inspired" by "Hey! Baby."

Bruce Channel was born in Jacksonville, Texas, on November 28, 1940. His parents worked in a tomato packing warehouse, and music was a popular hobby in their home. Bruce's father played harmonica and his two brothers played guitar. A cousin who came to live with them when Bruce was four taught him some chords. The family moved to Dallas during World War II, when Bruce's father became a machinist. When Bruce was a teenager the family moved 30 miles away to the more rural setting of Grapevine in east Texas. His father

presented him with a new Gibson guitar and said they should go to Shreveport to see about appearing on the "Louisiana Hayride" radio show. They drove 200 miles the following weekend to get there, and Bruce's father asked producer Tillman Franks to listen to his son. Franks liked what he heard and asked if Bruce was prepared to go on the show that night. He was, and he stayed with the show for six months.

Bruce's favorite vocal group at this time was the Platters, and he wrote a song he wanted to give to them, "Dream Girl." He also collaborated with a woman he knew, Margaret Cobb, and together they wrote "Hey! Baby." Margaret introduced Bruce to her friend Marvin Montgomery, who suggested they take their songs to a retired major in the air force, a record producer named Bill Smith in Fort Worth who had a taste of chart success with "Peanuts" by Rick and the Keens.

Major Bill wanted to cut an answer record to Ray Charles' "Hit the Road Jack" [see 98], and when Bruce approached him, he asked the young singer to record a demo of "Come Back, Jack." Then Major Bill asked Bruce what else he had to record, and Bruce showed him "Dream Girl" and "Hey! Baby." Major Bill didn't like the guitar intro on the lat-

ter, so he asked McClinton to play harmonica on the track, which was cut immediately. It took 15 minutes to record three takes.

Major Bill took the completed tape to a disc jockey convention in Nashville, where deals were usually signed. He cornered an important record company representative and asked him to listen to Bruce's tape. "I was going to play him 'Dream Girl,' but the tape started at the end of 'Hey! Baby,'" the Major remembers. The rep was so excited and wanted to buy it on the spot, but Major Bill took it and pressed his own copies on the LeCam label. The Major sent a copy to Mercury Records and got no response. When it started to get airplay on LeCam, the Major had a phone call from Irwin Steinberg of Mercury, who wanted to buy the master for their Smash Records subsidiary. The Major asked how much front money he was willing to pay, and Irwin said $500. The deal was made, and later that night the Major had a phone call from Randy Wood of Dot Records, who said "Hey! Baby" was hot and he wanted it. He offered $10,000. The offer was generous, but a few hours too late. Major Bill had given his word to Mercury Records and they released the song in the closing weeks of 1961.

## THE TOP FIVE
*Week of March 10, 1962*

1  **Hey! Baby**
   Bruce Channel

2  **Duke of Earl**
   Gene (Duke of Earl) Chandler

3  **Midnight in Moscow**
   Kenny Ball

4  **Don't Break the Heart
   That Loves You**
   Connnie Francis

5  **Let Me In**
   Sensations

# 106 Don't Break the Heart That Loves You MGM 13059
## CONNIE FRANCIS

*Writers: Benny Davis  Ted Murray*

*Producers: Arnold Maxin*
*Danny Davis*

*March 31, 1962*
*1 week*

AFTER George Franconero told his daughter to record the 1923 ditty "Who's Sorry Now" and it became her first hit, she trusted his opinion. So when George discovered that long-time songwriters Benny Davis and Ted Murray ("Baby Face," "I'm Nobody's Baby" and "There Goes My Heart") had written new songs, he recognized their hit potential and told his daughter to record "Don't Break the Heart That Loves You." It became her third number one single.

Connie continued her acting career while recording songs. She followed her first film, *Where the Boys Are*, with three other MGM movies: *Follow the Boys*, *Looking for Love* and *When the Boys Meet the Girls*.

Looking back on her motion pictures, Connie is clear that acting will never replace singing for her.

"If you've ever seen any of my movies, you know I'm not an actress....I was amateurish....I just never cared about (the films)....I used to keep a book of all the bad reviews because they were hilarious." When producer Allan Carr remade *Where the Boys Are* in 1984, he asked Connie to be in it, but she declined after reading the script.

By 1962, Connie's audiences consisted of adults as well as teenagers. While her first few hits established her popularity with younger people, it was songs like "Mama" that made her popular with older audiences. But the latter half of the sixties was a difficult time for Connie. Her last single to make the top 50 came in 1965, and since 1969 she hasn't made the chart at all.

The most difficult period of all was still to come. On November 8, 1974, she was appearing at the Westbury

Music Fair in New York. Shortly after returning to her second-floor room at the Howard Johnson's motel, Connie was the victim of a rapist. The attack made headlines all over the world, and an emotionally shattered Connie Francis found she couldn't sing anymore.

It took six years to recuperate, but in the fall of 1978, Connie made a successful comeback on "Dick Clark's Live Wednesday," singing a medley of her hits. What the audience didn't know is that Clark had her pre-tape the songs so she could lip synch to them. It was the only way she could get through the performance.

In March, 1981, another tragedy struck. Connie's brother was murdered at his New Jersey home. The press called it a gangland slaying.

"I really had to pull myself up by the boot straps for a change," Connie says. "I had been wallowing in self-pity and...fear...for seven years and I just decided (to go) back to work."

Connie's autobiography, *Who's Sorry Now*, was published in September, 1984. "After my brother's death, I decided that was something I wanted to do. I set about writing it with two ghost writers to begin with, and then I just felt what they wrote wasn't me, and no one would be able to tell the story the way I could, so I decided to write it myself.

"It was very cathartic in many ways. It helped me analyze my relationship with my father, which I really had never done fully before. It helped me put to bed my fear about the rape—it helped me to confront my brother's death."

## THE TOP FIVE
*Week of March 31, 1962*

1  **Don't Break the Heart That Loves You**
   Connie Francis

2  **Hey! Baby**
   Bruce Channel

3  **Johnny Angel**
   Shelley Fabares

4  **Dream Baby**
   Roy Orbison

5  **Midnight in Moscow**
   Kenny Ball

*Writers: Lee Pockriss*
*Lyn Duddy*

*Producer: Stu Phillips*

*April 7, 1962*
*2 weeks*

In the late 50s-early 60s, one of the most popular family situation comedies was "The Donna Reed Show." Anyone who didn't want to be a part of the Anderson or Cleaver families surely wanted to live with the Stones in Hilldale.

Dr. Alex Stone and his wife Donna had two children, Mary and Jeff. After the show's second season, producer Tony Owen (Reed's then-husband) told the two actors who played the Stone offspring they would record songs that would be written into the series' third season scripts, and Colpix, the record arm of Columbia Pictures, would release those songs.

Shelley Fabares and Paul Petersen were not thrilled. "Both Paul and I said it was a great idea, but we couldn't sing. I was adamant. I'm not a singer. I was a very good, very sweet little girl who was not raised to say no, so it took a lot for me to say I can't do that."

Owen wasn't prepared to take no for an answer. He arranged for Stu Phillips to make demos for Shelley and Paul, and Shelley was convinced hers was so bad the idea would be dropped. It wasn't. Shelley recorded two solo songs, "Johnny Angel" and "Where's It Going to Get Me." She recalls being absolutely terrified dur-

ing the session. What she remembers most is the calibre of the musicians (people like Glen Campbell and Hal Blaine) and the "gorgeous" voices of her backing vocalists, the Blossoms, led by Darlene Love [see 119—"He's a Rebel"].

"Johnny Angel" was written into a script of "The Donna Reed Show," as was Paul Petersen's song, "She Can't Find Her Keys." Both actors had several follow-ups; Petersen fared best with "My Dad," which went to number six and Shelley's only other hit was "Johnny Loves Me," which peaked at 21.

In June, 1964, Shelley married record producer Lou Adler. She departed "The Donna Reed Show" and Paul's sister, Patti, joined the show as an adopted, younger daughter. In 1965, Shelley was the first artist to release a record on the new Dunhill label, which was partly owned by Adler.

After "The Donna Reed Show," Shelley co-starred in three Elvis movies and *Ride the Wild Surf* with Fabian. In 1971, she starred as the wife of the terminally ill football star Brian Picolo in TV's "Brian's Song." Her television credits include starring roles in a number of television series, including "The Little People" with Brian Keith, "The Practice" with Danny Thomas, "Forever Fernwood" with Greg Mullavey, "Highcliffe Manor" with Stephen McHattie, "One Day At A Time" with Bonnie Franklin and "Coach" with Craig T. Nelson.

She was born Michele Fabares on January 19, 1944, and her family called her Shelley. Her aunt Nanette suggested she spell her last name Fabray, but she preferred the family spelling despite problems with pronunciation (Fah-bear-ay is correct).

## THE TOP FIVE

*Week of April 7, 1962*

1 **Johnny Angel**
Shelley Fabares

2 **Don't Break the Heart That Loves You**
Connie Francis

3 **Good Luck Charm**
Elvis Presley

4 **Slow Twistin'**
Chubby Checker

5 **Dream Baby**
Roy Orbison

# 108 Good Luck Charm RCA 7992
## ELVIS PRESLEY

*Writers: Aaron Schroeder
       Wally Gold*

*Producers: Steve Sholes
         Chet Atkins*

*April 21, 1962
2 weeks*

ELVIS PRESLEY had a number one single every year between 1956 and 1962, the only artist aside from the Beatles to top the charts for seven consecutive years until Mariah Carey set a new rock-era record by having at least one chart-topping hit for 11 consecutive years.

"Good Luck Charm," Elvis' 16th number one, was one of five songs recorded on October 15 and 16, 1961, at RCA's studios in Nashville. It went to number one just ten days after the premiere of Elvis' ninth film, *Follow That Dream*. It was to be his last number one song until 1969.

The hits didn't stop coming immediately. He continued to chart in the top 10, with hits like "She's Not You," "Return to Sender" and "(You're the) Devil in Disguise." After "Bossa Nova Baby" went to number eight at the end of 1963, Elvis only had one top ten single in the next five-and-a half years ("Crying in the Chapel" went to number three in 1965).

A majority of the singles released between 1964-1968 were either from motion pictures, or were unreleased tracks from the early 60s.

By 1968, Elvis was considered a relic of an earlier period. The Beatles were the top recording act in the world, the Supremes were the most successful American group and the charts were dominated by artists as diverse as the Monkees, the Doors and Simon and Garfunkel. A new Elvis single meant nothing to radio station music directors; Presley had very little airplay on his new releases between 1965-1968.

A one-hour television special on NBC changed everything. Col. Tom Parker announced in January, 1968, that Singer Sewing Machines would sponsor the special, to be produced and directed by Steve Binder.

Parker and Binder had different ideas of how to showcase Elvis. Parker envisioned a seasonal program designed around Christmas songs. Binder, who was responsible for "The T.A.M.I. Show," a videotaped rock concert featuring everyone from the Beach Boys to James Brown to the Rolling Stones, saw it differently. He felt it was Elvis' last chance to rejuvenate his career. He wanted a one-man show of Elvis performing live before an audience at the NBC studios in Burbank. He wanted big production numbers, with Elvis' name in lights 20 feet high. And he didn't want to end the show with a traditional Christmas song like Parker suggested, he wanted something with a message that people would remember long after the telecast.

During the months of pre-production, Binder won Elvis' confidence and was able to mount the special his way. Dressed in a black leather suit, Elvis performed his greatest hits—and then some—before invited audiences inside Studio 4 at NBC-Burbank on June 29. There were two performances, one at 6 p.m. and one at 8 p.m., and the final telecast combined segments from the two as well as other pre-taped numbers. The show closed with "If I Can Dream," a song written specifically by Earl Brown for the closing spot. The special was telecast December 3 and it did everything for Elvis that Binder wanted it to. "If I Can Dream" entered the Hot 100 at number 100 the week before the telecast. Five days after the airdate, it was number 40. By February 1, 1969, it had peaked at 12, the highest-charting Elvis single in almost four years.

## THE TOP FIVE
*Week of April 21, 1962*

1 **Good Luck Charm**
   Elvis Presley

2 **Johnny Angel**
   Shelley Fabares

3 **Mashed Potato Time**
   Dee Dee Sharp

4 **Slow Twistin'**
   Chubby Checker

5 **Young World**
   Rick Nelson

the girls prevented from recording for any other label. When all was settled in 1967, the group recorded "Last Minute Miracle" for Scepter, but it was not a hit, and it marked the end of their association with the label.

Doris (now Mrs. Doris Jackson) took a temporary retirement in 1968, reducing the group to a trio. As Shirley and the Shirelles, they had a brief, unsuccessful stint with Bell Records. Shirley (now Mrs. Shirley Alston), Micki and Beverly then recorded two albums for RCA.

Shirley left in 1975 to pursue a solo career. The group had signed a contract in 1961 which stipulated that any group member who left could not use the name Shirelles. So when Shirley billed herself as Shirley of the Shirelles, the other group members sued her. The judge permitted her to bill herself as the "former lead singer of the Shirelles."

Doris re-joined, and with Micki and Beverly continued to perform all over the country in concert. In a 1980 interview with Wayne Jones in *Goldmine*, Micki said, "We were four young ladies who respected and loved each other. We were the only family we had for a long, long time. So, there is nothing I would really change other than I wish the four originals were still together."

On June 10, 1982, following a performance in Atlanta, Micki Harris was going out to dinner with friends when she collapsed and died of a massive heart attack. The family held a service in Passaic, New Jersey. On February 4, 2000, Doris Jackson died of cancer in Sacramento, California.

*Writers: Luther Dixon*
*Florence Greenberg*

*Producer: Luther Dixon*

*May 5, 1962*
*3 weeks*

**T**HE SHIRELLES had two very successful follow-ups to their first number one single [see 83—"Will You Love Me Tomorrow"]. Florence Greenberg, owner of Scepter Records, still believed in their 1959 song "Dedicated to the One I Love" and re-released it. This time it surpassed its original chart peak of 83 and soared to number three. It remains a classic to this day, and was given a totally different arrangement by the Mamas and Papas in early 1967 (they bested the Shirelles by taking the song to number two).

Then came "Mama Said," which went to number four and was used in 1984 in a commercial for Mercury's Topaz automobile. The next single, "A Thing of the Past" only went to 41, but remains Shirley's favorite Shirelles song.

In late 1961 Luther Dixon found a Burt Bacharach-Hal David song called "I'll Cherish You" that he liked for the Shirelles, but he asked Bacharach for new lyrics. The song became "Baby It's You," and it was recorded so quickly that Shirley simply added her vocals to Bacharach's

instrumental demo. The other Shirelles were not at the recording session, and the male backing vocal heard on the track is Bacharach. The song peaked at number eight.

Their next single was recorded when they had five minutes of studio time left at the end of a session. Dixon and Greenberg wrote a song on the spot and the group recorded it in one take. The song was "Soldier Boy,' and it not only went to number one, it surpassed "Will You Love Me Tomorrow" to become their biggest seller.

Scepter Records flourished, thanks to the Shirelles, and added a subsidiary label, Wand. The artist roster expanded to include Dionne Warwick, Chuck Jackson, Maxine Brown and the Isley Brothers. Despite this success, Dixon decided to leave the company for Capitol Records.

The Shirelles only had one top 10 hit, "Foolish Little Girl," after Dixon's departure. With Dixon gone and the onslaught of British artists in 1964, The Shirelles' hit-making days were over. The Beatles covered two Shirelles songs, "Baby It's You" and "Boys," and Manfred Mann had a hit with their "Sha La La," but that was of little help to the Shirelles.

When they turned 21, they expected to receive trust fund money from Scepter. They didn't, and lawsuits ensued for several years, with

## THE TOP FIVE
*Week of May 5, 1962*

1 **Soldier Boy**
Shirelles

2 **Mashed Potato Time**
Dee Dee Sharp

3 **Johnny Angel**
Shelley Fabares

4 **Stranger on the Shore**
Mr. Acker Bilk

5 **Good Luck Charm**
Elvis Presley

# Stranger on the Shore ATCO 6217
## MR. ACKER BILK

*Writer: Acker Bilk*

*Producer: Dennis Preston*

*May 26, 1962*
*1 week*

**T**WENTY months before The Beatles invaded the United States and opened the floodgates for British acts to monopolize U.S. radio playlists and sales charts, a jazz clarinetist from Somerset, England became the first British artist to go to number one in America.

There have been 174 British singles to reach the number one spot on the Hot 100, but before the Beatles, Herman's Hermits, the Rolling Stones, Lulu, Elton John, the Police, Culture Club and Right Said Fred there was Mr. Acker Bilk and "Stranger on the Shore," the first British number one in the States.

A number of British artists who were very popular at home were having minor success in America. Cliff Richard, who has had 13 number one songs in England (third only to the Beatles and Elvis Presley) made the American top 30 in 1959 with "Living Doll," and had five more minor chart hits until finally breaking through in 1976 with "Devil Woman."

Actor/singer Anthony Newley managed to hit the lower regions of the chart four times between 1960-62, and Lonnie Donegan, a skiffle band singer from Scotland, had two impressive top 5 hits with "Rock Island Line" (1956) and "Does Your Chewing Gum Lose Its Flavor (On the Bedpost Over Night)" (1961). Marty Wilde, Helen Shapiro, Frank Ifield and Matt Monro also made

## THE TOP FIVE
*Week of May 26, 1962*

1  **Stranger on the Shore**
   Mr. Acker Bilk

2  **Soldier Boy**
   Shirelles

3  **Mashed Potato Time**
   Dee Dee Sharp

4  **I Can't Stop Loving You**
   Ray Charles

5  **Old Rivers**
   Walter Brennan

minor breakthroughs in America before the Beatles, but many artists, including Billy Fury, John Leyton, Eden Kane and Susan Maughan did not.

Considering the heavier rock sound of most of the 170 British hits that followed it, "Stranger on the Shore" is an unlikely contender for the title of "forerunner of the British Invasion." But its adult contemporary sound made it a perfect song to top the American chart in 1962.

The song was written and recorded by Bilk for an album commissioned by Atco Records called *Sentimental Journey*. It was originally titled "Jenny," after one of Bilk's children. The BBC wanted Bilk to play the title tune for a new children's TV series, "Stranger on the Shore," so "Jenny" was renamed and became the main theme for the program.

Released as a single in the United Kingdom, it did very well—peaking at number two. It fared even better in the States, although it did not give

Bilk a long-lasting American career. It is the only one of his four U.S. singles to penetrate the top 50.

Bilk was born January 28, 1929 as Bernard Stanley Bilk (his nickname Acker is rural slang for "mate"). His father was a preacher and his mother played the organ in church. In 1947, he fell asleep while on guard duty in Egypt and was sentenced to prison for three months. While incarcerated, he learned to play the clarinet. He formed a group, the Paramount Jazz Band, in 1958, and three years later starred on the "BBC Beat Show." He was easily recognized by his bowler hat.

It's appropriate that the British band Squeeze paid homage to Britain's first American chart-topper with a track on their 1982 album, *Sweets from a Stranger*. It was one of the rare times that the title of a number one song was totally (and deliberately) incorporated into another song. Side one, track four of the album is called "Stranger Than the Stranger on the Shore."

ABC-PARAMOUNT 10330 **I Can't Stop Loving You** 111

RAY CHARLES

*Writer: Don Gibson*

*Producer: Sid Feller*

*June 2, 1962*
*5 weeks*

PRODUCER Sid Feller wasn't sure what Ray Charles was up to when he called and asked to hear the greatest country songs from the past 20 years. But Feller gathered material and narrowed the field down to 150 songs, which he forwarded to Ray.

One of those songs had been composed and recorded by Don Gibson in 1958. It had been written in a house trailer in Knoxville, Tennessee on a hot afternoon. Gibson had no air conditioning—he also didn't have a microphone stand, so he fixed up a wire coat hanger. First he wrote "Oh Lonesome Me" (which became a top 10 song) and then he started writing a ballad without a title. The lyric "I can't stop lovin' you" stood out, so that's what Gibson called it. He had intended to give "Oh Lonesome Me" to George Jones and keep "I Can't Stop Loving You" for himself, but his publisher felt Gibson should record them both.

The same lyric stood out to Ray Charles four years later. After he heard the first two lines, Ray says he didn't have to hear the rest. He knew he would include the song on his album *Modern Sounds in Country and Western Music*.

In a 1973 interview with Ben-Fong Torres for *Rolling Stone*, Charles said: "...with ABC we had people saying, 'Hey man, gee whiz, Ray, you got all these fans, you can't do no country-western things. Your fans—you gonna lose all your fans.' Well, I said, '...I'll do it anyway.'...I didn't want to be a Charlie Pride...I'm not saying there's anything wrong with that. I'm just saying that was not my intent. I didn't want to be a country-western singer. I just wanted to take country-western songs. When I sing 'I Can't Stop Loving You,' I'm not singing it *country-western*. I'm singing it like *me*."

In fact, Larry Newton, an ABC-Paramount Records executive, has been quoted as saying, "When he wanted to record his first country and western album, we said to him, 'don't do it.' Even when the distributors got it, they said, 'what is this? A joke?'"

The distributors may have thought the album was a joke, but it sold more than a million copies and became the first gold album ABC-Paramount had ever released. It was so popular that Charles recorded *Modern Sounds in Country and Western Music, Vol. 2.*

In 1983, Charles signed with CBS Records in Nashville and recorded a country album, *Wish You Were Here Tonight*. He told *Billboard's* Kip Kirby that the LP "encompasses traditional country, and I've never really done that before. In the 60s, I did a lot of country songs, but I always made them sound contemporary. I'd add strings, give them a pop feel, so that way I got a lot of people into country for the first time."

## THE TOP FIVE
*Week of June 2, 1962*

1  **I Can't Stop Loving You**
   Ray Charles

2  **Stranger on the Shore**
   Mr. Acker Bilk

3  **Soldier Boy**
   Shirelles

4  **Lovers Who Wander**
   Dion

5  **Mashed Potato Time**
   Dee Dee Sharp

# 112 The Stripper MGM 13064
### DAVID ROSE AND HIS ORCHESTRA

*Writer: David Rose*

*Producer: Jesse Kaye*

*July 7, 1962*
*1 week*

DAVID ROSE was scoring a television show called "Burlesque" in 1958, starring Dan Dailey and Joan Blondell. Just before going on the air with a live broadcast, the producer suggested that a scene where the two stars argued behind a closed dressing room door needed something going on in the background. Rose said there should be a stripper on stage, as it was a burlesque house. "So I wrote eight measures of strip music and forgot about it," Rose explains.

Soon after, Rose was in the recording studio to make a string album. He had hired a brass section,

too, and at the end of recording, with ten minutes of studio time remaining, he had the musicians play "a funny piece of music with no title." He told them to clown around with it, and he had a recording made of it for each person in the orchestra to take home and show their family the beautiful "string album" they had been working on.

"It was all tongue-in-cheek, and I kept it at home and used to play it for people," Rose remembers. Friends said he should record and release it, but MGM Records said no. Label executives felt Rose was known for strings and could never release anything "as terrible as that."

Four years later, Rose was asked by MGM to quickly record a new version of the song "Ebb Tide" to help promote the MGM film *Sweet Bird of Youth*, starring Paul Newman and Geraldine Page. Rose recorded the song so fast there was no time to do a second track for the "B" side, so someone at MGM pulled an obscure, unreleased cut from the master files and scheduled it for the flip.

"Ebb Tide" may have been a pretty song, but Los Angeles disc jockey Robert Q. Lewis thought it would be funnier to play the other side. He thought it was so funny, that he played it over and over for 45

minutes. "Whoever would call and request a number, he said, 'coming right up' and instead of their request he would play this," says Rose.

That stunt helped make "The Stripper" the number one song in Los Angeles even before it debuted on the national chart. Rose still performs the song today at his many concerts around the world. "I played it in London at the Albert Hall. It had no place at all, but they yelled out for it, so I played it but I apologized to the Albert Hall."

Rose was born in London on June 15, 1910, and his family moved to Chicago when he was seven (Rose later became an American citizen). Rose's parents made him study the piano when he was a child. He joined his high school's dance orchestra and attended the Chicago College of Music, although he considers himself to be self-taught. He went to work for NBC Radio in Chicago as a pianist and arranger. In 1938, he formed an orchestra for the Mutual Broadcasting System in Hollywood, but at the last moment the orchestra was cut. He was left with only a string section. He decided he'd better learn to write for strings, and in 1944, recorded his first million-selling record, "Holiday for Strings."

In the 1950s Rose became a prolific composer of television theme songs, and at one time there were 22 series on the air with his music. He won Emmys for the music he wrote for the 1958 special "An Evening With Fred Astaire" and for "Bonanza."

Michael Landon asked him to be the musical director for "Little House on the Prairie" and a 1975 episode of that program marked Rose's 1000th television score. In 1984, Landon asked Rose to write the music for the "Highway to Heaven" series.

Rose's other passion was for trains. He received a toy locomotive at age seven that inspired his life-long interest. His home in California's San Fernando Valley had a thousand feet of track and 10 locomotives that burned coal and were capable of transporting up to 30 people. Sharp-eyed viewers would have spotted Rose playing a train engineer in a 1981 episode of "Little House on the Prairie."

Rose died on August 23, 1990, of heart disease.

## THE TOP FIVE
### *Week of July 7, 1962*

1. **The Stripper**
   David Rose & His Orchestra

2. **Roses are Red**
   Bobby Vinton

3. **I Can't Stop Loving You**
   Ray Charles

4. **Palisades Park**
   Freddy Cannon

5. **It Keeps Right on A-Hurtin'**
   Johnny Tillotson

EPIC 9505 **Roses Are Red (My Love)**
BOBBY VINTON

113

**Writers:** *Paul Evans*
*Al Byron*

**Producer:** *Bob Morgan*

*July 14, 1962*
*4 weeks*

**B**OBBY VINTON (born April 16, 1935 in Canonsburg, Pennsylvania) wanted to be a big band leader, like his father. He formed his own band in high school and while attending Duquesne University played at local dances and nightclubs. In the Army, he played trumpet in a military band and after leaving the service, appeared with a new band in an NBC variety show. In 1960, a Pittsburgh disc jockey named Dick Lawrence told Bobby that End Records was interested in him, and recorded Vinton singing "I Love You the Way You Are." Lawrence liked it so much

he took it to CBS instead, and the label, not wishing to offend an important DJ, signed Bobby to their subsidiary, Epic Records.

"They weren't really interested in my songs or me," says Bobby. "They just signed me and Lawrence held on to the tape." Bobby did record two albums of big band music for Epic, but they failed to sell. At a meeting with label executives, Bobby was told he was being dropped from the label. "I said 'no, no, you owe me two more sides,' and the lawyers looked at each other and they said, 'Excuse us, we have to go to the other room to discuss something.'

"They were figuring out how to get rid of me. I saw a pile of records that said 'reject pile,' and they still weren't back. I noticed the record player was turning, so I started to listen to some of the records they were throwing out and all of a sudden

I heard, 'Roses are red, my love, violets are blue.'

"When they came back, they said the band just wasn't making it. I said, 'I can sing a little, and there's a song you're throwing away that really sounds like something I would hear on the radio." They did owe Bobby another session, and agreed to let him cut two more songs, including "Roses Are Red."

Bobby recorded it as an R&B song. "It was the worst sounding thing you ever heard in your life," he remembers. "I'm not really a country singer, but I said we should do it country, and on the strength of the song I got a second shot at 'Roses Are Red.'" Epic agreed to another recording session and brought in new arrangements, strings and a vocal choir.

The single went to number one, the first for the Epic label. When the record sold a million copies, Bob Morgan became the first record producer to officially receive a gold record for acknowledgment of his contribution.

Bobby was hoping for another number one single with the follow-up, "Rain Rain Go Away," but hadn't counted on his old friend, Dick Lawrence. After the success of "Roses Are Red," Lawrence sold "I Love You the Way You Are" to a smaller label, Diamond Records, which released it to compete with "Rain Rain Go Away." Vinton found himself calling DJs around the country and asking them not to play his older record so his newer single would chart higher. "Rain Rain Go Away" peaked at 12, but there would be more number one singles for Vinton.

## THE TOP FIVE
*Week of July 14, 1962*

1 **Roses are Red**
Bobby Vinton

2 **The Stripper**
David Rose & His Orchestra

3 **I Can't Stop Loving You**
Ray Charles

4 **The Wah-Watusi**
Orlons

5 **Sealed With a Kiss**
Brian Hyland

## 114  Breaking Up Is Hard to Do  RCA 8046
### NEIL SEDAKA

*Writers: Neil Sedaka*
*Howard Greenfield*

*Producers: Al Nevins*
*Don Kirshner*

*August 11, 1962*
*2 weeks*

Who would have guessed that "Comma, comma, down-doo-be-doo-down down," would be one of the immortal phrases of rock and roll?

Probably not Mac and Eleanor Sedaka's neighbor, Mrs. Greenfield, who heard 13-year old Neil play piano in the lobby of the Kenmore Lake Hotel in Livingston Manor, New York. He had started to study the piano at age nine, and three years later was accepted as a student at the Juilliard Preparatory Division for Children. Mrs. Greenfield suggested that Neil collaborate on a song with her son, a 16-year-old poet named Howie.

Neil said he didn't know how to write songs, but Mrs. Greenfield had Howie knock on the Sedakas' door the next week anyway. After a few days, they had come up with their first composition: "My Life's Devotion." It was not a classic, but it had enough merit for Neil and Howie to continue writing together.

In 1952, Neil and his high school girlfriend Carol Klein (later to become Carole King) [see 294—"It's Too Late / I Feel the Earth Move"] heard a song on a pizza parlor jukebox. It was the Penguins' "Earth Angel," and it led Neil to suggest to Howie they write a rock and roll song. Howie was more into Lorenz Hart than doo-wop, but he went along with Neil and they wrote "Mr. Moon." Neil sang it at a high school talent show and describes the reaction in his biography, *Laughter in the Rain:*

"As I finished, the crowd went wild—the students exploded into something resembling a large-scale riot....For a few moments the sissy was a hero."

About a year after that, Neil teamed up with some high school friends to form a vocal group—the Tokens. They had a local New York hit, "I Love My Baby," before going their separate ways [see 102—"The Lion Sleeps Tonight"].

In his senior year, Neil won a piano competition judged by Arthur Rubinstein. After graduation, torn between classical and rock music, he enrolled at Juilliard. Still, he continued to write with Howard Greenfield, and they had several songs recorded by R&B singers, including Clyde McPhatter, Lavern Baker and the Clovers.

In 1958, Sedaka and Greenfield wrote a song called "Stupid Cupid." After being rejected by Hill and Range Music, they ran into songwriters Doc Pomus and Mort Shuman. They suggested Sedaka and Greenfield try a new publishing company, Aldon Music, owned by Al Nevins (a former member of the Three Suns) and a young man named Don Kirshner. Nevins and Kirshner were impressed enough to sign the two new songwriters to exclusive contracts.

Connie Francis [see 69—"Everybody's Somebody's Fool"] was hot on the charts with her first hit, "Who's Sorry Now," and Kirshner convinced her to listen to some Sedaka-Greenfield songs. Neil and Howie visited her New Jersey home and played some ballads, but she seemed disinterested. In desperation, Neil played a song already promised to the Sheppard Sisters. Connie loved it, said she would record it and asked Neil to play piano on the track—"Stupid Cupid."

The song peaked at number 14 on Billboard's Hot 100, but songwriting was not enough for Neil. He wanted to record his own material. He was unhappy with how Little Anthony and the Imperials recorded his song "The Diary," and Nevins suggested they take the song to RCA with Neil as the vocalist. Within a few days of meeting Steve Sholes, the same man who signed Elvis Presley to RCA, Neil was in a recording studio. "The Diary" matched "Stupid Cupid" by peaking at number 14.

Nine more chart singles followed, including "Oh! Carol" (written for Carol Klein), "Calendar Girl" and "Happy Birthday, Sweet Sixteen." Then Neil heard "It Will Stand," a paean to rock and roll by The Showmen. It inspired him to write a song that he says felt predestined. He came up with a title and brought it to Greenfield, who was not excited. A week later, Neil tried again and got a better reception. A recording session was arranged for "Breaking Up Is Hard to Do."

The night before, Neil couldn't sleep. He felt something was missing from the song. Then he suddenly had the missing part. He telephoned his arranger, Allan Lorber, at 12:30 in the morning to sing the newly discovered line: "Down-doo-be-doo-down-down, comma, comma..."

Neil was in England playing at the London Palladium when the song was released. His wife, Leba, sent him telegrams to inform him of the song's sales and chart progress. Then came a final cable, telling him the song had gone all the way to number one.

### THE TOP FIVE
*Week of August 11, 1962*

1  **Breaking Up is Hard to Do**
Neil Sedaka

2  **Roses are Red**
Bobby Vinton

3  **The Wah-Watusi**
Orlons

4  **Loco-Motion**
Little Eva

5  **Ahab the Arab**
Ray Stevens

Writers: *Gerry Goffin*
*Carole King*

Producer: *Gerry Goffin*

August 25, 1962
1 week

ONE of the popular myths of rock and roll is that Carole King and Gerry Goffin came home one day and found their babysitter, Eva, pushing a broom around the kitchen singing "The Loco-Motion."

"The fact of the matter is we knew she could sing when she came to work for us, and it was just a matter of time before we were going to have her sing on some of our demos," Carole explains in her "One to One" video.

Little Eva was born Eva Narcissus Boyd on June 29, 1945, in Belhaven, North Carolina. She moved to Brooklyn, New York and met a former IBM employee, Earl-Jean McCree, who was working with her friends Dorothy Jones and Margaret Ross as background singers for many of the top artists of the day, including Neil Sedaka, Tony Orlando, Mel Torme and most of the artists who worked with songwriters Goffin and King.

Gerry and Carole were churning out hits for Aldon Music, the publish-ing firm owned by Al Nevins and Don Kirshner. Goffin and King had given birth to their first daughter, Louise, in 1960, and now they were taking her to recording sessions where she would sit in a playpen and rock and roll while her parents worked (it must have rubbed off—Louise is still rock and rolling. She's recorded three albums so far). Realizing they needed a full-time babysitter, they asked their background singers if they had any friends who might like the job. Earl-Jean recommended her friend, Eva Boyd.

When Gerry and Carole wrote "The Loco-Motion," they asked Eva to sing on the demo, but not with the intent of releasing a record by her. The song was pitched to Dee Dee Sharp, who had just had scored with another dance song, "Mashed Potato Time." Her producers at Cameo Records turned "The Loco-Motion" down, but Kirshner liked Eva's sing-ing enough to release her version. It was the very first single on Kirshner's new label, Dimension Records.

Gerry produced the session and Carole did all the arrangements. She also sang backing vocals along with Dorothy, Margaret and Earl-Jean, who had been responsible for Eva's $35 a week job as the Goffin-King babysitter. Soon, the entire country was dancing the loco-motion. They certainly weren't doing it *before* the record came out. "There never was a dance called the loco-motion until after it was a number one hit rec-ord," says Carole. "Everyone said, 'how does this dance go,' so Little Eva had to make up a dance."

Little Eva's chart career was short-lived. Her next single, another Goffin-King production, was called "Keep Your Hands Off My Baby" and peaked at 12. "Let's Turkey Trot" did not inspire a national dance craze but did go to number 20. She recorded a duet with Big Dee Irwin, the stand-ard "Swingin' on a Star," that made the Top 40 in early 1963. Her final chart single was "Old Smokey Loco-motion" in June, '63. A few more Dimension singles like "What I Gotta Do" followed, and in later years Eva recorded for the Amy and Spring labels. Her sister, Idalia Boyd, had one release on Dimension, "Hula Hoopin'," that failed to chart.

In May, 1974, "The Loco-Motion" went to number one again, when producer Todd Rundgren convinced the members of Grand Funk [see 364] they should record the 1962 tune after he heard them having fun with the song's harmonies. The Goffin-King composition almost topped the chart again in 1988, when a single by Kylie Minogue peaked at number three. Produced by Mike Stock, Matt Aitken and Peter Waterman, Minogue's dance version sold well enough to reach number one on the Hot 100 Singles Sales chart.

Little Eva continued to make appearances at oldies shows until her health declined. She died of cervical cancer on April 10, 2003.

## THE TOP FIVE
*Week of August 25, 1962*

1 **Loco-Motion**
Little Eva

2 **Breaking Up is Hard to Do**
Neil Sedaka

3 **Things**
Bobby Darin

4 **You Don't Know Me**
Ray Charles

5 **Sheila**
Tommy Roe

## 116 Sheila ABC-PARAMOUNT 10329
### TOMMY ROE

*Writer: Tommy Roe*

*Producer: Felton Jarvis*

*September 1, 1962*
*2 weeks*

THOMAS DAVID ROE was born in Atlanta, Ga. on May 9, 1942. Among his boyhood friends were Joe South, Billy Joe Royal, Mac Davis and Ray Stevens. With fellow students at Brown High School, Tommy formed a band, the Satins, and played fraternity parties at the University of Georgia and Georgia Tech. When he was 16, he signed a two-year contract with a local southern company, Judd Records. In 1960 the label released a song called "Sheila" that Roe had written when he was only 14. Unfortunately, the label didn't have the resources to pull off a national hit.

While in the 11th and 12th grades, Tommy and his band played sock hops for a prominent Atlanta disc jockey, Paul Drew (the man who would become the influential chief programmer for the RKO radio chain in the late 60s). Drew introduced Tommy to Felton Jarvis, who liked Tommy's singing and signed him to ABC-Paramount Records.

Tommy played some of the songs he had written, and Jarvis liked the Buddy Holly-influenced "Sheila." Jarvis produced the session (with Jerry Reed on guitar), and, two years after it was a single on Judd, it was released on ABC-Paramount.

Meanwhile, Tommy had graduated from Brown High, and was earning $70 a week soldering wires for General Electric. He was still employed by G.E. when "Sheila" went into *Billboard*'s top 10. He had a call from ABC-Paramount executives, asking him to go on the road to promote "Sheila." Tommy said he couldn't give up his seniority, a chance for promotion and $70 a week. ABC advanced him $5,000 and Tommy hit the road.

"Sheila" went to number three on the British charts, so Tommy toured the United Kingdom. One of the supporting acts was the Beatles. On the flight home, Tommy was inspired to write "Everybody," which hit the American top 10 in late 1963.

Then Tommy joined the army, and was inactive while the Beatles and other British groups held American artists at bay. By the time he returned to civilian life in 1966, he was ready for another top 10 hit.

That was "Sweet Pea," a song Tommy says many people assume has hidden meaning. One radio station even ran a contest to have their listeners guess what the song was about, but Tommy says it's just a basic little story. His next single, "Hooray for Hazel," went even higher, peaking at number six.

Then, in the later 1960s, bubblegum music took over the charts, and Tommy was due for another number one song.

### THE TOP FIVE
*Week of September 1, 1962*

1 **Sheila**
Tommy Roe

2 **Loco-Motion**
Little Eva

3 **Breaking Up is Hard to Do**
Neil Sedaka

4 **You Don't Know Me**
Ray Charles

5 **Party Lights**
Claudine Clark

The group had been recording singles under a wide variety of pseudonyms and singing backing vocals for producer Crewe (for artists like Bobby Darin, Freddy Cannon and Danny and the Juniors).

An audition for a lounge in a New Jersey bowling alley didn't get them a job, but resulted in an important change. "We figured we'll come out of this with something," Gaudio says, "so we took the name of the bowling alley. It was called the Four Seasons."

The first single released under the new name was "Bermuda" on George Goldner's Gone Records in 1961. It failed to chart, but the group signed with the Chicago-based Vee Jay label, and their fortunes turned.

"Some songs come quickly and some songs take forever," Gaudio explains. " 'Sherry' was a quickie. It took 15 minutes. I was ready to leave for a rehearsal we were having, and I sat at the piano and it just came out. Not having a tape recorder in those days, the only way I could remember it was to put a quick lyric to it and remember the melody and the words together. I drove down to rehearsal humming it, trying to keep it in my mind. I had no intention of keeping the lyrics. To my surprise, everybody liked the lyrics so we didn't change anything."

Gaudio also recalls the first time he heard "Sherry" on the radio: "I was driving on the Westside Highway (in Manhattan) and I had to pull off the road. It was kind of a shock. At first I didn't associate it with our record. The first ten seconds just sounded interesting, then the bell rang!"

*Writer: Bob Gaudio*

*Producer: Bob Crewe*

*September 15, 1962*
*5 weeks*

To many, "Sherry" seemed like an overnight success for the Four Seasons. In four short weeks the group's chart debut climbed to the top of the Hot 100, making an impressive leap from 11 to one. In truth, lead singer Frankie Valli had been working for 10 years before "Sherry" became a hit, and he formed the nucleus of the Four Seasons as early as 1955.

Valli, born Francis Castelluccio on May 3, 1937, started working clubs in his native Newark, New Jersey in 1952. A year later he released his first solo single, "My Mother's Eyes," under the name Frankie Valley. Two years after that he joined with three members of the Variety Trio—Nick and Tommy DeVito and Hank Majewski—and formed the Variatones. A year later, they changed their name to the Four Lovers and hit the charts with "You're the Apple of My Eye," a song they performed on Ed Sullivan's show.

Subsequent releases did not chart. Valli recorded a solo effort in 1958 titled "I Go Ape," significant because it introduced him to the songwriter, Bob Crewe, who would become the Four Seasons' producer and co-writer. That same year, another New Jersey group, the Royal Teens, had a top three hit with "Short Shorts." Both groups appeared on a Baltimore TV show the same day, and that's how Valli met Royal Teen Bob Gaudio.

"We both happened to be from New Jersey, so we struck up a conversation," Gaudio remembers. "We didn't see each other for a couple of years. I departed the Royal Teens and took a job in a printing factory as a compositor. I got real nervous, because some people lost a few fingers, so I left. A mutual friend of a friend mentioned the Four Lovers were looking for a keyboard player, so I auditioned and started working with them."

DeVito was replaced by Charles Calello who was replaced by Gaudio; Majewski was replaced by Hugh Garrity who was replaced by Nick Massi. The Four Seasons line-up that would record "Sherry" was in place by 1961.

## THE TOP FIVE
*Week of September 15, 1962*

1  **Sherry**
   Four Seasons

2  **Sheila**
   Tommy Roe

3  **Ramblin' Rose**
   Nat King Cole

4  **Loco-Motion**
   Little Eva

5  **Green Onions**
   Booker T & the MG's

## 118 Monster Mash GARPAX 44167
### BOBBY 'BORIS' PICKETT AND THE CRYPT-KICKERS

*Writers: Bobby Pickett*
*Leonard Capizzi*

*Producer: Gary S. Paxton*

*October 20, 1962*
*2 weeks*

BOBBY PICKETT was a big Elvis Presley fan, so he was delighted when a friend of his who knew Elvis told him that the King had heard his hit single, "Monster Mash." Bobby asked his friend Melody what Elvis thought of his novelty song. "Well, he hates your record, Bobby," she told him. "He thinks it's the stupidest thing he ever heard." Bobby could only sputter, "Whoever liked Elvis anyway?!" Looking back on it, Bobby reconsiders. "I don't think he knew who Boris Karloff was, to tell the truth."

Bobby, born February 11, 1938, in Somerville, Massachusetts, first learned about Boris Karloff when he saw the actor's films. As a child, Bobby went to the movies a lot—his father managed a movie theater. In high school, Bobby was a jock.

After a stint in Korea as part of the Signal Corps, Bobby went home to Somerville. "I would enter these tal-ent contests. I did this shtick about Boris Karloff . . . and every time I'd do it, I'd win." Bobby stayed in Somerville for a year before moving to Hollywood to pursue an acting career. Soon after, his friend Lenny Capizzi also moved to California with three other Italian boys from Somerville. They formed a singing group, the Cordials, and asked Bobby to join.

"I asked Lenny if it would be O.K. if during the monologue of 'Little Darlin' I would do Boris Karloff. That inspired Lenny to say that would be a great voice for a novelty record." But Bobby wanted to act. He quit the Cordials and signed with an agent. Two weeks later, the agent died of a heart attack.

So Bobby called Lenny and suggested they do that novelty song after all. They met one Saturday to write. Bobby's original title was "Monster Twist," but Lenny thought the "Monster Mashed Potato" would be more *au courant*. "It came very easily and very fast," Pickett recalls. "In less than two hours we had the whole thing. We did it on a Wollensak tape recorder. Lenny took the reel over to Gary Paxton, and he said, 'We'll call it the "Mean Monster Mashed Potato." ' We decided that was too much."

Paxton produced the record. He created the sound of a coffin opening by putting a rusty nail in a 2″ by 4″ and pulling it out slowly with a hammer. The bubbling sounds came from blowing into a straw in a glass of water. The chains were dropped onto plywood planks on the floor. "When I reached the studio, on the corner of Highland and Franklin, we were booked just after a guy named Herb Alpert," says Bobby. "The Crypt-Kickers were Gary Paxton, a writing partner of his named Johnny McCrae and Ricki Paige, who was a session singer." The song was recorded in one take with one pick-up. "I was very prepared for it. I'd gone over it in my head. I guess I'd done it out loud in front of a mirror a couple of times. I walked in and felt real comfortable. Leon Russell was playing piano."

Paxton took the record to four major labels and was turned down by all of them. "I had no idea it would ever get played on the radio or be a hit," Bobby declares. Paxton pressed a thousand copies himself and drove around California, dropping off copies at radio stations. "By the time he drove back, they had played it. The phones lit up and he knew he had a hit. One of the labels that turned him down, London Records, called and said, 'We made a mistake.' And he made a deal with London."

"Monster Mash" proved to have amazing longevity. It re-entered the Hot 100 eight years later, on August 29, 1970, and peaked at 91. Almost three years after that, on May 5, 1973, it made a second re-entry, and this time went all the way to number 10.

### THE TOP FIVE
*Week of October 20, 1962*

1 **Monster Mash**
   Bobby (Boris) Pickett
   & the Crypt Kickers

2 **Sherry**
   Four Seasons

3 **Do You Love Me**
   Contours

4 **He's a Rebel**
   Crystals

5 **I Remember You**
   Frank Ifield

*Writer: Gene Pitney*

*Producer: Phil Spector*

*November 3, 1962*
*2 weeks*

THE CRYSTALS are credited with recording six top 20 hits for Phil Spector [see 46—"To Know Him Is to Love Him"] on his Philles label. It's one of the many ironies of rock music that their voices are not heard on their biggest hit, "He's a Rebel."

Philles Records was created in 1961 when, after success with the Paris Sisters' "I Love How You Love Me," producer Spector took up record executive Lester Sill's offer to finance a new label.

While in the offices of Hill and Range Publishing in New York, Phil met five teenage girls from Brooklyn: Dee Dee Kennibrew, Barbara Alston, Patricia Wright, LaLa Brooks and Mary Thomas. They were high school students who had been singing just for fun when they met songwriter Leroy Bates. They took their name from Bates' daughter, Crystal. They took their songs from Bates too, including "There's No Other (Like My Baby)" which Spector recorded as the "B" side of their first Philles single, "Oh Yeah Maybe Baby."

"There's No Other" proved to be the "A" side, peaking at number 20. For their next single, Spector talked songwriters Barry Mann and Cynthia Weil into giving him a song that had been written for Tony Orlando, who was hot with "Halfway to Paradise" and "Bless You." With a few changes in lyrics for gender, The Crystals recorded "Uptown" and it peaked at number 13.

Next, Phil recorded a Carole King-Gerry Goffin song for The Crystals, "He Hit Me (And It Felt Like a Kiss)." With lyrics like "He hit me, and I was glad" the song was destined for failure. But perhaps this record served another purpose—Phil wanted complete control of Philles Records for artistic as well as commercial reasons, and he wanted to win the label away from Sill and part-owner Harry Finfer. That may be why, in 1962, he signed a deal with Snuff Garrett at Liberty Records to be head of east coast A&R for the label.

While at Liberty, Phil heard a song written by an old friend, Gene Pitney, that Garrett was planning to record with Vikki Carr. Phil abruptly resigned and headed for the west coast with Pitney's demo. At Gold Star studios, he assembled arranger Jack Nitzsche, engineer Larry Levine and outstanding session musicians like drummer Hal Blaine, guitarist Larry Knechtel, percussionist Sonny Bono [see 181—"I Got You Babe"] and saxophonist Steve Douglas—all the musicians who would become the core of Spector's famous "Wall of Sound" production.

The only people he *didn't* have were the Crystals, who were still in New York. But it was a race against time, with the Vikki Carr version already completed and about to be released on Liberty. Phil recruited a trio of backing singers well known in the industry, the Blossoms [see 107— "Johnny Angel"]. Lead singer

Darlene Love, Fanita James and Gracia Nitzsche (Jack's wife) sang the vocals on "He's a Rebel."

Phil's version soared up the Hot 100 and Vikki Carr didn't make her chart debut until 1967, with "It Must Be Him." Phil bought out his other partners, and as part of the deal, promised they would share in the profits of the next two Crystals singles. The first, "He's Sure the Boy I Love," was also recorded by the Blossoms, and it went to number 11. The second was recorded by the real Crystals (now a quartet after Mary's departure), but Spector had the last laugh. It was called "(Let's Dance) The Screw" and was a five-minute sexually provocative song punctuated by Phil's lawyer saying, "Do the screw." It received no air play, was not commercially pressed and thus resulted in zero profits. Spector was now sole owner of Philles.

The authentic Crystals had two more top 10 hits, "Da Doo Ron Ron" and "Then He Kissed Me." But by the summer of 1963, Phil was working with another female group, the Ronettes (whose lead singer, Veronica, he would later marry) and many believe he lost interest in The Crystals.

Darlene Love and Fanita James recorded with Bobby Sheen as Bob B. Soxx and the Blue Jeans and had a top 10 single with a Spectorized "Zip-A-Dee Doo Dah." Darlene also recorded solo, and made the top 40 twice, with "(Today I Met) The Boy I'm Gonna Marry" and "Wait Til' My Bobby Gets Home."

## THE TOP FIVE
*Week of November 3, 1962*

1  **He's a Rebel**
   Crystals

2  **Only Love Can Break a Heart**
   Gene Pitney

3  **Do You Love Me**
   Contours

4  **Monster Mash**
   Bobby (Boris) Pickett
   & the Crypt Kickers

5  **All Alone Am I**
   Brenda Lee

## 120 Big Girls Don't Cry VEE JAY 465
### THE FOUR SEASONS

Writers: *Bob Crewe*
*Bob Gaudio*

Producer: *Bob Crewe*

*November 17, 1962*
*5 weeks*

"**B**IG GIRLS DON'T CRY" was a phrase uttered by Clark Gable in a movie, and it inspired songwriters Bob Crewe and Bob Gaudio to write the follow-up to "Sherry," the Four Seasons' first number one single. Five weeks after "Sherry" slipped from the top of the chart, "Big Girls Don't Cry" was in its place.

Actually, both songs were recorded at the same session, and it was a toss-up as to which would be released first. As it turned out, it didn't matter. They both established Frankie Valli's falsetto voice and the danceable rhythms of the group as the definitive East Coast sound, with its roots in doo-wop and R&B music of the fifties.

The Four Seasons may have the distinction of recording under more pseudonyms than any other group. During their struggling years, from 1956 to 1961, both the group and Frankie as a solo act recorded under more than 13 different names. Here is a chronological list of some of those pseudonyms:

*Variatones*
*Frankie Valli and the Travelers*
*Frankie Love and the Four Lovers*
*The Four Lovers*
*Frankie Tyler*
*Frankie Vally*
*Frankie Valle and the Romans*

### THE TOP FIVE
*Week of November 17, 1962*

1 **Big Girls Don't Cry**
Four Seasons

2 **Return to Sender**
Elvis Presley

3 **He's a Rebel**
Crystals

4 **All Alone Am I**
Brenda Lee

5 **Next Door to an Angel**
Neil Sedaka

*Billy Dixon and the Topics*
*Village Voices*
*The Topics*
*Eric Anthony*
*Turner Di Sentri* (Bob Gaudio)
*Alex Alda* (Bob Gaudio).

Even after they were considered to be America's most successful group, they resorted to a false name one more time. In 1965 they released a version of Bob Dylan's "Don't Think Twice" under the name The Wonder Who?, featuring an even higher-pitched than usual Frankie Valli.

"Big Girls Don't Cry" was very similar to "Sherry," but that didn't hurt its chances for success at all—in fact, the similarity no doubt contributed to its number one status.

"I didn't feel it was the freshest follow-up," Gaudio confesses. "After the success of 'Sherry,' we had to follow it up with something vaguely similar. The harmonies were structured differently, a little bigger." With their adrenalin flowing, the group became a little cocky, by their own admission. With two number one songs under their belt, could they do it again? It would not take very long to get an answer.

Writer: Joe Meek

Producer: Joe Meek

December 22, 1962
3 weeks

O N July 10, 1962, the United States launched the world's first communications satellite, Telstar, designed to relay television signals between the United States and Europe. During the week of December 22, 1962, London Records launched the first British group to have a number one single in America.

Mr. Acker Bilk was the first artist from England to go to the top of the U.S. chart [see 110—"Stranger on the Shore"], but the first British group—and the *only* British group until the Beatles—to go to number one in America was the Tornadoes.

The person most responsible for the eerie, otherworld sounds of "Telstar" was writer/producer Joe Meek. He became interested in radio and electronics as a child, and when he joined the Royal Air Force he worked as a radar technician. Later, he got a job as a sound engineer at · IBC Studios in London and then moved to Landsowne Studios, where he completely redesigned the studio. With the royalties he earned from writing the flip side of a Tommy Steele hit, Meek opened his own record company, Triumph, and produced his first British hit, Michael Cox' "Angela Jones." His first British number one was "Johnny Remember Me" by John Leyton. Meek also produced hits for Mike Berry, who was backed by a band called the Outlaws. Drummer Clem Cattini came to audi-

tion for the Outlaws in 1961. Instead Meek decided to form the nucleus of a new instrumental group he wanted to rival Britain's Shadows. Lead guitarist Alan Caddy came from another backing band, the Pirates. Then Meek added his protege, a German singer named Heinz Burt, who lived in Southampton and became the group's bass player; rhythm guitarist George Bellamy; and organist Roger LaVerne.

At first, the Tornadoes were a backing band for singer Billy Fury, but in 1962 Meek recorded them on their own. They cut their first single, "Love and Fury," at Meek's Caledonian Road studios in North London. It was not a hit. But "Telstar," their second single, went to number one in Britain on October 4, the fifth anniversary of the launching of the world's *first* artificial satellite, Sputnik I.

The Tornadoes managed a few more hits in Britain, but not in America. In 1963, Heinz left for a solo career as a vocalist. Soon after, Bellamy left, followed by Caddy and

LaVerne. Cattini, the only original member still in the group, finally quit, and the Tornadoes carried on with a completely different line-up from the group that recorded "Telstar."

On February 3, 1967, Meek apparently took his own life by shooting himself at his studio. What happened that day has never fully been explained, although friends have speculated that the date, the eighth anniversary of Buddy Holly's death, may not have been a coincidence. With Meek's death, the Tornadoes disbanded.

Four of the original Tornadoes (all except Caddy) recorded an updated version of "Telstar" in 1975, but it did not lead to a revival of the group. Bellamy has been running an independent record company, Caddy is in management, LaVerne works in advertising in Mexico, Cattini is a session musician who often plays on the BBC's "Top of the Pops" and Heinz, once a grocer's assistant, has worked in newspaper advertising and at a bakery.

## THE TOP FIVE
*Week of December 22, 1962*

1 **Telstar**
   Tornadoes

2 **Limbo Rock**
   Chubby Checker

3 **Return to Sender**
   Elvis Presley

4 **Bobby's Girl**
   Marcie Blane

5 **Big Girls Don't Cry**
   Four Seasons

# Go Away Little Girl COLUMBIA 42601
## STEVE LAWRENCE

*Writers: Gerry Goffin*
*Carole King*

*Producer: Al Kasha*

*January 12, 1963*
*2 weeks*

THE first number one single of 1963 was the fourth chart-topper for the writing team of Gerry Goffin and Carole King. This was an especially good year for Goffin and King, with over a dozen top 30 singles. Their biggest hits of the year were "One Fine Day" by the Chiffons, "Up on the Roof" by the Drifters, "Keep Your Hands Off My Baby" by Little Eva, "Hey Girl" by Freddie Scott and "Don't Say Nothin' Bad (About My Baby)" by the Cookies.

Four of Goffin and King's top 30 hits were recorded by Steve Lawrence, a popular television personality who had a trio of top 10 singles in 1960-1961. "Go Away Little Girl" was his first single on Columbia Records, and his only number one hit.

He was born Sidney Leibowitz on July 8, 1935 in Brownsville, an underprivileged section of Brooklyn. His father, Max, was a cantor and by age

eight, young Sidney was singing in his father's synagogue. His voice began to change at 11, and his father suggested he stop singing. Over the next three years, he studied piano and saxophone and started writing songs. He started singing again at assemblies and in the glee club while attending Thomas Jefferson High School. He came to the attention of local DJ Ted Brown, who sent him to work with the vocal coach who had trained Eddie Fisher and Kitty Kallen.

His first professional work was not singing, but accompanying his vocalist brother Bernie on the piano. When Bernie was drafted, Sidney decided to become a singer himself. He adopted the names of his nephews, Steve and Lawrence, and won first prize on "Arthur Godfrey's Talent Scouts"—an opportunity to appear on Godfrey's morning radio show for a week.

Steve signed with King Records in April, 1952, and made the chart with his first single, "Poinciana." His high school principal allowed him time off to make personal appearances, but Steve was so busy with his career that he left school before graduating.

In July, 1953, Steve Allen picked Lawrence over 50 other applicants to be a regular performer on his local variety show on WRCA, the NBC flagship station in New York. When that show evolved into "The Tonight Show" on the full network, Lawrence remained a regular for five seasons. Those appearances led to a new recording contract with Coral Records, and a top five hit in 1957, a cover version of Buddy Knox' "Party Doll" [see 19].

There was one more benefit from appearing on Steve Allen's shows. That's where Lawrence met singer Eydie Gorme, and after appearing on TV together for four years, they were married on December 29, 1957 in Las Vegas. In the July and August of 1958, they starred in their own series, a summer replacement for Steve Allen called "Steve Allen Presents the Steve Lawrence-Eydie Gorme Show."

Steve was drafted in the fall of 1958, and was stationed at Fort Myer, Virginia as the official vocalist for the United States Army Band. While in the service, he had two top 10 hits on ABC-Paramount ("Pretty Blue Eyes" and "Footsteps"). He then signed with United Artists Records and had one more top 10 hit ("Portrait of My Love").

He followed "Go Away Little Girl" with a Barry Mann-Cynthia Weil song ("Don't Be Afraid, Little Darlin'") and two more Goffin-King songs ("Poor Little Rich Girl" and "Walking Proud"). In the summer of 1963, he recorded a duet with Eydie ("I Want to Stay Here"), also penned by Goffin and King.

## THE TOP FIVE
*Week of January 12, 1963*

1 **Go Away Little Girl**
Steve Lawrence

2 **Telstar**
Tornadoes

3 **Limbo Rock**
Chubby Checker

4 **Hotel Happiness**
Brook Benton

5 **Pepino the Italian Mouse**
Lou Monte

VANGUARD 35017 **Walk Right In** 123
THE ROOFTOP SINGERS

*Writers: Gus Cannon*
*Hosie Woods*

*Producers: Erik Darling*
*Bill Svanoe*

*January 26, 1963*
*2 weeks*

Erik Darling was born in Baltimore, Maryland on September 25, 1933. His parents were both artists, and as a young boy, Erik listened to all types of music on the radio. At 16, Erik went to live with his mother in New York City. In Greenwich Village's Washington Square, he heard groups play the same kind of folk music he had heard on the Canadian radio show.

Erik hung out in Washington Square and learned to play banjo and guitar. When he was 18, he saw the Weavers in concert, and wanted to join a group like that to sing harmony. Five years later, Erik put together a quartet called the Tune Tellers. They disbanded and reformed as a trio, the Tarriers, which included Alan Arkin. The group was together for two years.

"Alan got fed up with the scene and wanted to go back to his original choice in life, to be an actor," Erik explains. Darling left the Tarriers eventually, but still had a desire to be in a group. He was one of the few people in America who knew how to play the five-string banjo, and when Pete Seeger left the Weavers in 1958, Erik was asked to take his place. He spent four-and-a-half years with the Weavers before going out on his own.

Then he heard a song on an old RCA album from 1930 by Gus Cannon and the Jugstompers, called "Walk Right In." "When I heard that song," says Erik, "I said to myself, that's a hit." He changed some lyrics ("Everybody's talking about a *two way woman*" became "*a new way of walking*") and recruited two friends to sing it with him.

The first was Bill Svanoe, a guitarist whose style was similar to Darling's. The second was Lynne Taylor, a jazz singer who had performed with Tommy Dorsey and Benny Goodman. Lynne already knew how to harmonize with Erik's voice; she loved to sing along while listening to his *True Religion* album.

Erik wanted to record "Walk Right In" with two 12-string guitars, but there weren't many to be found outside of pawn shops. He ordered two from the Gibson Guitar Company, and waited six months for them.

The record was a windfall for the song's writer, 79-year-old Gus Cannon, who was living in a little house by the railroad tracks in Memphis. He had almost frozen the previous winter, until he hocked his banjo for $20 worth of coal. It was the first time in 50 years his banjo was in someone else's hands. Gus not only earned publishing profits from "Walk Right In," but a recording contract with Stax Records.

The Rooftop Singers had two more chart entries ("Tom Cat" and "Mama Don't Allow"). "We had a certain problem in that the group was put together strictly for 'Walk Right In,'" Erik admits. "There's wasn't anything else that really fit...we never did come up with anything that was remotely as good." Still, they stayed together for four-and-a-half years. Today, Erik is a psychologist in Denver, interested in opening a counseling center. Bill is writing screenplays, and Lynne Taylor passed away in 1982.

## THE TOP FIVE
*Week of January 26, 1963*

1 **Walk Right In**
Rooftop Singers

2 **Hey Paula**
Paul & Paula

3 **Go Away Little Girl**
Steve Lawrence

4 **Tell Him**
Excitors

5 **The Night Has
a Thousand Eyes**
Bobby Vee

## 124 Hey Paula PHILIPS 40084
## PAUL AND PAULA

*Writer: Ray Hildebrand*

*Producer: Major Bill Smith*

*February 9, 1963*
*3 weeks*

"I WAS a college student at Howard Payne College in Brownwood, Texas," says Ray Hildebrand. "I was a lifeguard at the swimming pool, and the coach let me live in the gymnasium during the summer for free. For some reason, a song by Annette Funicello called 'Tall Paul' was in my head. I started writing a song about a boy named Paul and a girl named Paula. I worked on it for a couple of months, and I called it 'Paul and Paula.'"

Ray was attending Howard Payne on a basketball scholarship, and during school months he lived in a boarding house. The owner had a niece named Jill Jackson, who asked Ray to sing with her on a radio benefit for the American Cancer Society. They sang the tune Ray had written in the gym, and one of the DJs liked it so much, he taped it to play on his own show. When requests started coming in for the song, the DJ told Jill's mother the "kids" might have something. A basketball player who was a friend of Ray's told them to go see Major Bill Smith, a Fort Worth record producer who had just recorded a number one single for Bruce Channel [see 105—"Hey Baby"].

"We walked into this little radio station, KFJZ, with a recording studio in the basement," Ray remembers. "We waited all day to see this guy, but he was recording people all day long. At the last session, a black guy named Amos Milburn, Jr. didn't show up. We were standing there, and Major Bill said, 'What do you kids want?' We said we had these songs, and we sung them and he said, 'Let's record them. I'm paying these musicians for something, we might as well record the "Star Spangled Banner," but we're gonna record something!'"

Jill and Ray recorded "Hey Paula" in two takes—one would have done it, but Ray popped his "p's" on "Paula." After the recording session, they went back to their motel and signed contracts. Major Bill pressed the record on his own LeCam label,

and three months later he called Ray and asked if he had any clothes. "I said I didn't, so he sent me $500 and I went to Neiman-Marcus and spent it all on three suits. We took off to Atlanta where the record was starting to break out."

Shelby Singleton of Mercury Records was impressed with the sales in Atlanta, and bought the master for their newly acquired Philips Records. The only change he asked for was in the artists' names—he thought "Paul and Paula" would sell more records than "Jill and Ray." The record entered the Hot 100 on December 29, 1962, and topped the chart six weeks later.

Ray had originally written "Hey Paula" as a six-minute song, but part of it was edited out in the studio when Major Bill said it would be too long for a single. Ray took the deleted material, and with Jill's mother, turned it into the follow-up, titled "Young Lovers."

Despite the national success, Ray had "internal struggles" with the record business. He and Jill were touring with the "Dick Clark Caravan of Stars" when he suddenly decided to leave the tour. Clark had to go on stage the first night and sing with

Jill; Ray went to Oregon and hauled hay for a week while he organized his thoughts. Although he returned to "Paul and Paula" briefly, he finally decided his life as a Christian was of more value than his life as a singer. He married his college sweetheart and raised a family in Kansas City, where he still lives today. Jill is married and lives in the San Fernando Valley in Southern California. From time to time she telephones Ray and asks if he'd like to resume his career, but he politely and firmly declines.

## THE TOP FIVE
*Week of February 9, 1963*

1  **Hey Paula**
   Paul & Paula

2  **Walk Right In**
   Rooftop Singers

3  **The Night Has
   a Thousand Eyes**
   Bobby Vee

4  **Loop De Loop**
   Johnny Thunder

5  **Up on the Roof**
   Drifters

*Writers: Bob Crewe
           Bob Gaudio*

*Producer: Bob Crewe*

*March 2, 1963
3 weeks*

**W**HEN "Walk Like a Man" topped the chart on March 2, 1963, the Four Seasons became the first group in the history of the Hot 100 to have three consecutive number one singles*. The Four Seasons were the most successful group in America during 1962-1963, and for the 27-week period that began September 15, 1962, they occupied the number one position for 13 weeks.

They were so popular that during the summer of 1963, an American disc jockey discussing the British phenomenon of the Beatles described them as Britain's answer to the Four Seasons.

Riding the wave of success, the group increased its touring schedule, giving Bob Gaudio less time to write songs. As a result, the follow-up to "Walk Like a Man" was a cover version of Fats Domino's "Ain't That a Shame." It sounded like a Four Seasons record, but compared to the three previous hits, it was a failure, peaking at 22. The group's next single, "Candy Girl" backed with "Marlena," was a two-sided hit, with the "A" side going to number three. It was also an "outside" song, written by Larry Santos.

But trouble was brewing between the group and their label, Vee Jay. Until the Four Seasons became such a hot property, the Chicago-based label had a roster that primarily featured black artists. Gene Chandler gave the label their first number one single [see 104—"Duke of Earl"], but at one time or another the label also featured artists such as Jerry Butler, Jimmy Reed, the Dells, the Staple Singers, Gladys Knight and the Pips and Dee Clark.

Vee Jay was founded in 1953 by Vivian Carter and her husband, James C. Bracken. The first artists

they signed were the Spaniels and Jimmy Reed. Vivian's brother, Calvin Tollie Carter, was head of A&R and was responsible for signing many acts. He lent his middle name to one of the label's publishing companies and later, a subsidiary label.

The company's west coast sales manager, Randy Wood, first heard "Sherry" when Frankie Valli played him a dub over the phone. He liked the record and arranged a deal with the group's producer, Bob Crewe.

Thanks to the immediate success of "Sherry," Vee Jay was approached by EMI Records in England about one of their hits, "I Remember You" by Frank Ifield. Vee Jay took the record and with it, a five-year contract on an unknown EMI group who had not yet released their first British single. That group was the Beatles.

Contractual difficulties between the Four Seasons and Vee Jay resulted from disputes about royalty payments. A shake-up in Vee Jay's management, with vice-president Ewart Abner departing the label, did not help resolve the matter. From August to November of 1963 suits and countersuits were filed. The Four Seasons recorded a new single, "Dawn (Go Away)," but it was withheld from Vee Jay and released on their new label: Philips Records, distributed at the time by Mercury in the United States. "Dawn" hit the charts on February 1, 1964. During the first onslaught of Beatlemania, it held on to the number three position for three consecutive weeks while the Beatles, by this time also free of their Vee Jay committment, held the top two positions [see 143—"I Want to Hold Your Hand"].

**THE TOP FIVE**
*Week of March 2, 1963*

1 **Walk Like a Man**
   Four Seasons

2 **Ruby Baby**
   Dion

3 **Rhythm of the Rain**
   Cascades

4 **Hey Paula**
   Paul & Paula

5 **You're the Reason
   I'm Living**
   Bobby Darin

* Technically, the Four Seasons' run of three consecutive number one singles was interrupted by "Santa Claus Is Coming to Town," released after "Big Girls Don't Cry." It was intended as a holiday record, however, and its peak position of 23 should not affect the group's record of having three of their regular consecutive releases hit number one.

# 126 Our Day Will Come KAPP 501
## RUBY AND THE ROMANTICS

Writers: Bob Hilliard
       Mort Garson

Producer: Allen Stanton

March 23, 1963
1 week

Before Ruby Nash joined the Romantics as their lead singer, the four men who made up the group were known as the Supremes. Allen Stanton, an A&R man at Kapp Records who produced their sessions, told the group on a Friday they needed a new name, and by Monday he had come up with Ruby and the Romantics. It didn't sit well at first with the four male members, who thought that "Romantics" didn't project the right image for them.

Ruby Nash was born in Akron, Ohio, on June 15, 1934. She grew up listening to all kinds of music on the radio, but didn't start singing until she was a senior in high school. Then she formed a group with her sister and two other girlfriends, and they entered talent contests in Akron.

Meanwhile, the four male members of the group had sung together in their high school choir. The group consisted of Ed Roberts, first tenor; George Lee, second tenor; Leroy Fann, bass; and Ronald Moseley, baritone. After graduating from high school they decided to sing professionally. They went to New York and recorded for some small labels, but weren't able to come up with any hits. Fann heard Ruby sing and thought that a female vocalist might bring the group some success. He asked her to join them, and through arranger Leroy Kirkland, they won an audition with Kapp.

Ruby remembers the audition lasting from 5 to 11 PM. "Everyone in the group sang everything we knew," she says. It was Stanton who decided Ruby should be the lead vocalist.

Stanton first heard the song "Our Day Will Come" at the home of songwriter Bob Hilliard. Soon after, Ruby was in Stanton's office listening to material. The song's co-writer, Mort Garson, was there, and Ruby heard "Our Day Will Come." "I said that's gonna be a hit," Ruby recalls. "Let us do that song." Garson told her the song was going to be recorded by someone else. "Every day he played different songs and I kept saying let us hear that other song again. Finally, after a week, Mort said we could do it." Although Ruby didn't know it, Garson and Hilliard were reluctant to let an unknown group have their song. Stanton had to promise the songwriters that if the Ruby and the Romantics recording of the song didn't work out, he would record it with Kapp artist Jack Jones.

When the group went to cut "Our Day Will Come," it was the first time Ruby had ever been in a recording studio. Two different arrangements were recorded: a straight, pop version and one with a bossa nova rhythm. Stanton chose to release the latter, and Jones never got a shot at recording the song.

"Our Day Will Come" entered the Hot 100 on February 9, 1963, at number 79. Six weeks later it was number one. Although they never had another top 10 single, many of their songs were recorded by other artists. Eddie Holman changed the gender of "Hey There Lonely Boy" and took "Hey There Lonely Girl" to number two in 1970. The Marvelettes had a top 30 hit with "When You're Young and in Love" in 1967, and 17 years later the Flying Pickets had an *a cappella* hit with it in Britain. The Carpenters released "Hurting Each Other" in 1975 (it went to number two) and "Your Baby Doesn't Love You Anymore" in 1984.

Ruby and the Romantics broke up in 1971. "I really just got tired of all the traveling," Ruby had to admit. "Plus, I was married and my husband was tired of us being separated for so long. And I wanted to raise a family." Ruby settled in Akron, Ohio, and worked for AT&T. She considered singing again, but only with a group. For many years, she decided that she would wait until her two sons and her daughter were older before she would return to performing again. She kept in touch with two of the Romantics, who lived in New York. Ed worked in a bank and George drove a truck. Leroy Fann was killed in 1973.

"Our Day Will Come" was a hit again in 1975, when Frankie Valli [see 398—"My Eyes Adored You"] took it to number 11 on the Hot 100.

## THE TOP FIVE
*Week of March 23, 1963*

1 **Our Day Will Come**
  Ruby & the Romantics

2 **The End of the World**
  Skeeter Davis

3 **You're the Reason I'm Living**
  Bobby Darin

4 **He's So Fine**
  Chiffons

5 **Walk Like a Man**
  Four Seasons

*Writer: Ronnie Mack*

*Producers: Phil Margo*
*Mitch Margo*
*Hank Medress*
*Jay Siegal*

*March 30, 1963*
*4 weeks*

**M**ANY number one songs have been the subjects of lawsuits, but none have been as well publicized as "He's So Fine" vs. "My Sweet Lord." The winner: the estate of Ronnie Mack, the young composer who died shortly after "He's So Fine" went to number one. The loser: former Beatle George Harrison, who was told by a judge in 1976 that his number one song, "My Sweet Lord" [see 286], had been subconsciously copied from "He's So Fine."

The Chiffons were four female friends from Upper Manhattan and the Bronx. Judy Craig, Barbara Lee, Patricia Bennett and Sylvia Peterson often sang in the lunchroom at school,

so when songwriter Ronnie Mack asked them to record some of his tunes as demos, they gladly spent an hour at a midtown Manhattan studio where they recorded as many of Mack's songs as they could in the allotted time.

Busy with high school graduation and finding jobs, the girls forgot about their session with Mack, but he was visiting every New York record company he could to secure a contract. One day he was in the Mutual of Omaha building at Broadway and 54th, when he walked into the office of Phil Margo, Mitch Margo, Hank Medress and Jay Siegal. Better known as the Tokens [see 102—"The Lion Sleeps Tonight"], the four young men had signed a production deal with Capitol Records.

"He walked in right off the street, played three or four songs, and we said we must sign him," Phil Margo recalls. Their production budget exhausted, they used their publishing money to finance a recording session for the girls, who named themselves

the Chiffons. Not being able to afford musicians, the Tokens played all the instruments themselves. While recording "He's So Fine," the engineer suggested that the background singers' chant of "doo-lang, doo-lang, doo-lang" was cute and should come at the beginning of the song.

Capitol had first option on anything the Tokens produced, but they passed on the Chiffons. The Tokens were partial to the song "Oh My Lover" because it sounded like their first hit, "Tonight I Fell in Love." They tried 13 other labels, including MGM, Columbia and ABC-Paramount, but with no luck. Finally, they went to a smaller label, Laurie Records, that had success with Dion DiMucci [see 99—"Runaround Sue"]. The company's owners were so taken with "He's So Fine," they signed a deal on the spot.

Shortly after his song went to number one, Mack collapsed on the street and was taken to Roosevelt Hospital. He had been ill with Hodgkins' Disease, but had not told anyone. The Tokens presented him with a gold record in his hospital room, and soon after, the talented young songwriter died.

The Chiffons' next hit was "One Fine Day," written by Gerry Goffin and Carole King. The Tokens' heard the demo and liked it so much, they wiped the vocal off and recorded the Chiffons' over it. Their only other top 10 single was "Sweet Talkin' Guy" in 1966. After the Harrison trial, the Chiffons recorded "My Sweet Lord," but the novelty was not enough to win airplay.

## THE TOP FIVE
*Week of March 30, 1963*

1 **He's So Fine**
Chiffons

2 **Our Day Will come**
Ruby & the Romantics

3 **The End of the World**
Skeeter Davis

4 **South Street**
Orlons

5 **You're the Reason I'm Living**
Bobby Darin

# I Will Follow Him RCA 8139
## LITTLE PEGGY MARCH

Writers: *Jacques Plant*
*J.W. Stole*
*Del Roma*
*Arthur Altman*
*Norman Gimbel*

Producers: *Hugo Peretti*
*Luigi Creatore*

*April 27, 1963*
*3 weeks*

PEGGY MARCH was 15 years, one month and 13 days old when "I Will Follow Him" went to number one, making her the youngest female singer ever to have a number one single (she edged out Brenda Lee, who was 15 years, seven months and seven days old when "I'm Sorry" topped the chart). Peggy was 4'10" tall at the time, inspiring producers Hugo Peretti and Luigi Creatore to dub her Little Peggy March. "I said, 'please don't do that, please don't,'" she remembers. "They said it was cute. The one thing I never liked was to be made smaller than I was, but I had no say. When I turned 16, we officially dropped 'Little.'"

Although her family always called her Peggy, she was born Margaret Battavio in Lansdale, Pennsylvania. Her stage name, which she has since legally adopted, was taken from the month of her birth: March. She started singing at age two. She remembers watching artists sing on Perry Como's television show and dreaming she would do that one day. After winning a talent contest at age five, she began appearing on local radio and television shows.

She was always asked to sing at family gatherings, so it was not unusual that she sang at her cousin's wedding. A friend of the family, Russell Smith, heard her and spoke to her father about Peggy becoming professional. "Dad was not too happy about it. We had a very long talk and I said, 'I don't know if the opportunity will ever come up again, please let me do this.'"

Smith took Peggy to RCA, where she auditioned for Hugo and Luigi. Her piano player didn't show up, so she sang *a cappella*. She signed with the label in the spring of 1962 and released her first single, the title song from Sid Caesar's Broadway show, *Little Me*. "It was not a song I should have recorded," she says.

"Shortly after, 'I Will Follow Him' wound up on Hugo and Luigi's desk."

The song was already a big hit in France, where Petula Clark had recorded it under the name "Chariot." Arthur Altman and Norman Gimbel added English lyrics and Peggy recorded it in RCA's Studio A on 23rd Street in New York. It was released on January 22, 1963.

In Lansdale, Peggy listened to New York radio station WABC's countdown while washing the supper dishes. "I Will Follow Him" was stuck at number two for five weeks. "Finally, one night it made it to number one, for one week. Our house was ecstatic, but I do remember doing the dishes that night."

"I Will Follow Him" was an international hit, and Peggy toured Europe extensively and travelled to Japan. On her 19th birthday, secretaries at RCA took her out for a three-hour lunch. When she returned to the office, an angry Arnie Harris was waiting for her to keep an appointment she didn't know she had with him. He became her manager, and a year later they married.

In 1969 they moved to Germany, and stayed for 12 years. Peggy starred in TV shows and stage musicals, and recorded in German and English. On January 22, 1974, 11 years to the day after "I Will Follow Him" was released, her daughter Sandy was born.

While competing in a Majorca

song festival in 1971, a man from France introduced himself and thanked her for "I Will Follow Him." A puzzled Peggy asked why, and Paul Mauriat [see 237—"Love Is Blue"] revealed for the first time that he had written the song as an instrumental under the *nom-de-plum* Del Roma.

Peggy began songwriting in 1979. She's had two European number one singles: "Manuel Goodbye," co-written and sung by Audrey Landers (who played Afton Cooper in "Dallas") and "When the Rain Begins to Fall" by Jermaine Jackson and Pia Zadora. She and her family moved back to the States in 1981. But her popularity in Europe remained high, and she and Arnie continued to spend time in Munich, recording new albums in German.

## THE TOP FIVE
*Week of April 27, 1963*

1  **I Will Follow Him**
   Little Peggy March

2  **Can't Get Used to Losing You**
   Andy Williams

3  **He's So Fine**
   Chiffons

4  **Puff (The Magic Dragon)**
   Peter, Paul & Mary

5  **Baby Workout**
   Jackie Wilson

# If You Wanna Be Happy
## JIMMY SOUL

*Writers: Frank Guida*
        *Carmela Guida*
        *Joseph Royster*

*Producer: Frank Guida*

*May 18, 1963*
*2 weeks*

In "Sam Turns the Other Cheek," an episode of NBC's "Cheers," Sam Malone (Ted Danson) is confronted in the bar after closing time by an irate husband brandishing a gun. He's angry because Sam has been fooling around with his wife, and we're not sure how serious he is about shooting Sam. Neither is Sam, who eases the irate man into conversation. When the husband complains his wife is so beautiful that men are always throwing themselves at her, Sam commiserates and tells him it's just like the old song says:

"If you wanna be happy for the rest
        of your life,
Never make a pretty woman your
        wife,
So for my personal point of view,
Get an ugly girl to marry you."*

And with that, Sam takes the gun and puts it in his back pocket, accidentally shooting himself in the rear end.

"If You Wanna Be Happy" will probably never be the theme song of the National Organization of Women, but feminists weren't well-organized enough in 1963 to place any formal protest over the lyrics.

Frank Guida had already produced two other singers from Norfolk, Virginia: Gary U.S. Bonds [see 93—"Quarter to Three"] and Tommy Facenda ("High School U.S.A."). Guida was a fan of calypso music, having been to Trinidad, and decided to combine it with R&B music. The result was "Twistin' Matilda," a song he wrote in 1962. He found a local singer, James McCleese, to sing it, and gave him a new last name that said it all in one word: Soul.

In 1963, Frank teamed up with his wife Carmela and a friend, Joe Royster, to write a song based on the calypso melody, "Ugly Woman." The result was "If You Wanna Be Happy," which Jimmy Soul took all the way to number one.

Jimmy was born in Harlem in 1942. His parents moved to a farm in rural North Carolina, where he grew up listening to the circuit-rider preachers. When he was seven years old, Jimmy became a preacher himself. The family moved to Portsmouth, Virginia, and Jimmy continued to preach and sing with gospel groups. He toured the country with the Nightingales, a popular gospel singing group, but once back home he turned to the secular world of rock and roll.

He performed at the Azalea Gardens in Norfolk, where a one-week stand turned into several months' work. Jimmy was well-known on the Norfolk scene by the time he and Guida recorded "Twistin' Matilda."

Jimmy released "Treat 'Em Tough" as the follow-up to "If You Wanna be Happy." It was equally as enlightened, but the formula didn't work again and the song didn't chart. Jimmy entered the Army, and never made the chart again.

## THE TOP FIVE
### *Week of May 18, 1963*

1  **If You Wanna Be Happy**
   Jimmy Soul

2  **I Will Follow Him**
   Little Peggy March

3  **Puff (The Magic Dragon)**
   Peter, Paul & Mary

4  **Surfin' U.S.A.**
   Beach Boys

5  **Foolish Little Girl**
   Shirelles

# It's My Party
MERCURY 72119

### LESLEY GORE

Writers: John Gluck, Jr.
Wally Gold
Herb Wiener

Producer: Quincy Jones

June 1, 1963
2 weeks

THREE DAYS AFTER LESLEY Gore cele-brated her 17th birthday, "It's My Party" entered the Hot 100. Four weeks later it was the number one song in America. Lesley is the fourth-youngest solo female artist to top the chart, behind Little Peggy March [see 128—"I Will Follow Him"], Brenda Lee [see 71—"I'm Sorry"] and Tiffany [see 681—"I Think We're Alone Now"].

It was almost an "overnight suc-cess" for the Tenafly, New Jersey, high school student who had been singing for friends and relatives since she was a small child. "I was one of those little kids that you put up on a cocktail table and you didn't have to bother winding me up, I just loved to sing," Lesley told Dick Clark.

While attending the Dwight School for Girls, Lesley sang with a seven-piece band of college students. They played for a catering house in Queens, New York, where they would play a wedding in the morning, a bar mitzvah in the afternoon and a "sweet 16" party at night.

The band got their first paying job in Manhattan, at the Prince George Hotel. "They didn't want a girl vocalist on this particular evening," Lesley told Dick, "but I went down to watch and clap my hands and they asked me to get up and do one or two numbers, and it just happened that Quincy Jones was sitting in the little cocktail lounge that evening."

Quincy was a staff producer for Mercury Records, and label executive Irving Green liked Lesley's vocals well enough to sign her to the label.

In February, 1963, Quincy paid a visit to Lesley's home in Tenafly, armed with over 250 demos so they could select songs for her to record. The first one he played for her was "It's My Party," and that song was one of four she recorded on March 30 at Bell Sound in New York.

"I left the studio and forgot about the whole thing," she told Clark. "I had been warned that most often when record companies record an art-ist their record is shelved for maybe

years at a time."

Six days later, Lesley was driving home from school when she heard her recording of "It's My Party" on New York radio station WINS. "I nearly drove off the side of the road into a hydrant, and I stopped at a friend's house and called my mother and told her to try and get it on the radio."

The reason for the sudden release, according to Lesley, was that Mer-cury records had learned the Crystals [see 119—"He's a Rebel"] were about to record the song. Mercury rushed out test pressings of Lesley's version and received immediate airplay.

The record was officially released at the end of April. Its ascension on the charts was swift: it debuted at 60 and moved to 26, to nine, to one.

Lesley's second single continued the saga of Judy and Johnny: "Judy's Turn to Cry" peaked at number five. "She's a Fool" also peaked at five, and her next single came as close as anyone could to number one: "You Don't Own Me" was number two for three weeks, its move to the top halted only by the Beatles first number one single [see 143—"I Want to Hold Your Hand"].

"It's My Party" was the first number one single for producer Quincy Jones and for the engineer on the recording, Phil Ramone.

Lesley released 29 singles on Mercury, before she left the label in 1969. She released three singles on Bob Crewe's Crewe Records, in addition to a duet with Oliver ("Good Morning Sunshine") under the names of Billy

and Sue. Lesley recorded one album for Motown and an album for A&M in 1976 that reunited her with producer Quincy Jones and included the single "Immortality," as well as one on EMI-Manhattan that was a duet with Lou Christie.

Lesley has appeared on the Hot 100 since then—but as a writer, not an artist. She co-wrote two songs on the *Fame* soundtrack with her brother Michael (an Oscar winner for writing the title song from *Fame*), including Irene Cara's "Out Here on My Own," which peaked at number 19 in 1980.

"It's My Party" finally went to number one in Britain, but not by Lesley, who took the song to number nine in the United Kingdom in 1963. Dave Stewart and Barbara Gaskin updated the song in 1981 and topped the British chart for four weeks.

## THE TOP FIVE
*Week of June 1, 1963*

1 **It's My Party**
Lesley Gore

2 **If You Wanna Be Happy**
Jimmy Reed

3 **I Love You Because**
Al Martino

4 **Surfin' U.S.A.**
Beach Boys

5 **Da Doo Ron Ron**
Crystals

*Writers: Rokusuke Ei*
*Hachidai Nakamura*

*Producer: Koji Kusano*

*June 15, 1963*
*3 weeks*

**J**APAN is the world's second largest record market, but while some English-speaking artists do well in Japan, few Japanese artists are able to crack the American charts. In the entire rock era, only three Japanese artists have achieved any success at all in the States. Pink Lady, a female duo picked for stardom by NBC's one-time president Fred Silverman, made the top 40 in 1979 with "Kiss in the Dark." The Yellow Magic Orchestra, a trio specializing in synthesizer music, made it to number 60 the following year with "Computer Games." But the most successful Japanese artist by far, and the only one to have a hit sung in Japanese, was Kyu Sakamoto, who went to number one in June, 1963 with the mistitled "Sukiyaki."

The real title of the song is *"Ue O Muite Aruko,"* which translates "I Look Up When I Walk." Louis Benjamin, the head of Britain's Pye records, heard the song while visiting Japan on business in 1962, and brought it back for jazzman Kenny Ball to record. British DJs were not likely to be able to pronounce the real title, so Pye released the single under a Japanese name most people recognized: "Sukiyaki." As *Newsweek* pointed out, it was like releasing "Moon River" in Japan with the title "Beef Stew."

Ball's "Sukiyaki" went to number 10 in the United Kingdom in January, 1963. In America, disc jockey Rich Osborne of station KORD in Pasco, Washington, got hold of Sakamoto's original version and played it on his evening show. Audience reaction was immediate and the station started playing the song in heavy rotation. As it spread through Washington state, Capitol Records picked up distribution rights and released it under its British title of "Sukiyaki." It became the second song sung in a foreign language to top the Hot 100 ("Tequila" may be a Spanish word, but it doesn't count).

Kyu Sakamoto was born in the industrial city of Kawasaki, the ninth child of a Tokyo restuarant owner. Kyu started singing in jazz clubs while still a high school student, and failed to graduate. In 1959, still a pimply-faced adolescent, Kyu signed with a talent company in Tokyo that was looking for a "boy-next-door"

type. Toshiba Records signed him to a recording contract, and he was an immediate hit. By the time Capitol released "Sukiyaki" in the United States, Sakamoto had 15 singles and eight albums that were best-sellers in Japan. He had also appeared in ten movies and was a regular on seven different weekly television programs and two radio shows.

Two months after "Sukiyaki" hit the number one position, an English version by country singer Clyde Beavers entered Billboard's country chart and peaked at number 21. Another English translation, by the black female duo A Taste of Honey (also signed with Capitol Records), went all the way to number three in 1981. The song was a top 10 hit again in 1994 when 4 PM. managed to take it to number eight.

Sakamoto was one of 520 people who perished when a Japan Airlines 747 crashed into the side of a mountain near Tokyo on August 12, 1985. He was 43 years old.

## THE TOP FIVE
*Week of June 15, 1963*

1 **Sukiyaki**
   Kyu Sakamoto

2 **It's My Party**
   Lesley Gore

3 **You Can't Sit Down**
   Dovells

4 **Da Doo Ron Ron**
   Crystals

5 **I Love You Because**
   Al Martino

## 132   Easier Said Than Done   ROULETTE 4494
### THE ESSEX

*Writers: William Linton*
        *Larry Huff*

*Producer: Henry Glover*

*July 6, 1963*
*2 weeks*

It was not unusual for singers like Elvis Presley, Pat Boone, Frankie Avalon and Gary Troxel from the Fleetwoods to serve time in the Armed Forces while their careers were in full swing. There was even precedent for a group to form while in the service—the Dell-Vikings ("Come Go With Me") were all in the Air Force, stationed in Pittsburgh, Pennsylvania when they had a hit in 1957 with "Come Go With Me." But only one group had a number one single while all the members were serving their country. The Essex were in the United States Marine Corps at Camp LeJeune, North Carolina when "Easier Said Than Done" went to number one.

Walter Vickers and Rodney Taylor met while serving in Okinawa in 1961. When they returned to Camp LeJeune the following year, they met Rudy Johnson and Billie Hill. The four Marines started singing together, but the group wasn't complete until they heard another Marine, Anita Humes, singing at the Non-Commissioned Officers Club.

With Anita singing lead, the group was signed by George Goldner, whose Gone and End labels had been absorbed by Roulette Records. He liked the songs on their demo tape, but asked for some more upbeat material.

They turned to another Marine at Camp LeJeune, William Linton, who had been stationed with Vickers and Taylor in Okinawa. "I was working in the communications department," Linton recalls. "We had a bunch of teletype machines, and when they were running all together they had a beat. The sound of the teletype machines inspired the beat of 'Easier Said Than Done.'"

Linton wrote the song with Larry Huff, and the Essex recorded it—but they thought it would be the flip side of their first single, "Are You Going My Way," written by Rudy Johnson. In fact, most of the recording session was devoted to that song, with "Easier Said Than Done" rushed through in the last few minutes. The take was so short, parts of the song had to be spliced together to produce a finished master.

"The group did not like the song," Linton reveals. "They were more or less doing me a favor. There were other songs they liked better." As it turned out, it was Linton who did a favor for the Essex. "Easier Said Than Done" entered the Hot 100 at number 81 on June 8, 1963, and took only four weeks to reach number one.

The Essex made personal appearances in their Marine uniforms, and continued to record while in the service. Their next single, "A Walkin' Miracle," was a soundalike for "Easier Said Than Done;" it had the same beat with the chords reversed. It peaked at number 12, and only one more song, "She's Got Everything," was able to make the chart.

When Anita was discharged, she attempted a solo career. It was difficult for the Essex to maintain their career momentum, especially when they all got out of the service at different times. When all four male members returned to civilian life, they tried to carry on with a new lead singer, but with no success.

Anita re-enlisted in the Army; Rudy worked as a police officer; Billie has worked for a university; and William Vickers lapsed into a diabetic coma and died several years ago. "The last time we got together," Linton sadly notes, "was at his funeral."

### THE TOP FIVE
*Week of July 6, 1963*

1   **Easier Said Than Done**
    Essex

2   **Sukiyaki**
    Kyu Sakamoto

3   **Blue on Blue**
    Bobby Vinton

4   **Hello Stranger**
    Barbara Lewis

5   **It's My Party**
    Lesley Gore

Writers: *Jan Berry*
*Brian Wilson*

Producer: *Jan Berry*

*July 20, 1963*
*2 weeks*

JAN BERRY (born April 3, 1941) and Dean Torrence (born March 10, 1940) became close friends at University High School in West Los Angeles, where they discovered the shower room in the boys' gym provided a great echo for singing. They formed a group called the Barons with several friends, including first tenor Arnie Ginsberg. It was Arnie who discovered a stripper in downtown L.A. named Jennie Lee, and a trip to the "Follies Burlesk" on Main Street inspired the song "Jennie Lee," recorded in Jan's garage with two tape recorders, duplicating the echo effect of the showers.

While Dean went into the Army Reserves for six months, Jan signed with Arwin Records, owned by Doris Day and her husband, Marty Melcher. With Dean away, the record was released by "Jan and Arnie." When his active duty was finished, Dean returned and Arnie went into the Navy. Through producers Lou Adler and Herb Alpert, Jan and Dean signed with Dore Records and recorded "Baby Talk," a song that Beach Boy Mike Love says helped inspire their first record, "Surfin'."

After a few hits on Dore and one on Challenge Records, Jan and Dean signed to Liberty. They recorded "Linda," a song written in 1944 by Jack Lawrence about the daughter of a friend, little Linda Eastman, who would one day grow up and marry Paul McCartney. "Linda" was a change in style for Jan and Dean, their first song to have a "west coast" sound.

Meanwhile, the Beach Boys and Jan and Dean met while packaged together at record hops in southern California. The Beach Boys were a self-contained band, and they would play for themselves as well as backing up Jan and Dean.

Lou Adler, now their manager, suggested they do some surf songs, so they asked Brian Wilson, who had already written "Surfin'" and "Surfin' Safari," if he had any material. Dean remembers Brian playing two songs

for them: "He said, 'first of all, let me play you our new single'…and he plays 'Sweet Little Sixteen' but he's changed the words and he's called it 'Surfin' U.S.A.' 'That's great,' we said, 'Brian, why don't you give that to us?' We weren't able to talk him out of that one…but he said, 'I have another song…I started this one and I have a verse and chorus and that's about it' and he plays, 'two girls for every boy!' He said, 'it's called "Surf City." and if you want to finish it…I'll split the writing with you.' We re-arranged it somewhat and he came in and helped us sing a lot of the vocal parts."

At the same time, Brian gave Jan and Dean a song they liked even better than "Surf City." Called "Gonna Hustle You," it was full of "Papa-Doo-Ron-Rons." Although they recorded it, it wasn't released because radio wasn't ready for a song with "when summer comes, gonna *hustle* you" in the lyrics. A year later, Jan wrote new words and it became "The New Girl in School," the flip side of "Dead Man's Curve."

That song, about a fatal car crash, proved to be tragically prophetic. On Tuesday evening, April 19, 1966, Jan was driving down the Sunset Strip and lost control of his car, swerving into a parked truck. He was taken to UCLA Medical Center in critical condition, and he remained in a coma for months. He survived, but suffered brain damage and went through years of physical and mental rehabilitation. While Jan recuperated, Dean retired from performing and started a graphic design company, Kittyhawk Graphics.

Jan continued to make progress, and in 1973 the duo made an attempt at a comeback, lip-synching on stage to a recorded track. The audience reaction was hostile, dashing any hopes of resumed careers. Dean went back to Kittyhawk and Jan recorded some solo material. In 1974, Dean and a friend wrote a treatment for a film biography. It took four years to get it made, and in 1978 CBS telecast "Dead Man's Curve," starring Richard Hatch and Bruce Davidson. Reaction to the film was so positive that Mike Love asked Jan and Dean to join the Beach Boys for a tour. This time, they sang live and it was warmly received. Since that time, Jan and Dean have toured every spring and summer, while Jan continues to appear in smaller clubs all year round.

## THE TOP FIVE
*Week of July 20, 1963*

1 **Surf City**
Jan & Dean

2 **Easier Said Than Done**
Essex

3 **So Much in Love**
Tymes

4 **Tie Me Kangaroo Down, Sport**
Rolf Harris

5 **Memphis**
Lonnie Mack

## 134 So Much in Love PARKWAY 871
### THE TYMES

*Writers: Billy Jackson*
*Roy Straigis*
*George Williams*

*Producer: Billy Jackson*

*August 3, 1963*
*1 week*

THE TYMES are a Philadelphia quintet who had more in common with the romantic songs of Johnny Mathis than the typical R&B tunes of 1963. With the seashore sounds of waves rolling in, birds chirping and fingers snapping, "So Much in Love" sailed to the top of the chart in August, 1963.

The story of the Tymes begins in 1956, when George Hilliard and Norman Burnett met at summer camp. A few months later they formed a quartet, the Latineers, with friends Albert Berry and Donald Banks. They performed at record hops, local talent shows and at night clubs. In 1960, they added George Williams as lead singer and changed their name to the Tymes.

In April, 1963, the Tymes appeared on a talent show sponsored by radio station WDAS. Cameo/Parkway was Philadelphia's hottest record company, and a label executive heard the group and signed them to Parkway, the label that featured Chubby Checker.

George Williams wanted to record a romantic song called "The Stroll." He had written the melody and the first verse, and producer Billy Jackson and arranger Roy Straigis worked to finish the song. Jackson

### THE TOP FIVE

*Week of August 3, 1963*

1  **So Much in Love**
   Tymes

2  **Fingertips-Pt. 2**
   Little Stevie Wonder

3  **Surf City**
   Jan & Dean

4  **(You're the)**
   **Devil in Disguise**
   Elvis Presley

5  **Wipe Out**
   Surfaris

came up with the idea of adding the seashore noises, and changed the title to "So Much in Love."

For their next single, Jackson capitalized on their vocal similarity to Mathis and recorded Johnny's first chart record, "Wonderful! Wonderful!" Mathis' version had peaked at number 14; the Tymes bested him by going to number seven. One more single, "Somewhere" (not the *West Side Story* song), made the top 20, but by 1964 the Tymes were off the charts.

Two years later, the Tymes started their own Cameo-distributed label, with songwriters John Madara, Dave White and Leon Huff. Their label didn't have any hits, so Billy Jackson took them to MGM. When they failed to make it there, Jackson changed their image from "Mills Brothers" music to contemporary soul. They recorded an updated ver-

sion of "People" from *Funny Girl*, and it went to number 39.

Six more years would pass before they would chart again. At the end of 1973, Jackson took the Tymes into Philadelphia's Sigma Sound Studios and recorded new songs. He took them to Huff and his partner, Kenny Gamble, but they turned him down, so Jackson took the tapes to RCA Records, and the group was signed to the label. The first single, "You Little Trustmaker," was a worldwide hit, peaking at number 12 in the States and 18 in Britain. An album track, "Miss Grace," was released as a single with the more liberated title of "Ms. Grace," and it became their first and only number one song in Britain.

"So Much in Love" was sung by former Eagle Timothy B. Schmit on the soundtrack of *Fast Times at Ridgemont High* in 1982. It went as high as number 59 on the Hot 100.

TAMLA 54080 **Fingertips (Pt. II)**
LITTLE STEVIE WONDER **135**

*Writers: Henry Cosby*
*          Clarence Paul*

*Producer: Berry Gordy*

*August 10, 1963*
*3 weeks*

**T**HEY called him the 12-year-old genius. And though Stevie Wonder has grown older, the term "genius" still applies. The first of his nine number one singles was "Fingertips (Pt. II)," the second number one for Berry Gordy's Motown Records Corporation.

It was the first live single to go to number one, and it marked the first time that a single and the album it came from were both number one on *Billboard's* charts at the same time. During the three-week run of "Fingertips (Pt. II)" at the top of the singles chart, *Little Stevie Wonder– the 12-Year-Old Genius* moved to number one on the album chart.

"Fingertips" had been released the previous year on a studio album, *The Jazz Soul of Little Stevie.* Marvin Gaye played drums and piano on the LP, joined by Motown's top session musicians: James Jamerson on bass, Joe Hunter on piano, Earl Van Dyke

on organ, Thomas "Bean" Bowles on flute and Benny Benjamin on drums.

Stevie's first three singles ("I Call It Pretty Music, But the Old People Call It the Blues," "Little Water Boy" and "Contract on Love") failed to chart, but his performances on the company's Motortown Reviews were so exciting, Gordy decided to record him live.

"Fingertips" was seven minutes long on the *12-Year-Old Genius* album, and wasn't considered for a single. But the reaction was so positive, Gordy decided to divide it into two parts and release it as a 45. DJs across America preferred the second side, including the spontaneous cry of "What key? What key?" from a confused musician during a reprise.

Steveland Morris was born blind at birth on May 13, 1950 in Saginaw, Michigan. His father's last name was Judkins, a name Stevie later used as a songwriter. Along with his mother, sister and four brothers, Stevie moved to Detroit, where he sang in the Whitestone Baptist Church Choir.

The radio was a big influence on Stevie, who loved to listen to many of Detroit's stations. His first musical

instrument was a six-hole harmonica given to him by an uncle; later he would receive a toy set of drums, which the local Kiwanis Club would replace with real drums. A neighbor moved away and left Stevie her piano, on which he played music that sounded like his idol, Ray Charles.

By the time he was nine years old, Stevie had formed a duo with his best friend, John Glover. John told his cousin about Stevie's talent—and the cousin happened to be Ronnie White, newly signed to Tamla Records as one of the Miracles.

After hearing Stevie and John play, White introduced Stevie to Brian Holland, one of Motown's first staff producers. Holland was impressed enough to call his boss, Gordy, and interrupt a steak dinner to tell him to sign the 11-year-old singer.

Along with his sister Lucy and A&R employee Billie Jean Brown, Berry considered a stage name for his new artist. "Little" was a popular prefix for young stars like Little Willie John and Little Anthony, and Gordy considered Stevie the Little Wonder and Stevie Little Wonder before deciding on Little Stevie Wonder.

The first song Stevie recorded was "Thank You (For Loving Me All the Way)," a tribute to mothers. It wasn't released, but it wasn't long before he recorded *A Tribute to Uncle Ray*, an album of Ray Charles songs. Then followed his three uncharted singles and "Fingertips (Pt. II)," the first of 27 top 10 singles, all recorded for Berry Gordy's record company.

## THE TOP FIVE
*Week of August 10, 1963*

1 **Fingertips-Pt. 2**
   Little Stevie Wonder

2 **Wipe Out**
   Surfaris

3 **(You're the)**
   **Devil in Disguise**
   Elvis Presley

4 **Blowin' in the Wind**
   Peter, Paul & Mary

5 **So Much in Love**
   Tymes

**136** # My Boyfriend's Back SMASH 1834
## THE ANGELS

Writers: Robert Feldman
Jerry Goldstein
Richard Gottehrer

Producers: Robert Feldman
Jerry Goldstein
Richard Gottehrer

August 31, 1963
3 weeks

LIKE their predecessors the Shirelles, the Marvelettes, the Crystals and the Chiffons, the Angels carried on the tradition of girl groups. There was only one difference: the Angels were the first white girl group to have a number one record.

The Angels were three girls from New Jersey. Barbara Allbut (born September 24, 1940) and Phyllis "Jiggs" Allbut (born September 24, 1942) were sisters, and their friend Peggy Santiglia (born May 4, 1944) was lead singer of the group.

Barbara and Jiggs sang together in high school and started a group called the Starlets with a girl named Linda Jansen from Hillside, New Jersey. Barbara played piano and taught the other girls how to sing harmony. They would travel to New York to sing backing vocals for other artists. They also made demos, and one of them landed on a desk at Caprice Records. Jiggs dropped out of college and Barbara left Juilliard to sign with Caprice, and they recorded "'Til" for the label. They wanted a new group name, so they thought of a few and put them all into a hat. Out came "the Blue Angels," which was shortened to the Angels.

"'Til" proved to be a good debut song, going all the way to number 14 on *Billboard's* Hot 100. The follow-up, "Cry Baby Cry" went to 38. After this record, Linda left and was replaced by Peggy, who had been appearing on Broadway in *Do Re Mi* and recording commercials for radio station WINS in New York.

Near the end of 1962, the girls met the writing/producing team of Robert Feldman, Jerry Goldstein and Richard Gottehrer. Jiggs dated Jerry, and the Angels did demo work for the three producers. Feldman, Goldstein and Gottehrer wrote "My Boyfriend's Back" for the Angels, who were still under contract to Caprice. But people from Mercury

Records heard the song and bought the master for their Smash subsidiary.

"My Boyfriend's Back" entered the Hot 100 on August 31, 1963 at number 75, and in four weeks it was number one. The Angels had only two follow-ups that made the chart, "I Adore Him" and "Wow! Wow! Wee! (He's the Boy for Me)."

The Angels carried on through the sixties, with a supper club routine choreographed by Donna McKechnie, who would go on to star in Broadway's *A Chorus Line*. In 1969, the group started appearing in oldies shows, and two years later Peggy did some work as lead vocalist for Dusk, a sister group to Tony Orlando and Dawn [see 287—"Knock Three Times"].

There came a time when Barbara was ready to call it quits, so Jiggs and Peggy carried on with a new member, Lana Shan, appearing at oldies shows around the country.

The Feldman-Goldstein-Gottehrer team turned recording artists in 1965 and had a hit single, "I Want Candy," as the Strangeloves. While on the road, they discovered the McCoys and produced a number one song for them [see 185—"Hang on Sloopy"]. Goldstein went on to produce War, and Gottehrer produced Blondie before Mike Chapman, as well as some albums by Robert Gordon.

### THE TOP FIVE
*Week of August 31, 1963*

1 **My Boyfriend's Back**
Angels

2 **Hello Mudduh, Hello Fadduh**
Allan Sherman

3 **Fingertips-Pt. 2**
Little Stevie Wonder

4 **Candy Girl**
Four Seasons

5 **Blowin' in the Wind**
Peter, Paul & Mary

*Writers: Bernie Wayne*
*Lee Morris*

*Producer: Bob Morgan*

*September 21, 1963*
*3 weeks*

**B**OBBY VINTON's "blue period" was 1963. In the spring he had a hit with "Blue on Blue," and four months later he had his second number one single with the standard, "Blue Velvet."

After his success with "Roses Are Red (My Love)" [see 113], Vinton found songwriters bringing their latest tunes to his office in New York. A writer by the name of Burt Bacharach had an appointment to see Bobby, but before he came in, an associate of Vinton's suggested Bobby secure publishing rights to any songs he recorded. Enter Burt.

"I heard 'Blue on Blue' and my legs started to shake," Bobby laughs. "I said to myself, this is a number one record. But I'm real cool and I said to Burt, 'It's kind of nice, but I'm not really that excited. Maybe I'll throw it into an album for you if I can own the publishing.' He said, 'Gee, I'd love to give you the publishing, but I signed it away this morning to Famous Music and I don't think I can get it back. If I had known you would have liked it, I would have never given it to them.' He's walking out the door, toward the elevator, and I went running after him and said, 'Burt, I was kidding, that's a great song, I can't play games with you.'"

Producer Bob Morgan agreed, and Bobby remembers Burt being in the studio during the recording to do the

## THE TOP FIVE
*Week of September 21, 1963*

1  **Blue Velvet**
   Bobby Vinton

2  **My Boyfriend's Back**
   Angels

3  **If I Had a Hammer**
   Trini Lopez

4  **Heat Wave**
   Martha & the Vandellas

5  **Sally, Go 'Round the Roses**
   Jaynetts

arrangement. The result was a smash that just missed going to number one—it peaked at three. But it was so successful that Bobby decided to do an album of all "blue" songs, and in a bold move for 1963, decided to record it in Nashville.

"I picked songs like 'Blue Moon' and 'Blue Hawaii' and everything that was blue in the title. Al Gallico, a well-known music publisher, said I ought to do 'Blue Velvet.' He gave his secretary a dollar to run down to the music store and buy the sheet music."

An hour later, Bobby recorded

"Blue Velvet" with all-star musicians like Floyd Cramer, Boots Randolph, Grady Martin and Charlie McCoy. The song was done in two takes, and Bobby considered it a throwaway. He thought the hit would be "Am I Blue."

Epic Records began to get calls about "Blue Velvet," and told Vinton they wanted to release it as a single. "I said, 'that's not going to make it, we did that in ten minutes and it's too sweet and pretty and today the kids want rock.' They said O.K. and they put it out anyway. I didn't mind being wrong."

**138** ## Sugar Shack Dot 16487
### JIMMY GILMER AND THE FIREBALLS

*Writers: Keith McCormick*
*Faye Voss*

*Producer: Norman Petty*

*October 12, 1963*
*5 weeks*

THE number one single of 1963 was recorded in the same studio where Buddy Knox and Buddy Holly had recorded their chart-topping songs in the 1950s—Norman Petty's famed Clovis, New Mexico studio. Petty managed solo singer Jimmy Gilmer as well as the instrumental group the Fireballs, and he suggested they combine forces.

Gilmer was born in Chicago, but grew up in Amarillo, Texas, where he studied music at the Musical Arts Conservatory. He led a rockabilly band, the Jimmy Gilmer Combo, that played at high school and college dances in a 100-mile radius of Amarillo. The Combo's drummer, Gary Swaffert, also played drums for the Norman Petty Trio and was responsible for introducing Gilmer to Petty.

Jimmy met a band from Raton, New Mexico at Petty's studios, although he didn't work with them. They were the Fireballs, and they had gotten together when they were seniors in high school. They had two instrumental hits on the Top Rank label in 1959-1960 ("Torquay" and "Bulldog"), and after a major tour,

their lead singer suddenly quit.

"He left them at an awkward time," says Gilmer. "They had a tour scheduled in about two months in the midwest, and they were in desperate need of somebody to front the band. Norman Petty...suggested they contact me."

Gilmer joined the Fireballs, a decision that disappointed his parents because it meant leaving junior college. Jimmy spent the next two-and-a-half years touring and recording. There were still solo releases by Gilmer as well as records by the Fireballs. One of the projects they worked on was supplying new instrumental backings for some incomplete vocals by the late Buddy Holly.

In 1962, Gilmer had come off of a tour and was looking for new material. One source was Keith McCormack, a singer/guitarist with another Norman Petty band, the String-a-Longs. They had a national hit with a Petty instrumental, "Wheels," in 1961, and McCormack played seven songs for Gilmer. He chose three he thought would be suitable for the Fireballs.

Jimmy worked out arrangements for the songs and added them to the group's repertoire on their next tour. Over the next six months, one song in particular got an incredible response from audiences—the reaction was so great, they played it twice each show. "Because of the response we were receiving, we

decided to record it at the next convenient time."

The song was "Sugar Shack," and it was released in May of 1963. For the next four months, it sold well in Dallas, Albuquerque, and Oklahoma City, but couldn't seem to break through on a national basis. Their label, Dot, wanted to go with a new single, but station CKLW on the Detroit/Canada border started playing "Sugar Shack" and it spread throughout North America, debuting on the Hot 100 on September 21 at number 65. The next week it moved to 19, then to four and on October 12 it went to number one, where it remained for five weeks.

The follow-up, "Daisy Petal Pickin'," went to number 15. By 1967, Gilmer was spending time in Greenwich Village clubs, where he met songwriter Tom Paxton. He liked Paxton's "Bottle of Wine" enough to record it, but Dot Records didn't want to release it. "We believed in it so much, we asked for our release," Gilmer recalls. Randy Wood, president of Dot, granted it and the group signed with Atco Records. Released under the name "the Fireballs" because groups were popular, "Bottle of Wine" made the top 10.

Gilmer left the Fireballs in 1969 with the intention of moving to Los Angeles and starting a new band. Instead, he was hired by United Artists Music in Nashville and became vice-president of CBS Songs' southern operations. "It's given me a chance to help young writers and artists not make the same mistakes I made," he laughs.

### THE TOP FIVE
*Week of October 12, 1963*

1 **Sugar Shack**
Jimmy Gilmer & the Fireballs

2 **Be My Baby**
Ronettes

3 **Blue Velvet**
Bobby Vinton

4 **Cry Baby**
Garnet Mimms & the Enchanters

5 **Sally Go 'Round the Roses**
Jaynetts

Writers: *Mitchell Parish*
*Peter de Rose*

Producer: *Ahmet Ertegun*

*November 16, 1963*
*1 week*

**O**FTEN mistaken for husband and wife, Nino Tempo and his sister April Stevens both had successful solo careers before they teamed up to record together. They credit their mother—a beauty contest winner whose strict father wouldn't allow her to pursue a professional life—with motivating them to pursue show business careers.

Nino was performing in recitals at age three, and when he was seven, his mother took him to a Benny Goodman concert in Buffalo, New York, 30 miles from their Niagara Falls home. "Peggy Lee had just done a number...and my mom said, 'go up there and tell Mr. Goodman your grandfather bet you five dollars if you were any good you'd sing with his band,'" Nino recalls. An enchanted Goodman put the boy on a chair so he could reach the microphone, and he brought the house down with "Rosetta." Goodman liked it so much, he had Nino come back the next six nights and pull the same stunt.

The family moved to California, and April was shopping in Wallichs' Music City in Hollywood when a man asked if she was a singer. She thought he was flirting, but he owned a small record company and was looking for a vocalist. April recorded "No No No Not That" for him, which was the start of her solo career. She had a top ten single in 1951, "I'm in Love Again," and a hit single in 1959 with "Teach Me Tiger," a song the astronauts on board the space shuttle Challenger requested for a wake up call on April 6, 1983.

Nino picked up the clarinet after meeting Goodman, then became a jazz saxophonist. He was playing on a Bobby Darin session when he met Ahmet Ertegun of Atlantic Records. Ertegun asked if Nino did more than play sax, and Nino said he was thinking of putting an act together with his sister. Ahmet was a fan of April's singing, and went to the Tempo home for a spaghetti dinner—with a contract for them to sign.

April came up with the idea to record "Deep Purple," and Nino did the arrangement. "Nino was supposed to sing the second chorus by himself," explains April. "He didn't know the words, so I started speaking them to him." A friend who heard the demo thought April's "narration" sounded great. "It took me two months to convince my brother...he said he didn't want anyone talking while he was singing!"

April and Nino went into the studio to record the standard, "Paradise," and with 14 minutes left of studio time, told Ahmet they wanted to try "Deep Purple." He said it was impossible to finish in the time remaining, but Nino had quick words with the session musicians (including guitarist Glen Campbell) and the female back-up singers. "There was no rehearsal," says Nino. "We just talked about it for 30 seconds and recorded it. In 14 minutes, we got two takes."

A secretary at the studio told Nino "Deep Purple" would be a smash. It had some wrong chords, yodeling and a harmonica he wanted to replace, but Nino called Ahmet in New York and said he was sending the master just the way it was and it would be a hit. Two weeks passed, and Ahmet didn't call back. Finally, Nino telephoned and asked what he thought. Ahmet said it was the most embarassing thing April and Nino had ever recorded. "Deep Purple" went on the shelf and "Paradise" was released. It didn't make the Hot 100.

"I called Ahmet and said please give us our contract back," Nino confesses. "He said, 'I'll release one more record, and if it flops, you've got your contract back.'" Nino wanted to sign with his friend Phil Spector, who also thought "Deep Purple" would be big.

Ahmet agreed to release "Deep Purple," although he thought the flip side, "I've Been Carrying a Torch for You So Long That I Burned a Great Big Hole in My Heart" was the hit. He was wrong. "Deep Purple" knocked "Sugar Shack" out of number one, and the "B" side that Ahmet favored had to settle for being the longest title of any number one flip side, a record it would hold for almost 21 years.

## THE TOP FIVE

*Week of November 16, 1963*

1 **Deep Purple**
Nino Tempo & April Stevens

2 **Sugar Shack**
Jimmy Gilmer & the Fireballs

3 **Washington Square**
Village Stompers

4 **I'm Leaving It Up to You**
Dale & Grace

5 **It's All Right**
Impressions

# I'm Leaving It Up to You
MONTEL-MICHELE 921
## DALE AND GRACE

Writers: *Don Harris*
*Dewey Terry, Jr.*

Producer: *Sam Montel*

*November 23, 1963*
*2 weeks*

DALE AND GRACE followed April and Nino into the number one position, the first time a male-female duet succeeded another male-female duet at the top of the chart. Dale Houston was introduced to Grace Broussard by record producer Sam Montel, who owned his own Montel label for national releases, as well as three smaller labels named after his daughters (Michele, Stephanie and Debbie) for regional releases.

"Dale was a country and western piano player-singer from up around Ferriday, Louisiana," Montel explains. "He was playing in a small honky-tonk where Jerry Lee Lewis got started several years earlier. I went up and introduced myself and told Dale I had this idea about doing an old tune originally recorded in 1956 by Don and Dewey."

Sam found 19-year-old Grace in her native Prairieville, Louisiana, in the heart of cajun country. She idolized her older brother, Van, who had his own cajun band. She was earning $15 a week singing with Van's group when Montel invited her to come to his Baton Rouge studio and meet Dale.

At first, Sam tried to record "I'm Leaving It Up to You" as a solo by

Dale, but it sounded flat. So he matched them up and they recorded it as a duet. The record was released just locally on the Michele label, and Sam sent promo copies to radio stations. He received a call from Paul Berlin, the top disc jockey at KNUZ in Houston, telling him the record was the pick of the station's seven DJs.

"I said, 'Wait a minute, Paul, I'm going to change the violins because they're recorded in B-natural and they're supposed to be B-flat. I made a mistake.' He said, 'If you tell me you're gonna change anything on this record after seven experts say this is gonna be a number one song, you are crazy—or using reverse psychology.' I took his advice and never changed it."

The record went to number one in Houston and Sam decided to release it on his national label, Montel. Because the record was already a local hit on Michele, the distributor pressed them on the Montel-Michele label.

"I'm Leaving It Up to You" went to number one on the Hot 100 the week beginning November 17, 1963. Dale and Grace were on tour with Dick Clark's Caravan of Stars at the time. On Friday of that week, they were in Dallas, Texas, for an evening performance.

"In the morning, myself and Dick Clark, along with Dale and Grace, Bobby Rydell, Jimmy Clanton and Brian Hyland stood on the steps of

our hotel, and as President Kennedy's motorcade turned onto Elm Street we applauded the President and his wife. Three blocks later, the tragedy happened. We went back to our rooms and didn't find out about it until three hours later," Sam recalls, sadly. For four days, there was no music in the land.

For their second single, Dale and Grace recorded "Stop and Think It Over," a song distinguished by its extraordinarily long pause after the word "stop." It reached number eight and was the duo's only other hit.

They continued to tour and were in Fargo, North Dakota, when Sam received a phone call from Bobby Vee [see 97—"Take Good Care of My Baby"]. "They were spending the weekend with Bobby," Sam says. "He said I'd better come up. Dale was sick, bleeding internally. He and Grace were arguing a lot, and Bobby said they weren't speaking to each other."

Sam caught the next plane to Fargo and found Dale seriously ill. Dale was hospitalized. Grace told Montel she missed her family, her dogs and her home on the bayou. "I had an agreement with Dale and Grace that at any time they wanted to shut it down, all they had to do was call me. They had my word," says Sam.

When Dale recuperated, Sam recorded some tracks with him back in Baton Rouge. Grace agreed to record some solo tracks and have them overdubbed, but the feeling of a duet was missing and the idea was abandoned. Both singers recorded some solo tracks for Montel, but without any national success.

## THE TOP FIVE
*Week of November 23, 1963*

1  **I'm Leaving It Up to You**
   Dale & Grace

2  **Washington Square**
   Village Stompers

3  **Deep Purple**
   Nino Tempo & April Stevens

4  **Sugar Shack**
   Jimmy Gilmer & the Fireballs

5  **It's All Right**
   Impressions

*Writer: Soeur Sourire*

*Producer: Not Known*

*December 7, 1963*
*4 weeks*

ONE day in 1961, a beat-up Citroen pulled up in front of the Brussels office of Philips Records. The passengers were two nuns, and the older one spoke to executives at the record company. She indicated that her younger companion composed songs which the sisters would sing in the evenings at their retreats at the Fichermont Monastery. The songs were so popular with the young girls studying at the convent, the two sisters wondered if they could pay Philips Records to press a couple hundred copies of the songs to be given away as gifts.

It was the Christmas rush season, and the Philips executives politely said no. Three months later, the sisters telephoned and asked if this would be a good time to press up those copies. Philips agreed to a brief, non-commercial recording session.

Sister Luc-Gabrielle was accompanied by a chorus of four nuns and a new guitar. She recorded more than a dozen songs. The light, simple, uplifting melodies so impressed the Philips executives that they manufactured thousands of albums by *"Soeur Sourire"* (Sister Smile) and released them commercially in Europe. Because of its success throughout the continent, Philips released the album in America under the title "The Singing Nun." It didn't get any reaction until publisher Paul Kapp decided to release one of the album's songs,

"Dominique," as a single.

The song, which eulogizes the founder of the Dominican order, was written by Sister Luc-Gabrielle for her Mother Superior's Saint's Day. The Mother Superior approvingly told *Newsweek* that the song treated St. Dominic "with familiarity and a touch of impertinence." It made The Singing Nun an overnight celebrity, and helped prevent "Louie Louie" by the Kingsmen from going to number one.

"Dominique" was so popular, that the single and album both moved into the number one position on *Billboard's* singles and albums charts simultaneously. It was the first time in history anyone had accomplished this.

Sister Luc-Gabrielle appeared on the January 5, 1964 Ed Sullivan show from the convent, but only after the Archdiocese convinced the Mother Superior of Sullivan's good intentions. Despite the national publicity, "Dominique" was the only hit The Singing Nun ever had.

In 1966, Debbie Reynolds starred in a movie about The Singing Nun's life. It was a critical failure (but it did mark the first time a number one artist starred in the life story of another number one artist) [See 24 — "Tammy"].

Soon after the film's release, Sister Luc-Gabrielle left the convent. Under her real name, Jeanine Deckers, she became a secular missionary. On March 29, 1985, she and her friend Annie Pescher were found dead in their home in Belgium. In a note, Deckers said she had "lost all courage in the face of a losing battle with tax people."

*Debbie Reynolds as "the Singing Nun"*

## THE TOP FIVE
*Week of December 7, 1963*

1 **Dominique**
  Singing Nun

2 **I'm Leaving It Up to You**
  Dale & Grace

3 **Everybody**
  Tommy Roe

4 **Louie Louie**
  Kingsmen

5 **She's a Fool**
  Lesley Gore

# There! I've Said It Again Epic 9638
## BOBBY VINTON

**142**

*Writers: Redd Evans
Dave Mann*

*Producer: Bob Morgan*

*January 4, 1964
4 weeks*

"THERE! I'VE SAID IT AGAIN" by Bobby Vinton is one of the most significant number one singles of the rock era. Not because of anything inherent in the song or the artist, but because it signified the end of an era. Following it would be a dividing line almost as thick and inpenetrable as Bill Haley's "(We're Gonna) Rock Around the Clock." Music would never be the same again.

The years 1960-1963 were innocent years. Rock and roll didn't seem as rebellious as it had when it first burst on the airwaves in 1955. Critics of this new music were less vocal—perhaps they weren't as threatened by

"The Loco-Motion" and "Sherry" as they had been by *The Blackboard Jungle* and Elvis shaking his pelvis on Ed Sullivan's TV show.

The early 60s marked the rise of the songwriter, with writers like Gerry Goffin, Carole King, Neil Sedaka, Howard Greenfield, Barry Mann and Cynthia Weil churning out the hits.

And American artists like Bobby Vinton dominated the charts. From "Rock Around the Clock" to "There! I've Said It Again," only five number one songs were by non-American artists. Within six months, that figure would double. Many artists whose careers seemed unshakable would stop having hits all at once. Number one artists like Connie Francis, Chubby Checker, Pat Boone and the Shirelles would never even place a single in the top 20 again. It wasn't that they were doing anything wrong—there was simply a shift in

the musical world, led by one group, that made us all look at rock and roll in a completely different light. The time of the self-contained musical unit was coming. The time of lyrics with social weight and significance was coming.

For the record, the number one single that helped mark this dividing point was the third number one for Bobby Vinton (an artist whose career, unlike many others, would not suffer during the next 12 months). Vinton was appearing low on the bill at a Cincinatti rock concert when he saw a long-haired, bearded DJ he found intimidating.

"He was smiling at me," Bobby recalls, "and he was screaming something as I was walking on to the stage. His face was red and he said, 'Come here!' I asked, 'What is it,' and he said, 'If you sing "There! I've Said It Again" you'll have a number one record.' That just shocked me—I mean why a DJ on stage before a concert, especially one looking like he looked, would even know a song like "There! I've Said It Again" or be concerned about me...it stayed with me for a week.

"I still remember that recording session. It was about ten after seven and I sang it one time, and it was a quarter after seven. The session was supposed to go to ten o'clock and I said, 'that's it. I could sing this all night, but it's not going to get any better. It's a hit just the way it is, goodnight everybody.'"

"There! I've Said It Again" was number one for four weeks. Then came the Beatles, and suddenly, everything changed.

## THE TOP FIVE
*Week of January 4, 1964*

1 **There! I've Said It Again**
Bobby Vinton

2 **Louie Louie**
Kingsmen

3 **Dominique**
Singing Nun

4 **Since I Fell For You**
Lenny Welch

5 **Forget Him**
Bobby Rydell

*Writers: John Lennon*
*Paul McCartney*

*Producer: George Martin*

*February 1, 1964*
*7 weeks*

It MUST HAVE seemed to manager Brian Epstein that the Beatles were never going to make it in America. For over a year, his charges had been a British phenomenon, selling millions of records on EMI's Parlophone label. But Brian just couldn't get EMI's American Company, Capitol Records, interested in the Beatles. Capitol declined to release the Beatles' first four British singles because, as a label executive informed Epstein, "we don't think the Beatles will do anything in this market."

"I Want to Hold Your Hand" was written by John Lennon and Paul McCartney in the basement of a house owned by the family of Jane Asher, Paul's actress girlfriend. The song was meant to have an American gospel sound, and it was the record Brian thought would finally break the Beatles in the United States. "I Want to Hold Your Hand" was recorded on October 19, 1963, along with the British flip side, "This Boy." It was scheduled for release in the United Kingdom on November 29.

Brian took a demo copy of the record with him when he flew to New York on November 5, just one day after the Beatles performed for the Queen Mother at the annual Royal Command Performance variety show.

One of Brian's appointments in Manhattan was with Brown Meggs, director of eastern operations for Capitol Records. Meggs heard something in this song that he felt had been missing in the songs that Capitol had declined to release: "Love Me Do" [see 148], "Please Please Me," "From Me to You" and "She Loves You" [see 144]. An American release date of January 13, 1964, was scheduled.

Before he left New York, Brian also went to the Delmonico Hotel, where he had an appointment with a man he had previously met in London. The gentleman had come to Britain to scout talent, and had experienced Beatlemania first hand, stuck in a crowd at Heathrow Airport while the Beatles were returning from a trip to Sweden. By the time Brian boarded the plane for the trip home to England, he had signed a deal with Ed Sullivan to feature the Beatles on two consecutive live telecasts, February 9 and 16.

"I Want to Hold Your Hand" had an advance order of 940,000 copies in Britain. It entered the chart on December 5 and went to number one the following week, where it remained for five weeks.

America was not going to wait until January 13 for Capitol to release the single. Carroll Baker, a disc jockey at radio station WWDC in Washington, D.C., obtained a British 45 from a BOAC airline stewardess and became the first American to broadcast "I Want to Hold Your Hand." The reaction was immediate and spread quickly to Chicago and then St. Louis, where other radio stations obtained copies of the song. Capitol advanced the release date to December 26, and increased the press run from 200,000 copies to one million.

Americans saw the Beatles for the first time eight days later when Jack Paar featured film clips of them on his weekly Friday night show. Suddenly, there was a media explosion. *Life, The New York Times*, CBS, the Associated Press and *The Washington Post* all assigned reporters to file stories on the Beatles.

Brian Epstein had arranged for the group to play the Olympia Theatre in Paris, to try and break them in France, the only European country that hadn't submitted to their charms. They were ensconced in their rooms at the George V hotel when Brian received the news: "I Want to Hold Your Hand" had gone to number one in America.

It remained on top of the Hot 100 for seven weeks, the first single to do so since "Tossin' and Turnin'" [see 94] by Bobby Lewis in 1961. With worldwide sales of 15 million, "I Want to Hold Your Hand" was the best-selling British single until Elton John's "Candle in the Wind 1997."

The importance of "I Want to Hold Your Hand" cannot be overestimated. Next to "(We're Gonna) Rock Around the Clock" [see 1], it is the most significant single of the rock era, permanently changing the course of music. The influence of the Beatles has been felt by every artist who has followed them, and it is not difficult to imagine that as the centuries pass, their songs will be the classical music of tomorrow.

## THE TOP FIVE
*Week of February 1, 1964*

1  **I Want to Hold Your Hand**
   Beatles

2  **You Don't Own Me**
   Lesley Gore

3  **Out of Limits**
   Marketts

4  **Surfin' Bird**
   Trashmen

5  **Hey Little Cobra**
   Rip Chords

## 144 She Loves You SWAN 4152
### THE BEATLES

*Writers: John Lennon*
*Paul McCartney*

*Producer: George Martin*

*March 21, 1964*
*2 weeks*

SHE LOVES YOU followed "I Want to Hold Your Hand" into the number one position, the first time an artist had two consecutive chart-toppers since Elvis Presley in 1956 [see 15— "Love Me Tender"]. America was in the throes of Beatlemania, a phenomenon that had manifested itself in Britain when "She Loves You" topped the chart there.

The screaming and rioting had begun on their third national tour of Britain, with American singer Roy Orbison [see 91—"Running Scared"]. But the full impact of the Beatles wasn't felt until they appeared on the popular television show "Sunday Night at the London Palladium" on October 13, 1963, two days after "She Loves You" was certified gold in the United Kingdom. The street outside the theater had been mobbed with fans all day, and when the Beatles left the theater with program host Bruce Forsyth, there were riots as the police tried to restrain the crowds. Newspaper photographers captured the mayhem on film and the next day, the press called it "Beatlemania."

America wasn't quite ready to succumb. You would have had to read all the way down page 32 of the September 21, 1963, issue of *Billboard* to notice the listing under Four-Star Singles ("awarded new singles with sufficient commercial potential in their respective categories to merit being stocked by dealers") for a new release by the Beatles called "She Loves You," issued on Swan Records with the catalogue number 4152. Murray the K played it on radio station WINS in New York, where it placed third in a field of five new singles on his weekly listeners' poll.

But 1963 was not to be the year of the Beatles in America. After EMI's American label, Capitol, turned down "Please Please Me," manager Brian Epstein licensed it to Vee Jay records of Chicago. Released on February 25, the record was such a high priority with the label that the artists' name was misspelled "The Beattles" on the label.

"From Me to You," released in May, fared little better. It received enough airplay on radio station KRLA to reach number 31 on the playlist, but nationally it merely bubbled under at number 116. After two failures in a row, Brian Epstein leased "She Loves You" to the Philadelphia-based Swan Records, but the label did no better than Vee Jay.

"She Loves You" was first heard by millions of Americans when Jack Paar screened film footage of the Beatles on his television program on January 3, 1964. The next day, people who didn't recall the name of the song or the group did remember the words, "yeah, yeah, yeah."

After Capitol Records broke the Beatles in America with "I Want to Hold Your Hand," Swan Records reactivated "She Loves You." The single entered the Hot 100 at number 69 on January 25, 1964, and succeeded "I Want to Hold Your Hand" at number one eight weeks later.

"She Loves You," featuring John Lennon and Paul McCartney singing lead, with George Harrison joining them on harmony, was recorded at Abbey Road studios on July 1, 1963. Paul and John had written the song in Yorkshire, England, while touring the country by bus.

John and Paul played the song for producer George Martin on their acoustic guitars. It was Martin who suggested they start with the chorus of "She loves you, yeah yeah, yeah . . ." instead of going right into the first verse. "The idea of having the sixth chord when it finishes was George Harrison's," Paul has said. "And George Martin said, 'That's funny, that's very old fashioned.' And we said, 'Yes, but it's nice, isn't it?' and he said, 'Yes, okay.' "

"She Loves You" charted again in June, 1964, when Swan Records released a German version of the song, *"Sie Liebt Dich,"* by the Beatles. It entered the Hot 100 at 97 and departed the following week.

### THE TOP FIVE
*Week of March 21, 1964*

1 **She Loves You**
Beatles

2 **I Want to Hold Your Hand**
Beatles

3 **Please Please Me**
Beatles

4 **Dawn (Go Away)**
Four Seasons

5 **Fun, Fun, Fun**
Beach Boys

*Writers: John Lennon
       Paul McCartney*

*Producer: George Martin*

*April 4, 1964
5 weeks*

"CAN'T BUY ME LOVE" established five remarkable chart records, four of which still stand today. The only one to fall is the biggest leap to number one. After 38 years, the 27-1 move of the Beatles' "Can't Buy Me Love" was surpassed by an incredible 52-1 jump [see 926—"A Moment Like This"].

Here's what the Beatles achieved:

**1.** *Greatest Monopoly of the Top Five.* With the sudden success of The Beatles on Capitol Records, their former labels realized what a goldmine they had in their catalogs. So many Beatles records were issued on so many labels, that on April 4, 1964, the Beatles held the top five positions on the Hot 100 (see box). No one had

ever done anything even close to this before, and it is doubtful the conditions will ever exist for anyone to do it again. The week before, the Beatles held the top four positions, and with the ascension of "Can't Buy Me Love" into the number one slot, they had a hammerlock on the top five.

**2.** *Greatest Monopoly of the Hot 100.* Before the Beatles, the highest number of concurrent singles by one artist on the chart was nine. This was accomplished on December 19, 1956, by Elvis Presley. That record stood for seven years. The Beatles surpassed Elvis' total on March 28, 1964, with 10 singles on the Hot 100. On April 4, two more Beatles' songs debuted, giving them a total of 12. And on April 11, with "Can't Buy Me Love" in its second week at number one, the Beatles occupied 14 positions on the chart. This record-breaking achievement was accomplished thanks to the following titles, which joined "Can't Buy Me Love" on the April 11 survey:

2. Twist and Shout
4. She Loves You
7. I Want to Hold Your Hand
9. Please Please Me
14. Do You Want to Know a Secret
38. I Saw Her Standing There
48. You Can't Do That
50. All My Loving
52. From Me to You
61. Thank You Girl
74. There's a Place
78. Roll Over Beethoven
81. Love Me Do

**3.** *Biggest Leap to Number One.* In the entire history of the Hot 100, only a few songs have managed to jump to the top of the chart from outside of the top 10. The first single to leap to number one from a position outside the top 20 was "Can't Buy Me Love," which debuted at number 27 and then pole vaulted to number one in its second chart week.

**4.** *Most Consecutive Number One Singles.* "Can't Buy Me Love" immediately succeeded "She Loves You," which directly followed "I Want to Hold Your Hand" at number one. This broke the record established by Elvis Presley when he had two consecutive number one singles in the second half of 1956 with "Don't Be Cruel / Hound Dog" and "Love Me Tender."

**5.** *Largest Advance Sale.* The conditions were exactly right for "Can't Buy Me Love" to rack up the greatest advance sales order of any single in history. It was the official Capitol Records follow-up to "I Want to Hold Your Hand," itself one of the most successful singles in the history of the charts. When released on March 16, 1964, "Can't Buy Me Love" was only available as a single and wouldn't be released on an album until the soundtrack of *A Hard Day's Night* was issued in July. So no one should have really been surprised when this single had an international advance order of 2,100,000 copies.

When people are asked what the greatest Beatles single of all time is, they usually mention "Hey Jude," "Let It Be," or "I Want To Hold Your Hand." They do not often think of "Can't Buy Me Love." And yet, for all the amazing records it established that have lasted for more than 30 years, perhaps "Can't Buy Me Love" should stand as one of the Beatles' very greatest achievements.

**THE TOP FIVE**
*Week of April 4, 1964*

1  **Can't Buy Me Love**
   Beatles

2  **Twist and Shout**
   Beatles

3  **She Loves You**
   Beatles

4  **I Want to Hold Your Hand**
   Beatles

5  **Please Please Me**
   Beatles

# 146 Hello, Dolly! Kapp 573
## LOUIS ARMSTRONG

*Writer: Jerry Herman*

*Producer: Mickey Kapp*

*May 9, 1964*
*1 week*

> *If it hadn't been for jazz, there wouldn't be no rock and roll.*
> LOUIS ARMSTRONG.

**I**F you were asked to select the artist most unlikely to usher the Beatles out of the number one position after they had three consecutive records that held the top spot for a combined 14 weeks, you might name a 63-year-old jazz trumpeteer from New Orleans who hadn't had a top 10 single in eight years. You might, but you'd be wrong.

Incredibly, Louis "Satchmo" Armstrong, one of the greats of the jazz world, whose music was as much a part of the twenties and thirties as the post-Beatles sixties, is the artist who brought a temporary halt to the Beatles' monopoly of the top of the charts. In doing so, he became the oldest artist (at age 63) to have a number one song.

The song was "Hello, Dolly!" written by Jerry Herman for Carol Channing's second act entrance in the Broadway musical of the same name. It is one of only two songs from a Broadway show to become number one in the rock era [see 253—"Aquarius/Let the Sunshine In"].

The musical opened on Broadway on January 16, 1964. Armstrong wasn't even aware of the show when he recorded the song, brought to him by someone at Herman's publishing company. It was just another track on an album of show tunes. Armstrong's biggest chart hit before "Hello, Dolly!" was a version of Berthold Brecht and Kurt Weill's "Mack the Knife" from the stage musical *A Threepenny Opera*. It was released in 1956, three years before Bobby Darin covered it [see 59], and it made the top 20.

But "Hello, Dolly!" was easily the best-selling record of his career, and it popularized not only Armstrong but the Broadway show. Five years later, Armstrong was deservedly cast in the motion picture of *Hello, Dolly!* in which he sang his hit tune to the film's leading lady, Barbra Streisand.

Armstrong was born on the 4th of July in 1900 in New Orleans to Willie and Mary Ann Armstrong. On New Year's Eve of 1913, Louis celebrated by firing his daddy's .38, a shot Louis believed was responsible for starting his career. He was arrested and sent to the Waif's Home for Boys, where music teacher Peter Davis took an interest in him. He made Louis the official school bugler and taught him to play the cornet.

It was in this school that Louis earned his lifelong nickname. The other kids called him "satchel-mouth" because of his big mouth, and the name was later contracted to "Satchmo."

When he left the school in 1917, Louis studied with Joe Oliver, a famous black trumpeteer. When "King" Oliver left Kid Ory's Band two years later, he had Louis replace him. Armstrong and Oliver were reunited in 1922 in Chicago, and four years later Armstrong was a headline attraction. It was in 1929 that Armstrong went to New York and played in "Connie's Hot Chocolates," where he introduced Fats Waller's "Ain't Misbehavin'."

Louis toured Europe in the 1930s, and his fame spread. In the late 30s, he started to appear in films, including *Pennies from Heaven, Cabin in the Sky* and, in 1956, *High Society* with Bing Crosby, Frank Sinatra and Grace Kelly.

Armstrong's recording career began in 1923, when he made his first disc as part of King Oliver's Jazz Creole Band. His first chart record was "That Lucky Old Sun" in October, 1949, which means it took 14 years and seven months from his first chart entry until he reached number one.

Louis Armstrong died on July 6, 1971, two days after his 71st birthday. In 1976, a statue of the jazz great was unveiled at Louis Armstrong Park in his hometown of New Orleans.

## THE TOP FIVE
*Week of May 9, 1964*

1  **Hello, Dolly!**
   Louis Armstrong

2  **Do You Want to Know a Secret**
   Beatles

3  **My Guy**
   Mary Wells

4  **Bits and Pieces**
   Dave Clark Five

5  **Can't Buy Me Love**
   Beatles

*Writer: William 'Smokey' Robinson*

*Producer: William 'Smokey' Robinson*

*May 16, 1964*
*2 weeks*

**M**ARY WELLS established a number of firsts for Motown. She was the first artist to record on the Motown label, the first to have William "Smokey" Robinson of the Miracles [see 285—"The Tears of a Clown"] for a writer/producer, the first to have a top 10 song on Motown ("The One Who Really Loves You") and the very first to give the label a number one song ("My Guy"). She was also the first major artist to leave the company, a bittersweet end to her Motown career.

Mary Esther Wells was born on May 13, 1943, in Detroit, Michigan, the youngest of three children. She started singing in church when she was three years old and excelled in the choir at Jefferson Junior High. At Northwestern High School, she became the choir's featured vocalist. She also sang with neighborhood doo-wop groups and idolized Jackie Wilson. She started writing songs, and came up with one she wanted Wilson to record.

She was just 17 years old when she asked a friend of a friend, Motown chief engineer Robert Bateman, to introduce her to Wilson's producer, Berry Gordy, Jr. She had no intention of becoming an artist herself, but she couldn't read or play music, so she sang her song for Gordy. He loved it, but said she

should record it herself, and signed her to a contract on the spot. Mary was thrilled to be signed to Tamla, the record company that was so hot with the Miracles and the Marvelettes. But Gordy told her he was starting a new label called Motown. Mary concealed her disappointment at being signed to an unknown label.

A few days later she was in the studio recording "Bye Bye Baby." Berry made her do 22 takes and by the final take her voice was hoarse, giving it a bluesy, gospel feeling. The record reached 45 on the Hot 100.

Mary's songwriting career came to a swift end. Gordy teamed her up with Smokey Robinson, who wrote and produced three top 10 hits in 1962—"The One Who Really Loves You," "You Beat Me to the Punch" and "Two Lovers." The next few singles did not do as well, and in late 1963 Mary became one of the first Motown artists to benefit from the writing and production of Brian Holland, Lamont Dozier and Eddie Holland. She recorded their "You Lost the Sweetest Boy," with the Supremes and Temptations singing backing vocals. It peaked at 22, and the Robinson-penned flip, "What's Easy for Two Is So Hard for One," was close behind at number 29.

Then came the song that would become Mary Wells' trademark for life. It was an instant classic, and hearing it for the first time, it was easy to predict that it would go to number one. The song, written and produced by Smokey, was "My Guy."

It managed to go to the top in the middle of the Beatles' chart sweep,

and it stayed there for two weeks until the Beatles pushed it out. The year was 1964 and Mary Wells, at the peak of her career, turned 21. It was time to renegotiate her contract with Motown.

Mary was now married to a Motown employee, Herman Griffin. He advised her to accept a large advance from 20th Century Fox Records rather than re-sign for a lower royalty payment with Gordy's company. Mary became the first major artist to exit Motown, a move that would not become more common until the mid-70s.

She had only minor success with 20th Century Fox, and over the next few years recorded for a number of labels, including Atco, Jubilee, Reprise and Epic. But "My Guy" was her last single to crack the Top 30.

Motown released a duet album with Marvin Gaye while "My Guy" was climbing up the charts, but there was never an official follow-up. A few years later, Motown released an album called "Vintage Stock" with some of the prospective follow-ups, including "When I'm Gone," which was recorded by Brenda Holloway after Mary left the company.

Mary later married Cecil Womack, (the brother of Bobby Womack), and together they collaborated on some of Mary's post-Motown work. They divorced in 1977. In the early1980s, Mary had discussions with Motown about returning, but ultimately no deal was concluded.

Diagnosed with throat cancer in August, 1990, Wells passed away on July 26, 1992, at the age of 49. A public memorial was held on July 30.

## THE TOP FIVE
*Week of May 16, 1964*

1 **My Guy**
  Mary Wells

2 **Hello, Dolly!**
  Louis Armstrong

3 **Love Me Do**
  Beatles

4 **Bits and Pieces**
  Dave Clark Five

5 **Do You Want to Know a Secret**
  Beatles

## 148 Love Me Do TOLLIE 9008
### THE BEATLES

*Writers: John Lennon*
*Paul McCartney*

*Producer: George Martin*

*May 30, 1964*
*1 week*

THE CORRECT ANSWER to the question, "Did Ringo Starr play drums on the single version of 'Love Me Do'?" depends on where you live. If you are a resident of Britain, the answer is yes. If you live in America, the answer is no.

"Love Me Do" was first recorded at Abbey Road studios on September 4, 1962. It was the second time the Beatles had recorded at Abbey Road. Their first visit to the studio was on June 6 of that year, a day studio manager Ken Townsend remembers vividly.

Townsend was involved in technical operations at the time. "I'd been working with George Martin in Cambridge when he mentioned the following week he had a group coming in called the Beatles. The session was booked from six til eight in the evening, and they were short of staff that night and asked me if I'd work on it."

Townsend and engineer Norman 'Hurricane' Smith (who would later record "Oh, Babe, What Would You Say?") were standing in the control room overlooking the studio when the four young men with long hair first walked in. "I remember Norman turned round to me and said, 'Good God, Ken, what the hell we got here?' I didn't realize that coming in there was the group that would be known around the world forever.

"We recorded several songs that evening. They weren't very brilliant, quite honestly, and the drummer was Pete Best. He was replaced the next time they came in, on the fourth of September, when Ringo Starr played the drums. They recorded 'Love Me Do,' and came back a week later on the 11th of September to record it again, when Ringo played the tambourine and a session drummer called Andy White was on drums."

On the first session, it took 17 takes to record "Love Me Do." Martin was unsure about Ringo's talent as a drummer. "I didn't rate Ringo very highly," Martin is quoted in Hunter Davies' biography *The Beat-*

les. "He couldn't do a roll—and still can't—though he's improved a lot since. Andy was the kind of drummer I needed. Ringo was only used to ballrooms. It was obviously best to use someone with experience."

Ringo didn't play drums on "P.S. I Love You" either. He was handed a pair of maracas while White handled the drumming. "I thought that's the end," Ringo said in Davies' biography, "they're doing a Pete Best on me . . . I was shattered."

When "Love Me Do" was released in Britain on October 5, Ringo felt a lot better—it was the take recorded September 4, featuring his drumming. The Andy White version was included on the *Please Please Me* album and was also used for the American single. The track featuring Ringo on drums wasn't released in America until it was included on the *Rarities* album in 1980.

The drums weren't the only instrument that figured prominently on the recording of "Love Me Do." John played harmonica on the song, inspired specifically by the work of Delbert McClinton on a number one single by Bruce Channel [see 105— "Hey! Baby"]. When Channel toured England in 1962, the Beatles were a support act on the bill. John told McClinton how much he liked his harmonica playing on the song, and asked him to show him how to play the intro.

"Love Me Do," written by John and Paul when they used to skip classes at Quarry Bank High School to work on their songs, became the first Beatles single to enter the British chart on October 11, 1962. Beatles' manager Brian Epstein purchased 10,000 copies to help it move up the survey. The record inched up the top 40, holding at number 27 until December, when it finally managed to peak at number 17.

Martin wanted the group to record Mitch Murray's "How Do You Do It" as a second single, but the Beatles insisted their own "Please Please Me" should be the follow-up. Although he recorded the Beatles singing "How Do You Do It," Martin finally agreed to release "Please Please Me." It went to number two. Martin produced Gerry and the Pacemakers singing "How Do You Do It" instead, and their version went to number one on April 11.

The song that knocked "How Do You Do It" off the top of the chart was the Beatles' first British number one single. It was their third release, "From Me to You," which entered the British chart on April 18, 1963. It moved into the number one position on May 2 and stayed for seven weeks.

In America, "Love Me Do," backed with "P.S. I Love You," first entered *Billboard's* Hot 100 at number 81 on April 11, 1964. It originally charted as an import, on the Capitol of Canada label. By May 9, *Billboard* listed the label as Tollie, a subsidiary of Vee Jay, the company that had released "Please Please Me" and "From Me to You" in America during the summer of 1963.

## THE TOP FIVE
*Week of May 30, 1964*

1 **Love Me Do**
Beatles

2 **Chapel of Love**
Dixie Cups

3 **My Guy**
Mary Wells

4 **Love Me With All Your Heart**
Ray Charles Singers

5 **Hello, Dolly!**
Louis Armstrong

*Writers: Jeff Barry
Ellie Greenwich
Phil Spector*

*Producers: Jerry Leiber
Mike Stoller
Jeff Barry
Ellie Greenwich*

*June 6, 1964
3 weeks*

In the first six months of 1964, only one American group had a number one single: the Dixie Cups, three female singers from New Orleans who were the first act to release a record on Jerry Leiber and Mike Stoller's new Red Bird label.

Although it only existed for two years, Red Bird is a much-collected, much-admired label for its extremely high ratio of hits and its talent roster. Aside from the Dixie Cups, it included the Shangri-Las [see 160 — "Leader of the Pack"], the Jelly Beans and (on the Blue Cat subsidiary) the Ad-Libs and Evie Sands. It was a haven for the girl group sound.

Leiber and Stoller started their first label, Spark Records, in 1952. It lasted three years and provided them with regional hits at best, but never a national chart record. With their final release, "Smokey Joe's Cafe" by the Robins, they realized they wanted to create records, not sell them, so they signed a production deal with Atlantic Records.

After achieving success with Elvis Presley [see 14—"Don't Be Cruel" / "Hound Dog"], the Coasters and Ben E. King, Leiber and Stoller again decided to start their own label in 1963. They formed Tiger Records, but had no success and considered folding the company. Instead, they brought in experienced label owner George Goldner as a partner, and from material already recorded, he selected the Dixie Cups' "Chapel of Love" as the first release for the new Red Bird label.

The Dixie Cups had been brought to Leiber and Stoller by Joe Jones, a New Orleans singer ("You Talk Too Much") who became their manager after seeing them perform at a talent show. Barbara Ann Hawkins, her sister Rosa Lee Hawkins and Joan Marie Johnson were going to be called Little Miss and the Muffets until a last-minute name change to the Dixie Cups. Leiber and Stoller put them under the guidance of the husband-and-wife writing team of Jeff Barry and Ellie Greenwich.

Ellie met Jeff at a Thanksgiving dinner at her aunt's house. Her aunt, through marriage, was Jeff's cousin, and he was at the dinner with his first wife. After that marriage was annulled, Jeff and Ellie started dating and writing songs together. They were married on October 28, 1962, and had an extremely successful year in 1963, writing with Phil Spector for the Ronettes and the Crystals, and recording themselves as the Raindrops.

One of the songs they had written for the Ronettes was "Chapel of Love," the final track on the "Presenting the Ronettes" album. Over Phil's objections, they cut it with the Dixie Cups. Leiber and Stoller were listed as producers, although their role may be better defined as "executive producers" while Jeff and Ellie did the main production work and Joe Jones did the arrangements.

Despite being the only American group to overcome the British monopoly and top the charts in the first half of 1964, the Dixie Cups did not have staying power. Their next single, "People Say," peaked at 12, followed by two-mid charters, "You Should Have Seen the Way He Looked at Me" and "Little Bell." "Iko Iko," a traditional New Orleans song recorded spontaneously with soda bottles and a box, reached number 20. When Red Bird folded its wings in 1966, the Dixie Cups signed with ABC Records, but never had another chart entry.

## THE TOP FIVE
*Week of June 6, 1964*

1  **Chapel of Love**
   Dixie Cups

2  **Love Me Do**
   Beatles

3  **My Guy**
   Mary Wells

4  **Love Me With All Your Heart**
   Ray Charles Singers

5  **Hello, Dolly!**
   Louis Armstrong

## 150

# A World Without Love  Capitol 5175
## PETER AND GORDON

*Writers: John Lennon*
*Paul McCartney*

*Producer: Norman Newell*

*June 27, 1964*
*1 week*

**P**ETER ASHER (born June 22, 1944 in London) and Gordon Waller (born June 4, 1945 in Braemaer, Scotland) met while attending the Westminster Boys School in London. They both played guitar and sang, and while their musical tastes were different— Peter preferred jazz and folk music and Gordon liked Elvis Presley and Buddy Holly—they found common ground in their appreciation of the Everly Brothers.

Calling themselves Gordon and Peter, they started playing at school parties, moved on to extracurricular engagements and eventually started appearing in local clubs.

One night at the Pickwick Club in London, they were asked by EMI recording manager Norman Newell to come in for an audition—and two weeks later they were signed to EMI.

Now they needed songs to record, so Peter turned to a friend who was dating his sister, Jane. The friend was Paul McCartney, who had already played a song for Peter that the Beatles didn't think was right for them. Paul had also offered it to Billy J. Kramer, but he decided not to record it. Peter said the song needed a bridge, but Paul never wrote one until the time came for the first EMI recording session. That song, "A World Without Love," was chosen to

be the first Peter and Gordon single. It is the first Lennon-McCartney song not recorded by The Beatles to go to number one.

The follow-up, "Nobody I Know," was also a Lennon-McCartney composition. In 1966 Peter and Gordon recorded McCartney's "Woman," written under the pseudonym "Bernard Webb" as an experiment to see if it would sell without the Lennon-McCartney name on it. The song became a hit before the media revealed McCartney's involvement.

Peter and Gordon's two other biggest hits were "Lady Godiva," a novelty song that Peter is not fond of, and "I Go to Pieces," written by Del Shannon [see 88—"Runaway"]. "We were on tour with The Searchers and Del Shannon in Australia," Peter recalls, "and Del was playing the song to The Searchers who he thought should do it and we overheard it. They decided not to do it, and we suggested that we should."

The duo broke up in 1967, mostly due to separate ambitions. Gordon wanted to record a solo album and Peter had more interest in producing other artists, starting with Paul

Jones after he departed Manfred Mann. That project was not successful, but it led McCartney to ask Peter (in 1968) to produce some acts for a new label the Beatles were starting. By the time the label— Apple Records—was organized, Peter was head of A&R. The first person he signed to Apple was James Taylor.

Peter left when Allen Klein came in to run the label and is best known today for his excellent production work with Taylor and with the person Peter describes as "the best girl singer in the world," Linda Ronstadt.

In the 70s, Gordon starred in a production of Tim Rice and Andrew Lloyd Webber's rock musical, *Joseph and the Amazing Technicolor Dreamcoat.* He is now married to an Australian woman he met while touring down under in the Peter and Gordon days. He hadn't seen her for 10 years after that initial meeting. They have two children and live in England. Peter lives in Los Angeles, but spends at least one month a year in London to visit his family. Peter says he still sees Gordon from time to time.

---

### THE TOP FIVE
*Week of June 27, 1964*

1  **A World Without Love**
   Peter & Gordon

2  **I Get Around**
   Beach Boys

3  **Chapel of Love**
   Dixie Cups

4  **My Boy Lollipop**
   Millie Small

5  **People**
   Barbra Streisand

CAPITOL 5174 **I Get Around**
BEACH BOYS

*Writer: Brian Wilson*

*Producer: Brian Wilson*

*July 4, 1964*
*2 weeks*

On the Fourth of July, 1964, the Beach Boys topped the Hot 100 with "I Get Around," the first number one single by an American male singing group in eight months. The timing was appropriate, for the Beach Boys were the embodiment of the all-American singing group, promoting little deuce coupes, surfin' U.S.A. and California girls. It was also prophetic timing—the Beach Boys often performed concerts on the Fourth of July.

Murry Wilson and Audree Neva Karthof were married in Los Angeles. Their first son, Brian Douglas Wilson, was born June 20, 1942. Murry was a songwriter, and before Brian was a year old he could hum along while his dad sang. At three, Brian could sing on key. By the time he was five, Brian had two younger brothers, Dennis (born December 4, 1944) and Carl (born December 21, 1946).

The family lived in Hawthorne, California, and Murry's sister, Emily Love, lived about 20 minutes away in Baldwin Hills. Her son, Mike, was just six months older than Brian and was close to all the Wilson brothers.

Brian was a senior in high school when he became friends with football teammate Al Jardine (born September 3, 1942, in Lima, Ohio). Jardine loved music too, especially the Kingston Trio. Brian invited him over to the house to sing with his brothers.

In the fall of 1961, Murry and Audree took off for a vacation in Mexico City, leaving the refrigerator well-stocked and money to buy more food when it became empty. The food money was spent on the rental of a standup bass, drums and a microphone. While their parents were away, the Wilson brothers, along with Mike and Al, went to see Hite and Doreen Morgan, Murry's music publishers, about recording a song. The Morgans were only interested in original material, and the group didn't have any. Dennis, the only one of the five who surfed, suggested

they write a song about surfing. They started to write a song right then and there in the Morgans' office, and took it home to polish it. Two days later, they were ready to record "Surfin'."

The Morgans took the boys to Keen Recording Studios, where they cut "Surfin'" and a second song written by Brian and Mike, "Surfin' Safari." Then the Morgans took the tapes to Herb Newman [see 11—"The Wayward Wind"], who owned the Candix label. He agreed to release "Surfin'" immediately.

The group needed a name. They had called themselves Carl and the Passions at a Hawthorne High School assembly, but now they were using the Pendletones, after a southern California status symbol, Pendleton shirts. Although many people are given credit, the Beach Boys have said that Candix promotion man Russ Regan was the one who suggested they call themselves the Beach Boys.

"Surfin'" was a local smash. Nationally, it peaked at 75. Newman didn't care for any of the other songs

the Beach Boys recorded, including "Surfer Girl," and declined to release a follow-up. In the spring of 1962, Murry brought a new tape of the Beach Boys to Nick Venet at Capitol Records. Venet played it for his boss, Voyle Gilmore, and an hour later Capitol agreed to sign the group.

"I Get Around" was their seventh Capitol single, following top ten hits like "Surfin' U.S.A." (a rewrite of Chuck Berry's "Sweet Little Sixteen"), "Be True to Your School" and "Fun, Fun, Fun." Brian had already written a number one single for his friends Jan and Dean [see 133—"Surf City"], but until "I Get Around," the Beach Boys had been shut out of the number one position every time.

During the recording of "I Get Around," Brian argued with his father in the studio about the production. The conflict ended with Brian shoving Murry, who never returned to the studio. Later, a tearful Brian would apologize and explain that he only wanted "I Get Around" to sound perfect.

"I Get Around" was the Beach Boys' first top ten hit in Britain. The group credits Mick Jagger for their initial success—after hearing them on a visit to the States, he went home and praised the band on British television.

### THE TOP FIVE
*Week of July 4, 1964*

1 **I Get Around**
Beach Boys

2 **My Boy Lollipop**
Millie Small

3 **Memphis**
Johnny Rivers

4 **Don't Let the Sun Catch You Crying**
Gerry & the Pacemakers

5 **People**
Barbra Streisand

## 152 **Rag Doll** PHILIPS 40211
### THE FOUR SEASONS

*Writers: Bob Crewe*
*Bob Gaudio*

*Producer: Bob Crewe*

*July 18, 1964*
*2 weeks*

**T**HE FOUR SEASONS scored their fourth number one single in the summer of 1964 with their first hit ballad, "Rag Doll." Writer Bob Gaudio remembers his inspiration for the song:

"I was coming down the Westside Highway, near 10th Avenue, where there is the longest traffic light of all time. When you stop for the light, a bunch of kids run out and clean your windows and get a couple of cents. I had come in one day going to a session and stopped at the light, and this little girl—I didn't realize it was a little girl right away—came over and was cleaning my windows.

"I saw her face—just the picture of her face and the clothes, tattered...with holes in her stockings and a little cap on her head. She finished cleaning and was standing by the window and I started searching my pockets. I didn't have any change at all. I thought, 'this is terrible, what am I going to do?' I found my money, and the smallest thing I had was a five dollar bill.

"There was a split second where I said, 'I can't give her a five dollar bill,' but I couldn't give her nothing. So I gave her the five dollar bill. The look on her face when I was pulling away—she didn't say 'thank you,' she just stood there with the bill in her hand and I could see her in the rear-

view mirror, just standing in disbelief in the middle of the street with the five dollars. And that whole image stayed with me, a rag doll was what she looked like.

"I spent a long time with that song. I did a good portion of it, music and lyrics, and could not finish it. I couldn't wind the story up. I called Bob Crewe. He and I spent about two weeks just coming up with a finish. We ran into a wall. I didn't think I'd get it at one point. We contemplated dumping it and saying it won't finish itself, let's put it away."

When they finally did finish it, Crewe and Gaudio wanted to release it as their next single instead of an album track that had been scheduled. It was Sunday and the group was leaving town on a tour the next day, so the song had to be recorded immediately. But they couldn't get into their normal studio and had to record in the basement of a demo studio on Broadway in Manhattan.

"We couldn't get our studio or our engineer, and were working with people we had never worked with before," says Gaudio. "We almost didn't get through with it."

For the next four years, the group consistently hit the top 20, with songs like "Save it for Me," "Big Man in Town," "Bye, Bye, Baby (Baby Goodbye)," "Let's Hang On," "Working My Way Back to You," "Opus 17 (Don't You Worry 'Bout Me)," "I've Got You Under My Skin" and "C'mon Marianne." The group left Philips Records briefly in 1969 to record one single for Crewe's own label, then returned to Philips for a final single.

There were also personnel changes. In 1965, Nick Massi departed and was replaced temporarily by arranger Charles Callelo and then by Joe Long. In 1971, Tom DeVito retired and the following year, Gaudio left the group: "I just woke up one morning and realized I'm not really a performer, I'm a writer. I never really considered myself a performer, I never felt good about it, I never felt I had anything to offer in that vein."

But he had offered the Four Seasons a quartet of number one singles, and he would continue to write and produce for them until they were back on top of the chart again.

### THE TOP FIVE
*Week of July 18, 1964*

1  **Rag Doll**
   Four Seasons

2  **Memphis**
   Johnny Rivers

3  **I Get Around**
   Beach Boys

4  **Can't You See**
   **That She's Mine**
   Dave Clark Five

5  **The Girl from Ipanema**
   Getz/Gilberto

CAPITOL 5222 **A Hard Day's Night**
THE BEATLES

Writers: John Lennon
        Paul McCartney

Producer: George Martin

August 1, 1964
2 weeks

"IT's such a period piece now," Paul McCartney responded when asked to comment on the motion picture *A Hard Day's Night* in a 1984 interview with Jan Etherington of Britain's *TV Times*. "I hate to say it but when you see the girls in their mini-skirts and white floppy hats it does look dated. I think the general opinion is that it was funny and entertaining, and I'm still proud of it."

The critics found it more than funny and entertaining. Andrew Sarris, the *Village Voice* film critic called the film "the Citizen Kane of juke box musicals."

The film's first working title was *Beatlemania*, rejected immediately by the Beatles. Paul suggested *What Little Old Man?*, but the producers wanted something more distinctive. Finally, the title was inspired by Ringo Starr. At the end of a strenuous day of filming, he leaned on the arm of a canvas director's chair and exclaimed, "It's been a hard day's night, that was!"

*A Hard Day's Night.* written by Liverpudlian Alun Owen, was meant to be a fictional account of two days in the Beatles' lives, beginning with a train departure from Liverpool and ending with a concert the following night. Director Richard Lester commented in Ray Coleman's *Lennon* biography, "The film was based on their lives living in small boxes, as prisoners of their own success. The concept came from John's reply to a question I asked him about a trip they'd made to Sweden. 'How did you like it,' I said. John said: 'Oh, it was a room and a car and a car and a room and a room and a car.' That became our signal of how to do *A Hard Day's Night*."

Production began March 2, 1964, on the platform of Paddington Station in London. On the first day of filming, George Harrison met model Patti Boyd, who had a small role as a schoolgirl on the train. It wasn't until the third day that Patti agreed to have dinner with George and romance blossomed quickly. They were married in January, 1966.

Lennon and McCartney began to write the songs for the film score while they were in Paris [see 143—"I Want to Hold Your Hand"]. They had a grand piano brought to their suite at the George V hotel. The film's title song, featuring double-tracked vocals by Lennon, and lead and harmony vocals by McCartney, was recorded on April 16. Nine days later, production wrapped on *A Hard Day's Night* and the Beatles moved on to other projects—topping the bill at the New *Musical Express* Pollwinners' Concert at Wembley, and filming a British television special, "Around the Beatles."

On Monday, July 6, more than 12,000 people were jammed into Piccadilly Circus in hopes of catching a glimpse of the Beatles as they attended the Royal World Premiere of *A Hard Day's Night* at the London Pavilion. Princess Margaret and the Earl of Snowdon attended the screening and the party afterwards at the Dorchester Hotel on Park Lane. The celebration stretched far enough into the night for Ringo to celebrate his 24th birthday on July 7. By the time the party ended, the morning newspapers containing the first reviews were on the streets. The *Daily Mail* said the Beatles were "as funny as the Marx Brothers," and the *Daily Mirror* critic, not a Beatles fan, admitted they were "cheeky, irreverent, funny, irresistable."

On the morning of July 10, the Beatles departed London by airplane to return home to Liverpool. The ten-mile route from the airport to the city center was lined with almost 200,000 cheering fans. After a reception at 7 p.m. that night in the Liverpool Town Hall, the official Northern Premiere took place at the Liverpool Odeon.

Two days later, the single of "A Hard Day's Night" entered the American Hot 100 at number 21. In just two short weeks, the single was sitting on top of the chart.

### THE TOP FIVE
*Week of August 1, 1964*

1 **A Hard Day's Night**
Beatles

2 **Rag Doll**
Four Seasons

3 **The Little Old Lady
(From Pasadena)**
Jan & Dean

4 **Everybody Loves Somebody**
Dean Martin

5 **Where Did Our Love Go**
Supremes

# 154 Everybody Loves Somebody REPRISE 0281
## DEAN MARTIN

*Writers: Irving Taylor*
*Ken Lane*

*Producer: Jimmy Bowen*

*August 15, 1964*
*1 week*

DEAN MARTIN's recording career had been cold for six years when, through a series of unusual circumstances, he recorded a radically new arrangement of "Everybody Loves Somebody," a song written in 1949 and recorded by several well-known artists without success.

In 1962, Dean signed with a brand new label, Reprise. The owner of the company was a good friend—Frank Sinatra. By the time Warner Brothers bought the label in 1963, the artist roster also included Sammy Davis, Jr., Trini Lopez, Nancy Sinatra [see 194—"These Boots Are Made for Walkin'"] and Rosemary Clooney.

Signed to the A&R department was Jimmy Bowen [see 19—"Party Doll"], who decided he wanted to pro-

duce Martin himself. He intended to record an album of contemporary material, but first Dean wanted to cut an album called *Dream With Me*, featuring the low-key, moody songs he performed in the lounge of Las Vegas' Sands Hotel during the late hours, after headlining the main room.

Bowen put together a small band of musicians and set up mood lighting in the studio to create the proper atmosphere. After recording 11 songs for the album, Dean balked at the twelfth selection. One more tune was needed to complete the LP, and Ken Lane, Dean's conductor and piano player, suggested "Everybody Loves Somebody," a song he had written with Irving Taylor.

Lane was living in a southern California guest house then, and after kicking around ideas with Taylor, wrote the song in 20 minutes. "I was working with Frank Sinatra in those years, and he recorded it around 1950," Lane explains. "Dinah Washington recorded it, Peggy Lee did it and so did three or four other people. It was picked as a big song, but it

didn't make it until Dean recorded it."

After he found out the song was 15 years old, Bowen found some of the older versions, including Dinah Washington's recording. With arranger Ernie Freeman, he worked out the contemporary sound he wanted and a few days later, Dean recorded "Everybody Loves Somebody" a second time.

At first, it looked like Bowen's effort was for naught. There was no action on the record and Reprise was ready to stop promoting it. Before they could take such a drastic action, radio stations in New Orleans and Worcester, Massachussetts, started playing the record. It spread to other stations around the country, and entered the Hot 100 on June 27, 1964, at number 72. Seven weeks later, Dean Martin displaced the Beatles from the top of the chart.

A series of hit singles in the same style followed, including "The Door Is Still Open," "Send Me the Pillow You Dream On" and "I Will." Lane credits the success of "Everybody Loves Somebody" with inspiring NBC to give Dean a weekly television series.

With "Everybody Loves Somebody" as its theme song, "The Dean Martin Show" debuted on Thursday, September 16, 1965, at 10 p.m., and ran for nine seasons. Ken Lane was the only supporting cast member who appeared on the series for all nine years.

In 1987, Martin's 35-year-old son Dino, who had performed in the pop trio Dino, Desi & Billy, was killed in a plane crash. On December 25, 1995, Martin died of acute respiratory failure in his Beverly Hills home. He was 78.

## THE TOP FIVE
*Week of August 15, 1964*

1 **Everybody Loves Somebody**
Dean Martin

2 **Where Did Our Love Go**
Supremes

3 **A Hard Day's Night**
Beatles

4 **Rag Doll**
Four Seasons

5 **Under the Boardwalk**
Drifters

*Writers: Brian Holland*
        *Lamont Dozier*
        *Eddie Holland*

*Producers: Brian Holland*
          *Lamont Dozier*

*August 22, 1964*
*2 weeks*

Four young girls growing up in Detroit wanted to sing. When they first got together as the Primettes in 1959, no one could have predicted they would become the most successful American singing group of all time, or that they had four very different destinies. One would quit almost immediately. One would still be leading the group 18 years later. One would die under tragic circumstances at age 32. And one would achieve fame of stratospheric proportions, becoming not just the most successful female singer of the rock era, but a world class superstar.

By the time the girls recorded "Where Did Our Love Go," they were a trio [see 159—"Baby Love"] known as the Supremes—or the "No-Hit Supremes," as the other artists at Motown uncharitably called them. Diana Ross, Mary Wilson and Florence Ballard had released eight singles with poor results, while artists like the Miracles [see 285—"The Tears of a Clown"] and the Marvelettes [see 101—"Please Mr. Postman"] were burning up the charts.

The girls were still the Primettes when they recorded their first song for the company, "After All." Two more numbers ("Who's Lovin' You," "Play a Sad Song") were recorded before the December 15, 1960, session that produced their first single, "I Want a Guy." Before he released it on the Tamla label, Gordy told the group to come up with a new name. Florence Ballard was at the company's Grand Boulevard office when a decision was needed. She was presented a list of possibilities and chose the only name that didn't end with "ette." When Ross and Wilson found out she picked the "Supremes," they were horrified. It sounded too masculine for their taste [see 126—"Our Day will Come"].

"I Want a Guy" did not make the Hot 100, nor did the follow-up, "Buttered Popcorn," featuring Florence

on lead vocal. For their third single, they were switched over to the Motown label—and they went all the way to number 95 with "Your Heart Belongs to Me." Next came the faster-paced "Let Me Go the Right Way," which peaked at 90. A ballad, "My Heart Can't Take It No More," didn't chart at all, but "A Breath Taking Guy" went to number 75 in the summer of 1963.

During the early part of 1964, Holland, Dozier and Holland wrote "Where Did Our Love Go"—but not for the Supremes. "Actually, 'Where Did Our Love Go' was for the Marvelettes, Dozier reveals. "Gladys Horton, their lead singer, was not that fond of the song. I played a little bit of it for her—we had the track already cut—but she just couldn't get into the 'baby, baby' and said, 'no way am I gonna sing any junk like that!'"

H-D-H took the song to the Supremes instead. "They were low on the totem pole and they wouldn't give us any lip because they couldn't afford to," Dozier says. "But Gladys

had told Diane, 'Hey, I wouldn't do that, girl, we turned it down.' They said, 'Wait a minute, what are we doing, getting rejects of the Marvelettes?' It was just one headache after another, but they did the song and they were quite disappointed with the outcome."

"Where Did Our Love Go" was recorded April 8, 1964. By the time the single was released in June, the Supremes were booked along with Motown artist Brenda Holloway ("Every Little Bit Hurts"), Gene Pitney and the Shirelles on Dick Clark's "Caravan of Stars." Diana, Mary and Florence didn't even get billing when the tour started—they were bunched in with "and others." As the tour progressed, audience reaction to "Where Did Our Love Go" grew louder and louder. The single had entered the Hot 100 at number 77 on July 11. Six weeks later it was number one, and the Supremes had moved from "and others" to the caravan's headline attraction. It was just a hint of what the next five-and-a-half years would bring.

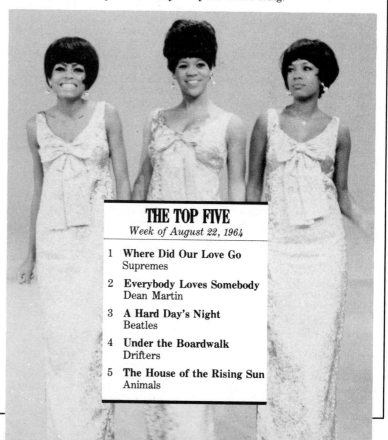

### THE TOP FIVE
*Week of August 22, 1964*

1   **Where Did Our Love Go**
    Supremes

2   **Everybody Loves Somebody**
    Dean Martin

3   **A Hard Day's Night**
    Beatles

4   **Under the Boardwalk**
    Drifters

5   **The House of the Rising Sun**
    Animals

# House of the Rising Sun  MGM 13264
## THE ANIMALS

*Writer: (Traditional) Alan Price*

*Producer: Mickie Most*

*September 5, 1964*
*3 weeks*

Eric Burdon was ten years old when he first heard "House of the Rising Sun," a traditional folk song recorded by Josh White. He found the melody haunting, and while the words didn't mean much to him, the music stayed in his mind.

Born Eric Victor Burdon in Newcastle-Upon-Tyne, an industrial city in the northeast of England, he developed an interest in black American music at an early age. A merchant seaman who lived downstairs from Eric's family brought back Perry Como and Frank Sinatra records from the United States, but Eric had heard Wynonie Harris' "Don't Roll Those Bloodshot Eyes at Me" and was more interested in R&B music. He would ask his neighbor to bring back Chuck Berry, Bo Diddley and Wilbert Harrison records.

He didn't originally intend to turn his love of music into employment. Burdon went to college to study set design, art and graphics. Frustrated at not finding work in the television and film industries, he finally decided to sing professionally.

Alan Price was also born in Newcastle. When he was 11, an illness kept him out of school for almost a year, and he spent the time learning to play his grandmother's piano. An early interest in jazz led to skiffle music which led to rock and roll, and by 1960 the Alan Price Combo, which also included lead guitarist Hilton Valentine, bassist Bryan "Chas" Chandler and drummer John Steel,

was a popular attraction in Newcastle clubs.

Burdon joined the combo in 1962 from a group called the Pagans, and the line-up that would record "House of the Rising Sun" was in place. The popular myth is that their audiences called the group "animals," resulting in the name change. Actually, Burdon and Steel were on the fringes of a local gang led by a flipped-out army vet who called himself Animal Hog. He was a symbol of rebellion to the lads and they borrowed his name for the group.

The Animals built up a following at Newcastle's Club-A-Go-Go, and recorded a four-track EP. They pressed 500 copies and sold all of them. Record producer Mickie Most saw them in Newcastle and urged them to move to London. He got them a job as the opening act for Chuck Berry's United Kingdom tour, and as a counterpoint to Berry's rock and roll they decided to include the slow, bluesy "House of the Rising Sun" in their act. Bob Dylan had recorded a version that refined some of the bawdy lyrics from the traditional version, and the Animals used Dylan's recording as a guide.

Most signed the group to EMI's Columbia label, and while Berry was playing Luton, the Animals loaded their instruments onto British Rail and went to London to record "House of the Rising Sun" at a Kingsway studio in two takes.

Columbia was reluctant to release the song because it ran over four minutes, anathema to tightly programmed radio stations. So the first single released was "Baby, Let Me Take You Home," based on a blues song called "Baby, Don't You Tear My Clothes" and also recorded by

Dylan. After it made the British top 30, Most convinced EMI they should follow it with "House of the Rising Sun." It became their only number one single in both Britain and America.

After the first American tour, Price realized he had a fear of flying and left the group. He put together the Alan Price Set, hung out with Dylan and appeared in his film *Don't Look Back*. He also scored the motion picture *O Lucky Man*.

Steel left after recording the single "Inside Out," then Chandler quit and the group officially ended. Chandler discovered Jimi Hendrix in a Greenwich Village club, the Cafe Wha. He brought him back to London and introduced him to Noel Redding. Later, Chandler discovered the British band Slade, which he managed for 12 years.

Burdon put together a new line-up of Animals and continued to record hits like "Help Me Girl" and "San Franciscan Nights." At one point, the new Animals included future Policeman Andy Summers [see 574—"Every Breath You Take"].

In 1969, Burdon met up with a black American group called Nite Shift. He changed their name to War and recorded one album with them (which included the hit "Spill the Wine") before they went out on their own.

The original Animals have had three reunions. In 1968 they did one show at Newcastle City Hall. They recorded an album for Chandler's Barn label in 1976, and at a press conference in 1983 announced they were reuniting to tour and record two albums for Miles Copeland's I.R.S. label.

## THE TOP FIVE
*Week of September 5, 1964*

1 **The House of the Rising Sun**
Animals

2 **Where Did Our Love Go**
Supremes

3 **Everybody Loves Somebody**
Dean Martin

4 **Because**
Dave Clark Five

5 **C'mon and Swim**
Bobby Freeman

MONUMENT 851. **Oh, Pretty Woman**
ROY ORBISON

**157**

*Writers: Roy Orbison*
*Bill Dees*

*Producer: Wesley Rose*

*September 26, 1964*
*3 weeks*

Here's one for the record books: in a 68-week period that began August 8, 1963, Roy Orbison was the *only* American artist to have a number one single in Britain. He did it twice, with "It's Over" on June 25, 1964, and "Oh, Pretty Woman" on October 8, 1964. The latter song also went to number one in America, making Orbison impervious to the chart dominance of British artists on both sides of the Atlantic.

Orbison was so popular in Britain that he toured the country in 1963. His opening act—although some nights they switched and Orbison opened the show—was the Beatles.

Many people wonder why Orbison is always seen wearing dark eyeglasses. It wasn't always so, and pictures of him taken before 1963 show him with clear lenses or no glasses at all. This "trademark" happened accidentally. While flying into Alabama for a performance, Roy left his regular glasses on the plane. He didn't realize he had his sunglasses on until evening, but by then he had no choice: he either had to wear the dark glasses or not see at all. Embarrassed, he went on stage wearing the sunglasses. The next day he flew to England for the Beatles tour and was forced to continue wearing dark lenses so he could see. Photographs taken of Roy with the Beatles ran in newspapers around the world. Although he didn't plan to have a new image, he was stuck with one and kept it.

"Oh, Pretty Woman" was written one afternoon while Roy's wife, Claudette, was shopping. As she was leaving the house, Roy asked if she needed some money. Songwriter Bill Dees interjected, "A pretty woman never needs any money," and thought that would make a good song title.

By the time Claudette returned, they had written "Oh, Pretty Woman."

It was Orbison's biggest American hit yet, and many thought there could only be better things ahead for the Texas balladeer. Instead, there was great personal tragedy.

Roy's string of nine top 10 singles ended with "Oh, Pretty Woman." He left Monument Records in 1965 and signed with MGM, a label that promised him more money as well as motion picture work. He never even made the top 20 again, and acted in only one film, *The Fastest Guitar Alive*.

But it was personal tragedy that would torment Orbison for the next several years. On June 7, 1966, he saw his wife Claudette die in a motorcycle accident. A couple of years later, a fire destroyed his home in Tennessee, killing sons Roy Jr. and Tony. Devastated by the loss of his family, Roy tried to block out the pain by constantly touring all over the world. Although he remarried in 1969 and started a new family, which included surviving son, Wesley, Roy did not perform in the United States again until 1977.

Two years later, he recorded a new album for Asylum, and in 1980, he recorded "That Lovin' You Feelin' Again," a duet with Emmylou Harris that won him his first Grammy. Virgin Records signed Orbison in 1987. A year later, he joined George Harrison, Bob Dylan, Tom Petty and Jeff Lynne in the Traveling Wilburys. On December 6, 1988, Orbison suffered a heart attack and was rushed to a hospital, where he died just after being admitted.

## THE TOP FIVE
*Week of September 26, 1964*

1 **Oh, Pretty Woman**
Roy Orbison

2 **Bread and Butter**
Newbeats

3 **The House of the Rising Sun**
Animals

4 **G.T.O.**
Ronny & the Daytonas

5 **Remember (Walkin'**
**in the Sand)**
Shangri-Las

# Do Wah Diddy Diddy ASCOT 2157
## MANFRED MANN

Writers: *Jeff Barry*
*Ellie Greenwich*

Producer: *John Burgess*

*October 17, 1964*
*2 weeks*

IF Jeff Barry and Ellie Greenwich could write a song titled "Da Doo Ron Ron," what could stop them from writing one called "Do Wah Diddy Diddy"?

In early 1963, Jeff and Ellie were writing a song for the Sensations, the Philadelphia group that had a hit with "Let Me In" the previous year. When they played a demo of the new tune, "What a Guy," for Jerry Leiber and Mike Stoller, the producers sent it to Jerry Blaine at Jubilee Records, who offered a recording deal to Jeff and Ellie. They released the record as the Raindrops, adding Ellie's younger sister to the album cover to create the illusion of a group.

After two hits (the follow-up was "The Kind of Boy You Can't Forget"), the Raindrops started to lose steam (their third single, "That Boy John," was dropped from radio station playlists when President John F. Kennedy was assassinated, even though the song was not about him).

"We were in the studio as the Raindrops taking one last chance at recording," explains Ellie. The song they chose was "Do Wah Diddy Diddy," which had failed when the Exciters ("Tell Him") recorded it. "Jeff and I really believed in that song. We got a call from Leiber and Stoller at the studio saying, 'You ought to forget about it. It was just

shipped by Manfred Mann.' We had finished recording it, but we never mixed it."

Manfred Mann is the name of a South African jazz pianist born Michael Lubowitz in Johannesburg on October 21, 1941. Manfred Mann is also the name of the British group he organized that had numerous personnel changes and incarnations through the 60s, 70s and 80s.

Manfred Mann (the man) moved to Britain in 1961, after studying at the Vienna State Academy and the Juilliard School of Music in New York. A year later he met drummer Mike Hugg and guitarist Mike Vickers, and they formed the Mann-Hugg Blues Brothers, a group that worked clubs in the south of England.

They signed with EMI's HMV label in 1963 as Manfred Mann and the Manfreds, but by the time their first instrumental single, "Why Should We Not?" was released, the name had been contracted to Manfred Mann. Before their next single, "Cock-a-Hoop" was issued, two new members vere added, both from a popular London group called the Roosters (which included future Rolling Stone Brian Jones).

The new recruits were bassist Tom McGuiness and lead singer Paul Pond, who changed his name to Paul Jones. Their first two singles failed to chart, but their third effort, "5-4-3-2-1," was adopted as the theme song for the British pop musič television series "Ready Steady Go!"—which helped propel the single to number five in the United Kingdom. After one more hit, "Hubble Bubble Toil and Trouble," they released Barry-Greenwich's "Do Wah Diddy

Diddy," which went to number one on both sides of the Atlantic.

Covering an American tune worked so well, the group did it again for their next single, the Shirelles' "Sha La La." During 1965 they recorded "Come Tomorrow," "Oh No Not My Baby" (a Gerry Goffin-Carole King song recorded by Maxine Brown) and "If You Gotta Go, Go Now," one of their first flirtations with Bob Dylan. By the time the year was over, Vickers had left to concentrate on playing jazz and McGuiness took over lead guitar, while Jack Bruce joined as bassist. Bruce left the following year to help form Cream and was replaced by Klaus Voorman (the man who designed the cover of the Beatles' *Revolver* album).

Jones struck out on his own in 1966, starred in the film *Privilege* and had some solo hits as well. He continued his acting career in the early 70s, and formed the Blues Band with McGuiness and Hughie Flint in 1980. His recent stage work includes "Guys and Dolls" at Britain's National Theatre and the West End production of "Pump Boys and Dinettes."

Candidates to replace Jones as lead singer included Rod Stewart, Long John Baldry and Wayne Fontana, but the winner was Mike D'Abo from Band of Angels. D'Abo handled the vocal duties on "The Mighty Quinn (Quinn the Eskimo)," a Dylan song that topped the British chart.

The group Manfred Mann finally split in 1969, but there was more music to come from the South African keyboardist, who would lead two more groups in the next decade [see 454—"Blinded by the Light"].

---

## THE TOP FIVE

*Week of October 17, 1964*

1  **Do Wah Diddy Diddy**
   Manfred Mann

2  **Dancing in the Street**
   Martha & the Vandellas

3  **Oh, Pretty Woman**
   Roy Orbison

4  **We'll Sing in the Sunshine**
   Gale Garnett

5  **Last Kiss**
   J. Frank Wilson
   & the Cavaliers

*Writers: Brian Holland*
*Lamont Dozier*
*Eddie Holland*

*Producers: Brian Holland*
*Lamont Dozier*

*October 31, 1964*
*4 weeks*

FOUR months earlier they had been the "No-Hit Supremes." When "Baby Love" became their second number one single [see 155—"Where Did Our Love Go"], the Supremes catapulted to the top of Motown's artist roster. They were the first of Berry Gordy, Jr.'s acts to achieve two chart-toppers and they did it in just over two months.

To trace the origin of the Supremes, one must begin with a singing group called the Primes. Eddie Kendricks, Paul Williams and Cal Osborne had moved from their native Birmingham, Alabama, to Cleveland, Ohio, where they were discovered by manager Milton Jenkins. He brought them to Detroit where they were named the Primes [see 168—"My Girl"].

Jenkins was interested in having a sister group that he could package with the Primes for personal appearances. He knew a 15-year-old girl who lived in the Brewster Projects, a government subsidized housing project. Although she was interested in becoming a nurse, Florence Ballard also wanted to sing and she accepted Jenkins' offer.

Mary Wilson attended the same school as Florence, but they didn't become friends until they competed against each other in a talent contest.

Florence recruited Mary into her new group and together they chose a third member who was a year older than they were, Betty Travis. But popular girl groups of the day like the Shirelles had four members, so the Primettes were not complete. Paul Williams is given credit for bringing another girl from the Brewster Projects to Jenkins' attention. Diane Ross had to ask her parents' permission to join the group.

Diane met with Williams and Kendricks in an apartment near Detroit's Flame Show Bar. The first song she learned was "The Night Time Is the Right Time." With rehearsals in full swing, Betty Travis' mother thought her daughter was not devoting enough time to her studies and pulled her out of the group. She was replaced by Barbara Martin, but soon Florence and Barbara were forced to leave as well because of bad grades.

Diane and Mary continued as a duo until Florence and Barbara could return. The Primettes were a quartet again when Diane asked her former neighbor Smokey Robinson [see 285—"The Tears of a Clown"] if he would introduce the group to his boss, Berry Gordy Jr. at Motown Records. Smokey invited the girls to sing for him in the basement of his girlfriend Claudette Rogers' home. They brought along their guitarist, Marv Tarplin, and sang their hearts out for Smokey. Robinson thought the Primettes were promising—but he liked Tarplin's guitar work enough to offer him a permanent job with Smokey's own group.

The Primettes had to find another way into Motown. They started hanging around Gordy's Hitsville U.S.A. offices and won an audition with the company through Robert Bateman, who had seen the girls win first prize at a talent contest in Windsor, Ontario. Gordy asked them to sing the Drifters' "There Goes My Baby." But Gordy wasn't that enthused—the Primettes weren't even out of high school yet.

Undaunted, the four girls auditioned for another Detroit record company, Lu-Pine. Owner Robert West signed them and had them sing background vocals for Eddie Floyd, then recorded two songs with the group: "Tears of Sorrow" with Ross on lead and "Pretty Baby" featuring Wilson's voice.

They earned some local airplay, but that was all. The Primettes returned to the company they really wanted to sign with, but Gordy still wasn't ready to take them on. He let them hang around, and opportunities were presented: they did the handclaps for a Marvin Gaye song, and the backing vocals for blues singer Mable John. In J. Randy Taraborelli's biography *Diana*. Mable recalls discussing Diane with Berry: "...back then he didn't seem to have any special plans for her one way or the other. We agreed that Diane was the type of kid who probably knew what she wanted and how she was going to get it....he didn't really want to do anything with her, but somehow she made him see that she was destined for stardom."

## THE TOP FIVE
*Week of October 31, 1964*

1 **Baby Love**
Supremes

2 **Do Wah Diddy Diddy**
Manfred Man

3 **Last Kiss**
J. Frank Wilson & the Cavaliers

4 **We'll Sing in the Sunshine**
Gale Garnett

5 **Dancing in the Street**
Martha & the Vandellas

# 160 Leader of the Pack RED BIRD 10-014
## THE SHANGRI-LAS

**Writers:** *George 'Shadow' Morton*
*Jeff Barry*
*Ellie Greenwich*

**Producers:** *George 'Shadow' Morton*
*Jeff Barry*
*Ellie Greenwich*

*November 28, 1964*
*1 week*

"THERE were two songs in my whole career that I actually walked out of the studio and...had a gut feeling (they) would be number one," says songwriter Ellie Greenwich. "'Chapel of Love' [see 149] was one and 'Leader of the Pack' was the other."

The Shangri-Las were two sets of sisters from Queens, New York. Mary and Betty Weiss and twins Marge and Mary Ann Ganser met at Andrew Jackson High School and started singing together. They signed a contract with Artie Ripp and Kama Sutra Productions, then moved over to the Red Bird label for their first hit, "Remember (Walking in the Sand)."

"Leader of the Pack" was a girl-meets-boy (she met him at the candy store), girl-falls-for-boy (he turned around and smiled at her, you get the picture?), boy-dies-in-motorcycle-crash (and now he's gone) epic. Like the crying of the sea gulls and lap of the waves in "Remember," sound effects were put to their best use in "Leader of the Pack." The revving of the motors, the screeching of the

brakes and the sudden crashing of two vehicles helped make the single an unforgettable classic.

"We even had one of the guys in the studio, an (engineer) named Joey Veneri, (bring in) his motorcycle, which we put into an echo chamber in the hall and miked it," Ellie recalls. "We actually used his stepping on the gas to get the motor going."

Jeff and Ellie also remember how difficult it was for the Shangri-Las to record the song. Lead singer Mary Weiss was 16 when she recorded "Leader of the Pack." Jeff recalls her being inhibited by the studio and the microphone she had to face. "I was sitting across the mike from her, kind of mouthing the words with her and letting her feel free to let it out emotionally. She was crying, you can hear it on the record."

"The girls weren't easy to work with," Ellie agrees, adding that it required "spoonfeeding, mothering, big sistering and reprimanding to get them to do it. But they did come through."

The Shangri-Las' records did well in Britain, and the group was flown over for a promotional tour. Sixteen-year-old Mary was too young to go, which may explain why most British sources cite Betty as lead singer.

The group often appeared in the U.S. as a trio—at one point Betty was angry enough to leave, and another time Marge was absent. After Mary Ann died of encephalitis in 1971, the Shangri-Las continued to appear at

rock and roll revival shows as a trio. In 1994, Marge was diagnosed with breast cancer. She died on July 28, 1996, in the Bronx.

The song "Leader of the Pack" lived on in pop culture. A parody, "Leader of the Laundromat" by the Detergents (featuring lead vocals by Ron Dante, who would later fill the same role for the Archies), was a top 20 hit. Bette Midler recorded "Leader of the Pack" on her first album, *The Divine Miss M.* The song became the title tune in a Broadway musical devised around the songs of Barry and Greenwich. With Ellie as the star of the show, *Leader of the Pack* played six performances at the Bottom Line in Greenwich Village in January, 1984. With Michael Peters as director, the show opened on Broadway at the Ambassador Theatre in March, 1985.

## THE TOP FIVE
*Week of November 28, 1964*

1 **Leader of the Pack**
Shangri-Las

2 **Baby Love**
Supremes

3 **Come a Little Bit Closer**
Jay & the Americans

4 **She's Not There**
Zombies

5 **Ringo**
Lorne Greene

*Writers: Don Robertson
Hal Blair*

*Producer: Joe Reisman*

*December 5, 1964
1 week*

LORNE GREENE's face is recognized by more than half a billion people around the world. By conservative estimates, that is the number of people in more than 80 countries who have watched an episode of "Bonanza," the classic western television series in which Greene starred as Ben Cartwright, patriarchal owner of the Ponderosa. The series ran on NBC for 14 years, and was rated the number one program for three consecutive seasons, beginning in 1964.

Lorne Greene's voice is recognized by a lesser number of people, but only because those living in non-English speaking countries heard the voice of Ben Cartwright dubbed into their own language. It was his deep, powerful baritone voice, once known as the "Voice of Doom," that helped propel "Ringo" to number one on December 5, 1964.

Greene was only the second Canadian to top the American chart, after Paul Anka [see 25—"Diana"]. Born in Ottawa, Ontario, Canada, on February 12, 1915, Greene's first experience with music came when he was 10 years old. "I studied violin for five years to please my mother," he confesses. "She decided I was going to be a concert violinist. She dragged me to concerts . . . . I knew deep in my heart this was not for me. I wanted to play with the other kids." One day, while playing softball, Lorne went to catch a ball and fell over a rock. "Eighteen stitches later, I was out of the violin business."

Greene studied drama at Queen's University in Ontario, then won a fellowship to the Neighborhood Playhouse School of the Theatre in Manhattan. Returning to Canada in the spring of 1939, he tried to enlist in the armed forces as World War II was breaking out in Europe. The military wasn't interested in him, so he auditioned for a radio announcing job with the Canadian Broadcasting Company. In January, 1940, he replaced Charles Jennings (father of ABC news anchor Peter Jennings) as the chief news broadcaster for the CBC.

For the next three years, his commanding voice brought nothing but bad news to Canadian listeners, earning him the title "Voice of Doom." Finally, at the end of 1942, a successful campaign in Africa brought the first good news of the war and he was renamed the "Voice of Canada."

The Canadian Army finally accepted him in 1943, and after his discharge he returned to broadcasting and founded the Academy of Radio Arts, a broadcasting school whose students included Leslie Nielsen and James Doohan (Engineer Montgomery Scott of the starship Enterprise).

His broadcasting experience led him to invent a stopwatch that counted backwards, for announcers who needed to know the time remaining until the end of a program. During a visit to New York City in 1953 to demonstrate the watch for an NBC executive, Greene had a chance meeting with producer Fletcher Markle, who cast him in the American television program "Studio One." He continued to work in television and on stage, and made 12 motion pictures between 1954-1958.

A guest appearance in "Wagon Train" caught the eye of producer David Dortort, who asked Greene to star as Ben Cartwright in "Bonanza." The first western series to be televised in color, the program made its debut on September 12, 1959. It survived a laughable first episode, damning reviews and two years of

poor ratings to become America's favorite show.

As "Bonanza" reached its peak of popularity in 1964, a producer at RCA suggested the Cartwrights record an album. NBC-TV and RCA Records were both subsidiaries of RCA Corporation and a Christmas LP featuring the voices of Michael Landon, Dan Blocker, Pernell Roberts and Greene was issued. "It wasn't terribly good," Lorne admits, "but we sold a lot of copies." It was successful enough that RCA signed Lorne to a recording contract. When a second Bonanza cast album, *Welcome to the Ponderosa*, was recorded, Lorne was asked to look over a poem with six verses. "By the end of the fourth stanza, I got chills," Lorne recalls. He knew before he recorded it that the story of a sheriff who saves the life of gunman Johnny Ringo could be a big hit.

Lorne was emcee for a ceremony on Prince Edward Island that was attended by Queen Elizabeth II when he received an urgent phone call from RCA in New York. A Lubbock, Texas, disc jockey had played "Ringo" from the album and created such a demand for it, that RCA pressed 1,200 copies of the song as a 45 and shipped them to Texas. They sold out in one day.

After "Ringo," Lorne recorded seven albums for RCA. "Bonanza" remained on the air until January 16, 1973. Greene starred in three more series: "Griff," "Battlestar Galactica" and "Code Red." He was scheduled to begin work on the TV movie "Bonanza: The Next Generation" when he died of respiratory complications on September 11, 1987. He was 72.

## THE TOP FIVE
*Week of December 5, 1964*

1 **Ringo**
Lorne Greene

2 **Mr. Lonely**
Bobby Vinton

3 **Leader of the Pack**
Shangri-Las

4 **She's Not There**
Zombies

5 **Baby Love**
Supremes

## Mr. Lonely EPIC 9730
### BOBBY VINTON

*Writers: Bobby Vinton*
*Gene Allen*

*Producer: Bob Morgan*

*December 12, 1964*
*1 week*

MANY artists who had been popular before the Beatles found it impossible to have hits in 1964, but not Bobby Vinton. "Mr. Lonely" became his fourth number one single and preceded a list of 16 more top ten records. The man whose "There! I've Said It Again" had been deposed by "I Want to Hold Your Hand" believes the Beatles contributed to his success.

"In a way, they may have helped me because they wiped out all of my competition. There were no more male singers in America. I was lucky to hold on because I was coming up with good songs," Bobby says.

He returned the favor to many British groups. Bobby's manager was Allen Klein. "He was a good investor and I was saving a lot of money, and doing very well for a pop artist. So the English groups would come in and talk to me." Klein ended up handling affairs for the Animals and Herman's Hermits, then the Rolling Stones and finally, the Beatles.

As for "Mr. Lonely," it was a long time between recording session and hitting the top spot on the Hot 100. When Bobby had his do-or-die recording session that produced his first number one song [see 113—

"Roses Are Red (My Love)"], he recorded *two* songs. The other one was "Mr. Lonely."

According to Bobby, executives at Epic Records didn't really think he was a singer just because he had a hit with "Roses Are Red..." They still saw him as the big band leader he had intended to be. They had another artist, who Bobby prefers not to name, that they thought was a great singer.

"I'm driving in my car one day listening to the radio, and I hear 'Mr. Lonely' the way I wrote it and arranged it, but it wasn't my voice, it was his. So I called Epic Records and said, 'That's my song, it should be the follow-up to 'Roses Are Red.' And they said, 'Come on, you're not really a singer and he is. You're hot now, but this song could kick off a new artist.'"

"Mr. Lonely" was not a hit for this unnamed artist, but Bobby had moved on to "Rain Rain Go Away," and forgot about "Mr. Lonely" until it was time to put a greatest hits album together. He had 11 songs and needed one more, so he added the song that he thought should have been a hit for him. It started to get airplay and was finally released as a single.

In 1974, Bobby left Epic and found it difficult to get a new label deal with a song he had written that was partially sung in Polish. Jay Lasker at ABC Records heard it and said it would sell a million copies. He was right. "My Melody of Love" went to number three and earned a gold record, and its success led to a syndicated TV series, "The Bobby Vinton Show," that aired from 1975-1978.

### THE TOP FIVE
*Week of December 12, 1964*

1  **Mr. Lonely**
   Bobby Vinton

2  **She's Not There**
   Zombies

3  **Ringo**
   Lorne Greene

4  **Come See About Me**
   Supremes

5  **I Feel Fine**
   Beatles

Writers: *Brian Holland*
*Lamont Dozier*
*Eddie Holland*

Producers: *Brian Holland*
*Lamont Dozier*

December 19, 1964
*2 weeks*

"COME, SEE ABOUT ME" was the third single from the Supremes' album *Where Did Our Love Go*. It was also the third consecutive number one single for the Supremes, making them the first American group to pull three chart-toppers from one LP. "Come See About Me" was recorded July 13, 1964, and released on October 27, *before* "Baby Love" went to number one. Its early release didn't prevent "Baby Love" from sitting on top of the Hot 100 for four weeks, the longest run of any Supremes single.

The sudden release of "Come See About Me" was ordered when Berry Gordy, Jr., learned that New York-based Scepter Records was releasing a cover version of the song by female singer Nella Dodds on their Wand label. Motown had been planning to issue the song as a 45 anyway, but they brought forward the release date in time to have the Supremes' single debut on the Hot 100 the same week as Dodds' version. It was never

a contest—the Supremes entered the chart at number 66 on November 14, while Dobbs came on at number 87. A week later, the Supremes jumped to 31 while Dodds crept to 84. The following week Dodds peaked at 74 while the Supremes went to number 13. From that position they moved to eight, to four and then to number one.

The writing/producing team of Brian Holland, Lamont Dozier and Eddie Holland "put their noses to the grindstone" to come up with material for the Supremes when they realized "Where Did Our Love Go" [see 155] was going to be such an enormous hit, according to Dozier. "'Come See About Me' and 'Baby Love' were recorded in the same (two) weeks after we found out 'Where Did Our Love Go' was such a big smash. Brian came up with this melody for 'Baby Love' and I came up with 'Come See About Me.'"

The Supremes were hitting the chart so fast, there was no time to record demos, Dozier explains. "We would just cut tracks. I'd come up with an idea, Brian and I would finish it off and then run downstairs and cut the track with the band. A lot of times we didn't even have a title. Then we'd bring it back up and Eddie and I would sit there and bounce things around and (ask) what is this track saying? Then we would come up with a title and finish it off." At

this point, the Supremes were not offering any arguments when presented with a new Holland-Dozier-Holland song, as they had when they first heard "Where Did Our Love Go."

The names Holland-Dozier-Holland became as familiar to fans of the Supremes as Lennon-McCartney and George Martin were to Beatles fans. "The chemistry between the three of us working was just very rare, because there are a lot of thoughts and everybody wants to do their own thing, but somehow we just clicked. We went into these songs with the idea of making the best possible music we could make," Dozier remembers.

By the end of 1964, the Supremes were becoming a very visible act. Three days after "Come See About Me" was released, they performed the song—along with their first two number one hits at a taping of *The T.A.M.I. Show*, a rock and roll extravaganza that also starred the Rolling Stones, James Brown, the Beach Boys, Chuck Berry, the Miracles, Lesley Gore, Marvin Gaye, Gerry and the Pacemakers, Billy J. Kramer and the Dakotas and hosts Jan and Dean. The electronically recorded event was released theatrically in 1965.

"Come See About Me" spent one week at number one, then dipped to number two for three weeks while the Beatles' "I Feel Fine" topped the chart. "Come See About Me" then returned to number one for an additional week. During its interim run at number two, the Supremes made their first appearance on "The Ed Sullivan Show" on December 27.

## THE TOP FIVE
*Week of December 19, 1964*

1 **Come See About Me**
Supremes

2 **I Feel Fine**
Beatles

3 **Mr. Lonely**
Bobby Vinton

4 **She's Not There**
Zombies

5 **Ringo**
Lorne Greene

## 164 I Feel Fine CAPITOL 5327
## THE BEATLES

*Writers: John Lennon*
*Paul McCartney*

*Producer: George Martin*

*December 26, 1964*
*3 weeks*

**B**ETWEEN the weeks of January 18 and October 24, 1964, the Beatles placed 28 different titles on the Hot 100, more chart entries than any other artist has ever achieved in a comparable period. The list includes their regular Capitol releases, as well as re-issues on a host of labels: Swan, Vee Jay, MGM, Tollie, Capitol of Canada and Atco. The *Billboard* Hot 100 for the week of October 31 was the first chart since January 18, when "I Want to Hold Your Hand" debuted, not to feature a Beatles single ("Matchbox" fell off the chart from number 52 the week of October 24).

For five consecutive weeks, the Beatles remained off the Hot 100. But they had recorded two songs for single release in early October, and on December 5, "I Feel Fine" and "She's a Woman" entered the Hot 100 at numbers 22 and 46, respectively. This brought their total number of

chart entries for the calendar year to 30, an all-time record.

The "A" side of the single was "I Feel Fine," written by John Lennon in the studio at Abbey Road. The distinctive opening, featuring a single note of feedback, marked the first use of such a device. Responding to a question about which Beatle songs were written by John and which were written by Paul McCartney, Lennon told David Sheff about "I Feel Fine" in a *Playboy* interview: "That's me, including the guitar lick with the first feedback ever recorded. I defy anybody to find an earlier record—unless it is some old blues record from the twenties—with feedback on it."

In the *Lennon* biography, author Ray Coleman explains, "Lennon's musical experiments were encouraged by George Martin and the other three Beatles, notably the first recorded use of feedback on 1964's 'I Feel Fine.' Lennon had a small studio at Kenwood, where he tinkered with tape recorders and fragments of songs, the results of which would manifest themselves the following year."

"I Feel Fine," featuring lead vocals by John, harmony by Paul and a lead guitar duet by both of them,

was first played in America by radio station KRLA in Los Angeles. The station obtained a copy on November 6 and began airing it once an hour. Program director Reb Foster told *Billboard:* "We've received calls from Florida, New York, St. Louis, Denver and Cleveland stations, offering us money and queries about where we picked up the single. We don't feel we are (doing anything illegal) in breaking the record." Capitol Records asked the station to refrain from playing the single or passing it on to any other station.

John Rooke at KQV in Pittsburgh, Pennsylvania, gave the song its first East Coast airplay on November 11, and sent a copy to sister station WABC in New York. After its "official" release, "I Feel Fine" surged up the Hot 100, moving from 22 to 5 to 2, reaching the top spot the week of December 26. Because *Billboard* charted "B" sides separately at this time, "She's a Woman" moved up the Hot 100 under its own power, from 46 to 29 to 14 to number four, making it the highest charting Beatles "B" side to date.

"She's a Woman" was also composed in the studio—but by Paul. It's an R&B influenced-rocker, somewhat removed from the ballads many people associate with McCartney.

"I Feel Fine" became the Beatles' sixth number one single in both America and Britain. In the U.K., it was only available as a single and was purposely not included in the *Beatles for Sale* album, released December 4. In the United States, "I Feel Fine" and "She's a Woman" were both available in the album *Beatles '65*, released on December 15.

### THE TOP FIVE
*Week of December 26, 1964*

1  **I Feel Fine**
   Beatles

2  **Come See About Me**
   Supremes

3  **Mr. Lonely**
   Bobby Vinton

4  **She's a Woman**
   Beatles

5  **She's Not There**
   Zombies

*Writer: Tony Hatch*

*Producer: Tony Hatch*

*January 23, 1965*
*2 weeks*

PETULA CLARK was an international star, popular in her native Britain as well as Australia, Canada and all of Europe. However, she was a virtual unknown in America when "Downtown" soared to the the top of the Hot 100, making her the first British female of the rock era to have a number one single in the United States. (Vera Lynn topped the American chart in 1952 with "Auf Wiederseh'n Sweetheart").

Petula had moved to Paris after marrying Claud Wolff, publicity director for the French Vogue label, in 1961. She had a succession of hits sung in French, including "Ya Ya Twist" and "Chariot," which was later translated into English and became a number one hit for Peggy March [see 128—"I Will Follow Him"]. Tony Hatch, who worked for Pye Records in Britain, produced Petula's French hits, and arrived one day in 1964 with a batch of new songs for her to record.

He suggested it was time for her to record in English again, and she said she would only if she could find the right song. Tony had just written a new melody and played it for Petula while she went into the kitchen to make some tea. When she heard the music, she came running out to the living room and told Tony it was a great tune, and if he could write suitable lyrics to match his title of "Downtown," she would record it.

Released first in Britain, it became a number two hit. In America, where she had released a number of unsuccessful singles between 1951-1962, Petula had her first chart record. "Downtown" entered the Hot 100 on December 19, 1964, at number 87 and was number one five weeks later.

Petula Sally Olwen Clark was born in Epsom, Surrey on November 15, 1932. Her parents were both nurses, but her father harbored secret ambitions to be an actor and her Welsh mother, who died at the age of 38, was a natural singer. At age three Pet was singing in church with her mother in Wales, and when she was nine, her father arranged for her to sing on a BBC Radio show, "It's All Yours." During a rehearsal an air raid siren sounded, and the producers asked if someone would sing to calm the audience. Young Pet volunteered and sang "Mighty Like a Rose," a song she was asked to sing again when the show went on the air.

During World War II she appeared on over 500 radio programs, and had her own show on BBC, "Pet's Parlour." She began recording at age 17, and her first record, issued only in Australia, was a 78 rpm version of "Music, Music, Music." Her first British release was "Put Your Shoes on Lucy" in 1949.

The following year she starred in her first British television series and signed with the Polygon label. Her first British chart record came in 1954, with "The Little Shoe maker," and her first rock and roll record was "With All My Heart" in 1957. Her

first number one single in Britain was "Sailor," an English language version of an Austrian song, "Seemann." Lolita, a German singer, had a hit in Europe with the original version and went top five with it in America in 1960.

The follow-up to "Downtown" was another Tony Hatch song, "I Know a Place." It went to number three, making Petula Clark the first female vocalist in the rock era to have her first two chart entries make the top three of *Billboard's* Hot 100. It was a record that would stand until 1984 [see 589—"Time After Time"].

## THE TOP FIVE
*Week of January 23, 1965*

1 **Downtown**
Petula Clark

2 **You've Lost That Lovin' Feelin'**
Righteous Brothers

3 **Love Potion Number Nine**
Searchers

4 **I Feel Fine**
Beatles

5 **Come See About Me**
Supremes

## 166 You've Lost That Lovin' Feelin' PHILLES 124
### THE RIGHTEOUS BROTHERS

*Writers: Phil Spector*
*Barry Mann*
*Cynthia Weil*

*Producer: Phil Spector*

*February 6, 1965*
*2 weeks*

Two friends from Orange County in Southern California gave new meaning to the term "blue-eyed soul." Bill Medley and Bobby Hatfield were called "righteous brothers" by black marines who saw them perform at the Black Derby in Santa Ana. On their first number one single, Medley and Hatfield formed a perfect union with their producer and writers to create a classic song that will be covered by singers for centuries to come.

The team responsible for "You've Lost That Lovin' Feelin'" consisted of singers Medley and Hatfield, who adopted the marines' "Righteous Brothers" as their name; husband-and-wife songwriters Barry Mann and Cynthia Weil, who spent their formative years working for Al Nevins and Don Kirshner at Aldon Music; and producer Phil Spector, often referred to as a "creative genius" by rock historians, and not without good reason.

The Righteous Brothers' roots lie in two groups: the Paramours, which featured Santa Ana's Bill Medley, and the Variations, which included Anaheim's Bobby Hatfield. A mutual friend, John Wimber, was working in

Las Vegas and wanted to form a group that would keep him home in California. He approached Bill and his guitar player from the Paramours, and Bobby and his drummer from the Variations. Together they formed a new version of the Paramours.

Medley was a songwriter, and the group included his "Little Latin Lupe Lu" in their act. It was so popular at the Rendezvous Ballroom in Balboa, California, that a local record company asked Bill and Bobby if they wanted to record it. Fans who wanted to buy the record were all told to go to the same store. Suddenly, that shop had sold more than two thousand copies of the single. By lucky chance, the store reported its sales figures each week to Los Angeles radio station KRLA. Impressed by such a large sales report, the music director asked for a copy to be sent over immediately. The station used the song in the background of a commercial for a record hop, and a hit single was born.

The Righteous Brothers signed with Moonglow Records and had two more hits: "Koko Joe" (written by Sonny Bono [see 181—"I Got You Babe"]) and "My Babe." In 1964, they appeared at the Cow Palace in San Francisco with ten other acts, including the Ronettes. The Ronettes' producer, Phil Spector, was conducting the band for the entire show, and was very impressed with the Righteous Brothers. He bought the

remaining two-and-a-half years of their contract from Moonglow and signed them to his Philles label.

Phil asked Barry and Cynthia to fly to California and write a song for the Righteous Brothers. They checked in to the Chateau Marmont on Sunset Strip and rented a piano. After hearing "Little Latin Lupe Lu" and "My Babe," they decided to write the boys a ballad. Inspired by their favorite song at the time, "Baby I Need Your Lovin'" by the Four Tops [see 177—"I Can't Help Myself (Sugar Pie Honey Bunch)"], Barry and Cynthia wrote a song with the dummy lyrics "You've lost that lovin' feelin'," but Phil liked those words and decided to keep them. The song was completed at Phil's house, where Mann, Weil and Spector wrote the bridge together.

The first time Barry heard the completed record, with Medley's deep-voiced introduction, was over a telephone. "When Phil played it for me over the phone, I said, 'Phil, you have it on the wrong speed!'" Barry laughs.

After the success of "You've Lost That Lovin' Feelin'," Bill and Bobby were signed by producer Jack Good to join Bobby Sherman, Glen Campbell, Leon Russell and Donna Loren in the resident cast of ABC-TV's "Shindig."

"You've Lost That Lovin' Feelin'" is one of a handful of number one singles to make the top 20 three separate times: Dionne Warwick [see 380—"Then Came You"] took the song to number 16 in 1969 and Daryl Hall and John Oates [see 457—"Rich Girl"] went to number 12 in 1980.

### THE TOP FIVE
*Week of February 6, 1965*

1 **You've Lost That Lovin' Feelin'**
Righteous Brothers

2 **Downtown**
Petula Clark

3 **The Name Game**
Shirley Ellis

4 **This Diamond Ring**
Gary Lewis & the Playboys

5 **Hold What You've Got**
Joe Tex

*Writers: Al Kooper*
*Bobby Brass*
*Irwin Levine*

*Producer: Snuff Garrett*

*February 20, 1965*
*2 weeks*

THANKS to the guidance of producer Snuff Garrett and arranger Leon Russell, Gary Lewis and the Playboys put together an enviable string of hits between 1965-1966 that began with their only number one single, "This Diamond Ring."

Gary Lewis, the son of comedian Jerry Lewis, was born July 31, 1946, in New York City. Gary's fourteenth birthday gift from his father was a set of drums. With several friends, he formed a band, and they successfully auditioned for Disneyland in 1964.

At this point, Lewis and Garrett tell different stories of how they met. According to Gary, Snuff and his family happened to be in the park one day and heard the band play. After. one of their sets, he approached them about recording for Liberty Records.

Snuff remembers it this way: "I had two idols growing up. One was Roy Rogers, who's become like a father to me. The other one became my neighbor, Jerry Lewis. I idolized him in my younger years. One day Lou Brown, Jerry's piano player and

conductor, said Gary's working at Disneyland with a group. He said, 'Would you like to go out and see them sometime?' I said, 'Not really, the drive to Disneyland doesn't thrill me.'"

A couple of weeks later, Gary and the band were rehearsing at the Paramount lot in Hollywood, and Brown invited Snuff again. "They weren't very good," Snuff confides. "They sounded like any other group I've ever heard. But then I got to thinking, if I could do a record with Gary and get Jerry to help me promote it, it might do well."

Snuff, who had produced Bobby Vee [see 97—"Take Good Care of My Baby"] for Liberty Records, suggested a song that Vee had turned down: "This Diamond Ring." Gary's mother used her household money to finance the recording session, which featured Russell on keyboards and Hal Blaine on drums.

"Gary wasn't a very good singer," says Snuff. "I used to mix him with other singers. When I got through mixing him, he sounded like Mario Lanza." Snuff called disc jockey Murray the K in New York and asked him to play "This Diamond Ring." In exchange, Snuff promised that Gary Lewis and the Playboys would come back and do Murray's next live concert. The record broke in New York. Snuff asked Jerry Lewis to call Ed

Sullivan about booking the group on his show, and Jerry picked up the phone on the spot and called Ed. A few weeks later, the group performed on Sullivan's show.

At the end of 1966, Gary was drafted into the United States Army. He was bitter about having his career interrupted, and when the military suggested he form a band and entertain troops, he said he'd rather handle supplies. He spent two years in Korea as a clerk/typist.

When he returned to public life, American musical tastes had changed. The Playboys had disbanded and attempts at putting together a new group were not successful.

## THE TOP FIVE
*Week of February 20, 1965*

1 **This Diamond Ring**
Gary Lewis & the Playboys

2 **You've Lost That Lovin' Feelin'**
Righteous Brothers

3 **Downtown**
Petula Clark

4 **My Girl**
Temptations

5 **The Name Game**
Shirley Ellis

## 168 My Girl GORDY 7038
THE TEMPTATIONS

*Writer: William "Smokey" Robinson*
*Ronald White*

*Producers: William "Smokey" Robinson*
*Ronald White*

*March 6, 1965*
*1 week*

**A**FTER recording several singles written and produced by Motown founder Berry Gordy, Jr., the Temptations were teamed up with the leader of the Miracles, William "Smokey" Robinson [see 285—"The Tears of a Clown"], who wrote the song that made the Tempts the first male Motown group to achieve a number one single. "My Girl," one of the songs that led Bob Dylan to call Smokey "America's greatest living poet," and a companion piece to Mary Wells' "My Guy" [see 147], was also the first number one for the Motown subsidiary that bears Gordy's name.

The Temptations were the result of a merger of two groups: the Primes and the Distants. Both groups shared the same manager, Milton Jenkins, and when each group suffered defections, the survivors were brought together to form a quintet named the Elgins.

Eddie Kendricks and Paul Williams lived near each other in Birmingham, Alabama, where they organized a group called the Cavaliers with friends Cal Osborne and Willy Waller. They moved to Cleveland, Ohio, and were discovered by Jenkins, who suggested they move to Detroit. Eddie, Paul and Cal made the move and became the Primes. Soon after, Jenkins decided they should have a sister group and helped form the Primettes [see 159—"Baby Love"].

Otis Williams, who grew up on a farm in Texarkana, Texas, as Otis Miles, moved to Detroit in 1950. Seven years later, he was singing street-corner harmony with a friend, Elbridge Bryant. In 1959, Williams and Bryant formed a group with a friend from Northwestern High School, Melvin Franklin (born David English), his cousin Richard Street and Albert Harrell. They called themselves the Elegants, the Questions and finally the Distants when they signed a recording contract with the Northern label. Street was the lead vocalist on

### THE TOP FIVE
*Week of March 6, 1965*

1. **My Girl**
   Temptations
2. **This Diamond Ring**
   Gary Lewis & the Playboys
3. **You've Lost That Lovin' Feelin'**
   Righteous Brothers
4. **The Jolly Green Giant**
   Kingsmen
5. **Eight Days a Week**
   Beatles

their first single, the Otis Williams-penned "Come On." After a couple of records that didn't fare well, Street and Harrell departed (Street formed another Motown group, the Monitors, and returned to the Temptations in 1971), and Jenkins brought in Kendricks and Paul Williams to form the Elgins.

The Elgins were signed to Berry Gordy's new Miracle label, but before their first release ("Oh Mother of Mine") in August, 1961, Otis Williams and Motown employee Bill Mitchell came up with a new group name, the Temptations. After one more release on Miracle, the group was shifted to the new Gordy label.

Smokey's association with the Temptations began with "I Want a Love I Can See," and when that record floundered, Bryant decided the Temptations were never going to make it. He quit the group and was replaced by a singer from Meridian, Mississippi, who was signed to Motown as a solo artist: David Ruffin. The new line-up recorded Smokey's "The Way You Do the Things You Do" with Kendricks on lead vocals, and had their first hit.

After two more singles featuring Kendricks ("I'll Be in Trouble" and "Girl (Why You Wanna Make Me Blue)"), Smokey turned to Ruffin for lead vocal duties on "My Girl."

The Miracles and the Temptations were appearing together at the Apollo Theater in Harlem when Smokey recorded the rhythm track for "My Girl." It was a song he intended to record with his own group, but the Temptations heard it and pleaded with Smokey to cut the song with them. Smokey finally agreed and rehearsed the group for a week in their top floor dressing room. They returned to Detroit and recorded "My Girl" on December 21, 1964. The single debuted on *Billboard's* Hot 100 on January 16, 1965 at number 76 and went to number one on March 6.

Smokey wrote and produced four more hits for the Temptations ("It's Growing," "Since I Lost My Baby," "My Baby" and "Get Ready") before turning over the reins to Norman Whitfield, who would produce three more number one singles for the Temptations over the next six years [see 259—"I Can't Get Next to You"].

CAPITOL 5371 **Eight Days a Week**
THE BEATLES

169

*Writers: John Lennon*
*Paul McCartney*

*Producer: George Martin*

*March 13, 1965*
*2 weeks*

"EIGHT DAYS A WEEK" was the first British single to go to number one in America and not make the chart in its own country. Of course, there was a good reason—"Eight Days a Week" was never released as a single in Britain.

It was only owing to the peculiar release pattern established in America that "Eight Days a Week" came out as a 45. The song was recorded for the *Beatles for Sale* album in the United Kingdom, released December 4, 1964. It was considered for single release, along with "No Reply" and "I'm a Loser," but was passed over in favor of "I Feel Fine" [see 164], which became the Beatles' sixth number one single in both Britain and America.

Beatles albums in the United Kingdom and the United States remained disparate until the 1967 release of *Sgt. Pepper's Lonely Hearts Club Band.* Until then, British albums always contained more tracks than their American counterparts, resulting in enough left-over material to create interim, patchwork American LPs.

This pattern began with the very first Beatles album, *Please Please Me* released in the U.K. on March 22, 1963. Vee Jay issued the album in the United States on July 22, 1963, with two tracks ("Please Please Me" and "Ask Me Why") deleted. During the first wave of Beatlemania, the album was re-released, with the two deleted tracks added and "Love Me Do" [see 148] and "P.S. I Love You" discarded instead.

The soundtrack album *A Hard Day's Night* continued the pattern. The British LP included all of the songs from the film, plus five titles that had been written for the film but not included in the soundtrack. The American equivalent, released on the United Artists label, included instrumental versions of Beatles' songs and deleted the five extra tracks, which turned up on Capitol's next album, *Something New*, along with some of the songs from *A Hard's Day's Night*. It made for another patchwork LP.

At this point, there was only one song that hadn't appeared on an American album—"I'll Be Back," from the British *A Hard Day's Night* LP. A similar release pattern could have begun at this point, but like most other British albums of the day, *Beatles for Sale* contained 14 tracks, and the standard count for American LPs was 12. *Beatles' 65* only contained 11 songs—eight of them from *Beatles for Sale.*

Americans who couldn't obtain an import copy of *Beatles for Sale* had to wait two months to hear the first two unreleased tracks: "Eight Days a Week" and "I Don't Want to Spoil the Party" were released as a single and entered the Hot 100 at number 53 on February 20, 1965. "Eight Days a Week," featuring a double-tracked lead vocal by John Lennon and an unusual guitar fade-in, became the Beatles' seventh American number one single three weeks later, while "I Don't Want to Spoil the Party" peaked at number 39.

The non-release of "Eight Days a Week" in the U.K. meant British fans had to wait almost five months after the release of "I Feel Fine" for another Beatles single. The long wait caused complaints that there were too few Beatles' records being released in Britain. Manager Brian Epstein answered the criticism in *Billboard:* "I think that the Beatles produce as many records as most artists on average. The reason why more people are asking for more records is that there is obviously a greater demand for Beatles' material. In my experience many artists have been damaged by over-exposure on record."

Two important events in the lives of the Beatles took place just before "Eight Days a Week" topped the American chart. Ringo Starr became the second Beatle to wed (John Lennon married Cynthia Powell on August 23, 1962) when he took Maureen Cox for his bride. The wedding took place February 11 in London, with John Lennon and George Harrison in attendance. Paul McCartney was on holiday in North Africa with his girlfriend Jane Asher, and was informed of the surprise wedding by reporters.

On February 22, the Beatles departed London's Heathrow Airport for the Bahamas, the first location for their second motion picture [see 182—"Help!"].

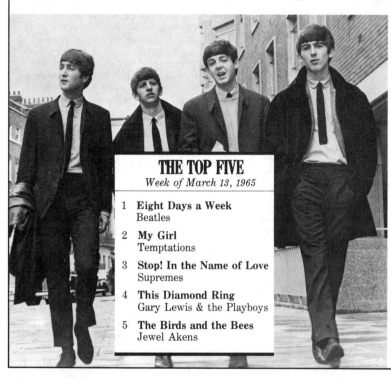

**THE TOP FIVE**
*Week of March 13, 1965*

1  **Eight Days a Week**
   Beatles

2  **My Girl**
   Temptations

3  **Stop! In the Name of Love**
   Supremes

4  **This Diamond Ring**
   Gary Lewis & the Playboys

5  **The Birds and the Bees**
   Jewel Akens

# 170 | Stop! In the Name of Love MOTOWN 1074
## THE SUPREMES

*Writers: Brian Holland*
*Lamont Dozier*
*Eddie Holland*

*Producers: Brian Holland*
*Lamont Dozier*

*March 27, 1965*
*2 weeks*

**W**HEN the Supremes released "Stop! In the Name of Love" in February, 1965, their fans were waiting to see if they could do it again. Could they follow three consecutive number one singles with a fourth, and become the first group in the history of the Hot 100 to have four chart-toppers in a row? The answer came during the week of March 27: Yes.

Lamont Dozier remembers the incident that gave him the idea for the song. "I was arguing with my girlfriend. (I) said, "Stop in the name of love" and we both started laughing and stopped arguing. I said, 'What did I say?' and she said, 'Something about stop in the name of love.' "

Personal relationships were just one source of song ideas, according to Lamont. "A couple of titles came out of *TV Guide*. 'Ask Any Girl' was an old movie. I couldn't have a decent conversation with anyone because everything was, 'What did you say?' People would say, 'That crazy boy's

walking around with songs in his head all the time; he can't carry on a decent conversation because he's looking for material.' When I went to the movies, I couldn't enjoy the movie for looking for a line. Something would trigger me and I would get up to go (find) a piano. It's almost a curse."

The Supremes had recorded "Stop! In the Name of Love" on January 5, 1965, in Detroit. Soon after, they were winging their way to Europe for the first Motortown Revue to hit the continent.

It was already apparent to Mary Wilson and Florence Ballard that the star of the Supremes was Diana Ross. Tempers flared, egos conflicted, and though the girls loved each other like sisters, there were early warning signs of trouble. "We weren't even talking to each other by the time we got to Europe," Diana is quoted in J. Randy Taraborrelli's biography *Diana*. "The pace of everything had gotten to us, I think. It was hard work and we were so young it sort of surprised us, coming so fast and all. Berry was on that tour with us and I decided that we had all better sit down and regroup like adults. Everybody was spreading apart and doing their own thing. We were having misunderstandings and all kinds of little arguments. We knew that the

Supremes would break up someday just like any other group in the world, but we had just gotten started and it was so good. I didn't want it to end."

While touring England, the famous hand movement for "Stop! In the Name of Love" was invented. The Supremes were booked for a live television show but had no choreography prepared for their new single. They ducked into a men's room with Paul Williams and Melvin Franklin of the Temptations and Berry Gordy to come up with the well-known move that resembles a police officer halting traffic.

## THE TOP FIVE
*Week of March 27, 1965*

1 **Stop! In the Name of Love**
Supremes

2 **Can't You Hear My Heartbeat**
Herman's Hermits

3 **The Birds and the Bees**
Jewel Akens

4 **Eight Days a Week**
Beatles

5 **King of the Road**
Roger Miller

TOWER 125 # I'm Telling You Now
### FREDDIE AND THE DREAMERS

*Writers: Freddie Garrity*
*Mitch Murray*

*Producer: John Burgess*

*April 10, 1965*
*2 weeks*

THE British Invasion began with the Merseybeat groups: the Beatles, Gerry and the Pacemakers and Billy J. Kramer and the Dakotas. In the year that followed, the focus shifted from Liverpool to London (the Rolling Stones, Manfred Mann), Newcastle (the Animals) and Manchester, thrust into the spotlight by the clown antics of Freddie and the Dreamers.

The image of Freddie leaping into the air to "do the Freddie" on television's "Shindig" and "Hullabaloo" is indelibly stamped on the mind of any 60s teenager.

"I'm Telling You Now" was a two-year-old hit when it reached American shores. In Britain, Freddie and the Dreamers made their first chart appearance in May, 1963, with a cover version of James Ray's 1962 American hit, "If You Gotta Make a Fool of Somebody," which charted as high as number three. The follow-up was "I'm Telling You Now," the group's biggest United Kingdom hit, peaking at two.

By the time "I'm Telling You Now" was released in the U.S., Freddie and the Dreamers had racked up five more British hits.

Freddie Garrity was born in Manchester on November 14, 1940. During the late 50s, Freddie sang with a local skiffle group, the Red Sox. He also worked as an engineer and a milkman. He continued delivering milk door-to-door while singing with the John Norman Four and the Kingfishers, a group that also included guitarist Roy Crewsdon. The Dreamers evolved from this group and eventually also included bassist Peter Birrell, drummer Bernie Dwyer and guitarist Derek Quinn.

The group became well known in Manchester by appearing on radio's "Beat Show" in early 1961. In October, they started to get national attention when they made their television debut on the BBC's "Let's Go." They spent the next few months touring England, appearing at the Leyton Baths, the Dreamland in Margate and Stevenage's Locarno. In late 1962, they were signed to the (British) Columbia label, distributed by EMI.

EMI's American label, Capitol Records, released the group's singles in the States on their new Tower subsidiary. But by the time "I'm Telling You Now" had an American release, the band had signed with Mercury Records in the United States. While Tower was releasing old material like "I'm Telling You Now" and "You Were Made for Me," Mercury was simultaneously releasing newer songs, such as "I Understand (Just How You Feel)"

and "Do the Freddie."

Freddie and the Dreamers had their final chart entries in both Britain and America at the end of 1965. They worked in clubs and cabarets for the next few years, and released a final album in 1970, a children's LP titled *Oliver in the Overworld*. The official split came in 1972, with Freddie and Peter moving on to host a children's television series, "The Little Big Time."

Freddie and the Dreamers came back in 1976, with Garrity as the only original member. They toured Australia and America, and continue to work today throughout Britain, occasionally appearing on television. Freddie continues to work in pantomime, a British traditional form of children's play that draws large family audiences each Christmas.

## THE TOP FIVE
*Week of April 10, 1965*

1  **I'm Telling You Now**
   Freddie & the Dreamers

2  **Stop! In the Name of Love**
   Supremes

3  **Can't You Hear My Heartbeat**
   Herman's Hermits

4  **Shotgun**
   Jr. Walker & the All Stars

5  **The Birds and the Bees**
   Jewel Akens

## 172 Game of Love FONTANA 1509
### WAYNE FONTANA AND THE MINDBENDERS

*Writer: Clint Ballard, Jr.*

*Producer: Not Known*

*April 24, 1965*
*1 week*

BEFORE he adopted the name Wayne Fontana, Glyn Ellis (born October 28, 1945, in Manchester, England) was advised by a school counselor to find a secure job, like a train driver. But it was too late—Ellis was already hooked on music, having formed his own skiffle band, the Velfins.

He dropped out of school and spent his days as an apprentice telephone engineer, but at night he performed with his first semi-professional group, the Jets, in Manchester's pubs and clubs. He adopted the name Wayne Fontana not from the label which would one day sign him, but from Elvis Presley's drummer, D.J. Fontana.

The Jets were playing at Manchester's Oasis Club when the manager arranged an audition for them with Jack Baverstock, a producer for Philips/Fontana Records.

The night of the audition, only Wayne and bass player Bob Lang showed up; certain disaster was averted when two friends in the audience, guitarist Eric Stewart and drummer Ric Rothwell, agreed to help out. Baverstock liked what he heard and in early 1963 the group was signed to Fontana. A horror film playing at the local cinema inspired Wayne to name his group the Mindbenders.

Their first British single was released in July, 1963, and featured Fats Domino's "My Girl Josephine" (retitled "Hello Josephine") on one side and Bo Diddley's "Roadrunner" on the other. It reached number 46 in the British chart, but the next two singles, cover versions of the Coasters' "Love Potion No. 9" and the Gladiolas' "Little Darlin'," failed to chart.

They continued to record covers of American tunes, including Ben E. King's "Stop, Look and Listen" and Gene Chandler's "Duke of Earl," but their first breakthrough at home was a version of Major Lance's "Um Um Um Um Um Um," which went to number five in the fall of 1964.

In America, where even musicians from Manchester were said to have the "Liverpool sound," "Game of Love" was the group's first single. It peaked at number two in Britain, but followed Manchester's Freddie and the Dreamers into the number one spot on the Hot 100 on April 24, 1965.

Together, Wayne Fontana and the Mindbenders had only one more stateside hit, the mid-chart single "It's Just a Little Bit Too Late." By the end of 1965, disagreements over musical directions caused a split. Wayne's solo career produced four U.K. chart entries, including "Pamela Pamela" which peaked at number 11, but he never made the Hot 100 again.

The Mindbenders fared better, recording "A Groovy Kind of Love," written by Toni Wine and Carole Bayer (Sager). It went to number two in Britain and America. The Mindbenders appeared in the film and on the soundtrack of *To Sir With Love*, but by the end of 1968 the group disbanded. Lang has a stereo equipment business and Rothwell is an antiques dealer. Stewart did session work until he formed Hotlegs with Graham Gouldman, Kevin Godley and Lol Creme. After one hit, "Neanderthal Man," the group became 10cc, who went to number two in 1975 with "I'm Not in Love."

Wayne Fontana owns the Mindbenders name now, and still performs in England, although he hasn't released any recorded material since the 1976 single "The Last Bus Home." He appeared at a concert celebrating BBC Radio 1's 15th birthday in 1982, where he sang "Game of Love."

## THE TOP FIVE
*Week of April 24, 1965*

1  **Game of Love**
   Wayne Fontana &
   the Mindbenders

2  **Mrs. Brown You've Got
   a Lovely Daughter**
   Herman's Hermits

3  **I'm Telling You Now**
   Freddie & The Dreamers

4  **I Know a Place**
   Petula Clark

5  **Stop! In the Name of Love**
   Supremes

*Writer: Trevor Peacock*

*Producer: Mickie Most*

*May 1, 1965*
*3 weeks*

"MRS. BROWN YOU'VE GOT A LOVELY DAUGHTER" entered *Billboard's* chart at number 12, the highest debut on the Hot 100 for any single to date. When it went to number one two weeks later, it completed a Mancunian hat trick, being the third number one single in a row for a group from Manchester, England. Liverpool may have produced the Beatles, but Manchester could lay claim to native-born groups like the Hollies, Freddie and the Dreamers and Wayne Fontana and the Mindbenders.

Herman's Hermits were much more successful in the United States than at home. In 1965, their chart domination was so strong, they had seven new entries on the Hot 100 in one calendar year. For six weeks, they had three songs in the top 30. The rush of Hermits records wasn't exactly planned; with "Can't You Hear My Heartbeat" moving down the chart, MGM chose to release "Sil-

houettes," an updating of the Rays' 1958 hit. Radio stations played it, but there was an even more enthusiastic response for "Mrs. Brown You've Got a Lovely Daughter," a cut from the album *Introducing Herman's Hermits*. MGM was forced to issue it as a single, and it's pre-release popularity was so great that the high chart entry position was assured.

"Mrs. Brown . . ." sounds like it might have been an old vaudevillian song from the London music hall days, but it was written in 1963 by Trevor Peacock and sung by actor Tom Courtenay in a British television play. Despite its enormous American success, "Mrs. Brown . . ." was never released as a single in Britain.

In 1967, the group starred in an MGM film, *Mrs. Brown You've Got a Lovely Daughter*, with actor Stanley Holloway, who portrayed Alfred P. Doolittle in *My Fair Lady*. The soundtrack included a new version of the title song.

The lead singer of Herman's Hermits was Peter Noone, born Peter Blair Denis Bernard Noone on November 5, 1947 in Liverpool. His father was a semi-professional musician who enrolled his son at the Manchester School of Music, where Peter studied music, singing and

drama. He worked as an actor, becoming a child star in the United Kingdom from his roles in the series "Knight Errant" and "Coronation Street," a long-running British soap opera.

Peter started playing music with a Manchester band, the Cyclones, who changed their name to the Heartbeats. Record producer Mickie Most saw Peter on "Coronation Street" and thought he resembled a young John F. Kennedy. The rest of the Heartbeats thought he looked more like Sherman, boy companion to Mr. Peabody (of Way-Bac machine fame) on "The Bullwinkle Show," and when producer Most approached them about recording, they changed their name to Herman and the Hermits, and later, Herman's Hermits.

The group roster changed during the metamorphosis from Heartbeats to Hermits, and the line-up that recorded "Mrs. Brown . . ." included guitarists Derek Leckenby and Keith Hopwood, bassist Karl Green and drummer Barry Whitwam. Most sources agree that the Hermits didn't actually play on their studio recordings, where the musical duties were handled by Jimmy Page and John Paul Jones, who would one day be the first two members of Led Zeppelin.

Herman's Hermits' first single for Most was "I'm Into Something Good," a Gerry Goffin-Carole King tune originally recorded by Earl Jean, lead singer of the Cookies. It was the Hermits' only British number one single, and also the only British number one for Goffin and King.

## THE TOP FIVE
*Week of May 1, 1965*

1. **Mrs. Brown You've Got a Lovely Daughter**
   Herman's Hermits

2. **Game of Love**
   Wayne Fontana &
   the Mindbenders

3. **I Know a Place**
   Petula Clark

4. **I'm Telling You Now**
   Freddie & the Dreamers

5. **I'll Never Find Another You**
   Seekers

# 174 Ticket to Ride CAPITOL 5407
## THE BEATLES

*Writers: John Lennon*
*Paul McCartney*

*Producer: George Martin*

*May 22, 1965*
*1 week*

SHARP-EYED BEATLE fans received their first clue to the title of the Beatles' second film when they bought a copy of "Ticket to Ride." The fine print under the writing credit for Lennon-McCartney read, "From the United Artists Release *Eight Arms to Hold You.*"

The Beatles never did write a song called "Eight Arms To Hold You," although a song by that title did appear in the 1985 film *The Goonies.* John Lennon wrote "Help!" [see 182], which became the movie's title song.

Lennon was responsible for writing "Ticket to Ride," a song the Beatles recorded in February, 1965, before leaving for the Bahamas to begin production of the film that would eventually be titled *Help!* John sang lead, with backing vocals by Paul McCartney and George Harrison. "Ticket to Ride" is the first Beatles single to feature McCartney on lead guitar, a responsibility usually handled by Harrison (McCartney also played lead guitar on "Another Girl," included in the *Help!* soundtrack and recorded around the same time as "Ticket to Ride").

Lennon wrote the flip side of "Ticket to Ride," titled "Yes It Is," and was featured on lead vocals, accompanied by John and George.

"Ticket to Ride" entered the Hot 100 at number 59 on April 24, 1965. "Yes It Is" debuted the following week at number 71. "Ticket to Ride" stalled on its way to the top, moving 58 to 18 to 3 to 3. It overcame Herman's Hermits' "Mrs. Brown You've Got a Lovely Daughter" the week of May 22 and became the Beatles' eighth number one single, remaining on top of the chart for just a solitary week. "Yes It Is" only managed to climb as high as number 46.

Three weeks after "Ticket to Ride" was number one, Queen Elizabeth II celebrated her birthday, an event marked by the annual announcement of new Members of the Order of the British Empire. On June 12, 1965, it was announced that the John Lennon, Paul McCartney, George Harrison and Ringo Starr were to receive MBEs. A wave of protests from more conservative holders of the MBE hit Buckingham Palace and the government of Prime Minister Harold Wilson. Some previous awardees returned their MBE medals.

"We thought getting the MBE was as funny as everybody else thought it was," John is quoted in Hunter Davies' biography *The Beatles.* ". . . We all met and thought it was daft . . . All we did when we were waiting in the Palace was giggle. We collapsed, the whole thing was so funny. There was this Guardsman telling us how to march, how many steps and how to curtsey when we met the Queen. We knew in our hearts she was just some woman, yet we were going through it all. We'd agreed to it."

On August 13, 1965, the Beatles' began their second tour of America. This tour was shorter than the first, lasting just 17 days. The highlight took place on August 23 when the Beatles played Shea Stadium in New York. There were more than 55,000 people in the audience, and the performance grossed $304,000, establishing a world record for one concert.

## THE TOP FIVE
*Week of May 22, 1965*

1 **Ticket to Ride**
Beatles

2 **Mrs. Brown You've Got a Lovely Daughter**
Herman's Hermits

3 **Count Me In**
Gary Lewis & the Playboys

4 **Help Me Rhonda**
Beach Boys

5 **I'll Never Find Another You**
Seekers

*Writer: Brian Wilson*

*Producer: Brian Wilson*

*May 29, 1965*
*2 weeks*

"HELP ME RHONDA," featuring the lead voice of rhythm guitarist Al Jardine, was originally a track on *The Beach Boys Today* album under an alternate spelling, "Help Me Ronda."

Jardine was a charter member of the Beach Boys, but he had quit the group after "Surfin' " was released on Candix Records. He had planned a secure future for himself as a dentist, and being in a rock and roll band that would probably break up after a few months of success was diverting him from that goal.

After "Surfin' U.S.A." was a top three single, Brian called Jardine and asked if he'd like to tour with the Beach Boys. He returned from his East Coast studies and re-joined the group permanently.

"Help Me Rhonda" entered the Hot 100 at number 80 on April 17, 1965. Just eight days earlier, Bruce Johnston became the sixth Beach Boy. The need for a new Beach Boy became apparent after Brian Wilson had a nervous breakdown on a flight to Houston on December 23, 1964. In his book *The Beach Boys*, John Tobler quotes Brian:

"I was run down mentally and emotionally because I was running around, jumping on jets from one city to another on one night stands, also producing, arranging, singing, planning, teaching, to the point where I had no peace of mind and no chance

### THE TOP FIVE
*Week of May 29, 1965*

1  **Help Me Rhonda**
   Beach Boys

2  **Ticket to Ride**
   Beatles

3  **Back in My Arms Again**
   Supremes

4  **Mrs. Brown You've Got
   a Lovely Daughter**
   Herman's Hermits

5  **Wooly Bully**
   Sam the Sham & the Pharaohs

to actually sit down and rest or think. . . . The plane had only been in the air five minutes when I told Al Jardine I was going to crack up any minute, but he told me to cool it. Then I started crying, I put a pillow over my face and began screaming and yelling. . . .

Brian's doctors advised him to stop touring to prevent further mental and physical damage. Aside from the stress, Brian suffered a hearing loss in his right ear, and the amplified music was causing further damage. During the recording of *The Beach Boys Today*, Brian broke the news that he would no longer tour with the Beach Boys.

For six months, his replacement on the road was guitarist Glen Campbell [see 415—"Rhinestone Cowboy"], but he never really fit in with the group, and when an illness forced him to drop out of a tour, he was replaced by Bruce Johnston.

Johnston (born June 27, 1944, in Peoria, Illinois) grew up in Santa Monica, California. By the time he was 16, he had worked with Richie Valens, Sandy Nelson and Bobby Vee [see 97—"Take Good Care of My Baby"]. He played in a band with Phil Spector, who asked him to show up for a recording session one night. Bruce was too young to drive and couldn't come, but the song recorded that evening became a number one hit [see 46—"To Know Him Is to Love Him"]. With his friend Terry Melcher, he formed a duo (Bruce and Terry) that recorded songs ("Custom Machine," "Summer Means Fun") that sounded like they came from the Beach Boys' songbook. He also produced and sang lead vocals on the Rip Chords' "Hey Little Cobra."

The first song Johnston recorded with the group was the follow-up to "Help Me Rhonda," called "California Girls." It sounded like a number one single, but it couldn't overcome Sonny and Cher [see 131—"I Got You Babe"] and the Beatles [see 182—"Help!"]. It stalled at number three.

# 176 Back in My Arms Again MOTOWN 1075
## THE SUPREMES

*Writers Brian Holland*
*Lamont Dozier*
*Eddie Holland*

*Producers: Brian Holland*
*Lamont Dozier*

*June 12, 1965*
*1 week*

*How can Mary tell me what to do,*
*When she's lost her love so true?*
*And Flo, she don't know,*
*'Cause the boy she loves is a Romeo...*\*

IF Diana Ross' singing partners had been named Emily and Hortense, it might have proven more difficult for songwriters Brian Holland, Lamont Dozier and Eddie Holland to work them into "Back in My Arms Again." Fortunately, Mary and Flo seemed to fit right in and provided an inside joke for Supremes' fans.

Recorded December 1, 1964—before "Stop! In the Name of Love"—"Back in My Arms Again"

entered the Hot 100 at number 68 on May 1, 1965. Six weeks later it became the Supremes' *fifth* consecutive number one single. To date, the Supremes are the only American group to have five consecutive chart-toppers. The only groups that have surpassed that total are the Beatles and the Bee Gees, with six consecutive number ones each.

By the summer of 1965, the two most powerful forces in rock and roll were the sounds of Liverpool and Detroit. Many people have tried to define the Motown sound. One of the best descriptions comes from Adam White, former editor of *Billboard*: "A bedrock bass line; an emphatic beat accentuated by tambourines; pounding percussion and piano tracks; saxophone-driven brass charts; shrill *femme* backup vocals in the classic call-and-response mode of gospel performances; and those swirling, riff-reinforcing strings of the Detroit Symphony."

Motown's highly-polished rhythm and blues helped to break down the barriers between white music and black music. Listening to a Supremes single like "Back in My Arms Again," one didn't think of it in terms of sounding black or sounding white. Diana Ross talked about the acceptance of the Supremes by white audiences with Gerri Hirshey, author of *Nowhere to Run*: "Someone said, and I agree with him, that the Supremes were such a crossover for young black and white males in our country because there were three black girls and they could openly enjoy them and even lust for them—without thinking what color they were."

Six weeks after "Back in My Arms Again" was number one, the Supremes made one of the ultimate crossovers—headlining at one of America's top venues, the Copacabana in Manhattan. Trained by Motown's army of charm school teachers, choreographers, make-up artists and fashion experts, the Supremes made their debut at the Copa on July 29, 1965. The critics loved the show as much as the opening night audience. J. Randy Taraborrelli quotes Diana's reaction in his biography, *Diana*: "I think what stands out in my mind most about the Copa is the feeling of respect that we'll never forget from those audiences. To be appreciated, to be respected...after you've worked so hard at it, dreamed about it for so long, was just a wonderful experience. It was the beginning of everything for us. We made it where it really counted...at the Copa!"

## THE TOP FIVE
### *Week of June 12, 1965*

1 **Back in My Arms Again**
Supremes

2 **Wooly Bully**
Sam the Sham & the Pharoahs

3 **Crying in the Chapel**
Elvis Presley

4 **I Can't Help Myself
(Sugar Pie Honey Bunch)**
Four Tops

5 **Help Me Rhonda**
Beach Boys

MOTOWN 1076 **I Can't Help Myself (Sugar Pie, Honey Bunch)** 177
THE FOUR TOPS

*Writers: Eddie Holland*
*Lamont Dozier*
*Brian Holland*

*Producers: Brian Holland*
*Lamont Dozier*
*Eddie Holland*

*June 19, 1965*
*2 weeks*

THE FOUR TOPS performed and recorded together for more than 40 years without any change in their original line-up. No other group with a number one single can make that same boast.

Their first chart-topper, "I Can't Help Myself (Sugar Pie, Honey Bunch)" was written by Eddie Holland, Lamont Dozier and Brian Holland while that trio was in the middle of an unprecedented hot streak with the Supremes, and was the first Motown single to succeed another Motown 45 at number one [see 176—"Back in My Arms Again"].

Lead vocalist Levi Stubbs recorded "I Can't Help Myself" and was unhappy with the results after a couple of takes, but producer Brian Holland insisted it was perfect. Levi was promised he could try again the next day, but there was no recording session the next day. "I Can't Help Myself" was released just as Brian heard it after the second take.

Levi Stubbs, Abdul "Duke" Fakir, Lawrence Payton and Renaldo "Obie" Benson were friends growing up in the North End section of Detroit. They played ball together, but they all sang with different groups. At high school parties, it was not unusual for someone to take the latest Ruth Brown record off the turntable and have someone get up

and sing. One night in 1954, a girl they all knew asked the four of them to sing together. Levi handled the lead while the others sang backing vocals, and it sounded so good, they met the next day at Duke's house where they rehearsed some songs and decided to form a quartet.

They called themselves the Four Aims and sang in local clubs until they signed with Chess Records in 1956. Their name was too similar to the Ames Brothers, and when their musical conductor asked how they picked the Four Aims, Duke replied they were "aiming" for the top. Their conductor suggested they call themselves the Four Tops.

Their lone Chess single, "Kiss Me Baby," failed and they signed with Red Top Records, where they had one more failure. Columbia Records signed the Four Tops and Aretha Franklin at the same time, but while Aretha lingered at the label for years without a smash hit, the Tops stayed for only one release, "Ain't That Love," in 1960.

In their native Detroit, Berry Gordy was just starting Motown Records and asked the group if they would like to sign with him. Being with a new black record company based in Detroit was the farthest thing from their minds, when New York conglomerates like CBS were interested in them. But after unproductive terms with record companies big and small, the Four Tops watched Motown grow with artists like Mary Wells, the Miracles and Marvin Gaye and decided to go back and see if Gordy was still interested in them.

He was, and paid them the $400 they asked for to sign a contract. The Four Tops were assigned to the

Workshop label and recorded a jazz album, *Breaking Through*. They also sang backing vocals for other Motown artists, and can be heard prominently on one of Holland-Dozier-Holland's first productions for the Supremes, "When the Lovelight Starts Shining Through His Eyes."

The Four Tops were with Motown for a year without any successful results. One night in 1964 they were playing at a Detroit club popular with Motown artists, the 20 Grand, when Brian Holland called and asked them to come to the studio when they finished working. It was 2 a.m. when Eddie Holland sang "Baby I Need Your Loving" for them, the song they recorded that night. It was the Tops' first Hot 100 hit, reaching number 11. They had two follow-ups in the same vein, "Without the One You Love" and "Ask the Lonely," when Holland-Dozier-Holland gave them "I Can't Help Myself," a song that defines "the Motown sound" in two minutes and 43 seconds.

## THE TOP FIVE
*Week of June 19, 1965*

1 **I Can't Help Myself (Sugar Pie Honey Bunch)**
Four Tops

2 **Mr. Tambourine Man**
Byrds

3 **Wooly Bully**
Sam the Sham & the Pharaohs

4 **Crying in the Chapel**
Elvis Presley

5 **Back in My Arms Again**
Supremes

## 178 Mr. Tambourine Man COLUMBIA 43271
### THE BYRDS

*Writer: Bob Dylan*

*Producer: Terry Melcher*

*June 26, 1965*
*1 week*

BEFORE the Byrds recorded "Mr. Tambourine Man," there was folk music and there was rock music. Electrifying Bob Dylan's song with a 12-string Rickenbacker guitar, the Byrds created an amalgam of folk rock music that influenced and spawned a generation of musicians and supergroups, including Crosby, Stills and Nash; the Eagles; the Flying Burrito Brothers; and the New Riders of the Purple Sage.

Jim McGuinn was inspired to get his first electric 12-string guitar after he saw George Harrison play one in *A Hard Day's Night*. It was during that summer of 1964 that McGuinn met Gene Clark at the Troubadour in Los Angeles.

McGuinn went on to tour with the Chad Mitchell Trio, and then played 12-string guitar and banjo for Bobby Darin, who included several folk songs in his Las Vegas act. McGuinn played on sessions for Judy Collins and Hoyt Axton, but once he was aware of the Beatles he knew he wanted to form his own group.

Clark had played in a Kansas City high school band called the Sharks, and then worked with a folk group in that city, the Surf Riders. Still 17, he joined the New Christy Minstrels and was with them for a year until he, too, heard the Beatles and knew he wanted to pursue a different musical course.

McGuinn and Clark teamed up with David Crosby, who had been working as a solo artist after spending some time with Les Baxter's Balladeers, a folk quartet that entertained while Baxter's orchestra took their break. Crosby introduced McGuinn and Clark to A&R man Jim Dickson, who produced some demos for them under the name the Jet Set.

To play bass, Dickson recruited Chris Hillman, who played bluegrass mandolin with his own band, the Hillmen. Crosby found drummer Mike Clarke and with all five members in place, they recorded new demos which would eventually be released on an album called *Preflyte*.

Thanks to Dickson, the quintet recorded a single for Elektra Records, "Please Let Me Love You." A label executive suggested their name, the Beefeaters, which was quickly abandoned when their option to record an album wasn't picked up. Dickson then signed the group to Columbia Records, a label that hadn't ventured very far into·the new wave of rock and roll that had begun with the Beatles.

Columbia's youngest producer was Terry Melcher, son of singer Doris Day, and he was assigned to work on the Byrds' first album. In the first batch of demos the band recorded, they had included "Mr. Tambourine Man," a song Dickson urged them to cut after Dylan had given him a dub of it.

For their first Columbia album, "Mr. Tambourine Man" was re-recorded, but the group did not play on the track. Without the luxury of unlimited studio time, Dickson and Melcher hired the best session musicians they could find—guitarists Leon Russell and Glen Campbell, drummer Hal Blaine and bassist Larry Knechtel. The only Byrd playing on the track is McGuinn, who added his electric 12-string Rickenbacker and sang lead while Crosby and Clark added harmony vocals.

### THE TOP FIVE
*Week of June 26, 1965*

1 **Mr. Tambourine Man**
Byrds

2 **I Can't Help Myself
(Sugar Pie Honey Bunch)**
Four Tops

3 **Wooly Bully**
Sam the Sham & the Pharaohs

4 **(I Can't Get No) Satisfaction**
Rolling Stones

5 **Wonderful World**
Herman's Hermits

*Writers: Mick Jagger*
*Keith Richard*

*Producer: Andrew Loog Oldham*

*July 10, 1965*
*4 weeks*

THE YEAR WAS 1965, the place was a hotel room in Clearwater, Florida, and the man having trouble sleeping was Keith Richard, lead guitarist and co-songwriter of the Rolling Stones. Insomnia has its benefits, and the reward for the restless Stone that night was a chord progression that came to his fingers. The next morning, when he played the guitar riff back on his portable cassette recorder for songwriting partner Mick Jagger, he offered some words to go with it: "I can't get no satisfaction."

"That was just a working title," Keith told Philip Norman, author of the Rolling Stones biography *Sym-*

phony for the Devil. "I never thought it was anything commercial enough to be a single." Fortunately, no one else agreed. On May 10, 1965, the Stones checked in to Chess studios in Chicago, where they recorded four songs for their *Out of Our Heads* album plus the first take of "Satisfaction." The next day, they flew to Los Angeles and completed the song during an 18-hour recording session at RCA studios in Hollywood.

"We were very comfortable there," remembers Andrew Loog Oldham, the Stones' manager and producer at the time. With Dave Hassinger on the board, the song rolled out fast and smooth. "As there'd already been a bash made, they knew where to put the meat and potatoes. When they're right, they go very easily," says Oldham. "I never had any doubts about it." Keith continued to argue that the song wasn't strong enough for an "A" side—he wanted his riff, which he acknowledged was inspired by Martha and the Vandellas' "Dancing in the Street," to be played by a horn section. But his misgivings were overruled and "Satisfaction" became the Rolling Stones' first number one single in America.

The British quintet was formed during the early 60s blues/trad jazz scene in London, and they took their name from a Muddy Waters song. The nucleus of the group, Mick Jagger (born Michael Phillip Jagger on July 26, 1943, in Dartford, England) and Keith Richard (born Keith Richards on December 18, 1943, in

Dartford, England), first met at Maypole County Primary School. They met again when Mick was attending the London School of Economics and Keith was a student at Sidcup Art School. Keith joined Mick's group, Little Boy Blue and the Blue Boys, which also included original Rolling Stone bassist Dick Taylor.

Brian Jones (born Lewis Brian Hopkins-Jones on February 28, 1942 in Cheltenham, England) was singing with Alexis Korner's Blues, Incorporated, an outfit that later included drummer Charlie Watts (born June 2, 1941, in the London district of Islington). Brian started his own band, which included pianist Ian Stewart, who would also become a charter Rolling Stone. Mick and Keith started jamming with Korner and were introduced to Jones and Stewart.

Mick had become the vocalist for Blues, Incorporated, by the time they were invited to guest on the BBC's "Jazz Club" radio show. But the program's budget only allowed for six of the seven members of the band, so Jagger was not invited to join the broadcast. While Korner and company were jamming on the radio, Jagger put a group together to fill in for Blues, Incorporated, at the Marquee Club. The date was July 12, 1962, and the line-up of Jagger, Richard, Jones, Taylor, Stewart and drummer Mick Avory marked the first-ever appearance of the Rolling Stones. Avory and Taylor departed soon after, to be replaced by drummer Tony Chapman and bassist Bill Wyman (born October 24, 1936, in London). By January, 1963, Chapman left and Watts had taken his place.

## THE TOP FIVE
*Week of July 10, 1965*

1 **(I Can't Get No) Satisfaction**
Rolling Stones

2 **I Can't Help Myself (Sugar Pie Honey Bunch)**
Four Tops

3 **Mr. Tambourine Man**
Byrds

4 **Wonderful World**
Herman's Hermits

5 **Wooly Bully**
Sam the Sham & the Pharaohs

# 180

## I'm Henry VIII, I Am  MGM 13367
### HERMAN'S HERMITS

*Writers: Fred Murray*
*R.P. Weston*

*Producer: Mickie Most*

*August 7, 1965*
*1 week*

AFTER the success of their first number one single [see 173—"Mrs. Brown You've Got a Lovely Daughter"], Herman's Hermits searched for another song with the same music-hall sound of turn-of-the-century London. Actually, "Mrs. Brown..." just sounded like an old song, but had been written only two years before the Hermits recorded it. For a sequel, the group found an authentic music hall song written in 1911 by Fred Murray and R.P. Weston and popularized by Cockney comedian Harry Champion. It was the infectious "I'm Henry VIII, I Am," a song too ethnic to make the British chart, despite its number one success in America.

MGM was releasing Herman's Hermits singles so fast that the actual follow-up to "Mrs. Brown..." was a new version of Sam Cooke's "Wonderful World," which entered the Hot 100 just six weeks after "Mrs. Brown..." did. "I'm Henry VIII, I Am" entered the chart on July 3, 1965, and was on top five weeks later.

Before 1965 ended, the group had two more hits: "Just a Little Bit Better," which peaked at seven, and "A Must to Avoid" (written by American songwriters P.F. Sloan and Steve Barri for the film *Hold On*), which peaked at eight.

Herman's Hermits continued to

have hits in America for three more years. Despite being labelled a teenybopper group that only appealed to adolescents, they worked with some of Britain's most respected musicians and writers. Aside from working with Jimmy Page and John Paul Jones in the studio, the Hermits recorded songs by Ray Davies of the Kinks ("Dandy"), Donovan ("Museum") and fellow Mancunian Graham Gouldman ("No Milk Today"), who would later be a part of 10cc.

Their final top 10 single was 1967's "There's a Kind of Hush," and their final American chart appearance was "Sleepy Joe" in 1968. In Britain, they had seven more chart hits, before fading from the scene in 1970 with "Lady Barbara," which credited the group as Peter Noone and Herman's Hermits.

The final split was not amicable. Noone took legal action to prevent the group from using the name Herman's Hermits, but lost. They did reunite with Noone for a 1973 tour with the Searchers, Gerry and the

Pacemakers, Billy J. Kramer and the Dakotas, and Wayne Fontana and the Mindbenders, which culminated with an SRO concert at Madison Square Garden. After that tour, the group—minus Herman—recorded for Buddah Records as Herman's Hermits.

Peter pursued a solo career and had one hit single in the United Kingdom, a version of David Bowie's "Oh You Pretty Thing" which featured Bowie on piano. Peter moved to the south of France with his wife, Mirelle, and wrote songs that were recorded by artists such as Debby Boone and Deniece Williams. Later, he moved to New York and opened a clothing boutique, and by the early 1980s was performing again with a group called the Tremblers. After they split, Peter recorded a solo album for a label owned by Beach Boy Bruce Johnston [see 175—"Help Me Rhonda"]. In 1982, he received good reviews for his portrayal of Frederic in the London West End staging of Gilbert and Sullivan's *The Pirates of Penzance*.

## THE TOP FIVE
### Week of August 7, 1965

1  **I'm Henry VIII, I Am**
   Herman's Hermits

2  **(I Can't Get No) Satisfaction**
   Rolling Stones

3  **What's New Pussycat?**
   Tom Jones

4  **Save Your Heart For Me**
   Gary Lewis & the Playboys

5  **I Got You Babe**
   Sonny & Cher

*Writer: Sonny Bono*

*Producer: Sonny Bono*

*August 14, 1965*
*3 weeks*

Sᴀʟᴠᴀᴛᴏʀᴇ Pʜɪʟʟɪᴘ Bᴏɴᴏ met Cher-ilyn Sakisian LaPierre at a coffee shop next to radio station KFWB in Hollywood. It was a popular hang-out for folks in the record business, and Bono had been working in the industry for several years. Born in Detroit (February 16, 1935), his family moved to Inglewood, California, when Sonny was a teenager. He had wanted to sing since he was a youngster, and wrote his first song while working as a stockboy in a grocery store. It was inspired by a new brand of cookies, Koko Jo, and years later the Righteous Brothers had a local hit with "Koko Joe" in Los Angeles.

In 1957, Sonny went to work for Specialty Records, where he wrote and produced for Don and Dewey, and Larry Williams. Among his early, memorable songs are "She Said Yeah," recorded by Williams and later covered by the Rolling Stones; and "Needles and Pins" which he co-wrote with Jack Nitsche for Jackie DeShannon. It was an international hit in 1964 for the Searchers.

When Sonny met Cher, he was working for producer Phil Spector. "I was a general flunky for Phillip," says Sonny. "I was his West Coast promotion man, I sang background and I hired the musicians and back-ground singers." Sonny knew that Cher (she was 16, but told him she was 18) wanted to sing, and brought her to Spector sessions to join him in backing vocals. Among the classic recordings they worked on were "Da Doo Ron Ron" by the Crystals, "Be My Baby" by the Ronettes and "You've Lost That Lovin' Feelin'" [see 166] by the Righteous Brothers, as well as Spector's legendary Christmas album, *A Gift for You.*

Sonny asked Phil to produce records for Cher, but aside from one obscure single, "Ringo, I Love You" released under the name Bonnie Jo Mason on Annette Records, Spector declined.

Sonny then borrowed $135 to produce his own session for Cher at RCA's Hollywood studios. At the last minute, a nervous Cher asked Sonny to sing on the record with her, so "Baby Don't Go" was recorded as a duet. Bono took the completed track to Spector. "The best way I knew how to tell if a record was a hit or not was to play it for Phil. If Phil wanted to buy it, you knew you had a hit." Spector offered Sonny $500 for half of the publishing rights.

At the same time, Cher was signed to Imperial as a solo artist. Her first release was "Dream Baby," a Spector soundalike released under her real name, Cherilyn. Meanwhile, Ahmet Ertegun at Atlantic was interested in signing both of them. Reprise had several of their songs, but no contracts had been signed, so as "Sonny and Cher" they went to Atco Records.

Their first single was to be "Sing C'est la Vie," but it was relegated to the flip side of "Just You," a Spec-torish ballad. Next came a song written in their Laurel Canyon home. "I Got You Babe" was recorded quickly, and Sonny was sure it was a smash. He sent the recording to Ertegun in New York, and Ahmet called to say how much he loved the new single—"It's Gonna Rain." Sonny was thunderstruck—that was the flip side. "I said, 'Ahmet, get serious!'"

Ahmet was not to be persuaded. He was going to release "It's Gonna Rain." Sonny headed him off at the pass by taking "I Got You Babe" to radio station KHJ in Hollywood, where program director Ron Jacobs promised to play it once an hour, if he could have it exclusively. He did, and it was an immediate smash.

On November 13, 1987, Sonny and Cher appeared together on "Late Night With David Letterman." After much coaxing from Dave, the couple sang "I Got You Babe" for the first time in 10 years. "It was a really nice way to bring it full circle," Cher said in *People* magazine. "Sonny got emotional just watching me sing. People could finally see there is no animosity."

On January 5, 1998, Rep. Sonny Bono (R-Palm Springs) was killed when he crashed into a tree while skiing at a resort in South Lake Tahoe, Calif. He was 62.

## THE TOP FIVE
*Week of August 14, 1965*

1  **I Got You Babe**
   Sonny & Cher

2  **(I Can't Get No)**
   **Satisfaction**
   Rolling Stones

3  **Save Your Heart For Me**
   Garry Lewis & the Playboys

4  **I'm Henry VIII, I Am**
   Herman's Hermits

5  **What's New Pussycat?**
   Tom Jones

# Help! CAPITOL 5476
## THE BEATLES

*Writers: John Lennon*
*Paul McCartney*

*Producer: George Martin*

*September 4, 1965*
*3 weeks*

"**W**HEN *Help!* came out in '65, I was actually crying out for help," John Lennon told David Sheff in a 1980 interview for *Playboy*. "Most people think it's just a fast rock 'n' roll song. I didn't realize it at the time; I just wrote the song because I was commissioned to write it for the movie. But later, I knew I really was crying out for help. It was my fat Elvis period. You see the movie: He—I—is very fat, very insecure, and he's completely lost himself. And I am singing about when I was so much younger and all the rest, looking back at how easy it was . . . I was fat and depressed and I *was* crying out for help."

In an interview with Jann Wenner of *Rolling Stone* conducted December 8, 1970, in New York City, Lennon described "Help!" and "Strawberry Fields Forever" [see 220] as "personal records." "They were the ones I always considered my best songs," John said. "They were the ones I really wrote from experience and not projecting myself into a situation and writing a nice story about it." Later in the interview, Lennon said of "Help!": "The lyric is as good now as it was then. It is no different, and it makes me feel secure to know that I was that aware of myself then. It was just me singing 'Help,' and I meant it. I don't like the recording that we did; we did it too fast trying to be commercial."

"Help!" was recorded April 13, 1965. The single entered the Hot 100 at number 41 on August 7, 1965, two weeks before the film premiered in New York. On September 4, "Help!" became the Beatles' ninth American chart-topper.

*Help!* was directed by Richard Lester, the man who guided the Beatles through their first film, *A Hard Day's Night* [see 153]. Filmed in color in the Bahamas, the town of Obertauren in Austria, the Salisbury Plain in England and a London soundstage, the movie also starred Leo McKern, Eleanor Bron, Victor Spinetti and Roy Kinnear. Walter Shenson was producer and the script was credited to Marc Behm and Charles Wood.

The plot revolved around Ringo, intended victim of a madcap scientist willing to go to any extreme to recover a ring from the drummer's finger. Figuring prominently in the story was the eight-armed God Kali, an ominous figure that helped inspire the double-entendre original title of the film, *Eight Arms to Hold You* [see 174—"Ticket to Ride"]. The soundtrack included the previous single "Ticket to Ride," as well as five new songs: "The Night Before," "You've Got to Hide Your Love Away," "I Need You," "Another Girl" and "You're Going to Lose That Girl" (listed as You're Gonna Lose That Girl" on the American soundtrack album).

"Help!" had its Royal World Premiere on July 29. *Billboard* reported in the August 14 issue: "About 10,000 screaming fans mobbed London's Piccadilly Circus Thursday when the Beatles arrived for the premiere of *Help!*, their second movie. Some 200 police attempted to restrain the crowd. Ambulances were summoned to take away the casualties as 14 girls fainted. The quartet received louder cheers than Princess Margaret, the chief guest in the star-studded audience."

*Help!* had its American premiere on August 3. There would be more Beatle movies: *Magical Mystery Tour* had its premiere on British television on December 26, 1967; the animated *Yellow Submarine* opened in 1968; and the documentary *Let It Be* [see 271] chronicled the last days of the Beatles.

There was to be a third Beatles feature after *Help!* but it never materialized. As *Billboard* reported in the December 11, 1965 issue: "Plans for the Beatles third film are grinding to a halt. The group set aside three months in the spring to make the picture, but as yet no story has been approved. The Beatles were supposed to film Richard Condon's western novel *A Talent for Loving*, partly on location in Spain beginning around April 1, but the group has found preliminary scripts unacceptable. Producer Walter Shenson, who will again make the film for United Artists, commented, 'It's not even sure that we will do *A Talent for Loving* now; with the present situation we would be lucky to get it going in April.'"

## THE TOP FIVE
*Week of September 4, 1965*

1 **Help**
 Beatles

2 **Like a Rolling Stone**
 Bob Dylan

3 **California Girls**
 Beach Boys

4 **Unchained Melody**
 Righteous Brothers

5 **It's the Same Old Song**
 Four Tops

*Writers: P.F. Sloan*
*Steve Barri*

*Producers: P.F. Sloan*
*Steve Barri*

*September 25, 1965*
*1 week*

*"McGuinn and McGuire were just*
*getting higher.*
*In L.A., you know where that's at..."*
*CREEQUE ALLEY**

**B**ARRY MCGUIRE EARNED HIS mention in the Mamas and the Papas' "Creeque Alley" after he brought them to Dunhill Records owner Lou Adler, who was immediately taken with the group's harmonies and songs. He signed them and had them sing backing vocals for McGuire's album before recording their own hits [see 198—"Monday, Monday"].

McGuire was one of the first artists signed to the newly-formed Dunhill label. He had been with the New Christy Minstrels since they were organized by Randy Sparks in 1962, and had sung lead on their hits "Green, Green" and "Saturday

Night." He had also written "Greenback Dollar," a hit for the Kingston Trio.

Adler turned to his staff writers, Philip "Flip" Sloan and Steve Barri, to come up with material for McGuire to record. Sloan and Barri were accustomed to writing songs on assignment: they could write surfing songs, hot rod songs, whatever was needed. At one point, they had recorded their own album of surf songs as the Fantastic Baggys and had a Southern California hit with "Tell 'Em I'm Surfin'," but Barri was a reluctant performer and preferred his role as a writer/producer.

In 1965, Bob Dylan broke through commercially, and as his "Like a Rolling Stone" climbed the charts, there was suddenly a market for "protest songs." Strongly influenced by Dylan, Sloan wrote "Eve of Destruction" and brought it to Barri, who suggested they play it for Adler.

"Lou liked it, but not as much as a few other things we had written for Barry," Steve remembers. "It was really done as a 'B' side." Adler told Sloan and Barri to record McGuire's rough vocal on the instrumental track, so Barry could hear it before

he recorded the final mix.

"The next morning, we played it for (Dunhill vp) Jay Lasker, who loved it and thought it was a smash," Steve says. "We said...'Lou doesn't like this side as much as the other. We left the tape with Jay, which was a big mistake. He had some promotion guy take it over to KFWB."

Two hours later, Adler was driving to the office when he heard "Eve of Destruction" on the radio. KFWB had made it a pick of the week, and Adler was angry. He didn't know the song was finished. Actually it wasn't—KFWB was playing the rough mix. Barry never finished his vocals for "Eve of Destruction." The record that was released and went to number one on September 25, 1965, was the rough mix that Sloan and Barri put together at four o'clock in the morning.

"Eve of Destruction," which summed up ills both foreign and domestic in less than three minutes, was controversial enough to be banned by some radio stations, although many withstood a wave of conservative complaints about the lyrical content. John Madara and Dave White, songwriters responsible for hits like Danny and the Juniors' "At the Hop" [see 32], Lesley Gore's "You Don't Own Me" and Len Barry's "1-2-3," wrote a right-wing answer record, "Dawn of Correction," which they recorded as the Spokesmen.

While he gave Dunhill its first number one single, Barry's star faded after "Eve of Destruction." He only had two more chart entries, and in the '70s became a born-again Christian, recording some albums of gospel songs.

## THE TOP FIVE
*Week of September 25, 1965*

1  **Eve of Destruction**
   Barry McGuire

2  **Hang On Sloopy**
   McCoys

3  **You Were on My Mind**
   We Five

4  **Catch Us If You Can**
   Dave Clark Five

5  **Help**
   Beatles

# 184 Hang on Sloopy BANG 506
## THE MCCOYS

*Writers: Bert Russell*
*Wes Farrell*

*Producers: Bob Feldman*
*Jerry Goldstein*
*Richard Gottehrer*

*October 2, 1965*
*1 week*

RICK ZEHRINGER started playing music when he was nine years old, and as a teenager in Ohio formed a band with his younger brother Randy. When they moved to Indiana, neighbor Dennis Kelly made the group a trio. The first song Rick taught Dennis to play on the bass guitar was a song from a Ventures album called "The McCoy." Rick figured they could use that as a theme song, so they named the group the McCoys.

The name didn't last. In the tradition of the Bill Black Combo, the group decided to call themselves the Rick Z. Combo. A couple of record promoters liked the band but hated the name, so it was changed to Rick and the Raiders, and they released their first single, "You Know That I Love You," on the Sonic label.

Pianist/organist Ronnie Brandon joined the group, and when Dennis left for college, bass player Randy Hobbs was added. The group played proms, sock hops and local clubs, usually startling the headline acts because they knew the material so well. In 1965, the band—still called Rick and the Raiders—opened for the Strangeloves, a trio signed to a New York label, Bang Records. Bang Records was a new label that had originally been started by Bert Berns, Ahmet Ertegun, Neshui Ertegun and Gerald Wexler. Berns, born Burt Russell, was the writer of many rock hits, including "Twist and Shout," "Piece of My Heart," "Here Comes the Night," "Brown-Eyed Girl" and a 1964 hit for the R&B group the Vibrations, "My Girl Sloopy."

Berns thought the last song could be a hit if it was recorded by four guys with Beatle haircuts. He told the Strangeloves to keep an eye out on their tour for a group that would fill the bill. On the last night of the tour, the Strangeloves played Dayton. They had not found anyone to sing Bert's song. But their back-up band was Rick and the Raiders.

After the show, the Strangeloves asked Rick and his group if they'd like to go to New York the next day and record "My Girl Sloopy." Rick and Randy's parents were to start their vacation then, so 16-year-old Rick said yes.

By this time, Paul Revere and the Raiders were having some local success, so the group name had to be changed again. Looking through old family photo albums, one of their producers spotted a picture of the group in its earliest days with "the McCoys" written on the drum. He loved the name and said he would find an all-girl group called the Hatfields (he didn't).

Two other names were changed: "My Girl Sloopy" became "Hang on Sloopy" and Rick D. Zehringer dropped the "Z" to become Rick Derringer. He said the idea came to him in a dream, and he was inspired by the small picture of a derringer on the Bang Records label. He also wanted a name that would be similar to his own so his family could be proud of his success.

The McCoys had eight chart records on Bang, then switched to Mercury Records in 1968. A year later, their record fortunes faded, they became the house band for a popular Times Square nightclub, Steve Paul's Scene. In 1974, Rick released his first solo album on Blue Sky Records, a label owned by Steve Paul. His first hit single from the LP was "Rock and Roll, Hoochie Koo." In 1975, Derringer released his own version of "Hang on Sloopy," which peaked at number 94.

## THE TOP FIVE
*Week of October 2, 1965*

1 **Hang On Sloopy**
  McCoys

2 **Eve of Destruction**
  Barry McGuire

3 **Yesterday**
  Beatles

4 **Catch Us If You Can**
  Dave Clark Five

5 **You Were on My Mind**
  We Five

*Writers: John Lennon*
*Paul McCartney*

*Producer: George Martin*

*October 9, 1965*
*4 weeks*

"**Y**ESTERDAY" is actually the first solo single by a Beatle. John Lennon, George Harrison and Ringo Starr were not in the studio when Paul McCartney recorded his composition, playing an acoustic guitar and backed by a string quartet. In the 54th anniversary issue of *The Hollywood Reporter*, Rod Granger quoted McCartney talking about "Yesterday."

"I just fell out of bed and that was there. I have a piano by the side of my bed and just got up and played the chords. I thought I must have heard it the night before or something, and spent about three weeks asking all the music people I knew, 'What is this song?' I couldn't believe I'd written it."

Paul described the evolution of "Yesterday" to Paul Gambaccini in a 1974 *Rolling Stone* interview: "I did the tune first and wrote words . . . later. I called that 'Scrambled Egg' for a long time. I didn't have any words to it."

Producer George Martin suggested that Paul record the song with a string quartet. "I said, 'Are you kidding? This is a rock group.' I hated the idea," McCartney told Granger. "He said, 'Well, let's try it and if you hate it, we can just wipe it and go back to you and the guitar.' So I sat at the piano and worked out the arrangements with George, and we did it, and, of course, we liked it."

"Yesterday" was recorded during late May–early June of 1965, and first saw the light of day on side two of the British *Help!* soundtrack. The song was not included on the American album, but was released instead as a single, backed with a cover version of Buck Owens' "Act Naturally," featuring Ringo Starr on lead vocals.

"Yesterday" was not released as a Beatles single in Britain until 1976, when it peaked at number eight. Because the Beatles passed over "Yesterday" in 1965, Matt Monro released a cover version of it as a single, and it also peaked at number eight.

It was the first of over 2,500 cover versions of the song, making it the most covered song in history, according to *The Guinness Book of World Records*.

McCartney does not own the copyright on "Yesterday," and had to ask permission from the publisher to include it in his 1984 film *Give My Regards to Broad Street*. He told Jan Etherington of Britain's *TV Times* how he and director Peter Webb came up with the sequence that featured the song:

"When we were kids, if you had to walk to somebody's house, you always had your guitar with you, 'cos you were going to practice together. I was telling Peter that we would wander along singing songs and showing off to the girls on our way to John's house or mine, and Peter said, 'We could do a busking scene in the film.' So we use it as kind of dream sequence . . . The crew took me to Leicester Square one night, grotted me up with mud from the car park, ripped me jeans and stood me on a corner . . . So there I was, playing a lousy, honky-tonk version of 'Yesterday' and having money thrown at me by the unsuspecting public. The money I made went straight to the Seamen's Mission. An old Scottish drunk unloaded all his small change at my feet, put his arm round me and said, 'Awright, son, yer doin' greet.' "

## THE TOP FIVE
*Week of October 9, 1965*

1 **Yesterday**
Beatles

2 **Hang On Sloopy**
McCoys

3 **Treat Her Right**
Roy Head

4 **Eve of Destruction**
Barry McGuire

5 **The "In" Crowd**
Ramsey Lewis Trio

# 186 Get Off of My Cloud LONDON 9792
## THE ROLLING STONES

*Writers: Mick Jagger*
*Keith Richards*

*Producer: Andrew Loog Oldham*

*November 6, 1965*
*2 weeks*

"Get Off of My Cloud," the Rolling Stones' second American number one single [see 179—"(I Can't Get No) Satisfaction"], proved the English quintet was not a one-hit wonder among the many British pop groups vying for chart attention in 1965. Keith Richards told biographer Philip Norman, "It's difficult to realize what pressure we were under to keep turning out hits. Each single you made in those days had to be better *and* do better. If the next one didn't do as well as the last one, everyone told you you were sliding out. It got to be a state of mind. Every eight weeks you had to come up with a red-hot song that said it all in two minutes, 30 seconds."

"Get Off of My Cloud" was the eighth Stones single released in the U.S. The first two British 45s, cover versions of Chuck Berry's "Come On" and John Lennon/Paul McCartney's "I Wanna Be Your Man," were passed over in America. The third British single, a remake of Buddy Holly's "Not Fade Away," became their first American release, charting at number 48.

It was followed by the first song Mick Jagger and Keith Richards wrote together, "Tell Me (You're Coming Back)," which fared better on the Hot 100, peaking at number 24. A cover of the Valentinos' "It's All Over Now" did almost as well, reaching number 26. Then came the band's first top 10 single, "Time Is on My Side," a number six hit in the autumn of 1964. "Heart of Stone" went to number 19 and "The Last Time" climbed to number nine, but the Rolling Stones were not in the same class as the Beatles, yet. Their reign as the second most popular British group of the rock era didn't begin until "(I Can't Get No) Satisfaction" went to number one.

"Get Off of My Cloud" was the first disc to be issued under the Stones' renegotiated contract with Decca Records in the U.K. That pact reportedly gave the group the best royalty rate of the day. Scoring the coup was New York accountant Allen Klein [see 162—"Mr. Lonely"], introduced to the Stones by Andrew Loog Oldham to insure the band would receive all the money they could possibly earn from their artistic endeavors.

Klein's role was to organize the fall 1965 American tour so it would not be a repeat of their earlier U.S. tours. "They played state fairs in Texas with Bobby Vee, Diane Renay and a big fish tank in front of the stage where there'd been performing seals in the afternoon," according to Oldham. "Or there were shows where it was so bad, the promoters didn't show up."

Under Klein's direction, the band traveled by private plane or fleets of cars and vans, and lodged in hotels with tight security. The careful attention to logistics was crucial, as "Satisfaction" and "Get Off of My Cloud" had lifted the Stones into the rarefied strata of British supergroups. Upon their arrival in New York in October, the roofs of their Cadillac limousines were nearly crushed by the weight of young girls desperate to follow the Stones into their hotel. The plug had to be pulled on several concerts when the fainting, screaming fans alarmed local authorities unaccustomed to witnessing mass adulation of rock and roll musicians.

## THE TOP FIVE
*Week of November 6, 1965*

1  **Get Off of My Cloud**
   The Rolling Stones

2  **A Lover's Concerto**
   The Toys

3  **Yesterday**
   The Beatles

4  **Everybody Loves a Clown**
   Gary Lewis & the Playboys

5  **Keep On Dancing**
   The Gentrys

*Writers: Brian Holland*
*Lamont Dozier*
*Eddie Holland*

*Producers: Brian Holland*
*Lamont Dozier*

*November 20, 1965*
*2 weeks*

FOLLOWING their unprecedented fifth consecutive number one single [see 176—"Back in My Arms Again"], the Supremes released a track from their *More Hits by the Supremes* album as their new 45. "Nothing But Heart-aches" was anxiously watched by the group's fans to see if they could pull off the impossible and stretch their run of chart-toppers to six. This time, the answer was no. "Nothing But Heartaches," another in a series of Brian Holland, Lamont Dozier and Eddie Holland productions, didn't even make the top 10. It stalled at number 11.

"That was humiliating," Dozier admits. "That was considered a flop

for us. We had failed." Of course, it wasn't too bad when one considered that of the first eight Supremes singles, only one had climbed higher than number 75.

"We learned humility and we realized there is down side to everything. We were still kids and we were still learning about life. It helped us in our writing," says Dozier. The relative failure of "Nothing But Heartaches" did frighten the production trio. "We started frantically looking for new ideas. The question came up, (was it) time to shift the Supremes and give them to someone else. Well, what happened was they were opened up to other producers.

"Nobody came up with anything, and finally we pulled out another one—'I Hear a Symphony.' Brian was playing this melody...it was sounding sort of classical to me. Eddie took it and ran with the lyrics."

"I Hear a Symphony" was recorded September 22, 1965. It entered the Hot 100 on October 30 at number 39, the highest new entry position yet for a Supremes single.

Doubts about the Supremes' longevity were dispelled rapidly, as the record moved 39-12-5 to number one.

The next release was "My World Is Empty Without You," recorded October 28, 1965. It entered the Hot 100 on January 15, 1966, at number 78. Four weeks later it was in the top 10, and it seemed to have the momentum to carry it all the way to number one. Instead, it peaked the following week at number five.

Next came "Love Is Like an Itching in My Heart," recorded June 23, 1965, before "I Hear a Symphony" and "My World Is Empty Without You." It entered the Hot 100 at number 62 on April 30, 1966, and was in the top 10 just three weeks later. Then it stalled at nine, the first time the Supremes had two consecutive singles that failed to go to number one since before "Where Did Our Love Go."

Still, it was hardly the end of the Supremes. They had only collected half of their total of number one singles. The girls from the Brewster Projects were just beginning.

## THE TOP FIVE
*Week of November 20, 1965*

1 **I Hear a Symphony**
Supremes

2 **1-2-3**
Lon Barry

3 **Get Off of My Cloud**
Rolling Stones

4 **Rescue Me**
Fontella Bass

5 **Let's Hang On**
Four Seasons

**188** | # Turn! Turn! Turn! COLUMBIA 43424
THE BYRDS

Writer: Pete Seeger

Producer: Terry Melcher

December 4, 1965
3 weeks

NUMBER one songs like "The Yellow Rose of Texas" and "Michael" may have originated in the last century, but "Turn! Turn! Turn!" has them beat as being the number one single with the most ancient lyrics. Pete Seeger adapted the words from the Book of Ecclesiastes, making this the oldest chart-topper of the rock era.

The Byrds were playing their own instruments on "Turn! Turn! Turn!" their second number one single. It was only on their first number one [see 178—"Mr. Tambourine Man"] and one other track on their first LP where studio musicians were called in to expedite recording.

The Byrds followed "Mr. Tambourine Man" with another Bob Dylan song, "All I Really Want to Do." Unfortunately for them, their first single paved the way for many artists to record Dylan songs, and Cher [see 181—"I Got You Babe"] had chosen "All I Really Want to Do" for her first solo single to be released under the name of Cher. Both versions entered the Hot 100 on July 3, 1965, and while some bookmakers might have listed the odds in favor of the Byrds, the winner was Cher. She

took the song to number 15 while the Byrds faltered at number 40 (many stations gave airplay to the Byrds' "B" side, "I'll Feel a Whole Lot Better," but it didn't chart nationally).

"Turn! Turn! Turn!" was the band's third single. Jim McGuinn, an admirer of Seeger's, had already recorded a version of it when he played guitar on Judy Collins' third album. One day while travelling with the group on a tour bus, he started to play a rock version of the song. David Crosby added a twist of his own and some harmonies were added to come up with the final arrangement. It took more than 50 takes to produce the track that was released as a single.

"Mr. Tambourine Man" and "Turn! Turn! Turn!" were the only Byrds' singles to penetrate the top 10. Their fourth single, "Set You Free This Time" backed with "It Won't Be Wrong," peaked at 63. Next came "Eight Miles High," which was banned by many radio stations, because it was thought to be about drugs. The group insisted it was about travelling in an airplane to England, but the lack of airplay hurt and the song only reached number 14.

It was on the plane ride back from England in August, 1965, that Gene Clark discovered he had a fear of flying. He was the first Byrd to depart.

The Byrds continued as a quartet until October, 1967, when friction

between McGuinn and Crosby led to the latter's exit. Crosby objected to recording Gerry Goffin and Carole King's "Goin' Back," and McGuinn was not eager to record Crosby's "Triad," a song eventually cut by Jefferson Airplane and Crosby's next group, Crosby, Stills, Nash and Young.

Now a trio, the Byrds moved from folk-rock to country-rock for their next album, *The Notorious Byrd Brothers*. Clarke decided to quit and was replaced by Gram Parsons of the International Submarine Band on the next LP, *Sweetheart of the Rodeo*. Parsons left the group after five months on the morning they were to leave London for a tour of South Africa. When Chris Hillman left the Byrds two months later, he formed the Flying Burrito Brothers with Parsons. Gram Parsons was a seminal influence on the growing movement of California-based country rock, recording only two solo albums before his mysterious death at age 26 in 1973.

Jim McGuinn was the only original Byrd left by the end of 1968, and he was now Roger McGuinn, having committed to the Subud faith, a religion which allows an optional name change to suit the sound of the individual's soul.

With various changes in membership, the Byrds lasted until 1972, when McGuinn finally called a halt. A year later, the five originals members reunited for an album released on Asylum Records, but it was a one-time-only collaboration. In 1978, McGuinn, Clark and Hillman formed a band which recorded briefly for Capitol.

## THE TOP FIVE
*Week of December 4, 1965*

1 **Turn! Turn! Turn!**
  Byrds

2 **I Hear a Symphony**
  Supremes

3 **1-2-3**
  Len Barry

4 **Let's Hang On**
  Four Seasons

5 **I Got You (I Feel Good)**
  James Brown

*Writer: Robert Byrd*

*Producer: Dave Clark*

*December 25, 1965*
*1 week*

THE DAVE CLARK FIVE will long be remembered for hits like "Glad All Over," "Bits and Pieces" and "Because," although they weren't number one songs. The group's sole American chart-topper was a remake of Bobby Day's 1958 single "Over and Over," which he wrote under his real name, Robert Byrd.

The DC5 rode to American shores on the crest of the wave that brought the Beatles crashing onto our charts. Their timing was impeccable: in England, "Glad All Over" became their only British number one on January 16, 1964, just as the Beatles were breaking in America. And because "Glad All Over" had followed "I Want to Hold Your Hand" in the top spot, it appeared that the Dave Clark Five had toppled the Beatles and were the new British supergroup.

At this point in time, Americans assumed anyone with a British accent were neighbors of the Beatles in Liverpool. The Dave Clark Five were actually from the North London suburb of Tottenham, although an advertisement placed in *Billboard* by

Epic Records proclaimed that the group had "the Mersey sound with the Liverpool Beat." "Glad All Over" shot into the top 10 on March 21, 1964, and "Bits and Pieces" joined it there just three weeks later.

The group's roots go back to 1958, when drummer David Clark (born December 15, 1942) and his friend, guitarist Chris Walls, formed a group to raise money to finance their rugby team's trip to Holland. They advertised for musicians in the pop weekly *Melody Maker*. Successful applicants were rhythm guitarist Rick Huxley (born August 5, 1942) and a vocalist/saxophonist, Stan Saxon. Lead guitarist Mick Ryan made the group a quintet, and their first gig as "the Dave Clark Five featuring Stan Saxon" was at a Tottenham youth club.

Personnel continued to change over the next three years, and by 1961 the group that would go on to have 16 top 30 singles in America was intact: Huxley was now playing bass, Lenny Davidson (born May 30, 1944) played guitar and sang harmony, Denis Payton (born August 11, 1943) was on tenor sax, Michael Smith (born December 6, 1943) was lead vocalist and Walls, Saxon and Ryan had exited.

With Clark fully in charge of managing the group, they signed with a

small label and released an instrumental, "Chaquita," which was not dissimilar to The Champs' "Tequila." They also recorded for a subsidiary of Pye Records, before an A&R man from EMI's Columbia label saw them at the Tottenham Royal.

The DC5 worked with songwriter Mitch Murray for a short while, and recorded his "I Like It" before Gerry and the Pacemakers had a hit with it. Their first chart single in Britain was a cover version of a Motown song—The Contours' "Do You Love Me," which peaked at 30. The follow-up was "Glad All Over."

The group fared better in the States, where they had 11 top 30 entries by the time they recorded "Over and Over."

"Over and Over" only reached number 45 in Britain. The DC5 managed a few more hits in both countries, including the American top 10 single, "You Got What It Takes," but by 1968 their American career was over and two years later their British hits stopped coming.

They announced their break-up in August, 1970, but Clark and Smith continued recording as "Dave Clark and Friends" until 1973.

In 1986, Clark produced the musical *Time*, which had its world premiere at the Dominion Theatre in London on April 9. Cliff Richard starred in the production, which featured a holographic performance by Laurence Olivier. Clark co-wrote most of the music and lyrics for the show, and an album was released featuring vocals by Richard as well as Dionne Warwick and others. When Richard departed the cast, he was succeeded by David Cassidy.

## THE TOP FIVE
*Week of December 25, 1965*

1 **Over and Over**
Dave Clark Five

2 **Turn! Turn! Turn!**
Byrds

3 **I Got You (I Feel Good)**
James Brown

4 **Let's Hang On**
Four Seasons

5 **Sounds of Silence**
Simon & Garfunkel

## 190 The Sounds of Silence COLUMBIA 43396
### SIMON AND GARFUNKEL

*Writer: Paul Simon*

*Producer: Tom Wilson*

*January 1, 1966*
*2 weeks*

No one was more surprised than Paul Simon and Art Garfunkel when "The Sounds of Silence" went to number one. Paul had written the song in 1963, two years before recording it with just vocals and acoustic guitar for their first Columbia album, *Wednesday Morning, 3 a.m.* When the LP wasn't successful, Art returned to graduate school at New York's Columbia University and Paul returned to England, where he had first moved in 1964.

Meanwhile, a Boston radio station had selected one of the cuts from the album for airplay. The reaction to "The Sounds of Silence" was so positive, Columbia Records felt they would have a hit single, if they could electrify the instrumental track.

Tom Wilson, who produced the original recording, was in the studio with Bob Dylan on June 15, 1966, to record "Like a Rolling Stone." When that song was completed, Wilson asked the musicians to record one more track. With electric guitar, bass and drums he created a new backing rhythm track for "The Sounds of Silence."

In London, Paul had recorded a solo album, *The Paul Simon Songbook*, which featured several songs that would eventually be recorded by Simon and Garfunkel (including "I Am a Rock," "April Come She Will" and "A Most Peculiar Man"). He was producing an album for one Jackson C. Frank when he received a telephone call from New York informing him that "The Sounds of Silence" was the number one song in America.

Paul Simon (born November 5, 1942, in Newark, New Jersey) and Art Garfunkel (born October 13, 1942, in Queens, New York) first met in a sixth grade production of *Alice in Wonderland* at P.S. 164 in Forest Hills, New York. Paul played the white rabbit and Art was the Cheshire cat.

In 1955, they wrote a song together ("The Girl for Me"). With the Everly Brothers as role models, the two friends recorded a demo of "Hey, Schoolgirl" in 1957. An executive from Big Records heard them recording the song, and signed them to the label. The record was released under the pseudonyms of Tom (Graph) and Jerry (Landis), and it peaked on *Billboard's* chart at number 49. The pair made their television debut on Dick Clark's "American Bandstand," and it looked like the beginning of a promising career. But it was a false start, and

after two singles that flopped, they both went to college.

Paul majored in music at New York University and English literature at Queens College, where he met Carol Klein before she became Carole King [see 294—"It's Too Late" / "I Feel the Earth Move"]. With her help, Paul recorded demos for publishers, earning $15 a crack and learning about studio techniques. Art studied mathematics at New York University and architecture at Columbia.

They both continued to sing under a variety of aliases. Art recorded for Warwick Records as Artie Garr, and Paul just barely dented the Hot 100 twice—first as leader of Tico and the Triumphs with "Motorcycle" in 1962 (number 99) and then as Jerry Landis with "The Lone Teen Ranger" in 1963 (number 97). As Landis, he wrote "Red Rubber Ball," recorded in 1966 by the Cyrkle, and recorded "Carlos Dominquez," which he wrote under the name Paul Kane.

In early 1964, Simon and Garfunkel made the Greenwich Village coffee house circuit, starting with Gerde's Folk City. Before moving to England, Paul took one of his songs to Tom Wilson at Columbia. He signed Simon and Garfunkel to the label, and recorded the acoustic collection of Dylan songs, traditional folk tunes and original Simon compositions that became *Wednesday Morning, 3 a.m.*

"The Sounds of Silence" topped the chart for one week, then submitted to the Beatles' "We Can Work It Out." On January 22, "The Sounds of Silence" returned to number one for an additional week.

## THE TOP FIVE
*Week of January 1, 1966*

1 **The Sounds of Silence**
  Simon & Garfunkel

2 **We Can Work It Out**
  Beatles

3 **I Got You (I Feel Good)**
  James Brown

4 **Turn! Turn! Turn!**
  Byrds

5 **Over and Over**
  Dave Clark Five

*Writers: John Lennon
          Paul McCartney*

*Producer: George Martin*

*January 8, 1966
3 weeks*

THE songwriting credits for "We Can Work It Out" and its flip side, "Day Tripper," both read John Lennon-Paul McCartney. But unlike other collaborators, John and Paul often wrote their songs separately. An agreement made when they were both teenagers assured that all of their songs would be credited to Lennon-McCartney, no matter who actually wrote what.

"They did love each other very much throughout the time I knew them in the studio," producer George Martin says in Ray Coleman's *Lennon* biography. "But the tension was there mostly because they never really collaborated. They were never Rodgers and Hart. They were always songwriters who helped each other out with little bits and pieces. One would have most of a song finished, play it to the other, and he'd say, 'Well, why don't you do this?' "

In a 1980 interview with David Sheff for *Playboy,* Lennon talked about writing songs with McCartney: "You could say that he provided a lightness, an optimism, while I would always go for the sadness, the discords, a certain bluesy edge. There was a period when I thought I didn't write melodies, that Paul wrote those and I just wrote straight, shouting rock 'n' roll. But, of course, when I think of some of my own songs—"In My Life"—or some of the early stuff—"This Boy"—I was writing melody with the best of them.

"Paul had a lot of training, could play a lot of instruments. He'd say, 'Well, why don't you change that there? You've done that note 50 times in the song.' You know, I'll grab a note and ram it home. Then again, I'd be the one to figure out where to go with a song—a story that Paul would start. In a lot of the songs, my stuff is the 'middle eight,' the bridge."

One such song is "We Can Work It Out." Lennon told Sheff: ". . . Paul did the first half, I did the middle eight. But you've got Paul writing, 'We can work it out / We can work it out'—real optimistic, y' know, and me, impatient: 'Life is very short and there's no time / For fussing and fighting, my friend . . .' "

Paul sang lead on "We Can Work It Out," joined by John on the choruses. John played the harmonium and acoustic guitar while George Harrison played tambourine.

The song was recorded in early November, 1965, as was the "B" side, "Day Tripper." Featuring a lead vocal duet by John and Paul, the song was written by Lennon. The Beatles appeared on NBC-TV's "Hullabaloo" to lip-synch both songs, not surprising considering that their manager Brian Epstein hosted the "British Scene" segment of the program.

"We Can Work It Out" entered the Hot 100 at number 36 on December 18. "Day Tripper" debuted at number 56 the same week. "We Can Work It Out" became the Beatles' 11th number one single in America during the week of January 8, 1966. After two weeks at one, it slipped to number two while Simon and Garfunkel's "The Sounds of Silence" [see 190] returned for one more week at the summit. "We Can Work It Out" then took over the top spot once more for a final week. "Day Tripper" peaked at number five during the week of January 22. In Britain, the single became the Beatles' ninth chart-topper, and the first to have both sides listed at number one.

**THE TOP FIVE**
*Week of January 8, 1966*

1 **We Can Work It Out**
  Beatles

2 **The Sounds of Silence**
  Simon & Garfunkel

3 **She's Just My Style**
  Gary Lewis & the Playboys

4 **Flowers on the Wall**
  Statler Brothers

5 **Ebb Tide**
  Righteous Brothers

### 192 My Love WARNER BROTHERS 5684
### PETULA CLARK

*Writer: Tony Hatch*

*Producer: Tony Hatch*

*February 5, 1966*
*2 weeks*

WHEN "My Love" topped the Hot 100 on February 5, 1966, Petula Clark became the first British female to have *two* number one singles in America. After failing to make the American charts for 14 years, Petula Clark started a dazzling winning streak with "Downtown" [see 165] in January, 1965. That was the first of 15 consecutive top 40 hits in the United States, including "You'd Better Come Home," "Round Every Corner," "A Sign of the Times," "I Couldn't Live Without Your Love" and "Don't Sleep in the Subway."

"My Love" was the first song Petula recorded in America. Like Jimmy Dean's "Big Bad John" [see 100] it was written on an airplane, although this may be the first number one single written on a *transatlantic* flight. Petula and her record producer Tony Hatch flew to the States in November, 1965. He began writing the song over the North Pole and had it completed by the time they landed in Los Angeles, where Pet recorded it with an American studio orchestra.

Her successful American recording career led to her being cast in Hollywood films. Before she was cast in the 1968 musical *Finian's Rainbow* with Fred Astaire, she had turned down a part in an Elvis Presley film and the Patty Duke role in *Valley of the Dolls*. In 1969, she won the female lead in *Goodbye Mr. Chips*, opposite Peter O'Toole.

Her motion picture career really began in Britain, where she became a child star in 1943. She signed with the Rank Organization, and her first film was *Medal for the General*, released in 1944. She made 25 films for Rank, including *Vice Versa*, in which she played Anthony Newley's girlfriend and *Holiday Camp* where she was Jack Warner's daughter. She was given her first screen kiss in the 1950 film *Don't Ever Leave Me*.

It was a different kind of screen kiss that became controversial in 1968, the year Petula had her first American network television special. Scheduled for telecast on April 2 on NBC, the musical special was taped at the network's Burbank facility. During the final number, "On the Path to Glory," Petula kissed her guest star, Harry Belafonte. A representative of the sponsor, Chrysler-Plymouth, protested. A white woman kissing a black man would offend Southern viewers, he said, and he demanded the scene be cut. NBC refused and the innocent kiss was seen on network television (a few months later, William Shatner kissed Nichelle Nichols in the "Plato's Step-children" episode of "Star Trek," but the controversy had subsided after Petula kissed Harry).

Petula's last American top 40 hit was "Don't Give Up" in July, 1968. She left Warner Brothers for MGM, where she recorded a new version of Mary Wells' "My Guy" [see 147] in 1972. In 1976, Pet recorded a disco version of "Downtown," which was popular in British clubs, but failed to chart anywhere. Her last American chart entry was "Natural Love," recorded for the Scotti Brothers label in 1982.

In 1980, she starred on stage in London's West End in a revival of *The Sound of Music.*

## THE TOP FIVE
*Week of February 5, 1966*

1 **My Love**
Petula Clark

2 **Barbara Ann**
Beach Boys

3 **No Matter What Shape
(Your Stomach's In)**
T-Bones

4 **We Can Work It Out**
Beatles

5 **Lightnin' Strikes**
Lou Christie

MGM 13412 **Lightnin' Strikes** 193
LOU CHRISTIE

*Writers: Lou Christie*
*Twyla Herbert*

*Producer: Charles Calello*

*February 19, 1966*
*1 week*

**T**HERE'S always been an element of mystery about Lou Christie, thanks to his friendship with songwriting partner Twyla Herbert, a clairvoyant who is said to have accurately predicted which of their songs would become hits. Lou was a 15-year-old ninth grader when he first met her at an audition in the basement of a church in his hometown of Glen Willard, Pennsylvania. She was twice his age, and very flamboyant with her gypsy red hair. They hit it off immediately.

Born Lugee Geno Sacco on February 19, 1943, he was raised in an Italian-Polish family where singing was as natural as breathing and eating. He made his solo performing debut in the first grade, singing "Away in the Manger" as St. Joseph in a school play. With his sister Amy and other school friends, he later formed a group, the Crewnecks.

When he met Twyla, she needed a singer for her group, the Classics. He recorded "Close Your Eyes" with them in 1959, and a year later, sought out the arranger for the Pittsburgh-based Skyliners ("Since I Don't Have You"). Lennie Martin had Lugee and Amy sing backing vocals for one of his vocalists, then cut a record for their own group, Lugee and the Lions.

The name "Lou Christie" was an unexpected and disappointing surprise for Lugee Sacco, who learned about it when his first single for C&C Records, "The Gyspy Cried," was released. He had been working on a list of names when the company picked one for him and put it on the record without telling him. It took him 20 years to get used to it, he's said.

"The Gypsy Cried," featuring Lou's signature falsetto voice, was a local hit in Pittsburgh when New York-based Roulette Records picked it up. It was the first song written by Lou and Twyla, and it established him nationally, peaking at number 24 on the Hot 100. The follow-up, "Two

Faces Have I," was a bigger hit, reaching number six.

Lou was touring with Dick Clark's Caravan of Stars, where he became infatuated with the lead singer of an up-and-coming group, the Supremes. But he had to say goodbye to Diana Ross three days before the tour ended because he was called up for Army Reserve duty. He served six months at Fort Knox, a frustrating interruption of his career. He was determined to get out of the Army and have a number one song. The day he was discharged, he went home to Pittsburgh and called Twyla.

They collaborated on "Lightnin' Strikes," and Lou took it to his new label, MGM. They hated it, and Lou

has said that the president of the label threw the song into the wastebasket. Now managed by Bob Marcucci, the man who guided the careers of Fabian and Frankie Avalon [see 50—"Venus"], Lou moved to California to promote the record, which the company released anyway.

It debuted on the Hot 100 at number 93 on December 25, 1965, and took eight weeks to climb to the top of the chart. His next single, "Rhapsody in the Rain," was so controversial, entire radio chains banned it and Lou was forced to go back into the studio and change some sexually suggestive lyrics. While the idea may seem tame today, in 1965 radio wasn't ready for a young teenage couple making love to the rhythm of a car's windshield wipers (hey, nobody ever said "Lightnin' Strikes" was about the weather).

Despite some engaging singles like "Painter" and "If My Car Could Only Talk to Me," Lou didn't have any more hits on MGM. After a short, unproductive term with Columbia, he moved to Buddah Records and made the top 10 with Tony Romeo's "I'm Gonna Make You Mine," a song that featured Linda Scott ("I Told Every Little Star") and songwriter Ellie Greenwich on backing vocals.

Lou lived in London for a few years, where he married British beauty queen Francesca Winfield. In the past few years, he has toured the rock and roll oldies circuit, where he closes his act with a mean version of "Since I Don't Have You."

## THE TOP FIVE
*Week of February 19, 1966*

1  **Lightnin' Strikes**
   Lou Christie

2  **These Boots are Made For Walkin'**
   Nancy Sinatra

3  **Up Tight**
   Stevie Wonder

4  **My Love**
   Petula Clark

5  **My World is Empty Without You**
   Supremes

## 194 These Boots Are Made for Walkin' REPRISE 0432
### NANCY SINATRA

*Writer: Lee Hazlewood*

*Producer: Lee Hazlewood*

*February 26, 1966*
*1 week*

NANCY SINATRA's "These Boots Are Made for Walkin' " has more in common with the aggressive tone of songs by Pat Benatar and Tina Turner [see 593—"What's Love Got to Do With It"] than with female singers of the '60s like Lesley Gore [see 130—"It's My Party] and Connie Francis [see 69—"Everybody's Somebody's Fool"]. Lesley was independent enough to sing "You Don't Own Me" and Connie sang "My Heart Has a Mind of Its Own," but somehow you knew they weren't going to trample you with their boots.

Not that Nancy would, either. "The image created by 'These Boots Are Made for Walkin' isn't the real me," she said during the production of a 1970 television special, "The Many Moods of Perry Como." " 'Boots' was hard, and I'm as soft as they come."

Nancy Sinatra was one of the first artists signed to her father Frank's new label, Reprise, in 1961. A full-page ad in the August 14 issue of *Billboard* introduced her first single, "Cufflinks and a Tie Clip," promising "the biggest DJ tumult in years is about to begin!" They were right about the tumult, they were just five years off. Nancy continued to release singles like "Tonight You Belong to Me" and an updating of Cole Porter's "True Love," and she had some success in Italy, Japan, Holland and South Africa, but none at home. She had her first Hot 100 chart entry in 1965 with "So Long Babe," which reached a forgettable number 86.

She married and divorced Tommy Sands, and released 15 singles by the time she put herself in the hands of writer/producer Lee Hazlewood.

According to *Time* magazine, Hazlewood lectured Nancy: "You're not a sweet young thing. You're not the virgin next door. You've been married and divorced. You're a grown woman. I know there's garbage in there somewhere." Garbage, *Time* elaborated, meant "pain, heartbreak, worldliness."

Hazlewood wrote and produced "These Boots Are Made for Walkin' "

for Nancy, and the result was an international number one song. In Great Britain, Nancy was the first American female vocalist to have a number one single since Connie Francis' "Stupid Cupid" in 1958.

Nancy Sinatra, the oldest of Frank and Nancy Sinatra's three children, was born June 8, 1940, in Jersey City, New Jersey. She was still a child when her parents moved

to southern California, and Nancy attended University High School in West Los Angeles. For a year-and-a-half, she majored in economics at the University of Southern California, but all the time she had been studying piano, voice, dance and drama.

The world had first heard of Nancy when she was five years old; that's when her father recorded a song written about her, "Nancy with the Laughing Face." A re-introduction came in 1959, when she made a guest appearance on a television special starring her father and Elvis Presley. After "These Boots . . ." she was a frequent television guest, and in 1967 starred in her own TV special, "Movin' With Nancy."

She also starred in motion pictures, including *For Those Who Think Young, Get Yourself a College Girl* and *The Oscar*. She co-starred and sang with Elvis in *Speedway*.

Her second biggest solo hit was the follow-up to "These Boots . . .", "How Does That Grab You, Darlin'," went to number seven. "Sugar Town" went to number five in 1967, the same year that Nancy started recording duets with Hazlewood ("Summer Wine," "Jackson") and her father [see 222—"Somethin' Stupid"].

But it was thanks to "These Boots . . ." that Nancy developed an identity of her own, something some children of celebrities find difficult to accomplish. "Almost all of my life I was Frank Sinatra's daughter," she said. "Then for five years I was Tommy Sands' wife or the sister of Frank Sinatra, Jr. Suddenly, I was somebody on my own."

### THE TOP FIVE
*Week of February 26, 1966*

1 **These Boots are Made For Walkin'**
Nancy Sinatra

2 **Lightnin' Strikes**
Lou Christie

3 **The Ballad of the Green Berets**
S/Sgt. Barry Sadler

4 **Uptight**
Stevie Wonder

5 **My World is Empty Without You**
Supremes

RCA 8739 **The Ballad of the Green Berets** 195

### S/SGT. BARRY SADLER

*Writers: Barry Sadler*
*Robin Moore*

*Producer: Andy Wiswell*

*March 5, 1966*
*5 weeks*

PRESIDENT JOHN F. KENNEDY created an army combat unit called the Special Forces in 1961. They soon came to be known by the distinctive cap which was a part of their uniform: the green beret. On December 18, 1965, one of their members, S/Sgt. Barry Sadler, recorded a tribute to his fellow soldiers. It was released on January 11, 1966, while America was embroiled in the Vietnam war, and was an immediate success. It sold more than a million copies in the first two weeks, and became RCA's fastest-selling single of all time. It was the number one single of 1966, according to *Billboard*.

Sadler was born in New Mexico, but moved frequently with his parents. His father was a plumber and his mother a waitress, but their passion was gambling and they often pulled up stakes to travel to find the best action.

After high school, Sadler fooled around with the drums, but didn't take up music as a profession. He enlisted in the Air Force and served for four years. After his discharge in 1962, he learned to play guitar and formed a group, playing in clubs and bars around New Mexico. The work was not lucrative, and exhausted of funds, he decided to return to the military. This time he tried the Army, enlisting in their airborne school. He trained for a year as a combat medic and won his green beret.

He was still interested in music and started writing songs while stationed at Fort Sam Houston in Texas. He was sent to Vietnam, where his fellow soldiers showed little interest in his singing or his songs. He often sat by himself, strumming his guitar and singing his own compositions.

His Vietnam duty was cut short when he fell into a booby trap while on patrol. A *pungi* stake, fashioned from sharpened bamboo and dipped in poison, pierced his leg. Lapsing in and out of consciousness, he treated the wound himself. He was eventually rescued, but suffered a permanent scar and a numb feeling in his leg.

Back in the States, Sadler recuperated. A friend suggested he write a song about the Special Forces, and Sadler composed a 12-verse lyric. He submitted the song to publisher Chet Gierlach, who showed it to a friend, Robin Moore, author of *The Green Berets*.

Moore thought the song had potential and with Sadler, rewrote and edited it. It was recorded on a small budget and released just for the military. It proved so popular that Moore took the track to RCA. The company agreed to finance a full recording session, complete with orchestra.

After the song became an immediate smash, Moore's publisher asked Sadler to pose for the cover of the paperback edition of *The Green Berets*. More than 1,500,000 copies were printed with Sadler's face.

Stationed at Fort Bragg, North Carolina, Sadler was given leave to make appearances on Ed Sullivan and Jimmy Dean's network television shows. The song was also an international success, so popular in West Germany that East Germany banned all airplay on its government-controlled radio stations. A report in the East German youth newspaper *Junge Welt* complained that despite the official ban, the song was played at dances and teenagers were often heard singing it.

Sadler's *Ballads of the Green Berets* album also sold well, but a follow-up single called "The A-Team" fizzled and Sadler's career on the pop charts came to an end. He eventually re-enlisted in the Army and later did some acting work.

On September 7, 1988, Sadler was shot in the head as he got into a taxi in Guatemala, where he was reportedly training anti-communist Contra fighters. He suffered brain damage in the incident and was hospitalized in various facilities over the next 14 months. He died on November 5, 1989, at a hospital in Murfreesboro, Tennessee.

### THE TOP FIVE
*Week of March 5, 1966*

1 **The Ballad of the Green Berets**
S/Sgt Barry Sadler

2 **These Boots are Made For Walkin'**
Nancy Sinatra

3 **Lightnin' Strikes**
Lou Christie

4 **Listen People**
Herman's Hermits

5 **California Dreamin'**
Mamas and Papas

# 196 (You're My) Soul and Inspiration VERVE 10383
## THE RIGHTEOUS BROTHERS

*Writers: Barry Mann*
*Cynthia Weil*

*Producer: Bill Medley*

*April 9, 1966*
*₃ weeks*

**A**FTER writing the Righteous Brothers' first number one single [see 166—"You've Lost That Lovin' Feelin'"], songwriters Barry Mann and Cynthia Weil were asked by producer Phil Spector to write the follow-up. They were in the middle of writing "(You're My) Soul and Inspiration" when they suddenly stopped.

"Barry and I felt we were copying from ourselves," Cynthia explains. "We said, 'Phil, this isn't as good, we don't want to finish the song. So Phil turned to Carole and Gerry."

Carole King and Gerry Goffin, that is, who wrote "Just Once in My Life" as the sequel to "You've Lost That Lovin' Feelin'." "Just Once in My Life" reached a respectable number nine on the Hot 100, so Medley and Hatfield recorded another Goffin-King song, "Hung on You." This time, disc jockeys preferred the flip side, Spector's production of a 1950s tune, "Unchained Melody." Displeased that program directors liked the old song better, Spector decided he would give them exactly what they want and *only* record pop standards for the Righteous Brothers. "Ebb Tide" went to number five, but "The White Cliffs of Dover" failed to chart.

## THE TOP FIVE
*Week of April 9, 1966*

1 **(You're My) Soul and Inspiration**
Righteous Brothers

2 **Daydream**
Lovin' Spoonful

3 **19th Nervous Breakdown**
Rolling Stones

4 **Bang Bang (My Baby Shot Me Down)**
Cher

5 **The Ballad of the Green Berets**
S/Sgt. Barry Sadler

When MGM offered to pay one million dollars for the Righteous Brothers' contract in 1966, Spector sold it and turned his attention to Ike and Tina Turner. Signed to MGM subsidiary, Verve, Medley and Hatfield had to come up with new material.

Barry and Cynthia had played part of "Soul and Inspiration" for Bill before abandoning the song. He telephoned the songwriters and asked them to complete it for the Righteous Brothers to record. "We said you don't want it, it's a second rate 'Lovin' Feelin'," says Cynthia. As a favor to Bill, they finished the song and Bill produced a Spectorized version of it. "He made this terrific record," Cynthia admits, "but it will always be 'Lovin' Feelin' sideways to me."

Bill and Bobby found it difficult to follow-up "Soul and Inspiration," and in 1968, the duo split up. Medley pursued a solo career, scoring some mid-chart placements with "Brown Eyed Woman" and "Peace, Brother, Peace." Hatfield formed a new Righteous Brothers with Jimmy Walker of the Knickerbockers ("Lies"), but neither act achieved the success of the original Righteous Brothers.

In 1974, Bill and Bobby re-teamed and recorded "Rock and Roll Heaven," an ode to departed rock stars written by Alan O'Day [see 469—"Undercover Angel"]. It was their only hit and they parted ways again, coming back together for the 20th anniversary telecast of Dick Clark's "American Bandstand" in 1981 and for the duo's 30th anniversary in 1983.

ATLANTIC 2321 **Good Lovin'**
THE YOUNG RASCALS  **197**

Writers: *Rudy Clark*
*Arthur Resnick*

Producers: *Tom Dowd*
*Arif Mardin*

April 30, 1966
1 week

THE YOUNG RASCALS evolved from Joey Dee's Starliters [see 103—"Peppermint Twist - Part 1"], circa 1964. Keyboardist Felix Cavaliere, percussionist Eddie Brigati and guitarist Gene Cornish were in Dee's backing band when the New Jersey singer left the Peppermint Lounge to open his own club, the Starliter. Eddie's older brother, David, had been one of the original Starliters when "Peppermint Twist" was number one.

Before he played for Dee, Cavaliere (born November 29, 1943) was the only white member of the Stereos, a group from his native Pelham, New York. They had a top 30 hit with "I Really Love You" in late 1961. Felix became a pre-med student at Syracuse University, but two years later was back in Manhattan to pursue a musical career.

When they had played "Peppermint Twist" once too often, Felix, Eddie and Gene decided to form their own group. Felix and Eddie had both played in bands with Dino Danelli, a jazz drummer who at 15 years of age had toured with Lionel Hampton. They invited Dino to become the fourth member of a group they planned to call the Rascals. They rehearsed all through the closing months of 1964, and by January, 1965, were ready to debut their act at the Choo Choo Club in Eddie's home town of Garfield, New Jersey. By July they were booked to play the Barge, a floating discotheque at the Hamptons in Long Island. Sid Bernstein, the promoter who brought the Beatles to Shea Stadium, caught their act and became their manager. He signed them to Atlantic Records in 1965, and their first single, "I Ain't Gonna Eat Out My Heart Anymore," was a mid-charter in February, 1966.

Before that single was released, the band learned they couldn't call themselves the Rascals, because there was already a group known as the Harmonica Rascals. Without their knowledge, the name "Young Rascals" was selected for them and their first 45 was released under that name. Cavaliere would have preferred almost any other adjective, but Young it was, leading to much confusion with the Little Rascals.

The Young Rascals were heavily influenced by R&B music, and became leading exponents of blue-eyed soul. For their second single, they covered "Good Lovin," a song by the Olympics that had peaked at number 81 the year before. They felt the original version lacked excitement and energy, so they concentrated on arranging a version that would keep people on the dance floor. They worked it into their act before going into a recording studio to cut it. Not totally satisfied with their final version, they wanted to improve upon it, but Atlantic released it anyway. It debuted on the Hot 100 on March 12, 1966 and went to number one seven weeks later.

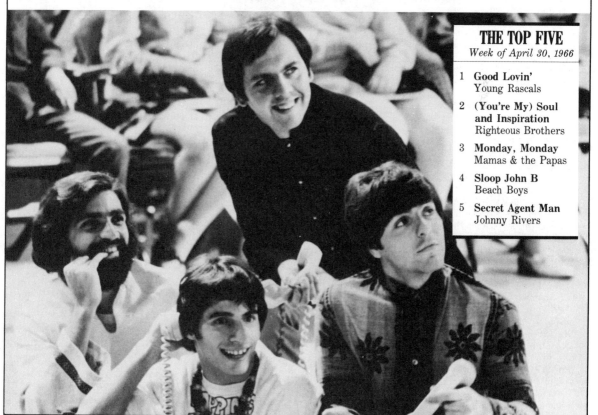

## THE TOP FIVE
*Week of April 30, 1966*

1  **Good Lovin'**
   Young Rascals

2  **(You're My) Soul
   and Inspiration**
   Righteous Brothers

3  **Monday, Monday**
   Mamas & the Papas

4  **Sloop John B**
   Beach Boys

5  **Secret Agent Man**
   Johnny Rivers

## 198 Monday, Monday DUNHILL 4026
### THE MAMAS AND THE PAPAS

*Writer: John Phillips*

*Producer: Lou Adler*

*May 7, 1966*
*3 weeks*

"MONDAY, MONDAY" was the first song recorded by a fully sexually integrated group to go to number one. Prior to the Mamas and the Papas, the only co-ed groups that had number one hits were groups like the Platters, the Fleetwoods and Ruby and the Romantics, which featured just one member of the opposite sex.

Having two men and two women in the group was not the only distinction for the Mamas and the Papas, whose outrageous dress and beautiful harmonies brought them media attention and radio airplay on their first hit, "California Dreamin'."

Their 1967 hit "Creeque Alley" detailed the origins of the group, but for those who don't still have that 45 in their collection, here's a biographical reminder of how John, Michelle, Cass and Denny came together:

*John Phillips*, born August 30, 1935, on Parris Island, South Carolina, was in the Journeymen, a folk trio that included Scott McKenzie (who would record John's "San Francisco (Be Sure to Wear Flowers in Your Hair)" in 1967).

*Dennis Doherty*, born November 29, 1941, in Halifax, Nova Scotia, Canada, was a member of another folk trio, the Halifax Three. While on a tour associated with ABC-TV's "Hootennany U.S.A." show, the Halifax Three opened for the Journeymen. One night, near the end of the tour, John wanted to know what the opening act sounded like, and heard Denny's voice for the first time.

*Ellen Naomi Cohen*, born September 19, 1941, in Baltimore, Maryland, was nicknamed Cassandra by her father. Adopting the stage name of Cass Elliot, she recorded two albums with another trio, the Big Three, which also featured her first husband, James Hendricks. When the Big Three and the Halifax Three broke up, Denny and Cass formed a new group with guitarist Zal Yanovsky. That group, with the addition of John Sebastian [see 205—"Summer in the City"] on harmonica, became the Mugwumps.

*Holly Michelle Gilliam*, born June 4, 1945, in Long Beach, California, wanted to be a model when she met John at the Hungry i in San Francisco in 1961. When the Journeymen and the Mugwumps disbanded in 1964, John and Michele, now married, formed the New Journeymen with Denny to fulfill contract obligations.

The group coalesced in California, where all four members eventually ended up after leaving the Virgin Islands. They lived with a friend, Barry McGuire [see 183—"Eve of Destruction"], who had just signed with Dunhill Records. He introduced them to his producer, Lou Adler,

who signed them after hearing the songs that would form their first album, *If You Can Believe Your Eyes and Ears*. Adler asked them to sing backing vocals for Barry's album, which included John's composition of "California Dreamin.'" Later, they would wipe off Barry's vocals and add their own.

A group name was needed, and the leading contender was the Magic Circle. But while watching a television documentary about the Hell's Angels, John heard one of the members tell the interviewer, "Some people call our women cheap. We call them mamas."

Dunhill issued the first single from the album, "Go Where You Wanna Go," but a dream caused Adler to recall it immediately and release "California Dreamin'" instead. While that single was out, radio stations started playing "Monday, Monday" from the album. By the time it was released as a single, it was so popular that it sold more than 150,000 copies the first day.

It was a song that John had to force the other members to record. Cass, Denny and Michelle disliked it, as did Adler. But John prevailed and it was the last song recorded for the album. For years, John maintained he had no idea what the song meant.

The group broke up in 1968 and re-formed briefly in 1971. Elliot performed at the London Palladium on July 29, 1974, and died that night in her flat of a massive heart attack. John was hospitalized in early 2001 and died of coronary arrest at UCLA Medical Center in Los Angeles on March 18.

### THE TOP FIVE
*Week of May 7, 1966*

1  **Monday, Monday**
   Mamas & the Papas

2  **Good Lovin'**
   Young Rascals

3  **Sloop John B**
   Beach Boys

4  **(You're My) Soul
   and Inspiration**
   Righteous Brothers

5  **Kicks**
   Paul Revere & the Raiders

ATLANTIC 2326 **When a Man Loves a Woman** 199
PERCY SLEDGE

*Writers: Cameron Lewis*
*Arthur Wright*

*Producers: Quin Ivy*
*Marlin Greene*

*May 28, 1966*
*2 weeks*

Percy Sledge describes "When a Man Loves a Woman" as a "happy accident" in Gerri Hirshey's *Nowhere to Run*. "Wasn't no heavy thought to it," he tells her, "I was just so damned *sad*."

The song began as an improvisational cure for the blues. Percy was working as an orderly at Colbert County Hospital, not far from his hometown of Leighton, Alabama. He also sang at Gallillee Baptist Church and was a member of the Esquires Combo, a group that performed in local clubs.

One night, while singing with his group, Sledge was so upset about a broken affair that he couldn't manage to sing the usual repertoire of Smokey Robinson and Beatles songs. He asked bassist Cameron Lewis and organist Arthur Wright to play something in any key. Out poured his emotions, coalescing into a song that would come to be known as "When a Man Loves a Woman."

Later, when he was in a happier frame of mind, Percy worked on the song and came up with a polished version that he took to Quin Ivy, one of the movers and shakers in the music industry in Alabama. Ivy was a local disc jockey in Sheffield who owned a record store and a recording studio.

## THE TOP FIVE
*Week of May 28, 1966*

1  **When a Man Loves a Woman**
   Percy Sledge

2  **A Groovy Kind of Love**
   Mindbenders

3  **Monday, Monday**
   Mamas and the Papas

4  **Paint It Black**
   Rolling Stones

5  **Rainy Day Women #12 & #35**
   Bob Dylan

Intent on pursuing a solo career, Sledge auditioned for Ivy in his record shop, Ivy's Tune Town. Percy won him over with the plaintive "When a Man Loves a Woman." Ivy not only wanted to record Percy, he wanted that song.

A generous Sledge had given songwriting credit to Lewis and Wright, and the song was recorded with Ivy's co-producer and recording engineer, Marlin Greene, on guitar, and many of Rick Hall's Muscle Shoals musicians from his Fame studios filling in on other instruments.

It was Hall who suggested to his friends at Atlantic Records that they pick up Sledge's master. They released it in early 1966, and on April 9 it debuted on the Hot 100 at number 100. Seven weeks later, Atlantic Records scored their third number one single.

"When a Man Loves a Woman" was Percy's only top 10 hit. His next single, "Warm and Tender Love," peaked at 17, and his second-biggest single, "Take Time to Know Her," peaked at 11 in the spring of 1968. He continued to record for Atlantic until 1973, always working with his friends in Alabama until the very last single, "Sunshine," which was recorded in Philadelphia. This turned out to be a brief departure from home, as the following year he signed with Phil Walden's Capricorn label, based in Georgia, and had his final Hot 100 entry with "I'll Be Your Everything," which peaked at number 62.

## 200 Paint It Black LONDON 901
### THE ROLLING STONES

*Writers: Mick Jagger
Keith Richard*

*Producer: Andrew Loog Oldham*

*June 11, 1966
2 weeks*

"PAINT IT BLACK" started as a comedy track, Keith Richard admitted in *Rolling Stone.* "Bill (Wyman) was playing an organ, doing a take-off of our first manager (Eric Easton) who started his career as an organist in a cinema pit." But the nihilistic, brooding song took an innovative turn for 1966, using a sitar as lead instrument. "Brian (Jones) playing the sitar makes it a whole other thing," Keith added. *Melody Maker* agreed, hailing "Paint It Black" as "a glorious Indian raga-riot that will send the Stones back to number one."

Written during a March, 1966, tour of Australia and recorded at RCA's studios in Hollywood, "Paint It Black" was included on American copies of *Aftermath* instead of "Mother's Little Helper," a song that scandalized England with its saga of suburban drug abuse. *Aftermath* marked a turning point for the

Stones; it was their first album to be exclusively written by Jagger and Richard.

Mick and Keith came to the sessions not with completed arrangements, but sketches of songs, leaving the instrumentation to compatriates Wyman, Jones and Charlie Watts. "They never go the easy route," engineer Dave Hassinger explained in the LP's liner notes, "from the moment Mick and Keith run a song down to the rest of the group—to Brian deciding on an acoustic or electric guitar, or something more bizarre—to Bill sorting out a bass pattern—to Charlie laying down the tempo—to their friend Jack Nitzsche (always on the dates) or road manager Stu (Ian Stewart) picking out chords on piano, organ, harpsichord or anything else that happens to be lying around."

Several of the songs on *Aftermath* had been intended for a previous, unreleased album, *Could You Walk on Water,* that remained in the vaults of the British Decca recording company because, a spokesman said, the label "would not issue it with that title at any price." The 14 tracks on the British *Aftermath* brought the

album's total time to 52 minutes, 23 seconds, making it one of the lengthiest rock albums ever issued. The American equivalent featured just 11 songs for 42 minutes, 51 seconds.

During the summer of 1966, the Stones encountered the same chaos on their American tour they had experienced in Australia, New Zealand and Europe earlier in the year. The final date was in Hawaii on July 25. Although no one realized it at the time, it was the last appearance of the original Rolling Stones in the United States.

Brief vacations intervened before a British jaunt in the fall. On September 23, 1966, the Royal Albert Hall concert was momentarily halted after three minutes when screaming girls attacked Jagger on stage. The event is preserved in audio on the *Got Live If You Want It* album and on video in an accompanying documentary film. The concert drove home the Stones' unpopularity with members of the ruling class. A ban was imposed on pop concerts at the Albert Hall and the public who had attended the Stones concert there never heard the results, as Decca didn't release the live album in Britain.

### THE TOP FIVE
*Week of June 11, 1966*

1  **Paint It Black**
   Rolling Stones

2  **Did You Ever Have
   to Make Up Your Mind?**
   Lovin' Spoonful

3  **I Am a Rock**
   Simon & Garfunkel

4  **When a Man Loves a Woman**
   Percy Sledge

5  **A Groovy Kind of Love**
   Mindbenders

*Writers: John Lennon
Paul McCartney*

*Producer: George Martin*

*June 25, 1966
2 weeks*

When "Paperback Writer" moved from 15-1 the week of June 25, 1966, it made the second biggest leap to number one in what was then the eight-year history of the Hot 100. The only single to make a bigger jump to pole position prior to "Paperback Writer" was also a Beatles hit: "Can't Buy Me Love" had rocketed 27-1 the week of April 4, 1964 [see 926—"A Moment Like This"].

John Lennon was the paperback writer of the Beatles. His first book, *In His Own Write*, was published in 1964. *The Times* of London said it was, "worth the attention of anyone who fears for the impoverishment of the English language and the British imagination."

Still, it was Paul who wrote "Paperback Writer" and he sings lead, with vocal harmonies by John Lennon and George Harrison.

The flip side, "Rain," was written by Lennon at the studio in his Kenwood home and featured John on lead vocals with harmony by Paul and George. John took the master tape home and accidentally played it backwards. He liked the effect so much, he incorporated it into the ending of the song, in which his vocal line, "Rain, when the rain comes they run and hide their heads" is heard backwards.

"Paperback Writer" was released in Britain on June 10. Just before the single was released, the Beatles had posed for a photo session wearing white butcher smocks, with pieces of raw meat and dismembered childrens' dolls strewn about. One of the photographs from this session was used in the press advertisement for "Paperback Writer."

The same photo was first seen by the American public ten days later when another Capitol compilation album, *Yesterday and Today*, was released. The cover caused a wave of protest and the "butcher sleeve" was quickly withdrawn. With no time to spare, Capitol prepared an innocent photo of the Beatles collected around a steamer trunk, and pasted the new

sleeve directly over the old. The offending cover could still be detected through Ringo's jacket, and existing copies of the album with both covers intact are rare collector's items today.

The Beatles faced more adverse publicity in America during the summer of 1966. On March 4, the *Evening Standard* in London had printed an interview with Lennon by Maureen Cleave. In the course of their conversation, John had said, "Christianity will go. It will vanish and shrink. I needn't argue about that. I'm right and I will be proved right. We're more popular than Jesus now. I don't know which will go first—rock 'n' roll or Christianity. Jesus was all right but his disciples were thick and ordinary. It's them twisting it that ruins it for me."

There was no adverse reaction to Lennon's comments until the American magazine *Datebook* published them out of context on July 29. Two days later, radio stations in Birmingham, Alabama, banned all Beatles records and a national furor arose. A bonfire was organized by radio station KLUE in Longview, Texas, so listeners could burn their Beatles records. In South Carolina, the Grand Dragon of the Ku Klux Klan attached a Beatles record to a wooden cross and set it on fire.

The timing couldn't have been worse. The Beatles began their third American tour in the middle of this

controversy. Under pressure, John apprehensively faced the American press in Chicago to clarify his remarks and apologize. He explained: "I believe in God, but not as one thing, not as an old man in the sky. I believe that what people call God is something in all of us . . . I wasn't saying the Beatles are better than God or Jesus . . . I could have said TV or the cinema or anything popular and I would have gotten away with it."

The morning after the Texas bonfire, KLUE's transmission tower was struck by lightning, damaging their equipment, rendering the news director unconscious and knocking the station off the air.

---

## THE TOP FIVE
*Week of June 25, 1966*

1 **Paperback Writer**
Beatles

2 **Strangers in the Night**
Frank Sinatra

3 **Paint It Black**
Rolling Stones

4 **Did You Ever Have to Make Up Your Mind?**
Lovin' Spoonful

5 **I Am a Rock**
Simon & Garfunkel

# 202 Strangers in the Night REPRISE 0470
## FRANK SINATRA

*Writers: Bert Kaempfert*
*Charlie Singleton*
*Eddie Snyder*

*Producer: Jimmy Bowen*

*July 2, 1966*
*1 week*

THE NUMBER ONE SONG on the first singles chart published by *Billboard* was "I'll Never Smile Again" by Tommy Dorsey, featuring vocals by Frank Sinatra. The date was July 20, 1940. Sinatra's final chart entry in his lifetime was his cover of Liza Minnelli's "Theme from New York, New York," which peaked at number 32 in 1980 and made its last appearance on the Hot 100 the week of July 19, giving Sinatra a chart span of 40 years to the day.

His only solo number one single of the rock era was "Strangers in the Night," a song that interrupted the reign of the Beatles' "Paperback Writer." "Strangers in the Night" went to number one just 18 weeks after Nancy Sinatra topped the chart [see 194—"These Boots Are Made for Walkin'"], and just over nine months before Frank and Nancy became the only father-daughter duo to have a number one single [see 222—"Somethin' Stupid"]. Sinatra was the third artist to have a number one song on his own label, Reprise, following Dean Martin [see 154—"Everybody Loves Somebody"] and Nancy.

The man who helped find "Strangers in the Night" for Sinatra was his producer, Reprise A&R man Jimmy Bowen [see 19—"Party Doll"]. Publisher Hal Fine brought Bowen some instrumental tracks written for the soundtrack of *A Man Could Get Killed* by German composer Bert Kaempfert. Kaempfert had already recorded a number one single [see 82—"Wonderland by Night"] and written another [see 95—"Wooden Heart"]. When Bowen heard one of Kaempfert's melodies, he immediately stopped Fine. Bowen told him if he could come up with English lyrics for the song, Sinatra would record it.

It took a few months for the lyrics to be written, but a publisher's job is to get as many recordings of a song as possible and earn money for the writer (and the publisher!). By the time Bowen received the lyrics, Bobby Darin and Jack Jones were

recording it, too. Bowen had three days notice of the Jones' single being released.

Bowen called arranger Ernie Freeman and asked him to come up with an arrangement for Sinatra quickly. On the third day, a Monday, Bowen had a full orchestra in place at 5 p.m. Three hours later, Sinatra arrived to record "Strangers in the Night." He had his finished vocal track on tape by 9 p.m., and within 24 hours radio stations across America were playing the Sinatra version.

Exactly one month before "Strangers in the Night" topped the Hot 100, it went to number one in Britain for three weeks. It was succeeded by the Beatles' "Paperback Writer," which was number one simultaneously in the United States and the United Kingdom.

Francis Albert Sinatra was born on December 12, 1915, in Hoboken, New Jersey. He sang in the glee club at Demarest High School. He dropped out of school to become a professional singer, but at his mother's insistence went to work for the *Jersey Journal*, where he worked his way up from copy boy to sportswriter. He continued to sing in local clubs, and with some friends formed

a group, the Hoboken Four. They won first prize on "Major Bowes Amateur Radio Hour."

In June, 1939, bandleader Harry James was listening to radio station WNEW's "Dance Band Parade" when he heard a voice that attracted his attention. The singer was not identified on the broadcast, but the band playing belonged to Harry Arden and the show originated from the Rustic Cabin in Englewood, New Jersey. The next night James went to the Rustic Cabin, found the singer was named Frank Sinatra, and offered him a job as vocalist for $65 a week.

Sinatra had already made his first recording, a demo disc, in February. He recorded "Melancholy Mood" and "From the Bottom of My Heart" with James' orchestra on July 13, and those songs became his first official record release.

In December, Tommy Dorsey offered Sinatra a job at $100 per week, and James consented to let Sinatra out of his contract. With Dorsey's band, Sinatra appeared in the film *Las Vegas Nights*, singing "I'll Never Smile Again."

Sinatra's status as America's first teen idol was established after his 1942 concerts with Benny Goodman at New York's Paramount Theater. In 1943 he signed with Columbia Records, and remained with the label until 1953. His career seemed to be slowing down until he was cast in the motion picture *From Here to Eternity*, for which he won an Oscar for Best Supporting Actor in 1954. Then he switched to Capitol and had 23 chart records before switching to his own label, Reprise Records.

---

## THE TOP FIVE
*Week of July 2, 1966*

1 **Strangers in the Night**
Frank Sinatra

2 **Paperback Writer**
Beatles

3 **Red Rubber Ball**
Cyrkle

4 **Paint It, Black**
Rolling Stones

5 **You Don't Have
to Say You Love Me**
Dusty Springfield

*Writers: Jeff Barry*
*Ellie Greenwich*

*Producer: Henry Glover*

*July 16, 1966*
*2 weeks*

TOMMY JAMES (born Thomas Gregory Jackson on April 29, 1947, in Dayton, Ohio) was just two years old when his mother bought him a record player and some 78 rpm records. "I just played everything I could get my hands on," Tommy remembers. "When I was three years old, I started to play the ukulele—the guitar was too big for me. When I was nine I bought my first guitar and taught myself how to play it. I moved on the next year to an electric guitar."

Tommy was 11 when his family moved to Niles, Michigan. Enrolled in a new, larger school, he fulfilled his desire to put a rock group together. With friends from the school band, he formed the Shondells while still in the seventh grade. At the same time, Tommy went to work in a record store and met people from a wholesale distributor who owned a recording studio. At the tender age of 12, Tommy James took the Shondells into the studio and cut his first record, "Long Pony Tail." He had 500 copies pressed and distributed locally.

Jack Douglas, a disc jockey at WNIL in Niles, was interested in starting a regional record label. After he heard "Long Pony Tail," he asked Tommy if his group had more material to record.

Tommy had heard a song performed by a group in a club in South Bend, Indiana. "I really only remembered a few lines from the song, so when we went in to record it, I had to make up the rest of the song. I just pieced it back together from what I remembered."

The song was "Hanky Panky," originally recorded in 1963 by Jeff Barry and Ellie Greenwich as the Raindrops [see 158—"Do Wah Diddy Diddy"]. They were in the middle of a recording session when they realized they needed a "B" side for a single, so they went out to the hall and wrote "Hanky Panky" in 20 minutes.

Tommy's version was released on Douglas' Snap Records, and sold well in the tri-state area of Michigan, Indiana and Illinois. Without national distribution, the record's popularity didn't extend beyond those borders, and the song died a natural death. Tommy graduated from high school and spent the summer of 1965 on the road in Chicago and the Midwest. By December he was out of work, and was sitting at home feeling sorry for himself when he received a phone call from a disc jockey in Pittsburgh. The

## THE TOP FIVE
### *Week of July 16, 1966*

1   **Hanky Panky**
    Tommy James & the Shondells

2   **Wild Thing**
    Troggs

3   **Red Rubber Ball**
    Cyrkle

4   **You Don't Have
    to Say You Love Me**
    Dusty Springfield

5   **Paperback Writer**
    Beatles

DJ had found a two-year-old copy of "Hanky Panky" and had been playing it on the air. As a result, someone had bootlegged 80,000 copies of the single and had been selling them in local stores.

Tommy asked the Shondells to fly to Pittsburgh, but according to him, they were no longer interested. Tommy went by himself and was invited to appear on local television shows and perform in clubs. "I had no group, and I had to put one together really fast. I was in a Pittsburgh club one night, and I walked up to a group that was playing that I thought was pretty good, and asked them if they wanted to be the Shondells. They said yes, and off we went." The quartet, known as the Raconteurs until Tommy recruited them, consisted of bassist Mike Vale, drummer Pete Lucia, keyboardist Ronnie Rosman and guitarist Eddie Gray.

Tommy took the original master of "Hanky Panky" to New York, where he sold it to Roulette Records. "The amazing thing is, we did not re-record the song," he says. "I don't think anybody can record a song that bad and make it sound good. It had to sound amateurish like that. I think if we'd fooled with it too much we'd have fouled it up."

If Tommy was surprised that the song was a number one hit, songwriter Jeff Barry was equally shocked. "I was surprised when it was *released,*" Jeff laughs. "As far as I was concerned, it was a terrible song. In my mind it wasn't written to be a song, just a "B" side. I was kind of ashamed of it when it first came out, but then I found out what a big hit it was and maybe it had something I just didn't see."

# 204 Wild Thing
FONTANA 1548/ATCO 6415
## THE TROGGS

*Writer: Chip Taylor*

*Producer: Larry Page*

*July 30, 1966*
*2 weeks*

THE TROGGS foreshadowed music's new wave of the '70s with songs like "Wild Thing," written by an American songwriter, Chip Taylor. The group had to choose between two songs to record in 1966—John Sebastian's "Did You Ever Have to Make Up Your Mind?" and Taylor's "Wild Thing." In his book *Where Did You Go to, My Lovely?*, Fred Dellar quotes Reg Presley on his first reaction to "Wild Thing": "I looked at the lyrics—'Wild thing...you make my heart sing...you make everything groovy'...and they seemed so corny that I thought, 'Oh God, what are they doing to us?'"

In 1965, four young men from Andover, Hampshire, England, formed a group called the Troglodytes, as in cave dwellers. The original line-up included bricklayer Reg Ball on bass, Ronnie Bond on drums, Tony Mansfield on guitar and lead vocals and Dave Wright on guitar. Mansfield and Wright left and were replaced by Chris Britton and

Pete Staples, who had belonged to a group called Ten Foot Five. A reluctant Reg became the new lead vocalist and they were soon discovered by producer Larry Page. Their first single, "Lost Girl," was written by Reg and released on CBS. It wasn't a hit. Reg changed his last name to Presley and the group signed with Fontana Records in England.

An appearance on the British television program "Thank Your Lucky Stars" helped bring them national attention, and their first United Kingdom hit, "Wild Thing," was aided by suggestive lyrics and the unusual sound of Presley's ocarina. "Wild Thing" went all the way to number two in Great Britain; its American release went one position higher.

There was an unusual problem with the American release, however. Two record labels, Fontana and Atco, both claimed ownership of the Troggs' recordings and both released singles. "Wild Thing" is the only number one single to have a simultaneous release on two different labels.

The group's American career was short-lived. In 1968, they had a top ten song, "Love Is All Around," a pretty ballad that was miles away from the sleaziness of "Wild Thing."

In Britain, they were constantly plagued by objections to their lyrics. In "I Can't Control Myself," Reg sang, "Her slacks were low and her hips were showing," and radio stations shied away from airplay.

The song "Wild Thing" lives on, however. It has been covered over the years by artists from Jimi Hendrix to X. Shortly after the Troggs' version went to number one in America, writer Chip Taylor produced a satiric version by "Senator Bobby," a soundalike for Robert F. Kennedy, that made the top 20.

## THE TOP FIVE
*Week of July 30, 1966*

1 **Wild Thing**
Troggs

2 **Hanky Panky**
Tommy James & the Shondells

3 **Lil' Red Riding Hood**
Sam the Sham & the Pharaohs

4 **The Pied Piper**
Crispian St. Peters

5 **I Saw Her Again**
Mamas & the Papas

*Writers: John Sebastian*
*Steve Boone*
*Mark Sebastian*

*Producer: Erik Jacobsen*

*August 13, 1966*
*3 weeks*

"SUMMER IN THE CITY" was originally a poem written by Mark Sebastian, whose brother John was in the Lovin' Spoonful. Mark showed it to his brother, who thought the beginning of it wasn't exciting enough. He loved the chorus, though, and asked Mark if he'd let him try to write a grittier beginning with more tension. Lovin' Spoonful bassist Steve Boone had a piece written for piano that hadn't fit into any other song, but seemed to work here.

When the song was finished, John said it sounded like George Gershwin—"An American in Paris." "It sounded like traffic," he recalls. "We hired an old sound man, obviously from the radio era, and he had old acetates of traffic jams and car horns. We listened for hours to various traffic jams and car horns and selected the ones we wanted. We found a pneumatic hammer...to provide the payoff for that section and put it all together."

In 1964, John Sebastian was excited by the Beatles and was inspired to put his own four-man rock and roll band together. "On the very night the Beatles played 'The Ed

Sullivan Show,' I was meeting Zal Yanovsky for the first time at Cass Elliott's house. We watched that show, then sat down and played together for two, three hours, after which we both went to our separate corners. Cass, who was always a wonderful go-between, would keep going to Zally and say, 'you know, he really wants to play with you,' and coming back to me and saying, 'Zally loved the way you play.' I would say Cass is quite responsible for how fast our relationship grew in those early days."

John and Zal were recruited into the Mugwumps, which also featured future mama and papa [see 198—"Monday, Monday"] Cass Elliott and Denny Doherty. "I would sit on one side of the stage and play little blues licks that weren't part of the arrangement," Sebastian confesses. "The manager felt this was counter-productive and I was fired as being a bad influence on Zally. I waited six months and the Mugwumps died a natural death."

Meanwhile, Sebastian wandered through the South, meeting folk artists and bluesmen, including Mississippi John Hurt. One of Hurt's songs included the lyric, "I love my baby by the lovin' spoonful."

Back in Greenwich Village, John and Zal met Steve Boone and Joe Butler, two rock and rollers that Sebastian thought would give credibility to the new group he wanted to organize.

The Lovin' Spoonful recorded "Do You Believe in Magic" as a demo record. "No record company in New York City was interested because we didn't sound like anything that had come before, nor did we sing with Liverpool accents. Phil Spector came down one evening to see the band. The next night everyone from the Brill Building was there...from out of that we got a record contract."

Released as their first single on the Kama Sutra label, "Do You Believe in Magic" went to number nine on the Hot 100. "You Didn't Have to Be So Nice" peaked at 10, then the next two singles ("Daydream" and "Did You Ever Have to Make Up Your Mind?") reached number two. "Summer in the City" was the group's fifth single.

Zal left in 1967, and was replaced by Jerry Yester (whose brother Jim was in the Association [see 208—"Cherish"]). A year later, Sebastian departed for a solo career [see 434—"Welcome Back"]. The Lovin' Spoonful carried on for a few months with new lead singer Joe Butler, but without the two founding members the band had lost its soul and its will to live.

## THE TOP FIVE
*Week of August 13, 1966*

1 **Summer in the City**
Lovin' Spoonful

2 **Lil' Red Riding Hood**
Sam the Sham & the Pharaohs

3 **They're Going to Take Me Away, Ha-Haa!**
Napoleon XIV

4 **Wild Thing**
Troggs

5 **The Pied Piper**
Crispian St. Peters

## 206 Sunshine Superman EPIC 10045
### DONOVAN

*Writer: Donovan*

*Producer: Mickie Most*

*September 3, 1966*
*1 week*

WHETHER he deserved it or not, Scottish-born Donovan was tagged a Bob Dylan imitator by the press, an inference he was stuck with until Dylan came to Britain and the two met at Dylan's hotel. After a day of camaraderie, the two artists emerged from the hotel obvious friends, and the media's attitude toward Donovan shifted to a more favorable stance.

It's easy to see why the Donovan of 1965 was considered to be a copy of Dylan. He wore a denim cap, played a harmonica attached to a neck harness and sang what sounded like folk songs. As Donovan's music evolved, and as his image changed from wandering minstrel to flower child, the distinction between him and Dylan became much clearer.

Donovan Phillip Leitch was born February 10, 1946, in Maryhill, a small town on the edge of Glasgow, Scotland. His family moved to Hatfield in England when he was 10. Five years later he left school to travel around the countryside. He met another traveller, Gypsy Dave, and they wandered through England and the Continent, passing a hat for money as Donovan played guitar and Gypsy Dave played the kazoo.

Donovan was 18 when he returned to London, and a quick series of events propelled him into the public eye. Peter Eden saw him performing at a club, became his manager, and arranged for him to record some demos. The producers of the British television series "Ready Steady Go" heard the tapes and signed him for an appearance. The reaction was so great they brought him back the following week, when he was spotted by executives of Pye Records, who signed him to a recording contract.

His first single, "Catch the Wind," performed well on both sides of the Atlantic, and Donovan was invited to appear on American television's "Shindig." After two more folk-oriented singles ("Colours" and "The Universal Soldier"), he sought out pop producer Mickie Most.

"He was . . . getting labelled as a bit of a Dylan copy, and he came to

see me," says Most in *The Record Producers* by John Tobler and Stuart Grundy. "He played me this song "Sunshine Superman" and it had a very different color to it from the way it is on record." Most tells how John Cameron and Spike Heatley wrote the arrangement for "Sunshine Superman," and adds, "We went into the studio at two o'clock on a Sunday afternoon, and by five o'clock it was finished.

"I enjoyed working with him because he was very good at performing his own songs in the studio, and because he was a writer, I didn't have to keep going to America looking for songs, all I had to do was go up to his cottage in Hertford, which was much cheaper and much less aggravation."

Due to legal problems, "Sunshine Superman" was in the can for seven months before it was released. Donovan had left his previous manager, and a December 4, 1965, story in *Billboard* revealed that "American business manager Allan Klein" was negotiating a new pact between Donovan and Most. Two weeks later, another *Billboard* story stated that Donovan's business manager denied any agreement with Most. In Janu-

ary, 1966, the British Pye label deleted "Sunshine Superman" from their release schedule due to the legal entanglement. It wasn't until July 23 that the Donovan-Most pact was announced and "Sunshine Superman" was released in America. Donovan was worried that the lapse of time might hurt the song's chances. It entered the Hot 100 on July 30 at number 90. Donovan's fears were unwarranted; on September 3 the song was number one. The single wasn't issued in Britain for another five months. Released a full year after it had been recorded, it still did well, peaking at number three.

Donovan's next single was "Mellow Yellow," widely misconstrued as an instruction manual for smoking bananas. Paul McCartney could be heard whispering "mellow yellow" throughout, a fair exchange since Donovan had joined in the shipboard fun of "Yellow Submarine."

Donovan continued to have hit singles through the '60s, including "There Is a Mountain," "Hurdy Gurdy Man" and "Atlantis." His career was more erratic in the '70s. He enjoyed periods of semi-retirement in Ireland and surfaced occasionally to compose soundtrack music for films like *If It's Tuesday, It Must Be Belgium*; *The Pied Piper* and *Brother Sun, Sister Moon*. There were albums, but *7-Tease* and *Cosmic Wheels* didn't have the impact of his earlier work. In 1980, Donovan appeared at the Edinburgh Festival, then toured France and Germany. He performed at a London Palladium concert for children's charities, and periodically releases an album of new material.

### THE TOP FIVE
*Week of September 3, 1966*

1 **Sunshine Superman**
Donovan

2 **Summer in the City**
Lovin' Spoonful

3 **See You in September**
Happenings

4 **You Can't Hurry Love**
Supremes

5 **Yellow Submarine**
Beatles

*Writers: Brian Holland*
*Lamont Dozier*
*Eddie Holland*

*Producers: Brian Holland*
*Lamont Dozier*

*September 10, 1966*
*2 weeks*

BRIAN HOLLAND came up with the melody and Eddie Holland thought of the title for the Supremes' ninth number one single, "You Can't Hurry Love." "We were trying to reconstruct 'Come See About Me' in a way, and somehow it turned into 'You Can't Hurry Love,'" explains Lamont Dozier. "It was basically a gospel feel we were after."

"You Can't Hurry Love" entered the Hot 100 at number 66 on August 13, 1966. Although it followed two Supremes singles that didn't go to number one ("My World Is Empty Without You," "Love Is Like an Itching in My Heart"), it was an upwardly mobile record, moving 66-28-7-4 then to number one. In its second week at number one, it prevented the Beatles' "Yellow Submarine" from taking charge of the top spot.

In Britain, the Supremes' version of "You Can't Hurry Love" peaked at number three, putting it in a three-way tie for their second biggest single in the United Kingdom. "Baby Love" is their only British number one; "Where Did Our Love Go" and "Stoned Love" also went to three. "You Can't Hurry Love" did eventually become a British number one—in early 1983, thanks to a recording by Phil Collins [see 586—"Against All Odds (Take a Look at Me Now)"] that Dozier thinks is one of the best cover versions of a Supremes song.

Diane Ross was born March 26, 1944, at Women's Hospital in Detroit, the second child of Fred and Ernestine Ross. Her parents had chosen the name Diane, but a clerical error by a hospital staff member resulted in "Diana" appearing on the birth certificate—a name that Diane would choose for herself only after becoming a Supreme.

Late in 1950, with three more children in the family, Ernestine was stricken with tuberculosis. She was sent to a hospital in Holland, Michigan, to recover while her five children were sent to her sister, Beatrice, in Bessemer, Alabama. "My grandfather—Rev. William Moton—was minister of the Bessemer Baptist Church," Diana has recalled. "I sang in his choir and maybe that's when I realized I loved to sing."

Healthy again, her mother moved home and the children returned from Bessemer, with Aunt Bea along to help out. Diane graduated into Dwyer Junior High School, and on her 14th birthday, the Ross family moved into a three-bedroom apartment in a new division of the Brewster-Douglas Projects, government subsidized housing for low income families.

Diane was accepted into Cass Technical High School, which required its students to have a "B" average to enroll. She studied fashion design and was also active on the swim team. One day before Christmas vacation began in 1961, Diane played the first Supremes record, "I Want a Guy," for her classmates. Her friend Barbara Allison recalled the event for J. Randy Taraborrelli in his *Diana* autobiography:

"She was very nervous because she didn't know how we would receive it. We were quite impressed and Diane was kind of embarassed by that. She was a little silly and nervous because this was her first record for Tamla. And when everybody in the class started complimenting her on the song, well, she just didn't know what to do with herself. She came just a little unglued!"

Her career as a singer wasn't established yet. Although Berry Gordy, Jr., had released "I Want a Guy," he hadn't signed the Supremes to a recording contract. Diane signed her contract on January 15, 1961, but a year-and-a-half later, with no hits to her credit, she took a job as a busgirl in the cafeteria of Detroit's leading department store, Hudson's.

**THE TOP FIVE**
*Week of September 10, 1966*

1  **You Can't Hurry Love**
   Supremes

2  **Sunshine Superman**
   Donovan

3  **Yellow Submarine**
   Beatles

4  **See You in September**
   Happenings

5  **Summer in the City**
   Lovin' Spoonful

# Cherish VALIANT 747
## THE ASSOCIATION

*Writer: Terry Kirkman*

*Producer: Curt Boettcher*

*September 24, 1966*
*3 weeks*

THE ASSOCIATION 's roots can be traced back to a meeting between a salesman (Terry Kirkman) and a sailor (Gary Jules Alexander) at the home of a pediatrician in Honolulu in 1964.

Kirkman, born in Salinas, Kansas, had been playing music since he was 14, when he performed with a polka band in a Basque restaurant. For five years, he played at "beatnik" coffee houses in California with Frank Zappa. He was selling business forms in Hawaii when he met Alexander, who was serving in the Navy. Alexander, born in Chattanooga, Tennessee, was a high school dropout who became proficient at rhythm, bass and lead guitar. They agreed to meet again after Alexander was discharged from the navy.

Back on the mainland, Kirkman and Alexander met up in early 1965. They formed a 13-man group called the Men in Los Angeles. They played folk-rock blended with jazz, and made their debut at the Troubadour, a popular Melrose Boulevard club owned by Doug Weston. An argument during a rehearsal led to a sudden exodus of seven Men, and the six remaining members took refuge at Terry Kirkman's house to consider their future.

Determined to continue as a musical unit, the surviving Men sought a new name. The Aristocrats was suggested, but when Terry Kirkman's wife, Judy, went to look up the definition in the dictionary, she found another word on the same page that seemed more appropriate: the Association.

In addition to Kirkman and Alexander, the Men who became the Association included drummer Ted Bluechel, Jr., bassist Brian Cole, percussionist Russ Giguere and rhythm guitarist Jim Page. When Page left soon after, he was replaced by Jim Yester.

The Association developed a large southern California following by appearing at the Ice House, a night club that had locations in Pasadena and Glendale. They released one single on Jubilee Records ("Babe I'm Gonna Leave You"), but were then turned down by every major label who heard their first album, which included "Cherish." Finally, they were signed to Valiant Records, a label founded by Barry DeVorzon, Billy Sherman and Budd Dolinger in 1960. The label was owned by Four Star Television and distributed by Warner Brothers Records.

Their first Valiant release was a Bob Dylan song, "One Too Many Mornings." It did well in Los Angeles, where the group had many fans, but didn't place on *Billboard's* Hot 100. Their first national hit was "Along Comes Mary," a song many people interpreted as a drug reference to marijuana. Reactions to this charge were varied. Some radio stations were reluctant to play the song, while others considered the inference too vague to have any credibility. During an appearance at Disneyland, the group was warned by the Orange County Sheriffs Department not to perform the tune, but three weeks later the sisters of Marymount College named it the song of the year, obviously seeing "Mary" in a different light.

While some expected the next single to be "Enter the Young" from the group's first album, *And Then . . . Along Comes the Association*, the band wisely chose "Cherish," a Terry Kirkman composition.

Kirkman had written "Cherish" in just over a half-hour. He had already written the word on a pad of paper three weeks earlier, but had been unable to write the song then. Mike Whelan, who had gone from the Men to the New Christy Minstrels, liked the song and added it to that group's repertoire. In an interview with Marty Natchez in *Goldmine*, Kirkman explains how Whelan almost recorded the song first: "He had an offer from a Denver-based production company to record it as a single. They were going to buy the song from me for $1,000. Well, I thought I had found manna from heaven! When that deal fell through, I was disappointed beyond my wildest dreams."

"Cherish" was recorded in a garage converted into a studio by arranger Gary Paxton [see 70—"Alley Oop"]. Kirkman and Alexander played on the track, but studio musicians filled in for the other members, who only supplied their vocal talents. Originally written as a slow ballad, Paxton and producer Curt Boettcher speeded up the tempo. The song was three minutes and 25 seconds long, edited down to 3:13 for the single. Concerned that radio stations would be frightened off by the length, the single's running time was listed as an even three minutes.

"Cherish" debuted on the Hot 100 on August 27, 1966, at number 66. Four weeks later it was number one.

## THE TOP FIVE
*Week of September 24, 1966*

1 **Cherish**
Association

2 **You Can't Hurry Love**
Supremes

3 **Sunshine Superman**
Donovan

4 **Yellow Submarine**
Beatles

5 **Bus Stop**
Hollies

*Writers: Eddie Holland
Lamont Dozier
Brian Holland*

*Producers: Brian Holland
Lamont Dozier
Eddie Holland*

*October 15, 1966
2 weeks*

AFTER their first number one single [see 177—"I Can't Help Myself (Sugar Pie, Honey Bunch)"] written by Brian Holland, Lamont Dozier and Eddie Holland, the Four Tops needed a follow-up *immediately*. Their success on Motown inspired Columbia, a label they had been signed to briefly in 1960, to re-release "Ain't That Love," and Motown was afraid that would spoil the chances of a hit sequel.

Holland-Dozier-Holland wrote the fastest hit of their career with "It's the Same Old Song," a ditty some critics mused was, indeed, the same old song. Its similarity to "I Can't Help Myself" was striking and it may be that very similarity that helped make it such a big hit. The Four Tops were hustled into a studio on a Thursday and on Monday the new single was released. "It's the Same Old Song" was the fifth biggest single of their career, charting at number five on the Hot 100.

Holland-Dozier-Holland were a regular hit factory, stamping out top 10 hits for the Supremes and the Four Tops at the same time. After "It's the Same Old Song" left the Columbia single in the dust (it was on the Hot 100 for one week, at number 93), the Tops released "Something About You," "Shake Me, Wake Me (When It's Over)" (both top 20 hits) and "Loving You Is Sweeter Than Ever" (which only went to number 45).

Something was needed to re-energize the Four Tops, and Holland-Dozier-Holland came up with another number one single, "Reach Out, I'll Be There." Like "I Can't Help Myself," it was recorded in a couple of takes. The group didn't pay much attention to it, assuming it was just another track for their next album.

Soon after, Berry Gordy called the group into his office and told them to be prepared for the biggest hit of their career. Duke Fakir remembers trying to figure out which song Gordy meant. When the Motown founder said "Reach Out," Duke had to think back to which song had that title. The group assumed it was a pep talk and didn't place too much faith in Gordy's prediction. Two weeks later, when almost every radio station in the country was playing "Reach Out, I'll Be There," the Tops realized Gordy had been right.

The song established them internationally. In Britain, where they had failed to crack the top 20, even with "I Can't Help Myself," they were suddenly number one.

The next two singles were in a similar vein to "Reach Out." "Standing in the Shadows of Love" peaked at six and "Bernadette" at four. The Tops recorded two more Holland-Dozier-Holland singles ("7 Rooms of Gloom" and "You Keep Running Away") before turning to cover versions of other hits ("Walk Away Renee" and "If I Were a Carpenter"). There was only one more H-D-H single recorded by the Four Tops ("I'm in a Different World") before the songwriting team that had written their biggest hits left Motown over royalties disputes. Other producers tried to come up with hits for the group, but only Frank Wilson's "Still Water (Love)" and a cover version of "It's All in the Game" [see 43] cracked the top 30.

Finally, in 1972, the Four Tops made the difficult decision to leave Motown. They were in the midst of negotiations with Dunhill Records when label president Jay Lasker asked the writing/producing team of Dennis Lambert and Brian Potter to play the two songs they had written for the group. When the Four Tops heard "Keeper of the Castle" and "Ain't No Woman (Like the One I've Got)," they stopped negotiating and signed immediately. The former song went to number ten and the latter soared to number four, an impressive comeback.

Unfortunately, they were the only top 10 hits at Dunhill. Label personnel changes and a sale to parent company ABC probably hurt the Tops, and they eventually left. They were off the charts for almost five years when they signed with Polygram's Casablanca label and went to number 11 with "When She Was My Girl."

On June 20, 1997, second tenor Lawrence Payton died of liver cancer in Southfield, Michigan, at the age of 59. The group had been intact ever since its founding in 1954, and the surviving members elected not to replace their long-time friend. They decided instead to continue as a trio known simply as the Tops.

## THE TOP FIVE
*Week of October 15, 1966*

1 **Reach Out I'll be There**
Four Tops

2 **Cherish**
Association

3 **96 Tears**
? (Question Mark)
& the Mysterians

4 **Last Train to Clarksville**
Monkees

5 **Psychotic Reaction**
Count Five

## 210 96 Tears CAMEO 428
### ? (QUESTION MARK) AND THE MYSTERIANS

*Writer: Rudy Martinez*

*Producer: Not Known*

*October 29, 1966*
*1 week*

THE secret identity of the lead singer for the Mysterians was the biggest mystery about "96 Tears," a song now acknowledged as a forerunner of punk rock, a movement spearheaded in the '70s by artists like Patti Smith and the Sex Pistols.

The singer's true identity may have been a mystery in 1966, but it's no secret today. Behind the sunglasses he never removed, Question Mark, known more commonly as ?, was Rudy Martinez. Rudy was born in Mexico and raised in Michigan's Saginaw Valley, as were his fellow Mysterians: lead guitarist Robert Balderrama, keyboardist Frank Rodriquez, bassist Frank Lugo and drummer Edward Serrato.

The song "96 Tears" was written four years before the group came together. They were known as XYZ when they played for the first time in Adrian, Michigan. Rudy had written a poem titled "Too Many Teardrops." Set to music by the band, it was a favorite with the audiences at Mount Holly hall. The group's manager, Lilly Gonzalez, formed a record label, Pa-Go-Go, especially for the group. The song "96 Tears" and its flip side, "Midnight Hour," were recorded in her living room, which provided some unusual acoustics.

The Mysterians thought "Midnight Hour" was the hit side, but ? knew he had a big hit on his hands with "96 Tears." He promoted the single in Flint, Saginaw and Bay City, Michigan. Despite the lack of radio airplay, it started to sell in stores. Finally, Bob Dell of radio station WTAC in Flint broke the record. When CKLW, a major Detroit station, started playing it, the record came to the attention of Neil Bogart, then president of Cameo Records in Philadelphia. He bought the master from Pa-Go-Go to release nationally.

In his fanzine *Who Put the Bomp?*, editor Greg Shaw said,

"Question Mark and the Mysterians fulfilled the dreams of every punk band—a national number one hit— and with a home recording at that! On paper, '96 Tears' is nothing; songs don't come any simpler. But the performance was perfect, and the record became an instant classic."

One of the song's attributes that has merited attention the past two decades has been its acclaimed use of the Farfisa organ. It was a surprise, then, when Martinez revealed in a 1982 *Goldmine* interview with Jeff Tamarkin that the group used a *Vox* organ, not a *Farfisa.*

? and the Mysterians followed "96 Tears" with "I Need Somebody," backed with "8-Teen." The latter song was a hit for Alice Cooper in 1971 under the title "Eighteen." There were three more ? and the Mysterians singles on Cameo, but none came close to matching the success of "96 Tears."

In 1967, Bogart started a new label, Buddah Records. He signed the production team of Jerry Kasenetz and Jeff Katz, and their Super-K productions specialized in bubblegum artists like the 1910 Fruitgum Company ("Simon Says," "Indian Giver") and the Ohio Express ("Yummy Yummy Yummy," "Chewy Chewy"). ? and the Mysterians released one single on the subsidiary Super-K label, "Hang In." It's the last recorded product by the group.

Garland Jeffreys revived "96 Tears" in 1981, taking it to number 66 on the Hot 100. That encouraged Martinez to put together a new band of Mysterians and hit the road again.

## THE TOP FIVE
*Week of October 29, 1966*

1 **96 Tears**
   ? (Question Mark)
   & the Mysterians

2 **Last Train to Clarksville**
   Monkees

3 **Reach Out I'll be There**
   Four Tops

4 **Poor Side of Town**
   Johnny Rivers

5 **Walk Away Renee**
   Left Banke

Writers: *Tommy Boyce*
*Bobby Hart*

Producers: *Tommy Boyce*
*Bobby Hart*

November 5, 1966
1 week

No one ever expected Richard Chamberlain to perform heart surgery, or William Shatner to pilot an Apollo mission, but the entire world was appalled that the Monkees didn't play their own instruments. It's a fact that Michael Nesmith and Peter Tork had musical ability, but along with Mickey Dolenz and Davy Jones, they were simply hired as actors to portray a rock and roll band. The distinction between reel life and real life was blurred because the Monkees records were competing in the marketplace with non-fictional groups like the Beatles, the Beach Boys and the Rolling Stones.

And compete they did. "Last Train to Clarksville" was released on August 16, 1966, two weeks and six days before the series premiered on NBC (the official premiere date was September 12, but NBC "previewed" the first episodes of two series, "The Monkees" and "Star Trek," the week of September 5). The single made its first appearance on the Hot 100 the same week that the series premiered, and was number one eight weeks later. Clearly, it didn't matter to the more than one million people who bought "Last Train to Clarksville" if Mickey could play the drums or not.

Credit for the concept of the Monkees goes to producers Bert Schneider and Bob Rafelson, who combined the zaniness of the Beatles' *A Hard Day's Night* with the Marx Brothers and sold the idea to NBC. At first, the producers considered building a show around the Lovin' Spoonful [see 205—"Summer in the City"], but when that didn't work they placed an advertisement in the Hollywood trade paper *Daily Variety*. The headline read, "Madness!! Auditions" and the copy asked for "Folk and Rock Musicians-Singers for Acting Roles in a New TV Series. Running parts for four insane boys, age 17-21."

Legend has it that 437 people answered the ad. Among them were Danny Hutton, later to be one of Three Dog Night [see 277—"Mama Told Me (Not to Come)"]; songwriter Paul Williams; former star of "The Donna Reed Show" Paul Petersen; and Stephen Stills, who was rejected because his teeth and hair weren't perfect.

Stills had a friend who strongly resembled him, except he had better teeth and hair. So Stills told Peter Tork about the casting call, and Tork became one of four successful applicants.

Screen Gems, the Columbia Pictures' production company that filmed the series, owned a new record label, Colgems, and a publishing company, and put both to good use. Publisher Don Kirshner was asked to find songs for the Monkees to record. Kirshner turned to his roster of talented songwriters for material, which explains why the Monkees recorded songs written by Gerry Goffin-Carole King, Neil Diamond, Neil Sedaka, David Gates, Barry Mann-Cynthia Weil and Tommy Boyce-Bobby Hart.

Boyce and Hart wrote the theme song for the series as well as "Last Train to Clarksville." Hart got the idea for the song after hearing the Beatles' "Paperback Writer" [see 201] for the first time and mistakenly thinking the Beatles were singing something about a "last train." When he realized that had nothing to do with the song, he decided to write his own tune around those words. Bobby picked a favorite Arizona town for the train's destination, and Clarksville became the fourth American city (after Kansas City, New Orleans and El Paso) to be mentioned in the title of a number one song.

Michael, Peter, Mickey and Davy spent 12 hours a day on a Columbia soundstage filming the series, leaving little time for recording. That, and the production company's doubts about their musical talent, led to studio musicians being hired to lay down the tracks for the Monkees' songs. Glen Campbell, Leon Russell, Hal Blaine and Louie Shelton were among the top Los Angeles session musicians who worked on the Monkees' material. For "Last Train to Clarksville," as well as all the tracks on their first two albums, the Monkees were only expected to come in and lay down their vocals. The fact that Screen Gems wanted the Monkees' musical non-involvement kept a secret led to eventual friction between the production company and the band, that erupted as a full-scale controversy in the press.

## THE TOP FIVE
*Week of November 5, 1966*

1 **Last Train to Clarksville**
   Monkees

2 **96 Tears**
   ? (Question Mark)
   & the Mysterians

3 **Poor Side of Town**
   Johnny Rivers

4 **Reach Out I'll be There**
   Four Tops

5 **Dandy**
   Herman's Hermits

**212**

# Poor Side of Town  IMPERIAL 66205
## JOHNNY RIVERS

*Writers: Johnny Rivers*
*Lou Adler*

*Producer: Lou Adler*

*November 12, 1966*
*1 week*

"POOR SIDE OF TOWN" was the only top 40 Johnny Rivers hit that he wrote himself. Rivers admits he was afraid of releasing any of his own compositions as singles because he was having so much success with songs written by other people. He knew it would be a big risk to release something he had written, but with nine chart records to his credit, Rivers took a gamble which paid handsomely. "Poor Side of Town" became his first—and only—number one single.

John Ramistella was born on November 7, 1942, in New York City. His family moved to Baton Rouge, Louisiana, when he was three, giving him a chance to see people like Fats Domino entertain at his junior high school.

When he was 15, Johnny returned to New York City to visit an aunt. Determined to meet Alan Freed, Johnny stood in front of radio station WINS' offices, waiting for the well-known disc jockey to show up for his air shift. When Freed arrived, Johnny introduced himself, and was told to come back the next day. Freed liked Johnny's songs and arranged for him to be signed to George Goldner's Gone/End Records.

Freed suggested Johnny use a shorter last name, and based on his bayou upbringing by the Mississippi River, came up with Johnny Rivers. Although he released a single on Gone, Johnny was never comfortable recording with New York musicians and returned to Louisiana. For a time, he lived in Nashville, where he became friendly with Roger Miller. Back home, he met two musicians from Shreveport, guitarist James Burton and bassist Joe Osborn. They worked with Ricky Nelson, and Rivers submitted a song which Nelson recorded, "I'll Make Believe."

In 1958, Johnny decided to fly to Los Angeles to meet Ricky. He fell in love with southern California, and couldn't get the Golden State out of his mind when he returned to Baton Rouge. Work with Louis Prima's band led him to Las Vegas and Lake Tahoe, and by 1961 he made a permanent move to Los Angeles.

He roomed with Jimmy Bowen [see 19—"Party Doll"], who gave Johnny some studio work. At the end of 1963, Johnny was appearing at Gazzarri's on La Cienega Boulevard, building up a sizeable following that lined up outside each night to enter the small club. A few months later, a man named Elmer Valentine told Johnny that if he would sign with him, he would open a club on Sunset Boulevard called the Whisky-a-Go-Go. Johnny's fans faithfully followed him to the new club. At the same time Johnny was meeting record producer Lou Adler.

Adler signed Johnny to Imperial Records, and Rivers was ecstatic to be on the same label as Fats Domino and Ricky Nelson. A live album was recorded at the Whisky. The songs were the same ones Johnny had been playing in Baton Rouge for years, songs like Chuck Berry's "Memphis" and "Maybelline," which became Johnny's first two Imperial singles.

"Memphis" spent two weeks at number two on the Hot 100, establishing Rivers as a national star.

Following "Poor Side of Town," Johnny returned to covering other artists' material. For his next single, he had to choose between "By the Time I Get to Phoenix," a song written by Jimmy Webb, whom he had signed to his publishing company, and "Baby I Need Your Lovin'," the Four Tops [see 177—"I Can't Help Myself (Sugar Pie, Honey Bunch)"] hit. He picked the latter, and followed that with another Motown hit, "The Tracks of My Tears."

In 1966, when renewing his contract with Imperial, Johnny asked for and got his own label. Soul City Records became a hot property in 1967, thanks to the Fifth Dimension [see 253—"Aquarius/Let the Sunshine In"]. That same year, Johnny helped organize and served on the board of directors of the Monterey Pop Festival.

Johnny's last top 10 hit was "Swayin' to the Music (Slow Dancin')," a Jack Tempchin composition released in 1977.

### THE TOP FIVE
*Week of November 12, 1966*

1  **Poor Side of Town**
   Johnny Rivers

2  **Last Train to Clarksville**
   Monkees

3  **96 Tears**
   ? (Question Mark)
   & the Mysterians

4  **Good Vibrations**
   Beach Boys

5  **Dandy**
   Herman's Hermits

thing was so much tighter. When we locked into a groove it was hellacious. The key thing was that we all grew up together and had this Detroit way of approaching music."

Another of the elements in the Supremes' success were the two women who mostly sang background vocals for Diana Ross, although Mary Wilson says she never felt like a background singer until the group changed its name to Diana Ross and the Supremes [see 223—"The Happening"].

"It has always bothered me when people refer to me as 'just' a background singer," Wilson told Thomas Ingrassia for a *Goldmine* interview. "...The Supremes were a *group*, and every position was important. So I never saw myself as *just* a background singer. When people ask about that, I tell them that I was the *star* in the background."

Mary Wilson was born March 6, 1944, in Greenville, Mississippi, the eldest of three children. "My father was a laborer who lost a leg, had two heart attacks and died when I was 14," Mary said in a 1968 interview. "I didn't know him very well. I lived with my aunt and uncle until I was 11. I thought they were my parents. My aunt worked at a cleaners and my uncle at an auto plant. I did for myself, alone in the house. I would sit by the window and just look out. I wasn't looking at anything particular, just dreaming. I was so skinny that my clothes didn't fit and I didn't want to go out. But I'm sort of glad I grew up the way that I did. I learned how to be alone and I learned how to be with people and still keep my privacy."

*Writers: Brian Holland*
    *Lamont Dozier*
    *Eddie Holland*

*Producers: Brian Holland*
    *Lamont Dozier*

*November 19, 1966*
*2 weeks*

"You Keep Me Hangin' On" was a conscious effort by Brian Holland, Lamont Dozier and Eddie Holland to create a rock and roll record for the Supremes. By merging rock with rhythm and blues, they gave the Supremes a harder sound than their previous singles—and they also gave them their eighth chart-topper.

"You Keep Me Hangin' On" was recorded June 30, 1966. It entered the Hot 100 at number 68 on October 29 and moved like lightning: 68-27-7 to number one. In its first week on top of the chart, it presided over a unique top five: it was the first time in the history of the Hot 100 that all five positions were filled by songs that either had been or would be number one [see The Top Five].

The Motown sound continued to evolve in the latter half of the '60s— records like "You Keep Me Hangin' On" and the Four Tops' "Reach Out, I'll Be There" [see 209] represented a new direction for Holland-Dozier-Holland. One of the elements that remained constant during the '60s was the band of session musicians responsible for the Motown sound. Artists like Diana Ross, Stevie Wonder and Marvin Gaye enjoyed the limelight, but the men who made the music remained anonymous except to the devoted fans who cared enough to find out who the men behind the hits were.

The core of Motown's studio band was a group known as the Funk Brothers. "Those guys had to be the best ever," Dozier acknowledges. Led by keyboardist Earl Van Dyke, the band also included bassist James Jamerson, drummers Benny Benjamin and Uriel Jones, guitarist Robert White and keyboardist Johnny Griffith.

"You could compare our rhythm section to anything else happening at the time and we were just better," Griffith told Nelson George in a *Musician* interview. "The Motown

## THE TOP FIVE
*Week of November 19, 1966*

1 **You Keep Me Hangin' On**
Supremes

2 **Good Vibrations**
Beach Boys

3 **Winchester Cathedral**
New Vaudeville Band

4 **Last Train to Clarksville**
Monkees

5 **Poor Side of Town**
Johnny Rivers

# 214 Winchester Cathedral FONTANA 1562
## THE NEW VAUDEVILLE BAND

*Writer: Geoff Stephens*

*Producer: Geoff Stephens*

*December 3, 1966*
*3 weeks*

THE NEW VAUDEVILLE BAND was the concoction of Geoff Stephens, a British composer who had written hits like "Tell Me When" for the Applejacks and "The Crying Game" for Dave Berry. Stephens was born October 1, 1934, in New Southgate, London. He taught French, English and religious studies in Southend, Essex, England, then left the field of education to work in an advertising agency. He was employed by the BBC as a writer, and one day saw a newspaper advertisement for a music publishing job.

Stephens was hired and worked for two years as a staff songwriter. His office was in Denmark Street, London's answer to Tin Pan Alley, and one day he was staring at a calendar hung on the wall. Above the days of the month was a picture of Winchester Cathedral. Looking at the Gothic architecture of the medieval church, Stephens was moved to write a song about the cathedral.

Being a fan of the music from the vaudeville era, Stephens decided to write his song in that style. To make sure the vocal was an accurate recreation of the 1930s sound he wanted, Stephens sang "Winchester Cathedral" himself. Session musicians were used to provide the instrumental track.

Sung through a megaphone, the record sounded more like Rudy Vallee than Herman's Hermits (who would later record Stephens' "There's a Kind of Hush"). Its unusual sound may have helped make it such a big hit in both countries. In the United Kingdom, it peaked at number four, but in America it went all the way to

the top. It debuted on the survey October 29, 1966, and was number one five weeks later. After one week, it gave way to the Beach Boys. On December 17, it rebounded from three back to the number one spot for two additional weeks.

After the record's international success, a "real" New Vaudeville Band was organized. Henry Harrison, a drummer from Watford who had belonged to a defunct British R&B group, Cops 'n' Robbers, was recruited. So was lead guitarist Mick Wilsher, trombonist Hugh "Shuggy" Watts, saxophonist Robert "Pops" Kerr, bassist Neil Korner and pianist Stan Heywood. Singer Alan Klein was brought in to handle lead vocals. He adopted the moniker "Tristram, seventh Earl of Cricklewood."

The New Vaudeville Band had two more singles, "Peek-a-Boo" and "Finchley Central," named for the stop on the London Underground. Neither came close to duplicating the success of "Winchester Cathedral."

When their British success faded, the band toured North America extensively. They spent a year at the Aladdin Hotel in Las Vegas before returning to Britain. With some change in membership, the band veered away from 1930s music and became popular playing cabarets.

Winchester Cathedral is one of a number of British landmarks that have been immortalized in song. Two of the rock era's biggest hits, the Beatles' "Penny Lane" [see 220] and Gerry Rafferty's "Baker Street," were about geographical locations in Britain.

## THE TOP FIVE
*Week of December 3, 1966*

1  **Winchester Cathedral**
   New Vaudeville Band

2  **Good Vibrations**
   Beach Boys

3  **You Keep Me Hangin' On**
   Supremes

4  **Devil With a Blue Dress On & Good Golly Miss Molly**
   Mitch Ryder & the Detroit Wheels

5  **Mellow Yellow**
   Donovan

CAPITOL 5676 **Good Vibrations**
BEACH BOYS

Writers: *Brian Wilson*
*Mike Love*

Producer: *Brian Wilson*

*December 10, 1966*
*1 week*

"**M**Y MOTHER used to tell me about vibrations," Brian Wilson explained in a 1976 *Rolling Stone* interview. "I didn't really understand too much of what she meant when I was a boy. It scared me, the word 'vibrations'—to think that invisible feelings, invisible vibrations existed scared me to death. But she told me about dogs that would bark at people, but wouldn't bark at others, that a dog would pick up vibrations from some people that you can't see, but you can feel. And the same thing happened with people."

"Good Vibrations" was Brian Wilson's pop symphony. It was the most expensive, elaborate single ever produced when it was released in October, 1966. Brian has estimated the cost at $16,000, unheard of in the mid-60s for one 45 rpm record. But "Good Vibrations" wasn't just another piece of seven-inch plastic. It was a masterpiece.

The early months of 1966 were spent working on a new Beach Boys album. Inspired by the production work of Phil Spector, *Pet Sounds* was a quantum leap over anything Brian had produced before.

It was after he completed *Pet Sounds* that Brian began working on "Good Vibrations." It was recorded in 17 sessions over a period of six months, at four different recording studios. The first session was completed at Western Recorders, where most of the Beach Boys' hits had been cut. Engineer Chuck Britz, who was there for the first live recording of "Good Vibrations," has said that the final version sounded the same as that first recording.

Carl described the evolution of the song to Himes: " 'Good Vibrations' has a lot of texture on it because we did so many overdubs. We'd double or triple or quadruple the exact same part, so it would sound like twenty voices. When I first heard it, it was much rougher sound; it had more *whomp* to it. Instead of making it bigger, bulgier and more raucous as Phil Spector might have, Brian refined it and got it more even-sounding. He had the idea of 'I'm picking up good vibrations,' but Michael didn't write the lyrics until the very last minute."

After recording at Western, Brian laid down overdubs at RCA, Gold Star and Columbia studios. "Every studio has its own marked sound," Brian said in *Rolling Stone*. "Using the four studios had a lot to do with the way the final record sounded." Among the unusual instruments Brian used were a cello and a theremin, an electronic instrument first heard on the soundtrack of the 1945 film *Spellbound*. The song continued to grow as Brian worked on it.

There were four "final" mixes of "Good Vibrations." The third mix was ready to go to Capitol when Brian changed his mind at the last minute and mixed it one more time.

An international public acknowledged Brian's creation. "Good Vibrations" entered the Hot 100 on October 22, 1966, at number 80. On December 10, it interrupted the three-week chart-topping run of "Winchester Cathedral." "Good Vibrations" went to number one in Britain on November 17.

It didn't seem possible at the time, but "Good Vibrations" turned out to be the last Beach Boys' single to make the top 10 until "Rock and Roll Music" went to number five in 1976. Emotional problems, a change of record label, an evolution of music—they may be some of the reasons the group sold fewer records. No matter what they released, their fans were still happy to hear "Surfin' U.S.A." and "California Girls." When Capitol issued the double-album *Endless Summer*, with early Beach Boys' hits, it sold far better than their newer material.

## THE TOP FIVE
*Week of December 10, 1966*

1  **Good Vibrations**
   Beach Boys

2  **Mellow Yellow**
   Donovan

3  **Winchester Cathedral**
   New Vaudeville Band

4  **Devil With a Blue Dress On
   & Good Golly Miss Molly**
   Mitch Ryder & the Detroit Wheels

5  **You Keep Me Hangin' On**
   Supremes

# 216 I'm a Believer COLGEMS 1002
## THE MONKEES

*Writer: Neil Diamond*

*Producer: Jeff Barry*

*December 31, 1966*
*7 weeks*

THE MONKEES first number one single [see 211—"Last Train to Clarksville"] was a big hit, but publisher Don Kirshner thought they hadn't reached their full sales potential. He called his friend Jeff Barry and asked him to find a follow-up song that would sell *millions* of copies. Barry was working with songwriter Neil Diamond [see 282—"Cracklin' Rosie"] at the time, having "discovered" him singing in a Greenwich Village coffee house, and Barry thought Diamond's song "I'm a Believer" would be right for the Monkees.

"Right" is an understatement. The single had an advance order of 1,051,280 copies, the highest advance sales on a 45 for RCA (which manufactured and distributed Colgems) since Elvis Presley. "I'm a Believer" entered the Hot 100 at number 44 on December 10, 1966, and went to number one three weeks later. It remained in the top spot for seven weeks, the longest-running number one since the Beatles' "I Want to Hold Your Hand" [see 143].

"I'm a Believer" established the Monkees as international stars. "Last Train to Clarksville" had failed in Britain because the series wasn't on the air yet. Its debut coincided with the release of "I'm a Believer," which went to number one in the United Kingdom ("Last Train . . ." subsequently entered the British chart). In the March 11, 1967, edition of *Billboard*, reports from England, Holland, Germany, France and Belgium told of the widespread popularity of the Monkees under the headline, "Europe's Gripped by Monkeesteria."

The four members of the Monkees all had differing degrees of involvement in show business before they answered the *Daily Variety* advertisement placed by Screen Gems.

*George Michael Dolenz* was born March 8, 1945, in Tarzana, California. He followed in the footsteps of his father (actor George Dolenz), and at the age of 11 was cast in the lead of the television series "Circus Boy"

(using the stage name Mickey Braddock), which premiered on NBC September 23, 1956, and ran for two seasons. He took guitar lessons as a teenager, and after high school studied architectural drawing at Los Angeles Trade and Technical College. In his late teens he had guest roles in the television series "Mr. Novak" and "Peyton Place." He learned to play the drums only after being assigned to the instrument by the producers of "The Monkees."

*David Thomas Jones* was born December 30, 1946, in Manchester, England. His father, a railroad engineer, never fulfilled his own dreams of becoming a performer. Young Davy left school when he was 14 1/2 to work at a racetrack, and had ambitions of becoming a jockey (his adult height is five-foot-three). He met a theatrical agent who owned horses, and was sent on an audition for the stage production of *Oliver*. He won the role of the Artful Dodger, and was later asked by American producer David Merrick to join the Broadway cast. He signed a contract with Columbia Pictures and recorded for their Colpix record label, a predecessor to Colgems. He was a contract player with Columbia when he auditioned for "The Monkees."

*Robert Michael Nesmith* was born December 30, 1942, in Houston, Texas. He grew up in Farmer's Branch, near Dallas, and first took up the saxophone. After a firecracker exploded in his hands, he switched to guitar for therapy. After a stint in the Air Force, he attended college in San Antonio and became involved in the folk music scene. He was briefly in a band with Michael Murphey ("Wildfire"), until he moved to Los Angeles in 1964. There he hosted the Monday night hootenannys at the

Troubadour, where Randy Sparks (of the New Christy Minstrels) saw him and invited him to join a folk band, the Survivors. He also recorded for Colpix, under the name Michael Blessing. Sparks noticed the ad in *Daily Variety* and suggested to Nesmith that he apply.

*Peter Halsten Thorkelson* was born February 13, 1944, in Washington, D.C. He was raised in Connecticut, where his father taught economics at the University of Connecticut. Peter took up the ukulele, guitar and five-string banjo, and decided to become a folksinger after two unsuccessful attempts at enrolling in college. In Greenwich Village he found a job accompanying the Phoenix Singers, and after touring with them for six months headed west to California. His first job was washing dishes at the Golden Bear club in Huntington Beach, but he was soon accompanying Stephen Stills. When Stills failed the Monkees audition because of his teeth and hair, he told his look-alike, Peter Tork, to try out.

## THE TOP FIVE
*Week of December 31, 1966*

1 **I'm A Believer**
   Monkees

2 **Snoopy vs. the Red Baron**
   Royal Guardsmen

3 **Winchester Cathedral**
   New Vaudeville Band

4 **That's Life**
   Frank Sinatra

5 **Sugar Town**
   Nancy Sinatra

*Writers: Jim Holvay*
*Gary Beisber*

*Producer: Not Known*

*February 18, 1967*
*2 weeks*

**M**OST people asked to name a rock group from Chicago would be hard-pressed to name anyone but Chicago [see 446—"If You Leave Me Now"]. While the Windy City is more known for Chicago blues than pop groups, it has produced its share, including the Cryan' Shames, the Mob and the group that preceded Chicago on the Hot 100 by almost three years, the Buckinghams.

The group came together on the north side of Chicago. Originally known as the Pulsations, the line-up in 1965 included lead singer Dennis Tufano, guitarist Carl Giammarese, bassist Nicholas Fortuna (later known as Nicky Fortune), keyboardist Dennis Miccoli and drummer Jon (Jon Jon) Paulos.

Their first local success was appearing in the 13 episodes of the "All Time Hits Show," broadcast on WGN-TV. Someone at the station suggested they change their name, and in the midst of the British invasion it was not surprising they chose something as Anglicized as the Buckinghams (the Baker Street Irregulars was considered).

They played neighboring towns and states and recorded their first single, a cover version of the Drifters' "Sweets for My Sweet," for the Spectra Sound label. In 1966, they were signed to a Chicago label, USA, where their first release was James Brown's "I'll Go Crazy," a song that Brown placed on the Hot 100 in February of that year. There were two more singles, including a version of the Beatles' "I Call Your Name," before "Kind of a Drag."

The song was written by Jim Holvay and Gary Beisber of the Mob, and was on a demo tape Holvay had given the band. "Kind of a Drag" entered the Hot 100 on December 31, 1966, at number 90. Seven weeks later it was number one, a surprising feat for a small, independent label.

USA couldn't hold on to the Buckinghams very long. They were wooed away by Columbia Records, who teamed them up with James William Guercio, the man who would go on to produce Blood, Sweat and Tears and Chicago for the same label. While USA released the official follow-up, "Lawdy Miss Clawdy," Columbia issued "Don't You Care." It was no contest. The former faltered at number 41 while the latter shot to number six. In their early days with CBS, Miccoli left the group and was replaced by Martin Grebb.

The Buckinghams had a relatively short career. They placed only four more songs on the chart: "Mercy, Mercy, Mercy," "Susan," "Hey Baby (They're Playing Our Song)" and "Back in Love Again."

Guercio and the band parted ways in 1968, and two years later the Buckinghams disbanded. Tufano and Giammarese signed as a duo with Lou Adler's Ode Records and had one chart entry in 1973, "Music Everywhere," which peaked at 68.

Fortuna became a session musician, Grebb played with the Fabulous Rhinestones and eventually toured with Chicago. Poulos became a manager, handling several acts, including Tufano and Giammarese and the Boyzz. Poulos was 32 years old when he died on March 26, 1980, of drug-related causes.

After their duo broke up, Dennis moved to Los Angeles to pursue acting. He had a role in Cheech and Chong's *Up in Smoke*. Later, he collaborated with lyricist Bernie Taupin [see 328—"Crocodile Rock"] on one of Taupin's albums. Carl sang on commercials.

*Made in Chicago*, a double album of greatest hits plus some new material, was released in 1975, but the Buckinghams remained inactive until a 1981 reunion of Tufano, Giammarese and Fortuna plus two new members at the annual ChicagoFest.

"We held back from putting the band together before, because it was a sacred kind of thing for us," Tufano told Moira McCormick for a *Goldmine* story. "The Buckinghams were special to us, and we never wanted to take it out on the road just to do it because we knew the name would bring in money."

---

## THE TOP FIVE
*Week of February 18, 1967*

1  **Kind of a Drag**
   Buckinghams

2  **I'm a Believer**
   Monkees

3  **Ruby Tuesday**
   Rolling Stones

4  **Georgy Girl**
   Seekers

5  **(We Ain't Got) Nothin' Yet**
   Blues Magoos

## 218

# Ruby Tuesday LONDON 904
## THE ROLLING STONES

*Writers: Mick Jagger*
*Keith Richards*

*Producer: Andrew Loog Oldham*

*March 4, 1967*
*1 week*

"LET'S SPEND THE NIGHT TOGETHER" was the intended "A" side of the first Rolling Stones single of 1967, but American radio stations were reluctant to broadcast its blatantly sexual message. So was Ed Sullivan, who had no desire to help stoke the Stones' reputation as the dirty bad boys of rock and roll. When they appeared on his live television program January 15 to promote their new single, he insisted they change the words to the less specific "Let's Spend Some Time Together."

Did the band accede to his request? "I never said 'time.' I really didn't," Mick told Jonathan Cott in a 1968 interview for *Rolling Stone*. "I said, mumbled, 'Let's spend some mmmmm together.' They would have cut it off if I had said 'night.'"

Radio station program directors couldn't ask Jagger to change the words, so they flipped the disc and played the cool, pastoral lament of "Ruby Tuesday," allegedly named for a famous groupie. The song, highlighted by the haunting recorder of Brian Jones, became the Stones' fourth American number one.

Neither song were favorites of the band. They were both included in the recorded-on-the-run *Between the Buttons* LP, which Jagger disdained in *New Musical Express*. "The only

decent song on the album was 'Back Street Girl.' The rest of it is more or less rubbish."

The Stones spent 10 laborious months of 1967 recording their next album, *Their Satanic Majesties Request*, at the Olympia Studios in the west London suburb of Barnes. During these sessions, the growing rift between the Stones and Andrew Loog Oldham became irreparable and the connection was severed. Producing chores were left to the group's discretion and the managerial reins were passed to Allen Klein.

Injected with the revolutionary spirit of 1968's Parisian student riots and the Chicago Democratic Convention demonstrations, the Stones reacted with hard hitting rock and roll. An American, Jimmy Miller, manipulated the board while four of the five group members created *Beggars Banquet*. "Brian played on some, not all of it," Mick qualified. "(He) wasn't around towards the end. What we didn't like was that we wanted to play again on stage and Brian wasn't in any condition to play."

Not that the Stones were setting off on any major campaigns. To promote *Beggars Banquet* they planned a television spectacular, "The Rolling Stones Rock 'n' Roll Circus."

Between the fire eaters, clowns and knife throwers, guest stars like the Who, Jethro Tull and a one-time only superjam band of John Lennon, Eric Clapton, Keith Richards (now sporting his plural last name) and Mitch Mitchell of the Jimi Hendrix Experience cavorted alongside their hosts. But Jagger reportedly didn't like the way he looked, so the film was permanently shelved.

During the production of the program, observers noted Brian Jones' growing inability to function within the band. His dependencies on drugs and alcohol left him in a condition described by an eyewitness as "dire" and "really pathetic." On June 9, 1969, it was officially announced that Brian was leaving the band—presumably over creative differences. He was replaced by Mick Taylor.

To introduce Taylor to the public, the Stones scheduled a free concert in London's Hyde Park for July 5. Two days earlier, Brian Jones was found dead at the bottom of the swimming pool on his Cotchford Farm in Hartfield, England. The official coroner's report called it "death by misadventure," citing high levels of alcohol and barbituates in his system. More than 250,000 people showed up in Hyde Park for the emotion-laden concert, which the Stones dedicated to their fallen comrade.

### THE TOP FIVE
*Week of March 4, 1967*

1 **Ruby Tuesday**
Rolling Stones

2 **Love is Here and Now You're Gone**
Supremes

3 **Kind of a Drag**
Buckinghams

4 **Baby, I Need Your Lovin'**
Johnny Rivers

5 **Georgy Girl**
Seekers

MOTOWN 1103 **Love Is Here and Now You're Gone**
THE SUPREMES

*Writers: Brian Holland*
*Lamont Dozier*
*Eddie Holland*

*Producers: Brian Holland*
*Lamont Dozier*

*March 11, 1967*
*1 week*

"LOVE IS HERE AND NOW YOU'RE GONE" featured the sexy speaking voice of Diana Ross. It was Eddie Holland's idea to write passages for Diana to talk through rather than sing, a technique she would put to good use on many future hits [see 281—"Ain't No Mountain High Enough"]. "'Talk singing' is what we used to call it," explains Lamont Dozier. We realized she was quite dramatic at it. She would start singing these songs and if they touched her emotionally, she would just cry and sing right on the spot. She was a natural, so it was no big surprise that she went into the movie business. Diana's future seemed to be unlimited."

Sadly, the opposite was true for another Supreme. Florence Ballard was born June 30, 1943, in Detroit, Michigan. She came from a large family—her parents Jessie and Lurlee had 13 children in all. Her father played the guitar and encouraged his daughter to sing. When he died, the family supported Florence's interest in music, although she was also considering nursing as a career until the Primes' manager, Milton Jenkins, asked her if she would like to form a female group, the Primettes.

As 1966 came to a close, Florence was increasingly unhappy about remaining in the background while Diana's star grew bigger·and brighter. Flo sang lead on the group's second single, "Buttered Popcorn," but it was quickly apparent to everyone—including Berry Gordy, Jr.— that Diana had the most commercial voice and should rightfully be the group's lead singer.

The tension became worse when "People," the one song Flo was allowed to sing in the stage act, was dropped. Flo was accused of gaining too much weight and of drinking to excess. She denied the charges, but missed shows in New Orleans and Montreal, forcing Diana and Mary to appear as a duo.

Mary Wilson realized for the first time that Florence was seriously considering leaving the Supremes after a press conference in which they were kept waiting in another room while Diana met reporters. "Flo and I sat up and cried that night because we realized this beautiful thing was really about to split up," Mary told Jeffery Wilson in a 1983 interview.

In early 1967, a search was implemented for a possible replacement for Ballard. Diana recalled that Cindy Birdsong, a member of Patti LaBelle and the Bluebelles [see 399—"Lady Marmalade"], bore some resemblance to Flo. Cindy was brought to Detroit from her native Camden, New Jersey, to audition as a "stand-in" for Florence.

Just three weeks after "Love Is Here and Now You're Gone" fell off the Hot 100, Birdsong was given 36 hours notice that she was to appear on stage with the Supremes for the first time. The event was a benefit for the United Negro College Fund and the UCLA School of Music. Los Angeles radio station KHJ sponsored the concert, held at the Hollywood Bowl on April 29. The Supremes headlined a bill that included the Fifth Dimension, Buffalo Springfield, Brenda Holloway, Johnny Rivers and the Seeds.

Florence was still a Supreme, and appeared with the group after the Hollywood Bowl concert. Engagements at the Copacabana in New York and the Cocoanut Grove in Los Angeles featured the original line-up, but the problems were not solved, and an unhappy ending was just around the corner.

## THE TOP FIVE
*Week of March 11, 1967*

1 **Love is Here and Now You're Gone**
Supremes

2 **Ruby Tuesday**
Rolling Stones

3 **Baby, I Need Your Lovin'**
Johnny Rivers

4 **Kind of a Drag**
Buckinghams

5 **Penny Lane**
Beatles

# Penny Lane CAPITOL 5810
## THE BEATLES

*Writers: John Lennon*
*          Paul McCartney*

*Producer: George Martin*

*March 18, 1967*
*1 week*

On AUGUST 29, 1966, the Beatles concluded their third American tour with a concert at Candlestick Park in San Francisco, California. It was the quartet's final live performance ever. From that day forward, Beatles' performances were restricted to the studio.

John Lennon spent the next couple of months on location in Germany and Spain, starring as Private Gripweed in Richard Lester's *How I Won the War*. After production wrapped, John returned to London. On November 9, he was invited to the Indica Art Gallery by owner John Dunbar for a private preview of an exhibition called "Unfinished Paintings and Objects." While wandering through the unusual exhibit, John met the artist: a woman dressed entirely in black. Her name was Yoko Ono.

A month later, the Beatles began recording their next album, *Sgt. Pepper's Lonely Hearts Club Band*. The first three songs recorded for the LP were "Penny Lane," "Strawberry Fields Forever" and "When I'm Sixty-Four." As the album evolved, the concept changed and the first two songs were dropped. They were released instead as a single in February, 1967. Both songs were about actual locations in Liverpool, and there was purposefully no indication as to which was the "A" side. The intention was to let the strongest side win out.

On February 25, 1967, "Strawberry Fields Forever" entered the Hot 100 at 83, two places higher than "Penny Lane." By the second week, the contest was decided. "Penny Lane" moved up 49 places, to number 36, while "Strawberry Fields Forever" went to number 45. By March 18, "Penny Lane" was the Beatles' 13th number one single and "Strawberry Fields Forever" had climbed to 11. It would eventually peak at eight. In Britain, the single only reached number two, the first new Beatles single since "Please Please Me" in

1963 not to go to number one in that country.

" 'Penny Lane' is a bus roundabout in Liverpool," Paul has explained, "and there is a barber's shop showing photographs of every head he's had the pleasure to know—no, that's not true, they're just photos of hairstyles, but all the people who come and go stop and say hullo. There's a bank on the corner so we made up the bit about the banker in his motor car. It's part fact, part nostalgia for a place which is a great place, blue suburban skies as we remember it, and it's still there."

Paul sings lead vocal on the song, backed by John. John and producer George Martin both play piano, George Harrison plays conga drum and provides the firebell and Ringo, of course, is on drums. Augmenting the sound are David Mason and Phillip Jones of the London Symphony Orchestra, who play piccolo trumpet and trumpet, respectively. Promotional copies of "Penny Lane" distributed to radio stations ended with seven notes of piccolo trumpet played by Mason. Commercial copies sold in stores did not include this ending, making the DJ copies rare collectors items. "Penny Lane" was only available in a monaural recording in America until the 1980 *Rarities* album was released. The recording of "Penny Lane" on this album is in true stereo and includes the missing seven piccolo trumpet notes.

"Strawberry Fields Forever" also has an unusual recording history.

John didn't like the first recording of the song and asked George Martin to come up with a string arrangement for a second recording. Then he asked Martin to edit together the first half of the first recording and the second half of the second recording. They were in different keys and tempos, but Martin speeded up the second recording by five per cent and was able to edit them together to produce a final version.

At the end of the song, a mischievious Lennon says, "Cranberry sauce," later interpreted as "I bury Paul," a supposed clue in the "Paul is dead" mystery. In *The Beatles on Record*, J. P. Russell points out that a Morse code message is tapped out after John sings, "Let me take you down . . ." The message consists of the letters "J" and "L."

## THE TOP FIVE
*Week of March 18, 1967*

1  **Penny Lane**
   Beatles

2  **Happy Together**
   Turtles

3  **Baby, I Need Your Lovin'**
   Johnny Rivers

4  **Love is Here and
   Now You're Gone**
   Supremes

5  **Ruby Tuesday**
   Rolling Stones

*Writers: Gary Bonner*
*Alan Gordon*

*Producer: Joe Wissert*

*March 25, 1967*
*3 weeks*

Gary Bonner and Alan Gordon, former members of a band called the Magicians, had been turned down by all the artists they had approached about recording their song, "Happy Together." By the time the Turtles heard it, the dub was so worn out, it was practically unlistenable. Still, there was something in the song that attracted them and they started playing it on stage, finally recording the basic track in 15 takes in January, 1967.

The membership of the Turtles changed several times during their six years together, but what remained constant was the leadership of Howard Kaylan and Mark Volman, two friends who sang together *a cappella* in their high school choir.

Kaylan (*nee* Howard Lawrence Kaplan) was born June 22, 1947, in New York City. Volman was born April 19, 1947, in Los Angeles. They both grew up in Westchester, California, and attended different junior high schools. Unknown to them both, they studied with the same private clarinet teacher. One night at a 10th grade sock hop, Mark saw a familiar-looking sax player wailing away with the Crossfires. It was his friend Howard from choir, who had joined a local band called the Nightriders in 1961. The outfit included bass player Chuck Portz and guitarist Al Nichol, and they added drummer Don Murray and became the Crossfires.

Volman wanted very badly to join the group. Only one problem: there wasn't anything he could do. They paid him five dollars a night to play tambourine, sing a couple of songs and help set up the equipment. Tired of earning such a meager salary, he bought an alto sax, learned how to play it, and became an official member of the group.

The Crossfires' popularity spread to other nearby communities, and by 1963 they released their first single, "Dr. Jekyll and Mr. Hyde." A year later, "One Potato Two Potato" was released on Lucky Token. when 1965 began, they added rhythm guitarist

Jim Tucker and became the house band at the Revelaire in Redondo Beach, a club owned by KRLA disc jockey Rebel Foster. By June, the group felt they were not progressing and decided to call it quits.

Club manager Bill Utley told Foster the bad news, who responded by inviting two record distributors who had worked for Liberty to see the Crossfires. Ted Feigan and Lee Laseff were looking for artists to sign to their new label, White Whale, and after seeing the Crossfires twice, they had their first act.

They did suggest the group search for a new name. Influenced by many British groups, especially the soft vocals of Zombies' lead singer Colin Blunstone, they considered Six Pence. Foster came up with "Tyrtles," spelled *a la* the Byrds, but the band went for Turtles spelled the old-fashioned way.

White Whale wanted a folk-rock group, so the Turtles searched the Bob Dylan songbook and recorded "It Ain't Me Babe." Listening to the KHJ countdown in their car one night, they were ecstatic to learn the song debuted in the top 10 on the station's Boss 30. Within a few weeks, the song was top 10 nationally.

The group had turned down P.F. Sloan's "Eve of Destruction" [see 183] before Barry McGuire recorded it, but they did record Sloan's "Let Me Be" and "You Baby." "Happy Together" was their sixth chart single, and it entered the Hot 100 at number 79 on February 11, 1967. Six weeks later it was number one. The follow-up, "She'd Rather Be With Me," was also written by Bonner and Gordon and was the group's second biggest single, peaking at number three.

Among the people who drifted in and out of the Turtles between 1965-1970 were drummer John Barbata, who replaced Murray before "Happy Together," and went on to drum for Crosby, Stills and Nash, and Jefferson Starship; bassist Chip Douglas, who replaced Portz and eventually left the band himself, only to come back and produce some of their tracks; bassist Jim Pons, who came from the Leaves to replace Douglas; and drummer John Seiter, formerly of Spanky and Our Gang, who replaced Barbata.

By 1970 there were no more personnel changes. The Turtles broke up permanently, with lawsuits ensuing between members of the band and executives of White Whale.

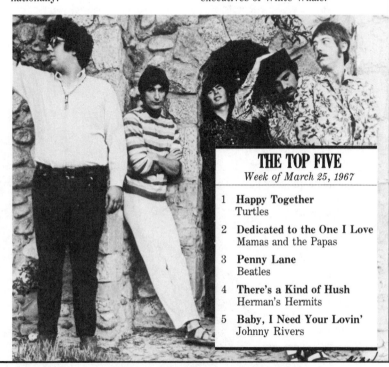

### THE TOP FIVE
*Week of March 25, 1967*

1  **Happy Together**
   Turtles

2  **Dedicated to the One I Love**
   Mamas and the Papas

3  **Penny Lane**
   Beatles

4  **There's a Kind of Hush**
   Herman's Hermits

5  **Baby, I Need Your Lovin'**
   Johnny Rivers

## 222 Somethin' Stupid REPRISE 0561
### NANCY AND FRANK SINATRA

*Writer: C. Carson Parks*

*Producers: Jimmy Bowen*
*Lee Hazlewood*

*April 15, 1967*
*4 weeks*

NANCY SINATRA and her father, Frank, had both achieved their own solo number one singles [see 194—"These Boots Are Made for Walkin'" and 202—"Strangers in the Night"] before their duet, "Somethin' Stupid," topped the Hot 100 on April 15, 1967. It's the only father-daughter duet to ever go to number one. The only other father-daughter team to both have number one singles are Pat Boone [see 92—"Moody River"] and his daughter Debby [see 475—"You Light Up My Life"].

"Somethin' Stupid" was a collaborative effort by Frank's producer, Jimmy Bowen, and Nancy's producer, Lee Hazlewood, who found the song, written in 1966 by C. Carson Parks. Hazlewood gave the song to Nancy, Bowen told Bob Gilbert and Gary Theroux in *The Top Ten.* "She showed it to her dad. Frank thought it was perfect for the two of them—a sure hit—and they wanted to cut it right away. Since I was producing Frank at the time, and Lee was working with Nancy, Lee and I became co-producers on this particular track.

"The session itself was hilarious. It was on the first eight-track equipment any of us had used—a brand-new board at Western Records in Hollywood. Eddie Bracken was our engineer, the greatest there was,

especially back in the days of three-track and four-track. He arranged the studio so that Frank and Nancy would be looking in the control room at us, side by side, the entire time. Hè also set up a producer's desk with two talk-back mikes, and a couple of name plates, you know, making kind of a light thing of it. That was because everyone was worried there'd be a lot of tension between Hazlewood and me. But we got the session done. I think it took about four takes. It was one of those that went real smooth."

Bowen told Gilbert and Theroux that some people at Reprise thought it was a mistake for father-and-daughter to sing a love song. One executive told Frank what he thought, and Sinatra told him not to worry. Sinatra was right—the record sailed to number one without a second thought about the lyrics.

Nancy and Frank had two follow-up singles to "Somethin' Stupid." Then Nancy recorded several duets with Lee Hazlewood ("Jackson," "Some Velvet Morning"), until he started his own record company and began recording with Ann-Margret. Nancy continued to chart on the Hot 100 through 1969 as a solo artist.

Frank did not return to the top 20 after "Somethin' Stupid," but then he hardly needed a hit record to maintain career momentum. His biggest post-1967 hits include "Cycles," "My Way" and the "Theme from 'New York, New York,'" an anthem to Manhattan originally sung by Liza Minelli in her film *New York, New York.*

### THE TOP FIVE
*Week of April 15, 1967*

1 **Somethin' Stupid**
   Nancy Sinatra & Frank Sinatra

2 **Happy Together**
   Turtles

3 **This is My Song**
   Petula Clark

4 **Bernadette**
   Four Tops

5 **A Little Bit Me,
   A Little Bit You**
   Monkees

*Writers: Brian Holland*
*Lamont Dozier*
*Eddie Holland*
*Frank DeVol*

*Producers: Brian Holland*
*Lamont Dozier*

*May 13, 1967*
*1 week*

"**T**HE HAPPENING" established two firsts and a series of lasts for the Supremes. It was the first single to feature a fourth writing credit following the names of Brian Holland, Lamont Dozier and Eddie Holland. It was also the first Supremes single to be the title tune of a motion picture. It was the last single to feature the name "the Supremes." It was the last of 10 number one singles written and produced by Holland, Dozier and Holland. And it was the last number one single that Florence Ballard recorded.

The extra writing credit belonged to Frank DeVol, composer of the soundtrack music for *The Happening*.

"The Happening" was the 18th chart record for the Supremes, and the last to feature that name. Berry Gordy, Jr., announced that Diana Ross would be elevated to star billing, and the group would henceforth be known as "Diana Ross and the Supremes." Mary Wilson says as soon as the name was changed, she was certain that Diana's departure was a *fait accompli*.

"The Happening" was the 10th and final number one single by the

Supremes written and produced by Holland-Dozier-Holland. The three creative geniuses had established the Motown sound with records like "Baby Love," "Stop! In the Name of Love" and "You Can't Hurry Love." But they believed they weren't being paid enough royalties for their work, and they regretted the changes at Motown. "We were happy for the company getting so big, but there's always a price," says Dozier. "You lose that intimate feeling. The buildings got bigger and the communications got smaller. People drifted apart."

Holland-Dozier-Holland wrote three more singles for Diana Ross and the Supremes: "Reflections," which peaked at number two; "In and Out of Love" (number nine) and "Forever Came Today" (number 28). Then they departed, turning their attentions to their own labels, Invictus and Hot Wax, and an artist roster that included Freda Payne, the Chairmen of the Board and the Honey Cone [see 293—"Want Ads"].

Dozier knew the Supremes would carry on without him. "We figured they would just go on. There was ample production talent to keep them afloat. We didn't think they would fall apart."

But at first, it was rough going. Nickolas Ashford and Valerie Simpson [see 281—"Ain't No Mountain High Enough"] wrote and produced the first non-Holland-Dozier-Holland Supremes single, "Some Things You Never Get Used To." It went to number 30, the lowest-charting

Supremes single since before "Where Did Our Love Go."

The most dramatic change for the Supremes was the departure of original member Florence Ballard. Halfway through an engagement at the Flamingo Hotel in Las Vegas, Florence was dismissed from the trio. That night, she was flown to Detroit and admitted to Ford Hospital to recover from exhaustion. Cindy Birdsong [see 219—"Love Is Here and Now You're Gone"], who had filled in for Flo at a Hollywood Bowl concert, officially became a Supreme.

Florence married Thomas Chapman, a former Motown employee, on February 29, 1968. A week later she signed with ABC Records and released two singles, "It Doesn't Matter How I Say It" and "Love Ain't Love." They were not successful and she did not record again for the label. Over the next few years, lawsuits between Ballard and Motown ensued, and by 1975 Florence was separated from her husband and receiving financial aid from the government to help feed her three children. There was some good news that year—she won a settlement of $50,000 against one of her lawyers and went off welfare. She was asked to sing at a benefit at Ford Auditorium on June 25 and received a standing ovation. A reconciliation with her husband seemed possible.

But on February 21, 1976, an overweight Florence Ballard complained that her arms and legs felt numb. She was taken to Mount Carmel Mercy Hospital, and the next morning she was dead at age 32 of cardiac arrest.

## THE TOP FIVE
*Week of May 13, 1967*

1 **The Happening**
Supremes

2 **Sweet Soul Music**
Arthur Conley

3 **Somethin' Stupid**
Nancy Sinatra & Frank Sinatra

4 **Groovin'**
Young Rascals

5 **A Little Bit Me,**
**A Little Bit You**
Monkees

## 224 Groovin' ATLANTIC 2401
### THE YOUNG RASCALS

*Writers: Felix Cavaliere*
*Eddie Brigati*

*Producers: Not Known*

*May 20, 1967*
*4 weeks*

ALTHOUGH their first two singles were cover versions of songs by other writers, the Young Rascals became inspired by the Beatles to write their own songs. It was a bold move, considering they had achieved a number one single by recording an Olympics tune [see 197—"Good Lovin'"]. "You Better Run," the band's third single release, was written by group members Felix Cavaliere and Eddie Brigati. It reached number 20 on the Hot 100, a disappointment considering they had just topped the chart.

Felix wrote the fourth single, "Come on Up," by himself. Its peak position of 43 caused the group's label, Atlantic, to become slightly nervous about the future of the Young Rascals. But Cavaliere felt the song's only problem was that it was ahead of its time, and likens it now to what Jimi Hendrix was doing around this period.

Before he wrote the group's fifth single, Felix fell in love. That made all the difference, he's said, and he was in top creative form when he penned "I've Been Lonely Too Long." It went to number 16 in early 1967 and paved the way for the next single.

It was a love song, written by two guys (Felix and Eddie) who worked all week long and could only see their girlfriends on Sundays. And what could be better than "Groovin'," on a Sunday afternoon? The single, with a Felix Cavaliere vocal not dissimilar to his idol, Ray Charles, erased any doubts Atlantic might have had about the Young Rascals. It entered the hot 100 at number 79 on April 22, 1967 and was number one four weeks later. It held on to the number one position for two weeks, gave way to another Atlantic single [see 225—"Respect"] for two weeks, then returned to the top for two more weeks.

"Groovin'" was the first of only two singles to chart in Britain, peaking at number eight. The band had already played some top English venues the year before, when they attracted members of the Beatles, the Rolling Stones, the Animals and other British beat groups who were fascinated by the New York group's brand of white R&B.

The two records that followed "Groovin'" both made *Billboard*'s top 10. "A Girl Like You" went to 10 and "How Can I Be Sure" reached number four. The latter song was inspired by Cavaliere's impending marriage. Brigati was not pleased about the upcoming wedding, according to Felix, who was having his own doubts and expressed them in "How Can I Be Sure."

The final single to bear the name "Young Rascals" was issued at the end of 1967. "It's Wonderful" was a voyage into psychedelia, a direct descendant of the Beatles' *Sgt. Pepper's Lonely Hearts Club Band*. It marked the transition from ordinary love songs to material of a higher spiritual nature, a result of the band's interest in Swami Satchidananda's Integral Yoga Institute.

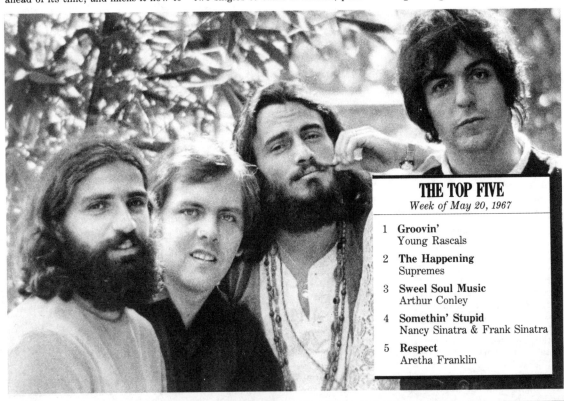

### THE TOP FIVE
*Week of May 20, 1967*

1  **Groovin'**
   Young Rascals

2  **The Happening**
   Supremes

3  **Sweel Soul Music**
   Arthur Conley

4  **Somethin' Stupid**
   Nancy Sinatra & Frank Sinatra

5  **Respect**
   Aretha Franklin

*Writer: Otis Redding*

*Producer: Jerry Wexler*

*June 3, 1967*
*2 weeks*

ARETHA FRANKLIN languished on Columbia Records for six years, recording show tunes with lush orchestral arrangements, before Jerry Wexler encouraged Atlantic Records chief Ahmet Ertegun to sign her and let her unleash her soul.

Ertegun was not easily convinced. He knew Aretha was capable of being a great artist, but her Columbia Records weren't selling. In John Tobler and Stuart Grundy's *The Record Producers*, engineer Tom Dowd recalls Jerry Wexler telling Ertegun, "We've got these rhythm sections down south, and I've got a hunch that...she's not singing as well as when she was singing gospel songs."

At Wexler's insistence, Atlantic purchased a new four-track recorder for Rick Hall's Fame studios in Muscle Shoals, Alabama, in time for Aretha's first recording session. Wexler, Dowd and Arif Mardin recorded "I Never Loved a Man (The Way I Love You)" and part of "Do Right Woman—Do Right Man" in Muscle Shoals. The former was released as a single and immediately proved Wexler's point. The record soared to number nine on the Hot 100, a major achievement considering only one of Aretha's previous eight Columbia chart entries had reached the top 50.

With "I Never Loved a Man..." bulleting up the chart, Atlantic needed an album from Aretha. A rhythm section from Memphis was flown to Atlantic's New York studios, and the album was completed within a week. Dowd recalls in *The Record Producers*: "We just did it by the seat of our trousers—she'd sit down at the piano, play a song . . . we were doing Aretha in gospel/blues tradition, unlike the elegant production things she had been doing at Columbia."

One of the songs recorded that week was "Respect" written by Otis Redding [see 238—"(Sittin' on) The Dock of the Bay"], a song Dowd had engineered on *Otis Blue*. "During that week when we had to cram an album together, Aretha said that she liked that song, and she started run-

ning it in, although her sister Carolyn was instrumental in the tempo aspect of it, the way they did it with the 'R-E-S-P-E-C-T' lines. . . . It just went by very easily," says Dowd.

Following "Respect," Aretha Franklin earned her title "Lady Soul" by having six consecutive top 10 singles on Atlantic, including "Baby I Love You," "(You Make Me Feel Like) A Natural Woman" (written by Gerry Goffin, Carole King and Jerry Wexler) and "Chain of Fools." She continued with the label until the late '70s, when she signed with Arista. In 1982, producer Luther Vandross brought her back to the top 30 after an eight-year absence with "Jump to It."

Aretha Franklin was born March 25, 1942, the daughter of Rev. C.L. Franklin. The family moved to Detroit when Aretha was two, and her father became pastor of the 4,500-member New Bethel Baptist Church. Her mother, gospel singer Barbara Siggers, deserted her husband and five children when Aretha was six, and died four years later. Aretha's mother-figures were Mahalia Jackson and Clara Ward, who sang in her father's church and were frequent guests in the Franklin home along with Sam Cooke [see 30—"You Send Me"] and James Cleveland.

As a 12-year-old, Aretha sang solo in her father's church, and two years later joined him on the road for his evangelistic tours. Rev. C.L. Franklin recorded gospel albums for Chess records, and encouraged Aretha's secular career.

John Hammond, the Columbia A&R man who during his long career, brought artists as diverse as Billie Holiday, Bob Dylan and Bruce Springsteen to the company, first heard Aretha's voice on a demo of "Today I Sing the Blues," written by Curtis Lewis. Hammond was more interested in the vocal than the songwriting, and when Jo King, Aretha's manager, invited him to a hear Aretha rehearse at a Manhattan recording studio, he rushed over and signed her. He couldn't foresee that the label, under the direction of A&R chief Mitch Miller [see 2—"The Yellow Rose of Texas"], would try to blanch her soul by having her record songs like "Swanee" and "Rock-a-Bye Your Baby With a Dixie Melody."

---

## THE TOP FIVE

*Week of June 3, 1967*

1  **Respect**
   Aretha Franklin

2  **Groovin'**
   Young Rascals

3  **I Got Rhythm**
   Happenings

4  **Release Me**
   **(And Let Me Love Again)**
   Engelbert Humperdinck

5  **Creeque Alley**
   Mamas and the Papas

## 226  Windy  WARNER BROTHERS 7041
## THE ASSOCIATION

*Writer: Ruthann Friedman*
*Producer: Bones Howe*

*July 1, 1967*
*4 weeks*

"**W**INDY " was one of 22 songs on a demo tape submitted by writer Ruthann Friedman to producer Bones Howe. "'Windy' was written as a waltz in 3/4 time," says Howe. "I loved that song—I thought it was wonderful. But we couldn't put out a waltz." A new arrangement was written, with four beats to the bar, and the Association came up with their second number one.

Howe, the engineer on the Mamas and the Papas' recordings [see 198—"Monday, Monday"], was brought in to produce the Association's third album after their second LP, *Renaissance*, failed to sell as many copies as Valiant Records expected. That album had been produced by Jerry Yester, brother of the Association's Jim Yester. Originally, Howe was approached to engineer the third album and "keep an eye" on producer Yester.

Howe refused. "I said, 'I can't be a policeman. If you don't like him, I'd love to produce the album. But on this basis, I will not work on this project." Two weeks later, with Yester off the project, the group's manager called and asked Howe to produce. He agreed, providing he could have a "strong say" in selecting material, and could use studio musicians, with the Association providing just the vocals.

Before recording "Windy" and the album *Insight Out*, the Association had a change of labels and guitarists. Warner Brothers bought Valiant Records in April, 1967. Valiant's financial status had been shaky until the Association broke through, and as a result of their success, the label grossed over a million dollars in 1966. Warner Brothers' primary purpose in buying the label was to secure the Association.

In the liner notes of the group's first album, '*Teen* magazine editor Phyllis Burgess wrote, ". . . Gary who doesn't smoke, drink or eat meat . . . would like to travel to India to 'study the mystic religious life there.'" It wasn't puffery, it was true. Founding member Gary Jules

### THE TOP FIVE
*Week of July 1, 1967*

1  **Windy**
   Association

2  **Groovin'**
   Young Rascals

3  **Little Bit O' Soul**
   Music Explosion

4  **San Francisco (Be Sure to Wear Flowers in Your Hair)**
   Scott McKenzie

5  **She'd Rather Be With Me**
   Turtles

Alexander left the Association after the *Renaissance* album to study meditational philosophy in India. He was replaced by Larry Ramos, a Hawaiian native who had grown up in Los Angeles. Ramos came to the Association from the New Christy Minstrels, and shared lead vocals on "Windy" with Russ Giguere.

"Windy" was recorded in a marathon session that began in the early hours of the afternoon. The group was due in Virginia the next day, and had a plane to catch at 8:30 the following morning. The session was completed just after 6:30 a.m. As the dawn was breaking, Russ and Larry's voices were so burned out, they were supported by all the visitors present to record the multi-layered vocal chorus ending of the song. Songwriter Ruthann Friedman can be heard in the fade of the record, singing counter harmony.

After "Windy," the Association had two more top 10 singles. "Never My Love" held on to the number two spot for two weeks, and "Everything That Touches You" reached number 10.

Alexander returned to the group in 1969, in time to record the title tune for the film *Goodbye, Columbus*. The group continued to record until 1973. On August 2 of that year, bassist Brian Cole died of a drug overdose. His death was the catalyst for the dissolution of the Association.

During the 1970s, Yester worked in computers, Alexander produced films, Giguere became a comedy writer, Ramos surfed and Bluechel put together a new group and toured as the Association. Kirkman worked on the production staff of television's "Name That Tune," and in 1980 Home Box Office asked him to help put together a reunion of the original Association for a cable TV special. On September 26, the Association reunited for the first time in over six years.

The Association stayed together to record two singles for Elektra, but an album was never issued. Yester left again in 1983, and then Bluechel and Kirkman departed, leaving Russ Giguere and Larry Ramos to carry on.

*Writers: Robbie Krieger*
*Ray Manzarek*
*John Densmore*
*Jim Morrison*

*Producer: Paul Rothchild*

*July 29, 1967*
*3 weeks*

---

Two months after they graduated from the film school at UCLA, Jim Morrison and Ray Manzarek happened to meet on the beach in Venice, California. Manzarek asked Morrison what he had been doing since graduation and Jim read the lyrics to one of the songs he had written, "Moonlight Drive." "I'd never heard lyrics to a rock song like that before," Manzarek told Digby Diehl. "We talked a while before we decided to get a group together and make a million dollars."

Morrison (born December 8, 1943, in Melbourne, Florida) was the son of a career Navy officer who had to move his family often. After graduating from George Washington High School in Alexandria, Virginia, Jim moved to St. Petersburg, Florida, to attend junior college. He transferred to Florida State University for a year, then dropped out. In 1964 he moved to Los Angeles and attended UCLA, where he selected a name for an imaginary band he wanted to form someday. Aldous Huxley's *The Doors of Perception* served as inspiration, as did a passage written by William Blake: "There are things that are known and things that are unknown, in between the doors."

After Manzarek and Morrison

agreed to organize a group, they recruited two other members to complete the quartet. "I was involved in Maharishi meditation," Ray told Ray Townley in *Down Beat*, "and in my class...were John (Densmore) and Robbie (Krieger). We all got together and the music was incredible and it was as simple as that."

Densmore (born December 1, 1945, in Los Angeles) first played drums in a jazz band while attending University High School in West Los Angeles. He attended five different colleges and changed his major from literature to anthopology before meeting Manzarek in meditation class. Krieger (born January 8, 1946, in Los Angeles) had taken up guitar as a teenager and joined a jug band while attending the University of California at Santa Barbara. He transferred to UCLA to major in physics and psychology and played in different folk and blues groups before attending the same meditation class.

The Doors became the house band at the Whisky-a-Go-Go on the Sunset Strip, where Jac Holzman, founder of Elektra Records, first saw them. Paul Rothchild witnessed their Whisky performances, too, and wanted to produce an album that would be an "aural documentary" of their live act.

Their first album, *The Doors*, yielded a single, "Break on Through,"

that failed to chart. Another track on the album was more popular, but at six minutes and 50 seconds, Elektra considered "Light My Fire" too lengthy to issue as a 45. In spite of their wishes to see the long version released, the Doors agreed to their label's demand for a newly recorded, shorter version. Unhappy with the result, the Doors settled for having Rothchild edit a sizeable chunk out of the instrumental break. Ironically, once "Light My Fire" topped the Hot 100, many radio stations preferred to play the longer version, which remains an airplay staple today.

"Light My Fire" established the reputation of both the group and its charismatic lead singer, although Morrison's contribution to the number one hit was minimal. Krieger has explained the genesis of the song: "Ray had the idea for the opening part, which was the real hook. Jim helped me out on some of the lyrics...and the beat was John's idea."

The Doors did not create "Light My Fire" with the intention of releasing it as a single. "We always made an album as an album; we never really tried to make singles," Densmore clarified in *The Doors* biography by John Tobler and Andrew Doe. "We'd make the album, then we might think, 'OK, what might be commercial for AM play?'"

## THE TOP FIVE
*Week of July 29, 1967*

1 **Light My Fire**
Doors

2 **I Was Made to Love Her**
Stevie Wonder

3 **Windy**
Association

4 **Can't Take My Eyes Off You**
Frankie Valli

5 **A Whiter Shade of Pale**
Procol Harum

# 228 | All You Need Is Love · CAPITOL 5964
## THE BEATLES

*Writers: John Lennon*
*Paul McCartney*

*Producer: George Martin*

*August 19, 1967*
*1 week*

On June 1, 1967, the Beatles officially released what many consider to be the greatest album ever recorded—*Sgt. Pepper's Lonely Hearts Club Band.* There were no singles released from the album, but 24 days later an estimated audience of 400 million people watched the Beatles record "All You Need Is Love" in cavernous Studio One at Abbey Road studios. The studio was large, but not large enough to accomodate all those people—the recording was telecast live via satellite to 26 nations around the world on a unique six-hour television program, "Our World," broadcast as part of the Canadian Expo '67.

The Beatles had been selected by the BBC to be Britain's participants in the program. "All You Need Is Love" was written in May, and the first instrumental track was recorded June 14 at Olympic Studios in the southwest London suburb of Barnes. John Lennon played harpsichord, Paul McCartney played string bass with a bow, Ringo Starr played drums and George Harrison played violin for the first time in his life.

They produced a 10-minute backing track that day, then completed the instrumental work at Abbey Road, where they played their normal instruments, with George Martin playing piano. For the telecast, an orchestra consisting of two trumpets,

two trombones, two saxophones, four violins, two cellos and an accordion were brought in. The members of the orchestra were asked to wear white dinner jackets while the Beatles wore the psychedelic clothing they were associated with during the *Sgt. Pepper* era.

The Beatles invited many of their friends to the studio to form a chorus for backing vocals. Mick Jagger, Keith Richard, Brian Jones, Keith Moon, Donovan, Graham Nash, Jane Asher, Marianne Faithfull, Patti Harrison and Gary Leeds were all in attendance.

Producer Martin suggested they begin the song with the *Marseillaise*, the French national anthem. It was also Martin's idea to include a fragment of Glenn Miller's "In the Mood," resulting in a copyright payment to the song's publisher. The Beatles included "Greenseleeves" and a piece of their own "She Loves You" [144].

The six-minute version seen on the "Our World" telecast was not released as a single. After the program, John recorded his vocal track again for a final take. It was then edited down to four minutes and released around the world. In America, "All You Need Is Love" entered the Hot 100 at number 71 on July 22, 1967. Four weeks later it became the Beatles' 14th number one single.

The flip side, "Baby You're a Rich Man," entered the Hot 100 at number 64 on July 29 and rose to number 34. It was originally intended to be two different songs—"One of the Beautiful People," written by John, and "Baby You're a Rich Man," written by Paul. Melded together, the song was destined for the soundtrack of *Yellow Submarine* until the Beatles decided it belonged on the "B" side of "All You Need Is Love." John sings lead vocal, backed by Paul and John. John plays the clavioline, a keyboard-amplifier hybrid, at the beginning of the song.

During the week that "All You Need Is Love" was number one in America, Mrs. Queenie Epstein was visiting her son Brian in London. Her 10-day visit ended August 24 and she returned to Liverpool. The next afternoon, Brian drove to his country home in Sussex to spend the Bank Holiday weekend with friends. That evening, he changed his mind and returned home to London. On Sunday afternoon the 32-year-old manager of the world's most successful recording group was dead of an accidental drug overdose.

It was years later than John Lennon admitted, "The Beatles were finished when Eppy died. I knew, deep inside me, that that was it. Without him, we'd had it."

## THE TOP FIVE
*Week of August 19, 1967*

1. **All You Need Is Love**
   Beatles
2. **Light My Fire**
   Doors
3. **Pleasant Valley Sunday**
   Monkees
4. **I Was Made to Love Her**
   Stevie Wonder
5. **Baby I Love You**
   Aretha Franklin

CAPITOL 5950 **Ode to Billie Joe** **229**
BOBBIE GENTRY

*Writer: Bobbie Gentry*

*Producers: Kelly Gordon*
*Bobby Paris*

*August 26, 1967*

*4 weeks*

It was 3:00 a.m. when Bobbie Gentry woke up, inspired to write a song for her first Capitol album. A sentence scribbled on a pad of paper supplied the seed: "Billie Joe McAllister jumped off the Tallahatchee Bridge." From that line grew not only a song, but a lyrical mystery that puzzled listeners for years. What did Billie Joe and his girlfriend throw off the bridge, and why did Billie Joe kill himself the next day by jumping off the bridge?

Those who wondered about such matters missed the point of the song, according to Gentry. "The song is sort of a study in unconscious cruelty. But everybody seems more concerned with what was thrown off the bridge than they are with the thoughtlessness of people expressed in the song—and what was thrown off the bridge really isn't that important.

"Everybody…has a different guess about what was thrown off the bridge—flowers, a ring, even a baby. Anyone who hears the song can think anything they want…but the real 'message' of the song, if there must be a message, revolves around the nonchalant way the family talks about the suicide. They sit there eating their peas and apple pie and talking, without even realizing that Billie Joe's girlfriend is sitting at the table, *a member of the family*."

The atmosphere in "Ode to Billie Joe" is based on Bobbie's upbringing in the Mississippi Delta. She was born Roberta Lee Streeter on July 27, 1944, into a Southern Baptist family in Chickasaw County, Mississippi. She lived on her grandparents' dirt farm until she was six, when she moved to Greenwood, Mississippi.

She taught herself to play piano by watching Ginny Sue, the pianist at Pleasant Grove Baptist Church. But Ginny Sue only played the black keys, and that's how Bobbie learned to play at age seven.

At 13, she moved to Palm Springs, California, with her mother. A year later, she saw Jennifer Jones

in the film *Ruby Gentry*, and decided she preferred Gentry as a last name over Streeter. After high school, Bobbie studied philosophy at UCLA and music at the Los Angeles Conservatory of Music, supporting herself through secretarial work.

By 1966, she was appearing with her own vocal and dance group in Las Vegas. She wrote all of their material, and decided to seek out a publisher for her songs. She made a demo record of "Mississippi Delta" and took it to publisher Larry Shayne, who played it for Kelly Gordon at Capitol Records. To Bobbie's surprise, Capitol wanted her as an artist as well as a songwriter.

"Ode to Billie Joe" was recorded on July 10, 1967, in Studio C in the Capitol Records tower on Vine Street in Hollywood. It took less than an hour to record the track, with Bobbie accompanying herself on the guitar. Later, Gordon asked arranger Jimmie Haskell to add violins and cellos. The result was a song that ran more than seven minutes long. Capitol shortened the track and put it on the flip side of "Mississippi Delta."

"Those involved felt it had a number of drawbacks," Gentry has said. "They said it was too long, that it couldn't be categorized and aimed at a specific audience, that I was a female vocalist and soloist and this was the day of group singers." Despite Capitol's relegation of "Ode to Billie Joe" to the "B" side, radio discovered it and disc jockeys around the country started playing it. It debuted on the Hot 100 on August 5, 1967, and was number one three weeks later.

"I figured the South would enjoy Billie Joe. I can't say I anticipated the immediate national acclaim and certainly not the international response." The record charted in many countries, including Britain. The BBC invited Gentry to host her own series, originating in London. Armed Forces radio asked her to host a weekly show for GIs overseas.

"Ode to Billie Joe" was such a strong number one single, it prevented Diana Ross and the Supremes' "Reflections" from moving to the top of the chart. Bobbie Gentry won three Grammys for her hit, and became a regular headliner in Las Vegas. She married Bill Harrah, president of the Desert Inn Hotel, on December 18, 1969. After their divorce, she married singer Jim Stafford ("Spiders and Snakes") on October 15, 1978.

For those who continued to wonder what Billie Joe McAllister did throw off the Tallahatchee Bridge, an answer of sorts came in 1976, when the song was adapted into a motion picture starring Robby Benson and Glynnis O'Connor. According to the film, Billie Joe threw his girlfriend's rag doll over the bridge and committed suicide the next day because he was unsure of his sexual preference. Despite the film's revelation, many preferred to still consider the song's lyrical mystery unsolved.

Bobbie Gentry sang a new version of the title tune, which was released on Warner Brothers. It entered the Hot 100 along with a new pressing of the original Capitol single, and both remained on the chart simultaneously for four weeks.

## THE TOP FIVE
*Week of August 26, 1967*

1 **Ode to Billie Joe**
  Bobbie Gentry

2 **All You Need Is Love**
  Beatles

3 **Pleasant Valley Sunday**
  Monkees

4 **Light My Fire**
  Doors

5 **Baby I Love You**
  Aretha Franklin

*Writer: Wayne Carson Thompson*

*Producer: Dan Penn*

*September 23, 1967*
*4 weeks*

WAYNE CARSON THOMPSON , a Grammy-winning songwriter for "Always on My Mind," credits his father with inspiring "The Letter." "My dad had the first line," Thompson explains. "He was a songwriter of sorts. He would come up with ideas and pass them on to me, and say, 'If you can do anything with this, then go ahead.' 'Give me a ticket for an aeroplane' was all he had. I took that one line and wrote the rest of the words and the melody."

Thompson's friend, Chips Moman, ran the American Recording Studios in Memphis, Tennessee. Moman had hired Dan Penn to write and produce at ARS. "He had this little ol' rock and roll band he liked the sound of—they didn't even have a name," Thompson recalls.

The rock and roll band were five friends who had played in different groups while attending high school in Memphis. Lead singer Alex Chilton (born December 28, 1950) was the youngest member of the group—just 16 when they recorded "The Letter." The other four members were lead guitarist Gary Talley, bassist William Cunningham, drummer Daniel Smythe and keyboardist John Evans. A Memphis disc jockey introduced the band to Penn, who decided to record them at ARS.

Songwriter Thompson was there for the session, playing guitar. The group still didn't have a name. "One of the guys said, 'Well, let's have a contest and everybody can send in fifty cents and a box top.' Dan looked at me and I looked at him, and he said, 'Hell, that sounds great,' and named 'em the Box Tops."

Thompson remembers not liking the Box Tops' arrangement the first time he heard it. "I listened to it, and said I don't like it cause the boy don't sing high enough. Dan said, 'Well, it's a hit record.' Then he added the jet and I thought he'd lost his mind. And it was still only one minute and 58 seconds long. I left the country on a USO Tour. Six weeks later I got back and the damn thing was number four in the nation."

The Box Tops recorded another Thompson song, "Neon Rainbow," for a follow-up. It only went to number 24 on the Hot 100, and at that point, Smythe and Evans left the group to return to college. They were replaced by Thomas Boggs and Rick Allen, respectively, and the re-organized Box Tops released "Cry Like a Baby," which became the group's second-biggest hit, peaking at number two.

The Box Tops never returned to the top 10. "Choo Choo Train," "I Met Her in Church," "Sweet Cream Ladies, Forward March" and "I Shall Be Released" all failed to make even the top 20. In 1969, the group recorded another Thompson song, "Soul Deep," which peaked at number 18.

After their final chart entry in 1970, the Box Tops split up and Chilton pursued a solo career. "Alex moved to New York, where he got his chops together both as a guitarist and as a songwriter," Jon Tiven writes in the liner notes for the Rhino Records release, *The Box Tops Greatest Hits*. "Unable to get his solo career off the ground in Manhattan, he returned to Memphis where he cut a solo LP at Ardent Studios using session musicians . . . but his producer was unable to come up with anything but a singles deal which Chilton rejected."

Chilton teamed up with Chris Bell, a friend from his schooldays in Memphis. Bell had almost been a Box Top, but wasn't able to make the first recording session and so missed the opportunity. Chilton and Bell formed a band called

Big Star and released the album *#1 Record*. Bell left before the second album, *Radio City*, and was killed in a 1978 car crash. Years after the band broke up, a third album was released. Chilton recorded a solo album, *Like Flies on Sherbert*, and produced recordings for two bands: the Cramps and Panther Burns.

After that point Alex Chilton was not heard from again for some time, but then he resurfaced in New Orleans in the mid-1980s, gigging in some local clubs. In 1993, Chilton and Jody Stephens, the drummer for Big Star, played a reunion concert at the University of Missouri. A live album was issued. Chilton continued to record in the '90s, releasing such albums as *Clichés* (1994) and *Man Called Destruction* (1995). In 1996, Chilton and Stephens, together with Jonathan Auer and Ken Stringfellow of the Posies, toured once again as Big Star.

---

### THE TOP FIVE
*Week of September 23, 1967*

1 **The Letter**
  Box Tops

2 **Ode to Billie Joe**
  Bobbie Gentry

3 **Come Back When You Grow Up**
  Bobby Vee

4 **Reflections**
  Diana Ross and the Supremes

5 **Never My Love**
  Association

*Writers: Don Black*
*            Mark London*

*Producer: Mickie Most*

*October 21, 1967*
*5 weeks*

Marie McDonald McLaughlin Lawrie was 14 years old when she was discovered by Tony Gordon singing with the Gleneagles in a small Glasgow night club. He told his sister, Marian Massey, about his discovery and suggested she manage the young singer. It was Marian who came up with a new name for Marie, but only after hours of rejecting possible choices. "She actually gave up, and then said, 'I'll tell you one thing, she's a real lulu of a kid.' I think she picked up that expression in America. I said that's a daft name, a cartoon. But it's been very lucky for me," says the woman known the world over as Lulu.

The Gleneagles became the Luvvers, and their first single, featuring Lulu singing a cover of the Isley Brothers' 1959 hit "Shout," made the U.K. top 10. The Beatles loved the recording and thought she was a black singer from America. The public tagged her the "Scottish Brenda Lee."

Massey's sister, Felice, worked for a film agent and kept an eye open for scripts for Lulu. When she read *To Sir With Love,* she informed Marian, who contacted director James Clavell. He agreed to attend a Beach Boys concert in London that featured Lulu on the bill. "Marian said that when he saw me jump on the stage, he said, 'We definitely have to have her in the film.' They gave me a small part and asked me to sing the title song."

Once production was underway, Lulu's part was expanded. The five-foot-two singer remembers being intimidated at first by six-foot-four Sidney Poitier. Meanwhile, the producers came up with a number of candidates for the title song.

"I hated them," says Lulu. "I said to my friend Mark London, 'They're going to make me sing those rotten songs and it will be awful. Why don't you write the songs?'" London declined, thinking his work would never be considered. Lulu insisted, and the Canadian composer wrote the music in five minutes. The next day, lyricist Don Black provided the words. "I was over the moon. I just knew it was going to be a great song," Lulu remembers.

In June, 1967, Epic Records released a Lulu single in the U.S. "The Boat That I Row" was a cover of a Neil Diamond song. Relegated to the B-side, to Lulu's dismay, was "To Sir With Love." But American DJs preferred

the flip, and by September the film theme had entered the Hot 100. Oddly, the song was never released in the U.K. as a single, and thus never charted. The song was also not nominated for an Academy Award, causing Lulu and her manager to protest the snub.

Lulu had three more chart singles on Epic: "Best of Both Worlds," "Me, the Peaceful Heart" and "Morning Dew," all in 1968. The following year she represented the U.K. at the Eurovision Song Contest with "Boom Bang-a-Bang," which tied for first place. The single peaked at number two in the U.K., her biggest hit to that date.

That same year, Lulu signed with Atlantic Records' Atco imprint and recorded two albums in Muscle Shoals, Alabama, produced by Jerry Wexler, Tom Dowd and Arif Mardin. Her single "Oh Me Oh My (I'm a Fool for You Baby)" went to number 22 on the Hot 100.

In Britain, she peaked at number three in 1974 with a remake of David Bowie's "The Man Who Sold the World" on Polydor. She recorded for the Chelsea and Alfa labels, and resurfaced in 1993 on the Dome label. In October of that year she finally achieved her first U.K. number one, teaming up with British boy band Take That on a new version of Dan Hartman's "Relight My Fire."

Her reputation as a songwriter grew when Tina Turner recorded "I Don't Wanna Fight." She also wrote her own 1999 single, "Hurt Me So Bad." She sailed into the millennium with more hits on the British chart, including "Where the Poor Boys Dance" in 2000 and a duet with Ronan Keating on a remake of Bob Seger's "We've Got Tonight" in 2002.

## THE TOP FIVE
*Week of October 21, 1967*

1  **To Sir With Love**
   Lulu

2  **The Letter**
   The Box Tops

3  **Never My Love**
   The Association

4  **How Can I Be Sure**
   Young Rascals

5  **Expressway to Your Heart**
   Soul Survivors

# 232 Incense and Peppermints UNI 55018
## STRAWBERRY ALARM CLOCK

*Writters: John Carter*
*Tim Gilbert*

*Producers:Frank Slay*
*Bill Holmes*

*November 25, 1967*
*1 week*

JOHN Carter was an English major at the University of Colorado when he wrote a song for his college roommates, who were in a band called Rainy Daze. "That Acapulco Gold" was a West Coast hit and reached number 70 on *Billboard's* Hot 100, the first chart hit for MCA's new Uni label. It was the first song Carter had ever written, and because of his initial success, producer Frank Slay sent him an instrumental track and asked him to complete a song for a new group, Thee Sixpence.

Carter put together "Incense and Peppermints." As the lyrics stated, they were just "meaningless nouns," but they rhymed. Sort of. Carter mailed the finished song back to Slay, and two months later was invited to observe the recording session in California. "It was the first time I met the band," he recalls, "and they resented the fact that someone had written a song to their track." The group thought the song would be adequate as a "B" side for their first

single, so they didn't bother to object when Carter told the lead singer he was wrong for the song. Carter picked another member of the band to sing "Incense and Peppermints."

The next day, Carter returned for the recording of the "B" side (or, if you were a member of the band, what you thought would be the "A" side). The singer he had chosen for "Incense and Peppermints" was gone. "I said, 'Where's the guy who sang yesterday?' They said, 'He was just a friend of ours; we brought him in because we knew he could sing the high harmony parts." The friend was not heard from again, although the group didn't mind leaving his vocal on the track for "Incense and Peppermints"—it was just a "B" side.

The single was released on a small label, All-American Records. When the group looked in *Billboard* to find the review of the single, they were shocked to find two other records had been released that week by the Syxpence and the Sixpence. They decided to abandon Thee Sixpence and choose a new name. Turning the page to the Hot 100, one of the group members closed his eyes and put his finger down on "Strawberry Fields Forever" by the Beatles [see 220].

By the time Uni Records picked up the recording, the group had settled on Strawberry Alarm Clock.

"Incense and Peppermints" entered the Hot 100 at number 88 on September 30, 1967, and became Uni's first number one single eight weeks later.

In concert, drummer Randy Seol sang the hit because his voice most closely resembled the long-departed former friend. Seol must have craved attention—he played the bongos with his hands on fire. The other members of the band—lead guitarist Edward King, rhythm guitarist Lee Freeman, keyboards player Mark Weitz, and bassists Gary Lovetro and George Bunnell—recorded several more singles for Uni, but only "Tomorrow" made the top 30.

After the group broke up, King joined southern rockers Lynyrd Skynyrd and co-wrote their number eight hit, "Sweet Home Alabama," in 1974. King left and was replaced by Steve Gaines, who was killed along with his sister Cassie and Ronnie Van Zant in a plane crash in 1977.

A 1982 newspaper ad for an appearance by the Strawberry Alarm Clock at a Los Angeles club attracted the eye of Lee Freeman, who knew nothing about the group getting back together. He went to the club and found out it was a ruse to reunite the Strawberry Alarm Clock. As a result, some members of the band had a brief comeback.

## THE TOP FIVE
*Week of November 25, 1967*

1 **Incense and Peppermints**
Strawberry Alarm Clock

2 **To Sir, With Love**
Lulu

3 **The Rain, the Park & Other Things**
Cowsills

4 **Soul Man**
Sam & Dave

5 **Daydream Believer**
Monkees

COLGEMS 1012 **Daydream Believer**
THE MONKEES

233

*Writer: John Stewart*

*Producer: Chip Taylor*

*December 2, 1967*
*4 weeks*

MOUNTING criticism of their failure to play their own instruments and frustration over lack of creative control over their own careers led to a Monkees rebellion in 1967. At a Manhattan press conference, Michael Nesmith went public with his criticism of Screen Gems and Don Kirshner. At a meeting with his production company, an angry Nesmith put his fist through a door to demonstrate his anger ("That could have been your face," Michael said to an executive who suggested Nesmith could be suspended).

Screen Gems granted the Monkees more creative control, and Kirshner was taken off the project. Starting with their third album, *Headquarters*, the four Monkees became more involved with selection of material and playing on their own tracks. Chip Douglas, who had worked with the Turtles [see 221—"Happy Together"], was brought in to do production work. The Monkees continued to record songs by Screen Gems writers, including Gerry Goffin-Carole King ("Pleasant Valley Sunday," "The Porpoise Song"), Barry Mann-Cynthia Weil ("Shades of Grey," "Love Is Only Sleeping") and Tommy Boyce-Bobby Hart ("Words," "I'll Spend My Life With You").

The follow-up to "Daydream Believer," "Valleri," was the last top 10 single for the Monkees. NBC cancelled the series at the end of the 1967-1968 season, after 59 episodes. When production ended, series producer Bob Rafelson wrote a film script for the group with actor Jack Nicholson. *Head* was perhaps too confusing for the Monkees' younger fans, resulting in a critical success and a commercial failure.

On April 14, 1969, NBC telecast a one-hour special, "33 1/3 Revolutions Per Monkee." It marked the end of Tork's involvement with the Monkees. The Monkees carried on as a trio for a year, then Nesmith quit. Linda Ronstadt had already recorded his song, "Different Drum," with the Stone Poneys, and Dot Records had released his big band album, *The Wichita Train Whistle Sings*. Micky

Dolenz and Davy Jones continued as a duo, briefly and unsuccessfully.

After the demise of the Monkees, Nesmith signed with RCA and had a hit with "Joanne" (number 21 in October, 1970). He relocated to Carmel, California, and organized the Pacific Arts Corporation. Originally a record label, it expanded into a video company after producing a video for his single, "Rio." In 1982, Nesmith won the first Grammy for a video.

Micky Dolenz worked as a producer/director in England. He was invited to star in a stage production of Nilsson's *The Point* in 1976 and remained in the country to produce a children's television series.

Dolenz and Jones attempted to reform the Monkees in 1975, teaming up with songwriters Tommy Boyce and Bobby Hart for an album and a tour. The real Monkees revival took place in 1986, buoyed by a marathon showing of their television episodes on MTV. Manager David Fishof put together a 20th anniversary tour, first approaching Peter Tork with the idea. The two of them flew to England where Dolenz was continuing his directing work and Jones was appearing in a London revival of *Godspell*. After 14 transatlantic trips, Fishof persuaded three-quarters of the Monkees to reunite for the summer tour.

Meanwhile, Arista Records was putting together a new greatest hits package for the anniversary. When they learned of the tour, they asked for some new material. Dolenz and Tork recorded three new tracks, including "That Was Then, This Is Now," which peaked at number 20 in August, 1986.

## THE TOP FIVE
*Week of December 2, 1967*

1 **Daydream Believer**
Monkees

2 **The Rain, the Park,**
**& Other Things**
Cowsills

3 **Incense and Peppermints**
Strawberry Alarm Clock

4 **To Sir With Love**
Lulu

5 **I Say a Little Prayer**
Dionne Warwick

## 234 Hello Goodbye CAPITOL 2056
### THE BEATLES

*Writers: John Lennon*
*Paul McCartney*

*Producer: George Martin*

*December 30, 1967*
*3 weeks*

In Britain, "Hello Goodbye" was number one for seven weeks, tying "From Me to You" as the longest-running Beatles chart-topper. In America, "Hello Goodbye" spent three weeks at one, while its surreal flip side, "I Am the Walrus," only managed to reach number 56, the lowest ranking for any charted "B" side of a Beatles number one single.

The Beatles began recording "Hello Goodbye" on October 2, 1967, in the middle of production for their *Magical Mystery Tour*. Written by Paul, "Hello Goodbye" was not meant for the soundtrack of the film, although an excerpt of it is heard at the end. Paul McCartney is the lead vocalist, and is joined on backing vocals by John Lennon and George Harrison. Paul plays piano, bongos and conga drum; John plays organ in addition to lead guitar; George plays lead guitar and tambourine; and

Ringo Starr plays drums and maracas. Session musicians played the two violas heard near the end of the song.

The flip side of "Hello Goodbye" was one of six songs written for *Magical Mystery Tour*. "I Am the Walrus," written by John Lennon, was inspired by Lewis Carroll's poem "The Walrus and the Carpenter" from *Alice in Wonderland*. Lennon talked about the song with David Sheff for a 1980 *Playboy* interview: "To me, it was a beautiful poem. It never occurred to me that Lewis Carroll was commenting on the capitalist and social system. I never went into that bit about what he really meant, like people are doing with the Beatles' work. Later, I went back and looked at it and realized that the walrus was the bad guy in the story and the carpenter was the good guy."

Lennon was "sitting in an English garden" in his Weybridge home when he heard the two-note wail of a police siren that suggested the meter of the song: "Mis-ter ci-ty p'lice-man, sit-ting, pret-ty p'lice-man in a row." Lennon explained some of the lyrics to Sheff: "Part of it was putting down Hare Krishna....The reference to 'elem'ry penguin' is the elementary,

naive attitude of going around chanting, 'Hare Krishna,' or putting all your faith in any one idol. I was writing obscurely, *a la* Dylan, in those days."

John sings lead vocal, backed by Paul and George. John plays the Mellotron at the beginning of the song, Paul plays bass, George is on tambourine and Ringo handles drums. Session musicians were brought in to play the eight violins, four cellos and three horns. The Michael Sammes Singers provide the lines at the end: the three boys sing, "Oompah, oompah, stick it up your jumpah" and the three girls sing, "Everybody's got one." One of the tracks was BBC Radio, recorded live during the session. Lennon used whatever happened to be on the air at the time, including a broadcast of *King Lear*: "Sit ye down father, rest you."

Jeff Lynne of the Electric Light Orchestra has said that "I Am the Walrus" is his all-time favorite song. The use of cellos in a rock song specifically inspired him to organize ELO, a group that blended classical elements with rock and roll.

*Magical Mystery Tour* was sold to the BBC, which telecast the film in black and white on December 26. Universally panned by the critics, the film wasn't shown in America until years later, when it made the rounds of the "art theaters."

"Hello Goodbye" entered the Hot 100 at number 45 on December 2, 1967, and became the Beatles' 15th number one single just four weeks later.

### THE TOP FIVE
*Week of December 30, 1967*

1  **Hello Goodbye**
   Beatles

2  **I Heard it Through the Grapevine**
   Gladys Knight & the Pips

3  **Daydream Believer**
   Monkees

4  **I Second That Emotion**
   Smokey Robinson & the Miracles

5  **Woman, Woman**
   Union Gap

PAULA 282 **Judy in Disguise (With Glasses)**
JOHN FRED AND HIS PLAYBOY BAND

**235**

*Writers: John Fred*
*Andrew Bernard*

*Producers: John Fred*
*Andrew Bernard*

*January 20, 1968*
*2 weeks*

JOHN FRED GOURRIER (born May 8, 1941, in Baton Rouge, Louisiana) remembers the first time he heard *Sgt. Pepper's Lonely Hearts Club Band*. "I just brought *Sgt. Pepper's* home, and we had a job that night in New Orleans. I was in my room shaving. I'd never heard "Lucy in the Sky with Diamonds." When it came on, I thought he was saying "Lucy in disguise with diamonds." That's the first time it hit my mind, those Beatles were so clever! When I looked at the album it said "Lucy in the sky," and then I was totally disappointed."

Within a few months, John Fred turned his disappointment into a number one song that, ironically, knocked the Beatles off the top of the chart.

The sight of hundreds of girls wearing sunglasses on the beach in Florida started John Fred thinking about lyrics for a bass line he already had in his head. The song John Fred came up with was called "Beverly in Disguise (With Glasses)." The final inspiration came from a television commercial for Playtex living bras

("Cross your heart, with your living bra . . .")

When John Fred and writing partner Andrew Bernard brought the finished song (named for Judy instead of Beverly) to the rest of the band, they weren't enthusiastic about recording what they thought was a bubblegum song. They also didn't care for John Fred's ending, where he playfully narrates, "I guess I'll just take your glasses."

"I said, 'why don't we try to cut a rock and roll track,'" John Fred recalls. "It was like a satire of rock and roll. Everybody laughed about it." The track was recorded at the Robin Hood Brians studio in Tyler, Texas. Bernard played a New Orleans rhythm piano and a sitar was added. Within two weeks of the record's release, John Fred and His Playboy Band were getting calls from agents and television shows all over the country who wanted to book them for appearances.

Most people thought the group was a brand-new outfit, but they had formed in 1956, when 15-year-old John Fred Gourrier went to a party where a live band was playing. The singer was hoarse that night and John Fred joined the band to sing a couple of Fats Domino songs. He was asked to join the group permanently, but his father (Fred Gourrier, who played third base for the Detroit Tigers) was reluctant to give permission. John Fred joined anyway.

It was a year after the introduc-

tion of *Playboy* magazine, so someone suggested they call themselves the Playboys. The group played at high schools and recreation centers, and were unpopular with some parents because they were a white band playing "race" music. One of the songs they performed was "Shirley," a song John Fred wrote with Playboy Tommy Bryan. It was a regional hit in the south and went to number 82 on *Billboard's* Hot 100 in March, 1959. To John Fred's surprise, Shakin' Stevens recorded it in 1982, and took it to number five in Britain.

His parents had always stressed education, and John Fred dropped out of singing from 1960-1964 to attend college. He had a basketball scholarship to Louisiana State University, but it didn't take him long to get back into music. With a new group of Playboys (Ronnie Goodson, Charlie Spinosa, Jimmy O'Rourke, Harold Cowart, Tommy DeGeneres and Joe Miceli, plus Andrew Bernard), he was signed to Stan Lewis' Jewel label, based in Shreveport.

After two albums as "John Fred and His Playboys," Gourrier decided to alter the name of the band. Although he had had first dibs on the "Playboys" name, Gary Lewis and the Playboys [see 167—"This Diamond Ring"] were so popular that John Fred thought it would be less confusing to change the name. The group became known as John Fred and His Playboy Band in time for a new single, "Agnes English." It bubbled under the Hot 100 for five weeks. Another change found the band transferred to Jewel's sister label, Paula.

## THE TOP FIVE
*Week of January 20, 1968*

1 **Judy in Disguise (With Glasses)**
John Fred & his Playboy Band

2 **Chain of Fools**
Aretha Franklin

3 **Hello Goodbye**
Beatles

4 **Woman, Woman**
Union Gap

5 **Green Tambourine**
Lemon Pipers

## 236 Green Tambourine BUDDAH 23
### LEMON PIPERS

*Writers: Paul Leka*
*Shelley Pinz*

*Producer: Paul Leka*

*February 3, 1968*
*1 week*

NOVICE songwriter Shelley Pinz, lyrics tucked under her arm, was visiting music publishers in the 1650 Broadway building when she encountered a young man she didn't know in an elevator. It was still legal to smoke in elevators in those days, and he offered her a cigarette. "No, I wouldn't like to have a cigarette," she told him, "but I would like to have a music writer."

The young man, who was Stan Costa, nephew of record producer Don Costa, took Shelley to the office of Circle Five Productions and introduced her to a man who could write music: Paul Leka. "I never saw anybody with so many lyrics," Leka recalls with amusement. "We ended up writing about 20 songs together."

After that first batch of songs, Shelley saw a newspaper article that intrigued her. It was about an elderly gentleman in England who played music in front of a bank. He was a literal one-man band, playing all his instruments by himself. On the ground in front of him was a tambourine, to collect donations from passers-by. The image of a tambourine filled with money made Shelley think of a "green tambourine."

After Paul wrote the music for the song, he took it around to various publishers and was turned down by a dozen of them. Finally, the song was heard by an employee of a new label, Buddah Records. Gary Cannon (a.k.a. Gary Katz, who would go on to produce Steely Dan) liked "Green Tambourine" and played it for his boss, Bob Reno. He thought it would be a smash and played it for label president Neil Bogart.

Bogart needed an artist to record the song. He called Leka and explained there was a group the label was about to drop. Leka was to fly to their hometown of Oxford, Ohio, and play the song for them. If they decided to record it, their option would be picked up. If they declined, they were history.

"It was a strange meeting," Leka

remembers. "I played the song on an upright piano they had, and asked them what they thought. They were more into psychedelic songs. They went into the other room, and came out and said they really didn't like the song."

Leka wrestled with his conscience. Should he tell the group the consequences of their decision? "I said, 'I don't know if I should say this—you're being dropped from the label. Bob Reno and Neil Bogart are determined to record this song. You're gonna be dropped if you don't record this.' They said they would think about it. I flew back (to New York) the same day and told Bob they didn't like it. The next day they called and said they'd record it."

Paul returned to Oxford to rehearse the group, then took them to Cleveland Recording Studios to cut the song. He searched all over town for an upright piano, and finally found one he could rent at a music store.

He flew back to New York with the recording. Reno asked him to come directly to his apartment to play the track. "My production wasn't good at all," Paul confesses. The problems included the drum track, the lack of strings and the voice of lead singer Ivan Browne, which Leka

describes as "nasal." Reno told Leka not to play it for anyone else until the strings were added.

A new drum track and the addition of cellos transformed the recording, and Bogart had 250 masters pressed and distributed to radio stations, informing them they had a hot-off-the-press exclusive. Three days of telephone calls and telegrams followed, and the promotion worked. "Green Tambourine" entered the Hot 100 on December 16, 1967, at number 68. Seven weeks later it became Buddah's first number one single. During the following year, the label became known for its bubblegum music, releasing hits like "Yummy Yummy Yummy" by the Ohio Express and "Simon Says" by the 1910 Fruitgum Co.

The Lemon Pipers didn't want to be associated with that bubblegum image, although they continued to record songs like "Rice Is Nice" and "Jelly Jungle (Of Orange Marmalade)" with Leka. Finally, the group—consisting of lead guitarist William Bartlett, bass guitarist Steve Walmsley, drummer William Albaugh, keyboards player R. G. Nave and lead singer Browne—produced their own album. They did not make the chart again.

*Writers: Andre Popp*
*Pierre Cour*

*Producer: Not Known*

*February 10, 1968*
*5 weeks*

"LOVE IS BLUE " by Paul Mauriat is the only American number one single to originate in France. The Singing Nun recorded "Dominique" [see 141] in French, but she was from Belgium and recorded her song there.

Mauriat had been to the top of the Hot 100 once before, but not as an artist, and not under his own name. Using the pseudonym Del Roma, he wrote "Chariot," a French instrumental that eventually garnered English lyrics and became "I Will Follow Him" [see 128], a number one single for Little Peggy March.

Mauriat did not write "Love Is Blue." Andree Popp wrote the music and Pierre Cour wrote the words in 1967, and the song was selected as Luxembourg's entry in the annual Eurovision Song Contest.

The Eurovision contest, a subject of much ridicule and interest throughout the continent, began in 1956.

Each year, the nations of Europe have internal contests to determine their national entry. These finalists then compete against each other in a televised contest watched by millions of people throughout Europe. Each year, the contest is hosted by the nation that won the previous year. The most famous group to be launched by a Eurovision win is Abba [see 458—"Dancing Queen"], who took top honors for Sweden in 1974 with "Waterloo."

Vicky Leandros sang Popp and Cour's composition in the 1967 Eurovision contest, held in Vienna, Austria. But 1967 wasn't to be the year for Leandros or Luxembourg. The song placed fourth. The British entry, Sandie Shaw's "Puppet on a String," was the winner (Vicki won for Luxembourg in 1972 with *"Apres Toi"*).

Vicki's recording of *"L'amour est Bleu"* was not a particularly hot seller, even though she recorded it in 19 different languages. Mauriat covered the song and included his instrumental version on the album *Blooming Hits*. Released as a single in the United States, it timidly entered the Hot 100 at number 99 on

January 6, 1968.

It was not a likely candidate for a number one record. No instrumental had topped the Hot 100 in more than five years. But "Love is Blue" proved irresistable to American listeners, and five weeks after its debut it was sitting on top of *Billboard's* singles chart, the first number one instrumental since the Tornadoes' "Telstar" [see 121].

The song "Love Is Blue" was so popular, that on February 24, there were four versions on the Hot 100. Mauriat was comfortable in the number one slot, followed by Al Martino at number 57, Claudine Longet at 97 and Manny Kellem at 100. In 1969, the Dells incorporated the song into a medley, "I Can Sing a Rainbow/Love is Blue," which went to number 22.

"Love Is Blue" was Mauriat's only top 50 hit. He had two more chart entries, "Love in Every Room" (number 60) and "Chitty Chitty Bang Bang" (number 76).

Paul Mauriat grew up in a musical family. His father, a postal inspector in Marseille, loved to play classical piano and violin. Paul began studying music at age four. When he was 10, the family moved to Paris. Paul studied at the *Conservatoire* and formed his first orchestra when he was 17, touring Europe's concert halls. Returning to Paris, he became known for arranging, conducting and producing recording sessions for many French artists. When "Love is Blue" became an international hit, Mauriat toured the United States and made appearances on American television.

## THE TOP FIVE
*Week of February 10, 1968*

1 **Love is Blue**
Paul Mauriat

2 **Green Tambourine**
Lemon Pipers

3 **Spooky**
Classics IV

4 **Judy in Disguise (With Glasses)**
John Fred & his Playboy Band

5 **Chain of Fools**
Aretha Franklin

## 238 (Sittin' On) The Dock of the Bay VOLT 157
### OTIS REDDING

*Writers: Otis Redding*
*Steve Cropper*

*Producer: Steve Cropper*

*March 16, 1968*
*4 weeks*

IT looked like 1967 was going to be Otis Redding's year. Aretha Franklin recorded his song "Respect" [see 225], and took it to number one. Thousands of people in the audience impulsively rushed toward the stage and started dancing when Otis gave an electrifying performance at the Monterey Pop Festival, exposing his talent to many white fans for the first time. His protege, Arthur Conley, had a number two single with a song Otis co-wrote, "Sweet Soul Music." The British pop weekly newspaper *Melody Maker* published their annual readers' poll on September 23, and Redding was named the world's best male vocalist, ending Elvis Presley's eight-year run.

On December 7, 1967, Otis went into the Memphis recording studios of Stax/Volt Records and recorded "(Sittin' On) The Dock of the Bay". Three days later, his private twin-engine Beechcraft plane crashed into the icy waters of fog-shrouded Lake Monoma, near Madison, Wisconsin, killing Otis Redding, the pilot, his valet and four members of the Bar-Kays.

Three months later, "(Sittin' On) The Dock of the Bay" became the first posthumous number one single, and Otis Redding finally received the widespread public acclaim he had never experienced during his lifetime. The song later won two Grammys, for Best R&B Male Vocal Performance and Best R&B Song.

Otis was born on September 9, 1941, in Dawson, Georgia, where his father was a Baptist minister. Otis grew up singing in church choirs, and when he was still a child the family moved to Macon, Georgia.

Otis got a job as valet and part-time singer for a local group, Johnny Jenkins and the Pinetoppers. In 1962, Otis drove the group to the Stax offices in Memphis where they had an audition with label owner Jim Stewart. Otis wasn't there to sing, but with 20 minutes of studio time left he was allowed to record two songs. The first reminded Stewart too much of Redding's idol, Little Richard, who was also from Macon. The second was the ballad "These Arms of Mine," which didn't excite Stewart, but he decided to release it anyway. It was Redding's first chart entry.

More pop and R&B hits followed, including "Pain in My Heart," "Security," "Mr. Pitiful," "I've Been Loving You Too Long (To Stop Now)," "Respect" and, in a bid to win a wider pop following, a cover version of the Rolling Stones' "(I Can't Get No) Satisfaction" [see 179].

A Stax/Volt tour of Europe helped spread Otis' fame, especially in Britain and France. Then came the Americans' turn, when shortly after midnight on a Saturday night, last-of-the-bill Otis Redding took the stage at the Monterey Pop Festival. It had been a long day and the audience was falling asleep, when suddenly Otis woke them all up with a rousing rendition of "Shake," a song originally recorded by his other idol, Sam Cooke. Otis' Monterey performance has become legendary, and afterwards, he wrote "(Sittin' On) The Dock of the Bay" while in a houseboat near Sausalito, California.

Otis was 26 years old when he died. Over 4,000 people attended his funeral in Macon. The pallbearers were Johnnie Taylor, Joe Tex, Percy Sledge, Don Covay, Solomon Burke, Joe Simon and Sam Moore of Sam and Dave.

In 1980, Otis' sons, Dexter and Otis III, formed a band with their cousin, Mark Locket, called the Reddings. They released a version of "(Sittin' On) The Dock of the Bay," and it reached number 55 on the Hot 100, the first time that a number one single was covered by an artist's offspring.

### THE TOP FIVE
*Week of March 16, 1968*

1 **(Sittin' On)**
 **The Dock of the Bay**
 Otis Redding

2 **Theme from**
 **"The Valley of the Dolls"**
 Dionne Warwick

3 **Love is Blue**
 Paul Mauriat

4 **Simon Says**
 1910 Fruitgum Company

5 **Just Dropped In (To See What**
 **Condition My Condition Was**
 **In)**
 First Edition

UNITED ARTISTS 50283 **Honey**
BOBBY GOLDSBORO

239

*Writer: Bobby Russell*

*Producers: Bob Montgomery
Bobby Goldsboro*

*April 13, 1968
5 weeks*

BOBBY GOLDSBORO wrote most of his own hits that charted on the Hot 100, including "See the Funny Little Clown," "Little Things" and "It's Too Late." A song he didn't write, "Honey," was his biggest hit ever.

"Honey" was written by Bobby Russell, who also penned "Little Green Apples" (recorded by O. C. Smith), "The Joker Went Wild" (recorded by Brian Hyland) and a number one song for his then-wife Vicki Lawrence [see 331—"The Night the Lights Went Out in Georgia"].

Inspiration struck one night when he had planned to go out for the evening, so Russell stayed home to write "Honey." The idea for the tune began with a tree in Russell's front yard. He suddenly noticed how much it had grown in the last four years ("See the tree, how big it's grown . . .) and the song developed from there.

The first person to record it was Bob Shane, one of the founding members of the Kingston Trio [see 45—"Tom Dooley"]. "I heard the Shane record, but I thought a lot of the lyrics were covered up by the arrangement, so we had Russell come over and play it on a guitar," Bobby told Jim Bickhart in a *Billboard* interview. "Bob Montgomery and I flipped over it and asked if we could do it. Russell told us we would have to promise not to release it as a competing single. We agreed to wait four weeks."

"The session on 'Honey' was unreal. We cut it right the first take, tried it again just to see if something was wrong, and it came out just as well the second time. So we went with the second take . . . we didn't even have to remix the track."

Only two of Bobby's 25 chart records reached the top ten: his first for United Artists, "See the Funny Little Clown," which peaked at nine in 1964, and "Honey," which entered the Hot 100 on March 23, 1968 at number 64 and was number one just three weeks later. Surprisingly, it was his first country hit. Although Bobby was raised in the South and

listened to a lot of country music while growing up, he was ignored by country radio until "Honey."

Bobby Goldsboro was born in Marianna, Florida, on January 18, 1941. When he was in the ninth grade, his family moved to Dothan, Alabama, where Bobby had two loves: baseball and music. He played baseball all through high school, intending to be a major league ball player. It was only when he went to Auburn University that he realized his 120-pound weight didn't make him big enough to play in the major leagues.

His interest in music started when he was 12. A friend had received a ukulele as a gift, but couldn't play it very well. Bobby would strum it when he visited his friend, and soon was playing so well that his parents bought him a guitar for Christmas. He accompanied songs he heard on the radio, and put together a band in high school, the Webbs. Looking back, Bobby says they weren't very good—but they were the only band around.

The band stayed together in college, and soon they were taking in $1,200 a week just playing on weekends. During Bobby's sophomore year, the Webbs were asked to back-up Roy Orbison [see 91—"Running Scared"] on some local college dates.

A few months later, when he returned to the area, Orbison again requested the Webbs as his back-up band. This time he asked if they would like to go on a national tour with him. Bobby's parents wanted him to continue at Auburn University, but Goldsboro left before his junior year to tour with Orbison.

Bobby toured with Roy for two-and-a-half years, singing harmonies and co-writing songs with him. Laurie Records signed Goldsboro as a solo artist and released his first chart record, "Molly," which reached number 70 at the beginning of 1963. A few months later, United Artists signed Bobby and released "See the Funny Little Clown."

As the record moved up the Hot 100, Orbison told Bobby he should hit the road on his own. If it didn't work out, Orbison said he would take him back. Bobby's first solo performance was at a Veterans of Foreign Wars club in Binginton, New York. It was snowing like crazy, and only 80 people showed up to hear him sing. But as "See the Funny Little Clown" moved up the chart, his audiences grew and he knew he would not be going back to work for Orbison.

"Honey" established Bobby as a major star. He became a frequent guest on television talk shows, including "The Tonight Show Starring Johnny Carson" and "The Mike Douglas Show," which he co-hosted for a week. In 1972, Bobby went into production on a half-hour syndicated music series. There were 78 episodes made between 1972-1975.

---

## THE TOP FIVE
*Week of April 13, 1968*

1. **Honey**
   Bobby Goldsboro

2. **Young Girl**
   Union Gap Featuring
   Gary Puckett

3. **(Sittin' On)
   The Dock of the Bay**
   Otis Redding

4. **Cry Like a Baby**
   Box Tops

5. **(Sweet Sweet Baby)
   Since You've Been Gone**
   Aretha Franklin

## 240 Tighten Up ATLANTIC 2478
### ARCHIE BELL AND THE DRELLS

*Writers: Archie Bell*
*Billy Butler*

*Producer: Skipper Lee Frazier*

*May 18, 1968*
*2 weeks*

ARCHIE BELL missed the opportunity to experience first hand the euphoria of having a number one single in America. While "Tighten Up" was reigning over the Hot 100, Archie was in a West German hospital, recovering from being shot in the leg while serving in Vietnam. He received letters and phone calls from the Drells telling him how well they were doing at home. "I remember telling the guys in my unit that the guy singing on Armed Forces Radio was me. No one really believed me at the time," says Archie.

He pleaded with military officials to allow him to return home and reap the benefits of a hit record. The best Archie could manage, however, was 15-day passes that gave him enough time to fly to New York and record follow-up singles with his band. including "I Can't Stop Dancing" and "(There's Gonna Be a) Showdown."

During one visit home, Archie's mother was ill and his stay was extended to 30 days, giving him time to tour with the Drells. That helped put a stop to the counterfeit groups who were appearing all over the country, taking advantage of the fact that the real Drells weren't able to go out on the road. "There was no TV exposure, so there was no chance for people to see who we were," Archie

laments. "There was even a group out of Nashville, nine white guys (posing as) Archie Bell and the Drells."

"Tighten Up" was originally recorded as a demo in 1964, and was all but forgotten when Archie was drafted on May 12, 1967. Just before he was to leave for his tour of duty in Vietnam, his roommate Billy Butler came home and found a depressed Archie lying on the couch. To cheer him up, Billy did a little dance and when Archie asked what the dance was, Billy told him it was the "Tighten Up."

The next day, Archie Bell and the Drells had a recording session scheduled so they would have material to release while Bell was in Vietnam. Archie dusted off "Tighten Up" and found the original demo outdated, so the group recorded a new version. Archie added an unusual introduction, telling the world the group was Archie Bell and the Drells from Houston, Texas. He explains why he felt the intro was necessary:

"When (John F.) Kennedy was assassinated, I heard a disc jockey say, 'nothing good ever came from Texas,' so I wanted people to know

that we were from Texas and we were good."

"Tighten Up" became a local hit in the Lone Star state. New York-based Atlantic Records bought the record for national distribution, but label executives thought the flip side, "Dog Eat Dog," was the hit. "We finally convinced the people in New York to turn it over," says Archie. Four months later, Atlantic started pushing "Tighten Up." It entered the Hot 100 on March 30, 1968, at number 81. Seven weeks later, with Archie recuperating from his leg wound in West Germany, it was number one.

Archie was discharged on April 19, 1969, but the momentum of his career was gone. "(There's Gonna Be a) Showdown" went to number 21, the last time Archie Bell and the Drells made the top 50. They remained with Atlantic until 1970, and their final chart entry, "Dancing to Your Music," was on the Glades label. In 1975 they signed with Philadelphia International Records, and under the guidance of Kenny Gamble and Leon Huff the men from Houston met the sound of Philadelphia for some successes on the black music chart.

---

### THE TOP FIVE
*Week of May 18, 1968*

1 **Tighten Up**
Archie Bell & the Drells

2 **Mrs. Robinson**
Simon & Garfunkel

3 **Honey**
Bobby Goldsboro

4 **The Good, the Bad And the Ugly**
Hugo Montenegro, His Orchestra & Chorus

5 **Beautiful Morning**
Rascals

*Writer: Paul Simon*

*Producers: Paul Simon*
         *Art Garfunkel*
         *Roy Halee*

*June 1, 1968*
*3 weeks*

THE GRADUATE is a frozen moment of the 1960s. It is a motion picture that specifically evokes memories of a troubled year, 1968. In the summer, the riots at the Democratic Convention in Chicago were an outlet for a smouldering rage that had been building since the assassinations of Martin Luther King, Jr., and Robert F. Kennedy in the spring.

On the day RFK was shot in Los Angeles, the number one single in America was "Mrs. Robinson." Another hero was gone, and the prophetic lines in Paul Simon's song echoed the loss:

*"Where have you gone, Joe DiMaggio?*
*A nation turns its lonely eyes to you . . ."\**

Dustin Hoffman starred in *The Graduate* as Ben Braddock, a young man advised to take up plastics as a career by Mr. Robinson, father of the girl he loves (Katharine Ross) and husband of the woman who first seduces him—Mrs. Robinson (Anne Bancroft).

*The Graduate* was the second motion picture directed by Mike Nichols, after *Who's Afraid of Virginia Woolf*. A popular comedian when he teamed with Elaine May in the 1950s, he became a popular Broadway director starting in 1963 with *Barefoot in the Park*. Nichols wanted a Simon and Garfunkel score for *The Graduate*, but while Simon was writing new material, Nichols had other ideas. Paul explained it years later in a *Musician* interview:

"While I was writing a whole score for the film, Mike Nichols was using existing material to fill in the places where the score was supposed to be, and the more he lived with it, the more he decided that that material was absolutely appropriate, so the only new song that made it into there was 'Mrs. Robinson.' "

The soundtrack of *The Graduate* includes familiar Simon and Garfunkel songs like "Scarborough Fair/Canticle" and "April Come She Will." Two versions of "Mrs. Robinson" appear on the album, both different from the cut that appears on the *Bookends* album, which Simon and Garfunkel were recording while working on *The Graduate*.

"Mrs. Robinson" exemplifies the vocal style of Simon and Garfunkel. In a 1972 *Rolling Stone* interview with Jon Landau, Paul talked about how that harmony was recorded: "Simon and Garfunkel's vocal sound was very often closely worked-out harmony, doubled, using four voices, but doubled right on, so that a lot of times you couldn't tell it was four voices....'Mrs. Robinson' was four voices."

"Mrs. Robinson" was the second number one single for Simon and Garfunkel. They followed their first [see 190—"The Sounds of Silence"] with two top 10 singles, "Homeward Bound" (number five) and "I Am a Rock" (number three). The next four singles all made the top 30, but Simon has been quoted as not being fond of any of them: "The Dangling Conversation," "A Hazy Shade of Winter," "At the Zoo" and "Fakin' It."

## THE TOP FIVE
*Week of June 1, 1968*

1  **Mrs. Robinson**
   Simon & Garfunkel

2  **The Good, the Bad And the Ugly**
   Hugo Montenegro, His Orchestra & Chorus

3  **Beautiful Morning**
   Rascals

4  **Tighten Up**
   Archie Bell & the Drells

5  **Honey**
   Bobby Goldsboro

\*Lyrics copyright 1967 Charing Cross Music. Used with permission.

### 242 This Guy's in Love With You A&M 929
#### HERB ALPERT

*Writers: Burt Bacharach*
*Hal David*

*Producers: Herb Alpert*
*Jerry Moss*

*June 22, 1968*
*4 weeks*

"THIS GUY'S IN LOVE WITH YOU" was the first number one single for the artist, Herb Alpert; the label, A&M Records; and the writers, Burt Bacharach and Hal David.

By the time "This Guy's in Love With You" entered the Hot 100 on May 18, 1968, Alpert had charted 17 singles, all of them instrumental. The first was "The Lonely Bull," a top 10 hit in 1962. The song had been written under the title "Twinkle Star" by a friend, Sol Lake, and recorded in Alpert's garage. Alpert added a mariachi sound and crowd noise from a Tijuana bullfight, then Alpert's friend and business partner, Jerry Moss, suggested the record be released by "Herb Alpert and the Tijuana Brass."

The Brass had one more top 10 single, "A Taste of Honey," and a succession of number one albums. They were still popular in 1968 when Alpert was given his own special on CBS Television, scheduled for broadcast on April 22. "I wanted to use my wife somehow," Alpert told *Newsweek*. "The idea came up, why not sing her a song?" Over 50 were submitted, and Alpert chose one with music by Burt Bacharach and lyrics by Hal David: "This Guy's in Love With You." The sequence was taped on location at the beach in Malibu, with Alpert singing the tune to his (first) wife, Sharon. The day after the telecast, thousands of viewers telephoned CBS and asked where they could buy the song. The single was released the following day.

Although it was his first vocal to chart, Alpert had sung on record before. "Tell It to the Birds" was a local hit in Los Angeles when released under the name "Dore Alpert" in 1962. Dot Records paid $500 to pick it up for national distribution, and that money helped finance the recording of "The Lonely Bull."

Alpert was born March 31, 1935, in Los Angeles. Everyone in the family was musical: his father played the mandolin, his mother the violin, his sister the piano and his brother the drums. Alpert took up the trumpet when he was eight. At Fairfax High School, he thought he would be a jazz musician, but couldn't develop a distinctive style of his own. His career plans were interrupted by a two-year Army hitch; stationed at the Presidio in San Francisco, he played trumpet and bugle and performed taps more times than he cares to remember.

Out of the service, he became a session musician. He was popular with film composers and played for several motion pictures. His trumpet can be heard on the soundtrack of *The Ten Commandments*, in which he had a cameo role. In 1957, he met Lou Adler and they collaborated on some songs. They were hired as staff writers for Keen Records, where they wrote "(What a) Wonderful World" with Keen's major artist, Sam Cooke [see 30—"You Send Me"].

A year later, they produced several tracks for Jan and Dean [see 133—"Surf City"], including their first hit, "Baby Talk." They worked briefly for Larry Uttal at Madison Records, where they produced Dante and the Evergreens' version of "Alley Oop" [see 70].

In 1962, Alpert and Moss formed A&M Records. Aside from the Tijuana Brass, a group that only existed in the studio until Alpert put together a real band in 1965, the early artist roster included the Baja Marimba Band, Chris Montez, and Sergio Mendes and Brasil '66. The label was so successful that in September, 1966, Alpert and Moss paid one million dollars cash to buy the CBS studio lot at Sunset and LaBrea in Hollywood. Once owned by Charlie Chaplin, in the 1950s the studio was home to "Perry Mason" and "the Adventures of Superman."

Later, the label signed British artists like Procol Harum, Joe Cocker and Cat Stevens. During the 1970s, the label's best-selling acts were the Carpenters [see 278—"(They Long to Be) Close to You"] and Peter Frampton. Supertramp, Styx [see 517—"Babe"], the Police [see 574—"Every Breath You Take"] and Joe Jackson also sold millions of records.

Alpert released only two more vocal singles after "This Guy's in Love With You." "To Wait for Love," also composed by Bacharach-David, and "Without Her," written by Harry Nilsson [see 307—"Without You"] both failed to crack the top 50.

Less than a year after Alpert took "This Guy's . . ." to number one, Dionne Warwick [see 380—"Then Came You"] recorded it as "This Girl's in Love With You," which peaked at number seven.

### THE TOP FIVE
*Week of June 22, 1968*

1  **This Guy's in Love With You**
   Herb Alpert

2  **MacArthur Park**
   Richard Harris

3  **Mrs. Robinson**
   Simon & Garfunkel

4  **Yummy, Yummy, Yummy**
   Ohio Express

5  **The Look of Love**
   Sergio Mendes & Brasil '66

*Writer: Philemon Hou*

*Producer: Stewart Levine*

*July 20, 1968*
*2 weeks*

Hugh Masekela was introduced to jazz at the age of 13, when he saw Kirk Douglas in *Young Man With a Horn*, a film biography of Bix Beiderbecke. "I was in a little trouble in boarding school," Masekela confesses. "The chaplain, Father Trevor Huddleston, asked me, 'What do you really want to do? You're only 13 and we can't expel you.' I said, 'Father, if I can get a trumpet, I won't bother anybody anymore.' He bought a second-hand trumpet and I found a teacher from the Johannesburg Municipal Native Brass Band. In two weeks I was playing songs from *Young Man With a Horn.* I was obsessed."

Hugh Ramapolo Masekela was born April 4, 1939, in Wilbank, South Africa, the son of a famous sculptor. He was raised by his grandmother until he was old enough to attend school, and learned to play piano when he was seven. His mentor, Father Huddleston, was deported back to England by the South African government because of his civil rights activities. In 1959, Huddleston

helped Masekela win a scholarship to the Royal Academy of Music in London. A year later, friends in America like Miriam Makeba helped him win a four-year scholarship to the Manhattan School of Music in New York. "Miriam Makeba and Harry Belafonte mostly paid for my fees and I worked part-time for Belafonte's music publishing company. I also got to work with his music director, the late Hugo Montenegro ("The Good, the Bad and the Ugly")."

In 1963, Masekela met Tom Wilson, who had been working with Bob Dylan and Simon and Garfunkel. Wilson produced a live Masekela album for MGM Records, *The Americanization of Ooga Booga,* which combined the traditional music of South Africa with a modern American sound. "MGM forgot to pick up my option," recalls Masekela. "Universal wanted to start a record company. They had a group called Strawberry Alarm Clock [see 232— "Incense and Peppermints"]. They felt they needed a catalogue artist. My second album I did for Uni was recorded live at the Whisky a Go Go on the Sunset Strip. The following album was *The Promise of a Future,* which has 'Grazing in the Grass.'"

Masekela explains how he found that song: "I was in Zambia to visit my

sister at the beginning of 1968. It was the first time I'd been in southern Africa in 10 years. A friend of mine who wrote a lot of songs laid a tape on me." Back in the States, while recording *The Promise of a Future,* Masekela needed one more song. His tenor sax player liked one of the songs on the tape and suggested they try it.

"The record took us about half an hour to make and it was just a filler," says Masekela. "When we finished the album we called Russ Regan, who was the head of Uni at the time, to come and listen to the LP. He walked in and the first thing we played him was the song that we had just finished. And he said, 'This is a smash!' We didn't know what a 'smash' was. Six weeks later, it was rushing up the charts. It was really a surprise hit."

After his instrumental version of "Grazing in the Grass" was number one, Masekela heard from a lot of people who wanted to write lyrics for the song. "Steve Allen wanted to do a vocal," Masekela remembers. "We had about 70 offers." A chef at Shelley's Manne-Hole jazz club in Los Angeles played a version of the song for Masekela. "He said, 'I know you're getting a lot of offers, and I'm just a cook here, but I want you to dig this.' It knocked us out. We said, 'This is the one.' We gave them the license." The version Hugh liked so much was by an L.A.-based quartet that had evolved from the Hi-Fi's, the group that spawned the Fifth Dimension. The Friends of Distinction took their vocal version of "Grazing in the Grass" to number three in June 1969. Masekela admits, "We didn't know it was going to be such a big smash."

## THE TOP FIVE

*Week of July 20, 1968*

1 **Grazing in the Grass**
   Hugh Masakela

2 **Lady Willpower**
   Gary Puckett & the Union Gap

3 **Jumpin' Jack Flash**
   Rolling Stones

4 **This Guy's in Love With You**
   Herb Alpert

5 **The Horse**
   Cliff Nobles & Co.

## 244 Hello, I Love You ELEKTRA 45635
### THE DOORS

*Writers: Jim Morrison*
*Ray Manzarek*
*Robbie Krieger*
*John Densmore*

*Producer: Paul Rothchild*

*August 3, 1968*
*2 weeks*

THE DOORS' second album, *Strange Days*, was as brilliant as their first, but when they returned to Sunset Studios in early 1968, they found themselves falling victim to what Robbie Krieger termed "the third album syndrome" in the biography *The Doors* by John Tobler and Andrew Doe. "Usually a group will have enough songs in their repertoire to record one or maybe two albums. Then what'll happen is they go on tour and they don't have time to write any more stuff. By the third album you find yourself trying to write stuff in the studio and it shows."

The group planned to fill one side of the LP with Jim Morrison's recitation of his epic poem, "Celebration of the Lizard," but sessions were continually scratched as the singer's intemperance made work impossible. John Densmore threw his drumsticks across the room one night in frustration and announced he was opting out of the band. "I was just frustrated," he recalled in *The Doors.* "Maybe I was trying to say to Jim, 'don't be so self-destructive.'" To fill the void, the band thumbed through Morrison's old poems written on his Venice rooftop the summer after he graduated from UCLA film school. Adam Holzman (son of Elektra Records' founder Jac Holzman) discovered "Hello, I Love You."

Jim had written it in Venice one afternoon as he and Ray watched a thin, young black girl walking down the beach. "Actually, I think the music came to my mind first and then I made up the words to hang onto the melody," Morrison explained in *No One Here Gets Out Alive* by Jerry Hopkins and Danny Sugarman. "I could hear it and since I had no way of writing it down musically, the only way I could remember it was to try and get words to put to it. And a lot of times I would end up with just the words and couldn't remember the melody."

The songs for the third album, *Waiting for the Sun*, hadn't been rehearsed in concert yet and the recording process required innumerable takes. Easily distracted, Morrison became bored and renewed his interests in poetry and film. The former led to several published volumes of his works and the latter to a promotional video clip for the single "The Unknown Soldier."

But the demands of pop stardom were creating an increased ennui in Jim's psyche that began to show in concert. On May 10, 1968, he incited a Chicago audience to riot and escaped through backstage doors as the crowd fought with police and stomped the stage and equipment into twisted, vandalized debris. Another riot followed three months later in New York.

Subsequent rioting foreshadowed the infamous "Miami incident," which took place March 1, 1969. Morrison was convicted of public profanity and indecent exposure during his performance at the Dinner Key auditorium. As a result, promoters became reluctant to book the band and local authorities refused them permits to play. Worse, the group's relationships with their label and producer Paul Rothchild deteriorated, until the latter exited during sessions for the *L.A. Woman* album. Engineer Bruce Botnick took over.

The four members of the group were taking a sabbatical when 27-year-old James Douglas Morrison died in Paris on July 2, 1971. Official cause of death was listed as heart attack induced by respiratory problems. The public is not alone in wondering about the mysterious circumstances surrounding Morrison's death.

"I don't know to this day how the man died and in fact I don't even know if he's dead," Manzarek said in a 1973 *Sounds* interview. I never saw the body and nobody ever saw Jim Morrison's body...it was a sealed coffin. So who knows, who knows how Jim died?"

The Doors' mystique did not die. Francis Ford Coppola included their music in *Apocalypse Now*; an album of Morrison reading his poetry was released posthumously; and in 1985 a videocassette of the Doors went on sale. His legendary status would have pleased Morrison. According to *The Doors*, he declared early on: "I see myself as a huge fiery comet, a shooting star. They'll never see anything like it ever again and they won't be able to forget me—ever."

### THE TOP FIVE
*Week of August 3, 1968*

1 **Hello, I Love You**
Doors

2 **Classical Gas**
Mason Williams

3 **Stoned Soul Picnic**
Fifth Dimension

4 **Grazing in the Grass**
Hugh Masekela

5 **Hurdy Gurdy Man**
Donovan

ATLANTIC 2537 **People Got to Be Free**
THE RASCALS

**245**

*Writers: Felix Cavaliere
Eddie Brigati*

*Producers: The Rascals*

*August 17, 1968
5 weeks*

Iɴ the spring of 1968, the Rascals convinced their record label that they could legally drop the dreaded adjective "Young" from their name and return to their original moniker, the Rascals. Most corporate entities are reluctant to change the name of a successful product, Datsun/Nissan notwithstanding. But the loss of the superfluous "Young" didn't hurt the Rascals a bit. They followed their second number one single [see 224— "Groovin'"] with "A Beautiful Morning," a soundalike song that went to number three.

But the spring of 1968 brought two assassinations that affected Felix Cavaliere as deeply as they did most Americans. Cavaliere found it difficult to cope with the losses of Rev. Martin Luther King, Jr., and Sen. Robert F. Kennedy. He expressed his feelings by writing "People Got to

Be Free" with Eddie Brigati. According to Felix, Jerry Wexler at Atlantic Records was reluctant to release a political song, as he thought it could harm the career of the Rascals. But Felix prevailed, insisting the song was important and needed to be released. It entered the Hot 100 at number 64 on July 20, 1968, just six weeks after Robert Kennedy was murdered. It went to number one four weeks later and stayed there for five consecutive weeks, becoming the Rascals' biggest hit.

Their next single, "A Ray of Hope," was written for Sen. Ted Kennedy and was meant to be an artistic as well as sequential follow-up to "People Got to Be Free." The record peaked at number 24 and elicited a thank you letter from Teddy.

In 1969, the Rascals began a decline they never recovered from. Internal tension manifested itself in their recordings, and songs like "Heaven," "See" and "Carry Me Back" could not make the top 25. Brigati, the man that Cavaliere considered to be the soul and spirit of the Rascals, quit at the beginning of 1970. Gene Cornish quit the following year and the group left Atlantic for

Columbia.

The composition of the Rascals changed radically, with original members Cavaliere and Dino Danelli joined by Buzzy Feiten (from the Paul Butterfield Blues Band), Robert Popwell (who had played guitar on sessions for Aretha Franklin, Bob Dylan and Eddie Floyd, among others) and Ann Sutton (a backing vocalist trained in opera who had been singing with various soul groups).

There were two albums for Columbia, but only one single, "Love Me," made the pop chart, and it just squeaked in at number 95. In 1972 the Rascals formally called it quits. Felix recorded three solo albums (the first was produced by Todd Rundgren) and produced sessions for Laura Nyro and a female group, Deadly Nightshade. Dino and Gene formed a new group, Bulldog, which evolved into Fotomaker. Eddie Brigati recorded an album with his older brother, David. In 1980, Cavaliere had a top 40 single with "Only a Lonely Heart Sees" and two years later Danelli recorded with Steve Van Zandt as one of Little Stevens' Disciples of Soul.

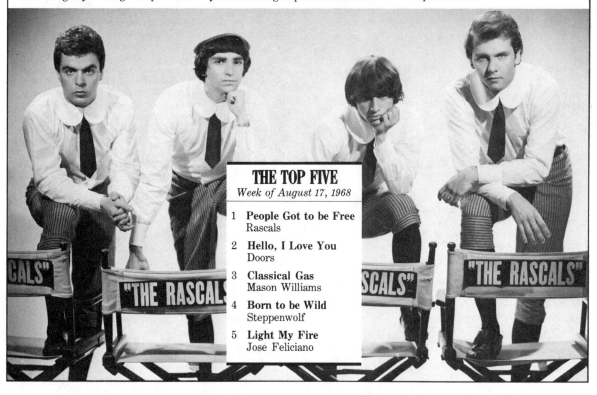

**THE TOP FIVE**
*Week of August 17, 1968*

1 **People Got to be Free**
Rascals

2 **Hello, I Love You**
Doors

3 **Classical Gas**
Mason Williams

4 **Born to be Wild**
Steppenwolf

5 **Light My Fire**
Jose Feliciano

# 246   Harper Valley P.T.A.   PLANTATION 3
## JEANNIE C. RILEY

*Writer: Tom T. Hall*

*Producer: Shelby Singleton, Jr.*

*September 21, 1968*
*1 week*

"HARPER VALLEY P.T.A." debuted at number 81 and then rocketed 74 places to number seven, holding the record for the biggest jump in Hot 100 history until the week of April 3, 1999, when Shanice took a 75-point leap from 91-16 with "When I Close My Eyes."

Tom T. Hall had been selling songs for almost 10 years in Nashville, but was not particularly well known by the public. Born in Olive Hill, Kentucky, Hall based "Harper Valley P.T.A." on a real confrontation between a young widow and a local P.T.A. group that objected to her manner of dress, social drinking and friendliness with the town's men folk.

Shelby Singleton, Jr., the man who bought Sun Records from Sam Phillips, heard a demo of "Harper Valley P.T.A." sung by Alice Joy, a singer with the Marty Robbins show. Singleton liked the song but thought Joy's voice was too soft. He held on to the tune for six months, searching for a sassier vocalist.

Paul Perry, a disc jockey at WENO who worked part time in Singleton's publishing firm, played Shelby a demo tape of a young singer from Anson, Texas, named Jeannie Carolyn Riley. She had moved to Nashville in 1966 and worked as a secretary while recording demos. Shelby knew she had the voice for "Harper Valley P.T.A." and called the publisher to make sure they had no objection to an unknown singer recording Hall's song.

When Jeannie met Shelby for the first time, she had reservations about recording "Harper Valley P.T.A." She said she wanted to have a country hit, not a pop hit, but Singleton assured her the record would be a big hit on the country chart as well. Unsure about Jeannie's commitment to the song, Shelby booked studio time for her and another artist, Royce Clark, at the same time. Jeannie showed up, and both singers cut two songs on the night of Friday, July 26, 1967.

After the first take, someone sug-

gested changing the line, "That's the day my mama put down the Harper Valley P.T.A." "Rowan and Martin's Laugh-In" had popularized "sock-it-to-me," so Jeannie sang "my mama socked it to the Harper Valley P.T.A."

Singleton was shipping records within 24 hours, and it was an instant hit, selling 1,750,000 copies in two weeks. The song established Hall as a major Nashville writer and won him a recording contract with Mercury Records.

Jeannie C. Riley never made the top 50 on the pop chart again, but consistently made the country top 10 with hits like "The Girl Most Likely" and "There Never Was a Time." "Harper Valley P.T.A." was such a big hit, that Jeannie found it hard to shake the image of the song's protagonist, although she did become a born again Christian in 1972.

The song has had a longer life than anyone could have imagined. A film based on the lyric's storyline was produced in 1978 starring Barbara Eden. NBC telecast the movie on February 24, 1980, and much to the network's surprise, the A.C. Nielsen report issued the following Tuesday listed *Harper Valley P.T.A.* as the number one show of the week. In those days, the network was consistently in third place to ABC and CBS, and relished any ratings victory.

To no one's amazement, within days NBC had announced that Barbara Eden would star in a weekly series based on the film. "Harper Valley P.T.A." premiered on January 16, 1981, 12 years and four months after the song was number one.

## THE TOP FIVE
*Week of September 21, 1968*

1   **Harper Valley P.T.A.**
Jeannie C. Riley

2   **People Got to be Free**
Rascals

3   **Hey Jude**
Beatles

4   **Hush**
Deep Purple

5   **1, 2, 3 Red Light**
1910 Fruitgum Company

APPLE 2276 **Hey Jude**
THE BEATLES  **247**

*Writers: John Lennon*
*Paul McCartney*

*Producer: George Martin*

*September 28, 1968*
*9 weeks*

"HEY JUDE," the first record released on the Beatles' own Apple label, was the group's most successful chart single. It was number one for nine weeks, longer than any other Beatles chart-topper. It also established two other records. The first, which it still holds, is for time. At seven minutes and 11 seconds, it is the longest song to ever go to number one. The second is for its entry position on the Hot 100. It entered the chart at number 10 on September 14, 1968, the highest charting single on the Hot 100 to this date.

There have been many guesses as to the identity of the person Paul McCartney is addressing in the song. And there are probably many answers.

One such answer came from McCartney, in a 1973 interview with Paul Gambaccini for the BBC and *Rolling Stone*. "I happened to be driving out to see Cynthia Lennon. I think it was just after John and she had broken up, and I was quite mates with Julian. He's a nice kid, Julian. And I was going out in me car just vaguely singing this song, and it was like 'Hey, Jules.' I don't know why, 'Hey, Jules.' It was just this thing, you know, 'Don't make it bad / Take a sad song . . .' And then I just thought a better name was Jude. A bit more country and western for me. In other words, it was just a name. It was just like 'Hey Luke' or 'Hey Max' or 'Hey Abe,' but Jude was better."

John Lennon had his own thoughts about "Hey Jude," and he revealed them to David Sheff in a 1980 *Playboy* interview: "He said it was written about Julian. He knew I was splitting with Cyn and leaving Julian then. He was driving to see Julian to say hello. He had been like an uncle. And he came up with 'Hey Jude.' But I always heard it as a song to me. Now I'm sounding like one of those fans reading things into it . . . Think about it: Yoko had just come into the picture. He is saying,

'Hey Jude,'—'Hey John.' Subconsciously, he was saying, go ahead, leave me. On a conscious level, he didn't want me to go ahead."

Others have suggested that Paul was speaking about himself, offering self-consolation after breaking up with Jane Asher. In a September 1968, interview with Jonathan Cott for *Rolling Stone*, John spoke about what was then the Beatles' brand-new single: "Well when Paul first sang 'Hey Jude' to me—or played me the little tape he'd made of it—I took it very personally. Ah, it's me! I said. It's *me*. He says, no, it's *me*."

John helped Paul complete the song at Paul's house on July 26, 1968. The following Monday, they rehearsed it with George Harrison and Ringo Starr at Abbey Road. The song was recorded Tuesday night, but the next day they went to Trident Studios and recorded a second version. After the instrumental track was completed, Paul added his solo vocal, then George and John sang harmony vocals. Paul had wanted to include a full, one-hundred piece orchestra, but he gave producer George Martin short notice and had to settle for 40 musicians, who completed their work the night of August 1. Aside from playing music, they clapped and joined in on the chorus for the four-minute fade of "na, na,

na, na na na na." A final remix was produced the following day and in the afternoon the first acetate recording was ready.

The flip side of "Hey Jude" was the fourth recorded version of "Revolution," a song John wrote about the student riots in America and Europe during the summer of 1968. This side charted as high as number 12 on the Hot 100. A slower version of the song appears on *The Beatles*, more commonly known as "the white album."

On December 21, with the Beatles' "Hey Jude" falling from six to 11 on the American chart, Wilson Pickett's soulful cover version debuted at number 90. It eventually peaked at 23.

## THE TOP FIVE
*Week of September 28, 1968*

1 **Hey Jude**
  Beatles

2 **Harper Valley P.T.A.**
  Jeannie C. Riley

3 **People Got to be Free**
  Rascals

4 **Hush**
  Deep Purple

5 **Fire**
  Crazy World of Arthur Brown

## 248 Love Child MOTOWN 1135
### DIANA ROSS and the SUPREMES

*Writers: Pam Sawyer*
*R. Dean Taylor*
*Frank Wilson*
*Deke Richards*

*Producers: Berry Gordy, Jr.*
*Frank Wilson*
*Henry Cosby*
*Deke Richards*
*R. Dean Taylor*

*November 30, 1968*
*2 weeks*

Dᴵᴬᴺᴬ Ross, Mary Wilson and Cindy Birdsong introduced "Love Child" on "The Ed Sullivan Show." Their glamorous outfits, make-up and wigs were discarded in favor of an earthier look—sweat shirts, cut-offs and bare feet, in keeping with the lyrics of their new single. "Love Child" was different from Supremes' hits like "Baby Love" and "You Can't Hurry Love"—the lyrics were more socially aware, a trend that would continue with Motown songs like "Cloud Nine" by the Temptations and "Living for the City" by Stevie Wonder. When "Love Child" became the Supremes' eleventh chart-topper, it proved the group could go to number one even without the talent of Brian Holland, Lamont Dozier and Eddie Holland.

Songwriter Deke Richards recalled the creation of the song for J. Randy Taraborrelli in *Diana*: "Berry put together some very strong forces...and locked us up in the Ponchartrain Hotel in Detroit until we came up with a hit song. He would check with us every now and then, asking, 'Did you get it? Did you get it?' Eventually, we got it. Berry was also very instrumental with the melody lines and structure, but he never took credit for it." Actually, none of the producers received credit by name. The label copy stated the record was produced by "the Clan."

The end of 1968 was a productive time for Diana Ross and the Supremes. They released four albums in two months, one of which was the soundtrack to their NBC television special "TCB," with the Temptations. The program demonstrated how far the two groups had come since they were the Primes and the Primettes in 1959 [see 159—"Baby Love"].

At the same time, the Supremes and the Temptations recorded a single, "I'm Gonna Make You Love Me," a cover version of a Madeline Bell song. Eddie Kendricks of the Temptations recorded his lead vocal in Detroit and Diana recorded hers in Los Angeles. The song peaked at number two.

The Supremes followed "Love Child" with another socially relevant single, "I'm Livin' in Shame." Also introduced on "The Ed Sullivan Show," it was more maudlin than "Love Child," but with good reason. Diana admitted in her stage act that the song was based on the Lana Turner film *Imitation of Life*. It was schmaltzy but it sounded great. It went to number 10.

Next came the "The Composer," written by Smokey Robinson. The single peaked at 27 and was followed by the Aquarius-influenced "No Matter What Sign You Are," which at 31 was the group's lowest-rated single since "A Breath-Taking Guy" in 1963.

### THE TOP FIVE
*Week of November 30, 1968*

1 **Love Child**
   Diana Ross & the Supremes

2 **Hey Jude**
   Beatles

3 **Magic Carpet Ride**
   Steppenwolf

4 **Those Were the Days**
   Mary Hopkin

5 **Abraham, Martin and John**
   Dion

*Writer: Norman Whitfield*
*Barrett Strong*

*Producer: Norman Whitfield*

*December 14, 1968*
*7 weeks*

"**I** HEARD IT Through the Grapevine" by Marvin Gaye stands as the Motown single with the fourth-longest run at the number one position, behind Diana Ross and Lionel Richie's "Endless Love" (nine weeks) and Boyz II Men's "End of the Road" (13 weeks) and their "I'll Make Love to You" (14 weeks). "I Heard It Through the Grapevine" entered the Hot 100 at number 34 on November 23, 1968, and became number one just three weeks later. For the week ending December 14, the Motown Record Corporation accomplished the unprecedented feat of capturing the top three spots on the Hot 100 [see The Top Five]. Incredibly, the company managed to hold onto those top three positions for four consecutive weeks (with "I'm Gonna Make You Love Me" by Diana Ross & the Supremes and the Temptations moving to number three on January 4, 1969).

It surprised some people that Motown would release Marvin's version of "Grapevine" so soon after Gladys Knight and the Pips took the song to number two in December, 1967. But Marvin's recording was a dramatic re-working of the song by producer Norman Whitfield. Actually, Marvin's vastly different arrangement of "Grapevine" was recorded *before* Gladys and the Pips cut it, although Gaye was not the first Motown artist to record the song.

They rarely get credit for it, but Smokey Robinson and the Miracles [see 285—"The Tears of a Clown"] were the first act to record Norman Whitfield and Barrett Strong's "I Heard It Through the Grapevine." It was eventually released on the *Special Occasion* album, around the same time the company released Marvin's *In the Groove* LP, which contained his similarly arranged version. But Marvin wasn't even the second artist to record "Grapevine." The Isley Brothers, who signed with Motown in 1966 and had a number 12 single with "This Old Heart Of Mine," recorded it after the Miracles, but their version remains hidden away in the Motown vaults.

"I Heard It Through the Grapevine" is one of the most active songs in the hyperactive catalogue of Jobete Music, the publishing division of Motown. It has appeared on the Hot 100 a total of six times. In August, 1968, King Curtis' instrumental version went to number 83. Creedence Clearwater Revival's 11-minute epic from *Cosmo's Factory* was edited for a single belatedly released in 1976; it peaked at number 43. Roger (Troutman) took "Grapevine" to number 79 in 1981. And the California Raisins (with the voice of Buddy Miles), featured in a TV commercial, peaked at 84 in January, 1988.

The song has also been recorded by other Motown artists, notably the Temptations [see 259—"I Can't Get Next to You"] and the Undisputed Truth, both groups falling under the aegis of producer Whitfield. The list of non-Motown artists who have chosen to record "Grapevine" includes Ike and Tina Turner, Paul Mauriat, and Elton John, who released a live

version on a British 12-inch single in 1984.

"I Heard It Through the Grapevine" was the 18th Marvin Gaye single to make the Hot 100 and his first number one. His first three Tamla releases ("Let Your Conscience Be Your Guide," "Mister Sandman" and "Soldier's Plea") failed to chart. It was his fourth single, "Stubborn Kind of Fellow," that brought national attention to the son of an apostolic minister from Washington, D.C. [see 342—"Let's Get It On"]. "Stubborn Kind of Fellow" peaked at number 46 in December, 1962, and featured the backing vocals of three young women who would score their own hit five months later: Martha and the Vandellas ("Come and Get These Memories" entered the Hot 100 on April 6, 1963).

Marvin continued to chart in the early '60s with "Hitch Hike" (number 30), "Pride and Joy" (10), "Can I Get a Witness" (22), "You're a Wonderful One" (15), "Try It Baby" (15) and "Baby Don't You Do It" (27). He returned to the top 10 at the beginning of 1965 with "How Sweet It Is (To Be Loved By You)," written and produced by Brian Holland, Lamont Dozier and Eddie Holland.

There were two more top 10 hits: "I'll Be Doggone" and "Ain't That Peculiar" (both peaked at number eight). Six consecutive singles failed to make the top 20, including the first single released from *In the Groove*, "Chained." Then radio airplay forced the release of a second single from the album, and "I Heard It Through the Grapevine" became part of Motown history.

---

## THE TOP FIVE
*Week of December 14, 1968*

1  **I Heard It Through the Grapevine**
   Marvin Gaye

2  **Love Child**
   Diana Ross & the Supremes

3  **For Once in My Life**
   Stevie Wonder

4  **Abraham, Martin and John**
   Dion

5  **Who's Making Love**
   Johnnie Taylor

**250** **Crimson and Clover** ROULETTE 7028
TOMMY JAMES AND THE SHONDELLS

### THE TOP FIVE
*Week of February 1, 1969*

1 **Crimson And Clover**
Tommy James & the Shondells

2 **Everyday People**
Sly & the Family Stone

3 **Worst That Could Happen**
Brooklyn Bridge

4 **Touch Me**
Doors

5 **I Heard It Through the Grapevine**
Marvin Gaye

*Writers: Tommy James*
*Peter Lucia*

*Producer: Tommy James*

*February 1, 1969*
*2 weeks*

"I DON'T THINK there's anything scarier than having a number one record and not knowing why," says Tommy James, who was as surprised as anyone when a three-year-old recording became his first chart-topper [see 203—"Hanky Panky"]. "There was no blueprint to follow, especially after a fluke record like 'Hanky Panky.'"

After the unexpected success of "Hanky Panky," James met producers Bo Gentry and Ritchie Cordell in New York. Gentry sat down at a piano and played "I Think We're Alone Now" for James, who knew he had found another hit song. It went to number four in the spring of 1967. A number of Gentry-Cordell hits followed, including "Mirage," "Gettin' Together" and "Mony Mony."

"I realized in 1968, after 'Mony Mony,' that I was at the end of the road with Bo and Ritchie," Tommy says. He had been writing songs since he was eight years old, and decided he would write and produce for the Shondells. "It was very

important that we made that move. I don't know what instincts made me—things were going very well.

" 'Crimson' and 'clover' were two of my favorite words that I put together. We had the title before we had the song. When I wrote with the Shondells, it was different than when I wrote with Bo and Ritchie—a different energy flow. 'Crimson and Clover' was part of the psychedelia of the late 1960s," Tommy maintains.

"Crimson and Clover" entered the Hot 100 at number 85 on December 14, 1968. Seven weeks later it was number one. "We had to come up with our own sound," says Tommy. "We finally did that with 'Crimson and Clover.'" The group's next two hits followed in the same groove: "Sweet Cherry Wine" checked in at number seven, and "Crystal Blue Persuasion" held at number two for three weeks. " 'Crystal Blue Persuasion' is my favorite single," Tommy claims. "The title came right out of the Bible. 'Crystal blue' meant truth. I said, 'What a title, I only wish it meant something!'"

In 1970, Tommy collapsed on stage in Alabama. He was hospitalized for several weeks, and then quit performing. "I was just really spent. I had been going for five years, full tilt. I bought a farm in

upstate New York and retired at age 23." After six months of living on 3,000 acres of land, Tommy was ready to return to show business. "I went in to the studio to do a record by myself, "Tighter and Tighter." The tracks were already laid down, but when I went to do the lead vocal, I froze. I literally was scared of failure. I went to the microphone and freaked out. I went directly to the telephone and called up people I knew from Brooklyn, a group called Alive and Kicking." Tommy produced them singing "Tighter and Tighter," and the record went to number seven in the summer of 1970.

That success helped restore Tommy's confidence, and he embarked on a solo career, sans Shondells. His biggest hit was "Draggin' the Line," which peaked at number four in the summer of 1971. He remained with Roulette through 1974. His next hit single didn't come until 1980, when he signed with Millennium and scored with the autobiographical "Three Times in Love."

"Crimson and Clover" was a top 10 hit again in 1982, when Joan Jett and the Blackhearts [see 553—"I Love Rock 'n Roll"] took it to number seven. Their version was produced by Tommy's former producer, Ritchie Cordell.

EPIC 10407 **Everyday People**
SLY AND THE FAMILY STONE

**251**

*Writer: Sylvester Stewart*

*Producer: Sly Stone*

*February 15, 1969*
*4 weeks*

PSYCHEDELIA belonged to California—San Francisco in particular. Its laid back, peace-love-and-good-vibrations atmosphere flowered some of the most innovative music of the late '60s. It wasn't just garden variety pop but rock and roll of all hues by the Jefferson Airplane, Grateful Dead, Country Joe and the Fish, Janis Joplin, Moby Grape, Quicksilver Messenger Service and an armlength list of others. One whose step was slightly quicker than his compatriots was ex-disc jockey Sylvester Stewart, who traded his radio microphone for a stage model when he created Sly and the Family Stone. In 1968 they added another species to the San Francisco hotbed—"psychedelic soul."

It was much earlier, though, at the age of four, that Sly (a schoolboy nickname) first saw the inside of a recording studio; with his family, a gospel group called the Stewart Four, he sang "On the Battlefield for My Lord." Childhood equalled rhythm and music. "That's all I had to play with. No toys," he's said. He found pop music by the time he reached his senior year in Vallejo, California, when he recorded "Yellow River" as a member of the Viscanes, a vocal quintet. Vallejo Junior College taught him music composition, which helped him write and produce for Autumn Records. Among his credits there: Bobby Freeman's "C'mon and Swim" and the Beau Brummels' "Laugh, Laugh" and "Just a Little."

Working behind the scenes didn't fully satisfy Sly's ambition, so after attending radio announcing school for three months, he found a niche on the airwaves—first at KSOL, then at KDIA. "I was into everyone's records. I'd play Dylan, Hendrix, James Brown back to back, so I didn't get stuck in any one groove." He became one of the Bay Area's most popular on air personalities, but spinning records was not the same as making them. With a high school friend, trumpet player Cynthia Robinson, he formed a group called the Stoners. Not satisfied with the group's sound, he took Cynthia and moved on to a more ambitious project: he recruited Larry Graham (bass), Jerry Martini (sax), Gregg Errico (drums), brother Freddie (lead guitar) and sister Rosie (electric piano) to form Sly and the Family Stone.

In an era of jeans and tie-dyed performance apparel, Sly and the Family Stone were incongruous. Clive Davis, president of Columbia Records during Sly's run of hits, wanted the artist's music to appeal to the underground audience, whose twin Meccas were the Fillmore East and West. In his book, *Clive: Inside the Record Business*, Davis writes, "Sly at that time made no compromise to the Fillmore mentality. His stage act included costumes, unusual hair-dos and stylized body movements. He was a dedicated musician and I knew that he was serious about his work. But I thought the glitter was a mistake. You look too much like a Las Vegas act, I said, the kids don't know how to take it."

Of course, they did, beginning with "Dance to the Music," a number eight hit in the spring of 1968. Sly's third single was "Everyday People," the first of three number one records. Its educational, gospel message of brotherhood, couched in dance funk, helped him reach the wider audience he'd been seeking. "What I write is people's music. I want everybody, even the dummies, to understand what I'm saying. That way they won't be dummies anymore," he reasoned.

## THE TOP FIVE
*Week of February 15, 1969*

1 **Everyday People**
Sly & the Family Stone

2 **Crimson And Clover**
Tommy James & the Shondells

3 **Touch Me**
Doors

4 **Build Me Up Buttercup**
The Foundations

5 **Worst That Could Happen**
Brooklyn Bridge

**252** **Dizzy** ABC 11164
TOMMY ROE

Writers: *Tommy Roe*
         *Freddy Weller*

Producer: *Steve Barri*

*March 15, 1969*
*4 weeks*

Aᴛᴛᴇʀ writing and producing hits like Barry McGuire's "Eve of Destruction" [see 183] for Dunhill Records, the team of P.F. Sloan and Steve Barri went their separate ways. Sloan wanted to be a recording artist, and Barri, happy to work as a writer/producer, connected with groups like the Grass Roots. When parent company ABC Records bought out its subsidiary label, Dunhill, Barri was asked by label executives if he would stay and work with ABC artists.

"I was always a big Tommy Roe fan," Barri explains, "because he reminded me a lot in the early days of Buddy Holly. Buddy and the Everly Brothers were the two artists I loved more than anyone else and were the biggest influence in my life of becoming a fan of rock and roll music."

Barri wanted to move Tommy away from the bubblegum sound he

had achieved with hits like "Sweet Pea" and "Hooray for Hazel," and take him back to the Buddy Holly sound that had given him his first number one single [see 116—"Sheila"].

Barri produced three tracks for Tommy. Two of them were similar to "Sheila" and the third had that bubblegum sound—"Dizzy." That was the song Barri liked the least, and Roe liked the most.

Tommy had written it with Freddy Weller, a hometown friend from Atlanta who was one of Paul Revere's Raiders [see 295—"Indian Reservation"]. Tommy had appeared on Dick Clark's "Where the Action Is," a weekday show that featured the Raiders as regulars. In 1968, Tommy was touring with Dick Clark's Caravan of Stars when he showed the chorus of "Dizzy," a song he was having trouble completing, to Weller, who helped finish it.

After the Buddy Holly-type tracks he recorded with Barri failed, Tommy suggested they try "Dizzy" as the next single. They hadn't finished recording it, and Barri felt something was missing from the mix. He thought the song needed a different touch, and asked arranger Jimmie

Haskell to add strings. "That was unique at the time," says Barri. "It was one of the main ingredients that made the record so popular. 'Dizzy' came to life for me when we put the violins on."

Despite the record's bubblegum sound, it became Roe's biggest hit ever, entering the Hot 100 at number 86 on February 1, 1969, and moving to number one six weeks later, where it stayed for four weeks.

The follow-up to "Dizzy" was "Heather Honey," which peaked at number 29. His last top 10 hit was "Jam Up and Jelly Tight," another bubblegum-sounding single, which went to number eight in early 1970. That summer, he toured the country with childhood friends Billy Joe Royal and Joe South. Tommy had one more top 30 hit, a cover of Lloyd Price's "Stagger Lee" [see 49], which charted at number 25 in the fall of 1971.

In a 1979 interview in *Los Angeles* magazine, Tommy looked back at the aftermath of "Dizzy" and the success that followed: "All artists want to outdo themselves, but how did I top 'Dizzy,' which sold six million records? . . . I lived in a beautiful Malibu beach house, the ultimate in the California dream, but in my mind it was foggy every day. I needed a cleansing, so I went home to Georgia, back to the people who knew me when I wasn't anybody."

Roe stayed home for four years before returning to Los Angeles with a more positive, upbeat attitude. He signed with Warner/Curb Records, but a single called "Dreamin' Again" did not return him to the charts and he went home again to play in local clubs.

---

## THE TOP FIVE
*Week of March 15, 1969*

1  **Dizzy**
   Tommy Roe

2  **Proud Mary**
   Creedence Clearwater Revival

3  **Everyday People**
   Sly & the Family Stone

4  **Build Me Up Buttercup**
   The Foundations

5  **Traces**
   Classics IV

SOUL CITY 772 **Aquarius/Let the Sunshine In**
THE FIFTH DIMENSION

253

*Writers: James Rado*
*Gerome Ragni*
*Galt MacDermot*

*Producer: Bones Howe*

*April 12, 1969*
*6 weeks*

JAMES RADO, GEROME RAGNI and Galt MacDermot were not kidding when they proclaimed, "this is the dawning of the age of Aquarius." It takes 25,868 years for the Earth to pass through the influence of all 12 signs of the zodiac, and as the 20th century came to a close, the world moved out of the Piscean age, a dark period that brought with it war, famine and misery, into the age of Aquarius, a time of humanity, love and light.

The three composers ushered in the Aquarian age with a hit musical, *Hair*, which opened off-Broadway at the New York Public Theatre on October 29, 1967, and moved to the Biltmore Theatre on Broadway on April 29, 1968, where it remained for 1,742 performances. Only two Broadway musicals provided number one singles during the rock era: *Hello, Dolly!* with a version of the title tune by Louis Armstrong [see 146] and *Hair*, which dominated the Hot 100 on May 10, 1969, with the Fifth Dimension's "Aquarius/Let the Sunshine In" in the number one position and the Cowsills' version of "Hair" in

second place. Two more hit singles grew from *Hair*—Oliver's "Good Morning Starshine" peaked at three, and Three Dog Night's "Easy to Be Hard" went to four.

The Fifth Dimension, a Los Angeles-based group who were once known as the Versatiles [see 261—"Wedding Bell Blues"], were appearing at the Americana Hotel in 1968, when Billy Davis, Jr., went shopping one afternoon. He inadvertently left his wallet in a cab, but the next passenger found it and kindly called Billy with the good news. The man turned out to be one of the producers of *Hair*, and a grateful Billy invited him and his wife to come to the Americana to see the Fifth Dimension. In return, the producer invited the group to see *Hair*.

Although they were not sitting together, they were all so taken with Ronnie Dyson's performance of the show's opening number, "Aquarius," that before they left the theater they all agreed it was a song they had to record.

Back in California, producer Bones Howe was not impressed with their choice. "I said it's half a song," Bones recalls. "They said, 'you gotta see it on stage.' I said it's an introduction, it needs something on the back end." Bones suggested a gospel-like sing-a-long would be appropriate, but it wasn't until he went to New York to see *Hair* that he realized the last three bars of "The Flesh Fail-

ures," a song subtitled "Let the Sunshine In," would be perfect. The audience joined in and sang the same line over and over: "Let the sunshine in, the sunshine in."

Despite the misgivings of the group, and arranger Bob Alcivar, Bones suggested they take the two pieces and "put them together like two trains." Drummer Hal Blaine helped provide the link with a couple of bars of eighth-notes and tom-toms, and the instrumental tracks were completed in Los Angeles. Bones then recorded the vocals in Las Vegas, where the group was appearing with Frank Sinatra at Caesars Palace.

The finished product was over seven minutes long, so Bones edited it down to four minutes and 50 seconds for a single. Bill Drake of Los Angeles radio station KHJ heard it and asked Bones to meet him at Martoni's, a popular Hollywood restaurant for the music industry [see 181—"I Got You Babe"]. He told Bones the single was too long to play on the radio and asked to make an edit. "He said, 'if you don't feel you can cut the record down, I'll go with it. Everyone in the country will play it. If you can find a way to shorten it to three minutes, you'll get twice as much airplay,'" Bones recalls. He produced two different edited versions, one just under three minutes and one just over.

"Aquarius/Let the Sunshine In" was *Billboard's* second biggest single of 1969. The songs were included in the 1979 motion picture version of *Hair*, directed by Milos Forman.

## THE TOP FIVE
*Week of April 12, 1969*

1 **Aquarius/**
**Let the Sunshine In**
Fifth Dimension

2 **You've Made Me So Very**
**Happy**
Blood, Sweat & Tears

3 **Dizzy**
Tommy Roe

4 **Galveston**
Glen Campbell

5 **Time of the Season**
Zombies

## 254 Get Back APPLE 2490
### THE BEATLES WITH BILLY PRESTON

*Writers: John Lennon*
*Paul McCartney*

*Producer: George Martin*

*May 24, 1969*
*5 weeks*

ONLY two human beings on the planet have ever shared label billing with the Beatles. The first was Tony Sheridan, and only by virtue of the fact that long before they were popular, the Beatles had backed him up on several tracks [see 82—"Wonderland by Night"]. When they were re-issued in the first wave of Beatlemania, the label credit read "Tony Sheridan with the Beatles." The second was an American keyboard player.

"I didn't even know until the record was out that they had put my name on it," explains Billy Preston. It was something that I could have never asked for or no manager could negotiate, just something they felt for me."

"Get Back," the 17th Beatles single to go to number one, has a strange recording history. It was John's idea to record their next album "live" in the studio without any overdubbing or technical wizardry. Paul suggested that they film the recording of the album, and on January 2, 1969, the Beatles began rehearsals at Twickenham Studios for a proposed two-part television special. George Harrison walked out of the sessions on January 10, and the TV specials were abandoned. Instead, the Beatles decided to film the recording of the album for a motion picture, which became the *Let It Be* movie, released in 1970.

George went to see Ray Charles perform at the Royal Festival Hall and saw an old friend on stage: Billy Preston, whom the Beatles had met in Liverpool in 1962 when he toured with Little Richard. George returned to the Apple Studios sessions and brought Billy with him. The Beatles invited him to spend the next two weeks recording and filming with

them, and on "Get Back," Paul told Billy to take a solo on the electric organ.

The BBC previewed the single "Get Back" on Easter Sunday. But before copies were released the following Friday, the Beatles stopped the presses from rolling and re-mixed the track once more. The single became the first and only Beatles' 45 to enter the British charts at number one.

"Get Back" made an impressive debut in America as well, entering the Hot 100 at number 10, tying "Hey Jude" as the second-highest new entry of all time to this date.

A full-page ad in *Billboard* promoted the single with the headline "The Beatles as nature intended," and the copy added, "It's the first Beatles record which is as live as can be, in this electronic age."

Promotional copies of the *Get Back* album were released to American and British DJs, but commercial copies for the public were never pressed. Allen Klein, the newly appointed manager of the Beatles' business affairs, thought the album needed more work, but the group lost interest and eventually John suggested that Phil Spector produce the final mix. The result was the *Let It Be* album, which provoked controversy among fans and critics over which was better: George Martin's spare production or Spector's string-laden final product.

While "Get Back" was number one, the Beatles quickly released another single: "The Ballad of John and Yoko," which was recorded on April 22 by John and Paul without George and Ringo. John and Paul were both married in March—Paul to Linda Eastman on March 12 in London and John to Yoko Ono on March 20 on Gibraltar. The song chronicled John's marriage to Yoko, their quest for peace and problems with the media. It peaked at number eight, the only Beatles' single on Apple not to go to number one.

Many people have been called "the fifth Beatle," but if anyone deserves the title, it's Billy Preston [see 337—"Will It Go Round in Circles"]. Rumors that the Beatles considered asking him to join the group were confirmed later in a book written by John, but it would not be long before there would be no Beatles to join.

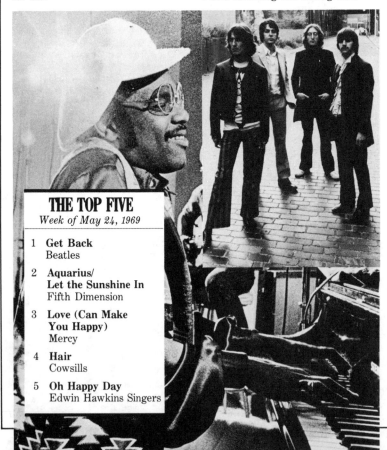

### THE TOP FIVE
*Week of May 24, 1969*

1 **Get Back**
Beatles

2 **Aquarius/**
**Let the Sunshine In**
Fifth Dimension

3 **Love (Can Make**
**You Happy)**
Mercy

4 **Hair**
Cowsills

5 **Oh Happy Day**
Edwin Hawkins Singers

## RCA 0131 Love Theme from 'Romeo and Juliet' 255
### HENRY MANCINI

*Writer: Nino Rota*

*Producer: Joe Reisman*

*June 28, 1969*
*2 weeks*

HENRY MANCINI was America's most pre-eminent film composer. He won more Oscars and Grammys than any other pop artist, and his scores graced motion pictures such as *Breakfast at Tiffany's, Days of Wine and Roses,* the Pink Panther series, *Victor/Victoria* and *The Music Box,* among many others. Ironically, his only number one single was from a film score that he didn't write himself.

One night in late 1968, Mancini went to see Franco Zeffirelli's *Romeo and Juliet,* starring 17-year-old Leonard Whiting and 16-year-old Olivia Hussey. The film opened to widespread critical acclaim, including praise for Nino Rota's score. "I liked the picture very much," says Mancini, "and in the background was this lovely piece of music. I left the movie very impressed with the score, and I started asking...why this hasn't been recorded."

Mancini finally discovered there had been one recording of the main theme, which disappeared without a trace. He decided to arrange his own version, and include it in an album he was recording at the time, *A Warm Shade of Ivory.* Another song Mancini decided to include was "The Windmills of Your Mind," written by Michel Legrand with Alan and Marilyn Bergman for the motion picture *The Thomas Crown Affair,* starring Steve McQueen and Faye Dunaway. Because "Windmills . . ." looked like a sure bet to win the Oscar that year, Mancini suggested to RCA they release that track as a single. Asked to suggest a flip side, Mancini chose "Love Theme from 'Romeo and Juliet'" because it was short and might earn some airplay on its own.

What Mancini didn't expect was for the record to seriously compete with Jimi Hendrix, the Beatles and the Rolling Stones for airplay on top 40 radio. But an Orlando, Florida, top 40 station started playing it one night, and received so many requests that they put the song into heavy airplay rotation. From there, the record spread to other top 40 stations.

Mancini recalls that there was

"heavy resistance" to the record at some stations. "It was very soft for its time. Some of the big (stations) refused to put it on until it became number one, because it wasn't a hard rocker."

"Love Theme from 'Romeo and Juliet'" is Mancini's only top 10 single. His most famous composition, "Moon River," peaked at number 11 in 1961. He first charted with "Mr. Lucky," the theme song from the television series starring John Vivyan, in 1960. His best-known television theme is "Theme from 'Peter Gunn,'" from the Blake Edwards-produced series starring Craig Stevens.

Mancini served as a staff composer for Universal Pictures from 1952 to 1958, scoring over 150 motion pictures (including *The Glenn Miller Story, The Benny Goodman Story,* the Francis the Talking Mule series and the Bonzo series, including some that starred former president Ronald Reagan). He had already done some work for producer Blake Edwards when he bumped into Edwards at the studio barbershop one day. In a casual conversation, Blake asked if Mancini would compose the music for "Peter Gunn." Mancini's original jazz score was quite innovative in a medium that had been content to import canned

music from Europe for most series. His work for "Peter Gunn" earned two Grammys in the first year of those awards. He eventually went on to win a total of 20 Grammys.

Henry Mancini was born on April 16, 1924, in Cleveland, Ohio. He grew up in the steeltown of Aliquippa, Pennsylvania, and when he was eight years old his father suggested he learn to play the flute. At 13, he studied piano and by 15, he was making his own arrangements.

After high school he enrolled at Juilliard in New York, a move that saved his life. In his freshman year he was drafted as a resident of New York. Had he been drafted from his hometown, he would have been with a division that was wiped out at the Battle of the Bulge.

Following three years of military service, Mancini joined the postwar Glenn Miller Band. Singing with the band's vocal group, the Meadowlarks, was a woman named Ginny O'Connor. She and Henry were married in 1947. The arranger for the band, Jerry Gray, helped Mancini to get the job with Universal in California.

In the '80s, Mancini wrote the title theme for the "Newhart" television series and recorded an album with Johnny Mathis, *The Hollywood Musicals.* He also re-recorded some of his greatest hits for Denon and was elected to the Songwriters Hall of Fame. In 1990, he returned to RCA Victor and released four albums in four years.

On June 14, 1994, Mancini died at his home in Los Angeles from complications of liver and pancreatic cancer. He was 70 years old.

---

### THE TOP FIVE
*Week of June 28, 1969*

1 **Love Theme from "Romeo & Juliet"**
Henry Mancini & Orchestra

2 **Bad Moon Rising**
Creedence Clearwater Revival

3 **Get Back**
Beatles

4 **Too Busy Thinking About my Baby**
Marvin Gaye

5 **One**
Three Dog Night

## 256    In the Year 2525 (Exordium & Terminus)    RCA 0174
### ZAGER AND EVANS

*Writer: Rick Evans*

*Producers: Denny Zager*
          *Rick Evans*

*July 12, 1969*
*6 weeks*

Rick Evans wrote "In the Year 2525" in the year 1964, when he was a member of a Lincoln, Nebraska, band called the Eccentrics. The quintet had been formed by Denny Zager, a native of Wymore, Nebraska, after he graduated from high school in 1961. Zager had been looking for a guitarist for the Eccentrics when he spotted Rick playing in a talent show at Wesleyan University.

By the time Rick had written "In the Year 2525," Denny had split from the Eccentrics and formed another group, the Devilles. He stayed with them for four years. During that time, Rick couldn't get the Eccentrics interested in recording "In the Year 2525." By 1968, Zager and Evans were both disappointed with their groups and quit to form a duo based in Lincoln.

"We were looking for uptempo material, because most of the stuff we did was ballads," Denny explains. " 'In the Year 2525' was pulled out of the hat, and we said, 'let's put it on stage.' I didn't go nutty over the song, because it really wasn't the style I wanted to do."

Denny wrote a new arrangement of the song for two people to sing, and they added it to their repertoire. They were appearing at a motel lounge in Lincoln at the time. "The reason we recorded it," Denny says, "was because we got so many requests for it." They invested $500 and recorded the song at a studio in Odessa, Texas. They had one thousand copies pressed up on their own label, Truth Records, and distributed the single themselves to radio stations and record stores. A local station added the song to its playlist,

### THE TOP FIVE
*Week of July 12, 1969*

1   **In the Year 2525**
    **(Exordium & Terminus)**
    Zager & Evans

2   **Spinning Wheel**
    Blood, Sweat & Tears

3   **Good Morning Starshine**
    Oliver

4   **Love Theme from**
    **"Romeo & Juliet"**
    Henry Mancini & Orchestra

5   **One**
    Three Dog Night

helping to make it a smash in Lincoln and Omaha even before it got to RCA Records.

Jerry Weintraub of Management III heard the song and flew to Lincoln to meet Zager and Evans. He negotiated a contract with RCA for the duo and signed to be their manager. The record was an instant smash. It entered the Hot 100 on June 21, 1969, at number 72. Three weeks later it was number one.

During its second week at the top, *Time* ran a story on Zager and Evans. Of "In the Year 2525," the article suggested: "This futuristic ballad sounds as though it were composed by a computer at the Rand Corporation." Actually, the very human Rick Evans had composed the song in a half-hour.

Much has been made of the fact that Zager and Evans are "one-hit-wonders." After "In the Year 2525" went to number one, they never had another single make the Hot 100. Denny explains that he made up his mind while "In the Year 2525" was a hit that it wasn't the type of song he wanted to be known for, and he had already decided to quit the duo before the record fell off the chart.

Zager and Evans have remained friends and communicate via telephone a couple of times a year. Rick is living in Lake Tahoe, California, where he continues to write songs and appear in clubs. Denny has returned to private life, and while he'd prefer to put "In the Year 2525" behind him, he finds it difficult to forget. Just recently, a friend pointed out to him that he was the subject of a question in *Trivial Pursuit*.

LONDON 910 **Honky Tonk Women**
THE ROLLING STONES

*Writers: Mick Jagger*
*Keith Richards*

*Producer: Jimmy Miller*

*August 23, 1969*
*4 weeks*

A MONTH before the death of Brian Jones [see 218—"Ruby Tuesday"], the Rolling Stones commenced work on the *Let It Bleed* album. Though he was unreliable at best and a helpless mess at worst, Jones did participate in the sessions. He even pulled himself together to appear before Jean Luc Goddard's cameras, as the French filmmaker captured the Stones at work in the studio for his semi-documentary, *Sympathy for the Devil (One Plus One)."*

Released as a single the day after Jones' funeral, "Honky Tonk Women" entered the Hot 100 on July 19, 1969, and became the Stones' fifth American chart-topper five weeks later. Only its flip side, "You Can't Always Get What You Want," appeared on *Let It Bleed*. In its place was a raucus, nasal, hillbilly rendition called "Country Honk." The original version of the barroom drinking song had appeared three months earlier on the greatest hits collection, *Through the Past Darkly (Big Hits Vol. 2)*.

*Let It Bleed* went on sale one day before the Stones traipsed into New York for a Madison Square Garden concert. For the first time since 1966, "the greatest rock and roll band in the world" put their talent onstage in America, a move that was financially

and artistically necessary. They had their new rhythm guitarist, Mick Taylor, to showcase, as well as the flinty maturity required to overcome their pop origins. Just as important was their mounting unhappiness with Allen Klein's handling of their business affairs. A band that had made millions found their pockets amazingly empty.

To organize the tour, they borrowed the Who's road manager, Peter Rudge, and Klein's nephew, Ronnie Schneider. They set forth that fall with the most elaborate traveling rock and roll circus to date— also the most expensive, at $4.50-$7.50 a ticket. The price angered critics, especially Ralph Gleason, who attacked the Stones in the *San Francisco Chronicle* for their alleged greed and exploitation of their black opening acts (B.B. King, Ike and Tina Turner) by not sharing with them a percentage of the profits.

"Can the Rolling Stones really need all that money?" Gleason asked. "It says they despise their audience." The condemnation was reprinted in *Rolling Stone*, where it reached Mick Jagger's eyes, spurring him to search for a statement that would effectively counteract the charge. Remembering the success of the Hyde Park memorial to Brian Jones, and further prodded by the summer's Woodstock gathering, Jagger elected to stage a free outdoor concert in Gleason's part of the world—the Bay Area. Where to hold the show was a problem, with numerous sites considered and rejected. Just 24 hours before the

starting time, organizers settled on the Altamont Raceway.

Santana, Jefferson Airplane, the Flying Burrito Brothers and Crosby, Stills, Nash and Young joined the Rolling Stones for the day-long event on December 6, but peace and love were in short order. Hired as security guards, members of Hell's Angels were involved with numerous scuffles among the crowd of 300,000, culminating in the death of a young black spectator. Meredith Hunter waved a gun at the stage and was stabbed by a flock of Angels. The violence was preserved on celluloid by Albert and David Maysles, brothers who had been hired to document the Stones' tour. The startling footage was later seen by filmgoers at the climax of *Gimme Shelter*.

## THE TOP FIVE
*Week of August 23, 1969*

1 **Honky Tonk Women**
Rolling Stones

2 **A Boy Named Sue**
Johnny Cash

3 **Crystal Blue Persuasion**
Tommy James & the Shondells

4 **Sweet Caroline (Good Times Never Seemed So Good)**
Neil Diamond

5 **In the Year 2525 (Exordium & Terminus)**
Zager & Evans

## 258 Sugar, Sugar
CALENDAR 1008
### THE ARCHIES

*Writers: Jeff Barry*
*Andy Kim*

*Producer: Jeff Barry*

*September 20, 1969*
*4 weeks*

THE ARCHIES never toured, never appeared with Ed Sullivan and were never interviewed by the press. The Archies also never existed.

The Archies were as fictional as the characters who have appeared in the Archie comic strip and book since John L. Goldwater created them in 1942. Filmation Studios produced a Saturday morning animated show based on the strip in 1968, and Don Kirshner (guiding light behind the Monkees' early hits) was hired to supervise the music for the series. He put together a group of studio musicians and hired Ron Dante to sing lead vocals.

Dante started working for Kirshner at the age of 16. His musical career had started early: at 11, he fell out of a tree and broke his arm. A doctor recommended exercises for his wrist, so his father bought him a guitar. A year later, Ron formed a rock band, the Persuaders.

Working for Kirshner's Aldon Music, the young Dante was in awe of the songwriting teams who worked out of that office: Gerry Goffin-Carole King, Barry Mann-Cynthia Weil and Neil Sedaka-Howard Greenfield. Ron sang on many of the demos written by those teams, and then co-wrote songs with some of them.

In 1968 he concentrated on a solo performing career, but couldn't find anyone who wanted to record him. When Kirshner asked him to anonymously sing lead on the Archies sessions for scale, he gladly accepted.

Kirshner asked Jeff Barry, the man who had produced "I'm a Believer" [see 216] for the Monkees, to write and produce the Archies' records. The Archies' first single release in September, 1968, was "Bang-Shang-a-Lang," a song that seemed to fit in with Barry's earlier works, "Da Doo Ron Ron" [see 470] and "Do Wah Diddy Diddy" [see 158]. It reached a respectable number 22 on the Hot 100, but the next single, "Feelin' So Good (Skooby-Doo)," didn't crack the top 50.

Barry wrote the Archies' third single with Andy Kim [see 377—"Rock Me Gently"], a Canadian artist who had been recording for Barry's Steed label. "Sugar, Sugar" entered the Hot 100 on July 26, 1969, and was number one eight weeks later. It sold over three million copies and was the number one single of 1969, according to *Billboard*.

There were only two vocalists on the single, although it sounds like Archie, Betty, Veronica, Jughead, Moose and all their friends are singing together. Dante multi-tracked his voice and was aided by Toni Wine, who also sang several parts. Wine did not appear on subsequent Archies' singles like "Jingle Jangle" and "Who's Your Baby?" possibly because

she was unhappy at not being paid royalties on a single that sold more than three million.

The Archies were not the first dummy group fronted by Dante. In 1964, he was the voice of the Detergents, and hit the top 20 with "Leader of the Laundromat," a parody of the Shangri-Las [see 160—"Leader of the Pack"]. While he was the Archies, he also signed with Decca Records as the Cuff Links and recorded "Tracy," a single that was in the top five simultaneously with "Sugar, Sugar."

Dante did not remain anonymous in the '70s. A popular singer on commercials, he was called to a session with Melissa Manchester and Valerie Simpson to record a jingle for a new soft drink, Tomboy. The drink tasted like rust and failed in its test market, but Dante struck up a friendship with the jingle writer, Barry Manilow, and produced his first number one single [see 389—"Mandy"].

The Archies have been the subject of much disdain from critics for the bubblegum sound of their records, but as Dante and Barry have pointed out, there was a large audience for that type of music. "Sugar, Sugar" survived the Archies to have several interesting cover versions. Less than a year after the Archies went to number one, Wilson Pickett recorded it and reached number 25 on the Hot 100. In Britain, Jonathan King recorded it under one of his many anonymous names, Sakkarin. And Dante, who recorded on his own in the '70s, sang an updated version and released it under his own name.

### THE TOP FIVE
*Week of September 20, 1969*

1 **Sugar, Sugar**
Archies

2 **Honky Tonk Women**
Rolling Stones

3 **Green River**
Creedence Clearwater Revival

4 **A Boy Named Sue**
Johnny Cash

5 **Easy to be Hard**
Three Dog Night

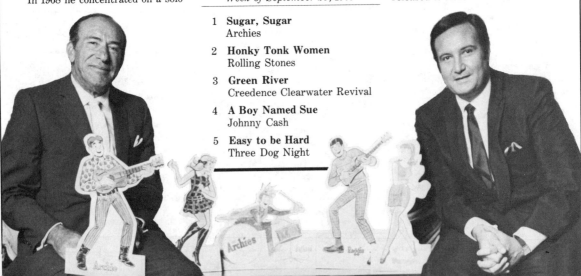

# I Can't Get Next to You
## THE TEMPTATIONS

**259**

*Writers: Norman Whitfield
Barrett Strong*

*Producer: Norman Whitfield*

*October 18, 1969
2 weeks*

THE TEMPTATIONS followed their first number one single [see 168—"My Girl"] with five top 10 hits. Their career was in high gear when David Ruffin, who shared lead vocals with tenor Eddie Kendricks, left the group in the summer of 1968. Producer Norman Whitfield made a drastic change in the direction of the group, added a new lead singer, and made the next phase of the Temptations' carrer even more successful.

Dennis Edwards was born February 3, 1943, in Birmingham, Alabama. His father was a minister, and Dennis sang in his church when he was just two years old. Then his father moved to Detroit and opened a new church there, and the family followed. Dennis studied piano and composition at the Detroit Music Conservatory and became lead singer for a gospel group, the Crowns of Joy.

Sam Cooke's transition from spiritual to secular music [see 30—"You Send Me"] inspired Dennis to follow the same course, and after a stint in the Army, he came home and formed an R&B group, Dennis Edwards and the Firebirds.

Motown's best-known bass guitar player, James Jamerson, arranged an audition for Dennis with label founder Berry Gordy, Jr. A nervous Edwards sang Lou Rawls' "Love Is a Hurtin' Thing," and was signed to the company as a solo artist. Before he could record for the label, he was asked to fill in for the ailing lead singer of the Contours ("Do You Love Me"). Dennis toured with the group for a year and recorded one single, "It's So Hard Being a Loser."

Then he reactivated Dennis Edwards and the Firebirds, a group that now sounded like Sly and the Family Stone [see 251—"Everyday People"]. Motown executives said the timing wasn't right for such a group so a frustrated Dennis met with writer/producers Brian Holland, Lamont Dozier and Eddie Holland, who had broken away from the company and were starting their own Invictus and Hot Wax labels [see 293—"Want Ads"]. Holland, Dozier, and Holland were interested in signing the group to Invictus, and Dennis asked Motown for his release.

A few days later, Dennis was called to the executive offices—to be told of his release from the company, he assumed. Instead, he was asked if he'd like to join the Temptations.

As Edwards took Ruffin's place, Whitfield re-shaped the sound of the group—ironically, he used the sound of Sly and the Family Stone for a role model. The first single featuring Edwards as lead singer was the Norman Whitfield-Barrett Strong composition "Cloud Nine," which went to number six at the beginning of 1969.

Whitfield and Strong wrote two more socially conscious songs for the Temptations, "Runaway Child, Running Wild" (number six) and "Don't Let the Joneses Get You Down" (number 20). In the summer of 1969, they returned to affairs of the heart, in a powerful single that gave all five Temptations a turn at singing lead. "I Can't Get Next to You" entered the Hot 100 at number 84 on August 16, 1969, and became the group's second number one single nine weeks later.

## THE TOP FIVE
*Week of October 18, 1969*

1 **I Can't Get Next to You**
Temptations

2 **Hot Fun in the Summertime**
Sly & the Family Stone

3 **Sugar, Sugar**
Archies

4 **Jean**
Oliver

5 **Little Woman**
Bobby Sherman

## 260   Suspicious Minds   <small>RCA 9764</small>
### ELVIS PRESLEY

*Writer: Mark James*

*Producers: Chips Moman*
    *Felton Jarvis*
    *Elvis Presley*

*November 1, 1969*
*1 week*

live performance was as acclaimed as his television special. Jerry Hopkins, who wrote the *Elvis* biography, was in the audience that night and describes the excitement:

FROM the February 1, 1969, issue of *Billboard*: (Memphis)—Elvis Presley and a contingent of RCA recording technicians quietly slipped in here last week and recorded a 16-tune session at American Record Studios. In the only recording studio interview granted by Presley since he joined RCA, he said: "This is where it all started for me. It feels good to be back in Memphis recording."

These were the first recording sessions for Elvis after his triumphant NBC Television special, telecast December 3, 1968 [see 108—"Good Luck Charm"]. He hadn't recorded in Memphis since a Sun session in July, 1955 (with the exception of the Million Dollar Quartet recording [see 17—"Too Much"]). The marathon session that began January 13, 1969, and lasted 10 days, was originally scheduled for Nashville, but a last-minute switch found Elvis at the American Recording Studio. (ARS was well-respected in the industry. The Box Tops recorded their number one single [see 230—"The Letter"] there. Other hit singles cut at ARS include B.J. Thomas' "Hooked on a Feeling" and Dusty Springfield's "Son of a Preacher Man" from her *Dusty in Memphis* album. Wilson Pickett, Joe Tex and Dionne Warwick recorded there, too).

The Memphis sessions were incredibly productive for Elvis. In the 10-day period, he recorded "In the Ghetto," "Don't Cry Daddy" and a tune written by Mark James, "Suspicious Minds." "In the Ghetto," which entered the Hot 100 in May, became Elvis' first top 10 single since "Crying in the Chapel," three years earlier.

"Suspicious Minds," with backing vocals by Ronnie Milsap and Jeannie Greene, was released in September, 1969. Elvis had already introduced the song on stage on July 26, when he made his first live concert appearance in eight years, at the Hilton Hotel in Las Vegas. His return to

"Elvis sauntered to center stage, grabbed the microphone from its stand, hit a pose from the fifties—legs braced, knees snapping almost imperceptibly—and before he could begin the show, the audience stopped him cold. Just as he was to begin his first song, he was hit in the face with a roar. He looked. All two thousand people were on their feet, pounding their hands together and whistling, many of them standing on their chairs and screaming."

Ten days after his Hilton engagement ended, "Suspicious Minds" entered the Hot 100 at number 77. Seven weeks later it became Elvis' 17th and final number one single. It was the end of a record run—between 1956-1969, he topped the chart for a total of 79 weeks, more than any other artist.

He continued to have hits through

1972. "Don't Cry Daddy," released after "Suspicious Minds," peaked at six. "Kentucky Rain," recorded at a second Memphis session that took place February 17-22, reached number 16. "Burning Love," recorded in Nashville at the end of March, 1972, just missed becoming Elvis' 18th number one. It stalled at number two on October 28, and was prevented from reaching the summit by Chuck Berry [see 321—"My Ding-a-Ling"].

After his Hilton triumph, Elvis resumed a full touring schedule in the early 70s. He remained on North American soil, and Elvis fans in other countries had to settle for a television special, "Aloha from Hawaii Via Satellite," telecast live to Japan on January 14, 1973, and seen in other countries (including the United States) as late as April.

Elvis' final session in a recording studio took place March 9-12, 1975, at RCA's Hollywood studios. After that he recorded at Graceland twice, and on June 19-21, 1977, the final Elvis Presley recordings were made at his concerts in Omaha and Rapid City, Nebraska. Five days later, Elvis gave his last performance in Indianapolis, Indiana.

On August 16, 1977, Elvis was found unconscious in the bathroom off his bedroom at Graceland. An ambulance rushed him to Baptist Memorial Hospital, but it was too late. At 3:30 p.m. Eastern Standard Time, the world learned that Elvis Presley was dead at age 42.

The banner headline on the August 17 edition of the *Memphis Press-Scimitar* read, "A Lonely Life Ends on Elvis Presley Boulevard."

---

## THE TOP FIVE
*Week of November 1, 1969*

1. **Suspicious Minds**
   Elvis Presley

2. **Wedding Bell Blues**
   Fifth Dimension

3. **Sugar, Sugar**
   Archies

4. **I Can't Get Next to You**
   Temptations

5. **Baby It's You**
   Smith

*Writer: Laura Nyro*

*Producer: Bones Howe*

*November 8, 1969*
*3 weeks*

"WEDDING BELL BLUES" was the Fifth Dimension's second number one song, but it was recorded as a joke and never meant for single release. The group had done well with songs written by Bronx composer Laura Nyro, taking "Stoned Soul Picnic" and "Sweet Blindness" into the top 15 in 1968, so it was not unusual for them to record Nyro's "Wedding Bell Blues" for their *Age of Aquarius* album. Producer Bones Howe suggested Marilyn McCoo record it because she was engaged to group member Billy Davis, Jr., and the song conveniently begins, "Bill, I love you so, I always will . . ."

At the time, Bones reveals, Marilyn was not an experienced lead singer. In fact, he had to make 22 splices in the recording of "Wedding Bell Blues" to come up with a final take. But Bones believed so strongly in her talent, he continued to use her as lead vocalist.

Bones was a big fan of Laura Nyro's, and had heard her version of "Wedding Bell Blues" on KHJ, where it was a top 30 hit in the summer of 1967. He met Laura at the Monterey Pop Festival, where the miscast singer gave a disastrous performance and returned to New York. David Geffen found her at her parents' home and offered to manage her. He coaxed her into the studio, where Laura recorded the album *Eli and the 13th Confession*. Geffen brought

Howe a demo of the album, suggesting "Stoned Soul Picnic" for the Fifth Dimension. He warned Howe he'd have to wait until Columbia Records decided what Laura's first single from the LP would be. When "Eli's Coming" was released by Nyro, Bones recorded "Stoned Soul Picnic" and "Sweet Blindness" with the Fifth Dimension.

After "Aquarius/Let the Sunshine In" went to number one, Neil Sedaka and Howard Greenfield's "Workin' on a Groovy Thing" was released as the follow-up. At the same time, radio stations started playing "Wedding Bell Blues" from the album. Al Bennett, head of Liberty Records (the label that distributed Soul City), refused to release "Wedding Bell Blues," insisting it would not be a hit. Even Marilyn agreed, thinking it was too soon after Laura's hit version of the same song. Bennett was presented with a Tin Ear Award when it went to number one.

The Fifth Dimension evolved from a quintet known as the Hi-Fi's. Lamonte McLemore was photographing the Miss Bronze California contest in 1963 when Florence LaRue was crowned the winner by the previous year's title-holder, Marilyn McCoo. Lamont and Marilyn were both interested in singing, and with three other people formed the Hi-Fi's

and toured with Ray Charles. Two members of the group, Harry Elston and Floyd Butler, left to form the Friends of Distinction ("Grazing in the Grass," "Love or Let Me Be Lonely"). After the Ray Charles tour, Marilyn went to work as a department store executive trainee, and spent time as a youth job developer in Watts, California. Lamont returned to his photography. When Billy Davis, Jr., called him up and said he was thinking of signing with Motown as a solo artist, the two friends got together with opera-trained Ron Townsend and discussed forming a new vocal group that would include Marilyn. They wanted another female singer, so Lamont called Florence, who was teaching at Grant Elementary School in Hollywood. They decided to call themselves the Versatiles.

When Johnny Rivers signed them to his Soul City label, he insisted the name was out-of-date and told the group to select a more modern-sounding name. Townson and his wife, Bobette, came up with the Fifth Dimension, which everyone liked immediately. Their first two chart singles were "Go Where You Wanna Go" (a Mamas and Papas song) and "Another Day, Another Heartache," but the song that brought them fame was Jimmy Webb's "Up, Up and Away."

## THE TOP FIVE
*Week of November 8, 1969*

1 **Wedding Bell Blues**
   Fifth Dimension

2 **Suspicious Minds**
   Elvis Presley

3 **Come Together**
   Beatles

4 **I Can't Get Next to You**
   Temptations

5 **Baby It's You**
   Smith

## 262 Come Together / Something APPLE 2654
### THE BEATLES

*Writers: John Lennon
        Paul McCartney /
        George Harrison*

*Producer: George Martin*

*November 29, 1969
1 week*

THE BEATLES achieved their first two-sided number one single thanks to a *Billboard* policy change that took effect while "Come Together" and "Something" were listed as separate chart entries. When the Hot 100 was first introduced on August 4, 1958 [see 40—"Poor Little Fool"], it was standard operating procedure to rank "A" and "B" sides of the same single in separate chart positions.

Operating under this set of rules, "Something" and "Come Together" debuted on the Hot 100 at 20 and 23, respectively, on October 18, 1969. Two weeks later, "Come Together" had surpassed "Something," as the two titles held down positions 10 and 11. The week of November 15, "Come Together" was number two and "Something" was number three. A week later, the former had fallen to seven while the latter held at three.

It looked like neither side had enough strength to go to number one. But beginning with the Hot 100 of November 29, *Billboard* altered its method of compiling the chart, ranking both titles of double-sided hits in the same position. As a result, "Come Together" and "Something" both moved to the top of the chart for one week, becoming the first double-sided number one single since Elvis Presley's "Don't" and "I Beg of You" [see 33] in early 1958.

"Come Together" and "Something" were both from *Abbey Road*, the final Beatles album to be recorded (although the previously recorded *Let It Be* had a later release). "Come Together," written by John Lennon, was the last song recorded for the album. "Something," written by George Harrison, was the first Harrison composition to be released as an "A" side of a Beatles single.

In his book *I Me Mine*, George discussed the evolution of his number one song: " 'Something' was written on the piano while we were making the white album. I had a break while Paul was doing some overdubbing so I went into an empty studio and began to write. That's really all there is to it, except the middle took some time to sort out! It didn't go on the white album because we'd already finished all the tracks. I gave it to Joe Cocker a year before I did it.

"It's probably got a range of five notes which fits most singers' needs best. This I suppose is my most successful song with over 150 cover versions. My favorite cover version is the one by James Brown—that was excellent. When I wrote it, in my mind I heard Ray Charles singing it, and he did do it some years later. I like Smokey Robinson's version too."

Indeed, "Something" has charted on the Hot 100 four times, more than any other Beatles chart-topper. After Harrison took it to number one in November, 1969, the song charted again in 1970 by Shirley Bassey (number 55) and Booker T. and the M.G.'s (76), then again in 1974 by Johnny Rodriguez (85).

"Come Together" has charted three times in all. After the Beatles original topped the chart, Ike and Tina Turner took it to number 57 in 1970, and an Aerosmith version reached number 23 in 1978.

By the time "Come Together" and "Something" were released, the first Beatle solo single had already charted. On June 1, 1969, the sixth day of their bed-in at the Queen Elizabeth Hotel in Montreal, John and Yoko recorded "Give Peace a Chance" with friends Tommy and Dick Smothers, Derek Taylor, Murray the K and Timothy Leary. The single was released in July by the "Plastic Ono Band," and went to number 14 on the Hot 100. Less than two years later, all three other Beatles would also have solo chart entries.

In Britain, "Something" and "Come Together" only went to number four, the lowest ranking for a new Beatles single since their first chart record, "Love Me Do" [see 148], went to number 17 in early 1963. In America, the double-sided hit became the Beatles' 18th number one single, surpassing the total of 17 number ones for Elvis Presley [see 260—"Suspicious Minds"].

### THE TOP FIVE
*Week of November 29, 1969*

1 **Come Together/Something**
Beatles

2 **And When I Die**
Blood, Sweat & Tears

3 **Wedding Bell Blues**
Fifth Dimension

4 **Take a Letter Maria**
R. B. Greaves

5 **Na Na Hey Hey
Kiss Him Goodbye**
Steam

FONTANA 1667 **Na Na Hey Hey Kiss Him Goodbye**
STEAM

**263**

*Writers: Gary De Carlo*
*Dale Frashuer*
*Paul Leka*

*Producer: Paul Leka*

*December 6, 1969*
*2 weeks*

Hastily recorded and mixed in a single evening, "Na Na Hey Hey Kiss Him Goodbye" was designed to be so inferior that disc jockeys would immediately recognize it as the "B" side it was intended to be. Fate had other plans.

After producing a number one single for the Lemon Pipers [see 236—"Green Tambourine"], Paul Leka joined Mercury Records. He convinced the label's new A&R head Bob Reno to sign Gary De Carlo, a friend from Paul's hometown of Bridgeport, Connecticut, to a recording contract. Paul had played piano for a local group, the Chateaus, that had included De Carlo. For Mercury, Paul recorded four songs with Gary and took them to Reno. He thought all four deserved to be "A" sides. Rather than put two of them on the same single and risk splitting airplay, Reno asked Leka to go back into the studio with De Carlo and quickly record a new flip side.

The day of the session, Paul's friend Dale Frashuer dropped by the studio. Also a former member of the Chateaus, Dale had written many songs with Paul that had never been recorded. Dale's visit prompted Paul to dig through their old material, and together they found an uptempo ballad they had composed in 1961, "Kiss Him Goodbye." They started recording at Mercury Sound Studios at 6 p.m., without a full complement of musicians. Instead, Paul spliced together a drum track from one of Gary's four songs and played keyboards himself.

"Kiss Him Goodbye" was only two minutes long, and Paul wanted to record something longer than four minutes, to further discourage DJs from playing it. "I said we should put a chorus to it," Paul recalls. "I started writing while I was sitting at the piano, going 'na na na na, na na na na...' Everything was 'na na' when you didn't have a lyric." Someone else added "hey hey hey."

By 1 a.m. the track was done, but the vocal track included the dummy lyrics. "We agreed it was just a 'B' side and said the hell with it, let's leave those lyrics in. We fattened it up by singing it a couple more times.

"When we came out of the studio at five in the morning, it looked like there was a big fire. There was a manhole, and someone said, 'Wow, look at all the steam!' I put that in the back of my head for a group name," says Paul.

A day later, an employee at the mastering lab called Paul. The track was so long, he couldn't make a good pressing of it without the record skipping. He asked Paul if he could shorten it, and Paul suggested he fade it out earlier. Meanwhile, Reno heard it and said it sounded too good for a "B" side. He told Leka that Mercury had to release so many records per year on its Fontana subsidiary, and he wanted "Na Na Hey Hey Kiss Him Goodbye" as a separate single.

"It was an embarassing record," Paul confides. "Not that Gary sang it badly. But compared to his four songs, it was an insult." Paul consulted with Gary and Dale, and the three agreed that "Na Na Hey Hey Kiss Him Goodbye" could come out under an assumed group name on Fontana while Gary's own singles—under his stage name of Garrett Scott—would be released on Mercury.

Paul remembered the manhole incident and came up with Steam for a group name. To everyone's amazement, "Na Na Hey Hey Kiss Him Goodbye" soared up the Hot 100, while all four of Gary's singles bombed. Now the label needed an album and a group who could tour under the name Steam.

Paul and Dale pulled out some more songs from their 1961 songwriting days and composed some new ones, all in Gary's key. Unhappy at the strange turn of events that left his own records at the starting gate while "Na Na Hey Hey" streaked to number one, Gary refused to record any more songs for a Steam album. Instead, Paul recruited a group from Bridgeport and turned them into Steam.

---

## THE TOP FIVE
*Week of December 6, 1969*

1 **Na Na Hey Hey**
**Kiss Him Goodbye**
Steam

2 **Leaving on a Jet Plane**
Peter, Paul & Mary

3 **Come Together/Something**
Beatles

4 **Take a Letter Maria**
R. B. Greaves

5 **Down on the Corner/**
**Fortunate Son**
Creedence Clearwater Revival

## 264 Leaving on a Jet Plane WARNER BROTHERS 7340
### PETER, PAUL AND MARY

Writer: John Denver

Producers: Albert B. Grossman
            Milt Okun

December 20, 1969
1 week

PETER, PAUL AND MARY'S final single was their first and only number one hit. They had come close in 1963 with two consecutive releases that peaked at number two—"Puff the Magic Dragon" and "Blowin' in the Wind."

"Leaving on a Jet Plane" was written by John Denver [see 360—"Sunshine on My Shoulders"]. Mary liked the song enough to record it on the group's Album 1700, but it wasn't planned for single release until radio airplay encouraged Warner Brothers to issue the song as a 45.

Peter, Paul and Mary first met in New York City's Greenwich Village in 1961. Peter Yarrow had studied art at the High School of Music and Art in Manhattan. While majoring in psychology at Cornell University, he took a sabbatical and moved to the Village.

Albert Grossman saw Peter singing at the Cafe Wha and became his manager. "It was his thought that we could make a group with a particular kind of configuration that would allow the individual talents to be exposed...he thought in terms of a woman's voice and a comedic element," Peter remembers. Noel Paul Stookey, who had led a collegiate

rock group called the Birds of Paradise when he attended Michigan State, was working as a stand-up comedian at the Gaslight Club, across the street from the Cafe Wha. "I had seen Paul perform as a solo," says Peter. "I felt intuitively he would be a very good person for the other male in the group. Albert approached him, but Paul said he wasn't interested."

Grossman suggested that given time, Stookey would change his mind. Meanwhile, Grossman and Yarrow were visiting the Folklore Center when Peter noticed a photograph on the wall of a beautiful, energetic-looking blonde woman. He learned she was Mary Travers, who had done some folk singing on a Pete Seeger record as a member of the Song Swappers and appeared briefly on Broadway in a Mort Sahl musical, The Next President.

"She and I met together, just the two of us. It was interesting when we sang, but it wasn't anything special. But we went over and joined Paul in his apartment in the East Village and...there was magic in the room. The first song we sang was 'Mary Had a Little Lamb.'"

There followed an intense seven-month period of rehearsals. Grossman brought in Okun to develop material, arrange songs and arbitrate decisions for the three individuals. Their first public performance was at the Bitter End club in 1961, where Peter and Paul each did solo sets, followed by a

dozen songs from the trio. They were appearing at the Blue Angel when Warner Brothers Records announced in the February 3, 1962, issue of Billboard they had signed the group.

Their first single, "Lemon Tree," hit the charts in May. "If I Had a Hammer" made the top 10 in the autumn. "Puff the Magic Dragon," released in early 1963, was their first top two hit. Many people falsely believed it was a song about drugs. " 'Puff' never was anything except a song about the innocence of childhood and the sadness of the passing of that kind of innocence we all feel," Paul clarifies.

The breakup of the trio came in 1971. "It had become a 10-year period of living out of each others' back pockets," Mary told Thomas K. Arnold in Goldmine. "We needed some distance; we needed to form an identity of our own. (The) catalyst was that Paul had become a reborn Christian and really felt that being on the road for the length of time we were...was not really the way he wanted to lead his life."

All three members recorded solo albums in the early '70s, and appeared in concert together for presidential candidate George McGovern in 1972. In 1978 they performed in concert at Survival Sunday, an anti-nuclear rally at the Hollywood Bowl. Since then the trio has been touring and recording. They released an album in 1983 on their own label and signed with Gold Castle Records in 1986, yielding an LP No Easy Walk to Freedom.

## THE TOP FIVE
### Week of December 20, 1969

1  **Leaving on a Jet Plane**
   Peter, Paul & Mary

2  **Someday We'll be Together**
   Diana Ross & the Supremes

3  **Down on the Corner/**
   **Fortunate Son**
   Creedence Clearwater Revival

4  **Na Na Hey Hey**
   **Kiss Him Goodbye**
   Steam

5  **Raindrops Keep Falling**
   **on my Head**
   B. J. Thomas

MOTOWN 1156 **Someday We'll Be Together**
DIANA ROSS AND THE SUPREMES
**265**

Writers: *Jackie Beavers*
*Johnny Bristol*
*Harvey Fuqua*

Producer: *Johnny Bristol*

December 27, 1969
1 week

THE final number one song of the 1960s was by the most successful American group of the decade—of the entire rock era, in fact. "Someday We'll Be Together" was the twelfth number one single for Diana Ross and the Supremes, and their final release before Diana left to pursue a solo career.

"Someday We'll Be Together" had been written nine years earlier by Johnny Bristol and Jackie Beavers, two friends who had served in the military together. They were two of the youngest soldiers on base and became close friends. After being discharged, they wrote "Someday We'll Be Together."

"I was young, romantic and married at the time," Bristol answers when asked what inspired him to write the song. "I was on the road quite often, and so was Jackie, who was also married." They recorded the song as a duet, and it was released on Harvey Fuqua's Tri-Phi label by "Johnny and Jackie." When Tri-Phi was absorbed by Motown, Bristol signed on as a writer and producer. The only singing he did was on demo recordings, as Berry Gordy assured him he was more valuable to the company as a writer.

He filed away "Someday We'll Be Together" in a corner of his mind, thinking it would be a hit for someone, someday. As the end of the '60s approached, Bristol thought it was time to revive the duo of Johnny and Jackie, and took a tape of "Someday We'll Be Together" to Gordy.

"He said, 'Oh, this is a smash for the Supremes!' Bristol recalls. "His decisions were usually pretty right on. He and I went into the studio with Diana." And only Diana. Although this was the last single by Diana Ross and the Supremes, in strictly technical terms this was a solo effort by Diana Ross. Mary and Cindy do not appear on the record at all, their roles of backing vocalists assumed by Maxine and Julia Waters.

There is also a male singer prominently featured on the track—Johnny Bristol. "That was Berry Gordy's decision," explains Bristol. "Diana was getting a little tired in the studio, and he and I could see we weren't getting the feeling from her that we wanted. I suggested if I went in the other booth and sang with her, just sort of gave her a little inspiration, that it might spark a little more feeling. Gordy liked what I did so much, he said he was going to keep it on."

Johnny was able to see Diana Ross and the Supremes sing "Someday We'll Be Together" on Ed Sullivan's show, the last of 20 appearances they made with Ed. But Johnny didn't attend the group's final performance, which began at 11:54 p.m. on January 14, 1970, on stage at the Frontier Hotel in Las Vegas. As she began the last song of the set, a

six-minute rendition of "Someday We'll Be Together," Diana reassured everyone, including herself, "It's alright . . ."

At the conclusion of the song, after speeches by Nevada Senator Howard W. Cannon and the entertainment manager of the hotel, Diana brought her replacement, Jean Terrell, up on stage. Jean would sing lead on a string of Supremes hits in the '70s, including "Up the Ladder to the Roof," "Stoned Love" and "Nathan Jones," but the Supremes would never have another number one single.

Terrell remained with the group through 1973's "Bad Weather." Before that, Cindy Birdsong departed, and was replaced by Lynda Laurence. Scherrie Payne, sister of Freda, took over lead duties and Cindy returned briefly. When she left again, her place was taken by Susaye Greene. Mary Wilson, the only constant during this period of change, remained with the group until the end. She spent most of 1984 writing her biography, *Dreamgirl: My Life As a Supreme.*

Despite their promise, the Supremes did not come back together for 12 years. Diana, Mary and Cindy were reunited for the first time professionally during the production of NBC's special celebrating the 25th anniversary of Motown Records. Eyewitnesses at the taping were surprised when Diana appeared to shove Mary away from the microphone, but Mary dismissed it later, saying she was sure it was nothing personal.

## THE TOP FIVE
*Week of December 27, 1969*

1 **Someday We'll be Together**
Diana Ross & the Supremes

2 **Leaving on a Jet Plane**
Peter, Paul & Mary

3 **Raindrops Keep Falling on my Head**
B. J. Thomas

4 **Down on the Corner/ Fortunate Son**
Creedence Clearwater Revival

5 **Na Na Hey Hey Kiss Him Goodbye**
Steam

# Raindrops Keep Fallin' on My Head SCEPTER 12265
## B.J. THOMAS

*Writers: Burt Bacharach*
*Hal David*

*Producers: Burt Bacharach*
*Hal David*

*January 3, 1970*
*4 weeks*

THE night before he was to record "Raindrops Keep Fallin' on My Head" for the soundtrack of *Butch Cassidy and the Sundance Kid*, B.J. Thomas was ordered by his doctor not to use his voice for two weeks. He was suffering from laryngitis—probably picked up on a 15-day tour he had just completed. B.J. pleaded with the doctor, explaining that had to record a song for a new Paul Newman movie the next day. The doctor finally agreed to treat his throat again, then gave Thomas some medication to keep it lubricated.

The following day, B.J. did five takes of the song before writer/producer Burt Bacharach was satisfied. Later, B.J. said if he had been asked to record one more take, his throat wouldn't have made it. An executive from 20th Century Fox present at the recording session congratulated B.J. on sounding so much like Paul Newman, and asked how he thought of using such a raspy voice.

A few weeks later, his throat healed, B.J. flew to New York to record the single version of "Raindrops Keep Fallin' on My Head." His voice was crystal clear this time, and at this session Bacharach added the "da-da-da-da-da" tag.

B.J. Thomas was not the producers' first choice to record "Raindrops . . ." Pop history books agree that Bob Dylan was asked to record the song, but Bacharach says that is not true. He recalls showing the film to Ray Stevens [see 274—"Everything Is Beautiful"] in hopes he would sing the title song. "He liked the picture, but it just wasn't the career move he wanted to make. I think he also had an album in the can that would have conflicted," Bacharach explains.

Dionne Warwick brought Thomas to Bacharach's attention. Bacharach and David wrote all of Dionne's mid-'60s hits, and Thomas was signed to the same label as Dionne, Scepter Records. Dionne took a copy of B.J.'s "Hooked on a Feelin'" to Burt and suggested he write and produce for him. Burt signed Thomas to a management contract, and agreed that if Dylan rejected the song, B. J. could record it.

"Raindrops . . ." was Bacharach-David's second number one single of the rock era [see 242—"This Guy's in Love With You"]. It won the Academy Award for best song, only the second number one song of the rock era to do so [see 3—"Love Is a Many Splendored Thing"].

Billy Joe Thomas was born in Hugo, Oklahoma. The family moved often, but finally settled in Roseburg, Texas, near Houston. B.J.'s early musical influences were both country and R&B: Hank Williams, Ernest Tubb and Jackie Wilson. The first record he bought was "Miss Ann" by Little Richard. At 14, B.J. joined the church choir and also sang in his high school choral group. While still in high school, he joined a group called the Triumphs and they had a local hit with "Lazy Man." On July 4, 1965, the band had a date at a state park in Houston, where they were seen by Charles Booth, owner of Pacemaker Records.

He signed B.J. Thomas and the Triumphs to his label and released their first album. One of the tracks was Hank Williams' "I'm So Lonesome I Could Cry," which Thomas recorded for his father. He never thought he'd have a hit with an old country song, but a Houston disc jockey named Bob White thought it was a smash and gave it airplay.

Pacemaker released it as a single, and New York-based Scepter Records picked it up for national distribution. The song peaked at number eight on the Hot 100 during the spring of 1966. After a few disappointing follow-ups, B.J. reached the top 30 with "The Eyes of a New York Woman" in 1968, and went to number five with "Hooked on a Feeling" in early 1969.

## THE TOP FIVE
*Week of January 3, 1970*

1 **Raindrops Keep Falling on my Head**
   B. J. Thomas

2 **Leaving on a Jet Plane**
   Peter, Paul & Mary

3 **Someday We'll be Together**
   Diana Ross & the Supremes

4 **Down on the Corner/ Fortunate Sun**
   Creedence Clearwater Revival

5 **Na Na Hey Hey Kiss Him Goodbye**
   Steam

Writers: *Freddie Perren*
*Fonce Mizell*
*Deke Richards*
*Berry Gordy, Jr.*

Producers: *Freddie Perren*
*Fonce Mizell*
*Deke Richards*
*Berry Gordy, Jr.*

*January 31, 1970*
*1 week*

**F**OUR weeks after Diana Ross and the Supremes had their twelfth and final number one single, the Jackson Five ushered in a new decade with their first number one, "I Want You Back." The five young brothers were the symbol of a new era at Motown.

"I Want You Back" was not written specifically for the Jackson Five. Freddie Perren and Fonce Mizell had just moved to California and were introduced to Motown by Deke Richards. The three collaborators were sitting in Richards' well-furnished apartment one day. Deke was playing the guitar, accompanied by Fonce on bass and Freddie on piano, and they started playing a riff for a song they called "I Wanna Be Free."

They thought it would be a perfect song for Gladys Knight and the Pips to record. Perren, Mizell and Richards were asked to be on standby while producer Hal Davis was recording; if he didn't use up his three hour recording time, they could have the rest of the session to record their track.

Davis only needed an hour-and-a-half, so the three writers went to the Sound Factory studio on Selma Avenue in Hollywood and produced their instrumental track. Fifteen minutes into the session they knew they had something special.

Deke suggested they ask Berry Gordy to record it with Diana Ross. When they approached Gordy, he listened to the track and came up with a different idea. He told them he had just signed five kids from Gary, Indiana, and suggested rewriting the words to "I Want You Back" for them.

Joe and Katherine Jackson raised their nine children in Gary. They had married when Joe was 16. He dreamed of being a professional musician, and when his children were very young, he and his two brothers had an R&B group called the Falcons. Gary was a steel mill town, and when the Falcons didn't bring in enough money to support a family, Joe went to work as a crane operator at a steel plant.

One night, Joe came home and discovered his second oldest son, Toriano Adaryll Jackson (Tito), had been fooling around with the guitar he played in the Falcons. After giving Tito a whipping, Joe wanted to know how well his son could play. Rather well, as it turned out. When his brothers joined in by singing, Tito suggested they form a family act and turn professional.

The three eldest brothers formed a trio. Sigmund Esco (Jackie), Jermaine LaJaune and Tito were joined later by Marlon David and Michael Joe. Youngest brother Randy would one day fill in for Jermaine, and sisters Maureen (Rebbie), LaToya and Janet would concentrate on their own careers later. A woman in their neighborhood suggested the name Jackson Five, and the family bought as many instruments as they could afford. When they had no money left to buy drums or a piano, they recruited cousins Johnny Jackson and Ronnie Rancifer, who already owned those instruments.

Michael was just five years old when the group played their first professional gig at a Gary nightclub. They were only paid eight dollars, but the coins and bills tossed on stage totalled over $100. They travelled in their Volkswagen van to neighboring cities, including Chicago, where they were often the opening act at the Regal Club for Motown superstars like the Temptations, the Miracles, and Gladys Knight and the Pips.

"I Want You Back" was the only single released from their first album. It entered the Hot 100 on November 15, 1969, at number 90. On January 31, 1970, the song began a four-week run at the top.

## THE TOP FIVE
*Week of January 31, 1970*

1 **I Want You Back**
   Jackson Five

2 **Venus**
   Shocking Blue

3 **Raindrops Keep Falling on my Head**
   B. J. Thomas

4 **Whole Lotta Love**
   Led Zeppelin

5 **Without Love (There is Nothing)**
   Tom Jones

## 268 Venus COLOSSUS 108
### SHOCKING BLUE

*Writer: Robbie van Leeuwen*

*Producer: Robbie van Leeuwen*

*February 7, 1970*
*1 week*

"**V**ENUS" is the biggest-selling single to originate from Holland and the first of two Dutch songs to top the American chart. Although it shares a title with a number one song by Frankie Avalon [see 50], "Venus" is an original composition by Dutch musician Robbie van Leeuwen.

Van Leeuwen was the guitarist for a popular Dutch group of the mid-'60s, the Motions. Like Golden Earring, Q '65 and the Outsiders, they were one of the leading "beat acts" of the '60s in Holland, according to *Billboard's* Dutch correspondent, Willem Hoos. Robbie was more introverted than Motions founder Rudy Bennett, who had an explosive personality. Their differences led Robbie to form his own group in 1967—Shocking Blue.

Joining Van Leeuwen in the group were drummer Cor van Beek, bass player Klaasje van der Wal and lead singer Fred de Wilde, who had been the vocalist for a mid-'60s cult pop group from The Hague, Hu and the Hilltops. In the spring of 1968, Shocking Blue were signed to Dureco, an independent company in the Netherlands. The group's first single, "Lucy Brown Is Back in Town," was released on the company's Pink Elephant label and went to number 21 on the Dutch top 40.

A couple of months later, Shocking Blue's manager Cees van Leeuwen (no relation to Robbie) and music publisher Willem van Kooten attended a party celebrating the success of Golden Earring's first number one song in Holland. A band known as the Bumble Bees, fronted by female singer Mariska Veres, performed at the party, and the two men thought she would be a perfect addition to Shocking Blue.

Mariska, half-Hungarian and half-German, had often sung with her father, who played violin in a gypsy orchestra. She recorded a solo single called "Topkapi" before she was asked to join Shocking Blue. She replaced De Wilde as lead singer on the group's second 45, "Send Me a Postcard Darling," which went to

number 11 on the Dutch chart.

One more single, "Long Lonesome Road," was released, and it went to number 17 in Holland. Then came "Venus," recorded on a two-track machine at Soundpush Studio in Blaricum, a small city 20 miles east of Amsterdam. "Venus" peaked at number three on the Dutch chart in the summer of 1969. It did go to number one, however, in Belgium, then France, Italy, Spain and Germany.

Jerry Ross, an American producer, was just starting a new label in America, and picked up the rights to three Dutch singles: "Ma Belle Amie" by the Tee Set, "Little Green Bag" by the George Baker Selection and "Venus." The first to debut on the Hot 100 was "Venus," which entered the chart at number 77 on December 13, 1969. It went to number one eight weeks later.

"Venus" was the only Shocking Blue hit to make the American top 40. "Mighty Joe" peaked at 43 and "Long Lonesome Road" went to 75. In Holland, "Venus" re-entered the top 40 because of its American success—and peaked at number three again. But the group did have two number one singles in their own country, "Mighty Joe" and "Never Marry a Railroad Man." They continued to chart with songs like "Hello Darkness," "Shocking You," "Blossom Lady" and "Inkpot." Robbie tried to write another song that would be an American hit, but was never able to match the success of "Venus." His depression led to quar-

rels within the group, and the members of Shocking Blue went their separate ways in 1974.

Robbie surprised the Dutch music industry, according to Hoos, when he returned in 1976 with Galaxy Lin, a group much more folk and jazz oriented than Shocking Blue. Their album was a critical success and a commercial failure. A year later, Robbie produced some solo singles for Mariska, but also with little success.

At the end of 1984, Shocking Blue decided to reunite for two concerts at a "Back-to-the-Sixties" festival. After the festival, rumors circulated that Robbie, Mariska, Cor and a new bass player would once again record as Shocking Blue.

### THE TOP FIVE
*Week of February 7, 1970*

1 **Venus**
Shocking Blue

2 **I Want You Back**
Jackson Five

3 **Raindrops Keep Falling on my Head**
B. J. Thomas

4 **Thank You (Falettin Me be Mice Elf Agin)/ Everybody is a Star**
Sly & the Family Stone

5 **Without Love (There is Nothing)**
Tom Jones

EPIC 10555 **Thank You (Falettin Me Be Mice Elf Agin)/Everybody Is a Star**
SLY AND THE FAMILY STONE

*Writer: Sylvester Stewart*

*Producer: Sly Stone*

*February 14, 1970*
*2 weeks*

Like so many other '60s bands, Sly and the Family Stone were immortalized at Woodstock. Songs like "You Can Make It If You Try," "I Want to Take You Higher" and "Stand!" became anthems for a counterculture looking to music for its direction. The positivism expressed in Sly's simple messages reinforced young people of all races. It attracted, as well, the attention of the Black Panthers, who, according to David Kapralik (former CBS executive and Sly's first manager), wanted to enlist the artist for their own propaganda purposes.

"During that period . . . Sylvester Stewart had enormous pressures on him to align himself with the voices of despair and nihilism," Kapralik stated in a 1971 *Rolling Stone* article. "I pulled with all my energy to keep him from becoming a spokesman for those things. The poor kid was torn apart." Adding to the fray were internal band frictions with family members and assassination threats. The pressures were too heavy on a 25-year-old just beginning to cope with the demands and changes brought about by sudden fame. The symptoms of a bleeding ulcer appeared, though Sly never actually developed the ulcer. What he did develop was a drug habit. Said Kapralik, "One of the clinical ways to ease the pain is cocaine."

Clive Davis viewed the change from the presidential chair at Columbia Records. "As often happens, Sly began to live very well," he assesses in his biography, *Clive: Inside the Record Business.* "It was different from his earlier days, when he worked seven days a week and whenever I saw him coming out of a recording studio, he was literally running to another appointment, looking intense and preoccupied. Now that he was successful, he was into exotic cars and jewelry, expensive homes, private planes, glittering women."

The toll was beginning to show on the road. A retinue of hangers-on not only overloaded the efficiency of the operation but also cut into its solvency. The public wasn't protected from the chaos of Sly's affairs, either, especially in the concert arena. Two and three hour delays became usual, when the star bothered to appear at all. Angry ticket holders revolted, rioting in Chicago and at the Newport Jazz Festival in 1971, where drunken attendees broke down fences and stormed the stage in a hail of lightning and thunder. Such irresponsibility and the lawsuits it inevitably aroused had a severe impact on the artist's wallet. "Sly has lost more money in two years than the average rock group would have earned in that period of time," declared attorney Peter Bennett, in charge of Kapralik's business matters at the time.

The maelstrom manifested itself creatively. After "Hot Fun in the Summertime," a number two hit in the summer of 1969, Sly could only muster one single during a two-year period: the double-sided hit, "Thank You (Falettin Me Be Mice Elf Agin)" and "Everybody Is a Star." It entered the Hot 100 at number 59 on January 3, 1970, and went to number one six weeks later. It would be another 18 months before Sly would publicly reveal his conflicts, on the album *There's a Riot Goin' On.*

## THE TOP FIVE
*Week of February 14, 1970*

1 **Thank You (Falettin Me be Mice Elf Agin)/ Everybody is a Star**
Sly & the Family Stone

2 **I Want You Back**
Jackson Five

3 **Raindrops Keep Falling on my Head**
B. J. Thomas

4 **Venus**
Shocking Blue

5 **Hey There Lonely Girl**
Eddie Holman

## 270 Bridge Over Troubled Water COLUMBIA 45079
### SIMON AND GARFUNKEL

*Writer: Paul Simon*

*Producers: Paul Simon*
*Art Garfunkel*
*Roy Halee*

*February 28, 1970*
*6 weeks*

THERE had always been an element of tension in the relationship between Paul Simon and Art Garfunkel, hidden from public view by compromise and a friendship that began when they were in the sixth grade. But during the recording of *Bridge Over Troubled Water*, one of the most successful albums of the rock era, the age of compromise ended and the break-up of the best-selling duo since the Everly Brothers [see 28—"Wake Up Little Susie"] began.

"During the making of *Bridge Over Troubled Water* there were a lot of times when it just wasn't fun to work together," Simon told Jon Landau in a 1972 *Rolling Stone* interview. "It was very hard work, and it was complex. I think Artie said that he felt that he didn't want to record, and I know I said I felt that if I had to go through these kinds of personal abrasions, I didn't want to continue to do it."

While the album was being recorded, Garfunkel was busy filming *Catch-22*, directed by Mike Nichols (*The Graduate*). "On several tracks on *Bridge* there's no Artie at all,"

says Simon in *Rolling Stone*. "It's a Simon and Garfunkel record, but not really . . . there are many songs where you don't hear Simon and Garfunkel singing together. Because of that the separation became easier."

The title track from the album was written during the summer of 1969. Paul and his wife Peggy were renting a house with Garfunkel on Blue Jay Way, the same house in Los Angeles where George Harrison had been inspired to write "Blue Jay Way." Paul wrote it on his guitar and had it transposed for piano by arranger Jimmie Haskell. There were only two verses written before they went into the studio, where Garfunkel suggested a third verse be added. To this day, Paul feels the final verse does not match the first two.

The instrumental track was completed in Los Angeles, then Paul and Art returned to New York to record the vocals. At first, Garfunkel was reluctant to sing "Bridge Over Troubled Water." Paul recalls in *Rolling Stone*:

"He didn't want to sing it himself....He felt I should have done it. And many times I think I'm sorry I didn't do it. Many times on a stage ...when I'd be sitting off to the side...and Artie would be singing 'Bridge,' people would stomp and cheer when it was over, and I would think, 'That's my song, man. Thank you very much, I wrote that

song'...in the earlier days when things were smoother I never would have thought that, but towards the end when things were strained I did. It's not a very generous thing to think, but I did think that."

One more disagreement sealed the breakup of Simon and Garfunkel. Art refused to record a song Paul had written for the album, "Cuba Si, Nixon No." Paul didn't want to record a Bach chorale track that Art favored. There was no compromise, so they released the LP with 11 songs instead of 12.

Despite the six Grammys won by the album and single of "Bridge Over Troubled water," there was some relief in not continuing, Simon told Landau. "Having a track record to live up to and the history of successes had become a hindrance. It becomes harder to break out of what people expect you to do. From that point of view, I'm delighted I didn't have to write a Simon and Garfunkel follow-up to 'Bridge Over Troubled Water,' which I think would have been an inevitable letdown for people."

Although there would be temporary reunions, there was never to be another studio album of new material from Simon and Garfunkel. Their respective careers enjoyed different degrees of success in Britain and America. In the United Kingdom, Garfunkel scored two number one singles ("I Only Have Eyes for You," "Bright Eyes"), while in America Simon had a solitary solo number one single [see 428—"50 Ways to Leave Your Lover"].

### THE TOP FIVE
*Week of February 28, 1970*

1 **Bridge over Troubled Water**
Simon & Garfunkel

2 **Thank You (Falettin Me be Mice Elf Agin)/**
**Everybody is a Star**
Sly & the Family Stone

3 **Travelin' Band/**
**Who'll Stop the Rain**
Creedence Clearwater Revival

4 **Hey There Lonely Girl**
Eddie Holman

5 **No Time**
Guess Who

"A" side of a single. At one point, it was scheduled for release as a Plastic Ono Band 45, backed with "What's the New Mary Jane." Assigned a British catalogue number of Apples 1002, the single was withdrawn and John Lennon issued "Instant Karma (We All Shine On)" instead.

"Instant Karma" entered the Hot 100 on February 28, 1970, three weeks before "Let It Be." The two singles were in direct competition, with "Instant Karma" holding its peak position of number three the week "Let It Be" moved to number one.

With a John Lennon single on the chart, perhaps it wasn't so surprising when the news that the Beatles were breaking up made headlines around the world on April 10. "Let It Be" was the number one song in America, and its title offered an unintentional message to Beatle fans.

Looking back on the evolution of the Beatles, from their earliest days at the Cavern Club in Liverpool to the latter stage of their career, when they had become the biggest band in the history of Western civilization, it's easy to see now that they were in truth no longer a group by 1970. They were four individuals who had matured personally and professionally to a point where the dissolution of the group was inevitable. It was time for each Beatle to control his own destiny, to make his own music. No matter how much the rest of the world wanted the Beatles to remain together forever, it was time to let it be.

*Writers: John Lennon*
*Paul McCartney*

*Producers: George Martin*

*April 11, 1970*
*2 weeks*

"LET IT BE" MADE a spectacular debut on the Hot 100. When it opened at number six, it was the highest new entry of all time to this date. Despite its lofty first-week position on March 21, 1970, the single didn't become the Beatles' 19th number one until three weeks later. It was held at bay by Simon and Garfunkel's "Bridge Over Troubled Water."

The single release of "Let It Be" was produced by George Martin. The song was recorded in January, 1969, before the sessions that resulted in the *Abbey Road* album and the group's previous number one single [see 262—"Come Together" / "Something"]. "Let It Be" was written by Paul McCartney for his late mother, Mary, although the "mother Mary" in the song has often been interpreted in a religious light. Paul sings a solo

vocal and plays piano. John Lennon, George Harrison and Ringo Starr all play their regular instruments (lead guitar, bass guitar and drums) and Billy Preston [see 254—"Get Back"] guest stars on organ.

A different version of the song appears on the album *Let It Be*. This is the Phil Spector remix, which includes brass instruments and a choir overdubbed, as well as different arrangements for John and George's guitar playing.

The album was originally to be titled *Get Back* and was scheduled to be released in December, 1969. A month later, with the album delayed because of internal problems in the Beatles' Apple company, Britain's *New Musical Express* reported the album title might be changed to *Let It Be*, after the Beatles' forthcoming single. The 45 was released March 11, 1970, and the album followed two months later.

The flip side of "Let It Be" was a strange concoction called "You Know My Name (Look Up the Number)." Different sources cite the recording date as 1967 or 1968; what is certain is that the song was considered for an

## THE TOP FIVE
*Week of April 11, 1970*

1 **Let It Be**
The Beatles

2 **ABC**
Jackson 5

3 **Instant Karma (We All Shine On)**
John Ono Lennon

4 **Spirit in the Sky**
Norman Greenbaum

5 **Bridge Over Troubled Water**
Simon and Garfunkel

**272** **ABC** MOTOWN 1163
THE JACKSON FIVE

*Writers: Freddie Perren*
*Fonce Mizell*
*Deke Richards*
*Berry Gordy, Jr.*

*Producers: Freddie Perren*
*Fonce Mizell*
*Deke Richards*
*Berry Gordy, Jr.*

*April 25, 1970*
*2 weeks*

IF "ABC" sounded like a school lesson, it was. Former schoolteacher Freddie Perren's role as producer of the Jackson Five was not so different from his teaching days. "I still do teach in a sense, when I work with groups like the Jackson Five," says Perren. "To produce the way I produce, there is an element of teaching, because you have to teach them the song the way you want it sung, so they know it before they begin to express it themselves."

And if "ABC" sounded like its predecessor [see 267—"I Want You Back"], it was. "The music of 'ABC' is the chorus of 'I Want You Back,'" Perren confesses. "All we did was take that music and keep playing it, adding a couple of steps to it. We cut the track for 'ABC' before 'I Want You Back' was really a big hit."

It was a Motown tradition for a follow-up to resemble the song it succeeded. "Baby Love" [see 159] and "It's the Same Old Song" [see 177—"I Can't Help Myself (Sugar Pie Honey Bunch)"] were incredible records, but both sounded like the singles that had come directly before. As those records insured chart longevity for the Supremes and the Four Tops, "ABC" gave the Jackson Five a second consecutive number one single. The media started to pay close attention to the five brothers from Gary, Indiana, realizing for the first time they were not one-hit wonders.

One story reported often in the media was that Motown superstar Diana Ross had discovered the group and brought them to Gordy's attention. It's true that the Jackson Five were the opening act for Diana Ross and the Supremes during a fall, 1969, show at the Forum in Inglewood, California, and it's also true that the group's first album was titled *Diana Ross Presents the Jackson Five*, but in recent years all parties involved have denied that Diana actually found the group.

"No, I didn't discover them," Diana said in a *Rolling Stone* interview. Motown artists Bobby Taylor and Gladys Knight are acknowledged as early boosters of the Jackson Five, and they apparently told Gordy about the brothers from Gary. Diana did figure in the group's destiny, however. After they were signed to Motown, the five Jacksons moved to Hollywood for a year of rehearsals. During that time, some of the Jacksons lived with Gordy and the others, including Michael, lived in Diana's home.

"He won me over the first time I saw him," Diana told *Newsweek*. "I saw so much of myself as a child in Michael. He was performing all the time. That's the way I was. He could be my son."

"ABC" entered the Hot 100 on March 14, 1970, at number 41. Six weeks later it pre-empted the Beatles' "Let It Be" as the number one song in the nation. "ABC" is in a five-way tie for the shortest title of any number one single. Its co-title holders are Frankie Avalon's "Why" [see 62], Edwin Starr's "War" [see 280] and Michael Jackson's "Ben" [see 320] and "Bad" [see 680].

## THE TOP FIVE
*Week of April 25, 1970*

1 **ABC**
Jackson Five

2 **Let It Be**
Beatles

3 **Spirit in the Sky**
Norman Greenbaum

4 **Instant Karma**
**(We All Shine On)**
John Lennon

5 **American Woman/**
**No Sugar Tonight**
Guess Who

RCA 0325 **American Woman / No Sugar Tonight** 273
GUESS WHO

Writers: *Randy Bachman*
*Burton Cummings*
*Garry Peterson*
*Jim Kale/*
*Randy Bachman*

Producer: *Jack Richardson*

*May 9, 1970*
*3 weeks*

**I**N 1965, before legislation was passed requiring a certain percentage of airtime be given to native artists, Canadian musicians found it difficult to crack radio playlists in their own country. To avoid that prejudice, Winnipeg band Chad Allen and the Expressions elected to leave their name off their new single, "Shakin' All Over." As far as anyone in Canada knew, the song was by a new, anonymous band called Guess Who. The name stuck.

Five years later, the Guess Who would lead the emigration of Canadian groups south to the U.S. charts with "American Woman." This, their only number one hit, capped an 11-year odyssey that began in their home town. Winnipeg's favorite sons were Mickey Brown and the Velvetones, who not only played all the

best clubs but broadcast live on the radio. One of their original instrumental songs was "Randy's Rock," named for their lead guitarist, Randy Bachman. Friendly competition for the Velvetones were Allan and the Silvertones, who began incorporating Shadows and Cliff Richard material into their set, music that was previously unheard of in Winnipeg. Bachman was intrigued enough to defect, bringing along drummer Garry Peterson to join Allan Kobel (vocals), Jim Kale (bass) and Brian Ashley (piano).

The new quintet set two priorities—changing their name and getting a record contract. Kobel christened himself Chad Allen and his cohorts became the Reflections. Canadian-American Records signed them and released two singles. The debut was spoiled by a mixup in master tapes which incorrectly listed "I Just Didn't Have the Heart" as "Tribute to Buddy Holly" on the first few hundred pressings, forcing record stores to crudely paste a corrected label on their copies. Still, the moderate success of their singles was sufficient to warrant American release, and interest the Canadian label Quality to ink the group.

"Shakin' All Over" followed, reaching number 22 on the Hot 100 in July, 1965. The Guess Who toured the States as part of a performing package with the Turtles, Eddie Hodges and the Crystals. During the tour Ashley developed an escalating case of stage fright that eventually forced him to leave the group. Replacing him was another Winnipeg singer, Burton Cummings, who traded lead vocals with Allen until the strain on the latter's voice caused *him* to retire too. Bachman and Cummings' song, "These Eyes " was released as a single by the band's new label, RCA, in 1969, and finally the Guess Who were on their way.

Their third album, *American Woman*, contained both sides of their number one single, "American Woman" and "No Sugar Tonight." The single entered the Hot 100 at number 46 on March 21, 1970, and climbed to the top of the chart seven weeks later.

The group only had two more top 10 hits, "Share the Land" in 1970 and "Clap for the Wolfman" in 1974. It wasn't failure that led to the group's dissolution, but success. Bachman had left in 1970, and later formed Bachman-Turner Overdrive [see 382—"You Ain't Seen Nothing Yet"] with brother Robin and Fred Turner. After myriad changes, Cummings called a halt to the Guess Who in 1975 and established a solo career with "Stand Tall," a number 10 hit in January, 1977. Bachman and Cummings got the original line-up back together in 1983 to record an album, and after that Kale headed up his own version of the band.

## THE TOP FIVE
*Week of May 9, 1970*

1   **American Woman/**
    **No Sugar Tonight**
    Guess Who

2   **ABC**
    Jackson Five

3   **Let It Be**
    Beatles

4   **Vehicle**
    Ides of March

5   **Spirit in the Sky**
    Norman Greenbaum

# 274 | Everything Is Beautiful BARNABY 2011
## RAY STEVENS

*Writer: Ray Stevens*

*Producer: Ray Stevens*

May 30, 1970
2 weeks

GROWING up in Clarkdale, Georgia, Ray Stevens (born Ray Ragsdale on January 24, 1941) heard country music artists like Kitty Wells, Lefty Frizell and Ernest Tubb on the juke box at the municipal swimming pool. His father, a cost engineer, was transferred to Atlanta when Ray was 10, giving the youngster a chance to listen to a wide variety of R&B singers, including Ruth Brown, the Drifters, LaVern Baker and the Clovers. Influenced by both country and R&B music, Ray started writing songs and turned professional at 17, when Atlanta publisher Bill Lowery helped him get a contract with Prep, a subsidiary of Capitol Records.

His first recording, "Silver Bracelet," wasn't very successful, so he tried a novelty song, "Sergeant Preston of the Yukon." It showed signs of taking off, until Capitol received a letter from King Features, owner of the Sergeant Preston character. Stevens had failed to get permission to use their hero in his song, and the record had to be pulled off the market.

Ray met Mercury Records executive Shelby Singleton when he was a regional promotion man. When the label promoted Singleton to record producer, he relocated to Nashville and signed Stevens to the

label. He also hired Ray to assist Jerry Kennedy in A&R. Ray recorded his first single for Mercury, "Jeremiah Peabody's Poly Unsaturated Quick Dissolving Fast Acting Pleasant Tasting Green and Purple Pills," then moved to Nashville himself. His next Mercury single, "Ahab the Arab," went to number five on the Hot 100, establishing Ray as a novelty artist. He recorded comedy records for the next six years.

In 1966, Ray switched to Monument Records, and for the first time, had a top 30 hit with a serious song. "Mr. Businessman," written to vent his frustration at being cheated in a business deal, peaked at number 28.

In 1969, Roger Miller introduced Ray to Andy Williams' brother, Don Williams. Soon after, Andy signed Ray as an artist for his new label, Barnaby. Ray made frequent appearances on Williams' weekly NBC variety series, and proved popular enough that NBC asked him to host a summer replacement series for Williams in 1970.

In the spring of 1970, Ray was preparing for his first Barnaby

recording session. "I wanted a big song that could be a hit and also be the theme song for the television show. My piano was in the basement of the house we lived in, and I just chained myself to the piano and didn't come out until I had written 'Everything Is Beautiful.'"

To underscore the optimism of the song, Ray took a portable tape recorder to his daughters' school, Oak Hill Elementary in Nashville. His youngest daughter was in kindergarten, and she was excused to join her sister's second grade class in the school auditorium, where the children sang the chorus of "Everything is Beautiful." Later, their voices were added to Ray's vocal track.

"Andy Williams Presents Ray Stevens" made its network debut on Saturday, June 20, 1970, at 7:30 p.m. It was an eccentric, fast-paced show, produced by Williams' producers, Chris Bearde and Alan Blye. The series' regulars included Cass Elliott [see 198—"Monday, Monday"] and Lulu [see 231—"To Sir, With Love"]. The final segment was telecast August 8, 1970.

## THE TOP FIVE
*Week of May 30, 1970*

1  **Everything Is Beautiful**
   Ray Stevens

2  **American Woman /
   No Sugar Tonight**
   Guess Who

3  **Love on a Two-Way Street**
   The Moments

4  **Cecilia**
   Simon and Garfunkel

5  **Up Around the Bend /
   Run Through the Jungle**
   Creedence Clearwater Revival

# The Long and Winding Road/For You Blue

APPLE 2832

**THE BEATLES**

*Writers: John Lennon*
*Paul McCartney*
*George Harrison*

*Producer: Phil Spector*

*June 13, 1970*
*2 weeks*

"THE LONG AND WINDING ROAD" began in the seaport town of Liverpool, the birthplace of four young men who met through one twist of fate or another, and formed a band because they loved rock and roll. They had dreams of fame, but not in their wildest dreams could they have imagined what the future held for them. Even when "I Want to Hold Your Hand" went to number one in America, even when they occupied the top five positions on the Hot 100, they did not dare believe their career would last longer than a few years.

"The Long and Winding Road" was the 20th and final number one single for the Beatles. As of June, 1970, the Fab Four had accumulated more chart-toppers than any other act. Elvis Presley had amassed 17 and the Supremes had 12. Ironically, the Beatles, Elvis and the Supremes all had their final number one hit singles in an eight-month period between November, 1969, and June, 1970 [see 260—"Suspicious Minds" and 265—"Someday We'll Be Together"]. By 2003, the Beatles still had more number ones than any other artist.

"The Long and Winding Road," which was not released as a single in Britain, was a track from the *Let It Be* album. The single entered the Hot 100 at number 35 on May 23, 1970, while the single "Let It Be" was number six. Backed with George Harrison's "For You Blue," Paul McCartney's "The Long and Winding Road" moved 35-12-10 and then jumped to number one. It was the second double-sided chart-topper for the Beatles, and the second number one for Harrison [see 262—"Come Together" / "Something"].

Only two Beatles were present in the studio for the recording of "The Long and Winding Road." Paul played piano and sang a solo vocal. John Lennon played bass guitar. The original version as they recorded it can only be heard on bootleg Beatles albums. The album track and single release were produced by Phil Spector [see 254—"Get Back"], who overdubbed an orchestra, complete with strings, and a backing choir of female singers.

Philip Norman related in *Shout!* what happened after the Beatles heard Spector's production work: "An acetate went to each Beatle accompanied by a long letter from Spector, justifying what he had done but assuring them he could make whatever changes they wished. When Paul McCartney played the acetate, he was stunned. His ballad, "The Long and Winding Road," had been remixed by Spector, then dubbed with a violin and horn section and topped with a sickly celestial choir. Paul tried to contact Spector, but could not. He wrote to (Beatles manager) Allen Klein, demanding the restoration of his original version, but to no avail.

George Harrison made no comment on Spector's production mix of "For You Blue." He didn't have to—he asked Phil to produce his first solo album, *All Things Must Pass*, which was statement enough. "For You Blue" featured a solo vocal from George, who played acoustic guitar. John played steel guitar, Paul played bass and piano, and Ringo Starr played drums.

Just as "Someday We'll Be Together" was an appropriate final single for the Supremes, "The Long and Winding Road" summed up the state of the Beatles in 1970. The break-up of the group has already been announced [see 271—"Let It Be"] but somehow it didn't seem final just yet. Many believed that there would only be a temporary lull, that after experimenting with solo careers the four Beatles would come together once more. As time passed and it became obvious the dream was over, fans held on to an undying hope that there would be a Beatles reunion. Despite denials, rumors of an impending worldwide satellite broadcast, or a charity concert, or an unexpected surprise get-together, continually cropped up. It was only on December 8, 1980, that the world tragically realized the Beatles would never play together again [see 534—"(Just Like) Starting Over"].

## THE TOP FIVE
*Week of June 13, 1970*

1 **The Long and Winding Road/ For You Blue**
Beatles

2 **Which Way You Goin' Billy?**
Poppy Family

3 **Everything Is Beautiful**
Ray Stevens

4 **Get Ready**
Rare Earth

5 **Love on a Two Way Street**
Moments

**276** **The Love You Save** MOTOWN 1166
THE JACKSON FIVE

*Writers: Freddie Perren*
*Fonce Mizell*
*Deke Richards*
*Berry Gordy, Jr.*

*Producers: Freddie Perren*
*Fonce Mizell*
*Deke Richards*
*Berry Gordy, Jr.*

*June 27, 1970*
*2 weeks*

W HEN "The Love You Save" moved into the number one position on *Billboard's* Hot 100 on June 27, 1970, the Jackson Five became the first artists of the rock era to have their first three chart releases reach number one.

"After two platinum singles, Berry Gordy kept saying, 'What about the follow-up?'" Freddie Perren recalls. "He wasn't worried, but he really wanted to bring the third one home. We really didn't have that third one yet." Deke Richards, Fonce Mizell and Perren came up with several ideas, but none of them seemed right for the third Jackson Five single. Finally they wrote a song about watching out for traffic, and with some minor adjustments in lyrics, it became a song about "a girl who was

a little too fast for her age." The three writer/producers recorded their own demo one night and were satisfied enough to want Gordy to hear it. But he was busy elsewhere, so they went to their regular studio, the Sound Factory in Hollywood, to record the track. Gordy dropped in while they were recording.

"He would never come to a tracking session," says Perren. "He would usually come after. We hadn't finished it yet, we were still working on parts of it. He stayed 15 minutes and half-way through said, 'you guys got it. I'm not worried anymore.' And he walked out."

Like its two predecessors, "The Love You Save" listed its writing and production credits as "The Corporation," a name as anonymous as "The Clan" [see 248—"Love Child"]. Perren, Mizell and Richards had planned to release their own albums as the Corporation. Looking back on those early days with Motown, Perren speculates that the company may have preferred the anonymity of "The Corporation" over singling out any individual writer or producer; the pain of the Holland-Dozier-Holland split was still being felt.

Producing the Jackson Five's first three singles was not Perren's first association with the group. He was

playing piano for Jerry Butler at the Regal Theater in Chicago when the brothers were the opening act. It was near the end of June, 1968, and the group was having regional success with a pre-Motown single, "I'm a Big Boy Now."

"Michael was tiny," Perren remembers. "I felt so sorry for him, because it was a nightclub. I said this little kid's gonna go out and they're gonna murder him. Michael went out there and brought the house down. I wish we had gone on first."

### THE TOP FIVE
*Week of June 27, 1970*

1 **The Love You Save**
Jackson Five

2 **Mama Told Me (Not to Come)**
Three Dog Night

3 **Ball of Confusion (That's What the World is Today)**
Temptations

4 **The Long and Winding Road/ For You Blue**
Beatles

5 **Hitchin' a Ride**
Vanity Fare

*Writer: Randy Newman*

*Producer: Richard Podolor*

*July 11, 1970*
*2 weeks*

THAT mama. First she said there'd be days like this. Then she said love don't come easy, it's a game of give and take. Then there was this great party, but mama told me not to come (she said that ain't the way to have fun). And who said father knows best?

Three Dog Night sold lots of albums and grossed five million dollars a year from touring, but mainly they were a hit singles machine. Between 1969-1975 they had 21 chart entries, and 11 of those made the top 10. One of the primary reasons for their success was their ability to recognize new songwriters before the public did. Ironically, they were constantly slammed by the rock press for not writing their own material; instead, the critics should have thanked them for being among the first to record works by Harry Nilsson [see 307—"Without You"], Laura Nyro, Elton John [see 328—"Crocodile Rock"] and Bernie Taupin, Leo Sayer [see 450—"You Make Me Feel Like Dancing"] and Randy Newman.

Artists had been recording Randy Newman songs since 1962, when Gene McDaniels sang "Somebody's Waiting" on the flip side of "Spanish Lace." During the next few months, Newman's songs were recorded by the Fleetwoods ("They Tell Me It's Summer") and Jackie DeShannon ("Did He Call Today, Mama?"). Gene Pitney, the O'Jays, Cilla Black and Jerry Butler all recorded Randy's songs long before anyone knew who he was.

Newman's first top ten hit was "Simon Smith and the Amazing Dancing Bear," which Alan Price [see 156—"The House of the Rising Sun"] took to number four in Britain during 1967. That same year, Price's compatriot Eric Burdon recorded three Newman songs on the *Eric Is Here* album: "I Think It's Gonna Rain Today," "Wait Till Next Year" and "Mama Told Me (Not to Come)."

Before he helped organize Three Dog Night [see 291—"Joy to the World"], singer Cory Wells heard

"Mama Told Me (Not to Come)" by Burdon and also the original version by Newman, who had recorded it on one of his albums. At the time, Wells' own band, the Enemies, had broken up and he had gone to Tempe, Arizona, to start a new group. He included "Mama Told Me" in their repertoire.

Wells tried to persuade Three Dog Night to record "Mama Told Me (Not to Come)" right from the start, but the rest of the group had heard Newman sing it and didn't think it was very commercial. Wells persisted, and by their third album, *It Ain't Easy*, the other six members of the band finally agreed to give it a try.

"Mama Told Me (Not to Come)" is the only number one song written by Newman. His own recording of "Short People" came close—it peaked at number two in early 1978.

By the time "Mama Told Me (Not to Come)" went to number one, Nilsson and Nyro had already reaped rewards from having their songs recorded by Three Dog Night. The group's first single, "Nobody" (recorded previously by Kim Weston), failed to make the Hot 100. Another track from their first album, "Try a Little Tenderness," was their breakthrough song, peaking at number 29 in the spring of 1969. The third single from the LP was the title track, "One," written by Nilsson. It was only after Three Dog Night's single entered the Hot 100 that Harry had success on his own, start-

ing with Fred Neil's "Everybody's Talkin'," a song heard on the soundtrack of *Midnight Cowboy*.

Next came "Easy to Be Hard," a song from Broadway's *Hair*. The group's fifth single was "Eli's Coming," written by Nyro. Its appearance on the Hot 100 coincided with two other Nyro cover versions: "And When I Die" by Blood, Sweat and Tears and "Wedding Bell Blues" by the Fifth Dimension [see 261], helping to establish Laura as one of the hottest songwriters of the day.

Three Dog Night included Elton John and Bernie Taupin's "Lady Samantha" on their second album, *Suitable for Framing* and gave Leo Sayer a boost in America by taking a cover version of his British hit "The Show Must Go On" to number four in 1974.

## THE TOP FIVE
*Week of July 11, 1970*

1 **Mama Told Me (Not to Come)**
Three Dog Night

2 **The Love You Save**
Jackson Five

3 **Ball of Confusion (That's What the World is Today)**
Temptations

4 **Ride Captain Ride**
Blues Image

5 **Band of Gold**
Freda Payne

**278**  **(They Long to Be) Close to You** A&M 1183
CARPENTERS

Writers: *Burt Bacharach*
*Hal David*

Producer: *Jack Daugherty*

*July 25, 1970*
*4 weeks*

RICHARD CARPENTER was three-and-a-half years older than his sister, Karen. As they were growing up in New Haven, Connecticut, Richard became interested in his father's extensive record collection. The first song Richard remembers hearing on the radio was "Music, Music, Music" by Teresa Brewer. He took his first music lessons when he was 12, playing pop tunes while studying classical piano. With two older friends, he found work playing music in a local pizza joint, a job interrupted by the family's move to Downey, California, in 1963.

In his senior year at Downey High School, Richard joined the marching band as an alternative to gym class, and was also pianist in his teacher's own band. When Karen entered high school, the idea of running around the track early in the morning appalled her, and she asked if she could join the band, too. She had never played an instrument, so the glockenspiel was suggested. After a brief fling, she expressed interest in the drums and was told by the band director that wasn't "normal." That's all Karen needed to hear.

Within two weeks, her father bought her a drum set and Karen took to it immediately.

At the same time, Richard was enrolled at California State College at Long Beach, where he sang in the *a cappella* choir under the direction of

Frank Pooler (who would later write the lyrics for the Carpenters' holiday classic, "Merry Christmas Darling"). Richard became friends with music major Wes Jacobs, who played tuba and bass fiddle. With Karen on drums, they formed a jazz trio and entered the 1966 Battle of the Bands at the Hollywood Bowl. They performed "The Girl from Ipanema" and "Iced Tea" and won first prize. Neely Plumb, an A&R man from RCA, was there and offered them a contract.

They cut four sides, but while Plumb saw possibilities in rock and roll tuba, others at RCA didn't. The songs were never released and the Carpenter Trio was dropped from the label's artist roster.

Jacobs left for Juilliard (and later joined the Detroit Symphony). Richard put together another group, Spectrum, which included fellow choir member John Bettis. Karen took over lead vocal duties, while continuing to play the drums. Spectrum produced an audition tape that made the rounds of record labels, but they were rejected everywhere and the band dissolved.

Certain they had talent, Richard persevered. Experimenting with multi-tracked voices, he and Karen recorded another tape in the North Hollywood garage/studio of session musician Joe Osborn. A friend of his passed it on to record producer Jack Daugherty, who gave it to Herb Alpert, [see 242—"This Guy's in Love With You"] co-owner of A&M Records. The label had turned Spectrum down, but Alpert liked Karen's voice and signed the Carpenters.

The first album, *Offerings*, included the first single, a new arrangement of the Beatles' "Ticket

to Ride" [see 174]. Songwriter Burt Bacharach went to A&M's other owner, Jerry Moss, and mentioned he had heard "Ticket to Ride" on the radio and loved it. When Moss told Bacharach that the group singing it was also signed to A&M, Burt asked if the Carpenters would open for him at a charity benefit for the Reiss-Davis Clinic, to be held at the Century Plaza Hotel. Burt requested that Richard arrange a medley of Bacharach songs, and Richard began to search for some of Burt's obscure tunes.

While rehearsing on an A&M soundstage, Richard was approached by Herb, who suggested a Burt Bacharach-Hal David song from 1963. Burt had wanted Herb to record it himself, but Alpert wasn't comfortable singing, "So they sprinkled moon dust in your hair..." Herb told Richard about an earlier Dionne Warwick version, but suggested he not listen to it until he came up with his own arrangement.

The song did not fit into Richard's medley, but the lead sheet sat on his electric piano, and as the days passed, Richard couldn't get the melody out of his head. Finally, Richard and Karen went into the studio and recorded it. Richard felt the title "They Long to Be Close to You" was too long, so he shortened it by putting the first four words in parentheses.

After recording the song, Alpert asked Richard how he thought the song would do. Carpenter predicted it would either be number one or the biggest stiff the label had ever released.

## THE TOP FIVE
*Week of July 25, 1970*

1  **(They Long to Be)**
   **Close to You**
   Carpenters

2  **Mama Told Me (Not to Come)**
   Three Dog Night

3  **Band of Gold**
   Freda Payne

4  **The Love You Save**
   Jackson Five

5  **Make It With You**
   Bread

*Writer: David Gates*

*Producers: David Gates*
*James Griffin*
*Robb Royer*

*August 22, 1970*
*1 week*

FOLLOWING the Carpenters into the number one position was another group cast in the same adult contemporary music mold, Bread. The three members of this soft-rock band were David Gates, James Griffin and Robb Royer. After their first LP failed to rise above number 100 on *Billboard's* album chart, Mike Botts joined to make Bread a quartet.

The group was discouraged when the first album flopped, but that didn't sour them on making dough. Collectively, the members of Bread were well-connected into the Los Angeles music scene, and their friends in the industry gave them much support to continue. They decided to record one more album before considering a break-up. The first four songs recorded included "Make It With You," a track they were convinced would be a big hit. David Gates had written and produced hits for other people, but hearing "Make It With You" on the radio was the first time his own voice was on a hit record, and he found it

exhilarating.

Gates was born on December 11, 1940, in Tulsa, Oklahoma. His father directed the band and orchestra for the local high school, but suggested his son find a lucrative profession, like being a lawyer, and keep music as a hobby. David was not to be persuaded. He formed a band (which included his girlfriend's brother, Leon Russell) that backed up artists like Chuck Berry and Carl Perkins when they came to town. He also recorded some singles and formed a record distribution company.

When David heard of Leon's success in Hollywood, working with artists such as Ricky Nelson, he decided to follow. After six hungry months, he began to work regularly as a session musician, playing on demos for Jackie DeShannon and Randy Newman. Johnny Burnett recorded one of David's songs, and although it wasn't a hit, it inspired Gates to keep writing.

In 1968, his friend Leon Russell recommended that David produce an album for Griffin and Royer, who had formed a duo called Pleasure Faire. Griffin was from Memphis, and learned classical guitar before taking up rock and roll in high school. He was signed to Reprise and recorded one album, *Summer Holiday*, which didn't take off. Royer played several instruments, but was studying drama

in college when he joined Pleasure Faire.

Griffin, Royer and Gates decided to form a trio. Pleasure Faire evolved into Bread, and they were signed to Elektra. In 1970, Griffin and Royer wrote "For All We Know," for the film *Lovers and Other Strangers*. under the assumed names of Arthur James and Robb Wilson. The song won an Oscar and was recorded by the Carpenters.

After "Make It With You" made it big, the band went back to their first album and re-recorded "It Don't Matter to Me," which peaked at number 10. Although they tried recording upbeat material like "Let Your Love Go" and "Mother Freedom," they could only reach the upper portion of the Hot 100 with their softer songs, such as "If," "Baby I'm-A Want You" and "Everything I Own."

The line-up shifted in 1971 when Royer left to write screenplays. He was replaced by ace session musician Larry Knechtel, who had played on many number one singles, including "Mr. Tambourine Man," "This Diamond Ring" and "Bridge Over Troubled Water."

By 1973, Bread had grown stale and the four members mutually decided to disband. Gates recorded several solo albums and had his biggest hit with the title tune for Neil Simon's *The Goodbye Girl*. Griffin recorded a solo album for Polydor and Knechtel went back to session work. A brief Bread reunion in 1976 produced the top 10 single "Lost Without Your Love," and by 1978 the group had gone their separate ways again.

## THE TOP FIVE
*Week of August 22, 1970*

1  **Make It With You**
   Bread

2  **(They Long to Be)**
   **Close to You**
   Carpenters

3  **Spill the Wine**
   Eric Burdon & War

4  **War**
   Edwin Starr

5  **In the Summertime**
   Mungo Jerry

## 280 War GORDY 7101
### EDWIN STARR

*Writers: Norman Whitfield*
*Barrett Strong*

*Producer: Norman Whitfield*

*August 29, 1970*
*3 weeks*

EDWIN STARR toured Britain for the first time in 1966 after his single "Stop Her on Sight (S.O.S.)" became a top 40 hit in the United Kingdom. The single was issued on Polydor in Britain, although at home he was signed to the Detroit-based Ric-Tic label—or at least, he thought he was.

After completing his tour of England, Edwin flew directly to New York to appear at the Apollo Theater with Motown's Temptations [see 168—"My Girl"]. When he arrived, one of the Tempts welcomed him to the "family." Edwin wondered what family he was being welcomed to, and was told he was now a Motown artist. Ric-Tic, along with its parent label, Golden World, had been purchased outright by Motown.

Edwin found that hard to believe, and immediately telephoned the Golden World office in Detroit. The receptionist answered, "Motown Record Corporation," and he knew for certain he had a new family.

Unfortunately, family members do not always agree, and Edwin found himself involved in contract negotiations that stretched out for two-and-a-half years. During that frustrating time period, he did not record anything. Finally, in late 1968, he appeared on a local television show, "20 Grand," named after a popular Detroit nightclub frequented by Motown artists. Edwin sang a song he had written in 1965 called "Twenty-Five Miles." Some people from Motown saw him on the show and asked if he'd like to record the song. Ironically, he had already been told by other people at the company that the song had no potential.

Released on Motown's Gordy label, the record peaked at number six on the Hot 100 in the spring of 1969. Motown released an album, *25 Miles*, which contained the follow-up single, "I'm Still a Struggling Man." The title proved prophetic, as that record only made it to number 80.

At this time, the Temptations were being produced by Norman Whitfield. In early 1970 they released

a single of "Psychedelic Shack," written by Whitfield and his partner, Barrett Strong. An album titled after the single contained another Whitfield-Strong composition, "War."

Motown received hundreds of letters, many from college students, urging them to release "War" as a single. The company had other priorities for the Temptations, including a new single, "Ball of Confusion (That's What the World Is Today)." Thinking there was hit potential in "War," Whitfield asked Starr if he'd like to record it. Edwin had included a couple of Whitfield songs in the *25 Miles* album and agreed to work with the producer. He hadn't recorded anything for six months, and was happy to get back into the studio.

"War" entered the Hot 100 on July 11, 1970, at number 72. Seven weeks later it was number one. Vietnam was not mentioned anywhere in the lyrics, but it's no coincidence that the song was a hit while the United States was embroiled in an unpopular war.

Starr won a Grammy for Best Male R&B Vocal Performance for "War." The follow-up was another Whitfield-Strong composition, "Stop the War Now," but Edwin was unhappy about recording such a sim-

ilar song. It peaked at number 26 in early 1971. Starr remained with Motown through the mid-'70s, moving over from the Gordy label to Soul.

Edwin Starr was born Charles Hatcher on January 21, 1942, in Nashville, Tennessee. He was three years old when his family moved to Cleveland, Ohio. During study hall periods at Cunard Junior High School, he and several friends would sit in strategic places around the room and sing all the vocal parts to "Why Do Fools Fall in Love." The teachers weren't crazy about it, but Edwin enjoyed singing so much he got together with four of his friends after school to put a group together, the Future Tones.

They entered a local talent contest on a television show hosted by "Uncle Jake" and won five weeks in a row. First prize was a Sealy Postrapedic mattress, which the group had to somehow split five ways. Edwin's career plans were interrupted by military service, and when he was discharged two-and-a-half years later, he found the other group members had little interest in singing professionally. Edwin sang in Cleveland clubs and was spotted by band leader Bill Doggett ("Honky Tonk"), who asked Edwin to tour with him.

In 1993, a re-recording of "War" charted at number 69 in the U.K., where Starr remained popular, especially with fans of "northern soul" music. Starr had moved to Britain in the early 1980s, where he continued his recording career and toured extensively in the U.K. and Europe. He was 61 when he died in Nottingham, England, on April 2, 2003, of a heart attack.

## THE TOP FIVE
*Week of August 29, 1970*

1. **War**
   Edwin Starr

2. **Make It With You**
   Bread

3. **(They Long to Be) Close to You**
   Carpenters

4. **In the Summertime**
   Mungo Jerry

5. **Spill the Wine**
   Eric Burdon & War

*Writers: Nickolas Ashford
Valerie Simpson*

*Producers: Nickolas Ashford
Valerie Simpson*

*September 19, 1970
3 weeks*

Dᴵᴬᴺᴬ Rᴏss had a lot to live up to with her first single as a solo artist. As lead singer of the Supremes, she had amassed an incredible total of 12 number one singles (more than any- one except the Beatles and Elvis Presley), starting with "Where Did Our Love Go" [see 155] in 1964 and ending with "Someday We'll Be Together" in 1969 [see 265].

Even if they didn't feel it in their hearts, Diana and the new Supremes were now competitors, as far as the public was concerned. Fans of Diana Ross and the Supremes were anxious to see who would have the biggest hits, and who would go to number one first—if anyone.

The contest started off with sur- prising results. The Supremes were the first to place a single on the Hot 100. With Jean Terrell singing lead, "Up the Ladder to the Roof" entered the chart on March 7, 1970. Although it didn't go to number one, it did reach number 10, a respectable show- ing for a brand-new lead singer. Diana's long-awaited first single made its debut on April 25, 1970. "Reach Out and Touch (Somebody's Hand)" was written and produced by Nick- olas Ashford and Valerie Simpson. It didn't receive the wide acceptance of "Up the Ladder to the Roof," and only reached number 20. Not a bad showing for a new artist, but disap- pointing for a woman who had hit the top of the chart 12 times (despite its chart position, "Reach Out . . ." has become an anthem for Diana, a con- cert staple all these years that she still uses to get the audience to hold hands and sing along with her).

In the summer of '69, Berry Gordy turned to an outside producer, Bones Howe, to produce Diana's first solo album. Bones had been at the helm of number one singles for the Association [see 226—"Windy"] and the Fifth Dimension [see 253— "Aquarius/Let the Sunshine In"]. He suggested Diana be treated as "the black Barbra Streisand," and pro- duced four tracks for her, including

Laura Nyro's "Stoney End" and "Time and Love," songs that Strei- sand would record herself the following year.

Before Howe could complete the LP, he was dropped from the project and Motown staffers Ashford and Simpson were asked to produce Diana's first solo album. Among their song selections were two hits they had written for Marvin Gaye and Tammi Terrell, "You're All I Need to Get By" and "Ain't No Mountain High Enough."

The latter was Marvin and Tammi's first chart entry in 1967, and had peaked at 19. Nick wrote the lyric when he first moved to New York. Walking down a Manhattan thoroughfare, he was determined that New York City would not get the best of him, and the words "Ain't no mountain high enough" popped into his head. He quickly called Valerie and they finished the song in a short time.

For Diana Ross, they came up with a completely new concept for the song. "We thought Diana had such an interesting speaking voice," Valerie explains. "We thought it was very sexy and wanted to incorporate that into the production."

"Ain't No Mountain High Enough" was altered from a boy-girl duet to a long narrative with a rousing, exalt- ing climax that featured Valerie's gospel backing vocals. "We felt the

slow build worked well, and by not singing the actual chorus until the very end, we thought it added drama and suspense."

Ashford and Simpson were excited when they delivered the fin- ished master to Berry Gordy. "We presented it to him and he wanted to change the whole thing around, and start with the chorus and forget all the slow build and drama, just to get to the point. We had to fight him on that because he really wanted to change it." They prevailed, and their final version of "Ain't No Mountain High Enough" was exactly six min- utes long, far too long for single release.

On first listening to the *Diana Ross* album, it was impossible not to be captivated by the startling arrangement of "Ain't No Mountain High Enough." As Motown had not provided an edited version, radio sta- tions around the country made their own edits and added the album cut to their playlists. Whether Gordy origi- nally intended to release "Ain't No Mountain High Enough" as Diana's second single will never be known, because the heavy airplay forced Motown to edit the song down to three minutes and 15 seconds and issue it as a 45.

"Ain't No Mountain High Enough" entered the Hot 100 on August 8, 1970, at number 70. Six weeks later it knocked "War" out of number one, only the third time in the rock era that one Motown song had displaced another at the top of the chart [see 177—"I Can't Help Myself" and 249— "I Heard It Through the Grapevine"].

---

## THE TOP FIVE
*Week of September 19, 1970*

1  **Ain't No Mountain
   High Enough**
   Diana Ross

2  **War**
   Edwin Starr

3  **Lookin' Out my Back Door/
   Long as I Can See the Light**
   Creedence Clearwater Revival

4  **Patches**
   Clarence Carter

5  **Julie, Do Ya Love Me**
   Bobby Sherman

**282** **Cracklin' Rosie** UNI 55250
**NEIL DIAMOND**

*Writer: Neil Diamond*
*Producer: Tom Catalano*
*October 10, 1970*
*1 week*

NEIL DIAMOND first cracked the number one position as a writer, thanks to the Monkees [see 216—"I'm a Believer"]. Three years and 10 months later, he toppled Diana Ross off her mountain to reach the summit on his own with "Cracklin' Rosie." It's not a song about a girl named Rosie, but a tune inspired by a story Neil heard while visiting Canada. A medical missionary there related the tale of an Indian tribe that had more men than women. The men who did not have women would buy bottles of rose wine, and the bottles of wine would become their women for the weekend (don't ask, just enjoy the song).

Neil Diamond was born January 24, 1941, in Brooklyn, near Coney Island. His interest in music goes so far back, he doesn't remember a time when he didn't want to play music. His father was a soldier, and he was stationed in Cheyenne, Wyoming, when Neil was three. It was just three years later when the family returned to Brooklyn.

Neil was a student at Erasmus High School, and when he was 16, attended a summer camp in upstate New York where Pete Seeger performed. "Some of the kids had actually written a song and they played it for him and I kinda sat back and watched, and I became aware of the possibility of actually writing a song," Diamond told Ben Fong-Torres in a 1976 *Rolling Stone* interview. "And the next thing, I got a guitar when we got back to Brooklyn, started to take lessons and almost immediately began to write songs."

"I took to writing songs to satisfy my need for expression, to gain acceptance and recognition," he said in 1971. "What I remember most about my childhood was the constant moving from school to school. Under the circumstances, making friends was difficult and keeping them was impossible. I was pretty much an outsider most of the time. I was never accepted. That's why I took to writing so passionately."

He received a fencing scholarship to New York University and was a pre-med student, with a major in biology and a minor in chemistry. The idea of becoming a doctor did enter his mind. "I was trying to be practical. While it's great to dream you're going to make it as a songwriter or singer, very few people do. You have to be realistic about how you're going to make a living." He dropped out of school and had a succession of staff writing jobs for different publishers. None of them worked out, so he finally rented a storage room above Birdland, a jazz nightclub in Manhattan. He bought an upright piano for $35 and spent a year writing songs.

He made some early recordings; first for Duel Records as "Neil and Jack," a duo he formed with Jack Parker, then for Columbia Records. He was also performing in Greenwich Village coffee houses, where he met husband-and-wife songwriters Jeff Barry and Ellie Greenwich [see 149—"Chapel of Love"]. They took him to Atlantic Records, where Jerry Wexler expressed great interest. At the time, Atlantic was financing a new

label run by Bert Berns, and Wexler helped Berns sign Diamond as one of the first artists on the roster of Bang Records.

Before he released any singles on Bang, Neil had his first top 20 hit. Jay and the Americans recorded Neil's "Sunday and Me," which peaked at number 18 in 1965. Neil's first single for Bang, "Solitary Man," did well in certain regions of the country, but wasn't a national hit.

His next single, "Cherry, Cherry" went top 10 and established Neil as a singer/songwriter. He recorded a few more hits for Bang ("You Got to Me," "Girl, You'll Be a Woman Soon," "Thank the Lord for the Night Time" and "Kentucky Woman"). Meanwhile, other artists were recording his material, notably Lulu ("The Boat That I Row") and Deep Purple ("Kentucky Woman").

Neil left Bang in 1968 and signed with MCA's Uni label. He moved from Brooklyn to California, an experience that would one day become part of the song "I Am...I Said."

Neil's first three singles for Uni failed to go higher than number 50. "Brother Love's Travelling Salvation Show" was next; it peaked at 22. The follow-up, "Sweet Caroline (Good Times Never Seemed So Good)," went to four and was his biggest single to date. "Cracklin' Rosie," from the album *Tap Root Manuscript* was Neil's ninth single on Uni. It was not his first song about wine. Two years earlier, he had a chart record with "Red Red Wine," a song that UB40 took to number one in Britain in 1983 [see 710].

---

### THE TOP FIVE
*Week of October 10, 1970*

1 **Cracklin' Rosie**
   Neil Diamond

2 **I'll Be There**
   Jackson 5

3 **Candida**
   Dawn

4 **Ain't No Mountain High Enough**
   Diana Ross

5 **All Right Now**
   Free

This particular tune was natural. I first heard it on just the keyboards. I loved the melody—the title was already 'I'll Be There,' and I thought it needed some lyric help."

With Willie Hutch, Davis and West re-wrote the song and took a chance on recording the instrumental track. They hadn't completely resolved the problem of new lyrics when they played it for Gordy. "Berry liked it instantly," Davis remembers. Gordy started writing lyrics and helped finish the song. "The next thing you know, we're in the studio with Michael and the kids," Davis laughs.

"I'll Be There" became the biggest-selling Motown single to date. When it went to number one, it gave the Jackson Five the unique distinction of being the only group in the history of the Hot 100 to have their first four entries go to number one.

The Jacksons were not to have another number one single as a group. Perren and Mizell re-wrote "Mama's Pearl," and it followed "I'll Be There," peaking at number two for two weeks. A Clifton Davis song, "Never Can Say Goodbye," came next, and that peaked at number two for three weeks. "Maybe Tomorrow" broke the run of top 10 singles, but just temporarily. "Sugar Daddy" was next, and that went to 10.

There was only one more Motown top 10 single for the group: Davis' "Dancing Machine" in 1974. In 1975, the Jackson Five left Motown for Epic Records. Jermaine Jackson, who married Berry Gordy, Jr.'s, daughter, Hazel, did not leave—yet. He stayed with Motown until 1984, when he signed with Arista.

---

Writers: *Berry Gordy, Jr.*
*Hal Davis*
*Willie Hutch*
*Bob West*

Producer: *Hal Davis*

*October 17, 1970*
*5 weeks*

---

**A**FTER three number one singles in an uptempo, "soul bubblegum" groove, it was a bold move for Berry Gordy, Jr., to allow his young charges from Gary, Indiana, to record a ballad. But producer Hal Davis had found the right song, and Berry passed over an early version of "Mama's Pearl" written by Freddie Perren and the rest of the Corporation [see 267—"I Want You Back"] in favor of "I'll Be There."

Gordy's judgment was flawless. "I'll Be There" entered the Hot 100 on September 19, 1970, at number 40. Four weeks later it went to number one and stayed there for five weeks, making it the most successful Jackson Five single of all time.

Although it hadn't been apparent until now, there were two factions at Motown competing to write for and produce the Jackson Five. Freddie Perren and Fonce Mizell were part of the Corporation, and they seemed to be winning the "battle" by coming up with the first three Jacksons singles—chart-toppers all. But writer/producer Hal Davis was a contender, too. In the early '60s, Davis met Berry Gordy at a West Coast record conference. Gordy was interested in opening a Hollywood branch office for his Detroit record corporation, and hired Davis and Marc Gordon, the man who would one day manage the Fifth Dimension [see 253—"Aquarius/ Let the Sunshine In"], to run an office. Based in the 6290 Sunset Boulevard building at the corner of Sunset and Vine, Davis signed the company's first Los Angeles-based artist, Brenda Holloway ("Every Little Bit Hurts," "When I'm Gone"). After she became successful, Davis wrote and produced for Detroit-based artists, starting with Stevie Wonder.

Davis met the Jackson Five as soon as they signed with Motown. As head of the West Coast office, he picked them up at the airport when they arrived in Los Angeles for a year of intense rehearsals before recording their first record and going on the road.

Soon after the Jacksons came to Motown, Davis received a song written by a friend of his, Bob West. The song had also gone to Motown's A&R department, but they hadn't shown much interest—especially since it was unlikely the Jackson Five would be recording ballads for their singles.

But Davis felt differently. "Very few tunes have come along in my lifetime that I knew were just natural.

---

## THE TOP FIVE
*Week of October 17, 1970*

1 **I'll Be There**
Jackson 5

2 **Cracklin' Rosie**
Neil Diamond

3 **Green-Eyed Lady**
Sugarloaf

4 **All Right Now**
Free

5 **We've Only Just Begun**
Carpenters

## 284 I Think I Love You BELL 910
### THE PARTRIDGE FAMILY

*Writer: Tony Romeo*

*Producer: Wes Farrell*

*November 21, 1970*
*3 weeks*

THE MONKEES' first single [see 211—"Last Train to Clarksville"] went to number one two months to the day after the series premiered on NBC. The Partridge Family beat that record. Their series debuted on ABC September 25, 1970, and "I Think I Love You" reached number one four days shy of two months later.

The stars of "The Partridge Family" were Shirley Jones and David Cassidy, and they were the only two members of the cast who actually appeared on the records. Susan Dey, Danny Bonaduce, Suzanne Crough and Jeremy Gelbwaks (later replaced by Brian Forster) were talented young actors, but were not hired for their musical ability.

Shirley Jones, born March 31, 1934, in Smithton, Pennsylvania, was singing at age three. She had plans to study veterinary medicine, until she won the title of Miss Pittsburgh. She went to New York, where her vocal coach arranged an audition with Rodgers and Hammerstein. They gave her a small role in their Broadway production of *South Pacific*, which led to a starring role in the motion picture version of *Oklahoma*.

After she was cast in the lead of "The Partridge Family," the producers searched for an actor to play her eldest son. "They were very frightened about hiring David because they knew he was my stepson, and they didn't know what our relationship was. They didn't know (if) we hated each other…so they came to me very sheepishly said, 'we tested David and we really feel he's best for the role, but how do you feel about it?'"

Shirley thought it was wonderful. David, born April 12, 1950, in New York City, grew up in West Orange, New Jersey, with his father, actor Jack Cassidy, and mother, Evelyn Ward. When they divorced, David went to live with his mother in California.

"I didn't get to know him until he became an adult," says Shirley, who married Jack Cassidy in 1956. "We've really based our love and friendship on an adult relationship as opposed to me being his mother."

Still, that was her role in the series. In the recording studio, she admits to playing a small part. "I did very little in the recording sessions. I literally was the background vocals for David. It was very unusual for me. I never thought I'd have a gold record. Of course, I didn't do much to get it," she laughs, "but nevertheless it hangs on my wall and I'm very proud of it."

In the first episode of the series, the Partridge children ask their mother to help with a recording session in their garage. They record the song "I Think I Love You," sell it to a record company and have a number one record. Life imitated art, when "I Think I Love You" became a real hit, topping the Hot 100 for three weeks beginning November 21, 1970.

The series ran for four seasons and made David Cassidy an international teen idol. Records by the Partridge Family (including "Doesn't Somebody Want to Be Wanted" and "I'll Meet You Halfway") continued to chart until 1973.

An infrequent visitor to "The Partridge Family" set was Shirley's son, David's half-brother Shaun Cassidy [see 470—"Da Doo Ron Ron"]. His mother advised him to pursue an acting career before recording, but Shaun was convinced he could duplicate his brother's success. He was right, and Shirley and Shaun remain the only mother and son to both have number one singles.

### THE TOP FIVE
*Week of November 21, 1970*

1 **I Think I Love You**
Partridge Family

2 **We've Only Just Begun**
Carpenters

3 **I'll Be There**
Jackson 5

4 **The Tears of a Clown**
Smokey Robinson
& the Miracles

5 **Fire and Rain**
James Taylor

Writers: Henry Cosby
       William 'Smokey' Robinson
       Stevie Wonder

Producers: Henry Cosby
        William 'Smokey'
        Robinson

December 12, 1970
2 weeks

T HE MIRACLES almost went to number one with their second single for Berry Gordy, Jr.'s Tamla label, "Shop Around." That record entered the Hot 100 on December 12, 1960, and peaked at number two. By an odd coincidence, they would have to wait exactly ten years for their first number one single: "The Tears of a Clown" was the number one song in America on December 12, 1970.

It was only an odd twist of fate that gave the Miracles their first number one. They had recorded "The Tears of a Clown" on a 1967 album, *Make it Happen*. Stevie Wonder and Henry Cosby had written the instrumental track, but were unhappy with the lyrics they wrote for it. They asked Smokey to take the track and see if he could come up with a new set of lyrics. The sound of a calliope in the instrumental made Smokey think of Pagliacci the clown, and he wrote new lyrics based on that theme.

Three years later, British Motown executive John Marshall was looking for a follow-up to a re-release of "The Tracks of My Tears" and discovered the Miracles had another "Tears" song in their catalogue. "The Tears of a Clown" was released as a single in

the United Kingdom only, and to everyone's amazement it went to number one, the first and only British chart-topper for the Miracles.

A month after it went to number one in Great Britain, Motown was preparing a new American single for the group when Gordy suggested they follow their British counterparts and release "The Tears of a Clown" instead. "It sold a million copies here and 900,000 in England, and it really surprised us because we didn't like the song at first," group member Bobby Rogers told Dick Clark.

Smokey Robinson, Ronnie White, Pete Moore and Bobby Rogers met as early as 1954 and started singing as the Matadors. They auditioned for Jackie Wilson's manager, who turned them down because they sounded too much like the Platters [see 13—"My Prayer"]. Another man present at the audition was impressed enough to sign the group. That man was Berry Gordy, Jr.

In 1958, Smokey, Berry and Jackie Wilson's cousin, Tyrone Carlo, wrote an answer song to the Silhouettes' "Get a Job." It was titled "Got a Job," and released on End Records. Unhappy with the amount of royalties he received on the record, Berry leased the next Miracles single, "Bad Girl," to Chess Records. It was the group's first chart entry, peaking at number 93 at the end of 1959.

The greater amount of the royalties still went to Chess, not to Gordy, so Smokey helped convince Berry he should start his own record company. Gordy borrowed $800 and the

Motown Record Corporation was born. The Miracles were the first group signed to the Tamla label, and their first single was "Way Over There." Smokey's wife, Claudette, was an original member, but she quit touring and eventually left the group to take care of her family.

In 1967, the group became known as Smokey Robinson and the Miracles, around the same time the company's leading female act became Diana Ross and the Supremes [see 223—"The Happening"]. By 1970, Smokey was ready to leave the group. He was tired of touring, and wanted to be home with his two-year-old son and newborn daughter. He would have carried out his plan, except the group had the biggest hit of their career with "The Tears of a Clown," and he was persuaded to stay.

In 1972, he followed through with his decision and embarked on a solo career. Billy Griffin took his place as lead singer of the Miracles [see 430—"Love Machine (Part 1)"]. At first, Smokey found it almost impossible to have a hit on pop radio—his first 11 solo singles failed to make the top 25. Finally, at the beginning of 1980, "Cruisin'" broke the streak by going to number four. After Kim Carnes recorded Smokey's "More Love," Robinson took a couple of new songs to her producer, George Tobin, for Carnes to record. Tobin was no longer working with Carnes, and suggested Smokey record "Being With You" himself. He did, and it went to number two for three weeks in 1981, held out of the number spot by Kim Carnes' "Bette Davis Eyes" [see 543].

## THE TOP FIVE
*Week of December 12, 1970*

1  **The Tears of a Clown**
   Smokey Robinson &
   the Miracles

2  **I Think I Love You**
   Partridge Family

3  **Gypsy Woman**
   Brian Hyland

4  **One Less Bell to Answer**
   Fifth Dimension

5  **I'll Be There**
   Jackson 5

## 286   My Sweet Lord/Isn't It a Pity   APPLE 2995
### GEORGE HARRISON

*Writer: George Harrison*

*Producers: George Harrison*
*         Phil Spector*

*December 26, 1970*
*4 weeks*

"MY SWEET LORD" was the first solo Beatles single to go to number one. George Harrison was also the first Beatle to release a solo recording—the soundtrack to Joe Mussot's film *Wonderwall*. The album, *Wonderwall Music*, was released in Britain on November 1, 1968, 28 days earlier than John Lennon's first musical project away from the Beatles, *Unfinished Music No. 1–Two Virgins*.

George wrote "My Sweet Lord" while touring with Delaney and Bonnie ("Soul Shake," "Never Ending Song of Love") in December, 1969. Before recording it himself, George gave the song to Billy Preston [see 337—"Will It Go Round in Circles"], and produced it for his *Encouraging Words* album on Apple. Billy's version was scheduled to be released as a single in September, 1970, and was assigned the British catalogue number Apple 29, but was withdrawn. Two months later, Harrison's "My Sweet Lord," produced by George with Phil Spector, was released in America to precede his triple album, *All Things Must Pass*. In Britain, "My Sweet Lord" wasn't released until January 15, 1971, a month-and-a-half following *All Things Must Pass*.

In his book *I Me Mine*, George revealed, "I was inspired to write 'My Sweet Lord' by the Edwin Hawkins Singers' version of 'Oh Happy Day.' I thought a lot about whether to do 'My Sweet Lord' or not, because I would be committing myself publicly and I anticipated that a lot of people might get weird about it. Many people fear the words 'Lord' and 'God'—makes them angry for some strange reason."

Some people, including the publisher of a number one song by the Chiffons [see 127—"He's So Fine"], found what they thought was another inspiration for "My Sweet Lord." A lawsuit claiming George had plagiarized the song, written by the late Ronnie Mack, was filed.

A story in the March 6, 1971, issue of *Billboard* stated that royalty payments to Harrison had been halted all over the world until settlement of the dispute. That didn't come until more than five years later, when United States District Court Judge Richard Owen ruled in New York that Harrison was guilty of copyright infringement. The judge conceded that Harrison did not deliberately plagiarize "He's So Fine."

"Nevertheless," Owen said, "it is clear that 'My Sweet Lord' is the very same song as 'He's So Fine.' Under the law, this is infringement of copyright, and is no less so even though it may have been subconsciously accomplished."

George discussed the lawsuit in *I Me Mine*: "I wasn't consciously aware of the similarity between 'He's So Fine' and 'My Sweet Lord' when I wrote the song as it was more improvised and not so fixed, although when *my* version of the song came out and started to get a lot of airplay people started talking about it and it was then I thought, 'Why didn't I realize?'. It would have been very easy to change a note here or there, and not affect the feeling of the record."

After Judge Owen's ruling, George wrote "This Song," in order "to exorcize the paranoia about song writing that had started to build up in me," Harrison explains in *I Me Mine*. "I still don't understand how the courts aren't filled with similar cases—as 99 percent of the popular music that can be heard is reminiscent of something or other."

Even after the case was settled, it wasn't over for George. Former Beatles manager Allen Klein purchased the publishing rights to "He's So Fine" and along with it, the right to continue to sue for damages. George summed up his feelings: "I even tried to give 'My Sweet Lord' away to get the thing settled—just let 'em have it; it doesn't matter to me. I've never had any money from it—it's always been in escrow—and as far as I'm concerned the effect the song has had far exceeds any bitching that's been going on between copyright people; it's just greed and jealousy and all that."

Two novelty songs resulted from the lawsuit. The Chiffons recorded a version of "My Sweet Lord," and British entrepeneur Jonathan King ("Everyone's Gone to the Moon") released a version of "He's So Fine" that had the exact arrangement of George's "My Sweet Lord."

"My Sweet Lord" has the distinction of being the only solo Beatle number one single to be a double-sided hit. There were two versions of "Isn't It a Pity" on *All Things Must Pass*. The longer take, running seven minutes and 10 seconds, was placed on the flip side of "My Sweet Lord." In *I Me Mine* George explains the song "is about whenever a relationship hits a down point—instead of whatever other people do (like breaking each other's jaws) I wrote a song. It was a chance to realize that if I felt somebody had let *me* down, then there's a good chance *I* was letting someone else down. We all tend to break each other's hearts, taking and not giving back—isn't it a pity."

## THE TOP FIVE
*Week of December 26, 1970*

1   **My Sweet Lord/Isn't it a Pity**
    George Harrison

2   **One Less Bell to Answer**
    Fifth Dimension

3   **The Tears of a Clown**
    Smokey Robinson &
    the Miracles

4   **Knock Three Times**
    Dawn

5   **Black Magic Woman**
    Santana

*Writers: L. Russell Brown*
*Irwin Levine*

*Producers: Hank Medress*
*Dave Appell*

*January 23, 1971*
*3 weeks*

Tony Orlando has had two separate recording careers. In 1961, Epic Records billed him as a teenage idol, and two of his singles ventured into the top 40: "Halfway to Paradise," written by Gerry Goffin and Carole King [see 294—"It's Too Late / I Feel the Earth Move"] and "Bless You," written by Barry Mann and Cynthia Weil.

Tony's second, more successful career started as a fluke. In 1970, while he was working for April-Blackwood Music, the publishing arm of CBS, he reluctantly agreed to sing lead vocal on a song he was certain would fade into obscurity. Instead, "Candida" soared to number three on the Hot 100, and Tony was asked to record the follow-up, "Knock Three Times."

The Tony Orlando story begins in the Hell's Kitchen section of Manhattan, where he was born Michael Anthony Orlando Cassivitis of Greek and Puerto Rican heritage on April 3, 1944.

His neighborhood was tough, but Tony preferred singing with a doo-wop group to fighting with a gang. With the Five Gents, he knocked on record company office doors to no avail. When the rest of the guys dropped out, Tony persevered, and at age 13 was hired to sing demos for publishers. He met Don Kirshner at Aldon Music and was teamed up with Carole King. One of the demos he recorded for her was "Halfway to Paradise," which Kirshner sold to Epic Records.

The follow-up, "Bless You," went to number 15 on the Hot 100 in the autumn of 1961. But then the hits stopped coming, and by 1963 Tony considered himself a has-been. He married that year, and with a family to support, went to work for music publisher Robbins, Feist and Miller. He learned all about publishing and producing demos, and was hired away by April-Blackwood in 1968. He worked with writers like James Taylor [see 296—"You've Got a Friend"] and Laura Nyro, and reported to Clive Davis.

Then one day he was approached by record producers Hank Medress, former member of the Tokens [see 102—"The Lion Sleeps Tonight"], and Dave Appell. They had a song called "Candida" performed by a group named Dawn (named after Stacy Dawn Siegal, daughter of Tokens member Jay Siegal). They also had a problem: Bell Records liked the song,

but didn't care for the lead singer.

Tony decided to record the song as a favor to Medress and Appell, but only because he never expected to hear the song again. When he did hear it eight weeks later, it was in heavy rotation on every New York radio station. Even after he recorded the follow-up, "Knock Three Times," Tony hadn't met background singers Telma Hopkins and Joyce Vincent Wilson. They were living in California, where they recorded the backing vocals separately from Tony.

Meanwhile, Bell Records was desperate to have a real-live act to promote Dawn's records. Pseudo-Dawns were appearing all over America as well as in Britain, where "Knock Three Times" also went to number one.

Tony asked Telma if she and Joyce would be interested in becoming Dawn for real. "I really was not looking to go on the road with anyone," she recalls. "But he was so persistent. He said, 'What would it take for you to at least be interested in trying it?' I sat there and thought what can I tell this man that will get him off my back? He was really starting to get on my nerves. Joyce and I had always dreamed of going to Europe. I said, 'I'd like a first-class trip to Europe. That would make me interested.'"

A few days later, Tony called Telma's bluff. The first tour would be in Europe with first class accommodations. She called Joyce, who was about to be married. "I said, 'You're going to have to stop the wedding because we're going to Europe.' We rehearsed for two weeks and were on the road for seven years."

## THE TOP FIVE
*Week of January 23, 1971*

1  **Knock Three Times**
   Dawn

2  **My Sweet Lord/Isn't it a Pity**
   George Harrison

3  **One Less Bell to Answer**
   Fifth Dimension

4  **Lonely Days**
   Bee Gees

5  **Black Magic Woman**
   Santana

288

# One Bad Apple  MGM 14193
## THE OSMONDS

*Writer: George Jackson*

*Producer: Rick Hall*

*February 13, 1971*
*5 weeks*

DESPITE being seen in millions of homes each week on "The Andy Williams Show," it took the Osmond brothers almost eight years to make a hit record. But once they started, they racked up an impressive 11 million-selling discs in one year, a record unmatched by any other artist.

The five brothers—Alan, Wayne, Merrill, Jay and Donny—had recorded for Williams' label, Barnaby, and MCA's Uni Records before label president Mike Curb signed them to MGM. Five other brothers from Gary, Indiana, had been burning up the charts with four consecutive number one singles [see 283—"I'll Be There"], so it was logical that Curb put his quintet in the hands of Rick Hall, owner of the popular Fame studios in Muscle Shoals, Alabama, home for many R&B artists.

One of Hall's staff writers, George Jackson, had already written "One Bad Apple," and Hall knew it would be a perfect song to break the Osmonds on the charts. He was right. The song, which invited inevitable comparisons to the Jackson Five, debuted on the Hot 100 on January 2, 1971, at number 78, and went

to number one six weeks later.

The Osmonds began as a quartet in 1959, in their hometown of Ogden, Utah. George and Olive Osmond observed "family night" every Monday, a custom popular in the Mormon religion. In a 1976 interview, Olive explained, "The church encourages talent, beginning with such things as singing, sports and speeches when the children are small. That's how the four boys got started singing together. Our church brings children out of their private shells, but it's a gradual, family process. So we push whoever is in front and the rest of us divide the work necessary to keep the front runners in first place and the family strong."

There are two older Osmond brothers, Virl and Tommy. Virl suffers a 40 per cent hearing loss and Tommy has almost no hearing at all. Although their mother taught them to speak, the entire family is conversant in sign language. Virl and Tommy would eventually handle family business matters while their younger siblings performed.

Alan, Wayne, Merrill and Jay learned barber shop quartet harmony, and in 1962 their father took them to Los Angeles in hopes of auditioning for Lawrence Welk [see 84—"Calcutta"]. According to Donny, Welk said he was too busy to see the boys. To help ease their disappointment, George turned the trip into a

vacation and took his family to Disneyland. The four young brothers were dressed alike, and caught the eye of the Dapper Dans, a professional barber shop quartet performing on Main Street. The Dans asked the boys if they could sing in harmony. An impromptu performance on Main Street led to a meeting with the park's talent booker, and the Osmond Brothers were signed to appear in the "Disneyland After Dark" show.

A few weeks later, Jay Williams saw them perform at Disneyland and told his son Andy he should sign the boys for his new NBC television series. The Osmonds made their debut on December 20, 1962, singing "I'm a Ding Dong Daddy from Dumas" and "Side by Side." On December 10, 1963, one day after his sixth birthday, Donny joined his brothers on the show. He soloed on "You Are My Sunshine."

The Osmonds stayed with Andy Williams until his last show in May, 1967, then appeared on Jerry Lewis' variety series from September, 1967, to May, 1969.

Osmondmania ruled from 1971-1974. During those years, the brothers had 10 chart entries, while Donny, Marie and youngest brother Jimmy also made the Hot 100. Their teenybopper appeal faded by the mid-1970s, and the final chart entry of the decade for any Osmond was in 1978.

The Osmonds disbanded in the summer of 1980. While Donny dropped out of recording, the four elder brothers reformed in 1982 as a country act, recording for Mercury and then Warner Brothers.

## THE TOP FIVE
*Week of February 13, 1971*

1  **One Bad Apple**
   Osmonds

2  **Knock Three Times**
   Dawn

3  **Rose Garden**
   Lynn Anderson

4  **I Hear You Knocking**
   Dave Edmunds

5  **Lonely Days**
   Bee Gees

COLUMBIA 45314 **Me and Bobby McGee**
JANIS JOPLIN **289**

Writer: *Kris Kristofferson*

Producer: *Paul Rothchild*

March 20, 1971
2 weeks

**S**HE was a bawdy, hard-drinking Texas mama who swore like the boys and savaged her white vocal chords to sing the blues. When friends suggested her health could not withstand her rowdy lifestyle, she replied, "Maybe I won't last as long as other singers, but I think you can destroy your now worrying about tomorrow." Janis Joplin will never have to worry about tomorrow. She was found dead in her room at the Landmark Motel in Hollywood on the evening of October 4, 1970, a victim of a heroin overdose.

She hadn't completed recording her *Pearl* album when she died. Released in January, 1971, it yielded the second posthumous number one single of the rock era [see 238—"(Sittin' on) The Dock of the Bay"]. "Me and Bobby McGee" was written by actor, singer, Rhodes scholar and songwriter Kris Kristofferson, who tagged along with his friend Bobby Neuwirth to what Myra Friedman, in her Joplin biography *Buried Alive*, calls "the great Tequila bash" in the spring of 1970. Kristofferson stayed to become Janis' beau for a short time and left behind his song for his feather-boaed girlfriend.

Janis Joplin was born January 19, 1943, in the conservative oil refinery town of Port Arthur, Texas. "I was a sensitive child," she revealed in

## THE TOP FIVE
*Week of March 20, 1971*

1 **Me and Bobby McGee**
   Janis Joplin

2 **She's a Lady**
   Tom Jones

3 **Just My Imagination
   (Running Away with Me)**
   Temptations

4 **One Bad Apple**
   Osmonds

5 **For All We Know**
   Carpenters

David Dalton's biography, *Janis*. "I had a lot of hurts and confusions. You know, it's hard when you're a kid to be different, you're full of things and you don't know what it's about."

To *Rolling Stone* she elaborated: "I was always outrageous. I got treated very badly in Texas. They don't treat beatniks too good in Texas." Her earliest artistic interests were painting and poetry, but those were quickly abandoned when a friend introduced her to jazz at 17 and she sent away for some Leadbelly and Odetta records. Her stay at college, where she learned to be a keypunch operator, was brief. Her refusal to bend to the middle-American norm sent her running off to the West Coast where she finally landed in a Haight-Ashbury rehearsal pad, right in the center of the 1966 San Francisco hippie culture. Unhappy in California, she went to Austin, Texas, and sang with a country and western outfit.

Back in San Francisco, the house band at the Avalon Ballroom was looking for a female singer. A friend of the group remembered Joplin and contacted her in Texas. She returned to California in June, 1966, to join Big Brother and the Holding Company.

An album on Mainstream, highlighted by the single "Down on Me," brought the group some attention, but it was their explosive performance at the Monterey Pop Festival in 1967 that cemented their national reputation. Signed to Columbia Records, they released the *Cheap Thrills* album and a single, "Piece of My Heart," that went to number 12 in the autumn of 1968. Before the year was over, Joplin exited the band along with guitarist Sam Andrew. Her first solo album, *I Got Dem Ol' Kozmic Blues Again Mama!* was released in September, 1969. A brief semi-retirement followed, then Janis put together the Full Tilt Boogie Band to work on the album that would become *Pearl*, Janis' nickname.

Her death in October, 1970, was the second loss for the music world in a three-week period. On September 18, Jimi Hendrix died of an accidental barbiturate overdose in London. Joplin and Hendrix were both just 27 when they died. Both left behind musical legacies that will survive the changing trends of pop music. Janis' live performances have been captured on film for those who missed the real thing; both the *Monterey Pop* documentary and the *Janis* biopic are cinematic proof of her raw talent.

# 290 Just My Imagination (Running Away With Me) GORDY 7105
## THE TEMPTATIONS

*Writers: Norman Whitfield
Barrett Strong*

*Producer: Norman Whitfield*

*April 3, 1971
2 weeks*

"JUST MY IMAGINATION (RUNNING AWAY WITH ME)" was the 17th chart record produced for the Temptations by Norman Whitfield. Although Smokey Robinson was the group's primary producer in the early part of their career (he wrote and produced their first number one single [see 168—"My Girl"], Whitfield worked with the group as early as 1964 when he produced "Girl (Why You Wanna Make Me Blue)," which featured the lead voice of tenor Eddie Kendricks.

Smokey's association with the Temptations continued through 1966 with "Get Ready," another Kendricks lead vocal. Later that year, Whitfield became the Temptations' full-time producer, beginning with "Ain't Too Proud to Beg." That song, along with hits like "Beauty Is Only Skin Deep" and "(I Know) I'm Losing You," were co-written with Eddie Holland, the man responsible (along with Lamont Dozier and Brian Holland) for number one hits by the Supremes

and the Four Tops.

Whitfield and Holland's association continued through the 1967 Temptations song "(Loneliness Made Me Realize) It's You That I Need." That same year, Whitfield teamed up with a new lyricist, Barrett Strong.

The first Whitfield-Strong collaboration to hit the chart was "I Wish It Would Rain," a number four hit for the Temptations in the early part of 1968. From that point on, Whitfield and Strong were a hot property. They gave the Temptations eight more top 30 hits in a row, beginning with "I Could Never Love Another (After Loving You)." When David Ruffin left the group, Whitfield and Strong gave the Tempts a new direction with the socially conscious "Cloud Nine," a song reminiscent of the style of Sly and the Family Stone.

The socially relevant songs continued with "Runaway Child Running Wild" and "Don't Let the Joneses Get You Down." Then Whitfield and Strong gave the Temptations their second number one single [see 259—"I Can't Get Next to You"], and followed it with "Psychedelic Shack" and "Ball of Confusion (That's What the World Is Today)." The formula started to wear thin with "*Ungena Za Ulimwengu* (Unite the World),"

the first Tempts song to miss the top 30 since "I'll Be in Trouble" in 1964.

Perhaps it was that single's relative failure that encouraged Whitfield to return to the mid-'60s sound of the Temptations. Eddie Kendricks, whose tenor voice had given the group their first hit in 1964 with "The Way You Do the Things You Do," was recruited to sing one of the prettiest Motown ballads ever written.

"We needed to do something a little different," Strong admits. "We had thought of 'Just My Imagination' a year or two before we recorded it, but the timing wasn't right. Norman asked me, 'What was that the song we were messing around with a year ago?' I played it on the piano and he said, 'Meet me in the studio because I'm gonna record it today.'"

"Just My Imagination" entered the Hot 100 at number 71 on February 6, 1971, and went to number one eight weeks later, giving the Temptations their third number one single. But by that time, there were two more defections from the group. Kendricks, whose clear tenor voice graced "Just My Imagination," was gone, apparently to embark on a solo career [see 348—"Keep on Truckin'"]. Paul Williams, who had formed the Primes with Kendricks and sung lead on early Temptations hits like "I Want a Love I Can See" and "Don't Look Back," was also out of the group. An alcoholism problem had become more serious, and a liver ailment forced him to retire. Difficulties with his marriage and finances added more pressure, and on August 17, 1973, the 34-year-old singer committed suicide.

## THE TOP FIVE
*Week of April 3, 1971*

1 **Just my Imagination (Running Away With Me)**
Temptations

2 **Me and Bobby McGee**
Janis Joplin

3 **For All We Know**
Carpenters

4 **She's a Lady**
Tom Jones

5 **What's Going On**
Marvin Gaye

*Writer: Hoyt Axton*

*Producer: Richard Podolor*

*April 17, 1971*
*6 weeks*

Elvis Presley's first number one single [see 10—"Heartbreak Hotel"], co-written by Mae Axton, topped *Billboard's* Best Sellers in Stores chart on April 21, 1956. Exactly 15 years later, Mae's son Hoyt claimed the same honor, when his song "Joy to the World," recorded by Three Dog Night, was the number one song in the land. Mae and Hoyt are the only mother-and-son songwriters to have both written number one tunes.

Hoyt originally wrote "Joy to the World" for a children's animated television special, "The Happy Song." The show never went into production, so Hoyt took the individual songs from the score and tried to place them independently. He had toured with Three Dog Night as their opening act, so one day he just showed up in the recording studio and played "Joy to the World" for them. Cory Wells didn't think it sounded like a hit, but the rest of the band loved it and decided to record it. When Hoyt heard their version, he was disappointed and was convinced it would never sell. Five weeks after it debuted on the Hot 100, it was number one. It remained on top for six weeks and became the best-selling single of all time for both the group and their record company, Dunhill. "Joy to the World" was *Bill-*

## THE TOP FIVE
*Week of April 17, 1971*

1 **Joy to the World**
   Three Dog Night

2 **What's Going On**
   Marvin Gaye

3 **Just My Imagination
   (Running Away With Me)**
   Temptations

4 **She's a Lady**
   Tom Jones

5 **Another Day/Oh Woman Oh
   Why**
   Paul McCartney

*board's* number one single of 1971.

Three Dog Night was not a trio, but a septet of vocalists and musicians who had all worked professionally before joining as a unit. Danny Hutton (born September 10, 1942, in Buncrana, Ireland) worked for Walt Disney Productions before he moved over to Hanna-Barbera, where he recorded voices for animated programs and was signed to the company's new record label as an artist. He released "Roses and Rainbows" in 1965, then signed with MGM Records, where he recorded "Funny How Love Can Be."

Meanwhile, in Los Angeles, Cory Wells (born February 5, 1942, in Buffalo, New York) was the lead vocalist for the Enemies, the house band at the Whisky-A-Go-Go.

Tired of working with the Enemies, Wells asked Hutton if he'd be interested in teaming up to record, but Hutton wanted to concentrate on a solo career and declined.

About a year and a half later, Hutton was driving by the Ambassador Hotel in Los Angeles when he noticed a display of classic cars on the front lawn. An automobile enthusiast,

Hutton was inspired by the sight of each individual car being an integral part of the overall display. He thought it would be interesting to try the same thing with a group, where all the singers and musicians were leads. He called Cory, and they conspired to secretly audition their friend Chuck Negron (born June 8, 1942, in the Bronx, New York) by inviting him over to sit around the piano and sing some songs. Negron, who started singing at the Apollo Theater in Harlem when he was just 14, had a high, tenor voice that blended well with Cory's soulful sound and Danny's rougher, pop vocals.

To form Three Dog Night, the three vocalists recruited four musicians: lead guitarist Mike Allsup, organist Jim Greenspoon, bassist Joe Schermie and drummer Floyd Sneed.

And the group name? As any Australian knows, if it's cold in the outback, you sleep with one dog to keep you warm. If it's a very cold night, you need two dogs. And when the mercury dips so low that your blood turns to ice, that's a three dog night.

# Brown Sugar   ROLLING STONES 19100
## THE ROLLING STONES

292

*Writers: Mick Jagger
         Keith Richard*

*Producer: Jimmy Miller
May 29, 1971
2 weeks*

THE TURN of the decade marked a change in the public perception of the Rolling Stones. Once reviled as too scruffy and dirty for decent folk, they became the ruling rock elite, gentlemen of leisure, members of the international jet set.

Mick Jagger, Keith Richard (reverting to a singular last name), Charlie Watts and Bill Wyman underscored that status by leaving England and setting up housekeeping in the south of France. The move was prompted by Britain's exorbitant tax laws, which sliced over 90 per cent of their income into the crown's pot. With more of their earnings in their pockets, the Stones came to enjoy the *emigre* life.

Epitomizing their ascendancy to respectability was the wedding of Mick Jagger to Bianca Perez Mora Macias, a Nicaraguan beauty with ambassadorial roots on both sides of her family tree. Among the luminaries who attended the civil ceremony at the Hotel de Ville in St. Tropez on May 12, 1971, were Paul and Linda McCartney, Ringo Starr, Eric Clapton, Keith Moon, Roger Vadim, Nathalie Delon, Stephen Stills, Brigitte Bardot and the Queen's cousin, Lord Litchfield, snapping society shots.

Though they had become fodder for the gossip columnists, the Stones

still retained a *soupcon* of outrage, which they chose to literally display on their album, *Sticky Fingers*. Andy Warhol designed the cover, the waist-to-knees portion of a well-endowed male in jeans (rumored to be the artist's underground film superstar Joe Dallesandro), with a real zipper at the crotch.

Originally the package was scheduled to have a balloon pop out when the zipper was undone, but the additional touch was deemed too costly. Another Warhol creation was the band's new logo, a red, open mouth with tongue sticking out. The immediately identifiable image set the tone for the group's latest venture, Rolling Stones Records. To distribute their own label, they selected Atlantic Records, since their long tempestuous association with British Decca had expired with the contract.

The first release under the new agreement was "Brown Sugar," recorded at the Muscle Shoals studios in December, 1969. The song was simultaneously interpreted as a racist, sexist slur as well as referring

to Mexican heroin. Jagger added to the confusion by scrambling the vocals, which were deliberately mixed down into the instrumental track. In doing so, he was taking Fats Domino's advice, "You should never sing the words out very clearly," a philosophy to which the Stones lead singer adhered on more than one occasion.

Recording and social climbing were not enough to satisfy Mick Jagger's restless energy. The film world had already knocked on his door several times. After Jean Luc Goddard's documentary *Sympathy for the Devil (One Plus One)*, Jagger went to Australia to star as bandit *Ned Kelly*. In 1970, Jagger starred in Nicholas Roeg's psychological study, *Performance*. It depicted what many had come to believe represented the Stones' off-stage existence—a decadent, drug and sex sodden trail that could only lead to tragedy. Jagger as Turner, a burnt out rock star, trades identities with a small time hood, initiating him into the darker pleasures of the show business mystique.

## THE TOP FIVE
*Week of May 29, 1971*

1  **Brown Sugar**
    Rolling Stones

2  **Joy to the World**
    Three Dog Night

· 3  **Never Can Say Goodbye**
    Jackson 5

4  **Want Ads**
    Honey Cone

5  **It Don't Come Easy**
    Ringo Starr

*Writers: General Johnson*
*Greg Perry*
*Barney Perkins*

*Producer: Greg Perry*

*June 12, 1971*
*1 week*

WHEN BRIAN HOLLAND, LAMONT DOZIER AND EDDIE HOLLAND left Motown after producing a string of number one hits for Diana Ross and the Supremes [see 223—"The Happening"] and the Four Tops [see 209—"Reach Out, I'll Be There"], they formed their own company and signed artists to two labels—Invictus, distributed by Capitol, and Hot Wax, distributed by Buddah.

Not surprisingly, the first two groups Holland-Dozier-Holland worked with were a female trio and a male quartet—the Honey Cone and the Chairmen of the Board. Edna Wright, Carolyn Willis and Shellie Clark teamed to sing backing vocals for Burt Bacharach on a 1969 television special starring Andy Williams. Edna asked her friend Eddie Holland to watch the show, and he suggested they form a group. The Honey Cone had the very first single released on Hot Wax, "While You're Looking for Sugar."

Edna began her professional career in 1960, singing with a gospel group from Los Angeles, the COGIC (Church of God in Christ) singers. Through her sister, Darlene Love [see 119—"He's a Rebel"], Edna met record producer Phil Spector.

Spector associate Jack Nitzsche produced the first record featuring Edna as lead vocalist—"Yes Sir, That's My Baby" by Hale and the Hushabyes, a pseudonymn for an aggregation that included Sonny and Cher, Jackie DeShannon and Brian Wilson.

Between 1965-1967, Edna recorded several singles as Sandy Wynns, including a minor hit called "A Touch of Venus." She continued to work as a background singer, first for Johnny Rivers and then for Ray Charles, who asked her to join the Raelettes.

Carolyn Willis had been a member of the 1964 girl group the Girlfriends ("My One and Only Jimmy Boy") and also did some work with Spector's Bob B. Soxx and the Blue Jeans. She worked often as a backing vocalist for artists like Lou Rawls and O. C. Smith. Shellie Clark moved from Brooklyn to Los Angeles when she won a scholarship to the University of Southern California. She worked as an Ikette for Ike and Tina Turner and sang backing vocals for Little Richard and Dusty Springfield.

The Honey Cone recorded for almost two years on Hot Wax without a major hit. Meanwhile, Holland-Dozier-Holland's other label, Invictus, had scored a couple of top three hits—"Give Me Just a Little More Time" by the Chairmen of the Board and "Band of Gold" by Freda Payne.

The lead singer on "Give Me Just a Little More Time" was General Johnson, who had written and sung lead on "It Will Stand," a 1961 hit for the Showmen. Brian Holland had been interested in his talent since a re-issue of "It Will Stand" went to number one in Detroit in 1964, but his voice was too similar to Levi Stubbs of the Four Tops to bring him to Motown. When Invictus and Hot Wax were created, H-D-H signed Johnson to a contract and brought him to Detroit, where he lived in Lamont Dozier's house.

But Holland-Dozier-Holland were the primary songwriters in their company, and Johnson had to prove his writing talent. He teamed up with Greg Perry to write "Somebody's Been Sleeping (In My Bed)" for the Hot Wax group 100 Proof Aged in Soul. The record went to number eight in the fall of 1970.

Then Johnson and Perry wrote a song they thought would be right for a female singer, "Stick-Up." It was rejected, so they changed the chord progression and came up with new lyrics: "Wanted, young man, single and free. . ." The song was "Want Ads." First it was recorded with an Invictus group, Glass House, featuring lead vocals by Freda Payne's sister Scherrie (later a member of the Supremes). Unhappy with that version, Johnson and Perry had Freda give it a try. That didn't work either, so they recorded it a third time, with the Honey Cone.

"Want Ads" entered the Hot 100 at number 79 on April 10, 1971. Nine weeks later it was number one. For a follow-up, the group recorded "Stick-Up," which peaked at number 11. They had two more hits, "One Monkey Don't Stop No Show—Part 1" (number 15) and "The Day I Found Myself" (number 23).

## THE TOP FIVE
*Week of June 12, 1971*

1 **Want Ads**
Honey Cone

2 **Brown Sugar**
Rolling Stones

3 **Rainy Days & Mondays**
Carpenters

4 **It Don't Come Easy**
Ringo Starr

5 **Joy to the World**
Three Dog Night

## 294 It's Too Late/I Feel the Earth Move ODE 66015
### CAROLE KING

Writers: Toni Stern
       Carole King

Producer: Lou Adler

June 19, 1971
5 weeks

By THE TIME HER two-sided hit "It's Too Late" and "I Feel the Earth Move" reached pole position, Carole King had already written four number one singles. By May, 1974, she had eight number one hits to her credit, more than any other female songwriter at that time.

During the summer of 1971, Carole began to enjoy tremendous acceptance as a recording artist. Her *Tapestry* album was number one for 15 weeks and went on to sell more than 15 million copies worldwide. She won four Grammys that year, including Best Album, Song of the Year, Record of the Year and Best Female Vocalist.

Carol Klein was born in Brooklyn on February 9, 1942. She took piano lessons from her mother when she was four, and in high school she wrote music for a quartet she formed, the Co-Sines. In 1958 she met Gerry Goffin at Queens College in New York. They were dating and writing songs at the same time. Carole's first single as an artist was "Baby Sittin'," released on the ABC-Paramount label in March, 1959. A year later she released "Oh Neil," an answer record to "Oh Carol," a song written about her by her high school boyfriend, Neil Sedaka.

Carole and Gerry's real success came when they went to work for

### THE TOP FIVE
*Week of June 19, 1971*

1  **It's Too Late/**
   **I Feel the Earth Move**
   Carole King

2  **Rainy Days & Mondays**
   Carpenters

3  **Want Ads**
   Honey Cone

4  **Brown Sugar**
   Rolling Stones

5  **It Don't Come Easy**
   Ringo Starr

Don Kirshner and Al Nevins' Aldon Music. Carole composed music for Gerry's lyrics as they worked alongside other famous songwriting teams like Barry Mann-Cynthia Weill and Neil Sedaka-Howard Greenfield.

Goffin and King's first success was the Shirelles' "Will You Love Me Tomorrow" [see 83], a number one single in 1961. A complete list of their songs is far too long to print here, but some of their biggest hits include number one singles for Bobby Vee [see 97—"Take Good Care of My Baby"], Little Eva [see 115—"The Loco-Motion"] and Steve Lawrence [see 122—"Go Away Little Girl"] plus other hits like "Up on the Roof" by the Drifters, "I'm Into Something Good" by Herman's Hermits, "Just Once In My Life" by the Righteous Brothers, " "(You Make Me Feel Like) A Natural Woman" by Aretha Franklin, "Don't Bring Me Down" by the Animals, "Hi-De-Ho" by Blood, Sweat and Tears and "Chains," recorded by the Cookies in 1962 and covered by the Beatles a year later.

Carole's biggest pre-"Tapestry"

success as a vocalist came in 1962, when she recorded a demo for Bobby Vee. Kirshner liked her singing so much, he didn't give Vee a chance to record it. He released Carole's version on his Dimension Records label. The song, "It Might As Well Rain Until September," peaked at number 22 in America and number three in Britain.

In 1968, Carole and Gerry ended their marriage, and both moved to California separately. With Danny Kortchmar and Charles Larkey, she formed a group called the City. They recorded an album for Lou Adler's new Ode label.

In an October, 1970, interview, Carole said she was hesitant about writing lyrics for the first time for fear of "revealing" herself. "I didn't want people to interpret what I wrote, I think I have a block against that. People can point to a phrase in lyrics." She also said, "I want to make LPs. I don't want to be a star." Five months later *Tapestry* was released. Carole's life changed forever.

COLUMBIA 45332 **Indian Reservation (The Lament of the Cherokee Reservation Indian)** **295**

THE RAIDERS

*Writer: John D. Loudermilk*

*Producer: Mark Lindsay*

*July 24, 1971*
*1 week*

**P**AUL REVERE AND THE RAIDERS were the first rock group signed to Columbia Records. The year was 1963 and the label was more oriented to Andy Williams and Steve Lawrence than rock and roll, which explains why the group's "Louie Louie" single was only a hit in the Pacific Northwest while the Kingsmen's version became the national hit.

The band came to national prominence when Dick Clark signed them to be regulars in his daily afternoon music show filmed on location, "Where the Action Is." The series debuted on June 27, 1965, and three months later the group's first Columbia hit, "Steppin' Out," debuted on the Hot 100.

Paul Revere and the Raiders had nine top 20 hits before the decade was over, and while they're remembered as a '60s band, they had their biggest hit in 1971 with "Indian Reservation." At the time, it was the biggest-selling single in Columbia Records' history.

Don Fardon's recording of "Indian Reservation" was number three in

Britain when a Columbia Records executive told Lindsay he should record the song. " 'Indian Reservation' was going to be a [solo] Mark Lindsay single," Lindsay reports. "I'd had 'Arizona' [number 10 in February, 1970] before that. Jack Gold suggested I record it. At the time the Raiders had no material out there. As the producer of the Raiders, and I also produced 'Indian Reservation,' it was my choice to put it out under the name Raiders. I'm about one-sixteenth Cherokee, so I suppose there was something that prompted me to tell about the injustice."

Revere first organized a group in his native Caldwell, Idaho, in 1958. He had been a barber and a drive-in restaurant owner. The tall, skinny kid who delivered buns from a local bakery was Mark Lindsay. who had played in bands like Freddy Chapman and the Idaho Playboys. A lawnmower accident when he was four years old left Mark with a missing tip of his left index finger. Because of the injury, years later his guitar teacher suggested he try a different instrument. Revere needed a saxophone player in his band, the Downbeats, so Lindsay hocked his guitar and bought a sax, and listened to an album by the Champs [see 34 — "Tequila"] for inspiration before auditioning for Revere.

The group signed with Gardena Records, where a label executive suggested Paul's real name was too good a gimmick not to use. For two weeks, the band was known as Paul Revere and the Nightriders, but they thought it sounded like a "cowboy" band, so they changed to the patriotic-sounding Paul Revere and the Raiders. Their single, "Like Long Hair," reflected Revere's inspiration, the boogie woogie piano of Jerry Lee Lewis.

After that 1961 single, Revere was drafted and the group broke up for a couple of years. Lindsay went to Hollywood but two years later moved to Portland, Oregon, where the band re-formed.

One Friday afternoon, Revere and Lindsay were walking down the street when they stopped to stare at the window of a costume shop. Three mannequins were dressed in Revolutionary War outfits, and they thought it would be clever to rent the costumes and wear them after intermission at a college dance they were playing Saturday night. The crowd went crazy and the costumes became a permanent part of the act.

The band enjoyed success in the latter half of the '60s with "Just Like Me," "Kicks," "Hungry" and "Good Thing." In 1968, Paul and Mark hosted their own television series, "Happening '68." Lindsay had some solo hits in 1969-70 ("Arizona," "Silver Bird") and in 1970 the group shortened their name to the Raiders. A year later, "Indian Reservation" became their last top 20 single.

### THE TOP FIVE
*Week of July 24, 1971*

1 **Indian Reservation**
Raiders

2 **It's Too Late/**
**I Feel the Earth Move**
Carole King

3 **You've Got a Friend**
James Taylor

4 **Don't Pull Your Love**
Hamilton, Joe Frank & Reynolds

5 **Mr. Big Stuff**
Jean Knight

# You've Got a Friend WARNER BROTHERS 7498
## JAMES TAYLOR

*Writer: Carole King*

*Producer: Peter Asher*

*July 31, 1971*
*1 week*

" *'You've Got a Friend' was not written*
*for James . . . . It was one of*
*those moments when I sat down at the*
*piano and it wrote itself from some*
*place other than me.*"
— *CAROLE KING*

**T**WO weeks after her double-sided hit of "It's Too Late" and "I Feel the Earth Move" was number one, songwriter Carole King was back on top of the chart with "You've Got a Friend," one of the songs included on her multi-million selling LP *Tapestry*. But Carole didn't release "You've Got a Friend" as a single. Her close friend James Taylor did, and it is his only number one song.

Taylor and his producer Peter Asher [see 150—"A World Without Love"] recorded the album *Sweet Baby James* just a few blocks away from the studio where Carole and her producer, Lou Adler, were recording *Tapestry*. Carole and James were long-time friends; they met through Danny Kortchmar, a boyhood friend of James' who was in a group called the City with Carole. In the spring of 1971, James did a 27-city tour of America with Carole as his opening act.

James was born March 12, 1948, in Boston. His father Issac became dean of the medical school of the University of North Carolina, and his mother Trudy, who devoted time to raising her children, was a lyric soprano. James' brothers Alex and Livingston and his sister Kate were interested in music, and all went on to record their own albums.

The family spent their summers at Martha's Vineyard, where James, at 15, met Kortchmar. With Danny on harmonica and James on guitar, they won a local hootenanny contest. Back in North Carolina at boarding school, James formed a group with Alex called the Fabulous Corsairs. At 17 he became severely depressed and had himself committed to the McLean Psychiatric Hospital in Belmont, Massachussetts. During his 10-month stay he began to write songs.

Then he went to New York and joined Kortchmar's group, the Flying Machine. They played Greenwich Village clubs until their break-up, caused in part by Taylor's addiction to heroin. Attempting to break his drug habit, James moved to London in 1968. Kortchmar had once played in a band called the Kingbees who had backed up Peter and Gordon, and Danny told James to call Peter, now head of A&R for the Beatles' Apple label. Taylor brought Asher a demo tape.

"I liked the tape a lot," Asher recalls. "He was the first person I signed." James recorded one album for Apple, with Paul McCartney and George Harrison sitting in on one track. But James could not kick his heroin habit, and he returned to America and entered Austin Riggs, a mental hospital in Stockbridge, Massachussetts. Asher left Apple and came to the States, where he signed James to Warner Brothers Records.

"Fire and Rain," written about his drug habit and a friend who committed suicide, broke from the album. A cover story in the March 1, 1971, issue of *Time* and the release of "You've Got a Friend" from the *Mudslide Slim and the Blue Horizon* album helped establish James as a star. "You've Got a Friend" won two Grammys—one for James (Best Pop Male Vocal Performance) and one for Carole (Song of the Year).

James married Carly Simon [see 326—"You're So Vain"] on November 3, 1972. With Carly, he had two chart singles: cover versions of Charlie and Inez Foxx' "Mockingbird" and the Everly Brothers' "Devoted to You." In 1982, Carly filed for divorce.

## THE TOP FIVE
*Week of July 31, 1971*

1 **You've Got a Friend**
James Taylor

2 **Indian Reservation**
Raiders

3 **It's Too Late/**
**I Feel the Earth Move**
Carole King

4 **Mr. Big Stuff**
Jean Knight

5 **Draggin' the Line**
Tommy James

ATCO 6824 # How Can You Mend a Broken Heart
## BEE GEES

*Writers: Barry Gibb*
*Robin Gibb*

*Producers: Robert Stigwood*
*Barry Gibb*
*Maurice Gibb*
*Robin Gibb*

*August 7, 1971*
*4 weeks*

"NEW YORK MINING DISASTER, 1941 (HAVE YOU SEEN MY WIFE, MR. JONES )," the first Bee Gees single to be released in America, fooled many listeners who thought they were hearing a new song by the Beatles. "Bee Gees" was assumed to be short for some mysterious name like "Beatles Group." As it turned out, Barry, Maurice and Robin Gibb were not the Beatles, although they would one day star in a motion picture based on the album *Sgt. Pepper's Lonely Hearts Club Band*.

"How Can You Mend a Broken Heart" must have been a sweet reward for the brothers Gibb when it moved to the top of the Hot 100 on August 7, 1971, for the group had broken up in December, 1969, after performing together for over 13 years.

Hugh and Barbara Gibb were living on the Isle of Man when their first son, Barry, was born on September 1, 1947. Twin brothers Maurice and Robin were born December 22, 1949, in Manchester, England.

Just after their youngest brother Andy [see 472—"I Just Want to Be Your Everything"] was born, the family emigrated to Brisbane, Australia. Barry, Maurice and Robin appeared at local speedways, singing between races. Two men with the initials B.G. helped accelerate their careers. Speedway organizer Bill Goode heard one of their tapes and asked his friend Bill Gates, a disc jockey, to play their songs on the radio. After an 18-month run as the house band at a Queensland club, they won their own television series and were signed to Australia's Festival Records.

They relocated to Sydney, and after a succession of top 10 singles in Australia, the brothers told their parents they wanted to return to England. At first their father was upset and threatened to cancel their passports. He suddenly changed his mind and booked passage home, sending copies of the Bee Gees' Australian LP to management companies in England, including NEMS, which once handled the Beatles.

In the London office of NEMS, Robert Stigwood received the album and liked what he heard. The Bee Gees were back on British soil for less than 24 hours when Stigwood arranged an audition for them at the Seville Theatre in London. He signed them to a five-year contract. As they released their first album, they were a quintet: the three Gibbs plus drummer Colin Peterson and guitarist Vince Melouney, both Australians.

In America, their first five singles made the top 20—but not the top 10. They finally broke through with "I've Gotta Get a Message to You" and "I Started a Joke," two consecutive top 10 singles in 1968. A year of touring the world and extensive television appearances followed. In December, 1968, Melouney left. It was only the first sign of dissension.

Along with success came family infighting, excessive drinking and a fast life style. By 1969, Robin and Maurice were not speaking to each other, and Robin split the group. He recorded a solo album, *Saved by the Bell*, and refused his father's request to resolve the brotherly conflict.

The Bee Gees continued as a trio, until August, 1969, when Barry and Maurice announced Peterson's departure. The *Cucumber Castle* album featured the two remaining brothers, but no hits. Barry and Maurice were both planning to record solo albums when Robin reconciled with them and rejoined the group. Robin told *Time* magazine, "If we hadn't been related, we would probably never have gotten back together."

The first product from the reunited brothers was *2 Years On*, which included their biggest single yet. "Lonely Days" went to number three. It was followed by "How Can You Mend a Broken Heart," a song Barry and Robin had written for Andy Williams to record. When he passed on it, they decided to record it themselves. It became the first of nine number one singles for the Bee Gees.

## THE TOP FIVE
*Week of August 7, 1971*

1 **How Can You Mend a Broken Heart?**
Bee Gees

2 **Mr. Big Stuff**
Jean Knight

3 **Take Me Home, Country Roads**
John Denver

4 **Draggin' the Line**
Tommy James

5 **You've Got a Friend**
James Taylor

# Uncle Albert/Admiral Halsey APPLE 1837
## PAUL AND LINDA MCCARTNEY

*Writers: Paul and Linda McCartney*

*Producers: Paul and Linda McCartney*

September 4, 1971
1 week

Asked if any of the characters in his songs—persons like Michelle and Eleanor Rigby—were real people, Paul McCartney told interviewer Paul Gambaccini: " 'Uncle Albert' was. I did have an Uncle Albert who used to quote the bible to everyone when he got drunk. He used to read from the Bible. It was the only time he ever read the Bible, but it was when he was drunk. He died a few years ago and he was a good man."

"Uncle Albert/Admiral Halsey" was the second number one single by a former Beatle [see 286—"My Sweet Lord/ Isn't It a Pity"]. It was a track from Paul and Linda McCartney's *Ram* album, released as a single two-and-a-half months after the LP. It was the only single from the album, and it was not released in Britain, where the lone track pulled for release as a 45 was "The Back Seat of My Car," which reached number 39.

*Ram* was the second album from Paul. The first, simply titled *McCartney*, had no singles released from it, although many thought "Maybe I'm Amazed" was a perfect candidate. The first album had been released in April, 1970, a date that alarmed the other Beatles, who thought it was scheduled too close to the release of *Let It Be*. McCartney discussed the conflict with Gambaccini for a 1974 *Rolling Stone*

## THE TOP FIVE
*Week of September 4, 1971*

1  **Uncle Albert/Admiral Halsey**
   Paul & Linda McCartney

2  **How Can You Mend
   a Broken Heart**
   Bee Gees

3  **Smiling Faces Sometimes**
   Undisputed Truth

4  **Spanish Harlem**
   Aretha Franklin

5  **Go Away Little Girl**
   Donny Osmond

interview: "There was some hassle at the time. We were arguing over who had mentioned a release date first. It was all a bit petty. I'd pegged a release date, and then *Let It Be* was scheduled near it. I saw it as victimization, but now I'm sure it wasn't."

In February, 1971, Paul released his first solo single. "Another Day" backed with "Oh Woman Oh Why" reached number five on the Hot 100. The former listed writing credits for Paul and Linda McCartney, as did "Uncle Albert/Admiral Halsey." Sir Lew Grade, who then owned Northern Songs, the company that published McCartney's songs, said Linda was incapable of songwriting and initiated a lawsuit.

"Lew Grade suddenly saw . . . that I was now claiming that I was writing half my stuff with Linda, and that if I was writing half of it she was entitled to a pure half of it, no matter whether she was a recognized songwriter or not," McCartney told Gambaccini. ". . . I thought that whoever I worked with, no matter what the method of collaboration was, that person, if they did help me on the song, should have a portion of the song for helping me. I think at the time their big organization suddenly

thought, 'Hello, they're pulling a fast one, they're trying to get some of the money back,' whereas, in fact, it was the truth." Eventually, the suit was dropped and Sir Grade's company produced McCartney's 1973 television special, "James Paul McCartney."

Life began for James Paul McCartney on June 18, 1942, in Liverpool's Walton Hospital. His mother Mary had worked in the maternity ward where he was born, and his father Jim was a trumpet player who had once led Jim Mac's Band. Paul's first musical interest was in his father's instrument, and he took lessons on the trumpet. Paul had just turned 14 when his mother died unexpectedly. Soon after, his father bought him a guitar for 15 pounds. Paul had the guitar restrung so he could play it left-handed.

On July 6, 1957, Paul want to the Woolton Parish Church Fete and saw a group called the Quarrymen play. That day, he met John Lennon for the first time. They both shared an interest in music, and Lennon was impressed enough with McCartney's guitar playing on the song "20 Flight Rock" to invite him to join the Quarrymen, the group which evolved into Johnny and the Moondogs, the Silver Beatles and the Beatles.

*Writers: Gerry Goffin*
*Carole King*

*Producer: Rick Hall*

*September 11, 1971*
*3 weeks*

THE first song in the rock era to be number one by two different artists is "Go Away Little Girl," which first hit the top spot in 1963 when Steve Lawrence [see 122] recorded it. Producer Rick Hall made a wise selection when he had Donny Osmond record it again in 1971, because songwriter Carole King [see 294—"It's Too Late" / "I Feel the Earth Move"] was the hottest artist of the year, thanks to her *Tapestry* album. Many artists recorded Carole King songs in 1971, including James Taylor [see 296—"You've Got a Friend"].

Donald Clark Osmond was born December 9, 1957, while Sam Cooke's "You Send Me" [see 30] was the number one song in the nation. He was the seventh son of George and Olive Osmond, and he began his singing career early. Four of his older brothers were already entertaining at church functions when four-year-old Donny asked his mother to buy him some Andy Williams albums. He remembers singing along with Andy's vocals. Once his parents noticed he had the desire to sing, they let him join his brothers in the act. By shifting from four-part to five-part harmony, the Osmonds moved away from a barber shop sound to something more modern.

After years of failure in the recording field, the Osmonds broke through in 1971 with their first chart entry, a number one single [see 288—"One Bad Apple"]. The teen magazines ran articles on the entire group, but they singled out Donny for special attention. It was logical that he should record on his own.

The Osmonds did record other people's material, like Joe South's "Yo-Yo," but they also wrote their own songs, such as "Crazy Horses" and "Down by the Lazy River."

Donny followed his chart debut of "Sweet and Innocent" with a long run of cover versions of earlier hits.

After "Go Away Little Girl," he tried another Gerry Goffin-Carole King song from 1963, Freddie Scott's "Hey Girl." Then came covers of Paul Anka's "Puppy Love," Nat "King" Cole's "Too Young," Frankie Avalon's "Why" [see 62] and Johnny Mathis' "The Twelfth of Never." All made the top 20.

Donny also recorded duets with his sister Marie. They preferred cover versions as well, updating Dale and Grace's "I'm Leaving It Up to You" [see 140], Tommy Edwards' "Morning Side of the Mountain" and April and Nino's "Deep Purple" [see 139]. In 1976, ABC-TV rewarded the brother and sister with their own television series, which lasted for three seasons.

The series was still on the air when Donny married Debra Glenn of Provo, Utah. Those who remember six-year-old Donny Osmond singing on "The Andy Williams Show" may find it hard to believe he now has four boys of his own.

He kept away from the recording studio for a long time, but kept himself busy. He starred in a revival of the musical *Little Johnny Jones*, although the show closed after opening night on Broadway. He directed a television special for Grover Washington, Jr. and headed his own production company. In 1988, Donny signed with Virgin Records in the U.K. Capitol picked him up for America, and his single "Soldier of Love" peaked at number two, his highest chart ranking since "Go Away Little Girl."

## THE TOP FIVE

*Week of September 11, 1971*

1 **Go Away Little Girl**
Donny Osmond

2 **Spanish Harlem**
Aretha Franklin

3 **Smiling Faces Sometimes**
Undisputed Truth

4 **Ain't No Sunshine**
Bill Withers

5 **Uncle Albert/Admiral Halsey**
Paul & Linda McCartney

# 300 Maggie May/Reason to Believe MERCURY 73224
## ROD STEWART

**Writers: Rod Stewart**
**Martin Quittenton/**
**Tim Hardin**

**Producer: Rod Stewart**

*October 2, 1971*
*5 weeks*

"**M**AGGIE MAY," the tale of a school-boy's not-so-fondly remembered sexual initiation, was almost excluded from Rod Stewart's *Every Picture Tells a Story* album. A last minute addition to the LP, it was not a prime candidate for a single. The original "A" side was Tim Hardin's ballad, "Reason to Believe." It entered the Hot 100 at number 98 on July 17, 1971. But both sides of the 45 caught the fancy of radio programmers and listeners, and by its fifth week on the chart, "Maggie May" was listed as the "B" side. The following week, the titles were reversed, with "Maggie May" moving from 62 to 46 as the official "A" side. Six weeks later the double-sided smash was number one. The same week, *Every Picture Tells a Story* went to number one on the album chart. Accolades from the music press followed, like being named "Rock Star of the Year" by *Rolling Stone*. Rod was firmly established as a new face on the scene.

Actually, he was an old Face, having joined the aggregation consisting of Ronnie Lane, Ron Wood, Kenny Jones and Ian McLagen in 1969. But

the Faces didn't achieve commercial success in America until after "Maggie May," when "Stay With Me" went to number 17 in early 1972.

Roderick David Stewart was born January 10, 1945. The only one of Robert and Elsie Stewart's five children to be born in London, he nevertheless was instilled with a passion for things Scottish. He began his love affair with music as a child, listening to his father's Al Jolson records, but his family thought his love of football would lead to a pro career. His father even coerced him into signing with the Brentford team, but his career only progressed as far as cleaning out the lockers and blacking the players' boots.

Music was always in Rod's soul, from his first skiffle group at 14 to the Kool Kats. He learned to play banjo, then guitar, developing a taste for folkies like Woody Guthrie and Jack Elliot and, as he recalled in a *Musician* interview, "turning into a leftist Marxist type. I skipped across Europe with just a guitar singing songs like 'Cocaine All Around My Brain.'" Bob Dylan's debut was a turning point for Stewart.

"From there on, I decided I'd become a beatnik, hair right down the back." The nomadic phase lasted two years before he was kicked out of Spain for vagrancy. "I smartened up, cut me hair off and became a mod. Didn't play the guitar anymore. Used to hang out in London when the Yard-birds used to be a local dance band."

One of Stewart's favorite haunts was Eel Pie Island, and to get home to Highgate at night, he had to take a train. Waiting at Twickenham station one evening, singing the blues, he was overheard by Long John Baldry who offered him a singing spot with the Hoochie Coochie Men. It beat his day job, digging graves, and though, out of shyness, he would often sing with his back to the audience, Rod became a voice on the soon-to-boom London music scene (although he had been in the recording studio before—playing harmonica on Millie Small's 1964 hit, "My Boy Lollipop").

Shotgun Express and Steampacket were the next stops, but neither group lasted. He commiserated with his friend, Jeff Beck. "Jeff had been fired from the Yardbirds, I'd been fired from Steampacket," Rod recounted in *Musician*. He became the vocalist for the Jeff Beck Group and was featured on two albums, *Truth* and *Beck-Ola*, along with guitarist Ron Wood. When Beck sacked Wood, Stewart left too and they both joined the Faces.

Rod was also concentrating on a solo career, begun in 1966 with a recording of Sam Cooke's [see 30—"You Send Me"] "Shake." "I was really into Sam Cooke. He's probably the biggest influence on my life," Stewart has declared.

Mercury signed Rod as a solo artist in July, 1968. Two LPs, *The Rod Stewart Album* and *Gasoline Alley* enjoyed moderate success before the double-whammy number one of "Maggie May" / "Reason to Believe" and *Every Picture Tells a Story*.

## THE TOP FIVE
*Week of October 2, 1971*

1  **Maggie May/Reason to Believe**
   Rod Stewart

2  **Go Away Little Girl**
   Donny Osmond

3  **The Night They Drove Old Dixie Down**
   Joan Baez

4  **Superstar**
   Carpenters

5  **Ain't No Sunshine**
   Bill Withers

# Gypsys, Tramps and Thieves
## CHER

*Writer: Bob Stone*

*Producer: Snuff Garrett*

*November 6, 1971*
*2 weeks*

PRODUCER Snuff Garrett has worked with many artists, including Bobby Vee [see 97—"Take Good Care of My Baby"], Gary Lewis and the Playboys [see 167—"This Diamond Ring"] and Vicki Lawrence [see 331—"The Night the Lights Went Out in Georgia"], but "Gypsys, Tramps and Thieves" remains one of his two all-time favorite singles that he's produced. The other is "Old Rivers," a number five hit for Walter Brennan in 1962.

Like "Old Rivers," "Gypsys, Tramps and Thieves" is a story-song, and it's exactly what Garrett was looking for when Cher was signed to Kapp Records in 1971. He had known Sonny and Cher for a long time, both from his days at Liberty Records—when Cher recorded solo singles for the Imperial subsidiary—and from living next door to the couple in the affluent Bel Air suburb of Los Angeles.

Johnny Musso of Kapp Records thought that Garrett and Cher would work well together and decided to team them up. "I knew exactly what I was looking for," Snuff maintains. "I wanted a song along the lines of 'Son-of-a Preacher Man,' a story-type song." A writer named Bob Stone met with one of Garrett's staff members and asked if he could meet personally with Snuff. He told Snuff he didn't have a handle on what the producer was looking for and asked him to elaborate. "He came back the next day with a song called 'Gypsys and White Trash,'" says Snuff. A simple re-write turned it into "Gypsys, Tramps and Thieves."

It was an important release for Cher. Her last solo appearance on the Hot 100 had been almost four years earlier, with "You Better Sit Down, Kids." Her first solo single to make the chart, "All I Really Want to Do," preceded the debut of the first charted Sonny and Cher single [see 181—"I Got You Babe"] by one week. Until "Gypsys, Tramps and Thieves," her biggest hit on her own had been "Bang Bang (My Baby Shot Me Down)," which peaked at number two in April, 1966. After recording on Imperial for four years, she recorded some solo singles for Atco, the label that released Sonny and Cher's biggest hits, but none of those 45s made the chart.

"Gypsys, Tramps and Thieves" entered the Hot 100 at number 88 on September 18, 1971, and was number one seven weeks later. Its success followed the debut of "The Sonny and Cher Comedy Hour" on CBS, which premiered August 1, 1971, as a summer series. The show opened with an antagonistic banter between Sonny and Cher, a routine they had perfected in their night club act. Fred Silverman, then head of programming for CBS, saw them at the Americana Hotel in New York and thought they might work well on a variety series. He arranged for them to be substitute hosts on "The Merv Griffin Show" and satisfied with their performance, offered them their own series. The summer tryout earned high enough ratings for Silverman to bring the program back in December, 1971, as a weekly prime time offering.

## THE TOP FIVE
*Week of November 6, 1971*

1 **Gypsys, Tramps and Thieves**
Cher

2 **Theme from "Shaft"**
Isaac Hayes

3 **Maggie May/**
**Reason to Believe**
Rod Stewart

4 **Imagine**
John Lennon
Plastic Ono Band

5 **Yo-Yo**
Osmonds

# 302 Theme from 'Shaft' ENTERPRISE 9038

ISAAC HAYES

*Writer: Isaac Hayes*

*Producer: Isaac Hayes*

*November 20, 1971*
*2 weeks*

ISAAC HAYES' "Theme from 'Shaft'" was the third number one single to win an Academy Award for Best Song. The first two winners were Sammy Fain and Paul Francis Webster's "Love Is a Many-Splendored Thing" [see 3] and Burt Bacharach and Hal David's "Raindrops Keep Fallin' on My Head" [see 266].

Hayes had already made his mark as a songwriter with partner David Porter when he was invited to a meeting with MGM executives to discuss a property they had acquired, the novel *Shaft*. The studio wanted black film artists to make a film about a black hero. Hayes thought he would be considered for the lead role and agreed to compose the film score. Instead, he received a telephone call a few weeks later informing him that Richard Roundtree had been cast as Shaft and production was underway.

He had committed himself to writing the music, so he fulfilled his obligation. Released as a single, an edited version of the main theme entered the Hot 100 on October 16, 1971, and was number one five weeks later.

The song was given an elaborate presentation on the 1972 Oscar telecast. Hayes dramatically rose from the depths below stage in swirls of smoke and steam, his powerful black body attired in chains. It was a long way from "Whatever Will Be, Will Be."

Hayes was a session player for the Stax-Volt labels in Memphis before releasing his own records on the companies' Enterprise subsidiary. He played on all of Otis Redding's hits, and teamed up with songwriter David Porter to compose songs for Sam and Dave ("Soul Man," "Hold On! I'm a Comin'") and Carla Thomas ("B-A-B-Y"). After having a substantial amount of champagne at a Stax Christmas party, Hayes went into the studio with drummer Al Jackson and bassist "Duck" Dunn to see what they could come up with on tape. The results were dramatic re-workings of pop hits like "Misty," prefaced by long monologues and punctuated by some original jazz arrangements. The

songs were released on an album, *Presenting Isaac Hayes*. Although it wasn't a big seller, it led to a second album, *Hot Buttered Soul*.

Hayes was born August 20, 1942, in Covington, Tennessee. His mother died a year-and-a-half later and Isaac was raised by his grandparents, who were sharecroppers on a farm. They made sure he attended church and by age five he was singing in the choir.

He was an avid listener to the radio, especially to Rufus Thomas on WDIA, although he also listened to country music. He taught himself to play piano and organ and moved to Memphis when he was a teenager, where he played in several bands like Valentine and the Swing Cats, the Teen Tones and Sir Isaac and the Doodads. He idolized Sam Cooke [see 30—"You Send Me"] and when Cooke was hospitalized in Memphis, Isaac managed to sneak into his hospital room and catch a glimpse of the

singer with a thermometer in his mouth before a nurse asked him to leave.

He was originally hired at Stax to fill in on keyboards while Booker T. Jones was away at college. Hayes' first session for the Memphis label was for Otis Redding in July, 1965, when "Respect" and "I've Been Lovin' You Too Long" were recorded.

After his success with *Shaft*, he was asked to score a couple of blax-ploitation films, *Tough Guys* and *Truck Turner*. He guest starred in an episode of "The Rockford Files" with Dionne Warwick and recorded an album with her, *A Man and a Woman*. Later, he recorded a duet album with Millie Jackson and co-wrote "Deja Vu" for Warwick.

After 1974's "Joy - Pt. 1" he found it difficult to make the top 30, until he signed with Polydor in 1979. His re-working of Roy Hamilton's "Don't Let Go" went to number 18 in 1980.

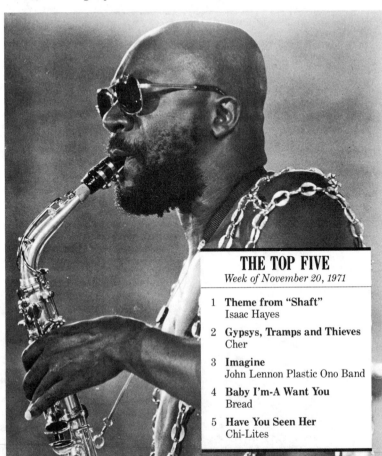

## THE TOP FIVE

*Week of November 20, 1971*

1 **Theme from "Shaft"**
Isaac Hayes

2 **Gypsys, Tramps and Thieves**
Cher

3 **Imagine**
John Lennon Plastic Ono Band

4 **Baby I'm-A Want You**
Bread

5 **Have You Seen Her**
Chi-Lites

EPIC 10805 **Family Affair**
SLY AND THE FAMILY STONE

**303**

*Writer: Sylvester Stewart*

*Producer: Sly Stone*

*December 4, 1971*
*3 weeks*

Lawsuits, fines for being late at concerts (or not showing up at all), illness, management battles and lack of new material were slowly chipping away at the popularity of Sly and the Family Stone. In 1970, 26 of his 80 scheduled appearances were cancelled; in 1971 the figures were 12 out of 40. To add to Sly's woes, Columbia Records, frustrated at the length of time it was taking him to complete a new studio album, suspended his contract.

"He was so far behind schedule that I was getting worried that his contract would expire and he'd sign with someone else for the large advance he was seeking," explained Clive Davis, former president of the label, in his biography *Clive: Inside the Record Business*. The financially strapped artist asked for a quarter-of-a-million dollar mortgage payment on his sumptuous Los Angeles home (formerly owned by John Phillips of the Mamas and the Papas), but was evicted when the money didn't come through.

One of the places where Stone channeled his frustration was his music. For two years he experimented, parking a camper outside the studio and recording at whim. He stood up engineers or picked at the guitar to the tune of $140 for each hour of studio time. David Kapralik, then his manager, defended Sly in *Rolling Stone*, instructing, "Sylvester

Stewart does not create 'product.' Sylvester Stewart is an innovator, a source of new fusions, new concepts. Ya don't turn them out like you turn out pizzas. They're life statements."

Finally, Sly emerged with an album Kapralik defined as "ripping into his soul," *There's a Riot Goin' On*. Its centerpiece was the single "Family Affair," the musician's own emotional explanation of the strife swirling around him. His manager claimed he was being chopped into pieces by several factions, including his family. Sly obliquely countered in *Rolling Stone*, "They may be trying to tear me apart, but I don't feel it. Song's not about that. Song's about a family affair, whether it's a result of genetic processes or a situation in the environment."

"Family Affair" was the highest new entry on the Hot 100 for the week ending November 6, 1971. The first new Sly and the Family Stone single in 18 months, it debuted at 50 and made a swift ascension, moving 50-21-8-5 to number one. It was the last single from the group to chart in

the top 10. "Runnin' Away," the follow-up, reached number 23. "If You Want Me to Stay," released in the summer of 1973, was Sly's last hit, peaking at 12.

Though he periodically improved his concert appearance record, Sly's career never returned to the heights it had achieved in the late '60s.

Compatriot Bobby Womack ("Lookin' for a Love") talked Stone into seeking treatment for his drug problem in 1984, then asked him to perform on a two-month tour. Womack, who recorded with his brothers as the Valentinos ("It's All Over Now") before a solo career on Minit Records, gives Sly credit for giving him an education in production during *There's a Riot Goin' On*, to which Womack contributed a couple of guitar tracks while absorbing engineering techniques. "He went a lot further in his career than I have, than I have ever to reach," Womack told Lee Hildebrand in *Pulse!* "He fell a lot lower but it's just because he became overtaken by drugs and the pressure."

## THE TOP FIVE
*Week of December 4, 1971*

1  **Family Affair**
   Sly & the Family Stone

2  **Theme from "Shaft"**
   Isaac Hayes

3  **Baby I'm-A Want You**
   Bread

4  **Have You Seen Her**
   Chi-Lites

5  **Gypsys, Tramps and Thieves**
   Cher

## Brand New Key NEIGHBORHOOD 4201
### MELANIE

**304**

Writer: Melanie Safka

Producer: Peter Schekeryk

December 25, 1971

3 weeks

**A** SIMPLE, '30s-sounding tune about a young girl who gets "a brand-new pair of roller skates" brought singer/songwriter Melanie Safka her greatest hit—and, ultimately, her biggest headache.

Born February 3, 1947, in New York City, of Ukranian-Italian parentage, Melanie cut her musical teeth as a teenager performing in New Jersey clubs and Greenwich Village coffee shops. A classic high school outcast, she was often punished for wearing sandals in violation of the school dress code.

Melanie also studied acting at the Academy of Fine Arts in New York, and while hunting for an audition one day at 1690 Broadway, she was misdirected to the office of Buddah Records. As the story goes, label president Neil Bogart took one look at the irresistible, moon-faced teenager carrying a guitar, auditioned her, introduced her to her future producer and husband Peter Schekeryk, and signed her up.

Such is the stuff of music biz legends—but Melanie's career as a sweet-sounding folkie didn't really take off until she performed at the legendary Woodstock Festival in 1969. As rain poured down, the drenched multitude responded by lighting hundreds of candles. She watched them glow in the darkness. Inspired by this happening,

Melanie evoked the spirit of peace and love in a number six hit in the summer of 1970, "Lay Down (Candles in the Rain)," recorded with the Edwin Hawkins Singers. After two more singles on Buddah ["Peace Will Come (According to Plan)" and "Ruby Tuesday"], Melanie and husband Schekeryk started their own label, Neighborhood Records. Her first single for the label, "Brand New Key," had been composed in 15 minutes and was intended to be an uptempo interlude she could slip into concerts when she got tired of singing about "the trials of man."

Though Melanie knew that the "key" and "lock" were prime Freudian symbols, she was still unprepared for the barrage of interpretations that greeted the song. In fact, some misguided radio stations went so far as to ban it from the airwaves.

"Brand New Key" entered the Hot 100 at number 87 on October 30, 1971, and reached the number one position eight weeks later. It was a Christmas present in disguise. Its

incredible popularity forced her to reassess herself and her "Woodstock generation" image. "I've suffered in the categorization that I fell in," she once said. "Yummy, yummy, goody, goody, Melanie, Melanie . . . . So it was very difficult because of that categorizing of a person and freezing you in a moment of time...giving you a phrase and a sentence and a photograph and that's supposed to represent what you are. A person who writes and creates all the time needs more."

Tired of being seen as "a sicky sweet person singing sicky sweet songs," Melanie quit performing. She withdrew to her home in South Jersey and gave birth to two children. In 1975, she ended her self-imposed exile and emerged as a mature adult singing mature adult songs for Atlantic, Midsong International and then Tomato Records. But during her hiatus the times had changed—and Melanie could never recapture the fans who somehow had also left their innocence behind.

### THE TOP FIVE
*Week of December 25, 1971*

1 **Brand New Key**
Melanie

2 **Family Affair**
Sly & the Family Stone

3 **American Pie**
Don McLean

4 **An Old Fashioned Love Song**
Three Dog Night

5 **Got to be There**
Michael Jackson

United Artists 50856 **American Pie** **305**
DON McLEAN

*Writer: Don McLean*

*Producer: Ed Freeman*

*January 15, 1972*
*4 weeks*

"I CAN'T necessarily interpret 'American Pie' any better than you can," Don McLean told *Life* magazine reporter P. F. Kluge in 1972. But McLean did provide an important clue about his eight minute, 27 second melange of pop music and recent history. "Buddy Holly [see 26—"That'll Be the Day"] was the first and last person I ever really idolized as a kid. Most of my friends liked Elvis Presley. More of them liked Presley than Holly. But I liked Holly because he spoke to me. He was a symbol of something deeper than the music he made. His career and the sort of group he created, the interaction between the lead singer and the three men backing him up, was a perfect metaphor for the music of the '60s and for my own youth."

References to Holly abound in the song: "I can't remember if I cried/When I read about his widowed bride/But something touched me deep inside/The day the music died."* There was little doubt that the day the music died was February 3, 1959, the day Holly was killed in a plane crash along with Richie Valens and J. P. Richardson, the Big Bopper. Elvis Presley, the Beatles, Bob Dylan, the Rolling Stones all take the stage before the song ends with an elegy to the '60s.

Too long to fit onto one side of a single, "American Pie" was divided into two parts for release as a 45.

## THE TOP FIVE
*Week of January 15, 1972*

1 **American Pie**
   Don McLean

2 **Brand New Key**
   Melanie

3 **Let's Stay Together**
   Al Green

4 **Sunshine**
   Jonathan Edwards

5 **Family Affair**
   Sly & the Family Stone

But the song was too powerful to be abbreviated, and a majority of radio stations played only the complete version. "American Pie" made its first appearance on the Hot 100 at number 69 on November 27, 1971. Seven weeks later it was number one.

Born October 2, 1945, in suburban New Rochelle, New York, McLean's participation in sports and rigorous childhood activities were limited by asthma. He immersed himself in music, specifically Little Richard, Frank Sinatra and Holly. Aside from a brief stint as a paper boy, alluded to in "American Pie," McLean always made his living as a musician, a profession he firmly elected to follow at 15 when his father died.

Playing the banjo and guitar at parties while an undergraduate at Iona College and Villanova University led to working with folk artists Josh White and Pete Seeger, who tapped him for the prestigious Hudson River Sloop restoration benefit. That was in 1968, the same year McLean was named "Hudson River Troubadour" by the New York State Council on the Arts. Winning the title meant touring the entire length of the river, performing three concerts each day, five days a week, for six weeks and getting to know nearly every town along the Hudson.

His first album, *Tapestry*, was produced by Jerry Corbitt of the Youngbloods ("Get Together") and rejected by 34 labels before Mediarts finally released it in 1970.

When United Artists Records purchased Mediarts, McLean quickly became their most successful new artist with the album *American Pie*. McLean claimed he never knew how commercial the song was, just that he had written a masterpiece.

All the attention on McLean created a backlash, which prevented subsequent singles like "Vincent" (a tribute to artist Vincent Van Gogh) and "Dreidel" from fulfilling their potential. After "Wonderful Baby" in 1975, McLean didn't return to the Hot 100 again until 1981, when he went to number five with a cover version of Roy Orbison's [see 91—"Running Scared"] "Crying." Though his recording is sporadic, McLean still performs regularly, usually with just banjo and guitar—although he has fronted everything from bluegrass to rock bands to orchestras like the Israeli Philharmonic.

Concerts also bring to light the full range of his songwriting output, with "Castles in the Air" and "And I Love You So" becoming recognized as McLean compositions. Songwriting is cathartic for him, he says, demanding all his energies. Still, he sees himself as an all-around entertainer, interpreting other people's compositions as sensitively as his own.

# 306 Let's Stay Together HI 2202
## AL GREEN

*Writers: Al Green*
*Willie Mitchell*
*Al Jackson*

*Producer: Willie Mitchell*

*February 12, 1972*
*1 week*

TODAY, Al Green is a minister at the Full Tabernacle Church in Memphis, but in the first half of the '70s he was America's sexiest soul singer, burning up the charts with top 10 hits like "You Ought to Be With Me," "I'm Still in Love With You" and "Look What You Done for Me." Before he recorded his number one single, "Let's Stay Together," his roots were in gospel music. "I was raised on it," he told interviewer Geoffrey Himes. "It was put into my cornbread. I ate it. My mother and my father, they were Baptists. We were raised in church, and we sang at home....I was raised on the sound of Sam Cooke [see 30—"You Send Me"] and the Soul Stirrers."

Al Green was born April 13, 1946, in Forrest City, Arkansas. His parents, Robert and Cora, moved to Grand Rapids, Michigan, when Al was nine. With brothers Robert, Walter and William he sang gospel songs as the Green Brothers.

With high school friends Palmer James, Curtis Rogers and Gene Mason, Al formed a pop group, the Creations, in 1964. They played the "chitlin' circuit" in the midwest for three years and recorded some local hits on the Zodiac label. James and Rogers formed their own record company, Hot Line Music Journal, in 1967. They wrote a song, "Back Up Train," and recorded it with a re-organized group that included Al's brother Robert and a friend, Lee Virgins. Released under the name Al Greene and the Soul Mates, it went to number 41 on the Hot 100 in early 1968.

But Al never had a proper follow-up and the label folded. A year later, he was booked to play a club in Midland, Texas, the same night as Willie Mitchell, leader of a Memphis band and head of A&R for Hi Records. Mitchell had just been made vice president of Hi by owner Joe Cuoghi. Willie asked Green if he'd like to come to Memphis to record with his band, which included drummer Al Jackson of Booker T. and the MGs. Green replied that he didn't care much for Memphis.

But Mitchell was persistent. Two weeks later he called Al in Grand Rapids and asked if he'd changed his mind about Memphis. Al said he hadn't, but he'd come anyway. When he got to the studio, he was surprised to overhear Jackson tell Mitchell that Green was a genius—and just as surprised to hear Mitchell answer that he wasn't.

Mitchell did believe in his talent, though, and set a goal: he gave himself 18 months to make Green a star. The first single was a cooled-down, breathy version of the Temptations' "I Can't Get Next to You" [see 259], which went to number 60.

Right from the beginning, Green established a pattern of combining original hit singles with cover versions of pop hits like "Light My Fire," "How Can You Mend a Broken Heart" and "For the Good Times." He didn't forget his musical upbringing, always including religious songs like "God Is Standing By" and "Jesus Is Waiting" on his albums.

His single "Sha-La-La (Make Me Happy)" was moving toward the top 10 when a personal tragedy struck on October 25, 1974. Green was taking a shower in his home outside of Memphis when a former girlfriend burst in, poured boiling hot grits over him and then killed herself with his gun. Green suffered second-degree burns on his back, stomach and arm. Many credit this incident with Green's ultimate spiritual transformation, but the singer denied it in his interview with Himes:

"I was born again in 1973....It wasn't an incident that did it. No. People are silly when they write that. Nothing happened to bring me to Christ except coming into the knowledge of Christ and being transformed in mind and spirit on a particular morning....I'm a gospel singer now, and when it happened to me, I was singing rock 'n' roll."

## THE TOP FIVE
*Week of February 12, 1972*

1 **Let's Stay Together**
   Al Green

2 **American Pie**
   Don McLean

3 **Without You**
   Nilsson

4 **Precious and Few**
   Climax

5 **Never Been To Spain**
   Three Dog Night

RCA 0604 **Without You** `307`
NILSSON

*Writers: Pete Ham*
*Tom Evans*

*Producer: Richard Perry*

*February 19, 1972*
*4 weeks*

A DRUNKEN night of revelry and a trip to England to work with producer Richard Perry lifted Nilsson to number one status in 1972.

Harry Edward Nelson III was born on June 15, 1941, in the Bushwick section of Brooklyn, New York. In the early '50s his family relocated to southern California's San Fernando Valley where Harry attended parochial school. After graduation, he took a night job supervising the computer processing department at Security First National Bank in Van Nuys. By day, he wrote songs, sang demos for music publishers and hawked his songs to recording studios, producers and record labels.

Mercury Records signed him in the early '60s and released an unsuccessful single, "Donna," under the pseudonym Johnny Niles. He switched over to Capitol, where he recorded more solo singles and sang lead with the New Salvation Singers.

The first song Nilsson ever sold was cowritten with Scott Turner. Entitled "Travelin' Man" (not the Ricky Nelson song), Harry sold it to Randy Sparks and the New Christy Minstrels for five dollars. Harry's big break came when Phil Spector gave two of his songs ("Paradise," "Here I Sit") to the Ronettes and one ("This Could Be the Night") to the Modern Folk Quartet. With a nod from a powerful producer like Spector, the floodgates opened and Harry Nilsson, the songwriter, was in demand.

Harry's writing credits showed up on albums by the Turtles; Rick Nelson; Lulu; Blood, Sweat and Tears; and Mary Hopkin. The bank lost Harry to music forever the day he turned on the radio and heard the Monkees sing his song "Cuddly Toy."

Nilsson signed with RCA in 1967 and recorded his first album, *Pandemonium Shadow Show*, which included cover versions of the Beatles' "You Can't Do That" and "She's Leaving Home." John Lennon heard the LP and dubbed Nilsson his "favorite American singer." In fact, Nilsson developed a close friendship

with John, who produced Harry's 1974 *Pussy Cats* album. Nilsson would also become best buddies with Ringo Starr, and together they produced a 1974 film and soundtrack called *Son of Dracula*.

In 1968 Otto Preminger asked Nilsson to write the score for *Skidoo*, a film starring Jackie Gleason and Carol Channing. Harry's growing reputation as a songwriter took a quantum leap a year later when Three Dog Night [see 277—"Mama Told Me (Not to Come)"] took his song "One" to number five in June. Two months later, Nilsson had his first chart hit on his own—with a song written by Fred Neil. "Everybody's Talkin'," recorded on Nilsson's second album *Aerial Ballet*, went to number six, thanks to its inclusion in the soundtrack of *Midnight Cowboy*. Nilsson had submitted his own song for the Dustin Hoffman-Jon Voigt film, but the producers preferred the Neil tune. Undaunted, Harry

released "I Guess the Lord Must Be in New York City" as his second single, and it peaked at 34 in November, 1969.

Harry diversified, writing the music for Bill Bixby's "The Courtship of Eddie's Father" series (including the theme, "Best Friend"), and the story and score for an animated television special, "The Point." That soundtrack yielded Harry's third chart single, "Me and My Arrow," number 34 in May, 1971.

Gathering material for his *Nilsson Schmilsson* album, Harry was listening to records and having more than his share to drink at a friend's house when he heard "Without You" for the first time. "After sobering up the next day, I said, 'What was that Lennon tune we were listening to last night?' " Nilsson told Dick Clark in an interview for his syndicated "Rock, Roll and Remember" radio series. "We went through a bunch of (Beatles) albums and couldn't find it. Finally I said, 'No! It wasn't the Beatles. It was another group. It was Grapefruit or something.' We finally looked and we realized it was Badfinger—Pete Ham and Tom Evans. I took it to Richard Perry and said, 'I think this should be a number one hit.' I wish I had written it, in a way. But then again, it's not what I write."

Tragically, Ham committed suicide in 1975, as did Evans eight years later. Nilsson suffered from diabetes, and his health declined after a heart attack on Valentine's Day of 1993. He died in his sleep at his home in Southern California on January 15, 1994, at the age of 52. Two days earlier, he had finished recording his first new album since 1976.

## THE TOP FIVE
*Week of February 19, 1972*

1 **Without You**
  Nilsson

2 **Let's Stay Together**
  Al Green

3 **Hurting Each Other**
  Carpenters

4 **Precious and Few**
  Climax

5 **Never Been to Spain**
  Three Dog Night

## 308 Heart of Gold REPRISE 1065
### NEIL YOUNG

*Writer: Neil Young*

*Producers: Elliot Mazer*
*Neil Young*

*March 18, 1972*
*1 week*

In 1972, rock superstar Neil Young went "searchin' for a heart of gold." What he found at the end of the trail was a chart-topping single, his only solo 45 to penetrate the top 30.

One of pop music's most acclaimed and enigmatic performers, Neil Young (born November 12, 1945, in Toronto, Canada) played in several rock bands while still in high school in Winnipeg. He returned to Toronto in the '60s, where he met Stephen Stills and Richie Furay. With Rick James ("Super Freak," "Give It to Me Baby"), Young formed a band called the Mynah Birds. When they split up, Young headed for California with the group's bassist, Bruce Palmer. Reunited with Stills and Furay in Los Angeles, they organized Buffalo Springfield, a west coast band (also including drummer Dewey Martin) that successfully blended the best elements of folk, rock and country.

With the Springfield, Young showed himself to be a singer/song-writer of considerable prowess, contributing such memorable tunes as

"Broken Arrow," "Mr. Soul" and "I Am a Child." One of the keys to the band's success was having five strongly-willed individuals—which also led to its demise. After coping with the conflicts inherent in group recording, Young resolved to work alone. But Stephen Stills had joined ex-Byrd David Crosby and ex-Hollie Graham Nash in a superstar trio, and by 1970 Young was lured into adding his name to the corporation: Crosby, Stills, Nash and Young.

After charting with singles like "Woodstock" (number 11) and "Teach Your Children" (number 16), the quartet broke up in 1971. Young once again embarked on an unpredictable career as a single artist, often backed by Crazy Horse. Young's first three solo albums provided FM radio with some of the early '70s' most unforgettable anthems of love, innocence and alienation—"The Loner," "Sugar Mountain," "Cinnamon Girl" and "Everybody Knows This Is Nowhere."

Young once described his music as being about "the frustrations of not being able to attain what you want." "Heart of Gold," culled from his fourth solo album, *Harvest*, is a perfect expression of the brooding, idiosyncratic artist at the height of his quest.

"I was in and out of hospitals for

the two years betwen *After the Gold Rush* (his third LP) and *Harvest*," Young told *Rolling Stone* in 1975. "I have one weak side and all the muscles slipped on me. . . . I recorded most of *Harvest* in a brace. That's a lot of the reason it's such a mellow album. I couldn't physically play an electric guitar."

Recorded in 1971 in Nashville, "Heart of Gold" featured back-up vocals by Linda Ronstadt and James Taylor. A reflection of those unsettled times, the single entered the Hot 100 at number 62 on February 5, 1972. Six weeks later it was number one.

Not that Young, whom critic John Rockwell once called "the quintessential hippie-cowboy loner," exactly felt at home in such a lofty position. As he put it in his notes for his 1977 retrospective LP *Decade*, "This song put me in the middle of the road. Travelling there soon became a bore so I headed for the ditch. A rougher ride but I saw more interesting people there."

Actually, "Heart of Gold" was never intended for single release. "We went into the studio to cut the album," Young told Ray Coleman of *Melody Maker*, "and I guess we were hot that night and it was a good cut but it's gone now. I've seen a few artists who've got hung up on the singles market when they've really been albums people. . . . It's easy to do, but if you're wise, you stay with being what you really are. . . . I just hope there is not a single off my next album."

With typical irony, he once told *Rolling Stone*, "One day Neil Young will write a happy song. But I'll probably sell it to TV for a commercial."

## THE TOP FIVE
*Week of March 18, 1972*

1 **Heart of Gold**
Neil Young

2 **A Horse With No Name**
America

3 **Lion Sleeps Tonight**
Robert John

4 **Without You**
Nilsson

5 **Everything I Own**
Bread

WARNER BROTHERS 7555 **A Horse With No Name**
AMERICA
**309**

*Writer: Dewey Bunnell*

*Producer: Ian Samwell*

*March 25, 1972*
*3 weeks*

Gerry Beckley, Dewey Bunnell. and Dan Peek were all sons of American military personnel based in England when they met at London's Central High School in Bushey Park. The school was primarily for children of military families, although there were children who had parents employed by private corporations as well as the American embassy. Gerry, Dewey and Dan were all interested in music and had played in various other bands before forming a five-man unit called the Daze.

Gerry, born in Texas, started playing the piano when he was three years old. A year later he started taking lessons, but as his father was transferred so often, he had a number of teachers over the next six years. At 15, he started playing bass in school bands. One of his groups won a talent contest and was rewarded with a recording session.

While Gerry was off recording, Dan's father found jobs for Dan and Dewey in the cafeteria on base. Before forming the Daze, the three would-be musicians also worked in a tire warehouse and a storage area, operating forklifts.

Gerry's father was the commanding officer at the base and he handed the three boys their high school diplomas in 1969. Dan took off for college but returned a year later. With two members from the Daze departed, the three friends decided to put together an acoustic trio. They wrote their own songs and eventually auditioned for Jeff Dexter, a concert promoter who ran a popular London club called the Roundhouse. He liked the group and booked them as the opening act for many of the headliners who played at the venue, including Pink Floyd [see 523—"Another Brick in the Wall"].

Legend says the trio picked their name from an Americana-brand jukebox in a London pub. But the name America meant more than the logo on a jukebox to them, it was their homeland—even if it was a place they hadn't lived in for very long.

Dexter's friend Ian Samwell was a staff producer at the London office of Warner Brothers Records and he beat out offers from Atlantic and DJM Records to sign the group. By the time they recorded their first album, they were well-known in London for their Roundhouse appearances, but complete unknowns in America.

They finished recording their first LP and couldn't decide what the first single should be. Gerry's composition "I Need You" seemed to be first choice but before it could be released they went back into the studio and recorded one more song. Written by Dewey, it was inspired by a homesickness for America and the desert countryside he remembered when he lived briefly at Vandenberg Air Force base near San Luis Obispo, California. The song was "A Horse With No Name."

Released in America, the song entered the Hot 100 on February 19, 1972, at number 84. As it moved up the chart, the group came home to America for the first time in many years and toured as the opening act for the Everly Brothers [see 28—"Wake Up Little Susie"], one of the sources of inspiration for America's own harmonies. They finished the tour in Los Angeles and returned to Britain before "A Horse With No Name" went to number one on March 25, 1972.

## THE TOP FIVE
*Week of March 25, 1972*

1 **A Horse With No Name**
America

2 **Heart of Gold**
Neil Young

3 **Lion Sleeps Tonight**
Robert John

4 **Puppy Love**
Donny Osmond

5 **Mother and Child Reunion**
Paul Simon

## 310 The First Time Ever I Saw Your Face ATLANTIC 2864
### ROBERTA FLACK

Writer: Ewan MacColl

Producer: Joel Dorn

April 15, 1972
6 weeks

SOME SONGS are instant hits and others take time—years, in some cases, to prove their full potential. "The First Time Ever I Saw Your Face" belongs to the latter category. It was one of eight songs recorded in 10 hours by a newly-signed recording artist for her 1969 disc debut, giving literal interpretation to the album's title, *First Take*. But Roberta Flack had no trouble giving a perfect presentation of the folk tune (written by Ewan MacColl for his wife, Peggy, sister of Pete Seeger), since it was one the pianist/singer performed regularly in a Washington, D.C., restaurant during Sunday afternoon brunches.

Three years and two albums later, Clint Eastwood was filming a suspense thriller about a disc jockey, set at the Monterey Jazz Festival. When he wanted to underscore a particularly romantic scene with Donna Mills in *Play Misty for Me*, he remembered the slow, majestic fire of the song and phoned Flack for permission to include it in the movie. Film fans ran from theaters to record

stores asking for the song, which Atlantic quickly rushed into their hands after slicing 66 seconds from its five minute, 21 second length to accommodate top 40 radio airplay. At 33 years old, after being involved with music for 24 years, Roberta Flack scored her first commercial success.

"The First Time Ever I Saw Your Face" debuted on the Hot 100 at number 77 on March 4, 1972, and took just six weeks to sail to number one. It remained there for six weeks, the longest-running chart-topper by a solo female artist since "The Wayward Wind" by Gogi Grant in 1956 [see 11]. Roberta Flack was born February 10, 1939, in Asheville, North Carolina. By the time she was four, her parents, two sisters, brother, grandmother, aunt and uncle had relocated to a two-bedroom basement apartment in Arlington, Virginia, not far from the nation's capital. Papa Loren was a draftsman while mama Irene worked as a cook, domestic and organist at the African Methodist Episcopal Zion Church. When Irene fell ill, 13-year-old Roberta took over for her, receiving four dollars a month to play behind the choir. That same year, Roberta took second place honors in a statewide piano contest, having developed her keyboard prow-

ess on a lime green upright her dad rescued from a junkyard.

Skipping several grade levels, the prodigy won a scholarship to Howard University, entering at 15 years old to study piano and voice. "I thought I was gonna be the first short black concert pianist," the 5'2" Flack told *Rolling Stone*.

Switching to music education, she graduated in three years to teach in an all-black Farmville, North Carolina, school. "I was hired to teach English literature and I ended up having to teach basic grammar to twelfth graders," she grimaced in the *Washingtonian*. Her other subjects were math and, of course, music. After a year she entered the Washington school system and, in 1962, began moonlighting at Georgetown's Tivoli restaurant, playing for the opera singers who congregated there.

It was at a benefit that jazz maestro Les McCann saw Flack and was stunned by the performance. "Her voice touched, tapped, trapped and kicked over every emotion I've ever known," he remembered on the liner notes for *Quiet Fire*. Signed to Atlantic himself, he telephoned label chief Ahmet Ertegun and producer Joel Dorn to arrange an audition. Roberta arrived with 600 songs under her arm, played 42 of them in three hours and laid down 39 song demos in nine hours of studio time. Her reward was a year's contract and, later on, a win for herself and songwriter MacColl when "The First Time Ever I Saw Your Face" won Grammys for Record of the Year and Song of the Year.

### THE TOP FIVE
*Week of April 15, 1972*

1  **The First Time Ever
   I Saw Your Face**
   Roberta Flack

2  **A Horse With No Name**
   America

3  **I Gotcha**
   Joe Tex

4  **Rockin' Robin**
   Michael Jackson

5  **Heart of Gold**
   Neil Young

*Writer: Eugene Record*

*Producer: Eugene Record*

*May 27, 1972*
*1 week*

THE CHI-LITES waited patiently for 12 years to get a number one single on the Hot 100. The group was formed as a quintet in 1960 by Marshall Thompson, a Chicago native who had played drums at the Regal Theater for artists like Major Lance, the Dells and the Flamingos. Thompson and group member Creadel Jones had sung together in a local outfit, the Desideros. The other three members—Eugene Record, Clarence Johnson and Robert "Squirrel" Lester—had been part of another vocal group, the Chantours.

The five men took the name Hi-Lites and signed with Mercury, where a single called "Pots and Pans" failed to clean up. They lost their label deal and their name—another group had claim to it first. "We figured that if we added a 'C' to the front of our name that'd give us an original name *and* identify us from coming from Chicago," Thompson told one writer.

As Marshall and the Chi-Lites, they recorded for James Shelton, Jr.'s Daran and Ja-Wes labels and developed a following in the Windy City. Re-signed to Mercury, they released two singles on the Blue Rock subsidiary—and were dropped again. In 1967, the group signed with the Dakar production company, which secured a deal with MCA. Changing their name permanently to just the Chi-Lites, they made the Hot 100 for the first time in the spring of 1969 with "Give It Away," on MCA's Brunswick label.

Thompson recalled, "1969 was when we first made it....We went and bought some new suits, went out on

the road. All of a sudden a record company was interested in us. Eugene was getting some big successes (writing for fellow Brunswick artist Barbara Acklin). Eugene was always a good writer. Some of the things we record now he wrote years ago when he was a nobody."

As the group's falsetto-voiced lead singer and astute producer, Record gave the Chi-Lites a romantic sound that critic Vince Aletti dubbed "neo-classical." Record also supplied them with a series of sweetly soulful hits that made the bottom third of the Hot 100: "Let Me Be the Man My Daddy Was," "I Like Your Lovin' (Do You Like Mine)" and "Are You My Woman (Tell Me So)."

But the Chi-Lites still wanted a major crossover hit to establish the group as stars in the pop market. "We all figured that we needed to

### THE TOP FIVE
*Week of May 27, 1972*

1 **Oh Girl**
Chi-Lites

2 **I'll Take You There**
Staple Singers

3 **The First Time Ever
I Saw Your Face**
Roberta Flack

4 **Look What You Done For Me**
Al Green

5 **Candy Man**
Sammy Davis Jr.

broaden our sound," said Thompson. "Up until then we'd choose mainly ballads. Sweet things. There was a lot of unrest and injustice in the world and we all felt that artists couldn't ignore that situation and just sing about love. So Eugene wrote this uptempo number called '(For God's Sake) Give More Power to the People'. . . . We *knew* it'd be a big one."

And they were right. It peaked at number 26 in May, 1971. Just six months later they topped it with a return to their familiar sentimental turf. "Have You Seen Her" soared to number three. Then "I Want to Pay You Back (For Loving Me)" hiccoughed at 95, but their next release was "Oh Girl," a beautiful tune which, through skillful production and Record's memorable vocalizing, touched a universal chord. Wrote critic Joe McEwen, "The Chi-Lites stark portrait of excessive male vulnerability was unlike that of even the Moments and Delfonics, two other groups who exercised melancholy with great effect. Record highlighted his thin tenor with the most plainting production techniques: a forlorn harmonica on 'Oh Girl,' windstorms on '(The) Coldest Days of My Life.' While this type of pathos was occasionally overwrought, often it was quite dramatic and effective . . ."

The Chi-Lites only had one more top 30 hit after "Oh Girl." The joyous "Stoned Out of My Mind" (on love, of course) squeaked in to number 30 in the fall of 1973. Three years later, Record left the group temporarily for a solo career on Warner Brothers Records. He returned and worked with the group as they recorded for Chi-Sound and Private I Records.

### 312

# I'll Take You There   STAX 0125
## THE STAPLE SINGERS

*Writer: Alvertis Isbell*

*Producer: Al Bell*

*June 3, 1972*
*1 week*

Roebuck "Pop" Staples hails from the rural, blues-rooted Mississippi delta. During the depression, he moved to Chicago with his wife Oceola, where by days he worked in a steel mill and at night sang gospel with his musically gifted family. In the early '50s, Pop officially organized the Staples Singers, which featured son Pervis (who would leave the group in 1971) and daughters Cleo, Mavis and Yvonne, with the patriarch himself accompanying them on guitar.

Eventually the Staples—sparked by Mavis' spirit-lifting lead vocals—became headliners on the gospel music circuit. "At that time gospel music was much more popular than it is today," Mavis told Vernon Gibbs in *Essence* magazine, "and we would appear with eight or ten other gospel acts. We could easily fill a 10,000-seat auditorium or armory doing two shows a day, especially in the South."

In the mid-'50s, the Staples Singers began recording traditional gospel music, first for the small United label and then for Chicago-based Vee Jay Records, which released the gospel smash, "Uncloudy Day." Pop experimented with a secular, soul-oriented sound, and in June, 1967, the Staples had their first Hot 100 record, "Why? (Am I Treated So Bad)," which lasted

## THE TOP FIVE
### Week of June 3, 1972

1  **I'll Take You There**
   Staple Singers

2  **Oh Girl**
   Chi-Lites

3  **The First Time Ever
   I Saw Your Face**
   Roberta Flack

4  **Candy Man**
   Sammy Davis Jr.

5  **Sylvia's Mother**
   Dr. Hook and the
   Medicine Show

just one week on the chart, at number 95. Signed to Epic Records, they also recorded cover versions of Bob Dylan and Woody Guthrie songs, and did a dynamite rendition of Buffalo Springfield's "For What It's Worth."

Critics screamed "sell out," but Pop insisted to Gibbs, "We didn't do it for the money. Since we made the move, a lot of groups have come up to us and said, 'I'm going to do the same thing you did and get me some of that rock money.' But what usually happens is that they can't make it in the pop field, and they can't go back to the church circuit. Once you leave the church, you can't go back..."

In keeping with the changing times, the Staples sang about peace on Earth and the sanctifying power of universal love. "We always tried to do material that was inspirational and uplifting in addition to whatever else it was," Pop said in *Essence*, "and I guess the deejays picked up on that. We were accepted for that, and even after we started doing material that wasn't strictly gospel, we've always tried to make music that is affirmative, happy music that makes a positive point. Our aim is to get across a message while we're entertaining people. We want people to

enjoy the music, but we also want them to hear the lyrics and hear our message—love."

The family made an important move in July, 1968—they signed with Memphis-based Stax Records.

Steve Cropper was their first Stax producer, and he gave them a number 27 hit in April, 1971, with "Heavy Makes You Happy (Sha-Na-Boom Boom)," written by Jeff Barry and the late Bobby Bloom. Bell produced the album *Be Altitude: Respect Yourself*. It was the title track, "Respect Yourself," that was the real breakthrough for the Staple (the final 's' was long gone) Singers. It peaked at number 12 in December, 1971.

The second single from the album took them to the pinnacle of the pop chart. "I'll Take You There" made its first appearance on the Hot 100 at number 63 on April 8, 1972, and became the group's first number one single eight weeks later.

It had been a long, hard climb from the Mississippi delta to the top of the chart. But Pop kept it all in perspective and never forgot for an instant who made it happen. "It pleased God to put a guitar in my hands and a song on the lips of my children," he said, "and we aim to please God through our music."

MGM 14320 **Candy Man**  **313**
SAMMY DAVIS, JR

*Writers: Anthony Newley*
*Leslie Bricusse*

*Producers: Mike Curb*
*Don Costa*

*June 10, 1972*
*3 weeks*

"CANDY MAN" was the first song heard in the children's musical *Willie Wonka and the Chocolate Factory*, a 1971 motion picture directed by Mel Stuart from a script by Roald Dahl, based on his novel *Charlie and the Chocolate Factory*. Gene Wilder starred as the eccentric owner of a candy factory who devises a scheme to find an honest, loving child to take over his work.

The musical score for the film was written by Anthony Newley and Leslie Bricusse, long-time collaborators whose credits included the Broadway shows *Stop the World, I Want to Get Off* and *The Roar of the Greasepaint–The Smell of the Crowd*. They also wrote the lyrics for John Barry's "Goldfinger," and Newley had written the music for the autobiographical motion picture *Can Heironymus Merkin Ever Forget Mercy Humppe and Find True Happiness?*, in which he starred with his ex-wife, Joan Collins.

The song "Candy Man" is sung in *Willie Wonka and the Chocolate Factory* by Aubrey Woods, who plays Bill, a candy store owner who sells sweets to neighborhood children. Newley was so appalled at his singing, he offered to play the role himself if producers Stan Margulies and David Wolper would re-shoot the

scene. They declined and Newley was convinced the song would never become a hit because of what he considered to be a dreadful performance in the film.

Newley hadn't counted on Mike Curb, president of MGM Records, coming up with the idea of recording the song with Sammy Davis, Jr. Two of Davis' biggest hits in the rock era had come from Broadway shows: "I've Gotta Be Me" was from *Golden Rainbow* and "What Kind of Fool Am I?" was from Newley and Bricusse's *Stop the World.*

Curb and Don Costa produced an instrumental track and asked Davis to sing the vocal. He disliked the song at first, according to Newley, but consented to record it anyway. The result was not the kind of song top 40 radio usually played. In fact, many rock stations refused to play the song at all, and "Candy Man" made it to number one based on heavy airplay from stations that featured what is now known as "adult contemporary" music—or "easy listening," as it was labelled in 1972.

"Candy Man" is the biggest pop hit of Davis' multi-faceted career. He was born December 8, 1925, in New York City. His parents were vaudeville performers in his uncle Will

Mastin's "Holiday in Dixieland," and by the time he was four years old, Sammy was performing with his uncle and father in the Will Mastin Trio.

Sammy was a regular nightclub performer until 1943, when he entered the Army. During World War II he was a member of the special services unit, producing shows and performing. When he returned to civilian life, he rejoined the family act. They opened at Slapsie Maxie's in Hollywood in April, 1946. The act played Las Vegas, Chicago and the Copa in New York. In 1954, Sammy signed a recording contract with Decca. On November 11 of that year, he was driving from Las Vegas to Los Angeles for a recording session when he was involved in an automobile accident, resulting in the loss of one eye.

His acting talents came to the fore in the 1950s. He was cast in the lead of *Mr. Wonderful* on Broadway, a role which led to film work. He starred in *Anna Lucasta* with Eartha Kitt and made a series of films with the "rat pack" of Frank Sinatra [see 202—"Strangers in the Night"], Dean Martin [see 6—"Memories Are Made of This"], Peter Lawford and Joey Bishop. These included *Oceans 11, Sergeants Three* and *Robin and the Seven Hoods.* Sinatra started his own label, Reprise, in 1961 and signed Davis as his first artist.

Sammy appeared on many television variety series and guest starred in episodes of "Ben Casey," "The Rifleman" and "Lawman." In 1966, he had his own variety series on NBC, "The Sammy Davis, Jr., Show." Because of a prior contract with ABC, he couldn't appear in three segments of his own series. He was a regular performer on "NBC Follies," a musical variety series that lasted for four months in 1973 and starred in a comedy-drama movie for television, "Poor Devil." From 1975-1977 he hosted his own talk show, "Sammy and Company." He has also been a guest star in situation comedies, most notably "All in the Family," "Diff'rent Strokes" and "Gimme a Break."

Davis died of throat cancer on May 16, 1990. He was 64 years old. Quincy Jones wrote a moving tribute to the performer, published the following month in *Rolling Stone.*

## THE TOP FIVE
*Week of June 10, 1972*

1 **Candy Man**
   Sammy Davis Jr.

2 **I'll Take You There**
   Staple Singers

3 **Oh Girl**
   Chi-Lites

4 **Song Sung Blue**
   Neil Diamond

5 **Sylvia's Mother**
   Dr. Hook and the
   Medicine Show

## 314 Song Sung Blue UNI 55326
### NEIL DIAMOND

*Writer: Neil Diamond*

*Producers: Tom Catalano*
*Neil Diamond*

*July 1, 1972*
*1 week*

WHEN Neil Diamond sang "Song Sung Blue" on his February 21, 1977, NBC-TV special, he invited celebrity members of the audience up on stage to join in for some of the choruses. Helen Reddy [see 324—"I Am Woman"] did just fine but Henry Winkler choked up until Diamond suggested he get into character and sing it as the Fonz. One vocalist had to be edited out of the telecast: Mayor Tom Bradley of Los Angeles was running for re-election at the time, prompting the network to be concerned about giving his opponents equal time.

The NBC special had been taped at Diamond's September, 1976, concerts at the Greek Theatre in Los Angeles, scene of his triumphant *Hot August Night* live album in 1972. Lee Margulies of the *Los Angeles Times* called the special "a smashing bit of television, full of exuberance."

The 1976 Greek Theatre concerts where the special was taped were part of a return to live performing for Diamond. The famed "Hot August Nights" concerts, taped just one month after "Song Song Blue" topped the Hot 100, were followed by a 20-concert stand at the Winter Garden Theatre in New York. At the end of that run, Diamond announced he was taking a leave of absence from performing.

"I felt strongly about taking a sabbatical," Diamond told Barbra Zuanich of the *Los Angeles Herald-Examiner*. "I wanted a normal human existence. I wanted to remove myself from celebrity status...to do things people take for granted, like driving my son to school and having breakfast with my wife. I wanted to re-establish personal relationships with family and friends...to be home for birthdays and Christmas. To make up for times I wasn't around...to stop seeing my life as a juggling act."

As it turned out, the sabbatical lasted 40 months, finally broken by his first-ever concerts in Australia and New Zealand. Back home in the United States, he opened the $10 million Aladdin Theater for the Performing Arts in Las Vegas on July 4, 1976.

"I had secretly hoped when I finished at the Winter Garden that I would never have to come back and perform," Diamond said in an interview with Robert Hilburn of the *Los Angeles Times*. "I was exhausted. But then I got itchy about wanting to be in front of an audience again. I wanted to test myself again. Besides, being on stage is a real upper."

Diamond followed "Song Sung Blue" with two top 20 hits on Uni, "Play Me" and "Walk on Water." Uni was short for Universal and at the end of 1972 the label identity was dropped, along with Decca and Kapp, in favor of an MCA label. Diamond had two more uneventful singles on MCA, then left the company for a five million dollar contract with Columbia Records.

His first two singles for Columbia were from his score for the motion picture *Jonathan Livingston Seagull*. Neither "Be" nor "Skybird" are among Diamond's most memorable hits. His third Columbia single, "Longfellow Serenade," went to number five.

Ironically, his best run of hits would be released on Capitol, the label that issued the soundtrack for *The Jazz Singer*, a 1980 release starring Diamond and featuring his music. Neil had three consecutive top 10 hits from the film: "Love on the Rocks" (number two for three weeks), "Hello Again" (number six) and "America" (number eight).

### THE TOP FIVE
*Week of July 1, 1972*

1  **Song Sung Blue**
   Neil Diamond

2  **Candy Man**
   Sammy Davis Jr.

3  **Outa-Space**
   Billy Preston

4  **Lean on Me**
   Bill Withers

5  **Too Late to Turn Back Now**
   Cornelius Brothers & Sister Rose

*Writer: Bill Withers*

*Producer: Bill Withers*

*July 8, 1972*
*3 weeks*

BILL WITHERS was a musical late bloomer. He didn't start singing professionally until he was 32, and when he signed his first record contract, he was manufacturing toilet seats for Boeing 747s.

Withers was born July 4, 1938, in the small mining town of Slab Fork, West Virginia. He was the youngest of six children and his father died when he was very young. Raised by his mother and grandmother, Bill dropped out of school after he finished the ninth grade.

He spent nine years in the Navy, where he underwent speech therapy to overcome a stuttering problem. After his discharge, he delivered milk, then worked for the Ford Motor Company and IBM. In his spare time, he wrote songs. By 1967, he was confident enough in his ability as a songwriter to move to Los Angeles and record some demo tracks. He was only earning about $3.50 an hour working for Lockheed Aircraft but he spent $2,500 to make the demos. Despite his heavy investment, not one record company or publisher expressed any interest. Bill didn't give up his day job—in fact, it was at this point that he started manufacturing toilet seats for 747s.

He took up guitar at this time and in early 1970, Clarence Avent of Sussex Records introduced Withers to Booker T. Jones, leader of the famed Memphis group Booker T. and the M.G.'S ("Green Onions, "Time Is Tight"). Withers wrote new material and Booker T. produced an album, *Just as I Am*, for Sussex. Playing lead guitar on the album was Stephen Stills.

The first single from the LP, "Ain't No Sunshine," went to number three in September, 1971, and won a Grammy for Best R&B Song. Next came "Grandma's Hands," which was a mid-chart record at number 42. In 1972, Withers recorded a second album, *Still Bill*, which included "Lean on Me." He was still working in the aircraft factory when he wrote the song, and claims the friendships he formed there and the willingness

of his co-workers to help each other out were direct inspiration for the song.

"I had a rural background and an urban international adulthood," Bill has said, explaining why his songs were so popular.

In Britain, other artists were more successful with his songs. "Ain't No Sunshine" was a U.K. hit for Michael Jackson, who took it to number eight in 1972. Although Withers' version of "Lean on Me" charted at number 18, it was a bigger hit by the pop group Mud, peaking at number seven in 1976. It was an even bigger hit in 1987 for Club Nouveau [see 662], who went to number three in the British chart with their updated version. In America, Club Nouveau's single topped the Hot 100, making "Lean on Me" the fourth song in the rock era to be taken to number one by two different artists.

Withers had one more big hit on Sussex, "Use Me," which spent two weeks at number two in the fall of 1972. Subsequent Sussex singles failed to make the top 30, and Bill ended up in a legal dispute with the label. "This kind of legal hassle, if it drags on, can really stop you musically," Withers told Dennis Hunt of the *Los Angeles Times* in 1975. "I have to compose before I record and I have a very hard time being creative when I'm worried about bus-

iness problems. That's the way I am.

"In order to write, you have to be vulnerable and open. I haven't been vulnerable often in the last few years. The part of my mind I write with has been closed off a lot of the time. If you're paranoid you don't write much because all you can think about is what's making you paranoid."

Withers also discussed his late acceptance of himself as a singer with Hunt: "Not too long ago, I admitted to myself for the first time that I am a singer and a person who makes music. For a long time I didn't really accept my new career. It was like I was on vacation from the factory and at some point I would have to take my tool box and go back to work."

Withers, who married actress Denise Nicholas, eventually signed with Columbia Records. That company bought his old masters when Sussex folded. His only hit single for his new label was "Lovely Day," which went to number 30 in early 1978. Three years later, Bill sang lead vocal on "Just the Two of Us," a Grover Washington, Jr., single that spent three weeks at number two.

Withers put his career in perspective in an interview with Leonard Feather of the *Los Angeles Times*: "When I was repairing airplanes, that was a vital gig, because you can lose a lot of lives if that job isn't done properly. Even when I was working on bathroom seats, this was at least constructive. I challenge anybody: I won't sing for a month and you don't go to the bathroom for a month and let's see...who comes off with less misery."

## THE TOP FIVE
*Week of July 8, 1972*

1 **Lean on Me**
Bill Withers

2 **Outa-Space**
Billy Preston

3 **Song Sung Blue**
Neil Diamond

4 **Too Late to Turn Back Now**
Cornelius Brothers & Sister Rose

5 **Candy Man**
Sammy Davis Jr.

# 316  Alone Again (Naturally)  MAM 3619
## GILBERT O'SULLIVAN

*Writer: Gilbert O'Sullivan*

*Producer: Gordon Mills*

*July 29, 1972*
*6 weeks*

"ALONE AGAIN (NATURALLY)" was such a convincing song, it was widely assumed that it was the story of Gilbert O'Sullivan's life. Not so, says the Irish born singer. "None of the situations in the song ever happened to me," he told Paul Gambaccini in a 1973 *Rolling Stone* interview. "I've never been stood up at a church because I've never gotten close to getting married. My father is dead, but I didn't cry when he died. I distinctively remember that because I was the only one in the family who didn't. I was never close to him. And my mother I love very much, but she's not dead."

Raymond Edward O'Sullivan was born in Waterford in the republic of Ireland. When he was 13, his family moved to Swindon, England. He attended art college, where he was a member of two bands, the Doodles and the Prefects. Influenced by the Beatles as much as Cole Porter, he started writing his own songs. He had a choice of going into graphic design or pursuing a career in music, but the decision was easy for him.

It's unlikely anyone thought he was really named Gilbert O'Sullivan, but there were people who assumed he picked the name himself. "My name is still Ray O'Sullivan," he told Gambaccini. "I would never change my name to Gilbert. No way. I don't

like it. I couldn't be a Gilbert."

The man who did change it was Gordon Mills, the consummate manager who transformed a Welsh rocker going under the name Tommy Scott into an international star named Tom Jones, and a singer from Leicester, England, named Arnold George Dorsey into a suave balladeer known as Engelbert Humperdinck.

Mills, a former Welsh harmonica champion, built a $40 million empire around Jones and Humperdinck. O'Sullivan sent Mills a demo tape and a photograph of himself, dressed in knee-length trousers, a waistcoat, hob-nail boots and a funny cap that only partially hid his punchbowl haircut. It was a photo designed to attract attention and it worked. Later, O'Sullivan admitted he would have shaved his head bald if that's what it would have taken to interest a manager of Mills' stature.

Mills liked the songs and his curiosity was aroused by the strangely-dressed singer. "I couldn't believe it," Mills told *Time*. "He looked like a young Charlie Chaplin." Mills signed him and changed his name from Raymond to Gilbert. He allowed his new client to retain his Chaplinesque image for his first British album, but

when "Alone Again (Naturally)" entered the Hot 100 on June 17, 1972, Mills decided O'Sullivan needed a better image for America.

As the song went to number one on July 29 (it had peaked at three in the United Kingdom), Gilbert O'Sullivan was appearing on American television in his new get-up, a preppy look highlighted by a collegiate sweater with a big "G" on the front. "A college sweater can be sexy," Mills told *Time*. "It hugs the shoulders."

O'Sullivan quickly followed "Alone Again (Naturally)" with a song written about Mills' youngest daughter, "Clair." It went to number two in America and number one in Britain. "Out of the Question" only went to 17, followed by "Get Down," number seven in America and number one in Britain. His last Hot 100 entry was "Happiness Is Me and You" in the spring of 1974. O'Sullivan continued to be managed by Mills until a legal dispute found them suing each other. In 1982, a British court ruled in favor of O'Sullivan, finding he had not received all the income he had earned. By this time, O'Sullivan was signed with Epic Records and had reached the British top 20 with a 1980 single, "What's in a Kiss?"

## THE TOP FIVE
*Week of July 29, 1972*

1  **Alone Again (Naturally)**
   Gilbert O'Sullivan

2  **Brandy (You're a Fine Girl)**
   Looking Glass

3  **Too Late to Turn Back Now**
   Cornelius Brothers & Sister Rose

4  **(If Loving You is Wrong)**
   **I Don't Want to be Right**
   Luther Ingram

5  **Daddy, Don't You**
   **Walk So Fast**
   Wayne Newton

*Writer: Elliot Lurie*

*Producers: Mike Gershman*
*Bob Liftin*
*Looking Glass*

*August 26, 1972*
*1 week*

"**I** HAD a high school sweetheart named Randy," says the leader of Looking Glass, Elliott Lurie (born August 19, 1948, in Brooklyn, New York). "When I was free-associating with the lyric, that came in, but it never sang as well as Brandy. So we changed it quickly."

Lead guitarist/singer Lurie, keyboards player Larry Gonksy and bassist Pieter Sweval met as students at New Jersey's Rutgers University in the late '60s and formed the nucleus of the original Looking Glass. They were a hard-rocking outfit playing frat parties and beer joints, and they struggled to keep themselves afloat after graduation.

But the lack of work forced the young musicians to disband after a year. Lurie and Gonsky went on to play in a group called Fake Fun, while Sweval and drummer Jeffrey Grob formed a band called Tracks. "Then after a few months," Lurie recalls, "the original guys got back together. We decided we were going to give a real try at writing material and getting a recording contract.

"All of us rented a big old farmhouse in Western New Jersey," he continues. "We rehearsed there, continued playing bars and did showcases in Manhattan." After nearly two years of continued efforts, however, Looking Glass still found

## THE TOP FIVE
*Week of August 26, 1972*

1 **Brandy (You're a Fine Girl)**
Looking Glass

2 **Alone Again (Naturally)**
Gilbert O'Sullivan

3 **Long Cool Woman**
Hollies

4 **I'm Still in Love With You**
Al Green

5 **Hold Your Head Up**
Argent

itself stuck as a bar band in the hinderlands. Then a mutual friend introduced them to manager Mike Gershman, who liked what he heard and set up a showcase performance for CBS Records President Clive Davis. "We played at the old Cafe a Go Go," says Lurie, "and Clive Davis liked the show—and especially liked 'Brandy.' " Davis signed the group to Epic Records.

Various producers, including Booker T. and the M.G.s' guitar whiz Steve Cropper, took a shot at producing Looking Glass, but nothing clicked until the band and Gershman decided to produce themselves. The first piece of material they worked on was Lurie's composition, "Brandy (You're a Fine Girl)."

" 'Brandy' was one of the songs that I wrote at the farm," says Lurie. "While I was working on it, everything was not in place and Larry Gonsky and I decided that it was really worth finishing. So he would continually play it for me and I would try and fill in the remaining lyric.

"Sandy Linzer originally produced the rhythm track on 'Brandy' and helped arrange it, but we parted ways . . . because we considered his approach a little too 'bubble-gum' for our tastes. So we re-recorded the song with engineer Bob Liftin (owner of New York's Regent Sound Studios)."

Harv Moore of radio station WPGC in Washington, D.C., broke "Brandy," and within three weeks, the record was number one in the nation's capital. The single entered the Hot 100 at number 68 on June 17, 1972, and replaced Gilbert O'Sullivan's "Alone Again (Naturally)" at the top just 10 weeks later. After a lone week at number one, "Brandy (You're a Fine Girl)" yielded to "Alone Again (Naturally)," which returned to the top of the chart for two more weeks.

Looking Glass only had one further chart entry, the mellow-sounding "Jimmy Loves Mary-Anne," number 33 in September, 1973. "Part of the problem that I saw with the group," Lurie concedes, "was that 'Brandy' was not really typical of our live repertoire. We were a lot more of a hard-rock band than that record signified. When we went on tour, people who liked 'Brandy' were often disappointed with the over-all show because we didn't really sound like the record. It was heavily overdubbed with strings and horns, and we were basically a guitar, piano, bass and drum rock 'n' roll band."

Lurie pursued a solo career, but without any chart hits. He turned his attention to supervising music for motion pictures and in 1985 produced the soundtrack for the John Travolta-Jamie Lee Curtis film, *Perfect.*

**318** # Black and White DUNHILL 4317
## THREE DOG NIGHT

Writers: *David Arkin*
          *Earl Robinson*

Producer: *Richard Podolor*

*September 16, 1972*
*1 week*

IN 1954, the United States Supreme Court handed down its landmark decision banning segregation in the public schools. Nearly 20 years later, Three Dog Night scored its third number one single with a song written in response to that ruling.

"Our idea was to celebrate the event," says Earl Robinson, who composed "Black and White" in 1955 with David Arkin, the late father of actor Alan Arkin. "We had no idea that it would reach out as it did eventually." Robinson's songwriting career extends over 50 years; he is also known for composing the memorable union ballad "Joe Hill" and the epic "Ballad for Americans," immortalized by Paul Robeson.

In the late '50s, Sammy Davis, Jr. [see 313—"Candy Man"], recorded "Black and White," backed by

## THE TOP FIVE
*Week of September 16, 1972*

1 **Black and White**
  Three Dog Night

2 **Baby Don't Get Hooked on Me**
  Mac Davis

3 **Alone Again (Naturally)**
  Gilbert O'Sullivan

4 **Saturday in the Park**
  Chicago

5 **Back Stabbers**
  The O'Jays

another classic Robinson composition, "The House I Live In," for a limited edition EP issued by the Anti-Defamation League of B'nai B'rith. But the song did not receive a commercial release until the Jamaican group Greyhound cut a reggae version in 1971.

While on a European concert tour, members of Three Dog Night heard Greyhound's single on a Dutch radio station. "When I eventually met Three Dog Night," says Robinson, "they told me, 'We knew this was going to be a hit immediately.' Of course, both they and (Greyhound) changed the style from the way we originally wrote it. They made it like an 'A-A-B-A-B-A' song," he explains, "whereas we wrote it as five verses with quite a bit more content. To give you an idea, the second verse of our version runs, 'Their robes were black/Their heads were white/The schoolhouse doors were closed so tight/Nine judges all set down their names/To end the years and years of shame.'

"They condensed the most communicable parts of it into a single song number," continues Robinson. "You might call it a more unified

whole, although Dave and I liked our arrangement better than theirs. But of course, we were delighted that they did it," he chuckles, "because the Robinson family ate for a year afterwards."

"I got called by CBS in the late '50s or early '60s," Robinson says, remembering another special use for "Black and White." "I was on CBS often in the early '40s, but it had been a long time since they called me. You see, I had gone through the blacklist (in the McCarthy era). At any rate, now they wanted to clear a song of mine that they called 'The Ink is Black.'

"And what were they doing with it? Well, it was to be part of a film about an American sort of Peace Corps in French Guinea helping the locals build a recreation hall. They were using this song to teach them how to speak English. And it appeared in the film several times with a blackboard and a pointer. And it went, 'The ink is black/The page is white . . .' ".

Three Dog Night's "Black and White" entered the Hot 100 at number 61 on August 12, 1972, and made a swift ascension: 61-47-23-14-9 to number one. The group had two more top 10 hits, "Shambala" (number three in July, 1973) and Leo Sayer's "The Show Must Go On" (number four in May, 1974). Their 21st and final chart entry was " 'Til the World Ends," number 32 in August, 1975.

COLUMBIA 45618 **Baby Don't Get Hooked on Me**
MAC DAVIS

**319**

*Writer: Mac Davis*

*Producer: Rick Hall*

*September 23, 1972*
*3 weeks*

M AC DAVIS had written hits for Bobby Goldsboro [see 239—"Honey"], Elvis Presley [see 260—"Suspicious Minds"], O.C. Smith and Kenny Rogers [see 533—"Lady"] and the First Edition before he got around to writing one for himself.

"My producer, Rick Hall, asked me to write a 'hook' song, one with a repeat phrase which is singles oriented," Davis explained in a 1973 *Billboard* interview. "So I came up with this phrase and melody line, 'baby don't get hooked on me.' Hall tells me, 'Now that sounds like a number one record. Let's cut it.' Hell, I hadn't even written it yet. So the band made up a skeleton chord progression. I wrote the song that night and we cut it the next day. I thought it was super-egotistical and pretentious, but Columbia released it as a single anyway."

He was born on January 21, 1942, in Lubbock, Texas. At 10, his father made him sing in the church choir. He didn't form his first rock band until he was a college student in Atlanta, working for the Georgia State Board of Probation during the day and taking classes at night. The band was called the Zotz, and they performed at a roller rink, specializing in Jimmy Reed songs. They also recorded a single, "Rock a Bongo," for a local label.

The Zotz were not going anywhere, so Mac quit the group and

## THE TOP FIVE
*Week of September 23, 1972*

1  **Baby Don't Get Hooked on Me**
   Mac Davis

2  **Black and White**
   Three Dog Night

3  **Saturday in the Park**
   Chicago

4  **Back Stabbers**
   The O'Jays

5  **Alone Again (Naturally)**
   Gilbert O'Sullivan

went to work as a regional promotion man for Vee Jay Records. He promoted the label's artists, including Jimmy Reed, Gene Chandler [see 104—"Duke of Earl"] and the Four Seasons [see 117—"Sherry"], for four-and-a-half years, then transferred to Liberty Records in the same capacity. More interested in songwriting than promoting records, he earned a transfer to Liberty's publishing office in Hollywood.

Before long, two of his songs were recorded: "You're Good for Me" by Lou Rawls and "Within My Memory" by Glen Campbell. In 1968, Elvis recorded four of Davis' songs, "In the Ghetto," "Memories," "Don't Cry Daddy" and "A Little Less Conversation."

To avoid confusion with Mack David, songwriting brother of Hal David, Mac used his son's name, Scott Davis, as well as Mac Scott Davis, for his writing credits. After Elvis took "In the Ghetto" into the top 10, other artists wanted to record Davis' songs. His early hits included "Little Green Apples" and "Friend, Lover, Woman, Wife" by O. C. Smith, "Somethin's Burnin'" by Kenny Rogers and the First Edition and "Watching Scotty Grow," a song about his son, by Bobby Goldsboro. By the time the Smothers Brothers

featured him in the "Poet's Corner" segment of their television series, he was going by Mac Davis.

He was a frequent guest star on television programs in 1970, appearing with Glen Campbell, Red Skelton and Johnny Cash. In 1971 he opened for Nancy Sinatra [see 194—"These Boots Are Made for Walkin'"] in Las Vegas and received such rave reviews that he was signed as a headliner for the Sahara hotels in Vegas and Lake Tahoe. Columbia Records signed him in 1971, and NBC-TV asked him to host his own 90-minute late night special, "I Believe in Music" (his theme song, which became a hit in 1972 for the group Gallery).

Although his chart fortunes faded after a trio of top 15 hits ("One Hell of a Woman," "Stop and Smell the Roses" and "Rock 'n Roll (I Gave You the Best Years of My Life)"), he remained a popular television attraction. On May 20, 1980, he starred in a one-hour prime time NBC show, "The Mac Davis 10th Anniversary Special: I Still Believe in Music."

He left Columbia Records for Casablanca in 1979, the same year he began concentrating on acting. He made his motion picture debut in *North Dallas Forty* with Nick Nolte. He also starred in *Cheaper to Keep Her* and *The Sting II*.

# 320 Ben MOTOWN 1207
## MICHAEL JACKSON

*Writers: Don Black*
   *Walter Scharf*

*Producers: Freddie Perren*
    *Fonce Mizell*
    *Deke Richards*
    *Berry Gordy, Jr.*

*October 14, 1972*
*1 week*

IN APRIL, 1985, animal rights advocates congregated on the Kennedy Space Center in Florida as the space shuttle Challenger was launched with its crew of astronauts, monkeys and 24 experimental rats. The demonstrators were there to protest the government's plan to kill the rats and conduct autopsies in the name of science.

Anyone who saw *Ben*, the 1972 chiller about an ailing youngster who befriends the leader of a pack of rats, would have to be more than a little upset at the murder of a few of these furry creatures. For that hit movie, a sequel to 1971's *Willard*, generated not only terror, but also a tender love song from the boy to the rodent.

At one point in the picture, little Danny, the revenge-filled hero, sits down at the piano and, taking a break from the mayhem, composes a song for his rat pal. "Ben, the two of us need look no more," he croons, "Ben, we've both found what we're looking for . . ."

"I had just finished work on another film," says composer Walter Scharf, "and was going away for a rest when the people at (the studio) sent me the script to *Ben*. They needed a song to be used in the last few minutes of the film." Scharf, whose extensive credits include the National Geographic and Jacques Cousteau television specials, admits, "the terms were so good that I just couldn't pass it up."

Scharf asked Londoner Don Black [see 231—"To Sir, With Love"] if he'd be interested in writing the words to "Ben." "Walter knew I'd written the lyrics to 'Born Free,'" recalls Black. "Since that was about a lion, I suppose he figured I'd be a good choice to write about a rat."

It was Black who suggested Michael Jackson sing the theme song for *Ben*. "When Michael saw the song, he was anxious to do it," Black continues. "He's quite an animal lover—very sensitive, you know. He enjoys anything that crawls or flies."

Michael's first solo recording entered the Hot 100 just a couple of weeks shy of two years after the debut of the Jackson Five's first hit [see 267—"I Want You Back"]. "Got to Be There" peaked at number four in December, 1971, followed by a remake of Bobby Day's "Rockin' Robin," number two in April, 1972. "I Wanna Be Where You Are" reached number 16 in July, 1972, and was followed by "Ben." The title theme debuted on the Hot 100 at number 85 and took 10 weeks to go to number one.

There is a sad postscript to the saga of "Ben." In early 1985, a young English lad named Ben was dying of a terminal disease. During his last days, British radio stations flooded the airwaves with the song as a tribute to his brave struggle.

## THE TOP FIVE
*Week of October 14, 1972*

1 **Ben**
 Michael Jackson

2 **Use Me**
 Bill Withers

3 **Everybody Plays the Fool**
 Main Ingredient

4 **Burning Love**
 Elvis Presley

5 **Go All the Way**
 Raspberries

CHESS 2131 **My Ding-a-Ling**
CHUCK BERRY

## THE TOP FIVE
*Week of October 21, 1972*

1 **My Ding-A-Ling**
Chuck Berry

2 **Use Me**
Bill Withers

3 **Burning Love**
Elvis Presley

4 **Everybody Plays the Fool**
Main Ingredient

5 **Nights in White Satin**
Moody Blues

*Writer: Chuck Berry*

*Producer: Esmond Edwards*

*October 21, 1972*
*2 weeks*

WHEN first contact is made between humans beings and life forms from another world, it's possible the aliens will have already heard the music of Chuck Berry. Even as you read this, a copper phonograph record sprayed with gold and attached with titanium bolts to the side of Voyager I is speeding through the galaxy, bearing a 120-minute recorded message from the people of Earth to whatever civilization finds it. The record contains greetings in many different human languages, blips that can be decoded into black-and-white and color photographs and 90 minutes of music, ranging from the first movement of Bach's Brandenburg Concerto No. 2 to "Johnny B. Goode" by Chuck Berry.

It's one of the crazier quirks of the rock era that "My Ding-a-Ling," a forgettable rude novelty song, is Chuck Berry's only number one single. The man who shaped the future of rock and roll with seminal tunes like "Sweet Little Sixteen" and "Roll Over Beethoven" had to wait 17 years for his first chart-topper.

"My Ding-a-Ling" was recorded

live at the 1972 Arts Festival in Lanchester, England. The origin of "My Ding-a-Ling" is up for grabs. Dave Bartholomew recorded the song in 1952 and takes writing credit for it; Berry recorded it in 1958 under the euphemistic title "My Tambourine," and also takes writing credit for it.

Charles Edward Anderson Berry was born October 18, 1926, in San Jose, California. The teenaged Berry was sent to reform school for three years on a burglary charge. He then worked at General Motors and studied hairdressing before forming a trio that became popular in St. Louis clubs while Berry also worked as a beautician.

In 1955, Chuck went to Chicago and heard Muddy Waters play. He asked to sit with the blues master, and Waters was impressed enough to suggest that Berry audition for Leonard Chess, head of the Chess record label. Chuck played two songs for Chess. The first was the bluesy "Wee Wee Hours," and the second was a strange blend of country and R&B music called "Ida Red." Chuck liked his blues number better but Chess preferred the rockin' "Ida Red." He suggested a slight alteration in the lyrics, changing the name "Ida Red" to the name of a cow in a children's story, "Maybellene."

Chess didn't want to settle for an R&B hit, he wanted to conquer the pop (read white) charts. He enlisted

the aid of disc jockey Alan Freed, who gave the record heavy airplay. He also received a co-writing credit on the song. "Maybellene" was a crossover hit, peaking at number five on the pop chart in 1955.

Berry certified his status as a rock and roll legend during the next three years, charting in the top 10 with "School Day," "Rock and Roll Music," "Sweet Little Sixteen" and "Johnny B. Goode." He unveiled his famous "duck walk" at an Alan Freed show at the Paramount Theater in Brooklyn. He opened his own club in St. Louis and starred in four rock and roll movies, including *Go Johnny Go* and *Rock Rock Rock*. In 1959, Berry brought a 14-year-old girl from Texas to work as a hat check girl in his club. When she was fired, she accused Berry of molesting her, and he was arrested under the Mann Act, which forbids transporting a minor across state lines for sexual purposes. Berry's first trial was so racist it was thrown out by a higher court. After a second trial, he was sentenced to two years in the federal penetentiary in Indiana.

When he was released in 1964, his marriage and career seemed to be over. A year before, Brian Wilson had taken Berry's "Sweet Little Sixteen" and converted it into "Surfin' U.S.A." for the Beach Boys [see 151—"I Get Around"]. Berry's freedom coincided with the very beginning of the British Invasion, and most of the new groups included Chuck Berry songs in their repertoires. The Rolling Stones' very first single was Berry's "Come On," and the Beatles recorded both "Roll Over Beethoven" and "Rock and Roll Music."

## 322 I Can See Clearly Now EPIC 10902
### JOHNNY NASH

*Writer: Johnny Nash*

*Producer: Johnny Nash*

*November 4, 1972*
*4 weeks*

JOHNNY NASH has assumed many identities in his long recording career—teen idol, middle-of-the-road ballad singer, soul crooner and reggae superstar.

Born on August 19, 1940, in Houston, Texas, Nash sang lead in the choir at Progressive New Hope Baptist Church. He once competed in a local talent show, with first prize being a spot at the Apollo Theater in Harlem, but lost out to an aspiring soul singer, Joe Tex ("I Gotcha," "Hold What You've Got"). Just into his teens, Johnny starred in "Matinee," a local variety show, breaking the color barrier on Texas television.

An appearance on "Arthur Godfrey's Talent Scouts" led the 16-year-old Nash to a stint with Godfrey that lasted seven years. With his warm personality and smooth high tenor voice, Nash scored a string of easy listening hits for ABC-Paramount, including "A Very Special Love" (number 23 in early 1958), "Almost in Your Arms" (number 78 at the end of 1958) and "As Time Goes By" (number 43 in the spring of 1959). With Paul Anka and George Hamilton IV, he recorded "The Teen Commandments" (number 29 in early 1959).

During the early '60s, Nash recorded Sam Cooke-influenced pop and show tunes for Warner Brothers,

Argo and MGM. His biggest success during this period was "What Kind of Love Is This," a Nash composition recorded by Joey Dee and the Starliters [see 103—"Peppermint Twist-Part 1"] that went to number 18 in October, 1962. Later in the decade, Nash and partner Danny Simms started the New York-based JoDa Records, later changed to Jad. For the fledgling label, Johnny produced Sam and Bill's 1965 soul hit, "For Your Love." At the same time, he was also playing supper clubs to pay his rent.

Nash first journeyed to Jamaica in 1957 while on location for a Burt Lancaster movie, *Take a Giant Step*. In 1968, he went back to Kingston to record the reggae-flavored "Hold Me Tight," a number five hit in November, 1968. He used the beat but didn't subscribe to the Rastafarian faith, which inspired reggae.

In 1969, Johnny duplicated the soul-reggae formula with "You Got Soul" and an updating of Sam Cooke's "Cupid." Although neither made the American top 30, both enjoyed top 10 success in Britain, encouraging Nash to move to London in 1971, where he signed with CBS Records.

By this time, Nash had hired a down-on-his-luck reggae singer named Bob Marley to work as a songwriter. Among the classic Marley contributions for Nash were "Stir It Up" and "Guava Jelly." Using the money he earned from songwriting, Marley started the Tuff Gong label, on which he eventually launched his legendary career with the Wailers.

In 1972, Nash again returned to Jamaica to cut his biggest record ever. With some of Marley's mates backing him up, he recorded "I Can See Clearly Now." Released in America, the song entered the Hot 100 at number 84 on September 9, 1972, and moved to number one eight weeks later.

*Newsday* rock critic Robert Christgau described the Nash-penned song as "the kind of record that can get you through a traffic jam." With its positive message and infectious rhythms, Christgau went on to call it, "Two minutes and 48 seconds of undiluted inspiration." In keeping with his new reggae image, Johnny took off his tux for personal appearances and began wearing tailored, well-faded denim jackets, covered with badges and patches.

### THE TOP FIVE
*Week of November 4, 1972*

1  **I Can See Clearly Now**
   Johnny Nash

2  **Nights in White Satin**
   Moody Blues

3  **My Ding-A-Ling**
   Chuck Berry

4  **Freddie's Dead
   (Theme from "Superfly")**
   Curtis Mayfield

5  **Burning Love**
   Elvis Presley

GORDY 7121 **Papa Was a Rollin' Stone**
THE TEMPTATIONS

**323**

*Writers: Norman Whitfield*
*Barrett Strong*

*Producer: Norman Whitfield*

*December 2, 1972*
*1 week*

**F**OUR months before the Temptations' "Papa Was a Rollin' Stone" entered the Hot 100, labelmates the Undisputed Truth were struggling up the chart with their version of the Norman Whitfield-Barrett Strong composition. Peaking at number 63, that recording was all but forgotten when the Temptations reached number one for the fourth time in their career.

It had long been a popular Motown practice for songs in the company's Jobete publishing catalogue to be recorded by several different artists on the label's roster. "I Heard It Through the Grapevine" [see 249] was recorded not just by Marvin Gaye and Gladys Knight and the Pips, but by the Miracles, the Isley Brothers, the Temptations and the Undisputed Truth.

Producer Whitfield often cut his songs with different acts, but the Temptations and the Undisputed Truth seemed exceptionally susceptible to this intramural effort. On the Undisputed Truth's four Gordy albums, at least 10 songs were at one time recorded by the Temptations, including the group's biggest hit, "Smiling Faces Sometimes" (number three in September, 1971).

Although it wasn't originally their song, the Temptations have made "Papa Was a Rollin' Stone" an integral part of their repertoire. Lead singer Dennis Edwards remembers being upset the first time he heard the lyrics, "It was the third of September/That day I'll always remember/Cause that was the day my daddy died." Edwards' father, a preacher rather than a rolling stone, had passed away on the third of September and the singer found the words upsetting. Dennis admits now that he hated the record when he first heard it, but changed his opinion later. The fact that it won a Grammy didn't hurt. Oddly, the Grammy was for best R&B Instrumental. The song was so long on the album (11 minutes, 45 seconds) that the "B" side of the edited single was just an instrumental passage.

"Papa Was a Rollin' Stone" was the first Temptations chart-topper featuring tenor Damon Harris, who replaced Eddie Kendricks [see 348—Keep on Truckin' "]. Original member Richard Street [see 168—"My Girl"] returned after the death of Paul Williams. More changes happened in the '70s: Glenn Leonard took Harris' place in 1975, and Edwards left—temporarily, as it turned out—in 1976, to be replaced by Louis Price. But the last Temptations' hit was "Masterpiece" (number seven in April, 1973), and a 1976 album *The Temptations Do the Temptations*, in which they wrote all of their own songs, failed to produce a chart single.

With only two original members (Otis Williams and Melvin Franklin) still in the group, the Temptations parted ways with Motown in 1977.

They recorded two albums for Atlantic, but even the production magic of Norman Harris and Brian Holland couldn't make a single appear on the Hot 100. Four years after their departure, the Temptations were wooed back to Motown with "Power," a song Berry Gordy had co-written especially for them. Dennis Edwards returned and stayed through the Temptations/Four Tops tour that resulted from the 1983 NBC Motown's 25th anniversary special .

When Edwards left again, he was replaced by Ali-Ollie Woodson, who sang lead on "Treat Her Like a Lady" (number 48 in February, 1985). Leonard left before the NBC special and was replaced by Ron Tyson, who made his debut with the group on the TV special. Edwards returned (and Woodson departed) in 1987, in time for the aptly titled *Together Again* LP.

## THE TOP FIVE
*Week of December 2, 1972*

1 **Papa Was a Rollin' Stone**
Temptations

2 **I Am Woman**
Helen Reddy

3 **I Can See Clearly Now**
Johnny Nash

4 **I'd Love You to Want Me**
Lobo

5 **If You Don't Know Me By Now**
Harold Melvin & the Blue Notes

## 324 | I Am Woman CAPITOL 3350
### HELEN REDDY

Writers: Helen Reddy
Ray Burton

Producer: Jay Senter

December 9, 1972
1 week

THERE are some moments in Grammy history that will never be forgotten, like Bette Midler accepting a Grammy from presenter Karen Carpenter, someone she took delight in poking fun at in her act. Like host Andy Williams asking Stevie Wonder, in a live hook-up from Africa, if he could see the telecast. And like Helen Reddy's acceptance speech after winning "Best Pop, Rock, and Folk Vocal Performance-Female" for "I Am Woman."

"I want to thank everyone concerned at Capitol Records," Helen told the audience in Nashville and the millions watching at home, "my husband and manager, Jeff Wald, because he makes my success possible, and God because She makes everything possible."

Her comments received just about the same reaction her song did—approval from feminists (both female and male) and shock from religious fundamentalists, who wrote letters to let her know what they thought.

"I Am Woman" became an anthem for the women's liberation movement in the '70s. "I'd been involved in the women's movement for about 10 months," says Helen, who had emigrated to the United States from her native Australia in 1966 [see 343—"Delta Dawn"]. "At that point, I was looking for songs that reflected the positive sense of self that I felt I'd gained from the women's movement. I couldn't find any. All I could find were these awful songs like, 'I am woman and you are man, I am weak so you can be stronger than,' so I realized the song I was looking for didn't exist, and I was going to have to write it myself."

Helen wrote the lyrics for "I Am Woman" and Ray Burton, an Australian musician who has since returned to his homeland because of immigration problems, set her words to music. "What I now refer to as the first draft of the song was on my first album," Helen explains.

"I sang that album as if my life depended on it," she said in a 1974 Billboard interview. "I wasn't all that pleased with the way the whole album sounded....I was particularly displeased with the way 'I Am Woman' came out. My producer was against using it in the first place; he thought it sounded too 'butch.'"

But the song didn't die. Producer Mike Frankovich wanted to use it as a theme song in a "women's lib" comedy he was filming, Stand Up and Be Counted. Unhappy with the original arrangement, Helen made some changes, as she told Jacoba Atlas in Melody Maker: "We re-recorded it and I added the last verse—it was always a little short." Helen also altered some lyrics, changing "I can face anything" to "I can do anything." She told Frankovich he could use the song in the film if he donated $1,000 each to Women's Centers in Los Angeles, New York and Chicago.

"A lot of people said it would be the end of my career," Helen says.

Undaunted, she was pleased when Capitol released it as a single. At this point her biggest hit had been her first release for the label, a cover version of Tim Rice-Andrew Lloyd Webber's "I Don't Know How to Love Him" from Jesus Christ, Superstar. It had peaked at 13, but Helen's next two singles ("Crazy Love," "No Sad Song") failed to break the top 50.

At first, it looked like "I Am Woman" would do no better. It entered the Hot 100 on June 24, 1972, at number 99. Three weeks later it fell off the chart, not to return until September 16, when it re-entered at number 87. Airplay did not come easy for the song. Helen describes what she calls the "typical DJ reaction: 'I can't stand this record! I hate this song! But you know, it's a funny thing, my wife loves it!'" Helen made frequent television appearances to sing the song. "Women started calling up radio stations and requesting it. Television forced radio to play it," she explains.

Helen and her husband Jeff refused offers to turn the song into a commercial for any product, despite the many requests from advertising agencies to the song's publisher, Almo Music. Helen did give the song to the United Nations for use during the International Women's Year, for a token fee of one dollar.

"The biggest thing about 'I Am Woman' is that I've had a chance to raise consciousness among American women en masse," Helen told Newsweek. "I get a special feeling when I sing it. It's a chest-beating song of pride. And it pleases me."

## THE TOP FIVE
### Week of December 9, 1972

1  **I Am Woman**
   Helen Reddy

2  **Papa Was a Rollin' Stone**
   Temptations

3  **If You Don't Know Me By Now**
   Harold Melvin & the Blue Notes

4  **I Can See Clearly Now**
   Johnny Nash

5  **You Ought to be With Me**
   Al Green

PHILADELPHIA INTERNATIONAL 3521 **Me and Mrs. Jones** 325
BILLY PAUL

*Writers: Kenny Gamble
Leon Huff
Cary Gilbert*

*Producers: Kenny Gamble
Leon Huff*

*December 16, 1972
3 weeks*

HELEN REDDY'S anthem of female liberation was knocked off the top of the charts by Billy Paul's soulful ballad about a steamy extramarital affair. It was the first number one single for Kenny Gamble and Leon Huff's Philadelphia International label, the third record company owned by the writer/producers.

Billy Paul had recorded for all three of Gamble and Huff's labels. Paul first met Gamble in 1967 at the Cadillac Club in Philadelphia. "I got talking to Billy about coming to Gamble Records," Kenny told Tony Cummings in *The Sound of Philadelphia*. "Billy had gone and recorded a few things on himself and he brought them to me. I told him he wanted three more sides to make an album. So we went in the studios and cut three things and we put them on the album *Feelin' Good at the Cadillac Club*."

The album was jazz-oriented and didn't fare well. "We decided to do something with a more up-to-date sound, with more musicians," Paul told Cummings. "Something that would venture a bit into R&B but without me losing my sound. We spent a lot of time working it out and came up with the album called *Ebony Woman*, which came out on Neptune."

A single was released, Billy's version of Simon and Garfunkel's "Mrs. Robinson" [see 241], but Neptune was distributed by Chess Records and after owner Leonard Chess' death, the label folded. When Gamble and Huff started Philadelphia International through CBS, they signed many of their former artists, including Billy Paul.

"We really wanted to get a big hit on Billy," Gamble explained to Cummings. "The problem was finding a balance between his natural jazz style and what was going down in soul music. The *Ebony Woman* album for Neptune had started getting Billy into a commercial groove and got a

lot of favorable reaction from the industry. So for Billy's next album, *Goin' East*, we extended the concept further. We took in outside influences—the Beatles, the Eastern thing—but we kept it rhythmic and we didn't try to smother Billy. We nearly had a hit with 'Magic Carpet Ride' from the album...and then we did Billy's *360 Degrees* album and it all came together with 'Me and Mrs. Jones.'"

Billy Paul was born Paul Williams on December 1, 1934, in Philadelphia. His family had a collection of 78 rpm records that he loved to listen to. "That's how I really got indoctrinated into music," he admits. "My mother was always...collecting records and she would buy everything from *Jazz at Philharmonic Hall* to Nat 'King' Cole." But female singers were the strongest musical influence on Billy.

"I think the reason behind that is because of my high range. The male singers who had the same range I did, when I was growing up, didn't do much for me. But put on Nina Simone, Carmen McRae or Nancy Wilson, and I'd be in seventh heaven. Female vocalists just did more with their voices, and that's why I paid more attention to them."

Billy was singing on Philadelphia radio station WPEN when he was 11, thanks to some help from a talented young neighborhood comedian, Bill Cosby. Billy studied at the West Philadelphia Music School and the Granoff Music School. "When I was 16, I played the Club Harlem in Philly and I was on the same bill as Charlie Parker," Billy told Cummings. "He died later that year. I was there with him for a week and I learned what it would normally take two years to pick up. Bird told me if I kept struggling I'd go a long way, and I've never forgotten his words."

Billy formed a trio with Sam Dockery and Buster Williams. He recorded his first single, "Why Am I," for Jubilee Records, but his career was interrupted by military service. When he was discharged, he recorded for New Dawn Records and filled in for an ailing member of Harold Melvin and the Blue Notes, the group that would one day have hits of their own on Philadelphia International ("If You Don't Know Me By Now," "The Love I Lost"). His next recording association would be with Gamble and Huff.

## THE TOP FIVE
*Week of December 16, 1972*

1 **Me and Mrs. Jones**
Billy Paul

2 **I Am Woman**
Helen Reddy

3 **If You Don't Know Me By Now**
Harold Melvin & the Blue Notes

4 **You Ought to be With Me**
Al Green

5 **It Never Rains in Southern California**
Albert Hammond

# You're So Vain ELEKTRA 45824
## CARLY SIMON

Writer: *Carly Simon*

Producer: *Richard Perry*

*January 6, 1973*
*3 weeks*

ONE of the greater lyrical mysteries of the rock era is the subject of Carly Simon's "You're So Vain." Speculation on the cad's identity runs from Warren Beatty to Mick Jagger, from Kris Kristofferson to Carly's former husband James Taylor [see 296—"You've Got a Friend"], whom she married on November 3, 1972. But the puzzle has never been solved.

Carly has never revealed the identity of the vainee, if indeed it is one person, but she has said who the song is *not* about. "It's definitely not about James," she said in a 1973 interview with Stuart Werbin for *Rolling Stone*, "although James suspected that it might be about him because he's very vain. No, he isn't, but he had the unfortunate experience of taking a jet up to Nova Scotia after I'd written the song. He was saved by the fact that it wasn't a Lear."

Carly commented to Werbin about a competition to determine who the song was written about: "The contest is run by this man in Los Angeles named Winkler, and he had his listeners call in to cast their ballots to who they thought the song was about. Kris Kristofferson is leading. A lot of people think it's about Mick Jagger and that I have fooled him into singing on it, that I pulled that ruse....But I can't possibly tell who it's about because it wouldn't be fair."

In an interview with her younger brother Peter for his book *Carly Simon Complete*, Carly voided the idea that "You're So Vain" was written about a specific individual: "I would say I had about three or four different people in mind when I wrote that song....I actually did think specifically about a couple of people when I wrote it, but the examples of what they did was a fantasy trip."

"You're So Vain" prominently features backing vocals by Mick Jagger. Carly first met Mick after deciding she'd like a career as a journalist. She thought Jagger would be a great subject for her first interview. "It was very strange, that first meeting," she said in *Rolling Stone*. "I expected

to look so much like him because people were always commenting on the resemblance. I expected to walk into a mirror. But then I didn't think we looked anything alike." Eventually, the idea of the interview was abandoned when they became friends and Carly felt she'd lost the objectivity she would need as an interviewer.

Carly told her brother Peter how Jagger came to sing backing vocals on "You're So Vain": "It was one of those things that just comes about sort of spontaneously. While we were doing the vocal on it, he just happened to call up the studio and ask if he could come down and visit. I said sure and asked if he'd like to sing back-up, and he seemed enthused with the idea. He had sort of a twang in his voice, and I got into it. I slurred into it toward the end of the session. I started hearing myself saying, 'You're so vine,' so on every successive verse I sang more 'vine' than 'vain.' I had fun that night, I enjoyed myself."

Much of the credit for "You're So Vain" goes to producer Richard Perry, although Carly admitted to Werbin that she was not enthused at first about working with him. "I was against the idea because...his work with Nilsson and Barbra Streisand was too slick for me, and I didn't want to have that kind of a sound."

Carly's association with Perry continued through three albums and her second most successful single, "Nobody Does It Better," from the James Bond film *The Spy Who Loved Me*.

"Richard's perfectionism on 'You're So Vain' got the rhythm track," she told Werbin. "We recorded the song three different times with three different drummers. We've got two pianos going on that track. Klaus Voormann was very instrumental on the sound of that track; just that opening bass sets the mood of a swaggering self-indulgent man to come prancing into the room with his hat."

Many of Carly's songs, like her very first hit "That's the Way I've Always heard It Should Be," reflect her childhood and family relationships. She was born June 25, 1945, in New York City, the third child of Richard and Andrea Simon. Her father was the co-founder of the Simon and Schuster publishing house and her mother had studied voice and stressed the importance of music to her children. The eldest child, Joanna, became a mezzo-soprano opera singer. While attending Sarah Lawrence College, Carly formed a duet with her other elder sister, Lucy. As the Simon Sisters, they recorded an album for Kapp and went to number 73 on the Hot 100 in 1964 with "Winkin', Blinkin' and Nod." Albert Grossman wanted to record Carly as the female Bob Dylan, but after cutting "Baby Let Me Follow You Down" with musicians like Robbie Robertson, Rick Danko, Mike Bloomfield and Al Kooper, the project was abandoned.

## THE TOP FIVE
*Week of January 6, 1973*

1 **You're So Vain**
Carly Simon

2 **Clair**
Gilbert O'Sullivan

3 **Me and Mrs. Jones**
Billy Paul

4 **Superstition**
Stevie Wonder

5 **Funny Face**
Donna Fargo

*Writer: Stevie Wonder*

*Producer: Stevie Wonder*

*January 27, 1973*
*1 week*

Nine years and five months had passed since Stevie Wonder first topped the *Billboard* chart [see 135—"Fingertips (Pt. II)"], but it had hardly been an uneventful decade for the man who had once been dubbed "the 12-year-old genius."

With the success of "Fingertips," Stevie became an integral part of the Motown family. And family it was for the boy who was just becoming a teenager. "Everyone over 11 was a parent," he recalled. "(Producer) Clarence Paul loved me like his own son. Esther Edwards, Berry Gordy's sister...all the musicians and artists watched over me. Wanda of the Marvelettes would always tell me when she thought I was eating too much candy. I wish kids today could have the same kind of caring expressed and shown to them."

By 1966, Little Stevie Wonder was no longer so little. He survived a producer's suggestion that he be dropped from the label when his four singles that followed "Fingertips" failed to make the top 20. With maturation, his voice changed and, with the turbulent times of the '60s, his choice of material underwent some changes, too. Just seven months after releasing the upbeat, danceable "Uptight (Everything's Alright)" (number three in February, 1966), he returned to the top 10 with Bob Dylan's pensive "Blowin' in the Wind."

By the end of the decade, Stevie had racked up nine top 10 hits for Motown, including "I Was Made to Love Her" (number two in July, 1967), "For Once in My Life" (number two in December, 1968) and "My Cherie Amour" (number four in July, 1969). Not yet 21, Stevie was receiving a weekly allowance, with his earnings put in trust until he came of age. When he reached adulthood and went to collect, he was shocked to learn that he was only entitled to one million dollars, after earning over 30 million dollars for the company.

That's when Stevie informed Ewart Abner, then president of Motown, that he wanted to control his own fate. In an unprecedented move for Motown, Stevie and his lawyer, Johanan Vigoda, successfully negotiated for Stevie to have his own production and publishing companies, staffed with his own people.

Stevie matured as a musician as well as a businessman. No longer content to produce formula hits, he explored new sounds. In 1971, Richie Havens ("Here Comes the Sun") introduced Stevie to Robert Margouleff and Malcolm Cecil, creators of the giant Tonto synthesizer. That led Stevie to New York City's Electric Lady studios, armed with synthesizer know-how, equipment and $250,000 of his own money. He emerged in March, 1972, with *Music of My Mind*. Although the album produced no top 30 singles, it marked an evolution in his music and established him as an artist to be taken more seriously than the "Little" Stevie Wonder of the early '60s.

Eight months later, Stevie issued the more complex, more mature *Talking Book* album. Thanks to Motown's insistence, Stevie had a second number one single.

Stevie's first choice for a 45 was "Big Brother," but Motown executives were adamant that "Superstition" would be a stronger release. A year earlier, Stevie had worked with guitar virtuoso Jeff Beck. The song "Superstition" had been written for Beck, and Stevie believed it was perfect for his sound. "My understanding was that Jeff would be releasing 'Superstition' long before I was going to finish my album; I was late giving them *Talking Book*," Stevie told Ben Fong-Torres in *Rolling Stone*. "Jeff recorded 'Superstition' in July, so I thought it would be out." Since Stevie hadn't finished "Big Brother" in time, Motown released "Superstition" just ahead of the LP. The single entered the Hot 100 at number 82 on November 18, 1972, and 10 weeks later moved to number one.

## THE TOP FIVE
*Week of January 27, 1973*

1. **Superstition**
   Stevie Wonder

2. **You're So Vain**
   Carly Simon

3. **Crocodile Rock**
   Elton John

4. **Your Mama Don't Dance**
   Loggins & Messina

5. **Why Can't We Live Together**
   Timmy Thomas

## 328 Crocodile Rock MCA 40000
### ELTON JOHN

*Writers: Elton John*
*Bernie Taupin*

*Producer: Gus Dudgeon*

*February 3, 1973*
*3 weeks*

In June, 1972, Elton John and his band members settled in at Strawberry Studios in France to begin sessions for *Don't Shoot Me, I'm Only the Piano Player*, an LP the artist later dismissed in *Rolling Stone* as "Elton John's disposable album. I think it's a very happy album, very ultra-pop." From that album came Elton's first number one single, one he described to the magazine as an amalgam of several early influences. "I always wanted to write one song, a nostalgia song, a rock and roll song which captured the right sounds. 'Crocodile Rock' is just a combination of so many songs, really. 'Little Darling,' 'Oh, Carol,' some Beach Boys, they're in there as well, I suppose. Eddie Cochran. It's just a combination of songs."

"I never wanted to do this in the first place. I only wanted to be a songwriter," Elton John told *Rolling Stone* during a 1976 interview in New York. In just 29 years he had traveled light years from his lifestyle in Pinner, Middlesex, England, where he was born on March 25, 1947, as Reginald Kenneth Dwight. The only child of ex-Royal Air Force trumpeter Stanley Dwight and his wife, Sheila, he had a distressing relationship with his father, one in which he remembers himself being "surpressed and petrified" in the biography *Elton John 'Only the Piano Player'*.

"I was never allowed to do this, that or the other (including kick a football in the garden—he might damage dad's rose trees) until my parents got divorced." That event occurred when he was 10 and already had six years of piano practice under his chubby belt. With his father gone there were no more arguments over the youngster's bent for music; it was encouraged by his mother, whose purchase of Elvis Presley's "Heartbreak Hotel" [see 10] "freaked out" her son. "The first thing I ever read about Elvis was in a barber's shop, and I couldn't believe it. I went on from there," he recounted. With his

pocket money he brought home records and picked out the melodies by ear. Formal lessons on the correct performance of classical exercises couldn't hold the interest of the kid who declared, "pop music was my whole life."

Nonetheless, he won a scholarship to the Royal Academy of Music when he was 11. Three years later he formed a band with his cousin's friend's boyfriend. A few years after that the two would form Reg's first money-making group, Bluesology. Bluesology's tour backing Major Lance garnered them similar employment with other bands all over Europe and, later, their own slot at the Cromwellian Club back home where Long John Baldry offered to end their pick-up status if they'd join him permanently.

*New Musical Express* advertised for "musicians to form new group" on June 17, 1967, a squib placed by Liberty Records. Reg replied after timorous deliberation, but botched the audition. To make the rejection less harsh, a Liberty exec suggested the pianist get in touch with a Lincolnshire lyricist named Bernie Taupin who was seeking a collaborator. The new songwriting team stealthily made their demos in Dick James Music studios during off hours. When the music publisher discovered their nocturnal activity he preferred 10 pounds per week and a steady job, causing Reg to make the final split from Bluesology and to change his name as well, befitting his new profession. Combining the first names of Bluesology member Elton Dean and John Baldry, he dubbed himself Elton John.

### THE TOP FIVE
*Week of February 3, 1973*

1 **Crocodile Rock**
   Elton John

2 **You're So Vain**
   Carly Simon

3 **Superstition**
   Stevie Wonder

4 **Why Can't We Live Together**
   Timmy Thomas

5 **Your Mama Don't Dance**
   Loggins & Messina

ATLANTIC 2940 **Killing Me Softly With His Song**
ROBERTA FLACK **329**

*Writers: Norman Gimbel*
*Charles Fox*

*Producer: Joel Dorn*

*February 24, 1973*
*5 weeks*

It STARTED out as "Killing Me Softly With His Blues," the feeling Don McLean [see 305—"American Pie"] engendered in singer Lori Lieberman when she caught him singing his number one hit at the Troubadour in Los Angeles. Songwriters Norman Gimbel and Charles Fox polished it into final form for Lieberman to record. Then Roberta Flack plugged in the stereo earphones on a TWA jet from Los Angeles to New York and flipped through the in-flight magazine. "I saw the picture of this little girl, Lori Lieberman, and the title of the song," she explained to *New Musical Express*. "I'm more interested in seeing who's the featured artist than hearing the music—just to see if I'm on there. But I'd never heard of Lori Lieberman, so I thought I'd see what she'd got going for her that I didn't have. Before I heard the song I thought it had an awfully good title, and when I heard it I really loved it."

Flack embellished the story for *High Fidelity*. "To tell you the truth, my ego got involved because for me, that song wasn't 'finished.' What I mean is, sometimes a song will be done by a Streisand or someone like that, and I simply feel that there's no need for me to do it. When something

## THE TOP FIVE
*Week of February 24, 1973*

1  **Killing Me Softly**
   **With His Song**
   Roberta Flack

2  **Dueling Banjos**
   Eric Weissberg and
   Steve Mandell

3  **Crocodile Rock**
   Elton John

4  **You're So Vain**
   Carly Simon

5  **Could It Be I'm**
   **Falling in Love**
   Spinners

has really been *done* there's nothing you can do—no matter how great you are yourself—to improve on it. But this song was not finished. By the time I got to New York I knew I had to do that song and I knew I'd be able to add something to it. My classical background made it possible for me to try a number of things with it. I changed parts of the chord structure and chose to end on a major chord. It wasn't written that way."

The perfectionist in Roberta kept her in the studio for three months, fiddling with little snatches here and there, tinkering mostly with the background vocals. She was a constant visitor to an Atlantic executive's office, punching and re-punching tapes of different mixes. The executive assured her that any of

the editions were a sure hit, but she insisted on continuing to fine tune. "I wanted to be satisfied with that record more than anything else," she stated emphatically in *Melody Maker*.

Her determination paid high dividends. "Killing Me Softly With His Song" was the highest new entry on the Hot 100 for the week ending January 27, 1973, debuting at number 54. It moved up in record time, from 54-34-15-5 to number one. Her second consecutive chart-topper [see 310—"The First Time Ever I Saw Your Face"], "Killing Me Softly" repeated her earlier Grammy feat by winning Record of the Year for Roberta and producer Joel Dorn, and Song of the Year for Gimbel and Fox. Flack won an additional Grammy for Best Pop Vocal—Female.

## 330 Love Train PHILADELPHIA INTERNATIONAL 3524
THE O'JAYS

*Writers: Kenny Gamble*
*Leon Huff*

*Producers: Kenny Gamble*
*Leon Huff*

*March 24, 1973*
*1 week*

T HE O'JAYS began as a duo, grew to a quintet and then shrank to a quartet. When their 13th chart single, "Love Train," went to number one, they were a trio.

Eddie Levert and Walter Williams were friends in elementary school in Canton, Ohio, when they formed a duo to sing gospel songs. In 1958, they joined with William Powell, Bobby Massey and Bill Isles and turned to secular music. They called themselves the Triumphs until 1961, when they signed with Sid Nathan's King Records and changed their name to the Mascots.

Four singles on King failed to make any noise and they were taken under the wing of a Cleveland disc jockey, Eddie O'Jay. He booked them into small clubs and introduced them to a record producer from Detroit, Don Davis. They recorded "Miracles" for the small Dayco label, and in appreciation for Eddie's guidance, changed their name to the O'Jays.

In 1963 they met producer H. B. Barnum, who signed the group to Los Angeles-based Imperial Records. "Barnum helped us with our vocals, and showed us the ins and outs of the music business," says Levert. "After a year he took us into the studio and we recorded 'Lonely Drifter.'"

## THE TOP FIVE
*Week of March 24, 1973*

1 **Love Train**
O'Jays

2 **Killing Me Softly**
**With His Song**
Roberta Flack

3 **Also Sprach Zarathustra (2001)**
Deodato

4 **Neither One of Us (Wants to**
**be the First to Say Goodbye)**
Gladys Knight & the Pips

5 **Last Song**
Edward Bear

That became their first chart entry, peaking at a humble number 93 in September, 1963. They had three more chart entries on Imperial, including "Lipstick Traces (On a Cigarette)." The group also did backing vocal work for other artists, including Nat "King" Cole, but by 1966 they were not having much luck with their recording career. Isles quit the group in August and the remaining four members moved back to Cleveland.

They were considering retirement when they were offered a contract with Bell Records. They had three more chart entries, then found their career cold again. They appeared at the Apollo Theater in Harlem with the Intruders, who were scoring hits on Kenny Gamble and Leon Huff's Philadelphia label, Gamble Records. The Intruders told Gamble and Huff to check out the O'Jays, and they did, signing them to their new label, Neptune Records.

"One Night Affair" was the first single released on Neptune. It was the first of three chart entries on the label, but before the O'Jays could build any momentum, the label folded. Once more, the O'Jays returned to Ohio without a record label. They were briefly reunited with Barnum and Massey quit the group to become a record producer.

Now a trio, the O'Jays kept in touch with Gamble and Huff, knowing the producers intended to start a new label, Philadelphia International, through CBS. According to Walter Williams, the group received offers from Motown and the new label started by Brian Holland, Lamont Dozier and Eddie Holland, called Invictus. But they turned both offers down in favor of returning to Philadelphia to sign with Gamble and Huff again.

One of the label's first releases was "Back Stabbers," which went to number three in the summer of 1972. It was the first O'Jays single to go higher than 40. The follow-up, "992 Arguments," came from the *Back Stabbers* album, and when Gamble and Huff returned to the album for a third single, they selected the final track on side two: "Love Train." It entered the Hot 100 at number 61 on January 20, 1973 and became the O'Jays first and only number one single on March 24.

For the next five years, the O'Jays were consistent hit-makers, charting with top 10 songs like "For the Love of Money," "I Love Music" and "Use Ta Be My Girl." There was one sad change in the group's line-up in 1976. William Powell was stricken with cancer that year. He quit touring, but continued to record with the group until his death on May 26, 1977. He was replaced by Sammy Strain, who had been a member of Little Anthony and the Imperials for 12 years.

BELL 45303 **The Night the Lights Went Out in Georgia**
VICKI LAWRENCE

`331`

*Writer: Bobby Russell*

*Producer: Snuff Garrett*

*April 7, 1973*
*2 weeks*

Vicki Lawrence is best known for her work in television, especially "The Carol Burnett Show" and "Mama's Family," and while she never concentrated on a singing career, she did have a number one record. The story of how she was discovered rivals the Lana Turner/Schwab's Drug Store fable, and better yet, it's completely true.

Vicki grew up in Inglewood, California, and her father's hobby was collecting autographed covers of *Time*. Perhaps that inspired Vicki to write so many fan letters to Hollywood stars. A lot of her friends told her that she resembled Carol Burnett, then one of the stars on the weekly Garry Moore TV series, and Vicki's mother urged her to write a fan letter to Carol.

In her letter, Vicki mentioned the resemblance and said she'd love to meet Carol one day. Carol's secretary selected the 10 best fan letters every week and showed them to Carol, and when she read Vicki's, she called her up and said she would like to come to a beauty pageant that Vicki had entered. Carol said she was very pregnant and didn't want any fuss, so she wouldn't see Vicki that night but would call her later for lunch. When Carol arrived at the Miss Fireball contest, the emcee excitedly rushed on stage, announced her presence and asked her to come up and crown the winner. Vicki was mortified and knew her career was over before it had begun.

But Carol graciously crowned the winner ("in an awful coat and a turban around her head," Vicki remembers), who turned out to be Vicki. Three weeks later Carol gave birth and Vicki dragged her boyfriend to the hospital, hoping she'd be admitted to Carol's room. The nurses assumed she was Carol's sister Chrissy and let her in without question. "She was very nice and said 'wait til I get my tummy back and we'll have lunch,'" says Vicki. A few weeks later, Carol's husband, producer Joe Hamilton, asked Vicki to meet them at CBS. He revealed then that Carol was beginning a new series the next fall and they wanted Vicki to play Carol's sister in an ongoing sketch.

The Emmy-winning series was on CBS from 1967-1978 and Vicki won her own Emmy during the show's ninth season. One of the running sketches in the show was the basis for the "Mama's Family" series, which began on NBC and then moved into syndication with new episodes.

During the early '70s, Vicki was briefly married to songwriter Bobby Russell. He wrote "The Night the Lights Went Out in Georgia," but didn't think much of it. Vicki told him it was a hit and recorded the demo in Nashville. The song was turned down by a number of artists, including Sonny Bono, who rejected it for Cher because it might offend listeners in the Southern United States (Vicki says Cher did not know Sonny turned the song down until years later). Producer Snuff Garrett decided to record the song with Vicki and in three hours they had a finished record. "Snuff changed the melody and made it sound eerier," she recalls.

As the song climbed up the chart, Vicki's marriage was disintegrating, and she says recording the album was a strain and brings up unpleasant memories. "I sort of got out of music after that."

## THE TOP FIVE
*Week of April 7, 1973*

1 **The Night the Lights Went Out In Georgia**
Vicki Lawrence

2 **Neither One of Us (Wants to be the First to Say Goodbye)**
Gladys Knight & the Pips

3 **Killing Me Softly With His Song**
Roberta Flack

4 **Ain't No Woman (Like the One I've Got)**
Four Tops

5 **Break Up to Make Up**
Stylistics

## 332    Tie a Yellow Ribbon Round the Ole Oak Tree    BELL 45318
### DAWN

*Writers: Irwin Levine*
*        L. Russell Brown*

*Producers: Hank Medress*
*         Dave Appell*

*April 21, 1973*
*4 weeks*

Tony Orlando, Telma Hopkins and Joyce Wilson were ready to go their separate ways by the end of 1972. Dawn's first two singles did well, with one of them even topping the Hot 100 [see 287—"Knock Three Times"], but their next three releases failed to make the top 20, and the three 45s after that failed to make the top 60. The financial strain of keeping the act on the road was so great they considered disbanding after one more recording session.

Then Telma received a telephone call from producers Hank Medress and Dave Appell asking her and Joyce to fly to New York to record a song they were very excited about. She remembers the evening they were scheduled to meet Tony at the studio. "I'll never forget it," she declares, "because 'Brian's Song' aired that night. We stayed home to watch Billy Dee Williams. We didn't go to the studio until after it aired. The music was already done when we walked in . . . the producers didn't care if we were late and I thought that was kind of odd." They didn't care because they knew nothing was

going to prevent "Tie a Yellow Ribbon Round the Ole Oak Tree" from becoming a hit record. "When we first heard it, we knew it was a hit," Telma confirms.

Orlando's first reaction was not as positive. "I thought it was corny," he told Tom Burke in *Rolling Stone*. "Hank Medress wanted 'Yellow Ribbon' on the (next) album. I didn't—except I found it was stuck in my head, I kept singing it around the house. Against my will, because my taste, musically, has always been what I *don't* necessarily do well, rhythm and blues. Fortunately, Hank . . . saw in 'Yellow Ribbon' . . . a nice satire of the American dream, that it gently kids the fact that we love stories about turmoil, lyrics with suspense, doubt about a happy ending, as long as we know we *are* gonna get the happy ending in the last line."

The song with the happy ending was based on a true story. A man who had served three years in prison for writing bad checks was returning home on a bus headed south on U.S. 17 in Georgia. He had written a letter to his wife saying that he would understand if she didn't wait for him, but if she still loved him, she could let him know by tying a yellow ribbon around the old oak tree in the city square of their hometown. As the bus rolled in to White Oak, Georgia, the driver slowed down so the man—and all the passengers—could see if she had signalled her inten-

tions. When the yellow ribbon was spotted, the man broke down and cried as the passengers cheered.

Wire services picked up the inspiring story and songwriters Irwin Levine and L. Russell Brown fashioned it into "Tie a Yellow Ribbon Round the Ole Oak Tree." The number one song for 1973, according to *Billboard*, it proved to be a turning point in the career of Tony Orlando and Dawn.

The trio performed the nominated song on the Grammys. Watching the broadcast was Fred Silverman, then head of programming for CBS Television. "We were only on the show for three minutes and 10 seconds," Tony told Bob Thomas of the Associated Press. "But Fred saw something in us that seemed promising. He asked our agent what we had done in television, and our agent sent him three shows we had done in England for BBC. Then he came to see us perform at Westbury, Connecticut." He liked them enough to give them a four-week summer tryout series, which led to a regular berth in the CBS prime time schedule in December, 1974. The series remained on the air until December 28, 1976.

"Tie a Yellow Ribbon Round the Ole Oak Tree," the second most-recorded song of the rock era with over one thousand cover versions [see 185—"Yesterday"], had a revival when the American hostages returned from Iran after 444 days in captivity. Yellow ribbons were displayed coast-to-coast to welcome them home.

---

### THE TOP FIVE
*Week of April 21, 1973*

1   **Tie a Yellow Ribbon Round the Ole Oak Tree**
Dawn

2   **The Night the Lights Went Out in Georgia**
Vicki Lawrence

3   **Sing**
Carpenters

4   **The Cisco Kid**
War

5   **Ain't No Woman (Like the One I've Got)**
Four Tops

TAMLA 54232 **You Are the Sunshine of My Life**
STEVIE WONDER    **333**

*Writer: Stevie Wonder*

*Producer: Stevie Wonder*

*May 19, 1973*
*1 week*

Less than four months after *Talking Book* yielded a number one single [see 327—"Superstition"], Stevie Wonder was back on top of the Hot 100 with another chart-topper, "You Are the Sunshine of My Life." Where the first single addressed the pettiness and destructiveness of superstitious beliefs, the second concentrated on pure love and adoration.

While Stevie was maturing as a musician and a businessman, he wasn't missing out on a social life. When he was 17 he had met a girl named Angie and wrote "I Was Made to Love Her" (number two in July, 1967) based on that affair. It took Stevie a little while to get the rest of the world to drop "Little" from his name, but marrying Syreeta Wright helped to hasten that process.

Syreeta was a secretary at Motown when she first met Wonder. She was also an aspiring singer. Motown producer Clarence Paul suggested Stevie write a song for her, but the finished tune was never released. The collaboration did lead, however, to love and marriage. Syreeta was instrumental in speeding up Stevie's spiritual growth. Although he had always believed in a higher power, Syreeta, who teaches transcendental meditation, brought a centeredness to Stevie's life. Although the marriage only lasted 18 months, their friendship continues.

(Stevie later married his secretary, Yolanda. Their firstborn, daughter Aisha Zakia (the names mean "strength" and "intelligence" in an African language), provided the inspiration for the song "Isn't She Lovely" on *Songs in the Key of Life*. They also have a son, Keita).

"You Are the Sunshine of My Life," featuring Stevie on most of the instruments, became an anthem to love and further broadened Stevie's appeal to the public. The song has not only been covered by artists like Frank Sinatra, Tom Jones, Andy Williams, Johnny Mathis and Liza Minelli, but has become standard Muzak elevator fare.

The song begins in a unique fashion for a Stevie Wonder song; two other singers are heard on the introduction before Wonder's voice comes in. Jim Gilstrap ("Swing Your Daddy") is the male voice, followed by a female vocalist, Gloria Barley.

"You Are the Sunshine of My Life" made its debut on the Hot 100 at number 76 on March 17, 1973. Nine weeks later it became Stevie Wonder's third number one single. When it won a Grammy for Best Pop Vocal Performance—Male, Stevie accepted by saying, "I would like to thank all of you for making this night the sunshine of my life."

A second award for the song was turned down. The National Association of Record Merchandisers named "You Are the Sunshine of My Life" Best Soul Song. At a UCLA symposium sponsored by *Billboard*, Stevie explained, "The song wasn't one that should be played for a special kind of people. All of us can feel love. When music is categorized, yet all of us can relate to it, I wouldn't be thankful for accepting it."

## THE TOP FIVE
*Week of May 19, 1973*

1  **You Are the Sunshine of My Life**
   Stevie Wonder

2  **Tie A Yellow Ribbon Round The Ole Oak Tree**
   Dawn

3  **Little Willy**
   The Sweet

4  **Frankenstein**
   Edgar Winter Group

5  **Daniel**
   Elton John

# 334 Frankenstein EPIC 10967
## EDGAR WINTER GROUP

*Writer: Edgar Winter*

*Producer: Rick Derringer*

*May 26, 1973*
*1 week*

JOHNNY WINTER, the albino rock-blues guitarist, had made quite a name for himself around his native Beaumont, Texas, leading a flashy teenaged band. Younger brother Edgar (born December 28, 1946) was happier fiddling with his keyboards and saxophone, performing in the background and toning down his image. But every so often he would tire of the "commercial sell-out," temporarily assemble a lounge lizard jazz band, expand his creative horizons, then rejoin his elder brother's high energy rock conglomerate. Columbia

Records anteed up $600,000 for Johnny's services and placed him on a national tour, which gave Edgar time in the solo spotlight each night.

"He needed a song to play when they said, 'Let's hear Edgar Winter, bring him out here,' " remembers Rick Derringer, who produced records for both brothers after fronting the McCoys [see 184—"Hang on Sloopy"]. "So he wrote this song called 'The Double Drum Solo,' just for a working name, and every night when he came out he'd bring down the house. At the end of the song he'd get to play sax, he'd get to play keyboards, he'd get to play drums—he'd get to play everything."

Soon Edgar was also under the Columbia umbrella, brought there by his brother's manager, Steve Paul. Compiling several of his Texas musi-

cian cohorts into a horn-based Southern roadhouse boogie band called White Trash, Edgar led them through two highly successful, critically acclaimed albums and a financially rewarding tour. He left his associate Jerry La Croix to carry on the name and tradition when his tastes began leaning more toward pop sounds and a glittery stage presentation. With Dan Hartman ("Instant Replay," "I Can Dream About You"), Chuck Ruff and Ronnie Montrose (replaced by Jerry Weems, who was replaced by Derringer) he formed the Edgar Winter Group.

"When it came time for Edgar to do his first band album, *They Only Come Out at Night*, he wanted to include that instrumental in the album," Rick explains. "Bill Szymczyk and I—I was the producer and he was the engineer—were really looking forward to doing that song. To us, we're musicians, the rest of the album was a little more predictable. The one thing that seemed like it was going to be fun was the instrumental. At one point in the project Edgar started to be nervous. 'Oh, I don't know, it's a little too crazy. Is this gonna be too jazzy, too out of context for the rest of the album?' All of us voiced our opinions immediately, saying, 'It's fantastic, it's gotta be on the record.' We went ahead and finished it; we did some editing to shorten it, as it was too long in the live form. The editing is where Edgar got the name 'Frankenstein,' through all the little cuts and stuff, all the patches in (the) master."

"Frankenstein" was originally the "B" side of "Hangin' Around," added so its sole songwriter could collect more royalties than on any of the LP's other co-authored tunes. However, disc jockeys were drawn to the unusual track and demanded yet a shorter version.

Entering the Hot 100 at number 98 on March 10, 1973, "Frankenstein" took 11 weeks to reach the top of the chart and spurred *They Only Come Out at Night* on to over 1.2 million sales, a figure that doesn't surprise its producer. "Usually you get flack," Derringer says, "but the one song where you perceive a lot of nervousness from the business itself is usually the one song the regular record buying public finds to be the most interesting song on the whole record."

### THE TOP FIVE
*Week of May 26, 1973*

1 **Frankenstein**
Edgar Winter Group

2 **My Love**
Paul McCartney & Wings

3 **Daniel**
Elton John

4 **Tie a Yellow Ribbon Round the Ole Oak Tree**
Dawn

5 **You Are the Sunshine of My Life**
Stevie Wonder

## THE TOP FIVE
*Week of June 2, 1973*

1 **My Love**
Paul McCartney & Wings

2 **Daniel**
Elton John

3 **Frankenstein**
Edgar Winter Group

4 **Pillow Talk**
Sylvia

5 **Tie a Yellow Ribbon
Round the Ole Oak Tree**
Dawn

*Writer: Paul McCartney*

*Producer: Paul McCartney*

*June 2, 1973*
*4 weeks*

**P**AUL McCARTNEY's post-Beatles solo career turned out to be a brief one. After a year on his own, a period that produced a number one single [see 298—"Uncle Albert/Admiral Halsey"] recorded with his wife Linda, Paul wanted to participate in the dynamics of a group again.

Denny Seiwell was a New York session musician who had played drums on McCartney's *Ram* album. He and Linda were Paul's first two recruits for the new band. Next came a Birmingham musician who had sung lead on a classic '60s British hit, "Go Now." Former Moody Blues man Denny Laine was recording his own solo LP when Paul called and asked if he'd like to be in a group. The solo album was dropped and Laine went to Scotland to be part of the unnamed

quartet that recorded the *Wild Life* album.

On September 3, 1971, Linda McCartney was in Kings College Hospital in London to give birth. Paul had intended to assist, as he had done when their daughter Mary was born, but a Caesarian section was required and Paul was not admitted to the operating room. "I sat next door in my green apron praying like mad," he told the London *Sunday Times*. "The name 'Wings' just came into my head." Later, Linda said he was thinking about the "Wings of an angel."

Wings made surprise appearances at universities around Britain, sometimes charging just 50 pence admission to startled students who couldn't believe the former Beatle was playing at such small venues. But the unannounced concerts gave Wings a chance to develop as a band without the critical eye of the press upon them. Guitarist Henry McCullough was added to make Wings a quintet. Their first two singles

released in America, "Give Ireland Back to the Irish" and "Mary Had a Little Lamb" backed with "Little Woman Love" failed to make the top 20.

Paul rebounded with "Hi, Hi, Hi," a rocker that peaked at number 10 in February, 1973. A month later, the new single from the band was released under the name "Paul McCartney and Wings," perhaps in reaction to the moderate sales of earlier Wings singles. The song was a sentimental ballad, "My Love," written by Paul for Linda.

Linda Louise Eastman was born September 24, 1942, in Scarsdale, New York. Her father, Lee, was a successful lawyer. While growing up, Linda declined to take piano lessons, but loved listening to rock and roll on the radio—especially to Buddy Holly, Chuck Berry and the Everly Brothers. After her mother was killed in a plane crash, Linda married—"a mistake," she later said. She had one child, Heather, before she was divorced.

She moved to Tucson, Arizona, and became interested in photography. Returning to New York, she went to work for *Town and Country* magazine as a receptionist and intercepted an invitation to cover a press party for the Rolling Stones aboard a boat on the Hudson River. Her photographs of the Stones established her reputation as a professional photographer.

On assignment to shoot the rock group Traffic in London in 1967, she was taken to see Georgie Fame play at the Bag O'Nails Club by Jimi Hendrix' manager, Chas Chandler [see 156—"House of the Rising Sun"]. Paul McCartney was there with some friends, and he and Linda gave each other the eye. After that first meeting, Paul visited Linda in New York, then vacationed in California with her. He asked her to come to England, and they lived together. "Neither of us talked about marriage," Linda told *Sounds*. ". . . we liked each other a lot, so being conventional people, one day I thought, 'O.K., let's get married—we love each other, let's make it definite.'" With Paul's brother Michael as best man and Heather as bridesmaid, Paul and Linda were married March 12, 1969, at the Marylebone Register Office.

## 336 Give Me Love (Give Me Peace on Earth) APPLE 1862
### GEORGE HARRISON

*Writer: George Harrison*

*Producer: George Harrison*

*June 30, 1973*
*1 week*

**F**OLLOWING George Harrison's first number one single [see 286—"My Sweet Lord" / "Isn't It a Pity"], Apple Records in America released "What Is Life," a song originally written for Billy Preston [see 337—"Will It Go Round In Circles"]. But George realized the song wasn't suitable for Preston and recorded it himself for his *All Things Must Pass* album. There was no follow-up single from the album in the United Kingdom; British fans had to wait until July, 1971, for George's next single, "Bangla-Desh," a song written after musician Ravi Shankar asked George to organize a charity concert to aid the starving people of that country.

On August 1, 1971, two concerts for Bangla-Desh took place at Madison Square Garden in Manhattan. The artist roster for this benefit included Ringo Starr, Bob Dylan, Eric Clapton, Leon Russell, Billy Preston, members of Badfinger and Harrison and Shankar. Almost a quarter of a million dollars was raised from the concerts alone; proceeds from the triple album and the movie that followed brought the total amount raised to fifteen million dollars. Legal problems prevented all of the funds actually reaching the people of Bangla-Desh; only a fraction of the amount raised went to feeding the people of that nation.

After the concert album was released in December, 1971, George did not release another new recording until the single "Give Me Love (Give Me Peace on Earth)," the only 45 to be released from his album *Living in the Material World*. George discussed the song briefly in his book *I Me Mine*: "Sometimes you open your mouth and you don't know what you are going to say, and whatever comes out is the starting point. If that happens and you are lucky—it can usually be turned into a song. This song is a prayer and personal statement between me, the Lord, and whoever likes it."

Following "Give Me Love," George had four more singles on Apple, then started his own label, Dark Horse. Although he made the top 20 with "Crackerbox Palace" in 1977 and "Blow Away" in 1979, he didn't have another major hit until 1981, when his tribute to John Lennon, "All Those Years Ago," held at number two for three weeks.

It *was* all those years ago that the George Harrison story began. He was born February 25, 1943, in Liverpool, the fourth child of Harold and Louise Harrison. George attended Dovedale Primary School, where he probably never met a fellow student who was three years older—Lennon. At 13, George bought his first guitar. The same year, he formed a group called the Rebels with his brother Peter and some friends.

In 1958, George met Paul McCartney. At the same time, Paul joined John Lennon's group, the Quarrymen. When George was introduced to John, he was challenged: "If you can play as good as Eddie Clayton, you're in." George played "Raunchy" on his guitar and was admitted to the Quarrymen.

Before forming Johnny and the Moondogs with John and Paul, George spent the autumn of 1959 working as an apprentice electrician at a Liverpool store, Blacklers. The following year, the 17-year-old Harrison went to Hamburg to work with John, Paul and Pete Best at the Indra Club. By December, George was deported for being under-age and not having resident or work permits.

### THE TOP FIVE
*Week of June 30, 1973*

1 **Give Me Love
(Give Me Peace on Earth)**
George Harrison

2 **My Love**
Paul McCartney & Wings

3 **Will It Go Round in Circles**
Billy Preston

4 **I'm Gonna Love You
Just a Little More Baby**
Barry White

5 **Kodachrome**
Paul Simon

A&M 1411 **Will It Go Round in Circles** 337

BILLY PRESTON

*Writers: Billy Preston*
*Bruce Fisher*

*Producer: Billy Preston*

*July 7, 1973*
*2 weeks*

AFTER he became the only American artist to share label billing with the Beatles [see 254—"Get Back"], Billy Preston was signed to Apple Records, where he recorded two albums. Up until that time he had been a keyboard player and a studio musician; now he was given the freedom to be a vocalist and co-produce his own material (with George Harrison, who recruited musicians like Eric Clapton, Ginger Baker and Keith Richard to play on Billy's sessions).

But when the Beatles' empire began to fall apart, Billy suggested he leave the label and did so with good wishes. Back in Los Angeles, he signed with A&M Records and recorded the album *I Wrote a Simple Song*. A&M released the title song as a single, but Preston preferred the instrumental "B" side, "Outa-Space." So did radio stations across the country, and that side peaked at number two.

With songwriting partner Bruce Fisher, Billy joked one day that he had a song but no melody. Those words became part of "Will It Go Round in Circles," Billy's first solo number one single. Thanks to its success, Fisher was able to resign his job in the mailroom at NBC in Burbank, California.

Billy was born September 9, 1946,

## THE TOP FIVE
*Week of July 7, 1973*

1 **Will It Go Round in Circles**
   Billy Preston

2 **Kodachrome**
   Paul Simon

3 **My Love**
   Paul McCartney & Wings

4 **Give Me Love**
   **(Give Me Peace on Earth)**
   George Harrison

5 **Bad, Bad Leroy Brown**
   Jim Croce

in Houston, Texas. He was raised in Los Angeles, where by the age of three he was playing piano. His mother was the organist for the Victory Baptist Church and Billy was asked to direct the church choir. He played the organ when Mahalia Jackson appeared at the church and watching that performance was the producer of the motion picture *St. Louis Blues*. He cast 10-year-old Billy as the young W.C. Handy, the man known as the "father of the blues." It was Preston's only film role until he appeared in the motion picture *Let It Be* with the Beatles.

Billy was signed to Sar Records, the label owned by Sam Cooke [see 30—"You Send Me"] and in 1962 Billy joined a gospel tour starring Cooke and Little Richard. When they arrived in England, they discovered it wasn't a gospel tour at all—the kids wanted to hear rock and roll. Billy played rock for the first time

and loved it. It was during this tour that he first met the Beatles, who asked him questions about America and one of their idols, Little Richard.

In 1965, Billy was playing clubs in Los Angeles when he was visited by Sounds Incorporated, the British band who backed Little Richard on the '62 tour. They brought television producer Jack Good to the club and he invited Billy to become the resident keyboard player on his "Shindig" series.

During a rehearsal for the show, Billy sat in for his idol, Ray Charles. When Charles heard Billy sing "Georgia on My Mind," he invited him to record on his next album. In 1967, Charles toured Europe and introduced Billy as the man he'd like to carry on the work he had started. It was a concert at the Royal Festival Hall that attracted George Harrison to Preston and led to his joining the Beatles on "Get Back."

# Bad, Bad Leroy Brown ABC 11359
## JIM CROCE

Writer: *Jim Croce*

Producers: *Terry Cashman*
*Tommy West*

*July 21, 1973*
*2 weeks*

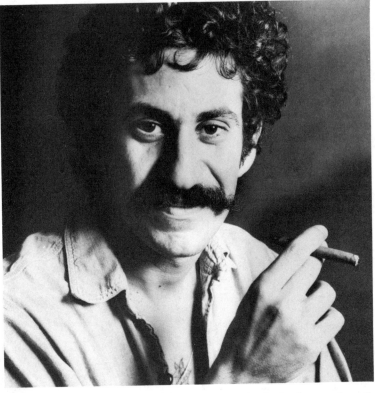

SOLDIER JIM CROCE was learning how to be a telephone lineman at Fort Dix, New Jersey, when he met the character who inspired his first number one single, "Bad, Bad Leroy Brown." "He stayed there about a week, and one evening he turned around and said he was really fed up and tired," Croce is quoted in *The Top Ten* by Bob Gilbert and Gary Theroux. "He went AWOL, and then came back to get his pay check. They put handcuffs on him and took him away. Just to listen to him talk and see how 'bad' he was, I knew some-day I was gonna write a song about him."

The reference to "meaner than a junkyard dog" also came from Croce's true-life experiences. During his days as a laborer, he used to frequent junkyards in search of car parts. There, he'd see dogs running through the yards with some heavy pieces of metal tied around their necks to "slow them down a bit." With that kind of leash, the dogs became real mean real quick, an image Croce stowed away for use in a song some day.

Born on January 10, 1943, in Philadelphia, Pennsylvania, Croce was an avid viewer of Dick Clark's "American Bandstand."

When he was 18, Jim had saved up enough money from his job at a local toy store to buy his first guitar,

a 12-string. While attending Villanova University, he was a disc jockey on a three-hour folk and blues show on the college radio station, and played with a series of bands he organized. After graduating college, he had a series of odd jobs, but kept working on his music in his spare time. He was an advertising salesman for a local black radio station, then switched to a variety of laborer jobs. On one of these projects, he smashed his finger with a sledge hammer. Though the finger was saved, he had to develop a unique way of guitar picking that didn't rely on use of the injured digit.

In 1966, he was married and with his wife, Ingrid, taught at a summer camp in Pine Grove, Pennsylvania.

While he was in college, Jim had become friends with Tommy West, who, with Terry Cashman, was an upcoming record producer. At Tommy's insistence, Jim and Ingrid moved to New York in 1967. There, Croce sang in coffeehouses and small clubs. He signed with Capitol Records and recorded an album with Ingrid that didn't sell very many copies.

Discouraged, the Croces returned to Pennsylvania and for the next two-and-a-half years, Jim and Ingrid did whatever they could to make ends meet. Jim kept writing songs while working as a truck driver. When he had completed six numbers, he recorded them on a cassette and sent it to Cashman and West. Pleased with his progress, they invited him to record the songs at the Hit Factory in Manhattan.

By 1972, ABC Records had signed Jim and issued his first album, *You Don't Mess Around With Jim*. The title track was released as a single and went to number eight on the Hot 100 in September. A second 45 from the LP, "Operator (That's Not the Way It Feels)," peaked at number 17 in December. His next album, *Life and Times*, yielded an initial single, "One Less Set of Footsteps," that only reached number 37 in March, 1973. It was the second single from that LP that did the trick—"Bad, Bad Leroy Brown" entered the Hot 100 at number 85 on April 21, 1973, and took over the top spot from Billy Preston 11 weeks later.

## THE TOP FIVE
### Week of July 21, 1973

1. **Bad, Bad Leroy Brown**
   Jim Croce

2. **Will It Go Round in Circles**
   Billy Preston

3. **Yesterday Once More**
   Carpenters

4. **Shambala**
   Three Dog Night

5. **Kodachrome**
   Paul Simon

*Writers: Al Kasha*
*Joel Hirschhorn*

*Producer: Carl Maduri*

*August 4, 1973*
*2 weeks*

IT was a Thursday, the 30th of March, in 1972, when songwriters Al Kasha and Joel Hirschhorn met with executive producer Irwin Allen at 20th Century Fox. He asked them to compose the love theme for his latest film, *The Poseidon Adventure*, starring Gene Hackman, Shelley Winters, Ernest Borgnine and Carol Lynley. Excited by the opportunity, Kasha and Hirschhorn asked how long they had to write the song. The answer: one day.

The production schedule called for the song to be recorded the following Monday, and Allen wanted to hear the completed tune on Friday. The two songwriters returned to Kasha's home and brewed up some strong, black coffee. "We were at the piano all night," Hirschhorn remembers. "We stumbled in the next morning. . . . They said, 'It's perfect!' "

The song they turned in that Friday was called "Why Must There Be a Morning After?" but Allen and director Ronald Neame wanted a more positive message in their "disaster" film. The title was changed to "The Morning After," and at one point the film's title was almost changed as well. The script was based on a little-known story by Paul Gallico, "The Poseidon Adventure," and the studio thought the public might not relate to the title.

Kasha and Hirschhorn went into the studio on the appointed Monday with "ghost singer" Renee Armand, who recorded a vocal track for Lynley to lip synch to in the film. Irwin Allen suggested Barbra Streisand would be a good choice to sing the theme song for release as a record. Dismissing that idea as unlikely, Kasha and Hirschhorn approached Russ Regan, then head of 20th Century Records, to locate a singer. "Before we knew it, out of (Regan's) own budget, he recorded the song," Kasha recalls.

A few months earlier, Regan had heard a demo tape of a secretary who was working part time as a folksinger. He liked her voice so much, that when "The Morning After" project came his way, he signed Maureen McGovern (born July 27, 1949, in Youngstown, Ohio) to the label and had her record it.

Kasha and Hirschhorn presented McGovern's recording to Allen. "He was very shaken by it," Kasha recounts. "He had never heard of this girl in his life . . . he asked us what we thought of it and we told him we loved it. We weren't just being Monday morning quarterbacks—we thought she captured the song beautifully."

"The Morning After" was nominated for an Academy Award for Best Song, but was considered a long shot against stronger contenders like Walter Scharf and Don Black's "Ben" [see 320], which had already been a number one hit for Michael Jackson. "I didn't expect to win," Hirschhorn admits. "I'm a nervous wreck at these things. When they announced the winner, my hands sweated off the gold plating on the Oscar. It turned silver!".

It was only after the extra attention the song garnered from winning an Academy Award that it became a hit. It started off slowly, debuting at number 99 on the Hot 100 dated June 23, 1973. Its chart progress sharply increased in its third week on the chart; it moved 99-86-42-29-20-9 to number one.

The Kasha-Hirschhorn-McGovern connection scored again two years later with the theme song from another Irwin Allen disaster film, *The Towering Inferno*. Performed by McGovern in the picture, "We May Never Love Like This Again" won the Academy Award for Best Song of 1974.

Reflecting on the success of "The Morning After," Kasha suggests, "It struck a chord of hope. It can be read as a personalized kind of song. It could be read as a love song. It could be read as a song for a person who's on alcohol or some kind of drug, 'there's got to be a morning after,' meaning getting through the night. . . . It's just a great song of hope."

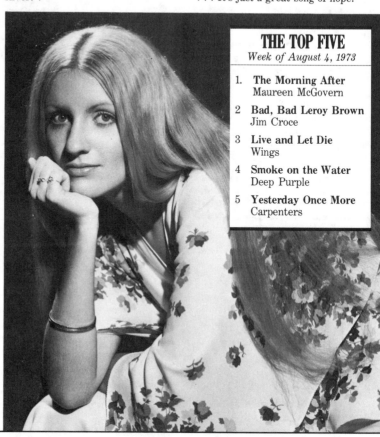

### THE TOP FIVE
*Week of August 4, 1973*

1. **The Morning After**
   Maureen McGovern
2. **Bad, Bad Leroy Brown**
   Jim Croce
3. **Live and Let Die**
   Wings
4. **Smoke on the Water**
   Deep Purple
5. **Yesterday Once More**
   Carpenters

## 340  Touch Me in the Morning  MOTOWN 1239
### DIANA ROSS

*Writers: Michael Masser*
*Ron Miller*

*Producers: Michael Masser*
*Tom Baird*

*August 18, 1973*
*1 week*

**B**ERRY GORDY, JR., was so unsure of how the public would react to Diana Ross' acting debut in *Lady Sings the Blues*, he wanted to have a number one single waiting in the wings in case her career needed a boost.

Instead of relying on experienced writers like Nick Ashford and Valerie Simpson [see 281—"Ain't No Mountain High Enough"], Motown executive Suzanne de Passe turned to a novice composer, Michael Masser. He was teamed with Motown veteran lyricist Ron Miller to write "Touch Me in the Morning."

"I felt that Michael's composition, which was brilliant, had all of the elements of a pop record, but it didn't have anything that was anywhere near rhythm and blues," Miller told J. Randy Taraborrelli in *Diana*. "I didn't want Diana to lose her base, so we ripped off a riff from Ashford and Simpson. One part is straight out of 'Ain't No Mountain High Enough.' And then we had her talking in parts, all of which we did to keep the identity she established with 'Mountain' and to add some soul to the record."

Miller described the construction of the song to Taraborrelli: "I had already dreamed up this title, 'Touch Me in the Morning,' but I didn't have the vaguest idea what it meant....So I analyzed Diane as a person. I said, 'Well, this girl is out on her own now.

### THE TOP FIVE
*Week of August 18, 1973*

1  **Touch Me in the Morning**
   Diana Ross

2  **Live and Let Die**
   Wings

3  **Brother Louie**
   Stories

4  **The Morning After**
   Maureen McGovern

5  **Let's Get It On**
   Marvin Gaye

She's an adult and a movie star. She's also a contemporary woman and...much more liberal about expressing her sexual values. Whereas once upon a time, only a man could say something like that, now a liberated woman like Diane could. However, though she's ostensibly a sophisticated woman, she's still crying inside to be touched in the morning.' It was just a very cold, calculated and wonderful job of crafting."

Miller felt Diana was emphasizing her movie career over recording plans, and was concerned when she arrived late for the "Touch Me in the Morning" session. "I knew she wasn't going to be up to her potential, so we had her record the song about 12 times. And then we went in and spent about 300 hours in the studio editing; there are not three syllables from one performance together on the final product."

"Touch Me in the Morning" was not released immediately after it was recorded. Instead, a single from *Lady Sings the Blues* was issued—"Good Morning Heartache" (number 34 in March, 1973). It was part of the plan to get the public to think of Diana as Billie Holiday—and to win her an Oscar as Best Actress. The ultimate winner was Liza Minnelli for *Cabaret*.

Following her loss, Diana went back in to the studio to re-cut "Touch Me in the Morning." The original single release was three minutes and 51 seconds, but some Motown staffers felt that was too long and an edited version at three minutes and 15 seconds was released. "No one was quite sure what to make of it," Masser said in *Diana*. "...Motown stuck with it, though, and what it needed was about three or four weeks of saturated airplay to make it happen. And then, of course, it happened all over and became the standard I like to think it is. I think it really helped legitimize Diana to a large, sophisticated audience."

"Touch Me in the Morning" entered the Hot 100 at number 89 on June 2, 1973. Twelve weeks later it followed another "morning" record [see 339—"The Morning After"] into the number one position.

*Writers: Errol Brown*
*Tony Wilson*

*Producers: Kenny Kerner*
*Richie Wise*

*August 25, 1973*
*2 weeks*

A COVER version of a British pop-reggae hit about an interracial marriage took a troubled American band to the top of the Hot 100 on August 25, 1973. The short story of Stories' meteoric rise and fall began in the late '60s when Michael Brown and Ian Lloyd were introduced by their violinist-fathers, who had been working together as session musicians.

Brown, a Brooklyn native, was the founding member and guiding force of the Left Banke, the chamber-rock group that scored with "Walk Away Renee" (number five in October, 1966) and "Pretty Ballerina" (number 15 in February, 1967). After those two hits, Brown recorded a couple of other songs with different personnel under the Left Banke's name, then re-grouped the band for one final chart entry, "Desiree."

When Brown met Lloyd (nee Ian Buonconciglio), he was looking to assemble a new group along clean, Beatlesque lines. He found the perfect front man in the charismatic, Seattle-born singer. Teaming up with guitarist Steve Love and drummer

Bryan Madey, they secured a record deal with Kama Sutra and released their first album in 1972.

Stories' self-titled debut album, which yielded a number 42 hit in the summer of 1972, "I'm Coming Home," sold well enough to merit a follow-up. But in the midst of the recording sessions, internal dissent caused Brown to write off his brain-child and leave the group.

To replace him, the remaining band members added Kenny Aaronson on bass and Ken Bichel on keyboards. Stories completed the 1975 LP, *About Us*, and as an afterthought covered a hit by the British rock/soul outfit Hot Chocolate called "Brother Louie."

Composed by Hot Chocolate's Errol Brown and Tony Wilson, "Brother Louie" was the tale of a black girl, her white boyfriend and his racist parents. The song's chorus ("Louie, Louie, Louie, Loo-aye") was strongly inspired by the Kingsmen's classic "Louie, Louie," written by Richard Berry. Hot Chocolate's original version went to number seven in the United Kingdom in the spring of 1973, but never made the American chart. Stories' driving version entered the Hot 100 at number 83 on June 23, 1973, and went to number one nine weeks later.

Not until early 1975 did Hot Chocolate make an impact in the American market with "Emma," a number eight hit. They also scored with "You Sexy Thing" (number three in February, 1976), "So You Win Again" (number 31 in September, 1977, but number one in England) and "Every 1's a Winner" (number six in February, 1979).

The enormous popularity of "Brother Louie" gave Stories enough momentum to sustain themselves with two less spectacular hits, "Mammy Blue" and "If It Feels Good, Do It." But the group did not have a storybook ending. Another round of squabbles broke the band up for good.

Ian Lloyd followed a solo career and had one mid-chart record, "Slip Away," in 1979. Three years earlier, British musicians Mick Jones and Ian MacDonald met at a Lloyd recording session, and went on to organize the hit-producing band Foreigner [see 601—"I Want to Know What Love Is"]. But that's another story.

**THE TOP FIVE**
*Week of August 25, 1973*

1. **Brother Louie**
   Stories

2. **Live and Let Die**
   Wings

3. **Touch Me in the Morning**
   Diana Ross

4. **Let's Get It On**
   Marvin Gaye

5. **The Morning After**
   Maureen McGovern

**342** ## Let's Get It On TAMLA 54234
MARVIN GAYE

Writers: *Marvin Gaye*
*Ed Townsend*

Producers: *Marvin Gaye*
*Ed Townsend*

*September 8, 1973*
*2 weeks*

"I CAN'T see anything wrong with sex between consenting anybodies," Marvin Gaye wrote in the liner notes to his 1973 *Let's Get It On* album. "I think we make far too much of it. After all, one's genitals are just one important part of the magnificent human body. I have no argument with the essential part they play in the reproduction of the species; however, the reproductive process has been assured by the pleasure both parties receive when they engage in it."

His reputation on the singles chart assured in the '60s, Marvin made his mark as an album artist with his eloquent 1971 LP about social issues, *What's Going On*. That album produced three hit singles—the title track, which held on to the number two position for three weeks; "Mercy Mercy Me (The Ecology)" (number four) and "Inner City Blues" (number nine).

There was not much room for doubt or interpretation as to what Marvin was talking about in *Let's Get It On*. He had moved from singing

about war, the ghetto and the environment to an erotic, sensual celebration of sex. His fans responded by giving him his second number one single [see 249—"I Heard It Through the Grapevine"].

Marvin Pentz Gay, Jr., was born April 2, 1939, in Washington, D.C. His father, the Rev. Marvin Gay, Sr., was an Apostolic preacher. Marvin started singing in his father's church at age three, and soon learned to play the organ. In 1957, he joined the Marquees and cut some tracks for the Okeh label with producer Bo Diddley.

Harvey Fuqua of the Moonglows saw them perform in a talent show, and thought they sounded remarkably like his own group. When the Moonglows broke up, Fuqua asked the Marquees to become the new Moonglows. The new group didn't match the success of the earlier incarnation, and the second generation Moonglows broke up as well. Harvey continued to work with Marvin, as he recalled for Aaron Fuchs and Dan Nooger in *Goldmine*:

"Marvin and I would sit at the piano for hours and hours. I showed him all the chords I knew. He was a great learner and musician and he expanded on those things and took it further." Fuqua went to work for Anna Records in Detroit, a label owned by Berry Gordy's sister, Anna Gordy. Marvin played drums on some

Anna releases, but never recorded for the label. He did fall in love with Anna, however, and they were married. Years later, their divorce would become the subject of the album *Here, My Dear*.

The founder of Motown first heard Marvin Gaye sing at a party held at a Detroit nightclub. "Berry Gordy wanted to record Marvin on his label," Fuqua explained in *Goldmine*, "and I thought it would be a good political move....So that's how he came to sign as an artist with Motown."

During his tenure at Motown, Marvin Gaye had 34 chart singles on his own. He had 15 more in duets with four different Motown female stars over an 11 year period. With Mary Wells, he had a double-sided hit in 1964, "What's the Matter With You Baby" backed with "Once Upon a Time." A couple of hits with Kim Weston, including "It Takes Two," followed. Marvin's most successful team-up was with Tammi Terrell, a Philadelphia native who sang with James Brown as Tammy Montgomery before signing with Motown. Marvin and Tammi took duets like "Your Precious Love" and "You're All I Need to Get By" into the top 10, but their partnership had a tragic ending. During a 1967 performance at Hampton-Sydney College in Virginia, Tammi collapsed into Marvin's arms. She was reportedly suffering from a brain tumor, and she died March 16, 1970. Marvin's final Motown duets were with Diana Ross in 1973-1974, resulting in two top 20 singles ("You're a Special Part of Me," "My Mistake (Was to Love You)").

---

## THE TOP FIVE
*Week of September 8, 1973*

1 **Let's Get It On**
Marvin Gaye

2 **Brother Louie**
Stories

3 **Delta Dawn**
Helen Reddy

4 **Say, Has Anybody Seen
my Sweet Gypsy Rose**
Dawn featuring Tony Orlando

5 **Touch Me in the Morning**
Diana Ross

*Writers: Alex Harvey*
*L. Collins*

*Producer: Tom Catalano*

*September 15, 1973*
*1 week*

HELEN REDDY was the fifth female vocalist to have a crack at "Delta Dawn" but she was the only one to capture the top spot on the Hot 100 with it. The song's co-writer, Alex Harvey, recorded it before any of the women had a chance. He included it on an album recorded for Capitol. One of the backing vocalists on his track was Tracy Nelson, lead singer for Mother Earth. With her group, Tracy performed "Delta Dawn" at the Bottom Line in Manhattan.

One of Tracy's admirers was Bette Midler. She came to the Bottom Line for several nights in a row, captivated by Tracy's treatment of "Delta Dawn." Bette included the song in her act at the Continental Baths and recorded it for her first Atlantic album, *The Divine Miss M.* Invited to appear on NBC's "The Tonight Show Starring Johnny Carson," she sang the song for a national audience.

Sitting at home watching Bette on television was record producer Billy Sherrill, who thought the song would be perfect for 13-year-old Tanya

Tucker. Her country version of "Delta Dawn" was released on MCA, and peaked at number 72 on the Hot 100 in 1972. The country success of "Delta Dawn" convinced producer Tom Catalano that the song could be a pop hit if recorded by the right female vocalist. He was about to produce an album for Barbra Streisand and recorded an instrumental track for her. She disliked the song and turned it down, leaving Catalano with a backing track and no singer. The song's publisher called manager Jeff Wald, who was looking for material for his client—and wife—Helen Reddy. Reddy agreed to do the song just in time—her single was released as a single by Bette was coming out to follow "Do You Want to Dance?" Atlantic flipped Bette's 45 to "Boogie Woogie Bugle Boy," and Helen's version entered the Hot 100 at number 86 on June 23, 1973. It went to number one 12 weeks later.

"Delta Dawn" was featured on Helen's album *Long Hard Climb.* It was an accurate title. She was born October 25, 1941, in Melbourne, Australia, daughter of show business veterans Max Reddy and Stella Lamond. Her father was a writer/producer and comedian; her mother was an actress in a popular Australian soap opera. Helen was just four when she first appeared on stage with her parents, at the Tivoli Theatre

in Perth. In 1966, she entered a talent contest sponsored by an Australian television station. She defeated 1,358 contestants to capture first prize: a trip to New York, $400 cash and an audition with Mercury Records.

Collecting the prize proved to be difficult, as Helen explained to Robert Hilburn of the *Los Angeles Times:* "It took phone calls virtually every day for four months before they finally made good their promise."

Once in New York, there were more problems, as Reddy told Hilburn. "Somebody from the record company took me to lunch, was pleasantly polite and wound up saying goodbye and hoping I had a lovely visit. There was no audition. I was told they had listened to a tape of my voice, sent from Australia, and while it was very nice, it wasn't for them. I learned later that even that was a lie. There had been no tape at all."

Helen sang where she could, even earning $25 for singing at a veterans' hospital. The night before her 25th birthday, she took stock: she had no permanent place to live, her assets amounted to $12 and she had return tickets to Australia she couldn't cash in. She decided to go home. On her birthday, friends gave her a surprise party, charging guests five dollars each to raise funds for Helen. A talent agent from the William Morris Agency crashed the party. His name was Jeff Wald and he didn't pay to get in. He did propose marriage four days later and Helen accepted.

They moved to Chicago, where Jeff took a job as talent booker at Mr. Kelly's, where Helen would fill in for artists who didn't show up for their dates. Then they moved to California, where Wald called Capitol executive Artie Mogull every day for five months until he agreed to let Helen cut one single. Mogull heard "I Don't Know How to Love Him" from *Jesus Christ, Superstar,* and urged Linda Ronstadt [see 393—"You're No Good"] to record it. She hated the song, so Mogull passed it along to Wald, who agreed to cut it as a "B" side for Helen's first Capitol single, "I Believe in Music." Disc jockeys preferred the flip side and helped make it a hit, leading Capitol to want an album from Helen, an LP that included an early version of her first number one song [see 324—"I Am Woman"].

## THE TOP FIVE
*Week of September 15, 1973*

1 **Delta Dawn**
Helen Reddy

2 **Let's Get It On**
Marvin Gaye

3 **Say, Has Anybody Seen my Sweet Gypsy Rose**
Dawn featuring Tony Orlando

4 **Loves Me Like a Rock**
Paul Simon

5 **We're an American Band**
Grand Funk

# 344 We're an American Band CAPITOL 3660
## GRAND FUNK

*Writer: Don Brewer*

*Producer: Todd Rundgren*

*September 29, 1973*
*1 week*

GRAND FUNK was the archetypal Midwestern power-trio of the early '70s. Long-haired, sweaty and unrestrained, they preached a brand of heavy-metal populism and were proud to call themselves "an American band."

Guitarist Mark Farner (born September 29, 1948, in Flint, Michigan) and drummer Don Brewer (born September 3, 1948, in Flint) were both members of the Pack, led by former Detroit disc jockey Terry Knight. Signed to the local Lucky Eleven label, they reached number 46 on the Hot 100 with a cover version of Ben E. King's "I (Who Have Nothing)" in January, 1967.

When Knight scattered the pack and moved to New York, Farner and Brewer teamed up with bassist Mel Schacher (born April 8, 1951, in Owosso, Michigan), who had played briefly in ? and the Mysterians [see 210—"96 Tears"]. They called Knight back from Manhattan to be their manager; he agreed to handle them if they gave him complete creative and financial control.

He named them Grand Funk Railroad, after Michigan's Grand Trunk Railroad. Before long, the clever promoter parlayed the band's explosive set at the 1969 Atlanta Pop Festival into a contract with Capitol Records. Their debut LP, *On Time*, set the pattern: excessive, ear-wracking rock and roll, or "the all-time loud white noise," as Rod Stewart called it.

Within a year, Grand Funk Railroad became one of rock's most colossal overnight successes—without the benefit of critical praise or radio airplay. They sold out New York's Shea Stadium in less than 24 hours, a feat which had taken the Beatles three weeks. Capitol estimated that it sold a Grand Funk album every four seconds. In 1970 alone, the band racked up five million dollars in sales.

While critics never found a justification for the group's staggering popularity, *Creem* writer Dave Marsh took a sociological approach to explain their mass appeal: "Grand Funk ARE an experience, meant to be lived, in which to participate," he wrote in 1971. "For they are in touch with what no one else is—the spirit of American youth, the children of the '70s."

Knight would have agreed with that assessment. "This group has got something its competitors don't have," he said. "You have to go to

people like Presley, the Beatles, the Stones and Sinatra to find it. Grand Funk says something to its audience that no other rock group says today. It is saying to its audience that, 'We are part of you. We are your voice.'"

And that voice, according to critic Greil Marcus, was one of "noise, anger, comradeship and rebellion." The Grand Funk audience, he wrote, was inarticulate. "They aren't looking for answers, they're looking for confirmation. This music is the possession of teenagers who want something of their own."

Disagreements between the three band members and Knight ultimately led to Grand Funk dumping their manager in March, 1972. A series of lawsuits ensued and the group turned their business affairs over to New York lawyer John Eastman (Linda McCartney's brother).

In creative control of their career for the first time, Mark, Don and Mel made several changes. They added long-time friend Craig Frost (born April 20, 1948, in Flint) on keyboards. They shortened their name to Grand Funk. And they hired studio wizard Todd Rundgren ("I Saw the Light," "Hello It's Me") to produce their first album of 1973, *We're an American Band*. Until the title track, written by Brewer, was released, no Grand Funk single had ever climbed higher than number 22 ("Closer to Home" in October, 1970).

Pressed on golden vinyl, "We're an American Band" entered the Hot 100 at number 83 on July 28, 1973. Nine weeks later, the rock anthem became Grand Funk's first chart-topper.

## THE TOP FIVE
*Week of September 29, 1973*

1 **We're an American Band**
Grand Funk

2 **Let's Get It On**
Marvin Gaye

3 **Half-Breed**
Cher

4 **Loves Me Like a Rock**
Paul Simon

5 **Delta Dawn**
Helen Reddy

MCA 40102 **Half-Breed**
CHER **345**

*Writers: Mary Dean*
*Al Capps*

*Producer: Snuff Garrett*

*October 6, 1973*
*2 weeks*

AFTER reviving the recording fortunes of Cher [see 301—"Gypsys, Tramps and Thieves"], producer Snuff Garrett was invited by Kapp Records head Johnny Musso to produce an album for Sonny and Cher. The result was their first top 10 single since 1967's "The Beat Goes On"—"All I Ever Need Is You" went to number seven in 1971. The follow-up, "A Cowboy's Work Is Never Done," went to eight. Garrett gave Cher another top 10 hit, "The Way of Love," but then disagreed with Sonny on the kind of material his wife should be recording. After Sonny turned down a Bobby Russell song that Snuff thought would be number one [see 331—"The Night the Lights Went Out in Georgia"], Snuff quit as their producer.

Lyricist Mary Dean didn't know that when she brought "Half-Breed" to Garrett. She had written the tale of the daughter of a Cherokee mother and a white father especially for Cher. "I said from the lyrics it's a smash for Cher and for nobody else," Garrett told Jay Grossman for a 1973 *Rolling Stone* story. "And I didn't even have Cher at the time. To me, nobody else could do that song but Cher—that was Cher's story. So I held the song and then it worked out that we got Cher back, but the song sat in my desk for about three, four months."

## THE TOP FIVE
*Week of October 6, 1973*

1  **Half-Breed**
   Cher

2  **Loves Me Like a Rock**
   Paul Simon

3  **Let's Get It On**
   Marvin Gaye

4  **We're an American Band**
   Grand Funk

5  **Higher Ground**
   Stevie Wonder

"Half-Breed" entered the Hot 100 at number 89 on August 4, 1973. Nine weeks later it became the second number one single for the new corporate entity MCA Records, which had absorbed its own subsidiary labels, Decca, Kapp and Uni.

The years 1971-1972 were prosperous for Sonny and Cher. Not only were they having hit records, but their CBS-TV series, "The Sonny and Cher Comedy Hour," was performing well, even when the network switched it from Monday nights at 10 p.m. to Friday nights at 8. They had successfully matured their image from their "hippy" days [see 181—"I Got You Babe"]. It was a conscious effort begun in 1967 to appeal to adults as well as teenagers, and it worked.

By the time "Half-Breed" hit the charts, the recording career of Sonny and Cher as a duo was over. Their last chart single, "Mama Was a Rock and Roll Singer, Papa Used to Write All Her Songs," struggled to number 77 in the spring of 1973.

"Cher wanted to be a solo act at every level," Sonny said in 1985. "I think all along she did. (Sonny and Cher) was a stepping stone to a goal she was seeking. I wanted to hang on to it and she wanted to end it. And it ended."

She had come a long way since Sonny had met her in a Hollywood coffee shop and brought her along to sing background on Phil Spector sessions. She was born Cherilyn Sakisian LaPierre on May 20, 1946, in El Centro, California. She grew up in Hollywood, where her mother was an actress. Cher sang in high school, and her mother enrolled her in acting classes with teacher Jeff Corey. Those classes would one day pay off with an Academy Award.

# 346 Angie ROLLING STONES 19105
## THE ROLLING STONES

### THE TOP FIVE
*Week of October 20, 1973*

1 **Angie**
Rolling Stones

2 **Half-Breed**
Cher

3 **Ramblin' Man**
Allman Brothers Band

4 **Let's Get It On**
Marvin Gaye

5 **Midnight Train to Georgia**
Gladys Knight & the Pips

---

*Writers: Mick Jagger*
*Keith Richard*

*Producer: Jimmy Miller*

*October 20, 1973*
*1 week*

THE ROLLING STONES had an eventful year in 1972. They freed themselves from manager Allen Klein, settling a $29 million lawsuit out of court; they mounted their most elaborate tour to date, the Stones Touring Party; they ended their tax exile in France and returned home to England; they were denied working visas in Japan and Australia because of drug problems; and a drug bust in England extended the list of countries where they were not welcome.

Jamaica held no ill will, though, and that's where the fivesome retreated to absorb Caribbean rhythms for their 1973 album, *Goat's Head Soup*. Mick Taylor claimed the title referred to a Jamaican delicacy of run-down goat scraped from the road and boiled up as an entree. The music was taken more nonchalantly, with

Keith Richard telling *New Musical Express*, "It's nothing I feel motivated to put on, but when it's on, it sounds good." Jagger remembers that it was delayed for two months because Atlantic had problems with the blatant title of a song about a groupie which ended up with the compromise title of "Star Star."

Of "Angie," he is quoted in *Mick Jagger in His Own Words*, "I used to write nearly all the words in that period. That was my contribution, though quite often Keith used to write the words until *Between the Buttons*. And then in a very modest way I started writing the tunes as well. 'Angie' is a kind of throw-back to the 'Back Street Girl' and 'Lady Jane' ballads which we used to do."

With a string arrangement by Nicky Harrison, and Nicky Hopkins on piano, "Angie" was the highest new entry on the Hot 100 for the week ending September 8, 1973. Debuting at number 75, the record took just six weeks to rise to the top.

During 1974, the Stones could not place a single in the top 10. Their three releases each placed one rung

lower than the other: "Doo Doo Doo Doo Doo (Heartbreaker)" went to 15 in February, "It's Only Rock 'n Roll (But I Like It)" was 16 in September and a cover version of the Temptations' "Ain't Too Proud to Beg" reached 17 in December.

Citing "musical differences," Mick Taylor resigned from the Rolling Stones in 1974. Several of Britain's best guitarists auditioned for the post, until Rod Stewart's Faces disbanded, leaving Ron Wood at loose ends. Keith's near twin, Wood was a natural choice to "guest" with the other four on their 1975 American tour. The following year he was made an official Rolling Stone, sealing his new identity with yet another trek to the States and 39 dates in Europe. The roadshow wound down at the Knebworth Festival in England, the first outdoor gathering the Stones had played since Altamont. Headlining a bill supported by Lynyrd Skynyrd, Todd Rundgren and 10cc, the newly aligned Stones turned in a lackluster performance. It did not go unnoticed, the London *Times* called them "old men . . . over the hills."

*Writer: Jim Weatherly*

*Producer: Tony Camillo*

*October 27, 1973*
*2 weeks*

Gladys Knight and the Pips reached the runner-up position on the Hot 100 twice during their Motown years. "I Heard It Through the Grapevine" spent three weeks at number two in December, 1967. The Jim Weatherly-penned "Neither One of Us (Wants to Be the First to Say Goodbye)" was number two for a couple of weeks at the end of March, 1973. It took a change of labels and titles and their 25th chart entry to put Gladys Knight and the Pips on top of the *Billboard* singles chart in October, 1973.

After eight years with Motown's Soul label, Gladys and the Pips went in search of greener pastures. They signed with New York-based Buddah Records and released "Where Peaceful Waters Flow," a ballad that was a medium-sized hit at number 28 in the summer of 1973. For their second single, they returned to the repertoire of Jim Weatherly.

The songwriter from Pontotoc, Mississippi, had recorded one of his own songs, "Midnight Plane to Houston," on Jimmy Bowen's Amos Records. "It was based on a conversation I had with somebody . . . about taking a midnight plane to Houston," Weatherly recalls. "I wrote it as kind of a country song. Then we sent the song to a guy named Sonny Limbo in Atlanta and

he wanted to cut it on Cissy Houston . . . he asked if I minded if he changed the title to 'Midnight Train to Georgia.' And I said, 'No, I don't mind. Just don't change the rest of the song.'" Cissy Houston, first cousin of Dionne Warwick and mother of Whitney Houston [see 620], took Weatherly's song into the R&B chart.

Weatherly's publisher forwarded the song to Gladys Knight and the Pips, who followed Houston's lead and kept the title "Midnight Train to Georgia." Their second single for Buddah, it debuted on the Hot 100 at number 71 and became the group's first number one hit eight weeks later.

Gladys Knight (born May 28, 1944 in Atlanta, Georgia) made her singing debut at age four at the Mount Mariah Baptist Church. Both her parents were singers in the Wings Over Jordan gospel choir, and with encouragement from her mother, seven-year-old Gladys appeared on Ted Mack's "The Original Amateur Hour" and won the first prize of $2,000 for singing Nat "King" Cole's "Too Young."

At her brother Merald's 10th birthday party, Gladys entertained the family by singing with Merald, her sister Brenda and cousins William and Elenor Guest. Another cousin, James "Pip" Wood, suggested they turn professional and lent them his nickname. Elenor and Brenda eventually chose married life over a career and were replaced by two more cousins, Edward Patten and Langston George.

Their first chart record, "Every

Beat of My Heart," went to number six in July, 1961. They recorded for Vee Jay and Fury Records, and after "Letter Full of Tears," a top 20 hit in early 1962, cousin Langston quit and Gladys Knight and the Pips continued as a quartet.

It wasn't a unanimous decision, the group signed with Motown in 1965 but they didn't score consecutive top 10 singles until they moved to Buddah. Following "Midnight Train to Georgia," they had three more top 10 singles: "I've Got to Use My Imagination," Weatherly's "Best Thing That Ever Happened to Me" and "On and On," from the film *Claudine*.

Legal complications in the late '70s prevented Gladys from recording with the Pips for three years. She recorded a solo album while the Pips released two albums on Casablanca. They were reunited on Columbia Records in 1980. Seven years later, they signed with MCA.

## THE TOP FIVE
*Week of October 27, 1973*

1  **Midnight Train to Georgia**
   Gladys Knight & the Pips

2  **Angie**
   Rolling Stones

3  **Half-Breed**
   Cher

4  **Ramblin' Man**
   Allman Brothers Band

5  **Keep on Truckin'**
   Eddie Kendricks

**348** **Keep on Truckin'** TAMLA 54238
EDDIE KENDRICKS

Writers: *Anita Poree*
*Frank Wilson*
*Leonard Caston*

Producers: *Frank Wilson*
*Leonard Caston*

*November 10, 1973*
*2 weeks*

THE VOICE of Eddie Kendricks had sold millions of records before he attempted a solo career. As the translucent tenor voice of the Temptations, Eddie had helped them achieve their first hit, "The Way You Do the Things You Do" (number 11 in April, 1964). While David Ruffin sang lead on the group's first chart-topper [see 168—"My Girl"], Eddie shared lead vocals with Dennis Edwards on the group's second number one [see 259—"I Can't Get Next to You"] and was lead soloist on the Temptations' third number one hit [see 290—"Just My Imagination (Running Away With Me)."

It was during the recording sessions for *The Sky's the Limit*, the album that included "Just My Imagination," that Eddie was preparing for his solo debut. Following the departure of David Ruffin in 1968, it looked like Eddie was choosing to go out on his own. "I never, ever wanted to leave the group," he candidly admits. "I never thought about leaving. The only reason I left is because I wasn't allowed to record on my own." Financial problems made it necessary to record a solo LP, Kendricks says, but he wanted to release that as a side project while remaining with the Temptations. Forced to choose between a group and a solo career,

he opted for the latter.

Performing solo was not new for the former Temptation. Born Edward James Kendricks on December 17, 1939, in Union Springs, Alabama, he was raised in Birmingham. With high school friend Paul Williams, he moved to Cleveland, Ohio, and formed a group called the Cavaliers. After that group broke up, Kendricks and Williams sang as solo artists, appearing in concert with dancer Caledonia Young.

Personal manager Milton Jenkins brought Kendricks and Williams to Detroit, where they became the Primes and eventually merged with another of Jenkins' groups, the Distants, to form the unit that would evolve into the Temptations.

Eddie had scored hits on the Gordy label as part of the Tempts and had a number two single on Motown, a Supremes/Temptations collaboration titled "I'm Gonna Make You Love Me," on which he shared lead vocals with Diana Ross. For his solo career, he moved to a third Motown subsidiary label, Tamla. While his first two albums did not produce a single that made the top 60, he was a hot attraction in New York discos, thanks to the songs

"Girl, You Need a Change of Mind" and "Date With the Rain." Those two numbers from his second LP were so popular in Gotham that Kendricks had to include them whenever he performed in Manhattan.

With his third solo album, Kendricks had a new manager and suddenly found his career in high gear. Producer Frank Wilson brought him a scratchy demo of a seven-minute song called "Keep On Truckin'." Eddie boasted, "I knew it was a hit because of the title. The old people used to truck when they were dancing. And I knew the trucking industry would embrace the record." Just to be sure that happened, the sound of a truck roaring down the highway was strategically mixed into the single.

"Keep on Truckin'" was the highest new entry on the Hot 100 for the week of August 25, 1973. Debuting at number 79, it took 11 weeks to rise to the top. Eddie followed it with "Boogie Down," a number two hit in 1974.

Kendricks' very last chart entry was a medley of two Temptations songs with Daryl Hall and John Oates and David Ruffin. Kendricks was 52 years old when he died of lung cancer in his hometown of Birmingham on October 5, 1992.

## THE TOP FIVE
*Week of November 10, 1973*

1 **Keep on Truckin'**
Eddie Kendricks

2 **Midnight Train to Georgia**
Gladys Knight & the Pips

3 **Angie**
Rolling Stones

4 **Heartbeat—It's a Lovebeat**
DeFranco Family

5 **Paper Roses**
Marie Osmond

*Writers: Richard Starkey*
*George Harrison*

*Producer: Richard Perry*

*November 24, 1973*
*1 week*

"**I**'M MOST happy—I guess we all are in a way—for Ringo's success," John Lennon told Tom Snyder in an interview for the "Tomorrow" show on NBC. "It always went 'round that Ringo was dumb, but he ain't dumb. But he didn't have that much of a writing ability and he wasn't known for writing his own material. And there was a bit of a worry that although he can make movies . . . how was his recording career gonna be?" Pausing to laugh, John concluded, "And in general, it's probably better than mine!"

In pure mathematical terms, Ringo Starr actually had the most successful solo career of any Beatle during the first half of the '70s. A look at chart statistics reveals that of his first eight singles released after the Beatles' break-up, seven made the top 10.

But it's not surprising the other Beatles were worried about how well he would do on his own. As the drummer for the Beatles, he was overshadowed by the writing of John Lennon and Paul McCartney, and George Harrison, and sang the fewest amount of lead vocals. Not that his songs were unpopular— "Yellow Submarine," "Boys," "I Wanna Be Your Man," "With a Little Help From My Friends" and "Act Naturally" all had many devotees, as did the first Beatles song composed

by Ringo, "Don't Pass Me By" on the double album *The Beatles.*

Ringo's first solo LP was *Sentimental Journey,* a collection of standards produced by George Martin and arranged by a roster of luminaries that included Paul McCartney, Quincy Jones, Elmer Bernstein, Maurice Gibb and Richard Perry. The first solo single by Ringo was the title track of his second album, *Beaucoups of Blues,* a country and western LP produced by Pete Drake in Nashville. That single spent five weeks on the Hot 100, only climbing as high as 87.

But the tide turned with Ringo's second single, "It Don't Come Easy." Written by Ringo and produced by George, it was a *bona fide* hit, peaking at number four in June, 1971. The follow-up, "Back Off Boogaloo," was also written by Ringo and produced by George. It went to number nine in May, 1972.

In early 1973, producer Richard Perry asked Ringo if he would like to be a presenter with Harry Nilsson at the Grammy Awards, originating that year in Nashville. Ringo had played

on drums on Nilsson's second LP, which Perry had produced, and accepted the invitation. "After Ringo telling me that he would do it, he phoned me back and said, 'Listen, I'm not going to Nashville just for the Grammy Awards. Remember you talked about going in the studio? Let's go in and see what happens.' So without any lawyers knowing anything about it, we came back to L.A., and in five days had recorded five tracks, which included the three major singles from the album, 'Photograph,' 'You're Sixteen' and 'Oh My My,' " Perry revealed in *The Record Producers* by John Tobler and Stuart Grundy.

George Harrison and John Lennon were in Los Angeles, and they became excited enough about the project to lend assistance. George, who co-wrote "Photograph" with Ringo, played 12-string acoustic guitar and sang harmony vocals.

"Photograph" was released as a single six weeks prior to the *Ringo* album. Debuting at number 74 on the Hot 100, it took only seven weeks to reach number one.

## THE TOP FIVE

*Week of November 24, 1973*

1  **Photograph**
   Ringo Starr

2  **Keep On Truckin'**
   Eddie Kendricks

3  **Top of the World**
   Carpenters

4  **Space Race**
   Billy Preston

5  **Heartbeat—It's a Lovebeat**
   DeFranco Family

350

# Top of the World A&M 1468
## CARPENTERS

*Writers: Richard Carpenter*
*John Bettis*

*Producers: Richard Carpenter*
*Karen Carpenter*
*Jack Daugherty*

*December 1, 1973*
*2 weeks*

"In a way, Karen was like my little sister," says John Bettis, who wrote the lyrics to Carpenters' hits like "Goodbye to Love," "Yesterday Once More" and the duo's second number one single, "Top of the World." "In a way, she was like my big sister. Obviously she was 'a' and 'the' voice for my words for a lot of years. So that carries an awful lot of baggage emotionally for me."

Bettis was part of a duo that per-formed in the same mid-'60s southern California folk circuit that produced Jackson Browne and the Nitty Gritty Dirt Band. But he knew the pair's days were numbered when he heard "The Sounds of Silence" [see 190], Simon and Garfunkel's 1966 chart-top-per, and "realized we couldn't compete with *that*." His partner, Maury Manseau, went on to form the mellow-rock Sunshine Company ("Happy," "Back on the Street Again").

In the fall of 1966, Bettis went off to California State College at Long Beach, where he joined the choir and met Richard Carpenter. When Bettis wrote a solo piece for the ensemble, Carpenter accompanied him during rehearsals. For the next two years, Carpenter and Bettis spent most of their time listening to records and writing songs. "It was just a writing

machine," Bettis says, "and I began to learn that I was basically a lyricist at heart. A lot of the songs we wrote back then are included on the first three Carpenters albums."

After college, Bettis ran hoot nights at a Berkeley folk club while the Carpenters signed with A&M and had their first number one single [see 278—"(They Long to Be) Close to You"]. For the group's fourth album, 1972's *A Song for You*, Bettis says, "Richard and I got together to write new songs because we had used up the old Long Beach State material."

One of the new songs Richard and John wrote was "Top of the World." "I had already written a song called 'Top of the World' with another part-ner," Bettis reveals. "Richard hadn't heard the song, but liked the title a lot. He came up with that introduc-tory lick which inspired a certain feel in it. And we just thrashed it out in a day. When we finished the song, Richard and I honestly did not realize that we'd written a hit. We thought it was a good album cut."

But while the Carpenters were on the road, the reaction to "Top of the World" convinced Richard it should be a single. Before it could be released, country singer Lynn Ander-son cut a cover version that went to the top of the country chart.

"In the back of Richard's mind," says Bettis, "it was already brewing as a single and he just wasn't pleased with the production on the album. Lynn's record was going up the coun-try chart while Richard was re-cutting the Carpenters' new version."

Bettis continued his longtime col-laboration with Carpenter, aware that he was still searching for a new musical direction since the tragic death of his sister. "I doubt that Richard will ever find another single voice that can be to him what Karen was. Just because that kind of magic would be *miraculous* to find again. Being without her was something we never contemplated. In terms of our writing, I still think we're adapting to it. I still find myself writing lyric ideas on bits of napkins and then shoving them away, saying, 'That's a Karen idea.' She was such a real per-son to me, and just like every other real person, she was varied. And just like every other creative person, she was very complex. But she was a delight, and I miss her very much."

## THE TOP FIVE
*Week of December 1, 1973*

1  **Top of the World**
   Carpenters

2  **Photograph**
   Ringo Starr

3  **Goodbye Yellow Brick Road**
   Elton John

4  **Space Race**
   Billy Preston

5  **Keep On Truckin'**
   Eddie Kendricks

Epic 11040 **The Most Beautiful Girl** 351
CHARLIE RICH

Writers: *Norro Wilson*
*Billy Sherrill*
*Rory Bourke*

Producer: *Billy Sherrill*

*December 15, 1973*
*2 weeks*

"THE SILVER FOX" waited 39 years to have a number one record. But with all the ups and downs in his checkered life and career, it sometimes seemed more like a hundred. Born December 14, 1932 in Colt, Arkansas, Charlie Rich developed an early love of blues and gospel singing as well as jazz piano. In the early '50s, the farmer's son served with the Air Force in Oklahoma, while moonlighting with a group called the Velvetones (featuring his wife Margaret Ann on vocals).

After his discharge, Rich returned to Arkansas and worked the farm with his father. "I wanted some security for my family," he explained to Robert Hilburn of the Los Angeles Times in 1974. "We had two kids and one on the way. I was still into music to some degree. If I had time, I'd play a gig around Memphis for $10 or $20 a night.

"After I had the family, however,

I didn't see how I could make a living in the music. There was always the idea in the back of my mind that if I could work it out, it would be nice, but the idea of making enough money through music seemed so remote." It all began to work out when Margaret Ann sent a tape of her husband's songs to saxophonist Bill Justis.

Justis, who had a number two hit with "Raunchy" in December, 1957, introduced Charlie to Sam Phillips of Sun Records in Memphis. Phillips recognized Charlie's talent, but told him to take some Jerry Lee Lewis records and come back when he'd learned how to rock. He was a good student, scoring in May, 1960, with a number 22 hit—the rockabilly classic "Lonely Weekends."

When Sun closed shop in the early '60s, Rich recorded briefly for RCA's Groove subsidiary. Then he signed with Mercury's Smash label in 1965, recording his second pop hit, "Mohair Sam" (number 21). An album for Hi Records took Charlie toward a more country-ballad format.

The transition from rockabilly singer to country crooner was complete when he joined the Epic stable in the late '60s. Working with producer Billy Sherrill, he recorded one of the most heart-wrenching working

class laments in country music, "Life Has Its Little Ups and Downs." It is a title that reflected Charlie's career.

The "ups" started in 1973 with "Behind Closed Doors," a single that went to number 15 on the Hot 100. His crossover success continued with "The Most Beautiful Girl," which cemented Charlie's position as a mass appeal, mainstream star. The record debuted on the Hot 100 at number 83 on September 29, 1973, and reached the summit 11 weeks later.

During the next two years, Rich continued hitting the pop chart with country-flavored hits like "There Won't Be Anymore" (number 18), "A Very Special Love Song" (number 11) and "Every Time You Touch Me (I Get High)" (number 19). But the "downs" were still to come, including a drinking problem and an inability to deal with stardom, all documented in Peter Guralnick's essay on Rich in his book *Feel Like Going Home*. He moved to Elektra in 1979 and placed two singles on the country chart, but was unable to duplicate his pop success of the mid-'70s.

On July 25, 1995, Charlie Rich and his wife of 43 years, Margaret Ann, watched their musician son Allan perform in Natchez, Mississippi. They were on their way home from Florida to Memphis when they stopped overnight at a motel in Hammond, Louisiana. But sadly Rich never made it home; he died that day of a blood clot on the lung. He was 62 years old. Sam Phillips declared in *Billboard*, "He will be remembered as a musician's musician, yet he was also a musician for all people, which is very difficult, if not impossible."

## THE TOP FIVE
*Week of December 15, 1973*

1 **The Most Beautiful Girl**
Charlie Rich

2 **Goodbye Yellow Brick Road**
Elton John

2 **Top of the World**
Carpenters

4 **Just You 'n' Me**
Chicago

5 **Time in a Bottle**
Jim Croce

# 352 Time in a Bottle ABC 11405
## JIM CROCE

*Writer: Jim Croce*

*Producers: Terry Cashman*
*Tommy West*

*December 29, 1973*
*2 weeks*

"**T**IME IN A BOTTLE" was one of 12 tracks on Jim Croce's first album, *You Don't Mess Around With Jim*, released in 1972. Atypical of the other songs on the LP, it had an almost British feel to it, thanks to the lead acoustic guitar of Maury Muehleisen. Because it was so different from the other cuts, it was never considered for release as a single. The album did yield two hits in 1972, the title track (number eight in September) and "Operator (That's Not the Way It Feels" (number 17 in December). Croce's next single was

taken from his second LP, *Life and Times*. When it went to number one [see 338—"Bad, Bad Leroy Brown"], no one had any intention of returning to the first album to mine more singles.

Until a fateful telephone call. "Elliott Abbot, who was Jimmy's manager, called me and said that interest had been expressed by David Wolper to use 'Time in a Bottle' on the soundtrack of a television film," explains Phil Kurnit, partners with Terry Cashman and Tommy West in their production company. The film was "She Lives," starring Desi Arnaz, Jr., and Season Hubley. Telecast September 12, 1973, on the ABC Movie of the Week, it told the story of a young woman dying of cancer. Producer Stan Margulies and director Stuart Hagman searched for an appropriate contemporary song to use as a theme in the film. They pur-

chased a stack of albums from a nearby record store and sat down to listen to all of them. When they heard the lyrics to "Time in a Bottle," they knew they had found the perfect song. After the broadcast, ABC affiliates all over the country received thousands of phone calls from listeners who wanted to know where they could buy the record.

The night the movie was telecast, Croce completed his third album, *I Got a Name*. Eight days later he gave a concert at Northwestern Louisiana University. A privately charted plane was waiting at the municipal airport at Natchitoches to take him to his next engagement, at another college 70 miles away. After an abortive take-off, the plane crashed into a tree. Jim Croce and five other people, including guitarist Maury Muehleisen, were killed.

Jim Croce was just 30 years old when he died. After years of struggling, he had experienced a year of intoxicating success. His music appealed to the head and heart, and once, during a concert, he analyzed his appeal, "I'm a kind of music psychologist, or a musical bouncer, or a live juke box. It depends on the audience."

After his death, "I Got a Name" was released as a single. It was used as a theme in the motion picture *The Last American Hero*. The week it peaked at number 10, "Time in a Bottle," a single at last, entered the Hot 100 at number 79. Six weeks later it was Croce's second number one single and the third posthumous number one of the rock era.

## THE TOP FIVE
*Week of December 29, 1973*

1 **Time in a Bottle**
Jim Croce

2 **The Most Beautiful Girl**
Charlie Rich

3 **Leave Me Alone**
**(Ruby Red Dress)**
Helen Reddy

4 **The Joker**
Steve Miller Band

5 **Goodbye Yellow Brick Road**
Elton John

Writers: *Steve Miller*
    *Ahmet Ertegun*
    *Eddie Curtis*

Producer: *Steve Miller*

January 12, 1974
1 week

WHEN STEVE MILLER, the rock super-star *Rolling Stone* dubbed "the man without a face," had his first number one single, he hung the gold record over his washing machine. The way he tells it, "As I do my underwear and socks I can consider 'the star' who wore them."

Miller was born in Milwaukee, Wisconsin, on October 5, 1943, but grew up in Dallas, Texas. At 12, he formed an R&B band that later featured vocals by another blue-eyed soul brother, Boz Scaggs. When the two attended the University of Wisconsin, they fronted a group called the Fabulous Night Trains that tore up the frat circuit with its hard-driving soul music.

After college, Miller drifted down to Chicago, and teamed up with keyboardist Barry Goldberg to form the Goldberg-Miller Blues Band. Moving to San Francisco in 1966, Miller started a band in four days, played a gig at the Avalon Ballroom, and became an immediate local favorite in those days of psychedelia.

When a record contract with Capitol seemed imminent, Scaggs returned from a folksinging stint in Sweden to join the group. The first two Steve Miller Band albums—*Children of the Future* and *Sailor*—combined straight-ahead blues with seamlessly produced, Beatlesque rock

suites. Many consider them Miller's finest work. In 1969, Scaggs left the band to pursue what would be a highly-successful solo career (recording hits like "Lowdown" and "Lido Shuffle").

Miller spent the early '70s playing some of the best rock music ever recorded, founded in the blues, grand-scaled and harmonically rich. Although he developed an enthusiastic following, he remained a relative unknown. "People tended to be fans of the albums," he said, "not of Steve Miller." He didn't break out as a mainstream superstar until his eighth LP, released in the autumn of 1973: *The Joker*.

"I never thought 'The Joker' was going to be a hit," Miller told *Guitar Player* in 1978. "I took the challenge; I said, 'Okay, it's got to be two-and-a-half minutes long, and it's got to play on top 40 radio, and it's got to follow a soul-disco symphony.' I always wanted to make singles; I like singles....So I just started taking that

two-and-a-half minute thing and started looking for sounds that record well....It's like a game, like a crossword puzzle. And as long as you get some tunes that've got feeling and soul and substance to them, there you go."

"The Joker" entered the Hot 100 at number 86 on October 20, 1973. Twelve weeks later it was number one. Although the album it came from was certified gold, Miller was uncertain about its commercial potential.

"That's how bright I am," Miller admitted in 1977. "I just decided, man, that it's not my gig, not my job so I said, 'You think there's a single on it? You're the guys that've gotta go out and...make people play it.' They were listening to it and some guy stood up—just like Brigham Young—and said, 'That's a hit!' They all just sort of stood up, with their fingers up in the air, and started marching around going, 'That's a hit!'"

## THE TOP FIVE
*Week of January 12, 1974*

1  **The Joker**
   Steve Miller Band

2  **Time in a Bottle**
   Jim Croce

3  **Show and Tell**
   Al Wilson

4  **Smokin' in the Boys' Room**
   Brownsville Station

5  **I've Got to Use
   My Imagination**
   Gladys Knight & the Pips

## 354 Show and Tell ROCKY ROAD 30073
### AL WILSON

Writer: Jerry Fuller

Producer: Jerry Fuller

January 19, 1974
1 week

AL WILSON knew he had found the right producer when Jerry Fuller drove 50 miles to hear him sing. Al was appearing at a small club in Chino, California, singing everything from rock and roll to ballads to rhythm and blues, six nights a week. Fuller could have auditioned Wilson by listening to tapes, but he wanted to hear the real thing, unencumbered by anyone else's production. At the end of his set, Wilson was invited to Fuller's office the following Friday morning, where Fuller showed him the lyrics to "Show and Tell." Wilson liked the words and asked to hear the melody. Fuller obliged by strumming it on a guitar, then handed Wilson a copy of Johnny Mathis singing the tune, which Fuller had just produced. Wilson thanked him, but declined to listen to Mathis' version until he had recorded it himself.

Wilson cut two songs with Fuller: "Show and Tell" and "Queen of the Ghetto," intended to be the "A" side. But the response to "Show and Tell" was so great, it quickly became the hit.

Al Wilson was born June 19, 1939, in Meridian, Mississippi. He sang in his church choir, formed a quartet to sing spirituals and also sang country and western songs. He realized he wanted to be a professional singer when he was in the Navy. He sang with a group on base and when he

was discharged in 1958, came to Los Angeles where he worked odd jobs as a dishwasher, mail carrier and janitor. He moved to the town of Victorville, then moved again to San Bernardino, where he joined a group called the Jewels. Changing their name to the Rollers, they went to number 80 on the chart with "The Continental Walk" in April, 1961.

Wilson left the group in 1962 and the following year worked as a drummer to support himself. His first big break came in 1966, when he met Marc Gordon, manager of the Fifth Dimension [see 253—"Aquarius/Let the Sunshine In"]. Gordon arranged an a cappella audition for Wilson with Johnny Rivers [see 212—"Poor Side of Town"], who was looking to sign artists for his Soul City label. Two years later, Wilson had his first solo chart record with "The Snake," which slithered up to number 27. He followed it with cover versions of

Johnny's "Poor Side of Town" and Creedence Clearwater Revival's "Lodi," but neither made the top 60.

In the early '70s, Gordon formed his own label, Carousel Records, and had a top three hit with "Precious and Few" by Climax. The label changed names to Rocky Road and Wilson was signed as an artist, giving the label its only number one hit with "Show and Tell." The single entered the Hot 100 at number 96 on October 20, 1973, and topped the chart 13 weeks later.

Fuller's "Touch and Go" was the follow-up, but it had a very similar sound and only managed to reach number 57. Wilson and O. C. Smith both released "La La Peace Song" in the fall of 1974, and Wilson won the cover battle, charting at number 30. The Rocky Road label folded and Wilson had one top 30 single on Playboy Records, "I've Got a Feeling (We'll Be Seeing Each Other Again)."

### THE TOP FIVE
Week of January 19, 1974

1 **Show and Tell**
Al Wilson

2 **The Joker**
Steve Miller Band

3 **Smokin' in the Boys' Room**
Brownsville Station

4 **I've Got to Use My Imagination**
Gladys Knight & the Pips

5 **You're Sixteen**
Ringo Starr

Writers: *Richard Sherman*
*Robert Sherman*

Producer: *Richard Perry*

*January 26, 1974*
*1 week*

PRODUCER Richard Perry worked with all four former Beatles while producing the *Ringo* album for the quartet's former drummer. "I would have to say that the entire Ringo involvement and the experience of making that album was the greatest thrill of my recording career, and one which I may never top," Perry told John Tobler and Stuart Grundy in *The Record Producers*. "Surely no session was more fun—the spirit of the recording, as they said, was 'A splendid time is guaranteed for all.' "

George Harrison participated in the album's first number one single [see 349—"Photograph"] as well as a John Lennon-authored track, "I'm the Greatest." George and John happened to be in Los Angeles while Ringo was working with Perry, and were eager to participate in the recording. A mere 6,000 miles didn't prevent Paul McCartney from getting involved.

"Quite coincidentally, Paul called and asked me to come to London to help supervise the musical tracks of his first TV special, because everything had to be re-recorded, and he wanted someone in the booth to help out the engineer, because TV engineers aren't that experienced in rock recordings," Perry related in *The Record Producers*. "And that was when we were going to London to continue work on Ringo's album, so it all came together very conveniently, and Paul was good enough to write a song for Ringo, and we had two or three wonderful nights of recording when he and Linda came down . . . in fact, the solo on 'You're Sixteen,' which sounds like a kazoo or something, was Paul singing very spontaneously as we played that track back, so he's singing solo on that."

"You're Sixteen" was the second single released from *Ringo*. It was the highest new entry on the Hot 100 the week of December 15, 1973, debuting at number 75. Just six weeks later, Ringo had his second number one.

It was the second time around for "You're Sixteen," originally a hit for Johnny Burnette. It peaked at number eight in December, 1960.

Richard Starkey was born during an air raid on July 7, 1940, in Liverpool. He was often ill as a child and spent at least three years in hospitals. His first musical outfit was the Eddie Clayton Skiffle Band and his first set of drums was a Christmas gift from his stepfather. He assumed the stage name of Ringo Starr while playing drums for a popular Liverpool group, Rory Storm and the Hurricanes. When they became a houseband at a club in Hamburg, Germany, Ringo met his future mates.

When Brian Epstein dismissed Pete Best from the Beatles on August 16, 1962, Ringo was invited to take his place. At the same time, Ringo was asked to join another successful Liverpool group, Kingsize Taylor and the Dominoes. Ringo took the offer with the best wage—25 pounds a week for being the Beatles' new drummer.

Ringo's success on the singles chart diminished in 1975 after ending his top 10 streak with "Oh My My," "Only You" and the two-sided hit, "No No Song" and "Snookeroo." He kept up an acting career that had started with *Candy* and *The Magic Christian*, impressing critics with his role in *That'll Be the Day*. During the filming of *Caveman* he met his second wife, Barbara Bach.

After Apple Records dissolved, Ringo recorded for Atlantic and Boardwalk Records in the United States. A 1983 LP, *Old Wave*, was released by RCA in Canada but did not come out in the U.S.

If you don't want to feel old, move on to "The Way We Were." Still with us? Ringo was the first Beatle to become a grandfather. Son Zak and his wife welcomed daughter Tatia Jayne Starkey on Sept. 7, 1985.

**THE TOP FIVE**
*Week of January 26, 1974*

1 **You're Sixteen**
Ringo Starr

2 **Show and Tell**
Al Wilson

3 **The Way We Were**
Barbra Streisand

4 **I've Got to Use
My Imagination**
Gladys Knight & the Pips

5 **The Joker**
Steve Miller Band

## 356 The Way We Were COLUMBIA 45944
### BARBRA STREISAND

*Writers: Marvin Hamlisch
Alan Bergman
Marilyn Bergman*

*Producer: Marty Paich*

*February 2, 1974
3 weeks*

EARLY in her career, a perceptive reviewer called Barbra Streisand an "original." Indeed, it would be difficult to find another entertainer who could match the breadth and scope of her achievements. A chronicle of her awards runs several pages, encompassing film, theater, live performances, television, records—even the best-dressed list.

Born with the traditional spelling of Barbara Joan Streisand on April 24, 1942, in Brooklyn, New York, her long, illustrious career began when she was a toddler. "My mother says I had lipstick smeared on my face and was acting on a dresser when I was two. She caught me before I fell. Maybe that was the first time I actually acted," she recalled. One of three children, her father died when she was 15 months old, leaving the family not "*poor* poor," but "we didn't have anything."

Her first exposure to Broadway was *The Diary of Anne Frank*, which she saw at age 14. "I thought I could go up on that stage and play any role without any trouble at all," was her reaction. Hustling as a theater usherette and switchboard operator, she applied herself to achieving her dream. "I was certain I'd be famous one day. When I'd tell my mother about it, she would say, 'How can you be famous? You're too skinny.' "

### THE TOP FIVE
*Week of February 2, 1974*

1 **The Way We Were**
  Barbra Streisand

2 **You're Sixteen**
  Ringo Starr

3 **Love's Theme**
  Love Unlimited Orchestra

4 **Show and Tell**
  Al Wilson

5 **Americans**
  Byron MacGregor

Mother also entreated daughter to acquire basic secretarial skills, but she refused, claiming, "I knew I had talent and I was afraid that if I learned how to type I'd become a secretary."

With her ambition and drive, Barbra had no reason to fear a dead-end office career. Winning a talent contest at 18 landed her a singing slot at Bonsoir, a Greenwich Village club, where her two-week engagement was extended to 11 weeks. Then she played the Blue Angel where producer David Merrick was impressed enough to offer her the ugly Jewish duckling role of Miss Marmelstein in *I Can Get It for You Wholesale* in 1962. New York and London theatrical triumphs in *Funny Girl* made her a full-fledged star.

Musicals were Streisand's entree into recording. Her contributions to the cast albums of *I Can Get It for You Wholesale* and *Pins and Needles* convinced Columbia Records that they had a major moneymaker in their studios, and they tendered a contract. Between 1964-1972 she placed 18 singles on the Hot 100, ranging from show tunes ("He Touched Me") to humorous pop songs ("Second Hand Rose") to compositions by contemporary writers like Carole King ("Where You Lead"). Her two biggest hits during these years were her first chart single, "People," from *Funny Girl* (number five in June, 1964) and Laura Nyro's "Stoney End" (number six in January, 1971).

She had to wait until 1974 for her first number one single, the title song from *The Way We Were*. The theme from this tear-jerker, in which Streisand and Robert Redford starred as a mismatched couple that audiences followed from college to marriage to divorce and beyond, debuted at number 92 on November 24, 1973. It didn't reach its full potential until the week of February 2, 1974, shortly after a new Streisand studio album featuring "The Way We Were" as its title song was released.

There were awards aplenty for the song, including a Grammy for Song of the Year to songwriters Marvin Hamlisch and Alan and Marilyn Bergman. The trio were also Oscar winners; "The Way We Were" was the fifth number one single of the rock era to win an Academy Award for Best Song.

gle, "I'm Gonna Love You Just a Little More Baby," peaked at number three in June. But he still had time to write and produce *Under the Influence of Love Unlimited*, the trio's debut album for 20th Century Records.

The first vocal single from the LP was "It May Be Winter Outside (But in My Heart It's Spring)," a song Barry had written and produced for Felice Taylor in 1967. It entered the Hot 100 on December 15, 1973, but two weeks earlier, the instrumental "Love's Theme" debuted at number 89. Eight weeks later it was number one. The song it segued into, "Under the Influence of Love," was eventually released as a single too, but it could only inch up to number 76 in May, 1974.

White was the conductor and arranger for the Love Unlimited Orchestra, although he never had a formal music lesson. "I can mix a song in 35 minutes that would take other people hours to complete. I have learned tricks in mixing and mastering that nobody knows, and the gifts I have in rhythm and countermelody would take nine years of college to learn."

White kept the Love Unlimited Orchestra active and charted four more singles on the Hot 100. The most successful was "Satin Soul," a number 22 hit in April, 1975. After leaving 20th Century, White released instrumental albums on his Unlimited Gold label, and in 1981 he teamed up with Glodean for an album of duets. The effort proved less successful than their marriage, which produced seven children.

*Writer: Barry White*

*Producer: Barry White*

*February 9, 1974*
*1 week*

**T**HE Love Unlimited Orchestra was the name Barry White invented for the 40-piece band he used to back the female singing trio Love Unlimited. But the studio musicians achieved a better chart average than the singers, starting with a number one instrumental, "Love's Theme."

The track was written as an overture for the girls' album, *Under the Influence of Love Unlimited*. As the first cut on the album, it segued directly into the vocal track "Under the Influence of Love." It was a sensation on the dance floor, as club DJs could play all eight minutes and 17 seconds of the two songs without lifting the needle—setting a trend that would become s.o.p. in discos.

Sisters Glodean and Linda Jones first sang in their church choir in San Pedro, California. When they joined their school choir, they became

friends with Diane Taylor. Each had planned a separate career out of the music field, but a fateful invitation to sing backing vocals at a recording session led them to producer Barry White [see 376—"Can't Get Enough of Your Love, Babe"]. When he heard their high-pitched harmonies, it was love at first listen.

"It was the greatest thing that ever happened to me," said White, who became their manager and mentor. "I devoted my heart, soul, talent and goals to the girls." It's true—later, he would even marry Glodean.

Taking the young women under his formidable wing, White undertook a three-year plan to mold them into superstars. His efforts paid off when he got them a recording contract with Uni Records. Their first single, the lushly romantic "Walkin' in the Rain With the One I Love," featured a cameo appearance by White as a voice on the telephone. The million-selling record peaked at number 14 in June, 1972.

White launched his own singing career with his sensual "pillow talk" vocal style in early 1973. His first sin-

---

## THE TOP FIVE
*Week of February 9, 1974*

1 **Love's Theme**
   Love Unlimited Orchestra

2 **The Way We Were**
   Barbra Streisand

3 **You're Sixteen**
   Ringo Starr

4 **Americans**
   Byron MacGregor

5 **Until You Come Back to Me
   (That's What I'm Gonna Do)**
   Aretha Franklin

# 358 Seasons in the Sun BELL 45432
## TERRY JACKS

*Writers: Jacques Brel
      Rod McKuen*

*Producer: Terry Jacks*

*March 2, 1974
3 weeks*

THE POPPY FAMILY sounded like they might have been Canada's answer to the Cowsills. Actually, the family consisted only of husband and wife Terry and Susan Jacks and they had two hits in 1970: "Which Way You Goin', Billy?" which peaked at number two, and "That's Where I Went Wrong," which managed to get to number 29.

Terry was born in Winnipeg, Manitoba, and Susan was born in Vancouver, British Columbia. Terry's family moved to Vancouver when he was a child. He grew up listening to American rock and roll records and spent the money he earned on his paper route buying Buddy Holly singles. He won an art scholarship in high school and intended to be an architect. At one point he considered following a professional golfing career. But he also spent time in the basement with his guitar pretending he was Roy Orbison, and music won out.

He formed a group called the Chessmen and they recorded in Nashville and Los Angeles. Aside from one hit in Vancouver, "The Way You Feel," the band was not very successful. While appearing on a Canadian television show with the Chessmen, Terry met another singer, Susan Pesklevits. They began a professional relationship (the Poppy Family) as well as a personal one (they were married).

They took the name Poppy Family at a time when groups were more popular than individual singers. Rather than release their first single under the name Susan Pesklevits, they decided to go with the Poppy Family.

The act and the marriage broke up in 1973. The Beach Boys asked Terry to work with them on a session and he suggested they record a song written by French composer Jacques Brel in 1961, "Le Moribond" ("The Dying Man"). Terry knew it from an English version by Rod McKuen that the Kingston Trio had recorded in 1964.

After recording it, the Beach Boys decided not to release it, and, mourning a friend who had died unexpectedly, Terry decided to cut it himself. He asked for permission to revise the final verse and give it a lighter feel, and the finished tape sat on a shelf in his basement for more than a year. One day while Jacks was considering what to release next, a newspaper delivery boy heard the tape and asked if he could bring his friends over to hear it. Their enthusiasm convinced Terry to release the song on his own Goldfish label. After it became a Canadian hit, Dave Carrico of Bell Records flew to Vancouver and secured the right to release the song in America.

The record topped the charts in Canada, England and America, with reported sales of over six million copies worldwide. Terry followed it up with another Brel song, "If You Go Away," which peaked at 68. On October 9, 1978, Brel died of cancer.

## THE TOP FIVE
*Week of March 2, 1974*

1 **Seasons in the Sun**
Terry Jacks

2 **The Way We Were**
Barbra Streisand

3 **Spiders and Snakes**
Jim Stafford

4 **Boogie Down**
Eddie Kendricks

5 **Jungle Boogie**
Kool & the Gang

*Writer: John Durrill*

*Producer: Snuff Garrett*

*March 23, 1974*
*1 week*

SNUFF GARRETT went to the story-song well one more time and came up with "Dark Lady,"a third number one single for Cher. John Durrill wrote it and recorded a demo for Snuff just before leaving for a tour of Japan with the Ventures. Listening to the song repeatedly, Garrett was unhappy with the third verse.

"She caught her boyfriend with the soothsayer (the dark lady of the title), and I decided she had to kill him. I couldn't find John. I called his booking agency and they said he was in Kyoto. I finally got a long distance call and heard a muffled voice on the other end—it was John calling from Japan. He said, 'You wanted me?' I said, 'Kill him! I want him dead in the third verse. You've got to send me new lyrics by telegram!' "

It was just over 24 hours later that Garrett received a stack of telegrams, each containing suggested new lines for the third verse. The song was rewritten and Cher recorded it in Los Angeles. It entered the Hot 100 at number 82 on January 19, 1974, and went to number one nine weeks later.

It was during the chart life of "Dark Lady" that Sonny and Cher's marital problems became public knowledge. They were still starring in a weekly variety series for CBS, taking pot shots at each other during the opening of each show. "The only difficult period I had with Cher was when we were still married," Sonny concedes. "We had split up, but we were pretending to be happily married with a kid. That was rough. After that, it was not rough at all."

Two days after their divorce became final, Cher married Gregg Allman. It was a stormy union, although it survived Cher's filing for divorce nine days after the marriage. Cher moved from MCA to Warner Brothers Records, where her recordings ranged from singles produced by Phil Spector (including a duet with Harry Nilsson) to an album of duets with husband Gregg.

Her marriage to Gregg did come to an end eventually and she was

later romantically linked with Gene Simmons of Kiss and rock musician Les Dudek, with whom she formed a rock band called Black Rose. They recorded one album, which failed to gain exposure on radio.

Her Casablanca single "Take Me Home" made the top 10 in May, 1979. After a recording hiatus of several years, Cher returned to the top 10 in 1987 with "I Found Someone," her first single for Geffen Records.

After their divorce, Sonny and

Cher had their own individual television series. "The Sonny Comedy Revue" debuted on ABC on September 22, 1974, and ran only until December 29. "Cher," a variety series with the emphasis on music, made its debut on CBS February 16, 1975. Its final telecast was January 4, 1976. A month later, a revived Sonny and Cher series returned to CBS in the same time period as Cher's show. They tried opening the show with the same put-downs that had marked their earlier, successful series, but as a divorced couple it just wasn't as funny. "The Sonny and Cher Show" disappeared from the network on August 29, 1977.

Cher has been most visible the past few years as an actress. She made her Broadway stage debut in *Come Back to the 5 and Dime, Jimmy Dean, Jimmy Dean*, directed by Robert Altman. The play was filmed for motion picture release. She had already appeared in films like *Good Times* and *Chastity*, but the critics and public really took notice of her in *Silkwood*, and the Academy of Motion Picture Arts and Sciences justifiably rewarded her with an Oscar nomination as Best Supporting Actress.

Just before the release of her 1985 film *Mask*, Harvard University's Hasting Pudding Club named her "Woman of the Year," an honor previously bestowed on people like Katharine Hepburn, Rosalind Russell, Angela Lansbury, Jane Fonda, Meryl Streep, Bette Midler and Joan Rivers.

"When you look at the people who have received this award, it's hard to take it less than seriously," she said.

## THE TOP FIVE
*Week of March 23, 1974*

1 **Dark Lady**
Cher

2 **Seasons in the Sun**
Terry Jacks

3 **Sunshine on my Shoulders**
John Denver

4 **Boogie Down**
Eddie Kendricks

5 **Mockingbird**
Carly Simon & James Taylor

# Sunshine on My Shoulders
RCA 0213

**JOHN DENVER**

360

Writers: *John Denver*
*Dick Kniss*
*Mike Taylor*

Producer: *Milt Okun*

*March 30, 1974*
*1 week*

"**P**EOPLE, lend me your ears as I sing why the world's a happy place," John Denver declared in *Seventeen* magazine. A graduate of the est training, John Denver was associated with cheery, optimistic songs like "Take Me Home, Country Roads," his first chart single and a number two hit in August, 1971. But when he sat down to write "Sunshine on My Shoulders," he didn't intend for it to be a happy song. "I was so down I wanted to write a feeling-blue song," he explained. "This is what came out." It seemed that he just couldn't help chronicling the positive side of existence. "That's how I feel," he continued. "It's a reflection of my own lifestyle."

Denver, who claimed to be more an entertainer than a songwriter, noted in *Seventeen*, "A lot of people object to the optimism in my music. But if you listen to my records, you hear about things that trouble me. Not every song I've written is 'Rocky Mountain High.' The reason I stay optimistic is that everything is new

every time I do it. I've never cut this record before. I've sung the same song a thousand times but I've never done the concert I'm going to do."

"I love to share my life with you. I am trying to communicate what is so in my life, the joy of living, " John told his fans from the stage of the Seattle Coliseum. It was this attitude that piqued Denver's critics, who blasted him for being corny, calculated and mechanical. "Simple, escapist fare," one called his music, but his supporters loved the euphoria and light, a contrast to the heavy, anti-war "message" songs of the late '60s and early '70s.

Henry John Deutschendorf, Jr., was born on New Year's Eve, 1943, in Roswell, New Mexico. An Air Force brat, his childhood was spent all over the southwest, but favorite times were spent on his grandmother's Oklahoma farm. The guitar his other grandmother had given him at age eight accompanied him everywhere. "I had kind of a lonely childhood," he recalled for the *Saturday Evening Post*. "I would stand in the lunch line with my guitar. Somebody would ask if I could play it. I didn't want them to be sorry they'd asked."

He took one year of lessons "to learn the basic chords," then joined a rock band in high school. Architecture was his official major at Texas

Tech, but in reality he spent more time playing than drawing. Folk music clubs drew him to Los Angeles midway through his junior year, where he renamed himself after his favorite city, as he explained to *Newsweek*, "I liked it because my heart longed to live in the mountains."

John Denver was selected out of 250 candidates to replace Chad Mitchell in the trio bearing his name, although producer Milt Okun later admitted, "he didn't sound especially good." During his three-year tenure with the trio he began writing songs, some of which he recorded for his first solo RCA album, *Rhymes and Reasons*. One of the tunes on that album became a number one hit for Peter, Paul and Mary [see 264—"Leaving on a Jet Plane"].

"Sunshine on My Shoulders" was his ninth single to chart. Only "Take Me Home, Country Roads" and "Rocky Mountain High" (number nine in March, 1973) had made the top 10. "Sunshine on My Shoulders" entered the Hot 100 at number 90 on January 26, 1974, and moved into the number one position nine weeks later.

A television movie using "Sunshine on My Shoulders" as a theme song was telecast on NBC during the 1974-1975 season. Starring Cliff DeYoung and Elizabeth Cheshire, it told the story of a widower raising his wife's daughter from an earlier marriage. The mother, who died of cancer, loved the song "Sunshine on My Shoulders." High ratings prompted a series, "Sunshine," which debuted March 6, 1975, and ran for three months.

## THE TOP FIVE
*Week of March 30, 1974*

1. **Sunshine on My Shoulders**
   John Denver

2. **Hooked on a Feeling**
   Blue Swede

3. **Seasons in the Sun**
   Terry Jacks

4. **Bennie and the Jets**
   Elton John

5. **Dark Lady**
   Cher

*Writer: Mark James*

*Producer: Bengt Palmers*

*April 6, 1974*
*1 week*

"**H**OOKED ON A FEELING" was originally a hit for B. J. Thomas [see 266—"Raindrops Keep Fallin' on My Head"], who recorded it at the American Recording Studios in Memphis. It was January of 1969 when Thomas took the song to number five, his biggest success to that date. Almost three years later, the song received a startling new arrangement from British entrepreneur Jonathan King.

Jonathan King is best remembered in the United States for his top 20 hit in 1965, "Everyone's Gone to the Moon." In Britain, he's remembered for a host of other reasons. He's the man who discovered Genesis, 10cc and the Bay City Rollers [see 423—"Saturday Night"]. He was president of his own label, UK Records. He ran for Parliament. He filed weekly reports from New York each Saturday afternoon on Radio 1 and he hosted "Entertainment, U.S.A.," a TV series filmed on location in the United States that kept British audiences informed about American show biz.

He has also recorded cover versions of American hits under a wide variety of assumed names, including 100 Ton and a Feather ("It Only Takes a Minute"), Bubblerock ("(I Can't Get No) Satisfaction") and 53rd and 3rd ("Chick-a-Boom"). "Hooked on a Feeling" was released under his own name and peaked at number 23 on the British chart in early 1972. It was a radical departure from the Memphis production of Chips Moman; the first thing one noticed was the opening chant, "ooga-chaga, ooga-ooga chaga." He wasn't talking about Chaga Khan, but nobody was quite sure what it meant.

The King arrangement was heard by Bengt Palmers, head of A&R for EMI Records in Sweden. He was working with a group known in their homeland as Bjorn Skiffs and Blablus, which translated as Blue Denim. Palmers suggested they incorporate the song into their stage act and the group performed it for four months before deciding to record it.

The song was released just for the Scandinavian market, where it became a big hit. When executives at EMI International heard it, they decided to try an American release.

An English name was needed for the group and Palmers suggested altering Blue Denim to Blue Swede. Their version of "Hooked on a Feeling" entered the Hot 100 at number 87 on February 16, 1974, and went to number one on April 6, making them the first Swedish group to top the American charts. Coincidentally, April 6 was the very same day that another group from Blue Swede's homeland won the Eurovision Song Contest, launching them on an international career that would make them the second Swedish group to have an American number one. The winning song was "Waterloo" and the group was Abba [see 458—"Dancing Queen"].

The members of Blue Swede were bassist Bosse Liljedahl, keyboardist Anders Berglund, saxophonist Hinke Ekestubbe, drummer Jan Guldback, guitarist Michael Areklew, trumpeteer Thomas Berglund and lead singer Bjorn Skiffs.

When Bjorn was 14, he started his own rock group, Slam Creepers. They became well known in Sweden but in 1969 Bjorn split for a solo career. Four years later he signed with EMI in Sweden. His first album for the label was called *Denim Jacket*.

When he decided to put a group together again in 1972, he contacted some of Sweden's top musicians from other bands and asked if they'd like to form a new group and start from scratch. Bjorn's *Denim Jacket* album was the inspiration for the group name Blablus.

Blue Swede had one more American hit in late 1974, a reworking of the Association's "Never My Love." The group broke up and Skiffs continued on his own. He was cast as the Arbiter for the studio recording of *Chess,* a musical written by Tim Rice (*Evita, Jesus Christ Superstar*) with Bjorn's countrymen Benny Andersson and Bjorn Ulvaeus of Abba. In the summer of 1996, Blue Swede reunited for a tour of Sweden.

## THE TOP FIVE
*Week of April 6, 1974*

1 **Hooked on a Feeling**
Blue Swede

2 **Bennie & the Jets**
Elton John

3 **Sunshine on My Shoulders**
John Denver

4 **Seasons in the Sun**
Terry Jacks

5 **The Lord's Prayer**
Sister Janet Mead

# Bennie and the Jets MCA 40198
## ELTON JOHN

*Writers: Elton John*
*Bernie Taupin*

*Producer: Gus Dudgeon*

*April 13, 1974*
*1 week*

With "Bennie and the Jets," the man who conquered the pop chart began his assault on soul. Not that he understood the appeal of a tubby white flamboyant dresser in glasses to that segment of record buyers. "What am I going to do on my next American tour? Play the Apollo for a week, open with 'Bennie' then say, 'Thanks, you can all go home now,' " Elton queried in *Rolling Stone*. But he was thrilled with the achievement. "I'm such a black record fanatic that to think I'm actually in the R&B chart means that even if it doesn't get any higher than (number) 34 I'm gonna stick it up and frame it." Eventually Elton hung a number 15 R&B record on his wall.

Like some of Elton's other million-selling singles, "Bennie and the Jets" was conceived in the peculiar collaborative style Elton John and Bernie Taupin evolved in their early days when they shared digs with the pianist's parents.

"Sometimes I'll come up with a title and I'll try to write a song around that," Taupin explained in *Rolling Stone*. "Other times I'll come up with a first line or a first two lines. Basically it takes me very little time to write a song. If I find myself taking more than an hour to do it I usually forget it and try something else. I like to work quickly; I never

## THE TOP FIVE
### Week of April 13, 1974

1 **Bennie and the Jets**
Elton John

2 **Hooked on a Feeling**
Blue Swede

3 **TSOP**
MFSB and the Three Degrees

4 **The Lord's Prayer**
Sister Janet Mead

5 **Come and Get Your Love**
Redbone

like to waste any time. I never write half a song and come back to it later at all. It all has to be done at once. I lose interest if I don't."

Delivering the several sheaves of lyrics under his arm, Taupin turns the task over to Elton who also works quickly. "If I am half an hour on one and it hasn't come by then, I move on," he's said. Not much time was ever wasted. "Reg has never failed to come up with a melody to my lyrics," Bernie elaborated. "There are some that we decide later on not to use but all come out as finished songs. It's amazing, you know, because Reg always writes a melody that's just perfect."

"I've never been involved with the lyrics," Elton said in *Billboard*. "Sometimes I would suggest the title to Bernie. I used to say to him, 'write a love song' or 'a song with a girl's (name) in it,' because I like songs in which you sing about someone so you can put a lot of emotion in them."

The songwriters were especially pleased with the 17 songs they authored to accompany "Bennie and

the Jets" on the double album *Goodbye Yellow Brick Road*. "It's far more musical, nothing like *Don't Shoot Me*," Elton previewed in a *Rolling Stone* interview.

The title track was the first single, and it held at number two for three weeks in December, 1973. The follow-up was intended to be the Taupin-John ode to Marilyn Monroe, "Candle in the Wind," but a black radio station in Detroit was giving heavy airplay to "Bennie and the Jets" and MCA decided that would make a better "A" side for America. The response to the label's decision was overwhelming. "Bennie and Jets" was the highest new entry on the Hot 100 for the week of February 16, 1974. Debuting at number 69, it took eight weeks to become Elton's second number one single. In Britain, "Bennie and the Jets" was relegated to the "B" side of "Candle in the Wind," which peaked at number 11. As Elton was leaving DJM Records to organize his own label in 1976, DJM belatedly released "Bennie" as an "A" side, but as a four-year-old single, it could only reach number 37.

*Writers: Kenny Gamble*
*Leon Huff*

*Producers: Kenny Gamble*
*Leon Huff*

*April 20, 1974*
*2 weeks*

MFSB (MOTHERS, FATHERS, SISTERS, BROTHERS) were the house band at Sigma Sound Studios, the recording facility owned by writer/producers Kenny Gamble and Leon Huff, the guiding lights behind Philadelphia International Records. The collection of almost 40 session musicians played on virtually every Philadelphia hit from Gamble-Huff and Thom Bell, including number one songs from Billy Paul [see 325—"Me and Mrs. Jones"] and the O'Jays [see 330— "Love Train"], as well as hits by the Delfonics, the Intruders, the Spinners and Harold Melvin and the Blue Notes, among others.

Gamble and Huff first met in a Philly band called the Romeos, which also included Roland Chambers, the guitarist of MFSB. Gamble and Huff became a writing/producing team in the mid-'60s, first experiencing success with the Intruders' "(We'll Be) United" on their own Gamble label in 1966. A year later they had a top five

hit with the Soul Survivors' "Expressway to Your Heart."

Before the decade was over, they would fashion hits for Jerry Butler ("Only the Strong Survive") and Dusty Springfield ("A Brand New Me"), all featuring the MFSB house band. In 1971, Gamble and Huff formed a new label, Philadelphia International, distributed by CBS. The sound of Philadelphia proved to be a real rival to Berry Gordy's sound of Detroit.

Helping Gamble and Huff to establish the sound of Philadelphia were the racially-mixed musicians who made up MFSB. Ronnie Baker played bass; Vince Montana was on vibes; Bobby Eli, Roland Chambers, Ron Kersey and Norman Harris were the guitarists; Earl Young played drums; Larry Washington handled percussion; Lenny Pakula was on organ; Zach Zachery played the saxophone; Ron Kersey was on keyboards; and Don Renaldo conducted. Bobby Martin handled arrangements.

Bobby Martin explained what happened next in Tony Cummings' *The Sound of Philadelphia*: "We all got together and planned an album. It wouldn't be a hard R&B album, or a

jazz album or an easy-listening album. It'd take in everything, every kind of music. When we finished it, we called the band MFSB and it came out on Philadelphia International in mid-'73.

"It was the "Soul Train" TV program which made things really happen. Don Cornelius, the program's producer, came down and saw us and asked us to work out a theme tune for his show. We did the tune and Kenny thought up the name 'TSOP.' We used the Three Degrees as voices at the end. Then . . . the demand grew for the release of the theme. At first we were a little reluctant to put it out, but we did, and of course it was a stone smash."

TSOP—The Sound of Philadelphia—continued to dominate the charts during the '70s, and at one point Gamble and Huff started a second label, called TSOP. One of the best exponents of TSOP were the Three Degrees, who had a number two hit at the end of 1974 with "When Will I See You Again." The female trio first recorded for the Philadelphia-based Swan label in the '60s, then for Warner Brothers, Metromedia and Neptune Records, a Gamble-Huff label that pre-dated Philadelphia International.

## 364 The Loco-Motion CAPITOL 3840
GRAND FUNK

*Writers: Gerry Goffin*
*Carole King*

*Producer: Todd Rundgren*

*May 4, 1974*
*2 weeks*

THE incongruity of a heavy metal band from Flint, Michigan, recording Little Eva's 1962 dance classic "The Loco-Motion" [see 115], should have been reason enough to catapult the record to number one.

Producer Todd Rundgren, who gave the Midwest rockers their first chart-topper [see 344—"We're an American Band"], heard the four Grand Funkers messing around with the song and having fun with its harmonies. He convinced them it should be a single.

Their blistering rendition entered the Hot 100 at number 82 on March 9, 1974. Eight weeks later, Rundgren's decision proved to be correct: "The Loco-Motion" became the second song of the rock era to become number one twice by different artists. Coincidentally, the first song to capture this honor, "Go Away Little Girl" (number one by Steve Lawrence [see 122] and Donny Osmond [see 299]), was penned by the same husband and wife songwriters, Gerry Goffin and Carole King.

Asked about the Grand Funk version of "The Loco-Motion," Gerry Goffin told Stewart Rhodes of *Rolling Stone,* "It's like a nice gift. It is kind of weird hearing it done in a different way, but you can still hear how it appeals to the kids."

"The Loco-Motion" was included in Grand Funk's tenth album, *Shinin' On.* The jacket featured a 3-D cover with star-shaped glasses and a 3-D poster inside. To support the LP, the four members of the band—Mark Farner, Don Brewer, Mel Schacher and Craig Frost—embarked on a whirlwind 40-city American tour. As a finale to the sold-out concerts, Grand Funk performed "The Loco-Motion" while a film of a train collision was projected behind them.

The band managed three successful follow-ups to their second number one single. The title track from *Shinin' On* went to number 11; "Some Kind of Wonderful" (not the Goffin-King song recorded by the Drifters) peaked at three and "Bad Time" went to four. After two more mid-chart singles for Capitol, the band shifted to MCA in 1976. By then, however, the end of the track was in sight, and the Funk threw in the towel later that year, after selling more than 20 million records.

"We surpassed all our goals and weren't having fun anymore," explained drummer Brewer. "We were burned out. We were at the point where being Grand Funk wasn't good anymore and we didn't want to cheat the public."

Guitarist Farner cut an inauspicious solo LP for Atco, then retreated to his isolated farm in northern Michigan, where he raised a family and started an alternative energy retail outfit. Meanwhile, Brewer and bassist Schacher fronted a rock/R&B outfit called Flint and also released an unsuccessful album.

But the lowering of the decibel level was not permanent. In 1981, the band was "called back into the line of duty," according to Farner. With a new bass player, Dennis Berringer, they returned to their ear-blitzing sound of yesteryear.

As Farner would put it, "People want the real thing. As long as there's room for sledgehammer rock and roll, there's room for Grand Funk Railroad."

## THE TOP FIVE
*Week of May 4, 1974*

1 **The Loco-Motion**
Grand Funk

2 **TSOP**
MFSB & the Three Degrees

3 **Bennie and the Jets**
Elton John

4 **Best Thing That Ever Happened to Me**
Gladys Knight & the Pips

5 **Dancing Machine**
Jackson 5

*Writer: Ray Stevens*

*Producer: Ray Stevens*

*May 18, 1974*
*3 weeks*

On APRIL 2, 1974, millions of viewers watching the Academy Awards saw a naked man streak past host David Niven on live television. Robert Opel, a 33-year-old advertising executive, was seized by security guards as he ran off stage but no charges were pressed. "I suppose it was bound to happen," Niven sighed, saying the man had revealed his "shortcomings." The next award presenter, Elizabeth Taylor, seemed a bit shaken as she told the audience, "That's a pretty hard act to follow. I'm nervous—that really upset me. I think I'm jealous!"

Opel had obtained a press pass, enabling him to stand backstage. He discarded his blue jumpsuit at the proper moment. "It just occurred to me," he explained to the *Los Angeles Times*, "that it might be an educative thing to do. You know, people shouldn't be ashamed of being nude in public. Besides—it's a hell of a way to launch a career."

Opel's career was only slightly shorter than the brief fad of streaking, which began on college campuses. Ray Stevens read an article about the phenomenon in a news magazine while on a flight from Nashville to Los Angeles. "It was a little bitty article about a college student who took off his clothes and ran through a crowd. The article called it 'streaking' and I said it had to be a great idea for a song.

"I made some notes and when I got to my hotel room I made some more notes. When I got home from the trip I dashed out a few lines. I intended to finish it whenever I could find the time. I didn't know it was going to be such a big fad. One morning I woke up and it was all over the news. Everywhere you turned, people were talking about streakers. So I built a fire under myself and went into the studio and rushed the record out.

"There were 15 other streaking records already on the market by the time I got mine out. There ended up being 35-40 streaking records altogether. Stores were setting up sections for the 'streaks of the week.

I got the jump on everybody, I think, by getting lucky and reading that article."

The single started getting airplay based on advance promotional copies. The novelty song won immediate response, and the single entered *Billboard*'s Hot 100 just five days after the Oscar telecast. Five weeks later it was number one.

"The Streak" branded Stevens a novelty singer once more. He had finally shaken that image after going to number one with a serious (but optimistic) song [see 274—"Everything Is Beautiful"]. He followed that with other non-novelty tunes, including "America, Communicate With Me" and "Turn Your Radio On."

After "The Streak," he recorded a parody of "Midnight Special" called "Moonlight Special." He also did a clever, uptempo updating of the pop standard "Misty" and took a satiric jab at Barry Manilow [see 389—"Mandy"] with "I Need Your Help, Barry Manilow." Under the unlikely name Henhouse Five Plus Two, he did a poultry-geist version of "In the Mood" (don't ask, you'd have to hear it).

For a singer identified with novelty songs, Stevens is an amazingly serious-minded man. In a 1969 interview, he said of himself, "A lot of insight comes from other people telling me things that I don't realize. One minute I know what I understand and then I don't. My whole attitude is one of trying to paint a broad picture of the scene. I don't try to narrow it down to any one area of life. I'm trying to be Ray Stevens. I realize that I am very complex. But I am slowly getting a picture of myself."

In 1984, Stevens signed with MCA Records and returned to the image he can't shake. "I've decided to go with the comedy image. That's how the majority of people perceive me, so that's how I'm gonna be for awhile. I'm gonna cut strictly comedy songs and see what happens."

## THE TOP FIVE
*Week of May 18, 1974*

1  **The Streak**
   Ray Stevens

2  **Dancing Machine**
   Jackson 5

3  **The Entertainer**
   Marvin Hamlisch

4  **The Loco-Motion**
   Grand Funk

5  **The Show Must Go On**
   Three Dog Night

# 366  Band on the Run APPLE 1873
## PAUL McCARTNEY AND WINGS

*Writer: Paul McCartney*

*Producer: Paul McCartney*

*June 8, 1974*
*1 week*

Paul McCartney followed his second post-Beatles chart-topper [see 335—"My Love"] with the theme song for the James Bond movie, *Live and Let Die*. Nominated for an Oscar for Best Song, "Live and Let Die" spent three weeks at number two in August, 1973. Oddly, it was prevented from reaching the top by three different number one singles: Maureen McGovern's "The Morning After" [see 339], Diana Ross' "Touch Me in the Morning" [see 340] and Stories' "Brother Louie" [see 341].

Next came "Helen Wheels," named after Paul's Land Rover. Peaking at number 10 in January, 1974, it was not meant to be included on the next Wings' album. But Capitol Records in America insisted the LP would sell more copies if the single were on it, and Paul consented to let American copies of *Band on the Run* contain "Helen Wheels."

Wings were scheduled to fly to Lagos, Nigeria, to record *Band on the Run*. But Henry McCullough and Denny Seiwell did not go to Africa. "They failed to turn up," Paul told Vic Garbarini in *Musician*, an interview that was later released as a commercial disc. ". . . I was left in the lurch at the last minute. It was literally an hour before we were getting into the plane to go on this trip to Africa . . . so we ended up just the three of us in Lagos and I played a lot of stuff myself. I played the

drums myself, the bass myself, a lot of guitar with Denny (Laine), did a lot of the vocals myself. I took a lot of control on that album. So it was almost a solo album. Almost."

The sudden departure of two Wings was just the first in a series of events that plagued the recording of *Band on the Run*. "We also had some strange things happen once we got there," McCartney told Robert Hilburn in a 1974 *Los Angeles Times* interview. "In Lagos, these guys were really sensitive about the idea of people ripping off their music. They couldn't understand why we had come to Lagos. We told them there was no dirty motive behind it. It's just that we thought it would be sunny. We thought it would be a sort of holiday while we recorded. That's all we wanted. But it turned out to be cloudy. It was the rainy season when we got there, so we blew it . . . to add to it all, we got held up at knife point over there and got robbed."

Despite the adverse conditions, the critics called *Band on the Run* McCartney's best solo album: "The best thing any of the Beatles have done since *Abbey Road*," said one. Two of the LP's songs had lyrics inspired by other people. Dustin

Hoffman told Paul that the last words reportedly spoken by artist Pablo Picasso were, "Drink to me, drink to my health, you know I can't drink any more." Challenged to write a song using those words, Paul did so while Hoffman watched. The result was "Picasso's Last Words (Drink to Me)." George Harrison was the source of the other inspired lyric. During a meeting of Apple's board of directors, a frustrated George uttered, "If we ever get out of here. . ."

Those words were the seed for the album's title track. But "Band on the Run" was not the first single chosen from the LP. "Jet," named for a McCartney dog (as was "Martha My Dear"), peaked at number seven in March, 1974. "Band on the Run" entered the Hot 100 on April 20, 1974, and became McCartney's third post-Beatles number one single seven weeks later.

*Band on the Run* also sparked comment for its star-studded cover. Sharing the glare of the prison yard spotlight with the three members of Wings are escapees James Coburn, Christopher Lee, boxer John Conteh, Member of Parliament Clement Freud, comedian Kenny Lynch and television host Michael Parkinson.

---

## THE TOP FIVE
### *Week of June 8, 1974*

1  **Band on the Run**
   Paul McCartney & Wings

2  **The Streak**
   Ray Stevens

3  **You Make Me Feel Brand New**
   The Stylistics

4  **Dancing Machine**
   Jackson 5

5  **Sundown**
   Gordon Lightfoot

ABC 11435 **Billy, Don't Be a Hero**
BO DONALDSON AND THE HEYWOODS **367**

*Writers: Mitch Murray*
*Peter Callander*

*Producer: Steve Barri*

*June 15, 1974*
*2 weeks*

"**B**ILLY, DON'T BE A HERO" was a tale about the Civil War, composed by two British songwriters. Mitch Murray had already scored a number one single in America with Freddie and the Dreamers [see 171—"I'm Telling You Now"] as well as hits by Gerry and the Pacemakers ("How Do You Do It," "I Like It"). His partner Peter Callander had written for Cliff Richard, Sandie Shaw and Tom Jones, among others. After collaborating for six years, they formed their own British company in 1974, Bus Stop Records. One of the first acts signed to the label was a group from Nottingham, Paper Lace.

Murray and Callander had half-written a song called "Billy Don't Be a Hero" when Peter's wife Connie saw Paper Lace win a talent contest on the television series "Opportunity Knocks." The writer/producers were looking for a strong lead singer to record the story-song and contacted the group through the "Opportunity Knocks" production office.

Paper Lace passed the audition, and Murray and Callander finished the song, adapting it for Paper Lace's style. Released in Britain on their own label, the single went to number one on March 16, 1974.

While the song was climbing the British chart, Murray and Callander were trying to make a deal for the song in the United States. They had already been disappointed with the reaction from Australia and New Zealand, where representatives of EMI had sent them a letter: "You've sent us quite a few records. This is the worst one you've sent us."

Negotiations dragged on in America while "Billy, Don't Be a Hero" closed in on the top spot in the United Kingdom. By the time Chicago-based Mercury Records bought the master, it was too late.

Producer Steve Barri had heard the Paper Lace version when it was offered to the label he worked for, ABC Records. Certain the song could be a hit in America, ABC Records chief Jay Lasker decided to cut a cover version. "We had signed Bo Donaldson and the Heywoods," Barri recalls. "We cut it that very night and had it out two or three days later."

The Heywoods had one previous chart single, "Special Someone," released on Artie Ripp's Family label in late 1972. It made an unimpressive showing at number 64. But the Heywoods, all from Cincinnati, Ohio,

had built up a tremendous following from their appearances on Dick Clark's "Action '73" television show. The group got its start after keyboards and trumpet player Bo Donaldson's mother, Bea Donaldson, went to work in Clark's Cincinatti office in August, 1966. Soon the Heywoods were touring on Clark's "Caravan of Stars," as the opening act for groups like the Rascals, the Raiders and Herman's Hermits.

Bo Donaldson and the Heywoods' version of "Billy, Don't Be a Hero" debuted on the Hot 100 on April 20, 1974, just one week ahead of Paper Lace's version. Many radio stations pitted the two records against each other on the air. One typical competition took place at WFIL in Philadelphia, where the Heywoods won in a landslide. The program director telephoned Bea Donaldson with the results. "He said he knew we had fans there, but he didn't realize they were crawling out of the woodwork."

Paper Lace had to settle for a peak position of 96, while Bo Donaldson and the Heywoods spent two weeks at number one. The Heywoods had one more hit record, "Who Do You Think You Are" (number 15 in September, 1974). Paper Lace had the last laugh just two months later [see 373—"The Night Chicago Died"].

## THE TOP FIVE
*Week of June 15, 1974*

1. **Billy, Don't Be a Hero**
   Bo Donaldson & the Heywoods

2. **You Make Me Feel Brand New**
   The Stylistics

3. **Sundown**
   Gordon Lightfoot

4. **The Streak**
   Ray Stevens

5. **Band on the Run**
   Paul McCartney & Wings

# Sundown REPRISE 1194
## GORDON LIGHTFOOT

*Writer: Gordon Lightfoot*

*Producer: Lenny Waronker*

*June 29, 1974*
*1 week*

"I DON'T know why I wrote my first song. I don't think the thought really struck me until I was about 17. It just came to me that people were writing songs that I was hearing constantly on the radio and I decided to try my hand at it," Gordon Lightfoot told *Billboard* in 1975.

Born on November 17, 1938, in Orillia, Ontario, Canada, on Lake Simcoe (80 miles north of Toronto), Lightfoot showed musical expertise as early as age 11. The principal of his elementary school was impressed enough with his young pupil's vocal ability to ask him to sing over the public address system on Parents Day. He won various local talent contests, but ultimately he found Orillia too limiting.

While reading *Down Beat* one day after graduating high school, he noticed an advertisement for the now-defunct Los Angeles-based Westlake College, which specialized in theory of jazz, orchestration and harmony. After 14 months in southern California, a homesick Lightfoot returned to Canada, working odd day jobs before becoming a music copyist. Writing romantic jazz piano pieces at the time, he saw Ian and Sylvia (Tyson) perform in a Toronto cafe in the early '60s. "When I saw that combination of folk and country music, I knew it was what I had been looking

## THE TOP FIVE
*Week of June 29, 1974*

1  **Sundown**
   Gordon Lightfoot

2  **Billy, Don't Be a Hero**
   Bo Donaldson & the Heywoods

3  **You Make Me Feel Brand New**
   The Stylistics

4  **Be Thankful for What You Got**
   William DeVaughn

5  **If You Love Me (Let Me Know)**
   Olivia Newton-John

for," Lightfoot told Robert Hilburn of the *Los Angeles Times*.

Continuing to pop up in various areas of the Toronto performing arts scene until 1963, Lightfoot settled into singing and playing his guitar. At the same time, he discovered the music of Bob Dylan. "He was moving into musical areas where angels feared to tread, so to speak. He was getting into areas that no one had ever explored before. Lyrically and musically, he had an extremely rural approach, which was partly in keeping with my influences," Lightfoot said in *Billboard*.

The Tysons were managed by Albert Grossman, who also represented Dylan and Peter, Paul and Mary [see 264—"Leaving on a Jet Plane"]. Grossman told Lightfoot that the trio were interested in recording his song "Early Morning Rain," and soon Lightfoot was also being managed by Grossman.

Signed to United Artists Records in the '60s, Lightfoot moved over to Reprise in 1970. He charted for the first time on the Hot 100 with "If You Could Read My Mind," a number five hit in February, 1971. His next three

chart entries failed to make the top 50, but then along came "Sundown."

The song was composed during one of Lightfoot's marathon writing sessions. In an April, 1975, *Billboard* interview, he disclosed, "I've been writing for deadlines for the last three years and 'Sundown' was one of a string of songs that I wrote when I lived on a farm out in King Township, just outside of Toronto. . . . I was getting off a tune every day out there. It certainly turned out to be a royal flush."

Asked to reveal the secret of the number one single's success, Gordon replied, "It's a down-the-middle rock 'n' roll type song with interesting lyrics. Besides that it had a nice groove to it. Of course, I was really quite pleased at the way it shot right up there. Another tremendous surprise was the way it crossed over into the country market."

In 1985, Lightfoot joined artists like Joni Mitchell, Neil Young and Bryan Adams to record "Tears Are Not Enough," the Canadian contribution to the fundraising campaign to feed the starving people of Africa [see 605—"We Are the World"].

*Writer: Wally Holmes*

*Producer: John Florez*

*July 6, 1974*
*1 week*

WALLY HOLMES, the man who founded the Hues Corporation, originally had a different name in mind for the black trio. "I wanted to call the group the Children of Howard Hughes, because I knew Hughes was single and he represented a conservative element. I was kind of wild in those days and I thought a fantastic thing would be to take a black group and call them the Children of Howard Hughes." But Holmes ran into a legal wall and was unable to incorporate Hughes' name into the group. "So, I came up with the idea of the Hues Corporation."

Holmes started the group with his body-surfing pal, Bernard St. Clair Lee Calhoun Henderson. They found H. Ann Kelly at a talent show in Los Angeles, and Karl Russell responded to notices placed in southern California record stores. Russell was soon replaced by singer Fleming Williams, and the Hues Corporation played local clubs with few results. Holmes booked them into the lounge at Circus Circus in Las Vegas. "All these

acts from all over the strip were coming over to this little funky lounge, seeing this group," Holmes recalls. Word of mouth spread and the group landed a record deal with RCA Records. Their first album, *Freedom for the Stallion*, yielded two singles, including the title track (number 63 in September, 1973).

"Rock the Boat" was one of the tracks on the LP. "It was not even considered for release," Holmes reports. "It was just an afterthought. It was put (on the album) like it had absolutely no chance of happening."

The intention was for Ann Kelly to sing lead vocal, but Holmes was encouraged by others not to use her. "Girl singers weren't happening then," he explains. Fleming Williams handled the lead vocal, but has never received proper credit for it because he left the group immediately after recording it and was replaced by Tommy Brown.

"You gotta remember Fleming . . . because he's the guy who sang that song," Holmes stresses. "He did an absolutely amazing job . . . there's a mouthful of words in the verses and this guy was able to make those verses swing."

RCA hired John Florez, the man who helped the Friends of Distinction ("Grazin' in the Grass," "Love or Let

Me Be Lonely") crossover to pop radio, to produce *Freedom for the Stallion*. But Holmes gives the credit for "Rock the Boat" to someone else. "John didn't know what to do with the song . . . I found this young guy from New York, Tom Sellers. He's the one who came up with the little bit of reggae beat . . . and what he did with that drum beat was a very important part of making the record happen. The rest is a mystery to me!"

*Freedom for the Stallion* was headed for the glue factory when RCA's David Kershenbaum went to see the band perform in Los Angeles. He noted the audience reaction to "Rock the Boat" and had the label release it as a single. "The record came out sometime in February and it's fair to say that by the middle of March, it was totally dead," Holmes recalls. "It was gone. Suddenly, when the record wasn't (being played) on any radio station, it sold 50,000 copies in New York City." "Rock the Boat" had become a hit in the dance clubs. "There was this mad, incredible rush to find the record. Disc jockeys were jumping on it and sending copies to disc jockeys they knew in other places."

Once radio started playing it, "Rock the Boat" sailed up the Hot 100, reaching number one just six weeks after its debut on May 25, 1974. But the Hues Corporation found it difficult to come up with another hit. "Rockin' Soul," the follow-up, peaked at 18. In 1977 they switched to Warner/Curb and had their last chart single, "I Caught Your Act" (number 92 in May, 1977).

## THE TOP FIVE
*Week of July 6, 1974*

1 **Rock the Boat**
Hues Corporation

2 **Sundown**
Gordon Lightfoot

3 **Billy, Don't be a Hero**
Bo Donaldson & the Heywoods

4 **Rock Your Baby**
George McCrae

5 **If You Love Me**
**(Let Me Know)**
Olivia Newton-John

T.K. 1004

# 370 Rock Your Baby
## GEORGE McCRAE

*Writers: Harry Wayne Casey
Richard Finch*

*Producers: Harry Wayne Casey
Richard Finch*

*July 13, 1974
2 weeks*

HARRY WAYNE CASEY and Richard Finch were struggling novices at Henry Stone's T.K. Records in Hialeah, Florida, when they wrote and produced George McCrae's "Rock Your Baby." Just 13 months later, Casey and Finch would record their own number one single with their group, KC and the Sunshine Band [see 414—"Get Down Tonight"].

Casey and Finch were still working in their respective warehouse and studio jobs at T.K. when they started fooling around in the studio, writing and producing for themselves and the other T.K. artists, like Betty Wright and Jimmy (Bo) Horne. "We had always done demos for other people," Casey told interviewer Jon Marlowe. "But one night we went into the studio to cut a whole finished track, but

the vocals (were) way too high for me to sing. Now we already had a record released at the time ("Sound Your Funky Horn"), so we decided to give the song to somebody else."

The track took less than an hour to complete, at a cost estimated by Finch and Casey at around $15. "It took us about 45 minutes to get the keyboard, bass and drum track down," Finch said in a 1974 *Billboard* interview. Casey added, "We used scrap tape and only had to pay Jerome Smith, the guitarist. I did keyboard and Rick was on bass and drums."

They took the track to Stone and his A&R chief, Steve Alaimo (who had a 1963 hit with "Every Day I Have to Cry"). "We went down to Henry's office and put the tape on, and he and Steve flipped over it and said not to change a single thing," Casey said.

They considered two male singers for the track, McCrae and Horne. Their decision was made for them when McCrae happened to walk into the studio the next day and hear the instrumental track. In two takes, he

had completed a vocal track.

"Rock Your Baby" entered the Hot 100 on June 1, 1974. Seven weeks later, it provided disco music with a one-two punch by following the Hues Corporation [see 369—"Rock the Boat"] into the number one position.

George McCrae, born October 19, 1944, in West Palm Beach, Florida, had put together a couple of groups in high school, the Fabulous Stepbrothers and the Jiving Jets. He spent four years in the Navy and organized a group there, too, called Atsugi Express.

George met his wife Gwen in the late '60s and after they were married, both were signed to Stone's Alston label. They recorded as a duo, but without much success. Finally, Gwen left the label to sign with Columbia. "I decided to study criminal justice and concentrate on Gwen's career," McCrae told *Billboard*. "The important thing at the time was that I had the responsibility of rearing a family, and it just wasn't happening for me in the music business. It wasn't an easy decision. After two years, I finally decided that I had to give it one more try. So I went to Steve Alaimo and asked him if he had any material that I could record."

"Rock Your Baby" was McCrae's only top 30 hit. In May, 1975, Gwen's recording of "Rockin' Chair" entered the Hot 100 and went to number nine. After they both had national hits, they recorded an album of duets. McCrae signed with Gold Mountain Records, an A&M-distributed label, in 1984. Based in Holland, George recorded new material in 1990.

## THE TOP FIVE
*Week of July 13, 1974*

1 **Rock Your Baby**
George McCrae

2 **Annie's Song**
John Denver

3 **Rock the Boat**
Hues Corporation

4 **Sundown**
Gordon Lightfoot

5 **Don't Let the Sun
go Down on Me**
Elton John

RCA 0295 **Annie's Song**
JOHN DENVER

**371**

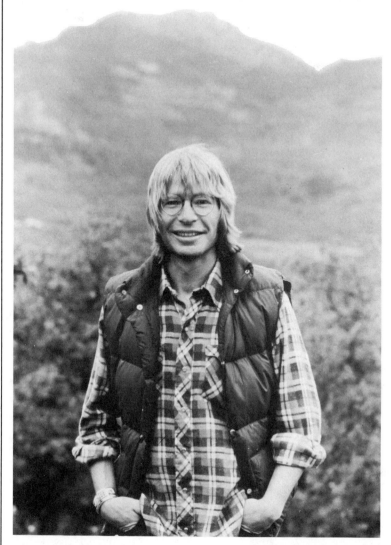

*Writer: John Denver*

*Producer: Milt Okun*

*July 27, 1974*
*2 weeks*

"I SING about America, about family, about the celebrations of life. I sing about what I know," John Denver has declared. In "Annie's Song," he made it perfectly clear how he felt about his college sweetheart, Ann Martell, whom he married in 1967. Written in 10 minutes on a ski lift, "Annie's Song" became a standard number for couples to marry to during the mid-'70s (the song is generic enough—Annie's name is not mentioned anywhere in the lyrics).

*People* magazine said the song "may be the most celebrated love ballad John Denver ever wrote." A 1979 story revealed that the near break-up of his marriage to his Minnesota-born wife is what "jolted" Denver into writing the song. "Admittedly 'insecure' and overwhelmed by John's staggering success during their 'tough' early years together, Annie, as well as John, had withdrawn into 'noncommunication,'" the article revealed.

"Finally, they actually separated, and a confused Denver fled their Aspen aerie for Switzerland. 'It was only six days, but felt like three months,' Annie recalls now. The crisis didn't end until a tearful long-distance call helped Annie 'really get clear that I loved him totally. What it came down to is that love is unconditional. We've had some bad times, but now we keep talking.'"

"Annie's Song" debuted on the Hot 100 during the week of June 1, 1974. Eight weeks later it became Denver's second consecutive number one single [see 360—"Sunshine on My Shoulders"]. "Annie's Song" almost made Denver a one-hit-wonder in Britain. His only solo single to ever chart in the United Kingdom, it went to number one on October 12, 1974 (four years later, Irish flutist James Galway took an instrumental version of "Annie's Song" to number three in Britain). Denver was rescued from being branded a one-hit-wonder by Placido Domingo. A duet between Denver and the Spanish vocalist, "Perhaps Love," went to number 46 on the British chart in early 1982.

"Annie's Song" ultimately ends on a sad note. The celebrated marriage ended in divorce in 1983. "I'd never had an experience like that ever before," Denver told Dennis Hunt of the *Los Angeles Times*. "The divorce was one of the most unhappy moments of my life. We were married 16 years. On the 15th anniversary we sat down and said, 'This isn't working out.' I had failed. I said, 'What you want from me is something I'm not able to give you, so you'd better look elsewhere.'"

Denver added, "I'd like to fall in love again, but I'm not sure that I ever will. I'm too busy to have a woman in my life. The last thing on my mind is finding a woman for a relationship. It wouldn't be that easy anyway—there's a lot I have to learn about women. Also, I'm pretty set in my ways now. That makes things even tougher."

## THE TOP FIVE
*Week of July 27, 1974*

1 **Annie's Song**
John Denver

2 **Don't Let the Sun Go Down on Me**
Elton John

3 **Rock and Roll Heaven**
Righteous Brothers

4 **Rock Your Baby**
George McCrae

5 **Rikki, Don't Lose That Number**
Steely Dan

## 372 Feel Like Makin' Love ALTANTIC 3025
### ROBERTA FLACK

*Writer: Eugene McDaniels*

*Producer: Rubina Flake*

*August 10, 1974*
*1 week*

ROBERTA FLACK'S third number one single did not come easily. Her producer of five years, Joel Dorn, departed the sessions for Flack's fifth album, *Feel Like Makin' Love*, in a flurry of dissension with Atlantic brass. The chair behind the board was taken over by a novice who quickly came and went, leaving Roberta without a producer. "I didn't know nothing about nothing," Flack stated in the *Aquarian*. "I had nobody to help me finish the album, so I did it myself. It was one of my worst experiences."

Dubbing herself Rubina Flake, she admitted she was not exactly a whiz at the job. "I knew what I wanted musically but I didn't know a lot of the technical things or the business aspects of producing. I learned the hard way," she admitted in the *Washington Post*. Despite their misgivings, Atlantic Records allowed her free reign, though she "spent a fortune" and took eight months to finish. "If you know what you're doing you can't spend too much time on an album, though you can certainly spend too much money," she defended in the *Aquarian*.

Utilizing the same process, it took her nearly three years to complete her next LP, *Blue Lights in the Basement*. Her schedule was also filled with other endeavors. The former operatic student who once directed an amateur performance of *Aida* worked on a linguistics doctorate from the University of Massachusetts, installing a computer in her Washington home to keep up with the program. In addition, she began acting, took dancing lessons, ran her own business, adopted a menagerie of 25 cats and dogs, and shed 42 pounds from her chunky-since-childhood frame. Plans had been laid for her to star in a film biography of Bessie Smith, but the project bogged down for lack of an adequate script or financing.

After "Feel Like Makin' Love," Roberta's biggest hit was "The Closer I Get to You," a track from the *Blue Lights in the Basement*

album that reunited her with former singing partner, Donny Hathaway. Their 1972 single, "Where is the Love," had peaked at five; this new effort spent two weeks at number two in May, 1978. Hathaway passed away less than a year later, on January 13, 1979.

An album of duets with Peabo Bryson in 1983 gave Roberta another top 20 hit, "Tonight, I Celebrate My Love." She and Bryson toured to promote the record—nothing, it seemed, could keep Flack off the road. Yugoslavia, Australia, Poland, New Zealand, Japan, Israel, Brazil, Africa, the European continent and, of course, North America were just some of the places she parked her piano for the night. In one not-so-atypical 24-hour span, she performed in Phoenix, Arizona, one evening and Barcelona, Spain, the next. Her home base shifted, too, to a seventh-floor co-op in New York City's famed and luxurious Dakota, while her animal family roamed a 33-acre purchase in New Jersey.

Films did utilize her services, but not in front of the cameras. She sang the title tracks for Joe Brooks' *If Ever I See You Again* and for the controversial *Making Love* in 1982, a film which included "Feel Like Makin' Love" in its soundtrack. Roberta was also the subject of a PBS special, "An Evening With Roberta Flack," taped at the Park West theater in Chicago.

More recently, Flack has been able to realize her dream of performing with symphony orchestras, describing the experience to the *Kansas City Times* as "a luxury, a rare kind of booking. Most singers who sing the kind of music I sing dream of singing with lots of strings behind them." She has also begun to compose her own material, having long been satisfied to interpret the songs of writers she respected. In 1984, Flack was honored with an hour-long musical tribute on the steps of New York's City Hall, one of several such accolades she has collected over the years for her social involvement as well as her contribution to the music world.

---

### THE TOP FIVE
*Week of August 10, 1974*

1 **Feel Like Makin' Love**
Roberta Flack

2 **The Night Chicago Died**
Paper Lace

3 **Annie's Song**
John Denver

4 **Don't Let the Sun
Go Down on Me**
Elton John

5 **Please Come to Boston**
Dave Loggins

MERCURY 73492 # The Night Chicago Died

## PAPER LACE

**373**

*Writers: Mitch Murray
            Peter Callander*

*Producers: Mitch Murray
             Peter Callander*

*August 17, 1974
1 week*

Mitch Murray and Peter Callander had no intention of having a second number one hit stolen from them [see 367—"Billy, Don't Be a Hero"] by an American group. Paper Lace's original version of "The Night Chicago Died" was rushed out in America before anyone else could record a cover version. But Murray believes the Bo Donaldson cover version of their first Paper Lace hit may have been a blessing in disguise. "'The Night Chicago Died' might not have been number one if 'Billy, Don't Be a Hero' had been a hit by Paper Lace," he suggests. "People took notice of us because we were beaten to the post. It made more of a story for DJs to talk about."

Nottingham, England, is known as the "lace city," and it was home to lead singer/drummer Philip Wright (born April 9, 1948). Along with bassist Cliff Fish (born August 13, 1949, in Ripley, Derbyshire), he formed Paper Lace in 1969. Joining within the next two years were lead guitarist Michael Vaughn (born July 27, 1950, in Sheffield, Yorkshire) and guitarist Chris Morris (born November 1, 1954, in Nottingham). They were the house band at a Rochdale club called Tiffany's, and made some television appearances on the BBC, first with host Terry Wogan and then on a pro-

gram called "Crackerjack."

In 1974, with rhythm guitarist Carlo Santanna (born June 29, 1947, in Rome) added, Paper Lace appeared on "Opportunity Knocks," a talent show broadcast on the BBC's rival, ITV. The group won first place. Watching their victory at home on television was Connie Callander, wife of writer/producer Peter Callander. She told her husband about the group, and along with his partner, Murray, set up an audition at their studio for Paper Lace.

Murray and Callander had half-completed a tune they wanted to record, and were looking for a group to cut it. It was a story-song, much like the number seven hit they wrote for Georgie Fame in 1968, "The Ballad of Bonnie and Clyde." The song was "Billy, Don't Be a Hero."

"The Night Chicago Died" followed in the story-song tradition. "Our research was a little bit slipshod," Murray admits. "We had a good example of bad research working well for us with 'Bonnie and Clyde.' We had 'dulap' bag instead of 'burlap' bag." A similar problem plagued "The Night Chicago Died." "We wrote this fictional story about Al Capone and his men having a shoot-out with the police, which of course never happened. And we used the phrase 'the East side of Chicago.'

They claim there is no 'east' side of Chicago!"

"The Night Chicago Died" only reached number three in Britain, even though it was specifically written for domestic consumption. "Our song was written for the English market," Murray says. "If you sit down and try to write an international hit, you get nowhere."

Once the record was a hit in America, the band's manager had a clever promotional idea. He thought. "The manager of the group naively wrote to Mayor (Richard) Daley, hoping that he was going to get congratulated . . . and when the boys went to the States they'd have a civic reception," Murray recalls. Instead of the key to the city, the group received what Murray terms "a rather rude letter." The Mayor ended it with, "And one more question . . . are you *nuts*?"

Paper Lace's American career ended seven months after it began. The follow-up to "The Night Chicago Died" was called "The Black-Eyed Boys," which peaked at 41. Soon after, the group listened to some bad advice and broke their contract with Murray and Callander's Bus Stop Records, hoping to get a large advance from another label. Lawsuits and countersuits ensued, with the band the loser in an out-of-court settlement.

### THE TOP FIVE
*Week of August 17, 1974*

1  **The Night Chicago Died**
   Paper Lace

2  **Feel Like Makin' Love**
   Roberta Flack

3  **(You're) Having My Baby**
   Paul Anka with Odia Coates

4  **Tell Me Something Good**
   Rufus

5  **Please Come to Boston**
   Dave Loggins

## 374  (You're) Having My Baby  UNITED ARTISTS 454
### PAUL ANKA with ODIA COATES

*Writer: Paul Anka*

*Producer: Rick Hall*

*August 24, 1974*
*3 weeks*

**P**AUL ANKA first went to number one in 1957 with "Diana" [see 25] and then again in 1959 with "Lonely Boy" [see 55]. When he returned to the top of the Hot 100 a full 15 years and two weeks later with "(You're) Having My Baby," he set a record for the longest gap between number one singles to this date.

"(You're) Having My Baby" was not without controversy. "We tested the song before its release and knew there would be flak," Anka told Paul Rosenfield in a 1975 *Los Angeles Times* interview. "But it's nothing compared to the acceptance. I wasn't putting women in a subservient position, for God's sake. Motherhood is a fact of life."

The National Organization of Women disagreed. They awarded Anka one of their annual "Keep Her in Her Place" awards. Ellen Peck, the founder of the National Organization for Non-Parents, said, "Were I 16 and pregnant, that song could keep me pregnant."

"It's the personal statement of a man caught up in the affection and joy of childbirth," Anka responded. Still, during a tour that followed the record's chart run, Anka acknowledged he made "a concession to women's lib" and changed the lyric to "having *our* baby," which altered the

viewpoint of the singer sufficiently to quiet any complaints.

Anka wrote "(You're) Having My Baby" for his wife and their four daughters while he was appearing in Lake Tahoe, California. Before composing the tune, he met a singer from Oakland, California, named Odia Coates. At the time, Anka was producing an album for Edwin Hawkins ("Oh Happy Day").

"I had called Edwin to ask his advice about a local deal offered to me," Odia explained in a *Billboard* interview, "and he said to forget about it, he'd talk to Paul about me. Later I got a call and he had set up an audition for me in Las Vegas, where Paul lives. I did 'Do You Wanna Dance' and Stevie Wonder's 'If You Really Love Me.' Paul was taken away by the songs but I didn't know that because he was very calm at the time. So I went on and continued my vacation and a week later gave Paul a call. And he said, 'Where have you been, I've been trying to reach you.'"

Paul wrote and produced a song for Odia, "Make It Up to Me in Love," leased to Buddah Records. "But we soon discovered Buddah wasn't going to do anything with the song. They had signed Gladys Knight, so who's Odia Coates?" she asked rhetorically.

Coates then signed with producer Rick Hall, who leased her recordings to Anka's label at the time, United Artists. She was in the studio with Anka when he was recording "(You're) Having My Baby" as a solo

effort. United Artists executive Bob Skaff was also there and he suggested Odia duet with Paul on the song.

Coates also sang with Anka on the follow-up single, "One Man Woman/ One Woman Man," which went to number seven in early 1975. She then charted at number 71 with a solo single, a cover version of Electric Light Orchestra's "Showdown." It was the last chart record for Coates, who was born in Vicksburg, Mississippi, and grew up in Watts, California. Her father was a pastor in the Beautiful Gates Church of God in Christ there. Odia sang in his church and became a member of the Southern California State Youth Choir. She turned professional in 1968, singing at a club in Sunnydale, California, while working during the day as a secretary for an aircraft company. Her next gig was in Batman's Cave at the Wayne Manor Club, where she worked with Sly and the Family Stone [see 251— "Everyday People"].

She worked with a band called Brotherly Love and then joined singer Merry Clayton in the Sisters Love. She was doing background singing when she made the fateful call to her friend Edwin Hawkins.

Anka had several chart successes in the latter half of the '70s, including "I Don't Like to Sleep Alone" (number eight), "(I Believe) There's Nothing Stronger Than Our Love" (number 15) and "Times of Your Life" (number seven), based on the Kodak commercial. In 1978, he left United Artists and returned to RCA, then signed with Columbia Records. Forty years after his first chart entry, he's as active as ever.

---

## THE TOP FIVE
*Week of August 24, 1974*

1  **(You're) Having My Baby**
   Paul Anka with Odia Coates

2  **The Night Chicago Died**
   Paper Lace

3  **Tell Me Something Good**
   Rufus

4  **Feel Like Makin' Love**
   Roberta Flack

5  **I Shot the Sheriff**
   Eric Clapton

*Writer: Bob Marley*

*Producer: Tom Dowd*

*September 14, 1974*
*1 week*

THOUGH HIS FANS WERE scrawling "Clapton Is God" across London walls as early as 1965, it took nearly a decade for the chart to echo the sentiment. Eric Patrick Clapp did it, not with the blues guitar that had defined him, but with a laid-back version of Jamaican Bob Marley's reggae confession, "I Shot the Sheriff." The hit single sprouted from *461 Ocean Boulevard*, an album that welcomed Clapton back from a successful two-year battle with heroin, cured through acupuncture. Named for the address of his white, tile-roofed Miami home while recording at Criteria Studios, the LP heralded a country-influenced, restrained direction that would typify Clapton's future solo works.

But it was the blues that first gripped the bricklayer's son, who was born March 30, 1945, in Ripley, England. Of his childhood, he recalled for the BBC's Paul Gambaccini, "I was the one that used to get stones thrown at me because I was so thin and couldn't do physical training very well." Raised by his grandparents, he foreswore studying stained glass window design in particular and courses at Kingston Art College in general to listen to Chuck Berry and Muddy Waters records. At the Ealing Club in London, he'd occasionally substitute for lead singer Mick Jagger in Blues, Incorporated, when he wasn't hustling meals as a street musician. The Yardbirds needed a replacement for Tony Topham in 1963 and drafted Clapton as their lead guitarist. Disillusioned with what he perceived as their abandonment of hardcore blues for popdom ("For Your Love" went top 10 in Britain and America), Clapton left his post to Jeff Beck and hauled building materials around a construction site with his grandfather before signing on with John Mayall's Bluesbreakers.

Though that job lasted just 14 months, with three months off for a Greek vacation, it established Clapton as Britain's top guitarist, created a hit album and inspired the graffiti.

"Very funny. Very strange. Nothing else was happening in England except me," was Eric's typical low key reaction.

After accomplishing all he could with the blues, Clapton found himself attracted to rock, and jammed occasionally with a bassist from Alexis Korner's Blues, Incoporated named Jack Bruce and the Graham Bond Organization's drummer, Ginger Baker. In July, 1966, they elected to put together "a blues trio, like Buddy Guy with a rhythm section," its guitarist told *Rolling Stone*. They called this first of the supergroups Cream, and in its two-year incarnation they released four albums and placed two singles in the top 10: "Sunshine of My Love" (number five in August, 1968) and "White Room" (number six in November, 1968).

Blind Faith, with Steve Winwood, Rick Grech and Ginger Baker, was Clapton's next aggregation. Their debut concert in Hyde Park drew almost 100,000 fans. Without a hit single, their first and only LP topped the album charts in Britain and America. During their sole United States tour, Clapton began playing along with the opening band, Delaney and Bonnie (Bramlett) and Friends.

With three of Delaney and Bonnie's "Friends," he formed Derek and the Dominos. "Layla," their number 10 hit from August, 1972, is an acknowledged rock classic and airplay staple of Album Oriented Rock radio stations. The song was named for Patti Boyd Harrison, formerly married to George, whom Clapton wed in 1979.

## THE TOP FIVE
*Week of September 14, 1974*

1  **I Shot the Sheriff**
   Eric Clapton

2  **(You're) Having My Baby**
   Paul Anka with Odia Coates

3  **Rock Me Gently**
   Andy Kim

4  **I'm Leaving It All
   Up to You**
   Donny & Marie Osmond

5  **Can't Get Enough
   of Your Love, Babe**
   Barry White

# 376 Can't Get Enough of Your Love, Babe 20TH CENTURY 2120
## BARRY WHITE

*Writer: Barry White*

*Producer: Barry White*

*September 21, 1974*
*1 week*

WHO would have guessed that the 11-year-old kid playing piano for Jesse Belvin on "Goodnight My Love" would grow up and have number one hit singles as a vocalist and leader of a 40-piece orchestra? Probably no one at that classic recording session, including young Barry White himself, who was paid $55 for his work that day.

Barry White was gigantic—in genius and girth. He weighed in at nearly 300 pounds, but he sure knew how to sell a song. Born September 12, 1944, in Galveston, Texas, White was raised by his mother in Los Angeles and began singing in the church choir when he was eight. He was a wild kid, but when he spent a couple of months in Juvenile Hall for stealing tires, he vowed never to see the inside of an institution again. By age 16, he was singing bass with a local group called the Upfronts.

"When I left school, I started learning about the record business, because I was hooked on music and trying to find out where I belonged," he said. At 17, he was hired as an arranger by Rampart Records. He had his first taste of success in 1964 when a song he arranged, Bob and Earl's "Harlem Shuffle," went to number 44. Two years later, his arrangement of "The Duck" by Jackie Lee peaked at number 14.

In 1967, while head of A&R for Los Angeles-based Mustang and Bronco Records, White wrote and produced "It May Be Winter Outside (But in My Heart It's Spring)" for Felice Taylor, a number 42 hit. That same year, Taylor had a number 11 hit in Britain with White's "I Feel Love Comin' On."

In 1969, he met the three women who would become Love Unlimited [see 357—"Love's Theme"], and three years later wrote and produced a million-selling single for them, "Walkin' in the Rain With the One I Love." "People always asked me how come I didn't record," Barry said, "but I was busy being a producer, writer, arranger and businessman—while knowing all the time that one day I would have to record and the time would be right."

The day came—three days after Russ Regan was named head of 20th Century Records. White had first met Regan at Loma Records, an R&B subsidiary of Warner Brothers. When Regan became head of Uni Records, White brought him Love Unlimited.

Regan agreed that the time was right for Barry to record his own material. His label debut, "I'm Gonna Love You Just a Little More Baby," went to number three in June, 1973. The company's fastest-selling single to that time, it helped shape White's hit-making persona. Combining a melodic tune with a memorable hook and steamy lyrics, White would croon in a seductive, half-sung, half-spoken baritone. This was backed by lush strings and a slow disco beat.

White's sweet and lowdown style proved irresistible, and before long, the self-proclaimed "prophet of love" had attracted millions of disciples. His biggest hit, "Can't Get Enough of Your Love, Babe," entered the Hot 100 at number 51 on August 3, 1974, and reached the top seven weeks later. The follow-up, "You're the First, the Last, My Everything," did almost as well, spending two weeks at number two in January, 1975. "What Am I Gonna Do With You," a number eight hit came next. Two years later, Barry had his final top 10 single, "It's Ecstasy When You Lay Down Next to Me."

In May, 2003, White was hospitalized in Los Angeles after a stroke. Battling kidney failure caused by high blood pressure, he died on the morning of July 4.

## THE TOP FIVE
*Week of September 21, 1974*

1  **Can't Get Enough of Your Love, Babe**
   Barry White

2  **Rock Me Gently**
   Andy Kim

3  **I Honestly Love You**
   Olivia Newton-John

4  **Nothing from Nothing**
   Billy Preston

5  **I Shot the Sheriff**
   Eric Clapton

*Writer: Andy Kim*

*Producer: Andy Kim*

*September 28, 1974*
*1 week*

ANDY KIM had a hot chart streak from 1968-1971, when he was signed as an artist to Jeff Barry's Steed label. He had a top 10 hit with a new version of the Ronettes' "Baby, I Love You," a song written by Jeff with his former wife Ellie Greenwich and Phil Spector. Andy also hit the top 40 with original songs like "How'd We Ever Get This Way" and "So Good Together," and returned to the Barry-Greenwich-Spector songbook to cover the Ronettes' "Be My Baby." His most rewarding success, in financial terms, was writing a number one song for the Archies [see 258—"Sugar, Sugar"] with Barry.

The Steed label folded and Kim recorded briefly for MCA, but from mid-1971 to mid-1974 Andy couldn't get a hit record. "I never mentally admitted defeat in spite of three years off the charts and 18 months between record contracts," Andy said in a 1974 *Billboard* interview. "It's true that you can be lonely at the top, but believe me, it's a lot lonelier when you're nowhere."

With his chart career as cold as the Canadian winter, the Montreal native formed his own label, Ice Records. He financed the recording session of "Rock Me Gently" himself. He could only afford to cut two sides and because he considered the second track good enough to be another "A"

## THE TOP FIVE

*Week of September 28, 1974*

1  **Rock Me Gently**
   Andy Kim

2  **I Honestly Love You**
   Olivia Newton-John

3  **Nothing from Nothing**
   Billy Preston

4  **Then Came You**
   Dionne Warwick and the Spinners

5  **Beach Baby**
   First Class

side, he put an instrumental version of "Rock Me Gently" on the flip side.

Andy played the completed track of "Rock Me Gently" for Stu Yahm, a former Steed promotion staffer who went to work for Capitol. He thought the song had potential and took it to label executives Al Coury and Bruce Wendell. They signed Kim to the label, resulting in Capitol's 30th number one single of the rock era. "Rock Me Gently" debuted on the Hot 100 on June 22, 1974, and took 14 long weeks to climb to number one. In addition to the pop airplay for the vocal side, many R&B stations played the instrumental "B" side.

With the success of "Rock Me Gently," Kim toured extensively, something he had shied away from during his Steed days. "Frankly, all my old hits were sped up on the tape, to make my voice sound higher for the pre-teen market," he revealed in *Billboard*. "That was one of the reasons I never did much touring. Kids who heard my records expected to see a 5'8" blond surfer. Instead they

got somebody 6'2" and dark. I went over best with their mothers who brought them to the shows."

Andy Kim was born Andrew Joachim on December 5, 1952. He was the third of four sons born to Lebanese parents who had emigrated to America in the early 1900s. He became interested in music while growing up in Montreal, and quit school at 16 to move to New York and pursue a songwriting career. He eventually met Jeff Barry and formed a successful songwriting team with him. Kim found it difficult to follow "Rock Me Gently" with another hit. "Fire, Baby I'm on Fire" was his next single. It peaked at number 28 and was his final chart entry. In 1981 he reunited with producer Michael Omartian and recorded under the pseudonym Baron Longfellow. Playing on the sessions were Steve Lukather and Mike Porcaro from Toto [see 567—"Africa"]. Released on his own Ice label, the album include an updated version of "Sugar, Sugar."

## 378 | I Honestly Love You MCA 40280
### OLIVIA NEWTON-JOHN

*Writers: Peter Allen*
*Jeff Barry*

*Producer: John Farrar*

*October 5, 1974*
*2 weeks*

PETER ALLEN intended to record "I Honestly Love You" himself. Jeff Barry, the songwriter responsible for number one hits by artists as diverse as the Dixie Cups, Manfred Mann and the Archies, was to produce Peter's first album for A&M, but didn't hear any hits in the tunes Allen had already written. "I had this idea for a song I thought would be great for a man to sing," Barry explains. "We wrote the song and made a demo and someone at the publishing office was going to see Olivia (Newton-John) with new material . . . and she loved it . . . she was the one who loved that song and wanted to record it. We decided to let (her) cut it instead of Peter. And no one else thought it was going to be a single. The label didn't want to put it out (but) radio demanded it."

"I flipped out when I heard it," Olivia confirmed in *Billboard*. "I was terrified that I would find out it had already been done." Allen didn't record it until years after it became Olivia's first number one single.

Olivia Newton-John was born September 26, 1948, in Cambridge, England, into an academic household. Her father, Bryn, a Welshman, had decided against a career as an opera singer to teach at King's College in Cambridge. He was following the scholarly lead of his father, Max

### THE TOP FIVE
*Week of October 5, 1974*

1  **I Honestly Love You**
   Olivia Newton-John

2  **Nothing from Nothing**
   Billy Preston

3  **Then Came You**
   Dionne Warwick and the Spinners

4  **Beach Baby**
   First Class

5  **You Haven't Done Nothin'**
   Stevie Wonder

Born, the Nobel Prize-winning German physicist who was Albert Einstein's best friend. Bryn, his wife, and daughters Rona and Olivia set sail for Australia when he was promoted to dean of Ormond College in Melbourne.

During the long boat ride, little Livvy lost her favorite toy, a stuffed shapeless animal she called Fluffy. "I guess somebody nicked it, some nasty little girl," a grown-up Newton-John reminisced years later in *Crawdaddy*. "I was very upset."

Early trauma behind her, the young emigre led a fairly uneventful childhood, writing songs on the family piano and picking out the "Tennessee" Ernie Ford discs [see 5—"Sixteen Tons"] from her father's thousands of classical records. Uneventful that is, until at 11, her parents divorced and, with mom, she moved into a Melbourne apartment. "My mother gave me an acoustic guitar when I was 13, which led me to Ian (her first boyfriend) and working in coffeehouses—on weekends only. Meanwhile I had been singing with three other girls in a group called the Sol Four; we did traditional jazz," she told *Crawdaddy*. That year she took top honors in a Hayley Mills lookalike contest, continuing her winning ways two years on when a

friend suggested she enter a talent search that offered a trip to England as a prize.

By now an established local television personality, Olivia was reluctant to cash her talent trophy, but did so at her mother's urgings. "She said it would broaden my, er, horizons," the singer recounted. So with "Go Show" buddy Pat Carroll, she lifted off for Blighty where they duetted in pubs for two years until Pat's visa expired.

Livvy stayed on, sliding into a regular spot on Cliff Richard's television series, then recording Bob Dylan's "If Not for You," her first American chart single (number 25 in September, 1971). Don Kirshner was intrigued by this "kewpie doll in knee sox," as he described her in *Crawdaddy*. "Then, when I heard her sing, I knew we could get a great, sweet sound out of her." Kirshner recruited Olivia for a foursome deliberately misspelled Toomorrow for a "dynamite film and music concept." It flopped, but ONJ's single, "Let Me Be There," became her first hit in the States (number six in February, 1974). It earned her a Grammy for Best Female Country Vocal. "It's probably the first time an English person won an award over Nashville people," the winner said upon receiving her award.

*Writers: Billy Preston
Bruce Fisher*

*Producer: Billy Preston*

*October 19, 1974
1 week*

**E**VEN after he had reached the number one position twice [see 254—"Get Back" and 331—"Will It Go Round in Circles"], Billy Preston had time to be a "studio musician" again. His credits could be found on albums by Barbra Streisand, Sly and the Family Stone, Carole King and former Apple labelmates George Harrison and Ringo Starr. In Jamaica, Billy met up with Mick Jagger, who invited him to tour with the Rolling Stones.

One night after the Stones tour, Billy was playing in a night club in Atlanta, Georgia. "They had a piano in my dressing room," he recalls, "and I was just playing around. I'd heard the saying 'nothing from nothing' before so I just started playing around with the chorus. I came home and got with Bruce Fisher, and he wrote the second verse. The saloon piano gave it character and I had a feeling it would be a hit because it was a sing-a-long kind of thing."

Preston's association with the Beatles was not over. He was appearing at the Roxy on the Sunset Strip in Los Angeles when a friend of Robert Stigwood's talked to him about a new film. Billy was cast as Sgt. Pepper in the ill-fated motion picture *Sgt. Pepper's Lonely Hearts Club Band*, which starred Peter

Frampton and the Bee Gees. Despite the presence of talent like Steve Martin, George Burns, Donald Pleasence and Frankie Howerd, the film earned a deserved shellacking from the critics. The record album fared no better, and some wags said it shipped gold and returned platinum.

In the middle of this critical holocaust, Preston was a shining beacon. His brief performance in the film was so electrifying, it seemed like it belonged in some other movie. "I was the last to shoot. They'd done the whole thing by the time I came in and I didn't know what the film was like at all."

Billy's song was one he should have known well—"Get Back," which

he recorded with the Beatles in 1969. "I got a chance to fly, in a harness, and the cranes lifted me up and brought me down. It was scary at first, then I got into it."

In 1978, Billy left A&M and signed with Motown Records. Songwriter Carol Connors [see 46—"To Know Him Is to Love Him"] wanted a duo to record a song she had written for the film *Fast Break*, so Motown executive Suzanne de Passe, who managed Billy as well as Syreeta Wright (formerly married to Stevie Wonder), put her two clients together. The result was "With You I'm Born Again," which went to number two in Britain and four in America.

## THE TOP FIVE
*Week of October 19, 1974*

1  **Nothing from Nothing**
   Billy Preston

2  **Then Came You**
   Dionne Warwick and the Spinners

3  **You Haven't Done Nothin'**
   Stevie Wonder

4  **I Honestly Love You**
   Olivia Newton-John

5  **Jazzman**
   Carole King

## 380 Then Came You ATLANTIC 3202
### DIONNE WARWICK and THE SPINNERS

*Writers: Sherman Marshall*
*Phil Pugh*

*Producer: Thom Bell*

*October 26, 1974*
*1 week*

TEAMING up Dionne Warwick(e) with the Spinners was a brilliant move by producer Thom Bell that gave both halves of the double-act their first number one single. "Then Came You" came about after the Spinners were asked by Dionne to be her opening act on a five-week summer theater tour, bringing the soul singing group into Las Vegas for the first time, a move Dionne felt was long overdue. Bell, who was producing the Spinners for Atlantic Records, suggested that Dionne duet with lead singer Phillipe Wynn(e) on "Then Came You." Dionne was signed to Warner Brothers Records at the time, Atlantic's sister label under the WEA corporate umbrella. With the exception of "Then Came You," Dionne's five years on Warner Brothers left her completely devoid of hits. This was in sharp contrast to her previous record.

Dionne first hit the charts with "Don't Make Me Over," released on Scepter Records at the end of 1962. She had been born Marie Dionne Warrick on December 12, 1940, in East Orange, New Jersey. Both her parents were involved with the music industry. Her father, a one-time Pullman porter and a chef, was director of gospel promotion at Chess Records. Her mother managed the Drinkard Singers, a church choir group for which Dionne played piano and occasionally sang. Along with her sister Dee Dee and their cousin Cissy Houston, Dionne formed a trio, the Gospelaires. Dionne was studying music education at the Hartt College of Music and supporting herself by doing background work on pop records with the Gospelaires.

Their earliest work was with Sam The Man' Taylor, Nappy Brown and Bobby Darin. Along with Doris Troy, they sang background at a fateful session— "Mexican Divorce,"

recorded by the Drifters and written by Burt Bacharach and Bob Hilliard for Atlantic Records (ironically, all four backing singers—Dionne, Dee Dee, Cissy (as part of the Sweet Inspirations) and Doris would end up recording for Atlantic themselves).

It was the first meeting between Dionne and Burt and it took place at the same time Bacharach was starting to work with Hal David. They brought Dionne in to sing backing vocals for artists like the Shirelles, Chuck Jackson and Tommy Hunt at Scepter Records, then signed her as a singer to the label. Her first hit came two years after she first met Burt—"Don't Make Me Over" went

to number 21 in early 1963. Dionne remained with Scepter through 1971, scoring eight top 10 hits, all written by Bacharach and David except for her highest charting Scepter single, "(Theme From) 'Valley of the Dolls,'" number two in 1968.

Always part of Motown's second division of artists, the Spinners decided to look for a new label deal. They were wooed by Stax and Avco, but their friend Aretha Franklin [see 225—"Respect"] suggested they sign with her label, Atlantic. While looking down the company's artist roster, producer Thom Bell noticed the Spinners' name had just been pencilled in, and decided he wanted to produce them. Their first single was intended to be "How Could I Let You Get Away," but disc jockeys wisely preferred the flip side, "I'll Be Around," which went to number three in the autumn of 1972.

Dionne Warwick (she dropped the "e" eventually) continued to flounder on Warner Brothers until she signed with Arista Records. Paired with writer/producer Barry Manilow [see 389—"Mandy"], she returned to the top five in 1979 with "I'll Never Love This Way Again."

### THE TOP FIVE
*Week of October 26, 1974*

1 **Then Came You**
Dionne Warwick and the Spinners

2 **You Haven't Done Nothin'**
Stevie Wonder

3 **You Ain't Seen Nothing Yet**
Bachman-Turner Overdrive

4 **Jazzman**
Carole King

5 **The Bitch is Back**
Elton John

vie's close friend and public relations person, Ira Tucker, recalled what he did for his friend in a 1974 issue of *Esquire*: "I knew that Stevie likes to listen to music really loud and I thought maybe if I shouted in his ear, it might reach him. The doctor told me to go ahead and try, it couldn't hurt. The first time I didn't get any response, but the next day I went back and I got right down in his ear and sang "Higher Ground". . . . His hand was resting on my arm and after a while, his fingers started going in time with the song. I said, 'Yeah! This dude is gonna make it.' "

Although the doctors stressed the need for rest and relaxation, it wasn't long before Stevie was working on new music from his hospital bed. By early 1974, he was back on stage. He jammed with Edgar Winter [see 334—"Frankenstein"] at New York's Bottom Line and surprised fans of Elton John when he joined Elton on stage in Boston for a rendition of the Stones' classic "Honky Tonk Women" [see 257].

Fully recovered by mid-July, Stevie was as active as ever. His *Fulfillingness' First Finale* LP became his first number one album since *Little Stevie Wonder–the 12-Year-Old Genius* in 1963. The first single from the album, "You Haven't Done Nothin'," featured the Jackson Five on backing vocals, and Wonder actually introduces the group in the song, "Jackson Five, sing along with me . . ." With all six Motown stars singing away, the single entered the Hot 100 at number 93 on August 3, 1974. Thirteen weeks later, Stevie Wonder had his fourth number one single.

*Writer: Stevie Wonder*

*Producer: Stevie Wonder*

*November 2, 1974*
*1 week*

Stevie Wonder followed *Talking Book* with an album that reinforced the music community's belief that here was a creative genius who was just beginning to reveal how great his true potential was. *Innervisions* was the first album on which Stevie wrote every song by himself. And with the exception of a few guest musicians, he once again played virtually every instrument on the LP.

One of the ways record companies introduce important new albums is to invite the press to a listening party, where they can eat, drink and merrily hear a major artist's new LP. The listening party for *Innervisions* departed from the norm. Since Stevie now had greater control over his product, thanks to the negotiations of 1971, he called the shots for the event. Invited guests were instructed to meet in Times Square, in the heart of Manhattan. There they were asked to don blindfolds as they boarded a waiting bus, which drove around the

city in a crazy, random pattern to throw off everyone's sense of direction. When the bus finally reached its destination, guests were led by hand through a recording studio and invited to *feel* musical instruments. Stevie explained, "the idea of the blindfolds was to try to give people an idea of what's happening in *my* mind. When you look at something, your hearing is distracted by your eyes." *Innervisions* contained three hit singles: "Higher Ground" (number four in October, 1973), "Living for the City" (number eight in January, 1974) and "Don't You Worry 'Bout a Thing" (number 16 in June, 1974).

Prior to the debut of *Innervisions* on *Billboard's* album chart, Stevie Wonder started a tour of America. On August 6, 1973, while travelling from Greenville, South Carolina, to Durham, a truck loaded with logs slammed on its brakes in front of the car Stevie was riding in. Several logs spilled out of the truck and crashed through the windshield of Wonder's car. Dozing in the passenger seat, Stevie was directly in the line of fire.

Despite the assurances of doctors at the hospital in Winston-Salem that Stevie would regain consciousness, he remained in a coma for a week. Ste-

## THE TOP FIVE
*Week of November 2, 1974*

1 **You Haven't Done Nothin'**
Stevie Wonder

2 **You Ain't Seen Nothing Yet**
Bachman-Turner Overdrive

3 **Jazzman**
Carole King

4 **The Bitch is Back**
Elton John

5 **Can't Get Enough**
Bad Company

**382** # You Ain't Seen Nothing Yet MERCURY 73622
BACHMAN-TURNER OVERDRIVE

*Writer: Randy Bachman*

*Producer: Randy Bachman*

*November 9, 1974*
*1 week*

"YOU AIN'T SEEN NOTHING YET" was a song intended for an audience of one. Songwriter Randy Bachman never wanted the public to hear the song he had composed especially for his brother Gary, the first manager of Bachman-Turner Overdrive. "He stuttered," Randy explains. "He had a speech impediment. We thought, just for fun . . . we'd take this song and I'd stutter and we'd send it to him. He'll have the only copy in the world of this song by BTO."

The tune began as an instrumental track inspired by the rhythm guitar of Dave Mason ("Only You Know and I Know"). BTO had already made the Hot 100 with two hits in 1974, "Let It Ride" (number 23 in April) and "Takin' Care of Business" (number 12 in August). They were in Seattle, Washington, recording their third album and had eight songs prepared. "But we had this ninth song," says Randy. "It was basically just an instrumental and I was fooling around . . . I wrote the lyrics, out of the blue, and stuttered through them."

When the album was completed, Charlie Fach of Mercury Records flew to Seattle to hear the finished product. After listening to the eight songs BTO recorded for the album, Fach complained that he "didn't hear that magic thing." "What's magic?" Randy parried. "It's magic when it gets airplay and people buy it. You can't plan magic." Fach asked if the band had anything else. Randy replied, "We have this one song, but it's a joke. I'm laughing at the end. I sang it on the first take. It's sharp, it's flat, I'm stuttering to do this thing for my brother." Fach asked Randy to play the song. "We did. Charlie smiled and said, 'That's the track. It's got a brightness to it. It kind of floats a foot higher than the other songs when you listen to it.' "

Randy agreed to include it on the album, but only if he could re-record the vocal. He went into the studio the next day. "I tried to sing it, but I sounded like Frank Sinatra. It didn't fit." Fach told him to leave it the way

it was, stuttering and all. When *Not Fragile* was released, radio stations jumped on "You Ain't Seen Nothing Yet" right away. "I started to hear it getting played and I was embarrassed. I'd turn the radio down. My wife would say to me, 'Look, at last, they're playing a song of yours like mad.' "

Fach kept calling with airplay reports, urging Bachman to permit the track to be released as a single. "And I refused for three weeks . . . I was producer, so I had final say on what went out. I woke up one day and asked myself, 'Why am I stopping this? Some of my favorite records are really dumb things like 'Louie, Louie' . . . so I said to Charlie, 'O.K., release it. I bet it does nothing."

"You Ain't Seen Nothing Yet" debuted at number 65 on September 21, 1974, and moved to the top of the Hot 100 seven weeks later. It was the first and only chart-topper for BTO, but Randy Bachman had been to the summit before as part of the Canadian group Guess Who [see 273—"American Woman" / "No Sugar Tonight"]. Bachman, a convert to Mormonism, left that group after 11 years when he realized, "After the final encore, I just didn't want to be with these guys." Wanting more control over his career, he took a year off and wrote some songs. "But I got restless right away. I'd just jam with any band that came into town." He struck out in a country and western direction with a group called Brave

Belt that included former Guess Who member Chad Allan and Randy's younger brother Robbie. Allen was replaced by another Bachman brother, Tim, and bass guitarist Fred Turner. Bachman-Turner Overdrive was born, named after the trade magazine of the trucking industry, *Overdrive*.

The father of eight children, Randy went on the road again with Bachman-Turner Overdrive in 1984. Looking back on "You Ain't Seen Nothing Yet," he reflects, "When it was all over, to realize that I could have a million-seller and a number one record without sitting down with mental giants like Paul McCartney and . . . saying, 'Let's write a number one song,'—you really can't. The magic is out of your hands."

## THE TOP FIVE
*Week of November 9, 1974*

1. **You Ain't Seen Nothing Yet**
   Bachman-Turner Overdrive

2. **Jazzman**
   Carole King

3. **Whatever Gets You Thru the Night**
   John Lennon

4. **Tin Man**
   America

5. **Back Home Again**
   John Denver

APPLE 1874 **Whatever Gets You Thru the Night**
JOHN LENNON

383

---

*Writer: John Lennon*

*Producer: John Lennon*

*November 16, 1974*
*1 week*

---

JOHN LENNON was the first Beatle to release a solo single, but was the last of the four to have a number one record on the Hot 100. "Give Peace a Chance" by the Plastic Ono Band was released in July, 1969, while the Beatles' "The Ballad of John and Yoko" was still climbing the chart; it reached number 14. "Cold Turkey," released four months later, was a song Paul McCartney did not want to record with the Beatles. The record peaked at number 30. "Instant Karma (We All Shine On)" was much more accessible. Produced by Phil Spector, it competed with "Let It Be" and went to number three in March, 1970. Lennon had five more

chart singles between 1971-1974, but only "Imagine" made any impact, also peaking at number three.

John was coping with the emotional stress of separation from Yoko Ono and his battle with the United States Immigration Service, which had ordered his deportation, when he recorded the *Walls and Bridges* album in his adopted home town of New York in the summer of 1974.

On one of the songs for the LP, Lennon was joined by a guest artist—Elton John. They recorded a new song John had written, "Whatever Gets You Thru the Night." Elton played piano and organ and sang backing vocals for Lennon, and was more convinced than John that the song would be a hit. During the recording session, Elton predicted the record would hit number one. "No, I'm out of favor here," Lennon is quoted in Ray Coleman's biography, *Lennon*. "It would be nice but

it's not a number one."

Elton insisted it was, and made a bargain with Lennon. If the song reached the top of the chart, Lennon would have to appear in concert with him. John was so sure he had not recorded a smash hit, he agreed. "Whatever Gets You Thru the Night" entered the Hot 100 at number 53 on September 28, 1974. Seven weeks later Lennon knew he had to make good on his promise.

He did so within two weeks. On Thanksgiving Night, 1974, Lennon made an unannounced appearance with Elton at Madison Square Garden. He turned down Elton's suggestion to sing "Imagine." "I didn't want to come on like Dean Martin, doing my classic hits," Coleman quotes him in *Lennon*. "I wanted to have some fun and play some rock 'n' roll. And I didn't want to do more than three because it was Elton's show." Together, they performed "Whatever Gets You Thru the Night," "Lucy in the Sky With Diamonds" and a song that Paul McCartney was primarily responsible for writing, "I Saw Her Standing There."

The latter song was released on the "B" side of Elton's "Philadelphia Freedom" [see 401]; the other two live recordings were not available until DJM Records in England issued them on a 12" single in 1981. They had taken on historical significance by then. The Madison Square Garden concert on November 28, 1974, marked the last time John Lennon would appear on stage.

## THE TOP FIVE

*Week of November 16, 1974*

1 **Whatever Gets You Thru the Night**
John Lennon

2 **Do It ('Til You're Satisfied)**
B.T. Express

3 **My Melody of Love**
Bobby Vinton

4 **Tin Man**
America

5 **Back Home Again**
John Denver

## 384  I Can Help  MONUMENT 8621
### BILLY SWAN

*Writer: Billy Swan*

*Producer: Chip Young*
*Billy Swan*

*November 23, 1974*
*2 weeks*

"I WROTE 'I Can Help' when Kris (Kristofferson) and Rita (Coolidge) bought me a little RMI organ for a wedding present," Billy Swan told Chet Flippo of *Rolling Stone*. "My wife had one of these little electric drummers . . . . So I was just sitting at the organ and . . . started playin' chords and pretty soon the words came out . . . . I did it in two takes and didn't even overdub the vocals— just stood up and played the organ and sang . . . . Some people call it a nostalgia song, but I don't think so. I just like the sound."

Swan had a multitude of interesting stops along the way to recording his own chart-topping single. He was born May 12, 1943, in Cape Giradeau, Missouri. He grew up listening to country stars like Hank Williams, Lefty Frizzell and Webb Pierce, then fell under the rock and roll influence of Jerry Lee Lewis, Buddy Holly and Elvis Presley.

The first song he ever wrote became a top 10 single. "I was 16 and wrote a poem in English class one day," he told Flippo. "A couple of years later Bill Black took it to Clyde McPhatter, who didn't like it but went ahead and cut it. That was 'Lover Please.' After that, I was spoiled. I figured show business was the easiest thing in the world."

Swan moved to Memphis to continue his career as a songwriter. "The

## THE TOP FIVE
*Week of November 23, 1974*

1  **I Can Help**
   Billy Swan

2  **Do It ('Til You're Satisfied)**
   B.T. Express

3  **My Melody of Love**
   Bobby Vinton

4  **Tin Man**
   America

5  **Longfellow Serenade**
   Neil Diamond

first thing I did was drive by Elvis' house," he recalled for Hilburn. I had been there before. Everybody down there used to stop by and see where he lived. I even remember one time sneaking into his yard and stealing a towel as a souvenir. I guess I hoped it would say 'Elvis' or something on it, but it just said Roosevelt Hotel.

"Anyway, I stopped by again as soon as I got to Memphis and started talking to Travis Smith. He's Elvis' uncle and he watched the gate . . . . I told him I was writing for Bill Black and looking for a place to stay . . . there was room at his place so I ended up living there . . . . I even ended up watching the gate sometimes late at night so Travis could go home for a bit."

Later, Swan relocated to Nashville and supported himself by working as a recording assistant at Columbia Records' studio. His duties included janitorial work, and when he quit during the recording of Bob Dylan's *Blonde on Blonde*, Swan gave his job to another songwriter, Kris Kristofferson.

Billy went on to produce "Polk Salad Annie" for Tony Joe White, and then Kristofferson made it big

and asked Billy to join his band. They toured the world, stopping at the Isle of Wight Festival in 1970. Returning to Nashville, Swan met Kinky Friedman and played rhythm guitar and sang harmony with his band, the Texas Jewboys. Around the same time, Swan met a woman who was looking for an apartment to rent in the building he lived in. Her name was Marlu and they were soon married.

While Marlu was expecting their first child, Billy was earning $75 a week working for a Nashville publisher. Kristofferson invited him to tour with his band again, and Billy took the job. Then producer Chip Young noticed that Billy's voice was similar to Ringo Starr's and decided to record a solo album with Swan.

Soon after his single hit number one, Swan was in Burbank, California, hosting NBC-TV's "The Midnight Special." His name was lit up in lights behind him. "It's sort of like a dream come true," he told Christopher Cabot of the Associated Press, "like the little boy in 'Johnny B. Goode,' whose mother says, 'Maybe someday your name will be in lights, saying "Johnny B. Goode" tonight.'"

*Writer: Carl Douglas*

*Producer: Biddu*

*December 7, 1974*
*2 weeks*

Biddu, an Indian-born producer living in London, was looking for a singer to record a tune by Brooklyn songwriter Larry Weiss [see 415—"Rhinestone Cowboy"] in the spring of 1974. Two years earlier, Biddu had composed the music for the film *Embassy* starring Richard (*Shaft*) Roundtree and through friends had met Jamaican singer Carl Douglas, whom he hired to sing the title song. Thinking that Douglas might be right for Weiss' "I Want to Give You My Everything," Biddu gave him a call.

The Weiss song was intended for the "A" side of a single, and Biddu needed something to record for the "B" side.

"I asked Carl if he had any lyrics," Biddu recalls. "He rattled off about four or five songs that he had written . . . one of the songs . . . had the lyrics for 'Kung Fu Fighting.' Since it was going to be a 'B' side, I said, 'Fine, we'll have a song called 'Kung Fu Fighting.' So I started working out some melody for it. Nothing was taken seriously."

With only 10 minutes of studio time left, "Kung Fu Fighting" was recorded quickly. "We did a lot of 'hoos!' and 'haas!' like someone giving somebody a karate chop," Biddu explains. He presented the Weiss song to Pye Records' A&R chief, who liked it, but wanted to hear the flip side as well. "It's just a fun thing," Biddu warned, but the label didn't laugh. They thought it was good enough to release as an "A" side. Biddu responded, "If you really think so, although I think it's the kind of song that might sell

20,000 records."

The record company thought it would do better than that. Karate was fashionable in the '70s, but kung fu was even bigger—Bruce Lee had popularized the ancient martial art at the box office. So Pye released the single in Britain and waited for the results.

"The first five weeks, we didn't get one play on radio," Biddu recollects. "It didn't sell one copy. And then suddenly, it just took off from the (dance) clubs and it went to number one all around the world."

"Kung Fu Fighting" was picked up for American release by 20th Century Records. The week that it yielded the number one position in Britain to John Denver's "Annie's Song" [see 371], it entered the *Billboard* chart at number 94. Eight weeks later it had battled its way to the top of the Hot 100.

Douglas, a former engineering student, only managed one follow-up in America, the similarly-constructed "Dance the Kung Fu," number 48 in March, 1975.

Biddu released several instrumental disco albums and produced another British number one hit, "I Love to Love (But My Baby Loves to Dance)" by Tina Charles. He returned home to India to compose music for films as well as recordings. Now living in London once more, he reflected on the international success of "Kung Fu Fighting." "If I had a theory why the record was a hit, I'd have more hits! You never know why a record is a hit. It had street appeal, I think. It was a bit of a novelty, but . . . it was a hit all over the world. Maybe it was just a good pop record without us knowing about it."

## THE TOP FIVE
*Week of December 7, 1974*

1 **Kung Fu Fighting**
Carl Douglas

2 **I Can Help**
Billy Swan

3 **When Will I See You Again**
Three Degrees

4 **Do It ('Til You're Satisfied)**
B.T. Express

5 **Cat's in the Cradle**
Harry Chapin

## 386 Cat's in the Cradle ELEKTRA 45203
### HARRY CHAPIN

*Writers: Harry Chapin*
*Sandy Chapin*

*Producer: Paul Leka*

*December 21, 1974*
*1 week*

Harry Chapin was rock's master storyteller. His songs were narrative prose set to music and he once said his compositions were "stories of ordinary people and cosmic moments in their non-cosmic lives."

"Cat's in the Cradle" was a story suggested by Chapin's wife, Sandy. He was touring when his youngest son was born and was unhappy about not being with Sandy for the birth. The song tells of a father and son who can't schedule time to be with each other—at any time during their lives.

Harry Chapin was born December 7, 1942, in New York City. His father, Jim, was a jazz drummer who worked with Tommy Dorsey and Woody Herman. Harry studied trumpet and sang in the Brooklyn Heights Boys' Choir, and with his brothers Tom and Stephen formed a folk group. Harry played guitar, banjo and trumpet.

Harry supported himself by working as a New York City cab driver. In 1969, he produced a documentary about boxing, *The Legendary Champions*, which was nominated for an Academy Award. He included some of his own songs in a second documentary, *Blue Water, White Death*.

With bassist John Wallace, guitarist Ron Palmer and cellist Tim Scott, he put together a new group and appeared at the Village Gate following evening performances of *Jacques Brel Is Alive and Living in Paris*. A review in the New York Times caught the attention of Elektra Records employee Ann Purtill, who saw him and insisted that label president Jac Holzman sign Chapin. On the lyric sheet of Chapin's first album, *Heads and Tales*, the words "Thank you, Ann Purtill" stand alone.

That album included "Taxi," a six-minute and 44-second story-song about a cab driver named Harry and a long-lost lover named Sue, who hails his taxi one night. Released as a single, the ballad reached number 24 in the spring of 1972. Despite the higher chart placement of "Cat's in the Cradle," the song most people associate with Chapin is the

more memorable "Taxi."

Chapin received a *Billboard* trendsetter award for his contribution to the narrative form. In 1975, "Cat's in the Cradle" was included in the score of a Broadway production, *The Night That Made America Famous*, a multi-media production that received two Tony nominations. In 1977, a musical revue of his songs, "Chapin," toured several cities. Chapin recorded on Elektra through 1979, his only other hit single being the tale of a morning DJ on "WOLD." In 1980, he signed with Neil Bogart's Boardwalk records and recorded a sequel to "Taxi," titled "Sequel." It continued the tale of Harry and Sue, and peaked at number 23, one notch higher than "Taxi."

Chapin performed about 200 concerts a year, half of them for political and social causes. He co-founded the World Hunger Fund and helped raise more than five million dollars to prevent people from dying of starvation. He also performed benefit concerts for the Multiple Sclerosis Foundation and for environmental and consumer causes.

He was scheduled to perform at a benefit concert on the night of July 16, 1981. At 12:27 that afternoon, he was driving into Manhattan for a business appointment when he changed lanes on the Long Island Expressway with his emergency blinkers flashing, apparently in an attempt to exit at the Jericho Turnpike. He was hit from behind by a tractor-trailer. The rear of Chapin's 1975 Volkswagen was crushed and sparks flew, igniting

the fuel tank. The driver of the truck freed Chapin from his seat belt and pulled him from the flaming wreckage, but Chapin was pronounced dead at Nassau County Medical Center at 1:05 p.m.

Harry Chapin's philanthropic work has been carried on by others. His brothers have performed memorial concerts in his name to raise money for the causes Harry supported. His manager, Ken Kragen, established a Harry Chapin Memorial Fund to continue his humanitarian efforts, especially "the eradication of world hunger." Kragen's work was successful enough to attract the attention of Harry Belafonte, who asked Kragen to become involved with the massive 1985 effort to attack the problem of hunger in Africa [see 605—"We Are the World".]

## THE TOP FIVE
*Week of December 21, 1974*

1 **Cat's in the Cradle**
Harry Chapin

2 **Kung Fu Fighting**
Carl Douglas

3 **Angie Baby**
Helen Reddy

4 **When Will I See You Again**
Three Degrees

5 **You're the First, the Last, my Everything**
Barry White

Writer: Alan O'Day

Producer: Joe Wisert

December 28, 1974
1 week

"**I**F I were going to teach a course on songwriting, I think I'd use 'Angie Baby' as my textbook," says Helen Reddy. It's a high compliment for the first number one song written by Alan O'Day [see 469—"Undercover Angel"].

"I was a little bit like a male 'Angie Baby,'" admits O'Day, "in that I used to sit alone a lot, being an only child, and listen to the radio and just kind of crawl into the songs. That was a lot of my entertainment."

The musical ancestor to "Angie Baby" was a Beatles song, according to O'Day. "The song 'Lady Madonna' by the Beatles just *killed* me. I thought, well, I'm gonna write a song about somebody who's growing up with the radio playing in the background of their life, with this rock and roll time we live in . . . there are songs for all of our emotions, and the radio really speaks for us in a way that nothing else does.

"But the heroine of my song came out real boring . . . at this point there was no 'Angie Baby,' just scraps of paper trying to work out something . . . so I took my ingenue and made her a little bit weird. The song started getting interesting. The weirder she got, the more interesting the song became."

"At another point, I went on one of my songwriting vacations down to Palm Springs. I stayed in this little motel. I had the idea of Angie becoming impregnated by this guy in the song and having a baby." Alan read a first draft of the idea to the woman who ran the motel, figuring that as someone removed from the record industry, her opinion would count more than some label executive. "She had heard the first part of the song and really liked Angie as a person. When I told her I was thinking about Angie going through this further trial and tribulation, she got kind of upset. She said, 'no, she's been through enough.'"

When he completed the song, his publisher, Warner Brothers Music, took the song to Cher, who had already recorded Alan's "Train of

Thought." It was not the first number one song to be rejected by Cher [see 331—"The Night the Lights Went Out in Georgia"]. Then the song went to Jeff Wald, who grabbed it for Helen.

Joe Wisert produced the song for Reddy. Alan says he "was one of the few producers who ever came back to me and asked me things about my demo and what I meant by the lyrics, so he would have a real understanding of the song when he went into the studio. That was impressive to me."

The lyrics of "Angie Baby" have

**THE TOP FIVE**
Week of December 28, 1974

1 **Angie Baby**
Helen Reddy

2 **Lucy in the Sky With Diamonds**
Elton John

3 **You're the First, the Last, my Everything**
Barry White

4 **Kung Fu Fighting**
Carl Douglas

5 **Cat's in the Cradle**
Harry Chapin

remained cryptic, even though Alan thought they were very clear. "I thought I spelled out what happened. It's a fantasy trip but it's real clear. And the very thing that made the song a hit was what happened to the guy in the song. I never intended it to be (a mystery)."

Still, neither Alan nor Helen will divulge what they think the ultimate outcome of the song is. Asked to explain the lyrics, Helen replies, "That's everybody's question . . . I'll never tell you." Alan will volunteer what Helen thought happened to Angie's mysterious visitor: "Helen Reddy said he turned into a sound wave."

But while he won't reveal his own idea of what happens at the end of the song, Alan tells the story of a phone call that woke him up at two in the morning: "I got a call from a disc jockey friend in Palm Springs when 'Angie Baby' was number one . . . he says, 'listen, I figured out who the guy was.'. . . he said he was a disc jockey . . . he was so excited. I'd never thought of that."

"Angie Baby," the second number one single in 15 months to mention the name Angie in the title [see 346—"Angie"], was Helen Reddy's third and final number one single. She made the top 10 one more time, with "Ain't No Way to Treat a Lady" in 1975. On July 18 of that year she became the first and only permanent host of "The Midnight Special" on NBC, the network that gave her an eight-week summer replacement show for Flip Wilson in 1973. She also starred in three films: *Airport '75* (as sort of a flying, singing nun), *Pete's Dragon* and the abysmal *Sgt. Pepper's Lonely Hearts Club Band.*

She continued to record for Capitol until 1979, then switched to MCA for two albums. Not currently signed to a label, she admits, "I certainly don't have the interest in music I once had. I'll always sing, but I would like that to be a smaller part of my life." Now divorced from husband Jeff Wald, she is writing a book about the history of her native Australia and is planning to do some acting in musical theater. In 1985, she went into a recording studio for the first time in two-and-a-half-years, although she is no longer writing songs and says it is hard to find good material.

# 388 Lucy in the Sky with Diamonds MCA 40344
ELTON JOHN

Writers: *John Lennon*
*Paul McCartney*

Producer: *Gus Dudgeon*

*January 4, 1975*
*2 weeks*

"I MET John last year," Elton John said of his introduction to John Lennon in Paul Roland's biography, *Elton John.* "Then when I was in New York getting off the SS France I saw him again and he said, 'Come down to my sessions.' So I did, and ended up doing, 'Whatever Gets You Thru the Night' [see 383] and 'Surprise' from the album. And he was going to L.A. to do a song which he had written for Ringo and I said, 'On the way back why don't you come up to Caribou? Cos we're gonna do 'Lucy in the Sky.' And he said 'sure.'"

"Lucy in the Sky with Diamonds" was the second number one single inspired by Julian Lennon [see 247—"Hey Jude"]. Lennon talked about the song's origin with David Sheff for a *Playboy* interview: "My son Julian came in one day with a picture he painted about a school friend of his named Lucy. He had sketched in some stars in the sky and called it 'Lucy in the Sky With Diamonds.' Simple."

Lennon was asked if the images in the song, which had the initials LSD, were drug-related. "The images were from *Alice in Wonderland*," he replied. "It was Alice in the boat. She was buying an egg and it turns into Humpty-Dumpty. The woman serving in the shop turns into a sheep and the next minute they are rowing in a rowing boat somewhere and I was visualizing that. There was also the image of the female who would someday come save me—a 'girl with kaleidoscope eyes' who would come out of the sky. It turned out to be Yoko, though I hadn't met Yoko yet. So maybe it should be 'Yoko in the Sky with Diamonds.'

"It was purely unconscious that it came out to be LSD. Until somebody pointed it out, I never even thought of it. I mean, who would ever bother to look at initials of a title? It's *not* an acid song."

The song first appeared on the Beatles' archetypal *Sgt. Pepper's Lonely Hearts Club Band* album in 1967. Although none of the songs on *Sgt. Pepper* were released as singles, Joe Cocker's first American chart single was a cover version of "With a Little Help from My Friends" (number 68 in December, 1968).

Elton John's "Lucy in the Sky With Diamonds" debuted on the Hot 100 at number 48 on November 30, 1974. When it became Elton's third number one single five weeks later, it also became the second John Lennon-Paul McCartney song not by the Beatles to top the chart [see 150—"A World Without Love"]. It also took the title of most successful Beatles cover version of the rock era. The runners-up include "The Fool on the Hill" by Sergio Mendes and Brasil '66 (number six, September, 1968), "I Saw Him Standing There" by Tiffany (number seven, April, 1988), "You Won't See Me" by Anne Murray (number eight, July, 1974), "Got to Get You Into My Life" by Earth, Wind and Fire (number nine, Septemer , 1978), "You've Got to Hide Your Love Away" by Silkie (number 10, November, 1965), and "We Can Work It Out" by Stevie Wonder (number 13, April, 1971).

BELL 45613 **Mandy**
BARRY MANILOW

**389**

*Writers: Scott English*
*Richard Kerr*

*Producers: Barry Manilow*
*Ron Dante*

*January 18, 1975*
*1 week*

BARRY MANILOW didn't think "Mandy" was a very special song the first time he heard it. Actually, it was still called "Brandy" then, and it had spent two weeks on the Hot 100 in March, 1972, when its lyricist, Scott English, reached number 91 with his version. "I was recording (my) second album and I was trying desperately to make hit records and break through," Manilow told Dick Clark. "I was doing boogies and I was doing rock and roll and I was doing introverted Jacques Brel type stuff, and Clive (Davis) showed me this . . . pleasant little song. I said, 'Oh, that'll just be an album cut,' and I did it as a favor. Who would know that this little album cut would turn out to be the beginning of my career?"

The original version was more uptempo, but Davis, who had just become the president of Bell Records (and would soon change the name to Arista), suggested it be recorded as a ballad. "He also wanted it for the single," Barry revealed in a 1975 *Billboard* interview. "I figured it was risky for new artists to release a ballad. But he said, 'This is a very special ballad, I'm telling you.' So I listened to him."

"Mandy" was the first Barry

## THE TOP FIVE
*Week of January 18, 1975*

1  **Mandy**
   Barry Manilow

2  **Please Mr. Postman**
   Carpenters

3  **Laughter in the Rain**
   Neil Sedaka

4  **You're the First,**
   **the Last, my Everything**
   Barry White

5  **Lucy in the Sky**
   **With Diamonds**
   Elton John

Manilow single to chart. Entering the Hot 100 at number 67 on November 16, 1974, it took nine more weeks to rise to the top.

Barry Manilow was born June 17, 1946, in Brooklyn, New York. "When he was two years old, I saw talent in Barry," his mother, Edna Manilow Murphy, has said. "We had the radio on all the time in our house…and he used to dance in his little diapers. When he was seven years old, I put an accordion in his hands. He played it beautifully . . . and later, we bought him a piano. He put his fingers on the piano, and forgot about the accordion."

His father had deserted the family when Barry was two. He was 13 when his mother remarried. "Willie Murphy changed the course of my life," Manilow said in *Seventeen* magazine. "Until he came along, I was being raised by people who were from the old country—Russia. What turned them on were horas and folk music. . . . Mom wasn't really into contemporary music, and nobody told

me there was jazz out there or show music. But the first thing Willie Murphy did was take me to a Gerry Mulligan concert. I'll never forget it; it was the biggest thing in my life."

His friends were turned on by Elvis Presley, but Barry couldn't care less about rock and roll. He was more interested in his stepfather's record collection, which included albums by June Christy, Chris Connor and Stan Kenton as well as Broadway cast albums like *The King and I* and *Carousel.*

At Eastern District High School in Brooklyn, Barry was voted best musician. He attended City College of New York briefly, but deciding that music would be his career, he switched to the New York College of Music, then was accepted at Juilliard. To pay the rent, he held down one in a series of odd jobs—he was employed in the mailroom at CBS Television in Manhattan, where on his daily rounds he dropped off the mail to programming chief Fred Silverman.

# Please Mr. Postman A&M 1646
## CARPENTERS

Writers: *Brian Holland*
*Robert Bateman*
*William Garrett*
*Georgia Dobbins*

Producers: *Richard Carpenter*
*Karen Carpenter*

*January 25, 1975*
*1 week*

**H**ISTORY repeated itself for the third time when the Carpenters' took "Please Mr. Postman" to the top of the Hot 100. The first Motown song to go to number one [see 101], "Please Mr. Postman" was the third chart-topper of the rock era to be number one twice by different artists. The first two songs to accomplish this unusual feat were "Go Away Little Girl" by Steve Lawrence [see 122] and Donny Osmond [see 299] and "The Loco-Motion" by Little Eva [see 115] and Grand Funk [see 364].

The Carpenters had released other singles that were cover versions, but all of them had been less obvious than "Please Mr. Postman" (with the exception of their very first 45, the Beatles' "Ticket to Ride" [see 174]). Songs like "Superstar" (Leon Russell), "Hurting Each Other" (Ruby and the Romantics) and "Sing" (from "Sesame Street") became better known by the Carpenters than their original recordings.

In an innovative move, Karen and Richard had strung together a rapid-fire succession of oldies but goodies on their *Now and Then* album, with a fictional DJ providing the connective tissue. Songs like "Johnny Angel" and "The End of the World" prompted some critics to suggest that Karen's voice was so-well suited to covering pop hits, she should consider doing it more often.

"Please Mr. Postman" was their first single to heed such advice. The first 45 pulled from their *Horizon* LP, it debuted on the Hot 100 at number 77 on November 23, 1974. Nine weeks later it became the third and final number one single of the Carpenters' career.

The follow-up, "Only Yesterday," was the last top 10 single (number four in May, 1975) for the duo. "Solitaire" and "There's a Kind of Hush (All Over the World)" made the top 20, but beginning in 1976 the Carpen-

ters entered a slump they found difficult to overcome. "Around the time of *Horizon* we started to get tired," Richard told Paul Grein in a 1981 *Billboard* interview. "It took a long time to do that album and I was wearing out."

The brother and sister took a self-imposed rest beginning in 1978. "I'd just had enough," Richard told Grein. "We'd always enjoyed our work, and when you get to a point that you're not enjoying it, you have to call a halt." Karen recorded a solo album in 1979 with producer Phil Ramone. After working on it for a year, the album was shelved in favor of a new LP with her brother. *Made in America* yielded their final top 20 single, "Touch Me When We're Dancing" (number 16 in August, 1981).

There were three more singles from the album, ending with another Marvelettes cover version, "Beechwood 4-5789," which paled in comparison with "Please Mr. Postman." Less than a year later, the world was shocked by the sudden death of Karen Carpenter at age 32. She was found unconscious at her parents' home in Downey, California, on the morning of February 4, 1983. Paramedics rushed her to Downey Community Hospital where she died of cardiac arrest at 9:51 a.m. PST.

"Karen had no idea how ill she was," Richard stated in a press release accompanying the *Voice of the Heart* album in November, 1983. "I believe in her heart of hearts she wanted to get better."

On the plump side as a child, Karen went on a diet in 1967 with the advice of her family physician. By 1975, she was suffering from anorexia nervosa, a disorder marked by compulsive dieting, often leading to serious health problems. At the time of her death, Karen had gained some weight back, and with it, some strength. The Los Angeles coroner said the cause of death was "heartbeat irregularities brought on by chemical imbalances asociated with anorexia nervosa."

### THE TOP FIVE
*Week of January 25, 1975*

1 **Please Mr. Postman**
Carpenters

2 **Laughter in the Rain**
Neil Sedaka

3 **Mandy**
Barry Manilow

4 **Fire**
Ohio Players

5 **Boogie On Reggae Woman**
Stevie Wonder

ROCKET 40313 **Laughter in the Rain**
NEIL SEDAKA

**391**

*Writers: Neil Sedaka*
*          Phil Cody*

*Producers: Neil Sedaka*
*            Robert Appere*

*February 1, 1975*
*1 week*

AFTER his first number one hit [see 114—"Breaking Up Is Hard to Do"], Neil Sedaka had some hungry years. By 1964, his singing career appeared to be over. He took a job as a staff writer for Don Kirshner at Screen Gems and with partner Howard Greenfield turned out a few hits, including "Workin' on a Groovy Thing" for Patti Drew and, later, the Fifth Dimension; "Puppet Man" for Tom Jones and the Fifth Dimension again; and "(Is This the Way to) Amarillo" for Tony Christie.

Around the same time that his high school girlfriend Carole King recorded "Tapestry," Neil tried for a comeback with an album titled "Emergence," released on the Kirshner label. Despite some critical approval, it failed to gain airplay or sales, and Sedaka and Greenfield decided to call an end to their long songwriting career. They wrote two more songs, including the sentimental "Our Last Song Together."

Through Kirshner, Neil met lyricist Phil Cody and they began writing together. Neil's agent, Dick Fox, suggested a trip to England might revive Sedaka's recording career. With wife Leba, daughter Dara and son Marc, Neil crossed the Atlantic and toured Great Britain, with an important date scheduled at the Royal Albert Hall in London. He won the audience over with his new songs, especially the finale, "Solitaire." The press loved him, too.

Personal manager Harvey Listberg suggested that while Neil was in Britain, he should record some songs at Strawberry Studios with a new group, Hotlegs (Graham Gouldman, Eric Stewart, Kevin Godley and Lol Creme). The result was the "Solitaire" LP, which did better in the United Kingdom than in the United States. That led to another album recorded with Hotlegs, now rechristened 10cc, at Strawberry Studios. Titled "The Tra-La Days Are Over," it was not released in America and a frustrated Neil decided to record his next album in Los Angeles.

British singer/producer Kenny Young recommended producer Robert Appere at Clover Studios on Santa Monica Boulevard. Before leaving London, Phil and Neil wrote a batch of new songs including "Laughter in the Rain."

An all-star band of session musicians played at the Los Angeles date, including Danny Kortchmar, Leland Sklar, Russ Kunkel and David Foster. Again, the album only had a British release. Although no American company was interested, a single from the album ("Laughter in the Rain") went to number 15 on the British chart.

Neil and Leba celebrated with a party at their London apartment. The guests included the Carpenters, Rod Stewart, Paul McCartney, the members of 10cc and two people who lingered until the end of the evening: Elton John and his manager, John Reid. Neil asked if they would like to sign him to their new American label, Rocket Records. Elton and Reid said yes and soon afterward Neil and Leba were visiting E.J. at the Caribou Ranch in Colorado to discuss Neil's first American release on Rocket.

The resulting album was a compilation of songs from the two albums recorded with 10cc and the LP produced by Appere in Los Angeles. The cover photo of Neil looking like he belonged in *The Godfather* inspired the title: "Sedaka's Back."

Neil chose "Laughter in the Rain" for the first single, but before it was released a cover version by Lea Roberts on United Artists Records started to get airplay. Not willing to let his American comeback slip away, Neil met with executives at MCA Records, distributor for the new Rocket label. They agreed to rush release "Laughter in the Rain" and within days it was a hit, bounding up the chart. During the week of February 1, 1975, it went to number one. It was the beginning of Neil Sedaka's *second* career.

## THE TOP FIVE

*Week of February 1, 1975*

1  **Laughter in the Rain**
   Neil Sedaka

2  **Fire**
   Ohio Players

3  **Boogie On Reggae Woman**
   Stevie Wonder

4  **You're No Good**
   Linda Ronstadt

5  **Pick Up the Pieces**
   Average White Band

## 392 Fire MERCURY 73643
### OHIO PLAYERS

Writers: *James Williams*
*Clarence Satchell*
*Leroy Bonner*
*Marshall Jones*
*Ralph Middlebrook*
*Marvin Pierce*
*William Beck*

Producer: *Ohio Players*

February 8, 1975
1 week

THE Ohio Players had been together for 15 years, in one incarnation or another, before they suddenly leaped out of obscurity to become one of the oldest, established, permanent "overnight successes" in the rock era.

Formed in Dayton, Ohio, in 1959, as Greg Webster and the Ohio Untouchables, they provided the vocal backing for the Falcons' 1962 R&B hit, "I Found a Love" (number 75 on the pop chart). The record is also notable for its impassioned lead vocal by 19-year-old Wilson Pickett. The Untouchables later released their own single for the Detroit-based Lu-Pine label, but soon disbanded.

However, two of the Untouchables—reedman Clarence "Satch" Satchell and bassist Marshall "Rock" Jones—decided to take another shot. Recruiting some local Dayton musicians, they put together a new ensemble called the Ohio Players. They worked as the house band for Compass Records, recording demo tapes on their own time. One of their tapes found its way to Capitol Records, and the Hollywood-based label signed the group in 1969.

Following the unsuccessful *Observations in Time* album, the Players pooled $400 for a trip to Nashville to record their next LP, *Pain*, which was released by Westbound Records of Detroit. Adopting an ultra-funky style strongly influenced by Sly Stone [see 251—"Everyday People"], the group began its ascent to the top with their first bona fide hit, "Funky Worm" (number 15 in May, 1973). Their three albums for the label featured pulsating rhythms and suggestive cover art, featuring a bald, scantily-clad female model in various poses of sexual bondage.

The Ohio Players were a study in democracy. Every one in the band contributed to each song. One might write lyrics, another the melody line, but each would make his impact. This approach worked so well because the Players saw few personnel changes in its glory days. Blessed with a crew of versatile musicians, the group often would use more than 20 instruments to get the sound it wanted.

When the Ohio Players switched to Mercury in 1974, their first album for the label, *Skin Tight*, outsold the three Westbound releases within three months. The title track became their biggest pop hit yet, peaking at number 13 in October, 1974.

The cover of their next album, *Fire*, revealed a gorgeous model wearing a fireman's helmet (and little else) and erotically fondling a horse. But if the artwork was hot, the sounds inside were blazing. Released in November, 1974, *Fire* was certified gold in two weeks. The title track entered the Hot 100 at number 73 on December 14, 1974, and moved to number one eight weeks later.

### THE TOP FIVE
*Week of February 8, 1975*

1 **Fire**
Ohio Players

2 **You're No Good**
Linda Ronstadt

3 **Boogie On Reggae Woman**
Stevie Wonder

4 **Pick Up the Pieces**
Average White Band

5 **Best of my Love**
Eagles

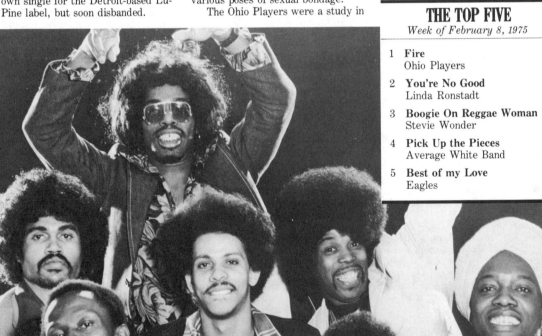

CAPITOL 3990 **You're No Good** **393**
LINDA RONSTADT

*Writer: Clint Ballard, Jr.*

*Producer: Peter Asher*

*February 15, 1975*
*1 week*

In the course of her career, Linda Ronstadt has sung country, folk, rhythm and blues, rock and roll, light opera and pop standards. The damn thing is she's done them all to perfection, succeeding with the public as well as the press no matter what style of music she chooses to sing at any given moment.

"She's about the best girl singer in the world in my prejudiced view," says her manager/producer, Peter Asher. "She can sing anything and does so incredibly well."

Ronstadt's commercial success kicked in after she teamed up with producer Asher, one half of the pop duo Peter and Gordon [see 150—"A World Without Love"]. "I first met her on one of my early trips to New York," Asher recalls. "I saw her at the Bitter End and liked her very much, and met her afterwards through some friends...later she was changing managers and asked me if I would be interested in managing her. I said I would be very interested, but I couldn't at that point because I'd just starting managing Kate Taylor, James' sister."

After one album, Kate returned to Martha's Vineyard and Peter became Linda's manager and producer in time to complete *Don't Cry Now*, her first album for Asylum Records. "We worked well together, so we decided to do the next (album) together, and that was *Heart Like a Wheel*," Peter explains. Linda still owed her previous record label, Capitol, one more album. They had their choice of her next three LPs and wisely decided to release *Heart Like a Wheel*. The album contained "You're No Good," a number one hit, and "When Will I Be Loved," which went to number two. Linda had been including "You're No Good" in her live show.

"I was certainly very keen on recording it," Asher says. "We recorded it a couple of different times to try and get it right. The first time we did it, it was a disaster. We had just hired the wrong people for it and later on we did it with Andrew Gold

playing most of the instruments, and that turned out to be the best way."

"You're No Good" established a pattern for Linda. With the exception of the new-wavish "How Do I Make You" in 1980 and "Somewhere Out There" in 1987, all of her top 10 singles have been cover versions of previous hits. After releasing the Everly Brothers' "When Will I Be Loved," her other top 10 hits included Martha and the Vandellas' "Heat Wave," Roy Orbison's "Blue Bayou," Buddy Holly's "It's So Easy," the Miracles' "Ooh [sic] Baby Baby" and Little Anthony and the Imperials' "Hurt So Bad."

Linda has taken musical risks, though, especially in the 1980s. She was cast as Mabel in the New York Shakespeare Festival production of Gilbert and Sullivan's *The Pirates of Penzance*, and *Newsweek* was effusive in its praise: "...she has not dodged the coloratura demands of her role (and Mabel is one of the most demanding parts in the G&S canon): from her entrance trilling 'Poor Wand'ring One,' it is clear that she is prepared to scale whatever soprano peaks stand in her way."

In 1983 she conquered another musical mountain by recording *What's New*, an album of pop standards produced by Nelson Riddle [see 8—"Lisbon Antigua"]. The project was so successful, she followed it

with two more installments of songs produced by Riddle.

Linda Maria Ronstadt was born on July 15, 1946, in Tucson, Arizona. Her father Gilbert, of Mexican, German and English heritage, owned "Ronstadt's Hardware Store" and loved to play his guitar for his three children. Along with her brother and sister, Linda formed the Three Ronstadts and sang at local functions. She left the University of Arizona in her freshman year to move to California, where she organized an acoustic rock band, the Stone Poneys, with friends Bob Kimmel and Ken Edwards. Their one hit, "Different Drum" (written by Michael Nesmith of the Monkees [see 211—"Last Train to Clarksville"]), was actually recorded by Linda with session musicians.

With the Stone Poneys disbanded, Linda fulfilled their contract obligations with another album for Capitol. Then she embarked on a true solo career, recording the album *Hand Sown, Home Grown* for Capitol. Her second solo LP, *Silk Purse*, produced the hit single "Long, Long Time." On her third album, *Linda Ronstadt*, her band included Don Henley and Glenn Frey, who went on to form the Eagles [see 395—"Best of My Love"]. Linda worked with producers Peter Boylan and J. D. Souther before connecting with Asher. "Peter was the first person willing to work with me as an equal," Linda told Cameron Crowe in *Rolling Stone*, "even though his abilities were far superior to mine. I didn't have to fight for my ideas....All of a sudden making records became so much more fun."

## THE TOP FIVE
*Week of February 15, 1975*

1 **You're No Good**
 Linda Ronstadt

2 **Pick Up the Pieces**
 Average White Band

3 **Best of my Love**
 Eagles

4 **Some Kind of Wonderful**
 Grand Funk

5 **Black Water**
 Doobie Brothers

# 394 Pick Up the Pieces ATLANTIC 3229
## AVERAGE WHITE BAND

*Writers: Roger Ball*
*Hamish Stuart*

*Producer: Arif Mardin*

*February 22, 1975*
*1 week*

HAILING from Scotland, the sextet that formed the Average White Band were raised on a steady diet of hot rhythm and blues, sweet Memphis soul and the classic Motown beat of the '60s. Out of this nourishing musical stew came a jazz-oriented, decidedly above-average sound so authentic that the fans of the AWB weren't confined by musical categorizations.

It was Bonnie Bramlett, one-half of the singing team of Delaney and Bonnie ("Soul Shake," "Never Ending Song of Love") that came up with the ironic—and highly-inaccurate—moniker for the Glasgow-based band. Bassist Alan Gorrie, sax player Roger Ball, guitarists Hamish Stuart and Onnie McIntyre, tenor sax player Malcolm "Molly" Duncan and drummer Robbie McIntosh scrounged out a meager living playing the European club circuit and American military bases in Germany. In 1973, the fledgling funk/soul group got a big break opening for Eric Clapton's comeback concert at the Rainbow Theatre in London, a show that included

Delaney and Bonnie on the bill.

Soon after the group sold their self-produced debut album, *Show Your Hand*, to MCA, and embarked on a no-frills American tour using second-hand equipment borrowed from the Who. Both the LP and tour bombed, however, and it wasn't until Jerry Wexler signed them to Atlantic Records in 1974 that the record-buying public caught up with AWB's enthusiastic, hard-driving soul sound.

"Pick Up the Pieces" was the tune that finally catapulted the Average White Band into the pop limelight. Written by Stuart and Ball, the funky Crusaders-like instrumental was lifted off the Arif Mardin-produced second album, *AWB*. The record featured volatile dual guitar work by Stuart and McIntyre, capped off with a memorable sax solo by Duncan.

"Pick Up the Pieces" was the highest new entry on the Hot 100 the week of December 7, 1974. Debuting at number 81, it took 11 weeks to reach the top. But the AWB's greatest triumph came on the heels of a bitter tragedy. Following an acclaimed American tour, Robbie McIntosh ingested a fatal dose of strychnine-laced cocaine at a party held for the band on September 22, 1974 in West Hollywood. He was found dead the next day, alone in his hotel room. The life of Alan Gorrie

was possibly saved due to the quick-thinking of another guest, Cher, who helped keep him from falling into a coma until the crisis passed.

Replacing McIntosh with a Brighton-based drummer, Steve Ferrone, the Average White Band dedicated their next album, *Cut the Cake*, to Robbie's memory. The title track, released as a single, was the group's second biggest hit, peaking at number 10 in June, 1975. The AWB became successful enough in the mid-'70s to turn their back on Scotland's tax laws and settle in the United States. It was a fitting move for a band that had found its musical roots in America before they had even arrived on her shores.

## THE TOP FIVE
*Week of February 22, 1975*

1. **Pick Up the Pieces**
   Average White Band

2. **Best of my Love**
   Eagles

3. **Some Kind of Wonderful**
   Grand Funk

4. **Black Water**
   Doobie Brothers

5. **Have You Never Been Mellow**
   Olivia Newton-John

*Writers: Don Henley*
*Glenn Frey*
*J. D. Souther*

*Producer: Glyn Johns*

*March 1, 1975*
*1 week*

A NEW strain of rock spread from Los Angeles in the early '70s. It grafted the instrumentation of country and bluegrass music onto the harmonies of California surfer rock, producing tender ballads and soft top-down pop about girls, cars and rock and roll. The nuclei of this genre were singer/songwriters, among them Jackson Browne, J. D. Souther and Warren Zevon, and their interpreters like Linda Ronstadt. But it was a single band whose name became synonymous with southern California country rock—the Eagles.

Curiously, not one of the four founders was a Californian by birth. Glenn Frey (born November 6, 1948, in Detroit) escaped Michigan's cold winters and musically stultifying frat and bar scene, bringing with him an R&B heritage, a Jack Kerouac quest for life and a sports vocabulary.

Blues and country were the sounds heard on the radio during the childhood of Don Henley (born July 22, 1947, in Gilmer, Texas), though his initial band forays were along rock lines. Nearly a college graduate, the love of language that led him to major in English literature emerged time and time again in Eagles' lyrics.

Stringed instruments—banjo, mandolin and pedal steel, as well as

the simple guitar, intrigued Bernie Leadon (born July 19, 1947, in Minneapolis, Minnesota), whose passion for country and bluegrass shaped the band's early direction. A car and cycle buff, Randy Meisner (born March 8, 1946, in Scottsbluff, Nebraska) preferred spending time with his family to playing bass in a rock and roll band.

Play, though, he did—as they all did—in bands like Poco, Dillard and Clark, the Flying Burrito Brothers, Rick Nelson's Stone Canyon Band, Longbranch Pennywhistle and the Stone Poneys. Linda Ronstadt [see 393—"You're No Good"] was preparing for a 1971 tour when her then-manager, John Boylan, extracted Frey, Leadon and Meisner from their affiliations. They were short a drummer until Frey recalled someone he'd met in the bar of the Troubadour, a favorite haunt for unemployed musicians in Los Angeles. He phoned Henley. "I was broke and here was a chance for $200 a week," Don told Robert Hilburn in the *Los Angeles Times*. While rooming together during the two-month tour, Frey and Henley decided to form their own band. With Leadon and Meisner as their partners, they released their initial album, *Eagles*, filled with pure, innocent country rock. Their next LP, *Desperado*, made it clear these were no relocated Nashville pickers with pretty four-part harmonies. The album was themed on old west outlaws and introduced the group's penchant for conceptual songwriting. For a time it attracted the attention of film director Sam Peckinpah, who

talked of turning the record into his next western, but discussions did not produce any celluloid results.

By the time the Eagles were ready to begin *On the Border*, a crisis of styles was beginning to brew. Glyn Johns, a producer chosen for his work with the Rolling Stones, Led Zeppelin and the Who, tended to extract the lush, melodic side of the band's double-edged music. Instead, they were pulled by the tougher, gut rock they experienced while touring with Joe Walsh. One night, he played them part of *The Smoker You Drink, The Player You Get*, his soon-to-be released album produced by Bill Szymczyk, a veteran of B. B. King and J. Geils Band recordings.

Szymczyk remembers the Eagles called him and said, "We want to rock." Though they had completed two-thirds of their sessions with Johns, including "Best of My Love," lock, stock and overdub moved to California to complete the LP under Szymczyk's guidance. To reinforce their new sound, they called in studio musician Don Felder, to add slide guitar to "Good Day in Hell." "He just blew us all away," enthused Frey. "It was about the best guitar work we'd ever heard." Two days later, Felder (born September 21, 1947, in Topanga, California) officially became the fifth Eagle.

Prior to "Best of My Love," only one of the seven Eagles' singles to chart had made the top 10 ("Witchy Woman" peaked at nine in November, 1972). "Best of My Love" entered the Hot 100 at number 83 on November 30, 1974, and became the Eagles' first chart-topper 13 weeks later.

## THE TOP FIVE
*Week of March 1, 1975*

1  **Best of my Love**
   Eagles

2  **Have You Never Been Mellow**
   Olivia Newton-John

3  **Black Water**
   Doobie Brothers

4  **My Eyes Adored You**
   Frankie Valli

5  **Some Kind of Wonderful**
   Grand Funk

# 396 Have You Never Been Mellow MCA 40349
## OLIVIA NEWTON-JOHN

*Writer: John Farrar*

*Producer: John Farrar*

*March 8, 1975*
*1 week*

WHEN Olivia's early singing partner Pat Carroll returned to Australia, it wasn't just to reminisce to friends about her show business fling. She married the guitarist of the "Go Show" band, John Farrar, and the couple hightailed it back to England, hooking up again with their old friend Olivia, whose career was on the rise. One reason for its continued ascendancy was John's steady hand in the producer's seat, and for Olivia's 1975 gold certified hit he even took up the composing pen.

The result was "Have You Never Been Mellow," the highest new entry on the Hot 100 the week of January 25, 1975. Debuting at number 63, the single took just six weeks to become Newton-John's second chart-topper. in the process, it also became one of her many country hits.

Beating in time with the correct pop pulse was no problem for the Farrar/Newton-John team, but placating Nashville was another kettle of musicians. "Appalachia? I've never heard of it. I sing easy listening, middle of the road music. . . . I sing new songs, old songs and country songs. I didn't think I would be considered a country singer. I was hoping for a hit record, no matter what it was," she would say to early interviewers. It was just this sort of old country, not honky tonk, dues-payin' country identity that angered certain members of the Country

Music Association when their fellows voted Olivia the 1974 Female Vocalist of the Year over competitors Loretta Lynn, Tammy Wynette, Dolly Parton and Tanya Tucker. So incensed were some members that they left the CMA and formed the Association of Country Entertainers. Said Johnny Paycheck at the time, "We don't want somebody out of another field coming in and taking away what we've worked so hard for."

Hurt by the furor, Olivia persevered, opening shows for Charlie Rich, playing places like the Dixie National Livestock Rodeo and deliberating on the proper wardrobe for county fair appearances (she decided on trousers because of the mud). She even had the nerve to play Nashville, though the concert was at the Municipal Auditorium and not the Grand Ole Opry. Later she would conclude, "I was a scapegoat at the time. In fact, Dolly Parton told me that the press blew the whole thing out of proportion . . . ."

The final hatchet-burying took place when she recorded in America for the first time and chose Nashville for the site. "We actually started recording in Los Angeles but it was an uncomfortable scene," she said in a local press conference. My producer and I were only going to do a single at first, but somewhere between L.A. and Nashville we found three great songs to go with the four we already had. So the session turned into an album." The disc, *Don't Stop Believin'*, turned out a number 33 single in the title track and earned her a gold album, her sixth in a row (her honors also include three platinum LPs).

ABC-TV helped Olivia realize the dream of having her own television special on November 17, 1976. The broadcast guest starred Elliot Gould, Lee Majors, Rona Barrett, Ron Howard, Tom Bosley, Lynda Carter and "lots of singing and dancing." It would be a direction the star would pursue in future endeavors.

---

## THE TOP FIVE
*Week of March 8, 1975*

1. **Have You Never Been Mellow**
   Olivia Newton-John

2. **Black Water**
   Doobie Brothers

3. **My Eyes Adored You**
   Frankie Valli

4. **Lady Marmalade**
   Labelle

5. **Lonely People**
   America

*Writer: Patrick Simmons*

*Producer: Ted Templeman*

*March 15, 1975*
*1 week*

Producer Ted Templeman, once a member of Harpers Bizarre ("The 59th Street Bridge Song (Feelin' Groovy)," "Anything Goes"), describes the origin of "Black Water." "Pat Simmons basically just wrote it as a song about the Mississippi River. I think he got the idea from when he was down there. He was just writing on his acoustic guitar. We laid it down on an acoustic guitar track with a rhythm machine, which in those days was pretty unheard of, and then we overdubbed the drums and the rest of it. . . . We had a breakdown in the center where

## THE TOP FIVE
*Week of March 15, 1975*

1 **Black Water**
Doobie Brothers

2 **My Eyes Adored You**
Frankie Valli

3 **Lady Marmalade**
Labelle

4 **Have You Never Been Mellow**
Olivia Newton-John

5 **Lovin' You**
Minnie Riperton

the vocals did an *a cappella* with no band. . . . (the producer of) Harper's Bizarre did the same thing for 'Feelin' Groovy' where he pulled the track out . . . so I stole the idea from my old producer."

"Black Water" was not so highly regarded when the album *What Were Once Vices Are Now Habits* was released. It was relegated to the flip side of the LP's first single, "Another Park, Another Sunday." "We never thought it was a single," Templeman confirms. "I didn't even know it. I'd like to tell you I did. Some little station started playing it in the South, and it started getting played around the country . . . it was just a self-made hit, a radio-made record."

Named after California slang for marijuana, the Doobie Brothers—none of whom are related to each other—got their start playing in Hell's Angels bars in northern California. The band's earliest influences were diverse. Drummer John Hartman had played with Moby Grape's Skip Spence. Singer and guitarist Patrick Simmons had been playing bluegrass and had started off his musical career in a folk trio with future Doobie Brother Tiran Porter. Early tours with Steely Dan and T-Rex taught them the finer points of

taking a show on the road. The quartet on the band's first album consisted of Hartman, Simmons, singer and lead guitarist Tom Johnston and bass guitarist Dave Shogren. Produced by Templeman and Lenny Waronker for Warner Brothers in 1970, the first LP was a dismal failure.

The Doobie Brothers decided to produce their own second album and spent a lot of money to get mediocre results. Warner Brothers was tempted to drop them from the label, but Templeman still believed in the band and volunteered to produce their third LP, *Toulouse Street*. That album contained the first hit single for the Doobies, "Listen to the Music" (number 11 in November, 1972).

The group's fourth album, *The Captain and Me*, was considered the group's real commercial breakthrough. "Long Train Runnin'" became the Doobies' first top 10 single (number eight in June, 1973).

Templeman offers an analysis of why "Black Water" was the Doobies' biggest hit to date. "Nobody was doing that kind of record with a vocal *a cappella*. It started off as an acoustic song, just an acoustic guitar for the first third of the record, then the drums come in. Records weren't like that on the radio. There were formula pop records then." Templeman doesn't consider the record perfect. "There's little things that speed up and slow down because we didn't stay right with the rhythm machine. But it's a pretty good record."

## 398 My Eyes Adored You PRIVATE STOCK 45003
### FRANKIE VALLI

*Writers: Bob Crewe*
*Kenny Nolan*

*Producer: Bob Crewe*

*March 22, 1975*
*1 week*

"**M**Y EYES ADORED YOU" was a tri-umphant return to the charts for Frankie Valli. He hadn't cracked the top 40 for almost seven years when he signed with Private Stock and gave both himself and the label their first number one singles.

He had topped the Hot 100 four times already as lead singer of the Four Seasons [see 117—"Sherry"], but his solo singles had always fallen short of that mark. Not too far short—"Can't Take My Eyes Off You" spent one week at number two in the summer of 1967. Most impor-tant, "My Eyes Adored You" revived the careers of Frankie Valli as well as the Four Seasons, who had their fifth number one single exactly one year after "My Eyes Adored You" [see 431—"December, 1963 (Oh What a Night)"].

After successful chart runs on Vee Jay and Philips, the Four Seasons signed with Motown in 1970. The choice was not so unusual; the group had done quite well on Vee Jay, a Chicago-based label that specialized in R&B acts. When the group went to Motown, they did so with the understanding that company founder Berry Gordy, Jr., would personally supervise their records. The reality turned out to be that Gordy was too involved with the motion picture *Lady Sings the Blues* starring Diana Ross to supervise the Four Seasons' career. It is a fact which Valli has publicly lamented, although he says he has nothing but admiration for Gordy and the company and would consider signing with the company today under the right circumstances.

The Four Seasons recorded an album titled *Chameleon*, released on the MoWest subsidiary. The critics liked it, but it was not a high priority item at Motown and the album pro-duced no hit singles (in 1975, a track titled "The Night" was released in the United Kingdom because of Valli's success with "My Eyes Adored You." It went to number seven, becoming the third biggest single for the Four Seasons in Britain at that time.

Valli also recorded some solo material for Motown, although noth-ing was released until he was having success on Private Stock. Ironically, "My Eyes Adored You" was a track recorded for Motown. It was originally titled "Blue Eyes in Georgia" when Bob Crewe and Kenny Nolan first wrote it, but when they played it for Valli it was altered to "My Eyes Adored You." Motown held onto the track for a year and a half without releasing it.

When the group's con-tract with Motown expired in 1973, Crewe, Gaudio and · Valli wanted the company to return just one track. They paid Motown four thousand dollars to buy back the rights to "My Eyes Adored You."

They shopped it around and were turned down by a number of labels, until Larry Uttal heard it. He had been ousted from Bell Records when Clive Davis was brought in to head the label, and was starting his own company, Private Stock.

"Larry sat down and listened to it, and rewound the tape in the mid-dle of the song," songwriter Nolan recalls. "He did that five times, and on the fifth play he said, 'I want that song.'"

Valli had recorded his first solo single, "My Mother's Eyes," before he joined the group that became the Four Seasons. He recorded under a wide variety of names [see 120—"Big Girls Don't Cry"], but adopted Valli from a country singer named Texas Jean Valley, who told people that Frankie was her "brother."

When the Four Seasons racked up three consecutive number one singles in 1962-1963, Frankie temporarily put his solo career on the back burner. He still believed he could have a solo career concurrent with the Four Sea-sons, and by 1966, was ready to try again. He released "(You're Gonna) Hurt Yourself," "The Sun Ain't Gonna Shine (Anymore)" and "The Proud One."

"Can't Take My Eyes Off You" was his fourth solo single of that time period, and he followed it with two more top 30 hits, "I Make a Fool of Myself" and "To Give (The Reason I Live)." At the same time, the Four Seasons were recording some offbeat singles (including Bob Dylan's "Don't Think Twice") as the Wonder Who, so there were weeks when Valli's voice was heard on three simul-taneous Hot 100 records.

### THE TOP FIVE
*Week of March 22, 1975*

1 **My Eyes Adored You**
Frankie Valli

2 **Lady Marmalade**
Labelle

3 **Lovin' You**
Minnie Riperton

4 **Black Water**
Doobie Brothers

5 **Have You Never Been Mellow**
Olivia Newton-John

40 with an R&B ballad, "Down the Aisle." They recorded for Parkway and Atlantic, but during the latter half of the '60s they were best known as the group Cindy Birdsong left.

Their fortunes changed in the '70s when they worked in England and met Vicki Wickham, who offered to manage them. After transforming their image and shortening the group name to a more contemporary Labelle, they released an album on Warner Brothers in October, 1971, that met with great critical acclaim. There was more praise for the second album, *Moonshadow*, which featured six songs written by Hendryx.

The rave reviews did not translate into hit records and they moved on to RCA. Their fusion of rock with R&B must have confounded radio station music directors, and their songs still failed to get airplay. They recorded an album with Laura Nyro, *Gonna Take a Miracle*, which included cover versions of Motown hits like "Jimmy Mack" and "You Really Got a Hold on Me." Then Labelle signed with Epic Records in June, 1974. Their first project for Epic was *Nightbirds*, an album recorded with producer Toussaint and his studio band, the Meters.

Released as the first single from the album, "Lady Marmalade" broke in the discos and then spread to radio. It entered the Hot 100 on January 4, 1975, at number 98 and went to number one 12 weeks later.

Labelle adapted a whole new space-age image but did not have another top 40 hit. After one more album, *Phoenix*, the three members couldn't agree on a musical direction and split the group.

---

*Writers: Bob Crewe
Kenny Nolan*

*Producer: Allen Toussaint*

*March 29, 1975
1 week*

---

**W**HEN "LADY MARMALADE" deposed "My Eyes Adored You" from the top of the charts, composers Bob Crewe and Kenny Nolan became the third songwriting team to succeed themselves at number one. The only collaborators who had accomplished this feat before were John Lennon and Paul McCartney [see 144—"She Loves You"] and Brian Holland, Lamont Dozier and Eddie Holland [see 177—"I Can't Help Myself (Sugar Pie Honey Bunch)"].

Nolan and Crewe had written "Lady Marmalade" in 1974, and recorded it on an album by "The Eleventh Hour," a studio group fronted by Kenny's vocals.

The song was written in pieces, Kenny explains. "I had one part of the song here and one part there, and it still needed something. Bob and I came up with the idea of 'Voulez-vous couchez avec moi ce soir.' It was like a puzzle that finally fit together."

"Lady Marmalade" was from New Orleans, and so was producer Allen Toussaint, who heard the Eleventh Hour track and decided to record it on Labelle. Labelle wasn't a New Orleans group; Patti Labelle, Nona Hendryx and Sarah Dash were from Philadelphia, where they formed the group in 1962 with New Jersey native

Cindy Birdsong, who left in 1967 to replace Florence Ballard in the Supremes [see 223 –"The Happening"].

Patricia Holt and Cindy Birdsong were friends in high school. "We used to listen to records on the radio and think, hey, we could do that," Patti told Tony Cummings in *The Sound of Philadelphia*. "So we got together with this high school group called the Ordettes. We'd sing at parties, things like that. That was around '59 or so. The other girls in the Ordettes weren't serious about music....In about '60 this promoter called Bernard Montague took two girls from the Del Capris, another local group— that was Sarah Dash and Nona Hendryx—and we formed a new group. That's when we met Bobby Martin and became the Blue Belles."

They signed with Newtown Records, and took their name from a subsidiary label, Bluebelle Records. Martin had produced a song called "I Sold My Heart to the Junkman" for a group called the Four Sportsmen on Newtown. It had failed, so Martin recorded the Blue Belles' vocals over the same instrumental track and released it. It went to number 15 on the Hot 100 in the spring of 1962.

"We enjoyed recording with Bobby," Patti told Cummings. "He tried to show us how to get a professional attitude to our music, but we were just young kids. We did a pile of records for Newtown and we worked real hard trying to get another hit." In 1963, the group changed its name to Patti LaBelle and the Blue Belles and made the top

---

## THE TOP FIVE
*Week of March 29, 1975*

1  **Lady Marmalade**
   Labelle

2  **Lovin' You**
   Minnie Riperton

3  **Philadelphia Freedom**
   Elton John Band

4  **Express**
   B.T. Express

5  **You Are So Beautiful**
   Joe Cocker

## 400 Lovin' You EPIC 50057
### MINNIE RIPERTON

Writers: *Minnie Riperton*
*Richard Rudolph*

Producer: *Stevie Wonder*

*April 5, 1975*
*1 week*

THE *PERFECT ANGEL* album was a perfect display piece for the powerful five-octave range of Minnie Riperton. Her number one single from that LP, "Lovin' You," was produced by Stevie Wonder [see 135—"Fingertips - Pt. 2"], and Wonder visited Minnie in the hospital the night before she died. "Well, the final person that I was waiting for has arrived, and everything will be alright now," she told him. Minnie Riperton died of cancer on July 12, 1979. She was just 31 years old.

She was born in Chicago on November 8, 1947, the youngest of eight children. Her mother loved to sing and encouraged Minnie to study music. At nine, she was singing in church, and a year later she went to Lincoln Center in the suburb of Oak-wood to study ballet and voice. She was studying opera when Raynard Miner and Rose Miller discovered her singing *a cappella* at Hyde Park High School. They were both involved with the Gems, a girl group signed to Chess Records. They brought Minnie to the label, and she worked as a receptionist as well as singing in the group.

She had to choose between joining the Junior Lyric Opera and touring with the Gems, and decided on the latter. The group backed up other Chess artists, including Fontella Bass and Etta James. They also released their own recordings until they broke up in 1966. Minnie stayed with Chess, first recording as Andrea Davis and then becoming one of the lead vocalists in Rotary Connection, an integrated group that combined R&B with psychedelic rock. They recorded six albums, covering songs like the Band's "The Weight" and Cream's "Sunshine of Your Love." When they disbanded in 1970, Minnie recorded a solo album, *Come to My Garden*, for Chess' Janus label. The next year

Riperton and her husband, Richard Rudolph, left Chicago and Chess behind for Gainesville, Florida. For two years, Minnie was "retired" from show business, and she spent the time raising her family and writing songs with Richard. But in 1973, she was tempted back into singing by Stevie Wonder, and she joined his backing vocal group, Wonderlove.

She toured with Wonder and sang on his *Fullfillingness' First Finale* album. In 1974, she was offered a contract by Don Ellis at Epic Records. After she signed, Wonder agreed to produce her first album for the label. The first single, "Reasons," failed to make the chart, and "Lovin' You" was released next. It entered the Hot 100 at number 80 on January 18, 1975, and went to number one 11 weeks later.

In 1976 Minnie learned she had cancer. She had a mastectomy that year, and became a spokesperson for the American Cancer Society. President Jimmy Carter honored her with the society's Courage Award, presented in a White House ceremony in 1977.

She continued to be treated for the disease, while remaining active as a performer and recording artist. In 1978 she left Epic and signed with Capitol, and while recording her first album for the label, *Minnie*, learned she had lymph cancer. The album was completed in February, 1979. After her death, Capitol released the posthumous *Love Lives Forever* album, with instrumental and vocal backing by many of the friends who loved her, including George Benson, Michael Jackson, Roberta Flack and Stevie Wonder.

### THE TOP FIVE
*Week of April 5, 1975*

1 **Lovin' You**
Minnie Riperton

2 **Philadelphia Freedom**
Elton John Band

3 **No No Song/Snookeroo**
Ringo Starr

4 **Express**
B.T. Express

5 **You Are So Beautiful**
Joe Cocker

*Writers: Elton John*
*Bernie Taupin*

*Producer: Gus Dudgeon*

*April 12, 1975*
*2 weeks*

IT all started with some tennis gear, a world champion and that good old Gamble-Huff style backbeat. Billie Jean King tells the story: "It was about a year after we'd started the World Team Tennis league. Elton was a big fan and when he was in town he'd come to the matches and holler and have a good time. I was player coach of the Philadelphia team, the Freedoms, at the time. So we had (tennis clothing designer and patriarch of the game) Ted Tingling custom make a Philadelphia Freedoms warm-up suit for Elton. We gave it to him, and as we were in the limo coming back from the matches he said, 'Billie, I'm going to write a song for you.' I said, 'Sure you are,' and he said, 'No, I mean it, just wait and see.'

"A couple months later we had the playoffs in Denver. Elton came because he'd been recording up at Caribou. He came back to the dressing room—I had a real important match to play—and was all excited, saying, 'You've got to listen to this

tape. This is it, the song I wrote for you. Do you like it?' So he played me a rough mix of 'Philadelphia Freedom' and of course, it was great. And when he got to the chorus he said, 'Listen to this part, the beat.' So I listened. 'Hear the beat?' he said. 'That's you when you get mad on the court.' "

Like his most recent number one, "Lucy in the Sky With Diamonds" [see 388], "Philadelphia Freedom" was recorded especially for release as a single. To make the 45 even more appealing to record collectors like himself (his collection numbers over 30,000 discs), Elton included his live duet with John Lennon [see 383—"Whatever Gets You Thru the Night"], "I Saw Her Standing There," on the flip side. "Philadelphia Freedom" was the highest new entry on the Hot 100 the week of March 8, 1975. It debuted at 53 and only took five weeks to become Elton's fourth chart-topper.

Chart positions, sales, promotion strategies, all these business aspects of the record industry had always occupied the artist's interests, so much that he started his own label, Rocket Records, in 1973. "I've always dreamed of having my own record company," he told *Rolling Stone*. "As a kid I used to watch the 78s when the labels were beautiful to look at,

I'd watch them go round." Bernie Taupin picked up the tale of Rocket Records' genesis. "In France (while recording *Don't Shoot Me, I'm Only the Piano Player*) the idea came about because (the band's guitarist) Davey Johnstone was going to make an album and he hadn't got a label to go out on."

"We went to a lot of companies but nobody would give us a reasonable deal," Elton continued. "So we were sitting around the table saying, what are we going to do, and I think it was me, actually, who said, 'Start our own label!' Because we'd all been drinking wine, we all said, 'Yeah.' Then we went to bed and all got up the next morning and said, 'Was everybody serious?' We all decided we were."

Distributed at first by MCA, then RCA, Rocket was never intended as a vehicle for its owner. After all, he set an industry precedent in 1974 when MCA shelled out $8 million for his contract. Rocket concentrated on artists like Neil Sedaka [see 391—"Laughter in the Rain"] and Kiki Dee [see 440—"Don't Go Breaking My Heart"] who both reached the apex of the Hot 100. There were some failures, too, like Rocket's first group, Longdancer. Elton assessed in 1973 that "Longdancer are not mind-shattering yet. They've got a long way to go." The band didn't have a chance to prove his theory but their guitarist, Dave Stewart, had to wait until he teamed up with a singing waitress named Annie Lennox before he had a chance to shatter minds with Eurythmics [see 575—"Sweet Dreams (Are Made of This)"].

## THE TOP FIVE
*Week of April 12, 1975*

1 **Philadelphia Freedom**
Elton John Band

2 **Lovin' You**
Minnie Riperton

3 **No No Song/Snookeroo**
Ringo Starr

4 **Express**
B.T. Express

5 **Poetry Man**
Phoebe Snow

# (Hey Won't You Play) Another Somebody Done Somebody Wrong Song ABC 12054

### B. J. THOMAS

*Writers: Chips Moman*
*Larry Butler*

*Producer: Chips Moman*

*April 26, 1975*
*1 week*

ONLY the technicality of a medley produced in Holland [see 544] prevents B. J. Thomas' "(Hey Won't You Play) Another Somebody Done Somebody Wrong Song" from being the number one single with the longest title. It remains a comfortable number two.

Thomas followed his first number one single [see 266—"Raindrops Keep Fallin' on My Head"] with a string of hits on Scepter Records before moving to ABC. "I Just Can't Help Believing," written by Barry Mann and Cynthia Weil, was his only other top 10 single in the first half of the '70s. Still, his other Scepter songs were popular on the radio, including the gospel-tinged "Mighty Clouds of Joy" and his anthem to pop music, "Rock and Roll Lullaby," featuring the twangin' guitar of Duane Eddy ("Because They're Young," "Forty Miles of Bad Road") and back-up vocals by the Chiffons [see 127—"He's So Fine"] and David Somerville of the Diamonds ("She Say (Oom Dooby Doom)," "Little Darlin' ").

Chips Moman, co-writer of "(Hey Won't You Play) Another Somebody Done Somebody Wrong Song," did not compose the tune for Thomas. It wasn't written with any singer in mind, but B. J. happened to be

offered it first. There was no special inspiration for the song—neither Moman nor Larry Butler had somebody do them wrong. "It's just like the guy who wrote 'Fly Me to the Moon' never had been to the moon," Moman points out. "You do have to have some imagination."

In his autobiography, *Home Where I Belong*, Thomas admits he barely remembers the recording session for his second number one hit. At the time, he was spending upwards of three thousand dollars a week to feed a drug habit that included addictions to Valium, cocaine and amphetamines. "It's a wonder I'm still alive," Thomas wrote in his autobiography, "considering how many times my bodily functions quit and someone had to revive me."

His marriage to his childhood sweetheart, Gloria, was virtually dissolved when he went to visit her and their daughter, Paige, in Fort Worth, Texas. During their separation,

Gloria had been converted to Christianity by two missionaries who lived nearby. In his book, B. J. recounts how his life was saved at midnight on January 28, 1976. He had hit rock bottom when Gloria took him to meet Jim and Micah Reeves. After talking with them, B. J. prayed privately for 20 minutes. Then he looked up at the clock. "The memory of seeing that secondhand sweep by the '12' will never leave me," he wrote.

Thomas began a drug-free life at that moment. His 1977 album, also called *Home Where I Belong*, was solid gospel and earned him a Grammy award. He went on to capture four more Grammys for his gospel music. His switch to religion hurt his status as a pop star. He was branded "born-again" and failed to get any more secular work. In 1983, he made a conscious effort to recapture his pop audience with the *New Looks* LP, followed by *The Great American Dream* in 1984.

---

### THE TOP FIVE

*Week of April 26, 1975*

1  **(Hey Won't You Play) Another Somebody Done Somebody Wrong Song**
   B.J. Thomas

2  **Philadelphia Freedom**
   Elton John Band

3  **He Don't Love You (Like I Love You)**
   Tony Orlando & Dawn

4  **Lovin' You**
   Minnie Riperton

5  **Supernatural Thing Part 1**
   Ben E. King

# He Don't Love You (Like I Love You)
## TONY ORLANDO AND DAWN

**403**

*Writers: Jerry Butler
      Clarence Carter
      Curtis Mayfield*

*Producers: Hank Medress
         Dave Appell*

*May 3, 1975
3 weeks*

AFTER 14 chart singles on Bell Records, including the biggest hit of their career [see 332—"Tie a Yellow Ribbon Round the Ole Oak Tree"], Tony Orlando and Dawn changed labels. "We moved to Elektra because someone very supportive of us moved to Elektra and we went with him," explains Telma Hopkins. That person was Steve Wax, a former promotion man at Bell who eventually became head of the Elektra label.

The original title of "He Don't Love You (Like I Love You)" was "He Will Break Your Heart." The first solo single for Jerry Butler after he left the Impressions, it peaked at number seven in December, 1960. The three composers of the song have all had their own successful careers. Butler, who earned the nickname "the Iceman" while working with Kenny Gamble and Leon Huff, has had 34 chart singles, including his biggest hit, "Only the Strong Sur-

vive" (number four in April, 1969).

Curtis Mayfield was a founding member of the Impressions with Butler. He went out on his own in 1970, scoring with two singles from the soundtrack of *Superfly.* Clarence Carter, a blind singer/guitarist from Montgomery, Alabama, had a string of chart singles from 1967-1973, including his two biggest hits, "Slip Away" (number six in October, 1968) and "Patches" (number four in September, 1970).

The Butler-Carter-Mayfield composition was the kind of R&B song Tony Orlando and Dawn preferred to sing. "It was my favorite song that we did," says Telma Hopkins. "We were all Jerry Butler fans." Their status as television and recording stars gave them more say in the material they recorded when they moved to Elektra.

Telma and her friend Joyce Wilson had given up their lucrative jobs singing backing vocals for some of the leading names in the R&B field when they were "coerced" by Tony into becoming Dawn [see 287—"Knock Three Times"]. Telma was 15 years old when she met Joyce. They were in rival backup groups in Detroit until Telma asked Joyce to work with her on a session for RCA. They dumped their respective groups, became best friends and still

live within 10 minutes of each other in Los Angeles.

Before working with Tony, their voices graced number one recordings like the Four Tops' "Reach Out, I'll Be There" [see 209] and Marvin Gaye's "I Heard It Through the Grapevine" [see 249].

The music stopped suddenly for Tony Orlando and Dawn on July 22, 1977. In the middle of a show at the Music Circus in Cohasset, Massachusetts, Tony stunned the audience—as well as Telma and Joyce—when he announced, "This is my last day as a performer. I am giving up show business in the name of Jesus Christ. I must give more time to my family." Shaken by the death of his 21-year-old sister Rhonda, a cerebral palsy victim, and the tragic suicide of his close friend Freddie Prinze, Orlando was emotionally exhausted. "He was crying from as far down deep as you can get. He was scared. We were all scared," his manager, Frank Lieberman, told *People.* After five months of what Orlando termed "heavy therapy," he returned to performing, but without Dawn.

Telma Hopkins concentrated on acting and won starring roles in the comedy series "Bosom Buddies," "Gimme A Break" and "Family Matters." Tony Orlando has followed an acting career as well, starring in the NBC-TV movie "Three Hundred Miles for Stephanie" and guest-starring in an episode of "The Bill Cosby Show" designed as a spin-off for a series starring Orlando.

## THE TOP FIVE
*Week of May 3, 1975*

1  **He Don't Love You
   (Like I Love You)**
   Tony Orlando & Dawn

2  **(Hey Won't You Play)
   Another Somebody Done
   Somebody Wrong Song**
   B.J. Thomas

3  **Before the Next
   Teardrop Falls**
   Freddy Fender

4  **Philadelphia Freedom**
   Elton John Band

5  **Chevy Van**
   Sammy Johns

**404**

# Shining Star COLUMBIA 10090
## EARTH, WIND & FIRE

*Writers: Maurice White*
*Philip Bailey*

*Producer: Maurice White*

*May 24, 1975*
*1 week*

EARTH, WIND and FIRE began as a mental image in a man's head. The man was Maurice White (born December 19, 1941), the musically prodigious son of a Memphis doctor. By 11, White was playing drums with a classmate, Booker T. Jones, who would later form the pioneer Memphis soul band, Booker T. and the M.G.'s ("Green Onions," "Time Is Tight"). Maurice was 16 when his family moved to Chicago, and against his father's wishes, he entered the Chicago Conservatory of Music, planning to become a music teacher.

In 1967, following a stint as a session musician at Chess Records, White joined the Ramsey Lewis Trio. He travelled to the Middle East while touring with the group and became a serious student of mysticism. Wanting to find a musical outlet for his new spiritual vision, he quit the Trio after three years and followed his dream to Los Angeles.

Using principles he discovered in a book called *The Laws of Success*, White held an image in his mind of the band he wanted to form. In fact, he even drew a detailed picture and hid it away. While looking through his astrological chart, White learned he had only earth, air and fire in his Sagittarius sign—and no water. Changing "air" to "wind," he had a name for the group he needed to find personnel for to bring his vision into reality.

The unit he finally assembled lived up to White's spiritual image. Most of the members were vegetarians and all regularly meditated together before performing to achieve a "oneness of mind." Three years later, when White took out the picture he had hidden, he found that he had, in fact, created his dream band.

Earth, Wind & Fire first recorded as a brassy, jazz-like band. But after Warner Brothers dropped the group from its roster in 1971, White began to rework the concept. Joining Columbia in 1973, the band began playing an exuberant dance music

that had life-affirming, often metaphysical lyrics wrapped around an exciting rhythm.

In 1975, the band released its sixth album, *That's the Way of the World*, which featured the vocal acrobatics of Philip Bailey (who would have his own solo career in 1985, reaching number two on the Hot 100 with "Easy Lover," a duet with Phil Collins [see 604—"One More Night"]). The LP was conceived as the soundtrack for a movie about an aspiring rock and soul band, portrayed by members of the group—Larry Dunn, Alan McKay, Ralph Johnson, John Graham, Andrew Woolfolk, Fred White, Verdine White and Philip and Maurice.

The first single from the album,

"Shining Star," entered the Hot 100 at number 86 on February 15, 1975. Their first six chart singles had failed to make the top 20, but lucky number seven, "Shining Star," moved to number one in its 15th week on the survey. In the gospel according to White, the song spoke of each person's potential to become a star in his or her own way. A disco smash, "Shining Star" earned Earth, Wind & Fire a Grammy for Best R&B Performance by a Vocal Group.

The band had five more top 10 singles, including John Lennon-Paul McCartney's "Got to Get You Into My Life" (number nine in September, 1978), a song they performed in the ill-fated movie, *Sgt. Pepper's Lonely Hearts Club Band.*

## THE TOP FIVE
*Week of May 24, 1975*

1  **Shining Star**
   Earth, Wind & Fire

2  **Before the Next**
   **Teardrop Falls**
   Freddy Fender

3  **Jackie Blue**
   Ozark Mountain Daredevils

4  **Only Yesterday**
   Carpenters

5  **Thank God I'm**
   **a Country Boy**
   John Denver

ABC/DOT 17540 **Before the Next Teardrop Falls** 405
FREDDY FENDER

*Writers: Vivian Keith*
*Ben Peters*

*Producer: Huey P. Meaux*

*May 31, 1975*
*1 week*

**F**REDDY FENDER had been playing his special blend of Tex-Mex R&B music for 20 years with just local success. Then he met producer Huey P. Meaux and recorded a 10-year-old song that he had heard sung by Charley Pride, "Before the Next Teardrop Falls." The single entered the Hot 100 at number 97 on February 1, 1975, and went to number one 17 weeks later.

Fender was born Baldermar Huerta on June 4, 1937, in San Benito, Texas. He traveled with his family through the southwest as a migrant farmworker and developed an early interest in music. He was just 10 when he started singing and a year later he learned to play the guitar, imitating country singers he heard on the radio. He started playing at local dances when he was 16 and in 1954 joined the Marines.

He played at USO clubs during his service years and when he was discharged in 1956, he put together a small group and started playing clubs and beer joints in Texas.

"I went to a recording studio to help a friend, but the owner liked me and signed me to Falcon Records," Freddy said in a 1975 *Billboard* interview. "I cut a number of regional hits, including a Spanish version of 'Don't Be Cruel,' and got on the charts on a lot of Chicano communities around the country." He also recorded "Wasted Days and Wasted Nights" in the late '50s, a song that he would record again in 1975 for the follow-up to "Before the Next Teardrop Falls."

Fender kept playing nightclubs although two unfortunate incidents should have been enough to discourage him from performing permanently. He became involved in an after-hours fight at a Corpus Christi club, leaving him with a broken nose and a knife wound in his neck. Fender talked about the second incident in *Billboard:* "In 1960, I was playing Baton Rouge when the police came up on the bandstand and busted me for grass. They'd gone through

the house I was staying in, found some seeds, and I ended up with a five-year jail sentence. I served three years, played my music on weekends and when I got out I continued to play."

After his release from prison, Freddy went home to Texas and worked in a recording studio as an engineer. He went to New Orleans and was the house singer at Poppa Joe's on Bourbon Street. In 1971, Freddy was back in Texas.

"I'd been going to college, studying sociology. I wanted to work with ex-convicts or juveniles, figuring that since I'd been in the pen, nobody was in a better position than me to do it. And I was working days as a mechanic."

All that changed when Freddy met Meaux in 1971. Meaux, a legend in Texas and Louisiana, had been responsible for hits like Jivin' Gene's "Breakin' Up Is Hard to Do," Joe Barry's "I'm a Fool to Care" and Barbara Lynn's "You'll Lose a Good Thing." He brought Fender to his Sugar Hill Studios in Houston, where they cut songs for Meaux' Crazy Cajun and Starflite labels, "Before the Next Teardrop Falls" was released on Crazy Cajun before Dot (bought by ABC Records) picked it up for national distribution.

Some may have expected the song to break on the country charts, but it

proved itself to be a pop hit as well. "I was a bit surprised myself," Fender told *Billboard* at the time. "I can understand why pop stations might not want to play it, because it sounds country. But I do not have a country voice. I think the way I sang it helped the crossover."

His re-recording of "Wasted Days and Wasted Nights" went to number eight in September, 1975. Fender found it hard to cope with fame, but in 1985 he successfully completed an alcohol and narcotic treatment program. In 1987 he made several appearances on "Hee-Haw," and the following year he played the role of Mayor Sam Cantu in Robert Redford's *The Milagro Beanfield War*.

## THE TOP FIVE
*Week of May 31, 1975*

1 **Before the Next Teardrop Falls**
   Freddy Fender

2 **Thank God I'm a Country Boy**
   John Denver

3 **How Long**
   Ace

4 **Only Yesterday**
   Carpenters

5 **Sister Golden Hair**
   America

# 406 Thank God I'm a Country Boy RCA 10239
## JOHN DENVER

*Writer: John Martin Sommers*

*Producer: Milt Okun*

*June 7, 1975*
*1 week*

ORIGINALLY recorded in the studio for the 1974 *Back Home Again* album, "Thank God I'm a Country Boy" was overshadowed by the huge impact of "Annie's Song" [see 371]. During that summer, John's concert performance at the Universal Amphitheater in southern California (which set a house record for selling out seven shows in 24 hours) was recorded for both television and disc. Written by Denver's back-up guitarist, the live version of the song entered the Hot 100 at number 82 on March 22, 1975, and became Denver's third chart-topper 11 weeks later.

The television special, "An Evening With John Denver," scored honors too, winning an Emmy as "Best Musical Variety Special" of the 1974-1975 season. In fact, the man who calls himself "Walter Mitty—a kind of Everyman who epitomizes America" couldn't do much wrong in 1975, capping his awards with the "Entertainer of the Year" title from the Country Music Association.

With the accolades rolling in, Denver could afford to take a little time off and indulge some of his interests outside the immediacy of making music. Concern for the mountains, which he said, "have obviously inspired my writing," and the environment at large spurred him to found the Windstar Foundation "to foster the concept of harmony in nature and provide a context for posi-

tive transformation in all areas of life."

From 1978-1980, he participated in the Presidential Commission on World and Domestic Hunger, and still is an enthusiastic promoter of the Hunger Project. He actively supports the Wilderness Society, Friends of the Earth, World Wildlife Fund, Environmental Action and Alaska Coalition, to select just a few of the associations that claim his time and sport his name on their advisory boards.

John's humanitarian activities sometimes spill over into his television specials. "The shows have a very intimate feeling," he explained. "They're the best I have ever done because they make an impact. I can talk about political as well as spiritual things." His love of flying (he is a licensed pilot) and involvement with the National Space Institute led to "The Higher We Fly," which reaped acclaim from the Houston Film Fes-

tival as well as the Aviation/Space Writers' Association's Earl Osborne Award. "John Denver's Alaska: The American Child," was cited by the United States Congress as a "distinguished television documentary."

"It's a critical time we live in," emphasized the singer and songwriter. "There's a real shift in consciousness taking place. There's an opportunity for musicians to become a catalyst. And I believe that we can turn this into a world not just for some of us but for all of us."

But he will always be associated with the Rocky Mountains and the city from which he took his name, so much so that Governor John Vanderhoof proclaimed him the poet laureate of Colorado. And every year he returns to his Aspen home to host his own Celebrity Pro/Am Ski Tournament. His explanation for the attraction? "When I get to the mountains, I'm happy," he said simply. "That's all there is to it."

---

## THE TOP FIVE
### *Week of June 7, 1975*

1 **Thank God I'm a Country Boy**
John Denver

2 **Sister Golden Hair**
America

3 **How Long**
Ace

4 **Bad Time**
Grand Funk

5 **Old Days**
Chicago

WARNER BROTHERS 8086 **Sister Golden Hair**
AMERICA

Writer: Gerry Beckley

Producer: George Martin

June 14, 1975
1 week

"SISTER GOLDEN HAIR" was from America's *Hearts* album. It was their fifth LP, following *America, Homecoming, Hat Trick* and *Holiday*, and preceding *Hideaway* and *Harbor*. If you sense a pattern developing here, you have a sharp eye. It was a coincidence at first, but became a conscious effort by the time *Holiday* rolled around. When they left Warner Brothers to sign with Capitol Records in 1980 they dropped the whole idea, except for a subtle jest with the *Silent Letter* album.

America followed their first number one single [see 308—"A Horse With No Name"] with two more top 10 efforts, "I Need You" and "Ventura Highway," a song written by Dewey Bunnell after travelling with his parents in the Oxnard/Ventura area of southern California and getting stranded with a flat tire near the freeway.

After their first album was produced in England by Ian Samwell and Jeff Dexter, the group recorded their next two LPs in America and produced their own tracks. After three singles failed to penetrate the top 30, the group turned to one of the rock era's most successful producers, George Martin. He agreed to produce their next album, but having heard how long it took America to record each LP, he insisted they travel to London and work on his home turf.

Wanting to impress the man who produced the Beatles, the group went into heavy rehearsals, so they would be prepared for Martin. It took only 15 working days to record *Holiday*, and Martin told them he might as well have taken a two-week holiday himself and recorded the album in California after all. That album produced America's biggest hits since "A Horse With No Name." The first single, "Tin Man," peaked at four and the follow-up, "Lonely People," went to five.

The band worked with Martin again on *Hearts*. The result was "Sister Golden Hair," which entered the Hot 100 at number 71 on April 5, 1975, and went to number one 10 weeks later.

America was reduced to a duo the following year, when Dan Peek left to pursue a solo career as a Christian artist. He signed with Lamb and Lion Records and had one Hot 100 entry in 1979, "All Things Are Possible."

Gerry Beckley and Dewey Bunnell did not consider replacing Dan. They continued as America, but found it difficult to come up with a hit single. It wasn't until their third Capitol album in 1982, *View from the Ground*, that they came up with "You Can Do Magic," written and produced by Russ Ballard. The song peaked at number eight.

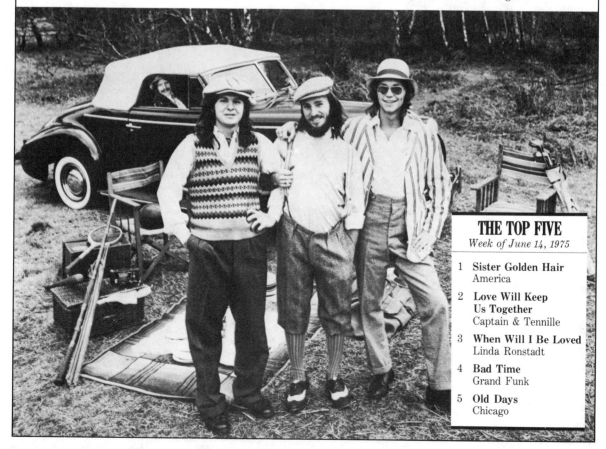

## THE TOP FIVE
*Week of June 14, 1975*

1 **Sister Golden Hair**
America

2 **Love Will Keep Us Together**
Captain & Tennille

3 **When Will I Be Loved**
Linda Ronstadt

4 **Bad Time**
Grand Funk

5 **Old Days**
Chicago

# Love Will Keep Us Together A&M 1672
## THE CAPTAIN AND TENNILLE

**408**

---

*Writers: Neil Sedaka*
*Howard Greenfield*

*Producer: Daryl Dragon*
*June 21, 1975*
*4 weeks*

---

DARYL DRAGON AND TONI TENNILLE first met in the lobby of the Marines Memorial Theater in San Francisco, California. Toni and Ron Thronson had written a musical about the environment called *Mother Earth* for the South Coast Repertory Theater, and in the summer of 1971 it was being presented by the American Conservatory Theater in San Francisco.

"We were going to move the musical down to the Huntington Hartford Theater in Los Angeles, and the keyboard player we had couldn't make the trip," Toni explains. "Daryl was recommended to me...and he was between Beach Boys' tours [see 151—"I Get Around"], so he flew up to San Francisco to meet me."

Toni remembers first seeing him, slumped in a seat dressed in dark blue from head to toe. "It wasn't love at first sight," she admits. "I don't believe in that. There was some kind of really strong vibration because I knew when I looked at him, in some way he would be important in my life." She liked his piano playing and he made her laugh, so she hired him on the spot.

When *Mother Earth* closed, the employee hired the employer: Daryl asked Toni if she'd like to work with the Beach Boys. They toured together for a season, Toni playing piano and singing vocal background while Daryl played all the other keyboards.

When the tour ended, they returned to Southern California and started working as a duo.

They found steady work at the Smoke House restaurant in Encino. "We were doing demo work at a small but good 16-track studio in Burbank," Toni said in a 1975 *Billboard* interview. "The owner said to pay us back he'd give us some studio time.

So we went in and recorded a song I wrote, 'The Way I Want to Touch You,' and the Beach Boys' 'Disney Girls.'"

Meanwhile, two disc jockeys from the San Fernando Valley saw them at the Smoke House and promised they would play their songs if they ever recorded anything. Toni and Daryl had 500 copies of "The Way I Want to Touch You" pressed on their own Butterscotch Castle label and sent it to radio stations themselves. The song started getting local airplay and was picked up for distribution by Joyce Records.

"We were . . . taking the record to labels," Daryl explained in *Billboard*, "but sort of halfheartedly." They received four offers from major labels, the last one being from A&M. "A&M was what we wanted, because they were the only ones who would let us produce ourselves, and because Herb Alpert and Jerry Moss had done the kind of thing I always wanted to do. But I was afraid because they have the Carpenters, (they didn't) need another female singer/male keyboardist team."

Daryl had no reason to worry. A&M signed them and they started work on their first album. It was almost completed when they realized they needed one more uptempo tune, something that would show off Daryl's keyboard playing. They were stumped until Kip Cohen of A&M's A&R department called them into his office and asked them to listen to a track from the *Sedaka's Back* album by Neil Sedaka [see 391—"Laughter in the Rain"]. They knew "Love Will Keep Us Together" was the right song for them as soon as they heard it. They spent two weeks coming up with a new arrangement, and when they played it for Alpert and Moss, everyone agreed they had a hit.

"Love Will Keep Us Together" entered the Hot 100 at number 98 on April 19, 1975. It went to number one nine weeks later and went on to win a Grammy for Record of the Year. Toni and Daryl recorded their entire first album in Spanish, releasing "Love Will Keep Us Together" ("Por Amor Viviremos") from that LP as a single. It charted on August 16, 1975, while the English original was still on the survey—the only occasion when two versions of a number one single were on the Hot 100 in different languages by the same artist.

## THE TOP FIVE
*Week of June 21, 1975*

1. **Love Will Keep Us Together**
   Captain & Tennille

2. **When Will I Be Loved**
   Linda Ronstadt

3. **Wildfire**
   Michael Murphey

4. **I'm Not Lisa**
   Jessi Colter

5. **Love Won't Let Me Wait**
   Major Harris

CAPITOL 4091 **Listen to What the Man Said**
WINGS

## THE TOP FIVE
*Week of July 19, 1975*

1 **Listen to What the Man Said**
Wings

2 **The Hustle**
Van McCoy & the
Soul City Symphony

3 **I'm Not in Love**
10 cc

4 **One of These Nights**
Eagles

5 **Please Mr. Please**
Olivia Newton-John

*Writer: Paul McCartney*

*Producer: Paul McCartney*

*July 19, 1975*
*1 week*

NEIL SEDAKA, whose "Love Will Keep Us Together" was knocked out of number one by Paul McCartney and Wings' "Listen to What the Man Said," had gracious praise for his chart successor. "A pop hit has to have certain hooks you can hang your hat on," Sedaka explained to *Time* magazine. "The hooks can be either musical or lyrical, but the best is a marriage of both words and music. McCartney does this. 'Listen to What the Man Said' is terrific."

The public agreed. The single entered the Hot 100 at number 65 on May 31, 1975. Seven weeks later, this teaser from the forthcoming *Venus and Mars* album became McCartney's fourth post-Beatles chart-topper. It was the first single by the group to appear on the Capitol label. Their previous single, "Junior's Farm" backed with "Sally G," had been the

last McCartney 45 on Apple.

The artist credit on "Listen to What the Man Said" listed only the group name "Wings," as the band's first two singles had done. In *Paul McCartney and Wings*, author Jeremy Pascall quotes McCartney saying that giving the group supporting credit was "an embarassment to me. It was never Paul McCartney and the Beatles, Paul McCartney and the Quarrymen or Paul McCartney and the Moondogs. Wings is quicker and easier to say and everybody knows I'm in the group anyway."

It was the Wings Mark Five lineup that recorded "Listen to What the Man Said." Reduced to a trio for the *Band on the Run* album [see 366], Wings expanded again when Paul went to Nashville to record some material for himself and produce an album for Peggy Lee, *Let's Love.* He asked 21-year-old guitarist Jimmy McCulloch to come to the States for the sessions. McCulloch had proven himself while making an album for Paul's brother, Mike McGear. A native of Glasgow, Scotland, he had been playing professionally since he

was 13. His credits included John Mayall's Bluesbreakers, Stone the Crows with Maggie Bell and a group called Blue, managed by Robert Stigwood. Invited to join Wings, a grateful McCulloch said, "I'm sick and tired of being in and out of bands. I want to get something down on record that's going to be appreciated instead of always being in new bands that so few people hear."

To find a drummer, Paul held auditions in London. The fifty applicants were narrowed down to five and then to two. The survivor was Geoff Britton, a Cockney lad who was also a karate expert. His tenure in Wings proved to be short—three songs into the *Venus and Mars* album, McCartney was looking for a replacement.

Joe English, born in Rochester, New York, was living in Georgia and getting ready to tour with Bonnie Bramlett when he was asked to come to Sea-Saint studios in New Orleans and work on the *Venus and Mars* sessions. While doing the final mixing in Los Angeles, Paul formally invited Joe to be a member of Wings.

# The Hustle AVCO 4653
## VAN MCCOY & the SOUL CITY SYMPHONY

*Writer: Van McCoy*

*Producers: Hugo Peretti*
*        Luigi Creatore*

*July 26, 1975*
*1 week*

VAN MCCOY was a talented writer, producer and arranger, well known and respected in the music industry long before the public became aware of him through his number one hit, "The Hustle." His death at age 35 shocked and saddened his many friends in the record business who knew he had much more to contribute to the music world.

McCoy didn't realize he had composed an international best-seller when he recorded "The Hustle" as one of the tracks on his album *Disco Baby.* "The album was specifically geared toward the discotheques because of the major role they play in getting a lot of new products started," McCoy told Vernon Gibbs in *Essence* magazine. "'The Hustle' was the last cut we did on the album, and we almost *didn't* do it. I was introduced to the hustle by a disc jockey (David Todd) at a New York City nightclub called the Adam's Apple. He'd been after me for a while to come and check out this new dance, but I just never had the chance so I sent one of my friends.

"When he came back, he showed me this very strange dance. It was something completely different from the you-do-your-thing-and-I-do-mine dances; it was people dancing together again. The hustle reminded me of ballroom dancing, and I love graceful dancing.

"I had recorded an entire album and my partner kept bugging me about doing something with the hustle. We had just one hour of studio time left, so I sat down and wrote whatever came into my head. Even after I finished 'The Hustle,' I wasn't excited because outside of the Latin market and the New York discos I wasn't aware of how popular the dance had become. I had no idea when I threw it together that it was going to be the hit it is."

"The Hustle" was McCoy's only single to make the top 40. Two years later, he was tired of being typecast as a disco artist. "Disco has played an important role in the development of

my career," he stressed in a *Billboard* interview. "But I am seeking greater versatility. I do not want to be forever locked into the image of the 'disco kid'; I no longer want to be packaged and marketed as a specific product. Rather, I would prefer the opportunity to evolve into the kind of entertainer I believe I am."

Van McCoy was born January 6, 1944, in Washington, D.C. His mother arranged piano lessons for him when he was four. He formed a duo with his older brother Norman, who played the violin. By the time he was 12, Van was writing songs. He gave up music as a teenager, mostly because his friends teased him about playing the piano. He didn't take it up again until he was a psychology major at Howard University.

While attending college, he sang with a local group called the Starlighters. Then he joined the Heartbeats and recorded for Gone/End Records. He moved to Philadelphia and, with an uncle, started a record label, Rockin' Records. He released his own song, "Hey Mr. DJ," which was picked up by Scepter Records. The label hired Van as an

A&R man and he wrote "Stop the Music" for the Shirelles. In 1962 he went to work for producers Jerry Leiber and Mike Stoller as a staff writer, and during the '60s wrote many pop hits, including "Giving Up" for Gladys Knight and the Pips, "Baby, I'm Yours" for Barbara Lewis and "When You're Young and In Love" for Ruby and the Romantics.

He started a production company and recorded his own album for Columbia Records. He continued to write songs for people like Aretha Franklin, Brenda and the Tabulations, Nancy Wilson and Tom Jones, and in 1970 wrote and produced a number 11 hit for the Presidents, "5-10-15-20 (25-30 Years of Love)." A year later he started to work with the Stylistics ("You Are Everything," "Betcha By Golly, Wow"), an association that teamed him up with producers Hugo and Luigi at Avco Records.

After his success with "The Hustle," a Grammy winner for Best Pop Instrumental, McCoy and partner Charles Kipps worked with David Ruffin ("Walk Away from Love") at Motown. Despite all his pop hits, McCoy's true love was classical music. "I like Beethoven, Wagner, Rachmaninoff, Dvorak and Tchaikowsky as much as I like Thom Bell and Gamble and Huff," he said in *Essence.*

He did compose soundtrack music for Mae West's *Sextette* and an NBC television movie, "A Woman Called Moses." On July 6, 1979, McCoy died of a heart attack in Englewood, New Jersey, exactly six months before his 36th birthday.

## THE TOP FIVE
*Week of July 26, 1975*

1  **The Hustle**
   Van McCoy & the
   Soul City Symphony

2  **I'm Not in Love**
   10 cc

3  **One of These Nights**
   Eagles

4  **Please Mr. Please**
   Olivia Newton-John

5  **Listen to What the Man Said**
   Wings

ASYLUM 45257 **One of These Nights** 411
EAGLES

*Writers: Don Henley*
*Glenn Frey*

*Producer: Bill Szymczyk*

*August 2, 1975*
*1 week*

**W**ITH their *One of These Nights* album, the Eagles solidified their new, aggressive, sinewy rock stance, relying heavily on electric guitar parts instead of banjo or pedal steel, and highlighting the soulful elements of the LP's songs. Recorded in Los Angeles and Miami, the entire project was helmed by Bill Szymczyk. "It wasn't all that difficult to get them into a new groove," he remembered. "Glenn Frey is an R&B fanatic and Don Henley is an excellent drummer with a great time sense."

Released as the first single from the album, the title track debuted on the Hot 100 at number 78 on May 31, 1975. Nine weeks later it became the second consecutive chart-topper for the Eagles. The album yielded two additional top five singles: "Lyin' Eyes" spent two weeks at number two in November and "Take It to the Limit" reached number four in March, 1976.

"Lyin' Eyes" won the Eagles' first Grammy, for "Best Pop Vocal Performance by a Duo, Group or Chorus." Another track from the LP, "I Wish You Peace," later engendered a feud between Don Henley and presidential daughter Patti (Reagan) Davis. Talking to the *Las Vegas Sun*, Davis reminisced about co-writing the song with Leadon, then her live-in partner. "I was very lucky," she said. "I made quite a bit of money and I still get royalties." The statement infuriated Henley, who shot off a letter to the paper, declaring that Bernie was responsible for most of the song and Davis' contribution was limited to a few words. Besides, he considered the tune "smarmy cocktail music and certainly not something the Eagles are proud of."

Continuing the band's gruelling treadmill of studio/live show workaholism, yet another tour ensued after the release of *One of These Nights*, their first to an international audience. The constant interaction of five divergent personalities fired some of the famed friction that came to characterize the group. Their manager, Irving Azoff, pointed out to Robert Hilburn of the *Los Angeles*

*Times*, "The Eagles talked about breaking up from the day I met them. There'd be one mini-explosion followed by a replacement in the band, then another mini-explosion followed by another replacement. You just had to step back and give things time to calm down."

Both the pace and musical direction alienated country/bluegrass steeped Bernie Leadon. Citing a desire to spend less time on the road, he became the first "mini-explosion" in late 1975, leaving to form the Bernie Leadon-Michael Georgiades Band.

Faced with a tour of Australia and the Orient, the Eagles needed to replace Leadon. They looked to their old friend, Joe Walsh, central figure for the James Gang, Barnstorm, and a soloist in his own right. If no previous action had convincingly presented their aim, the inclusion of a stinging, slam bang stylist like Walsh made the Eagles intent perfectly clear. Glenn Frey explained to *Musician*, "I had a lot of singing to do. I felt that for the benefit of the Eagles it was most important that we get a couple of blistering guitarists in there. After Bernie Leadon left, my role as a singer became much more important. I had to be in tune—all the time."

**THE TOP FIVE**
*Week of August 2, 1975*

1 **One of These Nights**
Eagles

2 **I'm Not in Love**
10 cc

3 **Jive Talkin'**
Bee Gees

4 **Please Mr. Please**
Olivia Newton-John

5 **The Hustle**
Van McCoy & the
Soul City Symphony

## 412 Jive Talkin' RSO 510
### BEE GEES

Writers: Barry Gibb
      Robin Gibb
      Maurice Gibb

Producer: Arif Mardin

August 9, 1975
2 weeks

ALTHOUGH the Bee Gees had reconciled their family differences before their first number one single [see 297—"How Can You Mend a Broken Heart"] in 1971, they were still musically lost in the first half of the '70s, unable to place six consecutive singles in the top 10. "We didn't know where we were going," Barry Gibb allowed in David Leaf's authorized biography of the group. "That's why it took so long to break through. We ended up doing dreary ballads, and that was totally wrong. (We) had a ballad hit with ". . . Broken Heart" and from that moment on Atlantic Records didn't want anything else but ballads. We seemed to be stuck in that mode."

One of the more depressing events of this low period was a series of shows at the Batley Variety Club in their home country of England. They performed their greatest hits to an audience that was more interested in getting drunk than hearing the Bee Gees.

With the Western world ignoring them, the Gibb brothers headed for Asia, where they always had a large following.

While struggling through the early '70s, they recorded Trafalgar, To Whom It May Concern and Life in a Tin Can, three albums that did nothing to increase their popularity. The lowest blow was Atlantic Records' refusal to release their next LP, A Kick in the Head Is Worth Eight in the Pants. Looking back on that self-indulgent effort, Barry told Dick Clark on "The National Music Survey," "When you write about yourself, it's introverted and it's death."

Some groups would have considered disbanding at this point, but the three brothers were not ready to call it quits. Their manager, Robert Stigwood, introduced them to Arif Mardin, one of Atlantic's top producers. As RSO was distributed by Atlantic, Mardin was available to work with the Bee Gees. He produced the Mr. Natural album, and while it didn't result in any hit singles, it opened up the Gibbs to a new sound.

Mardin took the Bee Gees away from Los Angeles and set up shop at Criteria Studios in Miami, Florida. Guiding and influencing their musical style, he had them concentrate on what was happening at top 40 radio and discos. And having established a good working relationship with the group, Mardin was asked to produce their next album, Main Course.

"Until Main Course, we still weren't bouncing off each other the way we should have been," Barry says in the Leaf biography. "When we got around to Main Course, we finally got into a way of thinking that suited the three of us, what we wanted to do and what we were going to do all the way. We were always split about that ever since the break-up. We could never really decide where we were going after that. And that's why all the music came out wrong."

Each evening, on their way to Criteria, the brothers would drive across the Sunny Isles Bridge, according to The Legend, an illustrated story of the Bee Gees by David English. The tires of their car made a "chunka-chunka" sound as they crossed some railroad tracks. One night Barry's wife, Linda, turned to her husband and said, "Hey, listen to that noise. It's the same every evening. It's our drive talking." Barry looked at her and started to sing a song that evolved into their second number one single, "Jive Talkin'."

But the Bee Gees were as cold as absolute zero, and there was not much chance that radio stations would get excited about a new single from the Gibbs. They repeated a trick they had used eight years earlier when their first single, "New York Mining Disaster 1941" was released. Promotional copies were issued on a white label with no identification of the artist.

Debuting at number 87 on May 31, 1975, "Jive Talkin'" took 10 weeks to top the Hot 100 and begin the Bee Gees' spectacular comeback.

## THE TOP FIVE
*Week of August 9, 1975*

1 **Jive Talkin'**
  Bee Gees

2 **I'm Not in Love**
  10 cc

3 **Please Mr. Please**
  Olivia Newton-John

4 **One of These Nights**
  The Eagles

5 **Someone Saved My Life Tonight**
  Elton John

PLAYBOY 6024 **Fallin' in Love**
HAMILTON, JOE FRANK AND REYNOLDS   **413**

*Writers: Dan Hamilton*
*Ann Hamilton*

*Producer: Jim Price*

*August 23, 1975*
*1 week*

Hamilton, Joe Frank and Reynolds evolved from the T-Bones, an instrumental combo that went to number three in 1966 with "No Matter What Shape (Your Stomach's In)," a tune used in an Alka-Seltzer commercial. In 1971 they had a number four hit, "Don't Pull Your Love," under their new name and by the time they recorded "Fallin' in Love" in 1975, they were actually Hamilton, Joe Frank and Dennison, although they were still recording as Hamilton, Joe Frank and Reynolds. Confused? Let's go back to the beginning.

Dan Hamilton was born in the rural community of Wenatchee, Washington, and grew up on his parents' farm. He moved to Los Angeles as a teenager and by the time he was 15 he was working steadily as a session musician for artists like the Ventures, Johnny Rivers, Chad and Jeremy, the Marketts and Jerry Lee Lewis. He worked on ABC-TV's "Shindig" music series, then put together the group of musicians who became known as the T-Bones.

Two of the T-Bones were Joe Frank Carollo and Tommy Reynolds. Carollo was born in Leland, Mississippi. After graduating from Leland High School, he majored in music at Delta State College in Cleveland, Mississippi. He was so busy playing gigs Thursdays through Mondays that he didn't complete college. He worked for a furniture company and then for IBM as an inventory control specialist. "It was a matter of survival—working at IBM simply meant the rent would be paid," he said. "I've even driven trucks to keep from starving and tried my damndest to avoid music. But it turns me on, and I had to get back into it."

Reynolds, a native New Yorker, learned how to play (and build) steel drums in the Caribbean. With Hamilton and Joe Frank, he left the T-Bones to form their own trio. They signed with Dunhill Records and the label released "Don't Pull Your Love."

Reynolds left the group in 1972 to become a minister in Texas. He was replaced by Alan Dennison, born in Marion, Ohio. His instruments included keyboards, electric flute and congas, and he explained that he didn't mind not having his name in the group's handle: "It's a name like any other group's name, an entity, and we're all equal parts of it."

The newly-composed trio found it hard to get a new label deal after their association with Dunhill ended. It was mid-1974 when Playboy Records signed them—a wise move, considering Hamilton, Joe Frank and Reynolds gave the label its first and only number one single.

A subsequent 45, "Winners and Losers," peaked at 21 in early 1976. After one more single, the group finally dropped Reynolds from the corporate masthead and gave Alan proper credit, changing the group's name to Hamilton, Joe Frank and Dennison. The change didn't have any effect on their chart fortunes: after two more singles that failed to rise higher than number 70, they disappeared from the Hot 100 forever.

## THE TOP FIVE
*Week of August 23, 1975*

1 **Fallin' in Love**
   Hamilton, Joe Frank
   & Reynolds

2 **One of These Nights**
   Eagles

3 **Get Down Tonight**
   K.C. & The Sunshine Band

4 **Jive Talkin'**
   Bee Gees

5 **Rhinestone Cowboy**
   Glen Campbell

# Get Down Tonight T.K. 1009
## KC AND THE SUNSHINE BAND

*Writers: Harry Wayne Casey*
*Richard Finch*

*Producers: Harry Wayne Casey*
*Richard Finch*

*August 30, 1975*
*1 week*

**KC** AND THE SUNSHINE BAND had already scored two hit records in Britain ("Queen of Clubs," "Sound Your Funky Horn") when they finally achieved success in their own country with "Get Down Tonight." It was the second number one single for both the T.K. label and writer/producers Harry Wayne Casey and Richard Finch [see 370—"Rock Your Baby"].

Casey (born January 31, 1951, in Hialeah, Florida) and Finch (born January 25, 1954 in Indianapolis, Indiana) were the heart of KC and the Sunshine Band. Casey, who lent his nickname KC to the group, worked in a retail record store in Hialeah, where he was responsible for ordering singles and albums. One of the places he picked up records from was Tone Distributors, a Hialeah company that also had its own record labels. One day the salesman for Tone invited Casey to visit the company's recording studios and meet Clarence Reid, who had scored a top 40 hit in 1969 with "Nobody But You Babe."

Casey gladly accepted, and the next time he needed to pick up records from Tone he went to see the studio. "Right then, there was a feeling that 'I want to be around here,'"

he remembers. "So I used to hang out there every day after work. I'd sit around for hours and hours. Finally they gave me a key to the door. I asked them for a job in the warehouse and they didn't have anything open."

Undeterred, Casey helped box records and did other odd jobs for no pay. He started to play keyboards on some sessions and was allowed to produce some records for a band by Betty Wright's manager, Willie Clark. About a year later, Rick Finch was hired to work in the studio for $46 a week. "He was very electronically inclined," says Casey. "He loved to tear things apart and fix them. We both seemed like underdogs (at the company) and I had some insight there was something greater there."

Casey and Finch spent their time in the studio after hours, writing and rehearsing material. At a wedding reception for Clarence Reid, they were fascinated by the Carribean band's "junkanoo" music, a blend of whistle flutes, steel drums and cowbells. Shortly after, Casey heard

those whistles again at a Timmy Thomas concert in Washington, D.C. Flying back to Florida, he started to write "Blow Your Whistle" on the plane. That song and "Sound Your Funky Horn" were recorded by Casey and Finch with studio musicians, but by the time they cut "Queen of Clubs," they put together an authentic Sunshine Band, which included guitarist Jerome Smith, drummer Robert Johnson and conga player Fermin Goytisolo.

Casey recalls the night he laid down his vocal track for "Get Down Tonight." "I couldn't believe it was such an incredible sound," he says. "I remember they must have played it back a hundred times and I couldn't believe it—it had that strange, mystical feeling, a feeling I had never felt before."

Because of their European success, KC and the Sunshine Band were not in the United States while the record was climbing the Hot 100. They arrived home in time to celebrate the single moving into the number one position on August 30, 1975.

## THE TOP FIVE
*Week of August 30, 1975*

1 **Get Down Tonight**
K.C. & The Sunshine Band

2 **Fallin' in Love**
Hamilton, Joe Frank
& Reynolds

3 **Rhinestone Cowboy**
Glen Campbell

4 **One of These Nights**
Eagles

5 **How Sweet It Is**
**(to be Loved by You)**
James Taylor

Writer: Larry Weiss

Producers: Dennis Lambert
Brian Potter

September 6, 1975
2 weeks

**G**LEN CAMPBELL waited a long time for a number one single of his own. He was associated with two groups that reached the chart summit, the Champs [see 34—"Tequila"] and the Beach Boys [see 151—"I Get Around"], but wasn't directly involved with their number one hits. He played guitar on a number one song for Frank Sinatra [see 202—"Strangers in the Night"], but couldn't claim any direct credit for that either.

Campbell's first chart entry was "Turn Around, Look at Me" on the Crest label in October, 1961. Two of his Capitol singles ("Too Late to Worry—Too Blue to Cry," and a cover version of Donovan's "The Universal Soldier") made the lower rungs of the chart in 1962 and 1965, respectively. He recorded John Hartford's "Gentle on My Mind" in 1967, but it only reached number 62 (it re-entered the Hot 100 the following year and went to 39). The first single that was a bona fide national hit was the Jim Webb-penned "By the Time I Get to Phoenix," which charted at number 26 at the end of 1967. Glen finally made the top 10 with Webb's "Wichita Lineman" in early 1968 and "Galveston" the following year. But it wasn't until September 6, 1975, that he scored the biggest hit of his career, "Rhinestone Cowboy," written by Larry Weiss.

Songwriter Weiss was signed as an artist to 20th Century Records, and released an album of his songs, *Black and Blue Suite*, in 1974. "Rhinestone Cowboy" was pulled as a single from the LP. It didn't chart, but it did receive heavy airplay on stations specializing in "easy listening" music.

"I think I first heard the song on KNX-FM in Los Angeles," Campbell said in a 1975 *Billboard* interview. "I called my secretary and said, 'I've got to get a song called "Rhinestone Cowboy" by somebody, I don't remember who.' Meanwhile, I stumbled into Al Coury's office at Capitol Records one day and he said he had a

record he wanted me to hear. And he played 'Rhinestone Cowboy.'"

Weiss, meanwhile, was depressed over the commercial failure of his album and was ready to rent a storefront and go into the furniture business. His hopes were renewed when he learned that Campbell was cutting his song. "'Rhinestone Cowboy' was among the first four (songs) we recorded," recalls Dennis Lambert.

Glen appeared on a telethon and sang "Rhinestone Cowboy." Paul Drew, programming director for KHJ radio in Los Angeles, happened to be watching the telethon and was enthused enough about the song to call Capitol and find out if Campbell had recorded it. "Paul Drew . . . took an acetate from my office of the record . . . and put that on the RKO chain before the pressed records were even available," explains Lambert. "In a sense, (he) forced everyone, Capitol primarily, to go into an even more accelerated rush release because now the record was on radio."

"Rhinestone Cowboy" entered the Hot 100 at number 81 on May 31, 1975. Fourteen weeks later it became Campbell's first number one song.

Even back then, Weiss had bigger plans for "Rhinestone Cowboy." His first idea was to turn it into a Broadway play, but the thought of moving back to New York convinced him to try another plan: Hollywood. He became involved in a development deal that expired after a year. Undaunted, Weiss took an ad in *Daily Variety* and *The Hollywood*

*Reporter* announcing that the song "Rhinestone Cowboy" would be made into a motion picture. That led to another development deal, with Quinn Martin. After a year-and-a-half, that deal fell through as well.

Weiss was discouraged by people who said *Midnight Cowboy* and *Urban Cowboy* were enough, the world didn't need a *Rhinestone Cowboy*. Besides, they said, the Robert Redford-Jane Fonda film *The Electric Horseman* had already used the imagery of his song. But Weiss remained tenacious, and when producer Howard Smith approached him and promised a film "that wouldn't embarrass the song," Weiss trusted him and signed another development deal. Smith got an agreement from Avco-Embassy to produce the film, and when the company was sold to Norman Lear, the project was the only one of 23 not to be dropped. Until they saw the re-write of the script.

Smith persisted, and finally, 20th Century Fox, the same company that owned the record label which released Weiss' "Rhinestone Cowboy," announced it would start production on a film called *Rhinestone*, starring Sylvester Stallone and Dolly Parton [see 537—"9 to 5"].

The teaming of Stallone and Parton should have been irresistible. It proved to be very resistible and the critics were not kind. The song "Rhinestone Cowboy" did not appear on the soundtrack album, but there was a credit for Weiss in the film: "Based on the song 'Rhinestone Cowboy' by Larry Weiss."

## THE TOP FIVE
*Week of September 6, 1975*

1  **Rhinestone Cowboy**
   Glen Campbell

2  **Fallin' in Love**
   Hamilton, Joe Frank
   & Reynolds

3  **Get Down Tonight**
   K.C. & The Sunshine Band

4  **At Seventeen**
   Janis Ian

5  **How Sweet It Is
   (to be Loved by You)**
   James Taylor

# 416 Fame RCA 10320
## DAVID BOWIE

*Writers: David Bowie*
*John Lennon*
*Carlos Alomar*

*Producers: David Bowie*
*Harry Maslin*

*September 20, 1975*
*2 weeks*

DAVID BOWIE is the ultimate chameleon of rock. It's been said he goes through musical styles faster than clothes. According to rock critic John Milward, "Bowie is a pop actor who conceived of his incarnations—pseudo-Dylan, ultragloss deco-rocker, soul brother—with a forethought that precluded losing himself in his fantasy. He could always move on to another role, or perhaps films; for David Bowie, rock was the ultimate mass-communications transformer.

David Robert Jones was born just after midnight on January 8, 1947, in the Brixton section of London. It was Elvis Presley's 12th birthday. On David's 12th birthday, he was already interested in music—studying the saxophone. He recorded with three different bands during the '60s: the King Bees, the Manish Boys and David Jones and the Lower Third. In 1966 he named himself after the Bowie knife to avoid confusion with Davy Jones of the Monkees [see 211—"Last Train to Clarksville"].

The "thin white duke" lived in a Buddhist monastery in Scotland, then worked with Lindsay Kemp's mime troupe. But he always had more than a passing fancy in wedding theatrics and rock. In 1969 he organized the Beckenham Arts Lab to combine theater and music; funding for the

## THE TOP FIVE

*Week of September 20, 1975*

1 **Fame**
   David Bowie

2 **Rhinestone Cowboy**
   Glen Campbell

3 **At Seventeen**
   Janis Ian

4 **I'm Sorry**
   John Denver

5 **Fight the Power Pt. 1**
   Isley Bros.

project came from David's contract with Philips Records.

His first chart single in Britain, "Space Oddity," entered the chart just seven weeks after Neil Armstrong became the first man to walk on the moon. It peaked at number five, but was re-issued in 1975, when it topped the British survey.

Taking the Velvet Underground as his model, Bowie began to develop the decadent persona that would flirt with transvestism and eventually metamorphose into the outrageous, orange-haired rocker known as "Ziggy Stardust."

Bowie's chart run in America began with "Changes," a number 66 hit in May, 1972. Although he didn't make the top 10, he did receive substantial airplay on "The Jean Genie" and "Rebel Rebel." He also produced hits for two other artists, Lou Reed ("Walk on the Wild Side") and Mott the Hoople ("All the Young Dudes").

In 1975, Bowie showed he had another surprise up his sleeve.

Checking into Philadelphia's Sigma Sound Studios, and backed by the city's top session musicians, he emerged as a born-again soul man. "It was a Polaroid album," Bowie said. "I took a snapshot of music in America as I saw it at the time." Titled *Young Americans*, this exercise in "plastic soul" (Bowie's term) produced a number 28 hit in the title track.

But it was the second single from the album that brought Bowie his first American number one. The song was "Fame," a joyous, disco-tinged melody that he dashed off in the studio with the help of guitarist Carlos Alomar and John Lennon, who can be heard singing near the end of the song.

"Fame" entered the Hot 100 at number 90 on June 28, 1975. It began a two-week stay at the top 12 weeks later. As an additional accolade, Bowie was invited to sing the song on the syndicated "Soul Train" television series, one of the first white guest stars on the program.

*Writer: John Denver*

*Producer: Milt Okun*

*September 27, 1975*
*1 week*

"JOHN DENVER, at 32, is the most popular singer in America," *Newsweek* proclaimed in 1976. And so he was, with three number one singles, three gold albums in a one-year period and a sold-out concert tour to his credit. As if his popularity needed any boosting, Denver had a two-sided smash during the summer of 1975.

"I'm Sorry" entered the Hot 100 at number 64 on August 16, 1975, and went to number one on its own six weeks later. But by that time, most radio stations in America were giving "Calypso," a celebration of the work done by marine pioneer Jacques Cousteau, equal airplay. In its ninth week on the Hot 100, positions were reversed and "Calypso" was listed as the "A" side.

Both tunes were from *Windsong,* an album that John said he wanted "to record the songs that the wind makes, to share her music with you in the same way that I am able to share mine. I hope that at some time in your life you'll be able to go someplace where it's quiet, to sit by a lake at the foot of a mountain and hear a storm come and go. There is beautiful, beautiful music there. All you have to do is listen."

Probably the most nature-inspired of all his albums, *Windsong* lent its name to John's newly-established rec-

ord label, formed, he said, to further Colorado musicians and his own self-taught knowledge of his craft. "It's always been my desire to learn all about everything I could, particularly about everything connected with the music business. I've been fortunate enough in my position to regularly run across great musical talent that I'll now be able to work with and help get the recognition they deserve." The Windsong stable included the co-writers of "Take Me Home, Country Roads," Bill and Taffy Danoff, who became the label's most successful act—the Starland Vocal Band [see 438—"Afternoon Delight"].

Following the success of "I'm Sorry" and "Calypso," Denver's chart domination began to wane. Turning to other endeavors, he made his feature film debut in 1977, co-starring opposite George Burns in *Oh God.* Politicians sought his counsel as well as his participation at campaign fund raisers.

He replaced Andy Williams as the host of the annual Grammy Awards show, then performed in concert and on television with entertainers that

ran the gamut from Beverly Sills, Itzhak Perlman and James Galway to the Muppets and Frank Sinatra.

For his entrance into the '80s, Denver chose to take his music beyond American shores, travelling to China and Russia, as well as Europe, the Far East, Australia, New Zealand and Latin America. In Japan, his show enticed the country's crown prince out of the palace to attend his very first pop concert. John's charitable activities encompassed a trip to Africa to publicize the food crisis there and act as spokesman for UNICEF's fundraising drive.

In February, 1984, he performed "The Gold and Beyond," the theme song he'd written for the Winter Olympics, on the slopes of Mt. Sarajevo, then joined ABC's announcers for some color commentary. On the personal front, he debuted some 15 years of landscape and wildlife photography with an exhibit at New York's prestigious Hammer Gallery. "Photography is absolute therapy for me, a real breakdown from all the stuff I'm thinking about," he confided to *People.*

Although he never reached the top 20 again after "Fly Away" in 1976, he became known for his interest in the environment and his love of flying. It was a clear, bright sunny afternoon on October 12, 1997 when he was practicing take-offs and landings in an experimental plane at Monterey Airport in California. He had just received permission from the tower to take the plane for a flight down the coast when the home-built single engine Long-EZ crashed into Monterey Bay. Denver was 53 when he died.

## THE TOP FIVE

*Week of September 27, 1975*

1 **I'm Sorry/ Calypso**
   John Denver

2 **Fame**
   David Bowie

3 **Rhinestone Cowboy**
   Glen Campbell

4 **Fight the Power Pt. 1**
   Isley Bros.

5 **Run Joey Run**
   David Goddes

## 418 Bad Blood ROCKET 40460
### NEIL SEDAKA

*Writers: Neil Sedaka*
*Phil Cody*

*Producers: Neil Sedaka*
*Robert Appere*

*October 11, 1975*
*3 weeks*

Neil Sedaka's comeback in the '70s was even more successful than his '60s career. In the short span of eight months, three songs that he wrote went to number one: "Laughter in the Rain" [see 391], "Love Will Keep Us Together" [see 408] and "Bad Blood."

The year 1975 was good for Sedaka. After a dry period of 11 years he was suddenly hot—he was signed to Elton John's new label, Rocket Records; he was starring on network television and appearing in Las Vegas; and he and other artists were topping the charts with his songs.

His Las Vegas career had a false start. Signed to be the opening act for the Carpenters at the Riviera Hotel, Neil was getting a better reception from the critics and audiences than Richard and Karen. One night, Sedaka introduced Dick Clark and Tom Jones in the audience. The next day he was asked to leave the show. He did, but not before signing a contract with the Riviera to return as a headliner.

The follow-up to "Laughter in the Rain" was "The Immigrant," a song Neil dedicated to John Lennon because of his problems with the United States government in obtaining permission to remain in America. The song peaked at 22 and another single from *Sedaka's Back* was released, "That's Where the Music Takes Me."

Neil waited for major radio stations to add his new single. Then came some good news: the influential RKO chain had added a new Neil Sedaka song to their playlists. The bad news was, it wasn't "That's Where the Music Takes Me." It was an album track from *Overnight Success*, a British LP that wasn't even released in the United States.

What may have influenced RKO programming chief Paul Drew to add the song was the fact that the owner of the record label was singing backing vocals. "Bad Blood" did not list him in the credits, but Elton John could clearly be heard on the track.

After he had written "Bad Blood" with Phil Cody, Sedaka suggested to producer Robert Appere that it could be recorded as a duet. Neil asked Elton to come to Clover Studios in Los Angeles to sing the backing vocal and he agreed.

The record was rush released by Rocket in America after the surprise airplay from RKO. While Neil may be primarily remembered for "Breaking Up Is Hard to Do," his most successful single is really "Bad Blood," which sold 1.4 million copies and was number one for three weeks.

With a couple of track changes, the *Overnight Success* album was retitled *The Hungry Years* for American release. Neil's follow-up to "Bad Blood" was a new arrangement of "Breaking Up Is Hard to Do." Instead of a 1962 pop song, it was transformed into a contemporary ballad. The new version went to number eight, and it is the only number one single to be re-recorded by the same artist and become a top 10 hit all over again.

After three more chart singles on Rocket, Neil signed with Elektra Records. His biggest success on the label was a duet with his daughter Dara, "Should've Never Let You Go." In 1983 he moved to MCA/Curb and again charted with Dara on a cover version of Marvin Gaye and Tammi Terrell's "Your Precious Love," making Sedaka one of a handful of artists whose chart careers span four decades.

### THE TOP FIVE
*Week of October 11, 1975*

1 **Bad Blood**
Neil Sedaka

2 **I'm Sorry/Calypso**
Denver

**Fame**
David Bowie

**Mr. Jaws**
Dickie Goodman

**Miracles**
Jefferson Starship

*Writers: Elton John*
*Bernie Taupin*

*Producer: Gus Dudgeon*

*November 1, 1975*
*3 weeks*

Neil Sedaka relinquished the number one position to his boss, Rocket Records owner Elton John. In effect, Elton was succeeding himself, as he not only owned the label Sedaka recorded for but sang backing vocals on his chart-topping "Bad Blood." It was typical of Elton's luck in 1975, the year everything he touched turned to gold.

"Island Girl" was his third number one single of 1975 and his fifth overall. Earlier in the year, he made recording history when his autobiographical LP, *Captain Fantastic and the Brown Dirt Cowboy*, became the first album to enter *Billboard's* chart at number one. Just five months later he repeated the feat with *Rock of the Westies*, the album that introduced his new band: Roger Pope (drums), James Newton Howard (keyboards), Kenny Passarelli (bass), Caleb Quayle (guitars), Ray Cooper (percussion) and Davey Johnstone (guitars). Johnstone participated in co-writing one *Rock of the Westies* cut while Cooper would assume more importance later in Elton's career.

Originally titled *Bottled and Brained*, the disc was supposed to gently break in the rookies with an "uptempo" group of selections. Unfortunately, the brilliant introspection of its predecessor overshadowed the

### THE TOP FIVE
*Week of November 1, 1975*

1  **Island Girl**
   Elton John

2  **I'm Sorry/Calypso**
   John Denver

3  **Miracles**
   Jefferson Starship

4  **Lyin' Eyes**
   Eagles

5  **They Just Can't Stop It
   (The Games People Play)**
   Spinners

happy tone, allowing critics to hack it to pieces. Even the creator later reflected in *Rolling Stone* that it "probably doesn't have much depth to it, but I kinda like it."

Second string as the songs may have been, Elton himself was more popular than ever, a phenomenon that began to manifest itself in his daily life. "I'm getting really cheesed off," he complained to *Rolling Stone*. "A couple of years ago I would deal with three or four fans outside the hotel and walk off down Lexington Avenue. Now it's impossible. I can't cope. I don't want to end up my life like Elvis. I want to be somebody who's active and involved with people and that means going outside. I even tried one of those disguises but that just doesn't work. I went to an amusement park on the tour and 13 people surrounded me for protection. I felt like the Pope."

One place Elton didn't mind crowds was in concert. He wound up 1975 with a two-day spectacular at Dodger Stadium in Los Angeles, the first that venue had allowed since outlawing rock shows after the Beatles played there in 1966. The performances capped a 15-date tour that had attracted over 250,000 people and grossed more than $2.2 million. At the same time, Los Angeles declared Elton John Day, with the man from Pinner getting his own star on Hollywood Boulevard. "I'm telling you, this is more nerve-wracking than a concert," he said as he accepted the honor. Following the memorable outdoor stand before 110,000 people at Dodger Stadium, the entertainer was ordered to bed by his doctors who deemed him about to drop from exhaustion. Gladly, he spent the next four months in Barbados.

**420** **That's the Way (I Like It)** T.K. 1015
KC and THE SUNSHINE BAND

Writers: *Harry Wayne Casey*
*Richard Finch*

Producers: *Harry Wayne Casey*
*Richard Finch*

*November 22, 1975*
*2 weeks*

Less than three months after their first number one single [see 414—"Get Down Tonight"], KC and the Sunshine Band returned to the top of the charts with "That's the Way (I Like It)."

The original recording of "That's the Way (I Like It)" was much more sensual than the version the public got to hear, according to KC. "I had to cool it down," he says, with some regret. "The 'ah-ha, ah-has' were more like a moaning and groaning, and I had to clean that up considerably. It was 1975 and I just thought it was a little risque. And I thought, 'boy, wait 'til my mother hears this one!' "

KC's mother might not have been so shocked. She was a long-time music fan, and while growing up in Hialeah, Casey listened to many of the R&B singles she bought. "My mother was into rhythm and blues

music and (the first song I heard) must have been a Jerry Butler record. She loved Jerry Butler, Nat 'King' Cole and of course, the Flamingos."

As he got older, Casey fell in love with the sound of Motown, especially Diana Ross and Marvin Gaye. "I like the stuff on Atlantic Records," he adds. "Aretha Franklin, the Rascals—(also) James Brown, Buddy Miles and the Chambers Brothers. I loved keyboard artists, like Joe Cocker, Leon Russell, Billy Preston. I liked Blood, Sweat and Tears for the brass sound. I liked rhythm, I liked percussion, I liked brass."

Casey's musical roots served him well in concert. Before his initial recording success, he had never played keyboards and sung at the same time, but he learned quickly when he had to go out on the road to promote his singles.

Steve Ditlea, writing in the *New York Times*, praised the live performances of KC and the Sunshine Band: "In person, they are one of the most exciting groups performing today. On stage KC becomes truly possessed by his rhythms, happily rocking from side to side as he stands hunched over his electric piano, skip-

ping across the floor, proselytizing his listeners to give in to the spirit of his fervent sound. This is no insecure Caucasian kid mimicking black inflections, exhorting a crowd to 'put your hands together.' Raised in the Pentecostal Church, KC has assimilated black music as if he were born to it. Like Elvis Presley a generation ago, KC has the stage presence and the musical ability to bridge the cultural chasm separating white performers and black listeners as well as between black music and white audiences."

## THE TOP FIVE

*Week of November 22, 1975*

1 **That's the Way (I Like It)**
K.C. & The Sunshine Band

2 **Fly, Robin Fly**
Silver Convention

3 **Who Loves You**
Four Seasons

4 **Island Girl**
Elton John

5 **The Way I Want to Touch You**
Captain & Tennille

*Writers: Silvester Levay*
*Stephan Prager*

*Producer: Michael Kunze*

*November 29, 1975*
*3 weeks*

A COTERIE of musicians existed in Munich in the mid-'70s who worked sometimes in adjoining studios, producing records that were successful around the world. Some of the names became well-known in the latter half of the decade, including Donna Summer and Giorgio Moroder; other names didn't become familiar until years later, like Keith Forsey [see 573—"Flashdance . . . What a Feeling"] and Harold Faltermeyer [see 672—"Shakedown"], who often worked together.

Two of the creative forces of the Munich musical connection were Silvester Levay and Michael Kunze. Levay was a studio musician until Kunze, impressed with his synthesizer work, asked him to arrange the sessions he was producing. A couple weeks after they started working together, Levay played some of the songs he had written for Kunze. Michael asked Silvester to add strings to one number called "Save Me" and record a demo of it.

Four hours later, with the addition of female background singers and a disco arrangement, they knew they had something special. Jupiter Records in Munich offered a deal for the song and they needed a group name. The session drummer, Forsey, suggested they use Levay's nickname, Silver,

and Silver Convention was born.

When "Save Me" became a European disco smash, an album had to be recorded. Before "Save Me," Levay had written another tune based on a riff he had in his head one morning upon waking. Kunze remembered it and suggested they use it for the LP. "I didn't know if it should go on the album," Levay confesses. But Kunze was convinced it would be a hit. "He said, 'I'm going to call this song "Run, Rabbit, Run."'" I wasn't so happy about it because of the Volkswagen Rabbit, but I didn't want to criticize him. The next morning, somebody up there must have heard my plea. I heard on Armed Forces Network a song, 'Run Rabbit.' It was just a half-hour before the girls were to come in and sing. I was very happy. I said to Michael that I had just heard a song called 'Run Rabbit' and in 30 seconds he said, 'O.K., let's do "Fly, Robin, Fly."'"

Recorded with the same set of anonymous background singers, "Fly, Robin, Fly" was a smash in the discos before it spread to radio. "Save Me" had not charted in America, but "Fly, Robin, Fly" debuted on the Hot 100 at number 87 on October 11, 1975, and soared to number one just seven weeks later. Silvester and Michael received a phone call from Bob Reno at Midland International Records

in the States informing them the song had gone to number one.

Unfortunately, the singers who had recorded as Silver Convention were about to adjourn. They could not come to terms and were replaced by three women signed to Jupiter Records. Penny McLean was recording her own solo LP, which included her disco hit, "Lady Bump." Ramona Wolf and Linda G. Thompson completed the new trio who became Silver Convention in time for their second American hit, "Get Up and Boogie" (number two in June, 1976).

The group had only one more chart entry, "No, No, Joe," number 60 in September, 1976. Linda Thompson left the group and was replaced by Rhonda Heath. Silver Convention continued to release albums in America through 1978 before plummeting back to obscurity.

Levay came to America after Donna Summer recorded his "Who Do You Think You're Foolin'" on her album *The Wanderer*. Working with Giorgio Moroder as arranger on his film work for *Flashdance*, *Scarface* and *Metropolis*, Levay was soon in demand as a composer. His themes have graced the television series "Airwolf," "Otherworld" and "Double Dare" as well as the motion picture *The Creator*, starring Peter O'Toole and Mariel Hemingway.

## THE TOP FIVE
*Week of November 29, 1975*

1 **Fly, Robin, Fly**
Silver Convention

2 **That's the Way (I Like It)**
K.C. & The Sunshine Band

3 **Island Girl**
Elton John

4 **The Way I Want
to Touch You**
Captain & Tennille

5 **Let's Do It Again**
Staple Singers

## 422 Let's Do It Again CURTOM 0109
### THE STAPLE SINGERS

*Writer: Curtis Mayfield*

*Producer: Curtis Mayfield*

*December 27, 1975*
*1 week*

MAVIS STAPLES was talking to a British reporter after the Staple Singers had their first number one single [see 312—"I'll Take You There"]. "You know, since we became 'stars,' whatever that is, it's been pretty hectic and everything moves kinda fast. 'Be What You Are,' 'I'll Take You There,' 'If You're Ready (Come Go With Me)'—our records are kinda funky but we still do message songs. But we had to move with the times."

The Staples were not the first black artists to jump from gospel to pop. Sam Cooke, Aretha Franklin and Al Green are among the many who made the successful transition. "Now we try to get across our message to a bigger audience, that's all. Two of our most exciting experiences...have been the 'Soul to Soul' and 'Wattstax' concerts. We can see our sound getting across to so many people....I don't think the message in our lyrics has changed since those times. Sure the beat's got harder. But the message is the same." And that message, according to Staples'

patriarch Roebuck "Pop" Staples, was, pure and simple, love."

With the demise of Stax Records, the Staple Singers moved on to Curtom. The label was owned by Curtis Mayfield, former lead singer for the Impressions ("People Get Ready," "Amen") and now a major solo artist in his own right.

Mayfield wrote and produced the exciting score to *Let's Do It Again*, a 1975 black action-comedy starring Sidney Poitier and Bill Cosby. The Staples' recording of the title song entered the Hot 100 at number 68 on October 25, 1975, and was the number one song in America just nine weeks later.

Pop admitted the slightly suggestive innuendo of the song—a plea from one partner to another to "do it again"—gave him some misgivings at first. "A little girl said to me, 'It sounds so much like sex. Is that where y'all comin' from now?' he recalled for Vernon Gibbs in *Essence*. "It knocked me out," he laughed.

The Staple Singers only placed one more single on the Hot 100 after "Let's Do It Again." Another track from the movie, "New Orleans," edged its way up to number 70. They continued to record for Warner Brothers, 20th Century and Private I, cutting a cover version of the Talking Heads' "Slippery People" for the latter.

"For as long as I can remember,

(Mom and Pop Staples) instilled in us that we must love and treat one another as sisters and brothers," Mavis told Gibbs. "Pop was very strict. He'd whip us good, and Mom would always leave it up to him. We've grown up with togetherness in the family. A lot of people have asked us, 'How do three sisters get along? How can you stay together like that?' It's just the way we were brought up." In the autumn of 2000, Roebuck "Pops" Staples fell in his home and suffered a concussion. He died on December 19 in the Chicago suburb of Dolton.

### THE TOP FIVE
*Week of December 27, 1975*

1 **Let's Do It Again**
Staple Singers

2 **Saturday Night**
Bay City Rollers

3 **That's the Way (I Like It)**
K.C. & The Sunshine Band

4 **Love Rollercoaster**
Ohio Players

5 **Theme from "Mahogany" (Do You Know Where You're Going To)**
Diana Ross

Writers: Bill Martin
      Phil Coulter

Producers: Bill Martin
         Phil Coulter

January 3, 1976
1 week

In the middle of 1975, it seemed like the Bay City Rollers were on their way to becoming one of Britain's all-time greatest hit-making bands. The level of hysteria they aroused in their fans hadn't been matched since the Beatles, and they had placed seven consecutive top 10 singles on the chart, including two consecutive number ones—a cover version of the Four Seasons' "Bye Bye Baby (Baby Goodbye)" and "Give a Little Love." It would have been hard to predict that by the end of 1977, the Rollermania phenomenon would be over, and they would not return to even the bottom rungs of the American or British charts.

For awhile, it looked as if they might not make it in America. They were idolized in the United Kingdom, successors to the teenybopper mantle they picked up from the Osmonds and David Cassidy. Signed to Bell Records in Britain, they were on the American company's artist roster when Clive Davis took over the label and changed its name to Arista.

He dropped most of the label's acts but the Bay City Rollers stayed. He tried releasing "Bye Bye Baby" in the United States—after all, it had been number one for *six* weeks in the United Kingdom, but it didn't make a dent in the Hot 100. All of their other British singles had failed in the States, too, so Davis used his intuition and went with an album track that he thought would be a good American single.

He was aided by top-notch promotion. The Scottish quintet appeared live via satellite on the premiere segment of ABC-TV's appropriately named "Saturday Night Live With Howard Cosell." Davis turned out to be right. "Saturday Night" became the first American chart entry for the Bay City Rollers, debuting on the Hot 100 at number 85 on October 11, 1975. Just 12 weeks later, the group started off 1976 with their first and only American chart-topper.

The Bay City Rollers soon had tartan-clad devotees in the States, just like they did back home. They scored another top 10 single, "Money Honey," and made frequent American television appearances on shows like "American Bandstand" and "The Midnight Special." Their chart fortunes dipped after their 1976 cover of Dusty Springfield's "I Only Want to Be With You," but by the summer of 1977 they had a comeback top 10 single with "You Made Me Believe in Magic."

The Bay City Rollers were all born in Edinburgh, Scotland. Brothers Alan and Derek Longmuir were attending Tynecastle School when they formed a group called the Saxons and started rehearsing in their parents' tenement apartment. They soon had a manager, Edinburgh band leader Tam Paton. They selected a group name by sticking a pin into a map—it landed in Bay City, Michigan, and they thought Bay City Rollers sounded like a good moniker.

They played for three years around Edinburgh, earning up to $55 a night. They were playing at the Caves Club in 1970 when an executive from Bell Records in London missed his flight back to London and caught their performance. They were signed to the label and had their first single, a cover version of the Gentrys' "Keep on Dancing," produced by Jonathan King. It went to number nine in Great Britain in 1971.

Guitarist Eric Faulkner joined the group after the success of "Keep on Dancing." Nobby Clarke and John Devine left the group at the beginning of 1973, and were replaced by lead singer Les McKeown and guitarist Stuart "Woody" Wood.

They were teamed up with writer/producers Bill Martin and Phil Coulter in 1974, paving the way for the beginning of Rollermania.

## THE TOP FIVE
*Week of January 3, 1976*

1   **Saturday Night**
    Bay City Rollers

2   **I Write the Songs**
    Barry Manilow

3   **Theme from "Mahogany"
    (Do You Know Where You're
    Going To)**
    Diana Ross

4   **Love Rollercoaster**
    Ohio Players

5   **Let's Do It Again**
    Staple Singers

**424** **Convoy** MGM 14839
C. W. McCALL

*Writers: C. W. McCall*
*Bill Fries*
*Chip Davis*

*Producers: Don Sears*
*Chip Davis*

*January 10, 1976*
*1 week*

CITIZEN BAND RADIOS were introduced in the United States in 1958, and for 15 years they were used almost exclusively by ham radio operators and farmers. In 1973, the Mid-East oil embargo changed all that. "The fuel shortage, the 55-mph speed limit and the truckers' strike were the events that lit the fuse," said Robert E. Horner, president and chief executive officer of E. F. Johnson Company, a leading manufacturer of CB radios.

CB radios, which are actually simpler versions of police two-way radios, were suddenly big business. In a 1975 article, *Time* predicted that CB radio "may be the fastest-growing communications medium since the Bell telephone." *Forbes* magazine, reporting CB sales of $350 million a year, predicted, "By 1980 enthusiastic CB makers are talking about sales of $1 billion." Instead, by 1980 the CB craze had gone the way of hula hoops and video games, passing fads that captured the attention of millions of people for a brief period of time.

Still, Americans were chattering away like mad on their CB radios when advertising agency director Bill Fries assumed the identity of C. W.

McCall and recorded "Convoy," a novelty song written in CB jargon. An English-speaking person not familiar with CBs might have assumed the song was written in a foreign tongue.

Fries was working at the Bozell and Jacobs advertising agency in Omaha when he created the character of "C. W. McCall" for an ad campaign for the Mertz Baking Company of Iowa. The campaign won a Cleo Award and was so popular, Fries recorded the commercial's theme song, "Old Home Filler-Up an' Keep on-a-Truckin' Cafe" and released it on a label he owned with partner Don Sears. After they sold 30,000 copies in three weeks, MGM Records picked up the song for national distribution and signed "C. W. McCall" to a recording contract.

Another single, "Wolf Creek Pass," went to number 40 in the spring of 1975. That June, Fries was listening to his CB while driving his jeep when a road sign inspired him to write the lyrics to "Convoy." Released the following winter, "Convoy" entered the Hot 100 on

December 6, 1975, at number 82 and moved to number one just five weeks later. It was the 16th and final number one song released on MGM Records. The label was purchased by Polygram Records and was used infrequently, mostly for soundtracks and adult contemporary artists like Jack Jones.

"Convoy" was irresistable enough to climb the charts in many other countries besides the United States. The tale of the "rubber duck" went to number two in Britain, long before CB radios were introduced in that country. "Convoy" also sold well in Canada, Australia and South Africa.

Fries was born November 15, 1928, in Audubon, Iowa. He played in the band at the University of Iowa, but became more interested in commercial art and went to work as a set designer at a local television station.

He kept his job at the ad agency, a clever move considering that after "Convoy" he only made the Hot 100 one more time: "There Won't Be No Country Music (There Won't Be No Rock 'n' Roll)" went to number 73 in the spring of 1976.

## THE TOP FIVE
*Week of January 10, 1976*

1 **Convoy**
C.W. McCall

2 **I Write the Songs**
Barry Manilow

3 **Theme from "Mahogany"**
**(Do You Know Where You're Going To)**
Diana Ross

4 **Love Rollercoaster**
Ohio Players

5 **Saturday Night**
Bay City Rollers

ARISTA 0157 **I Write the Songs** 425
BARRY MANILOW

*Writer: Bruce Johnston*

*Producers: Ron Dante*
*Barry Manilow*

*January 17, 1976*
*1 week*

ONE OF THE popular misconceptions of rock history is that Barry Manilow wrote "I Write the Songs." It's easy to see why people would assume he did—he *is* a songwriter, and he says it out loud for all to hear—"I Write the Songs." But not this one, nor any of his three number one singles.

The writer of "I Write the Songs" is Bruce Johnston, born in Peoria, Illinois, on June 27, 1944, and raised as Benjamin Baldwin. Transplanted to Santa Monica, California, when his father was made the president of a drug store chain owned by Justin Dart, he fell into the music business at 16 years old, playing piano in a band with Sandy Nelson. He recorded as part of the duo Bruce and Terry ("Summer Means Fun") with Doris Day's son, Terry Melcher, produced the Rip Chords ("Hey Little Cobra") and on April 9, 1965, officially became one of the Beach Boys [see 175—"Help Me Rhonda"].

Bruce was driving on the San Diego Freeway, working his way up the steep incline toward Mullholland Drive, when he got the idea for "I Write the Songs." He took the next offramp and returned home so he could work out the tune on the piano, and made a cassette of his new tune. He submitted it to a Japanese song festival, but it was rejected as being

unsuitable.

He played it for two friends who had worked with the Beach Boys and were looking for a record deal—Toni Tennille and her husband, Daryl Dragon [see 408—"Love Will Keep Us Together"]. Once they were signed to A&M, the Captain and Tennille included Bruce's song in their first LP, but didn't release it as a single.

In 1975, Johnston was producing David Cassidy [see 284—"I Think I Love You"] for RCA Records in Britain. David's first single for the label was "I Write the Songs," and it went to number 11. On a visit to London, Arista Records president Clive Davis heard the Cassidy version and thought it would be a perfect song for Manilow.

Recorded for the *Tryin' to Get the Feeling* album, "I Write the Songs" was the first single released from the LP. It debuted on the Hot 100 at number 48 on November 15, 1975, and made it to the top nine weeks

later. Johnston refers to Manilow's recording as "the definitive version."

There's another song that many people mistakenly assume was written by Manilow—the "You deserve a break today" commercial for McDonald's. The confusion bothered Manilow enough to prompt a letter to the press: "Over the years there's been some confusion about my involvement in the commercial industry. Before my records began to break, I participated in a few dozen jingles. I had a great time, learned a lot and moved on. Recently, I've begun to get credit for writing just about every jingle ever written. I guess that's because in my stage act, I don't stop and break down credits for all the jingles in my commercial medley." Manilow provided a list of jingles he wrote, which included Bowlene Toilet Cleaner, State Farm Insurance, Stridex and Band-Aids. His singing only credits included Pepsi, Jack-in-the-Box, Dr. Pepper and the famed Big Mac spot.

## THE TOP FIVE

*Week of January 17, 1976*

1 **I Write the Songs**
Barry Manilow

2 **Theme from "Mahogany" (Do You Know Where You're Going To)**
Diana Ross

3 **Convoy**
C.W. McCall

4 **Love Rollercoaster**
Ohio Players

5 **Fox on the Run**
Sweet

# 426 Theme from 'Mahogany' (Do You Know Where You're Going To) MOTOWN 1377
## DIANA ROSS

*Writers: Michael Masser*
*Gerry Goffin*

*Producer: Michael Masser*

*January 24, 1976*
*1 week*

FOLLOWING her triumphant acting debut in *Lady Sings the Blues,* Diana Ross had to find another vehicle that would confirm her status as a serious actress. Her next project was rumored to be a film called *A Couple of Swells,* and at one point she was being considered for *A Star Is Born,* a role that went to Barbra Streisand. Her second motion picture turned out to be *Mahogany,* the story of a fashion designer who becomes a model and risks her personal relationships for fame. But then, "Success is nothing without someone you love to share it with," or so Billy Dee Williams told her in the film.

Composer Michael Masser, co-writer of Diana's most recent number one single [see 340—"Touch Me in the Morning"] was given his first film assignment by Berry Gordy, Jr., founder of Motown and director of the film. "Berry said, 'Michael, this is probably going to be your best work because it's your first time around,'" Masser is quoted by J. Randy Taraborrelli in *Diana.* "After that, I sat and sat, just trying to figure out how I was ever going to pull this one off. I read a book on scoring and it had all of these real fancy words in it, but no meaning of music. So basically what I did was work it all out at home in front of a video machine. I played the entire film through with the dialogue turned off, so that I could get the feeling of expressions between Diana and Billy Dee. And then I watched the entire film over again, this time recording music right over the visuals. I'd play the piano anywhere I thought there should be music. I figured that if the sound was good on the piano in its basic form, then it could only sound as good or better when orchestrated. Rather than using a cerebral approach to the music, I used an emotional one and the result is the score you hear."

"Theme from 'Mahogany' (Do You Know Where You're Going To)" entered the Hot 100 at number 89 on November 1, 1975. When the Michael Masser-Gerry Goffin tune went to number one 12 weeks later, the song became Diana's third chart-topper as a solo artist. The week the song reigned on the *Billboard* chart, Motown staffers and many people in the music industry were shocked to find out the music screening committee of the Academy of Motion Picture Arts and Sciences had ruled the song "qualitatively ineligible" for an Oscar. That meant they just didn't think it was that good a song—and they had no intention of nominating it and even less intention of awarding it an Oscar.

A song's commercial potential is not a guarantee of an Oscar nomination, and reaching number one on the Hot 100 is not an assurance of consideration by the committee. But there were important voices in the music industry that expressed outrage at the committee's decision. "It's the best song to come out of Hollywood this year. Who are they kidding?" asked Clive Davis, president of Arista Records. "This is embarrassing to the entire entertainment community. There should be a petition process set up to bring the matter before the Academy."

In an unprecedented move, the music committee met again and rescinded their decision. There was still no guarantee the song would be included in the list of five nominees; all the committee was saying in effect was that they no longer considered the song terrible. But it *was* nominated, and some people believed it would emerge as the ultimate winner. Diana, in Europe for a tour on Oscar night, sang the nominated theme live via satellite from Amsterdam. The winning song was "I'm Easy" by Keith Carradine from *Nashville.*

## THE TOP FIVE
*Week of January 24, 1976*

1 **Theme from "Mahogany"**
   **(Do You Know Where You're**
   **Going to)**
   Diana Ross

2 **I Write the Songs**
   Barry Manilow

3 **Love Rollercoaster**
   Ohio Players

4 **Love to Love You Baby**
   Donna Summer

5 **I Love Music (Part 1)**
   O'Jays

Writers: *James Williams*
*Clarence Satchell*
*Leroy Bonner*
*Marshall Jones*
*Ralph Middlebrook*
*Marvin Pierce*
*William Beck*

Producer: *Ohio Players*

*January 31, 1976*
*1 week*

**W**ITH its first number one single [see 392—"Fire"], the Ohio Players finally overcame 15 years of struggle to become one of the hottest record and concert attractions in the music industry. But leader Clarence "Satch" Satchell was determined not to give in to the pressures of cutting a follow-up right away.

Satchell foresaw the danger of "going into the studio while everybody's thinking great schemes." Spontaneity was his thing, and if the Players lost that, they'd become what he termed "mechanical robots." To keep that from happening, the band always went into the studio without preconceived notions or prepared material. So private were their ses-

sions that only an engineer was allowed to join them.

"We just jam and let things happen naturally," Satchell told *Billboard* in 1975. "Afterwards, when we feel that we've got something, we'll add the finishing touches, vocals, mixes and effects. But first, it's gotta happen spontaneously." It took the group four hours to lay down their 1971 album *Pain* (which had cost $400 to produce) and three days to do the same for *Fire*.

Following a tour of 48 one-nighters, the Players went back in the studio and emerged with their hit-making, progressive soul groove still intact. The cover of *Honey*, the band's second LP for Mercury, again pictured a sexy model, this time dripping in the sticky substance.

*Honey* yielded a single, "Sweet Sticky Thing," that only reached number 33 in October, 1975. The second single from the album was the monster. It debuted on the Hot 100 at number 51 on November 15, 1975, and was sitting on top of the chart 11 weeks later.

The Ohio Players had come a long way, but not so far as to forget their roots. They were heavily involved in

community affairs in their home town of Dayton and regularly gave free concerts at their old high school. For their efforts, the city honored the group with "Ohio Players Day."

By now, the Players were a conglomerate, and to take care of business, they set up their own booking company, publishing firm and management subsidiary. But, as their leader Satchell kept stressing, "Music is still the main thing, and you can't choke off art for dollars."

Still, as the '70s wore on, Satch's fears had come to fruition. What had been the funkiest band in music lost its freshness and now just seemed to be going through the motions. They had indeed become "mechanical robots," grinding out lifeless riffs. And gradually dwindling record sales bore concrete witness to the loss.

In 1979, the Players switched to Arista for a one-shot album, and later tried to regain the magic in a stint with Neil Bogart's Boardwalk label. Though the band had changed to a more mainstream funk/pop fusion, this new, melodic sound never caught on. Ultimately, they slid back into obscurity that for one funky stretch they had risen above.

**THE TOP FIVE**
*Week of January 31, 1976*

1  **Love Rollercoaster**
   Ohio Players

2  **I Write the Songs**
   Barry Manilow

3  **Love to Love You Baby**
   Donna Summer

4  **You Sexy Thing**
   Hot Chocolate

5  **I Love Music (Part 1)**
   O'Jays

# 428

# 50 Ways to Leave Your Lover COLUMBIA 10270
## PAUL SIMON

*Writer: Paul Simon*

*Producers: Paul Simon*
*Phil Ramone*

*February 7, 1976*
*3 weeks*

IN 1970, Simon and Garfunkel decided that enough was enough, and dissolved their 13-year union that had produced three number one singles [see 270—"Bridge Over Troubled Water"]. Art Garfunkel pursued a critically acclaimed acting career (*Carnal Knowledge, Bad Timing*), while releasing carefully crafted hit LPs like *Angel Clare* and *Breakaway*. And Paul Simon? Well, he just kept on writing terrific songs.

Performing as a solo artist was not all that unique an experience for Simon. Early in his career, he had released records under such *nom de plumes* as Jerry Landis, Paul Kane and True Taylor, and in the mid-'60s had released a British album of his own material. But that was before "The Sounds of Silence" [see 190] so closely linked his name with Garfunkel's and cemented their partnership.

Now, at last, Simon was free to explore musical directions impossible within the framework of a duo. The first fruit of his post-Garfunkel period, 1972's *Paul Simon*, included Peruvian folk and Jamaican reggae sounds, and produced a pair of hit singles, "Mother and Child Reunion" (number four in March) and "Me and Julio Down by the Schoolyard" (number 22 in May). His second LP, *There Goes Rhymin' Simon*, yielded two number two hits: "Kodachrome," censored in Britain because it referred to a commercial product and in the United States because of the eighth word in the opening line, "When I think back on all the crap I learned in high school . . ."; and "Loves Me Like a Rock," featuring vocals by gospel stars the Dixie Hummingbirds.

In 1975, Simon and Garfunkel got together for the first time in five years to record "My Little Town," a number nine hit in December, 1975. The reunion effort was included on Simon's most personal album to date, *Still Crazy After All These Years*. Wrote *Rolling Stone's* Dave Marsh, "*Still Crazy* is a chronicle of experi-

ence, frequently using broken marriage as a metaphor (Simon's own longtime marriage had ended recently in divorce); it is Simon's most mature work, and his most musically sophisticated."

The album also found time to look at the humorous side of love and loss, as enumerated in the first single, "50 Ways to Leave Your Lover." As with many of his most popular tunes, Simon insisted that "50 Ways" was "just a fluke hit that I slipped into by accident." The single entered the Hot 100 at number 74 on December 20, 1975, and topped the chart seven weeks later.

As the decade wore on, Simon remained relatively quiet on the musical front. "Slip Slidin' Away," a new track from his *Greatest Hits, etc.* album, worked its way to number five in January, 1978. At the same time, he teamed up with Garfunkel and James Taylor on a remake of Sam Cooke's "(What a) Wonderful World," number 17 in March.

In 1977, Simon made his acting debut as Diane Keaton's producer/suitor in Woody Allen's Oscar-winning *Annie Hall*. Then in 1980, he jumped to Warner Brothers Records

and produced, scored and starred in *One-Trick Pony*. The soundtrack included a number six hit, "Late in the Evening." Simon didn't release another album until 1984's *Hearts and Bones*.

Not that he had been inactive. In September, 1981, an estimated half-million Simon and Garfunkel fans gathered in Central Park for an emotionally-charged reunion concert by the legendary duo. And in 1983, Simon had the force with him when he married actress Carrie Fisher.

---

## THE TOP FIVE
*Week of February 7, 1976*

1 **50 Ways to Leave Your Lover**
Paul Simon

2 **Love to Love You Baby**
Donna Summer

3 **You Sexy Thing**
Hot Chocolate

4 **I Write the Songs**
Barry Manilow

5 **Sing a Song**
Earth, Wind & Fire

*Writer: Barry DeVorzon*

*Producer: Steve Barri*
         *Michael Omartian*

*February 28, 1976*
*1 week*

COMPARED TO motion pictures, television has not been a rich field to mine number one singles, but during the rock era a number of songs introduced in television programs have appeared on the Hot 100. The first TV theme to reach the top of the pop singles chart was "TSOP" [see 363] from "Soul Train." But no prime time TV series had ever yielded a chart-topping single in the rock era until Steve Barri came up with the idea of recording the title theme from the ABC program "S.W.A.T."

The series made its debut on February 24, 1975, exactly one year before the theme song went to number one. Steve Forrest starred as the commanding officer of a Special Weapons and Tactics squad, which was assigned to handle violent situations, usually with innocent hostages involved. Rod Perry, Robert Urich, Mark Shera and James Coleman starred as the Vietman veterans who were assigned the key jobs on the S.W.A.T. team.

One of the series' most avid viewers was the six-year-old son of record producer Steve Barri, who with his partner P. F. Sloan had written and produced a number one single for Barry McGuire [see 183—"Eve of Destruction"]. "My son was always asking me if there was a record of the theme song. I couldn't find one," Barri explains. "I wanted to get him a record of it. One night I watched the show and liked the theme song. I though if we could do a dance version, it might be a real solid instrumental. I got Michael Omartian to do an arrangement on it, and we cut it as the Rhythm Heritage."

Barri used studio musicians on the track, including two who later had number one songs: Jeff Porcaro of Toto [see 567—"Africa"] and Ray Parker, Jr. [see 592—"Ghostbusters"]. Also playing on the track were lead guitarist Jay Graydon and bassist Scott Edwards.

The "Theme from 'S.W.A.T.'" was the second successful television theme Barri was involved with. He and Sloan had written "Secret Agent Man," which Johnny Rivers sang over the opening titles of Patrick McGoohan's 1965 CBS series, "Secret Agent." Rivers' theme song, which peaked at number three in the spring of 1966, was only heard in the American import version of the program, which had been titled "Danger Man" in its British run.

Prior to the success of the "Theme from 'S.W.A.T.,'" the highest-charting television theme had been "Hawaii 5-0" by the Ventures, which peaked at number four in the spring of 1969. Other TV theme songs that made the top 20 during the rock era include:

"Different Worlds" from "Angie" by
    Maureen McGovern (number 18)
"Batman" by the Marketts (number 17)
"Bonanza" by Al Caiola (number 19)
"Bad Boys" from "Cops" by Inner
    Circle (number 8)
"Three Stars Will Shine Tonight"
    from "Dr. Kildare" by Richard
    Chamberlain
"I'll Be There for You" from "Friends"
    by the Rembrandts (number 17)
"Theme from 'Greatest American Hero'
    (Believe It or Not)" by Joey
    Scarbury (number 2)
"Happy Days" by Pratt and McClain
    (number 5)
"The Theme from 'Hill Street Blues'"
    by Mike Post (number 10)
"Makin' It" by David Naughton
    (number 5)
"Miami Vice Theme" by Jan Hammer
    (number 1) [see 622]
"Peter Gunn" by the Ray Anthony
    Orchestra (number 8)
"The Rockford Files" by Mike Post
    (number 10)
"Zorro" by the Chordettes (number 17)

Two other television themes made the top 20; both were produced by Barri. The session musicians known as Rhythm Heritage recorded "Baretta's Theme (Keep Your Eye on the Sparrow)" from Robert Blake's series, a number 20 hit in the spring of 1976. The other was a number one single, John Sebastian's recording of the theme from Gabe Kaplan's "Welcome Back, Kotter" series [see 434].

Although they were released in conjunction with motion pictures, two television themes were top 20 hits in the '90s, both peaking at number seven. "Addams Groove" by Hammer, incorporating Vic Mizzy's original theme from "The Addams Family," was a hit in 1992. Adam Clayton and Larry Mullen of U2 updated Lalo Schifrin's "Theme from Mission: Impossible" in 1996.

In 1992, the song "How Do You Talk to an Angel" [see 812] from the series "The Heights" became the first number one single from a television show since Jan Hammer's "Miami Vice Theme" [see 622] in 1985.

## THE TOP FIVE
*Week of February 28, 1976*

1 **Theme from 'S.W.A.T.'**
   Rhythm Heritage

2 **50 Ways to Leave Your Lover**
   Paul Simon

3 **Love Machine (Part 1)**
   Miracles

4 **All By Myself**
   Eric Carmen

5 **December 1963**
   **(Oh What a Night)**
   Four Seasons

# 430 Love Machine Pt. 1 TAMLA 54262
## THE MIRACLES

*Writers: Warren 'Pete' Moore*
*William Griffin*

*Producer: Freddie Perren*
*March 6, 1976*
*1 week*

**W**HEN Smokey Robinson told his fellow Miracles in 1969 that he wanted to quit the group, no one believed him. As the lead singer and primary creative force behind their hits from "Shop Around" to "I Second That Emotion," Smokey was too valuable a resource to lose. Besides, he loved being a part of the group too much to leave. But Smokey longed to spend more time at home with his wife Claudette and their son. He promised he would stay until 1970.

By the end of 1970, a strange twist of fate gave the Miracles their first number one hit [see 285—"The Tears of a Clown"], and the group's sudden increase in popularity made Smokey reconsider. Still, his daughter was born that year, and now he had one more reason to stay off the road. In 1971, he again informed Pete Moore, Ronnie White and Bobby Rogers that he was definitely leaving the group.

It was during 1971 that the group met Bill Griffin, a Baltimore singer who grew up idolizing the Miracles. Invited to understudy Smokey, Griffin travelled all over the United States and Europe on the Miracles' farewell tour.

Smokey Robinson was listed as executive producer of their first album, *Renaissance*, but the line producers ranged from Marvin Gaye to Willie Hutch to Freddie Perren, the man who produced their first single without Smokey, "Do It Baby" (number 13 in October, 1974). But the Miracles needed more than one top 20 record to establish their new identity. An entirely new direction was needed.

"As writers we really haven't done anything since Bill joined the group," Moore explained in a 1975 *Billboard* interview. "We primarily wanted to concentrate on getting him acclimated....But our next album will have songs that we've written." That LP, *City of Angels*, finally cut the umbilical cord between the old and new Miracles. Featuring an array of new musical effects, including water

drums and synthesizers, the ambitious concept album examined the pleasures and pitfalls of the Hollywood star search.

Listened to in sequence, the songs told the story of a country girl named Charlotte who seeks fame and fortune in Los Angeles. When her boyfriend Michael follows her to the city of the Angels, he becomes the star. "Love Machine" is his ironic description of himself after becoming a celebrity.

Standing alone, "Love Machine" was a synthesizer-heavy, pulsing disco hit. Too long to release as a single, Motown divided it into two parts, and the first half became the hit side. "Love Machine Pt 1" entered the Hot 100 at number 90 on October 25, 1975. It took 19 weeks to reach

the top of the chart, and it remained on the Hot 100 for 28 weeks, making it the most successful single in the 16-year chart history of the Miracles.

It was also the last Miracles single to chart. In 1977, the group left Motown and signed with Columbia Records, adding Billy's brother Don to make the group a quintet. Griffin and Moore wrote all the tunes on their debut CBS album, *Love Crazy*, but the success of "Love Machine" was not repeated.

The last public appearance of the Miracles—reunited with Smokey Robinson—was on the Motown 25th anniversary special, telecast May 16, 1983. That same year, Billy Griffin recorded his first solo LP for Columbia, resulting in a top 30 single in Britain.

## THE TOP FIVE
*Week of March 6, 1976*

1  **Love Machine (Part 1)**
   Miracles

2  **All By Myself**
   Eric Carmen

3  **December 1963**
   **(Oh What a Night)**
   Four Seasons

4  **Theme from "S.W.A.T."**
   Rhythm Heritage

5  **Take It to the Limit**
   Eagles

*Writers: Bob Gaudio*
*Judy Parker*

*Producer: Bob Gaudio*
*March 13, 1976*
*3 weeks*

**W**HEN the Four Seasons returned to the Hot 100 after a five-year absence with "Who Loves You" in August, 1975, it seemed like a real comeback for a group that had been away a long time. Actually, it was almost a completely different group from the one that scored four number one singles from 1962-1964, and they hadn't really been away.

Their last top 30 single was a dramatic version of Gerry Goffin and Carole King's "Will You Love Me Tomorrow" in 1968. After parting ways with Philips Records in 1970, the group signed with Motown and released an album, *Chameleon*, on the MoWest subsidiary. The association with Motown proved disappointing and did not result in any American chart singles.

By the time "December, 1963" was released, the Four Seasons consisted of lead singer Valli *plus* four Seasons: Gerry Polci on drums and co-lead vocals, Don Ciccone (formerly of the Critters) on bass, John Paiva on guitar and Lee Shapiro on key-

boards. Adding support on keyboards was former group member and long-time writer, Bob Gaudio, who was also now the group's producer.

Gaudio's writing partner was Judy Parker, who would eventually become his wife. Their song, "December, 1963" was originally set 30 years earlier and was about the repeal of prohibition. "The lyrics were pretty bizarre, as I remember," Gaudio confesses. "Judy was never too happy with the lyric and Frankie was not overwhelmed. We cut the track, but we were planning on dropping it. Judy and I locked the doors for two days and changed it all. She worked on the lyric and I changed the melody, and out came 'Oh, What a Night.' "

And out came their first American number one single in 12 years and their first and only British number one single. It is their most successful record ever, an amazing accomplishment in 1976 for a group that most people assumed had peaked in the '60s.

It proved to be a short-lived return to the top, however. After three more singles that failed to make the top 30, the renaissance finally seemed to be over. The Four Seasons sound managed to live on in "Uptown Girl," a Billy Joel hit in 1983 that sounded like it really should have been recorded by the New Jersey quartet.

"What amazes me about that record," says Gaudio, "it's like everything we've ever done but like nothing we've ever done. That's a tribute to him, being able to accomplish the essence of the songs we were writing in those days. Yet, I think he did it with a freshness . . . he really took the next step."

In 1994, the Curb label re-released "December, 1963" with remixed vocals. The single returned to the Hot 100 in August and peaked at number 14. It remained on the chart for 27 weeks, bringing its total up to 54. That was the longest any single has remained on the Hot 100 until "Macarena" [see 849].

## THE TOP FIVE
*Week of March 13, 1976*

1 **December 1963 (Oh What a Night)**
Four Seasons

2 **All By Myself**
Eric Carmen

3 **Love Machine (Part 1)**
Miracles

4 **Take It to the Limit**
Eagles

5 **Dream Weaver**
Gary Wright

## 432 Disco Lady COLUMBIA 10281
## JOHNNIE TAYLOR

Writers: *Harvey Scales*
*Al Vance*
*Don Davis*

Producer: *Don Davis*

*April 3, 1976*
*4 weeks*

ONE OF THE RAREST, most precious metals on Earth is platinum. It's so rare, that all the platinum ever mined would only fill a 14-square-foot cube. Most people will only come in contact with platinum on the edge of a razor blade or in their automobile's catalytic converter. A select few will sell enough copies of a 45 rpm record and earn a platinum award from the Record Industry Association of America. The RIAA began certifying gold records in 1958 and the first million-selling single to be recognized was "Catch a Falling Star" by Perry Como [see 20—"Round and Round"]. As the record industry grew healthier, a new standard was needed to acknowledge larger sales. So in 1976, the RIAA created the platinum record certification, and the very first record to qualify was Johnnie Taylor's "Disco Lady."

"Disco Lady" was a hit right in the middle of the disco era, but that didn't mean you could dance to it. "A lot of people got 'Disco Lady' mixed up," according to Taylor. "They thought it was disco. It was not a disco tune. We were just *talking* about disco. Don Davis brought me 'Disco Lady.' It's one of the best records I ever made. Don said, 'Man, I got you a smash.' I said, 'Aw, you tell me that all the time.' "

Davis remembers Taylor's original reaction being less than enthusiastic. The demo, written as "Disco Baby," had been sitting on a shelf for a few years when Davis decided to rewrite the song and have Johnnie record it. After the final mix was completed, Taylor called to voice his objections. "He called me back and said the mix was terrible. He couldn't understand how we could put out a record that was mixed like that. I went back and listened to the record, and I called him back and told him he must be hearing it wrong, it was a great mix. We found out his turntable was on the wrong setting."

Within days of its release, Bruce Lundvall, then president of Columbia

Records, was sending bottles of Dom Perignon champagne to Taylor to celebrate the single's incredible sales. "I took a bath in some of it," Johnnie swears. "It makes your skin so smooth!" he laughs.

Johnnie Taylor was born in West Memphis, Arkansas, on May 5, 1937. His father, who was a Baptist minister in Battle Creek, Michigan, was a "mean harmonica player," according to Johnnie. "I get my talent from him."

Taylor started singing in church when his aunt suggested he do a recital on Easter Sunday. That led to traveling with the ministers, singing at revival shows. He became a member of a Kansas City gospel group, the Melody Masters. They opened for the famed Soul Stirrers, a gospel group that featured lead singer Sam Cooke [see 30—"You Send Me"], formerly of the Highway QCs.

In 1952, Johnnie moved to Chicago. When the Highway QCs decided to re-form, they invited Johnnie to be their new lead singer. Cooke turned to secular music and left the Soul Stirrers—and asked Johnnie to replace him as lead vocalist. "I guess we had some of the same qualities, and each group that he had been with recognized those qualities and wanted me to be with them," explains Taylor.

In California, Cooke started his

own label, Sar, and signed the Soul Stirrers as his first act. Encouragement from Cooke helped Johnnie make the difficult decision to leave gospel music behind for the world of secular music. He signed as a solo artist with Sam's company, releasing singles on both the Sar and Derby labels.

After Cooke's untimely death, his labels closed their doors. Johnnie returned home for a family visit to West Memphis, and on impulse dropped in at the offices of Stax Records in Memphis to see an old friend, executive vice president Al Bell. "We talked about old times...two weeks later I signed a contract."

Three years later, Johnnie had a pop smash on Stax, "Who's Making Love," which peaked at number five. He followed it with hits like "Take Care of Your Homework," "I Could Never Be President," "Jody's Got Your Girl and Gone" and one of his personal favorites, "I Believe in You (You Believe in Me)."

"I loved every minute I spent at Stax," Johnny answers when asked to recall the years he spent with the Memphis label. "We helped each other out at sessions. It was like family—everybody was happy." Taylor was at Stax during its peak, and he stayed until the very end, when the company went bankrupt. When it was all over, he signed with Columbia Records and released "Disco Lady" as his first single.

On May 31, 2000, Taylor died of a massive heart attack at his home in Dallas. Almost 7,000 people attended his funeral, including stars Aretha Franklin and Al Green.

---

## THE TOP FIVE
*Week of April 3, 1976*

1 **Disco Lady**
Johnnie Taylor

2 **Dream Weaver**
Gary Wright

3 **Lonely Night (Angel Face)**
Captain & Tennille

4 **Let Your Love Flow**
Bellamy Brothers

5 **Sweet Thing**
Rufus Featuring Chaka Khan

WARNER/CURB 8169 **Let Your Love Flow**
BELLAMY BROTHERS

**433**

*Writer: Larry E. Williams*

*Producers: Phil Gernhard*
*Tony Scotti*

*May 1, 1976*
*1 week*

DAVID BELLAMY, younger of the two Bellamy Brothers by four years, left his rural Florida home for California after Jim Stafford recorded one of his songs. "Spiders and Snakes" went to number three in early 1974, and Stafford's producer/manager, Phil Gernhard [see 80—"Stay"], was interested in developing David as a singer/songwriter.

Gernhard often used Neil Diamond's road band for recording sessions. Diamond toured infrequently and they were a tight band of musicians who played well together. One of Diamond's roadies was Larry Williams, an aspiring songwriter who gave one of his compositions to Gernhard. Phil liked "Let Your Love Flow" and decided to cut it with David on lead vocal. The results were disappointing, and the track was stored on a shelf.

A few months later, Gernhard and his partner, Tony Scotti, flew to Florida for the taping of a television special at Cypress Gardens. Stafford was scheduled to perform, but gathering storm clouds threatened to disrupt the location shooting with rain. Gernhard told Stafford's roadie to check the equipment quickly so they could tape the production number before the bad weather struck.

The roadie was Howard Bellamy, David's older brother. He needed a job, so Gernhard had hired him to "schlep things around" for Jim. "Tony and I were standing there talking, and this voice drifted across from the other side of the lake where they were set up to shoot, and before I put two and two together, I said that's the voice for 'Let Your Love Flow.' I turned around and it was Howard Bellamy."

When Howard finished a tour with Stafford, he was flown to California to go into the studio for the first time in his life. With assistance from brother David and Diamond's band, he spent a couple of sessions recording "Let Your Love Flow."

On the day of Howard's final session, Gernhard was about to go into the studio when his secretary handed him a copy of the song—just released on ABC/Dunhill by an R&B artist. Phil said he didn't want to hear it before he did the date with Howard. When he listened to it afterward he was satisfied he had produced the definitive version. Still, the idea of a competing record didn't sit well with record company executives, so the Bellamy Brothers' "Let Your Love Flow" was rush-released. It entered the Hot 100 at number 88 on January 31, 1976, and went to number one 13 weeks later.

Gernhard wasn't as surprised about the single going to number one as he was about a letter from a church council praising the song for its religious aspect. "What I envisioned was much more sensual than that," Gernhard admits. "I never thought about the religious aspects."

Howard and David told Dolly Carlisle in *People* magazine that the song was not beneficial to their careers. "Right after that, we hit bottom because we lost control," David explained. "We had people working for us we didn't know, and managers wouldn't let us do our own music." Howard added, "There were so many fingers in the pie, that there was no pie left." "We ended up in debt because of that record," David concluded.

They toured Europe for a couple of years after "Let Your Love Flow," then returned to the family homestead in Florida. They hired some local musicians to back them on a song, "If I Said You Had a Beautiful Body Would You Hold It Against Me," which topped the country chart and did well internationally.

The urban cowboy trend may have passed, but the Bellamy Brothers remained popular on the country charts, recording for MCA/Curb and then Atlantic. "We don't want to be a part of something that just comes and goes—like disco," Howard said in *People*. "We hated that. We're interested in longevity. There have been some terrible times, but now we've learned to ride with them."

## THE TOP FIVE
*Week of May 1, 1976*

1 **Let Your Love Flow**
Bellamy Brothers

2 **Right Back Where We Started From**
Maxine Nightingale

3 **Boogie Fever**
Sylvers

4 **Welcome Back**
John Sebastian

5 **Sweet Love**
Commodores

**434** ## Welcome Back REPRISE 1349
### JOHN SEBASTIAN

Writer: John Sebastian

Producers: Steve Barri
         John Sebastian

May 8, 1976
1 week

TEN weeks after "Theme from S.W.A.T." [see 429] topped the chart, another Steve Barri-produced television theme song went to number one: John Sebastian's "Welcome Back" from the ABC-TV situation comedy "Welcome Back, Kotter."

The series premiered September 9, 1975. Gabe Kaplan starred as a teacher who returned to his own high school to teach the toughest students, the "sweathogs." The four leading "sweathogs" were played by Lawrence Hilton-Jacobs, Ron Palillo, Robert Hegyes and John Travolta [see 484—"You're the One That I Want"], who became an international star while the series was still on the air. Travolta continued to play Vinnie Barbarino even after starring in Saturday Night Fever.

The producer of the series, Alan Sachs, mentioned to his agent that he was looking for a Lovin' Spoonful [see 205—"Summer in the City"], John Sebastian type of tune to be the program's theme song. The agent, Dave Bendet, also happened to be Sebas-

tian's agent at the time and brought his two clients together. "He was a Brooklynite and I was from Manhattan. We started insulting each other right away and got along great," Sebastian remembers of Sachs. "I read a 10-page synopsis of the storyline and later a first draft of the first episode. It seemed to me the relationship this teacher had with his students was not unlike the relationship I had with this producer, an antagonistic friendship.

"I wrote a song one afternoon that was just ghastly, and about four o'clock I got annoyed and threw it away. I wrote another song that was 'Welcome Back.'" The producers liked the song enough to change the series' name from "Kotter" to "Welcome Back, Kotter." Sebastian was relieved, as the only word he could rhyme with Kotter was otter.

Like most TV theme songs, "Welcome Back" lasted less than 60 seconds. When public demand for a record became so great that Warner Brothers Television suggested to Warner Brothers Records a single be released, Sebastian wrote a second verse. Although the song does not have the word "Kotter" anywhere in the lyrics or the title, the first pressings of the single were released as "Welcome Back, Kotter," to make sure everyone connected the song with the series.

"Welcome Back" applied not just to Gabe Kaplan but to John Sebastian, who was returning to the Hot 100 for the first time in over seven years. After he left the Lovin' Spoonful, he had one solo chart entry in 1969, "She's a Lady." He recorded a live album, which his record company wanted to release as a Lovin' Spoonful LP. Thinking that just a bit dishonest, Sebastian waited a year-and-a-half rather than let the company put out the album under false pretenses. Finally, Warner Brothers Records came to his rescue and volunteered to release the live album and take care of any legal hassles that would result. He was signed to the company's Reprise subsidiary, which released Cheapo Cheapo Productions Presents the Real Live John Sebastian.

Sebastian was born March 17, 1944, in New York City. His mother wrote scripts for radio shows and his father played classical harmonica. Their home in Greenwich Village found well-known guests dropping by, including Woody Guthrie and Burl Ives. Within a few blocks, Sebastian could walk to clubs and see artists like Lightnin' Hopkins and Mississippi John Hurt performing. "I was this neighborhood kid following these legends around, carrying their guitars," Sebastian wrote in a biography. "It was a magical time."

One summer Sebastian came home from camp and was invited to join the Even Dozen Jug Band, an outfit that included Maria Muldaur and Steve Katz. Next came the Mugwumps and then the band that made Sebastian famous, the Lovin' Spoonful.

---

### THE TOP FIVE
Week of May 8, 1976

1. **Welcome Back**
   John Sebastian

2. **Right Back Where We Started From**
   Maxine Nightingale

3. **Boogie Fever**
   Sylvers

4. **Fooled Around and Fell in Love**
   Elvin Bishop

5. **Silly Love Songs**
   Wings

CAPITOL 4179 **Boogie Fever**
THE SYLVERS

**435**

*Writers: Keni St. Lewis*
*Freddie Perren*

*Producer: Freddie Perren*

*May 15, 1976*
*1 week*

LIKE the Jackson Five and the Osmonds, the Sylvers were a family act. Various combinations of the nine brothers and sisters have made up the Sylvers over the years, from their earliest days singing as infants in their native Tennessee to their 1985 single, "Falling for Your Love," for Geffen Records.

The four eldest Sylvers were originally called the Little Angels. Olympia-Ann, Leon Frank III, Charmaine and James were encouraged by their mother, a former opera singer herself, to enter local talent contests. After proving themselves in Memphis, they were invited to appear on television with stars like Dinah Shore, Groucho Marx, Spike Jones and Danny Thomas. They also toured the United States and Europe as an opening act for Johnny Mathis and Ray Charles.

In 1971, younger siblings Edmund, Ricky and Foster became part of the act and the group signed with MGM's Pride label. Three singles charted on the Hot 100, but they were all bested by a solo effort from Foster, "Misdemeanor," which peaked at number 22 in July, 1973.

When Larkin Arnold, then vice president for Capitol Records, signed the Sylvers in 1975, he hired Motown veteran Freddie Perren to produce them. Perren helped write and produce three number one singles for the Jackson Five ("I Want You Back," "ABC," "The Love You Save") plus one for Michael Jackson ("Ben").

"I've been blessed to be able to work with families," says Perren, who has also worked with the brothers known as Tavares ("It Only Takes a Minute," "Heaven Must Be Missing an Angel"). "There's usually a thread that holds them together—a low, middle and high singer. God seems to have made a person for each part that needs to be sung."

The first time Perren heard the Sylvers, he knew he would be working with 24-carat material. "They were pure gold. I was blown away at the intricate harmonies they sang." The group had many of the same strengths as the early Jacksons, according to Perren, including a lead singer (Edmund) who was beginning to mature, but still had a youthful flavor to his voice.

Lyricist Keni St. James, one of Perren's oldest friends and collaborators, came to rehearsals and suggested they come up with a song using one of the popular words of the day, "boogie."

The funky tune that emerged, "Boogie Fever," featured all nine Sylvers, including the youngest sisters, Angelia and Pat. The single entered the Hot 100 at number 84 on February 14, 1976, and took 13 weeks to climb to number one. Perren says the song was successful because it appealed to kids and young adults. "You didn't need a PhD in music to understand what it was all about. People like to party, it had a recognizable and relatable lyric, the track was really pumping and it was released at the beginning of the disco thing."

The follow-up to "Boogie Fever," a confection called "Cotton Candy," had a short chart run, peaking at number 57. But the next single, "Hot Line," was the group's second biggest hit, peaking at number five in January, 1977.

Label deals with Casablanca and Solar followed, with Leon writing for many of the artists on the Solar roster. The Sylvers line-up that recorded for Geffen was a sextet, consisting of Foster, Ricky, James, Charmaine, Angelia and Pat.

### THE TOP FIVE
*Week of May 15, 1976*

1 **Boogie Fever**
Sylvers

2 **Welcome Back**
John Sebastian

3 **Silly Love Songs**
Wings

4 **Fooled Around and Fell in Love**
Elvin Bishop

5 **Love Hangover**
Diana Ross

## 436 | Silly Love Songs CAPITOL 4256
### WINGS

*Writer: Paul McCartney*

*Producer: Paul McCartney*

*May 22, 1976*
*5 weeks*

WINGS flew over America in 1976 and for the first time in 10 years, Paul McCartney appeared in concert on U.S. soil. With his previous band, he had last performed in the States on August 29, 1966, at Candlestick Park in San Francisco, California. The "Wings Over America" tour began the week "Silly Love Songs" burst into the top 10; the first date was May 3 in Fort Worth, Texas.

The band was playing the Capitol Center in Washington D.C. the day "Silly Love Songs" moved into the number one position on the Hot 100. Although it yielded to Diana Ross' "Love Hangover" for two weeks, "Silly Love Songs" returned to the top and stayed there an additional four weeks.

Linda McCartney talked about the tour with Robert Hilburn of the *Los Angeles Times.* "This tour has been a beauty for Paul. It has been the most positive thing that has happened to

him in years, and he works very much on positive vibes. When it's positive, he flowers. So, he's very much his old self again. He's got his thinking cap on again. He has got a team together in Wings and the audiences have accepted it. Seeing him on this tour, I can realize now what he had before the Beatles broke up. He had friendship and a creative community to work with. He could turn to John and say, 'Let's try this' or 'What about that?' It was all very positive. That's why it hit him so hard when the Beatles did break up. . . . Now, it's a high point again."

One high point on the tour for fans was the June 21 concert at the Forum in Inglewood, California. Near the end of the final number of the night, a man from the audience moved from his loge seat to the backstage area, and spontaneously grabbed a bouquet of flowers and ran on stage. He handed the flowers to guitarist Denny Laine, kissed Linda on the hand and took McCartney's bass. The audience cheered as old friends Ringo Starr and Paul McCartney embraced and walked off the stage together.

Of course, "Silly Love Songs" was

performed every night. *Time* magazine called it "the sort of tune that comes at the unwary out of car radios and open windows, attaching itself like a particularly stubborn lap cat. It will probably never go away. . . . It is a sort of refined disco tune, made for dancing and casual listening."

The song was written in reaction to the critics who said McCartney's music was lightweight. John Lennon, who accused his former collaborator of sounding like Engelbert Humperdinck, attacked Paul's "muzak" in the song "How Do You Sleep?"

But Paul, who ultimately had the most successful post-Beatles solo career, had no intention of changing his style. "I'm a fan of old-fashioned writing," he has admitted. "I do like rhyme, when it comes off. I hate silly rhymes, but when they work, they're the greatest little things in songwriting."

Not that Paul needed the vindication, but "Silly Love Songs" was the number one single of 1976, according to *Billboard*. That makes McCartney the only artist to be involved with three top singles of the year [see 143—"I Want to Hold Your Hand" and 247—"Hey Jude"].

### THE TOP FIVE
*Week of May 22, 1976*

1 **Silly Love Songs**
Wings

2 **Love Hangover**
Diana Ross

3 **Fooled Around and Fell in Love**
Elvin Bishop

4 **Boogie Fever**
Sylvers

5 **Get Up and Boogie**
Silver Convention

expect. There's even a part in there where she's laughing on the track. I didn't edit it because I wanted to keep that sense of spontaneity."

Diana is quoted by Taraborrelli on the session: "It was a spontaneous thing that we captured on record and if I had to go back in and do it again, I couldn't have. The music was me and I was the music. Things came out of my mouth that I didn't even expect."

Even with three number one singles, Diana's solo recording career was erratic in the '70s. In 1974, a depressing ballad called "Sleepin'" went dormant at number 70. That was followed by "Sorry Doesn't Always Make It Right," which was her first solo single to fail to make the Hot 100. She rebounded with a number one single [see 426—"Theme from 'Mahogany' (Do You Know Where You're Going To)"].

For a follow-up, Motown went with another ballad, "I Thought It Took a Little Time (But Today I Fell in Love)." The first single from the *Diana Ross* LP, it was moving slowly up the chart when people began to take notice of another track on the album, "Love Hangover."

Among those taking notice were the Fifth Dimension, who had reorganized since the departure of Marilyn McCoo and Billy Davis, Jr. Signed to ABC Records, the Dimension released a single of "Love Hangover."

Motown reacted quickly by rushing out Diana's single. Both versions entered the Hot 100 on April 3, 1976; Diana debuted at 78 and the Fifth Dimension came in at 95. Three weeks later the Fifth Dimension had peaked at number 80.

*Writers: Pam Sawyer*
*Marilyn McLeod*

*Producer: Hal Davis*

*May 29, 1976*
*2 weeks*

**I**N the '60s, *the* records to dance to were Motown records. "Baby Love," "Dancing in the Street," "I Can't Help Myself (Sugar Pie, Honey Bunch)," "This Old Heart of Mine," those were the songs you needed at a party if you wanted to dance. But in the decade that followed, the best dance music was no longer coming from Detroit. The disco movement was centered on the East Coast, and other cities provided the music people wanted to dance to—hits like "Rock the Boat," "Rock Your Baby" and "Get Down Tonight."

"No one really liked disco here at Motown," producer Hal Davis said in J. Randy Taraborrelli's biography, *Diana.* "The company wasn't heavily into it, so I figured I'd take advantage of that. When I did the track for 'Love Hangover,' I knew it was a hot track. But when I played it for Diana, well, she wasn't too sure

about it. She was used to singing more lush songs by producers like Michael Masser and the public sort of identified her with arrangements like 'Touch Me in the Morning' [see 340]. She liked the lyric to 'Love Hangover,' but people thought I was a little off for even suggesting that Diana do this song."

Davis went on to describe the evening that Diana recorded the Pam Sawyer-Marilyn McLeod song. "It was a late session; we started at about nine o'clock at night. I had it all planned out because I know how Diana is about atmosphere in the studio. So I told them to have some hot red lights put around and also a strobe light. Diana came in, took her shoes off, and got into it sort of slow. The song had two tempos, starting off kind of sultry, which was easy for her. But when we got to the disco part, I remember her laughing and saying, 'I can *not* do that!'

"So at that point, I had them turn the lights on and we had the place jumpin' like a disco. That's all she needed; she just took off after that. It turned out to be a lot of fun for her and she even improvised a little Billie Holiday in there that I didn't

# Afternoon Delight WINDSONG 10588
## STARLAND VOCAL BAND

*Writer: Bill Danoff*

*Producer: Milt Okun*

*July 10, 1976*
*2 weeks*

THE Starland Vocal Band was the creation of a clean-cut, all-American couple named Bill and Kathy "Taffy" Danoff. On the wings of angelic harmonies—and with a little help from a superstar-pal, they soared to the top of the Hot 100 on July 10, 1976, with "Afternoon Delight."

By the late '60s, folksinger Bill Danoff (born May 7, 1946, in Springfield, Massachusetts) was working nights as the light and sound man at the Cellar Door club in Washington, D.C. There, he met John Denver [see 360—"Sunshine on My Shoulders"], who was near the end of his stretch fronting the Chad Mitchell Trio. Soon Denver recorded Danoff's "I Guess I'd Rather Be in Colorado," and the friendship between them was cemented when they co-wrote the Rocky Mountain tycoon's first smash hit, "Take Me Home, Country Roads."

Meanwhile, Bill and his wife Taffy

(born Kathy Nivert on October 25, 1944, in Washington, D.C.) had been scuffling around the folk circuit fronting a quintet called Fat City, which gradually lost members until only the Danoffs remained. As "Bill and Taffy," they recorded a pair of RCA albums, *Pass It On* and *Aces.* Following their failure, Bill found himself making a difficult career decision.

"I was sitting around one night, writing and thinking what our next album should sound like," Bill told *Melody Maker.* "I was thinking of going in and cutting some singles in the hope that we could break through in that way. In the course of thinking about how to do them, I thought it might be a good idea with Jon (Carroll) and Margot (Chapman)." Pianist/singer Carroll had worked on the *Aces* LP, while vocalist Chapman was in one of Fat City's incarnations.

"I wasn't really looking to put a group together," he continued, "but I just thought that if we were going to have a group, it would be a good idea to have the four of us . . . I was thinking about the vocal idea, how we all got along and how it would work."

Calling themselves the Starland Vocal Band, the quartet finely-tuned

its rich pop harmony sound before becoming the first act signed by Denver to his new Windsong label. In November, 1975, during the recording of the group's debut album, Taffy delivered a baby. It was a favorable omen. Released as the first single, "Afternoon Delight" entered the Hot 100 at number 87 on May 8, 1976. Nine weeks later the Starland Vocal Band and Windsong Records had their first and only number one single.

According to an account in *Rolling Stone*, Taffy credited the song's creation to a culinary repast. "Bill wrote this after having lunch at Clyde's in Washington, D.C.," she explained to an audience before performing the song. "It seems Clyde's has a menu called 'Afternoon Delight' with stuff like spiced shrimp and hot Brie with almonds. So Bill ate it—the food, that is—and went home and explained to me what 'Afternoon Delight' *should* be."

Danoff acknowledged that audiences might find hidden meanings in the song. "I didn't want to write an all-out sex song," he told Dennis Hunt of the *Los Angeles Times*. "I just wanted to write something that was fun and hinted at sex. It was one of those songs that you could really have a good time writing."

The Danoffs thought they might have had a problem getting airplay on "Afternoon Delight," but few stations found it objectionable. "If the song had been banned it would have been a real injustice," Bill said in the *Times*. "The lyrics are subtle and sophisticated and not at all raunchy. It might have been banned years ago but not today."

## THE TOP FIVE
*Week of July 10, 1976*

1 **Afternoon Delight**
   Starland Vocal Band

2 **Kiss and Say Goodbye**
   Manhattans

3 **I'll Be Good to You**
   Brothers Johnson

4 **Shop Around**
   Captain & Tennille

5 **More, More, More (Part 1)**
   Andrea True Connection

COLUMBIA 10310 **Kiss and Say Goodbye**
MANHATTANS

**439**°

*Writer: Winfred 'Blue' Lovett*

*Producer: Bobby Martin*

*July 24, 1976*
*2 weeks*

CONTRARY to popular belief, the Manhattans did not name themselves after Gotham City. In *The Top Ten*, bass vocalist "Blue" Lovett told Bob Gilbert and Gary Theroux why the group originally known as the Dulcets changed their name: "It didn't sound that exciting; dulcets means 'melodic tones'—but how could you explain that to the public? We needed a catchy name that would last. So, with the cocktail theme in mind—not the borough of Manhattan—we picked the name Manhattans."

The original members of the group all grew up in Jersey City, New Jersey, but the Manhattans didn't take shape until Edward "Sonny" Bivins and Richard Taylor met in Germany while serving in the United States Air Force. When they returned stateside, they formed a '50s-style doo-wop group and added three singers from rival Jersey City bands—George Smith, Kenny Kelly and Lovett. A major turning point was entering a talent show at the

Apollo Theater in Harlem in 1964.

"On this particular night, we came in third," Lovett said in *The Top Ten*, "and a gentleman by the name of Joe Evans was there. He signed us to his label, called Carnival Records."

They made their debut on the pop chart with "I Wanna Be (Your Everything)," number 68 in March, 1965. They had no trouble getting R&B hits, but their next three chart singles failed to place higher than 90 on the Hot 100. In 1969 they switched to a King Records subsidiary, Deluxe, but still could not crack the pop market.

While touring Southern black colleges in 1970, they appeared on the same bill at North Carolina's Kittrell College with another group, the New Imperials. The Manhattans were impressed enough with singer Gerald Alston to ask him to join the group, but he declined. When George Smith died of a brain tumor later that year, Alston agreed to take his place.

In the latter half of 1972, the Manhattans signed with their third label, Columbia Records. With the backing of a major company like CBS, they were now able to become more involved in the production of their own records. Collaborating with Bobby Martin, a Gamble-Huff trained

producer at Philadelphia's Sigma Sound studios, the Manhattans reached the upper half of the Hot 100 for the first time with "There's No Me Without You" (number 43 in August, 1973).

But a top 10 record still eluded the group. "There were lots of songs I sat down and composed," Lovett told Gilbert and Theroux. "I did big arrangements on 'em, worked on 'em for a week, and nothing happened. A lot of times, I hear songs in my sleep. But I was too tired to get up and struggle in to where the piano was. But this particular night, I just couldn't lie there. I heard the melody. Everything was there. I got up about three o'clock in the morning and jotted down the things I wanted to say. I just put the words together on my tape recorder and little piano. I always thought that when you write slow songs, they have to have meaning. In this case, it's the love triangle situation we've all been through."

The song was "Kiss and Say Goodbye." It entered the Hot 100 at number 99 on April 17, 1976. Fourteen weeks later it was number one, and seven weeks after that it became the second single to be certified platinum [see 432—"Disco Lady"].

Columbia waited 14 months to release the song. Just as it was turning platinum, Richard Taylor left the group to devote himself to the Muslim faith. The Manhattans carried on, hitting number five in July, 1980, with "Shining Star." They had a hit on the black and adult contemporary charts in March, 1985, with a cover version of Sam Cooke's "You Send Me" [see 30], but it failed to go higher than number 81 on the Hot 100.

## THE TOP FIVE
*Week of July 24, 1976*

1 **Kiss and Say Goodbye**
Manhattans

2 **Afternoon Delight**
Starland Vocal Band

3 **I'll Be Good To You**
Brothers Johnson

4 **Moonlight Feels Right**
Starbuck

5 **Love is Alive**
Gary Wright

## 440  Don't Go Breaking My Heart  ROCKET 40585
### ELTON JOHN AND KIKI DEE

*Writers: Ann Orson*
*Carte Blanche*

*Producer: Gus Dudgeon*

*August 7, 1976*
*4 weeks*

THOUGH he'd topped the American chart with ease five previous times, Elton John had never possessed a number one single in his own country until he teamed with a singer from Bradford, Yorkshire, England who had once been signed to Motown Records.

Kiki Dee (born Pauline Matthews on March 6, 1947) recorded one LP for Motown, *Great Expectations*, resulting in her debut chart single, "Love Makes the World Go Round" (number 87 in April, 1971). Her destiny didn't lie in Detroit, however. British Motown executive John Reid went on to manage Elton John and introduced the two singers to each other. Signed to Rocket Records, Kiki had her first hit with "I've Got the Music in Me" (number 12 in November, 1974). Her next two singles failed to go higher than number 70.

"Don't Go Breaking My Heart," penned by Elton and Bernie under assumed names, marked Elton's first appearance on his own Rocket label and entered the Hot 100 at number 66 on July 3, 1976. Five weeks later it was the sixth number one for Elton and the first for Kiki. A video was produced at the recording session, and later Elton traded in Ms. Dee for Miss Piggy for a performance of the song on "The Muppet Show." After,

he declared in *Rolling Stone*, "I've achieved all my childhood ambitions."

Having done so, he stunned the world by electing to retire and devote his time to soccer as president of the Watford Football Club. "I've toured for six years and I'm fed up with having no base and constantly roaming around," he told *Melody Maker*. His enormous popularity was also a deciding factor. "It's got so big for me it's getting stupid. I cannot switch it off and it's beginning to be a little bit of a bore." The announcement was made at the end of a massive 1976 tour.

Of course, the retirement was not permanent. In 1978 he released his first album without Taupin, with whom he'd amicably split upon retirement. The LP established his songwriting collaboration with Gary Osborne. Elton decided to break his three-year touring hiatus with "a few dates," ending up performing (with just Ray Cooper for accompaniment) more than 100 concerts in 14 countries. One was the Soviet Union, where the eight concerts were filmed and later shown on British television as "To Russia With Elton." In 1980

he assembled a full-fledged rock and roll conglomerate and set off on a 40-date tour of the United States to promote his final MCA album, *21 at 33*.

Elton was one of the first artists to sign with Geffen Records, joining in 1981. He reteamed with Bernie Taupin, but his first six singles for the label (including "Empty Garden (Hey Hey Johnny)," a tribute to John Lennon) missed the top 10. The tide turned with the third single from *Too Low for Zero*. "I Guess That's Why They Call It the Blues" peaked at number four in January, 1984. His next single, "Sad Songs (Say So Much)," the first release from the *Breaking Hearts* album, went to number five in August, giving Elton his first two consecutive top 10 singles since 1975.

He "retired" again, performing what he said was his last worldwide tour in 1984. The show at Wembley Stadium just outside London was captured for *Elton John—Night and Day: The Nighttime Concert* and released on home video. Sixteen years would pass before his name would once again be listed on the Hot 100 at number one [see 803].

---

### THE TOP FIVE
*Week of August 7, 1976*

1  **Don't Go Breaking My Heart**
   Elton John & Kiki Dee

2  **Love is Alive**
   Gary Wright

3  **Moonlight Feels Right**
   Starbuck

4  **Let 'Em In**
   Wings

5  **You Should Be Dancing**
   Bee Gees

*Writers: Barry Gibb*
    *Robin Gibb*
    *Maurice Gibb*

*Producers: Barry Gibb*
    *Robin Gibb*
    *Maurice Gibb*
    *Albhy Galuten*
    *Karl Richardson*

*September 4, 1976*
*1 week*

AFTER reviving their wilting career with their first number one single in four years [see 412—"Jive Talkin"], the Bee Gees proved their comeback was no fluke. A second single from *Main Course*, "Nights on Broadway," sailed to number seven in December, 1975. It marked the first significant use of falsetto, which combined with their new, funky style, resulted in a distinctive sound that prompted even the critics to take notice of a band they had written off. A third single from *Main Course*, the balladish "Fanny (Be Tender With My Love)," went to number 12 in March, 1976.

Riding high on the wide acceptance of *Main Course*, the Bee Gees prepared to record a follow-up album with the same producer, Arif Mardin. But their manager, Robert Stigwood, had shifted the distribution of his RSO label from Atlantic to Polydor. Mardin was a "house producer" at Atlantic and was not allowed to work with artists recording for another label. The Bee Gees were thunderstruck—Mardin had been their ticket out of obscurity, and now he

was lost to them.

The Gibbs turned to producer Richard Perry, who had crafted number one singles for Nilsson, Carly Simon and Ringo Starr. But it was not a match made in heaven, and two days later they parted company.

Rudderless, the brothers decided their best plan of attack would be to re-create the environment that produced *Main Course*. During the recording of that LP, the Bee Gees had been impressed with the work of two men at Criteria Studios. Albhy Galuten, who had studied at the Berkeley School of Music, had been brought in to assist on engineering chores by his old friend Karl Richardson, the engineer and co-producer of the sessions. Albhy's solid background in music and Karl's technical expertise had been vital to the commercial success of *Main Course*, so the Gibbs added them to their production team.

Without Mardin's genius, Albhy's schooling was critical in communicating with the musicians on the new album, *Children of the World*. The

Bee Gees had never been formally trained in music, so they relied on Galuten to be their liaison with the orchestra. "We were a little scared because we were used to working with Arif," Maurice Gibb said in the group's authorized biography, written by David Leaf. "Now I've got great respect for Albhy and Karl as well. The things Arif brought out in us, they have perfected . . . to a better point and improved it more. We never used to experiment before. Now we might do the harmonies in voices, double them in falsettos, all sorts of things to get a different tone. We're mad perfectionists, and Albhy and Karl are both perfectionists as well. I don't think there's anyone who can beat them yet."

If the Bee Gees were worried about their chart fortunes without Mardin at the helm, their fears subsided when "You Should Be Dancing" was released as the first single from *Children of the World*. It entered the Hot 100 at number 67 on July 3, 1976, and nine weeks later became the Bee Gees' third number one single.

## THE TOP FIVE
*Week of September 4, 1976*

1 **You Should Be Dancing**
Bee Gees

2 **You'll Never Find Another
Love Like Mine**
Lou Rawls

3 **Let 'Em In**
Wings

4 **I'd Really Love
to See You Tonight**
England Dan & John Ford Coley

5 **(Shake, Shake, Shake)
Shake Your Booty**
K.C. & The Sunshine Band

# 442 (Shake, Shake, Shake) Shake Your Booty T.K. 1019
## KC AND THE SUNSHINE BAND

*Writers: Harry Wayne Casey
    Richard Finch*

*Producers: Harry Wayne Casey
    Richard Finch*

*September 11, 1976
1 week*

THERE were some critics who dismissed "(Shake Shake Shake) Shake Your Booty" as a piece of disco fluff. "To some it was a nonsense song," says KC, "but it had a lot more meaning and depth. I think during that time, a lot of people were afraid to open up, they were afraid what this one sitting next to them was going to say, or what their neighbor was doing. I remember doing concerts and seeing the entire crowd having a good time, and you'd see one or two people sitting there playing Mr. Big. There were several connotations to 'Shake Your Booty.' It could mean to get off your can and get out there and do it, in every area, not necessarily dancing—in your whole life."

"(Shake Shake Shake) Shake Your Booty" stands alone as the number one single with the most *repeated* word in its title. No other number one song dared to repeat the same word four times.

The gimmick of repeating words in a title has been used by some artists more than others. Abba [see 458—"Dancing Queen"] are masters of the art, having released singles like "Money, Money, Money," "Honey, Honey," "On and On and On," "Gimme! Gimme! Gimme! (A Man After Midnight)" and the all-time repetitive champ, "I Do, I Do, I Do, I Do, I Do."

While "Shake Your Booty" remains the clear winner among number one songs, it is followed closely by six titles that repeat the same word three times:

"I Want You, I Need You, I Love You"
"Turn! Turn! Turn!"
"Too Much, Too Little, Too Late"
"Say, Say, Say"
"Bills, Bills, Bills"
"Bump, Bump, Bump"

Elvis gets a special award for repeating two words three times each in "I Want You, I Need You, I Love You." There are seven number one songs that repeat two words twice. These multiple offenders include:

"Na Na Hey Hey Kiss Him Goodbye"
"Give Me Love (Give Me Peace on Earth)"
"He Don't Love You (Like I Love You)"
"You Don't Have to Be a Star (To Be in My Show)"
"All Night Long (All Night)"
"Get Outta My Dreams, Get Into My Car"
"(Everything I Do) I Do It For You"

There are 25 number one songs that repeat one word twice. There are too many to list here, but a careful perusal will reveal they range from Perry Como's "Round and Round" to "Maria Maria," a 2000 hit by Santana featuring the Product G&B.

The fact that 46 out of 933 number one singles repeat words in their titles is not enough proof that doubling up your *bon mots* is a surefire way to get to number one. Just ask the Kingsmen, who spent six weeks at number two with "Louie Louie," or the Blendells, who only reached number 62 with "La La La La La."

## THE TOP FIVE
*Week of September 11, 1976*

1 **(Shake, Shake, Shake) Shake Your Booty**
K.C. & The Sunshine Band

2 **You'll Never Find Another Love Like Mine**
Lou Rawls

3 **Play That Funky Music**
Wild Cherry

4 **I'd Really Love to See You Tonight**
England Dan & John Ford Coley

5 **A Fifth of Beethoven**
Walter Murphy & the Big Apple Band

EPIC 50225 **Play That Funky Music**
WILD CHERRY
**443**

*Writer: Robert Parissi*

*Producer: Robert Parissi*

*September 18, 1976*
*3 weeks*

IF the name Wild Cherry sounds like it belongs on a box of cough drops rather than on a record label, there's a good reason. Group leader Bob Parissi was in a hospital bed, anxious to go home and work with the first incarnation of his band. They were visiting him in his hospital room, and on their way out someone mentioned the group didn't have a name yet. "The first thing I saw was a box of cough drops," Parissi revealed in a 1976 *Billboard* interview. He was just fooling around when he said they could name the band after the flavor of the cough drops, but the rest of the group took him seriously.

The group was signed to the Brown Bag label, owned by Terry Knight of Grand Funk [see 344— "We're an American Band"]. Group personnel changed and eventually the band disintegrated. Parissi gave up music to manage a couple of Bonanza steakhouses, but the music he heard on the radio encouraged him to try it again, and he organized a completely new Wild Cherry.

The 1976 version of Wild Cherry consisted of lead guitarist Bryan Bassett, keyboard player Mark Avsec, bassist Allen Wentz and drummer Ron Beitle. They wanted to play rock, but it was the disco era, and they found themselves booked into places like the 2001 disco in Pittsburgh, Pennsylvania. Attempts to play harder music were countered by requests from patrons to "play that funky music."

Backstage, Parissi discussed with his band how they were going to play rock music and make the disco fans happy. Beitle told him to follow the customers' orders—"play that funky music, white boy." Parissi grabbed a bar order pad and wrote down the words.

The song he came up with was not intended for an "A" side. Wild Cherry recorded a cover version of "I Feel Sanctified" by the Commodores [see 487—"Three Times a Lady"], and Parissi thought it would be a hit. But Carl Meduri, who was forming a new record label with his partner Mike Belkin, preferred "Play That Funky Music." When their label, Sweet City Records, signed a deal with Epic, "Play That Funky Music" was one of their first releases.

"We're an electric funk people's band," Parissi explained in *Billboard*.

"We're trying to do a white thing to R&B music, adding some heaviness to it."

"Play that Funky Music" was the third single to be certified platinum by the RIAA, following Johnnie Taylor's "Disco Lady" [see 432] and the Manhattans' "Kiss and Say Goodbye" [see 439]. Wild Cherry had four more chart singles on Epic before breaking up in February, 1979.

## THE TOP FIVE
*Week of September 18, 1976*

1 **Play That Funky Music**
Wild Cherry

2 **(Shake, Shake, Shake) Shake Your Booty**
K.C. & The Sunshine Band

3 **I'd Really Love to See You Tonight**
England Dan & John Ford Coley

4 **A Fifth of Beethoven**
Walter Murphy & the Big Apple Band

5 **You'll Never Find Another Love Like Mine**
Lou Rawls

# A Fifth of Beethoven PRIVATE STOCK 45073
## WALTER MURPHY & THE BIG APPLE BAND

*Writer: Walter Murphy*

*Producer: Walter Murphy*

*October 9, 1976*
*1 week*

**B**EFORE pianist Walter Murphy scored in 1976 with his disco-tinged instrumental chartbuster, "A Fifth of Beethoven," he was an obscure Madison Avenue jingle writer with a crazy dream. A former arranger for Doc Severinsen and "The Tonight Show" orchestra, Murphy wanted to fuse classical themes to contemporary rhythms in a way that would stand pop music on its head.

Growing up in Manhattan, the young, conservatory-trained composer had been bowled over by two earlier rock hits based on music by Johann Sebastian Bach: "A Lover's Concerto" by the Toys in 1965 and "Joy" by Apollo 100 in 1972. Murphy wanted to duplicate their top 10 suc-

cess by hooking the same concept around a pulsating disco beat.

The experiment, as Murphy called it, was to take a symphonic theme, diametrically opposed to the current pop sound, and make a hit record out of it. To test his theory, Murphy made a demo tape of several classical and neo-classical works, which he shipped to every record company in New York City.

The response was underwhelming. In fact, the only song that generated even the remotest interest amongst the various labels was a self-produced and arranged rendition of Ludwig van Beethoven's *Symphony No. 5 in C Minor*, originally composed in 1807. Finally, Larry Uttal at Private Stock Records gave Murphy the go-ahead to celebrate the German composer in full-blown disco fashion.

Even though Murphy played nearly every instrument on "A Fifth of Beethoven," his record company cautioned that the record would stand

a much better chance if it was credited to a group rather than an individual. To the performer's chagrin, they came up with the moniker "Walter Murphy & the Big Apple Band," only to discover two days after release there already was a Big Apple Band. The name on the label was changed to "The Walter Murphy Band" then simply "Walter Murphy."

Neither Murphy nor his record company were prepared for the immediate nationwide response to his odd and very catchy music. In fact, he was so excited when he first heard "A Fifth of Beethoven" played on his car radio, he nearly plowed into a tree. Or so the story goes...

The single entered the Hot 100 at number 80 on May 29, 1976, and took 19 weeks to reach the top. Murphy's next single, "Flight '76," was based on Rimsky-Korsakov's "Flight of the Bumble Bee," but it only landed at number 44. A discofied version of George Gershwin's "Rhapsody in Blue" didn't make the chart at all, proving Murphy had taken the concept as far as it could (or should) go. His last chart single was a medley of "Themes from E.T. (The Extra Terrestrial)," which went to number 47 in 1982.

There is a footnote to Murphy's amazing success with "A Fifth of Beethoven." Early in 1977, the producers of a low-budget disco film starring a popular television teen idol contracted to use Murphy's number one single on the soundtrack. The movie was *Saturday Night Fever*, the teen idol was John Travolta and the soundtrack LP sold more than 25 million copies.

## THE TOP FIVE
*Week of October 9, 1976*

1 **A Fifth of Beethoven**
Walter Murphy &
the Big Apple Band

2 **Play That Funky Music**
Wild Cherry

3 **Lowdown**
Boz Scaggs

4 **Disco Duck (Part 1)**
Rick Dees & His Cast of Idiots

5 **If You Leave Me Now**
Chicago

RSO 857 **Disco Duck (Part 1)** 445
RICK DEES AND HIS CAST OF IDIOTS

*Writer: Rick Dees*

*Producer: Bobby Manuel*

*October 16, 1976*
*1 week*

Many Artists with number one songs to their credit have been employed in radio, but Rick Dees managed to top the Hot 100 while he was a full-time working disc jockey. Today, he handles morning drive on KIIS-FM in Los Angeles and hosts a nationally syndicated radio countdown show, "The Weekly Top 40." Back in the days of "Disco Duck," he was the morning DJ at WMPS in Memphis.

"I was working out in a gym in Memphis when disco was coming out, and I also worked in a club called Chesterfield's telling jokes and spinning records," says Dees. "The more I played the songs, the more I knew it might be time for a disco parody. One of the guys who worked out in the gym did a great duck voice, and I remembered a song called 'The Duck' (by Jackie Lee) back in the '60s, so I said, how about a 'Disco Duck'?

"I had mice in my apartment at the time, and I went home and put my feet up on the chair, because nobody likes to have their feet dangling down if there might be a mouse

nearby, and I wrote that song. It took me one afternoon. We went into the studio three months later—that's how long it took me to convince people to do the song."

Dees recorded his tune for Fretone Records, a local Memphis label owned by Estelle Axton, one of the founders of Stax Records. Dees had already released a single on Fretone, "The National Wet-Off," that had sunk without a trace. But "Disco Duck" really got down—starting in Birmingham, Alabama. As it spread throughout the South, Dees flew to Hollywood to sell the record to a major label.

"We talked to everybody in the business, and everybody passed on the song, except Al Coury (president of RSO Records). He said, 'Let me take it home and play it for my kids.'" They laughed at the song and Coury leased it for $3,500.

The record became a national hit, played everywhere except for Memphis. Rival stations wouldn't play it, for fear of promoting their competition. And Dees was forbidden to play the record on his own station. "I talked about it on my morning radio show, and the station manager came in and said, 'We think that's a conflict of interest. You're fired!'" Dees wasn't out of work long—he was hired by the station's prime com-

petitor, WHBQ-AM, owned by the RKO radio chain. In the spring of 1979, Dees was transferred to RKO's station in Los Angeles, KHJ. He remained there until the station switched to a country format, then was hired by KIIS. Aided by his wife Julie McWhirter Dees and a new cast of idiots, Dees is one of Southern California's most popular morning DJs.

Looking back on the national success of "Disco Duck," Dees says he was not surprised at how well the record sold. "I didn't know anything about the record business. I just thought you put out a song and it becomes a hit. Because of my being naive at the time, I thought it was gonna be a smash. Knowing what I know today, it's so hard to become number one. It takes a lot of luck and a lot of praying and a lot of good promotion people, plus a good song. I had no idea all those elements had to work in concert."

The follow-up to "Disco Duck" was inspired by the release of Dino DeLaurentis' re-make of *King Kong*, starring Jessica Lange. "Dis-Gorilla" went to number 56. A satire of Barry White [see 376—"Can't Get Enough of Your Love, Babe"], "Barely White," missed the Hot 100 but was popular in southern California. At the end of 1984, Dees returned to the chart with a single on Atlantic Records, "Get Nekked."

Born Rigdon Osmond Dees III in Memphis, the popular disc jockey hosted one season of the weekly television series "Solid Gold" and from July, 1990 to July, 1991 was host of ABC's late-night series "Into the Night."

---

## THE TOP FIVE
*Week of October 16, 1976*

1 **Disco Duck (Part 1)**
Rick Dees & His Cast of Idiots

2 **A Fifth of Beethoven**
Walter Murphy &
the Big Apple Band

3 **Lowdown**
Boz Scaggs

4 **If You Leave Me Now**
Chicago

5 **Play That Funky Music**
Wild Cherry

# 446 If You Leave Me Now COLUMBIA 10390
## CHICAGO

*Writer: Peter Cetera*

*Producer: James William Guercio*

*October 23, 1976*
*2 weeks*

CHICAGO, the metropolis, may be the "second city," but Chicago, the musical aggregation, has long reigned as America's premier jazz-rock ensemble. The group was first formed in 1967 as the Missing Links, an outfit that sported sharkskin suits and greasy pompadour hair-dos. Dropping that image, they called themselves the Big Thing and then the Chicago Transit Authority, a name they were forced to shorten when Mayor Richard Daley initiated a lawsuit. In their new identity, they were mining much the same territory as Blood, Sweat and Tears ("You've Made Me So Very Happy," "Spinning Wheel").

From the beginning, however, the band disputed the comparison. "Our roots are basically rock," singer-keyboardist Bobby Lamm pointed out in a *Down Beat* interview, "but we can and do play jazz. Blood, Sweat and Tears is basically a jazz-oriented combo that can play a lot of rock."

Living up to their name, all but Lamm hailed from the Windy City, and he moved there as a teenager. "We were friends before any of this (success) started happening," woodwind player Walter Parazaider told the New York *Post* in 1977. "Personally and musically, we're a family," Lamm said.

And just as tight. Throughout the years, Chicago had few personnel changes, with a rhythm section made up of Lamm, Peter Cetera on bass, Dan Seraphine on drums and Terry Kath on guitar, augmented by a horn trio of Parazaider on reeds, James Pankow on trombone and Lee Loughnane on trumpet. In 1974, they were joined by Brazilian percussionist Laudir Oliviera, and in 1978, Donnie Dacus became their lead guitarist after Kath died of an accidental self-inflicted gunshot wound.

The group's big break came when James William Guercio, a college friend who had moved to Los Angeles, became their manager and producer. Guercio was then influential at Columbia Records through his production work with the Buckinghams [see 217—"Kind of a Drag"]

and Blood, Sweat and Tears. He moved the members of Chicago Transit Authority to Los Angeles, paid their rent and found them work.

As the house band at the Whisky-a-Go-Go, they gained a strong local following and, with Guercio's help, signed with Columbia in 1969. They soared to superstardom by sticking to a well-honed formula of jazz-rock songs, funky licks and impeccable musicianship.

Although this combination proved unbeatable, Chicago never became the darlings of rock or jazz critics. In fact, the band was often villified as "purveyors of pap" and the "Mantovanis of rock." But Chicago looked the other way and kept a steady string of albums bouncing up the charts, all identified merely by Roman numerals.

"Our albums are simply documents of where we were playing at the time of their recording, nothing more," Lamm told Michael Ross of *Rock* "So any upward movement, any gains that have been made since the

first album, are purely unintentional. The music just happened that way."

For an album-oriented band, Chicago did not shrug off the singles market. Between 1970-1975 they scored 10 top 10 singles, including "25 or 6 to 4" (number four), "Saturday in the Park" (number three), "Just You 'N' Me" (number four) and "Old Days" (number five). Their *Chicago X* album provided their biggest single yet, "If You Leave Me Now," a beautiful, romantic ballad written by Cetera. It debuted on the Hot 100 at number 60 on August 14, 1976, and moved to the top of the chart 10 weeks later.

What is the secret to Chicago's long-term appeal? "Chicago is the most successful experiment in group therapy ever to go down in history," said Lamm in *Down Beat*. "There have been times when each of us wanted to walk away….(But) if somebody is obviously egoing out, there's six of us to deal with and we'll get together and give him a knuckle sandwich."

### THE TOP FIVE
*Week of October 23, 1976*

1 **If You Leave Me Now**
Chicago

2 **Disco Duck (Part 1)**
Rick Dees & His Cast of Idiots

3 **A Fifth of Beethoven**
Walter Murphy &
the Big Apple Band

4 **Lowdown**
Boz Scaggs

5 **Still the One**
Orleans

CAPITOL 4323 **Rock 'n Me** **447**
STEVE MILLER BAND

*Writer: Steve Miller*

*Producer: Steve Miller*

*November 6, 1976*
*1 week*

EVEN though he had the number one single in America [see 353—"The Joker"], Steve Miller still wasn't happy. With his personal and business life in shambles, something snapped. In a fit of rage, he threw all of his girlfriend's clothes into the fireplace. It was time, he would realize, to take a sabbatical.

Miller moved to a remote area near Medford, Oregon, and built himself a farm. The man once known as "the space cowboy" had become a reclusive plowboy. "It took me a year just to get back to my music," he told *Music Express*. Then, one day in 1976, he telephoned bassist Lonnie Turner and drummer Gary Mallaber and told them he was ready to record.

"So we went in and cut 22 tunes," he said. "We worked on them for a couple of weeks and came out with two albums." The sessions had gone so well because Miller knew exactly what he wanted the music to sound like. "It had to have some hot rock and roll, some heavy music, some light music, a lot of different textures."

Released in May, 1976, *Fly Like an Eagle* would yield three hit singles. The first, "Take the Money and Run," reached number 11 in July, 1976. "Rock 'n Me," the second single, was originally a throwaway tune composed for an isolated appearance at a British pop festival. Its catchy

## THE TOP FIVE
*Week of November 6, 1976*

1 **Rock 'n Me**
   Steve Miller Band

2 **Disco Duck (Part 1)**
   Rick Dees & His Cast of Idiots

3 **The Wreck of the
   Edmund Fitzgerald**
   Gordon Lightfoot

4 **If You Leave Me Now**
   Chicago

5 **Love So Right**
   Bee Gees

opening paid tribute to the late Paul Kossoff's intro to the classic Free single, "All Right Now."

"Yeah, it's a tack on the wall for Paul," Miller acknowledged. "I did one concert in the two years I was off the road. I went to London and played with Pink Floyd....It was a big, huge outdoor show so we needed a big rock and roll number that was really going to excite everybody. I just put it together and didn't think much about it, but they loved it. It knocked them out so we recorded it."

Whatever its genesis, "Rock 'n Me" was an immediate audience grabber. It didn't do too badly on the Hot 100 either, entering the chart at number 85 on August 14, 1976, and becoming Miller's second number one single 12 weeks later. The title track from the LP did almost as well. "Fly Like an Eagle" soared to number two for two weeks in March, 1977.

*Fly Like an Eagle* was the 33-year-old Miller's second solo production credit, and though he claims to be his own toughest critic, he admitted enjoying the triple challenge of being writer, musician and producer. As he told one interviewer in 1982, "My situation is similar to that of George Bernard Shaw when he describes this great hat stand next to his desk which has nine different hats: one for gardening, one for going to the cricket matches, etc. Next to my desk I've got five hats: one of them is the producer's hat, one of them is the stage show producer, one is songwriter, one is Steve Miller the guitar player and another one is the editor, the guy with the eraser....And since I'm such a harsh critic, I feel that I have a closer bond with my audience. They know if they buy my records, the quality will be high."

# 448 Tonight's the Night (Gonna Be Alright) WARNER BROTHERS 8262
## ROD STEWART

*Writer: Rod Stewart*

*Producer: Tom Dowd*

*November 13, 1976*
*8 weeks*

"WE PUT down 15 backing tracks at Cherokee Studios in Los Angeles and then got around to my singing. I couldn't sing. I just couldn't hit a note. The reason, if you ask me, is the smog. . . . So I went to Caribou Studios (in Colorado) to put down the vocals. Nice place, but I couldn't sing there either. At 9,000 feet above sea level, you're lucky if you can walk and still breathe," Rod Stewart told Cameron Crowe in *Rolling Stone*, giving an advance verbal peek at his album in progress, *A Night on the Town*. Rod and band subsequently migrated to Criteria Studios in Miami, home base of producer Tom Dowd, where, the singer assured Crowe, "We're really blazing now. This album is going to be great. Wait and see."

The seer in Stewart's Scottish background didn't let him down. Buoyed by not one but three hit singles, *A Night on the Town* turned platinum quickly, but the million sales didn't come without controversy. "Tonight's the Night (Gonna Be Alright)," which critic Greil Marcus admitted in the Paul Nelson-Lester Bangs biography *Rod Stewart*, is "a seduction song so transparent, helpless and forthright that not even a cynic can resist it," was much too diaphanous for top 40 radio. Citing the lyric, "Spread your wings and let

## THE TOP FIVE

*Week of November 13, 1976*

1  **Tonight's the Night (Gonna Be Alright)**
   Rod Stewart

2  **Disco Duck (Part 1)**
   Rick Dees & His Cast of Idiots

3  **The Wreck of the Edmund Fitzgerald**
   Gordon Lightfoot

4  **Love So Right**
   Bee Gees

5  **Muskrat Love**
   Captain & Tennille

me come inside" as too sexually explicit, program directors refused the song air time until their more liberated public demanded to hear it. If that wasn't enough uproar for one LP, the third single, "The Killing of Georgie," sensitively described the murder of a young homosexual, arousing mixed emotions from both gay and straight communities. Only "The First Cut is the Deepest," the second single from the album, proceeded up the chart without provoking anyone.

But then Rod Stewart had conducted his five years between chart-toppers [see 300—"Maggie May" / "Reason to Believe"] in a steady stream of contention. He was lead singer of the Faces but maintained a more successful solo career at the same time. The dual identity manifested itself in concert, where fans considered the conglomerate, which happened to contain some fairly sizeable egos on its own (Ronnie Lane, Ron Wood, Kenny Jones, Ian McLagan), just Rod's background band. The two sides of Rod were even more apparent when it came to vinyl, where he was signed to Warner Brothers as part of the Faces

and Mercury as a solo artist through 1974 (the companies had a legal wrangle over who owned the artist during his *Smiler* period). His dual artist status led to Stewart being accused of hoarding his best material for his solo discs, although Wood clarifies in *Rod Stewart*, "Songs written with him were with the Faces in mind *or* Rod in mind. We never used to scheme and say, 'Oh, we'll save this one.' " Nonetheless, the dissension first forced Ronnie Lane to defect in 1973, then put an end to the group for good in 1976.

A partial cause of the split was Rod's emigration from mother England to Los Angeles, a fact that endeared him to neither the tax man nor an up-and-coming generation of punk rockers. This particularly irked Stewart, who slammed back at the carpers in *Rolling Stone*. "They say, 'Well, Rod's gone to Hollywood with a movie star,' right? I come from the same background they do. In England all rock and roll comes from the working class. That's your only way of getting out of the rabble. I come from nothing. Then, all of a sudden I'm faced with a lot of glamorous women. What am I going to do?"

ABC 12208 **You Don't Have to Be a Star (To Be in My Show)** `449`

### MARILYN McCOO and BILLY DAVIS, JR.

*Writers: James Dean*
*John Glover*

*Producer: Don Davis*

*January 8, 1977*
*1 week*

In November of 1975, the husband-and-wife team of Marilyn McCoo and Billy Davis, Jr., took a step they had been thinking about for several years—they left the successful group they had been part of, the Fifth Dimension [see 261—"Wedding Bell Blues"], for solo careers. It was a decision they were able to make after taking the est training. ". . . through est I was able to strip away most of my negative feelings about myself and understand how I used them to keep me down or safe or inactive," McCoo told Alan Ebert in *Essence* magazine. "I began to understand *me*—that I was unique and not part of a mold and that I had every right to seek my own fulfillment. That freed me to do what I really wanted—to leave the group. Like Billy, I wanted to try new things."

Billy had his own reasons for leaving: "Singing background parts is fun, and an occasional solo is fine, but I have certain goals for myself that I cannot expect three or four other members to have for themselves. I also feel that I haven't had the chance to touch half the talent I've got."

The original intention was for Marilyn and Billy to have separate, solo careers. Otis Smith of ABC Records arranged for Marilyn to fly to Detroit and meet producer Don Davis, who had done important work at both Motown and Stax Records. Davis, who produced a number one single for Johnnie Taylor [see 432—"Disco Lady"], had recorded a half-dozen solo tracks with Marilyn when Billy decided their first project should be an album of duets.

Davis had a demo from songwriters James Dean and John Glover that he thought would be perfect for Marilyn and Billy. It wasn't written as a duet, but it was quickly re-arranged for the two of them to sing. "It's one of the few songs in my career where I tried to emulate the Motown sound," Davis admits. "So I made sure I got the session musicians I needed, like James Jamerson. I knew there was no way I wanted to

do this record without him."

Another priority was to produce a song that sounded contemporary. "I wanted to get away from any resemblance to the Fifth Dimension sound," Davis says. "I thought the Fifth Dimension had a great sound, but they needed something new and fresh." The record broke on black radio before it crossed over to pop, and although it was number one on the Hot 100, it won a Grammy in the category of Best R&B Vocal Performance by a Duo, Group or Chorus.

"You Don't Have to Be a Star" was the second McCoo and Davis single. The title track of their first album, "I Hope We Get to Love on Time," was released first, but only went to number 91. After "You Don't Have to Be a Star," the duo took "Your Love" to number 15. They only had one more chart single together, "Look What You've Done to My Heart," which peaked at 51.

Their success on the pop charts led to a summer variety series on CBS, "The Marilyn McCoo and Billy Davis, Jr. Show." It ran for six weeks, beginning June 15, 1977. Marilyn hosted the second season of the television series "Solid Gold," and signed to RCA as a solo artist. She released several singles, including a duet with Billy, but none of them charted.

## THE TOP FIVE
*Week of January 8, 1977*

1 **You Don't Have to be a Star (To Be in my Show)**
Marilyn McCoo & Billy Davis, Jr.

2 **You Make Me Feel Like Dancing**
Leo Sayer

3 **Tonight's the Night (Gonna Be Alright)**
Rod Stewart

4 **I Wish**
Stevie Wonder

5 **Car Wash**
Rose Royce

## 450 You Make Me Feel Like Dancing WARNER BROTHERS 8283
### LEO SAYER

*Writers: Leo Sayer*
*Vini Poncia*

*Producer: Richard Perry*

*January 15, 1977*
*1 week*

WHEN Leo Sayer first began working with producer Richard Perry, they spent some time rehearsing in the studio. "I just started singing that line, 'You got a cute way of talking,' and Richard immediately ran to the recorder, pushed the button and said, 'Look, let's take it,'" Sayer told Ben Fong-Torres of *Rolling Stone*. "Two months later I came back to Los Angeles and he played me back some stuff and said, 'That's number one!' I didn't even remember it."

Perry, who had already produced chart-toppers for Nilsson [see 307—"Without You"] and Carly Simon [see 326—"You're So Vain"], described "You Make Me Feel Like Dancing" for Fong-Torres: "It's full of syncopation, more like (Betty Wright's) "Clean Up Woman" (than disco). I hate disco music."

Sayer first gained recognition in America as a lyricist with a song he had taken to number two on the British chart. "The Show Must Go On," covered by Three Dog Night [see 277—"Mama Told Me (Not to Come)"], was a number four hit in the States in May, 1974. Sayer had been involved in the English music scene for several years prior to the release of his first hit. Born Gerard

Hugh Sayer on May 21, 1948, in Shoreham-by-the-Sea, England, he experienced a short career as a commercial artist, a nervous breakdown, a stint as a London street busker and being a substitute for singers who fell ill while performing in soul bands on United States Army bases.

His first band, while still in art college, was Terraplane Blues. In London he sang and played harmonica for a group called Patches. Influenced by Bob Dylan and blues artists Sonny Terry and Brownie McGhee, Sayer was more comfortable as a lyricist than a performer. In 1970, Patches entered a local contest, auditioning for Dave Courtney, former drummer for British singer Adam Faith ("It's Alright"). Courtney was impressed enough with Sayer to become his songwriting partner, creating melodies for his lyrics.

Courtney convinced Adam Faith to try his hand at artists' management and Sayer became his first client. Faith's wife thought Sayer looked like a little lion, prompting a

change of first names from Gerard to Leo.

Sayer recorded his first album at the studio owned by Roger Daltrey of the Who. Daltrey kept dropping in to listen to Sayer and Courtney's songs, then sat in on a couple of sessions and engineered part of the album. Daltrey was about to record his first solo album and asked Sayer if he had written any material that would be appropriate. The LP, produced by Courtney and Faith, had nine out of 11 cuts written by Courtney and Sayer.

After Sayer completed his autobiographical *Silverbird* album in 1973, he toured with Roxy Music to promote the LP and the single, "The Show Must Go On." His gimmick was appearing in a sad-faced clown costume and make-up inspired by the French film *Children of Paradise*. Critical reaction was favorable, but the image was not received well in America. He abandoned it for the next album, *Just a Boy*, which yielded his first American hit; "Long Tall Glasses (I Can Dance)" peaked at number nine in May, 1975. The third album, *Another Year*, was more somber, and Sayer told *Newsweek* in 1977 that the journals he wrote after his nervous breakdown provided the material for his first three albums.

Album number four, *Endless Flight*, was a departure in many ways. Recorded at Studio 55 in Los Angeles under the guidance of Perry, Sayer felt comfortable enough to break away from his own material for the first time. The title cut was written by Andrew Gold, and a cover version of Diana Ross and the Supremes' "Reflections" was featured (a cover of the Miracles' "The Tears of a Clown" was recorded but not included on the album). Sayer teamed up with new writing partners, including Barry Mann [see 166—"You've Lost That Lovin' Feelin'"] on "How Much Love" and Vini Poncia ("Do I Love You" by the Ronettes) on his number one single, "You Make Me Feel Like Dancing." One of the most important songs on the album was written by Albert Hammond and Carole Bayer Sager, and it would be released as the follow-up to "You Make Me Feel Like Dancing" [see 463—"When I Need You"].

## THE TOP FIVE
*Week of January 15, 1977*

1 **You Make Me Feel Like Dancing**
Leo Sayer

2 **I Wish**
Stevie Wonder

3 **Car Wash**
Rose Royce

4 **You Don't Have to be a Star (To Be in my Show)**
Marilyn McCoo & Billy Davis, Jr.

5 **Dazz**
Brick

Writer: Stevie Wonder

Producer: Stevie Wonder

January 22, 1977
1 week

BY THE SUMMER of 1976, the biggest guessing game in the record industry was trying to figure out the release date of Stevie Wonder's next album. Promised dates had come and gone, but Motown did not have an LP to deliver to stores. When August rolled around, it had been two years since the release of Stevie's *Fulfillingness' First Finale*, and some people were beginning to doubt if there would ever be an album. Just to assure everyone, Stevie took to wearing a T-shirt that announced, "We're almost finished!"

Anticipation for the project was so high, that when *Songs in the Key of Life* was finally released, it became only the third album in the history of *Billboard's* album chart to debut at number one (Elton John's *Captain Fantastic and the Brown Dirt Cowboy* and *Rock of the Westies* were the first two).

Stevie wrote on the lyric sheet, "Thank you everyone for being so patient!!" It was worth the wait. The double-album set was Wonder's finest, most mature work yet. "I'm sorry it took so long for *Songs* but then I'm not sorry because that's what I wanted to give you. The best I possibly can. And I did the best I can do," Stevie told a 1977 symposium at UCLA, sponsored by *Billboard*. "For *Songs* I wanted to come up with a title that would communicate what I wanted to do. It covers as much as I could vocally and what I wanted it to be."

The first single from the long-awaited album was "I Wish," the chronicle of a man's younger days when he was "a nasty little boy." "We were going to write some really crazy words for the song 'I Wish,'" Stevie revealed to David Breskin in *Musician.* "Something about 'The Wheel of '84.' A lot of cosmic type stuff, spiritual stuff. But I couldn't do that 'cause the music was too much fun—the words didn't have the *fun* of the track.

"The day I wrote it was a Saturday, the day of a Motown picnic in the summer of '76. God, I remember that 'cause I was having this really bad toothache. It was ridiculous. I had such a good time at the picnic that I went to Crystal Recording Studio right afterward and the vibe came

right to my mind: running at the picnic, the contests, we all participated. It was a lot of fun. . . . And from that came the 'I Wish' vibe. And I started talking to Gary (Olazabal) and we were talking about spiritual movements. 'The Wheel of '84,' and when you go off to war and all that stuff. It was ridiculous. Couldn't come up with anything stronger than the chorus, 'I wish those days (claps) would (claps) come back once more.' Thank goodness we didn't change that."

"I Wish" was the highest new entry on the Hot 100 for the week ending December 4, 1976, debuting at number 40. Seven weeks later it was the fifth Stevie Wonder single to go to number one.

*Songs in the Key of Life* was the first album released under Stevie's new contract, renegotiated by lawyer Johanan Vigoda with Motown in 1975. At the time, it was the most generous contract any artist had ever received, guaranteeing an income of $13 million over seven years, a royalty cut on record sales of more than 20 per cent and the freedom to choose which tracks from an LP would be released as singles. "I didn't feel that I was being greedy," Stevie has said. "It really is not important to me as much as it is important to me for my children, family and loved ones. I want them to be taken care of and to be well off."

And the public reaction? Well, any man who could produce a work like *Songs in the Key of Life* was entitled to anything he wanted, as far as the people were concerned.

## THE TOP FIVE
*Week of January 22, 1977*

1   **I Wish**
    Stevie Wonder

2   **Car Wash**
    Rose Royce

3   **You Make Me Feel Like Dancing**
    Leo Sayer

4   **Dazz**
    Brick

5   **You Don't Have to be a Star (To Be in my Show)**
    Marilyn McCoo &
    Billy Davis, Jr.

## 452 Car Wash MCA 40615
### ROSE ROYCE

*Writer: Norman Whitfield*

*Producer: Norman Whitfield*

*January 29, 1977*
*1 week*

"CAR WASH," the theme song from the movie of the same title, begins much the way a car starts out on its way to getting cleaned. First, there's the percussion, only the handclaps and drums. Then comes the bass and guitar, just as the brushes are working over the body. And as the car has been pulleyed along to the rinse stage, where the last bits of foam and grime are wiped from the surface, the instruments have moved into a crescendo of funky sound that gets and keeps you dancing.

"I tried to fit the mood of the music with the thing that was happening on the screen at the time," says Norman Whitfield, who wrote and produced the *Car Wash* soundtrack. "In one scene, for instance, you've got the owner's son trying to fit in with the rest of the men working on the line—only they're there out of necessity, not by choice, like him.

"Then, at another place, you've got the tension created when one of the guys tries to talk another out of holding the place up. And all the time the music has got to fit the mood."

New York-born Whitfield, long one of Motown's masterminds, composed five of the label's number one singles before moving on to create his own label. He co-wrote and produced Marvin Gaye's "I Heard It Through the Grapevine" [see 249] and Edwin Starr's "War" [see 280]. He began working with the Temptations in the mid-'60s, first assembling landmark records like "Ain't Too Proud to Beg" and "I Wish It Would Rain," then guiding them to a grittier, psychedelic-soul sound, heavily influenced by Sly and the Family Stone. His efforts paid off in three chart-toppers for the Temptations: "I Can't Get Next to You" [see 259], "Just My Imagination (Running Away With Me)" [see 290] and "Papa Was a Rolling Stone" [see 323].

In the early '70s, Whitfield put together eight male musicians as a recording and touring unit to back up the Temptations. On horns were Michael Moore, Freddie Dunn and Kenny "Captain Cold" Copeland. Kenji Chiba Brown was lead guitarist and Lequeint "Duke" Jobe played bass, with Mike Nash on keyboards, Terral "Powerpack" Santiel on percussion and Henry "Hammer" Garner on drums. Whitfield titled the ensemble Rose Royce and soon added a powerful female singer, Gwen Dickey, to handle lead vocals.

When he was hired to score *Car Wash*, Whitfield tabbed the new group to perform on the soundtrack, along with the Pointer Sisters. Featuring non-stop disco/funk music, the 1976 comedy captured a day in the life of a Los Angeles car wash, following the men who worked there and their eccentric customers.

"Car Wash" entered the Hot 100 at number 86 on October 23, 1976, and arrived at number one 14 weeks later. Rose Royce's next two singles were also from the film. "I Wanna Get Next to You" peaked at 10 and "I'm Going Down" did, right after it reached number 70. Their next three chart singles appeared on the Whitfield label, distributed by Warner Brothers. Their final chart entry, "Love Don't Live Here Anymore" (number 32 in February, 1979) has been covered often, most recently by Madonna [see 600—"Like a Virgin"].

## THE TOP FIVE
*Week of January 29, 1977*

1  **Car Wash**
   Rose Royce

2  **I Wish**
   Stevie Wonder

3  **Dazz**
   Brick

4  **You Make Me Feel
   Like Dancing**
   Leo Sayer

5  **Hot Line**
   Sylvers

ARIOLA AMERICA 7638  **Torn Between Two Lovers**
MARY MACGREGOR

**453**

*Writers: Phil Jarrell*
*Peter Yarrow*

*Producers: Peter Yarrow*
*Bary Beckett*

*February 5, 1977*
*2 weeks*

**M**ARY MACGREGOR always hated her number one single, "Torn Between Two Lovers," and still does to this day. "I think it's a real implausible situation," she explains. "A lady who wants to have her cake and eat it too. At the time I recorded the song, I was married and people thought I'd written it and wanted to know if *I* was 'torn.' It was real aggravating for me, although the success that it had was definitely not."

Actually, "Torn Between Two Lovers" was co-written by Phil Jarrell and Peter Yarrow of Peter, Paul and Mary [see 264—"Leaving on a Jet Plane"]. "It's very hard to know what inspired us to write it," says Yarrow. "It may have been a discussion which I had with my wife, who said she was very much moved by the dilemma in the novel *Dr. Zhivago* of a man loving two women at the same time. Originally it was written from the male perspective."

"Peter Yarrow thought it was a real good song for a woman to sing," she recalls. "But after we recorded it, he still wasn't sure what he was going to do with it. He talked about playing it for Anne Murray or Olivia Newton-John, people who were really happening then."

Instead, Yarrow brought the record to Jay Lasker, then head of the new Ariola America label, with Mary

as part of the package. "Jay immediately knew it was a big hit," says Yarrow. "I made a deal with him, for which I would've received nothing—except the cost of making the record—if it hadn't been a hit." In fact, the record's success was so unexpected that MacGregor didn't even have a deal with Ariola when it was released.

Although Mary can't stand the song, she acknowledges its universal appeal. "A lot of people are torn between two lovers," she says, "or have been, or will be." According to Yarrow, "I think the song got a lot of people angry or hit them in the heart. It was a contemporary statement."

"Torn Between Two Lovers" entered the Hot 100 at number 87 on November 20, 1976. When it reached number one 11 weeks later, it was the first chart-topper for Ariola America.

Her number one record had traumatic effects as well. Mary had been happily married for five years and had no intention of ever being unfaithful to her husband. But the

record's appeal soon put a devastating crimp in their relationship. "We were living on a ranch in Colorado," she recalls, "and my career didn't take up that much of my time. I was on the road for a couple of months out of the year. And maybe every other month, I would fly to Chicago or Nashville or Minneapolis to do a couple commercials, and be gone for a week. But when 'Torn Between Two Lovers' happened, it was like getting on an already fast-moving train. My life changed drastically, and my ex-husband just couldn't deal with it. I was gone a lot. It was just hard on both of us and we separated for a couple of years. During that time, I moved to L.A. and we eventually divorced."

Living on her central California ranch where she raises horses and writes songs, Mary looked back at her moment in the pop spotlight. She says the song ultimately proved to be a strain—"not because I was sleeping with someone else, but because I was living with my career instead of with him. But those things happen."

### THE TOP FIVE
*Week of February 5, 1977*

1 **Torn Between Two Lovers**
Mary MacGregor

2 **Car Wash**
Rose Royce

3 **Dazz**
Brick

4 **New Kid in Town**
Eagles

5 **Hot Line**
Sylvers

# 454 Blinded by the Light WARNER BROTHERS 8252
## MANFRED MANN'S EARTH BAND

*Writer: Bruce Springsteen*

*Producers: Manfred Mann and the Earth Band*

*February 19, 1977*
*1 week*

"BLINDED BY THE LIGHT" originally appeared on *Greetings from Asbury Park*, Bruce Springsteen's debut album for Columbia Records. It almost wasn't included on the LP, however. Not pleased with the first version of the album, label executives asked Springsteen to record a couple of songs which could be released as singles. "Blinded by the Light" was added, but since many of his band members had left town, Springsteen played most of the instruments on the track himself. "Spirit in the Night" was recorded at the same time.

Columbia was hoping for another Bob Dylan in Springsteen, and Peter Knobler's review in *Crawdaddy* helped. Knobler favorably compared "Blinded by the Light" with Dylan's "Like a Rolling Stone." Unfortunately, the single release of "Blinded by the Light," backed with

another song from the album called "The Angel," was a failure. Springsteen admired Dylan, but the comparisons didn't please him. He wanted to be a rock and roller rather than a folk poet. "Blinded by the Light," which Bruce no longer performs in concert, is typical of his early, rambling, more dramatic style which he later replaced with the more straightforward dramatically narrative songs which became hits for him.

There's some irony in Manfred Mann's success with the song. The original lead singer of Manfred Mann, Paul Jones, had a strong influence on Springsteen's style. Bruce even performed the old Manfred Mann song "Pretty Flamingo" at concerts, preceding it with a story about a girl he admired but never had the nerve to speak to. There are certain similarities between Jones' higher pitched voice and early Springsteen numbers like "Blinded by the Light." Later on, Springsteen dropped this smooth style for a rougher, more natural one.

Keyboard player Manfred Mann's biggest hits had been cover versions of American songs, like Jeff Barry

and Ellie Greenwich's "Do Wah Diddy Diddy" [see 158] and Bob Dylan's "The Mighty Quinn (Quinn the Eskimo)." But there were some lean years between hits. In 1969 Mann decided he wasn't interested in pop music anymore and formed a jazz-oriented group with the backward name Emanon. They evolved into Manfred Mann Chapter III, a group that recorded two unsuccessful albums. Thinking that pop music was the answer after all, Mann teamed up with singer/guitarist Mick Rogers, bassist Colin Pattenden and drummer Chris Slade to form Manfred Mann's Earth Band in 1971.

"Blinded by the Light" was their third chart single, following Randy Newman's "Living Without You" and Springsteen's "Spirit in the Night." Debuting on the Hot 100 at number 95 on November 20, 1976, "Blinded by the Light" took 13 weeks to reach the top. By the time it was a hit, two new guitarists—Chris Thompson and Dave Flett—had replaced Rogers. The Earth Band charted with two follow-ups, a re-release of "Spirit in the Night" (number 40 in June, 1977) and a cover version of Bob Dylan's "You Angel You" (number 58 in July, 1979).

**THE TOP FIVE**
*Week of February 19, 1977*

1  **Blinded by the Light**
   Manfred Mann's Earth Band

2  **New Kid in Town**
   Eagles

3  **Torn Between Two Lovers**
   Mary MacGregor

4  **Love Theme from "A Star Is Born" (Evergreen)**
   Barbra Streisand

5  **I Like Dreamin'**
   Kenny Nolan

ASYLUM 45373 **New Kid in Town**
EAGLES

**455**

*Writers: John David Souther*
*Don Henley*
*Glenn Frey*

*Producer: Bill Szymczyk*

*February 26, 1977*
*1 week*

"NEW KID IN TOWN" was the Eagles' first gold 45 as well as the initial release from their watershed *Hotel California* album. Entering the Hot 100 at number 48 on December 18, 1976, the single became the group's third chart-topper 10 weeks later.

Even the band's critics, and they included many of the music community's most influential writers, acknowledge *Hotel California* as the Eagles' finest work. Dave Marsh, in *The New Rolling Stone Record Guide*, wrote, "This is not to deny them their occasional moments of inspiration and insight (especially on *Hotel California*)," while *Village Voice* editor Robert Christgau conceded "this is their most substantial if not their most enjoyable LP" in his *Record Guide.*

Why did the rock press often exude contempt for the band? Kit Rachlis explained in the *Boston Phoenix.* "I dislike the Eagles with the same adolescent fervor that I reserved for the BMOC in my prep school and for many of the same rea-

sons: fear, politics, style, envy. If the Eagles weren't good at what they did—if they weren't so successful that they've come to epitomize southern California rock—they wouldn't be worth disliking so much. Which is part of their problem, because a band that arouses this much vitriol must be worth something."

Chief among the writers' complaints were the Eagles' allegedly misogynous belief "that the men have the power and the women don't," according to Rachlis, and the problems they were having coping with their own success. The band's defenders, notably Robert Hilburn of the *Los Angeles Times*, welcomed the songsters' viewpoint, stating they were "one of the few who came to grips with the self-absorption of the '70s....Using California as a metaphor for the nation, Henley and Frey wrote about the pursuit of the American dream, '70s style, using their own experiences in rock to convey the innocence ('New Kid in Town'), temptations ('One of These Nights') and disillusionments ('The Sad Cafe') of that pursuit. *Hotel California* examined their recurring theme with more precision, power and daring than ever."

The harsh words for the Eagles' work outside the coven weren't nearly as brutal as the ones within. "The one problem with the band is

that we have such high standards for making records, writing lyrics and performing that after a while it begins to take their toll on everybody's nerves," Don Felder told *Circus.* "But it's our goal to do the best job possible and as we go along every little part and piece of the operation gets refined. Glenn (Frey) uses a great analogy of building a table. You don't just slap some wood together and pour on some varnish, it takes years to sand it and find the right hinges because you are building a masterpiece. You are trying to create something that will be a mark of its time."

## THE TOP FIVE

*Week of February 26, 1977*

1 **New Kid in Town**
Eagles

2 **Love Theme from "A Star Is Born" (Evergreen)**
Barbra Streisand

3 **Blinded by the Light**
Manfred Mann's Earth Band

4 **Fly Like an Eagle**
Steve Miller Band

5 **I Like Dreamin'**
Kenny Nolan

## 456 Love Theme from 'A Star Is Born' (Evergreen) <small>COLUMBIA 10450</small>
### BARBRA STREISAND

*Writers: Barbra Streisand*
*Paul Williams*

*Producers: Barbra Streisand*
*Phil Ramone*

*March 5, 1977*
*3 weeks*

PRIOR to the title song from *A Star Is Born*, Barbra Streisand's composing credits were limited to one song. She explained how she came to co-author the million-selling single "Evergreen" with Paul Williams in James Spada's biography, *Streisand the Woman and the Legend*. "I was going through a period of feeling very inadequate because so many of our songstresses today write their own songs; and I thought, '. . . How talented they are to write their own songs and be able to sing them!' Then my guitar teacher—I wanted to play my own guitar in the movie—told me she wrote her own music and lyrics.

I remember getting very emotional and very insecure and very upset about it, because I thought, 'I only sing these songs that other people write.' I remember going into the bathroom and I started to cry. Jon (Peters) came into the bathroom and

told me that if I put my mind to it, I could write a song. So one day I was sort of bored during my guitar lesson—I wanted to play like Segovia and I can't—and I just started to fool around with chords. Instead of *A Star Is Born*, a song was born! It just came out of absolute impatience."

Unfortunately, the film didn't come so easily. From the beginning it was bucking odds. It was the third time this Hollywood chestnut had been put on the screen; its immediate predecessor was a fairly sainted version with James Mason and Judy Garland. To tamper with it verged on heresy, but executive producer Streisand and producer Jon Peters forged ahead, with Frank Pierson as writer/director and Kris Kristofferson playing a rock and roller whose alcoholic overindulgence smashes him from the pinnacle of success to suicide.

Fights on the set, middle-of-the-night script rewrites, editing on the Streisand/Peter home moviola and Pierson's candid expose of the above in *New York* magazine all added to the vitriol surrounding the project. One of the hardest scenes to capture was the concert where Kristofferson's character, John Norman Howard, is

to perform one number then roar offstage on a motorcycle. A real concert, starring Peter Frampton ("Show Me the Way," "I'm in You"), was staged at Sun Devil Stadium in Phoenix, Arizona, but the 70,000-strong crowd was so antsy after broiling in the sun for several hours that at one point they shouted for the production to stop its repetitive filming.

Streisand had to calm them down, then later performed her first chart hit ("People") and her first number one song [see 356—"The Way We Were"]. "Now I'll sing a song for you that I wrote myself," she announced. "I hope you like it. If you don't, I'll be crushed." With trepidation, she launched into the world premiere of "Evergreen." The overwhelming audience approval buoyed her confidence. "I'm really glad you like it because that's the first time I ever sang that song in front of people," she confided to the mass audience afterward.

Snubbed by the Academy of Motion Picture Arts and Sciences in almost every category, the film garnered only one nomination: for Best Song. Streisand and co-writer Paul Williams ("I Won't Last a Day Without You," "An Old Fashioned Love Song") accepted their awards. The Grammys were kinder, declaring "Evergreen" Song of the Year and Streisand's work to be Best Pop Vocal Performance, Female.

Kristofferson and Streisand were musically reunited in a 1984 video of her song "Left in the Dark." It was Streisand's initial video and Kristofferson portrayed a bartender to her cabaret singer.

### THE TOP FIVE
*Week of March 5, 1977*

1. **Love Theme from "A Star Is Born" (Evergreen)**
   Barbra Streisand

2. **New Kid in Town**
   Eagles

3. **Fly Like an Eagle**
   Steve Miller Band

4. **I Like Dreamin'**
   Kenny Nolan

5. **Blinded by the Light**
   Manfred Mann's Earth Band

*Writer: Daryl Hall*

*Producer: Chris Bond*

*March 26, 1977*
*2 weeks*

DARYL HALL and JOHN OATES met in a service elevator while trying to escape a fight between rival black gangs at a record hop in Philadelphia's Adelphi Ballroom. That fateful meeting encapsulizes several keys to the duo's unique personality—their southeastern Pennsylvania roots, a mixture of black and white cultures and music, and a career with more ups and downs than an elevator. In over 19 years together, Daryl and John have been stylistic chameleons, though at their core they always "basically tried to combine rhythm and blues and progressive music," Oates has insisted.

Doo-wop groups, the Temptations see 168—"My Girl" and the Stax/Volt sound were their earliest influences. In his pre-teen days, Daryl (born Daryl Franklin Hohl on October 11, 1948, in Philadelphia) would skip the piano lessons he hated and ride his bicycle to the heart of the black Chicken Hill ghetto across the bridge from his grandfather's farm in Pottsdown, Pennsylvania, so he could absorb the music.

Accordion lessons came first for John (born April 7, 1949, in New York City) but soon gave way to a teacher who showed him guitar chords on a three-string banjo. From the time he assembled his first Motown cover band in sixth grade, he made his living solely as a musician.

Both were leading their own groups (Daryl's was the Temptones and John's was the Masters) and attending Temple University at the time of the 1967 Adelphi Ballroom meeting, but it would take two years before they would officially team together and three more before their debut album, *Whole Oates*, would be released by Atlantic Records.

"Our first real record" is how Daryl and John categorize their second Atlantic LP, *Abandoned Luncheonette*. That album tagged them as blue-eyed soulsters, a reputation largely based on the single, "She's Gone." Written for Daryl's divorce from his wife Bryna and a New Year's Eve date that stood John up, the song would be recorded by Lou Rawls and Tavares before a re-issue of Hall and Oates' original rose to number seven in October, 1976.

The Todd Rundgren-produced *War Babies and Daryl Hall and John Oates*, their first album for RCA, followed. The latter LP spun out their first legitimate hit, "Sara Smile" (number four in June, 1976), even though Daryl didn't like the way his voice sounded on this ballad for his girlfriend Sara Allen. While the sound of the album caught the ear, the cover, by Mick Jagger's makeup designer Pierre LaRoche, captured the eye. "We decided that if we were going to put our faces on an album cover for the first time we wanted to do it in a big way," John explained in Nick Tosches' biography, *Dangerous Dances*. "Pierre said, in that French accent of his, 'I will immortalize you!' And he just about did. To this day it's the only album cover that people ask us about."

By the time they were ready to record *Bigger Than Both of Us* in the summer of 1976, New York's Greenwich Village had become their home, adding still another layer to their black/white, Philadelphia soul and rock fusion. But they flew to Los Angeles to work with producer Chris Bond and the best studio musicians available.

Though the songwriters believed "Do What You Want, Be What You Are" was the most commercial of the album's offerings, it fizzled out at number 39 in December, 1976. The second single from the LP, "Rich Girl," fared somewhat better, debuting at number 81 on January 22, 1977, and becoming the duo's first number one single nine weeks later.

Despite the title, it wasn't penned about a woman at all, but an ex-beau of Sara Allen's, heir to a fast food chain. "But you can't write, 'You're a rich boy' in a song, so I changed it to a girl," Daryl told *Rolling Stone*. A year or two later Daryl was flipping through a book about the notorious Son of Sam when he found out the killer "was motivated by 'Rich Girl.' It wasn't exactly a pleasant thing to know," he said with some understatement. The discovery was noted in "Diddy Doo Wop (I Hear the Voices)," a track on the *Voices* album that John jokingly referred to as "a song about an ax murderer."

## THE TOP FIVE
*Week of March 26, 1977*

1  **Rich Girl**
   Hall & Oates

2  **Love Theme from "A Star Is Born" (Evergreen)**
   Barbra Streisand

3  **Dancing Queen**
   Abba

4  **Don't Give Up On Us**
   David Soul

5  **Don't Leave Me This Way**
   Thelma Houston

# Dancing Queen ATLANTIC 3372
## ABBA

**Writers:** Benny Andersson
Stig Anderson
Bjorn Ulvaeus

**Producers:** Benny Andersson
Bjorn Ulvaeus

April 9, 1977
1 week

Most international artists would be thrilled to have an American track record that included a number one song, three other top 10 hits and nine additional singles that made the top 30. But the members of Abba consider America to be their only failure.

In the U.K., Abba scored nine number one hits (a total surpassed only by the Beatles, Elvis Presley, Cliff Richard, and Westlife) and had 18 consecutive top 10 singles.

The four members of Abba were all professional singers before they formed the quartet that has been called "the largest selling quartet in the history of recorded music." Bjorn Christian Ulvaeus (born April 25, 1945, in Gothenburg, Sweden) formed a folk band, the West Bay Singers, with friends from school. Record producer Stig Anderson heard them in 1963 and brought them to Stockholm. He renamed them the Hootenanny Singers and signed them as the first act on his new label, Polar Records. Bjorn's first successful composition was "Baby Those Are the Rules," which made the Swedish top 10.

Goran Bror Benny Andersson (born December 16, 1946, in Stockholm) chose not to follow in the footsteps of his father, a construction engineer. His interest in music led him to drop his job as a janitor and become the pianist for the Hep Stars, a band that scored 15 chart hits in Sweden, including a number one hit written by Benny, "Sunny Girl."

Bjorn and Benny met at a party in Vastervik, Sweden, in 1966. They decided to collaborate on songs and Bjorn toured briefly with the Hep Stars, but their writing partnership didn't flourish until the Hep Stars broke up in 1969. Around this time, Bjorn and Benny met two women who would be very important in their personal and professional lives.

Benny met Anni-Frid Lyngstad in Malmo, Sweden, where they were performing in different night clubs. Frida (born November 15, 1945, in

Narvik, Norway) moved to Eskilstuna, Sweden, near southwest Stockholm, when she was two. She was just 13 when she became the vocalist for a dance band and performed in song festivals in Japan and Venezuela before meeting Benny, whom she would marry 10 years later.

Bjorn fell in love with Agnetha Faltskog's voice when he heard her sing her own composition, "I Was So in Love," on the radio. Agnetha (born April 5, 1950, in Jonkoping, Sweden) sang professionally at 15 and was signed to CBS-Sweden two years later. She first met Bjorn when they were both invited to appear on the same television show being filmed on location. The four singers first performed together at the Festfolk Quartet in November, 1970. On July 7, 1971, Bjorn and Agnetha were married. Around this same time, Bjorn and Benny were hired by Stig to be producers at Polar Records. Benny and Bjorn recorded songs like "She's My Kind of Girl" and "Hello Old Man" with Agnetha and Frida singing background. The first song that featured the girls upfront was "People Need Love," released in America on Playboy Records by "Bjorn & Benny and Svenska & Flicka."

In 1972 and 1973, Benny and Bjorn entered songs in the Swedish competition to select an entry for the Eurovision Song Contest [see 237—"Love is Blue"]. "Better to Have Loved" and "Ring, Ring" were both passed over by the Swedish judges, but in 1974 their composition "Waterloo" became the Swedish entry in Eurovision. On April 6, at the Brighton Dome in England, at odds of 20-1, "Waterloo" won the contest—the first victory ever for Sweden.

"Waterloo" became an international hit, topping the charts in many

countries and peaking at number six in America. By this time, the group had a new name, thanks to Stig. "I couldn't be bothered to keep on saying all four names of the group...so I mixed up their initials and came up with Abba," he explained in a 1979 *Billboard* interview. "That didn't much please the two boys, because Abba is very similar to the name of a noted brand of pickled herring in Sweden."

After "Dancing Queen," Abba continued their American chart success with "Knowing Me, Knowing You," "Take a Chance on Me" and "The Winner Takes It All." By 1983, their status was hazy. Frida and Agnetha released solo albums and scored with respective hit singles, "I Know There's Something Going On" and "Can't Shake Loose." Benny and Bjorn teamed up with Tim Rice (*Jesus Christ, Superstar, Evita*) to write a stage musical, *Chess*. Two singles from that album were immediate hits: "One Night in Bangkok" by Murray Head made the American top 10 and "I Know Him So Well" by Elaine Paige and Barbara Dickson topped the British chart for four weeks.

## THE TOP FIVE
*Week of April 9, 1977*

1 **Dancing Queen**
Abba

2 **Don't Give Up On Us**
David Soul

3 **Don't Leave Me This Way**
Thelma Houston

4 **Rich Girl**
Hall & Oates

5 **Southern Nights**
Glen Campbell

PRIVATE STOCK 45129 **Don't Give Up on Us**
DAVID SOUL

**459**

*Writer: Tony Macaulay*

*Producer: Tony Macaulay*

*April 16, 1977*
*1 week*

AFTER David Soul's first album for Private Stock Records was released, he received a telephone call from Larry Uttal, president of the company. Uttal wanted Soul to meet with British songwriter Tony Macaulay and record a couple of his songs. "I talked to Tony from the stage of 'Starsky and Hutch' and he said, 'I can be over there on Wednesday.' I liked the way he talked to me on the phone so I just said, 'sure, come over,'" David recalls.

From their conversation, Soul knew he trusted Macaulay and would record his songs without even hearing them. It was the same way he chose the musicians he worked with—often hiring them based on intuition rather than listening to their music first.

Soul learned "Don't Give Up on Us" on Thursday and recorded it along with another Macaulay song on Friday, Saturday and Sunday. They were sweetened on Monday, mixed on Tuesday and on sale in Britain the following Friday. Only a minimal number of the *David Soul* albums had been pressed and these were pulled back so "Don't Give Up on Us" could be included.

More concerned with the recording process than having hits, David's goal had always been to have fun making music. But Private Stock was a singles-oriented company working hard to achieve top 10 records.

"Don't Give Up on Us" broke first in England, beginning a four-week run at number one on January 15, 1977. The song entered the American chart on January 29, debuting at number 74. It went to number one 11 weeks later. Looking back, Soul feels the only weakness in the recording is his vocal quality, which has improved since then. Although he never made the top 50 again in America, his British chart fortunes are quite impressive. "Going in With My Eyes Open" peaked at two, then "Silver Lady" became his second chart-topper. "Let's Have a Quiet Night In" went to eight and "It Sure Brings Out the Love in Your Eyes" reached number 12.

Although the casual viewer might have been surprised when one of the stars of television's "Starsky and Hutch" released a successful record, diehard David Soul fans knew their idol began his career as a singer. After dropping out of college he tried to support himself as a folksinger in the Midwest, opening for acts such as the Byrds, the Ramsey Lewis Trio and the Doors.

Wanting to try his luck in New York, he sent a picture of himself, his face covered by a ski mask, to the William Morris Agency. They were very interested. As a result, he appeared numerous times on "The Merv Griffin Show" and on "Shindig" as "The Covered Man." He expressed his philosophy on Merv's show with his first and only words, "My name is David Soul and I want to be known for my music." Although this gained Soul an entree to television, he became more known for the mask than his music. Eventually, he discarded his ski mask on Merv's show and revealed a handsome face.

Casting director Renee Valente saw Soul on a subsequent Merv Griffin show and cast him in "Here Come the Brides." By the time he was starring as Detective Ken Hutchinson in "Starsky and Hutch," he wanted to make sure a record company wanted him for his music and not because he was a well-known television personality. Uttal convinced him he would be taken seriously for his music.

He was born David Solberg on August 28, 1943, in Chicago, Illinois, and grew up in Germany where his father, a Lutheran minister, worked for a refugee organization. David's interest in music can be traced to his mother, a classical concert singer.

## THE TOP FIVE
*Week of April 16, 1977*

1 **Don't Give Up On Us**
David Soul

2 **Don't Leave Me This Way**
Thelma Houston

3 **Southern Nights**
Glen Campbell

4 **Hotel California**
Eagles

5 **The Things We Do For Love**
10 cc

## 460 Don't Leave Me This Way TAMLA 54278
### THELMA HOUSTON

Writers: *Kenny Gamble*
*Leon Huff*
*Cary Gilbert*

Producer: *Hal Davis*

*April 23, 1977*
*1 week*

As a child in Mississippi, Thelma Houston used to sit in the balcony of her local movie theater and fantasize about being a Hollywood star. When her mother, who picked cotton to support her three daughters, announced the family was moving to California, Thelma knew her dream was going to come true. "I always knew I was supposed to be there," she once said, "to be close to the people I saw every Sunday in the movies."

She missed by about 30 miles, as her family relocated to Long Beach. Thelma finished school, married, had two children, worked in health care and divorced. She joined a gospel group, the Art Reynolds singers, and after they recorded an album for Capitol and toured the country she gave serious consideration to a career in music.

She struggled on the edges of the Los Angeles music scene until the late '60s, when she was discovered at the Factory by Marc Gordon, manager of the Fifth Dimension [see 261—"Wedding Bell Blues"]. He helped her overcome lingering doubts about pursuing a career and signed her to Dunhill Records. Jimmy Webb wrote and produced her 1969 debut LP, *Sunshower*. According to Webb, Thelma manifested "everything great about the female black voice." Other, less partial critics, agreed, comparing

### THE TOP FIVE
*Week of April 23, 1977*

1  **Don't Leave Me This Way**
   Thelma Houston

2  **Southern Nights**
   Glen Campbell

3  **Hotel California**
   Eagles

4  **Don't Give Up On Us**
   David Soul

5  **The Things We Do For Love**
   10 cc

her to Aretha Franklin and Dinah Washington.

But the album failed to find an audience, and despite achieving her first chart single, Laura Nyro's "Save the Country" (number 74 in February, 1970), Houston soon found herself without a label. In 1971 she signed with Motown, which put out a self-named LP on its MoWest subsidiary. It also went nowhere, and for the next five years, Thelma recorded a few scattered singles, made a brief appearance on Motown's *The Bingo Long Traveling All-Stars and Motor Kings* soundtrack and was loaned out to a small label to record the *Pressure Cooker* album.

"All the while," wrote critic Russell Gersten in *The New Rolling Stone Record Guide*, "she was perfecting her own gospel-based pop style, which has a chilling precision and nuance of phrasing rare in soul music." But mostly she raised her two teenaged children, travelled on the soul club circuit and waited for that career-breaking hit.

"These have been tough years, full of disappointments," she admitted to Dennis Hunt of the *Los Angeles*

*Times*. "You release a record and you say, 'This is it.' But it's not. You release another one and go through the same thing. It's awful to have to rely on a hit record to get your career going but that's the way it is."

The waiting finally came to an end in 1976 when Thelma released her *Any Way You Like It* album for Tamla. Producer Hal Davis had heard Harold Melvin and the Blue Notes' "Don't Leave Me This Way" (featuring lead singer Teddy Pendergrass) at a party and had Thelma record a volcanic, disco-tinged version of it for the LP. Released as a single, it entered the Hot 100 at number 85 on December 18, 1976, and took a gradual journey to the top, arriving there 18 weeks later.

In an interview with the *Los Angeles Times*, Houston was understandably hard-put to explain just why it had taken her so long to break through. "(Before) the material was never right or something else wasn't right," she said. "I can't put my finger on what the problem has been. I don't want to blame anybody. I only know that I've been trying as hard as I can."

*Writer: Allen Toussaint*

*Producer: Gary Klein*

*April 30, 1977*
*1 week*

**W**HO should know better about "Southern Nights" than master New Orleans writer/producer/artist Allen Toussaint, the man responsible for southern hits like Lee Dorsey's "Ya Ya," Al Hirt's "Java," Barbara George's "I Know" and Jessie Hill's "Ooh Poo Pah Doo." Toussaint was connected with two number one singles prior to Glen Campbell's "Southern Nights." The first was by Ernie K-Doe [see 89—"Mother-In-Law"], which he wrote and produced; the second was by Labelle [see 399—"Lady Marmalade"], which he produced.

Toussaint, born in New Orleans on January 14, 1938, recorded infrequently, but he did release his own version of "Southern Nights" on a Warner Brothers album in 1975.

Campbell was born in the south, too, just three months after Toussaint. His birthdate is April 22, 1938,

and his birthplace is Delight, Arkansas. He is the seventh son of a seventh son, born into a family where everyone played some kind of musical instrument or sang. Glen was just four when he received his first guitar from Sears and Roebuck; two years later he would play on a live local radio show. He listened to all types of music—not just country, but to artists such as pianist George Shearing, singers Nat "King" Cole and Frank Sinatra, and guitarists Django Reinhardt and Tai Farlow. As a teenager, Glen joined his Uncle Dick Bill's band. In 1958, Glen formed his own group, Glen Campbell and the Western Wranglers. Two years later he moved to Los Angeles, where he became a popular session guitar player. Over the next five years he worked with artists like Bobby Darin, Dean Martin, Johnny Cash, Merle Haggard and two of his idols, Cole and Sinatra. By his own count, he played on 586 sessions in a one-year period.

He was a member of the Champs after they had a number one hit [see 34—"Tequila"], and in 1965 he was invited to tour with the Beach Boys

[see 151—"I Get Around"] for six months when Brian Wilson decided not to travel with the group. That same year, he was a frequent performer on the "Shindig" television series.

Once he had his own hits like "By the Time I Get to Phoenix" and "Gentle on My Mind," he became a popular guest star on variety series, especially "The Smothers Brothers Comedy Hour" on CBS. He was asked to star in a summer replacement series for Tom and Dick, "The Summer Brothers Smothers Show," which premiered June 23, 1968. The reaction to Campbell was so favorable, the network rewarded him with his own weekly prime time variety series, which began a three-year run on January 29, 1969.

Campbell had a brief run as a movie star, appearing in *True Grit* with John Wayne in 1969 and starring in the title role of *Norwood*, a 1970 release.

Between 1968-1980, Campbell recorded duets with four different female artists: Bobbie Gentry [see 229—"Ode to Billie Joe"], Anne Murray [see 492—"You Needed Me"], Rita Coolidge and Tanya Tucker. "Southern Nights" was Glen's last top 10 hit. He had three more chart entries on Capitol, and a final one on **Mirage Records**. He recorded for Atlantic/America, a country label run by Atlantic, then shifted to MCA Records.

There are lasting tributes to Glen Campbell in Tennessee and California. One of his guitars is on display at the Country Hall of Fame in Nashville; a star bearing his name shines on the Hollywood Walk of Fame.

---

## THE TOP FIVE
*Week of April 30, 1977*

1 **Southern Nights**
Glen Campbell

2 **Hotel California**
Eagles

3 **Don't Leave Me This Way**
Thelma Houston

4 **When I Need You**
Leo Sayer

5 **I've Got Love on my Mind**
Natalie Cole

## 462 Hotel California ASYLUM 45386
### EAGLES

*Writers: Don Felder*
*Don Henley*
*Glenn Frey*

*Producer: Bill Szymczyk*

*May 7, 1977*
*1 week*

Panic raged through Criteria Studios in Miami. There was always pandemonium in the halls whenever the Eagles recorded there, with the yelling and the fights and the horseplay, but this day there was more an element of fear, since the title song to the band's new album, the one they had devoted the last nine months of their blood and souls to, was in imminent danger of losing the concept that originally made it so compelling.

Don Felder had an idea. He was the one who constructed the song's basic elements, including the 12-string introduction and the solos at the end, back in Los Angeles on his four-track Teac tape deck. Calling his housekeeper, he sent her rummaging through the heaps of tapes in his home studio until she'd located the correct one, then had her play it to him over the phone while he recorded it on a professional Sony Walkman.

Back to Criteria he went, taking the cassette so he and Joe Walsh could re-learn all the guitar parts the band had liked in the first place.

When they listened to the final mix, the five Eagles were a little taken aback by what they'd produced, and especially wary about releasing something not in their familiar rock pocket as a single. It turned out to be their fourth chart-topper, entering the Hot 100 at number 72 on February 26, 1977, and moving to number one 10 weeks later. The LP would yield a final single, "Life in the Fast Lane," their first 45 to miss the top 10 since "James Dean" went to number 77 in October, 1974. It didn't miss by much, though—it peaked at number 11.

In April, 1977, the group started a tour of England, Scotland, Scandinavia and Europe, returning to the United States for a summer series of outdoor concerts in sports stadiums. During the last leg of the tour, bassist Randy Meisner decided he'd seen enough hotel rooms in his seven years as an Eagle and left for the quiet of Nebraska to recuperate and instigate a solo career. Three years later the title track of his *One More Song* album, featuring Henley and Frey on harmony vocals, revealed a "mythical tale" of his last night with the Eagles. On his own, Meisner placed three singles in the top 30 from 1980-1982, the most popular of which was "Hearts on Fire."

Following in Meisner's footsteps was the man who succeeded him in Poco, Timothy B. Schmit. "It's like a marriage and truly the most unified band I've ever been in," he told *Circus.* "We live with each other day in and day out so it has its Peyton Place-aspects too...they could have offered me a salary as a sideman but they didn't want that. My offer was to be a full partner in the Eagles' organization."

Schmit and his new brethren began sessions in February, 1978, at Bayshore in Miami for what would be the Eagles' final studio album, *The Long Run.* It took so long to finish that producer Szymczyk joked, "We ended up nicknaming it *The Long One.*" Eventually, the difficulties encountered in the tense two years would also lead to the band's dissolution.

### THE TOP FIVE
*Week of May 7, 1977*

1  **Hotel California**
   Eagles

2  **When I Need You**
   Leo Sayer

3  **Southern Nights**
   Glen Campbell

4  **Sir Duke**
   Stevie Wonder

5  **Don't Leave Me This Way**
   Thelma Houston

*Writers: Albert Hammond
       Carole Bayer Sager*

*Producer: Richard Perry*

*May 14, 1977
1 week*

"**I** WANT to be a success. I have giant ambitions," Leo Sayer confessed in a 1975 *Billboard* interview. "I want to be as important as Dylan. I want to leave my audience with the feeling that something important has gone on. I don't want to be just another rock 'n' roll singer or writer."

Leo Sayer's first number one single [see 450—"You Make Me Feel Like Dancing"] was still in the top 30 during the week of February 26, 1977, when his next release, "When I Need You," debuted at 81. While the former was an upbeat, disco-tinged pop number, the latter was a throwback to the poignant songs of his earlier albums. "I feel less a part of rock now than I did before," Sayer told Franc Gavin of *Rock Around the World* magazine in 1977. "As you get older you tend to take your heroes with you. You don't find many new ones. I owe the biggest debt to people like Bobby 'Blue' Bland, James Brown, the Staples, Sam Cooke, Jackie Wilson . . . some people think I'm falling into an R&B trip. Maybe not. It's still Leo Sayer music."

"When I Need You" was the second consecutive number one single from the Richard Perry-produced *Endless Flight* LP. Known for his work with Barbra Streisand, Nilsson, Ringo Starr and Carly Simon, Perry was considered a vocalist's producer. "Perry got me performing on records

rather than just writing songs and singing them," Sayer told *Newsweek*. "I've let go and it's changed my life."

Perry described their working relationship to *Rolling Stone*: "When I first started working with Leo, he came with a cassette of 12 new songs, none of which got recorded. That's a pretty heavy blow for an artist to be told that none of these songs are of any interest to me."

One of the songs Perry brought to Sayer was "When I Need You." The lyrics were by Carole Bayer Sager, whose credits include "A Groovy Kind of Love" and "Come in From the Rain" as well as the Broadway show *They're Playing Our Song*. The music was composed by Albert Hammond, best known for his number five hit in December, 1972, "It Never Rains in Southern California," and for writing "The Air That I Breathe" and "To All the Girls I've Loved Before."

Hammond called Sager for help with the song. "He was in desperate need of a lyricist," she relates. "He was recording an album for Columbia in a few weeks and the fellow that he originally wrote most of his songs with . . . was missing. So he came up to my apartment and he played me three melodies." One of them turned

out to be "When I Need You," a song Carole based on Albert's personal experiences. "Albert travelled a lot at the time and we were talking about the difficulties of being away from someone that you love."

Albert recorded "When I Need You" first, on a 1976 album, and Perry used that version as the prototype. "I think Richard actually cut the song twice because he wasn't happy with the first production, so he cut it with another rhythm section," Sager continues. "It was an easy song to write and often with myself anything that would be too easy I often discount as not being as good as something I labored over. Consequently I never thought very much of the song because it just seemed too simplistic to me. I don't think (Richard) really knew it was a hit either."

"When I Need You" turned out to be Sayer's biggest hit record. It was his first number one single in Britain, where he had hit the number two spot with three different singles. In America, it was his last top 10 single until his re-make of Bobby Vee's "More Than I Can Say" settled in at number two for four weeks in December, 1980.

## THE TOP FIVE
*Week of May 14, 1977*

1  **When I Need You**
   Leo Sayer

2  **Sir Duke**
   Stevie Wonder

3  **Hotel California**
   Eagles

4  **Southern Nights**
   Glen Campbell

5  **Couldn't Get It Right**
   Climax Blues Band

## Sir Duke TAMLA 54281
### STEVIE WONDER

*Writer: Stevie Wonder*

*Producer: Stevie Wonder*

*May 21, 1977*
*3 weeks*

**B**ORN SIGHTLESS, Stevie Wonder quickly discovered the pleasures of the radio at an early age. "I was greatly influenced by radio," he has said. "Detroit had the best cross section of music (and) different cultures." Among those early influences were the Coasters, the Five Royales, the Dixie Hummingbirds, Del Shannon, the Staples Singers and the artists recording for Berry Gordy, Jr.'s Motown Record Corporation, especially the Miracles and Mary Wells.

Stevie loved to listen to Detroit's black music station WCHB, particularly the program called "Sundown." That show gave him his first exposure to the R&B music he now calls "the old songs." Those tunes would later have a strong influence on his own work; one can hear echoes of Sam Cooke in "With a Child's Heart." Stevie's adoration for Ray Charles was manifested in the album *A Tribute to Uncle Ray*, an LP that Gordy thought would bring Stevie national attention by having the "12-year-old genius" perform songs from a well-known artist.

In 1964, Stevie suffered the second great trauma of that year (the first was when his voice changed) by missing the opportunity to meet another strong influence on his life, Dinah Washington. "She had expressed a desire to meet me," he explained years later, "but when I got off the tour in the South, she was performing. She passed away soon after . . ."

Stevie recognized yet another influence in 1968 when he recorded an instrumental album under the reverse name Eivets Rednow. That LP was a set of instrumental arrangements intended for a collaboration with one of his idols, legendary jazz guitarist Wes Montgomery. But Montgomery died in June of that year, and the dual effort was never realized.

The second single from *Songs in the Key of Life* was the latest in a series of musical acknowledgements to his heroes. "Sir Duke" was a tribute to Edward Kennedy Ellington,

the jazz genius who gained fame at the Cotton Club in Harlem during the '30s. Known for pop hits like "Mood Indigo," "Solitude" and "Sophisticated Lady," "Duke" Ellington passed away in 1974. Stevie's single also paid reverance to other important forerunners—Count Basie, Louis "Satchmo" Armstrong and Ella Fitzgerald.

"Sir Duke" was the highest new entry on the Hot 100 for the week ending April 2, 1977, coming in at 74. When it hit the top seven weeks later, it was the second consecutive number one single from *Songs in the Key of Life* and the sixth chart-topper of Stevie's career.

A month after the song hit the chart apex, Stevie discussed it at a UCLA symposium sponsored by *Billboard*. "I knew the title from the beginning but wanted it to be about the musicians who did something for us," he explained. "So soon they are forgotten. I wanted to show my appreciation."

"Sir Duke" was not the last Stevie Wonder song to pay tribute to an important figure in the artist's life. "Master Blaster (Jammin')," a number five hit in December, 1980,

was written about the leading exponent of reggae music, the late Bob Marley. Another track from the *Hotter Than July* album was "Happy Birthday," a plea for a national holiday to commemorate the birthday of civil rights leader, Rev. Martin Luther King. Stevie's wish came true in October, 1983, when the United States Senate mirrored the House of Representatives' majority vote to establish the third Monday of January as a holiday honoring King.

---

### THE TOP FIVE
*Week of May 21, 1977*

1  **Sir Duke**
   Stevie Wonder

2  **When I Need You**
   Leo Sayer

3  **Couldn't Get It Right**
   Climax Blues Band

4  **I'm Your Boogie Man**
   K.C. & The Sunshine Band

5  **Got to Give It Up, Pt. 1**
   Marvin Gaye

*Writers: Harry Wayne Casey*
*Richard Finch*

*Producers: Harry Wayne Casey*
*Richard Finch*

*June 11, 1977*
*1 week*

KC AND THE SUNSHINE BAND's hit streak extended into 1977 with the second track from their *Part 3* album to hit the top of the chart [see 442—"(Shake, Shake, Shake) Shake Your Booty"]. "I'm Your Boogie Man" was the group's fourth number one song, making them only the second group to have four number one singles in the seventies after the Jackson Five [see 283—"I'll Be There"].

"I'm Your Boogie Man" was not KC's original title for the song. When he first wrote it, the lyrics were "I'll be a son-of-a-gun, look what you've done" instead of "I'm your boogie man, that's what I am." He wasn't happy with the song and changed the meaning of the lyrics from being about a relationship gone bad to an ode to a disc jockey. "There was a double meaning there," KC confides. "There was the meaning that I would be there to help you, too."

On the *Part 3* album, "I'm Your Boogie Man" segued directly into

"Keep It Comin' Love." "That was intentionally done," KC explains. "It worked real well. I guess that was just an extension of saying, 'I'm your boogie man, keep it coming.' A lot of people start something, and when it gets to the point where they would hit—they stop.

"I had those feelings a lot of times during my apprenticeship—my five years of struggle," he adds. "There were days when you would feel, 'what am I doing this for?' and at the same time a little voice would say, 'don't you stop now.'"

"Keep It Comin' Love" peaked at number two in the autumn of 1977, and for the next two years, KC and the Sunshine Band couldn't get a top 30 hit. One of their older flip sides, "Boogie Shoes," was included in the motion picture *Saturday Night Fever*, causing T.K. to re-release it.

"Boogie Shoes" only managed to get to number 35 on the Hot 100, but there was some consolation in the fact that it was included in an album that sold over 25 million copies.

The group followed "Boogie Shoes" with their first non-original song. It was "It's the Same Old Song," a 1965 hit for the Four Tops [see 177—"I Can't Help Myself (Sugar Pie Honey Bunch)"]. "I didn't do anything tremendously different

with it," says KC. "I felt that (would have been) disrespectful. I put our sound to it, (but) I did try to stay as close to the original as possible." KC's next two singles failed to make the top 50, and KC blames T.K. for lack of promotion. "They weren't backing us at that time. I was getting ready to sign with new management, and I think they knew that and didn't want it to happen."

It was not over yet for KC and the Sunshine Band. They would extend their run of chart hits into the '80s with their first ballad in 15 chart entries [see 519—"Please Don't Go"].

---

### THE TOP FIVE
*Week of June 11, 1977*

1 **I'm Your Boogie Man**
   KC & The Sunshine Band

2 **Dreams**
   Fleetwood Mac

3 **Got to Give It Up, Pt. 1**
   Marvin Gaye

4 **Gonna Fly Now
   (Theme from "Rocky")**
   Bill Conti

5 **Feels Like the First Time**
   Foreigner

# 466 Dreams WARNER BROTHERS 8371
## FLEETWOOD MAC

*Writer: Stevie Nicks*

*Producers: Fleetwood Mac
Richard Dashut
Ken Caillat*

*June 18, 1977
1 week*

"I THINK one day John (McVie) and I will write a book on what's gone down," Mick Fleetwood told Robert Hilburn in the *Los Angeles Times*.

Having survived more personnel changes than Macy's, the 1977 members of Fleetwood Mac were experiencing emotional upheavals while recording *Rumours*, the album that had a 31-week run at number one and produced the band's only chart-topping single, "Dreams."

Keyboard player Christine McVie was separating from her husband, bass player John McVie. Drummer Mick Fleetwood was being divorced from a woman he would soon remarry. Guitarist Lindsey Buckingham was ending an eight-year relationship with singer Stevie Nicks. "It was a very difficult period for everyone," Buckingham confirmed to one reporter. ". . . there was a lot of tension, to put it mildly." The results of this anxiety was an LP that sold over 15 million copies for the edition of Fleetwood Mac that had been

together since 1975.

Only Mick and John, who had both played in John Mayall's Bluesbreakers, were part of the original Fleetwood Mac, formed in 1967. It was in April of that year that Aynsley Dunbar left the Bluesbreakers to join Rod Stewart in Jeff Beck's band. Replacing Dunbar was Mick Fleetwood, who joined Peter Green and John McVie. Fleetwood was fired from the group and Green quit shortly after. With lead guitarist Jeremy Spencer, they formed the first incarnation of Fleetwood Mac. McVie joined a month later. Just after their second album was released, Green suggested adding Danny Kirwan, giving the group three lead guitarists. In January, 1969, this line-up of Fleetwood Mac scored the group's only British number one single, the instrumental "Albatross."

Green departed in May, 1970, and later in the year, just before an American tour, John McVie's wife, pianist/vocalist Christine Perfect, gave up being a housewife to become part of Fleetwood Mac. Before her voluntary "retirement," she had been named *Melody Maker's* top female vocalist of 1969.

During the American tour, Spencer went missing for five days. By the time the band discovered his

whereabouts, he had joined a California sect called the Children of God. Green filled in for him until a permanent replacement was found—the group's first American citizen, Bob Welch. As the group took on more of a West Coast sound, there were still personnel changes to come. Kirwan was fired and Welch left. Bob Weston and Dave Walker had short tenures with the band, and in November, 1974, Fleetwood was in a Los Angeles supermarket when someone suggested he check out Sound City studios in Van Nuys. There, engineer Keith Olsen demonstrated the studio's capabilities by playing a tape of an album called *Buckingham Nicks*. Lindsey Buckingham and Stevie Nicks happened to be in an adjoining studio and came over to find out who was listening to their music. A few weeks later, Mick asked the two Americans to join the band.

It was this Anglo-American line-up that spent 10 days recording an album at Sound City. Titled simply *Fleetwood Mac*, it yielded three top 20 hits: "Over My Head," "Rhiannon (Will You Ever Win)" and "Say You Love Me." Their next LP, *Rumours*, did even better. It was the first album by a group to produce four top 10 singles: "Go Your Own Way," "Dreams," "Don't Stop" and "You Make Loving Fun."

TAMLA 54280 **Got to Give It Up, Pt. 1**
MARVIN GAYE
**467**

*Writer: Marvin Gaye*

*Producer: Art Stewart*

*June 25, 1977*
*1 week*

**D**ESPITE HIS fear of flying, Marvin Gaye agreed to appear in London in October, 1976, his first British performance in 10 years. "I saw that the English did understand me, and I understood them," Gaye told biographer David Ritz. "They're wilder than they let on."

Sold out concerts at the Royal Albert Hall and the London Palladium brought rave reviews from the British press. The Palladium concerts were recorded for a double album, but there was only enough material for three sides. Marvin needed to record something in the studio to fill up side four.

"He had this riff that seemed very danceable," producer Art Stewart told Ritz in *Divided Soul*. "He was doing crazy things like banging on a half-filled grapefruit juice bottle for rhythm. Well, I kept stuff like that on the track. Also people talking in the studio—that loose feeling."

Originally titled "Dancing Lady," Marvin told Ritz the inspiration for the song was Johnnie Taylor's "Disco Lady" [see 432]. "I love the way Johnnie sings, and I thought it was a fabulous song," Gaye said. "As good as disco ever got. I appreciated the picture of the super-sexy woman on the dance floor, though in my version I tried to give it a little twist."

Retitled "Got to Give It Up," the song ran 11 minutes and 48 seconds. "He left me alone to piece the song together," Stewart said. "On Christmas Day, 1976, after working on it for months, I ran it over to his house in Hidden Hills (California). He liked it but still wasn't sure—a typical Marvin reaction. Soon *everyone* was liking it."

"Got to Give It Up" was Gaye's last single for the Motown Record Corporation to make the Hot 100. Divorced from Anna Gordy Gaye, and living as a tax exile in Europe, Marvin left the company he had been part of for 20 years in the spring of 1981. A year of negotiations later, Marvin signed with Columbia Records.

His 1982 debut album for Columbia, *Midnight Love*, produced a number three single, "Sexual Healing." Mikal Gilmore, pop music critic of the *Los Angeles Herald Examiner*, said of the album, "*Midnight Love* was not merely an elegant, stylistic rebound, but also the most vividly hopeful and celebratory work of his career. Gaye wrote, arranged, produced and performed all of the music himself, and though, on the surface, it seemed merely a reprisal of the sex themes and rhythms of *Let's Get It On*, the singer clearly pursued physical and spiritual notions of fulfillment in the LP as if they were mutually inseparable ends."

"Sexual Healing" won two Grammys for Marvin Gaye, and it's no wonder he kissed the statuette during his acceptance speech. He had never won a Grammy before. One month and two days later, he reunited with old friends and sang "What's Going On" at the taping of Motown's 25th anniversary special.

On April 18, 1983, he began his final tour. When it ended in August, he returned to his parents' home on Grammercy Place in the Crenshaw District of Los Angeles. On April 1, 1984, one day before Marvin's 45th birthday, an argument between the singer and his father escalated into violence. Gaye was fatally shot twice in the chest. Paramedics rushed him to California Hospital Medical Center, but his heart had stopped beating and attempts at resuscitation failed. Marvin Gaye was declared dead at 1:01 p.m. PDT.

---

## THE TOP FIVE
*Week of June 25, 1977*

1 **Got to Give It Up, Pt. 1**
Marvin Gaye

2 **Gonna Fly Now (Theme from "Rocky")**
Bill Conti

3 **Undercover Angel**
Alan O'Day

4 **Feels Like the First Time**
Foreigner

5 **Lucille**
Kenny Rogers

## 468 Gonna Fly Now (Theme from 'Rocky') UNITED ARTISTS 940
BILL CONTI

*Writers: Bill Conti*
*Carol Connors*
*Ayn Robbins*

*Producer: Bill Conti*

*July 2, 1977*
*1 week*

CAROL CONNORS was a child prodigy on piano even before she recorded a number one hit with the Teddy Bears [see 46—"To Know Him Is to Love Him"] under her real name, Annette Kleinbard. "They wheeled a baby grand into my incubator," she deadpans.

With a friend named Ayn Robbins, she tried to create a show for Walt Disney Productions called "Cloud Nine." It didn't sell, but the studio liked the project enough to ask the pair to collaborate on the music for *The Rescuers*, resulting in an Oscar nomination for "Someone's Waiting for You."

At the time of the Oscar win, Sylvester Stallone was in production on "a little film about a boxer," as Carol describes it. Bill Conti had been hired to score the film and needed a lyricist. Connors and Conti shared the same agent, who suggested his clients work together.

"I remember sitting in a screening . . . with Sly," Carol says. (He was) sitting in front of us with John Avildsen . . . Frank (Stallone) had written a tune for *Rocky*. I think it was Ray Bradbury, I can't remember . . . (who) looked over to John at the end of the screening. Now remember, we're sitting in the back, I just happened to overhear this. He said, 'You will not only have a wonderful film, you will have an Academy Award film if you just get rid of that song.'

"I loved Frank's song, 'He had a Sunday punch that will put him into Monday,' it was a good song but it didn't really work for what they were trying to accomplish. So we got the job. There was a temporary track on the film. Bill had been signed to be the composer and was still making a decision for the theme song."

Conti met Connors and Robbins at Carol's house. He played the instrumental theme he wanted to use and asked his collaborators, "What do we do with that?" A few days later, Carol was taking a shower when the words "Gonna fly now . . ." came into her head. "I called Bill from the shower and said I knew what the words should be. He said, 'Where are you?' and I told him I was in the shower. 'Are you alone?' I said, 'Would I be calling you if I wasn't alone?' He said, 'Do me a favor, give me the lyrics before you electrocute yourself!' "

The completed song with full lyrics was submitted for the film, but the version heard in the final cut only contains 30 words. "I used to be embarassed that it was only 30 words," Carol declares. Her boyfriend at the time, Robert Culp, solved that problem. "He said, 'You and Aynnie captured in 30 words an entire concept of a film. What are you complaining about?' And from that day on I have not been ashamed of those 30 words."

The three songwriters attended the first screening of the film, held at MGM Studios in Culver City, California, for an audience of 200 sophisticated industry bigwigs. "Men were standing on their seats and screaming and women were yelling," Carol recalls. "Bill, Aynnie and I slouched in our seats. Bill looked over at both of us and said, 'I think it's a hit.' We never knew."

### THE TOP FIVE
*Week of July 2, 1977*

1   **Gonna Fly Now
    (Theme from "Rocky")**
    Bill Conti

2   **Undercover Angel**
    Alan O'Day

3   **Got to Give It Up, Pt. 1**
    Marvin Gaye

4   **Da Doo Ron Ron**
    Shaun Cassidy

5   **Looks Like We Made It**
    Barry Manilow

*Writer: Alan O'Day*

*Producers: Steve Barri*
*Michael Omartian*

*July 9, 1977*
*1 week*

Ed SILVERS, the president of Warner Brothers Music, called one of his leading songwriters into his office one day. He explained that the publishing company was starting its own label for its songwriters. Dubbed Pacific Records, it would be distributed by Atlantic Records, a sister subsidiary under the WEA corporate umbrella. And Silvers told Alan O'Day he wanted him to be the first artist signed to the label.

It's sometimes to an artist's advantage to be signed to a record company that is not connected to the artist's publisher, but O'Day trusted and respected Silvers and happily agreed to record for Pacific.

O'Day, who had written hits like "The Drum," recorded by Bobby Sherman; "Rock and Roll Heaven," recorded by Climax and then the Righteous Brothers; plus a number one single for Helen Reddy [see 387—"Angie Baby"], found he had to write for a new singer: himself. "I knew him well. I knew his vocal style. So I said sure, I can write for that guy," Alan recalls.

"There was a local hit on the radio called 'He Did Me Wrong, But He Did Me Right' by Patti Dahlstrom. In that song, she used the word 'undercover.' I thought it was a neat idea. I've always loved things about angels, too, so the words came together." The first verse had already been written when Alan hit upon the idea of an "undercover angel." The song blended fantasy and reality much the same way that his "Angie Baby" did.

The first recording session for "Undercover Angel" was produced by Tom Dowd. "We went into the studio with high hopes, but we ran into technical problems and we ran into my allergies," says Alan, who suffered through bronchial pneumonia as a child. The basic tracks were completed when Dowd left the project. "For all I knew, my record career was over at that moment."

Record producer Steve Barri [see 429—"Theme from 'SW.A.T.'"] was

asked by Silvers to meet with Alan to discuss producing him. "I always liked Alan's songs," Barri explains. "When he played 'Undercover Angel' as a demo, I said it was an absolute smash. Alan always did incredible demos." With co-producer Michael Omartian, Barri attempted to cut a final product that would be as close to the demo as possible.

The unusual echo on the song was improvised by Alan in the studio. He wanted something more than the standard tape echo, so he turned the tape recorder reel by hand, slightly speeding it up and slowing it down, so the echo changed pitch and had a spacey, distorted sound.

In spite of the song's hit status, some radio stations banned the song because of a supposed sexual innuendo. "Sure, it was sexual," admits Alan, "but like a child's version. Kids didn't have any trouble with it."

Alan O'Day was born October 3, 1940, in Hollywood, California. His father loved music and had a large collection of 78 rpm records, which now belong to Alan. An only child, six-year-old Alan would sit across the street from his parents' Mt. Washington home, looking out over the vistas of Los Angeles while playing songs on his toy xylophone. He would make up melodies of his own and by the time he was in the third grade, made an attempt at lyrics by writing a love poem to a girl in his class.

He was nine when his grandmother bought a piano. "It was the most important gift anybody ever gave me," he remembers fondly.

Because of his illness, the family moved to the Coachella Valley near Palm Springs, and Alan was attending Coachella Valley Union High School when he saw *The Blackboard Jungle* [see 1—"(We're Gonna) Rock Around the Clock"] for the first time. He fell in love with rock and roll and was in and out of three groups: the Imperials, the Shoves and the Renees.

He attempted Pasadena City College, but missed the rural atmosphere and transferred to San Bernadino City College. In 1960, he was invited to live in Burbank with a friend whose father ran a motion picture production company. Alan wrote music for a couple of low budget films they produced, and had his first song recorded: "Funky, Funky Feeling," which ended up as the "B" side of a Dobie Gray record.

Meanwhile, Alan had put together a trio and was playing in local clubs. He went to work for a recording studio for $1.50 an hour and met publisher Sidney Goldstein. They developed an instant friendship and Sidney asked to hear Alan's songs. "He ripped them apart, and it was a painful experience. I decided not to fight it. I decided to take direction. He ended up signing me to his company." Goldstein split Alan's publishing with Viva Music, headed by one Ed Silvers. Eventually Viva was purchased by Warner Brothers and Alan became a staff writer for Warner Brothers Music.

In 1985, Alan was asked to write the music for a new Jim Henson animated series for Saturday mornings, featuring the Muppet Babies.

## THE TOP FIVE
*Week of July 9, 1977*

1 **Undercover Angel**
Alan O'Day

2 **Da Doo Ron Ron**
Shaun Cassidy

3 **Looks Like We Made It**
Barry Manilow

4 **Gonna Fly Now**
**(Theme from "Rocky")**
Bill Conti

5 **I Just Want to be**
**Your Everything**
Andy Gibb

## 470 Da Doo Ron Ron WARNER/CURB 8365
### SHAUN CASSIDY

*Writers: Jeff Barry*
*Ellie Greenwich*
*Phil Spector*

*Producer: Michael Lloyd*

*July 16, 1977*
*1 week*

"IT was the first recording I ever bought," said Shaun Cassidy of the Crystals' "Da Doo Ron Ron," a 1963 classic produced by Phil Spector [see 119—"He's a Rebel"]. "When I was going to kindergarten and the first grade, the bus driver was always playing KHJ, Los Angeles' biggest top 40 station. The '60s music is where I've come from."

When his updated version of "Da Doo Ron Ron" was released, Cassidy was co-starring with Parker Stevenson in ABC's "The Hardy Boys." Such small screen exposure not only spurred his version of the 14-year-old song further up the Hot 100 than the original (which peaked at number three), but it made 18-year-old Shaun a teen idol. It was hardly an overnight success story, though—more like a 17-and-a-half year apprenticeship.

Born September 27, 1959, in Los Angeles, Shaun first tasted road life when he was six months old. He travelled with his singer/actor parents, Shirley Jones [see 284—"I Think I Love You"] and Jack Cassidy. What fine points of show business they didn't teach the youngster, his half-brother David did.

Music became a refuge for a sensitive 11-year-old stuck in a Pennsylvania boarding school. "I

hated it," he said years later. "Every night after dinner, I'd go into the music room, lock myself up with the piano and write songs about home and girls and things." At 13, his precocity surfaced in his first rock band, Longfellow. When he came back home to finish his education at Beverly Hills High School, he had another band, the Beverly Hills Brats.

An audition for Mike Curb landed 16-year-old Cassidy a Warner/Curb recording contract. Released initially in Europe and Australia, his debut album, *Shaun Cassidy*, yielded top 10 hits with "Morning Girl" and "That's Rock and Roll." The international success brought no immediate financial rewards. "All the money from the foreign sales was just enough to cover the cost of recording and promotion, so I didn't have any money. It was Christmas time and I needed to buy presents. So I got a job at Saks Fifth Avenue department store. I was an international star with a major recording contract, wrapping Christmas presents for pocket money."

"Da Doo Ron Ron" entered the Hot 100 at number 89 on May 14, 1977, and went to number one nine weeks later. It followed the Partridge Family's number one record by six years and seven months, making Shirley Jones and Shaun Cassidy the only mother-son combination to both have number one singles.

Two more top 10 hits followed: the American release of "That's Rock 'n' Roll" (number three) and "Hey Deanie" (number seven), both written by Eric Carmen. Cassidy continued his acting career, starring in the "Breaking Away" series after three years of "The Hardy Boys." Critics lauded Shaun's portrayal of a retarded youth in the 1979 television movie "Like Normal People." "It was nice to finally find out I was an actor," he declared. "I had to test myself, to push myself, because it's real easy to get comfortable in a mold."

In 1987, Cassidy was cast in ABC-TV's "General Hospital" as drifter Dusty Walker. The 28-year-old actor was no longer playing a teenager. "I'm too old," Cassidy said. "You can't go home again."

### THE TOP FIVE
*Week of July 16, 1977*

1 **Da Doo Ron Ron**
Shaun Cassidy

2 **Looks Like We Made It**
Barry Manilow

3 **Undercover Angel**
Alan O'Day

4 **I Just Want to be Your Everything**
Andy Gibb

5 **I'm in You**
Peter Frampton

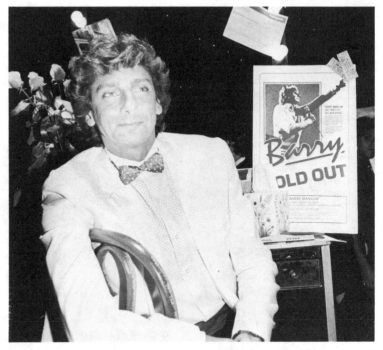

Writers: *Richard Kerr*
*Will Jennings*

Producers: *Ron Dante*
*Barry Manilow*

*July 23, 1977*
*1 week*

"LOOKS LIKE WE MADE IT" could well sum up the career of Barry Manilow. "Nobody was more surprised than I was when I became successful," he told interviewer Robyn Flans. "I was one of the millions of people sitting around waiting to find out who would be the next pop success since there really wasn't anybody on the horizon. I looked up one afternoon and realized it was me. . . . What a nice surprise, but it was terrifying. . . . No one is ever prepared for it."

It might have been hard to guess that the Brooklyn teenager who did not care for Elvis Presley would one day reach the peak of the same Hot 100 that the King topped 17 times.

At 22 years old, he was so desperate to get his music career going that he wrote to the *Playboy* adviser column asking what he should do. The magazine printed his letter and told him to "go sow your wild musical notes."

He had some experience already, writing an original score for an off-Broadway musical version of *The Drunkard* and working as musical director for WCBS-TV's "Callback!" series. He took *Playboy's* advice to heart and formed a musical duo with Jeanne Lucas. He was the piano player and arranger and she was the

## THE TOP FIVE
*Week of July 23, 1977*

1  **Looks Like We Made It**
   Barry Manilow

2  **I Just Want to be
   Your Everything**
   Andy Gibb

3  **Da Doo Ron Ron**
   Shaun Cassidy

4  **I'm in You**
   Peter Frampton

5  **My Heart Belongs to Me**
   Barbra Streisand

vocalist, until a club in Richmond, Indiana, booked them as a singing duet. On the plane trip to Richmond, Barry quickly learned how to sing "Georgy Girl" and "Somethin' Stupid."

Jeanne and Barry had a two-year run at Manhattan's Upstairs at the Downstairs, opening for Joan Rivers. Then Barry was asked to fill in as house pianist at the Continental Baths.

He took the job and in the spring of 1972, a red-headed dynamo named Bette Midler was booked to sing at the Baths. Barry soon became her musical director, arranger and pianist. When she signed with Atlantic Records, he co-produced and arranged her first two albums, *The Divine Miss M* and *Bette Midler*.

Meanwhile, Barry had played some of his songs for a friend, Ron Dante [see 258—"Sugar, Sugar"], who was also singing commercial jingles. They decided to record a demo tape together and between the two of them, came up with five thousand dollars to cut it. "It was really a toss-up as to who was going to sing, Ron or me," Barry told Merv Griffin. But Barry knew the words to the songs and sung them on the demo, and Bell Records offered him a deal if he

would agree to tour.

"I had never even considered fronting a band or being a soloist and when I was given the opportunity, I had a lot of thinking to do about it," Manilow told Robyn Flans. "I wanted to make that album because I just loved being in the studio, but I really wanted to be a composer, arranger or producer. I didn't want a singing career."

Coincidentally with Bell's request for him to tour, Midler asked him to be the musical director of her first national tour. He agreed, with the understanding that he would be allowed to sing three songs. He was given the unenviable position of opening the show's second act, following Bette's "Do You Want to Dance?"

"Looks Like We Made It" was composed by Richard Kerr, the man who wrote the music for Manilow's first number one single [see 389—"Mandy"], and lyricist Will Jennings [see 562—"Up Where We Belong"]. It debuted on the Hot 100 at number 88 on May 7, 1977, and became Barry's third chart-topper 11 weeks later. By January, 1981, Manilow had scored an impressive run of 18 consecutive top 40 hits, a string broken by "Lonely Together," a number 45 record in April, 1981.

# 472 I Just Want to Be Your Everything RSO 872

## ANDY GIBB

*Writer: Barry Gibb*

*Producers: Barry Gibb*
  *Albhy Galuten*
  *Karl Richardson*

*July 30, 1977*
*4 weeks*

SIX months before Hugh Gibb, his wife Barbara, daughter Leslie and sons Barry, Maurice and Robin were scheduled to move from Manchester, England, to Brisbane, Australia, Barbara gave birth to the fourth Gibb son, Andrew Roy, on March 5, 1958.

Nine years later, the Gibb family headed back to England in search of recognition for their three older sons' band, the Bee Gees [see 297—"How Can You Mend a Broken Heart"]. Moving into a two-family house in the London suburb of Hendon, the family's routine lifestyle was soon interrupted by the Bee Gees' first hit, "New York Mining Disaster 1941."

"I was going to a little school there," Andy said. "I knew they were sort of popular in Australia before we left, but to come home from school and find five or six hundred kids in the street, around the front door, and that was going on every day. And, actually, at the point of being 10 years old, you really don't think 'show business,' with the glitter and the stardom and the whole thing. I just accepted it. My brothers had to leave the house eventually. . . . It was unheard of, what was going on."

After three years in England, Hugh and Barbara Gibb took their youngest child and moved to the island of Ibiza, off the coast of Spain.

## THE TOP FIVE

*Week of July 30, 1977*

1  **I Just Want to be Your Everything**
   Andy Gibb

2  **I'm in You**
   Peter Frampton

3  **Looks Like We Made It**
   Barry Manilow

4  **My Heart Belongs to Me**
   Barbra Streisand

5  **Da Doo Ron Ron**
   Shaun Cassidy

Older brother Barry had given Andy his first guitar. At 13, Andy made his debut at a local tourist club. Because of his age and British citizenship, he received no salary, but he began to familiarize himself with performing publicly. Andy recalled, "That's when I met Tony Messina, my personal assistant. He got me my first gig, so to speak, playing in a wine bar to Swedish tourists, which was fun. The majority of these Swedish people, 90 per cent, were girls between 16 and 24 years old. Ah, yes. That was really fun. But I certainly became more aware vocally of what I could do and what I was suited to do, playing music." Gibb performed the current hits of the day and covered his brothers' hits of the '60s and early '70s.

Feeling uncomfortable under the repressive Franco regime, the Gibbs left Ibiza and moved to the Isle of Man in 1973, where Andy performed at the island's two main clubs. In 1975, brother Barry and manager Robert Stigwood suggested Andy return to Australia to gain greater attention for his music. He signed with ATA Records and released one song, "Words and Music." It became a huge Australian hit.

On the other side of the world, Stigwood and the Gibb family were impressed with 18-year-old Andy's

instant success and summoned him to North America. In Stigwood's Bermuda home, Andy signed a contract and started writing songs for his first RSO album.

"It was Barry who came up with the tune 'I Just Want to Be Your Everything,'" Andy is reported saying in *The Top Ten* by Bob Gilbert and Gary Theroux. "We needed a single and locked ourselves in a bedroom at (Stigwood's) big estate. I think we wound up writing four songs in two days. . . . The first day we came up with a nice ballad that was never used. Then, that afternoon, on his own, Barry came up with 'I Just Want to Be Your Everything.'"

During this Bermuda writing session, Barry and Andy also wrote "(Love Is) Thicker Than Water" [see 479], which Stigwood wanted to issue as the first single. Three days before the scheduled release date he changed his mind and put out "I Just Want to Be Your Everything." It was the lowest-ranking new entry on the Hot 100 the week of April 23, 1977, debuting at number 88. Ascending slowly, it made number one 14 weeks later. After three weeks it submitted to the Emotions' "Best of My Love." Dipping to two and then three, it made a startling return to the top four weeks after beginning its chart descent.

COLUMBIA 10544 **Best of My Love** 473
THE EMOTIONS

Writers: *Maurice White*
*Al McKay*

Producer: *Maurice White*

*August 20, 1977*
*5 weeks*

THOUGH the title was often confused with a number one hit by the Eagles [see 395—"Best of My Love"], the Emotions' "Best of My Love" belonged to an altogether different musical genre. Maurice White, leading light behind Earth, Wind and Fire [see 404—"Shining Star"], had composed the rhythm and a rough outline of the tune with Al McKay when he went into the studio to produce the singing trio. Lead singer Wanda Hutchinson learned the song from the demonstration tape, but had to jump her final vocals an octave higher than her usual register. It wasn't until she heard the song on the radio that she decided she was satisfied with her performance. Recorded during the heyday of disco, this "Best of My Love" whirled off dance club floors to the top of the Hot 100, earning a gold record for selling more than one million copies as well as a Grammy for Best R&B Vocal Performance by a Duo, Group or Chorus.

Reigning at disco's summit was a lengthy stretch from the Emotions' first vocalizings at Mt. Sinai Baptist Church in Chicago. There sisters Sheila, Wanda and Jeanette Hutchinson, with their father and mentor Joe, were known initially as the Hutchinsons, then the Heavenly

Sunbeams. In 1958 they debuted on television, then hosted a radio program of gospel music. Shortly thereafter they graduated to a weekly TV series on Sunday mornings. On tour, they met the Staple Singers [see 312—"I'll Take You There"], who brought them to Memphis-based Stax/Volt Records in 1968.

To emphasize their metamorphosis into a secular group they chose to call themselves the Emotions after a friend confided to Joe that the girls' voices elicited an emotional response in the form of spinal chills. Along the way, sister Pam replaced Jeanette, while the newly-monikered threesome delved into pop music under the aegis of Issac Hayes. Four of their Volt singles reached the Hot 100, but none placed higher than "So I Can Love You" (number 39 in July, 1969). They made a brief appearance in the 1973 *Wattstax* documentary, but when

### THE TOP FIVE
*Week of August 20, 1977*

1  **Best of my Love**
   Emotions

2  **I Just Want to be
   Your Everything**
   Andy Gibb

3  **(Your Love Has Lifted Me)
   Higher and Higher**
   Rita Coolidge

4  **I'm in You**
   Peter Frampton

5  **Easy**
   Commodores

Stax folded in 1975 they were without a record label.

They signed with Maurice White's Kalimba Productions and Columbia Records (Earth, Wind and Fire's label) snapped them up. *Flowers*, the initial White/Emotions collaboration, gave them a two-sided chart entry, "Flowers" / "I Don't Want to Lose Your Love," but it didn't make the top 50. Their next LP, *Rejoice*, turned platinum thanks to the single "Best of My Love," which debuted on the Hot 100 at number 82 on June 11, 1977. It succeeded Andy Gibb's "I Just Want to Be Your Everything" at number one 10 weeks later. After four weeks at the top, it was in turn replaced by "I Just Want to Be Your Everything," which made a dramatic return after falling to number three. Gibb's encore lasted one week, then the Emotions took over for one additional week.

Although they did not reach the top 40 again on their own, they did team up with Earth, Wind and Fire for the rousing "Boogie Wonderland" (number six in July, 1979).

A 1984 outing on Red Label Records, *Sincerely*, was followed by their 1985 debut on Motown, *If Only I Knew*. "We wanted to do something that reflected our musical growth over the years," explained Sheila. The record introduced Adrianne Harris as a replacement for Pam, who returned to college to finish her degree.

## 474 'Star Wars' Theme/Cantina Band  MILLENNIUM 604
MECO

*Writer: John Williams*

*Producers: Meco Monardo*
*Harold Wheeler*
*Tony Bongiovi*

*October 1, 1977*
*2 weeks*

ON May 25, 1977, Meco Monardo joined the people at a New York City theater who were lined up to see the opening day screening of a new film starring Mark Hamill, Carrie Fisher and Harrison Ford. Like millions of other fans seeing George Lucas' *Star Wars* for the first time, Meco thought the film was a *tour de force*. He loved the music—although he didn't think the main title theme, as performed by John Williams and the London Symphony Orchestra, was commercial enough to be a top 40 single.

Also like millions of others, Meco went back to see the film—11 times in all. By his last visit, he had conceived of a 15-minute disco treatment of several themes in the movie, including the music played by the Cantina Band in the bar on Tatooine. He also planned to include R2-D2 sound effects. He called Neil Bogart at Casablanca Records and explained his idea. Based on the tremendous success of *Star Wars*, Bogart agreed to Meco's idea without hearing any of his music.

Meco hired 75 musicians to play on the track, and played trombone and keyboards himself. The complete composition was released as part of an album and on a 12″ single. The original main title theme by the London Symphony Orchestra was

### THE TOP FIVE
*Week of October 1, 1977*

1  **"Star Wars" Theme/ Cantina Band**
Meco

2  **Keep It Comin' Love**
K.C. & the Sunshine Band

3  **Don't Stop**
Fleetwood Mac

4  **Best of my Love**
Emotions

5  **Strawberry Letter 23**
Brothers Johnson

released by 20th Century Records and entered the Hot 100 on July 9, 1977, less than two months after the film opened. Monardo was wrong about its commerciality; it raced up to number 10. But Meco's version, which debuted on the chart on August 6, raced past it to go to number one the week of October 1.

*Star Wars* went on to become the highest-grossing motion picture of all time, a record it temporarily lost to *E.T.* in 1982 but later regained with its 1997 re-release. Meco later recorded other film themes in his own style. He followed "'Star Wars' Theme/Cantina Band" with the "Theme from 'Close Encounters,'" which ran a close second to John Williams' original version (Williams went to number 13, while Meco was right behind him at number 18). Then came a medley of "Themes from 'The Wizard of Oz,'" a medley of themes from *The Empire Strikes Back* and "Love Theme from 'Shogun' (Mariko's Theme)."

Meco Monardo was born November 29, 1939, in Johnsonburg, Pennsylvania. His father played the trombone and taught Meco how to play. He was proficient enough to

join the high school band while he was still in sixth grade. In high school he formed his own Dixieland band, and after graduating in 1957, won a scholarship to the Eastman School of Music in Rochester, New York. He attended West Point, where he played in the Cadet Band, and learned about arranging from an Army sergeant. Returning to civilian life, Meco lived in New York City and was introduced to bandleader Kai Winding by a mutual friend, Chuck Mangione. Despite strong dislike for pop music, Meco worked for nine years playing all kinds of music.

"I was doing all these dumb ditty bop records that never came out," he told Romeo. He also earned a nice living arranging commercials, like a Neil Diamond spot for Coca Cola. In 1974 he co-produced his first pop hit, "Never Can Say Goodbye" by Gloria Gaynor [see 498—"I Will Survive"], followed by Carol Douglas' "Doctor's Orders."

His last single to appear on the Hot 100 was was "Ewok Celebration" in 1983, inspired by *Return of the Jedi*, giving Meco a hat trick of hit songs from the *Star Wars* trilogy.

WARNER/CURB 8455 **You Light Up My Life**
DEBBY BOONE

**475**

*Writer: Joe Brooks*

*Producer: Joe Brooks*

*October 15, 1977*
*10 weeks*

Pat AND Debby Boone were both twenty years old when they each had their first hit records. Pat was just two months shy of his twenty-first birthday when "Two Hearts" entered the chart on April 2, 1955. His daughter Debby was a mere three weeks away from turning twenty-one when "You Light Up My Life" debuted on the Hot 100 at number 71 on September 3, 1977. Six weeks later it had moved to number one and remained there for 10 weeks, the longest-running number one single since "Don't Be Cruel" [see 14] by Elvis Presley in August, 1956. Debby's hit was the first to have a 10-week run since the pre-rock-era days of October, 1948, when Dinah Shore's "Buttons and Bows" began its 10-week stay at the top. Aside from "Physical" [see 550], no other number one hit by a solo female artist managed to reign longer than 10 weeks until Whitney Houston's "I Will Always Love You" [see 813].

It was a stunning victory for Debby. Pat didn't top the Best Sellers in Stores survey until his 11th chart single [see 22—"Love Letters in the Sand"]. A rivalry between father and daughter made good copy, but Pat says it never existed. "Oh, I loved it!" he exclaims. "It was a sensational time. It brought back all the early excitement of my career, only it was doubly exciting because it was my daughter doing this. Lots of folks tried to see if there was some sort of professional jealousy or envy, and they just didn't understand how a father feels. Even Perry Como, who's a longtime friend, asked my manager once, 'Doesn't this sort of thing get under Pat's skin?' For her to surpass anything I'd ever done with her first record, I thought it was sensational."

The third of Pat and Shirley Boone's four daughters, Debby was born September 22, 1956, in Hackensack, New Jersey. She was four when her family moved to Los Angeles. Music was an important part of church, school and home life, and the sisters were often led in song while touring the country with their father. The Boone girls made their first professional appearance on Pat's television series in 1960.

Her teenage years were troubled, as Debby became a rebellious adolescent. It wasn't until after high school graduation that she fit into the family's conservative lifestyle. Choosing a career in music, Debby assumed the role of lead singer for the Boones. The four sisters signed with Motown Records. They left the label without having a hit, and moved to Warner/Curb, where their luckless streak continued. But label owner Mike Curb was keeping his ears open for a suitable song to launch Debby's solo career. He found it at a screening of *You Light Up My Life*, a film starring Didi Conn as a young singer trying to find fame as a recording artist. Conn's singing in the movie was lip-synched by a commercial jingle vocalist, Kacey Cisyk, who was destined to remain anonymous. Even the single released by Arista from the soundtrack listed the artist as "Original Cast" instead of her name.

Curb borrowed the instrumental track from writer/producer Joe Brooks and recorded Debby's vocal over it. "I flew to New York with my mother," Debbie recalled. "I recorded the song almost on a trial basis.

When we cut the record, my mother prayed the whole time I sang. When it was over, we looked at each other almost fearfully. We felt strange, like something was about to happen."

Years later, Debby disclosed that she was not thinking of a mortal man when she sang the song. "It wasn't a Christian song," she explained in *Billboard*, "although many people thought it was. However, mainly because the lyrics really lent themselves to how I felt about my relationship with the Lord, that's the way I chose to sing it. I never really thought anyone would know."

In addition to its stamina at number one, "You Light Up My Life" collected many honors, including an American Music Award for Favorite Pop Single and an Oscar for Best Original Song. Debby won a Grammy for Best New Artist.

Married to Gabriel Ferrer on September 1, 1979, Debby gave birth to son Jordan Alexander almost a year later. Jordan has three more siblings now, and mom has written a series of children's books. Debby has also starred in stage musicals including *Grease* (as tough-girl Rizzo) and *Meet Me in St. Louis.*

**THE TOP FIVE**
*Week of October 15, 1977*

1 **You Light Up My Life**
Debby Boone

2 **Keep It Comin' Love**
K.C. & the Sunshine Band

3 **Nobody Does It Better**
Carly Simon

4 **That's Rock 'n' Roll**
Shaun Cassidy

5 **"Star Wars" Theme/**
**Cantina Band**
Meco

# 476 How Deep Is Your Love RSO 882
## BEE GEES

*Writers:* Barry Gibb
    Robin Gibb
    Maurice Gibb

*Producers:* Barry Gibb
    Robin Gibb
    Maurice Gibb
    Karl Richardson
    Albhy Galuten

*December 24, 1977*
*3 weeks*

THE June 7, 1976, issue of *New York* magazine featured an illustration of a Manhattan crowd dancing the night away. The headline underneath the magazine's logo read, "Tribal Rites of the New Saturday Night by Nik Cohn."

"About six months before that story was published, Nik came to me," Robert Stigwood revealed in the Bee Gees' authorized biography, written by David Leaf. "I'd known him from his days in England. He told me he wanted to write a movie, or write a story for a movie, so I said, 'O.K. If you have an idea, come and see me again and we'll talk about it.' Six months later, I picked up *New York* magazine and saw this cover story and Nik's name. So I immediately read it. And I thought, 'This is a wonderful film subject.' So I called Nik up and said, 'You're crazy. You come to me about writing a story for

a picture. This is it.' And I made a deal with his agent in 24 hours to acquire the rights."

Meanwhile, across the Atlantic, the Bee Gees were settled in at the Chateau D'Herouville studios outside Paris. Elton John had made the place famous with his 1972 *Honky Chateau* LP and the Bee Gees wanted to record the follow-up album to *Children of the World* there. Unfortunately, the place had gone to seed. Determined to make the best of it, the Bee Gees recorded the first song for the proposed album, "If I Can't Have You," when they received a phone call from Stigwood. He told them to forget the studio album, he wanted a live LP to come out next. A few days passed and he telephoned again with a new directive. He needed four new songs for a film he was producing.

"We never saw any script," Barry said in Leaf's biography. "(Robert) said, 'It's about a bunch of guys that live in New York.'" The first song written after Stigwood's call was "How Deep Is Your Love," but it was meant for Yvonne Elliman, not the film. The Bee Gees were not even aware of a love scene in the film, but Stigwood heard the song and was adamant the Bee Gees record it themselves.

Stigwood arrived at the Chateau a couple of weeks later and gave the

brothers a very rough, verbal outline of the film's story. He stressed it was about a young guy who lives for Saturday night, when he can spend his weekly wages and go dancing. "So that's all we knew, except it was John Travolta playing the part," Maurice Gibb explained in the Bee Gees' biography. "We'd done 'If I Can't Have You' and 'How Deep Is Your Love' and we were thinking to ourselves, 'Wow! A disco film. Let's get into some good disco songs.' It took about two-and-a-half weeks to write them and put them down as demos. When Robert heard them, he said, 'You hit the nail right on the spot. That's perfect.' "

The Bee Gees remained in France while the film—titled *Saturday Night Fever*—was in production in the States. When Stigwood left the Chateau, he took with him the rough mixes of the songs that would be used in the picture as is.

"How Deep Is Your Love" was the first single issued from the soundtrack, prior to the actual release of the film. It entered the Hot 100 at number 83 on September 24, 1977, and moved into the number one position 13 weeks later. It remained in the top 10 for 17 consecutive weeks, the longest run of any single since the Hot 100 was initiated on August 4, 1958.

### THE TOP FIVE
*Week of December 24, 1977*

1 **How Deep is Your Love**
Bee Gees

2 **You Light Up My Life**
Debby Boone

3 **Blue Bayou**
Linda Ronstadt

4 **Back in Love Again**
LTD

5 **It's So Easy**
Linda Ronstadt

Writers: *Peter Beckett*
*John Charles Crowley*

Producers: *Dennis Lambert*
*Brian Potter*

*January 14, 1978*
*3 weeks*

WHEN "Baby Come Back" by Player followed the Bee Gees' "How Deep Is Your Love" at number one, it was the 19th time in the rock era that a record label succeeded itself at the top of the charts. But RSO was just getting started.

Player were originally signed to Dennis Lambert and Brian Potter's Haven Records, distributed by Capitol and then Arista. When Haven folded, Lambert and Potter took the group to RSO.

The origin of Player can be traced to a trendy Hollywood party where all the guests were expected to wear white. Peter Beckett, a guitarist from Liverpool, was gauche enough to wear jeans, and so was one other party-goer, John Charles Crowley III, a musician from Galveston Bay, Texas. Their similar manner of dress was reason enough to strike up a conversation; when they discovered they had similar musical interests, they agreed to get together for a jam session.

Beckett, who had been a member

of the American groups Friends and Skyband, agreed with Crowley that the session went well enough to pursue the idea of organizing a band. They found bassist Ronn Moss (who had played with the groups Count Zeppelin and the Fabled Airship, and Punk Rock) and drummer John Friesen (drummer and assistant musical producer for the Ice Follies), two musicians who had been friends in high school. The last addition was keyboard player Wayne Cook, who joined the group after they had taken the cover photograph for their first album.

Player completed that LP for Haven, but the label closed its doors before the album could be released. "The energy was there at the time," Beckett said in a 1978 *Billboard* interview. "We felt 'Baby Come Back' was a hit when we recorded it." The song was written by Beckett and Crowley after both had broken up with their respective girl friends. It took them about four hours to compose the tune, then they rehearsed in Crowley's garage/studio during a summery Los Angeles heat wave.

Lead vocalist Crowley explained in the same *Billboard* interview how they selected the name Player: "We saw the word on television when the players from the show were listed. We knocked off the 's' and went with it. I think the word holds a certain

ambiguity."

Critics were quick to cite "Baby Come Back" as being imitative of Daryl Hall and John Oates [see 457—"Rich Girl"]. Moss had a reply for them: "Most people who liken us to Hall and Oates haven't heard the rest of the album." Beckett added: "They label us for the sake of labelling. Everyone is likened to someone. We only sound like them in part."

Hall and Oates did have a longer chart life than Player. After "Baby Come Back," they took "This Time I'm in It for Love" to number 10. Two more RSO singles followed, but neither made a great impression. A 1980 Casablanca single and a 1982 RCA release both charted in the 40s.

## THE TOP FIVE
*Week of January 14, 1978*

1 **Baby Come Back**
Player

2 **How Deep Is Your Love**
Bee Gees

3 **Here You Come Again**
Dolly Parton

4 **You're in My Heart**
Rod Stewart

5 **Back in Love Again**
L.T.D.

## 478 Stayin' Alive RSO 885
### BEE GEES

Writers: Barry Gibb
    Robin Gibb
    Maurice Gibb

Producers: Barry Gibb
    Robin Gibb
    Maurice Gibb
    Karl Richardson
    Albhy Galuten

February 4, 1978
4 weeks

"SATURDAY NIGHT, SATURDAY NIGHT . . ." The phrase kept running through Robert Stigwood's mind. The basis for Stigwood's latest film project (he had produced *Tommy* and *Jesus Christ, Superstar* in the early '70s) was an article by fellow Briton Nik Cohn, entitled "Tribal Rites of the New Saturday Night." Years earlier, in Bermuda, Stigwood had heard the Bee Gees sing a number called "Saturday Night, Saturday Night." When he telephoned them at the Chateau D'Herouville studios to request four new songs for a film project he was working on, he asked that they record an eight-minute version of that song.

"Robert wanted a scene that was eight minutes long, where (John) Travolta was dancing with this girl," Barry is quoted in *The Top Ten* by Bob Gilbert and Gary Theroux. "It

would have a nice dance tempo, a romantic interlude and all hell breaking loose at the end. I said, 'Robert, that's crazy. We want to put this song out as a single, and we don't think the rhythm should break. It should go from beginning to end with the same rhythm, and get stronger all the way. To go into a lilting ballad just doesn't make sense.' The film got changed."

When Stigwood heard the initial demo of "Stayin' Alive," he objected, asking why it wasn't "Saturday Night, Saturday Night." "We said because there are so many bloody records out called 'Saturday Night.' It's corny; it's a terrible title," Maurice Gibb recalled in David Leaf's biography of the Bee Gees. "We said, 'Either it's 'Stayin' Alive' or we'll keep the song," Barry added.

"Stayin' Alive" it was, and it was the music heard in the electrifying opening of *Saturday Night Fever*, as Travolta's character, Tony Manero, struts down a New York City sidewalk. One week prior to the film's release, a 30-second teaser of the opening sequence was seen in theaters around the country, the pounding beat of "Stayin' Alive" playing under it. This brief coming attraction was enough to create a demand for the song, even though

the soundtrack album had not been released yet.

"Stayin' Alive" was issued as a single before "How Deep Is Your Love" [see 476] reached number one. It entered the Hot 100 at number 65 on December 10, 1977, and eight weeks later became the second consecutive chart-topper from *Saturday Night Fever*.

The soundtrack album went on to sell more than 25 million copies, making it not just the most successful soundtrack ever released, but the best-selling album of all time, a record that would stand until 1984 [see 571—"Beat It"].

### THE TOP FIVE
*Week of February 4, 1978*

1   **Stayin' Alive**
    Bee Gees

2   **Short People**
    Randy Newman

3   **Baby Come Back**
    Player

4   **We Are the Champions**
    Queen

5   **Love is Thicker than Water**
    Andy Gibb

RSO 883 **(Love Is) Thicker Than Water** 479
ANDY GIBB

*Writers: Barry Gibb*
*Andy Gibb*

*Producers: Barry Gibb*
*Albhy Galuten*
*Karl Richardson*

*March 4, 1978*
*2 weeks*

**A**FTER watching his brothers' success from the sidelines, 19-year-old Andy Gibb firmly established his own career with his second consecutive number one single, "(Love Is) Thicker Than Water." Initially planned by manager Robert Stigwood to be Andy's debut single, it was only a last minute change of mind that saw "I Just Want to Be Your Everything" [see 472] released first. Years later, the youngest Gibb revealed that he intuitively felt that if "(Love Is) Thicker Than Water" had been released first, it wouldn't have been a hit.

Both songs were written in Bermuda. When they were ready, Andy and eldest brother Barry headed to Miami's Criteria Studios to cut demos. Living in Australia at the time, Andy finished his work and headed home, but was only there two weeks when Stigwood asked him to return to Miami to record his first album, *Flowing Rivers*.

Bee Gees' co-producers Albhy Galuten and Karl Richardson were slated to produce Andy's LP, and Barry offered to serve as executive producer. Andy, who happily accepted his brother's offer, later told Dick Clark, "It was very easy for me because I had the finest producer to take care of me, to make sure every-

## THE TOP FIVE
*Week of March 11, 1978*

1  **Love is Thicker than Water**
   Andy Gibb

2  **Night Fever**
   Bee Gees

3  **Sometimes When We Touch**
   Dan Hill

4  **Emotion**
   Samantha Sang

5  **Lay Down Sally**
   Eric Clapton

thing went smoothly. So it was a very rewarding experience."

Helping enrich the experience was a guest star who performed anonymously on *Flowing Rivers*. While Gibb was recording the album, Eagles guitarist Joe Walsh [see 411—"One of These Nights"] was working in an adjoining studio. At Galuten and Richardson's invitation, Walsh dropped by to play guitar on "(Love Is) Thicker Than Water."

The Bee Gees and Andy had always been very conscious of record sales and chart activity, with Robin considered to be the "chart freak" of the family. Andy, who had been trained to monitor charts and sales as avidly, watched "(Love Is) Thicker Than Water" progress up the Hot 100. "It slowed down . . . we were all a little scared. There's lots of points where all the record people at RSO said they were a little worried that it was stopping. It didn't lose its bullet, but it really heavily lost its jump in sales activity. And then, for an equally strange reason, it just picked

up and nothing stopped it. So it was not predictable . . . but it's still a commercial song. . . . We believed in it. . . . I think the momentum of the first record obviously helped the second a little, but it was, again, a different record."

It is impossible to discuss Andy Gibb's career without noting the influence and impact of his brothers. In the Bee Gees authorized biography, Andy is quoted, "They have been the biggest influence and my biggest help. There's a magic when we work together. Imagine having the greatest singers and songwriters living under one roof . . . your roof. Their harmonies, their ballads, all influenced me greatly. I guess you could say I idolized the Bee Gees as a band and loved them as brothers."

With "(Love Is) Thicker Than Water," Andy surpassed his brother's initial chart achievements by having his first two chart singles reach number one. Impressive, yes, but Gibb wasn't through yet [see 485—"Shadow Dancing"].

# 480 Night Fever RSO 889
## BEE GEES

Writers: Barry Gibb
       Robin Gibb
       Maurice Gibb

Producers: Barry Gibb
          Robin Gibb
          Maurice Gibb
          Karl Richardson
          Albhy Galuten

March 18, 1978
8 weeks

THE BEE GEES continued their domination of the Hot 100 with their third consecutive number one single from the soundtrack of *Saturday Night Fever*. "Night Fever" was the fastest-rising single yet from the film. Debuting at number 76 on February 4, 1978, while "Stayin' Alive" [see 478] was still number one and "How Deep Is Your Love" [see 476] was still in the top 10, "Night Fever" was burning up the chart, moving 76-32-17-8-5-2 to number one. The week "Night Fever" moved to number eight, the Bee Gees' former two singles were still anchored in the top 10, making them the first group to have three songs in the top 10 simultaneously since the Beatles. And the week that "Night Fever" took over the top spot, "Stayin' Alive" resurged, moving from number six back to number two, where it remained for five weeks, turning platinum in the process. That made the Bee Gees the first group to have the top two songs on the Hot 100 since the Beatles last did it on April 25, 1964 [see 145—"Can't Buy Me Love"]. If those statistics weren't enough, the Bee Gees pulled off one more coup. For three consecutive weeks, they were responsible for writing and/or producing five records in the top 10. In addition to their own chart-toppers of "Night Fever" and "Stayin' Alive," they had written and produced "Emotion" for Samantha Sang. Barry had co-written and co-produced his brother Andy's former number one single, "(Love Is) Thicker Than Water" [see 479], and all three Gibbs had written Yvonne Elliman's "If I Can't Have You" [see 481], which was on its way to the top.

"Night Fever" also extended the record streak set by RSO Records—it was the fifth consecutive RSO single to top the *Billboard* chart, and brought the label's running total to 20 consecutive weeks at number one.

"Night Fever" was written before the film *Saturday Night Fever* had a title. In fact, it was the first title suggested by the Bee Gees, but Robert Stigwood rejected it as sounding too pornographic. Albhy Galuten, one of the record's producers, recalled in David Leaf's biography of the Bee Gees: "They spent a lot of time thinking of titles that would be evocative and represent the street scene of New York. That's where 'Stayin' Alive' and 'Night Fever' come from. They were both potential titles for the film, finely crafted to the meaning of the film."

Robin Gibb is quoted in Bob Gilbert and Gary Theroux' *The Top Ten*, "Stigwood . . . wanted to call the film *Saturday Night*. And we had already written the song 'Night Fever.' We told him we didn't like the title *Saturday Night*, and he said he didn't want to call the movie just *Night Fever*. So he thought it over for a while, called us back, and said, 'O.K., let's compromise. Let's call it *Saturday Night Fever*."

While the Bee Gees were writing the songs for the film in France, John Travolta was in training, working on dance routines back in the United States. The song he used was an older Bee Gees number from their *Main Course* album, "You Should Be Dancing [see 441], and when it came time to film his dance number for the movie, he didn't want to change songs. In the Bee Gees' biography, Maurice explained, "He didn't want to rehearse to another number, didn't want to start doing the same dance routine to a different song. It was supposed to be 'Night Fever' in that scene, but we didn't mind. It was an old hit of ours, but he made the song come alive again for us with that dance routine."

The first time the Bee Gees saw *Saturday Night Fever* complete with music was at the wrap party for Stigwood's next film, *Grease*. Sitting with Stigwood, director John Badham, John Travolta and Olivia Newton-John, the brothers watched a rough edit and Maurice recalled his reaction in Leaf's biography: "I thought, 'It's not the greatest story in the world, but it's an exciting film.'"

## THE TOP FIVE
*Week of March 18, 1978*

1 **Night Fever**
   Bee Gees

2 **Stayin' Alive**
   Bee Gees

3 **Emotion**
   Samantha Sang

4 **Lay Down Sally**
   Eric Clapton

5 **Love is Thicker than Water**
   Andy Gibb

*Writers: Barry Gibb*
*Robin Gibb*
*Maurice Gibb*

*Producer: Freddie Perren*

*May 13, 1978*
*1 week*

SHE started out as a fallen woman looking for a savior. She then redeemed herself in a stint with a fallen rock idol. But Yvonne Elliman was finally sanctified as a participant in disco's greatest hour.

Born December 29, 1951, in Honolulu, Hawaii, Yvonne learned how to play the piano from her father. She was part of a group in high school, We Folk, and after graduation she moved to London to try and find success in the music business. She was singing at a Kings Road club called the Pheasantry when Tim Rice and Andrew Lloyd Webber saw her and invited her to sing the role of Mary Magdalene for their rock opera *Jesus Christ, Superstar.*

When the album evolved into a stage production, Elliman stayed with the part for four years. Her original recording of "I Don't Know How to Love Him" was released as a single, and while it did respectably, charting at number 28 in June, 1971, it was surpassed by a cover version from Helen Reddy [see 324—"I Am Woman"].

In 1974 Yvonne relocated to New York for rehearsals of the Broadway production of *Jesus Christ, Superstar.* There she met Bill Oakes from Robert Stigwood's office and they were married soon after. Later that year, Elliman was at Criteria Studios in Miami, Florida, when Eric Clapton was recording *461 Ocean Boulevard* for RSO Records. He asked her to sing backing vocals on "I Shot the Sheriff" [see 375], which led to joining the heavyweight guitarist for his fabled comeback tour.

She was signed as an artist in her own right to RSO. Her *Rising Sun* LP was produced by Steve Cropper, but yielded no hit singles. Teaming up with producer Freddie Perren [see 267—"I Want You Back"], she recorded the *Love Me* album, which gave her two top 20 hits: the sizzling title track written by Barry and Robin Gibb and a remake of Barbara Lewis' "Hello Stranger."

She told *Rolling Stone* she felt "like a traitor" for leaving Clapton. "My voice doesn't lend itself to screaming," Elliman told the magazine. "It really prefers to sing love ballads. I'm a complete romanticist as well. I like appealing to women. I like pulling their heartstrings."

She almost got her chance to pull a few heartstrings. When the Bee Gees were asked to score *Saturday Night Fever*, they had already written "How Deep Is Your Love" [see 476] for Elliman, but Stigwood insisted the Bee Gees sing the ballad themselves.

Instead Yvonne was given the chance to belt out an uptempo disco tune, "If I Can't Have You." It entered the Hot 100 at number 89 on January 28, 1978. When it went to number one 15 weeks later, it established three records:

1. It was the fourth number one single from *Saturday Night Fever*, the only motion picture to produce that many chart-topping 45s.

2. It was the fourth consecutive number one single to be written by Barry Gibb, breaking the record set by John Lennon and Paul McCartney, who penned three consecutive number ones in 1964 [see 145—"Can't Buy Me Love"].

3. It was the sixth consecutive number one single for RSO Records. No other label has ever had more than two consecutive 45s reach the top of the Hot 100. RSO dominated the chart summit for 21 weeks in a row, and would log another 10 weeks at one before the last day of 1978.

## THE TOP FIVE
*Week of May 13, 1978*

1 **If I Can't Have You**
Yvonne Elliman

2 **The Closer I Get to You**
Roberta Flack &
Donny Hathaway

3 **With a Little Luck**
Wings

4 **Too Much, Too Little,
Too Late**
Johnny Mathis &
Deniece Williams

5 **Night Fever**
Bee Gees

## 482 With a Little Luck CAPITOL 4559
### WINGS

*Writer: Paul McCartney*

*Producer: Paul McCartney*

*May 20, 1978*
*2 weeks*

"WITH A LITTLE LUCK" was the follow-up to the most successful British single of Paul McCartney's career, including his tenure with the Beatles. The record sold 2.5 million copies in the United Kingdom, replacing the Beatles' "She Loves You" [see 144] as the best-selling single of all time in Great Britain (a record it held until 1984, when Band Aid's "Do They Know It's Christmas?" sold over three million copies). The title of this best-selling song is "Mull of Kintyre." It did not chart in America.

Paul wrote "Mull of Kintyre" as an anthem for Scotland because he loved living on his farm near Campbelltown, about 11 miles from the southern tip of the Scottish peninsula known as the Kintyre. Accompanying Wings on the recording are the 21 bagpipers of the Campbelltown Pipe Band. Not certain that the ballad would be a hit, Paul made sure the "B" side was a rocker. Originally titled "Love School," "Girls School" was inspired by advertisements for pornographic films. In the States, where one didn't know the Mull of Kintyre from the ice plains of Io,

"Girls School" was considered the "A" side. Peaking at number 33 in January, 1978, it was one of the lowest-charting singles of Wings' career.

"With a Little Luck" was recorded in a 24-track studio installed by the Record Plant on board the Fair Carol, a yacht anchored in the Virgin Islands. Paul had taken Wings there to record tracks for an album tentatively titled *Water Wings*. But after spending the month of May, 1977, in the Virgin Islands, the recordings were completed in London and the title was changed to *London Town*.

### THE TOP FIVE
*Week of May 20, 1978*

1 **With a Little Luck**
  Wings

2 **The Closer I Get To You**
  Roberta Flack &
  Donny Hathaway

3 **Too Much, Too Little,**
  **Too Late**
  Johnny Mathis &
  Deniece Williams

4 **You're the One That I Want**
  John Travolta &
  Olivia Newton-John

5 **If I Can't Have You**
  Yvonne Elliman

Jimmy McCulloch left Wings in September, and the four remaining members checked in to Abbey Road studios on October 25. By the time they completed their work there, drummer Joe English had left the group as well. Now a trio again, Wings completed *London Town* at George Martin's AIR Studios and at Abbey Road.

"With a Little Luck" was the highest new entry on the Hot 100 for the week of March 25, 1978. Debuting at number 70, it reached the top of the chart eight weeks later. It was the first single *not* on the RSO label to be number one since December 17, 1977 [see 475—"You Light Up My Life"].

Before "With a Little Luck" fell off the Hot 100, McCartney announced two new additions for Wings. Denny Laine had recommended them both—guitarist Laurence Juber and drummer Steve Holly. The first release for Wings Mark Seven was the single "Goodnight Tonight," an attempt at disco that McCartney almost didn't release. But second thoughts prevailed, and "Goodnight Tonight," the first McCartney record under his new North American deal with Columbia Records, peaked at number five in May, 1979.

Next came *Back to the Egg*, the final album released by Wings. While the LP's two singles ("Getting Closer," "Arrow Through Me") failed to make much of a chart impression, for many the highlight of the album was the "Rockestra Theme," featuring an assemblage of guest stars that included Dave Gilmour of Pink Floyd; John Bonham and John Paul Jones of Led Zeppelin; Pete Townshend of the Who; Ronnie Lane, once of the Small Faces; Gary Brooker, once of Procol Harum; and Hank Marvin of the Shadows.

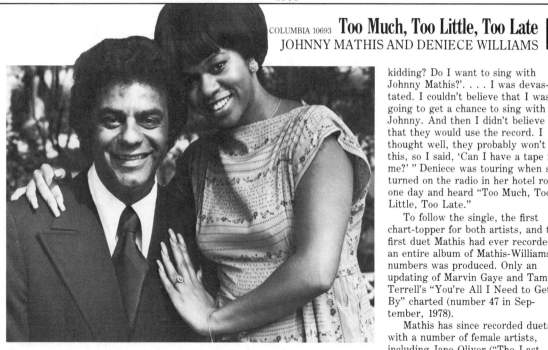

COLUMNS 10693 **Too Much, Too Little, Too Late**
JOHNNY MATHIS AND DENIECE WILLIAMS

**483**

Writers: *Nat Kipner*
*John Vallins*

Producer: *Jack Gold*

*June 3, 1978*
*1 week*

Johnny Mathis (born September 30, 1935, in San Francisco, California) made his first appearance on a *Billboard* chart on February 9, 1957, when "Wonderful! Wonderful!" made its debut. It remained on the survey for 39 weeks, the longest-running chart single until Paul Davis hit the 40-week mark with "I Go Crazy" on May 27, 1978. Mathis had little time to be upset about having his record broken—the following week he went to number one for the first time ever with "Too Much, Too Little, Too Late," a finely-crafted duet sung with Deniece Williams.

Mathis' highest ranking chart single prior to 1978 was the double-sided hit of "Chances Are" and "The Twelfth of Never," which reached number four on the Best Sellers in Stores chart in October, 1957. There were other classic singles—"It's Not for Me to Say," "Misty," "Gina"—romantic songs that helped make up *Johnny's Greatest Hits*, an album that remained on *Billboard's* LP chart for 490 weeks, another record Mathis held for years (until *Dark Side of the Moon* by Pink Floyd surpassed it).

While his name was assured a place in history, Mathis' chart career was in low gear in 1978. His last top 10 single had been "What Will My Mary Say" in 1963, and he hadn't even appeared on the Hot 100 since "Life Is a Song Worth Singing" in early 1974.

"Jack Gold, my producer, and I felt we had done as many good recordings as we could and couldn't figure out how we could do anything any better than we had already done, so we decided to try something different," Mathis divulged in a 1978 *Billboard* interview. "Jack had heard of Deniece and her success and knew how clever she was in the studio with background voices. . . . I grew up on R&B, jazz and classical music. So when we decided to try something different, we knew Deniece was big in the R&B area so I said, 'maybe we can get some of the R&B diehards to listen to some of my music.' We decided the best way was to get someone who was already accepted in that area and see what happens."

Deniece had sung with Stevie Wonder as part of the Wonderlove backing group, and had one hit single on her own before teaming with Mathis—"Free," number 25 in April, 1977. She describes how she and Mathis became a recording team: "I remember my manager saying the record company wants to know if you're interested in singing with Johnny Mathis and I said, 'Are you

kidding? Do I want to sing with Johnny Mathis?'. . . . I was devastated. I couldn't believe that I was going to get a chance to sing with Johnny. And then I didn't believe that they would use the record. I thought well, they probably won't use this, so I said, 'Can I have a tape for me?' " Deniece was touring when she turned on the radio in her hotel room one day and heard "Too Much, Too Little, Too Late."

To follow the single, the first chart-topper for both artists, and the first duet Mathis had ever recorded, an entire album of Mathis-Williams numbers was produced. Only an updating of Marvin Gaye and Tammi Terrell's "You're All I Need to Get By" charted (number 47 in September, 1978).

Mathis has since recorded duets with a number of female artists, including Jane Olivor ("The Last Time I Felt Like This" from *Same Time, Next Year*), former Harlette Paulette McWilliams ("Different Kinda Different"), Angela Bofill ("You're a Special Part of Me") and Dionne Warwick ("Friends in Love").

He reteamed with Williams on a re-working of the Major Harris song "Love Won't Let Me Wait," a song that did well on the Adult Contemporary chart just before Williams had her first number one single on her own [see 588—"Let's Hear It for the Boy"]. Mathis and Williams also recorded the theme song ("Without Us") for the long-running Michael J. Fox series, "Family Ties."

## THE TOP FIVE
*Week of June 3, 1978*

1  **Too Much, Too Little, Too Late**
Johnny Mathis &
Deniece Williams

2  **You're the One That I Want**
John Travolta &
Olivia Newton-John

3  **Shadow Dancing**
Andy Gibb

4  **With a Little Luck**
Wings

5  **Feels So Good**
Chuck Mangione

## 484 You're the One That I Want RSO 891
### JOHN TRAVOLTA AND OLIVIA NEWTON-JOHN

*Writer: John Farrar*

*Producer: John Farrar*

*June 10, 1978*
*1 week*

PACING the sitting room of her Sherry Netherlands hotel suite hours before her much-heralded 1977 debut at the Metropolitan Opera House in New York, Olivia Newton-John was perplexed. She'd had a stereo system installed in her quarters so she could listen and listen again to the Broadway cast album of *Grease*. She was also reading and re-reading the script for the film adaptation. Allan Carr, whom she met at a dinner party thrown by old friends Helen Reddy and Jeff Wald, had approached her about playing opposite John Travolta in the role of Sandy, and she was comfortable with the pony-tailed character's sweet and demure innocence, so close to her own public image. But she was unsure if her fans would believe the switch to leather-jacketed, gum-cracking biker moll at the end. "I just don't know about this," she fretted. "Maybe if I talk to John I'll feel better. I know he's in New York here shooting a movie. Can you get in touch with him for

me?" A phone call was arranged between Travolta's takes on *Saturday Night Fever*, and the conversation soothed her fears. Olivia Newton-John's first major film appearance would be in *Grease*.

Technically, it wasn't the first time she'd ever been before the cameras (that distinction belonged to the science-fiction musical disaster, *Toomorrow*). She had been anxious for a major Hollywood role. "But the scripts I was getting were so bad," she sighed in *People*. Even after accepting the challenge, Olivia insisted on taking a screen test, which she described in *Crawdaddy* as "a very nervous thing, at least for me, and I wasn't thrilled with my own performance. I kept thinking, 'Here I am, a singer wanting to be an actress, working with an actor who sings.' I was very mixed-up and frightened." To *People*, she explained she wanted the test because "I didn't want to go into something I couldn't handle or have something to say about. I was playing a naive girl but I didn't want her to be sickly."

Sickly was the last adjective anyone would apply to Livvy's portrayal of Sandy. Reflecting later in *Billboard*, she acknowledged, "*Grease* is the most important thing I've done.

Because I was playing a role I was able to try something different (in terms of a more powerful singing style). I would never have dreamt of it if not for the part. It was an excuse to do it and it worked."

The biggest song hits in the film *Grease* were especially written for the movie. The Newton-John/Travolta duet, "You're the One That I Want," was the first single released. It debuted on the Hot 100 at number 65 on June 10, 1978, and 10 weeks later it succeeded another duo, Johnny Mathis and Deniece Williams, at number one.

The team of Newton-John and Travolta were even more powerful in the U.K., where "You're the One That I Want" was number one for nine weeks and the follow-up, "Summer Nights," was number one for seven weeks. According to *The Guinness Book of Number One Hits*, that makes the duo the only chart act with more than one single to hit number one in Britain with every release. They also topped the chart with their first and last release and hit number one with their first two singles. They spent more than 15 weeks at number one in a calendar year, something only six other acts have ever done.

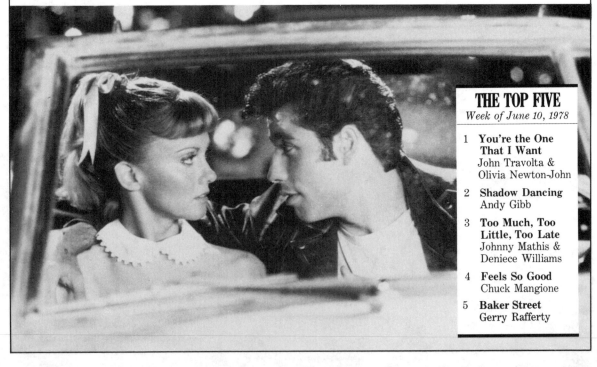

### THE TOP FIVE
*Week of June 10, 1978*

1  **You're the One That I Want**
   John Travolta &
   Olivia Newton-John

2  **Shadow Dancing**
   Andy Gibb

3  **Too Much, Too Little, Too Late**
   Johnny Mathis &
   Deniece Williams

4  **Feels So Good**
   Chuck Mangione

5  **Baker Street**
   Gerry Rafferty

RSO 893 **Shadow Dancing** 485
ANDY GIBB

"Shadow Dancing" debuted on the Hot 100 at number 69 and 10 weeks later began a seven-week run at the top. While it was the number one song in America, Andy's concert at Miami's *Jai Alai* fronton featured some surprise guests—the Bee Gees. It was the first concert performance with all four Gibbs and the sole live appearance of the Bee Gees during 1978.

Gibb followed the platinum-selling "Shadow Dancing" with three top 10 singles: "An Everlasting Love" (number five in September, 1978), "(Our Love) Don't Throw It All Away" (number nine in December, 1978) and "Desire" (number four in March, 1980). He also charted with two duets: "I Can't Help It" (number 12 in May, 1980) with Olivia Newton-John and a re-make of the Everly Brothers' "All I Have to Do Is Dream" (number 51 in September, 1981) with Victoria Principal, Pamela Barnes Ewing in "Dallas" and the subject of much media coverage because of her romance with Gibb.

Andy made his acting debut in the Los Angeles production of the Joseph Papp revival of Gilbert and Sullivan's *The Pirates of Penzance*. He later re-created the role of Frederic in the Canadian production.

Gibb hosted TV's "Solid Gold" series from 1981 until 1982. In January, 1988, he signed with Island Records. He was working on a new album when he was admitted to the John Radcliffe Hospital in Oxford, England, with severe stomach pains. On March 10, 1988, Andy died of an inflammatory heart virus.

Writers: Barry Gibb
Robin Gibb
Maurice Gibb
Andy Gibb

Producers: Barry Gibb
Albhy Galuten
Karl Richardson

*June 17, 1978*
*7 weeks*

**W**HEN "Shadow Dancing" went to number one, Andy Gibb became the first solo artist in the history of the Hot 100 to have his first three chart singles reach number one. The only chart acts that have surpassed this total are the Jackson Five [see 283—"I'll Be There"], who had their first four chart singles go to number one in 1970, and Mariah Carey [see 796—"Emotions"], whose first five singles all went to number one in 1990 and 1991. The Four Seasons started with three consecutive number ones, but they had already charted as the Four Lovers.

"Shadow Dancing" also extended the chart dominance of the Gibb family and the RSO label. It was the eighth RSO number one of 1978, an unprecedented total that would add another digit when Frankie Valli took a Barry Gibb song [see 488—"Grease"] to the top of the chart less than two months later.

As for the Gibb takeover of the chart, "Shadow Dancing" was the number one single of 1978, according to *Billboard*, presiding over a year-end top 10 that included the Bee Gees' "Night Fever" (number two), "Stayin' Alive" (number four) and "How Deep Is Your Love" (number six) as well as Andy's "("Love Is) Thicker Than Water" (number eight).

Andy wrote "Shadow Dancing" with his three older brothers in Los Angeles. "My brothers were making *Sgt. Pepper,* the movie," Andy would recall years later. "And one night, while we were relaxing, we sat down and we had to start getting tracks together for the (second) album. So we just literally sat down and in ten minutes, we had a group going, (singing) the chorus part. As it says underneath the song, we all wrote it, the four of us."

After recording part of the song at Wally Heider Studios in Los Angeles, Gibb returned to the home of the Bee Gees' hits, Criteria Studios, to record the *Shadow Dancing* album. Contributing to the LP were Eagles Joe Walsh and Don Felder. Producers Albhy Galuten and Karl Richardson also hired the same string musicians used by the Eagles on *Hotel California* [see 462] for the "Shadow Dancing" single.

### THE TOP FIVE
*Week of June 17, 1978*

1 **Shadow Dancing**
Andy Gibb

2 **You're the One That I Want**
John Travolta &
Olivia Newton-John

3 **Baker Street**
Gene Rafferty

4 **It's a Heartache**
Bonnie Tyler

5 **Too Much, Too Little,
Too Late**
Johnny Mathis &
Deniece Williams

## 486 Miss You ROLLING STONES 19307
ROLLING STONES

*Writers: Mick Jagger*
*Keith Richards*

*Producers: The Glimmer Twins*

*August 5, 1978*
*1 week*

THOUGH they'd been written off by a fickle rock press as lumbering dinosaurs, with "Miss You" the Rolling Stones proved they were far from extinct. Skewered by the stiletto steps of the disco era, pop radio found itself spinning a record that blended the band's essential rock with its newfound sound.

Not only was the Bob Clearmountain-remixed track "a very popular song," in the words of master-of-understatement Charlie Watts, it revitalized the over 15-year-old aggregation's image in the eyes of rock journalists. The Stones' music began to be influential again, as Watts aptly noted in *Musician*, "There's a load of 'Miss You's, aren't there?"

The prototype made its debut on the Hot 100 at number 76 on May 27, 1978, and worked its way to number

one 10 weeks later. It was the eighth Rolling Stones single to top the American chart. The album from which it was culled, *Some Girls*, sold over five million copies. For all their success, the Stones were making headlines in 1978 for other reasons. Many column inches were devoted to Mick Jagger's impending divorce from Bianca and his new relationship with Texas model Jerri Hall. Keith Richards was making even more unfortunate news.

Canadian authorities raided his Harbour Castle Hilton hotel room and arrested him for possession of both cocaine and heroin. Though he was allowed out on bail, Keith was virtually marooned in Toronto for weeks, deserted by his comrades after they'd finished their concerts at the El Mocambo club. Lawyers were able to manage a special visa to the United States with the proviso that Keith seek treatment for his heroin addiction from the Stevens Psychiatric Center in New York. He couldn't join the rest of the Stones in Paris where they were recording *Some Girls*, but had tapes flown in so he could contribute his parts. When the case came to trial in October, 1978, the judges defied speculation about a

harsh jail sentence and let the finally rehabilitated musician off on probation, stipulating that he and his band perform a special benefit concert for the blind.

Intact, the Rolling Stones embarked on a 1979 concert tour, cranking out *Emotional Rescue* the following year. The title track reached number three in September, 1980. Their 1981 album, *Tattoo You*, yielded "Start Me Up," which held at number two for three weeks in October. Two years later, they peaked at number nine with "Undercover of the Night" from the *Under Cover* LP.

A couple of solo efforts were released in the '80s. Bill Wyman followed his two mid-'70s outings with the soundtrack to the Ryan O'Neal film *Green Ice*, and scored a modest British hit with "(Si Si) Je Suis un Rock Star." He also collaborated with famed artist Marc Chagal on a book of photographs. Mick Jagger finally submitted to the solo LP bug in 1985, releasing *She's the Boss* in March. "Just Another Night" was the first single, followed by "Lucky in Love."

These departures did not signal an end to the 22-year saga of "the greatest rock and roll band in the world."

As soon as he finished promoting his album, Jagger flew to Paris to join the other four Stones in sessions for yet another new record.

### THE TOP FIVE
*Week of August 5, 1978*

1 **Miss You**
Rolling Stones

2 **Three Times a Lady**
Commodores

3 **Grease**
Frankie Valli

4 **Last Dance**
Donna Summer

5 **Shadow Dancing**
Andy Gibb

MOTOWN 1443 **Three Times a Lady**
COMMODORES

**487**

*Writer: Lionel Richie*

*Producers: James Carmichael and the Commodores*

*August 12, 1978*
*2 weeks*

LIONEL RICHIE was inspired to write "Three Times a Lady" at a party celebrating his parents' 37th wedding anniversary. "My father stood up and gave this wonderful speech about how he had been around my mother and spent years of ups and downs . . . and he's probably never taken the time to say, 'Thank you, Alberta, for all the years that you've spent with me and struggled with me,' and I said, 'My goodness, I'm in the same situation,' " Lionel told Dick Clark in a Mutual Broadcasting special. "I haven't taken the time to tell my wife thank you. How many other guys are in the same position? "

To observe the origin of the Commodores, one would have to return in a time machine to the campus of Tuskegee Institute in Alabama, in the first semester of the 1967-1968 academic year. That's when a freshman student named Thomas McClary who played the guitar, decided a good way to meet girls would be to form a band. He asked another freshman who brought his saxophone to school if he'd be interested. Lionel B. Richie, Jr., said he didn't really know how to play the sax, but he'd give it a try. With four other students, they entered a talent contest as the Mighty Mystics.

The top group on campus was the Jays, but they were seniors and were ready to graduate. When a couple of them decided to remain on campus and pursue higher degrees, they approached the Mystics about merging the two groups together. Included in this new hybrid were four future Commodores—McClary, Richie, trumpet player William King and keyboardist Milan Williams.

Arguments over a new name almost broke the group up before they started, but someone pointed out they were taking the matter too seriously, and a dictionary was thrown into the air to select a name at random. King's finger landed on the word Commodore, and for years after the group was grateful he had just missed the word Commode.

By the summer of 1968, the Commodores were the hottest group in Montgomery, Alabama. But they sought wider vistas. After they persuaded Lionel's parents to allow him to go to New York, the band ventured to Gotham City. There they met a public relations man who was also a marketing director for a liquor company. Benny Ashburn was persuaded to come to McClary's aunt's home to hear the Commodores play.

He got them a booking at a Harlem club called Smalls Paradise. After they conquered uptown, he moved them downtown to the Cheetah. But most important, he was becoming their mentor, their manager and their friend. They returned to their studies at Tuskegee Institute, while Benny got them bookings in Europe during the summer. The following year, drummer Walter Orange and bassist Ronald LaPread joined the group, finalizing the Commodores line-up that would be introduced to Suzanne de Passe, the woman responsible for finding an opening act for a 1971 tour by Motown's hottest group, the Jackson Five [see 267—"I Want You Back"].

The combination worked so well, the Commodores toured for two years with the Jacksons, culminating in a 1973 show at the Hollywood Bowl, just a few blocks from Motown headquarters. Although Berry Gordy, Jr., didn't attend, his children did— and they told their father he ought to sign the guys from Tuskegee to his label.

He did, but two years passed before the Commodores made their first recording for Motown. Under the guidance of producer James Carmichael, they cut four tracks. One of them was an instrumental called "Machine Gun," which became their first chart hit, peaking at number 22 in July, 1974. Three records later, they made the top 10 for the first time with "Sweet Love" (number five in April, 1976). Three more top 10 hits followed ("Just to Be Close to You," "Easy" and "Brick House") before "Three Times a Lady" entered the Hot 100 at number 73 on June 17, 1978. Eight weeks later the Commodores had their first number one single.

## THE TOP FIVE
*Week of August 12, 1978*

1 **Three Times a Lady**
Commodores

2 **Grease**
Frankie Valli

3 **Last Dance**
Donna Summer

4 **Miss You**
Rolling Stones

5 **Hot Blooded**
Foreigner

### 488 | Grease RSO 897
### FRANKIE VALLI

*Writer: Barry Gibb*

*Producers: Barry Gibb*
*Albhy Galuten*
*Karl Richardson*

*August 26, 1978*
*2 weeks*

ALMOST 16 years after his first number one single [see 117—"Sherry"], Frankie Valli topped the charts again with the title song from *Grease*, the most successful motion picture musical of all time.

As of the end of 1987, *Grease* was the 11th highest-grossing film of all time, according to *Variety*. If George Lucas and Steven Spielberg did not make movies, *Grease* would have been the number three box office attraction. But Lucas and Spielberg *do* make movies, and the top 10 films ahead of *Grease* as of the end of 1987 were:

1. *E. T. The Extra Terrestrial*
2. *Star Wars*
3. *Return of the Jedi*
4. *The Empire Strikes Back*
5. *Jaws*
6. *Ghostbusters*
7. *Raiders of the Lost Ark*
8. *Indiana Jones and the Temple of Doom*
9. *Beverly Hills Cop II*
10. *Back to the Future*

The soundtrack album of *Grease* established an important mark of its own. It is the second best-selling movie soundtrack of all time, with some 24 million copies sold, just behind the all-time best selling soundtrack, *Saturday Night Fever* [see 478—"Stayin' Alive"], with 25 million copies sold.

## THE TOP FIVE
*Week of August 26, 1978*

1  **Grease**
   Frankie Valli

2  **Three Times a Lady**
   Commodores

3  **Miss You**
   Rolling Stones

4  **Boogie Oogie Oogie**
   A Taste of Honey

5  **Hot Blooded**
   Foreigner

Valli's recording of the title track is the second number one single from the film [see 484—"You're the One That I Want"] and sold over three million copies itself, making the film *Grease* a financial windfall for Valli.

The single "Grease" was Valli's second solo number one [see 398—"My Eyes Adored You"]. He had two more big hits in 1975, "Swearin' to God," which peaked at six, and a remake of Ruby and the Romantics' "Our Day Will Come" [see 126], which charted at 11. He had two additional chart entries on the Private Stock label, but was without a company when Barry Gibb approached him about recording "Grease." Valli hadn't seen the film, but he knew the Broadway play was a huge success. After listening to Barry's song, he immediately agreed to record it.

Following his success with "Grease" on RSO, he signed with Warner Brothers in 1978 and with MCA in 1980. During this period, he also recovered his hearing after suffering for many years from otosclerosis, a rare disease that results in deafness. Valli went through three delicate ear operations to get his hearing back.

"Those years were a terrible strain for Frankie," his wife, Mary-Ann, has said. "For so long he missed all the little sounds that we take for granted....It got to where I had to scream at him just to be heard. When fans would come up to him, he wouldn't even know they were there....Then when new surgical procedures were finally developed, we kept getting conflicting reports from the specialists....It was terrifying....One day Frankie came to me and said, 'Okay, I've gambled before. I'm going to make sure of my odds and then I'm going to give it everything I've got.'"

Frankie took the risk and had the operations. He regained almost full hearing. He had memorized the Four Seasons act well enough to sing on stage without hearing the group play their music, but now for the first time in years, he could hear the Four Seasons performing on stage.

CAPITOL 4565 **Boogie Oogie Oogie**
A TASTE OF HONEY

**489**

Writers: *Janice Marie Johnson*
*Perry Kibble*

Producers: *Fonce Mizell*
*Larry Mizell*

*September 9, 1978*
*3 weeks*

IN 1971, keyboardist Perry Kibble and singer/guitarist Janice Marie Johnson found themselves unemployed and decided to work together. Taking their name from the song "A Taste of Honey," they added a pair of friends and found a gig at a beer joint in southern California.

They spent the next several years perfecting their act with a tour of duty that included stops at military bases all over Europe and the Far East. "We really paid our dues," said Janice Marie. When lead singer Gregory Walker quit in 1976 to join Santana, the remaining members decided it was time to settle on a permanent unit. A second female guitarist, Hazel Payne, was hired to complete the group.

A chance meeting with Larry and Fonce Mizell, hit-making producers for the Jackson Five [see 267—"I Want You Back"] and L.T.D. ("Love Ballad"), led to an audition with Capitol Records vice president Larkin Arnold. He liked what he heard and signed the group to a contract in 1978.

"Boogie Oogie Oogie" was written by Johnson and Kibble in response to an incident at an Air Force club. "We were knocking ourselves out," said Janice, "but getting no reaction from the crowd. In fact, they seemed to have contempt for two women who

thought they could front a band." Out of her rage for this brand of military chauvinism, she went home and wrote the stinging song.

"Boogie Oogie Oogie" entered the Hot 100 at number 82 on June 24, 1978. When it went to number one 11 weeks later, it became Capitol's 40th number one single, the first label to achieve this mark. Although A Taste of Honey won a Grammy for Best New Artist, they found it hard to follow-up the platinum-selling "Boogie Oogie Oogie." Fourteen months later, they had achieved only one additional chart record, "Do it Good," and that only went as high as number 79.

Eventually the group was reduced to a duo—Janice Marie on bass guitar and Hazel on guitar and keyboards. "That gives us a uniqueness from the beginning," said Hazel. "Also, we like to set the trend, not follow it."

In 1981, A Taste of Honey had a second smash with an unusual selection. They covered Kyu Sakamoto's number one hit from 1963 [see 131—"Sukiyaki"], but translated the original Japanese into English. The record was meant as a tribute to the country where the group had achieved its greatest glory. As part of their stage act, the women would wear kimonos and do fan dances.

"We can go to Japan and do a concert and they don't understand a word we're saying, but they can feel our vibrations," Janice told *Jet* in 1983. "It feels good to be appreciated for being a good entertainer without having to be under the gun of the black/white situation...(in Japan) they judge you on your music more than the color of your skin. That's one good thing disco had. It took away color."

## THE TOP FIVE
*Week of September 9, 1978*

1 **Boogie Oogie Oogie**
  A Taste of Honey

2 **Three Times a Lady**
  Commodores

3 **Hot Blooded**
  Foreigner

4 **Hopelessly Devoted to You**
  Olivia Newton-John

5 **Kiss You All Over**
  Exile

# 490 Kiss You All Over WARNER/CURB 8589
## EXILE

Writers: *Mike Chapman*
*Nicky Chinn*

Producer: *Mike Chapman*

September 30, 1978
4 weeks

"**K**ISS YOU ALL OVER" was the first American number one for Mike Chapman and Nicky Chinn, the songwriting team responsible for British hits by glitter era stars Suzi Quatro, Sweet, Mud and Gary Glitter. It was the first of four chart-toppers in an 11-month period for Chapman, an Australian who emigrated to England. He took his producing abilities for granted; as he told Jamie James in *Rolling Stone*: "If you can't make hit singles, you should...go chop meat somewhere."

Singer Jimmy Stokley, guitarist James Preston Pennington and keyboardist Buzz Cornelison were all members of the Fascinations, a popular band at Madison Central High School in Richmond, Kentucky, during 1963-1964. They changed their names to the Exiles in 1965 and played cover versions of popular hits at local clubs, but as Pennington admitted to James Curry in a 1985 *Pulse!* interview, "We were pretty bad, but everything we did you could dance to and we had a real wild front man. We were different. We had long hair and nobody else around here had that."

Persistence won them a spot on Dick Clark's "Caravan of Stars," first playing their own set and then backing artists like Brian Hyland and Tommy Roe. Other members of the band came and went, but the Stokley, Pennington and Cornelison core remained intact. Tommy James recommended the band to, Columbia

Records, but a 1969 recording of "Church Street Soul Revival" failed to ignite any interest.

After a brief stint with RCA's Wooden Nickel label, the group decided to write and perform their own material. Now a six-piece band, with the addition of keyboardist Marlon Hargis, drummer Steve Goetzman and bass guitarist Sonny Lemaire, the band sent demo tapes to influential people on the west coast.

Chapman, who moved from London to Los Angeles in 1975, mentioned to a friend at a party that he was looking for new groups to produce. The friend let him listen to a closetful of demo tapes, and Chapman liked the one by the Exiles best. He telephoned the group and although they had no idea who he was, they invited him to hear them play at the grand opening of an apartment complex in Lexington, Kentucky.

The acoustics were terrible, but Chapman liked the group enough to sign them. Their name was simplified to Exile and their first Chapman single, "Try It On," was released on Atco. It peaked at number 97 in March, 1977. As the band changed labels to Warner/Curb, Chapman sent them a demo of a song he had written, "Kiss You All Over," and told them to improvise with it. The tape was a spare production, with only three guitars, a drum beat and a vocal. The band made their version much funkier and Chapman was pleased with it.

Chapman described "Kiss You All Over" to Jim McCullaugh in *Billboard*. "It's a very unusual song and is very much about what music in the U.S. is all about in 1978. It's MOR soft rock, slightly disco though not pure disco, and has a sensuous lyric line that Americans love. Americans

are big lyric listeners and listen to every word. In Europe listeners are more into the atmosphere of a record and then they listen to the lyrics."

Another Chapman/Chinn song, "You Thrill Me," peaked at number 40. "How Could This Go Wrong" did; it only went to 88 and was the group's last pop hit. A 1980 album included "Take Me Down" and "The Closer You Get," both written by Pennington and new member Mark Gray and both later recorded by Alabama. After artists like Dave and Sugar, Janie Fricke and Kenny Rogers recorded their songs and made them country hits, Exile decided they might as well be a country band.

They took a year off and played the Rebel Room, a club inside a bowling alley owned by a friend of the band's in Lexington. They wrote songs, performed in the club and shopped for a new label. Signed to Epic, Exile earned their first country number one in early 1984 with "Woke Up in Love."

---

## THE TOP FIVE
*Week of September 30, 1978*

1 **Kiss You All Over**
Exile

2 **Boogie Oogie Oogie**
A Taste of Honey

3 **Hopelessly Devoted to You**
Olivia Newton-John

4 **Three Times a Lady**
Commodores

5 **Summer Nights**
John Travolta &
Olivia Newton-John

CHRYSALIS 2226 **Hot Child in the City**
NICK GILDER
**491**

*Writers: Nick Gilder*
*James McCulloch*

*Producer: Mike Chapman*

*October 28, 1978*
*1 week*

"**I**'M intrigued by sex," Nick Gilder confessed to *Rolling Stone*. "It's so much a part of everything we do, and we don't completely understand why we're doing it. It's our prime directive, almost, on this planet. Seek out and multiply, you know. I write stories around it because it intrigues people so much."

Nick Gilder fashioned one of his stories around the wasted life of a street-wise Lolita ("Drinking champagne is her pastime/Making love is her mainline") in "Hot Child in the City." His platinum-selling single debuted on the Hot 100 at number 88 on June 10, 1978, and took 20 more weeks to reach the top, longer than any other single that had come before.

"'Hot Child in the City' could well have been entitled 'Don't Bite the Apple,'" Gilder said in *Rolling Stone*. "I've seen a lot of young girls, 15 and 16, walking down Hollywood Boulevard with their pimps. Their home environment drove them to distraction so they ran away, only to be trapped by something even worse. It hurts to see that so I tried writing from the perspective of a lecher— in the guise of an innocent pop song."

The man *Rolling Stone* dubbed "the Nabokov of the jukebox" was born November 7, 1951, in London, England. When he was 10, his family moved to Vancouver, British Columbia, Canada. After attending

technical college, he teamed up with guitarist Jimmy McCulloch in 1971 to form a rock band called Sweeney Todd. They struggled in semi-obscurity until 1976 when London Records released "Roxy Roller," a sardonic tune about a groupie.

Gilder and McCulloch bowed out of Sweeney Todd due to internal squabbling, and travelled south to test their power-pop sound in the more lucrative waters of Los Angeles. They signed with Chrysalis Records, while their former label released a semi-new version of "Roxy Roller" in the United States, featuring a different lead singer and the original Sweeney Todd backing track.

When Chrysalis got wind of it, they obtained an immediate injunction that banned the record from further airplay and issued a new recording of the song by Gilder. To further complicate matters, a revamped Sweeney Todd went back in to the studio and recorded an entirely new version. As a result of the muddle, all three singles bombed.

After an aborted attempt to record with Beatles producer George Martin, Gilder teamed up with Stuart Alan Love in 1977 to produce his debut LP, *You Know Who You Are*. For his next effort, 1978's *City Lights*, Gilder was paired with glitter pop producer Mike Chapman to record three tracks in three days. One of them was "Hot Child in the City."

"I didn't think that track was strong enough to be the single," Chapman told Jim McCullaugh in a *Billboard* interview. "There was another track called 'All Because of Love' which I thought should be the single but Chrysalis president Terry Ellis felt 'Hot Child in the City' was stronger. He was right on that one."

Ellis' decision gave Chapman two consecutive number one singles as Gilder succeeded the Chapman-produced "Kiss You All Over" by Exile [see 490]. "It's like a dream come true," Chapman told McCullaugh. "I've wanted that kind of success in the U.S. for a long time and it's finally starting to happen."

## THE TOP FIVE
*Week of October 28, 1978*

1  **Hot Child in the City**
   Nick Gilder

2  **You Needed Me**
   Anne Murray

3  **Reminiscing**
   Little River Band

4  **MacArthur Park**
   Donna Summer

5  **Whenever I Call You "Friend"**
   Kenny Loggins

# 492 You Needed Me CAPITOL 4574
## ANNE MURRAY

*Writer: Randy Goodrum*

*Producer: Jim Ed Norman*

*November 4, 1978*
*1 week*

WHEN "You Needed Me" went to number one and became the biggest hit of Anne Murray's career, the singer had just returned to show business after a two-year hiatus. "One day I just sat down and said look, let's stop this," she remarked in a 1981 *Billboard* interview. "Let's say no to everything from now on. I need to have some breathing room. And it's made quite a difference."

Part of the reason for that hiatus was the birth of her first child, son William Stewart Langstroth, born in August, 1976. "I've always dreamed of a family," Murray told Jeff Wilson of United Press International after the birth of her second child, daughter Dawn. "It's nicer than I ever thought it would be."

Anne resumed her career with the album *Let's Keep It That Way*, produced by Jim Ed Norman. The first single from the LP, an updating of the Everly Brothers' "Walk Right Back," failed to dent the Hot 100. The follow-up was a song penned by Randy Goodrum, "You Needed Me." Murray, who does not write songs herself, said to a Las Vegas, Nevada, reporter in 1980, "When I find a song I like—I do it. There are times when I do a song for the first time, I know it's going to be a hit. That was true of 'You Needed Me.' I knew right away. I knew because the first few times I sang it I got all choked up. I couldn't even get through it."

## THE TOP FIVE
### Week of November 4, 1978

1 **You Needed Me**
  Anne Murray

2 **MacArthur Park**
  Donna Summer

3 **Reminiscing**
  Little River Band

4 **Double Vision**
  Foreigner

5 **Whenever I Call You "Friend"**
  Kenny Loggins

"You Needed Me" debuted on the Hot 100 at number 88 on July 15, 1978, and didn't reach the top until 16 weeks later. The first Anne Murray song to make the top five, it easily outdistanced her three other top 10 singles, "Snowbird" (number eight in September, 1970), "Danny's Song" (number seven in April, 1973) and a cover of the Beatles' "You Won't See Me" (number eight in July, 1974).

Anne Murray was born on June 20, 1947, in Springhill, Nova Scotia, Canada. Her parents were fans of Bing Crosby, Rosemary Clooney and Perry Como, singers who became her earliest influences. From her three oldest brothers, she learned about Broadway show tunes, country music and rock and roll, in that order. After studying the piano, 15-year-old Anne took voice lessons every Saturday from a teacher who lived 50 miles away.

While attending the University of New Brunswick in 1964, she auditioned for a Halifax television series, "Singalong Jubilee." Rejected at first, she was called back two years later and was invited to join a summer edition of the program by one of the producers, William Langstroth—the man who became her husband in 1975.

When autumn rolled around, Anne returned to college and graduated with a degree in physical education. She taught high school on Prince Edward Island for a year, even though the musical director of "Singalong Jubilee," Brian Ahern, wanted to record her. "I thought they were crazy," Anne has said of the people who thought she should record. "Singing was something you did in the bathtub and around bonfires. I felt there was no security in singing."

After a lot of persuasion, Ahern produced an album for a small Canadian label, Arc Records. Then he took her to Toronto to meet executives at the Capitol of Canada label. They signed her up and her first LP for the company included her debut single, "Snowbird," which received the first American gold record ever awarded to a Canadian female singer.

Her records have found homes on the Country and Adult Contemporary charts, but in 1981 Murray complained in *Billboard*, "I'm sick of ballads. . . . Everybody thinks I want to do ballads because that's all I've ever done, and I'm not saying that I want to do rock . . . just something uptempo. Nobody ever sends me other kinds of material."

*Writer: Jimmy Webb*

*Producers: Giorgio Moroder*
*Pete Bellotte*

*November 11, 1978*
*3 weeks*

Before Donna Summer recorded her discofied version of Jimmy Webb's "MacArthur Park," Richard Harris took the song to number two on the Hot 100 in June, 1968. But "Mac-Arthur Park" has a strange history that pre-dates the Harris version. In begins in the summer of 1967, when Webb wrote a 22-minute cantata that ended with a seven-minute coda called "MacArthur Park."

Bones Howe became friendly with Webb when they worked together on the Fifth Dimension's *Up, Up and Away* album. After that, Howe went to work producing the Association [see 208—"Cherish"] and Webb was hired by Johnny Rivers to produce the Fifth Dimension's concept LP, *The Magic Garden*. When problems arose between Webb and Rivers, Howe was asked to come in and produce the vocal tracks.

"We finished that album together," Howe notes. "During the last four weeks, Jimmy got this idea to do a cantata. He said . . . 'I'm gonna write a cantata, and it's gonna be 22 minutes long, and be the whole side of an album, and it'll be broken up into little pieces that could be singles.'" Webb suggested the Association would be the perfect group to record the cantata.

"Finally we got *The Magic Garden* album finished and he really dug into the cantata and worked on it full time after that . . . I set up a meeting with Jimmy and the Association. We were in studio three at Western, and he came in and . . . played on the piano through these pieces that he had worked and sang them and went back and played countermelodies, and showed them various things he had in mind for this cantata. It was just a wonderful piece of music. They listened and said, 'Because it's gonna take up the whole side of an album, we'd like to talk about it.' So Jimmy excused himself and walked out of the studio. They closed the door and somebody in the group—I don't remember who—said,

'Any two guys in this group could write a better piece of music than that.' I said, 'You guys are crazy. This is a wonderful concept' . . . they said, 'Yeah, but we'd have to give up the whole side of an album.' I said, 'This is a great possibility to go forward creatively and do something which nobody's ever done before.'"

It was left to Bones to break the news to Jimmy. "He was really crushed by it," Howe remembers. The Association wrote all their own songs for their *Birthday* album. "I kept saying to their manager, 'There's not one song here that's as good as the cantata that Jimmy brought in. We ought to go back to him.'" The answer was no. Webb took the last movement of the cantata—the seven-minute coda—and produced it for Richard Harris.

In 1978 Donna Summer released a double album, *Live and More*. The "Live" referred to the first three sides, which included her hits like "I Feel Love," "Love to Love You Baby" and the Oscar-winning "Last Dance" from *Thank God It's Friday*. The "More" referred to side four, a nonstop disco medley titled "MacArthur Park Suite" that began with an eight minute, 27 second version of Jimmy Webb's coda, then segued into "One of a Kind," "Heaven Knows" (the follow-up single) and a one minute, 32 second reprise of "MacArthur Park."

Edited down to three minutes and 53 seconds for release as a 45, "MacArthur Park" debuted on the Hot 100 at number 85 the week of September 9, 1978. Nine weeks later, Donna Summer bested Richard Harris and had her first number one single.

## THE TOP FIVE
*Week of November 11, 1978*

1 **MacArthur Park**
Donna Summer

2 **You Needed Me**
Anne Murray

3 **Double Vision**
Foreigner

4 **How Much I Feel**
Ambrosia

5 **Hot Child in the City**
Nick Gilder

## 494 You Don't Bring Me Flowers COLUMBIA 10840
### BARBRA STREISAND AND NEIL DIAMOND

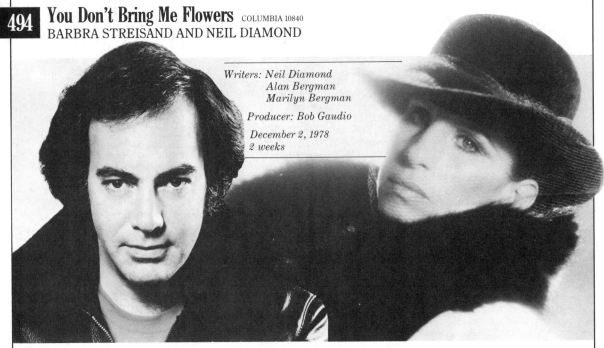

Writers: Neil Diamond
Alan Bergman
Marilyn Bergman

Producer: Bob Gaudio

December 2, 1978
2 weeks

GARY GUTHRIE was a particularly astute disc jockey. While spinning records for his WAKY-AM show in Louisville, Kentucky, he realized that not only had Barbra Streisand and Neil Diamond each included a version of "You Don't Bring Me Flowers" on their latest albums, they were both singing in the same key. To give his listeners an "exclusive," he spliced the two songs together to create a duet. When he played the tape on the air, the switchboard lit up with callers clamoring to hear it again, followed by record store owners besieged by customers wanting to buy their own copies.

Columbia Records heard about the Lousville ruckus, then suggested to both Brooklyn-born stars that they record the song together. Bob Gaudio, producer of Diamond's original version, had already mentioned to Neil when he first heard the Streisand version that it was in the same key, and wouldn't it be terrific if they could record it together.

"It wasn't an easy situation to try and coordinate two superstars in the same studio at the same time," Gaudio notes. But he scotched rumors that the two singers did not actually record their vocals at the same time. "I was there, so I know. That was done nose to nose, Barbra and Neil in the studio, just singing their little hearts out, with a piano. Neil's band was sitting outside in the lobby, in case the idea of just a piano and two voices singing was not the way to go. We were ready to bring in all the musicians, but as it turned out, there was a magical spell in that room. You just knew as soon as they opened their mouths, if we could get the record finished and out, we couldn't miss."

"You Don't Bring Me Flowers" was the highest new entry on the Hot 100 the week of October 28, 1978. Debuting at number 48, it needed only five more weeks to reach the summit. It was the third chart-topper for both artists. After its first week at number one, it yielded to Chic's "Le Freak," then returned for one more week at the top.

When the 1980 Grammy finalists were announced, "You Don't Bring Me Flowers" was nominated as Record of the Year and Streisand/Diamond were nominated as Best Pop Vocal Duo. At the awards, the two stars provided an electrifying moment when, unannounced, they entered the stage from opposite ends, microphones in hand, to sing the duet. Surprised, the glittering clan of record industryites applauded wildly throughout the performance, cheering and clapping without restraint at its climax. It was the first time Streisand had sung at the Grammys, and she had conquered her well-documented aversion to live appearances to do so. NBC anchorman Tom Bro-kaw, during a latter documentary on the awards show, commented after a replay of the performance, "When it's that good, it will live on for a long, long time."

Not everyone was pleased with Streisand and Diamond's success. Gary Guthrie filed a five million dollar breach of contract lawsuit against CBS, claiming they hadn't lived up to their agreement when he sold them the idea for the duet. Eventually, the royalty question was cleared up and the million-selling single helped propel Diamond's *You Don't Bring Me Flowers* and Barbra Streisand's *Greatest Hits, Volume II* to platinum status.

---

### THE TOP FIVE
*Week of December 2, 1978*

1 **You Don't Bring Me Flowers**
Barbra Streisand &
Neil Diamond

2 **MacArthur Park**
Donna Summer

3 **How Much I Feel**
Ambrosia

4 **Le Freak**
Chic

5 **I Just Wanna Stop**
Gino Vannelli

Writers: *Nile Rodgers*
*Bernard Edwards*

Producers: *Nile Rodgers*
*Bernard Edwards*

*December 9, 1978*
*5 weeks*

**W**HAT do Diana Ross, Duran Duran, Sister Sledge, Madonna, Debbie Harry, Carly Simon and David Bowie have in common? All have been beneficiaries of the writing and/or producing talents of the creative forces behind Chic, an all-American group with a French name and a high fashion image that became the leading exponent of disco in the closing months of the '70s.

Bernard Edwards (born October 31, 1952, in Greenville, North Carolina) and Nile Rodgers (born September 19, 1952, in New York City) first met in 1970. Just out of high school, the young men started playing together in jazz clubs and

## THE TOP FIVE
*Week of December 9, 1978*

1  **Le Freak**
   Chic

2  **MacArthur Park**
   Donna Summer

3  **You Don't Bring Me Flowers**
   Barbra Streisand &
   Neil Diamond

4  **I Just Wanna Stop**
   Gino Vannelli

5  **How Much I Feel**
   Ambrosia

beer joints in New York City. Two years later, they met drummer Tony Thompson and, aspiring to create a theatrical rock group like Roxy Music, formed a power-fusion trio called the Big Apple Band.

"Right from the start we had a concept for Chic," Rodgers told *Melody Maker* in 1979. "The music at that time was very much a secondary thing. We knew we had to have something that was international and interchangeable with the markets, while at the same time we had to be in with a music that was on the rise. At that time it was rock 'n' roll, and we thought we could make our concept work within its framework."

Rodgers and Edwards had a brief foray into new wave as Allah and the Knife-Wielding Punks, but the male-female structure of the new ensemble seemed totally unsuited to the blatantly macho rock world of the time.

"So we started to use our brains," Rodgers told Geoffrey Himes of *The Washington Post*. "What we wanted to do was make records. We didn't want to be a small band playing bar mitzvahs the rest of our lives. So we got into disco."

Rodgers elaborated in the *Melody Maker* interview: "When disco came in, it was like a gift from heaven. Discos gave us the perfect opportunity to realize our concept, because it wasn't about being black, white, male or female. Further, it would give us a chance to get into the mainstream. We wanted millions of dollars, Ferraris and planes—and this seemed like the way to            get them."

Not that they were particularly attracted to the new dance sound. Edwards, for one, confessed to *Melody Maker* that at first, he hated disco. "I got into it, though, and realized that if we did it our way, it'd be pretty good."

Rodgers and Edwards sold all their instruments and used the money to cut a few slick disco sides. These were turned down by every record company in New York City, including two rejections from Atlantic Records. Finally, Atlantic president Jerry Greenberg personally signed the group.

Chic was still in its formative stages when one of their rejected cuts, "Dance, Dance, Dance (Yowsah, Yowsah, Yowsah)" went to number six in February, 1978. Vocalist Norma Jean Wright left and singers Alfa Anderson and Luci Martin became the permanent voices of Chic.

The real breakthrough for Chic was their third single, "Le Freak." According to *New York Times* critic Stephen Holden, "'Le Freak' made Edwards and Rodgers the writer/producers of the hour and established their signature sound, a haunting, minimalist pop-funk built around the guitar and bass with a wash of strings and detached female voices carrying the lyrics."

"Le Freak" entered the Hot 100 at number 82 on October 28, 1978, and just six weeks later was Chic's first chart-topper. Certified platinum by the RIAA, it sold over four million copies and became the best-selling single        of all time on Atlantic                Records.

# 496 Too Much Heaven RSO 913
## BEE GEES

*Writers: Barry Gibb*
*Robin Gibb*
*Maurice Gibb*

*Producers: Barry Gibb*
*Robin Gibb*
*Maurice Gibb*
*Karl Richardson*
*Albhy Galuten*

*January 6, 1979*
*2 weeks*

CHARITIES were often the beneficiaries of the Bee Gees' generosity. On December 2, 1976, the Gibb brothers thanked the city that inspired "Nights on Broadway" by playing a sold-out concert at Madison Square Garden and donating all proceeds to the Police Athletic League of New York. They staged another benefit for the PAL at the premiere of their film, *Sgt. Pepper's Lonely Hearts Club Band*. But their biggest contribution to charity was yet to come.

In 1978, David Frost, an old pal of Bee Gees manager Robert Stigwood, approached United Nations Secretary-General Kurt Waldheim with the idea of having major pop stars donate earnings from songs to UNICEF, the agency dedicated to helping children around the world. Waldheim supported the concept, which came to be known as "Music for UNICEF." The Bee Gees helped Frost get the project started in Miami during March of 1978, when they promised to donate the royalties from their next single to UNICEF.

Describing the group as "not very political," Barry Gibb told Greg Mitchell in *Crawdaddy* that the Bee Gees wanted to participate in "Music for UNICEF" because they "consider children in need the most defenseless people on Earth."

The single that would be donated to UNICEF would come from the sessions for the next Bee Gees album. Under tremendous pressure to equal or better the track record set by *Saturday Night Fever*, which resulted in three consecutive number one singles [see 476—"How Deep Is Your Love," 478—"Stayin' Alive" and 480—"Night Fever"], the Bee Gees entrenched themselves at Critera Studios in Miami, Florida, for 10 months.

When they emerged, they had completed *Spirits Having Flown*. The first single featured the strings and vocal layerings characterisitc of the Bee Gees of the early '70s. Lush and smooth, "Too Much Heaven" was originally a more soulful ballad, but the final mix was slowed down half a step so that the bass is almost out of tune.

"Too Much Heaven" was the highest new entry on the Hot 100 the week of November 18, 1978. A lucky seven weeks later it became the seventh number one single for the Bee Gees. It was the number one song in America on January 10, 1979, the day NBC telecast "A Gift of Song—The Music for UNICEF Concert."

---

### THE TOP FIVE
*Week of January 6, 1979*

1 **Too Much Heaven**
Bee Gees

2 **Le Freak**
Chic

3 **My Life**
Billy Joel

4 **You Don't Bring Me Flowers**
Barbra Streisand & Neil Diamond

5 **I Love the Night Life**
Alicia Bridges

WARNER BROTHERS 8724 **Da Ya Think I'm Sexy?** `497`

ROD STEWART

Writers: Rod Stewart
        Carmine Appice

Producer: Tom Dowd

February 10, 1979
4 weeks

"I DON'T think it's in me to be domesticated. I'm still restless and need to get out and see what's going on," Rod Stewart asserted in *People*. His self-admitted penchant for "being very immature, a sucker for a pretty face and a pair of long legs," as he described to Paul Nelson in *Rolling Stone*, might not have always worked to his advantage in real life, but it did result in an international hit that topped charts in 11 countries, including the United States, where it was his third number one single. Even the 12" disco version achieved its own distinction, as reputedly the first 48-track disco mix.

Stewart's "singalong music," as his cowriter Carmine Appice labelled it, certainly struck a chord with the masses but to critics and lovers of his raspy raunch and roll, the defection to disco was unforgivable. Greil Marcus acidly assessed in *The Rolling Stone Illustrated History of Rock & Roll*, "Rarely has anyone betrayed his talent so completely (as Rod Stewart). Once the most compassionate presence in music, he has become a bilious self-parody—and sells more records than ever. There have been more albums since (*Smiler*)—huge hits, some of them, pandering, sleazy records, the humor forced, the sexiness burned down to everyone else's open shirt and stuffed crotch."

"Da Ya Think I'm Sexy?" also upset Brazilian songwriter Jorge Ben, but for a different reason. He claimed Rod had stolen part of the song from his composition "Taj Mahal," a tribute to the American blues singer who named himself after the Indian monument. There were no complaints from UNICEF, the United Nations agency to which all royalties were donated after the shock-haired blond entertainer performed the hit at the "Song for UNICEF" concert on his 34th birthday—January 10, 1979.

Rod surprised the legion of women who wanted to answer yes to

"Da Ya Think I'm Sexy?" just two months after its ascent to number one by marrying George Hamilton's ex-wife, Alana. Five years and two children later they parted, Stewart returning to his first love, music.

Tours to all parts of the world (including two headlining nights at the world's largest festival, Rock in Rio), continue to occupy his time, as does recording. Since "Da Ya Think I'm Sexy?" he has landed in the top 10 exactly 10 more times with "Passion," "Young Turks," "Infatuation," "Some Guys Have All The Luck," "Love Touch," "My Heart Can't Tell You No," "Downtown Train," "This Old Heart Of Mine," "Rhythm of My Heart" and "The Motown Song."

But for all his trappings—the beautiful women, the stable of expensive cars, the spectacular homes—Rod Stewart is still the rowdy north Londoner who tapes family reunions because they provide some of his best material and religiously tracks down British soccer scores from which ever global reference point he happens to alight. "When I left school, the only ambition I had was to play football," he stated in *Goldmine*. "But somewhere along the line I must have fallen in with the wrong people, who turned out to be the right people in the long run, and turned to music. I haven't regretted anything I've done."

## THE TOP FIVE

*Week of February 10, 1979*

1 **Da Ya Think I'm Sexy**
  Rod Stewart

2 **Y.M.C.A.**
  Village People

3 **Le Freak**
  Chic

4 **A Little More Love**
  Olivia Newton-John

5 **Fire**
  Pointer Sisters

**498** I Will Survive POLYDOR 14508
GLORIA GAYNOR

Writers: Dino Fekaris
    Freddie Perren

Producers: Dino Fekaris
    Freddie Perren

March 10, 1979
3 weeks

An inspiring anthem of defiance and freedom returned the deposed "Queen of the Discos" temporarily to her throne. One of seven children, Gloria Gaynor was born September 7, 1949, in Newark, New Jersey. By her early teens, she has already decided on a musical career. She credits her strong vocal delivery to an emulation of her favorite male performers, especially Frankie Lymon ("Why Do Fools Fall in Love," "Goody Goody").

"When Frankie was 13, I was eight, and I could sing exactly like him," she is quoted in *The Top Ten* by Bob Gilbert and Gary Theroux. "If you heard me from behind the door, you'd swear it was him." At 18, Gloria played her first professional gig, a one-week stint in Canada, but she admitted, "that was it. My career was at a standstill for almost six years."

In 1971, Gloria connected with a local Jersey band called the Soul Satrisfiers, and later started her own group, City Life, which was constantly in demand along the East Coast club circuit. While performing in New York City, she caught the ear of manager Jay Ellis, who quickly got her a record deal with Columbia. Her debut single, "Honey Bee," was played in the discos but failed to crossover to the pop chart.

With the release of her next single, a blazing remake of the Jackson Five's number two hit from 1971, "Never Can Say Goodbye," Gloria conquered the Hot 100 at last. The record charted at number nine in January, 1975. On her debut album, the songs "Honey Bee," "Never Can Say Goodbye" and a version of the Four Tops' "Reach Out, I'll Be There" [see 209] were segued together into a pulsating, side-long suite.

Based on the strength of her first LP and hit single, Gloria was crowned "Queen of the Discos" by the National Association of Discotheque Disc Jockeys at a "coronation" in Manhattan during March, 1975. But Queen Gloria's reign lasted only a year, her title bequeathed to a sensuous young rival, Donna Summer [see 504—"Hot Stuff"].

As her career slowed to a crawl, her personal life suffered setbacks as well. During a show in Europe, she fell and was later hospitalized for spinal surgery. At the same time, her mother passed away.

Released from the hospital, she teamed up with producers Dino Fekaris and Freddie Perren for a new album, *Love Tracks*. The first single released was "Substitute," but Gloria was more drawn to the "B" side because of its inspirational lyrics. It was a woman's defiant declaration of independence from her heartless lover, although the title seemed to sum up Gloria's strong resolve: "I Will Survive."

Eventually, discos and radio stations discovered there was a treasure on the flip side of "Substitute." The "A" side became "I Will Survive," and it entered the Hot 100 at number 87. Twelve weeks later Gloria Gaynor had her first number one single.

She found it difficult to find a song that could match "I Will Survive," and disappeared from the music scene. In 1983 she found an anthem similar to her number one single and took "I Am What I Am," the Act I finale from Broadway's *La Cage Aux Folles*, to the top 20 of the British chart.

### THE TOP FIVE
*Week of March 10, 1979*

1  **I Will Survive**
    Gloria Gaynor

2  **Da Ya Think I'm Sexy**
    Rod Stewart

3  **Tragedy**
    Bee Gees

4  **Fire**
    Pointer Sisters

5  **Heaven Knows**
    Donna Summer &
    the Brooklyn Dreams

Writers: *Barry Gibb*
*Robin Gibb*
*Maurice Gibb*

Producers: *Barry Gibb*
*Robin Gibb*
*Maurice Gibb*
*Karl Richardson*
*Albhy Galuten*

*March 24, 1979*
*2 weeks*

"Tragedy," an uptempo, passionate song featuring Barry Gibb on lead falsetto vocals, was the second consecutive number one single from *Spirits Having Flown*, stretching the total of Bee Gees' chart-toppers to eight. It was also the fifth consecutive number one for the Bee Gees, tying them with the Supremes [see 176—"Back in My Arms Again"] and placing them within striking distance of the Beatles' six consecutive number one singles.

Karl Richardson, co-producer of six of those Bee Gees hits, described Barry's singing in a *Circus* interview: "The control of Barry's voice is actually better in falsetto. On a powerful, complex song like 'Tragedy' the lead vocal has to stand out, and a lower range would have little impact and be harder to mix. The first time I heard 'Tragedy' was at Barry's house, with all three of the Bee Gees singing to an acoustic guitar. They even sang the explosion near the end which

ended up in the studio as five tracks of Barry cupping his hands over the microphone combined with (keyboardist) Blue Weaver hitting random notes on the bottom end of the piano, run through a product generator."

*Spirits Having Flown* was the first album on which the Gibb brothers were allowed all the time and money needed to produce exactly what *they* wanted. In David Leaf's authorized biography of the Bee Gees, Robin Gibb said, "We work a hell of a lot on our records. We're one of the hardest working teams of people in the business. We work hard to get what we want. We have always had the talent, but we surpressed it. We'd convinced ourselves we'd gone as far as we were going to go. Who is to say that you can't shatter barriers and go past the stars? Positive thinking is electric. It makes things happen. In our lives, we feel that there is no such thing as failure."

In the same biography, co-producer Albhy Galuten remarked that the Bee Gees' knowledge of recording techniques "seems to be unparalleled. They're far more talented in their ability to make records and communicate these messages and saying them right than anybody I've ever worked with. The only people who I feel even come close at this point would be Stevie Wonder and sometimes Paul McCartney. I think they're miles ahead at this point. *Saturday Night Fever* saw their blossoming as pro-

ducers. They've always been able to hear the difference, but now they have an active hand in being involved. They've taken the time to really get it right."

"The studio is my spaceship," Barry declared in the Bee Gees' biography. "I lose all sense of the outside world. I just turn into the music. It's a very satisfying sensation. I guess I have the studio personality, the patience and the perfectionism. The joy of writing a song on an acoustic guitar and watching it grow, fleshing it out until it sounds as my mind told me it should, that is what keeps me in there night and day. That moment when the song is realized is my payoff."

## THE TOP FIVE
*Week of March 24, 1979*

1 **Tragedy**
Bee Gees

2 **I Will Survive**
Gloria Gaynor

3 **What a Fool Believes**
Doobie Brothers

4 **Heaven Knows**
Donna Summer &
the Brooklyn Dreams

5 **Shake Your Groove Thing**
Peaches & Herb

# 500 What a Fool Believes WARNER BROTHERS 8725
## DOOBIE BROTHERS

*Writers: Michael McDonald
Kenny Loggins*

*Producer: Ted Templeman*

*April 14, 1979
1 week*

THE DOOBIE BROTHERS needed a personnel manager just to keep track of who was in and who was out of the band at any given moment. By the time they had their second number one single, the only original Doobies left were drummer John Hartman and singer/guitarist Patrick Simmons.

Bassist Tiran Porter and second drummer Michael Hossack had joined in time for the group's third album, *Toulouse Street*. Drummer Keith Knudsen came aboard for *The Captain and Me* LP. Jeff "Skunk" Baxter, who played guitar on the *What Were Once Vices Are Now Habits* album and then went on to play with Steely Dan ("Do It Again," "Reeling in the Years"), joined the Doobies as a full-time Brother in time for their 1975 tour. Co-founder Tom Johnston left the group five days into that tour because of a stomach ailment and Baxter suggested they replace him with another Steely Dan

session musician, keyboard player Michael McDonald. After 48 hours of grueling rehearsal in Louisiana, McDonald picked up where Johnston left off and was an instant Doobie.

The changes in personnel meant changes in musical styles. The Doobies moved away from a rock sound to slicker R&B, heavily influenced by McDonald. An accomplished songwriter, McDonald wrote "You Belong to Me" for Carly Simon and had been collaborating with Kenny Loggins [see 585—"Footloose"].

Producer Ted Templeman talks about the genesis of "What a Fool Believes." "Mike and Kenny wrote the song, and Kenny was putting it on his album. I loved the song, and so we decided to put it on ours. And we tried to cut it over and over and over and we couldn't get it to where it felt right. We must have cut that thing for five or six days straight. I finally—just to get the feeling right—ended up playing drums on it myself along with Keith Knudsen . . . I just wanted a sort of floppy feel and if you listen to it, it's really kind of a floppy record. It flops around, the drums aren't perfect, nothing's perfect on it . . . you know, a Rolling Stones record may not be perfect,

but it's got a feel to it."

Templeman acknowledges that McDonald is his favorite singer. "When I hear him singing those high parts, it just kills me." Unlike the Doobies' first chart-topper [see 397—"Black Water"], it wasn't a difficult decision to release "What a Fool Believes" as the first single from the *Minute by Minute* LP. "It just sounded like a hit," Templeman says. "It was pretty obvious."

The voting members of the National Academy of Recording Arts and Sciences gave their approval to "What a Fool Believes." It walked away with Grammys for Record of the Year and Song of the Year. McDonald won a Grammy for Best Arrangement Accompanying Vocalists, and *Minute by Minute* won a Grammy for Best Pop Vocal Performance by a Duo, Group or Chorus.

After completing a farewell tour in 1982, the Doobies decided to go their separate ways. Patrick Simmons and Michael McDonald each released solo albums, and the latter enjoyed several hit singles and LPs. The Doobies reunited in 1987 with Tom Johnston back in. They returned to the top 10 of the Hot 100 in 1989 with the single "The Doctor."

### THE TOP FIVE
*Week of April 14, 1979*

1   **What a Fool Believes**
    Doobie Brothers

2   **I Will Survive**
    Gloria Gaynor

3   **Knock on Wood**
    Amii Stewart

4   **Sultans of Swing**
    Dire Straits

5   **Music Box Dancer**
    Frank Mills

**Writers:** Eddie Floyd
Steve Cropper

**Producer:** Barry Leng

April 21, 1979
1 week

"**I**'VE never bought a disco record in my life," Amii Stewart told Paul Sexton in a 1985 *Record Mirror* interview. "And I don't *want* to buy one. When I go home and close that door I don't want my brains to be blown out. I go home and listen to Donald Fagen, Nik Kershaw, Phil Collins..."

Amii also admitted that her own number one single, a disco rendition of Eddie Floyd's "Knock on Wood," was not her favorite song of all time.

She was born Amy Stewart in Washington, D.C., the fifth of six children. Her father, who worked at the Pentagon and couldn't discuss his top secret work with his family, taught Amii to play music. At nine she took dance lessons, but her guidance counselors in junior high school tried to steer her away from a show business career. Her high school principal came to the rescue—he was her uncle—and arranged her class schedule so she could study dance in the afternoons.

There already was an Amy Stewart registered with Actor's Equity, so she changed the spelling of her first name to Amii. She attended Howard University in Washington, but left to work with the D.C. Repertory Dance Company, studying ballet and modern dance.

In 1975 she joined the touring company of *Bubbling Brown Sugar* in Florida, then joined the show on Broadway. A twist of fate brought her to London where she not only appeared in the show, but was assistant director.

While living in London, Amii met record producer Barry Leng. She was suffering from a cold when she auditioned for him, but he liked her singing anyway and produced "Knock on Wood" for her. Floyd's original recording, released on Memphis-based Stax Records, only went to number 28 in late 1966. Amii's updated version entered the Hot 100 on January 27, 1979, and went to number one 12 weeks later. The follow-up, a medley of the Doors' "Light My Fire" [see 227] and "137 Disco Heaven," stalled at number 69, but was a top five hit in Britain. In 1980, Amii recorded a duet of Mary Wells' "My Guy" [see 147] and the Temptations' "My Girl" [see 168] with Johnny Bristol [see 267—"Someday We'll Be Together"]. That single peaked at 63 in America and 39 in Britain.

Amii's most recent success was "Friends," which went to number 12 in Britain in early 1985. " 'Friends' is totally different from anything I've ever done, thank God," she said in *Record Mirror*. "You can't spend your life singing songs like 'Knock on Wood.' There's more melody now, you can dance as well as sit down....The disco era was a very good era for me, but it just wasn't geared for melody."

### THE TOP FIVE
*Week of April 21, 1979*

1 **Knock on Wood**
Amii Stewart

2 **I Will Survive**
Gloria Gaynor

3 **Heart of Glass**
Blondie

4 **Music Box Dancer**
Frank Mills

5 **What a Fool Believes**
Doobie Brothers

## 502 Heart of Glass CHRYSALIS 2295
### BLONDIE

*Writers: Deborah Harry*
*Chris Stein*

*Producer: Mike Chapman*

*April 28, 1979*
*1 week*

**B**LONDIE was so resigned to *not* having hit records, that when the disco-oriented "Heart of Glass" went to number one, members of the band found themselves apologizing for what bass guitarist Nigel Harrison called "compromise with commerciality." Lead singer and group leader Deborah Harry describes it differently. "I don't think being commercial is totally derogatory. I think that this was the most intriguing or interesting cut (on *Parallel Lines*) being that it was a crossover, and it . . . helped introduce new wave music in a more commercial way."

The single was such a big hit, it even warranted a party thrown by Andy Warhol at Studio 54. It was overwhelming for Harry, who tried unsuccessfully to escape the hordes of photographers who suddenly found her marketable. Guitarist Chris Stein, band co-leader and Harry's lover, told *Creem* magazine, "We didn't expect the song to be that big. We did it as a novelty item to put more diversity into the album. It's not selling out, it's only one song."

They had actually been performing a more funk-oriented version of the song years before it appeared on the *Parallel Lines* album. Harry recalls how the song was written: "It came very easily and very naturally, all at once. It just toppled into place. We had the music around for a while

### THE TOP FIVE
*Week of April 28, 1979*

1  **Heart of Glass**
   Blondie

2  **Reunited**
   Peaches & Herb

3  **Knock on Wood**
   Amii Stewart

4  **Music Box Dancer**
   Frank Mills

5  **I Will Survive**
   Gloria Gaynor

and I think Chris came up with the 'heart of glass' phrase . . . I was so tired of hearing girl singers write or sing about being beaten by love, and I just sort of said, well listen, I think there are a lot of girls who . . . walk away."

"Heart of Glass" and the rest of *Parallel Lines* were produced by glitter rock graduate Mike Chapman, who had already produced number one hits in America for Exile [see 490—"Kiss You All Over"] and Nick Gilder [see 491—"Hot Child in the City"]. A fan of Blondie's first three albums, he felt they could do better. Working with Chapman was very different from what the band was used to. Harry says, "It was diametrically opposite from working with Richard Gottehrer. He's very laid back and Mike is a real hot chili pepper and very energetic and enthusiastic. Mike would strive for the technically impeccable take so we would do take after take after take whereas Richard always went for the inspired take.

Despite its commerciality, "Heart of Glass" provided a problem for radio stations. Many objected to the lines, "Once I had a love and it was a gas/Soon turned out to be a pain in the ass." Stations who preferred not to play the original were provided

with a version in which a previous chorus without the offending word was substituted. Harry's reaction to the censorship: "I always go along with the idea that any kind of controversy causes excitement and more interest in the long run. That doesn't bother me."

Although Blondie had gone through some personnel changes [see 535—"The Tide Is High"], the line-up on "Heart of Glass" worked together smoothly. Along with Harry, Stein and Harrison were keyboard player Jimmy Destri, drummer Clem Burke and guitarist Frank Infante. Harry and Stein wrote together and separately, with the other members contributing songs as well.

Blondie had released several singles prior to "Heart of Glass," including "X Offender" and "In the Flesh" on Private Stock Records, an updating of Randy and the Rainbows' "Denise" retitled "Denis" and "Hanging on the Telephone," the first 45 from *Parallel Lines*. None of their singles made the Hot 100 until "Heart of Glass." The band was touring Italy and were in Milan when they found out the record had gone to number one in the States. How did it make Harry feel? "Great! I flipped out. We all got drunk—it was super."

*Writers: Dino Fekaris
Freddie Perren*

*Producer: Freddie Perren*

*May 5, 1979
4 weeks*

Peaches and Herb were a sweet soul duet of the '60s, but it was a '70s incarnation that reached the apex of the Hot 100.

After high school, Herb Feemster worked in a record store in his native Washington, D.C. It was January of 1965 when Van McCoy [see 410—"The Hustle"] walked in to the store to promote a female trio he was working with, the Sweet Things. Herb convinced McCoy to grant him an audition, and a week later the young record store employee was signed to a contract. McCoy took Herb and the Sweet Things to New York for their recording sessions, but while they were there, decided to use some extra studio time to record a duet with Herb and the lead singer of the Sweet Things, Francine Barker.

"We're in This Thing Together" was not doing very well when a disc jockey at radio station KATZ in St. Louis, Missouri, discovered he liked the "B" side better. "Let's Fall in Love" was soon moving up the Hot 100, peaking at 21 in March,1967.

Before the year was over, Peaches and Herb had three more hits: "Close Your Eyes" (number eight in May), "For Your Love" (number 20 in August) and "Love Is Strange" (number 11 in November). But in 1967, Francine stopped touring and was replaced by another Peaches on the road. Three years later, Herb

called it quits.

"One day we were off work and I was riding down the street in Washington," he related to Mary Campbell of the Associated Press. "I went in and took the exam for the Police Department. When they told me I had the job, I just quit Peaches and Herb and went to work for the city July 20, 1970. But I missed singing. That's why I'm back. In 1976 I started thinking Peaches and Herb could come back."

Linda Greene was home in Washington that year after working as a model. "I bumped into Van McCoy," she told AP, "and told him I was at home now and wished I could get into the record business. I thought I was ready to handle something like that." Van mentioned Linda's name to Herb's manager and the two singers met and hit it off.

Signed to MCA Records, the new-est Peaches and Herb recorded a McCoy-produced album which sank without a trace. It was only after they connected with producer Freddie Perren and signed with his MVP productions that the duo became hot again—*2 Hot*, in fact, as their album delineated. The first single, "Shake Your Groove Thing," was as disco-oriented as the title suggests and became the biggest Peaches and Herb hit yet, peaking at number five in March, 1979. The second single from the LP was in a completely different groove. As pretty as any ballad that Marvin Gaye and Tammi Terrell ever recorded, "Reunited" entered the Hot 100 on March 17, 1979, and shot to number one seven weeks later. Certified platinum, the single established Peaches and Herb as one of the hottest acts of 1979 and won them a berth on Bob Hope's three-hour special taped in China.

## THE TOP FIVE
*Week of May 5, 1979*

1 **Reunited**
Peaches & Herb

2 **Heart of Glass**
Blondie

3 **Music Box Dancer**
Frank Mills

4 **Knock on Wood**
Amii Stewart

5 **Stumblin' In**
Suzi Quatro & Chris Norman

# Hot Stuff CASABLANCA 978
## DONNA SUMMER

*Writers: Pete Bellotte*
*Harold Faltermeyer*
*Keith Forsey*

*Producers: Giorgio Moroder*
*Pete Bellotte*

*June 2, 1979*
*3 weeks*

IN the gospel according to Donna Summer, "God had to create disco music so that I could be born and be successful. I was blessed. I am blessed."

Born LaDonna Andrea Gaines on December 31, 1948, in Boston, Massachusetts, she had to fight for her identity among five sisters and a brother. Her weapon was music. At 10, idolizing Mahalia Jackson, she appeared with gospel groups in Boston-area churches.

Auditioning to replace Melba Moore in *Hair* on Broadway, she was offered a role in a road company production instead—in Munich, Germany. There, she married an Austrian actor, Helmid Sommer. Though they later divorced, she

Anglicized his surname and kept it for her stage name. When the musical closed, Donna remained in Europe with her daughter, Mimi. Some nights Donna would perform with the Vienna Folk Opera, in its productions of *Porgy and Bess* and *Showboat,* and the next afternoon she would be singing back-up vocals at MusicLand studios in Munich.

That's where she met Giorgio Moroder and Pete Bellotte, and the three collaborated on some recordings that failed to ignite any sparks. When one of them finally became a hit in France, Moroder sent a copy to Neil Bogart, founder of Casablanca Records in America.

Bogart played the 16-minute, 50-second orgasmic "Love to Love You Baby" at a party and was swamped with requests to repeat it. He decided to release it as a single on Casablanca (through a subsidiary label, Oasis), and in February, 1976, it went to number two.

Riding the disco phenomenon, Summer was tabbed with nicknames like "The First Lady of Lust" and "Disco's Aphrodite." "There were

times when I hated the image," she told Robert Hilburn of the *Los Angeles Times.* "...Reporters would come to interview me and I'd see them shaking as they opened their notebooks. They were so hyped up by the sex goddess image."

Unable to live with her fame and her image, Donna developed ulcers and landed in a California hospital. To find herself, she returned to Europe. "I needed time to think about things," she continued. "I made more records, but kept out of sight....The more I played, the more I found out about myself, the way I wanted to be on stage. I didn't want to be a fake image that I couldn't hold up 24 hours a day."

Donna became determined to demonstrate she was multi-talented. "I can sing songs like 'Love to Love You Baby,'" she pointed out to *Ebony* in 1977, "but I can also sing ballads, light opera, things from musical comedies, church hymns—all kinds of songs."

She was still the reigning queen of disco when she scored her first number one single [see 493—"Mac-Arthur Park"]. Trying to expand into other areas, she wanted to sing a rock song on her next album. Neil Bogart suggested she pass "Hot Stuff" along to Cher, but Donna insisted on recording it herself. Debuting at number 79 on April 21, 1979, the first single from her *Bad Girls* album was sitting on top of the Hot 100 a short six weeks later.

After one week at number one, "Hot Stuff" yielded to the Bee Gees' "Love You Inside and Out," then returned to the top for two more weeks.

## THE TOP FIVE
*Week of June 2, 1979*

1 **Hot Stuff**
Donna Summer

2 **Reunited**
Peaches & Herb

3 **Love You Inside Out**
Bee Gees

4 **We Are Family**
Sister Sledge

5 **Goodnight Tonight**
Wings

RSO 925 **Love You Inside Out**
BEE GEES

505

Writers: Barry Gibb
       Robin Gibb
       Maurice Gibb

Producers: Barry Gibb
          Robin Gibb
          Maurice Gibb
          Karl Richardson
          Albhy Galuten

June 9, 1979
1 week

"LOVE YOU INSIDE OUT" was a sta-tistically important single for the Bee Gees, helping them to rewrite the pop history books. It entered the Hot 100 at number 37 on April 21, 1979, and when it went to number one seven weeks later (interrupting Donna Summer's run at the top with "Hot Stuff"), it left four accomplish-ments in its wake:

1. It was the ninth number one single for the Bee Gees, tying them for fourth place on the list of artists with the most number ones. The top three: the Beatles (20), Elvis Presley (17), and Michael Jackson (12) tied with the Supremes (12).

2. It was the Bee Gees' sixth chart-topper in a row. The only other group to have six consecutive number one singles was the Beatles.

3. It was the third consecutive number one pulled from the *Spirits Having Flown* album, following "Too Much Heaven" [see 496] and "Tragedy" [see 499]. The Bee Gees also had three consecutive number one singles on *Saturday Night Fever:* "How Deep Is Your Love" [see 476], "Stayin' Alive" [see 478] and "Night Fever" [see 480]. Whitney Houston is the only other artist to have three con-secutive number one singles from two successive albums.

4. It brought the Bee Gees' total number of weeks spent at the top of the chart to 27, ranking them behind Elvis Presley, the Beatles, Michael Jackson and Paul McCartney.

It also brought a surprising end to the good chart fortunes of the Gibb brothers. The most successful group of the second half of the '70s, they became yesterday's heroes in the '80s. Their first two singles of the new decade, "He's a Liar" and "Liv-ing Eyes," ranked at 30 and 45 respectively on the Hot 100. Their work on the motion picture *Staying Alive*, the sequel to *Saturday Night Fever*, fared just slightly better. "The Woman in You" was their biggest hit of the first half of the '80s, peaking at number 24. The second single from the film, "Someone Belonging to Someone," petered out at number 49.

As cold as they were as artists, the Bee Gees remained white hot as writers and producers. Robin Gibb and the Bee Gees' keyboardist Blue Weaver wrote and produced "Hold on to My Love," a number 10 hit for Jimmy Ruffin in May, 1980 (Robin pursued a solo career in the '80s, reaching number one in Germany with "Juliet," included on his *How Old Are You?* album).

Barry produced the best-selling album of Barbra Streisand's career, *Guilty*, which included a number one single [see 532—"Woman in Love"] written by Barry and Robin. Dionne Warwick was the next beneficiary of a Barry Gibb production, and the Barry-Robin-Maurice Gibb composi-tion of "Heartbreaker" reached number 10 in January, 1983. Later that year, Kenny Rogers recorded his first RCA album, *Eyes That See in the Dark*, with Barry as producer. That resulted in another Barry-Robin-Maurice song going to number one [see 579—"Islands in the Stream"].

On January 8, 2003, Maurice Gibb was admitted to a Miami hospital for a blocked intestine. He went into cardiac arrest before undergoing abdominal surgery, and died four days later. The family held a private funeral on January 15.

## THE TOP FIVE
*Week of June 9, 1979*

1 **Love You Inside Out**
Bee Gees

2 **Hot Stuff**
Donna Summer

3 **We Are Family**
Sister Sledge

4 **Reunited**
Peaches & Herb

5 **Just When I Needed You Most**
Randy Vanwarmer

## 506 Ring My Bell JUANA 3422
### ANITA WARD

*Writer: Frederick Knight*

*Producer: Frederick Knight*

*June 30, 1979*
*2 weeks*

FREDERICK KNIGHT originally wrote "Ring My Bell" for 11-year-old singer Stacy Lattisaw, in anticipation that she would sign with his production company. "It was then a teenybopper type of song, about kids talking on the telephone." Knight told Bob Gilbert and Gary Theroux in *The Top Ten.* "It was conceived strictly for Stacy, because I believe a kid that young needs a special piece of material. 'Ring My Bell' was something real special and unique."

Stacy didn't sign with Knight; instead she went to Cotillion Records, an Atlantic subsidiary. "I had to rewrite 'Ring My Bell' when Anita did it," Knight said in *The Top Ten.* "The title was so catchy I kept that, but changed the lyrics. They kind of suggest that we play around, but I let the people make up their own meanings."

The record was produced in two days. Knight played all the percussion instruments, including a synthesized drum, one of the first chart songs to feature that effect.

Knight, an artist who had a hit record on his own ("I've Been Lonely For So Long") in 1972, sang backing vocals with Valerie Williams and Cheryl Bundy.

"Ring My Bell" entered the Hot 100 at number 90 on May 12, 1979, and went to number one seven weeks later. Before it topped the American chart, it was number one in Britain for two weeks.

Anita Ward was born in Memphis, Tennessee, the oldest of five children. She sang *a cappella* gospel in her church choir, where she was discovered by Chuck Holmes, who signed her to a management contract. Her early album work included an LP with the Rust College *A Cappella* Choir that featured opera singer Leontyne Price. Later, Anita released an album as part of a gospel quartet.

She supported herself by working as a substitute teacher in elementary schools, but her career received a big boost when Holmes introduced her to Knight. He arranged for her to be signed to Juana Records, one of the many labels distributed by Henry Stone's T.K. Records [see 414—"Get Down Tonight"]. At first, Knight was just going to record three songs with Anita, but he thought so highly of her, he agreed to produce an entire album.

All the tracks were completed when Knight decided the album needed one more uptempo tune. Overnight he rewrote "Ring My Bell" for Anita, who was not enthusiastic about recording the song. But she put herself in Knight's hands and became an international star.

Anita was a "one-hit-wonder" in Britain, where she never placed another single in the chart after "Ring My Bell." She almost duplicated that unwelcome feat in America, but was saved by "Don't Drop My Love," which worked its way up to number 87 in December of 1979.

## THE TOP FIVE
*Week of June 30, 1979*

1 **Ring My Bell**
  Anita Ward

2 **Hot Stuff**
  Donna Summer

3 **Bad Girls**
  Donna Summer

4 **We Are Family**
  Sister Sledge

5 **Chuck E's in Love**
  Rickie Lee Jones

*Writers: Donna Summer*
*Eddie Hokenson*
*Bruce Sudano*
*Joe 'Bean' Esposito*

*Producers: Giorgio Moroder*
*Pete Bellotte*

*July 14, 1979*
*5 weeks*

Casablanca Records didn't even wait for Donna Summer's "Hot Stuff" [see 504] to go to number one before releasing the follow-up single, "Bad Girls." The records were released so close together that "Hot Stuff" was still number two and climbing when "Bad Girls" entered the Hot 100 at number 55 on May 26, 1979. "Hot Stuff" was in its third week at number one when "Bad Girls" moved into the top five. And when "Bad Girls" became the third number one single of Donna Summer's career, "Hot Stuff" was still holding at number three. All in all, Donna Sum- mer had two singles in the top five for six consecutive weeks.

Both tracks were from her third consecutive double-LP (following *Once Upon a Time...* and *Live and More*), *Bad Girls*. Wrote Jim Miller of the *New Republic*: "On the cover of...*Bad Girls*, she poses as a Parisian hooker, cocky in a beret, her lips lying open in wait, her calling conveyed through the smoke-filled windshield of a car and the $50 bill brandished by its driver. But her stance is tough, uncompromising. Looking at the cover and listening to the music inside, you wouldn't want to bet on whether she's hoping to turn another trick, look for true love, or merely planning to roll the next bum who tries to take advantage of her."

Composed by Summer, her boyfriend (and future husband) Bruce Sudano, Eddie Hokenson and Joe "Bean" Esposito, "Bad Girls" is an explosive rock-disco song which, according to *Rolling Stone's* Stephen Holden, "cheerfully evokes the trash-flash vitality of tawdry disco dolls cruising down the main drag on a Saturday night."

Soon after, Donna renounced her image and proclaimed to the world that she had become a born-again Christian. "I went from poverty to riches, but when I got there, I found it wasn't so great," she testified. "I had neglected the spirit—my spiritual needs. I hadn't been to church in almost 10 years. I started crying like a baby. All the stuff that had been keeping me tense got released. I've gone down the wrong paths, had the life of sin and decadence, but I'm different now. It was the most wonderful experience of my life."

In early 1980, Donna further asserted her independence from the past by suing Casablanca Records, charging the label and its president, Bogart, with "undue influence, misrepresentation and fraud." Bogart released Donna from her contract and she signed with Geffen Records.

Creatively, Donna welcomed in the '80s with *The Wanderer*, an achingly personal statement of her soul's often troubled journey, which demonstrated her growing skills as a songwriter. The title track went to number three in November, 1980. She followed with 1982's *Donna Summer*, produced by Quincy Jones, which yielded a number 10 hit with "Love Is In Control (Finger on the Trigger)" and a cover version of Jon and Vangelis' "State of Independence," which only reached number 41.

Donna still owed her old label one more album. Her 1983 release, *She Works Hard for the Money*, was released on Mercury, which like Casablanca, was a Polygram-owned label. "The album was special from the outset," she said of her work with producer Michael Omartian. "Our meeting was divinely inspired and the Lord watched over us throughout the songs."

The title tune went to number three in August. A joyous celebration of the working woman, Donna was inspired to write it after encountering an exhausted worker named Onetta asleep at her post with the television blasting at Chasen's restaurant, on the border of Beverly Hills, California. Commented Donna, "She works hard for the money."

And so does Donna.

## THE TOP FIVE
*Week of July 14, 1979*

1 **Bad Girls**
   Donna Summer

2 **Ring My Bell**
   Anita Ward

3 **Hot Stuff**
   Donna Summer

4 **Chuck E's in Love**
   Rickie Lee Jones

5 **She Believes in Me**
   Kenny Rogers

**508** **Good Times** ATLANTIC 3584
CHIC

Writers: Nile Rodgers
Bernard Edwards

Producers: Nile Rodgers
Bernard Edwards

August 18, 1979
1 week

"**B**AD GIRLS" gave way to "Good Times" as Chic ascended to the top of the Hot 100 for a second time [see 495—"Le Freak"]. With each succeeding production, the Chic sound was growing more complex and sophisticated. To perfect their craft, leaders Nile Rodgers and Bernard Edwards found themselves spending more time in the studio. Atlantic had budgeted the first Chic LP at $35,000, and the two writer/producers had brought it in under budget, taking just three weeks. By the third album, *Risque*, the figures escalated to $160,000 and eight weeks.

But the effort was well worth it. Perhaps Chic's most fully realized creation, *Risque* yielded "My Feet Keep Dancing," "My Forbidden Lover" and the chart-topping "Good Times."

Success, however, bred slavish imitations of the group's trademark sound. Many people thought Queen's "Another One Bites the Dust" [see 531] was a direct copy of "Good Times." "Well, that Queen record came about because that bass player...spent some time hanging out with us at our studio," Edwards told *New Musical Express*. "But that's

O.K. What isn't O.K. is that the press...started saying that we had ripped *them* off! Can you believe that? 'Good Times' came out more than a year before, but it was inconceivable to these people that black musicians could possibly be innovative like that. It was just these dumb disco guys ripping off this rock 'n' roll song."

And it wouldn't be the only time that the Chic sound would be appropriated. "In the last year, we've been listenin' to the radio," Edwards told *Melody Maker* in 1981. "There's been at least 20 or 30 groups that have actually rewritten a tune or something around a tune that we wrote. We're not hassled, we don't go around yellin' and screamin' about it. But for some reason we're not respected as songwriters and producers in the rock areas, where we've influenced a lotta people."

With the end of the disco explosion, Chic added more ballads to its repertoire and took a harder dance-rock approach. Though the experiments were never less than interesting, the group seemed to be losing the old Chic magic. While their own hits were becoming rare, Rodgers and Edwards began to get more involved with writing and producing for other artists.

Their success rate has been remarkable. In tandem or separately, the two have produced hits for Sister Sledge ("He's the Greatest Dancer," "We Are Family"), Diana Ross [see 530—"Upside Down"], David Bowie

[see 572—"Let's Dance"], Duran Duran [see 590—"The Reflex"], Madonna [see 600—"Like a Virgin"], the Honeydrippers ("Sea of Love"), the Power Station ("Some Like It Hot") as well as records for Debbie Harry of Blondie ("Backfired"), Sheila B. Devotion ("Spacer") and original Chic vocalist Norma Jean ("High Society").

But, they admitted, juggling careers as artists and producers was sometimes a strain. "I'm standing onstage playing 'Good Times' and I'm thinking about 'Upside Down' or something, y'know," Edwards confessed to *Melody Maker*.

In 1980, critic Barry Cooper of the *New York Rocker* took a crack at explaining the Chic mystique, "...behind the lush string orchestrations and colorful polymelodies lies a raunchy pulse, a pulse that comes from the street, a gut-level instinct not necessarily sexual but raw and stripped of any phony trappings. That's why 'Good Times' had such broad appeal. The lyrics were easy and catchy (and ambiguous), but it was the *music*: that bass line like a jungle drum, that handclap like a heartbeat lifeline, allowing everyone to pour out their troubles on the dance floor."

Bernard Edwards and Nile Rodgers were in Japan on April 18, 1996, for a series of concerts with Steve Winwood and Sister Sledge when Edwards complained of feeling ill. He died that same night in his Tokyo hotel room at age 43. Chic drummer Tony Thomas called Edwards, "my best friend, my mentor, and one of the greatest people I've ever known."

## THE TOP FIVE
*Week of August 18, 1979*

1 **Good Times**
Chic

2 **My Sharona**
The Knack

3 **Main Event/Fight**
Barbra Streisand

4 **Bad Girls**
Donna Summer

5 **After the Love Has Gone**
Earth, Wind & Fire

CAPITOL 4731 **My Sharona** 509
THE KNACK

*Writers: Doug Fieger*
*Berton Averre*

*Producer: Mike Chapman*

*August 25, 1979*
*6 weeks*

EVER since the Beatles ushered in the era of modern pop, record company talent scouts have been searching for a successor. In 1979, potential heirs surfaced in the form of a Los Angeles quartet, the Knack. Comparisons started immediately, as the Knack's music was rooted in the original English invasion and was not part of the predominant disco scene. Furthering the analogy was the photograph on the back of their debut album, *Get the Knack*, where the foursome posed before television cameras in what looked like an outtake from *A Hard Day's Night*.

The memory of the original Fab Four was indelibly impressed on the memory of one young Beatles fan, Doug Fieger, who grew up to become the Knack's lead singer and rhythm guitarist. "The Beatles...changed my life," Fieger told Jeff Tamarkin in *Goldmine* magazine. "Me and my sister were watching Ed Sullivan and we begged my father to let us watch it on the big TV. He used to watch (another program) which was on at the same time. So we had to watch it on the TV in my sister's room. But I'll never forget it—especially Lennon. He was one of the most powerful and confident young people I'd ever seen."

Fieger and his cohorts, Berton Averre, Bruce Gary and Prescott Niles, didn't set out consciously to ape the Beatles. "We wanted to present a project along the lines of the bands in the '60s—not necessarily the Beatles but all those bands," the singer explained in *Goldmine*. "Our 11, 12 and 13-year-old souls were coming through in these songs."

Fieger told Tamarkin how "My Sharona" came to be: "Berton had this lick for a long time and we never worked on it. I had met this girl Sharona and fell very deeply in love with her—she was inspirational and moved me on a very basic level. I was just trying to put my feelings about her into the beat that Berton had come up with." The song compressed a sense of teenage sexual frustration into its stutter beat built on simple rock and roll. It took merely one afternoon to write, and the magnitutde of its success shocked its creators, all graduates of Los Angeles garage bands.

Outside the record industry, *Get the Knack* became known for its revival of power pop, but within, it was famous for its chart climbing speed and astonishing economics. Recorded virtually live with few overdubs, the album took just 11 days from start to final mix, costing a total of $18,000. Gold certification took 13 days, platinum less than a month and final sales topped over four million. "My Sharona" entered the Hot 100 at number 86 on June 23, 1979, and was certified gold by the time it reached number one nine weeks later. *Billboard* listed it as the number one single of 1979.

Not everyone loved the Knack, though, and their detractors massed as quickly as their supporters. One disgruntled San Francisco artist invented the "Knuke the Knack" kit. "Good Girls Don't," the band's follow-up single, peaked at 11. The biggest hit from their second LP (recorded in seven days for under $10,000) was "Baby Talks Dirty," which flickered out at number 38. After their third LP, *Round Trip*, the Knack broke up in 1982. In late '86, the Knack reformed with all four original members. They went back on the club circuit and played mostly new material.

## THE TOP FIVE
*Week of August 25, 1979*

1 **My Sharona**
  The Knack

2 **Good Times**
  Chic

3 **Main Event/Fight**
  Barbra Streisand

4 **After the Love Has Gone**
  Earth, Wind & Fire

5 **Bad Girls**
  Donna Summer

## 510  Sad Eyes  EMI-AMERICA 8015
### ROBERT JOHN

*Writer: Robert John*

*Producer: George Tobin*

*October 6, 1979*
*1 week*

Iᴛ's as if someone was testing Robert John's patience. When "Sad Eyes" went to number one, he set one record for longevity and tied another. John waited longer than any other artist for a number one record. From the time of his first appearance on the Hot 100 (as Bobby Pedrick, Jr.) on November 10, 1958, with "White Bucks and Saddle Shoes," to the time he topped the chart on October 6, 1979, was 20 years and 11 months. That record was eventually broken by Tina Turner [see 593—"What's Love Got to Do With It"].

"Sad Eyes" entered the Hot 100 at number 85 on May 19, 1979. When it arrived at the top 20 weeks later, it tied the record set by Nick Gilder [see 491—"Hot Child in the City"] for taking the longest amount of time to reach number one. John and Gilder's record was eventually broken by Vangelis [see 554—"Chariots of Fire"].

John's entire career has been a matter of waiting. Born Robert John Pedrick, Jr., in Brooklyn, New York,

he started vocalizing in street corner doo-wop groups. He was the lead singer on "My Jelly Bean," a regional New York hit by Bobby and the Consoles. He recorded for the Big Top and Verve labels, but national success eluded him. When his father died, he quit school and went to work as a production manager for trade magazines. Eventually he began to write songs with a partner, Mike Gately, and they were signed to a publishing company owned by Stan Catron and Lou Stallman. A Columbia Records staff producer, Dave Rubinson, liked their writing and John's voice on demos, and recorded "If You Don't Want My Love" (number 49 in June 1968). An album followed, and the John-Gately team had their songs recorded by Lou Rawls, Bobby Vinton and Blood, Sweat and Tears.

John met producer George Tobin, who was a fan of "If You Don't Want My Love." They collaborated on some singles for A&M that weren't hits and parted ways. In 1971 John recorded a cover of the Tokens' number one single "The Lion Sleeps Tonight" [see 102], produced by original Token Hank Medress. John was not enthusiastic about recording the song, but he couldn't afford to be too picky. Released on Atlantic Records, the song spent three weeks at

number three in March, 1972. "Even after 'Lion' . . . the company didn't have enough faith to let me do an album. I decided that if that's what happens after a number one song, then I just wasn't going to sing anymore," John told Steve Pond in *Rolling Stone.*

In 1978, Tobin called John from California. "I had him come out and he lived in my house," Tobin recalls. "He was actually a laborer in New Jersey at the time, carrying bricks on a construction job. I was looking for material for him and I heard a song called 'My Angel Baby' (by Toby Beau) and said, 'That's the kind of song Robert should be doing.' So we used that as a frame of reference. Robert wrote 'Sad Eyes' and rewrote it for about three months. Every time he'd write it I'd go, 'Nah, change this and change that.' We recorded another song first and it was bought by Ariola.

"Then we got dropped . . . but the president of EMI heard one of the Ariola records we had on a juke box in Florida. He told his business affairs guy to contact me and see about Robert's availability." The EMI executive telephoned for six weeks, but Tobin's secretary misunderstood who he was and the calls were not returned. "Finally one day I had to pick up the phone myself. And he wanted to know if I was interested in making a deal on Robert John. At that point I had been turned down by everybody; there was no one left to go to. I mean, I would have literally paid a couple of thousand bucks to get the record out there because we believed in it so much."

### THE TOP FIVE
*Week of October 6, 1979*

1  **Sad Eyes**
   Robert John

2  **Don't Stop 'Til
   You Get Enough**
   Michael Jackson

3  **Rise**
   Herb Alpert

4  **My Sharona**
   The Knack

5  **Sail On**
   Commodores

EPIC 50742 **Don't Stop 'Til You Get Enough**
MICHAEL JACKSON

**511**

*Writer: Michael Jackson*

*Producer: Quincy Jones*

*October 13, 1979*
*1 week*

"**H**E wasn't at all sure that he could make a name for himself on his own. And me, too. I had my doubts," producer Quincy Jones told the French publication *Actuel* in 1984.

Jones was referring to Michael's first solo LP in four years, the last being *Forever Michael*, recorded while he was still an integral part of the Jackson Five and the Motown family. In 1976, the Jackson Five switched to Epic Records and became the Jacksons; Michael had a solo deal with the label as well. By the end of 1978, the brothers had delivered their *Destiny* album and Michael was ready for a solo flight.

Quincy and Michael had worked together on Sidney Lumet's 1978 film *The Wiz*, with Michael playing the scarecrow to Diana Ross' Dorothy. Jones and Jackson had met before recording the soundtrack—Quincy remembers meeting 10-year-old

Michael at the house of Sammy Davis, Jr. and Michael recalls first meeting Q at a dinner for Muhammed Ali.

"One day, I called Quincy up to ask if he could suggest some great people who might want to do my album," Michael told *Melody Maker* in 1980. "It was the first time I fully wrote and produced my songs, and I was looking for somebody who would give me that freedom, plus somebody who's unlimited musically. Quincy calls me 'Smelly,' and said, 'Well, Smelly, why don't you let me do it?' I said, 'That's a great idea!' It sounded phoney, like I was trying to hint to that, but I wasn't. I didn't even think of that. But Quincy does jazz, he does movie scores, rock 'n' roll, funk, pop—he's all colors and that's the kind of people I like to work with. I went over to his house about every other day and we just put it together."

"It" turned out to be *Off the Wall*, an album that would ultimately sell nine million copies worldwide. The first single pulled from the LP was "Don't Stop 'Til You Get Enough." Debuting at number 87 on the Hot

100 dated July 28, 1979, the song began a slow chart ascent, losing its bullet at number 73. But it picked up steam and by its 11th week on the chart it was sitting comfortably on top.

Michael discussed the genesis of the song with Dick Clark on "The National Music Survey." "'Don't Stop 'Til You Get Enough' was written at home. I just came up with the melody. It's about forces and the power of love. Walking around the house, I started singing it and kept singing it. I went into a 24-track studio we have at home. I told (younger brother) Randy what to play on the piano. I did percussion and piano, and when I played it for Quincy, he loved it."

The references to "forces and the power of love" can be traced to Michael's allegiance to Jehovah's Witnesses, his mother's faith. Michael discussed his belief that he has been blessed with musical talents by God in a 1983 *Newsweek* interview. "The thing that touches me is very special. It's a message I have to tell. I start crying and the pain is wonderful. It's amazing. It's like God."

Michael talked about the divine inspiration in his songwriting in *Rolling Stone*. "I wake up from dreams and go, 'Wow, put *this* down on paper.' The whole thing is strange. You hear the words, everything is right there in front of your face. And you say to yourself, 'I'm sorry, I just didn't write this. It's there already.' And that's why I hate to take credit for the songs I've written. I feel that somewhere, someplace, it's been done and I'm just a courier bringing it into the world."

## THE TOP FIVE
*Week of October 13, 1979*

1 **Don't Stop 'Til You Get Enough**
Michael Jackson

2 **Rise**
Herb Alpert

3 **Sad Eyes**
Robert John

4 **Sail On**
Commodores

5 **My Sharona**
The Knack

### 512

# Rise A&M 2151
## HERB ALPERT

*Writers: Andy Armer*
*Randy Badazz*

*Producers: Herb Alpert*
*Randy Badazz*

*October 20, 1979*
*2 weeks*

"**R**ISE" was the first Herb Alpert single to appear on the Hot 100 in over five years. After 17 instrumental chart entries with the Tijuana Brass, he recorded a vocal effort that went to number one [see 242—"This Guy's in Love With You"]. His singing career was purposefully short, and he continued to chart with the Tijuana Brass until 1974. When he returned to the pop chart, he had a family member and television's most popular daytime drama to thank.

Randy Badazz suggested to his cousin Herb Alpert that he re-record his Tijuana Brass hits disco style, but Herb resisted, not keen on altering 17-year-old songs that had become pop standards. When the 3M Company loaned A&M Records a 32-track digital machine to experiment with, Herb finally agreed to go into the studio with Randy and try the idea.

Ten minutes into a discofied version of the 1962 hit "The Lonely Bull," Alpert realized the project would not work and called a halt. "It just sounded awful to me, I didn't want any part of it," Herb confessed to Dick Clark on United Stations' syndicated "Rock, Roll and Remember."

The musicians were already booked for three more sessions, so Herb told Randy they should try some other material. Randy gave his uncle a tape of songs he had written with a friend, Andy Armer, and Herb immediately liked one called "Rise." It was also a dance song, but Herb decided to slow it down from the standard 128 beats per minute to about 100 bpm, so "people could dance and hug each other at the end of the night."

The song was recorded live in A&M's Studio D. After the third take Alpert had goosebumps, and he leaned over to Randy and predicted, "I think we have a number one record."

Handclaps and another guitar were added to the final take and the song was released.

"Rise" debuted on the Hot 100 at number 83 on July 28, 1979, and rose slowly for the first three weeks. Then Jill Phelps, music director for ABC's number one daytime program, "General Hospital," decided to use "Rise" as the theme music to illustrate one of the series' most dramatic story-lines—the rape of Laura (Genie Francis) by Luke (Anthony Geary).

"Tony was very musical," says Phelps, who later was named producer of NBC's "Santa Barbara." "It was his idea to use 'Rise' for the rape scene. It was a suggestion he made walking up the stairs—he said, 'Hey, you ought to listen to Herb Alpert's 'Rise.' It had a very guttural, sensual beat . . . it was a wonderful thought."

The song was heard several times a week. "Every time Laura thought of the terrible rape by Luke it was played to evoke that memory," Phelps says. "Consequently, we used it constantly for a while. Then we turned the story around so that he was no longer the rapist and it became a whole other kind of love story, and that was no longer an appropriate piece of music."

The airplay on "General Hospital" helped the song rise even faster. Alpert succeeded Michael Jackson at number one on October 20.

In England, British club DJs failed to notice the imported American 12-inch pressings were recorded at 33 rpm, and played "Rise" at the wrong speed, making it sound much faster than even Randy had intended. As the song was instrumental, there were no clues to suggest they were wrong and "Rise" became a U.K. hit in its speeded-up version. In 1997, "Rise" rose again when the Notorious B.I.G. sampled the Alpert track in "Hypnotize" [see 854], which became a posthumous number one hit.

---

## THE TOP FIVE
*Week of October 20, 1979*

1 **Rise**
Herb Alpert

2 **Don't Stop 'Til You Get Enough**
Michael Jackson

3 **Pop Muzik**
M

4 **Sail On**
Commodores

5 **I'll Never Love This Way Again**
Dionne Warwick

SIRE 49033

# Pop Muzik
## M

**513**

*Writer: Robin Scott*

*Producer: M*

*November 3, 1979*
*1 week*

**M** WAS the secret identity of British pop musician Robin Scott. It was an alter ego he wishes he had kept secret. "At the time when I was putting the (record) sleeve together in Paris, I was thinking that I really needed a pseudonym which would create sufficient interest. I was looking out of the window and I saw this large 'M,' which you see all around Paris for the Metro, and I thought, 'Perfect. I'll take that. And the more people read into it, so much the better.' I should have never told anybody who I was."

"Pop Muzik" was a hit in his home country first, peaking at number two on May 12, 1979. Three months later it entered the Hot 100 at number 61. The single topped the *Billboard* chart the week of November 3, and was the first and only record by M to chart in America, making Scott's musical personality one of the rock era's one-hit-wonders. In Britain, M had three more chart hits, starting with "Moonlight and Muzak."

Scott describes the evolution of "Pop Muzik": "I was looking to make a fusion of various styles which somehow would summarize the last 25 years of pop music. It was a deliberate point I was trying to make. Whereas rock and roll had created a generation gap, disco was bringing people together on an enormous scale. That's why I really wanted to make a simple, bland statement, which was, 'All we're talking about basically (is) pop music.'"

Originally, Scott managed an R&B band, then worked with an all-girl group in Paris. Friends encouraged him to go out on his own, so he recorded a couple of songs, including "Pop Muzik." "That was the third version of that song," he explains. "When I first wrote the song I made a kind of rhythm and blues version, then I re-recorded it again and made a sort of funk version *a la* James Brown. Then finally I made the electronic version which it's famous for. (The third) definitely sounded quite different from anything that was around.

"I knew that the idea was very good, but it needed to be presented in a very fresh, startling way. It took six months, because I was having to persuade studios to part with what we call 'down time.' I didn't have any money, you see, and I just said, 'Look, maybe you'll give me some of your time, free, so that I can make a record and I'll give you a point or

percentage of whatever I make. That was the only way I could do it, so I had to sort of beg, borrow or steal the whole record.

"I was using the studio rather like the artist would use the canvas. The technology, which was changing all the time, proposed different ways of doing things. It's like a workshop situation where you build layer upon layer. I worked like that through sheer necessity because I didn't actually have a working band. I just had one or two people who I knew were talented, and I kind of put them together at different times." That way, Scott was able to overdub whichever musician was available that day.

"Electronic music was being employed for the first time in a commercial pop context, apart from perhaps Donna Summer's 'I Feel Love,' which was an inspiration to me. It had that kind of quirky machine-like feel which was to set a trend for the next few years. A machine is generating a pulse in perfect time, and so everybody follows the machine rather than following, say, the drummer who is always losing in a sense. Most music today is all based around the click of the bass drum or the synthesizer or whatever."

After his initial LP, which included "Pop Muzik," Scott released three more albums as M, none of which were successful. He then recorded two LPs with Japanese pop star and film actor Ryuichi Sakamoto (*Merry Christmas, Mr. Lawrence*). In 1985, Scott recorded a new album in London titled *The Kiss of Life*.

## THE TOP FIVE
*Week of November 3, 1979*

1 **Pop Muzik**
M

2 **Heartache Tonight**
Eagles

3 **Dim All the Lights**
Donna Summer

4 **Rise**
Herb Alpert

5 **Still**
Commodores

# 514 Heartache Tonight ASYLUM 46545
## EAGLES

Writers: Don Henley
      Glenn Frey
      Bob Seger
      J. D. Souther

Producer: Bill Szymczyk

November 10, 1979
1 week

"**W**E probably peaked on *Hotel California*," Don Henley assessed in an interview with Robert Hilburn of the *Los Angeles Times*. Joe Walsh agreed, admitting the album's success "made us very paranoid. People started asking us, 'What are you going to do now?' and we didn't know. We just kinda sat around in a daze for months." Glenn Frey declared, "Everything changed for me during *The Long Run*. There was so much pressure that Don and I didn't have any time to enjoy our friendship. We could talk about girls or football for awhile, but it wouldn't be long before we'd remember that we had to make a decision or that we had to get another song written for the next album."

To try and inject some freshness into the sessions, the Eagles broke in July, 1978, for a short tour, then recorded a seasonal single, a cover version of Charles Brown's "Please Come Home for Christmas," backed with the original "Funky New Year." It was released in November. The competition for self-expression was so intense, they nearly issued a double album. "We actually did about 18 songs before we honed it down," Frey revealed in *Musician*.

The first of three singles pulled from the album was "Heartache Tonight," written with assistance from friend J. D. Souther and Detroit's soulful rocker, Bob Seger ("Night Moves," "Still the Same"). It was the fastest-rising Eagles single ever, debuting at number 52 on October 6, 1979, and moving 52-15-9-7-2 to number one. It was the fifth and final chart-topper for the Eagles.

Like "The Mary Tyler Moore Show," the Eagles kept their vow to quit while they were on top. Frey explained their break-up in the *Los Angeles Times*, "I knew the Eagles were over halfway through *The Long Run*. I could give you 30 reasons why but let me be concise about it: I started the band, I got tired of it and I quit."

Each member has since issued at least one individual work, with varying degrees of acceptance. Ever the joker, Joe Walsh announced his candidacy for President in the 1980 election, prior to the release of his *There Goes the Neighborhood* LP and a solo tour. Felder contributed the title song to the soundtrack of *Heavy Metal*, then concentrated on his *Airborne* album. Timothy B. Schmit recorded a cover version of the Tymes' "So Much in Love" [see 134] for the soundtrack of *Fast Times at Ridgemont High*, then recorded the *Playing It Cool* album.

Frey and Henley have had the most successful post-Eagles careers. Glenn's first solo album was *No Fun Aloud* on Asylum, which produced a number 15 hit in November, 1982, "The One You Love." Disenchanted with the label, he switched to MCA, then headed by former Eagles manager Irving Azoff. *The Allnighter* album contained the "Sexy Girl" single and "Smuggler's Blues," a tune that so appealed to Michael Mann, executive producer of "Miami Vice," that he had an episode written around it and cast Frey as a spaced-out pilot. In 1985, Frey went to number two with both "The Heat Is On" (from *Beverly Hills Cop*) and "You Belong to the City" (another song from "Miami Vice").

Henley's first solo hit single should have been "Johnny Can't Read," but it stalled at number 42. "Dirty Laundry" did the trick, reaching number three in January, 1983. He switched from Asylum to Geffen, where his *Building the Perfect Beast* album yielded "The Boys of Summer" and "All She Wants to Do Is Dance," both top 10 singles.

After years of speculation, the Eagles finally got back together in December, 1993, to appear in Travis Tritt's video for "Take It Easy." That reunion then led to a "Hell Freezes Over" tour, to a live album on Geffen that debuted at number one and to the single "Get Over It."

## THE TOP FIVE
*Week of November 10, 1979*

1 **Heartache Tonight**
  Eagles

2 **Dim All the Lights**
  Donna Summer

3 **Still**
  Commodores

4 **Rise**
  Herb Alpert

5 **Pop Muzik**
  M

*Writer: Lionel Richie*

*Producers: James Anthony Carmichael and the Commodores*

*November 17, 1979*
*1 week*

THE COMMODORES' two biggest hits of 1979, both written by Lionel Richie, were inspired by married couples who were in the process of breaking up. "Sail On," which peaked at number four in October, was about the failing marriage of Richie's boyhood friend William "Smitty" Smith, who calls Lionel by his nickname, "Skeet." One night after the traumatic break-up, the two friends talked from 9 p.m. to sunrise. "Skeet mostly just listened," Smith told Roberta Plutzik, author of the *Lionel Richie* biography. "We cried, and when I walked out in the morning, I knew he was the old Skeet, and that he cared. Six months later he sent me the song, with the message that he'd written it with me in mind, and every line in 'Sail On' refers to something we talked over."

"Sail On" was still moving up the chart when the Commodores' next single, "Still," was rush-released. It debuted at number 68 the week of September 29 and moved quickly— "Sail On" was sitting in its peak position of four the week "Still" zoomed from 38 to 10.

"'Still' was the other side of the coin from 'Sail On' ", Richie told Dick Clark on a Mutual Broadcasting special. It was written about another couple, both good friends of Lionel, who were breaking up. "I admired their strength," Richie told Clark. "They decided that marriage was not the thing for them and they were probably destroying what they had in the first place, which was friendship. . . . They both sat down and said, 'Listen, we want to be friends, we said some things wrong, we've done some things wrong. Let's get a divorce and that way (we) can still be in love and still love (each other) as friends.' "

Working on outside projects like a Kenny Rogers LP [see 533—"Lady"] and a movie soundtrack [see 547— "Endless Love"] hastened the inevitable solo career of Lionel Richie [see 563—"Truly"]. His last single with the Commodores, "Oh No," peaked at number four in December, 1981. Reduced to a quintet, the Commodores' first two singles without Richie ("Why You Wanna Try Me," "Painted Picture") were their lowest-charting efforts in over seven years.

They recorded "Reach High," the theme song from the second season of NBC's "Teachers Only," a comedy series starring Lynn Redgrave, but that didn't improve their chart fortunes. Commodore William King expressed his frustration over Richie's departure in a 1985 interview with Dennis Hunt of the *Los Angeles Times*: "People gave Richie credit for everything. The world thinks he pro-

duced, arranged and wrote everything we did. We all built that sound. He wrote many of the hits but he didn't write all of them. But that didn't matter. People *thought* he did it all. So when he left nobody wanted to know about us. It was a rude awakening."

The Commodores lost their producer, James Anthony Carmichael, who chose to work with Richie on his solo projects. There was another loss in 1982 that affected the group personally and professionally. Their friend and manager Benny Ashburn died of a heart attack. "He was the glue," King told Hunt. "Losing Benny was more of a blow to the Commodores than if Richie had quit 20 times."

After two-and-a-half years without Lionel, the band lost charter member Thomas McClary to a solo career. They took on their first new member in 15 years, British singer J. D. Nicholas. Once a part of Heatwave ("Boogie Nights," "Always and Forever"), he moved to the United States in 1982 and found work singing backing vocals for Ray Parker, Jr., and Diana Ross, among others. Sharing lead vocals with drummer Walter Orange, Nicholas helped return the Commodores to the upper reaches of the Hot 100. "Nightshift," the title track from their LP and a tribute to the late Marvin Gaye and Jackie Wilson, stands as the third biggest hit of the Commodores career, having peaked at number three in April, 1985.

## THE TOP FIVE
*Week of November 17, 1979*

1 **Still**
Commodores

2 **Dim All the Lights**
Donna Summer

3 **No More Tears
(Enough is Enough)**
Barbra Streisand &
Donna Summer

4 **Babe**
Styx

5 **Heartache Tonight**
Eagles

## 516 No More Tears (Enough Is Enough) COLUMBIA 11125
### BARBRA STREISAND AND DONNA SUMMER

*Writers: Paul Jabara*
*Bruce Roberts*

*Producers: Gary Klein*
*Giorgio Moroder*

*November 24, 1979*
*2 weeks*

PAUL JABARA had long been a Barbra Streisand fan, going back to *Funny Girl* days when he'd sat, mesmerized, in front of the Broadway stage at least a dozen times. He was also the songwriter who had just turned out the Oscar-winning "Last Dance" for Donna Summer, from *Thank God It's Friday*. When Barbra, in her self-described tradition of being "an actress who sings," elected to perform the theme for her new boxing film co-starring Ryan O'Neal, *The Main Event*, Jabara's talents were solicited.

He talked about his excitement with James Spada in the biography *Streisand the Woman and the Legend*. "On the way over to Streisand's house to talk about *Main Event* I was an absolute wreck. I couldn't believe that I was actually going to be writing a song for her." He penned a ballad and an uptempo, dance number. Streisand chose the latter, then added a second segment called "Fight" to emphasize the movie's pugilist theme. When "The Main Event/Fight" peaked at number three in August, 1979, it was clear that Barbra was well on her way to mastering the pop idiom of the day, dance music.

When she went into the studio to record *Wet*, Streisand decided she wanted a concept disc, with each song based around water. Jabara pestered her to include a composition he had written with Bruce Roberts, "Enough Is Enough," but it lacked liquid. The songwriters tacked on the introduction, "It's raining, it's pouring, my love life is boring me to tears." At the urging of several intimates (including executive producer Charles Koppelman, producer Gary Klein, Jon Peters and Streisand's son Jason), Barbra hosted a lunch at her Malibu home for Donna Summer. Jabara popped a cassette into the recorder and out poured the melody authored as a duet for his extraordinary songstresses. "They both got excited," he told *Us* magazine. "Barbra kept asking, 'What part do I sing?' "

Overcoming their mutual nervousness was one of the biggest hurdles in realizing the effort. Jabara revealed, "Barbra and Donna were both intimidated by the other, and couldn't understand why the other person should be intimidated. It was crazy." Speculation in the press about explosions between the "dueling divas" amounted to naught. A concert the night before the recording session delayed Summer's arrival for two hours, eliciting the Streisand crack, "I haven't waited two hours for anybody!"

Rehearsal was a bit rocky, both women revving their vocal motors to the max. Donna even topppled from a stool when she tried to hold a note longer than her partner and lost her breath.

Once the tape began rolling, though, magic took over. Jabara described the session for *Us*: "There was Streisand, hands flaring, and Donna, throwing her head back—and they're both belting, sparking each other. It was a songwriter's dream. Seeing them on their stools opposite each other was so mind boggling, my head nearly turned 360 degrees, like Linda Blair's did in *The Exorcist*."

"No More Tears (Enough Is Enough)" entered the Hot 100 at number 59 on October 20, 1979, and moved impressively up the chart: 59–33–10–7–3 to number one. It was the fourth chart-topper for both women; Streisand had already scored a number one duet with Neil Diamond [see 494—"You Don't Bring Me Flowers"].

### THE TOP FIVE
*Week of November 24, 1979*

1  **No More Tears
   (Enough is Enough)**
   Barbra Streisand &
   Donna Summer

2  **Babe**
   Styx

3  **Still**
   Commodores

4  **Dim All the Lights**
   Donna Summer

5  **Heartache Tonight**
   Eagles

A&M 2188 **Babe**
STYX **517**

*Writer: Dennis DeYoung*

*Producer: Styx*

*December 8, 1979*
*2 weeks*

A SENSITIVE ballad written by a musician to his wife to express his feelings about separation became the sole number one single for one of America's most popular heartland rock bands, Styx.

Named after the river which, according to Greek mythology, dead souls are ferried across to reach Hades, Styx originated in Chicago in 1963 as a group called the Tradewinds. Dennis DeYoung (vocals, keyboards), twin brothers Chuck (bass) and John (drums) Panozzo and their friend Tom Nardini played in local bars, until Nardini left and the three remaining members enrolled in Chicago State University. Fellow student John Curulewski (guitar) joined the group, now known as TW4. A year later, James Young (guitar) was added and the group name was officially changed to Styx.

Signed to the Wooden Nickel label in Chicago, Styx went to number six in early 1975 with "Lady." A year later they switched to A&M Records and Curulewski was replaced by a crowd-pleasing guitarist-singer from Montgomery, Alabama, named Tommy Shaw.

With sold-out concert tours and best-selling albums like *Equinox*, *Crystal Ball*, *Grand Illusion* and *Pieces of Eight*, Styx eventually came to be voted America's favorite rock band in a Gallup poll—with overwhelming support from teenage girls. The 1979 *Cornerstone* LP yielded the band's biggest hit. Breaking from Styx' usual pattern of slick, progressive rock was an emotional, DeYoung-penned ballad called "Babe."

He wrote it as a personal message to his wife. "Being on the road for six years puts a strain on a relationship," Dennis says. "I wanted to tell her how much I missed her when I was gone." DeYoung recorded a demo of the song with the Panozzos, on which he sang all the vocal parts in his distinctively high, powerful voice.

Then he gave it to his wife of 15 years, Suzanne, as a birthday present. "The first time I heard 'Babe,'"

she says, "I knew it was as good as 'Lady,' if not better." Still, she was hesitant about her husband releasing the song as a Styx record. "I wasn't so sure I wanted to share our feelings with the world."

At the peak of their popularity, it would be a big gamble to release a straight ballad as a single. "Change is a scary thing for everyone," says DeYoung, adding that he takes his inspiration from the Beatles. "According to some people, you're either a rock and roll band, or you're not. And anybody who plays ballads was looked down upon by the radio establishment."

DeYoung finally convinced the other members of Styx they could have a hit with "Babe." So DeYoung *et al* went into the studio and tried to re-record the song. But no matter how hard they tried, they couldn't quite get it right. Instead they released the demo almost as is, adding only a guitar solo by Shaw.

"Babe" entered the Hot 100 at number 72 on October 6, 1979, and went to number one nine weeks later—nearly one year after DeYoung first presented it to his wife.

Following "Babe," "Why Me" (number 26) and "Borrowed Time" (number 64) were disappointing chart records. In 1981 the group returned

to the top 10 with "The Best of Times" (number three) and "Too Much Time on My Hands" (number nine). Two years later, they landed in the top 10 again with "Mr. Roboto" (number three) and "Don't Let It End" (number six).

At the end of 1984, DeYoung and Shaw recorded solo projects and Styx went into limbo. The band reformed in 1990 with Glen Burtnick replacing Shaw, who went into Damn Yankees. The new Styx went to number three in March, 1991 with "Show Me the Way."

## THE TOP FIVE
*Week of December 8, 1979*

1  **Babe**
   Styx

2  **No More Tears
   (Enough is Enough)**
   Barbra Streisand &
   Donna Summer

3  **Still**
   Commodores

4  **Please Don't Go**
   K.C. & the Sunshine Band

5  **Escape (Pina Colada Song)**
   Rupert Holmes

# 518 Escape (Pina Colada Song) INFINITY 50035
## RUPERT HOLMES

*Writer: Rupert Holmes*

*Producers: Rupert Holmes
        Jim Boyer*

*December 22, 1979
3 weeks*

THE age-old question "Do people listen to song lyrics?" was answered when Rupert Holmes' "Escape (Pina Colada Song)" became the last number one song of the '70s. A sophisticated wordsmith, Holmes' forte is fashioning clever songs that are three-minute mini-movies with good old fashioned beginnings, middles and endings.

"Escape" tells the story of a man so bored with his girlfriend that he answers an ad in the personal columns placed by a woman who likes pina coladas and getting caught in the rain. He responds with a personal ad of his own and they meet the next day in a bar. When she enters, he recognizes her immediately—because she's his girlfriend. "The guy's so vain, it never occurs to him that the girl was also bored," Holmes told interviewer Stephen Holden, "so when he meets her, it's kind of a comeuppance. She's the strong one, because she instigated the thing. Hopefully, they see each other in a new light."

Holmes also told Holden: "One of the reasons I liked writing 'Escape' was that, even though it's a light-hearted song, it has a point of view in its suggestion that we dispose of relationships too easily."

Holmes had to survive several label contracts before "Escape" made it to the top of the chart. He described his career as "the *Poseidon Adventure* of pop." He was signed to Epic Records in 1974 and recorded three albums for the label: *Widescreen*, *Rupert Holmes* and *Singles*. Despite ironic songs like "I Don't Want to Hold Your Hand," "Brass Knuckles" and "Terminal," he remained unknown—except to artists like Barry Manilow and Dionne Warwick, who recorded his material. And Barbra Streisand, who telephoned and asked for lead sheets on two of his songs. A meeting between Holmes and partner Jeffrey Lesser with Streisand resulted in their producing her *Lazy Afternoon* album. Holmes also wrote songs for the

soundtrack of *A Star Is Born*.

Meanwhile, Holmes asked for a release from Epic Records and moved home to England, producing albums for John Miles, Sparks, Sailor and the Strawbs. Returning to the States, Rupert signed with the fledgling Private Stock label. As his single "Let's Get Crazy Tonight" was moving up the Hot 100, the label folded.

Undaunted, Rupert signed with Infinity Records, helmed by his friend Ron Alexenburg and distributed by MCA. "Escape" was on its way to being the company's best-selling single when the label shut down. This time, "Escape" was too far up the chart to be stopped. MCA took over the record and moved Holmes to the parent label.

"Him" and "Answering Machine" were successful follow-ups to "Escape," and then Holmes signed with Elektra Records in 1981, but did

not come up with any hit singles.

Holmes was born in England, the son of an American G.I. and a British mother. The family moved to Nyack, New York, and at six years old Rupert wrote his first song, "Nobody Loves Me." He studied the clarinet, but rock and roll was frowned upon in the Holmes household and Rupert didn't become involved in contemporary music until he heard the Beatles. Then he formed a band in high school, the Nomads. He received a clarinet scholarship to the Manhattan School of Music and changed his major to composition. "Classical music for me was like wearing a tweed suit without underwear," he told Holden. "I wanted to get into a field where no one could say that you had no right to your opinion because you hadn't read the textbook."

He went to work for Lou Levy Publishing in the 1650 Broadway building, earning $45 a week. His biggest success was "Timothy," an offbeat song about two survivors of a mine disaster digesting the third ("Timothy, where on earth did you go..."). The Buoys took it to number 17 in early 1971.

That same year, Holmes was running to catch a train when he stopped to buy a book for his four-day journey from New York to Los Angeles. He picked up a copy of Charles Dickens' *The Mystery of Edwin Drood*. While working on other projects during the day, Holmes spent the hours between midnight and 5 a.m. turning *Drood* into a musical for the stage. He wrote the book, the music, the lyrics and 650 pages of orchestrations. In 1986, *The Mystery of Edwin Drood* won a Tony for Best Musical.

## THE TOP FIVE
### Week of December 22, 1979

1 **Escape (Pina Colada Song)**
   Rupert Holmes

2 **Please Don't Go**
   K.C. & the Sunshine Band

3 **Babe**
   Styx

4 **Send One Your Love**
   Stevie Wonder

5 **Still**
   Commodores

**Please Don't Go** **519**
KC AND THE SUNSHINE BAND

*Writers: Harry Wayne Casey*
*Richard Finch*

*Producers: Harry Wayne Casey*
*Richard Finch*

*January 5, 1980*
*1 week*

THE first number one single of the eighties was "Please Don't Go" by KC and the Sunshine Band. Their fifth chart-topper, it was a radical departure from their disco recordings of the latter '70s. "I was honestly getting a bit bored with (disco)," KC admits. "I love that type of music, but I thought people were starting to think there was no depth to me, that there was no variety."

It wasn't KC's original plan to veer off his disco course when he started work on the *Do You Wanna Go Party* album. In an April, 1979, interview with *Billboard's* Paul Grein, KC revealed, "We had a certain rhythm or beat going for awhile and then dance styles changed. But music's back to funk now and that's where our roots are." And so the title track, "Do You Wanna Go Party," was released as a single. It sauntered up to number 50 in the early summer. In August, the ballad "Please Don't Go" was released.

The song had been written in the middle of the recording sessions for *Do You Wanna Go Party*, KC reveals. "We were working on *Do You Wanna Go Party*, and while they were trying to get a guitar player, I just put my hands on the piano, and all of a sudden it started to come out. It was really beautiful. The rest of the guys came over and said, 'What's that?' I said, 'I don't know, it just started happening. And so we cut it. We stopped what we were doing and went right to that.'"

"Please Don't Go" entered the Hot 100 on August 25, 1979, at number 86. It began a long, slow move up the chart, sometimes inching up one or two places per week. It was 19 weeks later when it finally reached the summit and became the first number one single of the eighties.

It was also the last chart entry for KC and the Sunshine Band for four years. On January 15, 1982, KC was seven blocks from his home in Hialeah, Florida, when the car he was driving was hit head-on by another vehicle. He suffered a concussion and pinched a nerve on the right side of his body, causing him to lose all feeling in that area. He was confined to a wheelchair and had to learn to walk all over again. It was a difficult year of recuperation. "I go through a lot of pain, still, daily," he said in a 1984 interview.

Although he continued to record as KC and the Sunshine Band, the group dissolved and T.K. Records filed for bankruptcy. KC signed with Epic Records and released two albums under the group name and one solo effort, *Space Cadet*. A 1982 album, *All in a Night's Work*, contained a track titled "Give It Up." Epic's office in Ireland released that cut as a single and had some success with it; the British Epic label then released it, and the song became KC's first number one in the United Kingdom.

Surprisingly, Epic in America chose not to release it. That led to KC negotiating his release from the label and starting his own record company, Meca (for Musical Enterprise Corporation of America). He took the bold move of releasing "Give It Up" on Meca, and it peaked at number 18 in the spring of 1984—an impressive chart position for a record released on an independent label.

KC survived the "disco" years, although he regrets that name being applied to music. "I had always planned on having a long-range career, and never thought of being here today and gone tomorrow. I think dance or rhythm music never dies. I think a name (disco) died. A name that never should have been brought to the forefront, anyway. Because the type of music that was being played in the clubs was actually rhythm and blues music and not disco and not any other form. I had always been a little upset because the credit had not been given to rhythm and blues."

### THE TOP FIVE
*Week of January 5, 1980*

1 **Please Don't Go**
   K.C. & the Sunshine Band

2 **Escape (Pina Colada Song)**
   Rupert Holmes

3 **Rock With You**
   Michael Jackson

4 **Send One Your Love**
   Stevie Wonder

5 **Do That to Me One More Time**
   Captain & Tennille

## 520 Rock With You EPIC 50797
### MICHAEL JACKSON

*Writer: Rod Temperton*

*Producer: Quincy Jones*

*January 19, 1980*
*4 weeks*

WHILE gearing up to produce Michael Jackson's first solo LP since his departure from Motown, producer Quincy Jones located Rod Temperton, keyboardist for the British soul band Heatwave. Jones had been impressed with Temperton's "Boogie Nights," a number two single in November, 1977, and wanted his touch on the project.

"Quincy rang up and asked for songs for Michael," Temperton is quoted in Geoff Brown's biography of Michael Jackson. "I said it was impossible. I was doing the (third) Heatwave (album). Finally, he wrangled out of me that I would do one song." Rod flew to Los Angeles with his lone composition for the LP and ended up staying for the entire production, penning a total of three songs for the LP: "Rock With You," "Burn This Disco Out" and what became the title track, "Off the Wall."

Michael, who at one point considered producing the album himself, said in an interview with *Soul Teen* magazine: "I'm not sure I'm ready to be a record producer. I've only recently stepped into the role of solo artist." Explaining why he contacted Quincy Jones to produce the LP after their collaboration on *The Wiz*, Michael added, "When something works as well as it did with Quincy, I'm the type of person who says: 'Stay with what works.' So I started to hound Q."

### THE TOP FIVE
*Week of January 19, 1980*

1 **Rock With You**
   Michael Jackson

2 **Do That to Me One More Time**
   Captain & Tennille

3 **Escape (Pina Colada Song)**
   Rupert Holmes

4 **Coward of the County**
   Kenny Rogers

5 **Send One Your Love**
   Stevie Wonder

Not that Jones was opposed to working with Michael. Quincy told the French publication *Actuel* in 1984, "He had a real intensity. . . . People take him for a simpleton with a head full of silly songs, but he's a complex young man, curious about everything, who wants to go further and further. He behaves like an adolescent and, at the same time, like a wise old philosopher. I feel kind of responsible for him. I'm totally involved in his life, but at times, it's him who plays the role of father."

Michael consciously set out to produce a solo album that would not allow listeners to call it "another Jacksons album." In a 1980 *Billboard* interview, he explained, 'I said (to Quincy) I didn't want it to sound like a Jacksons album at all. And it's a lot different. The harmony sounds better and there's a lot of different styles on there." The two number one singles on the LP are evidence of those stylistic differences. "Don't Stop 'Til You Get Enough" [see 511] is a heavy, fast dance song, while "Rock With You" was at the other end of the musical spectrum: a ballad with smooth vocalizations and a dreamy beat.

The next two singles from the album, "Off The Wall" and "She's Out of My Life," both peaked at number 10, making Michael the first solo artist to have four top 10 singles from one LP. Prior to *Off the Wall*, the only group that had accomplished the same feat had been Fleetwood Mac [see 466—"Dreams"], who lifted four top 10 singles from *Rumours* in 1977. The soundtracks from *Saturday Night Fever* and *Grease* had both produced four top 10 singles, but by different artists.

All those records were yet to be broken. And the man who would break them was the very same man who had recorded *Off the Wall*, which turned out to be a dress rehearsal for the biggest-selling record of all time.

CASABLANCA 2215

# Do That to Me One More Time

## THE CAPTAIN AND TENNILLE

**521**

*Writer: Toni Tennille*

*Producer: Daryl Dragon*

*February 16, 1980*
*1 week*

"**I** REMEMBER having a talk with Karen Carpenter at the A&M office Christmas party," discloses Toni Tennille. "She said, 'They're forgetting what started this label and what made most of its money.' We felt they weren't interested in what we were doing." As A&M moved away from middle of the road artists and toward the British new wave scene—not an unsuccessful move for the label—the Captain and Tennille left the company that gave them their first number one single [see 408—"Love Will Keep Us Together"].

About a year before they departed A&M, Daryl Dragon and his wife Toni met Casablanca Records president Neil Bogart at a dinner party arranged by Norman Brokaw, their agent at William Morris. When they were ready to change labels,

Bogart was ready for them. Eager to lose Casablanca's image as a disco label, Bogart wanted an adult contemporary act and the Captain and Tennille filled the bill.

Toni knew "Do That to Me One More Time" would be a single even before she and Daryl recorded it. "We had just signed with Casablanca. Neil and his vice president, Bruce Bird, came over to our house in Pacific Palisades to hear some of our material we had gotten together for our first album. I had finished 'Do That to Me One More Time' and thought it was just a little tune—kind of nice, but it wasn't any big deal. We played all the other things we had in mind, including some other songs that were more powerful. At the very end I said, 'Well, I'll play you this little tune. It's not much, but it might make a good album cut.'

"So I sat down at the electric piano and played 'Do That to Me One More Time.' Neil said, 'That's a smash! There's no doubt in my mind, that's going to be your first single.'" After Bogart left, Toni sat down at

the piano to play the song again and re-evaluate it.

The slow, sensual song suited her voice perfectly. While not as rapidly paced as their bouncier hits like "Love Will Keep Us Together" and "Lonely Night (Angel Face)," it was not their first song with lusty lyrics. One didn't need a magnifying glass to read between the lines of "The Way I Want to Touch You" or "You Never Done It Like That."

"Do That to Me One More Time" did help create a new image for the Captain and Tennille, one they felt they needed after their ABC-TV variety series, which had run from September 20, 1976 to March 14, 1977. "Any woman can be a siren one minute and in pigtails the next," Toni told David Sheff in *People* magazine. "I am a very complex person with more than just the one facet that television played on." The show did not spoil the medium for Toni, who has since hosted a half-hour daily talk show and a pilot for a syndicated variety series, "Music of Your Life."

The Captain and Tennille followed "Do That to Me One More Time" with two mid-chart singles on Casablanca. After Neil Bogart passed away, they left the label. In 1984, Toni released a solo album of standards called *More Than You Know* on Mirage Records. While not as commercially successful as the Captain and Tennille's biggest hits, it did create enough interest in Toni as a solo singer to have her tour with big bands for concert performances. Combined with the time on the road appearing with the Captain, Toni finds herself spending too little time at home these days.

## THE TOP FIVE
*Week of February 16, 1980*

1 **Do That to Me One More Time**
Captain & Tennille

2 **Crazy Little Thing Called Love**
Queen

3 **Coward of the County**
Kenny Rogers

4 **Cruisin'**
Smokey Robinson

5 **Rock With You**
Michael Jackson

# 522 Crazy Little Thing Called Love ELEKTRA 46579
## QUEEN

*Writer: Freddie Mercury*

*Producers: Queen*
*Mack*

*February 23, 1980*
*4 weeks*

WHERE did Freddie Mercury write Queen's first number one hit? "I wrote the song languishing in my bath at the Munich Hilton," he reveals. Leaping from the tub, Mercury ran to his guitar and piano, which he used to set down the melody. After Mercury played the music for lead guitarist Brian May, bass guitarist John Deacon and drummer Roger Taylor in the studio, the band recorded the song with just a few quick run-throughs. For the first time on a Queen album, Mercury played guitar rather than just singing.

Freddie describes the process: "We arranged the song at band rehearsals the following day with me trying to play rhythm guitar. Everyone loved it so we recorded it. The . . . finished version sounded like the bathroom version. It's not typical of my work, but that's because nothing is typical of my work," says the man who lists Jimi Hendrix and Liza Minelli as his main influences.

Released in Britain first, the song peaked at number two, but almost didn't come out in America, according to Mercury. "We all felt it was a hit, except Elektra, who didn't want to release it." But American radio stations loved it, and imported copies to play. "That forced the single," says Freddie. "Crazy Little Thing Called Love" debuted on the Hot 100 at number 58 on December 22, 1979,

## THE TOP FIVE
*Week of February 23, 1980*

1 **Crazy Little Thing Called Love**
Queen

2 **Do That to Me One More Time**
Captain & Tennille

3 **Yes, I'm Ready**
Teri De Sario with K.C.

4 **Cruisin'**
Smokey Robinson

5 **Rock With You**
Michael Jackson

and began its reign at number one just nine weeks later.

The band was originally formed in 1971 in Middlesex and London around the nucleus of a band called Smile which had included May and Taylor. At first Queen avoided the club circuit, preferring to play at colleges, often only for invited guests at venues such as the College of Estate Management Hall. Eventually they moved into the Marquee Club. They struggled for two years until producers Roy Thomas Baker and John Anthony, who had heard a demo tape, decided they wanted to work with the band. Audition tapes were brought to many record companies, but it was EMI that finally signed the group to a contract. Chosen *Melody Maker*'s "Band of the Year" in a 1974 poll, Queen hit it big in Britain with their first single, "Seven Seas of Rhye," but didn't chart in America until the release of their second 45, "Killer Queen" (number 12 in May, 1975).

Queen's next single, "Bohemian Rhapsody," made it to number nine on its first release in the States, but in Britain it was number one for nine weeks beginning in November, 1975. After the death of Freddie Mercury, the song was reissued and returned to number one in the U.K. for five additional weeks at the end of 1991. With a total of 14 weeks at the top, it is in fourth place in the U.K. for longest-running number one song.

After working with Baker and producing themselves, Queen sought the assistance of a German producer known only as Mack for "Crazy Little Thing Called Love." The band had its own recording studio in Montreaux but found the atmosphere of Munich a lot more stimulating than that elegant Swiss resort town. Five years after it was a hit, Mercury said of "Crazy Little Thing Called Love," "I love it now as I did then, but it's easy to love the things that bring you money. I'm a loving person. Love was the inspiration for the song."

# Another Brick in the Wall

### PINK FLOYD

**523**

*Writers: Roger Waters*

*Producers: Roger Waters*
*Bob Ezrin*
*Dave Gilmour*

*March 22, 1980*
*4 weeks*

ACCORDING to one apocryphal story, a naive record company executive once greeted the British band known as Pink Floyd by asking, "Which one's Pink?" Needless to say, there is no "Pink" and no "Floyd," only four dedicated musicians whose lifestyle, according to producer Bob Ezrin, "is interchangeable with the president of just about any bank in England."

More than any other late-'60s band, Pink Floyd—Roger Waters on bass, Richard Wright on keyboards, Nick Mason on drums and David Gilmour on guitar (replacing founder Syd Barrett, who had a nervous breakdown)—realized the limitless possibilities of electronic sound against a spacey-rock background. With supreme craftsmanship and imagination, they fit together drone effects, intricate rhythmic patterns, sound collages and ultra-progressive rock.

Originally a band with a rabid but limited cult following, Pink Floyd found itself in rock's upper echelon by the mid-'70s. *Dark Side of the Moon*, Floyd's 1973 breakthrough album for Capitol's Harvest label, was on *Bill-*board's album chart longer than any other LP in history—logging 726 weeks by the beginning of May, 1988.

A switch to Columbia Records in 1975 produced another pair of smash albums, *Wish You Were Here* and *Animals*. The physically and emotionally exhausting *Animals* tour was source material for 1980's *The Wall*.

At the Montreal date, the cumulative effect of too many cities, too little sleep and too much adulation got to Waters. Something snapped and he spit on a fan in the front row. Later, he brooded about the incident and where Floyd's fame had brought him. Out of this dark night of the soul, he wrote the cycle of brutally revealing songs that became *The Wall*.

The "wall" in Waters' lyrics stands as a metaphor for Pink Floyd's gradual separation from its audience as the band's popularity soared. The double album is a stinging indictment of the mass crowd psychology that destroys the creativity of artists. Ironically, the first single from the album, "Another Brick in the Wall," became the group's biggest hit. Entering the Hot 100 at number 77 on January 19, 1980, it moved to

---

## THE TOP FIVE
### *Week of March 22, 1980*

1 **Another Brick in the Wall**
Pink Floyd

2 **Longer**
Dan Fogelberg

3 **Crazy Little Thing Called Love**
Queen

4 **Desire**
Andy Gibb

5 **Working My Way Back to You/Forgive Me, Girl**
Spinners

---

number one weeks later, and remained there for four weeks.

Waters originally composed the song as a simple tune with a single verse and chorus. He and Gilmour recorded the verse and then decided to get some teenagers to join in on the chorus. "I sent the tape to England," said Gilmour, then living in Los Angeles, "and got an engineer to summon some kids. I gave him a whole set of instructions—10 to 15 year olds from North London, mostly boys—and I said, 'Get them to sing as many ways as you like.'"

When the tape returned, Gilmour and Waters were bowled over. "The engineer filled up all the tracks on a 24-track machine with stereo pairs of all the different combinations and ways of singing with all these kids," Gilmour continued. "Originally, we were going to put them in the background, behind Roger and me singing on the same verse. But it was so good we decided to do them on their own."

In 1982, director Alan Parker (*Midnight Express*) shot a moderately successful film version of *The Wall*, starring Bob Geldof as "Pink."

By 1984, the band was inactive. Waters came out with a solo LP in 1984. In 1987, a Pink Floyd album called *A Momentary Lapse of Reason* was released by Gilmour, Mason and Wright, despite the fact that Waters had sued them to prevent them from using the name. "If one of us was going to be called        Pink Floyd, it's me,"Waters said in *Rolling Stone*.

## 524 Call Me CHRYALIS 2414
### BLONDIE

*Writers: Giorgio Moroder*
*Deborah Harry*

*Producer: Giorgio Moroder*

*April 19, 1980*
*6 weeks*

Giorgio Moroder, composer of the score for Paul Schrader's *American Gigolo*, originally sought Stevie Nicks of Fleetwood Mac to sing the title song for the film. When she turned him down, Moroder turned to Deborah Harry of Blondie, who agreed to write the lyrics and record the movie's theme. The result was "Call Me," the second chart-topper for Blondie and the number one single of 1980, according to *Billboard*.

"Giorgio had scored the entire picture," Harry recalls. "His lyrics suffer from his language change and he had a strange name (for the song), "Machine Man" or "Metal Man"or something like that. It had to do with the idea that the guy was a mechanical lover. You know, he was on call, so to speak. We went to the hotel where Paul was and they played us a video rough edition (of the film). The music was on the track with no lyrics, and we watched it and I went home and wrote the song immediately."

Working with Moroder was not that different from working with the equally disciplined Mike Chapman [see 502—"Heart of Glass"]. Of Moroder, Harry says, "He's very nice to work with, very easy, (but) I don't think he has a lot of patience with people who fool around or don't take what they do seriously. I think he's very serious about what he does and

### THE TOP FIVE
*Week of April 19, 1980*

1 **Call Me**
   Blondie

2 **Another Brick in the Wall**
   Pink Floyd

3 **Ride Like the Wind**
   Christopher Cross

4 **With You I'm Born Again**
   Billy Preston & Syreeta

5 **Special Lady**
   Ray, Goodman & Brown

he's intense and he's a perfectionist and he's very talented, so I think that people who are less talented or less concentrated bore him quickly . . . you really have to pay attention."

Harry was given complete creative freedom with the lyrics. Neither Schrader nor Moroder placed any restrictions on her. The actual recording process was fairly simple. The instrumental track was already recorded, so it only took Harry a couple of hours to record her vocals, including harmonies. She was very pleased with the results and how the song fit into the film perfectly. "I think it was very apropos."

Harry was especially pleased that "Call Me" was in a totally different style from other Blondie songs. Explaining why she took the risk of writing a song for a soundtrack designed to appeal to a wider audience than the one Blondie normally

attracted, she says, "We really tried to vary our music and we really tried not to mimic ourselves. Once you sort of establish a formula, (some people) stick with it because it's safe and people know and like it. We tried to be a little daring."

"Call Me" was only the third song from a soundtrack to top the year-end *Billboard* surveys. "To Sir, With Love" by Lulu [see 231] was the first in 1967, followed by Barbra Streisand's "The Way We Were" [see 356] in 1974. Two other songs associated with motion pictures have been number one singles of the year. Percy Faith's recording of "Theme from 'A Summer Place' " was the number one single of 1960, and Roberta Flack's "The First Time Ever I Saw Your Face" [see 310], included in the soundtrack of *Play Misty for Me*, was the top single of 1972.

Writer: Steven Greenberg

Producer: Steven Greenberg

May 31, 1980
4 weeks

THE disco machine was rapidly running out of fuel in 1980 when it received a surge of power from a bespectacled son of a storage magnate and the saxophonist daughter of a 3M chemist. Lipps, Inc. was the brainchild of young, Minneapolis-born songwriter/multi-instrumentalist Steven Greenberg. By age 15, Steven was pounding away as a rock drummer, and five years later he had written and produced his first record. He took it to Hollywood but was perceptive enough to realize he wasn't ready for the big time.

Returning home, Greenberg fought off pressure to join the family business. Instead he spent the next eight years honing his musical skills in local groups and as part of a popular singing duo, Atlas and Greenberg. Later, he launched a state-of-the-art mobile disco and was partnered in a production company that failed within a year. In 1979, Greenberg was ready to go for a hit record again. He wrote, produced and played all the instruments (except bass) on "Rock It," then pressed 500 copies to distribute in Minneapolis. Thanks to his self-promotion, the record topped the chart at local radio station KFMX.

That summer, Greenberg searched for a female singer to front a group called Lipps, Inc. Cynthia Johnson, a 24-year-old police department secretary, heard Steven was auditioning singers. She was singing on the weekends with a band, Flyt-Time, but wanted to try something new. Greenberg loved her voice and recorded a demo with her.

As a young girl, Cynthia had sung in the Mount Olivet Baptist Church, and at age eight had taken up the saxophone when her teacher ran out of "girls' instruments" for her to play. Her mother, a chemist at 3M, was horrified at this choice, so for 10 years Cynthia practiced in secret. Her saxophone skills later helped her win the Miss Black Minnesota U.S.A. title in 1976.

After rejections from many record companies, Bruce Bird at Casablanca expressed interest in Lipps, Inc.'s demo. "Bird called everyone in, from the secretaries to the vice presidents," Greenberg told Connie Singer in *People*, "and they were all packed into this little office dancing around. I'm in a corner, sweat pouring off my body, thinking this is what I've waited all my life for."

Lipps, Inc.'s debut album, *Mouth to Mouth*, was released in the fall of 1979. One of the songs on the LP was a hot dance tune featuring Greenberg's pumping rhythms and Johnson's searing vocals. Inspired by Greenberg's boredom with Minneapolis and his desire to move somewhere else, the song told of getting away to a "Funkytown." Released as the album's second single, it entered the Hot 100 at number 89 on March 29, 1980, and settled in at number one nine weeks later.

Although "Funkytown" was certified platinum by the RIAA, Lipps, Inc. could only make the singles chart one more time. A reissue of "Rock It" went to number 64.

Both Cynthia and Steven chose to remain in Minneapolis rather than seek fame in Los Angeles or New York. "I'm glad I live in Minnesota," Johnson said in *People*. "Nobody knows me. I can walk to the store." Steven echoed her sentiments. "I'm just sitting here in the Midwest writing music. Funk is a rhythm I hear."

## THE TOP FIVE
### Week of May 31, 1980

1 **Funkytown**
Lipps Inc.

2 **Call Me**
Blondie

3 **Coming Up (Live at Glasgow)**
Paul McCartney

4 **Don't Fall in Love
With a Dreamer**
Kenny Rogers
with Kim Carnes

5 **Sexy Eyes**
Dr. Hook

# Coming Up (Live at Glasgow) COLUMBIA 11263
## PAUL McCARTNEY

Writer: *Paul McCartney*

Producer: *Paul McCartney*

June 28, 1980
3 weeks

**P**AUL McCARTNEY ended the '70s on two triumphant notes. In the autumn of 1979, the *Guinness Book of Records* named him the most successful composer of all time. He was cited for writing 43 songs between 1962-1978 that sold over one million copies each; for accumulating 43 gold records with the Beatles, 17 with Wings and one with Billy Preston; and for having sold an estimated 100 million singles and 100 million albums. To commemorate his accomplishments, McCartney was presented with a medallion cast in rhodium by the British Minister of Arts at a ceremony held in London on October 24.

McCartney's other achievement in the fall of '79 was the fourth annual Buddy Holly Week [see 26—"That'll Be the Day"]. Through his MPL Communications, Paul had purchased the publishing rights to Holly's songs in the United States. "You've got to do something with money," McCartney explained to Paul Gambaccini in *Rolling Stone*. "You've got to invest it in something. I love songs . . . so now I'm a publisher and a businessman. . . . I love Buddy Holly, I've been crazy about him since I was a kid. And Lee (Eastman) rang up one day and said, 'Buddy Holly's publishing is up for sale.' "

McCartney told Gambaccini why he initiated the annual celebration,

---

### THE TOP FIVE
*Week of June 28, 1980*

1  **Coming Up (Live at Glasgow)**
   Paul McCartney

2  **Funkytown**
   Lipps Inc.

3  **The Rose**
   Bette Midler

4  **It's Still Rock and Roll to Me**
   Billy Joel

5  **Against the Wind**
   Bob Seger & the
   Silver Bullet Band

---

held each September. "I said let's have 'Buddy Holly Week'; let's have it on his birthday instead of his death day and just try to get people to play his music, 'cause there are kids who've never heard of him." For the 1979 celebration, Wings appeared at the Hammersmith Odeon with the Crickets and Paul invited Holly's widow, Maria, to London.

Buddy Holly was just one of ten stars McCartney portrayed in the video for "Coming Up." He also appeared as Frank Zappa, Ron Mael of Sparks, Andy Mackay of Roxy Music and a familiar looking character that McCartney referred to as "Beatle Paul." In an interview with Vic Garbarini for *Musician* that was later released on a commercial LP, McCartney revealed his feelings about playing himself: "I almost chickened out at the end . . . but once I did it and put on the old uniform . . . I didn't realize until a couple of days after, that I'd actually gone and broken the whole voodoo of talking about the Beatles. . . . It was

really like I'd gone back 20 years."

Paul sang lead vocal on "Coming Up" and played bass, synthesizers, piano, guitar and drums. It was the first solo Paul McCartney single to chart in America since the pre-Wings days of 1971. Wings' final appearance on record was *Concerts for the People of Kampuchea*, a double LP released in April, 1981. Wings didn't officially disband until April, 1981, although Steve Holly and Laurence Juber had departed some months before. Denny Laine worked with Paul on the 1982 album *Tug of War*.

Released in April, 1980, "Coming Up" (included on the solo *McCartney II* album) was moving up the Hot 100 when radio station programmers discovered their listeners preferred the "B" side. It was a live version of "Coming Up," recorded at the Glasgow Apollo in Scotland on December 17, 1979 with the Wings Mark Seven line-up. By the time the single reached number one, "Coming Up (Live at Glasgow)" was considered the "A" side.

COLUMBIA 11276 **It's Still Rock and Roll to Me** `527`

BILLY JOEL

Writer: Billy Joel

Producer: Phil Ramone

July 19, 1980
2 weeks

WILLIAM MARTIN JOEL was born May 9, 1949, in Hicksville, Long Island, New York, and it took a slow, hard climb and a lifelong love of music to get him out of those drab, working-class surroundings. At age four, Billy's parents enrolled him with a piano teacher who schooled him in the classics. But with the coming of Elvis Presley, the fledgling piano man quickly became hooked on rock and roll.

At 14, Billy started his first band, the Echoes, and before long was playing in all-night bars. Since his parents had divorced (and his German-born father had returned home), he helped support the family through music. He also became an amateur boxer, scoring 22 wins in 28 fights—and breaking his nose in the process.

By the late '60s, Billy had joined a popular Long Island band, the Hassles, which recorded a pair of flop albums for United Artists. Then he moved on to form a power-rock trio called Attila, which released one LP on Epic. To earn extra money, he painted a country club in Locust Valley and recorded a pretzel commercial with Chubby Checker [see 74—"The Twist"].

In 1972, after releasing his first solo album, Cold Spring Harbor, for Family Productions, Billy appeared at the Mar y Sol Festival in Puerto Rico. There, he was "discovered" by Columbia Records executives. When a legal hassle prevented him from signing with the company, a distressed Billy split to Los Angeles, where he worked incognito as a cocktail pianist named "Bill Martin."

Tracked down by Columbia in 1974, Billy recorded his Piano Man album, which yielded a number 25 hit with the title track. His next two LPs, Streetlife Serenade and Turnstiles, included favorites like "The Entertainer" and "New York State of Mind," and helped further expose his songs to a wider audience.

Billy first teamed up with producer Phil Ramone in 1977 for his breakthrough effort, The Stranger. The album spawned four consecutive hit singles in 1978: "Just the Way You Are" (number three in February), "Movin' Out (Anthony's Song)" (number 17 in May), "Only the Good Die Young" (number 24 in July) and "She's Always a Woman" (number 17 in October). Despite his success, Billy was irked by critics who insisted on describing him as a "pop crooner." Deciding to "throw a rock at the image people have of me," he recorded the hard-rocking Glass Houses in 1980, once again with producer Ramone. The rock that Billy threw scored a direct hit. "It's Still Rock and Roll to Me" became his first number one single, helping to push the LP past the five million unit plateau.

Some critics remained unimpressed. "Glass Houses is Joel's attempt to establish once and for all that he is a rocker to the core," wrote Dave Marsh in Rolling Stone, "which is a nearly diastrous error, not so much because he can't rock as because he is better at several other things. 'It's Still Rock and Roll to Me' may have redeemed the project commercially, but artistically the album fails, and as a career move, it was pointless."

Despite the critical barbs, the piano man from Hicksville drew four hit singles from this album as well, and before long Billy Joel would be on top of the chart again [see 577—"Tell Her About It"].

### THE TOP FIVE
*Week of July 19, 1980*

1  **It's Still Rock and Roll to Me**
   Billy Joel

2  **Coming Up (Live at Glasgow)**
   Paul McCartney & Wings

3  **Little Jeannie**
   Elton John

4  **Cupid/I've Loved You for a Long Time**
   Spinners

5  **Shining Star**
   Manhattans

# 528 Magic MCA 41247
## OLIVIA NEWTON-JOHN

*Writer: John Farrar*

*Producer: John Farrar*

*August 2, 1980*
*4 weeks*

Two years after *Grease*, Olivia Newton-John, the woman with the hyphenated last name (a combination of some set of forebear's names, "I can't remember which, but they go back a few generations") found herself with a multi-defined career. Singer, (occasional) songwriter, concert performer, defender of animal rights and now actress, all these adjectives split Livvy's identity. And now it was time to find another film script that would carry her screen career one step further. Reading the treatment for *Xanadu* tickled her fancy for the story and the lead character. Besides, the leading man was one of her idols. "I never thought I would get to sing and dance with Gene Kelly," she confided to Allison Steele in *After Dark*. "I had great fear and trepidation at the thought of dancing with him. But on the first day of rehearsals he put me at ease completely."

Another musical was absolutely on Olivia's agenda once she saw the pleasure *Grease* brought to people. "This musical fantasy appealed to me," she told Steele. "I'm concerned and saddened by conditions in the world now, and I hope that seeing *Xanadu* will provide pleasure and a chance for people to get away from their problems. If only for a little while." But how did she feel about the chances for the wild, multi-million dollar, special effects-laden production in which she appeared as one of the nine muses courted by a wealthy merchant (Kelly) and a punk rocker (Michael Beck)? "My stomach is in my mouth," she admitted.

Her gut instincts were right. *Xanadu* was what the star described as a "character-building" bomb. "I certainly wouldn't die of overexposure in *Xanadu*," she later laughed in *Billboard*. "Not enough people saw it. I don't regret it or anything I've done. I learned a lot and the music was successful. I would have been upset if the music flopped."

Indeed, the soundtrack was the only portion of the *Xanadu* project with redeeming financial value. It

teamed Olivia and her long-time producer/songwriter John Farrar with Jeff Lynne from the Electric Light Orchestra ("Telephone Line," "Don't Bring Me Down") on what she outlined to the Associated Press "we hope, will be the songs of the '80s. They're kind of an ethereal music,

written for the character I play. It's a new style for me, which I like. I try to grow each year."

The public's vote was clear: loved the music, hated the movie. The *Xanadu* soundtrack earned a platinum certification and yielded five top 20 singles:

1. "Magic" debuted on the Hot 100 May 24, 1980, and became Olivia's third number one single 10 weeks later.

2. "Xanadu," the title track, was a number eight hit for Olivia Newton-John and the Electric Light Orchestra. In Britain, where Felix Barker of the London *Evening News* called the film, "The most dreadful, tasteless movie of the decade. Indeed, probably of all time," the song went to number one.

3. "Suddenly," a romantic duet between Olivia and Cliff Richard, peaked at number 20.

4. "I'm Alive" by the Electric Light Orchestra, was a number 16 hit.

5. "All Over the World," also an ELO single, reached number 13.

Olivia's biggest benefit from her *Xanadu* experience was meeting actor/dancer Matt Lattanzi. "The first time I saw Matt he was roller-skating. Then he played the stand-in before there was a leading man and we became friends," she recounted to *People*. The two confirmed they were more than friends when they married in 1985, finally making moot the question Livvy had been hearing from interviewers since her career began—"So when are you going to settle down?"

## THE TOP FIVE
*Week of August 2, 1980*

1 **Magic**
 Olivia Newton-John

2 **It's Still Rock and Roll to Me**
 Billy Joel

3 **Little Jeannie**
 Elton John

4 **Cupid/I've Loved You For a Long Time**
 Spinners

5 **Shining Star**
 Manhattans

*Writer: Christopher Cross*

*Producer: Michael Omartian*

*August 30, 1980*
*1 week*

Christopher Cross was the success story of 1980. His debut album, *Christopher Cross*, yielded a single, "Ride Like the Wind," that spent four weeks at number two in May. Looking for a follow-up, his label favored a track called "I Really Don't Know Anymore," but Doobie Brother Michael McDonald [see 500—"What a Fool Believes"] was singing backing vocal on it as he had done on "Ride Like the Wind." McDonald's management company frowned on Cross depending on their client for two successive singles, so another track was selected: "Sailing."

It was not a bad choice. "Sailing" not only went to number one, it helped Cross sweep the Grammys with five big wins, including the top three awards: Song of the Year and Record of the Year for "Sailing," and Album of the Year for *Christopher Cross*. His other two trophies were for Best New Artist and Best Arrangement Accompanying Vocalist.

For all his success, the San Antonio singer had several obstacles to overcome even after he signed with a label. "With record business off, tight budgets and new wave happening, we had a lot going against us. But everything has sort of fallen into place," Cross told Rob McCorkle in *People*. Admittedly not the most handsome male singer to ever top the Hot 100, Cross told McCorkle that he wasn't relying on his looks to sell records. "When I'm old I'd like to be able to say all this happened because my music was good."

The first instrument young Christopher Geppert learned to play in his hometown of San Antonio, Texas, was a set of drums. Then he turned to guitar, encouraged by his father, a former musician. For a few years, Cross played with a band in Austin that covered other artists' hits, but he kept writing his own songs and occasionally trying them out with the band.

Cross sent audition tapes to Warner Brothers Records as early as 1975, but the Burbank, California, company showed little interest in the singer from San Antonio. Finally, Cross performed a live audition in Texas for Michael Ostin of Warners' A&R department. Ostin was won over and helped sign Cross to the label in 1978.

Cross brought his band along to record the album, which included some stellar guest names. In addition to McDonald, the credits listed Don Henley of the Eagles, Nicolette Larson and J. D. Souther. They were the kind of names that made people wonder who this "unknown" artist was to attract such luminaries to a debut album.

Even with such an impressive guest roster, the LP was held back from release for several months. Producer Michael Omartian explained the situation to Paul Grein in *Billboard*: "Maybe we were intimidated by the press predictions of a new wave onslaught. Everybody got a little gun-shy and said, 'Let's wait.' It turned out to be a very wise decision. The album came out in the January, 1980, release when nothing else was happening."

With "Ride Like the Wind" racing up the chart, Cross described that debut single to Stephen Holden of *Rolling Stone* as "all the cowboy movies I used to watch. When I was a kid, I really dug the Lone Ranger." He also told Holden, "I don't like rock and roll much anymore. We're not the new Jimi Hendrix. We're just a commercial pop band. I used to apologize for pop music, but I don't anymore."

Cross, who named his publishing company Pop 'n' Roll, was philosophical when he told Grein in a *Billboard* interview before the Grammy Awards, "If it stops right now and my second album comes out and goes down the tubes and I'm forgotten, I can still be on my deathbed and say, 'I put out an album that went double platinum and had a number one single and I was up for five Grammys. Now, what did you do?'"

## THE TOP FIVE

*Week of August 30, 1980*

1  **Sailing**
   Christopher Cross

2  **Upside Down**
   Diana Ross

3  **Magic**
   Olivia Newton-John

4  **Emotional Rescue**
   Rolling Stones

5  **Take Your Time**
   S.O.S. Band

## 530 Upside Down  MOTOWN 1494
### DIANA ROSS

*Writers: Bernard Edwards*
*Nile Rodgers*

*Producers: Bernard Edwards*
*Nile Rodgers*

*September 6, 1980*
*4 weeks*

DIANA ROSS began her third decade in the music business with the biggest hit of her career. "Upside Down" demonstrated its potential early; after debuting at number 82 on July 12, 1980, it took four weeks to rise to number 49. Then, in one gigantic leap, it skyrocketed to number 10. When it reached the top

of the Hot 100 on September 6, it stayed there for four weeks, longer than any of her solo number ones.

In 1980, Diana Ross was teamed up with the hottest production team of the year, Bernard Edwards and Nile Rodgers of Chic [see 495—"Le Freak"].

It had been four years since Diana had recorded a top 10 single. In fact, all of her singles in the '70s followed a strange pattern: they either went to number one or they missed the top 10 completely.

Diana was not pleased with the results of her sessions with Edwards and Rogers. She sounded more like a guest star on a Chic album than the center of attention on her own LP. After she heard the final mixes, she gave the two producers specific instructions on how she wanted the tracks remixed. Edwards and Rodgers made some slight changes and returned the tapes, suggesting that if she was still not happy she could remix them herself.

With assistance from Motown producer Russ Terrana, Diana did just that. She remixed every track, bring-

ing her vocals further forward. Nile Rodgers expressed his dismay in a *Billboard* interview. "I was shocked. I was furious and got on the phone right away and called Motown. I was asked to listen to the album and then talk to Diana. I calmed down and listened to the album about 10 times. Then I had to say, 'Hey! I know where they're coming from. I understand what they're doing.' But initially I was not prepared for that kind of shock. I'm not as happy as I would be if it was the way we mixed it, but I'm happy with the album because Diana is happy with it."

The two producers insisted that Ross and Terrana be given credit for the new mixes. "We don't want the public to assume that these are our mixes," Rodgers continued. "The basic problem was that we had two different concepts of what her voice should sound like. She hears her voice in one way and we hear it in another way. When it got to a point where she wanted her voice to sound a certain way, we couldn't take the responsibility for it because that's just not how we make records."

The Edwards-Rodgers LP, *diana*, went to number two on the *Billboard* album chart, making it the most successful solo LP of Diana's career. The follow-up single, "I'm Coming Out," ended the spell of only making the top 10 with a number one song. It peaked at five. The next 45 released was "It's My Turn," the title song from the Jill Clayburgh-Michael Douglas film. It also made the top 10 without going all the way, stopping at nine.

Diana left Motown in 1981 and signed with RCA for North America and EMI/Capitol for the rest of the world. Severing the ties with her long-time label did not mean ending her friendship with mentor Berry Gordy, but it was time for her to be in charge. She had a string of top 10 hits on RCA, including "Why Do Fools Fall in Love" and a tribute to Marvin Gaye written and produced by Lionel Richie, "Missing You." In 1989, Diana returned to Motown in North America after Gordy sold the company to MCA. "Workin' Overtime" missed the Hot 100, but peaked at number three on the Black chart. "When You Tell Me That You Love Me" also missed the Hot 100, but charted R&B as well as Adult Contemporary.

### THE TOP FIVE
*Week of September 6, 1980*

1  **Upside Down**
   Diana Ross

2  **Sailing**
   Christopher Cross

3  **Emotional Rescue**
   Rolling Stones

4  **All Out of Love**
   Air Supply

5  **Fame**
   Irene Cara

# Another One Bites the Dust 531
## QUEEN

*Writer: John Deacon*

*Producers: Queen*
*Mack*

*October 4, 1980*
*3 weeks*

AFTER listening to Queen's *The Game* album, Michael Jackson told his friend Freddie Mercury that the single should be "Another One Bites the Dust." When it was finally released as the third 45 from the LP, it turned out to be Queen's biggest hit of all time.

Most of Queen's hits had been written by Mercury ("Bohemian Rhapsody," "Killer Queen") or guitarist and keyboard player Brian May ("We Will Rock You," "Fat Bottomed Girls"). But "Another One Bites the Dust" was composed by bass guitarist John Deacon, whose only previous hit by the band had been "You're My Best Friend" (number 16 in July, 1976). Michael Jackson wasn't the only one who liked Deacon's song—both club and black radio station disc jockeys played the track off *The Game* LP while pop audiences were listening to the album's first two singles, "Crazy Little Thing Called Love" [see 522] and "Play the Game," which peaked at number 42.

"Another One Bites the Dust" was the highest new entry on the Hot 100 the week of August 16, 1980. Debuting at number 67, it took only seven weeks to become Queen's second number one single. Certified platinum, it remained on the chart for 31 weeks and was a tremendous hit on the black singles chart, holding at number two for three weeks—not bad for an outrageous band of British white boys with no R&B chart history.

The band had always been known for unique visuals on stage. In their earlier days, Mercury might appear in black leather, a dress or even a chiffon blouse designed by Zandra Rhodes, the well-known English designer famous for garments that look like dresses from *Gone With the Wind* and her rich punk look—expensive crepe dresses with holes and safety pins. By the time "Another One Bites the Dust" ruled the airwaves, Mercury had switched his stage persona from flowing outfits and long hair to a very short haircut and moustache.

A former art student, Mercury controlled all the graphics and artwork associated with the band. Brian May was as strong a personality and equally as individual. He constructed his original guitar himself out of wood from an old fireplace. Deacon was the band's expert on economics and electronics, while drummer Roger Taylor once studied to be a dentist.

Queen did not have another top 10 hit after "Another One Bites the Dust." They composed the music for Dino De Laurentiis' *Flash Gordon* starring Sam J. Jones, but the single release of the title theme fizzled out at number 42 in February, 1981. Later that year they teamed up with David Bowie [see 416—"Fame"] for a single, "Under Pressure," that ran out of steam at number 29. "Body Language" was their last hit, number 11 in June, 1982. In America, they switched from Elektra to Capitol in 1983, and their first single on their new label was "Radio Ga-Ga," number 16 in April, 1984.

On November 23, 1991, Freddie Mercury announced that he had AIDS. He issued a statement that said, in part, "I felt it correct to keep this information private to date in order to protect the privacy of those around me. . . . I hope that everyone will join with me . . . in the fight against this terrible disease." Mercury died the following day at age 45.

## THE TOP FIVE
*Week of October 4, 1980*

1 **Another One Bites the Dust**
Queen

2 **All Out of Love**
Air Supply

3 **Upside Down**
Diana Ross

4 **Give Me the Night**
George Benson

5 **Drivin' My Life Away**
Eddie Rabbitt

**532**

# Woman in Love COLUMBIA 11364
## BARBRA STREISAND

*Writers: Barry Gibb*
*Robin Gibb*

*Producers: Barry Gibb*
*Karl Richardson*
*Albhy Galuten*

*October 25, 1980*
*3 weeks*

Duets with Neil Diamond [see 494—"You Don't Bring Me Flowers"] and Donna Summer [see 516—"No More Tears (Enough Is Enough)"] had firmly re-planted Barbra Streisand at the top of the Hot 100. For her next partner, she looked no further than Dodger Stadium in Los Angeles where she attended a Bee Gees concert. At the same time, Barry was in search of projects outside the structure of the Gibb family. But when the opportunity to produce, write and sing with Streisand was extended, he nearly passed it up. Barry revealed in a *Billboard* interview: "I was an absolute nervous wreck before we started. Barbra is rumored to be a tough lady. I'd heard about the time 'Evergreen' was written and how Paul Williams was sent backwards

and forwards to write lyrics—and I was afraid that was going to happen to me."

Once he began, though, the Streisand fan discovered his fears were unfounded. "Apart from the fact that Barbra's a total professional, she's a very nice lady," he continued. "I'd have to say at least 80 per cent of the success of the record belongs to her."

Originally only half of the LP's nine songs were to be Gibb brothers' compositions, but Streisand so liked their first five submissions she requested more. No lyrics were rewritten at the interpreter's behest, however, she was hesitant about a portion of "Woman in Love." "She questioned the line, 'It's a right I defend/Over and over again,'" Barry said in *Billboard*. "At first she felt that it was a little bit liberationist; that it might be a little too strong for a pop song."

The sentiments weren't too strong for the public. "Woman in Love" entered the Hot 100 at number 49 on September 6, 1980, and became Streisand's fifth number one single seven weeks later.

"Woman in Love" was the first

single from the multi-platinum selling album *Guilty*, which Gibb produced. His duet with Barbra on the title track was an obvious choice for release, but it was deliberately held back when Streisand expressed concern about wearing out her teammate approach with the public.

"We and CBS felt that it was very important for the first single not to be a duet," delcared executive producer Charles Koppelman in *Billboard*. "We released the single five weeks before the album to make sure it took hold before everybody was exposed to the combined effort." An international number one in 12 countries, the LP had worldwide sales of over 20 million copies, making *Guilty* Barbra's best-selling album after 19 years and 35 LPs.

The next two singles to come from the album were duets with Barry Gibb. The title track peaked at number three and "What Kind of Fool" reached number 10. Streisand later returned to the top 10 in 1996 with "I Finally Found Someone," a duet performed with Bryan Adams.

Her next major project was the history-making *Yentl*. As the movie's director, author, star—not to mention the soundtrack's vocalist and co-producer—Streisand was the first woman in motion picture history to wear all those hats simultaneously. Such all-around involvement obviously scalloped Barbra's own personal mark onto this story of a young woman who breaks society's rules by entering the all-male world of Jewish education in the 1900s. At the same time, it allowed her to create a monument to her own father with a movie she termed an "obsession."

## THE TOP FIVE
### *Week of October 25, 1980*

1  **Woman in Love**
   Barbra Streisand

2  **Another One Bites the Dust**
   Queen

3  **He's So Shy**
   Pointer Sisters

4  **Upside Down**
   Diana Ross

5  **Real Love**
   Doobie Brothers

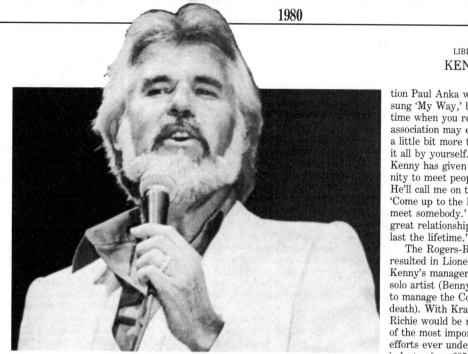

Writer: *Lionel Richie*

Producer: *Lionel Richie*

*November 15, 1980*
*6 weeks*

"THE IDEA was that Lionel would come from R&B and I'd come from country, and we'd meet somewhere in pop," said Kenny Rogers, explaining the origin of his biggest hit, "Lady," to *Billboard's* Paul Grein. "I hate to get stagnant, to do the same things over and over again," Rogers continued. "I was about to explode. I needed new input and that's where Lionel came in. I went to who I thought was the very best in that field. The Commodores have done what I've tried to do: they haven't limited themselves to any one area. I loved 'Three Times a Lady' [see 487]. I think that's probably one of the best records ever cut."

It wasn't the first foray into each other's musical territories for either Kenny or Lionel. "Sail On" by the Commodores was country-tinged, and not surprisingly, was covered by more than one country artist. As a result, Richie was admitted to the Country Music Association. Rogers told Grein, "I was raised in Houston in the middle of R&B. My main influences as a kid were Ray Charles and Sam Cooke and people like that."

Richie outlined the chronology of the collaboration to Grein. "The Commodores were preparing to go out on a 96-date tour, when our drummer (Walter Orange) had a motorcycle accident, forcing us to push back the tour for three to four weeks.

"Around that time, Kenny approached Jobete and they relayed his interest to me. I flew to Las Vegas to meet with him, and two weeks later the project was completed. At that first meeting I played a demo of 'Lady' and 'Goin' Back to Alabama,' a midtempo song I wrote that a little more in his country vein. I had written the skeleton of both songs—the melody and the hook—about two years ago.

"We cut both songs in the same night in an eight-and-a-half hour session. We kept it simple: there are only four rhythm musicians plus string and horn players. There are no gimmicks with Kenny, so the last thing you would ever want to do is put an arp or a synthesizer behind him. He doesn't need that: Kenny sells lyrics."

"Lady" was an important record for both Rogers and Richie. The first record of the '80s to place on all four of *Billboard's* singles charts (Hot 100, Black, Country and Adult Contemporary), it confirmed Rogers' status as a crossover superstar. For Richie, it was his first production work outside the Commodores and foreshadowed the amazing success he would enjoy as a solo artist [see 563—"Truly"].

Richie described the benefits he received from his partnership with Rogers to Grein: "It's the same situa-tion Paul Anka was in. He could have sung 'My Way,' but there comes a time when you realize that an outside association may enhance your career a little bit more than if you try to do it all by yourself. And working with Kenny has given me a great opportunity to meet people in the business. He'll call me on the phone and say, 'Come up to the house, I want you to meet somebody.' We've developed a great relationship that will probably last the lifetime."

The Rogers-Richie alliance resulted in Lionel signing with Kenny's manager, Ken Kragen, as a solo artist (Benny Ashburn continued to manage the Commodores until his death). With Kragen's assistance, Richie would be responsible for one of the most important humanitarian efforts ever undertaken by the music industry [see 605—"We Are the World"], a project that would involve Rogers as well.

Kenny Rogers' first chart entry on the Hot 100 was "Just Dropped In (To See What Condition My Condition Was In)," number five for the First Edition in March, 1968. It was the group's biggest hit of their 10 chart singles. Beginning his solo career with "Love Lifted Me," number 97 in March, 1976, Rogers accumulated four top 10 singles before "Lady," the most successful being "Coward of the County," number three for four weeks in January-February, 1980.

"Lady" made a powerful debut on the Hot 100 at number 39 on October 4, 1980. Six weeks later the single became the only solo number one of Rogers' recording career [see 579—"Islands in the Stream"].

## THE TOP FIVE
*Week of November 15, 1980*

1  **Lady**
   Kenny Rogers

2  **Woman in Love**
   Barbra Streisand

3  **The Wanderer**
   Donna Summer

4  **Another One Bites the Dust**
   Queen

5  **I'm Coming Out**
   Diana Ross

## 534 (Just Like) Starting Over GEFFEN 49604
### JOHN LENNON

*Writer: John Lennon*

*Producers: John Lennon*
*Yoko Ono*
*Jack Douglas*

*December 27, 1980*
*5 weeks*

SEAN TARO ONO LENNON was born on his father's birthday, the ninth of October, 1975. The happy event marked a major shift in the lives of Sean's parents. His father, John, began a five-year retirement from his profession. His mother, Yoko, ran the family's business from an office in their Manhattan apartment building, the Dakota.

During the five years that John Lennon lovingly toiled as a househusband, there were no new recordings released. His total attention and devotion was given to his son. "What I did was discover that I was John Lennon before the Beatles and would be afterward, and so be it," Lennon told Barbara Graustark of *Newsweek* in September, 1980.

Three months before Sean's fifth birthday, the family went to Bermuda for a vacation. There, John began to write songs again, starting with "Woman." During the next two weeks he and Yoko composed about 20 songs. When they returned to Manhattan, John and Yoko booked time at the Hit Factory studio, and on August 4, John Lennon ended his long hiatus from recording.

John and Yoko recorded *Double Fantasy* (named after a flower John saw in a botanical garden in Bermuda) without being signed to a record label. While some record companies asked to hear the LP before offering a deal, David Geffen volunteered to release the album without hearing a note.

The first taste of John's musical comeback reached the airwaves on October 24, when the single "(Just Like) Starting Over" was released. The song opened with the ringing of Yoko's personal wishing bell. "I put it on *Double Fantasy* to show the likeness and difference from 'Mother' to 'Starting Over,'" Lennon is quoted in Coleman's book. Of the single, John told David Sheff in *Playboy*: "It was the fifties-ish sound because I had never really written a song that sounded like that period, although that was my period, the music I identified with. So I just thought, why the hell not? In the Beatle days, that would have been taken as a joke. One avoided clichés. But now those clichés are not clichés anymore."

The news that Lennon was back

spread quickly. "(Just Like) Starting Over" made an impressive debut on the Hot 100 at number 38 on November 1, 1980 (Neil Diamond's "Love on the Rocks" was the highest new entry that week, coming in at 32).

*Double Fantasy* was released on November 17. The single moved erratically up the chart, from 38-32-10-9-8 to six, where it was positioned for the week ending December 6, 1980.

On December 8, 1980, John and Yoko worked late in the studio, mixing a song called "Walking on Thin Ice" which was to be part of a future album tentatively titled *Milk and Honey*. They returned home at 10:50 p.m. EST. In the interior courtyard of the Dakota, a voice called out. "Mr. Lennon?" John turned around and was shot five times. Two minutes later, a police car was rushing Lennon to Roosevelt Hospital where, despite best efforts to save his life, he died from a massive loss of blood.

The assassination of John Lennon affected millions of people as deeply as the loss of President John F. Kennedy in 1963. Yoko Ono asked for a 10-minute silent vigil at 2 p.m. EST on December 14. The silence was heard around the world.

"(Just Like) Starting Over," its title now a grim irony, was a posthumous number one single in America and Britain. As the days passed and the grieving millions let their sadness dissipate, or pretended to, the music remained. "Woman," "Watching the Wheels," then later "Nobody Told Me," were reminders that the music and soul of John Lennon were eternal. It is Yoko who said, "His spirit is in the world for ever."

### THE TOP FIVE
*Week of December 27, 1980*

1 **(Just Like) Starting Over**
John Lennon

2 **More Than I Can Say**
Leo Sayer

3 **Love on the Rocks**
Neil Diamond

4 **Lady**
Kenny Rogers

5 **Hungry Heart**
Bruce Springsteen

CHRYSALIS 2465 **The Tide Is High**
BLONDIE **535**

*Writer: John Holt*

*Producer: Mike Chapman*

*January 31, 1981*
*1 week*

AFTER a brief departure to work with Giorgio Moroder [see 524—"Call Me"], Blondie returned to the domain of producer Mike Chapman for their *Autoamerican* LP. The first single from the album, "The Tide Is High," resembled some of the songs in the *Parallel Lines* LP in both content and feeling—even though it was not written by any of the members of Blondie. "We had so many writers (in the band), we tried to stick with our own material,' says Deborah Harry.

But "The Tide Is High" was too good to resist. "It was on a compilation tape that someone gave us when we were in London," Harry remembers. "Chris (Stein) fell madly in love with the song, as did I, and we just decided to do it. We thought it was a potential hit song." It was the music more than the lyrics that appealed to them. "The musicality of it was just beautiful—beautiful melody, beautiful treatment. The harmonies on the original are very exciting."

The original was written by John Holt and recorded by the Jamaican band which featured him as lead singer, the Paragons. Blondie's version closely parallels the Paragons, since, unlike past Blondie songs, three extra percussionists and string and horn arrangements were used to evoke a West Indies sound. Harry points out one minor difference: "The harmonies are slightly different because theirs are men's voices, so

they were hitting some lower notes than I would hit."

There was not much question that it would be a single. "I think that it was just an obvious choice," says Harry. "The Tide Is High" debuted on the Hot 100 at number 81 on November 15, 1980, and became Blondie's third chart-topper 11 weeks later.

Deborah Harry was born July 1, 1945, in Miami, Florida. Adopted at three months old by Richard and Catherine Harry, she grew up in Hawthorne, New Jersey. She began her professional singing career in a folk-rock group, Wind in the Willows, who released an album on Capitol in 1968. She worked as a beautician, a Playboy bunny and a barmaid before joining the Stilettoes, a campy, new wave band featuring three female singers.

Chris Stein, born January 5, 1950, in Brooklyn, New York, joined the Stilettoes after graduating from the School of Visual Arts in New York City. When that band dissolved, Harry and Stein organized a new group, Angel and the Snakes, which evolved into Blondie. They became popular at CBGB, a club fashionable with punk rockers, and were signed to Private Stock Records with the

approval of major company stockholder Frankie Valli [see 398—"My Eyes Adored You"]. Along with Harry and Stein, the band was composed of bassist Gary Valentine, drummer Clem Burke and keyboardist Jimmi Destri.

Valentine departed and left Blondie a quartet for their next album, their first for Chrysalis, *Plastic Letters*. Harry feels Chrysalis was very supportive of the band, even if they weren't prepared for Blondie's surprises. "Sometimes they're shocked by what they hear, especially because we're always varying our style so much. (They'd say) 'Oh my God, what's this? What can we do with this? What is it?' That would happen sometimes. They tried hard. They were behind us. They worked to really market our things and they would listen to us well."

Harry was no less excited about her third number one single than her first. "You never get blase about that. It made it doubly exciting because we got all this response from the University of Alabama (and their football team), the Crimson Tide. They were calling us and playing the song at games and using it for a theme song. We just got a terrific amount of feedback."

---

## THE TOP FIVE
*Week of January 31, 1981*

1 **The Tide is High**
  Blondie

2 **(Just Like) Starting Over**
  John Lennon

3 **Celebration**
  Kool & the Gang

4 **I Love a Rainy Night**
  Eddie Rabbitt

5 **Every Woman in the World**
  Air Supply

# 536 Celebration DE-LITE 807
## KOOL AND THE GANG

*Writers: Ronald Bell*
*Kool and the Gang*

*Producers: Eumir Deodato*
*Kool and the Gang*

*February 7, 1981*
*2 weeks*

WHEN the American hostages returned home from 444 days of captivity in Iran on January 26, 1981, the uplifting anthem that greeted them was "Celebration," the first number one single for a Jersey City, New Jersey-based group that had been together for 17 years. "Celebration" was also the theme song of the 1981 Superbowl, and was heard during the traditional hoopla that followed the nomination of Presidential candidate Walter F. Mondale at the Democratic National Convention in July, 1984.

Kool and the Gang's origins date back to 1964, when 14-year-old bass player Robert "Kool" Bell started a group called the Jazziacs. Also featured in the aggregation were Robert "Spike" Mickens on trumpet, Dennis "D.T." Thomas on alto sax, George Brown on drums, Charles Smith on lead guitar and Ronald Bell, Robert's brother, on tenor sax.

"When the band first got together," Kool told *Rolling Stone*,

"we used to play jam sessions at a place called St. John's in Jersey City, and Pharaoh Sanders and Leon Thomas used to show up there." By the late '60s, the Jazziacs (later known as the SoulTown Band), had shifted direction and gathered a huge following on the Jersey circuit by laying a heavy R&B/funk beat over its jazz roots.

In 1969, "Kool and the Gang" was officially born. The group recorded the first of more than 25 singles for De-Lite Records. Their first, an instrumental titled "Kool and the Gang," only reached number 59 in November. They wouldn't break into the top 30 until October, 1973, when "Funky Stuff," from the *Wild and Peaceful* album, hit number 29. The next two singles from that LP were the band's biggest hits of the '70s: "Jungle Boogie" went to number four in March, 1974, and "Hollywood Swinging" peaked at six just four months later.

But with the emergence of disco, Kool knew it was time to produce a new sound—or perish. "It was a rough time," he told Steve Bloom in *Record*. "I guess you could call it a searching period for us." That search brought the band velvety-voiced lead singer James "J.T." Taylor and hit-making jazz producer/composer Eumir Deodato ("Also Sprach Zarathustra (2001)") for the smash album, *Ladies Night*.

"Deodato happened to be in the same studio we were working in," Kool recalled for *Rolling Stone*, "and we just started talking. We all came from a jazz background, so the chemistry was there. We talked about not being overcreative and Deo has the

same problem, so he kept saying, 'Let's not go way out to left field. Let's keep it simple and basic and clean.'"

*Ladies Night* spawned two hit singles in 1980, the title track (number eight in January) and "Too Hot" (number five in April). That success was topped with the release of the group's 16th chart single, "Celebration." "The Bible describes life as a celebration," Kool told Bruce D. Rhodewait of the *Los Angeles Herald Examiner*, "and the idea came from our celebration of our return to the music business." The eight-man outfit had plenty of reason to celebrate when their single entered the Hot 100 at number 87 on October 25, 1980, and rose to the top 15 weeks later. Their only number one single, it was certified platinum by the RIAA.

And the ensuing years have continued to give the Gang further cause for celebration ("Joanna" was a number two hit in February, 1984). "We all feel so positive about our direction and success," said Kool. "It's been a long time coming . . ."

## THE TOP FIVE
*Week of February 7, 1981*

1 **Celebration**
Kool & the Gang

2 **The Tide is High**
Blondie

3 **I Love a Rainy Night**
Eddie Rabbitt

4 **9 to 5**
Dolly Parton

5 **Passion**
Rod Stewart

*Writer: Dolly Parton*

*Producer: Gregg Perry*

*February 21, 1981*
*2 weeks*

DOLLY PARTON demonstrated all of her talents in *9 to 5*. Not only did she write and sing the title song, but she held her own while making her acting debut in the company of Oscar and Emmy winners, Jane Fonda and Lily Tomlin. As the dipsy secretary Doralee, subjected to continual harassment by her boss (Dabney Coleman), Parton made it clear she was more than the subject of a Johnny Carson or Joan Rivers joke. She showed just how far a simple country girl from Locust Ridge Hollow, Tennessee, could travel.

The fourth of Lee and Avie Lee Parton's 12 children, Dolly was born January 19, 1946, in a cabin on the banks of the Little Pigeon River. A family member recalled that "she began singing just about the same time she began talking." Her first guitar was an old mandolin, to which she added two bass guitar strings.

Songwriting began in Dolly's preschool days, when she would invent little stories and melodies and ask her mother to write them down. By the time she reached her teens she had already made one record, appeared on television and sung at the Grand Ole Opry.

Nashville was always Mecca for the ambitious singer. "I moved to Nashville in 1964," she said. "I graduated from high school on a Friday night and left early on Saturday morning," she told interviewer Richard Imamura. Relatives (including uncle Buck Owens) gave her a place to stay, but one of her first necessities was a trip to the laundromat. There she met her husband of 21 years, Carl Dean, a construction contractor.

Hot dog relish and mustard were about all Dolly subsisted on for a few lean weeks, even after landing her first record contract with Monument. It wasn't until 1967, when Porter Waggoner needed to replace the female singer in his road show, Norma Jean (who was leaving to get married), that Dolly's big break finally arrived.

Touring with Porter and appear-

ing on his syndicated television series brought Dolly to the attention of RCA Records. Country music fans discovered her long before the pop world, although two tunes ("Jolene," "Light of a Clear Blue Morning") sneaked into the lower region of the Hot 100 between 1974-1977.

She opted for wider horizons, seeking new management in Los Angeles. "I'm not leaving country," she reassured, "I'm just taking it with me." Recording Barry Mann and Cynthia Weil's "Here You Come Again" gave her a solid pop hit, registering at number three in January, 1978.

Acting seemed like the next logical step in her career. Of the time spent on the *9 to 5* set, Dolly recalled for Lesley Salisbury of *TV Times*, "I thought, 'This is goin' to be a breeze.' I never had a bad day on that film. I didn't really have to act, I just played myself, Dolly Parton, as a secretary."

Released as a single, the title song worked its way into the Hot 100 at number 73 on November 29, 1980. Twelve weeks later Dolly Parton had a number one record. After one week, "9 to 5" yielded to Eddie Rabbitt's "I Love a Rainy Night" for two weeks, then returned to the top spot for one additional week.

Dolly followed *9 to 5* with two other features. She played opposite Burt Reynolds in *The Best Little Whorehouse in Texas*, and co-starred with Sylvester Stallone in *Rhinestone*, based on a number one song by Glen Campbell [see 415—"Rhinestone Cowboy"]. The latter was her first project after an 18-month recuperation from stomach surgery for an ulcer-related problem.

## THE TOP FIVE

*Week of February 21, 1981*

1 **9 to 5**
Dolly Parton

2 **I Love a Rainy Night**
Eddie Rabbitt

3 **Celebration**
Kool & the Gang

4 **Woman**
John Lennon

5 **The Tide is High**
Blondie

## 538 I Love a Rainy Night ELEKTRA 47066
### EDDIE RABBITT

Writers: *Eddie Rabbitt*
*Even Stevens*
*David Malloy*

Producer: *David Malloy*

*February 28, 1981*
*2 weeks*

How Does A Boy born to an Irish family in Brooklyn, New York, and raised in East Orange, New Jersey, become a country music star? First, he joins the Boy Scouts of America. Then he goes on weekend camping trips with his troop, led by scoutmaster Tony Schwickrath, a.k.a. Texas Bob Randall. "On one of our hikes he pulled out a guitar and started playing some Johnny Cash and Bob Wills tunes," Eddie explained. "It was my first time to hear a guitar up close and I was fascinated. I asked him if he would teach me to play and that was the start. But I only learned two chords before Tony moved out of town, and from there I was on my own."

Eddie was already interested in music, thanks to his father Thomas Rabbitt, a refrigeration engineer who played the fiddle and accordion. He took his new-found knowledge of guitar and entered talent contests in New Jersey, then got a job singing at the Six Steps Down club in downtown Newark. He was paid $12 a night.

He moved on to the Hurricane Bar, but after four years he figured he'd never be discovered playing country music in Newark. He hopped on a Greyhound bus headed to Nashville, checked into a small hotel and took a long bath. While soaking

### THE TOP FIVE
*Week of February 28, 1981*

1 **I Love a Rainy Night**
  Eddie Rabbitt

2 **9 to 5**
  Dolly Parton

3 **Woman**
  John Lennon

4 **Celebration**
  Kool & the Gang

5 **Keep On Loving You**
  REO Speedwagon

in the water, he wrote a song, "Working My Way Up to the Bottom." A publisher bought it and Roy Drusky recorded it, and Eddie figured songwriting was going to be a cinch. Several months of rejection slips followed, and Eddie took a staff job at Hill and Range Music Publishing, earning $37.50 a week.

His first big break came in 1970 when Elvis Presley recorded a song he had written—"Kentucky Rain." "That legitimized me," Rabbitt told Dennis Hunt of the *Los Angeles Times*. "The doors that had been closed to me before were opened." His songs were recorded by other artists, including Ronnie Milsap, Dave & Sugar, Stella Parton, Tom Jones and Dr. Hook. Elektra Records signed him in 1974. After scoring some hits on the country chart, he made the Hot 100 for the first time in 1976 with "Rocky Mountain Music." His first big pop hit was the title song from *Every Which Way But Loose*, which peaked at number 30 in 1979. "Suspicions" went to number 13, and "Drivin' My Life Away," from the movie *Roadie*, hit number five in the latter half of 1980. The song will

be remembered long after the negative of the film crumbles into dust. "I haven't seen the film," Rabbitt admitted to *Billboard*'s Paul Grein. "It's probably buried in a time capsule somewhere."

The follow-up to "Drivin' My Life Away" was "I Love a Rainy Night." Rabbitt has around 300 "basement tapes" dating back 15 years, filled with scraps of lyrics and melodies. Listening to one of his tapes one day, he heard six seconds of a song fragment he had recorded 12 years earlier. It brought back the memory of sitting in a small apartment, staring out the window at one o'clock in the morning, watching the rain come down. He sang into his tape recorder, "I love a rainy night, I love a rainy night . . ." Twelve years later, upon hearing those words again, he completed the song.

Rabbitt followed "I Love a Rainy Night" with more pop hits, including "Step by Step" (number five) and "Someone Could Lose a Heart Tonight" (number 15). His last top 10 single was "You and I," a duet with Crystal Gayle that went to number seven at the beginning of 1983.

EPIC 50953 **Keep on Loving You**
REO SPEEDWAGON

**539**

*Writer: Kevin Cronin*

*Producers: Kevin Cronin*
*Gary Richrath*
*Kevin Beamish*

*March 21, 1981*
*1 week*

REO SPEEDWAGON took its name from a 1911 fire truck designed by maverick car maker Ransom Eli Olds. According to Kevin Cronin, (born October 6, 1951, in Evanston, Illinois), the band's lead singer and main songwriter, the group "didn't know the *Billboard* charts from a cookbook." But all that would change.

Like other Midwestern bands of the late '60s, such as the Bob Seger System or the Amboy Dukes (featuring Ted Nugent), REO was constantly on the road and eventually became regional superstars. "We've worked hard," Cronin told Don McLeese of the *Chicago Sun-Times*, "we played every single little bar, every single little town, every single high school in Illinois, Wisconsin and Michigan....We went out there and worked and beat the bushes, playing for everybody we could play for."

REO Speedwagon signed with Epic Records in 1971. Through 1976, the band released an album a year, each selling in the six-figure range, but none hitting higher than number 74 on *Billboard*'s LP chart. Never a darling of the critics, the Speedwagon was often dismissed as "faceless" and "formulaic."

Alan Niester termed it "one of America's least successful but long-lived bands commercially as well as aesthetically. Without a distinctive vocalist or material that's more than humdrum, REO Speedwagon has steadfastly maintained its stance as...a perennial opening act that's never quite qualified as a headliner."

In 1973, during production of the third LP, *Ridin' the Storm Out*, Cronin quit the band, citing "artistic differences" between him and the Speedwagon's hard-rocking guitarist Gary Richrath. "The most basic reason was immaturity," explained Cronin. "I was 20; Gary was 21....After the second album, Gary and I were having trouble with just what direction the band should go. The fact that we broke up was a blessing in disguise. There is creative tension there, but we learned that without creative tension, there is nothing. We learned to deal with it."

After an unsuccessful solo career, Cronin returned to the fold in time for the band's first million-seller, a live LP titled *You Get What You Pay For*. Conflicts resolved, Cronin got to work experimenting with a new type of song. "I realized that you can take a ballad and put the energy there," he said. "It doesn't have to be fast and loud; it can still be powerful."

REO's carefully crafted blend of hard-rock and high-energy ballads reached its zenith in late 1980 with the release of its 11th album, *Hi Infidelity*. The first single from the LP, "Keep on Loving You," entered the Hot 100 at number 88 on November 29, 1980. Sixteen weeks later it was number one, besting their previous high spot of number 56 for "Time for Me to Fly." The follow-up, "Take It on the Run," reached number five and a third single from the LP, "In Your Letter," went to number 20.

"The most gratifying thing for me is the peer recognition," Cronin said to the *Los Angeles Times*' Robert Hilburn. "I always had the feeling that no other band or performer in the world knew who we were. If they did know about us, I figured they probably didn't like us. We were never represented right on record. That's one of the things that was different this time," he added, referring to the production of *Hi-Infidelity*. "We've gotten better in the studio and we've improved as writers. If we had gone to number one with a crummy record, I'd be feeling pretty strange inside. But I love the album. It's what was in the back of my mind all those years. It's what kept us going."

## THE TOP FIVE
*Week of March 21, 1981*

1 **Keep On Loving You**
REO Speedwagon

2 **Woman**
John Lennon

3 **The Best of Times**
Styx

4 **9 to 5**
Dolly Parton

5 **Crying**
Don McLean

## 540 Rapture CHRYSALIS 2485
### BLONDIE

*Writers: Chris Stein*
*Deborah Harry*

*Producer: Mike Chapman*

*March 28, 1981*
*2 weeks*

"RAPTURE" was the first rap song many Americans had ever heard. Deborah Harry, Blondie's lead singer, describes its origin: "Rap was a local phenomenon that had been going on for about four or five years in the Bronx and Brooklyn. We used to go up to these rap parties, DJ sessions, and Chris (Stein) said, 'Hey, I've got this song that would be great for a rap song. Let's do it.'

"Chris gave me the idea for the rap. I guess that was really a co-authorship job, because I wrote the beginning of it and I wrote the verses of the song and then I wrote all the beginning of the rap. I know Chris wrote the part about eating the cars. You know, I actually have the original papers that were written and you can only tell by the original handwriting (who wrote what)."

Harry remembers the reaction of the rest of the band. "It took some getting used to for the guys. Thy really weren't solidly behind rap music at the time. It was very underground. They liked (the song) because it was interesting and funny and thematically it was correct for us and in line with what we did in the past. To me it's like a follow-up to 'The Attack of the Giant Ants.' The music was nice, the music's pretty, but (the band) weren't really sure about us doing a rap song. They thought it might have been a little too much." But innovation was important to Harry and Stein, so the song was recorded, with jazz saxophonist Tom Scott guest starring.

Harry says she would make some changes in the song if she re-recorded it today. "I think I would do the rap a little, what I would call tighter, more precise. To me it's a little bit off the beat. I only did one take on it and that was it. So if I were to do it again, I would have done a couple more takes."

Blondie performed the song live after recording it. "It's fun to do," Harry remarks. "We play with it a little. As I got more used to it, I would ad lib a little bit on the rap part." "Rapture" is Chris Stein's favorite Blondie hit, but Harry likes them all because each is so different from the other.

"Rapture" entered the Hot 100 at number 61 and became the group's third number one single eight weeks later. It was the second consecutive chart-topper from the *Autoamerican* LP. Harry then released a solo album, *Kookoo*, produced by Nile Rodgers of Chic [see 495—"Le Freak"]. Two singles ("Backfired," "The Jam Was Moving") failed to crack the top 40. Blondie regrouped for their final LP, *The Hunter*.

Harry has appeared in several films, including *Union City*, David Cronenberg's *Videodrome* and John Waters' *Hairspray*. She also starred off-Broadway in *Teaneck Tanzi*, an adaptation of a popular British play. Chris Stein, hospitalized with a genetic disorder called pemphigus, recovered from the long illness. With Chris feeling better, he and Debbie began collaborating on songs again. Three of their compositions ended up on Debbie's 1986 solo LP, *Rockbird*. The single "French Kissin'" peaked at number 57 in January, 1987. Retitled "French Kissin' in the U.S.A." for Britain, it was a much bigger hit there, going all the way to the top five on the popularity chart.

### THE TOP FIVE
*Week of March 28, 1981*

1 **Rapture**
Blondie

2 **Woman**
John Lennon

3 **The Best of Times**
Styx

4 **Keep On Loving You**
REO Speedwagon

5 **Crying**
Don McLean

Writers: *Janna Allen
Daryl Hall*

Producers: *Daryl Hall
John Oates*

*April 11, 1981
3 weeks*

Though they worked diligently, turning out albums and touring with annual clockwork efficiency, the fickle finger of fandom and hits did not point to Daryl Hall and John Oates immediately after their first number one single [see 457—"Rich Girl"]. "We had to see what we were," Daryl assessed in *Creem*, summing up the series of albums he and John Oates made to less than critical or commercial acclaim. "We made our mistakes in public, on record. We were in a learning process through the '70s, which were really not a very conducive time to do the kind of music we wanted to make."

Their main problem, as they saw it, was that their music had always been filtered through the ears of producers and the hands of session musicians unfamiliar with how the two thought and breathed. Besides, they wanted to capture the sound of New York ("the most conducive place to our creativity," according to John), so instead of camping in Los Angeles, they staked out Studio C at Electric Lady studios, not a five minute walk from their Greenwich Village apartments, in March of 1980. And they began producing their own record— finding it a tremendous relief because, as Daryl elaborated in *Billboard*, "We don't have to bother trying to communicate to other peo-

## THE TOP FIVE
*Week of April 11, 1981*

1 **Kiss On My List**
Hall & Oates

2 **Rapture**
Blondie

3 **The Best of Times**
Styx

4 **Woman**
John Lennon

5 **Just the Two of Us**
Grover Washington Jr.

ple. We always had a problem with it. That's one reason our sound kept changing so much, because the production style was changing so much." Added John, "The music on *Voices* is closer to the music we hear in our heads as we compose the songs."

The lack of a filtering process, plus recording with their own road band, proved to be the missing links in Hall and Oates' formula for hits. Not that the change was immediately apparent. The first single released, "How Does It Feel to Be Back," stopped at number 30 in September, 1980. Next came the first of four cover versions released as singles by Daryl and John, a remake of the Righteous Brothers' "You've Lost That Lovin' Feelin'" [see 166], which peaked at number 12 in November (the other covers are "Family Man," a medley of "The Way You Do the Things You Do" and "My Girl" and "Starting All Over Again").

It was the third single from *Voices* that went all the way to number one. "Kiss on My List" debuted at number 69 on the Hot 100 and took 11 more weeks to reach the top.

Janna Allen, younger sister of

Daryl's girlfriend Sara Allen, had never written a song before. But she had some lyrics and music, and when Daryl was visiting Los Angeles, they sat down at a borrowed Wurlitzer and banged it out. Suddenly, she found herself in the limelight with a song whose title was constantly mispronounced.

"People heard kiss on my lips instead of Kiss on My List,'" John pointed out to *Creem*, "because they didn't listen carefully." The lyrics were misunderstood, too. "It's an anti-love song," Daryl insisted. "It means that your kiss is only on the list of the best things, it's not the only thing. Everyone thinks it's 'I love you and without you I would die.' It's exactly the opposite of that."

If they didn't pick up the nuances, the general public did pick up on Hall and Oates' music. *Voices* turned platinum and yielded a fourth single, "You Make My Dreams," a number five hit in July, 1981. The success was particularly sweet for the duo. "We were vindicated," Daryl suggested in *Rolling Stone*. "We were accepted on our own terms." Just how far that acceptance would lead wouldn't be apparent until their next album.

# Morning Train (Nine to Five) EMI-AMERICA 8071
## SHEENA EASTON

*Writer: Florrie Palmer*

*Producer: Christopher Neil*

May 2, 1981
2 weeks

IF Sheena Easton had failed, she would have done so on national television in Britain. Sheena was given the chance of a lifetime when a BBC documentary show, "The Big Time," agreed to film a program about her quest for stardom. All she had to do was secure a recording contract and the producers would follow her for one year and document her success—or failure—as a pop star.

The BBC arranged Sheena's audition with EMI Records, but could offer no assurances the label would sign her. If the company passed, the documentary unit would search for another subject. With cameras rolling, Sheena sang for EMI's head of A&R, Brian Shepherd.

Shepherd later said he went to the audition with full intentions of not signing the unknown singer, but was overcome by her talent. Surprising everyone, including himself, he signed Sheena to EMI.

For one year, Sheena was filmed by "The Big Time." During those 12 months, she was paired up with producer Christopher Neil, who had succeeded with several British pop acts, including Dollar ("Who Were You With in the Moonlight"), Gerard Kenny ("New York, New York") and Paul Nicholas ("Heaven on the Seventh Floor"). Neil gave Easton a demo tape that included the songs

"Modern Girl" (which Neil had recorded himself, some 18 months earlier) and "9 to 5."

For Sheena's first single, EMI chose "Modern Girl." It was released before the documentary was shown on BBC. It meandered up to 56 on the British chart, a poor showing that disappointed Sheena, EMI and the program's producers. For the follow-up, "9 to 5" was released, just in time for the telecast of "The Big Time" in the summer of 1980. At the end of the program, the question of whether Sheena would make it or not was still unresolved.

But the power of television must never be underestimated. The program itself was the greatest promotion Sheena could receive. "9 to 5" suddenly took giant leaps up the chart, peaking at number three. While it was still moving up, "Modern Girl" came back to life and re-entered the chart, moving to number six. Sheena became the first female singer to have two singles in the British top 10 simultaneously since Ruby Murray in 1956, and the first British female singer to have her first two singles make the top 20.

Things began to move quickly for Sheena. She was invited to perform before the Queen Mother at the Royal Variety Show. She was asked to not only sing the title song but to appear in the opening credits of the James Bond film *For Your Eyes Only*. And on February 14, 1981, Sheena began her conquest of America when her first British hit, retitled "Morning Train (Nine to Five)" so as not to conflict with a current hit for

Dolly Parton [see 537—"9 to 5"], entered the Hot 100. Just 11 weeks later, it was number one, a factor which helped her win a Grammy for Best New Artist of 1981.

Sheena Easton was born on April 27, 1959, in Bellshill, near Glasgow, Scotland. She was the youngest of six children in a working class family and her father died when she was 10. As a teenager, Sheena heard her first Barbra Streisand record, and knew that she wanted to be a star.

She was accepted at the Royal Scottish Academy of Music and Drama and graduated in June, 1979, qualified to be a teacher of speech and drama. She had no intention of teaching, however. Sheena had joined her first band when she was 17, and two years later joined another group that had a regular gig in a hotel, so she could study without touring all over Scotland.

Sheena's first five American singles all made the top 30, but then she failed to make the top 50 with her next efforts. It was too early to count Sheena out—she rebounded with "We've Got Tonight," a duet with Kenny Rogers that was a top 10 hit and went to number one on the country singles chart. She returned to the top 10 with her own "Telefone (Long Distance Love Affair)," "Strut" and "Sugar Walls," a song co-produced by Prince [see 591—"When Doves Cry"] that placed in the top three on the black singles chart. And if successes on the pop, country and black charts were not enough, Sheena won a Grammy in 1985 for "Best Mexican-American Performance" for *Me Gustas Tal Como Eres*," a duet with Luis Miguel.

## THE TOP FIVE
### Week of May 2, 1981

1 **Morning Train (Nine to Five)**
Sheena Easton

2 **Just the Two of Us**
Grover Washington Jr.

3 **Being With You**
Smokey Robinson

4 **Angel of the Morning**
Juice Newton

5 **Kiss on my List**
Hall & Oates

EMI-AMERICA 8077 **Bette Davis Eyes** 543
KIM CARNES

*Writers: Donna Weiss*
*Jackie DeShannon*

*Producer: Val Garay*

*May 16, 1981*
*9 weeks*

ACTRESS Bette Davis, flattered by the rush of attention from Kim Carnes' recording of "Bette Davis Eyes," wrote letters to Carnes and songwriters Donna Weiss and Jackie DeShannon to tell them how much she appreciated being made "a part of modern times." Weiss recalls, "She thanked us and said now her grandson looked up to her and respected her. Then when we won the Grammy she sent us roses. It was fabulous."

But asked to reveal what—or who—*really* inspired her to write the song, Weiss replies, "Guess what. I've never told anybody that—and I can't. I know it sounds ridiculous but I can't tell the exact (derivation), aside from of course Bette Davis in— I think it was an old movie called *Jezebel*. The way she looked back then with white hair. But that's not really the inspiration for the song."

Weiss wrote the lyrics and DeShannon, who had top 10 hits with "What the World Needs Now Is Love" and "Put a Little Love in Your Heart," wrote most of the music. "I kind of helped with it a little," Weiss says. "I went over to Jackie's house one day with all the words—with too many words, as a matter of fact . . . it had more verses than we ended up having. We started work on it—it sounded real good, so I left her house. She called me the next morning real early and had it finished."

DeShannon recorded "Bette Davis Eyes" on her 1975 *New Arrangement* LP. It had a honky-tonky sound and bore little resemblance to the version produced in 1981 by Val Garay.

Kim Carnes wasn't crazy about the song when she first heard it. "I gave that song to Kim Carnes who told me it wasn't a hit," says George Tobin, who produced a top 10 single for Carnes, a 1980 cover version of the Miracles' "More Love." When Carnes turned to a new producer, Garay, Weiss sent her the song again. The songwriter was ecstatic with the results and attributes the success of the single to its innovative arrangement.

Asked who should get credit for the new arrangement of "Bette Davis Eyes," Kim Carnes told Dick Clark on "The National Music Survey" who was responsible. "It's Bill Cuomo, my synthesizer player who really came up with the new synthesizer feel, changing the chords. The minute he came up with that, then it fell into place. Everybody went, 'That's it! No shadow of a doubt!' "

"Bette Davis Eyes" entered the Hot 100 at number 80 on March 28, 1981, and reached the top of the chart seven weeks later. After five weeks at number one, it slipped to number two for one week while the medley by Stars on 45 had a week at the top. Then Carnes returned for an additional four weeks.

It remains the biggest hit in the career of the Los Angeles native who wrote her first song when she was just three years old. She started in the music business as soon as she graduated from high school, record-

ing demos for song publishers. After three years of playing small clubs, she was signed to Amos Records by Jimmy Bowen [see 19—"Party Doll"]. She moved to A&M and recorded three albums for the label, but did not produce any hit singles.

In 1978, Jim Mazza signed her as the first artist for a new label owned by Capitol/EMI. Dubbed EMI-America, the label soon was on the Hot 100 with Carnes' "It Hurts So Bad" (number 56 in March, 1979). Carnes' first real hit was "Don't Fall in Love With a Dreamer," a duet with Kenny Rogers from the *Gideon* concept LP, which Carnes and husband David Ellingson wrote.

"Bette Davis Eyes," number one in 21 countries and a double Grammy winner for Song of the Year and Record of the Year in 1981, was so successful that Kim found it impossible to follow. Only one of her subsequent solo singles rose higher than number 28 on the Hot 100. "What About Me," recorded with Kenny Rogers and James Ingram, did manage to reach number 15 in November, 1984, but a much-heralded duet with Barbra Streisand, "Make No Mistake, He's Mine," fizzled out at number 51 in January, 1985.

In April, 1985, Carnes confided to a television producer that she was no longer interested in how high her singles reached on the chart, and that she was resigned to never being able to match the success of "Bette Davis Eyes." Within four weeks of her admission, her single "Crazy in the Night (Barking at Airplanes)" debuted on the Hot 100 at number 65 and threatened to be her biggest hit since "Bette Davis Eyes."

## THE TOP FIVE
*Week of May 16, 1981*

1 **Bette Davis Eyes**
Kim Carnes

2 **Just the Two of Us**
Grover Washington Jr.

3 **Being With You**
Smokey Robinson

4 **Angel of the Morning**
Juice Newton

5 **Morning Train (Nine to Five)**
Sheena Easton

**544**

**Medley:** INTRO VENUS/SUGAR SUGAR/NO REPLY/I'LL BE BACK/DRIVE MY CAR/DO YOU WANT TO KNOW A SECRET/WE CAN WORK IT OUT/I SHOULD HAVE KNOWN BETTER/NOWHERE MAN/YOU'RE GOING TO LOSE THAT GIRL/STARS ON 45   RADIO RECORDS 3810

STARS ON 45

*Writers: Paul McCartney*
*John Lennon*
*Robbie van Leeuwen*
*Jeff Barry*
*Andy Kim*

*Producer: Jaap Eggermont*

*June 20, 1981*
*1 week*

**S**TARS ON 45 was the identity given to an aggregation of studio vocalists and musicians assembled by producer Jaap Eggermont in Holland to record a medley of songs inspired by a bootleg single.

Willem van Kooten, managing director of Red Bullet Productions, discovered a 12" bootleg single was being sold under the counter at various record shops in Holland for 30 guilders (about $10). The record was a medley of well known songs, performed by the original artists, edited together so it could be played in discotheques. One of the songs included in the medley was a song Van Kooten owned the copyright on, "Venus" by the Shocking Blue [see 268].

Neither Van Kooten nor the Dutch performing rights society could trace the source of the bootleg disc, and Van Kooten was justifiably angry at losing profits on the publishing of "Venus." He asked producer Jaap Eggermont, a former drummer for the Dutch pop group Golden Earring, if he could take the songs from the bootleg and create a similar medley of cover versions.

Eggermont was well-versed in medleys, as he had just produced a Dutch hit for a studio group dubbed Long Tall Ernie and the Shakers called "Golden Years of Rock & Roll," which included American oldies like "Wooly Bully," "Nut Rocker" and "At the Hop."

Eggermont selected some of the songs from the bootleg medley, like "Venus" and "Sugar Sugar," and added many more Beatles songs to make the Fab Four the focus of the track. He invited lead singers from well-known Dutch acts to record the songs. The stars of "Stars on 45" were the four gentlemen who provided the voices of the Beatles.

"Bas Muys seemed to be a duplicate of John Lennon," Eggermont explains, "which in the past didn't

help him very much. His appearance is really fundamental to the sound of the record." Okkie Huysdens sang the Paul McCartney vocals and Hans Vermeulen took the role of George Harrison.

Each song was recorded separately and edited later. "There must have been 20 edits in the single," Eggermont told *Billboard's* Dutch correspondent, Willem Hoos. "It was just before we went to computers, so all things were mixed manually. It was really complex for that time—we were lucky to have singers that could come so close."

The project was intended only for a 12" single release. "In the beginning we thought, this wasn't a record you could make a seven-inch of, the whole eleven-and-a-half minutes belonged together. It really surprised us that we could cut out a single and make it so successful."

The single topped the Dutch chart and spread to other European countries, including Belgium, West Germany, Switzerland, Austria and Spain, as well as territories around the world: Mexico, Canada, South Africa, New Zealand and the Philippines.

Fred Haayen, senior vice president of WEA International, was home in Holland for Christmas when he heard the Stars on 45 project. He took it back to America and played it for Dick Kline, who had just started his own label, Radio Records. Kline loved the medley and called publishers to clear all of the songs for use in the United States.

Clearance problems led to a couple of songs being deleted from the

U.S. single, and an identity crisis for the title of the song. In Europe, the single was known as "Stars on 45" and the "artist" was also Stars on 45. In Britain, the title of the song was "Stars on 45" but the "artist" was listed as Starsound. For American release, publishers insisted the titles of the songs in the medley be included in the title, resulting in a 41 word title that is the longest title of a number one song, as well as the longest title of any single to make the chart.

The Stars on 45 phenomenon started a medley craze that lasted for at least a year. In America, a medley of early Beach Boys songs went to number 12 in the summer of 1981, and a medley of songs from Beatles' movies also peaked at 12, in the spring of 1982.

Eggermont continued producing Stars on 45 medleys. Another Beatles medley peaked at 67 and a tribute to Stevie Wonder went as high as 28. In Britain, an Abba medley matched the number two chart position of the original Stars on 45 single. The latest incarnation of Stars on 45 is the Star Sisters, three females who recorded a medley of Andrews Sisters songs in 1984. Described as a cross between "white Pointer Sisters" and "three Madonnas," the Star Sisters are real people who can tour and record videos, unlike the anonymous performers of the first Stars on 45 single.

## THE TOP FIVE
*Week of June 20, 1981*

1   **Medley: Intro Venus/Sugar Sugar/No Reply/I'll be Back/ Drive My Car/Do You Want to Know a Secret/We Can Work it Out/I Should Have Known Better/Nowhere Man/You're Going to Lose That Girl/Stars on 45**
Stars on 45

2   **Bette Davis Eyes**
Kim Carnes

3   **Sukiyaki**
A Taste of Honey

4   **A Woman Needs Love**
Ray Parker Jr. & Raydio

5   **All Those Years Ago**
George Harrison

ARISTA 0604 **The One That You Love**
AIR SUPPLY
**545**

*Writer: Graham Russell*
*Producer: Harry Maslin*
*July 25, 1981*
*1 week*

Aɪʀ Sᴜᴘᴘʟʏ were the first of only three Australian bands to top the Hot 100 [see 561—"Who Can It Be Now?"], although the music press in Australia and America were often critical of the group because of their light, pop ballads. "Maybe the critics can't accept a successful band with romantic songs," founding member Graham Russell told Rob Hoerburger in a *Billboard* interview. "But if a critic wants to hear rock and roll, he should go see AC/DC."

The public obviously disagreed with the critics, as Air Supply placed seven consecutive singles in the top five, starting with "Lost in Love" in the spring of 1980 and extending through "All Out of Love," "Every Woman in the World," "The One That You Love," "Here I Am (Just When I Thought I Was Over You)," "Sweet Dreams" and "Even the Nights Are Better."

Air Supply came to life in Australia in 1976, although Russell was born June 1, 1950, in Sherwood, Nottingham, England. His mother died when he was 10 years old, and Graham retreated to a world of books, especially Charles Dickens and D.H. Lawrence. He wrote poems and song lyrics, and at 13 was told his father and new stepmother were moving to Australia. The night before their ship was to sail, Graham ran away from home and the family had no choice but to leave without him.

Graham lived with an uncle for the next three years and became the drummer for a local band. He couldn't persuade them to sing the songs he had written, and not wanting to grow up as a factory worker in industrial Nottingham, he listened to his sister's advice and joined his family in Melbourne. There, he joined another band that didn't want to perform his songs and went to work in a Kleenex factory. "I realized if I was going to play my music, I'd have to give up my drums," Graham has said. "So I sold my drum kit, took my acoustic guitar and started playing my own songs in coffee houses."

Graham saw an advertisement

announcing tryouts for a Melbourne production of *Jesus Christ, Superstar*, and won a part in the chorus—partially because he was the only person tall enough to fit into a costume left over from a previous production.

It was during the run of *Jesus Christ, Superstar* that Graham met fellow cast member Russell Hitchcock. Born on June 15, 1949, in Melbourne, Russell grew up in an industrial neighborhood.

He moved to Sydney and worked in a department store and then for a computer parts company. In 1976 he saw an ad for auditions for *Jesus Christ, Superstar* in Sydney. He missed the auditions, but learned there would be more in Melbourne. He took all his money and bought a plane ticket there, and won a role in the chorus over 300 competitors. "The first day of the show, 30 of us sang together, and I couldn't believe how beautiful it sounded. I instantly realized that it was what I should have been doing all my life."

Their first Australian single, "Love and Other Bruises," made the top three. The duo left *Jesus Christ, Superstar*, and supported by session musicians, opened for Rod Stewart on his Australian and American tours. Then Graham took six months off in Adelaide and wrote "Lost in Love" and "All Out of Love." After that respite, he returned home to Nottingham and wrote a rock opera

about Robin Hood, *Sherwood*. He spent the last of his money to attend a music industry conference in France and got food poisoning. Ill and depressed, he picked up an American trade paper and learned that Arista had picked up "Lost in Love" for the United States.

After their run of seven top five singles, Air Supply hiccoughed with "Young Love" and "Two Less Lonely People in the World," both of which peaked at number 38. In 1983 they formed an odd alliance with producer Jim Steinman [see 578—"Total Eclipse of the Heart"] and came up with a single that stayed at number two for three weeks, "Making Love Out of Nothing At All."

---

## THE TOP FIVE
*Week of July 25, 1981*

1 **The One That You Love**
Air Supply

2 **Bette Davis Eyes**
Kim Carnes

3 **Jessie's Girl**
Rick Springfield

4 **The Theme from "Greatest American Hero"**
Joey Scarbury

5 **Elvira**
Oak Ridge Boys

## 546  Jessie's Girl  RCA 12201
### RICK SPRINGFIELD

*Writer: Rick Springfield*

*Producer: Keith Olsen*

*August 1, 1981*
*2 weeks*

RICK SPRINGFIELD's "Jessie's Girl" was the number one song in America when the most important musical revolution of the '80s took place. On August 4, 1981, Warner Amex Satellite Entertainment Company introduced a new concept called Music Television. With an investment of over $20 million, Warner Amex was betting that MTV, a 24-hour-a-day cable television station broadcasting music videos, would return a handsome dividend. By its third year of operation, MTV not only had an operating profit of over $8.1 million but had put new life into the record industry.

It was appropriate that Rick Springfield was on top of the Hot 100 the day MTV made its debut. His television exposure on ABC-TV's "General Hospital" made him a perfect candidate for the new visual art. His fans already knew and loved him as Dr. Noah Drake when "Jessie's Girl" was released; his popularity on the daytime drama did not hurt his record sales.

Richard Lewis Springthorpe was born on August 23, 1949, in Sydney, Australia. He had the nomadic upbringing common to most military children before settling down in Melbourne. A temporary move to England when he was nine left an indelible imprint on the youngster. Not only was he ridiculed for his "funny" accent, which compounded his shyness, but the exciting sounds of Britain's embryonic music revolution were outside anything he'd experienced back home. The guitar he received as a 13th birthday present became the outlet for his frustrations, and soon he was spending more time fronting the Jordy Boys than doing his homework. School went by the boards for good when Rick joined Rock House.

Wackedy Wak came next, but Zoot was Springfield's most successful Australian band. It led to a solo hit in "Speak to the Sky," which caught the attention of Capitol Records in America. "I always knew I had to come over here," he told the New York *Daily News*. "At the time there was no movie industry or any significant record business. You'd play Sydney and Melbourne for 80 bucks then there were three other cities you could go to if you had the plane fare. The company would put your records in an envelope and send them to England and America and that was the end of it. Top bands would vie for a shot at a ticket overseas, but they'd all bomb once they got there. That was bad for the Australian ego."

Rick's own ego was bruised when Capitol traded on his good looks and marketed *Beginnings* to a pubescent audience. "It was a struggle between the press, which painted me as a teen or pre-teen idol, and the kind of music I wanted to play," he explained to *Billboard*. Nevertheless, "Speak to the Sky" marked his first appearance on the Hot 100, peaking at number 14 in October, 1972.

An LP recorded for Columbia called *Comic Book Heroes* was more to Rick's liking, but disappointed label executives who thought they were getting the next David Cassidy. Legal wranglings with his managers complicated by immigration hassles forced Springfield into three inactive years. "I had to do something, so I went to acting school."

His thespian talents were refined while he wrote the songs that would appear on *Wait for Night*, an album picked up by Chelsea Records just before the label folded. Stymied in music, his acting lessons paid off when he was signed to a contract by Universal, which cast him in "The Six Million Dollar Man," "Wonder Woman" and "The Rockford Files." The real life brown belt in *tae kwon do* played a karate-trained policeman on "The Incredible Hulk." He landed a recurring slot on "The Young and the Restless" and was signed to RCA Records two months before he was cast as the most eligible young doctor on "General Hospital."

### THE TOP FIVE
*Week of August 1, 1981*

1  **Jessie's Girl**
   Rick Springfield

2  **The One That You Love**
   Air Supply

3  **The Theme from "Greatest American Hero"**
   Joey Scarbury

4  **I Don't Need You**
   Kenny Rogers

5  **Elvira**
   Oak Ridge Boys

MOTOWN 1519 **Endless Love** 547
DIANA ROSS AND LIONEL RICHIE

*Writer: Lionel Richie*

*Producer: Lionel Richie*

*August 15, 1981*
*9 weeks*

LIONEL RICHIE'S EAGERNESS to compose the music for a motion picture wound up leading to one of the most successful singles of all time. Its nine-week reign at number one ensured it several entries in the record books. At the time of its chart domination, "Endless Love" was:

1. The most successful Motown single of all time. As a corporate entity, Motown had 47 number one singles to this date, 28 of them on the Motown label itself. "Endless Love" remained on top of the Hot 100 longer than any of them. The runners-up were Marvin Gaye's "I Heard It Through the Grapevine" (7 weeks) and the Jackson Five's "I'll Be There" (5 weeks).

2. The most successful soundtrack single to date. While Debby Boone's "You Light Up My Life" [see 475] had 10 weeks at number one, her version was not from the film (Kacey Cisyk vocalized the song in the movie for actress Didi Conn). Percy Faith's recording of "Theme from 'A Summer Place'" had nine weeks at the top, but that wasn't heard in the movie either. The runners-up in the soundtrack category were the Bee Gees' "Night Fever" from *Saturday Night Fever* (eight weeks), and Elvis Presley's "(Let Me Be Your) Teddy Bear" from *Loving You* and "Jailhouse Rock" from the film of the same name (seven weeks each). Bill Haley and His Comets' "(We're Gonna) Rock Around

### THE TOP FIVE
*Week of August 15, 1981*

1  **Endless Love**
   Diana Ross & Lionel Richie

2  **The Theme from "Greatest American Hero"**
   Joey Scarbury

3  **I Don't Need You**
   Kenny Rogers

4  **Jessie's Girl**
   Rick Springfield

5  **Elvira**
   Oak Ridge Boys

the Clock" and Pat Boone's "Love Letters in the Sand" are not eligible, as they existed prior to being included in *The Blackboard Jungle* and *Bernadine.*

3. The most successful duet up to that date. Many number one singles have resulted from the one-time-only pairing of two individually successful artists. Other duos are more career-oriented, such as the Everly Brothers, with their four-decade span of hits. But no duo had surpassed the nine-week run at number one by Diana Ross and Lionel Richie. The runners-up are "Ebony and Ivory" by Paul McCartney and Stevie Wonder (seven weeks), "Say, Say, Say" by Paul McCartney and Michael Jackson (six weeks), "Bridge Over Troubled Water" by Simon and Garfunkel (six weeks) and "In the Year 2525" by Zager and Evans (six weeks). Restricting this category to male-female duets, the runners-up would be Peaches and Herb's "Reunited," Elton John and Kiki Dee's "Don't Go Breaking My Heart" (four weeks) and Frank and Nancy Sinatra's "Somethin' Stupid" (also four weeks).

Lionel was still an integral part of the Commodores when he was asked to meet with producer Jon Peters and director Franco Zeffirelli, who were looking for an instrumental theme for their *Endless Love*, starring Brooke

Shields. They wanted something on the order of the theme from *Love Story*, and Lionel played them a piece of music he had written that hadn't been recorded by the Commodores.

Soon after, Zeffirelli changed his mind and decided he wanted the title song to have lyrics. Lionel agreed to write some. Then Zeffirelli called again, suggesting a female singer would be appropriate—someone like Diana Ross. Diana had just left Motown for RCA, but both labels agreed the two artists could record together.

But Diana's schedule didn't allow any time to fly to Los Angeles, and Richie was too busy with the next Commodores album and his work with Kenny Rogers [see 533—"Lady"] to leave the city. The problem was solved when Diana played Lake Tahoe, Nevada. Lionel agreed to meet her in Reno, about an hour away by automobile. Studio time was booked for 3 a.m., allowing Lionel to fly up after a recording session and Diana to drive in after her 1 a.m. show.

"This lady did not have any lyrics prior to the session," Richie told Dick Clark in a Mutual Broadcasting special. "She just had the melody. I said I'll bring the lyrics with me. At 3:30 in the morning we started singing. At five o'clock in the morning we had 'Endless Love' down on tape."

## 548 Arthur's Theme (Best That You Can Do) WARNER BROTHERS 49787
### CHRISTOPHER CROSS

Writers: Burt Bacharach
      Christopher Cross
      Carole Bayer Sager
      Peter Allen

Producer: Michael Omartian

October 17, 1981
3 weeks

DUDLEY MOORE, Liza Minnelli and Sir John Gielgud starred in the movie. Burt Bacharach, Christopher Cross, Carole Bayer Sager and Peter Allen wrote the song. The result: a box office hit, a number one single and an Oscar for Best Song.

Cross was the first and only person considered to sing the theme song for *Arthur*. "Oh yeah, no other choice," Burt Bacharach confirms. "We wanted him and what a logical move, too. Because the year before he'd won five Grammys, and it seemed like a good career move for him as well. Chris was in town, we had met him and we just said, 'Listen, you want to write this song with us?' It was pretty fast because I basically wrote it in one or two nights with Carole and Christopher.

"The line 'When you get caught between the moon and New York City' was a line from a song that (songwriter and performer) Peter (Allen) had written with Carole quite a few years ago, a song that had never been recorded. I guess Carole just asked Peter the next day if it was O.K. if she used this line. Christopher was over, and we just told him what we were doing and the three of us sat down and wrote the song. It was as simple as that. . . . I

had to have a tune that would fit the picture. It just couldn't be from scratch because I had been living with the picture, so I had . . . a general musical framework when we sat down to write and then we were able to adjust and change a few things here and there. The lyric took shape, then we heard Christopher singing and he sounded great on it, and it just worked out wonderfully."

"Arthur's Theme (Best That You Can Do)" was the eighth number one single of the rock era to win the Academy Award. "It was really the best feeling," Sager enthuses. "Being a songwriter all my life, I was surprised that it really had more of a jolt to it than anything connected with the record industry ever did. But I guess I've always felt that the ultimate achievement was when you win an Oscar. It's the most beautiful of statues—I mean it's the most beautiful award visually, I think. As a kid I grew up watching the Oscars on television and loving them and staying up late. It was just one of the

great nights, one of the most glamorous nights to view. So to win an Oscar I think was probably the most exciting achievement that I could experience in my career. It was just a terrific feeling and it happened to come five days before Burt and I were married. So winning with Burt made it all the better."

Bacharach agrees. "I was very happy, because it was great for Carole and myself to share that together, being that we loved each other."

"Arthur's Theme (Best That You Can Do)" was Cross' second number one single [see 529—"Sailing"] and an interim release between his first and second albums. That second LP, *Another Page*, yielded two disappointing chart singles ("All Right," "No Time for Talk"), but the day was saved when ABC-TV's "General Hospital" adopted "Think of Laura" as theme music for one of the daytime drama's most important characters. Released as the third single from *Another Page*, "Think of Laura" peaked at number nine in February, 1984.

### THE TOP FIVE
*Week of October 17, 1981*

1  **Arthur's Theme
   (Best That You Can Do)**
   Christopher Cross

2  **Endless Love**
   Diana Ross & Lionel Richie

3  **Start Me Up**
   Rolling Stones

4  **For Your Eyes Only**
   Sheena Easton

5  **Step By Step**
   Eddie Rabbitt

*Writers: Daryl Hall*
*Warren Pash*
*Sara Allen*
*Jana Allen*

*Producers: Daryl Hall*
*John Oates*

*November 7, 1981*
*2 weeks*

THOUGH *Private Eyes* was the ninth album they recorded together, John Oates told *Billboard*, "In a strange way, this is only our second album. We haven't stopped growing yet" and Daryl Hall elaborated, "It's an improvement on the ground that we broke with *Voices*. It's a lot more intense." It had taken 101 sessions over a four-month period at Electric Lady Studios to paste together the LP that was almost titled *Head Above Water*.

Much of the extra time was spent perfecting a new songwriting technique. "A lot of times we'll just come in with the basic idea of verse-chorus-verse musically, and I'll just sing something over it, words that don't make any real sense," Daryl illustrated in *Output*. "Then we'll come back and put the real lyrics in the song. It has worked real good for us because it keeps us from getting frustrated. We have it down now where we can go in the studio with incomplete songs and finish them there." The tunes, too, were becoming more compact. "I like to write short pieces now. We're editing ourselves all the time, chopping what we

consider dead wood out of songs and making them tight," he added in *Billboard*.

Personal relationships, as always, were at the core of *Private Eyes'* 11 tracks, songs that used intra-couple dynamics as metaphors for worldly concerns. Double entendre, innuendo and hidden meanings were all devices used to overlay love's simplicity with Daryl and John's more complex messages. "If you want to understand what we're talking about, read between the lines," Hall commanded. Laughed John, "Some people go to psychiatrist. We write songs."

They also toured, trekking exhaustively from coast to coast with the band they felt most comfortable around. It had taken most of the late '70s to find associates like guitarist G. E. Smith, drummer Mickey Curry and saxophonist Charlie DeChant (bassist Tom T-Bone Wolk would sign on later). The shows were stripped to a sharp, fine impact, simplified by

their 1979 series of club dates, and a nationwide round of high school concerts that were prizes for contests underwritten by Care Free Gum, one of the first-ever corporate tour sponsors. "It was the best thing we ever did in our lives," Daryl declared in *Billboard*. Oates added, "We were able to rearrange our performing style. The style you see now on stage came from that experience we got in the high schools and clubs.

And while the duo were fast becoming acknowledged pop kingpins, RCA finally released Daryl's solo album, *Sacred Songs*, that he recorded with Robert Fripp in the producer's seat. "I have lots of faces and all of them are honest faces," Daryl said. "When combined, they produce a study in opposites." The LP was certainly a departure from Hall and Oates' *Beauty on a Back Street* days, when it was recorded, but it fit right in with the direction the partners were now travelling.

## THE TOP FIVE

*Week of November 7, 1981*

1 **Private Eyes**
Hall & Oates

2 **Start Me Up**
Rolling Stones

3 **Arthur's Theme**
**(Best That You Can Do)**
Christopher Cross

4 **For Your Eyes Only**
Sheena Easton

5 **Tryin' to Live My Life**
**Without You**
Bob Seger & the
Silver Bullet Band

## 550 Physical MCA 51182
### OLIVIA NEWTON-JOHN

Writers: Steve Kipner
    Terry Shaddick

Producer: John Farrar

November 21, 1981
10 weeks

GREASE may have hinted to the public that there was more to Olivia Newton-John than her "girl-next-door" facade, but that image was truly shattered by "Physical." "I just wasn't in the mood for tender ballads. I wanted peppy stuff because that's how I'm feeling," she told *People*, explaining her sudden burst of gusto. "We thought it was a great title because of the keep-fit craze that is going on."

The song did become an aerobics class staple, but it was cited less for its health club sentiments than its sexual innuendo. "I think the song has a double entendre," its singer allowed. "You can take it how you want to. But it's meant to be in fun.

. . . It's not meant to be taken too seriously."

Some radio programmers did take it seriously, however, banning the record for its "suggestive lyrics." Explained one music director in *Billboard*, "Once the words sank in, it caused an uncomfortableness among listeners." The South African Broadcasting Corporation also censored the platinum-selling 45, insisting that the words "There's nothing left to talk about, unless it's horizontally" be omitted.

Yet such detractors proved to be merely a nagging flab on the single's fast rise to the top. Debuting as the highest new entry on the Hot 100 at number 66 the week of October 3, 1981, "Physical" took eight weeks to reach number one. When it arrived at the summit, it displayed tremendous stamina, remaining there for 10 weeks. At this point it tied Debby Boone's "You Light Up My Life" [see 475] as the second longest-running number one of the rock era. Only Elvis

Presley's "Don't Be Cruel" / "Hound Dog" [see 14], with 11 weeks to its credit, had a longer stay at number one by this date.

Accompanying the single and album of the same title was the entertainer's special, "Olivia Newton-John: Let's Get Physical," her fourth television extravaganza. It, and subsequent full-length home videos, have permitted her to cut down in recent years on the touring she never really enjoyed. She has also taken time to get more involved with animals, a passion that goes back to her childhood days when "I picked up strays all the time, but my mother was afraid of them and wouldn't let me keep them. As soon as I grew up I began taking them in" (she maintains five horses, eight dogs and several cats on her four-and-a-half acre Malibu property).

Animals are just one of the non-musical concerns Olivia has devoted her time to in recent years. With her "Go Show" partner (and producer John Farrar's wife) Pat Carroll, she owned Koala Blue, a boutique vending Australian wares in Los Angeles, and in 1984, she hosted a lavish bash for down-under Olympians.

Since "Physical" was named *Billboard's* number one single of 1982, Newton-John has returned to the top five an additional three times, with "Make a Move on Me" (number five in April, 1982), "Heart Attack" (number three in November, 1982) and "Twist of Fate" (number five in January, 1984) from the ill-fated *Two of a Kind*, her cinematic reunion with John Travolta.

### THE TOP FIVE
*Week of November 21, 1981*

1 **Physical**
Olivia Newton-John

2 **Private Eyes**
Hall & Oates

3 **Waiting for a Girl Like You**
Foreigner

4 **Start Me Up**
Rolling Stones

5 **Here I Am**
Air Supply

RCA 12357 **I Can't Go For That (No Can Do)** 551
DARYL HALL and JOHN OATES

*Writers: Daryl Hall*
*John Oates*
*Sara Allen*

*Producers: Daryl Hall*
*John Oates*

*January 30, 1982*
*1 week*

Daryl Hall and John Oates almost succeeded themselves at number one with the second single from their *Private Eyes* LP. All that got in the way was Olivia Newton-John's "Physical," which enjoyed a 10-week run at the top, allowing "I Can't Go For That (No Can Do)" to climb up the Hot 100 and become Hall and Oates' fourth chart-topper.

The song started out as a phrase, an intra-group expression among the Hall and Oates family, whenever any one of them found themselves pressured to go along with the crowd against their wishes. Late one night at Electric Lady Studios, after the real work on the *Private Eyes* album was finished, Daryl started fooling around on the synthesizer, singing a chorus left over from the *Voices* days. "We basically finished the song in the studio, right there," John disclosed. "We recorded all the instruments ourselves, except for the sax solo (later added by Charlie DeChant) and it just happened. It was just one of those very spontaneous things."

"The theme is sort of ongoing

with us, that people should think for themselves, do what they believe. They shouldn't act or do things just because other people do, or because the government says to do it or because their fathers and mothers say this is the right thing. People have to be able to assess each situation, based on their own beliefs, and not just follow along."

What started out as a private code became a public anthem, crossing all musical and color boundaries. The song entered the Hot 100 at number 59 on November 14, 1981, and was number one 11 weeks later. The song also appeared on the Adult Contemporary, Dance and Black charts. "I'm the head soul brother in the U.S.," Daryl noted in Nick Tosches' biography, *Dangerous Dreams*. "Where to now?"

Where they were headed was towards perfecting the sound they had begun 10 years earlier on *Abandoned Luncheonette*. "We've merged what some people might call mutually exclusive musical styles," said John. "On some songs we took modern dance beats and put them to rock and roll. By doing so we transcended at least some of the artificial barriers that separate people into factions, in addition to creating music you can move your head and body to. This is dance music." They later refined the name to rock 'n' soul, "rock and roll that comes from the heart," as Daryl put it.

The new style placed them in the

*World Book Encyclopedia* under the heading "Black Music." "I think it's kind of funny," laughed John. "I don't know, maybe people will remember us as famous black songwriters."

Actually, Hall and Oates had pointed the way their colleagues would follow, fusing the formerly unmixable elements of black and white music into songs that all races and radio playlists could embrace. One of Daryl's passions had always been to return to the colorblind stations of his youth, where he could flip the switch and hear a Smokey Robinson song that would segue into something from the Beatles. In "I Can't Go for That (No Can Do)," he had created a song that necessitated a new kind of radio, forerunner of the Urban Contemporary format that would become the mainstream of American pop.

The innovation was particularly satisfying to the duo. "I'd like to think we're seeing the first glimmer of hope that things are changing," John declared in Brad Gooch's biography, *Hall and Oates*. "If we have a crusade, it's bridging that gap, moving away from black/white polarization and getting music itself back to the sensibilities of the late '50s and early '60s.

Daryl had the last word: "I think there's going to be a return to a more integrated pop music. People seem more open-minded than they were in the 1970s, when pop music was about as racially segregated as it ever has been. That was bad for everybody, and especially bad for us."

## THE TOP FIVE
*Week of January 30, 1982*

1 **I Can't Go for That (No Can Do)**
Hall & Oates

2 **Waiting for a Girl Like You**
Foreigner

3 **Centerfold**
J. Geils Band

4 **Physical**
Olivia Newton-John

5 **Harden My Heart**
Quarterflash

## 552 Centerfold EMI-AMERICA 8102
### J. GEILS BAND

*Writer: Seth Justman*

*Producer: Seth Justman*

*February 6, 1982*
*6 weeks*

THE J. Geils Band first came together in 1967 when charismatic rock singer Peter Wolf (born Peter Blankfield on March 7, 1946 in the Bronx, New York) and drummer Stephen Jo Bladd (born July 13, 1942, in Boston, Massachusetts) left their group, the Hallucinations. They teamed up with a Boston-based trio named after its guitarist, Jerome Geils (born February 20, 1946, in New York City). The other members of the J. Geils Blues Band were harmonica whiz "Magic" Dick (born Dick Salwitz on May 13, 1945, in New London, Connecticut) and bassist Danny Klein (born May 13, 1946, in New York City). A year later the group dropped "Blues" from its moniker and added keyboardist Seth Justman (born January 27, 1951, in Washington, D.C.).

Atlantic Records signed the dynamic band in 1969, but from the start the Geils ensemble was not your average bunch of rough and tumble rock 'n' rollers. "We were asked to play Woodstock," Wolf told Jeff Tamarkin in *Goldmine*, "but we turned it down. We thought, 'Three days in the mud, who needs it?'

released from the band's 1981 *Freeze-Frame* album. "Centerfold" entered the Hot 100 at number 70 on November 7, 1981, and was top-of-the-chart 13 weeks later. Critics complained that to succeed the J. Geils Band sold out its traditional boogie sound and began pandering to the rock crowd, but as Wolf explained to Tamarkin, "We were always a rock 'n' roll band. We just had blues and R&B roots, but we never said we were a blues band.

*Freeze-Frame* produced two more singles: the title track peaked at number four and "Angel in Blue" stalled at 40. The album followed the lead of "Centerfold," spending four weeks at number one. That didn't necessarily fit in with the group's game plan, according to Wolf.

"I don't think the J. Geils Band's whole goal was to have a number one record," he told Bill Flanagan in *Musician*. "It was to make a good rock 'n' roll record and have some excitement. The charts tend to make people focus in on one, two, three, four. Anyone who feels that kind of achievement is going to solve anything is in for a disapointment....But

it's something you're glad happens. Being number one is an exciting thing. It was a great sense of accomplishment after all we'd been through."

Wolf, formerly a disc jockey on Boston's WBCN-FM and formerly married to Faye Dunaway, split from the J. Geils Band in the fall of 1983, the first personnel change for the group since Justman joined.

Working with writer/producer Michael Jonzun, Wolf's first solo album, *Lights Out*, yielded a number 12 single: the title track. The J. Geils Band carried on with Justman as lead singer, but didn't fare as well, just managing to reach number 63 with their first post-Wolf single, "Concealed Weapons."

### THE TOP FIVE
*Week of February 6, 1982*

1 **Centerfold**
J. Geils Band

2 **I Can't Go for That
(No Can Do)**
Hall & Oates

3 **Waiting for a Girl
Like You**
Foreigner

4 **Harden My Heart**
Quarterflash

5 **Turn Your Love Around**
George Benson

That's where we were at. There were a lot of bands that played around in T-shirts and no shoes on stage and we were into a very formal thing: suits, ties, ruffled shirts, a traditional lounge approach to our music. It was very black-oriented."

Between 1971-1977, the group placed six singles on the Hot 100, none charting higher than "Must of Got Lost," a number 12 hit in early 1975. In 1978 they switched to EMI-America where five more singles made the Hot 100, none reaching the top 30. "There's that old saying that if you just hang around and hang around, somehow your number's bound to come up," Wolf has said.

The number was one, and it came up at last when the first single was

*Writers: Jake Hooker
Alan Merrill*

*Producers: Ritchie Cordell
Kenny Laguna*

*March 20, 1982
7 weeks*

JOAN JETT created a problem for radio stations who wanted to place her music in a limited musical category. Contemporary Hit Radio stations found "I Love Rock n' Roll" too punk. New wave stations felt it was too rock. Adult contemporary stations thought it was more suitable for CHR. Joan came up with her own solution—by touring with the Blackhearts almost constantly since their formation in 1980, she created a demand for her music and specifically for "I Love Rock 'n Roll," a song listeners started requesting in droves. Finally, radio stations had to break down and play a Joan Jett record. "I ain't no punk rocker," she pointed out, "I play rock 'n' roll!"

"I Love Rock 'n Roll" was several years old when Joan released it on Neil Bogart's Boardwalk label. Originally recorded by Anglo/American band the Arrows as a "B" side of one of their British singles, the song was written by band members Jake Hooker and Alan Merrill as a response to the Rolling Stones' "It's Only Rock 'n Roll (But I Like It)." Hooker explains, "I know that they didn't really mean it in a derogatory way....It minimalized what I thought about rock and roll. My gut reaction on first hearing it was, 'What do you mean it's only

rock and roll but you like it? I love rock and roll!' And it sort of snowballed from there." The song took about half-an-hour to write with Hooker and Merrill collaborating on both lyrics and music.

"After we wrote it we knew it was a hit. We felt it was the best thing that we had ever written. We presented the song to Mickie Most who was our producer at the time and he (said), It's okay. It's not a hit." Most let them record it while he took a lunch break. The Arrows wanted it released as an "A" side, but the quality of the recording worked against it. The group still believed in the song, so they recorded a different version at Granada Television studios to sing in their British television series.

Joan Jett (born September 22, 1960, in Philadelphia) had played guitar with an all-girl band called the

## THE TOP FIVE
*Week of March 20, 1982*

1  **I Love Rock 'n' Roll**
   Joan Jett & the
   Blackhearts

2  **Open Arms**
   Journey

3  **Centerfold**
   J. Geils Band

4  **That Girl**
   Stevie Wonder

5  **Sweet Dreams**
   Air Supply

Runaways from 1975-1978. While touring England, they saw the Arrows perform the newer recording of the song on their TV series. Hooker received a phone call from Jett asking if he'd mind if they recorded the song. He responded, "Go ahead. Why not? You've got to do a better job than we did." But the Runaways didn't share Jett's enthusiasm for the song and she couldn't convince them to cut it.

After the Runaways broke up, Jett worked with producers Steve Jones and Paul Cook, ex-Sex Pistols. She recorded "I Love Rock 'n Roll," but it was only released in Holland as the flip side of an updated version of Lesley Gore's "You Don't Own Me." Jett formed the Blackhearts with lead guitarist Ricky Byrd, bass guitarist Gary Ryan and drummer Lee Crystal and toured Europe, since she felt American record companies wouldn't take her seriously because of the Runaways.

Returning to the United States, Joan shared a house with manager Kenny Laguna and his wife. Hooker kept asking Jett when she was going to record "I Love Rock 'n Roll" again. He brought producer Roy Thomas Baker to a Blackhearts concert on Staten Island, New York. Baker liked the band but only wanted to produce the one song. Laguna produced the entire album with Ritchie Cordell, and Jett recorded the song over again. The second version pleased Hooker very much. "That's exactly the way I always dreamed (the song) would be. The minute I heard it I had no doubts. I knew it was going to be number one."

In a 1984 *Bam* interview with Julie Panebianco, Joan said, "I'm really proud that 'I Love Rock 'n Roll' went to number one. People might expect me to be sick of it by now, the title and all, but when you sit there and look at that gold record and you think of your accomplishments—I mean to come back and do what we did is so incredible in itself that I can't believe it sometimes....We played a show for the Olympic athletes. An athlete from Sudan saw me, he was walking down the street in Olympic Village, and he yelled, 'I love rock 'n roll.' I don't think he even spoke English. The feeling that gave me, it's hard to explain to other people."

# Chariots of Fire POLYDOR 2189
## VANGELIS

*Writer: Vangelis*

*Producer: Vangelis*

*May 8, 1982*
*1 week*

**W**HEN the Oscar-winning Best Picture *Chariots of Fire* received the Academy Award for Best Original Score, the film's talented composer Evangelos Papathanassiou was fast asleep in London. A friend called him at 4 a.m. with the good news. "I'd been out late celebrating my birthday," Vangelis explained to Jerene Jones of *People*. "Over the phone I could hear the television and a big party in the background. This incredible thing was going on and *I* was in bed."

Raised in Athens, Greece, Vangelis (his stage name, a diminutive of his real first name, translates "angel that brings good news") was a musical prodigy who started composing at age four and by six was already giving public recitals. In the early '60s, the teenaged keyboard whiz was a Greek superstar with the group Formynx.

Following the right-wing military coup in his homeland, Vangelis was fleeing to England when the student riots in Paris broke out. He remained in France and teamed up with another expatriate, Demis Roussos, to form Aphrodite's Child. The flamboyant rock band scored a European smash in 1969 with "Rain and Tears."

After Aphrodite's Child broke up in the early '70s, Vangelis set out to establish himself as a serious composer and performer. He scored his

## THE TOP FIVE
*Week of May 8, 1982*

1  **Chariots of Fire**
   Vangelis

2  **Ebony and Ivory**
   Paul McCartney &
   Stevie Wonder

3  **I Love Rock 'n' Roll**
   Joan Jett & the Blackhearts

4  **Don't Talk to Strangers**
   Rick Springfield

5  **Freeze-Frame**
   J. Geils Band

first film, *L'Apocalypse des Animaux*, and in 1974, moved to London at last where he built a cavernous state-of-the-art synthesizer recording studio near Marble Arch. Initially, his explorations into the sound and structure of electronic pop music attracted little more than critical sneers. But he persevered through a series of moderately successful albums, including *Heaven and Hell* (which included music later used in Carl Sagan's "Cosmos" series for PBS), *Albedo 0.39*, *Spiral*, *Beauborg*, and *China*.

"I don't read or write music at all," Vangelis admitted to Kurt Loder, "but I play all the instruments, or I do it with a symphony orchestra, scoring on tape, dictating. It's the same thing, actually. Orchestration, composition, they teach these things in music schools, but there are some things you can never teach. You can't teach creation."

Once asked to replace Rick Wakeman as keyboardist in Yes [see 582—"Owner of a Lonely Heart"], Vangelis joined forces with Yes vocalist Jon Anderson in 1980. The pair's experiments in ambient music led to several popular albums for Polydor, including *Short Stories*, *The Friends of Mr. Cairo* (which yielded

the single "I'll Find My Way Home") and *Private Collection*.

But Vangelis had never composed music for a major film until producer David Puttnam signed him to score the true story of two obsessed runners preparing for the 1924 Paris Olympics. As Vangelis explained to *People*, he accepted the *Chariots of Fire* assignment because, "It's a nice, healthy, pure film. I like the Olympic Games and I did it for fun."

The first cut on the soundtrack LP was the music heard under the film's opening titles. Simply titled "Titles," it was released as a single but won little attention. Philadelphia-based Eric records released a cover version of the theme by the Assembled Multitude ("Overture from Tommy"), which perhaps goosed Polydor into promoting their original version. The single entered the Hot 100 at number 94 on December 12, 1981, and by its eighth week on the chart was sensibly re-titled "Chariots of Fire."

It had a long climb to the top—21 weeks, longer than any other single. It was the 24th instrumental to go to number one. It would be exactly three-and-a-half years until the next instrumental chart-topper [see 622—"Miami Vice Theme"].

COLUMBIA 02860 **Ebony and Ivory**
PAUL McCARTNEY AND STEVIE WONDER **555**

*Writer: Paul McCartney*

*Producer: George Martin*

*May 15, 1982*
*7 weeks*

"'EBONY AND IVORY' is supposed to say that people of all types could live together," Paul McCartney told Bryant Gumbel on NBC's "Today" show during a four-part interview telecast April 26-29, 1982. "It's just an idea that I had heard someone say once, you know the keyboard thing, you can play using just the black notes; or you can play using just the white notes, but combining them gives you great notes. That, I suppose, is a great analogy, I think that's a nice analogy."

While recording "Ebony and Ivory" for his *Tug of War* album, McCartney thought it would be a good idea to record the song as a duet with Stevie Wonder. McCartney had sent Stevie a message nine years earlier, when he wrote 'We love you' in braille in the upper left-hand corner of the back cover of his *Red Rose Speedway* album. This time, the word was passed along to the Motown superstar through Irv Beigel, a one-time employee of Berry Gordy's record company, who was working for Boardwalk Records when he ran into Wonder in Manhattan.

"(We) ran into each other downstairs in my office in New York," Stevie told Dick Clark on "The National Music Survey." "He said, 'You know, I was talking with Linda's father and they're telling me that Paul has written this song and he'd like to get a tape of it to you. . . . He told me it was called 'Ebony and Ivory.' "

Stevie suggested a tape be forwarded to his assistant, Keith Harris. "I listened to the song and I liked it very much," Stevie told Clark. "I liked what it was talking about. . . . I felt it was positive for everyone. It really—I won't say *demanded* of people to reflect upon it—but it politely *asks* the people to reflect upon life in using the terms of music . . . this melting pot of many different people."

Asked if he liked McCartney, Wonder replied, "I like him a lot. I think we have similar thoughts. I'm happy that we had a chance to meet each other for a greater period of time because it did . . . give me a little more insight on the Beatles, on his feelings and on his life."

While Paul and Stevie were together to record the song—on the island of Montserrat in the West Indies—they were nowhere near each other when the video was produced. It was only through the magic of videotape editing that they appeared to be performing together on the white and black keys of a piano.

With two high-powered talents collaborating on one single, it's not surprising that "Ebony and Ivory" debuted on the Hot 100 at number 29. Five weeks later it began a seven-week run at number one, the longest any McCartney post-Beatles single has remained at the top. Compared to the Beatles' list of number one singles, it matches the seven-week run of "I Want to Hold Your Hand" [see 143] and is only surpassed by the nine-week run of "Hey Jude" [see 247].

By the time "Ebony and Ivory" topped the British and American charts, Paul McCartney was listed in *Who's Who* after 15 years of deliberation. The entry under James Paul McCartney was 41 lines long and he was the only former Beatle listed. To an inquiry in 1969 as to why the Beatles were not included in the book of information on people of "influence and interest," the publishers replied: "There are so many Beatles and their reputations may not be altogether permanent."

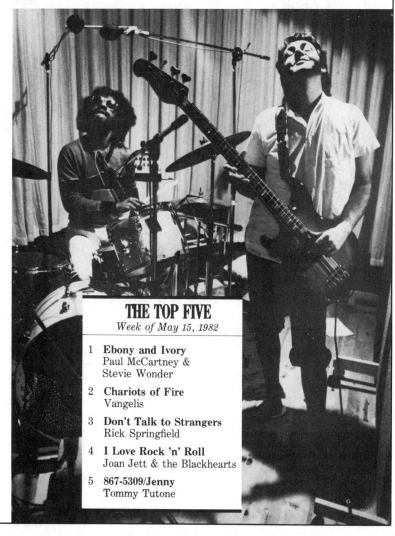

**THE TOP FIVE**
*Week of May 15, 1982*

1 **Ebony and Ivory**
Paul McCartney &
Stevie Wonder

2 **Chariots of Fire**
Vangelis

3 **Don't Talk to Strangers**
Rick Springfield

4 **I Love Rock 'n' Roll**
Joan Jett & the Blackhearts

5 **867-5309/Jenny**
Tommy Tutone

# 556 Don't You Want Me A&M 2397
## THE HUMAN LEAGUE

Writers: *Jo Callis*
*Phil Oakey*
*Philip Adrian Wright*

Producers: *Martin Rushent*
*The Human League*

*July 3, 1982*
*3 weeks*

"**D**ON'T YOU WANT ME," the first English synthesizer single to go to number one in America, gets the credit for opening up the Hot 100 to a British "mini" invasion of the '80s. Prior to the Human League's ascendancy to number one, English new wave bands found it hard to get a foothold in America. But in the wake of "Don't You Want Me," followed British groups like Culture Club and Dexy's Midnight Runners.

The original Human League had been formed in Sheffield, England, in 1977. Ian Craig Marsh and Martin Ware disbanded their group Future and reformed with the addition of vocalist Phil Oakey. Anxious to pro-

singers at a disco where they were dancing together. He brought them to the studio to record a couple of tunes, then convinced their parents to allow their high school age daughters to go off on a German tour which the band had committed to before their split.

"We're pretty amateurish for a big group," Oakey admitted to Dennis Hunt of the *Los Angeles Times*. "....We don't know anything about writing vocal arrangements or things like that, but we do them. It's hard for us to write them. When we get in the studio, it's hard for the girls to sing them. The way we work, it's amazing we get anything done."

Human League were originally signed to the independent Fast Records based in Edinburgh, Scotland, but were offered a contract by Virgin Records in London. Their first top 10 single in the United Kingdom was "Love Action (I Believe in Love)," the first 45 released from their *Dare* album. The follow-up, "Open Your Heart," also went top 10. The third single from *Dare* was "Don't You

mote an otherworldly image, the band took its name from "Starforce," a science-fiction game. The group split in 1980 with two of the members forming Heaven 17 while lead singer/synthesizer player Oakey and Philip Adrian Wright kept the band's name and added two male synthesizer players (Ian Burden, Jo Callis) and two female vocalists (Joanne Catherall and Susanne Sulley).

Oakey, the band's leader, is known for his eccentricities. When the two main musicians of the band left, Oakey decided showmanship was important, and decided to find two females who would dance as well as sing backing vocals. He found his

Want Me," which went to number one in Britain seven months before it topped the American chart.

It would take Human League two more years to release another album. In the interim, the singles "(Keep Feeling) Fascination" and "Mirror Man" kept them in the American top 30. While recording the *Hysteria* LP, the group battled with producer Martin Rushent, who left before the project was completed.

Oakey collaborated with Giorgio Moroder for a track on the *Electric Dreams* soundtrack and a solo album. In the near future he would be working with producers Jimmy Jam and Terry Lewis [see 652—"Human"].

*Writers: Frankie Sullivan*
*Jim Peterik*

*Producers: Jim Peterik*
*Frankie Sullivan*

*July 24, 1982*
*6 weeks*

THE blaring theme from a smash movie about a pugilistic survivor named Rocky gave a band called Survivor an imposing six-week reign as heavyweight champs of the chart. The story of Rocky's biggest fight yet—with "Clubber Lang" (played by the formidable Mr. T)—*Rocky III* would feature a different theme than the tune which had graced Rocky's two earlier incarnations [see 468—"Gonna Fly Now (Theme from 'Rocky')"].

For the latest installment, director/producer/star Sylvester Stallone decided to scuttle the earlier title song in favor of a more rock-oriented number. At one point, Queen's number one single "Another One Bites the Dust" [see 531] was a contender. But Stallone chose to commission a new song by a Chicago band that had yet to crack the top 30.

Keyboardist Jim Peterik, lead guitarist Frank Sullivan and singer David Bicker formed Survivor in 1978. It was a fitting name for the band. Peterik had been barely surviving in the music business since 1970 when, as a freshman at the University of Illinois, he joined a Blood, Sweat and Tears clone called the Ides of March. The group scored impressively with "Vehicle," a number two hit in May, 1970.

But many more ides were to pass before Peterik saw another big payday. In the early '70s, he recorded a largely-ignored solo album and made ends meet by performing jingles. Survivor became known throughout the Midwest soon after its formation and was signed to the Scotti Brothers label. In 1981, the trio was joined by bassist Stephan Ellis and drummer Marc Droubay.

Survivor managed to get three singles on the Hot 100, the most successful being "Poor Man's Son," number 33 in December, 1981. They never quite caught on until their hard-driving sound reached the ears of Stallone. "Tony (Scotti) had released a single by Sylvester's brother Frank a few years ago," Peterik explained to Dennis Hunt of the *Los Angeles Times*. "Tony knew about Sylvester wanting a title song for *Rocky III*, so he played him our last album (*Premonition*). Sylvester liked the beat and the drive of our music so he let us have a shot at writing the theme."

Stallone gave Peterik and Sullivan a cassette of the movie—and little direction. "He just said he wanted something with a strong beat," Peterik told Hunt. "He wanted a contemporary theme, something that

would appeal to the rock crowd. That's an audience he felt he didn't have then. He gave us a lot of leeway."

Within 90 minutes of seeing the rough cut of *Rocky III*, Peterik added, "We had fleshed out the song. We saw that phrase 'eye of the tiger' was repeated about six times. It was like a catch phrase. Rocky's trainer kept telling him he had to keep the eye of the tiger. So we just focused on that phrase."

On the soundtrack, tiger roars were added to the music, and at one point someone suggested they be tacked on to the single as well. "We said, 'No way!,' " Peterik said in the *Times*. "If the song doesn't roar itself, a little tiger roaring ain't gonna help."

According to Peterik, "The song, aside from being the theme of the movie, really sums up the band's attitude—we're out here to make our mark and you have to take that 'go-get-'em' approach. We call ourselves Survivor because we're all survivors of different bands and rock 'n' roll situations. It's a great feeling to watch Stallone in the movie, working out to 'Eye of the Tiger.' Just like the character he portrays, Survivor is still hungry for success."

## THE TOP FIVE

*Week of July 24, 1982*

1 **Eye of the Tiger**
Survivor

2 **Rosanna**
Toto

3 **Hurts So Good**
John Cougar

4 **Hold Me**
Fleetwood Mac

5 **Let It Whip**
Dazz Band

## 558 Abracadabra CAPITOL 5126
### STEVE MILLER BAND

*Writer: Steve Miller*

*Producers: Steve Miller*
*Gary Mallaber*

*September 4, 1982*
*2 weeks*

A CAPITOL Records employee who once got a peek at Steve Miller's royalty check couldn't believe his eyes. "It was over two million dollars," he said. "That's the largest check I've ever seen!" In 1976-1977, the durable performer was receiving those astronomical checks twice a year. And he didn't even have a manager to pay—he was taking care of business himself.

Miller's follow-up to *Fly Like an Eagle* was virtually a clone of the earlier LP because both were recorded at the same time. *Book of Dreams* yielded three hit singles in 1977: "Jet Airliner" (number eight in July), "Jungle Love" (number 23 in October) and "Swingtown" (number 17 in December).

By this time, Steve Miller had been recording nearly 10 years and had reached the pinnacle of success. Rock critic John Milward compared him to superbands Fleetwood Mac and Jefferson Starship. Like them, he wrote, "Miller was a prototype late-'70s rock phenomenon: a rocker who honed his craft in the '60s and bided his time until the market was right for his well-produced encyclopedia of riffs."

"The reason I continue to make music is the challenge," Miller observed, "which is why I continually grow. The challenge is to stay ahead of playing the old material too much. When you ask what the audiences expect from me, I think it's to deliver the songs that are their favorites, but still delight them with something new."

Following a four-year hiatus on his Oregon spread, Miller returned with an unsuccessful 1981 album of self-described "mood pieces" called *Circle of Love*. But the 38-year-old Miller would again demonstrate his resiliency. With *Abracadabra*, his 12th LP for Capitol, he returned to the crisp, melodic rock format

that had made him a star. "What's expected of me is short tunes," he told *Rolling Stone*. "They just want that four-minute fix."

On *Abracadabra*, Miller showed he had not lost the magic chord. The album's title track debuted on the Hot 100 at number 75 on May 29, 1982, and appeared at number one 14 weeks later. Miller described the LP as "basically a creative explosion by the drummer, Gary Mallaber, and the two new members of the band, guitarists Kenny Lewis and John Massaro."

Mallaber co-produced the album and co-wrote eight songs, while Lewis co-wrote three tunes and Massaro, four. "It's a new musical format for me," Miller pointed out, "because I usually write all the material I do. Now I'm enjoying input from other band members as well."

And Steve Miller, guitarist/songwriter/producer/superstar, saw no end in sight. "As the band grows," he said in 1982, "it's adding a lot of new creative ideas, and I'm enjoying the explosion. People have a tendency to wonder how you can play rock and roll for this long. Well, as a matter of fact, I'm just now coming into really having control over my medium....I know how to go into a studio and make a good record. I don't have the technical problems I had 10 years ago...and with the new members of my band, the production will continue to get better and better."

### THE TOP FIVE
*Week of September 4, 1982*

1 **Abracadabra**
Steve Miller Band

2 **Eye of the Tiger**
Survivor

3 **Hard to Say I'm Sorry**
Chicago

4 **Hold Me**
Fleetwood Mac

5 **Even the Nights are Better**
Air Supply

FULL MOON/WARNER BROTHERS 29979 **Hard to Say I'm Sorry** `559`
CHICAGO

*Writers: Peter Cetera*
*David Foster*

*Producer: David Foster*

*September 11, 1982*
*2 weeks*

Cʜɪᴄᴀɢᴏ was riding high in the '70s. The veteran jazz-rock fusion band had been recording for a decade and were more successful than ever, with 12 top ten singles racked up by 1977, including their first number one [see 446—"If You Leave Me Now"]. But with the accidental shooting death of lead guitarist and founding member Terry Kath on January 23, 1978, everything changed. After all, Terry was family. Deeply shaken, the band went on a brief hiatus.

Replacing Kath with Donnie Dacus on guitar and vocals, the septet regrouped and did its best to continue (Dacus remained with Chicago for just one year). But from 1978-1980, the highest position the band could reach on the Hot 100 was number 14 ("Alive Again," "No Tell Lover"). Five singles failed to make the top 40.

In 1981, Columbia Records unceremoniously dropped the group that had generated $160 million in album sales. But it was a sure thing that a band as durable and consistently innovative as the Windy City ensemble wouldn't stay down for long.

After a label switch to Full Moon/Warner Brothers in 1982, Chicago struck gold again with its 16th album and reasserted its position as one of rock's most popular bands. For *Chicago 16*, they were joined by guitarist Bill Champlin, the co-writer of Earth, Wind and Fire's number two hit from September, 1979, "After the Love Has Gone."

Describing the new, trimmed-down Chicago sound, keyboard player Bobby Lamm said it had an "upfront, immediate feel and, if anything. it's more of a group effort. I think ⸜ e of the big changes the band's been through recently is in collaborating; not just in the total sound, but in songwriting." The new LP yielded Chicago's biggest hit in six years, the theme song from a box office flop.

Set in the Greek isles, *Summer Lovers* portrayed a hot three-way relationship between a vacationing American couple (Daryl Hannah and Peter Gallagher) and a sexually adventurous French woman (Valerie Quennessen). The movie was directed by Randal Kleiser, who previously had helmed two consecutive smashes, *Grease* and *The Blue Lagoon*.

But this sun and sex-splashed *menage a trois* received pale marks from both critics and the moviegoing public. Chicago's contribution to the film, "Hard to Say I'm Sorry," had no apologies to make. Composed by bassist Peter Cetera (who had written the chart-topping "If You Leave Me Now") and producer David Foster, the romantic ballad entered the Hot 100 at number 75 on June 5, 1982. It seemed destined to peak at number five, a position it held for four consecutive weeks, before finally moving to number one in its 15th week on the chart. It·was the first number one single to sport the latest innovation in catalogue numbering: reverse order. Someone at corporate WEA (Warner-Elektra-Atlantic) headquarters figured out that if records were given catalogue numbers in descending order, the newest releases would show up at the beginning of a computer generated list instead of at the end. Starting with number 29999, Warner Brothers singles began counting down, presumably reaching number 00000 sometime in the next century.

The excitingly revitalized Chicago tapped a whole new generation of "Chicagophiles." Lamm observed in 1984, "A lot of our biggest fans these days are 18 to 25 year old. They're finding out about us for the first time. That's tremendously gratifying. It's great when what you're doing sounds fresh and new to people who've never heard it before. You get the feeling you're creating something that lasts."

## THE TOP FIVE

*Week of September 11, 1982*

1 **Hard to Say I'm Sorry**
Chicago

2 **Eye of the Tiger**
Survivor

3 **Abracadabra**
Steve Miller Band

4 **Jack and Diane**
John Cougar

5 **Even the Nights are Better**
Air Supply

# 560  Jack and Diane  RIVA 210
## JOHN COUGAR

*Writer: John Cougar Mellencamp*

*Producers: John Cougar Mellencamp
Don Gehman*

*October 2, 1982
4 weeks*

JOHN MELLENCAMP was born October 7, 1951, in Seymour, Indiana, a working-class burg right out of Bloomington. Not only was Seymour one of the most polluted areas of the country, but when Mellencamp was a teenager it also had the highest per capita murder rate in the nation.

"We were farmers, basically, of Dutch stock," Mellencamp said of his family. "My grandfather was a carpenter, never got past the third grade, could barely speak English. My dad became a vice president of an electrical company—one of those self-made guys. I'm the runt of the litter; everybody else has big muscles."

Young Mellencamp was a short, fat, loud-mouthed rebel. He was kicked off the high school football team for smoking. He hated authority figures with a passion and often got into fights. "You *had* to fight—your dignity depended on it," he recalled.

John was just 18 when he eloped with his 23-year-old pregnant sweetheart to Lousville, Kentucky. They moved in with her folks, and after she got a job with the phone company, he hung around the house—getting stoned, playing frisbee and writing songs. "It was 1971, and I *refused* to get a job," he told *Rolling Stone*. After putting up with him for 18 months, his in-laws threw him out.

In 1975, he went to New York, where David Bowie's manager, Tony DeFries, heard his demo tape and signed him to MCA Records. Mellencamp told writer Martin Torgoff what happened when his first album, *Chestnut Street Incident*, was released: "So I get the record finally—my first record—and it says *Johnny Cougar* on it! Nobody ever called me 'Johnny' my whole life, *ever*—and that's the name people in the Midwest know me by now because of that record. It's a ridiculous name but I'm stuck with it. It doesn't bother me that much anymore; I just laugh about it now."

After the album failed and he was dropped from the label, he severed his ties with DeFries. Under the guidance of Rod Stewart's then-manager, Billy Gaff, Cougar signed with Gaff's new label, Riva. He made the Hot 100 for the first time with "I Need a Lover," a number 28 hit in December, 1979. Moderate singles success followed, with "This Time" (number 27 in December, 1980) and "Ain't Even Done With the Night" (number 17 in May, 1981).

Then, in 1982, divorced and remarried, Cougar hit the jackpot with the *American Fool* album. The first single, "Hurts So Good," was number three with a bullet when the second single, "Jack and Diane," entered the Hot 100 at number 69 on July 24, 1982. Two weeks later, "Hurts So Good" moved into second place and remained there for four weeks. During the week of September 11, "Jack and Diane" zoomed from 11 to four while "Hurts So Good" slipped from seven to eight, giving John Cougar two hits in the top 10. When "Jack and Diane" went to number one the week of October 2, "Hurts So Good" while still holding in there at number 10.

"I had no idea 'Jack and Diane' would be like it was," Cougar told Christopher Connelly in *Rolling Stone*. "A lot of people think that chorus ('Life goes on/Long after the thrill of living is gone') is negative, but I don't. I think it makes people feel good to hear somebody else say, 'Hey...you can deal with it.'"

In 1983, John resisted his record company's suggestions and reverted to using Mellencamp as a last name. Now known as John Cougar Mellencamp, he had two top 10 singles, "Crumblin' Down" (number nine in November) and "Pink Houses" (number eight in February, 1984).

## THE TOP FIVE
*Week of October 2, 1982*

1  **Jack and Diane**
John Cougar

2  **Abracadabra**
Steve Miller Band

3  **Hard to Say I'm Sorry**
Chicago

4  **Eye of the Tiger**
Survivor

5  **You Should Hear How She Talks About You**
Melissa Manchester

COLUMBIA 02888 **Who Can It Be Now?** 561
MEN AT WORK

*Writer: Colin Hay*

*Producer: Peter McIan*

*October 30, 1982*
*1 week*

"WHO CAN IT BE NOW?" was the 12th number one to pose a question. Starting with the simple query "Why" from Frankie Avalon, the other leading musical questions of the rock era are: "Are You Lonesome Tonight?" "Will You Love Me Tomorrow?" "Where Did Our Love Go?" "Isn't It a Pity?" "How Can You Mend a Broken Heart?" "Will It Go Round in Circles?" "Have You Never Been Mellow?" "How Deep Is Your Love?" "Da Ya Think I'm Sexy?" and "Don't You Want Me?" There are, of course, no simple answers to these questions.

Another important question in 1982 was "Are you from Australia?" for suddenly things Australian were doing very well in the United States. Mel Gibson starred in *Mad Max*, the first of three films about the road warrior. Artists from Down Under were doing well on the Hot 100 as well. Air Supply, the Little River Band and Rick Springfield had already achieved top 10 singles in America when Men at Work joined them in the upper reaches of the chart.

Lead singer Colin Hay and lead guitarist Ron Strykert, both students at La Troube University in Melbourne, met at a band audition and discussed 12 string acoustic guitars. A few months later they decided to form a band. Keyboard and woodwind player Greg Ham, also studying at La Troube, was playing several instruments with a band called Sneak Attack and drummer Jerry Speiser was playing in a group called Numbers when they became two more Men at Work. Bass guitarist John Rees, who had been trained as a classical violinist and pianist, came aboard last.

Men at Work began their professional career by appearing every night in the pub at the Cricketers Arms Hotel in Melbourne. Experimenting with different musical styles, they spent a year-and-a-half playing in clubs and pubs before a CBS Records executive teamed them up with Peter McIan, an American record producer. Hay told *Rolling Stone* they were paying themselves $10 a week each at that time, with a $40 bonus at Christmas.

McIan produced the *Business as Usual* album and "Who Can It Be Now?" was released as the first single. The band toured America as a support act to Fleetwood Mac and were compared by the press to the

Police, the Cars and Traffic.

MTV adopted their video and helped break the single, which entered the Hot 100 at number 83 on July 10, 1982. It took 16 additional weeks to reach number one. As Rob Hoerburger pointed out in *Billboard*, "Who Can It Be Now?" was only the third debut single by a Columbia Records act to top the chart. The first two artists to have their first Columbia singles go to number one were Johnny Horton [see 54—"The Battle of New Orleans"] and the Byrds [see 178—"Mr. Tambourine Man"].

## THE TOP FIVE
*Week of October 30, 1982*

1 **Who Can It Be Now?**
Men At Work

2 **Jack and Diane**
John Cougar

3 **Eye in the Sky**
Alan Parsons Project

4 **I Keep Forgettin'
(Every Time You're Near)**
Michael McDonald

5 **Up Where We Belong**
Joe Cocker and
Jennifer Warnes

# 562 Up Where We Belong Island 99996
## JOE COCKER and JENNIFER WARNES

Writers: Jack Nitzsche
      Will Jennings
      Buffy Sainte-Marie

Producer: Stewart Levine

November 6, 1982
3 weeks

TROUBLED British rocker Joe Cocker and ex-flower child Jennifer Warnes had never met until the evening they recorded the Oscar-winning song from *An Officer and a Gentleman.* Just 30 days after director Taylor Hackford decided he wanted an original song for the end titles of his film, "Up Where We Belong" was a *fait accompli.*

With no time or money for an original score, Hackford relied on existing songs by his favorite artists for the soundtrack. Pat Benatar, Dire Straits and Van Morrison were among the contemporary pop singers included in the film. With the movie about to be released, Hackford knew he wanted a song written to close the film.

Lyricist Will Jennings was called in one Friday for a screening of the picture. He picked out two themes from Jack Nitzsche's background score and told Hackford he could write a title song based on them. Monday morning, the demo of "Up

Where We Belong" was sitting on Hackford's desk.

A friend of Hackford's was managing singer Jennifer Warnes, who had sung the Oscar-winning "It Goes Like It Goes" in *Norma Rae.* Hackford rejected the suggestion of using Warnes to sing the title song because he felt she had too sweet a sound. But when the friend suggested teaming her up with Joe Cocker, Hackford thought the duet could be very exciting.

Taylor showed the film to Island Records chief Chris Blackwell, who agreed that Cocker should sing the tune. The singer was on tour in the Pacific Northwest, but he flew to Los Angeles one afternoon and recorded the song with Warnes that evening. Then he hopped on a plane and resumed his tour.

*An Officer and a Gentleman* opened to rave reviews for stars Richard Gere, Debra Winger and Louis Gossett, Jr., who won an Oscar for Best Supporting Actor. True to its title, "Up Where We Belong" ascended to number one just 11 weeks after entering the Hot 100 at number 89 on August 21, 1982.

Cocker, the son of a social worker, was born in the northern England steeltown of Sheffield. Blessed with a fantastic set of lungs and a love of American R&B, he

recorded a demo with hometown lad Chris Stainton. Former Procol Harum producer Denny Cordell liked what he heard and cut Joe's debut album. His second single, a spine-chilling remake of the Beatles' "With a Little Help from My Friends" (featuring superstars Jimmy Page, Stevie Winwood and Albert Lee) topped the British chart in November, 1968.

Following an unforgettable performance at the Woodstock Festival, Cocker scored his first American hit with a re-make of the Box Tops' "The Letter" [see 230], which peaked at number seven in May, 1970. His next top 10 hit didn't arrive until 1975, when "You Are So Beautiful," written by Billy Preston [see 337—"Will It Go Round in Circles"] went to number five.

Jennifer Warnes, an Orange County, California, contemporary of Steve Martin, Diane Keaton and Jackson Browne, decided on a singing career when she was five years old. In the late '60s she became well-known through a featured part in the "tribal love-rock musical" *Hair* [see 253—"Aquarius/Let the Sunshine In"] and appearances on the Smothers Brothers' television show. Her recording career didn't kick in until 1977, when she signed with Arista Records and went to number six with "Right Time of the Night."

### THE TOP FIVE
*Week of November 6, 1982*

1 **Up Where We Belong**
Joe Cocker and
Jennifer Warnes

2 **Who Can it be Now?**
Men At Work

3 **Heart Attack**
Olivia Newton-John

4 **I Keep Forgettin'
(Every Time You're Near)**
Michael McDonald

5 **Jack and Diane**
John Cougar

*Writer: Lionel Richie*

*Producers: Lionel Richie
James Anthony
Carmichael*

*November 27, 1982
2 weeks*

LIONEL BROCKMAN RICHIE, JR., was born on June 20, 1949, in Tuskegee, Alabama. He grew up on the campus of the Tuskegee Institute, founded in 1881 by Booker T. Washington. Lionel's grandfather worked in the business office of the institute with Washington, and Lionel, with his parents and younger sister Deborah, lived with Richie's grandmother in a house across the street from the home of the college's president. Richie had the good fortune to be raised in a sheltered, intellectual community, filled with people of diverse backgrounds with varied philosophies and ideas. An appreciation of music was inspired by grandmother Adelaide, a popular music teacher in Tuskegee who was classically trained on piano. Lionel had been singing in the Episcopal Church

Choir, but found playing an instrument "sissy." Try as she would, Adelaide could not get Lionel to learn how to read music. It turned out to be irrelevant—Lionel had the gift of being able to play piano by ear.

Richie almost chose another profession over music. Deeply religious, he participated as an altar boy at the Episcopal Church and admired the church elders. He told Roberta Plutznik: "Father Jones and others were very influential men and, for many years, I couldn't think of doing anything better with my life than being like them."

Although he didn't pursue the priesthood as a profession, Lionel is quick to acknowledge God for songwriting inspiration. "I give credit to my co-writer because all I did was write down what He told me to write down," Richie told Robert E. Johnson in a 1985 *Ebony* interview. Richie said he prefers to write late at night. "From 11 (p.m.) to seven in the morning is a very wonderful time because, as they say, God isn't too worried with too many other folks."

It was Lionel's songwriting that propelled the Commodores [see 487—

"Three Times a Lady"] to the top of the Hot 100. With the group's success came press requests for interviews—with Richie. The attention on Lionel increased when he wrote and produced a number one hit for Kenny Rogers [see 533—"Lady"]. As he told one reporter in 1982, "In the articles, they ask 'Who wrote "Lady"?' I couldn't say 'we.' It was this guy over here, Lionel Richie wrote it."

For Richie, being singled out impacted negatively on the "team" structure of the Commodores. Though deeply committed to the men he calls his "brothers," he wanted to concentrate on his own music and continue working with other artists. The glare of the solo spotlight became too great when he wrote and recorded a number one hit with Diana Ross [see 547—"Endless Love"].

"Kenny Rogers just *sang* 'Lady,'" Lionel said in 1982. "I just wrote it and stayed over in the wings. (With) 'Endless Love' I was in front of 361 million people at the Oscars, singing live, *close up* . . . after that evening, life changed."

At a group meeting, Lionel and his fellow Commodores came to an inevitable decision. Lionel would leave the group and follow his own career. He recorded his first solo album for Motown over a nine-month period. The studio piano must have been a talisman: "The piano I played was an old brown beat up one. It turned out to be the piano Carole King used on *Tapestry*."

The album's first single, "Truly," debuted at number 60 on the Hot 100 dated October 9, 1982. Seven weeks later Lionel had his fourth number one—and the first of his new career.

## THE TOP FIVE

*Week of November 27, 1982*

1 **Truly**
  Lionel Richie

2 **Gloria**
  Laura Branigan

3 **Heart Attack**
  Olivia Newton-John

4 **Up Where We Belong**
  Joe Cocker and Jennifer Warnes

5 **Heartlight**
  Neil Diamond

## 564 Mickey CHRYSALIS 2638
### TONI BASIL

Writers: Nicky Chinn
Mike Chapman

Producers: Greg Mathieson
Trevor Veitch

December 11, 1982
1 week

Toni Basil took a circuitous route to the top of the Hot 100. "Mickey" was originally part of one of the first music video cassettes, *Word of Mouth*. When it was released in the pre-MTV days of 1980, there was no suitable outlet for the song in America. Released simultaneously as a record and video in other countries, there was enough reaction to boost the single "Mickey" into the top five in New Zealand, to number one in Australia and number two in Britain, where it was released on the Radialchoice label.

The record was rejected by most American labels, including Chrysalis. But with the growing popularity of music videos on television, "Mickey" became a hit in Los Angeles based on import sales. With the record registering in the top five on radio station KIQQ, Chrysalis was convinced to take a chance.

Basil was not so sure, though. She was afraid her two-year-old song would be *passé*, but she had nothing to worry about. The video for "Mickey," complete with real cheerleaders, created a visual image of Basil that she credits with helping to sell the record.

The original Nicky Chinn-Mike Chapman song was called "Kitty," but after Basil came up with the

### THE TOP FIVE

*Week of December 11, 1982*

1  **Mickey**
   Toni Basil

2  **Gloria**
   Laura Branigan

3  **Maneater**
   Hall & Oates

4  **Truly**
   Lionel Richie

5  **The Girl is Mine**
   Michael Jackson &
   Paul McCartney

cheerleader concept and added the chants, she changed the title. A one-time cheerleader herself, Toni remembered watching young kids in her neighborhood try out their cheerleading routines and based her choreography on that memory. Having done only two live shows as a singer prior to the release of "Mickey," Basil relied on the video and television appearances to promote the song, rather than touring.

Debuting on the Hot 100 at number 83 on September 4, 1982, "Mickey" took 14 weeks to reach the top. Prior to her fame as a recording artist, Basil was best known as an actress and choreographer. Her film credits include *Village of the Giants*, *Head*, *Five Easy Pieces*, *American Graffiti* and the role of the prostitute with Peter Fonda in *Easy Rider*. In the early '70s she helped create the well-known street dancing troupe the Lockers and worked with them for

several years. She choreographed David Bowie's *Diamond Dogs* tour and Bette Midler's back-up singers, the Harlettes. She also worked on videos for "Saturday Night Live" and the Talking Heads. Working on 8mm and 16mm films gave her the technical background she needed to combine music and visuals.

She followed the platinum success of "Mickey" with "Shoppin' From A to Z," number 77 in March, 1983. A second album, *Toni Basil*, yielded a single called "Over My Head."

Basil has since concentrated on other people's videos, receiving another MTV nomination for choreographing Bette Midler's "Beast of Burden" with guest star Mick Jagger. Toni also choreographed Tina Turner's "Better Be Good to Me" video; and choreographed, directed and co-produced Linda Ronstadt's video for "You Took Advantage of Me."

Writers: *Daryl Hall*
*John Oates*
*Sara Allen*

Producers: *Daryl Hall*
*John Oates*

December 18, 1982
*4 weeks*

LAMONT DOZIER remembers the first time he heard Daryl Hall and John Oates' "Maneater." He was excited by the introduction, because he thought they had done a cover version of one of his songs, "You Can't Hurry Love" [see 207]. It turned out to be a Hall and Oates original, despite the very similar intro, but Dozier was accustomed to hearing pieces of his '60s Motown songs in contemporary material. And a month later, a white male vocalist would release the old Supremes favorite anyway—Phil Collins [see 604—"One More Night"] had a top 10 hit with it.

"Maneater" came to life in John Oates' 12th floor apartment when John and Daryl were looking for new material. John pulled out a chorus, written with a reggae beat, that he

had never polished into a full-fledged song. Sitting at the piano, Hall changed the beat a little, added a verse, and "Maneater"was born. It was the first single released from the duo's elemental album, $H_2O$. "$H_2O$ is a good indicator of where we're headed," John declared in *Rockbill*. "It's more spontaneous than *Private Eyes* and a little more dancified. It's very band-oriented and the production is very streamlined. We've gone through pains to make every instrument mean something."

"The chemistry worked for Hall and Oates, and "Maneater" entered the Hot 100 at number 65 on October 16, 1982. Nine weeks later it was Hall and Oates' fifth chart-topper. It was also their biggest British hit ever.

Though Hall and Oates' records did well on their own, they were all so individual that audiences didn't link the body of work to the two artists. The missing particle was the visual, melding sight with sound so that Daryl and John's faces would become identified with their voices. Establishing an image was something they had tried to do for years, but with the advent of the music video, they found the answer.

The earliest of their videos dated back to 1973—a "perverse" clip of "She's Gone," produced by John's sister, Diane Oates. By the time MTV began operating on August 4, 1981 [see 546—"Jessie's Girl"], Hall and Oates' technique was refined, and they became charter artists on the new cable network. During the last week of recording at Electric Lady, they opened the studio to MTV's cameras, which filmed a documentary on the making of $H_2O$, allowing viewers a rare peek at how hit songs are born.

Though the video of "Maneater" prompted angry yelps for its "misogynous" depiction of a jaguar superimposed on a woman's face, and Daryl and John themselves found the need to put each single on film an increasingly objectionable chore, they acknowledged the difference video had made to their career. "It's not as simple as me being the melodic one or John being the one with the moustache," Daryl asserted. "I think our image is much more straight forward. People realize we're committed and serious musicians, we make music we believe in and it comes from the heart. I'd rather listen than look, but video is here and my job is to figure out a way to best use it." One of the results neither partner had counted on was their loss of anonymity. "I can hardly walk down the street without people constantly stopping, screaming, staring," John noted in the biographical *Dangerous Dances* by Nick Tosches.

## THE TOP FIVE

*Week of December 18, 1982*

1 **Maneater**
Hall & Oates

2 **Mickey**
Toni Basil

3 **Gloria**
Laura Branigan

4 **The Girl is Mine**
Michael Jackson &
Paul McCartney

5 **Truly**
Lionel Richie

## 566 Down Under COLUMBIA 03303
### MEN AT WORK

Writers: Colin Hay
       Ron Strykert

Producer: Peter McIan

January 15, 1983
4 weeks

"DOWN UNDER" was an unabashedly Australian song which almost needed a translation of its odd language. Now scores of Americans understand that Vegemite is a pretty vile brewer's yeast bread spread, but they buy it anyway for sentimental value. "We're proud to be Australians and we keep pushing that angle," keyboardist Greg Ham said in Bam magazine. "I mean even if we suddenly decided to become Americanized, I don't think we could get away with it. The American press will make quite sure we remain something exotic, and the Australian press generally tends to savage any Australian that starts to lose their identity."

The original version of "Down Under" was much simpler, using only a flute and guitar. Producer Peter McIan felt that wasn't commercial enough, and added more instruments and gave it a reggae-ska feel. "Down Under" isn't an Australian anthem, Ham has said. "It tells a story about Australians who have been abroad and come back home. The absurd Australian abroad. Fortunately for us, the song is all things to all peo-ple." Wayne Robins, writing in Long Island, New York's Newsday, described the record as "the first hit song in recent memory that belongs to everyone."

Billboard Australian correspondent Glenn Baker told Bam why he thought Men at Work were so popular in other countries. "What Men at Work have done is to draw together the various threads of interest that have existed overseas for two decades on different levels. (They) were a catalyst for this, giving the whole scene a focus and possibly giving it a rock respectability that appeals to both radio programmers and the public—something Air Supply, LRB (Little River Band) and AC/DC do not have. The Men are perfect for American pop. They're melodic, contemporary and humorous, and they're effectively telling the world that there are more good things coming from down under."

The band's first number one single [see 561—"Who Can It Be Now?"] was still in the top 10 when "Down Under" entered the Hot 100 at number 79 on November 6, 1982. Ten weeks later it was the second Men at Work single to go to number one. It spent three weeks at the top, yielded to Toto for one week, then returned for one additional week.

Men at Work's international success was capped by having the number one single and album (Business as Usual) in America and Britain all at the same time, the first instance of total United States-United Kingdom chart domination since Barbra Streisand teamed up with Barry Gibb [see 532—"Woman in Love"].

Winners of the Best New Artist Grammy, Men at Work carried on by releasing the Cargo album and three additional singles in 1983: "Overkill" (number three in June), "It's a Mistake" (number six in August) and "Dr. Heckyll and Mr. Jive" (number 28 in October). Drummer Jerry Speiser and bass guitarist John Rees departed and session musicians sat in for them on Men at Work's third album, Two Hearts, and its single, "Everything I Need."

### THE TOP FIVE
*Week of January 15, 1983*

1 **Down Under**
   Men At Work

2 **The Girl Is Mine**
   Michael Jackson/
   Paul McCartney

3 **Dirty Laundry**
   Don Henley

4 **Maneater**
   Daryl Hall & John Oats

5 **Sexual Healing**
   Marvin Gaye

COLUMBIA 03335 **Africa** 567
TOTO

*Writers: David Paich*
*Jeff Porcaro*

*Producer: Toto*

*February 5, 1983*
*1 week*

Over the years, the members of Toto have offered various explanations of the genesis of the group's name. The most repeated story is that it came from the name of Dorothy's dog in *The Wizard of Oz*. In another version, it is the Anglicized form of lead singer Bobby Kimball's real surname, Toteaux. Whatever the real reason, Toto became one of the most commercially successful, critically panned groups of the '80s.

Toto began when 16-year-old David Paich, son of film composer Marty Paich, and 13-year-old Jeff Porcaro started a Jimi Hendrix-influenced band called Rural Still Life. Based in California's San Fernando Valley, the outfit was soon headlining at Grant High School functions. When Jeff graduated, bassist David Hungate arranged a gig for him as drummer for Sonny and Cher [see 181—"I Got You Babe"]. Still in school, Steve Lukather and Jeff's younger brother, also named Steve, kept Still Life active.

In 1973, Jeff quit working with the Bonos to join Steely Dan ("Do It Again," "Reeling in the Years"), in time for the *Katy Lied* album. Meanwhile, the other Valley boys began getting a lot of work as Los Angeles session musicians, playing with the likes of Aretha Franklin; Elton John;

Earth, Wind & Fire; Jackson Browne; and Barbra Streisand. When Paich and Porcaro worked together on Boz Scaggs' smash 1976 LP, *Silk Degrees*, they decided it was time to give up the lucrative studio work and form a band with the two Steves, Hungate and another Porcaro brother, Mike.

"Everybody knows how hard it is to be a group," Jeff told Robyn Flans in *Bam*, "but we knew we had to take the chance, make a sacrifice...and starve." But not for too long. Signed by Columbia Records, the group had a number five single the first time out with "Hold the Line." It turned out to be the only Toto single that would make the top 10 for over three years.

Dave Marsh of *Rolling Stone* dismissed Toto's music as "all chops and no brains. Formula pop songs, singing that wouldn't go over in a Holiday Inn cocktail lounge." Other critics agreed, describing the band's work as "state-of-the-bland" and "about as real as a Velveeta-orange polyester leisure suit."

"These (critics) are dimwitted idiots," Jeff fumed in *Bam*, "and I dare any publication to include a list of the writer's credentials beside the interview or review. Is he a musician? What is his background, and what gives him the right to say this, besides that he's an illiterate, garbage-headed pig?"

With or without critical support, the group had a hit in July, 1982, with "Rosanna," a song that sat in the number two spot for five weeks. From the same album, *Toto IV*, came

the follow-up, "Make Believe," which only reached number 30. It was the third single, "Africa," that finally lifted Toto to the top of the chart. Making its debut at number 75 on October 30, 1982, it was 14 weeks later when "Africa" became the only continent to be mentioned in the title of a number song.

Toto dominated the 1983 Grammy Awards, winning in six categories, including Record of the Year ("Rosanna") and Album of the Year (*Toto IV*). "I was shell-shocked," Lukather said in *Bam*. "...I would have thought (Don) Fagen's album *The Nightfly* would have won. That's one of my all time favorite albums."

Kimball's defection for a solo career in 1984 brought new lead singer Dennis "Fergie" Frederiksen into the group. The group did not repeat the success of "Africa" or *Toto IV* with their new album, "Isolation."

## THE TOP FIVE
*Week of February 5, 1983*

1 **Africa**
   Toto

2 **Down Under**
   Men At Work

3 **Sexual Healing**
   Marvin Gaye

4 **Baby, Come to Me**
   Patti Austin

5 **Shame on the Moon**
   Bob Seger & the
   Silver Bullet Band

## 568 Baby, Come to Me QWEST 50036
### PATTI AUSTIN AND JAMES INGRAM

*Writer: Rod Temperton*

*Producer: Quincy Jones*

*February 19, 1983*
*2 weeks*

"GENERAL HOSPITAL," the ABC-TV series that A. C. Nielsen listed as the number one show in daytime television from 1982-1984, is responsible for more hit singles than any other daytime drama. The program's use of recorded music to underscore storylines has resulted in two number one singles and another top 10 hit.

Herb Alpert [see 512—"Rise"] was the first beneficiary of "General Hospital's" musical medicine. "Think of Laura" by Christopher Cross [see 548—"Arthur's Theme (Best That You Can Do)"] was enhanced by its inclusion in the series. And actors Rick Springfield [see 546—"Jessie's Girl"] and Jack Wagner ("All I Need," number two in December, 1984) were both members of the cast when they had their biggest hits.

"Baby, Come to Me" was already dead when "General Hospital" resuscitated it. The Patti Austin-

James Ingram duet had entered the Hot 100 at number 81 on April 24, 1982. Two weeks later it peaked at number 73, and two weeks after that it was off the chart. Then Jill Phelps, music director for the daytime drama, had a request from producer Gloria Monty to find some appropriate music for a love scene between the character of Luke (Anthony Geary) and a new woman who had entered his life after his main love interest in the show, Laura (Genie Francis), had left.

As soon as the song was heard on the show, letters and phone calls started coming in, demanding to know the name of the song. Phelps, later producer of NBC's "Santa Barbara," explains, "My daughter and the daughter of Howard Rosen, who was . . . the public relations guy over at Warner Brothers, went to school together. And (Rosen) said to me, 'Hey, this came up at a business meeting . . . what's this about 'Baby, Come to Me'? He arranged for it to be re-released and then it started to get a lot of airplay on the radio. So, it was a conspiracy of Warner Brothers and 'General Hospital.'"

Issued with a new catalogue number, "Baby, Come to Me" re-entered the Hot 100 at number 91 on October 16, 1982, and 18 weeks later was the number one song in America.

Patti Austin had been performing since her debut at the Apollo Theater at the age of five, when she was introduced by Dinah Washington. The daughter of jazz trombonist Gordon Austin, Patti then toured with Sammy Davis, Jr., and by the time she was 16 had appeared on television with Bobby Darin, Connie Stevens and Ray Bolger. After graduating high school she was signed to United Artists Records. By 19, she was steadily employed as a commercial jingles singer. At one point, she could be heard on commercials for four soft drinks, three hamburger chains and on-air promos for all three major television networks. She moved to the jazz-oriented CTI Records, then Columbia, and in 1982 cut her debut LP for Quincy Jones' Qwest label, *Every Home Should Have One*.

Her guest star on "Baby, Come to Me" was James Ingram, who met Quincy when the producer was impressed with the singer's voice on a demo of Barry Mann and Cynthia Weil's "Just Once." Ingram had recorded it as a favor. "I never thought I was a real singer," he has said, "but I figured I'd be good enough for demos." Austin and Ingram both contributed vocals to Jones' LP, *The Dude*, before recording "Baby, Come to Me." They teamed up again for the theme from the movie *Best Friends*, "How Do You Keep the Music Playing" (number 45 in July, 1983).

---

### THE TOP FIVE
*Week of February 19, 1983*

1 **Baby, Come to Me**
Patti Austin

2 **Down Under**
Men At Work

3 **Shame on the Moon**
Bob Seger & the
Silver Bullet Band

4 **Stray Cat Strut**
Stray Cats

5 **Africa**
Toto

*Writer: Michael Jackson*

*Producers: Quincy Jones*
            *Michael Jackson*

*March 5, 1983*
*7 weeks*

"**H**E'S taken us right up there where we belong," Quincy Jones told *Time* magazine for a cover story on Michael Jackson. "Black music had to play second fiddle for a long time, but its spirit is the whole motor of pop. Michael has connected with every soul in the world."

That might be because every soul in the world purchased a copy of *Thriller.* Or so it seemed—the album has passed the 40-million mark and is the best-selling record of all time, period. Among its precedent-shattering achievements: 37 weeks at number one on the *Billboard* album chart, longer than any contemporary rock or pop LP (only the cast album of *South Pacific* at 69 weeks and the *West Side Story* soundtrack at 54 weeks had longer runs at the top) and seven top 10 singles, a record later matched only by Bruce Springsteen *(Born in the U.S.A.)* and Janet Jackson *(Rhythm Nation 1814).*

It is impossible to reflect on the music of 1983 without thinking of a Michael Jackson song, his musical presence so dominated the charts that year. The first single, a duet with Paul McCartney called "The Girl Is Mine," peaked at number two in January, 1983. The impact of *Thriller* was first felt when the LP's second single, "Billie Jean," debuted on the

Hot 100 at number 47 during the week of January 22, 1983. When it reached number one six weeks later, Michael Jackson became the first artist in the history of *Billboard's* charts to simultaneously top the singles and album charts in both pop and black categories. For good measure, *Thriller* was also number one on the dance/disco chart. One week later, "Billie Jean" and *Thriller* were number one on their respective charts in Britain, giving Michael a worldwide sweep.

If Michael felt any pressure to match the achievement of his previous solo album, *Off the Wall,* he needn't have worried. He did have a lot to live up to; that album yielded two chart-topping singles [see 511— "Don't Stop 'Til You Get Enough" and 520—"Rock With You"] and a total of four top 10 singles.

The music on "Billie Jean" sounded far removed from Michael's world of exotic animals and Disneyana. It had a basic rhythm line performed by Jackson on a drum machine. Late into the recording, drummer Leon Ndugu Chancler was brought in to enhance the "punch" of the song. He said in *Musician,* "I was placed in a room by myself, so

there was no (sound) leakage. Both Michael and Quincy came in to suggest things for the two or three hours it took to cut the track. I played through it about eight to ten times."

The other dominant feature of "Billie Jean" is the bass line, suggested by Michael. Louis Johnson of the Brothers Johnson ("Strawberry Letter 23," "Stomp!") told *Musician* about working on the song with Michael. "He had me bring all my guitars to see how they sounded playing the part. I tried three or four basses before we settled on the Yamaha. It's really live, with a lot of power and guts." Veteran jazz musician Tom Scott received no credit, but played a lyricon solo in the background of the mix. Engineer Bruce Swedien recalled in *Musician:* "It was Quincy's idea to weave this thread into the thing. It was a last minute overdub thing. Quincy calls it 'ear candy.' It's just a subliminal element that works well."

Michael's vocal on "Billie Jean" was recorded in one amazing take. The end result of all this work: a single that remained at number one for seven weeks, shattering Michael's previous record of five weeks [see 283—"I'll Be There"].

## THE TOP FIVE
*Week of March 5, 1983*

1  **Billie Jean**
   Michael Jackson

2  **Shame on the Moon**
   Bob Seger & the
   Silver Bullet Band

3  **Stray Cat Strut**
   Stray Cats

4  **Do You Really Want
   to Hurt Me**
   Culture Club

5  **Hungry Like The Wolf**
   Duran Duran

## 570 Come on Eileen MERCURY 76189
### DEXYS MIDNIGHT RUNNERS

*Writers: Kevin Rowland*
*Jimmy Patterson*
*Kevin Adams*

*Producers: Clive Langer*
*Alan Winstanley*

*April 23, 1983*
*1 week*

WHEN British guitarist Kevin Rowland was young, his Irish-Catholic relations taught him that sex was "dirty." Years later, the former altar boy recalled those sentiments in a catchy tune that propelled Rowland and his "Celtic Soul Brothers" to number one.

In the high-spirited song, Rowland examines carnal love as he learned it in his guilt-ridden youth. "I quite like the idea of sex being dirty," he admitted to Paolo Hewitt in a 1982 *Melody Maker* story. "What's the point of me going on about how sex is beautiful? I've heard it a million times, you know."

A one-time candidate for priesthood, Rowland disclosed the autobiographical nature of the song. "It is about somebody, a girl who I grew up with basically, and it's absolutely true all the way along....And

there was a time, about 14 or 15, it was a funny thing, sex came into it and our relationship had always been so clean. It seemed at that time to get dirty and that's what it's about. I was really trying to capture that atmosphere." Then, lest any of his fans worry about him, Rowland quickly added, "I don't honestly think that sex is really dirty now."

The Birmingham-bred Rowland organized Dexys Midnight Runners in 1978. At first, he adopted a street gang look for the band, inspired by Robert DeNiro's street hustler in *Mean Streets*. According to Rowland, "It was a very spiffy look, very Italian...that hot sweaty thing surrounded the music at that time. I felt it was a very smoky image."

The sound itself had a Stax Records/Van Morrison-influenced soul flavor, heavy on horns.

Dexys' second

British single, "Geno" (a tribute to Geno Washington, a star of the '60s British club scene), went to number one. But after expressing contempt for the music press in full-page ads in Britain's weekly rock journals, the first incarnation of Dexys Midnight Runners split up. Rowland regrouped in 1981 with an entirely new look for the band. They wore ponytails, track suits and soccer boots, and in a spirit of puritanical fervor, they jogged to rehearsals and banned alcoholic beverages at their shows.

After a lean year, Rowland came up with yet another image and sound for Dexys. Now dressed in scruffy overalls, sandals and bandanas, the group teamed up with some fiddlers known as the Emerald Express and became born-again Celtic soulsters. The album *Too-Rye-Ay* reflected this new musical direction. Discarding the group's emblematic brass sound for acoustic strings and a wistful look back at adolescence, Rowland and company came up with "Come on Eileen," their second British number one single. Eight months later, Dexys knocked Michael Jackson's "Billie Jean" off the top of the Hot 100 and held his "Beat It" at bay to become number one in America.

"I promised myself that if 'Come on Eileen' didn't do well I'd find another way of making money," Rowland confessed to Lesley White in a 1982 interview for *The Face*. "I don't want to be in a loser group, touring round everywhere, suffering for my art....It doesn't mean a thing because if the music doesn't relate to people and win success, it's a waste of time."

## THE TOP FIVE
*Week of April 23, 1983*

1 **Come On Eileen**
Dexys Midnight Runners

2 **Beat It**
Michael Jackson

3 **Mr. Roboto**
Styx

4 **Jeopardy**
Greg Kihn Band

5 **Billie Jean**
Michael Jackson

EPIC 03759 **Beat It** | 571
MICHAEL JACKSON

*Writer: Michael Jackson*

*Producer: Quincy Jones*

*April 30, 1983*
*3 weeks*

**P**AUL GREIN reported the latest achievement for the former lead singer of the Jackson Five in his "Chartbeat" column in the April 30, 1983, issue of *Billboard*: "Michael Jackson's 'Beat It' jumps to number one on this week's Hot 100, just one week after 'Billie Jean' [see 569] ended its seven-week stay on top. That one-week gap between number one records is the shortest any act has had since the Beatles went one better and actually replaced themselves at number one in 1964.

Just two weeks earlier, with "Beat It" moving to number five and "Billie Jean" holding at number one for a seventh week, Grein pointed out that Michael was the first artist of the '80s to simultaneously have two hits in the top five. Only four artists had accomplished this feat in the '70s, Grein said: Donna Summer ("Hot Stuff," "Bad Girls"), Linda Ronstadt ("Blue Bayou," "It's So Easy"), the Bee Gees ("Stayin' Alive," "Night Fever") and Olivia Newton-John ("Hopelessly Devoted to You," "Summer Nights").

Album oriented rock stations that couldn't find room on their playlists for most black artists felt comfortable playing "Beat It" even before it was released as a single, thanks to the

searing solo guitar work by one of hard rock's premier guitarists, Eddie Van Halen [see 584—"Jump"].

Eddie almost missed the opportunity to work with Michael, because of a telephone that wasn't working properly. Intermittent equipment problems resulted in two calls in a row where Eddie couldn't hear the party on the other end. By the third call, he was aggravated enough to utter a couple of expletives into the mouthpiece. Eddie told *Musician* what he then heard: " 'This is Quincy, Quincy Jones.' I say, '. . . I'm sorry, I get so many crank calls that I didn't know.' He asked, 'You know, there's this song we'd like you to do, are you up for it?' "

Van Halen was definitely up for it. So much so that he accepted no pay for his contribution to "Beat It." "I didn't care, I did it as a favor," Eddie said in *Musician*.

Jackson's vocals match Van Halen's guitar playing for intensity. Engineer Bruce Sweiden talked about Michael's rigorous vocal training during the recording of *Thriller*: "During that period, every day—I don't just mean one day a week or something— every day that Michael records vocals, he's at his vocal coach's place at 8:30 in the morning. So when he comes in, he's ready to go."

Adding to the popularity of "Beat It" was the $160,000 video of the song that Michael bankrolled and Bob Giraldi directed. "The theme of my song is about two gangs coming together to rumble, to fight," Jackson

told reporter Barry Daniels. "And my objective is to tell them to turn the other cheek. It's like I'm coming in between them saying, 'Hey, man, don't fight! These guys are your brothers!' "

Jackson and *Dream Girls* assistant choreographer Michael Peters fashioned the dancing sequences in the video, winning praise from Bob Fosse and Gene Kelly. But *Time* magazine reported the ultimate tribute, from a man who used to watch Michael ride his bicycle around their neighborhood when the youngster was in the Jackson Five. "He is a wonderful mover," Fred Astaire said. "He makes these moves up himself and it is just great to watch. I think he just feels that way when he is singing those songs . . . Michael is a dedicated artist. He dreams, thinks of it all the time."

## THE TOP FIVE
*Week of April 30, 1983*

1 **Beat It**
Michael Jackson

2 **Come On Eileen**
Dexys Midnight Runners

3 **Jeopardy**
Greg Kihn

4 **Mr. Roboto**
Styx

5 **Der Kommissar**
After the Fire

572

# Let's Dance EMI-AMERICA 8158
## DAVID BOWIE

*Writer: David Bowie*

*Producers: David Bowie*
*Nile Rodgers*

*May 21, 1983*
*1 week*

FOLLOWING his first number one single [see 416—"Fame"], David Bowie made an impressive screen debut as an alien from a drought-ridden planet in *The Man Who Fell to Earth*. But suddenly, he confessed, "I went to pieces. I wasn't pulling anything together. So I went to Jamaica with my band and did a tour, half of which I can't remember. It was a fantasy world."

In the mid-'70s, Bowie moved to the Turkish quarter of Berlin and began a trilogy of dark, disjunctive collaborations with rock experimentalist Brian Eno (formerly of Roxy Music). He says his recuperation period took him two to three years.

"Even today," he admitted, "I sometimes get up and think, 'Well, I'm going to live this day as if it were the last day of my life.' Then about three o'clock in the afternoon, I think perhaps there is a future after all. But I don't have the kind of problems I used to have. I've learned to relax and be my present age and my present condition....It doesn't seem such an alien place to be."

Bowie's American chart performance in 1980-1981 was nowhere near as successful as his British performance. "Ashes to Ashes" was his second United Kingdom chart-topper, following a re-issue of "Space Oddity" in 1975. "Under Pressure," a collaboration with Queen, also went to number one in Britain. For Christmas, 1982, RCA released "Peace on Earth/Little Drummer Boy," a duet with Bing Crosby, that peaked at number three in the U.K.

Bowie's choice in the early '80s seemed to be acting. He gave impressive performances in two films, *The Hunger* and *Merry Christmas, Mr. Lawrence*, and on Broadway he won rave notices for starring in *The Elephant Man*. Although Mick Jagger opined that Bowie had found it necessary to "forfeit" his musical career to achieve success in movies, he was soon to show he had not lost his hit-making touch.

In 1983, Bowie signed with EMI in a deal worth a reported $10 million to the singer. For *Let's Dance*, his debut album for the label, he teamed up with producer/guitarist Nile Rodgers of Chic [see 495—"Le Freak"], the man already responsible for smash dance singles by Diana Ross [see 530—"Upside Down"], Sister Sledge ("He's the Greatest Dancer," "We Are Family") and Sheila B. Devotion ("Little Darlin'"). Featuring Bernard Edwards, another cornerstone of the Chic organization, on bass, the collaboration produced Bowie's most accessible music since *Young Americans* in 1975.

"*Let's Dance* is probably the simplest album I've ever done," said the new, "normal" Bowie. "In fact, it was quite complex to put together, but I hope the overall impression is that it's the most positive, emotional, uplifting album I've made in a long time." The title track was the first single released. It debuted on the Hot 100 at number 54 on March 26, 1983, and became Bowie's second American chart-topper eight weeks later. Two more hits followed: "China Girl" checked in at 10 and "Modern Love" reached number 14. Bowie's 1984 album, *Tonight*, provided just one hit single, "Blue Jean" (number eight). With no successful follow-ups, EMI-America had to rely on "This Is Not America," from the soundtrack of *The Falcon and the Snowman*, to return David to the top half of the chart. The collaboration between Bowie and the Pat Metheny Group peaked at number 32 in March, 1985.

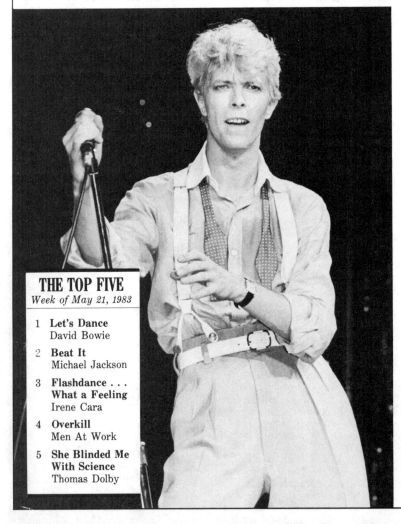

## THE TOP FIVE
*Week of May 21, 1983*

1 **Let's Dance**
David Bowie

2 **Beat It**
Michael Jackson

3 **Flashdance . . .**
**What a Feeling**
Irene Cara

4 **Overkill**
Men At Work

5 **She Blinded Me**
**With Science**
Thomas Dolby

CASABLANCA 811-440-7 **Flashdance...What a Feeling** 573
IRENE CARA

*Writers: Irene Cara*
*Giorgio Moroder*
*Keith Forsey*

*Producer: Giorgio Moroder*

*May 28, 1983*
*6 weeks*

IRENE CARA'S two biggest hits are both motion picture themes. "Fame," written by Dean Pitchford and Michael Gore [see 130—"It's My Party"], was the title song for Alan Parker's motion picture and was nominated for an Academy Award. "Flashdance...What a Feeling," composed by Irene with Giorgio Moroder and Keith Forsey, topped the Hot 100 on May 28, 1983. Ten months later, Irene won an Oscar when "Flashdance" was named Best Song by the motion picture academy.

Cara's first big break was being cast as Coco Hernandez in *Fame*, the motion picture that spawned the hit television series (Erica Gimpel played Coco in the TV version). The film made Irene an international star, and the title song became an anthem for teenagers determined to succeed in the performing arts.

Cara didn't appear in *Flashdance*. But Irene was invited to sing the title song, a project that found her teamed with Donna Summer's producer, Giorgio Moroder.

Critics suggested that Irene's vocals on "Flashdance" sounded very much like Summer [see 504—"Hot Stuff"]. "I hesitated using Giorgio as a producer, because I didn't need people giving me flack that I was using Donna Summer's producer," Cara told interviewer Richard Laermer.

In *Songwriter Connection*, Cara suggested to reporter Parvene Michaels the comparison to Summer was sexist. "There are so many records made by male artists today that sound alike. But nobody makes an issue of that. That's why I'm very supportive of other female artists, especially those trying to make their own statement and not be controlled. Trying to do what they want instead of being somebody else's Barbie doll. There are too many people in this business who just want you to look pretty and sing. That's the last thing I consider I do."

The lyrics to "Flashdance...What a Feeling" were written by Cara and Forsey while they were driving to a recording session (the word "flashdance" doesn't actually appear anywhere in the lyrics). "I came up with the original idea about talking about the feeling of dance," Irene told Michaels. "Keith elaborated on it, saying, 'dancing for my life.' 'What a feeling' as a metaphor about a dancer, how she's in control of her body when she dances and how she can be in control of her life."

Irene started performing when she was seven. "I come from a family of performers," she told Jay Merritt in a 1980 *Rolling Stone* interview. "My father is a musician, so is my brother, and I have a great-aunt who plays five instruments. My mother always wanted to be in show business, but her parents discouraged her. So when I started performing for the mirror, she enrolled me in dancing, singing and piano lessons....I didn't have to go to school, graduate and then go, 'What am I going to do.' I knew from the beginning."

Her first professional work was appearing on Spanish-language radio and television shows in New York. A year later, at age eight, she made her Broadway debut playing an orphan in *Maggie Flynn*, starring Jack Cassidy and Shirley Jones [see 284—"I Think I Love You"]. She also appeared in an ABC-TV documentary about music, "Over 7." By the time she was 10, her vocal talents were well known enough to win her an invitation to

sing at a tribute to Duke Ellington in Madison Square Garden, alongside Roberta Flack [see 310—"The First Time Ever I Saw Your Face"] and Sammy Davis, Jr. [see 313—"Candy Man"].

At 12, she started writing song lyrics, strongly influenced by writers like Carole King, Valerie Simpson, Ellie Greenwich and Joni Mitchell.

She made her film debut in the 1975 release *Aaron Loves Angela*, then won the lead role in the motion picture *Sparkle*, about three sisters striving for a singing career in the early '60s. Before *Fame* was released in 1980, Cara had two important television roles. She played Bertha Palmer, grandmother of Alex Haley, in "Roots: The Next Generation" and then played a cult member in "The Guyana Tragedy: The Story of Jim Jones."

After the title tune from *Fame* made her a star on the pop charts, she released another song from the movie, "Out Here on My Own," which peaked at number 19. "Anyone Can See," the title track from her debut solo album, failed to crack the top 40, but "Flashdance...What a Feeling" put her on top of the Hot 100 for the first time.

### THE TOP FIVE
*Week of May 28, 1983*

1 **Flashdance . . .**
   **What a Feeling**
   Irene Cara

2 **Let's Dance**
   David Bowie

3 **Overkill**
   Men At Work

4 **Time**
   Culture Club

5 **She Blinded Me**
   **With Science**
   Thomas Dolby

## 574 Every Breath You Take A&M 2542
### THE POLICE

*Writer: Sting*

*Producers: Hugh Padgham*
*The Police*

*July 9, 1983*
*8 weeks*

WITH an eight week run at number one, the Police's "Every Breath You Take" tied the Bee Gees' "Night Fever" [see 480] for the second-longest running number one by a British group, runners-up only to the Beatles' "Hey Jude" [see 247]. The song, influenced by the emotional lyrics of James Taylor, the reggae rhythms of Bob Marley and the jazz background of lead singer Sting, was *Billboard's* number one single of 1983. It was also one of the most difficult ones to record on the group's *Synchronicity* album, guitarist Andy Summers informed Christopher Connelly in a 1984 *Rolling Stone* article. An elaborate synthesizer section had been discarded so as not to distract from the song's simplicity. Sting told Connelly that it was not intended to be the sweet love song that many people believed it was. "I consider it a fairly nasty song," he said. "It's about surveillance and ownership and jealousy."

The three individuals who make up the Police were all involved in music before they came together as a band in 1977. Gordon Sumner (born October 2, 1951, in Wallsend, England), who was nicknamed Sting from a yellow and black jersey he liked to wear, had other jobs too—ditch digger, teacher, civil servant—before playing with a jazz group called Lost Exit in Newcastle. Then he met drummer Stewart Copeland (born July 16, 1952, in Virginia), son of an American CIA agent who had been raised in the Middle East. After attending college in California, he moved to England and became a member of Curved Air. They broke up in 1976 and the following year, Copeland and Sting formed the Police with guitarist Henri Padovani. Stewart formed Illegal Records with his brother Miles and released the band's first single, "Fall Out," in May, 1977.

Then Andy Summers (born December 31, 1942, in Blackpool, England) joined as a second guitarist. Soon after, Padovani departed for Wayne County's Electric Chairs. A trio once more, the newly aligned Police played their first gig at Rebecca's Club in Birmingham on August 18, 1977. In the early part of 1978 they were signed to A&M and the Copelands' label, now known as

I.R.S, became an A&M distributed label.

Their first record album, *Outlandos d'Amour*, cost less than four thousand pounds to produce. Against the advice of their record company, the Police conducted an equally low-budgeted tour of America and built a following that forced the American arm of A&M to release the LP in the United States. The debut single, "Roxanne," charted at number 32 in the spring of 1979.

Their British breakthrough came first; "Can't Stand Losing You" went to number two in the summer of 1979 and "Message in a Bottle" from *Reggatta de Blanc* became the first of five British number ones in the early fall. In America, real success didn't come until January, 1981, when the first single from *Zenyatta Mondatta*, "De Do Do Do, De Da Da Da" went to number 10. "Don't Stand So Close to Me" did likewise, then "Every Little Thing She Does Is Magic" became their biggest hit yet, peaking at number three in December, 1981.

The singles that followed "Every Breath You Take" continued the good fortunes of the Police. "King of Pain" (number three), "Synchronicity II" (number 16) and "Wrapped Around Your Finger" (number eight) were all from *Synchronicity*, an album recorded in a swift six weeks in Montserrat, France.

It turned out to be their final studio album. Foreshadowing the break-up of the band, Sting said in a 1983 *Musician* interview, "We are not joined at the hip; we are not a three-headed Hydra.... We each have our own contributions to make."

### THE TOP FIVE
*Week of July 9, 1983*

1 **Every Breath You Take**
  The Police

2 **Electric Avenue**
  Eddy Grant

3 **Flashdance . . . What a Feeling**
  Irene Cara

4 **Never Gonna Let You Go**
  Sergio Mendes

5 **Too Shy**
  Kajagoogoo

RCA 13533 **Sweet Dreams (Are Made of This)**
EURYTHMICS **575**

*Writers: Annie Lennox*
*David Stewart*

*Producer: David A. Stewart*

*September 3, 1983*
*1 week*

IF Eurythmics need to be defined by a single word, it would be obsessions. Dave Stewart was always obsessed by something. As a kid in the northern England town of Sunderland, it was sports—roller skating, pole vaulting, skiing, running and football. "When I was 12 I broke my knee in a match and was in hospital for ages," he reminisced. "I got so fidgety with nothing to do that someone brought me a guitar, which of course was fatal." Three years later he attended his first rock concert, given by a medieval madrigal outfit, the Amazing Blondel, and was so fascinated he stowed away in the group's van. His parents let him stay, abandoning him to the life of a roadie and rock musician. He formed Longdancer, one of the first bands signed to Elton John's Rocket Records label, then scuffled through a series of musical and romantic alliances, "having adventures" across Europe. He came back to London for surgery on a lung damaged during a serious car crash in Germany and met a fellow Sunderland musician, Peet Coombes. One night they had dinner in a restaurant where the meal was served by an unemployed singer named Annie Lennox.

"The first words Dave said were, 'Will you marry me?' I thought he was a serious nutter!" laughed the ex-waitress. "But from that night on, we were inseparable." The restaurant job was just one source of income for the boilermaker's daughter from Aberdeen, Scotland. But then swapping identities was second nature to the only child who spent much of her time alone, "having lots of fantasies drifting off into a dream world."

In the real world, Annie played the flute and set off for London at 17 to study the instrument (piano and harpsichord, too) at the Royal Academy of Music. A misfit, she quit just before final exams to write Joni Mitchell/Joan Armatrading type songs and to sing the Stax/Volt records she'd heard back in Aberdeen.

Stewart and Lennox moved in together, and with Coombes formed the Tourists in 1977. In a strange coincidence, they became the third act to take the song "I Only Want to Be With You" to number four on the British chart; both Dusty Springfield and the Bay City Rollers had achieved the exact same chart position with the song. But after recording two albums; touring Europe, Australia and America (in Dolly Parton's tour bus); and suing their British record label, Logo, the Tourists had little to show for their efforts. In Bangkok, they decided they'd had enough.

"The day Dave and I ended our romantic relationship, Eurythmics began," asserted Annie. Designed as a nuclear duo that would work with an ever-changing series of musicians, they recorded *In the Garden*, then dragged their gear around Britain in an old Volvo for a series of do-it-yourself live shows during the bitter British winter of 1981. Dave's lung collapsed and Annie had a nervous breakdown. A few months later, with new Dave Stewart songs, they tried again, assembling a makeshift studio in a London warehouse.

"Sweet Dreams (Are Made of This)" was recorded there on an eight-track machine. "We used so many different textures. It sounded so sophisticated but often we had to wait for the timber factory downstairs to turn off their machinery before we could record the vocals."

Subsequent singles have kept Annie's constantly changing image in the public eye. "Love Is a Stranger," "Here Comes the Rain Again," "Who's That Girl?" and "Right By Your Side" preceded their work on the soundtrack of *1984*, starring Richard Burton (in his last screen appearance) and John Hurt. At the last minute, director Michael Radford had substituted music by Dominic Muldowney. Compounding their problems with this soundtrack, American radio stations found the content of the "Sexcrime (Nineteen Eighty-Four)" single objectionable and gave it little airplay.

**THE TOP FIVE**
*Week of September 3, 1983*

1 **Sweet Dreams
(Are Made of This)**
Eurythmics

2 **Maniac**
Michael Sembello

3 **Every Breath You Take**
The Police

4 **Puttin' on the Ritz**
Taco

5 **She Works Hard
for The Money**
Donna Summer

## 576 Maniac CASABLANCA 812-516-7
### MICHAEL SEMBELLO

*Writers: Michael Sembello*
*Dennis Matkosky*

*Producers: Phil Ramone*
*Michael Sembello*

*September 10, 1983*
*2 weeks*

HORROR film fanatic Michael Sembello wrote a tender ode about a maniac hacking off people's arms, a song he thought would make a good title tune for an upcoming *Halloween*-type movie. When his friend Phil Ramone called and asked if Michael had anything suitable for the upcoming *Flashdance* motion picture, Sembello sent a demo tape without realizing that "Maniac" was included. Ramone called back and said his favorite song on the tape was—what else?—"Maniac." The original, sinister lyrics were toned down at the request of studio executives to become a warm-up anthem for welder-cum-dancer Jennifer Beals, and "Maniac" became the second number one single from the film [see 573—"Flashdance...What a Feeling"].

Sembello's name was new to the public, but he was hardly the latest "overnight" sensation. Born in Philadelphia, he first landed a position as Stevie Wonder's guitarist at the tender age of 17. He performed on every Wonder album from 1975-1979, and their close working relationship resulted in a Grammy for their collaboration, "Saturn."

Sought after as a session musician *par excellence*, Sembello was soon performing with and writing material for pop luminaries like Diana Ross,

Michael Jackson, Donna Summer, Art Garfunkel, Jeffrey Osborne and Sergio Mendes. After leaving Wonder, he moved to Los Angeles, where he later married Cruz Baca, one of Mendes' back-up singers.

Sembello credits his success as a solo artist and producer to his song "Mirror, Mirror," a number eight hit for Diana Ross in early 1982. Sembello had originally given the tune to an associate of the Pointer Sisters, convinced it would be perfect for their intricate three-part harmonies. Much to his surprise, however, the song was rejected as "a hokey nursery rhyme."

"That was the turning point of my life," Sembello told *Billboard's* Paul Grein. "Before that, I was the most cordial guy. If someone said my song sucked, I'd think, 'Maybe they're right; I'll go home and change it.' But that motivated me to get off my ass and stop being so submissive. I went overnight from being a Hindu to being a barbarian. You have to do a lot of pursuing in this business. I come from 10 or 15 years of hard labor in the training camps of Hollywood studios. I tried seriously to

get a deal for six or seven years. It didn't matter that I'd written some hits. It didn't matter that I'd been a sideman with Stevie Wonder for seven years. I really believe you're better off coming in off the street without anybody knowing anything about you."

Sembello followed "Maniac" with an album on Warner Brothers, *Bossa Nova Hotel*, a fusion of R&B and Latin music. Showing admirable restraint, he refused to rush back into the studio and manufacture a "Maniac" clone. As he explained to Debi Fee in *Rock & Soul*, " 'Maniac' was a great song for me and I was very proud when it reached number one because I've been struggling a long time. But hey, let it die. 'Maniac' was just a song and now I'm on to the next and I don't want to rip off the record-buying public by doing a carbon-copy of 'Maniac' just to make some money. I'm an artist and I'm happiest while creating. I'm really a recluse who just likes to stay in his studio and produce music." But, he added, "unfortunately I have to earn money. I learned to cope and survive."

### THE TOP FIVE
*Week of September 10, 1983*

1 **Maniac**
   Michael Sembello

2 **Sweet Dreams (Are Made of This)**
   Eurythmics

3 **The Safety Dance**
   Men Without Hats

4 **Puttin' on the Ritz**
   Taco

5 **Tell Her About It**
   Billy Joel

COLUMBIA 04012 **Tell Her About It** `577`
BILLY JOEL

*Writer: Billy Joel*

*Producer: Phil Ramone*

*September 24, 1983*
*1 week*

Following the multi-platinum successes of *The Stranger, 52nd Street* and *Glass Houses*, Billy Joel found himself perched at the summit of the pop heap. He took a break from the road and started work on his most ambitious album yet.

"I feel like I almost died making *The Nylon Curtain*," he said. "The thing you don't have control over is writing—you have to pull it out of yourself, stretch yourself...you pace the room with something like the dry heaves, having no control over the muse, horrified that it won't come. You're always in the desert looking for the oasis, and all that's out there with you is the piano, this big, black beast with 88 teeth. You have to lay your guts on the table and go through them 11 times on an album. Fifty thousand packs of cigarettes later, you start getting it."

While working on *The Nylon Curtain*, Billy had an actual brush with death when his motorcycle collided with a car on Long Island. "Right before I hit," he recalled, "I had a flood of images, jumbled up thoughts. I thought I was going to die and I...thought, 'You can't do this to me, I'm not ready to die.'"

Billy came out of the accident with a series of fractures that necessitated extensive surgery. But it didn't stop him from completing the album, an examination of his and his generation's "American experience—guilt, pressures, relationships and the Vietnam syndrome."

Billy's next album, *An Innocent Man*, found the singer/songwriter in a more positive frame of mind. "On every album I adopt a different sort of character," he explained, "and the character on this album is sort of a sweet person who is in love and feeling good. It's a guy enjoying the courtship rituals—making out, dating, slow dancing—and the insecurities that go with it—the gamut of passions that come with romance."

To convey this "innocent" atmosphere, Billy turned to the spirit and styles of his favorite '50s and '60s performers—the Drifters, Otis Redding, James Brown, Little Anthony and the Imperials and especially the Four Seasons. But whereas Joel says "singers like Frankie Valli were always going to give up their life for the girl," the songs on *An Innocent Man* reflected a less naive decade trying to face the anxieties at the heart of romance.

"I'm not living in the past," he insisted. "I'm celebrating *today*. I'd never have had the fire if I'd never hung out with the wild boys and heard the old magic." The first single pulled from the album was "Tell Her About It," for which he filmed an innovative video showing Billy on "The Ed Sullivan Show." The point of the song was to show how important it is "to communicate your feelings to somebody you're in love with, despite the insecurity that brings."

"Tell Her About It" made an impressive debut on the Hot 100 at number 38 on July 30, 1983. Eight weeks later it became his second number one single [see 527—"It's Still Rock and Roll to Me"]. There were many more singles to come from *An Innocent Man*—five more, to be exact. "Uptown Girl," his prenuptial love letter to girlfriend Christie Brinkley, held at number three for five weeks. Joel had never penetrated the British top 10 before, but this Four Seasons-influenced song went to number one in the United Kingdom and was the second best-selling single of 1983, behind "Karma Chameleon" [see 583].

Billy's subsequent hits from *An Innocent Man* included the title track (number 10), "The Longest Time" (number 14), "Leave a Tender Moment Alone" (number 27) and "Keeping the Faith" (number 18). While the last title was moving up the Hot 100, the Downtown Boy and his Uptown Girl tied the knot aboard a 145-foot yacht in the middle of New York Harbor.

## THE TOP FIVE
*Week of September 24, 1983*

1 **Tell Her About It**
  Billy Joel

2 **Total Eclipse
  of the Heart**
  Bonnie Tyler

3 **The Safety Dance**
  Men Without Hats

4 **Maniac**
  Michael Sembello

5 **Making Love Out of
  Nothing at All**
  Air Supply

### 578 Total Eclipse of the Heart COLUMBIA 03906
#### BONNIE TYLER

*Writer: Jim Steinman*

*Producer: Jim Steinman*

*October 1, 1983*
*4 weeks*

Bonnie Tyler severed all ties with her managers in 1981. Ronnie Scott and Steve Wolfe had written and produced "It's a Heartache" for Tyler, a number three record in 1978, but found it hard to duplicate that success. "Don't talk to me about those days," she told Chas De Whalley when he interviewed her for *Kerrang!* magazine. "I didn't have any control over what I was doing at all. I was signed to a production company and the guys who managed me were also songwriters. So they'd only let me record *their* material. I didn't have any choice.

"Before I signed with them I had my own band at home called Mumbles and we used to do raunchy soul stuff by people like Rufus, Chaka Khan and Tina Turner. But they wanted me to sing country songs because they were aiming at the Nashville album market. Some of their material was quite good, I suppose, but after I'd had seven flops in a row over a two year period my heart went out of it. When my contract expired, I just walked out."

Signed to new management, Bonnie was given the freedom to select songs and a new producer. "I'd always been a big fan of Phil Spector and that huge sound he used to get," Bonnie said. "The only producer who can get that epic sound nowadays is Jim Steinman, so when I was asked about possible producers, he was top of my list, though I didn't really think he'd do it. Other people who I thought would be good were Phil Collins, Jeff Lynne and Alan Tarney."

CBS Records approached Steinman about producing Bonnie, but he was working on a movie project and declined. "I also had a sneaking suspicion he thought the whole idea was completely ridiculous but then, one day, he called up out of the blue and said that if I hadn't found a producer he was really interested."

Bonnie flew to New York to meet Steinman at his apartment. "He played me Blue Oyster Cult's 'Going Through the Motions' and Creedence's 'Have You Ever Seen the Rain,' Bonnie told Sandy Robertson in *Sounds*, "and he says now that if I hadn't liked them he'd have known the whole thing wouldn't work. Then he played 'Total Eclipse of the Heart' on a grand piano for me. When he plays he practically knocks it through the floor, he's incredible! He won't give you it on tape, he has to tell you the big story and play it for you with Rory Dodd singing and the whole thing."

Both "Total Eclipse" and the next song Steinman played for Bonnie, "Faster Than the Speed of Night," evolved from theme music Steinman had written for a movie, *Small Circle of Friends*.

Steinman, the man responsible for writing and producing Meat Loaf's dramatic epic, *Bat Out of Hell*, put together an all-star band for the recording of "Total Eclipse of the Heart." The roster of musicians included drummer Max Weinberg and keyboard player Roy Bittan, both from Bruce Springsteen's E Street Band; guitarist Rick Derringer [see 184—"Hang On Sloopy"]; and Dodd, who sang the haunting background vocals of "turn around..."

"Total Eclipse of the Heart" went to number one in the United Kingdom first. When the LP *Faster Than the Speed of Night* entered the British chart at number one, Bonnie became the first female singer to go straight in at one in the U.K.

Several months passed before Columbia records decided to release the single in the United States. In the intervening time, songwriter Dean Pitchford heard an Australian copy of the single and decided to ask Bonnie to record a song for the soundtrack of his film *Footloose* [see 585]. Long before "Total Eclipse" entered the Hot 100, Bonnie agreed to cut "Holding Out for a Hero," written and produced by Steinman.

Bonnie Tyler was born June 8, 1953, in Skewen, South Wales, near Swansea. Along with her brothers and sisters, she loved listening to the Beatles, the Dave Clark Five and the Swinging Blue Jeans, but was especially enamored of Motown. She won a local talent contest when she was 17, and quit her job in a candy store to sing in Welsh nightclubs. After a year-and-a-half of performing, she developed nodules on her throat. She rested her voice and the nodules disappeared, only to recur twice. In 1976 she had an operation to remove them, leaving her with a huskier voice that reminds some of a female Rod Stewart.

While appearing at the Townsman Club in Swansea, she was seen by Scott and Wolfe, who asked her to record their composition "Lost in France." It became a top 10 single in Britain at the end of 1976. A year later, "It's a Heartache" went to number four on the British chart and was picked up for American release by RCA Records.

---

### THE TOP FIVE
*Week of October 1, 1983*

1  **Total Eclipse of the Heart**
   Bonnie Tyler

2  **Tell Her About It**
   Billy Joel

3  **The Safety Dance**
   Men Without Hats

4  **Making Love Out of Nothing at All**
   Air Supply

5  **(She's) Sexy and Seventeen**
   Stray Cats

*Writers: Barry Gibb*
*Robin Gibb*
*Maurice Gibb*

*Producers: Barry Gibb*
*Karl Richardson*
*Albhy Galuten*

*October 29, 1983*
*2 weeks*

Signed to RCA in a deal that put more than $20 million in his pocket, Kenny Rogers tapped Barry Gibb to produce the first album for his new label. "A couple of years ago, I was going to make an album on which I would sing duets with several people: Dolly Parton, Willie Nelson, Barry Gibb and others," Rogers told David Rensin in a 1983 *Playboy* interview. "But it never panned out. When my project with (Lionel) Richie was done and I was looking around for new collaborators, I remembered a song Barry had sent me that turned out to be a decent country hit for him. So I called him."

For one of the songs on *Eyes That See in the Dark*, Rogers recruited another RCA recording artist to be his singing partner. Dolly Parton was the fourth female singer to chart in a duo with Rogers. "Don't Fall Love With a Dreamer," sung with Kim Carnes, was a number four hit in May, 1980. "What Are We Doin' in Love" with Dottie West went to number 14 in June, 1981. Seven months before "Islands in the Stream," Kenny teamed with Sheena Easton for a cover version of Bob Seger's "We've Got Tonight," which peaked at number six.

"Islands in the Stream," the first single released from the album, entered the Hot 100 at number 58 on August 27, in 1983, and took nine weeks to journey to number one. Both Kenny [see 533—"Lady"] and Dolly [see 537—"9 to 5"] had garnered just one chart-topper each on their own prior to combining forces.

The rewards for "Islands in the Stream" were great. In addition to topping the country and Adult Contemporary charts, the song won an American Music Award for Best Country Single (Kenny Rogers has 18 AMAs, more than any other solo artist) and was named Vocal Duet of the Year and Single Record of the Year by the Academy of Country

Music. It was the only single in 1983 to achieve platinum status.

The collaboaration produced such great results that Kenny and Dolly recorded a Christmas album together in 1984, then packaged a dual American tour the following spring. Kenny guest starred on Dolly's 1985 *Real Love* LP, duetting on the title cut.

"Islands in the Stream" was miles away from Kenny's first chart entry, the psychedelic "Just Dropped In (To See What Condition My Condition Was In)," a top five hit for the First Edition in 1968. Rogers was one of the New Christy Minstrels in 1966 when, unhappy with that troupe's

inertia, he quit along with Terry Williams, Mike Settle and Thelma Camacho to form the First Edition.

Kenneth Ray Rogers (his birth certificate reads Kenneth Donald Rogers), born August 21, 1938, in Houston, Texas, has excelled in many other areas besides singing. He's an author, having penned *Making It With Music* with Len Epand. He's developed his acting skills, achieving high ratings for his television films "The Gambler" and "The Gambler II." In 2000, Rogers had his first chart single in 15 years when "Buy Me a Rose" peaked at number 40 on the Hot 100.

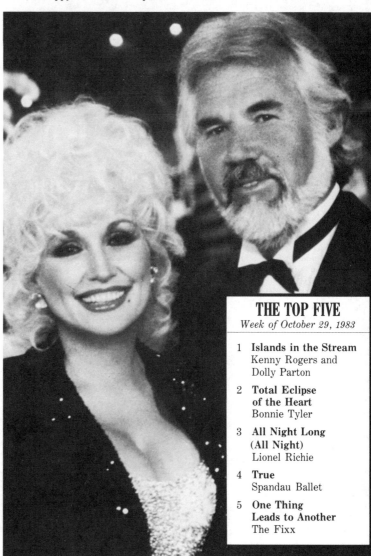

**THE TOP FIVE**
*Week of October 29, 1983*

1 **Islands in the Stream**
Kenny Rogers and
Dolly Parton

2 **Total Eclipse
of the Heart**
Bonnie Tyler

3 **All Night Long
(All Night)**
Lionel Richie

4 **True**
Spandau Ballet

5 **One Thing
Leads to Another**
The Fixx

# 580 All Night Long (All Night) MOTOWN 1698
## LIONEL RICHIE

*Writer: Lionel Richie*

*Producers: Lionel Richie*
*James Anthony*
*Carmichael*

*November 12, 1983*
*4 weeks*

In approaching his first solo album, Lionel Richie heeded advice Berry Gordy, Jr., gave the Commodores when they first signed with Motown. Lionel told a reporter in 1982: "Berry said, 'Listen, take three steps *back* and develop a following. And then, once you get somebody listening to your music, then you can take them anywhere you want to take them.' "

*Lionel Richie* did just that. The singer/songwriter stayed within the acceptable confines of a "Commodores" sound, but still established himself as a distinct solo artist. The album's first single hit number one [see 563—"Truly"] and confirmed Richie's status as an individual.

On his second album, *Can't Slow Down*, Richie explored new territory. One song was a joyous celebration with Carribean influences and lots of partying, "All Night Long (All Night)." Paul Sexton of *Record Mirror* asked Richie about the words, "Tom bo li de say di moi ya, yeah, jambo, jumbo." Lionel replied, "If you go back and try to find out what it means, it's like most of (Bob) Marley's chants, they don't really mean anything, but you know what they mean—you know what I'm saying? It's an old Jamaican chant." To perfect the pronunciation of the Jamaican words, Richie located an unusual source. He told *USA Today*, "I was worried about getting the right words and about pronouncing them right. My wife's gynecologist is Jamaican, so for a week I was after him. Finally he said, 'Look, Lionel, I'm right in the middle of an appointment, can we talk later?' "

"All Night Long (All Night)" entered the Hot 100 at number 62 on September 17, 1983, and worked its way to number one eight weeks later. In early 1984, Lionel received a request to perform at the closing ceremonies of the Olympic Games in Los Angeles. His televised appearance would be seen by more than 2.6 billion people in 120 countries. Richie hesitated: superstardom was here and he was shaken. He consulted with his friend Kenny Rogers [see 533—"Lady"].

Rogers told Richie's biographer, Roberta Plutznik, "Lionel's problem is like that of every person who is new to superstardom. They think fans and producers are going to hate them if they say no. It's just not true. People understand. I said to Lionel, 'You have a tremendous responsibility to yourself.' "

The initial request had been for Richie to perform with other artists. But when Diana Ross and Michael Jackson passed, the Olympic Committee had a new offer for Richie: to sing "All Night Long (All Night)" solo. He couldn't say no.

Described by the producer of the event, David Wolper, as an evening of "majesty . . . inspiration . . . emotion," the closing ceremonies were more like *Close Encounters of the Third Kind* than a climax to a sporting competition. Wolper secured a replica of the *Close Encounters* alien mothership and had it descend into the stadium, depositing a 10-foot high alien near the Olympic torch. His arms stretched out in a gesture of friendship and a two-minute laser extravaganza followed, concluding with the illumination of a center stage, revealing Lionel Richie and 200 break-dancers. He sang an extended version of "All Night Long" (including a special verse in honor of the Olympics) as athletes from all nations joined him on stage.

The event can best be summed up with Lionel's well-known one-word exclamation: "Outrageous!"

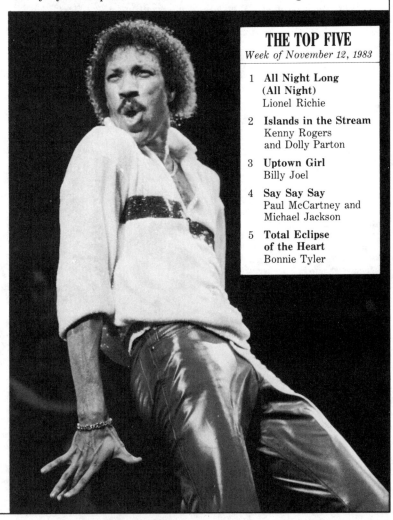

### THE TOP FIVE
*Week of November 12, 1983*

1 **All Night Long (All Night)**
Lionel Richie

2 **Islands in the Stream**
Kenny Rogers
and Dolly Parton

3 **Uptown Girl**
Billy Joel

4 **Say Say Say**
Paul McCartney and
Michael Jackson

5 **Total Eclipse of the Heart**
Bonnie Tyler

COLUMBIA 04168 **Say, Say, Say** 581
PAUL McCARTNEY AND MICHAEL JACKSON

*Writers: Paul McCartney*
*Michael Jackson*

*Producer: George Martin*

*December 10, 1983*
*6 weeks*

BY the time they recorded "Say, Say, Say," Paul McCartney and Michael Jackson had recorded between them 37 number one singles. You didn't need a computer to predict that "Say, Say, Say" had every chance of hitting the top as well. The single entered *Billboard's* Hot 100 on October 15, 1983, at number 26, the highest new entry since John Lennon's "Imagine" debuted at number 20 on October 23, 1971. Eight weeks after its debut, "Say, Say, Say" was number one.

In an interview recorded for "Paul McCartney: The Beatles and Beyond," a three-hour radio special broadcast on the Mutual Radio Network, Paul explained how the two artists decided to collaborate: "Michael originally rang me up on Christmas day . . . and I didn't believe it was him. I didn't think it was Michael . . . eventually I said, 'Is that really you?' He was laughing on the phone, he said, 'You don't believe me, do you?' "

Once identities were established, Michael told Paul why he was calling. "It turned out that he . . . fancied coming over to England. I think he had some time off, and he fancied trying to write some stuff with me. I said well, you know, great. Let me think about it . . . and I thought about it and thought well, why not? I

## THE TOP FIVE

*Week of December 10, 1983*

1  **Say, Say, Say**
   Paul McCartney and
   Michael Jackson

2  **All Night Long (All Night)**
   Lionel Richie

3  **Uptown Girl**
   Billy Joel

4  **Say It Isn't So**
   Hall & Oates

5  **Love is a Battlefield**
   Pat Benatar

admire him a lot, I really like his singing and his dancing and his musical abilities."

The first record released by McCartney and Jackson was "The Girl Is Mine," a track on Michael's *Thriller* LP. The first single from the album, it spent three weeks at number two in January, 1983. Two more McCartney-Jackson collaborations appeared on Paul's *Pipes of Peace* album: "Say, Say, Say" and "The Man." George Martin, producer of *Pipes of Peace*, talked about working with Michael on "The National Music Survey," hosted by Dick Clark: "He actually does radiate an aura when he comes into the studio, there's no question about it. . . . He's not a musician in the sense that Paul is, he's not a great keyboard player, or guitar player . . . but he does know what he wants in music and he has very firm ideas."

"Say, Say, Say" was on the Hot 100 concurrently with "P.Y.T. (Pretty Young Thing)," the sixth single from *Thriller*. That gave Michael a total of seven top 10 singles in a

calendar year, the most anyone has achieved since the Beatles logged 11 top 10 hits in 1964.

McCartney's follow-up to "Say, Say, Say" was "So Bad," a track from *Pipes of Peace* that only managed to reach number 23 in February, 1984. Curiously, the flip side, the title track from the album, was the "A" side in Britain, where it became McCartney's first solo number one single in his home country.

McCartney closed out 1984 with his first feature-length motion picture since *Let It Be.* The critics didn't care much for *Give My Regards to Broad Street,* but it did produce a hit single in "No More Lonely Nights" (number six in December, 1984).

In November of 1984, Paul returned to the city of his birth to receive a long overdue honor. The city council presented him with the Freedom of Liverpool award in a ceremony at the Picton Library. "I have never seen him so nervous," Linda McCartney told a reporter. "He was like he was on his wedding day."

## 582 Owner of a Lonely Heart ATCO 99817
### YES

*Writers: Trevor Rabin*
*Jon Anderson*
*Chris Squire*
*Trevor Horn*

*Producer: Trevor Horn*

*January 21, 1984*
*2 weeks*

A FAMILY tree illustrating the history of Yes would be one of the more complicated genealogies of the rock era, taking the group from its 1968 origin in London to its 1984 triumph on the American Hot 100.

Vocalist/percussionist Jon Anderson and bassist Chris Squire met at a pub popular with the music industry in 1968. They formed a band with guitarist Peter Banks, keyboardist Tony Kaye and drummer Bill Bruford. Opening for Cream's farewell concert in November, the band was hailed by critics as the next supergroup.

Banks was replaced by Steve Howe and the group had their first chart single in America, "Your Move" (number 40 in December, 1971). Then Kaye departed and Rick Wakeman, formerly of the Strawbs, brought his complex musical style to Yes. The group had their biggest American hit yet, "Roundabout" (number 13 in April, 1972). Bruford was the next defector, leaving for King Crimson. Alan White, a session drummer who had played in the Plastic Ono Band with John Lennon, became the new-

est Yes man. Wakeman departed, was replaced by Patrick Moraz, and then returned. Anderson went his own way and Yes made the most radical change yet, absorbing Trevor Horn and Geoff Downes, who as the Buggles had scored a British number one, "Video Killed the Radio Star."

That incarnation of Yes recorded one album and broke up. Squire and White recorded on their own, then approached South African guitarist Trevor Rabin about forming a new band, to be called Cinema. Rabin, a classically-trained musician, had been a star in his own country as part of a band called Rabbit. Unhappy with apartheid, he moved to England in 1977. He recorded as a solo artist for Chrysalis without great success, but turned down a chance to join Downes and Howe in Asia ("Heat of the Moment"). He passed up a solo contract with RCA to become part of Cinema.

Kaye became the fourth member of Cinema and Horn, who had been producing artists like ABC ("The Look of Love") and Dollar ("Give Me Back My Heart"), was brought in to produce the *90125* album, named after its catalogue number. Rabin used some of his solo material as the basis for the album, but something was missing. The group approached Anderson, who agreed to join them. They re-recorded some of the tracks with Anderson replacing Rabin on vocals. At this point, it seemed ridiculous to call the band Cinema when

they had unintentionally re-formed Yes.

The new Yes was more pop-oriented than the band of old, which was often criticized for being overindulgent and pretentious. "The other night Jon was telling me that in the old days the crowd was 99 per cent guys, with long hair and beards, but now the crowd is hipper," Rabin told Dennis Hunt in the *Los Angeles Times.*

While still including old Yes songs in their concerts, Rabin told Hunt, "We bring a new sound and style to it. I think most of the old fans have accepted the fact that Yes isn't what it used to be. But I'm sure there are some who resent the changes. We can't really worry about those people. We hate to lose them, but what can we do?"

### THE TOP FIVE
*Week of January 21, 1984*

1 **Owner of a Lonely Heart**
Yes

2 **Say Say Say**
Paul McCartney and
Michael Jackson

3 **Karma Chameleon**
Culture Club

4 **Talking in Your Sleep**
The Romantics

5 **Break my Stride**
Matthew Wilder

*Writers: George O'Dowd
        Jon Moss
        Roy Hay
        Mikey Craig
        Phil Pickett*

*Producer: Steve Levine*

*February 4, 1984
3 weeks*

OVER LUNCH at the San Lorenzo restaurant in London, Boy George discussed the cryptic "Karma Chameleon" with Robert Hilburn of the *Los Angeles Times*: "It's so stupid when people say that the song isn't about anything. It's about this terrible fear of alienation that people have, the fear of standing up for one thing. It's about trying to suck up to everybody, 'Oh yes, I agree with you.' What we're saying in the song is, if you aren't true, if you don't act like you feel, then you get karma—justice. That's nature's way of paying you back."

"Karma Chameleon" was Culture Club's biggest record in their homeland as well as their only number one single in America. In Britain, it was number one for five weeks and the best-selling 45 of 1983. In America, it was their fifth consecutive top 10 single. The first two American releases, "Do You Really Want to Hurt Me" and "Time (Clock of the Heart)," both peaked at number two on the Hot 100. When "I'll Tumble 4 Ya," also from their first LP *Kissing to Be Clever*, went to number 9, they became the first act since the Beatles to pull three top 10 singles from a debut album (an achievement that

was surpassed a few months later by Cyndi Lauper [see 589—"Time After Time"]).

Considering the amount of media coverage given to Boy George, it's easy to forget that Culture Club is a band made up of four people. George told Stephen Holden of the *New York Times*: "Our name came from the fact that we're four people from four different cultures, myself being Irish, Jon (Moss) being Jewish, Mikey (Craig) being of Jamaican descent and Roy (Hay) being a very English boy."

George Alan O'Dowd was born in South London on June 14, 1961, while the number one song in America was "Travelin' Man" by Ricky Nelson [see 90]. Asked why he first started wearing make-up, George told ABC-TV's Barbara Walters: "When I was in school, I found the whole environment...very boring and I realized there wasn't really any way you could say to people look at me...unless you were violent or agressive there was no way of being heard and it was my way I suppose of getting attention in the beginning."

George's first musical incarnation was Lieutenant Lush, recruited to sing with Bow Wow Wow by manager Malcolm McLaren. A photo of George with Bow Wow Wow's lead vocalist Annabella in the *New Musical Express* caught the eye of Mikey Craig (born February 15, 1960, in the Hammersmith section of London). A mutual friend introduced them, and with John 'Suede' they formed a band, the Sex Gang Children (a name since passed on to another group). Another friend suggested that

George contact drummer Jon Moss (born September 11, 1957, in Wandsworth, London), who had played with bands as diverse as Phone Bone Boulevard, Eskimo Norbert and the Clash. When 'Suede' was fired, auditions were held for a new guitarist, and the winner was Roy Hay (born August 12, 1961, in Southend, London).

The first gig took place in October, 1981, at Crocs, a club in Rayleigh, Essex. When they returned to Crocs two months later, they were seen by Danny Goodwin of Virgin Records, who offered them a chance to record a demo tape—which led to their signing with the label. Their first two British singles ("White Boy," "I'm Afraid of Me") failed to chart, but once "Do You Really Want to Hurt Me" became their first British number one in October, 1983, Culture Club was ready for cameras to go crazy.

## THE TOP FIVE
*Week of February 4, 1984*

1 **Karma Chameleon**
  Culture Club

2 **Owner of a Lonely Heart**
  Yes

3 **Talking in Your Sleep**
  The Romantics

4 **Joanna**
  Kool & the Gang

5 **Break my Stride**
  Matthew Wilder

## 584 Jump WARNER BROTHERS 29384
### VAN HALEN

*Writers: Edward Van Halen*
*Alex Van Halen*
*Michael Anthony*
*David Lee Roth*

*Producer: Ted Templeman*

*February 25, 1984*
*5 weeks*

Eddie Van Halen wrote the music for "Jump" two years before David Lee Roth agreed to write the lyrics and record it. "Man, there is so much music, so many snippets of good riffs and bad riffs—who knows what is getting thrown out after awhile?" Roth asked in *Musician*.

Producer Ted Templeman remembers the first time he heard the instrumental track that became "Jump." "Eddie wrote this thing on synthesizer. I really hadn't heard it for a long time, then he laid it down one night in the studio they have at Ed's house. I went in the next day, I heard it and it just killed me. It was perfect. And I played it for the people at Warner Brothers, just the track, there wasn't a song, it was just his synthesizer part. And everybody at Warners flipped out and we went in and cut the track the same way, almost identical."

Roth told *Musician* how he came up with the lyrics for "Jump" and the other songs on the band's *1984* album: "I wrote them in the back of a 1951 Mercury lowrider. I'd call up Larry the roadie, he'd show up after lunch, we'd hop in the car and go driving all through the Hollywood Hills, up the Coast highway, through the San Fernando Valley. I'd sit in back and write the words for whatever music I had on the cassette. Every hour and a half or so, I'd lean over the front seat and say, 'Lar, what do you think of this?' He's probably the most responsible for how it came out."

Van Halen had charted 11 singles on the Hot 100 without going top 10. A cover version of Roy Orbison's "Oh, Pretty Woman" [see 157] was their biggest hit (number 12 in April, 1982). "Jump" was an out-of-the-box smash, debuting at number 47 and hitting number one six weeks later.

Eddie (born January 26, 1957) and Alex Van Halen (born May 8, 1955) moved from their native Holland to Pasadena, California, in 1968. Trained in classical music as children, they turned to rock and roll once they were living in America. At first Eddie played the drums and Alex played the guitar, but they switched instruments and formed a band at Pasadena High School called Mammoth. Michael Anthony (born June 20, 1955, in Chicago) attended nearby Arcadia High School and led a rival band before joining the Van Halens. David Lee Roth (born October 10, 1955, in Bloomington, Indiana) was a student at Pasadena's Muir High School, and played in another local teenaged band.

"But I wanted to get serious about it," he told Robert Hilburn in a 1978 *Los Angeles Times* interview. "I wanted to be in a real band, make records, travel and do all that stuff. The Van Halens were always around. We were arch rivals, so it was only natural that we should eventually get together."

They shook the staid city of Pasadena with their hard rock and played local clubs in Van Nuys, Glendora and Redondo Beach. Gene Simmons of Kiss helped them make a demo tape and told Warner Brothers about them. As a result, company chairman Mo Ostin and producer Templeman caught their act at the Starwood club and signed them to a contract.

After the success of "Jump," David Lee Roth stepped out for a solo project. With Carl Wilson's assistance, he covered the Beach Boys' "California Girls" and matched their chart peak position of number three. A disciple of Al Jolson ("I learned all his greatest hits by the time I was seven. And ever since I've known that I would make music onstage"), Roth next released a medley of "Just a Gigolo/I Ain't Got Nobody," which cracked the top 15 in May, 1985.

### THE TOP FIVE
*Week of February 25, 1984*

1 **Jump**
Van Halen

2 **Karma Chameleon**
Culture Club

3 **99 Luftballons**
Nena

4 **Girls Just Want to Have Fun**
Cyndi Lauper

5 **Thriller**
Michael Jackson

Writers: *Kenny Loggins*
*Dean Pitchford*

Producers: *Kenny Loggins*
*Lee DeCarlo*

*March 31, 1984*
*3 weeks*

**T**HE first number one soundtrack single of 1984 was the title tune from *Footloose*, sung by Kenny Loggins. Before the year was over, the films *Against All Odds*, *Purple Rain*, *Ghostbusters* and *The Woman in Red* would also provide chart-topping singles. And for the first time during the rock era, all five songs nominated for an Oscar for Best Song would be number one singles [see 596—"I Just Called to Say I Love You"].

Screenwriter Dean Pitchford knew right from the beginning of his project that he wanted Kenny Loggins, who had already recorded Pitchford's "Don't Fight It," to sing the main title theme to *Footloose*. "It felt to me he was like the voice of the country, America," Pitchford told Dick Clark on "The National Music Survey." "It felt raucous and joyous and there was a hopefulness in what he was doing."

Pitchford, an Oscar winner with Michael Gore for writing "Fame" in 1980, worked for two years on the script for *Footloose*. "(Loggins) persevered wih me through script after script after script. He read all the revisions. He'd make notes and we'd talk about the characters. . . . He was very much around when the whole thing was coming together."

Just prior to their writing the song "Footloose," both men suffered setbacks. Loggins walked off a darkened stage in Provo, Utah, and broke some ribs. Pitchford came down with a virulent form of flu. But there was a deadline to meet for writing the song. Kenny recovered enough to perform and headed to Lake Tahoe, Nevada, for a concert. Dean, suffering through a 103° temperature and strep throat met him there.

"I couldn't let Kenny know (I was sick) because I didn't want him to say, 'Whoa! He's got strep throat and I have a show to do'. . . . So it was a very funny scene because Kenny would come to my hotel room and he'd sit there (wincing in pain from the mending ribs) and I was sitting in the corner, trying desperately not to look like I was running a temperature. . . . Somehow we wrote

'Footloose' in four days in this unbelievable pain."

The two songwriters were certain they had a hit when Loggins included the song in his concert performances before the film was released. "The crowds instantly got into it," Loggins recalled, "even though they'd never heard the song before."

Loggins, born January 7, 1948, in Everett, Washington, moved to Seattle with his family and then to Alhambra in southern California. While attending Pasadena City College, he realized he wanted to pursue music professionally. He played with a band called Second Helping, then got a job with a music publisher. He toured briefly with the Electric Prunes ("I Had Too Much to Dream Last Night") and started writing songs. His first hit was "House at Pooh Corner," recorded by the Nitty Gritty Dirt Band in 1971. In September of that year, Loggins signed with Columbia Records and met ex-Buffalo Springfield member Jim Messina. They decided to work together on Kenny's first solo LP, but they both recognized Loggins' need for guidance and Messina sat in on the recording. The result: *Kenny Loggins With Jim Messina: Sittin' In*. Their partnership lasted from 1972-1975 and resulted in 10 chart singles, with "Your Mama Don't Dance" (number four in January, 1973) being the most successful.

Going their separate ways in 1975, Loggins charted on his own with hits like "This Is It" and "I'm Alright," from *Caddyshack*. He also found one-time-only partners like Stevie Nicks ("Whenever I Call You Friend") and Steve Perry ("Don't Fight It").

## THE TOP FIVE
*Week of March 31, 1984*

1 **Footloose**
  Kenny Loggins

2 **Somebody's Watching Me**
  Rockwell

3 **Jump**
  Van Halen

4 **Here Comes The Rain Again**
  Eurythmics

5 **Girls Just Want to Have Fun**
  Cyndi Lauper

## 586   Against All Odds (Take a Look at Me Now)   ATLANTIC 89700
### PHIL COLLINS

*Writer: Phil Collins*

*Producer: Arif Mardin*

*April 21, 1984*
*3 weeks*

PHIL COLLINS rearranged his tour schedule so he would be available when the Academy of Motion Picture Arts and Sciences asked him to sing his Oscar-nominated song "Against All Odds (Take a Look at Me Now)" during the 57th annual Academy Awards ceremony. He needn't have bothered—the call never came.

"It's a terrible mistake. I'm dumbfounded," was the comment from *Against All Odds* director Taylor Hackford to *Daily Variety*. "As the original composer and a fabulous performer, I think it's only fitting that he do the song." Gary Le Mel, senior vice president of music for Columbia Pictures, echoed Hackford's sentiments. "Why wouldn't they want to use the real thing?" he queried. "I can only imagine they don't understand who Phil Collins is, how big he is. The producers of the (Oscar) show are all older guys."

Le Mel was apparently correct. Larry Gelbart, writer and co-producer of the awards telecast, had already responded to a letter from Paul Cooper, vice president of Atlantic Records, who suggested Collins for the show. "Thank you for your note regarding Phil Cooper," Gelbart wrote. "I'm afraid the spots have already been filled." Kathy Orloff, head of publicity for Columbia Pictures, told *Daily Variety* that when Oscar producer Gregory Peck called her to see if Ray Parker, Jr., would sing his nominated song [see 592— "Ghostbusters"], she mentioned that Collins would be available, too. "He didn't seem to know who Phil Collins was," she said.

Two days later, *Daily Variety* quoted Peck: "We know Phil Collins and we admire Phil Collins. It's just that we decided early on that we would not be using five recording artists....It's pure showmanship. We want variety." Peck told the *Los Angeles Times* that the Academy had no interest in promoting recording artists and preferred to use film people (apparently he didn't realize Collins had been an extra in the concert scenes of *A Hard Day's Night*).

*Daily Variety* also reported that Cher [see 301—"Gypsys, Tramps and Thieves"] was the first choice to sing "Against All Odds" on the telecast, but declined because she was busy promoting her film *Mask*. Finally selected was Ann Reinking (*All That Jazz, Annie*), who lip synched the song while performing a dance routine. Collins watched from the audience.

There was no question about who was Hackford's first choice to sing the title song for the film, which starred Jeff Bridges and Rachel Ward. Hackford told Dick Clark in an interview for "The National Music Survey": "Phil was my only choice." When a deal was signed with Atlantic Records to release the soundtrack, Hackford looked down their artist roster and chose Collins. "I wanted him to do it. At the time it was very difficult, because he was on tour with Genesis [see 604—"One More Night"]. His solo career and his Genesis career were very separate and I had to do a lot of convincing. I flew to Chicago—they were performing at a big amphitheatre in Chicago—I saw the concert, I met him, I went to his hotel room, I showed him the film and he did want to do it after we talked."

Collins wrote the song and record producer Arif Mardin recorded the strings and piano tracks in New York. When Collins was in Los Angeles on the Genesis tour, he came into a studio and laid down his vocal track and a drum track in one day. Hackford calls the entire affair "a textbook case of designing a song to fit a film, designing the lyrics to reflect what the film is, having the title of the song be the title of the film—and when it went out into the marketplace, I think it decidedly helped the film. People heard it and liked the song, they identified it with the film and they came to see the film."

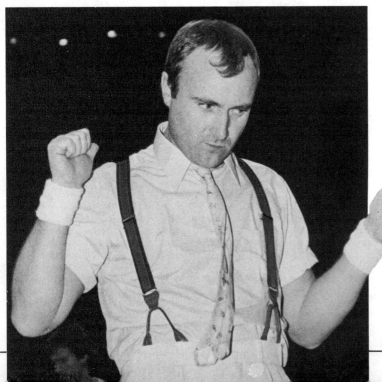

### THE TOP FIVE
*Week of April 21, 1984*

1. **Against All Odds (Take a Look at Me Now)**
   Phil Collins

2. **Footloose**
   Kenny Loggins

3. **Hello**
   Lionel Richie

4. **Hold Me Now**
   Thompson Twins

5. **Miss Me Blind**
   Culture Club

*Writer: Lionel Richie*

*Producers: Lionel Richie*
*James Anthony*
*Carmichael*

*May 12, 1984*
*2 weeks*

Lionel Richie told a reporter in 1982 how he developed as a ballad writer: "If you can imagine a Commodores album session and every guy brings in 10 songs. Somebody's got to be first and somebody's got to be last. Over the years, I made myself the last person to present the songs. Normally, everybody would bring in an uptempo song and I'd always say, 'This album needs one slow song.' That's how the slow songs came into play."

"Hello" was another ballad in the Lionel Richie tradition of love and positive sentimentality. The song had been written initially for his first solo LP, *Lionel Richie*, but was rejected despite the protests of Lionel's wife, Brenda Richie, and Rita Leigh, assistant to producer James Anthony Carmichael. "Hello" almost didn't make it onto Richie's second album, *Can't Slow Down*, but this time

Brenda insisted it be included.

The video for "Hello" was surprising and innovative. Richie and manager Ken Kragen contacted Bob Giraldi, television commercial wizard and the director of videos for Michael Jackson's "Beat It," Pat Benatar's "Love Is a Battlefield" and Paul McCartney and Michael Jackson's "Say, Say, Say." Giraldi had also directed Lionel's "Running with the Night" video, which whetted Richie's appetite for acting. In "Hello," Richie plays a drama teacher, Mr. Reynolds, who falls in love with a student he sees in class. Loving her from a distance, he cannot bring himself to express his love. When he drops in on a sculpture class, he discovers his love has sculpted a bust of how she sees him. The twist: she is blind.

"Hello" is the sixth number one single of Lionel's career. That total includes two with the Commodores, one with Diana Ross and two on his own. Every one of his eight solo singles have made the top 10, beginning with "Truly" [see 563] and continuing through 1983's "You Are" (number four in March), "My Love" (number five in June), "All Night Long (All Night)" [see 580] and 1984's "Running with the Night" (number seven in

February), "Stuck on You" (number three in August) and "Penny Lover" (number eight in August).

The awards for Lionel Richie have not stopped coming. *Can't Slow Down* won a Grammy for Album of the Year; ASCAP named him the Writer of the Year; and he walked away with six trophies at the American Music Awards in 1985, the second year in a row he had been the sole host of the three-hour telecast. The first time he hosted the AMAs, the program became the highest-rated music awards show of all time.

The financial rewards for Richie keep coming, too. In 1984, Richie signed a contract with the soft drink corporation Pepsico for a reputed $8.5 million. In return, Richie wrote songs and performed in Pepsi's television commercials. In negotiating the deal, Richie was promised that Pepsico would join him in contributing to charitable organizations. Richie told Robert E. Johnson in a January, 1985, interview for *Ebony*: "I want to make more than music. I want to make statements and I also want to make changes in areas such as minority education. For a long time, I have had an interest in talented kids with no opportunities. Unlike a lot of corporations that merely pay lip service, Pepsi has signed on the dotted line to do something about it."

Richie's social commitment went further than his concern for education. In 1985, he was a major force behind the union of recording artists who raised millions of dollars to help feed the starving people of Africa and America [see 605—"We Are the World"].

## THE TOP FIVE
*Week of May 12, 1984*

1 **Hello**
  Lionel Richie

2 **Against All Odds**
  **(Take a Look at Me Now)**
  Phil Collins

3 **Hold Me Now**
  Thompson Twins

4 **Let's Hear It For The Boy**
  Deniece Williams

5 **Love Somebody**
  Rick Springfield

## 588 Let's Hear It for the Boy COLUMBIA 04417
### DENIECE WILLIAMS

*Writers: Tom Snow*
*Dean Pitchford*

*Producer: George Duke*

*May 26, 1984*
*2 weeks*

"LET'S HEAR IT FOR THE BOY" was the second number one single from the soundtrack of *Footloose*, a motion picture that produced five top 40 hits, a record matched only by *Xanadu* and *Saturday Night Fever*. It's also the first solo number one single for Deniece Williams, who topped the chart in a duet with Johnny Mathis in 1978 [see 483—"Too Much, Too Little, Too Late"].

Anyone who saw "Footloose" would agree the song perfectly matched its sequence, where Kevin Bacon taught an awkward Christopher Penn how to dance. But for eight months of production, another song was slated to be used for this scene, and it was only a last minute change by screenwriter and lyricist Dean Pitchford that inserted the Deniece Williams song into the soundtrack.

As for the original song, Pitchford explains: "Everyone loved it at the beginning, but like any hit song played for eight months, we all grew tired of it and wanted new blood. I went back to Tom Snow and said, 'Tom, we have to do it again.' One night I went to his house for dinner and we worked late. I said I wanted something uplifting, a girl singing about how good her boyfriend is, even though he trips over his own two feet, and she gets to the point

### THE TOP FIVE
*Week of May 26, 1984*

1 **Let's Hear It For The Boy**
Deniece Williams

2 **Hello**
Lionel Richie

3 **Time After Time**
Cyndi Lauper

4 **Against All Odds
(Take a Look at Me Now)**
Phil Collins

5 **Oh, Sherrie**
Steve Perry

where she says, 'let's hear it for the boy!'" Suddenly, Pitchford and Snow knew they had something. They worked the rest of the night writing the song.

Pitchford had almost worked with Williams on the title song for Tom Selleck's film, *High Road to China*—except in the final print, there was no title song. He invited her and producer George Duke to hear the song for *Footloose*.

"We heard the song and liked it. Everyone else had seen the film," says Deniece, who hadn't. "They explained the storyline to me and we did it."

The first recording did not match Dean's expectations for the song. "Deniece sang it very girlish. I think she took the 'boy' very seriously. I called her and said, 'Deniece, this is not a girl, this is a woman!' But Deniece was now in New York, and had to fly back to Los Angeles to re-record the song. Because of deadlines, she was rushed from the airport, without having time to pick up her luggage, to the recording studio. It was 11 p.m. on the west coast, but Deniece was on east coast time.

"In 20 minutes, she recut it brilliantly," says Pitchford. "When she finished we all looked at each other,

and knew this is what it was meant to be."

But Deniece had to wait for the premiere of the film to know where her song was placed. "I sat there the whole time on pins and needles," she laughs. "By the time they got to my song, I thought it was incredible. If I had come to the film without the music in and they asked me what segment I wanted my song to be in, I would have chosen that segment."

Although some critics in metropolitan cities claimed the film's premise of dancing being banned in a rural, midwestern town rang false, Deniece doesn't agree. "I'm a product of that same type of environment. *Footloose* is really a story closely knitted to my growing up in Indiana in a very religious environment and wanting to do something different. I had had a couple of successes and still didn't know whether or not I wanted this career. It came from thinking I was doing something wrong against God."

Deniece says she finally had the realization that "He had given me this talent to do exactly what I'm doing. It's a gift, and I think it would be worse if I weren't using it. But that...was really a long time in coming."

# Time After Time
### CYNDI LAUPER

**589**

*Writers: Cyndi Lauper*
*Rob Hyman*

*Producer: Rick Chertoff*

*June 9, 1984*
*2 weeks*

"I'M not *trying* to be different," Cyndi Lauper told *Newsweek*, the magazine that called her a "new-wave Gracie Allen." "I'm just saying it's OK to be yourself, and if you have a few quirky things, that's OK, too."

It was a lesson hard-learned. Growing up in Queens, New York, Cyndi didn't understand the creativity burning inside her and simply thought she was crazy or stupid. Or both. It would be a long time before she would know herself well enough to tell Kurt Loder in *Rolling Stone*: "I always wanted to make world music—to say something that's worth sayin' and really touch humanity. That's why I'm here."

Cyndi's first taste of international success came with "Girls Just Want to have Fun," an ebullient song that went to number two on the Hot 100 and branded her in the eyes of some as a clever novelty who would fade after one hit. But there were emotions and dreams yet to be revealed. Her next single was the poignant "Time After Time," composed in the studio with keyboardist Rob Hyman. It was the last song written for Cyndi's *She's So Unusual* LP. The autobiographical video that accompanied the song featured the cast of Cyndi's life: her mother, Catrine Domenique; her boyfriend/manager, Dave Wolff; and her "mentor," Cap-

tain Lou Albano of the World Wrestling Federation, an organization that would profit as much as anyone from Cyndi's fame.

Cynthia Lauper was born June 20, 1953, in Boulevard Hospital in Queens, just a few miles from her parents' home in the Williamsburg section of Brooklyn. When her parents divorced, five-year-old Cyndi went to live in Queens with her mother, older sister Elen and younger brother Butch.

Her school years were difficult, and 17-year-old Cyndi decided to leave home and hitchhike through Canada with her dog, Sparkle. That adventure was followed by a year of art studies at a Vermont college, but that didn't fulfill Cyndi's creative needs either.

She returned to New York and sang with Doc West, a band from Long Island. She also worked as a secretary, sold karate lessons and walked horses at Belmont Park. Then she joined another Long Island band, Flyer, and continued singing cover versions of Rod Stewart and Janis Joplin songs until her voice gave out.

Doctors told her she would never sing again, but a friend suggested she see a vocal coach, Katie Agresta. After a year of training, Cyndi recovered her voice.

Lauper was singing at a Manhattan club in 1978 when she was introduced to musician John Turi. They formed a group, Blue Angel, and were signed to Polydor Records. A debut album in 1980 attracted critical raves, but disagreements with their manager and record label led to a break-up of the band. Cyndi sang at a Japanese piano bar and worked in an upper west side boutique called Screaming Mimi's, where she found the fashions to her liking.

During this period she met Wolff, who became her manager and signed her to CBS' Portrait label.

The winner of a Grammy for Best New Artist of 1984, Lauper's subsequent singles helped set new records. When "Time After Time" went to number one, she became the first female since Petula Clark [see 165—"Downtown"] to have her first two chart entries make the top three. The follow-up, "She Bop," went to number three and thus bested Petula's achievement. When Cyndi's next single, "All Through the Night," went to number five, she became the first artist in the rock era to pull four top 10 singles from a debut album.

## THE TOP FIVE
### *Week of June 9, 1984*

1  **Time After T ime**
   Cyndi Lauper

2  **Let's Hear It For The Boy**
   Deniece Williams

3  **Oh, Sherrie**
   Steve Perry

4  **The Reflex**
   Duran Duran

5  **Sister Christian**
   Night Ranger

**590** **The Reflex** CAPITOL 5345
DURAN DURAN

*Writer: Duran Duran*

*Producers: Alex Sadkin*
*Ian Little*
*Duran Duran*

*June 23, 1984*
*2 weeks*

RECORDED originally for their *Seven and the Ragged Tiger* album, "The Reflex" sounded too much like an album track to release as a single, according to Duran Duran co-founder Nick Rhodes. Always inspired by the sleek style of Chic [see 495—"Le Freak"], the band turned to Nile Rodgers to remix the song for single release. The result: their first American number one.

Duran Duran was formed in 1978 as a reaction to the punk-drenched British rock scene. Led by Rhodes (synthesizer and rhythm box) and John Taylor (then lead guitar), they quickly became a big attraction in their hometown of Birmingham. Performing mostly at the chic Barbarellas club, the band appropriately took their name from the villain in Jane Fonda's 1968 movie Barbarella (second choice for a moniker was R.A.F.).

When the bass player and lead singer left the group, Nick and John recruited drummer Roger Taylor (no relation to John). Inspired by Roger's Chic-fashioned drumming, John swapped his guitar for a bass and the band went searching for a new singer and a "live-wire" guitarist. During the next couple of years, they went through 10 singers and 20 guitarists.

Recalled Rhodes, "It was a hellish experience."

An advertisement in *Melody Maker* attracted guitarist Andy Taylor (no relation to John or Roger), who fit in perfectly with the band's developing "New Romantic" image of frilly clothes and semi-funky sounds. Meanwhile, Duran Duran signed with a pair of enterprising brothers, Paul and Michael Berrow, who had just opened the Rum Runner disco, a clone of Manhattan's Studio 54.

Still, the group had no lead singer—until a Rum Runner barmaid suggested her ex-boyfriend, a drama student at Birmingham University named Simon John Charles Le Bon. Sporting shades and pink leopard-skin trousers, Simon walked into rehearsal the next night and emerged as Duran's official lead singer.

Complete at last, the new Duran Duran were a hit at the 1980 Edinburgh Festival, and were signed to EMI the following year. Although the band immediately achieved superstar status in its native England, Duran fell on its face in America.

And then suddenly, MTV began playing the group's innovative videos ("Hungry Like the Wolf" was filmed in Sri Lanka and the award-winning "Rio" on the Caribbean island of Antigua). "Before that, radio wouldn't play us," Rhodes told Dennis Hunt of the *Los Angeles Times*. "But the reaction was so good on MTV that we got picked up by radio stations (in the United States). We always knew that all we needed was major exposure over here."

Aided by the heavy video play, Duran Duran became one of the most fanatically popular bands of the '80s, with female adulation approaching the intensity of Beatlemania. The band's string of top 10 hits included "Is There Something I Should Know" (number four), "Union of the Snake" (number three) and "New Moon on Monday" (number 10).

In 1985, Andy and John took a brief respite from Duran Duran and teamed up with singer Robert Palmer, and Tony Thompson and Bernard Edwards of Chic, to form the Power Station. John told Kim Freeman in *Billboard* that the project was a "good opportunity to improve our musical perspective." The one-time-only collaboration produced a top 10 single, "Some Like It Hot," but did not spell the end of Duran Duran. In addition to singing the title song for the James Bond film *From a View to a Kill*, Duran Duran recorded their fourth album under the production aegis of Bernard Edwards.

## THE TOP FIVE
*Week of June 23, 1984*

1 **The Reflex**
Duran Duran

2 **Time After Time**
Cyndi Lauper

3 **Let's Hear It For The Boy**
Deniece Williams

4 **Dancing in The Dark**
Bruce Springsteen

5 **Self Control**
Laura Branigan

WARNER BROTHERS 29286 **When Doves Cry** `591`
PRINCE

*Writer: Prince*

*Producer: Prince*

*July 7, 1984*
*5 weeks*

**F**EW PERFORMERS in recent rock annals have engendered the peculiar mix of controversy, mystique and popularity created by Prince Rogers Nelson, who once preferred to be known only by his forename because he "hated" his last. Termed at various times a prodigy, sinner, saint, genius or dictator, much of the confusion about his identity stemmed from his unwillingness to grant interviews.

Many answers to the puzzle were revealed in his closely autobiographical 1984 film debut, *Purple Rain*, though it's still a task separating fact from the fictional screenplay Prince fashioned with director Albert Magnoli.

Born June 7, 1960, to John and Mattie Nelson, the youngster spent his first 10 years in Minneapolis, Minnesota, with a musician father and a mother who had been a singer in his band. Music fascinated Prince at the early age of five. Still, the first time he could freely experiment on dad's piano was after his father moved out.

The teenaged Prince began a migratory home existence. "I ran away for the first time because of problems with my stepfather. I went to live with my real father, but that didn't last too long because he's as stubborn as I am. I lived with my aunt for a while. I was constantly running from family to family." Eventually he wound up in the basement of Bernadette Anderson, whose son, Andre Cymone, was Prince's best friend and later band mate. Outfitting the cellar in rabbit fur and mirrors, the visitor holed up there after finishing high school at age 16, writing as many as three or four songs a day. They were "sexual fantasies," as he described them to Barbara Graustark in *Musician*, "All fantasies. Because I didn't have anything around me . . . there were no people. No anything. When I started writing, I cut myself off from relationships with women."

He also taught himself guitar, keyboards, drums and just about any other instrument he could get his hands on (over 27 in all) so that when a local producer offered to trade free studio time for Prince's expertise on a commercial, the one-man band rapidly conceived his own demonstration tapes. Eventually they solicited him for a recording contract with Warner Brothers, the only company that would agree to the unknown 18-year-old's stipulation that he produce his record debut. *For You* ran ridiculously over its $100,000 budget, but the label still issued three more LPs to a steadily growing cult fascinated by the artist's twin themes of sex and loneliness.

*Purple Rain* was the first album on which Prince sought the collaboration of his band, formed for a 1978 tour. Written after the film was finished, "When Doves Cry" was recorded in Los Angeles at Sunset Sound. Engineer Peggy McCreary told *Musician*, "He doesn't make records like other people. He doesn't have any set hours and he doesn't have any set way of doing things. Nothing is normal." Prince eschews the usual recording technique of laying down basic tracks for several songs, overdubbing, vocal recording, then mixing as the final stage. "Prince does not do things that way," McCreary's engineer husband David Leonard elaborated in *Musician*. "He'll go into the studio with a song in his mind, record it, overdub it, sing it and mix it all in one shot, start to finish.

"When Doves Cry," the first single released from *Purple Rain*, debuted on the Hot 100 at number 57 on June 2, 1984, and took just six weeks to go to number one. *Billboard*'s year-end report revealed it was the number one single of 1984.

## THE TOP FIVE
*Week of July 7, 1984*

1 **When Doves Cry**
Prince

2 **Dancing in The Dark**
Bruce Springsteen

3 **Jump (For My Love)**
Pointer Sisters

4 **Self Control**
Laura Branigan

5 **The Reflex**
Duran Duran

# 592 Ghostbusters ARISTA 9212
## RAY PARKER, JR

*Writer: Ray Parker, Jr.*

*Producer: Ray Parker, Jr.*

*August 11, 1984*
*3 weeks*

"It's hard to write a song where your main objective is to use the word 'ghostbusters,'" Ray Parker, Jr., admitted to Craig Modderno for a *USA Today* story. "There aren't many words that rhyme with it." Parker did manage to write the theme song for one of the highest-grossing comedies of all time, an achievement which earned him an Academy Award nomination. "I figured the best thing to do was to have somebody shout, 'ghostbusters!' In order for that to work, I had to have something before it or after it. That's when I came up with the line, 'Who you gonna call?' I wanted to make a simple, easy song people could sing along with and not have to think about."

Ray was actively looking for a film project to work on—or star in—but nothing he screened raised his interest. "Then at the last minute, here comes *Ghostbusters*," he told Dick Clark in an interview for Mutual Broadcasting's "The National Music Survey." "They showed me the film and said, 'we have about 60 songs for this already, but we don't like any of them. Can you come up with one?'" The producers wanted something that was happy and funny with simple lyrics. Within two days, Ray had written and recorded the title song.

The next thing he knew, director Ivan Reitman (*Stripes*) was filming a video for the song, with cameo appearances by Carly Simon, Danny DeVito, Melissa Gilbert, Chevy Chase, Peter Falk and John Candy. The stars of *Ghostbusters*, Bill Murray and Dan Aykroyd, played their characters in the video, with Murray breakdancing on the streets of Manhattan.

"Ghostbusters" was the first number one single for Parker, whose chart career began in 1978 with the top 10 single "Jack and Jill." As leader of a group of musicians known as Raydio, Parker had two more top 10 hits, "You Can't Change That" and "A Woman Needs Love (Just Like You Do)." Going solo, he scored another top 10 single, "The Other Woman." But his musical career started long before he started having hit records under his own name.

Born in Detroit on May 1, 1954, Ray learned to play the clarinet when he was in first grade. He knew how to play several other instruments by the time he picked up the guitar at age 12. As a teenager, he toured with the Spinners and played in the house band at Detroit's 20 Grand club, where he backed artists like Stevie Wonder, the Temptations and Gladys Knight and the Pips. He became a prolific studio musician, working mostly for Brian Holland, Lamont Dozier and Eddie Holland's Invictus and Hot Wax labels. He played on sessions for Freda Payne, the Chairmen of the Board and a number one hit for the Honey Cone [see 293—"Want Ads"].

In 1972, Stevie Wonder asked Ray to join him on a tour with the Rolling Stones. After working on Wonder's *Talking Book* and *Innervisions* albums, Parker moved to Hollywood. He became a popular studio guitarist there, working with Barry White, Boz Scaggs, Gene Page and Labelle. His first success as a songwriter came when Rufus and Chaka Khan recorded his "You Got the Love," a number 11 hit in the closing months of 1974.

Ray switched over to Geffen for the *After Dark* album in 1987, and released *I Love You Like You Are* on MCA in 1991.

## THE TOP FIVE
*Week of August 11, 1984*

1 **Ghostbusters**
Ray Parker, Jr.

2 **When Doves Cry**
Prince

3 **State of Shock**
Jacksons

4 **What's Love Got to Do With It**
Tina Turner

5 **Sad Songs (Say So Much)**
Elton John

CAPITOL 5354 **What's Love Got to Do With It** `593`
TINA TURNER

*Writers: Terry Britten*
*Graham Lyle*

*Producer: Terry Britten*

*September 1, 1984*
*3 weeks*

TINA TURNER FIRST APPEARED on the Hot 100 with "A Fool in Love," recorded with her husband Ike. The single debuted on August 29, 1960. Twenty-four years later—to the week—Tina had her first number one single, "What's Love Got to Do With It." That set a new record for the longest amount of time between an artist's first appearance and their first number one hit, besting the previous record of 20 years and 11 months, set by Robert John [see 510—"Sad Eyes"].

Tina was born on November 26, 1939, in Nutbush, Tennessee. Her family's Baptist minister named her Annie Mae Bullock, and she grew up picking cotton on the plantation where her father was caretaker. Her parents divorced when she was a teen-ager, and Annie Mae went to live with her mother in St. Louis.

There was an after-hours night club called the Club Manhattan, and the hottest band in St. Louis played there—Ike Turner's. Annie Mae's sister was dating the drummer in the band and one night he came to the table and teased his girl with the microphone. Annie Mae grabbed the mike and started singing, and that's how she met Ike Turner, married him and launched a career as Tina Turner ("I chose Tina because it didn't sound very good—'Ladies and gentlemen, Annie Mae.' It had a sound—Ike and Tina.")

Ike and Tina had some R&B hits in the '60s, and in early 1966 they appeared in a filmed rock show, "The TNT Show." The musical director was Phil Spector, who was so impressed with Tina that he signed the duo to his label, Philles Records. That resulted in a song that many critics believe is one of the highlights of both Phil and Tina's career—"River Deep, Mountain High," written by Jeff Barry, Ellie Greenwich and Spector.

In 1969, Ike and Tina signed with Blue Thumb Records, which issued a couple of bluesy soul albums that had mild success. They hit the peak of

their career together in the early '70s with Liberty Records and their biggest hit to date, a version of Creedence Clearwater Revival's "Proud Mary" that accelerated from "nice and easy" to "nice and rough" in three minutes and 15 seconds.

In 1973 the duo recorded the autobiographical "Nutbush City Limits," and a year later, Tina began making solo recordings. In 1975, film director Ken Russell cast her as the Acid Queen in the motion picture version of The Who's rock opera, *Tommy*.

Tina told USA Today reporter Steve Pond that she and Ike got along for the first seven years, but the marriage began to decay in the next seven years. Tina told Pond: "I didn't plan to leave, but finally there was one last bit of real violence and I walked." She had 36 cents, a gasoline charge card and the clothes she was wearing. She went to a Ramada Inn in Dallas, where the hotel manager gave her his best suite. Tina paid him back two years later.

She called Ann-Margret, who starred in *Tommy*, and asked her to buy an airline ticket to Los Angeles for Tina. She spent six months with Ann-Margret while Ike searched for her frantically. In 1976, they were divorced.

For eight years, Tina worked nine months out of 12 touring and earning enough money to pay off past debts. In

1982, the British band Heaven 17 asked Tina to participate in an album project by the British Electric Foundation. Greg Walsh and Martyn Ware produced a track for Tina—a new version of the Temptations' "Ball of Confusion." When Tina signed with Capitol Records, she turned to Walsh and Ware and asked them to produce a single. Their choice: an updating of Al Green's classic "Let's Stay Together." The song went top five in Britain and top 30 in America.

When it came time to record an album, Tina's manager, Roger Davies, brought in several producers. One of them was British songwriter Tery Britten. Tina heard his demo of "What's Love Got to Do With It," and hated it. She said so. "He said that when a song is given to an artist it's changed for the artist. He said for me he needed to make it a bit rougher, a bit more sharp around the edges. All of a sudden, just sitting there with him in the studio, the song became mine."

And number one. And the winner of Grammys for Record of the Year, Song of the Year, Pop Vocal Performance-Female and Rock Vocal Performance-Female. It was worth the wait.

### THE TOP FIVE
*Week of September 1, 1984*

1 **What's Love Got to do With It**
Tina Turner

2 **Missing You**
John Waite

3 **Stuck on You**
Lionel Richie

4 **Ghostbusters**
Ray Parker, Jr.

5 **When Doves Cry**
Prince

## 594 Missing You  EMI-AMERICA 8212
### JOHN WAITE

Writers: *John Waite*
        *C. Sandford*
        *M. Leonard*

Producers: *John Waite*
          *David Thoener*
          *Gary Gersh*

*September 22, 1984*
*1 week*

WHEN John Waite wrote "Missing You" he was "in the middle of a lot of personal stuff . . . I couldn't really explain or get the better of." It was written quickly, almost improvised, in a bedroom in Los Angeles. Someday he would like to release the demo version, which he believes has a superior vocal on it. "I was trying to sing this lyric and I'm just making it up as I go along. And it got to the point where it was really explaining a lot about myself, what I was thinking, what was on my mind that I didn't really want to admit to. Because if you admit to things like that you really just fall to pieces, I think. Guys especially try to maintain some sort of balance and strength by not admitting to it. I was saying, 'I'm alright' because I had to get the record finished. 'Missing You' is pure word association. I think all really great poetry or good rock and roll lyrics are all quite subconscious and that certainly was. It was like sleep-walking."

A former art student from Lancaster, England, Waite (born July 4, 1955) has been playing bass guitar and harmonica, and singing with rock and jazz bands since he was 14 years

old. In 1976 he co-founded the Babys, a name chosen as an ironic statement for a band playing raucous music.

From the beginning, the Babys were heavily marketed. Although the band was English, there was little effort spent on promoting them at home. They went right for the United States. The group spent $10,000 to make a video, an unusual concept for 1975, and used it to help them get a deal with Chrysalis Records. The label in turn used the video to help promote the band. The Baby's first big single, "Isn't It Time" (number 13 in December, 1977), was sung by Waite and foreshadowed his solo material, although it was in a very different style from the rest of the Babys' music.

Even in those days, Waite knew

### THE TOP FIVE
*Week of September 22, 1984*

1   **Missing You**
    John Waite

2   **Let's Go Crazy**
    Prince and the
    Revolution

3   **She Bop**
    Cyndi Lauper

4   **What's Love Got
    to do With It**
    Tina Turner

5   **Drive**
    The Cars

what was important to him. As he told Jim Jozlowski in *Rock Around the World* magazine, "When you come right down to it, being a great musician means nothing more than being proficient. To say something simply and mean it and to express it melodically means so much more."

After three albums, internal disputes broke the Babys up. Jonathan Cain went into Journey ("Who's Crying Now," "Open Arms") and the other members found work elsewhere. "I was the last person to make it out of the Babys," Waite told Jeff Sewald in *Bam*. "...And I think I was the least likely to succeed, too. I'm the most dangerous. I have a lot more personality....I moved to New York and took it from there. I think they were looking for security and I was looking for the truth."

John's first solo single, "Change," was more popular as a video than as a record. "Missing You," the first single from his second solo album, *No Brakes*, proved to be a more popular video than "Changes," and was given heavy rotation on MTV.

Television and video continue to be important to Waite. He sang bits of "Missing You" on the "Paper Dolls" series, in which he played himself for three episodes. He originally wanted to adapt some footage from the English rock film *Privilege* into his stage act for the TV show, but ABC's Broadcast Standards department found the bondage theme inappropriate.

Having a number one song changed Waite's life. "Missing You" exorcised the feelings he had toward the woman he lived with in the Lake District of England and it also changed his feelings about himself. "I was so proud, utterly proud of myself and the people that were involved in that song when it got to number one because it was so unselfconsciously put together and so honestly written. I think you have to be excellent to get to number one. I think there's never been a bad song that's got to number one. You can't buy it. I've always found it very hard to take a compliment. But I don't say no, I'm not very good anymore. I say thank you. Because I was number one and I think that really helps me now to consider myself in some ways worthy of success and worthy of being an artist, and maybe worthwhile."

*Writers: Prince and the Revolution*

*Producers: Prince and the Revolution*

*September 29, 1984*
*2 weeks*

KLEIG lights swept the sky in front of Mann's Chinese Theater. It was a traditional, old-fashioned Hollywood premiere, with television cameras greeting the famous faces filing from the block-long line-up of limousines through the gaudy doors to view the town's latest cinematic extravaganza. But there was a definitely different air about the crowd gathered there in July, 1984, than in the days when the celebrities whose cement-enshrined hands and feet decorating Mann's sidewalk performed their art for the theater's patrons.

This night the cameras belonged to MTV and the luminaries—John Cougar Mellencamp, Quiet Riot, Little Richard, Devo, the Talking Heads, Lionel Richie, Stevie Nicks, Christopher Cross, Kiss—were more familiar with concert stages than wide silver screens. They had collected to pay homage to a 5'2", 26-year-old with ringlets of hair, clad in a purple lame trenchcoat. He was the star, screenwriter and composer of the film they were about to witness—*Purple Rain.*

Even before the soundtrack's first single went to number one [see 591—"When Doves Cry"], the headline in the *Los Angeles Herald-Examiner* claimed, "Prince delivers the best rock film ever made." The newspaper's pop music critic, Mikal Gilmore, had dropped in to a sneak

preview at a San Diego, California, theater and wrote an early review: "Prince fills the screen like the threat and promise that he is, inspiring the audiences in San Diego to the kind of uncalculated sexual hysteria I haven't heard since the Beatles tore across the opening frames of *A Hard Day's Night.*" Comparing the film to *Citizen Kane* at one point, Gilmore concludes that Prince "dominates the screen with all the allure, menace and vulnerability that made Marlon Brando so irrefutable in *The Wild One*, and for anybody expecting merely high-tech concert fare or sexual peacockery, his performance will prove astonishing and unforgettable."

And the music wasn't too bad, either. "When Doves Cry" was in its fifth and final week at number one when "Let's Go Crazy" debuted on the Hot 100 at number 45. Eight weeks later, it became the second single from the film to top the chart. Three more singles were pulled from the soundtrack: the title track (number two in November, 1984), "I Would Die 4 U" (number eight in February, 1985) and "Take Me With U" (number 25 in March, 1985). The album *Purple Rain* dominated *Billboard's* LP chart for 24 weeks and was the number one album for 1984.

The public couldn't get enough of the Bible-reading health food devotee who sang of religion and sex. More than 1,692,000 tickets to his five-month 1984-1985 concert tour were sold; in Washington, D.C., alone, 130,000 were snapped up in under 10 hours. Graduates of Prince's musical tutelage in Minnesota—Vanity, Apollonia 6, Sheila E., the Time—spun into their own popular orbits. Grammys, American Music Awards, gold and platinum honors and even an Oscar for Best Original Song Score for *Purple Rain* poured down on him.

At the end of his 32-city tour, Prince announced he was retiring from live performing. The retreat harkened back to his days in Bernadette Anderson's basement; it was one that he'd hinted at for over three years, despite assuring biographer Jon Bream in *Prince: Inside the Purple Reign* that his difficulty in opening up to people was something "I've been trying to work on a lot lately within myself. That's one of my weaknesses—sometimes I won't talk to people at all."

The last single from *Purple Rain* had hardly fallen off the Hot 100 when Prince launched a new assault: *Around the World in a Day* hit the album chart at 14 and running.

## THE TOP FIVE

*Week of September 29, 1984*

1 **Let's Go Crazy**
Prince and the Revolution

2 **Missing You**
John Waite

3 **Drive**
The Cars

4 **She Bop**
Cyndi Lauper

5 **I Just Called
to Say I Love You**
Stevie Wonder

## 596 I Just Called to Say I Love You MOTOWN 1745
### STEVIE WONDER

*Writer: Stevie Wonder*

*Producer: Stevie Wonder*

*October 13, 1984*
*3 weeks*

"STEVIE WONDER is in every sense of the word . . . an absolute genius," Dionne Warwick told Dick Clark on Mutual Broadcasting's "The National Music Survey." Warwick, who suggested that the producers of *The Woman in Red* ask Wonder to score the Gene Wilder film, elaborated, "We're quite aware of the fact that Steveland is blind. He came in to 'watch' the film, to see it. And I tell you, he *saw* the film. There's no way in the world that you can write the pieces of music that he wrote, for the sequences he wrote for, so directly."

Wonder's pattern over the past few years has been to take his time with his album projects. His 1976 LP, *Songs in the Key of Life*, took so long to produce that Stevie took to wearing a T-shirt that assured, "We're almost finished!" [see 451—"I Wish"]. Stevie didn't have that luxury on *The Woman in Red*. "He was under a deadline by the motion picture company," explains Jay Lasker, then president of Motown Records. "Orion Pictures held up the final prints, and they were down to the last minute when he finally delivered it to them."

Not that Lasker was enthusiastic about the project when he heard the first three songs Wonder wrote for the film. "When he first presented it to me, I really tried to discourage his doing the soundtrack because he was just about ready to deliver his new

LP which he had been working on for four years. And I didn't think the three songs he had done were very good. So he went back and did some more songs, of which 'I Just Called to Say I Love You' was one. The single is probably going to be the biggest single in the history of Stevie Wonder. This is the record I picked and said I wanted out as a single."

"I Just Called to Say I Love You" was a worldwide smash. It began its conquest of the international charts in America when it debuted on the Hot 100 at number 58 on August 18, 1984. Eight weeks later it became the eighth American number one for Wonder. Amazingly, when it went to number one in Britain, it was Stevie's first chart-topper there. He had managed to get to number two on four different occasions, and to number one in a duet with Paul McCartney [see 555—"Ebony and Ivory"], had never reached the apex on his own.

The best honor was yet to come for the man who had already won 15 Grammys. When the 1984 Academy Award nominations were announced, the name Stevie Wonder was included on the select list of nominees. The competition was tough—for the first time in the rock era, all five nominees had been number one on

the Hot 100. In fact, all five songs had topped the chart in a seven-month period beginning March 31, 1984.

Going up against "I Just Called to Say I Love You" were two songs from *Footloose* [see 585—"Footloose" and 588—"Let's Hear It for the Boy"], and first-time nominees Phil Collins [see 586—"Against All Odds (Take a Look at Me Now)"] and Ray Parker, Jr. [see 592—"Ghostbusters"]. The odds tipped in Stevie's favor when the Hollywood Foreign Press Association honored him with a Golden Globe. On March 25, Stevie's long-time friend Diana Ross performed his song on the Oscarcast, and minutes later, the winner of Best Original Song was announced: Stevie Wonder for "I Just Called to Say I Love You," the eleventh number one single of the rock era to win an Oscar.

Wonder accepted his first Oscar on behalf of Nelson Mandela, imprisoned black leader of the African National Congress. The following day, the state-owned South African Broadcasting Corporation banned all Stevie Wonder songs from the airwaves.

"If my being banned means people will be free, ban me mega-times," Stevie told United Press International.

### THE TOP FIVE
*Week of October 13, 1984*

1 **I Just Called to Say I Love You**
Stevie Wonder

2 **Let's Go Crazy**
Prince and the Revolution

3 **Drive**
Cars

4 **Hard Habit to Break**
Chicago

5 **Lucky Star**
Madonna

JIVE/ARISTA 9199 **Caribbean Queen (No More Love on the Run)** 597
BILLY OCEAN

*Writers: Keith Diamond*
*Billy Ocean*

*Producer: Keith Diamond*

*November 3, 1984*
*2 weeks*

THE original recording of "Caribbean Queen (No More Love on the Run)" was g.u.—a familiar abbreviation for any California boy who's fallen in love with a New York girl. It stands for geographically undesirable, and it's an appropriate description of the single Billy Ocean released in Britain in the summer of 1984, "European Queen (No More Love on the Run)."

The record didn't even generate enough excitement to get a negative response. There was simply no response at all, and the single, the first recorded by Billy for his new label, Jive, disappeared without a trace.

There had been a 12" disco version, however, and for that release, Billy's manager suggested the song be revised to "Caribbean Queen." There was no need to record the entire song over; it was simple enough just to drop the word "Carib-

bean" into all the right places. Someone at Jive suggested a third version, "African Queen," would round out the 12" single, and that was recorded as well.

When it came time to release a 45 in America, label executives decided not to go with "European Queen," which had already proved itself a failure in Europe. So "Caribbean Queen" was issued instead, and it became Billy's first American chart entry since "Love Really Hurts Without You," a number 22 hit in May, 1976.

"We thought it was great when it went into the Hot 100 at 85; we thought even if it doesn't go any further, at least it's a foot in the door," Ocean told Paul Sexton of *Record Mirror*. Further is exactly where it went—12 weeks after its debut, it was number one, the first for both Ocean and the Jive label.

Born in Trinidad, Billy demonstrated an interest in music as early as age four, when a friend of his mother's gave him a toy ukulele for Christmas. He was seven when his family moved to the East End of London—six children crowded into two bedrooms while their parents slept downstairs. He still loved the

calypso music of his native country, but now he was exposed to new musical influences.

His parents wanted him to attend college like his siblings, but he was more interested in being a professional musician. As a compromise, he took a course in tailoring and worked on Savile Row during the day while singing with groups like Shades of Midnight and Dry Ice at night. After a year, he was fired from his tailoring job and decided to pay full attention to music.

He teamed up with producer Ben Findon and was signed to GTO Records in England. "Love Really Hurts Without You" was number two in Britain, followed by two top 20 hits, "L.O.D. (Love on Delivery)" and "Stop Me (If You've Heard It All Before)." Although he couldn't get another American hit, "Red Light Spells Danger" reached number two in the United Kingdom in April, 1977. His name was kept alive in America by a big 1981 R&B hit, "Nights (Feel Like Getting Down)." It was released on Epic, which had absorbed a few GTO artists when that label shut down.

Signed to Jive, he was teamed with Trinidad-born producer Keith Diamond. His album, *Suddenly*, was recorded in New York and yielded two hit singles after "Caribbean Queen." "Loverboy," written with producer Robert John "Mutt" Lange (Foreigner, the Cars), went to number two in February, 1985, and the title track cracked the top 15 in May.

## THE TOP FIVE
*Week of November 3, 1984*

1 **Caribbean Queen**
**(No More Love On The Run)**
Billy Ocean

2 **I Just Called**
**to Say I Love You**
Stevie Wonder

3 **Purple Rain**
Prince

4 **Hard Habit to Break**
Chicago

5 **Wake Me Up**
**Before You Go-Go**
Wham

# 598 Wake Me Up Before You Go-Go COLUMBIA 04552
## WHAM!

*Writer: George Michael*

*Producer: George Michael*

*November 17, 1984*
*3 weeks*

DURING the era of *Saturday Night Fever*, George Michael and Andrew Ridgeley were two teenagers living in Bushey, near the North London suburb of Watford. Just 16 and 17 years old, they loved to party at the discos. One night, when George came round to Andrew's house to go out for the evening, he was waiting for his friend to finish getting ready in the bathroom when he noticed a sign over his bed. He figured that Andrew put it on his door when he wanted his mother to wake him up before she left for work. The sign read: "Wake me up-up before you go-go."

When Andrew finally came out of the loo, George told him the saying would make a great line in a song—or even a great title for a song. Andrew explained the sign was a mistake—he had accidentally written the word "up" twice, so he purposely compounded the error by writing "go" twice. The mistake turned into an international million-selling single in 1984, and the record that finally broke Wham! in America.

Michael and Ridgeley first met in school in their home town of Bushey. George was just 12 years old and entering the second year of a comprehensive school where Andrew was already a student. "The teacher ordered me to sit next to this horrible little boy, who then took charge of me," George laughingly recalled to Dick Clark on "The National Music Survey."

George had wanted to be a pop star since the time he was seven years old. He took his first tentative steps the year Andrew left school. They spent a year and a half in the Executives, a ska-band modelled after popular groups of the day like the Specials and Selecter. The music they made wasn't great, but they began writing songs together.

Unemployed, they went on the dole for nine months. They wrote a song about their lifestyle called "Wham Rap" and included it on a demo tape, along with another song written in 1981, "Careless Whisper" [see 602]. Those two tunes convinced

Mark Dean, the young founder of the British independent label Inner Vision to sign the duo, now named Wham! like their rap. Although that song didn't do well the first time around, their second 45 made it big: "Young Guns (Go For It)," picked up by Columbia Records for the States, where it failed to match its British success.

After a re-release of "Wham Rap" did well at home, "Bad Boys" was another British hit, and another American failure. George and Andrew were getting frustrated at not making it in the country that inspired all of their music in the first place—Michael was heavily into '60s Motown music and Ridgeley loved Elvis Presley and the Everly Brothers, artists his mother used to listen to.

But there were pockets of support in America. "Bad Boys" had made the top 10 on Los Angeles radio station playlists, and when "Wake Me Up Before You Go-Go" went to number one in the United Kingdom during the summer of 1984,

southern California was ready for a new Wham! single. This time, so was the rest of the nation. "Wake Me Up Before You Go-Go" entered the Hot 100 at number 80 on September 8, 1984, and topped the chart 10 weeks later.

"There's always the question, are we selling America to the Americans?" Michael pointed out to David Thomas of *Rolling Stone*. "I know it sounds ridiculous, but we've taken in all the stuff that they've fed us for the past 20 years, and I think we're perfectly capable of giving it back to them."

### THE TOP FIVE
*Week of November 17, 1984*

1. **Wake Me Up Before You Go-Go**
   Wham

2. **Purple Rain**
   Prince

3. **Caribbean Queen (No More Love On The Run)**
   Billy Ocean

4. **I Feel For You**
   Chaka Khan

5. **I Just Called to Say I Love You**
   Stevie Wonder

albums before. We wrote all the lyrics together, along with some help from Sara Allen as in the past, but this time we didn't go into the studio with finished songs, mostly ideas. It had a snowballing effect.

The first single, "Out of Touch," is a typical example. Beginning as a "big band" chorus in John's home studio, it gained a verse when Daryl got hold of it in the studio. To enhance the urban feeling they wanted to capture, they asked *Beat Street* soundtrack producer Arthur Baker for assistance with mixing and production. His input helped supply the finishing touch for what Hall terms a "coming out" album.

"Out of Touch" entered the Hot 100 at number 48 on September 29, 1984. Ten weeks later it became Hall and Oates' sixth number one single. "Method of Modern Love," the follow-up, peaked at number seven in February, 1985, the 15th Hall and Oates single to make the top 10. "Some Things Are Better Left Unsaid" was the third single released from *Big Bam Boom.*

The biggest problem Hall and Oates faced in the flush of their success was keeping their music fresh. "Most artists try to avoid cliches, but it's pretty hard to avoid them if you, yourself, end up being one," Daryl expressed in *Rolling Stone.* To *Creem,* he declared, "I've got enough money. I don't care about anything except making great music. I never have, really. Our only pressure is self-induced and whether we can improve on what we've done already. That's all." Concluded John, "It's a challenge."

*Writers: Daryl Hall*
*John Oates*

*Producers: Daryl Hall*
*John Oates*
*Bob Clearmountain*

*December 8, 1984*
*2 weeks*

**T**wo years after they recorded their *H₂O* album [see 565—"Maneater"], Daryl Hall and John Oates returned to Electric Lady Studios in New York to record their *Bim Bam Boom* studio album for RCA. In the interim, the label issued *Rock 'n Soul Part 1,* a collection of greatest hits plus a couple of new songs. Those two tunes both turned out to be top 10 hits: "Say It Isn't So" remained at number two for four weeks in December, 1983, and "Adult Education" checked in at number eight in April, 1984.

That was the month that the Recording Industry Association of America confirmed what *Billboard* and *Newsweek* had already declared—that Daryl Hall and John Oates were

the most successful duo in the history of recorded music. The RIAA issued a report citing the pair as the world's most certified duo, with a total of 19 gold and platinum awards.

The formula Hall and Oates had perfected beginning with their *Voices* album was still in good working order, but in 1984 Daryl and John had a vague, uneasy feeling it was time to try something new. Daryl duetted with Elvis Costello on the audio and video versions of "The Only Flame in Town," then produced his song "Swept Away," a number 19 hit for Diana Ross in October. John preferred to spend time on the racetrack driving Formula Fords and on the slopes skiing.

When it came time to begin sessions for *Big Bam Boom,* some deep thought had been put into how this different direction could best manifest itself. "Both John and I went through a lot of evaluation and re-evaluation while making this album," Hall explained to *Output.* Oates elaborated, "It's much more of a collaborative effort than any of the

## THE TOP FIVE
*Week of December 8, 1984*

1 **Out of Touch**
Hall & Oates

2 **Wake Me Up Before You Go-Go**
Wham

3 **I Feel For You**
Chaka Khan

4 **The Wild Boys**
Duran Duran

5 **All Through The Night**
Cyndi Lauper

# Like a Virgin
### MADONNA

SIRE 29210

**Writers:** *Billy Steinberg*
 *Tom Kelly*

**Producer:** *Nile Rodgers*

*December 22, 1984*
*6 weeks*

NILE RODGERS did not want Madonna to record "Like a Virgin." "I liked the melody a lot, because the tune was catchy, but I didn't think that the lyric 'like a virgin' was such a terrific hook," the producer told Steve Pond in the *Los Angeles Times*. "It just didn't seem like, you know, the all-time catch phrase. But after about four days I couldn't get the song out of my head, and I said, 'You know, Madonna, I really apologize, because if it's so catchy it stayed in my head for four days, it must be something. So let's do it.'"

The song was not only not written for Madonna, it was not even written for a female singer. "The idea for that song came from personal experience," lyricist Billy Steinberg said in the *Los Angeles Times*. "I wasn't just trying to somehow get that racy word *virgin* in a lyric. I was saying . . . that I may not really be a virgin—I've been battered romantically and emotionally like many people— but I'm starting a new relationship and it just feels so good, it's healing all the wounds and making me feel like I've never done this before, because it's so much deeper and more profound than anything I've ever felt."

Steinberg, who wrote Linda Ronstadt's top 10 hit from 1979, "How Do I Make You," penned "Like a Virgin" with Tom Kelly. Michael Ostin of Warner Brothers Records' A&R department was invited to Kelly's house to hear their demos.

"It was a fluke" is how Ostin described the fateful events that led to Madonna hearing the song. "I was there mostly to hear what Billy and Tom were up to in their own career, and they played me four or five tunes, all really nice," Ostin told Pond. "Then they said, 'Listen, we've got this other tune, and we don't really know what to do with it—it's not right for us, and we don't know what artist would be appropriate.' They played me 'Like a Virgin,' and it just so happened that the next day I had a meeting with Madonna to dis-

cuss her next album. The lyrics, the groove of the song—I just thought it would be perfect for her, and it was an uncanny coincidence that I was going to be seeing her the next day and she was on my mind. When I played it for Madonna she went crazy, and knew instantly it was a song for her and that she could make a great record out of it."

Madonna's biggest hit prior to "Like a Virgin" was "Lucky Star," number four in October, 1984. She had also charted with "Holiday" and "Borderline," but it was "Like a Virgin" that established her as a major artist, debuting on the Hot 100 at number 48 on November 17, 1984, and moving to number one five weeks later.

Madonna Louise Veronica Ciccone was born August 16, 1958, in Detroit, Michigan. The number one song in America was "Poor Little Fool" by Ricky Nelson [see 40]. Named after her mother, who died when Madonna was six, the singer moved to New York City and worked in a Times Square doughnut shop before winning a dance scholarship with Alvin Ailey. She fled to Paris to pursue a singing career and sang back-up vocals for Patrick Hernandez ("Born to Be Alive"). Home again, she was

aided by New York DJ Mark Kamins, who helped remix a demo tape that got her signed with Sire Records.

Winning rave reviews for her role in *Desperately Seeking Susan*, Madonna dominated the Hot 100 in 1985, charting as many as three singles at once. Before "Like a Virgin" fell off the chart, "Material Girl" went to number two and "Crazy for You" from *Vision Quest* was moving up fast, on its way to number one [see 606]. Waiting in the wings were two more singles from the *Like a Virgin* album: "Angel" and "Dress You Up."

## THE TOP FIVE
*Week of December 22, 1984*

1 **Like a Virgin**
 Madonna

2 **The Wild Boys**
 Duran Duran

3 **Out of Touch**
 Hall & Oates

4 **Sea of Love**
 Honeydrippers

5 **Cool It Now**
 New Edition

ATLANTIC 89596 **I Want to Know What Love Is**
FOREIGNER    **601**

Writer: *Mick Jones*

Producers: *Alex Sadkin*
           *Mick Jones*

*February 2, 1985*
*2 weeks*

"WHEN we found out we went number one, we really celebrated," Mick Jones told Ethlie Ann Vare in *Pulse!* "This is our first number one single. People seem to think we've had millions of number one singles, but we never had. We've had number one albums, and we had number two singles."

Jones wasn't kidding. Foreigner's "Waiting for a Girl Like You" moved into the runner-up position on November 28, 1981, and remained there for 10 weeks, longer than any prior number two hit. It was prevented from reaching the number one spot by Olivia Newton-John's athletic chart-topper [see 550—"Physical"].

"Waiting for a Girl Like You" was a ballad, not typical for a group whose earlier hits included heavier rockers such as "Feels Like the First Time" (number four in June, 1977), "Hot Blooded" (number three in September, 1978) and "Double Vision" (number two in November, 1978). Jones told Paul Grein in *Billboard* that the success of "Waiting for a Girl Like You" was not a factor in releasing the balladish "I Want to Know What Love Is" as the first single

from *Agent Provocateur*. "That was the one thing I was sort of dubious about—the fact that people might think we'd gone soft or something. I certainly want to retain the rock image. We just put this out because the song was so strong, and because it was coming out at Christmas, and it had the right kind of mood."

Not all the members of Foreigner agreed that "I Want to Know What Love Is" would make such a good single. "We worried that it might do irreparable damage to our rock image," said lead singer Lou Gramm. Bassist Rick Wills described the tune as "fluffy."

Foreigner had cast guest stars in leading roles before (Jr. Walker played sax on "Urgent" and Thomas Dolby brought his synthesizers to the sessions for the *4* album), so it was not a surprise to find some people dropping in for "I Want to Know What Love is." Tom Bailey of the Thompson Twins ("Hold Me Now," "Doctor! Doctor!") guested on the entire album, and was joined on the first single by *Dream Girls* star Jennifer Holliday ("And I Am Telling You I'm Not Going") and the New Jersey Mass Choir.

"I had met Tom Bailey before, and we talked about doing something together," Jones told Vare. "Jennifer Holliday was luck. She happened to be in the studio the night we were recording 'I Want to Know What Love Is.' She was a real inspiration for everybody." The single debuted

on the Hot 100 at number 45 and moved to the top of the chart eight weeks later.

The man responsible for organizing Foreigner is Mick Jones (born December 27, 1944, in London), who was first turned on to music by his father's Les Paul and Mary Ford records. The first single Mick bought was "It's So Easy" by Buddy Holly, and as a teenager, Jones worked in a record store in Woking, Surrey. In 1961, he was part of a British group called Nero and the Gladiators, who had two minor chart hits. After that, Jones lived in Paris for six years, working with singer Johnny Halliday. Back in England, he was part of Spooky Tooth and then emigrated to America, where he worked with the Leslie West Band.

Foreigner began to take shape when Mick met Ian McDonald (born June 25, 1946, in London), who had worked with King Crimson, at a recording session for Ian Lloyd, formerly of Stories [see 341—"Brother Louie"]. They decided to form a band and recruited two native New Yorkers, keyboardist Al Greenwood and bassist Ed Gagliardi. Jones met drummer Dennis Elliott (born August 18, 1950, in London) at a session for Ian Hunter, and invited him into the band. Then Jones heard two albums by a band called Black Sheep and liked their lead singer—Lou Gramm (born May 2, 1950, in Rochester, New York). His audition tape became the demo that landed Foreigner with Atlantic Records. McDonald and Greenwood departed in 1980 and Rick Wills who had been playing with a revived Small Faces, joined to make the group a quartet.

## THE TOP FIVE
*Week of February 2, 1985*

1  **I Want to Know What Love Is**
   Foreigner

2  **Easy Lover**
   Philip Bailey

3  **Careless Whisper**
   Wham! featuring George Michael

4  **You're the Inspiration**
   Chicago

5  **Lover Boy**
   Billy Ocean

# 602 Careless Whisper COLUMBIA 04691
## WHAM! FEATURING GEORGE MICHAEL

Writers: George Michael
       Andrew Ridgeley

Producer: George Michael

February 16, 1985
3 weeks

GEORGE MICHAEL had plenty of time to think while working as an usher in a local cinema in his hometown of Bushey. Just 16, he found the job boring and spent his free time writing song lyrics. One day, while riding on a bus, he thought up the melody to a song he called "Careless Whisper." It would become a truly international number one four years later—in England, America, and even in the People's Republic of China.

"It's very naive when you listen to it, but it still stands up, even if it does sound a little immature in some ways," Michael told reporter Daryl Morden. "We made up for that, I think, by making sure the production and arrangement didn't sound simplistic."

In Britain, "Careless Whisper" was released as a solo single by George. In America, where Wham! finally broke through in December, 1984, with their first number one single [see 598—"Wake Me Up Before You Go-Go"], "Careless Whisper" was released under the name "Wham! Featuring George Michael." It was the highest new entry on the Hot 100 for the week ending December 22, 1984. Debuting at number 37, it took only eight weeks to become the group's second American chart-topper.

"We knew it was off-tangent with the rest of what we'd been doing, that's why it was a solo single," Michael told Morden. "It was put on the album to show that there was no question of a split, and also because it's going to sell the record."

Wham!'s international status jumped up a few notches when they became the first major Western rock band invited to perform behind the Great Wall. The invitation came from the Youth Federation of China and the Minister of Culture in Canton.

More than 12,000 people attended the April 7, 1985, concert at the People's Gymnasium in Peking. Three days later, Wham! performed for 5,000 people at the 100-year-old Opera House in Canton. Tickets were sold for the equivalent of $1.60 each, with proceeds going to charity and cultural funds. Each ticket buyer received a free cassette of the Make It Big LP. Although Western albums are not available for sale in the People's Republic, the Chinese people were already familiar with Wham!'s music, thanks to five Cantonese cover versions of "Careless Whisper."

Wham!'s good chart fortunes continued after "Careless Whisper." In Britain, they had another number one single with "Freedom," and in December, 1984, peaked at number two with the seasonal "Last Christmas." That holiday offering was kept out of number one by "Do They Know It's Christmas?" by Band Aid, the original British effort to raise funds to help feed the starving people of Africa [see 605—"We Are the World"]. George was one of the vocalists featured on that single.

In America, Wham! followed "Careless Whisper" with another number one single [see 608—"Everything She Wants"]. Did all this success affect Wham!? Some people suggested that the band was arrogant and overconfident even before they had hit records.

"I put on a hard front," George admitted to Dennis Hunt of the Los Angeles Times, who found the singer "chilly" at the beginning of their luncheon interview, which Hunt thought would not survive the shrimp cocktail. But as they talked, George transformed into a friendly, cheerful chap. "I want to make sure nobody walks on us," George continued. "If you let people think they can walk all over you, they will. If they're not sure they can walk on you they won't try it. So I come off tough. I don't like doing it. It makes people think I'm difficult. I'm not, really."

Later in the interview, Michael went as far to say he is really "perfectly shy." He said, "If I acted like this shy person, this nice young kid, this innocent idealist who liked everybody and believed what everybody told him, I'd be slaughtered. I wish it wasn't that way, but it is. So I have to hide the real me sometimes. It's for survival."

### THE TOP FIVE
*Week of February 16, 1985*

1 **Careless Whisper**
Wham! featuring George Michael

2 **I Want to Know What Love Is**
Foreigner

3 **Easy Lover**
Philip Bailey

4 **Lover Boy**
Billy Ocean

5 **Method of Modern Love**
Hall & Oates

*Writer: Kevin Cronin*

*Producers: Kevin Cronin*
*Gary Richrath*
*Alan Gratzer*

*March 9, 1985*
*3 weeks*

"**T**HE greatest thing about having (another) number one record," Kevin Cronin told John Milward of *USA Today*, "is that it finally puts to rest the notion that we were a one-hit-wonder."

It had taken REO Speedwagon 10 years after signing with Epic Records to achieve their first chart-topper [see 539—"Keep On Loving You"]. Although that record and the follow-up, "Take It on the Run" (number five in May, 1981), came from a number one album, *Hi-Infidelity*, the group's future on the chart was far from assured.

"Success did change us, and it wasn't a good change." Cronin admitted to Michael Goldberg in *Rolling Stone*. "It's almost like a drug. When you get real high, you have to come down eventually." Down is where they went with their next album, *Good Trouble*, which Kevin describes as "half-baked."

"A lot of people did think we were washed up," Cronin told Goldberg. But the band knew better. They spent two months in the studio working on their next LP, *Wheels Are Turning*, when they called a halt to production. Of the 25 songs they had written between themselves, they suddenly realized only four or five were suitable for the album. They cancelled the studio time they had

booked and went their separate ways to come up with new material.

Cronin's destination was the relatively unspoiled Hawaiian island of Molokai. While writing new songs, he also worked on a tune he had started 10 years earlier but had never finished. "I guess the reason I couldn't finish it was because I hadn't figured out what I wanted to say," Cronin commented in *Rolling Stone*. Describing the song to Dick Clark on "The National Music Survey," Cronin said it is about "that moment in time where . . . it gets to be too painful to be where you are and you know you have to change . . . but change is hard . . . and you overcome that fear of change."

The rest of REO described it in other terms. "That stupid ballad" was what they called the song before it entered the Hot 100 at number 46 and sped to number one seven weeks later.

REO's membership has been intact since 1975, the year Cronin returned after a three-year hiatus. Since then, keyboardist Neal Doughty, bassist Bruce Hall, drummer Alan Gratzer, guitarist Gary

Richrath and Cronin have remained a cohesive unit. Ego trips were dispensed with long ago. "None of us are foolish enough now to think we're the kingpin of this organization," Cronin told Kim Freeman in *Billboard*.

REO Speedwagon was already rolling when Cronin joined. He was living in Chicago when he started the "Musicians Referral Service," an organization that helped put bands looking for musicians in touch with musicians looking for bands. After the first REO album was released, Richrath called the service anonymously, searching for a new lead singer. He was unwilling to divulge the name of the band because the original lead singer hadn't been informed of the pending change. Kevin pressed him to reveal which band he was in, then told Gary to come to his apartment and meet a new lead singer. When Gary arrived, Kevin sang an Elton John song and handed him a demo tape. Within a week, Cronin was the new lead singer of REO Speedwagon and was leaving Chicago for the band's hometown of Champaign, Illinois, to begin rehearsals.

---

## THE TOP FIVE
*Week of March 9, 1985*

1 **Can't Fight This Feeling**
REO Speedwagon

2 **Careless Whisper**
Wham! featuring George Michael

3 **The Heat is On**
Glenn Frey

4 **California Girls**
David Lee Roth

5 **Material Girl**
Madonna

# One More Night ATLANTIC 89588
## PHIL COLLINS

Writer: *Phil Collins*

Producers:*Phil Collins*
　　　　　*Hugh Padgham*

*March 30, 1985*
*2 weeks*

IRONICALLY, Phil Collins' "One More Night" was the number one song in America on the evening of the 57th annual Academy Awards ceremony—a night that saw Collins sitting in the audience while Ann Reinking performed his Oscar nominated song, a tune that had been his first number one [see 586—"Against All Odds (Take a Look at Me Now)"]. The Academy of Motion Pictures Arts and Sciences may not have known who Phil Collins was, but the rest of the world did.

Phil Collins was born January 31, 1951, in London. A child actor, he appeared in British television commercials and played the Artful Dodger in a West End production of *Oliver*. As a 19-year-old lad living in the West London suburb of Chiswick, he noticed an ad in the weekly pop paper *Melody Maker*. "Tony Stratton-Smith requires drummer sensitive to acoustic music," it read. Collins was not inexperienced—he had recorded an album, *Ark 2*, as part of a band called Flaming Youth. He called Stratton-Smith, founder of Charisma Records, and passed the audition—for Genesis, an English art band that had been formed in 1966 by students from the exclusive Charterhouse School.

Collins was the group's fourth drummer by the time he joined in 1970. Along with Tony Banks, Mike Rutherford, Peter Gabriel and Steve Hackett, Collins recorded Genesis' third album, *Nursery Cryme*. The band's popularity continued to grow around the world as it released more albums: *Genesis Live*, *Selling England by the Pound* and *The Lamb Lies Down on Broadway*. In August, 1975, lead singer Gabriel publicly announced a decision he had made seven months earlier to leave the group.

The critics said it was the end of Genesis, but no one else heard a death knell. Collins stepped out from his drums to become the new lead singer. After the departure of Hackett in 1977, Genesis continued as

a trio and achieved commercial success on the American Hot 100 for the first time. "Follow You Follow Me" became their first single to break into the top 30 in the spring of 1978.

Collins' led the group into the top 20 with "Misunderstanding" in the summer of 1980, although he felt his primary job with the group was still being their drummer. "I only sing in Genesis because we don't have another singer," he told Bill Milkowski in *Down Beat*. "And I sing my own things because I write them....Whatever else I am, I'm a drummer first."

While still a vital part of Genesis, Collins released his first solo album, *Face Value*, in 1981. Derk Richardson, interviewing Phil for *The Record*, asked what motivated the decision to do a solo project. "My divorce" was the answer. After a 1978 Genesis tour, Phil returned home and found his marriage was over. He thought moving to Vancouver with his wife would solve their problems; Rutherford and

Banks told him to sort out his marriage while they recorded solo projects.

After two months in Vancouver, Phil returned to England alone. "Mike and Tony were doing their own albums and I had nothing to do," Collins told Richardson. Collins wrote music and recorded it on an eight-track machine at home. Suddenly, he realized he had material for a solo album. "Like the album made itself without me knowing it. There was never any conscious time where I sat down and said, 'Right, I'm going to do an album.' It just sort of crept up behind me."

His first two singles, "I Missed Again" and "In the Air Tonight," both coincidentally peaked at number 19. The first single from his second album, *Hello I Must Be Going*, was an accurate cover version of the Supremes' "You Can't Hurry Love" [see 207]. It went to number 10 in America and number one in Britain. Two more tracks from the same LP were released: "I Don't Care Anymore" (number 39) and "I Cannot Believe It's True" (79).

After time out to produce a solo album for Frida of Abba [see 458—"Dancing Queen"] which resulted in a top 15 single ("I Know There's Something Going On"), and playing drums for Robert Plant's *Pictures at Eleven* album, Collins went to work on a third solo LP, *No Jacket Required*. Following his successful title song for *Against All Odds*, his popularity in America was sufficient to send both *No Jacket Required* and "One More Night" to number one simultaneously on their respective *Billboard* charts.

## THE TOP FIVE
*Week of March 30, 1985*

1　**One More Night**
　　Phil Collins

2　**Material Girl**
　　Madonna

3　**Can't Fight This Feeling**
　　REO Speedwagon

4　**Lover Girl**
　　Teena Marie

5　**We Are the World**
　　USA for Africa

COLUMBIA 04389 **We Are the World**
USA FOR AFRICA 605

*Writers: Michael Jackson*
*Lionel Richie*

*Producer: Quincy Jones*

*April 13, 1985*
*4 weeks*

ON Good Friday, April 5, 1985, at 3:50 p.m. Greenwich Mean Time, the world listened to one song. Some 5,000 radio stations around the globe—in North America, in Europe (including East Germany), in Asia (including the People's Republic of China), in Africa—simultaneously played "We Are the World," the remarkable effort by American recording artists to raise money to help feed the starving people of Africa and the United States.

"This all started with a phone call from Harry Belafonte," Ken Kragen, president of the United Support of Artists for Africa foundation, said in *Billboard*. The singer telephoned Kragen with the idea of staging a concert by black performers to raise money for Africa. Kragen felt a concert would not raise enough money. "So we began to discuss alternatives. I suggested an American version of Band Aid."

Band Aid was the name adopted by the union of British artists who recorded "Do They Know It's Christmas?" That effort, organized by Bob Geldof of the Boomtown Rats, sold over three million copies in Britain alone.

Belafonte acknowledged Band Aid's groundbreaking effort in *Billboard*. "After the success of Band Aid, and particularly Bob Geldof, it was obvious that USA for Africa was an idea whose time had come."

Kragen, owner of a personal management and television production company, telephoned his client Lionel Richie to discuss the idea. The next day, Lionel's wife Brenda was shopping in the same store as Stevie Wonder. She had him call her husband immediately about working on a project. Kragen meanwhile asked Quincy Jones to produce, and Jones asked Michael Jackson to contribute.

"Deciding to do the recording on the night of the American Music Awards, January 28th, was perhaps the key decision that I made," Kragen told *Billboard*. "It was a perfect way to make sure that I could get the maximum number of artists to take part. I knew that a number of key artists would be at the American Music Awards. I also knew that there were certain artists who would attract the others into the project: Michael, Lionel, Stevie, Bruce Springsteen."

At first, Lionel and Michael wanted to write a simple song, not an international anthem. Then they considered the artists involved and the effect the song would have on the world, and they knew they had to write something that would not just be a song for 1985, but a song for all time. Richie discussed the writing of "We Are the World" in *Billboard*. "I'll tell you honestly—I can't really say how the

## THE TOP FIVE
*Week of April 13, 1985*

1 **We Are the World**
   USA for Africa

2 **One More Night**
   Phil Collins

3 **Crazy for You**
   Madonna

4 **Nightshift**
   Commodores

5 **Material Girl**
   Madonna

song came about. Neither one of us saw the other put his hands on the keyboard. That's how we write. He brought in an idea, I brought in an idea; we went back, we listened, and then we smashed both ideas together. The music came first. As for the lyrics . . . It just kind of flowed. . . . I'd throw out a line, Michael would come back with a greater line—the same one, with the words changed around differently—and I'd change his line, and finally we got this wonderful line. . . . And it actually only took us about two-and-a-half hours to nail it, after three days of preparation."

The instrumental tracks were recorded first, then Quincy sent demo tapes to each artist involved in the project with the admonition to "check their egos at the door." Jones elaborated in *Billboard*: "I put that line in a letter I sent to all the artists before they got there, and everybody understood. . . . Oh, there were little murmurs beforehand that the song 'is not rock 'n' roll' . . . but once we got to the session, I was sure that every-

thing would totally even itself out and bring everyone into a euphoric state, and that's what happened."

The 45 artists began arriving at A&M Studios in Hollywood at 10 p.m. The name of each soloist was written on a piece of tape on the floor. There were six microphones in all, arranged in a semi-circle. After the chorus, featuring all of the artists, was recorded, the soloists performed their vocals. By 8 a.m. the following morning, Lionel and Quincy were the only two musicians left in the studio.

"We Are the World" arrived in record stores on Thursday, March 7. Over 800,000 copies were shipped. By the weekend they were gone. "It was phenomenal . . . unbelievable," Richard Petipas, singles buyer for Tower Records in West Hollywood, told the *Los Angeles Times*.

"We Are the World" entered the Hot 100 on March 23 at number 21. Three weeks later it was number one, the fastest-rising chart-topper since Elton John's "Island Girl" in November, 1975. As *Billboard's* Paul Grein pointed out in his "Chartbeat" column, 1985 became the eighth consecutive year that Lionel Richie had written a number one song.

On May 16, Columbia Records Senior Vice President Al Teller handed Ken Kragen a royalty check for $6.5 million. There was much more to come—over 7.3 million singles and 4.4 million albums had been sold. Less than a year after "We Are the World" had been released, total estimated worldwide sales of related products, including T-shirts, videotapes, sweatshirts and posters, was approximately $44 million.

The artists who participated in the recording of "We Are the World" are: Dan Aykroyd, Harry Belafonte, Lindsey Buckingham, Kim Carnes, Ray Charles, Bob Dylan, Sheila E., Bob Geldof, Daryl Hall and John Oates, James Ingram, Jackie Jackson, LaToya Jackson, Marlon Jackson, Michael Jackson, Randy Jackson, Tito Jackson, Al Jarreau, Waylon Jennings, Billy Joel, Cyndi Lauper, Huey Lewis and the News, Kenny Loggins, Bette Midler, Willie Nelson, Jeffrey Osborne, Steve Perry, the Pointer Sisters, Lionel Richie, Smokey Robinson, Kenny Rogers, Diana Ross, Paul Simon, Bruce Springsteen, Tina Turner, Dionne Warwick and Stevie Wonder.

## 606 Crazy for You GEFFEN 29051
### MADONNA

Writers: *John Bettis*
*Jon Lind*

Producer: *John "Jellybean" Benitez*

*May 11, 1985*
*1 week*

LYRICIST John Bettis and his songwriting partner Jon Lind were more than a little shocked when they found out who was going to sing the ballad they had written for the film *Vision Quest*.

"I was on vacation out in the desert, and Joel Sill (then an executive in charge of music for Warner Brothers Pictures) called and said Phil Ramone was in love with the song and wanted to cut it on Madonna," Bettis recalls with a laugh. " 'Borderline' was out at the time and I said, 'Excuse me? This is for *Madonna*? Really? Can she sing a song like this?' Jon and I were surprised at the choice of artist at the time, if you want to know the truth."

Bettis and Lind had written "Crazy For You" after receiving a copy of the *Vision Quest* script from Sill. "In reading the script, the place I wanted to write a song for was the first time that the two main characters, a young boy and a girl who's a boarder at the house, dance together at a club," Bettis elaborates. "We were noodling around and ('Crazy for You') was something that Jon was singing over that section of the song. It was really descriptive of the scene in the film.

Some time elapsed before they received the call from Sill letting them know that Madonna was going to sing their composition. "We went to one of the sessions, and, to be honest, that particular session didn't go all that well," Bettis continues. "Jon and I were depressed about the way the song had come out. We heard nothing else about it, and we were a little nervous the song was going to be dropped from the picture."

"I went to England to work on the film *Legend* with Jerry Goldsmith," says Bettis. "When I got home, Jon Lind called me and said, 'Have you heard the new record of "Crazy for You"? I've got a single here for you.' I said, 'What are you talking about? A single? What?' So I went over to his house and he played me a brand new version of it (with) a new arrangement. We owe a big debt of gratitude to a guy named Rob Mounsey, because

he completely rearranged the original track and added the background vocals and really made a hit record out of it."

The man who brought Mounsey in to arrange the new recording was the producer John "Jellybean" Benitez. "It was the first time I ever produced a ballad," Jellybean says. "Prior to that I had only produced dance/pop songs or dance songs. It was the first time I ever produced a live session, as opposed to having synthesizers and drum machines do everything.

"I was tense because I had never done a record like this," admits Jellybean, who produced "Holiday" on Madonna's first album. "Everything I did was totally on instinct. I tried to make the song stand on its own, but at the same time work in the two scenes (in which) it was used in the movie."

Jellybean notes that the song was important to Madonna. "She had just (charted with) 'Like a Virgin' [see 600] and 'Material Girl.' This song really opened up radio as far as Adult Contemporary was concerned. I think people saw that she could really do other things."

Bettis was happy to collect his second number one song [see 350—

"Top of the World"], but he had his doubts that "Crazy for You" would make it to the top after being stuck at number two for three weeks in a row. "(Going to number one) surprised me very much because we were out at the same time 'We Are the World' was out. Jon and I (said), 'If you gotta lose to something, it might as well be that. Luckily enough, the final week of the upward surge of the record, we topped 'We Are the World,' which lets you know how hot the song and how hot the artist were."

### THE TOP FIVE
*Week of May 11, 1985*

1 **Crazy for You**
Madonna

2 **We Are the World**
USA for Africa

3 **Don't You (Forget About Me)**
Simple Minds

4 **Rhythm of the Night**
DeBarge

5 **One Night in Bangkok**
Murray Head

*Writers: Keith Forsey*
*Steve Schiff*

*Producer: Keith Forsey*

*May 18, 1985*
*1 week*

JIM KERR'S comments in the press about "Don't You (Forget About Me)" were not what you would expect from someone who had just experienced his first American number one single. "(The lyrics) sound pretty inane to me," he told Dennis Hunt in the *Los Angeles Times*. "Sometimes I play it and I just puke. Other times I play it and I think, Hey, this is nae bad!" he exclaimed to Merle Ginsberg in *Rolling Stone*. "I don't think there was much soul bared in that song," he commented to Tim deLisle in *Creem*. "I would never use lyrics, I don't think, like 'vanity . . . insecurity and baby' and stuff," he said in *BAM*.

Later, Kerr would soften his criticism. "I wouldn't write a line like 'Don't you forget about me,' " he told Dick Clark on "The National Music Survey." "I'm more liable to write a line like 'Do forget about me.' So I will always have trouble with that line." What about words like vanity, insecurity and baby? Would he write those? "Maybe I would now but I certainly wouldn't have then." Kerr did give Clark some kind words about the tune: "That song really opened a lot of doors here for us."

Of course, no one forced Jim Kerr and the other members of Simple Minds to record "Don't You (Forget About Me)." It was only the second song the band recorded that they did not write. (The first was a cover of Lou Reed's "Street Hassle.") The song

was specifically written for the soundtrack of the John Hughes film *The Breakfast Club*, the ultimate brat pack movie, starring Emilio Estevez, Anthony Michael Hall, Judd Nelson, Molly Ringwald and Ally Sheedy.

Simple Minds were not composer Keith Forsey's first choice to sing the track. "The original guy I had in mind was Bryan Ferry," Forsey admits. "(He) turned it down. But Simple Minds, they could pull it off as well; it sounds like a song they could do. Simple Minds turned it down."

So Forsey had the movie screened for them, and the band simply changed their minds. Forsey has read Kerr's comments in the press. "The things he said about me (were) not really the way it was. He said he's never sung 'baby' in his life, and he kind of put the lyrics down. I told him the first thing I do with any artist when I've written a song . . . (is tell) them) if they can't sing it or if they don't believe it, it's gonna sound horrible. . . . If you don't like what we've got, then change (it), make it work for you. And that's exactly what I said to Jim. He went away (for) two (or) three days, came back, (and said) 'no, I love it.' That's it. He didn't (change) anything."

Still, don't look for Simple Minds to record anything like it again in the future. "If we started doing songs like that it would be the death of us in the long run," Kerr told Dennis Hunt. "We don't deal in formula music. We're into improvising and doing the unexpected."

Whatever Kerr ultimately thinks of "Don't You (Forget About Me)," it stands as Simple Minds' first American hit after seven years of recording.

Simple Minds, named after a lyric in David Bowie's "Jean Genie," first performed together in Kerr's native Glasgow, Scotland, in 1978. It was just a year after Kerr and fellow Simple Mind Charlie Burchill had a punk outfit called Johnny & the Self-Abusers, who recorded briefly for Britain's Chiswick label. The British arm of Arista Records signed Simple Minds to the Zoom label, and three albums later the group switched to Virgin Records.

Simple Minds' breakthrough single in the United Kingdom was "Promised You a Miracle," which hit number 13 in the spring of 1982. The line-up has had minor changes through the years. In 1985, the band consisted of Kerr, Burchill, keyboardist Mick MacNeil, drummer Mel Gaynor and bass player John Giblin, who replaced charter member Derek Forbes.

Simple Minds' next chart single after "Don't You (Forget About Me)" was "Alive and Kicking" (from *Once Upon a Time*), which peaked at number three in December, 1985.

## THE TOP FIVE
*Week of May 18, 1985*

1 **Don't You (Forget About Me)**
Simple Minds

2 **Crazy for You**
Madonna

3 **One Night in Bangkok**
Murray Head

4 **Everything She Wants**
Wham!

5 **Smooth Operator**
Sade

**608** **Everything She Wants** COLUMBIA 04840
WHAM!

Writer: George Michael

Producer: George Michael

May 25, 1985
2 weeks

WITH "Everything She Wants," Wham! became the first chart act since the Bee Gees [see 505—"Love You Inside Out"] to pull three number one singles from one album. *Make It Big* yielded "Wake Me Up Before You Go-Go" [see 598], "Careless Whisper" [see 602] and "Everything She Wants," a trio of singles that topped the Hot 100 in a six-month period between November, 1984, and May, 1985.

George talked about "Everything She Wants" in the Fall, 1985, issue of *ASCAP in Action:* "It's the only song I've written that successfully came from a backing track first. I wrote the Linn drum pattern and found a synthesizer program I liked and wrote the backing track in one evening, took it back to the hotel, and wrote the vocal in a hotel room the next morning. Because it was thrown together that way, I never looked at it as a single 'til everybody started saying it was great."

George elaborated on the lyrics to Dick Clark on his syndicated radio

countdown show: "It's a lyric about a man who is six or eight months into a marriage which obviously isn't going well. He's faced with the 'happy' news of an arriving baby. So he's in that situation where he can't back out. (The song) talks about the situation (in which) many men find themselves, working really hard to support a family . . . and see it as a kind of trap. It's a situation I've seen. . . . It's not the kind of thing I usually write about. Our lyrics are usually a lot closer to the kind of pop lightweight lyric we enjoy . . . but it's a departure, and I think it worked."

There was one more single from *Make It Big.* "Freedom," a number one single in the United Kingdom, peaked at number three in America in September, 1985. That fall, George Michael told partner Andrew Ridgeley and managers Jaz Summers and Simon Napier-Bell that Wham! had come to an end. "We always said that there'd be no Wham! past the point where we were not enjoying it," Michael later told Steve Gett in *Billboard.* "It became a very restrictive thing, and I felt I was ready to do other things musically. The directions I wanted to go in had nothing to do with the original concept of the group."

The press reports on the split made

it clear that Ridgeley's musical role in the group had been smaller than most people realized. Gett asked Michael how much Andrew actually contributed to Wham! "Originally, quite a lot. But by *Make It Big* he was contributing very little, partially through laziness and partially through accepting that what I was doing at the time was going to be so huge commercially that neither of us thought there would be any point in trying to collaborate when it would just dilute what I was doing. It was very difficult for him to even try to contribute, knowing that I had a very fixed goal in my mind musically."

There were still more Wham! singles to come, even after the split was announced. "I'm Your Man" peaked at number three in February, 1986. That was followed by a George Michael solo number, "A Different Corner," which went to number seven in June. The following month, the final Wham! LP was released. The American version was titled *Music from the Edge of Heaven,* and it contained "I'm Your Man" and "A Different Corner" as well as "The Edge of Heaven" (number 10 in August) and "Where Did Your Heart Go?" (number 50 in November). According to *Rolling Stone,* Ridgeley appeared on only two of the tracks on the album, a live recording of "Blue" from the China tour and "Wham! Rap '86," a remix of a 1983 song.

Wham! gave their final concert at Wembley Stadium on June 28, 1986. Their first single had entered the British chart the week of October 16, 1982, and their last single entered the American chart exactly four years later.

---

## THE TOP FIVE
*Week of May 25, 1985*

1 **Everything She Wants**
Wham!

2 **Don't You (Forget About Me)**
Simple Minds

3 **Everybody Wants to Rule the World**
Tears for Fears

4 **Axel F**
Harold Faltermeyer

5 **Smooth Operator**
Sade

MERCURY 880 659 7  **Everybody Wants to Rule the World**
TEARS FOR FEARS                                **609**

*Writers: Roland Orzabal*
*Ian Stanley*
*Chris Hughes*

*Producer: Chris Hughes*

*June 8, 1985*
*2 weeks*

CURT SMITH and Roland Orzabal met when they were 13-year-olds living in Bath, a popular tourist town about 100 miles west of London. Both were middle sons from broken homes, and both loved music. "We had the same sense of humor and we were the same height so we got on," Roland told Marc Levine in *Rock Beat.* "I'd been playing the guitar and writing songs since I was a wee lad and Curt was a closet vocalist. I heard him sing in the bedroom along to a (Blue Oyster Cult) record and it sounded great and I asked him to join our band." They were self-described "heavy metal freaks," and they played cover versions of songs by Led Zeppelin and Slade.

The two boys remained friends, although they followed different paths. Curt went to college while Roland formed a folk duo. But Curt, still a troubled teen, was arrested for stealing cameras from his school.

"Somebody handed me a copy of (Arthur Janov's) *Primal Scream* at 17, while I was doing a lot of soul-searching," Roland told reporter Michael Snyder. "It was well-written and provided a lot of simple answers for me, so I thought Curt might see some sense in it." Curt did, as he related to Cary Darling in *BAM*: "I read *The Primal Scream*, and it seems very obvious to me that what he was talking about is that your upbringing affects your life. You live in the past all the time, because those things that (affected you) when you were young affect you now."

When they were 19, Curt and Roland joined with friends Steve Buck, Andy Marsden and John Baker to form the group Graduate. Precision Records released a single, "Elvis Should Play Ska," but Curt and Roland wanted a stronger voice in the direction the group would take, and the band split up. They called themselves History of Headaches before taking the name Tears for Fears, a chapter heading in Janov's book *Prisoners of Pain.*

Their friend Dave Lord turned them on to synthesizers and introduced them to keyboardist Ian Stanley. Stanley and drummer Manny Elias, of the group Interview, became the third and fourth members of Tears for Fears. Their first album, *The Hurting*, was strongly inspired by Janov's theories. The British press thought they were too morose; the British public gave them three top five singles: "Mad World," "Change" and "Pale Shelter."

Looking toward their next album, the group released a single, "The Way You Are." It peaked at number 24 in Britain, and Curt and Roland felt they needed to change direction or their next LP would be *The Hurting II*. They took a few months off and came up with some of the material that would be recorded for their second album, *Songs From the Big Chair.*

They needed a final song to complete the album, and had three from which to choose. Producer Chris Hughes liked a half-finished song that Roland had been working on. "I really didn't think it was any good," Orzabal told Gary Graff of the Knight-Ridder newspaper chain. "It sounded so very un-Tears for Fears to me." Hughes suggested Orzabal complete the lyrics and a guitar line, and "Everybody Wants to Rule the World" was recorded in three days—a remarkable feat, considering it had taken four months to record "Shout" [see 614] and "Head Over Heels." "We added a few things and made some changes,"

Orzabal explained to Graff. "I really like the guitar line. And it came together so quick—I really do love it now."

"The reason we did it was to get an American hit," Curt confessed to Jim Sullivan in *USA Today.* "(It) sounded American because it's, like, *drive* music, and a lot of Americans love that." While "Shout" was the first single from the album in most other countries, "Everybody Wants to Rule the World" was purposely selected as the first single for America.

The song was rerecorded in 1986 as "Everybody Wants to Run the World," the musical theme for Sport-Aid, a Bob Geldof-supported charity event that continued the work of Live Aid [see 612—"A View to a Kill"].

### THE TOP FIVE
*Week of June 8, 1985*

1  **Everybody Wants to Rule the World**
Tears for Fears

2  **Everything She Wants**
Wham!

3  **Axel F**
Harold Faltermeyer

4  **Suddenly**
Billy Ocean

5  **Heaven**
Bryan Adams

# 610 Heaven A&M 2729
## BRYAN ADAMS

*Writers: Bryan Adams*
      *Jim Vallance*

*Producers: Bryan Adams*
         *Bob Clearmountain*

*June 22, 1985*
*2 weeks*

BRYAN ADAMS' "Heaven" ascended to the top of the Hot 100 two years after it was first recorded for the film *A Night in Heaven*, which starred Christopher Atkins as a male stripper. Danny Goldberg, hired by producer Gene Kirkwood to be the music supervisor for the movie, had arranged for A&M Records to release the soundtrack album. "When we sat down to think about who might be on the soundtrack, I suggested Bryan Adams, who at that point had *Cuts Like a Knife*, which (had) sold about 100,000 (copies)," explains Jeff Gold, former assistant to Jerry Moss, co-founder of A&M Records.

"Bryan was just starting to happen," Goldberg agrees. "He was not at all a big name yet, but it was clear to people who were paying attention that he was going to be somebody."

"We sent (Bryan) a script, and to be honest, he wasn't very impressed with it," says Gold. "But we asked him to . . . write a song anyway. He sent me a demo of a song he and Jim Vallance literally put together in a day. He wrote the song in Vancouver and demoed it in Jim's basement studios. (He) sent it to us and we flipped out—we thought it was great. So great, in fact, that we wanted him to record it. He was really reticent about it because he didn't feel strongly about the script. I was dispatched with Danny Goldberg to go to Columbia, South Carolina, show him a rough cut of the film and get him to record the song."

Adams was ill when they arrived. He watched the rough cut in his tour bus. "He wasn't real impressed with the movie, nor were we, but I think as a favor to Jerry Moss he decided he would record this song, 'Heaven,' " Gold says.

By the time the film and soundtrack album were released, Adams' career had heated up. "The film was a colossal failure," Gold acknowledges. "But Bryan was so hot, and *Cuts Like a Knife* had exhausted a long run in the charts . . . so a lot of AOR (album-oriented rock) stations picked up on

this song." Top 40 stations also added "Heaven" to their playlists.

Guy Zapoleon, program director of KZZP in Phoenix, Arizona, was one of the first to play "Heaven" off the soundtrack LP. "Listening to (the) new releases, I kept (hearing) this song and I got chills," he remembers. "The more I heard it, the more I knew this was a number one record. When it came time to (add new songs) that particular week, I (said) I'm going to give this record a shot. It just took off. Every source of research I could find showed it was a number one record." Zapoleon says he "started screaming at the vice president of promotion at A&M Records, Charlie Minor, to release 'Heaven' as a single." But it didn't happen.

"We thought it might be smart to save this, to put (it) out as a track on his next record and at least have a built-in demand item in addition to whatever hit single we would get," Gold explains. "Run to You" and "Somebody" were the first two singles from Adams' next LP, *Reckless*. "By that time there was a huge outcry to put out 'Heaven' as the third single," says Gold. Adams was reluctant but gave his consent. "(He) grew to like the song more than he had initially," Gold reports.

Adams was born in Kingston, On-

tario. His father worked for the British and Canadian military and then the United Nations, so between the ages of 6 and 12 Bryan lived in many different countries, including Israel, Portugal and Austria. When he returned to Canada, he was ready to rock and roll. "My hair was really long, and my attitude was that school just made no sense. . . . In high school, I was too far into my music to even pay attention to girls," he told Steve Pond in *Rolling Stone*.

Bryan was 17 when he met Jim Vallance at a music store. Vallance, formerly of the band Prism, was looking for a singer to record a demo. The two decided to write together. "I tried to be really tactful, but Bryan was an unruly young fellow, and the song ideas were just unstructured and undisciplined. So we pretty much scrapped anything he and I had been working on independently and started working together," Vallance told Pond.

At first Adams thought he and Vallance would form a duo, but he soon realized that his older, more conservative partner was happier working behind the scenes. They sent out many demo tapes before A&M Records offered Adams one dollar to record four songs. "I couldn't find anyone else to give me a break, so that's the one I took," Adams said.

His first single for A&M, "Let Me Take You Dancing," was a hit in the discos. "It was originally written as a pop song," Adams told Christopher Connelly in *Rolling Stone*. "Then they remixed it in New York and jacked it up to a million beats a minute. I remember getting the tape in the mail; I just about fell off my face."

## THE TOP FIVE
### *Week of June 22, 1985*

1 **Heaven**
   Bryan Adams

2 **Sussudio**
   Phil Collins

3 **Everybody Wants to
   Rule the World**
   Tears for Fears

4 **Raspberry Beret**
   Prince

5 **A View to a Kill**
   Duran Duran

*Writer: Phil Collins*

*Producers: Phil Collins*
            *Hugh Padgham*

*July 6, 1985*
*1 week*

"SUSSUDIO" WAS PHIL COLLINS' third consecutive number one single, making him the fifth male vocalist to accomplish this feat in the rock era. His predecessors: Elvis Presley (with five in a row), Andy Gibb, Michael Jackson (who also had five) and George Michael (with four).

"Sussudio" was the second single released from the *No Jacket Required* LP, and the second number one from that album [see 604—"One More Night"]. "When I first started writing stuff for the new album, I said to myself I want to write some different kind of songs, because I didn't want to be known as a miserable sod," Collins said in a recorded interview. "A lot of my songs are not necessarily miserable but they're about a certain aspect of relationships which isn't . . . the most optimistic. So I decided to do some dance-orientated songs."

The result, "Sussudio," was criticized in the British rock press for sounding too much like Prince—specifically like the song "1999." "I loved that song, I bought it when it first came out and I used to listen to it on the road," Collins noted. "I just took the tempo . . . I locked it into the drum machine. That was the end of it . . . I'd love to sound like Prince . . . I'm a big Prince fan."

Collins addressed the criticism in a *Rolling Stone* interview with Rob Hoerburger. "If anyone thinks I'm ripping off specific songs, that is up to them, but I'm not plagiarizing black music. 'Sussudio' was changed once because it was starting to sound a bit *too* much like Prince. I could never write a song like Prince, because I'm not from that environment. I'm a white guy from Hounslow in London. Because of my love of R&B and the fact that I surround myself with black musicians, music critics think I'm trying to convince people that I'm a half black. I have never been under any misconception of who I am or where I come from."

What exactly is "Sussudio"? The word itself is one Collins made up to verbalize the drum roll he uses on the track. As for the remaining lyrics, he described the song's content in *Record Mirror*: "It is about everything and yet it is about nothing. Seriously, it's about a younger man's fantasy for an older woman. Because she smiles at him he automatically thinks she fancies him and she becomes the object of his masturbatory fantasies. It's a song I'm sure people will identify with. It's like the first tumble on a sofa with your first girl or clambering around in the back of the car."

Between "Against All Odds (Take a Look at Me Now)" and "One More Night," Collins produced an album for Philip Bailey of Earth, Wind and Fire [see 404—"Shining Star"]. The single from that LP, "Easy Lover," was a duet between the two Phils and peaked at number two in February, 1985. "(Collins) definitely has soul," Bailey told John Milward in *USA Today*, "and not just because he's singing more rhythm and blues. . . . He's got feeling, conviction and the ability to sell a song." The Bailey/Collins duet was also a hit on black radio, peaking at number three on the *Billboard* Hot Black Singles chart. "Easy Lover" paved the way for "Sussudio," which went to number eight on the Hot Black Singles chart.

Some feared that Collins' success on his own might lead to his departure from Genesis, the art-rock band he joined in 1970. In an October, 1986, interview in *Playboy*, Collins may have fueled speculation: "If someone told me I had to choose between Genesis and my solo career, I'd choose my solo career; I'm totally responsible for it. But I don't have to choose. . . . It's good fun to have both."

The fun lasted almost ten more years. In April, 1996, Collins announced his departure from Genesis. Rather than remain a duo, Mike Rutherford and Tony Banks conducted a search for a new vocalist. Fourteen months later, the group announced that 28-year-old Ray Wilson would take Collins' place.

## THE TOP FIVE
*Week of July 6, 1985*

1 **Sussudio**
   Phil Collins

2 **A View to a Kill**
   Duran Duran

3 **Raspberry Beret**
   Prince

4 **Heaven**
   Bryan Adams

5 **The Search Is Over**
   Survivor

## A View to a Kill CAPITOL 5475
### DURAN DURAN

Writers: *Duran Duran*
*John Barry*

Producers: *Bernard Edwards*
*Jason Corsaro*
*Duran Duran*

*July 13, 1985*
*2 weeks*

IT'S A TRADITION: a new James Bond film means a new James Bond theme song. But it took 20 years and almost six months from the time the first Bond soundtrack single charted until 007 brought home a number one song with "A View to a Kill," the title song from Roger Moore's final Bond movie.

Until Duran Duran hit the top of the Hot 100, the most successful Bond singles were Paul McCartney's "Live and Let Die" from the film of the same name and Carly Simon's "Nobody Does It Better" from *The Spy Who Loved Me*. Both spent three weeks at number two. Chronologically, here are the Bond themes from the officially-sanctioned Bond movies that have appeared on the Hot 100:

"Goldfinger," Shirley Bassey (number eight in March, 1965)
"Thunderball," Tom Jones (number 25 in January, 1966)
"You Only Live Twice," Nancy Sinatra (number 44 in July, 1967)
"Diamonds Are Forever," Shirley Bassey (number 57 in March, 1972)
"Live and Let Die," Wings (number two in August, 1973)
"Nobody Does It Better," Carly Simon

from *The Spy Who Loved Me* (number two in October, 1977)
"For Your Eyes Only," Sheena Easton (number four in October, 1981)
"All Time High," Rita Coolidge from *Octopussy* (number 36 in August, 1983)
"A View to a Kill," Duran Duran (number one in July, 1985)
"If You Asked Me To," Patti LaBelle from *License to Kill* (number 79 in October, 1989)
"Die Another Day," Madonna (number eight in November, 2002)

There were two Bond films not produced by Cubby Broccoli. *Casino Royale* included Dusty Springfield's "The Look of Love" (number 22 in January, 1967) and Herb Alpert's recording of the title song (number 27 in May, 1967). A cover version of "The Look of Love" by Sergio Mendes and Brasil '66 went to number four in July, 1968. And Lani Hall recorded the title song from Sean Connery's return to the role as Bond in *Never Say Never Again* in 1983, but it did not chart.

"A View to a Kill" provided Duran Duran with their second number one single [see 590—"The Reflex"]. It also marked the temporary split of the band into two units. "It was a hard record to make," Nick Rhodes told Dennis Hunt in the *Los Angeles Times*. "We had just come off this tour. No one was delighted with the *Seven and the Ragged Tiger* album. There was a lot of tension in the studio. It was obvious that we were either going to take a break from

Duran or make a dreadful album."

Rhodes elaborated on the band's problems to Hunt: "Around the time we did 'A View to a Kill,' we started to have musical differences. John and Andy wanted to go off and do heavier rock. That's why they did Power Station. Simon and I wanted to do something more experimental and abstract."

While John Taylor and Andy Taylor recorded *The Power Station* album with vocalist Robert Palmer [see 634—"Addicted to Love"], the other three Durans (Simon LeBon, Nick Rhodes and Roger Taylor) formed Arcadia and recorded *So Red the Rose*, which included the single "Election Day" (number six in December, 1985). When Duran Duran did come back together, they were reduced to a trio. Roger Taylor left for health reasons and Andy Taylor left to concentrate on a solo career.

## THE TOP FIVE
*Week of July 13, 1986*

1 **A View to a Kill**
Duran Duran

2 **Sussudio**
Phil Collins

3 **Raspberry Beret**
Prince

4 **The Search Is Over**
Survivor

5 **Would I Lie to You?**
Eurythmics

*Writer: Daryl Hall*

*Producer: Laurie Latham*

*July 27, 1985*
*1 week*

**B**ACK in 1981, Daryl Hall's and John Oates' first self-produced album, *Voices*, yielded a number one hit [see 541—"Kiss on My List"]. Four years and three months later, another song from that album topped the Hot 100— "Everytime You Go Away," in a version by British pop star Paul Young.

It was Young's first American number one; he had already topped the British chart with a cover version of Marvin Gaye's "Wherever I Lay My Hat (That's My Home)." In fact, his first five American chart singles were all cover versions: in addition to the Daryl Hall and Marvin Gaye songs, he recorded Jack Lee's "Come Back and Stay," John Hurley's and Ronnie Wilkins' "Love of the Common People" and Elliot Randall's "I'm Gonna Tear Your Playhouse Down," an R&B hit for Ann Peebles.

Young explained to Billy Cioffi in *Music Connection* why so many of his single releases were cover versions: "I don't think I write singles. Which is why so many of our singles are covers. I want to search out and find great songs, I want to be the kind of artist who can go out and choose quality songs, in the same way Rod Stewart did with Tim Hardin's 'Reason to Believe' . . . people think I'm old-fashioned by covering other people's tunes, but it's really the other way around. People have been writing and covering their own tunes for 20 years now and it's about time they changed."

Daryl Hall might have been unhappy to read Merle Ginsberg's interview with Paul Young in *Rolling Stone*, where the singer commented, "I'd never cover a song I think there's a definitive version of." But in an interview in *Music Connection*, Hall gave Young credit for coming up with a commercial rendition of "Everytime You Go Away." "I never thought of it any other way than the way it was till Paul Young did it," Hall said. "I was just doin' a kind of gospel/soul song; that was all I had in mind for it. I was really surprised to hear the production they did because it kept the elements but commercialized it—made it sound like a pop record."

Paul Antony Young was born on January 17, 1956, in Luton, Bedfordshire, England. He took up the piano at age 14. Two years later he was hired at the same Vauxhall automobile manufacturing plant where his father worked, and in his free time he played bass guitar for local bands. In 1978 he was a member of Streetband, who signed with Logo Records and reached number 18 on the British chart with a novelty song called "Toast." "There I was, trying to hang on to me English accent, though I'd been listening to a lot of soul. It came out quite weird," Young said in *Newsweek*.

The next band Young was in proved more popular, although they never had a chart single. The Q-Tips, an eight-piece unit, played over 700 gigs in three-and-a-half years. "It was only then that I really found my voice," Young said. "There's nothing that improves your voice more than hearing it coming back at you night after night over the foldback on a *live* stage."

Muff Winwood, head of A&R for CBS Records in Britain (and brother of Steve Winwood) liked the band but didn't think they had commercial potential. He signed Young to a solo deal at the end of 1981. "They were confused about my direction," Young told Hilburn. "I think they kind of had in mind to push me in a poppy, lightweight soul direction."

Young collaborated with Q-Tips keyboard player Ian Kewley to write two original songs for his first album, *No Parlez*. The remaining songs were cover versions. "Wherever I Lay My Hat" failed to duplicate its British success in America; the single peaked at number 70 in October, 1983. "I expected (the album) to do here what it did in Europe," Young said in *Rolling Stone*. "When that didn't happen, I was left sort of up in the air. It began to get to me." In *Newsweek*, Young said: "It's especially important to me that America knows what I'm doing is good, because 90 percent of my influences are American."

"Everytime You Go Away" let America know that what Paul Young was doing was good. And as the summer of 1985 ended, Paul was joined by Daryl Hall on a New York stage for an extended duet of their number one song.

## THE TOP FIVE
*Week of July 27, 1985*

1 **Everytime You Go Away**
Paul Young

2 **Shout**
Tears for Fears

3 **You Give Good Love**
Whitney Houston

4 **A View to a Kill**
Duran Duran

5 **If You Love Somebody Set Them Free**
Sting

## 614   Shout   MERCURY 880 294 7
### TEARS FOR FEARS

---

*Writers: Roland Orzabal*
       *Ian Stanley*

*Producer: Chris Hughes*

*August 3, 1985*
*3 weeks*

---

Tears for Fears' second American single from *Songs From the Big Chair* gave them their second American number one: "Shout." Their first single [see 609—"Everybody Wants to Rule the World"] had only taken a week to record. "Shout" and its follow-up, "Head Over Heels," consumed the first half of the eight months it took to record the entire LP.

The first four months were "a teething period," according to Roland Orzabal. "It really paved the way for the rest of the album. We found it quite difficult being a bit more direct, a bit tougher. . . . In the past we'd been too modest, too subtle."

Their first album, *The Hurting*, had been strongly influenced by the works of Arthur Janov, author of *The Primal Scream*. The title of their second LP came from an NBC-TV miniseries starring Sally Field. "The idea for the title was from a film called *Sybil*," Curt Smith said on the TV program "Hollywood Insider." "It's about a girl with 14 different personalities. . . .

And her analyst has this very large chair, that when she regresses back to certain personalities in her past, she always wants to sit with her analyst in this big chair. It's the place where she feels comfortable; not scared of anyone; not frightened about what the outside world thinks of her."

Although "Shout" took a long time to record, it did not take long to compose the song. "We had a chorus—and that was the only thing we had," recalls Roland. "We knew it was a good chorus. We decided we needed a verse and I said, 'I can't think of anything . . . I need to go home.' Chris (Hughes, their producer) said, 'You've got an hour, try and do something.' Ian Stanley, our keyboard player, pointed me in the right direction. He showed me a few notes . . . and then it came, just like that."

Roland explained "Shout" to reporter Peter Standish: " 'Shout' works on a couple of levels. The easiest to understand is quite simply, it's about making a noise. Making your opinions known about how you feel about what's going on socially, politically, things that disturb you. One thing that disturbed an awful lot of people . . . was the installment of American nuclear weapons in England . . . that frightened an awful lot of people, including myself."

"But I don't really think we're trying to do much more with our music than sell a few records," Roland told Ron Young in the *San Antonio Light*. "Certainly many of our songs have a message. But ultimately people don't listen."

Roland confirmed to Todd Everett in the *Los Angeles Herald-Examiner* that the band intended to have *Songs From the Big Chair* sell more copies than *The Hurting*: "With this album, we sat down and agreed that we were going to try to sell a lot of records. We went so far as to pick out what we called the 'money tracks,' the potential hit singles, and work a lot on them, then throw the rest of the album down. Now that attitude's pretty hardheaded and the album is more commercially oriented, but I think it's benefitted from that approach."

The band was obviously not unhappy to score two consecutive charttoppers in America. "Because it's that kind of pie-in-the-sky pipe dream to have a number one in America," Roland told Standish. "Having said that, though, a number one in England has been elusive so far. We've been number one in virtually every territory apart from England. I'm glad that we've been number one in the States. I'm glad that we've achieved that. At least it gets it out of the way."

The band also used *Songs From the Big Chair* to establish that they were not as depressingly serious as some might have assumed from listening to *The Hurting*. "I think we have a lot of humor in what we do," Curt has said. "It's not Z.Z. Top, but we do smile, you know."

## THE TOP FIVE
*Week of August 3, 1985*

1 **Shout**
  Tears for Fears

2 **Everytime You Go Away**
  Paul Young

3 **If You Love Somebody**
  **Set Them Free**
  Sting

4 **You Give Good Love**
  Whitney Houston

5 **Glory Days**
  Bruce Springsteen

high school teacher who turns the band down. Howe: "So we needed the riff . . . finally he sent us just the basic instrumental track with dummy lyrics. He hadn't even finished the song. So in the movie we were never able to get to the part where the vocal starts, because we didn't have a lyric. I extended the intro and Marty with his band plays this intro and just at the moment where he's going to sing, Huey cuts him off." Huey's comment in the film: "I'm afraid you're just too darn loud." ·

The final tracks from Huey arrived in the nick of time. "We went right up to a couple of days before the final mix of the movie before we had the finished version of 'The Power of Love,' " says Howe.

Zemeckis found the only scene where the song would work. "He said the only place this works at all is coming out of the doctor's place and the skateboard ride to school. . . . If we put it any closer to the audition then it's going to be the same song on top of itself," explains Howe, who says that not everyone liked "The Power of Love." "There were a lot of people who were saying, 'It's a terrible record; "Back in Time" is the hit record.' I said it's a smash, it's a wonderful record."

"The Power of Love" was the first number one single for Huey Lewis and the News. They first charted with "Do You Believe in Love" (number seven in April, 1982), from their second album, *Picture This*. Their third album, *Sports*, yielded four consecutive top 10 singles between the fall of 1983 and the fall of 1984: "Heart and Soul," "I Want a New Drug," "The Heart of Rock and Roll" and "If This Is It."

Writers: *John Colla*
*Chris Hayes*
*Huey Lewis*

Producers: *Huey Lewis and the News*

August 24, 1985
2 weeks

**B**ONES HOWE produced number one songs for the Association [see 226—"Windy"] and the Fifth Dimension [see 253—"Aquarius/Let the Sunshine In" and 261—"Wedding Bell Blues"] before going into the business of supervising music for motion pictures. He was music supervisor and sound designer on the film *The Adventures of Buckaroo Banzai*. Neil Canton, co-producer of that film, was asked to produce a movie for Steven Spielberg's Amblin Entertainment production company. Canton told Howe he should audition to be the music supervisor for the film, which was about a kid who goes back in time 30 years and meets his parents as teenagers.

Canton said the producers would want music from 1985 as well as 1955. "I went home and did my music research, which really wasn't that difficult, because I was in the music industry in 1955," says Howe, who read the script and met with the producers. They hired him to supervise the music for *Back to the Future*.

"They had already decided they wanted Huey Lewis to write something original for the picture," Howe

remembers. "They were using 'I Want a New Drug' (as a temporary track)." The film went into production and Huey viewed some of the dailies. He met with Spielberg along with director/co-writer Robert Zemeckis, producer/co-writer Bob Gale and Canton. "They made a heavy duty pitch to Huey about doing this. Huey said he had a great idea for a song. The song was called "In the Nick of Time." He told us a little bit about it and everybody said, 'Oh, that's wonderful.' But we were in negotiations with Huey's manager and lawyers forever. In the meantime he had a commitment to finish this song with Ry Cooder."

So Huey gave "In the Nick of Time" away to another film—*Brewster's Millions*, starring Richard Pryor. It was sung by Patti LaBelle over the end titles. "We thought we were going to get that song," Howe says. "Everybody was really upset about it. But Huey said, 'Don't worry. I'm writing a great song for the end of the picture called "Back in Time." It'll work great for the end titles.' "

Working in Hollywood, Howe maintained a telephone relationship with Huey as the singer recorded material in Marin County in northern California. A deadline was approaching: for an early scene in the film, Michael J. Fox as Marty McFly was supposed to audition with his rock band for a high school dance. The inside joke was that he was playing a Huey Lewis song, and Huey would play the part of a

## THE TOP FIVE
*Week of August 24, 1985*

1 **The Power of Love**
Huey Lewis and the News

2 **Shout**
Tears for Fears

3 **Never Surrender**
Corey Hart

4 **St. Elmo's Fire
(Man in Motion)**
John Parr

5 **Freeway of Love**
Aretha Franklin

**616** ## St. Elmo's Fire (Man in Motion) ATLANTIC 89541
JOHN PARR

*Writers: David Foster*
*John Parr*

*Producer: David Foster*

*September 7, 1985*
*2 weeks*

**D**AVID FOSTER was not pleased to find out that his deadline for completing the soundtrack to the movie *St. Elmo's Fire* was moved up a month and 10 days. "That presented hideous problems," he recalls. "The older you get . . . the more you don't want to work 18 hours a day. . . . Then somebody tells you that the head of Columbia Pictures says, 'I think this is the hit movie of the summer and I want it out the day the kids get out of school.'"

Foster's protest failed to move anyone; he had a strict deadline and anything not ready by that date would be left out of the film. Initially he was angry. Then he realized the decision to release the movie earlier would benefit the film. "But it did make for long hours, and it meant when John Parr and I got together to write the theme, we only had one day to write it in. . . . We looked at each other and the first song we came up with was called 'Dirty Pictures.' That didn't work for the picture at all. We brought the director over. He said, 'Well, I love this song, but can't you get the title *St. Elmo's Fire* in there somewhere?' So we hit it again the second day and we just looked at each other. I was really depressed, because we couldn't come up with it. And this was not just a song in the movie; this was the title song." Foster remembered a tune he had done with Alice Cooper: "From the Inside." Something clicked. "In 10 minutes we had the song."

Foster invited Parr to sing the title theme based on his single "Naughty Naughty," which had peaked at number 23 in March, 1985. "David had a short list of people he wanted to work with on the film," says Parr. "I was on the list. . . . There was resistance from Columbia (Pictures) because I was virtually unknown to them. It was really David who said he wanted to work with (me)."

Parr had only seen clips from *St. Elmo's Fire* by the time he co-wrote the song. The real inspiration came from a video Foster showed him about Rick Hanson, a paraplegic athlete who was on a 25,000 mile wheelchair journey around the world to raise funds for spinal cord research. "I was instantly brimming over with ideas," says Parr. "We were vague enough with the lyric that the people involved with *St. Elmo's Fire* thought it was about the movie."

The song was Parr's first hit in his native Britain. Raised in Doncaster, England, he left home at age 15. After traveling through Europe, he returned home to play clubs and wine bars. In the autumn of 1980, he was caught in the middle of a "semi-riot" at the Rainbow club in London. "I was an innocent bystander and I got hurt," Parr remembers. "A lot of people were taken backstage. John Wolff, who at that time was managing The Who, was taking care of people. At that point, I could remember nothing more than being at that concert."

Suffering from partial amnesia, Parr was taken to Wolff's home and lived there for awhile. "He was looking for something to take on after The Who." He offered Parr a chance to record some demos in his studio and secured him a publishing contract.

Soon he was writing for artists like Meat Loaf and Roger Daltrey. Then he signed with Atlantic Records for North America and Phonogram for the rest of the world. "Naughty Naughty" was his first chart single, and it entered the Hot 100 in the closing weeks of 1984.

Parr has had difficulty following up "St. Elmo's Fire (Man in Motion)." "Love Grammar" peaked at 89 and "Blame It on the Radio" peaked one notch higher at 88.

Historical footnote: as Paul Grein noted in his "Chartbeat" column in *Billboard*, the week of September 7, 1985, was the first time in the rock era that songs from motion pictures held the top three positions on the Hot 100. In addition to Parr's title song from *St. Elmo's Fire*, "The Power of Love" by Huey Lewis and the News (from *Back to the Future*) and "We Don't Need Another Hero" by Tina Turner (from *Mad Max Beyond Thunderdome*) rounded out the top three.

---

## THE TOP FIVE
*Week of September 7, 1985*

1 **St. Elmo's Fire (Man in Motion)**
John Parr

2 **The Power of Love**
Huey Lewis and the News

3 **We Don't Need Another Hero (Thunderdome)**
Tina Turner

4 **Freeway of Love**
Aretha Franklin

5 **Summer of '69**
Bryan Adams

WARNER BROTHERS 28950 **Money for Nothing** 617
DIRE STRAITS

Writers: *Mark Knopfler*
*Sting*

Producers: *Mark Knopfler*
*Neil Dorfsman*

September 21, 1985
3 weeks

"**M**ONEY FOR NOTHING" may have been the most controversial number one song of 1985. Some people, including members of the press, objected to Mark Knopfler's use of the word "faggot" in the lyrics. Knopfler told reporter Liz Derringer how he was inspired to write the song in an appliance store on the Upper East Side of New York City: My wife Lourdes and I went to look at some kitchen stuff in this store, and there was a wall of TV sets . . . they had all this kitchen stuff in the front. There was

some, like, *blockhead* who was talking about the acts, because all of the TVs were tuned to MTV. He was . . . coming out with these classic lines. I went back to the custom kitchen part of the store and asked for a pen and paper, and started writing the song down at this kitchen table."

Knopfler elaborated to Bill Flanagan: "I wanted to use a lot of the language that the real guy actually used when I heard him, because it was more real. It just went better with the song, it was more muscular."

Knopfler discussed the backlash against the song with Stephen Holden of the *New York Times*. "The same thing happened when Randy Newman recorded 'Short People,' a song that was clearly about the stupidity of prejudice," Knopfler said. "An editor of *Gay News* in England attacked the song. What surprises me is that an intelligent journalist can misunderstand it."

Not everyone in America who listened to the song on the radio heard Knopfler's references to "little faggot." Warner Brothers Records provided edited versions of the song that deleted the epithet.

The songwriting credits for the song list a reluctant collaborator. Sting [see 574—"Every Breath You Take"] was on vacation in Montserrat in the West Indies while Dire Straits were there to record *Brothers In Arms*. Dropping by for dinner one evening, Sting was invited to add his vocals to the song on the refrain, "I want my MTV," which was sung to the Police's tune

"Don't Stand So Close to Me." Sting's publishing company insisted on sharing in the profits of the song. John Illsley, bass player for Dire Straits, told Robert Allen: "Sting said that it was completely ridiculous, but you know what record companies are like. So he gets a credit on the song."

Mark Knopfler was born August 12, 1949, in Glasgow, Scotland. When he was six the family moved to Newcastle, and by age 15 Knopfler had his first electric guitar. After two years of studying journalism in college, he went to work for the *Yorkshire Evening Post*, where his last assignment was writing an obituary for Jimi Hendrix. He spent a couple of months in an R&B group called Brewer's Droop, and then started a band called Cafe Racers.

Knopfler soon formed a new band with his younger brother David, David's roommate Illsley and Pick Withers, a drummer at Dave Edmunds' studio. At their first gig, a punk festival in 1977, they borrowed the name Cafe Racers. A friend of Withers suggested Dire Straits, based on their financial standing, and they adopted it in time for their second gig.

In late 1977, a demo tape that included "Sultans of Swing" was sent to BBC disc jockey Charlie Gillett at Radio London. He liked it enough to play it on his "Honky Tonk" show. One of the listeners was John Stainze, from the A&R department at Phonogram, who beat out several other record companies to sign the band. Later the group signed with Warner Brothers for North America, and the first single, a new recording of "Sultans of Swing," peaked at number four in April, 1979.

In July, 1980, David Knopfler left the group. Withers departed in 1982 after recording the *Love Over Gold* LP. By the time *Brothers in Arms* was released, the line-up of Dire Straits included Mark Knopfler, John Illsley, keyboardists Alan Clark and Guy Fletcher and drummer Terry Williams. Flute/sax player Chris White and second guitarist Jack Sonni joined later.

Knopfler's work includes activity outside of Dire Straits. He wrote "Private Dancer," the title tune of Tina Turner's comeback LP in 1984, and he has composed film scores for *Local Hero, Cal, Comfort and Joy* and *The Princess Bride*.

## THE TOP FIVE
*Week of September 21, 1985*

1  **Money for Nothing**
   Dire Straits

2  **Cherish**
   Kool and the Gang

3  **St. Elmo's Fire
   (Man in Motion)**
   John Parr

4  **We Don't Need Another
   Hero (Thunderdome)**
   Tina Turner

5  **Don't Lose My Number**
   Phil Collins

## 618 Oh Sheila MCA 52636
### READY FOR THE WORLD

**Writers:** *Melvin Riley*
*Gordon Strozier*
*Gerald Valentine*

**Producers:** *Ready for the World*

*October 12, 1985*
*1 week*

WHICH woman's name has appeared most often in the title of a number one song? Not popular names like Mary, Barbara or Linda. Three names have appeared twice in the titles of number one hits. First there was "Angie," immortalized by the Rolling Stones [see 346] and Helen Reddy [see 387]. Then came "Sheila," as in Tommy Roe's hit [see 116] and the single by Ready for the World. Finally, there's Paul Anka's "Diana" [see 25] and Michael Jackson's "Dirty Diana" [see 702].

Six young men from Flint, Michigan, make up Ready for the World. Melvin Riley (lead vocals, rhythm guitar, piano), Gordon Strozier (lead guitar, bass, drums), Gregory Potts (keyboards), John Eaton (bass), Gerald Valentine (drums) and Willie Triplett (percussion) got together after they graduated from high school. Melvin and Gordon were performing in one band and Willie and John were in another. As the two bands were competitors, Melvin was aware of the other potential members' musical talents and recruited them to be together in one band.

They considered several names for the group, including Private Boys' School, Plain Boy and Ice Connection. They wanted a group name that symbolized their music, and they settled on a moniker that came from the lyrics of one of their songs, "Ceramic Girl": "So nonchalant, laid back and ready for the world."

The six musicians went into a studio in Flint and recorded some songs for a demo tape. A local disc jockey, Charles "Mojo" Johnson at WJLB, gave them some airplay and introduced them to a management company. The demo tapes were sent to various record companies, and while there were many positive responses, no one was willing to sign the band to a contract. So they formed their own record company, Blue Lake Records, named for nearby Lake Michigan. They went to a Detroit studio to cut their first single, "Tonight," and called in a friend from Flint, Bernard Terry, to help them produce the track.

The group members personally visited record stores in their hometown to convince them to stock their single. Nick's Disco Shack was the first outlet to order the record. Eventually, "Tonight" sold well enough in Michigan to attract the attention of Jheryl Busby at MCA Records. He signed the band and released "Tonight" nationally. The group wanted to follow that with an uptempo single, but MCA selected another ballad, "Deep Inside Your Love."

Their third MCA single was "Oh Sheila." The group's Prince-like sound on the song caused many to assume that Sheila was Sheila E., the vocalist/percussionist whose mentor is Prince. "Sheila isn't anybody," Riley explained to Dennis Hunt of the *Los Angeles Times.* "I made her up."

Riley denied to Hunt that the band intended to sound like Prince. "I'm flattered that we're compared to a great artist like him. But we didn't try to sound like him. I sound like me, not Prince. I can't worry about what these negative people are saying. Fans are buying our records."

And what did the man who originally put "Sheila" on top of the chart think about the Ready for the World hit? Tommy Roe recalls the first time he heard "Oh Sheila." "I was in Minneapolis. Bobby Vee and I were doing a tour. We were driving alone in Bobby's van and this song comes on, 'Oh, Oh Sheila,' and I thought my goodness, it sounds like my record. I got my guitar out and started playing along with it, and, sure enough, it's almost the same chord progression as 'Sheila.' Of course, the melody's completely different. It's a great record—that's two number ones for the girl named Sheila. She should be pleased."

### THE TOP FIVE
*Week of October 12, 1985*

1 **Oh Sheila**
Ready for the World

2 **Money for Nothing**
Dire Straits

3 **Take on Me**
a-ha

4 **Saving All My Love for You**
Whitney Houston

5 **Part-Time Lover**
Stevie Wonder

WARNER BROTHERS 29011 **Take on Me** **619**
a-ha

*Writers: Pal Waaktaar*
*Mags Furuholem*
*Morten Harket*

*Producer: Alan Tarney*

*October 19, 1985*
*1 week*

W HEN "Take on Me" went to number one, a-ha was credited with being the first Norwegian group to top the American chart. True, they were the first *group* from Norway to go to number one on the *Billboard* Hot 100, but the honor of being the first Norwegian to be number one in America must go to someone else. Anni-Frid Lyngstad, better known as Frida, was born in Narvik, Norway, before moving to Eskilstuna, Sweden, at the age of two. Later (much later) she would be part of the most successful Scandinavian group of all time, Abba [see 458—"Dancing Queen"].

Magne (Mags for short) Furuholem of a-ha suggests that his native country is not the ideal environment for struggling young rock musicians. "Norway is sort of like heaven," he told Dennis Hunt of the *Los Angeles Times*. "There's little poverty. We all come from stable middle-class backgrounds. Just about everybody lives comfortably. It's a safe and pleasant place. If you stay there you just get lazy. We needed a sense of urgency. We had to go off and struggle, to force ourselves to be creative. We simply had to get the hell out of Norway."

In the Oslo suburb of Manglerud, Mags became friends with Pal Waaktaar when they were 12 years old. Pal, who began creating songs when he was 10, was writing in English by the time he wrote his second song.

Pal and Mags played together in a number of bands, and as early as age 14 they knew that one day they would have to move to London. They were playing school dances and club dates in a group called Britches when they met singer Morten Harket, a Uriah Heep fan who had also been in a number of local bands. Morten was asked to join them in the move to London. "I wanted to, but due to some mutual misunderstanding we lost contact and they thought I didn't want to go," he explains.

In London, Pal and Mags worked with British musicians but were unhappy with the results. "They came

back (to Norway) for me to join them again," says Morten. "We spent four months in Norway to get the act together, to see that it actually worked, that the chemistry was right. Then we left for England. We arrived in January, 1983, and spent the next two years there. It was exciting—we wanted to compete with English bands on their level."

After their move to Britain in 1983, the three musicians took their homemade demo tapes to the A&R departments at various companies but were unable to stir up any interest. Several months later their finances were drained, and Mags returned home to earn money so he could record more demos.

Back in London, the trio booked recording time at Rendezvous Studios, where they usually worked from 4 A.M. to 10 A.M. The studio manager, John Ratcliff, was impressed enough to play their music for Terry Slater, a former member of EMI's A&R department. Ratcliff and Slater offered to manage the band and arranged a showcase for the record industry. The group didn't have work permits, so they hadn't played any live gigs in Britain until that night. Their audience included executives from RCA, CBS and EMI, as well as Warner Brothers' talent scout Andy Wickham, who signed the band.

They took the name a-ha. "Originally we were trying to find a Norwegian word that people would be able to say in English," Mags told David Fricke in *Rolling Stone*. He

saw a song in Pal's notebook called "A-Ha." "It was a terrible song, but a great name. I mean, you say it, 'aha,' all the time."

Tony Mansfield produced their first album, but when the single "Take on Me" failed they went back into the studio with producer Alan Tarney (Cliff Richard, Leo Sayer) to rerecord the track. It still failed to catch fire until the American arm of Warner Brothers hired Steve Barron to direct a part live, part animated video. MTV loved it, and it received heavy rotation on the cable music channel (and went on to win many video awards).

The song had its origins in the early days of the band. "The theme from 'Take on Me' is the very first thing I heard (Pal and Mags) play together when I joined them," remembers Morten. "I said right away, 'that's going to be a hit.'"

## THE TOP FIVE
*Week of October 19, 1985*

1 **Take on Me**
a-ha

2 **Saving All My Love for You**
Whitney Houston

3 **Part-Time Lover**
Stevie Wonder

4 **Oh Sheila**
Ready for the World

5 **Miami Vice Theme**
Jan Hammer

# Saving All My Love for You ARISTA 9381
## WHITNEY HOUSTON

Writers: *Michael Masser*
*Gerry Goffin*

Producer: *Michael Masser*

*October 26, 1985*
*1 week*

WHITNEY HOUSTON made her recording debut in 1979, singing lead vocals on "Life's a Party," the title track for the Michael Zager Band's second album for the Private Stock label. Whitney was just 15 and Zager wanted to sign her to a recording contract, but her mother said no.

Mother knew all about the record business. Emily "Cissy" Drinkard Houston turned professional at age six when she joined the family gospel singing group, the Drinkard Sisters. Later she would organize an R&B quartet called the Sweet Inspirations, who sang backing vocals for Elvis Presley and Aretha Franklin.

As Minister of Music at the New Hope Baptist Church in Newark, New Jersey, Cissy was present when her eight-year-old daughter sang her first hymn in church, "Guide Me, O Thou Great Jehovah." "I think I got my emotion from gospel singing, from my mom instilling it in me at an early age," Whitney told Miles White in *USA Today*. There were other influences, including first cousin Dionne Warwick and her mother's close friend Aretha, known as "Auntie Ree".

Two years after the Zager album, Whitney signed a management contract with Gene Harvey and Seymour Flics. There were offers from labels like Epic, Elektra and Arista, but Harvey turned them down. "The most important thing was for Whitney to continue to develop as an artist in an unhurried way, unpressured way," Harvey said in the *Los Angeles Times*.

Whitney pursued a modeling career, took acting lessons and sang backing vocals for her mother's live appearances. Eventually she won a solo spot in her mother's shows, singing the Michael Masser-Gerry Goffin composition, "Greatest Love of All" [see 636]. She won roles in TV series like "Silver Spoons" and "Gimme a Break" and had photo spreads in magazines such as *Seventeen, Glamour* and *Cosmopolitan*. There were occasional recording guest appearances, including "Memories" on the *One Down* album by Material and "Eternal Love" on the *Paul Jabara and Friends* LP.

In 1983, Gerry Griffith, director of R&B music in the A&R department at Arista Records, arranged for Whitney to audition for label president Clive Davis. "Clive sat there poker-faced," Flics said in *Time*. "He said thank you and left. The next day we got an enthusiastic offer." Although she recorded duets with Teddy Pendergrass and Jermaine Jackson, her debut solo LP, *Whitney Houston*, did not appear until February, 1985. "It was a matter of searching for the right material and producers," Harvey told Paul Grein. "It was Clive's philosophy and ours that we not push this girl out there right away. We decided to wait and do the best job that we could, and if it took a little longer, so be it."

The first single from the LP was "You Give Good Love," written by LaLa and produced by Kashif. "We wanted to establish her in the black marketplace first," Clive Davis told Grein. "Otherwise, you can fall between cracks, where top 40 won't play you and R&B won't consider you their own. . . . We felt that 'You Give Good Love' would be at the very least a major black hit, though we didn't think it would cross over as strongly as it did." The single went to number three on the pop singles chart the week of July 27, 1985.

The next single was Masser and Goffin's "Saving All My Love for You," originally recorded by Marilyn McCoo and Billy Davis, Jr., [see 449—"You Don't Have to Be a Star (To Be in My Show)"] for their first CBS album. "I altered the song somewhat," explains Masser, who produced both versions. "I took out the second bridge, changed some things . . . and told Gene Harvey, 'That's the single. It's a torchy song; that's going to be your first number one.' "

---

## THE TOP FIVE
*Week of October 26, 1985*

1 **Saving All My Love for You**
Whitney Houston

2 **Part-Time Lover**
Stevie Wonder

3 **Take on Me**
a-ha

4 **Miami Vice Theme**
Jan Hammer

5 **Head Over Heels**
Tears for Fears

TAMLA 1808 **Part-Time Lover** 621
STEVIE WONDER

*Writer: Stevie Wonder*

*Producer: Stevie Wonder*

*November 2, 1985*
*1 week*

"PART-TIME LOVER" was the ninth number one for Stevie Wonder, tying the Motown artist with the Bee Gees and Paul McCartney at this point in time for fourth place among artists with the most number ones. In November, 1985, the leaders in this category were the Beatles (20), Elvis Presley (17) and the Supremes (12).

Some people might argue that Stevie could top that list if he just wouldn't wait so long to complete an album. "Part-Time Lover" was the first single from the LP *In Square Circle*, Stevie's first all-new studio album since *Hotter Than July* in 1980. "Five years is much too long to spend on making an album. We disagree tremendously on that. He could have had two or three albums out in that time," said Motown founder Berry Gordy in *Rolling Stone*.

"One of the first things you have to learn is that you can't base your life on other people's expectations," Stevie said in the *Los Angeles Times*. "I've basically taken the position that all I can do is my best. At the same time, you have the responsibility to accept nothing less than the best you can do. The only real pressures come from business matters—meetings, contracts, deadlines. But you have to accept that as part of your life. The biggest enemy is the deadline; the need to have your album done by a certain date. The only real deadline you should have is your own excitement. Your heart tells you when you're finished with a record."

Stevie told David Nathan in *Pulse* that the time he takes to record an album has nothing to do with his ego. "I don't get off on people waiting for my music. The whole idea of timing is important to me. I don't think that there is any comparison but people didn't rush Stravinsky or Beethoven! Music is my way of expressing myself, making a statement, the sum of my experiences in life. I'm not one of these people who feels that I have to make a new musical statement every six months. . . . I won't put out an album just to have one out there in the marketplace. It has to reflect my

musical development and I admit that I'm a perfectionist so I have to feel that it's right."

Stevie told Nathan about writing the songs for *In Square Circle*. "Sure, a lot of the songs I write are from my own direct experiences. I remember when I was breaking up with this girl and I was like, seeing this *other* girl. I came home and some guy called up and disguised his voice, tried to sound like one of her girlfriends to see if she was around." Nathan speculated that Stevie was talking about "Part-Time Lover." "Well, let's say that after I wrote that, I thought about how many people might get into trouble behind that song!" Stevie exclaimed.

Those who thought "Part-Time Lover" sounded like another Motown song were not wrong. As Stevie told Cary Darling in *Bam*: "When I first heard 'Part-Time Lover,' I thought of 'You Can't Hurry Love.' Uh-huh. It's a combination of 'You Can't Hurry Love' and, more so, 'My World Is Empty (Without You).' "

"Part-Time Lover" was the first single to go to number one on five

*Billboard* charts: the Hot 100, Hot Black Singles, Hot Adult Contemporary, Hot Dance/Disco Club Play and Hot Dance/Disco 12-inch Singles Sales. And coming just one week shy of 22 years and 3 months after Stevie's first number one single, "Part-Time Lover" established Stevie as the artist with the longest span of number ones to date.

### THE TOP FIVE
*Week of November 2, 1985*

1 **Part-Time Lover**
Stevie Wonder

2 **Miami Vice Theme**
Jan Hammer

3 **Saving All My Love for You**
Whitney Houston

4 **Head Over Heels**
Tears for Fears

5 **Take on Me**
a-ha

## 622 Miami Vice Theme MCA 52666
### JAN HAMMER

Writer: *Jan Hammer*

Producer: *Jan Hammer*

*November 9, 1985*
*1 week*

"**M**IAMI VICE" made its network television debut on September 16, 1984, and became an instant hit with the critics. Ratings popularity built steadily during the first season, and by summer reruns the series was firmly entrenched in A. C. Nielsen's top 10. It remained there until its third season, when NBC placed it against the CBS show "Dallas." The success of "Miami Vice" is attributable to many things, including the series' stylish sets and costumes and its unique blend of music and visuals.

Many of the television critics who praised the show in its first season made reference to the series' music, a combination of songs by artists like Glenn Frey, Phil Collins and Kate Bush and original music by Jan Hammer, the former keyboardist for the Mahavishnu Orchestra.

Hammer left his native Czechoslovakia in 1968, just before the Russian invasion. He had studied classical music composition at the University of MUSE Art in Prague, and once in the United States he enrolled in the Berklee College of Music in Boston. Six months later he dropped out and, at age 22, became pianist, arranger and composer for the Sarah Vaughan Trio. Two years after that, he relocated to Greenwich Village and fell in with a group of jazz musicians that included John McLaughlin, Billy Cobham, Rick Laird and Jerry Goodman. They formed the Mahavishnu Orchestra in 1971, recorded three jazz fusion albums and eventually broke up. Hammer then turned to jazz rock, working with artists such as Al Di Meola, Carlos Santana and Stanley Clarke. He was a sideman on Jeff Beck's world tour in 1976–77, and in 1979 he formed his own rock group, Hammer. He later recorded two albums (*Untold Passion* and *Here to Stay*) with Neal Schon, guitarist for Journey.

Hammer's next endeavor was scoring films. In 1983 he composed his first soundtrack, commissioned for the movie *A Night in Heaven* [see 610— "Heaven"] "Matching music to film is something I never studied," Hammer

told Bill McIlvaine in *BAM*. "The only real education I got was working with John Avildsen, the director of *A Night in Heaven*. That was the best school, because he's one of the best at editing. He showed me a lot about how to focus on a scene, who to focus on, whether to focus on the character or the emotion, or on the mood or atmosphere. After that, you just follow your instincts."

In March of 1984, Hammer was having meetings at various studios in Hollywood, when a friend introduced him to producer Michael Mann. Mann described his new project: "Miami Vice." "I 'clicked' instantly with the look and the feel of the show," Hammer told Brian Chin in a *Billboard* interview. "Just from the first few descriptions, I was able to play (Mann) something."

Hammer scored the pilot, and when NBC picked up "Miami Vice" as a series, Mann asked him to compose about 20 minutes of original music every week. "Other shows recycle music and use stuff over and over," Hammer told Dennis Hunt in the *Los Angeles Times*. "They take the show's theme and restate it a thousand different ways. I could do the same thing

. . . but I prefer writing all new music for every show. That freshness is important . . . but I've created a monster for myself. It's incredibly hard work."

Hammer did not read the script for each episode; about two weeks before air date he received a rough cut on three-quarter inch video tape. "I sit down and watch like a viewer, get caught up in the drama, and rely on that to goose me into action," he said in *USA Today* during the series' original run. The two or three pop songs heard in each episode had already been chosen and were on the tapes that Hammer received.

The composer was given complete freedom by Mann. "I can get adventurous and interesting because I have no one telling me what to do," Hammer said in the *Los Angeles Times*.

When MCA released the soundtrack album *Miami Vice*, it was easy to predict that Glenn Frey's "You Belong to the City" would be a hit (it peaked at number two). The long shot was Hammer's main title theme, which became the third prime time television series theme to top the Hot 100 [see 429—"Theme from S.W.A.T." and 434—"Welcome Back"]. It also became the 25th instrumental number one of the rock era, and the first since Vangelis' "Chariots of Fire" [see 554] in May, 1982.

A further surprise: the *Miami Vice* soundtrack LP went to number one and stayed there for 11 weeks, making it the most successful TV soundtrack of all time. Hammer received a congratulatory phone call from Henry Mancini, whose *The Music from Peter Gunn* was the previous record-holder—number one for 10 weeks in 1959.

---

## THE TOP FIVE
*Week of November 9, 1985*

1 **Miami Vice Theme**
   Jan Hammer

2 **Part-Time Lover**
   Stevie Wonder

3 **Head Over Heels**
   Tears for Fears

4 **You Belong to the City**
   Glenn Frey

5 **We Built This City**
   Starship

GRUNT 14170 **We Built This City**
STARSHIP

Writers:  Bernie Taupin
          Martin Page
          Dennis Lambert
          Peter Wolf

Producers: Dennis Lambert
           Peter Wolf
           Jeremy Smith

November 16, 1985
2 weeks

**B**ERNIE TAUPIN first met Martin Page at a lunch arranged by a publisher. Looking for a collaborator with a contemporary feel, Taupin took home an album Page's band, Q-Feel, had recorded. It included the track "Dancing in Heaven (Orbital Be-Bop)," a song that almost made the Hot 100 in 1983. "He listened to some of the tracks and then called me back a week after and said, 'This feels good to me, I'm ready to go. I've got a couple of lyrics I'd like to try out on you and see how it feels.' The first two lyrics he gave me were 'We Built This City' and 'These Dreams' [see 631]," Page recalls.

Page wrote music for "We Built This City" and recorded a demo for it at home in his 16-track studio. The demo circulated for six months, according to Page. "There'd been a lot of interest in the song. I believe the Motels half cut it and decided it wasn't quite right for them."

The demo was sent to Dennis Lambert, Peter Wolf and Jeremy Smith, who were set to produce the first album by the rechristened Starship. "We all agreed we loved that tune," Lambert says. "We said this song just lacks the punch of having a real chorus. We felt if we could find that special chorus or write it, it would be terrific. So we bounced off (Martin and Bernie) what we should do about it and they said, 'Well, go ahead. See what you guys can do.' And Peter and I sat down and restructured it and wrote a chorus to the tune that I think made it a very viable, very commercial hit-oriented tune."

The song was not written specifically for Starship. "I wrote 'We Built This City' from a Q-Feel perspective," Page told Ethlie Ann Vare in Billboard. "I wrote it for my band; I wrote it for me. I write my best songs when I'm writing without thinking about the artist, but thinking about what *I* would want to perform, what I would feel proud of."

The original song was not oriented to San Francisco. "Bernie and I feel it's every city," Page confirms. "We didn't write it about San Francisco. In the middle of the demo when the radio DJ comes in, I had a police call that I picked up off the radio which I used. Our demo was a little darker . . . it was a *Blade Runner* situation where you're in a city where rock and roll is being stopped by a corporation. Starship brightened it up with the radio programmer (talking about) sunny days in San Francisco."

"None of us had ever met Bernie or Martin," Grace Slick told Dave Zimmer in *Bam*. "But it sure sounded like they'd written the song with us in mind. We laughed when we first heard it, because so many of the lines hit home."

"We Built This City" was the first number one song for Starship, an accomplishment that eluded the band's former incarnations, Jefferson Airplane and Jefferson Starship. In 1967, the Airplane's first two singles both charted in the top 10: "Somebody to Love" peaked at number five in June and "White Rabbit" went to number eight in July. Over the next five years,

the Airplane had six more chart singles, including "Ballad of You & Me & Pooneil," "Volunteers" and "Pretty As You Feel," but none made the top 40.

Reorganized as Jefferson Starship, their first single was released in 1974. "Ride the Tiger" petered out at number 84, but the next single, "Miracles," became the band's biggest hit to date, peaking at number three in October, 1975. Their only other top 10 single was "Count on Me," which climbed to number eight in May, 1978.

## THE TOP FIVE
*Week of November 16, 1985*

1  **We Built This City**
   Starship

2  **You Belong to the City**
   Glenn Frey

3  **Miami Vice Theme**
   Jan Hammer

4  **Head Over Heels**
   Tears for Fears

5  **Part-Time Lover**
   Stevie Wonder

# 624 Separate Lives ATLANTIC 89498
## PHIL COLLINS and MARILYN MARTIN

*Writer: Stephen Bishop*

*Producers: Arif Mardin*
*    Phil Collins*
*    Hugh Padgham*

*November 30, 1985*
*1 week*

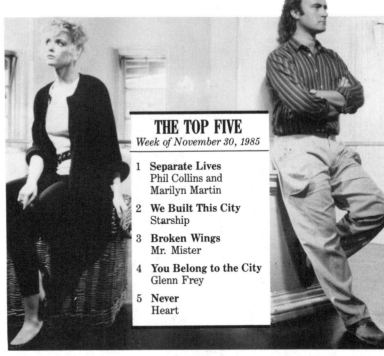

**THE TOP FIVE**
*Week of November 30, 1985*

1 **Separate Lives**
Phil Collins and
Marilyn Martin

2 **We Built This City**
Starship

3 **Broken Wings**
Mr. Mister

4 **You Belong to the City**
Glenn Frey

5 **Never**
Heart

MISCONCEPTION NUMBER 1: Phil Collins wrote "Separate Lives" for the Taylor Hackford film *White Nights*. It was easy to assume that Collins penned "Separate Lives" because he had written and performed the title song for Hackford's *Against All Odds* [see 586] and had been nominated for an Academy Award for that number one hit. But it was Stephen Bishop who wrote "Separate Lives," and the song dates back to 1982, when Hackford described the plot of *White Nights* to Bishop.

"I don't usually go on rough ideas," Bishop told Ethlie Ann Vare in *Billboard*, "but this sounded interesting, so I went ahead and did it. Then the movie kept getting turned down by the studios and I got tired of waiting. I ended up giving the song to Phil Collins and at some point, apparently either Taylor or Atlantic found out Phil was going to cut it, and they did it directly with him. I'm sure a lot of people now think Phil wrote the song."

Bishop gives partial credit for inspiration to his former girlfriend, actress Karen Allen (*Starman*). She broke up with him in 1981. "She thought it was a song about love," Bishop said in *People*. "But to me it's a song about anger."

The experience of writing "Separate Lives" was cathartic, according to Bishop. "It was emotional, very emotional writing," he said in *SongTalk*. "I've got the original draft, and I wrote it so deliberately that my pen just engraved itself into the paper."

Bishop was nominated but did not win an Oscar for "Separate Lives," losing to another song from *White Nights*, one written by Lionel Richie [see 626—"Say You, Say Me"]. Bishop has been a prolific writer of songs for films. In 1978 he wrote and recorded the title song for *Animal House*, which he claims should have been a hit. "The record company released it three months after the movie," he said in *Billboard*. "Here everyone was running around yelling 'toga, toga, toga,' and it was right there on the record,

but the record wasn't out." Bishop also wrote "It Might Be You" for *Tootsie*. That song peaked at number 25 in May, 1983.

Misconception Number 2: Crystal Gayle joined Phil Collins for a duet on "Separate Lives." "People think it's Crystal Gayle singing," Marilyn Martin acknowledged to Dennis Hunt in the *Los Angeles Times*. Martin was virtually unknown when she was selected to record the song with Collins. The Louisville, Kentucky, native had her first big break in 1983 when she sang backing vocals on an album by Joe Vitale, drummer for singer Joe Walsh. Walsh heard Martin sing and later invited her to sing backing vocals for him on tour. Stevie Nicks was headlining the tour, and she asked Martin to sing backing vocals for her as well. That led to touring with Kenny Loggins and singing background vocals on his number one single [see 585—"Footloose"].

In 1983, Martin and her husband, recording engineer Greg Drollman, moved to Los Angeles, where Marilyn was hired to sing on Nicks' *Rock a Little* LP. Doug Morris, president of Atlantic Records, was at a session and liked Marilyn enough to sign her to record her own album for Atlantic. But before she could begin work on

that project, she was asked to sing with Collins. "Doug thought my voice would blend well with Phil's," she told Hunt. "Phil had the final say on who would sing with him. They sent him a tape of my work and he said OK."

Prior to the recording, Martin met Collins backstage after one of his shows. At that point, she was in awe of the popular vocalist. "I was very intimidated at first," she admits. "The thought of trying to be on the same level with somebody like Phil was incredibly intimidating. But he and Arif (Mardin) were so kind. They let me know . . . if they didn't think I could do the job, I wouldn't be there in the first place."

After the song went to number one, Martin expressed some regrets to Hunt. "I'm not ungrateful for what it's done for me. I have nothing against the song. The only problem is that it's a ballad. I don't want to be classified as a singer who sings these quiet ballads. . . . I wouldn't sing a song I didn't like. 'Separate Lives' is great for what it is. It's just that I prefer singing another kind of song."

Martin had that chance when she recorded her LP *Night Moves*, released in early 1986. The title track was the first single; it peaked at number 25 in March.

Writers: *Richard Page*
*Steve George*
*John Lang*

Producers: *Paul DeVilliers*
*Mr. Mister*

December 7, 1985
2 weeks

"**S**TEVIE WONDER has talked about this river that runs by him and the creative process; that he really doesn't have anything to do with it, it's just there," explains Richard Page, who has personally worn out three copies of Wonder's *Fulfillingness' First Finale*. "If he can become a part of that river of thought and creativity, then it comes through him as a channel. I feel like I've only experienced that a couple of times, where the song happened effortlessly, and ("Broken Wings") was one of them."

"Broken Wings" was written in 20 minutes by Page, Mr. Mister keyboardist Steve George and Page's cousin John Lang. ("Unfortunately John doesn't play an instrument or he would probably be in the band," Page says.) The three composers were at Page's Southern California home. "We weren't there to write. The drum machine was going. I started with the bass line. Before I knew it, the song was done. It just sort of happened and luckily I had the tape machine on."

"Broken Wings" was one of three songs on a demo tape that the band gave to RCA Records when they were lobbying to produce themselves. But the label did not plan to release it as the first single from Mr. Mister's second album, *Welcome to the Real World*. The band was told that an uptempo track would have a better chance of making the chart. "We just felt it was the best track on the record," Page told Roy Trakin of *USA Today*. "That was our criteria, rather than looking for what would best fill the marketplace."

It was a different strategy than the band had used for their first RCA album, *I Wear the Face*. "The first album . . . was kind of a premeditated attempt at having a hit song," Page admitted to Tom Popson of the *Chicago Tribune*. "We were kind of starved for a hit. We tried to tailor-make a couple of songs for the marketplace, tried to fit the radio format—all stuff that doesn't work, which I found

out the hard way. We were listening to a lot of songs at the top of the charts. It's embarrassing to even say that. It's so unartistic, just a desperate attempt at having a hit. I'll never, ever do that again. But it was a good learning experience for us about writing what's real and meaningful rather than trying to blast the public with a hit song."

"Broken Wings" was not an immediate hit. "It was out there 12 or 13 weeks before it even hit the charts, and most songs are dead after 12 weeks if they haven't hit the charts," Page told Popson. "We thought, 'Oh, no, it's dying.' But the song became popular in a couple of places like Minneapolis and Denver. The record company went right for the throat as soon as they found those pockets within the country."

After Mr. Mister's own version of "Broken Wings" went to number one, a jazz version was recorded by Miles Davis. "We were recording recently in Los Angeles and we heard him rehearsing it in another room," drummer Pat Mastelotto told Walter Berry of the Associated Press. "Miles was playing the tape back and forth, teach-

ing his band the song. It knocked us out. We couldn't believe it. I mean, Miles Davis!"

A final footnote for those who need convincing that history repeats itself: The song that was number one on the Hot 100 exactly 10 years to the week before "Broken Wings" was "Fly, *Robin*, Fly" [see 421] by Silver Convention. And exactly 10 years before that, the number one song was "Turn! Turn! Turn!" [see 188] by the *Byrds*.

## THE TOP FIVE
*Week of December 7, 1985*

1 **Broken Wings**
   Mr. Mister

2 **Separate Lives**
   Phil Collins and Marilyn Martin

3 **We Built This City**
   Starship

4 **Never**
   Heart

5 **Say You, Say Me**
   Lionel Richie

## 626 Say You, Say Me MOTOWN 1819
### LIONEL RICHIE

*Writer: Lionel Richie*

*Producers: Lionel Richie*
*James Anthony*
*Carmichael*

*December 21, 1985*
*4 weeks*

"SAY YOU, SAY ME" was the second number one single from Taylor Hackford's film *White Nights*, which starred Mikhail Baryshnikov as a Russian defector who happens to be the world's greatest ballet star and Gregory Hines as an American soldier who defects to the Soviet Union. Lionel Richie's tune, which won the Oscar for Best Original Song, topped the Hot 100 just three weeks after Stephen Bishop's composition "Separate Lives" [see 624].

*White Nights* is only the sixth motion picture of the rock era to produce more than one number one single. The first was *Saturday Night Fever*, which holds the record for the most number one songs from a movie. The films and the number one songs they included are:

1. *Saturday Night Fever.* "How Deep Is Your Love" [see 476], "Stayin' Alive" [see 478] and "Night Fever" [see 480] by the Bee Gees and "If I Can't Have You" by Yvonne Elliman [see 481]. "Night Fever" and "If I Can't Have You" mark the only time two songs from the same film were number one consecutively.

2. *Grease.* "You're the One That I Want" [see 484] by John Travolta and Olivia Newton-John and "Grease" [see 488] by Frankie Valli.

3. *Flashdance.* "Flashdance . . . What a Feeling" [see 573] by Irene Cara and "Maniac" [see 576] by Michael Sembello.

4. *Footloose.* "Footloose" [see 585] by Kenny Loggins and "Let's Hear It for the Boy" [see 588] by Deniece Williams.

5. *Purple Rain.* "When Doves Cry" [see 591] by Prince and "Let's Go Crazy" [see 595] by Prince and the Revolution.

6. *White Nights.* "Separate Lives" [see 624] by Phil Collins and Marilyn Martin and "Say You, Say Me" by Lionel Richie.

Lionel was originally asked by Hackford to write the title song for *White Nights*. "We showed him the film and he loved it," says Gary LeMel, who at the time was head of Columbia Pictures' music department. "He definitely wanted to write a title song. A couple of weeks later I heard back from (Lionel's manager) Ken Kragen (who) said, 'Look, he can't seem to write anything called "White Nights," but he's written something that he thinks is one of the better things he's written and it fits the picture perfectly.'" Hackford and LeMel listened to the demo of "Say You, Say Me." They agreed that it was perfect for the movie.

One problem: they couldn't include the song on the soundtrack album, which Atlantic Records was releasing. "Lionel was supposed to deliver his (new) solo album to Motown on a certain date," explains LeMel. "Motown would not allow us to have 'Say You, Say Me' on the soundtrack but they agreed to release it as a single in time to promote the picture . . . as things turned out, Lionel (didn't) finish his album for almost a year. . . . The movie didn't suffer . . . (but) the soundtrack album would have sold more had (the song) been on (it)."

Lionel's *Dancing on the Ceiling* LP wasn't released until August, 1986. The delay was so long that the title was changed from *Say You, Say Me* in favor of the next single from the album. "Dancing on the Ceiling" peaked at number two in September. "Love Will Conquer All" went to number nine in November and "Ballerina Girl" reached number seven in February, 1987. When "Se La" failed to go higher than number 20 in May, it was the first single of Lionel's solo career that failed to make the top 10.

Richie had one more chart single on Motown. "Do It to Me" reached number 21 in June, 1992. Two months later, Richie left his long-time label home and signed with Mercury. But he didn't chart again until 1996. On January 30 of that year, he performed his new single "Don't Wanna Lose You," on ABC-TV's "The American Music Awards." The song peaked at number 39 on the Hot 100 in May.

On April 8, 2003, Richie was the celebrity judge on the popular TV series "American Idol." The theme was something he was very familiar with—*Billboard*'s number one hits. On June 20, 2003, Richie was honored with a star on Hollywood's Walk of Fame.

### THE TOP FIVE
*Week of December 21, 1985*

1 **Say You, Say Me**
Lionel Richie

2 **Broken Wings**
Mr. Mister

3 **Party All the Time**
Eddie Murphy

4 **Alive and Kicking**
Simple Minds

5 **Separate Lives**
Phil Collins and Marilyn Martin

*Writers: Burt Bacharach*
*Carole Bayer Sager*

*Producers: Burt Bacharach*
*Carole Bayer Sager*

*January 18, 1986*
*4 weeks*

"**T**HAT'S WHAT FRIENDS ARE FOR" was one of five songs written by Burt Bacharach and Carole Bayer Sager for the film *Night Shift*, a 1982 release starring Henry Winkler, Michael Keaton and Shelley Long. The other Bacharach-Sager songs were performed in the film by Quarterflash, Al Jarreau, the Pointer Sisters and Bacharach himself. "That's What Friends Are For" was recorded by Rod Stewart. It was the first Bacharach song Stewart had ever recorded.

"It felt like Rod could put a little edge on the song that might make it very attractive," explains Sager. Stewart produced the recording himself. "Burt and I were not very happy with the record," she adds. "The record company didn't want to consider it as a single for Rod because they thought it was too soft. The song quietly disappeared into oblivion."

But not permanently. In 1983, television producer Aaron Spelling commissioned Bacharach and Sager to write the theme song for the series "Finder of Lost Loves." After he heard the song, Spelling suggested Bacharach ask Dionne Warwick to record it. "Burt has subsequently related to me that he was reluctant to call," says Dionne. "We hadn't spoken in 10 years . . . we had seen each other (at) benefit functions and awards shows . . . but he stayed in his dressing room, I stayed in mine. . . . So to pick up a phone and call me again after that length of time . . . was hard to do."

Dionne agreed to listen to "Finder of Lost Loves." "I loved it. He came over and we set a key and recorded . . . it was wonderful. It was a very emotional reunion. . . . it was nice to giggle again together and to be the friends that we were." The writing team of Burt Bacharach and Hal David gave Dionne 33 chart songs between 1962 and 1971. When Bacharach and David split, Dionne sued them for not fulfilling a contractual obligation.

When Bacharach and Sager were scheduled to produce material for Warwick in 1985, Carole remembered the song "That's What Friends Are For" and asked Burt to play it for Dionne. "She thought it might make a good duet with Stevie Wonder . . . she had recently turned him on to doing *The Woman in Red* [see 596—"I Just Called to Say I Love You]," explains Carole. "We cut the track and Dionne sounded wonderful on it. The day that Stevie came in to do his vocal, Elizabeth Taylor came down to the studio with our friend Neil Simon. They were just mesmerized by the performance."

Taylor's presence in the studio gave Sager an idea. "I'm a friend of Elizabeth and I know how active she is in AIDS research. It just hit me that this song was so poignant, and wouldn't it be incredible if we donated the proceeds to AmFar (American Foundation for AIDS Research)."

Taylor was overwhelmed at the suggestion, Sager says. Bacharach, Warwick and Wonder were also taken with the idea. They decided to add another vocalist, and Dionne said she would like to sing with Gladys Knight. "We put Gladys on and it still needed one more singer, one more punch at the end (for) that final chorus," Sager says. "It was Clive Davis who suggested Elton John. Clive had become very involved with the record by then." Davis, president of Arista Records, agreed to donate the record company's proceeds to AmFar as well.

Elton was sent a copy of the recording-in-progress and flew to Los Angeles to complete the track. "That's What Friends Are For" entered the Hot 100 on November 9, 1985. Ten weeks later it was number one. It was Warwick's second number one song [see 380—"Then Came You"]; both songs were collaborations with other artists. It was the fifth number one for Bacharach; the third for Sager.

## THE TOP FIVE
*Week of January 18, 1986*

1 **That's What Friends Are For**
   Dionne and Friends

2 **Say You, Say Me**
   Lionel Richie

3 **Party All the Time**
   Eddie Murphy

4 **Alive and Kicking**
   Simple Minds

5 **I Miss You**
   Klymaxx

628

# How Will I Know ARISTA 9434
## WHITNEY HOUSTON

*Writers: George Merrill*
*Shannon Rubicam*
*Narada Michael Walden*

*Producer: Narada Michael Walden*

*February 15, 1986*
*2 weeks*

WHEN Whitney Houston's "How Will I Know" dislodged Dionne Warwick's "That's What Friends Are For" from the top of the *Billboard* Hot 100, it marked the third time in the rock era that an artist succeeded a blood relative at number one. In 1978, Andy Gibb replaced his older brothers, the Bee Gees, at number one [see 479—"(Love Is) Thicker Than Water"] and two weeks later the Bee Gees reciprocated, knocking Andy off the top of the chart [see 480—"Night Fever"].

First cousins Whitney and Dionne might not have had back-to-back number one songs if "How Will I Know" had been recorded by the artist for whom the song had been written. Songwriters George Merrill and Shannon Rubicam, signed to A&M Records as Boy Meets Girl, were asked by label executive John McClain to submit songs for Janet Jackson.

"(Janet) and her management passed on the song," reports Merrill. "We were pretty upset because we thought it was perfect for her at the time. We had written it completely with her in mind."

Brenda Andrews at Almo-Irving

Music, Merrill and Rubicam's publisher, played the song for Gerry Griffith, who at the time was director of R&B music in the A&R department at Arista Records. He was looking for material for Whitney's first album. "We had a lot of R&B-based tunes, we had a few ballads, but we didn't have a pop crossover song," says Griffith. "So when I heard 'How Will I Know,' I said this is absolutely perfect. I played it for Clive (and) he fell in love with it."

Andrews let the two writers know that Griffith was very interested in the song for Whitney Houston. "I wasn't very familiar with her family background," Merrill confesses. "I didn't realize that even at that time there was a pretty big industry buzz about her future."

Neither did producer Narada Michael Walden, who was busy working with Aretha Franklin [see 664—"I Knew You Were Waiting (For Me)"] on the *Who's Zoomin' Who?* album. "Gerry called and begged me to produce this song for Whitney Houston," says Walden. "I had no idea who Whitney Houston was; none of us knew who Whitney Houston was." Walden had worked with Griffith on previous Arista projects, including albums for Angela Bofill and Phyllis Hyman. "I explained to Gerry the Aretha record was a very important album . . . and it wasn't the kind of thing we wanted to take time out of. He persuaded me to listen to the song and give it serious thought."

Walden listened and wanted to make some changes. He asked Merrill and Rubicam for permission and they said no. "I called Gerry back and said this whole thing is not going to happen," Walden recalls. "First of all, the songwriters don't want me to touch their song and second of all, I don't know who Whitney Houston is. I don't have time to mess with her."

A second phone call to George and Shannon, with a request for them to write more lyrics to a verse that Walden had composed, did the trick. "It was a pretty different version from our demo," says Merrill. "At first listening we didn't really get it."

"It turned out fine," says Rubicam. "The reason we balked at first was that we hadn't ever co-written with anybody like that . . . we didn't know Narada and we had never spoken with him before. We weren't used to the idea of someone changing (our) song . . . now it's easier to let go, but at that time it was hard to be flexible."

Walden completed the instrumental tracks at his Tarpan Studios in San Rafael, California, and then flew to New York to record Whitney's vocals. That was completed in one day. The next day Whitney's mother, Cissy Houston, came in to sing background vocals. "I asked Whitney to sing on the background session," Walden says. "She was reluctant because she wanted to enjoy hearing her mother sing. I said, 'No, get out there and sing,' so she did. The background sounds incredible. . . . Clive Davis heard the mix and immediately proclaimed it a 10, which is outrageous for him, because he doesn't like anything!"

## THE TOP FIVE
*Week of February 15, 1986*

1 **How Will I Know**
Whitney Houston

2 **When the Going Gets Tough, the Tough Get Going**
Billy Ocean

3 **Burning Heart**
Survivor

4 **Kyrie**
Mr. Mister

5 **That's What Friends Are For**
Dionne and Friends

Writers: *Richard Page*
*Steve George*
*John Lang*

Producers: *Paul DeVilliers*
*Mr. Mister*

*March 1, 1986*
*2 weeks*

Like Mr. Mister's first number one single [see 625—"Broken Wings"], "Kyrie" was written quickly and effortlessly. "I don't remember writing it," says Richard Page. "It just happened."

The song was written a year before it was recorded. "We were on tour with Adam Ant," drummer Pat Mastelotto recalled for Robyn Flans. "Rich (Page) brought the song up to our hotel room. He couldn't figure out which beat to use. Because the song is in a certain groove, you can either play it double time or in half time. Originally, it had a kind of a Latin beat, an Al Jarreau feel. . . . On that song, we did a quick demo where I played the drums instead of programming them. The final track turned out very close to that original demo."

Page thought the word *Kyrie* was Latin. "I've been corrected," he says. "It's Greek, probably one of the oldest written words we have in our world next to Sanskrit." *Kyrie eleison* translates "Lord have mercy." "There's a lot of power in those words," Page continues. "(The song) is a prayer, basically. It's not that we're subscribing to any Christian dogma; I don't want to be pigeonholed as a Christian band because that's not what we're

about at all. . . . It helps me; I get a lot of power from meditation, from being still and realizing that what I'm doing is insignificant compared to the universe . . . that's what the song is all about."

Religion and music were strong influences on Page when he was growing up. His father was a Presbyterian choirmaster, and his mother directed the Phoenix Boys Choir to which Page and Steve George belonged. They attended high school together, and during that time George played keyboards and saxophone for a local group called Andy Hardy. When their vocalist left to become a Jehovah's Witness, Page replaced him. The band got a gig in Las Vegas, but after a few weeks Page left to attend the School of Performing Arts in San Diego, California. George stayed with the group, which moved to Los Angeles and worked the restaurant and bar circuit.

Reunited, Page and George teamed up with Page's cousin John Lang to write songs. Page and George formed a band, Pages, and were signed by A&R executive Bobby Colomby to Epic Records. Two albums for Epic and one for Capitol failed to sell well, and while planning a fourth album they decided to regroup.

Instead of starting a new band, they took up session work, sang background vocals and wrote songs for a great number of artists, including Michael Jackson, Kenny Loggins, Patti LaBelle, Rick Springfield, the Pointer Sisters, the Village People and Donna Summer. The work was lucrative but not satisfying, so in 1982

Page and George decided to form Mr. Mister.

Steve Farris was the first and only guitar player to audition for the group. Finding a drummer was not as easy; finally Pat Mastelotto, who often worked with producer Mike Chapman, was hired as the fourth Mister. "Pat was supposed to bring a bass player to his audition, but the guy didn't make it," Page told Walter Berry of the Associated Press. "There was a bass there in the studio, so I picked it up and started playing it." Instead of looking for a fifth member of the group, Page decided he'd be the band's bass player. "We figured four guys were better than five anyway."

Mr. Mister played a showcase at S.I.R. Studios in Los Angeles in the spring of '82 and were signed to RCA in June. Their first chart single, "Hunters of the Night," peaked at number 57. The group might have split apart then if Page had accepted the invitation he received to replace Bobby Kimball as lead singer of Toto. "I turned it down," Page told Dennis Hunt of the Los Angeles Times. "I wanted to make it in my own band, from scratch. Joining an established band didn't interest me."

Then came a more tempting offer—to replace Peter Cetera [see 643—"Glory of Love"] in Chicago. "It's like somebody handing you a million dollars," Page told Hunt. "It was a flattering offer. I got it before our record started to happen. But it would have been empty for me to be in Chicago. I didn't want to spend years singing 'Only the beginning . . .' I just didn't want to leave my band then. I had a feeling we had a hit record this time."

## THE TOP FIVE
*Week of March 1, 1986*

1 **Kyrie**
Mr. Mister

2 **How Will I Know**
Whitney Houston

3 **Sara**
Starship

4 **Living in America**
James Brown

5 **The Sweetest Taboo**
Sade

# 630   Sara  GRUNT 14253
## STARSHIP

**Writers:** *Ina Wolf*
        *Peter Wolf*

**Producers:** *Dennis Lambert*
          *Peter Wolf*
          *Jeremy Smith*

*March 15, 1986*
*1 week*

**THE TOP FIVE**
*Week of March 15, 1986*

1  **Sara**
   Starship

2  **These Dreams**
   Heart

3  **Kyrie**
   Mr. Mister

4  **Secret Lovers**
   Atlantic Starr

5  **How Will I Know**
   Whitney Houston

" 'SARA' has a special meaning for me because my wife's name is Sara," explains Mickey Thomas of Starship.

"Sara" was written by the husband-and-wife team of Ina and Peter Wolf (no, not the Peter Wolf who left the J. Geils Band for a solo career). They had recorded an album for Motown's rock label Morocco as Wolf and Wolf, and a later album for Warner Brothers as Vienna (Wolf's hometown). Peter had been the arranger on Jefferson Starship's *Nuclear Furniture* album in 1984 and was associate producer on the Commodores' hit "Nightshift" with Dennis Lambert.

"Sara" was the second number one single for Starship in four months, easily making this the most successful incarnation of the group in terms of the Hot 100. The complex roots of the band go back to San Francisco in 1965, when Marty Balin and Paul Kantner met at a local club called the Drinking Gourd. They formed Jefferson Airplane with Jorma Kaukonen, Skip Spence, Signe Anderson and Bob Harvey, later replaced by Jack Casady. On August 13, they played their first major gig at the Matrix Club, and before the year was over they were signed to RCA.

Anderson left in the summer of '66 to have a baby and was replaced by the female singer from the Great Society, another San Francisco band. Grace Slick had already recorded "Somebody to Love" and "White Rabbit" with that band, which included her husband Jerry Slick and her brother-in-law, Darby Slick.

Skip Spence left the Airplane to form a new band, Moby Grape, and was replaced by Spencer Dryden. The resulting line-up remained intact until 1970, when Dryden left for the New Riders of the Purple Sage and was replaced by Joey Covington. Grace later became pregnant by Kantner, and the Airplane temporarily ran aground. Casady and Kaukonen went off to form their own entity, obliquely named Hot Tuna.

During this period, Slick and Kantner recorded the LP *Blows Against the Empire*, which featured guest appearances by David Crosby, Graham Nash and Jerry Garcia. The artist billing was "Paul Kantner and Jefferson Starship." It was the first use of the name, and not directly related to the Jefferson Starship that would form in February, 1974.

The new line-up included Slick, Kantner, John Barbata (the Turtles' former drummer, who had played on the Airplane's 1972 LP, *Long John Silver*). Craig Chaquico (a 19-year-old guitarist who first worked with Slick and Kantner on their *Sunfighter* album), David Freiberg (a bass player who appeared with the Airplane during their final days) and Papa John Creach (Hot Tuna's violinist). Pete Sears, a British keyboardist and bass player, joined the group a few months later. Marty Balin made a cameo appearance on the first album, *Dragon Fly*, and then joined the group in time

for the *Red Octopus* album.

Balin and Slick both left in 1978, and a year later Mickey Thomas received a telephone call inviting him to come on board as lead singer. Thomas had sung the lead vocal on Elvin Bishop's "Fooled Around and Fell in Love" (number three in May, 1976). "I attended rehearsals in Paul Kantner's living room in San Francisco. My style seemed to fit in comfortably and naturally with what they were doing at that time," Thomas says.

There were more personnel changes: Barbata was replaced by Aynsley Dunbar of Journey, who in turn departed in 1982, to be replaced by Donny Baldwin. Slick returned permanently in 1981. Kantner made a bitter departure in June, 1984, laying claim to the band's name. The remaining members agreed to drop "Jefferson" and paid Kantner a settlement. Freiberg left during the recording of the newly-named Starship's first album, *Knee Deep in the Hoopla*.

CAPITOL 5541 **These Dreams**
HEART

**631**

*Writers: Bernie Taupin*
*Martin Page*

*Producer: Ron Nevison*

*March 22, 1986*
*1 week*

Sᴵx Mᴏɴᴛʜs before the album *Heart* was released, producer Ron Nevison outlined his strategy for the group to Paul Grein in *Billboard.* "I really like what Heart does," he commented. "I just think they need to do it better than they've done it in the last couple of years, and not change."

Longtime Heart guitarist Howard Leese admitted to Brian McTavish in *The Kansas City Star,* "We were getting lazy . . . and the girls never were really open to doing songs by other writers until Ron Nevison said, 'Well, when's the last time you guys wrote a hit?' Everybody looked at each other and went, 'Hmmmmm.' "

Heart had four consecutive platinum albums between 1976 and 1978 and then two gold albums in 1980. The next two LPs failed to crack the 500,000 sales barrier. "I thought they were a bit humbled by their past failures," Nevison said in *Modern Recording & Music.* "So it was fairly easy for me to go in. . . . The fact is that the band was going down the tubes. I had to make a commercial album. . . . Heart had about 20 songs, and . . . only a few were really good. We had to augment that with outside material."

Nevison had produced an album for songwriter Peter Wolf, who was called to Canada to assist with the recording of *Heart* (his credit: synthesizers, acoustic piano and creative input). Peter told songwriter Martin Page he was going to be working with Starship and Heart and asked if he had any songs for those groups.

Page had been collaborating with Bernie Taupin and had two of their songs in mind. One was "We Built This City" [see 623] and the other was "These Dreams." "I put the cassette of the demo in Peter's hand while we were doing a Maurice White solo record," Page recalls. "He called me from a plane and said, 'I just love "These Dreams." Let me take it to the band.' . . . I think there was a little concern when Ron Nevison wasn't convinced it was the right style. But then Peter played it for the band." Heart loved the song and wanted to record it.

"Bernie Taupin and Martin Page wrote a monster with that one," says Nancy Wilson, the sister who usually does *not* sing lead vocals on Heart songs. "When I heard the song, I thought, (they) wrote that for me, didn't (they)? When I sang it, I had a really bad cold. Oddly enough, parts of it sounded really good that way . . . we went back later . . . and we did most of it when I was well. I tried to recreate some of the raspiness in it, which we kept, too. So part of it is me

trying to recreate being ill," she laughs. "Ron said, 'Can't you just get sick again?' "

With a change in producers and a change in record labels (from Epic to Capitol), Heart began their most successful chart run ever. The first single from *Heart,* "What About Love?," peaked at number 10. Then "Never" peaked at number four and became their biggest hit to date (and marked the first time they had scored two consecutive top 10 hits). The third single from the LP was "These Dreams," Heart's first number one.

In the liner notes for the album, "These Dreams" is dedicated to Sharon Hess, a 21-year-old fan who spent a couple of weeks with the band before she died of cancer on Nancy Wilson's birthday.

## THE TOP FIVE
*Week of March 22, 1986*

1 **These Dreams**
   Heart

2 **Sara**
   Starship

3 **Secret Lovers**
   Atlantic Starr

4 **Rock Me Amadeus**
   Falco

5 **R.O.C.K. in the U.S.A.**
   John Cougar Mellencamp

# Rock Me Amadeus  A&M 2821
## FALCO

Writers: *Rob Bolland*
*Ferdi Bolland*
*Falco*

Producers: *Rob Bolland*
*Ferdi Bolland*

*March 29, 1986*
*3 weeks*

MANY composers have been immortalized in song during the rock era. Beethoven was paid homage by both Chuck Berry ("Roll Over Beethoven") and Eurythmics ("Beethoven [I Love to Listen To]"). The group ABC recorded a tribute to Smokey Robinson ("When Smokey Sings"). And Donna Summer wanted to have "Dinner With Gershwin" in a 1987 release written by Brenda Russell. Austrian rock singer Falco made certain that Wolfgang Amadeus Mozart received due honors when he recorded "Rock Me Amadeus," an international hit that went to number one in Germany before it topped the chart in America on March 29, 1986.

"I was really impressed with the movie *Amadeus* and the way (director) Milos Forman translated the rococo person (into) today's terms," Falco replies when asked what inspired him to write a song about his countryman. "If Mozart were alive today, he wouldn't be making classical music; he'd be an international pop star. And I felt it was time to write a song about him."

Falco was born Johann Holzel on February 19, 1957, in Vienna, Austria. The number one song in America at the time was "Too Much" by Elvis Presley. It wouldn't be long before the boy, called Hans or Hansi by his family, would be involved with music: by age four he was already playing the piano. But neither his father, an engineer, nor his mother, a traveling saleswoman, offered him encouragement to make a living as a musician. He told Jonathan Cooper in *People* magazine that his parents were "never close to the idea that I make a profession of it. They wanted to see me with a doctor in front of my name, didn't matter what kind."

After spending a year at the Vienna Music Conservatory, Holzel moved to West Berlin and sang for a jazz-rock band. One day he was watching a ski jump competition on television and was impressed with skier Falco

Weisspflog. Altering the "k" to a "c," Holzel called himself Falco Sturmer and then Falco Gutteherr and, finally, just plain Falco.

He returned to Vienna in 1978. Two years later his song "Ganz Wien" became a local underground hit. It wasn't played on the radio because of the lyric that translates, "All Vienna is on heroin today." "There was a very hard-core (drug) scene in Vienna that had a lot to do with the environment. . . . The song was very much anti-drugs—it was pointing out there is no future to that scene," Falco told Robert Hilburn of the *Los Angeles Times*.

In 1981, Falco wrote and recorded "Der Kommissar," a rap-like record recorded in German. "I did it to make the German language more comfortable to rock," he told reporter Jim Reid. "People would tell me that rap was strictly a black thing, but I don't care about color definition on records."

"Der Kommissar" made *Billboard*'s Dance/Disco chart in 1983, peaking at number 10. But it was an English language version of the song, by the British group After the Fire, that was the real American chart hit; it peaked at number five.

"It was hard after that record," Falco told Hilburn. "Everyone was . . . saying, 'What are you doing (on the charts), being out of Vienna? You are an absolutely one-hit wonder.' But the important things in a career, I have found, are the downs, not the

highlights. I think a lot of talented artists broke down after the first real huge hit. They just panic."

Falco didn't panic; he kept recording. "Der Kommissar" was included on his first American album, *Einzelhaft* ("Incarcerated"). His second LP, *Junge Roemer* ("Young Romans") didn't produce any hits. So on to *Falco 3* and new producers, Dutch brothers Rob and Ferdi Bolland.

Falco had one more hit on the Hot 100 when "Vienna Calling" peaked at number 18 in 1986. He was 40 years old when he died on February 6, 1998. On vacation in the Dominican Republic, Falco was driving an SUV that pulled out onto a highway and crashed into a bus.

---

## THE TOP FIVE
*Week of March 29, 1986*

1  **Rock Me Amadeus**
   Falco

2  **These Dreams**
   Heart

3  **Secret Lovers**
   Atlantic Starr

4  **R.O.C.K. in the U.S.A.**
   John Cougar Mellencamp

5  **Kiss**
   Prince and the Revolution

Writers: Prince and the Revolution

Producers: Prince and the Revolution

April 19, 1986
2 weeks

THE week that "Kiss" reached the pinnacle of the Hot 100, the single in the runner-up position was "Manic Monday" by the Bangles [see 656—"Walk Like an Egyptian"]. The songwriting credit on the Bangles song was given to "Christopher," but that was one of many *noms de plume* for the Minneapolis-born Prince Rogers Nelson. Prince thus became the fifth songwriter (or songwriting team) to hold down the top two positions on the *Billboard* singles chart. The others:

1. In 1956, Elvis Presley was listed as songwriter of both "Don't Be Cruel" [see 14] and "Love Me Tender"[see 15].

2. John Lennon and Paul McCartney were in the top two positions with "I Want to Hold Your Hand" [see 143] and "She Loves You" [see 144] for six consecutive weeks in 1964.

3. The Gibb brothers—Barry, Robin and Maurice—also held down the top two spots more than once during 1978.

4. Jim Steinman wrote both "Total Eclipse of the Heart" [see 578] by Bonnie Tyler and "Making Love Out of Nothing At All" by Air Supply, the top two songs on the Hot 100 the week of October 8, 1983.

The name "Christopher" referred to Christopher Tracy, the character Prince played in the film *Under the Cherry Moon*. The *Parade* album was an unofficial soundtrack to the movie, and it featured the song "Christopher Tracy's Parade."

Prince was dubbed a *wunderkind* so often by the press that his band, the Revolution, decided to shorten the name to just plain "Kid." Prince put together his first touring band in 1978, but these musicians didn't work with him in the studio very much until the *Purple Rain* album in 1984. Two years earlier, Prince had come up with the name "the Revolution."

Andre Cymone (nee Anderson), Prince's friend from childhood, was an original member of the Revolution. He played bass for Prince until 1981, when he left for a solo career. He was replaced by another Minneapolis musician, Mark Brown, who released his debut solo album for Motown in February, 1988, as Brownmark.

Gayle Chapman was keyboardist for Prince until 1980. Her replacement was Lisa Coleman, daughter of famed studio percussionist Gary Coleman. Dez Dickerson played guitar in the Revolution until 1983. His replacement was Wendy Melvoin, daughter of acclaimed jazz keyboardist Mike Melvoin, and Lisa Coleman's roommate.

Matt Fink, also known as Dr. Fink, was the other keyboardist for the Revolution. Rounding out the group was drummer Bobby Z (nee Rivkin), brother of David Z, an engineer/producer who worked on Prince's first demo tape and did the vocal arrangements on "Kiss."

*Parade* was the third album to be released by Prince and the Revolution. *Purple Rain* yielded two number one singles [see 591—"When Doves Cry" and 595—"Let's Go Crazy"]. *Around the World in a Day* produced two top 10 singles: "Raspberry Beret" (number two in July, 1985) and "Pop Life" (number seven in September). The first single from *Parade* was the chart-topping "Kiss." That was followed by "Mountains" (number 23 in July, 1986) and "Anotherloverholenyohead" (number 63 in August).

Prince dismissed the Revolution before releasing his next album, *Sign 'O' the Times*. The title track was the first single, peaking at number three in April, 1987. Then came "If I Was Your Girlfriend" (number 67 in June), "U Got the Look" (number two in October), "I Could Never Take the Place of Your Man" (number 10 in February, 1988) and the "B" side of that single, "Hot Thing," which began an independent climb up the Hot 100 just as the "A" side reached its peak.

## THE TOP FIVE
*Week of April 19, 1986*

1 **Kiss**
Prince and the Revolution

2 **Manic Monday**
Bangles

3 **Addicted to Love**
Robert Palmer

4 **Rock Me Amadeus**
Falco

5 **West End Girls**
Pet Shop Boys

## 634 Addicted to Love ISLAND 99570
### ROBERT PALMER

*Writer: Robert Palmer*

*Producer: Bernard Edwards*

*May 3, 1986*
*1 week*

ROBERT PALMER'S first number one single, "Addicted to Love," was almost released as a duet with one of his favorite singers, Chaka Khan ("I Feel for You," "I'm Every Woman"). "I bumped into her at a club," Palmer told Dennis Hunt in the *Los Angeles Times*. "We hit it off immediately . . . she's the one singer I've always wanted to sing with. I told her I was recording and she wanted to come to the studio. She showed up and we sang this song together that I was working on. The record sounded great."

Unfortunately, not many people would hear it. "Politics intervened," Palmer continued. "Her people said it was a conflict of interest. She'd have three singles out at the same time." So Khan's vocals were erased from the master tape. She was listed in the credits for the vocal arrangement, however. "She deserves credit for what she contributed."

Even without Khan's vocals, the song became Palmer's most successful American single. He told Dick Clark why he wrote the song. "There was a lot of concern throughout the media about various substances, and . . . a lot of people I was working with were going off to farms to get healthy and do all the various therapies. It strikes me that it's not the substance, it's the personality. It's the addictive personality that's the problem. If you're an addictive personality, it doesn't matter what's around, you're gonna get hooked on it. Food, alcohol . . . current substances, whatever they are. . . . I just thought it was a facetious kind of thing, being addicted to love."

The song came to Palmer in his sleep. "It woke me up," he said in *People* magazine. "I just dreamed the tune. I woke up and hummed it into my tape recorder. A lot of times when that happens, it's just nonsense. But in the morning I listened to it and I *knew* I'd caught one."

Just 13 months before "Addicted to Love" debuted on the Hot 100, Palmer had his first top 10 single with "Some Like It Hot," recorded by the Power Station. Palmer was already working

on his *Riptide* LP at home in the Bahamas when he received a tape from John Taylor of Duran Duran [see 590—"The Reflex"]. Along with fellow band member Andy Taylor and former members of Chic [see 495—"Le Freak"] Bernard Edwards and Tony Thompson, John was planning a one-off collaboration to be recorded between Duran Duran albums. "John sent me a cassette with 30 yards of G minor and told me to add melody and lyrics," Palmer told Roy Trakin of *Bam*. "I related to the groove immediately. Originally, they were going to call in different singers for each track, but they liked what I had done, so I ended up being on the whole record."

There were three chart singles from *The Power Station* album. "Get It On" and "Communication" followed "Some Like It Hot" into the Hot 100. " 'Communication' was the first time I'd met Bernard Edwards—or heard of him, actually," Palmer told Rob Tannenbaum in *Musician*. "After I finished that vocal . . . I left him a cassette of the stuff I'd been working on and said I was looking for some help. He was up for it, so we started on that right away." Edwards was hired to produce *Riptide* and brought along many of the musicians who worked on the Power Station project, including Andy Taylor and Tony Thompson.

Palmer and Power Station came to a parting of the ways when they asked him to join them on tour. "They insisted there would never be a tour nor another album," Palmer said in *Bam*. "So it did come as a bit of a shock to learn they were going to play live. We did get together and talk about it, but my head was into doing my own record." Power Station recruited Michael des Barres to handle lead vocals on tour, and Palmer completed *Riptide*. The album yielded another hit in a cover version of Cherelle's "I Didn't Mean to Turn You On," which peaked at number two in November, 1986.

### THE TOP FIVE
*Week of May 3, 1986*

1 **Addicted to Love**
  Robert Palmer

2 **West End Girls**
  Pet Shop Boys

3 **Kiss**
  Prince

4 **Why Can't This Be Love**
  Van Halen

5 **Harlem Shuffle**
  The Rolling Stones

EMI-AMERICA 8307 **West End Girls** 635
PET SHOP BOYS

*Writers: Neil Tennant*
*Chris Lowe*

*Producer: Stephen Hague*

*May 10, 1986*
*1 week*

A CHANCE meeting in a hi-fi store on Kings Road in the Chelsea district of London led to the formation of the Pet Shop Boys, the third British male duo to top the American chart in an 18-month period.

It was August, 1981, when Neil Tennant made the fateful journey to his neighborhood stereo shop. "They were making a lead to plug my synthesizer into my hi-fi system," he remembers. "They were welding it together downstairs, so I was just hanging around waiting for them to finish. Chris (Lowe) was buying a stylus for his record player and we started talking about keyboards and synthesizers. A couple of days later he came round to my house to look at my synthesizer and we started writing songs."

Tennant had moved to London from North Gosforth, a suburb of Newcastle Upon Tyne. His degree was in history, but he had also been involved with a theater group, had played cello in the school orchestra and had been part of a rock band named Dust. In London, he had been an editor for Marvel Comics (*The Fantastic Four*, *The Amazing Spider-Man*); his job had been to anglicize the dialogue. Lowe was born in Blackpool and had

studied architecture at Liverpool University. He also had a musical background playing trombone and piano. He had been one of seven members of a band called One Under the Eight.

Armed with two cassette recorders, Tennant and Lowe did some early recording in Neil's apartment and then worked at a friend's studio in Camden. Tennant had a day job: he was an editor for a weekly British pop magazine, *Smash Hits*. In August, 1983, the magazine assigned him to go to New York and interview the Police [see 574—"Every Breath You Take"], a band he was not particularly fond of. He used the opportunity to meet his favorite record producer, Bobby "O" Orlando. Impressed with Tennant's intimate knowledge of his work, Bobby "O" offered to produce a session with Tennant and Lowe.

They spent four hours in a studio and recorded "West End Girls." It was released in 1984 and was a hit in Belgium and France. Issued on Epic Records in Britain, it failed to chart, but Los Angeles radio stations got hold of the import 45 and made the song a local hit.

By the end of 1984, the relationship with Bobby "O" had soured. Tennant and Lowe got involved in a legal dispute with their producer, which prevented them from recording for anyone else for a year. In March of 1985, they were signed to EMI's Parlophone label in Britain, and a single called "Opportunities (Let's Make Lots of Money)" was released. It failed, and Tennant and Lowe went

back into the studio with producer Stephen Hague to record a new version of "West End Girls."

Lowe was reluctant to rerecord the song, but Tennant thought it was a good idea. "In Britain, no one had heard the first version," Tennant explains. "We didn't have the rights to rerelease it. That was frustrating."

The new, improved "West End Girls" was released in the United Kingdom in October, 1985. It went to number one on the British chart before reaching the same position on the American Hot 100.

"I thought it would be quite good to write a rap song a bit like 'The Message' by Grandmaster Flash," Neil replies when asked why the group recorded "West End Girls" in the first place. "Only an English rap, because no one ever raps in English accents. They always rap in New York street accents. The song is a contrast between the East End of London, which is kind of a tough area, and the West End, a glamorous nighttime area with clubs and cinemas. People run away from their everyday pressures of life into the atmosphere of a city at night."

The name Pet Shop Boys has caused some consternation in the press, but Tennant explained the true origin in the British rock weekly *Melody Maker*. "One of the newspapers said that it's New York slang for rent boys who are into S&M, but if it is, it's news to me. We did genuinely call ourselves after some friends we had who worked in a pet shop in Ealing. . . . If it has got that slightly dubious connotation then it's quite amusing but it's certainly not deliberate."

## THE TOP FIVE
*Week of May 10, 1986*

1 **West End Girls**
Pet Shop Boys

2 **Addicted to Love**
Robert Palmer

3 **Greatest Love of All**
Whitney Houston

4 **Why Can't This Be Love**
Van Halen

5 **What Have You Done for Me Lately**
Janet Jackson

*Writers: Michael Masser*
*Linda Creed*

*Producer: Michael Masser*

*May 17, 1986*
*3 weeks*

WHEN Whitney Houston auditioned for Clive Davis, president of Arista Records, one of the songs in her 30-minute set was Michael Masser's and Linda Creed's "Greatest Love of All."

The audition was set up by Gerry Griffith, who was then director of R&B music in the A&R department of Arista. A jewelry designer friend of Griffith's had passed him a tip that Bruce Lundvall was about to sign Whitney Houston to Elektra Records. Griffith, who had seen Whitney perform when she was just 15, was interested enough to call Whitney's manager, Gene Harvey. "He said, 'You're in luck, because we haven't signed a contract with Elektra, and she's appearing at Seventh Avenue South with her mother tomorrow night. Why don't you come down and see her?' " Griffith recalls.

"She was the most phenomenal, original talent I had seen in years. I set up a showcase for Clive, I said (to him), 'I'm not even going to ask you. I'm setting up a showcase for this young lady. You will be absolutely blown away, Clive.' " Griffith's boss couldn't argue with that. He signed Whitney to Arista and called his friend, composer Michael Masser.

The first time Masser encountered Whitney Houston, the singer was performing at Sweetwater's in New York. "I was walking in a little bit ahead of Clive and she was singing my song 'Greatest Love of All' right when I was walking in. It blew my mind," Masser remembers.

The song was originally written for the film *The Greatest*, the story of Muhammad Ali. Masser traveled to Jerusalem to write the song. "I went to Jerusalem because I wanted to get the essence of why men like Muhammad Ali take the stands that they do and give up everything." Masser wrote some songs for the film with Gerry Goffin, but chose to write "Greatest Love of All" with Linda Creed, whose previous collaborations with Thom Bell included numerous hits for the Spinners and the Stylistics. "I hooked up with Linda and we worked pretty intensely. She had just gotten out of

surgery for breast cancer."

Masser chose George Benson to record the song for the soundtrack of the film. The track was issued as a single on Arista, but it was not a major hit, peaking at number 24 in October, 1977.

Whitney's recording of "Greatest Love of All" was included on her debut album, but not with enthusiasm from Clive Davis, according to arranger Gene Page. "(Masser) had two songs that Clive loved and two that Clive hated," he told Len Chandler in the Los Angeles Songwriters Showcase *Musepaper*. "Michael put his foot down. He said, 'If you want me to do this album you have to do these.' " The two songs Clive disliked were "Saving All My Love for You" [see 620] and "Greatest Love of All," according to Page. Davis thought the former was too old-fashioned and felt that the latter had not been a hit for Benson. "Michael said he wouldn't do anything if Clive turned down those two tunes. This girl's an unknown and Michael had a track record of hits, so of course, he got his way."

"Greatest Love of All" must not have been seen as a potential hit. "It was never intended to be a single," Masser confirms. It was relegated to the "B" side of "You Give Good Love," the album's first 45. But radio airplay forced its release as the fifth single from the LP, following "You Give Good Love," "Saving All My Love for You," "Thinking of You" and "How Will I Know."

"Greatest Love of All" gave Whitney three number one songs from one LP, the first time a solo female artist ever accomplished that feat.

Michael and drove to the home of Jamie Foley, director of *At Close Range*. When he arrived, Foley and Penn told him that Madonna had suggested he write the score for the film. She had also asked who was going to sing the song, since it was written for a man to sing. But there was no question in Leonard's mind that she was the only person who should sing "Live to Tell."

"We recut the song, but we used the (same) vocal. She only sang it once (for the demo) and that was the vocal we used because it was so innocent and so shy. She had a legal pad in her hand and . . . you can hear the paper. It's as raw as raw can be and that's part of what gave it all its charm."

"Live to Tell" was released prior to *True Blue*. When it went to number one, it was only the fifth single in eight years to top the Hot 100 and not be available on an album, according to Paul Grein's Chartbeat column in *Billboard*. (The others are: "Too Much Heaven," the Bee Gees [see 496]; "Pop Muzik," M [see 513]; "Crazy Little Thing Called Love," Queen [see 522]; and "Say You, Say Me," Lionel Richie [see 626]. As with "Live to Tell," all appeared on albums that were released *after* the singles were number one.) "Live to Tell" was also Madonna's second number one single from a motion picture, following "Crazy for You" [see 606] from *Vision Quest*.

"Live to Tell" was a showstopper on Madonna's *True Blue* tour, and at a benefit concert at Madison Square Garden to raise money for medical research for AIDS, she dedicated the song to the memory of her friend, artist Michael Burgoyne.

*Writers: Madonna*
*Patrick Leonard*

*Producer: Patrick Leonard*

*June 7, 1986*
*1 week*

PATRICK LEONARD had just finished the Jacksons' Victory tour when his manager asked if he was interested in being musical director for Madonna's Virgin tour. At first he said no, but then he talked to Madonna on the phone, found her charming and agreed to do the two-month tour.

By the time the tour was over, Madonna had asked Leonard and Stephen Bray to write songs with her and co-produce her next album, *True Blue*.

"Madonna agreed to write some lyrics for a song I was going to write for a film that Paramount was doing," Patrick explains. "My managers represented the guy who was directing the film; it was his first film. I saw a little piece of the movie and I had the script. I wrote a theme, and I said, 'What if I could get Madonna to write the lyrics for it?' "

The movie was called *Fire With Fire*. "It was a love story (set at) a girls' school and a boys' prison, somewhere in the mountains around Vancouver," Leonard remembers, although he never saw the completed film. Paramount passed on his music. "They just didn't think that this theme was any good. (They thought) I wasn't going to be capable of (scoring) the film."

Leonard told Madonna that the people at Paramount didn't want the theme. "She said, 'This song would be great for Sean's new movie.' She wrote the lyrics—she just wrote them on the spot, which is what we always do. I don't think we've ever taken more than three hours to complete a song from start to finish. She sang it on the demo only once and left with the cassette. That day I went to work with Michael Jackson on some transcriptions for material he was writing for the *Bad* album. The phone rang at Michael's and it was Sean (Penn). He said. 'I'm over at the director's house and Madonna just brought the song over. We love it and we'd like to talk to you about it.' "

Patrick finished his work with

# 638 On My Own MCA 52770
## PATTI LaBELLE and MICHAEL McDONALD

*Writers: Burt Bacharach*
*Carole Bayer Sager*

*Producers: Burt Bacharach*
*Carole Bayer Sager*

*June 14, 1986*
*3 weeks*

" 'ON MY OWN' has a kind of wonderfully bizarre history to it," says songwriter Carole Bayer Sager, who wrote the song with her husband Burt Bacharach. "We wrote it slowly, very slowly. Burt had the melody for a while. I had a hard time putting lyrics to it. We played it for Patti (LaBelle) in various stages of writing it. She loved it. She said, 'When it's finished, I'll cut it.' "

Burt and Carole wanted to produce the song, but producer Richard Perry was already working with Patti, and he wanted to record it with her. The two songwriters paid a visit to the studio while Perry was cutting the track and were disappointed with the result. "We didn't think he had a handle on it," says Carole. "I think Richard tried to cut the track twice . . . he finally decided he loved the song but (it) wasn't coming together for him. So he was going to dump it. We asked Sandy Gallin, Patti's manager and a close friend of ours, "Would it be

OK if we took a shot at cutting it?' "

Bacharach and Sager produced the track with a live band. "After we cut the tracks, Patti put her vocal on and we still weren't sure about it. I still heard it as a duet. It was crying out for a male voice."

Patti returned home to Philadelphia and Carole called Michael McDonald to see if he would be interested in singing on two different tracks they were producing for Patti—"On My Own" and "Sleep With Me Tonight." McDonald listened to both tracks. "I thought I would do the best job on 'On My Own,' " McDonald told Mary Campbell of the Associated Press. "And they told me it was not going to be the single." McDonald said he had "long since used up my allowed number of lead vocal outside projects with Warner Brothers," his record label. Because "On My Own" was not scheduled to be a 45, his record company consented to him guest starring with Patti on MCA.

LaBelle and McDonald never met in the studio. She remained in Philadelphia while he recorded his vocals in Los Angeles. At first, McDonald's contribution was merely a cameo performance. "It certainly couldn't be considered a duet," explains Carole. "His entrance wasn't until three-quarters through the record. He didn't

come in until after the bridge. When everyone heard it they said, 'What are you, crazy? Michael and Patti are extraordinary together. Can't you put him on earlier in the record?' Then the question was, since it wasn't presented to him that way, would he come back and sing some more? He loved it, so he did."

"I sang to Patti's voice on tape," McDonald told Campbell. "When you're together, live, there's certain energy you can attain. But there's a tendency to just move ahead and not spend time with details. Everybody is going with the performance. Here, I got to go in and fix some lines, and she did, too. I think it's cheating, in one respect, but it can only make it better."

Patti completed her debut album for MCA, *Winner in You*. Label president Irving Azoff loved "On My Own" and wanted it to be the first single. "Not everyone at Warner Brothers thought it was a hit," says Sager. "Lenny Waronker (label president) did not think it was a hit. He said later . . . that he loved it. But Irving Azoff . . . felt strongly about the record and somehow they worked it out."

The two artists filmed a video for the song, but they still didn't meet. "We filmed it bicoastally," Patti told Christopher Vaughn in *The Hollywood Reporter*. "Mike was in Los Angeles and I did my part . . . in New York." As "On My Own" went to number one on the *Billboard* Hot 100, LaBelle and McDonald met for the first time—at NBC Studios in Burbank, where they performed the song on "The Tonight Show Starring Johnny Carson."

## THE TOP FIVE
*Week of June 14, 1986*

1 **On My Own**
  Patti LaBelle and
  Michael McDonald

2 **Live to Tell**
  Madonna

3 **I Can't Wait**
  Nu Shooz

4 **There'll Be Sad Songs
  (To Make You Cry)**
  Billy Ocean

5 **Crush on You**
  The Jets

*Writers: Wayne Brathwaite*
*Barry J. Eastmond*
*Billy Ocean*

*Producers: Barry J. Eastmond*
*Wayne Brathwaite*

*July 5, 1986*
*1 week*

**B**ARRY EASTMOND played keyboards and synthesizers on Billy Ocean's *Suddenly* album, and he co-wrote the song "Dancefloor" on that LP. Clive Calder, president of Jive Records, liked his work well enough to invite him back for Billy's second Jive album, *Love Zone*. This time, Calder wanted him to produce the album, along with Wayne Brathwaite.

Eastmond, Brathwaite and Ocean co-wrote eight of the nine tracks on the *Love Zone* album, including "When the Going Gets Tough, the Tough Get Going," from the Michael Douglas-Kathleen Turner film *The Jewel of the Nile*. Released as a single before the LP came out, that soundtrack song peaked at number two on the Hot 100 in February, 1986. "There'll Be Sad Songs (To Make You Cry)" was also released before the album came out, and it became Ocean's fifth top five single in 20 months as well as his second number one [see 597—"Caribbean Queen (No More Love on the Run)"].

"There'll Be Sad Songs" was one of the first tracks written for the album, according to Eastmond. "I had the music in my head for a little while. It seemed perfect for Billy. The lyrics came out of a story my wife told me about a friend of hers. She had just

broken up with the fellow she had been going out with for years. There was a particular song that always made her think of her boyfriend. She was at a party given by her new boyfriend and the song came on and reminded her of the old boyfriend. She broke down . . . we thought that was an interesting story so we wrote the song around it." Ironically, the song that made her cry was a Billy Ocean song, "Suddenly" (number four in June, 1985).

The next two singles released from the album were also written by Eastmond, Brathwaite and Ocean. The title track, "Love Zone," peaked at number 10 in September, and "Love Is Forever" went to number 16 two months later.

Success on the American pop chart did not change Billy Ocean, born Leslie Sebastian Charles in Trinidad. He had used several stage names while appearing in London pubs as a 19-year-old, including Joshua, Big Ben and Sam Spade. He told Bob Andelman of the *Tampa Tribune* how he chose the name Billy Ocean: "When I left Trinidad, there (was) a football team in the Village called Ocean 11. But they got their name, in turn, from an old film with Frank Sinatra and

Sammy Davis, Jr., (*Oceans 11*). When I went to England, I hit on the name Ocean, forgetting that there was a football team or that there was a film."

Signed to the GTO label in England, Ocean was still installing windshield wipers at a Ford plant when his first chart hit, "Love Really Hurts Without You," was released. "I was on the job when I heard that song on Radio Luxembourg," he told Steve Dougherty in *People* magazine. "I felt so good, because I knew I was free to leave. So I left."

There was an almost four-year gap between Billy's final GTO single and his first hit for Jive. "Eventually, songs began to develop again, without forcing, by nurturing ideas and letting them grow. Soon I had enough songs to begin my career all over again. I can't say I'm glad things went the way they did. I don't think I was really ready then for the kind of success I'm having now. Those years prepared me."

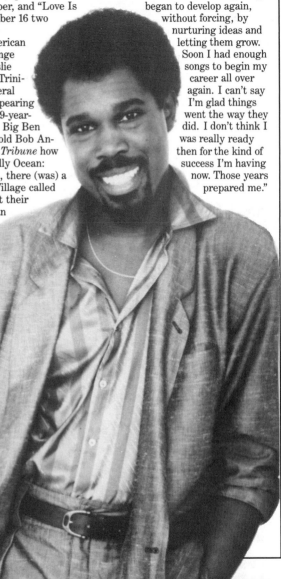

## THE TOP FIVE
*Week of July 5, 1986*

1  **There'll Be Sad Songs**
   **(To Make You Cry)**
   Billy Ocean

2  **Holding Back the Years**
   Simply Red

3  **Who's Johnny**
   El DeBarge

4  **No One Is to Blame**
   Howard Jones

5  **Nasty**
   Janet Jackson

# 640 Holding Back the Years ELEKTRA 69564
## SIMPLY RED

*Writers: Mick Hucknall*
*Neil Moss*

*Producer: Stewart Levine*

*July 12, 1986*
*1 week*

"CATHY'S CLOWN" by the Everly Brothers was the number one song in America on June 8, 1960, the day Mick Hucknall was born in Manchester, England. His father was a barber. His mother left the family when he was two years old, so Mick was raised by his Aunt Nellie and, in turn, her four daughters. One of Aunt Nellie's daughters, Sheila, took young Mick to see *A Hard Day's Night*. He became a self-described Beatles fanatic.

He was 12 when he bought his first single, "Doobedood'ndoobe, Doobedood'ndoobe, Doobedood'ndoo" by Diana Ross. (Fifteen years later she would ask him to write a song for her. He would come up with a much shorter title: "Shine.") His strongest influences were the sounds of Detroit (Tamla-Motown) and Memphis (Stax-Volt). At 14 he became a club DJ in Manchester, where he played James Brown and reggae music by bands like Big Youth and Burning Spear.

He enrolled in art school, but music was still a primary part of his life. When he was 17 he formed a band, the Frantic Elevators, that combined punk with R&B. They played at a bar called Eric's. The manager, Roger Eagle, told local talent booker Elliot Rashman about Hucknall's group. Rashman showed up at a Manchester Polytechnic gig to hear the band play. "I heard this voice, and I was like a drowning man, in reverse—I saw not my past, but my future flash in front of me. I thought, 'This is an incredible voice, a voice that has everything but has yet to be formed.'" Rashman told Fred Schruers in *Musician*.

The Frantic Elevators stayed together for three years. Then Hucknall put together another band that Eagle thought should be called either Concrete Wig or Corn Gods. Hucknall had another idea. "Originally, I just wanted to call the group Red, because it was originally going to be a solo thing," he told Bill Bentley in the *L.A. Weekly*. "I wanted to name it after my red hair, really. And Simply came in when my manager (Rashman) was making phone calls and being asked what the band was called, and he'd say, 'Simply "Red".'"

The current line-up of Simply Red played its first gig on June 15, 1985. Drummer Chris Joyce had been in a punk band called Fast Breeder and then helped form the group Durutti Column. Bassist Tony Bowers left Durutti Column with Chris for a new band, the Mothmen. Keyboardist Fritz McIntyre learned to play piano in his father's church. Guitarist Sylvan Richardson was brought in by McIntyre to replace Dave Fryman. Trumpet player Tim Kellett joined the band right out of the Royal Northern College of Music.

For their first single, Simply Red recorded a song Hucknall discovered while he was spinning records in clubs: "Money's Too Tight (To Mention)" by the Valentine Brothers. A hit in England, it was released as the first single in America in August, 1985, but failed to crack the Hot 100.

"Holding Back the Years," described as autobiographical, was the second single. Hucknall was 19 when he wrote it with Neil Smith, guitarist for the Frantic Elevators. Their original version is hard to find and Hucknall only has one copy himself. Simply Red's recording of the song entered the Hot 100 on April 5, 1986, and hit the top of the chart 14 weeks later. "Money's Too Tight (To Mention)" was rereleased as a follow-up, and it peaked at number 28.

Hucknall's soulful vocals brought him drubbings in the British press. But praise came from other quarters. The group was asked to be an opening act for James Brown. And not only did Diana Ross request a song, but Lamont Dozier, who helped write 10 number one singles for the Supremes, agreed to write some songs with Mick. They spent a day in Los Angeles at Dozier's house writing two songs for the *Men and Women* album. "When something like that happens," Hucknall told Roger Morton, "it's difficult to control your ego, to stay sane."

## THE TOP FIVE
*Week of July 12, 1986*

1 **Holding Back the Years**
Simply Red

2 **Invisible Touch**
Genesis

3 **There'll Be Sad Songs
(To Make You Cry)**
Billy Ocean

4 **Nasty**
Janet Jackson

5 **Who's Johnny**
El DeBarge

Writers: *Phil Collins*
*Mike Rutherford*
*Tony Banks*

Producers: *Genesis*
*Hugh Padgham*

*July 19, 1986*
*1 week*

**O**N June 28, 1986, past and present members of Genesis accounted for seven positions on the Hot 100 as either artists or producers. The current line-up of Genesis entered the top 10 that week with "Invisible Touch," and former member Peter Gabriel also entered the top 10 with "Sledgehammer." The song "No One Is to Blame" by Howard Jones, produced by Phil Collins, moved up to number five. Collins' solo effort, "Take Me Home," was in its final week on the chart, having peaked at number seven. Mike Rutherford had two singles on the chart with his other band, Mike + the Mechanics: "All I Need Is a Miracle" was moving down after peaking at number five, and the follow-up, "Taken In," debuted that week. Finally, former member Steve Hackett and his

new assemblage, GTR, was at number 21 with "When the Heart Rules the Mind."

This chart domination continued when "Invisible Touch" moved into the number one position on July 19, 1986. That same week, Gabriel's "Sledgehammer" moved to number two. It marked the first time that singles by a group and a former member of that group held down the top two positions on the Hot 100. It was also the first time that a group went to number one *after* a member of that group had his own solo number one single [see 586— "Against All Odds (Take a Look at Me Now)"]. Usually the process works in reverse, with solo singers scoring number one hits only after they had done so as a member of a group.

"Invisible Touch" was Genesis' 13th chart single, but only their second to make the top 10. "Your Own Special Way" was their first chart single, entering in 1977; it peaked at number 62. "That's All!" peaked at number six in February, 1984. But by the time "Invisible Touch" was released, Genesis' drummer and lead singer Phil Collins had amassed seven top 10 singles, including three number ones.

When Genesis came together to record the *Invisible Touch* LP, it was to be their first album since *Genesis* in 1983 and their first together since Collins had become a superstar. The lead singer described the origin of the song "Invisible Touch" in a recorded interview: "We were working on another song and Mike (Rutherford) started playing that guitar riff . . . as soon as he started playing that I started singing, 'she seems to have an invisible touch.' At that moment we just knew that was a great hook, and then we just sort of wrote a song around it."

Tony Banks elaborated on the construction of the song in that same interview: "Improvising the rhythm of ('Invisible Touch') came out of when we were doing 'The Last Domino' . . . (we) started playing this riff which . . . seemed to be good on its own and had a different character from what we were going for on the rest of that. . . . At one point (we were) thinking of incorporating the two, but I'm glad we didn't because I think 'Invisible Touch" makes a nice concise piece."

The *Invisible Touch* album produced five top 10 singles. "Throwing It All Away" and "Land of Confusion" both peaked at number four, followed by "Tonight, Tonight, Tonight" and "In Too Deep," which both reached number three. By the time the latter fell off the Hot 100, it was more than a year after "Invisible Touch" had peaked at number one.

To trace the genesis of Genesis, one would have to go back to the early summer of 1966, when four students at the posh English "public" school (the equivalent of a private school in America) formed a songwriting collective.

## THE TOP FIVE
*Week of July 19, 1986*

1 **Invisible Touch**
Genesis

2 **Sledgehammer**
Peter Gabriel

3 **Nasty**
Janet Jackson

4 **Danger Zone**
Kenny Loggins

5 **Holding Back the Years**
Simply Red

# Sledgehammer GEFFEN 28718
## PETER GABRIEL

*Writer: Peter Gabriel*

*Producer: Daniel Lanois*

*July 26, 1986*
*1 week*

Tony Banks, Mike Rutherford, Anthony Phillips and Peter Gabriel were members of two different bands in 1966. Gabriel and Banks were in the Garden Wall, and Rutherford and Phillips were in the Anon. Gabriel briefly joined an R&B cover band, the Spoken Word, after seeing Otis Redding and trumpet player Wayne Jackson at the Ram Jam Club, a legendary ska/R&B underground saloon in the south London area of Brixton. That night, Gabriel "decided that I wanted to be a musician for life."

In the winter of 1967 the four students and another named Chris Stewart joined forces as Genesis, so named by Charterhouse alumnus Jonathan King. (Employed by the Decca label in Britain, King had also been involved in the early careers of 10cc and the Bay City Rollers.) With a new drummer, John Silver, Genesis released their first single ("The Silent Sun") in Britain on February 22, 1968. Their debut album, *From Genesis to Revelation*, was released 13 months later. Soon after this, John Mayhew joined Genesis as their new drummer.

In 1970, Mayhew and Phillips left Genesis, and the group signed with the British Charisma label. A new drummer was found via a newspaper ad: Phil Collins got the job [see 604—"One More Night"]. Guitarist Steve Hackett joined soon after.

The line-up remained stable until the end of 1974. That year, film director William Friedkin asked Gabriel to work on a film, and Peter was interested enough to take a week off from working on the album *The Lamb Lies Down on Broadway*. "Genesis, at that time, were not into anyone having extracurricular activities—unlike today," Gabriel told Steve Pond in *Rolling Stone*.

That same year, Peter's wife Jill gave birth to their first child, Anna. She was born with an infection developed in the womb and was not expected to live. Gabriel withdrew from the world of rock and roll—and Genesis. For the next six months, Jill thought Peter was going mad. In August, 1975, Gabriel made the official announcement that he was leaving Genesis.

Between 1977 and 1982, Peter Gabriel released four albums, all titled *Peter Gabriel*. The fourth LP was called *Security* only in America, at the insistence of Geffen Records. "I originally thought I would avoid titles and make my records like magazines," Gabriel told Timothy White in *Spin*. "When you look at home at a pile of magazines, you remember them usually by the picture on the cover; I wanted it to look like a body of work."

Gabriel broke the run of eponymously titled albums in 1986 with the release of *So*. "The new record has a universal title so that people won't end up buying the same record twice. I'm quite happy that that's happened, because there's a little change in style—I wanted the album to be elemental, alive, unselfconscious."

The first single from the LP, "Sledgehammer," featured a brass section led by Wayne Jackson, whom Gabriel had seen that fateful night at the Ram Jam Club. In his press biography, Gabriel described "Sledgehammer" as "an attempt to recreate some of the spirit and style of the music that most excited me as a teenager—'60s soul. The lyrics of many of those songs were full of playful sexual innuendo and this is my contribution to that songwriting tradition. It is also about the use of sex as a means of getting through a breakdown in communication."

Gabriel spent eight painful 16-hour days lying under glass with his head supported by a steel pole to film the video for "Sledgehammer." "I think the song would have fared okay, 'cause it did seem to work well on the radio," he said in *Rolling Stone*. "But I'm not sure that it would have been as big a hit, and I certainly don't think the album would have been opened up to as many people without the video. Because I think it had a sense of both humor and of fun, neither of which were particularly associated with me. I mean—wrongly in my way of looking at it—I think I was seen as a fairly intense, eccentric Englishman."

---

## THE TOP FIVE
*Week of July 26, 1986*

1 **Sledgehammer**
   Peter Gabriel

2 **Danger Zone**
   Kenny Loggins

3 **Invisible Touch**
   Genesis

4 **Nasty**
   Janet Jackson

5 **Glory of Love**
   Peter Cetera

WARNER BROTHERS 28662 **Glory of Love**
PETER CETERA

**643**

*Writers: Peter Cetera*
*David Foster*
*Diane Nini*

*Producer: Michael Omartian*

*August 2, 1986*
*2 weeks*

Peter Cetera wrote and sang lead vocals on both of Chicago's number one singles [see 446—"If You Leave Me Now" and 559—"Hard to Say I'm Sorry"]. Still, the question was asked (as it often is whenever any major player leaves a group): Who would be more successful, Chicago without Peter Cetera or Peter Cetera without Chicago?

At first, it looked like no contest. While Cetera scored immediately with "Glory of Love," Chicago fared poorly with the first single from *Chicago 18*. It was a newly recorded version of "25 or 6 to 4" and it peaked at number 48. Cetera scored again with his second single and then Chicago stormed up to number three with "Will You Still Love Me?"

Cetera was with Chicago for 18 years. In 1982 he released a solo LP, *Peter Cetera*, that peaked at 143 on the album chart. When he was ready to record his second solo album, the other members of Chicago were not thrilled.

"I didn't quit," Cetera told Dick Clark on "Countdown America." "I was given my walking papers by the group. In effect, (they) fired me. I tried to leave when we were in our down period, right around *Chicago 15*." The group was in a relative slump during this period: after five consecutive number one albums and two that came close, they had four albums in a row that failed to make the top 10.

Cetera told the band and his record label that if his first solo album was a hit he would leave Chicago. "When record companies hear that, they say . . . 'this guy is not leaving this group . . . we have 10 times the amount of money invested in the group than we do in this person who thinks he can go solo' . . . the album sold about 16 or 17 copies because the record company just did not want me out there on my own."

But the band's fortunes took an upswing in 1982, and there was touring to be done. "When it came time for me to do my solo album . . . they wanted to tour some more and do the next album," Cetera told Clark. "They said, 'You have to go on the road and if you don't . . . we're gonna have to get somebody else.' I couldn't believe that . . . I think it was a management decision to 'let's scare the living bejesus out of Peter Cetera because we all know . . ., he would never take the step.' . . . And it was exactly the out I was looking for. . . . Had the guys not made that move I probably would've still been in the group."

While working on the *Solitude/Solitaire* album, Cetera met with Jerry and Bob Greenberg, president and executive vice president, respectively, of the new United Artists record label. One of the company's first projects was a soundtrack for *The Karate Kid II*.

"Initially, I played them a more uptempo song I had "(They Don't Make 'Em Like They Used To," which ended up on *Solitude/Solitaire*), which they liked. But they told me they were looking for a ballad," Cetera told Steve Gett in *Billboard*. "So I said, 'Well, I've got something that's not quite finished.' I sang them a few bars, they flipped over it and took me to see the movie."

Cetera had to finish the song but hit a writer's block. He was mumbling incoherently to the music when his wife Diane thought she heard him sing "Glory of Love." He hadn't, but Diane helped him finish the song. It was their first professional collaboration.

If "Glory of Love" hadn't been chosen for the soundtrack of *The Karate Kid II*, it probably would not have been a single. "I would never have picked 'Glory of Love' . . . because I did not want to come out with a ballad first," Cetera told Clark.

## THE TOP FIVE
*Week of August 2, 1986*

1 **Glory of Love**
   Peter Cetera

2 **Sledgehammer**
   Peter Gabriel

3 **Danger Zone**
   Kenny Loggins

4 **Papa Don't Preach**
   Madonna

5 **Invisible Touch**
   Genesis

# Papa Don't Preach SIRE 28660
## MADONNA

*Writers: Brian Elliot*
*Madonna*

*Producers: Madonna*
*Stephen Bray*

*August 16, 1986*
*2 weeks*

" 'PAPA DON'T PREACH' is a message song that everyone is going to take the wrong way," Madonna predicted to Stephen Holden in the *New York Times*. "Immediately they're going to say I am advising every young girl to go out and get pregnant. When I first heard the song, I thought it was silly. But then I thought, wait a minute, this song is really about a girl who is making a decision in her life. She has a very close relationship with her father and wants to maintain that closeness. To me it's a celebration of life."

Madonna was right. Everyone had something to say about the song, from Tipper Gore, founder of the Parents Music Resource Center, to Gloria Allred, an attorney from Los Angeles committed to sexual equality. Allred said that Madonna should "make a public statement noting that kids have other choices, including abortion, or if she doesn't want to make that statement, then she has the responsibility to make another record supporting the opposite point of view."

Gore, head of the Washington Wives group that vigorously protested explicit sexual lyrics, said she thought the song was important because it "discusses, with urgency, a real predicament which thousands of unwed

teenagers face in our country. If it fosters discussion about pregnancy between teens and their family, then I think it's all to the good."

Songwriter Brian Elliot, who composed "Papa Don't Preach" with "additional lyrics" by Madonna, commented to Jay Padroff in *Music Connection*, "The Pro-Life League has decided that 'Papa Don't Preach' is a rallying cry for them. All around the country, their offices have adopted my song. Strangely enough, Tipper Gore . . . who used to condemn Madonna, has applauded the song's urgency and sensitivity. Of course, I'm really glad this happened *after* the fact because I was a little worried that had Tipper Gore given her public support of the song earlier on, it might have *killed* it."

Elliot, who recorded one album for Warner Brothers, was producing ses-

sions for a new artist named Cristina Dent. He took the tape to Michael Ostin in the A&R department at Warner Brothers. "He liked the first song, but he completely fell out over 'Papa Don't Preach,' " Elliot told Padroff. "He played it back a number of times, and I had a very strong feeling that we had something happening at that point."

Ostin later asked if he could play the song for Madonna, and Elliot consented. Then Ostin called again: Madonna loved the song and wanted to record it. "At that point, Cristina and I had been working together for six months or so. I felt that the song was strong enough to make it and do something for Cristina—to get *that* career rolling. But I was persuaded by a great many people that to have Madonna cut the song would be an astute move for everybody. It would bring a lot of credibility and visibility and economic autonomy for me and everything I was doing—and move my career ahead by four or five years in a six-month span."

Elliot asked Madonna's management if he could go to the studio and listen to her version of the song. He was given a time to be at the studio when Madonna wouldn't be there. "I'm listening to it for the first time and I hear, 'Well, did I wreck your song?' And I turned around and there she is. . . . We had a *spirited* discussion at that point about certain interpretations of lines, and it was resolved to the mutual delight of all concerned."

Elliot did not stay out of the controversy created by the song. "If Madonna has influenced young girls to keep their babies, I don't think that's such a bad deal," he told Patrick Goldstein of the *Los Angeles Times*. "I've heard from all sorts of people that I'm a voice for the New Right and a minion of right-to-life groups. But I had no ambitions for this to be adopted by any special interest groups. I don't have any banner to wave. I just wanted to make this girl a sympathetic character. As a father myself, I'd want to be accessible to my children's problems."

## THE TOP FIVE
*Week of August 16, 1986*

1 **Papa Don't Preach**
   Madonna

2 **Glory of Love**
   Peter Cetera

3 **Mad About You**
   Belinda Carlisle

4 **Higher Love**
   Steve Winwood

5 **We Don't Have to
   Take Our Clothes Off**
   Jermaine Stewart

ISLAND 28710 **Higher Love** 645
STEVE WINWOOD

*Writers: Steve Winwood
Will Jennings*

*Producers: Russ Titelman
Steve Winwood*

*August 30, 1986
1 week*

STEVE WINWOOD made his chart debut the week of March 5, 1966, with "Keep on Running" by the Spencer Davis Group. Twenty years, five months and three weeks later he had his first number one single, "Higher Love."

Winwood was born May 12, 1948, in Great Barr, a suburb of Birmingham, England. His father managed an iron foundry and played a variety of instruments in his own band. The family had a piano in the parlor, and Steve took to playing it at age five.

When he was 14 he joined his brother's group, the Muff Woody Jazz Band, and within a year he and brother Muff met up with a lecturer named Spencer Davis at the University of Birmingham. Along with drummer Pete York, they formed a four-piece R&B-influenced band that had hits on both sides of the Atlantic. On the American chart, their two biggest hits came in 1967: "Gimme Some Lovin' " (number seven in February) and "I'm a Man" (number 10 in May).

That didn't stop him from quitting the band. "The reason I left the Spencer Davis Group in 1967 was because I didn't want to continue playing and singing songs that were derivative of American R&B," he told Timothy White in *Musician*. "I'd begun to make younger friends like Dave Mason, who was working for Spencer Davis as a roadie, and (Jim) Capaldi, who was the lead singer in a group I'd jammed with called Deep Feeling. And I sang some blues stuff briefly with Eric (Clapton), Jack Bruce on bass, Paul Jones played harp . . . we were called the Powerhouse. When Jim, Dave, Chris Wood and I went up to the Berkshire cottage in 1967 to start Traffic, it was the result of a lot of enthusiastic planning and time spent playing together informally."

Traffic first played psychedelic pop

music. When Mason left, Winwood took the band in a jazzier, more soulful direction. After three albums (*Mr. Fantasy, Traffic,* and *Last Exit*), it looked like Traffic had come to the end of its road. Winwood teamed up with Eric Clapton, Ginger Baker and Ric Grech to form the "supergroup" Blind Faith, but the foursome only stayed together for one album. Next Winwood played briefly in Ginger Baker's Air Force. He then started work on a solo album to be called *Mad Shadows*; the project turned into a Traffic reunion LP titled *John Barleycorn Must Die*. Traffic continued until 1974.

Winwood's first solo album, *Steve Winwood*, was released in 1977. *Arc of a Diver* followed three years later and produced a hit single: "While You See a Chance" (number seven in April, 1981). That was the first collaboration between Winwood and lyricist Will Jennings, a former English teacher who went to Nashville to write songs in 1971. Winwood's publisher arranged for a meeting between the two. The meeting resulted in Jennings going to Winwood's home in Gloucestershire, England, in 1980. After writing "While You See a Chance," they collaborated on three other songs for *Arc of a Diver*. A year later, they finished nine songs that were recorded for the *Talking Back to the Night* album. Their partnership continued, yielding five of the eight songs on Winwood's third solo LP, *Back in the High Life*, including the first single "Higher Love."

"He had demo tracks worked up on the tune," says Jennings, who came up with the title but recalls little of the songwriting process. "When I get away from the writing of a song, there's not a lot I remember," he confesses. "You go off into a dream and hope you come back with something good, and it's all magic."

Producer Russ Titelman, who recorded *Back in the High Life* in New York, talked about the recording of "Higher Love" with Timothy White: "Both of us were ecstatic after Chaka (Khan) did her fireworks on 'Higher Love' but the real capper there came when her drummer, John Robinson, sat down and began to add the acoustic drums to the track. . . . John's phenomenal sticking and timbale-style tom-tom playing at the close of 'Higher Love' were so hot, we decided to take that portion of the track and move it up to *begin* the record."

## THE TOP FIVE
*Week of August 30, 1986*

1 **Higher Love**
Steve Winwood

2 **Venus**
Bananarama

3 **Papa Don't Preach**
Madonna

4 **Take My Breath Away**
Berlin

5 **Dancing on the Ceiling**
Lionel Richie

## 646 **Venus** LONDON 886-056-7
### BANANARAMA

Writer: *Robbie van Leeuwen*

Producers: *Mike Stock*
*Matt Aitken*
*Pete Waterman*

September 6, 1986
1 week

**W**HEN Siobahn Fahey, Sarah Dallin and Keren Wood formed the British girl group Bananarama in 1979, "Venus" was one of the first songs in their repertoire. "When we first got together . . . and were rehearsing in a basement, we were trying out various old songs," Fahey said on the United Stations Radio Network. "That was one of the songs we used to sing and it always sounded great. But we wouldn't record it for years because we wanted to do our own songs . . . so that people would take us seriously. But then we stopped worrying about whether people took us seriously or not . . . we just thought, it's a great song, let's do it. And it proved to be a good idea!"

It did indeed, giving Bananarama a number one song in America, a level of success they have not yet achieved in their own country. The original version of "Venus" by the Dutch group Shocking Blue hit number one on February 7, 1970 [see 268]. That makes "Venus" the fourth song of the rock era to be number one twice by two different artists, following "Go Away Little Girl," "The Loco-Motion" and "Please Mr. Postman."

Bananarama's origin can be traced to Bristol, where Sarah and Keren were schoolmates. They moved to London together and found a flat on Denmark Street, home to many of Britain's leading music publishers. Downstairs was a rehearsal hall used by a punk band called the Professionals, which included Steve Jones and Paul Cook, formerly of the Sex Pistols.

Keren went to work at the BBC while Sarah attended the London School of Fashion, where she met fellow fashion journalism student Siobahn. "All the other girls looked like secretaries," Siobahn told Rob Patterson. "We looked scruffy, to put it mildly . . . we gravitated toward each other."

Siobahn's sister's boyfriend worked for an independent British label called Demon, and persuaded one of the company's owners, Clark Banks, to finance a demo for the trio. Paul Cook agreed to co-produce the track, a cover version of Black Blood's "Aie a Mwana." That song helped them choose their name. "We just wanted a silly name that expressed enjoyment and lightheartedness," Siobahn told Jon Young. "Our first single was sung in Swahili, so we thought of something tropical—bananas—and added 'rama' 'cause it sounded silly." In another interview, Siobahn said the "rama" came from Roxy Music's "Pyjamarama." "Sometimes we've regretted calling ourselves that," she said. "It's not the easiest name to spell or pronounce, around the world."

"Aie a Mwana" attracted the attention of Fun Boy Three, a popular British band that had splintered off from the Specials, FB3 invited Bananarama to join them on the single "It Ain't What You Do," which went to number four on the British chart. Fun Boy Three then guest starred on Bananarama's next single, a cover version of the Velvelettes' Motown track "He Was Really Sayin' Some-thin'."

For their next recordings, Bananarama teamed up with producers Tony Swain and Steve Jolley (Spandau Ballet). Songs like "Shy Boy" and "Robert DeNiro's Waiting" were hits in the United Kingdom, but the group didn't get an American hit until "Cruel Summer" was heard in the film *The*

*Karate Kid.* That helped it reach number nine in September, 1984.

"Venus" was produced by the British hit-making team of Mike Stock, Matt Aitken and Pete Waterman, who have also produced artists like Dead or Alive ("You Spin Me Round [Like a Record]") and Rick Astley ("Never Gonna Give You Up"), as well as Bananarama's *Wow!* album and its hit single, "I Heard a Rumour" (number four in October, 1987).

"We changed Bananarama," Waterman said in *Record Mirror*. "They were a bit dowdy and a bit of a joke. Now they're so sexual, it's unbelievable. They've grown up into the eighties very well. . . . I love working with them. Bananarama are my Supremes."

### THE TOP FIVE
*Week of September 6, 1986*

1 **Venus**
Bananarama

2 **Take My Breath Away**
Berlin

3 **Higher Love**
Steve Winwood

4 **Dancing on the Ceiling**
Lionel Richie

5 **Friends and Lovers**
Carl Anderson and Gloria Loring

COLUMBIA 05903 **Take My Breath Away**
BERLIN **647**

*Writers: Giorgio Moroder*
*Tom Whitlock*

*Producer: Giorgio Moroder*

*September 13, 1986*
*1 week*

DID Berlin's manager, Perry Watts-Russel, have faith that "Take My Breath Away" would be the band's biggest hit ever? "When it just barely came into the Hot 100, he said there's no chance," says Terri Nunn, lead singer of the group. "He said, 'If this goes top five, I'll get a Mohawk.' He told so many people that MTV decided to film it. We waited 'til it went top three. He was sitting in the chair when we got the phone call that it went to number one."

"Take My Breath Away" was heard by many people who had never heard the album-oriented-rock group Berlin before. "We hadn't written anything up to that point that could be played on adult contemporary stations," explains Nunn. "It was shocking for me, because the first station I heard it on was something my mother listens to."

"Take My Breath Away" was the second song written by Giorgio Moroder and Tom Whitlock for the Tom Cruise film *Top Gun*. The first was "Danger Zone." Both songs were given to Berlin. "Giorgio wanted 'Danger Zone' to be a duet," says Nunn. "But we all liked 'Take My Breath Away' more." Kenny Loggins ended up recording "Danger Zone," and it was the first single released from the soundtrack. It peaked at number two.

Whitlock listened to Giorgio's music for "Take My Breath Away" before he wrote the lyrics. "I hopped in my car and was driving home into Hollywood. By the time I got home I had written the lyric. The title was a phrase that had been running through my mind, in terms of asking for that kind of awe, something so striking that you can't breathe."

Whitlock had been working on the score for *Top Gun* as assistant engineer. He had seen most of the movie by the time he wrote the songs. "The love scene was reshot to our song after the fact. It wasn't nearly as poetic (so) they went back and shot it to match the song."

Nunn recalls recording "Take My Breath Away": "Giorgio originally had a strange arrangement on it which I

personally liked. But he had both the record company and the movie company asking him to be as normal in arrangement as possible. So he couldn't be as experimental as he would have liked."

"Take My Breath Away" won the Oscar for Best Original Song of 1986, making it the 13th number one of the rock era to win an Academy Award.

Berlin's beginnings can be traced to an accident John Crawford had when he was a sophomore in high school. He was confined to bed after breaking his leg in a basketball game. He used his recuperation period to learn to play the guitar, and later he formed a band with a couple of friends from Orange County, California. He didn't care for the sound of most Los Angeles bands at the time, so he wanted an international name for his band that would suggest decadence and mystery. He chose Berlin.

In 1979, Crawford advertised for a lead singer, and Terri Nunn responded. She had worked in her family's record store in Reseda, California, and had been fairly successful as an actress, winning roles in TV programs like "Lou Grant" and

"Mary Hartman, Mary Hartman."

She auditioned for 25 bands altogether, and 24 of them offered her a job. But Berlin was the group she wanted to join. She was eventually hired, and remained with the band for less than a year before she left. Crawford replaced her with Virginia Macalino, then broke up Berlin and started another group called Fahrenheit. In 1981 he reformed Berlin and invited Nunn back.

In the spring of 1982, the six-piece band recorded an EP, *Pleasure Victim*, for a small, independent label. Geffen Records signed the band and rereleased the EP and the group's first chart single, "Sex (I'm a . . .)." Eventually, Berlin was reduced to a trio, consisting of Crawford, Nunn and drummer Rob Brill.

Berlin did not find a successful follow-up to "Take My Breath Away," which was their only 45 released on Columbia. Their next single, "Like Flames," burned out at number 82. "When ('Take My Breath Away') went to number one, it seemed like a very beneficial thing," Watts-Russel told Paul Grein in the *Los Angeles Times*. "And it *was* useful in the short term. But it hasn't been particularly useful in terms of the career of the band. It alienated (album-oriented-rock) radio stations, which considered the song too top 40. The problem has been that Berlin has not been fully accepted at either format. We don't have anything against the song. It's just that the nature of the song was not representative of the identity of the band. The lesson here is that if you're going to have a big hit, it better be with a song that is truly representative of who you are and how you want to be perceived."

## THE TOP FIVE
*Week of September 13, 1986*

1 **Take My Breath Away**
 Berlin

2 **Dancing on the Ceiling**
 Lionel Richie

3 **Stuck With You**
 Huey Lewis and the News

4 **Friends and Lovers**
 Gloria Loring & Carl Anderson

5 **Venus**
 Bananarama

**648** ## Stuck with You CHRYSALIS 43019
### HUEY LEWIS AND THE NEWS

*Writers: Chris Hayes*
*Huey Lewis*

*Producers: Huey Lewis and the News*

*September 20, 1986*
*3 weeks*

HUGH ANTHONY CREGG III was born July 5, 1950, in New York, and he grew up in Mill Valley, California. When he was supposed to begin his freshman year as an engineering student at Cornell University his father advised him to take a year off and travel through Europe.

He hitchhiked around the continent and learned to play harmonica. Back in the States, music became his first love, but he ran a landscaping business and a yogurt distributorship before joining a country-rock band called Clover in 1972. They had already recorded a couple of albums for Fantasy Records when Cregg and keyboard player Sean Hopper came on board.

For the next four years, Clover played the same small circuit of clubs. In 1976 they had a gig at the Palomino in North Hollywood, California. The British band Dr. Feelgood was in town for a label convention, and along with manager Jake Riviera and singer Nick Lowe they caught Clover's act. Riviera and Dave Robinson had founded the Stiff Records company in Britain and signed Clover to a management deal.

Riviera brought the band to England, where Clover backed Elvis Costello on his first album, *My Aim Is True*. But the Sex Pistols were just breaking and punk, not country rock, was selling. Clover returned home. Back in Marin County, guitarist John McFee was recruited to take Jeff Baxter's place in the Doobie Brothers and Clover disbanded. But the mystique surrounding Clover's success in England gave Lewis the freedom to run the Monday night jam sessions at Uncle Charlie's in Corte Madera, California.

Offered some free studio time by Patty Gleason of the Different Fur studio, Lewis recorded a dance version of the theme from *Exodus*, dubbed "Exo-Disco." Called back to England to play harmonica on Nick Lowe's *Labour of Lust* and Dave Edmunds' *Repeat When Necessary* albums, Lewis let Riviera listen to the *Exodus* spoof. He thought it was terrible enough to be a hit and negotiated a $6,000 deal with Phonogram Records. Lewis took the money back to the States to record a demo tape, which Gleason sent to Pablo Cruise manager Bob Brown.

Brown was thinking about returning to his former line of work in the stock market when he received the tape from a band called Huey Lewis and American Express. He hated their cover version of the Supremes' "Stop! In the Name of Love" but liked the other two songs well enough to sign them. Later, Brown found out that Huey didn't really have a band, just a group of friends who jammed at Uncle Charlie's every Monday night.

The friends—bassist Mario Cipollina, saxophonist Johnny Colla, drummer Bill Gibson, lead guitarist Chris Hayes and keyboardist Sean Hopper (from Clover)—coalesced into the News and were signed with Huey to Chrysalis Records.

After the success of their *Sports* album [see 615—"The Power of Love"], Huey and the band members felt the pressure to come up with another multi-platinum album. After six months of struggling with new material, Bob Brown called Chris Hayes to tell him they still needed a hit tune. Hayes told Michael Goldberg in *Rolling Stone* what he said to Brown: "God, Bob, I don't know. I've got a lot of things going. My wife's pregnant right now. But let me see what I can do." One six-pack and three hours of studio time later, Hayes had written the music for "Stuck with You."

## THE TOP FIVE
*Week of September 20, 1986*

1 **Stuck with You**
Huey Lewis and the News

2 **Dancing on the Ceiling**
Lionel Richie

3 **Friends and Lovers**
Gloria Loring and Carl Anderson

4 **Take My Breath Away**
Berlin

5 **Words Get in the Way**
Miami Sound Machine

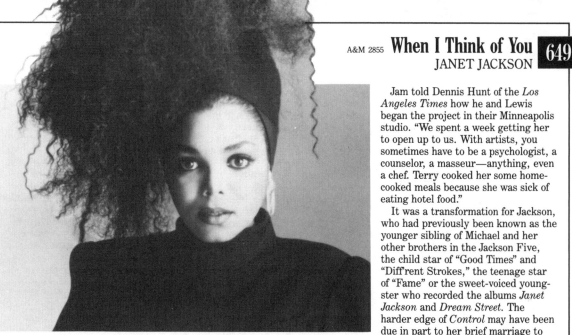

Writers: *James Harris III*
*Terry Lewis*
*Janet Jackson*

Producers: *Jimmy Jam*
*Terry Lewis*

October 11, 1986
*2 weeks*

"**I** SAW the Time in concert back when I was 16," Janet Jackson recalled in a *Spin* article by J. C. Stevenson. "It was in Chicago and they were great. And sooooo nasty. I was sitting out in the audience next to my mom, and I got so embarrassed that I had to move a few seats away from her." Perhaps Janet might have not been so embarrassed if she had been able to look into a crystal ball and see that in several years Time players Jimmy Jam (James Harris III) and Terry Lewis would produce her multi-platinum album *Control* and the number one single "When I Think of You."

Jam and Lewis played keyboard and bass, respectively, in the Time, a Minneapolis band that also included (at different times) Jesse Johnson, Alexander O'Neal and Morris Day. Prince helped them secure a record contract and took artistic control of the group. When Jam and Lewis were late for a gig because of a snowstorm in Atlanta, where they had been producing a session for the S.O.S. Band, Prince fined them $900 each and a few days later fired them from the Time.

"It devastated me," Lewis told Michael Goldberg in *Rolling Stone*. "I

didn't think I'd miss being famous or making money; I'd miss being with the fellas." But it became an opportunity for the two longtime friends. "Until that point," Jam told Mark Rowland in *Musician*, "producing was just something to do for fun. But that forced us to take it more seriously."

In a short time, Jam and Lewis wrote songs and produced sessions for the Force M.D.s ("Tender Love"), Cherrelle ("I Didn't Mean to Turn You On," later covered by Robert Palmer, and "Saturday Love," a duet with Alexander O'Neal) and Patti Austin ("The Heat of Heat"), among others. They were being called the Gamble and Huff [see 325—"Me and Mrs. Jones"] of the '80s when John McClain of A&M Records arranged for them to produce Janet Jackson's third album for the company.

Jam and Lewis had already composed the tracks for *Control* before McClain contacted them about working with Jackson. The tunes were written for Sharon Bryant, who had sung with Atlantic Starr [see 668—"Always"] until a bitter split. She decided the music was too rambunctious for her first solo effort. "Sharon just wanted a different feeling, I guess," Janet told Stevenson in *Spin*, "so Jimmy and Terry saved the tracks. What you hear on the album is the result of a lot of jamming that they did right there in the studio. All the music is pretty much them. But the lyrics, the vocal arrangements, the keyboards and synthesizers, that's where I came in."

Jam told Dennis Hunt of the *Los Angeles Times* how he and Lewis began the project in their Minneapolis studio. "We spent a week getting her to open up to us. With artists, you sometimes have to be a psychologist, a counselor, a masseur—anything, even a chef. Terry cooked her some home-cooked meals because she was sick of eating hotel food."

It was a transformation for Jackson, who had previously been known as the younger sibling of Michael and her other brothers in the Jackson Five, the child star of "Good Times" and "Diff'rent Strokes," the teenage star of "Fame" or the sweet-voiced youngster who recorded the albums *Janet Jackson* and *Dream Street*. The harder edge of *Control* may have been due in part to her brief marriage to James DeBarge of the singing DeBarge family. The marriage was annulled after six months. Without those events, "The album wouldn't have been the same. I don't know what it would have been like," Jackson said in *Bam*. The album was made without assistance from anyone else in the Jackson family. "I wanted the public to like my album because of *me*," Janet said, "and I wanted to prove that to myself."

The first five singles from *Control* all made the top five, each in a different position. "What Have You Done for Me Lately" peaked at number four, while "Nasty" went to number three. "When I Think of You" made Janet and Michael the first siblings to both have solo number one singles. "Control" reached number five, and "Let's Wait Awhile" went as high as number two.

## THE TOP FIVE
*Week of October 11, 1986*

1  **When I Think of You**
   Janet Jackson

2  **Don't Forget Me
   (When I'm Gone)**
   Glass Tiger

3  **Two of Hearts**
   Stacey Q

4  **Throwing It All Away**
   Genesis

5  **Typical Male**
   Tina Turner

# 650 | True Colors PORTRAIT 06247
### CYNDI LAUPER

*Writers: Tom Kelly*
*Billy Steinberg*

*Producers: Cyndi Lauper*
*Lennie Petze*

*October 25, 1986*
*2 weeks*

CYNDI LAUPER approached her second album, *True Colors*, under the shadow of the dreaded "sophomore jinx." Her first LP, *She's So Unusual*, had produced four consecutive top five songs in 1984: "Girls Just Want to Have Fun" (number two in March), "Time After Time" [see 589] (number one in June), "She Bop" (number three in September) and "All Through the Night" (number five in December). In July of 1985, she went to number 10 with the song "The Goonies 'R' Good Enough" from the soundtrack of *The Goonies*.

"We're not at all afraid of the sophomore slump," Dave Wolff, Cyndi's manager/fiancé, told Steven Dupler in *Billboard*. He also defended the choice of "True Colors" as the first single from the album. "There was a certain group of people that was surprised we elected to choose a ballad, but it's really a multiformatted song. 'Girls' helped establish Cyndi's persona, then 'Time After Time' deepened that image. Now that she's an established star, we felt we could go with a song like 'True Colors,' which has many shades to it."

Aside from cover versions of "What's Going On" and "Iko Iko," the title track was the only song on the *True Colors* LP that Cyndi didn't have a hand in writing. Tom Kelly and Billy Steinberg, who scored their first number one song when Madonna released "Like a Virgin" [see 600], wrote "True Colors," but not with any specific artist in mind.

"We usually write pretty fast," says Kelly, "(but) 'True Colors' from start to finish was probably the longest song we ever wrote." Steinberg wrote the lyrics first, then Kelly wrote the music quickly. The first verse, as originally written, was too complicated, Steinberg admits. But he was also reluctant to abandon it. "Finally I agreed we do need new verse lyrics. Then the ordeal started of trying to write them." The two songwriters would meet and Tom would play the intro on the piano. "I would just plug my ears and get mad," says Billy. "I'd stand up and say, 'I don't want to hear that, don't play that!"

"I'd get mad at him," Tom says. "I said, 'This is a great song, let's finish it.' We had an opportunity to pitch a song to George Martin for Kenny Rogers. Without even telling (Billy) I . . . sent the song over there and forgot about it." A few days later Kelly was awakened at 9 A.M. by a phone call. The person on the other end spoke with a British accent and identified himself as George Martin. Tom thought it was a joke, but when he remembered he had sent the song to Martin he woke up quickly. Martin liked the song but wanted simpler lyrics. "Even at the prospect of having a song for Kenny Rogers—and George loved it, he was really emphatic if we'd get it right he wanted to do it—I still couldn't get Billy going."

The demo was also sent to Don Grierson, then in the A&R department at Capitol. "Without even telling us, he played the song for Anne Murray. Apparently she didn't like it," says Steinberg, who finally completed the new lyrics with some help from Kelly. Their manager, John Baruck, sent the demo to Lennie Petze, who was co-producing Cyndi's second album. Petze called the writers to let them know that Cyndi wanted to record the song.

"It's the kind of song where somebody could sit down and sing (it) to a little kid," says Kelly. "That's how universal it should be. Cyndi . . . sings it like a little kid. It's got this childlike innocence to it."

## THE TOP FIVE
*Week of October 25, 1986*

1 **True Colors**
Cyndi Lauper

2 **Typical Male**
Tina Turner

3 **When I Think of You**
Janet Jackson

4 **I Didn't Mean to Turn You On**
Robert Palmer

5 **Heartbeat**
Don Johnson

*Writer: Tom Scholz*

*Producer: Tom Scholz*

*November 8, 1986*
*2 weeks*

Prolific is not a word that comes to mind when one thinks of Boston, the hard-pop band that completes a new album every eight years or so. Boston founder Tom Scholz is a self-admitted perfectionist.

Boston's eponymously titled debut album, released in 1976, was seven years in the making. The second LP, *Don't Look Back*, was issued a mere two years later, but Scholz later said it was unfinished at the time. Eight years later, *Third Stage* came out.

"Amanda," the first song written for the album, was completed in 1980. "I must admit that when I started it, there was a motivation to show that I could do it again, strictly an ego motivation," Scholz said in *Musician*. "But once I got 'Amanda' done, I felt I had to complete the album in a way that would do justice to that song, because I wasn't expecting it to work out that well. It set a standard for everything else I had to do."

That same year, Scholz created a new company called Scholz Research and Development. "I started it so I'd have some place to work, so that the music wouldn't be a job," the former Polaroid engineer and MIT graduate said in a 1986 *Time* interview. Through his company, Scholz developed a paperback book-sized guitar amplifier

called a Rockman. Sales of the Rockman helped finance the recording of *Third Stage*. "It took six years to produce *Third Stage*," Scholz said in *Time*. "When I first started working on the project, I'd put in 50 to 60 hours a week. During the last two years I really had to drive myself to go down to the basement and finish it."

Scholz, who has his own studio in the basement of his home in a suburb of Boston, might have been distracted from album work by other matters, such as a protracted legal battle with his former label, the CBS-owned Epic Records. Tired of waiting for the third Boston album, CBS froze the band's royalties earned from their first two albums and filed a $20 million lawsuit, alleging breach of contract on a five-album, ten-year deal. Scholz filed a countersuit and CBS asked for an injunction preventing Boston from signing with MCA Records. U.S. District Court Judge Vincent L. Broderick refused to issue the restraining order, and Boston was allowed to record for their new label.

By the time *Third Stage* was completed and the first single released, many people had already heard an unfinished version of the song. "A bootleg of 'Amanda' got released two or three years before the record came out," Boston vocalist Brad Delp told reporter Keith Zimmerman. "At first we thought that was going to be disastrous, but in a backhanded way, it turned out to have a somewhat positive effect. We found that, on every station that had managed to get

hold of it, it was the top requested song. It was the last thing we would have planned to do, and I don't know how it ever got out to people. MCA certainly made sure it didn't stay out long. If we had any fears about being accepted (after a long absence), I think that sort of relieved them."

Delp first met Scholz in 1970 at a club in Revere Beach, north of Boston. Scholz, originally from Toledo, Ohio, was looking for a vocalist for a band and the two musicians started working together. When it came time to sign a management deal three years later, Delp didn't feel right about it and left the group. "I didn't see Tom for a year or so," Delp told Elianne Halbersberg. "They had another singer for a while, and I had projects, but none were satisfying. I came home from a movie and there was a note from Tom in my mailbox saying, 'We're working on demos, if you're interested.' I was so ready by that time to go back! It wasn't the money—we were recording more than playing. . . . Shortly after we were back together, we worked up demos that were the basis for the *Boston* album."

The original line-up of Boston also included guitarist Barry Goudreau, bassist Fran Sheehan and drummer Sib Hashian. During the eight-year gap between *Don't Look Back* and *Third Stage*, they departed at various times. The liner notes for *Third Stage* credit Scholz with: "lead guitar, rhythm guitar, acoustic guitar, grand piano, electric pianos, bass guitar, Hammond organ, theater organ, some drums, guitar 'violins,' rocket ignition, thunderstorms and unidentified flying objects."

## THE TOP FIVE

*Week of November 8, 1986*

1 **Amanda**
   Boston

2 **I Didn't Mean to Turn You On**
   Robert Palmer

3 **True Colors**
   Cyndi Lauper

4 **Human**
   Human League

5 **True Blue**
   Madonna

# 652 Human A&M 2861
## HUMAN LEAGUE

Writers: *James Harris III*
*Terry Lewis*

Producers: *Jimmy Jam*
*Terry Lewis*

*November 22, 1986*
*1 week*

"**I** THINK music's gotten very boring in Britain over the last three or four years, and the most exciting record I'd heard in a long time was by a group called Change," Phil Oakey of the Human League told Dick Clark on his weekly radio show, "Countdown America." "The LP was produced by Jimmy Jam (James Harris III) and Terry Lewis. I found out . . . they were (producing) Cherelle and the S.O.S. Band. I think the S.O.S. Band are really wonderful, definitely one of my favorite bands. The guy who runs urban music at A&M in Los Angeles, John McClain, said, 'How would you like Jimmy and Terry to produce you?' and we went, 'Eh?' because we thought they didn't produce anyone when they didn't write the songs."

Oakey and bass player Ian Burden flew to Minneapolis to meet Jam and Lewis at their Flyte Tyme studios and agreed to have them produce the *Crash* LP. The band had already been working on the album in England with producer Colin Thurston, who had produced the Human League's first album. "We worked with him for nine months and then we realized it just

wasn't turning into a really good dance record. So we split with Colin and went with Jimmy and Terry," Human Leaguer Joanne Catherall said in *Only Music*.

Working with Jam and Lewis was a learning experience for the Human League. "It was the first time we said. 'You are the producer, we are the artists, we'll stand back and let you do what you want,' " Oakey said. "Jimmy and Terry brought us down to Earth. That had been our problem on the previous LP . . . we were doing a lot of talking instead of getting on with it. . . . In the same time that it used to take us to record a bass drum off a drum machine, they would have recorded half an album."

Oakey co-wrote six of the ten songs on *Crash*, not including the first single, "Human." "I think one of the things we learned from them was a sort of realism, and for a couple of years we haven't been writing those good songs . . . we'd be silly to turn down good songs, especially when they're written for us by a couple of guys that we like very much. We shall write better songs next time, though."

"Human" sounded as if it had been written by the Human League, and not by someone outside the band. "I think they listened to our records and they tried to fit a record to us, which I think they did very well . . . as an outsider hearing the song, I think it's a fantastic record. It's the best ballad since 'You've Lost That Lovin' Feelin'. "

Terry Lewis talked about the song with Michael Goldberg of *Rolling Stone*. "With 'Human,' I think the lyrics came out of just thinking about relationships. Men always express that they go out and do what they have to do, and they come and the woman forgives them and everything is wonderful. But a woman never speaks up. She'll go do her do (have an affair) and tiptoe back home, and you never know it. So I thought it would be cool to have this little twist where the woman comes in and says, 'Yeah, that's cool. You were human. I forgive you. . . . While you were gone, *I* was human too.' "

Lewis talked about recording "Human" in *Hits* magazine. "We had the tune . . . when Phil came to town. It was finished musically, but not lyrically or melodically. So we worked with Phil for two or three weeks and the lyrics and the melody came along and so we tried it. No one thought Phil would be able to sing it. Because Phil, by nature, is a mechanical singer and this was not a mechanical song. It took a whole week to get that song out of Phil, just the vocal, because he was not accustomed to singing with that kind of feeling that a ballad needs. We just did it over and over until he started feeling it. Because after you sing if for a while, you can understand and start to relate to it."

"Human" gave Jam and Lewis their second chart-topper, just five weeks after Janet Jackson took "When I Think of You" [see 649] to number one. The song brought Human League back to the top of the Hot 100 four years and four months after their first trend-setting number one single [see 556—"Don't You Want Me"].

## THE TOP FIVE
*Week of November 22, 1986*

1 **Human**
Human League

2 **Amanda**
Boston

3 **True Blue**
Madonna

4 **You Give Love a Bad Name**
Bon Jovi

5 **Take Me Home Tonight**
Eddie Money

MERCURY 884-953-7 **You Give Love a Bad Name** 653
BON JOVI

*Writers: Jon Bon Jovi*
*Richie Sambora*
*Desmond Child*

*Producer: Bruce Fairbairn*

*November 29, 1986*
*1 week*

JOHN BONGIOVI was born on March 2, 1962, (the number one song in America was "Duke of Earl" by Gene Chandler), in Perth Amboy, New Jersey. He grew up in Sayreville and was playing in garage bands by the time he was in junior high. At 14, he asked a lounge guitarist who moved into the neighborhood to give him lessons so he could meet "chicks."

In high school, he formed a cover band called the Atlantic City Expressway with his friend David Rashbaum. Bongiovi didn't go on to college but held down jobs in a junkyard, a fast food restaurant and a Kinney's Shoe Store, where he was fired for playing the radio too loud. His cousin, Tony Bongiovi, ran the Power Station recording studio in New York and had produced records for Aerosmith, the Ramones and the Talking Heads. Jon (he dropped the "h") went to Manhattan to work at the studio.

"I had a broom and a pot of coffee and I was the gofer," he told Keeps. "For 50 bucks a week for two years I slept on the floor in his place and learned about the music business. . . . The people that I met through the Power Station helped me in the business. It was a good experience."

Jon was able to record in the studio in the off hours, and with some help from musicians like Roy Bittan of the E Street Band, he soon had over 50 tracks. One of them was his own composition "Runaway." In 1983, radio station WAPP in New York picked up the song for their *Homegrown* LP, and

it was played by some album-oriented rock stations around the country.

Bongiovi had a hit record but no band. He asked his friend Dave Rashbaum (now named David Bryan) to play keyboards. He also recruited bassist Alec John Such from a local band, Phantom's Opera, and a drummer Tico Torres from Franke and the Knockouts [see 683—"(I've Had) The Time of My Life"]. Lead guitarist Richie Sambora, who played with Such in a New Jersey band called the Message, completed the group of five musicians.

Derek Shulman of PolyGram Records signed the band to the Mercury label. They all agreed to anglicize Jon's last name as the group name, so fans would recognize that "Runaway," included on Bon Jovi's first LP, was by the same person who recorded it on the *Homegrown* hit. "Runaway" peaked at number 39 on the Hot 100 in April, 1984. Their second LP, *7800° Fahrenheit*, produced a couple of mid-chart singles, "Only Lonely" and "In and Out of Love."

For their third album, the group turned to producer Bruce Fairbairn (Loverboy, Honeymoon Suite). They also wanted to collaborate with an outside writer who could turn out material that would bring the band a wider audience—specifically, more females. Paul Stanley of the group Kiss recommended Desmond Child, who had had a 1979 Hot 100 chart single, "Our Love Is Here to Stay" (by Desmond Child and Rouge).

"I got a lot of resistance," Child told Susan Orlean in *Rolling Stone*. "Jon didn't want to try those new rhythms. He thought it sounded too Michael Jackson. It took a tremendous leap of maturity for him to let that in." One of

the songs co-written with Child was "You Give Love a Bad Name," the first single released from *Slippery When Wet*.

Sambora talked about writing the song in *Music Connection*: "Jon, Desmond Child and I were sitting there talking, and the title was the first thing that came up. Jon said something like, 'How about "You Give Love a Bad Name"?' and I said, 'Ah-hah!' I think the riff came in next. We wrote the chorus first with the riff, put in the verses, and that was it. It took one day."

Fairbairn continues the story: "I remember Jon picking me up at the hotel. (He) said, 'Man last night we nailed this song that I think is a smash.' The title sounded great right off the bat. When the band learned it and we listened to it, we all had a real good feeling because of the changes and the chorus. It had that accessible (feel) to it. We worked it from there, building up the big vocal parts and coming up with the guitar parts that made the song special. When you finish the song and actually mix it, you say, 'Well, this is the best that we can do. God only knows if the kids are going to like it.' "

## THE TOP FIVE
*Week of November 29, 1986*

1  **You Give Love a Bad Name**
   Bon Jovi

2  **Human**
   Human League

3  **True Blue**
   Madonna

4  **The Next Time I Fall**
   Peter Cetera and Amy Grant

5  **Hip to Be Square**
   Huey Lewis and the News

## 654 | The Next Time I Fall FULL MOON 28597
### PETER CETERA and AMY GRANT

*Writers: Bobby Caldwell*
*Paul Gordon*

*Producer: Michael Omartian*

*December 6, 1986*
*1 week*

IT took Chicago almost 13 years after their chart debut to garner two number one singles. Former Chicago member Peter Cetera took six months, and he did it with his first two chart singles as a solo artist [see 643—"Glory of Love"].

"The Next Time I Fall" was written by Bobby Caldwell (who had a 1979 hit, "What You Won't Do for Love") and Paul Gordon. "Bobby was aware that Peter was looking (for songs) so we did try to mold it (for) him. It was also possibly for Chicago—we really wanted to fit it into that school," explains Gordon.

He elaborated on the construction of the song in an interview published in *Words & Music*. "I came over to Bobby's apartment; he'd just moved in and his furniture consisted of a coffee table and a DX-7. And we just started playing around with some ideas—we probably went through several different musical ideas until we arrived at the skeleton of 'Next Time I Fall.' "

They came up with a chord progression, but didn't have any lyrics or a title. "After the first session we had an entirely different chorus, musically, and it wasn't until the next session that Bobby came up with the music for the new chorus. We zeroed in on that and stuck it together with the verse we'd already written. We worked pretty quickly. . . . We got the music together to a point where we were satisfied and got out a blank page in the notebook, and sat in two chairs and looked at each other and said, 'Where do we go with this?' "

The music came easier than the words, Gordon said. "Lyrics, especially in a collaboration, can be a very tough thing. We came up, finally, with some compromises that we both made to each other and came out with a strong lyric."

Caldwell sang on the demo, which was recorded in one day. "We didn't write it as a duet," Gordon said. "When the demo was made Bobby sang lead vocal, and it always sounded like one vocal straight through. When we heard they were making it as a

duet we thought, 'That's interesting, I wonder how they're going to pull *that* off?' "

"I always wanted to do a duet," Cetera told Dick Clark on "Countdown America." "The choice of Amy Grant (was) totally left field." Cetera admitted his motive for singing with Grant to Howard and Sandy Benjamin of the Interview Factory. "Choosing Amy Grant . . . was a total career move. I wanted to use somebody that people would go, 'What?' Through a process of elimination, all of a sudden she appeared. It was . . . wonderful."

Amy Grant would agree with that assessment. "It was an amazing opportunity for me," she acknowledges. "Even though we had fine record sales and exceptional concert attendance, I never had a song make it on the radio. (Where) I have a kind of silent, grass roots following, Peter, from years of singing, has a visible radio following and shared that with me."

Grant, best known for her successes in Christian music, was born in Augusta, Georgia, on November 25, 1960. She grew up in Nashville and started writing songs at age 14. A year later, record producer Brown Bannister heard a tape of her songs and played it over the telephone for Stan Moser, head of the contemporary religious music label Word Records. He signed her to the label, and Grant recorded eight albums for him before recording a more secular LP, *Unguarded.*

Amy was visiting a girlfriend in Atlanta when she got the phone call asking her if she'd like to record a duet with Cetera. "I was floored. I

mean, I've listened to his stuff from the time I was very young—which he didn't want to hear about," she laughs. Grant first heard the song when Caldwell played his demo over the phone. "Then, just to make sure that I could sing it in the register they wanted, they sent me Peter's vocal. I was on the road and just flew in for the day to do the recording."

Grant was still touring when the single was released and didn't follow its progress on the *Billboard* Hot 100. "I remember getting back home to Nashville. My husband and I were driving in the car and I casually said, 'Gee, I was really hoping that song would do something; I hope the guys at the office aren't let down.' I was talking to fill space and thinking the song hadn't done well. My husband looked at me and said, 'I don't think you should feel so bad about a number one song!' "

### THE TOP FIVE
*Week of December 6, 1986*

1 **The Next Time I Fall**
   Peter Cetera and Amy Grant

2 **You Give Love a Bad Name**
   Bon Jovi

3 **Hip to Be Square**
   Huey Lewis and the News

4 **The Way It Is**
   Bruce Hornsby and the Range

5 **Walk like an Egyptian**
   Bangles

## RCA 5023 The Way It Is   655
### BRUCE HORNSBY AND THE RANGE

Writer: *Bruce Hornsby*

Producer: *Bruce Hornsby*
          *Elliot Scheiner*

*December 13, 1986*
*1 week*

"**I**'M sorry, I just don't think it's commercial," said Bruce Hornsby. Surprisingly, he was discussing his number one single, "The Way It Is," with Steve Pond of *Rolling Stone*. "I like to go for a sort of anthemic thing, a big chorus. But this is a very even-running song. It doesn't reach the highs and lows that I think of as desirable, almost, in songwriting."

It's not the first time Hornsby has been wrong about his music. "I didn't think the music I was making would interest any major labels," he told Bob Doerschuk in *Keyboard*. "It was just piano, bass, drums, a little synth pad and vocals. I didn't think it was your typical radio formula and I still don't."

Hornsby, a native of Williamsburg, Virginia, stands 6′4″ and had a keen

interest in basketball in school. But there were strong musical influences in his family. His grandfather played organ in a theater and supervised music in the public schools in Richmond. Bruce's father played sax with his brother's band, Sherwood Hornsby and the Rhythm Boys. There was a seven-foot Steinway piano in the Hornsby's living room that attracted Bruce's interest.

While Bruce was in college he formed the Bruce Hornsby Band with his older brother Bobby and a friend, drummer John Molo, who is now in Bruce Hornsby and the Range. Michael McDonald of the Doobie Brothers caught one of the band's sets at a local Steak and Ale. The next night he brought some of the Doobies to sit in, and he offered to introduce Bruce to people in Los Angeles if he would move out west.

Hornsby made the move to Hollywood in 1980 with his brother John as a songwriting partner. McDonald introduced them to Jeff Baxter, a former member of Steely Dan and the

Doobie Brothers. Ronnie Vance of 20th Century Fox's music publishing company heard the Hornsby brothers play at a showcase set up by Baxter. Vance liked what he heard and hired the brothers as staff writers.

"They'd come to us and say, 'Write us a song that sounds like "Physical" for Laura Branigan. Write us a song like "Slow Hand" or "He's So Shy," ' whatever was the real hot stuff that they could get recorded by other people. (We) found we were neither very good at it, nor had much interest in the whole process," Bruce told Robyn Flans in *Pulse*. The brothers also wrote music for films: "We wrote a couple of disco songs for a gay bar scene in *Making Love*. We were terrible at it," Bruce said in *Rolling Stone*.

Bruce recorded demos with producer David Foster and played in Sheena Easton's band for two years. He became friendly with Huey Lewis, who wanted one of Hornsby's songs for an early LP, but Bruce wanted to keep the song for himself. Later, Huey would take another of Bruce's songs to the top of the Hot 100 [see 661— "Jacob's Ladder"].

Frustrated with trying to fit in with the latest trend, Hornsby recorded a four-song demo tape that included "The Way It Is." The song "was written lyrics first and the music later," Hornsby said in *Keyboard*. "I remember being in my garage and coming up with this little lick that I liked. I kept playing it over and over again. And the melody? It's very strange. I'm not trying to be mysterious about it, but I just can't really remember how I wrote it."

Hornsby heard from his friend Pete Harris that Windham Hill Records was starting a new label for vocalists, so he sent them the demo tape "because I thought no major label out there would have any interest, since it was such an organic sounding tape," Hornsby told Bill Forman in *Bam*. "They offered me a deal for it, and I was just elated." But Bruce's attorney played the tape for some major labels, and Paul Atkinson at RCA liked what he heard. "I chose not to sign with Windham Hill because they weren't really interested in the rock side of what we were doing," Hornsby said in *Pulse*. "With RCA, I was able to make the total record I wanted to make. They were interested in all of me, not just one side."

### THE TOP FIVE
*Week of December 13, 1986*

1  **The Way It Is**
   Bruce Hornsby and the Range

2  **Walk Like an Egyptian**
   Bangles

3  **Hip to Be Square**
   Huey Lewis and the News

4  **The Next Time I Fall**
   Peter Cetera and Amy Grant

5  **Everybody Have Fun Tonight**
   Wang Chung

## 656 Walk Like an Egyptian COLUMBIA 06257
### BANGLES

*Writer: Liam Sternberg*

*Producer: David Kahne*

*December 20, 1986*
*4 weeks*

LIAM STERNBERG first thought of the title "Walk Like an Egyptian" while crossing the English Channel on a ferry boat. He wrote the phrase down in his notebook, and on his next visit to Los Angeles recorded a four-track demo of the song.

The demo, featuring the vocals of Marti Jones, was completed by January, 1984. Sternberg, an Akron, Ohio, native living in London, played the demo for Toni Basil [see 564—"Mickey"], who turned it down.

Bangles producer David Kahne received a tape from Peer Southern Publishing with two songs on it. He had been asked to consider the first song on the cassette, "Rock and Roll Vertigo," a candidate for the Bangles' second album, *Different Light*. "But whoever made the copy put 'Walk Like an Egyptian' first," Kahne says. "So I was listening to 'Walk Like an Egyptian' but thinking it was the other song . . . I really liked the demo . . . Marti sang it with an offhand quality I thought was really great."

Sternberg, who wrote and produced Rachel Sweet's first album for Stiff Records, was familiar with the Bangles, having seen them at a small club on Ventura Boulevard in California's San Fernando Valley. He loved the group's version of his song: "It was everything I had in mind, only better."

"Walk Like an Egyptian," the number one single for the year 1987 according to *Billboard*, was the third release from *Different Light*. "Manic Monday," written by Bangles aficionado Prince under the pseudonym "Christopher" [see 633—"Kiss"], peaked at number two in April, 1986. The next single, "If She Knew What She Wants," composed by Jules Shear, faltered at number 29 in July.

All four of the Bangles hail from Southern California. Sisters Vicki and Debbi Peterson grew up in Northridge. Susanna Hoffs was raised on the west side of Los Angeles. Michael Steele spent her formative years in Newport Beach.

Vicki formed her first band when she was in the ninth grade. Her songs were reminiscent of the '60s, strongly influenced by her favorite groups the Beatles and the Hollies. The band needed a drummer, so Vicki bought her sister a drum set.

Susanna's interest in music grew stronger after she graduated from the University of California at Berkeley in 1981. Returning to Los Angeles, she placed an ad in a weekly newspaper, the *Recycler*, that read, "Band members wanted: Into the Beatles, Byrds and Buffalo Springfield." It was one month after the assassination of John Lennon, and as a result of the ad, Susanna had a long telephone conversation with the Peterson sisters about that tragedy. The three women met in Susanna's garage, and with Annette Zalinskas on bass, formed a band called the Colours. The name was changed to the Supersonic Bangs and then shortened to the Bangs. They released a single, "Getting Out of Hand," on their own Downkiddie label. Playing at smaller clubs in Los Angeles, they became part of the "Paisley Underground," a loose-knit collection of psychedelic and folk-rock influenced groups.

Miles Copeland signed the Bangs to a management deal, released an EP and booked them as an opening act for the English Beat. An East Coast group called the Bangs threatened legal action if they continued to use the name, so while driving to Las Vegas they thought of possible new names and hated all of them. Finally, over dinner at a Mexican restaurant, somebody scrawled Bang-less on a napkin, and the Bangles were born.

In 1983, CBS Records offered to sign the quartet. That was a cue for Zalinskas to depart; she wanted to sing lead and the others were more interested in her bass playing. She joined the country punk outfit Blood on the Saddle. Her replacement was Michael Steele, known as Micki Steele when she was the original lead singer for the all-girl band the Runaways.

The Bangles' first album for CBS, *All Over the Place*, didn't produce any chart singles, although "Hero Takes a Fall" and "Going Down to Liverpool" won airplay on some album-oriented rock stations. But it did set the stage for *Different Light* and the hit singles "Manic Monday" and "Walk Like an Egyptian."

## THE TOP FIVE
*Week of December 20, 1986*

1 **Walk Like an Egyptian**
Bangles

2 **The Way It Is**
Bruce Hornsby and the Range

3 **Everybody Have Fun Tonight**
Wang Chung

4 **Notorious**
Duran Duran

5 **Shake You Down**
Gregory Abbott

COLUMBIA 06191 **Shake You Down** 657
GREGORY ABBOTT

*Writer: Gregory Abbott*

*Producer: Gregory Abbott*

*January 17, 1987*
*1 week*

"**I** THINK I might have coined a new phrase," Gregory Abbott laughs. "Now I hear women saying, 'Yeah, he really shook me down last night,' or 'I'd sure like to shake him down.' The song was my attempt to express how men feel when they see a women they like. Emotionally, the phrase 'shake you down' made sense to me, and when I repeated it to a lady friend of mine, she definitely understood what I was saying. So that became the hook of the song."

"Shake You Down" was Abbott's first single for CBS Records. It went to number one on the black singles chart in October, 1986, just one week after making its debut on the Hot 100. It wasn't originally scheduled to be Abbott's first single. "I Got the Feelin' (It's Over)," one of three songs that helped Abbott get a deal with CBS, was earmarked to be the first release.

Abbott was born in Harlem. His father, from Antigua, worked for the post office. His mother, from Venezuela, gave him his first piano lessons. She also arranged for her son to sing in the St. Patrick's Cathedral Choir (until his voice changed—"just like Menudo, they threw me out").

He got his undergraduate degree in psychology at Boston University and his master's at California State University at San Francisco. He earned tuition money by playing with different bands at college dances, fraternity parties and local clubs. "That was also a training period for me. At that time, though, I didn't know if I'd make music my main objective."

He went on to do graduate work in literature at Stanford. He also taught educational psychology, English and various courses in black studies at UC Berkeley. Abbott stopped working on his doctorate to pursue a music career. "I did most of the course work for a Ph.D.," he told Mary Campbell of the Associated Press. "I stopped because music began to become more and more important to me. I started taking it more seriously and wanted to make this a profession. I also learned how to produce records. . . . I met Marvin Gaye, who had a 24-track studio. He

taught me how to function in a studio. . . . I moved to L.A. and really got more heavily into music. I began to write songs. I lived there four or five years." During this period, his then-wife Freda Payne ("Band of Gold") recorded four of his songs on her albums *Stares and Whispers* and *Supernatural High*.

Abbott returned home to Manhattan and went to work as a researcher for a Wall Street brokerage. "I needed a job," he told Campbell. "I had been fascinated by Wall Street. At night I'd be uptown putting together my tapes in recording studios. Some investment bankers saw me listening to my Walkman. They were curious. I let them hear it. Seeing I was serious about what I was doing, they took (a) financial interest in me. They financed a recording studio in my home. They also financed a label, Gramercy Park Records."

Abbott produced other artists for his label but soon turned his attention to himself. "People would often ask who was singing on the demos I'd worked on," he explained to David Nathan of the *Los Angeles Herald-Examiner*. "I figured that it couldn't hurt to produce myself. After all, I know the artist in question pretty well—and I think he knows how to take direction."

Abbott spent three years writing songs for himself. "I was determined

not to go rushing out there with any old kind of stuff. So I waited till I had three songs that I felt really represented me the way I wanted to be heard." He recorded 40 songs on tape and chose the three best to submit to CBS. "I guess I'm like a studio junkie. Some people spend their money on vacations, clothes and so on. I'm just fascinated by . . . the studio."

It was his uncle, record executive Mike Abbott, who brought Gregory to the attention of Charles Koppelman's The Entertainment Company. "They're the ones who got the deal with CBS," Abbott told Nathan. The label agreed that Abbott could produce his own album. "What I most appreciated was that they trusted me."

## THE TOP FIVE
*Week of January 17, 1987*

1  **Shake You Down**
   Gregory Abbott

2  **C'est La Vie**
   Robbie Nevil

3  **Notorious**
   Duran Duran

4  **Walk Like an Egyptian**
   Bangles

5  **At This Moment**
   Billy Vera and the Beaters

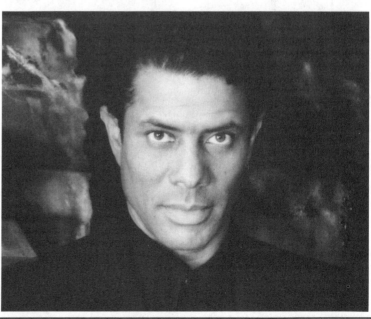

**658** | ### At This Moment RHINO 74403
BILLY VERA AND THE BEATERS

*Writer: Billy Vera*

*Producer: Jeff Baxter*

*January 24, 1987*
*2 weeks*

ONE FRIDAY night, Michael Weithorn wandered into a Los Angeles club called "At My Place" to catch a popular local act, Billy and the Beaters. Weithorn, a supervising producer/writer for NBC-TV's "Family Ties," took special note of one song he thought would work as a musical backdrop for a romance between characters played by Michael J. Fox and Tracy Pollan.

"He called me up and said, 'There's a song we heard you do (that) we want to use on our show.' They didn't even know the name of it," explains Billy Vera (born William McCord, Jr., in Riverside, California on May 28, 1944). "I said, 'Oh, that's called "At This Moment." Call Warner Brothers (Music) and they'll make a deal with you.' "

Weithorn had already considered other songs that were better known, but the rights to them were too expensive. He made the deal, and "At This Moment," which had peaked at number 79 when it was released on Alfa Records in September, 1981, was played during both segments of a two-part "Family Ties" episode broadcast during the 1985–86 season.

"I've learned the difference between a winner and a loser," says Vera. "When opportunity knocks, a winner answers the door. I saw this as an opportunity." Vera knew that his band had a strong enough local following that Los Angeles area record stores could sell their albums, if they had any in stock. He considered contacting a British label, Charly, about reissuing his older material but then made a call to an L.A.-based label. "I talked to Richard Foos at Rhino Records and managed to convince him . . . that he wouldn't lose any money." By the time Rhino licensed the masters from Tokyo-based Alfa, the "Family Ties" episodes had already been rerun.

The group's fans did buy copies of the album *By Request*, but fate was not finished with "At This Moment." Unbeknownst to Billy, the song was heard again in a new "Family Ties" episode the following season. NBC logged over 9,000 telephone calls inquiring about the song. "People

started calling radio stations requesting the song . . . and the next thing you know, the record starts jumping up the charts."

On January 24, 1987, "At This Moment" moved to the top of the Hot 100, just 19 years and one month after Vera made his first appearance on the chart with "Storybook Children."

Vera had written "At This Moment" four years before its 1981 release. Billy recorded a demo of the song, but nothing happened with it. While playing at a New Jersey Holiday Inn, he met songwriter Larry Brown [see 332—"Tie a Yellow Ribbon Round the Ole Oak Tree"]. They decided to collaborate, and Dolly Parton's version of their "I Really Got the Feeling" went to number one on the country chart.

The success of the Parton single brought about the publishing deal with Warner Brothers Music and a move to Los Angeles. Ed Silvers, head of Warner Brothers Music at the time, fell in love with "At This Moment" and brought it to Dionne Warwick and Olivia Newton-John. Both came close to recording it, but not close enough.

"While I was writing . . . I started Billy and the Beaters just to have some fun," Vera explains. "At first we

weren't doing any of my songs, and someone said . . . 'Why don't you do "At This Moment?" ' " Not long after, the band was signed to Alfa, a Japanese recording label that wanted an American presence. "I Can Take Care of Myself," the first single, peaked at number 39 in June of 1981. The follow-up was "At This Moment." Three weeks after a second album was released, Alfa closed down their American arm and Billy and the Beaters were without a label, a condition that existed until the belated success of "At This Moment."

SIRE 28508 **Open Your Heart** 659
MADONNA

*Writers: Madonna*
*Gardner Cole*
*Peter Rafelson*

*Producers: Madonna*
*Patrick Leonard*

*February 7, 1987*
*1 week*

Madonna's "Open Your Heart" moved up the Hot 100 simultaneously with Cyndi Lauper's "Change of Heart." But what Cyndi doesn't know is that songwriters Gardner Cole and Peter Rafelson wrote "Open Your Heart" with her in mind. "She never heard it," Cole reveals. At one point, the Temptations were under consideration to perform the tune. "(They) put the song on hold. Benny Medina, who was at Motown at the time, called Peter up and asked us if he could cut the song with the Temptations. Well, about a week later we found out that Madonna had already cut it. Once the Temptations heard that Madonna had cut the song they didn't have any interest in it any longer."

Cole and Rafelson wrote "Open Your Heart" as a rock and roll song, although the original title was "Follow Your Heart." "I got the title idea from a local health food restaurant," Cole explains, referring to Follow Your Heart in Canoga Park, California. The two songwriters spent a year writing and perfecting the tune. "Peter and I usually write very quickly. It's usually a day or two a song, but for some reason this didn't really hit us as a hit song. We didn't give up on it. We just kept working on it over the course of a year. Thank God we did."

Cole's manager, Bennett Freed, was working with Madonna's management when they were looking for material for her. "He gave her two or three songs and 'Open Your Heart' was the song that I thought would be the least likely song she would choose. The original version didn't really fit into what Madonna was doing at that time. . . . I thought she was going to stick with 'Holiday' and . . . what she was already doing. But this song was a step forward for her, it was a different area—more rock and roll than I thought she would want to go."

Freed called Cole to let him know Madonna had recorded the song. "Madonna redid some of the lyric ideas and, (with) Patrick Leonard, changed

the arrangement around. Pat and her put a . . . bass line underneath the song and got it into a rock and roll dance area instead of just rock and roll. The original song was more pop/rock than dance. Pat and her just cut it into a dance song."

Even after it was recorded, Cole was not certain that it would ever be heard. "It was the first song that was cut on the *True Blue* album. It made me nervous as a writer, because a lot of times the very first song that gets cut doesn't make it in the long run. But the song ended up making the album, which really opened up a lot of doors for me."

As a result of the success of "Open Your Heart," Cole was signed as an artist to Warner Brothers Records and formed a writing partnership with the producer of the song, Patrick Leonard. Their first four songs were taken by Jody Watley, Nile Rodgers, Chaka Khan and Marilyn Martin.

"Open Your Heart" was the third number one single from *True Blue*. It followed "Live to Tell" [see 637] and "Papa Don't Preach" [see 644]. The

next single was the title track, "True Blue," which peaked at number three. Madonna followed "Open Your Heart" with "La Isla Bonita," a song originally written by Patrick Leonard for Michael Jackson. When the song was turned down, Madonna completed the lyrics and recorded it. "La Isla Bonita" was the fifth consecutive top five single from *True Blue*, peaking at number four in May, 1987.

## THE TOP FIVE
*Week of February 7, 1987*

1 **Open Your Heart**
Madonna

2 **At This Moment**
Billy Vera & the Beaters

3 **Livin' on a Prayer**
Bon Jovi

4 **Change of Heart**
Cyndi Lauper

5 **Touch Me (I Want Your Body)**
Samantha Fox

## 660 Livin' on a Prayer MERCURY 888-184-7
### BON JOVI

*Writers: Jon Bon Jovi*
*Richie Sambora*
*Desmond Child*

*Producer: Bruce Fairbairn*

*February 14, 1987*
*4 weeks*

LESS THAN three months after scoring their first number one single [see 653—"You Give Love a Bad Name"], Bon Jovi returned to the top of the Hot 100 with "Livin' on a Prayer." It was a stunning achievement for the heavy metal band that had never made the top 30 of the singles chart until they released *Slippery When Wet*.

They began the project by bringing in a new producer. "I was listening to my compact disc in my room, trying to pick out the third single off the *7800°* album, and I threw in a cassette of a band called Black 'n' Blue," Jon Bon Jovi told reporter Sylvie Simmons. "I liked it so much production-wise that I put on our CD again and I said, 'Wait a minute! This doesn't sound as good as that cassette! What's the matter?' And that's when I realized it was time for a change. So I met up with the producer and he just had that same Jersey gutter attitude as us."

Which is odd, because Bruce Fairbairn was from Vancouver, British Columbia, in Canada. "I got a call from Derek Shulman, who is the A&R guy responsible for Bon Jovi at PolyGram," Fairbairn recalls. "He asked me if I'd be interested in working with Jon....I hadn't really been a big fan of Bon Jovi. I'd hear a couple of their songs on the radio, but I hadn't really followed the group." Fairbairn talked with Jon on the phone and then flew to New Jersey to meet the band.

"One of my priorities was getting better songs," Fairbairn says. "While their previous record had been good, I felt that the songs weren't as strong as they could be. Specifically, they didn't have songs on their records that were radio-oriented. They'd been selling most of their records based on their live shows.

"So first of all I went after the songs and then I went after the performances of the band. I found (them) to be excellent players. If anything, their last record really sold them short. The other (objective) was to get Jon singing lead well . . . I had heard from

different people that he wasn't that good a singer. When I first heard him sing . . . he had real good soul, he had good pitch and he had (a) great feel. I (told him), 'You're capable of doing a really strong album vocally, let's try and push it a bit and see how far we can take it.' "

Production of the album went quickly, according to Fairbairn. "We set the band up live in the studio and recorded all the tracks. . . . It only took us six or seven days to cut all the tracks, and from there we had time to work on the vocals and we did some work on the keyboard parts and fixed up a few guitar solos. The record only took us six weeks from start to finish."

"Livin' on a Prayer" was one of over 35 songs that could have been included on the album, and it almost didn't make the final cut. "Jon wasn't that excited about it," Fairbairn notes. In an interview for the *Denver Post*, Jon said, "When we wrote 'Livin' on a Prayer,' I said to Richie (Sambora), 'Maybe we can get this on a soundtrack or something,' because I never thought it was right for the band."

"I really heard the lyric in that song as being something that spoke to a lot of people," says Fairbairn, "so I liked it for that and I fought for the song. At some point it looked like it might not make the record. I convinced Jon

and Richie that it was worth hanging in there, and sure enough, it started to develop. We were digging around in Richie's guitar effects box. . . . I grabbed hold of this old tube and up comes this talk box, and I thought, 'Stick this in, I haven't heard one of these since the (Peter) Frampton album'. . . . We worked on the harmonies and the chorus and everything we did to it made the song better. By the (time) we finished it, everybody had the feeling that (it) was going to be a single. I thought it could be the biggest single on the record . . . as it turned out, it was. I'm glad I hung on to the song."

Writers: *Bruce Hornsby*
*John Hornsby*

Producers: *Huey Lewis and the News*

*March 14, 1987*
*1 week*

**D**ON'T believe the story that Huey Lewis met Bruce Hornsby [see 655— "The Way It Is"] while playing golf. It's a tale that's often been told to the press, but it isn't true. Their meeting actually dates back to 1981 when Huey's publisher heard a song that was a tongue-in-cheek look at sorority life called "Let the Girls Rock." The publisher thought it would be perfect for Huey, a former prep school student. "Huey did like the song and wanted to meet the writers," explains Bruce's collaborator, his brother John. "In this case, not only the guy who had written it but who had recorded the demo: Bruce. They just hit it off and have continued to be friends and consult each other on a lot of projects."

Despite their budding friendship, Huey didn't get to record "Let the Girls Rock." "Bruce and I thought that our record deal and success was just around the corner," says John. "That was a naive thought, of course, but we turned Huey Lewis down . . . for what would have been a place on his album *Sports*. We kicked ourselves for not having given him the song on that album, so we didn't turn him down next time."

Next time turned out to be in 1986, when Huey Lewis and the News were in the studio to record *Fore!*, the follow-up album to *Sports*. "Bruce and I wrote 'Jacob's Ladder' about the same time as we wrote 'Every Little Kiss,' " John recalls. "We had just enough songs for our album that we had to hold one over for the next album, and we decided to hold 'Jacob's Ladder.' Meanwhile, Huey was looking for material for his album and he had listened to our demo of 'Every Little Kiss' and 'Jacob's Ladder.' He said, 'You guys didn't record it; do you mind if we give it a shot for *Fore!?*' At the time, Bruce and the Range had not even released their album. We had no idea whether it would go over at all, so to have Huey Lewis ask to use one of our songs was something we were definitely not going to turn down."

Did the Hornsby brothers regret giving away a number one song? "We had no misgivings," John says honestly. "We know we made the right decision. We're happy for Huey and we're happy that (the song) gave us some credibility as songwriters." Huey's version differed greatly from Bruce's, according to John. "Bruce's demo was piano-oriented. Huey's was a rock guitar version. Bruce's had more of an R&B flavor to it."

John was still studying law at the University of Virginia when he wrote "Jacob's Ladder" with Bruce in the summer of 1985. "This was long before all the Jim and Tammy Faye Bakker stuff came down and Pat Robertson running for President," John notes. "There's no one media evangelist who inspired it. The title is a Biblical allusion to the ladder to Heaven— there's a Christian hymn of the same name. To us, the song is really about one person's personal goal, which is stated in the words, 'All I want from tomorrow is just to get it better than today.' On the other hand, it does deal with certain media evangelists who preach . . . 'Sing along, send money, join the chosen few.' "

John describes the writing of the song: "Bruce came up with the hook lines . . . and then we sat down together and talked about what we wanted some of the specifics to be about . . . I took the rest of it. I think he had a basic set of chords in mind . . . a basic groove and rhythm. I spent a couple of weeks (working) hard to try and say (the message) in a way that wasn't hitting people over the head and wasn't preaching at them. I decided to take a kind of rock and roll, 'Honky Tonk Women' approach to it. . . . I wanted to make it a fun song to sing."

John and Bruce Hornsby have continued to write songs together, even though John lives in Virginia and Bruce is based in Los Angeles. "We do a lot over the phone," John says. "I usually fly to Los Angeles for a couple of weeks at a time, and we do that about five or six times a year."

## THE TOP FIVE
*Week of March 14, 1987*

1  **Jacob's Ladder**
   Huey Lewis and the News

2  **Somewhere Out There**
   Linda Ronstadt and James Ingram

3  **Let's Wait Awhile**
   Janet Jackson

4  **Livin' on a Prayer**
   Bon Jovi

5  **Lean on Me**
   Club Nouveau

## 662 Lean on Me WARNER BROTHERS 28430
### CLUB NOUVEAU

*Writer: Bill Withers*

*Producers: Jay King*
*Thomas McElroy*
*Denzil Foster*

*March 21, 1987*
*2 weeks*

"LEAN ON ME" is the fifth song of the rock era to reach number one in versions by two different artists, following "Go Away Little Girl" [see 122 and 299], "The Loco-Motion" [see 115 and 364], "Please Mr. Postman" [see 101 and 390] and "Venus" [see 268 and 646]. The first three were originally number one songs in the '60s; like "Venus," "Lean on Me" was a cover version of a '70s hit.

Jay King, the son of a registered nurse and a city worker, was voted "Most Unlikely to Succeed" in high school before he dropped out in the 11th grade. He was 18 when he joined the Air Force. Stationed in Anchorage, he was discharged for fighting with an officer. He remained in Alaska as a legislative aid to a state senator. While there, he promoted an Anchorage concert by Con Funk Shun, an R&B group from his hometown of Vallejo, California. Back in high school, Jay had submitted his own material for Con Funk Shun to record; in Alaska, the group suggested he return home and record some of his own demos.

Through Fenton Pilate, a member of Con Funk Shun, King met Denzil Foster and Thomas McElroy. They released a couple of songs on the independent Triangle label, and their failure persuaded King to start his own record label. He received a demo tape from three songwriters: Marcus Thompson, Alex Hill and Mike Marshall. One of the songs was called "Rumors," and King liked it enough to pass it on to Con Funk Shun. When they turned it down, King called the songwriters and suggested they record it themselves.

Marcus said he didn't want to be an artist, according to King. Two days passed and Marcus called back, agreeing to record the song. King went into the studio with Thompson, Hill, Marshall, Foster and McElroy, now christened the Timex Social Club. He also brought in vocalist Valerie Watson, whose grandmother once lived across the street from King. "I sold my furniture and my car to raise money to get the record pressed, manufactured and distributed," King told Dick Clark on "Countdown America."

Released in February, 1986, "Rumors" failed to ignite. An independent promoter suggested they focus on Texas, and K104 in Dallas became the first station to break the song. By June, the record was a hit all over the nation. King says that two months earlier, the Timex Social Club had agreed to sign a three-year contract

with him. "Next day they signed a deal with another guy," King said in *Rock Express*. "They were told I wouldn't be able to pay them and that he was a better guy. They signed over all their money to this guy and basically left me. . . . I re-changed all of 'Rumors.' . . . I should have got the writer's credit, but I wouldn't take it because I was trying to be fair."

Foster and McElroy stayed with King and formed a new group. "We did it out of necessity, as opposed to desire," King said in *Rock Express*. "I learnt so much about the business and I can't help but be happy about what has happened to me."

The new group, which included Valerie Watson and Samuelle Prater, considered several names, including Jett Sett and Nouveau Riche. King's lawyer suggested the latter had a negative connotation, so the group settled on Club Nouveau—intended or not, a definite statement about the Timex Social Club.

King credits Foster and McElroy with the idea of recording Bill Withers' "Lean on Me." "It was a tit for tat kind of deal," King told Dick Clark. "I had a song called 'Let Me Go' that I wanted to do and they wanted to redo 'Lean on Me.' We knew we had to make the record new again."

King told *Rock Express* that Bill Withers contacted him after their version of "Lean on Me" went to number one. "He sent a telegram saying congratulations, thank you, and that he'd like to meet us. . . . I had admired him. He leaves music open enough for you to interpret in many different ways. Even back then, with 'Lean on Me,' I think it was just acoustic guitar, a drum and vocals."

### THE TOP FIVE
*Week of March 21, 1987*

1 **Lean on Me**
Club Nouveau

2 **Let's Wait Awhile**
Janet Jackson

3 **Nothing's Gonna Stop Us Now**
Starship

4 **Mandolin Rain**
Bruce Hornsby & the Range

5 **Somewhere Out There**
Linda Ronstadt & James Ingram

*Writers: Diane Warren*
*Albert Hammond*

*Producer: Narada Michael Walden*

*April 4, 1987*
*2 weeks*

"NOTHING'S GONNA STOP US NOW" was the third number one single for Starship, following "We Built This City" [see 623] and "Sara" [see 630]. It was the second number one single for songwriter Albert Hammond [see 463—"When I Need You"] and for producer Narada Michael Walden [see 628—"How Will I Know"]. And it was the first for songwriter Diane Warren, who also wrote "Rhythm of the Night" for DeBarge.

"A couple of friends introduced Diane and I," Hammond explains. "We had lunch one day and then we didn't see each other for four months. And then one day out of the blue Diane called and said, 'Remember me?' Since then we've written a lot of songs together."

Hammond had scored a number five hit in 1972, "It Never Rains in Southern California," on Mums Records. That's where he met Joel Sill, who went on to become head of music for Warner Brothers Pictures. He left that position to work with producer/

director Taylor Hackford [see 562—"Up Where We Belong"]. It was Sill who sent copies of the script for the film *Mannequin* to Hammond and Warren.

"We liked it and wanted to write an uptempo, positive song," says Diane. It took one day to write "Nothing's Gonna Stop Us Now." They recorded a demo. "I brought it to Teri Muench, a friend of mine in the A&R department at RCA Records," Diane continues. "I brought it to her to see what she thought of the song." The song was not written with any particular artist in mind, but two sets of duos were being considered by the filmmakers: John Parr and Laura Branigan and a re-teaming of Patti LaBelle and Michael McDonald [see 638—"On My Own"].

While Diane sat in Muench's office with A&R head Paul Atkinson, Teri came up with the idea of having Grace Slick and Mickey Thomas record the song. The demo was sent to Starship and it was received enthusiastically. Peter Wolf, who was one of the producers of the *Knee Deep in the Hoopla* LP, didn't have the same reaction. He was asked to produce the song for Starship but turned it down based on the demo.

Narada Michael Walden, who had worked with artists like Whitney Houston and Aretha Franklin, heard

the demo and loved it. "It was really good, big and broad," Narada recalls. "It had a lot of echo on it. Immediately, I thought of Phil Spector. (I thought) this is my big change to impress the world with my Phil Spector imitation. So I said, 'I'll do it.'"

Starship was on tour at the time, so Walden employed musicians he had used while recording Whitney and Aretha. A former drummer for the Mahavishnu Orchestra, Walden paid particular attention to the drum track. "We went in the studio with Dave Frazier and 'Bongo' Bob, who does a lot of percussion programming for me. We got great drum sounds on my Simmons kit: all electric drum sounds. I really think those sounds helped make that record a hit. I got so much joy entering the consciousness of Donny Baldwin . . . I thought to myself, 'How would Donny approach this song?' And I played very strong fills, very strong backbeats, that I knew he'd be proud of."

When Starship's tour finished, Grace Slick went to Walden's studio to lay down vocal tracks. "Initially I was having Grace sing Mickey's parts, the low parts . . . it was just too low for Grace . . . Donny Baldwin was in the room and he said, 'I think Grace could sing the high part.'" Walden agreed, and brought Mickey Thomas in the next day to complete the vocal duet.

"For the final Phil Spector touch, we brought in all the friends who work at the studio and this new group we're putting together, Girlfriend, an all-girl band. They all came in and grabbed bells and shakers and whistles. We shook all these things and got that big wall of sound thing happening. . . . I'm really proud of that production."

## THE TOP FIVE
*Week of April 4, 1987*

1 **Nothing's Gonna Stop Us Now**
Starship

2 **Lean on Me**
Club Nouveau

3 **Tonight, Tonight, Tonight**
Genesis

4 **Let's Wait Awhile**
Janet Jackson

5 **Come Go With Me**
Expose

**664** ## I Knew You Were Waiting (For Me) ARISTA 9559
### ARETHA FRANKLIN and GEORGE MICHAEL

*Writers: Simon Climie*
*Dennis Morgan*

*Producer: Narada Michael Walden*

*April 18, 1987*
*2 weeks*

Aretha Franklin and Clive Davis at the same time."

CAN a Nashville songwriter with more than 20 country number ones to his credit and a British pop star team up to write hit records? Ask Aretha Franklin, who scored her first number one single in 19 years and 10 months [see 225—"Respect"]. Or ask George Michael, who went to number one in America for the fourth time. Or ask producer Narada Michael Walden, who became the eighth producer in the rock era to have back-to-back number one hits* [see 663—"Nothing's Gonna Stop Us Now"].

Dennis Morgan was born in Tracy, Minnesota, and hitchhiked to Nashville when he was 16. He has had more than 600 of his songs recorded, and about 70 of them have been hits on the country chart.

On September 22, 1983, Morgan was at the Royal Albert Hall in London to see the long-awaited reunion of the Everly Brothers [see 68—"Cathy's Clown"]. He was also looking for someone new to write songs with. "I'd make two or three trips a year trying to find (someone)," he explains. "I was just experimenting. I had this instinct inside of me saying there's more than just Nashville and the country market. I want to write all kinds of tunes."

After the Everly Brothers show, Morgan went to a popular London club called Stringfellows to hang out with his friends, including Phil Everly. There he met Simon Climie, a British songwriter who has since put together a pop duo, Climie Fisher, with Rob Fisher of Naked Eyes. "We started writing, and 'I Knew You Were Waiting (For Me)' was the third song we wrote together," Morgan reports. "That was one of those songs that came out of mid-air—a gift from above, if you will. I came up with the title and we were off and running. We pitched it to Tina Turner and also to

*The other producers who had back-to-back number one songs prior to Walden are: Lee Gilette, who did it twice [see 5, 6, 8 and 9]; George Martin [see 143, 144 and 145]; Holland-Dozier-Holland [see 176 and 177]; Barry Gibb-Karl Richardson-Albhy Galuten [see 478, 479 and 480]; Mike Chapman [see 490 and 491]; Quincy Jones [see 568 and 569]; and Phil Ramone [see 576 and 577].

The song was not written specifically as a duet, and Simon's demo, recorded in London, was for one voice. Morgan first learned that Aretha would be recording the song with George Michael when Climie's publisher in Los Angeles told him that Clive was interested in having these two artists perform it together.

Producer Narada Michael Walden had helped Aretha return to the top 10 (after an 11-year absence) with "Freeway of Love" (number three in August, 1985) and "Who's Zoomin' Who" (number seven in November of that same year). He cut the instrumental tracks for "I Knew You Were Waiting (For Me)" at his Tarpan Studios in San Rafael, California. "The lead vocals were cut in Detroit," Walden recounts. "Aretha knocked her stuff out in a matter of hours and we went on and did some of her ad-libs just for the heck of it, and she was done.

"The next day George Michael flew in bright and early on the Concorde from England. He was very excited about singing with Aretha, the queen of soul. It was a lifelong ambition of his. I (can) understand him being a little nervous. He (sang) his heart out. I was very satisfied with what I was getting—extremely satisfied—but George . . . wanted to go on. . . . I said. . . . 'I know you're not used to

being produced . . . but we should really stop.' George (said), 'I'm not used to someone really producing me. Only one guy's ever produced me, and that was for "Do They Know It's Christmas" (by Band Aid)' . . . so he looked at me with those innocent virgin eyes, like he'd never been told, 'you oughta stop, kid.'

"The next day Aretha and George came together for the big heavyweight championship fight . . . it was really a memorable moment. And fortunately . . . a lot of that magic is in that record . . . they worked side by side kicking each other and just pushing it and made it happen."

VIRGIN 99481 **(I Just) Died in Your Arms** 665
CUTTING CREW

*Writer: Nick Van Eede*

*Producers: Terry Brown*
*John Jansen*
*Cutting Crew*

*May 2, 1987*
*2 weeks*

LYRICIST NICK VAN EEDE should bronze the note pad he uses to scribble down thoughts. One day, while reading the British rock paper *Sounds*, he noticed an article about the band Queen [see 522—"Crazy Little Thing Called Love"] going into the studio to record their new album. The reporter called them a "cutting crew," as in a "recording band." Van Eede wrote down the description.

The note pad came in handy again one night while Van Eede was making love to his girlfriend. Out came the words "I just died in your arms." "I actually remember saying that," admits Van Eede, who promptly leaned over and wrote down the phrase. Never know when it might become part of a song someday.

Van Eede turned professional when he was 18, touring with artists like Leo Sayer, David Essex and Hot Chocolate. "I used to support them, just me and my acoustic guitar and kazoo," Van Eede told Stuart Husband. "I think my greatest triumph . . . was playing with Slade in Poland."

Later, Van Eede toured Canada with his own band, the Drivers. Opening for them were a native group called Fast Forward. Van Eede was impressed with their guitarist, Kevin Macmichael, and on some nights of the tour Macmichael played in both bands. Macmichael had formed his first group, the Martian Minstrels, when he was only 12. "I remember on February 7, 1964, watching the Ed Sullivan show when suddenly I felt lightning all around me. It was a feeling of purpose never before experienced in my young life," Macmichael told Randi Mitnick in *RockFile* about his first visual contact with the Beatles.

"I had been looking for, however clichéd it sounds . . . all my musical life to find somebody who could take my . . . songs and give them a little bit of class and majesty that (I) wasn't able to do," Van Eede told Dick Clark on "Countdown America." "There was a symbiosis there, but putting all that aside, we became friends. I went

home to England. (There were) lots of expensive telephone conversations, where I kept begging him (to) get out of Canada, come back to England. In fact, that didn't work, so eventually I moved back to Toronto."

For a year and a half, Van Eede slept on friends' couches and asked Macmichael to come to Toronto to write songs together. But Macmichael continued to tour with his band, and one day Van Eede phoned him and said he was fed up with waiting. "Two days later he called me and said his group had driven their tour van off the edge of a mountain and rolled it over about 10 times. All the people in his band were hurt, some quite seriously, except for Kevin, who kicked in the back window and crawled from the wreckage."

They made London home base and gave themselves one year to sign a recording contract. Two more members were recruited: drummer Martin (Frosty) Beedle had been playing in a cabaret band on the QE2 and decided to join Cutting Crew when he was mugged during a shore leave in Portugal; bass player Colin Farley had been living in a castle in Spain and working as a session musician.

Van Eede and Macmichael felt they

had paid their dues in earlier bands, and they didn't want to tour for three years hoping some record label might sign them someday. So they staged a showcase at a recording studio in London and invited representatives from many different labels. All the reps showed up, and within three months contracts were signed with Siren Records, part of the Virgin Records group.

In 1987, Virgin reestablished its presence in America with its own label, and Cutting Crew gave the new entity its first number one song.

## THE TOP FIVE
*Week of May 2, 1987*

1 **(I Just) Died in Your Arms**
Cutting Crew

2 **Looking for a New Love**
Jody Watley

3 **Don't Dream It's Over**
Crowded House

4 **La Isla Bonita**
Madonna

5 **Sign 'O' the Times**
Prince

# 666 With or Without You ISLAND 99469
## U2

*Writers: U2*

*Producers: Daniel Lanois*
*Brian Eno*

*May 16, 1987*
*3 weeks*

In 1985, the promoter of U2's concert in Denver, Colorado, told the lead singer, "Bono, I think you might be the biggest group in the world right now for a lot of people, but remember: you still haven't written a 'Hey Jude,'" Robert Hilburn reported in the *Los Angeles Times.*

It may not have been number one for seven weeks, as "Hey Jude" was [see 247], but "With or Without You" held on to the top of the *Billboard* Hot 100 for three weeks and gave U2 their breakthrough song in America.

U2 began with a note posted by a 14-year-old student on the bulletin board at Mount Temple Comprehensive School in Dublin, Ireland. Larry Mullen had been playing drums since he was nine. His parents gave him a 15-dollar toy drum and his father suggested he get a group together, so he put up the notice looking for fellow students willing to form a rock band. "Stories simplify how big a step that was at the time," Adam Clayton said in *Time.* "That one action of Larry's has affected the rest of his life and, indeed, everyone's." Less than a week after Mullen's note appeared, a group of students gathered at his parents' house to run through some Rolling Stones songs.

"During the course of the afternoon, I saw that some people could play," Mullen said in *Time.* "The Edge (David Evans, nicknamed later by Bono, who said, 'The edge is the border between something and nothing') could play. Adam just *looked* great. Big bushy hair, long caftan coat, bass guitar and amp. He talked like he could play, used all the right words, like 'gig.' I thought this guy *must* know how to play. Then Bono (Paul Hewson, who got his nickname from a sign advertising Bono Vox of O'Connell Street, a hearing aid store in Dublin) arrived, and he meant to play the guitar, but he couldn't play very well, so he started to sing. He couldn't do that either. But he was such a charismatic character that he was in the band anyway, as soon as he arrived. I was in charge for the first five minutes, but as soon as Bono got there, I was out of a job."

Names like Feedback and the Hype were considered, but a local musician suggested U2, as in the high altitude spy plane (like the one Francis Gary Powers was flying over the Soviet Union when he was shot down). Seeking a manager, they persuaded a commercial director who managed a local band to come see them play. Paul McGuinness only agreed to go so he could turn them down but upon seeing the band he reacted positively. "Edge's playing was quite unique," he told James Henke in *Rolling Stone.* "And Bono, he just looked the audience in

the eyes as if to say, 'I dare you to look back.' And all I had ever seen before were performers who look out over the audience at some imaginary spot."

U2 played a lot of dates opening for other Irish bands. After winning a rock group competition, they were signed by CBS for Ireland only. Their first record was *U23*, an EP with three songs. CBS passed on signing the band for the rest of the world, so Bono distributed tapes of various U2 concerts to sympathetic music journalists. British rock weeklies like *Sounds* and *New Musical Express* wrote kindly of the band, but that didn't produce a record label deal.

The foursome played some showcases in London without generating any interest. So they went home and toured Ireland, ending with a concert at a 2,000-seat stadium in Dublin. Bill Stewart of Island Records saw the show, and in 1980, U2 were signed.

## THE TOP FIVE
*Week of May 16, 1987*

1 **With or Without You**
   U2

2 **Looking for a New Love**
   Jody Watley

3 **(I Just) Died in Your Arms**
   Cutting Crew

4 **La Isla Bonita**
   Madonna

5 **The Lady in Red**
   Chris de Burgh

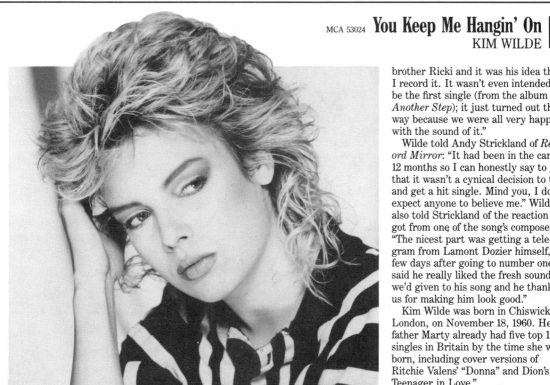

*Writers: Brian Holland*
      *Lamont Dozier*
      *Eddie Holland*

*Producer: Ricki Wilde*

*June 6, 1987*
*1 week*

In the first 31 years of the rock era, three songs climbed to number one in two versions by different artists: "Please Mr. Postman" [see 101 and 390], "The Loco-Motion" [see 115 and 364] and "Go Away Little Girl" [see 122 and 299]. In the 32nd year of the rock era, three more songs went to number one for the second time: "Venus" [see 268 and 646], "Lean on Me" [see 315 and 662] and "You Keep Me Hangin' On," originally a hit in 1966 by the Supremes [see 213] and brought back in 1987 by British pop singer Kim Wilde.

"You Keep Me Hangin' On" also became the first song in the history of the Hot 100 to have three different versions chart in the top 10. Vanilla Fudge's "psychedelic" version peaked at number six on August 31, 1968.

In all, five versions of "You Keep Me Hangin' On" have charted on the Hot 100, making it the most covered Supremes song of all time. The other two versions were by Wilson Pickett (number 92 in 1969) and Jackie De-Shannon (in a medley that peaked at number 96 in 1970). A total of 15 cover versions of Supremes songs have charted on the Hot 100. Kim Wilde and Vanilla Fudge's "You Keep Me Hangin' On" are the two most successful. The next eight, in descending order, are:

"Where Did Our Love Go" (in a medley with "Tainted Love") by Soft Cell (number 8 in 1982)
"You Can't Hurry Love" by Phil Collins (number 10 in 1983)
"Where Did Our Love Go" by Donnie Elbert (number 15 in 1971)
"Come See About Me" by Jr. Walker & the All Stars (number 24 in 1968)
"Stop! In the Name of Love" by the Hollies (number 29 in 1983)
"The Happening" by Herb Alpert (number 32 in 1967)
"Forever Came Today" by the Jackson Five (number 60 in 1975)
"Where Did Our Love Go" by the J. Geils Band (number 68 in 1976)

Surprisingly, Kim Wilde says she was unaware of the song's previous success (the Supremes' version peaked at number eight in Britain). "I really wasn't aware that the song had gone top 10 even once. It's a favorite of my brother Ricki and it was his idea that I record it. It wasn't even intended to be the first single (from the album *Another Step*); it just turned out that way because we were all very happy with the sound of it."

Wilde told Andy Strickland of *Record Mirror*: "It had been in the can for 12 months so I can honestly say to you that it wasn't a cynical decision to try and get a hit single. Mind you, I don't expect anyone to believe me." Wilde also told Strickland of the reaction she got from one of the song's composers: "The nicest part was getting a telegram from Lamont Dozier himself, a few days after going to number one. It said he really liked the fresh sound we'd given to his song and he thanked us for making him look good."

Kim Wilde was born in Chiswick, London, on November 18, 1960. Her father Marty already had five top 10 singles in Britain by the time she was born, including cover versions of Ritchie Valens' "Donna" and Dion's "A Teenager in Love."

Growing up, Kim was a self-described "naughty schoolgirl." She used the family's real surname "Smith" so her classmates wouldn't know she was the daughter of a famous pop star. Later, she and her mother sang backing vocals for her dad. Her brother Ricki recorded some teenybop songs in 1974, like "Teen Wave" and "I Wanna Go to a Disco." Ricki and Marty wrote all of the songs for Kim's debut album, including her first single hit, "Kids in America." It went to number two in the United Kingdom and was the first of five top 20 songs there. "Kids in America" appealed to the kids in America, too, where it reached number 25 in 1982.

## THE TOP FIVE
*Week of June 6, 1987*

1 **You Keep Me Hangin' On**
   Kim Wilde

2 **Always**
   Atlantic Starr

3 **Head to Toe**
   Lisa Lisa and Cult Jam

4 **The Lady in Red**
   Chris de Burgh

5 **With or Without You**
   U2

## 668 Always WARNER BROTHERS 28455
### ATLANTIC STARR

Writers: *Jonathan Lewis*
*David Lewis*
*Wayne Lewis*

Producers: *David Lewis*
*Wayne Lewis*

*June 13, 1987*
*1 week*

"**A**LWAYS" was written five years before it was recorded, according to Wayne Lewis, who wrote the song along with his brothers, Jonathan and David. "We wanted to use it before, but our producer James Carmichael, who is Lionel Richie's producer, decided that it wasn't the right time," Wayne says. "He wanted us to hold on to it. We ended up never using it with him . . . it worked out perfectly. I guess there is a time for everything."

Wayne details the origin of the song: "My brother Jonathan came up with a chord progression that was kind of hymnal, but with a country-western edge and also an R&B edge—a mixture of all three. He wanted me to collaborate with him, so I came up with the melody and the story line."

"Always" was the first single released from the band's premier album for Warner Brothers, *All in the Name of Love*. But the Lewis brothers weren't sure it should be the first release. "We wanted to have a dance song first. Benny Medina from Warner Brothers convinced us it should be our first single. We went along with him

for a lot of different reasons, and it turned out to be the perfect single."

Reaching the top of the Hot 100 was a great reward for a group that had survived a bitter split and a loss of their record label. In the mid-'70s, the three Lewis brothers were playing in separate bands in their native White Plains, New York. Along with members of their respective groups, they formed Atlantic Starr in 1976. Two years later, they were signed to A&M Records. In 1982 they had their first pop hit with "Circles," which peaked at number 38.

It was during the recording of their 1983 album *Yours Forever* that the nine-member group split into two factions. The three Lewis brothers and percussionist Joe Phillips were opposed by the other five members, including female vocalist Sharon Bryant. "All of a sudden everybody had their own ideas about concepts and directions," Wayne told Dennis Hunt of the *Los Angeles Times*. "There was a tug of war in all directions." As a result of the conflict, producer James Carmichael quit after recording *Yours Forever*.

Wayne told Hunt that A&M froze the band's royalties and dropped the group from its roster because of the friction. "There was no money coming in. Money was held up from the summer of '84 to the end of '84. Our houses and our cars were in danger. We were inspired into doing *something* about our situation. Actually, we

were scared into acting."

The three brothers and Phillips found a new vocalist, Barbara Weathers, from Greensboro, North Carolina. They met her while on a tour of the south and had planned to record some demos for her even before adding her to the group. They also produced themselves. "We'd always worked with other producers before and would usually only produce our own demos. We were just waiting for our time. And it came," Wayne said.

Atlantic Starr's final album for A&M, *As the Band Turns*, clicked with the release of the fourth single, "Secret Lovers." Sung as a duet (as was "Always"), it peaked at number three on March 22, 1986.

### THE TOP FIVE
*Week of June 13, 1987*

1  **Always**
   Atlantic Starr

2  **You Keep Me Hangin' On**
   Kim Wilde

3  **Head to Toe**
   Lisa Lisa and Cult Jam

4  **In Too Deep**
   Genesis

5  **I Wanna Dance with Somebody
   (Who Loves Me)**
   Whitney Houston

Writers: *Full Force*

Producers: *Full Force*

June 20, 1987
1 week

"HEAD TO TOE" almost sounds like a Motown hit from the '60s, specifically a Supremes song. But there's another, more subtle influence in the song as well. "We consider ourselves (musical) historians," says Bowlegged Lou, a.k.a. Lou George, of the group Full Force. "We went back to the old Motown days . . . we went back to Diana Ross and the Supremes . . . listen to 'Head to Toe.' Of course you hear the full Motown feel, but underneath it you've got some hard-driving drums, which is the Full Force sound. You've heard of Lulu. She did the song 'To Sir With Love' [see 231]. We went into that song also . . . when people hear it, they say, 'it sounds like something I know,' but they really can't put their finger on it unless we tell them."

The six men known as Full Force are responsible for putting together Lisa Lisa and Cult Jam. Full Force can trace their beginnings to 1970, when Lucien George formed a trio made up of his three sons, Brian, Paul Anthony and Lou. He called them the Amplifiers and had them play amateur night at the Apollo. They grew up playing music, sometimes joined by friend Mike Hughes and cousins Gerry Charles, Junior (Shy Shy) Clark and Curt Bedeau. When Lou went to Kingsborough Community College, he became friends with the student body president, Steve Salem.

Salem saw the George brothers play at a local club and was invited over to their house. "B (Brian) started playing the drums around this time and started jamming with the cousins around the corner," Salem told John Leland in *Spin*. "I know his father was really upset about him playing the drums, because he felt the lead singers were the ones who got the attention. He wanted B to be up front with his brothers. At that point the father decided to integrate the band with the singers, and that was where the cousins came in. They formed Full Force. This was in like '78. The father asked me to co-manage the group, and I said right then, 'yes.' "

Full Force was turned down by virtually every record label, according

to Salem, so in 1983 he decided the group should produce other artists. The result was "Roxanne, Roxanne," a top 10 dance hit for the rap band UTFO (Untouchable Force Organization). Salem told Leland what happened next: "B-Fine and myself, we were on the phone one day and we said, 'Let's create a new group.' New Edition was out at the time, so I said, 'They're doing the Jacksons, let's do the Supremes, let's get three girls.' So he went back and wrote 'I Wonder If I Take You Home' and 'Can You Feel the Beat?' And then we started auditioning girls."

Mike Hughes, who switched from playing music with Full Force to being a roadie, had plans of his own. "I had an idea if I found a female vocalist and maybe some musicians that I would form my own band through Full Force. I met Spanador (Alex Mosely) a year prior to that playing gigs around town and realized he was a good musician."

Hughes also met 16-year-old Lisa Velez. The youngest of 10 children, Lisa lived in the Hell's Kitchen section of Manhattan. She was sneaking out of her family's apartment to spend her evenings at the Fun House, a hip Manhattan nightclub that was a hangout for rappers and breakdancers. "I was working at Benetton, folding sweaters," Lisa said in *Spin*. "I was gonna do anything possible to get discovered, that way I could sing. I found out that Madonna was hanging

out at the Fun House, and that's how she was discovered by Jellybean, so I started going to the Fun House. It was a young atmosphere, no liquor served in the place at all, so I kinda liked it. I used to dance a lot, but I was always aware of where I was turning, so I would watch and find out who's who, where's where."

Hughes invited Lisa to the George family home in East Flatbush to audition. Her older brother Raymond said she couldn't go unless he went with her. But at 9:30 one evening, without telling Raymond, Lisa and Mike Hughes took the D train to Brooklyn for her fateful audition [see 679—"Lost in Emotion"].

---

## THE TOP FIVE
*Week of June 20, 1987*

1  **Head to Toe**
   Lisa Lisa and Cult Jam

2  **Always**
   Atlantic Starr

3  **I Wanna Dance With Somebody (Who Loves Me)**
   Whitney Houston

4  **In Too Deep**
   Genesis

5  **Diamonds**
   Herb Alpert

# 670 | I Wanna Dance With Somebody (Who Loves Me) ARISTA 9598
## WHITNEY HOUSTON

**Writers:** *George Merrill*
*Shannon Rubicam*

**Producer:** *Narada Michael Walden*

*June 27, 1987*
*2 weeks*

WHITNEY HOUSTON scored her fourth number one single with a song by George Merrill and Shannon Rubicam, the songwriters who had written one of her earlier chart-toppers [see 628—"How Will I Know"]. Merrill and Rubicam, both natives of Seattle, first met when they were among the singers hired to perform at the wedding of Susan Boeing of the famous airline family. "George was still in high school at the time and I had graduated, which meant I hardly gave him a second thought," Shannon laughs. "I was singing a duet with somebody and George was singing background vocals. We actually met at the reception."

There was no hint of a future songwriting collaboration at that time, although George admits to being romantically smitten. A few months after the wedding gig, when George's two-man band Sparrow needed a female singer, Shannon won the audition. Sparrow eventually broke up, but George and Shannon stayed together and spent four years writing songs

and mailing out demos. During that time, they worked with producer Thom Bell and at one point wrote songs for Deniece Williams. They also sang background vocals on her number one hit [see 588—"Let's Hear It for the Boy"].

The couple moved to Los Angeles and signed on as songwriters for Almo-Irving Music, the publishing arm of A&M Records. Soon after, they were signed to the A&M label itself as recording artists. They called themselves Boy Meets Girl and released an album. A single, "Oh Girl," climbed to number 39 in May, 1985, just two months after Whitney Houston's first album debuted on the *Billboard* chart.

Following George's and Shannon's success with "How Will I Know," Clive Davis and Roy Lott of Arista Records asked them to write another uptempo song for Whitney. The songwriters found inspiration while they were at Whitney's concert at the outdoor Greek Theater in Los Angeles. "She had just finished singing 'How Will I Know' and we just happened to look up (while) people were clapping and a star was falling," Shannon remembers. "We both saw it, so I pulled out my little note pad and wrote 'Waiting for a Star to Fall' and then (later) wrote a song around it. We sent it off to her and they passed on it."

The couple did not have time to get depressed—they were busy with other things in their personal lives, including the birth of their daughter. They were encouraged by Brenda Andrews at Almo-Irving to write another song for Whitney. It took only a couple of days to complete a second submission. "I pictured somebody single wishing that they found that special person for themselves," says Shannon. "It wasn't, 'I wanna go down to the disco and dance,' really. It was, 'I wanna do that dance of life with somebody.' That was the thought. So we sent our demo version of it to Clive and he loved it."

Producer Narada Michael Walden didn't have the same reaction. "I thought it was too country and western," he explains. "It reminded me of a rodeo song with Olivia Newton-John singing. I love Olivia Newton-John, but for Whitney Houston . . . I felt . . . there's gotta be some way I can make it . . . funkier. . . . I slept (on it), dreaming about it, (I'd) wake up in the morning thinking about it, running, playing tennis (wondering), what am I gonna do with this dang song? So (we) just jumped in the water and . . . lo and behold, a magic record was born. . . . Whitney just knocked it out and then I knew we had a good record."

Merrill and Rubicam didn't hear the finished version until Clive Davis invited them to a listening party at the Los Angeles office of Arista Records, where the label president announced that "I Wanna Dance with Somebody" would be the first single from Whitney's second album, and predicted that it would go all the way to number one.

## THE TOP FIVE
*Week of June 27, 1987*

1 **I Wanna Dance With Somebody (Who Loves Me)**
Whitney Houston

2 **Head to Toe**
Lisa Lisa and Cult Jam

3 **In Too Deep**
Genesis

4 **Alone**
Heart

5 **Always**
Atlantic Starr

Writers: *Billy Steinberg*
*Tom Kelly*

Producer: *Ron Nevison*

*July 11, 1987*
*3 weeks*

**H**EART scored their second number one with "Alone," the first single from their *Bad Animals* album. Like their previous chart-topper [see 631—"These Dreams"], "Alone" was composed by outside writers. Billy Steinberg and Tom Kelly, who had already written two previous number one songs [see 600—"Like a Virgin" and 650—"True Colors"], collaborated on the song five years before Heart heard it. Signed to Epic Records, Steinberg and Kelly recorded the song as i-Ten on the LP *Taking a Cold Look*.

"I was doing some background singing for Ron Nevison, (who) was producing Survivor," Kelly recalls. "As I was on my way out the door after a session, he said, 'I'm getting ready to do Heart. What we really need is a power ballad.' I thought of 'Alone.' "

Steinberg wasn't crazy about the idea. "The way it was recorded on the

i-Ten record, I *hated* it. It had a really great verse (but) something about the chorus bothered me. It bothered me so much I felt the song was totally disjointed; you couldn't even salvage it. I figured that's a song better forgotten."

Kelly talked Steinberg into submitting "Alone" to Nevison. "But he wanted to submit our old version of it." says Steinberg, who adamantly refused. A new demo was recorded. "In re-demoing it, we rewrote the first line of the chorus," Steinberg explains. "That made a world of difference lyrically and melodically. The i-Ten version had bombastic guitar power chords, which really made the song awful. We were in such a hurry to do a quick demo for (Heart) to hear the song that we demoed it with just a drum machine, bass and synthesizers. We left out guitars entirely. All of a sudden the song sounded pretty good. It took another jump because Ann sang it so phenomenally well."

"Alone" and "These Dreams" might never have happened if Ann and Nancy Wilson had called it quits after two relatively unsuccessful albums.

The history of Heart dates back to

1963, when brothers Roger and Mike Fisher and friend Steve Fossen formed a group called the Army in Seattle. The name was changed to White Heart, and Ann Wilson joined in 1970. The band relocated to Vancouver, British Columbia, in 1972. Nancy joined in 1974, the same year the name was shortened to Heart. Guitarist Howard Leese was added a year later. His friend, producer Mike Flicker, introduced them to Sheldon Siegel, who had his own label in Canada called Mushroom Records. He offered to sign Ann to a solo deal, but she insisted he take the entire band or nothing.

Heart's debut album, *Dreamboat Annie*, produced the top 10 single "Magic Man." But in 1977 the group filed a lawsuit against Mushroom Records, charging breach of contract. They signed with Portrait, a CBS subsidiary, and recorded the *Little Queen* album. A Seattle district court judge ruled that Mushroom could release an LP, *Magazine*, that Heart had left incomplete. The suit was settled out of court and Heart finished *Magazine*. Later in 1978 they released a second Portrait album titled *Dog & Butterfly*.

A shift in personnel took place in 1980 during the recording of the *Bebe Le Strange* album. Romances between Ann Wilson and Roger Fisher and Nancy Wilson and Mike Fiher ended. The brothers departed the band. Bassist Mark Andes (Spirit, Jo Jo Gunne, Firefall) and drummer Denny Carmassi (Montrose, Gamma ) joined the Wilson sisters and Leese. That lineup remained stable until Andes left in 1993 and Carmassi departed in 1994.

## THE TOP FIVE
*Week of July 11, 1987*

1 **Alone**
Heart

2 **I Wanna Dance With Somebody (Who Loves Me)**
Whitney Houston

3 **Shakedown**
Bob Seger

4 **Songbird**
Kenny G

5 **Don't Disturb This Groove**
The System

## 672 Shakedown MCA 53094
### BOB SEGER

---

*Writers: Harold Faltermeyer*
*Keith Forsey*
*Bob Seger*

*Producers: Harold Faltermeyer*
*Keith Forsey*

*August 1, 1987*
*1 week*

---

GLENN FREY had the most successful single on the *Beverly Hills Cop* sound-track: "The Heat Is On" peaked at number two on March 16, 1985. He might have had a number one single on the *Beverly Hills Cop II* sound-track; he was the first choice to record Harold Faltermeyer and Keith Forsey's song, "Shakedown." But Glenn didn't like the lyrics, and with nine days left to go before the song was to be recorded for the soundtrack, Frey came down with laryngitis. He called his friend (and former Eagles manager) Irving Azoff, president of MCA Records, to tell him he couldn't record "Shakedown."

"I was the first person Irving called," Bob Seger remembers. "I had finished a tour and was just sitting around." Azoff told Seger he wanted him to record a song for Eddie Murphy's sequel to *Beverly Hills Cop*. Seger received the track on a Friday. He kept the lyrics of the chorus ("Shakedown, breakdown, you're busted") but wrote new verses. "There were a lot of lyrics about working undercover. I didn't like them, so I threw them all out. I decided to write

it my way and they trusted my judgment." On Monday night he went over to Azoff's house and sang a verse and a half. "He said he loved it and told me to finish it." Four days later the song was complete and three days after that the track was recorded and mixed.

Robert Clark Seger was born on May 6, 1945, in Dearborn, Michigan. Bob grew up in Ann Arbor, where his father Stewart was a medic for the Ford Motor Company and a part-time band leader. After his father left the family, young Seger, his mother Charlotte and his brother George were forced to give up their middle-class surroundings for the poor side of town. "After my mom and brother turned in for the evening and the Michigan stations had shut down or reduced their power, the 50,000 watts of good ol' WLAC in Nashville would come beaming through on my teeny transistor earphone," Seger told journalist Timothy White. "I'd listen to . . . James Brown and the Famous Flames, or Garnet Mimms and the Enchanters doing 'Cry Baby.' "

In 1961, Seger convinced a disc jockey at WPAG in Ann Arbor to play a demo he recorded with his band, the Decibels. "The Lonely One" had been recorded in the basement of Max Crook [see 88—"Runaway"]. But Seger's recording career didn't start moving until he met Eddie "Punch" Andrews, a local promoter. Andrews released records by the Mushrooms, an act that included a native of Royal Oak, Michigan, named Glenn Frey (their "Such a Lovely Child" was written and produced by Seger) and Bob

Seger and the Last Heard. In 1965, Seger recorded "East Side Story," which was picked up by Cameo-Parkway Records. Three years later he signed with Capitol. "But most people don't realize that I was almost signed to Motown," Seger revealed to White.

Capitol did not maintain much momentum on Seger and in 1972 he left the label for a Warner Brothers/Reprise subsidiary. Warners rejected the *Beautiful Loser* album, but Capitol picked it up and re-signed Seger in 1975. A year later, the *Live Bullet* album, the first released by Bob Seger and the Silver Bullet Band, established Seger as a mainstream act.

Between 1976 and 1982, Seger hit the top 10 of the singles chart six times, with songs like "Night Moves," "Still the Same" and "Against the Wind." Most successful was "Shame on the Moon" (four weeks at number two). When "Shakedown" went to number one, Seger received a congratulatory phone call. "Glenn Frey called me up and said, 'At least we kept the money in Michigan!' "

---

### THE TOP FIVE
*Week of August 1, 1987*

1 **Shakedown**
Bob Seger

2 **I Still Haven't Found What I'm Looking for**
U2

3 **Alone**
Heart

4 **I Want Your Sex**
George Michael

5 **Rhythm Is Gonna Get You**
Gloria Estefan and Miami Sound Machine

# I Still Haven't Found What I'm Looking For

ISLAND 99430

U2

**673**

*Writers: U2*

*Producers: Daniel Lanois*
*Brian Eno*

*August 8, 1987*
*2 weeks*

LESS than three months after they went to number one on the Hot 100 for the first time [see 666—"With or Without You"], U2 returned to the top of the chart with their second single from *The Joshua Tree*, "I Still Haven't Found What I'm Looking For."

The album, U2's sixth to hit the chart, was named after the gnarled trees that grow in desert areas of the southwestern United States. The Mormons gave the tree its name because its configuration suggested the Biblical passage about Joshua pointing to the Promised Land. Bono made light of the album name in a *Rolling Stone* interview: "It's not exactly *Born in the Joshua Tree* or *Dark Side of the Joshua Tree*. It sounds like it would sell about three copies."

Instead, it was the first U2 album to make the top 10 of the American LP chart, let alone go to number one. And 1987 was the year of U2, with the band reaching superstar status as confirmed by a cover story in *Time*.

"We knew the album had the potential to be important," bassist Adam Clayton said in *Rock Express*, "but getting it to that state was soul-destroying. We worked incessantly on the songs; we recorded some of them about seven different ways and then sorted through for the best arrangement. . . . We recorded the songs live off the floor, and only added to it when it was almost finished. A lot of the guide vocals sounded so good we just left them on."

Lead singer Bono is not so certain about the band's status. "I can't really work out why anyone would buy a U2 record," he told Colin Irwin. "When I listen to it I just hear all the mistakes . . . mostly I think the instrumentation is good. But I don't like the way I've sung on any of the records. I don't think I'm a good singer, but I think I'm getting to *be* a good singer. On *Unforgettable Fire* I think something broke in my voice, and it's continuing to break on *The Joshua Tree*, but there's much, much more in there . . . for years I really wasn't sure who I was, or who U2 were, or really if

there was a place for us. People say U2 are self-righteous, but if ever I pointed a finger, I pointed it at myself."

The self-righteous charge may have something to do with the band's spirituality. Three of the four (Bono, the Edge and Larry Mullen) are self-described "committed Christians." "I'm really interested in and influenced by the spiritual side of Christianity, rather than the legislative side, the rules and regulations," the Edge said in *Rolling Stone*.

"That's a funny thing about rock," Bono said to Robert Hilburn of the *Los Angeles Times*. "Spirituality is a topic that is taboo for some people, but I don't think what we are saying is of interest only to Christians. I hate a lot of what I see—people who go around claiming they have the only answer and they are free from sin. It's such a sham when people go around holding the Good Book to their breast or holding the baby up to the TV. It's tragic that people have turned faith into an industry. It's also tragic that the name of Jesus, which is precious to me, gets trampled on. They use it like a little badge."

Mullen elaborated in *Time*: "I am a

Christian and not ashamed of that. But trying to explain my beliefs, our beliefs, takes away from it. I have more in common with somebody who doesn't believe at all than I do with most Christians." And Clayton, the only one of the four who has not made a claim to be a Christian, said in that same interview that for the press "religion was an easy angle, a hook to hang a story on. We all believe in much the same things but don't express ourselves in the same way."

## THE TOP FIVE

*Week of August 8, 1987*

1 **I Still Haven't Found What I'm Looking For**
U2

2 **I Want Your Sex**
George Michael

3 **Shakedown**
Bob Seger

4 **Heart and Soul**
T'Pau

5 **Luka**
Suzanne Vega

## 674 Who's That Girl SIRE 28341
### MADONNA

Writers: *Madonna*
*Patrick Leonard*

Producers: *Madonna*
*Patrick Leonard*

August 22, 1987
1 week

WHEN MADONNA needed songs for her third motion picture, *Slammer*, she called Patrick Leonard and Stephen Bray, who had written and produced her *True Blue* album. "She said she needed an uptempo song and a downtempo song," says Leonard, who produced and wrote the music for one of Madonna's previous number one singles [see 637—"Live to Tell"]. "She came over on a Thursday and I had the chorus. She went in the back room with a cassette of that. I worked out the rest of the parts, she finished the melody, she went back in the back room (and) she finished the rest of the lyrics. She came out and said, 'We'll call it "Who's That Girl," and I think it's a better title for the movie than *Slammer* so we'll change the name of the movie, too.' "

Leonard agreed that it made a better title. The next day they wrote a second song for the film, "The Look of Love," in similar fashion. With Bray, Madonna wrote two more songs for the film: "Causing a Commotion" (number two in October, 1987) and "Can't Stop."

"Who's That Girl" was recorded in one day, according to Leonard. "She sang it once and that was it. We put guitars on it and percussion the next day." "Who's That Girl" became Madonna's sixth number one single. All her chart-toppers came in the '80s, giving her more number ones during this decade than anyone else to date.

Madonna's relationship with the motion picture industry wasn't limited to recording songs for soundtracks. She was also in demand as an actress. Her first starring role was in *Desperately Seeking Susan*, which co-starred Rosanna Arquette. Director Susan Seidelman talked about Madonna in a *People* interview: "She is an incredibly disciplined person. During the (nine-week) shoot we'd often get home at 11 or 12 at night and have to be back on the set by 6 or 7 the next morning. Half the time the driver would pick Madonna up at her health club. She'd get up at 4:30 to work out first."

Madonna might have had a number one single from the soundtrack of this film if "Into the Groove" had been released as a single. It was only available as the "B" side of the 12-inch single of "Angel." Madonna's record company chose not to release it so it wouldn't compete with "Angel," which was already moving up the Hot 100.

In her second film, *Shanghai Surprise*, Madonna played a quiet young missionary from Massachusetts who fell in love with a small-time con man. Her co-star was the actor she first met while filming the video for "Material Girl," her husband Sean Penn. "We didn't actually plan on working on the film together," Madonna told British reporters at a film press conference that was also attended by executive producer George Harrison. "(Sean) had just finished a film and was looking for another movie to do and I'd just finished working on my record and I was looking for a movie to do. I read the script and loved it and asked him to read it for his opinion. He also liked the male role, so we looked at each other and thought maybe this would be a good one to do together." The critics were not kind to *Shanghai Surprise*, and the film did not do well.

The critics were equally unenthusiastic about Madonna's third film, *Who's That Girl*. Madonna played Nikki Finn, described in a press release as "a feisty, free-spirited femme destined to take her place among the screen's great comic heroines." Madonna talked about the music she wanted for the film: "I had some very specific ideas in mind, music that would stand on its own as well as support and enhance what was happening on screen and the only way to make that a reality was to have a hand in writing the tunes myself . . . (the) songs aren't necessarily about Nikki, or written to be sung by someone like her, but there's a spirit to this music that captures both what the film and the character are about, I think."

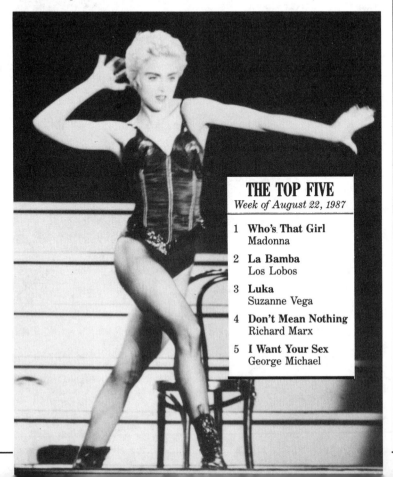

### THE TOP FIVE
*Week of August 22, 1987*

1 **Who's That Girl**
   Madonna

2 **La Bamba**
   Los Lobos

3 **Luka**
   Suzanne Vega

4 **Don't Mean Nothing**
   Richard Marx

5 **I Want Your Sex**
   George Michael

SLASH 28336 **La Bamba**
LOS LOBOS **675**

*Writer: Ritchie Valens*

*Producer: Mitchell Froom*

*August 29, 1987*
*3 weeks*

In his short lifetime, Ritchie Valens released only two singles. The first, "Come On, Let's Go," peaked at number 42 on November 24, 1958. The second was a two-sided hit. The "A" side, "Donna," peaked at number two on February 23, 1959. The "B" side, "La Bamba," peaked at number 22 on February 2, 1959. The next day, Valens was killed in the same plane crash that took the life of Buddy Holly and the Big Bopper.

In 1987, *La Bamba* was the title of the film biography of Ritchie Valens, produced by Taylor Hackford [see 562—"Up Where We Belong"] and written and directed by playwright Luis Valdez (*Zoot Suit, I Don't Have to Wear No Stinkin' Badges*). It was Valdez who made the final decision to record new music for the film rather than use Valens' own recordings. Los Lobos were among the musicians chosen for the movie.

Curt Sobel, music editor of the film, elaborated on some of the problems of recording the music for Jack Mathews in the *Los Angeles Times*: "An actor can only go so far (with lip-syncing), he can get you in the ballpark. Lou (Diamond Phillips) did a great job. He practiced constantly. But when everything was shot, there was still a lot of work to do." Sobel and a guitar instructor were on the set for all of Phillips' musical scenes, both to coach the actor and advise Valdez which takes would match up with Los Lobos'

music. Phillips would record a verse at a time, singing to Los Lobos' pre-recorded tracks. "The lips and voice are never perfectly synchronized," Sobel told Mathews. "You have to find the exact spot where the actor begins a word and put the beginning of the music right there."

As music editor, Sobel was required to lengthen or shorten the music to match Phillips' lip movements and guitar strumming. To facilitate this, Los Lobos recorded each instrument and David Hidalgo's lead vocals on separate tracks.

"La Bamba" was a song often performed by Los Lobos. Singer/guitarist Cesar Rosas described the song's origin to Paul Sexton in *Record Mirror*: " 'La Bamba' probably goes back 200 years. It means 'wedding song' and it's still used in the state of Veracruz for marriages. The guy puts on this six-foot sash and the couple do this beautiful dance. They put this thing on the floor and use their feet to make a bow with it . . . when Ritchie Valens sang it, he didn't know what he was singing about . . . because he didn't have the Spanish."

Valens' sister Connie confirmed that fact for Gregg Barrios in the *Los Angeles Times*. "Ritchie never spoke in Spanish because his dad never did." She explained that Valens' inspiration for recording "La Bamba" came from his childhood, when he heard the song performed at family gatherings. His mentor, Dickie Cota, taught him to strum a guitar and sing the song in Spanish. Valens did not first hear the song in a Tijuana brothel, as depicted in the film.

Los Lobos were a perfect choice to record the music for *La Bamba*. The

band's origins can be traced to an East Los Angeles junior high school, where Hidalgo introduced himself to Rosas. The original band members included drummer Louie Perez, bassist Conrad Lozano (who had been a member of Tierra, an East L.A. band that had charted on the Hot 100 with "Together") and Frank Gonzales (who left the band in 1976); they had all been in different bands before they decided to play together. Their first gig was at a local VFW Hall, and they were told to have a group name by that night. "I knew this great folk band from Mexico called Los Lobos that had albums out," Rosas told Mark Rowland in *Musician*. "So I said, 'Hey, how about "Los Lobos, from East L.A."?' "

In 1981, Hidalgo and Perez went to see the Blasters at the Roxy in Los Angeles. They hung around afterward to meet the band, and Dave Alvin remembered seeing Hidalgo in a public television documentary. The Blasters eventually recommended the group to their record label, Slash.

## THE TOP FIVE
*Week of August 29, 1987*

1 **La Bamba**
  Los Lobos

2 **Who's That Girl**
  Madonna

3 **Don't Mean Nothing**
  Richard Marx

4 **Luka**
  Suzanne Vega

5 **Only in My Dreams**
  Debbie Gibson

<table>
<tr><td>676</td><td></td></tr>
</table>

# 676 | I Just Can't Stop Loving You  EPIC 07253
## MICHAEL JACKSON and SIEDAH GARRETT

*Writer: Michael Jackson*

*Producer: Quincy Jones*

*September 19, 1987*
*1 week*

SIEDAH GARRETT was the last to know she would be recording a duet with Michael Jackson for his long-awaited follow-up to *Thriller*.

Actually, Michael's first choice for a singing partner for "I Just Can't Stop Loving You" had been Barbra Streisand, but she "didn't like it," according to a *Rolling Stone* quote of Michael's manager Frank Dileo. "I knew the song was a hit—with or without Barbra," Dileo added. Whitney Houston was also mentioned as a possible partner, but that didn't work out either.

Enter Garrett, whose credits include recording an album with a group called Plush and a duet with Dennis Edwards of the Temptations, "Don't Look Any Further," which peaked at number two on the black singles chart in 1984. She first met producer Quincy Jones when she auditioned for a vocal group he was putting together. The group turned out to be Deco, and

Siedah and four men were chosen out of 800 singers who tried out. They recorded the music for the *Fast Forward* soundtrack that Quincy was working on.

Garrett started writing songs while a member of Deco. "The guys in the group wanted a publishing deal along with their recording contract. I'd never written a song before in my life!" she exclaims with a laugh. "So I was sort of pushed into writing."

When Deco dissolved, Siedah was signed to a solo recording contract with Quincy's label, Qwest. In May of 1987 she was invited to Quincy's house along with some other songwriters and was told that Quincy was looking for songs for Michael's forthcoming album. The next day Siedah met with one of her writing partners, Glen Ballard, to work on songs for her own album project.

"He said to me, 'Let's try to write a song for Michael,' and I gave him this 'I'm really disappointed' look. But I said O.K. The result was "Man in the Mirror" [see 694], a song which Quincy and Michael loved. Siedah was invited to sing backing vocals.

"Then a few days later I got another call from Quincy. I was called back (to

the studio) and I thought we were gonna finish." Meanwhile, she had received a tape from Quincy. "It's not unusual for me to get a tape from Quincy's office because people send him songs for me to sing. The only thing different about this demo that didn't register at the time is that it was Michael Jackson singing."

Arriving at the studio, Siedah expected to find the Winans gospel group and Andrae Crouch's choir. "The only people in the studio are Bruce Swedien, Quincy, Michael and me. So I said, 'Maybe I'm early. Maybe they're running a bit late, I'll just wait.' Quincy said to me, 'Did you get the tape?' I said I got the tape. He said, 'Did you listen to the song?' I said I listened to the song. He said, 'Can you sing the song?' I said I can sing the song. He said, 'Well, go sing it.'"

"I walked over to the other side of the studio where there's two mike stands, music on either side, Michael Jackson on this end of the microphone, me on the other end, and *that's* when I knew we were doing a duet."

"I Just Can't Stop Loving You" was the first single released from *Bad*. On first listening, it was difficult to hear that it was a duet. Michael's and Siedah's voices sounded so similar, one had to look at the liner notes on *Bad* to see who was singing which part.

"When we were doing it, I didn't realize how much we were sounding alike," Garrett explains. "Michael is a vocal chameleon; he can sound like anybody. I think he was trying to blend with me. Quincy was sitting back, closed his eyes and said he'd be damned if he could tell which one of us was which."

## THE TOP FIVE
*Week of September 19, 1987*

1 **I Just Can't Stop Loving You**
  Michael Jackson
  and Siedah Garrett

2 **Didn't We Almost Have It All**
  Whitney Houston

3 **La Bamba**
  Los Lobos

4 **Here I Go Again**
  Whitesnake

5 **When Smokey Sings**
  ABC

*Writers: Michael Masser*
*Will Jennings*

*Producer: Michael Masser*

*September 26, 1987*
*2 weeks*

**W**HITNEY HOUSTON and composer Michael Masser both had their fifth number one single with "Didn't We Almost Have It All." Lyricist Will Jennings was only one behind. His previous chart-toppers were for Barry Manilow [see 471—"Looks Like We Made It"], Joe Cocker and Jennifer Warnes [see 562— "Up Where We Belong"] and Steve Winwood [see 645— "Higher Love"].

Jennings, born in Tyler, Texas, had written poetry for years and taught English at Tyler Junior College and the University of Wisconsin-Eau Claire. In 1971 he moved to Nashville and began writing songs for country artists.

Jennings later moved to Los Angeles. His publisher, Lance Freed at Almo-Irving Music, introduced Jennings to British composer Richard Kerr. Their first collaboration was "Somewhere in the Night," which made the Hot 100 three times: first by Batdorf and Rodney (number 69 in December, 1975), next by Helen Reddy (number 19 in February, 1976) and finally by Barry Manilow (number nine in February, 1979).

Arista Records had particular good fortune with Jennings' songs. "Looks Like We Made It" by Manilow was on Arista (and was number one exactly

ten years and two weeks before "Didn't We Almost Have It All," also on Arista). And Whitney's cousin, Dionne Warwick, signed with Arista in 1979 and had her first hit on the label with Jennings and Kerr's "I'll Never Love This Way Again" (number five in October, 1979).

"Didn't We Almost Have It All" took a long time to write, according to Jennings. "It seems like Michael Masser and I worked off and on for years on that song. I don't know how many times I rewrote bits and pieces of the tune." Jennings worked on it in many different locales, including England and Nashville. "I remember distinctly that we ran (up) over two hundred dollars worth of phone calls from a hotel in Nashville . . . of course, it was well worth it in the end."

The same week that "Didn't We Almost Have It All" moved to the top of the singles chart, Michael Jackson's *Bad* became the sixth LP in history to enter the album chart at number one. It was a feat that Whitney had accomplished just 13 weeks earlier with her second album, *Whitney*. She was the first female artist to ever have an album debut at number one. The first six albums to enter the *Billboard* LP chart at number one are:

1. *Captain Fantastic and the Brown Dirt Cowboy* by Elton John on June 7, 1975.
2. *Rock of the Westies* by Elton John on November 8, 1975.
3. *Songs in the Key of Life* by Stevie Wonder on October 16, 1976.
4. *Bruce Springsteen and the E Street Band Live/1975–85* on November 29, 1986.
5. *Whitney* by Whitney Houston on June 27, 1987.
6. *Bad* by Michael Jackson on September 26, 1987.

## THE TOP FIVE
*Week of September 26, 1987*

1 **Didn't We Almost Have It All**
Whitney Houston

2 **Here I Go Again**
Whitesnake

3 **I Just Can't**
**Stop Loving You**
Michael Jackson and
Siedah Garrett

4 **I Heard a Rumour**
Bananarama

5 **Lost in Emotion**
Lisa Lisa and Cult Jam

### 678 Here I Go Again GEFFEN 28339
#### WHITESNAKE

Writers: *David Coverdale*
*Bernie Marsden*

Producer: *Keith Olsen*

*October 10, 1987*
*1 week*

"**H**ERE I GO AGAIN" first charted in Britain in November, 1982, in an earlier incarnation. "I wrote the song in Portugal in 1981," says Whitesnake leader and founder David Coverdale. "We recorded it on an album (*Saints and Sinners*) later that year. However, I was totally disappointed (in it). It was the last album by the original Whitesnake. This album was not released in the U.S., so the song remained undetected for a long time." Coverdale says he re-recorded the song at the request of John David Kolodner of Geffen Records.

"I wanted to have a more positive backing track," Coverdale replies when asked what was different about the newer recording. "The only thing that stands up on the original version is the emotional security of the vocal performance. There's a very limp performance from some very exceptional musicians."

David Coverdale, born September 21, 1951, in Saltburn-by-the-Sea, Yorkshire, England, started singing for the same reason Ricky Nelson did—to impress a girl [see 40—"Poor Little Fool"]. He joined her brother's band, but he was still in school and intended to become an art teacher. He had a day job selling clothes in a boutique.

In 1973 he spied an ad in *Melody Maker* for the band Deep Purple ("Hush," "Smoke on the Water"). They were looking for a lead singer to replace Ian Gillan. Coverdale got drunk and recorded a version of "Everybody's Talkin' " and sent it to the band along with a photograph. "I didn't expect to get the gig," Coverdale told Daina Darzin in *Circus*.

He did get it, however. Coverdale became lead singer and wrote many of the group's songs beginning with their eleventh chart album, *Burn*. "The years I spent with Deep Purple were extremely valuable," Coverdale said in *Metal Mania*. "I was introduced to the world of songwriting, touring, recording and working with a full-time professional band." Coverdale left Deep Purple in March, 1976, shortly before the group disbanded.

### THE TOP FIVE
*Week of October 10, 1987*

1 **Here I Go Again**
   Whitesnake

2 **Lost in Emotion**
   Lisa Lisa and Cult Jam

3 **Carrie**
   Europe

4 **I Heard a Rumour**
   Bananarama

5 **U Got the Look**
   Prince

Contractually, Coverdale couldn't tour for two years. During that time he recorded two solo albums, the first of which was titled *White Snake*. In 1977, David started putting together the band that would become Whitesnake.

Whitesnake made its first appearance at the Sky Bird Club on February 23, 1978. The band went through numerous personnel changes between its debut and its first number one single. Among those who were part of the group at one time or another were Jon Lord and Ian Paice (both former members of Deep Purple), Mick Moody, Mel Galley, Dave Dowle, Bernie Marsden, Cozy Powell, Neil Murray, Aynsley Dunbar and John Sykes. In October, 1985, the latter three joined Coverdale and producer Mike Stone in Vancouver, British Columbia, to record the *Whitesnake* LP.

The sessions were soon interrupted when Sykes returned to England when Phil Lynott, his bandmate in Thin Lizzy, died unexpectedly. Coverdale lost his voice and discovered a deviated septum. Medication didn't help and he

was ordered to have surgery and six months rest. When Stone suggested someone else do the lead vocals, Coverdale fired him. Following a recuperative period, Coverdale brought in a new producer, Keith Olsen, and a new line-up of musicians: guitarist Adrian Vandenberg, Mark Andes and Denny Carmassi of Heart and other session players recruited specifically to finish the album. They completed the LP begun by the former members of Whitesnake, and "Here I Go Again" was polished in December. "I re-did the guitars and the solo and other bits and pieces on the album that needed tidying up," Vandenberg said in *Guitar World*.

For the video of the first single from the album, "Still of the Night," Coverdale retained Vandenberg and added three more musicians: Vivian Campbell on guitar, Rudy Sarzo on bass and Tommy Aldridge on drums. After filming the video, Coverdale invited them to become the permanent members of Whitesnake. "But no matter who's in the band," he said in *Hit Parader*, "as long as I'm around there will be a Whitesnake."

COLUMBIA 07267

# Lost in Emotion

## LISA LISA and CULT JAM

**679**

Writers: *Full Force*

Producers: *Full Force*

*October 17, 1987*
*1 week*

Lisa Velez and Mike Hughes walked about a mile from the subway station to the George home for Lisa's audition [see 669—"Head to Toe"]. "Lisa came walking in the basement all nervous, 'cause the six of us are pretty big guys," recalls Bowlegged Lou, a.k.a. Lou George, of the group Full Force. "I'm pretty sure she was afraid, but we're very lovable guys. The first thing my brother Paul Anthony told her was, 'You're very pretty,' so that kind of broke the ice."

Lisa sat on a stool and sang some songs written by Hughes. "They weren't that hot," Lou laughs. "Back then she was singing off-key, but we knew . . . she wasn't familiar with the songs he wrote. I was in the back laughing (and) crying because they were that terrible. Before she left we said, 'Hey, listen, sing something that we all know.' So she sang 'For Your Eyes Only.' That's what got it for her."

Lou and his brothers loved the way Lisa sang the James Bond tune. "She sang it with such little girl innocence," he explains. "That was what we were looking for. We weren't looking for a Patti LaBelle or a Gladys Knight or an Olivia Newton-John. We were looking for a young girl so that when she sings a song, a lot of little girls all over the world can hear her and imitate her voice . . . so whenever they hear Lisa sing, they can sing along with her. After Lisa, we auditioned some other girls, but we knew we found the right one when she sang 'For Your Eyes Only.' "

Lisa was signed to a management and production deal with Full Force and found her name doubled to Lisa Lisa. "I thought it was fun," she said in *Spin.*

Mike Hughes got his wish to be part of the act; he and Alex Moseley, nicknamed Spanador, became Cult Jam. At first, the new group was signed to Personal Records, a New York label. That company licensed "I Wonder If I Take You Home" to CBS for a European compilation album called *Breakdancing.* "The import got back to New York and the DJs went on it," explains Hughes. CBS in America picked up the single and released it.

Lisa was still working at Benetton's in New York. "I was folding sweaters and a friend of mine called and said, 'They're playing your song on the radio.' " Lisa thought she was joking, but she tuned to the station anyway. "It was playing and I started jumping and yelling. I was really excited. I was saying, 'It's me! That's me!' and people were (looking at me) like, 'What's wrong? Is she crazy?' "

"I Wonder If I Take You Home" topped the *Billboard* Hot Dance/Disco chart. On the Hot 100, it peaked at number 34 in August, 1985. The follow-up, "Can You Feel the Beat?," reached a disappointing number 69 in December. The third single from their debut LP proved to be their biggest hit yet. "All Cried Out," a change-of-pace ballad, went to number eight in October, 1986.

Lisa Lisa and Cult Jam's second album, *Spanish Fly*, proved to be the band's breakthrough LP. "Head to Toe" topped the Hot 100 in June, 1987. "My brother put together 'Head to Toe' and he thought it would be a good idea to have another song that was Motown-influenced," Bowlegged Lou says.

As "Head to Toe" was inspired by the records of the Supremes, "Lost in Emotion" was influenced by Mary Wells [see 147—"My Guy"]. Lou was playing her greatest hits album one day. "(The song) playing was 'Two Lovers.' And right after 'Two Lovers' came 'You Beat Me to the Punch.' So what we did is made ("Lost in Emotion") a combination of 'Two Lovers' and 'You Beat Me to the Punch.' We didn't steal the riffs; all we did was get the flavoring of it. We have a xylophone and some bells . . . because back in the Motown days they always used those simple instruments. They used real tambourines. The xylophone that you hear is a real xylophone. What we did was put it through an AMS, which is a computerized keyboard. If you listen to the end of the song it (sounds) like an 'I Love Lucy'-type thing."

## THE TOP FIVE
*Week of October 17, 1987*

1. **Lost in Emotion**
   Lisa Lisa and Cult Jam

2. **U Got the Look**
   Prince

3. **Carrie**
   Europe

4. **Bad**
   Michael Jackson

5. **Causing a Commotion**
   Madonna

# Bad EPIC 07418
## MICHAEL JACKSON

680

*Writer: Michael Jackson*

*Producer: Quincy Jones*

*October 24, 1987*
*2 weeks*

" **B**AD' is a song about the street," Michael Jackson wrote in his autobiography, *Moonwalk*, published in April, 1988. "It's about this kid from a bad neighborhood who gets to go away to a private school. He comes back to the old neighborhood when he's on a break from school and the kids from the neighborhood start giving him trouble. He sings, 'I'm bad, you're bad, who's bad, who's the best?' He's saying when you're strong and good, *then* you're bad."

It was producer Quincy Jones who suggested Martin Scorsese direct the video for "Bad," the second single and title track of Michael's follow-up album to *Thriller* [see 569—"Billie Jean"]. Michael's preference was for George Lucas or Steven Spielberg, but manager Frank Dileo agreed that Scorsese was an excellent choice.

The script for the video, written by Richard Price, was inspired by a true story. Edmund Perry, a young student from Harlem, left home to attend a prep school, Phillips Exeter Academy. In 1985, Perry was shot to death by a plainclothes police officer in New York who said Perry tried to mug him.

The "Bad" video was first shown in a half-hour special broadcast on CBS August 31, 1987, the same day the *Bad* album was released.

Michael talked about the recording of the *Bad* album in *Moonwalk*. "Why did it take so long to make *Bad*?" he

asked. "The answer is that Quincy and I decided that this album should be as close to perfect as humanly possible. A perfectionist has to take his time; he shapes and he molds and he sculpts that thing until it's perfect. He can't let it go before he's satisfied; he can't.

"If it's not right, you throw it away and do it over. You work that thing till it's just right. When it's as perfect as you can make it, you put it out there. Really, you've got to get it to where it's just right; that's the secret. That's the difference between a number 30 record and a number one record that stays number one for weeks. It's got to be good."

Michael also explained how he and Quincy work together. "I write the songs and do the music and then Quincy brings out the best in me. That's the only way I can explain it. Quincy will listen and make changes. . . . He'll guide me on and help me create and help me invent and work on new sounds, new kinds of music."

Their relationship is not always harmonious, Michael admitted. "And we fight. During the *Bad* sessions we disagreed on some things. If we struggle at all, it's about new stuff, the

latest technology."

Michael addressed the issue of competing against himself, specifically the biggest-selling LP of all time, *Thriller*. "There was a lot of tension because we felt we were competing with ourselves. It's very hard to create something when you feel like you're in competition with yourself because no matter how you look at it, people are always going to compare *Bad* to *Thriller*. You can always say, 'Aw, forget *Thriller*,' but no one ever will."

The single "Bad" entered the Hot 100 at number 40 the same week that the album's first release went to number one [see 676—"I Just Can't Stop Loving You"]. "Bad" topped the chart five weeks later, making it the fastest rising number one single since "We Are the World" [see 605], which hit the top just three weeks after its debut.

"Bad" is in a five-way tie for the shortest title of a number one song in the rock era. Two of the other four also feature lead vocals by Michael Jackson: "ABC" and "Ben." The other two three-letter titles are "Why" by Frankie Avalon and "War" by Edwin Starr.

## THE TOP FIVE
*Week of October 24, 1987*

1  **Bad**
   Michael Jackson

2  **Causing a Commotion**
   Madonna

3  **U Got the Look**
   Prince

4  **Lost in Emotion**
   Lisa Lisa and Cult Jam

5  **I Think We're Alone Now**
   Tiffany

MCA 53167 **I Think We're Alone Now**
TIFFANY

**681**

*Writer: Ritchie Cordell*

*Producer: George Tobin*

*November 7, 1987*
*2 weeks*

TIFFANY DARWISCH was born October 2, 1971, making her the first artist with a number one song to be born in the 1970s.

Tiffany says she was two years old when her cousin Darla taught her to sing "Delta Dawn." By the time she was five, she had declared to her mother that she was going to be a singer. She first performed in public at age nine, when her stepfather urged her to sing with the Country Hoedowners at a barbecue in her hometown of Norwalk, California. The band liked her and invited her to join them for other local gigs on weekends.

She started singing country songs but switched over to pop when some of the themes seemed too adult for her. "I couldn't sing 'My baby left me and my life is over' and have anyone believe me, because I was 12 years old," she explains with a giggle.

That's how old she was when she met producer George Tobin. She was recording a demo in one room of his studio in the San Fernando Valley while he was producing Smokey Robinson in another room. Someone told Tobin he should come and listen to the powerful voice of the 12-year-old singer and, reluctantly, he did. "I walked in and . . . listened to this incredibly powerful voice," Tobin recalls. "I suggested we keep in touch . . . and I waited about a year (before) I started to record her when she was almost 14."

Tobin cut 48 sides for Tiffany's first album. Four of those songs were remakes, including the Tommy James and the Shondells hit "I Think We're Alone Now" (number four in April, 1967). "It's probably one of my five favorite records," Tobin proclaims. "I've always loved the song. I wanted to do it because I was making records in that time period and knew (songwriter) Ritchie Cordell . . . we all basically worked in the same building: 1650 Broadway (in New York City)."

While Cordell was working with Tommy James, Tobin was a staff producer for Musicor Records, working with artists like Gene Pitney. Tiffany, of course, was not even born yet. "She

had never heard the song before," says Tobin, who thought it was perfect for his young protégée.

"I didn't hate it, but I wasn't crazy about it either," Tiffany admits. "He asked me to trust him and tell him what I thought after he laid down the tracks. A week later, I listened to the tracks and it sounded like a completely different song. It had great lyrics, it was fun to sing and I ended up liking the song."

It took almost a year to record the songs for Tiffany's debut album. Tapes were sent to record companies but the responses were not enthusiastic. So Tobin invited label executives to his studio to hear Tiffany live. The showcases resulted in several offers and Tobin picked MCA. The label came up with an innovative promotion: they sent Tiffany on a tour of shopping malls in 14 different cities. The young artist sang to prerecorded tapes and caught the attention of teenagers, their parents and even their grandparents. A single, "Danny," was released, but Tobin claims it was only issued so people who heard Tiffany sing in the malls would have something to buy; MCA never intended to promote it.

The story of Tiffany might have ended right there, were it not for Lou Simon, program director of KCPX in Salt Lake City, Utah. Simon listened to the album and heard a track he thought was a hit: "I Think We're Alone Now." Music director Evan

Lake agreed and played it on his show; telephone reaction was strong. DJ Morgan Evans played it in the afternoon and the station was deluged with calls. Simon called MCA and suggested they release the song as a 45. "They said, 'We're just not into the project, thank you anyway.' I knew if I badgered them hard enough, they'd come around." Simon provided research and sales data to MCA to convince the label of the song's hit potential. "It took four or five weeks but the single finally came out," Simon says.

No one was more surprised that the song went to number one than songwriter Cordell. "It was very foreign to me. It just wasn't the same song. All I can say is I don't argue with number one records," says Cordell.

---

## THE TOP FIVE
*Week of November 7, 1987*

1 **I Think We're Alone Now**
Tiffany

2 **Causing a Commotion**
Madonna

3 **Mony Mony**
Billy Idol

4 **Little Lies**
Fleetwood Mac

5 **Bad**
Michael Jackson

## 682 Mony Mony CHRYSALIS 43161
### BILLY IDOL

*Writers: Tommy James*
*Ritchie Cordell*
*Bobby Bloom*
*Bo Gentry*

*Producer: Keith Forsey*

*November 21, 1987*
*1 week*

"THAT'S A SONG I was trying to write for two years," Ritchie Cordell says. "I knew ('Mony Mony') had to be a song that had a title like 'Sloopy' or 'Patches' or one of those girl's names that didn't need a last name. I kept bugging Tommy about it." When the Shondells needed a hit record in England, Cordell was puzzled about what to write because he had never been there. "I just knew . . . that they liked real sloppy stuff, real stuff from the gutter. Then one day Tommy said to me, 'What do you think about MONY?' I said, 'What's MONY?,' and he pointed out his window. There was the Mutual of New York building. I still didn't understand what he meant by MONY but when I looked up it was blinking in two flashy segments, MONY-MONY, MONY-MONY. It sounded like magic, so I grabbed my guitar."

More than 13 years after Tommy James and the Shondells made the song a hit, Billy Idol recorded it. "That was the first song Billy and I ever worked on together (with Billy) as a solo artist," producer Keith Forsey remembers. "It was Billy's idea to record it. I thought it was a great idea. He had just finished with Generation X and came to New York." Forsey had produced the final album by Generation X, the British punk band that Idol had helped form in 1977. That album "didn't actually sell millions," Forsey admits. "It was pretty much a flop. So the (record) company didn't want to use me anymore. But Billy thought we got on real well together so he phoned me up and said, 'Let's record "Mony Mony." ' I said, 'Yeah, let's do it.' "

"One of the things I first did when I came to America was phone Keith up to do 'Mony Mony,' which is a Tommy James song I did for fun," Idol confirms. "It was one of the first records I ever had sex to with a young lady and it was great, you know. It was one of those songs you always heard

in the mid-'60s. It was a kind of disco as well as a rock and roll song—there's something really great about it." The song was lighter than most of the material Idol had been recording with Generation X. "I wanted to do something that was uncomplicated and fun (where) I could relax and not really have to worry. . . . (It's) for the dance clubs. It's just a good, fun record."

The song was included in *Don't Stop*, an EP released in America in 1981. Idol didn't have his first American chart single until 1982, when "Hot in the City" peaked at number 23. "White Wedding" and "Rebel Yell" both made the top 50, but it was "Eyes Without a Face" that gave Idol his first real American hit—it peaked at number four in July, 1984. "To Be a Lover" was almost as big, going to number six in December, 1986. It was a new, live recording of "Mony Mony" recorded over two nights in Seattle, Washington, that finally gave Idol an American number one.

Billy Idol was born William Broad on November 30, 1955. His family moved often when he was a child, not only around the South of England but to distant shores as well: Idol spent four years living on Long Island, New York. Back in Britain, he joined with

other friends living in Bromley to follow the Sex Pistols from gig to gig. Along with Tony James, he formed his own punk band, Chelsea, which evolved into Generation X. He decided not to use his real last name. "When I started out, everyone seemed to be adopting these names," he told Robert Hilburn in the *Los Angeles Times*. "Johnny Rotten, Sid Vicious. I wasn't really Rotten or Vicious or Nasty, so I wanted something a bit more funny— yet something that seemed real rock 'n' roll . . . something that acknowledged my ambition."

At first, he considered Billy Idle. "That's because one of my school reports when I was a kid said, 'William is idle,' " he told the *Los Angeles Times*' Dennis Hunt. ". . . When I looked back on it, I thought what a great thing to be. . . . I considered the name Idle but then I said, 'Why not Idol?' That makes more sense in this business."

Generation X's last single was "Dancing With Myself," which was popular in New York dance clubs, paving the way for Idol's move to America and the beginning of his solo career. "I came looking for new people to play with," Idol told Parke Puterbaugh in *Rolling Stone*. "I'd been hanging out in London for ages; it was a closed scene." In New York, Idol formed a songwriting partnership with Steve Stevens, whose searing guitar work became an Idol trademark.

And thanks to Idol's recording of "Mony Mony," Ritchie Cordell had two consecutive number one songs. It was the first time that two remakes of songs originally recorded by the same artist were number one back-to-back.

### THE TOP FIVE
*Week of November 21, 1987*

1 **Mony Mony**
Billy Idol

2 **(I've Had) The Time of My Life**
Bill Medley and Jennifer Warnes

3 **Heaven Is a Place on Earth**
Belinda Carlisle

4 **I Think We're Alone Now**
Tiffany

5 **Brilliant Disguise**
Bruce Springsteen

*Writers: Frank Previte*
*John DeNicola*
*Donald Markowitz*

*Producer: Michael Lloyd*

*November 28, 1987*
*1 week*

REMEMBER Franke and the Knock-outs? They had a top 10 single in 1981, "Sweetheart," on Jimmy Ienner's Millenium label. Ienner remembered them, and when he needed some songs for the soundtrack of the movie *Dirty Dancing*, he called his friend Franke Previte in New Brunswick, New Jersey, and asked him to submit something.

Reports Previte: "I said, 'I'd love to, but I'm right in the middle of working on another project.' He said, 'I suggest you get on this because if you get a song in this movie, it's going to change your life.' I have to say he was right!"

Ienner gave him a rough idea of the movie's plot and asked for a tune that started slow, ended up fast and had a mambo beat. "They wanted it to be seven minutes long," Franke recalls. "I never wrote a song that long in my life." Franke called his friend John DeNicola and asked him to co-write the song with him. DeNicola only had a four-track recorder, so he asked Don Markowitz if he could use the eight-track recorder in his New York City apartment. Markowitz contributed the drum rhythm and some chords and was given songwriting credit.

Franke played the instrumental track for Ienner over the phone, and was told to go ahead and write the melody and the lyrics. "I was driving along the Garden State Parkway on my way to record my other project, and the lyrics just came to me. I started to sing the words 'the time of my life' and I scribbled them on an envelope in the car. I write a lot in the car!"

Previte and DeNicola also wrote "Hungry Eyes" for the movie, and Franke was hoping to record one of the two songs himself. But when Ienner mentioned that he was thinking of Bill Medley for "The Time of My Life," Franke was happy to have one of his all-time favorite singers perform the tune.

Medley, on the other hand, was not excited about recording another

soundtrack single. He had teamed up with Gladys Knight to sing "Loving on Borrowed Time" for the soundtrack of Sylvester Stallone's *Cobra*. "I thought a Stallone movie couldn't miss," Medley told Dennis Hunt in the *Los Angeles Times*. "With a hit movie, the title song has a real good shot to make it. When the movie flopped and the single flopped, that took the heart out of me. I wasn't that eager to do another soundtrack song, especially for a small movie with an unknown cast. Odds were against this movie becoming a hit."

Ienner was insistent. "He told me I was the only one he could hear singing that song," Medley said. "We went back and forth over this for two months. He wouldn't take no for an answer." Medley was also reluctant to travel to New York for the recording session while his wife Paula was almost ready to give birth. When the session was moved to Los Angeles and Jennifer Warnes was selected to record the song with him, Medley reconsidered. "I'd never met Jennifer before, though I'd been a fan of hers for years," Medley told Jim Washburn in the *Orange County Register*. It turned out they were both from the same part of Southern California. "I didn't even know she was an Orange County girl until we were in the studio together. It turned out to be the fastest song that I've recorded in the last 15 years. It just came together immediately."

The single was Medley's third number one and Warnes' second. All of their previous chart-toppers had been duets: Medley's with Bobby Hatfield as the Righteous Brothers [see 166—"You've Lost That Lovin' Feelin' " and 196—"(You're My) Soul and Inspiration"] and Warnes' with Joe Cocker [see 562—"Up Where We Belong"]. Medley established two records with this single. The 22 years and 10 months between "You've Lost That Lovin' Feelin' " and "(I've Had) The Time of My Life" gave Medley the longest span of number one singles in the rock era to this date. And the 21 years and seven months between "Soul and Inspiration" and "The Time of My Life" is the longest gap of time *between* number one singles in the rock era.

## THE TOP FIVE
*Week of November 28, 1987*

1 **(I've Had) The Time of My Life**
Bill Medley and Jennifer Warnes

2 **Heaven Is a Place on Earth**
Belinda Carlisle

3 **Mony Mony**
Billy Idol

4 **Should've Known Better**
Richard Marx

5 **Faith**
George Michael

# Heaven Is a Place on Earth  MCA 53181

## BELINDA CARLISLE

**684**

Writers: *Rick Nowels*
*Ellen Shipley*

Producer: *Rick Nowels*

*December 5, 1987*
*1 week*

LOOKING back, Belinda Carlisle can understand how her parents might have been worried about the oldest of their seven children, who was "dressed in trashbags sitting on bus stops in Calabasas (California) waiting for my dad to pick me up. They were horrified. They saw where I was living, at the Canterbury, which was like a punk commune. They didn't understand that at all. It didn't get much better when I moved down to a place called Disgraceland with a bunch of friends."

Somehow, the Carlisles' oldest daughter had changed from a high school cheerleader to an Iggy Pop fan. In 1978 that path led to the Go-Go's, a band described in one text as "a comically inept all-girl punk novelty set." "At first, it was a serious joke," Belinda admits. "We didn't know how to play; we didn't know how to write songs. As time went on we realized there was some natural talent in the band. We asked Charlotte (Caffey) to join the band so she could show us how to plug our guitar cords into the amplifiers."

Belinda became the lead vocalist by default. "I didn't want to be the singer. I wanted to play bass. Bass was already tapped. I said, 'What's left?' They said drums or singing. I certainly didn't want to play drums because I'm much too lazy."

During a tour of the United Kingdom opening for the group Madness, the Go-Go's recorded an early version of "We Got the Beat" for the Stiff label. Back home, I.R.S. signed them to a contract; "Our Lips Are Sealed" (number 20 in December, 1981) and a new "We Got the Beat" (number two in April, 1982) were their first two hits, along with a number one LP, *Beauty and the Beat*.

After seven chart singles and three albums, the Go-Go's announced their breakup at a press conference on May 10, 1985. "When you stop growing artistically, it's time to try something else," Carlisle told the assembled reporters. She also mentioned she would start work on a solo album. *Belinda*

entered the chart on June 7, 1986, and included the hit single "Mad About You" (number three in August).

For her second solo LP, Belinda interviewed several candidates for producer and chose Rick Nowels, who co-wrote Stevie Nicks' "I Can't Wait." Nowels' writing partner, Ellen Shipley, flew to California from New York to write songs for Belinda. "We started brainstorming concepts and Ellen mentioned the title 'Heaven on Earth,' " Nowels remembers. "I thought that was a good concept for Belinda. . . . I started singing 'Heaven is a place on Earth,' which I thought was a slightly fresher title." Two cross-country trips and two months later, they had a song.

Back in Los Angeles, they spent another month recording the track with Belinda. "We actually finished a first version of it," Nowels said. "All along I knew there was a great chorus, but I was always a little uncomfortable with the verse."

Nowels played the rough mix for Shelly Yakus at A&M Studios, who agreed that the verse sounded like it belonged in some other song. So Nowels asked Shipley to fly to Los Angeles and rewrite the song with him. Three days later it was complete and there was only one thing left to do: tell Belinda she would have to record the song again. "I was very

nervous about breaking this to her," Nowels admits, "because I put her through a lot of changes to get her to sing the other vocal."

"He played the new version on the piano for me," Belinda confirms. "I said, 'It's better than the one we have,' so we had to record it all over again . . . the verses and the bridge were totally different."

Joining Belinda on the anthemic chorus were Nowels, Shipley and two women involved with previous number one singles: Michelle Phillips of the Mamas and the Papas [see 198—"Monday, Monday"] and Diane Warren, who co-wrote a number one single for Starship [see 663].

## THE TOP FIVE

*Week of December 5, 1987*

1 **Heaven Is a Place on Earth**
  Belinda Carlisle

2 **(I've Had) The Time of My Life**
  Bill Medley and Jennifer Warnes

3 **Faith**
  George Michael

4 **Should've Known Better**
  Richard Marx

5 **Is This Love**
  Whitesnake

COLUMBIA 07623 **Faith**
GEORGE MICHAEL    **685**

*Writer: George Michael*

*Producer: George Michael*

*December 12, 1987*
*4 weeks*

**A**FTER three number one singles with Wham!, George Michael was saddled with a bubblegum image no serious musician could stand. With the break-up of his partnership with Andrew Ridgeley [see 608—"Everything She Wants"], George moved on to the business of recording his first solo album, a project designed to demonstrate his maturity.

Before that record was released, there was a soulful duet with Aretha Franklin, which displayed another facet of George's talent and gave him another number one song [see 664—"I Knew You Were Waiting (For Me)"]. Six weeks after that single topped the *Billboard* Hot 100, "I Want Your Sex" made its debut. Released in advance of the album, the controversial song was included in the *Beverly Hills Cop II* soundtrack.

"We were concerned that people would overreact to it," Michael's manager Michael Lippman told Paul Grein in the *Los Angeles Times*, "so we decided to put it in a very safe environment, to take a little edge off it and to soften any kind of controversy."

George talked about the song in a *Musician* interview with Rob Tannenbaum. "I was nervous with 'I Want Your Sex' that I would be too far in front of the album and it would get lost again. If I'd had any real idea about the controversy that it caused, I would have realized I didn't need a . . . movie. . . . It was a compromise I didn't need to make, and it convinced me that I should not compromise with things when I don't want to."

"I Want Your Sex" was banned from the BBC, re-edited three times by MTV and refused airplay by many radio stations in the United States. The diminished airplay hurt the song's performance on the Hot 100, where it stalled at number two. On *Billboard's* ranking of the top 40 songs by sales only, "I Want Your Sex" was number one for two weeks.

Intentionally or not, the song did help transform George's image. "That was a turning point in the way people perceive George Michael as an artist," co-manager Rob Kahane told Grein.

"It was the first time since I've been involved in George's career that people were asking serious questions about his music."

Nine months after "I Want Your Sex" was on the chart, George looked back and assessed the impact of the single. "As Americans like to say, the hoopla, the fuss, was way out of proportion with the fact that it was just a pop record," he says. "But I think it was not really so much to do with the pop record as to do with the general atmosphere about censorship and AIDS and all the issues surrounding it. It seemed like for a month I was a sex spokesman for young people. And I sure don't know why anyone would be asking me. I just wrote a song about my particular view on one angle of relationships and it was just blown way out of proportion. No doubt though, it sold a few records."

Press reports on George's first solo album indicated it might be titled *Kissing a Fool*. But when it was released, it was named after the next single, "Faith." George was asked how the title came about. "I've seen some quite imaginative interpretations," he allows. "The most obvious one was that I was a born-again Christian. Actually, the reason is simply that it represents the way I feel at the moment. It's kind of another word for my hope and optimism. You know, faith to me is just really such a strong word and the more I got into the idea of the song being the single, the more I liked the idea of using it as the title track."

## THE TOP FIVE
*Week of December 12, 1987*

1  **Faith**
   George Michael

2  **Heaven Is a Place on Earth**
   Belinda Carlisle

3  **Should've Known Better**
   Richard Marx

4  **(I've Had) The Time of My Life**
   Bill Medley and Jennifer Warnes

5  **Is This Love**
   Whitesnake

# So Emotional ARISTA 9642
## WHITNEY HOUSTON

Writers: *Billy Steinberg*
*Tom Kelly*

Producer: *Narada Michael Walden*

*January 9, 1988*
*1 week*

"So Emotional" was Whitney Houston's sixth consecutive number one song. Or it wasn't, strictly speaking. Counting only singles that actually charted on the Hot 100, it was definitely her sixth consecutive number one song, a feat previously accomplished only by the Beatles and the Bee Gees.

The technicality is that between "Saving All My Love for You" [see 620] and "How Will I Know" [see 628], Arista released "Thinking About You" as a single. Some chart historians don't count this single, as the label promoted it to radio stations with an urban music format and not to mainstream pop stations. Nevertheless, it exists, and it did peak at number 10 on the *Billboard* Hot Black Singles chart.

"So Emotional" was the final song recorded for the *Whitney* album. Clive Davis, president of Arista Records, called songwriters Billy Steinberg and Tom Kelly, who had already written number one songs for Madonna [see 600—"Like a Virgin"], Cyndi Lauper [see 650—"True Colors"] and Heart [see 671—"Alone"]. He told them that 10 songs had been recorded for Houston's second album and he was looking for one more uptempo song.

Steinberg and Kelly did not have Whitney in mind when they sat down to write "So Emotional," a song they had titled just plain "Emotional." "Whenever we try to write a song for somebody, we usually end up writing something stupid and contrived, so it's best when we (just write)," explains Kelly. "I started playing a bass line as we typically do with a drum computer and Billy had this lyric. We started doing this real Prince type of thing. As the song evolved, we thought . . . it would be good for (Whitney)."

The song was "conceived, written and demoed in a couple of days," Kelly adds. "Our demo is really fun," says Steinberg. "Tom and I are both big Prince fans. (He's) a real inspiration. He's one of the few writers . . . on the cutting edge. Our demo really had a Prince vibe to it." The demo was sent off to Clive Davis and he reacted

immediately. "Clive gave us the impression he liked the song right off," says Steinberg. "He went to bat for the song. Clive is the kind of guy that has tremendous confidence in his own taste. If we send him a song and he doesn't like it . . . he'll say, 'Next time, don't send your "B" material.' He'll be direct but one does not feel insulted. The nice thing is he'll respond immediately. He'll either call or write a note the very day he gets it."

When producer Narada Michael Walden received the song, it was already retitled "So Emotional." He cut the tracks in two days at his Tarpan Studios in San Rafael, California, then flew to New York to have Whitney record the vocals. With the rest of the album already recorded, she was scheduled to come in and make some minor changes in the songs she had already tracked. Narada asked Whitney to record "So Emotional" before making the vocal fixes on the older songs. Her voice wasn't warmed up, according to Narada, but she recorded almost 90 per cent of the song that day. That's unusual, says Walden, who credits the fresh performance to the fact that Whitney recorded it in one session.

While still in New York, Walden

played the track for Clive, who loved it right away. It was harder for Steinberg and Kelly to feel the same way. "If you fall in love with (your) version of your song, and you're used to hearing it the way you conceived it . . . it's always hard to get used to," Kelly explains. "We thought (the demo) was real nasty and funky. It had a real biting side to it. When we first heard hers, it took awhile to get used to it. I kept thinking it was too slow. I called Clive a couple of times and said, 'You really ought to speed it up.' Now we love it."

## THE TOP FIVE
### *Week of January 9, 1988*

1  **So Emotional**
   Whitney Houston

2  **Got My Mind Set on You**
   George Harrison

3  **Faith**
   George Michael

4  **Is This Love**
   Whitesnake

5  **The Way You Make Me Feel**
   Michael Jackson

DARK HORSE 28178 **Got My Mind Set on You** 687

GEORGE HARRISON

Writer: *Rudy Clark*

Producers: *Jeff Lynne*
*George Harrison*

*January 16, 1988*
*1 week*

Georgе Harrison first topped the Hot 100 the week of February 1, 1964, with the Beatles' "I Want to Hold Your Hand" [see 143]. Two weeks shy of 24 years later, Harrison was once again at number one with "Got My Mind Set on You," the first single from his *Cloud Nine* album. That gave Harrison the longest span of number one singles in the rock era, beating a record set just seven weeks earlier by Bill Medley [see 683—"(I've Had) The Time of My Life"].

"Got My Mind Set on You" ended a five-year absence for Harrison from the Hot 100. After a string of 11 consecutive top 40 records between "My Sweet Lord" [see 286] in 1970 and "All Those Years Ago" in 1981, Harrison slipped a bit with a 1982 release, "Wake Up My Love" (number 53 in December), from the commercially unsuccessful *Gone Troppo* LP. The song that returned him to the chart after a period of filmmaking (*Time Bandits, Shanghai Surprise*) and gardening was an inspired choice, an R&B track from a James Ray album that George bought in America in 1963.

"In the very early '60s our manager, Brian Epstein, had his two NEMS—North End Music Stores—shops at Charlotte and Whitechapel Streets in Liverpool, and he made it his policy to have at least one copy of every record that came out in England," George told Timothy White in *Musician*. "We used to go through all the records in the two shops, and that's why the Beatles records in those very early days were made up of both all the obvious things we liked, like Chuck Berry and Little Richard, but also things which were obscure. Most of them were American records, but a lot were not even known there! We did a James Ray song, 'If You Gotta Make a Fool of Somebody' (number 22 in January, 1962), in our show for years. . . . So I came here to America in 1963—*before* the Beatles came here—and I bought that James Ray album that had 'If You Gotta Make a Fool of Somebody.' The album itself was really terrible, but the best three songs

were written by this guy who discovered James Ray, a former mailman named Rudy Clark. Clark wrote 'It's Been a Drag' and 'Got My Mind Set on You Part One/Part Two'—although it didn't have any break in between. If you listen to the song now it's very different from how I've done it. I've updated it and changed the chords, because I preferred it the way I heard it in my head. Clark and Ray's version of it was coming out of the old jazz/swing era, and it has these horrible screechy women's voices singing those backup parts.

"I did that song because Jim Keltner got this drum pattern going one day that was a cross between swing and rock. Gary Wright turned around and said, 'Hey! Doesn't that remind you of that song, "Got My Mind Set on You"?' I was so surprised that anybody else had *ever* heard that tune!"

Harrison explained why he chose self-described Beatle fan Lynne as his producer in a *Rolling Stone* interview with Anthony DeCurtis: "I was thinking for a number of years about who I could work with—who I'd have great respect for and trust and who would

respect me too, because, I mean, I've been around a bit. I didn't want some flash young producer who'd disregard anything to do with my past." Dave Edmunds ("I Hear You Knocking," "Girls Talk") arranged for a meeting between Harrison and Lynne. After suffering from cancer for three years, George Harrison died of metastatic non-small lung cancer in Los Angeles on November 29, 2001. Flags in the city of Liverpool were lowered to half-mast.

## THE TOP FIVE
*Week of January 16, 1988*

1 **Got My Mind Set on You**
George Harrison

2 **So Emotional**
Whitney Houston

3 **The Way You Make Me Feel**
Michael Jackson

4 **Need You Tonight**
INXS

5 **Could've Been**
Tiffany

**688** ## The Way You Make Me Feel EPIC 07645
### MICHAEL JACKSON

*Writer: Michael Jackson*

*Producer: Quincy Jones*

*January 23, 1988*
*1 week*

"THE WAY YOU MAKE ME FEEL" was the third consecutive number one single from Michael Jackson's *Bad* album. It was the first time in his career, both as a soloist and as a member of the Jackson Five, that Michael was able to pull three number one singles from one album, a feat already accomplished by artists like the Supremes, the Bee Gees, Wham! and Whitney Houston. Michael's *Off the Wall* and *Thriller* LPs both produced two number one singles each.

"The Way You Make Me Feel" affected Jackson's chart statistics in many important ways at the time of its release.

1. It was Michael's ninth solo number one single, putting him in a four-way tie for fourth place among the artists with the most number one singles of the rock era. The list includes the Beatles (20), Elvis Presley (17) the Supremes (12) and with nine each, the Bee Gees, Paul McCartney, Stevie Wonder and Michael Jackson.

2. Counting his hits with the Jackson Five, it was Michael's 13th number one single. Lumping solo efforts with group efforts for all artists, this places Michael seventh on the list of career totals for the rock era. Ahead of him: Paul McCartney (29), George Harrison (23), John Lennon (22) Ringo Starr (22), Diana Ross (18) and Elvis Presley (17).

### THE TOP FIVE
*Week of January 23, 1988*

1. **The Way You Make Me Feel**
   Michael Jackson

2. **Need You Tonight**
   INXS

3. **Could've Been**
   Tiffany

4. **Got My Mind Set on You**
   George Harrison

5. **Hazy Shade of Winter**
   Bangles

3. "The Way You Make Me Feel" was Michael's seventh number one single of the 1980s, giving him the most number ones of the decade to this date. Right behind him with the most number ones of the '80s were: Madonna (6), Whitney Houston (6), Daryl Hall and John Oates (5), Lionel Richie (5), Phil Collins (4), Blondie (3), Huey Lewis and the News (3), Paul McCartney (3), Prince (3), Starship (3), Wham! (3) and Stevie Wonder (3).

4. With this single, Michael became only the fourth male vocalist in the rock era to put together a string of three consecutive number one singles.

5. This song increases Michael's span of number one singles to 17 years and 51 weeks—stretching from January 31, 1970, (when "I Want You Back" went to number one) to January 23, 1988. That is the sixth longest span of number one singles in the rock era. The record was set just one week previously.

The longest spans of number one singles in the rock era are: George Harrison (23 years, 11 months—from "I Want to Hold Your Hand" to "Got My Mind Set on You"); Bill Medley (22 years, 10 months—from "You've Lost That Lovin' Feelin' " to "(I've Had) The Time of My Life"): Stevie Wonder (22 years, three months—from "Fingertips (Pt. II)" to "Part-Time Lover"); Paul McCartney (19 years, 10 months—from "I Want to Hold Your Hand" to "Say, Say, Say"); Aretha Franklin (19 years, 10 months—from "Respect" to "I Knew You Were Waiting (For Me)".

6. This single also set a record for producer Quincy Jones, giving him the longest span of number one singles for a producer—a span that is longer than that of any artist in the rock era. Quincy's first number one single was Lesley Gore's "It's My Party" [see 130], which topped the Hot 100 the week of June 1, 1963. That gives Quincy a span of number one singles that covers 24 years and seven months.

After Quincy, the producers with the longest spans of number one singles in the rock era are: George Martin (19 years, 10 months—from "I Want to Hold Your Hand" to "Say, Say, Say"); Hugo Peretti and Luigi Creatore (17 years, 10 months—from "Honeycomb" to "The Hustle"); George Harrison (17 years—from "My Sweet Lord" to "Got My Mind Set on You"); Burt Bacharach (16 years, five months—from "Raindrops Keep Fallin' on My Head" to "On My Own"); Phil Gernhard (15 years, four months—from "Stay" to "Let Your Love Flow"); Don Costa (14 years, 9 months—from "Diana" to "Candy Man"); Michael Masser (14 years, one month—from "Touch Me in the Morning" to "Didn't We Almost Have It All"); Allen Toussaint (13 years, 10 months—from "Mother-in-Law" to "Lady Marmalade"); and Stevie Wonder (12 years, nine months—from "Superstition" to "Part-Time Lover").

ATLANTIC 89188 **Need You Tonight** 689
INXS

Writers: *Andrew Farriss*
*Michael Hutchence*

Producer: *Chris Thomas*

*January 30, 1988*
*1 week*

INXS' "Need You Tonight" was the first American number one single for an Australian band in five years. Only two other Australian groups had ever topped the Hot 100: Air Supply was the first, in 1981 [see 545—"The One That You Love"] and Men at Work reached the summit twice, in 1982 [see 561—"Who Can It Be Now?"] and 1983 [see 566—"Down Under"].

Lead singer Michael Hutchence was born in Hong Kong of Australian parents. He was 12 when they moved back home to a working class neighborhood in Sydney, where he became friends with a fellow student, Andrew Farriss. It was Andrew who was working at becoming a rock musician. "I was never musical," Hutchence told Jock Baird in *Musician*. "I was just really interested in it and loved it."

In 1975, with his parents divorced, Hutchence and his mother moved to North Hollywood, California. Just 16, he didn't become involved with the Los Angeles music scene. "I was sort of a hermit," he told Dennis Hunt in the *Los Angeles Times*. "I spent the better part of nine months in my room, writing and listening to music."

A year later, he moved back to Sydney and found Andrew playing in a band with Garry Beers, a bassist he met through a classified ad. Andrew's younger brother Jon joined the group as a drummer. The eldest Farriss brother, Tim, was playing guitar in a group with Pengilly. When that outfit broke up, Tim suggested he and Kirk

join Andrew's group.

In 1978, Jon Farriss and his parents moved away to Perth, on the West Coast of Australia. The rest of the band followed. "I thought it was pretty strange at the time," Hutchence conceded to Ian Dickson in *Record Mirror*. "But I was 17 and I didn't know any better. . . . Jonny was still at high school and his parents moved to Perth. We thought that was the end of Jonny. But he was so good that we started talking about it, and thought maybe it would be good to go to Perth and not have any influences around us. It's a cheap place to live and we reckoned we could rent a . . . big house and rehearse all day."

A roadie suggested they call themselves "In Excess," and they adapted his idea into INXS, pronounced "in excess" and not "inks." After living in Perth for 10 months, they returned home to Sydney. They made their live debut as INXS on September 1, 1979, at the Oceanview Hotel in Toukley. Eight months later their first single, "Simple Simon," backed with "We Are the Vegetables," was released on an independent label, Deluxe Records. Their first album came out the following October.

INXS toured their homeland extensively and released a second LP, *Underneath the Colours*, in October, 1981. After touring New Zealand in January, 1982, they recorded a song titled "The One Thing." That became their first American chart single, peaking at number 30 in May, 1983. Before recording their third album, Michael, Andrew and Kirk took a pilgrimage to America and Britain to find new inspiration and consider where INXS would go next. That third LP, *Shabooh Shoobah*, was their first album released in America.

On the way to record their fourth album in London, the group met producer Nile Rodgers, who asked if they would be interested in recording with him. Tim, who was a big fan of Rodgers' work with Diana Ross and David Bowie, was ecstatic. The result was the track "Original Sin," which featured backing vocals by Daryl Hall. After completing the album *The Swing* with producer Nick Launay in England, the group turned to Chris Thomas to produce their fifth effort, *Listen Like Thieves*.

"What You Need" from that album was INXS' first major American hit, peaking at number five in April, 1986. Thomas also produced the band's sixth album. Hutchence told Darryl Morden, "Andrew came up with this riff and I had some lyrics that seemed to suit it. We were in Hong Kong at the time, and we went into this little studio and did about five or six songs. 'Need You Tonight' was one of them."

On November 22, 1997, Hutchence was found dead in his hotel room in Sydney, Australia. The local police said it was a suicide.

## THE TOP FIVE
*Week of January 30, 1988*

1 **Need You Tonight**
INXS

2 **Could've Been**
Tiffany

3 **Hazy Shade of Winter**
Bangles

4 **The Way You Make Me Feel**
Michael Jackson

5 **Seasons Change**
Exposé

## 690 Could've Been MCA 53232
## TIFFANY

*Writer: Lois Blaisch*

*Producer: George Tobin*

*February 6, 1988*
*2 weeks*

**W**ITH "Could've Been," Tiffany became the youngest female singer to have two consecutive number one singles since Brenda Lee [see 71—"I'm Sorry" and 78—"I Want to Be Wanted"]. Although Tiffany was 17 years old when "Could've Been" went to number one, she was only 13 when she recorded it.

It was originally cut as a demo by Los Angeles songwriter Lois Blaisch. "I had a very miserable three-month period, and at the end of this (time) I met the man of my dreams, who proceeded to tell me everything I wanted to hear," Blaisch says, detailing the origin of the song. "I fell deeply into infatuation/love with this guy, who about a month later, wound up dating somebody else. . . . I was extremely broken-hearted and one night . . . I couldn't sleep and I was crying. Through my tears I was looking at the flowers he had given me, which were wilting. (In) my depression I wrote 'Could've Been.' "

Blaisch was playing at a club called the Hungry Hunter in Thousand Oaks, California, when Bradley Schmidt came to hear her sing. He loved the songs he heard that night, including "Could've Been," and asked for a demo tape to give to producer George Tobin.

Tobin invited her to come to his studio to audition. She brought an acoustic guitar and just played one song—"Could've Been." "He asked me to play it over and over," she remembers. "I played it three times for him." Tobin loved the song. "He asked me if I would come in that night and make a piano vocal (recording). It came out so great that the next morning he called up the players in Kim Carnes' backup band . . . he proceeded to cut the track that is now Tiffany's track. That was my demo that now has Tiffany's voice on it. Tiffany copied my version phrase for phrase, exactly the way I sang it. He's changed it a little bit, put another guitar solo on and sped it up a little, but it's the same track."

"I loved the song," Tobin says. "I bought the publishing . . . I sent the song to Crystal Gayle, to Dolly Parton—to probably every female country and pop act in the world at least twice. No one ever bid on the song."

The demo that Gale, Parton and others like Natalie Cole heard was by Tiffany. "I sent it out to everyone . . . managers to producers to artists. I played it for every A&R guy in Los Angeles that I could find, every guy in New York . . . (I) never got anybody to react to that song, ever."

Still, Tobin believed in the song. So did his young protégée. "I loved the song the first time I heart it," Tiffany says. "I could relate to the lyrics. I played it for a couple of my friends and for my mom, and they loved it, too." Tiffany recorded the song in one take. " 'I Think We're Alone Now' is a great song to dance to, but it doesn't show that I can sing. 'Could've Been' is a song that demonstrates my vocal ability."

Under other circumstances, the song might have demonstrated Lois Blaisch's singing ability. "MCA loved the version that George played them with me singing on it," the songwriter explains. "George offered me a production deal and I was advised by an attorney not to accept the deal. For monetary reasons they suggested I hold out for a better deal."

Blaisch was still planning to record her own material but was ecstatic that Tiffany had taken "Could've Been" to the top of the *Billboard* chart. It was Blaisch's first song to make the Hot 100, although other compositions had sold well: "Keep on Tryin' " was on Disney's *Mousercise* album and "Rainbow Land" was on the *Rainbow Brite* LP.

While enjoying the success of a hit single, Blaisch kept one secret to herself: she didn't tell the man who broke her heart that his actions resulted in a number one song.

### THE TOP FIVE
*Week of February 6, 1988*

1 **Could've Been**
Tiffany

2 **Hazy Shade of Winter**
Bangles

3 **Need You Tonight**
INXS

4 **Seasons Change**
Exposé

5 **I Want to Be Your Man**
Roger

Writer: Lewis A. Martineé

Producer: Lewis A. Martineé

February 20, 1988
1 week

THE debut album by Exposé, *Exposure*, was released February 10, 1987. On the afternoon of February 10, 1988, producer Lewis A. Martineé and the three female singers in Exposé received a phone call from Dave Jurman at Arista Records to let them know that "Seasons Change," the fifth single from the LP, would be number one on the next *Billboard* Hot 100.

It was a triumph for both Martineé and the group, which was actually the second edition of Exposé. The trio's mentor and guiding force is Martineé, a Cuban-born Miami disc jockey who started hanging out in recording studios in 1978. In 1982 he put some local bands together and wrote songs for them. In 1984 he came up with the concept of a female singing trio.

Martineé wrote a song called "Point of No Return" and recorded the instrumental track. Then he hired three Miami-based session singers to handle the vocals. Laurie Miller, Sandeé Casanas and Ale Lorenzo were the original members of Exposé. Released through Martineé's company, Pantera, "Point of No Return" became a hit in the Miami dance clubs.

Martineé credits Jurman with signing the band to Arista. "I was in Miami at the end of 1984," says Jurman, the national director of dance music promotion for Arista. "The record came to my attention . . . I felt (it) could cross over (and) be a big national

hit. I brought the record to the attention of people here at Arista and the group was signed." Rereleased on Arista, "Point of No Return" peaked at number 19 on the *Billboard* Hot Dance/Disco 12-Inch Singles Sales chart in August, 1985. The next single, "Exposed to Love," also peaked at 19, in January, 1986.

With two respectable showings on the dance chart, it was time to record an album. The three female vocalists began work on their debut LP. A source from Arista Records who asked to remain anonymous told Dennis Hunt of the *Los Angeles Times* that the label felt the original Exposé didn't have enough star potential and that label head Clive Davis didn't think dance-oriented acts had any longevity, anyway. According to the source, the three original singers were fired.

Martineé undertook a search to find three new members for Exposé. A friend told him about a singer named Jeanette Jurado in California, so he flew to Los Angeles to hear her sing. Jurado, who first sang with her high school choir, had been singing with a top 40 band called New Breeze for three years. She accepted Martineé's offer and began recording material for the *Exposure* album even before the other two women were signed. Jeanette sang lead on "Seasons Change," and was the only member of Exposé when it was recorded.

Next to join was Gioia (pronounced Joya) Bruno (nee Carmen), born in Italy and raised in New Jersey. She was performing with the Gee Whiz Band in a Miami nightclub when Martineé discovered her. All but two of

the songs had lead vocals recorded when Martineé completed the trio with Ann Curless, who graduated from the University of Miami with degrees in music and music merchandising.

The first single from the new Exposé, "Come Go With Me," crossed over to the Hot 100 and peaked at number five in April, 1987. Clive Davis suggested that the trio rerecord "Point of No Return." With Jeanette's lead vocal, the song became a pop hit, matching the first single by peaking at number five in August. Two months later, "Let Me Be the One," featuring Gioia on lead, peaked at number seven.

After four dance-oriented singles, the ballad "Seasons Change" was released. It was the trio's fourth consecutive top 10 single, making them the first group in history to pull four top 10 hits from a debut album.

## THE TOP FIVE
*Week of February 20, 1988*

1 **Seasons Change**
   Exposé

2 **What Have I Done to Deserve This?**
   Pet Shop Boys with Dusty Springfield

3 **Could've Been**
   Tiffany

4 **Father Figure**
   George Michael

5 **Hungry Eyes**
   Eric Carmen

# Father Figure COLUMBIA 07682
## GEORGE MICHAEL

*Writer: George Michael*

*Producer: George Michael*

*February 27, 1988*
*2 weeks*

GEORGE MICHAEL'S third single from his *Faith* album was the sixth number one single of his career. He had three chart-toppers as half of Wham! and one with Aretha Franklin before reaching the summit on his own [see 685—"Faith"]. "Father Figure" returned him to the top of the *Billboard* Hot 100.

"The initial concept was completely different from the way the song turned out," George replies when asked about the genesis of the song. "In fact, the initial concept for 'Father Figure' was to make it a kind of mid-tempo dance track. And what happened was I wanted to hear something in my mix so I happened to cut out the snare on the board and suddenly it changed the whole entire mood of the track. Suddenly it just seemed really dreamy. And this was halfway through writing it—because I was writing the song as I was going along in the studio. And I just thought, well, hey, this is actually much better! So I worked the rest of the feel of the track around this kind of spacey type sound. And it ended up, in my mind, being the most original sounding thing on the album."

"Father Figure" entered the Hot 100 on January 16, 1988. It was the highest debut of the week, at number 49.

## THE TOP FIVE
*Week of February 27, 1988*

1  **Father Figure**
   George Michael

2  **What Have I Done to Deserve This?**
   Pet Shop Boys with Dusty Springfield

3  **She's Like the Wind**
   Patrick Swayze featuring Wendy Fraser

4  **Never Gonna Give You Up**
   Rick Astley

5  **Hungry Eyes**
   Eric Carmen

"Faith" was still in the top 10, sitting at number nine. Six weeks after its debut, "Father Figure" was number one.

The song continued George's transformation from bubblegum pop star to serious musician. "When (a) group has as strong an image as Wham! did, you feel restricted by it," George contends. "You do feel that if you try to do anything which is very personal, it tended to clash personality-wise with what Wham! was supposed to be. Wham! really was much more me as a 16, 17-year-old. Much more Andrew's (Ridgeley) input as well, from the personality angle. And then suddenly that restriction was lifted. I realized I had the freedom to write exactly what I wanted to write. And (I) set about doing that."

Elaborating on that theme to Judy Wieder, George said, "It's nerve-wracking. When you're given the freedom to do what you like because you're no longer part of a group, you're also given the freedom to make mistakes. I don't think I've made mistakes with this album. I think it's very honest, very much a progression that people can follow and enjoy. If I'm wrong, well, that will be tough because it's all down to me now."

George also emphasized to Wieder that he had control over his own career, in every aspect. "All professional decisions have always been mine. The more I learn how to do something, the more I have to be the one to do it. The video thing is a good example. Once I learned how to do it, I pretty much did and still do all the directing and editing. I like my decisions. I've been pleased with the results. How can I work for months on something musically and then just hand it over to someone else to produce or film? I know a lot of artists can do that, but I can't. I can't even hand over my songs for other artists to record. I've been asked to work with Barbra Streisand and other artists that I'm quite flattered about, but I still write very few songs and they're so personal to me. To be very honest with you, and I hope this never happens, the only way I could just turn my stuff over to someone else is if I were to become less possessive about my music."

*Writers: Mike Stock*
*Matt Aitken*
*Pete Waterman*

*Producers: Mike Stock*
*Matt Aitken*
*Pete Waterman*

*March 12, 1988*
*2 weeks*

RICK ASTLEY was born February 6, 1966, in Newton-le-Willows, a small, rural town located between Manchester and Liverpool in England. No one in his family—including his parents, two brothers and a sister—was involved with music professionally, but there was a piano in the house which his mother played very well. Rick sang in a church choir in Manchester and took piano lessons. His interest in music heightened when he was in school.

"Our form room, where we went for registration at school, was the music room, and there was a drum kit set up (in it). I just had to go one day and that was it. I had to sell my biking leather to buy my first drum kit," he laughs. With some friends from school, he formed a band called Give Way.

He was still behind the drums when he joined his second band, called FBI. They played local clubs and pubs and concentrated on cover versions of songs by the Beatles and the Shadows. "I started writing my own songs, so we gradually started to play more and more original material. I became the singer because I was writing most of the songs. It was just a natural progression." Rick also modestly admits he was a better singer than the bass player. "I've always had this low tone and this style of singing."

The band found a couple of managers. One of them knew Pete Waterman, who was just forming a production team with Mike Stock and Matt Aitken. (This team would go on to produce hit records for Bananarama [see 646—"Venus"] and Dead or Alive ["You Spin Me 'Round like a Record"].) Waterman was invited to hear FBI at a showcase held in Warrington at a private social club for the employees of a company called Monks.

"He liked my vocals but wasn't all that interested in the band because we were still very young," Rick continues. "(Waterman) offered me a deal, and a few months after thinking it over I decided to take him up on his offer." Rick went to meet everyone at Waterman's company, PWL. At first he would spend one or two days a week at the studio. "Eventually I was offered a job at PWL to work as a tape op, which is basically a tea boy who's learning the engineering profession. I did that for about 10 months."

While learning the technical aspects of recording—and making the tea as well—Rick was also working on his own demos. "We played a tape to one of the people at RCA, Peter Robinson in the A&R department. He didn't believe it was me singing," says the shy vocalist with the boy-next-door looks. "So we brought him round to the reception at PWL recording studios and I sang for him . . . and then he was convinced."

Astley's first performance on vinyl was an uncredited duet with singer O'chi Brown on "Learning to Live (Without Your Love)," recorded in the summer of 1986. In October, he cut "Never Gonna Give You Up," which would turn out to be his first single. Stock, Aitken and Waterman held it back from release until they thought it would be a good time for a new artist to hit the chart. RCA issued the single on July 27, 1987. Rick was on a tour of radio stations and clubs ("I sang in a place that was no bigger than your average living room") when the record went into the British top 75. It moved quickly to number one and stayed there for five weeks; it became the number one single of 1987 in the United Kingdom.

## THE TOP FIVE
*Week of March 12, 1988*

1 **Never Gonna Give You Up**
Rick Astley

2 **Father Figure**
George Michael

3 **She's Like the Wind**
Patrick Swayze featuring Wendy Fraser

4 **I Get Weak**
Belinda Carlisle

5 **Endless Summer Nights**
Richard Marx

# 694 Man in the Mirror EPIC 07668
## MICHAEL JACKSON

**Writers:** *Siedah Garrett*
*Glen Ballard*

**Producer:** *Quincy Jones*

March 26, 1988
2 weeks

MICHAEL JACKSON was the first solo artist in chart history to pull four number one singles off one album. "Man in the Mirror" was the fourth single from *Bad*, making that only the second LP ever to yield a quartet of chart-topping songs. There were four number one singles on *Saturday Night Fever*: three by the Bee Gees and one by Yvonne Elliman.

"Man in the Mirror" also extended the many records Michael set with his previous number one single [see 688—"The Way You Make Me Feel"]. It was Michael's 10th solo number one, putting him in fourth place among artists with the most number one songs. It was his eighth chart-topper of the '80s, the most number ones of the decade to this date. It stretched his span of number one singles to 18 years and two months. It also lengthened Quincy Jones' span of number one hits as a producer to 24 years and nine months.

"Man in the Mirror" was one of only two songs on *Bad* not written by Michael. Siedah Garrett, who duetted with Jackson on the first single from the album [see 676—"I Just Can't Stop Loving You"], wrote "Man in the Mirror" with Glen Ballard. In May of 1987, Siedah was invited to a meeting of songwriters at Quincy Jones' house. "The meeting was at 11 o'clock and I didn't get there 'til 12 because I got lost," Siedah remembers. "So I take my notes as to . . . what he wants in this next song for Michael, because he hadn't found all the songs yet. He said, 'We need another smash for Michael's album. I just want hits, that's all I want.' " Siedah made an appointment with Ballard for the following day to write songs for her own album.

When they got together, Siedah told Glen about the meeting at Quincy's home, and Ballard suggested they work on a song for Michael. "I sat down and started playing a figure on the keyboard and Siedah opened up her notebook," Ballard told Paul Zollo in *SongTalk*. "I started singing a verse idea melodically. I heard her singing something about a 'man in the mirror,' and I said, 'That's great. I love that.' So the first time I heard the title it was actually in the song."

They recorded a demo and had it finished on a Friday night. Siedah recalls, "Something said to me, call Q . . . tell him what you have. I (told him), 'This is highly irregular, but I cannot wait until Monday for you to hear this song.' " Quincy was in a meeting but told her to come over anyway. "The front door opens and there's 12 guys sitting at his dining room table in business suits with clipboards . . . they're having this big meeting about some movie Q's gonna do." Siedah gave him the song and asked that he call her back as soon as possible.

"He calls me four hours later and he says, 'Uhh, I don't know.' " Then Jones laughed and told her the song was incredible—but. "He said, 'I've been playing Michael songs for two years. We've been in the studio for 11 months. I don't know if he's going to take this song. But don't worry, if he doesn't do it on this record, we'll do it on (yours).' "

A few days later, Quincy told Siedah that Michael would cut "Man in the Mirror." A week after that, Quincy called Siedah from the studio and said that Michael wanted to make the bridge longer. Quincy told her he would bring in the Winans and the Andrae Crouch Choir to sing backing vocals—and that he'd squeeze Siedah in there, too. "On the day of the session," says Siedah, "just before the Winans left and before the choir came in, Michael came in . . . and I extended my hand to shake Michael's hand, and . . . he pulls me to him and kisses me on the cheek, and of course externally I'm very cool, and my heart's going, 'Omigod! Omigod! I've just been kissed by Michael Jackson!'"

## THE TOP FIVE
*Week of March 26, 1988*

1 **Man in the Mirror**
Michael Jackson

2 **Endless Summer Nights**
Richard Marx

3 **Never Gonna Give You Up**
Rick Astley

4 **Out of the Blue**
Debbie Gibson

5 **Get Outta My Dreams,
Get Into My Car**
Billy Ocean

*Writers: Robert John "Mutt" Lange*
*Billy Ocean*

*Producer: Robert John "Mutt" Lange*

*April 9, 1988*
*2 weeks*

**F**AST FACTS With Which You Can Amaze Your Friends: All three of Billy Ocean's number one singles have exactly eight words in the title [see 597—"Caribbean Queen (No More Love on the Run)" and 639—"There'll Be Sad Songs (To Make You Cry)"]. Furthermore, his singles that did not go to number one have titles that range from one word ("Loverboy," "Suddenly") to nine words ("When the Going Gets Tough, The Tough Get Going"), but none of them have eight words. Coincidence or Conspiracy? You Be the Judge.

The eight words that make up the title of Billy's third number one single caused some controversy in England, where the song was recorded. Billy

talked about "Get Outta My Dreams, Get Into My Car" in an interview on the United Stations Radio Network: "It's an English phrase . . . (It's) the same country that invented the language (and) when they heard it, thought it was dirty. I can't say the whole country, but (some people in) radio. In fact, it almost wasn't played. We had to re-edit; we had to do an edit on the intro . . . cut out some of the grunts and groans. . . . To me, it was harmless. It's a stream of words.

"I think part of the problem they foresaw," Billy said frankly, "was it could encourage perverts to molest little children . . . or encourage . . . men picking up prostitutes. I'd have preferred the original version . . . because I wouldn't do anything intentionally sexually offensive."

Billy explained that while growing up as a teenager in England, none of his friends drove automobiles. Most of them drove scooters around, but Billy felt that "Get Outta My Dreams, Get Onto My Scooter" just wouldn't cut it

as a song.

"Get Outta My Dreams, Get Into My Car" was produced and co-written by Robert John "Mutt" Lange, who also worked with Billy on "When the Going Gets Tough, the Tough Get Going." Ocean has also worked with writer/producers Wayne Brathwaite and Barry Eastmond. "Working with Mutt is different to how I work with Wayne and Barry," Ocean said. "Wayne and Barry tend to start the projects and I do a lot more running around . . . making demos. With Mutt it's more a case of . . . get the idea and we develop it there and then, which is a good way to work. It's a good way for me to work, considering I've got direction, considering I've got people around me (who) know what they're doing. And (I'm) not just left on my own . . . doing it like that with a certain amount of urgency, you create . . . adrenalin flowing . . . once you put it down . . . you haven't got to come back and try and recreate that bit of magic you've got in the demo."

Ocean enjoys the idea of collaborating with other people. "Different people bring out different things in you, and you bring out different things in them. On top of that, you bring out something totally new. More important, that takes the strain off you . . . why go through all that when you've got people around you. It's like refusing help."

Despite having three number one singles, Ocean didn't take his chart success lightly. "With so many records being released a week, to have a record anywhere on the chart is a tremendous amount of luck. It's like a blessing," he told Bob Andelman.

## THE TOP FIVE
*Week of April 9, 1988*

1 **Get Outta My Dreams, Get Into My Car**
Billy Ocean

2 **Man in the Mirror**
Michael Jackson

3 **Out of the Blue**
Debbie Gibson

4 **Devil Inside**
INXS

5 **Where Do Broken Hearts Go**
Whitney Houston

## 696 | Where Do Broken Hearts Go ARISTA 9674
### WHITNEY HOUSTON

*Writers: Frank Wildhorn*
*Chuck Jackson*

*Producer: Narada Michael Walden*

*April 23, 1988*
*2 weeks*

SONGWRITER Frank Wildhorn was driving in a car with his wife Rebecca in 1984 when he heard "Hold Me," a duet by Teddy Pendergrass and a then-unknown Whitney Houston. "I remember saying that's a voice I would like to write for," Wildhorn says. "When you write the kind of things I write, you want to write for those kinds of people." Four years later, Wildhorn and songwriting partner Chuck Jackson wrote Whitney's seventh consecutive chart single to go to number one, breaking the record of six set by the Beatles and the Bee Gees.

"Where Do Broken Hearts Go" was the fourth number one single from the *Whitney* album.

Wildhorn, a New Yorker who attended the University of Miami and the University of Southern California, signed with Chrysalis Publishing and had about 80 songs recorded over a five-year period. One of the first was called "One More Night," recorded by a singer named Donna Washington. It was produced by Chuck Jackson, who had also written and produced hits for Natalie Cole, including "This Will Be" and "I've Got Love on My Mind." Wildhorn liked what Jackson did with the Donna Washington song, and suggested they collaborate.

Jackson called Wildhorn soon after to tell him he had come up with a title: "Where Do Broken Hearts Go." Wildhorn liked it. "I sat there at the piano," Frank recalls, "and in about 40 minutes, 90 per cent of the sketch of the song was done. I called (Jackson) back and said, 'You gotta come over here tonight because I think we've got something.'" The song was completed the same night, and a simple demo, with just a piano, drum machine and one vocal, was recorded.

Cherie Fonorow, who worked at Chrysalis and then moved over to PolyGram's music publishing company in New York, submitted the song to Clive Davis at Arista. "Clive really liked the song, but he needed a bridge," says Wildhorn, who obliged and sent the song back to Davis. "From what I understand, it was one of the first songs chosen for the album. Knowing (it was for) Whitney's project, there must have been 50,000 songs submitted after (ours). So every week it was, 'Do we still have it?' We were going through hell."

Arista placed a hold on the song, but other artists—including Smokey Robinson—wanted to record it, according to Wildhorn. Uncertain if the song would make the final cut for Whitney's album, the songwriters weren't sure what to do. Eventually, they learned their song would indeed be on the album.

Fonorow was attending a Rock and Roll Hall of Fame dinner in New York in January of 1988 when Clive Davis called her over to his table. Just a few hours earlier, he had disclosed the title of Whitney's next single to the producers of "The American Music Awards," because she was scheduled to perform it on their telecast. Davis congratulated Fonorow—he had chosen "Where Do Broken Hearts Go." Fonorow thanked him and excused herself to go to the ladies' room. There she found a telephone and called Wildhorn in Florida to tell him the good news.

Narada Michael Walden, producer of Whitney's seventh consecutive chart single to go to number one, was pleased for the young superstar. "Whitney's seventh number one in a row is not only a great achievement in the outer world, but a most significant achievement in the inner worlds," says Walden, a disciple of the guru Sri Chinmoy. "There are seven lower worlds and seven higher worlds," Walden continues. "With Whitney's seventh in a row, she takes all of us to that seventh higher world. This is the place that all broken hearts go for inner nourishment, inner satisfaction, inner and outer peace."

### THE TOP FIVE
*Week of April 23, 1988*

1 **Where Do Broken Hearts Go**
Whitney Houston

2 **Devil Inside**
INXS

3 **Get Outta My Dreams,**
**Get Into My Car**
Billy Ocean

4 **Wishing Well**
Terence Trent D'Arby

5 **Girlfriend**
Pebbles

*Writers: Terence Trent D'Arby*
*Sean Oliver*

*Producers: Martyn Ware*
*Terence Trent D'Arby*

*May 7, 1988*
*1 week*

" '**W**ISHING WELL' was written when I was in a half-asleep, half-awake state of mind," Terence Trent D'Arby told Robin Smith in *Record Mirror*. "I like the feel of the words on that song. Actually, most of my lyrics are written in about 10 minutes."

"Wishing Well" was the second single released from the debut album, *Introducing the Hardline According to Terence Trent D'Arby*. "I want this album to leave a taste in your mouth that's as wholesome as your mum's best apple pie," D'Arby told Smith.

Born in New York City on March 15, 1962, D'Arby was raised in a strict Pentecostal home, where he was forbidden to listen to any music except for gospel. A neighborhood friend's mother used to buy her son a new single each week, and one day seven-year-old Terence was galvanized by the latest purchase: "I Want You Back" by the Jackson Five.

"You can't believe what those (Jackson Five) records meant to me," D'Arby told Robert Hilburn of the *Los Angeles Times*. "I had been singing in church and there was something about singing that made me know it was what I was meant to do. But I kept thinking, even as a child, that there was something else, besides gospel, to sing and then I heard the Jackson Five and it was like a whole new world opening up for me. It was like I had found my own world."

Like his brothers and cousins, D'Arby saw the 1976 Olympics and developed an interest in boxing. He enrolled at the University of Central Florida as a journalism major, but boxing scouts from the Army recruited him for a three-year hitch. While stationed in Germany, he started singing with a group called the Touch, and one day went AWOL for a gig. He was discharged from the Army and sent home, but he returned to Germany to continue with the band. He stayed with them for three years and left to travel through Europe. Eventually, he settled in England.

The U.K. division of CBS Records

**THE TOP FIVE**
*Week of May 7, 1988*

1 **Wishing Well**
Terence Trent D'Arby

2 **Anything for You**
Gloria Estefan and Miami
Sound Machine

3 **Angel**
Aerosmith

4 **Where Do Broken Hearts Go**
Whitney Houston

5 **Pink Cadillac**
Natalie Cole

signed him and paired him up with producer Howard Gray (The Cure, Scritti Politti) to record a couple of songs. "If You Let Me Stay" was his first single in Britain and America. Then Martyn Ware (Heaven 17) was brought in to produce nine more tracks to complete the album.

D'Arby's press interviews in England created the image of an arrogant star who wasn't afraid to call himself a genius. He said his first LP was "the most brilliant debut album from any artist this decade" and claimed it was a better work than *Sgt. Pepper's Lonely Hearts Club Band*.

When he arrived in America, D'Arby talked about his press clippings with Hilburn. "You've got to realize that I said a lot of (outrageous) things in England," he said. "A lot of it was what I truly believed, but a lot of it was exaggerated to make a point. You have to hit people over the head to make them notice, and I did it. I know how to play the game. But now I'm worried that a lot of people in America think I am some kind of hype because of all that has been written in England—and I'm very serious about my music and my career. I don't want to be just the latest curiosity."

# 698 | Anything for You EPIC 07759
## GLORIA ESTEFAN AND MIAMI SOUND MACHINE

*Writer: Gloria M. Estefan*

*Producer: Emilio Estefan*

*May 14, 1988*
*1 week*

"THE main thing people always ask me is, 'How come you write these (sad) ballads when supposedly you're happily married and you're very happy . . . and I am,'" emphasizes Gloria Estefan. "But I think that's where the artist uses his creative license. I might have experienced these feelings a while back or maybe vicariously through somebody else, maybe friends of mine that have gone through a similar thing. I think the artist always writes from within, from the soul, and even if you didn't experience it yourself, you have to feel how would people in this situation feel, and how would they say it. I always try to write very conversationally, and think how would someone want to say it to someone else and then I try to make it more musical."

Gloria Estefan and Miami Sound Machine's first number one single, "Anything for You," was the final song recorded for their album *Let It Loose*. The ballad was cut with piano and vocals and the group considered leaving it like that. But as they listened to it, they decided it needed a new arrangement. Returning home to Miami after a tour, the band went immediately into the studio and worked to complete the song.

The origin of Miami Sound Machine can be traced back to 1973, when Cuban-born Emilio Estefan was em-

ployed in the marketing division of Bacardi. For fun, he also played his accordion in local restaurants for tips. A friend at work asked him to play at a private party. They wanted to have dancing, so they suggested that Emilio bring a drummer and some other musicians.

Estefan invited two people recommended by his music teacher—a 17-year-old drummer named Enrique (Kiki) Garcia and a 15-year-old bass player, Juan Marcos Avila. The host was impressed with the group and suggested they keep working together. He also gave them a name: Miami Latin Boys.

Over the next year, the band played more local dates and built up a reputation. Meanwhile, Gloria and some friends put a band together one night for a party, and Emilio was asked to give them some friendly advice. Three months after that one-shot performance, Gloria's mother dragged her reluctant daughter to the wedding of a friend. The band playing at the reception was the Miami Latin Boys. Emilio recognized Gloria and asked her to sing a couple of songs with them.

Emilio told Gloria there were no bands in Miami with a female vocalist, and invited her to join the group. It didn't fit in with her plans to go to school, so she turned him down. He told her to think about it and call him,

but she didn't return the call. Two weeks later he invited Gloria and her family to come see the band play and meet Emilio's family.

With her mother's support, Gloria decided it would be alright to just join the band on weekends and keep working on her psychology degree at the University of Miami. Soon after, Gloria was collaborating on songs and recording with the group. Their first single, *"Renecer,"* was released on a Miami label, Audio Latino.

A year later, she and Emilio started dating. In 1978, just as the band was taking off internationally, they were married. In 1979, Miami Sound Machine financed the recording of an album, which was eventually released by CBS for the Latin market. After recording some bilingual albums, with one side in English and one side in Spanish, CBS International decided the group should only record in Spanish.

In 1984, Miami Sound Machine had their first crossover hit. Recorded in English, "Dr. Beat" went to number six on the British chart. The same crossover success occurred in America in February, 1986, when "Conga" peaked at number 10. "Anything for You," their eighth chart single, was recorded in three different versions: all-English, all-Spanish and a combination of the two, in "Spanglish."

---

## THE TOP FIVE
### *Week of May 14, 1988*

1  **Anything for You**
   Gloria Estefan and Miami Sound Machine

2  **Shattered Dreams**
   Johnny Hates Jazz

3  **Wishing Well**
   Terence Trent D'Arby

4  **One More Try**
   George Michael

5  **Pink Cadillac**
   Natalie Cole

COLUMBIA 07773 **One More Try** 699
GEORGE MICHAEL

*Writer: George Michael*

*Producer: George Michael*

*May 28, 1988*
*3 weeks*

"ONE MORE TRY" was George Michael's seventh number one single in three-and-a-half years [see 598—"Wake Me Up Before You Go-Go"] and his third consecutive number one from his *Faith* album.

Adam White, writing in *Rolling Stone*, pointed out that Michael's success on the black charts "reflects black/urban radio's continued willingness to include black-oriented records by white performers in their music mix—a trend begun in earnest during the disco radio explosion of the late '70s—as well as shrewd marketing by Michael's label, Columbia Records." White also mentioned that Michael wanted to be "fully briefed on the progress of *Faith* on the black charts."

While appearing in Frankfurt, Germany, Michael said, "One of the more remarkable things about my career in America has been that from day one black audiences accepted me, without a question, as a singer, songwriter and performer. They didn't really allow the stigma that was attached to wearing shorts and having the screaming get in the way. Credibility meant a different set of things in America and black acceptance was my consolation for America."

In an interview with Chris Heath, Michael called "One More Try" "the best thing I've ever done. (It's) about my attitude coming out of my last relationship and into this new one when I was pretty unwilling to be open to anything." In a biography issued by his record company, George acknowledged, "The best songs are my ballads. I will probably be remembered for my ballads over the next five or 10 years. While 'Careless Whisper' [see 602] was loved by many, it did nothing for me emotionally. Most likely because it seems like it's from another lifetime. On the other hand, 'One More Try' is a ballad very close to my heart. Many people compare the two. But for me, there is no comparison."

With seven number one singles to his credit, it's understandable that some might accuse Michael of being "commercial." He defended himself in an interview with the British magazine, Q. "I resent the fact that people think my song-writing is completely contrived and calculated," George said. "I only write in terms of commercial music because that's the way my mind works. You either have that sort of pop sensibility or feel for a commercial melody or you don't. You can't write songs on a business level. You just write songs the way they come out. Sure, you draw on influences but that's more often than not a subconscious process. Everybody does it."

George had his defenders in the press. The week "One More Try" went to number one on the *Billboard* Hot 100, Stephen Holden of the *New York Times* said, "If asked to nominate the one contemporary pop star most likely to be as successful 10 years from now as today, I'd cast my vote for George Michael. . . . (He) has everything a pop star requires for longevity. An avid student of American pop-soul music, he possesses a strong enough white voice to have held his own in a duet with Aretha Franklin [see 664— "I Knew You Were Waiting (For Me)"]. . . . At the same time, his voice has a vestigial teen-idol sob that complements his furry-eyebrowed, pugnosed good looks. . . . But the most important factors in Mr. Michael's longevity are his extraordinary skills as a songwriter, arranger and producer. Able to write in almost any contemporary pop style, he is not reliant upon other songwriters for his material or upon outside producers for a sound."

## THE TOP FIVE
*Week of May 28, 1988*

1 **One More Try**
George Michael

2 **Shattered Dreams**
Johnny Hates Jazz

3 **Anything for You**
Gloria Estefan and Miami Sound Machine

4 **Naughty Girls (Need Love Too)**
Samantha Fox

5 **I Don't Want to Live Without You**
Foreigner

## 700 Together Forever RCA 8319
### RICK ASTLEY

*Writers: Mike Stock*
*Matt Aitken*
*Pete Waterman*

*Producers: Mike Stock*
*Matt Aitken*
*Pete Waterman*

*June 18, 1988*
*1 week*

MIKE STOCK and Matt Aitken first met in 1978, when Stock had a band called Mirage. "I had to sack my guitarist, who was constantly drunk," Mike explains. "Through a mutual contact, Matt's name was given to me and he turned up one evening to do a gig." Mike had a house with a basement big enough to contain a studio, so the two of them started writing songs and honing their production techniques. They didn't record commercially, but did play live music on BBC Radio.

"When Matt and I got together, something jelled in the way we thought . . . we share a common ideal of what pop music's all about," says Mike. Their first hit was "Whatever I Do (Wherever I Go)," which Hazell Dean recorded and took to number four on the British chart. "A band called Dead or Alive heard that record and loved it so much they rang us up and asked if we'd produce them," Mike recalls. That led to Stock and Aitken's first number one hit in England, "You Spin Me Round (Like a Record)."

In 1984, Stock and Aitken teamed up with Pete Waterman, who had a partnership with producer Peter Collins (Musical Youth, Nik Kershaw). The new team of Stock-Aitken-Waterman soon became a hit-making fac-

### THE TOP FIVE
*Week of June 18, 1988*

1  **Together Forever**
   Rick Astley

2  **One More Try**
   George Michael

3  **Foolish Beat**
   Debbie Gibson

4  **Dirty Diana**
   Michael Jackson

5  **Make It Real**
   The Jets

tory, providing hits for Mel and Kim ("Showing Out"), Samantha Fox ("Touch Me [I Want Your Body]"), Bananarama [see 646—"Venus"] and even the late actor Divine ("You Think You're a Man").

After Waterman saw Rick Astley perform at a workingman's club [see 693—"Never Gonna Give You Up"], Stock and Aitken had a chance to meet the young singer. "The first we knew of Rick was when he came down to the studio," says Mike. "I can remember him coming to work here as a tape operator. . . . We knew he could sing . . . (but) we just thought of him as a guy working and making the tea. But that was deliberate in that we were getting to know him, and he was very shy and needed to come out for himself. He ended up making tea for the other pop stars we were working with, so he kind of came out of his shell a bit.

"When we first heard his voice, Matt and I were as surprised as most people," says Mike. Matt remembers what he thought when he first heard a demo tape Rick had recorded: "I wasn't quite sure whether I liked (his voice) or not, to be honest. The thing we had was a very bad recording. It

was a demo tape done in a small studio. It was not a particularly pleasing sound even though it was powerful. . . . We both knew instinctively he had a recognizable voice."

Working in the studio with the inexperienced singer was not easy at first, Matt remembers. "Rick hadn't had a lot of studio experience, although he had a lot of live experience. But it was with bands, and recording in a studio is quite a different thing. Rick's an inspirational guy and he tends to want to give his all. We had to give him the benefit of our experience and (correct) one or two things that weren't quite right, and he probably wasn't used to that at first."

"Together Forever" was designed to be an obvious successor to "Never Gonna Give You Up," although in Britain two singles interceded ("Whenever You Need Somebody," "When I Fall in Love"). "When we'd done all the other (tracks) we listened to them and thought . . . people have already bought 'Never Gonna Give You Up,'" says Mike. "What else is there on (the album) that really does compare? We thought we needed ('Together Forever') to get home to people what Rick could be."

ATLANTIC 89109 **Foolish Beat**
DEBBIE GIBSON **701**

*Writer: Deborah Gibson*

*Producer: Deborah Gibson*

June 25, 1988
*1 week*

**W**HEN SHE succeeded Rick Astley at the top of the *Billboard* Hot 100 with "Foolish Beat," Debbie Gibson became the second artist (after Tiffany) born in the '70s to have a number one single. And while Peggy March retained the honor of being the youngest female singer to have a number one hit [see 128—"I Will Follow Him"], 17-year-old Debbie became the youngest female to write, record *and* produce a number one song. The day the song dropped from number one, she graduated with honors from Calhoun High School in Merrick, Long Island.

Debbie was born August 31, 1970, to Joe and Diane Gibson. At age two she wanted to play the guitar, but her hands were too small, so her parents gave her a ukulele. She took up classical piano at four, and a year later, wrote her first song—"Make Sure You Know Your Classroom," an ode to entering kindergarten. At six, Debbie won a piano competition playing "Für Elise." She started appearing in musical productions like *The Sound of Music, Annie Get Your Gun* and *South Pacific*, and performed in the children's chorus of the Metropolitan Opera. When she was 12, Debbie entered a songwriting contest sponsored by WOR radio in New York and, competing against mostly adults, won the first prize of $1,000 with "I Come from America."

Her parents gave her a Casio synthesizer as a confirmation present, and Debbie soon had a 12-track studio in her garage. She dubbed it Root Beer Rag Studios, after a favorite Billy Joel song. At 13, she wrote "Only in My Dreams" and signed a management deal with entertainment lawyer Doug Breitbart. He agreed to accept her as a client with the provision that she wouldn't work professionally until she turned 16.

"During that period, there was time for her to do nothing but learn," Breitbart stressed in *Billboard*. "She spent time with different people going over everything from her lyrics to learning about arranging, programming, sequencing, basic engineering and producing."

Debbie, who says she can write a song in 10 or 15 minutes, had 200 songs in the hopper when Breitbart sent out demo tapes to various record companies. Some of them passed and others, like Atlantic, told her to keep in touch. Although personnel at the label changed, Debbie took Atlantic at their word. "An introduction was made at Atlantic to Larry Yasgar, who was the head of the dance department," Debbie explains. "He listened to probably 50 songs—because I was so young, they wanted to make sure that I wasn't a fluke."

Atlantic signed her for one 12-inch single. "They released 'Only in My Dreams' to the clubs, and I did track dates but always sang live, never lip-synched." Debbie played clubs for nine months, and her single was issued in 7-inch format. "Finally 'Only in My Dreams' hit the pop charts, and they decided to do an album," the singer recalls. *Out of the Blue* was recorded quickly to capitalize on the success of "Only in My Dreams," which peaked at number four in September, 1987. After the album was released, Atlantic issued "Shake Your Love" as a follow-up single. It also peaked at number four in December. Then the title cut, "Out of the Blue," went to number three in April, 1988.

The fourth single—released almost a year after "Only in My Dreams" entered the chart—was a ballad, "Foolish Beat." Debbie reveals, "I didn't write it about anything in particular because I wrote it before I ever had a boyfriend. I was just imagining what it would be like to have a love and then lose a love, which is kind of funny, being that I had never experienced it. What ends up happening sometimes is, I'll write a song and then I'll be able to relate to it a couple years later."

The chorus to "Foolish Beat" came to Debbie while she was traveling on an airplane. "I got up and went to the bathroom and started singing it and writing it. I wrote the verses when I got home." "Foolish Beat" is the only track on *Out of the Blue* that she produced by herself. "I had written a letter to George Michael, saying, 'I would love for you to produce this song,' because he's one of my favorite producers. I didn't get a response and I said, 'Fine, I'll produce it myself' . . . I was real happy with the demo and the way the basic idea sounded, so I thought I had a grip on what I wanted it to sound like."

## THE TOP FIVE
*Week of June 25, 1988*

1 **Foolish Beat**
Debbie Gibson

2 **Dirty Diana**
Michael Jackson

3 **Together Forever**
Rick Astley

4 **Make It Real**
The Jets

5 **The Flame**
Cheap Trick

## 702 Dirty Diana EPIC 07739
### MICHAEL JACKSON

*Writer: Michael Jackson*

*Producer: Quincy Jones*

*July 2, 1988*
*1 week*

"To me, a song like 'Dirty Diana' is a very surrealistic vignette; it's a one-act play," producer Quincy Jones told Alan DiPerna in *Music & Sound Output.* When this "one-act play" about rock-star groupies went to number one, Michael Jackson became the first person in chart history to pull five number one singles from one album. He did it with the first five releases from *Bad*: "I Just Can't Stop Loving You," "Bad," "The Way You Make Me Feel," "Man in the Mirror" and "Dirty Diana."

"Michael initially had about 66 songs," Jones told DiPerna. "But by the time I came in, it had been narrowed down to somewhere between 33 and 36 songs, which in many ways is like having nothing. Too much can be the same as too little. I had my eye on 10, maybe 12, of those 33 songs."

Jones explained why he thought *Bad* was different from *Thriller.* "It's all about contrasts, you know. We had a lot of highly textured, very sophisticated harmonic structures on a lot of the songs on *Thriller.* So it was fun to go the other way. And I'm sure we had that in mind when we were selecting the final songs we were going to use. 'Let's really get raw,' we thought, 'and make Michael dig into another side of himself.'"

Michael gave some insight into his philosophy of creating an album like *Bad* in his autobiography, *Moonwalk.* "We don't ever try to pander to the

### THE TOP FIVE
*Week of July 2, 1988*

1 **Dirty Diana**
Michael Jackson

2 **Foolish Beat**
Debbie Gibson

3 **The Flame**
Cheap Trick

4 **Make It Real**
The Jets

5 **The Valley Road**
Bruce Hornsby & the Range

fans," he wrote. "We just try to play on the quality of the song. People will not buy junk. They'll only buy what they like. If you take all the trouble to get in your car, go to the record store, and put your money on the counter, you've got to really like what you're going to buy. You don't say, 'I'll put a country song on here for the country market, a rock song for that market,' and so on. I feel close to all different styles of music."

Michael had included a rock song on his *Thriller* album. "Beat It" [see 571] featured Eddie Van Halen on guitar, and on *Bad*, Michael invited another rock guitarist to back him up. Steve Stevens, known best for his guitar work on Billy Idol's records, played on "Dirty Diana." He talked about accepting Michael's offer in *Melody Maker.* "I was just curious, man. I just wanted to see if he was gonna walk in with the mask on and all this! Working with Quincy Jones was great because he's a real jazz head and he's got these great expressions. Like, I'd be playing behind the beat maybe and he'd get on the talkback on the other side of the glass and say, 'Steve, uh, could you put a little more custard in your cone, man?' And here I am, white-boy guitar player, going, 'What *does* he mean?' 'Play ahead of the beat man, on top of the groove.' 'Oh, okay, yeah!'"

"Dirty Diana" extended Quincy Jones' span of number one records to 25 years and one month, stretching back to Lesley Gore's "It's My Party" [see 130] on June 1, 1963. That's the longest span of any record producer in the rock era. Jones foreshadowed his breaking away from Michael in a March, 1990 interview in *Rhythm & News.* "I don't know if there will be another collaboration with us," he said. "We worked together for 10 years. There's not much more to prove. I'm headed toward another direction. I think Michael should really do his own thing now." Michael would take that advice to heart [see 801—"Black or White"].

Michael's incredible string of number one hits from *Bad* did not stretch to six. Epic followed "Dirty Diana" with "Another Part of Me," a song that first appeared on the soundtrack of the Captain Eo attraction at Disneyland and EPCOT. It peaked at number 11, the first new solo Michael Jackson single not to make the top 10 since his Epic debut, "You Can't Win (Part 1)" from the soundtrack of *The Wiz* in February, 1979. The seventh and final single from *Bad* was "Smooth Criminal," which went to number seven in January, 1989. In Europe, Jackson released two more singles: "Leave Me Alone" and "Liberian Girl."

*Writers: Bob Mitchell*
*Nick Graham*

*Producer: Richie Zito*

*July 9, 1988*
*2 weeks*

"THE FLAME" marked a return to glory for the quartet known as Cheap Trick, although it was a song they hated when they first heard the demo. "The band didn't want to do it, so we had some pretty good arguments over it," producer Richie Zito recalls. "It became a little crusade for me. We recorded it one guy at a time because the band wasn't happy about it. I started with Robin (Zander) and a keyboard player. I figured if I was going to expose the band to this song, it had better be as right for him as I thought. It became screamingly obvious that the song was tailor-made for him. And then one by one the rest of the guys came in and did it. When they played it for the label and their manager, everyone told them how great it was. They started embracing it a little bit more—it became more Cheap Trick as the record progressed."

Nick Graham and Bob Mitchell had written songs in England for Sinitta, Toyah Wilcox and the group Imagination. "We were writing a song for Elkie Brooks," says Graham. "I was producing a track for her album of a song we'd written and she asked me to write another song. So Bob and I came up with 'The Flame,' and she didn't like it. Her record company went mad because they thought it was an amazing song. But she refused to record it, and we were already halfway through producing it for her. So I put a vocal on it myself, and we mixed it and sent it out to a few people."

The demo found its way to Don Grierson, a former Capitol Records executive hired to be senior vice president of A&R for Epic. Perusing the label's roster, he decided that Cheap Trick had been overlooked for too long. He asked Zito to produce a new album for the group. "The songwriters who wrote 'The Flame' and demoed it were certainly talented fellows," the producer acknowledges.

When "The Flame" was released as the first single from *Lap of Luxury*, Cheap Trick had not had a top 10 single since "I Want You to Want Me"

peaked at number seven in July, 1979. "I think it reaffirmed our faith in ourselves," bassist Tom Petersson told Keith Sharp in *Music Express*. "It was so good to have people say, 'Yeah, we like your music.' I think the band had kind of lost that sense of appreciation."

Cheap Trick's origin can be traced back to 1961, when guitarist Rick Nielsen, of Rockford, Illinois, had a succession of bands like the Phaetons, the Boyz, the Grim Reapers and then Fuse, which included Petersson. They had one album released on Epic in 1969. Another Rockford musician, Brad Carlson, later known as Bun E. Carlos, joined Fuse as a drummer. The group relocated to Philadelphia under the name Sick Man of Europe. They returned to Rockford and in 1973 formed Cheap Trick, adding vocalist Robin Zander of Loves Park, Illinois.

Epic signed the band in 1977 and released an eponymously titled album. After *In Color* and *Heaven Tonight*, the quartet recorded a live album in Japan meant only for release in that country. But *Cheap Trick at Budokan* was so popular as an import, Epic decided to issue it in the States. "I Want You to Want Me" had been released as a single twice previously; it was the live version from *Budokan* that gave them their first top 10 hit.

Cheap Trick remained strong through the rest of the '70s, but hit some rough times in the '80s. Petersson left after the George Martin-produced *All Shook Up* (and was replaced by Pete Comita, then by Jon Brant). Epic rejected an entire album in 1981. *One on One, Next Position Please* and *The Doctor* all failed to repeat former chart successes. But Petersson met up with his old bandmates while they were mixing *The Doctor* in 1986 and rejoined before *Lap of Luxury* was recorded.

Cheap Trick was looking for a new label deal when Grierson reaffirmed Epic's commitment. "The Flame" was the last song recorded for *Lap of Luxury*. And while the band wanted to step on the demo the first time they heard it, they learned to love the song. "We wish we'd written it because we know we had songs that were just as good," Nielsen told Cary Darling of *The Orange County Register*. "But to play 'What if?' is kind of silly. We're happy we had a success with it."

## THE TOP FIVE
*Week of July 9, 1988*

1  **The Flame**
   Cheap Trick

2  **Mercedes Boy**
   Pebbles

3  **Pour Some Sugar on Me**
   Def Leppard

4  **New Sensation**
   INXS

5  **Dirty Diana**
   Michael Jackson

## 704 Hold On to the Nights EMI-MANHATTAN 50106
### RICHARD MARX

*Writer: Richard Marx*

*Producers: Richard Marx*
*David Cole*

*July 23, 1988*
*1 week*

Growing up in Chicago, Richard Marx was surrounded by music: his mother was a singer, and his father was a jazz pianist who wrote and produced commercial jingles for clients like Peter Pan Peanut Butter and Nestle's Chocolate. "Music was flying through my house at all times, and my dad was responsible for writing 30-second hits," Marx told Steve Korté in *CD Review*. "My mom ended up singing on a lot of those things, and then I did it too when I was a little kid. It was a great training ground for me to be in the studio."

Before reaching his teens, Marx picked up the guitar, then found he preferred keyboards. At 15, his friends were interested in baseball, but Marx started writing songs to im-press girls in high school (it didn't work, he confesses). He loved song-writing, and made demo tapes to send to record companies. "One of the tapes wound up in Lionel Richie's hands," Marx told Pat Lewis.

Richie invited Marx to come to Los Angeles and offered him work singing backing vocals. Just 18 when he arrived in Southern California, Marx sang for Lionel on tracks like "You Are," "All Night Long (All Night)" [see 580], and "Running With the Night."

"After I had done Lionel's album, I had a long period of time where I didn't have anything to do," Marx told Korté. "It was pretty rough, but I started to take my songs around and get more background vocal session work, and little by little I became a session singer and songwriter and ar-ranger." With David Foster and Kenny Rogers, Marx co-wrote "What About Me?," which was recorded by Rogers with Kim Carnes and James Ingram. It went to number 15 in No-vember, 1984. Marx also co-wrote

"Crazy" for Rogers, as well as songs for Chicago and Philip Bailey.

He wasn't so well-received as an artist—every record company turned him down. Richard said in *People* that he hit a low point when David Foster "looked at me one day and said, 'You're never going to get a record. You're not an artist.' When you hear that from somebody you really care about, it's devastating. I felt like collapsing."

When Foster spoke at a songwriter's seminar in Canada, Marx attended and met A&R veteran Bobby Colom-by, who was working as an advisor to Manhattan Records. Colomby set up an appointment for Marx to audition for the head of the label. "I was real nervous," Marx told Robyn Flans in *Pulse!* "And Bobby said, 'Just sit down at the piano and play and sing.' I said, 'Bobby, what are you doing to me? I can't sing rock 'n' roll songs at the pi-ano.' I sat down and played one up-tempo thing that was really difficult to play on the piano and a rock and roll ballad . . . then I played the demo tape and Bruce Lundvall stood up and said, 'Welcome to Manhattan Records.'"

David Cole, whose credits included Bob Seger's *Like a Rock*, was called in to co-produce Marx' label debut. The first single, "Don't Mean Nothing," de-scribed the struggle of an aspiring musician, and peaked at number three in August, 1987. The follow-up, "Should've Known Better," reached number three in December. "Endless Summer Nights," the third single, went to number two in March, 1988.

Marx had his first number one hit with "Hold On to the Nights," the fourth single from his debut album. He was 22 when he wrote it.

### THE TOP FIVE
*Week of July 23, 1988*

1 **Hold On to the Nights**
Richard Marx

2 **Pour Some Sugar on Me**
Def Leppard

3 **New Sensation**
INXS

4 **Roll With It**
Steve Winwood

5 **The Flame**
Cheap Trick

**Roll With It**
STEVE WINWOOD

**705**

*Writers: Steve Winwood*
*Will Jennings*

*Producers: Steve Winwood*
*Tom Lord Alge*

*July 30, 1988*
*4 weeks*

"I WOULD never have believed someone who told me 10 years ago that I was going to have my biggest record ever when I was 40," Steve Winwood told Anthony DeCurtis in *Rolling Stone*. "Roll With It," released shortly after Winwood celebrated his 40th birthday on May 12, 1988, spent four weeks atop the *Billboard* Hot 100, the longest run of any number one single in 1988.

Winwood, who joined the Spencer Davis Group when he was 15, left that group in 1967 to form Traffic. When they signed with Island Records, Winwood began what would be a 20-year association with Chris Blackwell's label, taking him through the album *Back in the High Life* [see 645—"Higher Love"]. In 1987, Winwood signed a deal reportedly worth $13 million with Virgin Records. "I didn't say, 'I want to leave Island'—they were never excluded in any way," Winwood told Pete Clark in *Pulse!* "I just thought it was time to look at the options and see what other companies might do for me. I suppose changing record companies is a bit like changing insurance companies—there was no

lover's tiff involved, it's just a business arangement . . . it was simply time to go out and have a look."

Winwood asked Tom Lord Alge, an engineer on *Back in the High Life*, to produce his first album for Virgin, *Roll With It*. "Back in the High Life was a very successful album and we wanted to use various elements that we used on it," Winwood explained to Fred Goodman in *Rolling Stone*.

Having already recorded albums in Gloucestershire and New York, Winwood decided to record *Roll With It* in Toronto and Dublin. One of the songs recorded in the former city was the title track, "Roll With It," written with Will Jennings. Featuring Memphis Horns musicians Wayne Jackson on trumpet and Andrew Love on saxophone, the song reflected Winwood's growing interest in the musical history of the South. He moved to Tennessee after his marriage to Nashville native Eugenia Crafton in 1987.

"I think 'Roll With It' harks back to the music that I was listening to when I grew up and when I started playing music," Winwood told Goodman. "It's probably more like the kind of thing that I might have done with Spencer Davis." Winwood had been influenced by reading Peter Guralnick's *Sweet Soul Music*. "Nashville's generally known for its country music. But a lot of these (rhythm and blues) people are down there, and I started to explore and understand more of the history of

American music and of soul and '60s horn music."

The follow-up to "Roll With It" was "Don't You Know What the Night Can Do?" It peaked at number six in October, but not without some controversy. The song was licensed to Michelob, joining songs like Eric Clapton's "After Midnight" and Genesis' "Tonight, Tonight, Tonight" in the company's "The Night Belongs to Michelob" campaign. Some people charged Winwood with writing a song specifically to sell beer.

"There are two aspects to this," Winwood told DeCurtis. "The first one is whether the music that I'm doing is worse because they're involved in it. Are they paying me to write or to record something that's of inferior quality? I mean, I wrote a seven-minute song. Okay, they used 50 seconds of it. Fine. The edits were theirs, although I approved them . . . (the song) had the word 'night' in it, but so have other songs I've done. They knew that. There's no way that their involvement made me present a lower-quality product . . . The thing I want to do as a musician is to reach more people with my music. If they can use part of it on a commercial, then I'm reaching potentially more people."

The third single from *Roll With It*, "Holding On," peaked at number 11 in January, 1989. "Hearts on Fire" was next; it fizzled out at number 53 in April. In 1990, Winwood released the second album on his Virgin contract, *Refugees of the Heart*. All of the tracks were co-written with Jennings except for the lead-off single. "One And Only Man"—written with Winwood's ex-Traffic mate Jim Capaldi—peaked at number 18 in December.

## THE TOP FIVE
*Week of July 30, 1988*

1 **Roll With It**
Steve Winwood

2 **Hold On to the Nights**
Richard Marx

3 **Hands to Heaven**
Breathe

4 **Pour Some Sugar on Me**
Def Leppard

5 **Make Me Lose Control**
Eric Carmen

### 706 Monkey COLUMBIA 07941
### GEORGE MICHAEL

*Writer: George Michael*

*Producers: George Michael*
*Jimmy Jam*
*Terry Lewis*

*August 27, 1988*
*2 weeks*

"MONKEY" was the fourth consecutive number one single from George Michael's *Faith*. It entered the Hot 100 on July 9, 1988, and was number one seven weeks later. Including his hits as half of Wham!, it was the eighth chart-topper of his career.

The earlier number one hits were all self-produced, but for the single of "Monkey" George turned to Minneapolis-based producers Jimmy Jam and Terry Lewis, who had already produced number one hits for Janet Jackson [see 649—"When I Think of You"] and the Human League [see 652—"Human"]. Jam explains why they were called in. "On Janet Jackson's *Control* album, we did the first four remixes: 'What Have You Done for Me Lately,' 'Nasty,' 'When I Think of You' and the live version of 'Control.' In London, there was a release called *More Control*, which was the remixes we had done for the *Control* album. And there was a version of 'Nasty' on there that George Michael liked a lot. He liked it because he's into chords. But whenever you put chords on something, it's hard to make it funky. And he observed on the version of 'Nasty' that we had put chords on it (and) somehow kept the funk in. He said that 'Monkey' was a song he'd always envisioned as a little more melodic and had chords, but when he recorded it there was a deadline, and he didn't put the time into it that he wanted. So he said to us, 'If you were going to produce "Monkey," how would you do it?' "

But Jam and Lewis didn't remix the album track. "We totally recut the song from scratch," according to Jam. "We did the skeleton of the track in Minneapolis. Then we went to Los Angeles and George re-sang the vocals. We would have done it in Minneapolis, but he had been on vacation in the islands, and he didn't want to go from 90 degrees to 10 below zero. It took us about a week to do the vocals. He was in rehearsals for his tour, so between rehearsals he would run to the studio, do his thing for a couple of hours, go back to rehearsals, and so forth.

"After we got the vocals we needed, we actually sampled some of the vocals from the old version and combined them with the new version, which he sang a lot more funky." Returning home, Jam and Lewis discovered they didn't like the sound of the drum machine they had used on the track: they wanted "Monkey" to have more of a live sound. Jam, a former drummer, played drum pads for the track, and Vaughn Halyard, a Synclavier programmer, corrected some of the drum machine parts. "So the song has a very live feel to it. We knew he was going to do a live video for the song, so it worked out great. It was a lot of fun because George Michael is very talented—not only as a vocalist, but his conceptual ideas are great. He knows how he wants something to sound."

Although George had worked with producer Narada Michael Walden [see 664—"I Knew You Were Waiting (For Me)"], most of the time he produced his own records. "It's really hard to produce yourself," Jam contends. "I admire people who do it. We tend to like first takes and mistakes. I think it's cool to have a little bit of a mistake here or there, or a little bit of vulnerability in the vocals. A lot of times, we'll go for the feel of the vocal (rather) than the note, and I think that's what happened with his vocal. There are some—as he would call them—dodgy notes on there, but it doesn't matter. It fits what the track is doing, and I think it sounds great."

According to a CBS press release, "Monkey" was the first single in the company's history to be released in six different configurations: two each in vinyl, cassette and compact disc.

The follow-up to "Monkey" was "Kissing a Fool," the sixth single from *Faith*. It peaked at number five in November of 1988, making it the lowest-ranked track from the album ("I Want Your Sex," the initial release, peaked at number two).

## THE TOP FIVE
*Week of August 27, 1988*

1 **Monkey**
George Michael

2 **I Don't Wanna Go On With You Like That**
Elton John

3 **I Don't Wanna Live Without Your Love**
Chicago

4 **Sweet Child o' Mine**
Guns n' Roses

5 **Simply Irresistible**
Robert Palmer

GEFFEN 27963 **Sweet Child o' Mine**
GUNS N' ROSES

*Writers: Guns n' Roses*

*Producer: Mike Clink*

*September 10, 1988*
*2 weeks*

"SWEET CHILD O' MINE" was inspired by Erin Everly, daughter of Don Everly [see 28—"Wake Up Little Susie"], and girlfriend of Axl Rose at the time he wrote the song. "I had written this poem, reached a dead end with it and put it on the shelf," Axl stated in a press release. "Then Slash and Izzy got working together on songs and I came in, Izzy hit a rhythm, and all of a sudden the poem popped into my head. It just all came together. A lot of rock bands are too . . . wimpy to have any sentiment or any emotion in any of their stuff unless they're in pain. It's the first positive love song I've ever written, but I never had anyone to write anything that positive about, I guess."

Rose told Robert Hilburn of the *Los Angeles Times* that "the 'blue sky' line actually was one of my first childhood memories—looking at the blue sky and wishing I could disappear in it because it was so beautiful."

The single of "Sweet Child o' Mine" was an edit of the album track on *Appetite for Destruction*, and Rose expressed his feelings about the short version to Del James in *Rolling Stone*. "I hate the edit of 'Sweet Child o' Mine.' Radio stations said, 'Well, your vocals aren't cut.' My favorite part of the song is Slash's slow solo; it's the heaviest part for me. There's no reason for it to be missing except to create more space for commercials, so the

radio station owners can get more advertising dollars. When you get the chopped version of 'Paradise City' or half of 'Sweet Child' and 'Patience' cut, you're getting screwed."

Axl and Erin were married on April 27, 1990, at Cupid's Wedding Chapel in Las Vegas. On May 24, Rose filed for divorce, citing irreconcilable differences. The couple tried to get back together, but separated again. In January, 1991, Rose was granted an annulment. In discussing his anger against women with Kim Neely in *Rolling Stone*, he acknowledged, "I had an extremely volatile relationship with Erin."

Axl Rose was born and raised in Lafayette, Indiana, where he was known as William Bailey, the son of Sharon and L. Stephen Bailey. At five, he was singing in church. His Pentecostal parents forbade him to listen to evil music like rock and roll, but in sixth grade, Axl won a radio and listened to it secretly. As a teenager, he was considered a juvenile delinquent and was arrested more than 20 times. When he was 17, he learned that Stephen Bailey was his stepfather, and that his real father's last name was Rose. He decided to take the name W. Rose; at the suggestion of friends, he took the name Axl from one of the bands he was in. Later, he would legally change his name to W. Axl Rose.

One of Axl's best friends was guitarist Jeff Isabell, later known as Izzy Stradlin. They formed a punk band in

a town where the bars only featured country music or groups playing rock and roll covers. Izzy moved to Chicago and Indianapolis before settling in Los Angeles. On Easter of 1979, Axl knocked on Izzy's door after living in L.A. for a month. They eventually formed a band called Hollywood Rose. When they ran an ad for another guitarist in *The Recycler*, it was answered by Slash, born Saul Hudson in Stoke-on-Trent, England. His mother was Ola Hudson, a costume designer who worked with Diana Ross, David Bowie and the Pointer Sisters. His father was Anthony Hudson, an artist who designed album covers for Joni Mitchell and Neil Young.

Axl and Izzy turned Slash down at first. "We kept bumping into each other in clubs," Axl told Daina Darzin in *Circus*. "Then Izzy quit, we broke up, then Izzy was in L.A. Guns, Slash and Steve (Adler) had been playing with Duff (McKagan), that broke up, Duff moved across the street from Izzy, brought him in, and all of a sudden it was the same five guys."

They thought about calling themselves Heads of Amazon or AIDS before settling on Guns n' Roses. Teresa Ensenat and Tom Zutaut of Geffen Records' A&R staff found the band living in a seedy one-room apartment in Hollywood. Zutaut signed them to the label for a $75,000 advance—although the group continued to be courted by other labels because they enjoyed being taken out for dinner.

---

### THE TOP FIVE
*Week of September 10, 1988*

1 **Sweet Child o' Mine**
Guns n' Roses

2 **Simply Irresistible**
Robert Palmer

3 **Perfect World**
Huey Lewis and the News

4 **Monkey**
George Michael

5 **When It's Love**
Van Halen

## 708 Don't Worry, Be Happy
EMI-MANHATTAN 50146

BOBBY McFERRIN

*Writer: Bobby McFerrin*

*Producer: Linda Goldstein*

*September 24, 1988*
*2 weeks*

As a committed Democrat and supporter of Michael Dukakis in the 1988 Presidential race, Bobby McFerrin was not happy that Vice President George Bush was using his song "Don't Worry, Be Happy" as a campaign song. He asked his manager Linda Goldstein to file a protest, and she fired off a letter to Bush that read: "We were quite surprised at this unauthorized appropriation of Mr. McFerrin's rights. Indeed if anyone were to recognize the value of personal property rights, one would expect it to be the Republican Party. While we were amused that the Bush campaign would find its political philosophy reflected in the song 'Don't Worry, Be Happy,' we do not wish to have the composition associated with any presidential candidate." Even after the letter was sent, Goldstein reported getting a phone call from the White House asking McFerrin to accompany Bush in California and have dinner with him. On behalf of her client, she declined.

"Don't Worry, Be Happy" was the first *a cappella* song to reach number one on the *Billboard* Hot 100. "It was just something that I started improvising on, probably four or five years ago," McFerrin told Dick Clark on "Countdown America." "And I didn't have any lyrics—I just had the phrase 'Don't Worry, Be Happy.' Occasionally I would sing it in clubs and make up a

### THE TOP FIVE
*Week of September 24, 1988*

1. **Don't Worry, Be Happy**
   Bobby McFerrin

2. **Sweet Child o' Mine**
   Guns n' Roses

3. **I'll Always Love You**
   Taylor Dayne

4. **Simply Irresistible**
   Robert Palmer

5. **Love Bites**
   Def Leppard

lyric as I went along."

Bobby didn't plan to include it on his album *Simple Pleasures*, which at first was going to be made up of remakes of '60s songs. "I was working on another song and I got stuck. And I was looking for something to do to get unstuck. There was a piano close by and I started tinkling on 'Don't Worry, Be Happy.' My manager said, 'Why don't you work on that a little bit,' because it had been a song I had been in the process of writing for a few years and never really had something to finish it for."

The song has a light reggae touch to it, but McFerrin claims his vocal is not entirely Jamaican: "It's a cross between Jamaican and Juan's Mexican Restaurant just down the corner."

Soon after *Simple Pleasures* was released, Disney staffer Mitchell Leib and *Cocktail* music supervisor Carol Childs had lunch with Triad agent Joel Roman and told him they were looking for a Caribbean song for the film. Roman sent them a copy of McFerrin's album and recommended "Don't Worry, Be Happy." Leib played it for his boss, Chris Montan, senior vice president of music for Touchstone and Disney.

"We contacted EMI and said we would love to license it for our soundtrack," Montan says. "Bobby was still much more known as a jazz artist . . . not necessarily a top 40 type of artist. EMI was thinking it would be another nice means of exposure for him. I

don't think if you had put 10 people in a room, they would have ever said it was a number one song. Actually, it was becoming a hit about a week before the movie even came out. *Cocktail* put it over the top, but I also think it rang a universal chord with America. There were some floods going on at that point in Texas, and I was watching the news one night, and people were floating on the tops of the roofs of their houses holding up these big placards, 'Don't Worry, Be Happy.' When it gets into the vernacular of this society, you know you've got a big hit."

McFerrin was born March 11, 1950, in New York City. His father Robert was one of the first black singers at the Metropolitan Opera when he sang a major role in *Aida* in 1955. His mother Sara joined the voice department at Fullerton College when the family moved to Los Angeles. At six, Bobby began to study music theory. He formed the Bobby Mack Jazz Quintet in high school, and dropped out of college to play keyboards for the Ice Follies. He was thinking of becoming an Episcopalian minister when, in July, 1977, a voice inside of him said he should sing. He immediately found work performing in the piano bar of the Salt Lake City Hilton. Bill Cosby recommended him for a solo spot at the Playboy Jazz Festival in 1980 and later asked him to sing the theme for "The Cosby Show."

MERCURY 870 402-7 **Love Bites**
DEF LEPPARD

**709**

*Writers: Steve Clark*
*Phil Collen*
*Joe Elliott*
*Robert John "Mutt" Lange*
*Rick Savage*

*Producer: Robert John "Mutt" Lange*

*October 8, 1988*
*1 week*

DEF LEPPARD had to overcome so many crises in the life of the band that an April, 1992 cover story in *Musician* was accompanied by the banner, "The Curse of Def Leppard." The story was about their triumphs over adversity, including the amputation of their drummer's arm and the sudden death of their guitarist.

Def Leppard was born in the working-class city of Sheffield in South Yorkshire, England, in 1977, when vocalist Joe Elliott and guitarist Pete Willis joined Atomic Mass, a heavy-metal band led by bassist Rick Savage. Elliott, inspired to pursue a career in music at age 11 when he saw Marc Bolan on "Top of the Pops," suggested they change their name to Deaf Leopard. The band agreed, with an alteration in spelling. Steve Clark, a mate of Willis at Stannington College, joined the group as a second guitarist, and they specialized in cover versions of songs by Thin Lizzy and UFO.

Elliott's father loaned them enough money to record a three-track EP at Fairview Studios in Kingston-Upon-Hull. *Getcha Rocks Off* was released in November on their own label, Bludgeon Riffola. Drummer Rick Allen joined the group after the EP was recorded—at 15, he was the youngest

in a band where no one was older than 19.

After Radio Hallam played their EP, Def Leppard was invited to appear on John Peel's show on BBC's Radio 1. That led to Phonogram re-releasing the EP and offering Def Leppard a contract in August, 1979. Their first album, *On Through the Night*, was issued in March of 1980. The follow-up, *High 'n' Dry*, was produced by Mutt Lange, who also helmed the third album, *Pyromania*. That album gave Def Leppard their first Hot 100 entry, "Photograph," which peaked at number 12 in May, 1983. During the recording of *Pyromania*, Willis was fired by the group and replaced with Phil Collen, former guitarist with the punk glam-rock band Girl.

Def Leppard started work on their fourth album in 1984, renting a house in Dublin and installing a portable studio. Lange, who had just completed production of the Cars' *Heartbeat City*, was exhausted from a long period of work without a break. He told the band he would assist with pre-production, but wouldn't be available to produce the album.

The band turned to Jim Steinman, who wrote songs for Meat Loaf and produced epic wall-of-sound recordings for Bonnie Tyler [see 578—"Total Eclipse of the Heart"], Air Supply, Barry Manilow and Barbra Streisand. "Steve and Phil wanted to get rid of

Steinman after about three-and-a-half hours," Elliott said in *Pulse!* In December, they let him go, and decided to produce themselves after taking a break for Christmas.

On the last day of 1984, Rick Allen and his girlfriend went for a drive in his Corvette. A few miles out of Sheffield, Allen lost his temper and tried to pass another car on a sharp bend in the motorway. The Corvette turned over, and Allen's left arm was severed. While in the hospital, he was inspired to drum with his foot. "The day that Rick came back . . . was the day this band came back to life," Elliott said in *Rock Express*. "He was brilliant, so positive. It really inspired us to snap out of it and not let ourselves down."

Lange, meanwhile, had sufficiently rested and was back in the producer's chair. Elliott caught the mumps and temporarily lost his voice. Lange shattered his kneecap in an automobile accident. But by January, 1987, the sessions for *Hysteria* were complete. The fifth single from the album was the ballad "Love Bites," and it was the only track on *Hysteria* to feature keyboards. "Love Bites" debuted on the Hot 100 at number 52 the week of August 13, and eight weeks later, the song was number one.

On January 8, 1991, Steve Clark was found dead in his flat in the Chelsea section of London. The coroner's report listed cause of death as a fatal mixture of alcohol and drugs.

## THE TOP FIVE
*Week of October 8, 1988*

1 **Love Bites**
Def Leppard

2 **Red Red Wine**
UB40

3 **Don't Worry, Be Happy**
Bobby McFerrin

4 **Don't Be Cruel**
Cheap Trick

5 **One Good Woman**
Peter Cetera

## 710 Red Red Wine A&M 1244
### UB40

*Writer: Neil Diamond*

*Producers: UB40*
*Ray "Pablo" Falcone*

*October 15, 1988*
*1 week*

Guy ZAPOLEON, a program director with a reputation for picking hits, was working at KZZP-FM in Phoenix, Arizona in the summer of 1988 when two members of his staff, Todd Fisher and Gene Baxter, brought the song "Red Red Wine" by UB40 to his attention. "One of the things I've always used throughout my career is what I call 'Would've Been, Should've Beens,'" says Zapoleon. "If the current music wasn't up to snuff or even if that month's music wasn't up to snuff, I would dig into a pile of songs that I thought *should* have been a hit."

Zapoleon knew that the UB40 song had already charted at number 34 in

## THE TOP FIVE
*Week of October 15, 1988*

1  **Red Red Wine**
   UB40

2  **Love Bites**
   Def Leppard

3  **Groovy Kind of Love**
   Phil Collins

4  **Don't Be Cruel**
   Cheap Trick

5  **What's on Your Mind
   (Pure Energy)**
   Information Society

March, 1984, but felt it hadn't realized its true potential. So he started playing it again in 1988 on a Saturday night show called "Party Patrol." When the requests came in hot and heavy, he moved it to full-time rotation and the record took off.

Zapoleon urged A&M to re-release "Red Red Wine," but the label was resistant because they were busy promoting the band's latest album. When other radio stations around the country added "Red Red Wine" instead of the new single "Breakfast in Bed," the label decided to go with the older song.

"Red Red Wine" first appeared on the Hot 100 in April, 1968, when its composer recorded it. Released on Bang, Neil Diamond's version peaked at number 62. "We'd never heard of the Neil Diamond version," UB40's Robin Campbell reveals. "We had no idea Neil Diamond had anything to do with it. The only version we were aware of was the Tony Tribe version." Tribe, a Jamaican artist, recorded the song in 1969; in August of that year, it peaked at number 46 on the U.K. chart. UB40 recorded it on their first album of cover versions, *Labour of Love*.

All eight members of the British band UB40 grew up in Basall Heath, a poor area of Birmingham populated by West Indians, Asian Indians, blacks and whites. Most of the group were friends of Robin's younger brother, Ali. "From the age of 10, all I ever heard was reggae," Robin says.

Robin details the origin of the band: "Ali was the catalyst. He got injured in a bar fight—he had a pint glass smashed into his face." The incident

took place at the Red Lion pub on Ali's 17th birthday. He had 90 stitches on the left side of his face and a corneal implant. After a month in the hospital, he was awarded Criminal Injuries Compensation. "That's what started the band. When he got the money, he bought a set of drums and a couple of guitars, and we went from there."

The eight-member outfit named themselves after the registration form for the dole. "Unemployment Benefits, that's what the UB stands for," says Robin. "It's form 40. It's the identification card with your national insurance number on it so you can claim your unemployment benefits every week. It made a lot of sense to us . . . we were all unemployed. It wasn't even an idea of ours. A friend suggested it and it seemed very fitting."

UB40 had performed about 30 times when they got their break. "Chrissie Hynde of the Pretenders—she had a number one single at the time, 'Brass in Pocket,' in the U.K.—heard us playing in a pub in London and asked if we'd like to play on her tour," Robin recalls. "From playing pub gigs, we were suddenly on a national tour opening for a number one act. We recorded and released a single while we were on that tour." In the spring of 1980, UB40 had a two-sided hit in the U.K. with "King" (dedicated to Martin Luther King) and "Food for Thought" on the independent Graduate label, run by David and Susan Virr from their record store in Dudley in the West Midlands. A year later, the group formed their own label, DEP International, and on September 3, 1983, they topped the British chart with "Red Red Wine."

ATLANTIC 89017 **Groovy Kind of Love**

PHIL COLLINS

**711**

*Writers: Toni Wine*
*Carole Bayer Sager*

*Producers: Phil Collins*
*Anne Dudley*

*October 22, 1988*
*2 weeks*

PHIL COLLINS' acting career began when he was a youngster growing up in Chiswick, London. He was cast as the Artful Dodger in a stage production of *Oliver.* When his role in a children's film was cut to almost nothing, "I vowed never to do any more acting again," the drummer told Jay Sharbutt in the *Los Angeles Times.*

In 1984, Collins' song "In the Air Tonight" was heard in the soundtrack of the premiere of "Miami Vice." In 1986, series executive producer Michael Mann saw Collins in concert and created the role of Phil the Shill for an episode. When director David Green saw that episode of "Miami Vice" in London, he decided Collins should play the lead role in his film *Buster,* based on Buster Edwards' role in Britain's Great Train Robbery of 1963.

Collins didn't want to be involved in the music for the film's soundtrack, but changed his mind after asking his friend Lamont Dozier to participate [see 719—"Two Hearts"]. One of the songs on the soundtrack came to Phil via another friend, Stephen Bishop [see 624—"Separate Lives"]. "Stephen told this to me and so did Phil, so I know it's the gospel truth," says songwriter Toni Wine. "Stephen did a version of 'Groovy Kind of Love' and he wanted Phil to produce the song. So he did his own little demo of it. And Phil said, 'I love you, Bish, but I'd really love to do this song myself. In fact, I'm doing this movie *Buster* and it's the perfect time frame of where the movie takes place.' He did it for the movie and it was released as a single and it was huge. I love Stephen Bishop. I give him a million kisses and I thank him every day."

Toni was a teenager when her mother, a legal secretary at MGM Television in New York, told her daughter to go down to the fifth floor and visit the offices of MGM Records. "I met a bunch of people down there, and there were some people who asked me to do some demos for them . . . through Paul Kaufman [co-writer of "Poetry in Motion"] I met Donny Kirshner, and he signed me. He said that he thought I had something as a writer, and he loved my voice."

"I was signed at 15, which made me the youngest writer for Nevins/Kirshner and also the youngest writer signed to BMI." When she was 17, Toni was paired up with a high school English teacher just five years her senior as a writing partner. She hit it off immediately with Carole Bayer. "We wrote a bunch of songs and one of them was 'Groovy Kind of Love,'" Toni remembers. "It took 20 minutes to write that particular song. We were chuckling about the word 'groovy.' It was a new word and we jumped on it." Toni and Carole made a demo, and Kirshner submitted it to a British group he knew was looking for material. "We found out through Donny it was the Mindbenders' release. At the time we only knew . . . Wayne Fontana and the Mindbenders. Evidently Wayne split, and this would be their single." On June 4, 1966, Toni celebrated her birthday with a number one song—in another trade magazine. In *Billboard,* the song spent two weeks at number two.

When her publisher informed her that Collins had updated the song, Toni thought they were kidding. "It was unreal. I wanted to hear it . . . a friend of mine who was a disc jockey in Memphis got the record and called me live on the radio, which is dangerous because there's no telling what I could have said. I'm hearing it and I couldn't believe how great it was. It was as if I'd never heard the song before . . . his version is very intimate. And maybe that's why it does make me swallow hard even now when I hear it on the radio . . . it's a very touching record."

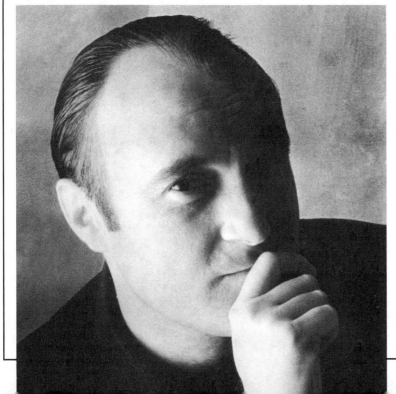

## THE TOP FIVE
*Week of October 22, 1988*

1 **Groovy Kind of Love**
Phil Collins

2 **Red Red Wine**
UB40

3 **What's On Your Mind (Pure Energy)**
Information Society

4 **Love Bites**
Def Leppard

5 **Wild, Wild West**
The Escape Club

## 712 Kokomo ELEKTRA 69385
### BEACH BOYS

*Writers: John Phillips*
*Mike Love*
*Terry Melcher*
*Scott McKenzie*

*Producer: Terry Melcher*

*November 5, 1988*
*1 week*

WHEN 1988 began, it wouldn't have been a good idea to bet that the Beach Boys would have a number one hit before the year was over. They hadn't had a top 10 single since 1976, or a number one song since 1966. They weren't even signed to a record label in 1988. Despite those odds, the Beach Boys had their fourth number one that year with "Kokomo," a song written for the Tom Cruise movie *Cocktail*.

When "Kokomo" went to number one, it gave the Beach Boys the longest span of number one hits in the rock era—24 years and four months elapsed between "I Get Around" [see 151] reaching number one and "Kokomo" going to the top of the chart. That beat the previous record of 23 years, 11 months and two weeks set by George Harrison [see 687—"Got My Mind Set on You"]. It also gave Terry Melcher the second longest span of number one hits as a producer—23 years, four months and one week, right behind Quincy Jones with 25 years and one month [see 702—"Dirty Diana"].

"I had been pitched the Beach Boys over the years, but I got a call from Terry Melcher, who was producing them, that he had a song he wanted us to hear," recalls Chris Montan, senior vice president of music for Touchstone

### THE TOP FIVE
*Week of November 5, 1988*

1 **Kokomo**
Beach Boys

2 **Wild, Wild West**
The Escape Club

3 **Groovy Kind of Love**
Phil Collins

4 **The Loco-Motion**
Kylie Minogue

5 **Bad Medicine**
Bon Jovi

and Disney. Dave Golden, then a William Morris agent, had been looking for movies that could use Beach Boys songs in their soundtracks and was instrumental in linking up the group with Montan.

"We read the script," says Mike Love of the Beach Boys. "I got the feeling and the mood of that section where Tom Cruise left New York for Jamaica. They played us the part of the film where the plane swoops in over Jamaica . . . we put in the tropical languid sounds of the steel drums and the congas. We flavored it like a tropical breeze.

"John Phillips came up with the word 'Kokomo.' He wrote the first verse: 'Off the Florida keys, there's a place called Kokomo/That's where we used to go to get away from it all.' But I changed it to 'That's where you wanna go.' He had another second verse, but I did a verse that I felt was compatible with the movie. That tense change was responsible in part for it appealing to a much wider demographic. The kids that voted it number one on the Nickelodeon channel didn't use to go anywhere—except maybe to nursery school. I came up with the 'Aruba, Jamaica' part. Terry Melcher came up with the 'Ooh, I wanna take you down to Kokomo/We'll get there fast, and then we'll take it slow' part, which Carl Wilson sang."

The Beach Boys, minus Brian

Wilson (who released a solo album in July, 1988), recorded a demo of the song. According to Moran, everyone who heard the demo loved it, "from the mailroom to the head of the costuming department. It was one of those universal songs."

"The funny thing," notes Love, "is that the powers-that-be at Elektra were initially against putting it out as a single. Finally it was issued as an Adult Contemporary single, and it built such a strong base of popularity that they finally turned it over to Contemporary Hit Radio. Ultimately, we got a letter from Disney Studios saying that in their opinion, it was 'Kokomo' that drove the album to the level of sales volume that it did attain."

Love believes that "Kokomo" helped broaden the audience for the Beach Boys. "It even got played on a major black AC station in Chicago. One of the reasons, I think, is because 'Smokey Joe's Cafe' (by the Robins) influenced me in the writing of the chorus. It has a kind of R&B groove to it." The Beach Boys' audience had already expanded when they recorded "Wipe Out" with the Fat Boys. "For a month or so, 'Wipe Out' was the number one requested song on MTV. That was outlandish for the Beach Boys and a bunch of kids from Brooklyn getting together and doing the world's first surf-rap tune—if you don't count 'Surfer Joe' by the Surfaris."

# Wild, Wild West
## THE ESCAPE CLUB

**713**

Steel remembers the day "Wild, Wild West" was written at Holliday's house. "We started off with a drum beat and we finished it within the day. It was a really quick song to write. I went home that night and wrote the lyrics . . . it wrote itself."

While Steel admits that "I didn't expect it to be a number one," he was shocked at the reaction of executives from the group's label. "We made that album for EMI in England; they paid for the album. They came down and heard 'Wild, Wild West' and said, 'Sorry, guys, we don't hear a hit.' By that time, we really believed in the song, so we started looking at other record companies. We knew it could be a hit. Atlantic saw it the same way . . . so we signed to them."

Although they had never charted at home in Britain, the Escape Club debuted on the *Billboard* Hot 100 on August 20, 1988, with "Wild, Wild West." "I thought it would be great if it's top 50 at first," says Steel. "(Then) I thought it would be great if it was top 40. Once it got in the top five, I was happy." Steel was in a London pub having a drink with a friend when he checked his answering machine at home and discovered he had the number one song in America. "I was *ecstatic* when it got to number one."

No one in the band had ever been to the States until they arrived to promote their hit. "We arrived in New York to do promotion and we got the big limo . . . we were driving over the bridge into Manhattan, seeing the skyline, and they were playing our song on the radio. It was an amazing feeling. I suddenly realized what we'd done. It was a huge country, and we had the number one single."

*Writers: The Escape Club*
*Producer: Chris Kimsey*

*November 12, 1988*
*1 week*

**W**HEN the British quartet called the Escape Club sang about the "Wild, Wild West," they weren't talking about the American frontier of the 19th century. "A lot of people thought it was about living in the Wild West," acknowledges lead singer Trevor Steel. "Actually, it was about living in the Western world when Thatcher was in power in England and Reagan was in power in the States. It was the idea that the whole Western world had become like a cowboy film, this big stand-off. Especially with Reagan in power, we found that quite amusing."

Along with guitarist John Holliday and bassist Johnnie Christo, Steel was raised in London. Drummer Milan Zekavica hailed from Leeds. Christo and Zekavica were playing in a band working the club circuit in London when they teamed up with Holliday and Steel to form the Escape Club.

The band released a single on an independent label and were booked on Channel 4's rock series "The Tube." That led to a deal with EMI and another single, "Rescue Me." Then came a tour with China Crisis and the Alarm and a debut album, *White*

*Fields*, which was not released in the United States. "The first album was rock-based. We ignored our influences . . . the fact that we all liked glam (rock). We were into a bit of dance and we tried to make a straight-down-the-line rock album. Unfortunately, at the time there was U2, Simple Minds— everybody was out doing the same thing, and we were just a small fish. It was time to sit back and think about what our influences really were."

The four members of the Escape Club decided to stop playing live and regroup before recording a second album. "We were playing to about 500 people per night, which isn't bad," Steel told Cary Darling in the *Orange County Register*. "But we got to a stage where we couldn't go any further because we weren't being played on the radio. With a reputation as a live band, you can only take that so far."

Through EMI, the band met producer Chris Kimsey, who had produced top 10 hits for the Rolling Stones ("Mixed Emotions," "Undercover of the Night") as well as chart singles for Peter Frampton ("I Can't Stand It No More") and the Psychedelic Furs ("Heartbreak Beat"). "Although we were trying to make a more accessible album this time, we wanted to keep the rock edge to it," Steel explains. "Chris had that rock background, especially with the Stones."

## THE TOP FIVE
*Week of November 12, 1988*

1  **Wild, Wild West**
   The Escape Club

2  **Kokomo**
   Beach Boys

3  **The Loco-Motion**
   Kylie Minogue

4  **Bad Medicine**
   Bon Jovi

5  **One Moment in Time**
   Whitney Houston

## 714   Bad Medicine   MERCURY 870 657-7
### BON JOVI

*Writers: Jon Bon Jovi*
*Richie Sambora*
*Desmond Child*

*Producer: Bruce Fairbairn*

*November 19, 1988*
*2 weeks*

"I HAVE this vision of taking Bon Jovi from the Beatles innocence of 'Yeah, yeah, yeah' to, like, *Sgt. Pepper*," Jon Bon Jovi told Lonn M. Friend in *Rip*. "That's where I am. When we did 'Bad Name' and 'Prayer' and 'Wanted,' it was great. It was wonderful. It's time now to move on, to *create* again. That's where I'm going. I want to think that's where the band's going, too."

After selling 13.5 million copies of *Slippery When Wet*, Bon Jovi returned to Little Mountain Sound Studios in Vancouver, British Columbia, to record their fourth album, *New Jersey*. Bruce Fairbairn was sitting in the producer's chair again, and Jon and

Richie Sambora collaborated once more with Desmond Child, the songwriter who worked with them on their first two number one hits, "You Give Love a Bad Name" [see 653] and "Livin' on a Prayer" [see 660].

"There was quite a bit of pressure on the band in terms of . . . trying to get the best songs possible," says Fairbairn. "When we made *Slippery*, it was a band struggling to make it from New Jersey, and there was that uneasiness about whether they're going to make it or not. Coming into *New Jersey*, they had a lot of confidence behind them, they were playing really well, and they were comfortable up at the studio in Vancouver. Everybody was still high from *Slippery*, and we had a lot of fun going into it."

Desmond Child was happy to be working with the band again. "We had common influences and references, so it was easy to agree on what we liked," he says. "And each person brought their own unique skill and sensibility to it. It was like a magic

combination—a lot of elements, not just me and Jon and Richie, but working with Bruce Fairbairn, and Bob Rock as the engineer."

Child found working on *New Jersey* a different experience than his first collaboration with Bon Jovi. "The first record was wonderful, because there was nowhere to go but up. Everyone was so fresh, they were innocent and so young. When I got together with them again for *New Jersey*, I was dealing with a whole other set of men. They really had matured, and also felt very pressured to beat the success they had last time. So it made the creative process much more difficult."

It was unusual for a group like Bon Jovi to be using an outside writer, according to Child. "It hadn't been common practice for rock bands to use outside writers, and they had gotten a lot of heat for doing so. But when I write with them, I think of myself as being in the band, and they think that way also. For *New Jersey*, they wrote for months without me; I think they felt like they had to prove they could do it on their own. They did have a number one song out of it without my influence [see 728—"I'll Be There for You"], so it's not like they can't. But it's just much easier when we write together, and I do think I bring something to the party."

Desmond came in at the last minute to work on *New Jersey*, and the band had already written a first draft of "Bad Medicine." "It was that one thing over and over again, and I came in and wrote that 'B' section that kind of lifted it. It was like a deceptive modulation. It sort of modulated down, then it modulated back up to the regular key, and it sounded like you went somewhere when you actually didn't. But it was one of those things where my fresh take on it helped the song move to another level."

Fairbairn remembers hearing the song for the first time when he was visiting Sambora's new home in New Jersey. "We were sitting around after dinner with a glass of wine and he played me 'Bad Medicine' on the acoustic and he said, 'Bruce, this is going to be a big song—I know it.' The chorus sounded great, and the verses were a little sketchy at that point. Sure enough, it came along when we started working the song up. When we recorded it, we had a really good feeling it was going to be a great song."

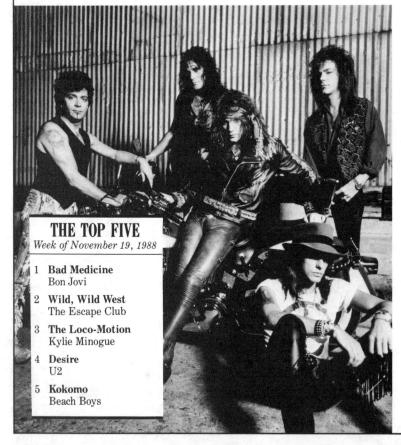

### THE TOP FIVE
*Week of November 19, 1988*

1. **Bad Medicine**
   Bon Jovi

2. **Wild, Wild West**
   The Escape Club

3. **The Loco-Motion**
   Kylie Minogue

4. **Desire**
   U2

5. **Kokomo**
   Beach Boys

EPIC 08034 **Baby, I Love Your Way/Freebird Medley (Free Baby)** **715**

WILL TO POWER

*Writers: Peter Frampton*
*Alan Collins*
*Ronnie Van Zandt*

*Producer: Bob Rosenberg*

*December 3, 1988*
*1 week*

Like Whitney Houston, Natalie Cole, Nelson and Wilson Phillips, Miami DJ Bob Rosenberg is a musical offspring. His mother, Gloria Mann, first hit the *Billboard* chart in 1955 with a version of "Earth Angel," and also charted with covers of "Teen Age Prayer" and "Why Do Fools Fall in Love."

Rosenberg, born in Philadelphia, attended high school and college in Florida. "I became a mobile DJ doing parties, bar mitzvahs and weddings and also worked in nightclubs," he says. "From there, I went to doing mixes on the radio." Rosenberg's edits were popular on Hot 105 in Miami.

He recorded a rap record, "Miami Vice," in 1985, but MCA frowned on his infringement of their copyright. He was attending a Winter Music Seminar in Ft. Lauderdale when he met Suzi Carr, who had co-written a couple of tracks for Miami Sound Machine's *Primitive Love*. "I was on one of the panels as a DJ and she was a local singer." She introduced herself, and Rosenberg told her he was looking for a vocalist.

He played her a song he had written called "Dreamin'." She didn't like the song, but agreed to sing backing vocals to his lead. Rosenberg released "Dreamin'" on his own Thrust label, and it became a regional hit in Miami.

It was picked up for national distribution by Epic Records, and the label asked Rosenberg if he had enough music for an album. "I said of course I do, but I didn't. That week I put my mind to music." He came up with another dance-club hit, "Say It's Gonna Rain," which featured Suzi on lead vocals.

He had all the songs for the album when he came up with the idea of a medley. "I was listening to music and a fan was on," he remembers. "And 'Baby, I Love Your Way' by Peter Frampton came on. From being a DJ, I hear correlations with different songs. And while the fan was on, I'm hearing 'Free Bird.'"

It was Christmas Day when Rosenberg decided to capture the Frampton/Lynyrd Skynyrd medley on tape. "Michael Caplan, the A&R guy from Epic, kept saying, 'Don't do it, the two songs together aren't going to work. If you want to do a remake, do one or the other—but don't put them together.'" Epic was not planning to release the medley as a single, "but I gave an advance tape to a radio station (in Miami), Power 96. They played it and a few other stations caught onto it, so Epic put it out."

Frampton's original recording of "Baby, I Love Your Way" peaked at number 12 in August, 1976; Lynyrd Skynyrd's "Free Bird" had gone to number 19 in January, 1975. Neither

act had ever had a number one single. Will to Power's medley entered the Hot 100 at number 97 the week of September 10, 1988, and went to number one 12 weeks later.

"I'm thrilled that someone covered it," Frampton announced in the *Los Angeles Times*. "I always thought it was a strong song. And it's definitely not hurting my situation. People can't seem to play the Will to Power record without saying, 'Oh yeah, remember the original' . . . having the song go to number one just gives me a very nice feeling to go upstairs to my little studio and write something else."

Will to Power was a trio when the medley hit number one, consisting of Rosenberg, Carr and a DJ known as Dr. J. When a second album, *Journey Home*, was released, Will to Power was a duo made up of Rosenberg and Elin Michaels, who had sung backing vocals on the first album.

Rosenberg explained the origin of the group name in the liner notes of *Journey Home*. "I borrowed the phrase from a friend of mine, Friedrich Wilhelm Nietzsche," he wrote. "He said, 'The first result of happiness is a sense of power . . . power contributes more to happiness than health, nourishment, home, entertainment. Even charity and self-sacrifice are motivated, paradoxically, by the same fixation, power.'"

## THE TOP FIVE
*Week of December 3, 1988*

1 **Baby, I Love Your Way/
 Freebird Medley (Free Baby)**
 Will to Power

2 **Look Away**
 Chicago

3 **How Can I Fall?**
 Breathe

4 **I Don't Want Your Love**
 Duran Duran

5 **Desire**
 U2

# 716 **Look Away** REPRISE 27766
CHICAGO

*Writer: Diane Warren*

*Producer: Ron Nevison*

*December 10, 1988*
*2 weeks*

**D**IANE WARREN was inspired to write "Look Away" after visiting a friend who worked in the building where they both had offices. "She had gotten divorced and remained friends with her husband," Diane explains. "I was in her office, and she was talking to him, telling him that she had met somebody else that she was going to marry. Even though they were still friends, I think on some level he thought they'd get back together. When she told him that it was really the end of the relationship, I thought, 'Wow, there's definitely a song here.' And I said to my friend, 'I hope you're not too mad at me, but I used your life here.' And that became 'Look Away.'"

Diane wrote the song from the man's point of view and submitted it to Chicago's management company. "Diane's demos always sound really good," producer Ron Nevison attests. "She uses Joe Turano, who's a great singer. Her demos are always very simple, but they always have great vocal performances."

Bass player Jason Scheff, who replaced Peter Cetera in 1985, received the demo after Chicago performed in Los Angeles. "The songs that last for me are the ones I don't get at first," he says. "I remember hearing 'Look Away' and thinking it's okay, but not

great. Thank God I'm not an A&R man."

When the band was ready to record *Chicago 19*, they asked Nevison, who had produced number one singles for Heart [see 631—"These Dreams" and 671—"Alone"] to take the producer's chair. Nevison wasn't able to schedule enough time for the entire project, but agreed to produce four tracks. Chas Sandford produced the rest of the album. "We thought it could be a nice idea to split it up with somebody else," says Scheff, "because Ron is primarily a rock and roll producer, and traditionally Chicago had . . . a diverse musical identity with all the different styles. All the singles ended up being Ron's, though, so it was a huge left turn for us.

"The first three singles on the album were Bill Champlin vocals. That was a great move for us, because it expanded our line-up as far as who we could use vocally. Up until then, it was really just that tenor sound of Peter Cetera. And with him making his own records, it was good for us to be able to release some songs with a different sound (like) Bill's voice. Then we wouldn't be saturating radio with Chicago-sounding songs."

Nevison, who followed David Foster as the group's producer, liked the idea of establishing a new sound for the group. "After David Foster, and after Peter Cetera left the group, I thought it was a perfect time to introduce the new voice who had been in the group for years, but had never really gotten a shot—Bill Champlin."

The first single from *Chicago 19*, "I Don't Wanna Live Without Your Love," peaked at number three in August, 1988. The follow-up was "Look Away," which entered the Hot 100 on September 24 and reached the top 11 weeks later. "You're Not Alone" was next; it went to number 10 in March, 1989. The fourth single, "We Can Last Forever," faltered at number 55 in June. A remixed version of the album's "What Kind of Man Would I Be?," featured on *Greatest Hits 1982–1989*, peaked at number five in February, 1990, while "Hearts in Trouble" (a cut from the soundtrack of *Days of Thunder*) petered out at number 75 in August. *Chicago Twenty 1*, released in 1991, proved a disappointment as far as hit singles: "Chasin' the Wind," the album's highest-charted single, stopped at number 39 in March.

---

## THE TOP FIVE
*Week of December 10, 1988*

1 **Look Away**
Chicago

2 **Baby, I Love Your Way/ Freebird Medley (Free Baby)**
Will to Power

3 **How Can I Fall?**
Breathe

4 **I Don't Want Your Love**
Duran Duran

5 **Giving You the Best That I Got**
Anita Baker

Writers: Bobby Dall
      C.C. DeVille
      Bret Michaels
      Rikki Rockett

Producer: Tom Werman

December 24, 1988
3 weeks

**B**RET MICHAELS first became interested in music as a child growing up in Harrisburg, Pennsylvania, when he heard his friend Brad Campbell play harmonica and acoustic guitar. "I was much too young to understand Bob Dylan," Michaels says. "I just loved the sound of acoustics, but as time rolled on . . . the first two albums I bought were *Led Zeppelin II* and *Lynyrd Skynyrd*. Probably my biggest inspiration for finally getting serious about (music) was when I went to see Sweet and Foghat playing together in 1977."

Michaels was in sixth grade when he had his first band. Lazer played covers of songs by Kiss and Aerosmith. At age 16, he met drummer Rikki Rockett, and they played in a band called the Spectres for three years before meeting bass guitarist Bobby Dall.

They entered the Miller High Life "Rock to Riches" battle of the bands, and came in second to a new-wave group called the Sharks. "The Sharks got the record deal and we said, 'That's it, let's go to California, where at least we have a fighting chance to play original material.'" Bret was the first to relocate, settling in Redondo Beach. "But I went to the Sunset Strip, and it blew my mind." He saw Mötley Crüe play the Whisky, and Billy Idol at the Roxy. "I thought, this is great, it's what I want to do, and it influenced me to keep writing original stuff." Bret moved back to Harrisburg, where the band played for a couple more years, saving their money for a permanent move to California.

Michaels, Rockett, Dall and guitarist Matt Smith left the East Coast in March of 1984. On the way to California, they found a new name for the band. "We formed it across the country on the way out," Michaels remembers. "We were thinking up names that we really dug . . . we came up with a billion of them. Finally, we just said, 'Poison—that's it.'"

The four musicians spent their first night in Los Angeles at the famed Tropicana motel on Santa Monica Boulevard. The money started to run out after two weeks, so they found a one-room apartment at the corner of Franklin and Whitley and spread their blankets on the floor. "We sold pencils and got bit-extra parts in movies, whatever we could do to get by," says Michaels. They started out at Club 88 and moved to Madame Wong's West before headlining the Troubadour. With Smith out and guitarist C.C. DeVille in, they were playing the Country Club in Reseda when executives from Enigma Records came to see them.

"All the other record labels at that point had turned us down, said (we're) not major-label material . . . everyone and their brother were signed but us." Enigma was known for taking chances on alternative music and hard-rock bands, and signed Poison in 1986.

The band made their debut on the *Billboard* Hot 100 with "Talk Dirty to Me," which peaked at number nine in May, 1987. In July of 1988, Poison had a number six hit with "Nothin' But a Good Time," the first single from their sophomore album, *Open Up and Say . . . Aah!* The follow-up was "Fallen Angel," number 12 in October. Then the rockers released "Every Rose Has Its Thorn."

"I was seeing a girl named Tracy," Bret responds when asked how the song was written. "We started to fall apart and the more successful our band got, the further apart our relationship got. We were playing Dallas at a club called the Ritz, with all of 24 people there to see us. We were staying at a really sleazy hotel across from the Ritz. I was in a laundry room where you wash your own clothes, sitting there with the washer and dryer, and it was kind of hot. It was just me and Rikki sitting there, talking and writing the song. I don't even know why the title came to me."

Not everyone was convinced the rock band would have a hit with an acoustic ballad. "We're not trying to be AC/DC and we're not trying to be Bob Dylan," Michaels professes. "But I have both those artists in my record collection. Why can't I have influences from both? Why can't I write a song that means something to me that's acoustic, then turn around and write 'Unskinny Bop' or 'Come Hell or High Water'?"

## THE TOP FIVE
*Week of December 24, 1988*

1   **Every Rose Has Its Thorn**
    Poison

2   **My Prerogative**
    Bobby Brown

3   **Look Away**
    Chicago

4   **Giving You the Best That I Got**
    Anita Baker

5   **Waiting for a Star to Fall**
    Boy Meets Girl

## 718 My Prerogative MCA 53383
BOBBY BROWN

*Writers: Gene Griffin*
*Bobby Brown*

*Producer: Gene Griffin*

*January 14, 1989*
*1 week*

**B**OBBY BARESFORD BROWN, born February 5, 1969, was 14 years old when he made his debut on the *Billboard* chart with "Candy Girl," recorded by the Boston-based teen group New Edition. He had made his stage debut even earlier—at three years old, when his mother took him to a James Brown concert at the Sugar Shack in Boston. "It was intermission, his band was playing music, and my mom pushed me onstage and told me to dance," Brown remembers. "That was the first time I was onstage."

Brown's mother and father, a school teacher and construction worker respectively, raised their son in the Orchard Park projects in Roxbury. In 1980, Bobby formed a group with four older friends: Ralph Tresvant, Ricky Bell, Michael Bivins and Ronald DeVoe. They sang a medley of Jackson Five songs at a talent contest where first prize was a recording session produced by Maurice Starr [see 732—"I'll Be Loving You (Forever)"]. A rap group won, but they weren't suited to the kind of material Starr wanted to record, and New Edition was given the prize. Starr signed them to the independent Streetwise label and molded them into an '80s version of the Jackson Five. While "Candy Girl" only went to number 46 in America, it went to the top of the British chart in May, 1983, right after Spandau Ballet's "True" and right before the Police's

"Every Breath You Take."

In 1984, New Edition split from Starr and signed with MCA. The producer made good his promise to put together a group of five white kids, but Starr and the members of New Edition endured years of legal hassles. "Cool It Now" was the first top 10 hit for New Edition, reaching number four in January, 1985. After the release of the *All for Love* album that year, Brown announced he was leaving New Edition for a solo career.

In 1986, MCA released Brown's first solo album, *King of Stage*. "It was really a solo New Edition album," Brown complains. "The voice was there, the voice they remember from 'Candy Girl.' It didn't work out for me. We had to regroup and find out what my identity was as a singer." The single "Girlfriend" reached number 57 on the Hot 100 in January, 1987. A year later, Brown completed production on a second album, *Don't Be Cruel*. He worked with a variety of producers, including L.A. Reid and Babyface and Gene Griffin. The title track, one of the L.A./Babyface songs, was the first single; it peaked at number eight in October, 1988. Oddly enough, while Brown's song was moving up the chart, so was

Cheap Trick's remake of Elvis Presley's "Don't Be Cruel."

The second single released from the album was "My Prerogative," produced by Gene Griffin. The credits on the record list Griffin and Brown as writers, although Brown has acknowledged that Teddy Riley and Aaron Hall of Guy had a strong hand in the development of the song. They both sang backing vocals; Riley, considered the inventor of New Jack Swing, played keyboards and helped mix the song. The lyrics referred to Brown's split from New Edition and his managers, as well as to the gossip that had been spread about him.

"My Prerogative" debuted on the Hot 100 the week of October 22, 1988, and was on top of the chart 12 weeks later. "Roni," the third single, peaked at number three in March, followed by another number three hit, "Every Little Step." Brown's next single was "On Our Own" from *Ghostbusters II*. He agreed to perform on the soundtrack in exchange for a small part in the film; he played a butler to the Mayor of New York. "On Our Own" reached number two in August, then Brown returned to the album for "Rock Wit'cha," which went to number seven in November.

### THE TOP FIVE
*Week of January 14, 1989*

1 **My Prerogative**
Bobby Brown

2 **Two Hearts**
Phil Collins

3 **Every Rose Has Its Thorn**
Poison

4 **Don't Rush Me**
Taylor Dayne

5 **Armageddon It**
Def Leppard

*Writers: Phil Collins
Lamont Dozier*

*Producers: Phil Collins
Lamont Dozier*

*January 21, 1989
2 weeks*

Pʜɪʟ Cᴏʟʟɪɴs was appearing at the Forum in Inglewood, California, and Tony Mandich of Atlantic Records invited songwriter Lamont Dozier to see the show and come backstage. "I had never gone to a Phil Collins concert," Dozier says. "Tony whispered (to Collins) I was there. Phil turned around and literally ran and jumped on me, put his arms around me—which took me by surprise, because Tony hadn't told me anything about Phil liking my music." Collins had already scored a top 10 single with a cover of Holland-Dozier-Holland's "You Can't Hurry Love," originally a hit for the Supremes [see 207].

"I found out that he had been, and still is, an avid fan of the Motown sound and the artists and the songs," Lamont continues. "So we struck up a relationship, and started to talk to each other periodically." One day, Dozier received a call from Collins saying he was in town working with Eric Clapton at Ocean Way Studios, and did he have any songs Eric might record? "Eric and I go back a long way, so I sent them over a song called 'Hung Up on Your Love.' He recorded that . . . then they asked me, 'Do you have another one?' I had the song 'Run' that I had just finished writing, so I said, 'This would be good for Eric.' I took it over, and before I could get home, Phil

had called my house and was talking to my wife when I walked through the door. They had already started recording the thing!"

Clapton recorded the two Dozier songs for his *August* album. "About a year later, a knock came on the door at 10:00 in the morning and it was Phil. He said, 'I'm doing this movie, *Buster*, and I want to concentrate on my acting. I don't want to have anything to do with the music. Would you do that—would you handle the music?'" Lamont readily agreed. "He told me it was a period piece and he needed '60s-type stuff. After hearing the story, I knew that the right music for that particular time was early Motown. I went to my old records to take myself back, because we move on. It took me about a week to get into the 'baby, baby's,' but it finally came back to me."

Dozier made some rough tracks in his own studio and flew to the *Buster* location in Acapulco to play the songs for Collins. "We were sitting in the room together and we turned our backs to each other to listen to the music. It was a stressful moment: I'm wondering what he's going to think of it, he's hoping that it's something he'll like, and that he won't have to tell me it's not right."

Collins told Dozier he was right on the button, and it was even more than he expected. One of the tracks was "Two Hearts." "I came up with the

feeling of the Motown '60s that I had a part in creating," relates Dozier. "I had listened to the way Phil approached 'You Can't Hurry Love'—since he'd picked that particular song, I knew that 'Two Hearts' would work for him."

Collins loved Dozier's material so much that he changed his mind about being involved with the music, and agreed to write lyrics. "That's what I was hoping for," the composer confesses, "because I told him, 'It would be almost sacrilege to make a movie and not have you write some of the stuff as well as sing it.'"

Two other Collins/Dozier collaborations appeared on the *Buster* soundtrack. Collins performed "Big Noise," and "Loco in Acapulco" was recorded by some old friends of Lamont's—the Four Tops. "The Tops were in Europe. They flew in to do this, and we finished it off at Ocean Way Studios. It was a big thrill for Phil, because he always wanted to work with the Tops. He played drums . . . and he was like a kid in a candy store."

Collins and Dozier formed a lasting mutual-admiration society. Phil returned the favor and collaborated with Dozier on his Atlantic album, *Inside Seduction*.

"Two Hearts," the second single from *Buster* to top the *Billboard* chart [see 711—"Groovy Kind of Love"], was the sixth number one for Collins.

---

## THE TOP FIVE
*Week of January 21, 1989*

1 **Two Hearts**
  Phil Collins

2 **Don't Rush Me**
  Taylor Dayne

3 **Armageddon It**
  Def Leppard

4 **My Prerogative**
  Bobby Brown

5 **When I'm With You**
  Sheriff

# 720 When I'm With You CAPITOL 44302
## SHERIFF

*Writer: Arnold Lanni*

*Producer: Stacy Heydon*

*February 4, 1989*
*1 week*

Sheriff, a Canadian quintet, broke up four years before "When I'm With You" went to number one on the *Billboard* Hot 100. And even though some members of the band wanted to re-unite and promote their chart-topping hit, it never happened.

Arnold Lanni's Italian family was shocked when he announced in 1979 he was dropping out of York University in Toronto to join a rock and roll band, Sheriff, which also included Wolf Hassell, Steve DeMarchi, Rob Elliott and lead vocalist Freddy Curci. They signed a deal with a production company which helped them pact with Capitol Records of Canada. When their debut album was released, the first two singles failed to catch fire. The third single was "When I'm With You." It entered the Hot 100 on May 14, 1983, and peaked at number 61 four weeks later.

Lanni wrote the song after meeting a woman he "flipped" over, Valerie Brown. It didn't take very long to compose the tune. "I sat down, put my coffee on the piano, tinkled some ivories, and four minutes later 80 percent of the song was written." For Valentine's Day, he played the song for Valerie and said, "I don't have anything, this is all I can really give you right now. It's yours."

Valerie loved the song—and married Arnold two years later. Meanwhile, Arnold played the song for the other members of Sheriff. "The band

really liked it, so we started playing it live. That was one of the last songs we recorded when we did the record. The producer said, 'Is there anything else?' I said, 'There's this song we play, it's kind of a wimpy song.' So we played it for him and he said, 'Yeah, that's kind of nice.'"

Lead singer Curci explains, "We were trying to establish ourselves as a rock act. They wanted to make it a rock band and shy away from the ballads, but a great song is a great song." Unhappy with his vocals, Curci was given a chance to re-record the song when it was being remixed for single release. "They had booked a couple of extra hours in the studio. I did the song in one take, including the last note at the end. Ten minutes later, the song was finished."

Lanni and Hassell formed a duo, Frozen Ghost, and signed with Atlantic. They charted with "Should I See," a single that peaked at number 69 in May, 1987. In the fall of 1988, Lanni received a phone call from a friend in Buffalo, New York, who told him his song was going to be a big hit. Lanni assumed his friend was talking about "Dream Come True," a new Frozen Ghost single. He was shocked to find out a station in Las Vegas had been playing "When I'm With You" as a current record and that other stations were starting to do the same, thereby encouraging Capitol to re-release the single.

"I didn't want to believe it," Lanni says. "The band had broken up, there's no video, the record company has punched holes in the album, it's deleted. They threw it out there . . . they didn't even call me to find out if I wanted to remaster it for CD."

Lanni was playing a gig at a high school in a small community in Northern Canada in February of 1989 when his brother Robert called to tell him that "When I'm With You" had gone to number one in America. In Toronto, Curci was working as a courier. He was delivering packages to an office when he heard "When I'm With You" on a radio in the background and started giggling. "The receptionist noticed I was laughing and said, 'What are you laughing at?' I said, 'If I tell you, you wouldn't believe me. Just sign the receipt.'" She insisted, so he asked her if she knew the song being played on the radio. She said she loved it, and Curci revealed that he was the singer. "She said, 'Sure, fella, you're trying to pick me up. I'll call security.'"

Curci and DeMarchi, along with three former members of Heart, were signed to EMI in 1990. Curci wanted to call the band Sheriff II, but settled for Alias. In November, 1990, they hit number two with their first chart single, "More Than Words Can Say."

## THE TOP FIVE
### *Week of February 4, 1989*

1 **When I'm With You**
Sheriff

2 **Straight Up**
Paula Abdul

3 **When the Children Cry**
White Lion

4 **Born to Be My Baby**
Bon Jovi

5 **Wild Thing**
Tone Loc

*Writer: Elliot Wolff*

*Producer: Elliot Wolff*

*February 11, 1989*
*3 weeks*

ON February 11, 1963, the number one song in America was "Hey Paula" by Paul and Paula. Twenty-six years later to the day, another Paula had the number one song in the nation with "Straight Up," the third single from her album *Forever Your Girl.*

Paula Abdul was born June 19, 1962. She grew up in North Hollywood, the second daughter of Harry and Lorraine Abdul. Her father, of Brazilian-Syrian heritage, sold livestock and her mother, a French Canadian Jew, worked as an assistant to film director Billy Wilder. Her parents separated when she was seven, the same age when Paula started performing, inspired by seeing Gene Kelly in *Singing in the Rain.* Her mother was trained as a concert pianist.

Her school friends were listening to Shaun Cassidy and the DeFranco Family, but Paula's musical horizons were expanded by her older sister Wendy, who preferred Carole King, Stevie Wonder and Joni Mitchell. At Van Nuys High, Paula was a cheerleader as well as senior class president. She appeared in a student film, *Junior High School.* Attending Cal State Northridge, she wanted to be a sportscaster like Jayne Kennedy. When a friend begged her to come with her and try out for a cheerleading position with the the Lakers, the Los Angeles basketball team, Paula reluctantly agreed.

Her friend didn't make the cut, but Paula became a Laker Girl and in her first season was named choreographer for the troupe. "I started getting calls at the Forum, asking who is the choreographer," says Paula. "After one of the games, several of the Jackson brothers, who were season ticket holders, told me they were getting ready to start their *Victory* tour (and asked) me to choreograph their first video."

John McClain of A&M Records complimented her after a Laker game and asked her to listen to some new tracks recorded by Janet Jackson. "I fell in love with the music and then I met Janet and we hit it off. I started working with her every day and applying what I had done with the Laker Girls. Neither of us knew the impact it would make." Paula was hired to be the choreographer on "The Tracey Ullman Show" for Fox Television and did a number of music videos for artists like Dolly Parton, Debbie Gibson and Warren Zevon. While working on the "Velcro Fly" video for ZZ Top, she mentioned to Jeff Ayeroff—then at Warner Brothers Records—that she would be interested in recording.

When Ayeroff was named head of Virgin Records in America along with Jordan Harris, Paula was one of the first artists he signed. Gemma Corfield, head of A&R for the label, sat down with Paula to choose songs for her first album.

One of the songs Corfield played for the singer was an eight-track demo of "Straight Up," written by Elliot Wolff. "I was working with another singer," Wolff explains. "I had spent about six months getting six songs together to get her a deal. We got her a deal, but then the record company hired a new A&R person and he didn't like the stuff I did, so I was completely out of the project. One of the songs was 'Straight Up.' The singer was dropped from Virgin before releasing an album and the A&R staffer lost his job."

The first single from *Forever Your Girl* was "Knocked Out," then "(It's Just) The Way That You Love Me" was issued. "(It's Just) The Way That You Love Me" was doing well on the R&B chart when KMEL in San Francisco started playing "Straight Up," forcing the label to make a choice—to either continue to promote "The Way That You Love Me" or redirect their energies toward "Straight Up." Their decision resulted in Paula Abdul's first number one hit.

## THE TOP FIVE
*Week of February 11, 1989*

1 **Straight Up**
Paula Abdul

2 **When I'm With You**
Sheriff

3 **Wild Thing**
Tone Loc

4 **Born to Be My Baby**
Bon Jovi

5 **When the Children Cry**
White Lion

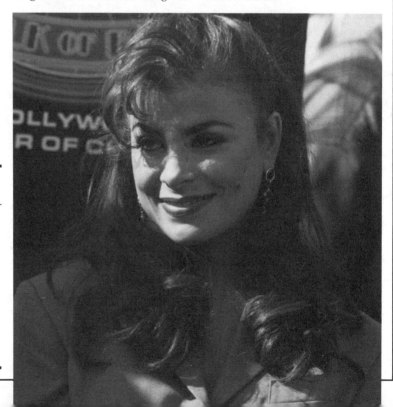

# Lost in Your Eyes ATLANTIC 88970
## DEBBIE GIBSON

*Writer: Deborah Gibson*

*Producer: Deborah Gibson*

*March 4, 1989*
*3 weeks*

DEBBIE GIBSON scored her second number one hit with the first single from her sophomore album, *Electric Youth.* "Lost in Your Eyes" entered the Hot 100 at number 42 the week of January 21, 1989, and quickly went to number one six weeks later. "It flew to number one so fast, I didn't even have time to think about it," the singer says. "I was tracking ("Foolish Beat"); it was really gradual, and you could kind of tell where it was headed. But 'Lost in Your Eyes' came out, and within a few weeks it was at the top, so it was pretty overwhelming."

"Lost in Your Eyes" had been in Debbie's repertoire for some time. "I did write that when the first album was out, and I was performing it on the first tour before it was recorded. It always got a really good response from the fans."

When asked if she wrote the song about a boyfriend, Debbie denies it. "Because I'd gone out with an actor who had particularly blue eyes, everyone thought I had written it about him. But I didn't—I didn't even know him when I wrote it."

Like her previous number one, "Lost in Your Eyes" was a ballad. "That's just the way it evolved," she explains. "I really wanted the piano to be the main focus, because I think if you have a strong song, you should let it speak for itself and not overproduce it. Both of those ballads had that simplicity."

## THE TOP FIVE
*Week of March 4, 1989*

1  **Lost in Your Eyes**
   Debbie Gibson

2  **The Lover in Me**
   Sheena Easton

3  **Straight Up**
   Paula Abdul

4  **The Living Years**
   Mike + the Mechanics

5  **You Got It (The Right Stuff)**
   New Kids on the Block

Debbie also savored the thrill of a number one album with *Electric Youth.* "It just goes to show you, you can never predict what the public's going to be into at any given time. It went number one and stayed there for weeks. I couldn't believe it. Which is funny for me, because I'm usually overconfident and then I get disappointed if it doesn't do what I had expected."

An even bigger thrill for Debbie was being acknowledged for her songwriting at the ASCAP Awards. "That was a highlight of my career. For a while, I felt like—pardon the pun—the new kid on the block, because I was among songwriters I looked up to and I won the award for the year. That was amazing."

The follow-up to "Lost in Your Eyes" was the title track from her album. "Electric Youth" peaked at number 11 in May, 1989. "No More Rhyme" was next, reaching number 17 in August. "We Could Be Together" was Debbie's first single to miss the top 30, stopping at number 71 in September.

For her third album, *Anything Is Possible,* Debbie teamed up with one of the rock era's best-known songwriters, Lamont Dozier. Paul Cooper at Atlantic suggested the collaboration because Debbie included a Motown medley in her concerts. Lamont's son brought his father to one of Debbie's shows, and Cooper asked if he would be interested in writing with Gibson.

"I had never co-written before, and I really didn't understand how people went about it," Debbie told Thom Duffy in *Billboard.* "I didn't know if they sat around a room and said, 'Okay, you finish this sentence.'" Four of the songs on the album were written by Gibson and Dozier, including "Anything Is Possible," which peaked at number 26 in January, 1991.

Although 1991 was a quiet year on the chart for Debbie, she began 1992 with an achievement in another field. On January 7, she stepped into the role of Eponine in the Broadway production of *Les Miserables.*

She had auditioned for the role in 1986, but didn't get it then because she couldn't hit all of the high notes. That wasn't a problem in 1992. Her stage credits actually began when she was five: she played the littlest elf in a repertory theater production of *The Elves and the Shoemaker.* With sisters Denise, Karen and Michele, Debbie later appeared in community theater musicals. She was also an extra in *Ghostbusters,* and was cast in commercials for Wendy's hamburgers and Oxydol detergent.

"I hope people forget that it's me, pop singer, up there," she told Patricia O'Hare of the New York *Daily News* on the eve of her opening in *Les Miserables.* "I love pop music, but it allows you to show only one side of yourself. This will be much more of me."

*Writers: Mike Rutherford
        B.A. Robertson*

*Producers: Christopher Neil
         Mike Rutherford*

*March 25, 1989
1 week*

Like the other two members of Genesis [see 641—"Invisible Touch"], guitarist Mike Rutherford enjoyed time away from the band in extracurricular activities. He released his first solo album, *Smallcreep's Day*, in 1979, and a follow-up, *Acting Very Strange*, in 1982. Three years later, Mike assembled drummer Peter Van Hooke, keyboard player Adrian Lee and singers Paul Carrack (Ace, Squeeze) and Paul Young (not the vocalist who recorded "Everytime You Go Away," but the former lead singer of the Manchester band Sad Cafe) and released an album as Mike + the Mechanics. "Silent Running (On Dangerous Ground)" and "All I Need Is a Miracle" were both top 10 singles in 1986. The former was written with B.A. Robertson, a Scotsman who recorded several hits in the U.K. in 1979-80, like "Bang Bang" and "Kool in the Kaftan."

"The first album was fairly experimental," Rutherford told Todd Everett. "I had some songs, but it was very much week by week. . . . My ambition was to have something outside Genesis that I could build on, rather than a casual project. I thought that if it did well, or at least got off the ground, I would continue it." With two top 10 singles, more than half a million albums sold and a successful tour, Rutherford's wish to continue the group was granted.

A second album, *Living Years*, was released in 1988. The initial single, "Nobody's Perfect," faded quickly on the Hot 100, peaking at number 63. Although it clocked in at a radio-unfriendly five minutes and 32 seconds, the obvious choice for a follow-up single was the title track, written by Rutherford and Robertson.

"Mike and I must have written about 40 songs together, and all of them pretty much came together the same way," Robertson attests. "We work on the music together, although the music is really more his domain, and then I usually write a lyric in isolation." For "The Living Years," a song about losing one's father before having the chance to say what is in one's heart, Robertson had a first verse written before his father passed away in 1986. The day it happened, he was at Mike Rutherford's house. "We were by ourselves and my father-in-law called. Mike came and said, 'Your father-in-law's on the telephone,' and I knew he had called to tell me that my father was dead."

Rutherford's father also passed away in 1986. Working with Rutherford on the song, Roberston remembers, "We were writing lots of music and none of it was coming together as a song. (So) we wrote the music around the first verse. The second verse I wrote in the car, driving from Guilford back to London." The last verse was written in Los Angeles. B.A. was working on a project for Disney and staying at the Sunset Marquis hotel. "It was getting down to the wire and Carrack had to do the vocal. I had to go back to England, I had to deliver a lyric. I went outside into the garden . . . and the verse came," Roberston says with great emotion.

Rutherford and Roberston watched "Nelson Mandela's 70th Birthday Party" concert that weekend and were touched by Eric Clapton's performance of "Wonderful Tonight," a song written about his ex-wife Patti. "He sung it with such dignity, and you felt part of it without ever feeling uncomfortable. It seemed to me . . . if Paul were able to impart the emotion with that same quality, then we would be okay."

## THE TOP FIVE
*Week of March 25, 1989*

1  **The Living Years**
   Mike + the Mechanics

2  **Eternal Flame**
   Bangles

3  **Girl You Know It's True**
   Milli Vanilli

4  **The Look**
   Roxette

5  **My Heart Can't Tell You No**
   Rod Stewart

# 724 Eternal Flame COLUMBIA 68533
## BANGLES

Writers: Susanna Hoffs
Billy Steinberg
Tom Kelly

Producer: Davitt Sigerson

April 1, 1989
1 week

THE BANGLES' second number one single was co-written by band member Susanna Hoffs with Billy Steinberg and Tom Kelly. It was the fifth number one song for a female vocalist written by the two men, following Madonna's "Like a Virgin," Cyndi Lauper's "True Colors," Heart's "Alone" and Whitney Houston's "So Emotional."

"I was a Bangles fan from their first album," Steinberg admits. "I went to see them perform at the Palace in Hollywood and met Susanna at that concert. We decided the three of us should try to write something together." Kelly continues: "We co-wrote with her after their first album. Nothing really came of it; what we wrote with her, she didn't record. But we established the writing relationship." Hoffs, Steinberg and Kelly composed "I Need a Disguise" for Belinda Carlisle's first album, Belinda.

"When we wrote 'Eternal Flame,' we wanted to write something Beatlesque and melodic," Tom explains. Billy adds, "The nice thing about working with Susanna is that she is a complete '60s fan, like Tom and I are—she loves all the songs by the Beatles and the Byrds. For us, 'Eternal Flame' was the Beatles meet the Byrds. In particular, it seems reminiscent of 'Here, There and Everywhere.'"

Billy recounts the two inspirations for the lyrics: "One was Susanna talking about when she and the Bangles were in Memphis. They went to Graceland. There was an eternal flame for Elvis. That made me think, when I was a child, I used to attend Sunday school at a local synagogue in Palm Springs. They used to walk us through there, and there was a little red light—like a little red Christmas light—that they called the eternal flame. I remember thinking that there was this flame that could burn forever. It seemed very mysterious. It was like thinking about how far the universe goes, those little things kids think about that blow their minds."

The song almost didn't make the final cut for the Everything album, according to Kelly. "It was different than everything else (on the album). They were trying very hard at that time to make an album that reflected their songwriting skills and their musicianship, and all of a sudden here was this ballad that required some different production values. It conflicted with their garage-band approach."

The first single released from Everything was "In Your Room," another composition by Hoffs, Steinberg and Kelly. It peaked at number five in January, 1989. "Eternal Flame," the follow-up, entered the Hot 100 on February 4 and was number one eight weeks later. There was only one more chart single, "Be With You," which hit number 30 in June. Four months later, the Bangles cut short their world tour and said they were "going on hiatus"

after nine years together. "For most of that time we had a tremendous loyalty to each other," Hoffs told Jean Rosenbluth in the Los Angeles Times. "We worked very hard and enjoyed a lot of success and got along really well compared to a lot of bands. But it got to a point where everyone in the band, I think, was feeling compromised. Each person had a certain vision of what they wanted to do artistically, and it seemed like none of us were being satisfied or getting off on what we were doing at the time."

Hoffs also confirmed what many believed: "The band is officially broken up, but I can maybe see working with one or all of them again. I mean, the Go-Go's are doing it . . . but it's really hard to say."

Hoffs was the first ex-Bangle to chart as a solo act on the Hot 100. The single "My Side of the Bed" from When You're a Boy peaked at number 30 in March, 1991.

## THE TOP FIVE
### Week of April 1, 1989

1 **Eternal Flame**
Bangles

2 **Girl You Know It's True**
Milli Vanilli

3 **The Look**
Roxette

4 **My Heart Can't Tell You No**
Rod Stewart

5 **The Living Years**
Mike + the Mechanics

*Writer: Per Gessle*

*Producer: Clarence Öfwerman*

*April 8, 1989*
*1 week*

PER GESSLE was at an Ian Hunter concert in Stockholm in January, 1989, when he heard a rumor that some radio stations in the States were playing a song by Roxette, the duo he had formed with Marie Fredriksson. "I didn't know which one, because we had just finished a Scandinavian tour and we were promoting 'Listen to Your Heart.'" He was on vacation in the Caribbean when a phone call came from his managers. "(They) told us 'The Look' had entered the *Billboard* chart at number 50. I've been a subscriber to *Billboard* since '81, so I know that going in at 50 is quite high."

It was a very high debut for an unknown band. But Roxette had some help from Dean Cushman, an American exchange student from Minneapolis who had seen one of the duo's concerts in Sweden. During a Christmas break he brought a copy of their CD *Look Sharp!* home with him and asked his local top 40 radio station, KDWB, to play it. Program director Brian Phillips thought the package looked interesting and set it aside. When Dean asked for his CD back, Phillips decided to listen to it first: "I had two DJs standing around. We put it on as a lark. And about a minute in . . . everybody said, 'Am I in a really good frame of mind or is this a number one record?'" Phillips decided to play it once and see if there was any reaction. "Within a couple of days, the record had become my pet project because I loved the way it sounded," says Phillips.

When his crosstown rival began a desperate search for "The Look," Phillips was certain it was a hit. He sent tapes of the song to stations in New York, Houston and Dallas. After influential KIIS-FM in Los Angeles added it, labels started calling Phillips to find out who the band was and how to contact them. Signed to EMI in Sweden, Roxette didn't have a deal for America. "EMI turned down the *Look Sharp!* album three months prior to this," Gessle says. "We were on our way to go somewhere else." Finally, Roxette signed with EMI for the

States. By this time, airplay was so heavy on "The Look" that it was able to make its high debut.

Gessle explains his inspiration for the song: "I wanted to write a ZZ Top-type of song. It turned out to be something totally different in the end, which is always the case. I never really thought it would be a big song. I had it around for a couple of months before I played it for Marie and Clarence Öfwerman, our producer. They both said, 'This is the best thing you've done in ages—you have to record it.'"

The lyrics of the song were written as dummy lyrics, but Gessle decided to keep them. "It's sort of a Marc Bolan-ish type of lyric, which I like. I really enjoy word games."

"The Look" went to number one for the week ending April 8, 1989—exactly 15 years to the week since the first Swedish number one in America, "Hooked on a Feeling" by Blue Swede [see 361]. It was also exactly 15 years since Abba [see 458—"Dancing Queen"] had won the Eurovision Song Contest with "Waterloo" on April 6, 1974.

"I'm a big Abba fan myself," admits Gessle, who co-wrote "Threnody" on Frida's *Something's Going On* album. "I think the big difference between Roxette and Abba is that we are much more rock-oriented than Abba was. Abba was more of a middle-of-the-road band, but if they had their heyday today, I think Abba would have been harder, too—contemporary music today is harder than it was in the '70s. Both Abba and Roxette are based on melodies and three-minute, 30-second songs."

The success of "The Look" was rewarding to Brian Phillips at KDWB. "Minneapolis really embraced the band," he says. "We got a fair amount of local press, so there was this local pride angle, and keep in mind, there are a tremendous number of Scandinavians in Minneapolis. I guess that's where my fear that it would only work in Minneapolis came from. What if I just hit some Scandinavian nerve with this thing, and it'll go to Los Angeles and not work at all? To say it sounds like a number one record is one thing, but when it actually went number one in *Billboard*, it was unbelievable."

**THE TOP FIVE**
*Week of April 8, 1989*

1  **The Look**
   Roxette

2  **Eternal Flame**
   Bangles

3  **Girl You Know It's True**
   Milli Vanilli

4  **She Drives Me Crazy**
   Fine Young Cannibals

5  **Like a Prayer**
   Madonna

## 726

# She Drives Me Crazy I.R.S. 53483
## FINE YOUNG CANNIBALS

*Writers: David Steele*
*Roland Gift*

*Producers: David Z*
*Fine Young Cannibals*

*April 15, 1989*
*1 week*

DAVID STEELE grew up on the Isle of Wight, where his mother took him at the age of nine to see Jimi Hendrix play at the Isle of Wight Festival. Eight years later he met Andrew Cox, a teenager from Birmingham who was working that summer making solar panels for his brother-in-law's company. He had a friend in tow, Dave Wakeling, and when they returned home they invited Steele to join them. Cox and Steele were 18 when they formed a band called the Beat in 1978 with Wakeling, Everette Morton and Ranking Roger.

The ska-flavored group had a number of top 10 singles in the U.K., including "Hands Off-She's Mine," "Mirror in the Bathroom," and a reggae version of Andy Williams' "Can't Get Used to Losing You." In America, where for legal reasons they were known as the English Beat, they did not manage to penetrate the Hot 100.

A few days after opening for David Bowie at Milton Keynes in 1983, Cox and Steele found out that the Beat was not going on when they read in a music paper that another record company had signed Wakeling and Roger as General Public. They decided their next group would be smaller and would spend less time touring. Advertising for a lead vocalist on MTV, they had almost 500 demo tapes sent their

---

## THE TOP FIVE
### Week of April 15, 1989

1  **She Drives Me Crazy**
   Fine Young Cannibals

2  **The Look**
   Roxette

3  **Like a Prayer**
   Madonna

4  **Eternal Flame**
   Bangles

5  **Girl You Know It's True**
   Milli Vanilli

---

way, but they didn't choose any of those singers. David saw someone on television that reminded him of the lead singer of the Akrylyx, a band from Hull that had supported the Beat on about 10 dates. Too shy to phone the lead singer themselves, Andy had his girlfriend place an introductory call.

The man on the other end of the line was Roland Gift, an actor and a musician who had played saxophone in a punk group from Hull called Blue Kitchen. When that band fizzled out, Gift took his sax to the Akrylyx and sang a couple of lead vocals as well. For a time, he even appeared in local pubs as half of a famous duo. "We thought it would be a good way to get some money, so we billed ourselves as the Righteous Brothers and played in this pub. Lots of people came and they got us instead of them," Gift says with a laugh. "The landlord didn't seem to mind . . . we didn't even do 'You've Lost That Lovin' Feelin'.'"

Gift moved to London and joined some friends in a blues band called Bones. He had sold the saxophone by this time and was singing lead vocals. He was with the Bones when the call came from Andy's girlfriend.

Gift agreed to join Steele and Cox in their new band that didn't have a name yet. "We'd been given the front cover of this magazine called *Blues and Soul* because they heard a demo tape . . . and they wanted to be the first to write about us," says Roland. "We did the interview but we still

didn't have a name. It made us more intriguing, more mysterious. . . . We had to come up with one quick." Andy took the name from the 1960 Robert Wagner-Natalie Wood film, *All the Fine Young Cannibals*, even though no one in the trio had seen it. "Still, to this day, we've never seen it," Gift reveals. "I might be disappointed if I saw it."

Executives from London Records in the U.K. saw the group perform "Johnny Come Home" on Channel 4's pop series "The Tube" and signed the band. That song was included on their debut album, as was a cover version of Elvis Presley's "Suspicious Minds" with Jimmy Somerville on backing vocals.

Three years passed between the recording of Fine Young Cannibals' first and second albums. In the interim, Cox and Steele wrote music for the John Candy-Steve Martin film *Planes, Trains and Automobiles* and produced tracks for the Wee Papa Girls and Pop Will Eat Itself. They also released a single in England as Two Men, a Drum Machine and a Trumpet.

The lead-off single from the Cannibals' second album, *The Raw & the Cooked*, was "She Drives Me Crazy," a song that took them six months to write. Originally called "She's My Baby," it was sung by Gift in his normal voice. "It didn't seem to be anything; I didn't enjoy singing it," Gift admits. After Steele changed the title and Gift tried singing it in a falsetto voice, the record clicked for the band.

SIRE 27539 **Like a Prayer**
MADONNA

**727**

Writers: *Madonna*
*Patrick Leonard*

Producers: *Madonna*
*Patrick Leonard*

April 22, 1989
3 weeks

Madonna had been absent from the Hot 100 for a year and a half when she released the first single from her album *Like a Prayer*. The title track debuted at 38 the week of March 18, 1989, and shot to number one five weeks later—making it the fastest-rising number one hit since Michael Jackson's "Bad" in 1987.

Madonna wrote and produced "Like a Prayer" with Patrick Leonard, who had collaborated on two of her previous chart-toppers, "Live to Tell" [see 637] and "Who's That Girl" [see 674]. Leonard remembers "Like a Prayer" being the first tune written for the album. "Originally it had bongos and Latin percussion, and we decided to eliminate that quickly," he says. "It was written and the lead vocal was recorded within about three hours. Most of the songs on that record were written just like that, in a few hours. . . . Once she came up with 'Like a Prayer,' we decided, 'We'll do this with a church organ and we'll add a choir to it, we'll add Andrae Crouch's choir later on.' It was that simple. It wasn't something that took weeks; this is something that took hours."

Madonna and Patrick met with Andrae Crouch to tell him what they had in mind. "He gets the choir together and they sort of wing it," says Leonard. "He knows what he's going to do and he knows what he's going to tell them . . . but I know he's making it up as he goes along. He's listened to it in his car and he's thought about what he's going to do . . . and it's very inspired."

Madonna talked about her religious upbringing with Becky Johnston. "I have a great sense of guilt and sin from Catholicism that has definitely permeated my everyday life, whether I want it to or not. And when I do something wrong, or that I think is wrong . . . if I don't let someone know I've wronged, I'm always afraid I'm going to be punished. I don't rest easy with myself. And that's something you're raised to believe as a Catholic."

Madonna told Johnston how the video of the song developed. "Originally, when I recorded the song, I would play it over and over again, trying to get a visual sense of what sort of story or fantasy it evoked in me. I kept imagining this story about a girl who was madly in love with a black man, set in the South, with this for-bidden interracial love affair. And the guy she's in love with sings in a choir. So she's obsessed with him and goes to church all the time. And then it turned into a bigger story, which was about racism and bigotry. . . . Then Mary Lambert got involved as the director, and she came up with a story that incorporated more of the religious symbolism I originally wrote into the song."

Before "Like a Prayer" was released, Madonna signed a one-year, $5-million contract with Pepsi-Cola which would include a series of commercials and sponsorship of Madonna's tour. The first commercial was scheduled to use the song "Like a Prayer." "I like the challenge of merging art and commerce," Madonna said in *Rolling Stone*. "The Pepsi spot is a great and different way to expose the record . . . the music will be playing in the background, and the can of Pepsi is positioned very subliminally."

The commercial had a different storyline than the video. For Pepsi, Madonna relived a birthday party from childhood. The two-minute commercial aired March 2, 1989, for the first and last time in the United States. Pepsi cited "consumer confusion" between the commercial and the video for "Like a Prayer." Fundamentalist groups threatened a boycott against the company because of what they considered to be Madonna's "blasphemous" video, but Pepsi said they arrived at their decision to pull the spot independently. Company spokesperson Todd McKenzie said, "If you've got an ad that has people confused, it's only logical to pull it." Pepsi did not ask for their money back, and Madonna did not offer.

## THE TOP FIVE
*Week of April 22, 1989*

1 **Like a Prayer**
Madonna

2 **She Drives Me Crazy**
Fine Young Cannibals

3 **The Look**
Roxette

4 **Funky Cold Medina**
Tone Loc

5 **I'll Be There for You**
Bon Jovi

# 728 I'll Be There for You MERCURY 872 564-7
## BON JOVI

*Writers: Jon Bon Jovi*
       *Richie Sambora*

*Producer: Bruce Fairbairn*

*May 13, 1989*
*1 week*

Bon Jovi followed "Bad Medicine" [see 714], the first number one single from their *New Jersey* album, with "Born to Be My Baby," a song producer Bruce Fairbairn thought would go higher than its chart peak of number three. "Boy, (that) should have been number one," he laments.

Co-writer Desmond Child says the title came from Richie Sambora. "It was meant to be a kind of folk-rock thing, more like a Springsteen anthem with jangly guitars and stuff like that. They gave it the 'Livin' on a Prayer' treatment, which I didn't agree with. It was still successful, but I would have preferred it if it had been a little slower."

For their third single from *New Jersey*, the band chose "I'll Be There for You," a song written by Sambora and Jon Bon Jovi. It debuted on the *Billboard* Hot 100 at number 82, and 10 weeks later it became Bon Jovi's fourth number one song.

"'I'll Be There for You' is one of those great personal ballads that Jon can get a hold of and when he sings it, his delivery is really outstanding," says Fairbairn. "You can't help but hear the song and get into it in a real personal way with him. It was a great song for them. Of course, a lot of things you never know, until you actually get them out there and see what the kids think about it."

Fairbairn says he produced *New Jersey* in the same fashion as the band's previous effort, *Slippery When Wet*. "I think we went about it the same way, the feeling being that it worked really well—so if it ain't broke, don't fix it. We naturally fell into a pretty similar kind of routine and a basically similar type of recording pattern."

The producer offers an analysis of Jon's performance on *New Jersey*: "He was singing with a lot more confidence. He knew what he had; he knew when he put his mind to it that he could sing with the best of them, and he really attacked the album with that kind of approach. When a singer goes in with that kind of confidence, you're definitely going to get good stuff."

There were two more singles from *New Jersey* after "I'll Be There for You." "Lay Your Hands on Me" peaked at number seven in July, 1989, and "Living in Sin" went to number nine in December.

Almost two years after *New Jersey* was released, Jon Bon Jovi completed a solo project, writing and recording songs for *Young Guns II*. That effort provided him with a number one song [see 764—"Blaze of Glory"]. Jon's working on his own fueled rumors that Bon Jovi might not record together again. But on December 23, 1990, the group played together for the first time since their 16-month, 237-date world tour ended in February. They played a charity benefit at the Count Basie Theater in Red Bank, New Jer-

sey, for the Monmouth County Arts Council and Holmdel's Sisters of the Good Shepherd. Eight days later, they headlined at the Tokyo Dome in Japan with Cinderella, the London Quireboys and Skid Row as supporting acts.

In March of 1991, Jon told Jeffrey Jolson-Colburn of the *Hollywood Reporter* that PolyGram, parent company of Mercury, was giving him his own label to run. "I haven't had a desk since I was in high school," the new CEO joked. Turning serious, he added, "This will be a label for artists by artists to give opportunities to musicians that deserve a shot."

Richie Sambora stepped out of the background and released a solo album, *Stranger in This Town*, in the summer of 1991. He told Melinda Newman in *Billboard* how difficult it was for him to write about the blues: "One day I was sitting in my house and I was thinking, how am I going to find the blues? I started to drink a little and I got into a good bottle of whiskey and I started to feel guilty about my life being so good." Then he remembered that Robert Johnson described the blues as, "I love my baby, my baby she don't love me." Sambora said, "That's the blues. Everybody's got that no matter what their economic state is."

Sambora told Newman he enjoyed being in the foreground. "This has been my dream ever since I was a kid. I know that this could be the beginning of a career beyond Bon Jovi. I'm starting a new relationship with the listener."

## THE TOP FIVE
*Week of May 13, 1989*

1 **I'll Be There for You**
Bon Jovi

2 **Like a Prayer**
Madonna

3 **Real Love**
Jody Watley

4 **Forever Your Girl**
Paula Abdul

5 **Soldier of Love**
Donny Osmond

VIRGIN 99230 **Forever Your Girl** **729**
PAULA ABDUL

*Writer: Oliver Leiber*

*Producer: Oliver Leiber*

*May 20, 1989*
*2 weeks*

On May 18, 1959, Wilbert Harrison's "Kansas City," written by Jerry Leiber and Mike Stoller, moved to the top of the *Billboard* Hot 100. Thirty years later to the day, the number one song in the country was Paula Abdul's "Forever Your Girl"—written and produced by Jerry's son, Oliver Leiber.

The younger Leiber, born February 12, 1961, idolized his father. "I wanted to be like him and fell in love with the excitement of what he did," Oliver explains. At first, he wasn't quite sure how his father earned a living. "My dad kind of lied to me. When I was younger, he said he was a drummer. And what I found out later on was that he really wasn't a musician, he was a lyricist."

At eight years old, while growing up on 74th Street on the West Side of Manhattan, Oliver picked out his first set of drums. "I never really wanted to be a songwriter," he says, "that's not what I set out to be." But he did write his first song at age 11. "Getting Mugged" was a three-chord, Buddy Holly-type of song, inspired by his fear of growing up in New York City.

Oliver left Manhattan at age 23 for Minneapolis. "I had a problem with chemical dependency and that landed me in a treatment facility in the Midwest in 1983," he elaborates. "That is where I rebuilt my life." After completing a 28-day course, he lived in a halfway house and was told to find work. Fortunately, Minneapolis was exploding as a hotbed of musical activity, thanks to Prince. "I played in a lot of top 40 bands as a drummer, and this opportunity opened up for a rhythm guitar player to go on tour with Alexander O'Neal." Oliver got the gig and met O'Neal's producers—his former bandmates in the Time, Jimmy Jam and Terry Lewis. Another Time member, Jesse Johnson, heard about Leiber and asked him to play with Ta Mara and the Seen, a band signed to A&M.

Oliver's manager, Don Brennan, suggested he work with another client, Paul Peterson. Known as St. Paul since he was part of the Paisley Park group the Family, Peterson was recording a solo album. Leiber and Peterson wrote a song called "Rich Man," which was released as a single by MCA. "Paul flew out to (Los Angeles) to make the video for 'Rich Man,' and the choreographer was Paula Abdul," Oliver explains.

Peterson gave Paula a tape of a song Oliver had written, "The Way That You Love Me." Oliver reports, "Apparently she hit the roof and said, 'I'm making this record and this is *exactly* the kind of stuff I want to do.'"

Meanwhile, Jerry Leiber had passed a copy of the same tape to Russ Titelman of Warner Brothers for Chaka Khan, who wanted to record it. "She was one of my idols," says Oliver, "and then this other unknown, obscure person, I thought her name was Abdula or something, was interested in it." Brennan suggested that if Chaka Khan had a hit with the song, no one would remember it came from Oliver. But if a new artist like Paula Abdul scored with it, people would want to know who made the record. Oliver took his advice, but said if he was going to sacrifice Chaka Khan cutting his song, he wanted Paula to record two of his songs.

The deal was signed, but Oliver didn't have a second song. "What I had was a rhythm track, and it was . . . very crude. I sent the rhythm track to 'Forever Your Girl' to Virgin and I sent it to Paula." The singer flew to Minneapolis along with Gemma Corfield of Virgin's A&R staff to check Oliver out. "It was after meeting Paula and getting a sense of her that I felt I had some sort of insight into what would work for her. She was very sweet, very innocent. So the music was written, but I wrote the lyrics to 'Forever Your Girl' after meeting Paula."

Leiber saved the tape from his answering machine of Paula calling him up to tell him the song had gone to number one on the Hot 100. "(She was) crying, hysterical, and told me not to tell the record company I knew, because she didn't want to ruin the surprise for them."

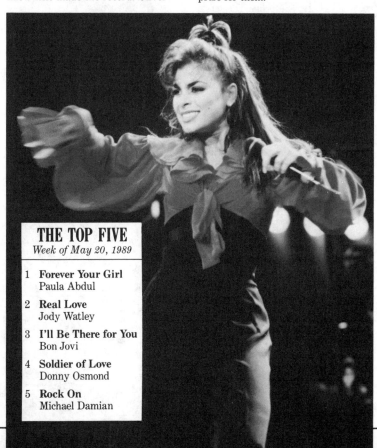

**THE TOP FIVE**
*Week of May 20, 1989*

1 **Forever Your Girl**
Paula Abdul

2 **Real Love**
Jody Watley

3 **I'll Be There for You**
Bon Jovi

4 **Soldier of Love**
Donny Osmond

5 **Rock On**
Michael Damian

## 730 Rock On CYPRESS 1420
### MICHAEL DAMIAN

*Writer: David Essex*

*Producers: Larry Weir*
*Michael Damian*
*Tom Weir*

*June 3, 1989*
*1 week*

MICHAEL DAMIAN WEIR was 11 years old when David Essex released "Rock On," a single that peaked at number five in March, 1974. "I loved the song since day one," Damian says. "It made such a strong impression on me as a child because it had such a rebellious and haunting vibe." Fourteen years later, Damian would record his own version of "Rock On" and surpass Essex' chart ranking on the Hot 100.

In April of 1988, on the weekend Damian turned 26, he decided to lay down the track for a new rendition of Essex' hit with his brothers Tom and Larry. It was recorded in Damian's 24-track recording studio in the garage of his home.

Damian grew up in a small town near San Diego, California. The second youngest of nine siblings—he has six sisters and two brothers—he learned to play the piano at age six when his mother, a classical pianist, gave him lessons at home. Along with his brothers and sisters, he formed a band called the Weirz, a progressive rock group that performed at San Diego dance clubs and marine bases in the '70s.

Initially, Damian played a B-3 Hammond organ and sang backing vocals for the band, but it wasn't long before his siblings realized the screams coming from the young girls in the audience were for Michael. They promoted him to lead vocalist when they moved to Los Angeles in 1978.

Soon afterward, Damian decided to pursue a solo career. In 1981 his cover version of Eric Carmen's "She Did It," released on LEG (a small label owned by his manager), inched up the Hot 100 to number 69. As a result, he was invited to perform the song on "American Bandstand." Damian says, "Dick Clark provided me with a great opportunity—the song really wasn't a hit."

The producers of "The Young and the Restless" were watching that day and they noticed Damian. "They saw me on 'American Bandstand,' auditioned me, and then wrote this whole character around a struggling young singer who is a waiter by day. It was funny because that's exactly what was happening to me in real life, so I went into the role playing myself."

Damian's real life continued to imitate his art. As he wrote songs that he performed on the show in his character of Danny Romalotti, he was signed in 1984 to CBS Records in Canada. Two albums were released in that country and Europe, but it would be several more years before he could convince a label in the United States to sign him.

His "Rock On" almost never rolled. It was tucked away in a closet for nine months after it was recorded because a number of labels didn't consider it commercial enough for radio to play it.

When film director Mark Rocco asked Tom and Larry Weir to write some music for the soundtrack of *Dream a Little Dream*, they decided on a whim to dig up "Rock On." "I remember the day we brought that tape to Mark," says Tom. "Larry and I were working on *Dream a Little Dream* and we went to drop the tape off and ended up playing 'Rock On' for him in our car. As soon as he heard it he said, 'This is cool' and grabbed the tape and said, 'We're going to put this in the movie.'"

"It was a complete surprise for me," adds Michael. "I remember my brother calling me and saying Mark wants to use 'Rock On' in his movie. I said, 'Where did he get it?'"

During a visit to Los Angeles, David Essex told *BAM* magazine how happy he was about the song's revival. "I'm very flattered that so many people still relate to the song," he commented. "Michael Damian's version is a lot more poppy than the way I originally recorded it. And when we met for the first time, he was very nervous. But once he realized I liked the way he did the song, we got on fine."

### THE TOP FIVE
*Week of June 3, 1989*

1 **Rock On**
Michael Damian

2 **Soldier of Love**
Donny Osmond

3 **Wind Beneath My Wings**
Bette Midler

4 **Patience**
Guns n' Roses

5 **I'll Be Loving You (Forever)**
New Kids on the Block

ATLANTIC 88972 # Wind Beneath My Wings
## BETTE MIDLER

Writers: *Larry Henley*
 *Jeff Silbar*

Producer: *Arif Mardin*

*June 10, 1989*
*1 week*

Bette Midler made her chart debut the week of December 23, 1972, with a remake of Bobby Freeman's "Do You Want to Dance" from her first album, *The Divine Miss M.* She followed that with her first top 10 single, a cover of the Andrews Sisters' 1941 hit, "Boogie Woogie Bugle Boy." During the next 16 years, Bette only had one other top 10 hit—the title song from her film *The Rose* (number three in June, 1980).

The singer, born in Paterson, New Jersey, on December 1, 1945, and raised in Hawaii, concentrated more on her motion-picture career in the '80s. After missteps with a filmed version of her *Divine Madness* concert and the critically-panned *Jinxed!*, she won plaudits for her role in the 1986 film *Down and Out in Beverly Hills.* The first in a series of films for Disney, it was followed by *Ruthless People* and *Outrageous Fortune.* But it wasn't until *Beaches* that Midler's musical talents were called upon, as they had been for *The Rose.*

"Everyone kept thinking, it's such a shame that they're only using a small portion of her talent," says Marc Shaiman, Midler's long-time musical arranger and music supervisor on *Beaches.*

When Shaiman and Midler first saw the script for *Beaches*, traditional songs were indicated wherever music was needed. Together, they decided what Bette would really sing in the film. For a scene near the end of the film, Shaiman suggested a song he had loved for a long time, "Wind Beneath My Wings."

The song had been written in 1982 by Jeff Silbar, a Nashville-based composer, and Larry Henley, former lead singer for the Newbeats ("Bread and Butter," "Run, Baby Run"). "Larry was signed to House of Gold Music, and I was the professional manager there," Silbar recalls. They had already teamed to write "He's a Heartache (Looking for a Place to Happen)," which went to number one on the country chart for Janie Fricke. Sitting down one day to write a song for Bob Seger, Silbar, a pilot, was inspired when he noticed that Henley had jotted down on his legal pad the phrase "Wind Beneath My Wings." "I knew we were going to write that song that day. He told me he had written a poem to his ex-wife years before with that title. We ended up using none of the poem, but based on the concept, we wrote the song." Henley wrote the lyrics, Silbar wrote the music, and a demo was recorded.

"Our publisher at the time, Bob Montgomery, heard our demo and felt like we had a hit," Silbar continues. "He championed the song. It was a year before it ever got recorded, then it got recorded 10 times. Originally, we played it for Kenny Rogers and Barry Manilow, yet the first time it was recorded, it was by Roger Whittaker. Then Sheena Easton recorded it, (and) Lou Rawls." Next came versions by Lee Greenwood and B.J. Thomas. "It was slated to be a Lee Greenwood single, and Gary Morris ran into the studio and put it out," says Silbar. "We had really not ever heard of Gary Morris; we were not too thrilled initially. Then it became a top five country record and Song of the Year in Nashville. Still feeling we had the big record to come, we let it cool off for a little bit, because we assumed it was too hot for somebody else to cover it pop." A version by Gladys Knight was released as "Hero."

In a meeting with Bette, her production partner Bonnie Bruckheimer and film director Garry Marshall, Shaiman, not trained as a vocalist, performed the song with his back turned to them. "When I turned around, they were all weeping, and everyone had to agree we were never going to beat that."

A remake of the Drifters' "Under the Boardwalk" was the first single released from the *Beaches* soundtrack. It failed to crack the Hot 100, and "Wind Beneath My Wings" was t e follow-up. It debuted on March 4 1989, and was number one 14 we ks later. Almost a year later, it won he Grammy for Song of the Year and Record of the Year.

---

## THE TOP FIVE
### *Week of June 10, 1989*

1 **Wind Beneath My Wings**
Bette Midler

2 **I'll Be Loving You (Forever)**
New Kids on the Block

3 **Every Little Step**
Bobby Brown

4 **Rock On**
Michael Damian

5 **Buffalo Stance**
Neneh Cherry

# 732 I'll Be Loving You (Forever) COLUMBIA 68671
## NEW KIDS ON THE BLOCK

*Writer: Maurice Starr*

*Producers: Maurice Starr*
*Michael Jonzun*

*June 17, 1989*
*1 week*

In 1981, Maurice Starr put together a quintet of five black kids from Boston and called them New Edition. Bobby Brown [see 718—"My Prerogative"], Ralph Tresvant, Ricky Bell, Michael Bivins and Ronald DeVoe first made the Hot 100 in May of 1983 with "Candy Girl" on the Streetwise label.

Starr told New Edition he was thinking of starting a group of five white kids, and they could headline together. But there never was a double billing, because after their first album, New Edition was wooed away by MCA Records, leaving Starr behind. Stunned at how he had been treated, Starr entered a period of depression. He heard industry talk that he had blown his one big chance.

"After my down period, I went to work," Starr recalls. "I got in my car and said, I'm going to find these five young white kids and put this group together. I stopped at a flower shop because Mother's Day was coming up. I saw this one young white kid . . . I said, 'Listen, how would you like to be a star? My name is Maurice Starr, and I used to work with New Edition.'" The teenager had never heard of New Edition, but Starr persevered. "I left my number and said, 'If you want to do this, give me a call; I won't take your number.' I got a call, all right—it was from the F.B.I." They wanted to know why a big black man was trying to pick up little white boys. "I knew then I had to find somebody white to help me find the kids." Starr turned to his long-time friend Mary Alford, a talent agent and personnel officer for the Massachusetts Department of Education.

"She brought about 30 kids to me over a period of a month, two months," says Starr. The first official New Kid was Mark Wahlberg [see 795—"Good Vibrations"]. Admittedly not a singer, and more interested in rap than the ballads Starr wanted to record, Mark dropped out of the group. His brother Donnie, discovered by Alford at Dorchester's Copley Square High School, remained in the

## THE TOP FIVE
### Week of June 17, 1989

1   **I'll Be Loving You (Forever)**
    New Kids on the Block

2   **Wind Beneath My Wings**
    Bette Midler

3   **Every Little Step**
    Bobby Brown

4   **Satisfied**
    Richard Marx

5   **Buffalo Stance**
    Neneh Cherry

New Kids and told Starr about his friend Danny Wood, and brothers Jordan and Jon Knight. A boy named Jamie Kelley completed the quintet, but Kelley's parents didn't want him exposed to show business at a young age, so he was replaced by Joe McIntyre before the first album was recorded.

"I knew I had the right guys," says Starr. "I knew it from day one." He produced a four-song demo for the group, who were then called Nynuk. Starr called his friend Larkin Arnold at Columbia Records, and told him he had a group that could really be big. Arnold hated the group name. One of the songs on the demo was a rap written by Starr and Donnie Wahlberg, "New Kids on the Block," which quickly replaced Nynuk as the group's monicker. "Cecil Holmes and Larkin together agreed this could be a big idea," according to Starr. "They signed New Kids on the Block to the black division of Columbia."

The first album was recorded in 1986. "Be My Girl" made it to number 90 on the Hot Black Singles chart, but the New Kids failed to dent the Hot 100. The second album, *Hangin'*

*Tough*, had a slow start. But then Randy Kabrich, program director of WRBQ-Tampa, started playing "Please Don't Go Girl," a song originally recorded by an earlier Starr group, Irving and the Twins. The New Kids' version peaked at number 10 in October, 1988. Five months later, "You Got It (The Right Stuff)" marched up to number three. The third single was "I'll Be Loving You (Forever)," a song Starr wrote for Smokey Robinson. "I was sitting down at the piano and could not think of a song. When I'm writing, a lot of times I'll just press all the keys down—anything to start making noise. It came together unconsciously, and I said, 'This would be great for Smokey Robinson.'" But Starr never showed the song to Smokey. "When it came to the New Kids, they were a priority. Every song I wrote was going to go to the New Kids. If it sounds like a hit to me, it's going to go to them. Later, I told Smokey the song was for him."

"I'll Be Loving You (Forever)" debuted on the Hot 100 on April 1, 1989. Eleven weeks later, it became the first number one single for the New Kids on the Block.

*Writer: Richard Marx*

*Producers: Richard Marx*
*David Cole*

*June 24, 1989*
*1 week*

Richard Marx was not concerned about the pressure of recording his sophomore album. "That pressure is pressure you put on yourself," he told Pat Lewis. "I've known certain people who have had successful first records, and their next record goes right in the toilet. Almost every time, it's been the pressure of coming up with new material. It's the notion that you have your whole life to write your first album, and only a few months to write the second. I write songs for a living, and that's what I do. I wrote most of my first album while I was recording it. 'Endless Summer Nights' and 'Should've Known Better' were the only old songs that I used. That was the kind of pressure I wanted."

Marx did have a lot to live up to. He was the first male vocalist to pull four top three singles from a debut album [see 704—"Hold On to the Nights"]. He wrote around 25 songs for *Repeat Offender* while touring to promote his first album; he recorded 15 of them, and narrowed the final choices down to 10 tracks. "This represents the best work that I've ever done and that I can possibly do right now," he told Lewis after delivering the master to EMI. "I wouldn't have changed any of the songs, written a different chorus here, or taken this song and placed it over there. I did everything the way I wanted to—now I just want to see

what people think of it."

His answer came quickly. "Satisfied," the first single from the album, made an impressive debut at number 39 the week of May 6, 1989. Seven weeks later, Marx had his second consecutive number one hit.

"'Satisfied' was the last song I wrote for the album," he told the Interview Factory. "It's the opposite of the first album. The first song I ever recorded was 'Don't Mean Nothing' and that was the first single. But this time, the album was pretty much finished (and) mixed, and I would listen to it and I would think, there's something missing . . . I've got this heart of rock and roll stuff that I'm really loving over here, and I've got this softer stuff . . . a ballad over here . . . (but) there's nothing right in the middle.

"So I wrote this song 'Satisfied,' and what I like most about it is that musically it sort of reminds me of the old Tubes song 'She's a Beauty' in its feel, and that's one of my favorite songs of all time. It's got that sort of dance, rock-and-roll party vibe about it. And the lyric is about never settling for second best, and trying to live each moment that you're not working your butt off to its fullest. I didn't want it to be like, 'Live every moment to its fullest,' because that's such a cliché. But I found myself promising to work really hard for a year and then take a month off—and when that month comes, I'm off doing this or doing that. Too many things have happened

to me in the last couple of years that have made me appreciate every moment that I live.

"I've always called myself a perfectionist, and it's a word that a lot of people use. I recently heard somebody say something about that which I really enjoyed, which is my new philosophy. All of us who call ourselves perfectionists, what is it that we do that's perfect? When I heard that line, I said, I'm never gonna call myself a perfectionist again. It's really true, I'm not easily satisfied, and that's why the song 'Satisfied' came so easily."

Included in the group singing background vocals on "Satisfied" were Richard's mother Ruth and his wife, actress Cynthia Rhodes. Marx was 19 when he was asked to write a song for the film *Staying Alive*, the sequel to *Saturday Night Fever*. Although none of Marx's work appears on the soundtrack album, he did meet one of John Travolta's female leads—Rhodes. She was seven years older than him, and recalled for *People* that she considered him "a really nice, sweet little boy, but he was so young." They met again at a party two years later, and she arranged for him to date some of her girlfriends—but all he would do was talk to them about Cynthia.

"After a couple of months, I convinced Cynthia that she and I should move to phase two," Marx said in *People*. They were married January 8, 1989. Their son Brandon was born September 11, 1990, in Los Angeles.

## THE TOP FIVE
*Week of June 24, 1989*

1 **Satisfied**
Richard Marx

2 **I'll Be Loving You (Forever)**
New Kids on the Block

3 **Buffalo Stance**
Neneh Cherry

4 **Baby Don't Forget My Number**
Milli Vanilli

5 **Good Thing**
Fine Young Cannibals

# 734

## Baby Don't Forget My Number
ARISTA 9781

MILLI VANILLI

*Writers: Frank Farian*
*Brad Howell*
*Bernd Berwanger*

*Producer: Frank Farian*

*July 1, 1989*
*1 week*

Rob Pilatus grew up in Munich. He was the son of a German strip-tease dancer and a black American soldier, but was given up for adoption and raised by a German couple. He worked as a DJ and a model, and gained notoriety as a breakdancer. He was good enough to be invited to an international breakdancing competition in New York in 1984.

Fabrice Morvan was born on the Caribbean island of Guadeloupe in the West Indies. His parents emigrated to Miami, and when his mother moved to Paris, Fab attended school there and excelled in athletics. He was training for a national trampoline competition when he injured his neck. Hearing that ballet was good exercise, Fab went to Los Angeles to attend classes. He loved to visit dance clubs at night, and on one particular occasion, met another black European who was visiting Los Angeles—Pilatus. Rob and Fab struck up a friendship and ended up back in Munich, where they earned money by appearing in videos and working in a local post office.

On January 1, 1988, Pilatus and Morvan accepted an invitation from German record producer Frank Farian to visit his studio in Frankfurt and hear a demo he had recorded of a song called "Girl You Know It's True." Farian was well-known in Europe for pro-

### THE TOP FIVE
*Week of July 1, 1989*

1  **Baby Don't Forget My Number**
   Milli Vanilli

2  **Good Thing**
   Fine Young Cannibals

3  **Satisfied**
   Richard Marx

4  **Buffalo Stance**
   Neneh Cherry

5  **If You Don't Know Me By Now**
   Simply Red

ducing Boney M, a West Indies quartet that scored nine top 10 singles in England. (In America, Boney M only managed four chart singles; the most successful was "Rivers of Babylon," which peaked at number 30 in August, 1978.)

"We got a call to come to his studio and we said, 'All right, that's it,'" Rob told Chuck Philips of the *Los Angeles Times*. "We were just dumb little kids, so we said, 'Let's go.' When we got to the studio, 'Girl You Know It's True' was just a demo and he asked us our opinion of it and if we could sing it and we said, 'Yeah, we could sing it.' And he said, 'Oh beautiful, I believe it, but next week we have shows to do, so don't worry, I'll make you into a millionaire.'"

"Girl You Know It's True" was included on the first Milli Vanilli album released in Europe. Issued on a small label, the LP was picked up by Arista for distribution in the United States. By the time "Girl You Know It's True" was released as a single in America, it had already been number three on the U.K. chart.

The song was actually a cover version. It was written by Bill Pettaway, a gas-station attendant from Annapolis, Maryland, along with Sean Spencer, Kevin Lyles, Rodney Holloman and Ky Adeyemo. They recorded "Girl You Know It's True" as Numarx, and released it on Studio Records. It was distributed in Germany, and be-

came popular there in dance clubs.

"Girl You Know It's True" established the Milli Vanilli name in America. The single went to number two on the Hot 100, peaking the week of April 1, 1989. Four weeks later, "Baby Don't Forget My Number" debuted at number 62; in its 10th week on the chart, it surpassed the first single by going to number one.

Milli Vanilli were not on the charts very long before the rumors started. In the fall of 1989, an American singer from Dallas named Charles Shaw told the media in Germany that he had sung the lead vocals on "Girl You Know It's True." He repeated the charges in an interview with New York's *Newsday*, and said that Rob and Fab were hired only for their looks.

Eight days later, Shaw retracted his statement. He issued a new one: "My manager, Mr. Andreas Glaner, was of the opinion that it would be a good public-relations gag for my new record if I declared that I sang the lead." Rob reacted to Jeff Giles of *Rolling Stone*: "Everybody ask me if I sing on this record. Even my *mother* ask me. I am very proud person, and this is embarrassing. Fabrice and I—I think we are big talents. We can sing as good as any other pop star in the top 10. But I have to go through this again and again, till I get cancer in my stomach and die."

Still, the rumors would not go away.

*Writers: David Steele*
*Roland Gift*

*Producers: Andy Cox*
*David Steele*
*Roland Gift*

*July 8, 1989*
*1 week*

THE second single from the Fine Young Cannibals' *The Raw & the Cooked* had actually been recorded long before "She Drives Me Crazy" [see 726], the first number one hit for the group.

Film director Barry Levinson (*Diner, Rain Man*) heard the trio's first album and liked their music enough to use it as a temporary soundtrack for his film *Tin Men* starring Richard Dreyfuss and Danny De-Vito. He asked Andy Cox, David Steele and Roland Gift if they would write original music for the film, about aluminum-siding salesmen working in Baltimore in 1963.

"We read the script and thought it was good," says lead singer Gift. "Then we went to have a viewing. He had finished the film and was editing when we saw it. We went to see if we'd like it enough to contribute the score." The group wrote four songs for the film, including "Good Thing."

Fine Young Cannibals ended up in the movie, playing a Baltimore soul band of the period. "He liked the way we looked," Gift says of Levinson. "We were in England doing the music, and when we were done, he got a studio and put in some extras, then filmed us and cut it into the film. He put us in at the last minute."

It wasn't Gift's only film role. "I used to do a lot of drama when I was younger," he says. "I used to be in a couple of groups that did plays, so I've always had an interest in that . . . I knew I'd be doing movies at some point." His work in *Tin Men* and some television parts led to his being cast in Stephen Frears' 1987 movie *Sammy and Rosie Get Laid*. Then Michael Caton-Jones cast him as Johnny Edge-combe in *Scandal*, based on the 1963 John Profumo affair.

The other Cannibals didn't have to worry about Gift opting out of the group for an acting career. "It's not as if they're solely producers and I'm solely an actor," Roland told Peter Johnson. "We've got the choice. We can make a decision on an artistic level, rather than on a purely financial level. Also, my singing and my acting feed each other. You're dealing with the same emotions; it's just a slightly different way of interpreting them. That's why I don't find it a problem, singing and acting. And also, it's good to take a break from one thing and do something else that's creative. I know a writer who will work on his script,

and by way of a rest, he'll work on his crossword. It helps his writing, and it also helps his crosswords."

There was no soundtrack released for *Tin Men*, so the four Fine Young Cannibals songs from the movie were available commercially for the first time when *The Raw & the Cooked* was released. The album also included "Ever Fallen in Love," their cover of a Buzzcocks tune which they had recorded for the film *Something Wild*.

Three of the newer tracks on *The Raw & the Cooked* were produced by David Z, whose previous credits included work with Jody Watley and Sheila E. The group had asked their record company to procure Prince as their producer—but it was more a stall for time than a genuine request. "I.R.S. was getting on our nerves, so it was a way of keeping them at bay," Gift confesses. David Z had worked with Prince as an engineer and arranger, and the trio was happy to work with him.

"Good Thing" debuted on the Hot 100 the week of May 6, 1989, at number 69; nine weeks later, the Fine Young Cannibals had their second chart-topping single. "Don't Look Back," the next track to be released, peaked at number 11 in October, 1989. "I'm Not the Man I Used to Be" reached number 54 in December, and "I'm Not Satisfied" petered out at number 90 in March, 1990.

**THE TOP FIVE**
*Week of July 8, 1989*

1 **Good Thing**
Fine Young Cannibals

2 **Baby Don't Forget My Number**
Milli Vanilli

3 **If You Don't Know Me By Now**
Simply Red

4 **Express Yourself**
Madonna

5 **Toy Soldiers**
Martika

# If You Don't Know Me By Now   ELEKTRA 69297
## SIMPLY RED

*Writers: Kenny Gamble*
*Leon Huff*

*Producer: Stewart Levine*

*July 15, 1989*
*1 week*

PRODUCER Stewart Levine was introduced to Simply Red when he was invited by Simon Potts to one of their first shows at a little college outside of London. It was January of 1985 and Levine, an American, had been living in the U.K. for about six months. "It was the days of demos. Everyone was sending demo tapes. I said, 'Listen to a band? See a band? No one's ever said that!'" he exclaims. "I went to see the show, and I was really impressed with Mick (Hucknall) in particular."

Levine produced Simply Red's first album *Picture Book*, and scored a number one single [see 640—"Holding Back the Years"]. The group's second album, *Men and Women*, was produced by Alex Sadkin, but the band remained friendly with Levine, and he returned for the third effort, *A New Flame*. Levine remembers discussing the songs that would appear on the album with Hucknall over a meal at a London restaurant, but doesn't recall who first suggested doing a remake of Harold Melvin and the Blue Notes' Philadelphia classic "If You Don't Know Me By Now," written and produced by Kenny Gamble and Leon Huff. "I think Mick did, and he thinks I did. A couple of glasses of wine later, he was singing it, and I was singing something."

Hucknall had included one remake on each of his first two albums: the

---

## THE TOP FIVE
*Week of July 15, 1989*

1  **If You Don't Know Me By Now**
   Simply Red

2  **Express Yourself**
   Madonna

3  **Good Thing**
   Fine Young Cannibals

4  **Toy Soldiers**
   Martika

5  **Baby Don't Forget My Number**
   Milli Vanilli

---

Valentine Brothers' "Money's Too Tight (To Mention)" was on *Picture Book*, and Cole Porter's "Ev'ry Time We Say Goodbye" was on *Men and Women*. "I think it's a challenge to do other people's songs from time to time," says Hucknall. "When you're writing from your point of view all the time, you're getting one side of it. When you're doing other people's songs, it's very good as a singer to expand your technique."

Hucknall admits to loving Harold Melvin's group and lead vocalist Teddy Pendergrass. "I used to dance to their music when I was about 13—my teenage period was the Philly sound." Still, Hucknall experienced some anxiety about covering a song by a vocalist of the caliber of Teddy Pendergrass.

"I find it terribly difficult to do covers," Levine confesses. "In the 25 years I've been producing records, I might have done a dozen covers. I felt 'If You Don't Know Me By Now' was a real piece of magic . . . such a great song to begin with. I didn't allow myself to listen to the original after we thought about doing it." The producer believes it is easier to remake a song where there isn't already a definitive version. That wasn't the case with the Gamble-Huff song: "You don't think of that song without thinking of Teddy Pendergrass."

After pre-production in Gallarate, Italy, Simply Red met Levine at Air

Studios in Montserrat in the West Indies to record *A New Flame*. "Mick was very nervous about the vocal on it," says the producer. "I didn't want too much orchestration, I wanted to keep it very simple. I remember the Philly record was produced to death—it was a great production. I went the other way and made it more sparse, a little bluesier and a little more organic. I think one of the big moves was to make it two-part harmony instead of a three-part harmony."

"If You Don't Know Me By Now" peaked at number two in the U.K., but Hucknall says he wasn't aware of the single's progress in the States. "My relationship with the record company at the time was close to awful. . . . the music did the work."

Levine also wasn't fully aware of the single's progress, but for different reasons. He was living in a rural area of upstate New York, and didn't have access to a pop radio station. Visiting a friend in Manhattan, Levine was on the way to see Spike Lee's *Do the Right Thing* with his two sons when a telephone call informed him that "If You Don't Know Me By Now" had moved to number one on the *Billboard* Hot 100. "I made a deal with my sons years before: anytime we go to number one, they get a hundred dollars." Levine says the movie was the most expensive one he had ever seen—the price of admission plus $200.

COLUMBIA 68747 **Toy Soldiers**
MARTIKA

**737**

*Writers: Martika*
*Michael Jay*

*Producer: Michael Jay*

*July 22, 1989*
*2 weeks*

"**I** always knew I needed to sing," says Marta Marrero Martinez, better known as Martika (adapted from the diminutive, Martica). "When I was two years old, I wanted to perform—I was asking my parents to let me go to dance and ballet class." Her parents, who emigrated from Cuba, raised Martika and her three older brothers in a bicultural section of Glendale, California. By the time she was 11, Martika was looking in the telephone directory for talent agents. At 12, she landed a role in the film version of *Annie*.

After working on the movie for three months, she found it difficult to find other roles. "I was getting a bit frustrated, so I got involved in a performance theater group in Los Angeles and spent three years with them. We ended up performing at the Roxy on Sunset for two years." Martika was in company of 15 kids, starring in a Sunday-afternoon review called "Let's Put On a Show."

"Some people had seen us perform at the Roxy and they developed a concept based on that for a TV pilot," Martika recalls. "We went to Utah and shot at the Osmonds' studio; I stayed in Donny's dressing room. It was very cool because I was about 14, and the show sold a year later as a series."

"Kids, Incorporated" lasted three seasons. During the production of that series, Martika crossed paths with a songwriter from Skokie, Illinois. A former music director for his college radio station, Michael Jay worked for Curtis Mayfield's Curtom label in Chicago before moving to Los Angeles. After being turned down by every label in town for a job in A&R, Michael discovered the Los Angeles Songwriters Showcase and decided to start his own publishing company, which led to a staff writer position at Famous Music.

Gloria Estefan and Stephanie Mills recorded his material, but Jay was also interested in producing his songs. "I was looking for months to find an artist I could do that with," he explains. Then he had lunch with his sister Lori Margulies, a production assistant on "Kids, Incorporated." "They were running overtime. I had to sit there and watch them tape a scene where Martika was singing. That was all I could talk about with my sister when we went to lunch. When we came back to the set, Lori introduced me to Martika's mother, who was

managing her career. Her mother and I hit it off, I met Martika, and we started doing some demos.

"When I first met her, Martika had no intention of being a songwriter. She wanted me to write the songs, then call her when it was time to come in the studio and do the vocals. One night, when we were having dinner at her house, she showed me this whole notebook of lyrics and phrases she had been writing. I couldn't believe how sensitive her lyrics were, how in-depth they were. It looked like they were written by a seasoned pro. So I decided we ought to write a song together."

Martika took Michael to the Whisky to see a friend of hers in a punk band called the Watch. "It was very underground and very dark," Martika describes. "It was a whole other scene from what Michael was used to, and I was into that scene." Jay picks up the story: "(The band) introduced the next song, and it was called 'Toy Soldiers.' It was 180 beats per minute, two chords, you couldn't understand any of the lyrics. But I walked out and thought 'Toy Soldiers' was a very cool title. In the parking lot, I started humming the chorus melody to 'Toy Soldiers' and sang it to Martika. I said, 'We have to get together and write this song tomorrow.'"

The next day, Jay asked if Martika could make the song mean something. "She was the one who came up with the idea about writing a song against drugs and drug addiction. Some of her friends were really involved . . . and it was really close to her at that time. The song was completely written in one-and-a-half days. We used a children's chorus on the record, which gave it a real cool atmosphere.

"Because the rest of the album is very pop/dance, we came into the studio and it was like having a party. But in order to get the vibe I wanted—that mystery in her voice and performance—we recorded the lead vocals beginning at midnight. She lit candles all around the studio, her entire family was there . . . it was a real solemn atmosphere."

## THE TOP FIVE
*Week of July 22, 1989*

1 **Toy Soldiers**
Martika

2 **Express Yourself**
Madonna

3 **If You Don't Know Me By Now**
Simply Red

4 **Batdance**
Prince

5 **So Alive**
Love and Rockets

## 738 Batdance WARNER BROTHERS 22924
### PRINCE

*Writer: Prince*

*Producer: Prince*

*August 5, 1989*
*1 week*

Prince went to the top of the *Billboard* Hot 100 for the fourth time with "Batdance," a pastiche of music, sounds and dialogue from *Batman*. Directed by Tim Burton, *Batman* starred Michael Keaton as Bob Kane's Caped Crusader from the pages of DC Comics. The film was a smash hit, earning $251 million domestically.

"We knew going in that *Batman* was going to be a franchise," says Gary LeMel, president of Warner Brothers Music. "We decided we wanted to have a superstar artist and we wanted to keep it in the family, meaning the family of labels. We started seeing dailies, and it so happened that the Joker character was dressed in purple. The cars were purple. It started to point to Prince. So we approached him; at that time, he was being managed by Albert Magnoli." Magnoli already had a relationship with Warner Brothers, having directed Prince's film *Purple Rain*, as well as the Sylvester Stallone-Kurt

Russell thriller *Tango and Cash*, for the studio.

"Albert loved the idea—thought it was great timing for Prince," LeMel continues. Magnoli told Chuck Arnold, "One thing that generally struck all the filmmakers involved with the motion picture and myself and Prince was the conflicting character that Batman was—the past haunting him and the present being irreconcilable; the desire to try to make amends with the Joker, but being unable to because the Joker is unable to cross that line."

In January of 1989, Prince took the Concorde to London to meet Burton on the set of *Batman* at Pinewood Studios and see some of the dailies. Burton had been playing Prince tapes in his car on the way to the studio, and was using "1999" and "Baby I'm a Star" on a temporary soundtrack.

Prince loved the set for Gotham City. He met Michael Keaton and Kim Basinger (starring as Vicki Vale) and watched a scene being filmed in the Batcave. Then he was invited to watch about 40 minutes of rough footage. According to LeMel, "He loved what he saw. He and Tim got along great. And there were three or four spots in the movie that were definitely song spots. They were written into the film—it

wasn't like we were trying to jam anything in. One thing Tim would never do is put something in that wasn't part of the fabric."

Prince canceled a scheduled vacation in Paris and went home to Minneapolis to write songs. Burton expected him to come up with a couple of numbers. "Prince wrote a lot of songs," recalls LeMel. "I went back to Minneapolis and he played me all the songs. He had written songs that were in places that were really 'score' places, yet they were brilliantly done. But Tim wanted the big *Batman* score, and the songs to be where they were supposed to be."

A month after Prince visited the London set, he played eight of his songs for Burton, all synchronized to film. Burton thought three pieces didn't work for the movie. He turned down an instrumental theme, as well as "Rave to the Joy Fantastic" and "200 Balloons," and asked Prince to come up with two more songs. Prince offered "Trust" and "Partyman."

The instrumental score for *Batman* was composed by Danny Elfman, leader of Oingo Boingo and composer of scores for *Pee Wee's Big Adventure* and *Beetlejuice* (both Burton movies). The abundance of music for the film led Warner Brothers to release two soundtracks. Prince's album, issued to coincide with the release of the movie, was titled *Batman: Motion Picture Soundtrack*. Elfman's disc, released two months later, was called *Batman: Motion Picture Score*.

Prince's soundtrack included the songs he had written for the movie that didn't make the final cut, like "Lemon Crush" and "The Arms of Orion," a duet with Sheena Easton. The single "Batdance" was also not heard in the movie. "'Batdance' was something Prince put together overnight," LeMel explains. "He called us and said, 'You gotta hear this.' We heard it and flipped out. We knew it would never be in the movie but everyone thought, what a great marketing tool for giving the public an insight into the film. At that point, people had seen the teaser trailer, but hadn't heard any of the dialogue."

To accompany the single, Prince shot a video in Los Angeles in which he played himself and Gemini, a half-Batman, half-Joker character. Fifteen dancers played multiple Batmans, Jokers and Vicki Vales.

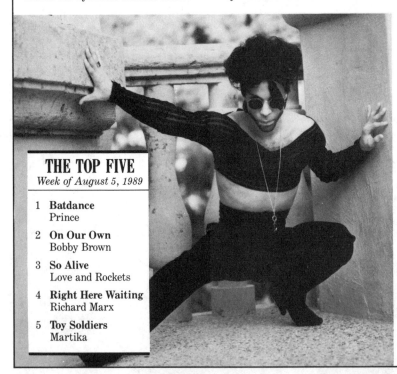

### THE TOP FIVE
*Week of August 5, 1989*

1 **Batdance**
  Prince

2 **On Our Own**
  Bobby Brown

3 **So Alive**
  Love and Rockets

4 **Right Here Waiting**
  Richard Marx

5 **Toy Soldiers**
  Martika

EMI 50219 **Right Here Waiting** 739
RICHARD MARX

Writer: *Richard Marx*

Producers: *Richard Marx*
*David Cole*

*August 12, 1989*
*3 weeks*

RICHARD MARX scored his third number one hit in a row with "Right Here Waiting," the second single from *Repeat Offender*. It was a song he resisted including on the album "because it was way too personal," he told the Interview Factory. "I didn't hear it as being a song I wanted to share with the world."

Marx had already written a power ballad with his friend Fee Waybill, and assumed that that song would satisfy the need to have a ballad on the second album. But then a series of events prevented him from seeing his wife, actress Cynthia Rhodes, for three months. She was in Africa on location for a film, and he was touring. They did plan to get together, but it didn't happen. Richard says the only way he was able to get through that period was to sit down and pour his feelings into a song. While visiting the home of his friend Bruce Gaitsch, Richard sat down and wrote "Right Here Waiting" in ten minutes.

Richard recorded a demo and sent it to Cynthia so she would know how much he missed her. "By accident, a couple of people heard the demo, just friends of mine, and they (fell) apart," Richard told Dick Clark on "Countdown America." "The main reason I didn't want to put it on the album is because . . . it would be like me writing her a love letter and then having it

printed in the *Globe*. . . . It was like an invasion of something that was really private. But then I realized that part of my job as a songwriter is to communicate with as many people as I can, and something that is that personal to me may be just as personal to somebody else in their own situation—which is exactly what happened."

There was one side effect of releasing the song that Marx didn't care for. "I set out to make such a strong rock album on *Repeat Offender*," he told the Interview Factory, "(but) the record company at the time really pushed the ballads . . . more than the rock songs. I felt that the lingering feeling was that the *Repeat Offender* album was a mellow record—because a lot of people still just buy singles, and if you base the album upon the singles, then that's probably true."

EMI continued to mine *Repeat Offender* for hits. "Angelia" peaked at number four in December, 1989. It was Marx' seventh top 10 hit in a row, his entire chart output. The top 10 streak was broken with the next single, "Too Late to Say Goodbye," which went to number 12 in March, 1990.

"Too Late to Say Goodbye" was followed by "Children of the Night," a number 13 hit in June.

"There's a foundation (called Children of the Night) in Los Angeles that's set up for runaway kids who've turned to prostitution or drug addiction," Marx told Steve Korté in *CD Review*. "These kids basically have no place to go. I got in touch with the head of the group because I'd heard she was trying to raise enough money to build a shelter for them. But because of the nature of the foundation, very few people will come forward and help. When I got wind of the problem, I told this woman, 'Look, I'd like to write a song about this. Maybe you can help me write the song by letting me meet some of these kids, and maybe I can help you. I'll give you whatever royalties the song makes.' So she hooked me up with a couple of children. When I went to do the record, I had a bunch of these kids from the street come into the studio to sing the last chorus. That's the big choir you hear." By 1991, Marx had donated $100,000 in royalties to Children of the Night.

## THE TOP FIVE
*Week of August 12, 1989*

1  **Right Here Waiting**
   Richard Marx

2  **On Our Own**
   Bobby Brown

3  **Batdance**
   Prince

4  **So Alive**
   Love and Rockets

5  **Once Bitten Twice Shy**
   Great White

# Cold Hearted
VIRGIN 99196

## PAULA ABDUL

*Writer: Elliot Wolff*

*Producers: Elliot Wolff*
*Keith Cohen*

*September 2, 1989*
*1 week*

Paula Abdul first heard Elliot Wolff's material when Virgin Records A&R chief Gemma Corfield played his composition "Straight Up" for the singer [see 721]. It was one of six songs Wolff had written for another artist signed to Virgin who was dropped before recording anything. "That was the only one they played Paula from that group of songs," says Wolff, a Washington, D.C. musician and former musical director for Peaches and Herb [see 503—"Reunited"]. "It's funny, I never thought to play them any of that other material. I didn't even think about it. I guess I like to keep going on, so when she asked me if I had another song for her, I wrote another song, which was 'Cold Hearted.'"

Abdul and Wolff both enjoyed their first number one single with "Straight Up." For a follow-up, Virgin released the title track from Paula's debut album, the Oliver Leiber-penned "Forever Your Girl" [see 729]. For the album's fifth single, Virgin returned to Elliot Wolff's material.

The writer/producer describes how he came up with "Cold Hearted": "I wrote it from the perspective of a woman." But is the song too harsh on men? "I've heard that said before. There was no conscious effort to do that. And if you know women, I guess you should know how they think. It's not so alien. There's not that much dif-

## THE TOP FIVE
*Week of September 2, 1989*

1  **Cold Hearted**
   Paula Abdul

2  **Right Here Waiting**
   Richard Marx

3  **Hangin' Tough**
   New Kids on the Block

4  **Don't Wanna Lose You**
   Gloria Estefan

5  **Angel Eyes**
   Jeff Healey Band

ference between guys and girls in terms of that subject."

Paula found that all of her producers on the first album had something in common about their work habits. "The hardest thing for me was the way the producers kept their hours—they never slept!" she exclaims. "A lot of the producers liked to work from night until morning. For me, it was difficult because I'm an early riser and I like to get up at 6:30, 7:00 in the morning. By the time it hits midnight, I'm dead. So I had to readjust my whole thinking." Recording the album at night, Paula was choreographing "The Tracey Ullman Show," Eddie Murphy's *Coming to America* and George Michael's *Faith* tour during the day.

Paula completed her vocals for the albums in a six-week period. "The songs themselves were thrown at Paula pretty fast," vocal trainer Evelyn Halus told Timothy White in *Billboard*. "We'd get them one day in instrumental or demo form, learn them together, get her vocal down, and then go back the next day and record it. Some of the stuff we learned in a single day and then recorded, like 'The Way That You Love Me.'"

Working in all areas of show busi-

ness was part of Paula's plan. "When I was growing up, I idolized the stars who could do it all—artist/entertainers like Gene Kelly, Judy Garland and Fred Astaire," she stated in a bio. "To be a star in their era, you had to excel in every area, and the all-around talent of those performers is what makes their films and recordings stand the test of time."

"Cold Hearted" entered the Hot 100 on June 24, 1989, and became Abdul's third consecutive number one hit 10 weeks later. As a follow-up, Virgin re-released Paula's second single, "(It's Just) The Way That You Love Me." Originally titled without the first two words, the parenthetical phrase was added to avoid confusion with Karyn White's "The Way You Love Me," which was climbing the chart at the same time. The first time around, the single's life was cut short because radio station KMEL in San Francisco started playing "Straight Up." Virgin executives decided at that time to promote "Straight Up" instead, and gave Paula her first number one hit. Following "Cold Hearted," the newly-released "(It's Just) The Way That You Love Me" peaked at number three in December, 1989.

COLUMBIA 68960 **Hangin' Tough**
NEW KIDS ON THE BLOCK

*Writer: Maurice Starr*

*Producer: Maurice Starr*

*September 9, 1989*
*1 week*

"IF there's one magic moment, it's when the kids got three standing ovations at the Apollo Theater," relishes Maurice Starr, producer and founder of the New Kids on the Block. "Right then and there, I felt I had a signal from God to say these kids are now ready."

Starr recalls getting the kids booked at the famed theater: "We walked the streets of Harlem together trying to get into different places. I happened to see Hal Jackson on the street. I followed him into an elevator and walked right into his office. I moved a couple of chairs back and said, 'If this ain't the greatest white group you've ever seen in your life, throw me out of here.' He thought I was crazy. He saw the group and thought they were fantastic, and immediately put them on at the Apollo."

Starr was willing to do whatever it took to make the five young men

mega-stars. "I begged for a tour with Tiffany—we got it." Opening for the teenaged Tiffany brought the New Kids attention not only from young female fans, but from people like Don Ienner, president of Columbia Records, who saw the Kids perform for the first time at the Westbury Music Fair in April, 1989. Midway through the tour, the acts switched positions and Tiffany became the opening act for the New Kids.

After the relative failure of the New Kids' first album for Columbia, the group was given another chance. "Cecil Holmes was generous to us, said he was going to put his neck on the line and give us another album at CBS," says a grateful Starr.

Writing the material for the New Kids' second album, Starr already had "Please Don't Go Girl," "You Got It (The Right Stuff)" and "I'll Be Loving You (Forever)" [see 732]. "We needed a song that symbolized what we were going through," says Starr. "So we talked, and I said I had an idea for a song called 'Hangin' Tough.'" The track became the title song for the album, and was the fourth single to be

released. It entered the Hot 100 on July 15, 1989; eight weeks later, it deposed Paula Abdul to become the New Kids' second consecutive number one single.

After sitting on top of the Hot 100 for one week, "Hangin' Tough" yielded to Gloria Estefan's "Don't Wanna Lose You." But it was still a great chart week for the New Kids. The fifth single from *Hangin' Tough*, "Cover Girl," was the highest new entry on the chart, debuting at number 62. The next highest debut was the New Kids' updating of the Delfonics' "Didn't I (Blow Your Mind)," which was also the flip side of "Hangin' Tough." A track from their first album, "Didn't I" debuted at number 68. The New Kids on the Block were the first group to have the top two debuts on the Hot 100 since the Beatles, who did it the week of October 18, 1969, with "Something" and "Come Together" [see 262].

By the week of September 30, all three of the New Kids' singles were in the top 40. It was the first time one artist had a trio of songs in the top 40 since the week of November 15, 1980, when Diana Ross had "Upside Down," "I'm Coming Out" and "It's My Turn" in the top 40 all at once.

Before the year was over, the New Kids released a Christmas single, "This One's for the Children." It peaked at number seven in January, 1990, and proceeds from the record were earmarked for United Cerebral Palsy. "This One's for the Children" gave the group a total of six top 10 singles in 1989—the last time an artist had that many top 10 hits in one year was 1983, when Michael Jackson had seven top 10 hits.

Sean Ross detailed the success of the New Kids at radio in *Billboard*. Steve Rivers, then program director of KIIS-FM in Los Angeles, told Ross that he was "*not* comparing the two groups musically. But for those of us who remember the early stages of Beatlemania, the enthusiasm is very similar. . . . Giving away (concert) tickets is the same as giving away a $100 bill. (Except) if you asked the kids which they'd rather have, they'd go for the tickets every time." At WHTZ in New York, where listeners could choose between tickets to a New Kids show and a Rolling Stones concert, 80 per cent of the winners chose the New Kids.

## THE TOP FIVE
*Week of September 9, 1989*

1  **Hangin' Tough**
   New Kids on the Block

2  **Cold Hearted**
   Paula Abdul

3  **Don't Wanna Lose You**
   Gloria Estefan

4  **Heaven**
   Warrant

5  **Right Here Waiting**
   Richard Marx

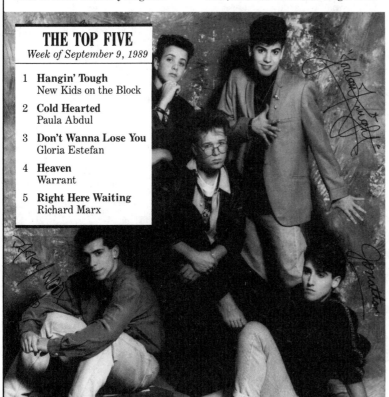

# Don't Wanna Lose You
EPIC 68959

## GLORIA ESTEFAN

*Writer: Gloria Estefan*

*Producers: Emilio Estefan
Jorge Casas
Clay Ostwald*

*September 16, 1989
1 week*

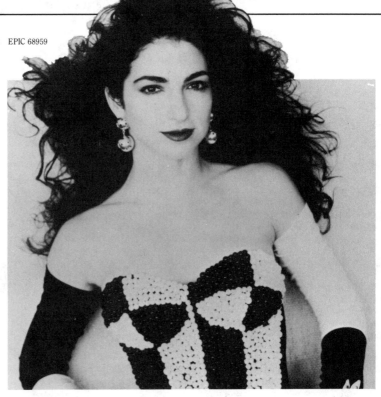

"DON'T WANNA LOSE YOU," the first single from the album *Cuts Both Ways*, was also the first single to list Gloria Estefan as a solo artist, as opposed to billing her as part of the Miami Sound Machine. "She's been the lead singer for years but no one knows her name," Emilio Estefan complained to Jefferson Graham in *USA Today*. "They always called her 'that girl from the Miami Sound Machine.' In the Grammys, she could only be nominated in the group category, not as a singer. This was the record company's idea, and I like it."

It also indicated that the original Miami Sound Machine was no more. Drummer Enrique "Kiki" Garcia, who co-wrote hits like "Conga" and "Rhythm Is Gonna Get You," was the last veteran member to leave in 1988.

Gloria wrote "Don't Wanna Lose You" for her husband. It was the last tune composed for *Cuts Both Ways* and, along with another ballad, "Here We Are," featured an arrangement by the singer. The single entered the *Billboard* Hot 100 at number 55 the week of July 8, 1989, and became Gloria's second chart-topper [see 698—"Anything for You"] 10 weeks later.

Nineteen-ninety started out as a good year for the Estefans. On January 22, Gloria was one of the hosts of the "American Music Awards," a Dick

Clark production for ABC-TV. On March 6, Sony Music presented the couple with a Crystal Globe, signifying more than five million albums sold outside the United States. (It was only the 24th such award handed out since the Crystal Globes were inaugurated in 1974.) And on Monday, March 19, Gloria, Emilio and their 10-year-old son Nayib met President George Bush in the White House. They discussed Gloria's anti-drug work as a White House photographer snapped away. A picture of the President with the Estefan family would later run in *People*.

The next afternoon, Gloria, Emilio and Nayib were aboard their tour bus, on their way to a performance in Syracuse, New York. A snowstorm in Pennsylvania snarled traffic on the interstate, and driver Ron "Bear" Jones brought the bus to a halt behind a jackknifed tractor-trailer near Tobyhanna in the Pocono Mountains. Suddenly, a speeding semi hit the tour bus from behind, sending it crashing into the stalled truck. Gloria, asleep in a bunk, was thrown violently to the floor. In pain, she called out for her husband to find their son. Emilio had cut his hand, but found Nayib. The boy had a broken collarbone.

"Nayib kept saying, 'Mommy, are you all right?'" Gloria remembers. "And I knew that I had to keep it together for his sake as well as mine. So

I focused on one thought: 'No, this is *not* going to happen! I'm going to do everything necessary to make myself strong, to make myself better than ever.'" As Emilio called for help on the bus phone, Gloria endured the painful wait by remembering her Lamaze training. She focused on a spot on the bus ceiling while breathing in and out. She was grateful for being able to feel pain—it meant her spinal cord had not been severed.

After being treated in a local hospital, Gloria and Emilio were airlifted by separate helicopters to the Hospital for Joint Diseases Orthopedic Institute in Manhattan. There Gloria underwent a four-hour surgery by Dr. Michael Neuwirth to insert two eight-inch metal braces to stabilize broken vertebrae. It wasn't until after the surgery that she was assured she would not be permanently paralyzed.

"She's not going to do much in the way of entertaining for three to six months," Dr. Harry Schmaltz announced. "It's a very serious injury and it's going to keep her out of commission for quite a while. She will need to wear a device to restrict movement during recovery."

The doctor's estimate was on the low side. Estefan did not appear on stage again until January, 1991, when she proved that she could come out of the dark.

## THE TOP FIVE
*Week of September 16, 1989*

1 **Don't Wanna Lose You**
Gloria Estefan

2 **Girl I'm Gonna Miss You**
Milli Vanilli

3 **Heaven**
Warrant

4 **Hangin' Tough**
New Kids on the Block

5 **Shower Me With Your Love**
Surface

# Girl I'm Gonna Miss You
## MILLI VANILLI

**743**

*Writers: Frank Farian*
*Dietman Kawohl*
*Peter Bischof-Fallenstein*

*Producer: Frank Farian*

*September 23, 1989*
*2 weeks*

Mɪʟʟɪ Vᴀɴɪʟʟɪ (a name that supposedly means "positive energy" in Turkish, but perhaps was just a defunct dance club in Berlin) scored their second number one single in America with "Girl I'm Gonna Miss You"—even as the rumors persisted that Rob Pilatus and Fabrice Morvan did not really sing on their records.

In a prophetic interview, Rob told *People* magazine, "Maybe we are going to stop being Milli Vanilli and go do our own music. Our people didn't want to have us so big as we are now. They created a monster."

Eight months later, those words had new meaning. Frank Farian, producer of the first Milli Vanilli album, called a press conference on November 14, 1990, to confirm the long-standing rumors that Rob and Fab did not sing a note as Milli Vanilli. He made the announcement after Rob and Fab had told him they wanted to actually sing on the second Milli Vanilli album and Farian had denied their request.

A day after Farian held his press conference, Rob and Fab spoke to Chuck Philips of the *Los Angeles Times*. "I feel like a mosquito being squeezed," Pilatus complained. "The last two years of our lives have been a total nightmare. We've had to lie to everybody. We are true singers, but that maniac Frank Farian would never allow us to express ourselves."

Farian (real name: Franz Reuther) retorted to Marc Fisher of *The Washington Post*: "I've never heard such a bad singer. They wanted to sing. They wanted to write songs. It never happened. They went instead to discos till 4:00 A.M. and slept all day." Farian said that he couldn't understand why people were upset at the revelation. "What was the betrayal? Did anyone in America believe that the Village People or the Monkees really sang themselves? The Archies? Please. Everyone's been doing it for 25 years."

The original singers turned out to be Brad Howell and John Davis, two former American soldiers who were not as photogenic as Rob and Fab. Howell gave his age as 45. The rapper on "Girl You Know It's True" was Charles Shaw, who had claimed to be the real Milli Vanilli as early as the fall of 1989, but then retracted his statement [see 734—"Baby Don't Forget My Number"]. At the end of 1990, Shaw claimed through friends that Farian had threatened him and banned him from his studio forever.

"I told Charles, 'You may not tell anyone you rapped,'" Farian told Fisher. "But threatening calls, that's something else. That he may not work here anymore, that's my decision. I told Shaw I wouldn't work with him if he said he was the voice of Milli Vanilli."

On November 19, 1990, the National Academy of Recording Arts and Sciences took back the Grammy Milli Vanilli won as Best New Artist. It was the first time in the 33-year history of the Grammys that an award had been rescinded. Academy President Mike Greene commented to Philips in the *Los Angeles Times*: "I hope this action signals loudly and clearly to producers, record companies and packagers that the academy cares deeply about this issue. I hope this revocation will make the industry think long and hard before anyone ever tries to pull something like this again." Greene said NARAS would not physically remove the trophy but would expect it to be returned. Rob and Fab's attorney, Alan Mintz, said before Greene made his announcement that the duo would return their statue.

When NARAS first announced the action it would take, there was no decision on what to do with the trophy. Rob and Fab suggested it be awarded to Howell, Davis and Shaw. Robert Hilburn of the *Los Angeles Times* listed all the options, including calling a new vote. He urged the Academy to present the Award to the runner-up in the voting—either Neneh Cherry, the Indigo Girls, Soul II Soul or Tone Loc. In the end, the Academy took the option of presenting no award in the Best New Artist category for 1989.

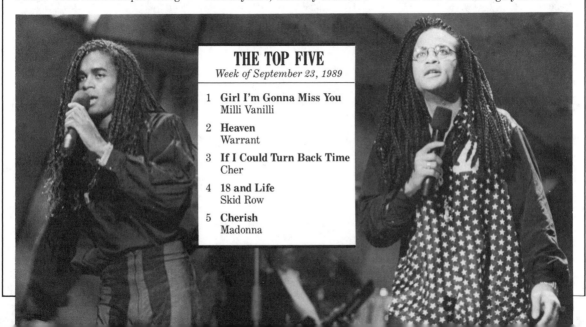

### THE TOP FIVE
*Week of September 23, 1989*

1  **Girl I'm Gonna Miss You**
   Milli Vanilli

2  **Heaven**
   Warrant

3  **If I Could Turn Back Time**
   Cher

4  **18 and Life**
   Skid Row

5  **Cherish**
   Madonna

## Miss You Much A&M 1445
### JANET JACKSON

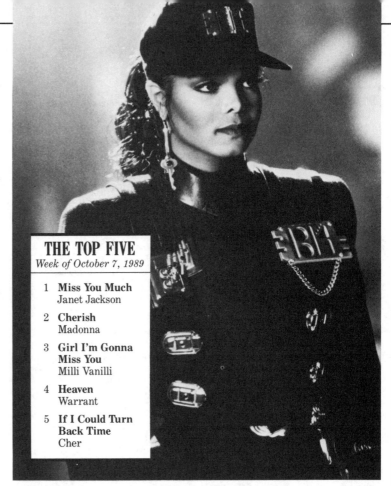

Writers: *James Harris III*
*Terry Lewis*

Producers: *Jimmy Jam*
*Terry Lewis*

*October 7, 1989*
*4 weeks*

**A**FTER the artistic and commercial success of *Control* [see 649—"When I Think of You"], Janet Jackson was under the same kind of pressure her brother Michael felt after releasing *Thriller*: what was she going to do next? The answer was her fourth album for A&M, *Rhythm Nation 1814*.

First, Janet had to settle the matter of who would produce the album. The logical choice was to return to Minneapolis and work with the two men who produced *Control*, Jimmy Jam and Terry Lewis.

"It happens in sports, but after a very successful record or a very successful season, you renegotiate," Jimmy Jam points out. "The reason it took so long in the negotiations was that we had decided because we were very close to Janet as friends, we would let the the lawyers and the managers take care of it and we wouldn't be involved. We would concentrate on the creative end of things. There were a lot of standstills, a lot of changes at A&M Records internally. Then she called me one day and said, 'Look, do you want to do the record or not?' I said, 'Well, of course we want to do the record. Do you want us to do the record?' And it was at that point she said, 'Well of course . . . let's just get this done.' We forcefully directed our attorneys and management to get a deal done—and magically, in two weeks, there was a deal."

Janet returned to Minneapolis in September, 1988, to begin the project. "She was very excited, and we were looking forward to it too," says Jimmy. Jam and Lewis had several tracks ready for Jackson to hear on her first day back at the Flyte Tyme studio. "I was working on the track to 'Miss You Much,' and she walked into the studio as I was putting down a keyboard part. I pointed at the keyboard and gave her the key of the song, and she ended up doing the string part that actually made the record. That was the way we started the album off.

"'Miss You Much' was the only song

### THE TOP FIVE
*Week of October 7, 1989*

1 **Miss You Much**
Janet Jackson

2 **Cherish**
Madonna

3 **Girl I'm Gonna Miss You**
Milli Vanilli

4 **Heaven**
Warrant

5 **If I Could Turn Back Time**
Cher

we already had a lyrical concept for, because we wanted a song to get started. We had no idea it would be the first single." Janet didn't record her lead vocals during this visit to Minneapolis. The producer explains: "The idea was to do the backgrounds first to get her voice back in tip-top singing shape, because she hadn't sung for probably two years."

After recording the backing vocals for several tracks, Janet returned home. Jam and Lewis worked on production while Janet wrote some lyrics. "It wasn't until after the Christmas holidays that we started back on the record again," says Jam. "We finally got back together around February of '89, and that's when we started working intensely on the project for the next four months."

The idea for the title to "Miss You Much" came from Jam's girlfriend. "She wrote me a letter and said at the end of it, 'Miss You Much' and I thought that was a cool title."

The concept for the album wasn't set when Janet recorded "Miss You Much." Jam elaborates: "The only se-

rious song we had at the beginning of the recording was 'The Knowledge.' We didn't have a clear picture of what we wanted the album to be conceptually. We (weren't) even thinking along the lines of a concept, intially; all we wanted was not to do *Control, Part Two*. So I think we were intent on trying to find different sounding songs than the *Control* album.

"Janet came up with the 'Rhythm Nation' concept. A lot of it had to do with watching TV. We're avid TV watchers, and we would watch BET, MTV . . . then switch over to CNN, and there'd always be something messed-up happening. It was never good news, always bad news. I think the thing that really triggered it was the Stockton playground murders, which really hit Janet hard. She loves kids." That led Janet, Terry and Jimmy to record "Livin' in a World (They Didn't Make)." "From that point on," Jam concludes, "we decided we should concentrate on doing some songs in that vein and we ended up with 'Rhythm Nation' and 'State of the World.' But the concept was her idea."

EMI 50223 ## Listen to Your Heart
### ROXETTE

Writer: *Per Gessle*

Producer: *Clarence Öfwerman*

*November 4, 1989*
*1 week*

"**I**F you've had the taste of a number one record, you want to have another one," Per Gessle of Roxette candidly admits. The Swedish duo's follow-up to their first chart-topper [see 725—"The Look"] was "Dressed for Success," which peaked at number 14 in July, 1989.

"Everyone said this (group) was going to be a one-hit-wonder," Gessle proclaims. "'The Look' was almost a novelty record. I know there were a lot of radio stations who didn't really believe in 'Dressed for Success'—not because they didn't like it, but because they thought success wasn't going to happen anymore."

The third single from Roxette's *Look Sharp!* was the ballad "Listen to Your Heart." "(That's) one of the rare occasions when I wrote the story about a very good friend of mine who went through a difficult divorce. We sat up all night discussing (his) problem. When it went to number one in the States, I got this fax from him telling me, 'Hey it's great—you and me and Marie are number one in America!'"

Gessle wrote the lyric first, then the music. "It's a traditional power ballad," he notes. "We wanted to loosen it up a bit at the end using trumpets and a horn section. We were really inspired by 'The Best of Everything' from *Southern Accents* with Tom Petty; Robbie Robertson did the arrangement for that. We really listened to that a lot."

Per Gessle and Marie Fredriksson were both well-known in their native Sweden before they came together as Roxette. Gessle doesn't remember their first meeting, but Marie says it took place in a rehearsal studio when they were working with their separate bands. "We were successful at the time and they were not, so they envied us," Gessle teases. His band was called Gyllene Tider, which translates as "Golden Times." They started out in 1978 by recording an EP of four songs. "It was the middle of the new wave, and there were so many bands. Everyone was sending cassettes to record companies, so we thought if we do a vinyl record, it (will) stand out. We presented it to all the record companies. Everyone hated it except EMI, which signed us immediately." The album went to number one in Sweden, as did the first single, the title of which translated as "The Girl At Television 2." Although Gessle started writing songs in English when he was 14, Gyllene Tider recorded all of their albums in Swedish, except for one called *The Heartland Café*.

Marie was half of a duo called Mama's Barn before recording three well-received solo albums. While Gessle was influenced by David Bowie, the Sweet, T. Rex and Mott the Hoople as well as Leonard Cohen and Joni Mitchell, Fredriksson's musical mentors included Billie Holiday, Ella Fitzgerald and Chick Corea.

In 1983, six of the songs from *The Heartland Café* were released in America on Capitol under the name Roxette. "Marie wasn't in the band, but she's singing backing vocals on the album because we were friends at the time," Gessle explains. The name of the band was taken from "Roxette," a single by the British group Dr. Feelgood.

Gyllene Tider broke up in 1984, exhausted as a band, according to Gessle. In 1986, Per and Marie recorded an album, released on EMI in Sweden, titled *Pearls of Passion*. They kept the name Roxette. "The whole intention of starting Roxette was that we wanted to do something in English and see if we could have a top 20 hit in Germany, and see how far (we could) go. We'd been touring and touring and had loads of success in Scandinavia. You get a little

bit fed up doing the same venues all the time." "Neverending Love"—a track from the album that featured both Per and Marie's voices—was released as a single. It was a hit in Germany, fulfilling Roxette's wish to expand beyond Scandinavia.

"Listen to Your Heart" was the first single to top the *Billboard* Hot 100 and not be available on a 7-inch vinyl single. It was released only as a cassette single, a harbinger of things to come. The follow-up was another *Look Sharp!* track, "Dangerous." It spent two weeks at number two in March, 1990, unable to dislodge Janet Jackson's "Escapade" from the top spot.

---

### THE TOP FIVE
*Week of November 4, 1989*

1  **Listen to Your Heart**
   Roxette

2  **Cover Girl**
   New Kids on the Block

3  **Miss You Much**
   Janet Jackson

4  **Sowing the Seeds of Love**
   Tears for Fears

5  **When I See You Smile**
   Bad English

# 746 When I See You Smile EPIC 69082
## BAD ENGLISH

*Writer: Diane Warren*

*Producer: Richie Zito*

*November 11, 1989*
*2 weeks*

"I didn't in all honesty think it was that great," Diane Warren says of her initial reaction to her song "When I See You Smile." "I started playing it for people. When I'm writing a song, I'll call people, or if someone's walking down the hall, I'll grab them and they can come in and listen. I was playing it for people and they loved it."

As Diane started to change her mind about the song, she sent it to an A&R staffer at Capitol Records, thinking it would be a good song for a group she heard was getting back together, Sheriff [see 720—"When I'm With You"].

When Sheriff's lead vocalist Freddie Curci heard the song, he didn't recognize the name Diane Warren. With the group reforming under the name Alias, Freddie had his own ballad, "More Than Words Can Say," in the can, and wanted to keep "When I See You Smile" for a future album. The publisher said he could have a 30-day hold on the song, but if Alias didn't record it, John Waite's new band was interested.

Don Grierson of Epic's A&R staff thought the song would be a smash for Waite, originally signed to Epic as a solo act after previous contracts with Chyrsalis and EMI [see 594—"Missing You"]. "I realized I didn't want to make another solo record and I would be happier doing something that had more of a gang feel to it, more of a band thing," Waite says.

Waite's manager suggested he team up with an old bandmate. Backstage at a Heart concert, Waite was reunited with Jonathan Cain from the Babys. "I swore I'd never go back with him," Waite affirms, "but I thought it might be a great diversion, something really different to go that route. We had changed. Since I'd last seen Jonathan, I'd been around the world five times . . . and of course, he'd been with Journey. We had gone in our different directions."

With another former member of the Babys, bassist Ricky Phillips, Waite and Cain went to work writing songs and playing in a small studio in San Francisco, about 10 miles from the home of ex-Journey guitarist Neal Schon. "He stopped by one day when we were recording some tunes and we needed a guitar player," Waite recalls. "Once Neal offered to help us out on guitar just to get us through the demos, everything semed to catch a light. It really got that terrific rebel kind of feeling."

Schon discovered drummer Deen Castronovo in Los Angeles, and recruited him to be the fifth member of Bad English. Waite explains the origin of the name: "There was a pool table next door to the studio, One on One Studios in Los Angeles. Between takes, we'd all run out and play pool." Bets started out small, for sushi and beer, but soon they were playing for $500 a game. Cain was reading a book about pool and came across the expression "english," meaning to put a spin on the cue ball to help set up the next shot. "Since a few of us really can't play pool and some of us really can, Bad English came from the expression of putting the wrong english on a cue ball," Waite clarifies.

Waite was a longtime friend of Diane Warren's, and had recorded her song "Don't Lose Any Sleep" on a previous album. Bad English had seven songs in the can when they met at producer Richie Zito's house to hold a conference call with Grierson to choose more material. "The band didn't want to do outside songs," says Waite. After the conference call, he insisted on recording "When I See You Smile."

Three days later, the backing track was cut. Waite recorded his vocals at Secret Sound, with the same microphone he used for "Missing You." "I sang it in two takes," he says. "Richie and the engineer rolled the tape, and I whipped through it." He wasn't satisfied with his performance, but Zito and Grierson were delighted. It was only after the album was pressed that Waite agreed with them.

"Forget Me Not," the first Bad English single, peaked at number 45 in August, 1989. "When I See You Smile," the follow-up, spent two weeks at number one. "Price of Love" was next, reaching number five.

The second Bad English album, *Backlash*, was their last—the group disbanded after that.

## THE TOP FIVE
*Week of November 11, 1989*

1 **When I See You Smile**
Bad English

2 **Listen to Your Heart**
Roxette

3 **Cover Girl**
New Kids on the Block

4 **Blame It on the Rain**
Milli Vanilli

5 **(It's Just) The Way That You Love Me**
Paula Abdul

*Writer: Diane Warren*

*Producer: Frank Farian*

*November 25, 1989*
*2 weeks*

FOR the seventh time in the rock era, a songwriter had back-to-back number one hits when "Blame It on the Rain" succeeded "When I See You Smile" at number one.* The Milli Vanilli single was the fourth chart-topper for composer Diane Warren, following Starship's "Nothing's Gonna Stop Us Now," Chicago's "Look Away" and Bad English's "When I See You Smile."

"Blame It on the Rain" was not written for the dreadlocked duo of Rob Pilatus and Fab Morvan. "I submitted it to the Jets," says Diane, "and then at the last minute they decided not to do it, which I'm happy about now—I wasn't happy then." Undaunted, Diane took her song elsewhere. "I submitted it to Clive Davis. I played the song for him, not knowing he needed songs for Milli Vanilli, because I didn't even know who they were."

Davis wanted to replace four songs from the European version of Milli Vanilli's debut album, titled *All or Nothing* on the Continent. For the

*The other writers who have had back-to-back number one songs are: John Lennon and Paul McCartney [see 143, 144 and 145]; Eddie Holland, Lamont Dozier and Brian Holland [see 176 and 177]; Bob Crewe and Kenny Nolan [see 398 and 399]; Barry Gibb [see 478, 479, 480 and 481]; Robin and Maurice Gibb [see 480 and 481]; and Ritchie Cordell [see 681 and 682].

American edition, he had producer Frank Farian record a cover version of the Isley Brothers' "It's Your Thing" and Diane's "Blame It on the Rain."

Diane and Clive usually had different ideas about who should record her songs. "I (would) submit a song for somebody big, like Whitney Houston, and he'd say, 'I don't want it for Whitney, but I want it for Exposé' or 'I want it for Taylor Dayne.' And I'd say, 'No, no, I want somebody big, I want Whitney.' Then these new artists would sell, like, three million copies and have all these hits. I'd kick myself in the head. So when Clive said, 'Milli Vanilli,' I said, 'Yeah, I trust you.'"

Asked how she feels about the revelation that Rob and Fab did not really sing "Blame It on the Rain," Diane responds, "Whoever sang it did a good job. I'm really proud of the song. It's a good record. I had heard that they didn't really sing, but I didn't know for sure because I'd never been in the studio with them. As a songwriter, I just give my songs to people. And when I found out I said, 'I'm still proud of the song, I made my contribution.'"

Record buyers were not as magnanimous. Consumers initiated class-action lawsuits against the group and their record company. When the scandal broke, Rob and Fab insisted that Arista Records was aware they did not sing on the album. Todd Headlee, who managed the group for Gallin Morey Associates, told the *Los Angeles Times*: "When I came on board, every record company official at Arista and BMG knew it. Everybody in the management company knew it. That's why most of their employees

are forced to sign a confidential clause binding them to stay silent."

Roy Lott, an executive vice president at Arista, told the *Times*: "There is no way that anyone ever could have known whether they sang or not. We are merely a distributor of their records in the United States. No one from Arista was ever in the studio when they recorded it. Rob and Fab and Frank (Farian) assured us that they sang on the record."

In June, 1991, a federal judge in Philadelphia refused to certify two multi-million-dollar class-action suits against Arista. That left 20 other similar cases pending around the country. In August, a Chicago judge threw out a proposed settlement to one of the class-action suits that would have seen Arista and its German parent company, BMG, issue rebates good on future purchases to consumers who bought the Milli Vanilli album. The judge said the company would have to do more than offer rebates.

On November 30, 1991, Rob Pilatus took a 6:00 A.M. walk onto the balcony of his room at the Mondrian Hotel on Sunset Strip in Los Angeles, and was dangling off the railing, nine stories up. He was heavily medicated, and had called the *Los Angeles Times* to tell them what he was doing. The newspaper alerted sheriff's deputies, who lured him back into his room.

Pilatus spent December in a drug rehabilitation center in Tucson, Arizona. In January of 1992, he confessed his embarrassment at the suicide attempt and stressed that it was not a publicity stunt. That same month, Rob and Fab finished recording a new album financed by Taj Records.

## THE TOP FIVE
*Week of November 25, 1989*

1 **Blame It on the Rain**
Milli Vanilli

2 **When I See You Smile**
Bad English

3 **Love Shack**
The B-52's

4 **(It's Just) The Way That You Love Me**
Paula Abdul

5 **We Didn't Start the Fire**
Billy Joel

# 748 We Didn't Start the Fire COLUMBIA 73021
## BILLY JOEL

*Writer: Billy Joel*

*Producers: Mick Jones*
*Billy Joel*

*December 9, 1989*
*2 weeks*

"WHEN I was going to school, one of my favorite subjects other than music was history," confesses Billy Joel. "Only I didn't like the way it was taught . . . the curriculum didn't leave any room for enjoying any of the history courses. I entertained the thought at one time of being a history teacher, but I didn't graduate high school. I didn't show up enough. I passed all the tests, but I was always absent because I was playing in bands. Who's gonna make an 8:00 homeroom when you've been gigging 'til 3:30 in the morning? At the end of my senior year in 1967 they said, 'Well, you gotta go to summer school.' I said, the hell with that, I'm not going to Columbia University, I'm going to Columbia Records."

Even though he didn't graduate from high school, Billy maintained his interest in history. "I think history is more than just dates and politicians and generals and presidents. I think a lot of it is popular culture, a lot of it is athletics, a lot of it is fashion . . . there's a lot more to history than just dates and names." His love of history proved useful while writing his third number one single, "We Didn't Start the Fire."

"I think, subconsciously, the idea came from the fact that I'd just turned 40," Joel explains. "The whole stim-

## THE TOP FIVE
*Week of December 9, 1989*

1 **We Didn't Start the Fire**
   Billy Joel

2 **Another Day in Paradise**
   Phil Collins

3 **Blame It on the Rain**
   Milli Vanilli

4 **(It's Just) The Way
   That You Love Me**
   Paula Abdul

5 **Don't Know Much**
   Linda Ronstadt f/Aaron Neville

ulus of writing it came from a conversation I was having with a guy who had just entered his 20s and was feeling a little depressed about the world situation. You gotta understand, this was '89, before the whole Iron Curtain came down. He was worried about AIDS . . . pollution . . . the situation in Red China." Billy says he was sympathetic at first to the would-be musician—until he told Billy that he was lucky because he grew up in the '50s, and nothing happened in the '50s.

"I said, 'Wait a minute, didn't you ever hear of Dien Bien Phu . . . the Hungarian freedom fighters . . . the Suez Canal crisis?' He never heard of any of this stuff. I started jotting these images down, these flashes of newspaper headlines that occurred to me. I actually tried to write them down in chronological order, like it was a mental exercise. It wasn't meant to be a record at the time." Billy was in the middle of recording his *Storm Front* album and didn't have all of the songs written yet.

"I went home and checked my encyclopedia to see how close I was to the chronology of events. As it turned out, I was almost dead on the money. I'd say about three or four changes came from reading the encyclopedia." Billy set the words to an old melody he had

already written that was originally titled "Jolene."

"What I wanted to do, lyrically, was sum up at the end of each of these years of names and faces and say, 'Hey, we didn't start this mess, we certainly did our best to make it better. It's not something we started and it's probably not something we're going to be able to finish. For the foreseeable future, this kind of craziness is going to go on and on. That's how life is.' When I finished writing this song, I didn't know it was going to be a hit."

Working in the studio for the first time with producer Mick Jones of Foreigner [see 601—"I Want To Know What Love Is"], Billy says the first approach to the song was too timid. "It needed a good kick in the ass to get it away from the pseudo-intellectual type of recording. It needed to be played like a rock and roll song. After that, we started perceiving that this might end up actually being a single."

The rapid-fire listing of names and events from 1949 forward brought mail from teachers who hailed the song as an educational aid. *Junior Scholastic* magazine included a cassette and lyric sheet in 40,000 copies. "Until they got the lyric sheet, some people thought 'trouble in the Suez' was 'trouble in the sewers,'" Billy laughs.

ATLANTIC 88774 **Another Day in Paradise**

PHIL COLLINS

*Writer: Phil Collins*

*Producers: Phil Collins*
*Hugh Padgham*

*December 23, 1989*
*4 weeks*

PHIL COLLINS, the man who sang lead vocals on eight number one hits in the '80s, had the final number one hit of the decade with "Another Day in Paradise."

It was the first single from his third solo album, . . . *But Seriously.* Collins reminded his critics and fans that it was his first true solo album in five years. "People think *Buster* was a solo project, they think the Genesis things are kind of mine . . . because I'm the singer," he said.

". . . *But Seriously* is the strongest thing I've done since *Face Value,*" Collins told J.D. Considine in *Musician.* "But it's still got the fun stuff on it. Things like 'Something Happened on the Way to Heaven' [a song Collins originally wanted to give to the Four Tops], 'Find a Way to My Heart,' are still the Phil Collins other people like or not."

Collins told Considine that after covering "Groovy Kind of Love" [see 711] for *Buster,* he felt he was becoming "a little more trivialized than I wanted to be. . . . I think maybe it's not so much a problem in America as in England. But I live in England, and you put your ear down to the ground and you hear what's going on. People are becoming a little bit too middle-of-the-road, maybe a little bit too Wayne Newton. And although that's going farther into the middle of the road than I would ever dare tread, there's that kind of reaction. I looked back at myself and said, 'This isn't really where I'm at, this is where people think I am.'

"So I sat down after *Buster* and started to write. At the end of a year and a half, I had all this material. We just chose the stuff that I liked the most, and when it came down to the first single, 'Another Day in Paradise' was chosen because it was a bit different from what had gone on before. It would bring people back to the starting line of remembering what I'm about. I write 'In the Air,' I'm quite capable of writing a 'Two Hearts,' but let's not forget I'm also doing this kind of stuff."

**THE TOP FIVE**
*Week of December 23, 1989*

1 **Another Day in Paradise**
Phil Collins

2 **Don't Know Much**
Linda Ronstadt f/Aaron Neville

3 **We Didn't Start the Fire**
Billy Joel

4 **Rhythm Nation**
Janet Jackson

5 **With Every Beat of My Heart**
Taylor Dayne

The working title for "Another Day in Paradise" was "Homeless." "When we were cutting the single in London, I crossed the road—I'd just come out (of) the studio . . . and this woman, I wouldn't have dreamed that she was going to say anything, this woman with two kids said . . . 'Give us some money, guv,' and obviously didn't have anywhere to go. . . . It's everywhere. . . . I remember when we played Washington . . . Washington was almost at a standstill and these people were trying to sleep on the grills where all the hot air was coming up, and you could see it was in the shadow of Capitol Hill. I thought it was an extraordinary sort of contradiction.

"What (the song) also deals with is people's awkwardness with it. When it happened to me, I just walked straight past. I thought, I'm doing the same thing as everybody else . . . I felt awkward. I didn't ignore her but at the same time I didn't stop and give her some money. . . . That's what the song deals with, people just sort of starting to pretend it's not happening."

Joining Collins on vocals for "Another Day in Paradise" was one of his heroes, David Crosby. "I just love him so much," Collins said. "I was in bands that did covers of Byrds and Crosby, Stills and Nash songs. I think he's the key member of that group, because he's the one who picks the odd notes out of the air and sings them." Collins wanted Crosby to guest star on *Face Value,* but the former Byrd couldn't make it to the studio. Collins and Crosby met for the first time at the Atlantic Records 40th Anniversary Concert at Madison Square Garden in 1988. Collins asked him if he would contribute some vocals to a couple of songs. "David did exactly what I expected him to do," Collins noted. "He just picked a few notes out of the air that I would never have thought of."

"Another Day in Paradise" debuted on the Hot 100 at number 43 the week of November 4, 1989; seven weeks later, it was number one. The next three singles from the album all made the top five: "I Wish It Would Rain Down" peaked at three in March, 1990. "Do You Remember?" and "Something Happened on the Way to Heaven" both reached number four, in June and October, respectively. The fifth single, "Hang in Long Enough," hit number 23 in January, 1991.

# How Am I Supposed to Live Without You COLUMBIA 73017
## MICHAEL BOLTON

*Writers: Michael Bolton*
*Doug James*

*Producer: Michael Omartian*

*January 20, 1990*
*3 weeks*

**M**ICHAEL BOLTON was surprised when he found out that Laura Branigan wanted to record a version of a song he had written with Doug James, "How Am I Supposed to Live Without You." The song had already been placed on hold by Arista's Air Supply [see 545—"The One That You Love"]. Deidre O'Hara of CBS Songs warned Branigan's management they would be wasting their time and money if they cut the track and then Air Supply released it. But Clive Davis wanted to change something in the chorus, according to Bolton, and the songwriter didn't want it changed. Air Supply never recorded the song; Branigan's version went to number 12 on the Hot 100 in October, 1983, and number one on the Adult Contemporary chart.

It was the first major hit for Bolton as a songwriter. He had composed his first song when he was 13, a sentimental country number called "Dreaming Dreams." His first important credit was getting Rex Smith to record one of his songs. He gained credibility when the Pointer Sisters recorded "Heartbeat." Kenny Rogers, Joe Cocker and Starship also recorded his songs before Branigan brought him to the upper reaches of the Hot 100.

In 1983, Bolton met Doug James—a songwriter whose credits included "After You" (recorded by Dionne War-

wick) and "Don't Tell Me, Tell Her" (recorded by Odyssey)—through O'Hara at CBS Songs. "She introduced us at the office in New York and showed us a room with a piano and said, 'You guys get in there,'" James remembers. "We spent the first part of the session telling jokes and getting to know one another. Finally, to break the ice, I sat down at the piano and Michael stood up behind me. I started to play, he started to sing, and we played ideas off one another. It was very much a collaborative effort both musically and lyrically. 'How Am I Supposed to Live Without You' was the first song I wrote with Michael, and the first song I wrote for CBS. We got the best part of it done in one session. It took, if my memory is correct, three sessions. We had the age-old problem—the second verse was tough as nails to write. It was very difficult."

James recalls Harvey Shapiro, who headed the East Coast office of CBS Songs, declaring the song a hit. After Air Supply put a hold on the song, "we were very excited because Air Supply was selling millions of records. We kept waiting for the thing to come out. One afternoon, I got a phone call from

Deidre saying, 'Congratulations, Laura Branigan's cutting your song this afternoon.' I was frantic because I hadn't done a lead sheet yet. But they went ahead and cut it from the tape."

Bolton's recording of the song is much more similar to the original demo, according to James. "When we first heard Laura's, we thought it was good, but it was not quite what we had envisioned. I love to hear her version—she's got a wonderful voice, and did a good job on it."

When Bolton and James wrote "How Am I Supposed to Live Without You," Bolton was steering away from ballads. "At the time, as a performer, he was more hard-rock," James confirms. Along with many others, James suggested he consider recording softer material.

Bolton, born in New Haven, Connecticut, on February 26, 1954, recorded his first single for Epic Records when he was just 15. He signed with RCA Records in 1975 and released two albums under his real name, Michael Bolotin. In the late '70s, he wrote some songs in upstate Massachusetts and was going to record them on his own, until his management at the time talked him into putting a group together. As part of the band Blackjack, he recorded two albums for Polydor that sounded more like Led Zeppelin or Bad Company than Michael Bolton.

Michael signed with a new manager in 1982; Louis Levin got him the publishing deal with CBS Songs, and a recording contract with Columbia. His debut for the label was a self-titled album released in 1983, followed by *Everybody's Crazy* in 1985. When that album failed, he decided hard rock was not for him.

Except for the single "Fools Game" (number 82 in May, 1983), Bolton didn't make an impact on the Hot 100 until "That's What Love Is All About" (number 19 in December, 1987). That was followed by a remake of Otis Redding's "(Sittin' On) The Dock of the Bay" (number 11 in March, 1988). The first single issued from his fourth album was the title track, "Soul Provider," which reached number 17 in September, 1989. The follow-up was "How Am I Supposed to Live Without You." It debuted on the Hot 100 on October 28, 1989—and 12 weeks later, it became the first single to go to number one in the '90s.

---

## THE TOP FIVE
### Week of January 20, 1990

1 **How Am I Supposed To Live Without You**
Michael Bolton

2 **Pump Up the Jam**
Technotronic f/Felly

3 **Another Day in Paradise**
Phil Collins

4 **Everything**
Jody Watley

5 **Downtown Train**
Rod Stewart

*Writer: Oliver Leiber*

*Producer: Oliver Leiber*

*February 10, 1990*
*3 weeks*

**A**FTER writing and producing two tracks for Paula Abdul [see 729—"Forever Your Girl"], Oliver Leiber received a call from Gemma Corfield of Virgin Records asking if he had a third song for Paula. "They needed a last track. I had this new machine, the MPC-60, which is a Linn drum machine-type thing, and I had done a two-bar pattern just to see how to work it. It was a bass line and the drum thing, and that was 'Opposites Attract.'" Leiber played it for Corfield over the phone. "I didn't even have the lyrics at that point, and Gemma (said), 'Sounds great! Can you do it?'"

Inspiration for the lyrics came while Leiber was driving his Camaro around a suburb of St. Paul, trying to find a friend's house. "My Camaro blew up and I coasted into a gas station. There was a McDonald's and a small mini-mall. I was killing time in the mini-mall and saw a used bookstore. It was full of drug store novels. I started reading the titles, and they were great! I asked for a piece of paper. I had about two hours, and I must have written down 300 titles, like *Dangerous Paradise, Liar's Moon, Boundary Lines* . . . and they had these horrible covers. One of them was *Opposites Attract*. The groove was in the computer back home, and I was broken down in Lakeville." When he finally was able to drive home, a friend accompanying him narrowed

the title choice down to "Opposites Attract." Leiber explains, "Usually the way I work with my songs is I come up with the title first and backtrack."

In creating the lyrics, Oliver was inspired by his relationship with the first love of his life. "I was this Jewish kid from New York—very hyper, very energetic—and she was this laid-back Norwegian girl from Fargo, North Dakota. I mean, she would put mayonnaise on a pastrami sandwich and she cooked stuff with that squeezable cheese, stuff you don't see in Jewish households. That relationship served as the source emotionally for all three songs ["Forever Your Girl," "(It's Just) The Way That You Love Me" and "Opposites Attract"]."

When it came time to record "Opposites Attract," Leiber called on the services of two singers he had worked with when recording the track "Obsessed" for the soundtrack of the Michael J. Fox film *Bright Lights, Big City*. He first met Tony Christian and Marv Gunn at a demo studio. They had been in a band called Mazarati, organized by Prince's bass player, Brownmark.

"When I was working with Paula, I wanted to add a little bit of soul," says

Leiber. "I brought (the Wild Pair) in on 'The Way That You Love Me' just to party . . . cause they're real spontaneous. Usually they both sing on the same mike, like Sam and Dave used to do. When I cut the vocals on 'Forever Your Girl,' I called them in to do backgrounds. Originally, 'Opposites Attract' wasn't written as a duet, but David Z heard the track and said it would be a great duet. The Wild Pair was a natural choice for me."

Leiber recorded Christian and Gunn in Minneapolis and Paula Abdul in Los Angeles. "I had the guys sing the whole song, because I really didn't know whose lines were whose at that time. When I started to see what lines would be hers, I muted the lines that they sang. They were never physically in the studio at the same time."

When Paula chose to work with the Family Stand for her second album [see 790—"Rush Rush"], Oliver moved on and produced tracks for a female singer named Stacy Earl, signed to RCA. Her second single for the label was Leiber's "Romeo and Juliet," recorded with the Wild Pair. At the same time, the duo was signed to Capitol Records and went into the studio with Leiber producing.

## THE TOP FIVE
*Week of February 10, 1990*

1 **Opposites Attract**
Paula Abdul w/the Wild Pair

2 **Two to Make It Right**
Seduction

3 **Downtown Train**
Rod Stewart

4 **Janie's Got a Gun**
Aerosmith

5 **How Am I Supposed to Live Without You**
Michael Bolton

# Escapade  A&M 1490
## JANET JACKSON

Writers: *Janet Jackson*
*James Harris III*
*Terry Lewis*

Producers: *Jimmy Jam*
*Terry Lewis*

*March 3, 1990*
*3 weeks*

AFTER "Miss You Much" held down
the top spot on the Hot 100 for four
weeks [see 744], Janet Jackson released the title track from her *Rhythm
Nation 1814* album. It peaked at number two the week of January 6, 1990,
unable to displace Phil Collins' "Another Day in Paradise." Two weeks
later, the album's third single, "Escapade," entered the *Billboard* chart at
number 37; six weeks later, it was
number one. During the song's first
week at the chart summit, Janet
opened "The Rhythm Nation World
Tour 1990" in Miami. It was her first
concert tour ever.

"Janet's a big basketball fan, a big
Lakers fan," Jimmy Jam specifies,
"and when she went to the games,
they would always play one of the
songs she liked, 'Nowhere to Run.'"
Janet wanted to record a new version
of the Martha and the Vandellas hit
from 1965 for *Rhythm Nation*. "I suggested that instead of doing a remake
of 'Nowhere to Run,' let's do something with that kind of feel to it, but
do our own song," says Jam.

Jam and his partner Terry Lewis
checked their "book of titles" to find
something appropriate. "Anytime we
hear a phrase or a saying, we write it
down as a title. We usually come up
with the music first, then we try to
think of a title that fits the way the

## THE TOP FIVE
*Week of March 3, 1990*

1  **Escapade**
   Janet Jackson

2  **Dangerous**
   Roxette

3  **Opposites Attract**
   Paula Abdul w/the Wild Pair

4  **Roam**
   The B-52's

5  **All or Nothing**
   Milli Vanilli

music sounds. And 'Escapade' we
thought was a cool word. It is kind of
old-fashioned—people don't really say
'Let's go on an escapade' anymore, but
it really worked with that track."

The instrumental track to "Escapade" had been one of the first recorded for the album, along with
"Miss You Much" and "Love Will
Never Do (Without You)." Jam continues the story of the song's creation:
"While she was sitting in one room
coming up with lyrics, I put it on the
24-track. We hooked the drum machine up. On my left hand I played the
bass, on the right hand I played the
chord. And it was just enough for her
to sing to, which we do a lot. Because
we like to let her sing to as minimum
of a track as we can do, then fill in the
track around her so that her part is
the main part of the song. With 'Escapade,' she sang it and we kept saying
we'll go back and redo the track . . .
we never redid the track.

"It's basically all drums. I don't even
think there's a mix of the drums, I
think all the drums are on one track.
There's a keyboard bass and another
thing, and that was it. All we added
were the overdubs, little bells . . . because we'd gotten so used to the feel
of the track, the mistakes and all, we

ended up leaving it the way it was."

"Escapade" was the second number
one single from *Rhythm Nation 1814*.
That was going one better than *Control*, which yielded only one chart-
topper [see 649—"When I Think of
You"]. Janet talked about the album's
theme that music and dance could
change the world with Jefferson
Graham of *USA Today*: "My mother
said that ever since she could remember, I've always been concerned with
other people before myself. I'm not
naive—I know an album or a song
can't change the world. I just want my
music and my dance to catch the audience's attention, and to hold it long
enough for them to listen to the lyrics
and what we're saying."

In April of 1990, as "Escapade" began its chart descent, Janet met President George Bush while in Dearborn,
Michigan for a concert. The President
was in town at the same time for a
fund-raiser, and both were at the Ritz
Carlton. Later that month, Janet received a star on the Walk of Fame in
Hollywood. Also in April, her next
single was released: "Alright" peaked
at number four in June. The fifth single from *Rhythm Nation 1814* was a
ballad—"Come Back to Me" spent two
weeks at number two in August.

ATLANTIC 88742 **Black Velvet** 753
ALANNAH MYLES

*Writers: Christopher Ward*
*David Tyson*

*Producer: David Tyson*

*March 24, 1990*
*2 weeks*

Aʟᴀɴɴᴀʜ Mʏʟᴇs recorded her vocals for "Black Velvet" on one of the hottest days of the year in her native Toronto. "It was about 99 degrees and it was very humid," she remembers. "I was in this basement studio with no air conditioning. It felt like (the song) needed to sound like it was Memphis on a hot sweaty day with flies buzzing around, and it was so hot you had to take your shirt off. And subsequently it was so hot I had to take my shirt off. I was wearing a bathing suit, of course."

When she first heard "Black Velvet," written by Christopher Ward and David Tyson, she thought the song was so good that she would not be the one to record it. "Even if I did, it wouldn't matter—somebody else was going to have a hit with it. I knew it was a special song. It broke my heart the minute I heard it, for fear I might not get the chance to have a success with this song because it was so beautiful."

Alannah was 11 when she took an interest in playing her mother's Spanish classical guitar and started singing. Four years later, heavily influenced by Leonard Cohen, Joni Mitchell and Joan Baez, she wrote her first song. At 19, she found an agent and performed at coffeehouses in Toronto.

Alannah met Christopher Ward at a party given by his sound engineer. Ward, signed to Warner Brothers in

Canada as an artist, was immediately attracted to Myles. "We became partners and ended up living together for about eight years," Ward elaborates. "I took her on tour as the opening act for my band and started writing songs for her."

Ward also worked as an actor with Second City and hosted an all-night video television show called "City Limits" in Toronto. When MuchMusic, the Canadian version of MTV, was launched, Ward was invited to become the channel's first VJ. "All the while, I was working on my songs and working on Alannah's career," he says.

Ward and Myles met record producer David Tyson in the mid-'70s. They collaborated on a three-song demo tape for Alannah. "We spent a lot of money on that and took it around to record comapnies," Ward recalls. Someone at Warner Brothers forwarded it to Tunc Erim, a senior A&R staffer at Atlantic Records in New York. "Tunc called me within 48 hours of us having sent the tape. I was in Vancouver in a hotel room, and he said, 'Christopher Ward, I think Alannah Myles is an international star. I want her on my label. Who's your lawyer?' We didn't even talk to anyone else . . . and (she's) the first artist he ever signed without meeting. He did it

based on the tape and a video."

Ward was inspired to write "Black Velvet" while on assignment for Much-Music. "They sent me to Memphis to cover the 10th anniversary of Elvis' death in the summer of 1987. We put me and a camera (operator) on a tour bus with 40 Elvis fanatics, which was an experience unto itself. I came to understand what the incredible passion was that these people had for this man, and what he really represented to them. We ended up calling the television special 'Mecca in Memphis.'

"As I was going down there on the bus, I had lots of time to think and make notes. At the same time, we were getting deeper and deeper into the South. I started to imagine what it was like when (Elvis) was a child growing up in the South, and that's why his mother is mentioned prominently. The crucial line in the song, at least for me, is 'a new religion that will bring you to your knees.' It's because in reading about the southern Fundamentalist preachers and the way that they would exhort members of the congregation, I realized in a flash that this was the same way Elvis exhorted his fans—there was a real parallel between that power of religion and the power that he possessed in bringing rock and roll to people."

## THE TOP FIVE

*Week of March 24, 1990*

1 **Black Velvet**
Alannah Myles

2 **Love Will Lead You Back**
Taylor Dayne

3 **Escapade**
Janet Jackson

4 **Roam**
The B-52's

5 **I Wish It Would Rain Down**
Phil Collins

# Love Will Lead You Back  ARISTA 9938

## TAYLOR DAYNE

*Writer: Diane Warren*

*Producer: Ric Wake*

*April 7, 1990*
*1 week*

Diane Warren's fifth number one song was "Love Will Lead You Back," a song she started writing in her hotel room during the first night of a trip to Russia. "I love that title," says the songwriter. "I like the idea of someone being strong enough to let somebody go, knowing in their heart they're going to come back. It takes a lot of strength, and I'm always attracted to songs with strong characters."

Diane remembers the day she gave the song to Arista Records chief Clive Davis. It was the same day she found out Tina Turner wasn't going to record another one of her compositions, "I'll Be Your Shelter," and Diane was mad. "So I said, 'Well, I'm going to show them. I'm going to get it cut by somebody else.' And I went to see Clive with that song and 'Love Will Lead You Back,' which was not in demo form yet. I played him 'I'll Be Your Shelter' and he freaked. He thought it would be good for Taylor Dayne . . . and I played him 'Love Will Lead You Back.' He was really moved by it and said, 'I want that song.' And I actually had it in mind for Whitney (Houston). . . . As soon as I demoed it, I sent it."

Producer Ric Wake was introduced to Diane Warren by Clive after recording Dayne's first album. "The demo was pretty sparse," Wake remembers. "I changed it around a lot. I added a whole different vibe with the harmonies. We used a guitar break."

The one thing that was always cool to me was the key change at the end—we kept that. When you hear the two versions, you hear a major difference."

Wake first heard the voice of Taylor Dayne when his friend Frank DeSaro handed him a tape and advised him to check it out. Wake didn't care for the song, but he did think that Dayne could sing. He went to the Russian nightclub in Brighton Beach where she was performing folk songs, liked the singer, and agreed to produce some songs for her.

Taylor was born July 3, 1962, the daughter of a rare coin dealer and an aspiring actress. She grew up in Baldwin, Long Island, and made her solo debut in the fourth grade belting out Jacques Brel's "Carousel." A Jimi Hendrix fan while attending Baldwin High School, she decided to take voice lessons and classical training. She spent two years in Felony, a Long Island band, and then another two years with a new wave band, the Next.

Dayne recorded under the name

Leslee (an adaptation of her real name, Lesley Wunderman). Wake produced two dance tracks—"I'm the One You Want" and "Tell Me You Can Love Me"—for an independent label, Megabolt. "We did two songs for that label, then the label dissolved," says Wake. "The very next record was 'Tell It to My Heart.'"

Dayne found that song herself by calling Chappell Music and asking for some throwaway songs that had been rejected by major artists. One of the numbers on the tape was "Tell It to My Heart." They released the song on another independent label.

"I had one person who offered me a deal if I could get a different singer," Wake recalls. "And then Clive Davis heard it. Andy Furman, the A&R guy at the time, called up and said (they) had to have it. I think Clive assumed that everybody wanted the record."

Davis told Dennis Hunt of the *Los Angeles Times*: "We signed her because she could *really* sing. We were impressed with the passion in her voice. We didn't want her to be categorized right away. We wanted to present a diversified picture of this artist. Just because she had one dance hit, she's not a dance artist. She can sing ballads and in different tempos. She's not one-dimensional."

Taylor's debut album, recorded quickly in six weeks, yielded four top 10 singles. "Tell It To My Heart" peaked at number seven in January, 1988. "Prove Your Love" equaled that chart placing in May. "I'll Always Love You" went to number three in September and "Don't Rush Me" ascended to number two in January, 1989. The first single from her sophomore album, *Can't Fight Fate*, was "With Every Beat of My Heart." It peaked at number five in December of 1989. "Love Will Lead You Back" entered the Hot 100 on January 27, 1990, and was number one 10 weeks later.

"That was exciting," says Wake, who along with Dayne was experiencing his first chart-topper. "I mean, when you get a number one in *Billboard*, that's it. For artists or producers, that means everything."

---

### THE TOP FIVE
*Week of April 7, 1990*

1  **Love Will Lead You Back**
   Taylor Dayne

2  **I'll Be Your Everything**
   Tommy Page

3  **All Around the World**
   Lisa Stansfield

4  **I Wish It Would Rain Down**
   Phil Collins

5  **Black Velvet**
   Alannah Myles

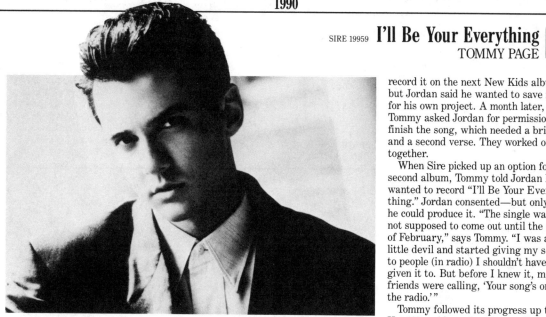

Writers: Jordan Knight
       Danny Wood
       Tommy Page

Producers: Jordan Knight
        Donnie Wahlberg
        Michael Jonzun

April 14, 1990
1 week

TOMMY PAGE grew up in West Caldwell, New Jersey, the third of four children born to Fred and Mimi Page. He started playing piano at age eight; he formed a rock band, Broken Promises, with his older brother Bill when he was 14, switching over to drums. "When I turned 17, we had our differences—he wanted to go more into rock and roll, and I wanted to go toward pop. So we split up and I moved to New York to go to NYU."

It was a drastic change of lifestyle for the young singer. "I was pretty miserable in my hometown," Tommy admits. In New York he became a "club kid," one of "the trendy kids coming in from Jersey (who) move to New York City and think they're really hip and cool and hang out in all the New York clubs. I would stay out every night 'til 5:00 in the morning.

"After going to NYU for six months, I got a job at Nell's, which was the hottest club in New York. I was a coatcheck boy downstairs in this little room hanging up everybody's coats. My room was right next to the DJ booth." Tommy made his own demos and had them pressed on acetate so the DJ could play them. He had

read a biography of Madonna that told how she was discovered by Mark Kamins, a DJ at the Danceteria, who helped her get a deal with Sire Records. The book had a photo of Kamins, and Tommy told the DJ at Nell's that if Kamins ever came in the club, to send him over to the coatcheck room.

Kamins brought Seymour Stein of Sire to Nell's one night after the premiere of Madonna's *Who's That Girl* in Times Square. Tommy played his demo of "Turning Me On" for them, and eventually Stein approved a deal for Tommy to record one song for the label. "Turning Me On" flopped in the States, but became a big hit in Asia, and the international department of Warner Brothers—Sire's parent—requested a Tommy Page album.

Tommy charted with a single, "A Shoulder to Cry On," and was asked to be the opening act for the New Kids on the Block/Tiffany tour. Tommy did not form a fast friendship with the five kids from Boston. "At first, I don't think we had much respect for each other," he says candidly. Lonely and bored on the tour, he sought out pianos in the lobbies of the hotels where he was staying. On several occasions, he noticed Jordan Knight of the New Kids watching from a distance. "This went on for a couple of weeks. We were at the Hyatt Hotel in Kansas City. And Jordan came over and said, 'Can I sit down on the bench?'"

Tommy played some songs he was working on, and asked Jordan if he had ever written anything; he started playing a ballad called "I'll Be Your Everything." Tommy suggested he

record it on the next New Kids album, but Jordan said he wanted to save it for his own project. A month later, Tommy asked Jordan for permission to finish the song, which needed a bridge and a second verse. They worked on it together.

When Sire picked up an option for a second album, Tommy told Jordan he wanted to record "I'll Be Your Everything." Jordan consented—but only if he could produce it. "The single was not supposed to come out until the end of February," says Tommy. "I was a little devil and started giving my song to people (in radio) I shouldn't have given it to. But before I knew it, my friends were calling, 'Your song's on the radio.'"

Tommy followed its progress up the Hot 100 and knew he was in a "horse race" with Phil Collins, Lisa Stansfield and Jane Child to get to number one. The night before the new chart was released, Tommy received a phone call from a label executive. "He said, 'Tommy, we are in major trouble—Jane Child is probably going to be number one.' One store report, one radio station playlist could make the difference. It was the worst night of my life."

Tommy's phone rang at 1:00 the next afternoon, at least an hour before the new chart was due. "I was shaking," recalls Tommy. "My dreams are going to come true or my nightmares are going to come true." Howard Klein, a vice president at the label, was on the other end. "All he said was, 'Tommy,' and I dropped the phone and screamed. Just from the tone of his voice . . . I started crying. I couldn't stand up."

## THE TOP FIVE
*Week of April 14, 1990*

1  **I'll Be Your Everything**
    Tommy Page

2  **Don't Wanna Fall in Love**
    Jane Child

3  **All Around the World**
    Lisa Stansfield

4  **Nothing Compares 2 U**
    Sinead O'Connor

5  **Love Will Lead You Back**
    Taylor Dayne

## 756 Nothing Compares 2 U
ENSIGN 23488
### SINEAD O'CONNOR

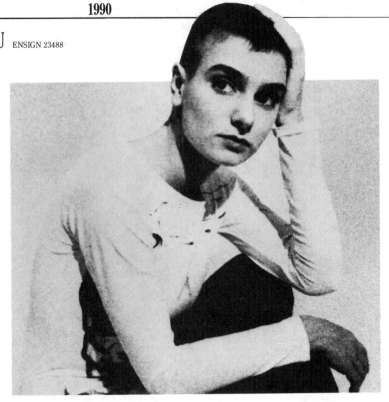

*Writer: Prince*

*Producer: Sinead O'Connor*

*April 21, 1990*
*4 weeks*

Sinead O'Connor was born in Glenageary, County Dublin, Ireland, on December 12, 1966, the third of four children. Her parents divorced when she was eight, and she was placed in a school run by Dominican nuns for adolescent girls with behavioral problems. When she was 14, a teacher at Mayfield College asked Sinead to sing at her wedding. The bride's brother, Paul Byrne, was the drummer for the Irish band In Tua Nua, and was impressed with the young singer. Later, Sinead would co-write the group's first single, "Take My Hand."

Sinead attended a boarding school at Waterford, then ran away to Dublin, where she attended college and performed at local pubs. She joined a group, Ton Ton Macoute, and met Fachtna O'Ceallaigh, who would become her manager and close friend.

In 1985, Nigel Grainge and Chris Hill of Ensign Records saw Ton Ton Macoute perform. "They were horrible," Grainge told Robert Hilburn of the *Los Angeles Times*. "Awful songs, awful playing, but she was interesting . . . this little student-type with baggy jersey and torn jeans, just singing to her feet for three-quarters of an hour with this amazing voice."

Grainge invited Sinead to come to London. She was happy to get away from Dublin and the memories of her mother, killed in a car crash that year. Grainge sent her into the studio with

### THE TOP FIVE
*Week of April 21, 1990*

1 **Nothing Compares 2 U**
Sinead O'Connor

2 **Don't Wanna Fall in Love**
Jane Child

3 **All Around the World**
Lisa Stansfield

4 **I Wanna Be Rich**
Calloway

5 **I'll Be Your Everything**
Tommy Page

Karl Wallinger, once a member of the Waterboys and later known as World Party. She recorded four songs, and Grainge signed her to his label. She rejected their idea of how she should look. "Chris Hill and Nigel Grainge wanted me to wear high-heel boots and tight jeans and grow my hair," Sinead told David Wild in *Rolling Stone*. "And I decided that they were so pathetic that I shaved my head so there couldn't be any further discussion."

Her early recordings included a song on the soundtrack of *Captive* and a debut single, "Troy." The follow-up, "Mandinka," went to number 17 in Britain. Her first album, *The Lion and the Cobra*, made the top 40 of the album charts in both the U.K. and the U.S.

O'Ceallaigh suggested Prince's "Nothing Compares 2 U," which Sinead recorded for her second album, *I Do Not Want What I Haven't Got*. Two days before making the video for the song, she permanently split with O'Ceallaigh. As a result, she would later say, her tears flowed easily while the cameras were operating.

"Nothing Compares 2 U" spent five weeks atop the U.K. singles chart before making its debut on the Hot 100 on March 17, 1990; five weeks later, it achieved similar chart status in America. Meanwhile, O'Connor signed with

a new manager, Steve Fargnoli. Ironically, his former client was Prince.

Sinead remained a hot media item for much of 1990 and 1991. She canceled an appearance on "Saturday Night Live" because she didn't want to appear with the host that week, Andrew Dice Clay. She refused to have "The Star Spangled Banner" play before her concert at the Garden State Arts Center in New Jersey. As a result, her music was banned from WHTZ in New York as well as other stations, and a New York state senator called for a boycott of her concerts. A clerk at the upscale Mrs. Gooch's market in Beverly Hills sang the national anthem to her while she shopped in the store and was fired for violating a store policy of not harassing customers. After attending the MTV Awards and the American Music Awards, Sinead withdrew from the Grammy Awards to call attention to the "false and destructive materialistic values" of the music industry. And after visiting Prince in December of 1990, she told the Irish music paper *Hot Press* that he had threatened to beat her and had left her stranded at 5:30 in the morning without a ride home (Prince said the incident never happened). Sinead told *Rolling Stone* that her encounter with Prince "spoiled ("Nothing Compares 2 U") completely for me."

*Writers: Madonna*
*Shep Pettibone*

*Producers: Madonna*
*Shep Pettibone*

*May 19, 1990*
*3 weeks*

"Vogue" was originally planned as the "B" side of "Keep It Together," the fifth single from Madonna's *Like a Prayer* album. After the title track went to number one [see 727], "Express Yourself" and "Cherish" both peaked at number two. The fourth single was "Oh Father," which broke Madonna's string of 17 consecutive top 10 singles by stalling at number 20. "It was the best song we'd ever done so far," co-writer and co-producer Patrick Leonard lamented in the *Chicago Tribune*. "It was a beautiful piece of music that resembles art in a big way." Madonna bounced back with "Keep It Together," which went as high as number eight. But the "B" side was not "Vogue."

Shep Pettibone, who wrote and produced "Vogue" with Madonna, remembers the reaction of people to the song the first time they heard it. "The record company went bananas, her manager went bananas. Everybody said, 'This is a major hit smash record—we're not going to lose it as a "B" side on "Keep It Together."' So it never became the 'B' side."

Pettibone, born in New York City, went to work at C.J.'s Record Store in Asbury Park, New Jersey, when he was 15. After finishing high school, he was hired to work at Sam Goody's in Manhattan. "That was boring, and I figured my next step was to become a club DJ, since I was always collecting music." Pettibone came up with the idea of remixing records to make them sound different, and soon his remixes were being played by Frankie Crocker on WBLS in New York.

Shep first met Madonna briefly when Mark Kamins was producing "Everybody" for her. He was also friendly with John "Jellybean" Benitez, who produced "Holiday" and "Crazy for You." Shep was asked to remix "True Blue" for a 12-inch single and "Into the Groove" for an album of dance remixes. "I made it a point to let her know what I could do," says Pettibone. "After that point, I became the person she wanted to remix her records.

"She really liked what I did on 'Express Yourself' and 'Like a Prayer,' so we jelled very well together. I was asked to come up with some music for a song. She liked it a lot, and she came to New York on the red-eye, very tired, and wrote most of the lyrics on the plane coming in."

Pettibone was surprised at the subject matter of the song. "Vogueing was in the underground clubs. It had been around for a while and it was also semi-passé. People were saying, 'What's the next thing? That's over.' She came in and said, 'I hope you don't mind, but I'm going to call the song "Vogue."'"

"Vogue" debuted on the Hot 100 at number 39 the week of April 14, 1990, and was number one five weeks later, matching the speed of "Like a Prayer." It was included on the album *I'm Breathless*, which bore the legend "Music from and inspired by the film *Dick Tracy*." "Vogue" was the exception. "It wasn't written for that movie or for that album," Pettibone acknowledges.

The remainder of the songs on *I'm Breathless* were sung in character. Three songs were actually from the Warren Beatty film: "Sooner or Later," "More" and "What Can You Lose," all written by Stephen Sondheim. "Sooner or Later" won the Oscar for Best Original Song, and Madonna won good critical notices for her role. She also won her share of media attention for a brief romance with the film's star.

## THE TOP FIVE
*Week of May 19, 1990*

1  **Vogue**
   Madonna

2  **Nothing Compares 2 U**
   Sinead O'Connor

3  **All I Wanna Do Is Make Love to You**
   Heart

4  **Hold On**
   Wilson Phillips

5  **Sending All My Love**
   Linear

**758**

# Hold On  SBK 07322
## WILSON PHILLIPS

Writers: *Chynna Phillips*
*Glen Ballard*
*Carnie Wilson*

Producer: *Glen Ballard*

*June 9, 1990*
*1 week*

Cʜʏɴɴᴀ Pʜɪʟʟɪᴘs, Carnie Wilson and her sister Wendy Wilson were in Japan, winning the Grand Prize at the Tokyo Song Festival for their first single, "Hold On," when the phone rang in Carnie's hotel room at 4:00 in the morning. It was Charles Koppelman, founder of the SBK label, calling to tell them "Hold On" was the new number one record in America. "It was one of the most incredible feelings I ever experienced," says Carnie. "I still remember the room, lying in bed, how everything looked and how I felt." What she didn't know was that 25 years ago on that very day, her father Brian had the number one song in America with "Help Me Rhonda" [see 175].

Chynna, Carnie and Wendy were childhood friends, all attending a Montessori school in Santa Monica and sharing the experience of having famous rock and roll parents. Carnie and Wendy were the daughters of Beach Boy Brian Wilson, and Chynna was the daughter of John and Michelle Phillips of the Mamas and the Papas. The three offspring even recorded a song together in 1973 when they were five and six years old, but "Take Me

Out to the Ballgame" by the Satellites was never released.

At 18, Chynna pursued an acting career, and had already been featured in *Some Kind of Wonderful*, *Caddyshack II* and the title role in the TV movie "Roxanne: The Prize Pulitzer" when she received a call from Owen Vanessa Elliott, daughter of the late Mama Cass. The younger Elliott had been raised by her aunt, singer Leah Kunkel, in Northampton, Massachusetts. Owen also wanted to be an actress, but she had an idea for an antidrug song that would feature the offspring of '60s artists. Chynna called her friends Carnie and Wendy and they tried harmonizing in Wendy's bedroom. "We were singing 'Dog and Butterfly' by Heart," Carnie recalls. "My mother came down and said, 'That sounds really good.' She couldn't believe it."

With Elliott, they had a meeting with producer Richard Perry, a longtime friend of Chynna's mother. After hearing them sing eight bars of Stevie Nicks' "The Wild Heart," Perry knew he wanted to take them into the studio. A couple of sessions later, it was obvious that Elliott's voice didn't fit with the other three, and Chynna asked her to bow out.

Perry wanted to record dance-oriented material with the trio, similar to the recordings he was making with the Pointer Sisters. "We said, 'We don't want to do dance music, we don't want to do teenybopper music,'" Carnie explains. Perry did work up a

dance track; according to Carnie, "We tried to do it but it sounded terrible. We said this is definitely not our bag." Perry introduced them to songwriter Glen Ballard, a native of Natchez, Mississippi, who started his career by working with Elton John and later co-wrote "Man in the Mirror" for Michael Jackson. Ballard heard the trio sing in three-part harmony, and thought their voices sounded great together.

"It was like love at first listen for me to hear the purity of the texture of their voices," Ballard recalls. "We immediately wrote some songs." A four-song demo was recorded, which included "Hold On," "Release Me" and "You're In Love," all future number one hits. Perry couldn't get a label interested, but Artie Mogull of SBK Productions liked the material, and, with Koppelman's approval, signed the women to a production deal. Then Perry was hired by Warner Brothers, and Wilson Phillips met with label executives Mo Ostin and Lenny Waronker. An offer was made, but the women felt they were being signed as a favor to Perry. They declined, and ended their relationship with the producer. When Koppelman and partner Marty Bandier formed SBK Records, Wilson Phillips were signed to the label.

Ballard wrote a musical track at one of their first sessions and kicked around some melodic ideas for it. "Chynna came in two or three days later with this lyric and it was 'Hold On,'" says Ballard. "Carnie added a couple of lines, and that was it. I had no input on the lyrics because it was something that Chynna was feeling and it poured out of her."

## THE TOP FIVE
*Week of June 9, 1990*

1  **Hold On**
   Wilson Phillips

2  **Vogue**
   Madonna

3  **Poison**
   Bell Biv DeVoe

4  **All I Wanna Do Is
   Make Love to You**
   Heart

5  **It Must Have Been Love**
   Roxette

*Writer: Per Gessle*

*Producer: Clarence Öfwerman*

*June 16, 1990*
*2 weeks*

"IT MUST HAVE BEEN LOVE" was written by Per Gessle in 1987. "We were doing promotion in Germany and went through hell because radio wouldn't play our records . . . they didn't know if (we) were top 40 or rock, and they couldn't decide. We fell between formats. Someone at EMI Electrola in Germany said, 'Why don't you write a Christmas song and try to get some airplay, because there aren't many Christmas records out this year.'" Gessle thought anything that would put Roxette on the radio was a good idea, so he went home and wrote a holiday ballad.

"I had a lyric which I transformed into a Christmas song. I wrote 'It Must Have Been Love' around it. We recorded it, and Germany didn't want it. It turned out to be our biggest hit in Sweden at the time." It wasn't included on any Roxette album, but was limited to a release as a Christmas single.

Then Per was contacted by Ron Fair of EMI Records and Chris Montan, senior vice president of music for Disney and Touchstone, regarding a new film starring Richard Gere and Julia Roberts. "When the *Pretty Woman* script first came out, it was not an obvious soundtrack picture," says Montan. "There was very little music indicated. I remember the day in the staff meeting when (Disney chairman) Jeffrey (Katzenberg) turned to me and said, 'Okay, so now what are we going

to do about the soundtrack?' And I said, 'What soundtrack?' and the rest was history.

"Ron and I knew we wanted Roxette to be one of our principal bands. We met with them first . . . and at that point they were out on a promotional tour, and they really didn't have time to write a new song for us. So they sent us all their demos and upcoming songs for their new album and old Swedish albums. . . . I heard 'It Must Have Been Love' in an old version and flipped for it . . . it was by far, I thought, the best thing we were being offered. So we told Per that we would love to include that on the soundtrack if he was willing to go back in the studio and update it a little bit."

Per explains: "We kept Marie's vocals from 1987, we just changed a small part." A "hard Christmas day" became "a hard winter's day." "We also had Christmas sounds at the beginning of the song. In the *Pretty Woman* version, it's more like a snare drum and the guitar parts. But at the time, nobody knew *Pretty Woman* was going to be such a massive hit. It was almost like a low-budget Hollywood movie— no big deal. If someone had told me ahead of time it was going to be one of the biggest films ever, it would be a different story.

"I heard the director really loved the song. I also heard he re-edited the movie to get it in there."

Montan enjoyed working with director Garry Marshall. "He was always open to us, though I think there were times where we were driving him crazy."

*Pretty Woman* turned out to be Disney's highest-grossing film of all time during its initial release. Per and Marie were invited to a screening of the film at the Disney lot in Burbank, California. "I was a little disappointed," notes Per. "You only heard 15 seconds of a David Bowie song. Our song was (heard for) almost a minute, but still, it was really edited." Per says he had never had a song included in a film before, and always thought, "Everything is going to circle around my song."

"It Must Have Been Love" bridged the gap between Roxette's *Look Sharp!* and *Joyride* albums. The track was the second single released from the *Pretty Woman* soundtrack, following Natalie Cole's "Wild Women Do." That song peaked at number 34 on April 14, 1990; a week earlier, "It Must Have Been Love" entered the Hot 100 at number 67, and 10 weeks later, it became Roxette's third number one single.

## THE TOP FIVE
*Week of June 16, 1990*

1 **It Must Have Been Love**
Roxette

2 **Hold On**
Wilson Phillips

3 **Poison**
Bell Biv DeVoe

4 **Step by Step**
New Kids on the Block

5 **Vogue**
Madonna

# Step by Step COLUMBIA 73343
## NEW KIDS ON THE BLOCK

*Writer: Maurice Starr*

*Producer: Maurice Starr*

*June 30, 1990*
*3 weeks*

**W**HEN the New Kids on the Block released the first single from their third album, *Step by Step*, they chose the title track. As an indication of their superstar status, it debuted at number 27 on the Hot 100, making it the highest debut (tied with M.C. Hammer's "U Can't Touch This") since "We Are the World" [see 605] entered the chart at number 21 the week of March 23, 1985. Two weeks after its lofty debut, "Step by Step" was in the top 10; two weeks after that, it began a three-week stay at number one.

Maurice Starr wrote "Step by Step" in 1986. "The first group that recorded the song was another group of mine from Boston, the Superiors," he reveals. Released on Motown, the single never charted. "The company thought it was a dud. Even some radio stations said it's not a hit record."

Starr was under pressure when he composed "Step by Step." "The group was coming to the studio but I didn't have a song for them. I had promised their manager Travis Gresham that I was going to have a song ready. About 10 minutes before they came in, I just dropped my fingers on the keyboard." He started to play some notes that sounded like steps.

"Step by Step" was still in the top 30 when the New Kids' next single was released. The Beatlesque "Tonight" debuted at number 37 on August 4, peaking at number seven. The third single from *Step by Step* was "Let's Try It Again," featuring Jordan Knight as a soundalike for Stylistics' lead singer Russell Thompkins, Jr. After nine consecutive top 10 singles, "Let's Try It Again" broke the string, peaking at number 53.

While the New Kids didn't have any chart hits in 1991, it was a profitable year on the road. *Forbes* placed them on top of the list of the highest-paid entertainers in the land, above Bill Cosby, Oprah Winfrey, Madonna and Michael Jackson. The Kids' estimated earnings for 1990-91 were $115 million. But on January 24, 1992, the New Kids' reputations were on the line, thanks to a lawsuit filed by Gregory McPherson, a University of Massachusetts music teacher. He charged breach of contract and creative infringement, and in statements to the *New York Post* alleged that Maurice Starr recorded many of the New Kids' vocals and the five members of the group lip-synched on stage. McPherson had been asked by the group's management company to put together a band for an appearance on "The Arsenio Hall Show" in February, 1989. He is listed as an "associate producer" and "string arranger" on the *Step by Step* album.

The New Kids responded to the charges by interrupting an Australian tour and postponing a Brisbane concert to fly to Los Angeles and sing live on "The Arsenio Hall Show." Before the group sang a medley of their hits and a new single, "If You Go Away," Hall spoke about the controversy with members of the audience, including Starr.

Reciting lyrics written on the plane from Australia, Donnie Wahlberg led a rap attack on their accuser: "I hear a little sucker say we don't sing on our records." In an interview with Hall, the New Kids admitted using recorded backing vocals during live performances and having Starr sing harmony on some recordings. They also acknowledged using a synthesizer called an Emulator on their first Arsenio Hall appearance to provide some backing tracks.

On February 10, the New Kids on the Block filed a civil suit against McPherson, accusing him of defamation for his statements published in the *New York Post*. In April, McPherson dropped his suit. He released a statement that read: "The allegations I made regarding New Kids on the Block lip-synching were untrue. They did sing lead on their vocals."

The New Kids returned to the Hot 100 with "If You Go Away," which peaked at number 16 in March, 1992. They sported a new name, although their identity was no secret—instead of New Kids on the Block, they called themselves NKOTB.

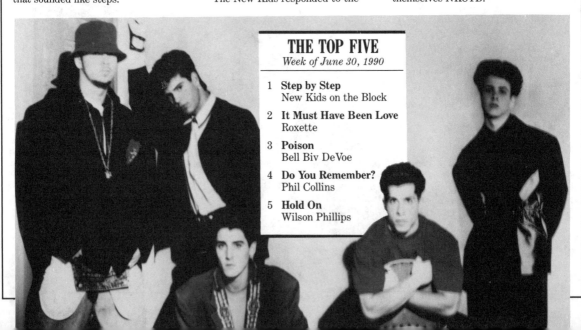

## THE TOP FIVE
*Week of June 30, 1990*

1 **Step by Step**
  New Kids on the Block

2 **It Must Have Been Love**
  Roxette

3 **Poison**
  Bell Biv DeVoe

4 **Do You Remember?**
  Phil Collins

5 **Hold On**
  Wilson Phillips

MCA 53831 **She Ain't Worth It**
GLENN MEDEIROS f/BOBBY BROWN

*Writers: Antonina Armato*
*Ian Prince*
*Bobby Brown*

*Producers: Denny Diante*
*Ian Prince*

*July 21, 1990*
*2 weeks*

GLENN MEDEIROS is the third artist with a number one single to be born in the '70s, following Tiffany and Debbie Gibson. Of Portuguese descent, Glenn was born June 24, 1970, and raised in the small town of Lawai on the island of Kauai in Hawaii. His fourth-grade teacher at Koloa Elementary School gave him an opportunity to sing and act in school productions as well as community theater.

The big break came when Glenn entered the "Brown Bags to Stardom" talent contest sponsored by radio station KMAI-FM (I-94). He chose a song written by Michael Masser and Gerry Goffin. "I was just listening to a George Benson album and I totally liked it," Glenn told Guy Aoki in *Music Connection*. "I might have heard it on the radio once or twice, but nothing happened to it." The song was "Nothing's Gonna Change My Love for You." Glenn won the local contest and was flown to Honolulu for the finals. He won the grand prize: $500 in cash and an opportunity to record his song.

Glenn recorded the Masser-Goffin tune in May, 1986, and KMAI added it to their playlist; within a few weeks, it was number one. Fortunately for Glenn, a visitor from Phoenix, Arizona, heard his song on the radio. "I needed a vacation, so I went to Hawaii," says Guy Zapoleon, then pro-

gram director of KZZP in Phoenix [see 710—"Red Red Wine"]. "I said, 'I don't want to talk to anybody, I don't want to be disturbed, because I'm really fried.' And sure enough, my friend Jay Stone, the program director of I-94, said, 'I've got a record, you've got to listen to it.'" Zapoleon loved the song, and promised Stone he would take it home to Phoenix and play it on the three-times-a-day feature called "Make It or Break It."

"After half a day's worth of airplay, people were calling in and dedicating the song to their loved ones," recalls the program director. "When people feel that strongly about a song . . . that's it."

Leonard Silver, head of Amherst Records in Buffalo, New York, was attending a record convention in Phoenix when he heard "Nothing's Gonna Change My Love for You" on KZZP. "They said it was the most requested single in Phoenix, and they said you couldn't buy it anywhere," noted Silver, who then flew to Hawaii and signed Medeiros to his label.

Medeiros made his debut on the Hot 100 the week of February 14, 1987. The single peaked at number 12, an impressive feat for a small, independent label. Released in the U.K. on London Records in 1988, "Nothing's Gonna Change My Love for You" spent four weeks at number one in July.

Exactly two years later, Medeiros had the number one song in the United States with "She Ain't Worth It," featuring Bobby Brown [see 718—"My Prerogative"]. The idea for the two artists to work together came from Rick James ("Super Freak"), who knew Leonard Silver. "Rick said he wanted me to work with this kid because he could really sing," says Brown. "I knew he had the potential of becoming a great artist. I loved the song that he did before, 'Nothing's Gonna Change My Love for You'—I used to sing it in my concert. When I found out he did that song, I really wanted to work with him."

Medeiros explains, "I had recorded 'She Ain't Worth It' and it was finished. We were going to throw a rap of some type on it." After Rick James talked to Bobby, he agreed to work on the song and wrote a rap in the studio. "It was about this girl I knew," Brown admits. "She still doesn't know."

Brown describes Medeiros as being "shy, kind of laid-back. I'm very energetic, always up. It was like working with Michael Jackson, like working with a shy person, trying to bring that rough side out of him. And I think we did a pretty good job of doing that on the song."

"She Ain't Worth It" debuted on the Hot 100 the week of May 19, 1990, and hit the top nine weeks later.

## THE TOP FIVE
*Week of July 21, 1990*

1  **She Ain't Worth It**
   Glenn Medeiros f/Bobby Brown

2  **Hold On**
   En Vogue

3  **Cradle of Love**
   Billy Idol

4  **Rub You the Right Way**
   Johnny Gill

5  **Vision of Love**
   Mariah Carey

## 762 Vision of Love COLUMBIA 73348
### MARIAH CAREY

Writers: *Mariah Carey*
*Ben Margulies*

Producers: *Rhett Lawrence*
*Narada Michael Walden*

*August 4, 1990*
*4 weeks*

MARIAH CAREY was born March 22, 1970, in New York City. Her mother Patricia named her after the song "They Call the Wind Mariah" from the Lerner and Loewe musical *Paint Your Wagon*. It's unlikely her mother was aware that on the day Mariah was born, the number one song in Britain was "Wand'rin' Star" by Lee Marvin—from *Paint Your Wagon*.

Mariah began singing early, when she was four years old. By six, she was writing poetry. Patricia was a vocal coach, a jazz vocalist and a singer with the New York City Opera, and Mariah's older brother and sister allowed their youngest sibling to listen to their Stevie Wonder, Gladys Knight and Aretha Franklin 45s.

When Mariah was 16, her brother paid for her to make a 24-track demo tape at a Manhattan studio. "We needed someone to play the keyboards for a song I had written with a guy named Gavin Christopher," Mariah remembers. "We called someone and he couldn't come, so by accident we stumbled upon Ben (Margulies). Ben came to the session, and he can't really play keyboards very well—he's really more of a drummer—but after that day, we kept in touch, and we just sort of clicked as writers."

Margulies had a studio set up at Bedworks, his father's cabinetry factory in Chelsea. Mariah was still a

high school student when she got together with Ben and wrote their first song, "Here We Go Round Again." "It was this real Motown thing," Ben remembers. "She wrote all the verses out. We were very excited because she sounded incredible. That was the beginning of the collaborating."

Mariah and Ben worked together for a couple of years on material, as she graduated high school and supported herself with jobs like waiting tables and checking coats. "The music kept us going," Margulies explains. "I didn't have much equipment, but we had a way of making demos sound incredible."

A friend of Mariah's who played drums for Brenda K. Starr mentioned that a back-up singer had quit, and suggested Mariah audition for the job. "I really didn't want to do it, but I said it's gotta be better than what I'm doing now," Mariah recalls. "So I went to the audition, and Brenda was such a great person." She was not only hired, she became close friends with Brenda.

Back in New York during a break in her tour, Brenda invited Mariah to attend a party thrown by CBS Records. Brenda handed Mariah's demo tape to CBS Records Group president Tommy Mottola, who listened to it in his limo on the way home. After hearing the first two songs, he went back to the party to find the singer. She had already left, and there was no phone number on the tape. Tommy spent the

weekend trying to track down Mariah, but Brenda's managers didn't know who she was and he had to wait until Monday. "I got this message that he had called and they wanted me to come to CBS Records, and I was so excited," says Mariah.

Rhett Lawrence, who had produced CBS artists like Johnny Kemp and Earth, Wind & Fire, was asked to fly to New York and listen to the demo tape. "They described her as a girl who was 18 and had the most incredible voice you've ever heard," Lawrence reports. "I literally got goosebumps on my arms when I heard her sing. I couldn't believe the power and maturity in her voice."

Carey went to Los Angeles to work with Lawrence. He heard a rough version of "Vision of Love," a song Mariah and Ben wrote right after she signed with Columbia. Described by Mariah as not so much a love song but a celebration of her life at that time, the demo sounded very different from what would be the finished product; according to Lawrence, "it was a different tempo at the time . . . a '50s sort of shuffle." Working with Ben and Mariah in the studio, Lawrence changed the tempo and used Mariah's vocals from the demo as a second vocal in the tag of the song. Released as Mariah's debut single, "Vision of Love" debuted on the Hot 100 the week of June 2, 1990, and was number one nine weeks later.

### THE TOP FIVE
*Week of August 4, 1990*

1 **Vision of Love**
Mariah Carey

2 **Cradle of Love**
Billy Idol

3 **Rub You the Right Way**
Johnny Gill

4 **The Power**
Snap!

5 **She Ain't Worth It**
Glenn Medeiros f/Bobby Brown

*Writers: Russ DeSalvo*
*Deena Charles*
*Robert Steele*

*Producer: Steve Peck*

*September 1, 1990*
*1 week*

Betty LeBron, lead singer of Sweet Sensation, studied opera at New York's High School of the Performing Arts and sang operatic material in 10 different languages to graduate. But it was a pop ballad that took her to the top of the *Billboard* Hot 100, giving the Atco label its seventh number one single and its first since "Owner of a Lonely Heart" by Yes in January, 1984 [see 582].

After graduation, Betty attended Satellite Academy, where she met accounting student Margie Fernandez, who had grown up on the Lower East Side of Manhattan. "After I left (the High School of the Performing Arts), I really had no interest in being a singer, because I was around people who were so competitive and they were much better," says Betty. "I was taking up liberal arts. I was taking accounting as well. I was going crazy—I hate math."

Betty and Margie both knew Joseph Malloy, better known as Romeo J.D. of the Boogie Boys. He had written a dance song, "Hooked on You," and thought Betty could sing it. She went into a studio with background singers and recorded it for Next Plateau Records. After the song was recorded, a group was put together consisting of Betty, Margie and her sister Maria.

"Our name was Sweet Temptation," Betty remembers. "It was printed on the label. And the day before the record was released, we got word from the Temptations' management company we couldn't use the name. We were stuck with Sweet Temptation on vinyl and didn't know what to do. We needed something that at least rhymed with temptation, and sensation came up." They were unaware that a previous group had charted under that name—"Sad Sweet Dreamer" was a number one hit in the U.K. and a number 14 hit in the U.S. for an octet from Manchester, England named Sweet Sensation.

"Hooked on You" reached number 64 on the *Billboard* chart in February, 1987. "We thought we could still go to school, (sing) on weekends, and it wouldn't interfere with anything," says Betty. "Then the record started happening in all the dance markets like Miami, New York and the West Coast. All of a sudden, we had to travel, and we had problems because we were in school. We started getting serious about it."

Signed to Atco Records, the Hispanic trio recorded an album and toured as an opening act for New Kids on the Block. "The first album was so danceable . . . I was afraid to follow that up," admits Betty, "but the pop field opened up to us, and I was nervous that our fans wouldn't appreciate it." One of their producers, Ted Currier, suggested they cover a Supremes song for the second album and they agreed on "Love Child" [see 248].

"Love Child" peaked at number 13 in May, 1990, besting by one position Sweet Sensation's biggest hit to date, "Sincerely Yours." The follow-up to "Love Child" was the ballad "If Wishes Came True."

Russ DeSalvo, co-writer of the song, says, "We wanted to write a sequel to 'Thinking of You,'" a hit he co-wrote for Sa-Fire. "We wanted a song about relationships. Although it's an unhappy situation, we wanted the chorus to reflect a positive feeling." Producer Steve Peck was looking for a crossover song and told DeSalvo that "If Wishes Came True" was it.

Betty thought the song was beautiful, but found it difficult to record. "I didn't know how to approach the song at first. When you get a girl who's so used to doing uptempo songs and jumping up and down, then give her something like this, you look at it and say, 'What do I do with this mess?'"

Sweet Sensation was on tour when "If Wishes Came True" was moving up the Hot 100. "We were very busy, constantly on the bus," Betty recalls. "We were busy watching movies in the back, so radio wasn't a big part of our trip. I didn't get the magazines like *Billboard* that we get when we're home. I remember we were in Pennsylvania and we had just gotten offstage. Our road manager took us into the bus and said, 'Your record just hit number one.' We cried for weeks. Every time somebody congratulated us, it was an extreme emotion."

## THE TOP FIVE
*Week of September 1, 1990*

1 **If Wishes Came True**
  Sweet Sensation

2 **Blaze of Glory**
  Jon Bon Jovi

3 **Unskinny Bop**
  Poison

4 **Release Me**
  Wilson Phillips

5 **Do Me!**
  Bell Biv DeVoe

# 764 Blaze of Glory  MERCURY 875 896-7
## JON BON JOVI

*Writer: Jon Bon Jovi*

*Producers: Danny Kortchmar*
*Jon Bon Jovi*

*September 8, 1990*
*1 week*

JOHN FUSCO, screenwriter for *Young Guns* and its sequel, *Young Guns II*, found a source of musical inspiration while he was penning the first film, about a young Billy the Kid and the pack of Regulators who rode with him.

"I heard the Bon Jovi song 'Wanted Dead or Alive' back while I was writing the first *Young Guns*," says Fusco. "I heard it on the radio and went out and bought the tape, and would play it every now and then while I was writing. Although I was playing a lot of period music, a lot of old banjo and bluegrass and music that was more indigenous to that period, 'Wanted Dead or Alive' gave me a blast of energy a couple of times a day. I think that helped me push for a contemporary feel for the picture. So I was a big fan of the song, and on the set of *Young Guns II* when Emilio (Estevez) mentioned that Bon Jovi was a fan of the movie, I told him about that experience and how 'Wanted Dead or Alive' was used as mood music during the writing process.

"He told Bon Jovi, and Bon Jovi said he was working on a song that he had sort of based on the script of *Young Guns II*. He had read the script. He travelled out to Galisteo, New Mexico, where we were filming, and wandered out onto the set with an old beat-up guitar. It was freezing that night—Emilio, Jon, and I went into Emilio's trailer, and Jon picked (the song) out on this old guitar and sang it."

Fusco found himself moved by "Blaze of Glory." "I did have some doubts, initially, about using a rock and roll song. I thought, 'Would a Bon Jovi song feel too anachronistic and work against us?' But I really loved the spirit of the song. I went to the set and got two of the producers, Paul Schiff and Irby Smith. We all crammed back into the trailer, Jon played it again, and they had the same response. After a short meeting, we decided we wanted to use the song in the end credits. Shortly after that, we grabbed Jon, threw him into the makeup room, squibbed him with special effects, and shot the hell out of him. I think we shot him 26 times in a scene in the movie."

Fusco describes Jon's scene: "There is a prison in the town of Lincoln called the Pit, which is based on the actual prison they had, just a huge hole dug in the ground covered with wooden slabs. The prisoners were just dumped in there—a real nasty place. Jon plays one of the prisoners in the Pit, and I do a little thing in there myself. If you watch the film, during the big escape, when Billy and the boys ride in disguised as the lynch mob and begin to shoot up the town, the Pit is shot open, the slabs fall back, and everybody starts to crawl out. The first two people who crawl out are Bon Jovi and me. We sneak up on a deputy. I grab him with my shackles around the neck, and Jon grabs his gun away from him. At that point, Jon is shot in slow motion, and flips over backwards into the Pit. He enjoyed it."

Just as the movie featured an all-star cast (Lou Diamond Phillips, Kiefer Sutherland and Christian Slater in addition to Estevez), Jon assembled an all-star roster of musicians to record the soundtrack, including Jeff Beck, Elton John and Little Richard. Jon was able to introduce Beck to one of his idols, Little Richard. "Beck was like a six-year-old," Jon told Toby Goldstein in *Circus*. "His fingers took over his body and he started playing 'Lucille.' And he knew he looked foolish and stopped. Jeff shook hands with Richard and said, 'You're the reason I'm in this business.' It was a great thrill for me to do that kind of favor for Jeff Beck."

"Blaze of Glory" entered the Hot 100 the week of July 21, 1990, and moved into the number one position seven weeks later. The song won the Golden Globe for Best Original Song. It was nominated in the same category for an Oscar, but lost to "Sooner or Later," the Stephen Sondheim song Madonna crooned in *Dick Tracy*.

## THE TOP FIVE
*Week of September 8, 1990*

1 **Blaze of Glory**
  Jon Bon Jovi

2 **Release Me**
  Wilson Phillips

3 **Do Me!**
  Bell Biv DeVoe

4 **Unskinny Bop**
  Poison

5 **If Wishes Came True**
  Sweet Sensation

*Writers: Wilson Phillips*

*Producer: Glen Ballard*

*September 15, 1990*
*2 weeks*

"'Release Me' was one of those pure moments of light," says producer Glen Ballard. He had participated in the writing of Wilson Phillips' first number one single [see 758—Hold On"], but Chynna Phillips and Carnie and Wendy Wilson wrote "Release Me" by themselves. "I loved it from the moment they played it for me," the producer says. "You listen to 'Release Me' and that's three-part harmony wall-to-wall, and it sounds like one voice. It's so tight and textured—that's my favorite thing that they've done. I'm as big a fan of that today as I was when I did the first arrangement on the demo."

Carnie explains the inspiration behind the song: "We were all going through this time with our boyfriends—it was like a joke. Breaking up, getting back together, breaking up. We all said, 'Let me go, that's it, I'm not going to come back to you anymore, I'm not going to take this.' I love the three-part harmony the whole way through the song. This is the first song we ever wrote together, music and lyrics."

Ballard calls it "the most fun record I ever cut. We cut it ensemble at 9:00 in the morning with an incredible rhythm section—Randy Kerber on piano, John Robinson on drums, Jimmy Johnson on bass, and Mike Landau on guitar. I had the arrangement written, and it was ready to go. We were just going to run it down, but we always put the red lights on. We recorded it, and they played it down. I said, 'I know I'm not supposed to do this, but I think it's a take—I think that's it.' And it was. I listened back to it and (said), 'Let's do another song.' It's never happened to me. . . . I knew it was a number one record."

SBK wanted "Release Me" to be the first Wilson Phillips single, but "Hold On" was eventually chosen. The second track issued from the album, "Release Me" entered the Hot 100 on June 30, 1990, and was number one 11 weeks later. The third single was "Impulsive," a song originally written for Japanese singing star Seiko. The Wilson Phillips version, the first single to feature Wendy on lead, peaked at number four in December.

Ballard, who co-wrote Michael Jackson's "Man in the Mirror" [see 694], describes how he records Wilson Phillips: "We don't use any tricks of any kind. We don't ever use

pitch changers, harmonizers, samplers, or any of that. They sing everything, and very often they sing together. Since there is so much harmony and so much texture on the records, we put them each on a separate microphone and have separate EQ for each of them, and let them sing together, which is sort of the magic of it. They work very hard in the studio, because they're perfectionists, and I am, too. We spend long hours making sure the textures are right."

Ballard says the first time Wilson Phillips records a song, "It's 99 percent right. We work a long time to get the extra one percent. Which probably doesn't matter to anybody, because the noise that comes out of their mouths is so pure and wonderful. We work out the harmonies usually before we even start singing.

"The whole is greater than the sum of their parts. I mean, there is this fourth voice I hear, this harmonic overtone that emerges when the three of them are singing together, that is scary to me sometimes. I know intellectually, from a musical standpoint, what they're singing, what parts are being sung, and how—but there's this unusual quality that emerges from the three voices together that's like nothing I've ever worked with. Carnie sings the lower parts, Wendy oftentimes will sing the highest parts, and a lot of times Chynna is in the middle. But that's a rule broken more often than kept, because they've all increased their range. They can sing lower and higher now than they could before—they really have matured as singers."

## THE TOP FIVE
*Week of September 15, 1990*

1 **Release Me**
Wilson Phillips

2 **Blaze of Glory**
Jon Bon Jovi

3 **Do Me!**
Bell Biv DeVoe

4 **Have You Seen Her**
M.C. Hammer

5 **Unskinny Bop**
Poison

## 766 (Can't Live Without Your) Love and Affection DGC 19689
### NELSON

*Writers: Matthew Nelson*
*Gunnar Nelson*
*Marc Tanner*

*Producers: Marc Tanner*
*David Thoener*

*September 29, 1990*
*1 week*

ONE day before their 23rd birthday, Matthew and Gunnar Nelson found out that the first single from their *After the Rain* album, "(Can't Live Without Your) Love and Affection," would be the new number one single on the *Billboard* Hot 100. It was the first time that one set of rock and roll offpsring replaced another at the top of the chart—the twin sons of Ricky Nelson [see 90—"Travelin' Man"] succeeded the daughters of Brian Wilson and the daughter of a Mama and a Papa.

Music was always encouraged in the Nelsons' household, along with anything artistic. As young children, they heard their father's Stone Canyon band rehearsing, and George Harrison lived next door for a time. When they were seven, Gunnar received a drum set and Matthew a bass guitar. They were almost 10 when they wrote their first song, "Feelings of Love."

"It was our birthday, and our parents told us we had a dentist's appointment after school," recalls Matthew. "So Mom picked us up and we went to this building, walked in, and it wasn't a dentist's office, it was a recording studio. All our instruments were set up. Dad was behind the glass waving to us and we recorded the song. So he actually produced our first song. It was really amazing."

### THE TOP FIVE
*Week of September 29, 1990*

1 **(Can't Live Without Your) Love and Affection**
Nelson

2 **Close to You**
Maxi Priest

3 **Release Me**
Wilson Phillips

4 **Blaze of Glory**
Jon Bon Jovi

5 **Praying for Time**
George Michael

At 13, the twins were chaperoned to nightclubs to play with their band. They rehearsed four hours a day and lived to play at Los Angeles spots like Madame Wong's, the Central and the Music Machine. Their music reflected their influences: Boston, Queen, the Eagles, Foreigner and Bad Company.

When Rick and Kris Nelson divorced, the twins found it difficult to continue playing music. "We were 14 years old, we couldn't drive, and she made us move all our gear to our dad's house to keep us from playing," Matthew told Jeffrey Ressner in *Rolling Stone*. On their 18th birthday, they moved in with their father.

Three months later, Matthew was driving to a friend's house on New Year's Eve to meet Gunnar when he turned on the radio and heard his dad's "Garden Party." When it ended, the disc jockey said it was a tribute to Ricky Nelson, who had been killed in a plane crash. Matthew thought it was a mistake, until he arrived and heard his friend's mother talking. He collapsed as Gunnar grabbed him.

The next day the twins moved into their own apartment. Soon after, they were the musical guests on "Saturday Night Live." On the plane ride home from New York, they made a major decision. "We looked at each other and there was a little voice screaming at us, 'This is not your time; this is not right,'" Matthew told Tom Green in *USA Today*. "Pop music wasn't what

we felt anymore. We fired the band before we hit the ground." They went through a period they describe as self-destructive. In 1987, they spent time in Australia, then returned to the States and met Marc Tanner, a songwriter who had recorded a couple of albums for Elektra.

The Nelsons contacted John Kalodner in Geffen Records' A&R department about getting a contract with the label. David Geffen sat in on their first meeting and reminded them that when they were two years old, he had visited their dad and joked that someday he would have his sons' publishing rights. Kalodner, in no rush to sign them, insisted on musical credibility for the twins, and they wrote and recorded some 56 demos over a three-year period. Finally, they burst into Kalodner's office with two acoustic guitars and played their songs. "He said he hadn't seen anyone do that since 1967," says Gunnar. Kalodner called the label's business affairs office and signed the Nelsons that day.

Nelson recorded *After the Rain* with a band that included guitarists Bret Garsed and Joey Cathcart, keyboard player Paul Mirkovich and drummer Bobby Rock. "(Can't Live Without Your) Love and Affection" began as an acoustic guitar riff Matthew came up with while looking at a photo of model Cindy Crawford in *Vogue*. "Do you think this might get me a date with her?" he asked Gunnar.

CHARISMA 98951 **Close to You** 767
MAXI PRIEST

Writers: Gary Benson
        Winston Sela
        Max Elliott

Producers: Geoffrey Chung
          Sly Dunbar
          Handel Tucker

October 6, 1990
1 week

THE first number one single on Charisma in the United States was "Close to You" by Maxi Priest, who believes he benefitted by being switched from Virgin Records to the Charisma label. Richard Branson, founder of the Virgin Group, announced the creation of a second U.S. record label on February 6, 1990. Phil Quartararo, named president of the New York-based Charisma Records, confirmed the initial roster would include T'Pau ("Heart and Soul"), When in Rome ("The Promise") and Maxi Priest.

Maxi Priest's first records in America were released on Virgin. He went to number 25 in January, 1989, with a reggae version of Cat Stevens' "Wild World." But the artist says that people at Virgin "were comparing me a lot with Ziggy Marley," son of the late Bob Marley and a Virgin artist himself. "Whenever (they discussed) promotion, they had to do stuff with Ziggy Marley first and then with me."

Born in London of Pentecostal Jamaican parents, the young Max Elliott was curious about his roots and became a devout Rastafarian at age 15. "I was also open to the Beatles, Phil Collins and the other pop out of England," he told Peter Ramjug. "And I was a great follower of guys like Smokey Robinson and Marvin Gaye."

As a teenager, Max created his own sound system in his mother's house and named it Gladiator Sounds. He built speaker cabinet boxes, then went to work for Saxon International, a mobile DJ system used by British and Jamaican reggae DJs. "I started to play the records, just rapping or deejaying over the 'B' sides," he told Don Snowden of the *Los Angeles Times*. "Gradually, I just started to sing around the sound system, and the people started to encourage me." He worked with well-known reggae stars like Smiley Culture, Tippa Irie and Philip "Papa" Levi. They were in the vanguard of DJs who were pioneering a new style of reggae whereby the DJs mixed self-created rhythm tracks with instrumentals taken from their favorite albums and topped off by their own vocals.

When he started working for Saxon, Max chose a new name for himself. He decided on Levi, after the priest of the Rastafarian Twelve Tribes of Israel. Then he met Papa Levi and deferred to him, changing his name to Maxi Priest.

Saxon's tapes were sent to Jamaica and reggae communities in America, so the name Maxi Priest was known even before he recorded his first record, "Hey Little Girl." It went to number eight on the U.K. reggae chart,

and did well in Jamaica. In 1985 he was signed to 10 Records, distributed by Virgin in the U.K., and recorded an album, *You're Safe*. Maxi made his debut on the British pop singles chart with "Strollin' On," number 32 in the spring of 1986. A second album, *Intentions*, was released later that year, and Priest made the U.K. pop chart with a reggae version of Van Morrison's "Crazy Love."

His third album, *Maxi*, was recorded in Jamaica with producers Sly Dunbar and Robbie Shakespeare. "It's a different world there," says the artist. "The musicians in Kingston live and breathe music. Hanging around the studio watching my heroes at work made me think there's something special about the way reggae is recorded in Jamaica. I felt I was an extended limb—a part of Jamaica that had grown in England."

*Maxi* was released in the U.S. as well, and contained "Wild World." It was the *Bonafide* album, though, that gave the singer his first number one single with "Close to You."

"The song was originally more like soul than reggae," says Maxi Priest, explaining why he wanted Sly Dunbar, Geoffrey Chung and Handel Tucker to produce it. "I used those producers to swing it back over. I think we got a nice balance between reggae, pop, and soul—it has all three of the elements in there."

## THE TOP FIVE
*Week of October 6, 1990*

1 **Close to You**
  Maxi Priest

2 **Praying for Time**
  George Michael

3 **(Can't Live Without Your) Love and Affection**
  Nelson

4 **Something Happened on the Way to Heaven**
  Phil Collins

5 **I Don't Have the Heart**
  James Ingram

# Praying for Time COLUMBIA 73512
## GEORGE MICHAEL

*Writer: George Michael*

*Producer: George Michael*

*October 13, 1990*
*1 week*

AFTER shedding his bubblegum Wham! image and achieving solo success with his *Faith* album, George Michael decided he'd had enough. Although he had wanted to be a pop star since the age of seven, George discovered that being a superstar made him miserable. The pressures of celebrity hit him hardest when he embarked on a 10-month tour to promote *Faith*. "I can remember the exact moment that I decided I must change my life," he told Robert Hilburn in the *Los Angeles Times*. "We (opened) the *Faith* tour in Japan, which was fine because they are reasonably quiet, and they listened to the music. But then we went to Australia, and the roof came off the first place we came to. The screaming. I thought, 'God, it is happening all over again. I'm not going to have a chance to really sing.' And I realized I had to do it for 10 months."

In the middle of the tour, George was forced to take a month off for emergency throat surgery to remove a cyst on his vocal chords. During the break, he decided to shift the focus from himself to his songs. "The only thing that really matters is making music that will still mean something to people in 20 or 30 years time," George commented. In *USA Today*, he said, "I'd set my sights on American superstardom and getting up there with Michael Jackson and Madonna and Prince, simply because my ego and my ambition needed a new challenge.

## THE TOP FIVE
### Week of October 13, 1990

1 **Praying for Time**
George Michael

2 **Close to You**
Maxi Priest

3 **I Don't Have the Heart**
James Ingram

4 **Ice Ice Baby**
Vanilla Ice

5 **Black Cat**
Janet Jackson

Once I was getting into that bracket . . . I realized I didn't want to be there. There was financial reward but no spiritual reward."

With the release of *Listen Without Prejudice, Vol. I*, George made good on his intentions. Instead of his face, the album cover depicted a photo of a crowded beach taken by 1940s photographer Weegee. George declined to do an extensive tour, and gave only three interviews to promote the album. Most surprising, the man who was a fixture on MTV refused to make a video for the album's first single, "Praying for Time." With George's consent, Columbia Records did release a video, but it simply presented the song's lyrics on a stark black background.

"Praying for Time," a ballad about the uncaring world he saw around him, showed George exploring a new social consciousness in his songwriting. "There comes a point where you have to write something which you have not written before, in which your interest in any particular topic or subject will inspire you. That's why, I suppose, eventually most lyricists do approach wider topics than sex and love."

George explained the roots of the song to Hilburn. The world, he said,

seemed like a "place where things are running out of time. Everything is getting more violent. You need more protection all the time and it has gotten so bad that people's general attitude is, 'What the hell? I think I am going to hold on to what I've got.' The key line for me is the one about it's hard to love, but there's so much to hate."

Before making *Listen Without Prejudice*, George went back beyond his soul roots and studied the '60s rock of the Beatles, the Rolling Stones and Joni Mitchell. "It made me decide to strip everything down. It was challenging, but it was also fun."

George told Kevin Connal how he came up with the album title: "What I was mostly talking about was that the album should be listened to by all types and races, and with an open mind. You see, I think radio and video in the last three or four years have veered very much into separate directions, one for white America and one for black America. I think it's quite an unhealthy trend."

"Praying for Time" debuted on the Hot 100 at number 41 the week of September 1, 1990. Six weeks later, it was the ninth number one for George—counting his hits with Wham!—or the sixth number one of his solo career.

WARNER BROTHERS 19911 **I Don't Have the Heart**
JAMES INGRAM

*Writers: Allan Rich*
*Jud Friedman*

*Producers: Thom Bell*
*James Ingram*

*October 20, 1990*
*1 week*

"I DON'T HAVE THE HEART" was the ninth single by James Ingram to make the upper half of the *Billboard* Hot 100, but the first one to be a solo effort by the singer from Akron, Ohio.

Ingram made his chart debut the week of August 15, 1981, with "Just Once," a Barry Mann-Cynthia Weil tune featured on Quincy Jones' album *The Dude*. It peaked at number 17. Like the follow-up, "One Hundred Ways," the label read "Quincy Jones featuring James Ingram."

His next chart single was "Baby, Come to Me," a duet with Patti Austin that went to number one in February, 1983 [see 568]. The follow-up duet was "How Do You Keep the Music Playing," which peaked at number 45. In December, 1983, "Yah Mo B There" debuted on the Hot 100; it was a duet with former Doobie Brother Michael McDonald. "What About Me?" featured vocals by Kenny Rogers, Kim Carnes and Ingram, and hit number 15 in November, 1984. Just over two years later, Ingram teamed up with Linda Ronstadt on another Mann-Weil tune, "Somewhere Out There" from the animated film *An American Tail*; an Oscar nominee, the song reached number two. In March, 1990, Ingram was featured along with Al B. Sure!, El DeBarge and Barry White on Quincy Jones' "The Secret Garden," which peaked at number 31.

## THE TOP FIVE
*Week of October 20, 1990*

1  **I Don't Have the Heart**
   James Ingram

2  **Black Cat**
   Janet Jackson

3  **Praying for Time**
   George Michael

4  **Ice Ice Baby**
   Vanilla Ice

5  **Close to You**
   Maxi Priest

Almost nine years after his chart debut, Ingram entered the Hot 100 the week of August 4, 1990, with "I Don't Have the Heart." It was the fourth single from his *It's Real* album, which had been released nearly a year and a half earlier.

The song, written by Allan Rich and Jud Friedman, found its way to Ingram through Benny Medina of Warner Brothers Records. "When I heard the song I immediately called the number that was on the tape," Ingram says. "I spoke to Allan and told him I loved the song and we were definitely going to do the song."

Rich remembers the phone call vividly. "I couldn't believe he was calling me at home. He said that the tape had been sitting there for over a year. He said, 'This is the first chance I've had to (listen to) my tapes, I've been so busy. This is the first song in several years that has made me weep.'"

Rich—a singer who used to open for Whitney Houston's mother Cissy in New York—moved to Los Angeles in 1980 to concentrate on songwriting. He waited tables in Beverly Hills and sold shoes at Venice Beach, where he was discovered by a producer. Howie Rice liked his songs, and soon Rich had his work recorded by Menudo, Patti LaBelle, Barry Manilow, Gladys Knight and Natalie Cole. Kathy

Spanberger at Peer Southern Music urged him to connect with a new writer she thought had talent. Rich agreed to meet Jud Friedman, another transplanted New Yorker.

"The first song we wrote together was 'I Don't Have the Heart,'" says Allan. Jud elaborates: "He told me the first verse and chorus over the phone . . . and I took it into the living room and sat down at my DX-7 and wrote it. It just poured out. Ultimately, we got together and finished the second verse and chorus bridge. I contributed some of the lyric."

Allan and Jud sent copies to everyone they thought might be interested; six months later, Ingram recorded it with producer Thom Bell. Rich and Friedman both list Bell as one of their idols. "I always had this dream that one day Thom Bell would produce me as a recording artist," says Allan, who was invited along with Jud to the recording session. "You hear a whole orchestra playing your song and Thom Bell conducting—it's a pretty momentous occasion in your life."

The week that James' version was released, another recording of the song was issued by Stacy Lattisaw. "The record company was not behind her," recalls Rich. "By some twist of fate, adult contemporary radio picked up on James' version."

# Black Cat A&M 1477
## JANET JACKSON

Writer: *Janet Jackson*

Producers: *Janet Jackson*
*Jellybean Johnson*

October 27, 1990
1 week

"BLACK CAT," Janet Jackson's fourth number one single, was a departure from her other hits. It was the first time she had sole writing credit on a single; it was produced by Jellybean Johnson instead of Jimmy Jam and Terry Lewis; and it was not pop or R&B—it was rock and roll.

Jam and Lewis were the producers of *Rhythm Nation 1814*, the album that included "Black Cat." "That was the last song recorded," says Jam. "We felt like we had everything we needed on the album, except we wanted to have a song that had more of a rock edge to it."

Janet had an idea for a song about a rebellious young man and sang the melody of "Black Cat" for Jimmy Jam. They laid down a rough track, and she came back the next day asking for help with the chorus and the verse. Jam told her the chorus should follow the guitar line and the verse should be another melody. "She had a bunch of different melodies, so we picked the two melodies that worked the best."

Jam then suggested to Janet, "'If you want to do something that's more rock, talk to Jellybean, because Jellybean is a closet rock-and-roller.' He's seriously into it." Jellybean confirms Jimmy Jam's opinion: "I'm a rock-and-roller. I made my name doing R&B drumming with the Time. I love heavy-metal music and rock and roll guitar,

so I was more than glad to do it."

Jimmy Jam says of Jellybean, "Bean gigs all the time locally—he sits in with all the bands, so he knows all the best players." Johnson asked a musician he had gigged with, Dave Barry, to play guitar on the track. "I've known Dave for a few years and I thought about guitar players, because I didn't want to chance doing this myself," says Jellybean. "I wanted it to be authentic rock and roll.

"I rocked it out, then Janet and I got together to do the vocals. Janet is a very nice, warm person, and she was receptive to my ideas. I played guitar for her on the *Control* album, on a song called 'You Can Be Mine,' so I had worked with her before."

"When she did the vocal," Jam reports, "it was funny, because I had tried to get her to sing a couple of the other vocals in her natural (voice) with kind of an edge on it. She didn't like the way her voice sounded. But for 'Black Cat,' that was exactly what was needed."

Johnson describes the process of recording the vocals: "One night I told her I wanted her to sound like a rock and roll queen on it—she usually uses one of her other voices to sing R&B funk. This, you wanted to be funky, but more rocked out. That was what I was trying to get her to do, and she did it in one or two takes."

The entire track was completed in less than a week and a half. "First, I

had Dave lay the tracks with a Rockman, but it didn't have that heavy-metal thing I wanted. I wanted it to compete with some of the heavy-metal things, so I went back and did it into the Marshall amp. I then had Dave double everything he did into the Marshall, and we used a mixture of the Rockman and the Marshall."

"Black Cat" debuted on the Hot 100 at number 37 the week of September 15, 1990. Six weeks later, it became the third single from *Rhythm Nation 1814* to hit number one.

Two guitarists from other groups guest-starred on remixes of the song. Vernon Reid of Living Colour and Nuno Bettencourt of Extreme [see 789—"More Than Words"] can be heard on different "Black Cat" tracks.

Prior to the release of the single, Janet was using a black leopard in her concert act. But after some fans voiced concern about the possible adverse effects of touring on the cat, Janet announced she would no longer employ the animal. "While the illusion with the cat was appreciated by most of the audience, if it caused even a few people to worry about the safety of the cat, it's not worth keeping it," she said in a statement. "I know how well the animal was treated by its trainer and my production staff. I love animals and would never do any harm, or allow anyone to do any harm, to one. Rather than let my fans worry, I would rather do without the cat."

---

## THE TOP FIVE
*Week of October 27, 1990*

1 **Black Cat**
Janet Jackson

2 **I Don't Have the Heart**
James Ingram

3 **Ice Ice Baby**
Vanilla Ice

4 **Giving You the Benefit**
Pebbles

5 **Love Takes Time**
Mariah Carey

*Writers: Vanilla Ice*
*Earthquake*
*David Bowie*
*Brian May*
*Freddie Mercury*
*Roger Taylor*
*John Deacon*

*Producer: Vanilla Ice*

*November 3, 1990*
*1 week*

Rᴏʙᴇʀᴛ Vᴀɴ Wɪɴᴋʟᴇ became the first rap artist to top the *Billboard* Hot 100 when "Ice Ice Baby" removed "Black Cat" from its perch atop the chart. But when SBK first released the single by Vanilla Ice, his real name was shrouded in mystery.

As was his life story. Vanilla Ice's biography claimed that he went to high school in Miami with Luther Campbell of 2 Live Crew, that he was a national motocross champion for Team Honda, and that his mother was a music professor at a Florida university. After reporters for the *Miami Herald* and the *Dallas Morning News* did some digging, a more accurate picture was formed. As a teenager, he lived in Texas as well as Florida, and attended many different schools, including one that Campbell attended.

He won some amateur motocross trophies and his mother, Beth Mino, taught music at a small college in Miami.

The origin of "Ice Ice Baby" can be traced back to 1987, when Tommy Quon, owner of the City Lights club in Dallas, discovered a white Camaro IROC parked in front of his marquee. He asked the driver, Robby Van Winkle, to move his car, but the brash young kid said he was coming inside to enter the talent contest and he didn't want his car ripped off. Quon let him leave it there.

"He wasn't that great as a rapper," Quon told David Handelman in *Rolling Stone*, "but he had that charisma, style. I signed him that night." It was Quon who surrounded the rapper with black dancers and let him open for City Lights headliners like Tone Loc, Paula Abdul and Public Enemy. Some demos were recorded, but they were turned down by every record company that heard them. Not discouraged, Quon decided he would release some recordings himself.

City Lights DJ Earthquake produced two of the tracks that Vanilla Ice recorded, and they were released back-to-back on Quon's Ultrax label. The "A" side was a reworking of Wild Cherry's "Play That Funky Music" [see

443]; the "B" side incorporated a chant by the black college fraternity Alpha Phi Alpha and the bass line from "Under Pressure," a song recorded by Queen and David Bowie. It was called "Ice Ice Baby."

Darrell J., a disc jockey at WAGH in Columbus, Georgia, liked the flip side better and played it on the air. When it topped the station's playlist, another station in Chattanooga, Tennessee, added it, and then some Dallas stations gave it airplay. Quon financed a video, which became the most requested number on Video Jukebox.

Atlantic Records was close to signing Vanilla Ice when SBK founder Charles Koppelman heard "Ice Ice Baby" over the phone. Eight minutes later, he said he would sign the artist if he could see the video. The next day, Vanilla Ice was an SBK artist, although he didn't immediately give up his day job, working at a car dealership managed by his stepfather.

He didn't have to keep the second job very long. "Ice Ice Baby" entered the Hot 100 on September 8, 1990, and was number one eight weeks later. It might have stayed at number one longer than a solitary week, but SBK deleted the single at the height of its popularity with hopes of selling more copies of *To The Extreme*. They eventually sold more than seven million albums.

"Play That Funky Music," released as a follow-up, peaked at number four in February, 1991. A month later, Ice was on the silver screen in a cameo role in *Teenage Mutant Ninja Turtles II: The Secret of the Ooze.* Before the year was over, Ice had the starring role in *Cool as Ice*, a film that quickly cooled at the box office.

## THE TOP FIVE
*Week of November 3, 1990*

1 **Ice Ice Baby**
   Vanilla Ice

2 **Black Cat**
   Janet Jackson

3 **Love Takes Time**
   Mariah Carey

4 **Giving You the Benefit**
   Pebbles

5 **I Don't Have the Heart**
   James Ingram

# 772 Love Takes Time COLUMBIA 73455
## MARIAH CAREY

**Writers: Mariah Carey**
**Ben Margulies**

**Producer: Walter Afanasieff**

*November 10, 1990*
*3 weeks*

COLUMBIA RECORDS literally stopped the presses for Mariah Carey's "Love Takes Time."

Mariah's debut album for the label was completed and being mastered when she wrote the song with Ben Margulies. "It was sort of a gospelish thing I was improvising, then we began working on it," Margulies relates. "It was on a work tape that we had . . . and we recorded a very quick demo. It was just a piano vocal demo—I played live piano, and she sang it."

Mariah was on a mini-tour of 10 states, playing acoustically with a piano player and three back-up singers. While on a company plane, she played the demo of "Love Takes Time" for Columbia Records president Don Ienner. "All the important guys were on the plane," Margulies recalls. "(Tommy) Mottola, Ienner, and Bobby Colomby." Mariah was told the song was a "career-maker," and that it had to go on the first album. Mariah protested—her album was already being mastered, and she intended this ballad for her next release.

The demo was sent to producer Walter Afanasieff. Born in São Paulo, Brazil, in 1958, Afanasieff grew up in San Francisco. He met producer Narada Michael Walden there in 1981, and first worked with him in the studio on Aretha Franklin's *Who's Zoomin' Who* album. When Mariah flew west to work with Narada on some tracks for her first album, Tommy Mottola and Don Ienner were impressed with Afanasieff's work and gave him an executive staff producer job with the label.

"I guess to see if he made the right choice, (Tommy) called me up one day," remembers Afanasieff. "He said, 'We've got this Mariah Carey album done, but there's a song that she and Ben Margulies wrote that is phenomenal, and I want to try everything we can to put it on the album.' I said, 'What do you want me to do?' and he said, 'You only have a couple of days, but are you ready to cut it?' I couldn't believe the opportunity that it was. I'd

never produced anything by myself up until that time."

The demo was very close to what Mottola wanted the finished product to be, according to Afanasieff. "We cut the song and the music and the basics in about a day—and the only reason is this deadline. It was do it or we were gonna miss out on the whole thing. We got the tape and recorded everything and we got on the plane and went to New York (and) did her vocals. She did all the backgrounds, practically sang all night. . . . We came back to the studio that afternoon, and we had to fix one line that we needed to get from Mariah. She fixed that one line very quickly, then (engineer) Dana (Jon Chappelle) and I got back on the plane with the tape, went back to the studio in Sausalito, and mixed it. So it was a three-day process: a day and a half for music, kind of like a day for vocals, and a day for mixing."

Afanasieff heard from Columbia executives as soon as they received the

mix. They wanted Mariah's vocal a little louder, so a remix was quickly completed. The producer asked if the song would still make the debut album, and was told, "We're going to do our best."

When the album was released, "Love Takes Time" was not listed on the cassette or compact disc. "(On) some of the original first copies of the record, they didn't have time to print the name of the song," Margulies laughs. "And so the song's on there, but it doesn't say that it's on there. It was a song that actually was strong enough to stop the pressing . . . I don't know if they had to throw away a few hundred copies."

After "Vision of Love" [see 762] had a four-week run at the top of the *Billboard* Hot 100, Columbia released "Love Takes Time" as a single. It debuted at number 73 (the same position that "Vision of Love" entered) the week of September 15, 1990, and became Mariah's second consecutive number one hit eight weeks later.

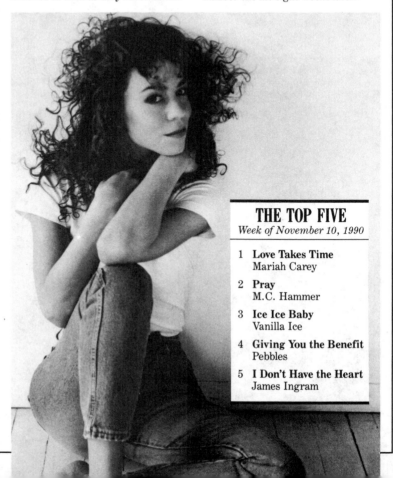

## THE TOP FIVE
*Week of November 10, 1990*

1 **Love Takes Time**
Mariah Carey

2 **Pray**
M.C. Hammer

3 **Ice Ice Baby**
Vanilla Ice

4 **Giving You the Benefit**
Pebbles

5 **I Don't Have the Heart**
James Ingram

Writers: *L.A. Reid*
*Babyface*

Producers: *L.A. Reid*
*Babyface*

*December 1, 1990*
*1 week*

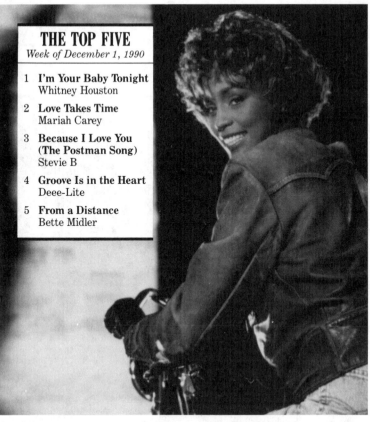

**THE TOP FIVE**
*Week of December 1, 1990*

1 **I'm Your Baby Tonight**
Whitney Houston

2 **Love Takes Time**
Mariah Carey

3 **Because I Love You
(The Postman Song)**
Stevie B

4 **Groove Is in the Heart**
Deee-Lite

5 **From a Distance**
Bette Midler

WHITNEY HOUSTON took a three-year break after recording her second album. By the time *I'm Your Baby Tonight* was released in 1990, she had accumulated seven consecutive number one singles on the *Billboard* Hot 100, a longer run than any other artist in the rock era [see 696—"Where Do Broken Hearts Go"].

Arista Records chief Clive Davis asked producers L.A. Reid and Babyface to work with Whitney on her third album. Antonio "L.A." Reid and Kenny "Babyface" Edmonds first met at the Zodiac club in Indianapolis, when Reid was playing there with his group, the Deele. Edmonds recalls, "After they finished their set, L.A. came down to my table and introduced himself." Each thought the other one was arrogant. "It was a band I would have liked to been in," Babyface admits. But he moved to Michigan and played in a top 40 cover band called the Crowd Pleasers. He wrote "Slow Jam" for Midnight Star, and was asked to attend the recording session.

Reid, meanwhile, had hooked up with Midnight Star and signed a production deal with them. Babyface was reunited with the Deele at the session. "It was a different kind of meeting," he says, "like, we should be working together." After he wrote some songs for the Deele and worked on their demos, L.A. invited Babyface to join the group. They made the Hot 100 debut in 1984 with "Body Talk" and had a top 10 hit in May, 1988, with "Two Occasions." By this time, Reid and Edmonds already had a song-writing and producing credit with another top 10 single, "Rock Steady" by the Whispers.

In a three-year period, L.A. and Babyface produced hits for Bobby Brown, Karyn White, Pebbles (who became Mrs. Reid) and After 7, a trio that included two of Babyface's brothers and Reid's cousin.

They had a long list of R&B credits when they went to work with Whitney. Some people suggested their main job was to re-establish her credibility with the black audience. "I would rather say to people that this new album is not different," Houston told Tom Green in *USA Today*. "It's just an extension of what Whitney has in store for them." She took exception to the idea that black people weren't listening to her anymore. "I get my flak like everybody else . . . but I'm just doing what I do best. I didn't plan on (selling 31 million albums). It just happened. I would think black people would be proud. . . . I don't sing music thinking this is black, or this is white . . . I sing songs that everybody's going to like."

Reid explains how the producers felt when they started working with the singer: "We wanted to come up with something that was different than anything Whitney had sung, so we approached it from that angle. We wanted to give her a new direction, and pick up where we felt she was lacking. We felt she needed more of a black base."

L.A. and Babyface had not met Whitney before they began the album.

"We wrote ("I'm Your Baby Tonight") among some other songs and when we had something, we asked her to come to Atlanta," Reid says. "We met with her and had dinner; we had a ball, and played the song for her. She was very happy."

L.A. describes the song as a shuffle, "sort of a cross between something that's a little jazzy and a little funky." About two weeks after they gave Whitney a tape of their demo, she was ready to record the number.

L.A. and Babyface discovered "I'm Your Baby Tonight" would be the album's title song "almost immediately after finishing," says Reid. "Once all of the material was recorded, it was pretty much decided then. We got a call that said, 'Guess what? You not only have the single, but you have the title track.'"

"I'm Your Baby Tonight" made a strong debut at number 42 the week of October 20, 1990. Six weeks later, Whitney Houston racked up her eighth number one hit. It was Reid and Babyface's first pop number one.

# Because I Love You (The Postman Song)
## STEVIE B

LMR 2724

*Writer: Warren Allen Brooks*

*Producer: Stevie B*

*December 8, 1990*
*4 weeks*

STEVEN BERNARD HILL was born and raised in Miami. A self-taught musician, he started a band in high school with Howard Johnson (later an A&M artist) called LUV, standing for Love, Unity and Virtue. Admittedly an average student as a college business major, Hill was a good tennis player and thought about turning pro. Then he started making money selling custom-lettered T-shirts. He also had a landscaping business and a car stereo shop, and saved up enough money to open a nightclub near his university in Tallahassee.

In 1980, Steven released "Sending Out for Love" on his own Midtown label, and in 1985 he formed a duo called Friday Friday with a friend, Warren Allen Brooks. Brooks had been interested in songwriting since the age of six. "I used to watch 'American Bandstand' and . . . I always wanted to get into music and writing," says the Tampa-born composer. Friday Friday released a single called "Boy Toy," then split up.

Stevie B opened his own recording studio in 1986. "I just worked hard, saved the money and did it," he said in *Billboard*. "By having my own place, I have the freedom to cut as many demos as I want to."

He grabbed rappers and other artists off the street and recorded them, releasing titles like "Pretty Girls" by the Miami Jam Crew and "I Need You"

by B.V.S.M.P. (Baby Virgo and the Simple Mind Persuaders). The latter single went to number three on the British chart in the summer of 1988. Meanwhile, Stevie B decided to turn his attention on himself. "I made a total commitment—I felt that I had a decent voice, and wasn't the ugliest guy in the world. So if I was packaged right as an artist, I could do all right."

Stevie released "Party Your Body" on his own label. Bill Tanner, program director of Power 96 in Miami, gave the record airplay and helped make it a local hit. Herb Moelis of LMR Records in New York heard the song, and signed Stevie B to his label.

Reissued on LMR, "Party Your Body" received significant club play in New York, San Francisco and Los Angeles as well as Miami. It peaked at number 69 on the Black Singles chart. The next Stevie B single, "Dreamin' of Love," was his Hot 100 debut, peaking at number 80 in May, 1988. His six successive singles also made the chart, with "Love and Emotion" (co-written with Brooks) going as high as number 15 in September, 1990.

Then LMR, which had been picked up for distribution by RCA, released "Because I Love You (The Postman Song)." It entered the Hot 100 on October 6, 1990, and nine weeks later, it was number one. "Because I Love You" was one of only three songs in 1991 to be number one for four weeks (after Sinead O'Connor's "Nothing Compares 2 U" and Mariah Carey's

"Vision of Love").

" 'Because I Love You' to me is a spiritual song," explains Brooks, the song's writer. "It was God talking to me, telling me that he loved me . . . it was like I had written him a letter . . . and he was telling me that he got my letter, that he cared, and that whenever I needed him, he'd be there. I turned it into a pop song where the audience thinks it's about a male/female relationship, but it's really about me and God having a personal relationship. I did the music first, then the lyrics."

Brooks had written the song years before. "Stevie B heard me sing it on the piano in 1985, and he would tell everybody, 'Listen to Warren's song—that could be a hit.' "

In February, 1991, Stevie B quietly signed a contract with Sony Music. Four months later, Lefrak-Moelis Records sued Sony in the New York State Supreme Court, alleging that the company exhibited a "pattern of predatory business practices," including the inducement to Stevie B to break his contract with LMR. A lawyer from LMR said that Stevie B had delivered three of the eight albums he agreed to record. In early November, a U.S. Bankruptcy Court judge in Fort Lauderdale, Florida, voided Stevie B's contract with LMR in favor of the Sony pact. On November 27, Sony asked a New York judge to dismiss the company from LMR's $150-million lawsuit.

---

## THE TOP FIVE
### Week of December 8, 1990

1 **Because I Love You
(The Postman Song)**
Stevie B

2 **I'm Your Baby Tonight**
Whitney Houston

3 **From a Distance**
Bette Midler

4 **Something to Believe In**
Poison

5 **Love Takes Time**
Mariah Carey

**Writers:** *Madonna*
*Lenny Kravitz*
*Ingrid Chavez*

**Producer:** *Lenny Kravitz*

*January 5, 1991*
*2 weeks*

AT THE END of 1990, Sire Records released *The Immaculate Collection*, an album featuring 15 of Madonna's hit singles from "Holiday" to "Vogue" [see 757], plus two new tracks, "Justify My Love" and "Rescue Me."

The former was released as a single, so it was only natural that Madonna would have a video to go with it. Directed by Jean-Baptiste Mondino, the video for "Justify My Love" proved to be even more controversial than the one for "Like a Prayer" [see 727], which drew the wrath of the Catholic Church. This one featured Madonna and her lover exploring erotic fantasies, including voyeurism, masturbation, some sadomasochism and bisexuality. It was even too hot for MTV.

"We respect her work as an artist and think she makes great videos," executives of the cable service said in a statement. "This one is just not for us." An MTV staffer was quoted, "This decision went all the way to the top. There was no way we could even edit this. I can't believe Madonna ever thought we would air it." Madonna responded: "Why is it that people are willing to go to a movie and watch someone get blown to bits for no reason, and nobody wants to see two girls kissing and two men snuggling?" But she did understand the music video

channel's position. "MTV has been good to me, and they know their audience," she told a reporter. "If it's too strong for them, I understand that." In another statement, she revealed she knew up front the video was probably too steamy for MTV. "Half of me thought I was going to get away with it," she said.

Within hours of the MTV decision, Warner/Reprise Video announced it would release "Justify My Love" as the first commercially-available video single. Bob Merlis, head of publicity for Warner Brothers, told Patrick Goldstein of the *Los Angeles Times*: "The plan to sell the clip only came about after we learned MTV wouldn't program the video."

The clip that proved too steamy for MTV was then telecast complete and uncensored on ABC-TV's "Nightline." Forrest Sawyer interviewed Madonna

about the brouhaha, and the late-night news program received its highest Nielsen rating of 1990. A 90-second excerpt aired on "Saturday Night Live," giving that series its highest rating of the season, according to the Nielsen overnights. "Entertainment Tonight" aired 60 seconds, and CNN's "Showbiz Today" aired 112 seconds—both received higher-than-normal ratings.

Months after "Justify My Love" was number one, another kind of controversy erupted over the song. Ingrid Chavez, a Minneapolis-based singer signed to Prince's Paisley Park label, sued Lenny Kravitz over the songwriting credits to the Madonna song. "It is truly unfortunate that after months of trying to amicably resolve the 'Justify My Love' issue, I've been left with no alternative but to place it in the hands of my attorneys," Chavez stated at the time the suit was announced. "The only words Lenny wrote were 'justify my love,' and Madonna changed one line," Chavez said in *Entertainment Weekly*. Chavez charged that most of the lyrics came from a letter she wrote but never mailed to Kravitz. The lawsuit alleged that Chavez received a $500 advance after Kravitz "pressured" her to sign an agreement surrendering credit and three-quarters of any royalties. Chavez told *USA Today*, "I signed the contract because I thought I could trust him. I agreed not to tell because he was afraid his wife would think we had a relationship going. . . . The bottom line is it's my style and my lyric. I should have gotten my name on it."

An out-of-court settlement was reached in Minneapolis on January 29, 1992, giving Chavez writing and co-publishing credit along with Kravitz and Madonna.

After "Justify My Love" was a hit, radio stations gave heavy airplay to "Rescue Me." But Sire issued the single too late. It had enough airplay to enter the Hot 100 at number 15, the fifth highest debut in chart history at the time. Yet by the time people could buy the single, airplay was diminishing, and the song peaked at number nine.

## THE TOP FIVE
*Week of January 5, 1991*

1 **Justify My Love**
Madonna

2 **Because I Love You
(The Postman Song)**
Stevie B

3 **From a Distance**
Bette Midler

4 **High Enough**
Damn Yankees

5 **Tom's Diner**
DNA f/Suzanne Vega

# 776 Love Will Never Do (Without You) A&M 1538

JANET JACKSON

Writers: James Harris III
        Terry Lewis

Producers: Jimmy Jam
          Terry Lewis

January 19, 1991
1 week

Janet Jackson collected her fourth number one hit from *Rhythm Nation 1814* with "Love Will Never Do (Without You)," the seventh track to be released as a single. With its chart placing, Janet became the first artist in the history of the *Billboard* Hot 100 to have seven top five hits from one album.

The track for "Love Will Never Do (Without You)" was one of the first ones cut by producers Jimmy Jam and Terry Lewis for *Rhythm Nation 1814*—even before Janet arrived at their Flyte Tyme studios in Minneapolis. "When we originally planned the song, we were thinking about doing it as a duet," Jam reveals. "We mulled around in our mind a whole lot of potential people. Prince, for one. We talked about either Johnny (Gill) or Ralph (Tresvant), people we were working with."

But there were no concrete plans to bring in a male partner. "We were just playing around with some ideas. So when she went in and sang the first verse, I said, 'Sing it low like some guy would sing it.' We just loved the way it sounded, and we said, 'Let's just leave it like this.' So she sings the first verse in this really low octave and goes up an octave on the second verse. The other thing that's nice is

## THE TOP FIVE

*Week of January 19, 1991*

1   **Love Will Never Do
    (Without You)**
    Janet Jackson

2   **Justify My Love**
    Madonna

3   **High Enough**
    Damn Yankees

4   **The First Time**
    Surface

5   **Sensitivity**
    Ralph Tresvant

there are a lot of intricate backgrounds that are going on, and she did all the parts herself. We like to do that with her, because it's important for it to be a Janet Jackson record, for her to sing all the parts."

Like "Miss You Much" [see 744], the background vocals for "Love Will Never Do (Without You)" were recorded first. "The backgrounds were a great way of getting her range back together and making her voice strong again. And also, of becoming familiar with the songs—after we got the backgrounds done, she couldn't wait to sing the lead."

Despite the fact that "Love Will Never Do" was the sixth number one song for producers Jam and Lewis, they still confess to being excited when their singles hit the top of the *Billboard* chart. "There's no other experience like being number one," Jam says. "It's not a happy 'I'm going out and celebrating' feeling, it's more a feeling of thank you to all the people that made it possible. Because I don't feel like we make hits—we make songs, the public makes hits. They are the ones who decide if a record is a hit

or not. We like the song when we leave the studio, but the public buys the record, the radio people play the record, and the retailer sells the record."

"Love Will Never Do (Without You)" was the last single A&M released from *Rhythm Nation 1814*. As a follow-up, the label promoted the track "State of the World" to radio, but did not issue a commercial single. After seven top five hits, label executives felt they would sell more albums if radio was playing a song that wasn't available as a single. As a result, "State of the World" received enough airplay to peak at number six on the Top 40 Radio Monitor but never made the Hot 100. Its commercial release would have assured Janet another place in chart history—she would have become the first artist to have eight top 10 hits from one album.

Jackson did make history of another kind on March 11, 1991, when she signed the largest recording contract ever announced. The $32-million, three-album deal with Virgin Records ended a bidding war between A&M, which enjoyed 12 top 10 hits with Janet, and Atlantic and Capitol.

COLUMBIA 73502 **The First Time**

SURFACE

777

*Writers: Bernard Jackson*
*Brian Simpson*

*Producers: Surface*

*January 26, 1991*
*2 weeks*

BERNARD JACKSON was only six years old when he picked up the telephone in his parents' home in Stamford, Connecticut, and dialed a number at random. He heard a woman's voice on the other end. "I started singing a James Brown song, and she said, 'I really like that. It sounds great and you should do it more often.' She's probably the reason why I'm singing. I didn't expect that response."

Bernard turned professional after visiting a cousin in the music business who lived in New York. In 1984, back in Stamford for a gig, he stopped to see his godfather, who told him that his nephew David was also in the music business, and that the two men should meet.

David Townsend, a former guitarist for the Isley Brothers, was the son of Ed Townsend, who had registered on the Hot 100 as an artist ("For Your Love" in June, 1958) and as a writer/producer (Marvin Gaye's "Let's Get It On" in September, 1973). David graduated from high school just as "Let's Get It On" was released and joined a band called Port Authority that included David "Pic" Conley. Tired of playing cover songs, Townsend and Conley decided to write their own material. David credits his father for giving him good advice about song-writing. "I think my father understood the formula for writing hit records. I used to be stubborn when I was young. I was into Hendrix, and my father said, 'That's nice, but this is how you do a hit record, here's the structure' . . . I understood him a lot better as I got older."

Townsend agreed to meet Jackson merely as a courtesy to his godfather. "But when I first heard Bernard, I was shocked," Townsend admits. "He was very talented. So I brought him out to Jersey to meet 'Pic.'"

Townsend, Conley and Jackson were hired as staff writers for EMI Music. They placed songs with New Edition ("Let's Be Friends") and Sister Sledge ("You're Fine"), then decided to relocate to Los Angeles. They called themselves Surface, taking the name from a duo Conley had performed in with singer Karen Copeland. Leonard Richardson of EMI Music heard a song called "Let's Try Again" and brought it to the attention of Larkin Arnold at Columbia Records. "He wanted to sign us immediately," says Bernard.

Surface's first album was released in 1987, and they peaked at number 20 on the Hot 100 with "Happy." In September of 1989, "Shower Me With Your Love" went to number five.

Bernard was visiting his friend Brian Simpson and his wife in their new California home when Brian brought out some sheet music for a song he had written in 1986. Bernard asked him to record the music on tape right away. "Around 4:00 in the morning, I took the tape in the bedroom and started writing," Bernard recalls. "It was a special song. It reminded me of Chicago, and I heard a little Earth, Wind and Fire in it. I heard drama."

"The First Time" was recorded in Simpson's garage, which was converted into a studio. A truck with a 24-track studio inside pulled up in front of the house. "We hooked up all the instruments into the truck, brought a microphone out of the truck into Brian's house, and I sang 'The First Time' right there in Van Nuys."

The first single from the *3rd Wave* album, "The First Time" entered the Hot 100 on November 3, 1990—and 12 weeks later, it became Surface's first number one hit.

Townsend, Conley and Jackson were asked to be presenters at the 1991 American Music Awards, broadcast live from the Shrine Auditorium in Los Angeles on January 28. "That day, we were number one for 'The First Time,'" says Townsend. "Everybody that was at the awards, all the celebrities, knew we were number one that week, and that enabled us to meet so many people. They were congratulating us, and it was overwhelming."

## THE TOP FIVE
*Week of January 26, 1991*

1 **The First Time**
Surface

2 **Love Will Never Do
(Without You)**
Janet Jackson

3 **Gonna Make You Sweat
(Everybody Dance Now)**
C + C Music Factory f/
Freedom Williams

4 **Sensitivity**
Ralph Tresvant

5 **High Enough**
Damn Yankees

# 778 Gonna Make You Sweat (Everybody Dance Now) COLUMBIA 73604
## C + C MUSIC FACTORY f/FREEDOM WILLIAMS

*Writers: Robert Clivillés*
*Frederick B. Williams*

*Producers: Robert Clivillés*
*David Cole*

*February 9, 1991*
*2 weeks*

DAVID COLE and Robert Clivillés met in 1985 in the sound booth at the underground club in Times Square called Better Days. Clivillés, a native of Manhattan, was a substitute DJ at the club and Cole—born in Johnson City, Tennessee, and raised in Passaic, New Jersey—was a teenager who took the bus into the city.

Cole got a job playing keyboards at the club, and they decided to work together professionally. "We were both musicians struggling to make it," Clivillés told Margy Rochlin in *Us*. "We thought we could do for ourselves what we were doing for other people." For their own label, David and Robert produced "It's Too Late," featuring the vocals of Tanya Wynn. They had a club hit with "Do It Properly" by 2 Puerto Ricans, a Blackman and a Dominican (Clivillés was one of the Puerto Ricans, and Cole was the black man). A follow-up, "Scandalous," was heard as background music on "Entertainment Tonight."

Clivillés and Cole became well-known in industry circles for remixing songs like Fleetwood Mac's "Big Love," Janet Jackson's "The Pleasure Principle" and Natalie Cole's "Pink Cadillac." In 1989, they put together a trio of female singers known as Seduction ("Two to Make It Right") and signed a deal with Larry Yasgar's Vendetta Records, distributed through A&M.

When Yasgar moved to the A&R department of Columbia Records, he signed Clivillés and Cole to produce a single with an option for an album. Cole had already released a single on Epic Records, "You Take My Breath Away," but it wasn't a hit. "As a result, I realized I couldn't be a performer and sit back and watch people mutilate things that I was involved in." So Cole and Clivillés decided not to emphasize their role as performers, but as producers. They formed C + C Music Factory with the idea that vocalists would come and go, but Clivillés and Cole would be the only permanent fixtures.

At Quad Recording Studios, they worked with an assistant engineer known as Freedom Williams. "He was pretty quiet, but when he spoke he had this really deep voice," says Cole. "This guy's got the perfect voice. I asked him what he did, and what did he really want to do. He said he wanted to be in the music industry, and I asked him could he rap." Clivillés and Cole were remixing Grace Jones' "Love on Top of Love," and Clivillés wanted to add a rap to it, so Freedom's voice was added to the track.

For their single deal with Columbia, the producers came up with "Gonna Make You Sweat (Everybody Dance Now)." The female singer belting out the line "Everybody Dance Now" was Martha Wash, a former member of Two Tons O'Fun and the Weather Girls. The video featured a much slimmer vocalist, Zelma Davis, lip-synching Martha's lines.

"From day one, Martha was to be a part of the C + C Music Factory," Cole explains. "We were trying to shop a solo deal for Martha. When Larry moved to Columbia, we realized this is the right deal. So we wanted to use C + C Music Factory as a launching pad . . . at the time we thought we could use Martha. At the time we didn't know she was doing Black Box." Wash, who had supplied vocals for some Seduction tracks, was also heard but uncredited on the Black Box hit "Everybody Everybody." Cole continues: "We called her to do the session—next thing you know, (there was) the lawsuit for Seduction."

Wash sued A&M for crediting her vocals on Seduction's "You're My One and Only True Love" to April Harris. She also sued RCA for not giving her the credit on the Black Box record, and Clivillés and Cole for leaving her name off the record and video of "Gonna Make You Sweat." "As I always say, if somebody is trying to burn down your house, do you invite them to dinner?" asks Cole.

David Cole was 32 when he died on January 24, 1995, from complications due to spinal meningitis. Clivilles completed projects the two had begun before Cole's death.

## THE TOP FIVE
*Week of February 9, 1991*

1 **Gonna Make You Sweat (Everybody Dance Now)** C + C Music Factory f/ Freedom Williams

2 **The First Time** Surface

3 **All The Man That I Need** Whitney Houston

4 **Play That Funky Music** Vanilla Ice

5 **Love Will Never Do (Without You)** Janet Jackson

with producer Narada Michael Walden to record the song.

Dean was visiting a friend in Montreal on the set of the film *If Looks Could Kill* when he received a message to call Clive in New York. "Clive is famous for this," Dean laughs. "He said, 'I just got the final mix on "All the Man That I Need." I want you to hear this, I think it's wonderful.'" Davis' office doesn't quite have a sophisticated sound system, and Dean was on a cellular phone as Clive lifted the receiver up to the speakers. "He came back on the phone and said, 'What do you think?'" Pitchford diplomatically replied, "What I heard sounds really good!"

Attempts to procure an advance copy of the *I'm Your Baby Tonight* album failed, as Whitney was adding a duet with Stevie Wonder at the last moment. Finally, Clive called and apologized for the long wait. He invited Pitchford to a listening party that evening at the Bel Air Hotel. "It would be the first chance I'd have to hear the song, so I threw on a suit and ran over to the hotel," recalls Dean, who finally heard the song on giant speakers and loved what he heard.

He remembers Maria Shriver pushing her way through the crowd to compliment him on the "gorgeous song." Then he was chatting with Luther Vandross, who produced one of the songs on the album. "He said, 'I love your song, it sounds so familiar. Where have I heard that song before?' And I said, 'Luther, you sang background vocals on it 11 years ago for Linda Clifford.'"

---

*Writers: Dean Pitchford*
*Michael Gore*

*Producer: Narada Michael Walden*

*February 23, 1991*
*2 weeks*

---

SEVEN weeks after Madonna claimed her ninth number one single [see 775—"Justify My Love"], Whitney Houston went to the top of the Hot 100 for the ninth time with a song originally written in 1981 for Linda Clifford.

Songwriters Dean Pitchford and Michael Gore worked with Clifford on the *Fame* soundtrack when she recorded their composition "Red Light." They wrote "All the Man That I Need" specifically for her, and Michael produced the track for her album *I'll Keep On Loving You*. Linda's version didn't chart, but in 1982 Sister Sledge recorded the song as a duet with David Simmons. It peaked at number 45 on the Hot Soul Singles chart, yet failed to make the Hot 100.

"I figured it was one of those songs that was probably going to be cut a number of times and not ever have its day," Pitchford says. Then, in late 1986, he was having dinner with Clive Davis. Though the two had been social friends for a long time, Dean had

never discussed business with the head of Arista Records before. "My publishers had always dealt with him. But this was the one night I said to him, 'I have a song I really should send you for Whitney. I've never done this before and I won't make a habit of it, but just listen to this.' He called as soon as he received it and said, 'I just got your lovely song, and I'd love to hold it for Whitney.'" Unfortunately, Whitney had just completed her second album. "He said, 'We won't be recording again for awhile.'"

It was a long wait. Arista mined the *Whitney* album for over a year, releasing five singles. Houston did not record for a two-year period, while Pitchford and Gore's publisher would receive requests from various singers for permission to record the song. "Every time somebody else would ask for the song, I'd call Clive and say, 'I won't show the song if you're still interested.' He said, 'I'm still interested.' It was a tremendous show of faith on both our parts," Dean professes.

Periodically, Dean would hear from someone who had been in Clive's office when the label head played the song and announced it would be on the next Whitney Houston album. "As long as Clive had that song, he never fell out of love with it," Pitchford says. Finally, Whitney went into the studio

---

## THE TOP FIVE
*Week of February 23, 1991*

1 **All the Man That I Need**
Whitney Houston

2 **Gonna Make You Sweat (Everybody Dance Now)**
C + C Music Factory f/
Freedom Williams

3 **One More Try**
Timmy T

4 **Someday**
Mariah Carey

5 **Where Does My Heart Beat Now**
Celine Dion

# 780 Someday COLUMBIA 73561
## MARIAH CAREY

Writers: *Mariah Carey*
*Ben Margulies*

Producer: *Ric Wake*

*March 9, 1991*
*2 weeks*

"SOMEDAY" was the third single released from Mariah Carey's debut album, and the third single to go to number one. "That started out as a bass line, sort of a drum-machine, almost hip-hop type groove," says co-writer Ben Margulies. "Now people call it new jack swing, but that stuff was going on before all these terms came about. It evolved out of an improvisational track with some very strong changes and a very strong harmonic structure. Mariah has an ability to improvise vocally and come up with great melody lines, great hooks. We generally work on a chorus first, but she would sing melody ideas through the verse sections and it came about that way."

Margulies explains how fast Mariah came up with the words: "In the amount of time that I would be playing around with the arrangement and coming up with some new change or something like that, she'd be sitting there writing out lyrics, then we'd demo it. I mean, we'd start turning the tape machine on, turning the computers on, and just start doing it."

"Someday" was one of four songs that Margulies and Carey included on the singer's demo tape. "All the demos that ended up going to CBS were very elaborate arrangements," Ben notes. "They were very close to what's on the album, if not almost exactly."

Tommy Mottola of CBS Records asked Anglo-American producer Ric Wake, who had been working with Arista artist Taylor Dayne [see 754—"Love Will Lead You Back"], to listen to Mariah Carey's demo. "It was obvious that she was great—she was amazing," says Wake, who met with Mottola on a Wednesday. The CBS Records Group president asked Wake if he could start working with Mariah on Thursday. "Mariah came over to my house the next day, we wrote 'There's Got to Be a Way,' and it went from there—we did four songs together."

One of the tracks that Wake produced was "Someday." "I loved that song right from the beginning," he acknowledges. "Tommy gave me a tape of 12 songs, and at the time, I think someone else was going to do it. It was up in the air, then Mariah called me up one day and said, 'I'd love you to do it if you want to do it.' It was great—I'm glad she called me.

"I remember the way that demo was; I wasn't sure how she wanted to do it. . . . We did it in about two, three hours."

Margulies liked the final version of their song "because it came off really simple and clean, and the point came across. Nothing was covered up. The original arrangement and production were very simple and funky. It had a simplicity to it that kind of drew you into it. To take it and make it too much of a production would have ruined the vibe of the song."

When she was first signed to Columbia, Mariah wanted to produce the album herself with Margulies. "I wasn't open to working with a superstar producer," she said in *Rolling Stone*. Ben elaborates: "You have your ideas and your creations, and sometimes it's difficult. You're seeing your songs come to fruition, but at the same time, you want to have a say in how your babies turn out. These things start out like the nucleus of the embryo of an idea. You sit down and start playing, improvising, and it comes to the point where it turns into a good demo; then you want to hear it. If you're a strong musician, or you're inclined to produce and arrange all that stuff, sometimes it's hard to hand over your creations like that. But it's inevitably what always happens, and you hope that people handle them with care."

"Someday" entered the *Billboard* Hot 100 at number 37 on January 19, 1991. Seven weeks later, Mariah Carey knocked Whitney Houston's "All the Man That I Need" off the top of the chart and moved in for a two-week stay.

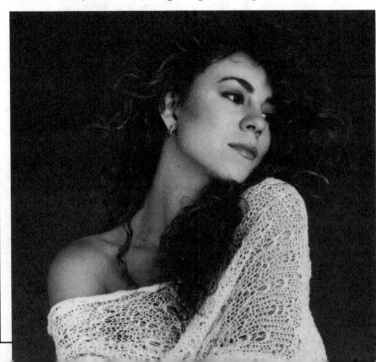

## THE TOP FIVE
*Week of March 9, 1991*

1 **Someday**
Mariah Carey

2 **One More Try**
Timmy T

3 **All the Man That I Need**
Whitney Houston

4 **Where Does My Heart Beat Now**
Celine Dion

5 **Show Me the Way**
Styx

Writer: Timmy T

Producer: Timmy T

March 23, 1991
1 week

TIMMY TORRES was born September 21, 1967, in Fresno, California. Music was a part of his childhood: he remembers watching his mother, a singer who once recorded backing vocals for a Jerry Lee Lewis session, play the piano and a Wurlitzer organ. Timmy taught himself to play both instruments, and started writing "little jingles" when he was 12.

His father lent him some money to place an advertisement in the Yellow Pages for his services as a magician and juggler. Timmy entertained at children's parties, producing and starring in his own cable TV series as a puppeteer when he was 14. "Herman and the Little People" aired every Monday in Fresno.

When he was 17, Timmy became more interested in music as a profession: "I wrote music for some local rappers here in town," he recalls, "(but) I didn't think that would be the road to take. I knew I could sing, and I always wanted to produce my own music." The rappers called him Timmy Tee.

The first song Timmy recorded professionally was "Time After Time." "I played all the instruments and programmed the drums; it cost me $181 to produce it at a local garage." That included $20 an hour for studio time, the price of the master reel and a dollar for a cassette.

"After I recorded it, I started playing the tape for people around town. I wrote the song for a girl I had been seeing; I gave her a copy of the song, and she was really impressed with it. So I started listening to what people were telling me, and I took it to the local radio stations here in town."

John Clay, program director for KYNO at the time, remembers Timmy showing up at the station with his single. "I promised him I would listen to the music at our music meeting," Clay says. "We listened to it and I just looked at the assistant music director and said, 'That's a smash!' So we put it on the radio. We got tons of calls immediately, and he became a local celebrity."

Timmy took off for Bakersfield on his motorcycle and delivered a copy to a station there, which agreed to play it. A San Diego station added it, and then Timmy hand-delivered a copy to Power 106 in Los Angeles—"a week later, some friends called and told me they were playing it." Soon program directors from all over the country were calling Timmy at home to procure their own copies. "I was going broke sending all these records," Timmy claims. Major labels were calling the program directors to find out how they could sign up this new recording artist. Timmy was most impressed with the call from Quality Records, a Canadian label opening a U.S. office under the guidance of Russ Regan, who once headed the Uni and 20th Century labels.

Quality wanted an album on the market as soon as possible. Timmy had several songs already written, including another one inspired by the same girlfriend, Cindy. "We broke up again. We weren't seeing each other for a couple of weeks, and I started thinking about her a lot—I wanted one more try." Timmy wrote the song in his parents' living room, and was encouraged by his mother's praise for the song. He recorded a slow and melodic version, using an old synthesizer that he bought at a yard sale for $80. "When I got the deal with Quality, I submitted 'One More Try,' but they said it was too long for radio. So I went in the studio again and made a second version. I put a piano in and shortened it." That version cost him only $200 to produce.

"I never thought it would go past number two," Timmy confesses (Mariah Carey was number one and Gloria Estefan was coming up fast). "I was on my way to Europe for the first time; it was a Wednesday, and the chart was coming out. I was on the plane with my manager, and we called the record company. They told me it went to number one—I was shouting and yelling on the plane."

## THE TOP FIVE
*Week of March 23, 1991*

1  **One More Try**
   Timmy T

2  **Someday**
   Mariah Carey

3  **Coming Out of the Dark**
   Gloria Estefan

4  **This House**
   Tracie Spencer

5  **Get Here**
   Oleta Adams

# 782 Coming Out of the Dark EPIC 73666

## GLORIA ESTEFAN

*Writers: Gloria Estefan*
*Emilio Estefan, Jr.*
*Jon Secada*

*Producers: Emilio Estefan, Jr.*
*Jorge Casas*
*Clay Ostwald*

*March 30, 1991*
*2 weeks*

"I FELT disconnected from my body, and there was excruciating pain when I tried to move my legs and feet," Gloria Estefan reports as she recalls the terrifying accident that threw her to the floor of her tour bus on a wintry day in March, 1990 [see 742—"Don't Wanna Lose You"]. "'Here it is,' I thought, 'the nightmare, the other shoe falling after this streak where everything was going so well.'"

As her fans around the world prayed for a speedy recovery, Gloria returned to Miami International Airport after recuperating for 10 days from surgery in New York. There were 200 people waiting to cheer the arrival of the private jet lent to her by singer Julio Iglesias.

She had received 400 stitches during the surgery and was sporting a 14-inch scar. The pain was so intense that she couldn't sleep for more than 45 minutes at a time. For three months, Estefan couldn't move without assistance, even to go to the bathroom. During that period, her husband Emilio didn't leave their home. Physical therapy began under the direction of personal trainer Ana Dalmastro. "At first she can only do swimming, stationary bicycle—no weights," the therapist told *Rolling Stone*. "Then we move to specific exercises. Before, when we would work out, she was very determined. And her goal then was only to lose weight, inches. Now she has a much more important goal: to go back to the stage."

By June, Gloria was able to think about music again. "I was apprehensive about getting back into writing, and I didn't know what would come out of it or if anything would," she related to Cary Darling of *The Orange County Register*. "My husband had been in one of the helicopters (the day of the crash) traveling from one hospital to the other. It was really dark and gray, and he was traumatized. He got this ray of light that hit him in the face, and he got the idea for 'Coming Out of the Dark.' About three months later, he came to me and said, 'When you start writing again, I have a song I want to co-write with you. (Later) when I came in, he was putting the melody to it, and when I sat there, it all poured out.'"

Gloria told Darling that she wasn't sure she was coming out of the dark until the summer. "It took that long for me to be unaided—to walk, go to the bathroom, get dressed. Up until that point, it was up in the air when I would recover, because there had been lots of nerve damage."

She recorded demos of new songs and sent them to the studio with Emilio. "I just could not feel down," the singer emphasizes. "I used everybody's prayers—I could feel that energy focused on me, and I used it. Most performers have to die to elicit such an outpouring of love. I was lucky to feel that, and it will touch me for the rest of my life."

Gloria says she resisted turning *Into the Light* into "the accident album." "I hate pity," she told Bruce Britt of the Los Angeles *Daily News*. "I'm very self-reliant and independent, and I'm used to that role. I don't like people feeling sorry for me. So I wrote 'Coming Out of the Dark' to let the people around me know how important they are to me. But that was as far as I wanted to go with the accident. I didn't want this to become 'the album on the accident.' What am I going to sing—'Oh, this bus hit me'?"

On March 1, Gloria began a world tour in Miami. "There was no way I could have started anywhere else," she comments. "I've just felt so much support and love that Miami had to be the first show. They'll also be forgiving—if I get choked up, they'll probably get choked up, too."

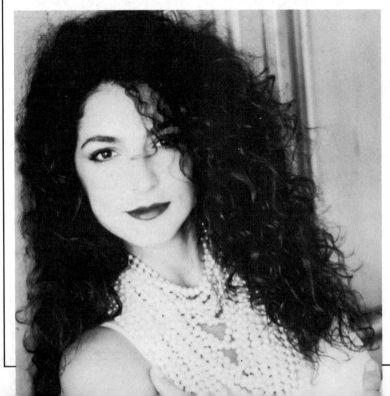

### THE TOP FIVE

*Week of March 30, 1991*

1 **Coming Out of the Dark**
Gloria Estefan

2 **One More Try**
Timmy T

3 **This House**
Tracie Spencer

4 **Hold You Tight**
Tara Kemp

5 **I've Been Thinking About You**
Londonbeat

RADIOACTIVE 54005 **I've Been Thinking About You**
LONDONBEAT **783**

*Writers: Willy Henshall
Jimmy Helms
George Chandler
Jimmy Chambers*

*Producer: Martyn Phillips*

*April 13, 1991
1 week*

**B**EFORE they had a number one hit with "I've Been Thinking About You," members of Londonbeat sang backing vocals for Tina Turner on *Break Every Rule*, as well as for Paul Young and for a band they've often been compared to, Fine Young Cannibals [see 726—"She Drives Me Crazy"].

Jimmy Helms, whose ancestry is Blackfoot Indian, was born in Florida. He moved to London in the '70s and had a top 10 in the U.K. with "Gonna Make You An Offer You Can't Refuse." He met Jimmy Chambers, a native of Trinidad, who had been part of the group DaDa in 1969 with Robert Palmer and Elkie Brooks. Helms and Chambers then hooked up with George Chandler, another American, who had emigrated from Atlanta. Chandler had been living in Italy as a member of the Four Kents, a quartet that recorded Four Tops hits in Italian.

The three singers decided to form a group and teamed up with guitarist Willy Henshall, who billed himself Willy M. A true Brit, Willy had been recording new-wave artists and dance records in New York, but was ready to come home and start up a new group. "Willy rang me up when he was looking for somebody to co-write songs with," Helms recalled to Edna Gunderson in *USA Today*. "I was a bit leery because you get a lot of calls like that that turn to nothing. But the four

of us got together the next evening, and there was something immediately magical about the association. We had the presence of mind to realize we were onto a good thing."

At that meeting in 1987, they promised that if they couldn't write a hit song in three hours, they would return to their day jobs. In 45 minutes, they composed "K.I.S.S.," the song that got Londonbeat a deal with the same management team that handled Eurythmics [see 575—"Sweet Dreams (Are Made of This)"]. Dave Stewart heard one of their tapes and signed them to his AnXious label in the U.K. "This band wouldn't have happened anywhere else in the world," Helms told William Shaw. "There's something very peculiar in the interpretation of what's gone on elsewhere that makes London like a laboratory." Chandler agreed; as he told Bob Mack, "One of the reasons we're called Londonbeat is simply to pay homage to the city. And we thought that to ever succeed in America, the fact that London is in the name might somehow be a plus."

They recorded an album, *Speak*, in Holland, and charted in Britain with the second song they wrote together, "9 A.M. (The Comfort Zone)," which peaked at number 21. The group found producer Martyn Phillips' phone number on a cassette, and asked him to produce their sophomore effort. After writing more than 40 songs for their second album, *In the Blood*, Londonbeat chose the best 12. "We agreed to be honest with ourselves and know when to throw a song in the waste bin," Helms told Gunderson. "After doing session work for years, you know in 10 minutes whether the song has any meat on the bone. We reached a point two-thirds into the album where we knew we'd have an interest-

ing result if we could maintain the momentum emotionally."

Chambers calls the group "a four-legged animal—each of us is capable of writing a song on his own. We find that together there is a chemistry that is unsurpassed. It's so magical, we thought that all compositions should be done by the four of us."

He describes the genesis of "I've Been Thinking About You": "We had a drum track, and Willy added a bass line to it. We started to kick it around and nothing was happening, so we each took a cassette copy of the track home. I had a cold and was sitting in my bedroom trying to think of something, and suddenly (it) came to me."

"I've Been Thinking About You" peaked at number two on the British chart before it was released in America on the Radioactive label. It entered the Hot 100 at number 52 on February 9, 1991, and captured the top spot on April 13. Chambers was in Spain promoting the album. When he returned to his hotel room, the telephone rang, and a friend told him he was number one in America.

---

## THE TOP FIVE
*Week of April 13, 1991*

1 **I've Been Thinking About You**
Londonbeat

2 **You're In Love**
Wilson Phillips

3 **Hold You Tight**
Tara Kemp

4 **Baby Baby**
Amy Grant

5 **Sadeness Part 1**
Enigma

## 784  You're In Love  SBK 07343
### WILSON PHILLIPS

*Writers: Wilson Phillips*
*Glen Ballard*

*Producer: Glen Ballard*

*April 20, 1991*
*1 week*

"YOU'RE IN LOVE" was the fourth single from Wilson Phillips' debut album. "I felt that if that song just got a chance, people would respond to it emotionally," says co-writer and producer Glen Ballard. "I think it was pretty unanimous from the record company (and) from the girls—the song had a certain magic to it."

Ballard describes how the song was written: "The girls had a verse, and I can remember sitting down in the demo room at MCA Publishing. They played 'Open the door and come in, I'm so glad to see you my friend,' and they played the first eight bars of the song, and that's all they had. From that, I had the idea to add the B-section and then a modulation into the chorus. Then I came up with the chorus. I'd been through a situation like that, and was reminded of the movie *Casablanca*. I'm no good at being noble, but to me, it was the idea that if you love somebody enough to let them go, it's really saying that you love them. Wendy, Carnie and Chynna really responded to that, and wrote the next verse and the bridge."

"You're In Love" entered the Hot 100 on February 9, 1991, at number 64 while the previous single, "Impulsive," was still on the chart. Ten weeks later, "You're In Love" became Wilson Phillips' third number one single.

Ballard credits SBK founder Charles Koppelman with providing ex-actly the right amount of support for Wilson Phillips. "He was intimately involved with everything we were doing; his comments were always constructive, specific, and right to the point, and always made the record better. He focuses on songs and understands the structure of songs—he's a song guy who got it from day one. He heard those four demos and said, 'This is it, this will be on the radio even though there's nothing like it.' He didn't have a second thought about it."

Writing in the 95th anniversary issue of *Billboard*, Koppelman stated that "Wendy and Carnie Wilson and Chynna Phillips make absolutely incredible music. I always say, if they were race horses I would syndicate them. I believe they are SBK Records' George Michael—our Madonna. They are the future."

Michelle Phillips—who was starring in "Knots Landing" when her daughter Chynna topped the Hot 100, and who'd visited the chart summit herself [see 198—"Monday, Monday"]—warned Chynna about the music industry when she first thought of teaming up with childhood pals Wendy and Carnie Wilson.

"I said, 'Why don't you just be a good little girl and just pursue your acting career?'" Michelle told Matt Roush in *USA Today*. "I remember feeling, this is going to be a terrible disappointment because the record business is so difficult. I was afraid for her. I thought people would say, 'Oh, here's the daughter of John and Michelle Phillips,' and they'd all be so snide."

Phillips told Roush it was no surprise that the three women sounded so great when they harmonized. "They were raised on it—not necessarily on our music, but singing harmonies. That's what we did in our house. Chynna was writing songs from the time she was four years old, and performing them. Carnie and Wendy, too."

Despite their success, Chynna revealed to Sean Mitchell in *USA Weekend* that "My only fear was that people weren't going to get it. Because when the album came out, rapping was huge—it still is. I just wasn't sure people's ears were ready for us." Chynna's fears were unfounded—the album sold eight million copies.

The trio's second album, *Shadows and Light*, was released in June, 1992. The first single was "You Won't See Me Cry." Two songs on the album dealt with their feelings about their respective fathers. Chynna wrote "All the Way from New York." She told Mitchell, "Who knows what runs through my dad's head and how he feels about his past?" Wendy and Carnie contributed "Flesh and Blood." "He never calls us," Wendy told Mitchell when asked about her father. "We don't have a relationship with him. We hope we will one day. It's so sad."

### THE TOP FIVE
*Week of April 20, 1991*

1  **You're In Love**
   Wilson Phillips

2  **Baby Baby**
   Amy Grant

3  **I've Been Thinking About You**
   Londonbeat

4  **Hold You Tight**
   Tara Kemp

5  **Joyride**
   Roxette

*Writers: Amy Grant*
*Keith Thomas*

*Producer: Keith Thomas*

*April 27, 1991*
*2 weeks*

**K**EITH THOMAS wrote the music for "Baby Baby," suggesting the title and the line "Ever since the day you put my heart in motion" to Amy Grant. The singer loved the music, but found it difficult to complete the lyrics. "The music really bowled me over, because it was part old Motown-sounding and part new," says Grant. "I worked on that lyric for months. Every time I tried to write a romantic lyric with the title 'Baby Baby,' it sounded like some overgrown football jock with no vocabulary trying desperately to be romantic."

Finally, Amy found inspiration from her daughter Millie, six weeks old at the time. "I'd been out in my car driving around— that's one place I write a lot. I came in through the back door, and I hadn't had any good luck at all working on that lyric. I saw her sweet little face; she was there with the babysitter. I sat down at the kitchen counter, and in less than ten minutes wrote the song to her. Suddenly, all the little silly phrases fit with the music, because it was to her."

When "Baby Baby" was issued as the first single from the *Heart in Motion* album, many people thought the

Christian singer was talking to a lover, an assumption bolstered by the video. "I think the song is really romantic, and I think that's great because not very many people have a baby to sing to," Amy says. "If you've got a great song that's so narrow in its scope, then not very many people can relate. I didn't even tell people for a long time what the song was written about. When the album came out, I thought when Millie's 50 years old, if she happens to drag out one of her fossil mother's albums, then it would be nice for her to know that the song was about her."

Grant first met Thomas at Word Records, the Christian label that released her albums until A&M made a distribution deal with the company. "I put together her first concert here in

town at Vanderbilt University and played keyboards," the producer notes. They stayed in touch through the years while Thomas worked at Word, where he was an avid fan of pop and R&B music. "I never did really listen to the Christian music, only because it wasn't as stimulating musically as what I wanted to do, and there were so many boundaries and limitations. If you wanted to get a song on the radio in the Christian-music industry, you couldn't put a guitar on it here or a sax on it there. I'm grateful for everything they did for me but I wanted to expand." Thomas met gospel singers BeBe and CeCe Winans when they were part of the PTL singers and produced *Heaven*, an album that broke them on the R&B charts.

"Amy had kind of reached her limit in the Christian-music industry, and she needed to expand her platform. She's gotten a lot of criticism— especially from the Christian-music people—but she's still the same person she was. She's still doing what she was doing, but in a bigger way."

After Thomas gave Grant the music and title of "Baby Baby," he didn't mind the wait for her to complete the song, since he was busy working on another project. Because of Keith's success with the Winans, Ed Eckstine of Polydor Records asked him to produce Vanessa Williams [see 806— "Save the Best for Last"].

When "Baby Baby" was completed, Thomas says A&M was not overly enthusiastic about it. "They sent it back. I don't think they really wanted it on the record, but since we had already cut it and spent the money, I think they were going to put it on there. At that point I got my manager involved, asking Amy if we could pull it off the record because I knew it was a hit and I wanted to get somebody else to do it." Instead, Thomas remixed the track and Mark Mazzetti of A&M told him it would be the first single.

Amy and Keith had different reactions to the dance-music remix the label issued. "I laughed my head off," says Amy. "I thought it was the most hysterical thing. . . . I think 'Baby Baby' is unique enough, but it could hold its own even with a completely different track." "I hate them," Keith grumbles. "If everything on the radio sounds alike, then there's no identity there and there's no musical integrity."

## THE TOP FIVE
*Week of April 27, 1991*

1  **Baby Baby**
   Amy Grant

2  **Joyride**
   Roxette

3  **You're in Love**
   Wilson Phillips

4  **I Like the Way
   (The Kissing Game)**
   Hi-Five

5  **Here We Go**
   C + C Music Factory f/Freedom Williams & Zelma Davis

# Joyride EMI 50342
## ROXETTE

*Writer: Per Gessle*

*Producer: Clarence Öfwerman*

*May 11, 1991*
*1 week*

"HAVING one number one in the States is more than enough in a person's life," says Per Gessle of Roxette. "But having four is incredible. Who could ask for more?"

Roxette scored their fourth American chart-topper when "Joyride" went to number one for the week ending May 11, 1991. That's three more number one hits than either of the previous two Swedish groups to hit the top of the chart, Blue Swede [see 361—"Hooked on a Feeling"] and Abba [see 458—"Dancing Queen"].

Gessle had two sources of inspiration for "Joyride." The first came from an interview with Paul McCartney that Per read in a magazine. "He said writing songs with John Lennon was a long joyride. At the time, we were in the middle of recording, and I was looking for a fun, positive title for the album. 'Joyride' seemed like a perfect word. At the same time, my girlfriend left me a note on my piano. She left to do some shopping. It was a note in Swedish saying, 'Hello, you fool, I love you.' That's a perfect chorus because it's a paradox. So it turned out to be yet another three-chord song, with a lot of 'Magical Mystery Tour' and T. Rex, all the roots put together."

The whistling in the song was Per's idea. "I had just seen *Life of Brian* with Monty Python, (which had) this song, 'Always Look on the Bright Side of Life,'" recalls Per, whistling a few bars from the Python tune. "I always wanted to have a whistling part in a song. I did the whistling myself. It's overdubbed 12 times, but I did it."

Per says his girlfriend probably doesn't remember the note that helped inspire the lyrics. "It's how songs happen. When you sit down and wait for inspiration or just fiddle around on the piano, nothing happens. But it's always coincidence. You hear a song on the radio and hear just the word that you've been looking for for three months, or you go to a movie and get something going on in your mind. It's like reading a book (or) talking to a friend—all these fluke things that happen that turn into good songs."

Gessle notes how Roxette has been maturing as a band. "It takes a lot of time to find your direction, which way you want to go. Even though we've been around for many years in Sweden before Roxette, we're still a young band: we've done three albums. When *Joyride* was written, I wrote 24 songs (and) we recorded 21 of them. I knew from the beginning which direction the album should go. I knew we wanted to make a harder album, get away from the dance-sequencing thing, which didn't fit us very well."

The role of their producer, Clarence Öfwerman, also changed over the years, according to Per. "When we started out, he did everything—he was the arranger, he played almost everything because everything was run through computers, as well as being the producer. Starting with the *Joyride* album, everything is more ready when we go into the studio, because I've got my own studio now, working with another engineer. When I made the demo for 'Joyride,' for instance, it sounded almost identical to the finished record. Clarence is really good at finding the perfect string sound or the perfect bass-guitar sound."

When the *Joyride* album was completed, Per and partner Marie Fredriksson picked the first three singles. They wanted to release "Joyride," followed by "Spending My Time" and then "Fading Like a Flower (Every Time You Leave)." They asked EMI which tracks the label wanted to release. According to Per, the label replied that "Europe (wanted) 'Fading Like a Flower' and America (wanted) 'Spending My Time.' We said no, we had to have an uptempo track. They thought it was risky with 'Joyride.'"

It turned out that Per and Marie were correct. In America, the follow-up to "Joyride" was "Fading Like a Flower," which peaked at number two in August. "Spending My Time" became their first chart single to miss the top 30 when it peaked at number 32 in January, 1992. The release of the fourth single from *Joyride*, "Church of Your Heart," coincided with Roxette's first tour of America.

## THE TOP FIVE
*Week of May 11, 1991*

1 **Joyride**
 Roxette

2 **Baby Baby**
 Amy Grant

3 **I Like The Way
 (The Kissing Game)**
 Hi-Five

4 **Here We Go**
 C + C Music Factory f/Freedom
 Williams & Zelma Davis

5 **Touch Me (All Night Long)**
 Cathy Dennis

# JIVE 1424 I Like the Way (The Kissing Game)
## HI-FIVE

**Writers: Teddy Riley**
**Bernard Bell**
**Dave Way**

**Producer: Teddy Riley**

*May 18, 1991*
*1 week*

How young is Tony Thompson, lead singer of Hi-Five? Young enough that he wasn't even born when "Philadelphia Freedom" by the Elton John Band and "Get Down Tonight' by K.C. and the Sunshine Band were number one on the *Billboard* chart. That young.

Thompson was born September 2, 1975, making him just 15 years old when he recorded "I Like the Way (The Kissing Game)." He was 12 when Ann Carli, senior vice president of development for Jive Records, met him in Waco, Texas. She had gone there to work on an album by a group called Ador that had been signed to Jive. The manager of Ador, Vincent Bell, played a tape for Ann and told her the vocalist was the cousin of the lead singer in Ador.

"I thought the tape was terrific," says Carli. "When I went to Waco to work on the Ador album, I was working out at the gym and these sneakered feet came over toward me by the rowing machine. It's a skinny little kid with the lead singer of the group we had signed. William, who was from the original group, said, 'This is my cousin, I told you all about him. I want you to meet him, and I want you to hear him sing.' And from that minute, I was sold. He was incredible. A

shy, skinny little kid, but he had a great voice. He sang me some songs in the car, and at his cousin's house. He sang something by the Deele, a church song—whatever came into his head."

Tony's managers at the time found other talented youngsters in Waco and Oklahoma City and formed a group called the Playmates that included Tony as well as Roderick Clark, Russell Neal and Marcus Sanders. Treston Irby, a teenager from the Bronx, joined later. The Playmates won a talent contest at the Waco Convention Center in 1987, where Tony was named "Voice of the Future."

Legal wrangles got in the way of Ador remaining with the label, but Tony's cousin, William Walton, was signed to Jive's publishing company. Vincent Bell and his partner Robert Ford worked with Walton on producing a demo tape for the youngsters, and Carli signed them to the label. She was also instrumental in teaming Hi-Five up with producer Teddy Riley, the young "father" of new jack swing. "The kids had met with Teddy early in the project, when the first stuff was being recorded," explains Ann. "Teddy has said repeatedly that he really loves the group—it was a fantastic match."

Bernard Bell, co-writer and co-producer of "I Like the Way (The Kissing Game)," met Riley through Lee Drakeford, lead singer of Today. Bell and Riley were working on an album for Guy, the group Teddy was in, at the same time they were producing tracks for Hi-Five.

Teddy and Bernard wrote the first single released from the album, "I

Just Can't Handle It." "It was so funky, we thought that one would do much better," Bernard admits. "In the beginning, we thought 'Kissing Game' is a great song, but most people won't appreciate it because it's so pretty."

Bell describes the "kissing game" as being like basketball. "The object of the game is to score as many baskets as possible. The kissing game is, like, to get as many kisses. Teddy has a knack about hooks and titles. We were talking about this game that we used to all play when we were little, how we would chase the girls and kiss them, so it was a young song. The guys were young, so we figured it might work. Teddy had the track, and me and Dave Way came up with the lyric."

Bernard enjoyed the sessions with the quintet. "Even though they were young, they were very professional. The sessions were late, so we were all kind of tired, ready to go home. I was surprised, because usually if you get five guys in a group, maybe one or two of them can really sing. But some of the other guys did some backgrounds, we did some backgrounds, and when Tony came in to sing lead, I was very impressed. He closed his eyes and he just sang."

"I Like The Way (The Kissing Game)" entered the Hot 100 at number 90 the week of February 23, 1991; 12 weeks later, Hi-Five were number one. The follow-up, "I Can't Wait Another Minute," peaked at number eight the week of August 31.

## THE TOP FIVE
*Week of May 18, 1991*

# I Don't Wanna Cry COLUMBIA 73743
## MARIAH CAREY

**Writers: Mariah Carey**
**Narada Michael Walden**

**Producer: Narada Michael Walden**

*May 25, 1991*
*2 weeks*

WHEN "I Don't Wanna Cry" went to number one, Mariah Carey became the first artist since the Jackson Five [see 283—"I'll Be There"] to have her first four chart singles top the *Billboard* Hot 100.

"I Don't Wanna Cry" was produced and co-written by Narada Michael Walden, who had already produced number one hits for Whitney Houston, Starship and Aretha Franklin and George Michael. The producer first heard about Mariah when he received a phone call from CBS Records Group president Tommy Mottola. "I promised when I was in New York, I would sit down and meet with her," says Walden, "and I did. She was very shy, and I asked her what she liked. She said she liked George Michael, so I got an idea of where she was coming from. Then we set up a day to actually go and write."

At this point, Narada had not heard Mariah's vocals. "The first time I heard her sing was in a writing session at the Hit Factory, where we

wrote some songs. After working on three or four songs, I wanted us to slow the tempo down. A big part of my raising as a kid are songs like (those recorded) by Chuck Jackson . . . 'I Don't Want to Cry,' 'Any Day Now,' those kind of really dramatic ballads, or 'When a Man Loves a Woman' by Percy Sledge, those 'crying' kind of ballads. I kind of pulled it down from the sky and started singing this thing to her, and she got into it."

Having worked with both Mariah Carey and Whitney Houston, Narada is in a unique position to compare the two singers who have been compared so often in the press. "Both are tremendous singers. Whitney comes more from being raised and singing in church—I mean, first-hand experience with her aunts and nieces, from her influence from Aretha as a little kid, from Dionne Warwick, and from her mother, the great Cissy Houston. She had all that to draw on. On Mariah's side, I know she's a great listener. She took to heart Aretha and a lot of great singers, from Gladys Knight on down.

"It's like the difference between, say, Carl Lewis and Ben Johnson, or Tommy Hearns and Sugar Ray Leonard. Both great track stars, both great boxers—and I'm honored to be able to work with both of them.

"Mariah is very astute in the studio, very picky. I don't mean to make it sound like a negative; for her, it's a positive, because she knows she wants to hear herself sound a certain way. For example, there's a lick on 'I Don't Wanna Cry' that I was really happy with, and I think at first she was, too. But after she lived with it, she wanted us to fix it. I don't even know if we fixed it twice or three times, but I had to fly the tape back to her in New York. She went in the studio, fixed that lick, and added other stuff onto it. I called her back and said, 'Look, I used your new lick on that one thing because you like it, but the other stuff you're adding on, you really don't need.' Then she gave in.

"I think a lot of that is what you experience when you're making your first album. You gotta remember, Mariah was 19, 20 years old, making her first album. She really wanted it to be special."

Narada found working with Mariah very similar to his experience with George Michael [see 664—"I Knew You Were Waiting (For Me)"]. "With George Michael, I actually had to have him stop singing, because he had me erase good vocals. He wanted me to keep going, and I said no, because I knew in my heart I already had it. The same thing with Mariah—I knew I had it. She feels if she sings more, maybe she'll go beyond it. And you know what? God bless her, in some cases, she does."

"I Don't Wanna Cry" jumped onto the Hot 100 at number 50 the week of April 6, 1991, just as "Someday" fell out of the top 10. Seven weeks later, Mariah returned to the top of the chart.

## THE TOP FIVE
*Week of May 25, 1991*

1  **I Don't Wanna Cry**
   Mariah Carey

2  **Touch Me (All Night Long)**
   Cathy Dennis

3  **More Than Words**
   Extreme

4  **I Like the Way**
   **(The Kissing Game)**
   Hi-Five

5  **Rhythm of My Heart**
   Rod Stewart

*Writers: Nuno Bettencourt
          Gary Cherone*

*Producer: Mike Wagener*

*June 8, 1991
1 week*

Gary Cherone and Nuno Bettencourt were sitting on Gary's porch when they wrote "More Than Words," an acoustic ballad that sent the hard-rocking band Extreme to the top of the *Billboard* Hot 100.

"Nuno had the music," says lead vocalist Cherone. "I remember being on the porch, hearing the cars go by, and it was a great sound effect. He was strumming on his guitar, and we were singing over normal neighborhood activity. It wasn't a nostalgia thing—people compare it to Simon and Garfunkel—it was just a pretty song, very simple. We decided we're not gonna change it, we're just gonna record it.

"I was sure the record company would want to add drums and this big production, and make it a power rock ballad. But no one said anything—we kept it the way it was. It got such a good reaction live. We did it on our first tour when the song wasn't even released, and we were getting write-ups about an acoustic ballad that no one knew."

Extreme was formed in Boston in 1985 when Cherone was in a band with drummer Paul Geary, and guitarist Bettencourt was in a rival band with bassist Pat Badger. Bettencourt was born in Portugal and lived in the Azores Islands. His family moved to Massachusetts in the '70s. "As a kid, I wanted nothing to do with music," he said in *Guitar Player*. "I was a jock and loved sports, especially hockey

and soccer. I was playing drums when I entered high school, and my brother Louie, who's an incredible guitarist, sat down with me a few times, trying to teach me how to play guitar." Bettencourt was a slow learner, and his brother became too frustrated to continue. "I knew he thought I was a loser, so just to feel better, I started learning songs a little bit at a time on my own. . . . In my sophomore and junior years, I dropped sports so I could play even more guitar."

The rival groups fought over communal dressing rooms one night, but later decided to come together in one new band. Nuno talked about accepting Cherone's offer in *Guitar Player*: "I couldn't believe it. The guy had never even heard me play! But we both got such good vibes from each other, and we were both into the same kinds of music."

Gary and Nuno stockpiled their songs and played dates in the Boston area, developing a large local following. They were named Outstanding Hard Rock/Heavy Metal Act at the Boston Music Awards in 1986 and 1987. Their managers owned a recording studio, so the band was able to take its time and record as much as they wanted. Nuno estimates they built up a catalog of 55 songs by the time A&R director Bryan Huttenhower signed them to A&M. "I always felt they had the potential to be huge," Huttenhower said in *Billboard*.

The label released the band's self-titled debut album in 1989; the first single was "Kid Ego," a song that would later make Cherone cringe. *Extreme*'s moderate sales were enough to support a second album, so Dokken/White Lion producer Michael Wagener was brought in to helm *Extreme II Pornograffitti*.

The album had a loose concept, based on a boy named Francis growing up in a violent, pornographic society. "Decadent Dance" and "Get the Funk Out" were released as singles. Cherone says he knew the former wouldn't be a hit, and radio would resist the double entendre of the latter. The album had fallen off the chart when A&M sent the third single to some Arizona radio stations. "More Than Words" entered the Hot 100 on March 23, 1991, at number 81.

In May, Extreme was touring Europe for the first time. "That was when it was climbing the chart," Gary recalls. "It hit the top 20, and we said, 'Imagine top 10!' Then it hit number nine for two weeks, and we thought it was peaking there." Meanwhile, friends and family members were calling from home to tell them how popular they were on the radio and MTV. "We couldn't comprehend it," Gary says. "We'd been touring, so we missed the success. When we went home and actually got our *Billboard*, we saw it was number one. It really hit home because every band—everybody—thinks about it."

## THE TOP FIVE
*Week of June 8, 1991*

1  **More Than Words**
   Extreme

2  **I Wanna Sex You Up**
   Color Me Badd

3  **Rush Rush**
   Paula Abdul

4  **I Don't Wanna Cry**
   Mariah Carey

5  **Love Is A Wonderful Thing**
   Michael Bolton

## Rush Rush CAPTIVE 98828
### PAULA ABDUL

*Writer: Peter Lord*

*Producers: V. Jeffrey Smith*
*Peter Lord*

*June 15, 1991*
*5 weeks*

Aᴦᴛᴇʀ recording a debut album that contained four number one hits [see 751—"Opposites Attract"], Paula Abdul had a lot to live up to with her second album of original material. "Coming off of the success of the *Forever Your Girl* album, I wanted to make an album that would take me to the next level," she confirms. "I didn't want to play it so safe that I would be making *Forever Your Girl, Part Two*. I was looking for some producers and songwriters who would help me take it to that next level. It was really important for me to grow in the period between the first and second album, and to take some risks, because I didn't want to feel stagnant and limited."

Accompanied by her managers Larry Tollin and Larry Frazin, Abdul attended a meeting in the office of Gemma Corfield, head of A&R for Virgin Records, to listen to demos submitted for her second album. After passing on a schmaltzy ballad and an anti-drug song, they heard a third submission, a song called "Rush Rush." During the violin break, Paula told Corfield she loved the song, and her managers concurred.

It was only then that the identities of the songwriters were revealed: Peter Lord and V. Jeffrey Smith, two-thirds of the group known as the Family Stand, an act signed to East West Records. Lord and Smith met through a mutual friend, Brooklyn-born

singer/writer/producer Will Downing. Lord and Smith teamed up to produce for Miki Howard, the Mac Band and Donna Allen before forming the Family Stand with Sandra St. Victor. They produced a group called Aftershock for Virgin, and impressed Corfield with their work. "She asked us to submit some songs for Paula, and the first thing we submitted was 'Rush Rush,'" recalls Lord.

"Sandra gave me the idea for the song," he continues, "because she dared me to write a simple song. We were joking around at the piano and I said, 'I can write a song like anybody else with nice pretty chords,' because she accused me of writing songs that make her scream all the time." Sandra concurs: "Every ballad or uptempo that they write, my part is always, 'Aaahhhhh!' 'Rush' was supposed to be my song, because I asked them to write me a song that I could sing real sweet to. Then he played it for Paula and she fell in love with it, so I ended up screaming again on our album."

Paula had plenty of time to learn the song. "'Rush Rush' was a song I received a year and a half (before recording it). I put it in my cassette deck in my car, heard the first eight bars, and knew that this was my song."

Peter was in the booth with her when she recorded it. "I was so nervous to sing 'Rush Rush' because I was afraid that I wouldn't be able to translate the song I loved so much

onto tape," says Paula. "I was squeezing Peter's hand, and he said, 'Just sing it—use your feelings right now, use those emotions.' There was magic to that song.

"I wanted to at least complete the song on tape, because I was getting ready to go shoot my album cover in London. I wanted to take it with me so I could get used to hearing it; I figured that when I came back, we could make changes. We ended up not making any changes."

Peter and Jeffrey were surprised that "Rush Rush" was the first single released from *Spellbound*, but Paula knew from the first time she heard it that it had to be the initial single, no matter what. "I remember walking into the record company and saying, 'I don't care what song makes it on the album, I want "Rush Rush" to be the first single.' I wanted it to be that much of a dramatic change and departure from the *Forever Your Girl* album." Virgin executives told her that she should finish the album and then decide. "But I'm really glad that 'Rush Rush' was the first single," Paula confides.

"Rush Rush" entered the *Billboard* Hot 100 at a lofty 36 on May 11, 1991; five weeks later it was number one, making it the fastest-rising single of Paula's career to that date. It remained on top for five weeks—the longest run at number one since Madonna's "Like a Virgin" [see 600] had a six-week stay in December, 1984.

*Writers: James Atkin*
*Ian Dench*
*Zac Foley*
*Mark Decloedt*
*Derry Brownson*

*Producer: Ralph Jezzard*

*July 20, 1991*
*1 week*

**F**OUR members of the British quintet known as EMF grew up in the Forest of Dean, in the west English countryside, on the border of Wales. "Nothing ever comes from there," drummer Mark Decloedt told Tony Fletcher in *DJ Times*. "It's a very working-class area where everybody lives from day to day, goes out on a weekend and gets drunk, gets married and has kids. All anyone dreams of is getting a flashy sports car and a nice house."

Decloedt was in a band with singer James Atkin while they were in high school. When Decloedt moved to London to follow a career in music, Atkin teamed up with bassist Zac Foley in another group. Keyboard player Derry Brownson operated a skateboard shop and then a clothing store. That store served as a base of operations for the four teenagers when they got together with Ian Dench; Ian had been in Apple Mosaic, a '60s-sounding band that had a deal with Virgin Records. "I've always had a white-rock background—the Smiths, Echo and the Bunnymen, that type of stuff," Dench told Gary Graff of the Knight-Ridder newspaper chain. "I was coming from that direction more than sort of hip-hop. But the hip-hop thing was all around us, and you couldn't help picking up on that, really."

They named themselves after a collection of groupies for New Order who were known as the Epson Mad Funkers (although a chant on the "B" side of "Unbelievable" suggests an alternative inspiration might have been the drug "ecstasy" and an epithet). A call to Nick Mander—a former manager of Decloedt's previous band who had taken a staff job in EMI's A&R department—helped EMF find management. After playing their fifth live gig, and before recording a demo, they were signed to EMI.

The single "Unbelievable" was recorded before the album *Schubert Dip*. "When I write songs," Dench told Moira McCormick, "I just stand there in front of a mirror with a guitar, imagine myself on some big stage and just go wild—the song is written in virtually five minutes." But that's not how "Unbelievable" was written. "Derry and I had had a heavy night out," Dench told Graff. "The next morning I was riding around on my bike, trying to clear my head out. It's an old postman's bike, and I was wobbling about as you might when you've been drunk the night before. Anyway, I was humming to myself, and the melody started coming out. That was it, really. It's funny that now it's sold a million copies."

"Unbelievable" peaked at number three on the U.K. chart. Since they were a band of good-looking young men, some members of the British press called them Britain's answer to the New Kids on the Block. "Being successful with our first single didn't do us any favors, in a way," Dench told McCormick. "Okay, so there's five of us, and we wear baseball caps. And we're young. It's a purely cosmetic comparison."

There were also comparisons to other bands from the Manchester rave scene, like Jesus Jones, Pop Will Eat Itself and Happy Mondays. "We all come from a rock background," Dench told Jim Richliano in *Billboard*. "But all of us would often go to the clubs and get into dance records. In a way, it seemed very natural for us, because we absorbed the things that were around us. We're not really funk, though; funk makes me think of Earth, Wind & Fire. We more or less combine the rock style of Led Zeppelin with the manic-punk/dance of groups like Killing Joke. Jesus Jones wasn't the first band to create this kind of sound. We and other Manchester bands were writing this kind of material before we even heard of them. And we're certainly not their protégés—we think they're a great band, but we would like to think that we're just from the same era, and not following in their footsteps."

"Unbelievable" entered the Hot 100 on April 13, 1991; 14 weeks later, EMF had the number one song in America.

## THE TOP FIVE
*Week of July 20, 1991*

1  **Unbelievable**
   EMF

2  **Rush Rush**
   Paula Abdul

3  **Right Here, Right Now**
   Jesus Jones

4  **(Everything I Do)**
   **I Do It for You**
   Bryan Adams

5  **P.A.S.S.I.O.N.**
   Rythm Syndicate

# 792 (Everything I Do) I Do It for You A&M 1567
## BRYAN ADAMS

*Writers: Bryan Adams*
*Robert John "Mutt" Lange*
*Michael Kamen*

*Producer: Robert John "Mutt" Lange*

*July 27, 1991*
*7 weeks*

A LOT OF ARTISTS had the opportunity to record the theme song from the much-anticipated motion picture *Robin Hood: Prince of Thieves*, starring Kevin Costner. "I felt it should be Marian's ballad rather than Robin's," says Michael Kamen, who scored the film. "I was interested to see if either Kate Bush or Annie Lennox wanted to do the song. Kate didn't feel it was for her, after thinking about it for a while; Annie wanted to sing it in Olde English, and was busy making a record of her own. So that didn't work out."

Kamen then turned the song over to David Kershenbaum, co-president of the Morgan Creek Music Group and the person in charge of music for the film. He oversaw the recording of a duet with different lyrics for Peter Cetera and Julia Fordham. When their demo was turned down, Lisa Stansfield expressed interest. "She wanted to sing the song and she was ready for it," says Kamen. "She was going to

write some lyrics and do it, but for some reason, Clive Davis decided he didn't want her involved in the movie."

Kamen was very happy with the ultimate decision to have Bryan Adams record the song. "He's got a lot of integrity," the composer enthuses. "He's a genuine rock and roller, so there's no question of it being a soppy ballad. And I love his singing. The only thing I had an argument with him (about) was a piano in the intro, because I had kept so-called modern-sounding instruments off the score. I wanted to include the orchestrations at the beginning of the ballad and let the orchestration turn into the vocal, and Bryan wanted the record kept intact."

Adams gave his point of view in *Q* magazine: "We had a great deal of trouble convincing Michael Kamen and the film company that our arrangement was going to work. They wanted to have more period instruments used on the score, so that it would blend in with the film. I said, 'We don't want lutes and mandolins on this—this is a pop record!' I think they're probably very pleased with the way things have turned out, but they still buried the song as far back in the film as possible, halfway through the credits—that's a reflection of how disappointed they were."

Kamen elaborated: "It wound up a little further down toward the end of the picture than it would ordinarily have wound up because we couldn't make the transition . . . what we joked about at the time was they were asking us to make a transition from C to C sharp and from 1195 to 1991 in the same breath."

Kamen, whose scoring credits include *Brazil* and the *Die Hard* and *Lethal Weapon* movies, grew up in New York and attended Juilliard. He studied classical music, but apprenticed as a rock and roller. "Sometime around that period, I'm talking 20-odd years ago, I came up with a little melody which I thought was very pretty, and filed away in the back of my head. I think I was writing a ballet at the time, and the choreographer didn't like the tune. Twenty years later, when I was writing the score for *Robin Hood*, I saw a piece of footage with Robin and Marian, (and) suddenly that theme came popping back." Kamen called Kershenbaum and told him he wanted that melody to be the main theme for *Robin Hood*. "I thought this was an opportunity to write the Robin Hood ballad for the 20th century."

The resulting collaboration between Kamen, Adams and Mutt Lange turned out to be the biggest-selling single since "We Are the World" [see 605]. It was number one for seven weeks on the Hot 100, longer than any song since the Police's "Every Breath You Take" [see 574] in 1983. In the U.K., Adams' single was number one for 16 weeks—the longest consecutive run at the top in British chart history.

## THE TOP FIVE
*Week of July 27, 1991*

1 **(Everything I Do)**
**I Do It for You**
Bryan Adams

2 **Right Here, Right Now**
Jesus Jones

3 **Unbelievable**
EMF

4 **P.A.S.S.I.O.N.**
Rythm Syndicate

5 **Summertime**
D.J. Jazzy Jeff and
the Fresh Prince

CAPTIVE 98752 **The Promise of a New Day**
PAULA ABDUL

Writers: *Peter Lord*
*Sandra St. Victor*
*V. Jeffrey Smith*
*Paula Abdul*

Producers: *V. Jeffrey Smith*
*Peter Lord*

September 14, 1991
1 week

AFTER writing "Rush Rush" [see 790] for Paula Abdul, V. Jeffrey Smith and Peter Lord of the group the Family Stand were asked to submit more material. "I was listening to other submissions from different producers and songwriters," says Paula. "I started working with the Family Stand, and it became such a strong rapport. They made me love what I'm doing so much that it was, like, 'Let's write some more.'"

Expressing her feelings about her new producers, Paula continues: "I was so fortunate to collaborate with the Family Stand. They really helped me pull from inside things I never knew that I had inside of me. All those fears of the sophomore jinx—'What if I can't top the last album?'—started to diminish, because I was having so much fun."

The first time Paula met the Family

Stand was at a party thrown by Gemma Corfield, head of A&R for Virgin Records. Peter sat at the piano that night and played a new song for her, "Blowing Kisses in the Wind." "We were doing our photo shoot for our last album down in Soho in New York City," Peter recalls. "I was walking with Sandra and started singing this song. That's how I got the idea. I thought it was a good title—we write from titles a lot of times."

The relationship between Paula and the members of the Family Stand continued to develop. "We got together and traded ideas." says Peter, "and the first idea Paula came up with was for 'Promise of a New Day.' We started working on it from suggestions by Paula, and took it from there. A few other songs we wrote like that also."

The Family Stand ended up writing and producing eight tracks for the album. "We wrote 'Rock House' and then it was, 'Great, let's write another one!'" Paula exclaims. "'Spellbound' came, and when we wrote 'Spellbound' together, I knew that it was going to be the title of my album, because the whole feeling was really magical."

*Spellbound* was the first album released on Captive Records, Paula's own label through Virgin Records. "It's great to have my . . . album be

the first act on Captive," Paula says. "Virgin Records has been wonderful in allowing me so much room to grow, giving me my own label deal, and letting me sign other artists. There's so much untapped talent out there to take under my wings."

"The Promise of a New Day" debuted on the Hot 100 at number 40 the week of July 20, 1991, the same week that "Rush Rush" fell from number one after a five-week run. Eight weeks later, Paula knocked Bryan Adams' multi-platinum "(Everything I Do) I Do It for You" off the top of the chart to rack up her sixth number one hit.

The third single from *Spellbound*, the ballad "Blowing Kisses in the Wind," debuted at number 47 the week of October 19 and peaked at number six the week of November 30. With "Blowing Kisses" still in the top 40, another track written by Peter, Jeffrey and Sandra was released. "Vibeology" entered the chart at number 65 the week of January 18, 1992; after three weeks at number 16 in February, it slipped down the chart, the first Paula Abdul single not to make the top 10 since the initial release of "(It's Just) The Way That You Love Me" in November, 1988.

For the fifth single from the album, Paula and Virgin chose another track written and produced by the Family Stand. "Will You Marry Me?" entered the Hot 100 at number 78 the week of April 4, 1992. The timing was perfect—it was released shortly after Paula and actor Emilio Estevez announced they would be married.

## THE TOP FIVE
*Week of September 14, 1991*

1 **The Promise of a New Day**
Paula Abdul

2 **I Adore Mi Amor**
Color Me Badd

3 **(Everything I Do)**
**I Do It for You**
Bryan Adams

4 **Motownphilly**
Boyz II Men

5 **Things That Make You Go**
**Hmmmm . . .**
C + C Music Factory f/
Freedom Williams

**794** **I Adore Mi Amor** GIANT 19204
COLOR ME BADD

Writers: *Color Me Badd*
*Hamza Lee*

Producers: *Royal Bayyan*
*Hamza Lee*

*September 21, 1991*
*2 weeks*

"ALL our lives, we've always looked in *Billboard* to see how the music was doing on the charts, and then to see our song on the chart with a bullet is incredible," Bryan Abrams, lead singer of Color Me Badd, said in a *Billboard* interview conducted before his group achieved the ultimate chart feat, a number one single.

Bryan's friendship with group member Kevin Thornton started in the sixth grade. Mark Calderon and Sam Watters were also elementary-school friends, and the four teenagers met when they attended Northwest High School in Oklahoma City. Bryan and Mark were competing against each other in the choir until they decided to join forces. Meshing old-fashioned doo-wop with new-wave hip-hop, they formed a quartet called Take One and made their debut at a high school talent show singing a Levi 501 Blues commercial.

The group became known for their spontaneous auditions. Attending a party one night, they discovered Ronnie Milsap was at a nearby function. They asked if they could sing *a cappella* for him, and he joined them in song. In a similar fashion, they met and auditioned for Huey Lewis, Sheila E., the O'Jays and Tony! Toni! Tone!

Their ultimate audition took place one night at the movie theater where Bryan and Kevin worked. Kevin was at the concession stand when he noticed someone who looked just like Jon Bon Jovi walk in. When he saw "Bon Jovi" written on the back of a bodyguard's jacket, he realized it was the real thing. He called the rest of the group to the theater. They waited through a double feature, then asked if they could sing *a cappella* for him. Jon asked if he could have a tape instead, but the group begged for 60 seconds of his time, and he consented. After hearing them sing, he invited them to go on before Bon Jovi's opening act, Skid Row, the next night. They played to a crowd of 15,000.

The quartet sneaked into a banquet for Oklahoma City high school students with perfect attendance so they could meet Kool and the Gang. After another "spontaneous" audition, Robert "Kool" Bell was impressed enough to introduce the group to managers Myles Sanders and Adil Bayyan. Sanders and Bayyan moved the

group to New York, where they spent a year and a half sleeping on the floor of a one-bedroom apartment. They returned periodically to Oklahoma City to write songs with Hamza Lee, whom they had met back in high school, when he was the musical director for the talent show they entered.

For one of the songs that ended up on their demo tape, "I Adore Mi Amor," the four members of Color Me Badd were inspired by a meeting with producers Jimmy Jam and Terry Lewis. "We admire them a lot," says Abrams. "At the time we met them, there was a rap tune out that was part-English, part-Spanish. We sang them an *a cappella* song and they said, 'Why don't you try something a little different.' They told us to try writing a tune with Spanish in it."

The foursome came up with a melody and sang it to Hamza—"We didn't have any words, we pretty much hummed," recalls Abrams. They went home to work on some lyrics while Hamza came up with a chord progression with a pop/rock feel. Once he heard the words, Hamza turned it into a ballad. "The next day," says Abrams, "we laid down the vocals. We were still reading off the paper—we'd just written the lyrics."

"I purposely made Sam's verse real moody and dark to match his husky voice," Lee explains. "I kind of brightened it up for Mark. His voice is, like, trumpety, kind of like Michael Jackson's. Kevin has a strong baritone voice, so his part is pretty much the busiest. I break it down for Bryan because he's a crooner-type. He has that nasal quality, a lot of strings floating around."

## THE TOP FIVE
*Week of September 21, 1991*

1 **I Adore Mi Amor**
Color Me Badd

2 **Good Vibrations**
Marky Mark and the Funky Bunch f/Loleatta Holloway

3 **Motownphilly**
Boyz II Men

4 **Emotions**
Mariah Carey

5 **Love of a Lifetime**
Firehouse

*Writers: Donnie Wahlberg*
*Mark Wahlberg*
*Spice*

*Producer: Donnie Wahlberg*

*October 5, 1991*
*1 week*

**M**ARK and Donnie Wahlberg, the two youngest children in a family of nine, were already well-known as street-corner breakdancers and rappers in their Dorchester, Massachusetts, neighborhood when producer Maurice Starr recruited them as the first two New Kids on the Block [see 732—"I'll Be Loving You (Forever)"]. "Me and Donnie were the only kids in the group at the time and we recorded a rap tune together," says Mark, who was 13 when he joined the group. "It's a Party" didn't capture Starr's attention; he was more interested in concentrating on ballads. "I was the only one who couldn't really sing," Mark explains, "so why go to vocal lessons and try to learn something that I'm not into? I decided to do my own thing."

School didn't hold any interest for Mark: his attendance was poor, and he dropped out during his freshman year. His own friends included getting into fights and shoplifting. While Donnie was becoming world-famous in New Kids on the Block, Mark was being arrested for assault and battery, charges later dismissed.

Donnie was on the road when he called home and promised to write a song for Mark, who was still rapping in the neighborhood. Mark didn't let him forget the promise, and when Donnie came home, they worked together late into the night writing music and lyrics.

The brothers produced a demo tape and sent it to record labels. Marc Benesch at Interscope Records had already worked with the New Kids when he was a senior vice president of promotion at Columbia Records. Benesch played the tape for his boss, Jimmy Iovine, who loved the song "Good Vibrations."

Interscope signed Mark, and he went into the studio with Donnie to come up with material for an album. Mark was hoping that "Wildside," a rap set to the music of Lou Reed's "Walk on the Wild Side," would be the first single, but the company decided on "Good Vibrations."

That track includes vocals sampled from Loleatta Holloway's "Love Sensation." "We talked to her," says Mark. "We set up a meeting with her and we got along so well, we asked if she wanted to be in the video." She also appeared with the band when they performed "Good Vibrations" on "The Arsenio Hall Show."

Holloway, born and raised in Chicago, started singing gospel in her mother's church choir when she was a little girl. She was part of a gospel group known as the Caravans, and appeared on stage in *Don't Bother Me, I Can't Cope* and *Your Arms Too Short to Box With God.* She made the top 10 of the Hot Soul Singles chart in 1975 with "Cry to Me," which was also her first entry on the Hot 100. "Love Sensation," written and produced by Dan Hartman, was a smash on the dance chart but never made the pop or R&B chart.

"They never stopped playing that song," says Loleatta. "It got to a point where it would be played in a 'mix,' so a lot of kids never knew who did it. Then they started sampling it. Samantha Fox was the first one I know who sampled it, on 'I Wanna Have Some Fun.'" The song was also sampled on the Black Box song "I Don't Know Anybody Else," a number 23 hit in February, 1991. "Good Vibrations" was the first single on which she was sampled that gave Loleatta billing on the label.

After achieving success with a number one single and a top 10 follow-up ("Wildside"), Mark changed his lifestyle. He received the equivalent of his high school diploma and was confirmed in the Catholic Church. He dropped "Marky Mark" and became Mark Wahlberg, actor. Critics liked him in Penny Marshall's 1994 film *Renaissance Man* and were more lavish with praise for his role as a porn star in *Boogie Nights.* Leading roles followed in *The Perfect Storm, Planet of the Apes* and *The Italian Job.*

## THE TOP FIVE
*Week of October 5, 1991*

1 **Good Vibrations**
Marky Mark and the Funky Bunch f/Loleatta Holloway

2 **I Adore Mi Amor**
Color Me Badd

3 **Emotions**
Mariah Carey

4 **Do Anything**
Natural Selection

5 **Love of a Lifetime**
Firehouse

# Emotions COLUMBIA 73977
## MARIAH CAREY

*Writers: Mariah Carey*
*David Cole*
*Robert Clivillés*

*Producers: David Cole*
*Robert Clivillés*
*Mariah Carey*

*October 12, 1991*
*3 weeks*

**M**ARIAH CAREY made chart history when "Emotions" went to number one on the *Billboard* Hot 100. She became the first artist to have her first five singles all make number one, breaking the record of four established by the Jackson Five [see 283—"I'll Be There"] 21 years earlier.

"Emotions," the title track from her second album, was one of four songs on the disc co-produced by the team of David Cole and Robert Clivillés, who had recently visited the top of the chart on their own as C + C Music Factory [see 778—"Gonna Make You Sweat (Everybody Dance Now)"].

Cole credited CBS Records Group president Tommy Mottola for suggesting the collaboration with Mariah. "Working with Mariah was, first of all, fun," he exclaimed. "Robert and I bounced off ideas. We came up with a whole bunch of grooves. If this worked, cool, if this doesn't work, next. And that's how we did the whole project. We would all come together and decide on what worked and what didn't.

"What was funny was both Robert and Mariah came up with the 'Emotions' groove separately. She had an idea for it and so did Robert. They

## THE TOP FIVE
*Week of October 12, 1991*

1  **Emotions**
   Mariah Carey

2  **Good Vibrations**
   Marky Mark and the Funky
   Bunch f/Loleatta Holloway

3  **Do Anything**
   Natural Selection

4  **I Adore Mi Amor**
   Color Me Badd

5  **Romantic**
   Karyn White

both had mentioned doing something similar to the (group) Emotions [see 473—"Best of My Love"]. I mean, the Emotions were an inspiration for the song 'Emotions,' there's no way to deny that or get around it. It definitely has the feeling from the Emotions, but we're not dumb enough to go and steal the damn record."

According to Cole, it was Mariah who came up with the song's title. "We thought maybe that's a bit much. And we all decided, 'No, why not?' There's nothing wrong with calling it 'Emotions' . . . it's a great name for a song."

The first song Cole and Clivillés worked on with Carey was "You're So Cold," which was being considered for the album's first single until they came up with "Emotions."

Cole talked about Mariah's octave range. "The high stuff? Oh, that's what she's known for. We had to include it, but as we started working, we decided we didn't want to use it as much as we could have. We didn't want it to become a gimmick instead of the fact that she could sing. But it's amazing. Listen to the very end of the song: she's hitting this very low note, and you compare that to the high notes that she hits. She's got an incredible range."

"Emotions" was Mariah's highest debut yet, leaping on to the Hot 100 at number 35 the week of August 31,

1991. Six weeks later, it was number one, where it remained for three weeks. For a follow-up, Columbia released "Can't Let Go," written and produced by Mariah and Walter Afanasieff [see 772—"Love Takes Time"].

"Mariah and I started writing together for the album a few months before starting to record," says Afanasieff. "I was doing Michael Bolton's album. And during the time that Michael would do a small little tour or take a break over the holidays, I would have the opportunity to write with Mariah." Soon they had a large collection of songs which they played for Columbia executives to see which ones should be recorded. "Can't Let Go," one of the first songs they had written, made the cut.

Afanasieff describes how their writing process usually unfolds: "Mariah stands next to me, I'm on the keyboard. I start playing a chord progression—or I'll start playing something on the keyboard—and she starts singing ideas, melodic ideas and lyrical ideas. We start feeding off each other: she starts singing to what I'm playing and I start playing to what she's singing. . . . She'll either come up with a few lyrical ideas right there and then go home and write a complete lyric, or she'll use the melody and write the lyric."

WARNER BROTHERS 19319 **Romantic**
KARYN WHITE

*Writers: Karyn White*
*Jimmy Jam*
*Terry Lewis*

*Producers: Jimmy Jam*
*Terry Lewis*

*November 2, 1991*
*1 week*

**K**ARYN WHITE, born and raised in Los Angeles, knew her direction in life at a very early age. She entered the Little Miss Ebony pageant when she was five. Around the same time, she saw Diana Ross in *Lady Sings the Blues* and told her mother Vivian that she wanted to be a star. "She believed me, that was the great thing about it," says Karyn.

Karyn sang for her church congregation, where her mother was the choir director. The aspiring singer took dance lessons as well as acting lessons, because she was determined to be an all-around entertainer. She was a cheerleader in high school, but quit because having to yell at football games was ruining her voice, something her classmates couldn't understand.

At 16, White auditioned in Los Angeles for a production of *Dreamgirls*, even though the company required actresses who were 18 or older. "I remember my mom taking me there. We had to do a dancing combination, then they cut you from there. I got all the way down to the last five girls. I was really scared, because I figured, how was I going to do that, I was in school—I couldn't tour." So she left without finding out if she would have been cast in the show.

Karyn started writing songs at 17, and a year later co-wrote "Automatic Passion," which was recorded by Stephanie Mills on her *Stand Back* album. When Jody Watley left Shalamar, White auditioned to replace her, but didn't get the job. In 1983 she joined the group Legacy, but after a brief stint, they booted her out because they didn't think her singing was commercial enough. The following year, she was hired to sing backing vocals for O'Bryan, an R&B singer who had one Hot 100 entry, "The Gigolo." But when his tour was over, Karyn was out of work.

Karyn's big break came when she recorded a demo at singer Michael Jeffries' studio in San Francisco. Michael Ostin and Benny Medina of Warner Brothers Records were looking for a vocalist to be featured on an album by fusion artist Jeff Lorber. Siedah Garrett [see 676—"I Just Can't Stop Loving You"] had been hired, but wasn't available. Karyn auditioned for the job, and was asked to sing on the album along with Jeffries.

"Michael Jeffries and I both signed with Warners with the option that if things went well, we'd become solo acts," Karyn told Steve Ivory in *Billboard*. "Michael got signed as a solo act too, but it just happened that 'Facts of Love' was the first single from Jeff's album, and it established me. I'm grateful to Jeff. I mean, there I was, with a hit single and my face in a video, all on his artist budget." "Facts of Love," with Karyn billed as a featured vocalist, reached number 27 in February, 1987.

That success led to more session work, backing artists like the Commodores, Julio Iglesias, Richard Marx, Ray Parker Jr., Bobby Brown and Sheena Easton. Karyn also recorded her own album for Warner Brothers, working with producers like L.A. Reid and Babyface. The first single from the album, "The Way You Love Me," peaked at number seven on the Hot 100 in February, 1989. Next came "Superwoman," a number eight hit in April, and "Secret Rendezvous," number six in August.

White did a guest duet with Michael Jeffries on his album, and met producers Jimmy Jam and Terry Lewis. Jimmy Jam recalls filming the video of the song: "I had my video camera with me, and I was filming a behind-the-scenes of making the video. I look back on that tape now and I can see that there's an obvious love connection between Karyn and Terry, but I really didn't take it as that at the time."

Karyn and Terry were married, and Jimmy Jam suggested they all work together. "'Romantic' was the first song we wrote for her," says Jimmy. "We ended up producing six songs and executive-producing the whole project." The project was Karyn's second album, *Ritual of Love*. Released as the first single, "Romantic" debuted on the Hot 100 the week of August 17, 1991. Eleven weeks later, Karyn displaced Mariah Carey from the top of the chart and scored her first number one pop single.

## THE TOP FIVE

*Week of November 2, 1991*

1 **Romantic**
   Karyn White

2 **Emotions**
   Mariah Carey

3 **Cream**
   Prince and the New Power
   Generation

4 **Do Anything**
   Natural Selection

5 **Can't Stop This
   Thing We Started**
   Bryan Adams

# 798 Cream PAISLEY PARK 19175
## PRINCE AND THE NEW POWER GENERATION

*Writers: Prince and the New Power
 Generation*

*Producers: Prince and the New Power
 Generation*

*November 9, 1991
2 weeks*

"I FELT we all needed to grow," Prince told Neal Karlen in *Rolling Stone* when asked why he broke up his former band, the Revolution [see 595— "Let's Go Crazy"]. "We all needed to play a wide range of music with different types of people. Then we could all come back eight times as strong. No band can do everything. For instance, this band I'm with now is *funky*. With them, I can drag out 'Baby I'm a Star' all night! I just keep switching gears on them, and something else funky will happen. I couldn't do that with the Revolution. They were a different kind of funky, more electronic and cold. The Revolution could tear up 'Darling Nikki,' which was the coldest song ever written. But I wouldn't even think about playing that song with *this* band."

This band was the New Power Generation, named after a song on the soundtrack of Prince's *Graffiti Bridge*. Tony Mosely, known as Tony M., first met Prince during the filming of *Purple Rain*. "We were extras on the *Purple Rain* set. He saw us dancing around, and he came up to me, Kirk Johnson, and Damon Dickson, and he said, 'I want you guys to do a few routines for the movie.'"

Tony formed a band with Kirk and Damon, and played the college circuit.

"I don't think we were really satisfied with just being dancers, because we looked around and saw the dancers in other bands never went on to do anything else after the dancing was over. We decided if we were going to have any longevity, we better pick up something else. So that's when we started working on our writing skills. I play guitar and keyboards; Kirk is a drummer and plays keyboards. *Graffiti Bridge* came along, and Prince asked us to choreograph that. Then he said, 'Hey, I'm going to form this band, the N.P.G., would you guys like to be a part of that?'

"The beginning stages of the New Power Generation started with *Graffiti Bridge*—that's the band we took over to Europe when we did the Nude Tour. Prince asked Rosie Gaines if she would like to be in it, and asked me if I'd mind rapping in it." Prince and the New Power Generation started writing songs while they were still in Europe. "When we got off the tour is when we really started recording the album," Tony notes.

*Diamonds and Pearls* was more of a collaboration between Prince and his musicians than previous albums had been, according to Tony M. "We were all in the studio together. Everybody got their headsets on and we were in there grooving. A lot of things came from just vibing off each other."

The first single from *Diamonds and Pearls*, "Gett Off," was bulleting up

the chart at number 31 when the second single, "Cream," debuted at number 46. "Gett Off" met with resistance at radio and reached number 21 the week of October 12, 1991, while "Cream" sailed to number one.

"'Cream' was done while we were in Europe," Tony recalls. "When we're on the road, he'll book studios and we'll go in and jam. And that was a vibe that the band, Levi Seacer, Jr., Sonny Thompson, and everybody else came up with. The message is, keep striving, keep pushing, and it will happen—perseverance."

Prince and Tony M. talked about adding rap to Prince's music even before the New Power Generation was formed. "I told him how I felt it was going to be perceived," says Tony. "He agreed with those assumptions that a lot of people are going to think that he's jumping on this bandwagon. I told him I was willing to put on the gloves and go for it."

Tony believes the N.P.G. coalesced as a band when they finished the Nude Tour. "Everything started coming together when we got back and we did 'Rock in Rio' in Rio De Janeiro. We did some showcases for Warner Brothers in Chicago. We did the Jack the Rapper convention in Atlanta—that was different for him, because that's on majority a hip-hop crowd, and no one expected him to do anything like that. I think that's when everything started tightening up for the band."

## THE TOP FIVE
*Week of November 9, 1991*

1 **Cream**
  Prince and the New
  Power Generation

2 **Romantic**
  Karyn White

3 **Can't Stop This Thing We
  Started**
  Bryan Adams

4 **Real Real Real**
  Jesus Jones

5 **When a Man Loves a Woman**
  Michael Bolton

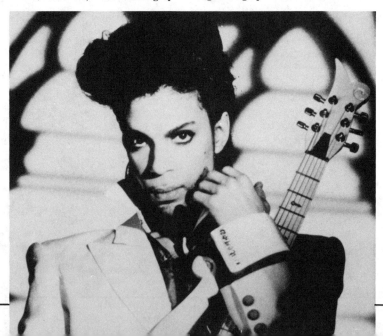

COLUMBIA 74020 # When a Man Loves a Woman

**799**

## MICHAEL BOLTON

Writers: *Cameron Lewis*
*Arthur Wright*

Producers: *Walter Afanasieff*
*Michael Bolton*

*November 23, 1991*
*1 week*

Growing up in New Haven, Connecticut, Michael Bolton was encouraged musically by his parents. His father was a ward chairman for the Democratic party, and his mother was a housewife whose own musical career had been discouraged by her husband. They rented a saxophone for Michael when he was eight, and at 11, Michael was performing at the local Jewish community center.

His taste in music was influenced by his older brother Orrin, who was a big Motown fan. Michael remembers one of the first singles his brother bought was Stevie Wonder's "Fingertips" [see 135]. Some of those soulful influences were obvious in Bolton's choices of cover songs on his albums. He included Otis Redding's "(Sittin' On) The Dock of the Bay" on his third album, *The Hunger*. Next came *Soul Provider*, with an updated version of Hoagy Carmichael's 1930 song "Georgia on My Mind," popularized in 1960 by Ray Charles. And on *Time, Love and Tenderness* Bolton included a new version of "When a Man Loves a Wo-

man," recorded in 1966 by Percy Sledge.

Walter Afanasieff, who produced the album with Bolton, remembers Columbia Records executives Tommy Mottola and Donnie Ienner visiting the studio to listen to some of the tracks they were recording. "We were all sitting there listening, and Michael said, 'I want to do another oldie remake.' Both Tommy and Donnie said, 'We know the perfect song for you, Michael.' And Michael had not told anybody he was going to do this song. He'd never told me, so it's the first time he was announcing his intention. I immediately thought, 'This guy should do "When a Man Loves a Woman"' but I didn't say anything. Tommy and Donnie, simultaneously, said, '"When a Man Loves a Woman."' Everybody heard each other say the same song. Michael stood up and said, 'That's the song I was going to do.' It was a perfect call."

Afanasieff, who first met Bolton through Kenny G, listened to the Percy Sledge version before recording it with Michael. In addition to producing the track, Afanasieff played organ on it. "The melody speaks for itself," he says. "Everybody who sings 'When a Man Loves a Woman' is going to sound like the original record melodically. We needed to capture the authenticity of it and relate to the newness of it. I've played that song for

so many years at so many weddings and so many clubs, and finally here I am recording it in the studio. We had the basics done and I put on my headphones and said, 'Man, turn off the lights.' The engineer played the tape loud, and I just played the B-3.

"When we finished the vocal, I thought it was perfect, but Michael wasn't really sold yet. He thought he could have sung it better." A couple of weeks after mixing the entire album, Bolton was in Los Angeles and called Afanasieff. He asked if Walter could fly down and book a studio so he could work on his vocals for "When a Man Loves a Woman."

The producer describes what happened: "We walked into the studio, set up the tape, sat there, listened to it, and he looks at me and says, 'Pretty good, huh?' I said, 'It's brilliant.' He said, 'Let's leave it alone and see what happens.'"

The first single from the album was the upbeat "Love Is a Wonderful Thing," which peaked at number four the week of June 1, 1991. The follow-up was the album's title track, Diane Warren's "Time, Love and Tenderness"; it went as high as number seven the week of September 14, 1991. "When a Man Loves a Woman," the third single, entered the Hot 100 at number 44 on October 12. Six weeks later, it became the seventh single of the rock era to be number one by two different artists [see 199], following "Go Away Little Girl," "The Loco-Motion," "Please Mr. Postman," "Venus," "Lean on Me" and "You Keep Me Hangin' On."

## THE TOP FIVE

*Week of November 23, 1991*

1 **When a Man Loves a Woman**
Michael Bolton

2 **Cream**
Prince and the New
Power Generation

3 **Set Adrift on Memory Bliss**
P.M. Dawn

4 **It's So Hard to Say
Goodbye to Yesterday**
Boyz II Men

5 **Can't Stop This Thing
We Started**
Bryan Adams

# 800 Set Adrift on Memory Bliss GEE STREET 866 094-4
## P.M. DAWN

Writers: Attrel Cordes
         Gary Kemp

Producers: P.M. Dawn

November 30, 1991
1 week

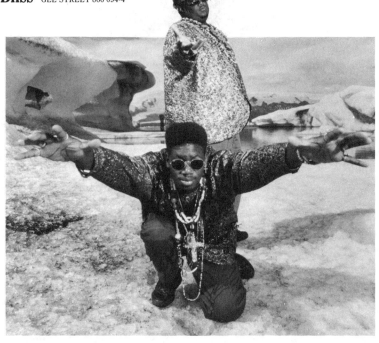

THE Hot 100, the definitive weekly ranking of the most popular singles in America, first appeared in *Billboard* on August 4, 1958. Prior to that date, *Billboard* published a number of separate surveys, including Best Sellers in Stores and Most Played by Jockeys. The Hot 100 melded sales and airplay information into one chart, and for over 30 years the information was gathered in a "human" fashion.

Sales reports from retail outlets were taken over the telephone by *Billboard* staffers, who would ask store managers and clerks to rank singles via a point system. Other people in the *Billboard* chart department would register airplay reports from key radio stations around the country. If a radio station listed a particular single at number one on its playlist, it would receive more points than a song ranked number two—even if the runner-up song was being played more often than the title in the pole position.

All of that changed the week of November 30, 1991, when the Hot 100 was ushered into the computer age. Under the guidance of Michael Ellis, Director of Charts for *Billboard*, a new system employing monitored airplay and piece counts became the methodology for ranking the nation's hottest 100 singles.

For the "new" Hot 100, sales data

## THE TOP FIVE
### Week of November 30, 1991

1  **Set Adrift on Memory Bliss**
   P.M. Dawn

2  **When a Man Loves a Woman**
   Michael Bolton

3  **Black or White**
   Michael Jackson

4  **It's So Hard to Say
   Goodbye to Yesterday**
   Boyz II Men

5  **Cream**
   Prince and the New
   Power Generation

was gathered by SoundScan, a company that uses bar-code scanning to determine the actual number of records sold throughout the country. Airplay information for the new Hot 100 was collected by Broadcast Data Systems. That division of BPI Communications, the publisher of *Billboard*, monitors songs played on the radio 24 hours a day, seven days a week, via an encoded audio "fingerprint." A third component of the new chart was airplay lists from smaller markets not monitored by BDS.

The first song to be number one under the new methodology was "Set Adrift on Memory Bliss" by P.M. Dawn, two brothers from Jersey City, New Jersey, who first found fame in Great Britain. Attrel and Jarrett Cordes—better known as Prince Be and DJ Minutemix—were recording the song "Comatose" when they heard Spandau Ballet's "True" in the studio. "It's so beautiful," says Prince Be. "I wanted Prince Be's version. I basically reincarnated the spirit of 'True' for me. I reshaped it as if I wrote it myself, creating 'Set Adrift on Memory Bliss.'"

Attrel and Jarrett were the two oldest of seven brothers. Their father, Attrel Cordes, Sr., died of pneumonia when Attrel was one year old. Their mother Janice, a devotee of mystic Edgar Cayce, remarried. The two brothers were guided into musical ca-

reers at a young age by their stepfather, Buck, a percussionist and founding member of Kool and the Gang [see 536—"Celebration"]. He gave a very young Attrel a copy of a Donovan record that helped inspire his musical vision. Their mother thought medicine would be a better career, although she later changed her mind.

Their Uncle Tim would bring home 45s he found on his rounds as a garbage collector, giving the two brothers a musical library that included Simon and Garfunkel, Sergio Mendes and Brasil '66, Nat King Cole, Dr. Buzzard's Original Savannah Band and the Beatles. By the time he was 10, Attrel was writing rap songs. After high school, he and Jarrett submitted some demos to Tommy Boy Records, but were rejected. Instead, they signed with a smaller label, Warlock, and issued a single called "Ode to a Forgetful Mind." Prince Be says candidly, "The record company didn't really believe in the project." One clue was the phrase someone had etched into the runoff groove: "Ode to a waste of vinyl."

Warlock licensed the record to a British company, Gee Street. The brothers liked how they were treated by the label, and signed with the company before it became a part of Island Records. "Set Adrift on Memory Bliss" was released in the U.K. first, where it peaked at number three.

EPIC 74100 **Black or White**
MICHAEL JACKSON

*Writer: Michael Jackson*

*Producers: Michael Jackson*
*Bill Bottrell*

*December 7, 1991*
*7 weeks*

IN December, 1969, Diana Ross and the Supremes garnered their 12th number one single, putting them in third place behind the Beatles and Elvis Presley as the artist with the most number one songs. The top three remained unchanged until 22 years later, when Michael Jackson went to the top of the *Billboard* Hot 100 for the 12th time as a solo artist with "Black or White," the lead-off single from his *Dangerous* album.

Jackson faced the same questions he did when *Bad* was released. Would it be as big as *Thriller*, the all-time bestselling record with 40 million copies sold worldwide? *Bad* may not have sold as many copies as *Thriller*, but it still managed to move a hefty 20 million copies around the world.

In the glare of media scrutiny, *Dangerous* had a fast start. It sold roughly 326,000 copies in its first week, well enough to debut at number one on the *Billboard* Top 200. "Black or White" was the fastest-rising single in 22 years, debuting at number 35, moving to number three in its second week, hitting the top in its third week. The last single to do that was "Get Back" by the Beatles.

It took almost four years to complete the sessions for *Dangerous*. "Michael started the day we finished *Bad*," producer Bruce Swedien told

Michael Goldberg in *Rolling Stone*. At first, Epic planned to release a greatest-hits package called *Decade* that would include four new songs. But when Michael had half an album done, that idea was shelved in favor of an entirely new album. Ultimately, around 60 songs were recorded. As Quincy Jones moved on to other projects [see 702—"Dirty Diana"], Michael turned to producers L.A. Reid and Babyface, but did not use any of their tracks on the album. The 14 tracks on *Dangerous* were produced by Teddy Riley, Bill Bottrell and Swedien.

Bottrell told Goldberg that "Black or White" was developed from a track intended for *Bad*. "That piece of music, the beginning part that Slash plays on, was first recorded at Michael's house," Bottrell said. "Michael asked me to dig it out of the vault in August of 1989. He had in mind to use it as the intro to 'Black or White.' It took a long time before we got Slash on it."

Bottrell described Michael's recording method to Goldberg. "He starts with an entire sound and song, musically. Usually he doesn't start with lyrics, but he hears the sound and the whole arrangement of the song in his head. I suppose there are exceptions, but this is generally the way it is. He fills in the lyrics later. He hums things. He can convey it with his voice like nobody. Not just singing the song's lyrics, but he can convey a feeling in a drum part or a synthesizer part.

He's really good at conveying those things."

The video for "Black or White" premiered simultaneously on the Fox Television Network, MTV and the Black Entertainment Television channel on November 14, 1991. Only those who watched the video that night saw the entire 11-minute epic directed by Jon Landis, for the next day Jackson responded to outraged fans and indignant journalists who found the last four minutes offensive. The footage of Michael rubbing his crotch, destroying a car and throwing a garbage can through a store window was excised. The superstar issued an apology, saying in part, "It upsets me to think that 'Black or White' could influence any child or adult to destructive behavior, either sexual or violent."

Michael missed the chance to surpass the Supremes when the second single from *Dangerous*, "Remember the Time," peaked at number three in March, 1992. Still, sales of *Dangerous* remained strong. In its first four months of release, it had sold 7.5 million copies worldwide.

It proved that Sony had made a good deal when they gave Michael the most lucrative contract in music history. In March of 1991, just a week after Janet Jackson was signed to Virgin in a $50-million deal, Sony Software announced that Michael's new deal had a "billion-dollar potential." It included an $18-million advance for *Dangerous*, a new record label called Nation Records with Michael as CEO, the highest royalty rate in the business and a deal for television and movie production under the auspices of the Jackson Entertainment Complex.

## THE TOP FIVE
*Week of December 7, 1991*

1 **Black or White**
Michael Jackson

2 **When a Man Loves a Woman**
Michael Bolton

3 **Set Adrift on Memory Bliss**
P.M. Dawn

4 **It's So Hard to Say Goodbye to Yesterday**
Boyz II Men

5 **All 4 Love**
Color Me Badd

## 802 All 4 Love GIANT 19236
## COLOR ME BADD

*Writers: Color Me Badd*
*Howard Thompson*

*Producer: Howie Tee*

*January 25, 1992*
*1 week*

AFTER Cassandra Mills of Giant Records signed Color Me Badd to the label, she asked producer Dr. Freeze if he could come up with a song like Bell Biv DeVoe's "Do Me!" for the group to sing on the soundtrack of the film *New Jack City*. "I asked him to watch the movie and pay close attention to the strip scene, since that was the segment the music would accompany," she told Jim Richliano in *Billboard*. Dr. Freeze brought her "I Wanna Sex You Up," which became Color Me Badd's debut single. It spent four weeks at number two in June, 1991.

Assisting Dr. Freeze in the studio was Howard Thompson, better known as Howie Tee. "He asked me if I could come in the studio and help him," says Tee, born in Birmingham, England, and raised in Jamaica and Brooklyn. He was taken with the group from their first meeting. "Those guys were real easy to work with; they sound terrific. I never knew a bunch of guys could sound like that at the drop of a dime if you ask them to do a harmony. It wasn't a situation where one guy had to do his note, then the other guy finds his note. They just knew their harmony."

Tee liked "I Wanna Sex You Up" but didn't know it would be a hit. "It had a real catchy hook, but I didn't think people would actually buy it. That track was real 'street.' The song sounded good, and apparently it worked."

The group called Tee when it was time to record their first album. "They needed a couple of tracks," he relates. "All I was doing was rap groups and rap artists." He had an instrumental track on tape. "I heard this record by Nancy Wilson called 'On Spinning Wheels' and I liked that groove. First I sampled it, and once I had the loop going, I played things over it so the sample could disappear." He played the track for Color Me Badd.

"Howie Tee had the track and we took it home," recalls lead singer Bryan Abrams. "The melody came right to us, and we wrote the lyrics in a matter of hours. It's one of the fastest songs we'd ever written."

The recording session for "All 4 Love" wasn't a rush job, according to Tee. "They took their time to do the vocals. There were a lot of times where Bryan would sing his lead to me and it was perfect, it was excellent, but he was never satisfied. Even the engineer would have to tell him it's fine. They like to make sure their vocals are right. If the energy that he was hearing is not there, he'll do it over. I wasn't rushing him—I wanted to make sure everybody was happy with what was going on."

"All 4 Love" exemplifies Color Me Badd's desire to meld an old sound with a new sound. "We started out singing *a cappella*, and when the hip-hop thing came out, we were really into that also," Bryan explains. "We wanted to get into that street sound, the hip-hop sound, but we wanted to keep the doo-wop—we didn't want to lose that once we got into music. I feel like we did that very well with most of

the tunes on the album; there's a lot of harmony going on."

"All 4 Love" debuted on the Hot 100 at number 37 the week of November 9, 1991, while the group's previous number one single, "I Adore Mi Amor" [see 794], was still on the chart. Eleven weeks later, Color Me Badd had their second consecutive number one hit.

The group followed "All 4 Love" with "Thinkin' Back," written with Hamza Lee and Troy Taylor. "When the tune was brought to me to do something with the music, I listened to somebody sing a verse," says Lee, a friend of the group's since their high school days in Oklahoma City. "I put the music together in about two hours. It was a cold night—January 4, 1990. We stayed up until 6:00 in the morning, recording a demo for it. When we finished that song, we listened to it over and over, we played it for everybody we knew. Everyone we played it for was just stunned."

---

### THE TOP FIVE
*Week of January 25, 1992*

1  **All 4 Love**
   Color Me Badd

2  **Can't Let Go**
   Mariah Carey

3  **Don't Let the Sun
   Go Down on Me**
   George Michael/Elton John

4  **Black or White**
   Michael Jackson

5  **Finally**
   Ce Ce Peniston

COLUMBIA 74086 **Don't Let the Sun Go Down on Me** 803
GEORGE MICHAEL/ELTON JOHN

*Writers: Elton John*
*Bernie Taupin*

*Producer: George Michael*

*February 1, 1992*
*1 week*

Gᴇᴏʀɢᴇ Mɪᴄʜᴀᴇʟ embarked on his
"Cover to Cover" tour in 1991. Although he sang some of his own hits
like "Careless Whisper" and "Faith,"
the majority of each concert was devoted to George's favorite songs from
the '70s and '80s, like David Bowie's
"Fame," McFadden and Whitehead's
"Ain't No Stoppin' Us Now" and Terence Trent Darby's "Sign Your Name."
In a video documentary, George
talked about why he loves singing
other people's hits: "One of the main
attractions of a song written by someone else is that there's nothing personal about it. There is some kind of
release for me in the middle of a performance to actually stop singing me
and just say, 'Right, this is an instrument and this is using it to the
best of my ability.'

"Range is something that again is a
very important consideration. That's a
very strong reason for me doing so
many Stevie Wonder covers. I've done
over various sets four or five Stevie
Wonder covers. And apart from the
fact that I consider him an incredible
writer . . . the key that he was writing for (in the '70s) is perfectly suited
to my voice, and somehow I've really
managed to get something out of his
songs live."

Another favorite source of cover
material for George was his friend,
Elton John. As a child, George avidly
collected Elton's albums. His friendship with Wham! partner Andrew
Ridgeley was originally cemented
when the two schoolmates discovered
they both owned and loved Elton's
double album *Goodbye Yellow Brick
Road.*

After George became famous, his
admiration for Elton's work became
mutual. On March 13, 1985, George
was the youngest person to be named
Songwriter of the Year at the annual
Ivor Novello awards in London—the
person making the presentation was
Elton John. The pair first recorded together that year for Elton's album *Ice
on Fire.* George appeared on the first
two singles, sharing lead vocals with
Elton on "Wrap Her Up" and singing

backgrounds on "Nikita." Elton returned the favor by playing piano on
"The Edge of Heaven," a Wham! single that peaked at number 10 in August, 1986. He also joined George
onstage in Honolulu on April 5, 1988,
for George's solo concert debut in the
U.S. They duetted on "Candle in the
Wind."

In March, 1991, George was performing at Wembley Stadium on the
"Cover to Cover" tour when Elton surprised him backstage. They spontaneously decided to do a duet and
picked "Don't Let the Sun Go Down
on Me," a song that George had performed at Live Aid in July, 1988, and
was already including in his set.

The song had appeared originally on
Elton's *Caribou* album in 1974. Elton
has described it as one of his three favorites that he's written, and mentions
the song was influenced by the Beach
Boys' "God Only Knows" and "Good
Vibrations."

A recording of "Don't Let the Sun
Go Down on Me" from the Wembley
concert was released as a single; it entered the Hot 100 at number 72 the
week of December 7, 1991. When it
went to number one eight weeks later,

it was the seventh number one hit for
both Elton and George (counting only
his post-Wham! hits).

While the Wembley track is featured
on the single, the footage in the video
is not from that same concert. "The
video for the single was actually shot
over several days," confirms Michael
Pagnotta, George's publicist. "It was
shot just prior to George's U.S. 'Cover
to Cover' tour, which began in October. It was shot in an airline hangar
in Burbank (California) where George
had been rehearsing; Elton came in
for a night, and they ran through the
song a couple times. Then the song
was filmed in its entirety live in Chicago in the middle of October as part
of that 'Cover to Cover' tour, and
when Elton came out from the wings,
the place went crazy."

The proceeds from the single were
divided among 10 different charities
for children, AIDS and education.
George recorded another cover of an
Elton John song in 1991. He sang "Tonight," from the *Blue Moves* album,
on *Two Rooms,* an all-star compilation
saluting the 25th anniversary of the
writing partnership of Elton John and
Bernie Taupin.

**THE TOP FIVE**
*Week of February 1, 1992*

1 **Don't Let the Sun
Go Down on Me**
George Michael/Elton John

2 **I Love Your Smile**
Shanice

3 **All 4 Love**
Color Me Badd

4 **Diamonds and Pearls**
Prince and the New
Power Generation

5 **Can't Let Go**
Mariah Carey

# 804 I'm Too Sexy CHARISMA 98671
## RIGHT SAID FRED

*Writers: Richard Fairbrass*
*Rob Manzoli*
*Fred Fairbrass*

*Producer: Tommy D.*

*February 8, 1992*
*3 weeks*

In THEIR native Britain, Right Said Fred's debut single held at number two for six weeks, unable to break Bryan Adams' 16-week stranglehold on the top of the chart [see 792—"(Everything I Do) I Do It for You"]. "Our domestic newspapers, which are always interested in grief, tried to turn it into a major feud, and tried to make it sound like we hated Bryan Adams," says Richard Fairbrass. "It didn't bother me at all until the newspapers started telling me that it should be bothering me. By the time 'Sexy' had dropped out of the charts, I started getting really irritated with Bryan Adams. But we got to number one in the U.S.—that more than made up."

The Fairbrass brothers grew up in Sussex. Fred wanted to play music; Richard wasn't sure what he wanted to do, so he got a bass guitar and joined his brother in a band. They moved to London in 1981. Richard remembers catching his reflection in a window while walking down the street. "On that day, it hit me: I looked a complete state. So I started working out. I used to be very skinny and a bit round-shouldered." He went to work in a gymnasium called the Dance Attic, and ended up managing it with Fred.

They attended the New Music Seminar in New York in 1987 and got a development deal with Capitol that expired without anything being recorded. Back in London, they gigged as an acoustic duo for three years. They got their name after their friend Katie Randall heard the 1962 top 10 U.K. hit "Right Said Fred" by Bernard Cribbins on the radio and called them up. "I think we went for it because we knew it was stupid," Richard laughs. "It had a good eccentric kind of English sound to it. I think if 'Sexy' hadn't happened, we would have changed it by now." When they decided to make a demo, they searched for a guitarist and found Rob Manzoli at a rehearsal hall in Putney.

After a couple of independent label deals fell through, they were at a friend's house working on a demo when they came up with a bass line they put into a computer. "We took a tea break and the computer was playing this loop round and round, and right out of the blue—I can't tell you where it came from—I started singing, 'I'm too sexy for my shirt' and we all fell about laughing.

"Fred was a little bit weird about it . . . he didn't think we should be frivolous. He thought we should crank on and do our serious music. So Rob and I convinced Fred after three or four days that we should pursue it. And I couldn't get the top line out of my head. We realized that although we had the verse and we had the basic lyrical idea, we didn't have a chorus. So we worked for a couple of weeks on a chorus, then Fred strung all the lyrics together. All I came up with were the 'I'm Too Sexy' bits—Fred did the rest of the lyrics, and Rob wrote the top line of the chorus." Before it was "I'm Too Sexy," the song was called "Heaven." "It was

a catalogue of things that a particular person was bothered by every single day of their life," Richard explains. "He was looking forward to moving on to another level, where life would be more civilized and peaceful." The theme for "I'm Too Sexy" came from the Dance Attic. "If you work in a gymnasium or a health club or a dance studio, you see so much posing and so much attitude going on," Richard points out. "We took the opportunity of using that as raw material to work the song around. It wasn't like we had a big beef against models—we just wanted to choose something to pin the song on." Fred and Richard used the rough mixes as a workout song at the gym. "The rough demo sounded pretty terrible," Richard says candidly.

A song plugger named Guy Holmes suggested they remix and re-edit the song, so they borrowed £1,500 and produced a new master with the help of DJ/producer Tommy D. Then Holmes took it to several major record companies in the U.K. "They said, 'This is rubbish, it's not a hit,' in the tradition of record company A&R men who cannot spot a hit if it disappears up their rear end," sneers Richard. Holmes offered to establish an independent label named Tug to release a single of "I'm Too Sexy."

According to Richard, "People didn't get the joke to start with. A few people actually thought I was talking about myself and taking the whole thing seriously. Once people saw the video, they realized it was all a spoof."

## THE TOP FIVE
*Week of February 8, 1992*

1  **I'm Too Sexy**
   Right Said Fred

2  **I Love Your Smile**
   Shanice

3  **Don't Let the Sun
   Go Down on Me**
   George Michael/Elton John

4  **Diamonds and Pearls**
   Prince and the New
   Power Generation

5  **All 4 Love**
   Color Me Badd

ATLANTIC 87580 **To Be With You** `805`
MR. BIG

Writers: Eric Martin
   David Grahame

Producer: Kevin Elson

February 29, 1992
3 weeks

WHEN Capitol Records dropped Eric Martin from their roster in 1987, the singer wrote a lot of new songs with the intention of recording another solo album for somebody else. "And then Billy Sheehan gave me a call out of the blue," Martin recalls. The date was March 4, 1988. "He said, 'I left David Lee Roth . . . I don't want to back anybody up. I want to have a real rock and roll band, bass, drums, guitar and vocals, just like Free, Humble Pie, Spooky Tooth—in that vein, (a) bluesy rock and roll band, and I've heard your voice. Let's start a band.'"

Martin had never met Sheehan before that phone call, but had seen him on MTV in Roth's "Yankee Rose" video. "After we hung up, I bought a bunch of records and he was always plastered over *Guitar Player* magazine." Sheehan came to San Francisco and met with Martin and his managers. Martin knew right away he wanted to team up with this "wild man." "I said, 'I guess the solo idea's out, let's go searching for a label'."

Guitarist Paul Gilbert and drummer Pat Tropey rounded out the band. "We spent eight days fooling around, and wrote practically the whole first album," says Eric. "We showcased it and everybody came, but everybody passed on it. We tried to get Atlantic Records to come, and they wouldn't

come." But based on the four musicians' reputations, the label signed the group on faith.

The band had a label deal but no name. "We had all kinds of weird names like 'Mars Needs Women,' 'The Evil Stepsisters'—we were gonna open for Cinderella," Eric laughs. "But our drummer Pat was looking through a bunch of rock and roll records and listening to bands that we wanted to have a spirit of, like Free." Tropey found a song by Free called "Mr. Big." "It was a coincidence, because Billy said when he was in the band Palace, he used to do a bass solo with that song."

"To Be With You" is a song that Eric had been hearing in his head for 15 years. The lyrics were inspired by a platonic girlfriend a few years his senior; she resembled Nico of the Velvet Underground, and read poetry to him after school in her dad's beat-up Mercedes Benz. "She always had boyfriends, she always wanted to find Mr. Right, and she could never find him," Martin reminisces.

About a year before Mr. Big was formed, Martin spent a couple of days writing with David Grahame, who had portrayed Paul McCartney in a production of *Beatlemania*. "My melody and lyrics were a little more folky, and he gave it the Beatles feel, the 'All You Need Is Love' type of sound." Martin didn't submit their song for the first Mr. Big album because "we were going for a straight-ahead, Van Halenesque rock and roll band. I didn't think Mr. Big wanted to break out and do a folk song."

At one point Martin did play it for

Gilbert, a big fan of the Beatles and Beach Boys as well as the Osmonds' "Crazy Horses." "But I had no idea that he then played it for Mr. Big," Martin confesses. "I came to rehearsal for our *Lean Into It* album and I was playing a bunch of songs, and they said, 'What about that acoustic song?'"

Martin thought his bandmates were kidding, but they weren't. After recording more than two dozen songs for their second album, the other members told Eric they wanted to record "To Be With You." It was the last song recorded, and the last song heard on the album. "Green-Tinted Sixties Mind" was the first single from the album. "To Be With You" wasn't scheduled to be a single until an AOR station in Lincoln, Nebraska, gave it heavy airplay as an album cut. It entered the Hot 100 the week of December 21, 1991—nine weeks later it was number one.

## THE TOP FIVE
*Week of February 29, 1992*

1 **To Be With You**
 Mr. Big

2 **I'm Too Sexy**
 Right Said Fred

3 **I Love Your Smile**
 Shanice

4 **Remember the Time**
 Michael Jackson

5 **Diamonds and Pearls**
 Prince and the New
 Power Generation

**806** ## Save the Best for Last WING 865 136-4
### VANESSA WILLIAMS

*Writers: Wendy Waldman*
*Jon Lind*
*Phil Galdston*

*Producer: Keith Thomas*

*March 21, 1992*
*5 weeks*

Most people did not know who Vanessa Williams was until they heard her sing "Happy Days Are Here Again" at the Miss America pageant in 1986, a performance that helped her become the first black Miss America in the history of the contest. Soon after, she became the first Miss America to resign in a sex-related scandal, when nude photographs of her were published in *Penthouse.* Anyone who thought her signing with Polygram's Wing label was based on her notoriety wasn't aware of a musical background that dates back to childhood.

Vanessa was born March 18, 1963, in Tarrytown, New York. She grew up in nearby Millwood, where her parents were music teachers. At five, Vanessa was playing piano, violin and flute, and later took up the French horn. "You have to have an exceptional ear to play the French horn," her father told *USA Today.* "That's why now she never sings off key."

Vanessa married Ramon Hervey, the public relations expert hired to handle her beauty-pageant resignation, on January 2, 1987. He became her manager and worked out a label deal with Ed Eckstine, then general manager of Wing. Her first album for the label, *The Right Stuff,* yielded five top 10 R&B hits as well as one top 10 hit on the pop chart, "Dreamin'."

For her second album, *The Comfort*

### THE TOP FIVE
*Week of March 21, 1992*

1 **Save the Best for Last**
   Vanessa Williams

2 **To Be With You**
   Mr. Big

3 **Tears in Heaven**
   Eric Clapton

4 **Remember the Time**
   Michael Jackson

5 **I'm Too Sexy**
   Right Said Fred

*Zone,* Vanessa recorded 25 tracks that were narrowed down to 14. "Running Back to You" was the first single; it peaked at number 18 in October, 1991. The title track was released next, but it stopped at number 62 in January, 1992. Vanessa's favorite song on the album was released as the third single.

"Save the Best for Last" was a title written down in a notebook kept by New York songwriter Phil Galdston. Working with writing partner Jon Lind [see 606—"Crazy for You"] in Los Angeles, they were struggling to write a song. "We went on one of our tangents, a half-hour detour into obscurity," Phil laughs. In those 30 minutes, they wrote the music to "Save the Best for Last" in one spontaneous stream of consciousness. Galdston mentioned he wanted to work on the lyric with Wendy Waldman, a singer/songwriter who had relocated from Los Angeles to Nashville.

A month later, when Galdston was on the way to Nashville, Lind reminded him to show Waldman "that little thing." "I thought it was really beautiful," says Wendy. "Phil said, 'I want to call it 'Save the Best for Last' and I said, 'What does that mean?'"

Galdston explains his intention: "My idea with this title was a reference to somebody hurting somebody at the very end of a relationship—it was cynical. And when I told Wendy that, she said, 'That's not right at all. It really has to be positive, because that's what the music sounds like to me. It's winning music, and it's got to have this surprise.' I said, 'Like kind of a "moon in June" kind of song,' and literally, she said, 'Like sometimes the snow comes down in June,' and I said, 'Oh yeah, sometimes the sun comes round the moon.'" Galdston protested it didn't make any sense, and Waldman replied it made perfect sense. "And the rest is history," Phil smiles.

"The demo was deliberately underproduced," Lind reports. "We didn't use a drum machine—just piano, sort of fretless bass sound, and strings. I produced Wendy's vocal; her rendering of the vocal was tremendous for the lyric." Waldman wanted to submit the song to all the pop divas. "I don't think it got to very many of them before it got to Ed Eckstine," Waldman says. "He put his foot down and said, 'We're cutting it. Don't show it to anyone else'."

*Writer: Jermaine Dupri*

*Producer: Jermaine Dupri*

*April 25, 1992*
*8 weeks*

**B**ABY RAPPERS Chris Smith (Mack Daddy) and Chris Kelly (Daddy Mack) were only 12 and 13 when they recorded "Jump," but their producer and mentor, Jermaine Dupri, was no stranger to youthful enthusiasm. He was only 12 himself when, impressed by Teddy Riley, he decided to become a record producer. At 14 he wrote his first song, for female rappers Silk Tymes Leather. He had also toured as a dancer with Whodini and Run-D.M.C. and worked as a DJ for rappers Fresh Set by the time he discovered Smith and Kelly in an Atlanta mall in 1990. Dupri was shopping with the women from Silk Tymes Leather when the two boys, looking for new sneakers, came up and asked for autographs.

The suburban youngsters reminded Dupri of himself at a younger age. "They were in the mall buying clothes and they were real fresh," he recalls. "I thought they were some teen stars I wasn't hip to. So I said, 'Who are you? What do you all do?' They said, 'No, we ain't no group.' Everybody else in the mall was looking at them the same way. People were paying attention. I said, 'If you have that captivation over people right now, if you had a record out, this might be ridiculous.'"

Dupri came up with a musical concept for the two longtime friends as well as a unique look: other kids wore their baseball caps backward, but Smith

### THE TOP FIVE
*Week of April 25, 1992*

1 **Jump**
  Kris Kross

2 **Save the Best for Last**
  Vanessa Williams

3 **Tears in Heaven**
  Eric Clapton

4 **Bohemian Rhapsody**
  Queen

5 **My Lovin' (You're Never Gonna Get It)**
  En Vogue

and Kelly wore their entire baggy outfits backward. Dupri's father, Michael Mauldin, was a former road manager for acts like Brick, the S.O.S. Band and Cameo, and he agreed to manage the youngsters, dubbed Kris Kross. Dupri produced a demo tape and was turned down by several labels before Joe Nicolo, head of the Columbia-distributed Ruffhouse imprint, took a chance in the spring of '91. The track that locked up the deal was "Lil' Boys in Da Hood." It revealed Kris Kross' unique perspective. Instead of singing about what was happening on the playground, they were dealing with adult themes like gang violence and drug problems, albeit without the profanity associated with gangsta rap.

Dupri spent two years working on the Kris Kross debut album, *Totally Krossed Out.* He got the idea for "Jump" while attending a concert. "I watched the crowd. I watched how people were just into jumping. Rappers had been doing it and I said we should make a record like this. I went home and wrote the song in an hour."

The single was released in February, 1992. Columbia's promotion team

delivered it to clubs and hip-hop radio shows. Pop and urban radio stations received the single a week later. And nothing happened. MTV added the video the second week in March. It wasn't until the third week in March that the single sold enough copies to debut on Billboard's Hot Rap Singles chart. An April 6 appearance on the Fox-TV series "In Living Color" is credited with a surge in sales and requests for the song at radio. The spike was recorded on the Hot 100, where "Jump" debuted at number 61 and dramatically jumped to number 12 in its second chart week. Two weeks later it was number one.

All involved with the recording reaped the benefits of its success. Mauldin was named president of the Columbia Record Group's black music division. Dupri started his own label, So So Def, scoring with Xscape and Da Brat. And Kris Kross fooled the critics who branded them as one-hit wonders by mining platinum with a second album, *Da Bomb,* and gold with a third, *Young, Rich & Dangerous.* They were 17-year-old veterans by the time their "Tonite's tha Nite" single peaked at number 12 in February, 1996.

# 808 I'll Be There COLUMBIA 74330
## MARIAH CAREY

*Writers: Berry Gordy, Jr.*
*Hal Davis*
*Willie Hutch*
*Bob West*

*Producers: Walter Afanasieff*
*Mariah Carey*

*June 20, 1992*
*2 weeks*

**W**HEN MTV ASKED Mariah Carey to star in one of their "Unplugged" shows, she had little experience performing live. "She was very young and very shy," confirms producer Walter Afanasieff. "So we put together a very easy show because of the rules of 'MTV Unplugged.' You can't do anything electric."

Two days before taping the show, Carey added one remake of an old hit to her repertoire. "I've been listening to Michael [Jackson] since I was a baby," she told Edna Gundersen of *USA Today*. "When he was a little boy, his singing was so angelic. It was unbelievable that such a voice could come from a child. He was a big influence on me." Carey chose the biggest Jackson 5 hit, "I'll Be There" [see 283], as the oldie she would perform on "Unplugged." She could have chosen almost anything, according to Afanasieff. "She actually knows every song ever written," he claims. "She's a walking encyclopedia of songs, from every Stevie Wonder song all the way to every Police record ever made. She carries around this 'hard disk' full of songs. And there's nothing she can't sing."

There were special advantages in selecting "I'll Be There," says Afanasi-

eff. "Having the young Michael Jackson be in the same sort of key as a female singer made it easy. Also making it easy was the fact that the Jackson 5 [recording had] one of the other brothers singing the almost-duet. It fell into place because here's Trey Lorenz standing next to her." Lorenz, from Florence, South Carolina, was a close friend and backing singer for Carey, and got his big break by joining her on "I'll Be There." That collaboration led to his own solo album for Columbia, with Carey producing six tracks. Her work on "Unplugged" helped her become a better producer, Carey told Melinda Newman in *Billboard*. "'Unplugged' taught me a lot about myself because I tend to nitpick everything I do and make it a little too perfect because I'm a perfectionist. I also learned a lot from working with Trey because when you're working with another singer and the singer's going, 'Oh I hate that, that sounds horrible,' and you're going, 'No, it's great,' that's what everyone always does to me. I'll always go over the real raw stuff and now I've gotten to the point where I understand that the raw stuff is usually better."

Carey's "I'll Be There," sounding very close to the original version by the

Jackson 5, was issued as a single by Columbia. That surprised Afanasieff. "We were thinking studio albums were the way for Mariah. And all of a sudden [the label] said, 'We've decided to release "I'll Be There" as a single,' and everyone said, 'This is going to postpone a new studio album,' which we were already starting to write and produce. But it was a pleasant departure. Once in a while it's really a joy to break away from the norm."

"I'll Be There" had been a milestone in the chart career of the Jackson 5. It was their fourth consecutive number one single, and made them the first act to reach the top of the Hot 100 with its first four releases. Ironically, Carey was the one to break that record, when "Emotions" [see 796] became her fifth consecutive number one. Out of her first 10 chart singles, only "Can't Let Go" and "Make It Happen" didn't reach the summit.

"I'll Be There" was the eighth song in the rock era to be number one by two different artists, following "Go Away Little Girl," "The Loco-Motion," "Please Mr. Postman," "Venus," "Lean on Me," "You Keep Me Hangin' On" and "When a Man Loves a Woman."

## THE TOP FIVE
*Week of June 20, 1992*

1. **I'll Be There**
   Mariah Carey

2. **Baby Got Back**
   Sir Mix-A-Lot

3. **Jump**
   Kris Kross

4. **Under the Bridge**
   Red Hot Chili Peppers

5. **My Lovin' (You're Never Gonna Get It)**
   En Vogue

*Writer: Sir Mix-A-Lot*

*Producer: Sir Mix-A-Lot*

*July 4, 1992*
*5 weeks*

**B**ORN IN SEATTLE, Anthony Ray grew up listening to the music of James Brown and Parliament-Funkadelic, but was also influenced by Kraftwerk, Gary Numan and Devo. Considering himself a "blue-collar" rapper, he became interested in the genre because he didn't like it. "I thought we spent a lot of time talking about how great we were: 'I'm awesome. I'm the bomb,' and blah blah blah. What if someone just told a common story that everybody could relate to? That's why I did songs like 'Posse on Broadway,' 'Beepers' and 'My Hooptie.'"

Those Sir Mix-A-Lot singles were released on the Nastymix label. Ray explains how he earned his moniker: "When samplers finally came along, it never occurred to me to steal somebody else's music. I would bust a beer bottle on the ground or shoot off guns—I would use anything. I've always assembled songs using funny, strange sounds. It's like my trademark—that's where I got the Mix-A-Lot tag." The rapper credits Greg Jones with starting his career. "He was the financial guy behind Nastymix and Ed Locke was the brains. It was back when independents ruled the whole rap game."

Legal hassles with Nastymix ensued at the same time his contract lapsed, and Sir Mix-A-Lot met with label executives from RCA, Chrysalis and Charisma. He wasn't aware that Rick Rubin from Def American was trying to get in touch with him. "He didn't know my number and he knew he was going to have a hard time getting it from Nastymix. So he had someone call Nastymix and say they were from *Right On* magazine. I'm expecting to do this interview at 4:00 with *Right On* and a lady on the phone says, 'Rick Rubin wishes to speak to you.' And I'm thinking, 'He works for *Right On* now? I thought he was doing a little bit better than that!'"

The artist was making a video for "My Hooptie" when he got the idea for "Baby Got Back." He explains, "A lot of the girls at the video were telling me they couldn't get parts because they were too fat. And I said, 'Too fat? Your waist is 23 inches. What are you talking about?' 'Yeah, but my ass is 38 inches.'" Admitting he's attracted to curvy women and not the "straight up and down 10-year-old boy look," the rapper said he still tried to make the song as nonsexist as possible. "But you couldn't do 'Baby Got Brains' and sell records."

Mix-A-Lot credits his manager Ricardo Frazer and Def American founder Rubin with choosing "Baby Got Back" for single release. "I said, 'Are you sure? I mean, we're doing a song about asses!' Then we won a Grammy for it. That won't happen again, I'll bet." Making the video for an ode to rear ends also presented challenges. The rapper credits director Adam Bernstein with giving the video a comedic edge without offending too many people. "Of course, it eventually got banned from MTV. But as much as I hate the fact that they banned it, I have to appreciate that they made that record. MTV and the Video Jukebox combined put radio on that record. Because initially radio ran from it."

The artist was surprised at the negative aspects of having a number one single. "The great thing about rap is that the fans have a tendency to say out with the old and in with the new. That's easy to accept when you're the new. But when you reach the pinnacle, there ain't nowhere else to go. There's no number zero. You're going down. Initially I had to readjust my ego. As far as the business is concerned, I had to understand that this is what has to happen in order for things to move on. And then I started to diversify, so now I'm doing many other things." That includes having his own studio in the Pacific Northwest, producing other artists and running his own label, Rhyme Cartel.

## THE TOP FIVE
*Week of July 4, 1992*

1 **Baby Got Back**
   Sir Mix-A-Lot

2 **I'll Be There**
   Mariah Carey

3 **Under the Bridge**
   Red Hot Chili Peppers

4 **Jump**
   Kris Kross

5 **If You Asked Me To**
   Celine Dion

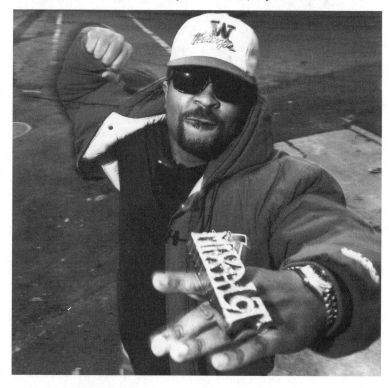

# 810 This Used to Be My Playground
SIRE 18822

MADONNA

Writers: *Madonna*
*Shep Pettibone*

Producers: *Madonna*
*Shep Pettibone*

August 8, 1992
1 week

IN 1943, CHICAGO Cubs owner P.K. Wrigley founded the All American Girls Professional Baseball League, in a contingency move to keep the sport of baseball alive in case the major leagues had to close down because of the Second World War. The women proved to be so popular that their stereotype-shattering league was active until 1954, and their exploits were retold years later in a documentary for PBS. In 1992, director Penny Marshall and screenwriters Lowell Ganz and Babaloo Mandell brought the story of the female baseball players to the big screen under the title *A League of Their Own.*

Music supervisor Jay Landers was working at Columbia Records when label president Don Ienner asked him to read the film's script. "I thought it was terrific and Michael Dilbeck, head of music for Columbia Pictures, and I decided we could put a good soundtrack together," Landers says. "Penny Marshall was very receptive to our musical ideas. And the one thing that made this record particularly easy to do was that everyone in the music community was such a big fan of Penny that we didn't need to go hat in hand to anyone, because they were all eager to help her."

Marshall's concept for the soundtrack was to have contemporary artists recording music of the period. "She wanted it to be very accurate to the actual time frame," explains Landers, so that a song from 1944 would not be heard in a scene taking place in 1943. "The picture is book-ended by modern day footage," adds the music supervisor. "So the film starts with a reunion and Carole King wrote the opening song. And Madonna was in the movie, so it was only natural to want her to sing a song. There was some early hesitation about whether she should step out of character so you suddenly hear Madonna's voice over the end titles, but ultimately there was enough separation between the character and Madonna that Penny, Mike and myself felt it would be okay."

Shep Pettibone recalls that he and Madonna had just completed work on their first ballad together, "Rain," when Marshall called her star and asked if she would record a song for the film. "Madonna said she really didn't have anything," says Pettibone. But the director wanted a ballad and they had just finished one that turned out well. "I came up with a track that night and Madonna came over the next day and said, 'I have an idea for it.'" Two days later, they had completed "This Used to Be My Playground." They sent the track off to Marshall for her reaction. "We immediately loved it," says Landers. "We all thought it would be a very successful record and we knew right away it would be perfect."

Recording the track was a new experience for Pettibone, as it was the first time he had worked with all live musi-cians. "We took the track and put a live drummer to it and live strings and live piano. We didn't have any strings written for the song [originally]. Jeremy Lubbock was chosen to do the arrangement on the strings and I think that had a lot to do with the final outcome of the song. He did a great job," says the producer.

Marshall completed her rough cut of the film but wasn't ready to show it to any of the actors yet. Landers was driving down Doheny Boulevard in Los Angeles with a copy of the film when a car pulled alongside his and he realized it was Madonna, driving herself somewhere. "I rolled down the window and held up the tape and said, 'You are so terrific in this movie! You're going to be so happy!' She chased me all the way down Doheny and at the next red light said, 'Who are you? Can I see the movie?' And I said, 'No, I'm sorry,' and drove away."

## THE TOP FIVE
*Week of August 8, 1992*

1 **This Used to Be My Playground**
Madonna

2 **Baby Got Back**
Sir Mix-A-Lot

3 **Baby-Baby-Baby**
TLC

4 **End of the Road**
Boyz II Men

5 **November Rain**
Guns N' Roses

MOTOWN 2178 **End of the Road** 811
BOYZ II MEN

*Writers: Babyface*
*L.A. Reid*
*Daryl Simmons*

*Producers: L.A. Reid*
*Babyface*

*August 15, 1992*
*13 weeks*

For 36 years, Elvis Presley held the record for the longest-running number one single of the rock era. His two-sided RCA release, "Don't Be Cruel"/ "Hound Dog," had ruled for 11 weeks and no one else had matched or surpassed that figure. Then along came Motown's Philly quartet, Boyz II Men, with a song produced by L.A. Reid and Babyface for the soundtrack of an Eddie Murphy movie. The 13-week reign of "End of the Road" shattered the King's record and made news all over the world. It's a good thing Babyface didn't keep the song for himself, as he almost did.

"End of the Road" was written specifically for Boyz II Men. Reid and Babyface wanted to work with the quartet and called Motown and the group's manager Michael Bivins. The song was also written specifically for *Boomerang*. "There was a scene I had in mind for it and it didn't get in that scene," says Babyface. "When I was close to finishing the song, L.A. and Daryl [Simmons] came in and helped me finish the lyrics. As it was being written, I kept thinking, 'This is a bad song.' I sang the demo. When I did, I thought, 'Maybe I can do this song.' It was certainly something I was considering, but then I thought Boyz II Men would take it further. That was probably one of the better feelings I've had in terms of handing a song over to somebody and watching them work it."

And the work went very quickly. "They had three hours to record the song," reports Reid. "We flew in from Atlanta to Philadelphia and went to the studio. When they got there, they told us, 'Tomorrow we have to be on tour.' So they did all the background vocals and all the individual lead vocals in three hours, which is unheard of. Well, not unheard of back in the Frank Sinatra or Nancy Wilson days, but now you take a day to do the background vocals, and then you think about it."

Shawn Stockman, Wanya Morris, Nathan Morris and Michael McCary met when they were students at the High School for Creative and Performing Arts in South Philadelphia. After performing in a school talent show, the four members seriously considered turning professional. In March, 1989, they sneaked into an invitation-only concert sponsored by radio station WUSL-FM. New Edition spin-off group Bell Biv DeVoe was performing, and the four students caught Michael Bivins as he was coming off stage. They spontaneously auditioned for him with an excerpt of New Edition's "Can You Stand the Rain." Impressed, Bivins gave Nathan his phone number. At a subsequent meeting in New York, Bivins agreed to be their manager and arranged for the group to be signed to Motown. Their name, Boyz II Men, was a further tribute to their idols, New Edition. That quintet had recorded a song called "Boys to Men" on their 1988 album *Heart Break*. Boyz II Men's first album, *Cooleyhighharmony*, yielded two singles that reached the top three: "Motownphilly," which spoke to their love of Motown music as well as the Philly sound they grew up with, and "It's So Hard to Say Goodbye to Yesterday," an *a cappella* remake of a G.C. Cameron song from the soundtrack of *Cooley High.*

The quartet's first number one single was "End of the Road." Babyface considers the song one of his very best. "As a writer, I always wanted to have one record that would be considered a classic. Not to sound vain, but I think that's my first classic. That's the first record I know will be played for a long time because of how those guys sing it."

| THE TOP FIVE |
| --- |
| *Week of August 15, 1992* |

| | | |
| --- | --- | --- |
| 1 | **End of the Road** Boyz II Men | |
| 2 | **Baby-Baby-Baby** TLC | |
| 3 | **This Used to Be My Playground** Madonna | |
| 4 | **Baby Got Back** Sir Mix-A-Lot | |
| 5 | **November Rain** Guns N' Roses | |

# How Do You Talk to an Angel
CAPITOL 44890

## THE HEIGHTS

Writers: Barry Coffing
    Steve Tyrell
    Stephanie Tyrell

Producer: Steve Tyrell

November 14, 1992
2 weeks

STEVE TYRELL had plenty of opportunities to work on soundtrack projects when he was head of A&R for Scepter Records in the '60s. In conjunction with songwriter Burt Bacharach, Tyrell's projects included *Alfie, Butch Cassidy and the Sundance Kid* and *Valley of the Dolls*. He was an established songwriter and producer by 1991, when he and George Duke were the supervising music producers on Robert Townsend's film for Twentieth Century-Fox, *The Five Heartbeats*.

That same year, another musically themed film, *The Commitments*, told the story of a group of working-class Irish youths who form a band. The success of the film inspired televison producer Aaron Spelling to come up with a weekly series for the Fox network about working-class American kids who form a band. When Spelling asked Fox executives to suggest a music supervisor for "The Heights," they told him about Tyrell's work on *The Five Heartbeats*.

Brought in at the very beginning of the project, Tyrell was involved before any actors were cast for the pilot. "Jamie Walters came in to audition in my studio and played a song called 'So Hot' on guitar," Tyrell recalls. "I imme-diately loved the sound of his voice and the hooky, bluesy licks. I called Spelling and said, 'You should hire this guy. He looks like James Dean and sounds like Bryan Adams. And he can act!'" Tyrell didn't know that Spelling already had an actor in mind to play the leader of the group. Shawn David Thompson won that role, but Walters was cast as Alex O'Brien, the shy lyricist with a crush on the female sax player.

Tyrell suggested to Tony Spiridakis, who created the series with Eric Roth, that the lyricist turn out to be a guitarist and a singer and that at the end of the pilot he be invited to join the band.

With his wife, Stephanie, and Barry Coffing, Tyrell wrote a song about the lyricist trying to express his romantic feelings. Stephanie came up with the title "How Do You Talk to an Angel." Soon after the pilot was filmed, Tyrell was at a party when a man stepped up to him and congratulated him on the song he had written for the show. "He said, 'I think it's a smash.' And I said, 'Man, you made my day.' He told me, 'I'm going to have my father-in-law call you' and went away." Curious, Tyrell asked another party guest who the man was. "And he said, 'That's Jamie Kellner, the head of Fox, you idiot!' And I said, 'Who's his father-in-law?' and he replied, 'Joe Smith.'" Tyrell knew who Joe Smith was: the president of Capitol Records. The next day, Smith called and wanted to know if Tyrell could have an entire soundtrack album ready to come out in the fall to coincide with the series' premiere.

It was only after all the songs were recorded that Capitol A&R exec Tim Devine agreed that "How Do You Talk to an Angel" should be the first single. To promote the series, the Fox network sent a DAT tape of the song to the program director of WEGX in Philadelphia. He added it immediately and it became the station's most requested song. Sister station Z100 in New York added it next, and the same thing happened. And Capitol hadn't even released the single yet.

The series premiered on August 27, 1992, to disappointing ratings. The premiere episode earned a 6.7 rating/12 share and never exceeded those numbers. By the time the single debuted on the Hot 100 in October, the series' rating average was 5.4/10. The record hit number one the week of November 14, becoming the first song from a TV series to hit the top of the Hot 100 since 1985 [see 622—"Miami Vice Theme"]. Less than a week after "Angel" fell from number one, the series' final episode was telecast.

"One thing I'm real proud of about the song is that it knocked off 'End of the Road,'" says Tyrell. "At the time that was the biggest record of all time and our little song from a TV show cruised right on up there and knocked it out of number one."

The Heights turned out to be one-hit wonders. Jamie Walters had a happier fate: he was cast in Spelling's "Beverly Hills 90210," and signed to Atlantic Records. In April, 1995, his single "Hold On" peaked at number 16 on the Hot 100.

## THE TOP FIVE
*Week of November 14, 1992*

1 **How Do You Talk to an Angel**
  The Heights

2 **End of the Road**
  Boyz II Men

3 **I'd Die Without You**
  P.M. Dawn

4 **If I Ever Fall in Love**
  Shai

5 **Sometimes Love Just Ain't Enough**
  Patty Smyth w/Don Henley

Writer: Dolly Parton

Producer: David Foster

November 28, 1992
14 weeks

As MUSIC supervisor on *The Body-guard*, Maureen Crowe had to find a song that would serve two purposes. Early in the film, Kevin Costner's former secret service agent takes Whitney Houston's superstar singer to a blue-collar bar, and the song playing on the jukebox had to illustrate the body-guard's workaday world to contrast it to the glamorous Hollywood lifestyle of Houston's character. Near the end of the film, after he has saved her life, she sings the song back to him as a tribute. The song originally selected was "What Becomes of the Brokenhearted," a number seven hit for Motown's Jimmy Ruffin in 1966. "I had demoed it and was ready to record it with Whitney," says producer David Foster.

"Initially the bar was playing oldies," explains Crowe. "It was going to be the original recording and then Whitney was going to do a version of it. And to be frank, the version wasn't really coming together." But they were still working on it when Paul Young released the same song from *Fried*

*Green Tomatoes*. Foster adds, "I picked up *Billboard* and there it was on the chart. We were due to go in the next day." Foster called Costner immediately and told him there was a problem. Costner requested that the producer wait 24 hours so the actor could find a replacement song.

Crowe asked film producer Jim Wilson to describe the bar to her. He told her it was a western bar, but they didn't want country music playing because it was in California. He still wanted an oldie, preferably a Motown song. Crowe told him, "Well, if it's oldies, it could also be the Eagles or Linda Ronstadt." The producer agreed, and Crowe put together a cassette with more Motown classics and a song that Linda Ronstadt recorded on her *Prisoner in Disguise* album, a remake of Dolly Parton's "I Will Always Love You."

Wilson and Costner made the final selection, and Foster, who wasn't familiar with the song, produced a demo for Houston to hear. "She loved it," says Foster, who then recorded the song with Houston in Miami. "It was a typical film thing where we did it with three cameras rolling at one time so she could do it live," explains Crowe. "We flew her band in. She only did five takes and the fourth take was the magic take. Kevin and I just jumped and David came out

of the truck and we all went up on stage and said, 'That was definitely it.'" At first the director didn't need the third verse of the song for the film, but then decided to have it recorded for a montage. Whitney went into the studio to record the third verse, which had been spoken in Parton's original recording and eliminated from Ronstadt's version.

Foster initally resisted Costner's request for an *a cappella* opening. "He said, 'It would be so great for my movie.' I said, 'Kevin, that's really a stupid idea. I'm not going to do it for the record.'" The actor asked if Foster would record it that way just for the film. "So then she's onstage in Miami and steps up to the mike and the whole place was captivated," Foster remembers. "I couldn't imagine putting music around it."

The record producer says Arista Records president Clive Davis loved the recording. "In fact, he loved the rough mix, and the rough mix is what (was released)." As the first single from the soundtrack to *The Bodyguard*, "I Will Always Love You" debuted on the Hot 100 at number 40. The next week it was number 12, and one week later it was number one. Parton's original recording had topped the country singles chart in June, 1974, and a re-recording from the soundtrack of *The Best Little Whore-house in Texas* also went to number one, in October, 1982.

Two weeks after Boyz II Men broke the 36-year-old record set by Elvis Presley's "Don't Be Cruel"/"Hound Dog" as the longest-running No. 1 single of the rock era, Whitney Houston began a run at the top of the Hot 100 that would result in a new champion. "I Will Always Love You" was the first single to be No. 1 for 14 weeks.

## THE TOP FIVE
*Week of November 28, 1992*

1 **I Will Always Love You**
   Whitney Houston

2 **How Do You Talk to an Angel**
   The Heights

3 **If I Ever Fall in Love**
   Shai

4 **Rump Shaker**
   Wreckx-N-Effect

5 **I'd Die Without You**
   P.M. Dawn

# A Whole New World (Aladdin's Theme) COLUMBIA 74751
## PEABO BRYSON and REGINA BELLE

*Writers: Alan Menken*
*Tim Rice*

*Producer: Walter Afanasieff*

*March 6, 1993*
*1 week*

Lyricist Tim Rice was in talks with the Walt Disney Studios as early as 1990 about a film version of *Evita*. "I met Jeffrey Katzenberg and told him I would really like to work in films because I've always preferred films to theater," Rice says. Disney executives invited him to act as a music consultant on a Dolly Parton film, *Straight Talk*, and then asked if he would like to write lyrics for a new animated feature about a lion.

At the Disney studios in Burbank, Rice got an advance look at a new film in production, *Beauty and the Beast*. "They said they had done all their hits so far with Alan Menken and Howard Ashman, but they wanted to get some new teams going," Rice recalls. He was asked who he would like to compose the music if he could choose anyone he wanted. Rice suggested two names: Elton John and Benny Andersson, one of his co-writers on *Chess*. Shortly after the deal with Elton was finalized and work had begun, Howard Ashman died of complications from AIDS. Menken and Ashman had been working on a new film, *Aladdin*, but the score was not complete. Rice was asked if he would like to partner with Menken, and worked on both films at the same time.

"The main thing missing was the big ballad," says the songwriter. "There wasn't a tune or anything." Rice and Menken collaborated at the latter's home in New York, but Rice had to be

## THE TOP FIVE
### Week of March 6, 1993

1. **A Whole New World (Aladdin's Theme)**
   Peabo Bryson & Regina Belle

2. **I Will Always Love You**
   Whitney Houston

3. **Ordinary World**
   Duran Duran

4. **Informer**
   Snow

5. **Nuthin' But a 'G' Thang**
   Dr. Dre

in London so Menken and Chris Montan, executive music producer for Walt Disney Feature Animation, flew to Britain and worked in Rice's home to write the song that would accompany Aladdin and Jasmine's magic carpet ride. Menken played some tunes he had written, and Rice came up with the title "A Whole New World." The song was completed quickly, but the film dictated some changes. "As I found with *The Lion King*, you write a song and there may be nothing wrong with it, but then the director decides that the sequence will be 30 seconds shorter or longer, and they must have a reference to a magic carpet ride at some point. There were lots of changes like that, but it sounded to me like a pretty good song." One thing that did not change was a lyric at the end that Rice included as a tribute to a childhood hero. "There was a wonderful British pop singer called Billy Fury. And one of his hits in England was 'A Wondrous Place.' It was a great, weird pop record, way ahead of its time. Lots of echoes and minimalist backing. Sort of Peggy Lee meets Chris Isaak. As a tribute to Billy Fury, I quite deliberately put in at the end of the song the line 'a wondrous place.'"

Rice was in the studio when Brad Kane and Lea Salonga recorded the version heard during the film. Then it was Montan's responsibility to find two pop recording artists to cut a version that would be released as a single.

"They were trying to get people like Barbra Streisand and George Michael," says Rice. "I was so glad in the end none of these people wanted to do it because we got two singers who are quite wonderful and who weren't automatic number ones. Imagine if it was Barbra Streisand and George Michael, you'd say yes, it was number one because it was them."

The singers were Peabo Bryson, who had recorded a duet with Celine Dion for *Beauty and the Beast*, and Regina Belle. Walter Afanasieff, who produced the Bryson-Dion recording, was asked to produce the Bryson-Belle track. Armed with the film clip, Menken's version at the piano and a pop-oriented piano demo by Robbie Buchanan, Afanasieff went into the studio. Bryson and Belle were in the studio at the same time to record their vocals. "When you're doing a duet, you create so much spirit together," says the producer.

As co-author of *The Guinness Book of Number One Hits* and *British Hit Singles*, Rice was particularly pleased to be part of chart history by ending the 14-week run of Whitney Houston's record-setting No. 1 hit, "I Will Always Love You." Three weeks after the single became the first song from a Disney animated film to top the Hot 100, Rice and Menken collected an Oscar for "A Whole New World," making it the 15th chart-topper to win an Academy Award for Best Original Song.

*Writers: Darrin O'Brien*
*Shawn Moltke*
*Edmond Leary*

*Producer: M.C. Shan*

*March 13, 1993*
*7 weeks*

"INFORMER" WAS the fifth reggae song to reach the pinnacle of the Hot 100, following "I Can See Clearly Now" by Johnny Nash, "The Tide Is High" by Blondie, "Red Red Wine" by UB40 and "Close to You" by Maxi Priest. When the Canadian dancehall rapper known as Snow hit pole position in America, he helped make chart history. During the very same week, "Oh Carolina" by Shaggy was number one in Britain, and it was the first time that two different reggae songs topped the charts on both sides of the pond.

Darrin Kenneth O'Brien grew up in a Toronto housing project. He heard a lot of R&B music because that's what his mother loved most. As a child, he also listened to Kiss and Ozzy Osbourne, but by the age of 10 he was more into "Rapper's Delight" by the Sugarhill Gang. "At 14, I got into reggae music because a lot of Jamaicans moved into my community," says the artist. "My next door neighbor's cousin would come up from New York every month and bring [reggae] tapes. I'd copy them and try to sing like them." But O'Brien wasn't looking to develop any kind of personal style. "I didn't really want to be a singer so I'd sing like other people. I'd imitate everybody else. Then around 19 years old I got my own style." He sang at basement parties and dances, usually drunk. In 1989

the high school dropout was charged with two counts of murder and sent to jail. The charges were later reduced, and he was acquitted. During his confinement, he wrote the song "Informer" about his experience of being framed for attempted murder.

Singing for his fellow inmates and getting their positive reaction made him think being a recording artist would be easy. After his release, he went to New York for the first time because his friend DJ Prince's girlfriend lived there. A demo tape came to the attention of rapper/producer M.C. Shan, who introduced him to Steve Salem and David Eng. They became O'Brien's managers. He was dubbed Snow because audiences fascinated with the white reggae artist called him "Snow White."

With M.C. Shan as producer, Snow recorded his *12 Inches of Snow* album for EastWest, and discovered it was hard work. "I thought you could just sing and do it. I didn't know you had to be perfect. 'Do it again. Do it again. Harmonize on that. Do that.' So I smashed a couple of headphones and a couple of booths. Other than that, it was fun. It was an experience for me because I had nothing else going for my life. I'd go home and drink and hang in the neighborhood." After completing the album, Snow was brought up on another assault charge and sent back to jail for eight months. "I said, 'I'll see

you guys later. Do what you want with the record.'"

EastWest released the rap-oriented "Lonely Monday Morning" as the first single, with no photo identification of the artist, just the name Snow. Label president Sylvia Rhone explained that the idea was to gain credibility in the ethnic market so Snow wouldn't be perceived as a "white boy trying to copy a black art form." The second single was "Informer," and it was originally targeted for reggae/dancehall and R&B audiences. During the 1992 Christmas season, WHQT (Hot 97) in New York added the record and it quickly became number one in requests.

Before going back to jail, Snow had filmed a video. The first time he saw it was from inside prison walls. The interactive music video channel The Box had added it, and the clip became the station's most requested video. At his manager's suggestion, a captioned version was produced so audiences could understand the lyrics.

His eight-month sentence at an end, Snow was immediately sent out on the road to promote "Informer." He remembers, "I was in Germany on a plane and Steve, my manager, says, 'Oh yeah, by the way, you went number one in *Billboard*.' I freaked out. I told the stewardess and she looked at me like I was crazy. I was 37,000 feet above the ground and it made me feel even higher."

## THE TOP FIVE
*Week of March 13, 1993*

1 **Informer**
Snow

2 **A Whole New World
(Aladdin's Theme)**
Peabo Bryson & Regina Belle

3 **Nuthin' But a 'G' Thang**
Dr. Dre

4 **Ordinary World**
Duran Duran

5 **I'm Every Woman**
Whitney Houston

## 816 Freak Me  KEIA/ELEKTRA 64654
### SILK

Writers: Keith Sweat
   Roy Murray

Producers: Keith Sweat
   T.H.

May 1, 1993
2 weeks

THE MEMBERS of Decatur, Georgia-based Silk got their big break in the summer of 1991 when they met manager Louise Ferguson. Her husband, Lonnie, was Keith Sweat's road manager. After hearing the group audition at her home, Louise invited them back the following week for a Fourth of July barbecue. "We get there and the buzz is that Keith Sweat is upstairs," recalls Gary Glenn, also known as "Big G" of Silk. "We meet him and shake his hand. And we go downstairs and stay out of his way." Some kids who knew they were a group asked the guys to sing, and they performed an *a cappella* version of "Greatest Love of All." Later that night, Sweat invited the group to meet him in a recording studio where he was working on a track for his *Keep It Comin'* album. "He asked us to listen to the song and harmonize on some background vocals. And we thought that was that."

But Sweat had more in mind. He invited Silk to join him on tour and sing backing vocals as well as some leads. When it came time to promote *Keep It Comin'*, Sweat included the group in his appearances on shows like Arsenio Hall's late night talk program. "I don't think we realized the magnitude of what we were doing," says Glenn. "We were just eager to show people that we could sing and that we had talent."

### THE TOP FIVE
*Week of May 1, 1993*

1  **Freak Me**
   Silk

2  **Informer**
   Snow

3  **Nuthin' But a 'G' Thang**
   Dr. Dre

4  **I Have Nothing**
   Whitney Houston

5  **Love Is**
   Vanessa Williams & Brian McKnight

Glenn was still employed at Domino's Pizza when the group began work on a sexually suggestive track called "Freak Me" for their debut album. The other members of the group—Timothy Cameron, Jimmy Gates, Jr., Gary Jenkins and Jonathan Rasboro—were concerned that Glenn would not like the song. "I was the 'choir boy,'" he laughs. Sweat held back the lyrics from Glenn until the group was in the studio, ready to record. "I heard what the lyrics were saying and everybody looked at me. I looked around the room and just dedicated myself to singing the song. I didn't think it would be a hit. I didn't want this to be how we're known." After Sweat gave the group a demo of their first album, scheduled for release on his own Keia label, Glenn played it for his cousin, who reacted immediately when he heard "Freak Me." He said, "This song is the hit."

Apparently label executives didn't agree, because the first single was "Happy Days." Glenn suggests that it was chosen "because it was a good uptempo song and Keith sang with us." While visiting Houston during the Christmas holidays, Glenn was surprised to hear "Freak Me" being played on different radio stations. "Every time

we changed the channel, it was the number one song. I was upset because 'Happy Days' wasn't being played. There was one station doing a countdown, and they said, 'The number one song is Silk.' And then comes 'Happy Days.' I thought, finally! And then it went right into 'Freak Me.'"

Back at work at Domino's in Atlanta, Glenn got a call from Sweat to let him know that the label was going with "Freak Me" as the second single. After six years of making and delivering pizzas, and even managing the store, Glenn left his job and watched "Freak Me" move up the Hot 100. It went to number two and stayed there for five weeks, held out of the top spot by Snow's "Informer." Glenn admits, "We were so green, we didn't know a lot about watching the charts back then. We were doing a video for 'Girl U for Me,' and after the shoot we went back to our trailer and there was a cake and champagne. They surprised us and said, 'You guys are number one. Congratulations!' The five of us got in our limo and that was the first moment the reality of this whole thing hit us. We said a prayer to God and toasted among ourselves and that was our moment. Our biggest moment."

VIRGIN 12650 **That's the Way Love Goes**
JANET JACKSON
**817**

*Writers: Janet Jackson*
*James Harris III*
*Terry Lewis*

*Producers: Jimmy Jam*
*Terry Lewis*
*Janet Jackson*

*May 15, 1993*
*8 weeks*

WHEN JANET JACKSON signed to Virgin Records in March, 1991, it was headline news. Her $32 million contract was the largest recording deal in history, although it was eclipsed soon after by her brother Michael when he signed a $50 million pact to remain with Epic Records. A little over two years after moving from A&M to Virgin, Janet released her first single under the new deal. "That's the Way Love Goes," a preview of her *janet.* album, debuted at number 14. A mere two weeks later, it was Janet's sixth number one on the Hot 100.

There had been a lot of legal wrangling between the managers of Jackson and her producers, Jimmy Jam and Terry Lewis, before recording began on her *Rhythm Nation* album [see 744—"Miss You Much"]. The mood was quite different going into *janet.*, according to Jimmy Jam. "It was pretty clear we wanted to work together. She came to Minneapolis and we had our first meeting to shape a direction for the record. We had written down an overview of things we felt would work well. She had done the same thing. And when we compared notes, we were 95 percent on the same page. So that was a good start."

The album reflected the lives of Janet and her producers. "We were all in very happy relationships and we were in love, not only with the people we were in relationships with, but with life in general. We'd been very successful professionally, and I think we were all feeling very satisfied with our personal lives, and that came out in the album. Also, she was fully a woman. When we did *Control* she was 18 or 19. *Rhythm Nation* was the thoughts of a girl realizing as a young adult you have to do something to make a change. And *janet.* was about a confident, sexy woman in touch with her feminine side. That was what she was feeling at that time, so our job was to enhance that."

"That's the Way Love Goes" began as a loop of a sample from James Brown's number one R&B hit from 1974, "Papa Don't Take No Mess." Jackson wasn't excited about the track the first time she heard it, so Jam and Lewis gave her a tape of it just as she was leaving for a Christmas vacation and asked her to listen to it for a couple of weeks. When she returned, she told the producers, "You know that track you did? I love it. It's absolutely the bomb." Janet came up with the title, and the first draft had the lovelorn tone one would expect from such a title. Then she called Jimmy Jam at 2 in the morning to tell him she was taking a different direction, casting the lyrics in a more seductive light.

Jam and Lewis needed permission from James Brown to sample his work, and assured him that as it was a Janet Jackson song, it would be all right. "He said, 'Oh no, I've got to see the lyrics and make sure it's okay,' because a bunch of rappers were taking his songs and putting all these foul lyrics on them. So we sent him the lyrics and he approved them," says Jimmy Jam.

Although it sounds like there are male voices chanting the title on the track, the producer asserts that Janet did all of the vocals. "That is her voice being electronically manipulated. I stuck it in a sampler and played around with it. When I played it back for her, she really liked it. We kept it in, but it wasn't part of the plan. Sometimes stuff like that just happens."

Jam and Lewis had a little bit of a fight with Virgin over which single to release first. "Everybody was talking about 'If,'" says Jimmy Jam. "To me, your first single should say, 'Welcome to the album. If you like this, check out the rest.' And we really felt 'That's the Way Love Goes' was in keeping with the spirit of the rest of the album. And since it went to number one, we proved that we were right!"

---

## THE TOP FIVE
*Week of May 15, 1993*

1 **That's the Way Love Goes**
Janet Jackson

2 **Freak Me**
Silk

3 **Love Is**
Vanessa Williams & Brian McKnight

4 **Informer**
Snow

5 **I Have Nothing**
Whitney Houston

**818** | **Weak** RCA 62521
SWV

*Writer: Brian Alexander Morgan*

*Producer: Brian Alexander Morgan*

*July 10, 1993*
*2 weeks*

THE SUCCESS OF female hip-hop groups like TLC and En Vogue inspired RCA to search for its own distaff outfit. Label executive Skip Miller hit platinum paydirt when he found SWV (Sisters With Voices), a trio of vocalists from Brooklyn and the Bronx who first sang together when they were 12 years old. In junior high, Cheryl (Coko) Gamble, Tamara (Taj) Johnson and Leanne (Lelee) Lyons called themselves Female Edition after their favorite group, New Edition.

Coko and Lelee turned to gospel music in high school, but when they decided to sing R&B, they reunited with Taj. Under the aegis of manager Maureen Singleton, they came to the attention of RCA and signed a multi-album deal. A majority of the tracks on their first album, *It's About Time*, were produced by Brian Alexander Morgan. A Wichita, Kansas songwriter and record producer transplanted to Sacramento, California, Morgan had been signed to Warner Brothers Records in 1987. Dropped from the label two years later, he concentrated on composing to survive. "I wrote a series of songs I thought were going to be for me; I was trying to shop a solo deal," he recalls. One of the songs, "Weak," was inspired by an artist Morgan knew in Sacramento. "Her name is Chanté Moore," he says. "I was unable to get into a relationship with her because she was with someone else. So I wrote the song

## THE TOP FIVE
*Week of July 10, 1993*

1  **Weak**
   SWV

2  **That's the Way Love Goes**
   Janet Jackson

3  **Whoomp! (There It Is)**
   Tag Team

4  **Can't Help Falling in Love**
   UB40

5  **Knockin' Da Boots**
   H-Town

about how I felt being around her." Without a record deal of his own, Morgan wanted to place the song with Charlie Wilson of the Gap Band so the group could record it, but he was unsuccessful. By 1992, the song was still unrecorded, and Morgan shifted tactics. He decided to target a specific artist and write for that person. Hooked up with Martha Wash, he wrote and produced "Give It To You," which became a dance hit on RCA. That led label exec Kenny Ortiz to team Morgan up with a group the label wanted to sign, SWV.

Morgan sent a tape of demos to the trio. "'Weak' was the last song on the tape," remembers Taj of SWV. "The way he recorded the tape, there was a big space before the song, so whenever we'd listen to the tape, we would never get to 'Weak' because we didn't think there were any more songs on the tape. So Brian said, 'Did you learn "Weak"?' and we said, 'What's that?' We listened to it and told him, 'How could you put

this so far back on the tape? This should have been the first song!' So we learned the song and recorded it in a day. We had a lot of fun working with Brian in the studio because he was as young as we were. We were just a bunch of kids cutting up in the studio, but getting the job done." Taj allows that Morgan was a perfectionist. "We stood in that booth forever. If he heard a little inkling of a flat note or if it was just a tiny bit sharp—nothing the average ear could hear—we'd have to get it right until he was satisfied."

The first single from the album was the original version of "Right Here," but it only climbed to number 92. The follow-up, "I'm So Into You," established SWV on the Hot 100 as the single peaked at number six. Then came "Weak," which had the strength to reach the top of the chart. The fourth single was a remix of "Right Here" that included excerpts from Michael Jackson's "Human Nature." The new combination spent three weeks at number two.

VIRGIN 12653 **Can't Help Falling in Love**
UB40

**819**

*Writers: George David Weiss*
*Hugo Peretti*
*Luigi Creatore*

*Producers: UB40*

*July 24, 1993*
*7 weeks*

**W**HEN UB40 RECORDED "Can't Help Falling in Love," it was for the soundtrack of a movie—but not the one it ended up in. "We were asked to record any Elvis tune for *Honeymoon in Vegas*," reports the band's Robin Campbell. "Our drummer, Jimmy, picked it just because he remembered it. We thought that they would really like it, but we weren't that pleased with it ourselves." What the eight members of UB40 didn't know was that about 200 other artists were also asked to contribute their remakes of Presley songs, so there were bound to be multiple versions for the producers to choose from. "Can't Help Falling in Love" ended up in the film, but by Bono of U2, not UB40.

Enter Tim Sexton, music supervisor for the film *Sliver.* He approached Virgin Records to release the soundtrack because they had several artists he wanted to use on the soundtrack, including UB40. "Primarily they had Massive Attack, who I was a fan of, and Enigma. The idea was to take a seductive, sexy sort of industrial rock approach, blending dance rhythms with a kind of hard-edged, odd sound that you wouldn't normally hear in a movie." Sexton agrees with critics who complained that unlike Ira Levin's original novel, the movie starring Sharon Stone, William Baldwin and Tom Berenger did not hold togeth-

er. "The best thing about the movie, if I say so myself, was the music. It became a character in the piece. We were going for stuff that was voyeuristic, and that's where Enigma and Massive Attack came in. And in the process, we had to find something we could take to radio. I needed a song that was radio friendly, and the UB40 song existed in the vaults at Virgin. I convinced [director] Philip Noyce to use it in the film."

If Sexton had not resuscitated the track, would UB40 have released it eventually? "I don't think we would have," says Campbell. "We were working on our own album at the time, *Promises and Lies,* which was all original material and we weren't in a hurry to put on a cover. We argued about it. Some of the band didn't want it on because they felt it wasn't representative of the rest of the album. I definitely wanted to put it on because I knew it was going to be a smash hit and I thought it would be stupid not to put it on."

"Can't Help Falling in Love" was one of several reggae tunes on the radio in 1993, along with "Bad Boys" by Inner Circle and "Flex" by Mad Cobra. "It was a sign that reggae had been discovered at last in America," says a grateful Campbell. "We'd been coming to the States for 16 years. And when we first played there, people would say, 'What kind of rock and roll do you play?' They never knew what it was called. If they didn't know Bob Marley, they'd say, 'Oh yeah, that calypso music.' I think if Marley hadn't died, it might have been a

different story, because he was on the verge of exploding in America. But there was nobody to take over. The march forward of reggae music was put back a giant step when he died. But it was a great feeling to be number one in America because there were so many reggae artists having success there."

The Elvis Presley recording of "Can't Help Falling in Love" peaked at number two the week of February 3, 1962, kept out of pole position by Joey Dee & the Starliters' "Peppermint Twist - Part I" [see 103]. The UB40 single is one of a handful of songs that reached number two the first time around and were subsequently number one when recorded by another artist. Included in this category are "I Heard It Through the Grapevine" (Gladys Knight & the Pips and Marvin Gaye), "MacArthur Park" (Richard Harris and Donna Summer) and "Don't Let the Sun Go Down on Me" (Elton John and George Michael with Elton).

## THE TOP FIVE
*Week of July 24, 1993*

1 **Can't Help Falling in Love**
UB40

2 **Weak**
SWV

3 **Whoomp! (There It Is)**
Tag Team

4 **That's the Way Love Goes**
Janet Jackson

5 **Knockin' Da Boots**
H-Town

## 820 Dreamlover COLUMBIA 77080
### MARIAH CAREY

Writers: *Mariah Carey*
*Dave Hall*

Producers: *Mariah Carey*
*Dave Hall*
*Walter Afanasieff*

*September 11, 1993*
*8 weeks*

**M**ARIAH CAREY had six number one hits to her credit when she went to work on her fourth album, *Music Box.* Her search for hot producers led to Dave Hall, a Mount Vernon, New York, native who had just finished a project with Mary J. Blige. "I loved what Dave was doing at the time," says Carey. "I wanted to do something that had a happy feeling, and that's really not Dave. It's very anti what he's about. So he said, 'Oh, you want to do that happy stuff? All right, all right.' He was not into doing it. Then we listened to a lot of loops and we used the 'Blind Alley' loop and I started singing the melody over it."

Carey explains what the 'Blind Alley' loop is: "It's from an old record. That's very low in the mix—you really can't even hear it. It was used on a rap record called 'Ain't No Half-Steppin'' by Big Daddy Kane and probably a lot of other things. But it never had this kind of a song over it. We built the song from there and I wrote the lyrics and the melody and Dave ended up liking it."

Hall also liked working with Carey. "My experience with Mariah was a good one. Some artists don't arrive on time and you sit in the studio waiting. But Mariah was always on time, very on point. She's a perfectionist. She knew exactly what she wanted to do when we got into the studio. We would lay down some ideas in the morning

### THE TOP FIVE
*Week of September 11, 1993*

1 **Dreamlover**
Mariah Carey

2 **Can't Help Falling in Love**
UB40

3 **Whoomp! (There It Is)**
Tag Team

4 **If**
Janet Jackson

5 **Runaway Train**
Soul Asylum

and she would go home with it that evening, until the next evening. We would get the hook down that night. She's pretty quick on that."

Hall explains that Carey did not have the title "Dreamlover" when they began working on the song. "The way I usually work is we do an untitled song. We'll grab the hook and we'll use that as the title," he says. Carey adds, "I wrote the verses first. I always do the melody first. Sometimes I'll have an idea for a lyric. If I'm collaborating with someone, I'll direct them in the direction that I'm going chordwise, because I get all these melody ideas and then I lose them if I don't have someone really good on keyboards right there with me. That's why I tend to collaborate because I lose the ideas by the time I figure out the chords. All these melody ideas just go."

Tommy Mottola, head of Sony Music Entertainment, as well as Carey's fiancé at the time, heard Hall and

Carey's take on "Dreamlover" and approached producer Walter Afanasieff about collaborating on the track. "Mariah and Dave did this loop thing and it was new to us pop producers at that time," says Afanasieff. "Their version of 'Dreamlover' was missing a lot of stuff. The spirit of the song was up but it wasn't hitting hard enough." Afanasieff reworked the drums, organ and keyboards. "The organ part and the hi-hat that I changed made it a little bit more swinging and a little bit more driving," says Afanasieff. "It put a whole different shade of colors to it."

"Dreamlover" proved to be Carey's biggest hit to date, topping the Hot 100 for eight weeks. "I love being able to make songs that a lot of people can relate to and a lot of people can sing along to, because that's what I do," says the artist. "I never go anywhere without the radio on. So I'm glad to be able to do this for a living."

MCA 54626 **I'd Do Anything for Love (But I Won't Do That)**
MEAT LOAF

*Writer: Jim Steinman*

*Producer: Jim Steinman*

*November 6, 1993*
*5 weeks*

**W**ITH WORLDWIDE SALES topping 30 million, the 1977 release *Bat Out of Hell* is one of the most enduring albums of the rock era, its 82 weeks on the *Billboard* album chart paling in comparison to its 450-plus-week stay on the British album chart, where it is the longest-charting album of all time. Still, Meat Loaf found it difficult to follow up his solo debut effort, and had a falling out with his longtime friend, songwriter Jim Steinman. Subsequent albums produced by Frank Farian, Tom Dowd and others did not fare as well and Meat Loaf, born Marvin Lee Aday, faced bankruptcy and the loss of his voice.

While recording the album *Bad Attitude* in 1984 at the Power Station, Meat ran into Steinman, who was producing Bonnie Tyler. "I hadn't seen him in four years and it was like nothing happened," the artist recalls. "He said, 'We should do another album. We should do the follow-up to *Bat.*'" Meat approached his record labels (Arista in the U.K. and RCA in the U.S.) about the idea and found no interest. Determined to reunite with Steinman, Meat asked for his release, but had to deliver one more album to complete his contract. *Meat Loaf Live* was released in Britain but not the States, and discussions began with Al Teller at CBS about a second *Bat* album. Teller moved over to MCA and Meat Loaf followed, but Steinman was now working with an act called Pandora's Box. A Virgin release

in 1989 included some of the songs meant for Meat, who wasn't thrilled. But Steinman promised him he had more songs.

Meat Loaf was signed to MCA in the States and Virgin for the rest of the world for two and a half years before he walked into a studio to record *Bat Out of Hell II: Back Into Hell.* He kept busy by playing over 200 dates a year, but in 1991 work on the project stopped. "We thought we were making a really good record and Jimmy said, 'I'm not going to finish this record with the managers you have.'" Meat Loaf heard the same thing from his wife, his business manager, his lawyer and a friend from Australia. He followed their advice and found a new manager and work resumed.

Meat Loaf first heard the song "I'd Do Anything for Love (But I Won't Do That)" in 1990 when Steinman came to his house for dinner. "I immediately said it was a great song, but we have to change the arrangement. I made him add verses and instrumentals. I always do that." Acknowledging that he assumes the role of a character for each of his songs, Meat Loaf (whose film acting credits include roles in *The Rocky Horror Picture Show* and *Roadie*) explains what role he played in "I'd Do Anything for Love." "Through my eyes,

it was a 14-year-old looking at this girl trying to figure out how to get up the nerve to go over and ask her out." The lyrics were the subject of much discussion, but the artist was surprised at the confusion over the meaning of the song. "It's so simple. The answer is right before every chorus. 'I'll never forget the way you feel right now. I'd do anything for love but I won't do that. I'll never stop dreaming of you every night of my life.' Everybody asks me (what it is about) and I always say, 'Did you listen to the song?'"

Edited down from its 12-minute running time on the album, "I'd Do Anything for Love" ran 5:08 as an American single. Meat Loaf was as surprised as anyone when it topped the Hot 100. "If you had said to me, 'I'll bet you a dollar you'll have a number one record,' I wouldn't have bet you. And it was number one in 25 countries."

Success was sweeter the second time around. "I was ready for it this time. Becoming a star or becoming rich have never been my goals. My goals were literally making the records, touring, doing the shows. I'm a worker bee. I'm not really a diva. I don't take myself seriously and I don't think everybody else should take me seriously. I like doing what I do and I think I do it well, so that's plenty."

## THE TOP FIVE

*Week of November 6, 1993*

1 **I'd Do Anything for Love (But I Won't Do That)**
Meat Loaf

2 **All That She Wants**
Ace of Base

3 **Just Kickin' It**
Xscape

4 **Again**
Janet Jackson

5 **Dreamlover**
Mariah Carey

# Again VIRGIN 38404
## JANET JACKSON

*Writers: Janet Jackson*
*James Harris III*
*Terry Lewis*

*Producers: Jimmy Jam*
*Terry Lewis*
*Janet Jackson*

*December 11, 1993*
*2 weeks*

JANET JACKSON looked stunning when she sang "Again" at the Academy Awards in March, 1994. But her 18-karat-gold necklace encrusted with 398 diamonds didn't bring her luck; the song, written by Jackson with producers Jimmy Jam (James Harris III) and Terry Lewis, was not destined to claim an Oscar. The statuette went to first-time winner Bruce Springsteen for "Streets of Philadelphia."

But there was no question who was the winner on the Billboard Hot 100. The Springsteen song peaked at number nine while "Again" was Jackson's seventh chart-topper. It was the second single from *janet.* to reach number one, and the first Jackson song from a movie to do so. "Again" was the closing ballad from *Poetic Justice*, directed by John Singleton. Jackson starred as a poet named Justice and won critical notice for her acting ability. She had been so successful in the record business that some had forgotten she was an actress first, with roles in TV series like "Good Times," "Diff'rent Strokes" and "Fame."

"Again" began with Jimmy Jam noodling on the piano. "Janet said, 'Oh, that's absolutely beautiful,'" the producer remembers. "But we didn't really do anything with it. We thought it was interesting but put it on the back burner and went about our business. When [the film producers] called and said they wanted a song for *Poetic Justice*, they said it needed to be a ballad, and be about her character and the character played by Tupac Shakur." Based on that request, Jackson wrote some lyrics and watched some footage from the film with Jam and Lewis. "As we were watching the movie I started playing some chords and it came around to the chords I had been messing with," says Jimmy Jam. Jackson took her lyrics home and shaped them around the chords. "That's how the song was done. It was partly the influence of the movie, and then it was a matter of putting those lyrical ideas with the chords that worked so well," explains Jimmy Jam.

Jam and Lewis brought in arranger Lee Blaskey to work on the session. "We're very lucky because we have two really great orchestras up here, the Minnesota Orchestra and the St. Paul Chamber Orchestra, and we're able to pull in most of their one and two chairs to do the sessions. We have 15-20 pieces and record them three or four times to make it sound bigger."

Janet's vocal was captured in one take, according to Jam. "She was going to sing it to me and I said, 'Why don't you just go in the booth and sing it? We'll put the scratch vocal on tape and then we'll tweak it.' She started singing and I let the tape roll. There was one line that says, 'Kind of late in the game' that she decided to change, from 'The ball is in your hands' to 'My heart is in your hands.'" The next day, another vocal take was recorded, but no subsequent recording had the same feel as Janet's first take.

The producer agrees that "Again" is one of Jackson's strongest vocals, eschewing the breathiness of some of her earlier ballads. "I think it's something she's more comfortable with as her voice gets better and stronger and as she feels more confident in her voice. It's all part of growing." Jam and Lewis enjoyed watching Jackson perform the song live, especially at the Oscar ceremony. "I got to play with her on the Academy Awards," says Jam. "It was a little bit scary because the orchestra was beautiful. Bill Conti was the conductor. But I hadn't played the song in about a year and a half. I'm sitting at the piano and there is a serious 80-piece orchestra of the best people and I'm thinking, 'I don't remember this song.' It was the weirdest thing, but somehow we got through it, and what a great experience!"

## THE TOP FIVE
*Week of December 11, 1993*

1 **Again**
   Janet Jackson

2 **I'd Do Anything for Love (But I Won't Do That)**
   Meat Loaf

3 **All That She Wants**
   Ace of Base

4 **Hero**
   Mariah Carey

5 **Shoop**
   Salt-N-Pepa

### THE TOP FIVE
*Week of December 25, 1993*

1  **Hero**
   Mariah Carey

2  **Again**
   Janet Jackson

3  **All That She Wants**
   Ace of Base

4  **I'd Do Anything for Love
   (But I Won't Do That)**
   Meat Loaf

5  **All for Love**
   Bryan Adams/
   Rod Stewart/Sting

*Writers: Mariah Carey
   Walter Afanasieff*

*Producers: Walter Afanasieff
   Mariah Carey*

*December 25, 1993
4 weeks*

IF "HERO" SOUNDS like it was meant to be heard over the end credits of a film, there's a good reason. Dustin Hoffman and Geena Davis starred in a movie for Columbia Pictures called *Hero*. Producer Walter Afanasieff recalls, "The people over at Epic Records were going to do the soundtrack for the film. They wanted to have Mariah sing the theme to it, but they didn't really think they could because at that time you couldn't get near Mariah to do anything filmwise. So they wanted to try the next best thing, which was to have us write something."

The film was screened for Afanasieff in Los Angeles and he was told that Gloria Estefan would probably be asked to sing a title theme. At the time, the producer was working with Carey on her *Music Box* album. "I went to New York and we were in the studio and came to a break. I was sitting at the piano and told Mariah about this movie. Within two hours, we had this incredible seed for this song, 'Hero.' It was never meant for Mariah to sing. In her

mind, we were writing a song for Gloria Estefan for this movie. And we went into an area that Mariah really didn't go into—in her words, it was a little bit too schmaltzy or too pop ballady or too old-fashioned as far as melody and lyrics."

The pair was almost finished writing the song when Tommy Mottola, president and COO of Sony Music Entertainment and Carey's fiancé (later her husband), walked into the studio. Hearing the song they were working on, he asked them what it was, and Carey replied, "This is a song for the film *Hero.*" Afanasieff recalls Mottola responding, "Are you kidding me? You can't give this song to this movie. This is too good. Mariah, you have to take this song. You have to do it."

Initially, Carey was guided by the subject of the film, but Afanasieff acknowledges that the artist made it a very personal song. After she decided not to give the song away, she completed the lyric and made it her own. The producer went back to the soundtrack people and told them, "You know what? I didn't come up with anything." Estefan never heard the tune originally meant for her, and the song that ended up in the soundtrack was "Heart of a Hero," written, produced and recorded by Luther Vandross.

Afanasieff and Carey came up with a couple of different versions of "Hero"

in the studio. "There was a simpler performance on tape and a more difficult one, with Mariah singing out more, with more licks. But we chose a happy medium. The song really calls for not anything really fancy. But she's always fighting the forces inside of her because she's her own devil's advocate. She wants to do something that's so over the top and use her talents and the voice she has. But she also knows she has to restrain herself and do what the music really calls for."

Before the song hit number one on the Hot 100, Carey announced that she was donating the proceeds from the sales of the single to the families of the victims of a December 7 shooting rampage on the Long Island Rail Road. Three days after the tragedy, Carey was on stage at Madison Square Garden when she dedicated "Hero" to the three men who subdued the gunman. Carey, who had been a frequent passenger on the LIRR rush-hour ride out of Penn Station, had been shocked by the senseless brutality of the incident. Afanasieff remembers the audience reaction: "We started playing the song, and there was a guy standing in the aisle and the light from the stage hit him. He was a grown man and he had tears streaming down his face. And I looked out and saw so many people crying and realized the power of the song."

## 824   All for Love   A&M 0476
### BRYAN ADAMS/ROD STEWART/STING

*Writers: Bryan Adams*
*Robert John "Mutt" Lange*
*Michael Kamen*

*Producers: Chris Thomas*
*Bryan Adams*
*David Nicholas*

*January 22, 1994*
*3 weeks*

'**B**RYAN ADAMS, Mutt Lange and I decided to repeat deliberately what we had done accidentally in *Robin Hood* to see if we could come up with a successful record with the three of us in the same room at the same time working on the same song," says Michael Kamen, composer of the score for *The Three Musketeers.* "With 'Everything I Do' [see 792] we were in three different cities and I had never met them."

The process began with a melody taken from the score. "My goal in working on a period film is always to evoke the period," says Kamen. The Alexandre Dumas novel is set in the time of King Louis XIII and his minister Cardinal Richelieu, in the first part of the 17th century. "I composed a score that was based on a French dance suite," explains Kamen, who then got together with Adams and Lange to write a song. "I would play the first part of the melody and then Mutt would suggest something. Bryan would be chucking away on the guitar or Mutt would and I was pounding on the piano."

Lange asked if the Three Musketeers had a motto, and Kamen reminded him it was, "All for one and one for all." Lange repeated it over and over and said, "It's pretty good, but I can't see them dropping their knickers for it

in Kansas." Kamen suggested they change it to "All for love." When the song was finished, Adams asked when the movie was coming out, and realized it would conflict with the release date for his greatest hits album and the single "Please Forgive Me." Kamen suggested, "Why don't we make the song with two other guys, and the three of you are the three musketeers." Adams called Sting, who agreed immediately. Filling the third spot proved more difficult. A couple of big names pulled out. Then Kamen sent a note to Luciano Pavarotti that read, "You started the Three Tenors and now we want three pop tenors and we'd like you to join us." He was unavailable, and Disney executives were concerned they weren't going to have a song ready in time. "So they made me meet with Jon Bon Jovi," Kamen reveals. He got together with Jon and Richie Sambora in Ibiza. "We wrote a killer song and he sent it to be produced long distance by Danny Kortchmar."

Kamen received a tape of the Bon Jovi song just as Adams called to say that Rod Stewart was in as the third musketeer. Mutt Lange was no longer available to produce it, so Adams lined up Trevor Horn, who then dropped out because of a conflicting commitment.

Time was running short. "We were mixing a reel a day and the film was nearly done and the song hadn't arrived," says Kamen. "Bryan and Sting did their vocals in London and then it was a question of nailing Rod to the floor long enough to get his vocal. Bryan flew to Los Angeles with the master and Rod interrupted his tour, touched down at LAX, and was escorted directly to the studio. He sang his

vocal and Bryan took off with the tape and mixed it with David Nicholas in Vancouver." With three days left before the final deadline, the contract for the three artists to appear on the same recording was still not finalized. "The deal between Bryan's end, A&M, Sting's people, Rod Stewart's people, and Disney and Polydor and Sony Music and Warner Brothers became one of the biggest bloodbaths I have ever been witness to," says Kamen. "Bryan would call me at four in the morning, 'It's off, man.' And then an hour later, 'It's on again.' And then my agent said, 'It's not gonna happen.' We all started becoming musketeers. It was worth fighting for. It was by the skin of our teeth that this song was physically completed and the deal was done and the master was sent to L.A. just in time to be dubbed into the final four minutes of the film before it was sent off to be duped and color corrected and sent to four million theaters all over the world."

---

### THE TOP FIVE
*Week of January 22, 1994*

1   **All for Love**
Bryan Adams/Rod Stewart/Sting

2   **Hero**
Mariah Carey

3   **Breathe Again**
Toni Braxton

4   **Again**
Janet Jackson

5   **All That She Wants**
Ace of Base

*Writers: Candy de Rouge*
 *Gunther Mende*
 *Jennifer Rush*
 *Mary Susan Applegate*

*Producer: David Foster*

*February 12, 1994*
*4 weeks*

S INGING IN A New York band and shopping her demos to all the major U.S. record labels wasn't working for Jennifer Rush, a native of Queens. Her parents lived in West Germany, where her father was an operatic tenor. He sent his daughter's demo tapes to some German -based labels and got positive reactions from Polydor and CBS. The latter company signed Rush and she relocated to Dusseldorf. The classically trained artist flopped with her first single, "Tonight," but then found herself chartbound in Germany with "25 Lovers" and "Ring of Ice." It was her fourth single that brought her international fame. The title: "The Power of Love."

"On that first album, I used a lot of lyrics I had written as poetry," says Rush. "I was working with people who didn't speak English, so I was fitting my poetry to their melodies." Recalling the inspiration for "The Power of Love," she says, "It's about my boyfriend, Steven, the second boyfriend I ever had in my life. We're still together. He was a bass player and he just graduated from Harvard."

When her first album was released, people took notice of "The Power of Love." Rush says, "There was something in that song that touched a lot of people." Despite the song's length of five minutes and 45 seconds, it hit num-

ber one in the U.K. the week of October 12, 1985, and stayed there for five weeks. With over a million copies sold, it became the best-selling single by a female artist to that date.

It was a different story in the U.S., where Air Supply released their version of "The Power of Love" first. It charted in August, 1985, and peaked at number 68, the first of the duo's singles to miss the top 40. Six months later, the Rush single debuted, but the song faltered at

number 57. In October, 1987, Laura Branigan entered the Hot 100 with her attempt at "The Power of Love." This time the song peaked at number 26, but it still wasn't the major hit it had been in many other countries.

In 1993, Quebec-born Celine Dion revived "The Power of Love." The chanteuse grew up in a small village, the youngest of 14 children. One of her brothers sent her demo tape to manager Rene Angelil, who signed the 12-year-old singer (and would marry her years later). After making an impression in her own country, she found international fame by representing Switzerland in the 1988 Eurovision Song Contest with "Ne Partez Pas Sans Moi," the winning song.

Dion didn't chart in the U.S. until 1990, when "Where Does My Heart Beat Now" entered the Hot 100. It was her first top 10 single, followed by "Beauty and the Beast" (with Peabo Bryson) and "If You Asked Me To." The lead-off single from her third domestic album, *The Colour of My Love*, was her remake of the Jennifer Rush song. She explains that the first time she heard the song, it gave her goosebumps, and she couldn't wait to record it. "It's not like we wanted to do it better than the original," she said in *Billboard*. "If you know you can bring some new emotion to it, it deserves to be done. For me, 'The Power of Love' has to be treated simply in the beginning, but by the end it's really powerful, so why not open the pipes? And if you want to open up and sing strong, you could not have a better song than 'The Power of Love.'"

Producer David Foster concurs. "I'm a sucker for holding out the big long money notes and she does it as well as anyone. I push her to the limit and get that extra half-tone or that extra oomph. I pride myself on working really hard on those vocals." Foster only had one problem with the singer, who spoke just a few words in English when they first met. "I was using the phrase 'bitchin' and she thought I was calling her a bitch. She really got upset."

Rush thinks that Dion did a "beautiful job" on the song. "Of course, I would have liked the shot in the States. My family, they don't quite get it. The retired aunt in Florida says, 'How could she do it?' and my boyfriend's parents called radio stations to complain."

## THE TOP FIVE
*Week of February 12, 1994*

1 **The Power of Love**
 Celine Dion

2 **All for Love**
 Bryan Adams/Rod Stewart/Sting

3 **Breathe Again**
 Toni Braxton

4 **Hero**
 Mariah Carey

5 **The Sign**
 Ace of Base

# The Sign ARISTA 12653
## ACE OF BASE

### THE TOP FIVE
*Week of March 12, 1994*

1 **The Sign**
  Ace of Base

2 **The Power of Love**
  Celine Dion

3 **Whatta Man**
  Salt-N-Pepa w/En Vogue

4 **Without You/**
  **Never Forget You**
  Mariah Carey

5 **So Much in Love**
  All-4-One

---

*Writer: Joker*

*Producers: Denniz Pop*
          *Joker*

*March 12, 1994*
*6 weeks*

JONAS BERGGREN, nicknamed Joker, and his younger sisters Jenny and Malin grew up in Gothenburg, on Sweden's west coast, where they studied classical music and sang in the church choir but had other musical influences as well. Their father, Göran, loved jazz and was also a fan of Abba's *Voulez-Vous* album. Jonas loved the synthesized sound of Vince Clarke (Depeche Mode, Yaz and later, Erasure) and in 1986, formed a group that went by the names Kallinin Prospect (after a Moscow street) and CAD (Computer Aided Disco) before settling on Tech Noir, inspired by the fictional Los Angeles disco in *The Terminator.* Jonas brought his sisters in to sing vocals, and in 1990, Kraftwerk fan Ulf Ekberg, known to his friends as Buddah, completed the foursome. Because people had difficulty pronouncing and remembering the name Tech Noir, the group changed its moniker to Ace of Base.

Ace of Base gave their first performance on August 6, 1990, but another group playing that night in Gothenburg got more attention: the Rolling Stones were in town. Over the next 18 months, the Swedish quartet continued to tour and recorded a demo tape. Ekberg describes the earliest version of the group as a cross between the German outfit Snap! and the eccentric rock duo known as the KLF. Turned down by Polar, the label that was home to Abba, and by other Swedish record companies, the group eventually signed to Mega Records, the Danish label that fostered the KLF's career. The first single, "Wheel of Fortune," caught on in Denmark and then Norway. As the song's popularity spread through Scandinavia, the German label Metronome licensed Ace of Base for the rest of Europe. The first single released outside of Scandinavia was "All That She Wants," which topped the charts in many countries before catching the ear of Richard Sweret, vice president of A&R for Arista. The American label launched the group with "All That She Wants" on September 6, 1993. The single missed the top spot on the Hot 100 and had to settle for a three-week run at number two.

Sweret was riding on a bus with Jonas in Stockholm when the Ace of Base leader sang him a new tune he intended to use as the lead-off single from the group's second album. The song was "The Sign." Sweret wanted the group to record it immediately. "Jonas realized he had nothing to lose if he cut it. He could use it for the second album or use it for the rest of the world, because at that point the [first] album hadn't come out in more than a few territories. When he did his rough mix of it, it was apparent that it was a very special song. He was so proud of it that he wanted it out."

"The Sign" was one of three new songs added to the *Happy Nation* album for American release, and based on the strength of the song, the album's title was changed to *The Sign.* Released as the follow-up to "All That She Wants," "The Sign" proved to have incredible staying power on the Hot 100. After a four-week run at number one, it dipped to number two while R. Kelly moved in with "Bump N' Grind." Following that single's four-week reign, "The Sign" posted another two weeks at the top.

The follow-up was another song that Sweret had asked to be added to the U.S. release of the album, but it was more difficult to convince the group to record it. The Diane Warren/Albert Hammond composition "Don't Turn Around" had already been released by Tina Turner, Neil Diamond and the reggae group Aswad. The latter had taken it to number one in Europe and the group thought it had been too big a hit to be recorded again. But the song had never made it big in the U.S., where the Ace of Base version was ultimately successful, peaking at number three.

Writer: R. Kelly

Producer: R. Kelly

April 9, 1994
4 weeks

**W**ITH SEVERAL critically acclaimed plays under his belt, theatrical producer and artists manager Barry Hankerson was auditioning talent for a new musical. Playwright Ron Millman, a good friend, told him about a young singer from Chicago, so Hankerson flew to the windy city to check out Robert Kelly. "He sang a Stevie Wonder song, 'Ribbon in the Sky,'" Hankerson remembers. "I saw quite a few people, but he was the standout." Still, Kelly wasn't cast in *The First Lady.* Hankerson heard Kelly's "raggedy little cassette" and signed the vocalist to a management contract. "I said, 'Let's forget the play. Let's go do an album.'"

Kelly had been singing his entire life. "I was determined to do this music because it was something I was born with," he explains. "I used to sing with my mother a lot. It was something I had to do. I would eat and sleep and drink and think and see and dream it. I knew I had to share my music with the world."

Hankerson had a longtime working relationship with Clive Calder, founder of Jive Records, and Kelly was quickly signed to the label. Thinking it would be easier to break a group instead of a solo artist, three dancers were recruited to back up Kelly and the first album, *Born into the '90s*, was released under the name R. Kelly and Public Announcement. Four singles charted on the Hot 100, but none made the top 30. The one that came closest was "Dedi-cated," which peaked at number 31 in May, 1993. Five months later, the first single from Kelly's second album debuted on the chart. The lusty "Sex Me (Parts I & II)" was a preview of the sexually charged *12 Play,* an album title that multiplied foreplay times three. The "Sex Me" record, with Kelly now listed as a solo act, peaked at number 20.

The follow-up single was based on a personal relationship. "At that time I was really into this girl that I wanted, and she didn't want me like I wanted her," Kelly laments. "That gave me the inspiration for 'Bump N' Grind.' I just went into the studio and wrote it. I didn't see anything wrong with it. She did."

The song was destined for the soundtrack to Albert and Allen Hughes' *Menace II Society,* starring Tyrin Turner and Jada Pinkett. "After hearing the song, we chose not to give it to the soundtrack," says Hankerson. "It got very political, because when you're breaking an act, you need to keep your music home. I've always had the view in the music business that soundtracks are great, and now that I have a label (Blackground), I'd sure like to get me one. But when you look at a soundtrack, you get two hot artists and they may drive a million sales on one album but they don't get paid but for that one single. So I've never been one to rush to do soundtracks unless the artist has multi-singles on the album. In this case they were looking for a song and Robert was new. When you have a new artist you have to be careful what you give away. People didn't like me very much when we said they couldn't have 'Bump N' Grind.'"

The *Menace II Society* soundtrack, released on Jive, peaked at number 11 on the Billboard album chart, but didn't yield any hit singles. "Bump N' Grind" debuted on the Hot 100 at number 59 on February 5, 1994. Nine weeks later, it was Kelly's first number one single. On Billboard's Hot R&B Singles chart, "Bump N' Grind" remained on top for 12 weeks, the longest any single has been number one since the chart first appeared on October 20, 1958. When Billboard tabulated its all-time charts for a 100th anniversary issue in November 1994, "Bump N' Grind" was listed as the number one R&B single of all time.

## THE TOP FIVE
*Week of April 9, 1994*

1  **Bump N' Grind**
   R. Kelly

2  **The Sign**
   Ace of Base

3  **Without You / Never Forget You**
   Mariah Carey

4  **The Power of Love**
   Celine Dion

5  **So Much in Love**
   All-4-One

## 828 I Swear BLITZZ/ATLANTIC 87243
### ALL-4-ONE

*Writers: Frank J. Meyers*
*Gary Baker*

*Producer: David Foster*

*May 21, 1994*
*11 weeks*

**G**ARY BAKER had already written hits like "Once Upon a Lifetime" for Alabama when his publisher suggested in 1988 he try writing some songs with Frank J. Meyers, whose credits included "You and I" for Eddie Rabbitt and Crystal Gayle. After the collaboration produced songs for Meyers' band, the Shooters, the two continued to write together and also became friends.

Baker came up with the idea for a song called "I Swear." He remembers, "I lived three hours from Frank and he was coming down that day to write. I called and said, 'I got this title. Throw it in your book and someday we'll work on it.'" Later that day, they took a break while writing at Fame Studios in Muscle Shoals, Alabama. Over lunch, Meyers told Baker he had already come up with a chorus for "I Swear." Meyers recalls, "I wrote the chorus on the way down to his house in my car. I get inspired driving. You talk to most writers and they'll tell you the same thing."

Both writers thought they had something special, but despite their feeling that they had written a great song, no one recorded it. Several artists put a hold on the song, including Kenny Rogers, but five years passed without a single recording. Meyers, who never cared much for the original demo, told

Baker, "If we can get another demo, we can get this song cut."

The first artist to hear the new demo was John Michael Montgomery. "I was supposed to write with him on a houseboat up in Kentucky, so I took the song to play for him. He wasn't sure at first," Meyers recollects. But Montgomery did record it, and on February 5, 1994, the Atlantic single became his second number one hit on Billboard's country chart. That's when Doug Morris, head of the label, called Rick Blackburn in the Nashville office and said he wanted to cut a pop version of the song.

Morris wanted the song for All-4-One, a quartet from Antelope Valley, California, that was coming off its first top 10 hit with a neo doo-wop remake of the Tymes' "So Much in Love" [see 134]. Tim O'Brien, founder of the Blitzz label, had originally recorded the song with another group. But that relationship soured, and O'Brien auditioned for someone else to record "So Much in Love." Jamie Jones, Tony Borowiak and Alfred Nevarez had been singing jingles for KAVS-FM when producer Gary St. Clair asked them to try out. They recruited a fourth, Delious Kennedy, to form a quartet. O'Brien was impressed enough to sign them to a single deal, and came up with a list of group names. The four members liked All-4-One, which reflected the group's multi-ethnicity.

When "So Much in Love" hit, All-4-One went back into the studio to record an album. The project was already completed when Morris called O'Brien and said he wanted to include "I Swear" on the album. David Foster had produced

one track for the album, and said yes when O'Brien asked him to record an additional song. In two days, Foster produced "I Swear" in his home studio. "It was obviously the next single," says O'Brien. "David did a phenomenal job. We put it on cassette and the same thing happened as with 'So Much in Love.' Radio stations played it. It became number one in requests in two or three days."

"I Swear" had a swift rise up the Hot 100, reaching the top just four weeks after it debuted. It became the first country number one hit to go to number one on the pop chart in a different version since Whitney Houston remade Dolly Parton's "I Will Always Love You" [see 813]. Like that extraordinary single from *The Bodyguard*, "I Swear" had a long visit at the top, remaining number one for 11 weeks.

### THE TOP FIVE
*Week of May 21, 1994*

1  **I Swear**
   All-4-One

2  **The Sign**
   Ace of Base

3  **I'll Remember**
   Madonna

4  **The Most Beautiful Girl
   in the World**
   ♀

5  **Bump N' Grind**
   R. Kelly

RCA 62870 **Stay (I Missed You)**
LISA LOEB & NINE STORIES

**829**

*Writer: Lisa Loeb*

*Producer: Juan Patiño*

*August 6, 1994*
*3 weeks*

**D**ALLAS-BORN Lisa Loeb listened to her clock radio when she was growing up and fell in love with the music of Olivia Newton-John, Queen and Elton John. After an early foray into songwriting, she took it up again in her sophomore year of high school. "It was like taking observations of what was going on around me and combining them with phrases and melodies and things that were going on in my head," she explains. "It felt comfortable. And luckily, from an early age I was encouraged by the people around me who were listening to music."

She majored in comparative literature at Brown University but spent a lot of time in the campus recording studio. She recorded, engineered and produced her own music and got together with other students to critique each other's work. She formed a duo with freshman roommate Liz Mitchell and got gigs in New York at the Bitter End and the Speakeasy. After graduation, Loeb became a solo act. She was looking for a percussionist when a friend from BMI brought Juan Patiño to her first acoustic show in Manhattan. Soon after they were recording material in Patiño's home studio.

After an argument with her boyfriend, Loeb went home and wrote a song called "Stay." She embellished the lyrics to make the tune more dramatic, and was also inspired when her friend from BMI told her that Daryl Hall was

looking for songs. "I'm a big fan of Hall and Oates," she says, "especially their older R&B-influenced Motown-type songs. And I thought, wow, they need a new 'Sara Smile.'" The opportunity to submit material to Hall fell through, but Loeb completed the song anyway.

With her band Nine Stories (named for a collection by J.D. Salinger), Loeb worked with Patiño to record nine songs in one day, including "Stay." Meanwhile, her Greenwich Village neighbor Ethan Hawke was acting in the film *Reality Bites* and asked her to write a song called "I'm Nothing" for the film. "I recorded it on a DAT in my apartment and sent it to the music supervisors. They liked it but thought it was too 'girly'—probably because I'm singing it. They used another person's 'I'm Nothing' but they were interested in more music. Within a few days Ethan came to see me play at the Cottonwood Cafe. He pulled me aside and said, 'What about that song "Stay"? That might be good.'" Hawke sent a tape of Loeb peforming the song to the film's music supervisor, Karyn Rachtman, as well as executive producer Stacy Sher and director Ben Stiller. A few days later, Loeb's band played a benefit for Hawke's theater company, and Stiller, in New York to screen a rough cut for studio execs, attended with some people

from the production crew. "They liked the song and later that week while I was at a temp job, I got a call on my machine. It was Ron Fair from RCA Records and he was wondering if they could use the song on the soundtrack. I told my lawyer, 'Call this guy!' and I quit my job."

At Fair's request, the band went to Los Angeles, where Loeb redid one vocal line and added a tambourine to the track. When the soundtrack was released, RCA sent the entire album to radio stations rather than selecting a single. KRBE in Houston jumped on "Stay," and then WPRT in New Jersey added it. As other stations added the track, RCA released it as a single and Hawke directed the video. To avoid confusion with other songs called "Stay," the title was altered. "We decided to add 'I Missed You,' a parenthetical, which I vowed I would never do, because I always see parentheticals in the Beatles' songbooks and I never understand how they picked that parenthetical as the parenthetical."

When "Stay (I Missed You)" reached the top of the Hot 100, Loeb was in a unique position of not having a label deal. Wooed by several majors, including RCA, she signed with Geffen and released the album *Tails*, which included her number one hit.

---

## THE TOP FIVE

*Week of August 6, 1994*

1 **Stay (I Missed You)**
Lisa Loeb & Nine Stories

2 **I Swear**
All-4-One

3 **Fantastic Voyage**
Coolio

4 **Can You Feel the Love Tonight**
Elton John

5 **Any Time, Any Place/**
**And On and On**
Janet Jackson

# 830 I'll Make Love to You MOTOWN 2257
## BOYZ II MEN

*Writer: Babyface*

*Producer: Babyface*

*August 27, 1994*
*14 weeks*

"THERE WAS A LOT of pressure going into the second album," acknowledges Nathan Morris of Boyz II Men. "In this industry you can be here today and gone tomorrow. We do what we do because we like to do it and we hope that people are satisfied with what we give them. If they are, we'll be around. If not, then we gotta go find another job."

The pressure was understandable, given the performance of their debut album, *Cooleyhighharmony*, and the soundtrack hit "End of the Road" [see 811]. With 13 weeks at the top, the single broke Elvis Presley's 36-year-old record for having the longest-running number one of the rock era. How could Boyz II Men possibly better that? And yet, they did, with "I'll Make Love to You," which held on to the top spot for 14 weeks, tying the rock era record to

that date held by Whitney Houston with "I Will Always Love You."

For their second album, Boyz II Men worked with a number of producers, including Dallas Austin, Jimmy Jam & Terry Lewis, Tony Rich and Babyface. Of the last name, Morris says, "He's a very creative individual and he's a good guy to work with because he's not just a producer. He's a vocalist as well, so he understands where you're trying to take the song vocally. Some producers, if they're not vocalists, don't know exactly what you may try to do with a song and they may be a little more precise in the way they want it to be. But he lets you add your own characteristics to the song."

Babyface was responsible for writing and producing "End of the Road," along with L.A. Reid and Daryl Simmons. When it came time to work on the group's next album, Babyface knew what to do. "'I'll Make Love to You' was really just me imagining what would be the next record for Boyz II Men. Something that would follow 'End of the Road' but not be exactly the same but

familiar enough where you could touch some of the same ingredients, so they don't make a total left turn from where they left off."

The group was concerned about going to that well once too often. "When we heard 'I'll Make Love to You,' we didn't know if we should put it out because it sounded a lot like 'End of the Road,' and we didn't know how people would react to it. Not that it wasn't a great song, just that we didn't want our fans to get bored. We wanted to give them something different. But the record company talked us into doing it and thank God it worked."

"I'll Make Love to You" and "Water Runs Dry" from the *II* album were recorded during the same two-day session in Los Angeles, according to Morris, who describes a typical Boyz II Men recording session: "When we hear a song, we start creating ideas as we hear it. We're a spontaneous group. One is singing his part while the other one is doing his background part. As far as the lead vocals, we go on feeling. Whoever's in the booth recording at the time, the other guys are adding in their two cents to give flavor to the song."

The combination of "End of the Road" and "I'll Make Love to You" gave Boyz II Men 27 weeks at the pinnacle of the Hot 100 with just two singles. It's no wonder that other groups have been imitating their sound. "We take it as a compliment," says Nathan. "We had to emulate someone to get to where we are as well. So it's not like, 'They're trying to sound like us.' If somebody can take something from us and add to it to make them successful, we don't have a problem with that."

---

## THE TOP FIVE
*Week of August 27, 1994*

1 **I'll Make Love to You**
Boyz II Men

2 **Stay (I Missed You)**
Lisa Loeb & Nine Stories

3 **Fantastic Voyage**
Coolio

4 **Wild Night**
John Mellencamp &
Me'Shell Ndegéocello

5 **I Swear**
All-4-One

MOTOWN 0244 **On Bended Knee**
BOYZ II MEN

**831**

Writers: *James Harris III*
*Terry Lewis*

Producers: *Jimmy Jam*
*Terry Lewis*

*December 3, 1994*
*6 weeks*

**W**HEN "ON BENDED KNEE" moved to number one the week of December 3, 1994, producers Jimmy Jam and Terry Lewis were disappointed. They were hoping the song that had been on top of the Hot 100 the previous week would remain in pole position. "We're pretty good friends with Babyface," says Jimmy Jam. "We were hoping 'I'll Make Love to You' would break the record. Motown said, 'Look, we couldn't hold it anymore.' It was a great run for the guys. They replaced themselves at number one. You can't write a better scenario than that."

If "I'll Make Love to You" had stayed number one for another week, it would have broken the 14-week record set by Whitney Houston's "I Will

Always Love You" [see 813]. Still, Boyz II Men couldn't be too unhappy. By succeeding themselves at the pinnacle, they became only the third chart act in the rock era to follow themselves at number one. The first was Elvis Presley. His two-sided hit, "Don't Be Cruel"/"Hound Dog" [see 14] gave way to "Love Me Tender" in November 1956. The Beatles topped that achievement by scoring three consecutive number one hits with "I Want to Hold Your Hand," "She Loves You" and "Can't Buy Me Love" [see 145] in 1964.

Jam and Lewis had not yet worked with Boyz II Men when they ran into the foursome at a City of Hope dinner honoring PolyGram group president/CEO Alain Levy in 1994. "We were backstage," Jam remembers. "The guys came up to us and said the song they sang when they auditioned for Michael Bivins was 'Can You Stand the Rain,' which was a cut we did for New Edition back in '89. They started singing it and said, 'It would be great if you did something on our album.' I said, 'You sold seven million last time out. I don't know

what we can do for you.'"

Later in the year, Boyz II Men attended the NBA All-Star Game in Minnesota and paid a visit to Jam and Lewis' studio. The Boyz played their new album for the producers and asked their opinion. "We said, 'It's great. We still don't see what you need us for,'" recalls Jam. "And they said, 'If you were going to add a song on the album, what would you add?'" The producers told them that their previous hit "End of the Road" had been a great "begging" song. "That kind of song is really effective and they didn't have a song like that." The group asked the producers to write them a "begging" song.

A couple of months later, Jam and Lewis called to tell the Boyz they had not only written a "begging" song, but came up with one that had "Can You Stand the Rain"-type lyrics. The title was "On Bended Knee," inspired by something Jam and Lewis' engineer Steve Hodge said over dinner one night. "Terry and I have what we call 'The Book of Titles.' Everytime I hear a phrase that I think will make a good title, it goes into the book."

Jam and Lewis observed first-hand the innate musical talent of Boyz II Men. "One of the things we pride ourselves on is that we write really nice harmonies. With these guys, we didn't need to write a harmony. I gave them a melody note and they just broke into harmony. I just said, 'Okay, let's go record.'" Jam compares Boyz II Men to the woman who has recorded most of his number one hits, Janet Jackson: "One of the things they have in common is they take a good song and elevate it to a whole other level. We're fortunate that we've worked with both of them because they make us look real good."

## THE TOP FIVE
*Week of December 3, 1994*

1  **On Bended Knee**
   Boyz II Men

2  **Here Comes the Hotstepper**
   Ini Kamoze

3  **Another Night**
   Real McCoy

4  **I'll Make Love to You**
   Boyz II Men

5  **Always**
   Bon Jovi

## 832 | Here Comes the Hotstepper COLUMBIA 77614
### INI KAMOZE

*Writers: Ini Kamoze*
*Salaam Remi Gibbs*
*Chris Kenner*
*Kenton Nix*

*Producer: Salaam Remi*

*December 17, 1994*
*2 weeks*

PRODUCER Salaam Remi had already completed remixes for tracks by Supercat, Mad Cobra and Shabba Ranks by the time he met dancehall reggae artist Ini Kamoze in 1991. Remi had plenty of experience producing rap artists, too, and brought a hip-hop sensibility to reggae when he recorded six demos with Kamoze to shop to record labels. Although one of those songs was the original version of "Here Comes the Hotstepper," the tapes didn't spark any interest and Kamoze returned home to Jamaica.

Remi continued to work on various reggae projects for Columbia Records, where he had contact with the label's A&R manager, Maxine Stowe. "She said she was doing a compilation called *Stir It Up* and asked if I had any songs," says Remi. He sent her four songs by Kamoze. "She was thinking of signing him, but it kind of wilted away." She did end up taking "Here Comes the Hotstepper" for the compilation, although Remi says the deal did not offer a lot of money. "Everybody said, 'Don't do it.' But at that point, I'd rather have had one song out somewhere rather than have demos sitting on a shelf that nobody would ever hear."

Remi was asked if he could come up with remixes of "Hotstepper." He explains, "At that point I did the remix

### THE TOP FIVE
*Week of December 17, 1994*

1 **Here Comes the Hotstepper**
Ini Kamoze

2 **On Bended Knee**
Boyz II Men

3 **Another Night**
Real McCoy

4 **Always**
Bon Jovi

5 **Creep**
TLC

that had 'Heartbeat' by Taana Gardner, because I was very familiar with that." Remi's father, Van Gibbs, had worked as an arranger for Gardner. Her "Heartbeat" single peaked at number 10 on *Billboard*'s Hot R&B Singles chart in 1981.

The initial reaction to the track was lukewarm, so Remi took it to FunkMaster Flex and Angie Martinez, two friends of his who worked as DJs for Hot 97 in New York City. Remi says the station was one of the first to play the track.

Early airplay helped sell singles, but the *Stir It Up* compilation wasn't really moving. Donnie Ienner, president of Columbia Records, and Maureen Crowe, then executive in charge of music for the label, pitched the song to director Robert Altman for his film *Pret-à-Porter*. "We were looking for a single for the film," Crowe explains, "and Robert loved the song." The remixed "Hotstepper" was the perfect backing track to one of the runway scenes in the movie, set in the world of the Paris fashion industry. By the time the film was released in the U.S., it had undergone a title change to *Ready to Wear*.

Remi thinks "Here Comes the Hot-

stepper" was such a big hit because it appealed to all generations. "It had 'Land Of 1000 Dances' from my grandparents' era; it had 'Murderer,' the chanting part which was very familiar for the reggae and West Indian community as well as the 'Heartbeat' sample which made it appeal to my parents' era. At the same time, there was nothing about it that would make a young person say, 'It sounds old.' It was intended to go all the way from the ghettos to the Grammys."

"Here Comes the Hotstepper" debuted on the Hot 100 the week of September 17, 1994, and hit the number one spot 13 weeks later, interrupting the six-week run of Boyz II Men's "On Bended Knee." The success of the single led to a bidding war for the unsigned Kamoze, as Columbia's option to sign the reggae artist expired just as the single began to move up the Hot 100. Giant, EastWest, Island, Atlantic, Mercury and even Columbia all wanted to add Kamoze to their roster. He ended up on EastWest, but his album was released without his hit single, because Columbia would not license "Hotstepper" to his new label.

*Writer: Dallas Austin*

*Producer: Dallas Austin*

*January 28, 1995*
*4 weeks*

WHEN L.A. REID AND Babyface asked Dallas Austin to meet three young women who had formed a new group, he couldn't help but laugh when he saw who they were. "Y'all are a group?" he said to Tionne "T-Boz" Watkins and Rozonda "Chilli" Thomas, who he knew from his high school days when they would all meet at a skating rink called Jellybean's. "I was known at the rink for music, because I would fly out of town and come back from California and a new record [I produced] would be out by Joyce Irby or Troop," says Austin, who was working with Another Bad Creation and Bell Biv DeVoe when he had his initial meeting with Watkins, Thomas and Lisa "Left Eye" Lopes, who had moved from Philadelphia to Atlanta. "I went in the studio instantly with them and before they had a concept of how they would look, I did five songs and it painted a picture of what these girls were about, even to their record label." Included in the first batch were socially conscious songs like "Ain't 2 Proud 2 Beg" and "What About Your Friends," both top 10 hits from the trio's debut album, *Ooooooohhh . . . On the TLC Tip.*

Austin was not surprised at TLC's success. "I knew from the way the songs were written they would reach a certain audience of girls who would relate to the same stuff that these three girls related to. You don't miss when you write from the perspective of the kids. If I have a little girl with an attitude, she's not the only little girl with attitude in the world." Austin has no difficulty writing from a woman's perspective. "A woman isn't scared to express the way she feels. There are so many different issues to deal with, within females. With a male, I think a lot of issues are coded." Austin says the first song he wrote where other people realized he could successfully write from a woman's point of view was TLC's "Creep."

"I had the track for six months," the producer remembers. "For two months, it was sitting on my computer. I made a tape of it and listened to it in my Jeep. And I was singing 'Creep' to it, riding around and singing and singing and singing." Austin was concerned that the hook was too corny, and didn't think the song was very good at this point. "After five months I couldn't get it out of my head so I recorded it." He thought it could work with the right lyrics. To write the words, Austin asked himself how he would feel if he was a woman whose man was seeing someone else. He liked the word "creep" because it had multiple meanings, like a guy who was weird or a guy who was sneaking around.

T-Boz, who says she enjoys recording with Austin and thinks of him as a brother, liked what "Creep" had to say. "We thought that was a good relation-ship to talk about because a lot of people don't admit that's how they feel—that their man's playing on them and they want to be with him so they seek attention elsewhere, but they really want to be with their guy." But Lopes, sentenced to five years probation for setting fire to her boyfriend's house, had some problems with the lyrical content. Austin explains, "The reason there's not a rap on it is because Lisa said, 'Dallas, I don't want this to offend people personally. I don't want it to interfere with my relationships. If he thinks I'm doing this, it's going to cause problems and I'm making a record out of it.' And I said, 'Hey man, that's what records are about. The biggest problem is maybe it is talking about you. It's harder to do something when you think you're telling on yourself.'"

## THE TOP FIVE
*Week of January 28, 1995*

1 **Creep**
TLC

2 **On Bended Knee**
Boyz II Men

3 **Another Night**
Real McCoy

4 **Always**
Bon Jovi

5 **Take a Bow**
Madonna

| 834 | **Take a Bow** MAVERICK 18000 |
| --- | --- |
|  | MADONNA |

*Writers: Babyface*
*Madonna*

*Producers: Babyface*
*Madonna*

*February 25, 1995*
*7 weeks*

THE *EROTICA* ALBUM explored the darker side of her personality, Madonna contends, while *Bedtime Stories* revealed a more romantic side. "I wanted a lot more of an R&B feel to this record," she said. "The idea going in was to juxtapose my singing style with a hard-core hip-hop sensibility and have the finished product still sound like a Madonna record. I began the process by meeting with the hip-hop producers whose work I most admired. It was important, if I were to use a variety of collaborators, that the end product sound cohesive and thematically whole. I wasn't interested in the variety pack approach."

Her search for R&B producers led to one of the most successful

writer/producers of the '90s. "I got a call from her camp wanting to set up a meeting first to see if there was any interest in working together," Babyface remembers. "I went to her record company and met with her and we got along fine." What do two superstars talk about when they first meet? "We talked about the weather, and the music we liked," the producer explains. "And we were both pleasantly surprised at each other's surroundings, in that she didn't have a whole gang of security and I wasn't traveling with a major posse either. It was refreshing to not have to go through that because a lot of younger producers that she worked with brought in major security and major posses. Some celebrities that I work with, it's such a major thing to get to them. So this was far more relaxing. After that, we decided to write together. She came over to my house—she'd drive herself. We went inside my writing room and just started going for it. We ended up writing two songs."

One of the songs was based on a

piece of music Babyface had already written. "I didn't know where to take it," he confesses. "Then I played it for Madonna and she immediately heard something in it. She clearly gave the song direction. We both wrote lyrics but she was the driving force. She was a great writing partner. She's very clever in her lyrics and very picturesque." They both agreed that the first line of the lyrics should be the title, even though the words "take a bow" were never repeated in the song.

When it came time to record the song, Babyface found he was nervous at the prospect of being in the studio with Madonna. He wondered if she would be too anal about recording. "Maybe too much of a perfectionist," he elaborates. "And you can go years in the studio if you're a perfectionist. I'm not that kind of a writer/producer. But it was very easy. And the mix was very easy, one of the quickest I've done. It was a joy."

"Take a Bow" was recorded with a full orchestra. It was the first time Babyface worked with live strings. "It was her suggestion, and it was Nellee Hooper who actually arranged [the strings]. She had worked with them many times before, but for me, it was a new experience. So I was learning new things. I had always thought about it, but had never done it."

Madonna had a good chart year in 1994, with "I'll Remember" from the film *With Honors* spending four weeks at number two, and "Secret," the first single from *Bedtime Stories*, peaking at number three. "Take a Bow" entered the Hot 100 the week of December 17, 1994, and reached the top at the end of February, 1995. It remained on top for seven weeks, easily becoming Madonna's biggest hit to date.

## THE TOP FIVE

*Week of February 25, 1995*

1 **Take a Bow**
Madonna

2 **Creep**
TLC

3 **On Bended Knee**
Boyz II Men

4 **Another Night**
Real McCoy

5 **Baby**
Brandy

Writers: *Montell Jordan*
*Oji Pierce*
*Ricky Walters*

Producers: *Oji Pierce*
*Montell Jordan*

April 15, 1995
*7 weeks*

**B**ORN IN LOS ANGELES on December 3, 1968, Montell Jordan grew up listening to his mother and grandmother's records, getting an education in Smokey Robinson & the Miracles, the Temptations, the Four Tops and the Spinners, "which is where I derived my harmonies and my ability to stack a lot of background vocals, because I always wanted to be in a group. And then I was influenced by Curtis Mayfield, Marvin Gaye and Quincy Jones." The young Jordan also wanted to be an illustrator, and studied the covers of albums by Earth, Wind & Fire and Parliament-Funkadelic.

He had sung gospel music in church for nine years, and by the time he was 17 and ready to graduate high school, he knew he wanted to pursue a career in music. He recorded demos and sang in talent shows, while majoring in communications and minoring in business at Pepperdine University in Malibu.

Success in music wasn't immediate. "It took me until I turned 26 before I landed a record deal," he says. A Los Angeles DJ named Paul Stewart played Jordan's demo tape for Def Jam founder Russell Simmons, who was looking for an R&B singer. Jordan was flown to New York to meet with Simmons and his friend Andre Harrell, founder of Uptown Records. "I ended up singing *a cappella* in the backseat of Andre's Range Rover in New York City. Andre said, 'I'd sign him,'" and Simmons did.

Another of Jordan's musical influences was Slick Rick. "Everybody was into M.C. Shan and Grandmaster Flash and I used to listen to Slick Rick. He told complete stories." At college fraternity parties, DJs would play Slick Rick's "Children's Story," which Jordan considers a hip-hop classic. "I wondered what would happen if I sang over that track, off *The Great Adventures of Slick Rick.* That's the song that comprised the sampled loop behind 'This Is How We Do It.' It took me approximately nine months to write that song and figure out how to make it a smash, because if you can't do it right, don't touch it! To redo somebody's song and not make it better or equally as good would be an injustice to the music. Oji Pierce and I came up with this universal idea. If you're in China, this is how they do it here. If you're from the ghetto, this is how they do it. If you're from New York, you do it like this. I think the reason the song was such a big smash with everybody was because everyone from different countries, gay, straight, whatever color, everybody has their individual way of doing what they do."

To record the crowd sounds heard on the track, Jordan invited 30 people to come to the studio. "I told everybody, 'Have a good time. Talk and do whatever you'd normally do at a party.' I had a lot of guys and girls who'd never met each other. We did six or seven tracks just with people's reactions. If you listen to the track, you can hear people screaming in the background and laughing. It was a party for real."

Jordan admits he wasn't all that much at ease in the studio. "It was my first album and I had not yet become comfortable with what was the best formula for me to record. I wasn't in control of that element because I was very unsure. Oji and I were placed in charge of this album and we didn't have a lot of A&R direction because Def Jam did not have adequate personnel who knew anything about R&B music. That's why on the first album there's a lot of variety—summertime music, ballads. It was kind of scattered."

When it came time to release the first single from his debut album, it was a toss-up between one of the first tracks recorded, "Somethin' 4 Da Honeyz," and one of the last, "This Is How We Do It." The latter was chosen, Jordan recalls, because, "It was a unanimous decision that we needed to put our best foot forward, to shoot the gun."

## THE TOP FIVE
*Week of April 15, 1995*

1 **This Is How We Do It**
Montell Jordan

2 **Red Light Special**
TLC

3 **Candy Rain**
Soul for Real

4 **Take a Bow**
Madonna

5 **Run Away**
Real McCoy

## 836 Have You Ever Really Loved a Woman? A&M 1028
### BRYAN ADAMS

*Writers: Bryan Adams*
*Robert John "Mutt" Lange*
*Michael Kamen*

*Producers: Robert John "Mutt" Lange*
*Bryan Adams*

*June 3, 1995*
*5 weeks*

AFTER TWO NUMBER ONE singles and two Oscar nominations, it's no wonder Bryan Adams, Mutt Lange and Michael Kamen wanted to work together again. "Bryan called and said, 'What are you working on?'" Kamen recalls. "I said, 'Well, there is a great film—an odd film. It's not *Robin Hood,* it's not Kevin Costner. It's not even *The Three Musketeers,* but it's a great film about love and it's a sweet story and a fabulous fantasy and we could come up with something great.'"

The film was *Don Juan DeMarco,* starring Johnny Depp and Marlon Brando. Kamen had worked with Bob Shaye of New Line Cinema before, and knew the film company's head of music, Toby Emmerich. Then he met the woman assigned to be the film's music supervisor. "When I said, 'Bryan Adams,' she said, 'We don't need Bryan Adams. We have another song.' Johnny Depp was sort of an alternative character at that time, and she was determined that she would use Tori Amos and Michael Stipe, which is a great idea. But she couldn't manage to get the film to either one of them, so they were going to make a song they would shoehorn in somewhere." Kamen protested to Shaye. "It was a pretty cool song, but it had nothing to do with the

### THE TOP FIVE
*Week of June 3, 1995*

1  **Have You Ever Really Loved a Woman?**
   Bryan Adams

2  **This Is How We Do It**
   Montell Jordan

3  **I'll Be There for You/
   You're All I Need to Get By**
   Method Man f/Mary J. Blige

4  **Total Eclipse of the Heart**
   Nicki French

5  **Water Runs Dry**
   Boyz II Men

film either lyrically or musically. I believe a film score and the story are inextricably linked and the theme of the movie should be the theme of the song, period."

Kamen composed the *Don Juan* score in Barbados. "There's a little dance the father and mother do when they first meet," Kamen explains. "It's a wonderful scene and I came up with a theme for them to dance to, a sort of Mexican folk tune. That was the melody of the chorus of 'Have You Ever Really Loved a Woman?'" Adams and Lange visited Kamen in Los Angeles and listened to the melodies he had written. Adams suggested tying two of them together and Kamen told him that was crazy, because "they were two completely different worlds and in different keys." Adams pointed out that one could be the verse and the other the chorus. "We went up to the studio and toughed it out and Bryan, Mutt and I had that goosebump, shivery feeling when we knew we had come up with something that was so delicious. This was a love song so tender and sweet and so evocative, to this day it makes women melt."

Adams came up with the lyrics after seeing the film. Then the composer

faced another problem. Director Jeremy Leven had fallen in love with a Linda Ronstadt song recorded in Spanish that he had been using as temporary music for the scene of the mother and father dancing. The film company had even licensed the song. Kamen called Leven and asked him to listen to Adams' demo. "Jeremy heard the song and asked me to leave the room, which made me really nervous," Kamen remembers. "Then he asked me to play it for him again and he asked me to leave the room again while he played it for himself. Then he called me back inside and said, 'This is a fantastic song. I will kill if they want to put anything but this song in my movie.'"

Kamen says that Adams' record label wasn't so certain the song would be a hit single. "Al Cafaro, the head of A&M, heard the song and dug it but wasn't sure because it was so different from anything that was around. He played it for a guy who doesn't have anything to do with the record industry—his personal trainer. Unbeknownst to Al, his trainer has been a friend of mine for 30 years. Mark said, 'That sounds like Kamen. That's great!'" A&M released the single and it quickly became Adams' fourth number one hit.

*Writers: Marqueze Etheridge
Lisa "Left Eye" Lopez
Organized Noize*

*Producers: Organized Noize*

*July 8, 1995
7 weeks*

Tionne "T-Boz" Watkins says that the uplifting message of "Waterfalls" meant a lot to her as well as other people she met. "It helped them get through their hard times. I met a lady who had AIDS and her husband had just died, and she was about to pass. Even if it's (through a) song, it makes you feel better to know that you made somebody feel better for five minutes of their life."

"Waterfalls" was written expressly for TLC, according to Rico Wade of Organized Noize. Along with his partners Patrick Brown and Raymon Murray, Wade was putting together a girl group called Organized Noize. When that act fell apart, they loved the name so much, they kept it for themselves. They produced a rap group managed by Pebbles, and then a Christmas song for TLC. Wade knew Tionne and Lisa "Left Eye" Lopes before they formed TLC with Rozonda "Chilli" Thomas. When someone he knew was holding auditions for a female group with a boyish look, Wade told his friends about the opportunity, which led to the formation of TLC. "Rico is the reason I started dressing baggy in the first place," says T-Boz. "He used to call me his little brother with lipstick. And Marqueze, who wrote 'Waterfalls,' I went to school with him and we always got kicked out of class together."

Marqueze Etheridge had been singing with the guys from Organized Noize, playing local gigs in Atlanta. He explains that "Waterfalls" was based on things he was going through as well as things people he knew were experiencing that he could relate to indirectly. "The song was like a blessing," says Etheridge. "It just came to me and I started singing it in the studio. We had musicians there and everyone was vibing on it. And it was like, 'Oh man, we've got to lay this down.'" The aquatic imagery he used in the chorus came to him immediately. "What's one of the most beautiful things in the world, but at the same time is one of the most deadliest? And I just thought, a waterfall, because it's wonderful to see but it's a dangerous force of nature. Just because everything looks good doesn't mean it's good for you."

Wade says that Organized Noize produced the track first, then called T-Boz in to hear it. "She loved it, so we cut the song and let L.A. Reid hear it. He loved it, and the rest is history." Watkins recalls that she recorded the song very quickly. "I came to the studio at 8 o'clock and sang two complete songs. One didn't make the album. And I left at one o'clock. It was so fast, it was like it was meant to be."

Etheridge kept his humility, even when his song went to number one on the Hot 100 and stayed there for seven weeks, giving the three members of TLC their biggest hit. "It caught me by surprise," says the songwriter. "Through it all, I still have my day job, working for the Marriot in the restaurant. And people say, 'Why haven't you quit yet?' It's not that it hasn't hit me. It's a blessing from God and I'm really thankful for it and I'm just trying to keep a level head and continue doing great music."

The only people who didn't fully enjoy the success of "Waterfalls" were the women in TLC, who declared bankruptcy in July, 1995. "We were going through so much stuff, it's almost like I feel I missed my time," says T-Boz. "I didn't feel it while it was happening. On the outside, it looked peachy." It took some time, but in November, 1996 TLC negotiated a new contract. "Everything's fine," says T-Boz. "No hard feelings. We were caught up in some bad contracts. So you have to crawl before you walk and sometimes you learn from your mistakes."

## THE TOP FIVE
*Week of July 8, 1995*

1 **Waterfalls**
TLC

2 **Don't Take It Personal
(Just One of Dem Days)**
Monica

3 **One More Chance/Stay with Me**
The Notorious B.I.G.

4 **Have You Ever Really Loved
a Woman?**
Bryan Adams

5 **Total Eclipse of the Heart**
Nicki French

## 838 Kiss from a Rose ZTT/SIRE 17896
### SEAL

*Writer: Seal*

*Producer: Trevor Horn*

*August 26, 1995*
*1 week*

"KISS FROM A ROSE" was one of the earliest songs Seal had written. "It started off as an experiment to see if I could build a track with lots of vocal overdubs on a small portastudio," says the artist, born Sealhenry Samuel in the Paddington section of London. "I really didn't know if it was any good. When I eventually signed with a record company and started making an album, my best friend told my producer about this song. But I didn't play it for him, because it wasn't necessarily right for the first record."

That first eponymously titled album was released in 1991. It yielded a top 10 single, "Crazy." It also contained a version of Seal's first U.K. hit, "Killer," written with Adam Tinley, known professionally as Adamski. "He was part of the rave culture," explains Seal. "He was kind of a newfangled Rick Wakeman in terms of keyboard playing. I used to see him at all these warehouse parties. He heard that I was a singer and one day we decided to do a song together." Their collaboration topped the U.K. singles chart in May, 1990 and led to a bidding war for Seal's talents. Producer Trevor Horn, initially not interested in signing the Nigerian vocalist to his ZTT label, changed his mind and offered him artistic freedom as well as money, and won out over several other U.K.-based labels.

The liner notes to Seal's second album, self-titled like the first, reveals

that it took two years, three months, a week and two days to produce. The first single was "Prayer for the Dying," but the album also contained "Kiss from a Rose." Normally reluctant to discuss the meaning of his songs, Seal allows, "There was obviously some kind of relationship that inspired the lyrics. But my songs seldom tend to be about one specific thing. I may use the concept of a relationship as a metaphor, but they tend to be about different things."

"Kiss from a Rose" almost didn't make it onto Seal's second album. "When we listened to all of the songs in sequence just before we put it out, I remember saying to Trevor, 'This song is too different. It doesn't sound like anything else on the album. It doesn't really fit.' And he said, 'Perhaps you're right.' Now the reason I said it is that I had a girlfriend at the time. She said she didn't think it fit. Not that she didn't like it, but it wasn't part of the concept. I got pre-release jitters and agreed with her. For about five minutes Trevor and I decided we weren't going to put it on the album. And then another friend of mine came to the studio and

heard it. She said, 'I liked the stuff I heard. Particularly that song that was something about a rose.' And Trevor turned to me and said, 'We're silly if we don't put this on it.'"

Steve Baker of Warner Brothers Records played "Kiss from a Rose" for Gary LeMel, president of music for Warner Brothers' movie division. "I flipped out over the song and thought it was perfect for *Batman Forever,*" says LeMel. "I played it for (director) Joel Schumacher, who immediately reacted and even said he wanted to shoot the video." Schumacher told Seal the song was perfect for a love scene between Bruce Wayne and Chase Manhattan. "It didn't work quite as well as the score worked in that one particular spot, so we put it at the end of the movie," says LeMel.

The first single from *Batman Forever* was U2's "Hold Me, Thrill Me, Kiss Me, Kill Me." Written expressly for the movie, it had a high debut but peaked at number 16. Released as the second single from the soundtrack, "Kiss from a Rose" soon surpassed the U2 single, reaching the top in its tenth chart week.

EPIC 78002 **You Are Not Alone**
MICHAEL JACKSON

*Writer: R. Kelly*

*Producers: R. Kelly*
*Michael Jackson*

*September 2, 1995*
*1 week*

THE ORIGINAL PLAN was for Michael Jackson to release a greatest hits album for Christmas, 1994, with a few new songs. After completing five tracks, he told Epic Records group chairman David Glew that he wanted to keep recording new material. Eventually he had an entire album of original songs, and *HIStory* became a two-CD set, half greatest hits and half new tunes. The first single, the two-sided "Scream" / "Childhood," did indeed make history when it debuted on the Hot 100 at number five, the highest new entry since the chart was initiated on August 4, 1958. The follow-up rewrote the record books. "You Are Not Alone" was the first single in chart history to enter the Hot 100 at number one.

R. Kelly [see 827—"Bump N' Grind"] thought Michael Jackson was kidding when he asked for a song. "Michael contacted my management. At first I thought he was playing, but it was serious. I was very honored, and I went into the studio and wrote a song right away, custom-made for him. I let Michael hear it over the phone." Kelly sent Jackson a copy of the song. "I actually imitated Michael when I sent it to him. He was laughing at me because I was imitating him."

Jackson flew to Chicago to collaborate with Kelly in the studio. "He's very easy to work with," says the man who wrote "You Are Not Alone," adding, "It amazed me because I work with a lot of people who haven't sold one album, and it'll be hard. But he was very easy, going along with everything I said." It took four days to complete the song. "We really wanted to get it right and concentrate on everything we could do to make history," says Kelly.

Jackson gives an emotional performance on "You Are Not Alone." Kelly explains, "Michael's a very passionate guy. He's got a lot of passion in his vocal chords. And I'm a very passionate guy, too. And then the song itself is really passionate because of the lyrics." Kelly was surprised that Jackson didn't request any changes in the song. "He was keen to leave it as it was, doing his vocals over mine. He even asked me to do the backgrounds with him."

The debut of "You Are Not Alone" at the top of the Hot 100 gave Jackson his 13th number one hit on the pop singles chart. For the previous four years, ever since his hit "Black or White" [see 801], Jackson had been tied with the Supremes in third place among artists with the most number one titles. "You Are Not Alone" broke him away from the pack, putting him in third place all by himself, behind the Beatles (20) and Elvis Presley (17). It was with some irony, therefore, that Diana Ross recorded "You Are Not Alone" as one of three new tracks on her collection of love songs, *Voice of Love*, released in the U.K. at the end of 1996.

The top five success of "Scream" and the number one status of "You Are Not Alone" must have come as welcome news to Jackson and everyone associated with the superstar. The *HIStory* album was his first work to be released after a slew of bad publicity, including a child molestation suit filed against him in 1993. Although the matter was settled out of court, it was uncertain how the public would react to a new Jackson record. "I don't think he's facing an image problem," Epic's Glew told *Billboard's* Melinda Newman at the time of the album's release. "I think the music will make the statement."

## THE TOP FIVE
*Week of September 2, 1995*

1 **You Are Not Alone**
Michael Jackson

2 **Gangsta's Paradise**
Coolio f/L.V.

3 **Kiss from a Rose**
Seal

4 **Waterfalls**
TLC

5 **Boombastic / In The Summertime**
Shaggy

## 840 Gangsta's Paradise
### COOLIO Featuring L.V.

MCA SOUNDTRACKS 55104

*Writers: Artis Ivey, Jr.*
*Larry Sanders*
*David Rasheed*
*Stevie Wonder*

*Producer: David Rasheed*

*September 9, 1995*
*3 weeks*

PRODUCERS Don Simpson and Jerry Bruckheimer relied on Kathy Nelson to supervise the music for their soundtracks. They didn't want the fact that she was working for MCA to get in the way of her putting together the music for *Dangerous Minds*, a Disney movie starring Michelle Pfeiffer as a former marine who becomes a teacher in a ghetto high school. "Initially there was some confusion over what direction the music would go in," Nelson reports. "They had temped the movie with more alternative music, which didn't work at all. I suggested that we do a very urban soundtrack. I brought Coolio in. He had just released a record called 'Fantastic Voyage' and I really liked the sound of his voice."

Nelson had never met Coolio when she invited him to view footage of the film in the editing room. She told him she wanted a song that could be a theme for the movie. "He loved the idea that the movie had a positive message, that it was about schools," says Nelson.

Soon after, Coolio was picking up a package from his manager at a studio and heard something that grabbed his attention. "I said, 'Damn, what is that?' because I'm a big Stevie Wonder fan, but this was a song I had never heard." Vocalist Larry Sanders, known as L.V. (Large Variety), was writing a song using the music from Wonder's "Pas-

time Paradise," a cut on the *Songs in the Key of Life* album. Coolio asked if he could work on it with him. He sat down and started writing on the spot, and the song was finished three hours later. Coolio thought the song would be perfect for *Dangerous Minds*. One problem cropped up immediately. "When we submitted the song to Stevie, he rejected it," says Coolio. "He told us we couldn't use 'Pastime Paradise' because I had a few vulgarities in the song and he wasn't with that. So I changed it. Once he heard the song, he thought it was incredible."

So did Nelson. "I was very excited. It didn't fit any of the trends happening in hip-hop or rap music at the time. And it was very different for Coolio. With 'Fantastic Voyage' everyone was expecting a fun party record from him. Instead they got this gothic, dramatic, much slower-paced song." The words weren't meant to represent Coolio's personal view of the world. "I thought it was actually too dark," he says. "People are still feeling like they're not in control of their lives, and 'Gangsta's Paradise' was not really my cry but the cry of some of these kids." Because of its theme, the artist thought the song would do well with urban stations. "I never had any idea it would go pop and

cross over and go worldwide. I didn't plan any of that. I just wrote a song that I felt good about."

Although the record became an international success, there was some resistance to it at first, says Nelson. "The turning point for me was when [Disney executive] Joe Roth, with encouragement from Bruckheimer and Simpson, decided to turn the whole campaign for the movie into a campaign with this song and this video. They immediately bought massive TV spots to promote the movie, which had our original Coolio and Michelle Pfeiffer video footage, along with clips from the movie."

"Gangsta's Paradise" opened a lot of doors for Coolio, the Compton rapper born Artis Ivey. He had been addicted to cocaine in the mid-'80s before he cleaned himself up and became a firefighter. One of the most memorable moments he recalls is performing the song with Stevie Wonder on "The Billboard Music Awards" in 1995. "I went to Stevie's studio and we changed the music so there would be room for him to sing. It didn't come to a head until I was actually on stage and he walked out from the back, singing. It gave me so much energy—I haven't felt that way about a performance for a long time."

---

### THE TOP FIVE
*Week of September 9, 1995*

1 **Gangsta's Paradise**
Coolio f/L.V.

2 **You Are Not Alone**
Michael Jackson

3 **Kiss from a Rose**
Seal

4 **Waterfalls**
TLC

5 **Boombastic / In The Summertime**
Shaggy

COLUMBIA 78043 **Fantasy**
MARIAH CAREY

**841**

*Writers: Mariah Carey*
*Chris Frantz*
*Tina Weymouth*
*Dave Hall*
*Adrian Belew*
*Steven Stanley*

*Producers: Mariah Carey*
*Dave Hall*
*Sean Combs*

*September 30, 1995*
*8 weeks*

"**I** HAD THE melody idea for 'Fantasy' and then I was listening to the radio and heard 'Genius of Love,' and I hadn't heard it in a long time," recalls Mariah Carey. "It reminded me of growing up and listening to the radio and the feeling that song gave me seemed to go with the melody and the basic idea I had for 'Fantasy.' I initially told Dave Hall about the idea and we did it." Issued as a single in 1982, "Genius of Love" by Talking Heads spin-off group Tom Tom Club peaked at number 32 on the Hot 100. "We called up the Tom Tom Club and they were really into it," says Mariah of her first single from the *Daydream* album.

Dave Hall, who also collaborated with Carey on "Dreamlover" [see 820], recalls that "Fantasy" was "a fun song to do. Mariah brought me 'Genius of Love' and I laid some strings on it and put it to a groove that I felt would really fit her. And that song didn't take us but a minute to do, because she really busted that out within two days. We did a rough copy and let (Sony Music Entertainment CEO) Tommy Mottola hear it and he loved it, so all we had to do was bring it back in and mix it down."

## THE TOP FIVE
*Week of September 30, 1995*

1  **Fantasy**
   Mariah Carey

2  **Gangsta's Paradise**
   Coolio f/L.V.

3  **You Are Not Alone**
   Michael Jackson

4  **Kiss from a Rose**
   Seal

5  **Runaway**
   Janet Jackson

The *Daydream* album reflected Mariah's love of hip-hop music. She took that influence one step further with "Fantasy," asking Sean "Puffy" Combs [see 853—"Can't Nobody Hold Me Down"] to helm a remix that emphasized the bass line more than the original pop version. Carey also invited Ol' Dirty Bastard from the Wu-Tang Clan to add some rap to the track.

"Fantasy" was an important step in Carey's career, and not just because the single was the second ever to debut at number one on the Hot 100, following Michael Jackson's "You Are Not Alone" [see 839], and the first by a female artist. The video for "Fantasy" marked Carey's debut as a director. "I'd done a lot of videos and wasn't always a hundred percent thrilled," she explains. "For the most part, I was never thrilled with the results, so I figured I would give it a shot." Carey earned high marks for the end result, which featured her Rollerblading in tight shorts, and a clown tied to a pole.

Three weeks after "Fantasy" entered the Hot 100 in pole position, the *Daydream* album repeated that feat on The Billboard 200. It was the first time that an artist had debuted at number one with an album and that album's first single. But more importantly for Carey, the experience of recording her sixth album was far different from making the first one. "I feel it's a lot easier now," she says. "When I think back to the first album, I wasn't used to the process of working with other people and producers, and I had a different role to play. I was like the guest of the producer in the studio, a kid that had a deal and was hoping to have some success. And now I feel more confident and more comfortable and more in control, because I am. I go in and do what I want. I sing by myself and if the co-producer chooses to come in at the end and give me some critique, that's fine and I'm really open to that. But I feel more free doing it the way I've been doing it for the last couple of albums."

842

# Exhale (Shoop Shoop) ARISTA 12885
## WHITNEY HOUSTON

*Writer: Babyface*

*Producer: Babyface*

*November 25, 1995*
*1 week*

**W**HEN SHE SIGNED to play the role of Savannah Jackson in the film adaptation of Terry McMillan's novel about the friendship of four very different African-American women, Whitney Houston wanted to concentrate on her acting, and had no plans to sing on the soundtrack. But that was before director Forest Whitaker recruited Kenny "Babyface" Edmonds to write and produce the music for *Waiting to Exhale.* "I was on tour with Boyz II Men in Anaheim, California," Babyface recalls. "Forest met me backstage and surprised me by asking me to consider doing the score as well as the soundtrack." When Babyface made his first visit to the set, Houston was still determined not to have any musical involvement in the film. "When she heard a song she liked, that's when she considered it," says the record producer. "'Count on Me' was the first song written and she ended up co-writing it with me."

Houston's previous film, *The Bodyguard* [see 813—"I Will Always Love You"], featured a multi-artist soundtrack, but Houston recorded the majority of the songs. Babyface took a different tack with *Waiting to Exhale.* "It was something Whitney and I talked about, but I always thought it should be [all] females. So it was a question of Whitney helping me to pick her favorite singers and people she would want to be involved on the project."

### THE TOP FIVE
*Week of November 25, 1995*

1 **Exhale (Shoop Shoop)**
Whitney Houston

2 **Fantasy**
Mariah Carey

3 **Gangsta's Paradise**
Coolio f/L.V.

4 **You Remind Me of Something**
R. Kelly

5 **Hey Lover**
LL Cool J

The roster of artists on the soundtrack was like a hall of fame of female R&B singers. "I got the chance to work with Chaka Khan, Patti LaBelle, Mary J. Blige and Brandy," enthuses Babyface. "It was a perfect opportunity to work with artists I hadn't had the chance to work with." Of the 16 songs on the soundtrack album, Houston only sang on three. "Count on Me" was a duet with her friend CeCe Winans, and "Why Does It Hurt So Bad" was a song Babyface had written for her two years earlier that she had never recorded. The first single from the soundtrack was the title song, "Exhale (Shoop Shoop)," which neatly summarized the movie's philosophy in three minutes and 24 seconds.

"When Whitney first heard the song, she figured I'd lost it—I couldn't come up with words anymore. And actually, she's right," Babyface says of the chorus that repeats "shoop shoop, shoop be doop." He explains, "I couldn't think of anything for that particular part. It felt like it should groove there.

But I knew it couldn't groove without any vocals, so I started humming along with it and that's what happened. The 'shoops' came. But they felt so good, I thought, 'Why not?' It doesn't have to mean anything."

"Exhale" was not the first time Babyface had worked with Houston in the studio. He and partner L.A. Reid had produced four tracks on her *I'm Your Baby Tonight* album, including the title track [see 773]. "It's always fun," says the producer. "Whitney and I are very close and we talk a lot. So when we get together, it's like family. It's always a good situation working in the studio with her."

Both the film and soundtrack were commercial successes. Budgeted at $15 million, the movie grossed over $66 million in the United States. The single "Exhale (Shoop Shoop)" was the third to debut at number one on the Hot 100, and was Houston's 11th chart-topper. That tied Houston with Madonna as the solo female artist with the most number one hits on the pop singles chart.

*Writers: Mariah Carey*
*Michael McCary*
*Nathan Morris*
*Wanya Morris*
*Shawn Stockman*
*Walter Afanasieff*

*Producers: Walter Afanasieff*
*Mariah Carey*

*December 2, 1995*
*16 weeks*

Superstar teamings are irresistible to radio programmers hungry for hits. It was inevitable that the pairing of Diana Ross and Lionel Richie would produce a number one song, just as there was no doubt that Paul McCartney and Stevie Wonder would capture the top spot, or that George Michael and Elton John would achieve pole position. So how could anyone doubt that Mariah Carey and Boyz II Men would achieve similiar success? In fact, they surpassed all other previous superstar match-ups, first by entering the Hot 100 at number one, and then by remaining there a record-shattering 16 weeks.

Carey says the idea for "One Sweet Day" was not inspired by the loss of one specific person in her life, but by several people she knew. "I told Walter [Afanasieff] the idea and started the usual process of me directing him as to what I'm hearing in my head and taking it from there—the two of us going to the bridge and developing the song. I had the first verse before I even sang it for Walter and the chorus was basically there. If I don't have the hook off the top of my head, it usually takes me a long time to get it, but that was really there. And then I stopped, because I

wanted to finish writing it with Boyz II Men."

Afanasieff elaborates, "At the time, Boyz II Men were the biggest thing out there. Through managers, we landed a meeting with the four guys to see if they would be interested. They loved the song. Mariah was in the studio singing it as the track was playing. She was singing the melody and one of the guys started singing the counter melody."

Nathan Morris of Boyz II Men was surprised at what he heard. "Mariah sang the verse she had already written. The lyrics and the idea and [a song I had written] coincided. Which was awkward, because I didn't know she was writing a song that pertained to what I was writing as well. I told her I had a song I had written two months earlier which was in the same vein." Afanasieff recalls what happened next: "We merged the two songs together lyrically, and a bit melodically, and that's why they're writers on the song."

The actual recording session was chaotic, the producer notes. "It was crazy! They had film crews and video guys. I'm at the board trying to produce. (Boyz II Men) are the busiest

guys in the world. Their managers and bodyguards are in the waiting room and it's 4:30 and they have until 7 o'clock. You've got four guys and you haven't even worked out their parts yet. So I was sweating. And these guys are running around having a ball, because Mariah and them are laughing and screaming and they're being interviewed. And I'm tapping people on the shoulder. 'We've got to get to the microphone!' They're gone in a couple of hours, so I recorded everything they did, praying that it was enough. After going home to my studio, I put the tracks together and did a rough blend of the four guys. And then Mariah went in and did some more voices to fill in a little bit, because it sounded like it's all Boyz II Men and there wasn't enough Mariah Carey on it."

Chart watchers all over the world had their eyes on the Hot 100 as "One Sweet Day" broke the 14-week record for remaining number one. "I didn't even focus on it until the very, very end," says Carey. "It's just not good. I don't think it's the right vibe to have. But it's definitely a blessing and I'm very grateful for it."

## THE TOP FIVE
*Week of December 2, 1995*

1 **One Sweet Day**
Mariah Carey & Boyz II Men

2 **Exhale (Shoop Shoop)**
Whitney Houston

3 **Hey Lover**
LL Cool J

4 **Fantasy**
Mariah Carey

5 **Gangsta's Paradise**
Coolio f/L.V.

## 844 Because You Loved Me 550 MUSIC 78237
### CELINE DION

Writer: Diane Warren

Producer: David Foster

March 23, 1996
6 weeks

DIRECTOR JON AVNET had a very strong idea about what he wanted in a song for his film *Up Close and Personal*, according to Kathy Nelson, President of Music for the Walt Disney Motion Picture Group. In her previous post at MCA Soundtracks, Nelson had worked with Avnet on *The War* and *Fried Green Tomatoes*, and based on her knowledge of the director's needs, hired four songwriters to come up with candidates for the vehicle starring Robert Redford and Michelle Pfeiffer. At the same time, word was out that Nelson was looking for a song for the movie, and publishers and songwriters were also submitting material. "We were looking for that perfect love song," says Nelson.

One of the composers asked to write specifically for the film was Diane Warren. "A lot of times if I'm asked to write a song for a movie, I want to write what I'd like to hear at the end of that movie," explains the songwriter. "So I saw the film and met with Avnet, and I talked to him about how I saw it and I talked to him about what he heard at the end. This was on a Friday, and on Saturday morning I went to my office and the song just came out. I started to write a chorus, and the chorus lyrically and musically wrote itself."

Although most people consider "Because You Loved Me" to be a romantic love song, Warren was

### THE TOP FIVE
*Week of March 23, 1996*

1  **Because You Loved Me**
   Celine Dion

2  **Nobody Knows**
   The Tony Rich Project

3  **Sittin' Up in My Room**
   Brandy

4  **Not Gon' Cry**
   Mary J. Blige

5  **One Sweet Day**
   Mariah Carey & Boyz II Men

thinking about her late father when she wrote it. "It was my way of thanking my dad, because he really believed in me, in my talent. And all those times I was discouraged when I was going to publishers, he'd always tell me to have faith in myself."

Warren didn't have an artist in mind when she wrote the song. One of the first artists Nelson contacted was Toni Braxton. "I knew she was finishing an album and thought she'd be a great artist and it would be a great opportunity, but they didn't feel the song was right for her." Celine Dion was not originally considered because Nelson knew her album *Falling into You* was complete and a first single had been chosen. But Dion had already recorded Warren songs like "If You Asked Me To" and "Nothing Broken But My Heart," and when she heard the song through Polly Anthony, head of the 550 Music label, she wanted to record it. "They loved it so much they changed course and changed the first single, and we did the whole campaign," says Nelson. The campaign was the advertising blitz for the film, which prominently featured Dion singing "Because You Loved Me." The song helped promote the movie and the movie helped promote the song. "It was like Celine Dion had a video in heavy rotation on every network," says Warren. "That's a once-in-a-lifetime exposure for an artist. I think that put her over the top. The combination of song and the exposure took her to superstar status."

As for the recording, Warren was thrilled with the final result. "It's better than what I heard in my mind," she confesses. "When someone like Celine sings your song or David (Foster) produces it, it's going to be better than you envisioned it. I lucked out on that," she said, just a few hours after waking up at 3 a.m. to watch the Oscar nominations announced on television. "I was so nervous, because you can't take anything for granted. I thought it would be nominated, but you don't know."

Of the five songs nominated from 1996, "Because You Loved Me" is the only one that went to number one. It topped the Hot 100 for six weeks, but fared even better on Billboard's Adult Contemporary chart, where it set a new record by remaining number one for 19 weeks.

COLUMBIA 78276 **Always Be My Baby**
MARIAH CAREY

**845**

*Writers: Mariah Carey*
*Jermaine Dupri*
*Manuel Seal*

*Producers: Mariah Carey*
*Jermaine Dupri*

*May 4, 1996*
*2 weeks*

**W**ITH "ALWAYS BE MY BABY," the third single from *Daydream*, Mariah Carey achieved her 11th number one hit, putting her in a three-way tie with Madonna and Whitney Houston as the solo female artist with the most number one hits to this date. "Always Be My Baby" also made Carey three for three, with all the singles from her fifth full-length studio album hitting the top of the Hot 100. There would be no more singles from the album after "Always Be My Baby," although "Forever" would become an airplay hit.

In her search to find producers to work with on *Daydream*, one of the people Carey turned to was Jermaine Dupri. She knew she wanted to collaborate with the Atlanta-based musician ever since she heard his production of "Jump" [see 807] for Kris Kross. He had also achieved success writing and producing for the female quintet Xscape ("Who Can I Run To") on his own So So Def label. "He's got a very distinct vibe," says Carey. "Jermaine, Manuel (Seal) and I sat down and Jermaine programmed the drums. I told him the feel that I wanted and Manuel put his hands on the keyboards and I started singing the melody. We went back and forth with the bridge and the B-section. I had the outline of the lyrics and started singing 'Always be my baby' off the top of my head."

Like other producers before him, Dupri was impressed with Carey's vocal abilities. "She can pretty much do anything with her voice," he says. "She's really strong vocally." Carey's talents extend to her backing vocals as well. On "Always Be My Baby," like many of her other songs, the backing voices take on some of the burden that instruments do in other artists' songs. "The background vocals are an important part of the whole picture for me," she explains. "That's why I like to do them myself a lot of the time, or at least initially I'll lay down the tracks. I'll double my voice or do a couple of tracks of my own voice. It's easy for me to match my voice. And then if I'm going to use other background singers, I'll let them go on top of mine. To me, on those kinds of records, the hook is really important. And I tend to do a lot of ad-libs, so it can get lost."

Less than a year after "Always Be My Baby" hit number one, Carey was back on the Hot 100—not as an artist, but as the head of her own label, Crave. The first single to be distributed by Crave to chart was "Head Over Heels" by the female R&B group Allure. "I've always wanted to help get new artists signed and I feel there's so much talent out there," says Carey. "I remember how it felt not knowing anybody, not knowing where to turn, and waiting to get noticed or signed. So Crave is a dream of mine. I'm trying to work with any of the artists who want my input or want help or want to collaborate. And it's cool for them because I'm a peer. I reached success at an early age and it's easy to relate to me as a friend, not just a record company person."

As for the name of the label, Carey isn't ready to reveal its true origin. "It came from a song I wrote that no one's ever heard. It's a secret. One day I'll talk about it."

**THE TOP FIVE**
*Week of May 4, 1996*

1 **Always Be My Baby**
Mariah Carey

2 **Because You Loved Me**
Celine Dion

3 **Nobody Knows**
The Tony Rich Project

4 **Ironic**
Alanis Morissette

5 **1, 2, 3, 4 (Sumpin' New)**
Coolio

## 846 Tha Crossroads RUTHLESS 6335
### BONE THUGS-N-HARMONY

Writers:Anthony Henderson
Charles Scruggs  Bryon McCane
Tim Middleton  Tony Cowan
Steven Howse  O'Kelly Isley
Marvin Isley  Rudolph Isley
Ronald Isley  Ernest Isley
Chris Jasper

Producer: D.J. U-Neek

May 18, 1996
8 weeks

THEY WERE FIVE young men growing up in a tough Cleveland neighborhood around East 99th Street and St. Clair Avenue. Layzie Bone and Flesh-N-Bone were siblings, Bizzy Bone was their stepbrother, Wish Bone was their cousin and Krayzie Bone was a lifelong friend. They loved the "old school" R&B that their parents listened to—artists like Marvin Gaye, Teddy Pendergrass, Rose Royce, Switch and DeBarge. In junior high, they were inspired by Run-D.M.C. to form a rap group, and called themselves the Band Aid Boys. They released a cassette of their music that sold well in Cleveland, but they couldn't seem to find the right manager, the right producer or the right record label. In 1992, they all took the same last name, Bone, because of the bone-deep bond between them. And a year later, on November 23, 1993, they boarded a bus headed away from the ghetto life and straight toward stardom. Next stop: Hollywood. Or at least close by.

They arrived in Visalia, California, where they knew some friends. Ready to audition for someone who could help them, they went to Tone Loc's house and rapped for him, but he wasn't interested. They called one of their heroes, Eric (Eazy-E) Wright, and he actually called them back. Sure, he'd love to listen to them, but he was heading out on the road with N.W.A. When the Bone brothers found out Eazy-E would be playing Cleveland, they headed back home.

They got a gig as an opening act for N.W.A. and met Eazy-E in his dressing room, where he took an instant liking to their music. He bought them bus tickets to return to California and gave them a couple of hundred dollars for spending money. Then he signed them to his own Ruthless label and executive produced an EP, Creepin' on Ah Come Up, which peaked at number 12 on The Billboard 200 in 1994. They were now called Bone Thugs-N-Harmony because they preferred to be known as thugs rather than gangstas, a term they associated with killing, and because they blended soft R&B harmonies with street rap.

Eazy-E put the group together with a producer, D.J. U-Neek, to record a full-length album. E. 1999 Eternal was released in August 1995 and entered the Billboard album chart at number one. It was a bittersweet victory for the rappers. Their mentor, Eazy-E, had died five months earlier, just shortly after announcing that he had AIDS. "Tha Crossroads" had originally been written as an elegy for one particular friend who had been gunned down in their Cleveland neighborhood, but for Bone Thugs-N-Harmony, the song was a tribute to all of their friends and family members who had been taken away too soon, including Eazy-E.

The single of "Tha Crossroads," a slight remix of the original recording, debuted at number two on the Hot 100. The following week it went to number one, the quickest move to the top since the Beatles took only two weeks to achieve pole position in 1964 with "Can't Buy Me Love" [see 145]. "Tha Crossroads" had an eight-week run at the top, making it the longest-running rap song at number one to this date since Kris Kross' "Jump" [see 807].

Their success resulted in the group starting its own label, Mo' Thugs. One of the first acts signed was the female trio Tré, who had guest-starred on "Tha Crossroads." The rappers' newfound wealth allowed them to give back to their own community, where they funded midnight basketball and contributed to an AIDS charity, Urban AID.

### THE TOP FIVE
*Week of May 18, 1996*

1  **Tha Crossroads**
   Bone Thugs-N-Harmony

2  **Always Be My Baby**
   Mariah Carey

3  **Because You Loved Me**
   Celine Dion

4  **Ironic**
   Alanis Morissette

5  **Nobody Knows**
   The Tony Rich Project

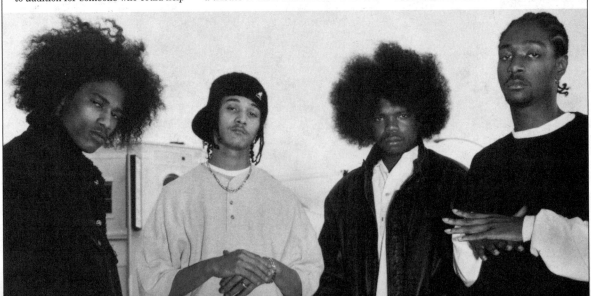

**How Do U Want It / California Love**

**847**

2PAC (Featuring KC & JOJO) and (Featuring DR. DRE & ROGER TROUTMAN)

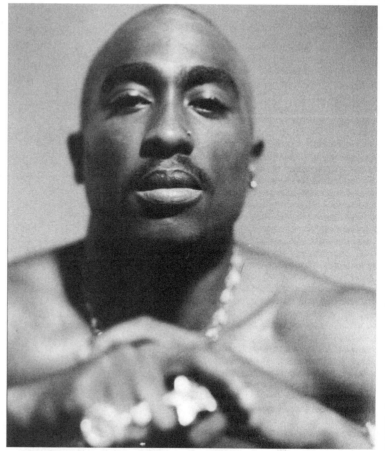

*Writers: Tupac Shakur*
*Johnny Jackson / Dr. Dre*
*Roger Troutman*
*Larry Troutman*
*Norman Durham*
*Woodrow Cunningham*

*Producers: Johnny "J" / Dr. Dre*

*July 13, 1996*
*2 weeks*

TUPAC SHAKUR was a man of conflicting images. He sang about gangstas and guns and was called a gangsta rapper, a label he denied. He was charged with sexual abuse, and with attacking film director Allen Hughes. Yet he won rave reviews for his acting in *Poetic Justice* and *Above the Rim,* and those who knew him best loved his sense of humor, and cited his creativity and sensitivity. Some even called him a "nice guy."

John Jackson, known in production credits as Johnny "J," was one of Shakur's best friends. They met after Shakur had completed work on *Poetic Justice,* introduced by a mutual friend named Big Syke. "I was working on his album and Pac heard some of the production I did and wanted to meet me," says Jackson. They collaborated on an album by Thug Life, a collection of rappers that included Syke and 2Pac. "It was wonderful working with 2Pac," says Jackson. "We were meant to be, because I was fast at laying music and he was quick at laying lyrics. When he got out of jail, and went to Death Row, he requested me."

While working on the *All Eyez on*

## THE TOP FIVE
*Week of July 13, 1996*

1  **How Do U Want It/**
   **California Love**
   2Pac (f/KC & JoJo) and
   (f/Dr. Dre & Roger Troutman)

2  **You're Makin' Me High/**
   **Let It Flow**
   Toni Braxton

3  **Tha Crossroads**
   Bone Thugs-N-Harmony

4  **Give Me One Reason**
   Tracy Chapman

5  **Macarena (Bayside Boys Mix)**
   Los Del Rio

*Me* album, Jackson played a track for Shakur that he had written three years before they met. Shakur liked it and asked Jackson to put it down on tape. "2Pac came up with the title and the lyrics. The music was all me—the beats, the melodies," Jackson says of the song that became "How Do U Want It." The producer adds, "Originally 2Pac was the one who sang the hook. And then after we listened to it for awhile, we said, 'Let's get someone else to sing the hook.'" Shakur suggested KC and JoJo from Jodeci. "The next thing I know," says Jackson, "they came in and did their thing." Shakur and Jackson worked at all hours of the day to complete the track as well as the album. "He was doing movies while we were cutting records," says the producer. "I would be laying music and he'd be somewhere filming. Then he'd meet me and do his vocals. We worked 24/7."

Jackson was attending his wife's high school reunion when he heard from Syke that 2Pac had been shot in Las Vegas. Jackson didn't believe the news until he and his wife called hospitals in the city and learned of 2Pac's condition. The 25-year-old recording artist and film actor had been in the front passenger seat of a car driven by the head of the Death Row label, Marion "Suge" Knight, when he was shot four times in an ambush near the Las Vegas strip. Six days later, on Friday, September 13, 1996, Shakur died of his wounds at 4:03 p.m. in the afternoon at University Medical Center. He would not be the only rapper to die in such a fashion [see 854—"Hypnotize"]. But his work would live on. In January 1997, Grammercy Pictures' *GRIDLOCK'd* opened, with Shakur receiving favorable notices for his role opposite actor Tim Roth in the comedy film. A soundtrack album including material by Shakur was released, with many more unreleased tracks from the prolific rapper waiting in the vaults.

# 848 You're Makin' Me High / Let It Flow  LAFACE 24160
## TONI BRAXTON

*Writers: Babyface/Bryce Wilson
Babyface*

*Producers: Babyface/Bryce Wilson
Babyface*

*July 27, 1996
1 week*

WHEN SHE WAS growing up in Severn, Maryland, Toni Braxton's conservative Apostolic minister father was so strict, she had to wait for him to go grocery shopping before she could watch "Soul Train." The tide had turned by the time she recorded "You're Makin' Me High," with its suggestive lyrics about sexual desire. Now her father was praying for his daughter's records to race up the Billboard charts.

With her sisters Traci, Towanda, Trina and Tamar, she recorded a single in 1990 called "The Good Life." The Braxtons auditioned for LaFace Records founders L.A. Reid and Babyface in Atlanta. "We thought Toni would be great as a solo artist," says Babyface. "It was a little touchy to go there because she was in a group with her sisters, but we thought that would be the best thing. The family handled it well." The first two songs Toni recorded for her new producers were "Give U My Heart," a duet with Babyface, and "Love Shoulda Brought You Home." Babyface reveals, "Those songs were meant for Anita Baker, but we couldn't get approval from her record company and Toni said, 'Hey, I'll sing them.' It was the best thing in the world for us and for her. We were lucky that Anita

said no." Both songs ended up on the *Boomerang* soundtrack and established Braxton's name on the Hot 100. Then her eponymously titled debut album went to number one and yielded three top 10 singles, "Another Sad Love Song," "Breathe Again" and "You Mean the World to Me."

Braxton's second album, *Secrets,* was released in June, 1996. "Doing a sophomore record after such a major debut, it's rough on anyone," concedes Babyface. "It took a little time to put it together because she did have a little pressure. She had to get in the right mindset before she could come all the way to the table. Once she started flowing with it, then it was fine." The first single, "You're Makin' Me High," was initially written by Bryce Wilson, half of the duo known as Groove Theory ("Tell

Me"). Wilson recorded the track in his basement studio and played it for Braxton and LaFace co-founder L.A. Reid. L.A. liked the music but not the lyrics. Wilson was on the road with Groove Theory when he received a phone call from Braxton saying she wanted something a little harder. "I told her I would send her some more tracks," says Wilson. "Actually, I sent her the tracks I had sent her before." Braxton loved one in particular, and Dallas Austin wrote lyrics to it. The song was titled "Nothing for You," but Reid felt it wasn't quite there yet. Braxton took it to Babyface, who suggested they bring Wilson back in. "Babyface had the hook and we worked on it for two or three days," says Wilson. When they finished, the track had provocative lyrics and a new title: "You're Makin' Me High." Babyface says, "It was sexy because Toni needed to do something a little more daring. She was fighting it a bit. She didn't know whether she should say those kinds of things. She didn't want to offend anybody. It was chancy, but it ended up working out."

The single's B-side also charted. "Let It Flow," Braxton's contribution to the *Waiting to Exhale* soundtrack, was already an airplay hit when the single was released. "We wanted to make sure it was on a single because we thought Toni did a great performance on it," says Babyface. "Initially I had 'Let It Flow' opening the film, but the director wanted it for another spot." As the composer of all the original songs on the *Exhale* soundtrack, it was up to Babyface to decide which female artist recorded which song. "I wrote specifically for the artist based on the scene and what it was about and who was the character in that particular scene."

Babyface enjoyed the experience of working in the studio with Braxton. "Toni is pretty easygoing. She doesn't like to spend a whole lot of time behind the mike. She likes to hit it and get it over with, so she stays there until she's done. She doesn't like to take breaks. If I think that her voice is worn a little bit, I have to fight her and say, 'Take a break.' She says, 'Nope, let's keep going.' I admire that about her."

## THE TOP FIVE
*Week of July 27, 1996*

1  **You're Makin' Me High/
   Let It Flow**
   Toni Braxton

2  **How Do U Want It/
   California Love**
   2Pac (f/KC & JoJo)/(f/Dr. Dre &
   Roger Troutman)

3  **Give Me One Reason**
   Tracy Chapman

4  **Macarena (Bayside Boys Mix)**
   Los Del Rio

5  **Twisted**
   Keith Sweat

Writers: *Antonio Romero Monge*
*Rafael Ruiz*

Producers: *Carlos De Yarza*
*Mike Triay*

*August 3, 1996*
*14 weeks*

"**M**ACARENA" WASN'T just a single, it was a phenomenon. It crept into every corner of our consciousness, captivating politicians, military generals, sports fans and record buyers all over the world, becoming the biggest dance craze since the Twist. It all began in Dos Hermanas, a southern Spanish town near Seville, where Antonio Romero and Rafael Ruiz were born in 1948. They were 14 when they started performing together. As Los Del Rio, they had recorded 31 albums of rumba-based music by the time "Macarena" debuted on the Hot 100. Their appeal was mostly to older Spaniards living in small towns.

In late 1992 they were at a party in Caracas, Venezuela, when Romero saw a beautiful woman flamenco dancing. He told her, "Give joy to your body, Macarena, for your body is there to give joy and good things." Macarena is the name of a neighborhood in Seville as well as a revered historical figure, so many young girls born in the city bear her name. The night of the party, Romero wrote the words to "Macare-

na." Los Del Rio recorded the song in early 1993 and included it on their album *A Mi Me Gusta.*

Sung entirely in Spanish, the original "Macarena" recording was popular in several countries before it caught on in Miami's South Beach. Jammin' John Caride, a DJ on Miami's Power 96, was getting requests to play it at the Baja Beach Club in Coconut Grove. He wanted to play it on the air, but station policy excluded songs not recorded in English. He persuaded assistant program director Kid Curry to let him play it at 1:30 in the morning. Curry raved about the song to program director Frank Walsh, who said he wanted an English remix ready in two days. Caride went to his friends Carlos De Yarza and Mike Triay, who had done production work on commercial jingles and recordings by artists like Menudo and 12 Gauge at their Bayside Studios (named after a book Triay had been reading that was published in Bayside, New York). De Yarza decided to bring the character of Macarena alive and let her speak in English. The lyrics were written and the melodies structured in one day. "It's a variation of the Los Del Rio melody," De Yarza explains. "It's not the same melody. A lot of people think the words are a translation, but it's a different song using the Los Del Rio chorus." Recording was scheduled for that night, but they couldn't locate studio singer Carla Ramirez. The next morning, fac-

ing a deadline, the production duo brought in singer Patricia Alfaro, who had worked with them on a jingle for a local Chrysler-Plymouth dealer, to record the vocals for "Macarena."

That afternoon, Power 96 was playing the remix of "Macarena," which soon became the most requested song in the station's history. Other radio stations requested their own copies, and soon De Yarza and Triay—dubbed the Bayside Boys by jocks at Power 96—were deluged with offers from major labels like Sony and Warner Brothers to release their remix. "We told the labels thank you, but we've used a piece of the original sound recording. It had to go to BMG." For the release of the RCA single in the U.S., the Bayside Boys gave the label a new, polished DAT mix of the song. So they were surprised when the single came out that it was their original demo, recorded for Power 96.

"Macarena" fell just shy of the top 40 portion of the Hot 100 in its first chart run. But once WKTU in New York added the record, it broke wide open. It returned to the Hot 100 and went to number one in its 33rd week, the latest in a chart run a single has ever reached the top. By the time "Macarena" fell off the chart, its 60-week run was the longest in Hot 100 history.

Despite the record's worldwide success, the Bayside Boys never got to meet Los Del Rio. "They seemed to have no interest," says De Yarza. "We wanted to get together with them." Triay adds, "We haven't even talked to them on the phone."

## THE TOP FIVE
*Week of August 3, 1996*

1 **Macarena (Bayside Boys Mix)**
Los Del Rio

2 **You're Makin' Me High/**
**Let It Flow**
Toni Braxton

3 **How Do U Want It/**
**California Love**
2Pac (f/KC and JoJo)/(f/Dr. Dre & Roger Troutman)

4 **Give Me One Reason**
Tracy Chapman

5 **I Can't Sleep Baby (If I)**
R. Kelly

## 850 No Diggity INTERSCOPE 97007
### BLACKSTREET (Featuring DR. DRE)

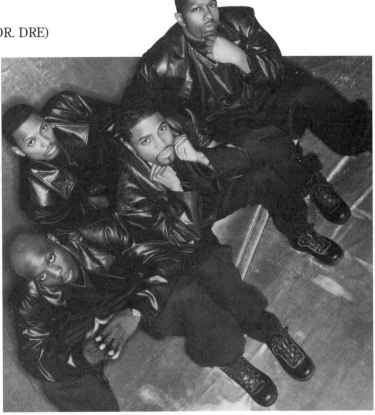

*Writers: Teddy Riley*
*Chauncey Hannibal*
*Lynise Walters*
*William Stewart*
*Dr. Dre*
*Bill Withers*

*Producers: Teddy Riley*
*William Stewart*

*November 9, 1996*
*4 weeks*

PRODUCER TEDDY RILEY could easily be a solo artist if he desired, but he's always chosen to be part of a group instead. "I feel like the power is in the team more than in one person," says the man acknowledged as the originator of the new jack swing sound, adding, "I'm a little afraid of getting out onstage by myself. I'm the shy one in the group." That explains why, after the breakup of his trio Guy, Riley plunged into another group, BLACKstreet.

The nucleus of the foursome is Riley and a friend he had known for 10 years, Chauncey Hannibal. Riley and Hannibal collaborated on some songs for Bobby Brown's 1992 album, *Bobby*, and then decided to form a new group. "Like Hall and Oates?" Hannibal asked. "No," Riley replied. "I want to do something like Boyz II Men but with a different sound, different style, different image, because we need more groups like that in the world." Riley's first choice for a name was the Flavor, but permutations of the name were copyrighted by Flavor Flav of Public Enemy. Riley and Hannibal kept writing songs for their new group and finally came up with BLACKstreet.

The line-up on the first album included David Hollister and Levi Lit-

### THE TOP FIVE
*Week of November 9, 1996*

1 **No Diggity**
BLACKstreet (f/Dr. Dre)

2 **It's All Coming Back to Me Now**
Celine Dion

3 **I Love You Always Forever**
Donna Lewis

4 **Macarena (Bayside Boys Mix)**
Los Del Rio

5 **Un-Break My Heart**
Toni Braxton

tle. Even though BLACKstreet had a top 10 hit with "Before I Let You Go" in 1994, Hollister and Little departed to pursue solo careers. Eric Williams and Mark Middleton were invited to join the quartet. Riley had wanted Williams in the first place, but he was in another group, Flex. Middleton was in a group called Brick City. Both men became available when their groups broke up.

Riley explains the genesis of BLACKstreet's number one hit. "What first gave me the idea of 'No Diggity' was a remix for a song on the first album called 'I Like the Way You Work.' LL Cool J and all of us did the remix, He was doing the rap. We were kidding around with some sayings and he said, 'I like the way you work it, no diggity, got to bag it up.' He kept saying that. But I didn't feel it as a rap. I felt it more as singing, like a chant. So we didn't use it then. About a year later we were working on this 'Grandma's Hands' sample. We kept playing with it and I kept putting beats to it." Riley knew he had a song everyone could dance to, but didn't think it should be the first single from BLACKstreet's second album. He played it for people like Heavy D and Dr. Dre, and got positive feedback about the track. "Dr. Dre

heard the song and fell in love with it," says Riley. "He said, 'Tell Teddy to let me be in the video.' I said let him be in the video and do a rap. That would be incredible. He did his rap and I edited it in because we had already mastered it without him." The female rapper on "No Diggity" is Queenpen, from Brooklyn. "I met her a long time ago," says the Harlem-raised Riley. "I needed a female vocalist but I told her I didn't have a record label. I said, 'When I get one, I will definitely get back to you.' And that's what happened with 'No Diggity.'" Riley has since signed Queenpen to his Lil' Man Records.

Interscope executives had no question about what to do with "No Diggity," the only track on the R&B-infused *Another Level* album with rapping on it. Riley says, "With Dr. Dre on it, the record company said it would have to be the first single." The record debuted at number 48 on the Hot 100 and jumped to number four in its second week. Three weeks later, it displaced the long-running "Macarena" from the summit. Riley was surprised when people told him how happy they were that "Macarena" was no longer number one. "I said, 'Why do you feel that way? That's a good song. My kids love it!'"

LAFACE 24200 **Un-Break My Heart**
TONI BRAXTON **851**

*Writer: Diane Warren*

*Producer: David Foster*

*December 7, 1996*
*11 weeks*

JUST 10 MONTHS after they ruled the Hot 100 with "Because You Loved Me" [see 844], songwriter Diane Warren and producer David Foster triumphantly teamed again for "Un-Break My Heart," the second number one single for sultry Toni Braxton. The song began with what Warren admits is an odd title. "It just flew into my head. I've never heard it said that way in my life. Everything's been said, but if you can twist it around slightly and come up with a new slant on it, and if you write it with a great melody, you'll probably have a great song."

Warren had her keyboard programmed to sound like an acoustic guitar and came up with a song that had a Spanish feel. "This key change happened, and as soon as I hit that, I thought, 'I'm on to something.'" Warren brought her work tape to Arista Records president Clive Davis not so much to pitch the song, but to get his opinion of it. She told him, "I don't really know what this song is. It's kind of strange. I don't know who it's for but I want you to hear it because I think it's pretty cool." Davis listened to the song and immediately said it should be recorded by Toni Braxton. Warren agreed, because she thought Braxton could communicate a "sadness" in her voice.

Armed with the demo, Foster paid a visit to Braxton's trailer on the set of a video shoot. LaFace co-founder Kenny "Babyface" Edmonds was there as well. "The demo was in a very low key, so I assumed I was going to raise the key to accommodate Toni's voice," explains Foster. "I said, 'Of course, I'll put it a few keys higher.'" Babyface protested, asking Foster to record Braxton in the same key as the demo. Foster responded, "But Kenny, she can't even sing down there. That's almost in a man's key." Kenny insisted, "No, it'll be great. It'll be really sexy." Considering that Babyface was speaking as the head of Braxton's record label, and not just another producer, Foster heeded the request. "And he couldn't have been more right. She sounds so sexy down there in this kind of man's range. And that gave us more room to shoot for the big notes in the chorus up top and really go for what I call the 'money notes.' She performed spectacularly, and L.A. Reid helped out with the background vocals at the end and made some suggestions. It was a real team effort."

One of Foster's previous productions had a strong influence on the sound of "Un-Break My Heart." He elaborates, "I'd just come off the Madonna song 'You'll See' that I wrote with her and produced, and I used Spanish guitar on that. I was kind of copying the Bryan Adams vibe from 'Have You Ever Really Loved a Woman?' I loved the Spanish guitar in that, so it's been a recent theme for me that I've used a few times. We're constantly searching for new ways to do the same thing. There's only 12 notes and 26 letters, so you gotta dig deep to be fresh and new and always creative."

Airplay on the original and a dance-mix version featured on "The Billboard Music Awards" and "The American Music Awards" contributed to long-lasting sales that kept "Un-Break My Heart" on top of the Hot 100 for 11 weeks. That, in spite of a review in *Entertainment Weekly* that asked how Braxton could record such a song. Warren bristles, "At the same time, he said, 'But Diana Ross would eat 10 cases of Haagen-Dazs for a song like that.' Is he saying that it's bad or . . . ?"

Whatever the reviewers said, Warren admits it's fun to be number one. "You want to be number one for as long as you can. It's good to be number one if it's one week. It's good to be number one if it's 11 weeks. It's a nice feeling to say it was a number one song (but) it doesn't make it a better or worse song."

## THE TOP FIVE
*Week of December 7, 1996*

1  **Un-Break My Heart**
   Toni Braxton

2  **No Diggity**
   BLACKstreet (f/Dr. Dre)

3  **Nobody**
   Keith Sweat f/Athena Cage

4  **Don't Let Go (Love)**
   En Vogue

5  **It's All Coming Back to Me Now**
   Celine Dion

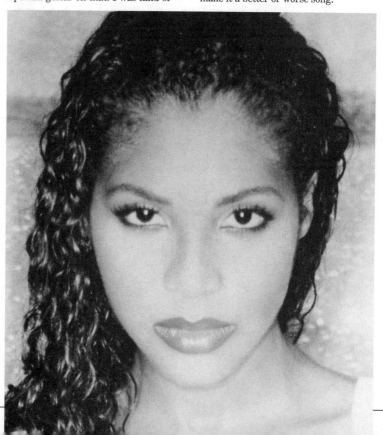

# 852 | Wannabe VIRGIN 38579
## SPICE GIRLS

*Writers: Spice Girls*
*Richard Stannard*
*Matt Rowe*

*Producers: Richard Stannard*
*Matt Rowe*

*February 22, 1997*
*4 weeks*

Fɪʀsᴛ, Sᴘɪᴄᴇ Gɪʀʟs stormed the charts in their native Britain. Their debut single, "Wannabe," went to number one. So did the follow-up, "Say You'll Be There." As did their third release, "2 Become 1." And when the group's fourth single, the two-sided "Who Do You Think You Are"/"Mama" topped the charts, they became the first act in U.K. chart history to have its first four singles hit number one. Just before that fourth single reached the pinnacle, the quintet conquered the U.S. with "Wannabe," ending the 11-week reign of Toni Braxton's "Un-Break My Heart" atop the Hot 100. The women seemed like overnight sensations, but actually they had been working hard for a long time to achieve their international success.

"It started about four years ago," confirms Melanie Chisholm, also known as "Sporty Spice." All of the women in the group had been working as dancers and singers since they were quite young. "Our paths have crossed at various auditions and we've done various jobs together," Chisholm continues. "But we did come together through an audition." Geri Halliwell, Melanie Brown and Victoria Addams attended that first audition with Chisholm and another woman. They had all answered an ad placed by a local talent manager in a newspaper, *The Stage.* He wanted to put together an all-female recording act. The women signed with him, but didn't stay long. "We weren't really happy with him, so we left and got Emma (Bunton) on board," explains Chisholm. "That's when we started writing our own material, and that's when Spice Girls actually formed."

Simon Fuller, manager of Annie Lennox and Cathy Dennis, wasn't looking for new acts but added the Spice Girls to his client roster. "What clinched it for me was that they had written their own material, and it was very strong," he told Dominic Pride in *Billboard.* "Coupled with the fact that they all had really strong individual charac-

ters, it was irresistible." Fuller brought the Spice Girls to executives at various London-based record labels, where the women sang *a cappella* or to a backing tape. While most labels expressed interest in the group, Fuller narrowed his choice to RCA and Virgin. "It was very exciting and competitive," Virgin's deputy managing director Ashley Newton told Pride. Virgin had a strong alternative roster, but no strong pop act. Spice Girls "brought something fresh, and we had a fresh perspective on pop music, as we don't have a history of it."

The Spice Girls went into the studio to complete their first album before any singles were released. "We always work with producers, because at the moment we haven't got the knowhow with technology," says Chisholm. "But we do a lot of work vocally. We always do a lot of the melodies and harmonies, and we always write all of our lyrics." Fuller teamed the women with two sets of producers, Paul Wilson and Andy Watkins, and Richard Stannard and Matt Rowe. The latter, known as Matt & Biff, helmed "Wannabe." Says Chisholm, "You know when you're in a gang and you're having a laugh and you make up silly words? Well we were having a giggle and we made up this silly word, zigazig-ha. And we were in the studio and it all came together in this song. It only took about 30 minutes to write and then we demoed it up fast. As soon as we recorded it, we knew we wanted it to be our debut single."

Chisholm answers quickly when asked what the highlight of the group's early career is. "Being number one in America. That's something we were always really determined to do, and we're ecstatic about it."

## THE TOP FIVE
*Week of February 22, 1997*

1  **Wannabe**
   Spice Girls

2  **Un-Break My Heart**
   Toni Braxton

3  **Can't Nobody Hold Me Down**
   Puff Daddy (f/Mase)

4  **I Believe I Can Fly**
   R. Kelly

5  **Don't Let Go (Love)**
   En Vogue

BAD BOY 79083 **Can't Nobody Hold Me Down**
PUFF DADDY (Featuring MASE)

*Writers: Sean "Puffy" Combs*
*Steve Jordan*
*Carlos Broady*
*Nashiem Myrick*
*Mason Betha*
*Greg Prestopino*
*Matthew Wilder*
*Sylvia Robinson*
*Melvin Glover*
*Clifton Chase*
*Edward Fletcher*

*Producers: Carlos Broady*
*Nashiem Myrick*
*Sean "Puffy" Combs*
*Stevie J.*

*March 22, 1997*
*6 weeks*

**W**HAT SEAN "PUFFY" COMBS really wanted to do when he was a student at Howard University in Washington, D.C., was sing, but he says it wasn't one of his talents. He didn't have the patience to write the rhymes he'd need if he was going to be a rapper, so that was also out of the question. He thought about being a dancer, and did a turn in a video for Fine Young Cannibals. That wasn't his destiny either. So he decided to tackle the business end of the record industry, and through his friendship with Heavy D managed to become an unpaid intern at Andre Har-

rell's Uptown Records in New York.

Twice a week, he caught the Amtrak train to Manhattan, hiding in the bathroom to avoid the train conductor, because he couldn't afford to buy a ticket. When he was 18, he got a paid position on Uptown's A&R staff, and worked his way up to vice president, shaping the careers of acts like Mary J. Blige and Jodeci. Ultimately, he clashed with Harrell over the hiring of a general manager for the label, and was dismissed. He was feeling depressed about his future when producer L.A. Reid, co-founder of LaFace Records, arranged for Combs to meet Arista Records president Clive Davis. Although other companies bid for his Bad Boy Entertainment, Combs signed a partnership deal with Arista. After a year of preparation, the Bad Boy label came on strong, charting with hits by Faith Evans, Craig Mack, Total, 112 and the Notorious B.I.G.

But the label's first number one single belonged to its founder. Combs had already charted on the Hot 100 as a featured artist on Lil' Kim's "No Time" when he released "Can't Nobody Hold Me Down." The title came from a line in Matthew Wilder's top five hit from 1985, "Break My Stride." The familiar musical hook was first heard on Grandmaster Flash and the Furious Five's seminal rap hit from 1982, "The Message." The rap came from a new act

signed to Bad Boy, a 19-year old named Mase. Combs first saw Mase at a party at the Hard Rock Cafe in Atlanta. After a spontaneous audition, Combs told the teenager he wanted to sign him to his label. "When I got back to New York, everybody found out I was about to join Bad Boy. I started getting offers from everywhere, everybody doubling the Bad Boy deal, tripling it, but my heart said Bad Boy." After appearing on a remix of 112's "Only You," Mase went to work on his own album. Combs suggested the time was right to release a track called "Can't Nobody Hold Me Down" immediately rather than waiting for Mase's album to be finished. "I didn't want to hold it," says Mase. "It might not be good a year from now when I was ready to come out. So I said, 'Let's go with it.'"

Just as Mase didn't like his rapping on the remix of the 112 track the first time he heard it, he had an initial negative reaction to "Can't Nobody Hold Me Down." He explains, "I did not originally like that beat. But Puff said, 'Just take my word for this one. It's going to be a hit.' I never thought it would be big so fast. I thought it would grow gradually and become big, but not instant out-of-the-box." The single reached the top of the Hot 100 in its ninth chart week, but having his first number one pop single as an artist and having the label's first pop number one was a bittersweet victory for the young label owner. Just three days before he learned that his single was on top of the chart, Combs had been accompanying his best friend and top-selling artist the Notorious B.I.G. to a party in Los Angeles sponsored by *Vibe* magazine when B.I.G., whose real name was Christopher Wallace, was fatally slain in a drive-by shooting.

## THE TOP FIVE
*Week of March 22, 1997*

1  **Can't Nobody Hold Me Down**
   Puff Daddy (f/Mase)

2  **Wannabe**
   Spice Girls

3  **You Were Meant for Me**
   Jewel

4  **Un-Break My Heart**
   Toni Braxton

5  **In My Bed**
   Dru Hill

## 854 Hypnotize BAD BOY 79092
### THE NOTORIOUS B.I.G.

*Writers: Sean "Puffy" Combs*
*Deric Angelettie*
*Ron Lawrence*
*Christopher Wallace*
*Andy Armer*
*Randy Badazz*

*Producers: Deric Angelettie*
*Ron Lawrence*
*Sean "Puffy" Combs*

*May 3, 1997*
*3 weeks*

WHEN HE WAS ALIVE, the Notorious B.I.G. only reached the number two position on the Hot 100. "One More Chance/Stay With Me" peaked in the runner-up slot the week of July 15, 1995. Eight weeks after he was gunned down in Los Angeles, the rapper earned a posthumous number one as "Hypnotize" hit pole position in its second week on the chart. It was the fifth posthumous chart-topper of the rock era, following Otis Redding's "(Sittin' On) The Dock of the Bay" [see 238], Janis Joplin's "Me and Bobby McGee" [see 289], Jim Croce's "Time in a Bottle" [see 352] and John Lennon's "(Just Like) Starting Over" [see 534]. Not counting the titles that debuted at number one, "Hypnotize" joined the Beatles' "Can't Buy Me Love" [see 145] and Bone Thugs-N-Harmony's "Tha Crossroads" [see 846] as the titles that took the shortest amount of time to reach the top. "Can't Buy Me Love" rocketed 27-1 in its second week, and "Tha Crossroads" and "Hypnotize" both debuted at number two and moved to number one the following week. To this date, the only singles to debut at number two were "Tha Crossroads," "Hyp-

notize" and Mariah Carey's "Always Be My Baby" [see 845].

"Hypnotize" displaced "Can't Nobody Hold Me Down" by Puff Daddy (featuring Mase) from the chart summit, giving Sean "Puffy" Combs back-to-back number one singles as writer and producer. It also gave Combs' Bad Boy label two consecutive number one hits, and with "Can't Nobody Hold Me Down" falling into second place, the top two titles on the Hot 100. It was only the second time that rap singles occupied the top two slots. On March 20, 1993, Snow and Dr. Dre led the list with "Informer" [see 815] and "Nuthin' But a 'G' Thang," respectively.

"Hypnotize," the first single from the Notorious B.I.G.'s ironically titled double-CD set *Life After Death*, had a familiar ring to it. That was because the music track sampled a title that had already been number one. That explained the writing credits for Randy 'Badazz' Alpert and Andy Armer. They were the composers of "Rise," a chart-topper for Randy's uncle, Herb Alpert [see 512]. "The really amazing thing to me is that the same people who were listening (and) buying the track on adult contemporary radio in 1979 now have kids who are grooving (and) buying the same track on rap/hip-hop radio in 1997," Randy says. "Substitute a legendary trumpet player with a legendary rapper

and you've bridged a generation."

The Notorious B.I.G. was Christopher Wallace, born to Jamaican parents in the Bedford-Stuyvesant section of Brooklyn on May 21, 1972. As early as the third grade he thought he might be interested in art, but he didn't grow up in a neighborhood that fostered such creativity. Hanging with gangs and selling crack was what a lot of kids did, and Wallace was no exception. He was 17 when he was arrested the first time. When he got out, he returned to the streets, but he also met a DJ named 50 Gran and discovered a talent for rhyming over his beats. An item about the young rapper appeared in the "Unsigned Hype" section of *The Source*, which led to a meeting with Combs. The first album was titled *Ready to Die*, but few realized that *Life After Death* was the second installment of a trilogy, designed to be completed with a third album, *Born Again*. It will never be recorded. Instead, the rapper was gunned down in the early morning hours of March 9, 1997, just a few minutes after leaving a party at the Peterson Automotive Museum in Los Angeles to celebrate the Soul Train Awards. Months after the incident, the murder remained unsolved and friends like Combs and family like Wallace's mother Voletta and former wife Faith Evans continued to mourn his loss.

### THE TOP FIVE
*Week of May 3, 1997*

1 **Hypnotize**
   The Notorious B.I.G.

2 **Can't Nobody Hold Me Down**
   Puff Daddy (f/Mase)

3 **You Were Meant for Me**
   Jewel

4 **For You I Will**
   Monica

5 **I Want You**
   Savage Garden

Writers: *Issac Hanson*
*Taylor Hanson*
*Zac Hanson*

Producers: *The Dust Brothers*
*Stephen Lironi*

*May 24, 1997*
*3 weeks*

Wᴴᴀᴛ's ᴀɴ "MMMBop"? A unit of time. The catchy pop song that made the Hanson brothers overnight sensations was about the fleeting nature of relationships, but the hook was originally a riff in another song. "MMMBop, bop, bop" was a scatlike ending of a different Hanson tune until they realized it was strong enough to become a song of its own. And when "MMMBop" hit the top of the Hot 100, Issac, Taylor and Zac Hanson became the first artists born in the '80s to have a number one hit.

Walker Hanson married his high school sweetheart, Diana, when they were both 19. He worked as a CPA and she stayed home to raise and home-school their first three children. The boys liked listening to the "oldies" in their father's record collection, and took up an interest in musical instruments and singing. They played state fairs and local events in Tulsa. In 1994, they took demos of their songs to the annual South By Southwest music conference held in Austin, Texas. Christopher Sabec, attorney for the Dave Matthews Band, liked them enough to become their manager. But 14 labels turned him down before Mercury A&R exec Steve Greenberg heard the tape. "It had this rough version of 'MMMBop' and I thought it was amazing," says Greenberg. "The lead singer's voice was tremendous and the song was so catchy. But I was totally

skeptical. I thought some adult was manipulating it. There must be adults playing the instruments or adults must have written the song and I bet that in real life the kids couldn't sing that well. I wasn't going to pursue it but the song stayed in my head. I went to see them perform live just so I could sleep at night after I passed on them."

Greenberg flew to Koffeeville, Kansas, to see Hanson perform at a town fair. He heard a live performance that was as outstanding as the tape, but still couldn't believe his ears. "I looked around the stage to see if there were tapes playing or DATs running in synch of if some adults were in the wings playing a keyboard, and none of that was happening. It was really these three guys being a wonderful garage band and right on the spot I said, 'I want to make a record with you.'"

The brothers had been resigned to the idea that a major label would want them to fit into an R&B dance groove, and that they would only be allowed to sing while studio musicians played. But Greenberg had other ideas. He wanted to keep the original garage band spirit and asked the Dust Brothers (Mike Simpson and John King) to produce Hanson. Knowing they wouldn't have time to produce the entire album, he

also asked Black Grape producer Stephen Lironi to work with the band.

"The demo stood out above and beyond anything we had received in a long while," says King. "We thought, 'This is a hit song.'" The Dust Brothers recorded the basic tracks for "MMM-Bop" in their home studio beginning in July, 1996. "We based it on some drums we had created and then had (Zac) overdub crashes and fills," King explains. But the Dust Brothers' schedule heated up when the album they produced for Beck was released, and it became difficult to finish the Hanson project. Lironi recorded the rest of the album and Greenberg waited for the Dust Brothers to finish "MMMBop." Finally, the A&R VP asked Simpson and King if Lironi could finish the track. "Stephen was the producer when the vocals were recorded and the over-dubs of all the instruments," says Greenberg. "Then we mixed it with Tom Lord-Alge and sent the Dust Brothers the tracks so we could get a mix out of them. I never thought we'd get one because they were so busy. But at the last minute, a mix appeared in the mail. Suddenly we had two finished versions of 'MMMBop,' so we put them both on the single. We started it in July and finished in November."

## THE TOP FIVE
*Week of May 24, 1997*

1   **MMMBop**
    Hanson

2   **Hypnotize**
    The Notorious B.I.G.

3   **Return of the Mack**
    Mark Morrison

4   **For You I Will**
    Monica

5   **Say You'll Be There**
    Spice Girls

## 856   I'll Be Missing You   BAD BOY 79097
### PUFF DADDY & FAITH EVANS (Featuring 112)

*Writers: Sting*
      *T. Gaither*
      *Faith Evans*

*Producers: Sean "Puffy" Combs*
         *Stevie J.*

*June 14, 1997*
*11 weeks*

SEAN "PUFFY" COMBS didn't just lose his label's main attraction when Christopher Wallace, a.k.a. the Notorious B.I.G. and Biggie Smalls, was fatally shot in Los Angeles. He also lost his best friend. "I was like the walking dead," Combs reflects on his emotional state in the days after the murder. "I wasn't talking. I wasn't doing anything." But he did attend to details in the aftermath of the rapper's death. "While I was dealing with all the funeral arrangements and was out of the loop on what was going on [at Bad Boy], one of my acts made a tribute record." That song, "We'll Always Love Big Poppa," was recorded by the Lox. "I said, 'I gotta do this, too,'" Puffy recalls. "I felt it was something that would help me."

Going into the studio to record "I'll Be Missing You" was a catharsis for the young label owner. "I was so used to talking to [Biggie] every day. I missed that. So when I made the record, I was finally able to talk to him. That's all it was, a conversation." Combs was inspired to sample a previous number one song while watching television. "I saw the Police video on MTV," he says of "Every Breath You Take" [see 574]. "That's always been one of my favorite songs. It's always

### THE TOP FIVE
*Week of June 14, 1997*

1   **I'll Be Missing You**
    Puff Daddy & Faith Evans (f/112)

2   **MMMBop**
    Hanson

3   **Say You'll Be There**
    Spice Girls

4   **Return of the Mack**
    Mark Morrison

5   **Hypnotize**
    The Notorious B.I.G.

made me cry. It always made me think of my father, in a good way." Combs had an affinity for older songs, even though he didn't collect records when he was growing up. "I listened to the radio. A lot of kids watched TV. I used to be on punishment a lot, so I used to get my TV privileges taken away. I was forced to listen to radio all the time. That's how I started knowing all of these hits from the '80s, because those are the records I listened to when I was on punishment." As big a hit as "Every Breath You Take" was—number one for eight weeks—"I'll Be Missing You" became an ever bigger hit, remaining on top for 11 weeks. "I get a lot of flack for sampling," Combs concedes. "People try to say it's uncreative or that's the only reason why the record is a success, but a lot of people are sampling out there and a lot of people aren't scanning," says the artist, referring to SoundScan's method of keeping track of record sales by scanning bar codes.

Combs collaborated on "I'll Be Missing You" with another of his Bad Boy artists, Faith Evans, who had been married to the Notorious B.I.G. "We're a family," says the man known as Puff Daddy. "It's not a joke or just there for publicity. We're around each other every second. She's in the studio with me every day, so that's not something unusual. I'm the leader of the family, so if I have an idea, everybody usually goes along with it. We all feel where each other is coming from, so she understood. She was helping me get through everything."

It was clear long before 1997 was over that Combs would be the number one producer of the year, thanks to his incredible run of hits. Still, he offered a candid assessment of his talent. "People ask when [rap music] is going to die. We're having number one records, so I've been beat up a lot by the critics. For the record, I can't say I'm the best producer out there, but I feel like I'm one of the best entertainers. When I'm producing a record, I'm not doing it selfishly, like I have to come up with this monumental new form of music. I'm just trying to make you dance. I make music because I want to make people dance."

BAD BOY 79100 **Mo Money Mo Problems**
THE NOTORIOUS B.I.G. Featuring PUFF DADDY & MASE

Writers: *Christopher Wallace*
*Sean "Puffy" Combs*
*Steve Jordan*
*Mason Betha*
*Bernard Edwards*
*Nile Rodgers*

Producers: *Stevie J.*
*Sean "Puffy" Combs*

August 30, 1997
2 weeks

**P**UFF DADDY AND the Notorious B.I.G.—Sean "Puffy" Combs and Christopher Wallace—wrote "Mo Money Mo Problems" about their own lives. "Having monetary success created jealousy and problems for us," says Combs. "It seems we didn't have any control over [those problems] unless we decided to run and hide and stay in the house. So we wanted people to know that we don't do this for the money, because the more money we come across, the more problems we see."

"Mo Money Mo Problems" was the second single from the Notorious B.I.G.'s double CD set *Life After Death,* and the second posthumous number one [see 854—"Hypnotize"] for the late rapper also known as Biggie Smalls. It is the only time in the rock era that an artist has had two posthumous chart-topping singles. "Mo Money Mo Problems" was the second consecutive number one title for Combs in his Puff Daddy identity, making him only the fourth act in the rock era to succeed himself at the top of the Hot 100, following Elvis Presley, the Beatles and Boyz II Men. The ascension of "Mo

Money Mo Problems" was also a coup for Combs' Bad Boy label. It became the first imprint since Motown in 1964 to have its first four chart-topping hits ("Can't Nobody Hold Me Down," "Hypnotize," "I'll Be Missing You" and "Mo Money Mo Problems") fall in the same calendar year. The coincidence was appropriate, as that same label also inspired Combs to feature artists from his Bad Boy roster on each others' hits. "(I'm) just following in the footsteps of Berry Gordy and Motown," he explains. "They piggybacked all their artists. When the Supremes were hot, they did something with Marvin Gaye and Michael Jackson and the Jackson Five. We all need each other to get to the next level."

Combs, who was with Biggie when the rapper was fatally shot, recalls his early impressions of Wallace. "I first saw his talent in his melodies. A lot of rappers rhyme, but they don't rhyme with melody. He had a lot of melody to his lyrics. His lyrics were almost like songs. Nobody's voice sounded like his, and the way he graphically described something, it made you feel like you were actually with him, in that room."

Combs also recalls how the late rapper worked in the studio. "He just sat in a chair. Imagine a studio and the music real loud, but the instrumental of the record playing for 20 hours straight and [he's] just sitting, not saying anything, not doing anything but maybe smoking a cigarette. Then all of a sudden, he gets up 20 hours later and goes into the booth and does the whole song. Didn't talk to you, never wrote down a lyric."

The writing credits for "Mo Money Mo Problems" include Bernard Edwards and Nile Rodgers. The creative core of Chic [see 495—"Le Freak"], the pair wrote and produced "I'm Coming Out" for Diana Ross, and that track is heavily sampled in the B.I.G. recording. "If I hear a song on the radio when I'm driving down the street, I'll remember it and use it," says Combs. "I've had success with a lot of records I sampled by recreating sounds and making them more up to date." Many of those sampled songs turned out to be bigger hits in the Combs' versions, such as Ross' original single of "I'm Coming Out," which peaked at number five.

## THE TOP FIVE
*Week of August 30, 1997*

1 **Mo Money Mo Problems**
The Notorious B.I.G.
f/Puff Daddy & Mase

2 **I'll Be Missing You**
Puff Daddy & Faith Evans (f/112)

3 **Quit Playing Games
(With My Heart)**
Backstreet Boys

4 **Semi-Charmed Life**
Third Eye Blind

5 **2 Become 1**
Spice Girls

**858**

# Honey COLUMBIA 78665
## MARIAH CAREY

*Writers: Mariah Carey*
*Sean "Puffy" Combs*
*Kamaal Fareed*
*Steve Jordan*
*Stephen Hague*
*Bobby Robinson*
*Ronald Larkins*
*Larry Price*

*Producers: Sean "Puffy" Combs*
*The Ummah*
*Stevie J.*
*Mariah Carey*

*September 13, 1997*
*3 weeks*

Mariah Carey is a huge fan of hip hop, according to Sean "Puffy" Combs, founder of Bad Boy Entertainment, who was asked by the artist to produce a couple of tracks for her *Butterfly* album. "She and [rapper] Q-Tip [of A Tribe Called Quest] had an idea and they asked me to come in and produce the record," says Combs. But his need for excellence kept him out of the one place you'd expect to find him. "A lot of people feel I'm overbearing, so I wasn't allowed in the studio when she did her vocals," he reveals. "I'm trying to work on that. I'm such a perfectionist, sometimes I don't give people the chance to breathe. So I've been banned from a lot of studios. Mariah [recorded "Honey"] until she thought it was perfect, like a hundred times. She gave me a hundred tracks to choose from."

Released as the first single from *Butterfly,* "Honey" was an instant hit, debuting at number one on the Hot 100. It was the sixth single to do so, and the

## THE TOP FIVE
*Week of September 13, 1997*

1  **Honey**
   Mariah Carey

2  **Mo Money Mo Problems**
   The Notorious B.I.G.
   (f/Puff Daddy and Mase)

3  **Quit Playing Games
   (With My Heart)**
   Backstreet Boys

4  **How Do I Live**
   LeAnn Rimes

5  **2 Become 1**
   Spice Girls

third by Carey after "Fantasy" [see 841] and "One Sweet Day" [see 843]. No other artist at this point in time had had even two singles debut at the top of the chart. "Honey" was also the single that broke Carey away from the pack. After "Always Be My Baby" [see 845], she was in a three-way tie with Madonna and Whitney Houston as the solo female artist with the most number one singles on the Hot 100. All three women had collected 11 chart-topping hits, but "Honey" put Carey out in front with 12. It also put her in a tie for fourth place with the Supremes among all artists for the most number one singles, behind the Beatles (20), Elvis Presley (17) and Michael Jackson (13). And it made her label, Columbia, the first to amass 80 number one hits in the rock era.

"Honey" also added impressive chart statistics to Combs' resumé. Along with Stevie J., it was his third consecutive number one on the Hot 100. It was only the third time in the rock era that a producer or production team had three chart-toppers in a row. George Martin gave the Beatles a hat trick in 1964 with "I Want to Hold Your Hand," "She Loves You" and "Can't Buy Me Love." And in 1978, Barry Gibb, Albhy Galuten and Karl Richard-

son were the producers on "Stayin' Alive" by the Bee Gees, "(Love Is) Thicker Than Water" by Andy Gibb and "Night Fever" by the Bee Gees. Sean and Stevie were responsible for producing "I'll Be Missing You," "Mo Money Mo Problems" and "Honey." That trio of hits gave the two producers another first: they were number one for the whole summer of 1997. No other producer or producers had ever been responsible for the top song on the Hot 100 for an entire season of the year.

On a more personal note, "Honey" was Carey's first single after the June, 1997 separation from her husband Tommy Mottola, the president and CEO of Sony Music Entertainment. The track, like the rest of *Butterfly,* revealed a more confident, mature and openly sensual woman than had been heard on previous albums. "I've come into my own as an artist," Carey told Elysa Gardner in the *Los Angeles Times.* "At this point I feel free enough to express what I'm really feeling, without using a smoke screen. . . . It's definitely an evolution for me." That evolution included a change of manager and attorney, and an exploration into acting in films and television for the 27-year-old superstar.

MOTOWN 860684 **4 Seasons of Loneliness**
BOYZ II MEN

**859**

Writers: *James Harris III*
*Terry Lewis*

Producers: *Jimmy Jam*
*Terry Lewis*

October 4, 1997
1 week

**B**ACK IN 1994, Boyz II Men ran into Jimmy Jam and Terry Lewis at the NBA All Star Game in Minneapolis and asked the writing/producing team for a song for their second album. Jam and Lewis came up with "On Bended Knee" [see 831]. Three years later, history repeated itself when the Boyz had another chance meeting with Jam and Lewis at the All Star Game in Cleveland. Shawn Stockman asked when the group could come to Minneapolis to work on some new material for their third album. The producers had just come up with an idea for a song called "4 Seasons of Loneliness" and Jimmy Jam realized it would be perfect for the Motown quartet.

Jam told Stockman the song was about the aftermath of a breakup, and how "every time the season changed, the things that had to do with the season would remind you of this girl. Like in the winter, when the snow fell, or in the spring when the flowers bloomed." Stockman liked the concept and wanted to hear the song. Jam and Lewis returned to their Flyte Tyme studios and completed the ballad. "The challenge was, do you put all four seasons in the chorus, or do you split it up," Jam explains. "Maybe you do two seasons in the first chorus and two seasons in the second. We kept going back and forth and decided we should put all four sea-

sons in each of the choruses. The only way to do that was to have a lot of words in the chorus."

Boyz II Men arrived in town, ready to hear the song. They were enthusiastic about the track, but doubtful about the chorus. To calm their fears, Jimmy asked them to try singing it, and promised to change the chorus if they didn't like it. After completing his vocal, Stockman took a break and then told the producers, "I totally get it. I can't get the song out of my mind."

It took a little more time to win over Motown's executives. But eventually the company told the group to pick the first single from *Evolution* themselves, and the Boyz chose "4 Seasons of Loneliness." Although Jimmy understands why the company was worried about a song with a hook that takes time to sink in, he thinks the audience is often underestimated when it comes to music. "Particularly women," Jam believes, "because women are into lyrics and they're into heartfelt emotions and I think that the melody of the song conveys a lot of emotion. . . . It's great that a song like that can work, particularly

right now when music is very sample driven."

Jam and Lewis were happy to work with Boyz II Men again, because they felt the four members had not allowed success to go to their heads. Jam observed they were even a little starstruck. The producer says the Boyz were very excited when they learned that Janet Jackson was working in an adjacent studio at the same time they were doing the final mix of "4 Seasons." When they finished at four in the morning, Jam led Shawn and group member Wayna Morris in to meet with Janet. "I said, 'Hey, do you mind if I play her just a rough of what we were doing?' It was really fun. She was totally blown away by their record and it was cool that she got to hear it and that she got to tell them how much she liked it," Jam recalls.

The rest of the world was also blown away by "4 Seasons of Loneliness." It debuted at number two on the Hot 100, then moved up to pole position the following week, replacing the quartet's former duet partner Mariah Carey [see 843—"One Sweet Day"] at number one.

## THE TOP FIVE
*Week of October 4, 1997*

1   **4 Seasons of Loneliness**
    Boyz II Men

2   **Honey**
    Mariah Carey

3   **You Make Me Wanna . . .**
    Usher

4   **How Do I Live**
    LeAnn Rimes

5   **Quit Playing Games
    (With My Heart)**
    Backstreet Boys

# 860 | Candle in the Wind 1997 / Something About the Way You Look Tonight

ROCKET 568108

## ELTON JOHN

*Writers: Elton John*
*Bernie Taupin*

*Producers: George Martin /*
*Chris Thomas*

*October 11, 1997*
*14 weeks*

On the morning of Sunday, August 31, 1997, Britain woke up to the most terrible news imaginable: Diana, Princess of Wales, had been killed in an automobile crash in Paris during the earliest hours of the morning. Her companion, Dodi Al-Fayed, was also dead, along with the driver of the car, Henri Paul. Only bodyguard Trevor Rees-Jones had survived. Over the next few days, there was a worldwide outpouring of grief over the death of the 36-year-old woman who had seemingly lived a fairytale life, although she lived it in the harsh spotlight of uninterrupted media scrutiny.

Just a few weeks earlier, Diana had attended the funeral of fashion designer Gianni Versace, where she was seen comforting a tearful Elton John. Now Elton would attend a funeral for another friend. One of Diana's sisters, Lady Sarah McCorquodale, invited Elton to sing at Diana's service in Westminster Abbey. Earliest reports were that Elton would sing his first hit, "Your Song," but Elton's preference was for a brand-new song. From England, he called Bernie Taupin in Los Angeles to make such a request and mentioned that radio stations all over the U.K. were playing "Candle in the Wind" in honor of Diana. Taupin misunderstood and thought Elton wanted new lyrics for

"Candle in the Wind." Feeling pressured to come up with quick results, Taupin took only two hours to rewrite the song originally composed in 1973 for *Goodbye Yellow Brick Road*. When he talked to Elton again, he realized his mistake, but both agreed the new "Candle in the Wind," written as a tribute from all the people of Great Britain, was most appropriate. Two days later, more than 2.5 billion people around the globe watched and listened as Elton performed the rewritten "Candle in the Wind" publicly for the first and only time. Tears flowed freely not just in the hallowed building, but in a multitude of nations.

At the end of the funeral service, Elton met producer George Martin at Townhouse Studios in West London to record the song. The first single from the album *The Big Picture* had already been scheduled for release; "Candle in the Wind 1997" would be joined by "Something About the Way You Look Tonight" for a two-sided hit that was released on Saturday, September 13, in the U.K. and Tuesday, September 23, in the U.S., where advance orders quickly reached the astounding figure of five million copies.

The original "Candle in the Wind" was written about the destruction of a Hollywood star. Like Princess Diana, Marilyn Monroe was also 36 when she died. That first version, which begins with the words, "Goodbye, Norma Jean," was released as a single in the U.K., where it peaked at number 11. In the U.S., "Candle in the Wind" was scheduled for single release, until an R&B station in Detroit added "Bennie and the Jets" [see 362] to its playlist. MCA execs decided that "Bennie and the Jets" would make a better single

for America. It became Elton's second number one hit on the Hot 100. When Elton returned to the MCA label after a stint with Geffen in the '80s, his homecoming single was a live version of "Candle in the Wind," recorded in Australia. That single peaked at number six on the Hot 100 in January, 1988.

With its rewritten lyrics bidding, "Goodbye, England's rose," proceeds from "Candle in the Wind 1997" were donated to Diana's favorite charities. The tribute single ultimately raised millions of dollars and rewrote the chart history books. It became the biggest-selling single of all time, displacing Bing Crosby's "White Christmas." The success of "Candle in the Wind 1997" helped extend Elton's stretch of having at least one title reach the top 40 portion of the Hot 100 every calendar year since his debut in 1970; the 30TK-year run, which ended in TKTK, is the longest on record. As an artist, Elton's span of number one hits expanded to 24 years, 11 months, and one week, dating back to "Crocodile Rock" [see 328]. As of this date, only Michael Jackson had a longer span of number one hits, stretching over 25 years, seven months, and one week. As a producer, George Martin's chart span of number one hits grew to 33 years, 11 months, and one week, dating back to the Beatles' "I Want to Hold Your Hand" [see 143]. That's the longest span for any producer in the rock era.

Impressive chart achievements, but the ultimate emotion is sadness when one thinks about the sudden, tragic death of a woman who cared so much about the disenfranchised and brought a human touch to the antediluvian monarchy.

## THE TOP FIVE

*Week of October 11, 1997*

1   **Candle in the Wind 1997 /**
    **Something About the Way**
    **You Look Tonight**
    Elton John

2   **4 Seasons of Loneliness**
    Boyz II Men

3   **How Do I Live**
    LeAnn Rimes

4   **You Make Me Wanna…**
    Usher

5   **Honey**
    Mariah Carey

COLUMBIA 78723

# Truly Madly Deeply
## SAVAGE GARDEN

**861**

*Writers: Darren Hayes*
*Daniel Jones*

*Producer: Charles Fisher*

*January 17, 1998*
*2 weeks*

**B**ORN IN BRISBANE, AUSTRALIA, Darren Hayes never had enough money to buy records, so he listened to hand-me-downs. "My influences were Fleetwood Mac's *Rumours*, Diana Ross & the Supremes' *20 Golden Greats*, Marvin Gaye, Hall and Oates. Those records became a part of the way I hear music and write music. I was listening to Berry Gordy productions when most kids were listening to new wave."

Through his school years, Hayes was certain he would become a singer and a songwriter. "I thought everybody wanted to do it. I learned to sing from imitating Michael Jackson and Stevie Wonder and Carole King. The reason I have such a strong falsetto is because I listened to a lot of female singers. As I got older, I got into bands and by the time I was in college, I was studying as a way to convince my parents that I wanted to have a serious career, when all I really wanted to do was make records."

Hayes responded to an ad in a music trade placed by Daniel Jones, who was looking for a vocalist for his band. Hayes got the job and when the band broke up, he and Jones remained friends and decided to work together as a duo. "We're both control freaks," explains Hayes. "He was an instrumentalist. I was a melodist and a lyricist." Under the name Crush, they sent out over a hundred demo tapes. An Australian manager named John Woodruff who worked with the Angels and Icehouse liked what he heard and financed production of an album. Inspired by the works of Anne Rice, Hayes and Jones changed their name to Savage Garden. "There's a theme in those books very similar to the theme in our music, where there are two agendas going on," says Hayes.

Savage Garden's first single, "I Want You," was a hit at home. "A consultant named Guy Zapoleon was in a conference in Australia and took this song back to the U.S.," Hayes recalls. "So by the time we started negotiating for a deal, we had an audition set up with Clive Davis and a meeting with [Columbia Records president] Donnie Ienner."

Hayes and Jones respected Davis, but were concerned he would exert too much control over them. When Columbia outbid Arista, the choice seemed obvious. "We delivered an album in its entirety and Columbia went with that record."

"I Want You" was also the first single in the U.S. It peaked at number four in May, 1997. The follow-up, "To the Moon and Back," stopped at number 37. For the third single, Columbia picked a song originally written as a bonus track. In its earliest demo form, it was titled "Magical Kisses." But the night before he recorded his vocals, Hayes sat in a café rewriting the lyrics. "It was about my wife. I had just been married six months. We'd been apart and I couldn't afford to fly back [to see her]. She drove down a couple of times to see me, but it was a difficult time." Inspired by a film about a love story that endured a lifetime (and more), Hayes named his song after the movie *Truly Madly Deeply.* "It was a 'wink-wink nudge-nudge' reference to a film I didn't think anyone had seen."

Hayes wanted to make the song a bonus track because he felt it was too personal. "I thought no one would want to listen to this sappy song about my love life. I thought, 'wouldn't it be cool to put this on as a hidden track?'" But producer Charles Fisher had other ideas. He told the duo it would be a smash hit.

"I was blasé about it," says Hayes. "I didn't even want to put backing vocals on it. It was just two vocals with an overlapping vocal. Charles produced it in a much more lush way and got me to sing those big backing vocals which I'm now known for, but back then it was the first time I'd done that. It was our first U.S. number one and it opened the whole world to Savage Garden. Thank God for that song."

## THE TOP FIVE
*Week of January 17, 1998*

1 **Truly Madly Deeply**
Savage Garden

2 **Together Again**
Janet Jackson

3 **Something About the Way You Look Tonight /**
**Candle in the Wind 1997**
Elton John

4 **How Do I Live**
LeAnn Rimes

5 **Been Around the World**
Puff Daddy & the Family

# Together Again
## JANET JACKSON

VIRGIN 38623

*Writers: Janet Jackson*
*James Harris III*
*Terry Lewis*
*René Elizondo, Jr.*

*Producers: Jimmy Jam*
*Terry Lewis*
*Janet Jackson*

*January 31, 1998*
*2 weeks*

"**I** FOUND OUT LATER that *The Velvet Rope* was a very trying album for Janet because she was going through a lot of emotional problems," says producer Jimmy Jam. "Going into the album, I didn't know that. I knew that the subject matter was going to be a little darker than the *janet.* album."

Producers Jimmy Jam and Terry Lewis had always found Jackson to be a diligent, punctual worker. So they were surprised when she called in sick for some sessions on *The Velvet Rope.* "But when we were in the studio working, she was very energetic," says Jam. "It was probably the smoothest album we had done, in the sense that we knew each other so well and there wasn't a lot of wasted energy or time going down the wrong path to find songs. But when she did interviews, she said, 'It was the toughest album I ever did,' and I'd think, what is she talking about?"

Jam credits Jackson with having the original idea for the song "Together Again." "It had a deep meaning for her because it was about a friend she had lost to AIDS, but as with all her songs, she tries to make it apply in a general sense to anybody. The idea was to make it a joyous song musically."

The song came together quickly, according to the producer. "She had the lyric, 'There are times when we look above and beyond' and knew the song would be called 'Together Again.' It came together just sitting in the studio. We had the whole format of the song in literally a half-hour, because she felt it right away. Sometimes I give her tracks and say, 'Live with this and see what you think.' This wasn't one where she said, 'Put that on tape for me. I'll live with it.' We had the arrangement, the [idea of] starting out slow and going fast. The melody was in place and the partial lyrics and then she wrote the rest of it."

Jam and Lewis produced two different versions of "Together Again." Jam recalls, "We did one where there was a long intro inspired by Donna Summer's 'Last Dance,' where it started off really slow before kicking into the beat. We thought it was a cool contrast, kicking into the more uptempo, house beat. We always figured radio would play the version that's immediately fast, but surprisingly enough, a lot of stations played the slow version."

On her *Velvet Rope* tour, Jackson sang "Together Again" as a finale. "She was looking for a different song to end the concert with, and in rehearsals she kept trying different songs," says Jam. "It kept coming around to 'Together Again' because of the energy it seemed to leave people with. She was going to start the song fast and I talked her into doing the slow intro because it sets the song up. Opening night, she tried it and when she hit the very first notes, the whole crowd started singing and practically drowned her out. It leaves the audience on a great high. It was nice to see the effect the song had. Everybody can relate to someone in their life passing away or feeling like they want to be together again with somebody. It ended up not only being a huge song in America, but worldwide."

While "Together Again" was the first hit from *The Velvet Rope,* the first song that went to radio was "Got 'Til It's Gone," based on Joni Mitchell's "Big Yellow Taxi." Jam says, "To me, Janet has always been one of those artists that bridges R&B and hip-hop and pop and rock. We really thought 'Got 'Til It's Gone' would be accepted across the board. We were surprised. Black radio took to it immediately and loved it and pop radio said, 'We'll wait until the next one comes out.'"

---

## THE TOP FIVE
*Week of January 31, 1998*

1. **Together Again**
   Janet Jackson

2. **Truly Madly Deeply**
   Savage Garden

3. **Nice & Slow**
   Usher

4. **How Do I Live**
   LeAnn Rimes

5. **Been Around the World**
   Puff Daddy & the Family

LAFACE 24290 **Nice & Slow**
USHER

*Writers: Jermaine Dupri*
*Manuel Seal*
*Usher Raymond*
*Brian Casey*

*Producer: Jermaine Dupri*

*February 14, 1998*
*2 weeks*

USHER RAYMOND WAS BORN October 14, 1978, in Chattanooga, Tennessee. His family moved to Atlanta when he was 12, but not before he recorded an album with a pre-teen quintet called NuBeginning. The young singer had a lot of musical influences. "If I was with my cousin, I was listening to LL Cool J. When I'd go to my grandmother's house, I'd listen to Donny Hathaway, Stevie Wonder, Marvin Gaye, Miles Davis and Fats Domino. So even though we were in the '80s, I got information from the '50s and the '60s, and it helped me mature, because kids are easy to influence at that age."

Relocated to Georgia, Usher entered the Atlanta Talent Search. "There were four individuals who went by the name of Brothers of Distinction. They put together a monthly talent show where everyone would perform no matter what age you were. I won it three months in a row. After the fourth month, they retired me."

It was through the talent search that Usher met L.A. Reid, founder of LaFace Records with Kenny "Babyface" Edmonds. Up until that point, Usher enjoyed singing but hadn't thought about it as a profession. "I never looked at it like that until after my first meeting with L.A. Reid and he asked me if I wanted to be a star, if I wanted to work for it. I told him yes."

Usher's first album for LaFace was released in 1994. There were no pop hits on the album, and just one song, "Think of You," reached the top 10 of the R&B chart. "That album allowed me to know which direction I should not go in and what I didn't want to do," Usher allows. "It had a lot to do with the fact that Puffy (Sean Combs) as executive producer wanted me to be something that I wasn't able to be at that age."

For his second album, LaFace teamed Usher with different producers, including Jermaine Dupri, who had done a remix on "Think of You." Dupri began the project by hanging out with Usher for a couple of weeks. "I was just seeing where he was at, whether he was still a young man in his mind or whether he was older, how he dealt with girls—just a lot of stuff that was going to be good for writing songs for an R&B artist," says the producer.

Usher confirms, "Jermaine allowed me to get involved by paying attention to my lifestyle. He wrote about what I experienced." Usher also got involved in the songwriting process for the first time. He co-wrote "You Make Me

Wanna...," which peaked at number two, and spent 11 weeks on top of the R&B chart. Usher also co-wrote the follow-up, "Nice & Slow," which became his first number one hit.

Dupri remembers how the song was born: "I told him, 'Usher, you need a ballad that's gonna knock out the world.' We got the track...the beat started going and out of nowhere the lyrics started popping into my head and once it started coming together like a puzzle, Usher added pieces to make it better. It was a hot collaboration. It took us about four hours to do that song."

Usher's contribution was based on his own life. "I was in love at the time and that was my daily routine after I came home from the studio. I'd pick up the telephone and call my girl and it went a little something like the beginning of the song."

Co-writer Manuel Seal, responsible for the guitar work in "Nice & Slow," recalls the goal was to find a middle ground for Usher. "We didn't want too good a guy like Michael Jackson and we didn't want too bad a guy like Bobby Brown. So we had to make [Usher] a nice guy but not too nice."

## THE TOP FIVE
*Week of February 14, 1998*

1 **Nice & Slow**
Usher

2 **Together Again**
Janet Jackson

3 **How Do I Live**
LeAnn Rimes

4 **Truly Madly Deeply**
Savage Garden

5 **Been Around the World**
Puff Daddy & the Family

# My Heart Will Go On 550 MUSIC 78825
## CELINE DION

*Writers: James Horner*
*Will Jennings*

*Producers: Walter Afanasieff*
*James Horner*

*February 28, 1998*
*2 weeks*

LYRICIST WILL JENNINGS WAS inspired by two female centenarians when he wrote the words to "My Heart Will Go On." The first was the character of Rose in James Cameron's film, *Titanic.* The other was ceramist Beatrice Wood, an artist from Ojai, California, that Jennings met at a premiere of a documentary about her life. "She spoke after the movie and shook all our hands when we walked by her. The notion that there could be a vibrant woman in her hundreds who had lived a passionate and romantic life and still be very much aware of the life she'd lived and the loves she'd had, helped with the inspiration."

Horner and Jennings had collaborated before, on soundtracks for *The Land Before Time, An American Tale: Fievel Goes West* and *Mighty Joe Young,* among others. When Horner called Jennings about writing a song for *Titanic,* he had to warn the wordsmith that Cameron absolutely didn't want a vocal performance for the movie. "James Cameron didn't want anything modern in his film," explains Walter Afanasieff, co-producer of Celine Dion's recording of "My Heart Will Go On." "It was a period piece and he wanted to be true to the music of the time."

In spite of Cameron's wishes, Horner summarized the script for Jennings and played the instrumental theme he had composed. "I started writing bits and pieces of the lyric immediately," says Jennings. "I revised and changed it over a period of a couple weeks." When the song was complete, Horner met with Dion and her manager/husband, René Angelil, in Las Vegas. "James has a choirboy's voice—imagine him sitting at the piano in her penthouse suite singing this song," says Jennings, who found out later that Dion didn't like the song immediately. "But René told her it was really good and she should listen. Next, she did something she never does—she did the demo with James in New York. Her entourage showed up, as well as Tommy Mottola and the people from

Sony. She sang it in one or two takes. All this is going on and James is still not presenting it to James Cameron."

Horner continued his scoring work on the film, while a negative buzz spread about the unseen work, unfairly comparing it to *Waterworld.* That's why, when Cameron showed up at the scoring stage, Horner asked if he was in good humor. Cameron said he was and Horner asked if he could play something for the director. "So they rolled the film and James played the demo against the ending," Jennings relates. "Cameron had to leave the room to compose himself."

With "My Heart Will Go On" set for the film, producer Afanasieff had to balance the needs of the artist, record company and the composer of the film. "It became very complicated because there were so many versions," he says. "I did use a little bit of what James Horner loved about the original demo, but we redid a lot of the vocals. Horner did another version with all of the drums and pop nuances and put that version at the end of the movie. The one I did is the one that got all the airplay, was released as the formal single, was the one that charted, was the one on Celine's album *Let's Talk About Love.* It didn't make any sense why the huge number one worldwide famous song wasn't actually in the movie."

"My Heart Will Go On" won the

Academy Award for Best Original Song. Two months earlier, it also picked up a Golden Globe. At that ceremony, Cameron asked Jennings if Horner had ever told him what the director had said when he collected himself and returned to the scoring stage after hearing the song for the first time. Jennings said no. "He asked, 'Who wrote that lyric?' because he said it was so perfect to continue the film after the ending. I told him I had some help because I had met Beatrice Wood in Ojai and I imagined Rose's feelings after spending time with Beatrice," says Jennings. "He just looked at me for a minute and said, 'Rose's character was inspired by Beatrice Wood.'"

## THE TOP FIVE
*Week of February 28, 1998*

1  **My Heart Will Go On**
   Celine Dion

2  **Nice & Slow**
   Usher

3  **Gettin' Jiggy Wit It**
   Will Smith

4  **Together Again**
   Janet Jackson

5  **Truly Madly Deeply**
   Savage Garden

COLUMBIA 79157 **Gettin' Jiggy Wit It**
WILL SMITH **865**

Writers: Will Smith
      Samuel Barnes
      Bernard Edwards
      Nile Rodgers
      Joe Robinson

Producers: Poke & Tone

March 14, 1998
3 weeks

YOU HAVE TO SMILE at the irony when looking back at the "New Faces" column in the December 1, 1988 issue of *Rolling Stone*. Writer Jeffrey Ressner profiled young rap duo D.J. Jazzy Jeff and the Fresh Prince, noting, "There has been some talk that the pair may appear in a new rap-oriented TV sitcom. A movie is also in the planning stages." That prediction certainly held true for Will Smith, who went on to star in the NBC-TV series "The Fresh Prince of Bel-Air," and then graduated to the silver screen, starring in box office smashes like *Independence Day* and *Men in Black*.

Smith's journey started in Philadelphia. In January, 1986, Jeff Townes was a DJ at a party and 17-year-old Smith stood up to do some spontaneous rapping. He wasn't new at it; he'd been rapping since he was 13. Less than nine months after they first met, the two rappers had their first single debut on *Billboard*'s R&B singles chart. Released on the independent Word-Up label under the name D.J. Jazzy & Fresh Prince, "Girls Ain't Nothing But Trouble" only managed to reach number 81. But it paved the way for a pact with Jive Records, and in 1988 Townes and Smith had two top 20 hits on the Hot 100: "Parents Just Don't Understand" and "A Nightmare on My Street."

"The Fresh Prince of Bel-Air," based on the life of manager Benny Medina, debuted on NBC September 10, 1990, and was on the network for six seasons. During the series' run, Smith made his film debut in *Where the Day Takes You* in 1992. The following year he received good notices for his role in *Six Degrees of Separation,* and then starred with Martin Lawrence in *Bad Boys,* before taking the lead role in the science fiction film *Independence Day.*

Smith made his first appearance without Jazzy Jeff on the Hot 100 in February, 1998, with a song produced by the duo of Poke & Tone, "Gettin' Jiggy Wit It." Born Jean Claude Olivier and Samuel Barnes, Poke & Tone had worked with Smith on the title song to *Men in Black.* That theme topped the Hot 100 Airplay chart for four weeks in 1997. The working relationship was successful and they got along well personally, so Poke & Tone continued to write and produce for Smith when he recorded his *Big Willie Style* album. Poke came up with a track and told Tone it might work for Smith. When they played it for him in the studio, Smith asked what the title was. "I said we should call it 'Gettin' Jiggy Wit It' and I started doing this cute dance," says Poke. "Everybody was laughing and we didn't know what to make of it, but once Will wrote the lyrics, Tone and I thought this might be the one. It

was magical. It was a cute terminology that everybody was using, being jiggy. It was a rap term from Brooklyn, in the streets, and we brought it to the mainstream. We should have patented it."

It would have been a moneymaker. Soon, "jiggy" was everywhere—written into an episode of "Seinfeld" and featured on an hour of Ricki Lake's talk show. "It was like the whole world got jiggy at that point," says Tone. "It's good and it's bad because we were getting invitations from different labels wanting us to do different artists...they wanted catchy hooks or phrases. We turned a lot of it down because we didn't want to be known just for that. That just happened to be a project that worked."

Poke and Tone were able to leave the world of "jiggy" behind, as was Smith. The producers helmed a number one hit for Destiny's Child [see 906 – "Independent Women Part I"] and Smith returned to the top of the Hot 100 with the title song from his 1999 film *Wild Wild West* [see 884].

## THE TOP FIVE
*Week of March 14, 1998*

1  **Gettin' Jiggy Wit It**
   Will Smith

2  **My Heart Will Go On**
   Celine Dion

3  **Nice & Slow**
   Usher

4  **No, No, No Part 2**
   Destiny's Child

5  **Truly Madly Deeply**
   Savage Garden

# 866  All My Life  MCA 55420
## K-CI & JOJO

*Writers: JoJo Hailey*
*Rory Bennett*

*Producers: JoJo Hailey*
*Rory Bennett*

*April 4, 1998*
*3 weeks*

"EVERYTHING WE KNOW ABOUT music came from church," says K-Ci Hailey, neé Cedric Hailey, and he isn't kidding. He and brother JoJo (given name: Joel) grew up in Charlotte, North Carolina, in a devoutly religious household. "Our parents were very strict with us. We had to go to church sometimes seven days a week." It was at church that the Hailey brothers heard about another pair of brothers who were also into gospel music. Mutual friends kept

telling them they should all hook up, so Donald ("DeVante Swing") and Dalvin DeGrate paid the Haileys a visit in their studio. "From that night on, we just clicked," says K-Ci. "We started making demos and one day Devante decided, 'Let's go to New York.' So we put our money together and took a chance."

The risk paid off. They auditioned for Uptown Records and were signed to the label. Jodeci (the name was constructed from their own first names) recorded three albums and had one top 10 hit on the Hot 100, a remake of Stevie Wonder's "Lately" that peaked at number four in 1993.

In 1996, K-Ci and JoJo earned a number one song away from Jodeci when they guest-starred with 2Pac on "How Do U Want It" [see 847]. A year

later, they released an album on their own, *Love Always...*, which yielded the single "All My Life." K-Ci says, "We always said if the Jodeci project became a success, we were going to branch off and do a duo. The group is still together."

Writing "All My Life" took two years, according to JoJo. "I came up with the melody but I had no words for it. Then one day my little girl walked into the studio and said, 'Daddy, I love you for the rest of my life,' and I knew those were the perfect words. So I started singing it and then I took it to Rory Bennett and he worked his magic and it came together."

K-Ci and JoJo met Bennett through Damon Jones, who was managing CeCe Peniston. Jones was looking for a duet partner for a track on Peniston's third album, and thought of K-Ci. Bennett suggested JoJo could do it, and Jones ending up managing K-Ci and JoJo and came up with the idea of JoJo writing with Bennett.

Recording "All My Life" followed the same pattern that K-Ci and JoJo used for all of their songs. "We do everything in the studio," says JoJo. "We never go home and sing to the tape. We'll learn the song in the studio. We start with K-Ci. He'll lay the basic track. I come in and do everything else in the middle and the top of the tracks. That's the blend. The chorus is our favorite part. We like to stack up harmonies over and over and over again. It's our little secret. We do take a lot of time with our backgrounds."

"All My Life" debuted on the Hot 100 the week of March 28, 1998 at number 15. The next week, it made one of the biggest jumps in history to number one.

## THE TOP FIVE
*Week of April 4, 1998*

1  **All My Life**
   K-Ci & JoJo

2  **Frozen**
   Madonna

3  **Nice & Slow**
   Usher

4  **My Heart Will Go On**
   Celine Dion

5  **No, No, No Part 2**
   Destiny's Child

*Writers: Kay Gee
Darren Lighty
Robert Huggar
Raphael Brown
Robert Ford
Den Z-il "D1" Miller
James Moore
Kurtis Walker*

*Producers: Kay Gee
Darren Lighty*

*April 25, 1998
5 weeks*

THE MINNEAPOLIS TRIO KNOWN as Next seemed like just another R&B vocal group when they charted with their first single, "Butta Love." It was pleasant, and sold well enough to be certified gold, but only reached number 16 on the Hot 100. Any notion that Next was average was dispelled with the release of their next single, "Too Close." Inspired by one of the earliest rap songs, "Christmas Rappin'" by Kurtis Blow, "Too Close" blew up and spent five weeks in pole position. The platinum single was *Billboard*'s top title of 1998.

Next can trace its origin to 1992, when brothers Terrance and Raphael Brown, as T-Low and Tweety, started their own group in Minneapolis. Their uncle, director of a gospel choir, introduced them to Robert Huggar [aka R.L.]. Huggar came from a musical family—his cousin was Philip Bailey of Earth, Wind & Fire. T-Low also had a musical connection: his godmother was Ann Nesby, who had charted on the Hot 100 as lead singer of Sounds of Blackness before having her own solo hits. Nesby acted as mentor to the trio in their early days, when they were known as Straight Forward.

Nesby's group was signed to the Perspective label, as was the Minneapolis funk group Lo-Key? At a local gig in 1994, the three guys met Lo-Key?'s keyboardist Lance Alexander and singer Prof T, who helped the group record a demo at Jimmy Jam and Terry Lewis' Flyte Tyme studios. The breaks kept coming—T-Low, Tweety and R.L. were shopping in a mall where they recognized Kay Gee of the rap outfit Naughty by Nature. "Tweety approached me and said they had a group," says Kay Gee, who asked them if they had a demo tape. They did, but not with them. He asked them to meet him that night at the club First Avenue so they could drop off their demo.

"It was good," says Kay Gee. "It was professionally done and more complete than a lot of demo tapes, because they worked with Lance and Prof." Kay Gee had his own imprint, Divine Mill, through Arista. He had already signed the duo Koffee Brown, and now he added Straight Forward to his roster, changing their name to Next. He invited T-Low, Tweety and R.L. to stay with him in New Jersey while they worked on their first album.

"My studio was in the back of my mother's house, in a carriage house. We sat there all day making beats. We went in early one day and worked on this beat, me and Darren Lighty, a keyboard player who worked with me. R.L. came down and I told him to write to this record. He was so young, he didn't know 'Christmas Rappin' by Kurtis Blow. I told him it was a classic and we were going to make an R&B record out of it. He was skeptical, but he did it. I told him it was going to be a number one record, and he said, 'I don't know.' At the same time, they liked the song, but they weren't used to doing uptempo records."

Kay Gee didn't sample "Christmas Rappin'." He says, "We played it live and changed it around. I heard that song all the time growing up. It brought brightness to the room or the car or wherever, and I felt if we put the right lyrics on top of that beat, we could bring that same magic back in the '90s."

## THE TOP FIVE
*Week of April 25, 1998*

1 **Too Close**
Next

2 **All My Life**
K-Ci & JoJo

3 **Let's Ride**
Montell Jordan f/
Master P & Silkk "The Shocker"

4 **Frozen**
Madonna

5 **You're Still the One**
Shania Twain

## 868 My All COLUMBIA 78821
### MARIAH CAREY

*Writers: Mariah Carey*
*Walter Afanasieff*

*Producers: Mariah Carey*
*Walter Afanasieff*

*May 23, 1998*
*1 week*

MARIAH CAREY APPROACHED the making of *Butterfly* the same way she had begun her previous albums. "The corporate world said it's time to go in and make another album," she explains. But it was not business as usual. "My personal life started taking a different turn and the songs reflected that. It was also the first time I was able to experiment with different types of producers who had inspired me, like Puffy and Stevie J. I was working with Walter Afanasieff again, but I was dictating a little bit more in terms of production. I was saying this has to be a little more sparse, we need to tone it down here. It was like the real me finally coming out."

It was a different experience for Afanasieff as well. "It doesn't help when a husband and wife start having problems that my hanging out with her or my hanging out with him doesn't make sense sometimes. Mariah and I got stuck in the middle. I needed to maintain a day-to-day, hour-to-hour, very strong relationship with Tommy [Motolla]. During that period, the beginning of their end, I had to stay away more than normal from her because she was going through a rough time. She felt that shutting her relationship with Tommy was also a cleansing of who she was. She felt that part of what she was dropping was the schmaltzy pop singer ballad kind of stuff he was adamant about. I had to make my exit and say, 'Mariah, you need to redefine yourself, that's fine. I'm here doing what I do and if and when you want to come back and do it again, I'm here.'"

One of the last tracks produced by Afanasieff for Carey was "My All." Carey recalls, "I had gone to Puerto Rico and was influenced by Latin music at that moment. When I came back, the melody was in my head. It was at a melancholy point in my life and the song reflects the yearning that was going on in me. It was like being in a situation but you want to break free and you can't, so you're confined yet you're releasing those emotions through the lyrics and the actual act of singing. That's why I think a lot of people felt very strongly about that song, because the emotion is clear when you listen to it."

Although Carey ultimately recorded "My All" in Afanasieff's San Francisco studio, they wrote the song in the studio in Carey's mansion in upstate New York. "It was one of the finest studios I've ever seen in anyone's home," says Afanasieff. "It's no longer there. I remember being in the back part of the studio where my keyboards were set up and we were sitting there late at night, writing. There was a new keyboard that had come out, the Trinity, and I was strolling through some sounds and came upon a particular sound from a steel acoustic guitar. I played these really beautiful chord changes that eventually led to 'My All.' She started singing and I started playing and we came up with the basis of the song. I put a little drum groove down and it was one of the easier songs to write with her."

The Spanish guitar sound on "My All" tapped into Carey and Afanasieff's roots, although Carey doesn't remember listening to a lot of Latin music when she was growing up. "I didn't spend much time with my paternal grandfather, who is the one who has Spanish in him, but I'm sure when I went to Queens to visit him, I would hear that music and subconsciously it was in me." Afanasieff was born in Brazil, but comes from a Russian background. "Hearing Russian music and Latin and Brazilian music my whole life, I went into an old-fashioned sort of Russian, Latin-Spanish chord progression melody, which was hardly being done."

### THE TOP FIVE
*Week of May 23, 1998*

1 **My All**
Mariah Carey

2 **Too Close**
Next

3 **I Get Lonely**
Janet Jackson
(f/ BLACKstreet)

4 **You're Still the One**
Shania Twain

5 **Everybody (Backstreet's Back)**
Backstreet Boys

Writers: *Rodney Jerkins*
*Brandy*
*LaShawn Daniels*
*Fred Jerkins III*
*Japhe Tejeda*

Producers: *Rodney Jerkins*
*Dallas Austin*
*Brandy*

*June 6, 1998*
*13 weeks*

I**T WASN'T JUST A** coincidence that the superstar duo of Brandy and Monica recorded a song with a very similar title to a hit by another superstar duo, Michael Jackson and Paul McCartney. Paris Davis, who worked in Atlantic's A&R department, recommended Brandy work with producer Rodney' Jerkins. It was David who made the suggestion to Jerkins as well as Monica's producer, Dallas Austin, about which song the two women should record. "Paris told me, 'Dude, you guys should do a song called 'The Boy Is Mine,' like when Michael and Paul did 'The Girl Is Mine,'" says Austin. "I think he told Rodney at the same time because he wanted either one of us to do it, or both. When the song came along, it was perfect for Monica and for Brandy because they had been going through this thing where people thought they didn't like each other."

Monica puts the kibosh on that rumor. "We didn't even know each other," she says. "I had never even seen

her before, because I listen to a lot of gospel music. From the time she was [first] released and I was [first] released, instantly people compared us and I never understood it. It's like they chose the two of us out of the bunch to put at odds. They never did it with me and Aaliyah, or Brandy and Aaliyah. It was always Brandy and Monica. That's why we took the song and brought humor to a situation that people had tried to make so serious. We thought it would be really funny to show us feuding in the video and then come together at the end, because we wanted people to let go of the idea of us not liking each other—but of course, they haven't."

The song wasn't based on real life, Brandy confirms. "But women do fight over men. A lot of people can relate to that. I was watching Jerry Springer one day and these women were fighting over one guy and I thought it was stupid. I thought it would be a great song. Rodney thought it would be a great idea." Brandy brainstormed with Jerkins and LaShawn Daniels. "We wanted to make the best song we could with the track that Rodney produced. We wanted to make the song an event, and we thought the only person who could pull it off was Monica. So I did it first. I sang the entire song by myself and I didn't like it by myself. I wanted to do it with somebody else. So we called her up."

Monica traveled to Los Angeles to record the song with Brandy. "We both realized after recording together that the fact that our voices were so different was the one thing that would make the song more dynamic," says Monica. "I had toned it down a notch because I have a really strong voice. We listened

after I got back to Atlanta and Brandy and I agreed, 'Do it your way and I'll do it my way and we'll blend them.' So here in Atlanta, Dallas produced me and then Rodney produced her in California and when we put them together, it sounded like we were in the same room."

Austin agreed that the two women should record separately. "I had to make Monica Monica on it. I didn't want it to turn into something where Monica's full character wasn't on it. It had to have their attitudes on it, and not just be them singing a song."

"The Boy Is Mine" was the first number one song on the Hot 100 for both artists. Brandy's previous best was the number two peak of "Sittin' Up in My Room" from *Waiting to Exhale* in 1996. Monica started her chart career with a number two song in 1995. Had "Don't Take It Personal (Just One of Dem Days)" gone to number one, 14-year-old Monica would have become the youngest female singer to top the Hot 100. By stopping in second place, the record set by 15-year old Peggy March in 1963 [see 128—"I Will Follow Him"] was left intact.

"The Boy Is Mine" remained in pole position for 13 weeks, making it the longest-running number one hit since Elton John's "Candle in the Wind 1997" [see 860].

## THE TOP FIVE
*Week of June 6, 1998*

1 **The Boy Is Mine**
Brandy & Monica

2 **Too Close**
Next

3 **You're Still the One**
Shania Twain

4 **My All**
Mariah Carey

5 **I Get Lonely**
Janet Jackson
(f/ BLACKstreet)

# 870 I Don't Want to Miss a Thing COLUMBIA 78952
## AEROSMITH

*Writer: Diane Warren*

*Producer: Matt Serletic*

*September 5, 1998*
*4 weeks*

WHEN "I DON'T WANT to Miss a Thing" entered the Hot 100 in pole position, no act had waited longer than Aerosmith from its first appearance on the chart to its first number one hit. The initial Aerosmith single to chart was "Dream On," which debuted the week of October 20, 1973. Almost 25 years later, Aerosmith was finally on top.

The band can trace its origin to a 1970 meeting between guitarist Joe Perry and singer Steven Tyler in New Hampshire. They formed a rock trio with bassist Tom Hamilton and then expanded by adding drummer Joey Kramer, who came up with the name Aerosmith. After relocating to Boston, the group added rhythm guitarist Brad Whitford. In 1972, Columbia Records' Clive Davis signed Aerosmith to the label. Nine albums later, the rock outfit shifted to the Geffen label, but in 1991 pulled a surprise by returning to the Columbia fold in a deal worth over $30 million. The pact wouldn't take effect until Aerosmith delivered three more albums to Geffen. Their final album for that label, *Get a Grip*, became their first number one

album when it was released in 1993. Four years later their first album under the new Columbia deal was finally issued. *Nine Lives* became their second chart-topping set. By 1998, Aerosmith had only racked up five top 10 hits on the Hot 100. The highest-ranked was the 1988 hit "Angel," which peaked at number three.

Meanwhile, Tyler's daughter, Liv, was establishing her credentials as an actress. She made her film debut at 17 in the 1994 release *Silent Fall*. Other roles followed, in movies like *Heavy* and *That Thing You Do!* In 1998 she was cast as Bruce Willis' daughter and Ben Affleck's fiancé in producer Jerry Bruckheimer's end-of-the-world disaster flick, *Armageddon*.

One of Bruckheimer's previous films, *Con Air*, included a Diane Warren song, "How Do I Live." The soundtrack featured Trisha Yearwood's vocals, substituted for an earlier version by LeAnn Rimes. "Both songs came out and people wanted me to pull both versions and I didn't do it," says Warren. "Jerry was pretty mad at me. I think he didn't want to work with me again."

Disney executive Kathy Nelson had been music supervisor on *Con Air* and was performing those duties for *Armageddon*. "Kathy believed I could write something great for the movie," says Warren. "I saw some of the scenes, especially the end where Bruce Willis' character dies. There was more emotion than usual for Jerry's movies; it was very touching. So I wrote 'I Don't Want to Miss a Thing.' I'd had the idea because I heard something that James Brolin said about Barbra Streisand, that he didn't want to go to sleep because he'd miss her. I kept that idea in mind."

Typical for Warren, she was not thinking of any particular artist when she wrote "I Don't Want to Miss a Thing." "When I demoed the song, it was very soft and more keyboard based. I thought, 'This is a good song for Celine Dion.' Which shows that songs are so malleable when they're quality songs." Warren had nothing to do with the selection of Aerosmith. "I've worked with them before, but I never thought they'd do a song they didn't write. I remember sitting down at the piano at the Sunset Marquis hotel, teaching Steven the song. Here's Steven Tyler singing in my ear—it was one of those moments."

Aerosmith's A&R person, John Kalodner, invited producer Matt Serletic to his office to hear the demo. When Serletic said how much he liked the song, Kalodner replied, "I want you to cut it with Aerosmith next week."

One week later, the band was at the Hit Factory in New York ready to record. "We did a lot of takes," says Serletic. "I'm really performance-driven. We go for it and we go for it and I'll figure it out later. And then working with Steven on backgrounds is astounding, because he knows that's when it's going to come alive."

Aerosmith's single was still on the Hot 100 when the song was covered by country artist Mark Chesnutt. "His producer Mark Wright has a deal with his kids," explains Warren. "When he drives them to school, he has six radio stations and they get one. He was driving them to school and they had their one station on and he heard 'I Don't Want to Miss a Thing.' He had a session with Mark Chesnutt that day and he said, 'I'm cutting this song today.' So it's one of those flukes that happen."

## THE TOP FIVE
*Week of September 5, 1998*

1 **I Don't Want to Miss a Thing**
   Aerosmith

2 **The First Night**
   Monica

3 **Crush**
   Jennifer Paige

4 **My Way**
   Usher

5 **The Boy Is Mine**
   Brandy & Monica

ARISTA 13522 **The First Night** 871
MONICA

*Writers: Jermaine Dupri*
*Tamara Savage*
*Marilyn McLeod*
*Pam Sawyer*

*Producer: Jermaine Dupri*

*October 3, 1998*
*5 weeks*

THE FIRST SONG TAMARA Savage wrote with Jermaine Dupri was "The First Night," which quickly became her first number one hit. Born in Ventura, California, Savage grew up in a musical family active in the Church of God in Christ. She wasn't allowed to listen to secular music, but she would secretly listen to the radio, where she heard songs she loved by Whitney Houston and the B-52's. While attending junior college in Riverside, California, she earned money by recording demos, which led to songwriting. She secured a manager, who introduced her to Big John Platt at EMI Music. He signed her to a publishing deal and took some of her songs with him on a trip to Atlanta.

"He called back the same day and said, 'I want to sign you,'" says Savage. Platt teamed Savage up with one of his writers, Warryn Campbell, and they came up with "When I Close My Eyes," recorded by Shanice. Then Platt sent Savage to Atlanta to work with Dupri, who recalls being in the studio with the new writer. "We needed a song for a young girl—but not too young—that all girls could relate to. I like to make songs that aren't for just one person; 10 people can listen to the song and they can all relate to what's going on in the record." Dupri says he came up with the phrase "the first night"

because, "That was happening to me. I found out girls don't really want to give it up on the first night."

Savage recalls that Dupri had the track, and she wrote the song based on a personal experience in New Orleans that she had just before arriving in Atlanta. "I was dating a guy and he wanted to get down on the first night. I write about whatever's going on with me and turn it into a song."

Savage recorded the vocal for the demo, but thought her publisher, Platt, didn't care much for the song. That's why she was surprised a day later when she found out that Clive Davis wanted "The First Night" for Monica, and that it was going to be her first single.

With Monica on board, Dupri wanted to continue a "tradition" she started with her first chart single, "Don't Take It Personal (Just One of Dem Days)." Dupri explains, "She had a crazy loop in that song. 'The Boy Is Mine' sounded a little bit adult for where my head was at at that point. I thought she needed something more ghetto from me, more of a street feeling." Dupri heard Diana Ross' "Love Hangover" [see 437] and knew that Marilyn McLeod/Pam Sawyer song was the one he wanted to sample for "The First Night."

Monica says her version was "one hundred per cent different" from the

demo. "As a vocalist, you should be able to stylize things and make them your own. But she did a great job with it," she says of Savage's vocals.

Monica Arnold was born October 24, 1980, in the College Park section of Atlanta. When she was two, she sang in the choir of the Jones Chapel United Methodist Church. Her talent was natural—she never took voice lessons. By the age of nine she was doing local talent shows, and when she was 12 she was discovered by producer Dallas Austin at a talent contest hosted by Atlanta DJ Ryan Cameron. "We found Another Bad Creation at one of his talent shows, so I went to check it out and hear her sing," says Austin. "I was blown away. I thought she was incredible." Austin signed her immediately and put her right in the studio. Her family wanted her to record songs like "Greatest Love of All," but that didn't match Austin's vision—or Monica's. "I was so tired of singing it," she confesses. "I sang it at least 3,000 times before I was able to switch to something different." Austin laid the groundwork with "Don't Take It Personal," which peaked at number two. "We gave her attitude and showed what her mentality was about. Then it was easy for people to see she had a real voice and a real talent."

## THE TOP FIVE

*Week of October 3, 1998*

1 **The First Night**
Monica

2 **I Don't Want to Miss a Thing**
Aerosmith

3 **One Week**
Barenaked Ladies

4 **Crush**
Jennifer Paige

5 **I'll Be**
Edwin McCain

# One Week REPRISE 17174
## BARENAKED LADIES

*Writer: Ed Robertson*

*Producers: Susan Rogers*
*David Leonard*
*Barenaked Ladies*

*October 17, 1998*
*1 week*

MAYBE THEY SHOULD HAVE called it "17 Weeks." But they didn't. They called it "One Week," and that's exactly how long the single by Barenaked Ladies topped The Billboard Hot 100.

Ed Robertson knew he wanted to be a musician the moment he started playing guitar in the fifth grade. He got his first band together when he was 14 but they concentrated on playing songs by Rush; he didn't start writing his own material until he was 16. He went to school with Steven Page from the fourth grade on, although they didn't become friends until years later, when they were counselors at a summer camp in Scarborough, Canada.

"Steve and I started singing together in our spare time at this camp and we realized we liked harmonizing and liked much of the same music. I was in a cover band called Three Guys From Berry. We were booked to play a fundraiser for a local food bank, and the cover band broke up. This woman from the food bank called and asked if we were still on for the fundraiser. And

I said, 'Ahhh…yes, but the name of the band has changed.' And I'm cycling through my head all these band names that Steve and I had discussed, even though we never intended to be a band. I said, 'The name of the band is now Barenaked Ladies.' And then I called Steve and said, 'Do you want to be in Barenaked Ladies with me?' So we did the fundraiser as a duo and we had so much fun playing together, we said we should do it again."

Robertson and Page did a few gigs as Barenaked Ladies, thinking each one would be the last. But they liked performing together so much they started writing more and more songs. "In the beginning it was all silliness and then we realized we liked the craft of writing and had a lot to say," Robertson explains. The duo made a demo tape that was turned down by all the major labels. They sold copies at gigs, hoping to recoup the $3,000 it cost to produce the tape. Booked to play a New Year's Eve show in Toronto in 1991, a controversy erupted over their name. "We went from selling 400 tapes a week from the stage to selling 14,000 copies because all of a sudden we were a major news story," says Robertson.

Barenaked Ladies became more popular in Canada and were signed by Seymour Stein to his Sire label, distributed through Reprise. When Stein departed for Elektra, he offered to take

the band with him, but told them they were well-liked by the staff at Reprise and would be better off staying on that label's roster. After making some minor chart inroads with the singles "The Old Apartment" and "Brian Wilson," the group, now a quartet, recorded "One Week."

"It was like the stuff we do live where Steve and I will just improv music off the top of our heads," says Robertson. "I had written the chorus to 'One Week' and I told Steve in the verses, I wanted to do a dancehall thing. I like the free-styling that we do, but when I try to write it, it's half-assed and crappy. So I kept putting off finishing it." Page suggested Robertson free style the song instead of writing it. "So I went home and pressed play on a video camera and made the song up off the top of my head. I transcribed it and e-mailed it to Steve and he e-mailed me back and said, 'It's done.' We all liked it and thought it was silly and were certain it would be a B-side or a bonus track."

Instead, "One Week" was the lead-off track on the group's *Stunt* album. "(Producer) Susan Rogers had a lot to do with making suggestions on how to sequence the record," says Robertson. "They decided it was going to be the single. A lot of times people bury their single because they're ashamed of it. We said, 'Let's kick it off with a bang!'"

## THE TOP FIVE
*Week of October 17, 1998*

1. **One Week**
   Barenaked Ladies

2. **The First Night**
   Monica

3. **I Don't Want to Miss a Thing**
   Aerosmith

4. **How Deep Is Your Love**
   Dru Hill f/Redman

5. **Crush**
   Jennifer Paige

RUFFHOUSE 78868 **Doo Wop (That Thing)** 873
LAURYN HILL

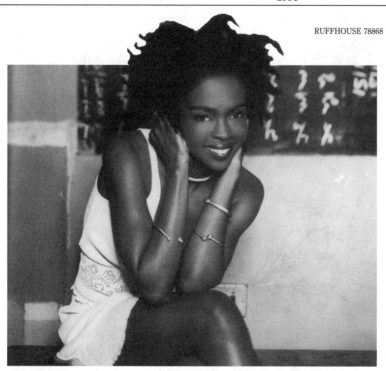

*Writer: Lauryn Hill*

*Producer: Lauryn Hill*

*November 14, 1998*
*2 weeks*

**W**HEN "DOO WOP (That Thing)" debuted at number one on the Hot 100 in November, 1998, Lauryn Hill became the first woman to be the sole recording artist, writer and producer on a chart-topping hit since March, 1989, when Debbie Gibson was the lone artist, writer and producer of "Foolish Beat" [see 722]. Not that Hill didn't find some resistance to the idea of her producing the parent album to "Doo Wop," *The Miseducation of Lauryn Hill.* When the album was just in the talking stage, it was reported that Wyclef Jean, one of Hill's comrades in the Fugees, would produce her first solo effort. At another point, RZA of the Wu-Tang Clan was mentioned as a possible producer.

"For some reason, women aren't taken seriously as thinkers and creators and arrangers and producers," Hill said in a *Playboy* interview. "The industry thinks there always has to be some man somewhere puppeteering the whole situation. It doesn't make you feel good as an artist when you are having conversations about your music and people don't take it seriously."

There was no problem with Hill's

work on *Miseducation* being taken seriously. Critics placed the album in the same category with seminal works like Marvin Gaye's *What's Going On* and Stevie Wonder's *Innervisions.* Those references were appropriate, as Hill was a student of 1960s and 1970s soul, ever since she found a box of her mother's precious 45s tucked away in the attic of their South Orange, New Jersey home. The collection included the Motown and Stax singles her mother loved, along with songs by Aretha Franklin, Al Green and Roberta Flack. Hill says she grew up trying to be Aretha.

On her seventh birthday, her mother took her to see the movie *Annie.* Hill memorized all the songs and sang them repeatedly, until her mother couldn't stand hearing that the sun would come out tomorrow. Young Lauryn also loved going to the Six Flags amusement park in Jackson, New Jersey, so she could sing Whitney Houston songs in the karaoke studio. When she was 12, Hill competed in the Amateur Night portion of the TV series "It's Showtime at the Apollo," singing an old Miracles favorite written by Smokey Robinson, "Who's Lovin' You." At 13, Hill and a friend from junior high, Prakazrel Michel, and his cousin, Wyclef Jean, formed a group they called the Fugees-Tranzlator Crew (Fugees was short for refugees). But music wasn't a clear choice as a profession yet. A role in

an off-Broadway production led to an agent, and she went out on auditions. In 1991, she had a running part on CBS-TV's "As the World Turns." That led to playing a troubled teen who rapped in *Sister Act II: Back in the Habit.* Finally, her acting career took a back seat as the Fugees were signed to the Ruffhouse imprint and released an album, *Blunted on Reality.* It didn't chart. Three years later, the follow-up, *The Score,* spent four weeks at number one on the *Billboard* album chart, fueled by airplay on a remake of Roberta Flack's "Killing Me Softly With His Song."

Despite the success of the second album, the Fugees did not record a follow-up. Wyclef Jean released his own solo effort in 1997, *Wyclef Jean Presents the Carnival Featuring Refugee Allstars.* "Pras" Michel's solo CD, *Ghetto Supastar,* entered The Billboard 200 the same week that "Doo-Wop (That Thing)" went to number one.

Hill's chart-topping song was interpreted as a message to other female artists, who relied more on their bodies than their minds, like rapper Lil' Kim. "I'm not dissing *them*—I'm dissing their *mind-set,*" Hill insisted in *Details.* "My music talks about a certain way of thinking, and if the cap fits, you know? I knew girls like Kim growing up—I might have even *been* one at a certain age—and there's a huge lack of self-esteem behind that thinking. I mean, when I was 14 I thought that if a guy didn't whistle at me, that meant I wasn't pretty. But either you mature past that or you get caught in the concept of, 'Oh, I have to show some ass, 'cause that's the only way I can feel beautiful.' Sex is cool, but it's only part of the story."

## THE TOP FIVE
*Week of November 14, 1998*

1. **Doo Wop (That Thing)**
   Lauryn Hill

2. **Lately**
   Divine

3. **The First Night**
   Monica

4. **One Week**
   Barenaked Ladies

5. **Because of You**
   98 Degrees

## 874 Lately PENDULUM 15316
### DIVINE

*Writers: Will Baker*
*Christopher Kelly*
*Pete Woodruff*

*Producers: John Howcott*
*Donald Parks*

*November 28, 1998*
*1 week*

JOHN HOWCOTT GREW UP in Indianapolis, Indiana, hometown of Kenny "Babyface" Edmonds. After playing in a couple of bands, Howcott went to work at a local studio as a recording engineer. That's where he met Emmanuel Officer of the gospel group Deliverance, and started writing songs with him. Officer had grown up with Babyface and moved to Atlanta to work with him. He encouraged Howcott to follow. In Atlanta, Howcott met Donald Parks at LaFace Records. That led to the formation of H.O.P. Productions, comprised of Howcott, Officer, and Parks. Their first project was to write songs for teen pop singer Jeremy Jordan.

H.O.P. fell apart when Officer moved to Los Angeles. Howcott and Parks formed a new company, Urban Vibe, and signed two writers from Indianapolis: Will Baker and Pete Woodruff. Baker's uncles had worked with Babyface when he was in a group called Manchild. When he was 12 years old, Baker visited the studio where Babyface and L.A. Reid's group the Deele recorded "Two Occasions." "That inspired me," says Baker. "When I reached 13, I knew what I wanted to do." Pittsburgh-raised Woodruff was on tour with Ready for the World [see 618—"Oh Sheila"] and settled in Indianapolis. Introduced through a mutual friend, Baker and Woodruff formed a songwriting team.

Baker's childhood friend Christopher Kelly collaborated with them on the song "Lately." "I wrote that song in about 35 minutes," says Baker. "We were in the studio and I was playing with this incredible guitar player. He showed me some different chords, and the hook immediately came into my head." The lyrics were inspired by personal experience. "It was about my high school days," says Baker. "My high school sweetheart took me on the merry-go-round of ups and downs. I ended up marrying her." The same day the song was written, a demo was recorded with vocalist Kiki Wyatt.

Shopping songs, Howcott met with the founder of the Pendulum label, Ruben Rodriguez. "The third song [we played for him] was 'Lately' and about eight bars in, he said, 'That's it! That's my first single!' So you've got to give him credit for having the ears to hear a hit," says Howcott.

Rodriguez was looking for material for three teenagers he had signed to his label. Kia Thornton, Nikki Bratcher and Tonia Tash were recruited by managers Nathan Garvin and Gillian Manigat to form Divine. "We were three girls from three different cities, and we just clicked," Bratcher told *Billboard*'s Chuck Taylor. "We ended up writing our own demo of six songs."

Divine traveled to Atlanta to record "Lately." Howcott recalls, "Will, Donald and I did the first vocal session with them. We didn't know if they could sing, so we took a chance. Thank God they could sing. They did a great job on the record."

A second session took place in New York where some of the vocals were re-recorded and background vocals were added. "We've always loved having the vocals in your face," says Howcott. "We take a lot of time to record our background vocals and get them really fat." A third recording session took place in Indianapolis, where Woodruff played a Hammond B3 organ. "Pete is a gospel organist and he put his signature on there and gave it a real southern feel," explains Howcott.

Nine months after recording "Lately," it still hadn't been released, and Baker thought it would never come out. "I was in my kitchen fixing lunch and watching videos like I do every day," the writer says. "I heard 20 seconds of a melody and I thought it was like something I would do." Baker shifted his gaze to the screen and saw Divine's video for "Lately." "We had no warning it was coming out and I froze." Then the song started doing well at radio. "For the first time ever, I opened up a *Billboard* magazine," says Baker. "I didn't even know what *Billboard* was." Baker looked at the bottom of the chart but couldn't find his song. Then he saw it had debuted at number 36 and was shocked. Howcott remembers when the song reached number two. "We had Lauryn Hill in front of us and I knew there was no way we were going to beat Lauryn Hill. Then we beat her. I felt like I was sitting in the audience with some popcorn watching this thing go!"

## THE TOP FIVE
*Week of November 28, 1998*

1 **Lately**
Divine

2 **Doo Wop (That Thing)**
Lauryn Hill

3 **Nobody's Supposed to Be Here**
Deborah Cox

4 **Because of You**
98 Degrees

5 **The First Night**
Monica

JIVE 42557 **I'm Your Angel** 875
R. KELLY & CELINE DION

Writer: R. Kelly

Producer: R. Kelly

December 5, 1998
6 weeks

CELINE DION HAD PAIRED with duet partners before. Her collaboration with Peabo Bryson on the title tune from *Beauty and the Beast* made the top 10 in 1992, and a team-up with Clive Griffin on an updating of "When I Fall in Love" sauntered into the top 30 in 1993. Her duet with Barbra Streisand on "Tell Him" registered on the Hot 100 Airplay chart in 1997. Her most successful duet, by far, was her partnership with R. Kelly on a song he wrote and produced, "I'm Your Angel." The duet ruled the Hot 100 for six weeks.

"I'm known for all of those ballads and holding a note forever," Dion told *Billboard*'s Chuck Taylor. "Maybe that's my trademark. But R. Kelly created this song and sent it to us and I thought it was sweet. The feelings were there without having to be dramatic. Hearing something different was very attractive to me—I love new moments."

Chicago-based R. Kelly traveled to Canada to record Dion. "I love R. Kelly," she professes. "Singing with him was a great moment for me. It was a quick moment; we recorded the song in Montreal. It's a great song and very refreshing in that it's not what people expect from me."

Looking at the Hot 100 as it was published in the December 5, 1998 issue of *Billboard*, it appeared that the song

jumped from 46-1, which would have qualified as the biggest leap to the top in the chart's history. But appearances can be deceiving. It was an illusory move, due to changes in chart policy implemented that week, the first week of the new chart year.

Since its inception on August 4, 1958, the Hot 100 has undergone many changes. Designed from the beginning as a chart that combined sales and airplay information, the formula for that blend has been altered over the years, as conditions at radio and retail have changed.

One of the most dramatic changes to the Hot 100 occurred the week of November 30, 1991, when new technologies provided by SoundScan and Broadcast Data Systems were put into play [see 800—"Set Adrift on Memory Bliss"]. But some would argue that changes implemented the week of December 5, 1998, were even more dramatic.

In the late 1990s, record companies took a new approach to

releasing singles. With little money to be made from the release of CD singles, label execs came to believe that sales of singles were eating into the more profitable sale of albums. They reasoned that if a single didn't exist, consumers would be forced to pay for an entire album, even if they only wanted one song.

As this belief became more prevalent, a number of album tracks found success at radio without having commercial singles available at retail. Songs like "Men in Black" by Will Smith, "Don't Speak" by No Doubt, "I'll Be There for You" by the Rembrandts and "Torn" by Natalie Imbruglia were ineligible for the Hot 100, because they were not available to purchase as singles. Yet, radio gave them so much airplay, they all topped the Hot 100 Airplay chart. It appeared that the Hot 100 was "out of touch," and that the chart no longer measured the most popular songs in the U.S.

The remedy was to allow these airplay-only tracks to appear on the Hot 100. As a result, the chart shifted from a singles chart to a song chart. As with most policy changes, it was not a rash decision, and was appropriate given changing market conditions. For months before the official changeover, *Billboard* compiled an unpublished "test chart," which was tabulated by the new rules. The Hot 100 that was published in the December 5, 1998, issue included data from the previous week's test chart in the "Last Week" column. So even though "I'm Your Angel" did not appear on the chart dated November 28, it appeared that the song had rocketed 46-1. In reality, the R. Kelly & Celine Dion duet debuted at number one.

## THE TOP FIVE
*Week of December 5, 1998*

1 **I'm Your Angel**
   R. Kelly & Celine Dion

2 **Nobody's Supposed to Be Here**
   Deborah Cox

3 **Lately**
   Divine

4 **Doo Wop (That Thing)**
   Lauryn Hill

5 **From This Moment On**
   Shania Twain

# 876 Have You Ever? ATLANTIC 84089
## BRANDY

*Writer: Diane Warren*

*Producer: David Foster*

*January 16, 1999*
*2 weeks*

Brandy and Monica both followed their chart-topping duet [see 869—"The Boy Is Mine"] with individual number one singles. Monica went first, as "The First Night" achieved pole position in October 1998. Three months later, Brandy's follow-up, "Have You Ever?" was sitting on top of the Hot 100.

"Have You Ever?" was the ninth number one hit for songwriter Diane Warren and the eighth for producer David Foster. Warren wrote the song on Christmas night. "I like to write on Christmas," she explains. "I'm Jewish. I remember being [in the studio] and coming up with the idea and thinking it was so real. Because 'Have you ever loved somebody so bad' is real. I thought it was a hit. A lot of times you've got to convince other people, but I sat down with David Foster and Brandy and she loved it and did it."

Foster remembers Warren asking him to work with Brandy, and that "Have You Ever?" stood out from the pack. "Diane had done an excellent demo," he says. "It was effortless to do the track, especially once Michael Thompson put on the guitars. I love the feel of it—there's nothing on there that's not necessary and nothing on there that doesn't add to it. It was one of the most perfect tracks I've ever done."

Foster's inspiration for the backing vocals came from listening to another

of Brandy's recordings, "Sittin' Up in My Room." He explains, "I really liked those background vocals. I wanted to get the same person to do them on our song, so I asked who it was and I found out it was all Brandy. I couldn't believe it! I have to say, I've never worked with anyone who could do backgrounds so easily. She could double it perfectly. It only took two hours and then she did a great job on the lead."

Brandy says doing the backing vocals is something she grew into. "I love doing backgrounds," she elaborates. "I love hearing my voice back about 45 times." She enjoyed working with Foster on the track. "He brought a lot out of me. He said, 'You have to hit the money notes.' Those are the notes that make you jump out of your seat. He brought the money notes out of me on 'Have You Ever?' and Diane Warren is so funny. She has this little bird she carries on her shoulder all the time and she's always talking back and forth to the bird. I was excited to work with David and Diane, and then to do a song so incredible was amazing."

Brandy Norwood was born February 11, 1979, in McComb, Mississippi. The family relocated to Los Angeles because of a job offer for her father from the Church of Christ. "He was minister of music, so that helped my brother and I because we were

around all the time," she says. Brandy sang in all of her father's choirs, and says she was strongly influenced by Whitney Houston. When she was 11, Brandy auditioned for Atlantic Records as part of a trio with twin sisters. The label liked Brandy's voice and told her to come back when she was 14. She made her Hot 100 debut at age 15 with "I Wanna Be Down," which peaked at number six. The follow-up, "Baby," went to number four in 1995.

Some fans of her first album already knew Brandy from her acting career. Three months after she signed with Atlantic, she was cast in the ABC-TV sitcom "Thea." When the show was cancelled, Brandy didn't mind—it gave her more time to concentrate on her recording career. But the experience served her well. In 1995, she was cast in the lead role of UPN's "Moesha." The series debuted in January, 1996 and lasted for six seasons. She also played the title role in a TV update of the Rodgers and Hammerstein musical "Cinderella" (starring opposite Whitney Houston), co-hosted "The American Music Awards" and earned a role in the 1998 horror film *I Still Know What You Did Last Summer.* Still, don't look for Brandy to choose between careers. "Acting is something I love and singing is definitely something I love, so I would love to do them both."

## THE TOP FIVE
*Week of January 16, 1999*

1  **Have You Ever?**
   Brandy

2  **Nobody's Supposed to Be Here**
   Deborah Cox

3  **I'm Your Angel**
   R. Kelly & Celine Dion

4  **...Baby One More Time**
   Britney Spears

5  **Lately**
   Divine

JIVE 42545  **...Baby One More Time**
BRITNEY SPEARS   **877**

*Writer: Max Martin*

*Producers: Max Martin
          Rami*

*January 30, 1999
2 weeks*

"**...B**ABY ONE MORE TIME" is the first elliptical title to top the Hot 100. The three dots that make up an ellipsis indicate something is missing, and that was the case with this Britney Spears song title. "I wanted the song to be called 'Hit Me Baby One More Time,'" explains Max Martin. "To me it was obvious that it meant 'so let's do it again' or 'try this once more.' But it was a big controversy. I was very naïve, thinking the Americans would accept that kind of a title. They were very scared radio would not play it, and they were probably right, since she was a debut artist."

She may have been a debut artist, but Spears had been preparing for a long time. She auditioned for a revival of "The Mickey Mouse Club" when she was eight, but was too young and wasn't asked to join the show until she turned 11. She competed on "Star Search" in 1992. "I've always had this strong motivation and drive," she says. "It wasn't until I was 16 that I realized I loved being on stage and I really wanted to sing and make a career out of it."

Lawyer Larry Rudolph arranged for Spears to meet Jeff Fenster, senior vice president for A&R at Jive Records. "I didn't have any demos," Spears explains. "I had the instrumental track to 'I Have Nothing' and sang it and sang 'The Star Spangled Banner' *a cappella*." Fenster signed the teenager and then made a phone call to Swedish producer Max Martin, who had already produced hits for the Backstreet Boys and Robyn. "I was in Florida and Jeff asked me to stop by the office in New York to meet this girl while I was in America," Martin recalls. "She was all dressed up. She was 16 at the time. She thought I was a 50-year old producer from the old school. I had really long hair at the time—I looked like Ozzy Osbourne," says the former heavy metal musician. "It was pretty obvious she had something, even though she was very quiet and very shy at the time."

Shortly after meeting Spears,

Martin returned to Sweden and wrote "...Baby One More Time." "I decided right after the song was done that it could work for her," he says. "I write on the Dictaphone. I came up with the melody first. I wrote the chorus—you just hum it in." Martin played the Dictaphone tape for his co-producer, Rami Yacoub. "Thanks to him, that song sounds the way it does," Martin acknowledges. "He is much more urban and R&B based than me. I'm more of a melody man. So he's a big reason that song turned out the way it did."

Growing up in the small town of Kentwood, Louisiana, Spears suddenly found herself flying to Sweden to record at Martin's Cheiron Studios. "I didn't know what to expect," she confesses. "It was my first time overseas. They had six songs...I had a week and I helped them write a little bit of a couple songs. It was a really important experience."

Martin remembers, "She came very well prepared. Since '...Baby One More Time' was the first song, we really didn't know where to take it. We just kept on recording. We tried a couple of different styles. After a while, I could hear her stomach growl in the microphone. I asked if she was hungry. We'd been going for eight hours. She said, 'No, I'm fine.' I said let's take a break, and she had three burgers."

"...Baby One More Time" marked the first collaboration between Martin and Rami. Martin had been collaborating with Dag Volle, known professionally as Denniz Pop. Volle passed away in August, 1998 after producing hits for the Backstreet Boys, Ace of Base, Rednex and Real McCoy. "Because this was the first time working with Max, I really wanted to do well," says Rami. "It was like a tryout. I know from Denniz Pop and Max's previous productions, when we do songs, there's kind of a nasal thing. With 'N Sync and the Backstreet Boys, we had to push for that mid-nasal voice. When Britney did that, she got this kind of raspy, sexy voice."

After the single was released, Spears was spending a lot of time on the road. Finally, she had a chance to go home. "I was in the car and they shut the doors and told me I was number one. I just wanted to be on the radio. I didn't think it would be on the *Billboard* charts! I was so excited, I wanted to cry."

### THE TOP FIVE
*Week of January 30, 1999*

1  **...Baby One More Time**
   Britney Spears

2  **Have You Ever?**
   Brandy

3  **Nobody's Supposed to Be Here**
   Deborah Cox

4  **I'm Your Angel**
   R. Kelly & Celine Dion

5  **Jumper**
   Third Eye Blind

# 878

## Angel of Mine
### MONICA
ARISTA 13590

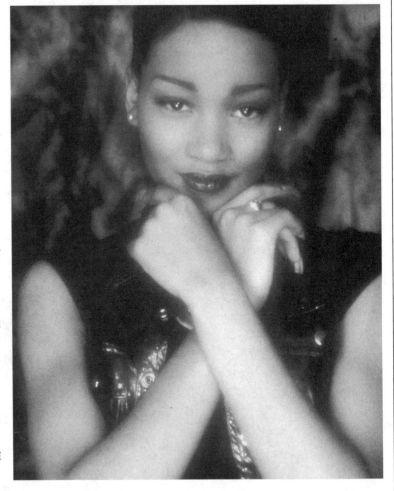

*Writers: Rhett Lawrence*
*Travon Potts*

*Producer: Rodney Jerkins*

*February 13, 1999*
*4 weeks*

THE BRITISH GIRL GROUP Eternal is a one-hit wonder in the U.S., where "Stay" peaked at number 19 in 1994. They fared much better at home in the U.K., where 12 of their 15 chart entries made the top 10, including a 1997 single, "Angel of Mine," which went to number four. Less than two years later, "Angel of Mine" was a number one song for a different artist and in a different country.

"Angel of Mine" was written in the U.S. by producer Rhett Lawrence and songwriter Travon Potts. After placing songs with some R&B artists, Potts had stepped away from a music career for a couple of years. When he returned, an engineer friend told him about an opening for a programmer at Lawrence's studio. "I think he didn't know I was a writer as well," says Potts. Lawrence gave him the freedom to write. "He gave me my own room and one day I lit a candle and started working on a music bed. I took it to Rhett and he wrote the hook and the first verse and I wrote the second verse and the bridge. Next thing we know, we have a song."

Lawrence explains, "The song is partially about my wife and partially about our little Pomeranian dog, who is the sweetest thing you can imagine. He was at the studio and I sat him down in a chair and looked at him every once in a while. I tried to write it from the perspective of total innocence." Lawrence usually spends a long time coming up with song titles. "You want it to capture the mood of the song," he says. "There were a hundred alternate titles for that song. I had a big pad of paper with a few pages of titles, and ["Angel of Mine"] jumped out."

Lawrence adds, "When the song was finished, I felt it had something really special, so I sent it to Clive Davis. He called me back the day he got it." Davis loved the song and put a hold on it, telling Lawrence he wanted him to record it with Monica. "Nine months went by. [Meanwhile] I had a number one song in several countries with Eternal. The song was "I Wanna Be the Only One." I wrote it with Bebe Winans. The song was so successful,

they needed something else to follow it up very quickly, for a greatest hits that was supposed to come out at Christmastime. There was a one-week deadline to record two songs." Eternal listened to a reel of Lawrence's songs and heard a snippet of "Angel of Mine." They asked if they could record it, and Lawrence explained that Clive had it on hold for Monica.

"I worked out an arrangement with Clive where I could record it on Eternal overseas and Monica had it exclusively for the U.S. Part of the arrangement was that someone else would cut the song with Monica while I cut it on Eternal. But the Monica track is more or less the same—a little different tempo, and that's it."

Monica, who likes to work quickly, recorded "Angel of Mine" in one day with producer Rodney Jerkins. "My voice was going through some different types of changes, so we made a lot of changes once we started working on it," she says. "I enjoyed it tremendously. To

this day I still love singing that song, and that's rare. Usually you get tired of singing the same song."

"Angel of Mine" became Monica's third number one song in less than nine months, making her the first artist to have that many chart-toppers in so short a time since Puff Daddy in 1997.

## THE TOP FIVE
*Week of February 13, 1999*

1  **Angel of Mine**
   Monica

2  **...Baby One More Time**
   Britney Spears

3  **Nobody's Supposed to Be Here**
   Deborah Cox

4  **Believe**
   Cher

5  **Have You Ever?**
   Brandy

*Writers: Brian Higgins*
*Stuart McLennen*
*Paul Barry*
*Steven Torch*
*Matthew Gray*
*Timothy Powell*

*Producers: Mark Taylor*
*Brian Rawling*

*March 13, 1999*
*4 weeks*

**E**VEN THOUGH "BELIEVE" BECAME the biggest hit of Cher's career, the single almost wasn't released in America. Because she was signed to Warner Brothers through the company's U.K. office, the U.S. arm of the label had little interest in the project. But Cher believed in the song and did her best to convince label execs it should be released. In the end, "Believe" was too strong to ignore, and once issued in the States, it gave Cher some new ink in the record books. She became the artist with the longest span of number one hits—33 years, seven months and three weeks, counting back to "I Got You Babe" [see 181] by Sonny & Cher in 1965.

"Believe" was recorded at Dreamhouse, a studio in Kingston, Surrey, England, home to Mark Taylor and Brian Rawling's Metro Productions. Rob Dickins, then chairman of Warner Brothers Records in the U.K., knew Taylor and Rawling from their work with Gina G ("Ooh Aah…Just a Little Bit") and Danni Minogue ("All I Wanna Do"), two artists signed to Warner's Eternal imprint. Dickins wanted to do a dance album with Cher, and asked Taylor and

Rawling to write a song for the project. They submitted "Dov'é L'Amore," written by Taylor with Paul Barry. The track was produced by Junior Vasquez in New York, but Dickins didn't care for it and asked Taylor and Rawling to do a new production. The Warner chief had another request for Taylor and Rawling. Dickins liked the chorus of a song called "Believe," written by Brian Higgins, Matt Gray, Stuart McLennen and Tim Powell, but wanted the rest of it reworked. Taylor and Rawling turned it over to Paul Barry and Steve Torch, who wrote new lyrics and melody for the verses and the middle eight.

"Cher made me rewrite a lot of the lyrics about four or five times because she wasn't happy with them," says Barry. "Initially, she thought they were too happy and she really wanted that darkness in there, a feeling of desperation. We wanted it to be that twisted feeling that you're going to go on, but you're not sure if you can pick yourself up off the ground."

The Metro staff enjoyed working with Cher in the studio. "She doesn't rate herself as a singer of any kind of caliber, which is a big mistake," says Taylor. "She really is a good singer." Barry adds, "She's a real trouper. She comes in and sings for three hours and gets tired quickly, but then she'll take a day off and come back and go at it again for three or four hours. Every time she sings a song, it gets slightly better. I think the vocals she did with

Mark were some of the best vocals she's ever done."

The most distinctive feature of "Believe" was the strange vocoder effect, recorded on a Digitech Talker. "It had just come out, so I literally got it that day and played around to see what it could do," says Taylor. "Because I was working on the Cher tracks at the time, I picked off a vocal and looped it around. The part I used was, 'Do you believe in life after love?' I was screwing around with it and took it to the max and thought it was a bit spectacular. Cher was coming in the next day to do some other vocals and I plucked up the courage to play it to her. I was terrified she was going to destroy me. But she absolutely loved it and we just put it where we thought it was right in the song, and she wanted me to delete the original vocal once we'd done that."

The special vocal processing didn't please everyone. "The record company wanted to take the effect off," says Barry. "Cher said, 'Over my dead body!' So it stayed." Rawling recalls that his team felt like they had something special. "The records we made with Gina G and Danni Minogue were good solid records, but this was a career record. It was enormously successful. We were on everyone's radar at that stage. It was really an exciting moment."

## THE TOP FIVE
*Week of March 13, 1999*

1 **Believe**
Cher

2 **Angel of Mine**
Monica

3 **Heartbreak Hotel**
Whitney Houston f/Faith Evans
& Kelly Price

4 **Angel**
Sarah McLachlan

5 **All I Have to Give**
Backstreet Boys

**No Scrubs** LAFACE 24385
TLC

*Writers: Kevin Briggs*
*Kandi Burruss*
*Tameka Cottle*

*Producer: She'kspere*

*April 10, 1999*
*4 weeks*

**K**ANDI BURRUSS WROTE HER first song when she was 14. "Our group Xscape had just met and I was meeting different producers. I would try to come up with melodies to their tracks. [My songs] weren't any good back then, but that's where I got started." Xscape was signed to Jermaine Dupri's So So Def imprint and had top 10 hits like "Just Kickin' It," "Understanding" and "The Arms of the One Who Loves You." After three albums, the group came apart at the seams. "We were having problems getting along," says Burruss. "We couldn't agree on anything. One of our members decided she wanted to go solo. If she wasn't in the group, I knew we weren't going to put out another album."

Burruss teamed up with another Xscape member, Tameka "Tiny" Cottle, to form a new duo. They called themselves KAT, as in Kandi and Tiny. This time, they were determined to have creative control. "I had a notepad with a bunch of ideas and concepts. I used to ask producers if I could write, but I guess they didn't think we could."

That changed when Kandi and Tiny's manager, Ian Burke, introduced them to producer Kevin Briggs, aka She'kspere. He had a track with lyrics already written. "I asked him, 'Do you mind if we have the track, because I think I can write a better song,'" says Burruss. "And he looked at me like, 'Yeah, right!' He gave me the track and I was riding in the car with it, because I come up with a lot of good ideas when I'm driving. I was thinking about some of my ex-boyfriends and I started talking about them. Scrubs was a term that me and all of my friends used."

Burruss came up with the first verse, the B section and the hook and brought the song to Cottle. "She laughed, 'Kandi, are you crazy?' She liked it, but she thought it was funny. So when we took it to She'kspere, I didn't know if he would like it, but he loved it." Briggs confirms, "She was really bashful about her writing. She sang the song and I said we've got something. This is hot! But there was no way anyone could have known that it was going to blow up to this type of magnitude."

Burruss continues, "Shortly after that, She'kspere played it for Dallas Austin and people at LaFace and they wanted it for TLC, even though we weren't trying to shop the song. We were trying to keep it for ourselves." It wasn't a difficult decision to give the song to TLC, says Burruss. "I always

wanted to write and it looked like a big opportunity. A lot of people write for themselves, but it's not often you get a chance to write something for another artist. So I said, 'Tiny, we need to give this song away.' She didn't know. I said, 'We can make plenty of songs. We can always write a better one.'"

Briggs made the decision to have Rozonda "Chilli" Thomas sing lead on "No Scrubs." "I thought the range would be too high for T-Boz, and I thought it would be a change to have Chilli sing lead because I hadn't heard that and I've always been a TLC fan. She was unsure of her singing ability, but we spent a night and a half on it and banged it out. We had some resistance from the other girls at one point, but we ended up working it out."

LaFace co-founder L.A. Reid told Burruss he was going to make "No Scrubs" the biggest hit of her career. "I was shocked it was going to be a single," she says. "I thought it was going to end up on the cutting room floor. Because they never had a song where T-Boz wasn't leading, I didn't expect it to be a single." Later, Burruss realized Reid was true to his word. "That song is the biggest of my career. It allowed me the opportunity to write for all the other people I've written for," says the woman whose songs have been recorded by Destiny's Child [see 883—"Bills, Bills, Bills"], Mariah Carey and Pink. "I realize now being the person in the front singing is not what it's about if you're trying to do this as a living. I did not realize how much songwriters made. When I showed my mom my checks, she said, 'You mean to tell me you got this just for that?'"

## THE TOP FIVE
*Week of April 10, 1999*

1 **No Scrubs**
TLC

2 **Believe**
Cher

3 **Every Morning**
Sugar Ray

4 **What's It Gonna Be?!**
Busta Rhymes f/Janet

5 **Heartbreak Hotel**
Whitney Houston f/Faith Evans & Kelly Price

C2 79124 **Livin' La Vida Loca** 881
RICKY MARTIN

**THE TOP FIVE**
*Week of May 8, 1999*

1 **Livin' La Vida Loca**
Ricky Martin

2 **No Scrubs**
TLC

3 **Kiss Me**
Sixpence None the Richer

4 **Every Morning**
Sugar Ray

5 **Believe**
Cher

*Writers: Robi Rosa*
*Desmond Child*

*Producers: Desmond Child*
*Robi Rosa*

*May 8, 1999*
*5 weeks*

**T**HERE ARE JUST A handful of television performances that could be considered defining moments in an artist's career, including the Beatles' first appearance on "The Ed Sullivan Show," Elvis Presley's comeback special in 1968, Michael Jackson's moonwalk on Motown's 25th anniversary special and Ricky Martin shaking his bon-bon while singing "The Cup of Life" on the Grammys in February 1999.

Martin wasn't unknown when he delivered that knock-out performance, but his profile was fairly low. He had served time in Menudo, the Puerto Rican boy band with a rotating roster

of teen singers; he starred in a Mexican soap opera, "To Reach a Star"; was cast in ABC-TV's "General Hospital"; and did a stint in the musical *Les Miserables* on Broadway. He recorded albums in Spanish and became a crossover star—almost everywhere except the U.S. His first Hot 100 entry, "Maria," stopped at number 88 and his 1998 World Cup soccer theme, "The Cup of Life," only managed to reach number 60 in its first chart run.

Writer/producer Desmond Child heard that Martin was going to record an album in English, and arranged a meeting with Joanna Effra of Columbia's A&R department. Martin's mentor, former Menudo singer Robi Rosa, and Martin's managers told Child they had been warned not to let him work with Ricky because he was a rock producer and didn't know anything about Latin music. Child thought that was ironic: "I'm Cuban, I grew up in Latin music and my mother is a Latin

music composer and my aunt is Latin music legend Olga Guitoz." Fortunately, Rosa and the managers said they weren't going to heed the "advice" about Child's rock credentials. "So it was almost on a dare that our enterprise began and there was chemistry between all of us from the start," says Child.

When Martin was chosen to record the World Cup theme, Child and Rosa wrote "La Copa De La Vida" sitting in the first class cabin of a plane on a flight from Los Angeles to Miami. Child explains, "Starting with 'Cup,' Robi and I created a fusion that was later to fuel the creation of 'Livin' La Vida Loca,' where we were combining Latin and Brazilian rhythms, Afro-Cuban and Brazilian rhythms, arena rock chant and the piano style called timbale which is associated with salsa music and danson, and an epic type of lyric."

Martin's manager, Angelo Medina, asked Child and Rosa to come up with another "Cup of Life," only this time with a "Spanglish" lyric. "I spent about three days working on that title," says Child. "I ran it by Robi, who flipped over the title, so we wrote the song around it. I felt the title embodied Ricky's zest for life and the kind of risk-taking that living a very fast life all over the world with crazy nights in different capitals of the world entails."

Child and Rosa's demo of "Livin' La Vida Loca" turned out to be the master. "We hired Randy Cantor to be our arranger and coaxed him into throwing in the kitchen sink," says Child. "We had everything from whistles to gongs and horns and rock guitar and Spanish piano. At the time, Frank Sinatra had passed away, so we were listening to Frank and swing. And I had this inspiration because Ricky reminded me of a Latin Elvis. So I had this vision of Ricky dressed like Elvis in a Las Vegas performance all in black, really moving and shaking. That's why we wrote the lyric and the swing of the melody like a Rat Pack-type song."

"Livin' La Vida Loca" began a string of number one hits for Latin artists on the Hot 100, with subsequent chart-toppers by Jennifer Lopez, Enrique Iglesias, Christina Aguilera and Santana. "It was an amazing moment," Child confirms. "Latin crossover had been dead in the water. The last hit was 'Just Another Day' by Jon Secada, which was seven years earlier."

# 882 If You Had My Love WORK 79163
## JENNIFER LOPEZ

---

*Writers: Rodney Jerkins*
*LaShawn Daniels*
*Cory Rooney*
*Fred Jerkins III*

*Producer: Rodney Jerkins*

*June 12, 1999*
*5 weeks*

---

JENNIFER LOPEZ ALREADY HAD a flourishing career when she recorded her first album. Born in the Bronx on July 24, 1970, she had studied singing and dancing when she was five years old. She continued dance classes after graduating high school, and got her first break in 1990 when she joined the sketch comedy series "In Living Color" as a Fly Girl. Acting jobs in TV movies and the series "Hotel Malibu" followed, and she was one of the dancers in Janet Jackson's video for "That's the Way Love Goes" [see 817]. That same year, she was cast in the film *My Family, Mi Familia.* Her list of movie credits grew quickly, with roles in *U-Turn, Money Train* and *Jack.* She earned praise from the critics for starring as the slain Tejana singer in *Selena,* and for playing opposite George Clooney in *Out of Sight.*

Firmly established as a film actress, Lopez still wanted a singing career. Sony Music chairman Tommy Mottola screened her performance in *Selena* and arranged a meeting with Lopez and a number of top producers, including Cory Rooney, Rodney Jerkins, Walter Afanasieff, Babyface and Ric Wake. "She was very impressed," says Rooney. "We went into the studio the very next day to record a song I played for her on the piano at the meeting."

While Lopez was recording the album that would be titled *On the 6,* Jerkins came up with an idea for a track. "Originally he had the groove for Michael Jackson and I heard it and said we should play around with it a little bit," Rooney recalls. "We went in the studio and kicked it around, but Jennifer wasn't too big on it. She wasn't sure if it was for her. But then me and LaShawn Daniels wrote the lyrics and the melodies out for her. Once we sang it to her, she jumped in the writing end of it. She really got into it, and we nailed it in one night."

Lopez voiced doubts about her singing ability, but her producers didn't share those feelings. "She took direction well," says co-writer Fred Jerkins, Rodney's older brother by seven years. "Shawn did the vocal production. He had her singing a lot better than she thought she could sing. He's a genius at what he does with vocal production, but she was a hard worker and wanted to be there."

Hopes were riding high on the Jerkins-produced track, "If You Had My Love." "It was her debut project, so it was super important for us to give her something we felt crazy about, because we knew she was a star in the movie industry, but the music business was untapped for her," says Fred Jerkins. "We knew if we could give her the right song that would be a big crossover song—not just an R&B song but one that could cross over to pop, her movie stardom would help accelerate the song to number one."

Rooney is lavish with praise for Lopez. "She is by far the most creative person I've come across in all of my collaborations with anybody," he proclaims. "She's very smart. She knows who she is. It makes everything I do pretty easy. She knows what it is that she's trying to portray or what message she's trying to get across."

The fact that she was a neophyte in the studio while recording "If You Had My Love" didn't hurt the project, according to Rooney. "I would always tell her that this is no different than her acting job. Forget technique. Just close your eyes and believe in every word you're singing. Don't worry about where you're standing or anything like that as far as positioning on the mic, because it's the job of the engineer to capture your voice. Just be you. Go into character for what this song is going to require and we'll pull off the rest."

Balancing two careers presented no problem for Lopez, Rooney believes. "I've never seen anyone shoot a movie all day and then show up at the studio full of energy and bursting at the seams, ready to go. She keeps everyone on their toes because she's so ready to do it."

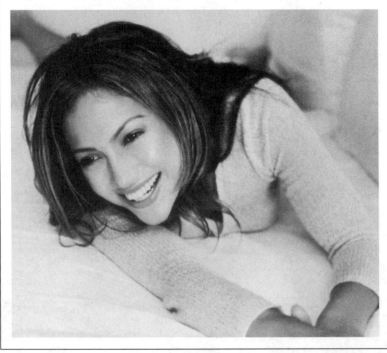

## THE TOP FIVE
*Week of June 12, 1999*

---

1  **If You Had My Love**
   Jennifer Lopez

2  **Livin' La Vida Loca**
   Ricky Martin

3  **No Scrubs**
   TLC

4  **Fortunate**
   Maxwell

5  **Where My Girls At?**
   702

their idea for the melody and that helped changed the girls' minds. "From that point on, we wrote about four songs that first trip," says Burruss. "They flew us back a second time to work with the girls and that's when 'Bills, Bills, Bills' came up. So we went from, 'We don't know if you're going to get on the record' to having five songs on their album."

Briggs and Burruss stopped in a grocery store during their second visit to Houston, and that's where Briggs came up with the hook, "Can you pay my bills, my bills, bills, bills?" Burruss said that sounded like the girls were gold diggers. "That's when I came up with the melody," she says. "The whole story is [something that] happened with this guy I dated. He was driving my car and I'm putting gas in it, and he's [using] my cell phone."

Burruss related those incidents to the members of Destiny's Child so they could work on the song together. "She'kspere kept humming the melody to the chorus," Knowles says of their writing session. "It was so catchy. We loved it. We knew it was a hit but we weren't sure of what the song was talking about. Why would we ask a guy to pay our bills? Only if he ran them up! We wrote the verses about him taking advantage of us even though nobody really paid attention to that part. People took it the wrong way."

Of all the songs he produced for the album *The Writing's on the Wall*, Briggs was confident that "Bills, Bills, Bills" would be the biggest hit. "Beyoncé is a phenomenal singer and at the time, she was just 17. I said to Kandi, 'She can really sing our songs. We can do things with an intricate melody and she can pull it off.'"

---

Writers: *Kandi Burruss*
*Beyoncé Knowles*
*LeToya Luckett*
*Kevin Briggs*

Producer: *She'kspere*

*July 17, 1999*
*1 week*

---

**K**ANDI BURRUSS KNEW SOMETHING about girl groups when she helped write "Bills, Bills, Bills," the first number one hit for Destiny's Child. Burruss had been a member of Atlanta-based Xscape, a quartet that never reached pole position, but did kick off its career with a number two hit in 1993, "Just Kickin' It."

Destiny's Child also started out as a quartet, but in Houston. That's where Beyoncé Knowles and Kelly Rowland grew up, along with LaTavia Roberson and LeToya Luckett. When they were just nine and 10, the four girls sang for the customers at the Headliners Hair Salon, owned by Beyoncé's mother, Tina. Her husband Matthew believed in the girls enough to quit his job to become their manager. Under the name Girls' Tyme, they competed on *Star Search*, but didn't win. The loss still stirs painful memories, but it was one

minor setback in a career of triumphs. In 1996, Destiny's Child was signed to Columbia Records. A year later, the single "No, No, No Part 2" made its debut on the Hot 100, ultimately peaking at number three.

Producer Kevin Briggs, known as She'kspere, had worked with female R&B groups TLC and Blaque when he was asked if he would like to produce Destiny's Child. "I didn't know much about them, but I was trying to do whatever it takes to establish my credibility as a producer and songwriter," he says. "I went to Texas and at first it was a little uncomfortable, because they weren't expecting to see Kandi."

Burruss recalls the awkward situation. "Kevin flew me down himself, so the girls didn't know I was coming. The label knew, but the group didn't. When I got there, they were looking like, 'What is she doing here?'" Briggs and Burruss were told there was only one slot open for a song on the second Destiny's Child album, so they knew they had to write something outstanding.

"Matthew wasn't expecting us to come up with anything," says Burruss. Briggs played the girls his track for a song called "Bugaboo," but when he left the room they told Burruss they weren't feeling the song. She presented

---

## THE TOP FIVE
*Week of July 17, 1999*

1 **Bills, Bills, Bills**
Destiny's Child

2 **If You Had My Love**
Jennifer Lopez

3 **Last Kiss**
Pearl Jam

4 **Genie in a Bottle**
Christina Aguilera

5 **Livin' La Vida Loca**
Ricky Martin

884

# Wild Wild West COLUMBIA 79157
## WILL SMITH Featuring DRU HILL & KOOL MOE DEE

*Writers: Stevie Wonder*
*Will Smith*
*Robert Fusari*
*Mohandas DeWese*

*Producer: Robert Fusari*

*July 24, 1999*
*1 week*

On SEPTEMBER 17, 1965, just two days after "Lost in Space" premiered on CBS, the network introduced another science-fiction/fantasy series, "The Wild, Wild West," starring Robert Conrad as special agent James West and Ross Martin as his sidekick, Artemus Gordon. The series ran four seasons, and eventually two television movies were made, the second airing in 1980. But that was not the end of the show. With TV series like "Star Trek" and "The Flintstones" turning into motion picture franchises, it was only a matter of time before someone brought "The Wild, Wild West" to the big screen.

Director Barry Sonnenfeld's film starred Will Smith as West. With Smith's title song from the Sonnenfeld-directed 1997 film *Men in Black* a proven airplay hit, it wasn't a big stretch to imagine the producers wanting a Smith song included on the soundtrack to *Wild Wild West*.

Omarr Rambert, Smith's A&R executive, asked writer/producer Rob Fusari if he had anything he wanted to submit for the soundtrack. Fusari had already worked on another project for Smith's Overbrook Productions, the album by "The Fresh Prince of Bel-Air" co-star Tatyana Ali. Fusari sent Rambert a dozen tracks. "They were all sample-oriented, because I knew that was Will's thing," says Fusari. "He took samples and did his rap and was very successful at it, so I wasn't going to send him anything that didn't have a sample." Fusari's tracks sampled hits by artists like AC/DC; Earth, Wind & Fire and Stevie Wonder. Smith took a liking to the track that sampled Wonder's "I Wish" [see 451].

Fusari suggested K-Ci and JoJo as guest artists. Smith wanted Dru Hill, and then added rapper Kool Moe Dee, who had a number 62 hit in 1988 with a song called "Wild, Wild West," as another featured artist. "It was an extremely expensive record to make," says Fusari. "Stevie Wonder took an advance of $500,000 just to use the sample. But it was a ball of fun. Making

that record was such a party. Will invited me to his house. We did the vocals in his new studio that he had just built. The atmosphere was so good working on that record, and I think you hear it on the song."

Fusari credits Smith for recording the vocals very quickly. "It's unbelievable. Will took two takes on the entire rap performance. I work with a lot of artists and it's rare when I'm fortunate enough to experience that. He came up with the bulk of the lyric and it was my job as producer to tweak it. It was never painstaking." On the second day of production, Fusari recorded Kool Moe Dee at Smith's home studio. Then Dru Hill recorded their parts at Right Track in Manhattan. "Sisqó came up with most of their vocal parts," says Fusari. When he arrived at the studio, Sisqó asked for a copy of the track with Smith's vocals. "He went outside for 20 minutes and came back and said, 'Let's go,'" Fusari remembers. "It was his first time hearing it and he had all the ideas ready to go."

On the last day of production, while mixing the song in Los Angeles, Smith said he wanted his wife to hear the track. "It was almost like she was the final O.K.," says Fusari. "I'm thinking, what if she hates it? It could kill this whole thing, all this work! It's his wife, he could take her opinion to heart." Jada Pinkett-Smith arrived at the studio and asked to hear the track. "Halfway through, she gets up out of her seat and starts dancing! Nothing was changed."

The movie *Wild Wild West* opened in theaters in the U.S. on July 4, 1999. With a $49.7 million opening weekend, it was the second-highest gross for a July 4th opening in history, runner-up only to the $50.2 million opening of Smith's *Independence Day* in 1996. The song "Wild Wild West" entered the Hot 100 the week of May 22, 1999, at a lofty number 32, more than a month before the release of the film. After a couple of weeks of rapid movement, the single slowed down, and was stuck at number eight for two weeks in a row when it suddenly catapulted to number one.

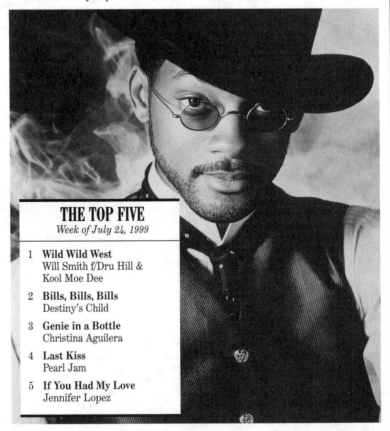

## THE TOP FIVE
*Week of July 24, 1999*

1  **Wild Wild West**
   Will Smith f/Dru Hill &
   Kool Moe Dee

2  **Bills, Bills, Bills**
   Destiny's Child

3  **Genie in a Bottle**
   Christina Aguilera

4  **Last Kiss**
   Pearl Jam

5  **If You Had My Love**
   Jennifer Lopez

*Writers: Steve Kipner*
*David Frank*
*Pam Sheyne*

*Producers: David Frank*
*Steve Kipner*

*July 31, 1999*
*5 weeks*

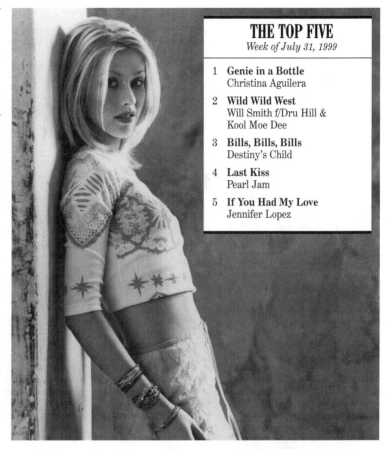

### THE TOP FIVE
*Week of July 31, 1999*

1  **Genie in a Bottle**
   Christina Aguilera

2  **Wild Wild West**
   Will Smith f/Dru Hill &
   Kool Moe Dee

3  **Bills, Bills, Bills**
   Destiny's Child

4  **Last Kiss**
   Pearl Jam

5  **If You Had My Love**
   Jennifer Lopez

THINKING THEY WOULD MAKE a good songwriting team, Carla Ondrasik of EMI Music introduced two of her writers to each other. The first song Steve Kipner and David Frank wrote together was "Into My Privacy," a hit for French singer Ophelie Winter. Frank had been collaborating with a couple of British songwriters, Andrew Frampton and Jodie Wilson. When a friend of theirs was coming over to the U.S., Frampton and Wilson suggested she ring up Kipner and Frank with the idea of writing as a trio. "She's from New Zealand, but had been living in England for a long time," says Frank. "Her name was Pam Sheyne."

The day of their songwriting appointment, Frank woke up in the middle of the night with an idea for a music track. "The muse smiled down on me, and when Steve and Pam came over, it was a very fluid process," says Frank. Kipner and Sheyne liked what they heard. "It's an eight-bar loop," says Frank. "That's what the song is, with a lot of different changes going in and out. Pam said, 'How about something like, "If you want to be with me,"' and Steve walked around with his arms waving and he started to sing the melody to the chorus." Kipner confirms, "It was that kind of energy—the song was just flying."

Frank continues, "I didn't know Pam that well, but I knew that Steve is a genius. I thought, what are the next [words after], 'If you want to be with me, there's a price to pay,' and I don't know how it happened, but I said, 'Like a genie in a bottle,' and Steve said, 'No, no, "I'm a genie in a bottle."'"

"It was really fast," Kipner picks up the story. "Pam is really a good singer, so we were all singing away. Instead of everyone trying to be intellectual, it was all very stream of consciousness. And before you knew it, the song was there. That's weird to me—sometimes songs just filter through and I think, where did that come from? Suddenly this thing exists. And there was no doubt this was a hit song."

There was one more element that had to fall into place. "When the song was finished, we were still calling it, 'If You Want to Be With Me,' which is stupid," laughs Kipner. "It was Christina's manager who said, 'You should call it "Genie in a Bottle,"'" says Frank.

The demo was sent out to A&R staffers the same day it was recorded. Responses came back quickly. "We knew there were certain people looking. Christina Aguilera was looking. We knew about Innocence, a group that was up and coming on RCA," says Frank. The songwriters felt they had a better chance of scoring an international hit if Innocence recorded the song because they were intended to be a sister group to 'N Sync.

Ron Fair from RCA's A&R department called the writers and said he wanted the song for Aguilera. "Christina wanted to start off her career with a ballad because Mariah had started with a ballad," says Fair. "I was adamant about grabbing the world's attention with a rhythmic song and wasn't so concerned about showing every aspect of her talent on the first song."

The writers knew Aguilera from her recording of "Reflection" on the *Mulan* soundtrack. "We thought she might be too much of a straight-ahead singer. But then she came over and sang the song for us and we were absolutely blown away. There was no doubt we had to have her do the song," says Frank.

The track from the demo was used for Aguilera's recording. "She put her voice over what the demo singer had done," says Kipner. "And then it was cleaned up. We put the vocal backing in." Frank continues, "She did all the backgrounds, all the leads." "We did them twice," says Kipner. "The first time it sounded fantastic but a little too hard-sounding and too powerful on the backgrounds. We wanted it to be a bit more innocent, so she's not in control— a little bit vulnerable, a little softer."

## 886 Bailamos OVERBROOK 97122
### ENRIQUE IGLESIAS

*Writers: Paul Barry*
*Mark Taylor*

*Producers: Mark Taylor*
*Brian Rawling*

*September 4, 1999*
*2 weeks*

ENRIQUE IGLESIAS WAS BORN May 8, 1975, in Madrid. His parents, singer Julio Iglesias and journalist Isabel Preysler, already had two children—a daughter, Chabeli, and a son, Julio José. When Enrique was three, his parents divorced. Five years later, fearing there was a plot in Spain to kidnap her children, Preysler sent them to live with their father in Miami. With their father absent for long periods because of his singing career, the children were raised by their nanny, Elvira Olivares.

Enrique enrolled at the University of Miami as a business major, but graduating from college was not his real goal. He didn't want his parents to interfere with his desire to pursue a musical career, so he kept it a secret from them. He recorded demos and sent them out to record companies posing as an unknown singer from Central America named Enrique Martinez. When Los Angeles–based Latin label Fonovisa signed Enrique to a three-album deal, his parents learned the truth. Collectively, Enrique's three Spanish-language albums for Fonovisa sold 14 million copies.

Fonovisa's deal with Enrique was for the U.S. and Mexico. International rights for non-Latin countries belonged to Universal. And that's how producers Mark Taylor and Brian Rawling, who had produced a number one hit for Cher [see 879—"Believe"], came into the picture. "We were approached by Steve Wolf, a friend of ours, who was helping out at Universal," explains Rawling. "He sent us a package and said they were looking for a record to break this guy internationally. They sent us the Spanish records, which were great. It was an intriguing offer."

Rawling and Taylor flew to Miami to see the young Iglesias in concert. "We were knocked out," says Rawling. "One song into the show, we looked at each other. It was like, 'This guy's got everything.' A couple of days later, we were in the studio recording him."

Songwriter Paul Barry wanted to write an English-language song for Enrique that would incorporate some Spanish. "I asked someone how to say 'Let Dance' in Spanish, and they said, 'Bailamos.' I put the accent on the wrong spot because I thought they said. 'Bai-la-MOS,' and of course, it's 'Bai-LA-mos.' It's funny, because Enrique says people tell him it's cool how the accent is on the third syllable. It's my ignorance."

Barry wrote the song with Taylor, who describes how they work together: "We both play guitars and keyboards, so we're sitting in a room with a guitar or keyboard, bashing stuff out. It's lyrics, melodies, music all coming one after the other. We usually start with either a melody idea or a title."

Barry sang the vocals on the demo of "Bailamos." When Iglesias recorded the song, a label deal wasn't in place. "He didn't have a deal with Interscope at that point," says Taylor. "It wasn't this enormous project or important priority act, so there were no heads of A&R coming down and tweaking. He got a deal with our finished record, and then all of a sudden he's signing a megadeal with Interscope and the record's a massive hit."

The Interscope deal, signed on June 27, 1999, was for six albums and was reportedly worth $44 million. "Enrique has the power and charisma that makes every artist that has the power to move people extraordinary," Interscope co-owner Jimmy Iovine told Chuck Taylor in *Billboard.*

A few months after recording "Bailamos," actor Will Smith saw Iglesias perform live in Los Angeles. Smith called the artist and asked him if he had anything to contribute to the soundtrack for *Wild Wild West.* Enrique sent over the recording of "Bailamos."

Taylor and Rawling say they were the last to know the song was going to be included in the soundtrack. "Aside from the fact we're on the other side of the world," says the U.K.-based Taylor, "once you've handed the record over, the communication breakdown starts. Eventually you see things in the press and hear things on the radio. We rarely get feedback from any record companies. Suddenly, it's a hit."

"Bailamos" was the second number one hit from *Wild Wild West,* rising to the top of the Hot 100 six weeks after Smith's title track [see 884]. Iglesias was the fourth Latin artist to reach pole position in the summer of 1999, following Ricky Martin, Jennifer Lopez, and Christina Aguilera.

### THE TOP FIVE
*Week of September 4, 1999*

1 **Bailamos**
Enrique Iglesias

2 **Genie in a Bottle**
Christina Aguilera

3 **Summer Girls**
LFO

4 **Unpretty**
TLC

5 **All Star**
Smash Mouth

Writers: *Dallas Austin*
*Tionne Watkins*

Producer: *Dallas Austin*

*September 18, 1999*
*3 weeks*

FIVE MOTHS AFTER scoring their first number one single from their *Fanmail* album, TLC were back on top of the Hot 100 with the follow-up, "Unpretty." Producer Dallas Austin reveals the origin of the song: "Tionne [Watkins] had a poem called 'Unpretty' and I thought the title was amazing. I said I should make one of those alternative pop songs, like a Natalie Imbruglia or an Ani DiFranco–type record."

Austin wrote lyrics based on Tionne's title, which also inspired him to write the music for the song. "Once I saw the title, I went to my keyboard and guitar and started playing melodies that would complement it. I didn't want it to be aggressive. I wanted it to be friendly—for a song called 'Unpretty' talking about how much you don't like stuff about yourself—so the message would come across to people with those kinds of problems or issues. I thought it would be unique to get it across in a sweet way."

Austin had no problem writing "Unpretty" from a woman's point of view—he had already done that successfully on TLC's first number one hit [see 833—"Creep"]. Austin, who had known the members of TLC before they formed a group, says, "When I write for TLC, I write for each one of the members. So when I do a Tionne part, it's different from what Chilli's part would be. When we first did 'Unpretty,' it was one of the most exciting records we'd ever done because it was different. And it still stayed along the lines of TLC having messages for people."

Austin thinks "Unpretty" is one of the most important songs he's written. "I've received letters from kids with cancer and different illnesses who say the record changed their perspective." The producer knew "Unpretty" would be a single from *Fanmail*, but he wasn't sure when. "Sometimes record companies get cold feet for things that aren't the norm of what the group has already done. All of us knew it would be a big record."

Austin credits Lisa "Left Eye" Lopes for the "brilliant" idea of using sign language in the video for "Unpretty." "It expanded the message even more. She was a very funny, caring person," he says of the woman who died April 25, 2002, in a car accident. Lopes was on vacation in Honduras, where she owned a condominium. She was a passenger in a rental car when the driver lost control of the vehicle and crashed.

"She was always funny," Austin recalls fondly. "When we were doing the first album, we used to have water fights in the studio. We took flour and catsup and mustard and all kinds of stuff and put it all over each other's faces. One time after I drenched her, she thought she'd take water and flour and pour it on my face so it would drip down and make a big mess on me. But she didn't put enough water in the flour. So when she came in the studio and dumped it on my head, it just stayed there, like a cake."

## THE TOP FIVE

*Week of September 18, 1999*

1 **Unpretty**
TLC

2 **Bailamos**
Enrique Iglesias

3 **Summer Girls**
LFO

4 **She's All I Ever Had**
Ricky Martin

5 **Genie in a Bottle**
Christina Aguilera

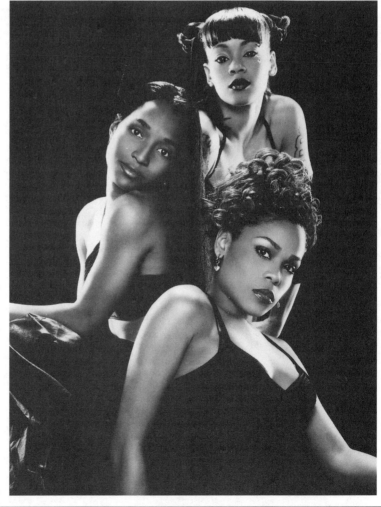

## 888 Heartbreaker COLUMBIA 79260
### MARIAH CAREY Featuring JAY-Z

Writers: *Mariah Carey*
*Shawn Carter*
*Shirley Elliston*
*Lincoln Chase*
*Narada Michael Walden*
*Jeffrey Cohen*

Producers: *Mariah Carey*
*Clue*

October 9, 1999
2 weeks

R*AINBOW* WAS MARIAH CAREY's final studio album of original material for Columbia, her label home since her debut in 1990. "In all honesty, it was like I have one more album here and I want to move on, because my personal life had changed. It was difficult for me to still be in the system, but it was a great outlet for me to be able to go into the studio and write a song like 'Petals,' which is one of my most personal songs and remains one of my favorites. I think [it has the most] honest lyrics I've ever written."

"Petals" wasn't a single. The label led with "Heartbreaker," produced by Carey with a friend she met through mutual acquaintances, DJ Clue. "He came up with the Stacy Lattisaw 'Attack of the Name Game' loop because he felt it was very much in my vein, like those happy kind of records. And when he came up with the 'It Ain't No Fun,' the remix, that's when I knew it was over. That's when I said this is

the hottest record I've ever done, in terms of a club record. That and 'Fantasy' with Ol' Dirty Bastard, because you can still go to clubs and hear them play that 'Heartbreaker' remix with Missy [Elliott] and [Da] Brat. I love collaborating with Clue." Carey is also effusive about her "Heartbreaker" partner, Jay-Z. "It's fun when you find people you can relate to and that you respect. Jay-Z is somebody I so admire as a writer and as an artist. We could be sitting in the studio and he could freestyle a rhyme that would be incredible just off the top of his head. He doesn't need pen and paper. I equate that to a singer who can pick up the mike and riff and ad-lib over a song and take you to a totally new place."

Carey recounts her inspiration for the "Heartbreaker" lyrics: "It was from the standpoint of girls who keep going back to that same guy and they can't help themselves. They know they're going to get hurt. I've been one of those girls, so I know there's a lot of them out there."

Providing backing vocals on "Heartbreaker" was someone Carey had known for a long time. Trey Lorenz was the male voice on her remake of the Jackson 5's "I'll Be There" [see 808]. "He's an amazing writer and singer," says Carey. "He's so influenced by old school stuff, yet he's so current. He's known me since before my first album, and he's a great, loyal friend."

There's a party atmosphere on the original version of "Heartbreaker" on the *Rainbow* album. But there wasn't a big crowd in the studio. "It's me, Clue and Jay-Z, and whatever other production things Clue put in," says Carey. "Being a DJ, he has a lot of different ideas for making atmospheric stuff on mix tapes."

"Heartbreaker" was Carey's 14th number one on the Hot 100, a total run up in just over nine years. With "Heartbreaker," she sailed past Michael Jackson's 13 chart-toppers to claim third place among artists with the most number ones. Only the Beatles (with 20) and Elvis Presley (with 17) had more than Carey, and she wasn't finished with pole position.

### THE TOP FIVE
*Week of October 9, 1999*

1 **Heartbreaker**
Mariah Carey f/Jay-Z

2 **Smooth**
Santana f/Rob Thomas

3 **Unpretty**
TLC

4 **Mambo No. 5 (A Little Bit of…)**
Lou Bega

5 **She's All I Ever Had**
Ricky Martin

ARISTA 13718 **Smooth**

**889**

SANTANA Featuring ROB THOMAS

*Writers: Rob Thomas*
*Itaal Shur*

*Producer: Matt Serletic*

*October 23, 1999*
*12 weeks*

THIRTY YEARS TO THE WEEK after making its first appearance on the Hot 100 ("Jingo"), Santana had its first number one hit. It was the longest anyone had waited from chart debut to reaching pole position.

Born in Autlan, Mexico, on July 20, 1947, Carlos Santana grew up in San Francisco. His father was a professional musician who had a strong influence on his son. After graduating from Mission High School, Carlos formed the Santana Blues Band. By the time Clive Davis signed them to Columbia, the name had been shortened to Santana. Their first album entered the *Billboard* chart in September, 1969, just a month after a critically acclaimed performance at Woodstock.

More than 20 years of albums followed, until Santana signed with the Polydor label in 1992. Later, Santana formed his own label, Guts and Grace, through Island Records. But his greatest chart achievements were yet to come. While on tour with Jeff Beck, Santana heard from his old friend Clive Davis, who wanted to know how the musician was doing. Santana mentioned he wanted out of his current label contract and Davis told him to call when the contract was up. In 1999, Davis once again signed Santana to a label deal, this time with Arista.

Manhattan-based songwriter Itaal Shur, who had written a 1996 top 10

R&B hit for Maxwell, "Ascension (Don't Ever Wonder)," heard that Santana was looking for songs for his first Arista album. He came up with the first draft of "Smooth," with lyrics that were considered too sexual. Evan Lambert of EMI Music Publishing called Rob Thomas of matchbox twenty and asked if he would work with Shur on the song. "He lived two blocks from me," says Thomas. "So I went over and he gave me the track he had written. My wife went out shopping and left me alone with it. By the time she came back, I had the chorus written. I went back to Itaal and the next day we had the demo done. But I wasn't supposed to sing. The original intent was that it would be my first foray into writing and not performing." Other names were considered for recording lead vocals, including George Michael, according to producer Matt Serletic. He and Davis suggested Thomas, and Santana agreed. Thomas explains, "Carlos, who had no idea who the hell I was, said, 'Does this guy sing? I like him. Can we get him?'" Thomas called his band to let them know. "If we had been on the road, there was no way I could have done it," he says. "But the timing was perfect."

Thomas thought he was going to show up at the studio and simply record his vocals. But Carlos was

there with all the members of Santana. "These are some of the best supporting musicians in the world," says Thomas, "and they played it one time through and then a second time, and that's the take on the record. Carlos overdubbed his guitar. There was a moment when I was cutting the scratch vocals in the booth and to my right is this band jamming and to my left is Carlos in the control room playing away and that was the first time it hit me. 'Wow, I'm working with Carlos! I'm actually jamming with him.'"

Serletic recalls making the track in San Francisco: "Those guys put a great demo together and it really helped shape the concept. We spent a lot of time working out the specifics of the arrangement and how it stops in the middle." After recording the band, Thomas' vocals and Carlos' guitar overdubs, Serletic and Thomas took Sunday off to go to Napa Valley. During the car ride back to the city, Serletic wrote the charts for the horns and recorded them the next day.

"Smooth" spent 12 weeks at number one. Other songs had spent 10, 11, 13, 14 and 16 weeks at the summit, but no song had ever completed its run at the top in 12 weeks. The single spent a record-setting 30 weeks in the top 10, an impressive feat considering only 10 number one titles in history had remained in the top 10 for 20 weeks or more. The previous record holder was Savage Garden's "Truly Madly Deeply" [see 861], which was in the top 10 for 26 weeks.

## THE TOP FIVE

*Week of October 23, 1999*

1 **Smooth**
   Santana f/Rob Thomas

2 **Heartbreaker**
   Mariah Carey f/Jay-Z

3 **Music of My Heart**
   'N Sync and Gloria Estefan

4 **Unpretty**
   TLC

5 **Mambo No. 5 (A Little Bit Of..**
   Lou Bega

# 890 What a Girl Wants RCA 65968
## CHRISTINA AGUILERA

*Writers: Shelly Peiken*
*Guy Roche*

*Producer: Guy Roche*

*January 15, 2000*
*2 weeks*

SHELLY PEIKEN's songwriting career got off to a great start when Taylor Dayne became the first artist to record one of her songs; "Carry Your Heart" appeared on *Tell It to My Heart*. "That was a lucky thing because her album went platinum," says Peiken. "It seemed like, 'This is going to be easy. All albums go platinum.' I was so wrong. It took a very long time to have a hit single in the States."

Peiken had plenty of songs recorded as album cuts, and some successful singles in other countries. Finally, her name appeared on the Hot 100 when she co-wrote Curtis Stigers' "You're All That Matters to Me," which went to number 98 and charted for one week in 1992. It wasn't until 1997 that she cracked the top 10, when she wrote "Bitch" with Meredith Brooks. That single peaked at number two. "We were knocking on that number one door and we couldn't get in," Peiken laughs. "At the same time, I was pregnant with my first and only wonderful child and I had

to step back and say maybe the universe is trying to tell me my number one is not a song. It's my child."

Peiken met a new songwriting partner, Tahiti-born Guy Roche, when he moved to Los Angeles from French Polynesia and produced demos for her. Later, his manager suggested they compose together. Peiken's normal m.o. was to take a track from a writer and drive around in her car to see if any lyrics would come to her. "I like the space and privacy of driving around in my car," says Peiken. "But I've never taken music from Guy and driven around. We're always in a room together. He's my good friend. I like being with him. The physical energy in a room with him is inspiring."

Peiken and Roche were sitting in a room one day when Roche played some music and Peiken sang to it. "I had a little cassette running, a work tape in case you can't remember something but you know it was good. A lot of hooks come out of making mistakes, and then you can't remember what you did. I went home that night and got into bed with my husband. I was listening to our work tape." Peiken asked her husband to listen to a little ditty that went, "What a girl needs, what a girl wants, whatever makes you happy and keeps you strong." She remembers, "I knew

there was a real gem there in a very raw form that was going to be something one day."

The song was completed and titled "What a Girl Needs," but it sat on the shelf for some time before it was pitched to Ron Fair of RCA's A&R department. Fair had signed Christina Aguilera to the label and was looking for material for her debut album. The RCA executive liked Peiken and Roche's song, but asked them to switch the word "needs" with "wants." Peiken recalls, "Guy and I looked at each other and said, 'I don't know, do we want to do this?' We took a leap of faith and followed Ron's suggestions. What he suggested felt right."

"What a Girl Wants" was the first song recorded for Aguilera's album, according to Fair. "It had a really strong hook, and when it was time to choose the next single, we re-recorded it because of the key. 'Genie in a Bottle' established the money spot of her voice. But the original version of 'What a Girl Wants' was done much lower, much smokier, much sultrier, and so the chorus didn't have the lift it needed. We changed the key and freshened up the rhythm and took a much more aggressive approach in re-recording it."

Peiken was home reading a *Winnie the Pooh* book to her daughter when a friend at Arista called to tell her "Smooth" had been knocked out of the number one spot by "What a Girl Wants." Peiken replied, "Don't get me wrong. I want to jump through the roof. But I'm reading a Pooh book to my daughter right now. When I put her to sleep at 8:30, I'm going to go wild. But I can't do it right now. She's still my number one over any number ones."

## THE TOP FIVE
*Week of January 15, 2000*

1 **What a Girl Wants**
Christina Aguilera

2 **Smooth**
Santana f/Rob Thomas

3 **Back at One**
Brian McKnight

4 **I Knew I Loved You**
Savage Garden

5 **I Wanna Love You Forever**
Jessica Simpson

COLUMBIA 78723    **I Knew I Loved You**   891

SAVAGE GARDEN

*Writers: Darren Hayes*
*Daniel Jones*

*Producers: Walter Afanasieff*
*Darren Hayes*
*Daniel Jones*

*January 29, 2000*
*4 weeks*

SAVAGE GARDEN'S FIRST NUMBER one hit, "Truly Madly Deeply" [see 861] was inspired by Darren Hayes' love for his wife. But the songs on the duo's second album, *Affirmation,*, were written about the breakup of his marriage. "There were songs about heartache and getting back on your feet but they weren't songs about 'I'm in love and the world is perfect' because the world wasn't perfect for me at that stage. We delivered the album and [Columbia Records president] Donnie Ienner listened to it and said, 'It's an artistic masterpiece. It's incredible. You've grown. You've matured. It's wonderful. [But] there's no "Truly Madly Deeply" in there.'"

Hayes is paraphrasing Ienner, because the label chief didn't deliver that message directly to the artists. "I probably would have stormed around the studio for two days saying, 'How dare he! Does Madonna have another "Holiday"?' It turns out that 20 years later she did and it was called 'Music.' But at the time, I just said, 'How can they expect me to repeat myself?'"

The message was delivered by producer Walter Afanasieff. His association with Savage Garden began when the duo was asked to write a song for the film *The Other Sister.* Ienner suggested to Hayes and Daniel Jones that they work with Afanasieff and arranged a

## THE TOP FIVE
*Week of January 29, 2000*

1   **I Knew I Loved You**
    Savage Garden

2   **What a Girl Wants**
    Christina Aguilera

3   **Smooth**
    Santana f/Rob Thomas

4   **Back at One**
    Brian McKnight

5   **Bring It All to Me**
    Blaque

conference call. "They started to ask me a lot of questions," the producer remembers, "and I said I'm not known to produce rock and roll acts. I'm stereotyped as a pop and maybe even a ballad producer." Hayes and Jones said they didn't want to work with someone like that; they were looking for an "edgy guy." Despite that, they agreed to visit the producer in his Bay Area studio. That led to recording "The Animal Song" for the soundtrack project. Ecstatic with the result, Hayes and Jones asked Afanaiseff to produce their entire second album.

It was after Afanasieff recorded 12 songs with Savage Garden and mixed them in his studio that he flew to New York and presented the album to executives at Columbia. That's when he was recruited to deliver the message about Ienner wanting another "Truly Madly Deeply." Afanasieff recalls, "Darren is a rebel. He likes to fight the establishment. So it was really difficult. I eased it into the conversation. And it was like a dare. He got a look in his eyes. I have this little writing room upstairs in my guest house where they were living. Darren looked over at Daniel and said, 'They want a "Truly Madly Deeply"? Alright, I'll give them one.' Ten minutes later they came back downstairs and

said, 'We did it. It's a song called "I Knew I Loved You."'"

Hayes and Jones had actually started four different songs in that 10-minute period, but they considered them so saccharine and calculated as to be laughable. Hayes was about to admit they couldn't come up with a song when Jones played some chords. Hayes asked him to repeat a certain chord, so Jones looped it. "And this song came out of me and it really healed my broken heart. It's such an innocent song and my way of relating to love at that time was to think about idealism and maybe the future."

Of course, when they came down from the listening room, Afanasieff didn't believe they had finished a new song. "I said, 'Come on, you just left the room.' Dan sat down at the piano and started playing the chords and Darren started singing, 'I knew I loved you before…' and I said, 'Wow! Pretty cool!'"

When Afanasieff was married on September 1, 2001, Hayes sang "I Knew I Loved You" at the wedding. "That was one of the highlights," says the producer, "to have Darren singing that song which made such perfect sense to dedicate to my new wife. It was an incredible moment."

# 892 Thank God I Found You COLUMBIA 79338
## MARIAH CAREY Featuring JOE & 98 DEGREES

*Writers: Mariah Carey
          James Harris III
          Terry Lewis*

*Producers: Jimmy Jam
            Terry Lewis*

*February 19, 2000
1 week*

WHAT IMPRESSED PRODUCERS Jimmy Jam and Terry Lewis most when they worked with Mariah Carey for the first time was that she knew exactly what she wanted, and she had intimate knowledge of their previous work. "She knew our catalog upside down," says Jimmy Jam. "She knew everything about us and what we'd done. She had written a song with Diane Warren called 'Can't Take That Away' and she said, 'You know how on the song "Again" you did the strings that sound like this and then on "On Bended Knee" you did a drum program that sounded like this.' She

could paint a total picture for us as to what she wanted the finished record to sound like."

Jam and Lewis didn't have a preconceived notion of what they wanted from Carey. "It wasn't like Janet [Jackson], where we all grew up together. Mariah had done her own thing and had been very involved with the arranging and production of her records, so we respected that and said, 'What can we do for you?' She would fly into town for five or six hours. We'd crank out a couple of songs. She'd get on a plane and fly to whatever was the next thing she was doing."

One night Jam and Lewis were at a Timberwolves game when they received a call from Carey's assistant, who told them she had an idea for a song and was arriving in Minneapolis at midnight. They met her at the studio at the appointed time. "She's got 'Thank God I found you' and that's about as much as she's got," Jam remembers. "She sang the melody. We usually have Big Jim Wright sit in on those kind of sessions to work out chords. He wasn't there so I had to work out the chords myself. So I'm playing and there was a part where I said, 'Man, what chord am I supposed to do here?' and Mariah has such a good ear, she sang me the chord."

Carey has a similar memory of that midnight session. "We just like sitting in a studio vibing off each other. 'Thank God I Found You' was a love song inspired by a relationship I was in at the time. I sang it to Jimmy and Terry and we put the song together from there. They

have been so inspirational to me throughout my life. Growing up, I listened to so many songs they have written which are classics."

At that late-night session, Jam and Lewis knew Mariah wanted male singers to join her on the track. "Our first choice when we wrote the song was K-Ci and JoJo. They were on a different record label and there were a lot of problems getting clearance for them to do it. We booked studio time and kept saying to them, 'Just come in and sing it. You could nail it in an hour. We'll worry about the politics later.'" It never happened. "So we thought about voices that would work with the song. Joe was a known entity in R&B but nowhere near the star he is now. From what we knew about Joe, he was a nice guy who would be there for the video and performances. That becomes important when you do duets, and his label was willing." Joe was flattered to be asked. "When she called me to come to the studio," says Joe, "I had no idea I would record at that moment, but I couldn't let the opportunity slip away. She sat in the control room while I was singing in the booth and it was amazing to have her sit there and watch her smile and be in her zone."

Jam and Lewis also wanted male harmonies on the track, and recruited the four members of 98 Degrees. "They had to do their part quickly and to this day the guys say, 'Sorry about the vocal.' But they came in and killed it. And Joe killed it. We always thought he had so much talent and should be bigger than he is. It was really a stepping stone for him to go on and do what he's done."

## THE TOP FIVE
*Week of February 19, 2000*

1 **Thank God I Found You**
  Mariah Carey f/
  Joe and 98 Degrees

2 **I Knew I Loved You**
  Savage Garden

3 **What a Girl Wants**
  Christina Aguilera

4 **Get It On…Tonite**
  Montell Jordan

5 **Smooth**
  Santana f/Rob Thomas

BNA 65957 **Amazed**
LONESTAR

**893**

We all thought it was a passionate song [that] people could relate to. But if you asked us then if it was going to do what it did, we wouldn't have had any idea."

After recording the song, Lonestar added "Amazed" to its live show to see how audiences would respond. McDonald improvised a new vocal lick for the live performance and called Huff, imploring him to go back into the studio to recut the song with this new addition. "I was doing another Megadeth album at the time when Richie called," says Huff. The producer didn't have a minute in his schedule, but trusted McDonald and agreed to meet him at 8:30 in the morning. "He came straight from the [tour] bus and we concocted a way to put that onto an existing mix so we wouldn't have to do it from scratch."

The first single from the *Lonely Grill* album was "Saturday Night," but radio was resistant and the label shifted gears so quickly, many people didn't realize there was a single before "Amazed." The song spent eight weeks at number one on the country chart and appeared on the Hot 100, peaking at number 24 before falling off. Then a pop remix was sent to top 40 stations. "Another track was made and I did re-sing it," says McDonald. "You can't have steel and fiddle in an Adult Contemporary format or a pop format. So you take a few things away and you add a few things." Brian Tankersley and Nick Stewart's pop remix helped "Amazed" return to the Hot 100 and begin its climb to the top. It was the first country song to achieve pole position since Kenny Rogers and Dolly Parton's "Islands in the Stream" [see 579] in 1983.

Writers: Marv Green
　　　Aimee Mayo
　　　Chris Lindsey

Producers: Dann Huff
　　　　Nick Stewart
　　　　Brian Tankersley

March 4, 2000
2 weeks

Marv Green, Aimee Mayo and Chris Lindsey had written in different combinations, until they decided to write songs as a trio. Green and Lindsey met Mayo at her home in Nashville's Green Hills one night. To set the mood, they lit candles and shared some wine. "We knew we wanted to write something emotional, something about communicating with someone you're really in love with," says Green. "We started working on the lyrical idea and it grew from the verse. We really started from the front to the finish." The trio began working at 6 p.m., and five hours later they had written one song, although they didn't know what to call it. "We walked into the demo session without a title," explains Green. "We were still arguing about the last part of the chorus as we were recording it. We actually had other lines in there that didn't even have the word 'Amazed' in it for awhile, but we settled on 'Amazed' by the time the session was done."

The songwriters didn't have a particular artist in mind for the song. The demo featured the voice of Bill Luther, who wrote "Let's Make Love" for Tim

McGraw and Faith Hill. "We pitched the song to McGraw first and someone in his camp passed on it and immediately we went to Lonestar with it," recalls Green.

The members of Lonestar all grew up in the Lone Star state of Texas, though the band came together in Nashville in 1992. "We all had other jobs at the time," says lead singer Richie McDonald. "I was working at a co-op mixing animal feed. Dean [Sams] was out at Opryland and Michael [Britt] was delivering pizzas and Keech Rainwater was managing a bar. We wanted to pay the bills doing something we loved and that was playing music." Lonestar hit the road, playing dates in Las Vegas and Reno, and traveling south to Florida and north to Canada. The band earned a solid reputation on the road but had to settle in Nashville to be noticed by a record label. In 1994, Lonestar became the house band at the Wildhorse Saloon and played there two weeks out of every month. That led to signing with BNA.

Lonestar kicked off its chart career with a number one hit on the country chart, "No News." But they had only two entries on the Hot 100, neither of which ranked higher than number 90, before the phenomenon of "Amazed." For their third album, the band worked with producer Dann Huff for the first time. "The four of us would sit around the table with Dann and Sam Ramage, the A&R person, and we'd have publishers bring songs in," says McDonald. "I remember the day 'Amazed' came in.

## THE TOP FIVE
*Week of March 4, 2000*

1　**Amazed**
　　Lonestar

2　**I Knew I Loved You**
　　Savage Garden

3　**Breathe**
　　Faith Hill

4　**Thank God I Found You**
　　Mariah Carey f/Joe &
　　98 Degrees

5　**Maria Maria**
　　Santana f/the Product G&B

# 894 Say My Name COLUMBIA 79342
## DESTINY'S CHILD

*Writers: Rodney Jerkins*
*Fred Jerkins III*
*LaShawn Daniels*
*Beyoncé Knowles*
*LeToya Luckett*
*Kelendria Rowland*
*LaTavia Roberson*

*Producer: Rodney Jerkins*

*March 18, 2000*
*3 weeks*

THE SECOND DESTINY'S CHILD album was recorded quickly, according to Beyoncé Knowles. "With *The Writing's on the Wall,* we did the whole album in about three weeks. Sometimes we did two songs a day. Some songs might take two days, but we've very, very quick in the studio." The girls worked with different producers, and recall how much fun they had being in the studio with Rodney Jerkins. "Rodney was a lot of fun to work with," confirms Kelly Rowland. Beyoncé adds, "It didn't feel like work. We had so much fun with Shawn and Rodney and his brother. It was like men and women getting together and talking about relationships. We had our debates. When you get women and men in the room and you're saying what men do and what women do, it's just fun. We laughed and we ate and we sang and we acted crazy and a great song came out of it."

That great song was the second number one hit for Destiny's Child, "Say My Name." Rodney Jerkins' brother, co-writer Fred Jerkins III, recalls how the track came together in California. "When we're working with an artist, whether the artist writes or it's just us writing, we sit down and vibe with them and try to figure out where they're at in their life, what's going on in their relationships, so we can cater to them."

When "Say My Name" was originally recorded, it had a different track, according to Jerkins. "After it was recorded, Rodney took the vocals and redid the track totally. It followed the vocals more. [The girls] loved the first track, but when they heard the second one, it blew them away."

"We were at a photo shoot for *The Writing's on the Wall* album the first time we heard the new mix of the song," says Rowland. "We ended up liking the remix better. Just to hear the hot new mix, we got even more amped about the album."

That album proved to be the swan song for half the members of Destiny's Child. LeToya Luckett and LaTavia Roberson, co-writers on "Say My Name," saw the video premiere of that song on BET and were surprised to find two other women lip-synching their parts. Farrah Franklin and Michelle Williams were the new members of the quartet. Luckett and Roberson filed a civil lawsuit against manager Matthew Knowles on March 15, 2000.

Franklin did not remain in Destiny's Child for very long. Five months after joining the group, she was out. There was no replacement this time; Beyoncé, Kelly and Michelle remained a trio.

## THE TOP FIVE
*Week of March 18, 2000*

1 **Say My Name**
Destiny's Child

2 **Amazed**
Lonestar

3 **Maria Maria**
Santana f/the Product G&B

4 **Breathe**
Faith Hill

5 **Bye Bye Bye**
'N Sync

*Writers: Wyclef Jean*
*Jerry Duplessis*
*Carlos Santana*
*Karl Perazzo*
*Raul Rekow*
*Marvin Moore-Hough*
*David McRae*

*Producers: Wyclef Jean*
*Jerry Duplessis*

*April 8, 2000*
*10 weeks*

Santana had to wait 30 years between the time of its chart debut and its first number one on the Hot 100. The wait for a second chart-topper was considerably shorter. Exactly three months after the final frame of the 12-week reign of "Smooth" [see 889], Santana was back on top with the follow-up, "Maria Maria."

Santana's *Supernatural* was filled with guest appearances—but then, who wouldn't want to work with the legendary Carlos Santana? Rob Thomas of matchbox twenty co-wrote and sang lead vocals on "Smooth." Eric Clapton played guitar on "The Calling." Dave Matthews sang on "Love of My Life."

And from the Fugees, Lauryn Hill joined forces with Santana on "Do You Like the Way." After Hill worked with Santana, her fellow Fugee Wyclef Jean also wanted to work on a track for the album.

Clive Davis, who signed Santana to Arista, played some finished tracks for Jean, who then teamed up with his cousin Jerry Duplessis to write and produce a song for *Supernatural.* Jean and Duplessis were both born in Haiti and both emigrated to the U.S. "We were playing music in church because my uncle, who was Wyclef's dad, was a preacher," says Duplessis, who worked with his first cousin on the Fugees' album *The Score.* "I'm always the shadow," says Duplessis. "I'm always behind Clef, which is where I like to be. We started writing songs around '88. We were living in a house where we had all kinds of instruments."

Duplessis also served as musical director for the Fugees on the road. It was during a tour that Davis asked Jean to work with Santana. "We went to San Francisco and met with Carlos and we created the beat in less than three hours," says Duplessis, recalling the origin of "Maria Maria." "All we

need is an MPC and an SB1200 drum machine and my bass guitar. I was at a drum machine creating the beat and Wyclef was on the keys getting a groove on. Soon we caught the vibe and said, 'Record it!'" The lyrics came from Jean's freestyling.

Duplessis remembers working with Carlos Santana in the studio. "When he touched that guitar, it was like listening to God talking. That's how good he is. He played on an electric guitar and then he played on an acoustic guitar, making it sound Spanish." The producers had met two young musicians known as the Product, and had signed them to a production deal (and later to Jean's own Yclef label, through Davis' J Records).

Billed as the Product G&B on "Maria Maria," the initials stood for Ghetto & Blues. "We're the product of the environment, two brothers caught up in a society where there is CPST—corruption, poverty, struggle and triumph," Sincere (born David McRae) told *Billboard's* Rashaun Hall.

Sincere and Money Harm (aka Marvin Moore-Hough) became friends when they were 13 on Long Island, N.Y. They met Jean through a twist of fate. Sincere called Sony Studios to talk to a friend, producer Al West. Pras of the Fugees answered the phone. "We ran six blocks in the cold to meet him," Sincere told Hall. Pras introduced them to Jean, and two weeks later, the two members of the Product were in San Francisco working with Jean and Santana on "Maria Maria." Sincere admitted, "We didn't even know who Santana was at the time."

At the 42nd annual Grammy Awards, "Maria Maria" was named Best Pop Performance by a Duo or Group with Vocal.

## THE TOP FIVE
*Week of April 8, 2000*

1 **Maria Maria**
Santana f/the Product G&B

2 **Say My Name**
Destiny's Child

3 **Breathe**
Faith Hill

4 **Amazed**
Lonestar

5 **Bye Bye Bye**
'N Sync

## 896 Try Again
### AALIYAH
BLACKGROUND 38722

*Writers: Timothy Mosley*
*Stephen Garrett*

*Producer: Timbaland*

*June 17, 2000*
*1 week*

ONCE THE POLICY WAS changed to allow airplay-only tracks to appear on the Hot 100 [see 875—"I'm Your Angel"], it was inevitable that one day an album cut that was not available as a commercial single would reach the top spot on the chart. Aaliyah made chart history when her song "Try Again" from the *Romeo Must Die* soundtrack achieved pole position based only on airplay. After the song was number one, a 12-inch vinyl single was issued, along with a 7-inch single.

Aaliyah Dana Haughton was born in Brooklyn and raised in Detroit. It was obvious to those who knew her as a child that she would become a performer. Her uncle, Barry Hankerson, managed artists and signed his niece as a client. By the time she was 11, she had already competed on "Star Search" and auditioned for Warner Brothers and MCA, though neither label signed her. When Hankerson added R. Kelly to his client roster, Aaliyah sang for him and he agreed to work with her. He wrote and produced "Back & Forth," a 1994 hit that peaked at number five on the Hot 100. Aaliyah was just 15, and newspapers reported she wed her producer, Kelly.

If the couple was married, it didn't last, and neither did their working relationship. Kelly had produced Aaliyah's first album, *Age Ain't Nothin' but a Number,* but wasn't involved on any of the tracks on her sophomore set, *One*

### THE TOP FIVE
*Week of June 17, 2000*

1 **Try Again**
 Aaliyah

2 **Breathe**
 Faith Hill

3 **Everything You Want**
 Vertical Horizon

4 **Be With You**
 Enrique Iglesias

5 **You Sang to Me**
 Marc Anthony

*in a Million,* released in 1996. Just 17 at the time, Aaliyah told J.R. Reynolds in *Billboard,* "I wanted to maintain my smooth street musical image but wanted to be funky and hot, yet sophisticated."

With two albums under her belt, and soundtrack contributions to films like *Anastasia* ("Journey to the Past") and *Dr. Dolittle* ("Are You That Somebody"), Aaliyah had a meeting with a film executive at Warner Brothers. They discussed possible film roles for her, and one project discussed was the script for a martial arts adventure, *Romeo Must Die.* "I had been wanting for a while to make the transition from music to film," Aaliyah told Rashaun Hall in *Billboard,* "and I real-

ly fell in love with it. Once I got the part, we began talking about the soundtrack and the direction it would take."

*Romeo Must Die,* with Jet Li in the lead male role, opened in theaters in 2000 and became a box office smash. The song from the film, "Try Again," had similar results on the chart. A year later, Aaliyah released her third album. *Aaliyah* had been recorded in Australia, while the singer was filming *Queen of the Damned. Aaliyah* debuted at number two on the *Billboard* album chart the week of August 4, 2001. Three weeks later, the 22-year-old star was killed in a plane crash in Marsh Harbour, the Bahamas, where she had been filming a video for the song "Rock the Boat."

INTERSCOPE 490366 **Be With You**
**ENRIQUE IGLESIAS** | **897**

*Writers: Enrique Iglesias*
*Paul Barry*
*Mark Taylor*

*Producers: Mark Taylor*
*Brian Rawling*

*June 24, 2000*
*3 weeks*

ENRIQUE IGLESIAS RECORDED THE vocals for his first number one hit [see 886—"Bailamos"] in Miami. Later in 1999, Iglesias traveled to the U.K. to promote "Bailamos" and to record the follow-up, "Rhythm Divine," written by the same people who wrote that first chart-topper, Paul Barry and Mark Taylor. "Paul and I wrote 'Rhythm Divine' specifically as a follow-up to 'Bailamos.' In hindsight, it was probably too much of a follow-up," admits Taylor. "It was the same kind of track, so much so that it didn't have the same magic that 'Bailamos' did. While Enrique was over [in England], we locked him away. He'd sit upstairs with Paul and I'd see how they were getting on."

Barry remembers sitting in his upstairs writing room with Iglesias, working on "Be With You." "It started with a verse. We tried to write something about him being on the road, and the isolation—looking out on the streets below and having the sense you've lost someone that you shouldn't have. You should have fought for them."

After completing the song in 20 minutes, Barry and Iglesias played it for Taylor, who says, "I loved it. I was the only person in the building who loved it. Maybe I could hear what I could do with it." Meanwhile, Iglesias went downstairs to the studio and recorded "Rhythm Divine."

That follow-up to "Bailamos" didn't fare nearly as well on the Hot 100, peaking at number 32 the week of January 22, 2000. Meanwhile, Iglesias had recorded "Be With You" on his next trip to England. Barry was surprised that Taylor and Rawling produced a dance track for the song. "I wasn't sure how that would work," he confides. "It was a bit of a gamble, but it still had the emotion, because the song was about loneliness and isolation. It had a darker edge to it, rather than just being a happy song. If you're going to go uptempo, you've got to be careful not to make it twee."

As Taylor explains, "It was always going to be a strange song because of that blend of the dance side of it. It's a very dancey song, but you could almost do it in half-time, a full-on ballad. That was my approach, where the vocal was sort of in slow motion on the top. With his vocal, he's got such a sound that it seems to set itself in the track." Taylor says that Iglesias usually runs down the entire song a few times when he records, and then they target specific parts. "He does manage to lose himself

in a song, which is great."

For the Spanish-flavored guitar parts, Taylor and Rawling turned to one of their session musicians. "Adam Phillips plays everything I can't play, [on] every record I do," says Taylor. "He's a young guy. He seems to hit the nail on the head. He's not a Spanish flamenco guitarist, just a regular guy from London."

In the U.K., where "Bailamos" peaked at number four and "Rhythm Divine" stopped at number 45, "Be With You" wasn't released as a single. "It was a true pop-dance record," says Rawling. "The funny thing for me was that it didn't come out in the U.K. That was one song I felt was a European smash."

Enrique finally had his first number one hit in the U.K. when "Hero" moved to the top spot in February, 2002. It was the first single from his sophomore English-language album, *Escape*. "I went to Miami because he'd been touring a lot," says Barry. "He asked if I could come there. We wrote what we thought would be the single, 'One Night Stand.' We had one last day, and we played Bruce Springsteen records—Enrique is a big fan of Springsteen and so am I. I had an idea to write a song about all the crazy things you'd say to someone. I had the line, 'Would you dance if I asked you to dance or would you laugh at me?' That was my original pitch to Enrique. From that, we started writing line after line, and 'Hero' came together quickly." In the U.S., where "Hero" became closely identified with the heroic efforts of firefighters and police officers after the terrorist attacks of September 11, 2001, the song peaked at number three.

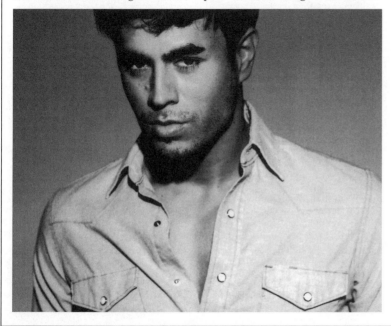

## THE TOP FIVE
*Week of June 24, 2000*

1 **Be With You**
Enrique Iglesias

2 **Try Again**
Aaliyah

3 **Everything You Want**
Vertical Horizon

4 **The Real Slim Shady**
Eminem

5 **Breathe**
Faith Hill

**898** Everything You Want  RCA 562846
VERTICAL HORIZON

*Writer: Matthew Scannell*

*Producers: Mark Endert*
          *Ben Grosse*

*July 15, 2000*
*1 week*

Born in Boston and raised in Worcester, Massachusetts, Matt Scannell was just two years old when he picked up his father's Spanish classical guitar and plucked the strings. "I was endlessly fascinated with it," he says. "When I was seven, I remember listening to the Cars' 'My Best Friend's Girl' on the radio. I was effectively playing along with the bass line because I was only playing one note." His parents arranged for lessons when he was 13. His teacher insisted he had to learn Bach if he also wanted to play Rush. While attending boarding school, he found a teacher who encouraged him to play pop music. It was during these high school years that he first had the urge to write his own songs.

His graduation present from his parents was a four-track recorder. "That was when I was able to experiment with different harmonies and pay attention to melody rather than worrying about the chords I was playing on the guitar," says Scannell. He majored in psychology at Georgetown University in the District of Columbia, where he met a Japanese major, Keith Kane, who played acoustic guitar. "I loved the sound of his voice," Scannell says. They recorded an album in a friend's studio and pressed up a thousand copies to sell, thinking they would last a lifetime. "Much to our surprise they sold, so we pressed up another thousand. It wasn't until we got to four thousand that we realized we should do another one." By the time they independently sold 70,000 CDs and attracted attention from major labels, the group was a quartet, including Sean Hurley (bass) and Ed Toth (drums). David Bendeth from RCA saw Vertical Horizon play at the South by Southwest conference in Austin and signed them.

Scannell was living in Greenwich Village when he wrote "Everything You Want." He remembers, "I was lying in bed and I heard a chord progression in my head. I keep a microcassette recorder on the side of the bed and sang what I heard to be a bass line. And then I realized I had this idea

buzzing through me. It's very much a buzzing sensation when a song is ready to come. You have to be receptive to music." Scannell got out of bed and completed the song quickly. Soon after, he demoed the song on the four-track recorder his parents had given him.

Through Bendeth at RCA, Vertical Horizon was teamed with producer Ben Grosse. "There were two things that intrigued me about working with the band," he says. "I liked the idea of taking a safe, straight-ahead soft rock band and making a train wreck—making them turn left a little bit. And when I met them I thought these were guys I would love hanging out with for three months." Grosse vividly remembers the first time he heard the demo of "Everything You Want." "Matt had that great chorus. I took that opening guitar and flipped it around, so there's a backward one and a forward one." When the rough mixes for the band's first RCA album were finished, Bendeth asked producer Mark Endert to rehash some songs before the final mix. "Ben is a wonderful producer," Endert acknowledges. "He comes from a straight-up rock background and I come from a pop background, so

it was a winning blend. I redid all of the bass lines because I like more movement in the bass. We redid some guitars. We left the heavy guitars for the chorus that Ben put on and redid cleaner guitars over the verses. Ben cut the vocals and we added some harmony vocals."

Looking back, Scannell admits, "I never felt that 'Everything You Want' would be what it became. It was a good song. I was very proud of it. But I had no idea what would happen with it."

## THE TOP FIVE
*Week of July 15, 2000*

1 **Everything You Want**
  Vertical Horizon

2 **Try Again**
  Aaliyah

3 **Be With You**
  Enrique Iglesias

4 **I Wanna Know**
  Joe

5 **It's Gonna Be Me**
  'N Sync

*Writer: Rob Thomas*

*Producer: Matt Serletic*

*July 22, 2000*
*1 week*

EXACTLY NINE MONTHS AFTER their first number one hit [see 889—"Smooth"], the writing and producing team of Rob Thomas and Matt Serletic was back on top of the Hot 100 with "Bent." This time the song wasn't for another artist, like Santana, but for Thomas' own group, matchbox twenty.

Thomas was born on a military base in Germany and was raised in South Carolina. He fell in love with music and songwriting at an early age. "I grew up loving people who told stories with their songs—sometimes just breaking down a moment and extrapolating on every little detail of it. Country songs have always done that and I think the trick is to be in the rock or pop world and keep that in mind."

In his early teens he was in a band that played songs like Duran Duran's "Hungry Like the Wolf" and Depeche Mode's "Master and Servant" as well as tunes by Richard Marx. "I was 14 so we'd play non-alcoholic teen bars. We played everything we listened to and everything that was on the radio." Later, Thomas put together a new band, Time of the Secret, with drummer Paul Doucette and bassist Brian Yale. Kyle Cook (lead guitar) and Adam Gaynor (rhythm guitar) completed the quintet. Their material found its way to producer Matt Serletic. "I was working on the second Collective Soul record down in Miami and two people sent me their tape," says Serletic. "My brother Dean, who was going to school in Miami, and a

woman I had worked with on a cruise ship. I played trombone and she was the hostess." Serletic was impressed by a song called "3 a.m." He met the band in Orlando, where the relocated group had issued a six-song EP to local stores, and felt Thomas could be a star. Two weeks later, he was working with the outfit, getting a new demo together and shopping them to labels.

Signed to Lava, Matchbox 20 released its first album, *Yourself or Someone Like You,* in 1997. The song "Long Day" was released to radio, but the band didn't break until a station in Birmingham, Alabama, started playing "Push."

Thomas was already working on the group's next album. "I started writing 'Bent' while we were on tour for *Yourself.* I had the chorus, and when I moved to New York City, I spent all my afternoons walking around, singing to myself, waiting for it to come to me. I would walk a few blocks and come up with a verse and I would run back to my apartment and write down my verse and record the melody. Then I'd go back out and walk a little while and finish writing. There's something great about not being tied to an instrument, going out and creating an entire song in your head, then putting it down."

"Bent" was inspired by his wife, says Thomas. "It takes a special person to be married to a songwriter. Some of

our worst fights are there on CD for her to have to listen to all the time." To Thomas, "Bent" implied "not fully broken." "It was like a co-dependent love song," he explains. "It's OK to be totally screwed up if you're both totally screwed up. You can go through life together that way. My wife and I are both a little askew and that's OK with us."

"Bent" was the first hit from the album *Mad Season* by a slightly renamed matchbox twenty—the group felt there were too many groups with numbers in the title, like Eve 6, Blink 182 and Eiffel 65. "The first record was all about getting the band together, and we had six weeks of intense practice," says Serletic. "The second record was, 'Let's go in the studio and see what happens.'" Thomas and Serletic rented a houseboat and spent two weeks with their wives at Lake Laneer, north of Atlanta, to shape the songs for *Mad Season.* "'Bent' was built and built and built," says Serletic. "There are three drum kits, one for the verse, a separate kit for the chorus and a third for the bridge, creating a sense of darkness. There's a ton of background vocals."

Thomas agrees, "On *Mad Season* we were calling ourselves the Matchbox Tabernacle Choir and we have an entire CD of the background vocals because we thought it was so funny."

## THE TOP FIVE
*Week of July 22, 2000*

1 **Bent**
matchbox twenty

2 **Everything You Want**
Vertical Horizon

3 **Try Again**
Aaliyah

4 **It's Gonna Be Me**
'N Sync

5 **I Wanna Know**
Joe

## 900

# It's Gonna Be Me  JIVE 42545
### 'N SYNC

*Writers: Max Martin*
*Rami*
*Andreas Carlsson*

*Producer: Rami*

*July 29, 2000*
*2 weeks*

I₸'S EASY TO SEE why some people consider the Backstreet Boys and 'N Sync to be rival groups. Both quintets started in Orlando, Florida; both were labeled boy bands; and both scored hits in Europe first before making it big at home. If the rivalry extended to the charts, then 'N Sync would have to be declared the winner on the Hot 100. While the Backstreet Boys never reached number one—their personal best is the number two ranking of "Quit Playing Games (With My Heart)"—the members of 'N Sync found themselves in pole position with their second hit from *No Strings Attached*, "It's Gonna Be Me."

Like that album's first hit, "Bye Bye Bye," "It's Gonna Be Me" was recorded in Sweden at the hit-making factory known as Cheiron Studios, where Max Martin and Rami had worked with Britney Spears on "...Baby One More Time" [see 877]. The connection between 'N Sync and Cheiron dated back to the group's first album, when Martin produced "I Want You Back," the first 'N Sync single to chart on the Hot 100.

The idea for "It's Gonna Be Me" started with Rami. "Sometimes when you're sitting at a table, you can't come up with anything, you're just blank. I was having a cup of coffee and I started to sing, 'Da da da da da.' I don't know why. And Max said, 'What is that?' We

started from there." Martin recalls, "Andreas and Rami continued on their own, working on verses, and then we met again. I had my own ideas and they had theirs and then we got back together a couple of weeks later and we finished it."

The partnership between Martin, Rami and Carlsson was very equal, in Martin's view. "Even though one guy might write more lyrics, you can always get a great idea from someone even though he might not be considered the best or fastest lyric writer. I think that was the reason everything turned out so well. There was a balance."

In his role as producer, Rami went into the studio with 'N Sync without knowing which singer would record which parts. "There are three strong singers in the group," he says. "But sometimes you record the bridge with two of them, because you're not really sure how it's going to sound when the production is finished, when you hear the song from beginning to end. So you always record more than you need and then I can choose later."

By the time "It's Gonna Be Me" topped the Hot 100 in 2000, 'N Sync had been together for five years. Lou Pearlman, the Svengali behind Backstreet Boys, was looking for another boy band. Chris Kirkpatrick decided to put a group together. First, he found 14-year-old Justin

Timberlake, a former cast member of "The Mickey Mouse Club." Timberlake had been collaborating on songs with another former Mouseketeer, JC Chasez. The fourth member to sign on was someone Kirkpatrick knew from performing at Universal Studios in Orlando—Joey Fatone. A bass singer was needed, and through their vocal coach from their "Mickey Mouse Club" days, they found Lance Bass.

Pearlman signed 'N Sync to his Trans Continental management firm, and in 1997 the group was offered a deal by execs from RCA, owned by the German company Bertelsman Music Group. Germany is where 'N Sync first hit the charts. In March, 1998, "I Want You Back" debuted on the Hot 100, eventually peaking at number 13. By the time the millennium rolled around, the fivesome's biggest hit was the soundtrack cut "Music of My Heart," recorded with Gloria Estefan. The single peaked at number two.

Martin and Rami both speak glowingly of the five members of 'N Sync. "They're great guys," says Rami. "Max and I wouldn't have worked so much with a group if it didn't work out socially. You can't work with someone that you don't like." Martin concludes, "They have a great spirit that I think even today you can feel when you see them. There's something about them that's just positive energy."

## THE TOP FIVE
### *Week of July 29, 2000*

1  **It's Gonna Be Me**
   'N Sync

2  **Bent**
   matchbox twenty

3  **Everything You Want**
   Vertical Horizon

4  **Try Again**
   Aaliyah

5  **I Wanna Know**
   Joe

*Writers: Montell Jordan
      Anthony "Shep" Crawford
      Kristin Hudson*

*Producer: Anthony "Shep" Crawford*

*August 12, 2000
2 weeks*

THE LINE MOST PEOPLE remember from *Jerry Maguire* is "Show me the money," uttered by Cuba Gooding, Jr. In second place is Renée Zellweger's "You had me from hello," which served as the title of a Kenny Chesney number one country hit from 1999. But when Kristin Hudson saw the film, the line that meant the most to her was another bit of dialogue that Tom Cruise delivers to Zellweger: "You complete me."

"Kristin came to me and said, 'You should write a song called "Incomplete,"'" says Montell Jordan, who is managed by Hudson. Jordan grew up in Los Angeles and attended Carver Missionary Baptist Church, where he met Anthony "Shep" Crawford. When Jordan got his label deal, he asked Crawford to be his music director. That led to collaborating as songwriters on tunes like "Nobody's Supposed to Be Here" by Deborah Cox and "Same Script Different Cast" by Whitney Houston.

Jordan and Crawford took Hudson's suggestion to heart. "We wanted to write a song that was very masculine about a guy who was sure of himself, but said that without the woman he loved, that was nothing. I think women love to hear that. They love to have a successful man, but they love to hear they are a necessity to make it all come true. It's like [they are] the missing part of the puzzle," says Crawford.

The ballad came together quickly. "I had the track when Montell came in and we kicked around some ideas," Crawford remembers. "Two or three hours later the song was written." The first artist to record "Incomplete" was Los Angeles–born Sam Salter, who had two minor hits on LaFace in 1997–98. But his version wasn't released, and a year went by before Jordan and Crawford heard that Sisqó of Dru Hill was recording a solo album.

Named after Druid Hill Park in their native Baltimore, the quartet known as Dru Hill first came together while the four members were still in high school. At first, they sang gospel, but later turned to secular music. They worked up an act while performing at the Fudgery, entertaining customers with music while making fudge. That led to competing in talent contests and an appearance at a BET event where they met Hiriam Hicks, then a senior vice president at Island Records. He asked Dru Hill to record a song for the *Eddie* soundtrack; "Tell Me" marked the group's first appearance on the Hot 100, where it went to number 18 in 1996.

Dru Hill received credit for a number one song by being featured on Will Smith's "Wild Wild West" [see 884]. But after recording two albums, the group devised a plan: each member would record a solo project before coming back together as Dru Hill. Mark "Sisqó" Andrews went first with *Unleash the Dragon*. The initial single,

"Got to Get It," peaked at number 40, but it was the "Thong Song" that made the album a smash. The infectious ditty about women's lingerie peaked at number three in May 2000. The follow-up was scheduled to be the title song from the album, but radio made its preference known by playing "Incomplete" instead.

"Incomplete" had a lot going against it. Sisqó's album was almost finished when Jordan played the song for label president Kevin Liles. Jordan says Liles promised he would see if Sisqó would record the song. "It was not like this was a smash record, it was kind of a favor," says Jordan. Sisqó told Crawford he wasn't feeling well when he showed up at the studio to record the song, and Crawford recalls that the artist wasn't as confident about "Incomplete" as its predecessor. "Sisqó played 'Thong Song' for me when we were getting ready to cut 'Incomplete.' He told me this was the record. He was dancing all around the studio, so I think he was very happy with ["Thong Song"]. He was a little nervous about 'Incomplete' coming after because it was a ballad and very much a different record."

Jordan and Crawford had no doubts about Sisqó's take on their song. "The beauty of when different people sing [the same] song is they bring their own element to it, and that's what Sisqó did," says Jordan. "When he gets to the ad-libs, he brought his own style of artistry to the song. It was not done exactly like the demo, but now I can't imagine it any other way."

## THE TOP FIVE
*Week of August 12, 2000*

1. **Incomplete**
   Sisqó

2. **Bent**
   matchbox twenty

3. **It's Gonna Be Me**
   'N Sync

4. **Jumpin', Jumpin'**
   Destiny's Child

5. **Try Again**
   Aaliyah

## 902 Doesn't Really Matter DEF JAM/DEF SOUL 562846
### JANET JACKSON

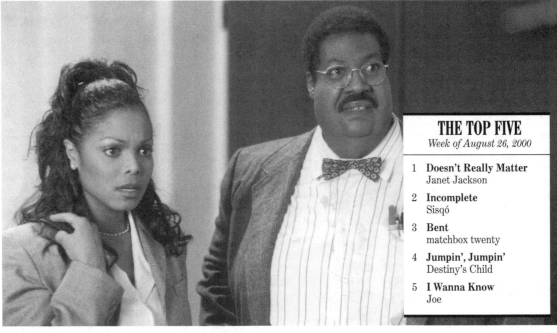

THE TOP FIVE

*Week of August 26, 2000*

1 **Doesn't Really Matter**
Janet Jackson

2 **Incomplete**
Sisqó

3 **Bent**
matchbox twenty

4 **Jumpin', Jumpin'**
Destiny's Child

5 **I Wanna Know**
Joe

Writers: *Janet Jackson*
         *James Harris III*
         *Terry Lewis*

Producers: *Jimmy Jam*
           *Terry Lewis*
           *Janet Jackson*

*August 26, 2000*
*3 weeks*

SEVEN YEARS AFTER RECEIVING critical raves for her role in the film *Poetic Justice*, Janet Jackson tried her hand at movie comedy. After auditioning for *The Nutty Professor II: The Klumps* with director Peter Segal, Janet felt she did a horrible job. She was called back to audition in full makeup and costume on a day that she was ill with the flu. "I think they wanted me to audition twice because they wanted to make sure they could separate the singer from this person on the screen who was in love with Sherman," Jackson says.

Jackson was cast as Professor Denise Gaines opposite Eddie Murphy. She was asked if she'd like to contribute a song to the film, and told the producers if she found the right song, she'd consider it. "The director of the movie came to Minneapolis," remembers producer Jimmy Jam. "He wasn't supposed to do this because he hadn't shown the movie to the people he was

supposed to show the movie to first, but he played it for us so we could get an idea of what it was. It was a fun movie but a very believable love story." Jam told Jackson he thought she was a good actress because he believed she loved Sherman Klump. That's when Jackson suggested that they should write a traditional love song but make it uptempo.

"The lyrical idea for 'Doesn't Really Matter' is totally hers, but the music and melody was something I had done with one of our drum programmers, Alex Richburg," says Jam. "I thought of it as a slow melody, but we sped it up. I gave Janet the tape. She was totally underwhelmed by it."

Jam and Lewis kept working on the track, but the deadline for inclusion in the film was quickly approaching. Jam liked the song and told Jackson so. She asked for the tape and said she would write the lyrics overnight. "We ended up with two different choruses," says Jam. "I wrote, 'Nutty, nutty, nutty, my love for you,' and she wrote, 'Doesn't really matter.' I always think it's cool if you can somehow work the title of the movie in, but you don't want it to be forced. The 'Doesn't really matter' chorus was better but she liked 'Nutty, nutty, nutty' and said we should put it at the end of the song. It would have been a bad idea to have done 'Nutty' through the whole song."

Jackson didn't give the final word that she liked the song and would record it until three days before it had to be completed for the soundtrack. The first day, she recorded the song in two takes. "We did some overdubs the second day and mixed it the third day and sent it out," says Jam. He and Terry Lewis submitted "Doesn't Really Matter" to the production company, along with another song, "Feels So Right." Jam explains, "When we were doing 'Feels So Right,' we were thinking it would work for the movie." Segal told Jam and Lewis that "Doesn't Really Matter" was a better lyrical fit with the film and felt like a summertime record, which is what he wanted. "I always tease Janet because I don't think she liked that record until it went to number one."

After being available on the soundtrack album for *The Nutty Professor II: The Klumps*, "Doesn't Really Matter" was also included on Jackson's *All for You* album, released in April, 2001. "We thought it would be cool to use the version she performed on the MTV Awards the year before the album came out, just to make it a little bit different," says Jam. "As a consumer, I always think artists should put their hit on there. No matter how old it is, people are going to enjoy it."

MAVERICK 562846

# Music
## MADONNA

Writers: Madonna
    Mirwais Ahmadzai

Producers: Madonna
    Mirwais

September 16, 2000
4 weeks

It was a sweltering day in July, 2000, when *Billboard* talent editor Larry Flick interviewed Madonna in her Los Angeles home. The artist was about to give birth—to her second child, as well as a brand-new studio album, *Music*. There was no air conditioning in the house, so Flick and Madonna sat near whirring fans and discussed the new CD as well as the first single, the title track.

"It's always a little nerve-wracking for me right before I share my work with the world," Madonna told Flick. "But that emotion is usually followed by a sense of accomplishment in doing the best job I can. With this new album, I feel like I've completed what I've set out to do—and that's a good, fulfilling feeling."

One of Madonna's biggest challenges with each new release is to reinvent herself—not just because her fans expect her to, but because an artist who sustains a career over decades must find new ways to express themselves. Flick touched on the subject with Madonna, asking what would be different between her previous album and the new release. "Everything in life moves in cycles," she replied. "There's a period where you're quiet, and there's a period where you explode. In the time leading up to *Ray of Light*, I was in a quiet space—making lots of discoveries and going through lots of changes. It was an introspective, questioning time. Then, almost without warning, I felt like I needed to explode. I didn't feel the need to be so introspective. I felt like dancing. And that's reflected in these songs."

One way to head in a new direction is to work with a new producer. To that end, Madonna enlisted a French musician, born in Switzerland to an Italian mother and an Afghani father. Mirwais Ahmadzai had been lead guitarist for the 1980s French pop band Taxi Girl, an outfit that blended punk, techno and disco. The group was a strong influence on French electronica bands like Daft Punk and Air. Taxi Girl came to the end of its road in 1987. Two years later, Ahmadzai played guitar in a more acoustic band, Juliette et les Independents. Eventually, Mirwais returned to the electronic scene, releasing the album *Disco Science* on an independent label in France in 1999. French photographer Stephane Sednaoui directed the video for "Disco Science," and passed a DAT along to Guy Oseary at Maverick Records in the U.S.

"I'm always searching for something new and edgy and undiscovered," Madonna told Flick. "I love to work with the weirdos that no one knows about—the people who have raw talent and who are making music unlike anyone else out there."

Initially, their collaboration looked like it was going to be difficult. Mirwais spoke only a little English, and Madonna just a little French. "The first couple of days we were recording, I wanted to rip my hair out. It didn't seem like there was any way for us to communicate." Mirwais' manager translated so artist and producer could speak to each other. As the two got to know each other better, tensions eased between Mirwais and Madonna. "I think he was nervous," she told Flick. "But I knew we would eventually click. I was intent on making it work, because I truly believe that man's a genius."

Madonna credits the producer with inspiring her to be open and vulnerable. "He's so incredibly smart and visionary. I listen to his stuff, and I think, 'This is the future of sound.'"

There was one glitch in the release of "Music" as a single. In May, 2000, an earlier mix was available for download on the internet. Some people accused Madonna of being responsible for the premature release. "Oh, please!" she exclaimed to Flick. "If I was going to leak my record, I would've put a better mix of it out there. I practically had a nervous breakdown when the track got out there. I wasn't even finished with the record when it happened…I don't want my whole album to be leaked. I don't care if you're my 83-year-old grandmother, you're not getting my record before I'm ready for you to have it."

## THE TOP FIVE
*Week of September 16, 2000*

1   **Music**
   Madonna

2   **Doesn't Really Matter**
   Janet Jackson

3   **Jumpin', Jumpin'**
   Destiny's Child

4   **Bent**
   matchbox twenty

5   **Incomplete**
   Sisqó

# 904 Come On Over Baby (All I Want Is You) RCA 65968
## CHRISTINA AGUILERA

*Writers: Johan Åberg*
*Paul Rein*
*Shelly Peiken*
*Ron Fair*
*Chaka Blackmon*
*Raymond Cham*
*Eric Dawkins*
*Christina Aguilera*
*Guy Roche*

*Producers: Celebrity Status*
*Ron Fair*

*October 14, 2000*
*4 weeks*

PAUL REIN HAD A HISTORY as a teen pop star in Sweden by the time he was looking for new studio space in the autumn of 1998. A friend suggested he try Eclectic Studios, owned by Anders Hansson. When Rein arrived at the studio to look it over, Johan Åberg was mixing a project. Hansson suggested that Rein and Åberg write together. A week later, Rein and Åberg met for a writing session, and the first song they composed was "Come On Over Baby," though at the time it was titled "All I Want Is You."

"We were in Johan's studio room at Eclectic when we wrote the song," says Rein. "The direction from Anders was to write something for the Spice Girls, something uptempo, happy and uplifting. We programmed an uptempo drumbeat and added a bassline, so I had something to sing to. Since singing is my big thing—I did a lot of touring during my pop star period back in 1986—I can find the right words to fit into the melody without sounding weird. You're always trying to find words that sound right within your specific melody line. Once I had a lot of words, I tried them on Johan. After we agreed on the lyrics, we did the chorus. Then we tried to find a verse that would build up to the chorus."

Pelle Lidell, then creative director at Air Chrysalis music publishing, thought "All I Want Is You" was a smash and played the song for Ron Fair, then in RCA's A&R department. Fair was looking for material for Christina Aguilera's first album. Rein and Åberg sent a 24-track tape with the music to Fair. "They used that tape in the studio and added Christina's vocals," explains Rein. Aguilera's original version of the song appeared on her debut album for RCA.

"Later, in the spring of 2000, we received a message from Ron that they wanted to make our song the next Christina single!" Rein exclaims. "But Ron wanted to update the music production, and wanted the lyrics to be sexier. Johan and I had a shot at changing the words, but we didn't come up with anything good."

Fair elaborates, "We always felt the hook of the song was really strong. But the original version was too ultra-pop for where Christina needed and wanted to go. She was feeling her legs in more of an R&B sense and singing more aggressive riffs, but we couldn't deny the hook. If you look at the production credits, there are nine writers. And you want to know something? That is a factual, true representation of who really wrote that record. All nine of us had a little hand in it."

At the end of the bridge of the newly recorded "Come On Over," there's a bit of a previous number one hit for Aguilera, "What a Girl Wants" [see 890], written by Shelly Peiken and Guy Roche. "The reason why we did that," says Fair, "is that our original concept for the single of 'Come On Over' was to make it a hybrid medley with 'Got to Be Real' by Cheryl Lynn. Because live in concert, in the middle of 'Come On Over,' they would go into 'Got to Be Real' and it was really exciting. But I couldn't clear the rights to 'Got to Be Real.'"

Three of the writers credited on the song are Chaka Blackmon, Eric Dawkins and Raymond Cham, who were also the producers known as Celebrity Status. "They did the new beat for the song," Fair explains. "I produced all the vocals and arranged the music. Shelly Peiken contributed to the lyrics and Christina contributed to the lyrics and the melody. Johan and Paul were very gracious to let us do this to their song. A lot of guys wouldn't. They realized this was their best chance to have a hit."

Rein vividly remembers it was ten to six in the evening and he was cooking pasta for his family when Lars Wiggman of Air Chrysalis called to tell him he was number one in the U.S. "It was a dream come true to see your own name printed on the Billboard Hot 100. The liquor stores close here at 6, so I rushed off to the nearest one I could find, which luckily was close to Eclectic. I bought two bottles of Bollinger and went to see Johan to celebrate."

## THE TOP FIVE
*Week of October 14, 2000*

1 **Come On Over Baby (All I Want Is You)**
Christina Aguilera

2 **Music**
Madonna

3 **Give Me Just One Night (Una Noche)**
98 Degrees

4 **Kryptonite**
3 Doors Down

5 **Most Girls**
Pink

*Writers: Mark Tremonti*
*Scott Stapp*

*Producers: John Kurzweg*
*Ron Saint-Germain*

November 11, 2000
1 week

Fɪʀsᴛ, Cʀᴇᴇᴅ ᴄᴏɴQᴜᴇʀᴇᴅ ᴛʜᴇ rock charts with tracks from the album *My Own Prison.* Then, with the release of a second album, *Human Clay,* Creed was ready for the Hot 100. "Higher" paved the way, peaking at number seven. Then, a sensitive song with lyrics written by Scott Stapp in anticipation of the birth of his first child, "With Arms Wide Open," found its way to pole position.

Stapp grew up in a strictly religious household run by his stepfather. He rebelled and ran away from home at 17, but years later acknowledged to his stepdad that being forced to write out Psalms and Proverbs from the Bible influenced his lyrics, in terms of being poetic and being able to open his mind to new thoughts.

Living in Tallahassee in 1994, Stapp was reunited with a friend from high school, Mark Tremonti. The day they ran into each other, they started writing songs. With drummer Scott Phillips, they formed a band and called themselves Naked Toddler. When bass player Brian Marshall came along, they evolved into Creed.

They found work at a live music bar in Tallahassee, Big Daddy's. Even though they weren't drawing large crowds and weren't the best live band, owner Jeff Hanson liked their songs and moved them into his larger venue, Floyd's Music Store. Hanson thought their songs were good enough to be played on the radio, but he couldn't prove his theory until the group recorded them. Hanson borrowed $2,000 to finance a recording session and asked producer John Kurzweg to see the band play at Floyd's. "He wasn't overly impressed," says Hanson.

"They were playing really heavy stuff," says Kurzweg. "It was real loud. It didn't have the finesse they were later able to conjure up." After a couple of visits to Floyd's, Kurzweg wasn't sure he wanted to produce Creed. But Hanson was persistent, and in June, 1996, sessions began at Kurzweg's home. "It was funny because they were all working day jobs and I couldn't get

all of them in the house at the same time," says the producer, who recorded the members of the band separately or in pairs. The final result was Creed's first album, *My Own Prison.* Hanson secured airplay on some Florida stations and pressed up 6,000 CDs. A lawyer arranged a showcase in New York and 14 labels showed up, but all of them passed. "I think they thought Creed was a grunge band," says Hanson. "Grunge was over. But I never thought of them as a grunge band." Back in Tallahassee, a dejected Creed played a set at a club called Bullwinkle's. Diana Meltzer from Wind-up had heard their independently pressed CD, saw the show that night, and signed the group to the label.

After the success of *My Own Prison,* Creed wanted to record their second album with Kurzweg. But Stapp couldn't go back to the producer's home because he was allergic to Kurzweg's cats, so Hanson found a home in Tallahassee that was feline-free and rented it for Kurzweg to set up a studio.

"With Arms Wide Open" was written by Stapp and Tremonti while the band was on the road. "The lyric drags you in immediately, and Scott's voice," says Kurzweg. "But the part that gave me chills the first time I heard it was the bridge." Stapp recorded five takes the first day and then another five takes a second day. Kurzweg doubled

Tremonti's guitar solo, one with a wah-wah and one without.

Ron Saint-Germain produced a pop remix of "With Arms Wide Open" with re-recorded guitars, and strings added. That helped secure radio airplay on top 40 stations. The song was number 10 in its 21st chart week when Creed announced the commercial release of a single, to benefit Stapp's With Arms Wide Open Foundation, whose mission was, "to promote healthy, loving relationships between children and their families." With a retail single available, "With Arms Wide Open" had enough sales and airplay to reach number one on the Hot 100.

## THE TOP FIVE
*Week of November 11, 2000*

1   **With Arms Wide Open**
    Creed

2   **Music**
    Madonna

3   **Kryptonite**
    3 Doors Down

4   **Come On Over Baby (All I Want Is You)**
    Christina Aguilera

5   **Independent Women Part I**
    Destiny's Child

## 906 Independent Women Part I COLUMBIA 79493
### DESTINY'S CHILD

Writers: *Samuel J. Barnes*
*Jean Claude Olivier*
*Cory Rooney*
*Beyoncé Knowles*

Producers: *Poke & Tone*
*Cory Rooney*
*Beyoncé Knowles*

*November 18, 2000*
*11 weeks*

"I WAS MAD BECAUSE PEOPLE misunderstood 'Bills' [see 883] and I was mad at my boyfriend at the time," says Beyoncé Knowles. "I was like, 'I don't need a man. I'm independent.' So I went in the studio by myself. I didn't tell anybody and I did the song. My dad heard it and he let the label hear it and they said, 'That's the soundtrack to *Charlie's Angels*. That's the first single.' So we went back in the studio. I went in with the girls and changed some of the words and made it fit the movie. It ended up being the single and it turned out to be our biggest song."

It didn't hurt that the people making *Charlie's Angels* were fans of Destiny's Child. "They had sold four million albums by the time they came across our radar," says John Houlihan, music supervisor for the movie. "Glen

Brunman, senior vice president of Sony Soundtrax, was the record company's point person on this project. He first identified the creative match of the group and the film. As luck would have it, Destiny's Child was changing from four members to three, and since there are three Charlie's Angels, we all sensed it was a great opportunity for them to come on strong with their new lineup and mirror our film."

"Independent Women" was produced by the Brooklyn-born team of Poke & Tone, neé Jean Claude Olivier and Samuel Barnes. They met in Los Angeles in 1987 while working on a project for Louski, an artist who never got a deal. They made a name for themselves producing hits for Mary J. Blige, Soul for Real and the Notorious B.I.G. They also produced "Men in Black" for Will Smith, and then helmed his number one hit, "Gettin' Jiggy Wit It" [see 865].

Poke & Tone already had a relationship with Sony Music before working with Destiny's Child. They had their own imprint, Trackmasters, and worked with the girl group Allure, signed to Mariah Carey's Crave label. "[Sony] wanted to use us on as many projects as possible," says Tone. Donnie Ienner, president of Columbia Records, told Poke & Tone about Beyoncé's idea

for "Independent Women" and that the song was destined for the *Charlie's Angels* soundtrack. "At first, it was supposed to be a remix, but we remade the record completely," says Poke. "We got together with Cory Rooney and made the track. I was executive vice president for urban music at Columbia so I had to stay in the office. Tone went out and got the vocals from Beyoncé. After we mixed it, that's when the magic came in and everybody started reacting to the record. We didn't understand how big it was going to be."

The first version of "Independent Women" ended up on the quartet's *Survivor* album, but because the second version was released first, the original was labeled Part II. After Brunman played the original version for Houlihan and director McG, the filmmakers asked if the song could be customized lyrically for the movie. "The next version was beyond our wildest dreams as far as nailing the feeling of the movie, the themes, the attitude," says Houlihan. "Not only was it a brilliant song on its own, but it was a brilliant marketing tool for the film. It not only incorporated the, 'Charlie, how do your Angels get down like that?' but the intro had shout-outs to the actresses. Instead of hiding they were doing a song for a film, they came right out of the gate and said, 'Here are these three stars. We respect them as women.' It was unabashedly proud of being associated with the film."

Producers Poke & Tone are not faint with their praise of Beyoncé. "People see her as a great singer," says Tone. "She might be underrated as a writer. I don't think people know she writes a lot of songs. I don't think many people know she wrote 'Independent Women.'"

### THE TOP FIVE
*Week of November 18, 2000*

1 **Independent Women Part I**
Destiny's Child

2 **With Arms Wide Open**
Creed

3 **Kryptonite**
3 Doors Down

4 **Music**
Madonna

5 **Most Girls**
Pink

Writers: Orville Burrell
　　　Ricardo Ducent
　　　Shaun Pizzonia
　　　Brian Thompson

Producer: Shaun Pizzonia

February 3, 2001
2 weeks

EIGHT YEARS AFTER TOPPING the U.K. singles chart with "Oh Carolina," Jamaican-born Orville Burrell, nicknamed Shaggy after the character in *Scooby-Doo*, had his first number one hit in the U.S. with "It Wasn't Me."

Shaggy spent his first 18 years in Jamaica, and while he listened to ska music on the radio and his grandmother's 7-inch vinyl singles, he had no other connection with music. When he moved to the U.S. and settled in the Flatbush section of Brooklyn, he hooked up with friends who were dancehall DJs and started writing rhymes. "It was just for fun," he says. "I never looked at this as a career because I went into the military." During his four years as a Marine, he'd drive between North Carolina and New York on the weekends to hit the reggae clubs and make some underground records. When he completed his military stint—including service in Kuwait during the Gulf War—he found himself with nothing to do, so he went back to the clubs and continued recording. A remake of a 1960 Jamaican hit by the Folkes Brothers called "Oh Carolina" was released by an independent company and picked up by the Greensleeves label in the U.K. "On the merits of that record, Ken Berry from Virgin Records offered me a deal," says Shaggy.

Virgin released "Oh Carolina" in the U.S., but it faltered at number 59. Two years later, the double-sided hit "Boombastic" / "In the Summertime" peaked at number three. When a second album on Virgin didn't sell well, Shaggy was dropped from the label. Almost a year later, producers Jimmy Jam and Terry Lewis asked Shaggy to record a song for the soundtrack to *How Stella Got Her Groove Back*. Shaggy wasn't sure if his contribution would make the album, but when he found out Janet Jackson would be featured on "Luv Me, Luv Me," he knew it was a lock. Shaggy did a promotional tour of radio stations to help attract airplay. "On the merits of me going out there and my work ethic, MCA offered me a deal."

Shaggy had a concept for a song based on a line from the Eddie Murphy film *Raw*. Sitting in his living room in Jamaica with Ricardo "RikRok" Ducent and Brian Gold, Shaggy collaborated on the words and melody for "It Wasn't Me." "[Shaun] 'Sting' [Pizzonia] had the beat. I came up with the chorus melody and Shaggy came up with the verses," recalls Ducent. "It was a typical routine. You have a beat playing in a minidisc player all day long and eat Jamaican beef patties. You talk a little, make a couple of jokes and write a line here or there and eat some more patties."

The demo was recorded in Shaggy's studio. "Funny, RikRok wasn't scheduled to sing on that song," says Shaggy. "His main forte was as a writer. He did the demo and we gave it to another artist and all these different issues came up. It wasn't going to make the album, so we gave it away to another artist and their record company heard it and didn't like it. So I took it back and Ricky's voice was already on it."

Ducent was asked to come to New York to record the final vocal. The difference in weather between Jamaica and New York gave him a cold. "I hadn't been doing many vocal exercises, so I was intimidated," says Ducent. "But it went smoothly. It took us a couple of hours and I forgot about it. Eight months later, Shaggy calls me and says 'It Wasn't Me' was number one in Hawaii. That's when we started watching the *Billboard* chart. It came in at 80-something. Then it was top 20 and top 10 and top five. It was number two for a while. Destiny's Child was number one with 'Independent Women.' They wouldn't go away, and you couldn't hate them because it was a great song. Finally we got to number one and I said, 'Damn, I got a number one song in *Billboard*. Ain't that something?'"

## THE TOP FIVE
*Week of February 3, 2001*

1　**It Wasn't Me**
　 Shaggy f/Ricardo "RikRok" Ducent

2　**Independent Women Part I**
　 Destiny's Child

3　**Ms. Jackson**
　 OutKast

4　**Don't Tell Me**
　 Madonna

5　**Love Don't Cost a Thing**
　 Jennifer Lopez

# Ms. Jackson LAFACE 24525
## OUTKAST

Writers: *Andre Benjamin*
*Antwan Patton*
*David Sheats*

Producers: *Earthtone III*

February 17, 2001
1 week

"WHEN I WAS A LITTLE kid, I'd listen to everything from Bob Marley to Bobby Womack to Tina Turner to the Police. I was a big fan of the Fat Boys, LL Cool J, Run-D.M.C. And by the time I got to high school my interest switched to Kate Bush, Guns n' Roses. Coming of age as an adult, I realized music was something I wanted to do," says Antwan Patton, better known as Big Boi.

Patton attended a performing arts high school in the borough of Atlanta known as East Point. So did Andre Benjamin. "We all became real close," says Patton. "A couple of our buddies from the same crew got caught up in some trouble. Me and Dre just stuck it out." Big Boi and Dre were in the tenth grade when they met the production team known as Organized Noize. "They taught us the ropes of production and how to make music and how to get your right tone together," says Patton. "We got into deep training, jogging around the block for a couple of miles, rapping, getting your breath right. Once we got serious, we had a chance to perform for LaFace. They turned us down two times. They didn't want to do rap music. Dr. Dre came out with *The Chronic* back then and they were in awe of how many records he sold. L.A. [Reid] thought about giving hip-hop a chance and gave us a shot."

Big Boi and Dre first called themselves Two Shades Deep, until some other students at their high school suddenly started calling themselves Four Shades Deep. "To keep from infringing on our own name, we looked in the dictionary. We found Misfits but there was already somebody with that name, so it was OutKast."

The duo made its first appearance on the Hot 100 in February, 1994, with "Player's Ball." While that song peaked at number 37, it spent six weeks at number one on the rap chart. OutKast didn't have a top 10 hit on the Hot 100 until "Ms. Jackson," a song recorded for their *Stankonia* album. "That was a very heartfelt song," says Big Boi. "Me

and Dre were both going through things so it was really a part of our life we felt like expressing. I think people felt it because the lyrics were real. We were talking about everyday situations the average Joe Schmo could relate to."

With Janet Jackson on the Hot 100 at the same time as "Ms. Jackson," those who didn't listen carefully might have thought the song was about the recording artist. "Jackson is such a common name among black folks and all people," says Big Boi. "It was just one of the most common names that people could relate to. Everyone knows a Ms. Jackson, a Mr. Williams or a Miss Jones."

Like most OutKast tracks, "Ms. Jackson" was unusual because it was sample-free. "We won't take somebody's whole song and do it over," acknowledges Big Boi. "But kick drums, snares and kind of psyched-out sound that we can create rhythm with, we'll do that, but you'll never know where it came from. It wouldn't be a 10 or 15-second sample. It would be a half-second, or a second or two of a beat, and then we chop it up and make our own music."

Big Boi and Dre produced their own number one song under the moniker Earthtone III. "We started out as writers, MCs, lyricists and then the production side came to us," says Big Boi. "If you have a person doing a movie and they write the script and they can also direct, act and do lighting, that makes it come across stronger. So for us to be able to produce and write and create the soundscape to our words, that's dangerous!"

## THE TOP FIVE
*Week of February 17, 2001*

1 **Ms. Jackson**
OutKast

2 **Stutter**
Joe f/Mystikal

3 **It Wasn't Me**
Shaggy f/Ricardo "RikRok" Ducent

4 **Again**
Lenny Kravitz

5 **Love Don't Cost a Thing**
Jennifer Lopez

Writers: *Roy Hamilton*
*Ernest Dixon*
*Trevant Hardson*
*Emandu Wilcox*
*Romye Robinson*
*Derrick Stewart*
*Stephen Boone*
*John Sebastian*
*Mark Sebastian*

Producers: *Allstar*
*Teddy Riley*
*Roy Hamilton*

*February 24, 2001*
*4 weeks*

**M**OST ONE-NAMED SINGERS have distinctive first names, such as Cher, Madonna or Sisqó. There isn't anyone who goes just by "Bill," or "Bob" or "Tom." But there is a Joe—born Joseph Thomas in Cuthbert, Georgia. So why is Joe just plain "Joe"? "It's me wanting to make a statement and say I'm just who I am," he explains. "I'm that guy who has an average name. I relate to a lot of people, and my music relates to a lot of people. It's just me."

Joe made a name for himself on the Hot 100 exactly one year before "Stutter" achieved pole position. During the third week in February of 2000, he shared the number one spot

with Mariah Carey [see 892—"Thank God I Found You"].

"Stutter" originated with songwriters Ernest Dixon and Roy Hamilton III (the grandson of Roy Hamilton, who charted on the Hot 100 in the '50s and '60s with "Don't Let Go" and "You Can Have Her"). Dixon and Hamilton met when both were signed to R. Kelly's production company as artists. When their association with the Chicago-based Kelly ended, Hamilton moved back to New Jersey. Dixon remembers, "We were driving from New York to New Jersey. I was listening to a Nas record and I started stuttering. I wondered what it would be like if you stuttered on a record." Dixon was told he couldn't, but was determined to try. By the time he arrived in New Jersey, he had a verse, the melody and a hook. "The next day I finished the second verse and the bridge and Roy came up with the track and we cut it in the studio."

The song was written for a woman to sing, although Dixon and Hamilton didn't have a specific artist in mind. "A lot of females we were interested in working with were recording albums at that time," says Hamilton. Dixon and Hamilton brought "Stutter" to producer Teddy Riley. "I wanted the song for my group, BLACKstreet," says Riley. "But we weren't coming out [with a new album] in time, so Roy brought the song to Clive Calder. Clive got it right away, and said it would be a great song for Joe."

After charting with singles on Mercury and Island, Joe was signed to the label Calder founded, Jive. Joe recorded his vocals for "Stutter" in one day. "Once he's set on what he wants to do, he'll practice before we come in, and the next thing you know, he's ready to lay the vocal," says Riley.

After recording the song with Riley, Joe came up for an idea for a remix and thought of asking Allstar to produce. "Sitting in a limo one night, I heard a

beat on the radio and I started singing along to it," says Joe. "That's where the idea [for the remix] came from, to merge what was an old school track from years ago for Quincy Jones, and then the Pharcyde used it. It was an incredible loop to use with that type of song."

While he's an R&B singer in the classic sense, Joe admits to being a fan of rap. "Mystikal is one of my favorite artists," he says of the man featured on "Stutter." "Not only does he have a lot of energy and style when he raps, but he says some very clever things."

## THE TOP FIVE
*Week of February 24, 2001*

1 **Stutter**
Joe f/Mystikal

2 **It Wasn't Me**
Shaggy f/Ricardo "RikRok" Ducent

3 **Love Don't Cost a Thing**
Jennifer Lopez

4 **Again**
Lenny Kravitz

5 **Ms. Jackson**
OutKast

## 910 Butterfly COLUMBIA 79549
### CRAZY TOWN

Writers: *Anthony Kiedis*
*Seth Binzer*
*Bret Mazur*
*Flea*
*John Frusciante*
*Chad Smith*

Producers: *Josh Abraham*
*Bret Mazur*

March 24, 2001
2 weeks

SETH BINZER AND BRET Mazur of Crazy Town both had families with musical connections. Binzer, known as Shifty Shellshock, is the son of Rollin Binzer, director of the concert film *Ladies and Gentlemen—the Rolling Stones* as well as the designer of album covers for artists like Chuck Berry and Buddy Miles. Mazur, a.k.a. Epic Mazur, had a grandfather who ran and owned nightclubs in New York. Mazur's father managed the Hassles, the group that featured Billy Joel, and was in charge of the music publisher April-Blackwood for five years. One of Mazur's father's friends was record producer Vini Poncia. As a youngster, Mazur asked his father what a record producer did, and was told, "It's like being the director of a movie. You kind of get to be a member of the band and you get in there and make a record with them." Mazur thought that was cool and was impressed by Poncia's black Blazer truck. "My dad took me to the studio with him and that led me to producing. I didn't want to become an artist until I had something to say myself."

Mazur worked with artists like Prince, Seal and Bell Biv DeVoe, but was also working on his own material with Binzer at the same time. He met Binzer while producing the Black Eyed Peas. Lead rapper Will made the introduction. "We hit it off immediately and started making music," says Mazur. "So while I'm producing and trying to pay the bills, we were moonlighting, making music that wouldn't come out for another three to five years."

Influenced by hip-hop, Mazur and Binzer formed the Brimstone Sluggers. "That was too limiting for us," says Mazur. "We were already putting live guitars on our tracks, so we knew we had to be a band. We had to find the right people." Binzer adds, "We didn't want to get a bunch of guys with instruments. We wanted guys who felt like

they were our buddies, like a crew that went to high school together."

While searching for the right musicians, they recorded demos. "Butterfly" was inspired by a relationship Binzer was in at the time. "We were writing songs like 'Lollipop Porn' when there was no girlfriend and all of a sudden I was in this relationship. I was in love and she was asking, 'What's up with all these lyrics? Is this what you're like?' So that made me come up with the concept of writing a song to her. Instead of writing a male chauvinistic song, I was going to write something sweet and nice to a girl I cared about. I was living with her and I'd started bringing home butterflies because she had a collection. I was thinking, what am I going to call this song and I'm lying on the bed looking at the ceiling and there's a big butterfly hanging over me. I had the beginning of the hook and that's all I had for a week. I was making a left onto Doheny off Santa Monica Boulevard and for some reason I said, 'You're my butterfly, sugar baby.' I called Bret because he's the guy who tells me if it's really stupid or really great." Mazur said he loved it and the demo was recorded that night.

The song includes a sample of an obscure Red Hot Chili Peppers song, "Pretty Little Ditty." Mazur says, "It's the only sample they've ever cleared. If we had to fight to get it cleared or they didn't like it, we would have come up with some other music. But we wanted

to stay true to our hip-hop origins and pay homage to a great band like the Peppers."

Crazy Town was signed to Columbia and Josh Abraham produced the final track. "The demo was a relaxed rap. Because the beat was so hype, I knew if Epic and Shifty got in everyone's face, it would be a lot more exciting. So the main thing we focused on was hyping up the vocals."

The album *The Gift of Game* was released in 1999, and the first two singles didn't chart. "Butterfly" entered the Hot 100 in January, 2001. "We were in Germany," says Mazur. "We got a phone call from our managers [that it was number one] and everybody came into my room and I went online to Billboard.com and pulled up the page."

### THE TOP FIVE
*Week of March 24, 2001*

1  **Butterfly**
   Crazy Town

2  **Angel**
   Shaggy f/Rayvon

3  **Stutter**
   Joe f/Mystikal

4  **Again**
   Lenny Kravitz

5  **Love Don't Cost a Thing**
   Jennifer Lopez

MCA ALBUM CUT **Angel**
SHAGGY Featuring RAYVON

**911**

Writers: *Ahmet Ertegun*
*Eddie Curtis*
*Chip Taylor*
*Steve Miller*

Producer: *Shaun Pizzonia*

March 31, 2001
1 week

Seven weeks after scoring his first number one song, Shaggy was back on top of the Hot 100 with "Angel." It was the first time since 1988 that an artist had two songs advance to number one during the first quarter of a calendar year. Shaggy was the first artist to do so since Michael Jackson did it with "The Way You Make Me Feel" and "Man in the Mirror."

There was a reason "It Wasn't Me" was released before "Angel," according to Shaggy. "We knew if you put 'Angel' out first it could easily be missed, because the industry is not going to take a chance on a record like that." Shaggy recalls the genesis of "Angel": "[Shaun] 'Sting' [Pizzonia] came to me with this beat, which was the Steve Miller bassline [from "The Joker"]. I don't know what Steve was thinking, but it's actually reggae. I did a world music kind of vibe on it." Shaggy and Pizzonia disagreed about how the track was turning out and so it was discarded. But Dave Kelly, one of the producers of the *Hotshot* album, thought it was worth pursuing. Working on the song in Jamaica, nothing was happening until Ricardo "RikRok" Ducent walked into the studio. "Out of frustration, I started humming anything that came into my head," says Ducent.

Shaggy concurs: "He was fooling around and sang, 'You're my angel in

the morning,' and we knew we should use that. So we changed the words to make it a little harder and I came up with the melody for the verse. All of us put words to it, and later on Ricky finished the end part."

None of Shaggy's compatriots are credited as songwriters. Ducent explains, "We're not listed because we used 'The Joker' beat and then we used 'Angel of the Morning.' Each party got 50 percent. Because we lost all publishing, we couldn't put our names on it." The names that were listed help make chart history. Chip Taylor, brother of actor Jon Voight and composer of "Angel of the Morning," originally a hit for Merrilee Rush & the Turnabouts and then Juice Newton, earned the longest span of number one hits for any songwriter in the rock era to this date. There were 34 years and eight months between his first chart-topper, "Wild Thing" by the Troggs [see 204], and Shaggy's "Angel." Also included in the writing credits are Eddie Curtis and Atlantic Records founder Ahmet Ertegun. That's because Steve Miller's "The Joker" included lyrics from the Clovers' "Lovey Dovey," written by Curtis and Ertegun.

Another name involved with "Angel"

is Barbados-born Rayvon. "Because it was such a poppy song, we needed to have an edge, and Rayvon's got that vocal with an edge to it. We gave the song to him and he came in and nailed it," says Shaggy.

Shaggy and Rayvon were both part of the reggae community in New York City, but didn't meet until they were both recording at the Living Room Studio in Flatbush. They first worked together on a remake of Air Supply's "All Out of Love" that was never released. "We met Shaun 'Sting' Pizzonia. I was doing some solo records and we kept doing stuff together. I also scored a record deal with Virgin due to songs like 'In the Summertime,' which was the B-side of 'Boombastic.' I did some hip hop rap with Funkmaster Flex." Like Shaggy, Rayvon's option wasn't picked up by Virgin.

Rayvon admits to keeping an eye on the charts. "I go to *Billboard* online to see what's happening. I was in England doing promotion for 'Angel' and I heard it hit number one in the U.S. I think it would have hit me harder if I was actually in the States. Then when it entered at number one in the U.K., I was in New York. But it was a nice feeling."

---

## THE TOP FIVE

*Week of March 31, 2001*

1 **Angel**
Shaggy f/Rayvon

2 **Butterfly**
Crazy Town

3 **All for You**
Janet Jackson

4 **Stutter**
Joe f/Mystikal

5 **Again**
Lenny Kravitz

## 912 All for You VIRGIN 97522
### JANET JACKSON

Writers: Janet Jackson
James Harris III
Terry Lewis
Wayne Garfield
David Romani
Mauro Malavasi

Producers: Jimmy Jam
Terry Lewis
Janet Jackson

April 14, 2001
7 weeks

**P**RODUCER JIMMY JAM FIGURES if Janet Jackson had recorded her *All for You* album a year earlier, it would have been filled with songs about sadness, anger and bitterness, as Jackson was going through her divorce from husband René Elizondo, Jr. "You go through all of those emotions and then you come out of it on the other side and say, 'I'm going to be okay and I have a lot of things to be thankful for,' and that was the overriding feeling in her life when we were making the album."

Before starting a new project with Jackson, producers Jimmy Jam and Terry Lewis get together with her and listen to a lot of older songs. One of the tracks Jam and Lewis played for Jackson before the *All for You* sessions was "The Glow of Love" by Change, with lead vocals by Luther Vandross. "She didn't know that song and I was really shocked," says Jam. "I was DJing at the time that record was out, so that was a huge song in my life and one that I have always wanted to sample and bring back for people to hear."

Jam thought the bright, funky sample of "Glow" was a perfect fit to Jackson's lyrics for "All for You." He says, "The lyric is about people meeting her and being intimidated about coming up to talk to her. It was very true-to-life. It was very positive and she was in a very comfortable place."

Jam contributed one line to the song. "I sent her home after she had done all the vocals. I had an idea for the line, 'All the girls at the party,' and I sang it. She loved it and sang it into her little voice recorder. She said she would come up with something and she ended up finishing the line. It came in the middle of the song and then her manager said it would be cool if the song started like that. So we reworked it with Alex Richburg, our drum programmer. He took the *a cappella* vocal and Steve Hodge, our engineer, put the

backward sweeping effect on it. It ended up being a huge hook in the song."

Jam thought the song should begin with Janet's voice. "We were able to do that by moving that piece to the beginning so when it came on the radio, the first thing you heard was her voice doing that little hook. That worked out really well."

Janet loved "All for You" from the beginning, unlike her previous single [see 902—"Doesn't Really Matter"]. Jackson was doing a photo shoot for a magazine at Jam and Lewis' studio. Jam asked her what track she wanted him to play, and Janet requested "All for You." "The session went on for 45 minutes. She kept saying, 'Play it again, play it again.' After the fifth play, the makeup artist, the camera assistant, the hairstylist and everybody is dancing around singing this song. At the end, Janet said, 'I'm going to say something. Don't think I'm crazy,' because we're not done with the record at this point. We had five or six songs to go. And she said, 'I think this is the first single. I know we're going to get some more songs and they're going to be really good, but this is the first thing I want people to hear from me when I do my first record after three or four years.'" Jackson's manager asked Jam

and Lewis for a copy of the song and immediately went to Virgin and played it for everyone. "The rest is history," Jam says with a smile.

After the label agreed "All for You" would be the first song sent to radio, Jam and Lewis overdubbed some more instruments on the track. They sent Jackson a copy of the latest version, and Janet called to say she loved what they did. Jam said he only did a couple of small things, but Jackson told him, "That keyboard thing totally makes it!" Jam adds, "Even when we were mixing the record, she kept telling me, 'You gotta turn up that keyboard stuff!'"

### THE TOP FIVE
*Week of April 14, 2001*

1 **All for You**
Janet Jackson

2 **Survivor**
Destiny's Child

3 **Angel**
Shaggy f/Rayvon

4 **Butterfly**
Crazy Town

5 **Missing You**
Case

INTERSCOPE 497066 # Lady Marmalade
## CHRISTINA AGUILERA, LIL' KIM, MYA & PINK
**913**

*Writers: Bob Crewe*
*Kenny Nolan*

*Producers: Missy Elliott*
*Rockwilder*
*Ron Fair*

*June 2, 2001*
*5 weeks*

Baz Luhrmann's vision for his musical film *Moulin Rouge* included his characters in 1900 Montmarte singing contemporary pop songs. And what better late 20th century tune for harlots to sing than Labelle's 1975 number one song, "Lady Marmalade" [see 399]? When the 2001 version of "Lady Marmalade" topped the Hot 100, it was the ninth song to be number one by two different artists, following "Go Away Little Girl," "The Loco-Motion," "Please Mr. Postman," "Venus," "Lean on Me," "You Keep Me Hangin' On," "When a Man Loves a Woman" and "I'll Be There."

Producer Missy Elliott recruited four 21st century performers to sing the new version of "Lady Marmalade." None of the four women were born when Labelle scored a number one hit with the Bob Crewe/Kenny Nolan song. Christina Aguilera is the youngest of the four, born December 18, 1980. Lil' Kim came into the world on July 11, 1975, four months after Labelle's recording reached the top. Mya was born October 10, 1979. And Pink was born one month earlier than Mya, on September 8, 1979.

Elliott asked Rockwilder to produce the song with her and Ron Fair. "To tell you the truth, I didn't like 'Lady Marmalade,'" says Rockwilder. "It's not that I didn't like the song, it's just that when I was a little kid, they played it so much. But after working with it, I finally realized what the song was about."

Lacing the track with samples, Rockwilder helped update the 1975 hit to fit in with the music of 2001. "We had to change Kim's verse to a hip-hop beat, because if she would have kicked it over that rhythm, I don't know how people would have taken it. We changed the beat around for her, and it made everything sound real funky when it got back to the 'Lady Marmalade' part."

Mya, who had already scored a number two hit with "Case of the Ex (Whatcha Gonna Do)" in the summer of 2000, was familiar with the original, but admits, "I took Spanish in school instead of French. Until I did the song, I didn't have a clue what it said or meant." She remembers the first day of recording: "We were all there and recorded our backgrounds. We alternated. It was a cool vibe. Missy, Rockwilder and Ron Fair were all there." Later, the four women recorded their lead vocals separately. "Different occasions, different studios, different days," says Mya. "Then we shot the video."

Mya welcomed the challenge of recording "Lady Marmalade" as part of a one-time-only quartet of solo artists. "It was competitive, because that's natural when you're with fellow artists. Nothing was cutthroat about it, but it pushed you and everybody brought out the best in themselves. I thought the key for me was higher than I usually sing, but it was great because people had never heard that register in my voice."

The success of the new version of "Lady Marmalade" helped rewrite the record books. By reaching the summit, it stretched songwriter Bob Crewe's span of number one hits to 38 years, seven months, and two weeks, dating back to his first chart-topper, the Four Seasons' "Big Girls Don't Cry" [see 120]. That bested the record set in March, 2001, when Chip Taylor had a songwriting credit on "Angel" [see 911] by Shaggy featuring Rayvon. Crewe's first hit as a songwriter on the *Billboard* pop singles chart was "Silhouettes" by the Rays in October, 1957. That gave Crewe a career chart span of 43 years and 10 months.

## THE TOP FIVE
*Week of June 2, 2001*

1 **Lady Marmalade**
Christina Aguilera, Lil' Kim, Mya & Pink

2 **All for You**
Janet Jackson

3 **Survivor**
Destiny's Child

4 **Hanging by a Moment**
Lifehouse

5 **Ride Wit Me**
Nelly f/City Spud

# 914 U Remind Me
ARISTA 13992
## USHER

*Writers: Anita McCloud
Eddie Clement*

*Producers: Eddie Clement
Jimmy Jam
Terry Lewis*

*July 7, 2001
4 weeks*

PRODUCER JIMMY JAM RAN into Usher backstage at the MTV Awards in September, 2000. They were both going through the press area doing interviews with radio stations when Usher asked Jimmy Jam if he would produce a song for him written by the members of 112. "We normally don't produce songs that we don't write," says Jimmy Jam. But Arista president L.A. Reid wanted Jimmy Jam and his partner Terry Lewis to bring acts to the label, and become involved with artists already on the roster. "It was exciting for us because we had never really done any Arista acts and TLC on LaFace was the only thing we'd ever done in that system. So the idea of having the chance to work with an Aretha Franklin or a Whitney Houston or an Usher or even a Sarah McLachlan or a Dido was very intriguing to us."

Jam and Lewis produced the 112-penned track, "Separated," for Usher. "The recording of that went really well, which led L.A. to say, 'Can you do another song with Usher?'" The artist flew to Minneapolis to work with Jam and Lewis in their studio. The first song recorded was "Can U Help Me." Arista's Reid was so impressed, he told Jam and Lewis he was delaying the album so they could write and produce more tracks. Reid also asked Jam and

## THE TOP FIVE
### *Week of July 7, 2001*

1  **U Remind Me**
   Usher

2  **Lady Marmalade**
   Christina Aguilera, Lil' Kim, Mya & Pink

3  **Hanging by a Moment**
   Lifehouse

4  **Peaches & Cream**
   112

5  **Let Me Blow Ya Mind**
   Eve f/Gwen Stefani

Lewis to work on "U Remind Me," a song that had been written by Eddie Clement and his sister, Anita McCloud. Reid had liked the demo, but wasn't enchanted with Usher's recording of it. He wanted Jam and Lewis to work with Usher on the vocals.

"Usher is very particular about what he sings," explains Jam. "He wants to be able to totally relate to a song and for some reason when he had done the vocal on that song, he sounded like he was distracted. It didn't work. So we redid the vocal. Usher felt very comfortable doing vocals with us. Terry, who I call the 'Vocal Master,' had a lot to do with that. It stems from when we had the privilege of working with Leon Sylvers. He taught us about doing vocals because at the time we could do tracks well. He told us, 'You're not really a producer until you can pull vocals off.' And that made us change our focus."

Jam and Lewis turned over their version of "U Remind Me" to Reid and the label head told them, "This song just went from being off the record to being the first single." Jam gives proper credit to Clement. "It's his concept. It was a wonderful song and a great

demo." Ironically, Clement never intended the song to go to Usher. He had his own group, Hustle Child, and had written a song for them called "Remember Me." L.A. Reid and Mark Pitts at Arista wanted that song, but Clement didn't want to give it up. So he wrote another song with his sister. When they finished "U Remind Me," they knew it was even better than "Remember Me," and wanted to hold on to it and give Reid the earlier song. "But L.A. said, 'I want "U Remind Me" and I guarantee you this is a number one record. Usher needs this for his project'," says Clement. "I'm a hungry young cat ready to get my break, so I said okay."

The next day, Clement and his sister were on a plane to Atlanta to work with Usher. "He's a sweetheart," says McCloud. "He took direction so well. He was eager to get it right and if he had to do something again, there wasn't any fuss. No temperament, no egotistical attitude at all. It was just so cool. It was a blessing to have Jimmy Jam and Terry Lewis on it. My first time out, I'm working with them. Everybody knew it was going to be a good song."

COLUMBIA 79622 **Bootylicious**
DESTINY'S CHILD `915`

*Writers: Beyoncé Knowles
    Robert Fusari
    Falonte Moore
    Stevie Nicks*

*Producers: Beyoncé Knowles
    Robert Fusari
    Falonte Moore*

*August 4, 2001
2 weeks*

Falonte Moore had several brushes with success in his early days in the music business. The writer/producer, born in Howardsville, Missouri, was in a group called 3XL that broke up. He spent time in Los Angeles working with LL Cool J. He sang in church with Ronald Isley and Angela Winbush. Through R.L. of Next, Moore met Arista Records president Clive Davis, who signed him to the label with Vernelle Sales as the duo Koffee Brown. Through his manager, he was introduced to Rob Fusari and they formed a partnership. Fusari was working on Will Smith's *Willennium* album and asked Moore to collaborate with him. "We had a chemistry, so we kept working together," says Fusari.

Fusari and Moore were working on a track that started with a drum groove on an MPC2000 sequencer when Fusari suggested they use a sample from Survivor's "Eye of the Tiger" [see 557]. Fusari dug through his CD collection and discovered he didn't have the song. "I had Stevie Nicks' greatest hits and remembered in 'Edge of Seventeen' there was a similar guitar part. It was late at night, so we just threw that in, thinking tomorrow we'd go out and get 'Eye of the Tiger.' But we put the track away and it sat around for six months. When I found out Destiny's Child was doing their third album, I was going through my tracks. I didn't think it was appropriate, but it was different from the rest of the stuff I was sending and I know Beyoncé likes different stuff. I never thought somebody would want to sing over it, but that's the one that turned out to be 'Bootylicious.'"

Beyoncé Knowles was on a flight to London when she was inspired to write lyrics to Fusari and Moore's track. "I was delirious from the long flight," she laughs. "It was a song of empowerment for people who didn't look like everyone in the magazines. They had a little meat on their bones, a little jelly. People still misunderstand the song. If someone says you need to lose weight or you don't look a certain way, you tell them you're too bootylicious for them."

Knowles loved the sample of "Edge of Seventeen." She says, "When I heard the Stevie Nicks sample, it made me want to dance. I couldn't stop moving and that title popped in my head." Later, Knowles had a chance to meet Nicks. "We had to get Stevie in the video."

Moore thought the idea of calling the song "Bootylicious" was "wild." He says, "It was a different style for Destiny's Child at the time. They were known as a clean-cut group. The first time I heard the song on the air was when I was in London. All day on television they were showing the video. So I knew it was going to be successful."

Fusari admits he changed his mind about the song, after not liking it at first. "It was fun, but I wasn't getting it. I didn't feel like it was going to be a hit. I got a call from the label that it was going to be the second single. Then I listened to it with different ears. My attitude about it changed quickly."

Moore found out the song was number one in an unusual way. "I was so busy on the road with Koffee Brown, I couldn't keep up with anything. I was doing a lot of traveling but I knew the song was big because people were talking about it and people had T-shirts that said, 'Bootylicious.' How I found out [it was number one] was from the first check I got in the mail."

"Bootylicious" was the fourth charttopper for Destiny's Child, putting them into a tie with TLC for second place behind the Supremes among girl groups with the most number one hits.

## THE TOP FIVE
*Week of August 4, 2001*

1 **Bootylicious**
  Destiny's Child

2 **Loverboy**
  Mariah Carey f/Cameo

3 **Hit 'Em Up Style (Oops!)**
  Blu Cantrell

4 **All or Nothing**
  O-Town

5 **U Remind Me**
  Usher

## 916 Fallin' J 21041
### ALICIA KEYS

*Writer: Alicia Keys*

*Producer: Alicia Keys*

*August 18, 2001*
*6 weeks*

Growing up in the Hell's Kitchen section of New York City, Alicia Keys started piano lessons at age seven—not because her mother said she had to take them, but because she wanted to. "Every time I saw a piano, I wanted to play it," she remembers. "I'd be fascinated by the way they would line up the pianos in those Baldwin or Steinway & Sons stores." Keys was talented enough to attend the Professional Performing Arts School in New York, graduating at 16.

Her first attempt at a musical career was a girl group called Ambition that varied from a trio to a quartet, but Ambition never got a record deal, and Keys concentrated on a solo career. Guided by manager Jeff Robinson, she met Michael Mauldin, head of black

music at Columbia Records. "He was a big supporter of being your own musician," says Keys. "Before that, a lot of other people just wanted you to look cute and sing over a hard beat. He actually cared that I wrote my own stuff." Mauldin signed the teenaged Keys to the label, but she languished there for four years without releasing anything, save one song on a So So Def Christmas collection produced by Mauldin's son, Jermaine Dupri.

Arista A&R exec Peter Edge had been following Keys' career, and brought her to the attention of label president Clive Davis, who saw Keys perform at a showcase. Davis wanted Keys for Arista, and paid Columbia a hefty sum for the rights to an album Keys has been working on while signed to the Sony imprint. "Columbia was going to try and give me a hard time about keeping music that I worked on, and I had a whole album already. So when I went to Arista, I had a lot of music." One of the songs that Keys had already worked on was "Fallin'," but Keys originally meant to give it to another artist. "There was this young girl at Columbia, about 11 years old, and I thought how crazy would it be for somebody young to sing this deep song about life and love and bring it across as if they lived it. Her name was Kimberly Scott. It wasn't like I started the song for her—it was just a thought I had." Keys kept working on the song and eventually realized it was not meant for Scott. "There was no question it was for me."

"Fallin'" was inspired by a real-life relationship. "It came from the feeling of when you really care about somebody and they can affect you in a way that can be so positive and negative, all at the same time. It was one of my first serious, deep relationships. I think your first one affects you even more so because you don't have the experience to know how to play it. You're tripping your way through it, and those hardships and good times and just growing is how 'Fallin'' developed."

Before she wrote the lyrics for the song, Keys composed the music. "I was in the studio mixing my record for Columbia. Because mixes would take forever, we'd pretty much live there. One day I was on the piano playing these arpeggiated chords. I kept playing and it was almost haunting me. Then it was almost as if the lyrics just came to it. I feel like it was already written."

Keys says she was experiencing a lot of tension in her life at the time, both personal and professional. "I was going through a lot. For those hours that it took to record the song, it was my chance to let out all my frustrations and my feelings. I remember feeling that way, like I had to get it out."

When Clive Davis left Arista and started his own J Records, he took Keys with him. Her album *Songs in A Minor* was released on J. The track "Girlfriend" was a contender for a single, but "Fallin'" was the preferred choice. By the time it was released to the public, Keys had lived with the song for three years. "Even when it was first written, it moved me," she says. "I heard it trillions of times and it would move me every time the same way. I feel like that means something special."

The single became J's first number one hit. The song has become a staple for "American Idol" contestants, and Keys was parodied on "Mad TV" and was surprised to be an answer on "Wheel of Fortune." "These are the things that make me laugh," she confides. "It's like, wow, how did that happen?"

### THE TOP FIVE
*Week of August 18, 2001*

1  **Fallin'**
   Alicia Keys

2  **Let Me Blow Ya Mind**
   Eve f/Gwen Stefani

3  **Hit 'Em Up Style (Oops!)**
   Blu Cantrell

4  **I'm Real**
   Jennifer Lopez f/Ja Rule

5  **Bootylicious**
   Destiny's Child

EPIC 79639    **I'm Real**

JENNIFER LOPEZ Featuring JA RULE

*Writers: Jennifer Lopez*
*Troy Oliver*
*Cory Rooney*
*L.E.S.*
*Jeff Atkins*
*Irv Gotti*
*Rick James*

*Producers: Troy Oliver*
*Cory Rooney*
*L.E.S.*

*September 8, 2001*
*5 weeks*

THERE ARE TWO SONGS by Jennifer Lopez called "I'm Real." The first one appeared on her album *J.Lo.* The track started as a loop from a DJ named L.E.S., a.k.a. Leshaun Lewis. Troy Oliver says he "freaked it up a little bit and twisted it around," and brought it to producer Cory Rooney. "We played it for Jennifer," says Rooney. "We were working on another song in the studio at the time and she said, 'While you guys are preparing this song, do you mind if I take the track and play around with some ideas?' On the first album, she had written with us, but she had never taken a track on her own and come up with ideas. So when she came back in the room 15 minutes later, she was almost shy. She said, 'I don't want anyone else to hear it. I want to sing it to you first.' She had worked out the whole chorus, the 'I'm real, what you get is what you see,' all of that. It was perfect. So I stopped what we were doing and recorded it on tape, so we could capture it while it was hot."

The single "Love Don't Cost a Thing" preceded the release of the album, and peaked at number three in February, 2001. The follow-up, "Play," only reached number 18. "We lost some momentum with the album because we released 'Play,'" says Rooney. "As a matter of fact, the album plunged on the chart. One problem was that R&B radio was not into Jennifer Lopez. They didn't believe in her. They said, 'Look, this girl does not make records for our stations, so why should we support her and believe in her?'" Rooney told Sony Music chief Tommy Mottola that the label needed to force radio to play Lopez. "So what we had to do was an old school trick I learned from Uptown Records. When Puffy said he invented the remix, he most certainly did. We did a remake of the song and I said we have to work with a person that radio cannot

refuse, which at the time was Ja Rule. We called Irv Gotti [founder of Murder Inc., Ja Rule's label]." Gotti said he had an idea for a track, and invited Rooney and Mottola to his studio in Soho. The elevator was broken, so Rooney and Mottola walked up 10 flights of stairs to meet with Gotti.

Rooney loved the track. "I came up with a melody and most people don't realize Ja Rule can write really good R&B melodies and songs as well as his rap stuff." Then Rooney told Ja Rule what he really wanted: "I need you to sing on this record with Jennifer, like a duet. Your verse has to be almost a singing verse." Rooney recalls how Gotti and Ja Rule reacted. "They laughed like you wouldn't believe. It took me 15 minutes to get the room focused again, because they tried to laugh me out of the room. I said, 'Now that you're finished laughing, I'm serious. If you look at every hit record you've had so far, Ja, it's you singing the choruses, and people have accepted that about you and this is what I want."

Once Ja Rule agreed to duet with Lopez, things moved quickly. "Jennifer was in Los Angeles and all of us were in New York," says Rooney. "So me and a couple of guys from my team and Irv and his guys jumped on a plane and we did the whole thing in 48 hours. We had a limo waiting for us outside of the studio so we could record the song, get it

all mixed, jump back in the limo with the tapes and come back to New York."

On the Hot 100, airplay of the original album track "I'm Real" and the remix were combined, per chart policy as it existed at that time. *Billboard* readers expressed complaints, because the two versions were two different songs that only shared a title. Chart policy was reconsidered, and beginning with songs that entered the chart in 2002, songs that were substantially different in melody were no longer counted as one title when computing airplay data. The first song to be affected by the new policy was P. Diddy's "I Need a Girl," with parts one and two charting separately.

---

## THE TOP FIVE

*Week of September 8, 2001*

1 **I'm Real**
Jennifer Lopez f/Ja Rule

2 **Fallin'**
Alicia Keys

3 **Someone to Call My Lover**
Janet Jackson

4 **Hit 'Em Up Style (Oops!)**
Blu Cantrell

5 **Let Me Blow Ya Mind**
Eve f/Gwen Stefani

918

# Family Affair MCA 155894
## MARY J. BLIGE

*Writers: Mary J. Blige*
*Melvin Bradford*
*Michael Elizondo*
*Camara Kambon*
*Luchana Lodge*
*Asiah Louis*
*Bruce Miller*
*Andre Young*

*Producer: Dr. Dre*

*November 3, 2001*
*6 weeks*

Mary J. Blige had peaked at number three (with Method Man on "I'll Be There for You/You're All I Need to Get By" in 1995) and number two (on "Not Gon' Cry" in 1996), but the Atlanta-born queen of hip-hop soul didn't have her first number one hit on the Hot 100 until she recorded "Family Affair" in 2001, almost nine-and-a-half years after she made her Hot 100 debut with "You Remind Me" in June, 1992.

Growing up in the projects in Yonkers, New York, Blige listened to the artists her mother loved, like Sam Cooke, the Isley Brothers and the O'Jays. As a child, Mary sang in her living room, using her hairbrush as a microphone. Her professional career began when she stepped into a karaoke-like studio in a shopping mall. She made a recording of her favorite song at the time, Anita Baker's "Caught Up in the Rapture." Her mother's boyfriend was working for General Motors and knew someone who knew someone who knew an artist who passed the tape to his manager. The next thing Mary knew, people were showing up at her home to hear her sing.

It took four more years to land a

## THE TOP FIVE
*Week of November 3, 2001*

1  **Family Affair**
   Mary J. Blige

2  **I'm Real**
   Jennifer Lopez f/Ja Rule

3  **Fallin'**
   Alicia Keys

4  **Differences**
   Ginuwine

5  **Hero**
   Enrique Iglesias

recording contract. But then the hits started coming quickly. By the time she recorded the *No More Drama* album, Mary had shared her darkest emotions with her fans. "We cried so much on the *My Life* album," she says. "We were so confused on the *Share My World* album. We went through a lot together and we almost died together, but I figured out a way to get us out of this private hell we're living in. The *No More Drama* album was about bringing the joy that I found to all those people who were crying with me."

One of the songs with a strong anti-hate message was "Family Affair." Co-writer Michael Elizondo remembers how the song was born. "A lot of the time me and Dr. Dre and Mel-Man [Melvin Bradford] and Camara Kambon get together and have writing days where we jam and come up with the skeleton of ideas. We archive them on DAT tapes and then come back to them. 'Family Affair' was intended for another artist that Dre had recently signed, a legendary rapper named Rakim. It was about six to eight months later that Mary J. heard it and decided she wanted to write something to it. She took the CD and her brother [Bruce Miller] was instrumental in writing it. We had the music and she wrote the lyric and melody and we fin-

ished the production on it after the vocals were done."

There was one extra step. After Dre heard Blige's vocals, he asked her to write a bridge for the song. "That's the most spiritual part of the song," says Blige, "because it's saying we don't need haters, we're just trying to love one another. We're here on this Earth together and we have to get along, so please leave your problems outside and try to make it work."

During the making of "Family Affair," artist and producer never got together. "I didn't work with Dr. Dre in person," explains Blige. "We were sending the track back and forth, because he was doing the *Training Day* movie at the time. We did the vocals and sent it to him to produce. He heard it over the phone, then touched it when he got his hands on it."

Earlier in her career, Blige didn't pay much attention to the *Billboard* charts. "Believe it or not, I just started checking what was going on," she says. "With *No More Drama* it was like, I need to see this with my own eyes, when they told me 'Family Affair' was number one for six weeks. I mean, it was the sixth week that I looked at the *Billboard* chart and said, 'Whoa, this is really real!' That's when it started and now, every now and then I peek in."

Writers: *Usher Raymond*
*Jermaine Dupri*
*Bryan-Michael Cox*

Producer: *Jermaine Dupri*

December 15, 2001
6 weeks

U MUST STAND FOR USHER, because the Atlanta-based singer had three consecutive hits from his album *8701* starting with the same letter. "U Remind Me" [see 914] was a number one hit, as was the follow-up, "U Got It Bad." Then came "U Don't Have to Call," which peaked at number three. With "U Remind Me" and "U Got It Bad," Usher was the only solo male artist to top the Hot 100 in 2001, and he did it twice.

Producer Jermaine Dupri describes "U Got It Bad" as a "one-hundred percent true story." He recalls, "We were working in the studio and Usher was in the recording booth. He couldn't get his performance together. It was because he had a girl in the studio. She was impeding our progress. She got him really upset, and then she left. Then she called him while he was in the studio. They got into some conversation and he couldn't finish his work." Dupri ordered Usher out of the studio, and when the artist asked why, Dupri replied, "We're going to do this later on. You got it completely too bad right now. You got it bad."

Usher took off. "When the door slammed, that title came back to me," says Dupri. "'You got it bad,' and I immediately started writing the song, thinking about how many people go through that situation. I just knew it was going to be big. When he came back to the studio, he said, 'You just wrote that from looking at me?' I told him that's where it comes from."

Working in the studio with Dupri was Bryan-Michael Cox, who had worked with Jagged Edge and written some songs for their *J.E. Heartbreak* album. Cox describes Dupri as "the initiator," explaining: "He initiates a lot of the songs. He'll have an idea. As the idea is developing, I'm adding things to it. He's humming a hook and we go back and forth. 'U Got It Bad' is special to me because Jermaine allowed me to express myself melodically. That's one track I initiated musically and Jermaine brought the lyrics and the whole production concept, where it started out with just a little piano idea I laid down. He built it from there and it became this massive song."

Cox enjoys working with Usher. "He's incredible. You don't even need to be there. Because he's an entertainer, people overlook the fact that he's a world-class singer. You don't have to tell him anything, he just knows what to do."

Dupri agrees. "Coaching him isn't that hard. I sing most of the songs to Usher and then he goes back in there and sings them the same way that I sing it. I'm not an amazing singer, but he imitates me in a way, but it sounds a hundred percent better than me." Dupri acknowledges Usher's growth since they first started working together. "At first he went in there just trying to hit notes that he never knew he could do. Now he knows his voice. He knows his falsetto. He knows when to use it and when not. He has really matured as a vocalist."

Usher returns the favor by talking about Dupri. "He's a party animal. If you work with him, you have to stay up. We'll be in the studio playing video games and listening to music, just having a good time. And I'm sitting there saying, 'Can we work now? We played video games all night. Let's work.' [Then he'll say] 'We've got to go to this one party.' But in all the conversations we have about relationships, he gets a chance to hear where I'm at and I get a chance to be familiar with him and loosen up. So by two o'clock in the morning, we come back to the studio and it just comes right out."

## THE TOP FIVE
*Week of December 15, 2001*

1 **U Got It Bad**
Usher

2 **Family Affair**
Mary J. Blige

3 **How You Remind Me**
Nickelback

4 **Hero**
Enrique Iglesias

5 **Turn Off the Light**
Nelly Furtado

# 920 How You Remind Me  ROADRUNNER 012053
## NICKELBACK

*Writers: Chad Kroeger*
*Nickelback*

*Producer: Rick Parashar*

*December 22, 2001*
*4 weeks*

As A CHILD IN HANNA, Alberta, Canada, Chad Kroeger couldn't resist pushing the keys every time he walked by a piano. "But I couldn't feel cool playing the piano, so I had to start playing the guitar," he says. "It's hard to run across the stage holding a piano."

Kroeger remembers writing his first song when he was 16. "It had a little bit of a folk feel to it, but it was funny. There were three different stories inside the song. I think it's going to be a hit somewhere down the road." Kroeger wasn't in a band when he wrote that first song—but his brother Mike and friend Ryan Peake were waiting for him to finish high school so he could join them on the road in a cover band. "We did that for about a year until it got boring playing other people's music and then we broke up," says Kroeger, who continued to write songs. "I didn't have anybody to sing them, so I stepped in. I showed the tunes to the other fellas and we came up to Vancouver and recorded them, and

away we went."

Nickelback had a plan. "We knew there are two types of bands that get signed," Kroeger explains. "There's the kind that has a buzz and you've got 15 different labels with deals on the table, or else you have to sell so many records on your own that it doesn't matter if you're four monkeys farting into a box...so we tried to be the four monkeys." Nickelback recorded an EP in 1997 and then an album called *The State* in 1999, released on their own label. The band, now including drummer Ryan Vikedal, handled their own promotion and distribution. "We took on everything ourselves, trying to make a big enough bang so we could get some record companies interested in us." The plan worked. Nickelback was signed to the Roadrunner label.

The quartet returned to Greenhouse Studios in Vancouver to record a new album. It was the same place they had recorded *The State*. "*Silver Side Up* was the first album we actually got to use someone else's money to make, which is really nice because you don't have to worry about money and time," says Kroeger.

Before they went into the studio, the band sent several new songs they had written to producer Rick Parashar. But one song was written the night

before a recording session. Kroeger recalls the inspiration: "I'd been living with a girl for a couple of years and the relationship was on its way down. I knew. She knew. One day, after I don't know how many fights, I went downstairs and was going to give her the 'f**k you' song and I wrote 'How You Remind Me.' It does sound like a love ballad, but if you finish the sentence, 'This is how you remind me of how I really am,' like you're a jerk, you're insensitive, all the unflattering things you hear throughout a day, that's what the song's about."

Parashar heard the song before the rest of the band. "I was driving to Vancouver and stopped at Chad's place and he played me that song. I was present at the rehearsal when the band first heard it. Usually I have a demo and I have all my notes and my ideas written out. With this one, I was more or less a coach, sitting on the sidelines watching them go through their thing. I sat back and let them hash things out. The next day we got down to the nitty gritty of structural things."

Kroeger remembers the song's evolution. "I didn't really play it for them. It was more, here's the verse and here's the choruses. Right away, Ryan Peake was coming up with lots of great ideas. The song really flew together."

### THE TOP FIVE
*Week of December 22, 2001*

1 **How You Remind Me**
Nickelback

2 **U Got It Bad**
Usher

3 **Family Affair**
Mary J. Blige

4 **Hero**
Enrique Iglesias

5 **Get the Party Started**
Pink

Writers: *Jeff Atkins*
*7 Aurelius*
*Irving Lorenzo*

Producer: *Irv Gotti*

*February 23, 2002*
*2 weeks*

"**H**E IS A BUNDLE of energy. I don't look at Ja Rule as a rapper," says writer/producer 7 Aurelius. "I look at him more like a musician who plays his instrument. I'll have a song and he'll come in and start vibing with it—just singing along, really melodic. He's a source of very deep, rich melodies. The interesting thing is, he never writes anything down. While recording, he does everything from memory. He'll do so many bars and go back. Irv [Gotti] helps him orchestrate things. Ultimately it's a great team—Ja Rule, Irv and myself."

The Ja in Ja Rule stands for Jeff Atkins, the real name of the rapper born in Hollis, Queens, New York. His earliest musical inspirations were the Stylistics, the O'Jays, Sam Cooke and Otis Redding. "My mom and grandma would play that stuff around the house," he says. But there were outside influences as well. "I used to see Run-D.M.C. riding down Hollis Avenue in a big Caddy. The glamour of it all and the fact that they weren't drug dealers showed me another way I could have that glamour, that swagger, and not be doing the drug thing all my life. That really opened my eyes."

In high school, the rapper was in a group, Cash Money Clique. He met Irv Gotti, who introduced him to rappers like Jay-Z and DMX. Ja Rule made his first appearance on the Hot 100 in 1998 as a featured artist on Jay-Z's "Can I Get a..." He was simply billed as Ja.

As Ja Rule, he charted with songs like "Holla" and "Between Me and You." In September, 2001, he was a featured artist on Jennifer Lopez' number one hit, "I'm Real" [see 917]. Six months later, he was in pole position again, this time as lead artist. The song "Always on Time" began as one of five instrumental tracks written by Aurelius. "I gave Ja Rule a CD of the music," says Aurelius. "He didn't take one I thought he was going to like. I said, 'Are you sure, man?' Then we let Irv hear it. He did not like it."

Ja Rule came up with the title "Always on Time." "If you listen to the track, it had these chords that just punch you right in the face," says Ja Rule. "I loved the track." But he had to act fast to keep it for himself. "The track was going out to Brandy so she could hear it and I grabbed it and did it."

At first, "Always on Time" was meant to be a solo effort by Ja Rule. Gotti told Aurelius he wanted to break Ashanti by featuring her on the song. Aurelius resisted at first, until he heard the result. "Ashanti is such a sweetheart," says Ja Rule. "She was always in the studio, being observant. This was my third album, and sometimes the record label people [insist on] using a big-name artist. 'Go get Beyoncé' or 'Go get this person' but I wanted this to be fresh and new and Ashanti was fresh and new."

"I wasn't prepared for everything to happen the way it did," says Ashanti. "Like my first [public] performance was on 'Saturday Night Live.' They told me a day before I had to do it that I was going to be with Ja Rule singing 'Always on Time.' It prepped me for my own thing." It was the success of the Ja Rule duet that propelled Ashanti's solo career. "We were getting such positive feedback," she says, "that Irv said, 'Let's see if we can make a record. It seems people like you.' So we recorded 'Foolish.'"

The success of "I'm Real" and "Always on Time" created a new sub-genre of music. "I feel I took the hip-hop duet somewhere else," says Ja Rule. "It was always an R&B and rap fusion. It was the rapper doing a 16-bar verse on an R&B record or maybe an R&B person singing the chorus. I do a little harmonizing when I rap, so I took it a little further. Ashanti is on the record just as much as I am."

## THE TOP FIVE
*Week of February 23, 2002*

1 **Always on Time**
Ja Rule f/Ashanti

2 **How You Remind Me**
Nickelback

3 **U Got It Bad**
Usher

4 **Ain't It Funny**
Jennifer Lopez f/Ja Rule

5 **In the End**
Linkin Park

# 922 Ain't It Funny EPIC 79639
## JENNIFER LOPEZ Featuring JA RULE

Writers: Jennifer Lopez
　　　　Cory Rooney
　　　　Irving Lorenzo
　　　　7
　　　　Jeff Atkins
　　　　Caddillac Tah
　　　　Osten Harvey, Jr.
　　　　Craig Mack

Producers: 7
　　　　Irv Gotti
　　　　Cory Rooney
　　　　Dan Shea

March 9, 2002
6 weeks

JUST AS THERE WERE two versions of "I'm Real" [see 917], there were two different tracks called "Ain't It Funny." And once the version of "I'm Real" with Ja Rule was a number one hit, there was only one way to go for the follow-up, according to producer Cory Rooney. "The question was, now that it worked so well, we need to do it again. Do we do it with someone else? I told Tommy [Mottola], 'If it worked for Roberta Flack and Donny Hathaway, then this should work for Jennifer Lopez and Ja Rule. Let's go for it.'"

The original recording of "Ain't It Funny" was inspired by Lopez' film, *The Wedding Planner*, according to Rooney, who recalls that he and Lopez watched scenes from the movie to come up with some music for the soundtrack. "There's a scene where Jennifer is driv-

ing on the road. She's the backseat passenger and Matthew McConaughey and Bridgette Wilson are in the front seat talking about the wedding. It made me feel like, 'Ain't it funny how some feelings you just can't deny and you can't move on even though you try.' All those words and those melodies just started coming to me."

After the idea for "Ain't It Funny" popped into his head, Rooney went home and roughed out the track and came up with a chorus. Then he worked with Lopez for an hour to finish the song. "We looked at the rough cut of the movie and pulled different thoughts and feelings. At the end of the day, the director felt 'Ain't It Funny' had too much Latin influence for the movie, because it had timbales. Jennifer really disagreed, but finally she said to use another song. They wanted 'Love Don't Cost a Thing,' which was a real R&B and pop type of record."

So why do a remix of "Ain't It Funny"? Rooney explains, "Because we had changed the sound of Jennifer Lopez [with "I'm Real"] and we didn't have anything else on the [*J.Lo*] album we could release as a single. We had to do another remix to keep the momentum going."

Enter Ashanti, who stopped off at Irv Gotti's studio in New York just to pick up a check. "Everyone was there and Ja [Rule] was on the floor playing video games, and they had the beat playing in the background. Chris Gotti,

who is Irv's brother, said 'Ja's supposed to be writing this record for J-Lo, but it doesn't look like he's going to be doing anything tonight. Why don't you go in there and see what's happening?' So that's exactly what I did," says Ashanti, who wrote two verses and demoed the new "Ain't It Funny" for Lopez.

Gotti and 7 Aurelius flew to Los Angeles to record the song with Lopez. "I flew out on September 10th," 7 remembers. "We were going to record it on the 11th. We had to postpone it because of everything that happened in New York."

When work resumed, Ashanti got a phone call in New York from Gotti in Los Angeles. He asked her to write another verse. "I had to write it over the phone and two-way Irv the lyrics," she recalls.

When "Ain't It Funny" advanced to number one, it gave Ja Rule two consecutive chart-toppers. He became the fifth artist in the rock era to have back-to-back number one hits, following Elvis Presley, the Beatles, Boyz II Men and Puff Daddy.

## THE TOP FIVE
*Week of March 9, 2002*

1　**Ain't It Funny**
　Jennifer Lopez f/Ja Rule

2　**Always on Time**
　Ja Rule f/Ashanti

3　**How You Remind Me**
　Nickelback

4　**In the End**
　Linkin Park

5　**Hey Baby**
　No Doubt f/Bounty Killer

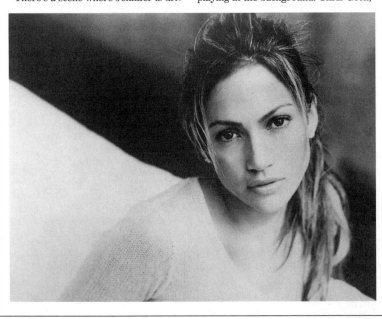

# Foolish
## ASHANTI

**923**

*Writers: Ashanti Douglas*
*Irving Lorenzo*
*Marcus Vest*
*Mark DeBarge*
*Etterlene Jordan*

*Producer: Irv Gotti*

*April 20, 2002*
*10 weeks*

"**M**Y DAD HAD ME listening to the Temptations, Blue Magic, Heatwave and the Delfonics. Growing up, I was listening to hip-hop and R&B," says Ashanti Douglas of her musical education. "I went to dance school. I did tap, jazz, ballet." Singing was another matter. "It was an accident how my mom found out I could sing. I was downstairs doing chores. My mom said, 'No radio, no television. It takes you too long when you're not paying attention.' So I'm vacuuming and she comes flying down the steps yelling at me, 'I thought I told you no radio.' And I said, 'Ma, that wasn't the radio. That was me singing.' She made me sing it again. She called my dad and then we started doing local talent shows not too far from my house and linked up with my co-manager and started shopping a deal."

Ashanti was only 14 when she wrote her first song. That was also the year she was signed to the Jive label. That deal and a subsequent one with Noontime/Epic didn't pan out. "It was bittersweet," she admits. "It was almost there, then we'd get a letdown. It hurt to keep going through the same thing. But I'd been doing it for too long. It didn't make sense to stop."

Through co-manager Linda Burke, Ashanti met Mario Baeza of AJM Records and recorded material in his studio. "Mario happened to know Irv Gotti, so he set up a meeting," Ashanti explains. She says the Murder Inc. label founder told her his company was strictly hip-hop and that he wasn't interested in an R&B artist. "I was persistent and kept coming to the office and the studio and he said, 'Alright, let me see what we can do.' I started writing and he got interested that way." Gotti found reasons to employ Ashanti. "Whenever I needed some singing on a hook, I'd call her," he told Rashaun Hall in *Billboard*. "Or I'd tell her to write something and she'd keep acing those tests. She had flow, bounce and content."

Meanwhile, writer/producer 7 Aurelius (Marcus Vest) had received a request from Craig Kallman of Atlantic Records for a song for British R&B singer Craig David. After laying down the music track, 7 Aurelius let Gotti hear it. Aurelius remembers, "One day I came in the studio and Irv said, 'Ashanti wrote something to the track. I think I'm going to call it "Foolish."'"

When Gotti first played the track for Ashanti, the singer protested, because it included a sample of DeBarge's "Stay With Me," which had already been sampled in "One More Time" by the Notorious B.I.G. Ashanti recalls, "I'm all amped to hear it. I said, 'Come on, Irv. That's Biggie Smalls. I don't want to come out as a new artist with one of Biggie's classic records. That's a lot of pressure.'" Gotti asked Ashanti to trust him. "He gave me the concept to write about a girl dealing with a guy who doesn't do the right thing but she stays with the guy. So I write it. I go in the vocal booth and do it. He comes back and he's screaming, 'I love it!'"

Gotti introduced Ashanti to the world by having her sing as a featured artist on Ja Rule's "Always on Time" [see 921]. She was also featured on Fat Joe's "What's Luv?" which peaked at number two. So her name was well-known by the time "Foolish" debuted. Those first three chart entries all occupied the top 10 of the Hot 100 at the same time, making Ashanti the first artist to have her first three chart titles appear in the top 10 simultaneously since the Beatles did it in 1964.

## THE TOP FIVE
*Week of April 20, 2002*

1 **Foolish**
Ashanti

2 **What's Luv?**
Fat Joe f/Ashanti

3 **Ain't It Funny**
Jennifer Lopez f/Ja Rule

4 **U Don't Have to Call**
Usher

5 **Girlfriend**
'N Sync f/Nelly

# 924 Hot in Herre
### NELLY
FO' REEL 015976

**Writers:** *Charles Brown*
*Nelly*
*Pharrell Williams*
*Chad Hugo*

**Producers:** *The Neptunes*

June 29, 2002
7 weeks

HE'S COME A LONG WAY from St. Louis, but Cornell Haynes, Jr. did not forget his roots, nor his friends. He was born in Texas, and lived in Spain with his mother and Air Force father before settling in St. Louis, Missouri. After getting into trouble at different schools, he moved with his mother to the University City suburb. In high school, he excelled in sports and it looked like he might have a future in professional baseball. But then he formed the rap crew St. Lunatics with pals Kyjuan, City Spud, Murphy Lee, Ali and Jason. Together, they scored a local hit in 1996 with "Gimme What Ya Got," a 12-inch single. "St. Louis didn't have a hip-hop scene," says Nelly. "We borrowed it from everybody else's. That's why the style is so universal, because I take aspects from every region of hip-hop—east coast, west coast and down south and that's how you get the Midwest sound."

Despite impressive sales and airplay in St. Louis, the St. Lunatics couldn't get a national break. When they were asked to guest star on an album by an artist named Kardan, the group felt that Nelly would stand out more if he did it on his own. When the track that featured him was heard on a mix tape by DJ Clue, Nelly was offered a deal with Universal Records.

His first album, *Country Grammar,* included the hit singles "(Hot S**t) Country Grammar," which peaked at number seven, and "Ride Wit Me," which featured City Spud and went to number three. The multi-platinum success of the first album was topped by the follow-up, *Nellyville.* The first song that went to radio was "Hot in Herre," just in time for summer. The track that suggested, "take off all your clothes" because the party's so hot, was produced by the Neptunes—Pharrell Williams and Chad Hugo.

Williams and Hugo were only 14 when they met in a summer school music class in Virginia Beach, Virginia. Hugo was playing saxophone and keyboards and Williams was a drummer who wrote lyrics and rapped. They

experimented with recording on four-track machines, and worked for Teddy Riley before going out on their own as the Neptunes.

Hugo and Williams kept running into Nelly's people and kept saying they should work together someday. When the day finally came, the Neptunes found Nelly easy to work with. "He knocks out his vocals in no time," says Hugo. "Everything he says is a hook, so despite how wordy it might seem, everyone knows the melody and the lyrics."

The Neptunes based the groove of "Hot in Herre" on "Bustin' Loose," a number one R&B hit for Chuck Brown & the Soul Searchers in February, 1979. Brown had come up with the song three years earlier. "It was just an idea that came to me," he said when interviewed for *The Billboard Book of Number One R&B Hits,* "a syncopation idea, a funky rhythm idea, and I kept hearing it, like an engine turning over in my head. It stayed with me, so I finally wrote a song out of that particular groove."

"A Tribe Called Quest, one of our favorite groups, used the same sample," says Hugo. "We always liked the groove, but we don't sample. We like

being inspired by old grooves. We wanted something simple and everything else was up to Nelly. His voice was the instrument added on top of the simple groove. It was minimal but it was perfect."

Nelly says it didn't take long to come up with the lyrics for "Hot in Herre" once the Neptunes played the track for him. "An idea just jumped in my head when I heard it. When I hear the beat, I usually get an idea right away. If I don't get an idea for the song right away, I usually skip the track."

## THE TOP FIVE
*Week of June 29, 2002*

1  **Hot in Herre**
   Nelly

2  **Without Me**
   Eminem

3  **Foolish**
   Ashanti

4  **I Need a Girl (Part One)**
   P. Diddy f/Usher & Loon

5  **Oh Boy**
   Cam'ron f/Juelz Santana

FO' REEL 019509 **Dilemma**
NELLY Featuring KELLY ROWLAND

**925**

Writers: *Kenny Gamble*
*Bunny Sigler*
*Nelly*
*Bam*
*Ryan Bowser*

Producers: *Bam*
*Ryan Bowser*

*August 17, 2002*
*10 weeks*

WHEN "DILEMMA" SUCCEEDED "HOT in Herre" at the top of the Hot 100, Nelly became the sixth artist in the rock era to collect two consecutive number one hits, following Elvis Presley, the Beatles, Boyz II Men, Puff Daddy and Ja Rule. Nelly was the third artist to accomplish this with his first two chart-toppers, after the Beatles and Puff Daddy.

Nelly had almost completed his *Nellyville* album when he heard a track composed by Bam (Antoine Macon) and Ryan Bowser in St. Louis. Bam and Bowser were playing Tetris one night when they came up with the idea for the song. "The track started with the melody," says Bam, who knew Nelly when he was still Cornell Haynes, Jr. ("Way back in the day before everybody got their deals, we started in the same studio," Bam explains.) "We sat down at the keyboard and messed around. After that, we added drums." Bam and Bowser had some of the lyrics when they played it for Nelly. "He's so creative and he's got so much energy flowing," says Bam. "He just hears [the music] and he writes. Sometimes it's on the spot. He helps you and pulls you through stuff."

The idea of using a sample of the classic R&B cut "Love, Need and Want You" from Patti

LaBelle's 1984 album *I'm in Love Again* came later. "We were listening to the track in the studio and I started humming the Patti LaBelle melody," says Bam. "Nelly heard it and said, 'What's that? What are you singing right there?'" Nelly told Bam and Bowser he wanted to include "Love, Need and Want You" in the track he had named "Dilemma."

"Once I heard it, I wanted to do something special with it," says Nelly. "I wanted to do something that nobody would think of, and that was the reason we brought Kelly [Rowland] into the picture. I thought getting her on a solo tip as opposed to getting her in the group [Destiny's Child] would be hot. Fortunately, it worked."

Rowland didn't believe Nelly wanted her to sing on the track when she first heard about his request. But she was happy to go into the studio to record her part, despite one misgiving. "I was very nervous," she confesses. "Because when you sing a Patti song, or any legend's song, you have to do it correctly." Rowland had a chance to hear from Patti directly when LaBelle was cast as her mother in the video for "Dilemma." Kelly recalls, "We were supposed to be working on the set and they were calling, 'Action!' and we were still chatting." La Belle told Rowland what a great job she did. "I was so happy she said that," says Rowland. "I felt that was the seal of approval, because I had been holding my breath until that moment."

Thanks to the use of "Love, Need and Want You," songwriters Kenny Gamble and Bunny Sigler are listed in the credits for "Dilemma." It was Gamble's sixth number one song over a

span of 29 years, 10 months and two weeks, dating back to Gamble's first chart-topper, Billy Paul's "Me and Mrs. Jones" [see 325]. That's the seventh longest span of number one hits by a songwriter in the rock era. The top three are Lincoln Chase (38 years, nine months and one week, from "Wonderland by Night" by Bert Kaempfert in Junauary, 1961, to "Heartbreaker" in October, 1999), Bob Crewe (38 years, six months and two weeks, from "Big Girls Don't Cry" by the Four Seasons in November, 1962, to "Lady Marmalade" by Christina Aguilera, Lil' Kim, Mya & Pink in June, 2001), and Chip Taylor (34 years and eight months, from "Wild Thing" by the Troggs in July, 1966, to "Angel" by Shaggy Featuring Rayvon in March, 2001). Gamble's career chart span as a songwriter on the Hot 100 is 38 years and two months, dating back to the November, 1964 debut of "The 81" by Candy & the Kisses.

## THE TOP FIVE
*Week of August 17, 2002*

1 **Dilemma**
Nelly f/Kelly Rowland

2 **Hot in Herre**
Nelly

3 **Complicated**
Avril Lavigne

4 **I Need a Girl (Part Two)**
P. Diddy & Ginuwine f/Loon, Mario Winans & Tammy Ruggeri

5 **Just a Friend 2002**
Mario

# 926 A Moment Like This RCA 60622
## KELLY CLARKSON

*Writers: Jorgen Elofsson
John Reid*

*Producers: Stephen Ferrera
Steve Mac*

*October 5, 2002
2 weeks*

FOLLOWING THE SUCCESS OF the TV series "Popstars," Britain's ITV broadcast the "Pop Idol" series, which debuted October 5, 2001. The show was a ratings success, and a record-setting 8.7 million people phoned in to vote for the final two candidates. The ultimate winner was 23-year-old Will Young, with 4.6 million votes. Runner-up was 17-year-old Gareth Gates, with 4.1 million votes. But the final outcome almost didn't matter. Young and Gates both went to number one in the U.K. with their debut singles as well as the follow-ups and a duet remake of the Beatles' "The Long and Winding Road." Third place Darius also topped the singles chart, and from the top 10 finalists, Rik Waller had a top 10 hit and Jessica Garlick was chosen to represent the U.K. at the 2002 Eurovision Song Contest.

It was inevitable that the successful British program would spawn an American version. Series creator Simon Fuller sold the concept to the Fox network in the U.S., and "American Idol" made its debut on June 11, 2002. Subtitled "The Search for a Superstar," the show retained many elements of the U.K. competition, as well as its acid-tongued judge, record executive Simon Cowell.

*American Idol* quickly whittled down its 100 plus contestants to 30, and then down to 10. In subsequent weeks, viewers voted off contestants until only Justin Guarini and Kelly Clarkson remained. On the final broadcast of the first season, shown live on Wednesday, September 4, 2002, the winner was announced: Kelly Clarkson. She reprised the song she and Justin had performed the night before: "A Moment Like This."

One of the people watching Clarkson's triumph at the Kodak Theater in Hollywood was Stephen Ferrera, senior vice president of A&R and staff producer for RCA. "My eyes welled up," he recalls. But when Kelly sang, he was also listening to the backing track, saying to himself, "Why didn't I fix that?" and "I could have done

that better," because the recording had been done in a very quick three days.

Ferrera became involved when RCA Records made the deal to release CDs from *American Idol.* Then–label head Bob Jamieson asked Ferrera to oversee the project. "The concept of bringing television in as a way to market and distribute music sounded amazing to me. In every other country in the world, that is the number one way it's done. In America, it hasn't been like that for many years."

Word went out to songwriters and music publishers that a song was needed for the ultimate winner. "The brief was we were looking not necessarily for a pop ballad," says Ferrera. "We were looking for a song that was going to be a postcard from the show, a memento in the same way as the closing song of the Olympics. It would contain the sentiment of the evening, and in subsequent hearings would bring you back to the excitement of what the show is all about."

The submissions were arriving three or four weeks before the live telecast of the last show in the season, giving Ferrera little time to sift through them all. But there was an obvious choice—"A Moment Like This," written by Jorgen Elofsson and John Reid. "When we finally isolated the song, there were four finalists and we had no way of knowing who was going to win," says Ferrara. "So we had to record the complete song with the four finalists. They all sing in different keys. We had to get string arrangements in four different keys and make four records." British producer Steve Mac was called in to work on the project, but was called back to the U.K. suddenly when his pregnant wife's due date arrived.

Ferrera and Mac had completed the vocals of the four finalists when Mac had to fly home. Tamyra Gray was eliminated, and Ferrera continued to reshape the track until Nikki McKibbin was voted off the show. "Then it was down to Justin and Kelly. I redid the backing track, because I knew it was down to their two specific styles. We cut the drums and guitars and put more keyboards on, and a new gospel

choir and had them both come in and recut their vocals to the new tracks." On the Thursday before Labor Day, each one had two hours to record their vocals. By Monday night both versions were ready to be mastered. On Wednesday night Clarkson was named the winner. Her single shipped the next day.

While she wasn't keen on the song the first time she heard it, Clarkson did grow to love "A Moment Like This." "It fit perfectly with the end of the show," she says. She was thrilled to learn that a 52-1 move on the Hot 100 gave her the biggest jump to the top in the chart's history. "I was so excited. They told me I broke a record and that was even cooler."

## THE TOP FIVE
*Week of October 5, 2002*

1 **A Moment Like This**
Kelly Clarkson

2 **Dilemma**
Nelly f/Kelly Rowland

3 **Gangsta Lovin'**
Eve f/Alicia Keys

4 **Complicated**
Avril Lavigne

5 **Cleanin' Out My Closet**
Eminem

*Writers: Marshall Mathers*
*Jeff Bass*
*Luis Resto*

*Producer: Eminem*

*November 9, 2002*
*12 weeks*

Marshall Mathers was a poor kid growing up in the Detroit suburb of Warren, Michigan. A high school dropout, he had a talent for rhyming and became a star in the hip-hop underground. In the film *8 Mile*, Mathers, better known as Eminem, plays Jimmy, a poor kid in Detroit who has a talent for rhyming and becomes a star in the hip-hop underground. Portraying a fictional version of himself won Eminem accolades for his acting; Richard Schickel wrote in *Time*, "His screen debut shows that he has it in him to become an authentic movie star. He's a kid with the ability to put a sullen but seductive face on an open heart."

In its first week of release, *8 Mile* topped the box office chart. It's a position Eminem was accustomed to, having topped The Billboard 200 with *The Marshall Mathers LP* and *The Eminem Show* and international singles charts with hits like "Stan" and "Without Me." But he didn't reach pole position on the Hot 100 until November, 2002, when "Lose Yourself," heard over the closing credits of *8 Mile*, settled in for a 12-week run, becoming the third longest-running number one hit from a soundtrack in the rock era, behind

Whitney Houston's "I Will Always Love You" [see 813] and Boyz II Men's "End of the Road" [see 811].

For his film *8 Mile*, director Curtis Hanson wanted a song written from the point of view of Eminem's character. On location in Detroit, Eminem had a makeshift studio in a trailer so he could work on the music for the movie. "That's where I first heard 'Lose Yourself,'" says co-writer and keyboardist Luis Resto. "It had been around for a little bit, maybe four months. He and Jeff [Bass] had come up with the primary riff—that guitar. Later, I heard earlier versions that were pretty different. One of the earlier versions was over a completely different rhythm. The chunk guitar was there but different guitar parts were there that I hadn't heard. We used it as one of the variations in the movie, a take-off of the theme."

When Resto first heard the track, lyrics were just being written. "He was searching for exactly what the verses needed to be talking about. He had the notion it was going to be locked into the flick, but it wasn't committed yet. I remember hearing the hook, 'Lose yourself in the moment,' then it would go off into a mumble because he hadn't completed it. We did a couple of keyboard parts and then next time he had a pretty full version of the lyrics. Marshall's lyrics are definitely controversial and some of the places he goes rubs people the wrong way. He's one of the most truthful cats I've ever met. He's not going to hold back. He means what he says and I

enjoy that about him. When I heard 'Lose Yourself,' it was such a positive statement and you could see how adept he is at writing."

There was still work to be done on the track. "He wanted to build the song," says Resto. "The song is one huge build. It's like he has orchestras going in his head—it's pretty wild to see how his head worked because I studied music at the University of Michigan and I'm very familiar with counterpoint. He never studied music and the way he communicated his ideas is by humming to you. So that's what I do—I hear them, I play them, and if one needs a bit of refinement, I do it. He either approves or disapproves. I gave my input, but that structure you hear on 'Lose Yourself' is really Marshall speaking. It's surprising how he can take three or four counter-thoughts and make them all work. He spits them out of his head one at a time, and it's the same with his raps."

The bulk of the recording was completed in two sessions, followed by some tweaking. "He will run down a vocal and do a take. He'll listen and he's pretty tough on himself to lay exactly where he wants it to lay. You'll have a main vocal and he'll do a double where you accent parts. He'll have a triple, a quad. After they are sounding pretty good to me, he will redo them all. When you hear the final product, you know he was right. I would have been flying with his first vocal because it sounds great, but he knows how he wants to ride the beat. It's just this razor sharp groove that he does when he raps."

## THE TOP FIVE
*Week of November 9, 2002*

1  **Lose Yourself**
   Eminem

2  **Dilemma**
   Nelly f/Kelly Rowland

3  **Work It**
   Missy "Misdemeanor" Elliott

4  **Hey Ma**
   Cam'ron f/Juelz Santana, Freekey
   Zekey & Toya

5  **A Moment Like This**
   Kelly Clarkson

## 928 Bump, Bump, Bump T.U.G. 79829
### B2K & P. DIDDY

*Writers: R. Kelly*
*Varick Smith*

*Producer: R. Kelly*

*February 1, 2003*
*1 week*

B2K's FIRST TWO SINGLES were big hits—but only on the sales chart. Radio didn't warm to "Uh-Huh," which went to number one on Hot 100 Singles Sales in January, 2002, but only reached number 37 on the Hot 100. A similar thing happened to the follow-up, "Gots ta Be," which peaked at number six on Hot 100 Singles Sales, but only went to number 34 on the Hot 100. The young R&B quartet broke down radio's resistance to grant them airplay with the first single from their second album, *Pandemonium.* "Bump, Bump, Bump," produced and co-written by R. Kelly, was a sales hit as well as an airplay hit, allowing the song to achieve pole position on the Hot 100.

The group started as a Los Angeles-based trio, consisting of J-Boog (Jarrell Houston), Raz-B (De'mario Thornton) and Lil Fizz (Dreux Frederic). Raz-B's cousin, Chris Stokes, managed the group and added Omarion (Omari Grandberry) as the fourth member. The quartet turned to current events to find a name. "It was 2000 and the whole Y2K thing was going on," says J-Boog. "We were Y2K at first but it didn't really mean anything. So we wondered what to change the Y to so it could fit with 2K. We decided to go through the alphabet. B was the second letter. It stands for Boys of the New Millennium." The group was discovered by Max Gousse, vice president of A&R for the Epic Record Group. "I had some talent searches in L.A. and the guys auditioned," says Gousse. "I was mesmerized the first time I saw them because of the chemistry they had and the bond they had as a group. It was clear they were going to be successful."

The *Pandemonium* album reflected the group's maturity. "When they were signed, they were 15," says Gousse. "By the time we marketed and promoted the first album, they had turned 17. So now you have 18-year-olds, and their perspective changes when they hit their late teens. They had a lot of things they wanted to say, so we got them in with producers and they wrote a good portion of the album."

One of the producers involved with

B2K's second album was R. Kelly. "David McPherson, who is the head of urban music at Epic, had a good working relationship with Robert since his Jive days," Gousse explains. "Kelly gave him a record and we made the call that it felt good for B2K. When the guys heard it, they loved it right away, and then we reached out to P. Diddy. He expressed an interest in working with the group from the first album after he saw the video. He was very impressed by their energy and dancing ability. We had discussions about who would fit the track and we felt that Diddy would be a natural fit, and he gladly obliged. He got involved with the recording—he participated in the mix."

P. Diddy enlisted a writer he had worked with, Varick Smith, to come up with his rap for "Bump, Bump, Bump." Smith had met Sean "P. Diddy" Combs at a taping of "The Tonight Show Starring Jay Leno" in 2001 and let the Bad Boy founder know he wanted to write for him. That led to work with Diddy as well as Faith Evans, and composing songs for the *Barbershop* soundtrack.

Smith was in Atlanta on a seven-hour stopover on his way to his home in the Little Haiti section of Miami when he wrote his part of "Bump, Bump, Bump." "B2K's lyrics were already done," he says. "There were only two verses and Puffy's part. I checked into a hotel and wrote the song in 10 minutes. You know what you

want Puffy to say and what he's going to respond to. At the same time, you want to be original and bring some creativity, so he can appreciate you as a writer. I know he wanted something sexy, because it was called 'Bump, Bump, Bump.' I had to stick with the concept of the song."

B2K recorded their part of the song in New York. "The guys were extremely excited about working with Robert," says Gousse. "He sent us the Pro Tools and we recorded the vocals with a few adjustments here and there, but overall it's pretty close to the demo he sent us." J-Boog adds, "It felt like the way it was done was tight. If we changed it, we could have ruined it, so we kind of imitated his voice a little bit and it turned out really good."

### THE TOP FIVE
*Week of February 1, 2003*

1 **Bump, Bump, Bump**
   B2K & P. Diddy

2 **Beautiful**
   Christina Aguilera

3 **Cry Me a River**
   Justin Timberlake

4 **I'm With You**
   Avril Lavigne

5 **All I Have**
   Jennifer Lopez f/LL Cool J

Writers: *Jennifer Lopez*
*Makeba Riddick*
*Curtis Richardson*
*Ron G*
*Lisa Peters*
*William Jeffrey*

Producers: *Cory Rooney*
*Ron G*
*David McPherson*

*February 8, 2003*
*4 weeks*

PRODUCER CORY ROONEY HAD completed work on Jennifer Lopez' *This Is Me... Then* album. Or so he thought. "Tommy Mottola called me, along with his guy at the label, Dave McPherson. Dave said, 'I know the album is finished and it's great. There's this one song I really think we're going to need.' Jennifer and I felt like we were done. Dave said, 'All I'm asking you to do is listen to it' and Tommy said, 'Cory, you have to structure this song, maybe rewrite some things and change some things around, but if you work with it, I think we can have a big record for Jennifer.'"

Rooney wondered what the problem was with the track, and thought Mottola and McPherson were preparing him to hate the song. "They let me hear it and it was really rough. I said, 'I really like it. Give me the tape.' I went right into the studio that same night and spent about three hours restructuring it and rewriting it. I called in [Makeba Riddick], the original lyricist, and she and I mapped it all out."

Before Mottola and McPherson told Rooney about the song, it began with a suggestion from an Epic promotion

staffer to McPherson, the label's executive vice president, about covering a Debra Laws song from 1981, "Very Special," written by William Jeffrey and Lisa Peters. Laws' single peaked at number 90 on the Hot 100, and number 11 on the R&B chart. Instead of covering the song, McPherson got together with producer Ron G, who came up with a new track that sampled "Very Special." "It took me one day," says Ron G. "One day to do the track and a day to mix it in my studio." McPherson then called Makeba Riddick, who had signed to Bad Boy as a writer and was on her way to Miami. She told McPherson he would have to call her back when she returned. "I didn't think he was serious," says Riddick. "Sure enough, the day I got back, he called and said he needed me to go in the studio that day."

With little time to spare, Riddick and her writing partner, Curtis Richardson, wrote the lyrics in 15 minutes. "That's a very personal song," says Riddick. "Curtis and I were both going through something when we wrote it."

The original title of the song was "I'm Good." McPherson notes, "She says that throughout the song. I thought it was too close to one of her other big hits, 'I'm Real.' One of the hooks in the song is 'all I have,' and that sounded like a good title."

Lopez hadn't heard the song yet when Rooney approached LL Cool J about guest starring on the track. "He's a longtime friend and my neighbor," says Rooney. "He and I met at Benihana's and I played him the record. He was blown away by it. I said this is a great thing for him, and he felt the same. He agreed to do it, and then we let Jennifer hear it. She was one of the last people to hear the record. She said it was a great song and she couldn't wait to do it." Lopez was in Philadelphia filming a movie, so she drove to New York City to meet up with LL Cool J and record the song with Rooney at the Hit Factory.

"All I Have" became Lopez' fourth number one hit, and the first for LL Cool J, born James Todd Smith in Queens, New York. His nickname stood for "Ladies Love Cool James." He was only 13 when he started sending out demos to record labels. Rick Rubin

signed the young rapper and released a 12-inch single of "I Need a Beat" as the very first Def Jam single in 1984, when LL Cool J was only 16. A year later, "I Can't Live Without My Radio" debuted on the R&B singles chart. LL Cool J made his Hot 100 debut the week of July 11, 1987, with "I'm Bad," which only went to number 84. His biggest hits before achieving pole position with "All I Have" were "Hey Lover" in 1995 and "Loungin" in 1996. Both peaked at number three. But LL Cool J was rewarded for his patience: from the time of his debut on the Hot 100 to his first number one hit, he had waited 16 years and seven months.

## THE TOP FIVE
*Week of February 8, 2003*

1 **All I Have**
Jennifer Lopez f/LL Cool J

2 **Bump, Bump, Bump**
B2K & P. Diddy

3 **Beautiful**
Christina Aguilera

4 **I'm With You**
Avril Lavigne

5 **Mesmerize**
Ja Rule f/Ashanti

## 930 In Da Club SHADY/AFTERMATH 497856
### 50 CENT

*Writers: Curtis Jackson*
*Andre Young*
*Michael Elizondo*

*Producers: Dr. Dre*
*Michael Elizondo*

*March 8, 2003*
*9 weeks*

A FORTUITOUS MEETING WITH Jam Master Jay of Run-D.M.C. changed the direction of Curtis Jackson's life. Born July 6, 1976, in South Jamaica, Queens, New York, Jackson was raised by his grandparents after his mother was murdered at age 23. His grandparents didn't know he was using and dealing drugs by the time he was 12. Seven years later he was running a local drug cartel. But fate had something else in store for the man who decided to call himself 50 Cent.

"I'm named after a gangster from the Fort Greene projects," he explains. "There was another 50 Cent ahead of me who was run-ning around the street. Me finding success as a rap artist is a dream that's bigger than anything that guy has ever done in his life but he'll be remembered because of that name."

50 Cent's life changed the day a friend of his was talking with Jam Master Jay. "I was able to work my way into the conversation. He wanted to find and develop a new artist and I told him I rap. He helped me develop my song structure, because I didn't know how to count bars or anything. My friends had turntables and we would buy singles and write our own lyrics to the instrumental, but we never stopped writing at 16 bars and made the chorus fit or have a four-bar chorus that repeats twice."

An album's worth of material was recorded, but Jam Master Jay was busy touring and wasn't able to focus on 50 Cent, who moved on to a deal with Columbia Records. "Three days before I was supposed to shoot a video for my single 'Thug Love' with Destiny's Child, I got shot. [The folks] at Columbia Records were afraid to work with me after I got shot."

The incident took place May 24, 2000. On his way to a tattoo parlor in Queens, 50 Cent was shot nine times. Miraculously, he survived, but carries a bullet fragment in his tongue, and a hole in his jaw gives him a distinctive slur. Dropped from Columbia, he worked on mix-tape albums for the independent G-Unit label. He sent tracks to Eminem's manager, and in June, 2002, Eminen and Dr. Dre signed 50 Cent to Shady/Aftermath. "Wanksta" was included in the *8 Mile* soundtrack.

Dr. Dre and Michael Elizondo had a track they wanted the group D-12 to record for *8 Mile*. "We were goofing around. It started with the pizzicato string sound," says Elizondo. The track didn't make it into the movie and went on the backburner. "We stored it on DAT and once 50 Cent's deal was solidified, he came into the studio. Dre played him a bunch of ideas and when he heard that track he said, 'Give me a notepad!'" says Elizondo. "He wrote ['In Da Club'], verses and choruses, in an hour. He recorded the bulk of his vocals that night as he wrote. While he was writing, we starting laying the idea to Pro Tools and built the track."

When it came time to choose his first single, there were a couple of tracks considered frontrunners. "The decision was made at the last minute," says Elizondo. 50 Cent met with Dre and Eminem, who favored "If I Can't." 50 Cent asked Dre which song he liked, and the producer replied, "In Da Club." 50 Cent says, "Dre and Em have both been able to sell records worldwide, so that humbles me and allows me to consider what they're saying."

## THE TOP FIVE
*Week of March 8, 2003*

1 **In Da Club**
50 Cent

2 **All I Have**
Jennifer Lopez f/LL Cool J

3 **Mesmerize**
Ja Rule f/Ashanti

4 **Miss You**
Aaliyah

5 **Cry Me a River**
Justin Timberlake

*Writers: Sean Paul Henriques*
*Steven Marsden*

*Producer: Steven Marsden*

*May 10, 2003*
*3 weeks*

Born in Kingston, Jamaica, on January 8, 1975, Sean Paul Henriques grew up listening to the music his mother loved—ballads by the Beatles, the Carpenters and Simon and Garfunkel. He heard the popular reggae hits of the day on the radio, while picking up some of the lesser-known tunes in the streets. "I used to sing along but never knew most of the words," he admits. As a teenager, he tried writing his own songs, with a modern influence. "I call hip-hop the cousin to dancehall music. I think people who listen to hip-hop should get the way I'm rhyming even though they don't know every word I say."

Sean's father knew the members of the popular Jamaican band Third World. "He took me to [Stephen] 'Cat' Coore, the guitar player. He was the first one to hear my music and say, 'That's really some good stuff.'" With Coore's encouragement, Sean spent a couple of years recording demos and trying to find a good home base. "I landed at Heartsong Recording Studio, doing little jingles and songs for sound systems. It blew up to the point where there was so much buzz on me, a producer recorded my song 'Baby Girl.'" That 1996 hit and "Infiltrate" in 1998 helped spread Sean Paul's reputation beyond the borders of Jamaica. After several more hit singles in the Caribbean, the VP label released his first album, *Stage One.* Two of his songs, "Deport Them" and "Hot Gal Today," appeared on *Billboard*'s Hot R&B/Hip-Hop Singles & Tracks chart.

While working at Penthouse Studios, Sean met a keyboardist for Buju Banton's band. "We call him 'Lenky' because he is skinny and lanky and long. His real name is Steven Marsden. We voiced a song a couple of years ago which didn't do too much, but it sealed up a relationship." Marsden built his own studio and recorded a multi-artist album titled *Diwali,* after a rhythm named for a Hindu festival of lights. The CD included "No Letting Go" by Wayne Wonder and "Get Busy" by Sean Paul. "I did some different overdubs on them to give each song a different identity," Marsden told *Billboard's* Rashaun Hall. "With Sean, I added more strings to give a more mystic feel to the track."

Sean Paul wrote the lyrics to "Get Busy" over two nights. "It was such an energized riddim," he says. "Everybody in Jamaica loved the clap-hand effect in the song. I thought, people want to dance. 'Get hot, get down, get busy.' That was the first line, so when the MC or DJ bring it in the dancehall, hopefully the ladies will get busy and start jumping around and screaming. Then I started to think about other words like, 'Crunked up and percolate' to try and make our audience in the U.S. understand some of the things I'm saying. If you say 'crunked up and percolate' you're talking about getting hyped up at a party. It's like a player's song in the chorus where I'm saying, 'It's all good girl, turn me on till the early morn, let's get it on.'"

Marsden liked the line, "Shake that thing," and thought it should be at the beginning. "I'm calling a lot of girls' names," explains Sean. "There's a girl I know named Kana, another named Annabella, another girl named Jodi, another named Rebecca. It was the perfect intro."

When "Get Busy" moved into pole position, Sean Paul became the fourth Jamaican-born artist to have a number one hit in the U.S. His predecessors were Carl Douglas [see 385—"Kung Fu Fighting"], Ini Kamoze [see 832—"Here Comes the Hotstepper"] and Shaggy [see 907—"It Wasn't Me"].

## THE TOP FIVE
*Week of May 10, 2003*

1 **Get Busy**
Sean Paul

2 **In Da Club**
50 Cent

3 **Ignition**
R. Kelly

4 **21 Questions**
50 Cent f/Nate Dogg

5 **Rock Your Body**
Justin Timberlake

# 21 Questions SHADY/AFTERMATH 080739
## 50 CENT Featuring NATE DOGG

Writers: *Curtis Jackson*
*Kevin Risto*
*Jimmie Cameron*
*Vella Cameron*

Producer: *Midi Mafia*

May 31, 2003
4 weeks

Asked if he thought people would be surprised that he included a softer song like "21 Questions" on his album *Get Rich or Die Tryin'*, 50 Cent candidly replies, "They're probably more surprised that I like women. Because in the past guys who do lyrics [with a] similar lyrical content to 50 Cent were so hard that they weren't able to say things that would make people feel like they were actually interested in women. They would make records that say, 'My ho's a trick,' like Snoop Dogg. I love Snoop's music, but that's the kind of material... they expect from 50 Cent. I'm not currently in a relationship, so those are the 21 questions I would be interested in asking a woman now."

"21 Questions" started as a beat composed by Canadian musician Kevin Risto, aka Dirty Swift of Midi Mafia. "We've got hundreds of beats," he explains. "That one I made in Brooklyn, for no particular reason. I came up with the guitar riff and the beat came out of it. It wasn't for any specific purpose." Risto came up with the idea of sampling a Barry White song, "It's Only Love Doing Its Thing," written by Jimmie and Vella Cameron. "When I made the beat, I was playing

with the intro to this Barry White song, the guitar part, and I chopped it up and made a different melody out of it. The sound was kind of gritty. I was going to have someone replay it, but the sample sounded really good, so we left it."

Risto gave the track to Dino Devaille, senior vice president of A&R for Universal Music. "He was looking to sign 50 Cent about a year before he did the Shady deal, when a few other labels were bidding for him. Dino passed some beats to him and he picked a few and '21 Questions' was one of them."

50 Cent elaborates, "They can give me 20 tracks on a CD and there'll be one that feels incredible to me and I'll do it. Like Midi Mafia, when I worked with his material, I made '21 Questions.' I told him, 'I'm going to use this one,' and he said, 'Are you sure?' I said, 'Yeah, it's a hit record.'" 50 Cent took the track and wrote the lyrics. "Some people like to write their lyrics before they even hear the record, but I like to write my lyrics to the music that I'm actually going to use it for. I start with the chorus, because the chorus is the song. That's what it's about. That and the opening statement. When I play a new artist's CD, he has 10 seconds on each song to catch my interest."

Risto first heard 50 Cent's completed track over the phone. "It sounded crazy. When he did the deal with Dre, Dre mixed the record and added Nate Dogg to the chorus. Originally it was 50 Cent singing the hook."

"21 Questions" became a hit while 50 Cent's previous number one [see 930—

"In Da Club"] was still in its prime. It wasn't originally scheduled to be the follow-up, according to Risto. "It was more of a female-friendly record. It was set to be the third single. They were trying to go with something more uptempo, but when the album came out, the amount of spins '21 Questions' was getting was doubling every week and it was charting. It was number one in Dallas before anybody was even working the record, so they had no choice."

When "21 Questions" broke out, Risto came up with an answer song that *really* was an answer song. "We thought of '21 Answers.' We got in touch with Lil' Mo and she did it immediately. We needed a rapper, and Free did it and it went straight to radio. Elektra took the record and stripped it on to Lil' Mo's new album and that was it."

---

## THE TOP FIVE
*Week of May 31, 2003*

1 **21 Questions**
 50 Cent f/Nate Dogg

2 **Get Busy**
 Sean Paul

3 **I Know What You Want**
 Busta Rhymes & Mariah Carey
 f/the Flipmode Squad

4 **Can't Let You Go**
 Fabolous f/Mike Shorey & Lil' Mo

5 **Ignition**
 R. Kelly

*Writers: Aldo Nova*
*Gary Burr*
*Chris Braide*

*Producer: Steve Mac*

*June 28, 2003*
*2 weeks*

**C**LAY AIKEN HAD ALREADY filled out his application to be a contestant on the reality series "The Amazing Race" when a friend convinced him he should try out for "American Idol" instead. Born in Raleigh, North Carolina, on November 30, 1978, Aiken had been singing since he was three years old—he would visit his mom at the Sears department store where she worked and stand on the carpet samples, vocalizing for a dollar. He sang with the Raleigh Boys Choir, and in church, and in high school musicals, but decided against going for a music degree in college in favor of studying special education. "I'm so not big on instability, and I did not want to knock on doors for the rest of my life and hope somebody would hear me," Aiken explains. He planned to study for six years, go for a Masters Degree, and figured by the time he was 50 he'd be a school principal.

An agency placed him with the Bubel family in Charlotte to work with their autistic son, Mike. Mike's mother is the one who told Aiken he should try out for "American Idol." "She kept bugging me. I said, 'Fine. I'll do it if you stop nagging me.'" Aiken went to an audition sponsored by the Fox affiliate in Charlotte. He didn't win, but Diane Bubel insisted he go to the Atlanta audition.

Co-executive producer Nigel Lythgoe told Aiken he was a crooner, and suggested he sing directly to Paula Abdul when he went before the judges the next day. But Abdul was absent, and Aiken sang Heatwave's "Always and Forever" for Simon Cowell and Randy Jackson. Cowell said Aiken didn't look like a pop star. Jackson liked his voice. He was through to Hollywood and the next round of auditions.

Aiken made it into the top 32, but when his group of eight competed, he wasn't voted into the top two. He was given a reprieve when the judges picked him for the "Wild Card" show, where he received the highest amount of votes, assuring him a place in the top 12. Week by week, contestants were voted off the show, and when there were only four left, they were taken to the Beverly Hills Hotel to meet the head of RCA and J Records, Clive Davis. The label president told Aiken and Ruben Studdard, Kimberley Locke and Josh Gracin he had two songs to play for them, and had assigned one song to two of them and the other to the remaining two. "Clive played 'This Is the Night' first and I got chills," says Aiken. "Remember, this is the first time that we had heard these songs and we're realizing this song is going to be the 'A Moment Like This' [see 926] of this year. I almost cried. It was such an amazing song. Then he played 'Flying Without Wings' and it was a great song and I loved it, but it didn't do what 'This Is the Night' did for me. And then he said, '"This Is The Night," the first song I played, I'm going to assign...' and I had my fingers crossed, 'Please God, let it be me.' He said, 'That's the song for Clay and Josh.' Yes!"

Studdard and Locke recorded "Flying Without Wings." Aiken went into a Southern California studio with producer Steve Mac and recorded "This Is the Night." The song had been written for the first season of the series at a songwriting camp run by Desmond Child. During one session, songwriters Aldo Nova, Gary Burr and Chris Braide were teamed up and wrote the song based on a melody composed by Nova. Braide sang the demo that Davis played for the final four contestants.

Gracin was voted off the show, and then Locke. On the final broadcast of the second season of "American Idol," Studdard won by a narrow margin. But then Cowell announced that Studdard and Aiken would both be releasing records, and that's when Aiken found out he was being signed to RCA. "This Is the Night" was released June 10, the same day Studdard's "Flying Without Wings" came out on J. Aiken's single sold almost 393,000 copies, the highest one-week total since Elton John's "Candle in the Wind 1997" [see 860]. "This Is the Night" debuted at number one on the Hot 100 and "Flying Without Wings" opened at number two, the first time in the history of the chart that the top two songs were new entries. Five weeks after it was released, Aiken's single was certified platinum by the RIAA.

## THE TOP FIVE
*Week of June 28, 2003*

1. **This Is the Night**
   Clay Aiken

2. **Flying Without Wings**
   Ruben Studdard

3. **21 Questions**
   50 Cent f/Nate Dogg

4. **Get Busy**
   Sean Paul

5. **Magic Stick**
   Lil' Kim f/50 Cent

# Debuts at Number One

| | | |
|---|---|---|
| You Are Not Alone | Michael Jackson | 1995 |
| Fantasy | Mariah Carey | 1995 |
| Exhale (Shoop Shoop) | Whitney Houston | 1995 |
| One Sweet Day | Mariah Carey & Boyz II Men | 1995 |
| I'll Be Missing You | Puff Daddy & Faith Evans (f/112) | 1997 |
| Honey | Mariah Carey | 1997 |
| Candle in the Wind 1997 / Something About the Way You Look Tonight | Elton John | 1997 |
| My Heart Will Go On | Celine Dion | 1998 |
| I Don't Want to Miss a Thing | Aerosmith | 1998 |
| Doo Wop (That Thing) | Lauryn Hill | 1998 |
| I'm Your Angel* | R. Kelly & Celine Dion | 1998 |
| This Is the Night | Clay Aiken | 2003 |

*"I'm Your Angel" appeared to move 46-1 on the Hot 100, but that was illusory. The song did not appear on the Hot 100 dated November 28, 1998, but was number one the following week. However, chart rules were changed the week of December 5, 1998, to allow songs that were not released as singles to chart. The numbers in the "last week" column were from a test chart that incorporated the new policy.

# The Biggest Jumps to Number One

| | | | |
|---|---|---|---|
| 52 to 1 | A Moment Like This | Kelly Clarkson | 2002 |
| 27 to 1 | Can't Buy Me Love | The Beatles | 1964 |
| 23 to 1 | The Boy Is Mine | Brandy & Monica | 1998 |
| 21 to 1 | U Remind Me | Usher | 2001 |
| 16 to 1 | Heartbreaker | Mariah Carey f/Jay-Z | 1999 |
| 15 to 1 | Paperback Writer | The Beatles | 1966 |
| 15 to 1 | All My Life | K-Ci & JoJo | 1998 |
| 14 to 1 | Say My Name | Destiny's Child | 2000 |
| 12 to 1 | Tequila | The Champs | 1958 |
| 12 to 1 | Uncle Albert/Admiral Halsey | Paul and Linda McCartney | 1971 |
| 12 to 1 | I Will Always Love You | Whitney Houston | 1992 |
| 11 to 1 | Sherry | The Four Seasons | 1962 |
| 11 to 1 | Walk Right In | The Rooftop Singers | 1963 |
| 11 to 1 | Come On Over Baby (All I Want Is You) | Christina Aguilera | 2000 |
| 10 to 1 | The Chipmunk Song | The Chipmunks w/David Seville | 1958 |
| 10 to 1 | Honey | Bobby Goldsboro | 1968 |
| 10 to 1 | The Long and Winding Road / For You Blue | The Beatles | 1970 |
| 10 to 1 | The Night the Lights Went Out in Georgia | Vicki Lawrence | 1973 |
| 10 to 1 | 50 Ways to Leave Your Lover | Paul Simon | 1976 |
| 9 to 1 | All Shook Up | Elvis Presley | 1957 |
| 9 to 1 | It's My Party | Lesley Gore | 1963 |
| 9 to 1 | My Love | Petula Clark | 1966 |
| 9 to 1 | Hello, I Love You | The Doors | 1968 |
| 9 to 1 | Black and White | Three Dog Night | 1972 |
| 9 to 1 | The Morning After | Maureen McGovern | 1973 |

# The Biggest Jumps to Number One

| 8 to 1 | In the Year 2525 (Exordium & Terminus) | Zager & Evans | 1969 |
|---|---|---|---|
| 8 to 1 | Island Girl | Elton John | 1975 |
| 8 to 1 | Tonight's the Night (Gonna Be Alright) | Rod Stewart | 1976 |
| 8 to 1 | "Star Wars" Theme/Cantina Band | Meco | 1977 |
| 8 to 1 | I Don't Wanna Cry | Mariah Carey | 1991 |
| 8 to 1 | I Swear | All-4-One | 1994 |
| 8 to 1 | No Scrubs | TLC | 1999 |
| 8 to 1 | Livin' La Vida Loca | Ricky Martin | 1999 |
| 8 to 1 | Wild Wild West | Will Smith f/Dru Hill & Kool Moe Dee | 1999 |

# The Biggest Falls from Number One

| 1 to 15 | Nothing from Nothing | Billy Preston | 1974 |
|---|---|---|---|
| 1 to 15 | Then Came You | Dionne Warwick and the Spinners | 1974 |
| 1 to 12 | The Sounds of Silence | Simon and Garfunkel | 1966 |
| 1 to 12 | Can't Get Enough of Your Love, Babe | Barry White | 1974 |
| 1 to 12 | Rock Me Gently | Andy Kim | 1974 |
| 1 to 12 | You Haven't Done Nothin' | Stevie Wonder | 1974 |
| 1 to 12 | You Ain't Seen Nothing Yet | Bachman-Turner Overdrive | 1974 |
| 1 to 12 | Whatever Gets You Thru the Night | John Lennon | 1974 |
| 1 to 11 | Theme from "Mahogany" (Do You Know Where You're Going To) | Diana Ross | 1976 |
| 1 to 10 | Two Hearts | Phil Collins | 1989 |
| 1 to 9 | Lean on Me | Bill Withers | 1972 |
| 1 to 9 | Let Your Love Flow | Bellamy Brothers | 1976 |
| 1 to 9 | Sir Duke | Stevie Wonder | 1977 |
| 1 to 9 | Lose Yourself | Eminem | 2003 |
| 1 to 8 | Young Love | Tab Hunter | 1957 |
| 1 to 8 | Laughter in the Rain | Neil Sedaka | 1975 |
| 1 to 8 | You're No Good | Linda Ronstadt | 1975 |
| 1 to 8 | My Eyes Adored You | Frankie Valli | 1975 |
| 1 to 8 | Shining Star | Earth, Wind & Fire | 1975 |
| 1 to 8 | Thank God I'm a Country Boy | John Denver | 1975 |
| 1 to 8 | Love Will Keep Us Together | The Captain & Tennille | 1975 |
| 1 to 8 | Bad Blood | Neil Sedaka | 1975 |
| 1 to 8 | December, 1963 (Oh, What a Night) | The Four Seasons | 1976 |
| 1 to 8 | Kiss and Say Goodbye | Manhattans | 1976 |
| 1 to 8 | Don't Go Breaking My Heart | Elton John & Kiki Dee | 1976 |
| 1 to 8 | On My Own | Patti LaBelle & Michael McDonald | 1986 |
| 1 to 8 | Bad Medicine | Bon Jovi | 1988 |
| 1 to 8 | Forever Your Girl | Paula Abdul | 1989 |
| 1 to 8 | Vision of Love | Mariah Carey | 1990 |
| 1 to 8 | Coming Out of the Dark | Gloria Estefan | 1991 |
| 1 to 8 | Gettin' Jiggy Wit It | Will Smith | 1998 |
| 1 to 8 | Maria Maria | Santana f/the Product G&B | 2000 |

# The Most Number Ones

## BY ARTIST

| | |
|---|---|
| The Beatles | 20 |
| Elvis Presley | 17 |
| Mariah Carey | 15 |
| Michael Jackson | 13 |
| Madonna | 12 |
| The Supremes | 12 |
| Whitney Houston | 11 |
| Janet Jackson | 10 |
| Bee Gees | 9 |
| Paul McCartney | 9 |
| Stevie Wonder | 9 |
| Elton John | 8 |
| The Rolling Stones | 8 |
| Diana Ross | 8 |
| Phil Collins | 7 |
| George Michael | 7 |
| Paula Abdul | 6 |
| Daryl Hall and John Oates | 6 |
| Boyz II Men | 5 |
| Cher | 5 |
| Eagles | 5 |
| The Four Seasons | 5 |
| KC and the Sunshine Band | 5 |
| Olivia Newton-John | 5 |
| Prince | 5 |
| Lionel Richie | 5 |
| Barbra Streisand | 5 |
| Bryan Adams | 4 |
| Christina Aguilera | 4 |
| Beach Boys | 4 |
| Blondie | 4 |
| Bon Jovi | 4 |
| John Denver | 4 |
| Destiny's Child | 4 |
| Celine Dion | 4 |
| The Jackson 5 | 4 |
| Jennifer Lopez | 4 |
| Puff Daddy/P. Diddy | 4 |
| Roxette | 4 |
| Rod Stewart | 4 |
| Donna Summer | 4 |
| The Temptations | 4 |
| TLC | 4 |
| Bobby Vinton | 4 |

## BY WRITER

| | | | |
|---|---|---|---|
| Paul McCartney | 32 | Jon Bon Jovi | 5 |
| John Lennon | 26 | Neil Diamond | 5 |
| Barry Gibb | 16 | Jermaine Dupri | 5 |
| Brian Holland | 15 | Bernard Edwards | 5 |
| Mariah Carey | 14 | Glenn Frey | 5 |
| Lamont Dozier | 14 | Bob Gaudio | 5 |
| James Harris III | 14 | Berry Gordy, Jr. | 5 |
| Terry Lewis | 14 | Ellie Greenwich | 5 |
| Robin Gibb | 13 | George Harrison | 5 |
| Eddie Holland | 13 | Don Henley | 5 |
| Maurice Gibb | 11 | Leon Huff | 5 |
| Michael Jackson | 10 | Tom Kelly | 5 |
| Madonna | 10 | Robert John "Mutt" Lange | 5 |
| Stevie Wonder | 10 | Michael Masser | 5 |
| Bernie Taupin | 9 | Nile Rodgers | 5 |
| Diane Warren | 9 | Carole Bayer Sager | 5 |
| Jeff Barry | 8 | Billy Steinberg | 5 |
| Gerry Goffin | 8 | Barrett Strong | 5 |
| Janet Jackson | 8 | Bryan Adams | 4 |
| Mick Jagger | 8 | Desmond Child | 4 |
| Carole King | 8 | John Denver | 4 |
| George Michael | 8 | Keith Forsey | 4 |
| Keith Richards | 8 | Per Gessle | 4 |
| Daryl Hall | 7 | Howard Greenfield | 4 |
| Elton John | 7 | Jerry Leiber | 4 |
| Babyface | 6 | Steve Miller | 4 |
| Burt Bacharach | 6 | Elvis Presley | 4 |
| Harry Wayne Casey | 6 | Deke Richards | 4 |
| Phil Collins | 6 | Cory Rooney | 4 |
| Bob Crewe | 6 | Richie Sambora | 4 |
| Richard Finch | 6 | Aaron Schroeder | 4 |
| Kenny Gamble | 6 | Neil Sedaka | 4 |
| Will Jennings | 6 | Paul Simon | 4 |
| Freddie Perren | 6 | Phil Spector | 4 |
| Prince | 6 | Mike Stoller | 4 |
| Norman Whitfield | 6 | Brian Wilson | 4 |

# The Most Number Ones

## BY PRODUCER

| | |
|---|---|
| George Martin | 23 |
| Jimmy Jam | 16 |
| Terry Lewis | 16 |
| Steve Sholes | 16 |
| Barry Gibb | 14 |
| Lamont Dozier | 13 |
| Albhy Galuten | 13 |
| Brian Holland | 13 |
| Karl Richardson | 13 |
| Quincy Jones | 12 |
| Walter Afanasieff | 10 |
| Mariah Carey | 10 |
| George Michael | 9 |
| Freddie Perren | 9 |
| Narada Michael Walden | 9 |
| David Foster | 8 |
| Maurice Gibb | 8 |
| Robin Gibb | 8 |
| Madonna | 8 |
| Stevie Wonder | 8 |
| Paul McCartney | 7 |
| Giorgio Moroder | 7 |
| Michael Omartian | 7 |
| Babyface | 6 |
| Steve Barri | 6 |
| James Anthony Carmichael | 6 |
| Harry Wayne Casey | 6 |
| Mike Chapman | 6 |
| Phil Collins | 6 |
| Gus Dudgeon | 6 |
| Richard Finch | 6 |
| Snuff Garrett | 6 |
| Berry Gordy, Jr. | 6 |
| Arif Mardin | 6 |
| Milt Okun | 6 |
| Hugh Padgham | 6 |
| Richard Perry | 6 |
| Lionel Richie | 6 |

| | |
|---|---|
| Norman Whitfield | 6 |
| Chet Atkins | 5 |
| Sean "Puffy" Combs | 5 |
| Jermaine Dupri | 5 |
| Bernard Edwards | 5 |
| John Farrar | 5 |
| Daryl Hall | 5 |
| Michael Masser | 5 |
| Fonce Mizell | 5 |
| Mickie Most | 5 |
| John Oates | 5 |
| Prince | 5 |
| Phil Ramone | 5 |
| Deke Richards | 5 |
| Nile Rodgers | 5 |
| Phil Spector | 5 |
| Bob Crewe | 4 |
| Jeff Barry | 4 |
| Don Costa | 4 |
| Luigi Creatore | 4 |
| Tom Dowd | 4 |
| Bruce Fairbairn | 4 |
| Lee Gillette | 4 |
| Rick Hall | 4 |
| Stevie J. | 4 |
| Dennis Lambert | 4 |
| Robert John "Mutt" Lange | 4 |
| Patrick Leonard | 4 |
| Stewart Levine | 4 |
| Hank Medress | 4 |
| Bob Morgan | 4 |
| Clarence Öfwerman | 4 |
| Andrew Loog Oldham | 4 |
| Hugo Peretti | 4 |
| Cory Rooney | 4 |
| Bill Szymczyk | 4 |
| Randy Wood | 4 |

## BY LABEL

| | |
|---|---|
| Columbia | 92 |
| RCA | 60 |
| Capitol | 50 |
| Epic | 40 |
| Atlantic | 38 |
| Motown | 37 |
| Warner Brothers | 36 |
| Arista | 32 |
| MCA | 29 |
| A&M | 26 |
| Mercury | 20 |
| EMI/EMI-America | 17 |
| RSO | 17 |
| ABC/ABC-Paramount | 16 |
| MGM | 16 |
| Tamla | 15 |
| Apple | 13 |
| Elektra | 13 |
| Virgin | 13 |
| Sire | 12 |
| Chrysalis | 10 |
| Jive | 9 |
| Reprise | 9 |
| Atco | 8 |
| Casablanca | 7 |
| Dot | 7 |
| LaFace | 7 |
| London | 7 |
| Bell | 6 |
| Decca | 6 |
| Liberty | 6 |
| Roulette | 6 |
| T.K. | 6 |
| Asylum | 5 |
| Curb | 5 |
| Dunhill | 5 |
| Geffen | 5 |
| Gordy | 5 |
| Island | 5 |
| United Artists | 5 |

# The Most Weeks at Number One

## BY ARTIST

| | | | |
|---|---:|---|---:|
| Elvis Presley | 79 | Christina Aguilera | 16 |
| Mariah Carey | 61 | Paula Abdul | 15 |
| The Beatles | 59 | Brandy | 15 |
| Boyz II Men | 50 | Phil Collins | 15 |
| Michael Jackson | 37 | George Michael | 15 |
| Janet Jackson | 33 | Daryl Hall and John Oates | 14 |
| Madonna | 32 | Los Del Rio | 14 |
| Whitney Houston | 31 | Andy Gibb | 13 |
| Elton John | 30 | Ja Rule | 13 |
| Paul McCartney | 30 | Barbra Streisand | 13 |
| Bee Gees | 27 | Donna Summer | 13 |
| Diana Ross | 23 | Ashanti | 12 |
| Monica | 22 | Toni Braxton | 12 |
| Santana | 22 | Cher | 12 |
| The Supremes | 22 | Eminem | 12 |
| Lionel Richie | 21 | Roberta Flack | 12 |
| Stevie Wonder | 21 | The Monkees | 12 |
| Puff Daddy/P. Diddy | 21 | Prince | 12 |
| Jennifer Lopez | 20 | Rob Thomas | 12 |
| Rod Stewart | 20 | Usher | 12 |
| Celine Dion | 18 | Bobby Vinton | 12 |
| The Four Seasons | 18 | All-4-One | 11 |
| Olivia Newton-John | 18 | Faith Evans | 11 |
| Bryan Adams | 17 | Guy Mitchell | 11 |
| Destiny's Child | 17 | 112 | 11 |
| Nelly | 17 | Simon and Garfunkel | 11 |
| The Rolling Stones | 17 | TLC | 11 |

## BY SONG

*16 weeks*

| One Sweet Day | Mariah Carey & Boyz II Men | 1995 |
|---|---|---:|

*14 weeks*

| I Will Always Love You | Whitney Houston | 1992 |
|---|---|---:|
| I'll Make Love to You | Boyz II Men | 1994 |
| Macarena (Bayside Boys Mix) | Los Del Rio | 1996 |
| Candle in the Wind 1997 / Something About the Way You Look Tonight | Elton John | 1997 |

*13 weeks*

| End of the Road | Boyz II Men | 1992 |
|---|---|---:|
| The Boy Is Mine | Brandy & Monica | 1998 |

# The Most Weeks at Number One

## BY SONG

*12 weeks*
| | | |
|---|---|---|
| Smooth | Santana f/Rob Thomas | 1999 |
| Lose Yourself | Eminem | 2002 |

*11 weeks*
| | | |
|---|---|---|
| Don't Be Cruel / Hound Dog | Elvis Presley | 1956 |
| I Swear | All-4-One | 1994 |
| Un-Break My Heart | Toni Braxton | 1996 |
| I'll Be Missing You | Puff Daddy & Faith Evans (f/112) | 1997 |
| Independent Women Part I | Destiny's Child | 2000 |

*10 weeks*
| | | |
|---|---|---|
| You Light Up My Life | Debby Boone | 1977 |
| Physical | Olivia Newton-John | 1981 |
| Maria Maria | Santana f/the Product G&B | 2000 |
| Foolish | Ashanti | 2002 |
| Dilemma | Nelly f/Kelly Rowland | 2002 |

*9 weeks*
| | | |
|---|---|---|
| Singing the Blues | Guy Mitchell | 1956 |
| Mack the Knife | Bobby Darin | 1959 |
| Theme from "A Summer Place" | Percy Faith | 1960 |
| Hey Jude | The Beatles | 1968 |
| Bette Davis Eyes | Kim Carnes | 1981 |
| Endless Love | Diana Ross & Lionel Richie | 1981 |

*8 weeks*
| | | |
|---|---|---|
| (We're Gonna) Rock Around the Clock | Bill Haley & His Comets | 1955 |
| Heartbreak Hotel | Elvis Presley | 1956 |
| All Shook Up | Elvis Presley | 1957 |
| Tonight's the Night (Gonna Be Alright) | Rod Stewart | 1976 |
| Night Fever | Bee Gees | 1978 |
| Every Breath You Take | The Police | 1983 |
| Jump | Kris Kross | 1992 |
| That's the Way Love Goes | Janet Jackson | 1993 |
| Fantasy | Mariah Carey | 1995 |
| Tha Crossroads | Bone Thugs-N-Harmony | 1996 |

# The Longest Waits from Debut of First Single to First Number One

| | |
|---|---|
| Santana | 30 years |
| Aerosmith | 24 years, 10 months, 2 weeks |
| Tina Turner | 24 years |
| Meat Loaf | 22 years, 5 months, 2 weeks |
| Johnny Mathis | 21 years, 3 months, 1 week |
| Robert John | 20 years, 10 months, 4 weeks |
| Steve Winwood | 20 years, 5 months, 4 weeks |
| Billy Vera | 19 years, 1 month, 3 weeks |
| Bob Seger | 18 years, 7 months, 2 weeks |
| David Rose | 18 years, 4 months, 2 weeks |
| Louis Armstrong | 18 years, 1 month |
| Sammy Davis, Jr. | 17 years, 9 months, 3 weeks |
| Chuck Berry | 17 years, 2 months |
| Lawrence Welk | 17 years, 1 week |
| Peabo Bryson | 16 years, 11 months, 3 weeks |
| Loleatta Holloway | 16 years, 9 months, 3 weeks |
| Bette Midler | 16 years, 5 months, 3 weeks |
| Roger Troutman | 15 years, 9 months, 1 week |
| LL Cool J | 15 years, 6 months |
| Johnny Nash | 14 years, 10 months, 1 week |
| Joe Cocker | 13 years, 11 months, 3 weeks |
| Glen Campbell | 13 years, 10 months, 1 week |
| Charlie Rich | 13 years, 9 months |
| Spinners | 13 years, 4 months |
| Labelle | 12 years, 11 months, 1 week |
| Kenny Rogers | 12 years, 9 months, 1 week |
| Gladys Knight & the Pips | 12 years, 5 months, 2 weeks |
| Peaches & Herb | 12 years, 5 months, 1 week |
| Johnnie Taylor | 12 years, 4 months, 1 week |
| Yes | 12 years, 3 months, 4 weeks |
| Dionne Warwick | 11 years, 10 months, 3 weeks |
| Manhattans | 11 years, 6 months, 1 week |
| Kool & the Gang | 11 years, 4 months, 4 weeks |
| Smokey Robinson & the Miracles | 11 years, 2 months, 1 week |
| Steve Lawrence | 10 years, 7 months |
| J. Geils Band | 10 years, 2 months |
| Boston | 10 years, 1 month, 3 weeks |

# The Longest Chart Spans of Number One Songs

## BY ARTIST (Career Totals)

*33 years, 7 months, 3 weeks*
CHER from "I Got You Babe" to "Believe"

*25 years, 7 months, 1 week*
MICHAEL JACKSON from "I Want You Back" to "You Are Not Alone"

*24 years, 11 months, 1 week*
ELTON JOHN from "Crocodile Rock" to "Candle in the Wind 1997" / "Something About the Way You Look Tonight"

*24 years, 4 months, 1 week*
THE BEACH BOYS from "I Get Around" to "Kokomo"

*23 years, 11 months, 3 weeks*
GEORGE HARRISON from "I Want to Hold Your Hand" to "Got My Mind Set on You"

*22 years, 10 months*
BILL MEDLEY from "You've Lost That Lovin' Feelin'" to "(I've Had) The Time of My Life"

*22 years, 4 months, 2 weeks*
ROD STEWART from "Maggie May" / "Reason to Believe" to "All for Love"

*22 years, 2 months, 3 weeks*
STEVIE WONDER from "Fingertips (Pt. II)" to "Part-Time Lover"

*19 years, 11 months*
ARETHA FRANKLIN from "Respect" to "I Knew You Were Waiting (For Me)"

*17 years, 1 month, 4 weeks*
DIANA ROSS from "Where Did Our Love Go" to "Endless Love"

*17 years*
PAUL ANKA from "Diana" to "(You're) Having My Baby"

JOHN LENNON from "I Want to Hold Your Hand" to "(Just Like) Starting Over"

*16 years, 3 weeks*
FRANKIE VALLI from "Sherry" to "Grease"

*15 years, 9 months, 2 weeks*
MADONNA from "Like a Virgin" to "Music"

*14 years, 7 months, 2 weeks*
JANET JACKSON from "When I Think of You" to "All for You"

*13 years, 6 months, 3 weeks*
THE FOUR SEASONS from "Sherry" to "December, 1963 (Oh, What a Night)"

*13 years, 6 months, 2 weeks*
ELVIS PRESLEY from "Heartbreak Hotel" to "Suspicious Minds"

*13 years, 2 months, 3 weeks*
NEIL SEDAKA from "Breaking Up Is Hard to Do" to "Bad Blood"

*13 years, 1 month*
THE ROLLING STONES from "(I Can't Get No) Satisfaction" to "Miss You"

*12 years, 4 months, 1 week*
MANFRED MANN from "Do Wah Diddy Diddy" to "Blinded by the Light"

*12 years, 2 months*
CHICAGO from "If You Leave Me Now" to "Look Away"

# The Longest Chart Spans of Number One Songs

## BY WRITER

*38 years, 9 months, 1 week*
LINCOLN CHASE from "Wonderland by Night" to "Heartbreaker"

*38 years, 6 months, 2 weeks*
BOB CREWE from "Big Girls Don't Cry" to "Lady Marmalade" (Christina Aguilera, Lil' Kim, Mya & Pink)

*34 years, 8 months*
CHIP TAYLOR from "Wild Thing" to "Angel"

*34 years, 7 months, 1 week*
JOHN SEBASTIAN and MARK SEBASTIAN from "Summer in the City" to "Stutter"

*31 years, 8 months, 3 weeks*
LUIGI CREATORE, HUGO PERETTI and GEORGE DAVID WEISS from "The Lion Sleeps Tonight" to "Can't Help Falling in Love"

*29 years, 11 months, 3 weeks*
PAM SAWYER from "Love Child" to "The First Night"

*29 years, 10 months, 2 weeks*
KENNY GAMBLE from "Me and Mrs. Jones" to "Dilemma"

*28 years, 7 months, 2 weeks*
STEVIE WONDER from "The Tears of a Clown" to "Wild Wild West"

*27 years, 2 months, 3 weeks*
AHMET ERTEGUN, EDDIE CURTIS and STEVE MILLER from "The Joker" to "Angel"

*26 years, 3 months, 1 week*
KENNY NOLAN from "My Eyes Adored You" to "Lady Marmalade" (Christina Aguilera, Lil' Kim, Mya & Pink)

*25 years, 6 months*
CAMERON LEWIS and ARTHUR WRIGHT from "When a Man Loves a Woman" (Percy Sledge) to "When a Man Loves a Woman" (Michael Bolton)

*25 years, 5 months, 3 weeks*
BRIAN HOLLAND from "Please Mr. Postman" (The Marvelettes) to "You Keep Me Hangin' On" (Kim Wilde)

*24 years, 11 months, 1 week*
ELTON JOHN and BERNIE TAUPIN from "Crocodile Rock" to "Candle in the Wind 1997" / "Something About the Way You Look Tonight"

*24 years, 9 months*
GERRY GOFFIN from "Will You Love Me Tomorrow" to "Saving All My Love for You"

*24 years, 5 months, 2 weeks*
LAMONT DOZIER from "Where Did Our Love Go" to "Two Hearts"

*24 years, 5 months*
BILL WITHERS from "Lean on Me" to "No Diggity"

*24 years, 1 month, 3 weeks*
STEVIE NICKS from "Dreams" to "Bootylicious"

*22 years, 9 months, 3 weeks*
EDDIE HOLLAND from "Where Did Our Love Go" to "You Keep Me Hangin' On" (Kim Wilde)

*22 years, 6 months, 1 week*
JOHN PHILLIPS from "Monday, Monday" to "Kokomo"

*22 years, 5 months, 1 week*
MARILYN MCLEOD from "Love Hangover" to "The First Night"

*22 years, 5 months*
BERRY GORDY from "I Want You Back" to ""I'll Be There" (Mariah Carey)

*21 years, 11 months*
MIKE LOVE from "Good Vibrations" to "Kokomo"

*21 years, 9 months, 3 weeks*
NEIL DIAMOND from "I'm a Believer" to "Red Red Wine"

*21 years, 8 months, 3 weeks*
RUDY CLARK from "Good Lovin'" to "Got My Mind Set on You"

*21 years, 8 months, 2 weeks*
HAL DAVIS, WILLIE HUTCH and BOB WEST from "I'll Be There" (The Jackson 5) to "I'll Be There" (Mariah Carey)

*19 years, 11 months, 2 weeks*
PAUL MCCARTNEY from "I Want to Hold Your Hand" to "Say, Say, Say"

# The Longest Chart Spans of Number One Songs

*19 years, 7 months, 2 weeks*
PHIL SPECTOR from "To Know Him Is to Love Him" to "Da Doo Ron Ron"

*19 years, 3 months, 3 weeks*
BERNARD EDWARDS and NILE RODGERS from "Le Freak" to "Gettin' Jiggy Wit It"

*18 years, 10 months*
TOMMY JAMES from "Crimson and Clover" to "Mony Mony"

*18 years, 2 weeks*
BURT BACHARACH from "This Guy's in Love With You" to "On My Own"

*17 years, 9 months, 1 week*
STEVE KIPNER from "Physical" to "Genie in a Bottle"

*17 years, 7 months*
ANDY ARMER and RANDY BADAZZ from "Rise" to "Hypnotize"

*17 years, 4 months, 4 weeks*
JOHN LENNON from "I Want to Hold Your Hand" to "Medley: Intro Venus…"

*17 years, 3 weeks*
JEFF BARRY from "Chapel of Love" to "Medley: Intro Venus…"

*17 years*
PAUL ANKA from "Diana" to "(You're) Having My Baby"

*16 years, 7 months, 1 week*
LEON HUFF from "Me and Mrs. Jones" to "If You Don't Know Me by Now"

ROBBIE VAN LEEUWEN from "Venus" (Shocking Blue) to "Venus" (Bananarama)

*15 years, 11 months, 2 weeks*
ALLEN TOUSSAINT from "Mother-in-Law" to "Southern Nights"

*15 years, 1 month, 3 weeks*
DAVID BOWIE from "Fame" to "Ice Ice Baby"

*15 years, 2 weeks*
HOWARD GREENFIELD from "Everybody's Somebody's Fool" to "Love Will Keep Us Together"

*14 years, 7 months, 2 weeks*
JAMES HARRIS III, TERRY LEWIS and JANET JACKSON from "When I Think of You" to "All for You"

*14 years, 7 months*
MADONNA from "Live to Tell" to "Music"

*14 years, 1 month, 3 weeks*
MICHAEL MASSER from "Touch Me in the Morning" to "Saving All My Love for You"

STING from "Every Breath You Take" to "I'll Be Missing You"

*13 years, 6 months, 3 weeks*
BOB GAUDIO from "Sherry" to "December, 1963 (Oh, What a Night)"

*13 years, 3 months, 3 weeks*
CAROLE KING from "Will You Love Me Tomorrow" to "The Loco-Motion" (Grand Funk)

*13 years, 2 months, 3 weeks*
NEIL SEDAKA from "Breaking Up Is Hard to Do" to "Bad Blood"

*13 years, 1 month, 2 weeks*
ROBERT BATEMAN, GEORGIA DOBBINS and WILLIAM GARRETT from "Please Mr. Postman" (The Marvelettes) to "Please Mr. Postman" (Carpenters)

ELLIE GREENWICH from "Chapel of Love" to "Da Doo Ron Ron"

*13 years, 1 month*
MICK JAGGER, KEITH RICHARDS from "(I Can't Get No) Satisfaction" to "Miss You"

*12 years, 7 months, 3 weeks*
JERRY FULLER from "Travelin' Man" to "Show and Tell"

*12 years, 6 months, 1 week*
DESMOND CHILD from "You Give Love a Bad Name" to "Livin' La Vida Loca"

*12 years, 3 months, 2 weeks*
MICHAEL JACKSON from "Don't Stop 'Til You Get Enough" to "Black or White"

*12 years, 3 months, 1 week*
BARRY GIBB and ROBIN GIBB from "How Can You Mend a Broken Heart" to "Islands in the Stream"

*12 years, 2 weeks*
DOLLY PARTON from "9 to 5" to "I Will Always Love You"

# The Longest Chart Spans of Number One Songs

## BY PRODUCER

*33 years, 11 months, 1 week*
GEORGE MARTIN from "I Want to Hold Your Hand" to "Candle in the Wind 1997"

*25 years, 1 month, 1 week*
QUINCY JONES from "It's My Party" to "Dirty Diana"

*24 years, 5 months, 2 weeks*
LAMONT DOZIER from "Where Did Our Love Go" to "Two Hearts"

*23 years, 4 months, 2 weeks*
TERRY MELCHER from "Mr. Tambourine Man" to "Kokomo"

*23 years, 1 month, 2 weeks*
ARIF MARDIN from "Good Lovin'" to "Wind Beneath My Wings"

*21 years*
STEWART LEVINE from "Grazing in the Grass" to "If You Don't Know Me By Now"

*17 years, 10 months*
LUIGI CREATORE and HUGO PERETTI from "Honeycomb" to "The Hustle"

*17 years, 1 month*
GEORGE HARRISON from "My Sweet Lord" / "Isn't It a Pity" to "Got My Mind Set on You"

*16 years, 6 months*
BURT BACHARACH from "Raindrops Keep Fallin' on My Head" to "On My Own"

*16 years, 4 months, 2 weeks*
DAVID FOSTER from "Hard to Say I'm Sorry" to "Have You Ever?"

*16 years*
THOM BELL from "Then Came You" to "I Don't Have the Heart"

*15 years, 5 months, 2 weeks*
PHIL GERNHARD from "Stay" to "Let Your Love Flow"

*14 years, 9 months, 2 weeks*
DON COSTA from "Diana" to "Candy Man"

JIMMY JAM and TERRY LEWIS from "When I Think of You" to "U Remind Me"

*14 years, 2 months, 3 weeks*
MICHAEL MASSER from "Touch Me in the Morning" to "Didn't We Almost Have It All"

*14 years, 1 month, 3 weeks*
MADONNA from "Papa Don't Preach" to "Music"

*13 years, 11 months, 2 weeks*
MICHAEL OMARTIAN from "Theme from S.W.A.T." to "How Am I Supposed to Live Without You"

*13 years, 10 months, 1 week*
ALLEN TOUSSAINT from "Mother-in-Law" to "Lady Marmalade" (Labelle)

*13 years, 1 month, 2 weeks*
PHIL SPECTOR from "To Know Him Is to Love Him" to "My Sweet Lord" / "Isn't It a Pity"

*12 years, 10 months, 2 weeks*
TOM DOWD from "Good Lovin'" to "Da Ya Think I'm Sexy?"

*12 years, 9 months, 2 weeks*
STEVIE WONDER from "Superstition" to "Part-Time Lover"

*12 years, 6 months, 2 weeks*
BOB CREWE from "Sherry" to "My Eyes Adored You"

*12 years, 6 months, 1 week*
SNUFF GARRETT from "Take Good Care of My Baby" to "Dark Lady"

*12 years, 6 months*
MICHAEL JACKSON from "Billie Jean" to "You Are Not Alone"

*12 years, 3 months, 1 week*
BARRY GIBB from "How Can You Mend a Broken Heart" to "Islands in the Stream"

*12 years, 3 months*
JOE REISMAN from "Round and Round" to "Love Theme from 'Romeo and Juliet'"

*12 years, 1 month, 3 weeks*
HANK MEDRESS from "He's So Fine" to "He Don't Love You (Like I Love You)"

# Title Index

# Writer Index

# WRITER INDEX

Brigati, Eddie
224 Groovin'
245 People Got to Be Free
Briggs, Kevin
880 No Scrubs
883 Bills, Bills, Bills
Bristol, Johnny
265 Someday We'll Be Together
Britten, Terry
593 What's Love Got to Do With It
Broady, Carlos
853 Can't Nobody Hold Me Down
Brooks, Joe
475 You Light Up My Life
Brooks, Warren Allen
774 Because I Love You (The
    Postman Song)
Brown, Bobby
718 My Prerogative
761 She Ain't Worth It
Brown, Charles
924 Hot in Herre
Brown, Errol
341 Brother Louie
Brown, L. Russell
287 Knock Three Times
332 Tie a Yellow Ribbon Round the
    Ole Oak Tree
Brown, Raphael Shawan
867 Too Close
Brownson, Derry
791 Unbelievable
Bruce, Gary
92 Moody River
Bryant, Boudleaux
28 Wake Up Little Susie
37 All I Have to Do Is Dream
Bryant, Felice
28 Wake Up Little Susie
37 All I Have to Do Is Dream
Bunnell, Dewey
309 A Horse With No Name
Burr, Gary
933 This Is the Night
Burrell, Orville
907 It Wasn't Me
Burruss, Kandi
880 No Scrubs
883 Bills, Bills, Bills
Burton, Ray
324 I Am Woman
Butler, Billy
240 Tighten Up
Butler, Jerry
403 He Don't Love You (Like I Love
    You)
Butler, Larry
402 (Hey Won't You Play) Another
    Somebody Done Somebody
    Wrong Song
Byrd, Robert
189 Over and Over
Byron, Al
113 Roses Are Red (My Love)

Caldwell, Bobby
654 The Next Time I Fall
Callander, Peter
367 Billy, Don't Be a Hero
373 The Night Chicago Died
Callis, Jo
556 Don't You Want Me
Cameron, Jimmie
932 21 Questions
Cameron, Vella
932 21 Questions
Campbell, Paul
102 The Lion Sleeps Tonight
Cannon, Gus
123 Walk Right In

Capizzi, Leonard
118 Monster Mash
Capps, Al
345 Half-Breed
Cara, Irene
573 Flashdance...What a Feeling
Carey, Mariah
762 Vision of Love
772 Love Takes Time
780 Someday
788 I Don't Wanna Cry
796 Emotions
820 Dreamlover
823 Hero
841 Fantasy
843 One Sweet Day
845 Always Be My Baby
858 Honey
868 My All
888 Heartbreaker
892 Thank God I Found You
Carlsson, Andreas
900 It's Gonna Be Me
Carmichael, Hoagy
79 Georgia on My Mind
Carpenter, Richard
350 Top of the World
Carter, Clarence
403 He Don't Love You (Like I Love
    You)
Carter, John
232 Incense and Peppermints
Carter, Shawn
888 Heartbreaker
Cartey, Ric
18 Young Love
Casey, Brian
863 Nice & Slow
Casey, Harry Wayne
370 Rock Your Baby
414 Get Down Tonight
420 That's the Way (I Like It)
442 (Shake, Shake, Shake) Shake
    Your Booty
465 I'm Your Boogie Man
519 Please Don't Go
Caston, Leonard
348 Keep On Truckin'
Cavaliere, Felix
224 Groovin'
245 People Got to Be Free
Cetera, Peter
446 If You Leave Me Now
559 Hard to Say I'm Sorry
643 Glory of Love
Cham, Raymond
904 Come On Over Baby (All I Want
    Is You)
Chambers, Jimmy
783 I've Been Thinking About You
Chandler, George
783 I've Been Thinking About You
Channel, Bruce
105 Hey! Baby
Chapin, Harry
386 Cat's in the Cradle
Chapin, Sandy
386 Cat's in the Cradle
Chapman, Mike
490 Kiss You All Over
564 Mickey
Charles, Deena
763 If Wishes Came True
Chase, Clifton
853 Can't Nobody Hold Me Down
Chase, Lincoln
82 Wonderland by Night
888 Heartbreaker
Chavez, Ingrid
775 Justify My Love

Cherone, Gary
789 More Than Words
Child, Desmond
653 You Give Love a Bad Name
660 Livin' on a Prayer
714 Bad Medicine
881 Livin' La Vida Loca
Chinn, Nicky
490 Kiss You All Over
564 Mickey
Christie, Lou
193 Lightnin' Strikes
Christopher, Gretchen
51 Come Softly to Me
Clark, Rudy
197 Good Lovin'
687 Got My Mind Set on You
Clark, Steve
709 Love Bites
Clement, Eddie
914 U Remind Me
Climie, Simon
664 I Knew You Were Waiting (For
    Me)
Clivillés, Robert
778 Gonna Make You Sweat
    (Everybody Dance Now)
796 Emotions
Cobb, Margaret
105 Hey! Baby
Cody, Phil
391 Laughter in the Rain
418 Bad Blood
Coffing, Barry
812 How Do You Talk to an Angel
Cohen, Jeffrey
888 Heartbreaker
Cole, David
796 Emotions
Cole, Gardner
659 Open Your Heart
Colla, John
615 The Power of Love
Collen, Phil
709 Love Bites
Collins, Alan
715 Baby, I Love Your Way/Freebird
    Medley (Free Baby)
Collins, Larry
343 Delta Dawn
Collins, Phil
586 Against All Odds (Take a Look
    at Me Now)
604 One More Night
611 Sussudio
641 Invisible Touch
719 Two Hearts
749 Another Day in Paradise
Color Me Badd
794 I Adore Mi Amor
802 All 4 Love
Combs, Sean "Puffy"
853 Can't Nobody Hold Me Down
854 Hypnotize
857 Mo Money Mo Problems
858 Honey
Connors, Carol
468 Gonna Fly Now (Theme from
    "Rocky")
Conti, Bill
468 Gonna Fly Now (Theme from
    "Rocky")
Cooke, Sam
30 You Send Me
Coots, J. Fred
22 Love Letters in the Sand
Cordell, Ritchie
681 I Think We're Alone Now
682 Mony Mony
Cordes, Attrel

800 Set Adrift on Memory Bliss
Cortez, Dave "Baby"
52 The Happy Organ
Cosby, Henry
135 Fingertips (Pt. II)
285 The Tears of a Clown
Cottle, Tameka
880 No Scrubs
Coulter, Phil
423 Saturday Night
Cour, Pierre
237 Love Is Blue
Covay, Don
85 Pony Time
Coverdale, David
678 Here I Go Again
Cowan, Tony
846 Tha Crossroads
Craig, Mikey
583 Karma Chameleon
Crawford, Anthony "Shep"
901 Incomplete
Creatore, Luigi
102 The Lion Sleeps Tonight
819 Can't Help Falling in Love
Creed, Linda
636 Greatest Love of All
Crewe, Bob
120 Big Girls Don't Cry
125 Walk Like a Man
152 Rag Doll
398 My Eyes Adored You
399 Lady Marmalade
913 Lady Marmalade
Croce, Jim
338 Bad, Bad Leroy Brown
352 Time in a Bottle
Cronin, Kevin
539 Keep on Loving You
603 Can't Fight This Feeling
Crook, Max
88 Runaway
Cropper, Steve
238 (Sittin' On) The Dock of the Bay
501 Knock on Wood
Cross, Christopher
529 Sailing
548 Arthur's Theme (Best That You
    Can Do)
Crowley, John Charles
477 Baby Come Back
Cummings, Burton
273 American Woman
Cunningham, Woodrow
847 California Love
Curtis, Eddie
353 The Joker
911 Angel

Dall, Bobby
717 Every Rose Has Its Thorn
Daniels, LaShawn
869 The Boy Is Mine
882 If You Had My Love
894 Say My Name
Danoff, Bill
438 Afternoon Delight
D'Arby, Terence Trent
697 Wishing Well
Darian, Fred
76 Mr. Custer
David, Hal
242 This Guy's in Love With You
266 Raindrops Keep Fallin' on My
    Head
278 (They Long to Be) Close to You
Davis, Benny
106 Don't Break the Heart That
    Loves You
Davis, Chip

# WRITER INDEX

**Mann, Kal**
23 (Let Me Be Your) Teddy Bear
**Manning, Dick**
57 The Three Bells
**Mannot, Marguerite**
9 Poor People of Paris
**Manzarek, Ray**
227 Light My Fire
244 Hello, I Love You
**Manzoli, Rob**
804 I'm Too Sexy
**Marcucci, Bob**
62 Why
**Maresca, Ernie**
99 Runaround Sue
**Margulies, Ben**
762 Vision of Love
772 Love Takes Time
780 Someday
**Markowitz, Donald**
683 (I've Had) The Time of My Life
**Marley, Bob**
375 I Shot the Sheriff
**Marsden, Bernie**
678 Here I Go Again
**Marsden, Steven**
931 Get Busy
**Marshall, Ed**
50 Venus
**Marshall, Sherman**
380 Then Came You
**Martika**
737 Toy Soldiers
**Martin, Bill**
423 Saturday Night
**Martin, Max**
877 …Baby One More Time
900 It's Gonna Be Me
**Martin, Eric**
805 To Be With You
**Martineé, Lewis A.**
691 Seasons Change
**Martinez, Rudy**
210 96 Tears
**Marx, Richard**
704 Hold On to the Nights
733 Satisfied
739 Right Here Waiting
**Masser, Michael**
340 Touch Me in the Morning
426 Theme from "Mahogany" (Do You Know Where You're Going To)
620 Saving All My Love for You
636 Greatest Love of All
677 Didn't We Almost Have It All
**Mathers, Marshall**
927 Lose Yourself
**Matkosky, Dennis**
576 Maniac
**May, Brian**
771 Ice Ice Baby
**Mayfield, Curtis**
403 He Don't Love You (Like I Love You)
422 Let's Do It Again
**Mayfield, Percy**
98 Hit the Road Jack
**Mayo, Aimee**
893 Amazed
**Mazur, Bret**
910 Butterfly
**McCall, C.W.**
424 Convoy
**McCane, Bryon**
846 Tha Crossroads
**McCary, Michael**
843 One Sweet Day
**McCartney, Linda**
298 Uncle Albert/Admiral Halsey

**McCartney, Paul**
143 I Want to Hold Your Hand
144 She Loves You
145 Can't Buy Me Love
148 Love Me Do
150 A World Without Love
153 A Hard Day's Night
164 I Feel Fine
169 Eight Days a Week
174 Ticket to Ride
182 Help!
185 Yesterday
191 We Can Work It Out
201 Paperback Writer
220 Penny Lane
228 All You Need Is Love
234 Hello Goodbye
247 Hey Jude
254 Get Back
262 Come Together
271 Let It Be
275 The Long and Winding Road
298 Uncle Albert/Admiral Halsey
335 My Love
366 Band on the Run
388 Lucy in the Sky With Diamonds
409 Listen to What the Man Said
436 Silly Love Songs
482 With a Little Luck
526 Coming Up (Live at Glasgow)
544 Medley: Intro Venus…
555 Ebony and Ivory
581 Say, Say, Say
**McCloud, Anita**
914 U Remind Me
**McCormick, Keith**
138 Sugar Shack
**McCoy, Rose Marie**
33 I Beg of You
**McCoy, Van**
410 The Hustle
**McCulloch, James**
491 Hot Child in the City
**McDaniels, Eugene**
372 Feel Like Makin' Love
**McDonald, Michael**
500 What a Fool Believes
**McFarland, J. Leslie**
67 Stuck on You
**McFerrin, Bobby**
708 Don't Worry, Be Happy
**McKay, Al**
473 Best of My Love
**McKenzie, Scott**
712 Kokomo
**McKuen, Rod**
358 Seasons in the Sun
**McLean, Don**
305 American Pie
**McLennen, Stuart**
879 Believe
**McLeod, Marilyn**
437 Love Hangover
**Medora, John**
32 At the Hop
**Meek, John**
121 Telstar
**Melcher, Terry**
712 Kokomo
**Mellencamp, John Cougar**
560 Jack and Diane
**Melson, Joe**
91 Running Scared
**Mende, Gunther**
825 The Power of Love
**Menken, Alan**
814 A Whole New World (Aladdin's Theme)
**Mercer, Johnny**

4 Autumn Leaves
**Mercury, Freddie**
522 Crazy Little Thing Called Love
771 Ice Ice Baby
**Merrill, Alan**
553 I Love Rock 'n Roll
**Merrill, Bob**
27 Honeycomb
**Merrill, George**
628 How Will I Know
670 I Wanna Dance With Somebody (Who Loves Me)
**Meyers, Frank J.**
828 I Swear
**Michael, George**
598 Wake Me Up Before You Go-Go
602 Careless Whisper
608 Everything She Wants
685 Faith
692 Father Figure
699 One More Try
706 Monkey
768 Praying for Time
**Michael-Cox, Bryan**
919 U Got It Bad
**Michaels, Bret**
717 Every Rose Has Its Thorn
**Middlebrook, Ralph**
392 Fire
427 Love Rollercoaster
**Middleton, Tim**
846 Tha Crossroads
**Migliacci, Franco**
41 Volare (Nel Blu Dipinto di Blu)
**Miller, Bruce**
918 Family Affair
**Miller, Den Z-il "D1"**
867 Too Close
**Miller, Frank**
6 Memories Are Made of This
**Miller, Ron**
340 Touch Me in the Morning
**Miller, Steve**
353 The Joker
447 Rock'n Me
558 Abracadabra
911 Angel
**Mitchell, Bob**
703 The Flame
**Mitchell, Willie**
306 Let's Stay Together
**Mizell, Fonce**
267 I Want You Back
272 ABC
276 The Love You Save
**Modugno, Domenico**
41 Volare (Nel Blu Dipinto di Blu)
**Moltke, Shawn**
815 Informer
**Moman, Chips**
402 (Hey Won't You Play) Another Somebody Done Somebody Wrong Song
**Monge, Antonio Romero**
849 Macarena
**Moore, Falonte**
915 Bootylicious
**Moore, James**
867 Too Close
**Moore, Robin**
195 The Ballad of the Green Berets
**Moore, Warren "Pete"**
430 Love Machine Pt. 1
**Moore-Hough, Marvin**
895 Maria Maria
**Morgan, Brian Alexander**
818 Weak
**Morgan, Dennis**
664 I Knew You Were Waiting (For Me)

**Moroder, Giorgio**
524 Call Me
573 Flashdance…What a Feeling
647 Take My Breath Away
**Morris, Lee**
137 Blue Velvet
**Morris, Nathan**
843 One Sweet Day
**Morris, Wanya**
843 One Sweet Day
**Morrison, Jim**
227 Light My Fire
244 Hello, I Love You
**Morton, George "Shadow"**
160 Leader of the Pack
**Mosley, Timothy**
896 Try Again
**Moss, Jon**
583 Karma Chameleon
**Moss, Neil**
640 Holding Back the Years
**Murphy, Walter**
444 A Fifth of Beethoven
**Murray, Fred**
180 I'm Henry VIII, I Am
**Murray, Mitch**
171 I'm Telling You Now
367 Billy, Don't Be a Hero
373 The Night Chicago Died
**Murray, Roy**
816 Freak Me
**Murray, Ted**
106 Don't Break the Heart That Loves You
**Myrick, Nashiem**
853 Can't Nobody Hold Me Down
**Mysels, Maurice**
12 I Want You, I Need You, I Love You

**Nakamura, Hachidai**
131 Sukiyaki
**Nance, Jack**
44 It's Only Make Believe
**Nash, Johnny**
322 I Can See Clearly Now
**Nelly**
924 Hot in Herre
925 Dilemma
**Nelson, Gunnar**
766 (Can't Live Without Your) Love and Affection
**Nelson, Matthew**
766 (Can't Live Without Your) Love and Affection
**Neuman, Klauss-Gunter**
82 Wonderland by Night
**Nevins, Al**
35 Twilight Time
**Nevins, Morton**
35 Twilight Time
**Newley, Anthony**
313 Candy Man
**Newman, Herb**
11 The Wayward Wind
**Newman, Randy**
277 Mama Told Me (Not to Come)
**Nickelback**
920 How You Remind Me
**Nicks, Stevie**
466 Dreams
915 Bootylicious
**Nini, Diane**
643 Glory of Love
**Nitzsche, Jack**
562 Up Where We Belong
**Nix, Kenton**
832 Here Comes the Hotstepper
**Nolan, Kenny**
398 My Eyes Adored You

# Producer Index

# Label Index

# Photo Credits

The task of collecting photographs to illustrate 48 years of rock-and-roll history was an enormous one. The editors gratefully acknowledge those who took the time and trouble to search through their Rolodexes, attics, and picture files so that we could meet our deadlines.

Courtesy of The Frank Driggs Collection: 1–45, 48–50, 52–56, 58, 59, 61, 69, 71–75, 77–79, 81, 83–88, 90–92, 94, 96–106, 108, 109, 111, 117, 119, 122, 124, 126 128, 130, 131, 133–137, 140, 151, 153–166, 168–182, 184–186, 188–191, 193, 194, 198, 199, 201, 203, 205–209, 212, 214–217, 221, 223–225, 227, 229, 230, 233, 234, 238, 239, 241–243, 246, 249, 251, 253, 255, 260, 261, 264, 265, 267, 269, 272, 280, 283, 284, 286, 288, 289, 293–299, 301–306, 310–315, 319–321, 324, 326, 328–330, 332, 334, 336, 340, 342–344, 347, 350, 351, 354, 356, 357, 360, 362, 364, 366, 367, 371, 372, 375–378, 382–384, 386, 387, 389, 391, 393–399, 401, 404, 408, 412, 415–419, 422, 423, 426, 428, 431, 432, 434, 435, 437–441, 446, 447, 450, 452, 454, 457–459, 461, 466, 470, 473, 475, 476, 478–482, 484, 486–489, 491, 493, 495, 496, 498, 500, 503, 507, 514, 517, 523, 525–527, 531, 534, 537–540, 549, 552, 554, 557, 559, 561, 567, 573, 575, 581, 584, 585, 589–591, 596, 598–600, 609, 620, 628, 636, 637, 651, 653, 661, 663, 685, 692.

Courtesy of Ebet Roberts: 259, 266, 270, 308, 323, 353, 388, 402, 425, 463, 467, 471, 472, 485, 492, 497, 504, 508, 509, 511, 518, 520, 522, 524, 529, 533, 535, 536, 541–543, 545, 546, 548, 550, 551, 553, 560, 563, 565, 566, 568–572, 574, 577, 580, 582, 583, 586, 587, 593–595, 604, 647, 660, 670, 696, 697.

Courtesy of The Michael Ochs Archive: 47, 70, 80, 82, 89, 95, 120, 121, 123, 125, 129, 132, 152, 167, 183, 187, 195–197, 200, 202, 204, 210, 211, 213, 218, 222, 226, 232, 235, 237, 244, 245, 250, 252, 254, 257, 258, 263, 268, 271, 282, 287, 291, 292, 300, 309, 316, 318, 322, 325, 327, 331, 339, 345, 346, 352, 358, 359, 363, 365, 369, 370, 374, 379–381, 392, 400, 403, 409, 410, 413, 414, 420, 424, 430, 433, 436, 444, 445, 448, 451, 455, 462, 464, 469, 474, 477, 483, 499, 501, 505, 506, 512, 515, 516 (Donna Summer), 555, 562, 576.

A&M Records: 556, 607, 610, 632, 649, 652; John Abeyta: 730; Jay Anning: 110; John Apostol: 93; Arista Records: 592, 597, 627 (Dionne Warwick), 639, 677, 686, 691, 695, 867, 869, 871, 878, 880, 889, 895, 908, 919; Atlantic Records: 611, 616, 624, 641, 689, 869 (Brandy), 876, 899, 931; *Billboard magazine:* 456, 494 (Barbra Streisand), 516 (Barbra Streisand), 532, 558; Blackground Records: 896; BNA Records Label: 893; Fred Bronson: 46, 76, 107, 192, 231, 240, 256, 307, 338, 368, 390, 421, 502, 521, 544; Jim Ed Brown: 57; Buddah Records: 236; Capitol Records: 335, 612, 631, 671, 672; CBS Records: 443, 494 (Neil Diamond); Gretchen Christopher: 51, 60; Chrysalis Records: 564, 615, 648, 682; Danny Clinch: 905; Columbia Records: 602, 608, 613, 656, 657, 664, 669, 679, 861, 865, 868, 870, 873, 881, 883, 891, 894, 906, 910, 915, 925 (Kelly Rowland); Attila Csupo: 654 (Amy Grant); Chris Cuffaro: 699; Dragon Records: 901; Elektra Asylum Records: 411, 640; EMI Manhattan: 635; EMI Records: 220, 228, 247, 262, 349, 355, 361, 510; Epic Records: 490, 603, 676 (Michael Jackson), 680, 688, 694, 698, 929, 875 (Celine Dion), 917 (Jennifer Lopez), 928; ESP Management: 601; Geffen Records: 642, 678; Jimmy Gilmer: 138; Bob Gruen/Star File: 735; Interscope Records: 886, 897, 927, 930, 932; Island Records: 634, 645, 666, 673; J Records: 916; Jive Records: 875 (R. Kelly), 877, 900, 909 (Mystikal), 909 (Joe); Kama Sutra Records: 341; LaFace Records: 863, 887, 914; MCA Records: 618, 622, 627 (Gladys Knight), 638 (Patti LaBelle), 667, 681, 690, 866, 907, 911, 918; Motown Records: 219, 248, 281, 285, 290, 348, 460, 530, 547, 621, 626; Mary MacGregor: 453; Murder Inc. Records: 917, 921 (Ashanti), 921 and 922 (Ja Rule), 923; Norby Walters Associates: 519; Bobby Pickett: 118; PolyGram Records: 614, 646; Portrait: 650; Pendulum Records: 874; Qwest Records: 676 (Siedah Garrett) (photo by Sam Emerson); RCA Records: 623, 625, 629, 630, 655, 683, 684, 693, 700 (photo by Mike Prior), 885, 890, 898, 904, 926; Reprise Records: 872; Rhino Records: 658; Herb Ritts: 644; Roadrunner Records: 920; Roc–A–Fella Records: 888 (Jay–Z); Lee Salem: 627 (Stevie Wonder); Lorraine Samuel: 753; David Seelig/Star File: 743; Showtime: 627 (Elton John); Sire Records: 606, 659, 674; Solters/Roskin/Friedman Inc.: 579; Sony Music: 922 (Jennifer Lopez); April Stevens: 139; Stone/Hallinan Associates: 468; T K. Records: 442, 465; Courtesy of Universal Pictures: 902; Universal Records: 925 (Nelly), 924; USA for Africa Foundation: 605 (photo by Harry Benson); Virgin Records: 665, 862, 912; Warner Brothers Records: 513, 617, 619, 633, 638 (Michael McDonald), 643, 654 (Peter Cetera), 662, 668, 675, 687, 879, 903; Vinnie Zuffante/Star File: 734, 747.